CHILTON®

FORD
SERVICE MANUAL
2012 EDITION
VOLUME II

Australia • Brazil • Japan • Korea • Mexico • Singapore • Spain • United Kingdom • United States

CHILTON®
Ford Service Manual
2010 Edition
Volume II

Vice President, Technology Professional Business Unit:
Gregory L. Clayton

Publisher, Technology Professional Business Unit:
David Koontz

Director of Marketing:
Beth A. Lutz

Senior Production Director:
Wendy Troeger

Production Manager:
Sherondra Thedford

Marketing Manager:
Jennifer Barbic

Marketing Coordinator:
Rachael Torres

Editorial Assistant:
Lisa Staib

Chilton Content Specialist:
Paula Baillie

Graphical Designer:
Melinda Possinger

Art Director:
Benj Gleeksman

Sr. Content Project Manager:
Mike Tubbert

Senior Editors:
Eugene F. Hannon, Jr., A.S.E.
Ryan Lee Price
Richard J. Rivele
Christine L. Sheeky

Editors:
Sherry Burdette
Maureen Lazarz
David G. Olson
Kyla Nyjordet
Lance Williams

ISBN-13: 978-1-4354-6160-4
ISBN-10: 1-4354-6160-6
ISSN: 1548-0887

Chilton
5 Maxwell Drive
Clifton Park, NY 12065-2919
USA

Cengage Learning is a leading provider of customized learning solutions with office locations around the globe, including Singapore, the United Kingdom, Australia, Mexico, Brazil, and Japan. Locate your local office at: **international.cengage.com/region**

Cengage Learning products are represented in Canada by Nelson Education, Ltd.

NOTICE TO THE READER

Printed in the United States of America
1 2 3 4 5 6 7 17 16 15 14 13 12

Table of Contents

Sections

10 Flex

11 Focus

12 Fusion, Milan, MKZ

13 MKS

14 MKT

15 Mustang

16 Ranger

17 Taurus

18 Transit Connect

DTC Diagnostic Trouble Codes

Model Index

Model	Section No.
F	
Flex	10-1
Focus	11-1
Fusion	12-1
M	
Milan	12-1
MKS	13-1
MKT	14-1
MKZ	12-1
Mustang	15-1
R	
Ranger	16-1
T	
Taurus	17-1
Transit Connect	18-1

USING THIS INFORMATION

Organization

To find where a particular model section or procedure is located, look in the Table of Contents. Main topics are listed with the page number on which they may be found. Following the main topics is an alphabetical listing of all of the procedures within the section and their page numbers.

Manufacturer and Model Coverage

This product covers 2010-2011 Ford Motor Company models that are produced in sufficient quantities to warrant coverage, and which have technical content available from the vehicle manufacturers before our publication date. Although this information is as complete as possible at the time of publication, some manufacturers may make changes which cannot be included here. While striving for total accuracy, the publisher cannot assume responsibility for any errors, changes, or omissions that may occur in the compilation of this data.

Part Numbers and Special Tools

Part numbers and special tools are recommended by the publisher and vehicle manufacturer to perform specific jobs. Before substituting any part or tool for the one recommended, you must be completely satisfied that neither your personal safety, nor the performance of the vehicle will be endangered.

ACKNOWLEDGEMENT

This product contains material that is reproduced and distributed under license from Ford Motor Company. No further reproduction or distribution of the Ford Motor Company material is allowed without express written permission from Ford Motor Company.

PRECAUTIONS

Before servicing any vehicle, please be sure to read all of the following precautions, which deal with personal safety, prevention of component damage, and important points to take into consideration when servicing a motor vehicle:

- Always wear safety glasses or goggles when drilling, cutting, grinding or prying.
- Steel-toed work shoes should be worn when working with heavy parts. Pockets should not be used for carrying tools. A slip or fall can drive a screwdriver into your body.
- Work surfaces, including tools and the floor should be kept clean of grease, oil or other slippery material.
- When working around moving parts, don't wear loose clothing. Long hair should be tied back under a hat or cap, or in a hair net.
- Always use tools only for the purpose for which they were designed. Never pry with a screwdriver.
- Keep a fire extinguisher and first aid kit handy.
- Always properly support the vehicle with approved stands or lift.
- Always have adequate ventilation when working with chemicals or hazardous material.
- Carbon monoxide is colorless, odorless and dangerous. If it is necessary to operate the engine with vehicle in a closed area such as a garage, always use an exhaust collector to vent the exhaust gases outside the closed area.
- When draining coolant, keep in mind that small children and some pets are attracted by ethylene glycol antifreeze, and are quite likely to drink any left in an open container, or in puddles on the ground. This will prove fatal in sufficient quantity. Always drain the coolant into a sealable container.
- To avoid personal injury, do not remove the coolant pressure relief cap while the engine is operating or hot. The cooling system is under pressure; steam and hot liquid can come out forcefully when the cap is loosened slightly. Failure to follow these instructions may result in personal injury. The coolant must be recovered in a suitable, clean container for reuse. If the coolant is contaminated it must be recycled or disposed of correctly.
- When carrying out maintenance on the starting system be aware that heavy gauge leads are connected directly to the battery. Make sure the protective caps are in place when maintenance is completed. Failure to follow these instructions may result in personal injury.
- Do not remove any part of the engine emission control system. Operating the engine without the engine emission control system will reduce fuel economy and engine ventilation. This will weaken engine performance and shorten engine life. It is also a violation of Federal law.
- Due to environmental concerns, when the air conditioning system is drained, the refrigerant must be collected using refrigerant recovery/recycling equipment. Federal law requires that refrigerant be recovered into appropriate recovery equipment and the process be conducted by qualified technicians who have been certified by an approved organization, such as MACS, ASI, etc. Use of a recovery machine dedicated to the appropriate refrigerant is necessary to reduce the possibility of oil and refrigerant incompatibility concerns. Refer to the instructions provided by the equipment manufacturer when removing refrigerant from or charging the air conditioning system.
- Always disconnect the battery ground when working on or around the electrical system.
- Batteries contain sulfuric acid. Avoid contact with skin, eyes, or clothing. Also, shield your eyes when working near batteries to protect against possible splashing of the acid solution. In case of acid contact with skin or eyes, flush immediately with water for a minimum of 15 minutes and get prompt medical attention. If acid is swallowed, call a physician immediately. Failure to follow these instructions may result in personal injury.
- Batteries normally produce explosive gases. Therefore, do not allow flames, sparks or lighted substances to come near the battery. When charging or working near a battery, always shield your face and protect your eyes. Always provide ventilation. Failure to follow these instructions may result in personal injury.
- When lifting a battery, excessive pressure on the end walls could cause acid to spew through the vent caps, resulting in personal injury, damage to the vehicle or battery. Lift with a battery carrier or with your hands on opposite corners. Failure to follow

these instructions may result in personal injury.

• Observe all applicable safety precautions when working around fuel. Whenever servicing the fuel system, always work in a well-ventilated area. Do not allow fuel spray or vapors to come in contact with a spark, open flame, or excessive heat (a hot drop light, for example). Keep a dry chemical fire extinguisher near the work area. Always keep fuel in a container specifically designed for fuel storage; also, always properly seal fuel containers to avoid the possibility of fire or explosion. Do not smoke or carry lighted tobacco or open flame of any type when working on or near any fuel-related components.

• Fuel injection systems often remain pressurized, even after the engine has been turned OFF. The fuel system pressure must be relieved before disconnecting any fuel lines. Failure to do so may result in fire and/or personal injury.

• The evaporative emissions system contains fuel vapor and condensed fuel vapor. Although not present in large quantities, it still presents the danger of explosion or fire. Disconnect the battery ground cable from the battery to minimize the possibility of an electrical spark occurring, possibly causing a fire or explosion if fuel vapor or liquid fuel is present in the area. Failure to follow these instructions can result in personal injury.

• The EPA warns that prolonged contact with used engine oil may cause a number of skin disorders, including cancer! You should make every effort to minimize your exposure to used engine oil. Protective gloves should be worn when changing oil. Wash your hands and any other exposed skin areas as soon as possible after exposure to used engine oil. Soap and water, or waterless hand cleaner should be used.

• Some vehicles are equipped with an air bag system, often referred to as a Supplemental Restraint System (SRS) or Supplemental Inflatable Restraint (SIR) system. The system must be disabled before performing service on or around system components, steering column, instrument panel components, wiring and sensors. Failure to follow safety and disabling procedures could result in accidental air bag deployment, possible personal injury and unnecessary system repairs.

• Always wear safety goggles when working with, or around, the air bag system. When carrying a non-deployed air bag, be sure the bag and trim cover are pointed away from your body. When placing a non-deployed air bag on a work surface, always face the bag and trim cover upward, away from the surface. This will reduce the motion of the module if it is accidentally deployed.

• Electronic modules are sensitive to electrical charges. The ABS module can be damaged if exposed to these charges.

• Brake pads and shoes may contain asbestos, which has been determined to be a cancer-causing agent. Never clean brake surfaces with compressed air. Avoid inhaling brake dust. Clean all brake surfaces with a commercially available brake cleaning fluid.

• When replacing brake pads, shoes, discs or drums, replace them as complete axle sets.

• When servicing drum brakes, disassemble and assemble one side at a time, leaving the remaining side intact for reference.

• Brake fluid often contains polyglycol ethers and polyglycols. Avoid contact with the eyes and wash your hands thoroughly after handling brake fluid. If you do get brake fluid in your eyes, flush your eyes with clean, running water for 15 minutes. If eye irritation persists, or if you have taken brake fluid internally, immediately seek medical assistance.

• Clean, high quality brake fluid from a sealed container is essential to the safe and proper operation of the brake system. You should always buy the correct type of brake fluid for your vehicle. If the brake fluid becomes contaminated, completely flush the system with new fluid. Never reuse any brake fluid. Any brake fluid that is removed from the system should be discarded. Also, do not allow any brake fluid to come in contact with a painted or plastic surface; it will damage the paint.

• Never operate the engine without the proper amount and type of engine oil; doing so will result in severe engine damage.

• Timing belt maintenance is extremely important! Many models utilize an interference-type, non-freewheeling engine. If the timing belt breaks, the valves in the cylinder head may strike the pistons, causing potentially serious (also time-consuming and expensive) engine damage.

• Disconnecting the negative battery cable on some vehicles may interfere with the functions of the on-board computer system (s) and may require the computer to undergo a relearning process once the negative battery cable is reconnected.

• Steering and suspension fasteners are critical parts because they affect performance of vital components and systems and their failure can result in major service expense. They must be replaced with the same grade or part number or an equivalent part if replacement is necessary. Do not use a replacement part of lesser quality or substitute design. Torque values must be used as specified during reassembly.

FORD

Flex

10

BRAKES 10-12

ANTI-LOCK BRAKE SYSTEM (ABS) 10-12
General Information 10-12
Precautions 10-12
Speed Sensors 10-12
Removal & Installation 10-12

BLEEDING THE BRAKE SYSTEM 10-14
Bleeding Procedure 10-14
Bleeding Procedure 10-14
Bleeding the ABS System 10-16
Brake Caliper Bleeding 10-15
Master Cylinder Bleeding 10-15

FRONT DISC BRAKES 10-16
Brake Caliper 10-16
Removal & Installation 10-16
Disc Brake Pads 10-16
Removal & Installation 10-16

REAR DISC BRAKES 10-17
Brake Caliper 10-17
Removal & Installation 10-17
Disc Brake Pads 10-18
Removal & Installation 10-18

CHASSIS ELECTRICAL 10-19

AIR BAG (SUPPLEMENTAL RESTRAINT SYSTEM) 10-19
General Information 10-19
Arming/Repowering the System 10-20
Disarming/Depowering the System 10-19
Service Precautions 10-19

DRIVE TRAIN 10-20

Automatic Transaxle Fluid 10-20
Drain and Refill 10-20
Front Driveshaft 10-23
Removal & Installation 10-23
Front Halfshaft 10-24
Removal & Installation 10-24
Rear Axle Assembly 10-26
Removal & Installation 10-26
Rear Differential Housing Cover 10-27
Removal & Installation 10-27
Rear Halfshaft 10-27
Removal & Installation 10-27
Rear Pinion Seal 10-29
Removal & Installation 10-29
Rear Stub Shaft Seal 10-30
Removal & Installation 10-30
Transfer Case Assembly 10-20
Drain & Refill 10-22
Removal & Installation 10-20

ENGINE COOLING 10-30

Coolant Pump 10-30
Removal & Installation 10-30
Engine Coolant 10-33
Draining Procedure 10-33
Filling and Bleeding With Radiator Refiller 10-34
Filling and Bleeding Without Radiator Refiller 10-34
Engine Fan 10-34
Removal & Installation 10-34
Radiator 10-37
Removal & Installation 10-37
Thermostat 10-39
Removal & Installation 10-39

ENGINE ELECTRICAL 10-41

BATTERY SYSTEM 10-43
Battery 10-43
Removal & Installation 10-43

CHARGING SYSTEM 10-41
Alternator 10-41
Removal & Installation 10-41

IGNITION SYSTEM 10-42
Firing Order 10-42
Ignition Coil-On-Plug 10-42
Removal & Installation 10-42
Spark Plugs 10-42
Removal & Installation 10-42

ENGINE MECHANICAL 10-43

Accessory Drive Belts 10-43
Accessory Belt Routing 10-43
Removal & Installation 10-43
Air Cleaner 10-45
Removal & Installation 10-45
Camshaft and Valve Lifters 10-45
Removal & Installation 10-45
Catalytic Converter 10-66
Removal & Installation 10-66
Charge Air Cooler 10-68
Cleaning 10-68
Removal & Installation 10-68
Crankshaft Front Seal 10-69
Removal & Installation 10-69
Cylinder Head 10-69
Removal & Installation 10-69
Engine Oil & Filter 10-78
Replacement 10-78
Exhaust Manifold 10-78
Removal & Installation 10-78
Intake Manifold 10-80
Removal & Installation 10-80
Oil Pump 10-83
Removal & Installation 10-83
Rear Main Seal 10-84
Removal & Installation 10-84
Turbocharger 10-85
Removal & Installation 10-85
Valve Covers 10-88
Removal & Installation 10-88

ENGINE PERFORMANCE & EMISSION CONTROLS 10-93

Camshaft Position (CMP) Sensor 10-93
Location 10-93
Removal & Installation 10-93
Catalyst Monitor Sensor 10-94
Removal & Installtion 10-94
Crankshaft Position (CKP) Sensor 10-94
Location 10-94
Removal & Installation 10-94
Cylinder Head Temperature (CHT) Sensor 10-95

Location....10-95
Removal & Installation....10-95
Fuel Rail Pressure (FRP) Sensor....10-95
Location....10-95
Removal & Installation....10-95
Heated Oxygen Sensor (HO2S)....10-96
Location....10-96
Removal & Installation....10-96
Intake Air Temperature (IAT) Sensor....10-98
Location....10-98
Removal & Installation....10-98
Knock Sensor (KS)....10-98
Location....10-98
Removal & Installation....10-98
Manifold Absolute Pressure (MAP) Sensor & Intake Air Temperature 2 (IAT2) Sensor....10-99
Removal & Installation....10-99
Powertrain Control Module (PCM)....10-99
Location....10-99
Removal & Installation....10-99
Throttle Position Sensor (TPS)....10-99
Removal & Installation....10-99
Turbocharger Boost Pressure (TCBP)/Charge Air Cooler Temperature (CACT) Sensor....10-100
Location....10-100
Removal & Installation....10-100
Variable Camshaft Timing (VCT) Oil Control Solenoid....10-100
Location....10-100
Removal & Installation....10-100

FUEL....10-101

GASOLINE FUEL INJECTION SYSTEM....10-101
Fuel Filter....10-102
Removal & Installation....10-102
Fuel Injectors....10-102
Removal & Installation....10-102
Fuel Pump....10-102
Removal & Installation....10-102
Fuel Rail....10-103
Removal & Installtion....10-103
Fuel System Service Precautions....10-101
Fuel Tank....10-105
Draining....10-105
Removal & Installation....10-106
Relieving Fuel System Pressure....10-101
Throttle Body....10-108
Removal & Installation....10-108

HEATING & AIR CONDITIONING SYSTEM....10-109
Blower Motor....10-109
Removal & Installation....10-109
Heater Core....10-109
Removal & Installation....10-109

PRECAUTIONS....10-12

SPECIFICATIONS AND MAINTENANCE CHARTS....10-3
Brake Specifications....10-7
Camshaft Specifications....10-5
Capacities....10-4
Crankshaft and Connecting Rod Specifications....10-5
Engine and Vehicle Identification....10-3
Engine Tune-Up Specifications....10-3
Fluid Specifications....10-4
General Engine Specifications....10-3
Piston and Ring Specifications....10-5
Scheduled Maintenance Intervals....10-8
Tire, Wheel and Ball Joint Specifications....10-7
Torque Specifications....10-6
Valve Specifications....10-4
Wheel Alignment....10-6

STEERING....10-110
Power Steering Gear....10-110
Removal & Installation....10-110
Power Steering Pump....10-113
Fluid Fill Procedure....10-114
Purging....10-114
Removal & Installation....10-113

SUSPENSION....10-115

FRONT SUSPENSION....10-115
Lower Control Arm....10-115
Lower Control Arm Bushing Replacement....10-116
Removal & Installation....10-115
Stabilizer Bar....10-116
Removal & Installation....10-116
Stabilizer Bar Link....10-117
Removal & Installation....10-117
Strut & Spring Assembly....10-118
Removal & Installation....10-118
Wheel Hub & Bearing....10-119
Removal & Installation....10-119
Wheel Knuckle....10-119
Removal & Insatllation....10-119

REAR SUSPENSION....10-120
Lower Control Arm....10-120
Removal & Installation....10-120
Shock Absorber....10-120
Removal & Installation....10-120
Spring....10-121
Removal & Installtion....10-121
Stabilizer Bar....10-122
Removal & Installation....10-122
Stabilizer Bar Link....10-123
Removal & Installation....10-123
Toe Link....10-123
Removal & Installation....10-123
Trailing Arm....10-123
Removal & Installation....10-123
Upper Control Arm....10-124
Removal & Installation....10-124
Wheel Hub & Bearing....10-126
Removal & Installation....10-126
Wheel Knuckle....10-127
Removal & Installation....10-127

SPECIFICATIONS AND MAINTENANCE CHARTS

ENGINE AND VEHICLE IDENTIFICATION

Engine							Model Year	
Code ①	Liters (cc)	Cu. In.	Cyl.	Fuel Sys.	Engine Type	Eng. Mfg.	Code ②	Year
W	3.5	213	6	MRFS ③	DOHC	Ford	A	2010
T	3.5	213	6	GTDI ④	DOHC	Ford	B	2011

① 8th position of VIN

② 10th position of VIN

③ 2-Speed Mechanical Returnless Fuel System (MRFS) with Sequential Multi-Port Fuel Injection (MFI)

④ Gasoline Turbocharged Direct Injection

25759_FLEX_C0001

GENERAL ENGINE SPECIFICATIONS

All measurements are given in inches.

Year	Model	Engine Displacement Liters (cc)	Engine ID/VIN	Fuel System Type	Net Horsepower @ rpm	Net Torque @ rpm (ft. lbs.)	Bore x Stroke (in.)	Com-pression Ratio	Oil Pressure @ rpm
2010	Flex	3.5 (3496)	W	MRFS ①	262@6250	248@4500	3.64X3.41	10.3:1	30@1500
		3.5 (3496)	T	GTDI ②	355@5700	350@3500	3.64X3.49	10.0:1	30@1500
2011	Flex	3.5 (3496)	W	MRFS ①	262@6250	248@4500	3.64X3.41	10.3:1	30@1500
		3.5 (3496)	T	GTDI ②	355@5700	350@3500	3.64X3.49	10.0:1	30@1500

① 2-Speed Mechanical Returnless Fuel System (MRFS) with Sequential Multi-Port Fuel Injection (MFI)

② Gasoline Turbocharged Direct Injection

25759_FLEX_C0002

ENGINE TUNE-UP SPECIFICATIONS

Year	Engine Displacement Liters	Engine ID/VIN	Spark Plug Gap (in.)	Ignition Timing (deg.)		Fuel Pump (psi)	Idle Speed (rpm)		Valve Clearance	
				MT	AT		MT	AT	Intake	Exhaust
2010	3.5 (3496)	W	0.051-0.057	N/A	①	65	N/A	①	0.0008-0.0027	0.0013-0.0320
	3.5 (3496)	T	0.035	N/A	①	65	N/A	①	0.0008-0.0027	0.0013-0.0320
2011	3.5 (3496)	W	0.051-0.057	N/A	①	65	N/A	①	0.0008-0.0027	0.0013-0.0320
	3.5 (3496)	T	0.035	N/A	①	65	N/A	①	0.0008-0.0027	0.0013-0.0320

N/A: Not Applicable

① Controlled by the Powertrain Control Module (PCM) and cannot be manually adjusted

25759_FLEX_C0003

CAPACITIES

Year	Model	Engine Displacement Liters	Engine ID/VIN	Engine Oil with Filter (qts.)	Transmission/axle (pts.) Auto.	Transmission/axle (pts.) Manual	Drive Axle (pts.) Front	Drive Axle (pts.) Rear	Transfer Case (pts.)	Fuel Tank (gal.)	Cooling System (qts.)
2010	Flex	3.5	W	5.5	18.8	N/A	N/A	2.43	1.13	19.0	11.1
		3.5	T	6.0	18.8	N/A	N/A	2.43	1.13	19.0	11.1
2011	Flex	3.5	W	5.5	18.8	N/A	N/A	2.43	1.13	19.0	11.1
		3.5	T	6.0	18.8	N/A	N/A	2.43	1.13	19.0	11.1

NOTE: All capacities are approximate. Add fluid gradually and ensure a proper fluid level is obtained.

N/A: Not applicable

25759_FLEX_C0004

FLUID SPECIFICATIONS

Year	Model	Engine Disp. Liters (VIN)	Engine Oil	Auto. Trans.	Drive Axle Front	Drive Axle Rear	Transfer Case	Power Steering Fluid	Brake Master Cylinder	Cooling System
2010	Flex	3.5 (W)	①	MERCON® LV	N/A	80W-90	75W-140	MERCON® V	DOT 3	②
		3.5 (T)	①	MERCON® LV	N/A	80W-90	75W-140	MERCON® V	DOT 3	②
2011	Flex	3.5 (W)	①	MERCON® LV	N/A	80W-90	75W-140	MERCON® V	DOT 3	②
		3.5 (T)	①	MERCON® LV	N/A	80W-90	75W-140	MERCON® V	DOT 3	②

DOT: Department Of Transpotation

N/A - Not Applicable

① 5W-20 Premium Synthetic Blend Motor Oil

② Motorcraft® Specialty Green Engine Coolant

25759_FLEX_C0005

VALVE SPECIFICATIONS

Year	Engine Displacement Liters	Engine ID/VIN	Seat Angle (deg.)	Face Angle (deg.)	Spring Test Pressure (lbs. @ in.)	Spring Free-Length (in.)	Spring Installed Height (in.)	Stem-to-Guide Clearance (in.) Intake	Stem-to-Guide Clearance (in.) Exhaust	Stem Diameter (in.) Intake	Stem Diameter (in.) Exhaust
2010	3.5	W	44.5	44.5	53 @ 1.45	1.900	1.450	0.0008-0.0027	0.0013-0.0032	0.2157-0.2164	0.2151-0.2159
	3.5	T	44.5	44.5	60 @ 1.45	2.170	1.450	0.0008-0.0027	0.0013-0.0032	0.2157-0.2164	0.2151-0.2159
2011	3.5	W	44.5	44.5	53 @ 1.45	1.900	1.450	0.0008-0.0027	0.0013-0.0032	0.2157-0.2164	0.2151-0.2159
	3.5	T	44.5	44.5	60 @ 1.45	2.170	1.450	0.0008-0.0027	0.0013-0.0032	0.2157-0.2164	0.2151-0.2159

25759_FLEX_C0006

CAMSHAFT SPECIFICATIONS

All measurements in inches unless noted

Year	Engine Displacement Liters	Engine Code/VIN	Journal Diameter	Brg. Oil Clearance	Shaft End-play	Runout	Journal Bore	Lobe Height Intake	Lobe Height Exhaust
2010	3.5	W	1.021-1.022	0.0029	0.0012-0.0066	0.0015	1.023-1.024	0.38	0.38
	3.5	T	1.021-1.022	0.0029	0.0012-0.0066	0.0015	1.023-1.024	0.35	0.36
2011	3.5	W	1.021-1.022	0.0029	0.0012-0.0066	0.0015	1.023-1.024	0.38	0.38
	3.5	T	1.021-1.022	0.0029	0.0012-0.0066	0.0015	1.023-1.024	0.35	0.36

25759_FLEX_C0007

CRANKSHAFT AND CONNECTING ROD SPECIFICATIONS

All measurements are given in inches.

	Engine		Crankshaft				Connecting Rod		
Year	Displacement Liters	Engine ID/VIN	Main Brg. Journal Dia.	Main Brg. Oil Clearance	Shaft End-play	Thrust on No.	Journal Diameter	Oil Clearance	Side Clearance
2010	3.5	W	2.6570	0.0010-0.0016	0.0039-0.0114	3	2.204-2.2050	0.0007-0.0021	0.0068-0.0167
	3.5	T	2.6570	0.0010-0.0016	0.0039-0.0114	3	2.204-2.2050	0.0007-0.0021	0.0068-0.0167
2011	3.5	W	2.6570	0.0010-0.0016	0.0039-0.0114	3	2.204-2.2050	0.0007-0.0021	0.0068-0.0167
	3.5	T	2.6570	0.0010-0.0016	0.0039-0.0114	3	2.204-2.2050	0.0007-0.0021	0.0068-0.0167

25759_FLEX_C0008

PISTON AND RING SPECIFICATIONS

All measurements are given in inches.

	Engine			Ring Gap			Ring Side Clearance		
Year	Displacement Liters	Engine ID/VIN	Piston Clearance	Top Compression	Bottom Compression	Oil Control	Top Compression	Bottom Compression	Oil Control
2010	3.5	W	0.0003-0.0017	0.0059-0.0098	0.0118-0.0216	0.0059-0.0177	0.0484-0.0492	0.0602-0.0610	N/A
	3.5	T	0.0003-0.0017	0.0067-0.0106	0.0118-0.0216	0.0059-0.0177	0.0484-0.0492	0.0602-0.0610	N/A
2011	3.5	W	0.0003-0.0017	0.0059-0.0098	0.0118-0.0216	0.0059-0.0177	0.0484-0.0492	0.0602-0.0610	N/A
	3.5	T	0.0003-0.0017	0.0067-0.0106	0.0118-0.0216	0.0059-0.0177	0.0484-0.0492	0.0602-0.0610	N/A

N/A - Not Available

25759_FLEX_C0009

TORQUE SPECIFICATIONS

All readings in ft. lbs.

Year	Engine Displacement Liters	Engine ID/VIN	Cylinder Head Bolts	Main Bearing Bolts	Rod Bearing Bolts	Crankshaft Damper Bolts	Flexplate Bolts	Manifold Intake	Manifold Exhaust	Spark Plugs	Oil Pan Drain Plug
2010	3.5	W	①	②	③	④	59	⑤	⑥	11	20
	3.5	T	①	②	③	④	59	⑤	⑦	11	20
2011	3.5	W	①	②	③	④	59	⑤	⑥	11	20
	3.5	T	①	②	③	④	59	⑤	⑦	11	20

① Step 1: 15 ft. lbs.
Step 2: 26 ft. lbs.
Step 3: Plus 90 degrees
Step 4: Plus 90 degrees
Step 5: Plus 45 degrees

② Step 1: 44 ft. lbs.
Step 2: Plus 90 degrees

③ Step 1: 17 ft. lbs.
Step 2: 32 ft. lbs.
Step 2: Plus 90 degrees

④ Step 1: 89 ft. lbs.
Step 2: Loosen 1 full turn
Step 3: 37 ft. lbs.
Step 4: Plus 90 degrees

⑤ Upper manifold: 89 INCH lbs.
Lower manifold: 89 INCH lbs.

⑥ Step 1: 15 ft. lbs.
Step 2: 18 ft. lbs.

⑦ Exhaust manifold stud: 106 inch lbs.
Exhaust manifold nuts Step 1: 11 ft. lbs.
Exhaust manifold nuts Step 2: 15 ft. lbs.

25759_FLEX_C0010

WHEEL ALIGNMENT

Year	Model		Caster Range (+/-Deg.)	Caster Preferred Setting (Deg.)	Camber Range (+/-Deg.)	Camber Preferred Setting (Deg.)	Toe-in (Deg.)
2010	Flex	F	0.75	+3.2	0.75	-0.60	+0.20+/-0.20
		R	—	—	0.75	-1.00	+0.24+/-0.20
2011	Flex	F	0.75	+3.2	0.75	-0.60	+0.20+/-0.20
		R	—	—	0.75	-1.00	+0.24+/-0.20

25759_FLEX_C0011

TIRE, WHEEL AND BALL JOINT SPECIFICATIONS

Year	Model	OEM Tires		Tire Pressures (psi)		Wheel	Ball Joint	Lug Nut
		Standard	Optional	Front	Rear	Size ①	Inspection	(ft. lbs.) ②
2010	Flex	P235/60R	①	40	40	18	NA	100
2011	Flex	P235/60R	①	40	40	18	NA	100

OEM: Original Equipment Manufacturer

PSI: Pounds Per Square Inch

NA: Information not available

① P235/55R H 19" Standard on the Limited models

② The Wheel Nut torque specification is for Clean, Dry Wheel Stud and Wheel Nut Threads

25759_FLEX_C0012

BRAKE SPECIFICATIONS

All measurements in inches unless noted

Year	Model		Brake Disc			Minimum Pad/Lining Thickness		Brake Caliper	
			Original Thickness	Minimum Thickness	Max. Runout	Front	Rear	Bracket Bolts (ft. lbs.)	Mounting Bolts (ft. lbs.)
2010	Flex	F	NA	1.122	0.002	0.118	—	111	44
		R	NA	0.394	0.002	—	0.118	81	21
2011	Flex	F	NA	1.122	0.002	0.118	—	111	44
		R	NA	0.394	0.002	—	0.118	81	21

F: Front

R: Rear

NA: Information not available

25759_FLEX_C0013

SCHEDULED MAINTENANCE INTERVALS

2010 Ford Flex - Severe

TO BE SERVICED	TYPE OF SERVICE	VEHICLE MILEAGE INTERVAL (x1000)											
		5	10	15	20	25	30	35	40	45	50	55	60
Spark plugs	Replace												✓
Automatic transaxle fluid	Replace						✓						✓
Engine coolant	Replace												
Halfshaft boots	Inspect	✓	✓	✓	✓	✓	✓	✓	✓	✓	✓	✓	✓
Rotate and inspect tires	Service	✓	✓	✓	✓	✓	✓	✓	✓	✓	✓	✓	✓
Drive belt(s)	Replace												
Drive belt(s)	Inspect	✓	✓	✓	✓	✓	✓	✓	✓	✓	✓	✓	✓
Air filter	Inspect	✓	✓	✓	✓	✓	✓	✓	✓	✓	✓	✓	✓
Air filter	Replace						✓						✓
Battery performance	Inspect	✓	✓	✓	✓	✓	✓	✓	✓	✓	✓	✓	✓
Cooling system & hoses	Inspect	✓	✓	✓	✓	✓	✓	✓	✓	✓	✓	✓	✓
Climate-controlled seat filter (if equipped)	Replace						✓						✓
Engine oil and filter	Replace	✓	✓	✓	✓	✓	✓	✓	✓	✓	✓	✓	✓
Exhaust system (Leaks, damage, loose parts & foreign material)	Inspect	✓	✓	✓	✓	✓	✓	✓	✓	✓	✓	✓	✓
Horn, exterior lamps, turn signals and hazard warning light operation	Inspect	✓	✓	✓	✓	✓	✓	✓	✓	✓	✓	✓	✓
Oil and fluid leaks	Inspect	✓	✓	✓	✓	✓	✓	✓	✓	✓	✓	✓	✓
Radiator, coolers, heater and airconditioning hoses	Inspect	✓	✓	✓	✓	✓	✓	✓	✓	✓	✓	✓	✓
Shocks struts and other suspension components for leaks and damage	Inspect	✓	✓	✓	✓	✓	✓	✓	✓	✓	✓	✓	✓
Windshield for cracks, chips and pitting	Inspect	✓	✓	✓	✓	✓	✓	✓	✓	✓	✓	✓	✓
Windshield wiper spray and wiper operation	Inspect	✓	✓	✓	✓	✓	✓	✓	✓	✓	✓	✓	✓
Fluid levels (all)	Top off	✓	✓	✓	✓	✓	✓	✓	✓	✓	✓	✓	✓
Brake system (Inspect brake pads/shoes/rotors/drums, brake lines and hoses, and parking brake system)	Inspect	✓	✓	✓	✓	✓	✓	✓	✓	✓	✓	✓	✓
Inspect wheels and related components for abnomal noise, wear, looseness or drag	Inspect	✓	✓	✓	✓	✓	✓	✓	✓	✓	✓	✓	✓
Cabin air filter	Inspect	✓	✓	✓	✓	✓	✓	✓	✓	✓	✓	✓	✓
Steering linkage, ball joints, suspension and tie-rod ends, lubricate if equipped with grease fittings	Inspect/ Lubricate	✓	✓	✓	✓	✓	✓	✓	✓	✓	✓	✓	✓
Transfer case fluid	Replace												✓
Rear differential fluid	Replace	every 150,000 miles											

For extensive idling and or low speed driving, change engine oil and filter every 5,000 miles, 6 months or 200 hours of engine operation.

25759_FLEX_C0014

SCHEDULED MAINTENANCE INTERVALS

2010 Ford Flex - Severe

TO BE SERVICED	TYPE OF SERVICE	VEHICLE MILEAGE INTERVAL (x1000)											
		5	10	15	20	25	30	35	40	45	50	55	60
Spark plugs	Replace												✓
Automatic transaxle fluid	Replace						✓						✓
Engine coolant	Replace												
Halfshaft boots	Inspect	✓	✓	✓	✓	✓	✓	✓	✓	✓	✓	✓	✓
Rotate and inspect tires	Service	✓	✓	✓	✓	✓	✓	✓	✓	✓	✓	✓	✓
Drive belt(s)	Replace												
Drive belt(s)	Inspect	✓	✓	✓	✓	✓	✓	✓	✓	✓	✓	✓	✓
Air filter	Inspect	✓	✓	✓	✓	✓	✓	✓	✓	✓	✓	✓	✓
Air filter	Replace						✓						✓
Battery performance	Inspect	✓	✓	✓	✓	✓	✓	✓	✓	✓	✓	✓	✓
Cooling system & hoses	Inspect	✓	✓	✓	✓	✓	✓	✓	✓	✓	✓	✓	✓
Climate-controlled seat filter (if equipped)	Replace						✓						✓
Engine oil and filter	Replace	✓	✓	✓	✓	✓	✓	✓	✓	✓	✓	✓	✓
Exhaust system (Leaks, damage, loose parts & foreign material)	Inspect	✓	✓	✓	✓	✓	✓	✓	✓	✓	✓	✓	✓
Horn, exterior lamps, turn signals and hazard warning light operation	Inspect	✓	✓	✓	✓	✓	✓	✓	✓	✓	✓	✓	✓
Oil and fluid leaks	Inspect	✓	✓	✓	✓	✓	✓	✓	✓	✓	✓	✓	✓
Radiator, coolers, heater and airconditioning hoses	Inspect	✓	✓	✓	✓	✓	✓	✓	✓	✓	✓	✓	✓
Shocks struts and other suspension components for leaks and damage	Inspect	✓	✓	✓	✓	✓	✓	✓	✓	✓	✓	✓	✓
Windshield for cracks, chips and pitting	Inspect	✓	✓	✓	✓	✓	✓	✓	✓	✓	✓	✓	✓
Windshield wiper spray and wiper operation	Inspect	✓	✓	✓	✓	✓	✓	✓	✓	✓	✓	✓	✓
Fluid levels (all)	Top off	✓	✓	✓	✓	✓	✓	✓	✓	✓	✓	✓	✓
Brake system (Inspect brake pads/shoes/rotors/drums, brake lines and hoses, and parking brake system)	Inspect	✓	✓	✓	✓	✓	✓	✓	✓	✓	✓	✓	✓
Inspect wheels and related components for abnomal noise, wear, looseness or drag	Inspect	✓	✓	✓	✓	✓	✓	✓	✓	✓	✓	✓	✓
Cabin air filter	Inspect	✓	✓	✓	✓	✓	✓	✓	✓	✓	✓	✓	✓
Steering linkage, ball joints, suspension and tie-rod ends, lubricate if equipped with grease fittings	Inspect/ Lubricate	✓	✓	✓	✓	✓	✓	✓	✓	✓	✓	✓	✓
Transfer case fluid	Replace												✓
Rear differential fluid	Replace	every 150,000 miles											

For extensive idling and or low speed driving, change engine oil and filter every 5,000 miles, 6 months or 200 hours of engine operation.

25759_FLEX_C0015

SCHEDULED MAINTENANCE INTERVALS

2011 Ford Flex - Normal

Service Item	Service Action	1	2	3	4	5	6	7	8	9	10	11	12	13	14	15
Engine oil & filter	Replace	✓	✓	✓	✓	✓	✓	✓	✓	✓	✓	✓	✓	✓	✓	✓
Spark plugs	Replace										✓					
Engine coolant	Replace										✓					✓
Halfshaft boots	Inspect	✓	✓	✓	✓	✓	✓	✓	✓	✓	✓	✓	✓	✓	✓	✓
Rear differential fluid	Replace															✓
Drive belt(s)	Inspect	✓	✓	✓	✓	✓	✓	✓	✓	✓	✓	✓	✓	✓	✓	✓
Drive belt(s)	Replace															✓
Transfer case fluid	Replace															✓
Automatic transaxle fluid	Replace															✓
Cabin air filter	Inspect	✓	✓	✓	✓	✓	✓	✓	✓	✓	✓	✓	✓	✓	✓	✓
Engine air filter	Replace			✓			✓			✓			✓			✓
Engine air filter	Inspect	✓	✓	✓	✓	✓	✓	✓	✓	✓	✓	✓	✓	✓	✓	✓
Cooling system, hoses, clamps & coolant strength	Inspect	✓	✓	✓	✓	✓	✓	✓	✓	✓	✓	✓	✓	✓	✓	✓
Battery performance	Inspect	✓	✓	✓	✓	✓	✓	✓	✓	✓	✓	✓	✓	✓	✓	✓
Climate-controlled seat filter (if equipped)	Replace			✓			✓			✓			✓			✓
Exhaust system (Leaks, damage, loose parts and foreign material)	Inspect	✓	✓	✓	✓	✓	✓	✓	✓	✓	✓	✓	✓	✓	✓	✓
Horn, exterior lamps, turn signals and hazard warning light operation	Inspect	✓	✓	✓	✓	✓	✓	✓	✓	✓	✓	✓	✓	✓	✓	✓
Windshield for cracks, chips and pitting	Inspect	✓	✓	✓	✓	✓	✓	✓	✓	✓	✓	✓	✓	✓	✓	✓
Windshield wiper spray and wiper operation	Inspect	✓	✓	✓	✓	✓	✓	✓	✓	✓	✓	✓	✓	✓	✓	✓
Fluid levels (all)	Top off	✓	✓	✓	✓	✓	✓	✓	✓	✓	✓	✓	✓	✓	✓	✓
Brake system (Pads/shoes/rotors/drums, brake lines and hoses, and parking brake system)	Inspect	✓	✓	✓	✓	✓	✓	✓	✓	✓	✓	✓	✓	✓	✓	✓
Inspect wheels & related components for abnomal noise, wear, looseness or drag	Inspect	✓	✓	✓	✓	✓	✓	✓	✓	✓	✓	✓	✓	✓	✓	✓
Cabin air filter (If equipped)	Replace		✓		✓		✓		✓		✓		✓		✓	
Steering linkage, ball joints, suspension, tie-rod ends, driveshaft and u-joints: lubricate if equipped with grease fittings	Inspect/ Lubricate	✓	✓	✓	✓	✓	✓	✓	✓	✓	✓	✓	✓	✓	✓	✓
Radiator, coolers, heater and air conditioning hoses	Inspect	✓	✓	✓	✓	✓	✓	✓	✓	✓	✓	✓	✓	✓	✓	✓
Rotate tires, inspect tread wear, measure tread depth and check pressure	Inspect/ Rotate	✓	✓	✓	✓	✓	✓	✓	✓	✓	✓	✓	✓	✓	✓	✓
Suspension components for leaks and damage	Inspect	✓	✓	✓	✓	✓	✓	✓	✓	✓	✓	✓	✓	✓	✓	✓

Oil change service intervals should be completed as indicated by the message center (Can be up to 1 year or 10,000 miles) If the message center is prematurely reset or is inoperative, perform the oil change interval at 6 months or 5,000 miles from your last oil change.

25759_FLEX_C0016

SCHEDULED MAINTENANCE INTERVALS

2011 Ford Flex - Severe

Service Item	Service Action	1	2	3	4	5	6	7	8	9	10	11	12	13	14	15
Engine oil & filter	Replace	✓	✓	✓	✓	✓	✓	✓	✓	✓	✓	✓	✓	✓	✓	✓
Spark plugs	Replace						✓						✓			
Engine coolant	Replace										✓					✓
Rear differential fluid	Replace															✓
Drive belt(s)	Inspect	✓	✓	✓	✓	✓	✓	✓	✓	✓	✓	✓	✓	✓	✓	✓
Drive belt(s)	Replace															✓
Transfer case fluid	Replace															✓
Automatic transaxle fluid	Replace			✓			✓			✓			✓			✓
Engine air filter	Inspect/	✓	✓	✓	✓	✓	✓	✓	✓	✓	✓	✓	✓	✓	✓	✓
Cooling system, hoses, clamps & coolant strength	Inspect	✓	✓	✓	✓	✓	✓	✓	✓	✓	✓	✓	✓	✓	✓	✓
Battery performance	Inspect	✓	✓	✓	✓	✓	✓	✓	✓	✓	✓	✓	✓	✓	✓	✓
Climate-controlled seat filter (if equipped)	Replace			✓			✓			✓			✓			✓
Exhaust system (Leaks, damage, loose parts and foreign material)	Inspect	✓	✓	✓	✓	✓	✓	✓	✓	✓	✓	✓	✓	✓	✓	✓
Horn, exterior lamps, turn signals and hazard warning light operation	Inspect	✓	✓	✓	✓	✓	✓	✓	✓	✓	✓	✓	✓	✓	✓	✓
Oil and fluid leaks	Inspect	✓	✓	✓	✓	✓	✓	✓	✓	✓	✓	✓	✓	✓	✓	✓
Shocks struts and other suspension components for leaks and damage	Inspect	✓	✓	✓	✓	✓	✓	✓	✓	✓	✓	✓	✓	✓	✓	✓
Windshield for cracks, chips and pitting	Inspect	✓	✓	✓	✓	✓	✓	✓	✓	✓	✓	✓	✓	✓	✓	✓
Windshield wiper spray and wiper operation	Inspect	✓	✓	✓	✓	✓	✓	✓	✓	✓	✓	✓	✓	✓	✓	✓
Halfshaft & U-joints	Inspect	✓	✓	✓	✓	✓	✓	✓	✓	✓	✓	✓	✓	✓	✓	✓
Fluid levels (all)	Top off	✓	✓	✓	✓	✓	✓	✓	✓	✓	✓	✓	✓	✓	✓	✓
Brake system (Pads/shoes/rotors/drums, brake lines and hoses, and parking brake system)	Inspect	✓	✓	✓	✓	✓	✓	✓	✓	✓	✓	✓	✓	✓	✓	✓
Inspect wheels & related components for abnomal noise, wear, looseness or drag	Inspect	✓	✓	✓	✓	✓	✓	✓	✓	✓	✓	✓	✓	✓	✓	✓
Cabin air filter	Inspect/	✓	✓	✓	✓	✓	✓	✓	✓	✓	✓	✓	✓	✓	✓	✓
Radiator, coolers, heater and air conditioning hoses	Inspect	✓	✓	✓	✓	✓	✓	✓	✓	✓	✓	✓	✓	✓	✓	✓
Rotate tires, inspect tread wear, measure tread depth and check pressure	Inspect/ Rotate	✓	✓	✓	✓	✓	✓	✓	✓	✓	✓	✓	✓	✓	✓	✓
Steering linkage, ball joints, suspension and tie-rod ends, lubricate if equipped with greases fittings	Inspect/ Lubricate	✓	✓	✓	✓	✓	✓	✓	✓	✓	✓	✓	✓	✓	✓	✓

Oil change service intervals should be completed as indicated by the message center (Can be up to 1 year or 10,000 miles) If the message center is prematurely reset or is inoperative, perform the oil change interval at 6 months or 5,000 miles from your last oil change.

For extensive idling and or low speed driving, change engine oil and filter every 5,000 miles, 6 months or 200 hours of engine operation.

25759_FLEX_C0017

PRECAUTIONS

Before servicing any vehicle, please be sure to read all of the following precautions, which deal with personal safety, prevention of component damage, and important points to take into consideration when servicing a motor vehicle:

- Never open, service or drain the radiator or cooling system when the engine is hot; serious burns can occur from the steam and hot coolant.
- Observe all applicable safety precautions when working around fuel. Whenever servicing the fuel system, always work in a well-ventilated area. Do not allow fuel spray or vapors to come in contact with a spark, open flame, or excessive heat (a hot drop light, for example). Keep a dry chemical fire extinguisher near the work area. Always keep fuel in a container specifically designed for fuel storage; also, always properly seal fuel containers to avoid the possibility of fire or explosion. Refer to the additional fuel system precautions later in this section.
- Fuel injection systems often remain pressurized, even after the engine has been turned **OFF**. The fuel system pressure must be relieved before disconnecting any fuel lines. Failure to do so may result in fire and/or personal injury.
- Brake fluid often contains polyglycol ethers and polyglycols. Avoid contact with the eyes and wash your hands thoroughly after handling brake fluid. If you do get brake fluid in your eyes, flush your eyes with clean, running water for 15 minutes. If eye irritation persists, or if you have taken brake fluid internally, IMMEDIATELY seek medical assistance.
- The EPA warns that prolonged contact with used engine oil may cause a number of skin disorders, including cancer. You should make every effort to minimize your exposure to used engine oil. Protective gloves should be worn when changing oil. Wash your hands and any other exposed skin areas as soon as possible after exposure to used engine oil. Soap and water, or waterless hand cleaner should be used.
- All new vehicles are now equipped with an air bag system, often referred to as a Supplemental Restraint System (SRS) or Supplemental Inflatable Restraint (SIR) system. The system must be disabled before performing service on or around system components, steering column, instrument panel components, wiring and sensors. Failure to follow safety and disabling procedures could result in accidental air bag deployment, possible personal injury and unnecessary system repairs.
- Always wear safety goggles when working with, or around, the air bag system. When carrying a non-deployed air bag, be sure the bag and trim cover are pointed away from your body. When placing a non-deployed air bag on a work surface, always face the bag and trim cover upward, away from the surface. This will reduce the motion of the module if it is accidentally deployed. Refer to the additional air bag system precautions later in this section.
- Clean, high quality brake fluid from a sealed container is essential to the safe and proper operation of the brake system. You should always buy the correct type of brake fluid for your vehicle. If the brake fluid becomes contaminated, completely flush the system with new fluid. Never reuse any brake fluid. Any brake fluid that is removed from the system should be discarded. Also, do not allow any brake fluid to come in contact with a painted surface; it will damage the paint.
- Never operate the engine without the proper amount and type of engine oil; doing so WILL result in severe engine damage.
- Timing belt maintenance is extremely important. Many models utilize an interference-type, non-freewheeling engine. If the timing belt breaks, the valves in the cylinder head may strike the pistons, causing potentially serious (also time-consuming and expensive) engine damage. Refer to the maintenance interval charts for the recommended replacement interval for the timing belt, and to the timing belt section for belt replacement and inspection.
- Disconnecting the negative battery cable on some vehicles may interfere with the functions of the on-board computer system(s) and may require the computer to undergo a relearning process once the negative battery cable is reconnected.
- When servicing drum brakes, only disassemble and assemble one side at a time, leaving the remaining side intact for reference.
- Only an MVAC-trained, EPA-certified automotive technician should service the air conditioning system or its components.

BRAKES

ANTI-LOCK BRAKE SYSTEM (ABS)

GENERAL INFORMATION

PRECAUTIONS

- Certain components within the ABS system are not intended to be serviced or repaired individually.
- Do not use rubber hoses or other parts not specifically specified for and ABS system. When using repair kits, replace all parts included in the kit. Partial or incorrect repair may lead to functional problems and require the replacement of components.
- Lubricate rubber parts with clean, fresh brake fluid to ease assembly. Do not use shop air to clean parts; damage to rubber components may result.
- Use only DOT 3 brake fluid from an unopened container.
- If any hydraulic component or line is removed or replaced, it may be necessary to bleed the entire system.
- A clean repair area is essential. Always clean the reservoir and cap thoroughly before removing the cap. The slightest amount of dirt in the fluid may plug an orifice and impair the system function. Perform repairs after components have been thoroughly cleaned; use only denatured alcohol to clean components. Do not allow ABS components to come into contact with any substance containing mineral oil; this includes used shop rags.
- The Anti-Lock control unit is a microprocessor similar to other computer units in the vehicle. Ensure that the ignition switch is **OFF** before removing or installing controller harnesses. Avoid static electricity discharge at or near the controller.
- If any arc welding is to be done on the vehicle, the control unit should be unplugged before welding operations begin.

SPEED SENSORS

REMOVAL & INSTALLATION

Front

See Figure 1.

1. Remove the wheel and tire.
2. Disconnect the wheel speed sensor electrical connector.
3. Remove the 2 scrivets and position aside the fender splash shield.

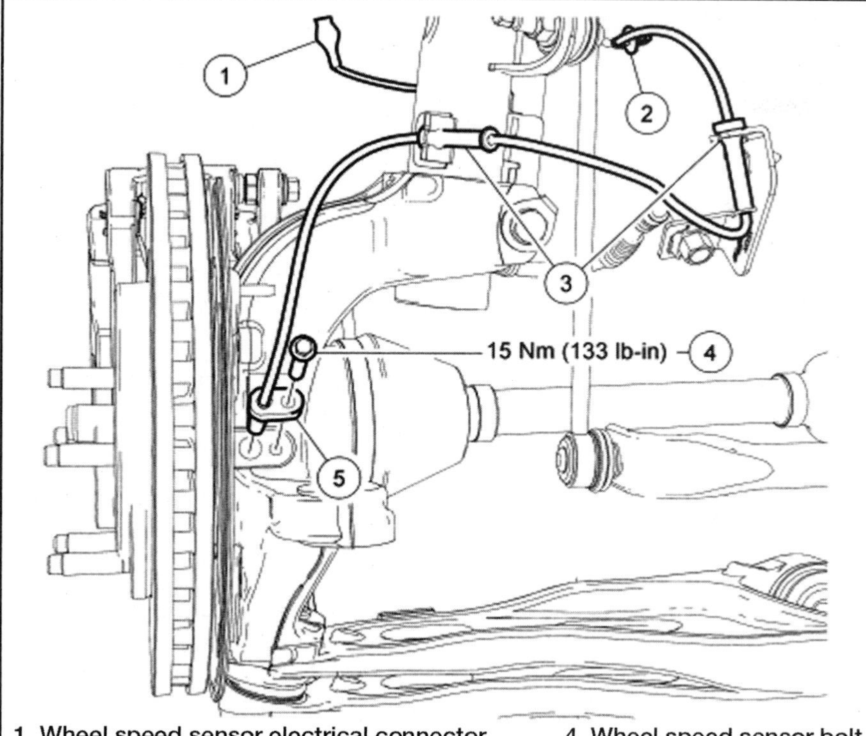

Fig. 1 Exploded view of the front wheel speed sensor

4. Remove the wheel speed sensor harness pin-type retainer.
5. Remove the 2 wheel speed sensor harness retainers.
6. Remove the bolt and the wheel speed sensor.

To install:

7. Install the wheel speed sensor, and install the bolt. Tighten the bolt to 133 inch lbs. (15 Nm)
8. Install the 2 wheel speed sensor harness retainers.
9. Install the wheel speed sensor harness pin-type retainer.
10. Install the 2 scrivets and reposition the fender splash shield.
11. Connect the wheel speed sensor electrical connector.
12. Install the wheel and tire.

Rear

See Figure 2.

➡Make sure to correctly route and secure the wheel speed sensor harness in the rear subframe assembly or damage to the harness may occur.

1. With the vehicle in NEUTRAL, position it on a hoist.
2. Disconnect the wheel speed sensor electrical connector.
3. Detach the 2 wheel speed sensor pin-type retainers.
4. Detach the 2 wheel speed sensor harness retainers.
5. Remove the wheel speed sensor bolt.
6. Remove the wheel speed sensor.

To install:

➡Make sure to correctly route and secure the wheel speed sensor harness in the rear subframe assembly or damage to the harness may occur.

7. Install the wheel speed sensor.
8. Install the wheel speed sensor bolt. Tighten the bolt to 133 inch lbs. (15 Nm).
9. Attach the 2 wheel speed sensor harness retainers.
10. Attach the 2 wheel speed sensor pin-type retainers.
11. Connect the wheel speed sensor electrical connector.
12. With the vehicle in NEUTRAL, lower the vehicle from hoist.

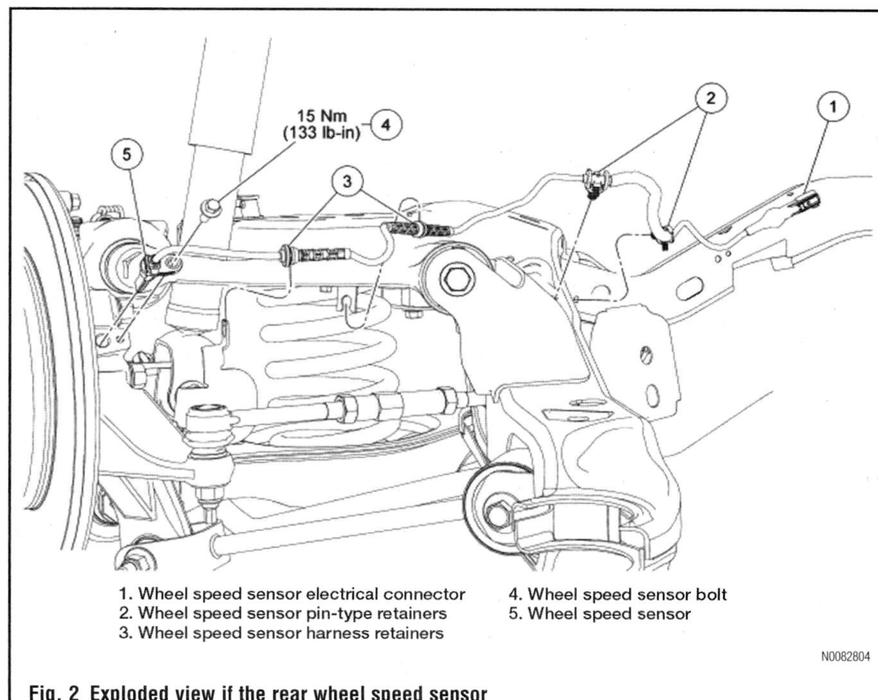

Fig. 2 Exploded view if the rear wheel speed sensor

BLEEDING PROCEDURE

BLEEDING PROCEDURE

Pressure Bleeding Procedure

See Figure 3.

✻✻ CAUTION

Do not use any fluid other than clean brake fluid meeting manufacturer's specification. Additionally, do not use brake fluid that has been previously drained. Following these instructions will help prevent system contamination, brake component damage and the risk of serious personal injury.

✻✻ CAUTION

Carefully read cautionary information on product label. For additional information, consult the product Material Safety Data Sheet (MSDS) if available. Failure to follow these instructions may result in serious personal injury.

✻✻ CAUTION

Do not allow the brake master cylinder to run dry during the bleeding operation. Master cylinder may be damaged if operated without fluid, resulting in degraded braking performance. Failure to follow this instruction may result in serious personal injury.

➡Do not spill brake fluid on painted or plastic surfaces or damage to the surface may occur. If brake fluid is spilled onto a painted or plastic surface, immediately wash the surface with water.

➡Pressure bleeding the brake system is preferred to manual bleeding.

➡The Hydraulic Control Unit (HCU) bleeding procedure must be carried out if the HCU or any components upstream of the HCU are installed new.

1. Clean all the dirt from around the brake fluid reservoir cap and remove the cap. Fill the brake master cylinder reservoir with clean, specified brake fluid.

➡Master cylinder pressure bleeder adapter tools are available from various manufacturers of pressure bleeding equipment. Follow the instructions of the manufacturer when installing the adapter.

2. Install the bleeder adapter to the brake master cylinder reservoir and attach the bleeder tank hose to the fitting on the adapter.

➡Make sure the bleeder tank contains enough specified brake fluid to complete the bleeding operation.

3. Open the valve on the bleeder tank. Apply 30-50 psi to the brake system.
4. Remove the RH rear bleeder cap and place a box-end wrench on the bleeder screw. Attach a rubber drain tube to the RH rear bleeder screw and submerge the free end of the tube in a container partially filled with clean, specified brake fluid.

➡Due to the complexity of the fluid path within the rear integral parking brake calipers, it is necessary to press and release the parking brake during the bleed procedure.

5. Loosen the RH rear bleeder screw. Leave open until clear, bubble-free brake fluid flows, then tighten the RH rear bleeder screw.
   - Press and release the parking brake 5 times.
   - Repeat until clear, bubble-free fluid comes out.
6. Tighten the RH rear bleeder screw. Tighten the rear bleeder screw to 89 inch lbs. (10 Nm).
   - Remove the rubber hose and install the bleeder screw cap.
7. Repeat Steps 5 and 6 for the LH rear brake caliper.
8. Continue bleeding the front of the system, going in order from the RH front brake caliper and then to the LH front brake caliper.
   - Tighten the front brake caliper bleeder screws. Tighten the front bleeder screw to 97 inch lbs. (11 Nm).
9. Close the bleeder tank valve and release the pressure. Remove the tank hose from the adapter and remove the adapter. Fill the reservoir with clean, specified brake fluid and install the reservoir cap.

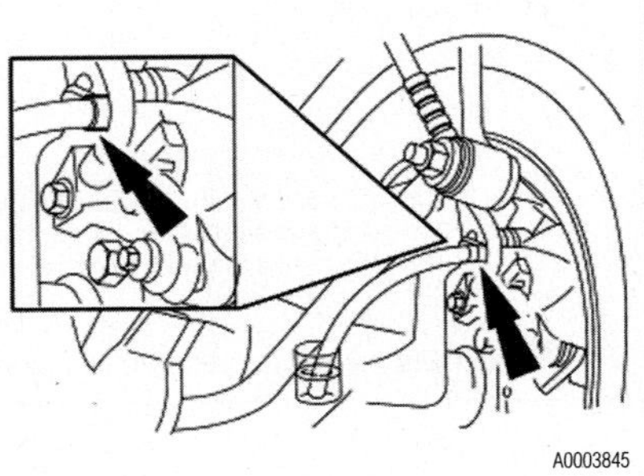

A0003845

Fig. 3 Right-hand rear bleeder cap and screw location

Manual Bleeding Procedure

See Figure 3.

✻✻ CAUTION

Do not use any fluid other than clean brake fluid meeting manufacturer's specification. Additionally, do not use brake fluid that has been previously drained. Following these instructions will help prevent system contamination, brake component damage and the risk of serious personal injury.

✻✻ CAUTION

Carefully read cautionary information on product label. For additional information, consult the product Material Safety Data Sheet (MSDS) if available. Failure to follow these instructions may result in serious personal injury.

✻✻ CAUTION

Do not allow the brake master cylinder to run dry during the bleeding operation. Master cylinder may be damaged if operated without fluid, resulting in degraded braking performance. Failure to follow this instruction may result in serious personal injury.

➡Do not spill brake fluid on painted or plastic surfaces or damage to the surface may occur. If brake fluid is spilled onto a painted or plastic surface, immediately wash the surface with water.

➡Pressure bleeding the brake system is preferred to manual bleeding.

➡The HCU bleeding procedure must be carried out if the HCU or any components upstream of the HCU are installed new.

1. Clean all the dirt from around the brake fluid reservoir cap and remove the cap. Fill the brake master cylinder reservoir with clean, specified brake fluid.

2. Remove the RH rear bleeder cap and place a box-end wrench on the bleeder screw. Attach a rubber drain tube to the RH rear bleeder screw and submerge the free end of the tube in a container partially filled with clean, specified brake fluid.

3. Have an assistant hold firm pressure on the brake pedal.

➡Due to the complexity of the fluid path within the rear integral parking brake calipers, it is necessary to press and release the parking brake during the bleed procedure.

4. Loosen the RH rear bleeder screw until a stream of brake fluid comes out. While the assistant maintains pressure on the brake pedal, tighten the RH rear bleeder screw.
   - Press and release the parking brake 5 times.
   - Repeat until clear, bubble-free fluid comes out.
   - Refill the brake master cylinder reservoir as necessary.

5. Tighten the RH rear bleeder screw to specification. Tighten the rear bleeder screw to 89 inch lbs. (10 Nm).
   - Remove the rubber hose and install the bleeder screw cap.

6. Repeat Steps 2 through 5 for the LH rear brake caliper.

7. Remove the RH front bleeder cap and place a box-end wrench on the bleeder screw. Attach a rubber drain tube to the RH front bleeder screw and submerge the free end of the tube in a container partially filled with clean, specified brake fluid.

8. Have an assistant hold firm pressure on the brake pedal.

9. Loosen the RH front bleeder screw until a stream of brake fluid comes out. While the assistant maintains pressure on the brake pedal, tighten the RH front bleeder screw. Tighten the front bleeder screw to 97 inch lbs. (11 Nm).
   - Repeat until clear, bubble-free fluid comes out.
   - Refill the brake master cylinder reservoir as necessary.

10. Tighten the RH front bleeder screw. Tighten the front bleeder screw to 97 inch lbs. (11 Nm).
    - Remove the rubber hose and install the bleeder screw cap.

11. Repeat Steps 7 through 10 for the LH front brake caliper bleeder screw.

Hydraulic Control Unit (HCU) Bleeding

➡Pressure bleeding the brake system is preferred to manual bleeding.

1. Follow the pressure bleeding or manual bleeding procedure steps to bleed the system.

2. Connect the scan tool and follow the ABS Service Bleed instructions.

3. Repeat the pressure bleeding or manual bleeding procedure steps to bleed the system.

MASTER CYLINDER BLEEDING

See Figure 4.

**** CAUTION**

Do not use any fluid other than clean brake fluid meeting manufacturer's specification. Additionally, do not use brake fluid that has been previously drained. Following these instructions will help prevent system contamination, brake component damage and the risk of serious personal injury.

**** CAUTION**

Carefully read cautionary information on product label. For EMERGENCY MEDICAL INFORMATION seek medical advice. Failure to follow these instructions may result in serious personal injury.

**** CAUTION**

Do not allow the brake master cylinder to run dry during the bleeding operation. Master cylinder may be damaged if operated without fluid, resulting in degraded braking performance. Failure to follow this instruction may result in serious personal injury.

➡Do not spill brake fluid on painted or plastic surfaces or damage to the surface may occur. If brake fluid is spilled onto a painted or plastic surface, immediately wash the surface with water.

➡When a new brake master cylinder has been installed or the system has been emptied, or partially emptied, it should be primed to prevent air from entering the system.

1. Disconnect the brake tubes from the master cylinder.

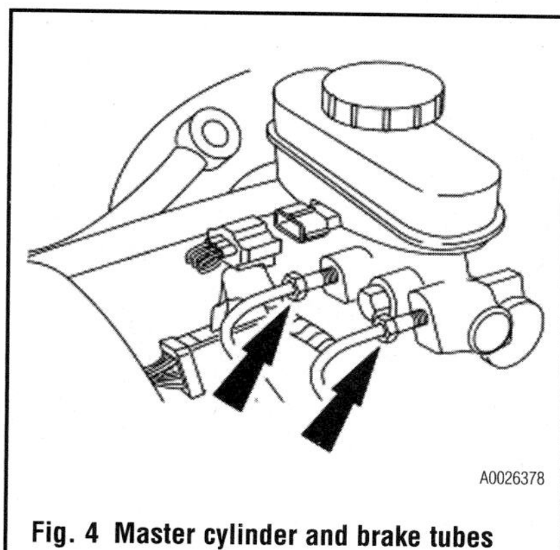

Fig. 4 Master cylinder and brake tubes

2. Install short brake tubes onto the primary and secondary ports with the ends submerged in the brake master cylinder reservoir.

3. Fill the brake master cylinder reservoir with clean, specified brake fluid.

4. Have an assistant pump the brake pedal until clear fluid flows from the brake tubes without air bubbles.

5. Remove the short brake tubes, and install the master cylinder brake tubes.

6. Bleed the brake system.

BRAKE CALIPER BLEEDING

See Figure 5.

**** CAUTION**

Do not use any fluid other than clean brake fluid meeting manufacturer's specification. Additionally, do not use brake fluid that has been previously drained. Following these instructions will help prevent system contamination, brake component damage and the risk of serious personal injury.

**** CAUTION**

Carefully read cautionary information on product label. For EMERGENCY MEDICAL INFORMATION seek medical advice. Failure to follow these instructions may result in serious personal injury.

**** CAUTION**

Do not allow the brake master cylinder to run dry during the bleeding operation. Master cylinder may be damaged if operated without fluid, resulting in degraded braking performance. Failure to follow this instruction may result in serious personal injury.

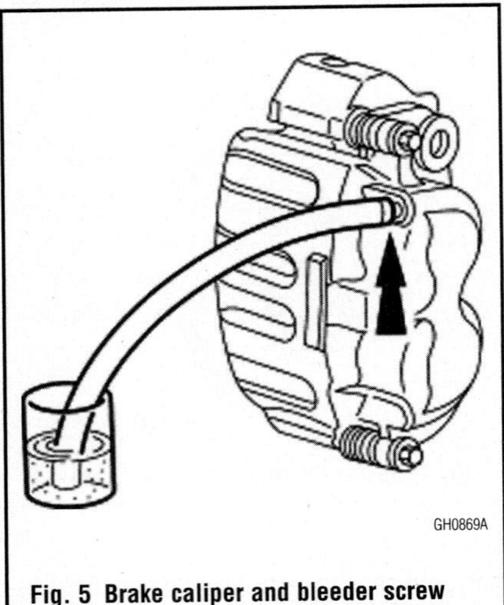

Fig. 5 Brake caliper and bleeder screw

➡Do not spill brake fluid on painted or plastic surfaces or damage to the surface may occur. If brake fluid is spilled onto a painted or plastic surface, immediately wash the surface with water.

➡It is not necessary to do a complete brake system bleed if only the disc brake caliper was disconnected.

1. Remove the brake caliper bleeder screw cap and place a box-end wrench on the bleeder screw. Attach a rubber drain hose to the bleeder screw and submerge the free end of the hose in a container partially filled with clean, specified brake fluid.
2. Have an assistant pump the brake pedal and then hold firm pressure on the brake pedal.

➡Due to the complexity of the fluid path within the rear integral parking brake calipers, it is necessary to press and release the parking brake during the bleed procedure.

3. Loosen the bleeder screw until a stream of brake fluid comes out. While the assistant maintains pressure on the brake pedal, tighten the bleeder screw.
   - If bleeding a rear brake caliper, press and release the parking brake 5 times.
   - Repeat until clear, bubble-free fluid comes out.
   - Refill the brake master cylinder reservoir as necessary.
4. Tighten the brake caliper bleeder screw, remove the rubber hose and install the bleeder screw cap.
   - Tighten the front brake caliper bleeder screws to specification. Tighten the front bleeder screw to 97 inch lbs. (11 Nm).
   - Tighten the rear brake caliper bleeder screws to specification. Tighten the rear bleeder screw to 89 inch lbs. (10 Nm).

BLEEDING THE ABS SYSTEM

For the Hydraulic Control Unit (HCU) Bleeding, it is preferred to use Pressure bleeding over the manual bleeding as outlined in this section.

BRAKES

FRONT DISC BRAKES

✲✲ WARNING

Dust and dirt accumulating on brake parts during normal use may contain asbestos fibers from production or aftermarket brake linings. Breathing excessive concentrations of asbestos fibers can cause serious bodily harm. Exercise care when servicing brake parts. Do not sand or grind brake lining unless equipment used is designed to contain the dust residue. Do not clean brake parts with compressed air or by dry brushing. Cleaning should be done by dampening the brake components with a fine mist of water, then wiping the brake components clean with a dampened cloth. Dispose of cloth and all residue containing asbestos fibers in an impermeable container with the appropriate label. Follow practices prescribed by the Occupational Safety and Health Administration (OSHA) and the Environmental Protection Agency (EPA) for the handling, processing, and disposing of dust or debris that may contain asbestos fibers.

✲✲ CAUTION

Do not use any fluid other than clean brake fluid meeting manufacturer's specification. Additionally, do not use brake fluid that has been previously drained. Following these instructions will help prevent system contamination, brake component damage and the risk of serious personal injury.

✲✲ CAUTION

Carefully read cautionary information on product label. For EMERGENCY MEDICAL INFORMATION seek medical advice. For additional information, consult the product Material Safety Data Sheet (MSDS) if available. Failure to follow these instructions may result in serious personal injury.

➡Do not spill brake fluid on painted or plastic surfaces or damage to the surface may occur. If brake fluid is spilled onto a painted or plastic surface, immediately wash the surface with water.

BRAKE CALIPER

REMOVAL & INSTALLATION

1. Remove the brake pads as outlined in this section.
2. Remove the brake caliper flow bolt and position the brake hose aside.
   - Discard the copper washers.
3. Remove the brake caliper.

To install:

4. Position the brake hose and install the brake caliper flow bolt.
   - Install new copper washers.
   - Tighten the bolt to 35 ft. lbs. (47 Nm).
5. Install the brake pads as outlined in this section.
6. Bleed the brake caliper as outlined in this section.

DISC BRAKE PADS

REMOVAL & INSTALLATION

✲✲ CAUTION

Always install new brake shoes or pads at both ends of an axle to reduce the possibility of brakes pulling vehicle to one side. Failure to follow this instruction may result in uneven braking and serious personal injury.

1. Check the brake fluid level in the brake master cylinder reservoir.
   - If required, remove the fluid until the brake master cylinder reservoir is half full.
2. Remove the wheel and tire.
3. Using a C-clamp, compress the pistons into the caliper housing.

➡Do not allow the brake caliper to hang from the brake hose or damage to the hose may occur.

4. Remove the 2 brake caliper guide pin bolts and position the caliper aside.
   - Support the caliper using mechanic's wire.
5. Remove the 2 brake pads and spring clips from the brake caliper anchor plate.
   - Discard the spring clips.

To install:

➡Do not allow grease, oil, brake fluid or other contaminants to contact the pad lining material, or damage to components may occur. Do not install contaminated pads.

➡If installing new brake pads, make sure to install all new hardware and lubricant supplied with the brake pad kit. Refer to the brake pad instruction sheet when applying lubricant.

6. Install the new spring clips and brake pads to the brake caliper anchor plate.
   - Apply equal amounts of specified lubricant to the brake caliper-to-brake pad contact points.

➡Make sure the caliper pin boots are correctly seated to prevent corrosion to the guide pins.

➡Make sure that the brake hose is not twisted when the caliper is positioned on the anchor plate to prevent abrasive damage.

7. Position the brake caliper onto the brake caliper anchor plate and install the 2 brake caliper guide pin bolts. Tighten the bolts to 53 ft. lbs. (72 Nm).
8. Install the wheel and tire.
9. If necessary, fill the brake master cylinder reservoir with clean, specified brake fluid.
10. Apply brakes several times to verify correct brake operation.

✱✱ WARNING

Dust and dirt accumulating on brake parts during normal use may contain asbestos fibers from production or aftermarket brake linings. Breathing excessive concentrations of asbestos fibers can cause serious bodily harm. Exercise care when servicing brake parts. Do not sand or grind brake lining unless equipment used is designed to contain the dust residue. Do not clean brake parts with compressed air or by dry brushing. Cleaning should be done by dampening the brake components with a fine mist of water, then wiping the brake components clean with a dampened cloth. Dispose of cloth and all residue containing asbestos fibers in an impermeable container with the appropriate label. Follow practices prescribed by the Occupational Safety and Health Administration (OSHA) and the Environmental Protection Agency (EPA) for the handling, processing, and disposing of dust or debris that may contain asbestos fibers.

✱✱ CAUTION

Do not use any fluid other than clean brake fluid meeting manufacturer's specification. Additionally, do not use brake fluid that has been previously drained. Following these instructions will help prevent system contamination, brake component damage and the risk of serious personal injury.

✱✱ CAUTION

Carefully read cautionary information on product label. For EMERGENCY MEDICAL INFORMATION seek medical advice. For additional information, consult the product Material Safety Data Sheet (MSDS) if available. Failure to follow these instructions may result in serious personal injury.

➡Do not spill brake fluid on painted or plastic surfaces or damage to the surface may occur. If brake fluid is spilled onto a painted or plastic surface, immediately wash the surface with water.

BRAKE CALIPER

REMOVAL & INSTALLATION

1. Release the parking brake cable tension as outlined in this section.
2. Disconnect the parking brake cable from the subframe bracket and the caliper.
   a. Position the parking brake cable aside.
3. Remove and discard the brake pads as outlined in this section.
4. Clean and inspect the disc brake caliper.
   a. If leaks or damaged boots are found, install a new disc brake caliper.
5. Disconnect the brake tube fitting from the brake flexible hose.

➡The brake caliper and brake flexible hose are removed as an assembly.

6. Remove the retainer clip from the brake flexible hose.

✱✱ WARNING

During installation, make sure that the brake flexible hose does not become twisted or damage to hose may occur.

To install:

✱✱ CAUTION

Do not use any fluid other than clean brake fluid meeting manufacturer's specification. Additionally, do not use brake fluid that has been previously drained. Following these instructions will help prevent system contamination, brake component damage and the risk of serious personal injury.

✱✱ CAUTION

Carefully read cautionary information on product label. For EMERGENCY MEDICAL INFORMATION seek medical advice. For additional information, consult the product Material Safety Data Sheet (MSDS) if available. Failure to follow these instructions may result in serious personal injury.

➡Do not spill brake fluid on painted or plastic surfaces or damage to the surface may occur. If brake fluid is spilled onto a painted or plastic surface, immediately wash the surface with water.

✱✱ WARNING

During installation, make sure that the brake flexible hose does not become twisted or damage to hose may occur.

➡**The brake caliper and brake flexible hose are removed as an assembly.**

7. Install the retainer clip to the brake flexible hose.
8. Connect the brake tube fitting to the brake flexible hose. Tighten the fitting to 150 inch lbs. (17 Nm).
9. Clean and inspect the disc brake caliper.
   a. If leaks or damaged boots are found, install a new disc brake caliper.
10. Install new brake pads as outlined in this section.
11. Connect the parking brake cable to the subframe bracket and the caliper.
   a. Reposition the parking brake cable.
12. Engage the parking brake cable tension as outlined in this section.
13. Bleed the caliper as outlined in this section.

DISC BRAKE PADS

REMOVAL & INSTALLATION

See Figures 6 and 7.

CAUTION

Always install new brake shoes or pads at both ends of an axle to reduce the possibility of brakes pulling vehicle to one side. Failure to follow this instruction may result in uneven braking and serious personal injury.

1. Check the brake fluid level in the brake fluid reservoir.
   a. If required, remove fluid until the brake master cylinder reservoir is half full.
2. Remove the wheel and tire.
3. Remove the brake caliper bolts.

➡**Do not allow the caliper to hang from the brake hose or damage to the hose may occur.**

➡**Care must be taken when servicing rear brake components without disconnecting the parking brake cable from the brake caliper lever. Carefully position the caliper aside using a suitable support or damage to the parking brake cable end fittings may occur.**

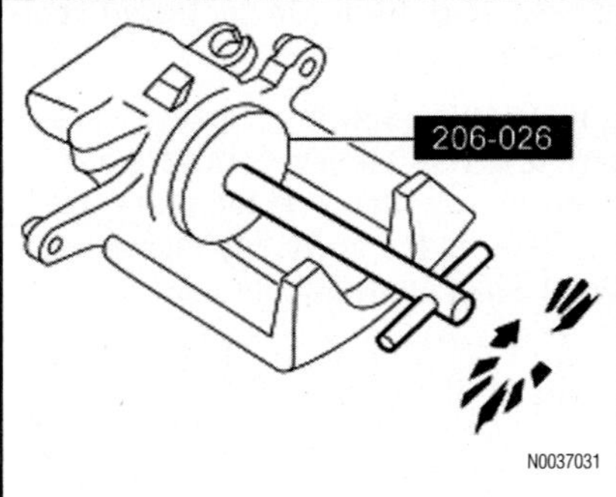

Fig. 6 Using a rear caliper piston adjuster, rotate the caliper piston clockwise to compress the piston into its cylinder.

4. Using hand force and a rocking motion, separate the brake caliper from the anchor plate. Position the brake caliper aside.
   a. Support the caliper with mechanic's wire.

➡**When the brake pads are separated from the brake caliper, new brake pads must be installed to prevent brake noise and shudder. The brake pads are one-time use only.**

5. Remove and discard the 2 brake pads and spring clips from the brake caliper anchor plate.

➡**Do not remove the anchor plate guide pins. The guide pins are press fit to the brake caliper anchor plate. If the guide pins are damaged, a new anchor plate must be installed.**

6. Inspect the brake caliper anchor plate assembly.
   a. Check the guide pins and boots for binding or damage.
   b. Install a new brake caliper anchor plate if it is worn or damaged.

To install:

➡**A moderate to heavy force toward the caliper piston must be applied. If sufficient force is not applied, the internal park brake mechanism clutch cone will not engage and the piston will not compress.**

7. Using the Rear Caliper Piston Adjuster (or equivalent such as OTC tool 7317A), rotate the caliper piston clockwise to compress the piston into its cylinder.

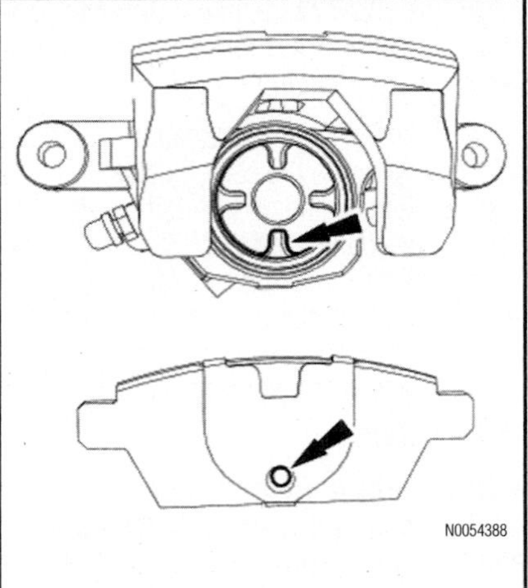

Fig. 7 Position the notch in the caliper piston so that it will correctly align with the pin on the backside of the inboard brake pad.

8. Clean the residual adhesive from the brake caliper fingers and piston using specified brake parts cleaner.
9. Position the notch in the caliper piston so that it will correctly align with the pin on the backside of the inboard brake pad.

➡**Do not allow grease, oil, brake fluid or other contaminants to contact the pad lining material, or damage to components may occur. Do not install contaminated pads.**

10. Install the new spring clips and brake pads to the brake caliper anchor plate.

➡**During installation, make sure brake flexible hose does not become twisted. A twisted brake hose may make contact with other components causing damage to the hose.**

11. Position the brake caliper and install the 2 bolts. Tighten the bolts to 24 ft. lbs. (33 Nm).
12. If necessary, fill the brake fluid reservoir with clean, specified brake fluid.
   a. Apply brakes several times to verify correct brake operation.
13. Install the wheel and tire.

GENERAL INFORMATION

WARNING

These vehicles are equipped with an air bag system. The system must be disarmed before performing service on, or around, system components, the steering column, instrument panel components, wiring and sensors. Failure to follow the safety precautions and the disarming procedure could result in accidental air bag deployment, possible injury and unnecessary system repairs.

SERVICE PRECAUTIONS

Disconnect and isolate the battery negative cable before beginning any airbag system component diagnosis, testing, removal, or installation procedures. Allow system capacitor to discharge for two minutes before beginning any component service. This will disable the airbag system. Failure to disable the airbag system may result in accidental airbag deployment, personal injury, or death.

Do not place an intact undeployed airbag face down on a solid surface. The airbag will propel into the air if accidentally deployed and may result in personal injury or death.

When carrying or handling an undeployed airbag, the trim side (face) of the airbag should be pointing towards the body to minimize possibility of injury if accidental deployment occurs. Failure to do this may result in personal injury or death.

Replace airbag system components with OEM replacement parts. Substitute parts may appear interchangeable, but internal differences may result in inferior occupant protection. Failure to do so may result in occupant personal injury or death.

Wear safety glasses, rubber gloves, and long sleeved clothing when cleaning powder residue from vehicle after an airbag deployment. Powder residue emitted from a deployed airbag can cause skin irritation. Flush affected area with cool water if irritation is experienced. If nasal or throat irritation is experienced, exit the vehicle for fresh air until the irritation ceases. If irritation continues, see a physician.

Do not use a replacement airbag that is not in the original packaging. This may result in improper deployment, personal injury, or death.

The factory installed fasteners, screws and bolts used to fasten airbag components have a special coating and are specifically designed for the airbag system. Do not use substitute fasteners. Use only original equipment fasteners listed in the parts catalog when fastener replacement is required.

During, and following, any child restraint anchor service, due to impact event or vehicle repair, carefully inspect all mounting hardware, tether straps, and anchors for proper installation, operation, or damage. If a child restraint anchor is found damaged in any way, the anchor must be replaced. Failure to do this may result in personal injury or death.

Deployed and non-deployed airbags may or may not have live pyrotechnic material within the airbag inflator.

Do not dispose of driver/passenger/curtain airbags or seat belt tensioners unless you are sure of complete deployment. Refer to the Hazardous Substance Control System for proper disposal.

Dispose of deployed airbags and tensioners consistent with state, provincial, local, and federal regulations.

After any airbag component testing or service, do not connect the battery negative cable. Personal injury or death may result if the system test is not performed first.

If the vehicle is equipped with the Occupant Classification System (OCS), do not connect the battery negative cable before performing the OCS Verification Test using the scan tool and the appropriate diagnostic information. Personal injury or death may result if the system test is not performed properly.

Never replace both the Occupant Restraint Controller (ORC) and the Occupant Classification Module (OCM) at the same time. If both require replacement, replace one, then perform the Airbag System test before replacing the other.

Both the ORC and the OCM store Occupant Classification System (OCS) calibration data, which they transfer to one another when one of them is replaced. If both are replaced at the same time, an irreversible fault will be set in both modules and the OCS may malfunction and cause personal injury or death.

If equipped with OCS, the Seat Weight Sensor is a sensitive, calibrated unit and must be handled carefully. Do not drop or handle roughly. If dropped or damaged, replace with another sensor. Failure to do so may result in occupant injury or death.

If equipped with OCS, the front passenger seat must be handled carefully as well. When removing the seat, be careful when setting on floor not to drop. If dropped, the sensor may be inoperative, could result in occupant injury, or possibly death.

If equipped with OCS, when the passenger front seat is on the floor, no one should sit in the front passenger seat. This uneven force may damage the sensing ability of the seat weight sensors. If sat on and damaged, the sensor may be inoperative, could result in occupant injury, or possibly death.

DISARMING/DEPOWERING THE SYSTEM

➡The air bag warning indicator illuminates when the correct Restraints Control Module (RCM) fuse is removed and the ignition is ON.

CAUTION

Always deplete the backup power supply before repairing or installing any new front or side air bag supplemental restraint system (SRS) component and before servicing, removing, installing, adjusting or striking components near the front or side impact sensors or the restraints control module (RCM). Nearby components include doors, instrument panel, console, door latches, strikers, seats and hood latches. Refer to the Component location section for location of the RCM and impact sensor(s). To deplete the backup power supply energy, disconnect the battery ground cable and wait at least 1 minute. Be sure to disconnect auxiliary batteries and power supplies (if equipped).

CAUTION

When performing service near the SRS/SIR (airbag) system components, all SRS/SIR precautions must be observed. Failure to do so could result in possible airbag deployment, unneeded SIR system repairs, personal injury or death.

CAUTION

The Supplemental Restraint System (SRS) must be fully operational and free of faults before releasing the vehicle to the customer.

1. Turn all vehicle accessories OFF.
2. Turn the ignition OFF.
3. At the Smart Junction Box (SJB), located below the left-hand side of the

instrument panel, remove the cover and the RCM fuse 32 (10A) from the SJB.

4. Turn the ignition ON and visually monitor the air bag warning indicator for at least 30 seconds. The air bag warning indicator will remain lit continuously (no flashing) if the correct RCM fuse has been removed. If the air bag warning indicator does not remain illuminated continuously, remove the correct RCM fuse before proceeding.

5. Turn the ignition OFF.

6. Disconnect the battery ground cable and wait at least one minute.

ARMING/REPOWERING THE SYSTEM

⁂ CAUTION

When performing service near the SRS/SIR (airbag) system components, all SRS/SIR precautions must be observed. Failure to do so could result in possible airbag deployment, unneeded SIR system repairs, personal injury or death.

1. Turn the ignition from OFF to ON.
2. Install RCM fuse 32 (10A) to the SJB and close the cover.
3. Connect the battery ground cable.
4. Prove out the SRS as follows:
    a. Turn the ignition from ON to OFF. Wait 10 seconds, then turn the back to ON and visually monitor the air bag warning indicator with the air bag modules installed. The air bag warning indicator will illuminate continuously for approximately 6 seconds and then turn off. If an SRS fault is present, the air bag warning indicator will:
    - fail to light
    - remain lit continuously
    - flash

    b. The flashing might not occur until approximately 30 seconds after the ignition has been turned from the OFF to the ON position. This is the time required for the RCM to complete the testing of the SRS. If the air bag warning indicator is inoperative and a SRS fault exists, a chime will sound in a pattern of 5 sets of 5 beeps. If this occurs, the air bag warning indicator and any SRS fault discovered must be diagnosed and repaired. Clear all continuous DTCs from the RCM and Occupant Classification System Module (OCSM) using a scan tool.

DRIVE TRAIN

AUTOMATIC TRANSAXLE FLUID

DRAIN AND REFILL

See Figure 8.

All Vehicles

1. With the vehicle in NEUTRAL, position it on a hoist.

➡If an internal problem is suspected, drain the transmission fluid through a paper filter. A small amount of metal or friction particles may be found from normal wear. If an excessive amount of metal or friction material is present, the transaxle will need to be overhauled.

2. Remove the transmission fluid drain plug and allow the transmission fluid to drain. Install the transmission fluid drain plug. Tighten the drain plug to 80 inch lbs. (9 Nm).

Vehicles Without 3.5L Turbo

3. Remove the transmission fluid level indicator. If the transaxle was removed and disassembled, fill the transaxle with 6.5 qt. of clean transmission fluid. If the main control cover was removed for in-vehicle repair, fill the transaxle with 4.5 qt. of clean transmission fluid.

Vehicles With 3.5L Turbo

4. Clean the area around the clamp that connects the Air Cleaner (ACL) to the ACL outlet pipe.

5. If equipped, remove the bolt cover.

➡Do not disconnect the Intake Air Temperature (IAT) sensor electrical connector.

6. Remove the ACL from the ACL bracket and the ACL outlet hose.
    a. Remove the wiring harness retainer from the ACL by pulling It up.
    b. Remove the 2 ACL bolts.
    c. Loosen the clamp.
    d. Pull up on the ACL to remove it from the 2 rubber grommets and position it aside with the IAT sensor electrical connector still connected.

7. With the IAT sensor connected, rotate the ACL 90 degrees to access the transmission fluid level indicator. Install the ACL in the outlet pipe and tighten the clamp. Tighten the clamp to 44 inch lbs. (5 Nm).

8. Remove the transmission fluid level indicator. If the transaxle was removed and disassembled, fill the transaxle with 6.2L (6.5 qt) of clean transmission fluid. If the main control cover was removed for in-vehicle repair, fill the transaxle with 4.3L (4.5 qt) of clean transmission fluid.

1. Wiring harness retainer
2. ACL bolts
3. Clamp
4. ACL

N0111070

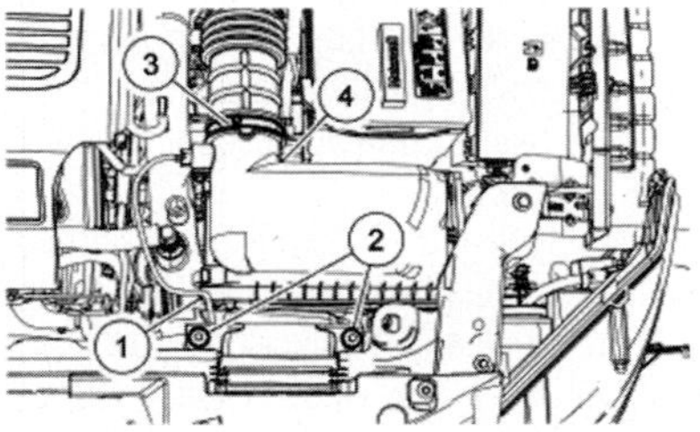

Fig. 8 Removal of the ACL bracket and the ACL outlet hose

All Vehicles

9. Start the engine and let it run for 3 minutes. Move the range selector lever into each gear position and allow engagement for a minimum of ten seconds. Check the transmission fluid level by installing and removing the transmission fluid level indicator. When installing the transmission fluid level indicator, be sure it is seated and rotate it clockwise to the locked position. Adjust the transmission fluid level.
    a. Correct transmission fluid level at normal operating temperature 180°F-200°F (82°C-93°C).
    b. Low transmission fluid level.
    c. High transmission fluid level.

Vehicles With 3.5L Turbo

10. Turn the engine off, loosen the clamp and remove the ACL assembly from the ACL outlet pipe and position it aside with the IAT sensor electrical connector connected.

11. Install the ACL.
    a. Position the ACL assembly in the ACL outlet pipe and push down to install it in the 2 rubber grommets. Tighten the clamp to 44 inch lbs. (5 Nm).
    b. Install the 2 ACL bolts. Tighten the bolts to 44 inch lbs. (5 Nm).
    c. Install the wiring harness retainer on the ACL.

12. If equipped, install the bolt cover.

TRANSFER CASE ASSEMBLY

REMOVAL & INSTALLATION

3.5L Engine, Except Turbo

See Figures 9 and 10.

1. With the vehicle in NEUTRAL, position it on a hoist.
2. Remove the RH halfshaft as outlined in this section.
3. Remove the RH catalytic converter as outlined in the Engine Mechanical Section.

➡To maintain the initial driveshaft balance, index-mark the driveshaft flange and the output flange.

4. Remove the 4 driveshaft-to-output flange bolts, then disconnect the driveshaft from the output flange. Position the driveshaft aside.
5. Remove the 5 Power Transfer Unit (PTU) support bracket bolts and the support bracket.
6. Position the engine roll restrictor aside.
   a. Remove the 2 engine roll restrictor-to-transaxle bolts.
   b. Loosen the rear engine roll restrictor bolt and pivot the roll restrictor downward.

➡Position a drain pan under the vehicle.

7. Remove the 5 PTU bolts. Pull the PTU outward and separate it from the transaxle. Rotate the output flange upward, then turn it and remove the PTU from the vehicle.
8. Using a small screwdriver remove and discard the compression seal.

To install:

➡A new compression seal must be installed whenever the Power Transfer Unit (PTU) is removed from the vehicle.

9. Using a suitable tool, install the new compression seal.
10. Position the PTU and install the 5 PTU bolts. Tighten the bolts to 66 ft. lbs. (90 Nm).
11. Position the PTU support bracket and install the 3 PTU support bracket-to-engine bolts. Tighten the bolts to 35 ft. lbs. (48 Nm).

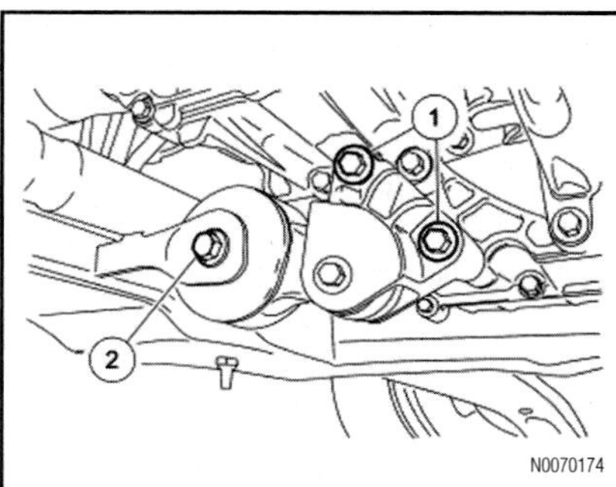

Fig. 9 Engine roll restrictor-to-transaxle bolts

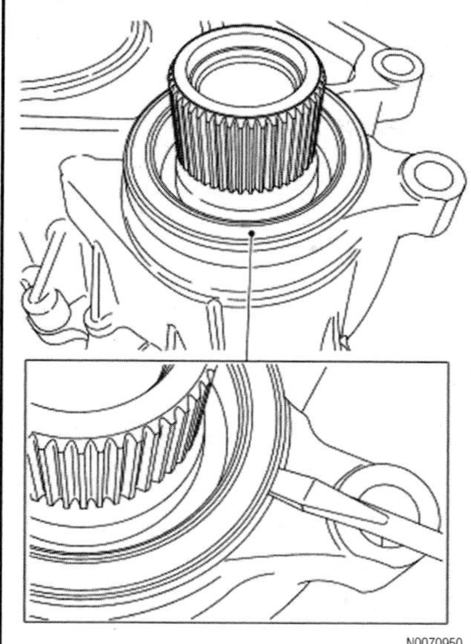

Fig. 10 Remove and discard the compression seal

12. Install the 2 PTU support bracket-to-transaxle bolts. Tighten the bolts to 35 ft. lbs. (48 Nm).
13. Position the engine roll restrictor to the transaxle and install the 2 bolts. Tighten the engine roll restrictor-to-transaxle bolts to 76 ft. lbs. (103 Nm), and tighten the rear engine roll restrictor bolt to 66 ft. lbs. (90 Nm).

➡Line up the index marks made during removal.

14. Install the 4 driveshaft-to-output flange bolts. Tighten the bolts to 52 ft. lbs. (70 Nm).
15. Install the RH catalytic converter as outlined in the Engine Mechanical Section.
16. Install the RH front halfshaft as outlined in this section.
17. Inspect the transmission fluid level and add clean, specified fluid as necessary.

3.5L Turbo Engine

See Figures 11 through 15.

1. With the vehicle in NEUTRAL, position it on a hoist.

➡Use a steering wheel holding device (such as Hunter® 28-75-1 or equivalent).

2. Using a suitable holding device, hold the steering wheel in the straight-ahead position.
3. Remove the 4 retainers and the underbody shield.

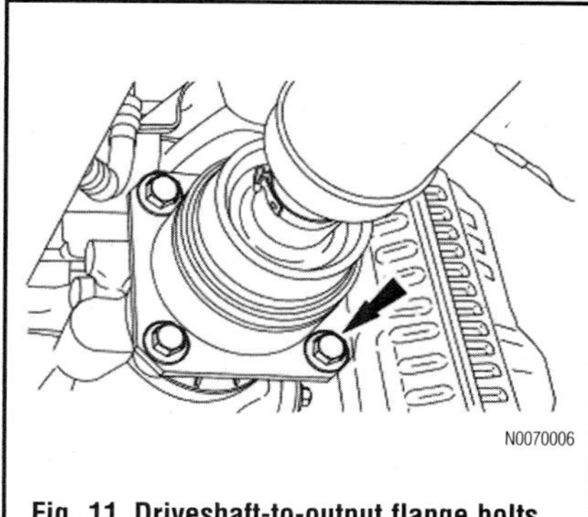

Fig. 11 Driveshaft-to-output flange bolts removal

4. Remove the RH halfshaft as outlined in this section.
5. Remove the RH catalytic converter as outlined in the Engine Mechanical Section.

➡To maintain the initial driveshaft balance, index-mark the driveshaft flange and the output flange.

6. Remove the 4 driveshaft-to-output flange bolts, then disconnect the driveshaft from the output flange. Position the driveshaft aside.

➡Do not allow the intermediate shaft to rotate while it is disconnected from the gear or damage to the clockspring may occur. If there is evidence that the intermediate shaft has rotated, the clockspring must be removed and recentered. Refer to the Chassis Electrical Section.

7. Remove the steering shaft bolt and disconnect the steering column shaft from the steering gear. Discard the bolt.
8. Remove the bolt and disconnect the 2 Electronic Power Assist Steering (EPAS) electrical connectors and the wiring retainer.

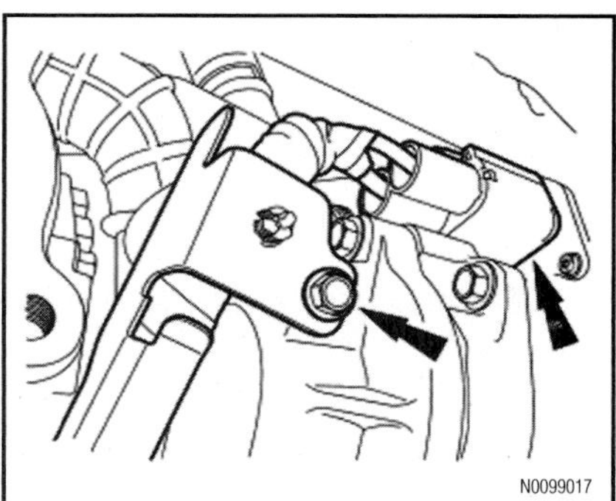

Fig. 12 Remove the bolt and disconnect the 2 Electronic Power Assist Steering (EPAS) electrical connectors and the wiring retainer

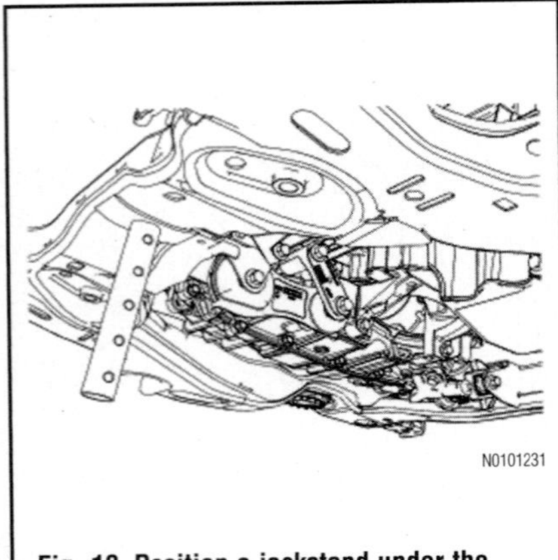

Fig. 13 Position a jackstand under the rear of the subframe

9. Remove the 3 bolts and the RH turbocharger lower bracket.
10. Remove the 3 bolts and the Power Transfer Unit (PTU) support bracket.
11. Position the rear engine roll restrictor aside in the following sequence.
   a. Remove the 2 engine roll restrictor-to-transaxle bolts.
   b. Loosen the engine roll restrictor-to-frame bolt and pivot the roll restrictor downward.
12. Remove the front engine roll restrictor bolt and position the engine roll restrictor aside.
13. Position a jackstand under the rear of the subframe.

➡**RH shown, LH similar.**

14. Remove the subframe bracket-to-body bolts.
15. Remove the subframe rear bolts and the subframe brackets. Discard the bolts.
16. Position a jackstand under the front roll restrictor bracket and raise the engine far enough to allow the PTU to be removed.

➡**Position a drain pan under the vehicle.**

17. Remove the 5 PTU bolts. Pull the PTU outward to separate it from the transaxle. Rotate the output flange upward, then turn it and remove the PTU from the vehicle.
18. Using a small screwdriver, remove and discard the compression seal.

To install:

➡**A new compression seal must be installed whenever the Power Transfer Unit (PTU) is removed from the vehicle.**

19. Using a suitable tool, install the new compression seal.

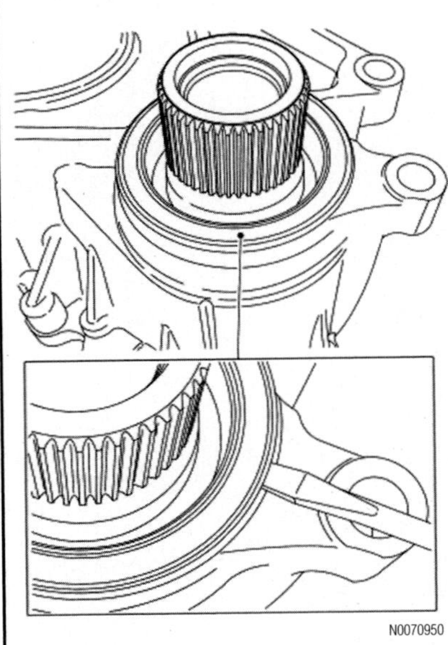

Fig. 14 Remove and discard the compression seal

20. Position the PTU and install the 5 bolts. Tighten the bolts to 66 ft. lbs. (90 Nm).
21. Lower the engine and remove the jackstand from the front of the roll restrictor.
22. Using the jackstand, raise the subframe into the installed position.
23. Position the subframe brackets and loosely install the 4 bolts.
24. Install the 2 subframe rear bolts. Tighten the bolts to 111 ft. lbs. (150 Nm).
25. Tighten the 4 subframe bracket-to-body bolts to 41 ft. lbs. (55 Nm).
26. Remove the jackstand from the subframe.
27. Position the front engine roll restrictor to the bracket and install the bolt. Tighten the bolt to 66 ft. lbs. (90 Nm).
28. Position the rear engine roll restrictor to the transaxle and install the 3 bolts. Tighten the engine roll restrictor-to-transaxle bolts to 76 ft. lbs. (103 Nm), and the rear engine roll restrictor bolt to 66 ft. lbs. (90 Nm).
29. Position the PTU support bracket in place and install the 3 bolts. Tighten the bolts to 35 ft. lbs. (48 Nm).
30. Install the RH turbocharger lower bracket and the 3 bolts.
31. Connect the 2 Electronic Power Assist Steering (EPAS) electrical connectors (1 shown) and attach the wiring retainer (not shown) and install the bolt Tighten the bolt to 80 inch lbs. (9 Nm).

➡**Do not allow the intermediate shaft to rotate while it is disconnected from**

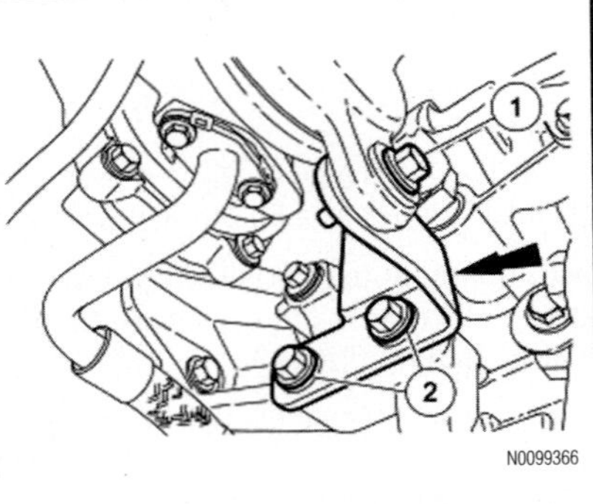

Fig. 15 Turbocharger lower bracket installation. Tighten the bolt (1) to 168 inch lbs. (19 Nm), and tighten the bolts (2) to 35 ft. lbs. (48 Nm)

the gear or damage to the clockspring may occur. If there is evidence that the intermediate shaft has rotated, the clockspring must be removed and recentered. Refer to the Chassis Electrical Section.

32. Install the steering intermediate shaft onto the steering gear and install a new bolt. Tighten the bolt to 15 ft. lbs. (20 Nm).

➡**Align the index marks made during removal.**

33. Install the 4 driveshaft-to-output flange bolts. Tighten the bolts to 52 ft. lbs. (70 Nm).
34. Install the RH catalytic converter as outlined in the Engine Mechanical Section.
35. Install the RH front halfshaft as outlined in this section.
36. Install the underbody shield and the 4 retainers.
37. Remove the locking device from the steering wheel.
38. Inspect the transmission fluid level and add clean, specified fluid as necessary.

DRAIN & REFILL

See Figure 16.

➡**A new Power Transfer Unit (PTU) must be installed any time the PTU has been submerged in water.**

➡**The Power Transfer Unit (PTU) is not to be drained unless contamination is suspected. To drain the PTU fluid, the PTU must be removed from the vehicle. The fluid that is drained may appear black and have a pungent odor. Do not mistake this for contaminated fluid.**

➡**Fill level checks are done in-vehicle only. Let the vehicle sit 10 minutes after the road test before checking the fluid level.**

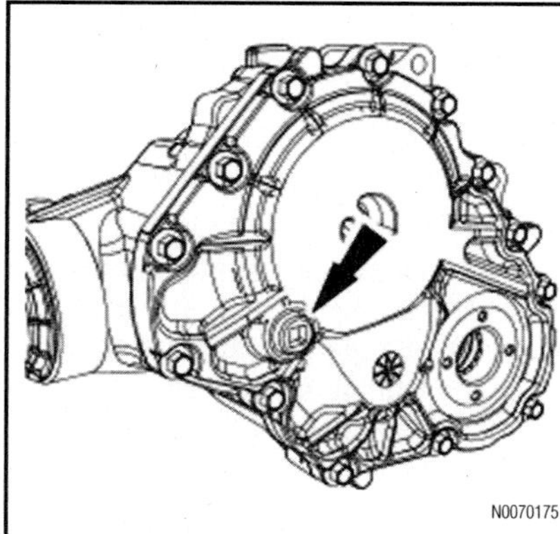

Fig. 16 Power transfer unit (PTU) fluid filler plug

1. With the vehicle in NEUTRAL, position it on a hoist.
2. Clean the area around the filler plug before removing.
3. Remove and discard the filler plug.
4. With the vehicle on a flat, level surface, fill the PTU with lubricant. The fluid must be even with the bottom of the fill opening. Fluid capacity is 18 oz.
5. Install a new filler plug. Tighten the plug to 15 ft. lbs. (20 Nm).

FRONT DRIVESHAFT

REMOVAL & INSTALLATION

See Figure 17.

➡All driveshaft assemblies are balanced. If undercoating the vehicle, protect the driveshaft to prevent overspray of any undercoating material.

1. The driveshaft assembly consists of the following:
   a. Rubber-isolated center support bearing
   b. CV joints at each end of the shaft
   c. U-joint at the center support
   d. Assembly balanced with traditional balance weights
   e. Lubed-for-life joints requiring no periodic lubrication
   f. Unique bolt and washer assembly for the rear CV joint
2. The driveshaft transfers torque from the Power Transfer Unit (PTU) to the rear axle. It is attached to the PTU flange with a CV joint. The 2-piece shaft is connected by a staked U-joint located rearward of the driveshaft center bearing and attached to the Rear Drive Unit (RDU) at the active torque coupling. The driveshaft joints allow the smooth continuous rotation of the driveshaft through the allowable angle planes and length variations required in normal vehicle operation. The driveshaft is always turning at front wheel speed. The driveshaft is not serviceable. A new driveshaft must be installed if worn or damaged.

➡Index-mark both driveshaft flanges.

3. With the vehicle in NEUTRAL, position it on a hoist.
4. Remove the muffler and tailpipe.
5. Remove the 4 exhaust support brace bolts and the exhaust brace.

➡Do not reuse the bolt and washer assemblies for the rear Constant Velocity (CV) joint flange. Install new assemblies or damage to the vehicle may occur.

6. Remove and discard the 3 Rear Drive Unit (RDU) pinion flange bolt and washer assemblies.
7. Separate the driveshaft CV flange from the RDU flange using a flat-blade screwdriver.

➡Do not reuse the Constant Velocity (CV) joint bolts. Install new bolts or damage to the vehicle may occur.

8. Remove and discard the 4 Power Transfer Unit (PTU) flange bolts.
9. Using a suitable prybar, separate the driveshaft flange from the PTU flange.
10. With the help of an assistant, remove the 2 outer center bearing bracket bolts and the driveshaft.
11. If necessary, remove the 2 inner center bearing bolts and remove the bracket.

➡If a driveshaft is installed and driveshaft vibration is encountered after installation, index the driveshaft. Refer to the General Information in this section.

To install:

➡If a driveshaft is installed and driveshaft vibration is encountered after installation, index the driveshaft. Refer to the General Information in this section.

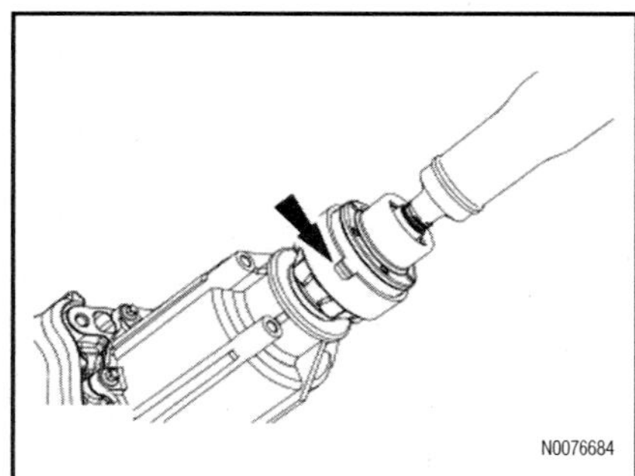

Fig. 17 Separate the driveshaft CV flange from the RDU flange using a flat-blade screwdriver in the area

12. If necessary, install the 2 inner center bearing bolts and install the bracket. Tighten the bolts to 15 ft. lbs. (20 Nm).
13. With the help of an assistant, install the 2 outer center bearing bracket bolts and the driveshaft. Tighten the bolts to 22 ft. lbs. (30 Nm).
14. Install the driveshaft flange to the PTU flange.
15. Install 4 New Power Transfer Unit (PTU) flange bolts. Tighten the bolts to 52 ft. lbs. (70 Nm).

➡Do not reuse the Constant Velocity (CV) joint bolts. Install new bolts or damage to the vehicle may occur.

16. Install the driveshaft CV flange to the RDU flange using a flat-blade screwdriver.
17. Install 3 New Rear Drive Unit (RDU) pinion flange bolt and washer assemblies. Tighten the bolt to 18 ft. lbs. (25 Nm).

➡Do not reuse the bolt and washer assemblies for the rear Constant Velocity (CV) joint flange. Install new assemblies or damage to the vehicle may occur.

18. Install 4 new exhaust support brace bolts and the exhaust brace. Tighten the bolts to 22 ft. lbs. (30 Nm).
19. Install the muffler and tailpipe.
20. With the vehicle in NEUTRAL, lower it from the hoist.
21. The driveshaft transfers torque from the Power Transfer Unit (PTU) to the rear axle. It is attached to the PTU flange with a CV joint. The 2-piece shaft is connected by a staked U-joint located rearward of the driveshaft center bearing and attached to the Rear Drive Unit (RDU) at the active torque coupling. The driveshaft joints allow the smooth continuous rotation of the driveshaft through the allowable angle planes and length variations required in normal vehicle operation. The driveshaft is always turning at front wheel speed. The driveshaft is not serviceable. A new driveshaft must be installed if worn or damaged.

➡Index-mark both driveshaft flanges.

22. The driveshaft assembly consists of the following:
   a. Rubber-isolated center support bearing
   b. CV joints at each end of the shaft
   c. U-joint at the center support
   d. Assembly balanced with traditional balance weights

e. Lubed-for-life joints requiring no periodic lubrication

f. Unique bolt and washer assembly for the rear CV joint

➡**All driveshaft assemblies are balanced. If undercoating the vehicle, protect the driveshaft to prevent overspray of any undercoating material.**

FRONT HALFSHAFT

REMOVAL & INSTALLATION

Left-Hand

See Figures 18 and 19.

1. With the vehicle in NEUTRAL, position it on a hoist.
2. Remove the wheel and tire.

➡**Apply the brake to keep the halfshaft from rotating.**

3. Remove the wheel hub nut.
    a. Do not discard at this time.

➡**Use care when releasing the lower arm and knuckle into the resting position or damage to the ball joint seal or Constant Velocity (CV) boot may occur.**

➡**Use the hex-holding feature to prevent the stud from turning while removing the nut.**

4. Remove and discard the lower ball joint nut.
    a. Separate the ball joint from the wheel knuckle.
5. Using the Front Wheel Hub Remover, separate the halfshaft from the wheel hub.
6. Pull the wheel knuckle outboard and rotate it toward the rear of the vehicle.

➡**The sharp edges on the stub shaft splines can slice or puncture the oil seal. Use care when inserting the stub shaft into the transmission or damage to the component may occur.**

7. Using the Slide Hammer and Halfshaft Remover, remove the halfshaft from the transmission.
8. Remove and discard the circlip from the stub shaft.
9. Inspect the halfshaft hub for wear or damage and install a new halfshaft, if necessary.
    a. Inspect the differential seal surface.
    b. Inspect the halfshaft bushing surface. If this surface is damaged, inspect the halfshaft bushing for damage.
    c. Inspect the differential side gear splines.

To install:

➡**The circlips are unique in size and shape for each shaft. Make sure to use the specified circlip for the application or vehicle damage may occur.**

10. Install the correct new circlip on the inboard stub shaft.

➡**After insertion, pull the halfshaft inner end to make sure the circlip is locked.**

11. Push the stub shaft into the transmission so the circlip locks into the differential side gear.
12. Rotate the wheel knuckle into position and insert the halfshaft into the wheel hub.
13. Position the lower ball joint into the wheel knuckle and install the new nut. Tighten the nut to 148 ft. lbs. (200 Nm).

➡**Do not tighten the wheel hub nut with the vehicle on the ground. The nut must be tightened to specification before the vehicle is lowered onto the wheels. Wheel bearing damage will occur if the wheel bearing is loaded with the weight of the vehicle applied.**

➡**Apply the brake to keep the halfshaft from rotating.**

14. Using the previously removed wheel hub nut, seat the halfshaft. Tighten the nut to 258 ft. lbs. (350 Nm).
    a. Remove and discard the wheel hub nut.

➡**The wheel hub nut contains a one-time locking chemical that is activated by the heat created when it is tightened. Install and tighten the new wheel hub nut to specification within 5 minutes of starting it on the threads. Always install a new wheel hub nut**

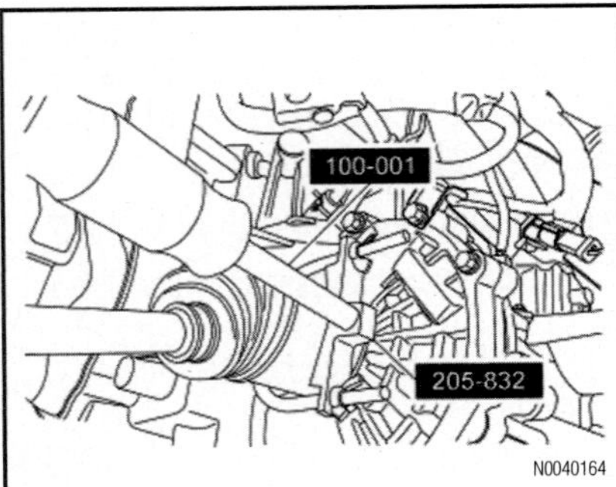

Fig. 18 Halfshaft from transmission removal

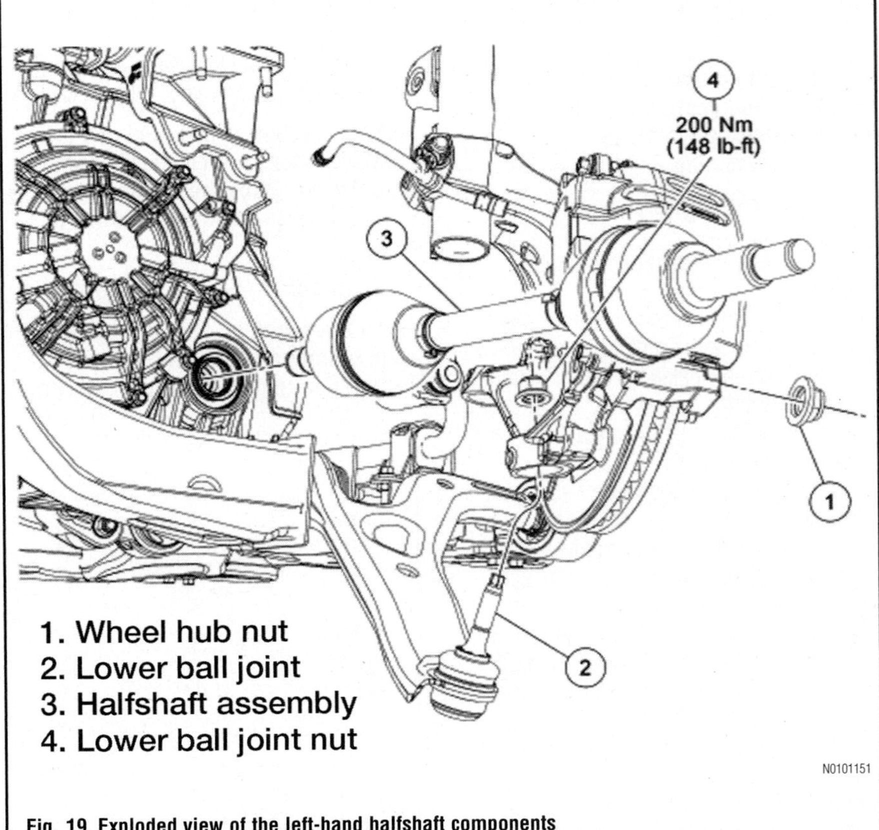

Fig. 19 Exploded view of the left-hand halfshaft components

after loosening or when not tightened within the specified time or damage to the components can occur.

➡Apply the brake to keep the halfshaft from rotating.

15. Install a new wheel hub nut. Tighten the nut to 258 ft. lbs. (350 Nm).
16. Install the front wheel and tire.

Right-Hand

See Figures 20 through 24.

All Vehicles

1. With the vehicle in NEUTRAL, position it on a hoist.
2. Remove the wheel and tire.

➡Apply the brake to keep the halfshaft from rotating.

3. Remove the wheel hub nut.
   a. Do not discard at this time.

All-Wheel Drive (AWD) Vehicles

4. Remove the front RH brake disc.

All Vehicles

5. Remove the bolt from the brake hose bracket.

➡Suspension fasteners are critical parts because they affect performance of vital components and systems and their failure may result in major service expense. New parts must be installed with the same part number or equivalent part, if replacement is necessary. Do not use a replacement part of lesser quality or substitute design. Torque values must be used as specified during reassembly to make sure of correct retention of these parts.

➡Use care when releasing the lower arm and knuckle into the resting position or damage to the ball joint seal or Constant Velocity (CV) boot may occur.

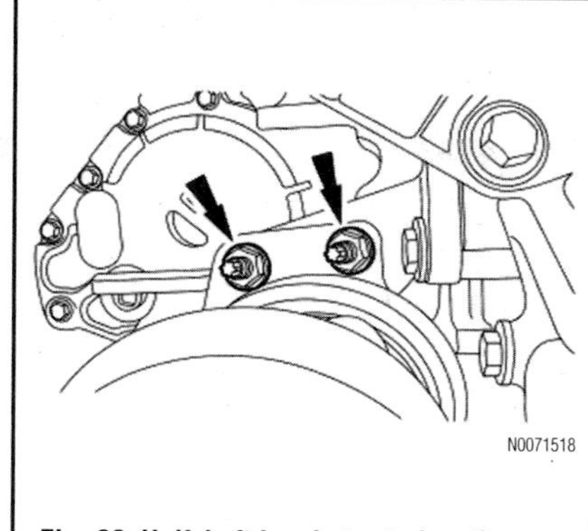

Fig. 22 Halfshaft bracket nuts location

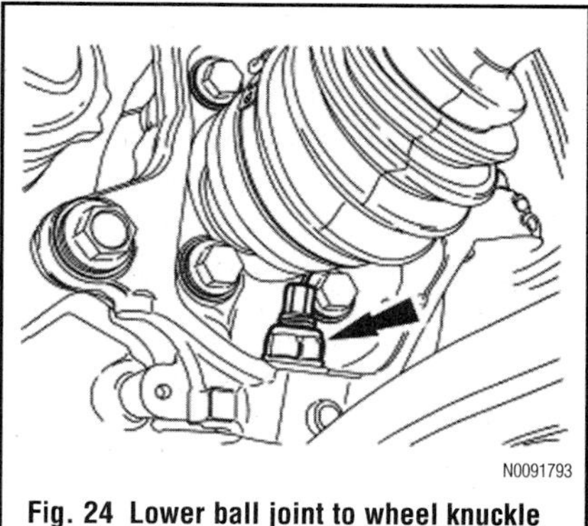

Fig. 24 Lower ball joint to wheel knuckle nut location

➡Use the hex-holding feature to prevent the stud from turning while removing the nut.

6. Remove and discard the lower ball joint nut.
   a. Separate the lower ball joint from the wheel knuckle.
7. Using the Front Wheel Hub Remover, separate the halfshaft from the wheel hub.
8. Pull the wheel knuckle outboard and rotate it toward the rear of the vehicle.
   a. Secure the wheel knuckle assembly.

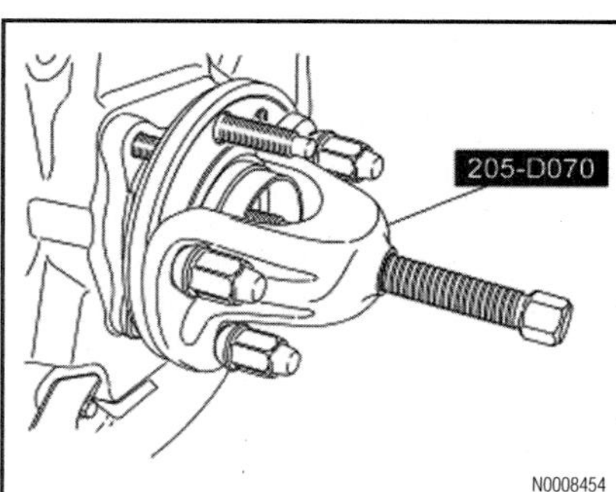

Fig. 20 Use the front wheel hub remover to separate the halfshaft from the wheel hub

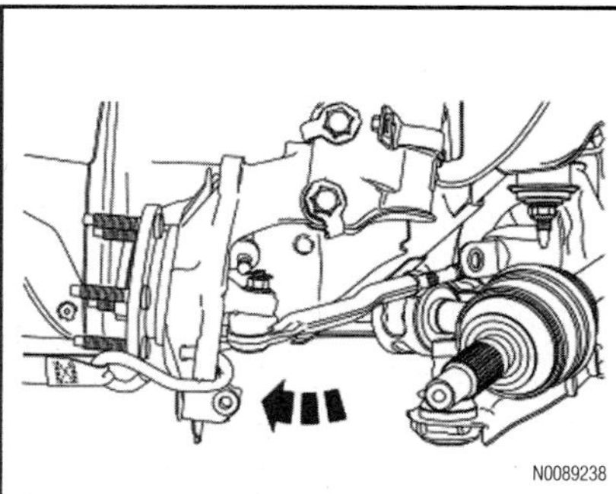

Fig. 21 Pull the wheel knuckle outboard and rotate it toward the rear of the vehicle

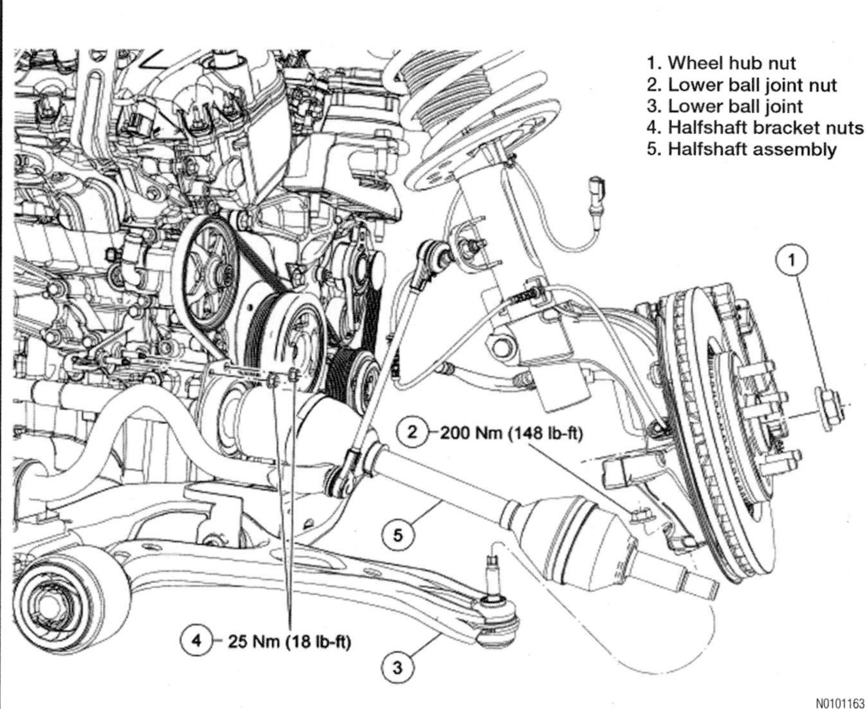

Fig. 23 Exploded view of the right-hand halfshaft components

9. Remove the 2 lower scrivets from the rubber shield and position the shield aside.

Without 3.5L Turbo

10. Remove the 2 halfshaft bracket nuts.
11. Remove the intermediate and halfshaft assembly.
    a. Inspect the intermediate shaft for pitting or damage in the seal contact area. Replace if necessary.
12. Inspect the halfshaft hub for wear or damage and install a new halfshaft, if necessary.
    a. Inspect the differential seal surface.
    b. Inspect the halfshaft bushing surface. If this surface is damaged, inspect the halfshaft bushing for damage.
    c. Inspect the differential side gear splines.

With 3.5L Turbo

13. Separate the halfshaft from the intermediate shaft and remove the halfshaft.

To install:

AWD vehicles

➡A new Power Transfer Unit (PTU) shaft seal must be installed whenever the intermediate shaft is removed or damage to the components can occur.

14. Install a new intermediate shaft seal and deflector as outlined in Transfer Case in this section.

With 3.5L Turbo

15. Install the halfshaft to the intermediate shaft.

Without 3.5L Turbo

16. Install the intermediate and halfshaft assembly and the 2 halfshaft bracket nuts. Tighten the nuts to 18 ft. lbs. (25 Nm).

All Vehicles

17. Rotate the wheel knuckle into position and insert the halfshaft into the wheel hub.
18. Position the lower ball joint into the wheel knuckle and install the new nut. Tighten the nut to 148 ft. lbs. (200 Nm).
19. Position the brake hose bracket and install the bolt. Tighten the bolt to 22 ft. lbs. (30 Nm).
20. Install the 2 scrivets in the rubber shield.

AWD Vehicles

21. Install the RH brake disc. For additional information, refer to Front Disc Brake.

All Vehicles

➡Do not tighten the front wheel hub nut with the vehicle on the ground. The nut must be tightened to specification before the vehicle is lowered onto the wheels. Wheel bearing damage will occur if the wheel bearing is loaded with the weight of the vehicle applied.

➡Apply the brake to keep the halfshaft from rotating.

22. Using the previously removed wheel hub nut, seat the halfshaft. Tighten the nut to 258 ft. lbs. (350 Nm).
    a. Remove and discard the wheel hub nut.

➡The wheel hub nut contains a one-time locking chemical that is activated by the heat created when it is tightened. Install and tighten the new wheel hub nut to specification within 5 minutes of starting it on the threads. Always install a new wheel hub nut after loosening or when not tightened within the specified time or damage to the components can occur.

➡Apply the brake to keep the halfshaft from rotating.

23. Install a new wheel hub nut. Tighten the nut to 258 ft. lbs. (350 Nm).
24. Install the wheel and tire.

Intermediate Shaft—3.5L Turbo

See Figure 25.

➡The intermediate shaft seal in the Power Transfer Unit (PTU) must be replaced whenever the intermediate shaft is removed or a leak may occur.

1. Remove the right halfshaft assembly.
2. Remove the 2 intermediate shaft support bracket bolts and the intermediate shaft.
3. Remove and discard the circlip from the outboard end of the intermediate shaft.

To install:

4. Install a new 1.181 in. (30 mm) circlip on the outboard end of the intermediate shaft.
5. Install a new intermediate shaft seal in the Power Transfer Unit (PTU) as outlined in this section.
6. Position the intermediate shaft in the PTU and engage the intermediate shaft splines with the PTU gears.

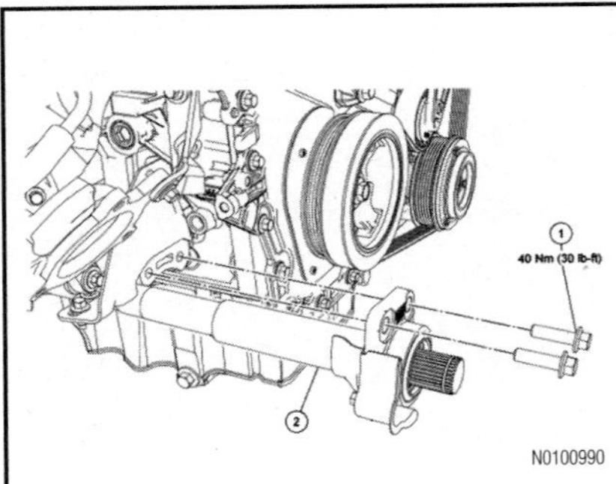

Fig. 25 Exploded view of the intermediate shaft components

7. Install the 2 intermediate shaft support bracket bolts. Tighten the bolts to 30 ft. lbs. (40 Nm).
8. Install the right halfshaft as outlined in this section.

REAR AXLE ASSEMBLY

REMOVAL & INSTALLATION

See Figures 26 and 27.

1. Remove the driveshaft assembly as outlined in this section.
2. Remove the rear halfshafts as outlined in this section.
3. Remove the stabilizer bar as outlined in the Suspension Section.
4. Position a suitable transmission hydraulic jack to the axle housing.
    a. Securely strap the jack to the housing.
5. Remove the 4 differential housing-to-front insulator bracket bolts.
6. Remove the 6 side insulator bracket-to-rear axle differential bolts.
7. Lower the axle to gain clearance to the Active Torque Coupling (ATC) electrical connector and disconnect the connector.
8. Remove the axle assembly.

To install:

➡If replacing the axle assembly, the 4X4 control module will need to be reconfigured with the new Active Torque Coupling (ATC) bar code information. If the new bar code information does not match the existing 4X4 control module information, driveline damage or drivability concerns can occur.

➡The ATC bar code can be found etched on the ATC wire harness connector of the new axle assembly.

➡Record the bar code identification number from the new axle assemblies wire harness connector.

9. Position the axle housing on a suitable transmission hydraulic jack.
    a. Securely strap the jack to the housing.
10. Raise the axle and connect the ATC electrical connector.
11. Install the 6 side insulator bracket-to-rear axle differential bolts. Tighten the bolts to 66 ft. lbs. (90 Nm).
12. Install the 4 differential housing-to-front insulator bracket bolts. Tighten the bolts to 66 ft. lbs. (90 Nm).
13. Install the stabilizer bar as outlined in the Suspension Section.

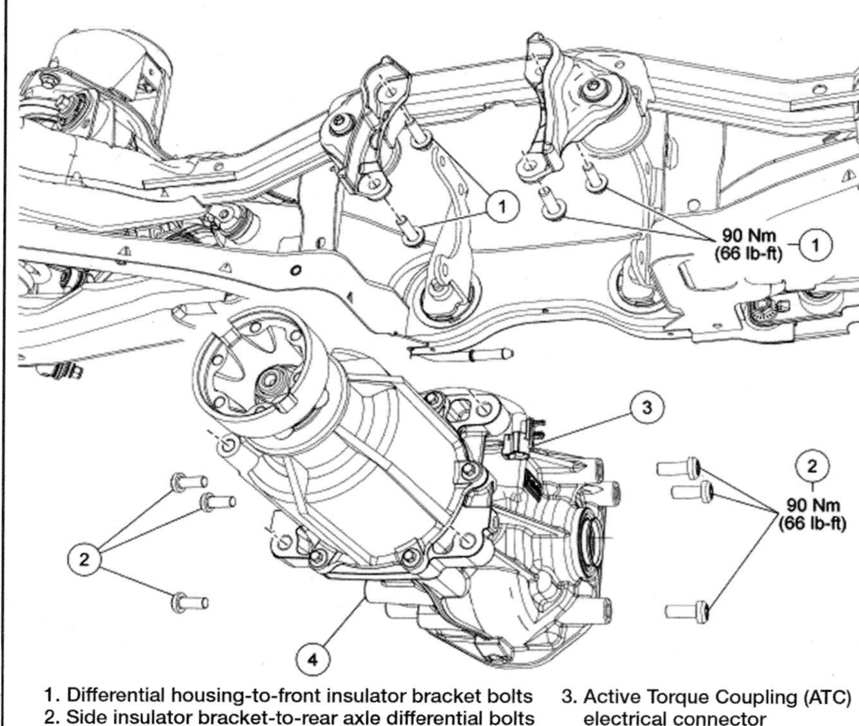

Fig. 26 Exploded view of the axle assembly

14. Install the rear halfshafts as outlined in this section.
15. Install the driveshaft assembly as outlined in this section.
16. Using the scan tool, program the 4-digit bar code information retrieved from the new axle assembly harness connector into the 4X4 control module using the ATC Bar Code Entry service function.
17. The scan tool will verify that the numbers entered are valid and display a message if the information is not correct.

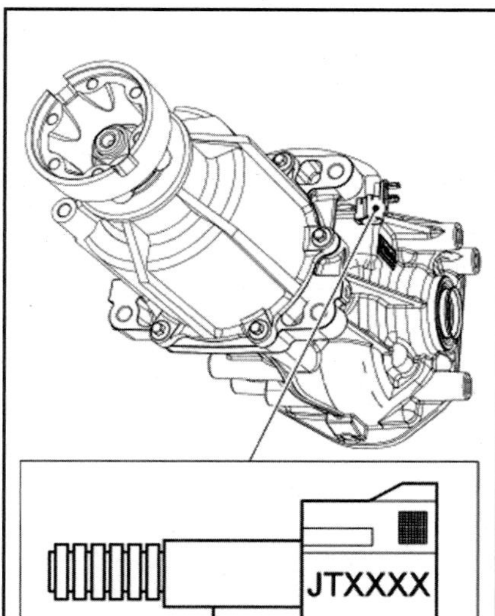

Fig. 27 Axle assemblies wire harness connector location

REAR DIFFERENTIAL HOUSING COVER

REMOVAL & INSTALLATION

1. With the vehicle in NEUTRAL, position it on a hoist.
2. If equipped, remove the exhaust insulator located near the differential housing cover using soapy water.

➡Drain the differential fluid into a suitable drain pan.

3. Remove the 10 bolts and the rear differential housing cover.
   a. Drain the differential fluid from the housing.

To install:

➡Make sure the machined surfaces on the rear axle housing and the differential housing cover are clean and free of oil before installing the new silicone sealant. The inside of the rear axle must be covered when cleaning the machined surface to prevent contamination.

4. Clean the gasket mating surfaces of the differential housing and the differential housing cover.

➡The differential housing cover must be installed within 15 minutes of application of the silicone, or new silicone must be applied. If possible, allow one hour before filling with lubricant to make sure the silicone has correctly cured.

5. Apply a new continuous bead of clear silicone rubber as shown in the illustration.
6. Install the differential housing cover and the 10 bolts. Tighten the bolts to 17 ft. lbs. (23 Nm).
7. Remove the filler plug and fill the rear axle with 2.43 pt. of rear axle lubricant, 0.118-0.196 inches below the bottom of the filler hole.
   a. Install the filler plug and tighten to 21 ft. lbs. (29 Nm).
8. If equipped, install the exhaust insulator located near the differential housing cover.

REAR HALFSHAFT

REMOVAL & INSTALLATION

See Figures 28 through 30.

➡Suspension fasteners are critical parts because they affect performance of vital components and systems and their failure may result in major service expense. New parts must be installed with the same part numbers or equivalent part, if replacement is necessary. Do not use a replacement part of lesser quality or substitute design. Torque values must be used as specified during reassembly to make sure of correct retention of these parts.

1. Measure the distance from the center of the wheel hub to the lip of the fender with the vehicle in a level, static ground position (curb height).
2. Remove the wheel and tire.
3. Remove the wheel hub nut.
   a. Do not discard at this time.

➡Do not allow the caliper to hang from the brake hose or damage to the hose can occur.

4. Remove and discard the 2 brake caliper anchor plate bolts and position the

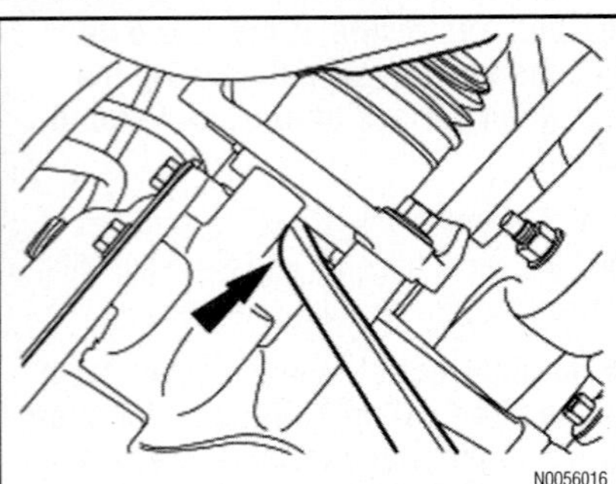

Fig. 28 Halfshaft inner CV joint from the differential removal

brake caliper and anchor plate assembly aside.

a. Support the brake caliper and anchor plate assembly using mechanic's wire.

➡Use the hex-holding feature to prevent the stabilizer bar link stud from turning while removing or installing the nut.

5. Remove and discard the stabilizer bar link upper nut and disconnect the link.

6. Remove and discard the toe link-to-wheel knuckle nut and disconnect the link.

7. Remove the wheel speed sensor bolt.

a. Disconnect the wheel speed sensor harness retainers and position the sensor and harness aside.

8. Position a screw-type jackstand under the lower arm.

9. Remove and discard the upper arm-to-wheel knuckle nut and bolt and disconnect the knuckle from the upper arm.

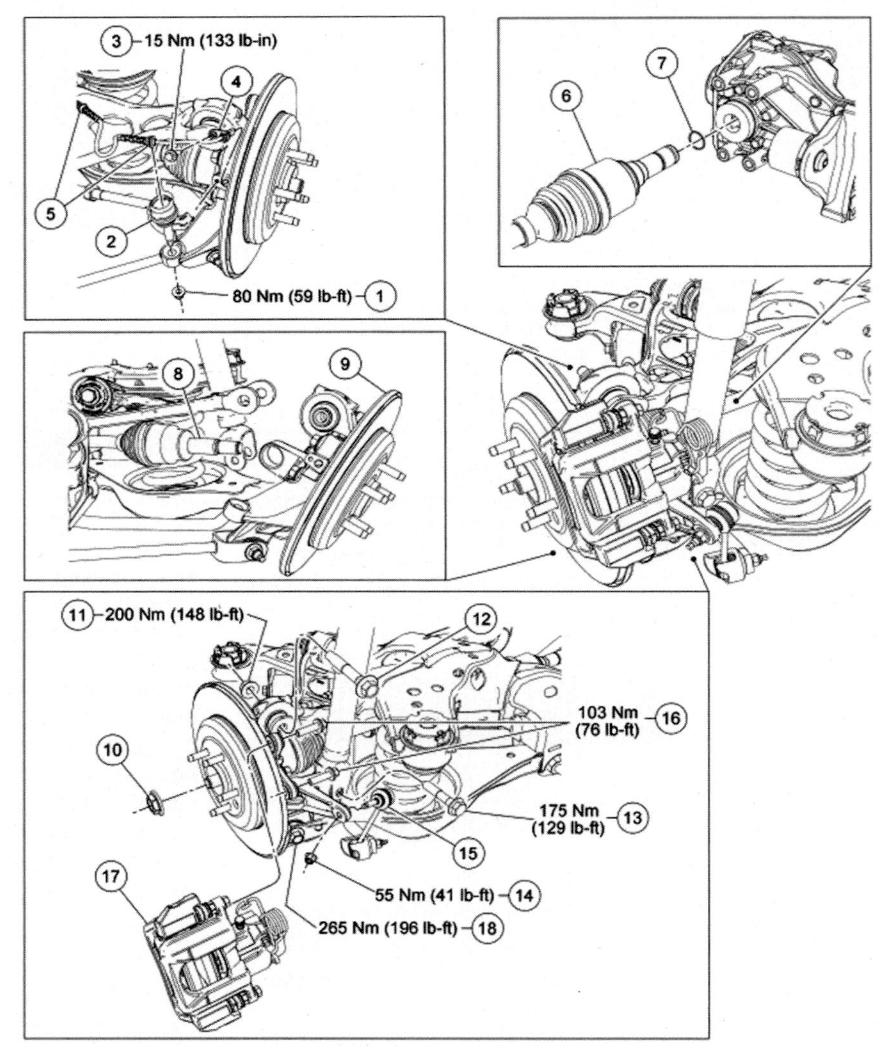

1. Toe link-to-wheel knuckle nut
2. Toe link
3. Wheel speed sensor bolt
4. Wheel speed sensor
5. Wheel speed sensor harness retainers (part of 2C190) (2 required)
6. Halfshaft inner CV joint
7. Circlip
8. Halfshaft outer CV joint
9. Wheel knuckle
10. Wheel hub nut
11. Upper arm-to-wheel knuckle nut
12. Upper arm-to-wheel knuckle bolt
13. Shock absorber lower bolt
14. Stabilizer bar link upper nut
15. Stabilizer bar link
16. Brake caliper anchor plate bolts (2 required)
17. Brake caliper anchor plate and caliper assembly
18. Lower arm-to-wheel knuckle bolt

N0097875

Fig. 29 Exploded view of the rear halfshaft

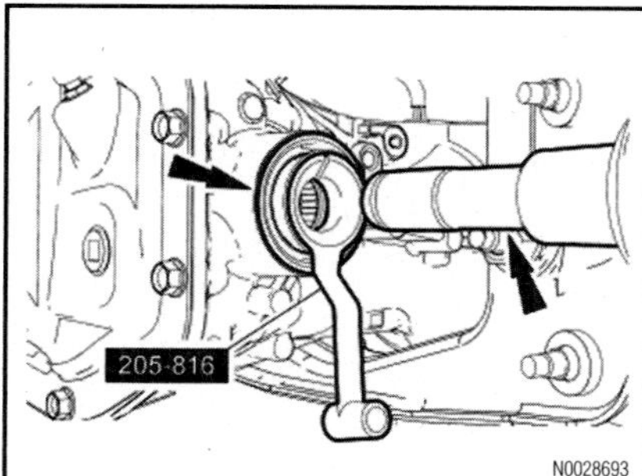

Fig. 30 Using the axle seal protector, install the halfshaft inner CV joint into the differential

10. Remove and discard the shock absorber lower bolt and disconnect the shock absorber from the knuckle bracket.
11. Loosen, but do not remove the lower arm-to-wheel knuckle bolt.
12. Using the Front Hub Remover, separate the halfshaft outer CV joint from the hub bearing.
13. Swing the wheel knuckle outward and remove the halfshaft outer CV joint from the hub bearing.

➡Do not damage the oil seal when removing the axle halfshaft from the differential.

14. Using a suitable pry bar, remove the halfshaft inner CV joint from the differential.
    a. Remove the halfshaft from the vehicle.
15. Remove and discard the circlip from the halfshaft.

To Install:

➡Before tightening suspension bushing fasteners, use a jackstand to raise the rear suspension until the distance between the center of the hub and the lip of the fender is equal to the measurement taken in the removal procedure (curb height).

➡The circlips are unique in size and shape for each shaft. Make sure to use the specified circlip for the application or vehicle damage may occur.

16. Install a new circlip on the halfshaft.
17. Using the Axle Seal Protector, install the halfshaft inner CV joint into the differential.
    a. Make sure the circlip locks in the side gear.
18. Swing the wheel knuckle inward and install the halfshaft outer CV joint through the hub bearing.
19. Position the wheel knuckle to the upper arm and loosely install a new nut and bolt.
20. Position the shock absorber and loosely install a new bolt.
21. Position the wheel speed sensor harness in the retainers and install the sensor and bolt. Tighten the bolt to 133 inch lbs. (15 Nm).
22. Position the toe link and loosely install a new toe link-to-wheel knuckle nut.
23. Position a suitable jackstand under the lower control arm at the shock and spring assembly attachment point and raise the rear suspension until the distance between the center of the hub and the lip of the fender is equal to the measurement taken in Step 1 of the procedure (curb height).

➡A slotted upper arm allows for the rear suspension camber to be adjusted by pushing inward or pulling outward on the wheel knuckle while tightening the upper arm-to-wheel knuckle nut.

24. With the wheel knuckle pushed inward for maximum negative camber, tighten the upper arm-to-wheel knuckle nut to 148 ft. lbs. (200 Nm).
25. Tighten the lower arm-to-wheel knuckle bolt to 196 ft. lbs. (265 Nm).
26. Tighten the shock absorber lower bolt to 129 ft. lbs. (175 Nm).
27. Tighten the toe link-to-wheel knuckle nut to 59 ft. lbs. (80 Nm).

➡Use the hex-holding feature to prevent the stabilizer bar link stud from turning while removing or installing the nut.

28. Connect the stabilizer bar link and install a new stabilizer bar link upper nut. Tighten the nut to 41 ft. lbs. (55 Nm).
29. Position the brake caliper and anchor plate assembly and install the 2 bolts. Tighten the bolts to 76 ft. lbs. (103 Nm).

➡Do not tighten the wheel hub nut with the vehicle on the ground. The nut must be tightened to specification before the vehicle is lowered onto the wheels. Wheel bearing damage will occur if the wheel bearing is loaded with the weight of the vehicle applied.

➡Apply the brake to keep the halfshaft from rotating.

30. Use the previously removed hub nut to seat the halfshaft. Tighten the nut to 258 ft. lbs. (350 Nm).
    a. Remove and discard the hub nut.

➡The wheel hub nut contains a one-time locking chemical that is activated by the heat created when it is tightened. Install and tighten the new wheel hub nut to specification within 5 minutes of starting it on the threads. Always install a new wheel hub nut after loosening or when not tightened within the specified time or damage to the components can occur.

➡Apply the brake to keep the halfshaft from rotating.

31. Install a new hub nut. Tighten the nut to 258 ft. lbs. (350 Nm).
32. Install the wheel and tire.
33. Check and if necessary, adjust the rear toe.

REAR PINION SEAL

REMOVAL & INSTALLATION

See Figure 31.

1. Remove the driveshaft as outlined in this section.
2. Using the Drive Pinion Flange Holding Fixture, hold the pinion flange and remove the nut.
    a. Discard the nut.
3. Index-mark the location of the pinion to the yoke.
4. Using the 2 Jaw Puller, remove the pinion flange.
5. Using the Torque Converter Fluid Seal Remover and Slide Hammer, remove the seal.

To install:

➡Make sure that the mating surface is clean before installing the new seal.

6. Using the Pinion Seal Replacer, install the seal.

➡Lubricate the pinion flange with grease.

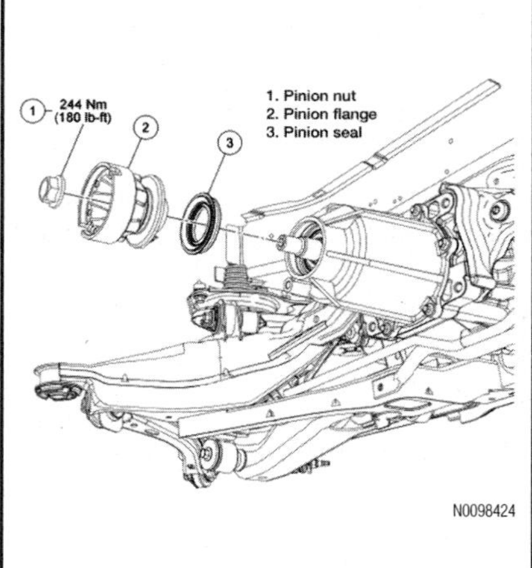

Fig. 31 Exploded view of the rear pinion seal

7. Line up the index marks and position the pinion flange.
8. Using the Drive Pinion Flange Holding Fixture, install the new pinion nut. Tighten the nut to 180 ft. lbs. (244 Nm).
9. Install the driveshaft as outlined in this section.

REAR STUB SHAFT SEAL

REMOVAL & INSTALLATION

See Figures 32 and 33.

➡The Rear Drive Unit (RDU) does not have stub shaft pilot bearings. It has stub shaft seals only.

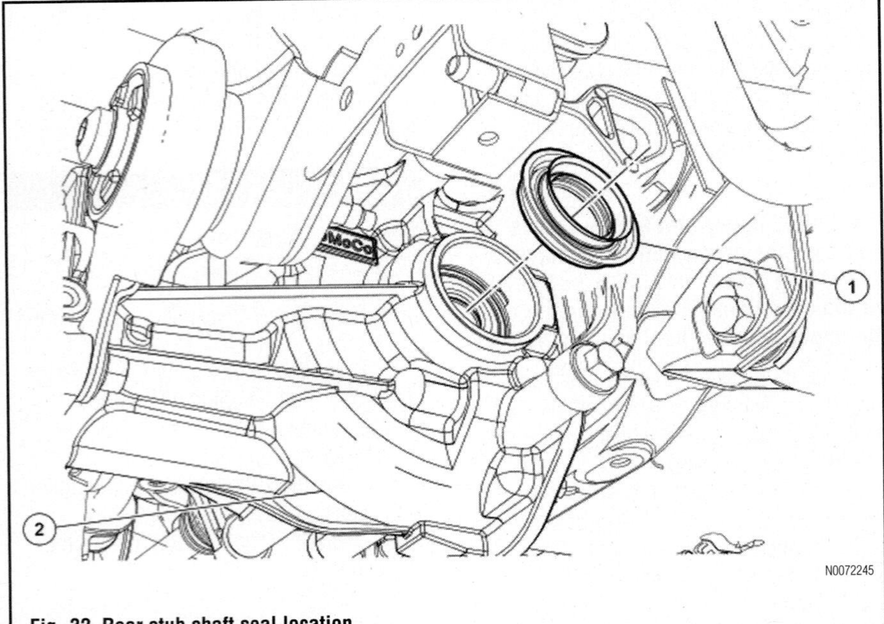

Fig. 32 Rear stub shaft seal location

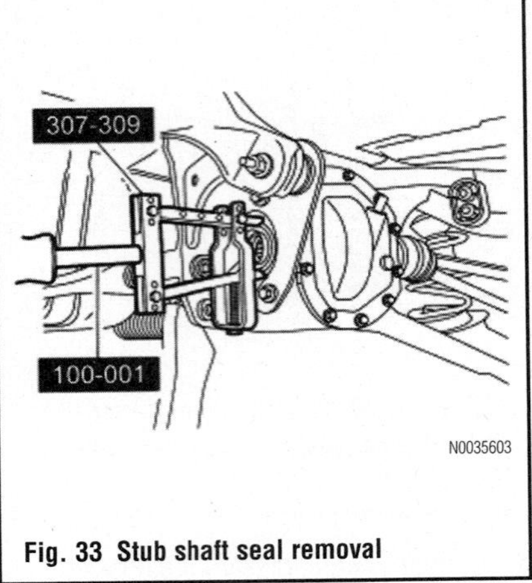

Fig. 33 Stub shaft seal removal

1. Remove the halfshaft assembly as outlined in this section.
2. Using the Torque Converter Fluid Seal Remover and Slide Hammer, remove the stub shaft seal.

To install:

➡Lubricate the new stub shaft seal with grease.

3. Using the Front Axle Oil Seal Installer and Handle, install the stub shaft pilot bearing housing seal.
4. Install the halfshaft assembly as outlined in this section.

ENGINE COOLING

COOLANT PUMP

REMOVAL & INSTALLATION

See Figures 34 through 49.

➡During engine repair procedures, cleanliness is extremely important. Any foreign material, including any material created while cleaning gasket surfaces, which enters the oil passages, coolant passages or the oil pan may cause engine failure.

➡On early build engines, the timing chain rides on the inner side of the RH timing chain guide. Late build engines are equipped with a different design RH timing chain guide that requires the timing chain to ride on the outer side of the RH timing chain guide. For service, all replacement RH timing chain guides will be the late build design.

All Vehicles

1. With the vehicle in NEUTRAL, position it on a hoist.
2. Drain the cooling system as outlined in this section.
3. Remove the engine front cover.
4. Remove and discard the engine oil filter.

Engines Equipped With Early Build RH Timing Chain Guides

5. Rotate the crankshaft clockwise and align the timing marks on the Variable Camshaft Timing (VCT) assemblies.

Engines Equipped With Late Build/Replacement RH Timing Chain Guides

6. Rotate the crankshaft clockwise and

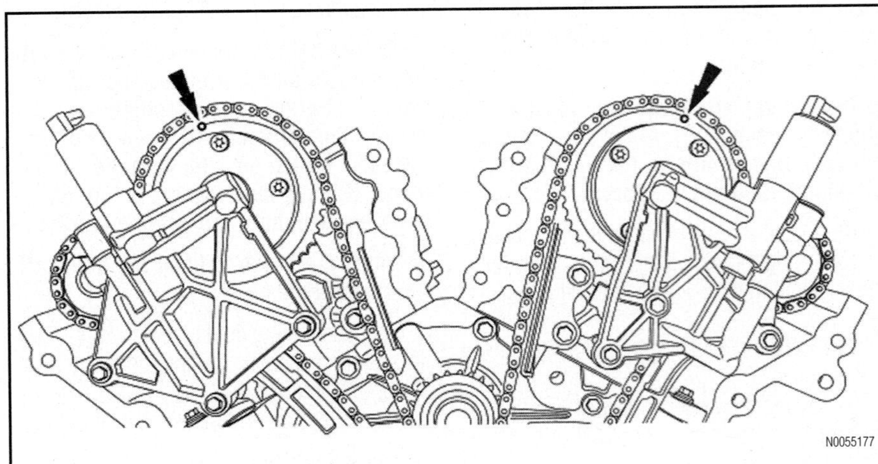

Fig. 34 Rotate the crankshaft clockwise and align the timing marks on the Variable Camshaft Timing (VCT) assemblies

Fig. 35 Rotate the crankshaft clockwise and align the timing marks on the Variable Camshaft Timing (VCT) assemblies

align the timing marks on the VCT assemblies.

All Vehicles

➡The Camshaft Holding Tool will hold the camshafts in the Top Dead Center (TDC) position.

7. Install the Camshaft Holding Tool onto the flats of the LH camshafts.

➡The Camshaft Holding Tool will hold the camshafts in the TDC position.

8. Install the Camshaft Holding Tool onto the flats of the RH camshafts.
9. Remove the 3 bolts and the RH VCT housing.
10. Remove the 3 bolts and the LH VCT housing.
11. Remove the 2 bolts and the primary timing chain tensioner.
12. Remove the primary timing chain tensioner arm.
13. Remove the 2 bolts and the lower LH primary timing chain guide.
14. Remove the primary timing chain.

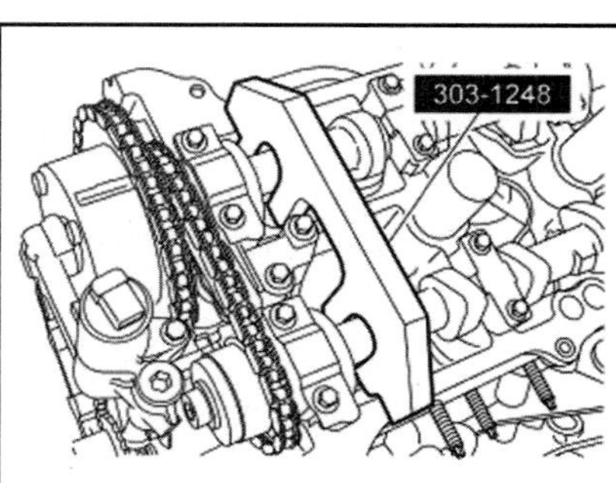

Fig. 36 Install the camshaft holding tool onto the flats of the LH camshafts, RH similar

15. Remove the 2 bolts and the upper LH primary timing chain guide.

Engines Equipped With Early Build RH Timing Chain Guides

16. Remove the RH primary timing chain guide lower bolt.

➡The RH primary timing chain guide must be repositioned to allow the coolant pump to be removed.

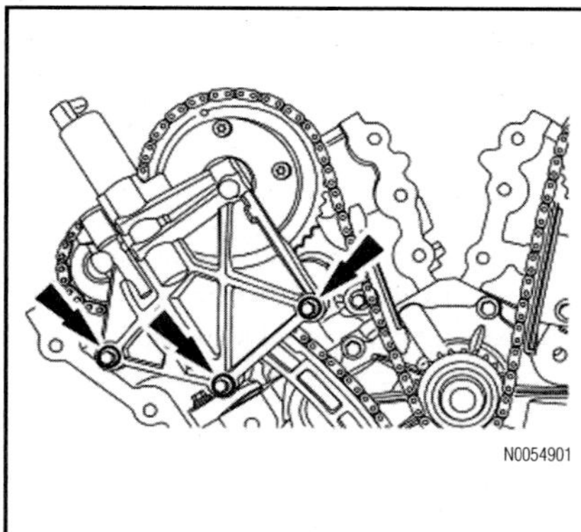
Fig. 37 RH VCT housing bolts, LH similar

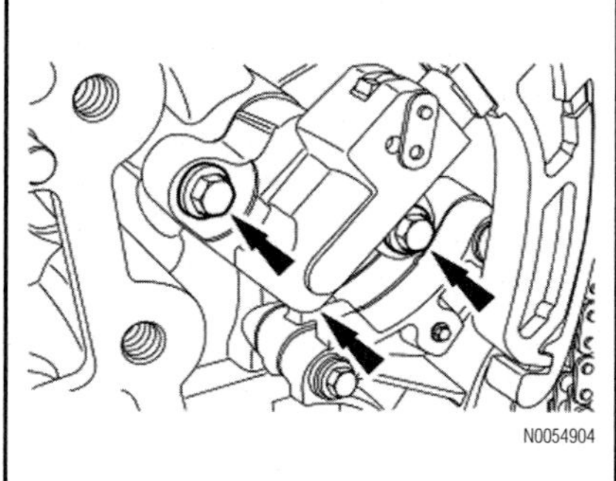
Fig. 38 Primary timing chain tensioner bolt location

17. Loosen the RH primary timing chain guide upper bolt.
    a. Rotate the guide and tighten the bolt.

Engines Equipped With Late Build/Replacement RH Timing Chain Guides

18. Remove the RH primary timing chain guide lower bolt.

➡The RH primary timing chain guide must be repositioned to allow the coolant pump to be removed.

19. Loosen the RH primary timing chain guide upper bolt.
    a. Rotate the guide and tighten the bolt.

All Vehicles

20. Place clean lint-free shop towels in the oil pan opening to prevent coolant from entering the oil pan during coolant pump removal.
21. Remove the 8 bolts and the coolant pump.

To install:

All Vehicles

➡Clean and inspect all sealing surfaces.

22. Install the coolant pump and the 8 bolts. Tighten the bolts to 89 inch lbs. (10 Nm).
23. Remove all of the shop towels from the oil pan opening.

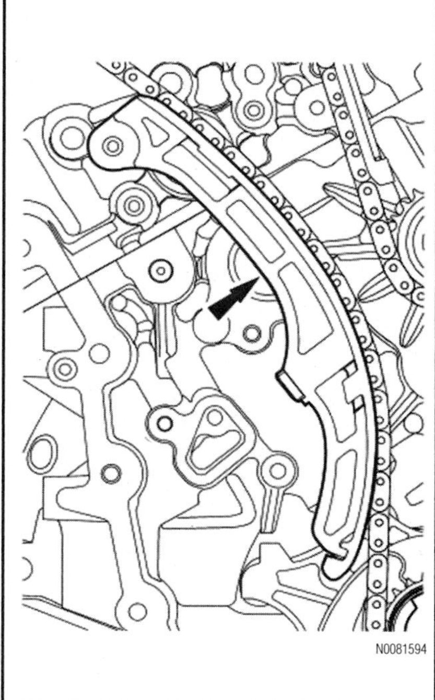
Fig. 39 Primary timing chain tensioner arm

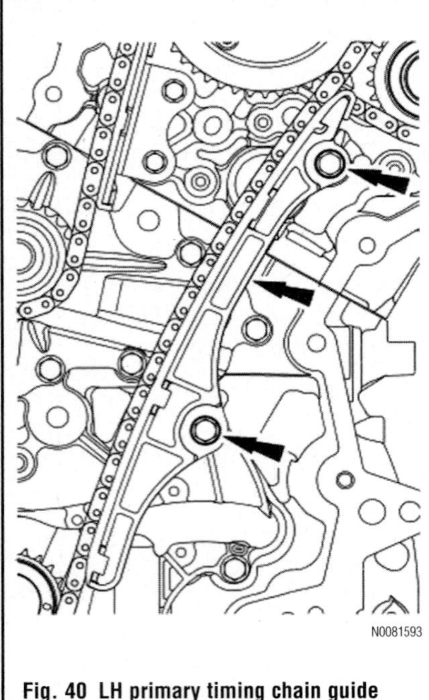

Fig. 40 LH primary timing chain guide

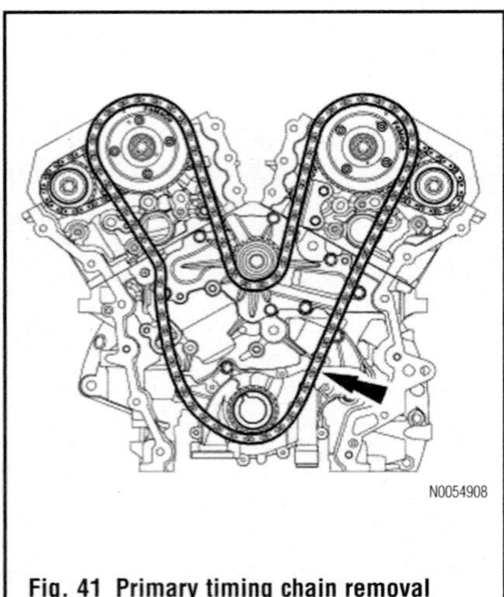

Fig. 41 Primary timing chain removal

➡Any coolant that has accumulated in the oil pan must be drained from the pan and any residual coolant cleaned from the front of the engine and oil pan. Failure to remove all traces of the coolant can result in oil contamination and severe engine damage.

24. Remove the oil pan drain plug and allow any accumulated coolant to drain.
   a. Remove any residual coolant from the front of the engine and the oil pan using regulated, compressed air and clean, lint-free shop towels.
   b. Install the oil pan drain plug. Tighten the drain plug to 20 ft. lbs. (27 Nm).

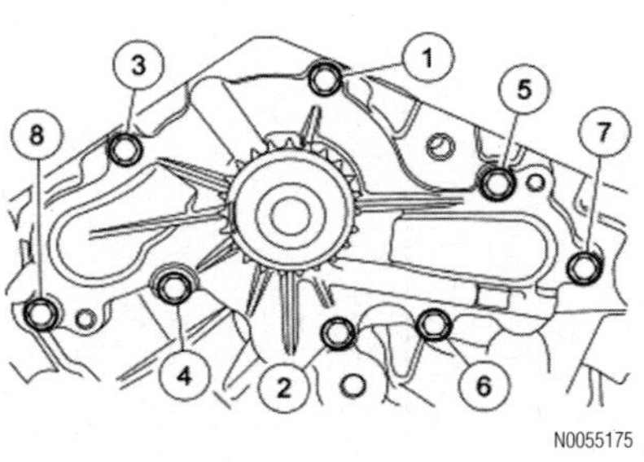

Fig. 42 Coolant pump removal & installation. Tighten the bolts in the proper sequence

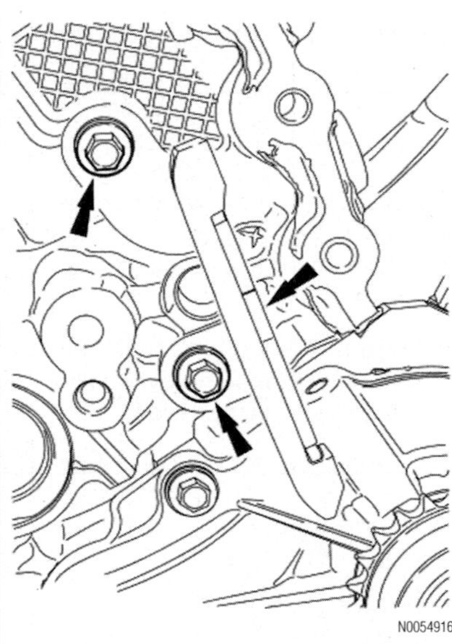

Fig. 43 RH primary timing chain guide upper and lower bolt locations. LH primary timing chain guide upper similar.

Engines Equipped With Late Build/Replacement RH Timing Chain Guides

25. Loosen the RH primary timing chain guide upper bolt.
   a. Position the RH primary timing chain guide and install the lower bolt. Tighten the bolts to 89 inch lbs. (10 Nm).

Engines Equipped With Early Build RH Timing Chain Guides

26. Loosen the RH primary timing chain guide upper bolt.
   a. Position the RH primary timing chain guide and install the lower bolt. Tighten the bolts to 89 inch lbs. (10 Nm).

All Vehicles

27. Install the primary timing chain with the colored links aligned with the timing marks on the VCT assemblies and the crankshaft sprocket.

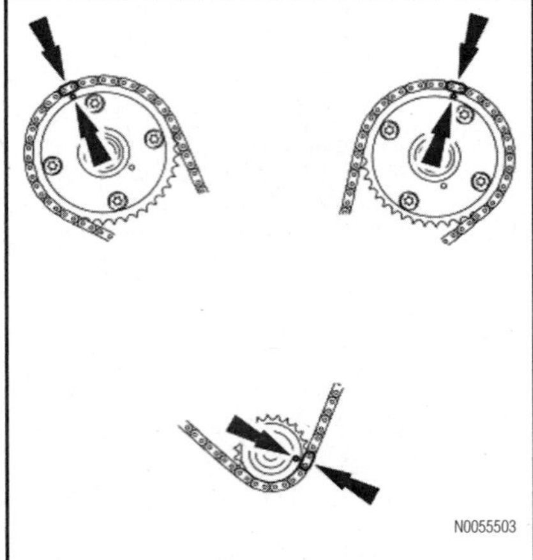

Fig. 44 Install the primary timing chain with the colored links aligned with the timing marks on the VCT assemblies and the crankshaft sprocket

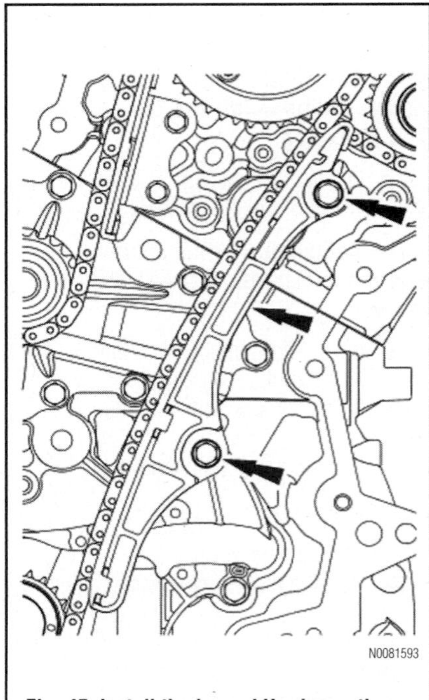

Fig. 45 Install the lower LH primary timing chain guide

28. Install the upper LH primary timing chain guide and the 2 bolts. Tighten the bolts to 89 inch lbs. (10 Nm).
29. Install the lower LH primary timing chain guide and the 2 bolts. Tighten the bolts to 89 inch lbs. (10 Nm).
30. Install the primary timing chain tensioner arm.
31. Reset the primary timing chain tensioner.
   a. Rotate the lever counterclockwise.

Fig. 46 Reset the primary timing chain tensioner arm

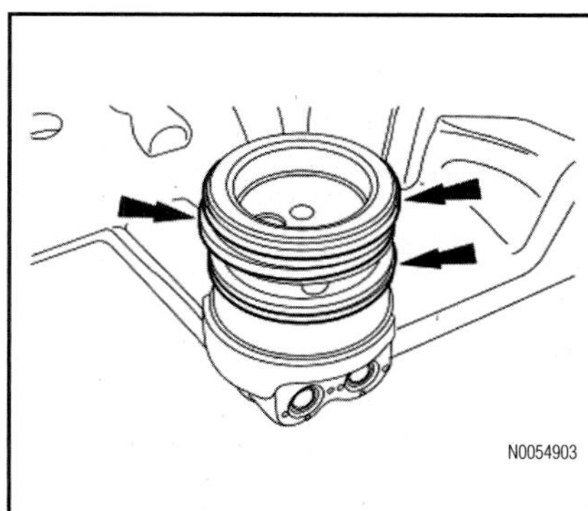

Fig. 47 Inspect the VCT housing seals for damage

b. Using a soft-jawed vise, compress the plunger.

c. Align the hole in the lever with the hole in the tensioner housing.

d. Install a suitable lockpin.

➡It may be necessary to rotate the crankshaft slightly to remove slack from the timing chain and install the tensioner.

32. Install the primary tensioner and the 2 bolts. Tighten the bolts to 89 inch lbs. (10 Nm).

a. Remove the lockpin.

33. As a post check, verify correct alignment of all timing marks.

34. Inspect the VCT housing seals for damage and replace if necessary.

➡Make sure the dowels on the VCT housing are fully engaged in the cylinder head prior to tightening the bolts.

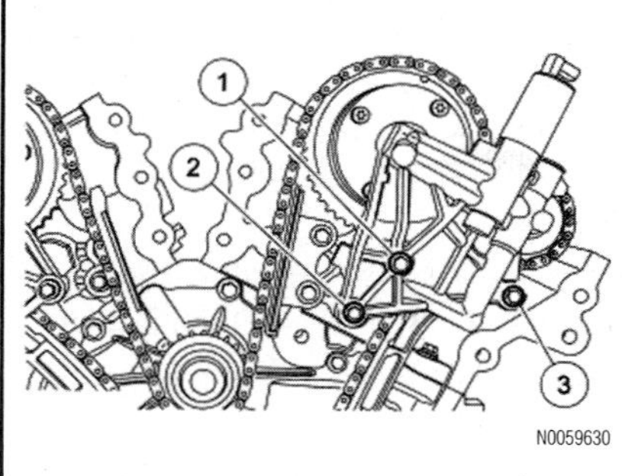

Fig. 48 Install the LH VCT housing and tighten the bolts in sequence shown

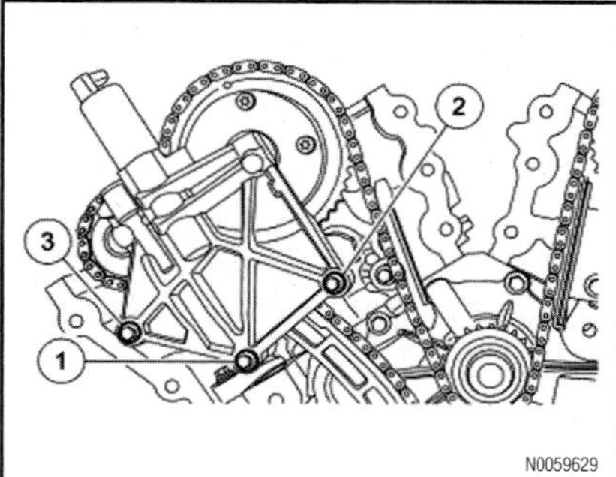

Fig. 49 Install the RH VCT housing and tighten the bolts in sequence shown

35. Install the LH VCT housing and the 3 bolts. Tighten the bolts to 89 inch lbs. (10 Nm).

➡Make sure the dowels on the VCT housing are fully engaged in the cylinder head prior to tightening the bolts.

36. Install the RH VCT housing and the 3 bolts. Tighten the bolts to 89 inch lbs. (10 Nm).

➡Lubricate the engine oil filter gasket with clean engine oil prior to installing the oil filter.

37. Install a new engine oil filter. Tighten the engine oil filter to 44 inch lbs. (5 Nm), and then rotate an additional 180°.

38. Install the engine front cover.

39. Fill and bleed the cooling system as outlined in this section.

ENGINE COOLANT

DRAINING PROCEDURE

See Figure 50.

⁂ CAUTION

Always allow the engine to cool before opening the cooling system. Do not unscrew the coolant pressure relief cap when the engine is operating or the cooling system is hot. The cooling system is under pressure; steam and hot liquid can come out forcefully when the cap is loosened slightly. Failure to follow these instructions may result in serious personal injury.

➡The coolant must be recovered in a suitable, clean container for reuse. If the coolant is contaminated, it must be recycled or disposed of correctly. Using contaminated coolant may result in damage to the engine or cooling system components.

➡The engine cooling system is filled with Motorcraft® Specialty Green Engine Coolant. Mixing coolant types degrades the corrosion protection of Motorcraft® Specialty Green Engine Coolant.

➡Genuine Mazda® Extended Life Coolant and Motorcraft® Specialty Green Engine Coolant are very sensitive to light. Do NOT allow these products to be exposed to ANY LIGHT for more than a day or two. Extended light exposure causes these products to degrade.

➡Stop-leak style pellets/products must not be used as an additive in this engine cooling system. The addition of stop-leak style pellets/products may clog or damage the cooling system, resulting in degraded cooling system performance and/or failure.

➡Less than 80% of coolant capacity can be recovered with the engine in the vehicle. Dirty, rusty or contaminated

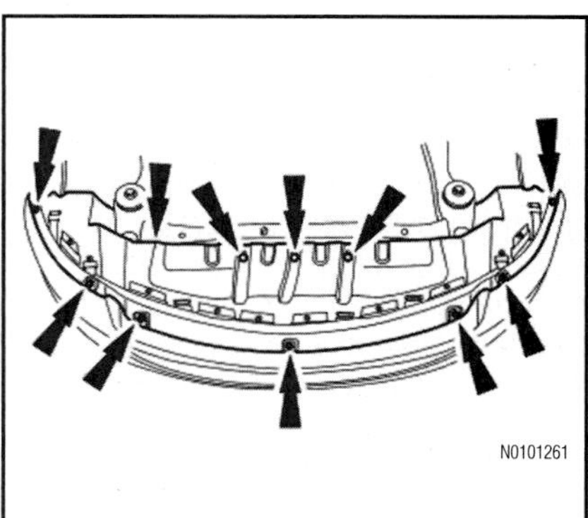

Fig. 50 Front splash shield bolt location

1. With the vehicle in NEUTRAL, position it on a hoist.

coolant requires replacement. Release the pressure in the cooling system by slowly turning the pressure relief cap one half to one turn counterclockwise to the first stop on the filler neck. When the pressure has been released, remove the pressure relief cap.

2. Remove the 7 bolts, 3 pin-type retainers and the front splash shield.
3. Place a suitable container below the radiator draincock. Open the radiator draincock and drain the coolant.
4. Close the radiator draincock.
5. Install the front splash shield, 3 pin-type retainers and the 7 bolts, when the cooling system or engine service is finished.

FILLING AND BLEEDING WITH RADIATOR REFILLER

See Figure 51.

1. Install the RADIATOR REFILLER and follow the manufacturer's instructions to fill and bleed the cooling system.
   a. Recommended coolant concentration is 50/50 ethylene glycol to distilled water.
   b. Maximum coolant concentration is 60/40 for cold weather areas.
   c. Minimum coolant concentration is 40/60 for warm weather areas.

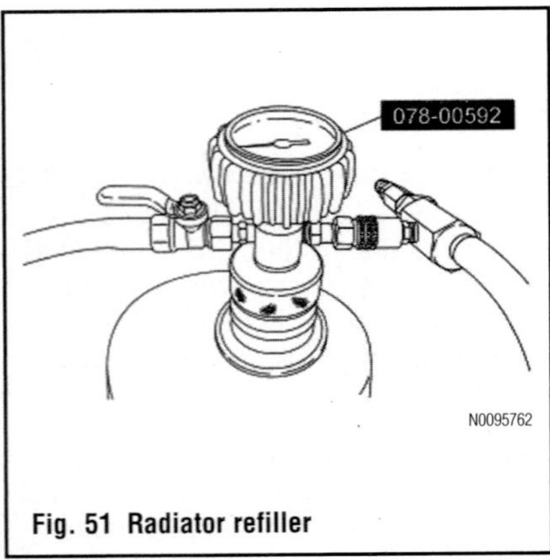

Fig. 51 Radiator refiller

FILLING AND BLEEDING WITHOUT RADIATOR REFILLER

➡Engine coolant provides freeze protection, boil protection, cooling efficiency and corrosion protection to the engine and cooling components. In order to obtain these protections, the engine coolant must be maintained at the correct concentration and fluid level. To maintain the integrity of the coolant and the cooling system:

➡Genuine Mazda® Extended Life Coolant and Motorcraft® Specialty Green Engine Coolant are very sensitive to light. Do NOT allow these products to be exposed to ANY LIGHT for more than a day or two. Extended light exposure causes these products to degrade.

➡Add Motorcraft® Specialty Green Engine Coolant to the cooling system.

➡Do not add alcohol, methanol or brine, or any engine coolants mixed with alcohol or methanol antifreeze. These can cause engine damage from overheating or freezing.

➡Ford Motor Company does NOT recommend the use of recycled engine coolant in vehicles.

➡Stop-leak style pellets/products must not be used as an additive in this engine cooling system. The addition of stop-leak style pellets/products may clog or damage the cooling system, resulting in degraded cooling system performance and/or failure.

1. Open the degas bottle cap and fill the degas bottle to 0.984 inch (25 mm) above the top of the COLD FILL RANGE.
   a. Recommended coolant concentration is 50/50 ethylene glycol to distilled water.
   b. Maximum coolant concentration is 60/40 for cold weather areas.
   c. Minimum coolant concentration is 40/60 for warm weather areas.
2. Close the degas bottle cap.
3. Turn the HVAC system to OFF.
4. Run the engine at 3,500 rpm for 30 seconds.

➡If the engine overheats or the fluid level drops below the top of the COLD FILL RANGE, shut off the engine and add fluid to 0.984 inch (25 mm) above the top of the COLD FILL RANGE once the engine cools.

5. Turn the engine off for 1 minute to purge any large air pockets.
6. Start the engine and let idle until the engine reaches normal operating temperature and the thermostat is fully open. A fully open thermostat can be verified by the radiator fan cycling on at least once.
7. Run the engine at 3,500 rpm for 30 seconds.
8. Run the engine at idle for 30 seconds.

➡If the engine overheats or the fluid level drops below the top of the COLD FILL RANGE, shut off the engine and add fluid to 0.984 inch (25 mm) above the top of the COLD FILL RANGE once the engine cools.

9. Turn the engine off for 1 minute.
10. Repeat Steps 7 through 9 a total of 10 times to remove any remaining air trapped in the system.

CAUTION

Always allow the engine to cool before opening the cooling system. Do not unscrew the coolant pressure relief cap when the engine is operating or the cooling system is hot. The cooling system is under pressure; steam and hot liquid can come out forcefully when the cap is loosened slightly. Failure to follow these instructions may result in serious personal injury.

11. Check the engine coolant level in the degas bottle and fill to 0.984 inch (25 mm) above the top of the COLD FILL RANGE when warm or to the top of the COLD FILL RANGE line when cold.
12. Install the degas bottle cap to at least one audible "click."

ENGINE FAN

REMOVAL & INSTALLATION

3.5L Engine, Except Turbo

See Figures 52 and 53.

1. With the vehicle in NEUTRAL, position it on a hoist.
2. Remove the Air Cleaner (ACL) assembly.
3. If equipped, detach the block heater wiring harness retainers from the engine wiring harness.
4. Disconnect the cooling fan motor electrical connector and detach the all the wiring harness retainers from the shroud.

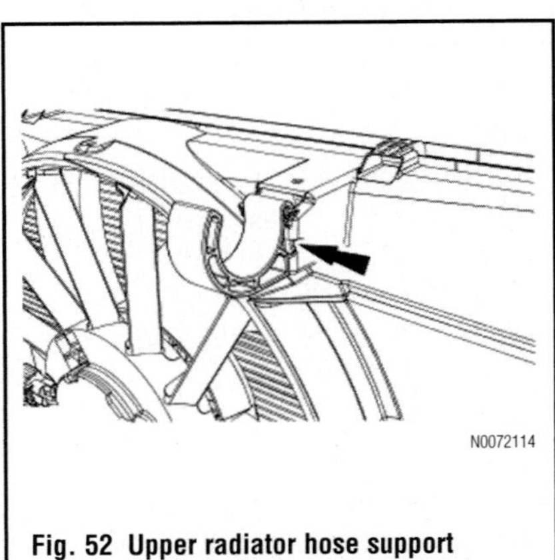

Fig. 52 Upper radiator hose support

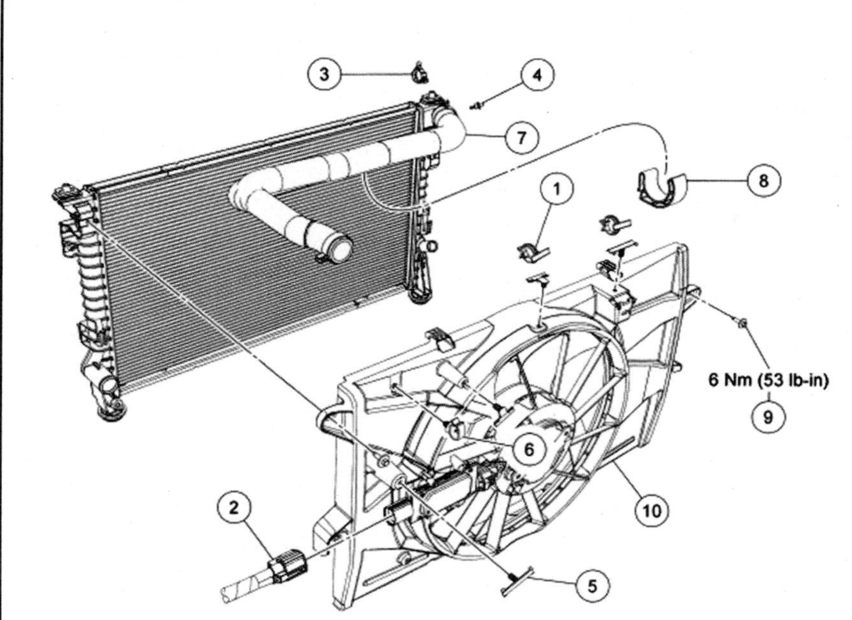

Fig. 53 Cooling fan motor and shroud—3.5L engine, except turbo

5. Detach the 2 wiring harness retainers from the radiator support.
6. Detach the hood release cable retainer from the cooling fan motor and shroud.
7. Detach the upper radiator hose from the cooling fan motor and shroud.
8. Release the tab through the access hole and remove the upper radiator hose support.
9. Remove the 2 bolts and the cooling fan motor and shroud.

To install:

10. Install the 2 bolts and the cooling fan motor and shroud. Tighten the bolts to 53 inch lbs. (6 Nm).
11. Engage the tab through the access hole and install the upper radiator hose support.
12. Attach the upper radiator hose from the cooling fan motor and shroud.
13. Attach the hood release cable retainer from the cooling fan motor and shroud.
14. Attach the 2 wiring harness retainers from the radiator support.
15. Connect the cooling fan motor electrical connector and detach the all the wiring harness retainers to the shroud.
16. If equipped, attach the block heater wiring harness retainers to the engine wiring harness.
17. Install the Air Cleaner (ACL) assembly.
18. With the vehicle in NEUTRAL, lower from hoist.

3.5L Turbo Engine

See Figures 54 through 56.

➡Whenever turbocharger air intake system components are removed, always cover open ports to protect from debris. It is important that no foreign material enter the system. The turbocharger compressor vanes are susceptible to damage from even small particles. All components should be inspected and cleaned, if necessary, prior to installation or reassembly.

1. With the vehicle in NEUTRAL, position it on a hoist.
2. Disconnect the cooling fan motor electrical connector.
3. Remove the 4 retainers and the underbody shield.

➡Index-mark the LH Charge Air Cooler (CAC) tube position for reference during installation.

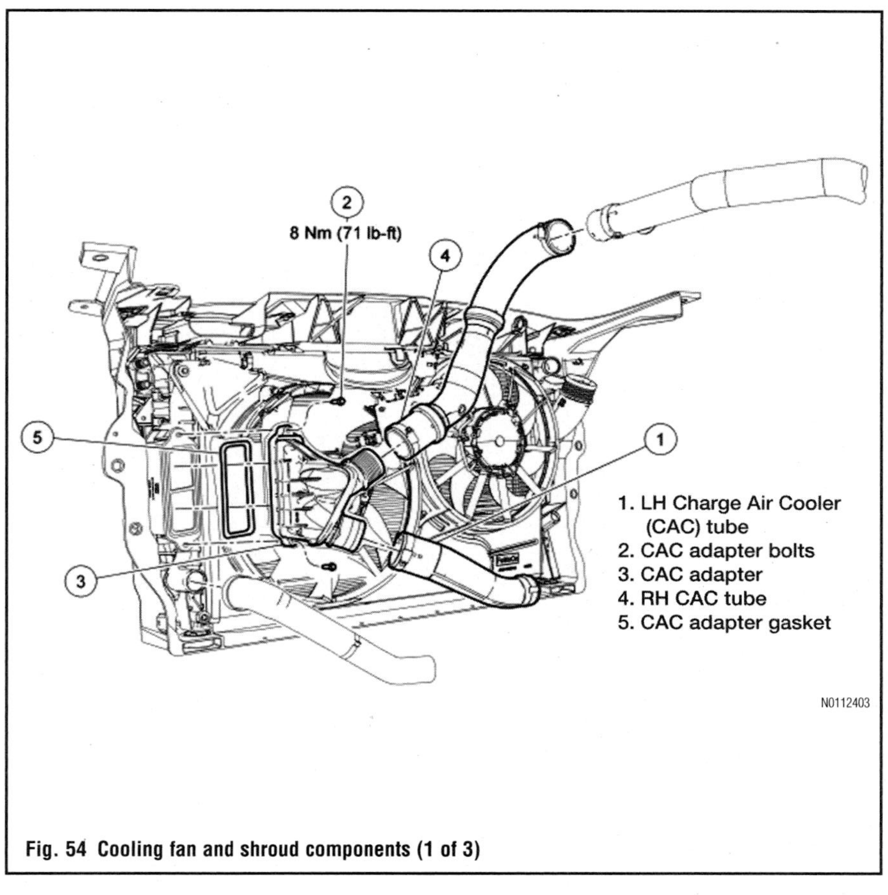

Fig. 54 Cooling fan and shroud components (1 of 3)

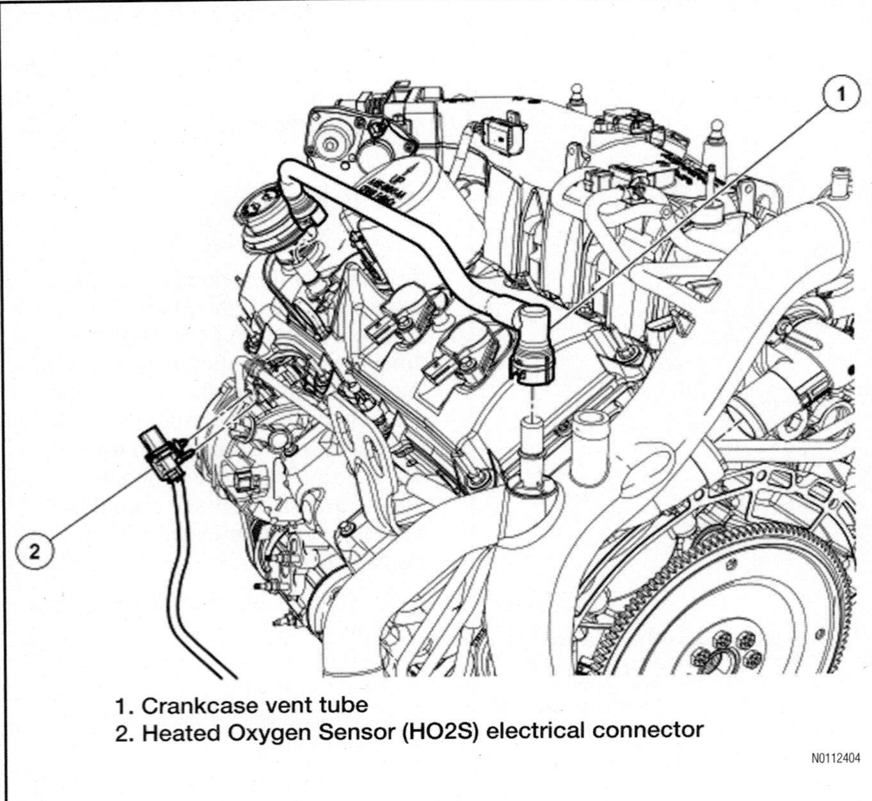

Fig. 55 Cooling fan and shroud components (2 of 3)

4. Working from below disconnect the LH CAC tube from the CAC adapter.
5. Remove the lower bolt from the CAC adapter.
6. Detach the lower radiator hose retainer from the cooling fan and shroud.
7. Remove the Air Cleaner (ACL) assembly and ACL outlet pipe.

➡Index-mark the RH CAC tube position for reference during installation.

8. Remove the RH CAC .
9. Remove the upper bolt and the CAC adapter.
   a. Inspect and install a new CAC adapter gasket, if necessary.
10. Disconnect the crankcase vent tube quick connect coupling and remove the crankcase vent tube.
11. If equipped, detach the block heater wiring harness retainers from the engine wiring harness.
12. Detach all the wiring harness retainers from the cooling fan and shroud and radiator grille support.
13. Disconnect the LH Heated Oxygen Sensor (HO2S) electrical connector.
    a. Detach the HO2S connector retainer from the bracket.
14. Remove the 2 bolts and the cooling fan motor and shroud.

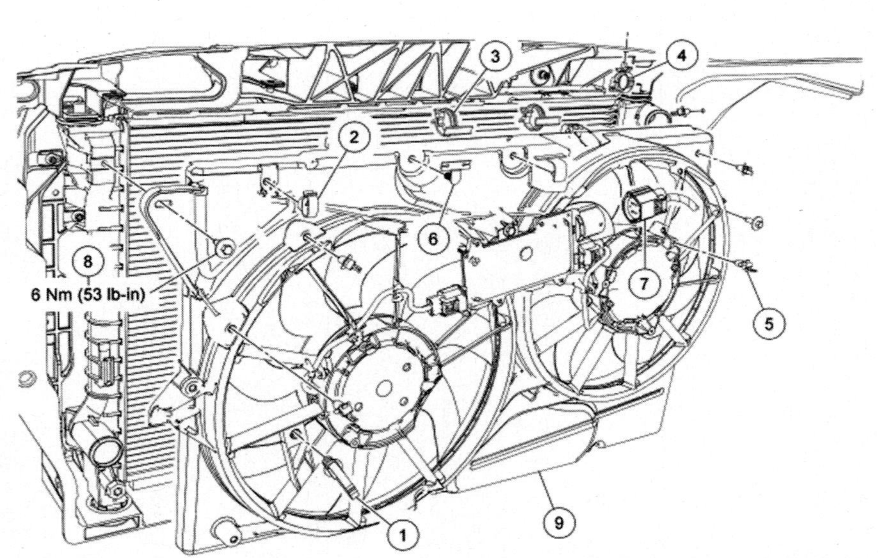

Fig. 56 Cooling fan and shroud components (3 of 3)

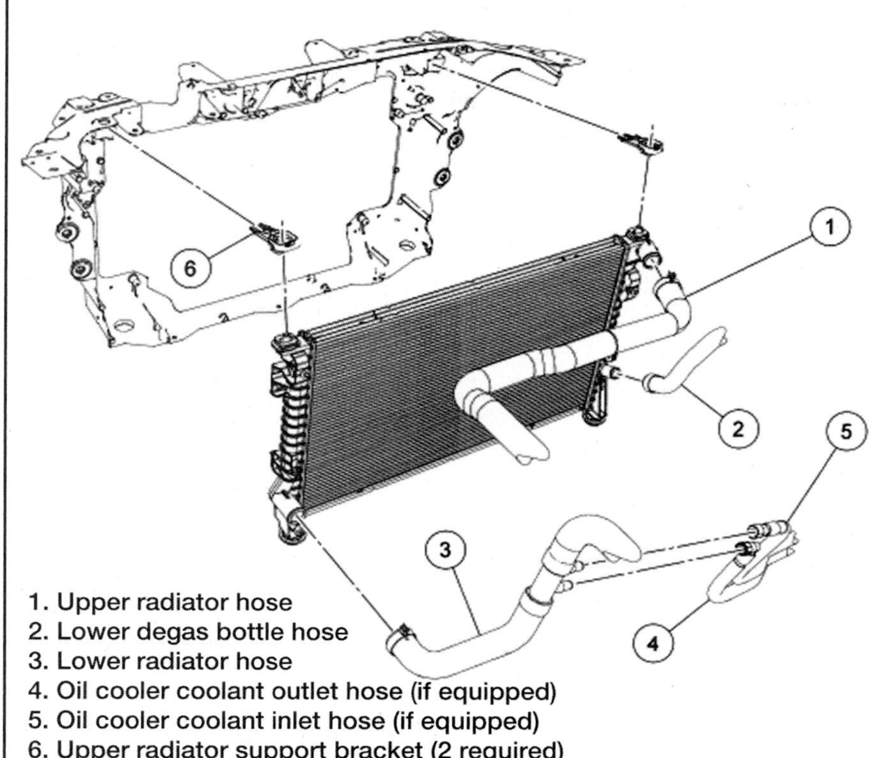

Fig. 57 Radiator components—3.5L (1 of 2)

To install:

15. Install the cooling fan motor and shroud and the 2 bolts. Tighten the bolts to 53 inch lbs. (6 Nm).
16. Connect the LH HO2S electrical connector.
    a. Attach the HO2S connector retainer to the bracket.
17. Attach all the wiring harness retainers to the cooling fan and shroud and radiator grille support.
18. If equipped, attach the block heater wiring harness retainers to the engine wiring harness.
19. Install the crankcase vent tube quick connect coupling. For additional information, refer to Fuel System - General Information.
20. Install the CAC adapter gasket, adapter and the upper bolt.
    a. Do not tighten the bolt at this time.
21. Install the lower bolt for the CAC adapter. Tighten the bolt to 71 inch lbs. (8 Nm).
22. Tighten the upper CAC adapter bolt. Tighten the bolt to 71 inch lbs. (8 Nm).

➡Align the marks for the RH CAC tube.

23. Install the RH CAC tube. Tighten the tube to 44 inch lbs. (5 Nm).
24. Install the ACL outlet pipe and ACL assembly.
25. Attach the lower radiator hose retainer to the cooling fan and shroud.

➡Align the marks for the LH CAC tube.

26. Connect the LH CAC tube to the CAC adapter. Tighten the tube to 44 inch lbs. (5 Nm).
27. Install the underbody shield and the 4 retainers.
28. Connect the cooling fan motor electrical connector.

RADIATOR

REMOVAL & INSTALLATION

3.5L Engine, Except Turbo

See Figures 57 and 58.

1. Drain the cooling system as outlined in this section.
2. Remove the cooling fan motor and shroud as outlined in this section.
3. Remove the front bumper cover.
4. Disconnect the upper radiator hose and lower degas bottle hose from the radiator.
5. Disconnect the lower radiator hose from the radiator.
6. Lift the tabs and remove the radiator support brackets and position the radiator toward the engine.
7. Remove the 2 A/C condenser bolts from the radiator and separate the condenser from the radiator.

➡Make sure the bottom radiator insulators are in place when installing the radiator.

8. Remove the radiator.

To install:

➡Make sure the bottom radiator insulators are in place when installing the radiator.

9. Install the radiator.
10. Install the 2 A/C condenser bolts to the radiator and separate the condenser to the radiator. Tighten the bolts to 53 inch lbs. (6 Nm).
11. Lift the tabs and install the radiator support brackets and position the radiator toward the engine.
12. Disconnect the lower radiator hose from the radiator.
13. Disconnect the upper radiator hose and lower degas bottle hose from the radiator.
14. Remove the front bumper cover.
15. Remove the cooling fan motor and shroud as outlined in this section.
16. Drain the cooling system as outlined in this section.
17. Fill and bleed the cooling system as outlined in this section.

3.5L Turbo Engine

See Figures 59 through 62.

➡Whenever turbocharger air intake system components are removed, always cover open ports to protect from debris. It is important that no foreign material enter the system. The turbocharger compressor vanes are susceptible to damage from even small particles. All components should be inspected and cleaned, if necessary, prior to installation or reassembly.

1. Drain the cooling system as outlined in this section.
2. Remove the cooling fan motor and shroud as outlined in this section.
3. Remove the front bumper cover.
4. Disconnect the Turbocharger Boost Pressure (TCBP)/Charge Air Cooler Temperature (CACT) sensor electrical connector.

➡Index-mark the Charge Air Cooler (CAC) outlet pipe position for reference during installation.

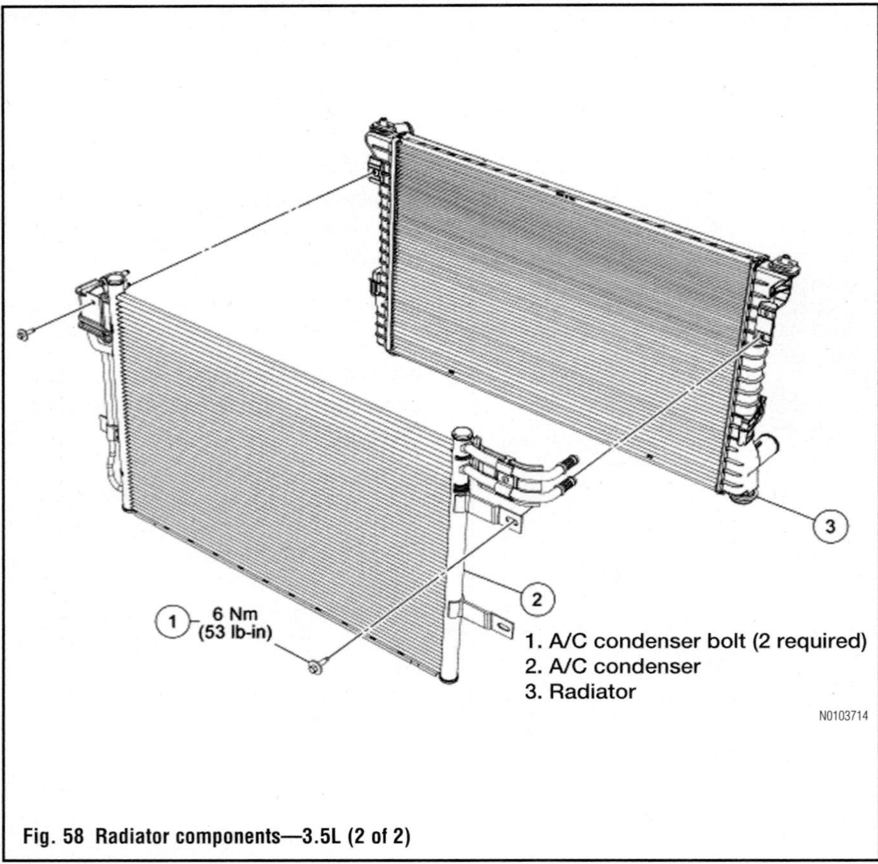

Fig. 58 Radiator components—3.5L (2 of 2)

5. Remove the CAC outlet pipe.
6. Disconnect the upper radiator hose and lower degas bottle hose from the radiator.
7. Detach the 4 radiator grille air deflector pin-type retainers and remove the RH and LH radiator grille air deflectors.
8. Remove the 2 A/C condenser bolts from the CAC and separate the A/C condenser from the CAC .
9. Lift the tabs and remove the radiator support brackets and position the radiator toward the engine.
10. Remove the 2 bolts and separate the CAC from the radiator.

➡Make sure the bottom radiator insulators are in place when installing the radiator.

11. Remove the radiator.

To install:

➡Make sure the bottom radiator insulators are in place when installing the radiator.

12. Install the radiator.
13. Install the 2 bolts and separate the CAC to the radiator. Tighten the bolts to 53 inch lbs. (6 Nm).

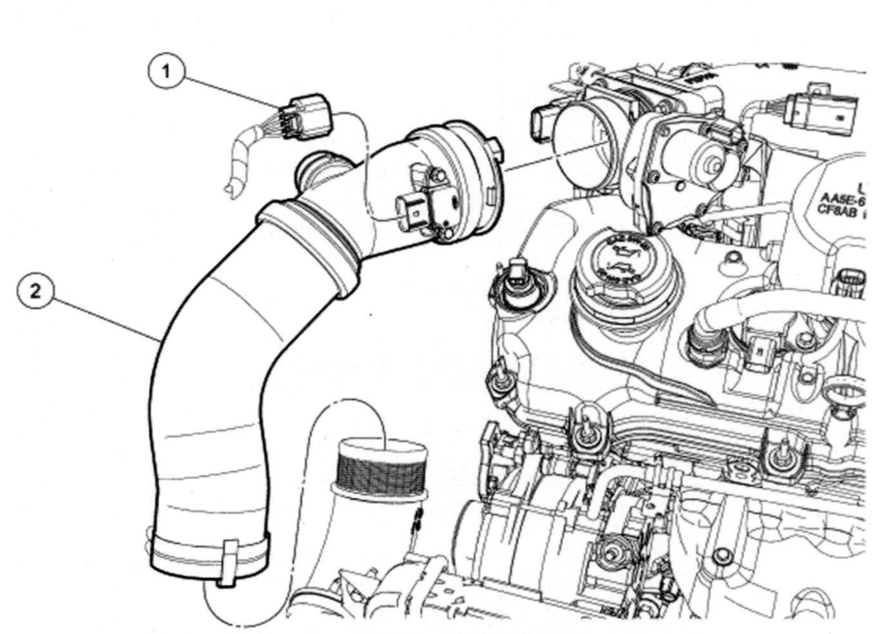

Fig. 59 Radiator components—3.5L Turbo (1 of 4)

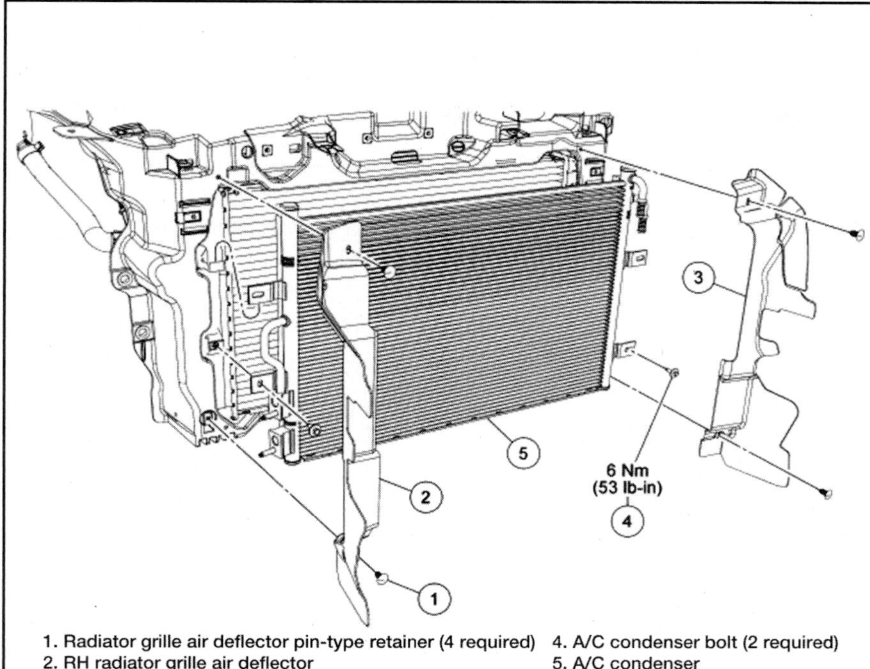

Fig. 60 Radiator components—3.5L Turbo (2 of 4)

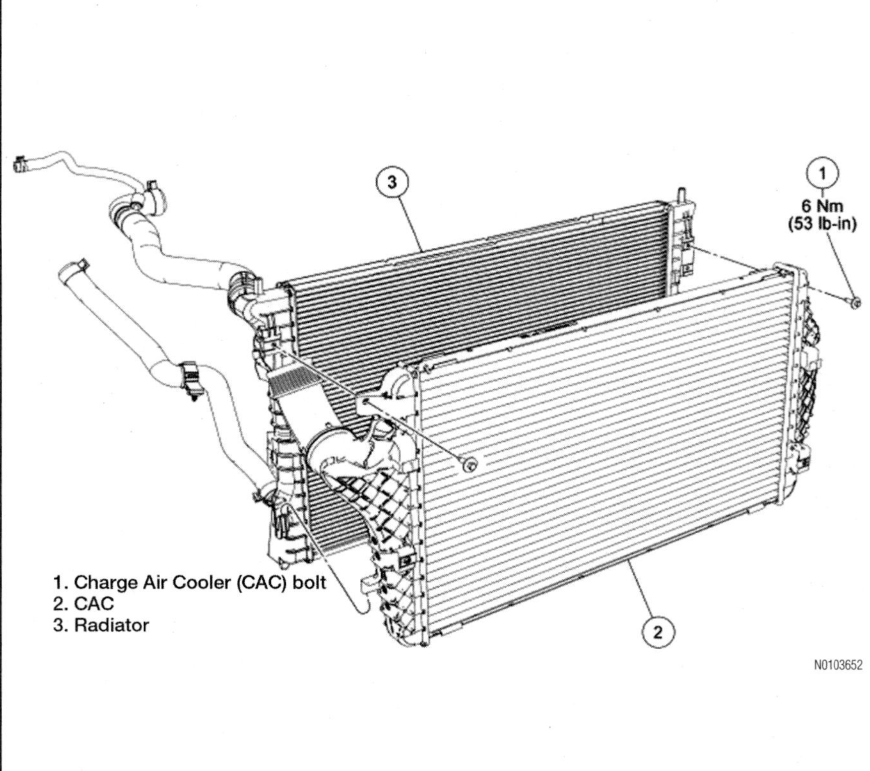

Fig. 61 Radiator components—3.5L Turbo (3 of 4)

14. Lift the tabs and install the radiator support brackets and position the radiator toward the engine.
15. Install the 2 A/C condenser bolts to the CAC and separate the A/C condenser to the CAC. Tighten the bolts to 53 inch lbs. (6 Nm).
16. Attach the 4 radiator grille air deflector pin-type retainers and install the RH and LH radiator grille air deflectors.
17. Connect the upper radiator hose and lower degas bottle hose to the radiator.
18. Connect the lower radiator hose to the radiator.

➡**Index-mark the Charge Air Cooler (CAC) outlet pipe position for reference during installation.**

19. Install the CAC outlet pipe. Tighten the outlet pipe to 44 inch lbs. (5 Nm).
20. Connect the Turbocharger Boost Pressure (TCBP)/Charge Air Cooler Temperature (CACT) sensor electrical connector.
21. Install the front bumper cover.
22. Install the cooling fan motor and shroud as outlined in this section.
23. Fill the cooling system as outlined in this section.

THERMOSTAT

REMOVAL & INSTALLATION

See Figure 63.

1. Drain the cooling system as outlined in this section.
2. Remove the engine Air Cleaner (ACL) outlet pipe.
3. Remove the 2 bolts and position aside the thermostat housing.
   a. On Gasoline Turbocharged Direct Injection (3.5L Turbo) vehicles, clean the bolts and apply Thread Sealant with PTFE before installing the bolts.
4. Remove the O-ring seal and thermostat.
   a. Clean and inspect the O-ring seal. Install a new seal if necessary.

➡**Genuine Mazda® Extended Life Coolant and Motorcraft® Specialty Green Engine Coolant are very sensitive to light. Do NOT allow these products to be exposed to ANY LIGHT for more than a day or two. Extended light exposure causes these products to degrade.**

➡**Lubricate the thermostat O-ring seal with clean engine coolant.**

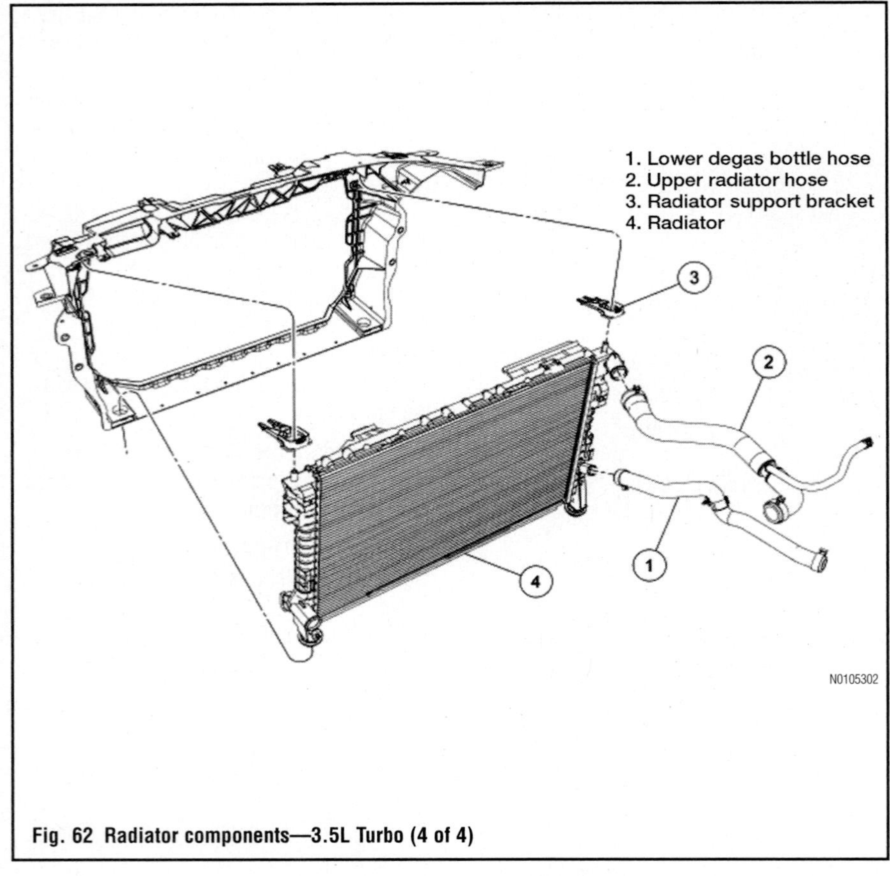

Fig. 62 Radiator components—3.5L Turbo (4 of 4)

To install:

➡Genuine Mazda® Extended Life Coolant and Motorcraft® Specialty Green Engine Coolant are very sensitive to light. Do NOT allow these products to be exposed to ANY LIGHT for more than a day or two. Extended light exposure causes these products to degrade.

➡Lubricate the thermostat O-ring seal with clean engine coolant.

5. Remove the O-ring seal and thermostat.
   a. Clean and inspect the O-ring seal. Install a new seal if necessary.
6. Remove the 2 bolts and position aside the thermostat housing.
   a. On Gasoline Turbocharged Direct Injection (3.5L Turbo) vehicles, clean the bolts and apply Thread Sealant with PTFE before installing the bolts. Tighten the bolts to 89 inch lbs. (10 Nm).
7. Remove the engine Air Cleaner (ACL) outlet pipe.
8. Drain the cooling system as outlined in this section.
9. Fill and bleed the cooling system as outlined in this section.

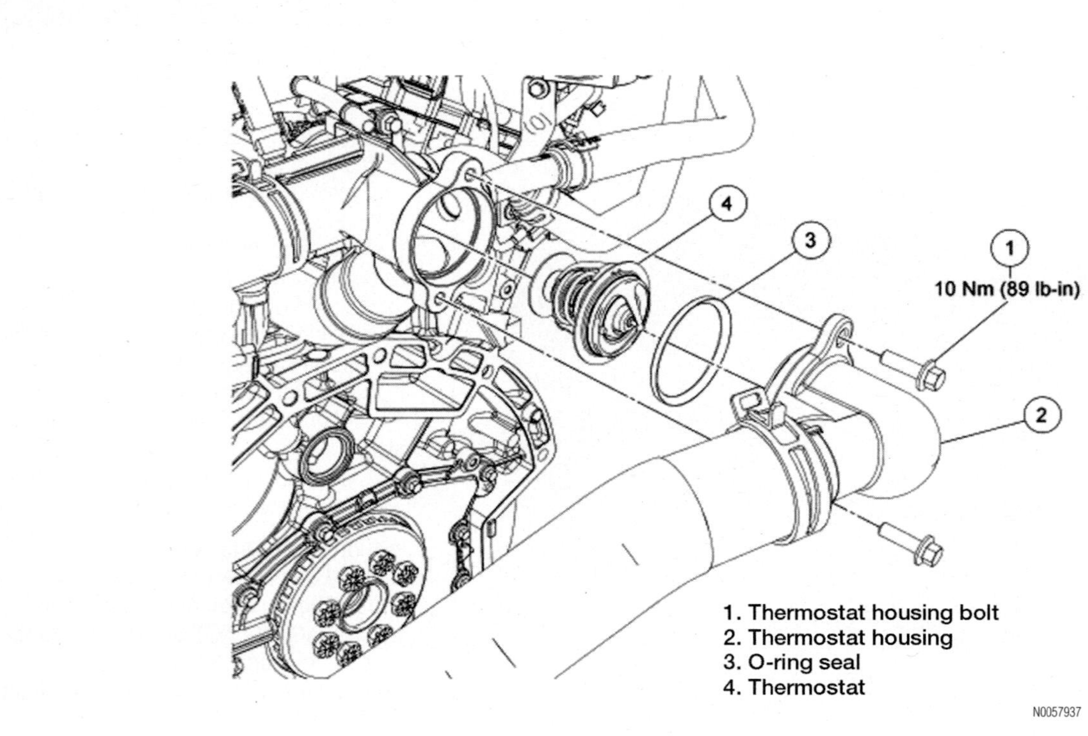

Fig. 63 Thermostat components (3.5L shown, 3.5L Turbo similar)

ALTERNATOR

REMOVAL & INSTALLATION

See Figure 64.

1. Disconnect the battery.
2. Remove the engine cover.
3. Position the alternator protective cover aside, remove the B+ nut and position the B+ terminal aside.
4. Disconnect the alternator electrical connector and position the harness aside.
5. For the 3.5L non-turbo engine, rotate the accessory drive belt tensioner and remove the accessory drive belt from the alternator.
6. For the 3.5L turbo engine, remove A/C compressor.
7. Remove the upper alternator nut and stud. Loosen the lower alternator bolt, and remove the alternator.

To install:

8. Position the alternator and install the lower alternator bolt.
   a. Hand-tighten the bolt at this time.
9. Install the upper alternator stud and nut. Tighten the stud to 71 inch lbs. (8 Nm), and the nut to 35 ft. lbs. (47 Nm).
10. Tighten the lower alternator bolt to 35 ft. lbs. (47 Nm).
11. Connect the alternator electrical connector and install the B+ nut. Tighten the nut to 150 inch lbs. (17 Nm).
12. Install the A/C compressor, if removed.
13. For the 3.5L non-turbo engine, rotate the accessory drive belt tensioner and install the accessory drive belt on the alternator.
14. Connect the alternator electrical connector and position the harness aside.
15. Reposition the alternator protective cover, and install the B+ nut and position the B+ terminal.
16. Install the engine cover.
17. Connect the battery cable.

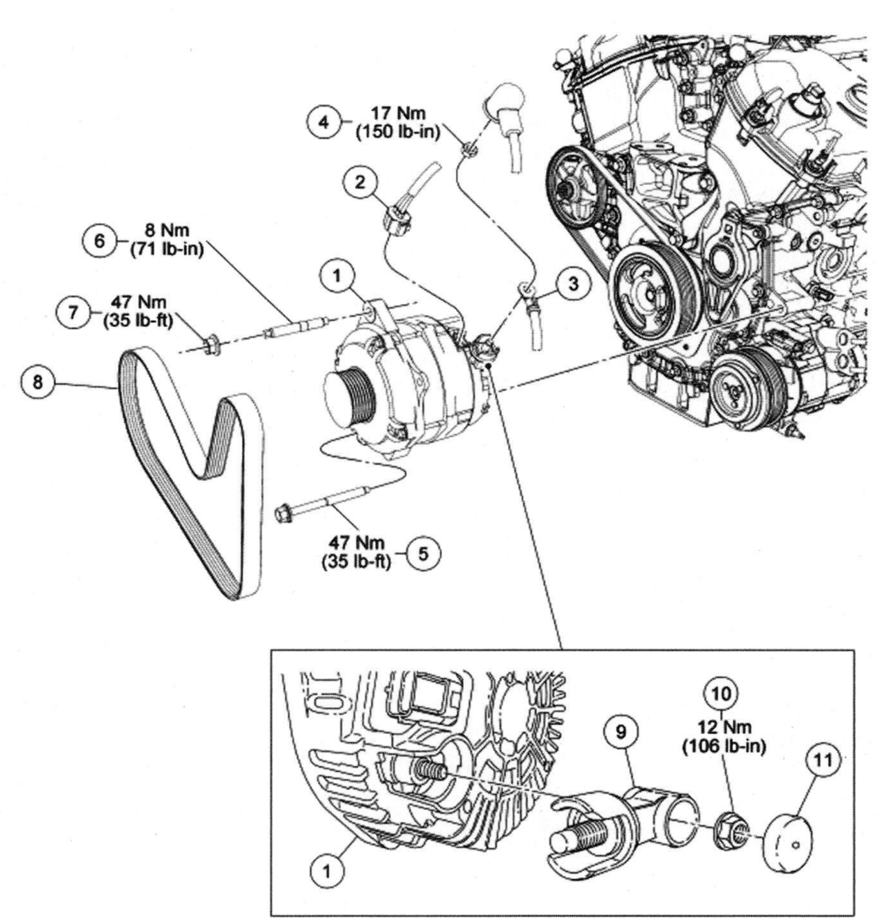

1. Generator
2. Generator electrical connector
3. Generator B+ terminal
4. Generator B+ terminal nut
5. Generator bolt
6. Generator stud (replace bolt)
7. Generator nut
8. Accessory drive belt
9. Radial arm adapter
10. Radial arm adapter nut
11. Radial arm adapter cap

N0106886

Fig. 64 Alternator components

FIRING ORDER

The Firing Order: 1-4-2-5-3-6

IGNITION COIL-ON-PLUG

REMOVAL & INSTALLATION

3.5L Engine, Except Turbo

LH Side

1. Disconnect the crankcase ventilation tube-to-valve cover fitting quick connect coupling and position aside.

RH Side

➡**The upper intake manifold must be removed to access the RH ignition coil-on-plugs.**

2. Remove the upper intake manifold as outlined in the Engine Mechanical Section.

Both Sides

3. Disconnect the 6 ignition coil-on-plug electrical connectors.

➡**When removing the ignition coil-on-plugs, a slight twisting motion will break the seal and ease removal.**

4. Remove the 6 bolts and the 6 ignition coil-on-plugs.
5. Inspect the coil seals for rips, nicks or tears. Remove and discard any damaged coil seals.
   a. To install, slide the new coil seal onto the coil until it is fully seated at the top of the coil.

To install:

Both Sides

6. Inspect the coil seals for rips, nicks or tears. Install any new coil seals.
   a. To install, slide the new coil seal onto the coil until it is fully seated at the top of the coil.

➡**When installing the ignition coil-on-plugs, a slight twisting motion will help ease installation.**

7. Install the 6 bolts and the 6 ignition coil-on-plugs. Tighten the bolts to 62 inch lbs. (7 Nm).
8. Connect the 6 ignition coil-on-plug electrical connectors.

RH Side

➡**The upper intake manifold must be removed to access the RH ignition coil-on-plugs.**

9. Install the upper intake manifold as outlined in the Engine Mechanical Section.

LH Side

10. Connect the crankcase ventilation tube-to-valve cover fitting quick connect coupling and position aside.
11. Apply a small amount of dielectric grease to the inside of the ignition coil-on-plug boots before attaching to the spark plugs.

3.5L Turbo Engine

See Figure 65.

LH Side

1. Remove the fuel injection pump noise insulator shield.
2. Disconnect the crankcase ventilation tube-to-valve cover fitting quick connect coupling.

Both Sides

3. Disconnect the 6 ignition coil-on-plug electrical connectors.

➡**When removing the ignition coil-on-plugs, a slight twisting motion will break the seal and ease removal.**

4. Remove the 6 bolts and the 6 ignition coil-on-plugs.

To install, tighten to 7 Nm (62 lb-in).

5. Inspect the coil seals for rips, nicks or tears. Remove and discard any damaged coil seals.

To install, slide the new coil seal onto the coil until it is fully seated at the top of the coil.

To install:

Both Sides

6. Inspect the coil seals for rips, nicks or tears. Install any new coil seals.
   a. To install, slide the new coil seal onto the coil until it is fully seated at the top of the coil.

Fig. 65 Crankcase ventilation tube-to-valve cover fitting quick connect coupling

➡**When installing the ignition coil-on-plugs, a slight twisting motion will ease installation.**

7. Install the 6 bolts and the 6 ignition coil-on-plugs. Tighten the bolts to 62 inch lbs. (7 Nm).
8. Connect the 6 ignition coil-on-plug electrical connectors.

LH Side

9. Connect the crankcase ventilation tube-to-valve cover fitting quick connect coupling.
10. Install the fuel injection pump noise insulator shield.
11. Apply a small amount of dielectric grease to the inside of the ignition coil-on-plug boots before attaching to the spark plugs.

SPARK PLUGS

REMOVAL & INSTALLATION

3.5L Engine, Except Turbo

1. Remove the 6 ignition coil-on-plugs as outlined in this section.

➡**Only use hand tools when removing or installing the spark plugs, or damage may occur to the cylinder head or spark plug.**

➡**Use compressed air to remove any foreign material in the spark plug well before removing the spark plugs.**

2. Remove the 6 spark plugs.
3. Inspect the 6 spark plugs.

To install:

4. Inspect the 6 spark plugs.

➡**Only use hand tools when removing or installing the spark plugs, or damage may occur to the cylinder head or spark plug.**

➡**Use compressed air to remove any foreign material in the spark plug well before installing the spark plugs.**

5. Install the 6 spark plugs. Tighten the spark plugs to 133 inch lbs. (15 Nm).
6. Install the 6 ignition coil-on-plugs as outlined in this section.
7. Adjust the spark plug gap as necessary to 0.051–0.057 inches.

3.5L Turbo Engine

1. Remove the 6 ignition coil-on-plugs as outlined in this section.

➡Only use hand tools when removing or installing the spark plugs, or damage may occur to the cylinder head or spark plug.

➡Use compressed air to remove any foreign material in the spark plug well before removing the spark plugs.

2. Remove the 6 spark plugs.
3. Inspect the 6 spark plugs.

To install:

4. Inspect the 6 spark plugs.

➡Only use hand tools when removing or installing the spark plugs, or damage may occur to the cylinder head or spark plug.

➡Use compressed air to remove any foreign material in the spark plug well before installing the spark plugs.

5. Install the 6 spark plugs. Tighten the spark plugs to 133 inch lbs. (15 Nm).
6. Install the 6 ignition coil-on-plugs as outlined in this section.
7. Adjust the spark plug gap as necessary to 0.032–0.038 inches.

ENGINE ELECTRICAL

BATTERY SYSTEM

BATTERY

REMOVAL & INSTALLATION

CAUTION

Batteries contain sulfuric acid and produce explosive gases. Work in a well-ventilated area. Do not allow the battery to come in contact with flames, sparks or burning substances. Avoid contact with skin, eyes or clothing. Shield eyes when working near the battery to protect against possible splashing of acid solution. In case of acid contact with skin or eyes, flush immediately with water for a minimum of 15 minutes, then get prompt medical attention. If acid is swallowed, call a physician immediately. Failure to follow these instructions may result in serious personal injury.

CAUTION

Always lift a plastic-cased battery with a battery carrier or with hands on opposite corners. Excessive pressure on the battery end walls may cause acid to flow through the vent caps, resulting in personal injury and/or damage to the vehicle or battery.

CAUTION

When directed to drive the vehicle as part of this test, drive the vehicle on a hard surface in an area without traffic to prevent a crash. Failure to follow these instructions may result in personal injury.

1. Disconnect the battery.
2. Remove the 2 nuts and the battery hold-down clamp.
3. Remove the battery.

To install:

4. Install the battery.
5. Install the 2 nuts and the battery hold-down clamp. Tighten the nuts to 27 inch lbs. (3 Nm).
6. Connect the battery.

ENGINE MECHANICAL

➡Disconnecting the negative battery cable may interfere with the functions of the on board computer systems and may require the computer to undergo a relearning process, once the negative battery cable is reconnected.

ACCESSORY DRIVE BELTS

ACCESSORY BELT ROUTING

See Figures 66 and 67.

Refer to the accompanying illustrations.

REMOVAL & INSTALLATION

Accessory Drive Belt

3.5L Engine, Except Turbo

➡Under no circumstances should the accessory drive belt, tensioner or pulleys be lubricated as potential damage to the belt material and tensioner damping mechanism will occur. Do not apply any fluids or belt dressing to the accessory drive belt or pulleys.

1. With the vehicle in NEUTRAL, position it on a hoist.
2. Working from the top of the vehicle, rotate the accessory drive belt tensioner clockwise and remove the accessory drive belt from the generator pulley.
3. Remove the 7 pin-type retainers and the RH splash shield.
4. Working from under the vehicle, remove the accessory drive belt.

To install:

CAUTION

Working from under the vehicle, position the accessory drive belt on all pulleys, with the exception of the generator pulley.

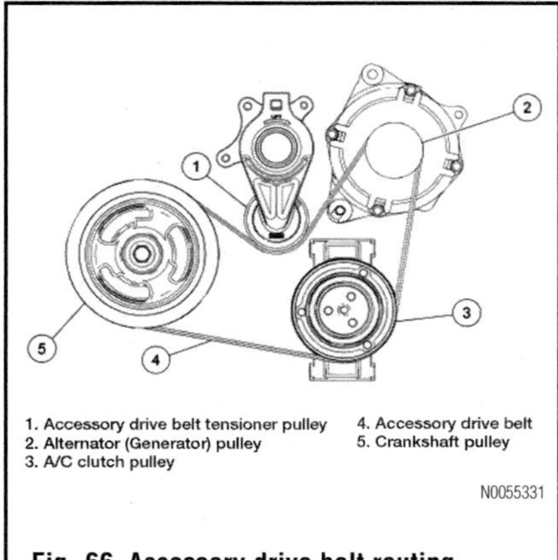

Fig. 66 Accessory drive belt routing

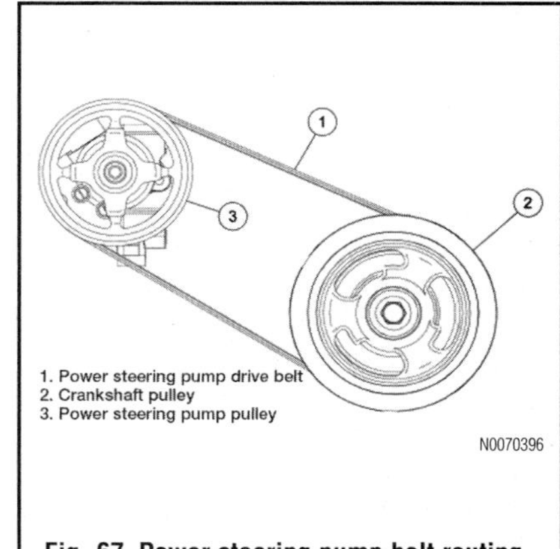

Fig. 67 Power steering pump belt routing

➡After installation, make sure the accessory drive belt is correctly seated on all pulleys.

5. Working from the top of the vehicle, rotate the accessory drive belt tensioner clockwise and install the accessory drive belt on the generator pulley.
6. Install the RH splash shield and the 7 pin-type retainers.

3.5L Turbo Engine

➡Under no circumstances should the accessory drive belt, tensioner or pulleys be lubricated as potential damage to the belt material and tensioner damping mechanism will occur. Do not apply any fluids or belt dressing to the accessory drive belt or pulleys.

1. With the vehicle in NEUTRAL, position it on a hoist.
2. Remove the RH front wheel and tire. For additional information, refer to Wheels and Tires.
3. Remove the 7 pin-type retainers and the RH splash shield.
4. Working from under the vehicle, rotate the accessory drive belt tensioner clockwise and remove the accessory drive belt.

To install:

5. Working from under the vehicle, position the accessory drive belt on all ulleys with the exception of the crankshaft pulley.

➡After installation, make sure the accessory drive belt is correctly seated on all pulleys.

6. Rotate the accessory drive belt tensioner clockwise and install the accessory drive belt on the crankshaft pulley.
7. Install the RH splash shield and the 7 pin-type retainers.
8. Install the RH front wheel and tire.

Power Steering Pump Belt

See Figures 68 through 71.

⁂ WARNING

Under no circumstances should the accessory drive belt, tensioner or pulleys be lubricated as potential damage to the belt material and tensioner damping mechanism will occur. Do not apply any fluids or belt dressing to the accessory drive belt or pulleys.

1. Working from the top of the vehicle, rotate the accessory drive belt tensioner clockwise and remove the accessory drive belt from the generator pulley.
2. Remove the RF wheel and tire.
3. Remove the 7 pin-type retainers and the RH splash shield.
4. Position the accessory drive belt off the crankshaft pulley.
5. Position the Stretchy Belt Remover on the power steering pump pulley belt.

➡Feed the Stretchy Belt Remover on to the power steering pump pulley approximately 90 degrees.

6. Turn the crankshaft clockwise and feed the Stretchy Belt Remover evenly on the power steering pump pulley.
7. Remove the power steering pump belt.
   a. Fold the Stretchy Belt Remover under the inside of the power steering pump belt as shown.

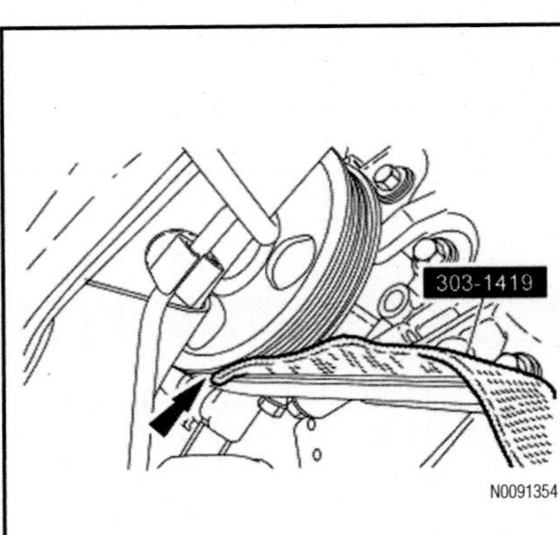

Fig. 68 Position the Stretchy Belt Remover on the power steering pump pulley belt

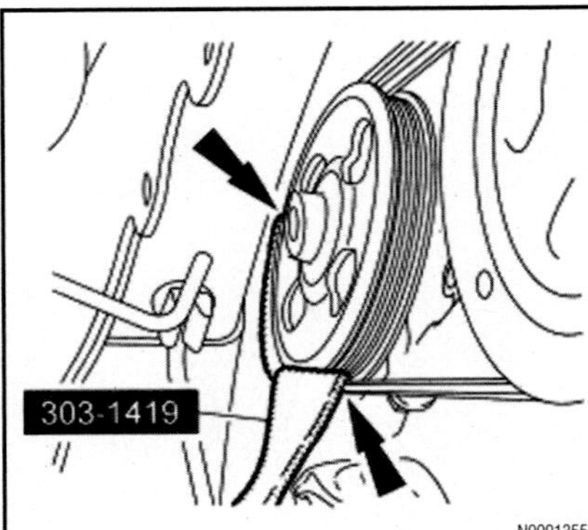

Fig. 69 Turn the crankshaft clockwise and feed the Stretchy Belt Remover evenly on the power steering pump pulley

   b. In one quick motion, firmly pull the Stretchy Belt Remover out of the RH fender well, removing the coolant pump belt.

To install:

8. Install the power steering drive belt on the crankshaft pulley.

➡After installation, make sure the power steering drive belt is correctly seated on the crankshaft and power steering pump pulleys.

9. Position the power steering drive belt around the Stretchy Belt Installer Tool and the power steering pump pulley. Make sure the belt is engaged with the power steering pump pulley and rotate the crankshaft clockwise to install the power steering drive belt.

Fig. 70 In one quick motion, firmly pull the Stretchy Belt Remover out of the RH fender well, removing the coolant pump belt

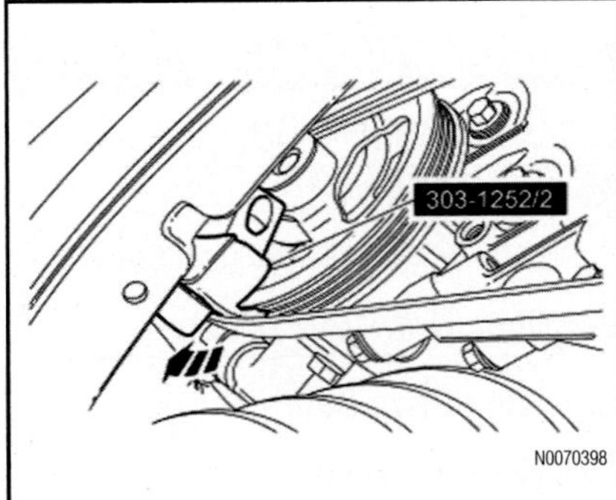

Fig. 71 Position the power steering drive belt around the Stretchy Belt Installer Tool and the power steering pump pulley. Make sure the belt is engaged with the power steering pump pulley and rotate the crankshaft clockwise to install the power steering drive belt

10. Position the accessory drive belt on the crankshaft pulley.

➡After installation, make sure the accessory drive belt is correctly seated on all pulleys.

11. Working from the top of the vehicle, rotate the accessory drive belt tensioner clockwise and install the accessory drive belt.
12. Install the RH splash shield and the 7 pin-type retainers.
13. Install the RF tire and wheel.

AIR CLEANER

REMOVAL & INSTALLATION

3.5L Engine, Except Turbo

1. Disconnect the Mass Air Flow (MAF) sensor electrical connector.
2. Loosen the clamp and disconnect the Air Cleaner (ACL) outlet pipe from the ACL.
3. Remove the 2 bolts from the ACL assembly.

➡No tools are required to remove the ACL assembly. Removal should be carried out using hands only.

4. Separate the 2 ACL feet from the rubber grommets and remove the ACL assembly.

➡Make sure that the 2 ACL feet are seated into the rubber grommets under the ACL assembly.

➡The ACL outlet pipe should be securely sealed to prevent unmetered air from entering the engine.

To install:

➡The ACL outlet pipe should be securely sealed to prevent unmetered air from entering the engine.

➡Make sure that the 2 ACL feet are seated into the rubber grommets under the ACL assembly.

➡No tools are required to install the ACL assembly. Installation should be carried out using hands only.

5. Install the 2 ACL feet to the rubber grommets and install the ACL assembly.
6. Install the 2 bolts to the ACL assembly. Tighten the bolts to 44 inch lbs. (5 Nm).
7. Connect the ACL outlet pipe to the ACL and Tighten the clamp. Tighten the clamp to 44 inch lbs. (5 Nm).
8. Connect the Mass Air Flow (MAF) sensor electrical connector.

3.5L Turbo Engine

➡Whenever turbocharger air intake system components are removed, always cover open ports to protect from debris. It is important that no foreign material enter the system. The turbocharger compressor vanes are susceptible to damage from even small particles. All components should be inspected and cleaned, if necessary, prior to installation or reassembly.

1. Disconnect the Intake Air Temperature 2 (IAT2) sensor electrical connector.
2. Release the IAT2 sensor wiring harness pin-type retainer from the Air Cleaner (ACL) cover.
3. Loosen the clamp and disconnect the ACL outlet pipe from the ACL .
4. If equipped, remove the bolt cover.
5. Remove the 2 bolts from the ACL assembly.

➡No tools are required to remove the ACL assembly. Removal should be carried out using hands only.

6. Separate the 2 ACL feet from the rubber grommets and remove the ACL assembly.

➡Make sure that the 2 ACL feet are seated into the rubber grommets under the ACL assembly.

➡The ACL outlet pipe should be securely sealed to prevent unmetered air from entering the engine.

➡Utilize the alignment features to make sure the ACL outlet tube is seated within 2 mm of the stops.

To install:

➡Whenever turbocharger air intake system components are installed, always cover open ports to protect from debris. It is important that no foreign material enter the system. The turbocharger compressor vanes are susceptible to damage from even small particles. All components should be inspected and cleaned, if necessary, prior to installation or reassembly.

➡Utilize the alignment features to make sure the ACL outlet tube is seated within 2 mm of the stops.

➡The ACL outlet pipe should be securely sealed to prevent unmetered air from entering the engine.

➡Make sure that the 2 ACL feet are seated into the rubber grommets under the ACL assembly.

➡No tools are required to install the ACL assembly. Installation should be carried out using hands only.

7. Install the 2 ACL feet from the rubber grommets and install the ACL assembly.
8. Install the 2 bolts from the ACL assembly. Tighten the bolts to 44 inch lbs. (5 Nm).
9. If equipped, install the bolt cover.
10. Connect the ACL outlet pipe to the ACL and Tighten the clamp. Tighten the clamp to 44 inch lbs. (5 Nm).
11. Engage the IAT2 sensor wiring harness pin-type retainer to the Air Cleaner (ACL) cover.
12. Connect the Intake Air Temperature 2 (IAT2) sensor electrical connector.

CAMSHAFT AND VALVE LIFTERS

REMOVAL & INSTALLATION

3.5L Engine, Except Turbo

See Figures 72 through 85.

⁂ WARNING

During engine repair procedures, cleanliness is extremely important. Any foreign material, including any material created while cleaning gasket surfaces, which enters the oil passages, coolant passages or the oil pan may cause engine failure.

⁂ WARNING

Early build engines have 11 fastener valve covers, late build engines have 9 fastener valve covers. Do not attempt to install bolts in the 2 empty late build valve cover holes or damage to the valve cover will occur.

➡On early build engines, the timing chain rides on the inner side of the RH timing chain guide. Late build engines are equipped with a different design RH timing chain guide that requires the timing chain to ride on the outer side of the RH timing chain guide. For service, all replacement RH timing chain guides will be the late build design.

All Camshafts

1. With the vehicle in NEUTRAL, position it on a hoist.
2. Recover the A/C system..
3. Remove the cowl panel grille.
4. Detach the brake booster vacuum hose retainer from the strut tower brace.
5. Remove the 4 nuts and the strut tower brace.
6. Release the fuel system pressure.
7. Remove the engine Air Cleaner (ACL) and ACL outlet pipe.
8. Remove the battery tray.
9. Disconnect the engine wiring harness electrical connector.
10. Remove the nut and disconnect the 2 power feed wires from the positive battery terminal.
11. Remove the nut and disconnect the ground cable from the negative battery terminal.
12. Drain the cooling system as outlined in the Engine Cooling Section.
13. Remove the LF wheel and tire.
14. Remove the accessory drive belt and the power steering belt as outlined in this section.
15. Remove the 3 pushpins, 7 screws and the front valance.
16. Disconnect the power steering cooler tube located at the left front subframe and drain the power steering fluid into a suitable container.
17. Remove the nut and disconnect the A/C tube.
    a. Discard the O-ring seal and gasket seal.
18. Remove the nut and the A/C tube.
    a. Discard the O-ring seal and gasket seal.
19. Remove the degas bottle as outlined in the Engine Cooling Section.
20. Disconnect the vacuum hose and the Evaporative Emission (EVAP) tube from the upper intake manifold.
21. Detach the EVAP tube pin-type retainer from the upper intake manifold.
22. Remove the EVAP canister purge valve as outlined in the Engine Performance & Emission Controls Section.
23. Disconnect the PCM and engine harness electrical connectors.
    a. Detach the wiring harness retainer.
24. Disconnect the 2 PCM electrical connectors.
25. Remove the engine wiring harness retainer from the bulkhead.
    a. Push the wiring harness retainer tab in.
    b. Slide the wiring harness up and out of the bulkhead.

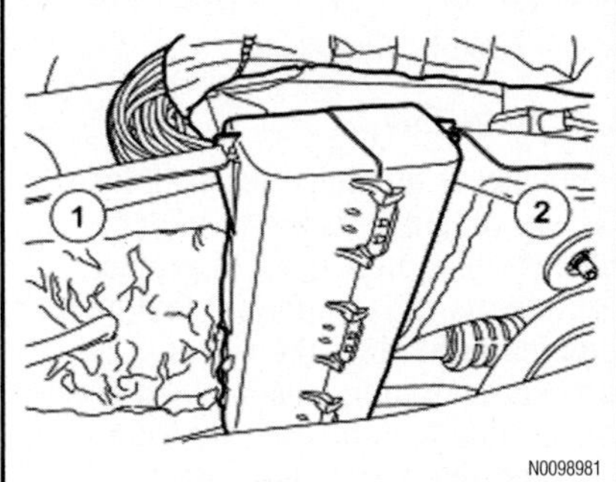

Fig. 72 Removal of the engine wiring harness retainer from the bulkhead

26. Disconnect the upper radiator hose, lower radiator hose and 2 heater hoses from the thermostat housing.
27. Disconnect the transaxle control cable from the control lever.
28. Disconnect the transaxle control cable from the shift cable bracket and detach the wiring harness pin-type retainer.
29. If equipped, detach the engine block heater harness from the radiator support.
30. Disconnect the A/C pressure switch and remove the nut and disconnect the upper A/C tube from the condenser.
    a. Discard the O-ring seal.
31. Disconnect the fuel supply tube from the fuel rail.
32. Detach the engine wiring harness retainer.
33. Detach the wire harness retainer from the RH valve cover stud bolt.
34. Remove the bolt and the ground cable from the engine.
35. Disconnect the hose from the power steering reservoir.

➡Use a steering wheel holding device (such as Hunter® 28-75-1 or equivalent).

36. Using a suitable holding device, hold the steering wheel in the straight-ahead position.

➡Apply the brake to keep the halfshafts from rotating.

37. Remove the RH and LH halfshaft nuts.
    a. Do not discard at this time.
38. Using the Front Wheel Hub Remover, separate the RH and LH halfshaft from the wheel hubs.
39. Remove the 2 lower scrivets from the rubber shield and position the shield aside.
40. Remove the bolt from the RH brake hose bracket.

WARNING

Do not allow the intermediate shaft to rotate while it is disconnected from the gear or damage to the clockspring may occur. If there is evidence that the intermediate shaft has rotated, the clockspring must be removed and recentered as outlined in the Chassis Electrical Section.

➡Index-mark the steering column shaft position to the steering gear for reference during installation.

41. Remove the bolt and disconnect the steering column shaft from the steering gear.
    a. Discard the bolt.
42. Remove the 4 Y-pipe-to-catalytic converter nuts.
    a. Discard the nuts.
43. Remove the 2 Y-pipe flange nuts.
    a. Detach the exhaust hanger and remove the Y-pipe.
    b. Discard the gaskets and nuts.

All-Wheel Drive (AWD) Vehicles

➡Index-mark the driveshaft for installation.

44. Remove and discard the 4 bolts and support the driveshaft with a length of mechanic's wire.

All Camshafts

45. Remove the drain plug and drain the engine oil.
    a. Install the drain plug and tighten to 20 ft. lbs. (27 Nm).
46. Remove and discard the engine oil filter.
47. Remove the Power Steering Pressure (PSP) tube bracket-to-steering gear bolt.
48. Remove the bolt, rotate the clamp plate clockwise and disconnect the PSP tube from the steering gear.

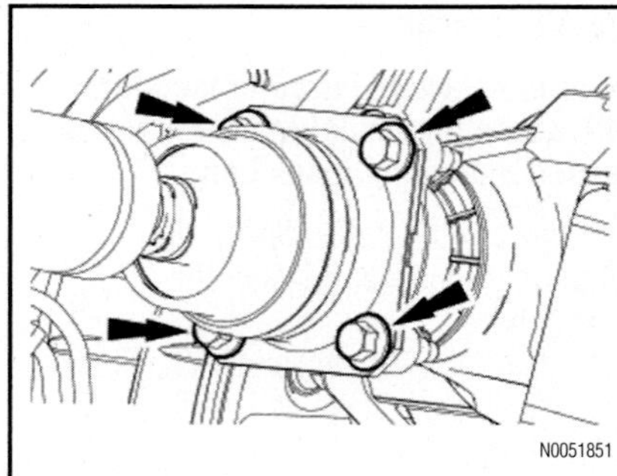

Fig. 73 Remove and discard the 4 bolts and support the driveshaft with a length of mechanic's wire

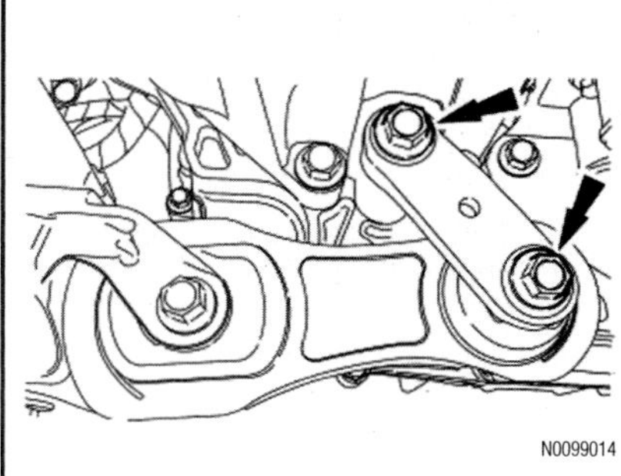

Fig. 74 Remove the 2 rear engine roll restrictor-to-transaxle bolts

a. Discard the O-ring seal.

49. Remove the 2 rear engine roll restrictor-to-transaxle bolts.

50. Remove the 2 front engine roll restrictor-to-transaxle bolts.

51. Remove and discard the upper stabilizer link nuts.

➡The hex-holding feature can be used to prevent turning of the stud while removing the nuts.

52. Remove and discard the tie-rod end nuts.

a. Separate the tie-rod ends from the wheel knuckles.

WARNING

Suspension fasteners are critical parts because they affect performance of vital components and systems and their failure may result in major service expense. New parts must be installed with the same part number or equivalent part, if replacement is necessary. Do not use a replacement part of lesser quality or substitute design. Torque values must be used as specified during reassembly to make sure of correct retention of these parts.

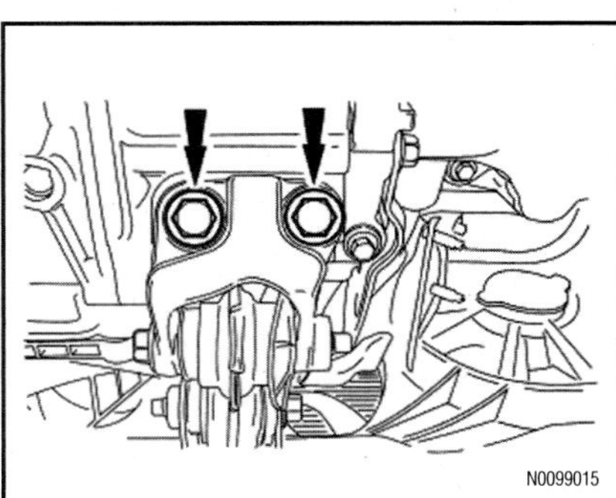

Fig. 75 Remove the 2 front engine roll restrictor-to-transaxle

WARNING

Use care when releasing the lower arm and knuckle into the resting position or damage to the ball joint seal or Constant Velocity (CV) boot may occur.

➡Use the hex-holding feature to prevent the stud from turning while removing the nut.

53. Remove and discard the lower ball joint-to-wheel knuckle nuts.

a. Separate the lower ball joints from the wheel knuckles.

54. Position the Powertrain Lift under the subframe assembly.

55. Remove the subframe bracket-to-body bolts.

56. Remove the rear subframe bolts and the subframe brackets.

57. Remove the front subframe bolts.

58. Lower the subframe assembly from the vehicle.

59. Pull the RH wheel knuckle outward and rotate it toward the rear of the vehicle.

a. Secure the RH wheel knuckle assembly.

60. Remove the 2 intermediate shaft bracket nuts.

61. Remove the intermediate and halfshaft assembly.

WARNING

The sharp edges on the stub shaft splines can slice or puncture the oil seal. Use care when inserting the stub shaft into the transmission or damage to the component may occur.

62. Using the Slide Hammer and Halfshaft Remover, remove the halfshaft from the transmission.

63. Remove and discard the circlip from the stub shaft.

64. Remove the 2 RH halfshaft support bracket studs.

65. Remove the 4 bolts and the RH halfshaft support bracket.

66. Remove the 2 secondary latches from the transmission fluid cooler tubes at the transmission fluid cooler thermal bypass valve.

67. Using the Transmission Cooler Tube Disconnect Tool, disconnect the transmission fluid cooler tubes from the transmission fluid cooler thermal bypass valve.

➡Position a block of wood under the transaxle.

68. Install the Powertrain Lift and Universal Adapter Brackets.

69. Remove the transaxle mount through bolt and nut.

70. Remove the bolt, 3 nuts and the transaxle mount bracket.

71. Remove the nut, bolt and engine mount brace.

72. Remove the 4 engine mount nuts.

73. Remove the 3 bolts and the engine mount.

74. Lower the engine and transaxle assembly from the vehicle.

75. Disconnect the PCV hose from the PCV valve.

76. Disconnect the Throttle Body (TB) electrical connector.

77. Detach the wiring harness retainers from the upper intake manifold.

78. Remove the upper intake manifold support bracket bolt.

79. Remove the wire harness pin-type retainer and the fuel tube bracket bolt from the upper intake manifold.

WARNING

If the engine is repaired or replaced because of upper engine failure, typically including valve or piston damage, check the intake manifold for metal debris. If metal debris is found, install a new intake manifold. Failure to follow these instructions can result in engine damage.

80. Remove the 6 bolts and the upper intake manifold.

a. Discard the gaskets.

81. Disconnect the RH catalyst monitor electrical connector.

82. Disconnect the RH Variable Camshaft Timing (VCT) solenoid electrical connector.

83. Disconnect the 3RH coil-on-plug electrical connectors.

84. Detach all of the wiring harness retainers from the RH valve cover and stud bolts.

85. Disconnect the LH VCT solenoid electrical connector.

86. Disconnect the 3 LH coil-on-plug electrical connectors.

87. Detach all of the wiring harness retainers from the LH valve cover and stud bolts.

88. Remove the 6 bolts and the 6 coil-on-plug assemblies.

89. Disconnect the PSP switch electrical connector.

90. Remove the PSP tube bracket-to-power steering pump bolt.

91. Remove the nut and the PSP tube bracket from the RH valve cover stud bolt.

92. Remove the 3 bolts and position aside the power steering pump.

93. Remove the 3 bolts and the accessory drive belt tensioner.

Early Build Vehicles

94. Loosen the 11 stud bolts and remove the LH valve cover.

a. Discard the gasket.

95. Loosen the bolt, the 10 stud bolts and remove the RH valve cover.

a. Discard the gasket.

Late Build Vehicles

96. Loosen the 9 stud bolts and remove the LH valve cover.

a. Discard the gasket.

97. Loosen the 9 stud bolts and remove the RH valve cover.

a. Discard the gasket.

All Vehicles

➡VCT solenoid seal removal shown, spark plug tube seal removal similar.

98. Inspect the VCT solenoid seals and the spark plug tube seals. Install new seals if damaged.

a. Using the VCT Spark Plug Tube Seal Remover and Handle, remove the seal(s).

99. Using the Strap Wrench, remove the crankshaft pulley bolt and washer.

a. Discard the bolt.

100. Using the 3 Jaw Puller, remove the crankshaft pulley.

101. Using the Oil Seal Remover, remove and discard the crankshaft front seal.

102. Remove the 2 bolts and the engine mount bracket.

➡Only use hand tools to remove the studs.

103. Remove the 2 engine mount studs.

104. Remove the 3 bolts and the engine mount bracket.

105. Remove the 22 engine front cover bolts.

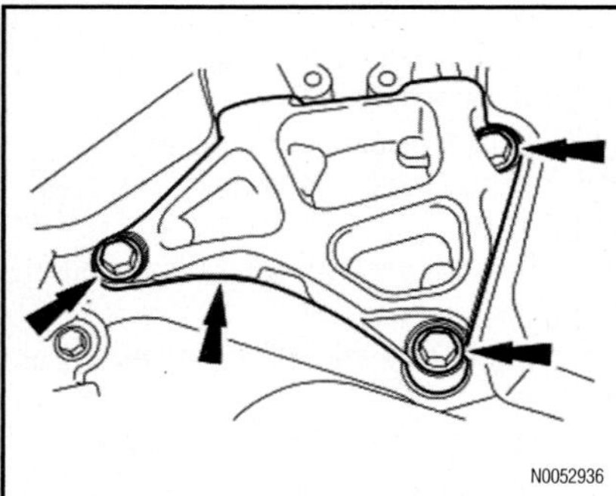

Fig. 76 Removal of the engine mount bracket bolts

106. Install 6 of the engine front cover bolts (finger tight) into the 6 threaded holes in the engine front cover.

a. Tighten the bolts one turn at a time in a crisscross pattern until the engine front cover-to-cylinder block seal is released.

b. Remove the engine front cover.

⁂ WARNING

Only use a 3M(tm) Roloc® Bristle Disk (2-in white, part number 07528) to clean the engine front cover. Do not use metal scrapers, wire brushes or any other power abrasive disk to clean the engine front cover. These tools cause scratches and gouges that make leak paths.

107. Clean the engine front cover using a 3M(tm) Roloc® Bristle Disk (2-in white, part number 07528) in a suitable tool turning at the recommended speed of 15,000 rpm.

a. Thoroughly wash the engine front cover to remove any foreign material, including any abrasive particles created during the cleaning process.

⁂ WARNING

Place clean, lint-free shop towels over exposed engine cavities. Carefully remove the towels so foreign material is not dropped into the engine. Any foreign material (including any material created while cleaning gasket surfaces) that enters the oil passages or the oil pan, may cause engine failure.

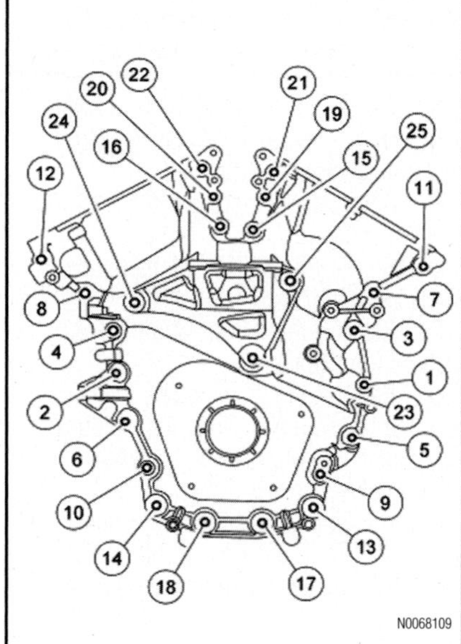

Fig. 77 Removal & installation of the 22 engine front cover bolts and the 3 engine mount bolts

⁂ WARNING

Do not use wire brushes, power abrasive discs or 3M(tm) Roloc® Bristle Disk (2-in white, part number 07528) to clean the sealing surfaces. These tools cause scratches and gouges that make leak paths. They also cause contamination that will cause premature engine failure. Remove all traces of sealant, including any sealant from the inner surface of the cylinder block and cylinder head.

108. Clean the sealing surfaces of the cylinder heads, the cylinder block and the oil pan in the following sequence.

a. Remove any large deposits of silicone or gasket material.

b. Apply silicone gasket remover and allow to set for several minutes.

c. Remove the silicone gasket remover. A second application of silicone gasket remover may be required if residual traces of silicone or gasket material remain.

d. Apply metal surface prep, to remove any remaining traces of oil or coolant and to prepare the surfaces to bond. Do not attempt to make the metal shiny. Some staining of the metal surfaces is normal.

e. Make sure the 2 locating dowel pins are seated correctly in the cylinder block.

Engines Equipped With Early Build RH Timing Chain Guides

109. Rotate the crankshaft clockwise and align the timing marks on the VCT assemblies.

Engines Equipped With Late Build/Replacement RH Timing Chain Guides

110. Rotate the crankshaft clockwise and align the timing marks on the VCT assemblies as shown.

All Camshafts

➡The Camshaft Holding Tool will hold the camshafts in the Top Dead Center (TDC) position.

111. Install the Camshaft Holding Tool onto the flats of the LH camshafts.

➡The Camshaft Holding Tool will hold the camshafts in the TDC position.

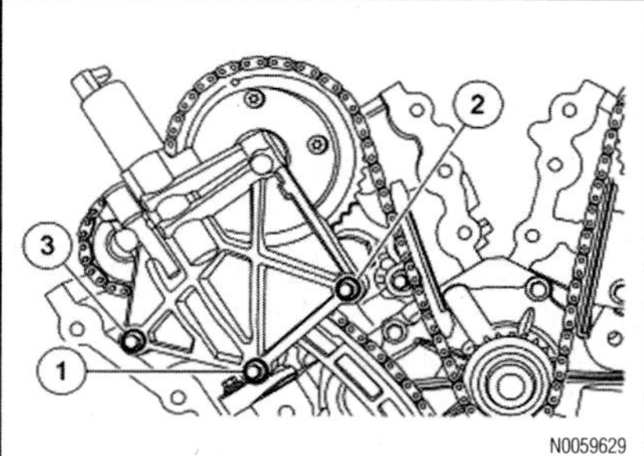

Fig. 78 Removal & installation of the RH VCT housing, and 3 bolts. Tighten in the sequence shown

112. Install the Camshaft Holding Tool onto the flats of the RH camshafts.
113. Remove the 3 bolts and the RH VCT housing.
114. Remove the 3 bolts and the LH VCT housing.
115. Remove the 2 bolts and the primary timing chain tensioner.
116. Remove the primary timing chain tensioner arm.
117. Remove the 2 bolts and the lower LH primary timing chain guide.
118. Remove the primary timing chain.

LH Camshafts

119. Compress the LH secondary timing chain tensioner and install a suitable lockpin to retain the tensioner in the collapsed position.

➡The VCT bolt and the exhaust camshaft bolt must be discarded and new ones installed. However, the exhaust camshaft washer is reusable.

120. Remove and discard the LH VCT assembly bolt and the LH exhaust camshaft sprocket bolt.
    a. Remove the LH VCT assembly, secondary timing chain and the LH exhaust camshaft sprocket as an assembly.

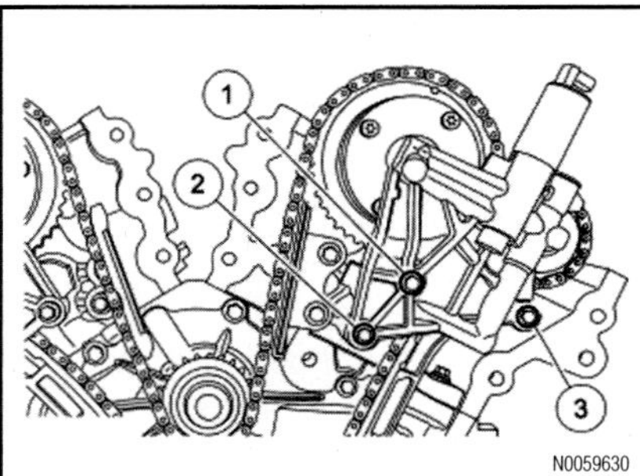

Fig. 79 Removal & installation of the LH VCT housing, and 3 bolts. Tighten in the sequence shown

➡When the Camshaft Holding Tool is removed, valve spring pressure will rotate the LH camshafts approximately 3 degrees to a neutral position.

121. Remove the Camshaft Holding Tool from the LH camshafts.

WARNING

The camshafts must remain in the neutral position during removal or engine damage may occur.

122. Verify the LH camshafts are in the neutral position.

➡Cylinder head camshaft bearing caps are numbered to verify that they are assembled in their original positions.

123. Remove the bolts and the LH camshaft bearing caps.
    a. Remove the LH camshafts.

RH Camshafts

124. Compress the RH secondary timing chain tensioner and install a suitable lockpin to retain the tensioner in the collapsed position.

➡The VCT bolt and the exhaust camshaft bolt must be discarded and new ones installed. However, the exhaust camshaft washer is reusable.

125. Remove and discard the RH VCT assembly bolt and the RH exhaust camshaft sprocket bolt.

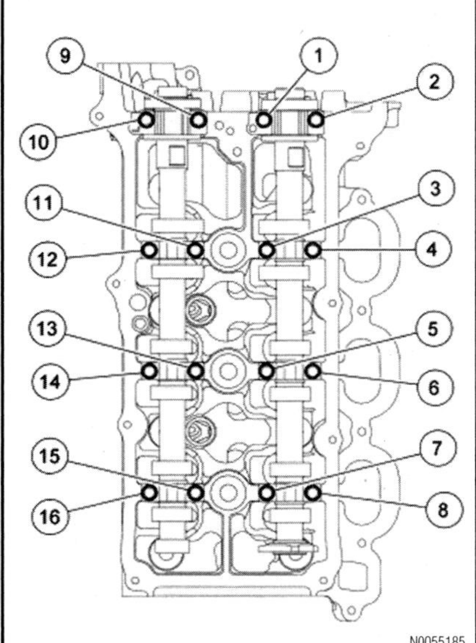

Fig. 80 Removal & installation of the LH camshaft bearing caps (8), and the bolts (16)

    a. Remove the RH VCT assembly, secondary timing chain and the RH exhaust camshaft sprocket as an assembly.
126. Remove the Camshaft Holding Tool from the RH camshafts.

WARNING

The camshafts must remain in the neutral position during removal or engine damage may occur.

127. Rotate the RH camshafts counterclockwise to the neutral position.

➡Cylinder head camshaft bearing caps are numbered to verify that they are assembled in their original positions.

128. Remove the bolts and the RH camshaft bearing caps.
    a. Remove the RH camshafts.

To install:

CAUTION

Do not smoke, carry lighted tobacco or have an open flame of any type when working on or near any fuel-related component. Highly flammable mixtures are always present and may be ignited. Failure to follow these instructions may result in serious personal injury.

WARNING

During engine repair procedures, cleanliness is extremely important. Any foreign material, including any material created while cleaning gasket surfaces that enters the oil passages, coolant passages or the oil pan, may cause engine failure.

WARNING

Early build engines have 11 fastener valve covers, late build engines have 9 fastener valve covers. Do not attempt to install bolts in the 2 empty late build valve cover holes or damage to the valve cover will occur.

➡On early build engines, the timing chain rides on the inner side of the RH timing chain guide. Late built engines are equipped with a different design RH timing chain guide that requires the timing chain to ride on the outer side of the RH timing chain guide. For service, all replacement RH timing chain guides will be the late build design.

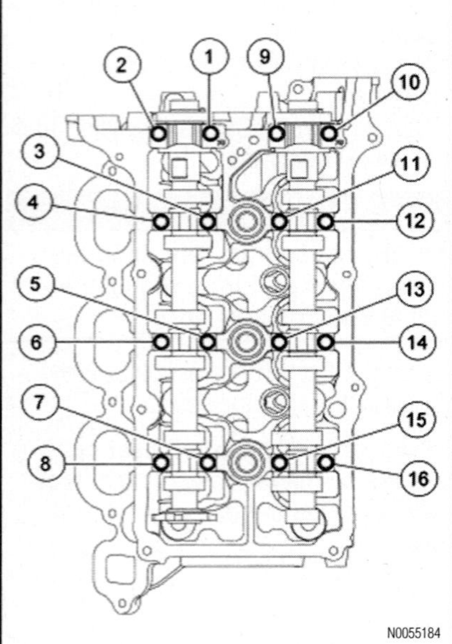

Fig. 81 Removal & installation of the RH camshaft bearing caps (8), and the bolts (16)

All Camshafts

⁂ WARNING

The crankshaft must remain in the freewheeling position (crankshaft dowel pin at 9 o'clock) until after the camshafts are installed and the valve clearance is checked/adjusted. Do not turn the crankshaft until instructed to do so. Failure to follow this process will result in severe engine damage.

129. Rotate the crankshaft counterclockwise until the crankshaft dowel pin is in the 9 o'clock position.

LH Camshafts

⁂ WARNING

The camshafts must remain in the neutral position during removal or engine damage may occur.

➡Coat the camshafts with clean engine oil prior to installation.

130. Position the camshafts onto the LH cylinder head in the neutral position.

➡Cylinder head camshaft bearing caps are numbered to verify that they are assembled in their original positions.

131. Install the 8 camshaft caps and the 16 bolts. Tighten the bolts to 89 inch lbs. (10 Nm).

RH Camshafts

⁂ WARNING

The camshafts must remain in the neutral position during removal or engine damage may occur.

➡Coat the camshafts with clean engine oil prior to installation.

132. Position the camshafts onto the RH cylinder head in the neutral position as shown.

➡Cylinder head camshaft bearing caps are numbered to verify that they are assembled in their original positions.

133. Install the 8 camshaft caps and the 16 bolts. Tighten the bolts to 89 inch lbs. (10 Nm).

All Camshafts

⁂ WARNING

If any components are installed new, the engine valve clearance must be checked/adjusted or engine damage may occur.

➡Use a camshaft sprocket bolt to turn the camshafts.

134. Using a feeler gauge, confirm that the valve tappet clearances are within specification. If valve tappet clearances are not within specification, the clearance must be adjusted by installing new valve tappet(s) of the correct size. Refer to Valve Clearance Check in this section.

LH Camshafts

➡Use a camshaft sprocket bolt to turn the camshafts.

135. Rotate the LH camshafts to the Top Dead Center (TDC) position and install the Camshaft Holding Tool on the flats of the camshafts.

136. Assemble the LH Variable Camshaft Timing (VCT) assembly, the LH exhaust camshaft sprocket and the LH secondary timing chain.

a. Align the colored links with the timing marks.

137. Position the LH secondary timing assembly onto the camshafts.

138. Install the new VCT bolt and new exhaust camshaft bolt and the original washer. Tighten in 4 stages.

a. Stage 1: Tighten to 30 ft. lbs. (40 Nm).
b. Stage 2: Loosen one full turn.
c. Stage 3: Tighten to 89 inch lbs. (10 Nm).
d. Stage 4: Tighten 90 degrees.

139. Remove the lockpin from the LH secondary timing chain tensioner.

RH Camshafts

➡Use a camshaft sprocket bolt to turn the camshafts.

140. Rotate the RH camshafts to the TDC position and install the Camshaft Holding Tool on the flats of the camshafts.

141. Assemble the RH VCT assembly, the RH exhaust camshaft sprocket and the RH secondary timing chain.

a. Align the colored links with the timing marks.

142. Position the RH secondary timing assembly onto the camshafts.

143. Install the new VCT bolt and new exhaust camshaft bolt and the original washer. Tighten in 4 stages.

a. Stage 1: Tighten to 30 ft. lbs. (40 Nm).
b. Stage 2: Loosen one full turn.
c. Stage 3: Tighten to 89 inch lbs. (10 Nm).
d. Stage 4: Tighten 90 degrees.

144. Remove the lockpin from the RH secondary timing chain tensioner.

All Camshafts

145. Rotate the crankshaft clockwise 60 degrees to the TDC position (crankshaft dowel pin at 11 o'clock).

146. Install the primary timing chain with the colored links aligned with the timing marks on the VCT assemblies and the crankshaft sprocket.

147. Install the lower LH primary timing chain guide and the 2 bolts. Tighten the bolts to 89 inch lbs. (10 Nm).

148. Install the primary timing chain tensioner arm.

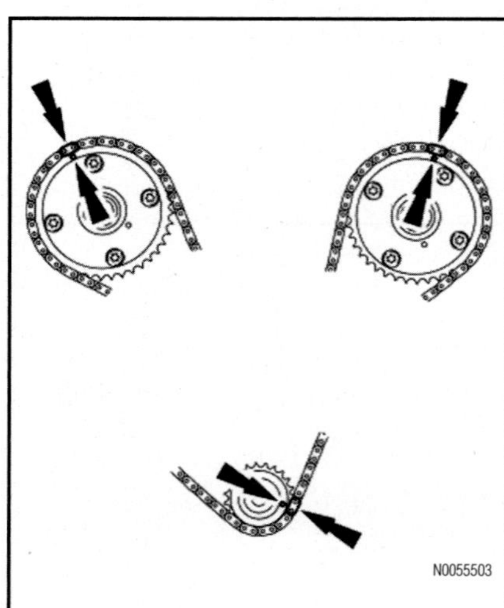

Fig. 82 Installation of the primary timing chain with the colored links aligned with the timing marks on the VCT assemblies

149. Reset the primary timing chain tensioner.

a. Rotate the lever counterclockwise.

b. Using a soft-jawed vise, compress the plunger.

c. Align the hole in the lever with the hole in the tensioner housing.

d. Install a suitable lockpin.

➡It may be necessary to rotate the crankshaft slightly to remove slack from the timing chain and install the tensioner.

150. Install the primary tensioner and the 2 bolts. Tighten the bolts to 89 inch lbs. (10 Nm).

a. Remove the lockpin.

151. As a post-check, verify correct alignment of all timing marks.

152. Inspect the VCT housing seals for damage and replace as necessary.

✱✱ WARNING

Make sure the dowels on the Variable Camshaft Timing (VCT) housing are fully engaged in the cylinder head prior to tightening the bolts. Failure to follow this process will result in severe engine damage.

153. Install the LH VCT housing and the 3 bolts. Tighten the bolts to 89 inch lbs. (10 Nm).

✱✱ WARNING

Make sure the dowels on the Variable Camshaft Timing (VCT) housing are fully engaged in the cylinder head prior to tightening the bolts. Failure to follow this process will result in severe engine damage.

154. Install the RH VCT housing and the 3 bolts. Tighten the bolts to 89 inch lbs. (10 Nm).

155. Install the Alignment Pins.

✱✱ WARNING

Failure to use Motorcraft® High Performance Engine RTV Silicone may cause the engine oil to foam excessively and result in serious engine damage.

➡The engine front cover and bolts 17, 18, 19 and 20 must be installed within 4 minutes of the initial sealant application. The remainder of the engine front cover bolts and the engine mount bracket bolts must be installed and tighten within 35 minutes of the initial sealant application. If the time limits are exceeded, the sealant must be removed, the sealing area cleaned and sealant reapplied. To clean the sealing area, use silicone gasket remover and metal surface prep. Failure to follow this procedure can cause future oil leakage.

156. Apply a 0.11 inch (3.0 mm) bead of Motorcraft® High Performance Engine RTV Silicone to the engine front cover sealing surfaces including the 3 engine mount bracket bosses.

a. Apply a 5.5 mm (0.21 in) bead of Motorcraft® High Performance Engine RTV Silicone to the oil pan-to-cylinder block joint and the cylinder head-to-cylinder block joint areas of the engine front cover in 5 places as indicated.

➡Make sure the 2 locating dowel pins are seated correctly in the cylinder block.

157. Install the engine front cover and bolts 17, 18, 19 and 20. Tighten the bolts to 27 inch lbs. (3 Nm).

158. Remove the Alignment Pins.

➡Do not tighten the bolts at this time.

159. Install the engine mount bracket and the 3 bolts.

✱✱ WARNING

Do not expose the Motorcraft® High Performance Engine RTV Silicone to engine oil for at least 90 minutes after installing the engine front cover. Failure to follow this instruction may cause oil leakage.

160. Install the remaining engine front cover bolts. Tighten all of the engine front cover bolts and engine mount bracket bolts in the sequence shown in 2 stages:

a. Stage 1: Tighten bolts 1 thru 22 to 89 inch lbs. (10 Nm) and bolts 23, 24 and 25 to 133 inch lbs. (15 Nm).

b. Stage 2: Tighten bolts 1 thru 22 to 18 ft. lbs. (24 Nm) and bolts 23, 24 and 25 to 55 ft. lbs. (75 Nm).

✱✱ WARNING

The thread sealer on the engine mount studs (including new engine mount studs if applicable) must be cleaned off with a wire brush and new Thread lock and Sealer applied prior to installing the engine mount studs. Failure to follow this procedure may result in damage to the engine mount studs or engine.

161. Install the engine mount studs in the following sequence.

a. Clean the front cover engine mount stud holes with pressurized air to remove any foreign material.

b. Clean all the thread sealer from the engine mount studs (old and new studs).

c. Apply new Thread lock and Sealer to the engine mount stud threads.

d. Install the 2 engine mount studs. Tighten the stud mounts to 15 ft. lbs. (20 Nm).

162. Install the engine mount bracket and the 2 bolts. Tighten the bolts to 18 ft. lbs. (24 Nm).

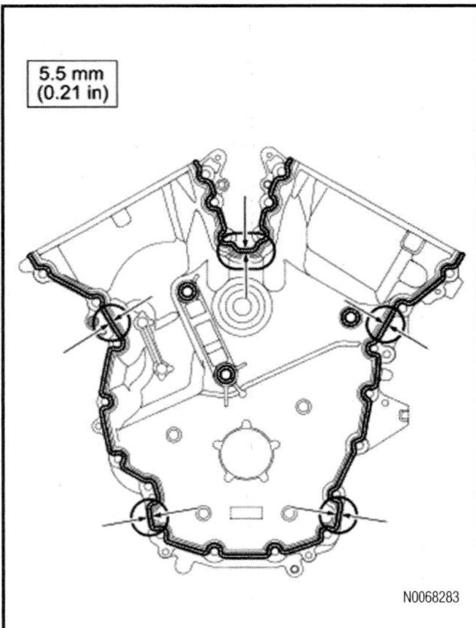

Fig. 83 Engine front cover silicone bead placement

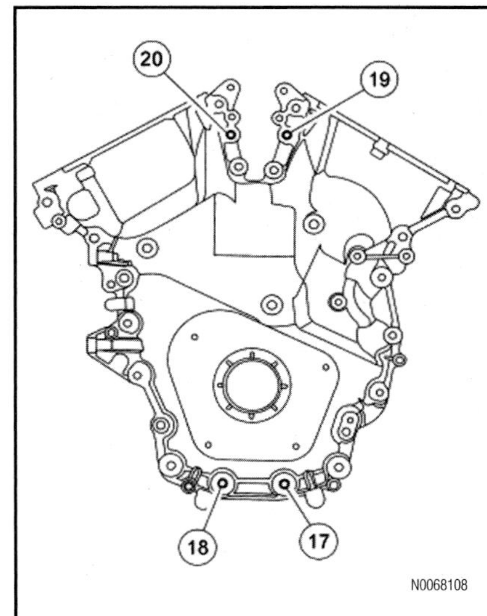

Fig. 84 Install the engine front cover and bolts 17, 18, 19 and 20. Tighten in sequence shown

➡**Apply clean engine oil to the crankshaft front seal bore in the engine front cover.**

163. Using the Crankshaft Vibration Damper Installer and Front Crankshaft Seal Installer, install a new crankshaft front seal.

➡**Lubricate the outside diameter sealing surfaces with clean engine oil.**

164. Using the Crankshaft Vibration Damper Installer and Front Cover Oil Seal Installer, install the crankshaft pulley.

165. Using the Strap Wrench, install the crankshaft pulley washer and new bolt and tighten in 4 stages.

a. Stage 1: Tighten to 89 ft. lbs. (120 Nm).

b. Stage 2: Loosen one full turn.

c. Stage 3: Tighten to37 ft. lbs. (50 Nm).

d. Stage 4: Tighten an additional 90 degrees.

166. Install the accessory drive belt tensioner and the 3 bolts. Tighten the bolts to 97 inch lbs. (11 Nm).

167. Install the power steering pump and the 3 bolts. Tighten the bolts to 18 ft. lbs. (25 Nm).

➡**Installation of new seals is only required if damaged seals were removed during disassembly of the engine.**

➡**Spark plug tube seal installation shown, VCT seal solenoid installation similar.**

168. Using the VCT Spark Plug Tube Seal Installer and Handle, install new VCT solenoid and/or spark plug tube seals.

**** WARNING**

Failure to use Motorcraft® High Performance Engine RTV Silicone may cause the engine oil to foam excessively and result in serious engine damage.

➡**If the valve cover is not installed and the fasteners tightened within 4 minutes, the sealant must be removed and the sealing area cleaned. To clean the sealing area, use silicone gasket remover and metal surface prep. Failure to follow this procedure can cause future oil leakage.**

169. Apply an 0.31 inch (8 mm) bead of Motorcraft® High Performance Engine RTV Silicone to the engine front cover-to-RH cylinder head joints.

Early Build Vehicles

170. Using a new gasket, install the RH valve cover, bolt and the 10 stud bolts. Tighten the bolts to 89 inch lbs. (10 Nm). Refer to the Valve Cover procedure for the proper sequence.

Late Build Vehicles

171. Using a new gasket, install the RH valve cover and tighten the 9 stud bolts. Tighten the bolts to 89 inch lbs. (10 Nm). Refer to the Valve Cover procedure for the proper sequence.

All Vehicles

**** WARNING**

Failure to use Motorcraft® High Performance Engine RTV Silicone may cause the engine oil to foam excessively and result in serious engine damage.

➡**If the valve cover is not installed and the fasteners tightened within 4 minutes, the sealant must be removed and the sealing area cleaned. To clean the sealing area, use silicone gasket remover and metal surface prep. Failure to follow this procedure can cause future oil leakage.**

172. Apply an 0.31 inch (8 mm) bead of Motorcraft® High Performance Engine RTV Silicone to the engine front cover-to-LH cylinder head joints.

Early Build Vehicles

173. Using a new gasket, install the LH valve cover and 11 stud bolts. Tighten the bolts to 89 inch lbs. (10 Nm). Refer to the Valve Cover procedure for the proper sequence.

Late Build Vehicles

174. Using a new gasket, install the LH valve cover tighten the 9 stud bolts. Tighten the bolts to 89 inch lbs. (10 Nm). Refer to the Valve Cover procedure for the proper sequence.

All Vehicles

175. Install the PSP tube bracket and nut to the RH valve cover stud bolt. Tighten the bolt to 62 inch lbs. (7 Nm).

176. Install the PSP tube bracket bolt. Tighten the bolt to 89 inch lbs. (10 Nm).

177. Connect the PSP switch electrical connector.

178. Install the 6 coil-on-plug assemblies and the 6 bolts. Tighten the bolts to 62 inch lbs. (7 Nm).

179. Attach all of the wiring harness retainers to the LH valve cover and stud bolts.

180. Connect the 3 LH coil-on-plug electrical connectors.

181. Connect the LH VCT solenoid electrical connector.

182. Attach all of the wiring harness retainers to the RH valve cover and stud bolts.

183. Connect the 3 RH coil-on-plug electrical connectors.

184. Connect the RH VCT solenoid electrical connector.

185. Connect the RH CMS electrical connector.

**** WARNING**

If the engine is repaired or replaced because of upper engine failure, typically including valve or piston damage, check the intake manifold for metal debris. If metal debris is found, install a new intake manifold. Failure to follow these instructions can result in engine damage.

186. Using a new gasket, install the upper intake manifold and the 6 bolts. Tighten the bolts to 89 inch lbs. (10 Nm).

187. Install the fuel tube bracket bolt to the upper intake manifold and install the wiring harness pin-type retainer. Tighten the bolt to 53 inch lbs. (6 Nm).

188. Install the upper intake manifold support bracket bolt. Tighten the bolt to 89 inch lbs. (10 Nm).

189. Attach the wiring harness retainers to the upper intake manifold.

190. Connect the Throttle Body (TB) electrical connector.

191. Connect the PCV hose to the PCV valve.

192. Raise the engine and transaxle assembly into the vehicle.

193. Install the engine mount and the 3 bolts. Tighten the bolts to 66 ft. lbs. (90 Nm).

194. Install the 4 engine mount nuts. Tighten the nuts to 46 ft. lbs. (63 Nm).

195. Install the engine mount brace, the nut and the bolt. Tighten the nut and bolt to 15 ft. lbs. (20 Nm).

196. Install the transaxle support insulator bracket, 3 nuts and the bolt. Tighten the nuts to 46 ft. lbs. (63 Nm), and the bolt to 41 ft. lbs. (55 Nm).

197. Install the transaxle support insulator through bolt and nut. Tighten the bolt to 129 ft. lbs. (175 Nm).

All-Wheel Drive (AWD)

➡**A new Power Transfer Unit (PTU) seal must be installed whenever the intermediate shaft is removed.**

198. Install a new PTU seal as outlined in the Drive Train Section.

All Camshafts

199. Connect the transaxle cooler tubes and install the 2 secondary latches.

200. Install the RH halfshaft support bracket and the 4 bolts.

a. Tighten the halfshaft support-to-cylinder block bolts to 30 ft. lbs. (40 Nm).

b. Tighten the catalytic converter-to-halfshaft support bolts to 15 ft. lbs. (20 Nm).

201. Install the 2 halfshaft support bracket studs. Tighten the studs to 89 inch lbs. (10 Nm).

WARNING

The circlips are unique in size and shape for each shaft. Make sure to use the specified circlip for the application or vehicle damage may occur.

202. Install the correct new circlip on the inboard stub shaft.

➡After insertion, pull the halfshaft inner end to make sure the circlip is locked.

203. Push the stub shaft into the transmission so the circlip locks into the differential side gear.

204. Rotate the LH wheel knuckle into position and insert the LH halfshaft into the wheel hub.

205. Install the intermediate and halfshaft assembly and the 2 bolts. Tighten the bolts to 18 ft. lbs. (25 Nm).

206. Rotate the RH wheel knuckle into position and insert the RH halfshaft into the wheel hub.

207. Using the Powertrain Lift, raise the subframe into the installed position.

208. Install the 2 front subframe bolts. Tighten the bolts to 148 ft. lbs. (200 Nm).

209. Position the subframe brackets and install the 4 bolts finger-tight.

210. Install the 2 rear subframe bolts. Tighten the bolts to 111 ft. lbs. (150 Nm).

211. Install the 4 subframe bracket-to-body bolts. Tighten the bolts to 41 ft. lbs. (55 Nm).

212. Position the ball joints into the wheel knuckles. Install the new ball joint nuts. Tighten the nuts to 148 ft. lbs. (200 Nm).

➡The hex-holding feature can be used to prevent turning of the stud while removing the nuts.

213. Install new tie-rod end nuts. Tighten the nuts to 111 ft. lbs. (150 Nm).

214. Install new upper stabilizer bar link nuts. Tighten the nuts to 111 ft. lbs. (150 Nm).

215. Install the 2 front engine roll restrictor-to-transaxle bolts. Tighten the bolts to 66 ft. lbs. (90 Nm).

216. Install the 2 rear engine roll restrictor-to-transaxle bolts. Tighten the bolts to 66 ft. lbs. (90 Nm).

217. Using a new O-ring seal, install the PSP tube onto the steering gear, rotate the clamp plate and install the bolt. Tighten the bolt to 18 ft. lbs. (25 Nm).

218. Install the PSP tube bracket-to-steering gear bolt. Tighten the bolt to 89 inch lbs. (10 Nm).

➡Lubricate the engine oil filter gasket with clean engine oil prior to installing the oil filter.

219. Install a new engine oil filter. Tighten the oil filter to 44 inch lbs. (5 Nm), and then rotate an additional 180 degrees.

AWD Vehicles

220. Line up the index marks on the rear driveshaft to the index marks on the PTU flange made during removal and install the 4 bolts. Tighten the bolts to 52 ft. lbs. (70 Nm).

All Camshafts

221. Using a new gasket, install the Y-pipe and install the 2 new nuts. Tighten the nuts to 30 ft. lbs. (40 Nm).

a. Attach the exhaust hanger.

222. Install the Y-pipe assembly and 4 new nuts. Tighten the nuts to 30 ft. lbs. (40 Nm).

WARNING

Do not allow the intermediate shaft to rotate while it is disconnected from the gear or damage to the clockspring may occur. If there is evidence that the intermediate shaft has rotated, the clockspring must be removed and recentered. Refer to the Chassis Electrical Section.

➡Align the index marks made during removal.

223. Install the steering intermediate shaft onto the steering gear and install a new bolt. Tighten the bolt to 17 ft. lbs. (23 Nm).

224. Position the RH brake hose bracket and install the bolt. Tighten the bolt to 22 ft. lbs. (30 Nm).

225. Position the rubber shield and install the 2 lower scrivets.

WARNING

Do not tighten the wheel hub nut with the vehicle on the ground. The nut must be tightened to specification before the vehicle is lowered onto the wheels. Wheel bearing damage will occur if the wheel bearing is loaded with the weight of the vehicle applied.

➡Apply the brake to keep the halfshaft from rotating.

226. Using the previously removed RH and LH wheel hub nuts, seat the halfshaft. Tighten the nuts to 258 ft. lbs. (350 Nm).

a. Remove and discard the wheel hub nuts.

WARNING

The wheel hub nut contains a one-time locking chemical that is activated by the heat created when it is tightened. Install and tighten the new wheel hub nut to specification within 5 minutes of starting it on the threads. Always install a new wheel hub nut after loosening or when not tightened within the specified time or damage to the components can occur.

➡Apply the brake to keep the halfshaft from rotating.

227. Install a new RH and LH wheel hub nut. Tighten the nut to 258 ft. lbs. (350 Nm).

228. Connect the hose to the power steering reservoir.

229. Install the oil level indicator.

230. Install the ground cable and bolt. Tighten the bolt to 106 inch lbs. (12 Nm).

231. Attach the wire harness retainer to the RH valve cover stud bolt.

232. Attach the engine wiring harness retainer.

233. Connect the fuel supply tube to the fuel rail.

234. Using a new O-ring seal, connect the upper A/C tube to the condenser and install the nut and connect the A/C pressure switch electrical connector. Tighten the nut to 133 inch lbs. (15 Nm).

235. If equipped, attach the block heater wiring harness retainer to the radiator and power steering tube.

236. Connect the transaxle control cable to the shift cable bracket.

237. Connect the transaxle control cable to the control lever.

238. Connect the upper radiator hose, lower radiator hose and heater hose to the thermostat housing.

239. Install the engine wiring harness retainer to the bulkhead.

a. Slide the wiring harness in the bulkhead.

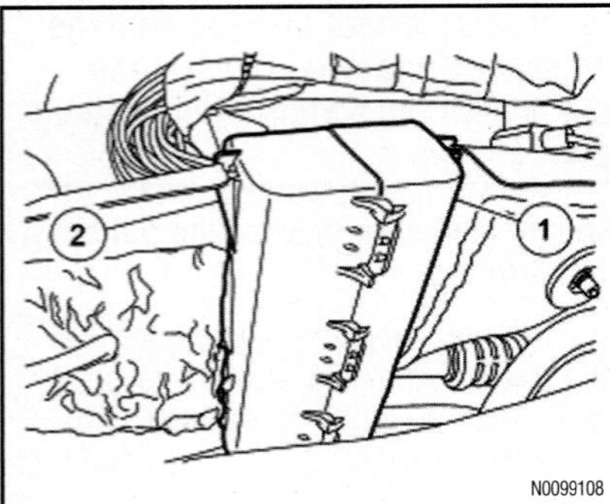

Fig. 85 Installation of the engine wiring harness retainer to the bulkhead

b. Make sure the wiring harness retainer tab is below the bulkhead lip.

240. Connect the 2 PCM electrical connectors.

241. Connect the PCM and engine harness electrical connectors.

a. Attach the wiring harness retainer.

242. Install the Evaporative Emission (EVAP) canister purge valve as outlined in the Engine Performance & Emission Controls Section.

243. Attach the EVAP tube pin-type retainer to the upper intake manifold.

244. Connect the vacuum hose and the EVAP tube to the upper intake manifold.

245. Install the degas bottle as outlined in the Engine Cooling Section.

246. Using a new O-ring seal and gasket seal, install the A/C tube and the nut. Tighten the nut to 133 inch lbs. (15 Nm).

247. Using a new O-ring seal and gasket seal, connect the A/C tube and install the nut. Tighten the nut to 133 inch lbs. (15 Nm).

248. Connect the power steering cooler tube.

249. Install the front valance, 3 pushpins and 7 screws.

250. Install the accessory drive belt and the power steering belt as outlined in this section.

251. Install the LF wheel and tire.

252. Connect the ground cable to the negative battery terminal and install the nut. Tighten the nut to 53 inch lbs. (6 Nm).

253. Connect the power feed wire to the positive battery terminal and install the nut. Tighten the nut to 53 inch lbs. (6 Nm).

254. Connect the engine wiring harness electrical connector.

255. Install the battery tray.

256. Install the engine Air Cleaner (ACL) and ACL outlet pipe.

257. Install the strut tower brace and the 4 nuts. Tighten the nuts to 26 ft. lbs. (35 Nm).

258. Attach the brake booster vacuum hose retainers to the strut tower brace.

259. Install the cowl panel grille.

WARNING

Do not expose the Motorcraft® High Performance Engine RTV Silicone to engine oil for at least 90 minutes after installing the engine front cover. Failure to follow this instruction may cause oil leakage.

260. Fill the engine with clean engine oil.

261. Fill and bleed the cooling system as outlined in the Engine Cooling Section.

262. Fill the power steering system as outlined in the Steering Section.

263. Recharge the A/C system.

3.5L Turbo Engine

See Figures 86 through 118.

CAUTION

Do not smoke, carry lighted tobacco or have an open flame of any type when working on or near any fuel-related component. Highly flammable mixtures are always present and may be ignited. Failure to follow these instructions may result in serious personal injury.

WARNING

During engine repair procedures, cleanliness is extremely important. Any foreign material, including any material created while cleaning gasket surfaces, which enters the oil passages, coolant passages or the oil pan may cause engine failure.

WARNING

Whenever turbocharger air intake system components are removed, always cover open ports to protect from debris. It is important that no foreign material enter the system. The turbocharger compressor vanes are susceptible to damage from even small particles. All components should be inspected and cleaned, if necessary, prior to installation or reassembly.

➡On early build engines, the timing chain rides on the inner side of the RH timing chain guide. Late build engines are equipped with a different design RH timing chain guide that requires the timing chain to ride on the outer side of the RH timing chain guide. For service, all replacement RH timing chain guides will be the late build design.

All Camshafts

1. With the vehicle in NEUTRAL, position it on a hoist.

➡Use a steering wheel holding device (such as Hunter® 28-75-1 or equivalent).

2. Using a steering wheel holding device, hold the steering wheel in the straight-ahead position.

3. Release the fuel system pressure.

4. Recover the A/C system as outlined in the Heating, Ventilation & Air conditioning.

5. Disconnect the LH Heated Oxygen Sensor (HO2S) electrical connector.

a. Detach the HO2S connector retainer from the bracket.

6. Remove the 4 retainers and the underbody shield.

7. Remove the 7 bolts, 3 pin-type retainers and the front splash shield.

8. Drain the cooling system as outlined in the Engine Cooling Section.

9. Remove the front wheels and tires.

10. Remove the 2 lower scrivets from the rubber shield and position the shield aside.

➡Apply the brake to keep the halfshafts from rotating.

11. Remove the RH and LH halfshaft nuts.

a. Do not discard at this time.

12. Using the Front Wheel Hub Remover, separate the RH and LH halfshaft from the wheel hubs.

13. Remove the bolt from the RH brake hose bracket.

14. Remove the LH and RH catalytic converters as outlined in this section.

15. Remove the 2 rear engine roll restrictor-to-transaxle bolts.

16. Remove the 2 front engine roll restrictor-to-transaxle bolts.

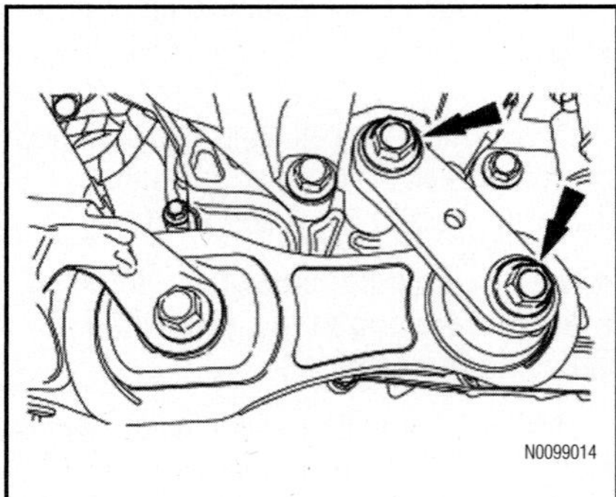

Fig. 86 Removal of the 2 rear engine roll restrictor-to-transaxle bolts

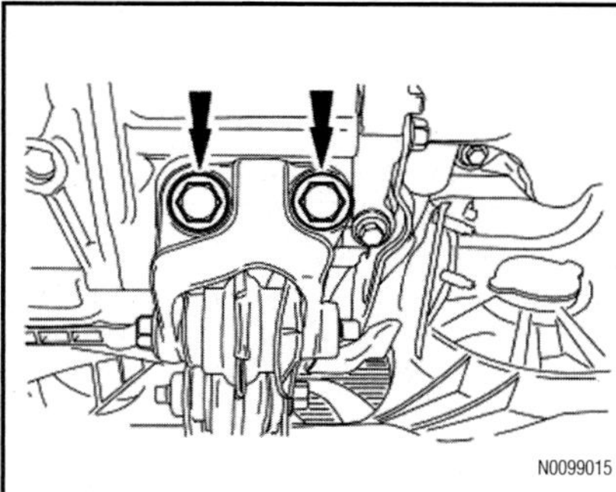

Fig. 87 Removal of the 2 front engine roll restrictor-to-transaxle bolts

17. Remove and discard the upper stabilizer link nuts.

➡The hex-holding feature can be used to prevent turning of the stud while removing the nut.

18. Remove and discard the tie-rod end nuts.
    a. Separate the tie-rod ends from the wheel knuckles.

✻✻ WARNING

Suspension fasteners are critical parts because they affect performance of vital components and systems and their failure may result in major service expense. New parts must be installed with the same part number or equivalent part, if replacement is necessary. Do not use a replacement part of lesser quality or substitute design. Torque values must be used as specified during reassembly to make sure of correct retention of these parts.

✻✻ WARNING

Use care when releasing the lower arm and knuckle into the resting position or damage to the ball joint seal or Constant Velocity (CV) boot may occur.

➡Use the hex-holding feature to prevent the stud from turning while removing the nut.

19. Remove and discard the lower ball joint-to-wheel knuckle nuts.
    a. Separate the lower ball joints from the wheel knuckles.

✻✻ WARNING

Do not allow the intermediate shaft to rotate while it is disconnected from the gear or damage to the clockspring may occur. If there is evidence that the intermediate shaft has rotated, the clockspring must be removed and recentered. Refer to the Supplemental Restraint System in the Chassis Electrical Section.

20. Remove the bolt and disconnect the steering column shaft from the steering gear.
    a. Discard the bolt.
21. Remove the bolt and disconnect the 2 Electronic Power Assist Steering (EPAS) electrical connectors, and the wiring retainer.
22. Position the Powertrain Lift under the subframe assembly.
23. Remove the subframe bracket-to-body bolts.
24. Remove the rear subframe bolts and the subframe brackets.
25. Remove the front subframe bolts.
26. Lower the subframe assembly from the vehicle.
27. Pull the RH wheel knuckle outward and rotate it toward the rear of the vehicle.
    a. Secure the RH wheel knuckle assembly.
28. Remove the 2 halfshaft bracket bolts.
29. Remove the intermediate and halfshaft assembly.
    a. Inspect the intermediate shaft for pitting or damage in the seal contact area. Replace if necessary.

✻✻ WARNING

The sharp edges on the stub shaft splines can slice or puncture the oil seal. Use care when inserting the stub shaft into the transmission or damage to the component may occur.

30. Using the Slide Hammer and Halfshaft Remover, remove the halfshaft from the transmission.
31. Remove and discard the circlip from the stub shaft.
32. Remove the cowl panel grille.
33. Detach the 2 brake booster vacuum hose retainers from the strut tower brace.
34. Remove the 4 nuts and the strut tower brace.
35. Disconnect the PCM and engine harness electrical connectors.
    a. Detach the wiring harness retainer.
36. Disconnect the 2 PCM electrical connectors.
37. Remove the engine wiring harness retainer from the bulkhead.
    a. Push the wiring harness retainer tab in.
    b. Slide the wiring harness up and out of the bulkhead.
38. Remove the nut and disconnect the A/C tube.
    a. Discard the O-ring seal and gasket seal.
39. Remove the nut and the A/C tube.
    a. Discard the O-ring seal and gasket seal.
40. Remove the degas bottle as outlined in the Engine Cooling Section.
41. Remove the engine Air Cleaner (ACL) and ACL outlet pipe.
42. Remove the noise generator. Refer to the Intake Air System Components as outlined in this section.
43. Disconnect the Turbocharger Boost Pressure (TCBP)/Charge Air Cooler Temperature (CACT) sensor electrical connector.
44. Loosen the 2 clamps and remove the CAC outlet pipe.
45. Remove the battery tray.
46. Disconnect the engine wiring harness electrical connector.
47. Remove the nut and disconnect the ground cable from the negative battery terminal.
48. Remove the nut and disconnect the power feed wires from the positive battery terminal.
49. Disconnect the brake booster vacuum quick connect coupling.
50. Disconnect the transaxle control cable from the control lever.
51. Disconnect the transaxle control cable from the shift cable bracket.
    a. Detach the wiring harness pin-type retainer.
52. Loosen the 2 clamps and remove the RH CAC tube.
53. Disconnect the 2 heater hoses from the intake manifold.
54. Remove the bolt and ground wire from the engine front cover.

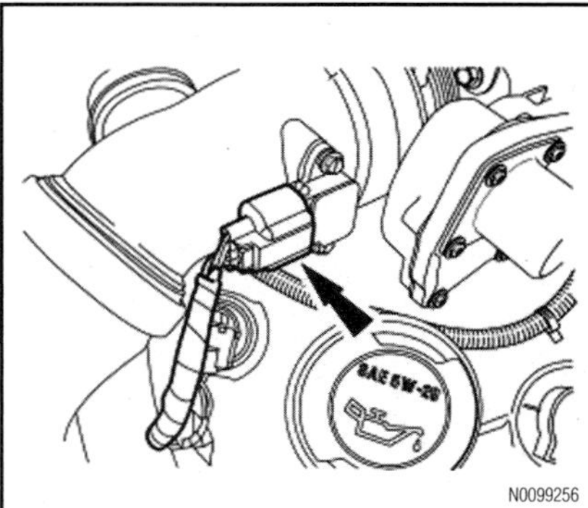

Fig. 88 Turbocharger Boost Pressure (TCBP)/Charge Air Cooler Temperature (CACT) sensor electrical connector

55. Disconnect the upper radiator hose from the intake manifold coolant tube.

56. If equipped, detach the engine block heater harness from the radiator support wiring harness.

57. Disconnect the Evaporative Emission (EVAP) tube quick connect coupling.

58. Disconnect the EVAP valve electrical connector and detach from the intake manifold.

59. Disconnect the quick connect coupling from the intake manifold and remove the EVAP tube assembly.

60. Disconnect the fuel supply tube as outlined in the Fuel System.

➡Index-mark the driveshaft for installation.

61. Remove and discard the 4 bolts and position aside the driveshaft.

62. Remove the drain plug and drain the engine oil. Install the drain plug and tighten the plug to 20 ft. lbs. (27 Nm).

63. Remove and discard the engine oil filter.

64. Remove the A/C tube bracket bolt from the rear of the compressor.

65. Remove the nut and disconnect the upper A/C tube from the compressor.

a. Discard the O-ring seal and gasket seal.

66. Loosen the clamp and disconnect the lower LH CAC tube from the LH turbocharger.

67. Detach the lower radiator hose retainer from the cooling fan and shroud.

68. Disconnect the lower radiator hose from the radiator.

69. Remove the 2 secondary latches from the transmission fluid cooler tubes at the transmission fluid cooler thermal bypass valve.

70. Using the Transmission Cooler Line Disconnect Tool, disconnect the transmission fluid cooler tubes from the transmission fluid cooler thermal bypass valve.

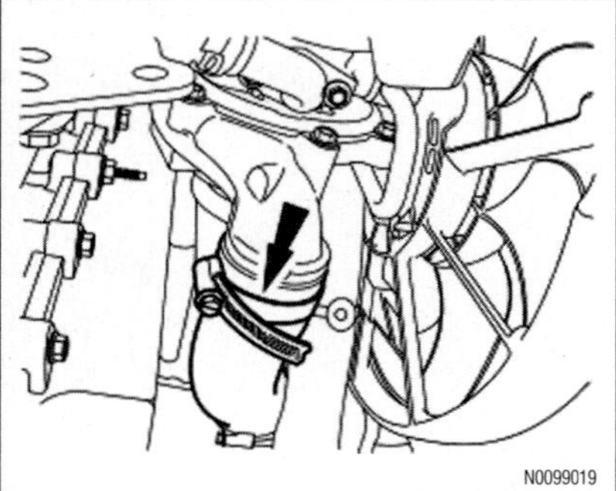

Fig. 89 Disconnect the lower LH CAC tube from the LH turbocharger

Fig. 90 Disconnect the transmission fluid cooler tubes from the transmission fluid cooler thermal bypass valve

71. Remove the 3 bolts and the RH turbocharger lower bracket.

72. Remove the 2 bolts and the RH halfshaft support bracket.

73. Remove the 3 bolts and the Power Transfer Unit (PTU) support bracket.

74. Remove the 5 bolts and the PTU .

➡Position a block of wood under the transaxle.

75. Install the Powertrain Lift and Universal Adapter Brackets.

76. Remove the 3 nuts and the bolt from the transaxle support insulator bracket-to-transaxle.

77. Remove the 4 engine mount nuts.

78. Remove the 3 bolts and the engine mount.

79. Lower the engine and transaxle assembly from the vehicle.

80. Disconnect the 2 quick connect couplings and remove the crankcase vent tube.

81. Remove the nut and the A/C tube from the compressor.

a. Discard the O-ring seal and gasket seal.

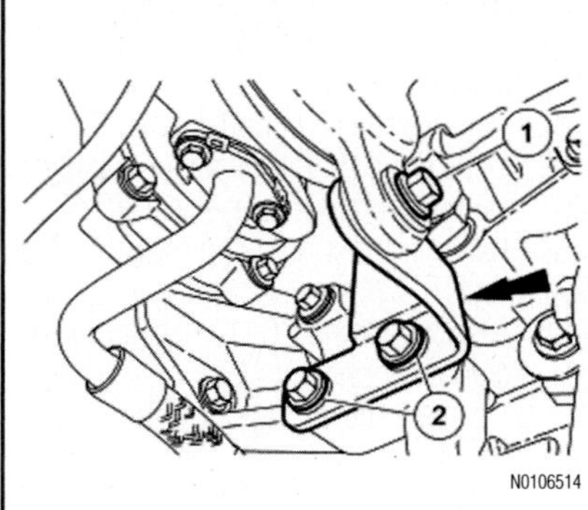

Fig. 91 RH turbocharger lower bracket. Tighten the "1" bolt to 168 inch lbs. (19 Nm), and the "2" bolts to 35 ft. lbs. (48 Nm)

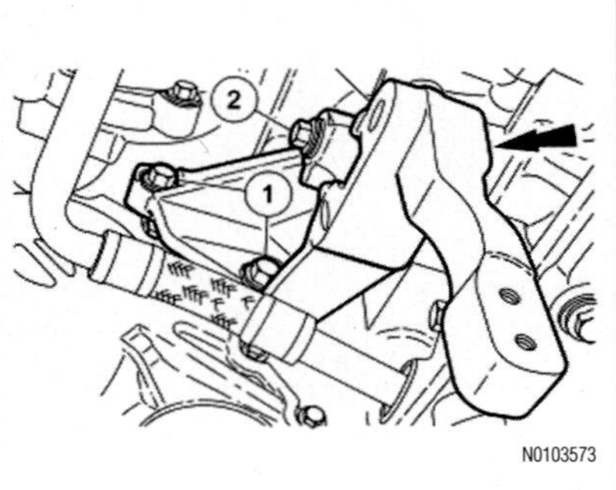

Fig. 92 Power Transfer Unit (PTU) support bracket. Tighten the "1" bolts to 35 ft. lbs. (48 Nm), and the "2" bolt to 52 ft. lbs. (70 Nm)

82. Disconnect the brake vacuum tube from the intake manifold.

83. Disconnect the 2 quick connect couplings and remove the PCV tube.

84. If equipped, disconnect the 2 heated PCV electrical connectors.

85. Disconnect the LH turbocharger bypass valve electrical connector.

➡Index-mark the hoses for installation.

86. Disconnect the turbocharger wastegate regulating valve hoses from the RH CAC tube and turbocharger wastegate regulating valve.

87. Loosen the clamp and remove the LH turbocharger intake tube from the LH turbocharger.

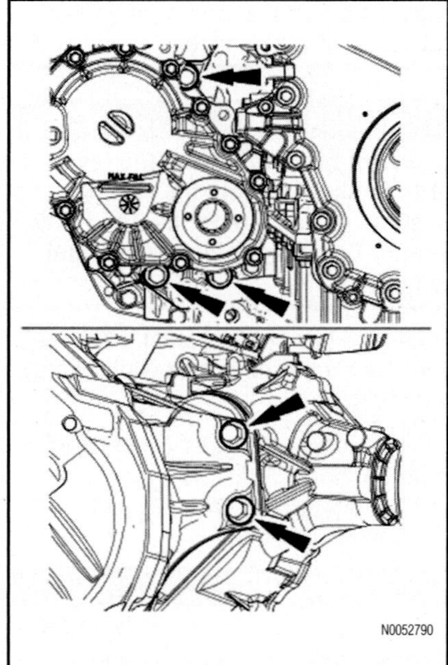

Fig. 93 PTU bolt location and removal

88. Disconnect the RH turbocharger bypass valve electrical connector.

89. Loosen the clamp and remove the RH CAC tube from the RH turbocharger.

90. Loosen the clamp and remove the RH turbocharger intake pipe from the RH turbocharger.

WARNING

The compression limiter bushing may fall out of the mounting bracket grommet on the turbocharger intake tube during service. Make sure the bushing is in place when reinstalling the tube or damage to the tube may occur.

91. Remove the nut from the RH valve cover stud bolt for the RH turbocharger intake tube.

WARNING

The compression limiter bushing may fall out of the mounting bracket grommet on the Charge Air Cooler (CAC) tube during service. Make sure the bushing is in place when reinstalling the tube or damage to the tube may occur.

92. Remove the RH CAC tube nut from the intake manifold and remove the RH CAC tube and turbocharger intake tube as an assembly.

93. Remove the noise insulator shield for the fuel injection pump and disconnect the electrical connector.

94. Disconnect the Throttle Position (TP) sensor and electronic TB electrical connectors.

95. Disconnect the LH Variable Camshaft Timing (VCT) solenoid electrical connector.

96. Disconnect the Engine Oil Pressure (EOP) electrical connector.

a. Detach the wiring harness retainer from the block.

97. Disconnect the 3 LH ignition coil-on-plug electrical connectors.

98. Remove the lower radiator hose from the thermostat housing.

99. Remove the engine cover mounting stud from the LH valve cover stud bolt.

100. Detach all the wiring harness retainers from the LH valve cover and stud bolts.

101. Remove the nut and the oil supply tube bracket from the LH valve cover stud bolt.

102. Remove the oil level indicator.

103. Detach and disconnect the 2 fuel injector wiring harness electrical connectors.

104. Disconnect the Manifold Absolute Pressure (MAP)/Intake Air Temperature 2 (IAT2) sensor electrical connector.

105. Disconnect the turbocharger wastegate regulating valve electrical connector.

106. Detach the 2 wire harness-to-intake manifold retainers.

107. Remove the fuel tube-to-engine front cover bracket bolt and position the fuel tube aside.

108. Disconnect the 2 turbocharger coolant hoses from the intake manifold.

WARNING

If the engine is repaired or replaced because of upper engine failure, typically including valve or piston damage, check the intake manifold for metal debris. If metal debris is found, install a new intake manifold. Failure to follow these instructions can result in engine damage.

➡**Note the routing of the 2 fuel rail wiring harnesses for installation.**

109. Remove the 12 bolts and the intake manifold.

a. Remove and discard the intake manifold, coolant crossover and thermostat housing gaskets.

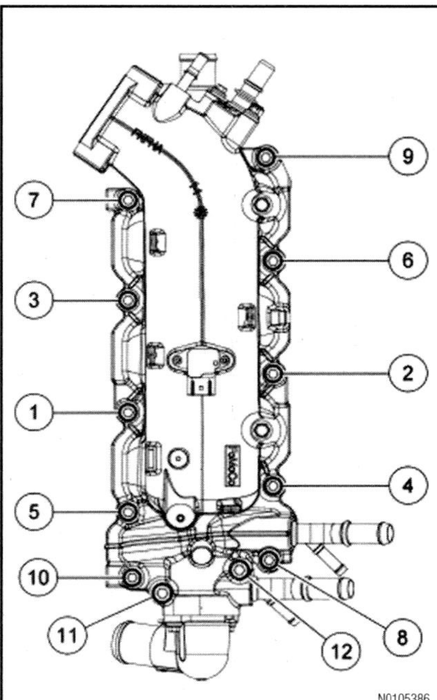

Fig. 94 Removal & installation of the intake manifold. Using a new intake manifold, coolant crossover and thermostat housing gaskets, install the intake manifold and 12 bolts. Tighten the bolts in the sequence shown to 89 inch lbs. (10 Nm)

b. Clean and inspect all sealing surfaces.

110. Disconnect the RH VCT solenoid electrical connector and detach the 2 wiring harness retainers.

111. Disconnect the 3 RH ignition coil-on-plug electrical connectors.

112. Detach all the wiring harness retainers from the RH valve cover and stud bolts.

Early Build Vehicles

113. Remove the nut for the high pressure fuel tube from the LH valve cover stud bolt.

Late Build Vehicles

114. Remove the high pressure fuel tube bolt from the LH cylinder head.

All Vehicles

➡**To release the fuel pressure in the high pressure fuel tube, wrap the flare nuts with a shop towel to absorb any residual fuel pressure during the loosening of the flare nuts.**

115. Remove the high pressure fuel tube flare nut from the fuel injection pump. Remove the 2 high pressure fuel tube flare nuts from the fuel rails and remove the high pressure fuel tube assembly.

116. Remove the 2 bolts and the fuel injection pump.

117. Remove the fuel injection pump mounting plate.

➡**Valve cover is removed for clarity.**

118. Remove the fuel injection pump roller tappet.

a. Inspect the fuel injection pump roller tappet.

➡**When removing the ignition coil-on-plugs, a slight twisting motion will break the seal and ease removal.**

119. Remove the 3 bolts and the 3 LH ignition coil-on-plugs.

➡**When removing the ignition coil-on-plugs, a slight twisting motion will break the seal and ease removal.**

120. Remove the 3 bolts and the 3 RH ignition coil-on-plugs.

121. Loosen the 10 stud bolts and remove the LH valve cover. Discard the gasket.

122. Loosen the 11 stud bolts and remove the RH valve cover. Discard the gasket.

➡**VCT solenoid seal removal shown, spark plug tube seal removal similar.**

123. Inspect the VCT solenoid seals and the spark plug tube seals. Install new seals if damaged.

a. Using the VCT Spark Plug Tube Seal Remover and Handle, remove the seal(s).

124. Rotate the accessory drive belt tensioner clockwise and remove the accessory drive belt.

125. Remove the 3 bolts and the accessory drive belt tensioner.

126. Using the Strap Wrench, remove the crankshaft pulley bolt and washer.

a. Discard the bolt.

127. Using the 3 Jaw Puller, remove the crankshaft pulley.

128. Using the Oil Seal Remover, remove and discard the crankshaft front seal.

129. Remove the HO2S connector bracket stud bolt from the engine front cover.

➡Only use hand tools to remove the studs.

130. Remove the 2 engine mount studs.

131. Remove the 3 bolts and the engine mount bracket.

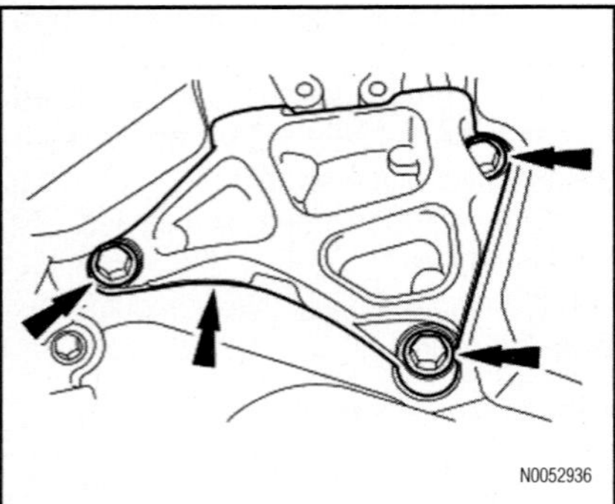

Fig. 95 Removal & installation of the engine mount bracket

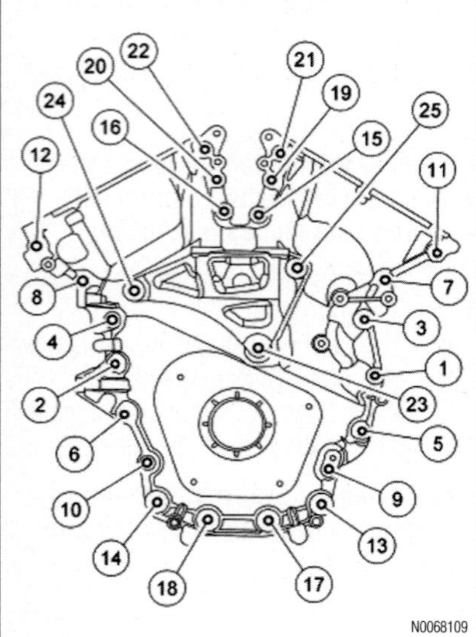

Fig. 96 Removal & installation of the engine front cover. Tighten the bolts in the sequence shown

132. Remove the 22 engine front cover bolts.

133. Install 6 of the engine front cover bolts (finger-tight) into the 6 threaded holes in the engine front cover.

a. Tighten the bolts one turn at a time in a crisscross pattern until the engine front cover-to-cylinder block seal is released.

b. Remove the engine front cover.

WARNING

Only use a 3M™ Roloc® Bristle Disk (2-in white, part number 07528) to clean the engine front cover. Do not use metal scrapers, wire brushes or any other power abrasive disk to clean the engine front cover. These tools cause scratches and gouges that make leak paths.

134. Clean the engine front cover using a 3M™ Roloc® Bristle Disk (2-in white, part number 07528) in a suitable tool turning at the recommended speed of 15,000 rpm.

a. Thoroughly wash the engine front cover to remove any foreign material, including any abrasive particles created during the cleaning process.

WARNING

Place clean, lint-free shop towels over exposed engine cavities. Carefully remove the towels so foreign material is not dropped into the engine. Any foreign material (including any material created while cleaning gasket surfaces) that enters the oil passages or the oil pan, may cause engine failure.

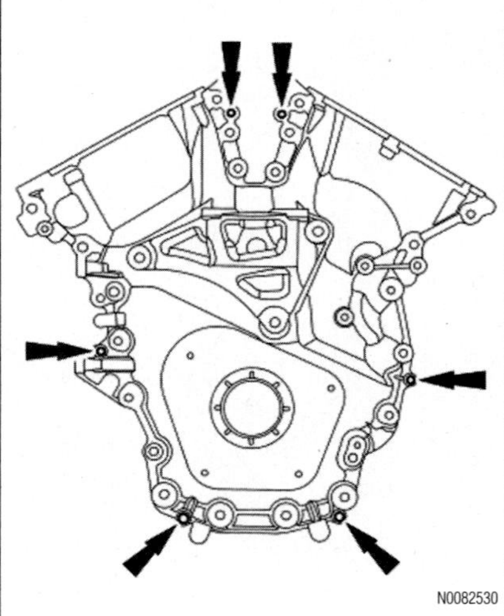

Fig. 97 Install 6 of the engine front cover bolts (finger-tight) into the 6 threaded holes in the engine front cover. Tighten the bolts one turn at a time in a crisscross pattern until the engine front cover-to-cylinder block seal is released

WARNING

Do not use wire brushes, power abrasive discs or 3M™ Roloc® Bristle Disk (2-in white, part number 07528) to clean the sealing surfaces. These tools cause scratches and gouges that make leak paths. They also cause contamination that will cause premature engine failure. Remove all traces of sealant, including any sealant from the inner surface of the cylinder block and cylinder head.

135. Clean the sealing surfaces of the cylinder heads, the cylinder block and the oil pan in the following sequence.

a. Remove any large deposits of silicone or gasket material.

b. Apply silicone gasket remover and allow to set for several minutes.

c. Remove the silicone gasket remover. A second application of silicone gasket remover may be required if residual traces of silicone or gasket material remain.

d. Apply metal surface prep, to remove any remaining traces of oil or coolant and to prepare the surfaces to bond. Do not attempt to make the metal shiny. Some staining of the metal surfaces is normal.

e. Make sure the 2 locating dowel pins are seated correctly in the cylinder block.

Engines Equipped With Early Build RH Timing Chain Guides

136. Rotate the crankshaft clockwise and align the timing marks on the VCT assemblies as shown.

Engines Equipped With Late Build/Replacement RH Timing Chain Guides

137. Rotate the crankshaft clockwise and align the timing marks on the VCT assemblies as shown.

All Camshafts

➡The Camshaft Holding Tool will hold the camshafts in the Top Dead Center (TDC) position.

138. Install the Camshaft Holding Tool onto the flats of the LH camshafts.

➡The Camshaft Holding Tool will hold the camshafts in the TDC position.

Fig. 98 Rotate the crankshaft clockwise and align the timing marks on the VCT assemblies—Early Build

139. Install the Camshaft Holding Tool onto the flats of the RH camshafts.
140. Remove the 3 bolts and the RH VCT housing.
141. Remove the 3 bolts and the LH VCT housing.
142. Remove the 2 bolts and the primary timing chain tensioner.
143. Remove the primary timing chain tensioner arm.
144. Remove the 2 bolts and the lower LH primary timing chain guide.
145. Remove the primary timing chain.

LH Camshafts

146. Compress the LH secondary timing chain tensioner and install a suitable lock-pin to retain the tensioner in the collapsed position.

➡The VCT bolt and the exhaust camshaft bolt must be discarded and new ones installed. However, the exhaust camshaft washer is reusable.

147. Remove and discard the LH VCT assembly bolt and the LH exhaust camshaft sprocket bolt.
   a. Remove the LH VCT assembly, secondary timing chain and the LH exhaust camshaft sprocket as an assembly.

➡When the Camshaft Holding Tool is removed, valve spring pressure will rotate the LH camshafts approximately 3 degrees to a neutral position.

148. Remove the Camshaft Holding Tool from the LH camshafts.

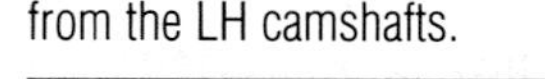

WARNING

The camshafts must remain in the neutral position during removal or engine damage may occur.

149. Verify the LH camshafts are in the neutral position.

➡Cylinder head camshaft bearing caps are numbered to verify that they are assembled in their original positions.

150. Remove the bolts and the LH camshaft bearing caps.
   a. Remove the LH camshafts.

RH Camshafts

151. Compress the RH secondary timing chain tensioner and install a suitable lock-pin to retain the tensioner in the collapsed position.

➡The VCT bolt and the exhaust camshaft bolt must be discarded and new ones installed. However, the exhaust camshaft washer is reusable.

152. Remove and discard the RH VCT assembly bolt and the RH exhaust camshaft sprocket bolt.
   a. Remove the RH VCT assembly, secondary timing chain and the RH exhaust camshaft sprocket as an assembly.

Fig. 99 Rotate the crankshaft clockwise and align the timing marks on the VCT assemblies—Late Build/Replacement

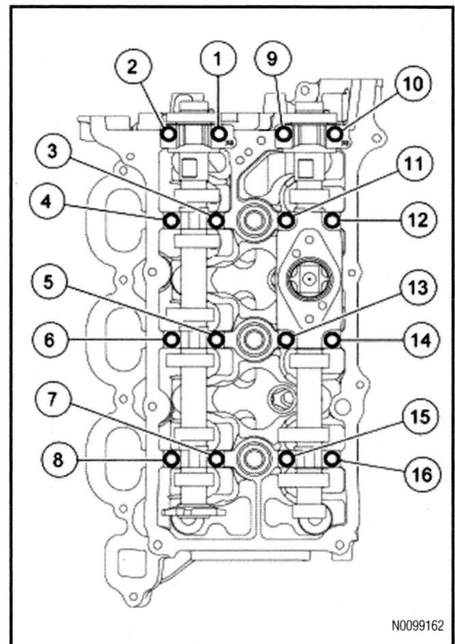

Fig. 100 Removal & installation of the LH camshaft 16 bolts and 8 caps. Tighten in the sequence shown

153. Remove the Camshaft Holding Tool from the RH camshafts.

⁂ WARNING

The camshafts must remain in the neutral position during removal or engine damage may occur.

154. Rotate the RH camshafts counter-clockwise to the neutral position.

➡Cylinder head camshaft bearing caps are numbered to verify that they are assembled in their original positions.

155. Remove the bolts and the RH camshaft bearing caps.
   a. Remove the RH camshafts.

To install:

⁂ CAUTION

Do not smoke, carry lighted tobacco or have an open flame of any type when working on or near any fuel-related component. Highly flammable mixtures are always present and may be ignited. Failure to follow these instructions may result in serious personal injury.

⁂ WARNING

Whenever turbocharger air intake system components are removed, always cover open ports to protect from debris. It is important that no foreign material enter the system. The turbocharger compressor vanes are susceptible to damage from even small particles. All components should be inspected and cleaned, if necessary, prior to installation or reassembly.

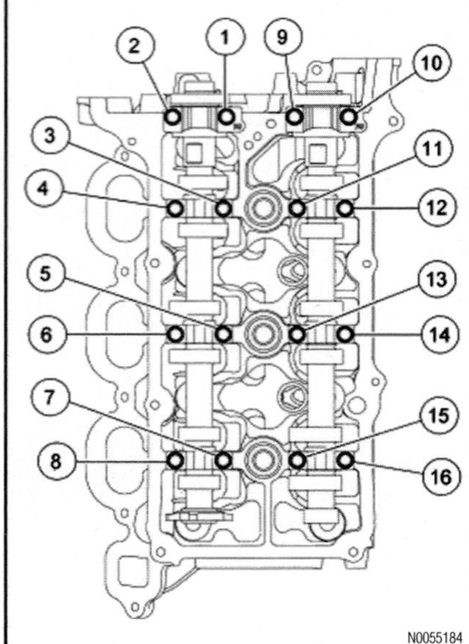

Fig. 101 Removal & installation of the RH camshaft 16 bolts and 8 caps. Tighten in the sequence shown

⁂ WARNING

During engine repair procedures, cleanliness is extremely important. Any foreign material, including any material created while cleaning gasket surfaces that enters the oil passages, coolant passages or the oil pan, may cause engine failure.

➡On early build engines, the timing chain rides on the inner side of the RH timing chain guide. Late build engines are equipped with a different design RH timing chain guide that requires the timing chain to ride on the outer side of the RH timing chain guide. For service, all replacement RH timing chain guides will be the late build design.

All Camshafts

⁂ WARNING

The crankshaft must remain in the freewheeling position (crankshaft dowel pin at 9 o'clock) until after the camshafts are installed and the valve clearance is checked/adjusted. Do not turn the crankshaft until instructed to do so. Failure to follow this process will result in severe engine damage.

156. Rotate the crankshaft counterclockwise until the crankshaft dowel pin is in the 9 o'clock position.

LH Camshafts

⁂ WARNING

The camshafts must remain in the neutral position during installation or engine damage may occur.

➡Coat the camshafts with clean engine oil prior to installation.

157. Position the camshafts onto the LH cylinder head in the neutral position.

➡Cylinder head camshaft bearing caps are numbered to verify that they are assembled in their original positions.

158. Install the 8 camshaft caps and the 16 bolts. Tighten the 16 camshaft bolts to 89 inch lbs. (10 Nm) in the proper sequence.

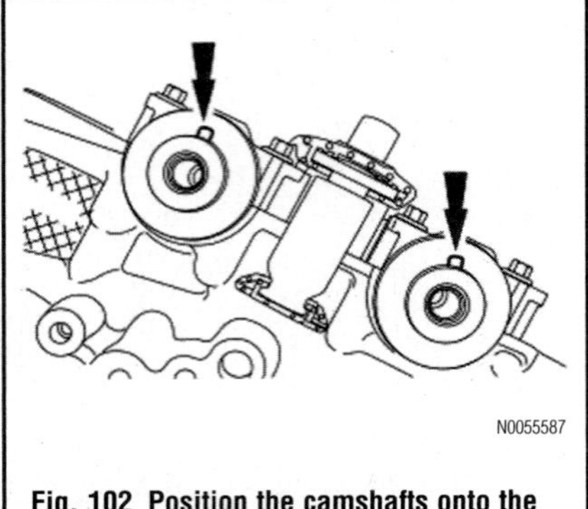

Fig. 102 Position the camshafts onto the LH cylinder head in the neutral position

RH Camshafts

⁂ WARNING

The camshafts must remain in the neutral position during installation or engine damage may occur.

➡Coat the camshafts with clean engine oil prior to installation.

159. Position the camshafts onto the RH cylinder head in the neutral position.

➡Cylinder head camshaft bearing caps are numbered to verify that they are assembled in their original positions.

160. Install the 8 camshaft caps and the 16 bolts. Tighten the 16 camshaft bolts to 89 inch lbs. (10 Nm) in the proper sequence.

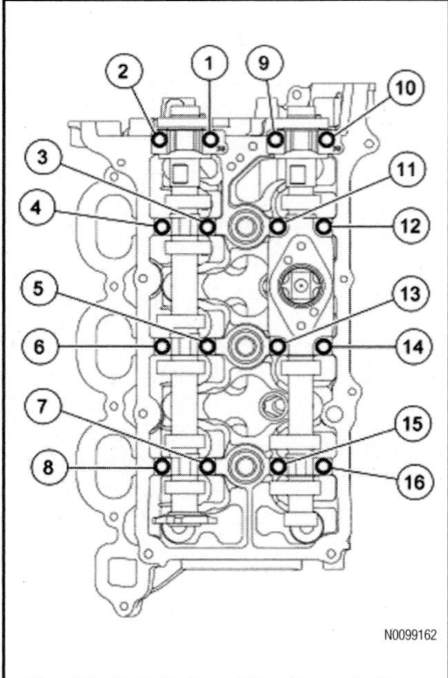

Fig. 103 Installation of the 8 camshaft caps and 16 bolts—LH camshaft

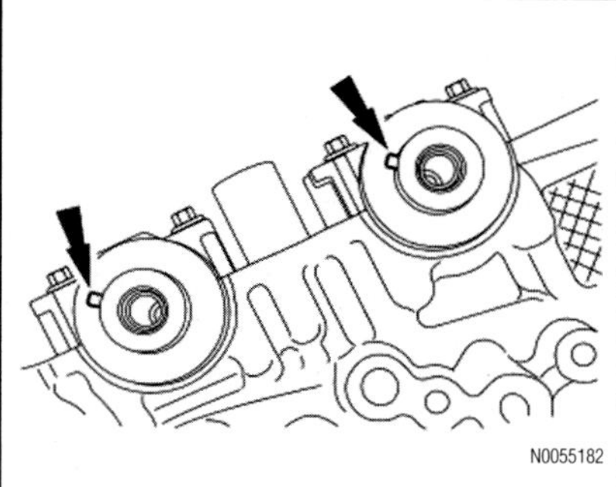

Fig. 104 Position the camshafts onto the RH cylinder head in the neutral position

All Camshafts

WARNING

If any components are installed new, the engine valve clearance must be checked/adjusted or engine damage may occur.

➡Use a camshaft sprocket bolt to turn the camshafts.

161. Using a feeler gauge, confirm that the valve tappet clearances are within specification. If valve tappet clearances are not within specification, the clearance must be adjusted by installing new valve tappet(s) of the correct size.

LH Camshafts

➡Use a camshaft sprocket bolt to turn the camshafts.

162. Rotate the LH camshafts to the Top Dead Center (TDC) position and install the Camshaft Holding Tool on the flats of the camshafts.

163. Assemble the LH Variable Camshaft Timing (VCT) assembly, the LH exhaust camshaft sprocket and the LH secondary timing chain.

a. Align the colored links with the timing marks.

164. Position the LH secondary timing assembly onto the camshafts.

165. Install 2 new bolts and the original washer. Tighten in 4 stages.

a. Stage 1: Tighten to 30 ft. lbs. (40 Nm).

b. Stage 2: Loosen one full turn.

c. Stage 3: Tighten to 89 inch lbs. (10 Nm).

d. Stage 4: Tighten 90 degrees.

166. Remove the lockpin from the LH secondary timing chain tensioner.

RH Camshafts

➡Use a camshaft sprocket bolt to turn the camshafts.

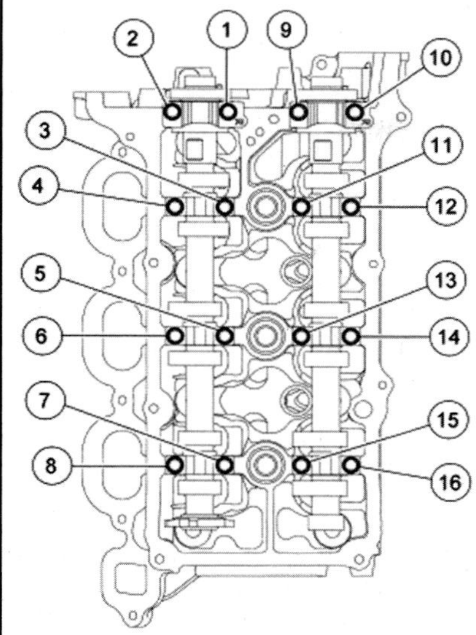

Fig. 105 Installation of the 8 camshaft caps and 16 bolts—RH camshaft

167. Rotate the RH camshafts to the TDC position and install the Camshaft Holding Tool on the flats of the camshafts.

168. Assemble the RH VCT assembly, the RH exhaust camshaft sprocket and the RH secondary timing chain.

a. Align the colored links with the timing marks.

169. Position the RH secondary timing assembly onto the camshafts.

170. Install 2 new bolts and the original washer. Tighten in 4 stages.

a. Stage 1: Tighten to 30 ft. lbs. (40 Nm).

b. Stage 2: Loosen one full turn.

c. Stage 3: Tighten to 89 inch lbs. (10 Nm).

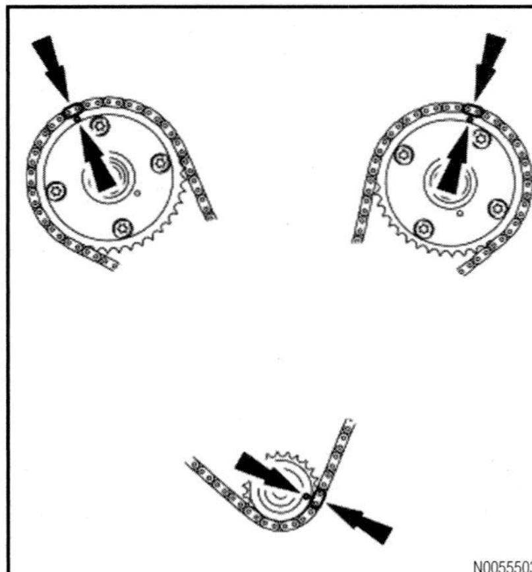

Fig. 106 Install the primary timing chain with the colored links aligned with the timing marks on the VCT assemblies and the crankshaft sprocket

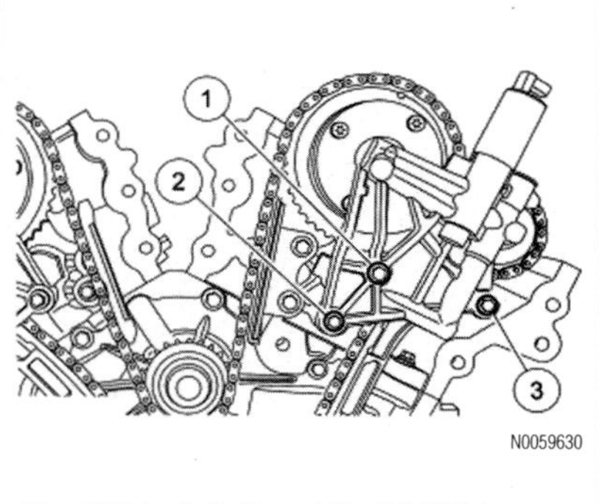

Fig. 107 Installation of the LH VCT housing and the 3 bolts

d. Stage 4: Tighten 90 degrees.

171. Remove the lockpin from the RH secondary timing chain tensioner.

All Camshafts

172. Rotate the crankshaft clockwise 60 degrees to the TDC position (crankshaft dowel pin at 11 o'clock).

173. Install the primary timing chain with the colored links aligned with the timing marks on the VCT assemblies and the crankshaft sprocket.

174. Install the lower LH primary timing chain guide and the 2 bolts. Tighten the bolts to 89 inch lbs. (10 Nm).

175. Install the primary timing chain tensioner arm.

176. Reset the primary timing chain tensioner.

a. Rotate the lever counterclockwise.

b. Using a soft-jawed vise, compress the plunger.

c. Align the hole in the lever with the hole in the tensioner housing.

d. Install a suitable lockpin.

➡It may be necessary to rotate the crankshaft slightly to remove slack from the timing chain and install the tensioner.

177. Install the primary tensioner and the 2 bolts. Tighten the bolts to 89 inch lbs. (10 Nm).

a. Remove the lockpin.

178. As a post-check, verify correct alignment of all timing marks.

179. Inspect the VCT housing seals for damage and replace as necessary.

WARNING

Make sure the dowels on the Variable Camshaft Timing (VCT) housing are fully engaged in the cylinder head prior to tightening the bolts. Failure to follow this process will result in severe engine damage.

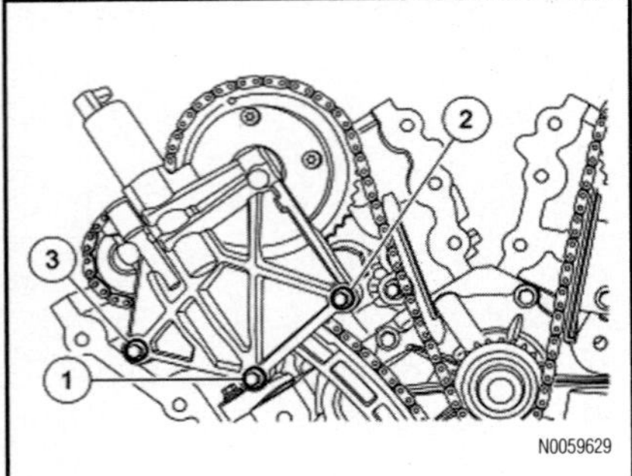

Fig. 108 Installation of the RH VCT housing and the 3 bolts

180. Install the LH VCT housing and the 3 bolts. Tighten the bolts to 89 inch lbs. (10 Nm).

WARNING

Make sure the dowels on the Variable Camshaft Timing (VCT) housing are fully engaged in the cylinder head prior to tightening the bolts. Failure to follow this process will result in severe engine damage.

181. Install the RH VCT housing and the 3 bolts. Tighten the bolts to 89 inch lbs. (10 Nm).

182. Install the Alignment Pins.

WARNING

Failure to use Motorcraft® High Performance Engine RTV Silicone may cause the engine oil to foam excessively and result in serious engine damage.

➡The engine front cover and bolts 17, 18, 19 and 20 must be installed within 4 minutes of the initial sealant application. The remainder of the engine front cover bolts and the engine mount bracket bolts must be installed and tightened within 35 minutes of the initial sealant application. If the time limits are exceeded, the sealant must be removed, the sealing area cleaned and sealant reapplied. To clean the sealing area, use silicone gasket remover and metal surface prep. Failure to follow this procedure can cause future oil leakage.

➡Apply a 0.11 inch (3.0 mm) bead of Motorcraft® High Performance Engine RTV Silicone to the engine front cover sealing surfaces including the 3 engine mount bracket bosses.

➡Apply a 0.21 inch (5.5 mm) bead of Motorcraft® High Performance Engine RTV Silicone to the oil pan-to-cylinder block joint and the cylinder head-to-cylinder block joint areas of the engine front cover in 5 places as indicated.

➡Make sure the 2 locating dowel pins are seated correctly in the cylinder block.

183. Install the engine front cover and bolts. Tighten the bolts to 27 inch lbs. (3 Nm).

184. Remove the Alignment Pins.

➡Do not tighten the bolts at this time.

185. Install the engine mount bracket and the 3 bolts.

WARNING

Do not expose the Motorcraft® High Performance Engine RTV Silicone to engine oil for at least 90 minutes after installing the engine front cover.

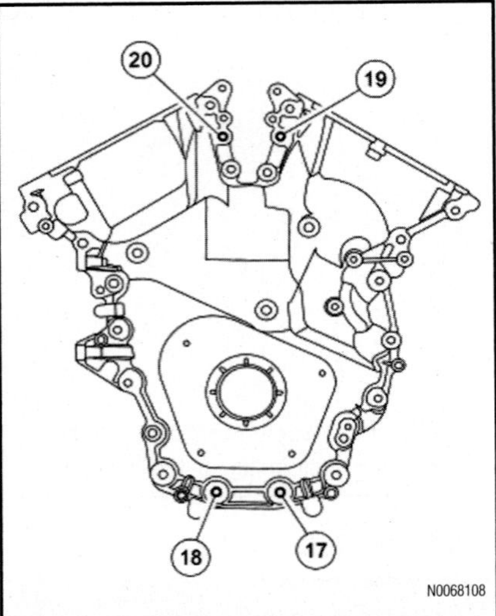

Fig. 111 Installation of the engine front cover bolts 17, 18, 19 and 20

Failure to follow this instruction may cause oil leakage.

186. Install the remaining engine front cover bolts. Tighten all of the engine front cover bolts and engine mount bracket bolts in the proper sequence.

a. Stage 1: Tighten bolts 1 thru 22 to 89 inch lbs. (10 Nm) and bolts 23, 24 and 25 to 133 inch lbs. (15 Nm).

b. Stage 2: Tighten bolts 1 thru 22 to 18 ft. lbs. (24 Nm) and bolts 23, 24 and 25 to 55 ft. lbs. (75 Nm).

WARNING

The thread sealer on the engine mount studs (including new engine

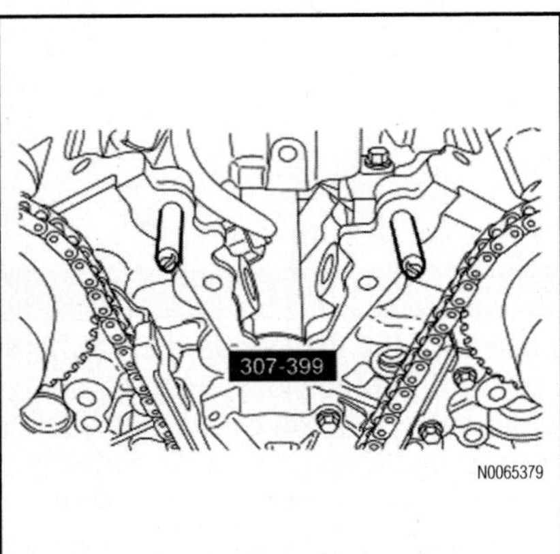

Fig. 109 Alignment pin location

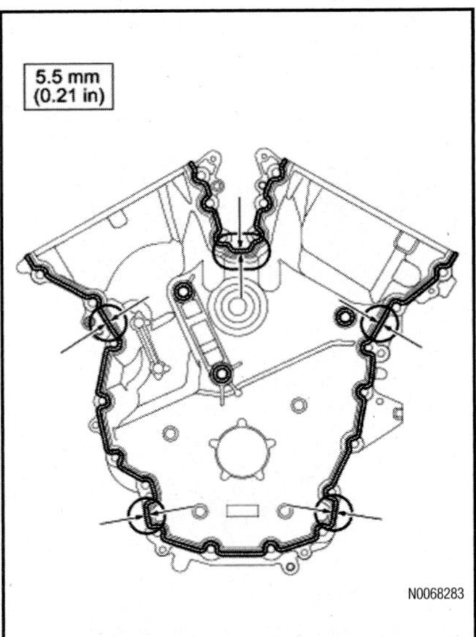

Fig. 110 Engine front cover silicone application locations

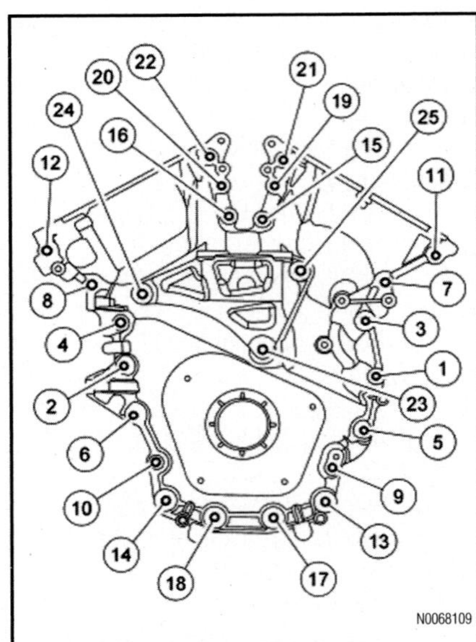

Fig. 112 Installation of the remaining engine front cover bolts

mount studs if applicable) must be cleaned off with a wire brush and new Thread lock and Sealer applied prior to installing the engine mount studs. Failure to follow this procedure may result in damage to the engine mount studs or engine.

187. Install the engine mount studs in the following sequence.
   a. Clean the front cover engine mount stud holes with pressurized air to remove any foreign material.
   b. Clean all the thread sealer from the engine mount studs (old and new studs).
   c. Apply new Thread lock and Sealer to the engine mount stud threads.
   d. Install the 2 engine mount studs. Tighten the studs to 15 ft. lbs. (20 Nm).
188. Install the Heated Oxygen Sensor (HO2S) connector bracket and stud bolt to the engine front cover. Tighten the bolt to 89 inch lbs. (10 Nm).

➡Apply clean engine oil to the crankshaft front seal bore in the engine front cover.

189. Using the Crankshaft Vibration Damper Installer and Front Crankshaft Seal Installer, install a new crankshaft front seal.

➡Lubricate the outside diameter sealing surfaces with clean engine oil.

190. Using the Crankshaft Vibration Damper Installer and Front Cover Oil Seal Installer, install the crankshaft pulley.
191. Using the Strap Wrench, install the crankshaft pulley washer and new bolt and tighten in 4 stages.
   a. Stage 1: Tighten to 89 ft. lbs. (120 Nm).
   b. Stage 2: Loosen one full turn.
   c. Stage 3: Tighten to 37 ft. lbs. (50 Nm).
   d. Stage 4: Tighten an additional 90 degrees.
192. Install the accessory drive belt tensioner and the 3 bolts. Tighten the bolts to 97 inch lbs. (11 Nm).
193. Rotate the accessory drive belt tensioner clockwise and install the accessory drive belt.

➡Installation of new seals is only required if damaged seals were removed during disassembly of the engine.

➡Spark plug tube seal installation shown, VCT solenoid seal installation similar.

194. Using the VCT Spark Plug Tube Seal Installer and Handle, install new VCT solenoid and/or spark plug tube seals.

✱✱ WARNING

Failure to use Motorcraft® High Performance Engine RTV Silicone may cause the engine oil to foam excessively and result in serious engine damage.

➡If the valve cover is not installed and the fasteners tightened within 4 minutes, the sealant must be removed and the sealing area cleaned. To clean the sealing area, use silicone gasket remover and metal surface prep. Failure to follow this procedure can cause future oil leakage.

195. Apply an 0.31 inch (8 mm) bead of Motorcraft® High Performance Engine RTV Silicone to the engine front cover-to-RH cylinder head joints.
196. Using a new gasket, install the RH valve cover and tighten the 11 stud bolts. Tighten the stud bolts to 89 inch lbs. (10 Nm). Refer to the Valve Cover procedure for torque sequence.

✱✱ WARNING

Failure to use Motorcraft® High Performance Engine RTV Silicone may cause the engine oil to foam excessively and result in serious engine damage.

➡If the valve cover is not installed and the fasteners tightened within 4 minutes, the sealant must be removed and the sealing area cleaned. To clean the sealing area, use silicone gasket remover and metal surface prep. Failure to follow this procedure can cause future oil leakage.

197. Apply an 0.31 inch (8 mm) bead of Motorcraft® High Performance Engine RTV Silicone to the engine front cover-to-LH cylinder head joints.
198. Using a new gasket, install the LH valve cover and tighten the 10 stud bolts. Tighten the stud bolts to 89 inch lbs. (10 Nm). Refer to the valve cover procedure for torque sequence.
199. Install 3 RH ignition coil-on-plugs and the 3 bolts. Tighten the bolts to 62 inch lbs. (7 Nm).
200. Install 3 LH ignition coil-on-plugs and the 3 bolts. Tighten the bolts to 62 inch lbs. (7 Nm).

➡The cam lobe for the fuel injection pump must be at Bottom Dead Center (BDC) for the fuel injection pump installation.

201. Using the crankshaft pulley bolt, turn the crankshaft until the fuel injection pump cam lobe is at BDC .

➡Valve cover is removed for clarity.

➡Apply clean engine oil to the fuel injection pump mounting pedestal bore.

202. Install the fuel injection pump roller tappet.

➡Apply clean engine oil to the fuel injection pump mounting plate seal.

203. Inspect the fuel injection pump mounting plate-to-valve cover gasket and replace if necessary.

➡Apply clean engine oil to the fuel injection pump mounting plate O-ring seals.

204. Inspect the 2 fuel injection pump mounting plate O-ring seals and replace if necessary.

➡Apply clean engine oil to the fuel injection pump O-ring seal.

205. Install the fuel injection pump on the fuel injection pump mounting plate.

➡Clean the fuel injection pump bolts and apply Thread Sealant with PTFE to the bolts.

➡Start the fuel injection pump bolts by hand then simultaneously tighten.

206. Install the fuel injection pump and the 2 bolts. Tighten the bolts to 89 inch lbs. (10 Nm), then tighten an additional 45°
207. Connect the high pressure fuel tube flare nut to the fuel injection pump. Connect the 2 high pressure fuel tube flare nuts to the fuel rails. Tighten the nuts to 22 ft. lbs. (30 Nm).

Late Build Vehicles

208. Install the bolt for the high pressure fuel tube to the LH cylinder head. Tighten the bolt to 53 inch lbs. (6 Nm).

Early build vehicles

209. Install the nut for the high pressure fuel tube to the LH valve cover stud bolt. Tighten the nut to 53 inch lbs. (6 Nm).

All Vehicles

210. Attach the wiring harness retainers to the RH valve cover and stud bolt.
211. Connect the 3 RH ignition coil-on-plug electrical connectors.
212. Connect the RH VCT solenoid electrical connector and attach the 2 wiring harness retainers.

✱✱ WARNING

If the engine is repaired or replaced because of upper engine failure, typically including valve or piston damage, check the intake manifold for metal debris. If metal debris is found, install a new intake manifold. Failure to follow these instructions can result in engine damage.

➡Make sure the fuel rail wiring harnesses are routed correct.

➡Installing the 2 long bolts first will aid in installing the intake manifold.

213. Using new intake manifold, coolant crossover and thermostat housing gaskets, install the intake manifold and the 12 bolts. Tighten the bolts to 89 inch lbs. (10 Nm). Refer to the Intake Manifold procedure for torque sequence.
214. Connect the 2 turbocharger coolant hoses to the intake manifold.
215. Position the fuel tube and install the fuel tube-to-engine front cover bracket bolt. Tighten the bolt to 89 inch lbs. (10 Nm).
216. Attach the 2 wire harness-to-intake manifold retainers.
217. Connect the turbocharger wastegate regulating valve electrical connector.
218. Connect the Manifold Absolute Pressure (MAP)/Intake Air Temperature 2 (IAT2) sensor electrical connector.
219. Connect and attach the 2 fuel injector wiring harness electrical connectors.
220. Install the oil level indicator.
221. Install the oil supply tube bracket on the LH valve cover stud bolt and install the nut. Tighten the nut to 71 inch lbs. (8 Nm).
222. Attach all the wiring harness retainers to the LH valve cover and stud bolts.
223. Install the engine cover mounting stud to the LH valve cover stud bolt. Tighten the bolt to 53 inch lbs. (6 Nm).
224. Install the lower radiator hose to the thermostat housing.
225. Connect the 3 LH ignition coil-on-plug electrical connectors.
226. Connect the Engine Oil Pressure (EOP) electrical connector.
    a. Attach the wiring harness retainer to the block.
227. Connect the LH VCT solenoid electrical connector.
228. Connect the Throttle Position (TP) and electronic Throttle Body (TB) electrical connectors.
229. Connect the fuel injection pump electrical connector and install the insulated cover.

✱✱ WARNING

The compression limiter bushing may fall out of the mounting bracket grommet on the Charge Air Cooler (CAC) tube during service. Make sure the bushing is in place when reinstalling the tube or damage to the tube may occur.

230. Install the RH Charge Air Cooler (CAC) tube and turbocharger intake tube as an assembly and install the RH CAC tube nut to the intake manifold. Tighten the nut to 53 inch lbs. (6 Nm).

✱✱ WARNING

The compression limiter bushing may fall out of the mounting bracket grommet on the turbocharger intake tube during service. Make sure the bushing is in place when reinstalling the tube or damage to the tube may occur.

231. Install the RH turbocharger intake tube to the valve cover stud bolt and install the nut. Tighten the nut to 53 inch lbs. (6 Nm).

➡Align the index marks for the RH turbocharger intake pipe.

232. Install the RH turbocharger intake pipe to the RH turbocharger and tighten the clamp. Tighten the clamp to 44 inch lbs. (5 Nm).

➡Align the index marks for the RH CAC tube.

233. Install the RH CAC tube to the RH turbocharger and tighten the clamp. Tighten the clamp to 44 inch lbs. (5 Nm).
234. Connect the RH turbocharger bypass valve electrical connector.

➡Align the index marks for the LH turbocharger intake tube.

235. Install the LH turbocharger intake tube to the LH turbocharger and tighten the clamp. Tighten the clamp to 44 inch lbs. (5 Nm).
236. Install the turbocharger wastegate regulating valve hoses to the turbocharger wastegate regulating valve and to the RH CAC tube.
237. Connect the LH turbocharger bypass valve electrical connector.
238. If equipped, connect the 2 heated PCV electrical connectors.
239. Install the PCV tube and connect the 2 quick connect couplings.
240. Connect the brake vacuum tube to the intake manifold.
241. Using a new O-ring seal and gasket seal, connect the A/C tube to the compressor and install the nut. Tighten the nut to 133 inch lbs. (15 Nm).
242. Install the crankcase vent tube and connect the 2 quick connect couplings.
243. Raise the engine and transaxle assembly into the vehicle.
244. Install the engine mount and the 3 bolts. Tighten the bolts to 66 ft. lbs. (90 Nm).
245. Install the 4 engine mount nuts. Tighten the nuts to 46 ft. lbs. (63 Nm).
246. Install the bolt and the 3 nuts to the transaxle support insulator bracket-to-transaxle. Tighten the bolt to 59 ft. lbs. (80 Nm), and the nuts to 46 ft. lbs. (63 Nm).

➡A new compression seal must be installed whenever the Power Transfer Unit (PTU) is removed from the vehicle.

247. Using a small screwdriver, remove the compression seal and discard.
248. Using a soft face hammer, install the new compression seal.
249. Position the PTU in place and install the 5 bolts. Tighten the bolts to 66 ft. lbs. (90 Nm).
250. Position the PTU support bracket in place and install the 3 bolts.
251. Install the RH halfshaft support bracket and the 2 bolts. Tighten the bolts to 30 ft. lbs. (40 Nm).
252. Install the RH turbocharger lower bracket and the 3 bolts.

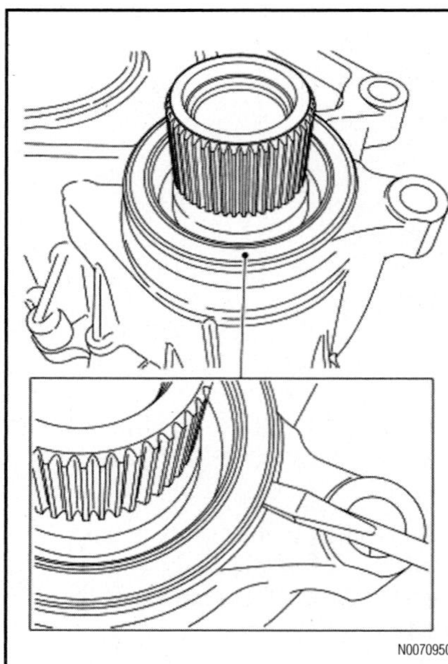

Fig. 113 Power Transfer Unit compression seal location

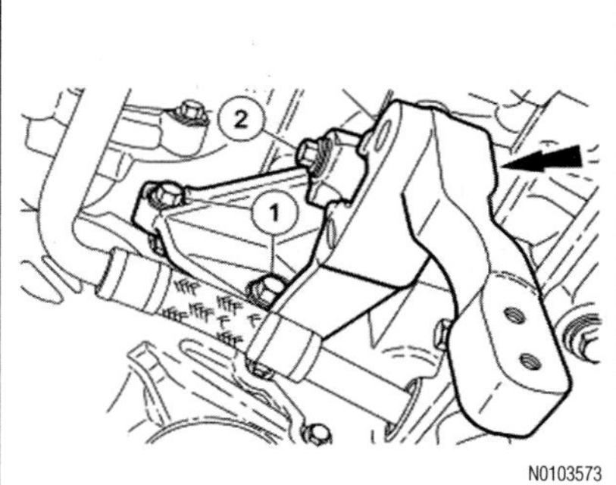

Fig. 114 PTU support bracket bolt installation. Tighten the "1" bolt to 35 ft. lbs. (48 Nm), and the "2" bolt to 52 ft. lbs. (70 Nm).

253. Connect the transaxle cooler tubes and install the 2 secondary latches.

254. Connect the lower radiator hose to the radiator.

255. Attach the lower radiator hose retainer to the cooling fan and shroud.

➡Align the index marks for the LH CAC tube.

256. Connect the lower LH CAC tube to the LH turbocharger and tighten the clamp. Tighten the clamp to 44 inch lbs. (5 Nm).

257. Using a new O-ring seal and gasket seal, install the upper A/C tube to the A/C compressor and install the nut. Tighten the nut to 133 inch lbs. (15 Nm).

258. Install the A/C tube bracket and bolt to the rear of the A/C compressor. Tighten the bolt to 18 ft. lbs. (25 Nm).

➡Lubricate the engine oil filter gasket with clean engine oil prior to installing the oil filter.

259. Install a new engine oil filter. Tighten the filter to 44 inch lbs. (5 Nm), and then rotate an additional 180°.

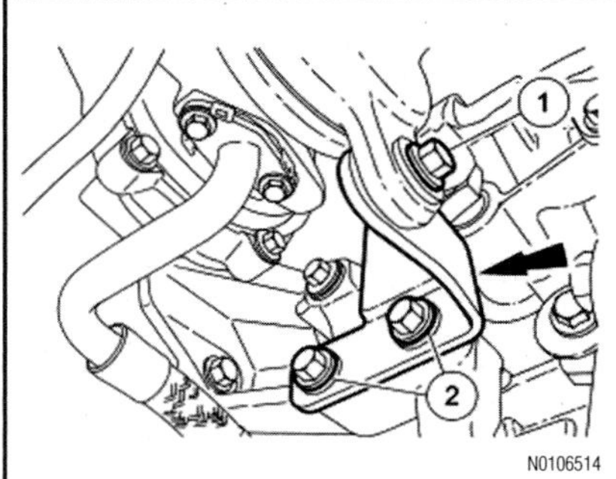

Fig. 115 RH turbocharger lower bracket installation. Tighten the "1" bolt to 168 inch lbs. (19 Nm), and the "2" to 35 ft. lbs. (48 Nm).

260. Line up the index marks on the rear driveshaft to the index marks on the PTU flange made during removal and install the 4 new bolts. Tighten the 52 ft. lbs. (70 Nm).

261. Connect the fuel supply tube.

262. Install the Evaporative Emission (EVAP) tube assembly and connect the quick connect coupling to the intake manifold.

263. Connect the EVAP valve electrical connector and attach to the intake manifold.

264. Connect the EVAP tube quick connect coupling.

265. If equipped, attach the engine block heater harness to the radiator support wiring harness.

266. Connect the upper radiator hose to the intake manifold coolant tube.

267. Install the ground wire and bolt to the engine front cover. Tighten the bolt to 89 inch lbs. (10 Nm).

268. Connect the 2 heater hoses to the intake manifold.

➡Align the index marks for the RH CAC tube.

269. Install the RH CAC tube and tighten the clamps. Tighten the clamps to 44 inch lbs. (5 Nm).

270. Attach the wiring harness pin-type retainer and connect the transaxle control cable to the shift cable bracket.

271. Connect the transaxle control cable to the control lever.

272. Connect the quick connect coupling to the brake booster.

273. Connect the power feed wires to the positive battery terminal and install the nut. Tighten the nut to 53 inch lbs. (6 Nm).

274. Connect the ground cable to the negative battery terminal and install the nut. Tighten the nut to 53 inch lbs. (6 Nm).

275. Connect the engine wiring harness electrical connector.

276. Install the battery tray.

➡Align the index marks for the CAC outlet pipe.

277. Install the CAC outlet pipe and tighten the clamps. Tighten the clamps to 44 inch lbs. (5 Nm).

278. Connect the Turbocharger Boost Pressure (TCBP)/Charge Air Cooler Temperature (CACT) sensor electrical connector.

279. Install the noise generator as outlined in Intake Air distribution and Filtering in this section.

280. Install the engine Air Cleaner (ACL) and ACL outlet pipe as outlined in Intake Air distribution and Filtering in this section.

281. Install the degas bottle.

282. Using a new O-ring seal and gasket seal, install the A/C tube and the nut. Tighten the nut to 133 inch lbs. (15 Nm).

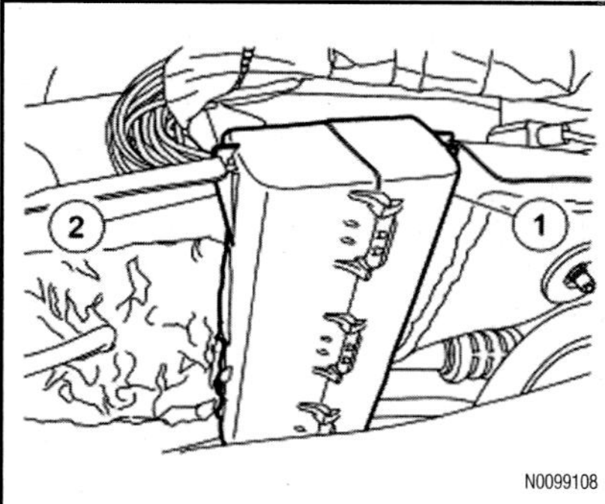

Fig. 116 Engine wiring harness retainer to the bulkhead installation

283. Using a new O-ring seal and gasket seal, connect the A/C tube and install the nut. Tighten the nut to 133 inch lbs. (15 Nm).

284. Install the engine wiring harness retainer to the bulkhead.

a. Slide the wiring harness in the bulkhead.

b. Make sure the wiring harness retainer tab is below the bulkhead lip.

285. Attach the wiring harness retainer and connect the electrical connector.

286. Connect the 2 PCM electrical connectors.

287. Install the strut tower brace and the 4 nuts. Tighten the nuts to 22 ft. lbs. (30 Nm).

288. Attach the 2 brake booster vacuum hose retainers to the strut tower brace.

289. Install the cowl panel grille.

WARNING

The circlips are unique in size and shape for each shaft. Make sure to use the specified circlip for the application or vehicle damage may occur.

290. Install the correct new circlip on the inboard stub shaft.

➡After insertion, pull the halfshaft inner end to make sure the circlip is locked.

291. Push the stub shaft into the transmission so the circlip locks into the differential side gear.

292. Rotate the LH wheel knuckle into position and insert the LH halfshaft into the wheel hub.

WARNING

A new Power Transfer Unit (PTU) shaft seal must be installed whenever the intermediate shaft is removed or damage to the components can occur.

293. Install a new intermediate shaft seal and deflector as outlined in this section.

294. Install the intermediate and halfshaft assembly and the 2 bolts. Tighten the bolts to 18 ft. lbs. (25 Nm).

295. Rotate the RH wheel knuckle into position and insert the RH halfshaft into the wheel hub.

296. Using the Powertrain Lift, raise the subframe into the installed position.

297. Install the 2 front subframe bolts. Tighten the bolts to 148 ft. lbs. (200 Nm).

298. Position the subframe brackets and install the 4 bolts finger-tight.

299. Install the 2 rear subframe bolts. Tighten the bolts to 111 ft. lbs. (150 Nm).

300. Tighten the 4 subframe bracket-to-body bolts to 41 ft. lbs. (55 Nm).

301. Connect the 2 Electronic Power Assist Steering (EPAS) electrical connectors and attach the wiring retainer and install the bolt. Tighten the bolt to 80 inch lbs. (9 Nm).

WARNING

Do not allow the intermediate shaft to rotate while it is disconnected from the gear or damage to the clockspring may occur. If there is evidence that the intermediate shaft has rotated, the clockspring must be removed and recentered.

302. Install the steering intermediate shaft onto the steering gear and install a new bolt. Tighten the bolt to 15 ft. lbs. (20 Nm).

303. Position the ball joints into the wheel knuckles. Install the new ball joint nuts. Tighten the nuts to 148 ft. lbs. (200 Nm).

➡The hex-holding feature can be used to prevent turning of the stud while installing the nuts.

304. Install new tie-rod end nuts. Tighten the nuts to 111 ft. lbs. (150 Nm).

305. Install new upper stabilizer bar link nuts. Tighten the nuts to 111 ft. lbs. (150 Nm).

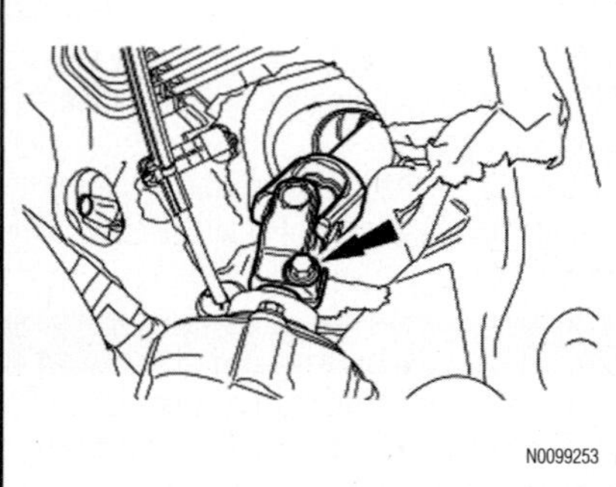

Fig. 117 Steering intermediate shaft to steering gear installation

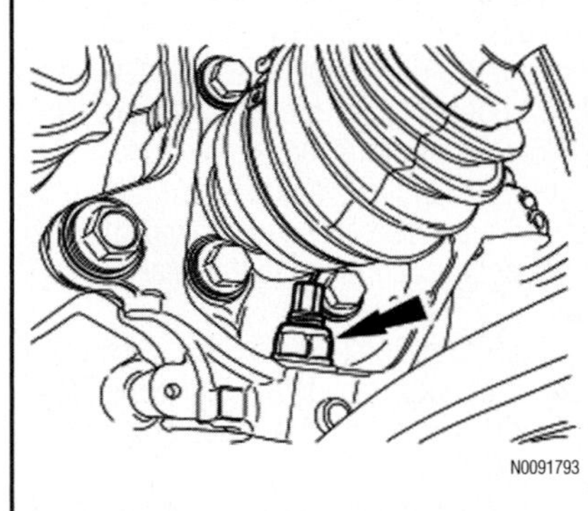

Fig. 118 Ball joints to wheel knuckles installation

306. Install the 2 front engine roll restrictor-to-transaxle bolts. Tighten the bolts to 66 ft. lbs. (90 Nm).

307. Install the 2 rear engine roll restrictor-to-transaxle bolts. Tighten the bolts to 66 ft. lbs. (90 Nm).

308. Install the RH and LH catalytic converters as outlined in this section.

309. Position the RH brake hose bracket and install the bolt. Tighten the bolt to 22 ft. lbs. (30 Nm).

WARNING

Do not tighten the wheel hub nut with the vehicle on the ground. The nut must be tightened to specification before the vehicle is lowered onto the wheels. Wheel bearing damage will occur if the wheel bearing is loaded with the weight of the vehicle applied.

➡Apply the brake to keep the halfshaft from rotating.

310. Using the previously removed RH and LH wheel hub nuts, seat the halfshaft. Tighten the nuts to 258 ft. lbs. (350 Nm).

a. Remove and discard the wheel hub nuts.

WARNING

The wheel hub nut contains a one-time locking chemical that is activated by the heat created when it is tightened. Install and tighten the new wheel hub nut to specification within 5 minutes of starting it on the threads. Always install a new wheel hub nut after loosening or when not tightened within the specified time or damage to the components can occur.

➡Apply the brake to keep the halfshaft from rotating.

311. Install a new RH and LH wheel hub nut. Tighten the nut to 258 ft. lbs. (350 Nm).

312. Install the 2 scrivets in the rubber shield.

313. Install the front wheels and tires.

314. Fill the engine with clean engine oil.

315. Fill and bleed the cooling system as outlined in the Engine Cooling Section.

316. Install the front splash shield, 3 pin-type retainers and the 7 bolts, when the coolant system or engine service is finished.

317. Install the underbody shield and the 4 retainers.

318. Connect the LH Heated Oxygen Sensor (HO2S) electrical connector.

a. Attach the HO2S connector retainer to the bracket.

319. Fill the engine with clean engine oil.

320. Refill the transaxle fluid as outlined in the Drive Train Section.

321. Recharge the A/C system.

CATALYTIC CONVERTER

REMOVAL & INSTALLATION

3.5L Engine, Except Turbo

Left-Hand

➡Always install new fasteners and gaskets. Clean flange faces prior to new gasket installation to make sure of correct sealing.

1. With the vehicle in NEUTRAL, position it on a hoist.
2. Disconnect the LH Catalyst Monitor Sensor (CMS) electrical connector.
3. Remove the exhaust Y-pipe.
4. Remove the 2 catalytic converter support bracket-to-transmission bolts.
5. Remove the 4 nuts and the LH catalytic converter.
    a. Discard the nuts and gasket.
6. Inspect the exhaust manifold studs for damage.
    a. If damaged, or if stud comes out when removing the nut, replace the stud.

To install:

➡Always install new fasteners and gaskets. Clean flange faces prior to new gasket installation to make sure of correct sealing.

7. Inspect the exhaust manifold studs for damage.
    a. If damaged, or if stud comes out when removing the nut, replace the stud. Tighten the nut to 18 ft. lbs. (25 Nm).

8. Install the 4 nuts and the LH catalytic converter.
   a. Discard the nuts and gasket. Using a new gasket and nuts, tighten the nuts to 30 ft. lbs. (40 Nm).
9. Install the 2 catalytic converter support bracket-to-transmission bolts. Tighten the bolts to 35 ft. lbs. (48 Nm).
10. Install the exhaust Y-pipe.
11. Connect the LH Catalyst Monitor Sensor (CMS) electrical connector.
12. With the vehicle in NEUTRAL, lower it from the hoist.

Right-Hand

➡Always install new fasteners and gaskets. Clean flange faces prior to new gasket installation to make sure of correct sealing.

1. With the vehicle in NEUTRAL, position it on a hoist.
2. Remove the exhaust Y-pipe.
3. Remove the RH Catalyst Monitor Sensor (CMS) as outlined in the Engine Performance & Emission Controls Section.
4. Remove the 2 bracket-to-RH catalytic converter bolts.
5. Remove the 4 nuts and the RH catalytic converter.
   a. Discard the nuts and gasket.
6. Inspect the exhaust manifold studs for damage.
   a. If damaged or if stud comes out when removing the nut, replace the stud.

To install:

➡Always install new fasteners and gaskets. Clean flange faces prior to new gasket installation to make sure of correct sealing.

7. Inspect the exhaust manifold studs for damage.
   a. If damaged or if stud comes out when removing the nut, replace the stud. Tighten the nut to 18 ft. lbs. (25 Nm).
8. Install the 4 nuts and the RH catalytic converter.
   a. Discard the nuts and gasket. Using a new gasket and nuts, tighten the nuts to 30 ft. lbs. (40 Nm).
9. Install the 2 bracket-to-RH catalytic converter bolts. Tighten the bolts to 15 ft. lbs. (20 Nm).
10. Install the RH Catalyst Monitor Sensor (CMS) as outlined in the Engine Performance & Emission Controls Section.
11. Install the exhaust Y-pipe.
12. With the vehicle in NEUTRAL, lower it from the hoist.

3.5L Turbo Engine

Left-Hand

➡Always install new fasteners and gaskets. Clean flange faces prior to new gasket installation to make sure of correct sealing.

1. With the vehicle in NEUTRAL, position it on a hoist.
2. Remove the LH Heated Oxygen Sensor (HO2S) as outlined in the Engine Performance & Emission Controls Section.
3. Remove the LH exhaust flexible pipe.
4. Disconnect the LH Catalyst Monitor Sensor (CMS) electrical connector.
5. Remove the 3 LH catalytic converter-to-turbocharger nuts and the catalytic converter.
   a. Discard the nuts and gasket.
6. Inspect the LH turbocharger-to-catalytic converter studs for damage.
   a. If damaged or if a stud comes out when removing the nut, replace the stud.

To install:

➡Always install new fasteners and gaskets. Clean flange faces prior to new gasket installation to make sure of correct sealing.

7. Inspect the LH turbocharger-to-catalytic converter studs for damage.
   a. If damaged or if a stud comes out when removing the nut, replace the stud. Tighten the nut to 18 ft. lbs. (25 Nm).
8. Install the 3 LH catalytic converter-to-turbocharger nuts and the catalytic converter.
   a. Discard the nuts and gasket. Using a new gasket and nuts, tighten the nuts to 30 ft. lbs. (40 Nm).
9. Connect the LH Catalyst Monitor Sensor (CMS) electrical connector.
10. Install the LH exhaust flexible pipe.
11. Install the LH Heated Oxygen Sensor (HO2S) as outlined in the Engine Performance & Emission Controls Section.
12. With the vehicle in NEUTRAL, lower it from the hoist.

Right-Hand

➡Always install new fasteners and gaskets. Clean flange faces prior to new gasket installation to make sure of correct sealing.

1. With the vehicle in NEUTRAL, position it on a hoist.
2. Remove the RH front wheel and tire.
3. Disconnect the RH Heated Oxygen Sensor (HO2S) electrical connector.
   a. Detach the HO2S electrical connector retainer from the bracket.
4. Remove the LH and RH exhaust flexible pipes.
5. Disconnect the RH Catalyst Monitor Sensor (CMS) electrical connector.
6. Remove the 3 RH catalytic converter-to-turbocharger nuts and the converter.
   a. Discard the nuts and gasket.
7. Inspect the RH turbocharger-to-catalytic converter studs for damage.
   a. If damaged or if a stud comes out when removing the nut, replace the stud.

To install:

➡Always install new fasteners and gaskets. Clean flange faces prior to new gasket installation to make sure of correct sealing.

8. Inspect the RH turbocharger-to-catalytic converter studs for damage.
   a. If damaged or if a stud comes out when removing the nut, replace the stud. Tighten the nut to 18 ft. lbs. (25 Nm).
9. Install the 3 RH catalytic converter-to-turbocharger nuts and the converter.
   a. Discard the nuts and gasket. Using a new gasket and nuts, tighten nuts to 30 ft. lbs. (40 Nm).
10. Connect the RH Catalyst Monitor Sensor (CMS) electrical connector.
11. Install the LH and RH exhaust flexible pipes.
12. Connect the RH Heated Oxygen Sensor (HO2S) electrical connector.
   a. Attach the HO2S electrical connector retainer to the bracket.
13. Install the RH front wheel and tire.
14. With the vehicle in NEUTRAL, lower it from the hoist.

Underbody

The production underbody catalytic converter and muffler assembly is serviced as one part. Refer to the Muffler And Tailpipe in this section.

Muffler And Tailpipe

See Figures 119 and 120.

⁂ WARNING

Do not use oil or grease-based lubricants on the isolators. They may cause deterioration of the rubber.

⁂ WARNING

Oil or grease-based lubricants on the isolators may cause the exhaust isolator to separate from the exhaust hanger bracket during vehicle operation.

All Vehicles

1. With the vehicle in NEUTRAL, position it on a hoist.
2. Support the muffler assembly with a suitable jackstand.

3.5L Non-Turbo

3. Remove the Torca® clamp nut.

WARNING

The resonator must be supported to prevent damage to the flexible pipe.

4. Using a length of mechanic's wire, support the resonator.

3.5L Turbo

5. Remove the 4 LH and RH exhaust flexible pipes-to-underbody catalytic converter nuts.
    a. Discard the nuts and gaskets.

All Vehicles

WARNING

Do not damage or tear the isolators during removal.

6. Using soapy water, separate the isolators and remove the muffler assembly from the vehicle.

To install:

3.5L Non-Turbo

7. Grind the spot weld and the tac weld from the Torca® clamp and remove the clamp.
8. Clean the uneven surface area and position the new Torca® clamp.

All Vehicles

➡Inspect and replace any isolators found to be damaged or torn during the removal process.

9. Install the muffler assembly in the isolators and support with a suitable jackstand.

3.5L Turbo

10. Install the new LH and RH exhaust flexible pipe-to-underbody catalytic converter gaskets and nuts. Tighten the nuts to 30 ft. lbs. (40 Nm).

3.5L Non-Turbo

➡Make sure the clamp position is no more than 1.08 inch (27.5 mm) or less than 1 inch (25.5 mm) from the inlet of the pipe.

11. Make sure the back of the slot is covered by the clamp and the button is fully seated inside the notch.
12. Tighten the Torca® clamp. Tighten the clamp to 41 ft. lbs. (55 Nm).

CHARGE AIR COOLER

REMOVAL & INSTALLATION

➡Whenever turbocharger air intake system components are removed, always cover open ports to protect from debris. It is important that no foreign material enter the system. The turbocharger compressor vanes are susceptible to damage from even small particles. All components should be inspected and cleaned, if necessary, prior to installation or reassembly.

1. Remove the radiator as outlined in the Engine Cooling Section.
2. Remove the Charge Air Cooler (CAC).

To install:

➡Whenever turbocharger air intake system components are removed, always cover open ports to protect from debris. It is important that no foreign material enter the system. The turbocharger compressor vanes are susceptible to damage from even small particles. All components should be inspected and cleaned, if necessary, prior to installation or reassembly.

3. Install the Charge Air Cooler (CAC).
4. Install the radiator as outlined in the Engine Cooling Section.

CLEANING

WARNING

Do not use a high-pressure power washer to clean the Charge Air Cooler (CAC) or damage to the CAC may occur.

➡Drain all contaminates such as coolant, fuel and oil prior to cleaning the Charge Air Cooler (CAC).

➡Thoroughly clean the joint clamp areas as well as the turbocharger connection, engine connection and the CAC connections, using metal brake parts cleaner.

1. Lay the CAC flat with the inlet and outlet ports pointing up.

➡Plug or cap the CAC openings prior to agitating.

2. Add an appropriate amount of commercially available detergent cleaner such as Simple Green Pro HD, or equivalent to the CAC . Follow the manufacturer's directions for cleaning. Fill the CAC to 40% of its volume with water.
3. Raise one end of the CAC and agitate it by hand for at least 5 minutes.
4. Raise the opposite end of the CAC and agitate it by hand for at least 5 minutes.
5. Drain the CAC .
6. Flush the CAC thoroughly with clean water.
7. Repeat Steps 1 through 6 until no contaminates are found in the flush water.
8. Allow the CAC to air dry.

➡The following leak test steps must be performed prior to installing the CAC .

9. Install the CAC Y-pipe, gasket and bolts. Tighten the bolts to 71 inch lbs. (8 Nm).

➡Use a commercially available kit, such as the SPX/OTC Charged Air Cooler Tester No. 5039, or equivalent.

10. Install the commercially available CAC cooler tester on the CAC following the manufacturer's installation instructions. Tighten the clamps to 44 inch lbs. (5 Nm).

CAUTION

Never exceed the specified pressure. Excessive pressure may cause the test adapter to blow off or may damage the charge air cooler (CAC). Failure to follow this instruction may result in serious personal injury.

11. Slowly apply air pressure to 22 psi.

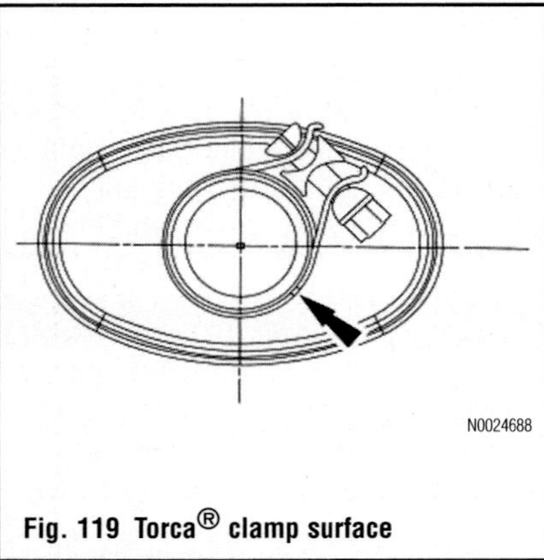

Fig. 119 Torca® clamp surface

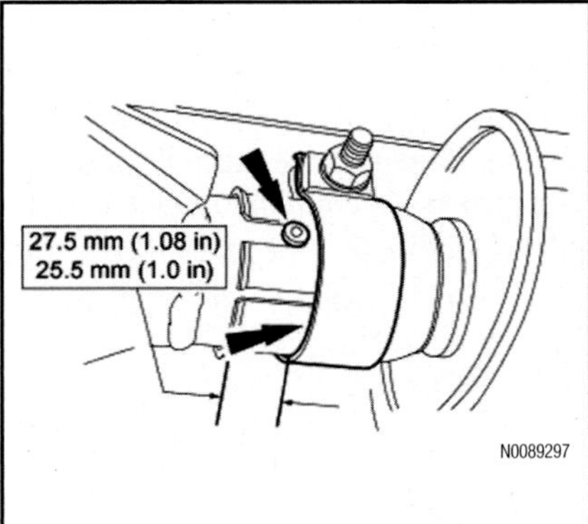

Fig. 120 Torca® clamp position

12. Let the CAC stand for a few minutes and note any loss in pressure.
  a. Release the air pressure.
13. Repeat Steps 11 and 12 as many times as necessary to verify the readings. The reading is considered verified when 3 consecutive tests show approximately the same pressure drop.
  a. If the pressure loss exceeds 1.5 psi per minute, install a new CAC . For additional information, refer to Charge Air Cooler in this section.

CRANKSHAFT FRONT SEAL

REMOVAL & INSTALLATION

1. With the vehicle in NEUTRAL, position it on a hoist.
2. Remove the crankshaft pulley.
3. Using the Oil Seal Remover, remove and discard the crankshaft front seal.
  a. Clean all sealing surfaces with metal surface prep.

To install:

➡Apply clean engine oil to the crankshaft front seal bore in the engine front cover.

4. Using the Front Crankshaft Seal Installer and Crankshaft Vibration Damper Installer, install a new crankshaft front seal.
5. Install the crankshaft pulley.
6. With the vehicle in NEUTRAL, lower it from the hoist.

CYLINDER HEAD

REMOVAL & INSTALLATION

3.5L Engine, Except Turbo

Left-Hand

See Figure 121.

⁂ WARNING

During engine repair procedures, cleanliness is extremely important. Any foreign material, including any material created while cleaning gasket surfaces, which enters the oil passages, coolant passages or the oil pan, may cause engine failure.

1. Remove the LH camshafts.
2. Disconnect the 6 fuel injector electrical connectors.
3. Disconnect the Cylinder Head Temperature (CHT) sensor electrical connector.
4. Disconnect the LH Camshaft Position (CMP) sensor electrical connector.
5. Remove the bolt and the LH CMP sensor.
6. Disconnect the LH Heated Oxygen Sensor (HO2S) electrical connector.
7. Disconnect the LH Catalyst Monitor Sensor (CMS) electrical connector.
8. Detach the wiring harness retainer from the rear of the LH cylinder head.
9. Remove the nut and disconnect the generator B+ cable.
10. Disconnect the generator electrical connector.
11. Remove the nut, bolt and the generator.
  a. Remove the generator stud.
12. Disconnect the Engine Oil Pressure (EOP) switch electrical connector and the wiring harness pin-type retainer.
  a. Remove the wiring harness from the engine.
13. Remove the 2 LH catalytic converter bracket bolts.
14. Remove the 4 nuts and the LH catalytic converter.
  a. Discard the nuts and the gasket.
15. Remove the 3 bolts and the LH exhaust manifold heat shield.
16. Remove the 6 nuts and the LH exhaust manifold.
  a. Discard the nuts and the exhaust manifold gasket.
17. Clean and inspect the LH exhaust manifold.
18. Remove and discard the 6 LH exhaust manifold studs.
19. Remove the LH cylinder block drain plug.
  a. Allow coolant to drain from the cylinder block.
20. Remove the 4 nuts and the RH catalytic converter.
  a. Discard the nuts and gasket.
21. If equipped, remove the heat shield and disconnect the block heater electrical connector.
  a. Remove the block heater wiring harness from the engine.
22. Remove the RH cylinder block drain plug or, if equipped, the block heater.
  a. Allow coolant to drain from the cylinder block.
23. Remove the coolant bypass hose from the thermostat housing.
24. Remove the 4 bolts and the fuel rail and injectors as an assembly.
25. Remove the 3 thermostat housing-to-lower intake manifold bolts.
  a. Remove the thermostat housing and discard the gasket and O-ring seal.

⁂ WARNING

If the engine is repaired or replaced because of upper engine failure, typically including valve or piston damage, check the intake manifold for metal debris. If metal debris is found, install a new intake manifold. Failure to follow these instructions can result in engine damage.

26. Remove the 10 bolts and the lower intake manifold.
  a. Discard the gaskets.
27. Remove the 2 bolts and the upper LH primary timing chain guide.
28. Remove the 2 bolts and the LH secondary timing chain tensioner.

➡If the components are to be reinstalled, they must be installed in the same positions. Mark the components for installation into their original locations.

29. Remove the valve tappets from the cylinder head.
30. Inspect the valve tappets.
31. Remove and discard the M6 bolt.

⁂ WARNING

Place clean, lint-free shop towels over exposed engine cavities. Carefully remove the towels so foreign material is not dropped into the engine. Any foreign material (including any material created while cleaning gasket surfaces) that enters the oil passages or the oil pan, may cause engine failure.

⁂ WARNING

Aluminum surfaces are soft and may be scratched easily. Never place the cylinder head gasket surface, unprotected, on a bench surface.

➡The cylinder head bolts must be discarded and new bolts must be installed. They are a tighten-to-yield design and cannot be reused.

32. Remove and discard the 8 bolts from the cylinder head.
  a. Remove the cylinder head.
  b. Discard the cylinder head gasket.

⁂ WARNING

Do not use metal scrapers, wire brushes, power abrasive discs or other abrasive means to clean the sealing surfaces. These tools cause scratches and gouges that make leak paths. Use a plastic scraping tool to remove all traces of the head gasket.

➡**Observe all warnings or cautions and follow all application directions contained on the packaging of the silicone gasket remover and the metal surface prep.**

➡**If there is no residual gasket material present, metal surface prep can be used to clean and prepare the surfaces.**

33. Clean the cylinder head-to-cylinder block mating surfaces of both the cylinder heads and the cylinder block in the following sequence.
   a. Remove any large deposits of silicone or gasket material with a plastic scraper.
   b. Apply silicone gasket remover, following package directions, and allow to set for several minutes.
   c. Remove the silicone gasket remover with a plastic scraper. A second application of silicone gasket remover may be required if residual traces of silicone or gasket material remain.
   d. Apply metal surface prep, following package directions, to remove any remaining traces of oil or coolant and to prepare the surfaces to bond with the new gasket. Do not attempt to make the metal shiny. Some staining of the metal surfaces is normal.
34. Support the cylinder head on a bench with the head gasket side up. Check the cylinder head distortion and the cylinder block distortion.

To install:

✱✱ WARNING

During engine repair procedures, cleanliness is extremely important. Any foreign material, including any material created while cleaning gasket surfaces that enters the oil passages, coolant passages or the oil pan, may cause engine failure.

35. Install a new gasket, the LH cylinder head and 8 new bolts. Tighten in the proper sequence in 5 stages:
   a. Stage 1: Tighten to 15 ft. lbs. (20 Nm).
   b. Stage 2: Tighten to 26 ft. lbs. (35 Nm).
   c. Stage 3: Tighten 90 degrees.
   d. Stage 4: Tighten 90 degrees.
   e. Stage 5: Tighten 90 degrees.
36. Install the M6 bolt. Tighten the bolt to 89 inch lbs. (10 Nm).

➡**The valve tappets must be installed in their original positions.**

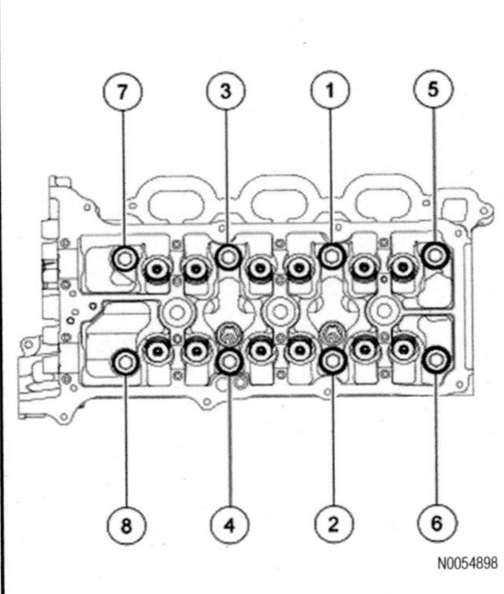

Fig. 121 LH cylinder head and tightening sequence

➡**Coat the valve tappets with clean engine oil prior to installation.**

37. Install the valve tappets.
38. Install the LH secondary timing chain tensioner and the 2 bolts. Tighten the bolts to 89 inch lbs. (10 Nm).
39. Install the upper LH primary timing chain guide and the 2 bolts. Tighten the bolts to 89 inch lbs. (10 Nm).

✱✱ WARNING

If the engine is repaired or replaced because of upper engine failure, typically including valve or piston damage, check the intake manifold for metal debris. If metal debris is found, install a new intake manifold. Failure to follow these instructions can result in engine damage.

40. Using new gaskets, install the lower intake manifold and the 10 bolts.
   a. Tighten in the proper sequence to 89 inch lbs. (10 Nm). Refer to the Intake Manifold procedure for the sequence.
41. Using a new gasket and O-ring seal, install the thermostat housing and the 3 bolts. Tighten the bolts to 89 inch lbs. (10 Nm).

✱✱ WARNING

Use O-ring seals that are made of special fuel-resistant material. The use of ordinary O-rings may cause the fuel system to leak. Do not reuse the O-ring seals.

➡**The upper and lower O-ring seals are not interchangeable.**

42. Install new fuel injector O-ring seals.
   a. Remove the retaining clips and separate the fuel injectors from the fuel rail.
   b. Remove and discard the O-ring seals.
   c. Install new O-ring seals and lubricate with clean engine oil.
   d. Install the fuel injectors and the retaining clips onto the fuel rail.
43. Install the fuel rail and injectors as an assembly and install the 4 bolts. Tighten the bolts to 89 inch lbs. (10 Nm).
44. Install the coolant bypass hose to the thermostat housing.
45. Install the RH cylinder block drain plug or, if equipped, the block heater. Tighten the drain plug to 30 ft. lbs. (40 Nm).
46. If equipped, install the block heater wiring harness onto the engine.
   a. Connect the block heater electrical connector and install the heat shield.
47. Using a new gasket, install the RH catalytic converter and 4 new nuts. Tighten the nuts to 30 ft. lbs. (40 Nm).
48. Install the LH cylinder block drain plug. Tighten the drain plug to 15 ft. lbs. (20 Nm), plus an additional 180°.
49. Install 6 new LH exhaust manifold studs. Tighten the studs to 106 inch lbs. (12 Nm).

✱✱ WARNING

Failure to tighten the exhaust manifold nuts to specification a second time will cause the exhaust manifold to develop an exhaust leak.

50. Using a new gasket, install the LH exhaust manifold and 6 new nuts. Tighten in 2 stages in the proper sequence (refer to Exhaust Manifold procedure):
   a. Stage 1: Tighten to 15 ft. lbs. (20 Nm).
   b. Stage 2: Tighten to 18 ft. lbs. (25 Nm).
51. Install the LH exhaust manifold heat shield and the 3 bolts. Tighten the bolts to 89 inch lbs. (10 Nm).
52. Using a new gasket, install the LH catalytic converter and 4 new nuts. Tighten the nuts to 30 ft. lbs. (40 Nm).
53. Install the LH catalytic converter bracket bolts. Tighten the bolts to 15 ft. lbs. (20 Nm).
54. Attach the Engine Oil Pressure (EOP) switch wiring harness pin-type retainer.
55. Install the stud, generator and the nut and bolt. Tighten the stud to 106 inch

lbs. (12 Nm), and tighten the nut and bolt to 35 ft. lbs. (48 Nm).

56. Connect the generator electrical connector.

57. Connect the generator B+ cable and install the nut. Tighten the nut to 150 inch lbs. (17 Nm).

58. Attach the pin-type wire harness retainer to the rear of LH cylinder head.

59. Connect the LH Catalyst Monitor Sensor (CMS) electrical connector.

60. Connect the LH Heated Oxygen Sensor (HO2S) electrical connector.

61. Install the LH Camshaft Position (CMP) sensor and the bolt. Tighten the bolt to 89 inch lbs. (10 Nm).

62. Connect the LH CMP sensor electrical connector.

63. Connect the Cylinder Head Temperature (CHT) sensor electrical connector.

64. Connect the 6 fuel injector electrical connectors (3 shown).

65. Install the LH camshafts.

Right-Hand

See Figures 122 and 123.

WARNING

During engine repair procedures, cleanliness is extremely important. Any foreign material, including any material created while cleaning gasket surfaces, which enters the oil passages, coolant passages or the oil pan, may cause engine failure.

➡On early build engines, the timing chain rides on the inner side of the RH timing chain guide. Late build engines are equipped with a different design RH timing chain guide that requires the timing chain to ride on the outer side of the RH timing chain guide. For service, all replacement RH timing chain guides will be the late build design.

All Vehicles

1. Remove the RH camshafts. For additional information, refer to Camshaft in this section.

2. Disconnect the RH Heated Oxygen Sensor (HO2S) electrical connector.

3. Disconnect the RH Camshaft Position (CMP) sensor electrical connector.

4. Remove the bolt and the RH CMP sensor.

5. Remove the bolt and the Power Steering Pressure (PSP) tube bracket from the RH cylinder head.

6. Remove the bolt and the ground wire.

7. Disconnect the 6 fuel injector electrical connectors (3 shown).

8. Disconnect the Cylinder Head Temperature (CHT) sensor electrical connector.

9. Disconnect the LH Catalyst Monitor Sensor (CMS) electrical connector.

10. Remove the 2 LH catalytic converter bracket bolts.

11. Remove the 4 nuts and the LH catalytic converter.

a. Discard the nuts and the gasket.

12. Remove the LH cylinder block drain plug.

a. Allow coolant to drain from the cylinder block.

13. Remove the 4 nuts and the RH catalytic converter.

a. Discard the nuts and gasket.

14. If equipped, remove the heat shield and disconnect the block heater electrical connector.

a. Remove the block heater wiring harness from the engine.

15. Remove the RH cylinder block drain plug or, if equipped, the block heater.

a. Allow coolant to drain from the cylinder block.

16. Remove the 3 bolts and the RH exhaust manifold heat shield.

17. Remove the 6 nuts and the RH exhaust manifold.

a. Discard the nuts and exhaust manifold gaskets.

18. Clean and inspect the RH exhaust manifold as outlined in this section.

19. Remove and discard the 6 RH exhaust manifold studs.

Engines Equipped With Early Build RH Timing Chain Guides

20. Remove the 2 bolts and the RH primary timing chain guide.

Engines Equipped With Late Build/Replacement RH Timing Chain Guides

21. Remove the 2 bolts and the RH primary timing chain guide.

All Vehicles

22. Remove the bolts and the RH secondary timing chain tensioner.

23. Remove the 2 bolts and the engine lifting eye.

➡Index-mark the location of the bracket on the cylinder head for installation.

24. Remove the bolt and the upper intake manifold support bracket.

25. Remove the coolant bypass hose from the thermostat housing.

26. Remove the 4 bolts and the fuel rail and injectors as an assembly.

27. Remove the 3 thermostat housing-to-lower intake manifold bolts.

a. Remove the thermostat housing and discard the gasket and O-ring seal.

WARNING

If the engine is repaired or replaced because of upper engine failure, typically including valve or piston damage, check the intake manifold for metal debris. If metal debris is found, install a new intake manifold. Failure to follow these instructions can result in engine damage.

28. Remove the 10 bolts and the lower intake manifold.

a. Discard the gaskets.

29. Disconnect and remove the CHT sensor jumper harness.

➡If the components are to be reinstalled, they must be installed in the same positions. Mark the components for installation into their original locations.

30. Remove the valve tappets from the cylinder head.

31. Inspect the valve tappets.

32. Remove and discard the M6 bolt.

WARNING

Place clean, lint-free shop towels over exposed engine cavities. Carefully remove the towels so foreign material is not dropped into the engine. Any foreign material (including any material created while cleaning gasket surfaces) that enters the oil passages or the oil pan, may cause engine failure.

WARNING

Aluminum surfaces are soft and may be scratched easily. Never place the cylinder head gasket surface, unprotected, on a bench surface.

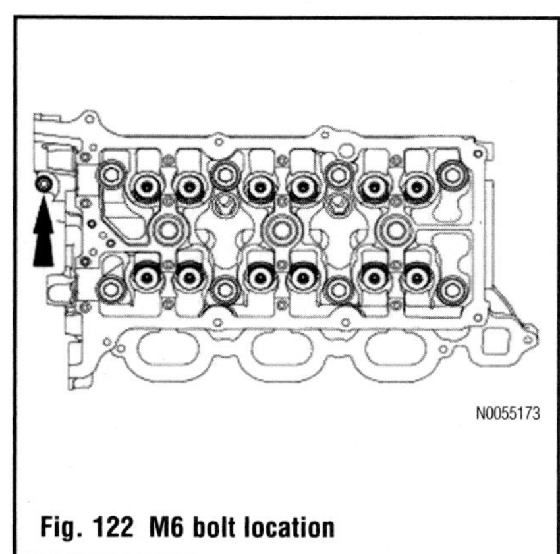

Fig. 122 M6 bolt location

➡The cylinder head bolts must be discarded and new bolts must be installed. They are a tighten-to-yield design and cannot be reused.

33. Remove and discard the 8 bolts from the cylinder head.
    a. Remove the cylinder head.
    b. Discard the cylinder head gasket.

➡Do not use metal scrapers, wire brushes, power abrasive discs or other abrasive means to clean the sealing surfaces. These tools cause scratches and gouges that make leak paths. Use a plastic scraping tool to remove all traces of the head gasket.

➡Observe all warnings or cautions and follow all application directions contained on the packaging of the silicone gasket remover and the metal surface prep.

➡If there is no residual gasket material present, metal surface prep can be used to clean and prepare the surfaces.

34. Clean the cylinder head-to-cylinder block mating surfaces of both the cylinder heads and the cylinder block in the following sequence.
    a. Remove any large deposits of silicone or gasket material with a plastic scraper.
    b. Apply silicone gasket remover, following package directions, and allow to set for several minutes.
    c. Remove the silicone gasket remover with a plastic scraper. A second application of silicone gasket remover may be required if residual traces of silicone or gasket material remain.
    d. Apply metal surface prep, following package directions, to remove any remaining traces of oil or coolant and to prepare the surfaces to bond with the new gasket. Do not attempt to make the metal shiny. Some staining of the metal surfaces is normal.
35. Support the cylinder head on a bench with the head gasket side up. Check the cylinder head distortion and the cylinder block distortion.

To install:

⁂ WARNING

During engine repair procedures, cleanliness is extremely important. Any foreign material, including any material created while cleaning gasket surfaces that enters the oil passages, coolant passages or the oil pan, may cause engine failure.

➡On early build engines, the timing chain rides on the inner side of the RH timing chain guide. Late built engines are equipped with a different design RH timing chain guide that requires the timing chain to ride on the outer side of the RH timing chain guide. For service, all replacement RH timing chain guides will be the late build design.

All Vehicles

36. Install a new gasket, the RH cylinder head and 8 new bolts. Tighten in the sequence shown in 5 stages:
    a. Stage 1: Tighten to 15 ft. lbs. (20 Nm).
    b. Stage 2: Tighten to 26 ft. lbs. (35 Nm).
    c. Stage 3: Tighten 90 degrees.
    d. Stage 4: Tighten 90 degrees.
    e. Stage 5: Tighten 90 degrees.
37. Install the M6 bolt. Tighten the bolt to 89 inch lbs. (10 Nm).

➡The valve tappets must be installed in their original positions.

➡Coat the valve tappets with clean engine oil prior to installation.

38. Install the valve tappets.
39. Install and connect the Cylinder Head Temperature (CHT) sensor jumper harness.

⁂ WARNING

If the engine is repaired or replaced because of upper engine failure, typically including valve or piston damage, check the intake manifold for metal debris. If metal debris is found, install a new intake manifold. Failure to follow these instructions can result in engine damage.

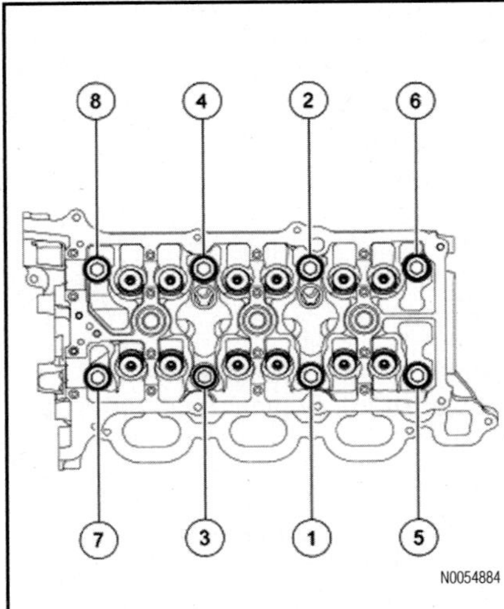

Fig. 123 RH cylinder head installation and tightening sequence

40. Using new gaskets, install the lower intake manifold and the 10 bolts. Tighten the bolts to 89 inch lbs. (10 Nm). Refer to the Intake Manifold procedure for the sequence.
41. Using a new gasket and O-ring seal, install the thermostat housing and the 3 bolts. Tighten the bolts to 89 inch lbs. (10 Nm).

⁂ WARNING

Use O-ring seals that are made of special fuel-resistant material. The use of ordinary O-rings may cause the fuel system to leak. Do not reuse the O-ring seals.

➡The upper and lower O-ring seals are not interchangeable.

42. Install new fuel injector O-ring seals.
    a. Remove the retaining clips and separate the fuel injectors from the fuel rail.
    b. Remove and discard the O-ring seals.
    c. Install new O-ring seals and lubricate with clean engine oil.
    d. Install the fuel injectors and the retaining clips onto the fuel rail.
43. Install the fuel rail and injectors as an assembly and install the 4 bolts. Tighten the bolts to 89 inch lbs. (10 Nm).
44. Install the coolant bypass hose to the thermostat housing.

➡Align the bracket with the index mark made during removal.

45. Install the upper intake manifold support bracket and the bolt. Tighten the bolt to 89 inch lbs. (10 Nm).
46. Install the engine lifting eye and the 2 bolts. Tighten the bolts to 18 ft. lbs. (24 Nm).
47. Install the RH secondary timing chain tensioner and the 2 bolts. Tighten the bolts to 89 inch lbs. (10 Nm).

Engines Equipped With Late Build/Replacement RH Timing Chain Guides

48. Install the RH primary timing chain guide and the 2 bolts. Tighten the bolts to 89 inch lbs. (10 Nm).

Engines Equipped With Early Build RH Timing Chain Guides

49. Install the RH primary timing chain guide and the 2 bolts. Tighten the bolts to 89 inch lbs. (10 Nm).

All Vehicles

50. Install 6 new RH exhaust manifold studs. Tighten the studs to 106 inch lbs. (12 Nm).

⁂ WARNING

Failure to tighten the exhaust manifold nuts to specification a second time will cause the exhaust manifold to develop an exhaust leak.

51. Using a new gasket, install the RH exhaust manifold and 6 new nuts. Tighten in 2 stages in the sequence shown in the Exhaust Manifold procedure:
    a. Stage 1: Tighten to 15 ft. lbs. (20 Nm).
    b. Stage 2: Tighten to 18 ft. lbs. (25 Nm).
52. Install the RH exhaust manifold heat shield and the 3 bolts. Tighten the bolts to 89 inch lbs. (10 Nm).
53. Install the RH cylinder block drain plug or, if equipped, the block heater. Tighten the bolts to 30 ft. lbs. (40 Nm).
54. If equipped, install the block heater wiring harness onto the engine.
    a. Connect the block heater electrical connector and install the heat shield.
55. Using a new gasket, install the RH catalytic converter and 4 new nuts. Tighten the nuts to 30 ft. lbs. (40 Nm).
56. Install the LH cylinder block drain plug. Tighten the drain plug to 15 ft. lbs. (20 Nm) plus an additional 180 degrees.
57. Using a new gasket, install the LH catalytic converter and 4 new nuts. Tighten the nuts to 30 ft. lbs. (40 Nm).
58. Install the 2 LH catalytic converter bracket bolts. Tighten the bolts to 15 ft. lbs. (20 Nm).
59. Connect the LH Catalyst Monitor Sensor (CMS) electrical connector.
60. Connect the CHT sensor electrical connector.
61. Connect the 6 fuel injector electrical connectors.
62. Install the ground wire and the bolt. Tighten the bolt to 89 inch lbs. (10 Nm).
63. Install the Power Steering Pressure (PSP) tube bracket and the bolt to the RH cylinder head. Tighten the bolt to 89 inch lbs. (10 Nm).
64. Install the RH Camshaft Position (CMP) sensor and the bolt. Tighten the bolt to 89 inch lbs. (10 Nm).
65. Connect the RH CMP sensor electrical connector.
66. Connect the RH Heated Oxygen Sensor (HO2S) electrical connector.
67. Install the RH camshafts as outlined in this section.

3.5L Turbo Engine

Left-Hand

See Figures 124 through 128.

⁂ WARNING

During engine repair procedures, cleanliness is extremely important. Any foreign material, including any material created while cleaning gasket surfaces, which enters the oil passages, coolant passages or the oil pan, may cause engine failure.

⁂ WARNING

Whenever turbocharger air intake system components are removed, always cover open ports to protect from debris. It is important that no foreign material enter the system. The turbocharger compressor vanes are susceptible to damage from even small particles. All components should be inspected and cleaned, if necessary, prior to installation or reassembly.

1. Remove the fuel rails.
2. Remove the LH camshafts as outlined in this section.
3. Disconnect the LH Camshaft Position (CMP) sensor electrical connector.
4. Remove the bolt and the LH CMP sensor.
5. Detach the wiring harness retainer from the rear of the LH cylinder head.
6. Remove the coolant tube bracket-to-cylinder head nut.
7. Remove the nut and disconnect the generator B+ cable.
8. Disconnect the generator electrical connector.
9. Remove the nut, bolt and the generator.
    a. Remove the generator stud.
10. Remove the 3 bolts and the LH exhaust manifold heat shield.
11. Disconnect the turbocharger wastegate regulating valve hose from the LH turbocharger assembly.
12. Remove the 2 bolts and the LH turbocharger oil return tube from the turbocharger.
    a. Remove and discard the gasket.
13. Remove the LH oil supply tube secondary latch.
14. Using the Spring Lock Coupling Disconnect Tool, remove the LH oil supply tube from the quick connect fitting.
    a. Inspect and if necessary, replace the quick connect fitting.
15. Remove the 2 coolant tube banjo bolts and the LH turbocharger coolant tubes and sealing washers.
    a. Discard the sealing washers.
16. Remove the LH turbocharger oil supply tube banjo bolt.
    a. Discard the sealing washer.
    b. Discard the oil supply tube filter.
17. Remove the 2 bolts and the lower LH turbocharger-to-cylinder block bracket.
18. Remove the 2 bolts and the upper LH turbocharger bracket-to-cylinder block bracket.
19. Remove the 8 LH exhaust manifold nuts and the exhaust manifold and turbocharger assembly.
    a. Discard the exhaust manifold gasket and nuts.
20. Clean and inspect the LH exhaust manifold as outlined in this section.
21. Remove and discard the 8 LH exhaust manifold studs.

⁂ WARNING

Do not use metal scrapers, wire brushes, power abrasive discs or other abrasive means to clean the sealing surfaces. These may cause scratches and gouges resulting in leak paths. Use a plastic scraper to clean the sealing surfaces.

22. Clean the exhaust manifold mating surface of the cylinder head with metal surface prep. Follow the directions on the packaging.
23. Remove the LH cylinder block drain plug.
    a. Allow coolant to drain from the cylinder block.
24. If equipped, remove the heat shield and disconnect the block heater electrical connector.
    a. Remove the block heater wiring harness from the engine.
25. Remove the RH cylinder block drain plug or, if equipped, the block heater.
    a. Allow coolant to drain from the cylinder block.
26. Remove the 2 bolts and the upper LH primary timing chain guide.
27. Remove the 2 bolts and the LH secondary timing chain tensioner.

➡If the components are to be reinstalled, they must be installed in the same positions. Mark the components for installation into their original locations.

28. Remove the valve tappets from the cylinder head.

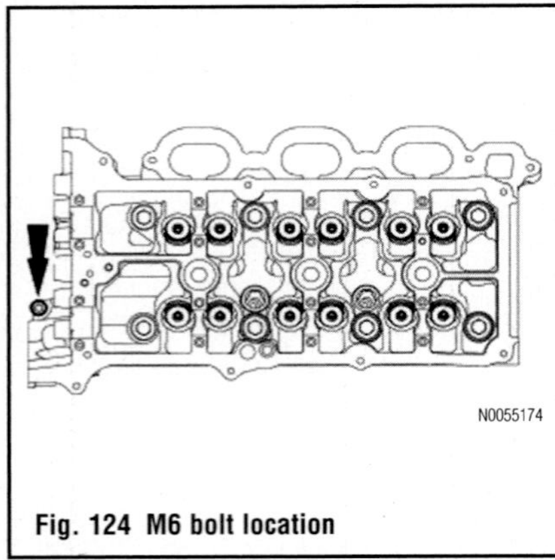

Fig. 124 M6 bolt location

29. Inspect the valve tappets as outlined in this section.

30. Remove and discard the M6 bolt.

WARNING

Place clean, lint-free shop towels over exposed engine cavities. Carefully remove the towels so foreign material is not dropped into the engine. Any foreign material (including any material created while cleaning gasket surfaces) that enters the oil passages or the oil pan, may cause engine failure.

WARNING

Aluminum surfaces are soft and may be scratched easily. Never place the cylinder head gasket surface, unprotected, on a bench surface.

➡The cylinder head bolts must be discarded and new bolts must be installed. They are a torque-to-yield design and cannot be reused.

31. Remove and discard the 8 bolts from the cylinder head.
   a. Remove the cylinder head.
   b. Discard the cylinder head gasket.

WARNING

Do not use metal scrapers, wire brushes, power abrasive discs or other abrasive means to clean the sealing surfaces. These tools cause scratches and gouges that make leak paths. Use a plastic scraping tool to remove all traces of the head gasket.

➡Observe all warnings or cautions and follow all application directions contained on the packaging of the silicone gasket remover and the metal surface prep.

➡If there is no residual gasket material present, metal surface prep can be used to clean and prepare the surfaces.

32. Clean the cylinder head-to-cylinder block mating surfaces of both the cylinder heads and the cylinder block in the following sequence.
   a. Remove any large deposits of silicone or gasket material with a plastic scraper.
   b. Apply silicone gasket remover, following package directions, and allow to set for several minutes.
   c. Remove the silicone gasket remover with a plastic scraper. A second application of silicone gasket remover may be required if residual traces of silicone or gasket material remain.
   d. Apply metal surface prep, following package directions, to remove any remaining traces of oil or coolant and to prepare the surfaces to bond with the new gasket. Do not attempt to make the metal shiny. Some staining of the metal surfaces is normal.

33. Support the cylinder head on a bench with the head gasket side up. Check the cylinder head distortion and the cylinder block distortion as outlined in this section

To install:

WARNING

During engine repair procedures, cleanliness is extremely important. Any foreign material, including any material created while cleaning gasket surfaces that enters the oil passages, coolant passages or the oil pan, may cause engine failure.

WARNING

Whenever turbocharger air intake system components are removed, always cover open ports to protect from debris. It is important that no foreign material enter the system. The turbocharger compressor vanes are susceptible to damage from even small particles. All components should be inspected and cleaned, if necessary, prior to installation or reassembly.

34. Install a new gasket, the LH cylinder head and 8 new bolts. Tighten in the proper sequence in 5 Stages:
   a. Stage 1: Tighten to 15 ft. lbs. (20 Nm).
   b. Stage 2: Tighten to 26 ft. lbs. (35 Nm).
   c. Stage 3: Tighten 90 degrees.
   d. Stage 4: Tighten 90 degrees.
   e. Stage 5: Tighten 90 degrees.

35. Install the cylinder head M6 bolt. Tighten the bolt to 89 inch lbs. (10 Nm).

➡The valve tappets must be installed in their original positions.

➡Coat the valve tappets with clean engine oil prior to installation.

36. Install the valve tappets.

37. Install the LH secondary timing chain tensioner and the 2 bolts. Tighten the bolts to 89 inch lbs. (10 Nm).

38. Install the upper LH primary timing chain guide and the 2 bolts. Tighten the bolts to 89 inch lbs. (10 Nm).

39. Install the RH cylinder block drain plug or, if equipped, the block heater. Tighten the drain plug to 30 ft. lbs. (40 Nm).

40. If equipped, install the block heater wiring harness onto the engine.
   a. Connect the block heater electrical connector and install the heat shield.

41. Install the LH cylinder block drain plug. Tighten the drain plug to 15 ft. lbs. (20 Nm) plus an additional 180°.

42. Install 8 new LH exhaust manifold studs. Tighten the studs to 106 inch lbs. (12 Nm).

WARNING

Failure to tighten the exhaust manifold nuts to specification a second time will cause the exhaust manifold to develop an exhaust leak.

43. Install a new gasket, LH exhaust manifold and turbocharger assembly and 8

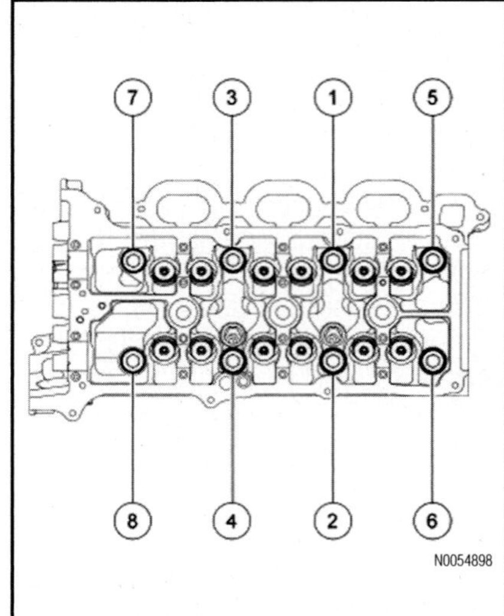

Fig. 125 LH cylinder head installation and tightening sequence

Fig. 126 LH exhaust manifold studs location

new nuts. Tighten the nuts in 2 stages in the following sequence:

a. Stage 1: Tighten to 133 inch lbs. (15 Nm).

b. Stage 2: Tighten to 15 ft. lbs. (20 Nm).

44. Install the upper turbocharger bracket-to-cylinder block and the 2 bolts.

a. Do not tighten the bolts at this time.

45. Install the lower turbocharger-to-cylinder block bracket and the 2 bolts.

a. Do not tighten the bolts at this time.

WARNING

The next 4 steps must be performed in order or damage to the turbocharger may occur.

46. Tighten the upper turbocharger bracket-to-turbocharger bolt. Tighten the bolt to 168 inch lbs. (19 Nm).

47. Tighten the upper turbocharger bracket-to-cylinder block bolt. Tighten the bolt to 18 ft. lbs. (25 Nm).

48. Tighten the lower turbocharger bracket-to-turbocharger bolt. Tighten the bolt to 168 inch lbs. (19 Nm).

49. Tighten the lower turbocharger bracket-to-cylinder block bolt. Tighten the bolt to 97 inch lbs. (11 Nm).

50. Install the oil supply tube filter, washer and bolt.

a. Install a new oil supply tube filter in the oil supply tube block.

b. Slide the new washer onto the oil supply tube block.

c. Install the banjo bolt into the oil supply tube block.

51. Install the LH turbocharger oil supply tube. Tighten the bolt to 26 ft. lbs. (35 Nm).

52. Using 2 new sealing washers, install the 2 LH turbocharger coolant tubes and the banjo bolts. Tighten the bolts to 27 ft. lbs. (37 Nm).

53. If necessary, install the LH cylinder head turbocharger oil supply quick connect fitting. Tighten the fitting to 142 inch lbs. (16 Nm).

➡Listen for audible click when installing the oil supply tube into the quick connect fitting.

54. Install the LH oil supply tube into the quick connect fitting.

55. Install the LH oil supply tube secondary latch.

56. Install a new gasket, turbocharger oil return tube and the 2 bolts. Tighten the bolts to 89 inch lbs. (10 Nm).

➡Make sure the turbocharger wastegate regulating valve hose does not contact the exhaust manifold heat shield.

57. Connect the turbocharger wastegate regulating valve hose to the LH turbocharger assembly.

58. Install the LH exhaust manifold heat shield and the 3 bolts. Tighten the bolts to 124 inch lbs. (14 Nm).

59. Install the stud, generator and the nut and bolt. Tighten the stud to 71 inch lbs. (8 Nm), and the nut & bolt to 35 ft. lbs. (47 Nm).

60. Connect the generator electrical connector.

61. Connect the generator B+ cable and install the nut. Tighten the nut to 150 inch lbs. (17 Nm).

62. Install the LH coolant tube bracket-to-cylinder head nut. Tighten the nut to 89 inch lbs. (10 Nm).

63. Attach the pin-type wire harness retainer to the rear of LH cylinder head.

64. Install the LH Camshaft Position (CMP) sensor and the bolt. Tighten the bolt to 89 inch lbs. (10 Nm).

65. Connect the LH CMP sensor electrical connector.

66. Install the LH camshafts as outlined in this section.

67. Install the fuel rails.

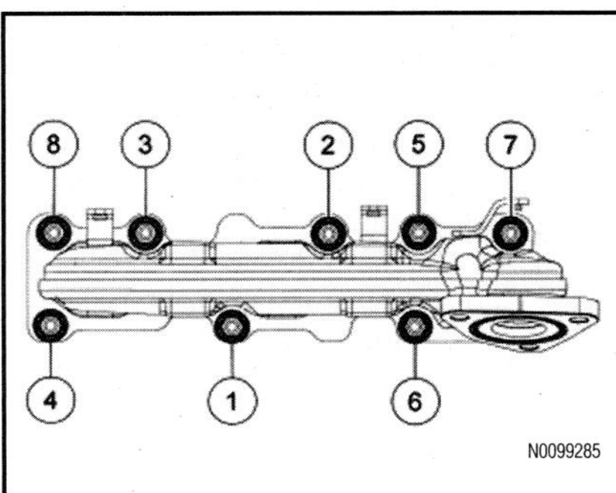

Fig. 127 LH exhaust manifold and turbocharger assembly installation

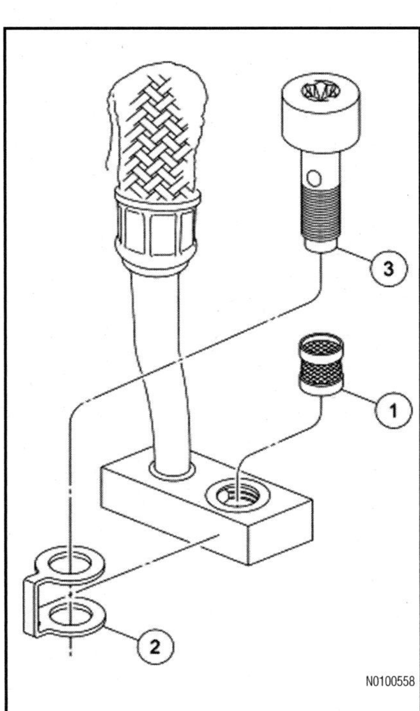

Fig. 128 Oil supply tube filter, washer and bolt

Right-Hand

See Figures 129 through 133.

WARNING

During engine repair procedures, cleanliness is extremely important. Any foreign material, including any material created while cleaning gasket surfaces, which enters the oil passages, coolant passages or the oil pan, may cause engine failure.

WARNING

Whenever turbocharger air intake system components are removed, always cover open ports to protect from debris. It is important that no foreign material enter the system. The turbocharger compressor vanes are susceptible to damage from even small particles. All components should be inspected and cleaned, if necessary, prior to installation or reassembly.

➡On early build engines, the timing chain rides on the inner side of the RH timing chain guide. Late build engines are equipped with a different design RH timing chain guide that requires the

timing chain to ride on the outer side of the RH timing chain guide. For service, all replacement RH timing chain guides will be the late build design.

All Vehicles

1. Remove the fuel rails.
2. Remove the RH camshafts as outlined in this section.
3. Disconnect the RH Camshaft Position (CMP) sensor electrical connector.
4. Remove the bolt and the RH CMP sensor.
5. Remove the bolt and the ground wire.
6. Remove the bolt and the radio capacitor from the RH cylinder head.
7. Disconnect the Cylinder Head Temperature (CHT) sensor electrical connector from the rear of the RH cylinder head.
8. Remove the 5 bolts and the 2 upper RH exhaust manifold heat shields.
9. Disconnect the turbocharger wastegate regulating valve hose from the RH turbocharger assembly.
10. Remove the 2 bolts and the turbocharger oil return tube from the RH turbocharger.
    a. Remove and discard the gasket.
11. Remove the oil supply tube secondary latch.
12. sing the Spring Lock Coupling Disconnect Tool, remove the RH turbocharger oil supply tube from the quick connect fitting.
    a. Inspect and if necessary, replace the quick connect fitting.
13. Remove the 2 coolant tube banjo bolts and the RH turbocharger coolant tubes and sealing washers.
    a. Discard the sealing washers.
14. Remove the coolant tube bracket-to-cylinder head bolt.
15. Remove the 3 bolts and the upper turbocharger-to-cylinder block bracket.
16. Remove the 3 exhaust manifold-to-turbocharger bolts and the turbocharger assembly.
    a. Discard the gasket and bolts.
17. Remove the RH turbocharger oil supply tube banjo bolt.
    a. Discard the sealing washer.
    b. Discard the oil supply tube filter.
18. Remove the 8 nuts and the RH exhaust manifold.
    a. Discard the nuts and exhaust manifold gaskets.
19. Clean and inspect the RH exhaust manifold as outlined in this section.
20. Remove and discard the 8 RH exhaust manifold studs.

WARNING

Do not use metal scrapers, wire brushes, power abrasive discs or other abrasive means to clean the sealing surfaces. These may cause scratches and gouges resulting in leak paths. Use a plastic scraper to clean the sealing surfaces.

21. Clean the exhaust manifold mating surface of the cylinder head with metal surface prep. Follow the directions on the packaging.
22. Remove the LH cylinder block drain plug.
    a. Allow coolant to drain from the cylinder block.
23. If equipped, remove the heat shield and disconnect the block heater electrical connector.
    a. Remove the block heater wiring harness from the engine.
24. Remove the RH cylinder block drain plug or, if equipped, the block heater.
    a. Allow coolant to drain from the cylinder block.

Engines Equipped With Early Build RH Timing Chain Guides

25. Remove the 2 bolts and the RH primary timing chain guide.

Engines Equipped With Late Build/Replacement RH Timing Chain Guides

26. Remove the 2 bolts and the RH primary timing chain guide.

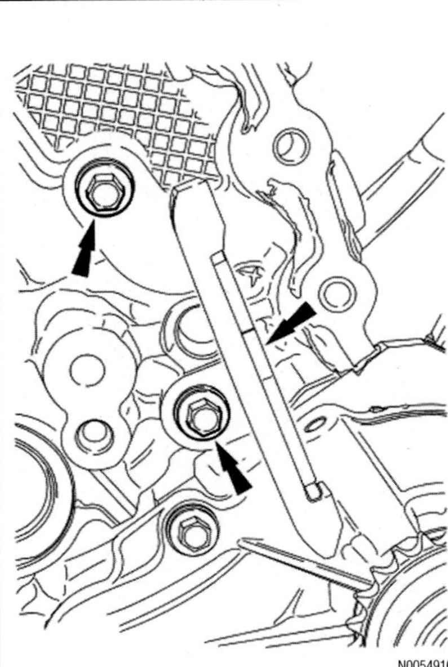

Fig. 129 Early build RH primary timing chain guide location

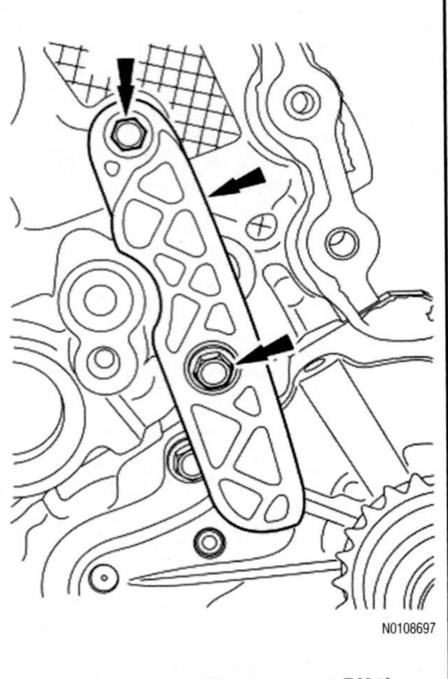

Fig. 130 Late build/Replacement RH timing chain guides

All Vehicles

27. Remove the bolts and the RH secondary timing chain tensioner.
28. Remove the 2 bolts and the RH engine lifting eye.

➡If the components are to be reinstalled, they must be installed in the same positions. Mark the components for installation into their original locations.

29. Remove the valve tappets from the cylinder head.
30. Inspect the valve tappets as outlined in this section.
31. Remove and discard the M6 bolt.

WARNING

Place clean, lint-free shop towels over exposed engine cavities. Carefully remove the towels so foreign material is not dropped into the engine. Any foreign material (including any material created while cleaning gasket surfaces) that enters the oil passages or the oil pan, may cause engine failure.

➡Aluminum surfaces are soft and may be scratched easily. Never place the cylinder head gasket surface, unprotected, on a bench surface.

➡The cylinder head bolts must be discarded and new bolts must be installed. They are a torque-to-yield design and cannot be reused.

32. Remove and discard the 8 bolts from the cylinder head.

a. Remove the cylinder head.

b. Discard the cylinder head gasket.

**** WARNING**

Do not use metal scrapers, wire brushes, power abrasive discs or other abrasive means to clean the sealing surfaces. These tools cause scratches and gouges that make leak paths. Use a plastic scraping tool to remove all traces of the head gasket.

➡Observe all warnings or cautions and follow all application directions contained on the packaging of the silicone gasket remover and the metal surface prep.

➡If there is no residual gasket material present, metal surface prep can be used to clean and prepare the surfaces.

33. Clean the cylinder head-to-cylinder block mating surfaces of both the cylinder heads and the cylinder block in the following sequence.

a. Remove any large deposits of silicone or gasket material with a plastic scraper.

b. Apply silicone gasket remover, following package directions, and allow to set for several minutes.

c. Remove the silicone gasket remover with a plastic scraper. A second application of silicone gasket remover may be required if residual traces of silicone or gasket material remain.

d. Apply metal surface prep, following package directions, to remove any remaining traces of oil or coolant and to prepare the surfaces to bond with the new gasket. Do not attempt to make the metal shiny. Some staining of the metal surfaces is normal.

34. Support the cylinder head on a bench with the head gasket side up. Check the cylinder head distortion and the cylinder block distortion as outlined in this section.

To install:

**** WARNING**

During engine repair procedures, cleanliness is extremely important. Any foreign material, including any material created while cleaning gasket surfaces that enters the oil passages, coolant passages or the oil pan, may cause engine failure.

**** WARNING**

Whenever turbocharger air intake system components are removed, always cover open ports to protect from debris. It is important that no foreign material enter the system. The turbocharger compressor vanes are susceptible to damage from even small particles. All components should be inspected and cleaned, if necessary, prior to installation or reassembly.

➡On early build engines, the timing chain rides on the inner side of the RH timing chain guide. Late build engines are equipped with a different design RH timing chain guide that requires the timing chain to ride on the outer side of the RH timing chain guide. For service, all replacement RH timing chain guides will be the late build design.

All Vehicles

35. Install a new gasket, the RH cylinder head and 8 new bolts. Tighten in the proper sequence:

a. Stage 1: Tighten to 15 ft. lbs. (20 Nm).

b. Stage 2: Tighten to 26 ft. lbs. (35 Nm).

c. Stage 3: Tighten 90 degrees.

d. Stage 4: Tighten 90 degrees.

e. Stage 5: Tighten 90 degrees.

36. Install the cylinder head M6 bolt. Tighten the bolt to 89 inch lbs. (10 Nm).

➡The valve tappets must be installed in their original positions.

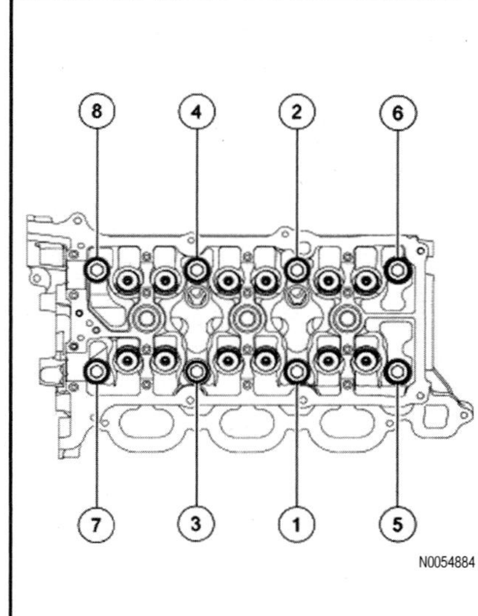

Fig. 131 RH cylinder head installation and tightening sequence

➡Coat the valve tappets with clean engine oil prior to installation.

37. Install the valve tappets.

38. Install the RH engine lifting eye and the 2 bolts. Tighten the bolts 18 ft. lbs. (24 Nm).

39. Install the RH secondary timing chain tensioner and the 2 bolts. Tighten the bolts to 89 inch lbs. (10 Nm).

Engines Equipped With Early Build RH Timing Chain Guides

40. Install the RH primary timing chain guide and the 2 bolts. Tighten the bolts to 89 inch lbs. (10 Nm).

Engines Equipped With Late Build/Replacement RH Timing Chain Guides

41. Install the RH primary timing chain guide and the 2 bolts. Tighten the bolts to 89 inch lbs. (10 Nm).

All Vehicles

42. Install the RH cylinder block drain plug or, if equipped, the block heater. Tighten the drain plug to 30 ft. lbs. (40 Nm).

43. If equipped, install the block heater wiring harness onto the engine.

a. Connect the block heater electrical connector and install the heat shield.

44. Install the LH cylinder block drain plug. Tighten the drain plug to 15 ft. lbs. (20 Nm), plus an additional 180 degrees.

45. Install 8 new RH exhaust manifold studs. Tighten the studs to 106 inch lbs. (12 Nm).

**** WARNING**

Failure to tighten the exhaust manifold nuts to specification a second time will cause the exhaust manifold to develop an exhaust leak.

46. Install a new gasket, RH exhaust manifold and 8 new nuts. Tighten in 2 stages in the proper sequence:

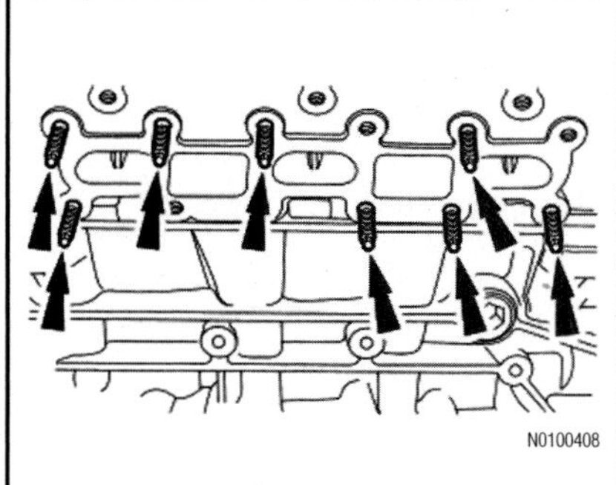

Fig. 132 RH exhaust manifold studs location

a. Stage 1: Tighten to 133 inch lbs. (15 Nm).

b. Stage 2: Tighten to 15 ft. lbs. (20 Nm).

47. Install the oil supply tube filter, washer and bolt.

a. Install a new oil supply tube filter in the oil supply tube block.

b. Slide the new washer onto the oil supply tube block.

c. Install the banjo bolt into the oil supply tube block.

48. Install the RH turbocharger oil supply tube. Tighten the bolt to 26 ft. lbs. (35 Nm).

49. Install a new gasket, the turbocharger and the 3 new exhaust manifold-to-turbocharger bolts. Tighten the bolts to 33 ft. lbs. (45 Nm).

50. Install the upper turbocharger-to-cylinder block bracket and the 3 bolts and position the bracket as far clockwise as possible and tighten the bolts in the following sequence:

a. Tighten the lower bolt to 19 ft. lbs. (26 Nm).

b. Tighten the upper bolt to 19 ft. lbs. (26 Nm).

c. Tighten the turbocharger bolt to 168 inch lbs. (19 Nm).

51. Using 2 new sealing washers, install the 2 RH turbocharger coolant tubes and banjo bolts. Tighten the bolts to 27 ft. lbs. (37 Nm).

52. Install the coolant tube bracket-to-cylinder head bolt. Tighten the bolt to 89 inch lbs. (10 Nm).

53. If necessary, install the RH cylinder head turbocharger oil supply quick connect fitting. Tighten the quick connect fitting to 142 inch lbs. (16 Nm).

➡Listen for audible click when installing the oil supply tube into the quick connect fitting.

54. Install the RH oil supply tube into the quick connect fitting.

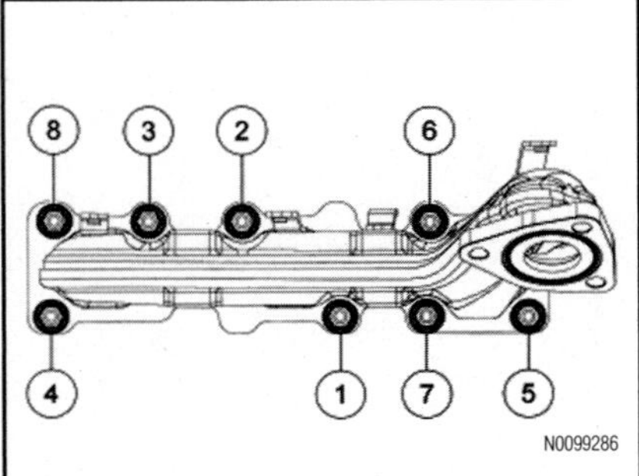

Fig. 133 RH exhaust manifold nuts location and tightening sequence

55. Install the oil supply tube secondary latch.

56. Install a new gasket and the RH turbocharger oil return tube and the 2 bolts. Tighten the bolts to 89 inch lbs. (10 Nm).

➡Make sure the turbocharger wastegate regulating valve hose does not contact the exhaust manifold heat shield.

57. Connect the turbocharger wastegate regulating valve hose to the RH turbocharger assembly.

➡Make sure the heat shield does not contact the wastegate arm.

58. Install the 2 upper RH exhaust manifold heat shield and the 5 bolts. Tighten the bolts to 124 inch lbs. (14 Nm).

59. Connect the Cylinder Head Temperature (CHT) sensor electrical connector to the rear of the RH cylinder head.

60. Install the radio capacitor and bolt to the RH cylinder head. Tighten the bolt to 89 inch lbs. (10 Nm).

61. Install the ground wire and the bolt. Tighten the bolt to 89 inch lbs. (10 Nm).

62. Install the RH Camshaft Position (CMP) sensor and the bolt. Tighten the bolt to 89 inch lbs. (10 Nm).

63. Connect the RH CMP sensor electrical connector.

64. Install the RH camshafts as outlined in this section.

65. Install the fuel rails.

ENGINE OIL & FILTER

REPLACEMENT

3.5L Engine, Except Turbo

1. With the vehicle in NEUTRAL, position it on a hoist.

➡Lubricate the engine oil filter gasket with clean engine oil prior to installing the oil filter.

2. Remove and discard the engine oil filter.

To install, tighten to 44 inch lbs. (5 Nm)and then rotate an additional 180 degrees.

3. Remove the 3 bolts and the oil filter adapter.

a. Discard the gasket.

4. Clean and inspect all sealing surfaces.

To install, tighten to 89 inch lbs. (10 Nm).

To install:

5. Clean and inspect all sealing surfaces. Tighten to 89 inch lbs. (10 Nm).

6. Install the 3 bolts and the oil filter adapter.

a. Discard the gasket.

➡Lubricate the engine oil filter gasket with clean engine oil prior to installing the oil filter.

7. Install and discard the engine oil filter. Tighten the filter to 44 inch lbs. (5 Nm) and then rotate an additional 180 degrees.

8. With the vehicle in NEUTRAL, lower it from the hoist.

3.5L Turbo Engine

1. With the vehicle in NEUTRAL, position it on a hoist.

2. Remove and discard the engine oil filter.

3. Remove the 3 bolts and the oil filter adapter.

a. Discard the gasket.

b. Clean and inspect all sealing surfaces.

To install:

4. Using a new gasket, install the oil filter adapter and the 3 bolts. Tighten bolts 89 inch lbs. (10 Nm).

➡Lubricate the engine oil filter gasket with clean engine oil prior to installing the oil filter.

5. Install a new engine oil filter. Tighten the filter to 44 inch lbs. (5 Nm) and then rotate an additional 180 degrees.

EXHAUST MANIFOLD

REMOVAL & INSTALLATION

3.5L Engine, Except Turbo

Left-Hand

See Figure 134.

1. Remove the LH catalytic converter as outlined in this section.

2. Remove the LH Heated Oxygen Sensor (HO2S) as outlined in the Engine Performance & Emission Controls Section.

3. Remove the 3 bolts and the LH exhaust manifold heat shield.

4. Remove the 6 nuts and the LH exhaust manifold.

a. Discard the nuts and gasket.

5. Clean and inspect the LH exhaust manifold as outlined in this section.

6. Remove and discard the 6 LH exhaust manifold studs.

⁂ WARNING

Do not use metal scrapers, wire brushes, power abrasive discs or

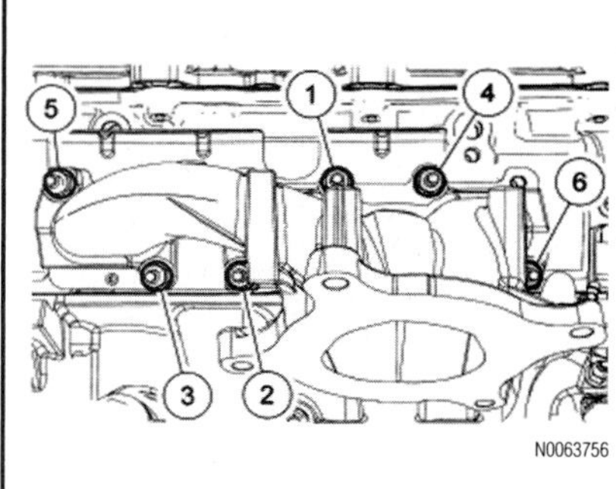

Fig. 134 LH exhaust manifold—3.5L engine, except turbo

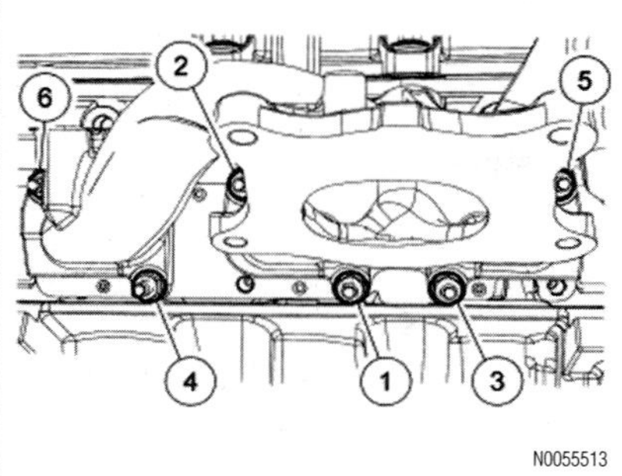

Fig. 135 RH exhaust manifold—3.5L engine, except turbo

other abrasive means to clean the sealing surfaces. These may cause scratches and gouges resulting in leak paths. Use a plastic scraper to clean the sealing surfaces.

7. Clean the exhaust manifold mating surface of the cylinder head with metal surface prep. Follow the directions on the packaging.

To install:

8. Install 6 new LH exhaust manifold studs. Tighten the studs to 106 inch lbs. (12 Nm).

⁂ WARNING

Failure to tighten the exhaust manifold nuts to specification a second time will cause the exhaust manifold to develop an exhaust leak.

9. Using a new gasket, install the LH exhaust manifold and 6 new nuts. Tighten the nuts in 2 stages in the proper sequence.
   a. Stage 1: Tighten to 15 ft. lbs. (20 Nm).
   b. Stage 2: Tighten to 18 ft. lbs. (25 Nm).
10. Install the LH exhaust manifold heat shield and the 3 bolts. Tighten the bolts to 89 inch lbs. (10 Nm).
11. Install the LH HO2S as outlined in the Engine Performance & Emission Controls Section.
12. Install the LH catalytic converter as outlined in this section.

Right-Hand

See Figure 135.

1. Remove the RH catalytic converter as outlined in this section.
2. Disconnect the RH Heated Oxygen Sensor (HO2S) electrical connector.
3. Remove the 6 nuts and the RH exhaust manifold.
   a. Discard the nuts and gasket.
4. Clean and inspect the RH exhaust manifold as outlined in this section.
5. Remove and discard the 6 RH exhaust manifold studs.

⁂ WARNING

Do not use metal scrapers, wire brushes, power abrasive discs or other abrasive means to clean the sealing surfaces. These may cause scratches and gouges resulting in leak paths. Use a plastic scraper to clean the sealing surfaces.

6. Clean the exhaust manifold mating surface of the cylinder head with metal surface prep. Follow the directions on the packaging.

To install:

7. Install 6 new RH exhaust manifold studs. Tighten to 106 inch lbs. (12 Nm).

⁂ WARNING

Failure to tighten the exhaust manifold nuts to specification a second time will cause the exhaust manifold to develop an exhaust leak.

8. Using a new gasket, install the RH exhaust manifold and 6 new nuts. Tighten in 2 stages in the proper sequence.
   a. Stage 1: Tighten to 15 ft. lbs. (20 Nm).
   b. Stage 2: Tighten to 18 ft. lbs. (25 Nm).
9. Connect the RH HO2S electrical connector.
10. Install the RH catalytic converter as outlined in this section.

3.5L Turbo Engine

Left-Hand

See Figures 136 through 138.

⁂ WARNING

Whenever turbocharger air intake system components are removed, always cover open ports to protect from debris. It is important that no foreign material enter the system. The turbocharger compressor vanes are susceptible to damage from even small particles. All components should be inspected and cleaned, if necessary, prior to installation or reassembly.

1. Remove the 2 top LH exhaust manifold heat shield bolts.
2. Remove the LH catalytic converter as outlined in this section.
3. Remove the bottom bolt and the LH exhaust manifold heat shield.
4. Remove the 2 bolts and the LH upper turbocharger bracket.
5. Loosen the 2 bolts for the LH lower turbocharger bracket.
6. Remove the 3 LH turbocharger-to-exhaust manifold bolts.
   a. Discard the gasket.
7. Remove the 5 top LH exhaust manifold nuts.
   a. Discard the nuts.
8. Remove the 3 bottom nuts and the LH exhaust manifold.
   a. Discard the nuts and gasket.
9. Clean and inspect the LH exhaust manifold as outlined in this section.
10. Remove and discard the 8 LH exhaust manifold studs.

⁂ WARNING

Do not use metal scrapers, wire brushes, power abrasive discs or other abrasive means to clean the sealing surfaces. These may cause scratches and gouges resulting in leak paths. Use a plastic scraper to clean the sealing surfaces.

11. Clean the exhaust manifold mating surface of the cylinder head with metal surface prep. Follow the directions on the packaging.

To install:

12. Install 8 new LH exhaust manifold studs. Tighten the studs to 106 inch lbs. (12 Nm).

⁂ WARNING

Failure to tighten the exhaust manifold nuts to specification a second time will cause the exhaust manifold to develop an exhaust leak.

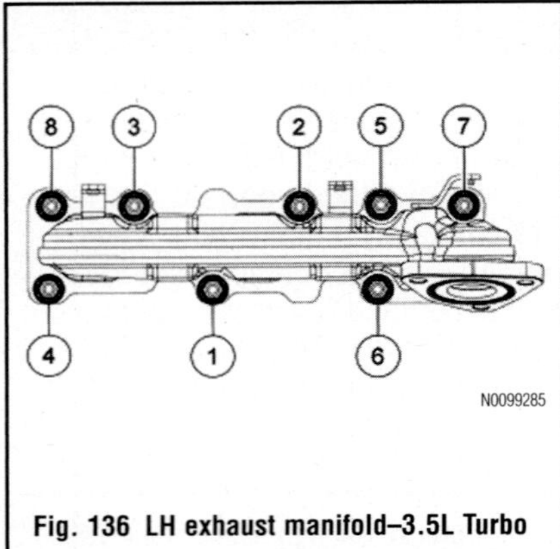

Fig. 136 LH exhaust manifold–3.5L Turbo

13. Install a new gasket, LH exhaust manifold and 8 new nuts. Tighten in 2 stages in the proper sequence.
a. Stage 1: Tighten to 133 inch lbs. (15 Nm).
b. Stage 2: Tighten to 15 ft. lbs. (20 Nm).
14. Install a new gasket and the 3 turbocharger-to-exhaust manifold bolts. Tighten the bolts to 33 ft. lbs. (45 Nm).
15. Install the upper turbocharger bracket and the 2 bolts.
a. Do not tighten the bolts at this time.

WARNING

The next 4 steps must be performed in order or damage to the turbocharger may occur.

16. Tighten the upper turbocharger bracket-to-turbocharger bolt. Tighten the bolt to 168 inch lbs. (19 Nm).
17. Tighten the upper turbocharger bracket-to-cylinder block bolt. Tighten the bolt to 18 ft. lbs. (25 Nm).
18. Tighten the lower turbocharger bracket-to-turbocharger bolt. Tighten the bolt to 168 inch lbs. (19 Nm).
19. Tighten the lower turbocharger

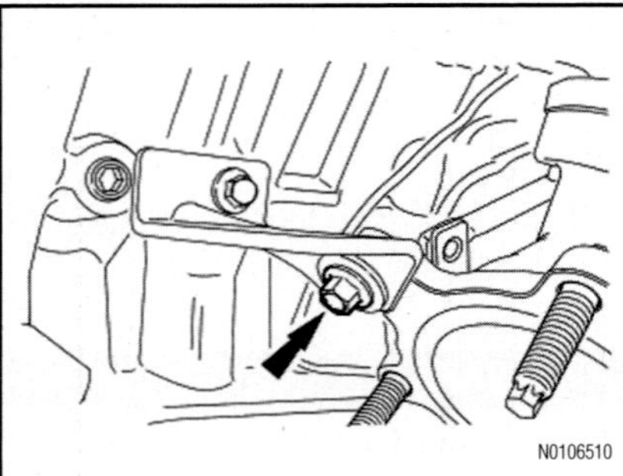

Fig. 137 Upper turbocharger bracket-to-turbocharger

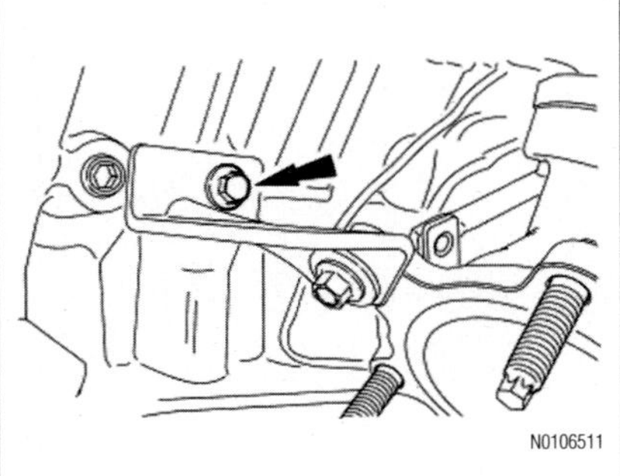

Fig. 138 Upper turbocharger bracket-to-cylinder block bolt

bracket-to-cylinder block bolt. Tighten the bolt to 97 inch lbs. (11 Nm).
20. Install the LH exhaust manifold heat shield and the bottom bolt.
a. Do not tighten the bolt at this time.
21. Install the LH catalytic converter as outlined in this section.
22. Install the 2 top LH exhaust manifold heat shield bolts. Tighten the bolts to 124 inch lbs. (14 Nm).
23. Tighten the LH exhaust manifold heat shield bottom bolt. Tighten the bolt to 124 inch lbs. (14 Nm).

Right-Hand

See Figure 139.

WARNING

Whenever turbocharger air intake system components are removed, always cover open ports to protect from debris. It is important that no foreign material enter the system. The turbocharger compressor vanes are susceptible to damage from even small particles. All components should be inspected and cleaned, if necessary, prior to installation or reassembly.

1. Remove the RH turbocharger.
2. Remove the 8 nuts and the RH exhaust manifold.
a. Discard the nuts and exhaust manifold gasket.
3. Clean and inspect the RH exhaust manifold as outlined in this section.
4. Remove and discard the 8 RH exhaust manifold studs.

WARNING

Do not use metal scrapers, wire brushes, power abrasive discs or other abrasive means to clean the sealing surfaces. These may cause scratches and gouges resulting in leak paths. Use a plastic scraper to clean the sealing surfaces.

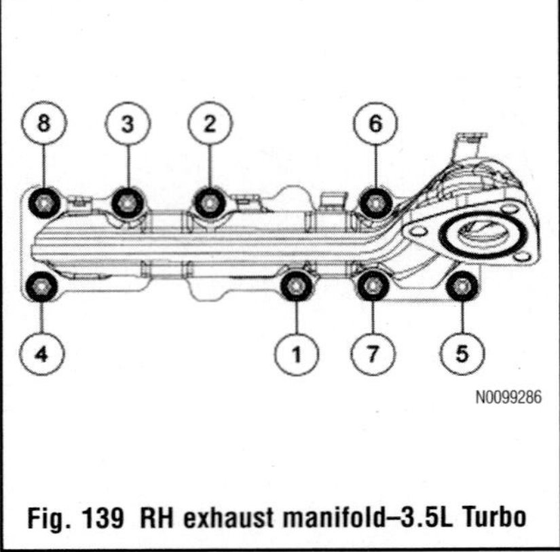

Fig. 139 RH exhaust manifold–3.5L Turbo

5. Clean the exhaust manifold mating surface of the cylinder head with metal surface prep. Follow the directions on the packaging.

To install:

6. Install 8 new RH exhaust manifold studs. Tighten the studs to 106 inch lbs. (12 Nm).

WARNING

Failure to tighten the exhaust manifold nuts to specification a second time will cause the exhaust manifold to develop an exhaust leak.

7. Install a new gasket, RH exhaust manifold and 8 new nuts. Tighten in 2 stages in the proper sequence.
a. Stage 1: Tighten to 133 inch lbs. (15 Nm).
b. Stage 2: Tighten to 15 ft. lbs. (20 Nm).
8. Install the RH turbocharger.

INTAKE MANIFOLD

REMOVAL & INSTALLATION

3.5L Engine, Except Turbo

Lower

See Figure 140.

WARNING

During engine repair procedures, cleanliness is extremely important. Any foreign material, including any material created while cleaning gasket surfaces that enters the oil passages, coolant passages or the oil pan, may cause engine failure.

1. Remove the fuel rail.
2. Drain the cooling system as outlined in the Engine Cooling Section.

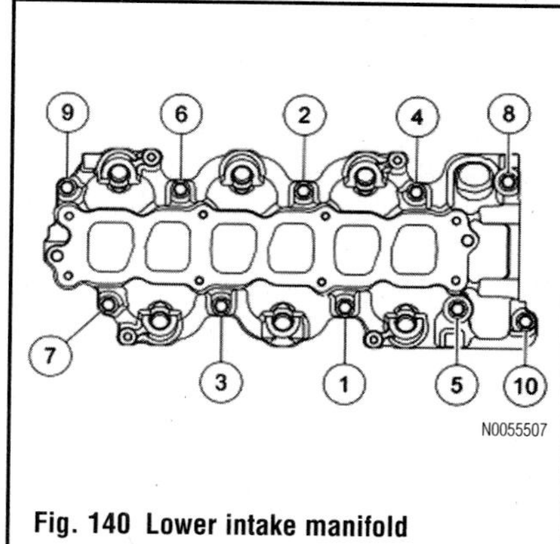

Fig. 140 Lower intake manifold

3. Remove the 3 thermostat housing-to-lower intake manifold bolts.
4. Remove the 10 bolts and the lower intake manifold.
   a. Remove and discard the intake manifold and thermostat housing gaskets.
   b. Clean and inspect all sealing surfaces.

To install:

⁂ WARNING

If the engine is repaired or replaced because of upper engine failure, typically including valve or piston damage, check the intake manifold for metal debris. If metal debris is found, install a new intake manifold. Failure to follow these instructions can result in engine damage.

5. Using new intake manifold and thermostat housing gaskets, install the lower intake manifold and the 10 bolts. Tighten the bolts in the proper sequence to 89 inch lbs. (10 Nm).
6. Install the 3 thermostat housing-to-lower intake manifold bolts. Tighten to 89 inch lbs. (10 Nm).
7. Install the fuel rail.
8. Fill and bleed the cooling system as outlined in the Engine Cooling Section.

Upper

See Figure 141.

1. Remove the Air Cleaner (ACL) outlet pipe as outlined in this section.
2. Disconnect the Throttle Body (TB) electrical connector.
3. Disconnect the Evaporative Emission (EVAP) tube from the intake manifold.
4. Detach the EVAP tube pin-type retainer from the upper intake manifold.
5. Disconnect the brake booster vacuum hose from the intake manifold.

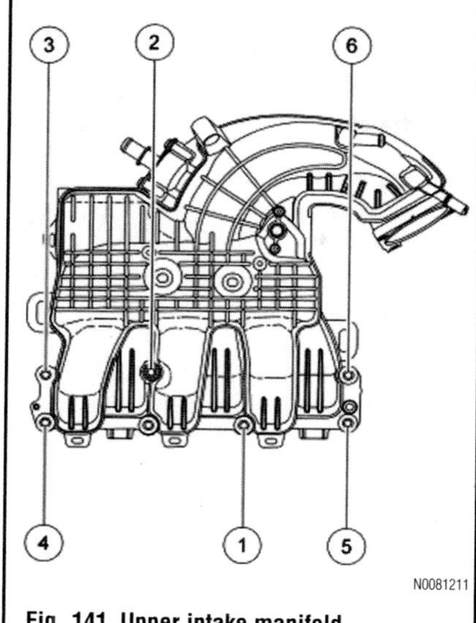

Fig. 141 Upper intake manifold

6. Disconnect the PCV tube from the PCV valve.
7. Detach the wiring harness retainers from the upper intake manifold.
8. Remove the upper intake manifold support bracket bolt.
9. Remove the fuel tube bracket bolt.
10. Remove the 6 bolts and the upper intake manifold.
    a. Remove and discard the gaskets.
    b. Clean and inspect all of the sealing surfaces of the upper and lower intake manifold.

To install:

⁂ WARNING

If the engine is repaired or replaced because of upper engine failure, typically including valve or piston damage, check the intake manifold for metal debris. If metal debris is found, install a new intake manifold. Failure to follow these instructions can result in engine damage.

11. Using new gaskets, install the upper intake manifold and the 6 bolts. Tighten the bolts in the proper sequence to 89 inch lbs. (10 Nm).
12. Install the fuel tube bracket bolt. Tighten the bolt to 53 inch lbs. (6 Nm).
13. Install the upper intake manifold support bracket bolt. Tighten the bolt to 89 inch lbs. (10 Nm).
14. Attach the wiring harness retainers to the upper intake manifold.
15. Connect the PCV tube to the PCV valve.
16. Connect the brake booster vacuum hose to the intake manifold.
17. Connect the EVAP tube to the intake manifold.
18. Attach the EVAP tube pin-type retainer to the upper intake manifold.
19. Connect the TB electrical connector.
20. Install the ACL outlet pipe as outlined in this section.

3.5L Turbo Engine

See Figure 142.

⁂ WARNING

During engine repair procedures, cleanliness is extremely important. Any foreign material, including any material created while cleaning gasket surfaces that enters the oil passages, coolant passages or the oil pan, may cause engine failure.

⁂ WARNING

Whenever turbocharger air intake system components are removed, always cover open ports to protect from debris. It is important that no foreign material enter the system. The turbocharger compressor vanes are susceptible to damage from even small particles. All components should be inspected and cleaned, if necessary, prior to installation or reassembly.

1. Drain the cooling system as outlined in the Engine Cooling Section.
2. Remove the Air Cleaner (ACL) outlet pipe as outlined in this section.
3. Disconnect the LH turbocharger bypass valve electrical connector.
4. Disconnect the LH turbocharger bypass valve hose from the RH Charge Air Cooler (CAC) tube.
5. Disconnect the turbocharger wastegate regulating valve hose from the RH CAC tube.
6. Disconnect the RH turbocharger bypass valve electrical connector.
7. Disconnect the RH turbocharger bypass valve hose from the RH turbocharger intake tube.

⁂ WARNING

The compression limiter bushing may fall out of the mounting bracket grommet on the Charge Air Cooler (CAC) tube during service. Make sure the bushing is in place when reinstalling the tube or damage to the tube may occur.

8. Remove the RH CAC tube nut from the intake manifold.
9. Loosen the clamp and remove the RH CAC tube.
10. Loosen the clamp and remove the RH CAC tube from the RH turbocharger.
11. Remove the noise generator.
12. Loosen the clamp and position CAC outlet pipe-to-Throttle Body (TB) aside.
13. Disconnect the Throttle Position (TP) sensor and electronic TB electrical connectors.
14. Disconnect the quick connect coupling Evaporative Emission (EVAP) tube from the intake manifold.
15. Detach the EVAP purge valve from the intake manifold.
16. Disconnect the brake booster vacuum hose from the intake manifold.
17. Remove the fuel tube-to-engine front cover bracket bolt and position the fuel tube aside.
18. Disconnect the PCV tube quick connect coupling from the intake manifold.
19. If equipped, disconnect the heated PCV valve electrical connector from the intake manifold.
20. Detach and disconnect the 2 fuel injector wiring harness electrical connectors.
21. Disconnect the Manifold Absolute Pressure (MAP)/Intake Air Temperature 2 (IAT2) sensor electrical connector.

➡Mark the location of each hose for installation.

22. Disconnect the 2 hoses from the turbocharger wastegate regulating valve.
23. Disconnect the turbocharger wastegate regulating valve electrical connector.
24. Detach the 2 wire harness-to-intake manifold retainers.
25. Detach the 2 wire harness retainer from the LH valve cover stud bolt.
26. Detach the 2 wire harness retainer from the LH valve cover.
27. Disconnect the 2 coolant heater hoses from the intake manifold.
28. Disconnect the 2 turbocharger coolant hoses from the intake manifold.
29. Disconnect the lower radiator hose from the thermostat housing.
30. Remove the bolt and ground wire from the engine front cover.
31. Disconnect the upper radiator hose at the intake manifold and position the hose aside.

➡Note the routing of the 2 fuel rail wiring harnesses for installation.

32. Remove the 12 bolts and the intake manifold.

a. Remove and discard the intake manifold, coolant crossover and thermostat housing gaskets.
b. Clean and inspect all sealing surfaces.

To install:

WARNING

If the engine is repaired or replaced because of upper engine failure, typically including valve or piston damage, check the intake manifold for metal debris. If metal debris is found, install a new intake manifold. Failure to follow these instructions can result in engine damage.

➡Make sure the fuel rail wiring harnesses are routed correctly.

➡Installing the 2 long bolts first will aid in installing the intake manifold.

33. Using new intake manifold, coolant crossover and thermostat housing gaskets, install the intake manifold and the 12 bolts. Tighten the bolts in the proper sequence to 89 inch lbs. (10 Nm).
34. Connect the upper radiator hose to the intake manifold.
35. Install the ground wire and bolt to the engine front cover. Tighten the bolt to 89 inch lbs. (10 Nm).
36. Connect the lower radiator hose to the thermostat housing.

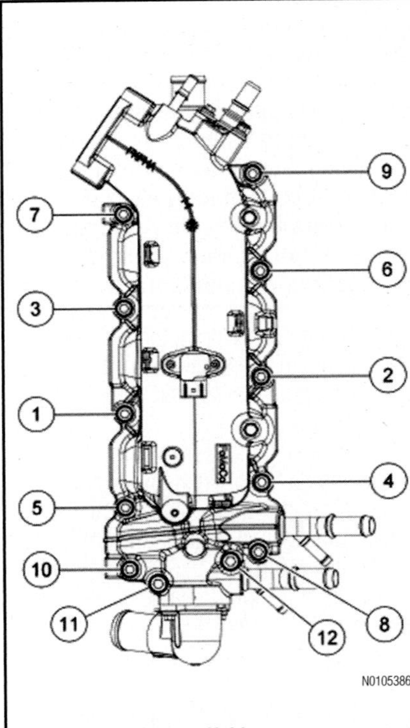

Fig. 142 Intake manifold

37. Connect the 2 turbocharger coolant hoses from the intake manifold.
38. Connect the 2 coolant heater hoses from the intake manifold.
39. Attach the 2 wire harness retainers to the LH valve cover.
40. Attach the 2 wire harness retainers to the LH valve cover stud bolt.
41. Attach the 2 wire harness-to-intake manifold retainers.
42. Connect the turbocharger wastegate regulating valve electrical connector.
43. Connect the 2 hoses to the wastegate control valve.
44. Connect the MAP/IAT2 sensor electrical connector.
45. Connect and attach the 2 fuel injector wiring harness electrical connectors.
46. If equipped, connect the heated PCV valve electrical connector.
47. Connect the PCV tube quick connect coupling to the intake manifold.
48. Position the fuel tube and install the fuel tube-to-engine front cover bracket bolt. Tighten the bolt to 89 inch lbs. (10 Nm).
49. Connect the brake vacuum tube to the intake manifold.
50. Attach the EVAP purge valve to the intake manifold.
51. Connect the quick connect coupling EVAP tube to the intake manifold.

➡Align the index marks for the outlet pipe.

52. Connect the TP sensor and electronic TB electrical connectors.

➡Align the index marks for the CAC outlet pipe.

53. Position CAC outlet pipe on the TB and tighten the clamp. Tighten the clamp to 44 inch lbs. (5 Nm).
54. Install the noise generator as outlined in this section.

➡Align the index marks for the RH CAC tube.

55. Install the RH CAC tube to the RH turbocharger and tighten the clamp. Tighten the clamp to 44 inch lbs. (5 Nm).

➡Align the index marks for the RH CAC tube.

56. Install the RH CAC tube and tighten the clamp. Tighten the clamp to 44 inch lbs. (5 Nm).

WARNING

The compression limiter bushing may fall out of the mounting bracket grommet on the Charge Air Cooler (CAC) tube during service. Make sure

the bushing is in place when reinstalling the tube or damage to the tube may occur.

57. Install the RH CAC tube and the RH CAC tube nut to the intake manifold. Tighten the nut to 53 inch lbs. (6 Nm).
58. Connect the RH turbocharger bypass valve hose to the RH turbocharger intake tube.
59. Connect the RH turbocharger bypass valve electrical connector.
60. Connect the turbocharger wastegate regulating valve hose to the RH CAC tube.
61. Connect the LH turbocharger bypass valve electrical connector and the turbocharger bypass valve hose.
62. Install the ACL outlet pipe as outlined in this section.
63. Fill and bleed the cooling system as outlined in the Engine Cooling Section.

OIL PUMP

REMOVAL & INSTALLATION

See Figures 143 through 149.

✲✲ WARNING

During engine repair procedures, cleanliness is extremely important. Any foreign material, including any material created while cleaning gasket surfaces, which enters the oil passages, coolant passages or the oil pan may cause engine failure.

➡On early build engines, the timing chain rides on the inner side of the RH timing chain guide. Late build engines are equipped with a different design RH timing chain guide that requires the timing chain to ride on the outer side of the RH timing chain guide. For service, all replacement RH timing chain guides will be the late build design.

All Vehicles

1. Remove the engine front cover as outlined in this section.

Engines Equipped With Early Build RH Timing Chain Guides

2. Rotate the crankshaft clockwise and align the timing marks on the Variable Camshaft Timing (VCT) assemblies.

Engines Equipped With Late Build/Replacement RH Timing Chain Guides

3. Rotate the crankshaft clockwise and align the timing marks on the VCT assemblies.

Fig. 143 Early Build RH Timing Chain Guides

All Vehicles

➡The Camshaft Holding Tool will hold the camshafts in the Top Dead Center (TDC) position.

4. Install the Camshaft Holding Tool onto the flats of the LH camshafts.

➡The Camshaft Holding Tool will hold the camshafts in the TDC position.

5. Install the Camshaft Holding Tool onto the flats of the RH camshafts.
6. Remove the 3 bolts and the RH VCT housing.
7. Remove the 3 bolts and the LH VCT housing.
8. Remove the 2 bolts and the primary timing chain tensioner.
9. Remove the primary timing chain tensioner arm.
10. Remove the 2 bolts and the lower LH primary timing chain guide.
11. Remove the primary timing chain.
12. Remove the crankshaft timing chain sprocket.
13. Remove the 2 bolts and the oil pump screen and pickup tube.
    a. Discard the O-ring seal.
14. Remove the 3 bolts and the oil pump.

To install:

15. Install the oil pump and the 3 bolts. Tighten the bolts to 89 inch lbs. (10 Nm).
16. Using a new O-ring seal, install the oil pump screen and pickup tube and the 2 bolts. Tighten the bolts to 89 inch lbs. (10 Nm).
17. Install the crankshaft timing chain sprocket.
18. Install the primary timing chain with the colored links aligned with the timing marks on the VCT assemblies and the crankshaft sprocket.

Fig. 144 Late Build/Replacement RH Timing Chain Guides

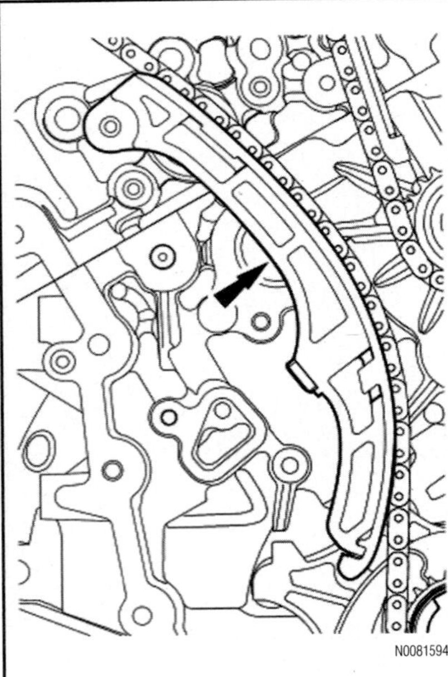
Fig. 145 Primary timing chain tensioner arm

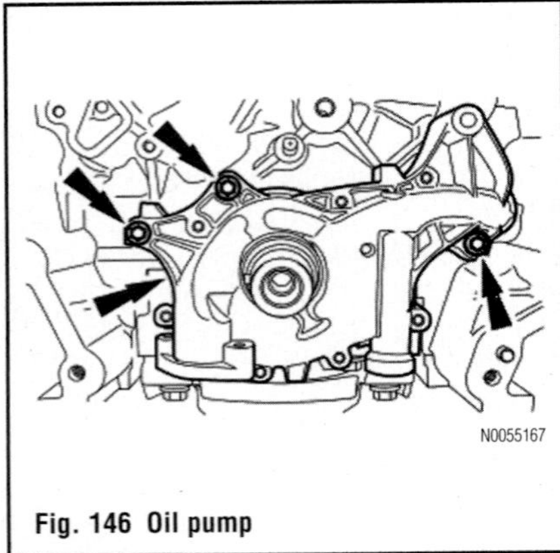
Fig. 146 Oil pump

Fig. 147 Install the primary timing chain with the colored links aligned with the timing marks on the VCT assemblies and the crankshaft sprocket

19. Install the LH primary timing chain guide and the 2 bolts. Tighten the bolts to 89 inch lbs. (10 Nm).

20. Install the primary timing chain tensioner arm.

21. Reset the primary timing chain tensioner.

a. Rotate the lever counterclockwise.

b. Using a soft-jawed vise, compress the plunger.

c. Align the hole in the lever with the hole in the tensioner housing.

d. Install a suitable lockpin.

➡It may be necessary to rotate the crankshaft slightly to remove slack from the timing chain and install the tensioner.

22. Install the primary tensioner and the 2 bolts. Tighten the bolts to 89 inch lbs. (10 Nm).

a. Remove the lockpin.

23. As a post-check, verify correct alignment of all timing marks.

24. Inspect the VCT housing seals for damage and replace as necessary.

⁂ WARNING

Make sure the dowels on the Variable Camshaft Timing (VCT) housing are fully engaged in the cylinder head prior to tightening the bolts. Failure to follow this process will result in severe engine damage.

25. Install the LH VCT housing and the 3 bolts. Tighten the bolts to 89 inch lbs. (10 Nm) in the proper sequence.

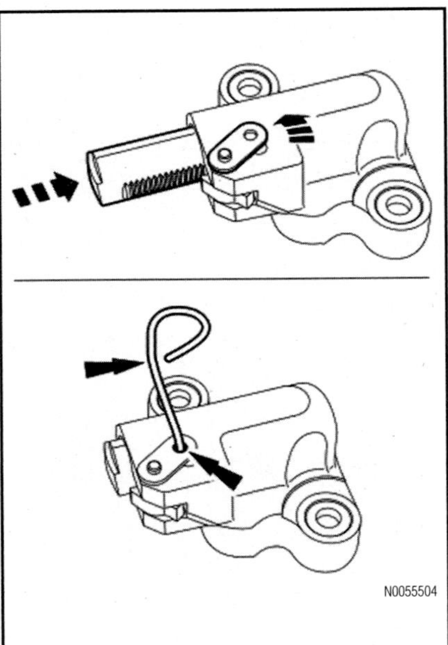
Fig. 148 Reset the primary timing chain tensioner

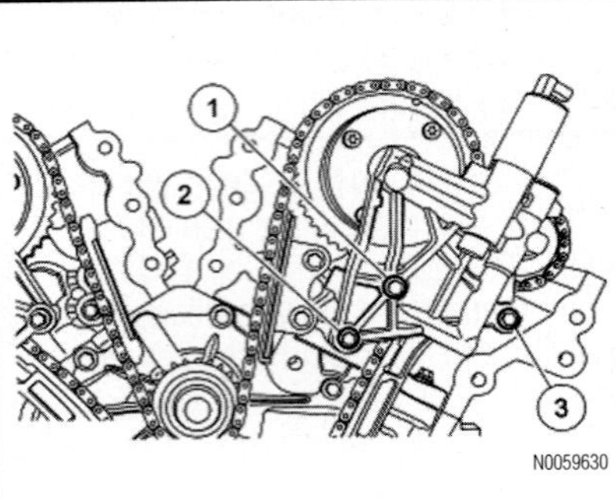

Fig. 149 Install the LH VCT housing and the 3 bolts

⁂ WARNING

Make sure the dowels on the Variable Camshaft Timing (VCT) housing are fully engaged in the cylinder head prior to tightening the bolts. Failure to follow this process will result in severe engine damage.

26. Install the RH VCT housing and the 3 bolts. Tighten the bolts to 89 inch lbs. (10 Nm) in the proper sequence.

27. Install the engine front cover as outlined in this section.

REAR MAIN SEAL

REMOVAL & INSTALLATION

3.5L Engine, Except Turbo

See Figure 150.

1. With the vehicle in NEUTRAL, position it on a hoist.

2. Remove the flexplate.

3. Remove the crankshaft sensor ring.

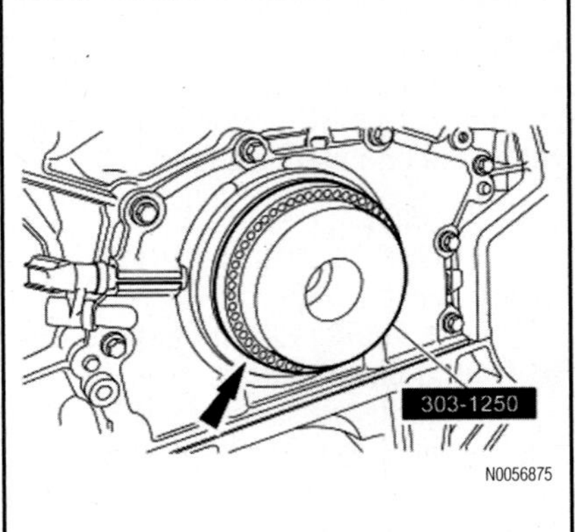

Fig. 150 Position the Rear Main Seal Installer onto the end of the crankshaft and slide a new crankshaft rear seal onto the tool

4. Using the Crankshaft Rear Oil Seal Remover and Slide Hammer, remove and discard the crankshaft rear seal.
5. Clean all sealing surfaces with metal surface prep.

To install:

➡Lubricate the seal lips and bore with clean engine oil prior to installation.

6. Position the Rear Main Seal Installer onto the end of the crankshaft and slide a new crankshaft rear seal onto the tool.
7. Using the Rear Main Seal Installer and Handle, install the new crankshaft rear seal.
8. Install the crankshaft sensor ring.
9. Install the flexplate.

3.5L Turbo Engine

See Figure 151.

1. Remove the flexplate.
2. Remove the crankshaft sensor ring.
3. Using the Crankshaft Rear Oil Seal Remover and Slide Hammer, remove and discard the crankshaft rear seal.
4. Clean all sealing surfaces with metal surface prep

To install:

➡Lubricate the seal lips and bore with clean engine oil prior to installation.

5. Using the Rear Main Seal Installer and Handle, install the new crankshaft rear seal.
6. Install the crankshaft sensor ring.
7. Install the flexplate.
8. Using the scan tool, perform the Misfire Monitor Neutral Profile Correction procedure, following the on-screen instructions.

TURBOCHARGER

REMOVAL & INSTALLATION

Left-Hand

See Figures 152 through 154.

⁂ WARNING

Whenever turbocharger air intake system components are removed, always cover open ports to protect from debris. It is important that no foreign material enter the system. The turbocharger compressor vanes are susceptible to damage from even small particles. All components should be inspected and cleaned, if necessary, prior to installation or reassembly.

1. With the vehicle in NEUTRAL, position it on a hoist.
2. Remove the Air Cleaner (ACL) assembly.
3. Disconnect the wastegate control valve hose from the LH turbocharger assembly.
4. Remove the 2 bolts from the top of the LH exhaust manifold heat shield.
5. Loosen the clamp and remove the LH turbocharger intake tube from the turbocharger.
6. Remove the LH turbocharger oil supply tube bolt and sealing washer.
   a. Discard the sealing washer and oil supply tube filter.
7. Drain the cooling system as outlined in the Engine Cooling Section.
8. Remove the LH catalytic converter as outlined in this section.
9. Remove the bottom bolt and the LH exhaust manifold heat shield.
10. Remove the 2 LH oil return tube-to-turbocharger bolts.
   a. Remove and discard the gasket.
11. Remove the LH turbocharger oil return tube from the oil pan.
   a. Discard the 2 O-ring seals.
12. Remove the 2 coolant tube banjo bolts and the LH turbocharger coolant tubes.
   a. Discard the sealing washers.
13. Loosen the clamp and remove the LH CAC tube from the LH turbocharger.
14. Remove the 3 exhaust manifold-to-LH turbocharger bolts.
   a. Discard the gasket and bolts.
15. Remove the 2 bolts and the lower LH turbocharger-to-cylinder block bracket.
16. Remove the upper LH turbocharger bracket-to-turbocharger bolt and the turbocharger assembly.

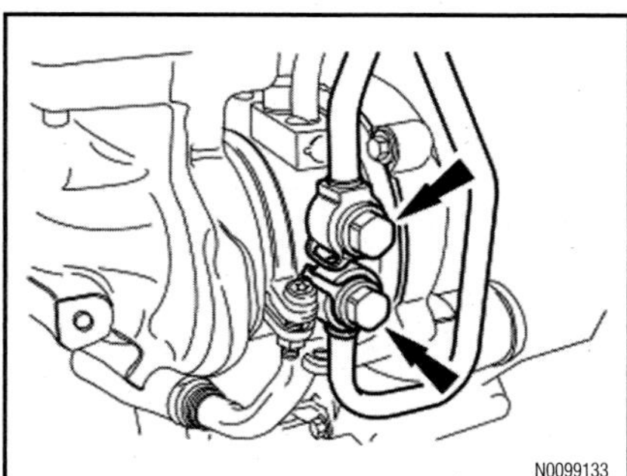

Fig. 152 Remove the 2 coolant tube banjo bolts and the LH turbocharger coolant tubes

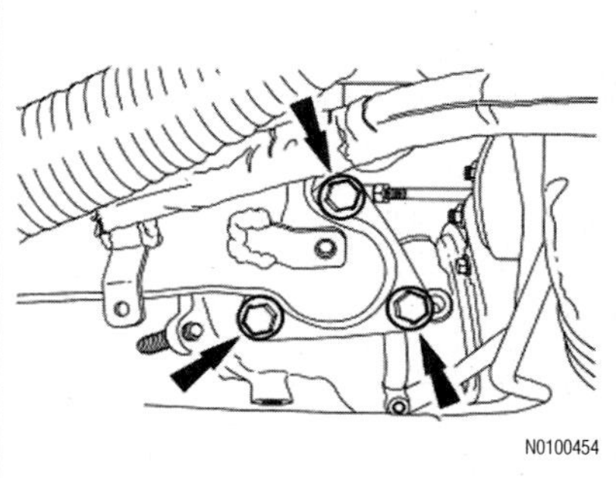

Fig. 153 Remove the 3 exhaust manifold-to-LH turbocharger bolts

To install:

⁂ WARNING

The upper LH turbocharger bracket bolt must be loosened in order to perform the tightening sequence or damage to the turbocharger may occur.

17. Loosen the upper LH turbocharger bracket bolt.
18. Install a new LH exhaust manifold-to-turbocharger gasket.
19. Install the turbocharger assembly and install upper LH turbocharger bracket-to-turbocharger bolt.
   a. Do not tighten the bolts at this time.
20. Install the lower LH turbocharger-to-cylinder block bracket and the 2 bolts.
   a. Do not tighten the bolts at this time.
21. Install the 3 new LH exhaust manifold-to-turbocharger bolts. Tighten the bolts to 33 ft. lbs. (45 Nm).

⁂ CAUTION

The next 4 steps must be performed in the order written or damage to the turbocharger may occur.

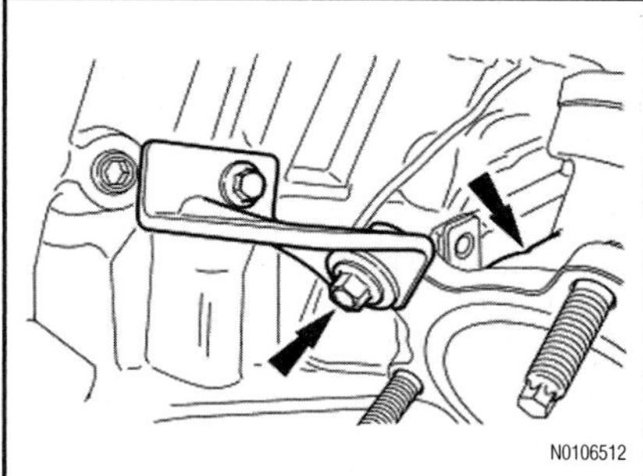

Fig. 154 Install the turbocharger assembly and install upper LH turbocharger bracket-to-turbocharger bolt

22. Tighten the upper LH turbocharger bracket-to-turbocharger bolt. Tighten the bolt to 168 inch lbs. (19 Nm).

23. Tighten the upper LH turbocharger bracket-to-cylinder block bolt. Tighten the bolts to 18 ft. lbs. (25 Nm).

24. Tighten the lower LH turbocharger bracket-to-turbocharger bolt. Tighten the bolt to 168 inch lbs. (19 Nm).

25. Tighten the lower LH turbocharger bracket-to-cylinder block bolt. Tighten the bolt to 97 inch lbs. (11 Nm).

➡Align the index marks for the LH CAC tube.

26. Install the LH CAC tube on the LH turbocharger and tighten the clamp. Tighten the clamp to 44 inch lbs. (5 Nm).

27. Using 2 new sealing washers, install the 2 coolant tube banjo bolts. Tighten the bolts to 27 ft. lbs. (37 Nm).

➡Lubricate the oil pan bore with clean engine oil.

28. Using 2 new O-ring seals, install the LH turbocharger oil return tube to the oil pan.

29. Using a new gasket, install the LH turbocharger oil return tube and the 2 bolts. Tighten the bolts to 89 inch lbs. (10 Nm).

➡Align the marks for the LH turbocharger intake tube.

30. Install LH turbocharger intake tube and tighten the clamp. Tighten the clamp to 44 inch lbs. (5 Nm).

31. Install the oil supply tube filter, washer and bolt.

a. Install the new oil supply tube filter in the oil supply tube block.

b. Slide the new washer onto the oil supply tube block.

c. Install the bolt into the oil supply tube block.

32. Install the LH turbocharger oil supply tube. Tighten the bolt to 26 ft. lbs. (35 Nm).

➡Make sure the turbocharger wastegate regulating valve hose does not contact the exhaust manifold heat shield.

33. Connect the wastegate control valve hose to the LH turbocharger assembly.

34. Install the LH exhaust manifold heat shield and the bottom bolt.

a. Do not tighten the bolts at this time.

35. Install the 2 top LH exhaust manifold heat shield bolts. Tighten the bolt to 124 inch lbs. (14 Nm).

36. Tighten the LH exhaust manifold heat shield bottom bolt. Tighten the bolt to 124 inch lbs. (14 Nm).

37. Install the LH catalytic converter as outlined in this section.

38. Fill and bleed the cooling system as outlined in the Engine Cooling Section.

39. Install the ACL assembly as outlined in this section.

Right-Hand

See Figures 155 through 164.

WARNING

Whenever turbocharger air intake system components are removed, always cover open ports to protect from debris. It is important that no foreign material enter the system. The turbocharger compressor vanes are susceptible to damage from even small particles. All components should be inspected and cleaned, if necessary, prior to installation or reassembly.

1. With the vehicle in NEUTRAL, position it on a hoist.

➡Use a steering wheel holding device (such as Hunter® 28-75-1 or equivalent).

2. Using a suitable holding device, hold the steering wheel in the straight-ahead position.

3. Remove the 4 retainers and the underbody shield.

4. Drain the cooling system as outlined in the Engine Cooling Section.

5. Remove the RH catalytic converter as outlined in this section.

6. Remove the front subframe.

7. Remove the RH turbocharger oil supply tube secondary latch.

8. Using a Spring Lock Coupling Disconnect Tool, remove the RH turbocharger oil supply tube from the quick connect fitting.

a. Inspect and if necessary, replace the quick connect fitting.

9. Remove the lower RH exhaust manifold heat shield bolt.

10. Loosen the clamp and remove the RH turbocharger intake pipe from the RH turbocharger.

11. Disconnect the turbocharger wastegate regulating valve hose from the RH turbocharger assembly.

12. Remove the 3 bolts and the RH turbocharger lower bracket.

13. Remove the 2 bolts and the RH turbocharger oil return tube from the turbocharger.

a. Remove and discard the gasket.

14. Remove the RH turbocharger oil return tube from the cylinder block.

a. Discard the 2 O-ring seals.

15. Remove the 2 coolant tube banjo bolts and the RH turbocharger coolant tubes.

Discard the sealing washers.

16. Detach the 2 vacuum hose retainers from the strut tower brace.

17. Remove the 4 nuts and the strut tower brace.

18. Disconnect the LH turbocharger bypass valve electrical connector and the turbocharger bypass valve hose.

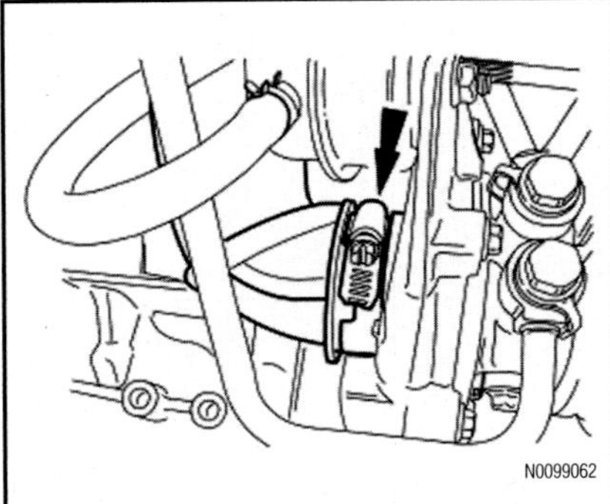

Fig. 155 Remove the RH turbocharger intake pipe from the RH turbocharger

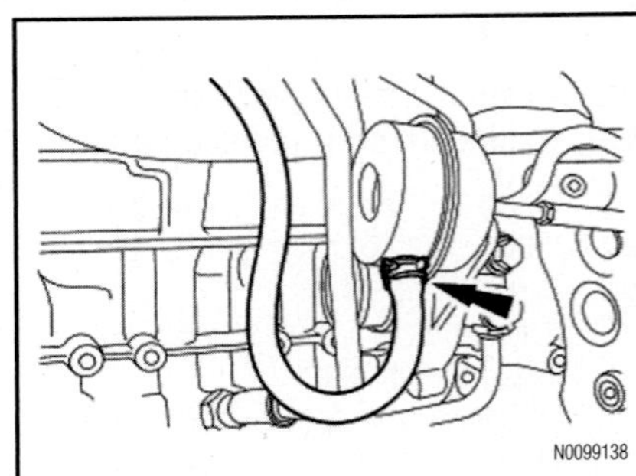

Fig. 156 Turbocharger wastegate regulating valve hose from the RH turbocharger assembly

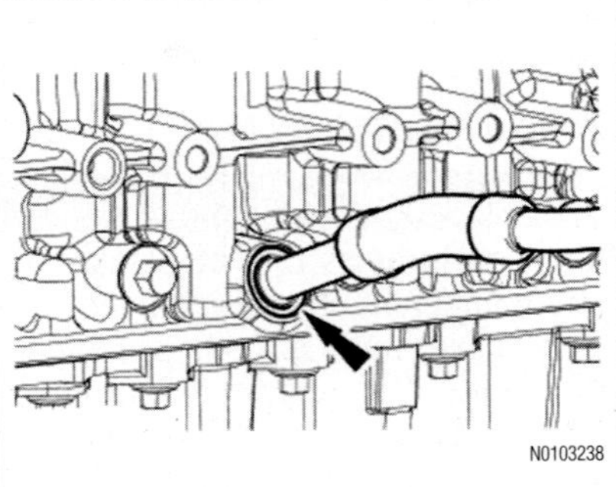

Fig. 157 Remove the RH turbocharger oil return tube from the cylinder block

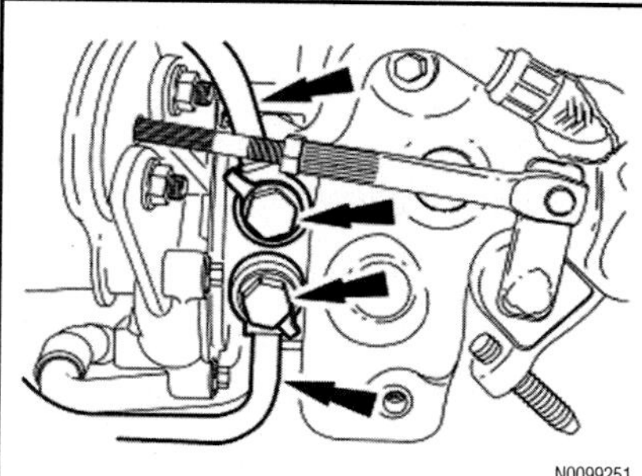

Fig. 158 Remove the 2 coolant tube banjo bolts and the RH turbocharger coolant tubes

19. Remove the turbocharger wastegate regulating valve hose from the RH Charge Air Cooler (CAC) tube.
20. Disconnect the RH turbocharger bypass valve electrical connector.
21. Disconnect the RH turbocharger bypass valve hose.
22. Remove the RH CAC tube nut from the intake manifold.
23. Loosen the clamp and remove the RH CAC tube.
24. Loosen the clamp and remove the RH CAC tube from the RH turbocharger.

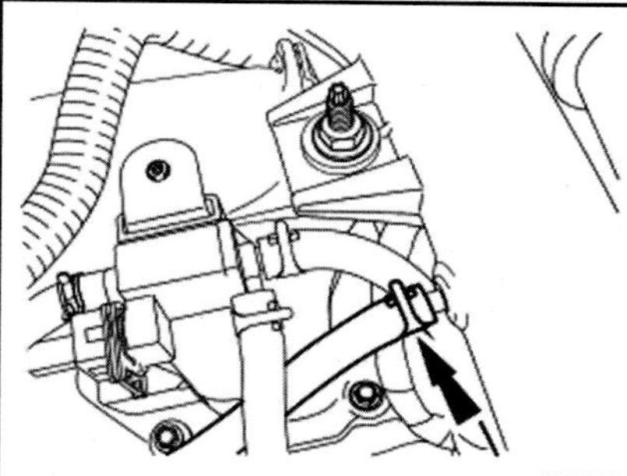

Fig. 159 Turbocharger wastegate regulating valve hose from the RH Charge Air Cooler (CAC) tube

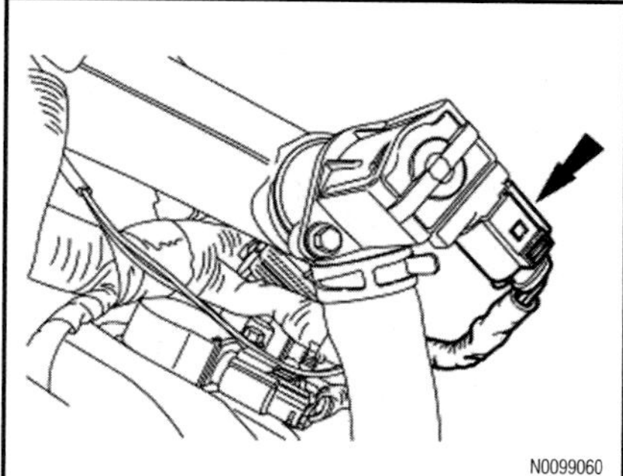

Fig. 160 RH turbocharger bypass valve electrical connector

25. Remove the 4 bolts and the 2 upper RH exhaust manifold heat shields.
26. Remove the 2 bolts and the RH engine lifting eye.
27. Remove the 3 RH exhaust manifold-to-turbocharger bolts.
    a. Discard the gasket.
28. Remove the upper RH turbocharger-to-cylinder block bracket bolt and the RH turbocharger assembly.
29. Remove the RH turbocharger oil supply tube banjo bolt.
    a. Discard the sealing washer and oil supply tube filter.

To install:

30. Install the oil supply tube filter, washer and bolt.
    a. Install the new oil supply tube filter in the oil supply tube block.
    b. Slide the new washer onto the oil supply tube block.
    c. Install the bolt into the oil supply tube block.
31. Install the RH turbocharger oil supply tube. Tighten the bolt to 26 ft. lbs. (35 Nm).

⁂ WARNING

The upper RH turbocharger bracket bolts must be loosened in order to perform the tightening sequence or damage to the turbocharger may occur.

32. Loosen the 2 bolts for the upper RH turbocharger-to-cylinder block bracket.
33. Install a new RH exhaust manifold-to-turbocharger gasket.
34. Install the RH turbocharger assembly and the upper RH turbocharger-to-cylinder block bracket bolt.
    a. Do not tighten the bolts at this time.
35. Install the 3 new RH exhaust manifold-to-turbocharger bolts. Tighten the bolts to 33 ft. lbs. (45 Nm).
36. Install the RH engine lifting eye and the 2 bolts. Tighten the bolts to 18 ft. lbs. (24 Nm).
37. Install the 2 upper RH exhaust manifold heat shields and the 4 bolts. Tighten the bolts to 124 inch lbs. (14 Nm).

➡Align the index marks for the RH CAC tube.

38. Install the RH CAC tube to the RH turbocharger and tighten the clamp. Tighten the clamp to 44 inch lbs. (5 Nm).

➡Align the index marks for the RH CAC tube.

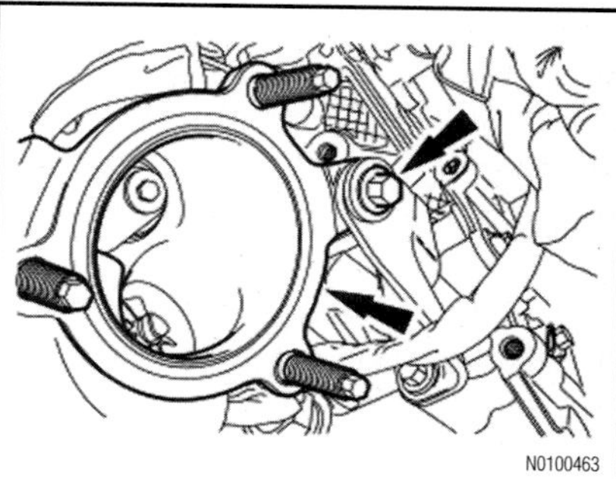

Fig. 161 Upper RH turbocharger-to-cylinder block bracket bolt and the RH turbocharger assembly

39. Install the RH CAC and tighten the clamp. Tighten the clamp to 44 inch lbs. (5 Nm).
40. Install the RH CAC tube and the RH CAC tube nut to the intake manifold. Tighten the nut to 53 inch lbs. (6 Nm).
41. Connect the RH turbocharger bypass valve hose.
42. Connect the RH turbocharger bypass valve electrical connector.
43. Install the turbocharger wastegate regulating valve hose to the RH CAC tube.
44. Connect the LH turbocharger bypass valve electrical connector and the turbocharger bypass valve hose.
45. Install the strut tower brace and the 4 nuts. Tighten the nuts to 22 ft. lbs. (30 Nm).
46. Attach the 2 brake booster vacuum hose retainers to the strut tower brace.
47. Position the upper RH turbocharger-to-cylinder block bracket as far clockwise as possible and tighten the bolts in the proper sequence as follows:
    a. Tighten the lower cylinder block bracket bolt to 19 ft. lbs. (26 Nm).
    b. Tighten the upper cylinder block bracket bolt to 19 ft. lbs. (26 Nm).
    c. Tighten the cylinder block bracket-to-turbocharger bolt to 168 inch lbs. (19 Nm).

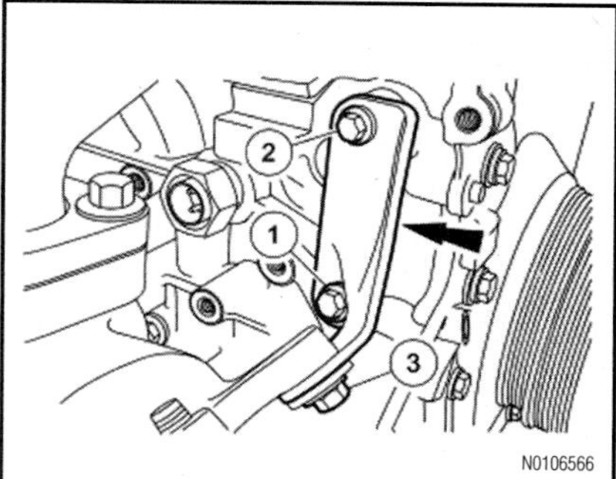

Fig. 162 Upper RH turbocharger-to-cylinder block bracket

48. Using 2 new sealing washers, install the 2 RH turbocharger coolant tube banjo bolts. Tighten the bolts to 27 ft. lbs. (37 Nm).

➡**Lubricate the cylinder block bore with clean engine oil.**

49. Using 2 new O-ring seals, install the RH turbocharger oil return tube in the cylinder block.

50. Install a new gasket and install the RH turbocharger oil return tube and the 2 bolts. Tighten the bolts to 89 inch lbs. (10 Nm).

51. Install the lower RH turbocharger bracket and the 3 bolts and tighten in proper sequence as follows:

a. Tighten the lower RH turbocharger bracket-to-turbocharger bolt to 168 inch lbs. (19 Nm).

b. Tighten the 2 lower RH turbocharger bracket-to-cylinder block bolts to 35 inch lbs. (48 Nm).

➡**Make sure the turbocharger wastegate regulating valve hose does not contact the exhaust manifold heat shield.**

52. Connect the turbocharger wastegate regulating valve hose to the RH turbocharger.

➡**Align the index marks for the RH turbocharger intake pipe.**

53. Install the RH turbocharger intake pipe to the RH turbocharger and tighten the clamp. Tighten the clamp to 44 inch lbs. (5 Nm).

54. Install the lower RH exhaust manifold heat shield bolt. Tighten the bolt to 124 inch lbs. (14 Nm).

➡**Listen for audible click when installing the oil supply tube into the quick connect fitting.**

55. Install the RH turbocharger oil supply tube into the quick connect fitting.

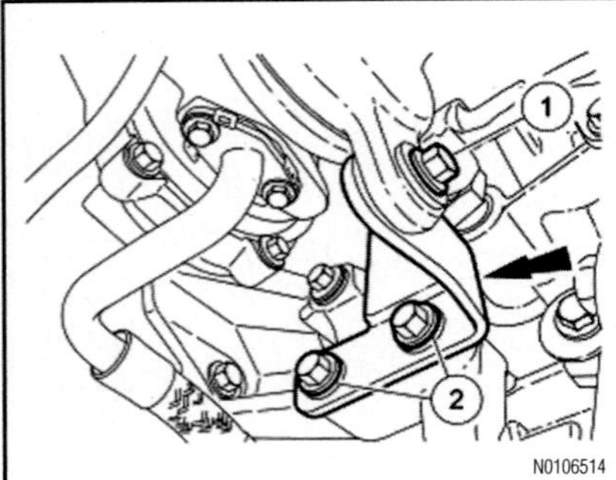

Fig. 163 Lower RH turbocharger bracket-to-cylinder block bolts

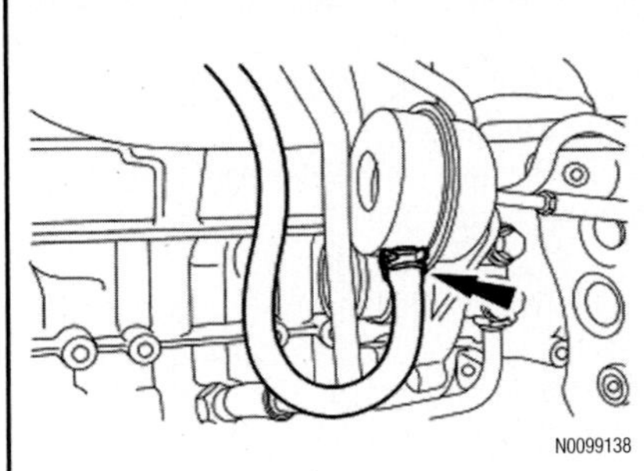

Fig. 164 Turbocharger wastegate regulating valve hose to the RH turbocharger

56. Install the RH turbocharger oil supply tube secondary latch.

57. Install the front subframe.

58. Install the RH catalytic converter as outlined in this section.

59. Fill and bleed the cooling system as outlined in the Engine Cooling Section.

60. Install the underbody shield and the 4 retainers.

VALVE COVERS

REMOVAL & INSTALLATION

3.5L Engine, Except Turbo

Left-Hand

See Figures 165 and 166.

WARNING

During engine repair procedures, cleanliness is extremely important. Any foreign material, including any material created while cleaning gasket surfaces that enters the oil passages, coolant passages or the oil pan, may cause engine failure.

WARNING

Early build engines have 11 fastener valve covers, late build engines have 9 fastener valve covers. Do not attempt to install bolts in the 2 empty late build valve cover holes or damage to the valve cover will occur.

All Vehicles

1. Remove the LH ignition coils as outlined in the Engine Electrical Section.

2. Remove the oil level indicator.

3. Disconnect the LH Variable Camshaft Timing (VCT) solenoid electrical connector.

4. Detach all of the wiring harness retainers from the LH valve cover stud bolts.

5. Disconnect the 3 LH fuel injector electrical connectors.

Early Build Vehicles

6. Loosen the 11 stud bolts and remove the LH valve cover.

a. Discard the gasket.

Late Build Vehicles

7. Loosen the 9 stud bolts and remove the LH valve cover.

a. Discard the gasket.

All Vehicles

➡**VCT solenoid seal removal shown, spark plug tube seal removal similar.**

8. Inspect the VCT solenoid seals and the spark plug tube seals. Remove any damaged seals.

a. Using the VCT Spark Plug Tube Seal Remover and Handle, remove the seal(s).

9. Clean the valve cover, cylinder head and engine front cover sealing surfaces with metal surface prep.

To install:

All Vehicles

➡**Installation of new seals is only required if damaged seals were removed during disassembly of the engine.**

➡**Spark plug tube seal installation shown, VCT solenoid seal installation similar.**

10. Using the VCT Spark Plug Tube Seal Installer and Handle, install new VCT solenoid and/or spark plug tube seals.

WARNING

Failure to use the correct Motorcraft® High Performance Engine RTV Silicone may cause the engine oil to foam excessively and result in serious engine damage.

➡**If the valve cover is not installed and the fasteners tightened within 4 minutes, the sealant must be removed and the sealing area cleaned.**

➡**To clean the sealing area, use silicone gasket remover and metal surface prep. Failure to follow this procedure can cause future oil leakage.**

11. Apply an 0.31 inch (8 mm) bead of Motorcraft® High Performance Engine RTV Silicone to the engine front cover-to-LH cylinder head joints.

Late Build Vehicles

12. Using a new gasket, install the LH valve cover and tighten the 9 stud bolts. Tighten the stud bolts to 89 inch lbs. (10 Nm) in the proper sequence.

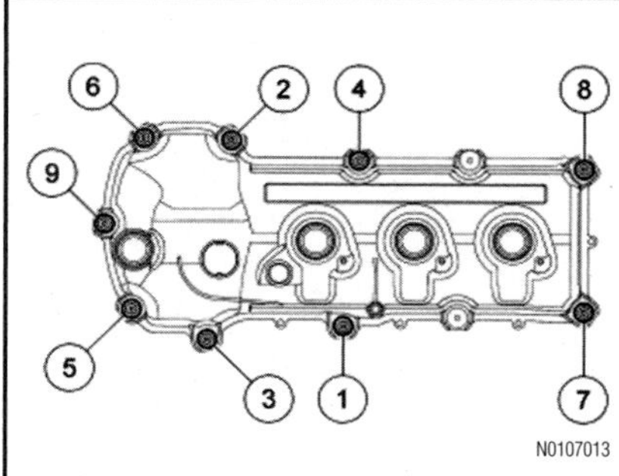

Fig. 165 LH valve cover tightening sequence—Late Build Vehicles

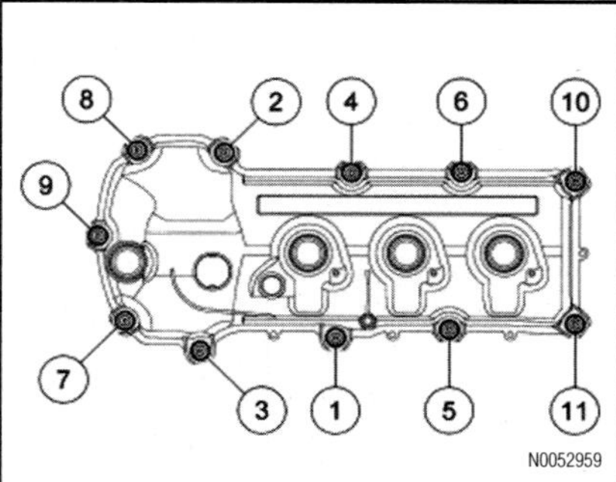

Fig. 166 LH valve cover tightening sequence—Early Build Vehicles

Early Build Vehicles

13. Using a new gasket, install the LH valve cover and tighten the 11 stud bolts. Tighten the stud bolts to 89 inch lbs. (10 Nm) in the proper sequence.

All Vehicles

14. Connect the 3 LH fuel injector electrical connectors.
15. Attach all of the wiring harness retainers to the LH valve cover stud bolts.
16. Connect the LH VCT solenoid electrical connector.
17. Install the oil level indicator.
18. Install the LH ignition coils as outlined in the Engine Electrical Section.

Right-Hand

See Figures 167 through 169.

✽✽ WARNING

During engine repair procedures, cleanliness is extremely important. Any foreign material, including any material created while cleaning gasket surfaces that enters the oil passages, coolant passages or the oil pan, may cause engine failure.

✽✽ WARNING

Early build engines have 11 fastener valve covers, late build engines have 9 fastener valve covers. Do not attempt to install bolts in the 2 empty late build valve cover holes or damage to the valve cover will occur.

All Vehicles

1. Remove the RH ignition coils as outlined in the Engine Electrical Section.
2. Detach and disconnect the RH Heated Oxygen Sensor (HO2S) electrical connector.
3. Detach and disconnect the RH Catalyst Monitor Sensor (CMS) electrical connector.
4. Disconnect the RH Variable Camshaft Timing (VCT) solenoid electrical connector.
5. Disconnect the 3 RH fuel injector electrical connectors.
6. Detach all of the wiring harness retainers from the RH valve cover stud bolts.
7. Remove the nut and the Power Steering Pressure (PSP) tube bracket from the valve cover stud bolt.

Early Build Vehicles

➡It is necessary to reposition the A/C tubes to remove the valve cover.

8. Loosen the bolt, the 10 stud bolts and remove the RH valve cover.
   a. Discard the gasket.

Late Build Vehicles

➡It is necessary to reposition the A/C tubes to remove the valve cover.

9. Loosen the 9 stud bolts and remove the RH valve cover.
   a. Discard the gasket.

All Vehicles

➡VCT solenoid seal removal shown, spark plug tube seal removal similar.

10. Inspect the VCT solenoid seals and the spark plug tube seals. Remove any damaged seals.
   a. Using the VCT Spark Plug Tube Seal Remover and Handle, remove the seal(s).
11. Clean the valve cover, cylinder head and engine front cover sealing surfaces with metal surface prep.

To install:

All Vehicles

➡Installation of new seals is only required if damaged seals were removed during disassembly of the engine.

➡Spark plug tube seal installation shown, VCT solenoid seal installation similar.

12. Using the VCT Spark Plug Tube Seal Installer and Handle, install a new VCT solenoid and/or spark plug tube seals.

✽✽ WARNING

Failure to use Motorcraft® High Performance Engine RTV Silicone may cause the engine oil to foam excessively and result in serious engine damage.

➡If the valve cover is not installed and the fasteners tightened within 4 minutes, the sealant must be removed and the sealing area cleaned. To clean the sealing area, use silicone gasket remover and metal surface prep. Failure to follow this procedure can cause future oil leakage.

Apply an 0.31 inch (8 mm) bead of Motorcraft® High Performance Engine RTV Silicone to the engine front cover-to-RH cylinder head joints.

Late Build Vehicles

13. Using a new gasket, install the RH valve cover and tighten the 9 stud bolts.

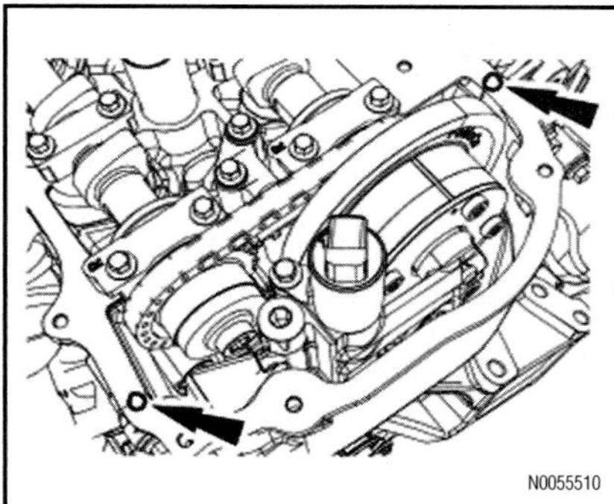

Fig. 167 Engine front cover-to-RH cylinder head joints

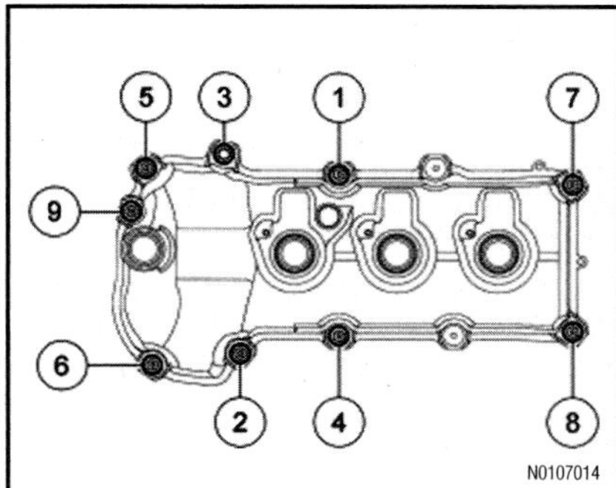

Fig. 168 RH valve cover—Late Build Vehicles

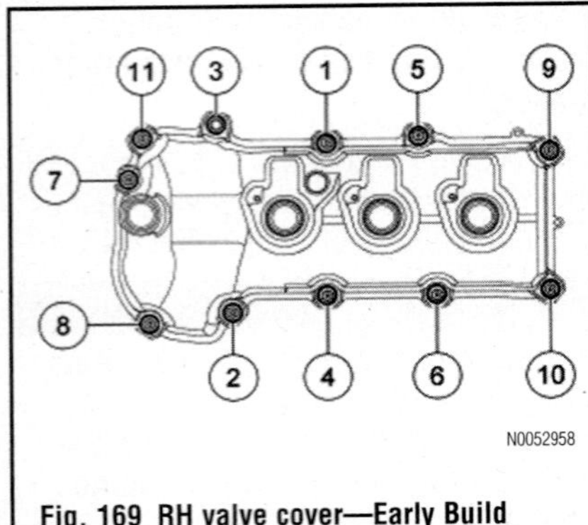

Fig. 169 RH valve cover—Early Build Vehicles

Tighten the stud bolts to 89 inch lbs. (89 Nm) in the proper sequence.

Early Build Vehicles

14. Using a new gasket, install the RH valve cover and tighten the bolt and the 10 stud bolts. Tighten the stud bolts to 89 inch lbs. (10 Nm) in the proper sequence.

All Vehicles

15. Install the PSP tube bracket on the valve cover stud bolt and install the nut. Tighten the nut to 62 inch lbs. (7 Nm).
16. Attach all of the wiring harness retainers to the RH valve cover stud bolts.
17. Connect the 3 RH fuel injector electrical connectors.
18. Connect the RH VCT solenoid electrical connector.
19. Connect the RH CMS electrical connector.
20. Connect the RH HO2S electrical connector.
21. Install the RH ignition coils as outlined in the Engine Electrical Section.

3.5L Turbo Engine

Left-Hand

See Figures 170 through 174.

WARNING

During engine repair procedures, cleanliness is extremely important. Any foreign material, including any material created while cleaning gasket surfaces that enters the oil passages, coolant passages or the oil pan, may cause engine failure.

WARNING

Whenever turbocharger air intake system components are removed, always cover open ports to protect from debris. It is important that no foreign material enter the system. The turbocharger compressor vanes are susceptible to damage from even small particles. All components should be inspected and cleaned, if necessary, prior to installation or reassembly.

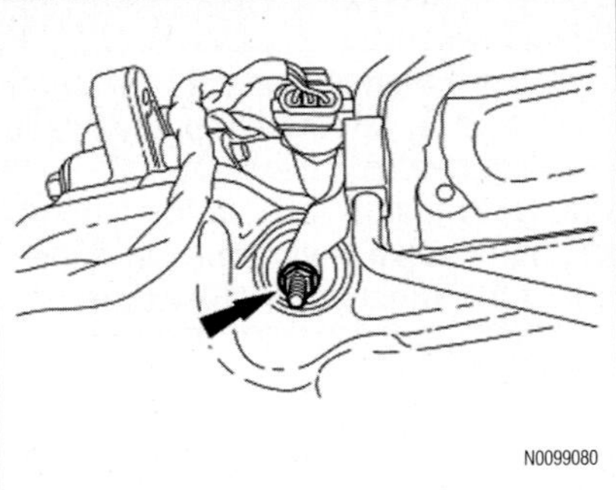

Fig. 170 High pressure fuel tube from the LH valve cover stud bolt

All Vehicles

1. Release the fuel system pressure as outlined in the Fuel System Section
2. Disconnect the Turbocharger Boost Pressure (TCBP)/Charge Air Cooler Temperature (CACT) sensor electrical connector.
3. Remove the noise generator as outlined in this section.
4. Loosen the 2 clamps and remove the Charge Air Cooler (CAC) outlet pipe.
5. Disconnect the 2 quick connect couplings and remove the crankcase vent tube.
6. Remove the fuel injection pump noise insulator shield.
7. Remove the oil level indicator.

Early Build Vehicles

8. Remove the intake manifold as outlined in this section.
9. Remove the nut for the high pressure fuel tube from the LH valve cover stud bolt.

➡To release the fuel pressure in the high-pressure fuel tubes, wrap the flare nut with a shop towel to absorb any residual fuel pressure during the loosening of the flare nuts.

10. Remove the high pressure fuel tube flare nut from the fuel injection pump. Remove the 2 high pressure fuel tube flare nuts from the fuel rails and remove the high pressure fuel tube assembly.

Late Build Vehicles

11. Remove the Throttle Body (TB).
12. Disconnect the LH turbocharger bypass valve electrical connector.
13. Disconnect the LH turbocharger bypass valve hose from the RH CAC tube.
14. Disconnect the turbocharger wastegate regulating valve hose from the RH CAC tube.

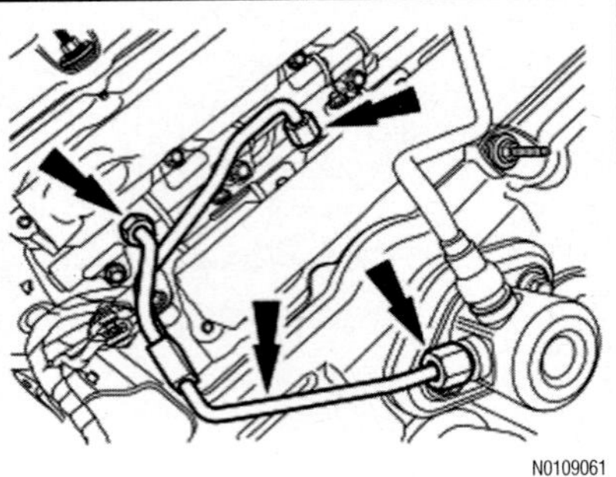

Fig. 171 Remove the high pressure fuel tube flare nut from the fuel injection pump. Remove the 2 high pressure fuel tube flare nuts from the fuel rails and remove the high pressure fuel tube assembly

15. Disconnect the RH turbocharger bypass valve electrical connector.
16. Disconnect the RH turbocharger bypass valve hose from the RH turbocharger intake tube.

WARNING

The compression limiter bushing may fall out of the mounting bracket grommet on the Charge Air Cooler (CAC) tube during service. Make sure the bushing is in place when reinstalling the tube or damage to the tube may occur.

17. Remove the RH CAC tube nut from the intake manifold.
18. Loosen the clamp and remove the RH CAC tube.
19. Loosen the clamp and remove the RH CAC tube from the RH turbocharger.

All Vehicles

20. Remove the fuel injection pump.
21. Disconnect the LH Variable Camshaft Timing (VCT) solenoid electrical connector.
22. Remove the engine cover mounting stud from the LH valve cover stud bolt.
23. Detach all of the wiring harness retainers from the LH valve cover stud bolts.
24. Remove the nut and the oil supply tube bracket from the LH valve cover stud bolt.
25. Disconnect the 3 LH ignition coil-on-plug electrical connectors.

➡When removing the ignition coil-on-plugs, a slight twisting motion will break the seal and ease removal.

26. Remove the 3 bolts and the 3 LH ignition coil-on-plugs.
27. Loosen the 10 stud bolts and remove the LH valve cover.
    a. Discard the gasket.

➡VCT solenoid seal removal shown, spark plug tube seal removal similar.

28. Inspect the VCT solenoid seals and the spark plug tube seals. Remove any damaged seals.

a. Using the VCT Spark Plug Tube Seal Remover and Handle, remove the seal(s).

29. Clean the valve cover, cylinder head and engine front cover sealing surfaces with metal surface prep.

To install:

All Vehicles

➡Installation of new seals is only required if damaged seals were removed during disassembly of the engine.

➡Spark plug tube seal installation shown, VCT solenoid seal installation similar.

30. Using the VCT Spark Plug Tube Seal Installer and Handle, install new VCT solenoid and/or spark plug tube seals.

✲✲ WARNING

Failure to use the correct Motorcraft® High Performance Engine RTV Silicone may cause the engine oil to foam excessively and result in serious engine damage.

➡If the valve cover is not installed and the fasteners tightened within 4 minutes, the sealant must be removed and the sealing area cleaned. To clean the sealing area, use silicone gasket remover and metal surface prep. Failure to follow these instructions can cause future oil leakage.

31. Apply an 0.31 inch (8 mm) bead of Motorcraft® High Performance Engine RTV Silicone to the engine front cover-to-LH cylinder head joints.

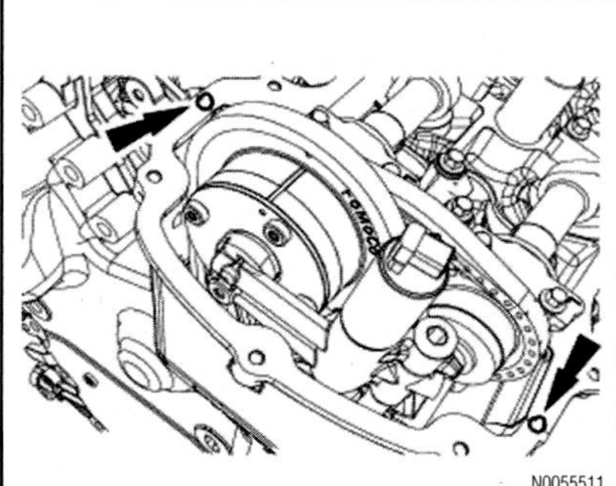

Fig. 172 Apply an 0.31 inch (8 mm) bead of Motorcraft® High Performance Engine RTV Silicone to the engine front cover-to-LH cylinder head joints

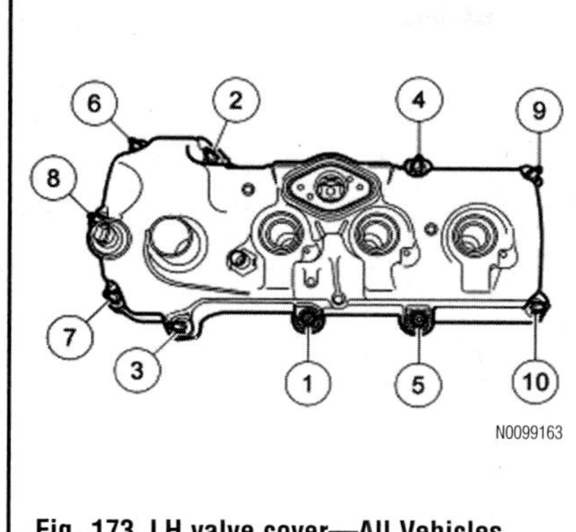

Fig. 173 LH valve cover—All Vehicles

32. Using a new gasket, install the LH valve cover and tighten the 10 stud bolts. Tighten the stud bolts to 89 inch lbs. (10 Nm) in the proper sequence.

33. Install 3 LH ignition coil-on-plugs and the 3 bolts. Tighten the bolts to 62 inch lbs. (7 Nm).

34. Connect the 3 LH ignition coil-on-plug electrical connectors.

35. Install the oil supply tube bracket on the LH valve cover stud bolt and install the nut. Tighten the bolt to 71 inch lbs. (8 Nm).

36. Attach all of the wiring harness retainers to the LH valve cover and stud bolts.

37. Install the engine cover mounting stud to the LH valve cover stud bolt. Tighten the bolt to 53 inch lbs. (6 Nm).

38. Connect the LH VCT solenoid electrical connector.

39. Install the fuel injection pump.

Late Build Vehicles

➡Align the index marks for the RH CAC tube.

40. Install the RH CAC tube to the RH turbocharger and tighten the clamp. Tighten the clamp to 44 inch lbs. (5 Nm).

➡Align the index marks for the RH CAC tube.

41. Install the RH CAC tube and tighten the clamp. Tighten the clamp to 44 inch lbs. (5 Nm).

✲✲ WARNING

The compression limiter bushing may fall out of the mounting bracket grommet on the Charge Air Cooler (CAC) tube during service. Make sure the bushing is in place when reinstalling the tube or damage to the tube may occur.

42. Install the RH CAC tube and the RH CAC tube nut to the intake manifold. Tighten the nut to 53 inch lbs. (6 Nm).

43. Connect the RH turbocharger bypass valve hose to the RH turbocharger intake tube.

44. Connect the RH turbocharger bypass valve electrical connector.

45. Connect the turbocharger wastegate regulating valve hose to the RH CAC tube.

46. Connect the LH turbocharger bypass valve electrical connector and the turbocharger bypass valve hose.

47. Install the Throttle Body.

Early Build Vehicles

48. Connect the high pressure fuel tube flare nut to the fuel injection pump and the 2 high pressure fuel tube flare nuts to the fuel rails. Tighten the nuts to 22 ft. lbs. (30 Nm).

49. Install the nut for the high pressure fuel tube on the LH valve cover stud bolt. Tighten the bolt to 53 inch lbs. (6 Nm).

50. Install the intake manifold as outlined in this section.

All Vehicles

51. Install the oil level indicator.

52. Install the fuel injection pump noise insulator shield.

53. Install the crankcase vent tube and connect the 2 quick connect couplings.

➡Align the index marks for the CAC outlet pipe.

54. Install the CAC outlet pipe and tighten the 2 clamps. Tighten the clamps to 44 inch lbs. (5 Nm).

55. Install the noise generator as outlined in this section.

56. Connect the TCBP/CACT sensor electrical connector.

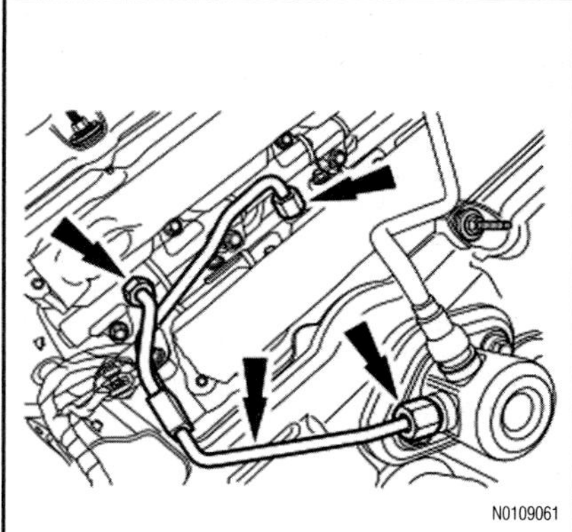

Fig. 174 High pressure fuel tube flare nut to the fuel injection pump and the 2 high pressure fuel tube flare nuts to the fuel rails

Right-Hand

See Figure 175.

⁂ WARNING

During engine repair procedures, cleanliness is extremely important. Any foreign material, including any material created while cleaning gasket surfaces that enters the oil passages, coolant passages or the oil pan, may cause engine failure.

⁂ WARNING

Whenever turbocharger air intake system components are removed, always cover open ports to protect from debris. It is important that no foreign material enter the system. The turbocharger compressor vanes are susceptible to damage from even small particles. All components should be inspected and cleaned, if necessary, prior to installation or reassembly.

1. Release the fuel system pressure.
2. Disconnect the LH turbocharger bypass valve electrical connector.
3. Disconnect the turbocharger bypass valve hose from the RH Charge Air Cooler (CAC) tube.
4. Remove the turbocharger wastegate regulating valve hose from the RH CAC tube.
5. Disconnect the RH turbocharger bypass valve electrical connector.
6. Disconnect the RH turbocharger bypass valve hose from the RH turbocharger intake tube.

⁂ WARNING

The compression limiter bushing may fall out of the mounting bracket grommet on the Charge Air Cooler (CAC) tube during service. Make sure the bushing is in place when reinstalling the tube or damage to the tube may occur.

7. Remove the RH CAC tube nut from the intake manifold.
8. Loosen the clamp and remove the RH CAC tube.
9. Loosen the clamp and remove the RH CAC tube.
10. Detach the 2 brake booster vacuum hose retainers from the strut tower brace and position aside.
11. Disconnect the fuel supply tube.
12. Remove the fuel tube-to-engine front cover bracket bolt and position the fuel tube aside.
13. Disconnect the RH fuel injector wiring harness electrical connector.
14. Disconnect the Evaporative Emission (EVAP) tube quick connect coupling.
15. Disconnect the EVAP valve electrical connector and detach from the intake manifold.
16. Disconnect the quick connect coupling from the intake manifold and remove the EVAP tube assembly.
17. Disconnect the 2 quick connect couplings and remove the PCV tube.
18. If equipped, disconnect the 2 heated PCV electrical connectors.
19. Disconnect the RH Variable Camshaft Timing (VCT) solenoid electrical connector and detach the 2 wiring harness retainers.
20. Disconnect the 3 RH ignition coil-on-plugs electrical connectors.
21. Detach all of the wiring harness retainers from the RH valve cover and stud bolts position aside.

➡When removing the ignition coil-on-plugs, a slight twisting motion will break the seal and ease removal.

22. Remove the 3 bolts and the 3 RH ignition coil-on-plugs.
23. Loosen the clamp and remove the RH turbocharger intake tube from the RH turbocharger intake pipe.

⁂ WARNING

The compression limiter bushing may fall out of the mounting bracket grommet on the turbocharger intake tube during service. Make sure the bushing is in place when reinstalling the tube or damage to the tube may occur.

24. Remove the nut from the RH valve cover stud bolt and position the RH turbocharger intake tube off the RH valve cover stud bolt.
25. Loosen the 11 stud bolts and remove the RH valve cover.
    a. Discard the gasket.

➡VCT solenoid seal removal shown, spark plug tube seal removal similar.

26. Inspect the VCT solenoid seals and the spark plug tube seals. Remove any damaged seals.
    a. Using the VCT Spark Plug Tube Seal Remover and Handle, remove the seal(s).
27. Clean the valve cover, cylinder head and engine front cover sealing surfaces with metal surface prep.

To install:

➡Installation of new seals is only required if damaged seals were removed during disassembly of the engine.

➡Spark plug tube seal installation shown, VCT solenoid seal installation similar.

28. Using the VCT Spark Plug Tube Seal Installer and Handle, install new VCT solenoid and/or spark plug tube seals.

⁂ WARNING

Failure to use Motorcraft® High Performance Engine RTV Silicone may cause the engine oil to foam excessively and result in serious engine damage.

➡If the valve cover is not installed and the fasteners tightened within 4 minutes, the sealant must be removed and the sealing area cleaned. ➡To clean the sealing area, use silicone gasket remover and metal surface prep. Failure to follow this procedure can cause future oil leakage.

29. Apply an 0.31 inch (8 mm) bead of Motorcraft® High Performance Engine RTV Silicone to the engine front cover-to-RH cylinder head joints.
30. Using a new gasket, install the RH valve cover and tighten the 11 stud bolts. Tighten the bolts to 89 inch lbs. (10 Nm) in the proper sequence.

⁂ WARNING

The compression limiter bushing may fall out of the mounting bracket grommet on the turbocharger intake tube during service. Make sure the bushing is in place when reinstalling the tube or damage to the tube may occur.

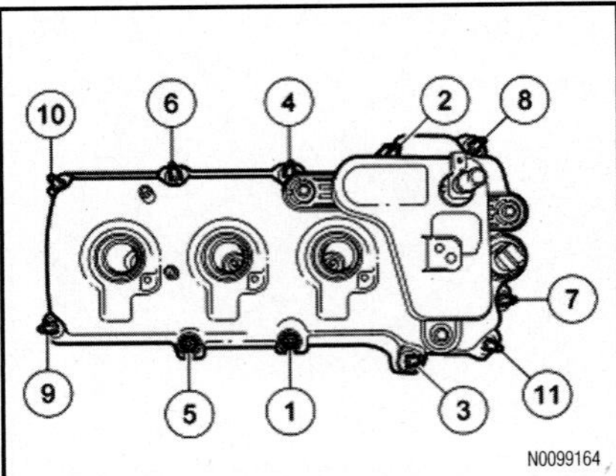

Fig. 175 Using a new gasket, install the RH valve cover and tighten the 11 stud bolts

31. Position the RH turbocharger intake tube and install the nut to the RH valve cover stud bolt. Tighten the bolt to 53 inch lbs. (6 Nm).

➡Align the index marks for the RH turbocharger intake tube.

32. Install the RH turbocharger intake tube to the RH turbocharger intake pipe and tighten the clamp. Tighten the clamp to 44 inch lbs. (5 Nm).
33. Install 3 RH ignition coil-on-plugs and the 3 bolts. Tighten the bolts to 62 inch lbs. (7 Nm).
34. Attach all of the wiring harness retainers to the RH valve cover and stud bolts.
35. Connect the 3 RH ignition coil-on-plug electrical connectors.
36. Connect the RH VCT solenoid electrical connector and attach the 2 wiring harness retainers.
37. If equipped, connect the 2 heated PCV electrical connectors.
38. Install the PCV tube and connect the 2 quick connect couplings.
39. Install the EVAP tube assembly and connect the quick connect coupling to the intake manifold.
40. Connect the EVAP valve electrical connector and attach to the intake manifold.
41. Connect the EVAP tube quick connect coupling.
42. Connect the RH fuel injector wiring harness electrical connector.
43. Position the fuel tube and install the fuel tube-to-engine front cover bracket bolt. Tighten the bolt to 89 inch lbs. (10 Nm).
44. Connect the fuel supply tube.
45. Attach the 2 brake booster vacuum hose retainers to the strut tower brace.

➡Align the index marks for the RH CAC tube.

46. Install the RH CAC tube to the RH turbocharger and tighten the clamp. Tighten the clamp to 44 inch lbs. (5 Nm).

➡Align the index marks for the RH CAC tube.

47. Install the RH CAC tube and tighten the clamp. Tighten the clamp to 44 inch lbs. (5 Nm).

⁂ WARNING

The compression limiter bushing may fall out of the mounting bracket grommet on the Charge Air Cooler (CAC) tube during service. Make sure the bushing is in place when reinstalling the tube or damage to the tube may occur.

48. Install the RH CAC tube and turbocharger intake tube as an assembly and install the RH CAC tube nut to the intake manifold. Tighten the nut to 53 inch lbs. (6 Nm).
49. Connect the RH turbocharger bypass valve hose to the RH turbocharger intake tube.
50. Connect the RH turbocharger bypass valve electrical connector.
51. Install the turbocharger wastegate regulating valve hose to the RH CAC tube.
52. Connect the turbocharger bypass valve hose to the RH CAC tube.
53. Connect the LH turbocharger bypass valve electrical connector.

ENGINE PERFORMANCE & EMISSION CONTROLS

CAMSHAFT POSITION (CMP) SENSOR

LOCATION

See Figures 176 and 177.

Refer to the accompanying illustrations.

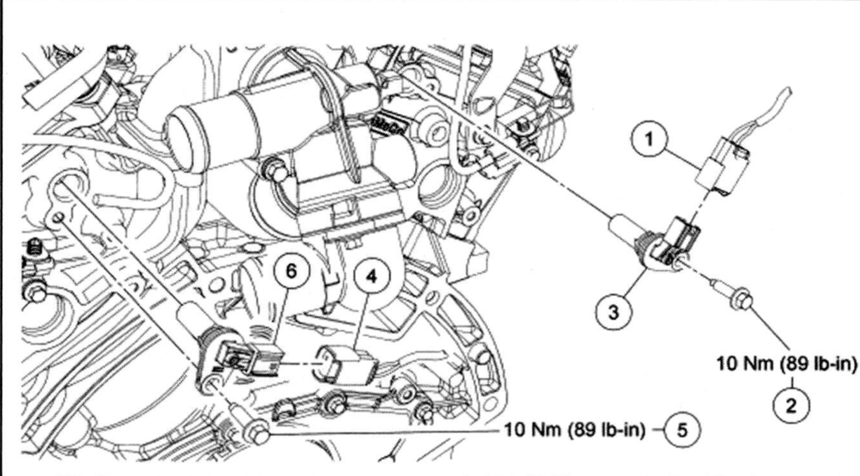

Fig. 176 Camshaft Position (CMP) sensor location—3.5L engine, except Turbo

REMOVAL & INSTALLATION

3.5L Engine, Except Turbo

1. Remove the Air Cleaner (ACL) outlet pipe and the ACL.
2. Disconnect the Camshaft Position (CMP) sensor electrical connector.
3. Remove the bolt and the CMP sensor.

➡Lubricate the CMP sensor O-ring seal with clean engine oil.

To install:

➡Lubricate the CMP sensor O-ring seal with clean engine oil.

4. Install the bolt and the CMP sensor. Tighten the bolt to 89 inch lbs. (10 Nm).
5. Connect the Camshaft Position (CMP) sensor electrical connector.
6. Install the Air Cleaner (ACL) outlet pipe and the ACL.

3.5L Turbo Engine

Both Sensors

1. Remove the Air Cleaner (ACL) outlet pipe and the ACL.

RH Sensor

2. Position the RH turbocharger intake tube aside as outlined in the Engine Mechanical Section.

LH Sensor

3. Position the LH turbocharger intake tube aside as outlined in the Engine Mechanical Section.

Both Sensors

4. Disconnect the Camshaft Position (CMP) sensor electrical connector.
5. Remove the bolt and the CMP sensor.

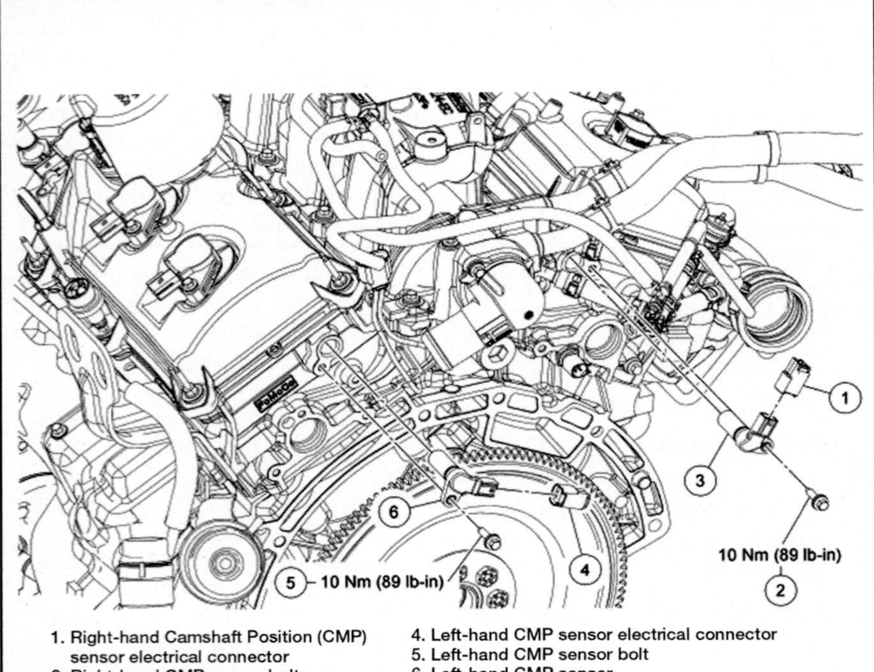

Fig. 177 Camshaft Position (CMP) sensor locations—3.5L Turbo engine

➡Lubricate the CMP sensor O-ring seal with clean engine oil.

To install:

➡Lubricate the CMP sensor O-ring seal with clean engine oil.

Both Sensors

6. Install the bolt and the CMP sensor. Tighten the bolt to 89 inch lbs. (10 Nm).
7. Connect the Camshaft Position (CMP) sensor electrical connector.

LH Sensor

8. Position the LH turbocharger intake tube as outlined in the Engine Mechanical Section.

RH Sensor

9. Position the RH turbocharger intake tube as outlined in the Engine Mechanical Section.

Both Sensors

10. Install the Air Cleaner (ACL) outlet pipe and the ACL.

CATALYST MONITOR SENSOR

REMOVAL & INSTALLTION

All Sensors

1. With the vehicle in NEUTRAL, position it on a hoist.

All Sensors Except The RH 3.5L Turbo Sensor

2. Disconnect the Catalyst Monitor Sensor (CMS) electrical connector.

RH 3.5L Turbo Sensor

3. Disconnect the CMS electrical connector.
   a. Detach the wiring retainer from the rear engine roll restrictor bracket.

All Sensors

➡If necessary, lubricate the sensor threads with penetrating and lock lubricant to assist in removal.

4. Using the Exhaust Gas Oxygen Sensor Socket, remove the CMS.
   a. Calculate the correct torque wrench setting for the following torque.

➡Apply a light coat of anti-seize lubricant to the threads of the CMS.

To install:

➡Apply a light coat of anti-seize lubricant to the threads of the CMS.

All Sensors

➡If necessary, lubricate the sensor threads with penetrating and lock lubricant to assist in installation.

5. Using the Exhaust Gas Oxygen Sensor Socket, install the CMS.
   a. Calculate the correct torque wrench setting. Tighten to 48 Nm (35 lb-ft).

RH 3.5L Turbo Sensor

6. Connect the CMS electrical connector.
   a. Attach the wiring retainer to the rear engine roll restrictor bracket.

All Sensors Except The RH 3.5L Turbo Sensor

7. Connect the Catalyst Monitor Sensor (CMS) electrical connector.

All Sensors

8. With the vehicle in NEUTRAL, lower from the hoist.

CRANKSHAFT POSITION (CKP) SENSOR

LOCATION

See Figure 178.

Refer to the accompanying illustration.

REMOVAL & INSTALLATION

All Vehicles

1. With the vehicle in NEUTRAL, position it on a hoist.

All Vehicles Except 3.5L Turbo

2. Remove the LH catalytic converter as outlined in the Engine Mechanical Section.
3. Remove the bolt, nut and the heat shield.

3.5L Turbo

4. Remove the LH turbocharger.
5. Remove the nut and the heat shield.

All Vehicles

6. Remove the rubber grommet cover.
7. Disconnect the Crankshaft Position (CKP) sensor electrical connector.
8. Remove the bolt and the CKP sensor.

To install:

All Vehicles

9. Install the bolt and the CKP sensor. Tighten the bolt to 89 inch lbs. (10 Nm).
10. Connect the Crankshaft Position (CKP) sensor electrical connector.
11. Install the rubber grommet cover.

3.5L Turbo

12. Install the nut and the heat shield. Tighten the nut to 89 inch lbs. (10 Nm).
13. Install the LH turbocharger.

All Vehicles Except 3.5L Turbo

14. Install the bolt, nut and the heat shield. Tighten the bolt to 89 inch lbs. (10 Nm).
15. Install the LH catalytic converter as outlined in the Engine Mechanical Section.

All Vehicles

16. With the vehicle in NEUTRAL, position it on a hoist.

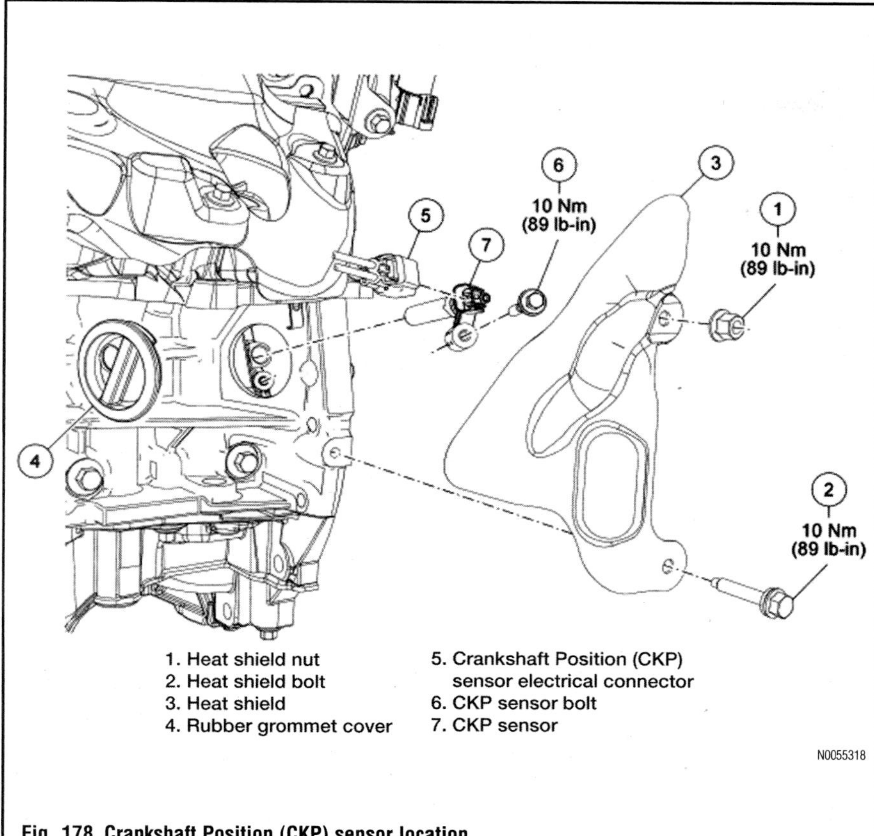

Fig. 178 Crankshaft Position (CKP) sensor location

3.5L Turbo

17. Using the scan tool, perform the Misfire Monitor Neutral Profile Correction procedure, following the on-screen instructions.

CYLINDER HEAD TEMPERATURE (CHT) SENSOR

LOCATION

See Figures 179 and 180.

Refer to the accompanying illustrations.

REMOVAL & INSTALLATION

3.5L Engine, Except Turbo

1. Remove the lower intake manifold as outlined in the Engine Mechanical Section.
2. Disconnect the Cylinder Head Temperature (CHT) sensor electrical connector.
3. Remove and discard the CHT sensor.

To install:

WARNING

Do not reuse the CHT sensor. Install a new sensor.

4. Install the CHT sensor. Tighten the sensor to 89 inch lbs. (10 Nm).
5. Connect the Cylinder Head Temperature (CHT) sensor electrical connector.
6. Install the lower intake manifold as outlined in the Engine Mechanical Section.

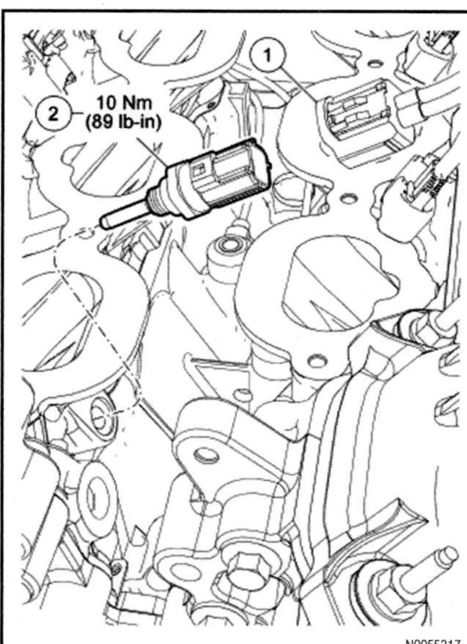

Fig. 179 Cylinder Head Temperature (CHT) Sensor electrical connector (1) and CHT sensor (2)—3.5L engine, except Turbo

3.5L Turbo Engine

1. Remove the Air Cleaner (ACL) outlet pipe and the ACL.
2. Remove the ACL-to-LH and ACL-to-RH turbocharger intake tubes.
3. Disconnect the Cylinder Head Temperature (CHT) sensor electrical connector.
4. Remove and discard the CHT sensor.

To install:

WARNING

Do not reuse the CHT sensor. Install a new sensor.

5. Install the CHT sensor. Tighten the sensor to 89 inch lbs. (10 Nm).
6. Connect the Cylinder Head Temperature (CHT) sensor electrical connector.
7. Install the ACL-to-LH and ACL-to-RH turbocharger intake tubes.
8. Install the Air Cleaner (ACL) outlet pipe and the ACL.

FUEL RAIL PRESSURE (FRP) SENSOR

LOCATION

See Figure 181.

Refer to the accompanying illustrations.

REMOVAL & INSTALLATION

CAUTION

Do not smoke, carry lighted tobacco or have an open flame of any type when working on or near any fuel-related component. Highly flammable mixtures are always present and may be ignited. Failure to follow these instructions may result in serious personal injury.

CAUTION

Before working on or disconnecting any of the fuel tubes or fuel system components, relieve the fuel system pressure to prevent accidental spraying of fuel. Fuel in the fuel system remains under high pressure, even when the engine is not running. Failure to follow this instruction may result in serious personal injury.

1. Release the fuel system pressure.
2. Disconnect the battery ground cable.
3. Remove the intake manifold as outlined in the Engine Mechanical Section.

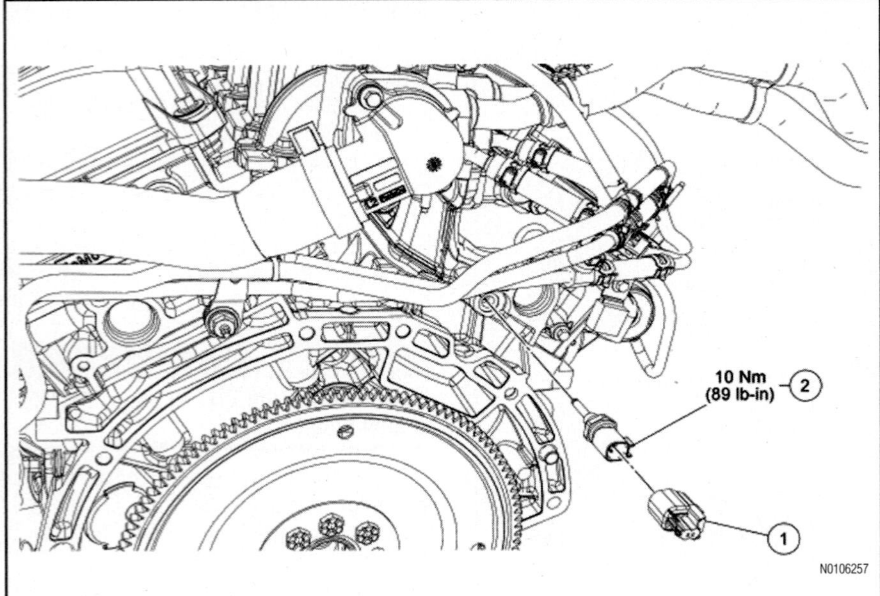

Fig. 180 Cylinder Head Temperature (CHT) Sensor electrical connector (1) and CHT sensor (2)—3.5L Turbo engine

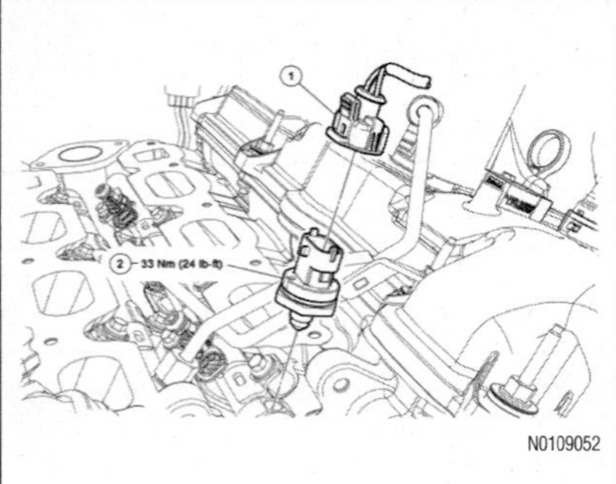

Fig. 181 Fuel Rail Pressure (FRP) Sensor electrical connector (1) and FRP sensor (2)

4. Disconnect the Fuel Rail Pressure (FRP) sensor electrical connector.
5. Remove the FRP sensor.

To install:

**** CAUTION**

Do not smoke, carry lighted tobacco or have an open flame of any type when working on or near any fuel-related component. Highly flammable mixtures are always present and may be ignited. Failure to follow these instructions may result in serious personal injury.

**** CAUTION**

Before working on or disconnecting any of the fuel tubes or fuel system components, relieve the fuel system pressure to prevent accidental spraying of fuel. Fuel in the fuel system remains under high pressure, even when the engine is not running. Failure to follow this instruction may result in serious personal injury.

6. Install the FRP sensor. Tighten the sensor to 24 ft. lbs. (33 Nm).
7. Connect the Fuel Rail Pressure (FRP) sensor electrical connector.
8. Install the intake manifold as outlined in the Engine Mechanical Section.
9. Connect the battery ground cable.
10. Pressurize the fuel system pressure.

HEATED OXYGEN SENSOR (HO2S)

LOCATION

See Figures 182 through 184.

Refer to the accompanying illustrations.

REMOVAL & INSTALLATION

See Figures 185 through 188.

All RH Sensors

1. With the vehicle in NEUTRAL, position it on a hoist.

RH 3.5L Turbo Sensor

2. Disconnect the Heated Oxygen Sensor (HO2S) electrical connector.
   a. Detach the HO2S electrical connector retainer from the bracket.

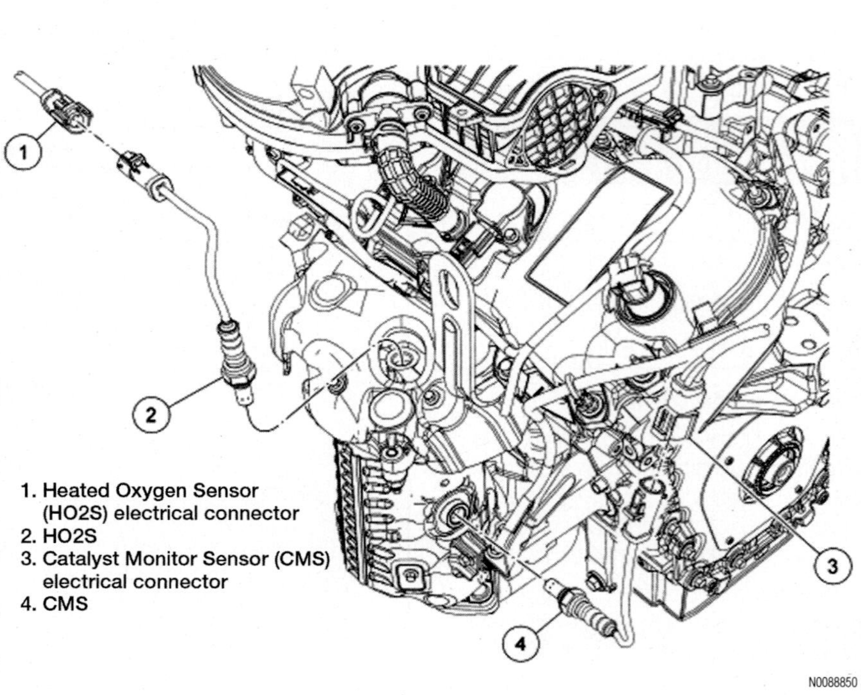

Fig. 182 Right-Hand Heated Oxygen Sensor (HO2S) and catalyst monitor sensor location—3.5L engine, except Turbo

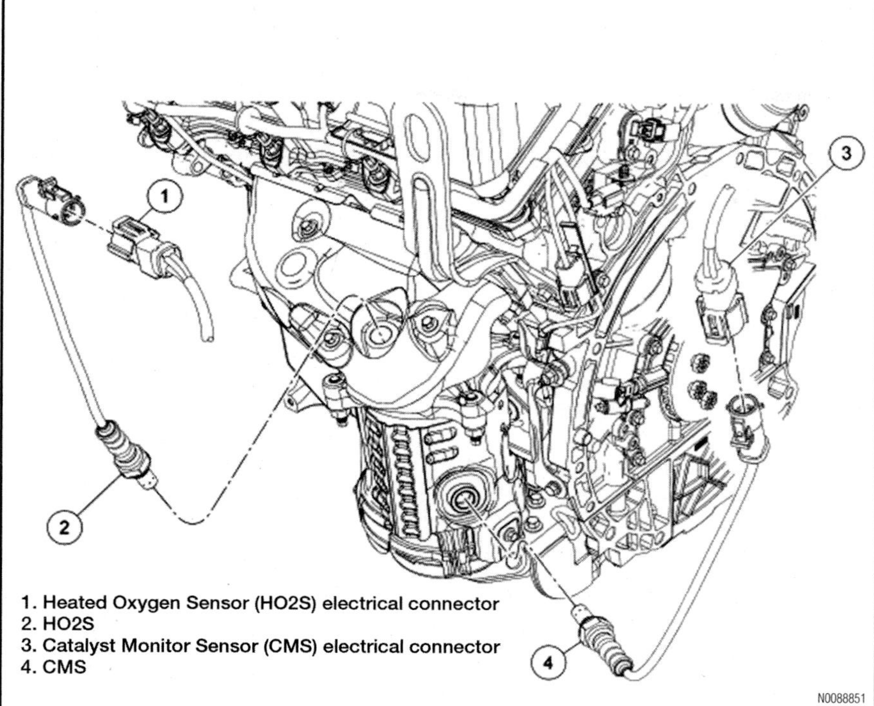

Fig. 183 Left-Hand Heated Oxygen Sensor (HO2S) and catalyst monitor sensor location—3.5L engine, except Turbo

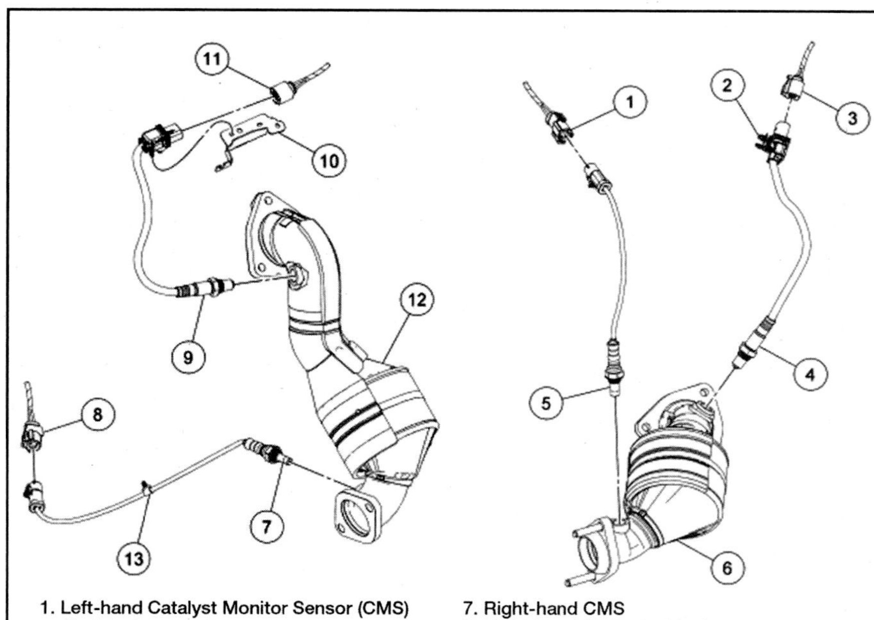

Fig. 184 Heated Oxygen Sensor (HO2S) and catalyst monitor sensor location–3.5L Turbo engine

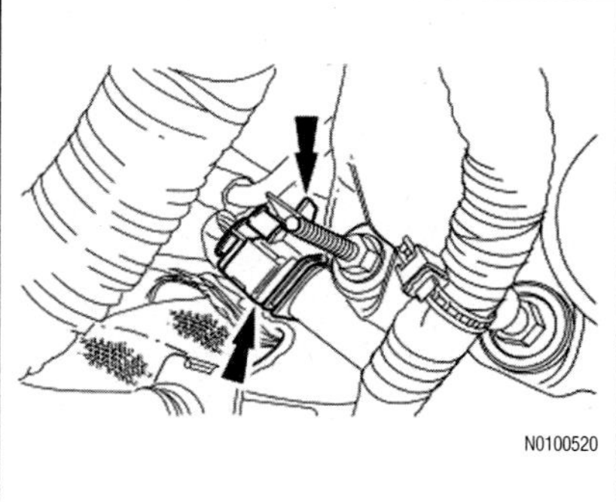

Fig. 185 Heated Oxygen Sensor (HO2S) electrical connector

LH 3.5L Turbo Sensor

3. Remove the 4 retainers and the underbody shield.
4. Disconnect the LH HO2S electrical connector.
   a. Detach the HO2S connector retainer from the bracket.

All Sensors Except Turbo

5. Disconnect the HO2S electrical connector.

All Sensors

➡If necessary, lubricate the sensor threads with penetrating and lock lubricant to assist in removal.

6. Using the Exhaust Gas Oxygen Sensor Socket, remove the HO2S.
   a. Calculate the correct torque wrench setting.

➡Apply a light coat of anti-seize lubricant to the threads of the HO2S.

To install:

All Sensors

➡Apply a light coat of anti-seize lubricant to the threads of the HO2S.

➡If necessary, lubricate the sensor threads with penetrating and lock lubricant to assist in removal.

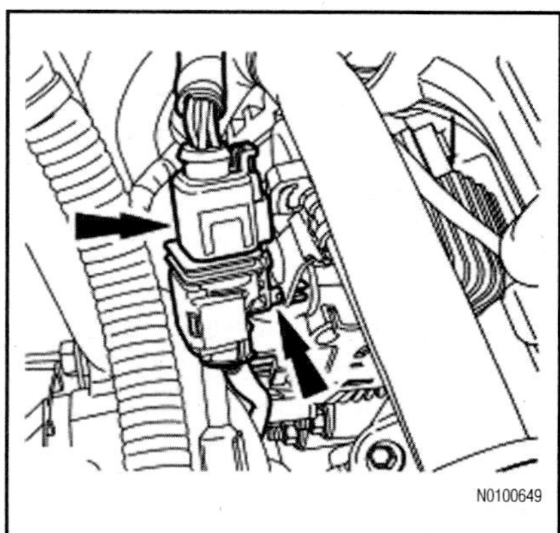

Fig. 186 LH HO2S electrical connector

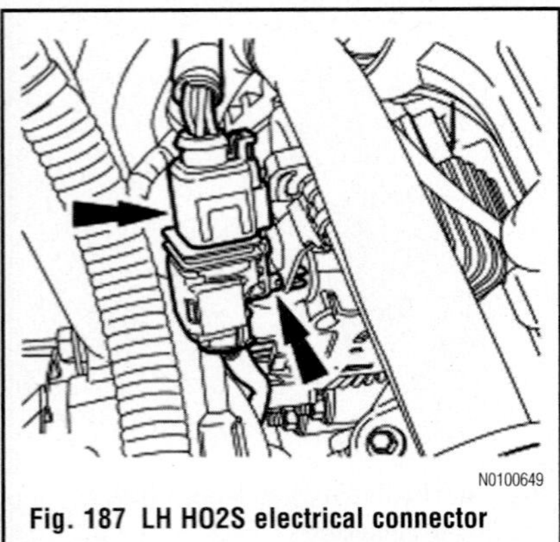
Fig. 187 LH HO2S electrical connector

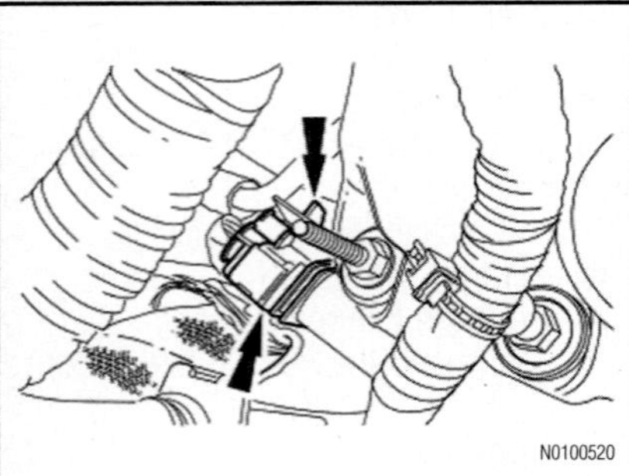
Fig. 188 Heated Oxygen Sensor (HO2S) electrical connector

7. Using the Exhaust Gas Oxygen Sensor Socket, install the HO2S.
   a. Calculate the correct torque wrench setting. Tighten the sensor to 35 ft. lbs. (48 Nm).

All Sensors Except Turbo

8. Connect the HO2S electrical connector.

LH 3.5L Turbo Sensor

9. Install the 4 retainers and the underbody shield.
10. Connect the LH HO2S electrical connector.
    a. Attach the HO2S connector retainer to the bracket.

RH 3.5L Turbo Sensor

11. Connect the Heated Oxygen Sensor (HO2S) electrical connector.
    a. Attach the HO2S electrical connector retainer to the bracket.

All RH Sensors

12. With the vehicle in NEUTRAL, lower it from the hoist.

INTAKE AIR TEMPERATURE (IAT) SENSOR

LOCATION

See Figure 189.

Refer to the accompanying illustration.

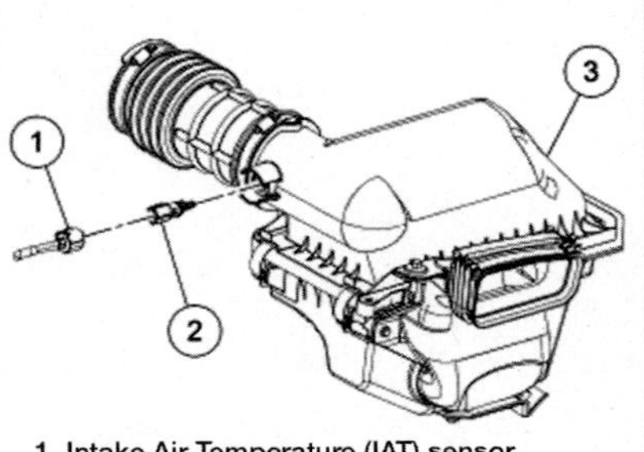

Fig. 189 Intake Air Temperature (IAT) sensor location

REMOVAL & INSTALLATION

1. Disconnect the Intake Air Temperature (IAT) sensor electrical connector.
2. Remove the IAT sensor.
   a. Lift the tab and turn the IAT sensor counterclockwise to remove.

To install:

3. Install the IAT sensor.
   a. Push the tab and turn the IAT sensor clockwise to install.
4. Connect the Intake Air Temperature (IAT) sensor electrical connector.
5. Make sure the IAT sensor tab is fully seated during installation.

KNOCK SENSOR (KS)

LOCATION

See Figures 190 and 191.

Refer to the accompanying illustrations.

REMOVAL & INSTALLATION

3.5L Engine, Except Turbo

1. Remove the thermostat housing as outlined in the Engine Cooling Section.
2. Remove the lower intake manifold as outlined in the Engine Mechanical Section.
3. Remove the coolant tube.
   a. Discard the O-ring seal.
4. Disconnect the Knock Sensor (KS) electrical connector.
5. Remove the 2 bolts and the KS.

To install:

6. Install the 2 bolts and the KS. Tighten to 15 ft. lbs. (20 Nm).
7. Connect the Knock Sensor (KS) electrical connector.
8. Install the coolant tube.
   a. Discard the O-ring seal.
9. Install the lower intake manifold as outlined in the Engine Mechanical Section.

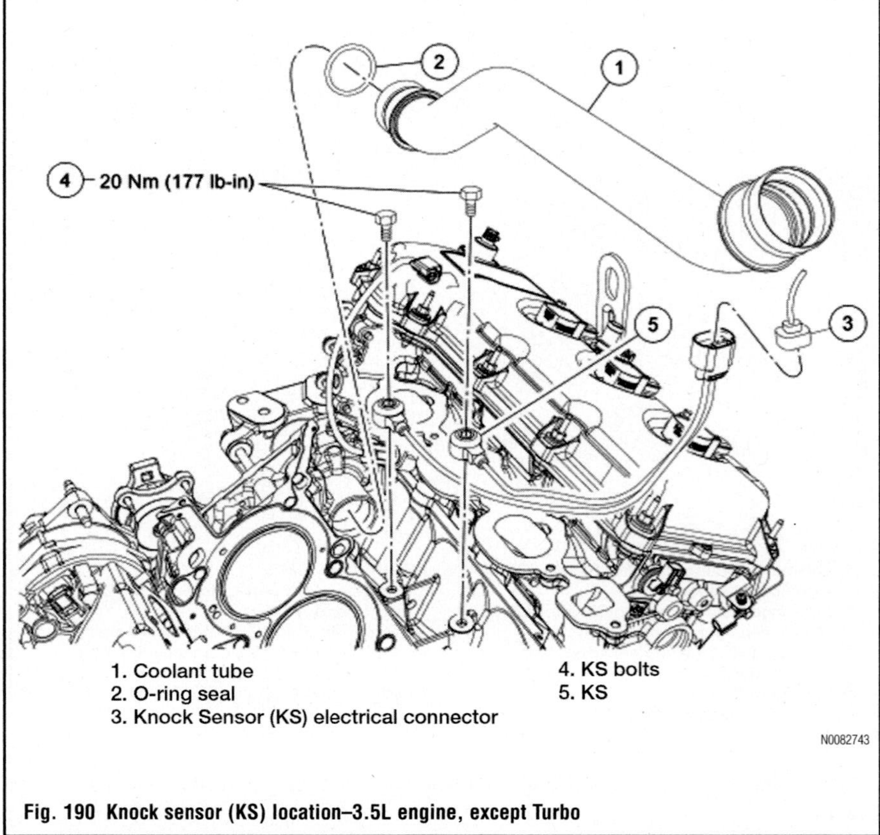

Fig. 190 Knock sensor (KS) location–3.5L engine, except Turbo

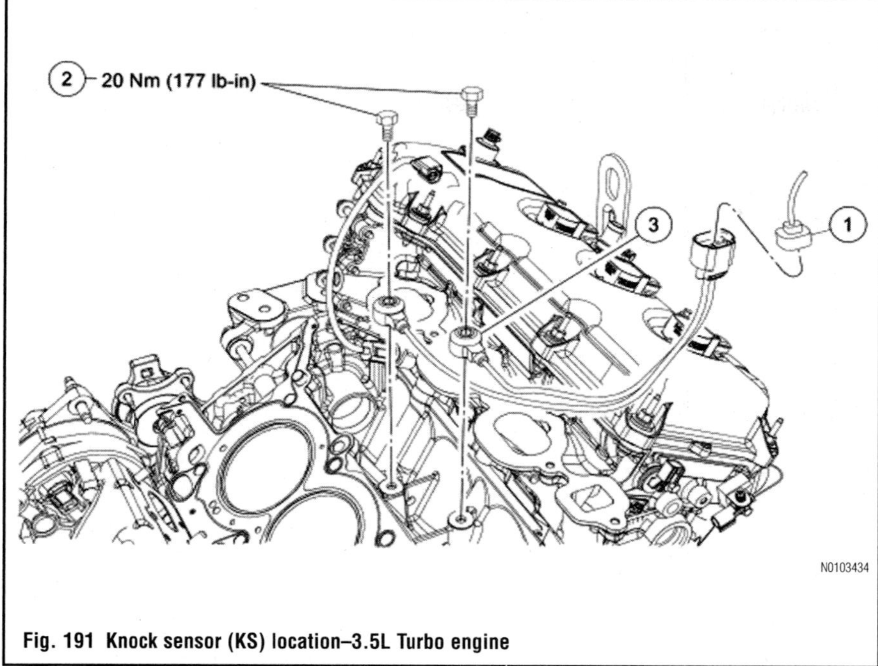

Fig. 191 Knock sensor (KS) location–3.5L Turbo engine

10. Install the thermostat housing as outlined in the Engine Cooling Section.

11. Lubricate the new O-ring seal with clean engine coolant.

3.5L Turbo Engine

1. Remove the coolant inlet pipe.
2. Remove the fuel rail.
3. Disconnect the Knock Sensor (KS) electrical connector.
4. Remove the 2 bolts and the KS.

To install:

5. Install the 2 bolts and the KS. Tighten the bolts to 15 ft. lbs. (20 Nm).
6. Connect the Knock Sensor (KS) electrical connector.
7. Install the fuel rail.
8. Install the coolant inlet pipe.

MANIFOLD ABSOLUTE PRESSURE (MAP) SENSOR & INTAKE AIR TEMPERATURE 2 (IAT2) SENSOR

REMOVAL & INSTALLATION

➡The Turbocharger Boost Pressure (TCBP)/Charge Air Cooler Temperature (CACT) sensor and the Manifold Absolute Pressure (MAP)/ Intake Air Temperature 2 (IAT2) sensor are not interchangeable.

1. Disconnect the MAP/IAT2 sensor electrical connector.
2. Remove the 2 screws and the MAP/IAT2 sensor.

To install:

3. Lubricate the MAP/IAT2 sensor O-ring seal with clean engine oil.
4. Install the MAP/IAT2 sensor and the 2 screws. Tighten the screws to 53 inch lbs. (6 Nm).
5. Connect the MAP/IAT2 sensor electrical connector.

POWERTRAIN CONTROL MODULE (PCM)

LOCATION

See Figure 192.

Refer to the accompanying illustration.

REMOVAL & INSTALLATION

➡PCM installation DOES NOT require new keys or programming of keys.

1. Retrieve the module configuration. Carry out the module configuration retrieval steps of the Programmable Module Installation (PMI) procedure.
2. Remove the cowl panel grille.
3. Disconnect the 3 PCM electrical connectors.
4. Remove the 2 nuts and the PCM.

To install:

5. Install the PCM and the 2 nuts. Tighten the nuts to 71 inch lbs. (8 Nm).
6. Connect the 3 PCM electrical connectors.
7. Install the cowl panel grille.
8. Restore the module configuration. Carry out the module configuration restore steps of the Programmable Module Installation (PMI) procedure.
9. Reprogram the Passive Anti-Theft System (PATS). Carry out the Parameter Reset procedure.
10. Using the scan tool, perform the Misfire Monitor Neutral Profile Correction procedure, following the on-screen instructions.

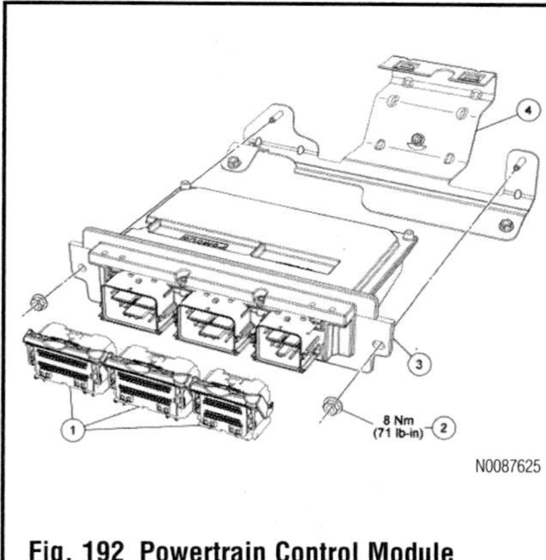

Fig. 192 Powertrain Control Module (PCM) location

THROTTLE POSITION SENSOR (TPS)

REMOVAL & INSTALLATION

See Figures 193 and 194.

1. Remove the Charge Air Cooler (CAC) outlet pipe as outlined in the Engine Mechanical Section.
2. Disconnect the Throttle Position (TP) sensor electrical connector.

⁂ WARNING

Do not put direct heat on the Throttle Position (TP) sensor or any other plastic parts because heat damage may occur. Damage may also occur if Electronic Throttle Body (ETB) temperature exceeds 248°F (120°C).

➡Do not use power tools.

3. Remove the TP sensor.
   a. Using a suitable heat gun, apply heat to the top of the Electronic Throttle Body (ETB) until the top TP sensor bolt ear reaches approximately 130°F (55°C), this should take no more than 3 minutes using an 1,100-watt heat gun. The heat gun should be about 1 inch (25.4 mm) away from the ETB .
   b. Monitor the temperature of the top TP sensor bolt ear on the ETB with a suitable temperature measuring device, such as a digital temperature laser or infrared thermometer, while heating the ETB .

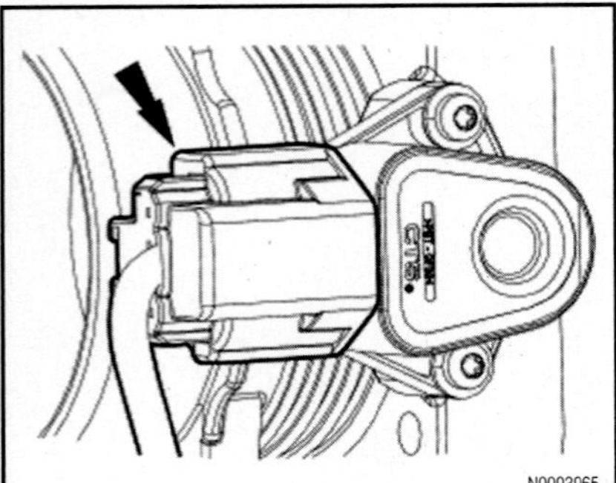

Fig. 193 Throttle Position (TP) sensor electrical connector

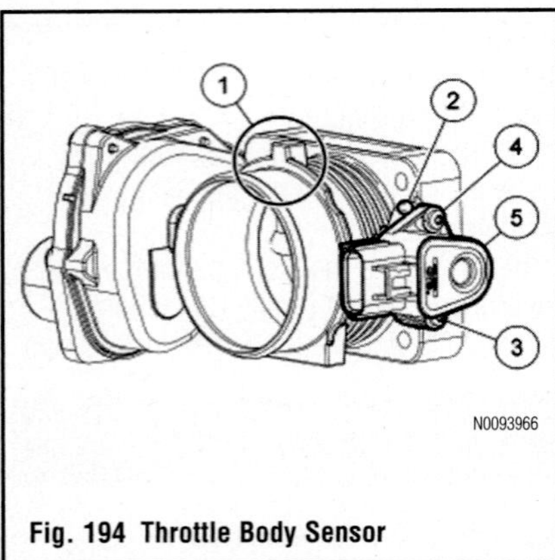

Fig. 194 Throttle Body Sensor

c. Using hand tools, quickly remove the bolt farthest from the heat source first and discard.

d. Using hand tools, remove the remaining bolt and discard.

e. Remove and discard the TP sensor.

To install:

➡When installing the new TP sensor, make sure that the radial locator tab on the TP sensor is aligned with the radial locator hole on the ETB .

➡Do not use power tools.

4. Install the new TP sensor.

a. Using hand tools, install the 2 new bolts. Tighten the bolts to 27 inch lbs. (3 Nm).

5. Connect the TP sensor electrical connector.

6. Install the CAC outlet pipe as outlined in the Engine Mechanical Section.

TURBOCHARGER BOOST PRESSURE (TCBP)/CHARGE AIR COOLER TEMPERATURE (CACT) SENSOR

LOCATION

See Figure 195.

Refer to the accompanying illustration.

REMOVAL & INSTALLATION

➡Turbocharger Boost Pressure (TCBP)/Charge Air Cooler Temperature (CACT) sensor and the Manifold Absolute Pressure (MAP)/Intake Air Temperature 2 (IAT2) sensor are not interchangeable.

1. Disconnect the TCBP/CACT sensor electrical connector.
2. Remove the 2 screws and the TCBP/CACT sensor.

To install:

3. Lubricate the TCBP/CACT sensor O-ring seal with clean engine oil.
4. Install the TCBP/CACT sensor and the 2 screws. Tighten the screws to 27 inch lbs. (3 Nm).
5. Connect the TCBP/CACT sensor electrical connector.

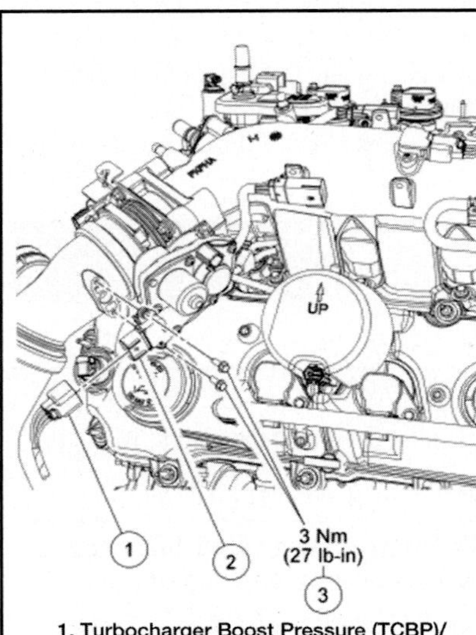

Fig. 195 Turbocharger Boost Pressure (TCBP)/Charge Air Cooler Temperature (CACT) Sensor location

VARIABLE CAMSHAFT TIMING (VCT) OIL CONTROL SOLENOID

LOCATION

See Figure 196.

Refer to the accompanying illustration.

REMOVAL & INSTALLATION

1. Remove the LH or RH valve cover as outlined in the Engine Mechanical Section.
2. Remove the bolt and the Variable Camshaft Timing (VCT) oil control solenoid.

To install:

3. Remove the bolt and the Variable Camshaft Timing (VCT) oil control solenoid. Tighten the bolt to 89 inch lbs. (10 Nm).
4. Remove the LH or RH valve cover as outlined in the Engine Mechanical Section.

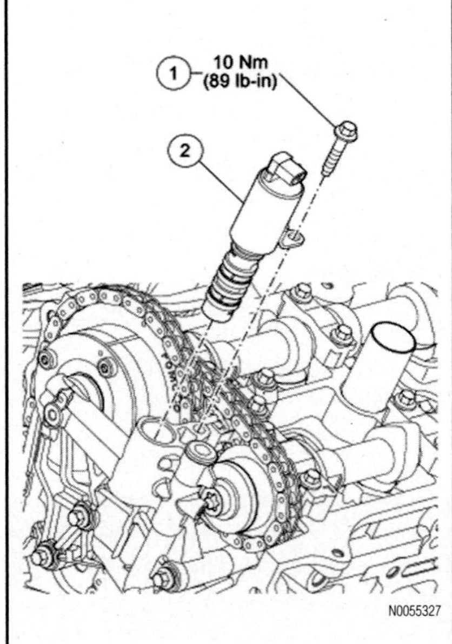

Fig. 196 Variable camshaft timing (VCT) oil control solenoid location. Variable camshaft timing (VCT) oil control solenoid bolt (1), VCT oil control solenoid (2)

FUEL SYSTEM SERVICE PRECAUTIONS

Safety is the most important factor when performing not only fuel system maintenance but any type of maintenance. Failure to conduct maintenance and repairs in a safe manner may result in serious personal injury or death. Maintenance and testing of the vehicle's fuel system components can be accomplished safely and effectively by adhering to the following rules and guidelines.

- To avoid the possibility of fire and personal injury, always disconnect the negative battery cable unless the repair or test procedure requires that battery voltage be applied.
- Always relieve the fuel system pressure prior to disconnecting any fuel system component (injector, fuel rail, pressure regulator, etc.), fitting or fuel line connection. Exercise extreme caution whenever relieving fuel system pressure to avoid exposing skin, face and eyes to fuel spray. Please be advised that fuel under pressure may penetrate the skin or any part of the body that it contacts.
- Always place a shop towel or cloth around the fitting or connection prior to loosening to absorb any excess fuel due to spillage. Ensure that all fuel spillage (should it occur) is quickly removed from engine surfaces. Ensure that all fuel soaked cloths or towels are deposited into a suitable waste container.
- Always keep a dry chemical (Class B) fire extinguisher near the work area.
- Do not allow fuel spray or fuel vapors to come into contact with a spark or open flame.
- Always use a back-up wrench when loosening and tightening fuel line connection fittings. This will prevent unnecessary stress and torsion to fuel line piping.
- Always replace worn fuel fitting O-rings with new Do not substitute fuel hose or equivalent where fuel pipe is installed.

Before servicing the vehicle, make sure to also refer to the precautions in the beginning of this section as well.

RELIEVING FUEL SYSTEM PRESSURE

See Figure 197.

CAUTION

Do not smoke, carry lighted tobacco or have an open flame of any type when working on or near any fuel-related component. Highly flammable mixtures are always present and may be ignited. Failure to follow these instructions may result in serious personal injury.

CAUTION

Do not carry personal electronic devices such as cell phones, pagers or audio equipment of any type when working on or near any fuel-related component. Highly flammable mixtures are always present and may be ignited. Failure to follow these instructions may result in serious personal injury.

CAUTION

Before working on or disconnecting any of the fuel tubes or fuel system components, relieve the fuel system pressure to prevent accidental spraying of fuel. Fuel in the fuel system remains under high pressure, even when the engine is not running. Failure to follow this instruction may result in serious personal injury.

CAUTION

When handling fuel, always observe fuel handling precautions and be prepared in the event of fuel spillage. Spilled fuel may be ignited by hot vehicle components or other ignition sources. Failure to follow these instructions may result in serious personal injury.

CAUTION

Always disconnect the battery ground cable at the battery when working on an evaporative emission (EVAP) system or fuel-related component. Highly flammable mixtures are always present and may be ignited. Failure to follow these instructions may result in serious personal injury.

➡Refer to Description and Operation, Intelligent Access with Push Button Start in the Chassis Electrical Section Passive Anti-Theft System (PATS) to review the procedures for achieving the various ignition states (ignition OFF, ignition in ACCESSORY, ignition ON and ignition START) on vehicles with this feature.

All Vehicles

➡The Fuel Pump (FP) control module is mounted to the panel behind the rear seat backrest cushion. The FP control module electrical connector can be accessed through the luggage compartment.

1. Disconnect the FP module electrical connector.
2. Start the engine and allow it to idle until it stalls.
3. Turn the ignition to the OFF position.

3.5L Turbo

➡On vehicles equipped with Gasoline Turbocharged Direct Injection (GTDI), it is necessary to release the high system fuel pressure prior to disconnecting a low pressure fuel tube quick connect coupling.

➡To release the fuel pressure in the high pressure fuel tube, wrap the flare nut with a shop towel to absorb any residual fuel pressure during the loosening of the flare nut.

4. Disconnect the high pressure fuel tube-to-fuel injection pump flare nut.

All Vehicles

5. When the fuel system service is complete, reconnect the FP control module electrical connector.

➡It may take more than one ignition cycle to pressurize the fuel system.

6. Cycle the ignition and wait 3 seconds to pressurize the fuel system.

➡Carry out an ignition ON engine OFF visual inspection for fuel leaks prior to starting the engine.

7. Start the engine and check for leaks.

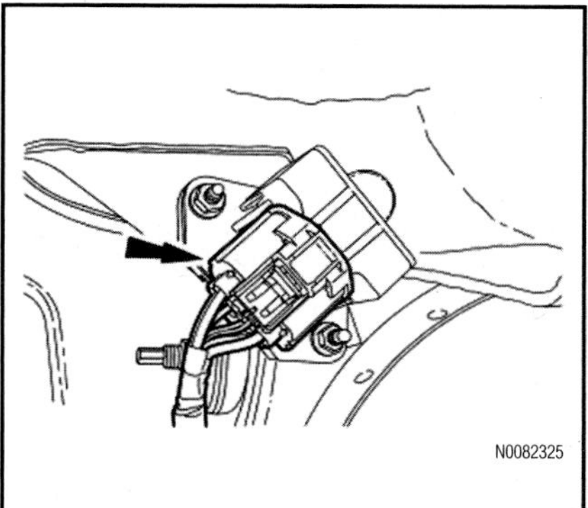

Fig. 197 FP control module electrical connector

FUEL FILTER

REMOVAL & INSTALLATION

A Lifetime Fuel Filter is used and serviced as part of the Fuel Pump (FP) module.

FUEL INJECTORS

REMOVAL & INSTALLATION

The fuel injectors are serviced with the fuel rail.

FUEL PUMP

REMOVAL & INSTALLATION

See Figures 198 and 199.

**** CAUTION**

Do not smoke, carry lighted tobacco or have an open flame of any type when working on or near any fuel-related component. Highly flammable mixtures are always present and may be ignited. Failure to follow these instructions may result in serious personal injury.

**** CAUTION**

Do not carry personal electronic devices such as cell phones, pagers or audio equipment of any type when working on or near any fuel-related component. Highly flammable mixtures are always present and may be ignited. Failure to follow these instructions may result in serious personal injury.

**** CAUTION**

Before working on or disconnecting any of the fuel tubes or fuel system components, relieve the fuel system pressure to prevent accidental spraying of fuel. Fuel in the fuel system remains under high pressure, even when the engine is not running. Failure to follow this instruction may result in serious personal injury.

**** CAUTION**

When handling fuel, always observe fuel handling precautions and be prepared in the event of fuel spillage. Spilled fuel may be ignited by hot vehicle components or other ignition sources. Failure to follow these instructions may result in serious personal injury.

**** CAUTION**

Always disconnect the battery ground cable at the battery when working on an evaporative emission (EVAP) system or fuel-related component. Highly flammable mixtures are always present and may be ignited. Failure to follow these instructions may result in serious personal injury.

All Vehicles

1. Release the fuel system pressure.
2. Disconnect the battery ground cable.
3. Remove the Fuel Pump (FP) module access cover.

➡Clean the FP module connections, couplings, flange surfaces and the immediate surrounding area of any dirt or foreign material.

4. Disconnect the FP module electrical connector.

➡Place absorbent toweling in the immediate surrounding area in case of fuel spillage.

5. Disconnect the fuel tank jumper tube-to- FP module quick connect coupling.
6. Attach the Fuel Storage Tanker tube to the FP module outlet fitting and remove one fourth (approximately 5 gallons) of the fuel from a completely full tank, lowering the fuel level below the FP module mounting flange.

All Vehicles

➡Carefully install the Fuel Tank Sender Unit Wrench to avoid damaging the FP module when removing the lock ring.

7. Install the Fuel Tank Sender Unit Wrench, remove the FP module lock ring.

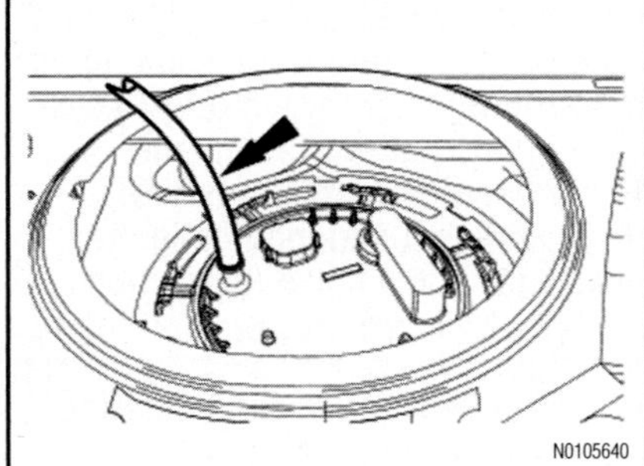

Fig. 198 Attach the Fuel Storage Tanker tube to the FP module outlet fitting and remove one fourth (approximately 5 gallons) of the fuel from a completely full tank, lowering the fuel level below the FP module mounting flange

AWD Vehicles

**** WARNING**

The Fuel Pump (FP) module must be handled carefully to avoid damage to the float arm.

8. Carefully lift the FP module out of the fuel tank allowing access and disconnect the FP module internal quick connect coupling.

All Vehicles

**** WARNING**

The Fuel Pump (FP) module must be handled carefully to avoid damage to the float arm.

➡The FP module will have residual fuel remaining internally, drain into a suitable container.

9. Completely remove the FP module from the fuel tank.

➡Inspect the surfaces of the FP module flange and fuel tank O-ring seal contact surfaces. Do not polish or adjust the O-ring seal contact area of the fuel tank flange or the fuel tank. Install a new FP module or fuel tank if the O-ring seal contact area is bent, scratched or corroded.

10. Remove and discard the FP module O-ring seal.

➡Make sure to install a new FP module O-ring seal.

➡To install, apply clean engine oil to the O-ring seal.

To install:

➡Make sure the alignment arrows on the fuel pump module and the fuel tank meet before tightening the FP module lock ring.

➡Tighten the FP lock ring until it meets the stop tabs on the fuel tank.

➡Make sure to install a new FP module O-ring seal.

➡To install, apply clean engine oil to the O-ring seal.

➡Inspect the surfaces of the FP module flange and fuel tank O-ring seal contact surfaces. Do not polish or adjust the O-ring seal contact area of the fuel tank flange or the fuel tank. Install a new FP module or fuel tank if the O-ring seal contact area is bent, scratched or corroded.

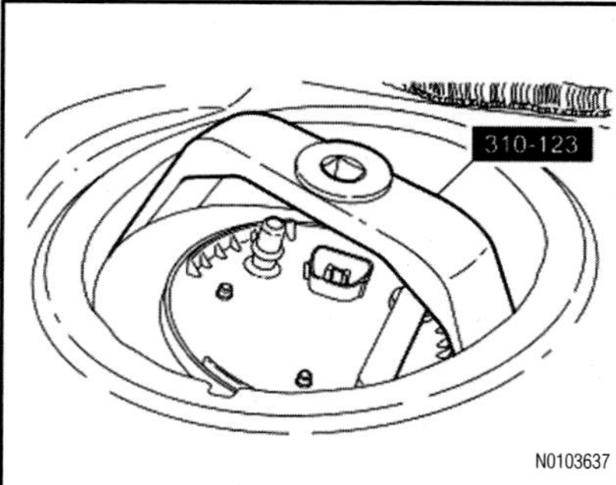

Fig. 199 Install the Fuel Tank Sender Unit Wrench, remove the FP module lock ring

Remove and discard the FP module O-ring seal.

WARNING

The Fuel Pump (FP) module must be handled carefully to avoid damage to the float arm.

➡The FP module will have residual fuel remaining internally, drain into a suitable container.

11. Completely install the FP module from the fuel tank.

WARNING

The Fuel Pump (FP) module must be handled carefully to avoid damage to the float arm.

12. Connect the FP module internal quick connect coupling, and carefully lower the FP module into the fuel tank.

➡Carefully install the Fuel Tank Sender Unit Wrench to avoid damaging the FP module when removing the lock ring.

13. Install the Fuel Tank Sender Unit Wrench, install the FP module lock ring.
14. Attach the Fuel Storage Tanker tube to the FP module outlet fitting and remove one fourth (approximately 5 gallons) of the fuel from a completely full tank, lowering the fuel level below the FP module mounting flange.

➡Place absorbent toweling in the immediate surrounding area in case of fuel spillage.

15. Disconnect the fuel tank jumper tube-to- FP module quick connect coupling.
16. Disconnect the Fuel Tank Pressure (FTP) sensor electrical connector.
17. Disconnect the fuel tank wiring harness electrical connector.

➡Clean the FP module connections, couplings, flange surfaces and the immediate surrounding area of any dirt or foreign material.

18. Disconnect the FP module electrical connector.
19. Remove the Fuel Pump (FP) module access cover.
20. Remove the rear seat lower cushion.
21. Disconnect the battery ground cable.
22. Release the fuel system pressure.

FUEL RAIL

REMOVAL & INSTALLTION

3.5L Engine, Except Turbo

CAUTION

Do not smoke, carry lighted tobacco or have an open flame of any type when working on or near any fuel-related component. Highly flammable mixtures are always present and may be ignited. Failure to follow these instructions may result in serious personal injury.

CAUTION

Before working on or disconnecting any of the fuel tubes or fuel system components, relieve the fuel system pressure to prevent accidental spraying of fuel. Fuel in the fuel system remains under high pressure, even when the engine is not running. Failure to follow this instruction may result in serious personal injury.

CAUTION

Do not carry personal electronic devices such as cell phones, pagers or audio equipment of any type when working on or near any fuel-related component. Highly flammable mixtures are always present and may be ignited. Failure to follow these instructions may result in serious personal injury.

CAUTION

Always disconnect the battery ground cable at the battery when working on an evaporative emission (EVAP) system or fuel-related component. Highly flammable mixtures are always present and may be ignited. Failure to follow these instructions may result in serious personal injury.

CAUTION

Clean all fuel residue from the engine compartment. If not removed, fuel residue may ignite when the engine is returned to operation. Failure to follow this instruction may result in serious personal injury.

1. Release the fuel system pressure.
2. Disconnect the battery ground cable.
3. Remove the upper intake manifold as outlined in the Engine Section.
4. Detach the fuel tube routing clips from the fuel rail.
5. Disconnect the fuel jumper tube-to-fuel rail spring lock coupling.
6. Disconnect the 6 fuel injector electrical connectors.
7. Remove the 4 fuel rail bolts.
8. Remove the fuel rail and injectors as an assembly.
9. Remove the 6 fuel injector clips and the 6 fuel injectors.
   a. Remove and discard the 12 fuel injector O-ring seals.

To install:

WARNING

Use O-ring seals that are made of special fuel-resistant material. The use of ordinary O-rings may cause the fuel system to leak. Do not reuse the O-ring seals.

➡The upper and lower fuel injector O-ring seals are similar in appearance, but are not interchangeable.

10. Install the new O-ring seals onto the fuel injectors and lubricate them with clean engine oil.
11. Install the 6 fuel injectors and the 6 fuel injector clips into the fuel rail.
12. Install the fuel rail and fuel injectors as an assembly.
13. Install the 4 fuel rail bolts. Tighten the bolts to 89 inch lbs. (10 Nm).
14. Connect the 6 fuel injector electrical connectors.
15. Connect the fuel jumper tube-to-fuel rail spring lock coupling. For additional information, refer to Fuel System—General Information.
16. Attach the fuel tube routing clips to the fuel rail.
17. Install the upper intake manifold as outlined in the Engine Section.
18. Connect the battery ground cable.

3.5L Turbo Engine

See Figures 200 and 201.

All Vehicles

⁂ CAUTION

Do not smoke, carry lighted tobacco or have an open flame of any type when working on or near any fuel-related component. Highly flammable mixtures are always present and may be ignited. Failure to follow these instructions may result in serious personal injury.

⁂ CAUTION

Do not carry personal electronic devices such as cell phones, pagers or audio equipment of any type when working on or near any fuel-related component. Highly flammable mixtures are always present and may be ignited. Failure to follow these instructions may result in serious personal injury.

⁂ CAUTION

When handling fuel, always observe fuel handling precautions and be prepared in the event of fuel spillage. Spilled fuel may be ignited by hot vehicle components or other ignition sources. Failure to follow these instructions may result in serious personal injury.

⁂ CAUTION

Before working on or disconnecting any of the fuel tubes or fuel system components, relieve the fuel system pressure to prevent accidental spraying of fuel. Fuel in the fuel system remains under high pressure, even when the engine is not running. Failure to follow this instruction may result in serious personal injury.

⁂ CAUTION

Clean all fuel residue from the engine compartment. If not removed, fuel residue may ignite when the engine is returned to operation. Failure to follow this instruction may result in serious personal injury.

⁂ CAUTION

Always disconnect the battery ground cable at the battery when working on an evaporative emission (EVAP) system or fuel-related component. Highly flammable mixtures are always present and may be ignited. Failure to follow these instructions may result in serious personal injury.

➡A clean working environment is essential to prevent dirt or foreign material contamination.

1. Release the fuel system pressure as outlined in this section.
2. Disconnect the battery ground cable.
3. Remove the intake manifold as outlined in the Engine Section.
4. Remove the fuel injection pump noise insulator shield.

Early Build Vehicles

5. Remove the high pressure fuel tube nut.

Late Build Vehicles

6. Remove the high pressure fuel tube bolt.

All Vehicles

➡To release the fuel pressure in the high pressure fuel tube, wrap the flare nuts with a shop towel to absorb any residual fuel pressure during the loosening of the flare nuts.

7. Loosen the 3 flare nuts and remove the high pressure fuel tube.
8. Disconnect the Fuel Rail Pressure (FRP) sensor electrical connector.

⁂ WARNING

It is very important to note the routing of the fuel charge wire harnesses on the fuel rails and index-mark the location of the tie straps prior to removal or damage may occur to the wire harnesses during installation.

➡Use compressed air and remove any dirt or foreign material from the cylinder head, block and general surrounding area of the fuel rail and injectors.

9. Cut, remove and discard the fuel charge wiring harness tie straps.

⁂ WARNING

Pull out the fuel rails in the direction of the fuel injector axis or damage may occur to the fuel injectors.

➡When removing the fuel rails, the fuel injectors may remain in the fuel rails but normally remain in the cylinder heads and require the use of a Fuel Injector Remover tool to extract.

10. Remove and discard the 6 bolts and remove the LH fuel rail.
11. Remove and discard the 6 bolts and remove the RH fuel rail.
12. Disconnect the 6 fuel injector electrical connectors and remove the 2 fuel charge wire harnesses.
13. Remove and discard the 6 upper fuel injector O-ring seals.
14. Remove and discard the 6 fuel injector clips.
15. Using the Slide Hammer and the Fuel Injector Remover, remove the 6 fuel injectors.

To install:

All Vehicles

➡A clean working environment is essential to prevent dirt or foreign material contamination.

➡Make sure to thoroughly clean any residual fuel or foreign material from the cylinder head, block and the general surrounding area of the fuel rails and injectors.

16. Using the Fuel Injector Brush, clean the fuel injector orifices.

⁂ WARNING

Do not attempt to cut the lower Teflon® seal without first pulling it away from the fuel injector or damage to the injector may occur.

➡Be very careful when removing the lower Teflon® seals, not to scratch, nick or gouge the fuel injectors.

17. Pull the lower Teflon® seal away from the injector with narrow tip pliers.
18. Carefully cut and discard the 6 lower fuel injector Teflon® seals.

➡Do not lubricate the 6 new lower Teflon® fuel injector seals.

19. Install the new lower Teflon® seals on the narrow end of the Arbor (part of the

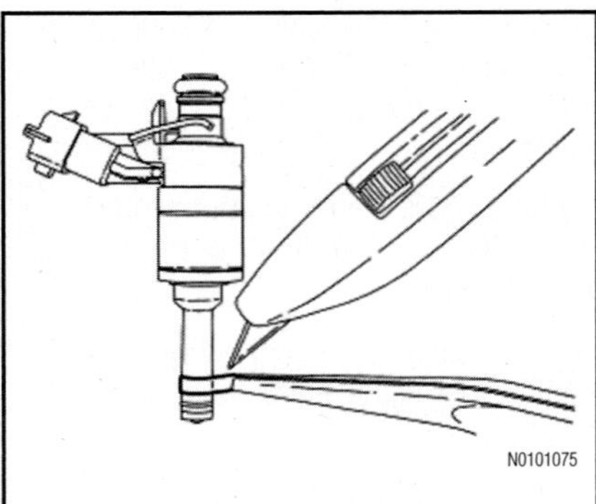

Fig. 200 Carefully cut and discard the 6 lower fuel injector Teflon® seals

Fuel Injector Seal Installer), then install the Arbor on the fuel injector tips.

⁂ WARNING

Once the Teflon® seal is installed on the Arbor, it should immediately be installed onto the fuel injector to avoid excessive expansion of the seal.

20. Using the Pusher Tool (part of the Fuel Injector Seal Installer), slide the Teflon® seals off of the Arbor and into the groove on the fuel injectors.

21. Place the Adjustment Ring (part of the Fuel Injector Seal Installer) beveled side first, over the fuel injector tip until it bottoms out against the fuel injector and turn 180 degrees.

a. After one minute, turn the Adjustment Ring back 180 degrees and remove.

⁂ WARNING

It is very important to note the routing of the fuel charge wiring harnesses on the fuel rails and index-mark the location of the tie straps prior to removal or damage may occur to the wire harnesses during installation.

22. Install the fuel charge wire harnesses and tie straps to the index-marked locations on the fuel rails. Start by attaching the first tie strap farthest down the wire harness and continue to the connector end of the harness, leaving ample slack between the fuel injectors.

23. Connect the FRP sensor electrical connector.

⁂ WARNING

Use fuel injector O-ring seals that are made of special fuel-resistant material. The use of ordinary O-ring seals may cause the fuel system to leak. Do not reuse the O-ring seals.

➡To install, apply clean engine oil to the 6 new upper fuel injector O-ring seals only. Do not lubricate the lower fuel injector Teflon® seals.

➡Inspect the fuel injector support disks and replace if necessary.

24. Install the 6 new upper fuel injector O-ring seals.

25. Install the 6 new fuel injector clips.

➡The anti-rotation device on the fuel injector has to slip into the groove of the fuel rail cup.

26. Install the 6 fuel injectors into the fuel rails and connect the 6 electrical connectors.

⁂ WARNING

It is very important to visually inspect the routing of the fuel charge wire harness to make sure that they will not be pinched or damaged between the fuel rail and the cylinder head during installation.

➡Tighten the bolts in a method that draws the fuel rail evenly to the head, preventing a rocking motion.

27. Install the 6 new bolts and the RH fuel rail assembly.

a. Push down on the fuel rail face above the injectors and begin tightening the outer bolts first and then proceed inward.

b. To install, tighten the bolts to 89 inch lbs. (10 Nm), and then tighten an additional 45 degrees.

⁂ WARNING

It is very important to visually inspect the routing of the fuel charge wire harness to make sure that they will not be pinched or damaged between the fuel rail and the cylinder head during installation.

➡Tighten the bolts in a method that draws the fuel rail evenly to the head, preventing a rocking motion.

28. Install the 6 new bolts and the LH fuel rail assembly.

a. Push down on the fuel rail face above the injectors and begin tightening the outer bolts first and proceed inward.

b. To install, tighten the bolts to 89 inch lbs. (10 Nm), and then tighten an additional 45 degrees.

➡To install, apply clean engine oil to the threads of the 3 high-pressure fuel tube flare nuts.

29. Install the high-pressure fuel tube and tighten the 3 flare nuts. Tighten the nuts to 22 ft. lbs. (30 Nm).

Early Build Vehicles

30. Install the high-pressure fuel tube nut. Tighten the nut to 53 inch lbs. (6 Nm).

Late Build Vehicles

31. Install the high-pressure fuel tube bolt. Tighten the bolt to 53 inch lbs. (6 Nm).

All Vehicles

32. Install the fuel injection pump noise insulator shield.

33. Install the intake manifold as outlined in the Engine Mechanical Section.

34. Connect the battery ground cable.

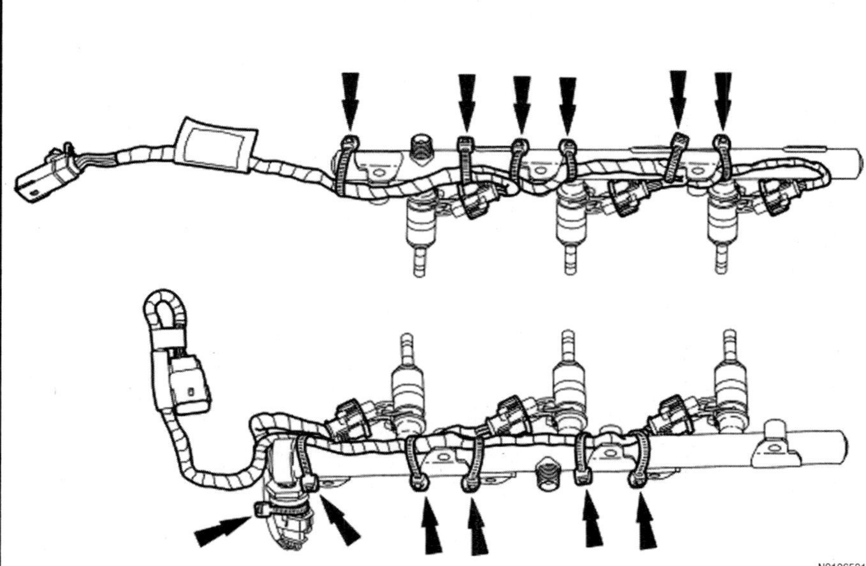

Fig. 201 Install the fuel charge wire harnesses and tie straps to the index-marked locations on the fuel rails. Start by attaching the first tie strap farthest down the wire harness and continue to the connector end of the harness, leaving ample slack between the fuel injectors

FUEL TANK

DRAINING

See Figures 202 through 208.

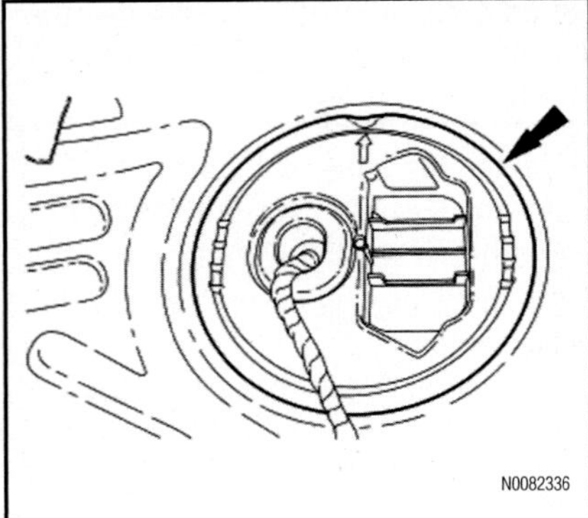

Fig. 202 Remove the Fuel Pump (FP) module access cover

CAUTION

Do not smoke, carry lighted tobacco or have an open flame of any type when working on or near any fuel-related component. Highly flammable mixtures are always present and may be ignited. Failure to follow these instructions may result in serious personal injury.

CAUTION

Do not carry personal electronic devices such as cell phones, pagers or audio equipment of any type when working on or near any fuel-related component. Highly flammable mixtures are always present and may be ignited. Failure to follow these instructions may result in serious personal injury.

CAUTION

When handling fuel, always observe fuel handling precautions and be prepared in the event of fuel spillage. Spilled fuel may be ignited by hot vehicle components or other ignition sources. Failure to follow these instructions may result in serious personal injury.

CAUTION

Always disconnect the battery ground cable at the battery when working on an evaporative emission (EVAP) system or fuel-related component. Highly flammable mixtures are always present and may be ignited. Failure to follow these instructions may result in serious personal injury.

CAUTION

Before working on or disconnecting any of the fuel tubes or fuel system components, relieve the fuel system pressure to prevent accidental spraying of fuel. Fuel in the fuel system remains under high pressure, even when the engine is not running. Failure to follow this instruction may result in serious personal injury.

1. Release the fuel system pressure as outlined in this section.
2. Disconnect the battery ground cable.
3. Remove the Fuel Pump (FP) module access cover.

➡Clean the FP module connections, couplings, flange surfaces and the immediate surrounding area of any dirt or foreign material.

➡Place absorbent toweling in the immediate surrounding area in case of fuel spillage.

4. Disconnect the fuel tank jumper tube-to- FP module quick connect coupling.
5. Attach the Fuel Storage Tanker tube to the FP module outlet fitting and remove one fourth (approximately 5 gallons) of the fuel from a completely full tank, lowering the fuel level below the fuel level sensor flange.
6. Remove the fuel level sensor access cover.

➡Clean the fuel level sensor connections, couplings, flange surfaces and the immediate surrounding area of any dirt or foreign material.

7. Disconnect the fuel level sensor electrical connector.
8. Disconnect the 2 fuel vapor tube-to-fuel level sensor quick connect couplings.

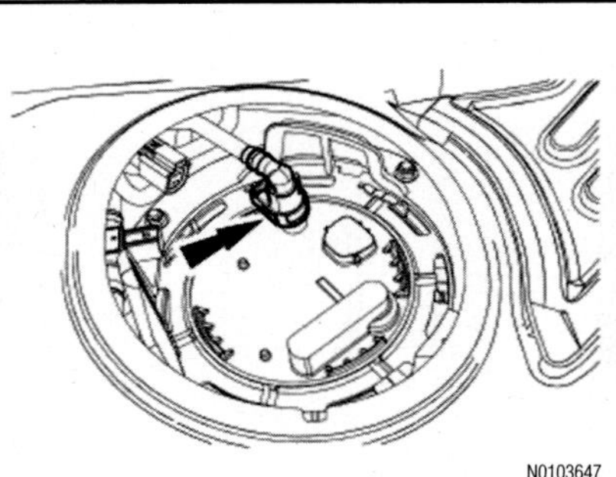

Fig. 203 Disconnect the fuel tank jumper tube-to- FP module quick connect coupling

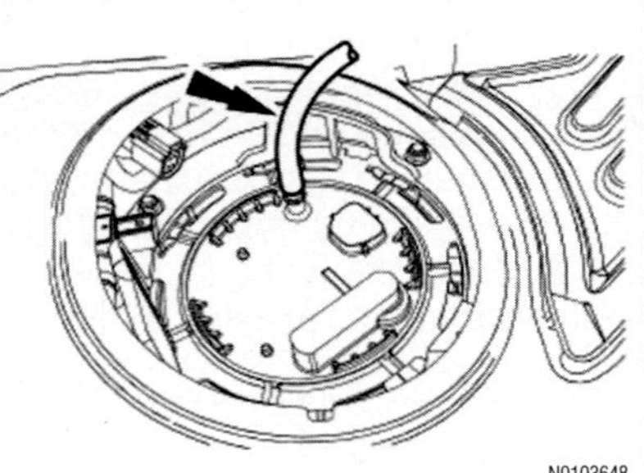

Fig. 204 Attach the Fuel Storage Tanker tube to the FP module outlet fitting and remove one fourth (approximately 5 gallons) of the fuel from a completely full tank, lowering the fuel level below the fuel level sensor flange

WARNING

Carefully install the Fuel Tank Sender Unit Wrench to avoid damaging the fuel level sensor when removing the lock ring.

➡Place absorbent toweling in the immediate surrounding area in case of fuel spillage.

➡Make sure to install a new fuel level sensor O-ring seal.

9. Install the Fuel Tank Sender Unit Wrench and remove the fuel level sensor lock ring.
10. Position the fuel level sensor aside, insert the tube from the Fuel Storage Tanker into the fuel level sensor aperture and remove as much of the remaining fuel as possible from the fuel tank.

REMOVAL & INSTALLATION

CAUTION

Do not smoke, carry lighted tobacco or have an open flame of any type when working on or near any fuel-related component. Highly flammable mixtures are always present and may be ignited. Failure to follow these instructions may result in serious personal injury.

CAUTION

Do not carry personal electronic devices such as cell phones, pagers or audio equipment of any type when working on or near any fuel-related component. Highly flammable mix-

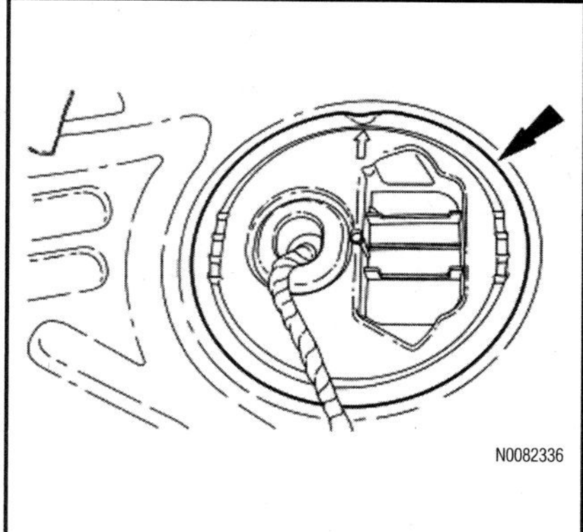

Fig. 205 Remove the fuel level sensor access cover

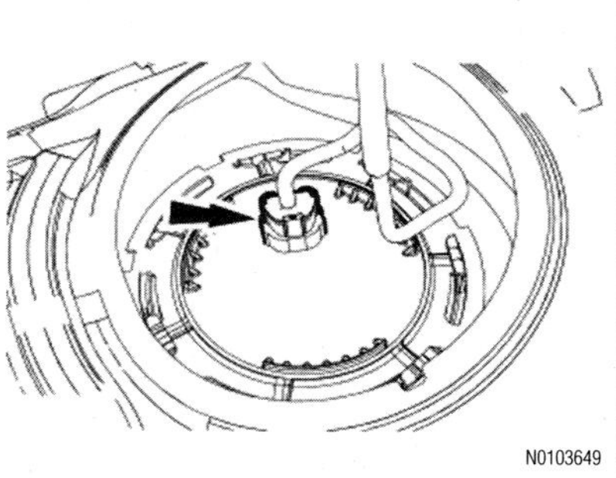

N0103649

Fig. 206 Disconnect the fuel level sensor electrical connector

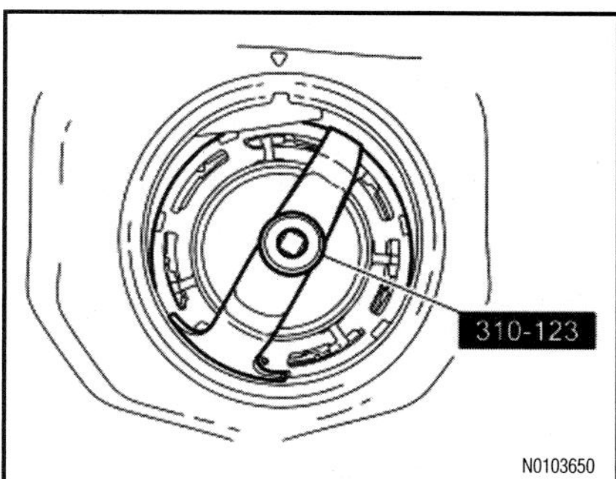

Fig. 207 Install the Fuel Tank Sender Unit Wrench and remove the fuel level sensor lock ring

tures are always present and may be ignited. Failure to follow these instructions may result in serious personal injury.

CAUTION

Before working on or disconnecting any of the fuel tubes or fuel system components, relieve the fuel system pressure to prevent accidental spraying of fuel. Fuel in the fuel system remains under high pressure, even when the engine is not running. Failure to follow this instruction may result in serious personal injury.

CAUTION

When handling fuel, always observe fuel handling precautions and be prepared in the event of fuel spillage. Spilled fuel may be ignited by hot vehicle components or other ignition sources. Failure to follow these instructions may result in serious personal injury.

CAUTION

Always disconnect the battery ground cable at the battery when working on an evaporative emission (EVAP) system or fuel-related component. Highly flammable mixtures are always present and may be ignited. Failure to follow these instructions may result in serious personal injury.

1. With the vehicle in NEUTRAL, position it on a hoist.
2. Remove the muffler and tail pipe.
3. Drain the fuel tank as outlined in the section.
4. Remove the driveshaft as outlined in the Drive Train Section.
5. Remove the Evaporative Emission (EVAP) canister.

➡Some residual fuel may remain in the fuel tank filler pipe after draining the fuel tank. Carefully drain any residual fuel into a suitable container.

6. Release the clamp and remove the fuel tank filler pipe hose from the fuel tank.
7. Disconnect the fuel vapor tube assembly-to-fuel tank filler pipe recirculation tube quick connect coupling as outlined in this section.
8. Disconnect the fuel tank jumper tube-to-fuel tube quick connect coupling as outlined in this section.
9. Release the fresh air hose vent cap and pin-type retainer from the body.
10. Position the Powertrain Lift under the fuel tank.
11. Loosen the 2 rear fuel tank strap bolts.
    a. Calculate the correct torque wrench setting for the following torque.
12. Remove the 2 front fuel tank strap bolts.

➡Do not bend or distort the fuel tank straps.

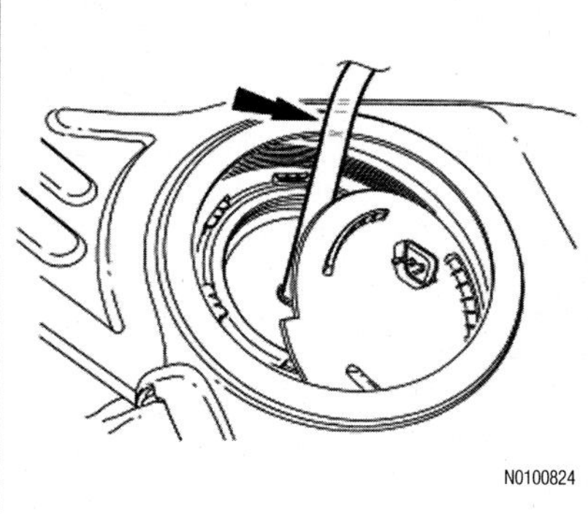

Fig. 208 Position the fuel level sensor aside, insert the tube from the Fuel Storage Tanker into the fuel level sensor aperture and remove as much of the remaining fuel as possible from the fuel tank

13. Release the 2 straps from the fuel tank and carefully position aside.
14. Carefully lower and remove the fuel tank from the vehicle.

To install:

CAUTION

Do not smoke, carry lighted tobacco or have an open flame of any type when working on or near any fuel-related component. Highly flammable mixtures are always present and may be ignited. Failure to follow these instructions may result in serious personal injury.

CAUTION

Do not carry personal electronic devices such as cell phones, pagers or audio equipment of any type when working on or near any fuel-related component. Highly flammable mixtures are always present and may be ignited. Failure to follow these instructions may result in serious personal injury.

CAUTION

Before working on or disconnecting any of the fuel tubes or fuel system components, relieve the fuel system pressure to prevent accidental spraying of fuel. Fuel in the fuel system remains under high pressure, even when the engine is not running. Failure to follow this instruction may result in serious personal injury.

⁂ CAUTION

When handling fuel, always observe fuel handling precautions and be prepared in the event of fuel spillage. Spilled fuel may be ignited by hot vehicle components or other ignition sources. Failure to follow these instructions may result in serious personal injury.

⁂ CAUTION

Always disconnect the battery ground cable at the battery when working on an evaporative emission (EVAP) system or fuel-related component. Highly flammable mixtures are always present and may be ignited. Failure to follow these instructions may result in serious personal injury.

15. Carefully lower and remove the fuel tank from the vehicle.

➡Do not bend or distort the fuel tank straps.

16. Engage the 2 straps to the fuel tank and carefully reposition.
17. Install the 2 front fuel tank strap bolts. Tighten the bolts to 26 ft. lbs. (35 Nm).
18. Tighten the 2 rear fuel tank strap bolts.
    a. Calculate the correct torque wrench setting for the following torque. To install, use a torque adapter and tighten the bolts to 26 ft. lbs. (35 Nm).
19. Position the Powertrain Lift under the fuel tank.
20. Engage the fresh air hose vent cap and pin-type retainer to the body.
21. Connect the fuel tank jumper tube-to-fuel tube quick connect coupling as outlined in this section.
22. Connect the fuel vapor tube assembly-to-fuel tank filler pipe recirculation tube quick connect coupling as outlined in this section.

➡Some residual fuel may remain in the fuel tank filler pipe after draining the fuel tank. Carefully drain any residual fuel into a suitable container.

23. Engage the clamp and install the fuel tank filler pipe hose to the fuel tank. Tighten the clamp to 27 inch lbs. (3 Nm).
24. Install the Evaporative Emission (EVAP) canister.
25. Install the driveshaft as outlined in the Drive Train Section.
26. Fill the fuel tank as outlined in the section.
27. Install the muffler and tail pipe.
28. With the vehicle in NEUTRAL, lower the vehicle from the hoist.

THROTTLE BODY

REMOVAL & INSTALLATION

3.5L Engine, Except Turbo

See Figure 209.

1. Remove the Air Cleaner (ACL) outlet pipe. For additional information, refer to Intake Air Distribution and Filtering.
2. Disconnect the electronic throttle control electrical connector.
3. Remove the 4 bolts and the Throttle Body (TB).
    a. Discard the TB gasket.

To install:

➡Install a new TB gasket

4. Install the 4 bolts and the Throttle Body (TB). Tighten the bolts to 89 inch lbs. (10 Nm).
5. Connect the electronic throttle control electrical connector.
6. Install the Air Cleaner (ACL) outlet pipe.

3.5L Turbo Engine

See Figure 210.

1. Disconnect the Throttle Position (TP) sensor electrical connector.
2. Disconnect the Throttle Actuator Control (TAC) electrical connector.
3. Loosen the clamp and disconnect the Charge Air Cooler (CAC) outlet pipe-to-Throttle Body (TB).
4. Remove the 4 bolts, the TB and the TP sensor shield bracket.
    a. Discard the TB gasket.

To install:

➡Install a new TB gasket.

5. Install the 4 bolts, the TB and the TP sensor shield bracket. Tighten the bolts to 89 inch lbs. (10 Nm).
6. Tighten the clamp and connect the Charge Air Cooler (CAC) outlet pipe-to-Throttle Body (TB). Tighten the clamp to 44 inch lbs. (5 Nm).
7. Connect the Throttle Actuator Control (TAC) electrical connector.
8. Connect the Throttle Position (TP) sensor electrical connector.

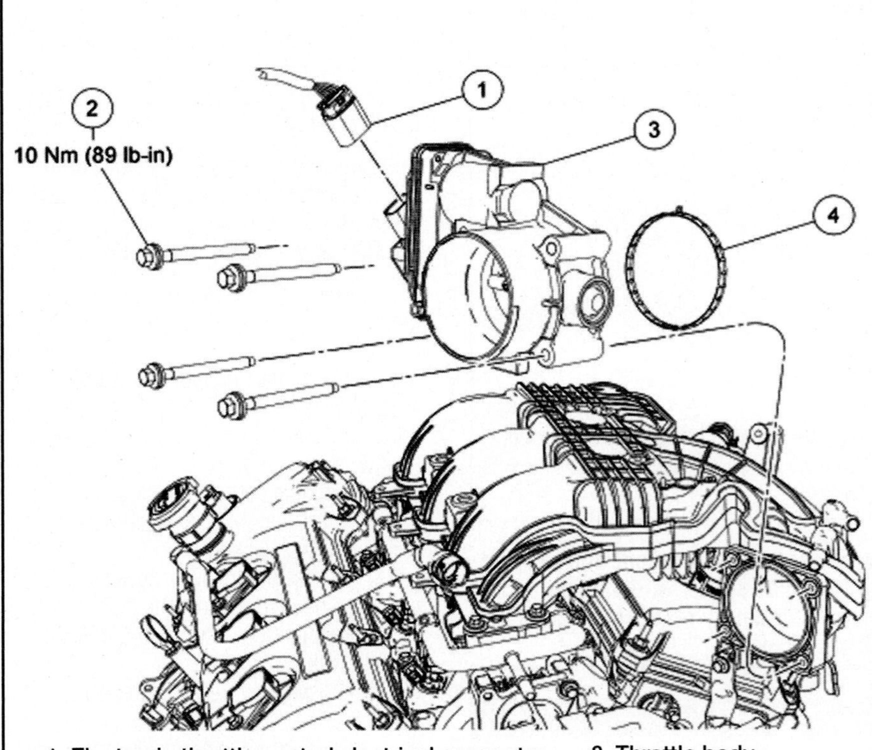

Fig. 209 Throttle Body—3.5L engine, except Turbo

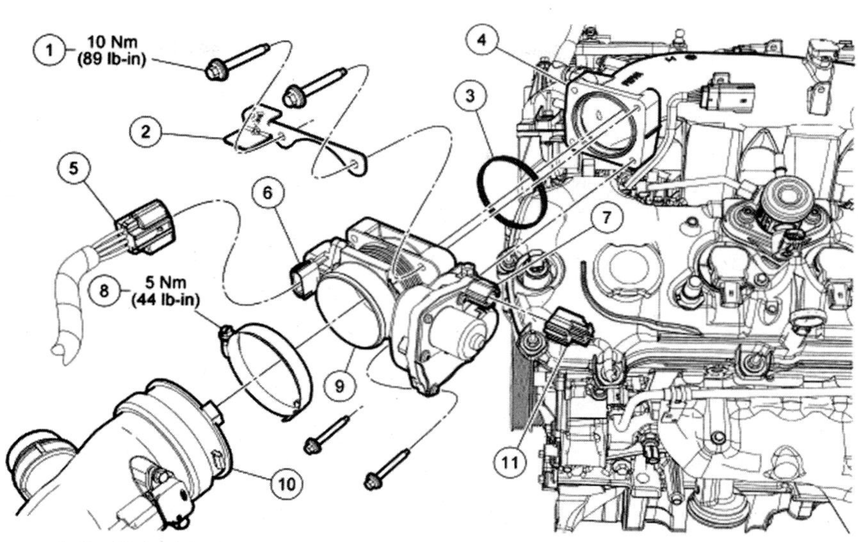

Fig. 210 Throttle Body–3.5L Turbo engine

HEATING & AIR CONDITIONING SYSTEM

BLOWER MOTOR

REMOVAL & INSTALLATION

See Figure 211.

1. Detach the RH scuff plate trim panel from the RH lower A-pillar trim panel.
2. Remove the RH lower A-pillar trim panel.
3. Remove the 2 RH lower instrument panel insulator pin-type retainers and the RH lower instrument panel insulator.
4. Disconnect the blower motor electrical connector.
5. Depress the 2 retaining tabs and detach the blower motor vent tube from the heater core and evaporator core housing.

➡The blower motor vent tube must be completely detached from the heater core and evaporator core housing to allow the blower motor to be rotated.

6. Rotate the blower motor counterclockwise to detach it from the heater core and evaporator core housing and remove the blower motor.

To install:

7. Install the blower motor, and rotate the blower motor clockwise to attach it to the heater core and evaporator core housing.

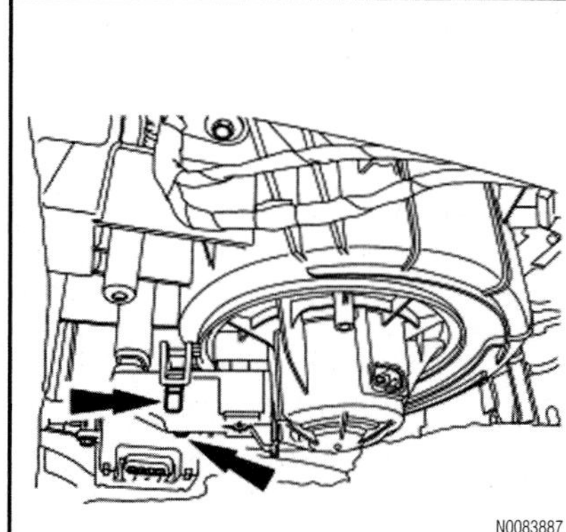

Fig. 211 Depress the 2 retaining tabs and detach the blower motor vent tube from the heater core and evaporator core housing

8. Position the tube upward to attach it to the heater core and evaporator core housing, and attach the 2 blower motor vent tube clips.
9. Connect the blower motor electrical connector.
10. Install the 2 RH lower instrument panel insulator, and install the 3 RH lower instrument panel insulator screws.
11. Install the RH lower A-pillar trim panel.
12. Attach the RH scuff plate trim panel to the RH lower A-pillar trim panel.

HEATER CORE

REMOVAL & INSTALLATION

➡If a heater core leak is suspected, the heater core must be pressure leak tested before it is removed from the vehicle.

1. Remove the heater core and evaporator core housing.
2. Remove the dash panel seal.

3. Remove the 3 heater core tube support bracket screws and heater core tube support bracket.
4. Remove the 10 plenum chamber screws and separate the heater core and evaporator housing.
5. Remove the heater core.

To install:

6. Install the heater core.
7. Install the 10 plenum chamber screws and separate the heater core and evaporator housing.
8. Install the 3 heater core tube support bracket screws and heater core tube support bracket.
9. Install the dash panel seal.
10. Install the heater core and evaporator core housing.

STEERING

POWER STEERING GEAR

REMOVAL & INSTALLATION

Electronic Power Assist Steering (EPAS)

See Figures 212 and 213.

➡Use a steering wheel holding device (such as Hunter® 28-75-1 or equivalent).

1. Using a suitable holding device, hold the steering wheel in the straight-ahead position.
2. Remove the wheels and tires.

⁂ WARNING

Do not allow the steering column to rotate while the steering column shaft is disconnected from the steering gear or damage to the clockspring may occur. If there is evidence that the steering column has rotated, the clockspring must be removed and recentered.

3. Remove the bolt and disconnect the steering column shaft from the steering gear.
   a. Discard the bolt.
4. Remove the 2 stabilizer bar link upper nuts.
   a. Discard the nuts.
5. Remove the 2 outer tie-rod end nuts and separate the tie-rod ends from the wheel knuckle.
6. Remove the 4 retainers and the underbody shield.
7. Remove the RH and LH exhaust flexible pipes.
8. Remove the 2 front and rear engine roll restrictor bolts.
9. Position the Powertrain Lift Table under the subframe.
10. Remove the 2 front subframe rearward bolts, the 4 support bracket bolts and the 2 subframe support brackets.
    a. Loosen the 2 front subframe forward bolts.
11. Lower the subframe to gain access to the steering gear.
12. Remove the wiring harness bracket bolt.
13. Disconnect the 2 Electronic Power Assist Steering (EPAS) electrical connectors and the wiring retainer.

➡Position the stabilizer bar to the full up position.

14. Remove the 2 steering gear bolts.
    a. Remove the steering gear from the RH side of the vehicle.

To install:

15. Position the steering gear and install the 2 bolts. Tighten the bolts to 122 ft. lbs. (165 Nm).
16. Connect the 2 EPAS electrical connectors and the wiring retainer.

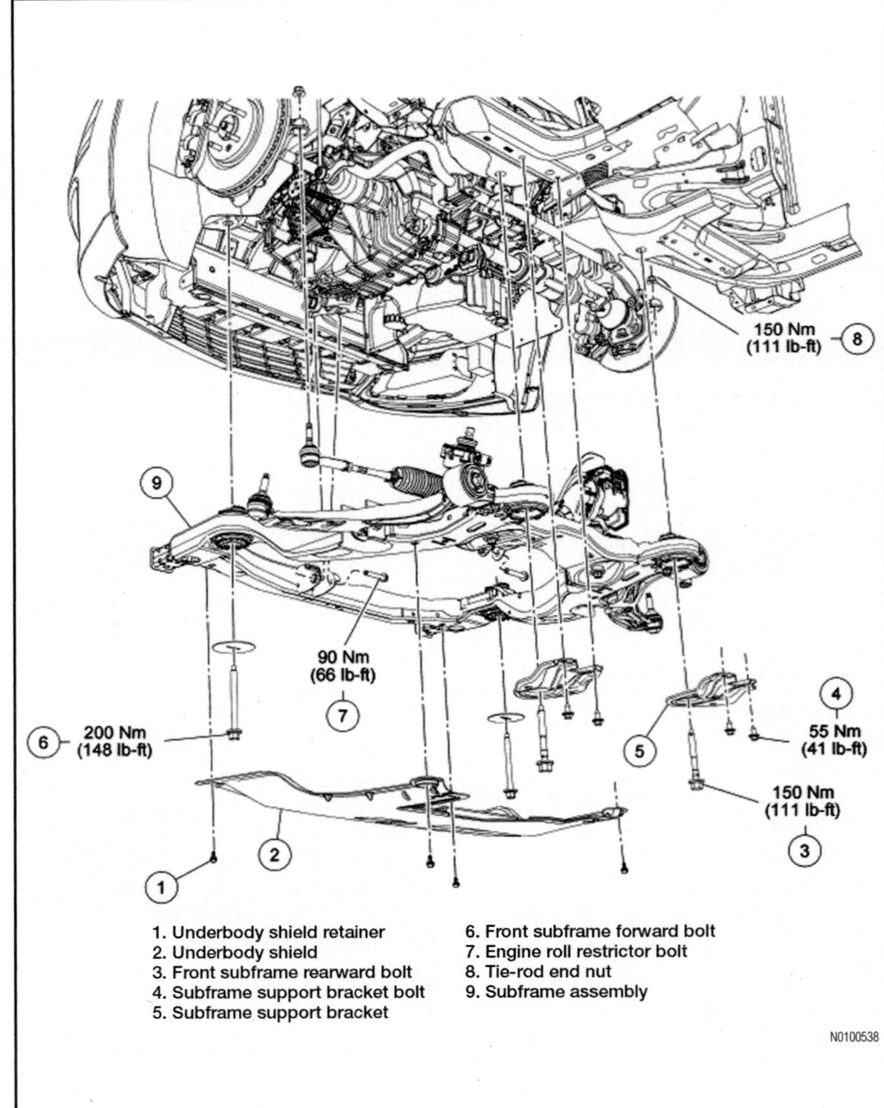

Fig. 212 Electronic Power Assist Steering (EPAS) (1 of 2)

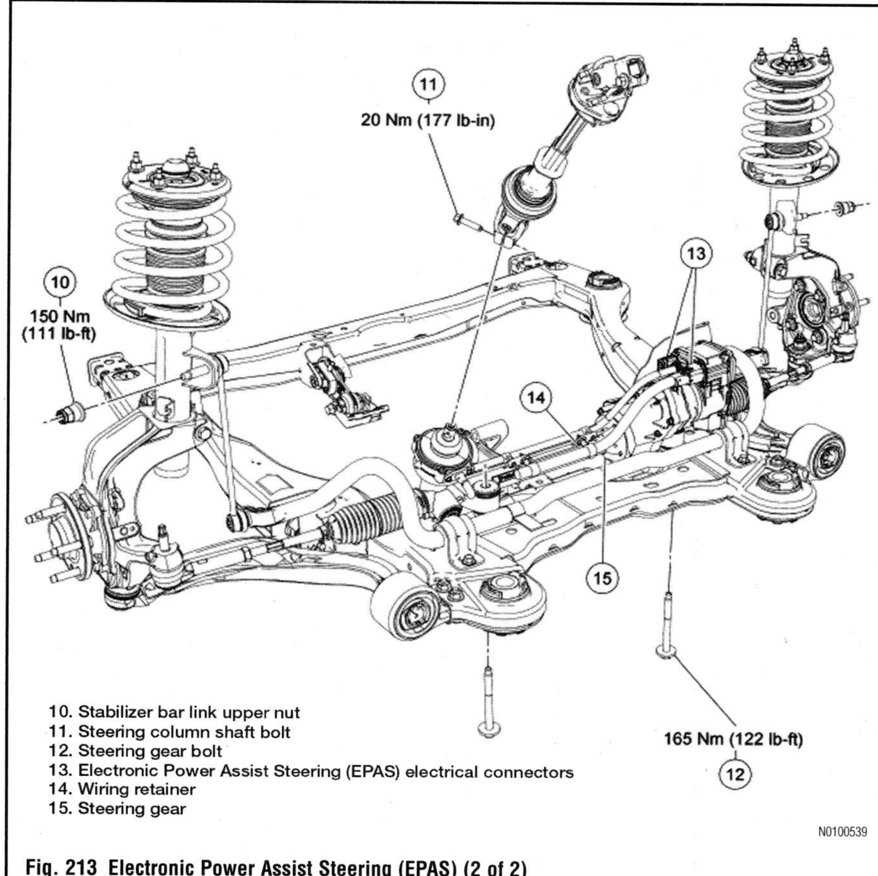

Fig. 213 Electronic Power Assist Steering (EPAS) (2 of 2)

17. Position the wiring harness bracket and install the bolt. Tighten the bolt to 80 inch lbs. (9 Nm).
18. Raise the subframe.
19. Position the 2 subframe support brackets and install the 4 bolts finger-tight.
20. Install the 2 front subframe rearward bolts. Tighten the rearward bolts to 111 ft. lbs. (150 Nm), and tighten the forward bolts to 148 ft. lbs. (200 Nm).
21. Tighten the 4 subframe support bracket bolts to 41 ft. lbs. (55 Nm).
22. Install the 2 front and rear engine roll restrictor bolts. Tighten the bolts to 66 ft. lbs. (90 Nm).
23. Install the RH and LH exhaust flexible pipes.
24. Position the underbody shield and install the 4 retainers.
25. Position the 2 outer tie-rod ends and install the nuts. Tighten the nuts to 111 ft. lbs. (150 Nm).
26. Connect the stabilizer bar links and install the 2 nuts. Tighten the new nuts to 111 ft. lbs. (150 Nm).

WARNING

Do not allow the steering column to rotate while the steering column shaft is disconnected from the steering gear or damage to the clockspring may occur. If there is evidence that the steering column has rotated, the clockspring must be removed and recentered as outlined in the Chassis Electrical Section.

27. With the locator on the input shaft correctly aligned, connect the steering column shaft to the steering gear and install the new bolt. Tighten the bolt to 15 ft. lbs. (20 Nm).
28. Install the wheels and tires.

Hydraulic Power Assist Steering (HPAS)

See Figures 214 and 215.

All Vehicles

WARNING

When repairing the power steering system, care should be taken to prevent the entry of foreign material or failure of the power steering components may occur.

➡Use a steering wheel holding device (such as Hunter® 28-75-1 or equivalent).

1. Using a suitable holding device, hold the steering wheel in the straight-ahead position.
2. Remove the wheels and tires.

➡The hex-holding feature can be used to prevent turning of the stud while removing the nut.

3. Remove the 2 tie-rod end nuts and disconnect the tie-rod ends from the wheel knuckles.
4. Remove the pressure line bracket-to-steering gear bolt.

WARNING

Whenever the power steering lines are disconnected, new O-ring seals must be installed. Make sure that the O-ring seals are installed in the correct order or a fluid leak may occur.

5. Remove the power steering line clamp plate bolt.
   a. Rotate the clamp plate and disconnect the pressure and return lines from the steering gear.
   b. Discard the 2 O-ring seals.

WARNING

Do not allow the steering column shaft to rotate while the lower shaft is disconnected or damage to the clockspring may result. If there is evidence that the shaft has rotated, the clockspring must be removed and recentered.

6. Remove the steering column shaft-to-steering gear bolt and disconnect the shaft from the steering gear.
   a. Discard the bolt.

➡The hex-holding feature can be used to prevent turning of the stud while removing the nut.

7. Remove and discard the 2 stabilizer bar link upper nuts.
   a. Position the stabilizer bar and links upward.

All-Wheel Drive (AWD) Vehicles

8. Remove and discard the 4 stabilizer bar bracket bolts.
   a. Position the stabilizer bar and links upward.

All Vehicles

9. If equipped, remove the steering gear heat shield-to-subframe pushpin.
10. Remove and discard the 2 steering gear nuts and bolts.
    a. Stage 1: Tighten to 30 ft. lbs. (40 Nm).

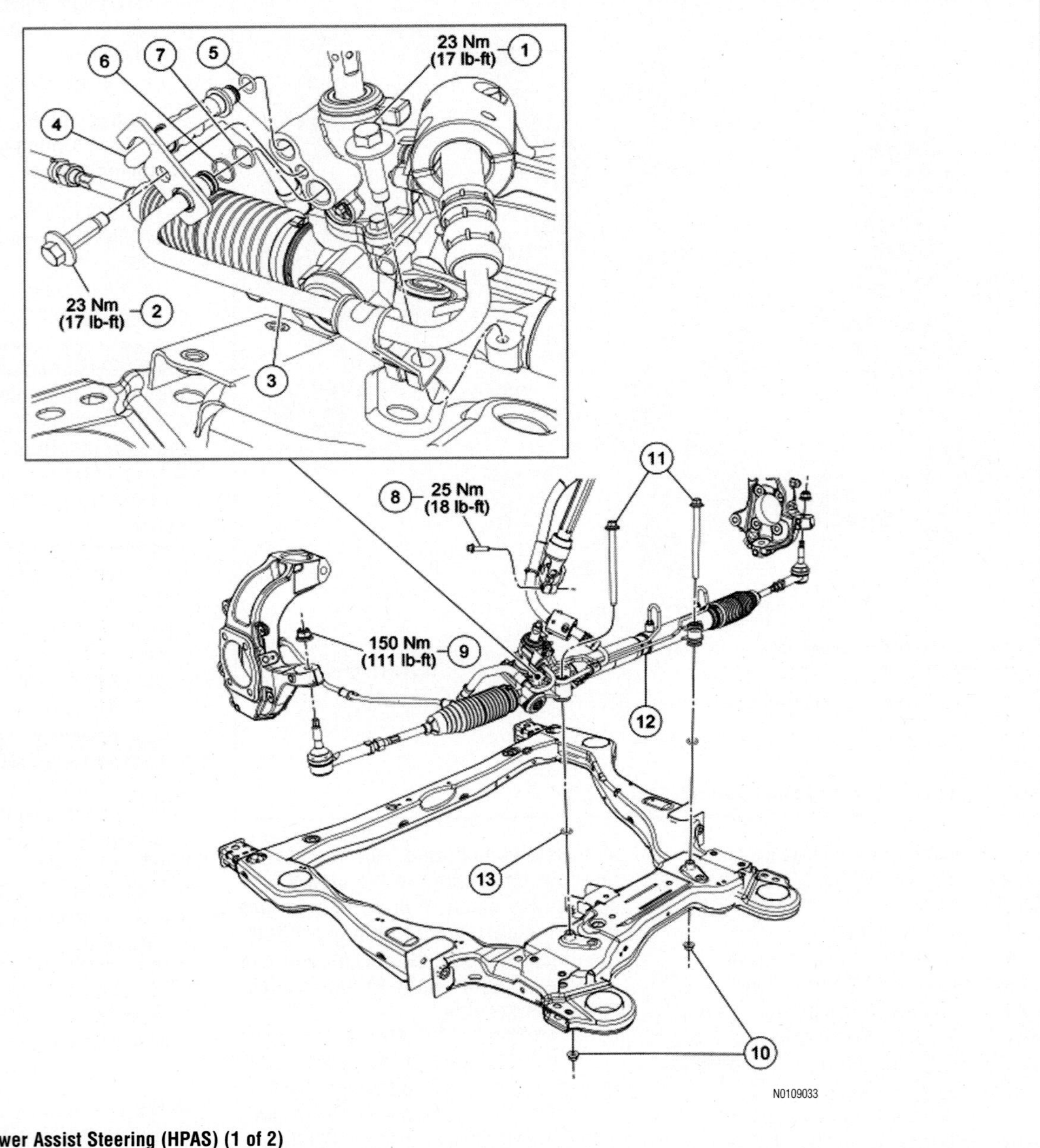

Fig. 214 Hydraulic Power Assist Steering (HPAS) (1 of 2)

b. Stage 2: Tighten an additional 180 degrees.

11. Remove the steering gear from the left side of the vehicle.

➡**NOTE: Whenever the power steering lines are disconnected, new O-ring seals must be installed.**

To install:

All Vehicles

➡**Whenever the power steering lines are disconnected, new O-ring seals must be installed.**

12. Install the steering gear to the left side of the vehicle.

13. Install and discard the 2 steering gear nuts and bolts.

a. To install, tighten the 2 new nuts and bolts in 2 stages:

b. Stage 1: Tighten to 30 ft. lbs. (40 Nm).

c. Stage 2: Tighten an additional 180 degrees.

14. If equipped, install the steering gear heat shield-to-subframe pushpin.

All-Wheel Drive (AWD) Vehicles

15. Install and discard the 4 stabilizer bar bracket bolts. Tighten the 4 new bolts to 41 ft. lbs. (55 Nm).

a. Position the stabilizer bar and links upward.

All Vehicles

➡**The hex-holding feature can be used to prevent turning of the stud while removing the nut.**

16. Install the 2 new stabilizer bar link upper nuts. Tighten the 2 new nuts to 111 ft. lbs. (150 Nm).

a. Position the stabilizer bar and links upward.

WARNING

Do not allow the steering column shaft to rotate while the lower shaft is disconnected or damage to the clockspring may result. If there is

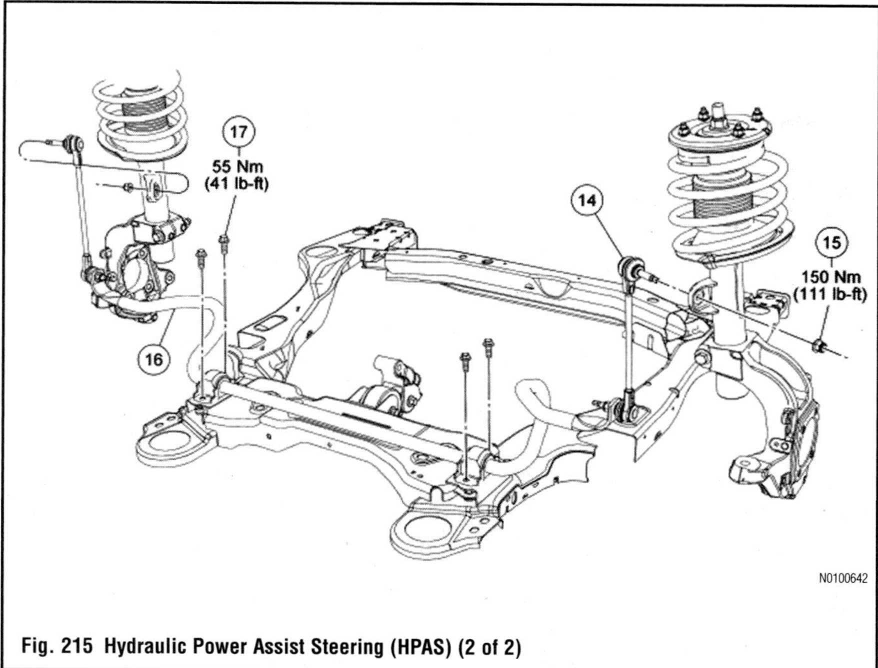

Fig. 215 Hydraulic Power Assist Steering (HPAS) (2 of 2)

evidence that the shaft has rotated, the clockspring must be removed and recentered.

17. Install the steering column shaft-to-steering gear bolt and connect the shaft from the steering gear. Tighten the new bolt to 18 ft. lbs. (25 Nm).

WARNING

Whenever the power steering lines are disconnected, new O-ring seals must be installed. Make sure that the O-ring seals are installed in the correct order or a fluid leak may occur.

18. Install the power steering line clamp plate bolt.
   a. Rotate the clamp plate and connect the pressure and return lines to the steering gear. Tighten the clamp to 17 ft. lbs. (23 Nm).
19. Install the pressure line bracket-to-steering gear bolt. Tighten the bolt to 17 ft. lbs. (23 Nm).

➡The hex-holding feature can be used to prevent turning of the stud while removing the nut.

20. Install the 2 tie-rod end nuts and connect the tie-rod ends to the wheel knuckles. Tighten the nuts to 111 ft. lbs. (150 Nm).
21. Install the wheels and tires.

WARNING

When repairing the power steering system, care should be taken to prevent the entry of foreign material or failure of the power steering components may occur.

➡Use a steering wheel holding device (such as Hunter® 28-75-1 or equivalent).

22. Using a suitable holding device, hold the steering wheel in the straight-ahead position.
23. Fill the power steering system.
24. Check and, if necessary, adjust the front toe.

POWER STEERING PUMP

REMOVAL & INSTALLATION

See Figures 216 through 219.

WARNING

While repairing the power steering system, care should be taken to prevent the entry of foreign material or failure of the power steering components may result.

1. With the vehicle in NEUTRAL, position it on a hoist.
2. Using a suitable suction device, siphon the power steering fluid from the power steering fluid reservoir.
3. Remove the 7 pin-type retainers and the RH splash shield.
4. Position the Stretchy Belt Remover on the power steering pump pulley belt.

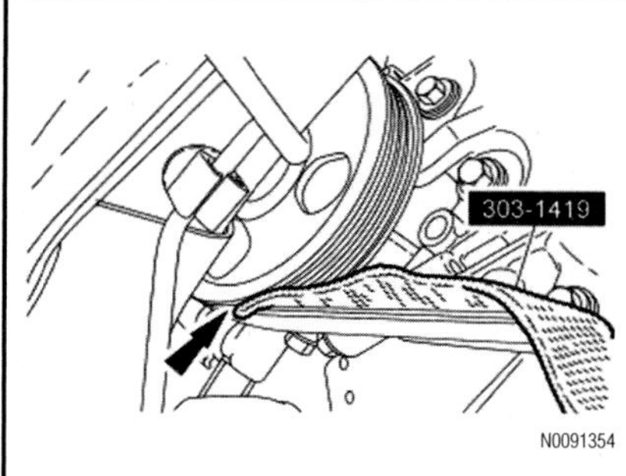

Fig. 216 Position the Stretchy Belt Remover on the power steering pump pulley belt

➡Feed the Stretchy Belt Remover onto the power steering pump pulley approximately 90 degrees.

5. Turn the crankshaft clockwise and feed the Stretchy Belt Remover evenly on the power steering pump pulley.
6. Remove the power steering pump belt.
   a. Fold the Stretchy Belt Remover under the inside of the power steering pump belt.
   b. In one quick motion, firmly pull the Stretchy Belt Remover out of the RH fender well, removing the power steering pump belt.
7. Release the clamp and disconnect the power steering fluid reservoir-to-pump supply hose from the power steering pump.
   a. Detach the supply hose retainer from the pressure line bracket.
8. Remove the pressure line bracket-to-engine bolt.
9. Remove the 3 power steering pump bolts.
10. Holding the power steering pump with a punch inserted into a mounting bolt cavity, disconnect the pressure line fitting-to-power steering pump.

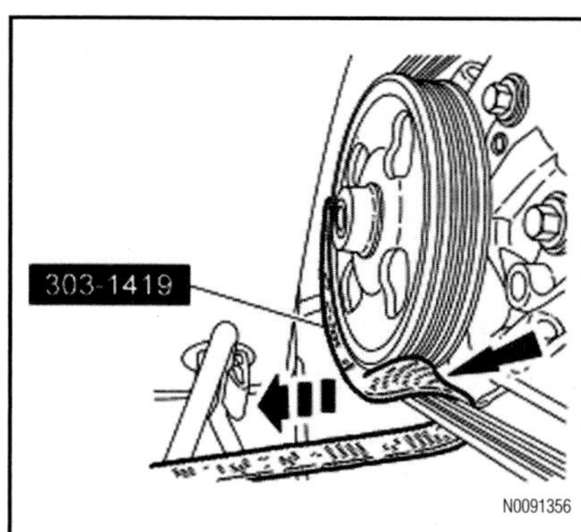

Fig. 217 Fold the Stretchy Belt Remover under the inside of the power steering pump belt

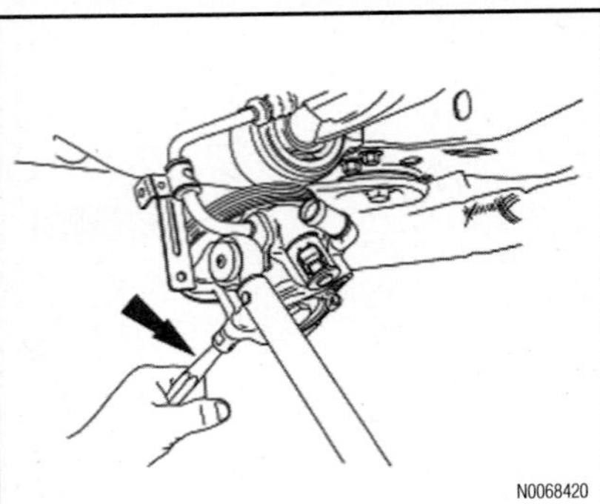

Fig. 218 Holding the power steering pump with a punch inserted into a mounting bolt cavity, disconnect the pressure line fitting-to-power steering pump

To install:

WARNING

A new Teflon® seal must be installed any time the pressure line is disconnected from the power steering pump or a fluid leak may occur.

11. Using the Teflon® Seal Installer Set, install a new Teflon® seal on the power steering pressure line fitting.
12. Holding the power steering pump with a punch inserted into a mounting cavity, connect the pressure line fitting-to-power steering pump.

Tighten the pressure line fitting to 55 ft. lbs. (75 Nm).

13. Position the power steering pump and install the 3 bolts. Tighten the bolts to 18 ft. lbs. (25 Nm).
14. Position the bracket and install the pressure line bracket-to-engine bolt. Tighten the bolt to 80 inch lbs. (9 Nm).

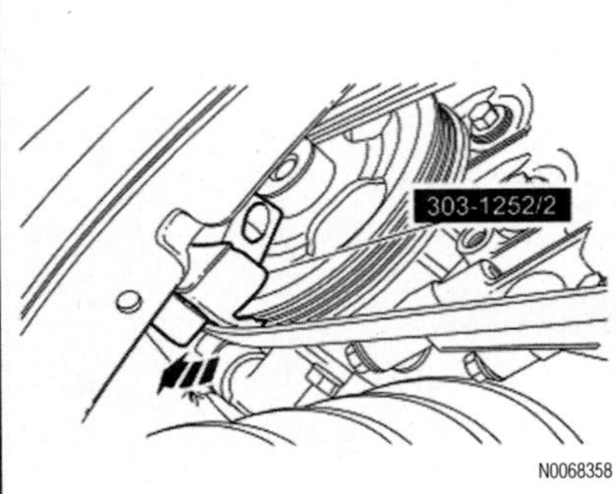

Fig. 219 Install the Stretchy Belt Installer Tool, between the power steering pump belt and pulley and turn the crankshaft bolt clockwise

15. Release the clamp and connect the power steering fluid cooler-to-pump supply hose.
    a. Attach the supply hose retainer to the pressure line bracket.
16. Using the Stretchy Belt Installer Tool, install the power steering pump belt onto the power steering pump pulley.
    a. Install the Stretchy Belt Installer Tool, between the power steering pump belt and pulley and turn the crankshaft bolt clockwise.
17. Install the RH inner fender splash shield.
18. Fill the power steering system.

PURGING

WARNING

If the air is not purged from the power steering system correctly, premature power steering pump failure may result. The condition may occur on pre-delivery vehicles with evidence of aerated fluid or on vehicles that have had steering component repairs.

➡A whine heard from the power steering pump can be caused by air in the system. The power steering purge procedure must be carried out prior to any component repair for which power steering noise complaints are accompanied by evidence of aerated fluid.

1. Remove the power steering reservoir cap. Check the fluid.
2. Raise the front wheels off the floor.
3. Tightly insert the Power Steering Evacuation Cap into the reservoir and connect the Vacuum Pump Kit.
4. Start the engine.
5. Using the Vacuum Pump Kit, apply vacuum and maintain the maximum vacuum of 20-25 in-Hg (68-85 kPa).
    a. If the Vacuum Pump Kit does not maintain vacuum, check the power steering system for leaks before proceeding.
6. If equipped with Hydro-Boost®, apply the brake pedal 4 times.

WARNING

Do not hold the steering wheel against the stops for an extended amount of time. Damage to the power steering pump may occur.

7. Cycle the steering wheel fully from stop-to-stop 10 times.
8. Stop the engine.
9. Release the vacuum and remove the Vacuum Pump Kit and the Power Steering Evacuation Cap.

➡Do not overfill the reservoir.

10. Fill the reservoir as needed with the specified fluid.
11. Start the engine.
12. Install the Power Steering Evacuation Cap and the Vacuum Pump Kit. Apply and maintain the maximum vacuum of 20-25 in-Hg (68-85 kPa).

WARNING

Do not hold the steering wheel against the stops for an extended amount of time. Damage to the power steering pump may occur.

13. Cycle the steering wheel fully from stop-to-stop 10 times.
14. Stop the engine, release the vacuum and remove the Vacuum Pump Kit and the Power Steering Evacuation Cap.

➡Do not overfill the reservoir.

15. Fill the reservoir as needed with the specified fluid and install the reservoir cap.
16. Visually inspect the power steering system for leaks.

FLUID FILL PROCEDURE

See Figure 220.

WARNING

If the air is not purged from the power steering system correctly, premature power steering pump failure may result. The condition can occur on pre-delivery vehicles with evidence of aerated fluid or on vehicles that have had steering component repairs.

1. Remove the power steering fluid reservoir cap.
2. Install the Power Steering Evacuation Cap, Power Steering Fill Adapter Manifold and Vacuum Pump Kit.

➡The Power Steering Fill Adapter Manifold control valves are in the OPEN position when the points of the handles face the center of the Power Steering Fill Adapter Manifold.

3. Close the Power Steering Fill Adapter Manifold control valve (fluid side).
4. Open the Power Steering Fill Adapter Manifold control valve (vacuum side).
5. Using the Vacuum Pump Kit, apply 20-25 in-Hg (68-85 kPa) of vacuum to the power steering system.

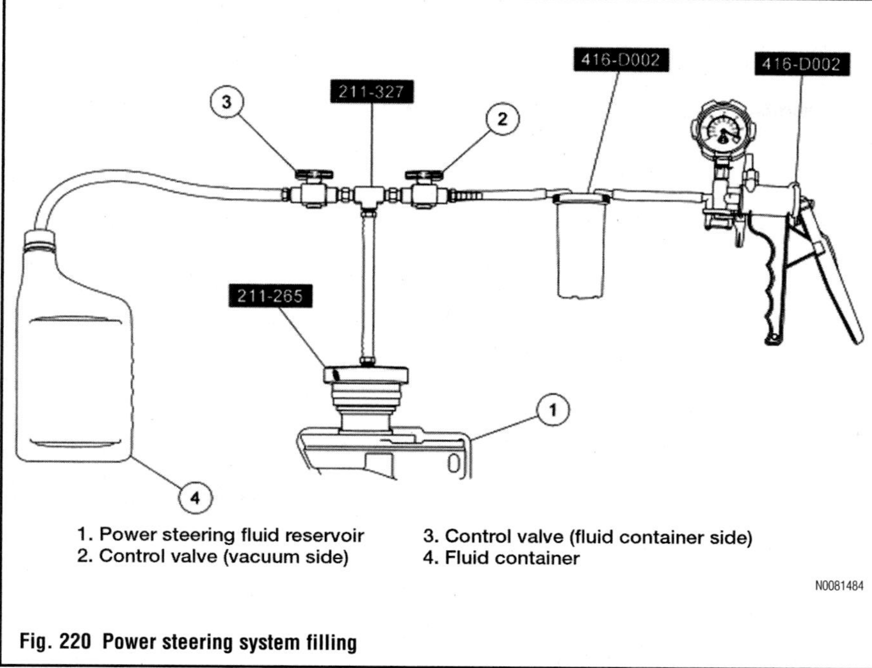

Fig. 220 Power steering system filling

6. Observe the Vacuum Pump Kit gauge for 30 seconds.
7. If the Vacuum Pump Kit gauge reading drops more than 0.88 in-Hg (3 kPa), correct any leaks in the power steering system or the Power Steering Evacuation Cap, Power Steering Fill Adapter Manifold and Vacuum Pump Kit before proceeding.

➡The Vacuum Pump Kit gauge reading will drop slightly during this step.

8. Slowly open the Power Steering Fill Adapter Manifold control valve (fluid side) until power steering fluid completely fills the hose and then close the control valve.
9. Using the Vacuum Pump Kit, apply 20-25 in-Hg (68-85 kPa) of vacuum to the power steering system.
10. Close the Power Steering Fill Adapter Manifold control valve (vacuum side).
11. Slowly open the Power Steering Fill Adapter Manifold control valve (fluid side).
12. Once power steering fluid enters the fluid reservoir and reaches the minimum fluid level indicator line on the reservoir, close the Power Steering Fill Adapter Manifold control valve (fluid side).
13. Remove the Power Steering Evacuation Cap, Power Steering Fill Adapter Manifold and Vacuum Pump Kit.
14. Install the reservoir cap.

WARNING

Do not hold the steering wheel against the stops for an extended amount of time. Damage to the power steering pump may occur.

➡There will be a slight drop in the power steering fluid level in the reservoir when the engine is started.

15. Start the engine and turn the steering wheel from stop-to-stop.
16. Turn the ignition switch to the OFF position.

➡Do not overfill the reservoir.

17. Remove the reservoir cap and fill the reservoir with the specified fluid.
18. Install the reservoir cap.

SUSPENSION

FRONT SUSPENSION

WARNING

Suspension fasteners are critical parts because they affect performance of vital components and systems and their failure may result in major service expense. New parts must be installed with the same part numbers or equivalent part, if replacement is necessary. Do not use a replacement part of lesser quality or substitute design. Torque values must be used as specified during reassembly to make sure of correct retention of these parts.

LOWER CONTROL ARM

REMOVAL & INSTALLATION

1. Remove the wheel and tire.

➡Use the hex-holding feature to prevent the stud from turning while removing the nut.

2. Using a crowfoot wrench, remove and discard the lower ball joint nut.

WARNING

Use care when releasing the lower arm and knuckle into the resting position or damage to the ball joint seal may occur.

3. Push the lower arm downward until the ball joint is clear of the wheel knuckle.
4. Remove and discard the lower arm forward bolt.
5. Remove and discard the lower arm rearward nuts and bolts.
   a. Install the new lower arm rearward bolts from the bottom of the lower arm bushing with the nuts on top.
6. If necessary, remove the lower arm rearward bushing. For additional information, refer to Lower Arm Bushing in this section.

WARNING

The lower arm forward bolt must be tightened with the weight of the vehicle on the wheels and tires or damage to the bushings may occur.

To install:

WARNING

Suspension fasteners are critical parts because they affect performance of vital components and systems and their failure may result in major service expense. New parts must be installed with the same part numbers or equivalent part, if replacement is necessary. Do not use a replacement part of lesser quality or substitute design. Torque values must be used as specified during reassembly to make sure of correct retention of these parts.

⁂ WARNING

The lower arm forward bolt must be tightened with the weight of the vehicle on the wheels and tires or damage to the bushings may occur.

7. If necessary, install the lower arm rearward bushing.
8. Install and use a new lower arm rearward nuts and bolts. Tighten the new nuts to 73 ft. lbs. (99 Nm).
    a. Install the new lower arm rearward bolts from the bottom of the lower arm bushing with the nuts on top.
9. Install and use a new lower arm forward bolt. Tighten the new bolt to 136 ft. lbs. (185 Nm).

⁂ WARNING

Use care when releasing the lower arm and knuckle into the resting position or damage to the ball joint seal may occur.

10. Push the lower arm upward until the ball joint is in the wheel knuckle.

➡Use the hex-holding feature to prevent the stud from turning while removing the nut.

11. Using a crowfoot wrench, install and use a new lower ball joint nut. Tighten the nut to 148 ft. lbs. (200 Nm).
12. Install the wheel and tire.

LOWER CONTROL ARM BUSHING REPLACEMENT

See Figures 221 and 222.

1. Remove the lower arm as outlined above.
2. Index-mark the bushing-to-lower arm position for reference during the installation procedure.

➡The Drive Pinion Bearing Cone Remover is used to secure the lower arm bushing while separating the bushing from the lower arm.

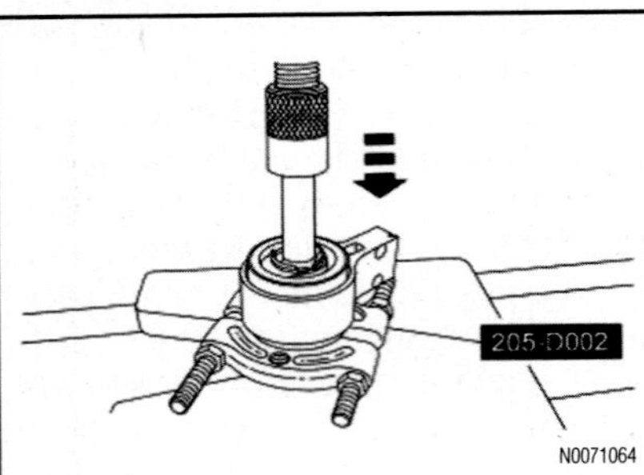

Fig. 221 Using the Drive Pinion Bearing Cone Remover, a suitable press and adapters, remove the lower arm bushing

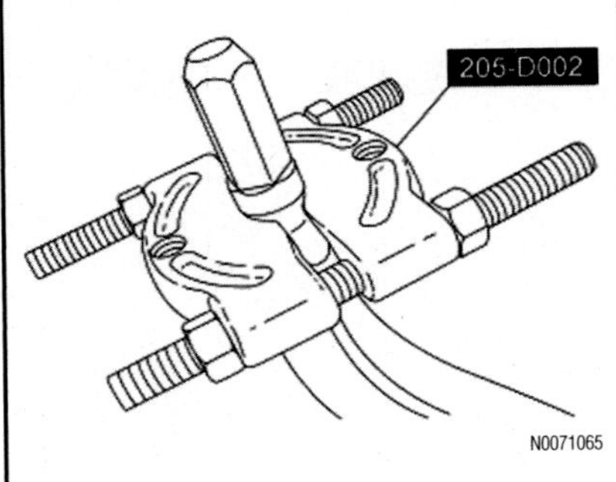

Fig. 222 Install the Drive Pinion Bearing Cone Remover onto the lower arm

3. Using the Drive Pinion Bearing Cone Remover, a suitable press and adapters, remove the lower arm bushing.

To install:

➡The Drive Pinion Bearing Cone Remover is used to clamp and hold the lower arm while installing the bushing.

4. Install the Drive Pinion Bearing Cone Remover onto the lower arm.
5. Transfer the index mark to the new lower arm bushing.

➡The Drive Pinion Bearing Cone Remover is used to clamp and hold the lower arm while installing the bushing.

6. Align the index marks and using the Drive Pinion Bearing Cone Remover, a suitable press and adapters, install a new lower arm bushing.
7. Install the lower arm.

STABILIZER BAR

REMOVAL & INSTALLATION

See Figures 223 through 225.

➡Make sure the steering wheel is in the unlocked position.

➡The stabilizer bushing and bracket are part of the stabilizer bar assembly. The stabilizer bar will not turn easily in the bushing.

All Vehicles

1. With the vehicle in NEUTRAL, position it on a hoist.
2. Disconnect the Heated Oxygen Sensor (HO2S) electrical connector and unclip the connector from the subframe.

All-Wheel Drive (AWD) Vehicles

3. Remove the exhaust Y-pipe.

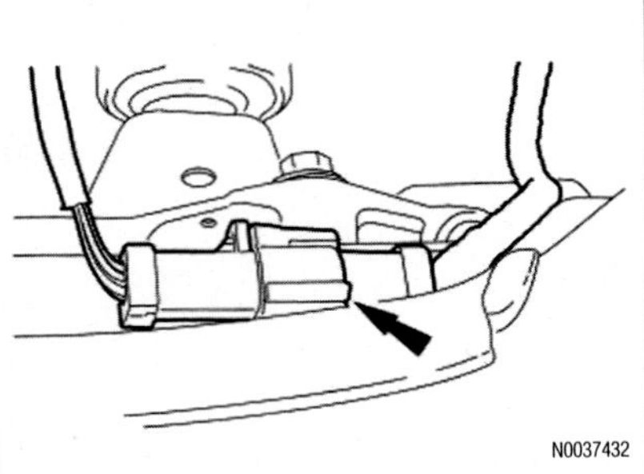

Fig. 223 Disconnect the Heated Oxygen Sensor (HO2S) electrical connector and unclip the connector from the subframe

All Vehicles

⁂ WARNING

Do not use power tools to remove the stabilizer bar link nut. Damage to the stabilizer link ball joint or boot may occur.

➡To remove the stabilizer bar link nut, first loosen the nut, then use the hex-holding feature to prevent the ball joint from turning while removing the stabilizer bar link nut.

4. Remove and discard the stabilizer bar link lower nuts.

➡No special tools are necessary to separate the tie rod from the front knuckle; use a mallet to loosen the joint.

5. Remove and discard both tie-rod end nuts and separate the tie-rod ends from the knuckles.

➡Install the new lower arm rearward bolts from the bottom of the lower arm bushing with the nuts on top.

6. Remove and discard the 4 lower arm rearward nuts and bolts.
7. Remove and discard the 2 lower arm forward bolts. Position both lower arms aside.
8. Using a suitable screw-type jackstand, support the rear of the subframe.
9. Remove the 2 steering gear nuts and bolts.
    a. Vehicles with Electronic Power Assist Steering (EPAS)
    b. Vehicles with Hydraulic Power Assist Steering (HPAS)
10. Remove and discard the 4 subframe bracket bolts.
11. Remove and discard the subframe forward bolts.
12. Remove and discard the subframe rearward bolts.

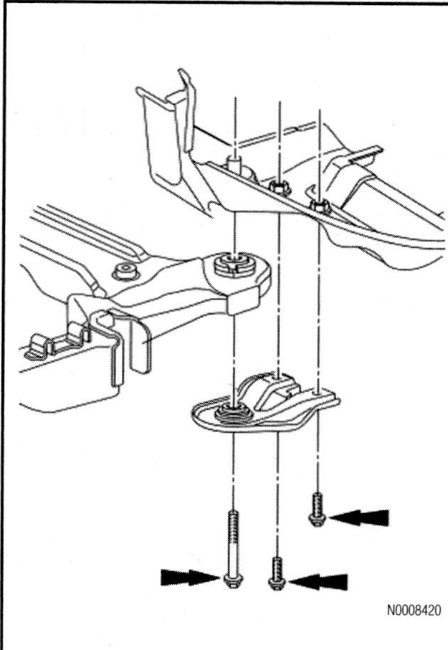

Fig. 224 Remove and discard the subframe rearward bolts

a. Vehicles with EPAS
b. Vehicle with HPAS

13. Lower the rear of the subframe approximately 21 inch (51 mm).
14. Remove and discard the LH and RH stabilizer bar bracket bolts.
15. Remove the stabilizer bar by guiding it between the subframe and the steering gear toward the RH side of the vehicle.

To install:

⁂ WARNING

Suspension fasteners are critical parts because they affect performance of vital components and systems and their failure may result in major service expense. New parts must be installed with the same part numbers or equivalent part, if replacement is necessary. Do not use a replacement part of lesser quality or substitute design. Torque values must be used as specified during reassembly to make sure of correct retention of these parts.

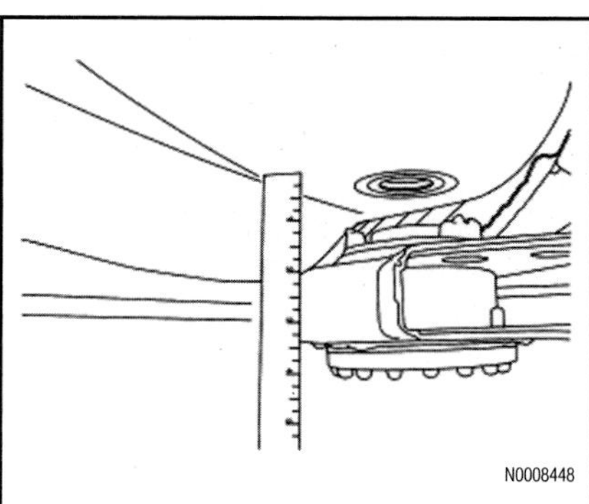

Fig. 225 Lower the rear of the subframe approximately 21 inch (51 mm)

➡Make sure the steering wheel is in the unlocked position.

➡The stabilizer bushing and bracket are part of the stabilizer bar assembly. The stabilizer bar will not turn easily in the bushing.

16. Install the stabilizer bar by guiding it between the subframe and the steering gear away from the RH side of the vehicle.

All Vehicles

17. Install and use new LH and RH stabilizer bar bracket bolts. Tighten the new bolts to 41 ft. lbs. (55 Nm).
18. Raise the rear of the subframe approximately 21 inch (51 mm).
19. Install and use new subframe rearward bolts.
    a. Vehicles with EPAS tighten the new bolts to 111 ft. lbs. (150 Nm).
    b. Vehicle with HPAS, tighten the new bolts to 130 ft. lbs. (175 Nm).
20. Install and use new subframe forward bolts. Tighten the new bolts to 148 ft. lbs. (200 Nm).
21. Install and use 4 new subframe bracket bolts. Tighten the new bolts to 41 ft. lbs. (55 Nm).
22. Install the 2 steering gear nuts and bolts.
    a. Vehicles with Electronic Power Assist Steering (EPAS), tighten the nuts to 122 ft. lbs. (65 Nm).
    b. Vehicles with Hydraulic Power Assist Steering (HPAS), tighten the new nuts to 86 ft. lbs. (117 Nm).
23. Using a suitable screw-type jackstand, support the rear of the subframe.
24. Install and use 2 new 2 lower arm forward bolts. Reposition both lower arms. Tighten the new bolts to 136 ft. lbs. (185 Nm).

➡Install the new lower arm rearward bolts from the bottom of the lower arm bushing with the nuts on top.

25. Install and use 4 new 4 lower arm rearward nuts and bolts. Tighten the new bolts to 73 ft. lbs. (99 Nm).

➡No special tools are necessary to separate the tie rod from the front knuckle; use a mallet to loosen the joint.

26. Install and new tie-rod end nuts and separate the tie-rod ends to the knuckles. Tighten the new nuts to 111 ft. lbs. (150 Nm).

⁂ WARNING

Do not use power tools to install the stabilizer bar link nut. Damage to the stabilizer link ball joint or boot may occur.

➡To install the stabilizer bar link nut, use the hex-holding feature to prevent the ball joint from turning while installing the stabilizer bar link nut, then tighten the nut.

27. Install and use new stabilizer bar link lower nuts. Tighten the new nuts to 111 ft. lbs. (150 Nm).

All-Wheel Drive (AWD) Vehicles

28. Install the exhaust Y-pipe.

All Vehicles

29. Connect the Heated Oxygen Sensor (HO2S) electrical connector and clip the connector to the subframe.
30. With the vehicle in NEUTRAL, lower from the hoist.

STABILIZER BAR LINK

REMOVAL & INSTALLATION

1. With the vehicle in NEUTRAL, position it on a hoist.

⁂ WARNING

Do not use power tools to remove the stabilizer bar link nuts. Damage to the stabilizer bar link ball joints or boots may occur.

➡To remove the stabilizer bar link nuts, first loosen the nuts, then use the hex-holding feature to prevent the stabilizer bar link ball joints from turning while removing the stabilizer bar link nuts.

2. Remove and discard the stabilizer bar link lower nut.
3. Remove and discard the stabilizer bar link upper nut.
4. Remove the stabilizer bar link.

➡To install the nuts, use the hex-holding feature to prevent the stabilizer link ball joints from turning while installing the nuts until snug. Finally, tighten the nuts using a socket and a torque wrench.

To install:

➡To install the nuts, use the hex-holding feature to prevent the stabilizer link

ball joints from turning while installing the nuts until snug. Finally, tighten the nuts using a socket and a torque wrench.

5. Install the stabilizer bar link.
6. Install and use a new stabilizer bar link upper nut. Tighten the new nut to 111 ft. lbs. (150 Nm).
7. Install and a new stabilizer bar link lower nut. Tighten the new nut to 111 ft. lbs. (150 Nm).

WARNING

Do not use power tools to remove the stabilizer bar link nuts. Damage to the stabilizer bar link ball joints or boots may occur.

➡To install the stabilizer bar link nuts, use the hex-holding feature to prevent the stabilizer bar link ball joints from turning while removing the stabilizer bar link nuts, and then tighten the nuts.

WARNING

Suspension fasteners are critical parts because they affect performance of vital components and systems and their failure may result in major service expense. New parts must be installed with the same part numbers or equivalent part, if replacement is necessary. Do not use a replacement part of lesser quality or substitute design. Torque values must be used as specified during reassembly to make sure of correct retention of these parts.

8. With the vehicle in NEUTRAL, lower from the hoist.

STRUT & SPRING ASSEMBLY

REMOVAL & INSTALLATION

See Figure 226.

CAUTION

Do not apply heat or flame to the shock absorber or strut tube. The shock absorber and strut tube are gas pressurized and could explode if heated. Failure to follow this instruction may result in serious personal injury.

CAUTION

Keep all body parts clear of shock absorbers or strut rods. Shock absorbers or struts can extend unassisted. Failure to follow this instruction may result in serious personal injury.

➡Make sure the steering wheel is in the unlocked position.

1. Loosen the upper strut mount nuts.
2. Remove the wheel and tire.

➡Do not discard the wheel hub nut at this time.

3. Remove the wheel hub nut.
4. Remove the brake disc (rotor).

➡No special tools are necessary to separate the tie rod from the front knuckle; use a mallet to loosen the joint.

5. Remove and discard the tie-rod end nut, then separate the tie rod from the wheel knuckle.
6. Remove and discard the stabilizer bar link upper nut.
7. Detach the wheel speed sensor harness from the strut.
8. Remove the bolt and the wheel speed sensor from the wheel knuckle. Position the wheel speed sensor aside.

➡Use the hex-holding feature to prevent the stud from turning while removing the nut.

9. Using a crowfoot wrench, remove and discard the lower ball joint nut.

WARNING

Use care when releasing the lower arm and knuckle into the resting position or damage to the ball joint seal may occur.

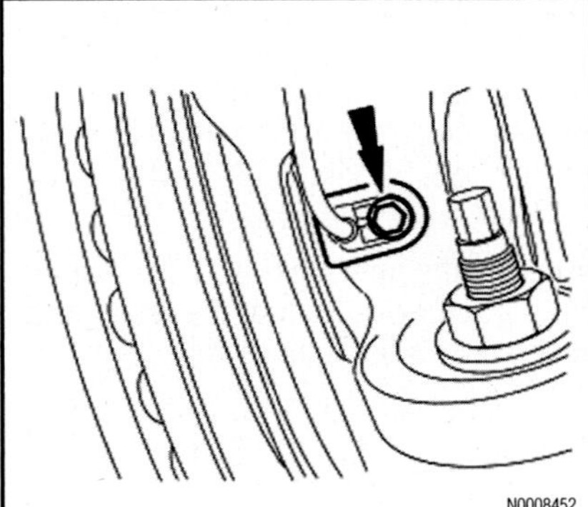

Fig. 226 Remove the bolt and the wheel speed sensor from the wheel knuckle. Position the wheel speed sensor aside

10. Push the lower arm downward until the ball joint is clear of the wheel knuckle.

WARNING

Do not allow the halfshaft to move outboard. Overextension of the tripod Constant Velocity (CV) joint may result in separation of internal parts, causing failure of the halfshaft.

11. Using the Front Wheel Hub Remover, press the halfshaft from the wheel bearing and hub. Support the halfshaft in a level position.
12. Remove and discard the 4 upper strut mount nuts.
13. Remove the wheel knuckle and the strut and spring as an assembly.
14. Remove and discard the strut-to-wheel knuckle nut and flagbolt.
15. Separate the strut and spring assembly from the wheel knuckle.

To install:

16. Position the wheel knuckle onto the strut and spring and install a new strut-to-wheel knuckle nut and flagbolt. Tighten the nut to 129 ft. lbs. (175 Nm).
17. Install the wheel knuckle and the strut and spring as an assembly.
18. Loosely install the 4 new upper strut mount nuts.
19. While supporting the halfshaft in a level position, install the halfshaft into the wheel bearing and hub.

WARNING

Use care not to damage the ball joint seal while installing the ball joint stud into the wheel knuckle.

20. Push the lower arm downward and install the ball joint stud into the wheel knuckle.

➡Use the hex-holding feature to prevent the stud from turning while installing the nut.

21. Using a crowfoot wrench, install the new lower ball joint nut. Tighten the nut to 148 ft. lbs. (200 Nm).
22. Position the wheel speed sensor and install the bolt. Tighten the bolt to 133 inch lbs. (15 Nm).
23. Attach the wheel speed sensor harness to the strut.
24. Install the new stabilizer bar link upper nut. Tighten the nut to 111 ft. lbs. (150 Nm).
25. Position the tie-rod end stud into the wheel knuckle and install a new tie-rod

end nut. Tighten the nut to 111 ft. lbs. (150 Nm).

26. Install the brake disc (rotor).

WARNING

Do not tighten the front wheel hub nut with the vehicle on the ground. The nut must be tightened to specification before the vehicle is lowered onto the wheels. Wheel bearing damage will occur if the wheel bearing is loaded with the weight of the vehicle applied.

➡Apply the brake to keep the halfshaft from rotating.

27. Using the previously removed hub nut, seat the halfshaft. Tighten the nut to 258 ft. lbs. (350 Nm).

28. Remove and discard the hub nut.

WARNING

The wheel hub nut contains a one-time locking chemical that is activated by the heat created when it is tightened. Install and tighten the new wheel hub nut to specification within 5 minutes of starting it on the threads. Always install a new wheel hub nut after loosening or when not tightened within the specified time or damage to the components can occur.

➡Apply the brake to keep the halfshaft from rotating.

29. Install a new hub nut. Tighten the nut to 258 ft. lbs. (350 Nm).

30. Install the wheel and tire.

31. Tighten the 4 upper strut mount nuts to 22 ft. lbs. (30 Nm).

WHEEL HUB & BEARING

REMOVAL & INSTALLATION

See Figure 227.

1. Remove the wheel knuckle.
2. Remove and discard the 4 wheel bearing and wheel hub bolts, then separate the wheel bearing and wheel hub from the wheel knuckle.

WARNING

The wheel knuckle bore must be clean enough to allow the wheel bearing and wheel hub to seat completely by hand. Do not press or draw the wheel hub and bearing into place or damage to the bearing may occur.

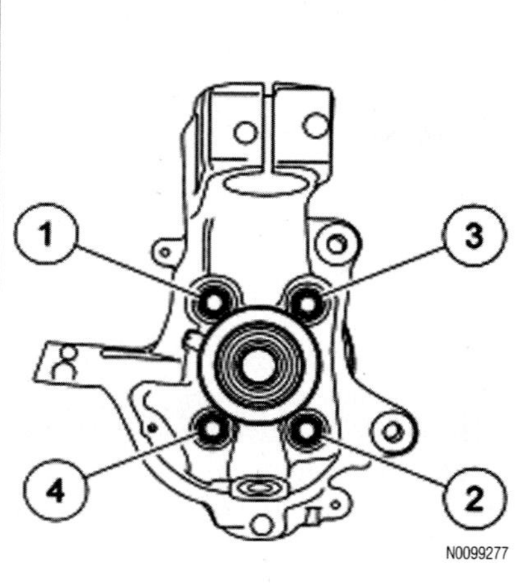

Fig. 227 Wheel bearing and wheel hub bolts location

3. Clean and inspect the knuckle bearing bore. If the wheel knuckle is cracked, install a new wheel knuckle.

➡Make sure the wheel hub-to-wheel knuckle mating surfaces are clean and free of any adhesive. Failure to clean the adhesive from both surfaces may cause bearing damage.

4. Using a clean shop towel, clean the wheel hub-to-knuckle mating surfaces.

To install:

WARNING

The wheel knuckle bore must be clean enough to allow the wheel bearing and wheel hub to seat completely by hand. Do not press or draw the wheel hub and bearing into place or damage to the bearing may occur.

5. Clean and inspect the knuckle bearing bore. If the wheel knuckle is cracked, install a new wheel knuckle.

➡Make sure the wheel hub-to-wheel knuckle mating surfaces are clean and free of any adhesive. Failure to clean the adhesive from both surfaces may cause bearing damage.

6. Using a clean shop towel, clean the wheel hub-to-knuckle mating surfaces.
7. Install separate the wheel bearing and wheel hub from the wheel knuckle, and then use 4 new wheel bearing and wheel hub bolts.
   a. To install, tighten the new bolts to 98 ft. lbs. (133 Nm).

WARNING

Suspension fasteners are critical parts because they affect performance of vital components and systems and their failure may result in major service expense. New parts must be installed with the same part numbers or equivalent part, if replacement is necessary. Do not use a replacement part of lesser quality or substitute design. Torque values must be used as specified during reassembly to make sure of correct retention of these parts.

8. Install the wheel knuckle.
9. Lubricate the hub-to-brake disc surface with anti-seize lubricant before installing the brake disc.

WHEEL KNUCKLE

REMOVAL & INSATLLATION

See Figure 226.

1. Remove the wheel and tire.

➡Do not discard the wheel hub nut at this time.

2. Remove the wheel hub nut.
3. Remove the brake disc (rotor).

➡No special tools are necessary to separate the tie rod from the front knuckle; use a mallet to loosen the joint.

4. Remove and discard the tie-rod end nut, then separate the tie rod from the wheel knuckle.
5. Remove the bolt and the wheel speed sensor from the wheel knuckle. Position the wheel speed sensor aside.

➡Use the hex-holding feature to prevent the stud from turning while removing the nut.

6. Using a crowfoot wrench, remove and discard the lower ball joint nut.
7. Push the lower arm downward until the ball joint is clear of the wheel knuckle.

WARNING

Do not allow the halfshaft to move outboard. Overextension of the tripod Constant Velocity (CV) joint may result in separation of internal parts, causing failure of the halfshaft.

8. Using the Front Wheel Hub Remover, press the halfshaft from the wheel bearing and hub. Support the halfshaft in a level position.
9. Remove and discard the strut-to-wheel knuckle nut and flagbolt.

10. Remove the wheel knuckle.
 a. If necessary, remove the wheel hub and bearing.

To install:

11. Position the wheel knuckle and install a new strut-to-wheel knuckle nut and flagbolt. Tighten the nut and flagbolt to 129 ft. lbs. (175 Nm).
12. While supporting the halfshaft in a level position, install the halfshaft into the wheel bearing and hub.

**** WARNING**

Use care not to damage the ball joint seal while installing the ball joint stud into the wheel knuckle.

13. Push the lower arm downward and install the ball joint stud into the wheel knuckle.

➡Use the hex-holding feature to prevent the stud from turning while installing the nut.

14. Using a crowfoot wrench, install the new lower ball joint nut. Tighten the nut to 148 ft. lbs. (200 Nm).
15. Position the wheel speed sensor and install the bolt. Tighten the bolt to 133 inch lbs. (15 Nm).
16. Position the tie-rod end stud into the wheel knuckle and install a new tie-rod end nut. Tighten the nut to 111 ft. lbs. (150 Nm).
17. Install the brake disc (rotor).

**** WARNING**

Do not tighten the front wheel hub nut with the vehicle on the ground. The nut must be tightened to specification before the vehicle is lowered onto the wheels. Wheel bearing damage will occur if the wheel bearing is loaded with the weight of the vehicle applied.

➡Apply the brake to keep the halfshaft from rotating.

18. Using the previously removed hub nut, seat the halfshaft. Tighten the nut to 258 ft. lbs. (350 Nm).
 a. Remove and discard the hub nut.

**** WARNING**

The wheel hub nut contains a one-time locking chemical that is activated by the heat created when it is tightened. Install and tighten the new wheel hub nut to specification within 5 minutes of starting it on the threads. Always install a new wheel hub nut after loosening or when not tightened within the specified time or damage to the components can occur.

➡Apply the brake to keep the halfshaft from rotating.

19. Install a new hub nut. Tighten the nut to 258 ft. lbs. (350 Nm).
20. Install the wheel and tire.

SUSPENSION

REAR SUSPENSION

**** WARNING**

Suspension fasteners are critical parts because they affect performance of vital components and systems and their failure may result in major service expense. New parts must be installed with the same part numbers or equivalent part, if replacement is necessary. Do not use a replacement part of lesser quality or substitute design. Torque values must be used as specified during reassembly to make sure of correct retention of these parts.

LOWER CONTROL ARM

REMOVAL & INSTALLATION

1. Measure the distance from the center of the wheel hub to the lip of the fender with the vehicle in a level, static ground position (curb height).
2. Remove the wheel and tire.

➡Use the hex-holding feature to prevent the stabilizer bar link stud from turning while removing the nut.

3. Remove both stabilizer bar link upper nuts and disconnect the links from the wheel knuckle.
 a. Discard the nuts.
4. Position a screw-type jackstand under the lower arm.
5. Remove and discard the lower arm-to-knuckle bolt and nut.

➡Do not remove the lower arm inner bolt at this time.

6. Loosen the lower arm inner bolt.
7. Lower the jackstand and remove the spring.
8. Remove the lower arm inner bolt and lower arm.
 a. Discard the bolt.

To install:

➡Before tightening the lower arm bolts, use a jackstand to raise the rear suspension until the distance between the center of the hub and the lip of the fender is equal to the measurement taken in the Removal procedure (curb height).

9. Position the lower arm and loosely install the new lower arm inner bolt.

➡Make sure the lower spring seat is properly positioned in the lower arm.

10. Install the spring and position the screw-type jackstand under the lower arm.

➡Do not tighten the lower arm nut at this time.

11. Raise the jackstand and loosely install the new lower arm-to-knuckle bolt and nut.
12. Using the jackstand, raise the rear suspension until the distance between the center of the hub and the lip of the fender is equal to the measurement taken in the Removal procedure (curb height).
13. Tighten the lower arm-to-subframe bolt to 159 ft. lbs. (215 Nm).
14. Tighten the lower arm-to-knuckle bolt to 196 ft. lbs. (265 Nm).

➡Use the hex-holding feature to prevent the stabilizer bar link stud from turning while removing the nut.

15. Position the stabilizer bar links and install 2 new stabilizer bar link upper nuts. Tighten the nuts to 41 ft. lbs. (55 Nm).

SHOCK ABSORBER

REMOVAL & INSTALLATION

See Figure 228.

1. Open the rear quarter trim panel storage compartment lid, remove the 4 screws and the storage compartment.
2. Remove and discard the shock absorber upper mount nut.
3. Remove the wheel and tire.

➡Use the hex-holding feature to prevent the stabilizer bar link stud from turning while removing or installing the nut.

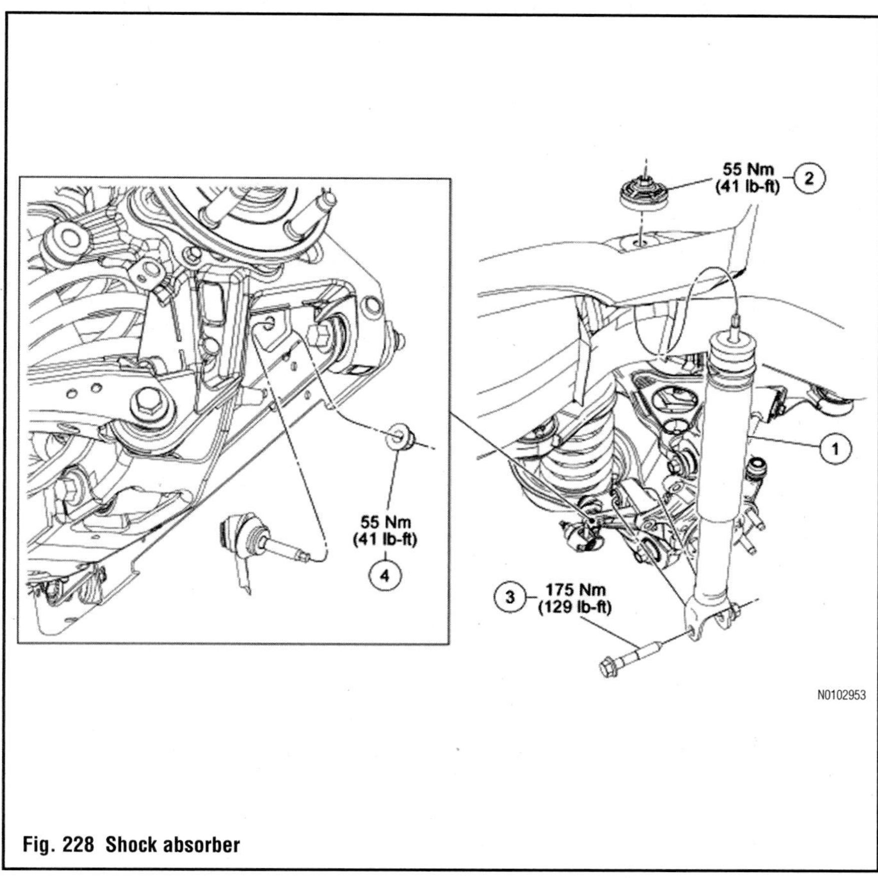

Fig. 228 Shock absorber

4. Remove and discard the stabilizer bar link upper nut and disconnect the link from the wheel knuckle.

5. Remove and discard the shock absorber lower bolt and remove the shock absorber.

To install:

6. Install and discard the shock absorber lower bolt and remove the shock absorber. Tighten the new bolt to 129 ft. lbs. (175 Nm).

➡Use the hex-holding feature to prevent the stabilizer bar link stud from turning while removing or installing the nut.

7. Install and discard the stabilizer bar link upper nut and connect the link to the wheel knuckle. Tighten the new nut to 41 ft. lbs. (55 Nm).

8. Install the wheel and tire.

9. Install and discard the shock absorber upper mount nut. Tighten the new nut to 41 ft. lbs. (55 Nm).

✻✻ WARNING

Suspension fasteners are critical parts because they affect performance of vital components and systems and their failure may result in major service expense. New parts must be installed with the same part numbers or equivalent part, if replacement is necessary. Do not use a replacement part of lesser quality or substitute design. Torque values must be used as specified during reassembly to make sure of correct retention of these parts.

10. Open the rear quarter trim panel storage compartment lid, remove the 4 screws and the storage compartment. Tighten to 44 inch lbs. (5 Nm).

SPRING

REMOVAL & INSTALLTION

See Figure 229.

1. Measure the distance from the center of the wheel hub to the lip of the fender with the vehicle in a level, static ground position (curb height).

2. Remove the wheel and tire.

➡Use the hex-holding feature to prevent the stabilizer bar link studs from turning while removing the nuts.

3. Remove and discard the 2 stabilizer bar link upper nuts.

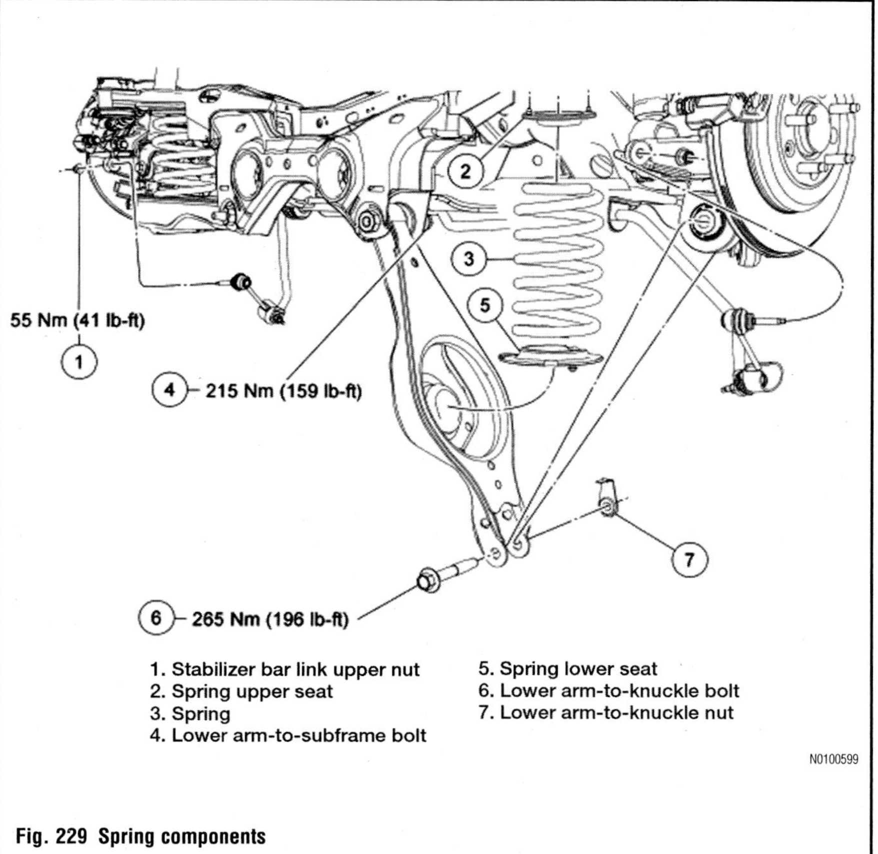

Fig. 229 Spring components

a. Position the stabilizer bar away from the lower arm.

4. Using a suitable jackstand, support the lower arm.

5. Loosen the lower arm-to-subframe bolt.

6. Remove and discard the lower arm-to wheel knuckle bolt.

7. Lower the jackstand and remove the spring.

➡**Make sure the lower spring seat is properly positioned in the lower arm.**

8. Inspect the upper and lower spring seats for damage and, if necessary, install new spring seats.

To install:

➡**Before tightening the lower arm bolts, use a jackstand to raise the rear suspension until the distance between the center of the hub and the lip of the fender is equal to the measurement taken in the Removal procedure (curb height).**

9. Install the spring and position the jackstand under the lower arm.

10. Raise the jackstand and loosely install a new lower arm-to-wheel knuckle bolt.

➡**Use the hex-holding feature to prevent the stabilizer bar link studs from turning while installing the nuts.**

11. Position the stabilizer bar and links and install 2 new stabilizer bar link upper nuts. Tighten the nuts to 41 ft. lbs. (55 Nm).

12. Using the jackstand, raise the rear suspension until the distance between the center of the hub and the lip of the fender is equal to the measurement taken in the Removal procedure (curb height).

13. Tighten the lower arm-to-wheel knuckle bolt to 196 ft. lbs. (265 Nm).

14. Tighten the lower arm-to-subframe bolt to 159 ft. lbs. (215 Nm).

15. Install the wheel and tire.

STABILIZER BAR

REMOVAL & INSTALLATION

See Figures 230 and 231.

➡**Use the hex-holding feature to prevent the stabilizer bar link stud from turning while removing or installing the nut.**

1. With the vehicle in NEUTRAL, position it on a hoist.

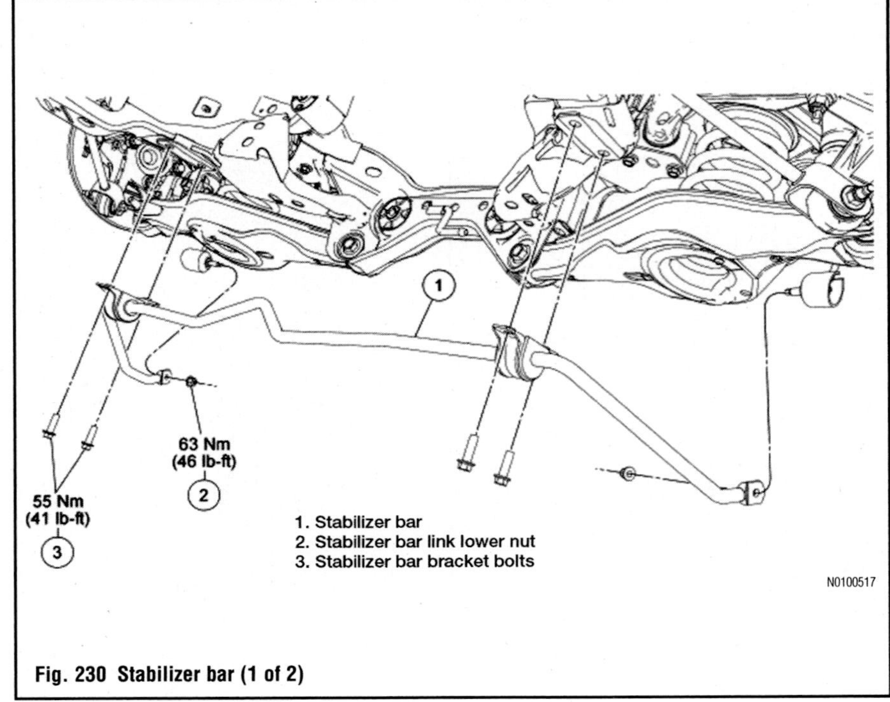

Fig. 230 Stabilizer bar (1 of 2)

2. Support the exhaust system with a suitable jackstand, disconnect the 2 muffler and tail pipe isolators and lower the exhaust approximately 2 inch (50.8 mm).

3. Remove and discard the 2 stabilizer bar link lower nuts.

4. Remove and discard the 4 stabilizer bar bracket bolts.

5. Remove the stabilizer bar.

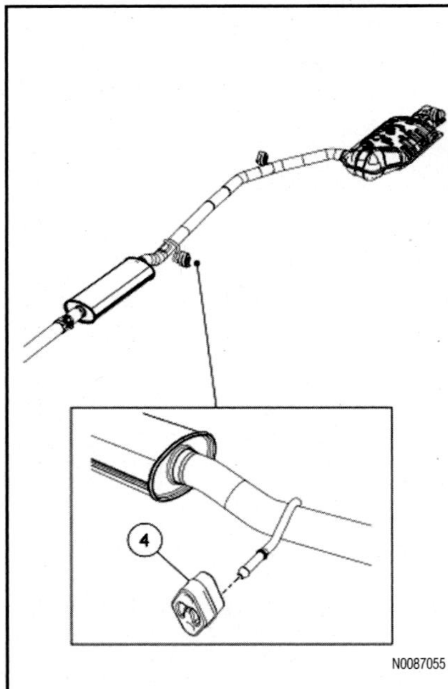

Fig. 231 Stabilizer bar (2 of 2). Muffler and tail pipe isolator (4)

To install:

6. Remove the stabilizer bar.

7. Remove and discard the 4 stabilizer bar bracket bolts. Tighten the new bolts to 41 ft. lbs. (55 Nm).

8. Remove and discard the 2 stabilizer bar link lower nuts. Tighten the new nuts to 46 ft. lbs. (63 Nm).

9. Support the exhaust system with a suitable jackstand, disconnect the 2 muffler and tail pipe isolators and lower the exhaust approximately 2 inch (50.8 mm).

WARNING

Suspension fasteners are critical parts because they affect performance of vital components and systems and their failure may result in major service expense. New parts must be installed with the same part numbers or equivalent part, if replacement is necessary. Do not use a replacement part of lesser quality or substitute design. Torque values must be used as specified during reassembly to make sure of correct retention of these parts.

➡**Use the hex-holding feature to prevent the stabilizer bar link stud from turning while removing or installing the nut.**

10. With the vehicle in NEUTRAL, lower it from the hoist.

STABILIZER BAR LINK

REMOVAL & INSTALLATION

➡Use the hex-holding feature to prevent the stabilizer bar link stud from turning while removing or installing the nut.

1. Remove and discard the stabilizer bar link lower nut.
2. Remove the stabilizer bar link upper nut and stabilizer bar link.
    a. Discard the nut.

To install:

3. Install the stabilizer bar link upper nut and stabilizer bar link.
    a. Tighten the new nut to 41 ft. lbs. (55 Nm).

⁂ WARNING

Suspension fasteners are critical parts because they affect performance of vital components and systems and their failure may result in major service expense. New parts must be installed with the same part numbers or equivalent part, if replacement is necessary. Do not use a replacement part of lesser quality or substitute design. Torque values must be used as specified during reassembly to make sure of correct retention of these parts.

➡Use the hex-holding feature to prevent the stabilizer bar link stud from turning while removing or installing the nut.

4. Install the stabilizer bar link lower nut. Tighten the new nut to 46 ft. lbs. (63 Nm).

TOE LINK

REMOVAL & INSTALLATION

See Figure 232.

1. Measure the distance from the center of the wheel hub to the lip of the fender with the vehicle in a level, static ground position (curb height).
2. Remove the wheel and tire.
3. Use a jackstand to raise the rear suspension until the distance between the center of the hub and the lip of the fender is equal to the measurement taken in Step 1 of the procedure (curb height).
4. Remove and discard the toe link-to-wheel knuckle nut.
5. Remove and discard the toe link-to-subframe bolt.

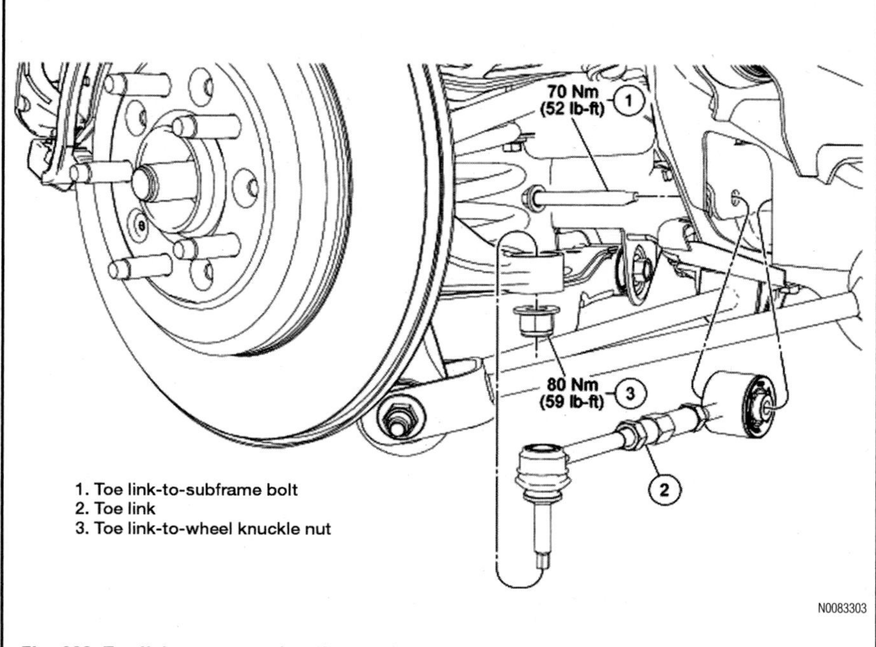

Fig. 232 Toe link component locations and torque values

To install:

6. Install and discard the toe link-to-subframe bolt. Tighten the new bolt to 52 ft. lbs. (70 Nm).
7. Install and discard the toe link-to-wheel knuckle nut. Tighten the new nut to 59 ft. lbs. (80 Nm).
8. Use a jackstand to raise the rear suspension until the distance between the center of the hub and the lip of the fender is equal to the measurement taken in Step 1 of the procedure (curb height).
9. Install the wheel and tire.

⁂ WARNING

Suspension fasteners are critical parts because they affect performance of vital components and systems and their failure may result in major service expense. New parts must be installed with the same part numbers or equivalent part, if replacement is necessary. Do not use a replacement part of lesser quality or substitute design. Torque values must be used as specified during reassembly to make sure of correct retention of these parts.

10. Measure the distance from the center of the wheel hub to the lip of the fender with the vehicle in a level, static ground position (curb height).

Check and, if necessary, adjust the rear toe.

TRAILING ARM

REMOVAL & INSTALLATION

See Figure 233.

1. Measure the distance from the center of the wheel hub to the lip of the fender with the vehicle in a level, static ground position (curb height).
2. Remove the wheel and tire.
3. Use a jackstand to raise the rear suspension until the distance between the center of the hub and the lip of the fender is equal to the measurement taken in Step 1 of the procedure (curb height).
4. Remove and discard the trailing arm-to-knuckle nut and bolt.
5. Remove and discard the trailing arm-to-subframe bolt.

To install:

6. Install and discard the trailing arm-to-subframe bolt. Tighten the new bolt to 122 ft. lbs. (165 Nm).
7. Install and discard the trailing arm-to-knuckle nut and bolt. Tighten the new nut to 66 ft. lbs. (90 Nm).
8. Use a jackstand to raise the rear suspension until the distance between the center of the hub and the lip of the fender is equal to the measurement taken in Step 1 of the procedure (curb height).
9. Install the wheel and tire. For additional information, refer to Wheels and Tires.

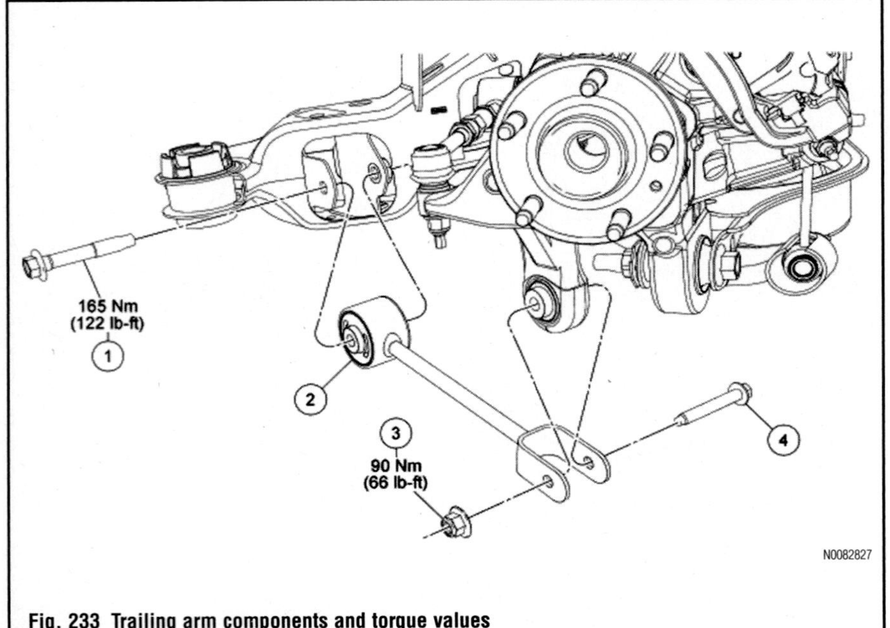

Fig. 233 Trailing arm components and torque values

⁂ WARNING

Suspension fasteners are critical parts because they affect performance of vital components and systems and their failure may result in major service expense. New parts must be installed with the same part numbers or equivalent part, if replacement is necessary. Do not use a replacement part of lesser quality or substitute design. Torque values must be used as specified during reassembly to make sure of correct retention of these parts.

10. Measure the distance from the center of the wheel hub to the lip of the fender with the vehicle in a level, static ground position (curb height).

UPPER CONTROL ARM

REMOVAL & INSTALLATION

See Figures 234 through 237.

1. Measure the distance from the center of the wheel hub to the lip of the fender with the vehicle in a level, static ground position (curb height).
2. Remove the rear wheels and tires.
3. Remove LH and RH parking brake cable bracket bolts.

⁂ WARNING

Do not allow the brake caliper to hang from the brake flexible hose or damage to the hose may occur.

4. Remove the 4 brake caliper anchor plate bolts and position the LH and RH brake caliper and anchor plate assemblies aside.
   a. Support the brake caliper and anchor plate assemblies using mechanic's wire.
5. Position screw-type jackstands under the LH and RH wheel knuckles.
6. Remove and discard the upper arm-to-knuckle bolt and nut.
7. Remove and discard the 2 upper arm-to-subframe rearward bolts.

➡Use the hex-holding feature to prevent the stabilizer bar link stud from turning while removing or installing the nut.

8. Remove and discard the LH and RH stabilizer bar link upper nuts and disconnect the links from the stabilizer bar.
9. Remove and discard the LH and RH lower shock bolts.
10. Remove and discard the 4 subframe bracket bolts.
11. Remove and discard the 2 subframe forward bolts and remove the 2 subframe brackets.
12. Remove and discard the 2 subframe rearward bolts and lower the subframe enough to allow removal of the upper arm forward bolt.
13. Remove and discard the upper arm-to-subframe forward bolt and nut.
    a. Remove the upper arm.
14. If service to the upper arm rearward bushing is required, remove the upper arm bushing bolt and remove the upper arm bushing.
    a. Discard the bolt.

To install:

➡Before tightening the shock absorber lower bolts and upper arm nut and bolts, use a jackstand to raise the rear

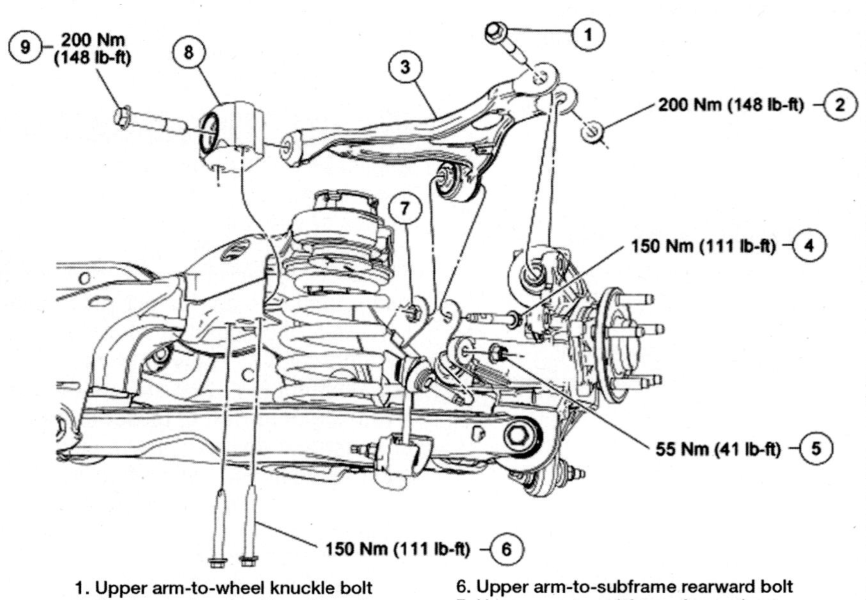

Fig. 234 Upper arm components (1 of 3)

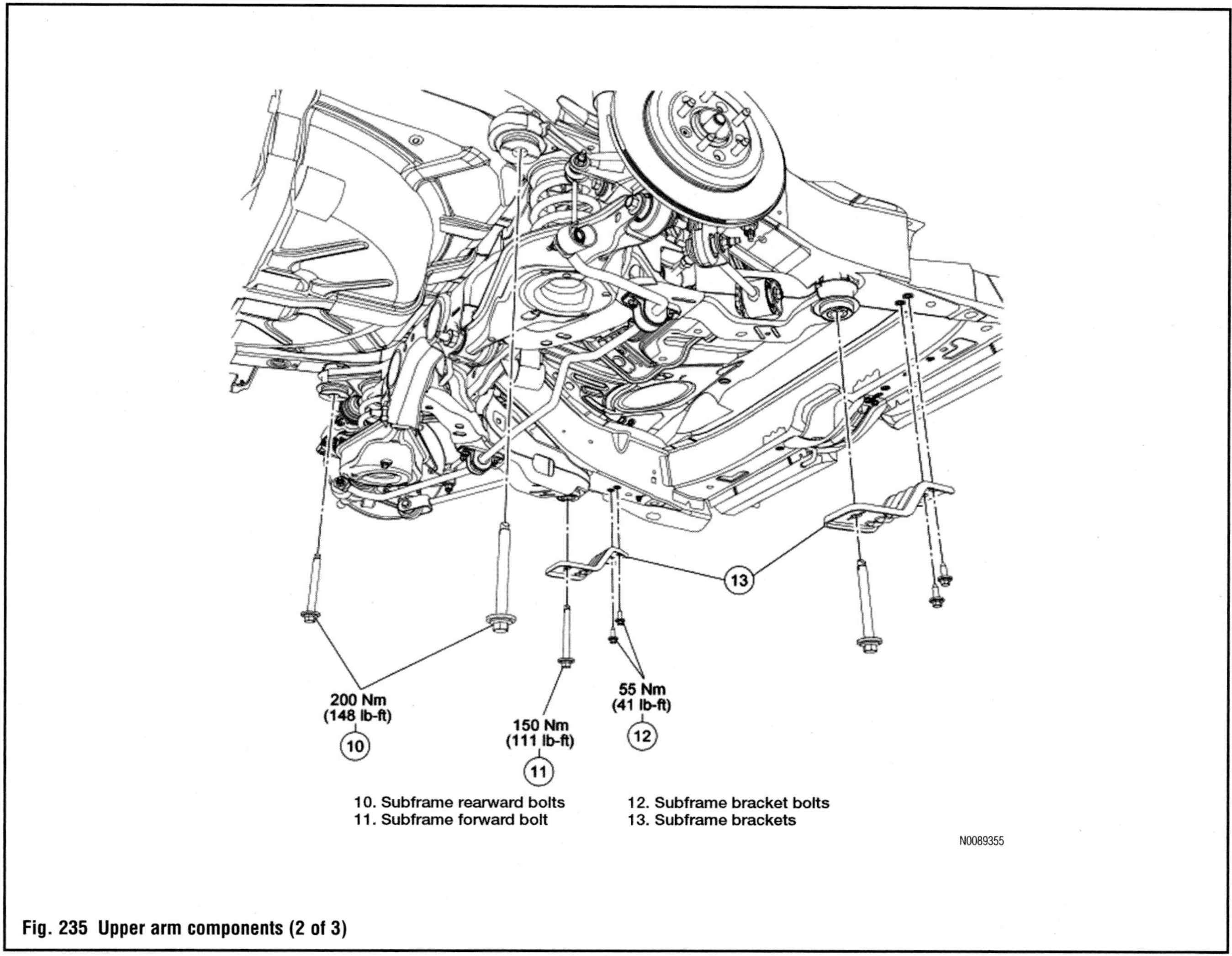

Fig. 235 Upper arm components (2 of 3)

suspension until the distance between the center of the hub and the lip of the fender is equal to the measurement taken in the Removal procedure (curb height).

15. If removed, install the upper arm bushing onto the upper arm in the following sequence.
   a. With the upper arm positioned so the top side is facing up and the upper arm bushing is positioned with the TOP OF PART facing up and the ARM TO THIS SIDE arrow is pointing toward the upper arm. Install the upper arm bushing.
   b. Install a new upper arm rearward bushing bolt and tighten to 148 ft. lbs. (200 Nm).
16. Position the upper arm and loosely install the new upper arm-to-subframe forward bolt and nut.
17. Raise the subframe and install 2 new subframe rearward bolts. Tighten the bolts to 148 ft. lbs. (200 Nm).
18. Position the 2 subframe brackets and install 4 new subframe bracket bolts. Tighten the bolts to 41 ft. lbs. (55 Nm).
19. Install 2 new subframe forward bolts. Tighten the bolts to 111 ft. lbs. (150 Nm).
20. Loosely install new LH and RH shock absorber lower bolts.

➡Use the hex-holding feature to prevent the stabilizer bar link stud from turning while removing or installing the nut.

21. Connect the LH and RH stabilizer bar links to the stabilizer bar and install the new nuts. Tighten the nuts to 41 ft. lbs. (55 Nm).
22. Loosely install 2 new upper arm-to-subframe rearward bolts.
23. Loosely install a new upper arm-to-knuckle bolt and nut.
24. Position the LH and RH brake caliper and anchor plate assemblies and install the 4 anchor plate bolts. Tighten the bolts to 76 ft. lbs. (103).
25. Install LH and RH parking brake cable bracket bolts. Tighten the bolts to 133 inch lbs. (15 Nm).
26. Using the screw-type jackstand, raise the rear suspension until the distance between the center of the hub and the lip of the fender is equal to the measurement taken in the removal procedure (curb height).
27. Tighten the upper arm-to-subframe forward bolt to 111 ft. lbs. (150 Nm).
28. Tighten the LH and RH shock absorber lower bolts to 129 ft. lbs. (175 Nm).
29. Tighten the 2 upper arm-to-subframe rearward bolts to 111 ft. lbs. (150 Nm).

➡A slotted upper arm allows for the rear suspension camber to be adjusted by pushing inward or pulling outward on the wheel knuckle while tightening the upper arm-to-wheel knuckle nut.

30. With the wheel knuckle pushed

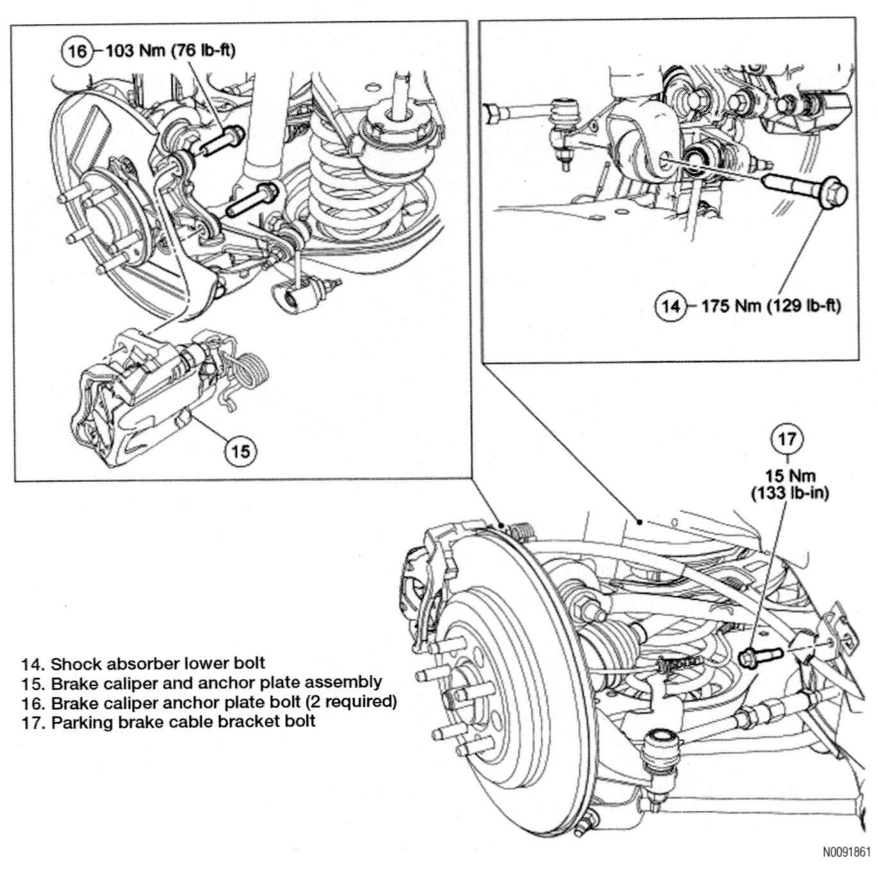

Fig. 236 Upper arm components (3 of 3)

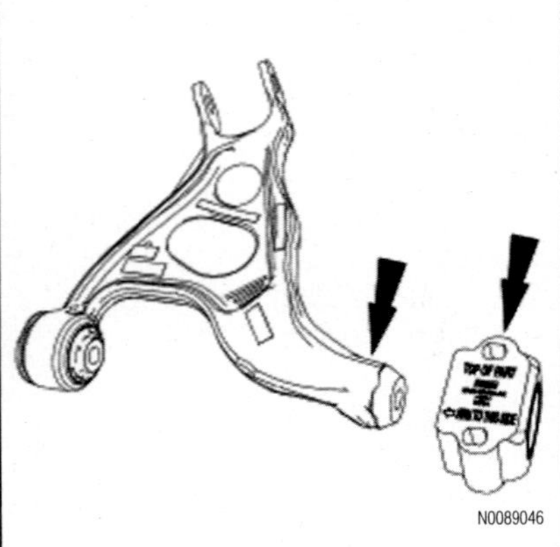

Fig. 237 With the upper arm positioned so the top side is facing up and the upper arm bushing is positioned with the TOP OF PART facing up and the ARM TO THIS SIDE arrow is pointing toward the upper arm. Install the upper arm bushing

inward for maximum negative camber, tighten the upper arm-to-wheel knuckle nut to 148 ft. lbs. (200 Nm).

31. Remove the 2 jackstands.
32. Install the rear wheels and tires.
33. Check and, if necessary, adjust the rear camber.

WHEEL HUB & BEARING

REMOVAL & INSTALLATION

See Figure 238.

All Vehicles

1. Remove the brake disc (rotor).
2. Remove the wheel speed sensor bolt and position the sensor aside.

All-Wheel Drive (AWD) Vehicles

➡Do not discard the nut at this time.

3. Remove the wheel hub nut.
4. Using the Front Wheel Hub Remover, separate the halfshaft from the wheel hub.

All Vehicles

5. Remove the 4 bolts and the wheel bearing and wheel hub.
   a. Discard the bolts.

⁂ WARNING

The wheel knuckle bore must be clean enough to allow the wheel bearing and wheel hub to seat completely by hand. Do not press or draw the wheel hub and bearing into place or damage to the bearing may occur.

⁂ WARNING

Make sure the wheel hub-to-knuckle mating surfaces are clean and free of any adhesive. Failure to clean adhesive from both surfaces may cause bearing damage.

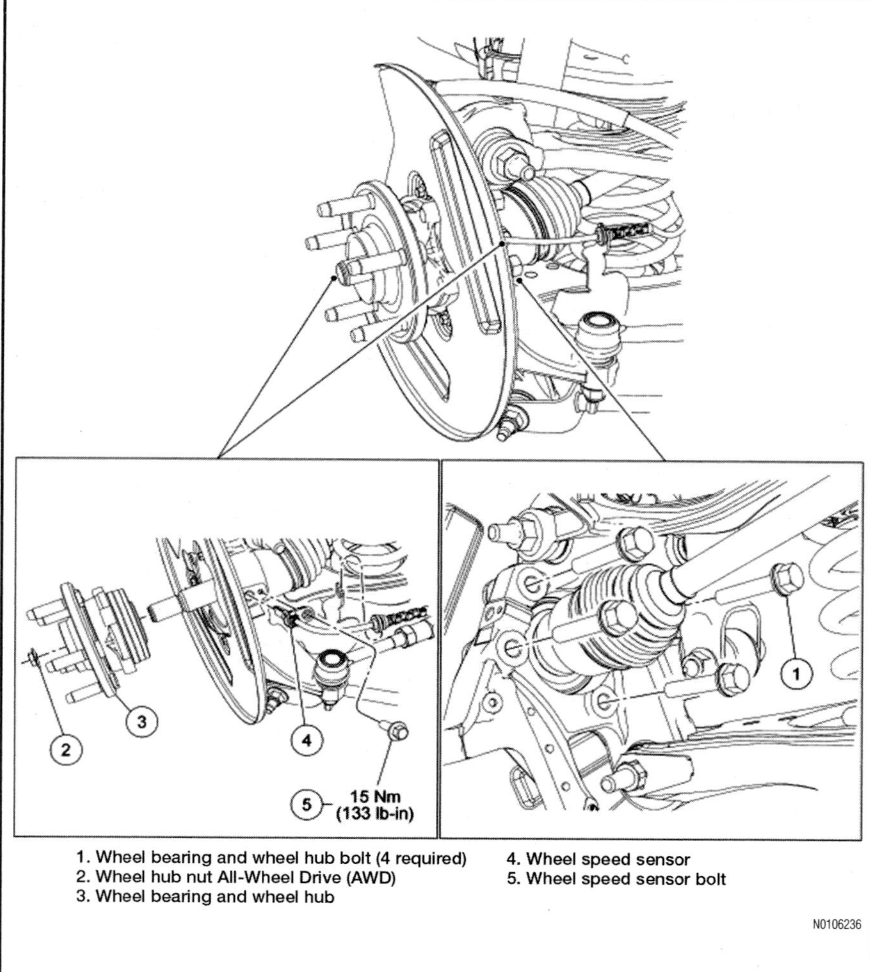

Fig. 238 Wheel bearing and wheel hub components. AWD shown, FWD similar

6. Using a clean shop towel, clean the wheel knuckle-to-mating surfaces and inspect the knuckle bearing bore.
   a. If the wheel knuckle is cracked, install a new wheel knuckle.

To install:

All Vehicles

7. Install the wheel bearing and wheel hub assembly.
8. Install the 4 new wheel bearing and wheel hub bolts. Tighten the bolts to 98 ft. lbs. (133 Nm) in a cross-pattern.
9. Install the brake disc (rotor).
10. Position the wheel speed sensor and install the bolt. Tighten the bolt to 133 inch lbs. (15 Nm).

AWD Vehicles

WARNING

Do not tighten the rear wheel hub nut with the vehicle on the ground. The nut must be tightened to specification before the vehicle is lowered to the ground. Wheel bearing damage will occur if the wheel bearing is loaded with the weight of the vehicle applied.

➡Apply the brake to keep the halfshaft from rotating.

11. Position the halfshaft in the hub and use the previously removed wheel hub nut to seat the halfshaft. Tighten the nut to 258 ft. lbs. (350 Nm).
   a. Remove and discard the nut.

WARNING

Install and tighten the new wheel hub nut to specification within 5 minutes of starting it on the threads. Always install a new wheel hub nut after loosening or when not tightening within the specified time or damage to the components may occur.

12. Install a new wheel hub nut. Tighten the nut to 258 ft. lbs. (350 Nm).

WHEEL KNUCKLE

REMOVAL & INSTALLATION

AWD Models

See Figures 239 through 241.

1. Measure the distance from the center of the wheel hub to the lip of the fender with the vehicle in a level, static ground position (curb height).
2. Remove the wheel bearing and wheel hub as outlined in this section.
3. Using a suitable jackstand, support the lower arm.
4. Remove and discard the trailing arm-to-wheel knuckle nut and bolt.

➡Use the hex-holding feature to prevent the stabilizer bar link stud from turning while removing or installing the nut.

5. Remove and discard the stabilizer bar link upper nut and disconnect the link.
6. Remove and discard the shock absorber lower bolt and disconnect the shock absorber from the knuckle bracket.
7. Remove and discard the toe link-to-knuckle nut.
8. Remove and discard the upper arm-to-wheel knuckle nut and bolt and disconnect the upper arm from the knuckle.
9. Remove and discard the lower arm-to-wheel knuckle nut and bolt.
10. Lower the jackstand, slide the knuckle off the toe link and remove the knuckle.
11. If necessary, remove the 3 brake disc shield bolts and remove the shield.

To install:

➡Before tightening suspension bushing fasteners, use a jackstand to raise the rear suspension until the distance between the center of the hub and the lip of the fender is equal to the measurement taken in the removal procedure (curb height).

12. If removed, install the brake disc shield. Tighten the 3 bolts to 133 inch lbs. (15 Nm).
13. Position the wheel knuckle onto the toe link and loosely install a new lower arm-to-wheel knuckle nut and bolt.
14. Loosely install a new toe link-to-knuckle nut.
15. Connect the shock absorber to the knuckle and loosely install a new shock absorber lower bolt.

➡Use the hex-holding feature to prevent the stabilizer bar link stud from turning while removing or installing the nut.

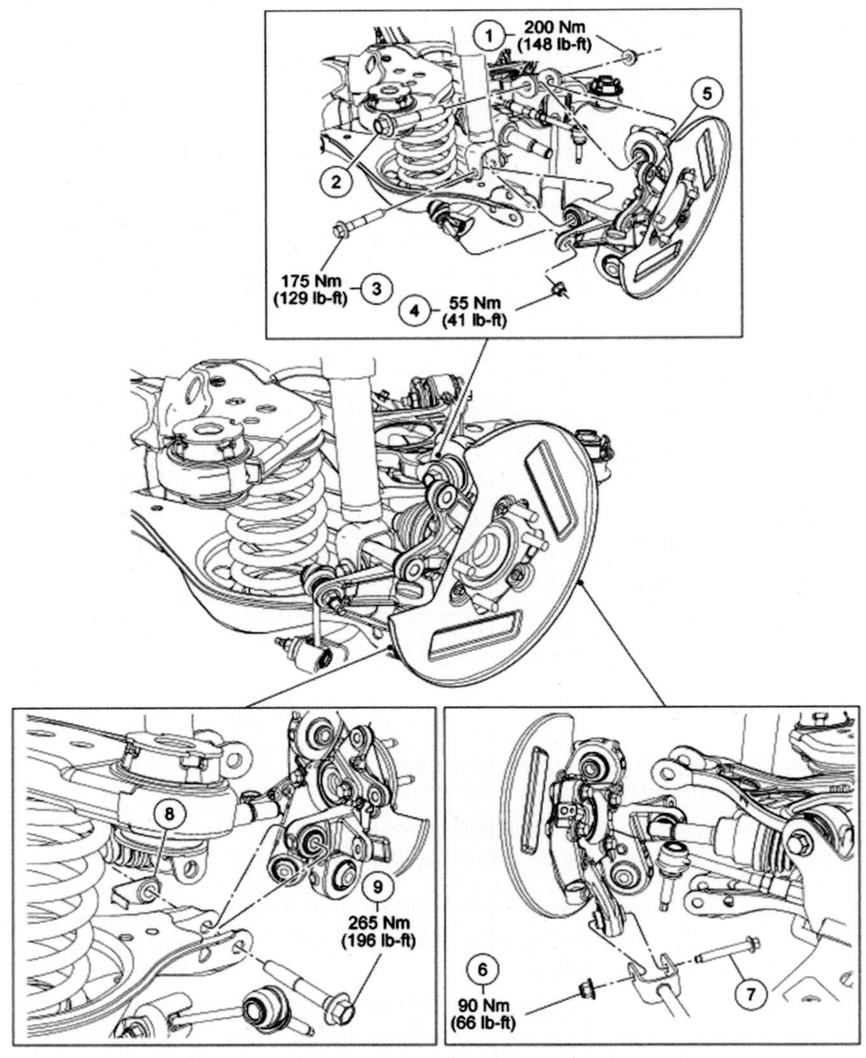

1. Upper arm-to-wheel knuckle nut
2. Upper arm-to-wheel knuckle bolt
3. Shock absorber lower bolt
4. Stabilizer bar link upper nut
5. Wheel knuckle
6. Trailing arm-to-wheel knuckle nut
7. Trailing arm-to-wheel knuckle bolt
8. Lower arm-to-wheel knuckle nut
9. Lower arm-to-wheel knuckle bolt

N0090810

Fig. 239 Wheel knuckle—AWD (1 of 3)

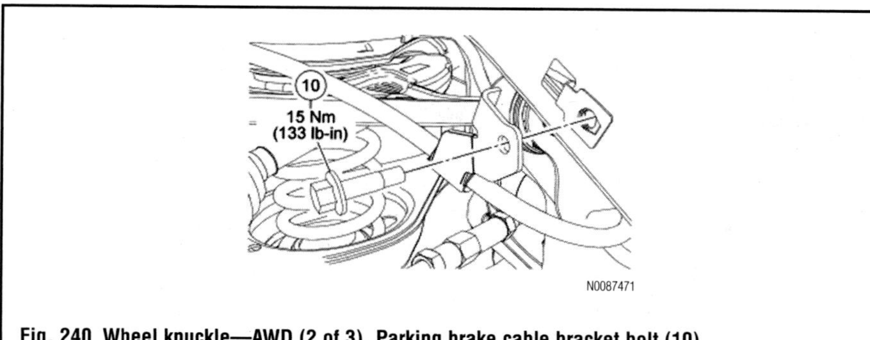

Fig. 240 Wheel knuckle—AWD (2 of 3). Parking brake cable bracket bolt (10)

16. Connect the stabilizer bar link and install a new stabilizer bar link upper nut. Tighten the nut to 41 ft. lbs. (55 Nm).
17. Loosely install a new trailing arm-to-wheel knuckle nut and bolt.
18. Raise the jackstand and loosely install a new upper arm-to-wheel knuckle nut and bolt.
19. Position a suitable jackstand under the lower control arm at the shock and spring assembly attachment point and raise the rear suspension until the distance between the center of the hub and the lip of the fender is equal to the measurement taken in Step 1 of the procedure (curb height).

➡A slotted upper arm allows for the rear suspension camber to be adjusted by pushing inward or pulling outward on the wheel knuckle while tightening the upper arm-to-wheel knuckle nut.

20. With the wheel knuckle pushed inward for maximum negative camber, tighten the upper arm-to-wheel knuckle nut to 200 Nm (148 lb-ft).
21. Tighten the lower arm-to-wheel knuckle bolt to 196 ft. lbs. (265 Nm).
22. Tighten the shock absorber bolt to 129 ft. lbs. (175 Nm).
23. Tighten the trailing arm-to-wheel knuckle nut to 66 ft. lbs. (90 Nm).
24. Tighten the toe link-to-wheel knuckle nut to 59 ft. lbs. (80 Nm).
25. Install the wheel bearing and wheel hub as outlined in this section.
26. Check and if necessary, adjust the rear toe.

FWD Models

See Figures 242 and 243.

1. Measure the distance from the center of the wheel hub to the lip of the fender with the vehicle in a level, static ground position (curb height).

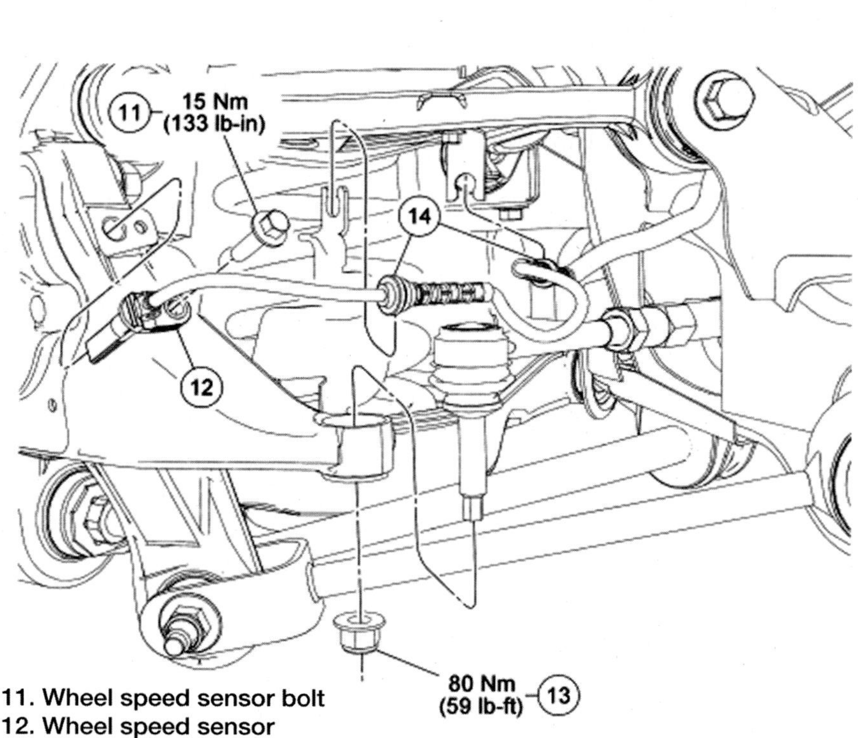

Fig. 241 Wheel knuckle—AWD (3 of 3)

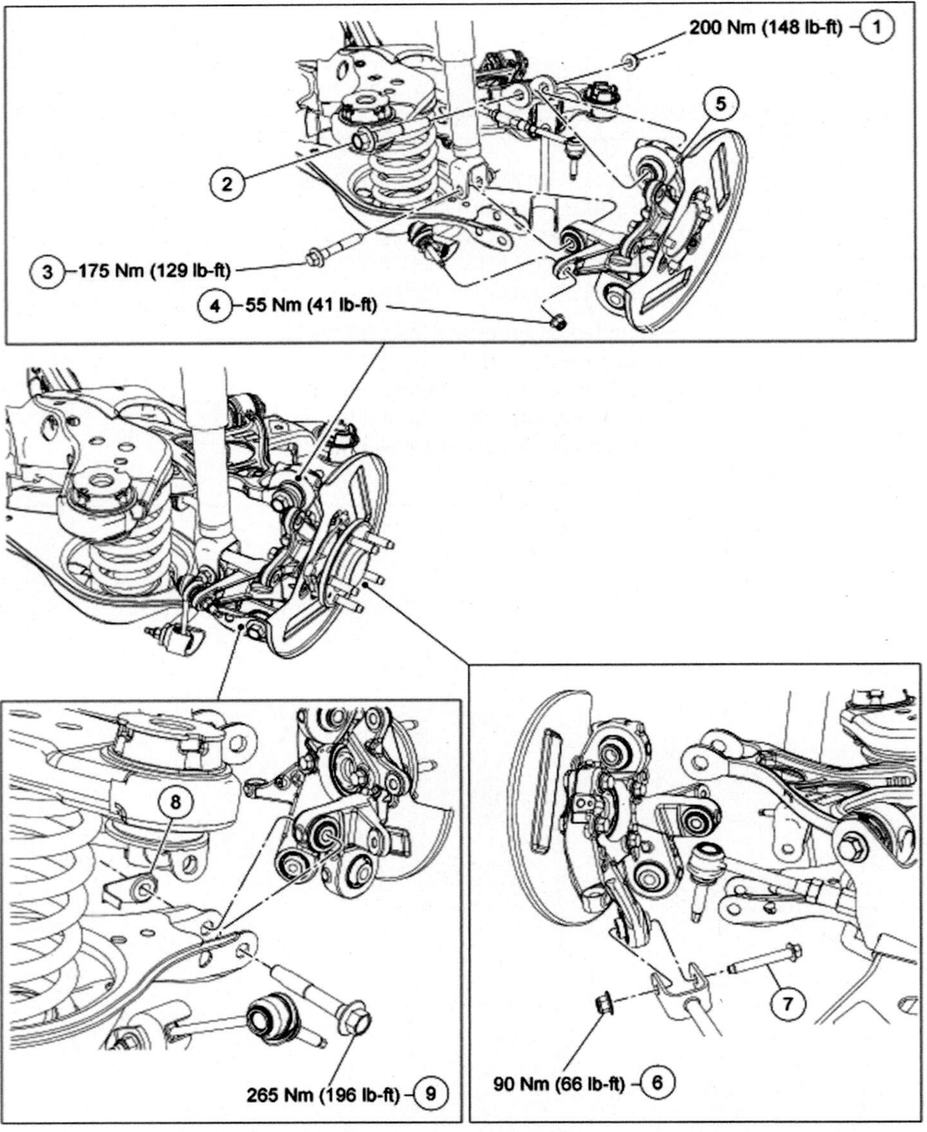

1. Upper arm-to-wheel knuckle nut
2. Upper arm-to-wheel knuckle bolt
3. Shock absorber lower bolt
4. Stabilizer bar link upper nut
5. Wheel knuckle
6. Trailing arm-to-wheel knuckle nut
7. Trailing arm-to-wheel knuckle bolt
8. Lower arm-to-wheel knuckle nut
9. Lower arm-to-wheel knuckle bolt

N0087434

Fig. 242 Wheel knuckle—FWD (1 of 2)

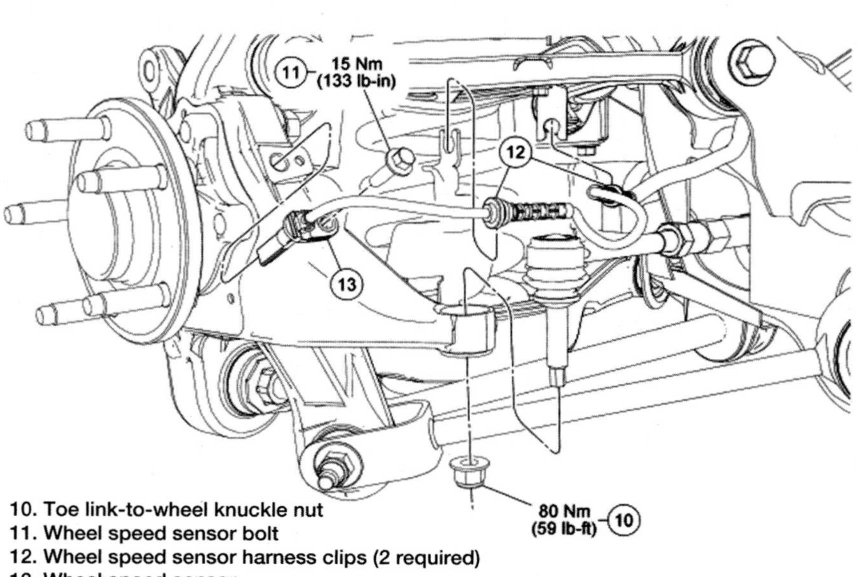

Fig. 243 Wheel knuckle—FWD (1 of 2)

2. Remove the wheel and tire.
3. Remove the brake disc (rotor).
4. Using a suitable jackstand, support the lower arm.
5. Remove and discard the trailing arm-to-wheel knuckle nut and bolt.

➡Use the hex-holding feature to prevent the stabilizer bar link stud from turning while removing the nut.

6. Remove and discard the stabilizer bar link upper nut and disconnect the link.
7. Remove and discard the shock absorber lower bolt and disconnect the shock absorber.
8. Remove the wheel speed sensor bolt, disconnect the harness and position the sensor and harness assembly aside.
9. Remove and discard the toe link-to-knuckle nut.
10. Remove and discard the upper arm-to-wheel knuckle nut and bolt and disconnect the upper arm from the knuckle.
11. Remove and discard the lower arm-to-wheel knuckle nut and bolt.
12. Lower the jackstand, slide the knuckle off the toe link and remove the knuckle.

To install:

➡Before tightening any suspension bushing fasteners, use a jackstand to raise the rear suspension until the distance between the center of the hub and the lip of the fender is equal to the measurement taken in the removal procedure (curb height).

13. Position the wheel knuckle onto the toe link and loosely install a new lower arm-to-wheel knuckle nut and bolt.
14. Loosely install a new toe link-to-knuckle nut.
15. Position the wheel speed sensor harness and install the wheel speed sensor and bolt. Tighten the bolt to 133 inch lbs. (15 Nm).
16. Connect the shock absorber to the knuckle and loosely install a new shock absorber lower bolt.
17. Connect the stabilizer bar link and install a new stabilizer bar link upper nut. Tighten the nut to 41 ft. lbs. (55 Nm).

➡Use the hex-holding feature to prevent the stabilizer bar link stud from turning while removing or installing the nut.

18. Loosely install a new trailing arm-to-wheel knuckle nut and bolt.
19. Loosely install a new upper arm-to-wheel knuckle nut and bolt.
20. Position a suitable jackstand under the lower control arm at the shock and spring assembly attachment point and raise the rear suspension until the distance between the center of the hub and the lip of the fender is equal to the measurement taken in Step 1 of the procedure (curb height).

➡A slotted upper arm allows for the rear suspension camber to be adjusted by pushing inward or pulling outward

on the wheel knuckle while tightening the upper arm-to-wheel knuckle nut.

21. With the wheel knuckle pushed inward for maximum negative camber, tighten the upper arm-to-wheel knuckle nut to 148 ft. lbs. (200 Nm).
22. Tighten the lower arm-to-wheel knuckle bolt to 196 ft. lbs. (265 Nm).
23. Tighten the shock absorber bolt to 129 ft. lbs. (175 Nm).
24. Tighten the trailing arm-to-wheel knuckle nut to 66 ft. lbs. (90 Nm).
25. Tighten the toe link-to-knuckle nut to 59 ft. lbs. (80 Nm).
26. Install the brake disc (rotor).
27. Install the wheel and tire.
28. Check and if necessary, adjust the rear toe.

FORD

Focus

11

BRAKES 11-10

ANTI-LOCK BRAKE SYSTEM (ABS) 11-10
General Information................ 11-10
Precautions........................ 11-10
Speed Sensors........................ 11-10
Removal & Installation........ 11-10
BLEEDING THE BRAKE SYSTEM 11-11
Bleeding Procedure................ 11-11
Bleeding Procedure 11-11
Bleeding the ABS System ... 11-13
Brake Line Bleeding............ 11-13
Fluid Fill Procedure 11-13
Master Cylinder Bleeding 11-12
FRONT DISC BRAKES........ 11-14
Brake Caliper.......................... 11-14
Removal & Installation........ 11-14
Disc Brake Pads..................... 11-14
Removal & Installation........ 11-14
PARKING BRAKE.............. 11-17
Parking Brake Cables............. 11-17
Adjustment 11-17
Parking Brake Shoes.............. 11-17
Removal & Installation........ 11-17
REAR DRUM BRAKES........ 11-15
Brake Drum 11-15
Removal & Installation........ 11-15
Brake Shoes........................... 11-16
Adjustment 11-17
Removal & Installation........ 11-16

CHASSIS ELECTRICAL 11-18

AIR BAG (SUPPLEMENTAL RESTRAINT SYSTEM) 11-18
General Information................ 11-18
Arming the System 11-19
Clockspring Centering........ 11-19
Disarming the System......... 11-18
Service Precautions............ 11-18

DRIVE TRAIN 11-20

Automatic Transaxle Fluid 11-20
Drain and Refill.................. 11-20
Clutch.................................... 11-23
Bleeding 11-23
Fluid Fill Procedure 11-24
Removal & Installation........ 11-23
Front Halfshaft........................ 11-24
Removal & Installation........ 11-24
Manual Transaxle Assembly 11-20
Removal & Installation........ 11-20
Manual Transaxle Fluid 11-22
Drain and Refill.................. 11-22

ENGINE COOLING........... 11-27

Engine Coolant....................... 11-27
Bleeding 11-28
Drain & Refill Procedure..... 11-27
Flushing............................. 11-28
Engine Fan 11-28
Removal & Installation........ 11-28
Radiator................................. 11-28
Removal & Installation........ 11-28
Thermostat 11-29
Removal & Installation........ 11-29
Water Pump 11-30
Removal & Installation........ 11-30

ENGINE ELECTRICAL 11-31

BATTERY SYSTEM............ 11-31
Battery................................... 11-31
Battery Reconnect/Relearn Procedure........................ 11-31
Removal & Installation........ 11-31
CHARGING SYSTEM 11-32
Alternator 11-32
Removal & Installation........ 11-32
IGNITION SYSTEM 11-33
Firing Order........................... 11-33
Ignition Coil 11-33
Removal & Installation........ 11-33
Ignition Timing....................... 11-33
Adjustment 11-33
Spark Plugs............................ 11-33
Removal & Installation........ 11-33
STARTING SYSTEM 11-34
Starter 11-34
Removal & Installation........ 11-34

ENGINE MECHANICAL...... 11-34

Accessory Drive Belts 11-34
Accessory Belt Routing....... 11-34
Adjustment 11-34
Inspection 11-34
Removal & Installation........ 11-34
Air Cleaner 11-35
Filter/Element Replacement... 11-35
Removal & Installation........ 11-35
Camshaft and Valve Lifters...... 11-36
Inspection 11-36
Removal & Installation........ 11-37
Catalytic Converter 11-39
Removal & Installation........ 11-39
Crankshaft Front Seal............. 11-40
Removal & Installation........ 11-40
Cylinder Head 11-41
Removal & Installation........ 11-41
Engine Oil & Filter 11-43
Replacement 11-43
Exhaust Manifold 11-44
Removal & Installation........ 11-44
Intake Manifold 11-44
Removal & Installation........ 11-44
Oil Pan 11-46
Removal & Installation........ 11-46
Oil Pump................................ 11-47
Removal & Installation........ 11-47
Piston and Ring...................... 11-48
Positioning 11-48
Rear Main Seal....................... 11-49
Removal & Installation........ 11-49
Timing Chain & Sprockets...... 11-51
Removal & Installation........ 11-51
Timing Chain Front Cover....... 11-50
Removal & Installation........ 11-51
Valve Covers 11-52
Removal & Installation........ 11-52
Valve Lash.............................. 11-53
Adjustment 11-53

ENGINE PERFORMANCE & EMISSION CONTROLS 11-54

Camshaft Position (CMP) Sensor 11-54

Location...11-54
Removal & Installation...11-54
Crankshaft Position (CKP) Sensor...11-54
Location...11-54
Removal & Installation...11-54
Cylinder Head Temperature (CHT) Sensor...11-56
Location...11-56
Removal & Installation...11-56
Heated Oxygen (HO2S) Sensor...11-56
Location...11-56
Removal & Installation...11-56
Knock Sensor (KS)...11-56
Location...11-56
Removal & Installation...11-56
Mass Air Flow (MAF) Sensor...11-57
Location...11-57
Removal & Installation...11-57
Powertrain Control Module (PCM)...11-57
Location...11-57
Parameter Reset Procedure...11-57
Programmable Module Installation (PMI) Procedure...11-58
Removal & Installation...11-57
Throttle Position Sensor (TPS)...11-58
Location...11-58
Removal & Installation...11-58
Vehicle Speed Sensor (VSS)...11-58
Location...11-58
Removal & Installation...11-58

FUEL...11-59

GASOLINE FUEL INJECTION SYSTEM...11-59
Fuel Filter...11-59
Removal & Installation...11-59
Fuel Injectors...11-59
Removal & Installation...11-59
Fuel Pump Module...11-60
Removal & Installation...11-60
Fuel System Service Precautions...11-59
Fuel Tank...11-61
Draining...11-61
Removal & Installation...11-61
Idle Speed...11-62
Adjustment...11-62
Relieving Fuel System Pressure...11-59
Throttle Body...11-62
Removal & Installation...11-62

HEATING & AIR CONDITIONING SYSTEM...11-63
Blower Motor...11-63
Removal & Installation...11-63
Heater Core...11-63
Removal & Installation...11-63

PRECAUTIONS...11-10

SPECIFICATIONS AND MAINTENANCE CHARTS...11-3
Brake Specifications...11-7
Camshaft Specifications...11-5
Capacities...11-4
Crankshaft and Connecting Rod Specifications...11-5
Engine and Vehicle Identification...11-3
Engine Tune-Up Specifications...11-3
Fluid Specifications...11-4
General Engine Specifications...11-3
Piston and Ring Specifications...11-5
Scheduled Maintenance Intervals...11-8
Tire, Wheel and Ball Joint Specifications...11-7
Torque Specifications...11-6
Valve Specifications...11-4
Wheel Alignment...11-6

STEERING...11-64
Power Steering Gear...11-64
Removal & Installation...11-64
Power Steering Pump...11-65
Bleeding...11-66
Fluid Fill Procedure...11-67
Removal & Installation...11-65

SUSPENSION...11-68

FRONT SUSPENSION...11-68
Control Links...11-68
Removal & Installation...11-68
Lower Ball Joint...11-68
Removal & Installation...11-68
Lower Control Arm...11-68
Removal & Installation...11-68
Stabilizer Bar...11-69
Removal & Installation...11-69
Steering Knuckle...11-70
Removal & Installation...11-70
Strut & Spring Assembly...11-72
Overhaul...11-72
Removal & Installation...11-72
Wheel Hub & Bearings...11-73
Adjustment...11-74
Removal & Installation...11-73

REAR SUSPENSION...11-74
Coil Spring...11-74
Removal & Installation...11-74
Lower Control Arm...11-75
Removal & Installation...11-75
Shock Absorbers...11-76
Removal & Installation...11-76
Testing...11-77
Stabilizer Bar...11-77
Removal & Installation...11-77
Upper Control Arm...11-78
Removal & Installation...11-78
Wheel Bearings...11-79
Adjustment...11-80
Removal & Installation...11-79
Wheel Knuckle...11-80
Removal & Installation...11-80

SPECIFICATIONS AND MAINTENANCE CHARTS

ENGINE AND VEHICLE IDENTIFICATION

Code ①	Engine: Liters (cc)	Cu. In.	Cyl.	Fuel Sys.	Engine Type	Eng. Mfg.
N	2.0	122	4	SFI	DOHC	Ford

Model Year: Code ②	Year
A	2010
B	2011

SFI: Sequential Multi-Port Fuel Injection

DOHC: Double Overhead Camshafts

① 8th position of VIN

② 10th position of VIN

25759_FOCU_C0001

GENERAL ENGINE SPECIFICATIONS

All measurements are given in inches.

Year	Model	Engine Displacement Liters	Engine ID/VIN	Fuel System Type	Net Horsepower @ rpm	Net Torque @ rpm (ft. lbs.)	Bore x Stroke (in.)	Com-pression Ratio	Oil Pressure @ rpm
2010	Focus	2.0	N	SFI	140@6,000	136@4,250	3.44 x 3.27	10.0:1	29-39@2,000
2011	Focus	2.0	N	SFI	140@6,000	136@4,250	3.44 x 3.27	10.0:1	29-39@2,000

SFI: Sequential Multi-Port Fuel Injection

25759_FOCU_C0002

ENGINE TUNE-UP SPECIFICATIONS

Year	Engine Displacement Liters	Engine ID/VIN	Spark Plug Gap (in.)	Ignition Timing (deg.)		Fuel Pump (psi)	Idle Speed (rpm)		Valve Clearance	
				MT	AT		MT	AT	Intake	Exhaust
2010	2.0	N	0.049-0.053	10B	10B	55	①	①	0.008-0.011	0.010-0.013
2011	2.0	N	0.049-0.053	10B	10B	55	①	①	0.008-0.011	0.010-0.013

NOTE: The Vehicle Emission Control Information label often reflects specification changes made during production. The label figures must be used if they differ from those in this chart.

B: Before Top Dead Center

① Idle speed is controlled by the PCM

25759_FOCU_C0003

CAPACITIES

Year	Model	Engine Displacement Liters	Engine ID/VIN	Engine Oil with Filter (qts.)	Transaxle (pts.) Auto.	Transaxle (pts.) Manual	Drive Axle (pts.) Front	Drive Axle (pts.) Rear	Transfer Case (pts.)	Fuel Tank (gal.)	Cooling System (qts.)
2010	Focus	2.0	N	4.5	14.0	4.0	N/A	N/A	N/A	13.0	5.3
2011	Focus	2.0	N	4.5	14.0	4.0	N/A	N/A	N/A	13.0	5.3

NOTE: All capacities are approximate. Add fluid gradually and ensure a proper fluid level is obtained.

N/A: Not Applicable

25759_FOCU_C0004

FLUID SPECIFICATIONS

Year	Model	Engine Disp. Liters	Engine Oil	Manual Trans.	Auto. Trans.	Drive Axle Front	Drive Axle Rear	Transfer Case	Power Steering Fluid	Brake Master Cylinder	Cooling System
2010	Focus	2.0	5W-20	①	Mercon® LV ATF	N/A	N/A	N/A	Mercon® V ATF	DOT 3	Motorcraft® Gold
2011	Focus	2.0	5W-20	①	Mercon® LV ATF	N/A	N/A	N/A	Mercon® V ATF	DOT 3	Motorcraft® Gold

DOT: Department Of Transportation

N/A: Not Applicable

① Full synthetic manual transmission fluid: XT-M5-QS

25759_FOCU_C0005

VALVE SPECIFICATIONS

Year	Engine Displacement Liters	Engine ID/VIN	Seat Angle (deg.)	Face Angle (deg.)	Spring Test Pressure (lbs. @ in.)	Spring Free-Length (in.)	Spring Installed Height (in.)	Stem-to-Guide Clearance (in.) Intake	Stem-to-Guide Clearance (in.) Exhaust	Stem Diameter (in.) Intake	Stem Diameter (in.) Exhaust
2010	2.0	N	45	45	①	1.768	1.492	0.0001	0.0001	0.2153-0.2159	0.2151-0.2157
2011	2.0	N	45	45	①	1.768	1.492	0.0001	0.0001	0.2153-0.2159	0.2151-0.2157

① Intake: 97.03 lbs.@0.35 inch; Exhaust: 93.34 lbs.@0.29 inch

25759_FOCU_C0006

CAMSHAFT SPECIFICATIONS

All measurements in inches unless noted

Year	Engine Displacement Liters	Engine Code/VIN	Journal Diameter	Brg. Oil Clearance	Shaft End-play	Runout	Journal Bore	Lobe Height Intake	Lobe Height Exhaust
2010	2.0	N	0.9820-0.9830	0.0010-0.0030	0.0030-0.0090	0.0010	0.9840-0.9850	0.3240	0.3070
2011	2.0	N	0.9820-0.9830	0.0010-0.0030	0.0030-0.0090	0.0010	0.9840-0.9850	0.3240	0.3070

25759_FOCU_C0007

CRANKSHAFT AND CONNECTING ROD SPECIFICATIONS

All measurements are given in inches.

Year	Engine Displacement Liters	Engine ID/VIN	Crankshaft Main Brg. Journal Dia.	Crankshaft Main Brg. Oil Clearance	Crankshaft Shaft End-play	Crankshaft Thrust on No.	Connecting Rod Journal Diameter	Connecting Rod Oil Clearance	Connecting Rod Side Clearance
2010	2.0	N	2.0460-2.0470	0.0007-0.0013	0.0080-0.0160	3	1.9670-1.9680	0.0010-0.0020	0.0760-0.1200
2011	2.0	N	2.0460-2.0470	0.0007-0.0013	0.0080-0.0160	3	1.9670-1.9680	0.0010-0.0020	0.0760-0.1200

25759_FOCU_C0008

PISTON AND RING SPECIFICATIONS

All measurements are given in inches.

Year	Engine Displacement Liters	Engine ID/VIN	Piston Clearance	Ring Gap Top Compression	Ring Gap Bottom Compression	Ring Gap Oil Control	Ring Side Clearance Top Compression	Ring Side Clearance Bottom Compression	Ring Side Clearance Oil Control
2010	2.0	N	0.0009-0.0017	0.0060-0.0120	0.0120-0.0180	0.0070-0.0270	0.0008-0.0013	0.0004-0.0011	0.0025-0.0054
2011	2.0	N	0.0009-0.0017	0.0060-0.0120	0.0120-0.0180	0.0070-0.0270	0.0008-0.0013	0.0004-0.0011	0.0025-0.0054

25759_FOCU_C0009

TORQUE SPECIFICATIONS

All readings in ft. lbs.

Year	Engine Disp. Liters	Engine ID/VIN	Cylinder Head Bolts	Main Bearing Bolts	Rod Bearing Bolts	Crankshaft Damper Bolts	Flywheel Bolts	Manifold Intake	Manifold Exhaust	Spark Plugs	Oil Pan Drain Plug
2010	2.0	N	①	②	③	④	⑤	13	⑥	9	21
2011	2.0	N	①	②	③	④	⑤	13	⑥	9	21

① Step 1: 44 inch lbs.
Step 2: 133 inch lbs.
Step 3: 33 ft. lbs.
Step 4: Plus 90 degrees
Step 5: Plus 90 degrees

② Apply engine oil to bolts
Step 1: 44 inch lbs.
Step 2: 18 ft. lbs.
Step 3: Plus 90 degrees

③ Step 1: 21 ft. lbs.
Step 2: Plus 90 degrees

④ Step 1: 74 ft. lbs.
Step 2: Plus 90 degrees

⑤ Step 1: 37 ft. lbs.
Step 2: 50 ft. lbs.
Step 3: 83 ft. lbs.

⑥ Step 1: 41 ft. lbs.
Step 2: 41 ft. lbs.

25759_FOCU_C0010

WHEEL ALIGNMENT

Year	Model		Caster Range (+/-Deg.)	Caster Preferred Setting (Deg.)	Camber Range (+/-Deg.)	Camber Preferred Setting (Deg.)	Toe-in (in.)
2010	Focus	F	0.75	+2.50	0.75	-0.50	0.00 +/- 0.20
		R	N/A	N/A	1.00	-1.00	0.36 +/- 0.20
2011	Focus	F	0.75	+2.50	0.75	-0.50	0.00 +/- 0.20
		R	N/A	N/A	1.00	-1.00	0.36 +/- 0.20

N/A: Not Applicable

25759_FOCU_C0011

TIRE, WHEEL AND BALL JOINT SPECIFICATIONS

Year	Model	OEM Tires		Tire Pressures (psi)		Wheel	Ball Joint	Lug Nut
		Standard	Optional	Front	Rear	Size	Inspection	(ft. lbs.)
2010	Focus	P195/60/R15	NA	①	①	NA	②	100
		P205/50/R16	NA	①	①	NA	②	100
		P215/45/R17	NA	①	①	NA	②	100
2011	Focus	P195/60/R15	NA	①	①	NA	②	100
		P205/50/R16	NA	①	①	NA	②	100
		P215/45/R17	NA	①	①	NA	②	100

OEM: Original Equipment Manufacturer

PSI: Pounds Per Square Inch

NA: Information not available

① Always refer to the owner's manual and/or vehicle label

② Replace if any measurable movement is found

25759_FOCU_C0012

BRAKE SPECIFICATIONS

All measurements in inches unless noted

			Brake Disc			Brake Drum Diameter			Minimum Pad/Lining Thickness		Brake Caliper	
Year	Model		Original Thickness	Minimum Thickness	Max. Runout	Original Inside Diameter	Max. Wear Limit	Maximum Machine Diameter	Front	Rear	Bracket Bolts (ft. lbs.)	Guide Pin Bolts (ft. lbs.)
2010	Focus	F	N/S	0.905	0.002	N/A	N/A	N/A	0.118	N/A	92	21
		R	N/A	N/A	N/A	N/S	8.030	N/S	N/A	0.147	N/A	N/A
2011	Focus	F	N/S	0.905	0.002	N/A	N/A	N/A	0.118	N/A	92	21
		R	N/A	N/A	N/A	N/S	8.030	N/S	N/A	0.147	N/A	N/A

F: Front

R: Rear

N/A: Not Applicable

N/S: Not Specified

25759_FOCU_C0013

SCHEDULED MAINTENANCE INTERVALS

Ford Focus - Normal

TO BE SERVICED	TYPE OF SERVICE	VEHICLE MILEAGE INTERVAL (x1000)												
		7.5	15	22.5	30	37.5	45	52.5	60	67.5	75	82.5	90	97.5
Accessory drive belt	Replace	Every 150,000 miles												
Engine oil & filter	Replace	✓	✓	✓	✓	✓	✓	✓	✓	✓	✓	✓	✓	✓
Engine coolant	Replace	At 6 years or 105,000 miles; then every 3 years or 45,000 miles												
Spark plugs	Replace												✓	
Engine air filter	Replace				✓				✓				✓	
Auto trans. fluid & filter	Replace	Every 150,000 miles												
Manual trans. fluid	Replace	Every 150,000 miles												
Cabin air filter (If equipped)	Replace		✓		✓		✓		✓		✓		✓	
Fuel filter (If equipped)	Replace				✓				✓				✓	
Halfshaft boots	Inspect	✓	✓	✓	✓	✓	✓	✓	✓	✓	✓	✓	✓	✓
Accessory drive belt	Inspect	✓	✓	✓	✓	✓	✓	✓	✓	✓	✓	✓	✓	✓
Cooling system, hoses, clamps & coolant strength	Inspect	✓	✓	✓	✓	✓	✓	✓	✓	✓	✓	✓	✓	✓
Engine air filter	Inspect	✓	✓	✓	✓	✓	✓	✓	✓	✓	✓	✓	✓	✓
Exhaust system (Leaks, damage, loose parts and foreign material)	Inspect	✓	✓	✓	✓	✓	✓	✓	✓	✓	✓	✓	✓	✓
Horn, exterior lamps, turn signals and hazard warning light operation	Inspect	✓	✓	✓	✓	✓	✓	✓	✓	✓	✓	✓	✓	✓
Oil and fluid leaks	Inspect	✓	✓	✓	✓	✓	✓	✓	✓	✓	✓	✓	✓	✓
Shocks struts and other suspension components for leaks and damage	Inspect	✓	✓	✓	✓	✓	✓	✓	✓	✓	✓	✓	✓	✓
Windshield for cracks, chips and pitting	Inspect	✓	✓	✓	✓	✓	✓	✓	✓	✓	✓	✓	✓	✓
Windshield wiper spray and wiper operation	Inspect	✓	✓	✓	✓	✓	✓	✓	✓	✓	✓	✓	✓	✓
Battery performance	Inspect	✓	✓	✓	✓	✓	✓	✓	✓	✓	✓	✓	✓	✓
Brake system (Pads/shoes/rotors/drums, brake lines and hoses, and parking brake system)	Inspect		✓		✓		✓		✓		✓		✓	
Inspect wheels and related components for abnomal noise, wear, looseness or drag	Inspect	✓	✓	✓	✓	✓	✓	✓	✓	✓	✓	✓	✓	✓
Cabin air filter (If equipped)	Inspect	✓	✓	✓	✓	✓	✓	✓	✓	✓	✓	✓	✓	✓
Radiator, coolers, heater and air conditioning hoses	Inspect	✓	✓	✓	✓	✓	✓	✓	✓	✓	✓	✓	✓	✓
Steering linkage, ball joints, suspension and tie-rod ends, lubricate if equipped with greases fittings	Inspect/ Lubricate	✓	✓	✓	✓	✓	✓	✓	✓	✓	✓	✓	✓	✓
Fluid levels (all)	Top off	✓	✓	✓	✓	✓	✓	✓	✓	✓	✓	✓	✓	✓
Rotate tires, inspect tread wear, measure tread depth and check pressure	Inspect/ Rotate		✓		✓		✓		✓		✓		✓	

25759_FOCU_C0014

SCHEDULED MAINTENANCE INTERVALS

Ford Focus - Severe

TO BE SERVICED	TYPE OF SERVICE	VEHICLE MILEAGE INTERVAL (x1000)											
		5	10	15	20	25	30	35	40	45	50	55	60
Accessory drive belt	Inspect	✓	✓	✓	✓	✓	✓	✓	✓	✓	✓	✓	✓
Accessory drive belt	Replace	every 150,000 miles											
Engine oil & filter	Replace	✓	✓	✓	✓	✓	✓	✓	✓	✓	✓	✓	✓
Spark plugs	Replace												✓
Engine coolant	Replace	At 6 years or 105,000 miles; then every 3 years or 45,000 miles											
Halfshaft boots	Inspect	✓	✓	✓	✓	✓	✓	✓	✓	✓	✓	✓	✓
Engine air filter	Inspect	✓	✓	✓	✓	✓	✓	✓	✓	✓	✓	✓	✓
Engine air filter	Replace						✓						✓
Cooling system, hoses, clamps & coolant strength	Inspect	✓	✓	✓	✓	✓	✓	✓	✓	✓	✓	✓	✓
Battery performance	Inspect	✓	✓	✓	✓	✓	✓	✓	✓	✓	✓	✓	✓
Exhaust system (Leaks, damage, loose parts and foreign material)	Inspect	✓	✓	✓	✓	✓	✓	✓	✓	✓	✓	✓	✓
Horn, exterior lamps, turn signals and hazard warning light operation	Inspect	✓	✓	✓	✓	✓	✓	✓	✓	✓	✓	✓	✓
Manual trans. fluid	Replace	every 150,000 miles											
Oil and fluid leaks	Inspect	✓	✓	✓	✓	✓	✓	✓	✓	✓	✓	✓	✓
Shocks struts and other suspension components for leaks and damage	Inspect	✓	✓	✓	✓	✓	✓	✓	✓	✓	✓	✓	✓
Windshield for cracks, chips and pitting	Inspect	✓	✓	✓	✓	✓	✓	✓	✓	✓	✓	✓	✓
Windshield wiper spray and wiper operation	Inspect	✓	✓	✓	✓	✓	✓	✓	✓	✓	✓	✓	✓
Fluid levels (all)	Top off	✓	✓	✓	✓	✓	✓	✓	✓	✓	✓	✓	✓
Brake system (Pads/shoes/rotors/drums, brake lines and hoses, and parking brake system)	Inspect			✓			✓			✓			✓
Inspect wheels and related components for abnomal noise, wear, looseness or drag	Inspect	✓	✓	✓	✓	✓	✓	✓	✓	✓	✓	✓	✓
Cabin air filter (If equipped)	Inspect	✓	✓	✓	✓	✓	✓	✓	✓	✓	✓	✓	✓
Cabin air filter (If equipped)	Replace			✓			✓			✓			✓
Radiator, coolers, heater and air conditioning hoses	Inspect	✓	✓	✓	✓	✓	✓	✓	✓	✓	✓	✓	✓
Rotate tires, inspect tread wear, measure tread depth and check pressure	Inspect/ Rotate	✓	✓	✓	✓	✓	✓	✓	✓	✓	✓	✓	✓
Steering linkage, ball joints, suspension and tie-rod ends, lubricate if equipped with greases fittings	Inspect/ Lubricate	✓	✓	✓	✓	✓	✓	✓	✓	✓	✓	✓	✓
Fuel filter (If equipped)	Replace			✓			✓			✓			✓
Auto. trans. fluid and filter	Replace						✓						✓

For extensive idling and or low speed driving, change engine oil and filter every 5,000 miles, 6 months or 200 hours of engine operation.

25759_FOCU_C0015

PRECAUTIONS

Before servicing any vehicle, please be sure to read all of the following precautions, which deal with personal safety, prevention of component damage, and important points to take into consideration when servicing a motor vehicle:

- Never open, service or drain the radiator or cooling system when the engine is hot; serious burns can occur from the steam and hot coolant.
- Observe all applicable safety precautions when working around fuel. Whenever servicing the fuel system, always work in a well-ventilated area. Do not allow fuel spray or vapors to come in contact with a spark, open flame, or excessive heat (a hot drop light, for example). Keep a dry chemical fire extinguisher near the work area. Always keep fuel in a container specifically designed for fuel storage; also, always properly seal fuel containers to avoid the possibility of fire or explosion. Refer to the additional fuel system precautions later in this section.
- Fuel injection systems often remain pressurized, even after the engine has been turned **OFF**. The fuel system pressure must be relieved before disconnecting any fuel lines. Failure to do so may result in fire and/or personal injury.
- Brake fluid often contains polyglycol ethers and polyglycols. Avoid contact with the eyes and wash your hands thoroughly after handling brake fluid. If you do get brake fluid in your eyes, flush your eyes with clean, running water for 15 minutes. If eye irritation persists, or if you have taken brake fluid internally, IMMEDIATELY seek medical assistance.
- The EPA warns that prolonged contact with used engine oil may cause a number of skin disorders, including cancer. You should make every effort to minimize your exposure to used engine oil. Protective gloves should be worn when changing oil. Wash your hands and any other exposed skin areas as soon as possible after exposure to used engine oil. Soap and water, or waterless hand cleaner should be used.
- All new vehicles are now equipped with an air bag system, often referred to as a Supplemental Restraint System (SRS) or Supplemental Inflatable Restraint (SIR) system. The system must be disabled before performing service on or around system components, steering column, instrument panel components, wiring and sensors. Failure to follow safety and disabling procedures could result in accidental air bag deployment, possible personal injury and unnecessary system repairs.
- Always wear safety goggles when working with, or around, the air bag system. When carrying a non-deployed air bag, be sure the bag and trim cover are pointed away from your body. When placing a non-deployed air bag on a work surface, always face the bag and trim cover upward, away from the surface. This will reduce the motion of the module if it is accidentally deployed. Refer to the additional air bag system precautions later in this section.
- Clean, high quality brake fluid from a sealed container is essential to the safe and proper operation of the brake system. You should always buy the correct type of brake fluid for your vehicle. If the brake fluid becomes contaminated, completely flush the system with new fluid. Never reuse any brake fluid. Any brake fluid that is removed from the system should be discarded. Also, do not allow any brake fluid to come in contact with a painted surface; it will damage the paint.
- Never operate the engine without the proper amount and type of engine oil; doing so WILL result in severe engine damage.
- Timing belt maintenance is extremely important. Many models utilize an interference-type, non-freewheeling engine. If the timing belt breaks, the valves in the cylinder head may strike the pistons, causing potentially serious (also time-consuming and expensive) engine damage. Refer to the maintenance interval charts for the recommended replacement interval for the timing belt, and to the timing belt section for belt replacement and inspection.
- Disconnecting the negative battery cable on some vehicles may interfere with the functions of the on-board computer system(s) and may require the computer to undergo a relearning process once the negative battery cable is reconnected.
- When servicing drum brakes, only disassemble and assemble one side at a time, leaving the remaining side intact for reference.
- Only an MVAC-trained, EPA-certified automotive technician should service the air conditioning system or its components.

BRAKES

ANTI-LOCK BRAKE SYSTEM (ABS)

GENERAL INFORMATION

PRECAUTIONS

- Certain components within the ABS system are not intended to be serviced or repaired individually.
- Do not use rubber hoses or other parts not specifically specified for and ABS system. When using repair kits, replace all parts included in the kit. Partial or incorrect repair may lead to functional problems and require the replacement of components.
- Lubricate rubber parts with clean, fresh brake fluid to ease assembly. Do not use shop air to clean parts; damage to rubber components may result.
- Use only DOT 3 brake fluid from an unopened container.
- If any hydraulic component or line is removed or replaced, it may be necessary to bleed the entire system.
- A clean repair area is essential. Always clean the reservoir and cap thoroughly before removing the cap. The slightest amount of dirt in the fluid may plug an orifice and impair the system function. Perform repairs after components have been thoroughly cleaned; use only denatured alcohol to clean components. Do not allow ABS components to come into contact with any substance containing mineral oil; this includes used shop rags.
- The Anti-Lock control unit is a microprocessor similar to other computer units in the vehicle. Ensure that the ignition switch is **OFF** before removing or installing controller harnesses. Avoid static electricity discharge at or near the controller.
- If any arc welding is to be done on the vehicle, the control unit should be unplugged before welding operations begin.

SPEED SENSORS

REMOVAL & INSTALLATION

Front Speed Sensor

See Figure 1.

1. Before servicing the vehicle, refer to the Precautions Section.
2. Raise and safely support the vehicle.
3. Remove the wheel and tire.
4. Remove the wheel speed sensor bolt.
5. Disconnect the wheel speed sensor electrical connector.
    - Remove the sensor by pulling the sensor grommets out of the clips.

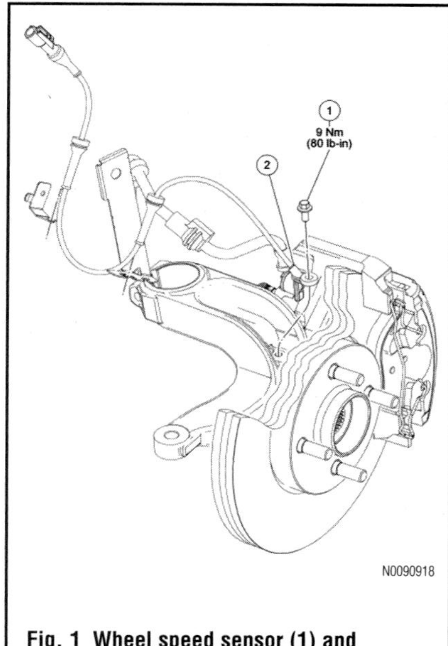

Fig. 1 Wheel speed sensor (1) and sensor bolt (2)—front

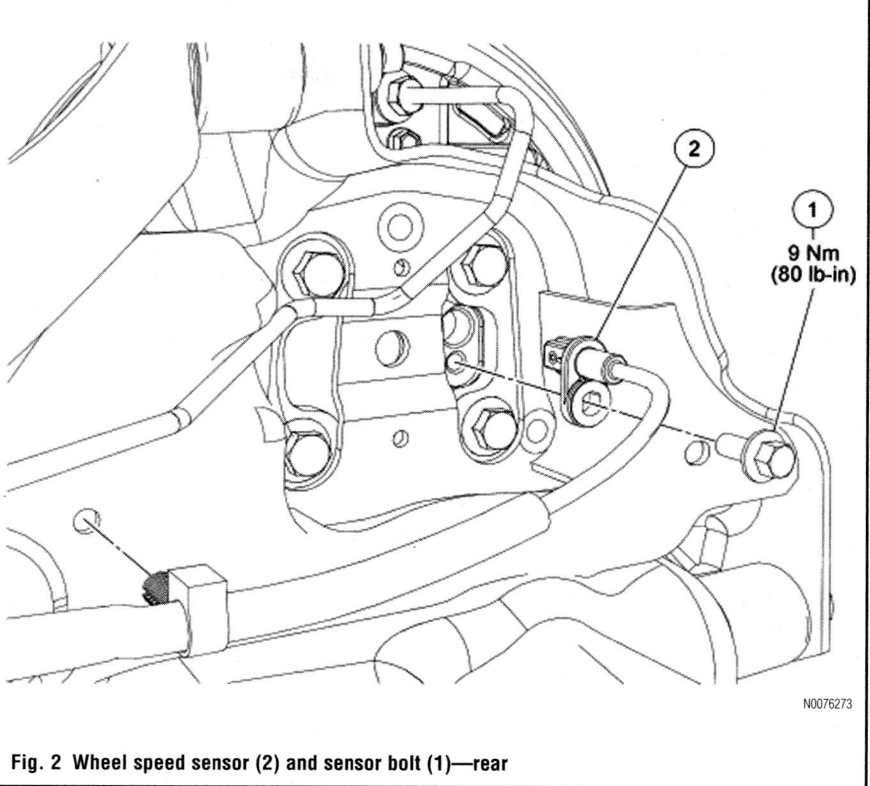

Fig. 2 Wheel speed sensor (2) and sensor bolt (1)—rear

To install:

6. Installation is the reverse of the removal procedure.
7. Tighten the wheel speed sensor bolt to 80 inch lbs. (9 Nm).

Rear Speed Sensor

See Figure 2.

1. Before servicing the vehicle, refer to the Precautions Section.
2. Raise and safely support the vehicle.
3. Place the vehicle in NEUTRAL.
4. Remove the wheel speed sensor bolt.

➡Not all the clips are part of the sensor assembly and may not be reusable.

5. Disconnect the wheel speed sensor electrical connector.
   - Remove the sensor by detaching the pin-type retainer and pulling the sensor grommets out of the clips.

To install:

6. Installation is the reverse of the removal procedure.
7. Tighten the wheel speed sensor bolt to 80 inch lbs. (9 Nm).

BRAKES — BLEEDING THE BRAKE SYSTEM

BLEEDING PROCEDURE

BLEEDING PROCEDURE

Manual Bleeding

✱✱ WARNING

Do not use any fluid other than clean brake fluid meeting manufacturer's specification. Additionally, do not use brake fluid that has been previously drained. Following these instructions will help prevent system contamination, brake component damage, and the risk of serious personal injury.

✱✱ CAUTION

Brake fluid contains polyglycol ethers and polyglycols. Avoid contact with the eyes. Wash hands thoroughly after handling. If brake fluid contacts the eyes, flush the eyes for 15 minutes with cold running water. Get medical attention if irritation persists. If taken internally, drink water and induce vomiting. Get medical attention immediately. Failure to follow these instructions may result in personal injury.

✱✱ WARNING

Do not allow the brake master cylinder to run dry during the bleeding operation. The master cylinder may be damaged if operated without fluid, resulting in degraded braking performance.

✱✱ WARNING

Do not spill brake fluid on painted or plastic surfaces or damage to the surface may occur. If brake fluid is spilled onto a painted or plastic surface, immediately wash the surface with water.

➡Pressure bleeding the brake system is preferred to manual bleeding.

1. Before servicing the vehicle, refer to the Precautions Section.
2. Clean all dirt from around the brake fluid reservoir cap and remove the filler cap.
3. Fill the brake master cylinder reservoir with clean, specified brake fluid.
4. Remove the RR bleeder screw cap and place a box-end wrench on the bleeder screw. Attach a rubber drain hose to the RR bleeder screw and submerge the free end of

the hose in a container partially filled with clean, specified brake fluid.

5. Have an assistant pump and then hold firm pressure on the brake pedal.

6. Loosen the RR bleeder screw until a stream of brake fluid comes out. While an assistant maintains pressure on the brake pedal, tighten the RR bleeder screw.

7. Repeat until clear, bubble-free fluid comes out.

8. Refill the brake master cylinder reservoir as necessary.

9. Tighten the RR bleeder screw to 71 inch lbs. (8 Nm).

10. Remove the rubber hose and install the bleeder screw cap.

11. Repeat the procedure for the LR, RF, and then LF bleeder screws.

Pressure Bleeding

**** WARNING**

Do not use any fluid other than clean brake fluid meeting manufacturer's specification. Additionally, do not use brake fluid that has been previously drained. Following these instructions will help prevent system contamination, brake component damage, and the risk of serious personal injury.

**** CAUTION**

Brake fluid contains polyglycol ethers and polyglycols. Avoid contact with the eyes. Wash hands thoroughly after handling. If brake fluid contacts the eyes, flush the eyes for 15 minutes with cold running water. Get medical attention if irritation persists. If taken internally, drink water and induce vomiting. Get medical attention immediately. Failure to follow these instructions may result in personal injury.

**** WARNING**

Do not allow the brake master cylinder to run dry during the bleeding operation. The master cylinder may be damaged if operated without fluid, resulting in degraded braking performance.

**** WARNING**

Do not spill brake fluid on painted or plastic surfaces or damage to the surface may occur. If brake fluid is spilled onto a painted or plastic surface, immediately wash the surface with water.

➡The Hydraulic Control Unit (HCU) bleeding procedure must be carried out if the HCU or any components upstream of the HCU are installed new.

➡Pressure bleeding the brake system is preferred to manual bleeding.

1. Before servicing the vehicle, refer to the Precautions Section.

2. Clean all dirt from the brake master cylinder filler cap and remove the filler cap.

3. Fill the brake master cylinder reservoir with clean, specified brake fluid.

➡Master cylinder pressure bleeder adapter tools are available from various manufacturers of pressure bleeding equipment. Follow the instructions of the manufacturer when installing the adapter.

4. Install the bleeder adapter to the brake master cylinder reservoir, and attach the bleeder tank hose to the fitting on the adapter.

5. Make sure the bleeder tank contains enough clean, specified brake fluid to complete the bleeding operation.

6. Open the valve on the bleeder tank.

7. Apply 30–50 psi (207–345 kPa) to the brake system.

8. Remove the RR bleeder screw cap and place a box-end wrench on the bleeder screw. Attach a rubber drain hose to the RR bleeder screw and submerge the free end of the hose in a container partially filled with clean, specified brake fluid.

9. Loosen the RR bleeder screw. Leave open until clear, bubble-free brake fluid flows, then tighten the RR bleeder screw to 71 inch lbs. (8 Nm).

10. Continue bleeding the rest of the system, going in order from the LR bleeder screw to the RF bleeder screw, ending with the LF bleeder screw.

11. Tighten the bleeder screws to 71 inch lbs. (8 Nm).

12. Close the bleeder tank valve. Remove the tank hose from the adapter and remove the adapter. Fill the reservoir with clean, specified brake fluid and install the reservoir cap.

MASTER CYLINDER BLEEDING

**** WARNING**

Do not use any fluid other than clean brake fluid meeting manufacturer's specification. Additionally, do not use brake fluid that has been previously drained. Following these instructions will help prevent system contamination, brake component damage, and the risk of serious personal injury.

**** CAUTION**

Brake fluid contains polyglycol ethers and polyglycols. Avoid contact with the eyes. Wash hands thoroughly after handling. If brake fluid contacts the eyes, flush the eyes for 15 minutes with cold running water. Get medical attention if irritation persists. If taken internally, drink water and induce vomiting. Get medical attention immediately. Failure to follow these instructions may result in personal injury.

**** WARNING**

Do not allow the brake master cylinder to run dry during the bleeding operation. The master cylinder may be damaged if operated without fluid, resulting in degraded braking performance.

**** WARNING**

Do not spill brake fluid on painted or plastic surfaces or damage to the surface may occur. If brake fluid is spilled onto a painted or plastic surface, immediately wash the surface with water.

➡When the brake master cylinder has been installed new or the system has been emptied or partially emptied, it must be primed to prevent air from entering the system.

1. Before servicing the vehicle, refer to the Precautions Section.

2. Disconnect the brake outlet tubes from the master cylinder.

3. Install short brake tubes onto the primary and secondary ports with the ends submerged in a container partially filled with clean, specified brake fluid.

4. Have an assistant pump the brake pedal until clear fluid flows from the brake tubes without air bubbles.

5. Remove the short brake tubes, and install the master cylinder brake tubes.

6. Tighten the brake tube fittings to specification:

a. Vehicles equipped with ABS, tighten to 150 inch lbs. (17 Nm).

b. Vehicles not equipped with ABS, tighten to 177 inch lbs. (20 Nm).

7. Bleed the brake system. Refer to Bleeding Procedure.

BRAKE LINE BLEEDING

Refer to Bleeding Procedure, Manual Bleeding or Pressure Bleeding.

BLEEDING THE ABS SYSTEM

**** WARNING**

Do not use any fluid other than clean brake fluid meeting manufacturer's specification. Additionally, do not use brake fluid that has been previously drained. Following these instructions will help prevent system contamination, brake component damage, and the risk of serious personal injury.

**** CAUTION**

Brake fluid contains polyglycol ethers and polyglycols. Avoid contact with the eyes. Wash hands thoroughly after handling. If brake fluid contacts the eyes, flush the eyes for 15 minutes with cold running water. Get medical attention if irritation persists. If taken internally, drink water and induce vomiting. Get medical attention immediately. Failure to follow these instructions may result in personal injury.

**** WARNING**

Do not allow the brake master cylinder to run dry during the bleeding operation. Master cylinder may be damaged if operated without fluid, resulting in degraded braking performance.

**** WARNING**

Do not spill brake fluid on painted or plastic surfaces or damage to the surface may occur. If brake fluid is spilled onto a painted or plastic surface, immediately wash the surface with water.

➡Pressure bleeding the brake system is preferred to manual bleeding.

1. Before servicing the vehicle, refer to the Precautions Section.
2. Follow the Pressure Bleeding or Manual Bleeding procedure steps to bleed the system.
3. Connect the scan tool and follow the ABS Service Bleed instructions.
4. Repeat the Pressure Bleeding or Manual Bleeding procedure steps to bleed the system.

FLUID FILL PROCEDURE

See Figure 3.

**** WARNING**

Do not use any fluid other than clean brake fluid meeting manufacturer's specification. Additionally, do not use brake fluid that has been previously drained. Following these instructions will help prevent system contamination, brake component damage, and the risk of serious personal injury.

**** CAUTION**

Brake fluid contains polyglycol ethers and polyglycols. Avoid contact with the eyes. Wash hands thoroughly after handling. If brake fluid contacts the eyes, flush the eyes for 15 minutes with cold running water. Get medical attention if irritation persists. If taken internally, drink water and induce vomiting. Get medical attention immediately. Failure to follow these instructions may result in personal injury.

**** WARNING**

Do not allow the brake master cylinder to run dry during the bleeding operation. Master cylinder may be damaged if operated without fluid, resulting in degraded braking performance.

**** WARNING**

Do not spill brake fluid on painted or plastic surfaces or damage to the surface may occur. If brake fluid is spilled onto a painted or plastic surface, immediately wash the surface with water.

1. Before servicing the vehicle, refer to the Precautions Section.
2. Clean all dirt from around the brake fluid reservoir cap and remove the filler cap.
3. Fill the brake master cylinder reservoir with clean, specified brake fluid.

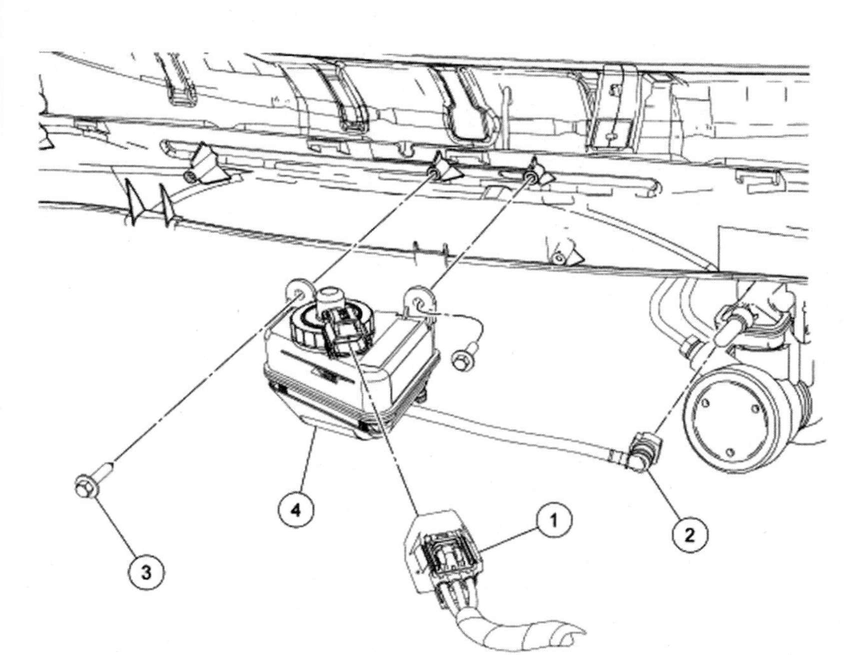

Fig. 3 View of brake fluid reservoir

⁂ CAUTION

Dust and dirt accumulating on brake parts during normal use may contain asbestos fibers from production or aftermarket brake linings. Breathing excessive concentrations of asbestos fibers can cause serious bodily harm. Exercise care when servicing brake parts. Do not sand or grind brake lining unless equipment used is designed to contain the dust residue. Do not clean brake parts with compressed air or by dry brushing. Cleaning should be done by dampening the brake components with a fine mist of water, then wiping the brake components clean with a dampened cloth. Dispose of cloth and all residue containing asbestos fibers in an impermeable container with the appropriate label. Follow practices prescribed by the Occupational Safety and Health Administration (OSHA) and the Environmental Protection Agency (EPA) for the handling, processing, and disposing of dust or debris that may contain asbestos fibers.

BRAKE CALIPER

REMOVAL & INSTALLATION

See Figure 4.

⁂ WARNING

Do not use any fluid other than clean brake fluid meeting manufacturer's specification. Additionally, do not use brake fluid that has been previously drained. Following these instructions will help prevent system contamination, brake component damage, and the risk of serious personal injury.

⁂ CAUTION

Brake fluid contains polyglycol ethers and polyglycols. Avoid contact with the eyes. Wash hands thoroughly after handling. If brake fluid contacts the eyes, flush the eyes for 15 minutes with cold running water. Get medical attention if irritation persists. If taken internally, drink water and induce vomiting. Get medical attention immediately. Failure to follow these instructions may result in personal injury.

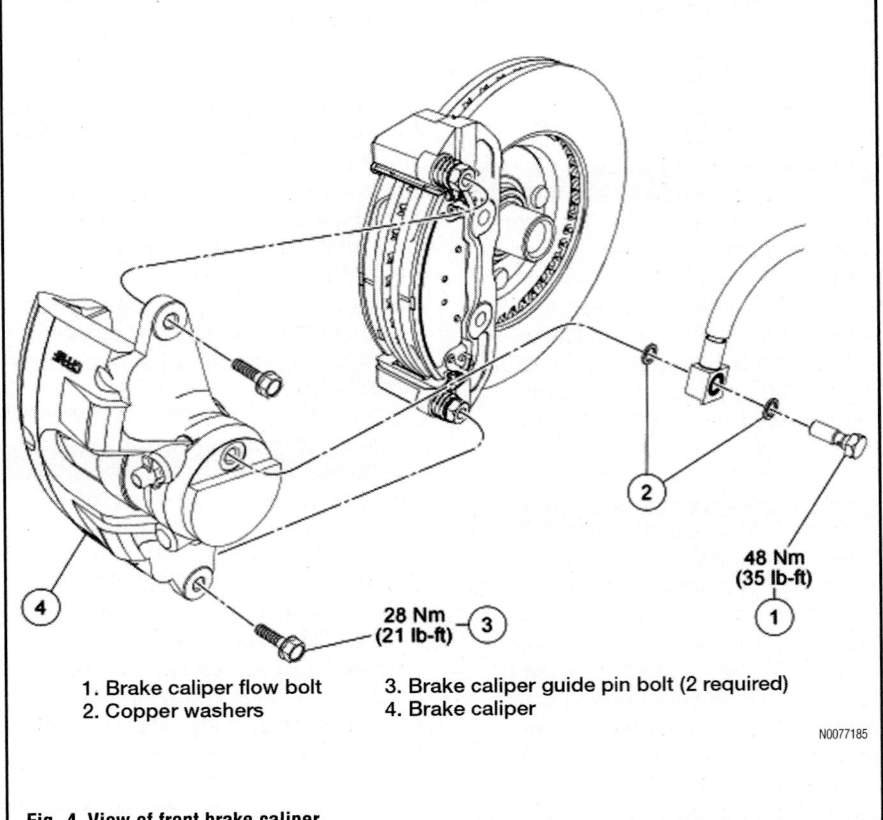

Fig. 4 View of front brake caliper

⁂ WARNING

Do not spill brake fluid on painted or plastic surfaces or damage to the surface may occur. If brake fluid is spilled onto a painted or plastic surface, immediately wash the surface with water.

1. Before servicing the vehicle, refer to the Precautions Section.
2. Raise and safely support the vehicle.
3. Remove the wheel and tire.
4. Remove the brake caliper flow bolt and position the brake flexible hose aside.

➡Cap the brake hose to prevent fluid loss and dirt contamination.

5. Remove the 2 brake caliper guide pin bolts and remove the brake caliper.

To install:

6. To install, reverse the removal procedure and note the following:
   - Install new copper washers
   - Tighten the 2 brake caliper guide pin bolts to 21 ft. lbs. (28 Nm)
   - Tighten the brake caliper flow bolt to 35 ft. lbs. (48 Nm)
7. Bleed the brake caliper. Refer to Bleeding Procedure.

DISC BRAKE PADS

REMOVAL & INSTALLATION

See Figure 5.

⁂ WARNING

Do not use any fluid other than clean brake fluid meeting manufacturer's specification. Additionally, do not use brake fluid that has been previously drained. Following these instructions will help prevent system contamination, brake component damage, and the risk of serious personal injury.

⁂ CAUTION

Always install new brake shoes or pads at both ends of an axle to reduce the possibility of brakes pulling vehicle to one side. Failure to follow this instruction may result in uneven braking and serious personal injury.

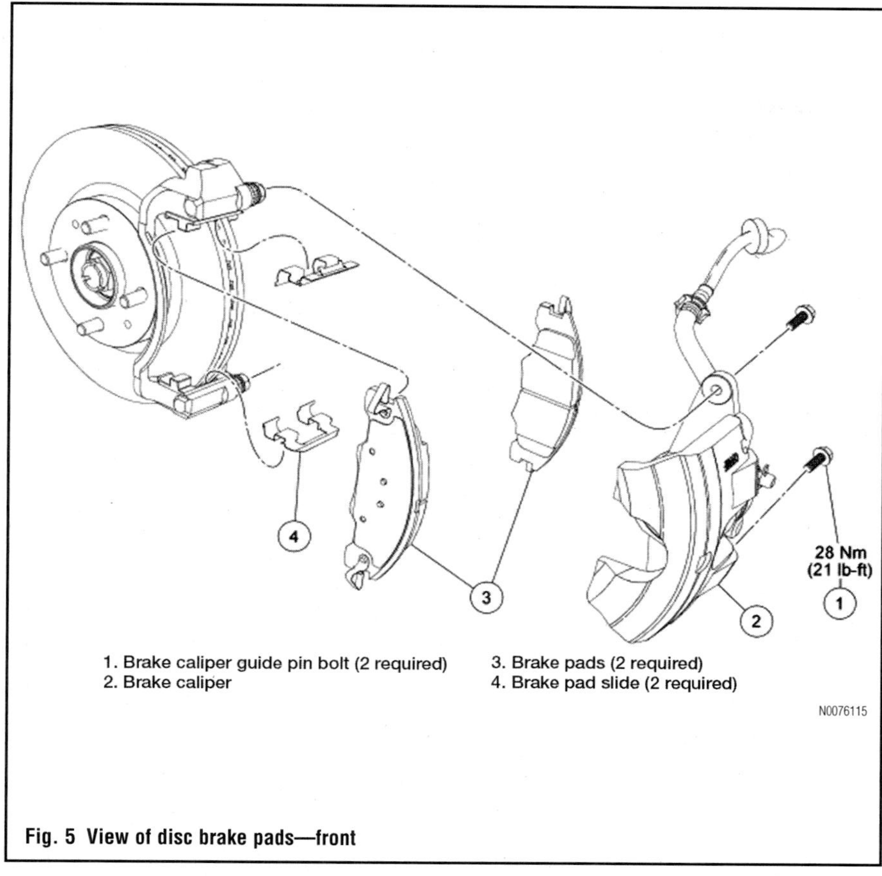

Fig. 5 View of disc brake pads—front

WARNING

Do not spill brake fluid on painted or plastic surfaces or damage to the surface may occur. If brake fluid is spilled onto a painted or plastic surface, immediately wash the surface with water.

1. Before servicing the vehicle, refer to the Precautions Section.
2. Check the brake fluid level in the brake master cylinder reservoir.

➡If required, remove the fluid until the brake master cylinder reservoir is half full.

3. Raise and safely support the vehicle.
4. Remove the wheel and tire assembly.

WARNING

Do not pry in the caliper sight hole to retract the pistons, as this can damage the pistons and boots. Do not allow the brake caliper to hang from the brake caliper flexible hose or damage to the hose can occur.

5. Remove the 2 brake caliper guide pin bolts and position the caliper aside. Support the caliper using mechanic's wire.
6. Remove the brake pads.

To install:

WARNING

Protect the caliper pistons and boots when pushing the caliper pistons into the caliper piston bores or damage to components may occur.

7. If installing new brake pads, using a C-clamp and a worn brake pad, compress the disc brake caliper pistons into the caliper.

➡The wear indicator is on the inner pad leading edge.

8. Install the new brake pads.
9. Reposition the caliper to the mounting bracket.
10. Tighten the guide pin bolts to 21 ft. lbs. (28 Nm).
11. Install the wheel and tire assembly. Tighten the wheel nuts in a star pattern to 100 ft. lbs. (135 Nm).
12. Apply brakes several times to verify correct brake operation.
13. Fill the master cylinder reservoir with specified brake fluid.
14. Road test the vehicle for proper operation.

BRAKES

REAR DRUM BRAKES

CAUTION

Dust and dirt accumulating on brake parts during normal use may contain asbestos fibers from production or aftermarket brake linings. Breathing excessive concentrations of asbestos fibers can cause serious bodily harm. Exercise care when servicing brake parts. Do not sand or grind brake lining unless equipment used is designed to contain the dust residue. Do not clean brake parts with compressed air or by dry brushing. Cleaning should be done by dampening the brake components with a fine mist of water, then wiping the brake components clean with a dampened cloth. Dispose of cloth and all residue containing asbestos fibers in an impermeable container with the appropriate label. Follow practices prescribed by the Occupational Safety and Health Administration (OSHA) and the Environmental Protection Agency (EPA) for the handling, processing, and disposing of dust or debris that may contain asbestos fibers.

BRAKE DRUM

REMOVAL & INSTALLATION

See Figure 6.

1. Before servicing the vehicle, refer to the Precautions Section.
2. Remove the wheel and tire assembly.
3. Remove and discard the dust cap.

WARNING

Do not use power tools to remove the wheel hub nut or damage to the spindle may occur.

➡If the bearing inner race(s) become separated from the bearing assembly,

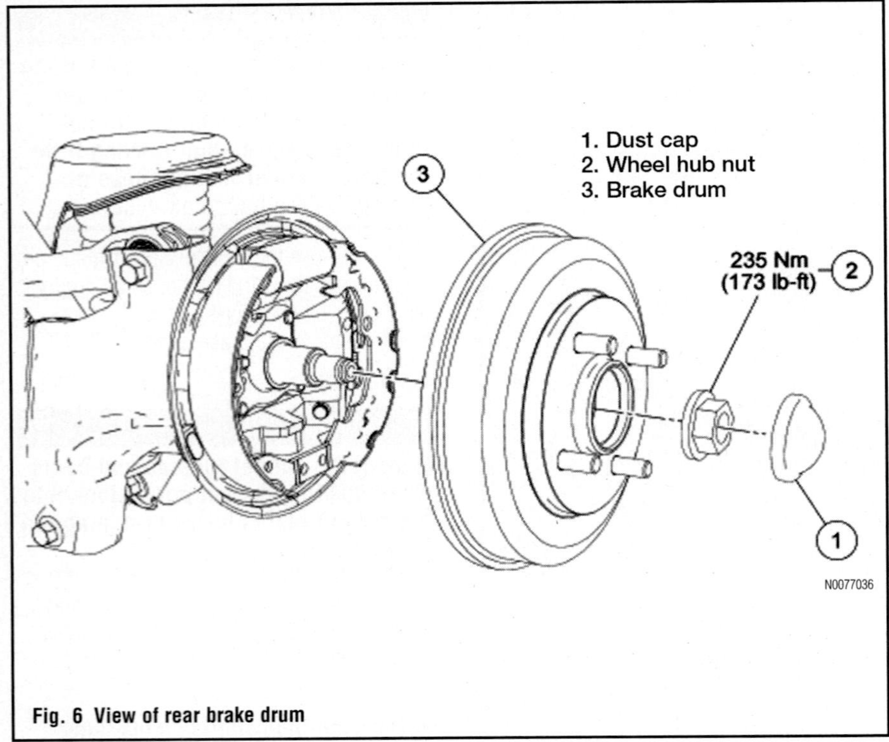

Fig. 6 View of rear brake drum

a new bearing must be installed. Reassembly and installation of the bearing that has become disassembled may result in bearing failure.

4. Remove and discard the wheel hub nut and remove the brake drum.

To install:

⁂ WARNING

Avoid impact on the wheel speed sensor ring and any contact between the sensor ring and a magnetic surface or damage to the sensor ring may occur. Make sure the wheel speed sensor ring is clean or sensor failure may occur.

⁂ WARNING

A new wheel hub nut must be installed or incorrect clamp load may occur resulting in wheel bearing failure.

5. Position the brake drum and wheel hub assembly and install a new wheel hub nut.
6. While rotating the brake drum in the opposite direction, tighten the wheel hub nut to 173 ft. lbs. (235 Nm).
7. Install a new dust cap.
8. Install the wheel and tire assembly. Tighten the wheel nuts in a star pattern to 100 ft. lbs. (135 Nm).

BRAKE SHOES

REMOVAL & INSTALLATION

See Figure 7.

1. Before servicing the vehicle, refer to the Precautions Section.
2. Remove the parking brake control boot.
   a. Release the boot clip.
   b. Lift the boot upward and over the parking brake control handle.
3. Move the parking brake control to the fully released position.
4. Relieve the tension on the parking brake cable by loosening the adjustment nut.
5. Remove the brake drum. Refer to Brake Drum, removal & installation.
6. Remove the hold-down clips and pins.

⁂ WARNING

Do not allow the wheel cylinder pistons to fall out of the wheel cylinder bore.

7. Disconnect the brake shoes from the wheel cylinder.
8. Using a suitable tool, hold the wheel cylinder pistons in place.
9. Release the shoes from the backing plate.
10. Disconnect the parking brake cable.
    a. Push the lever inward.
    b. Release the cable from the lever.
11. Remove the lower return spring.
12. Remove the upper return spring.
13. Remove the primary shoe from the strut and brake shoe adjuster.
    a. Pull the shoe outward.

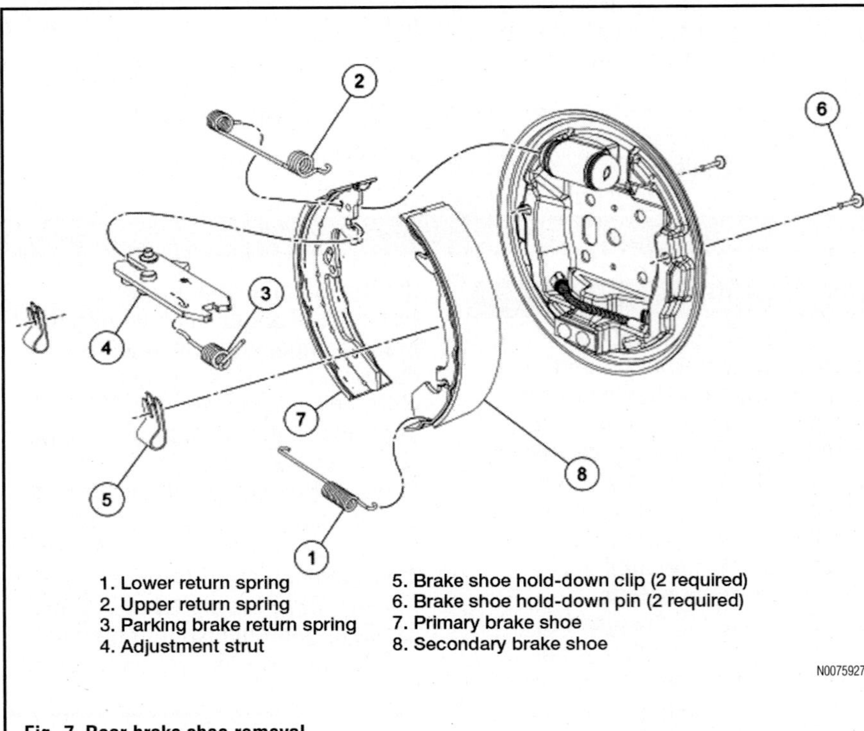

Fig. 7 Rear brake shoe removal

b. Disconnect the strut and adjuster.
c. Release the strut and adjuster.

⁂ CAUTION

The strut support spring is under tension.

14. Remove the secondary shoe from the support.
   a. Move the strut downward.
   b. Disconnect the parking brake return spring.

To install:

15. Make sure that all mating surfaces are free of foreign material.
16. Clean, check, and apply silicone grease to the brake shoe contact points on the brake backing plate.
17. To install, reverse the removal procedure and note the following:
   - The internal auto-adjuster must be set and the brake shoes centralized to the brake drum
   - Adjust the brake shoes
   - Adjust the parking brake cable

ADJUSTMENT

1. Before servicing the vehicle, refer to the Precautions Section.
2. Raise and support the vehicle so that the rear wheels are off the ground.

➡The internal auto-adjuster must be set and the brake shoes centralized to the brake drum.

3. With the aid of an assistant, rotate the rear wheel while applying the brake pedal 5 times.
4. Repeat Step 3 for the opposite rear wheel.
5. Carry out the parking brake cable adjustment.
6. Lower the vehicle.

PARKING BRAKE CABLES

ADJUSTMENT

See Figures 8 and 9.

➡The parking brake cables and rear brake shoes must be adjusted in sequence or a brake drag may occur causing excessive wear to the rear brake shoes.

⁂ WARNING

Do not use a prying device on the plastic edges of the parking brake control boot or damage to the boot or floor console trim panel may occur.

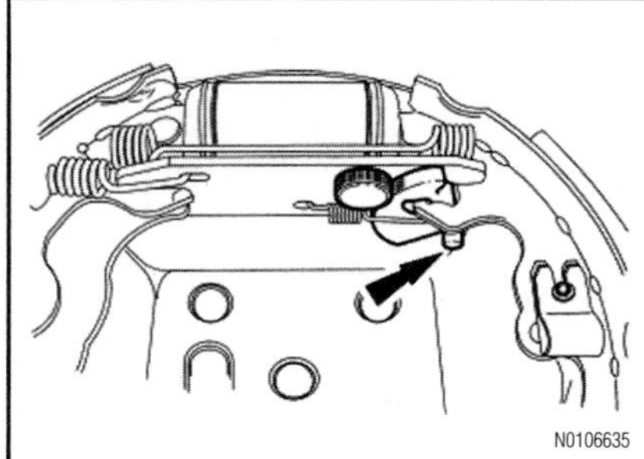

Fig. 8 Neutralize the brake shoe/parking brake auto-adjusters by pushing the retainer rod on the adjuster

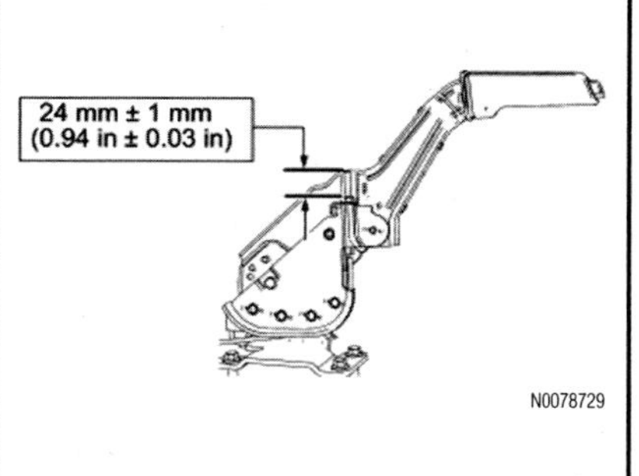

Fig. 9 Adjust the parking brake control adjustment nut as shown

1. Before servicing the vehicle, refer to the Precautions Section.
2. If applied, fully release the parking brake.
3. Using hand force only, pull upward on the front edge of the parking brake control boot trim.
4. Position the parking brake control boot forward until the trim tab clears the floor console trim panel.
5. Slide the parking brake control boot upward on the handle to gain access to the parking brake cable adjustment nut.
6. Loosen the parking brake cable adjustment nut until there is no tension in the cable.
7. Remove the rear brake drums. Refer to Brake Drum, removal & installation.
8. Neutralize the brake shoe/parking brake auto-adjusters (both sides) by pushing the retainer rod on the bottom of the adjuster toward the brake shoe backing plate.
9. Install the rear brake drums.
10. Apply the service brakes (brake pedal) 5 times.
11. Adjust the parking brake control adjustment nut.
12. Rotate the rear wheels to make sure the brake shoes do not drag.
13. Slide the parking brake control boot downward on the handle.
14. Position the parking brake control boot rearward, tucking the trim tab under floor console trim panel.
15. Push downward on the front edge of the parking brake control boot trim until it snaps into place.

PARKING BRAKE SHOES

REMOVAL & INSTALLATION

On drum brakes, the parking brakes utilize the regular service brakes. Refer to Rear Drum Brakes, Brake Shoes, removal & installation.

GENERAL INFORMATION

CAUTION

These vehicles are equipped with an air bag system. The system must be disarmed before performing service on, or around, system components, the steering column, instrument panel components, wiring and sensors. Failure to follow the safety precautions and the disarming procedure could result in accidental air bag deployment, possible injury and unnecessary system repairs.

SERVICE PRECAUTIONS

Disconnect and isolate the battery negative cable before beginning any airbag system component diagnosis, testing, removal, or installation procedures. Allow system capacitor to discharge for two minutes before beginning any component service. This will disable the airbag system. Failure to disable the airbag system may result in accidental airbag deployment, personal injury, or death.

Do not place an intact undeployed airbag face down on a solid surface. The airbag will propel into the air if accidentally deployed and may result in personal injury or death.

When carrying or handling an undeployed airbag, the trim side (face) of the airbag should be pointing away from the body to minimize possibility of injury if accidental deployment occurs. Failure to do this may result in personal injury or death.

Replace airbag system components with OEM replacement parts. Substitute parts may appear interchangeable, but internal differences may result in inferior occupant protection. Failure to do so may result in occupant personal injury or death.

Wear safety glasses, rubber gloves, and long sleeved clothing when cleaning powder residue from vehicle after an airbag deployment. Powder residue emitted from a deployed airbag can cause skin irritation. Flush affected area with cool water if irritation is experienced. If nasal or throat irritation is experienced, exit the vehicle for fresh air until the irritation ceases. If irritation continues, see a physician.

Do not use a replacement airbag that is not in the original packaging. This may result in improper deployment, personal injury, or death.

The factory installed fasteners, screws and bolts used to fasten airbag components have a special coating and are specifically designed for the airbag system. Do not use substitute fasteners. Use only original equipment fasteners listed in the parts catalog when fastener replacement is required.

During, and following, any child restraint anchor service, due to impact event or vehicle repair, carefully inspect all mounting hardware, tether straps, and anchors for proper installation, operation, or damage. If a child restraint anchor is found damaged in any way, the anchor must be replaced. Failure to do this may result in personal injury or death.

Deployed and non-deployed airbags may or may not have live pyrotechnic material within the airbag inflator.

Do not dispose of driver/passenger/curtain airbags or seat belt tensioners unless you are sure of complete deployment. Refer to the Hazardous Substance Control System for proper disposal.

Dispose of deployed airbags and tensioners consistent with state, provincial, local, and federal regulations.

After any airbag component testing or service, do not connect the battery negative cable. Personal injury or death may result if the system test is not performed first.

If the vehicle is equipped with the Occupant Classification System (OCS), do not connect the battery negative cable before performing the OCS Verification Test using the scan tool and the appropriate diagnostic information. Personal injury or death may result if the system test is not performed properly.

Never replace both the Occupant Restraint Controller (ORC) and the Occupant Classification Module (OCM) at the same time. If both require replacement, replace one, then perform the Airbag System test before replacing the other.

Both the ORC and the OCM store Occupant Classification System (OCS) calibration data, which they transfer to one another when one of them is replaced. If both are replaced at the same time, an irreversible fault will be set in both modules and the OCS may malfunction and cause personal injury or death.

If equipped with OCS, the Seat Weight Sensor is a sensitive, calibrated unit and must be handled carefully. Do not drop or handle roughly. If dropped or damaged, replace with another sensor. Failure to do so may result in occupant injury or death.

If equipped with OCS, the front passenger seat must be handled carefully as well. When removing the seat, be careful when setting on floor not to drop. If dropped, the sensor may be inoperative, could result in occupant injury, or possibly death.

If equipped with OCS, when the passenger front seat is on the floor, no one should sit in the front passenger seat. This uneven force may damage the sensing ability of the seat weight sensors. If sat on and damaged, the sensor may be inoperative, could result in occupant injury, or possibly death.

DISARMING THE SYSTEM

CAUTION

If a vehicle has been in a crash, inspect the Restraints Control Module (RCM) and the impact sensor (if equipped) mounting areas for deformation. If damaged, restore the mounting areas to the original production configuration. A new RCM and sensors must be installed whether or not the air bags have deployed. Failure to follow these instructions may result in serious personal injury or death in a crash.

CAUTION

To reduce the risk of accidental deployment, do not use any memory saver devices. Failure to follow this instruction may result in serious personal injury or death.

➡The air bag warning indicator illuminates when the correct Restraints Control Module (RCM) fuse is removed and the ignition is ON.

1. Before servicing the vehicle, refer to the Precautions Section.
2. Turn all vehicle accessories OFF.
3. Turn the ignition switch OFF.
4. At the Smart Junction Box (SJB), located below the LH side of the instrument panel, remove the cover and RCM fuse 32 (10A) from the SJB.
5. Turn the ignition switch ON and visually monitor the air bag warning indicator for at least 30 seconds. The air bag indicator will remain lit continuously (no flashing) if the correct RCM fuse has been removed. If the air bag indicator does not remain lit continuously, remove the correct RCM fuse before proceeding.
6. Turn the ignition switch OFF.

✱✱ CAUTION

Always deplete the backup power supply before repairing or installing any new front or side air bag Supplemental Restraint System (SRS) component and before servicing, removing, installing, adjusting, or striking components near the front or side impact sensors or the RCM.

7. To deplete the backup power supply energy, disconnect the battery ground cable and wait at least 1 minute. Be sure to disconnect auxiliary batteries and power supplies (if equipped).

ARMING THE SYSTEM

1. Before servicing the vehicle, refer to the Precautions Section.
2. Install the Restraints Control Module (RCM) fuse 32 (10A) to the Smart Junction Box (SJB) and install the cover.
3. Turn the ignition switch ON.

✱✱ CAUTION

Make sure no one is in the vehicle and there is nothing blocking or placed in front of any air bag module when the battery is connected. Failure to follow these instructions may result in serious personal injury in the event of an accidental deployment.

4. Connect the battery ground cable.
5. Prove out the Supplemental Restraint System (SRS) as follows:
   a. Turn the ignition switch from ON to OFF.
   b. Wait 10 seconds, then turn the ignition switch back to ON and visually monitor the air bag warning indicator with the air bag modules installed. The air bag warning indicator will light continuously for approximately 6 seconds and then turn off.
   c. If an air bag SRS fault is present, the air bag warning indicator will:
      - Fail to light
      - Remain lit continuously
      - Flash at a 5 Hz rate (RCM not configured)

➡The air bag warning indicator may not illuminate until approximately 30 seconds after the ignition switch has been turned from the OFF to the ON position. This is the time required for the RCM to complete the testing of the SRS. If the air bag warning indicator is inoperative and a SRS fault exists, a chime will sound in a pattern of 5 sets of 5 beeps. If this occurs, the air bag warning indicator and any SRS fault discovered must be diagnosed and repaired.

6. Clear all continuous DTCs from the RCM and Occupant Classification System Module (OCSM) using a scan tool.

CLOCKSPRING CENTERING

See Figure 10.

✱✱ CAUTION

Whenever working near any of the SRS components, such as the impact sensors, the air bag module, steering column, and instrument panel, disable the SRS. Refer to Disarming The System.

✱✱ CAUTION

Incorrect centralization may result in premature component failure. If in doubt when centralizing the clockspring, repeat the centralizing procedure. Failure to follow this instruction may result in personal injury.

✱✱ CAUTION

If installing a new clockspring, DO NOT remove the clockspring anti-rotation key until the steering wheel is installed. If the anti-rotation key has been removed before installing the steering wheel, the clockspring must be centered. Failure to follow this instruction may result in component damage and/or system failure.

1. Before servicing the vehicle, refer to the Precautions Section.
2. Rotate the clockspring inner rotor counterclockwise and carefully feel for the ribbon wire to run out of length with slight resistance. Stop rotating the clockspring inner rotor at this point.
3. Starting with the clockspring inner rotor, wiring, and connector in the 12 o'clock position, rotate the inner rotor clockwise through 4 revolutions to center the clockspring.
4. Verify that the clockspring is correctly centered by observing that after 4 revolutions:
   - The clockspring rotor window is in the 4 o'clock position and the yellow indicator shows in the window
   - The 2 arrows located on the inner and outer rotor of the clockspring line up in the 6 o'clock position
   - The clockspring inner rotor, wiring, and connector are in the 12 o'clock position

➡The clockspring inner rotor, wiring, and connector must be in the 12 o'clock position to install the steering wheel.

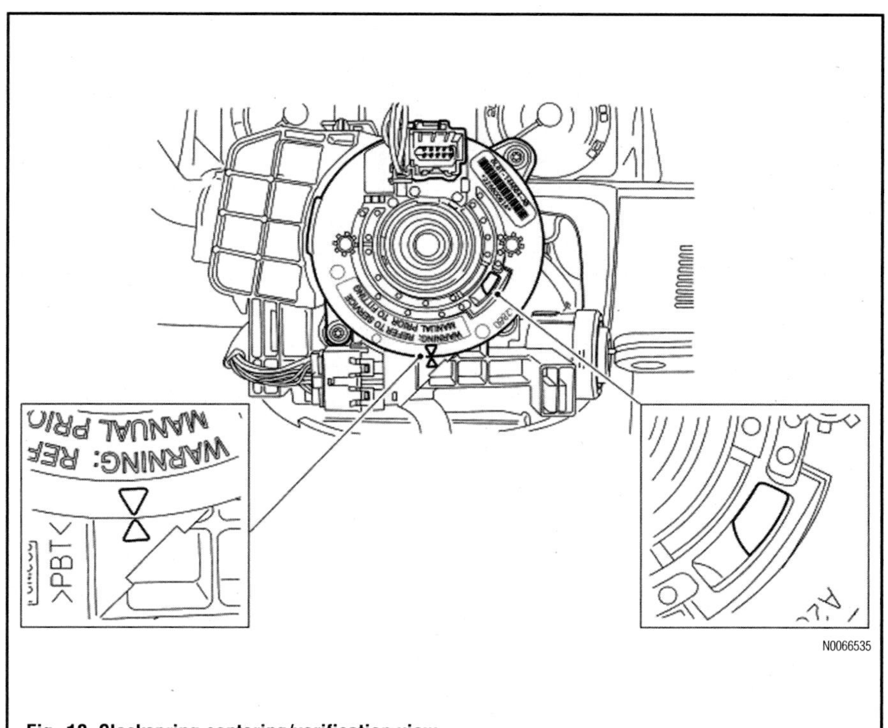

Fig. 10 Clockspring centering/verification view

DRIVE TRAIN

AUTOMATIC TRANSAXLE FLUID

DRAIN AND REFILL

See Figures 11 and 12.

WARNING

During this procedure, to prevent damage to the transaxle, do not run the engine above idle.

1. Before servicing the vehicle, refer to the Precautions Section.
2. With the vehicle in NEUTRAL, position it on a hoist.
3. Disconnect the transmission fluid cooler outlet tube from the transmission fluid cooler.
   a. Remove the transmission fluid cooler tube secondary latch.
   b. Slide the latch out of the transmission fluid cooler tube to the unlocked position.
   c. Remove the transmission fluid cooler tube from the transmission fluid cooler and position the transmission fluid cooler tube aside.
4. Attach a length of suitable drain hose to the transmission fluid cooler.
5. Insert the drain hose into a calibrated 10.5 qts. (10L) container.

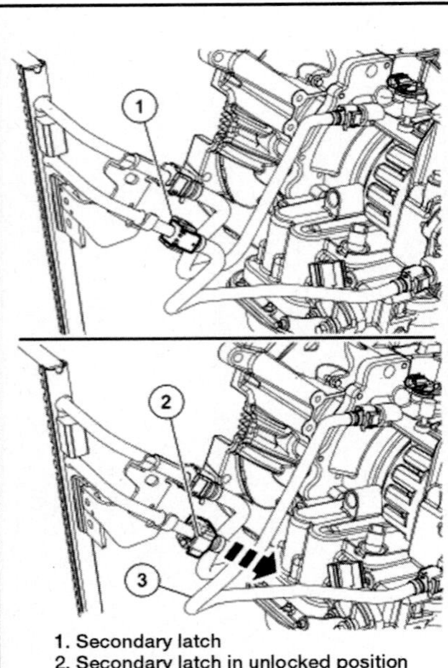

Fig. 11 Disconnect the transmission fluid cooler outlet tube from the transmission fluid cooler

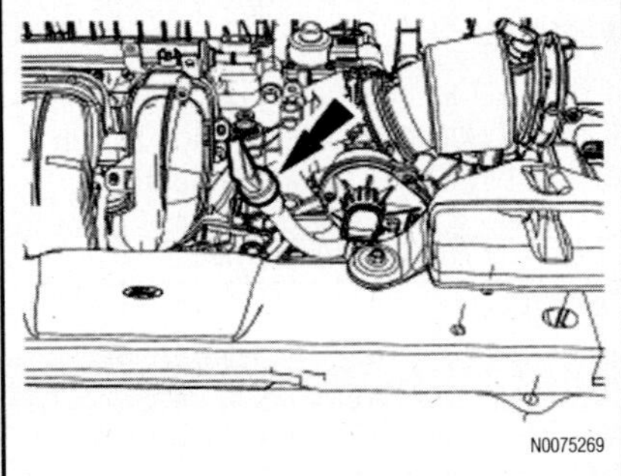

Fig. 12 Remove the transmission fluid level indicator

➡If the transmission fluid return rate is less than 1.0 qt. (0.95L) in 30 seconds, or if the return hose pulsates, check for restrictions at the pump, transmission fluid cooler or transmission fluid cooler tubes.

6. Run the engine at idle and pump out 3.17 qts. (3L) of transmission fluid.
7. Switch the engine OFF.
8. Remove the transmission fluid level indicator from the transmission fluid level indicator tube.
9. Add 3.17 qts. (3L) of transmission fluid to the transaxle.
10. Run the engine at idle and pump out 3.17 qts. (3L) of transmission fluid.
11. Switch the engine OFF.
12. Add 3.17 qts. (3L) of transmission fluid to the transaxle.
13. Run the engine at idle and pump out 3.17 qts. (3L) of transmission fluid.
14. Switch the engine OFF.
15. Remove the length of drain hose from the transmission fluid cooler.
16. Connect the transmission fluid cooler outlet tube to the transmission fluid cooler.
   a. Install the transmission fluid cooler outlet tube on the transmission fluid cooler until it bottoms out.
   b. Slide the latch into the transmission fluid cooler tube to the locked position.
   c. Install the transmission fluid cooler tube secondary latch.
17. Lower the vehicle.
18. Add 3.17 qts. (3L) of transmission fluid to the transaxle.
19. Install the transmission fluid level indicator into the transmission fluid level indicator tube.
20. Run the engine.
21. Check the transmission fluid level and fill to the proper level, as needed.

MANUAL TRANSAXLE ASSEMBLY

REMOVAL & INSTALLATION

See Figures 13 through 20.

1. Before servicing the vehicle, refer to the Precautions Section.
2. With the vehicle in NEUTRAL, position it on a hoist.
3. Remove the steering column shaft bolt.
4. Remove the battery. Refer to Battery, removal & installation.
5. Release the 2 wiring harness pushpins, then remove the 3 battery tray nuts and the battery tray.
6. Remove the intake air hose.
   a. Disconnect the crankcase ventilation hose.
   b. Disconnect the booster bleed hose.
   c. Loosen the clamps and remove the intake air hose.

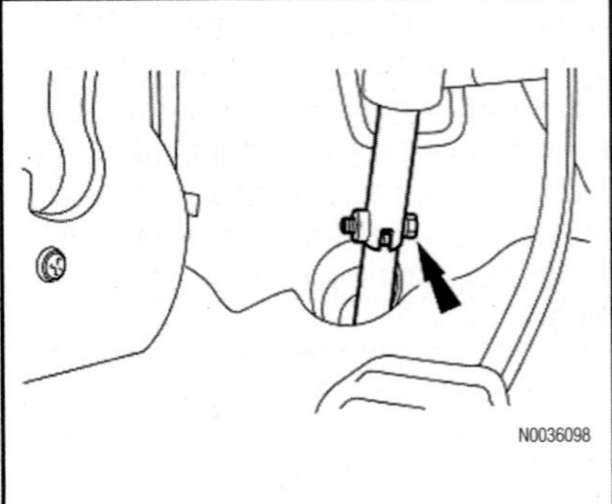

Fig. 13 Remove the steering column shaft bolt

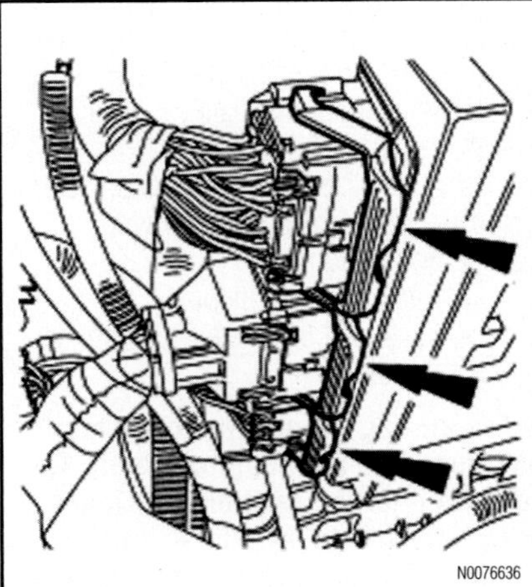

Fig. 14 Disconnect the PCM electrical connectors

7. Remove the 2 resonator bolts and the resonator.

8. Disconnect the PCM electrical connectors.

9. Remove the PCM bolt and nut and the PCM.

10. Remove the 3 PCM/battery support bracket bolts.

11. Install the Engine Support Bar and Adapters.

12. Remove the 5 LH transaxle support insulator nuts and the LH transaxle support insulator with the PCM/battery support bracket.

13. Remove the 3 LH transaxle support insulator bracket bolts and the LH transaxle support insulator bracket.

14. Disconnect the reverse lamp switch electrical connector.

15. Pressing the locking button, disconnect the gearshift cables from the transaxle.

16. Remove the gearshift cables from the bracket.

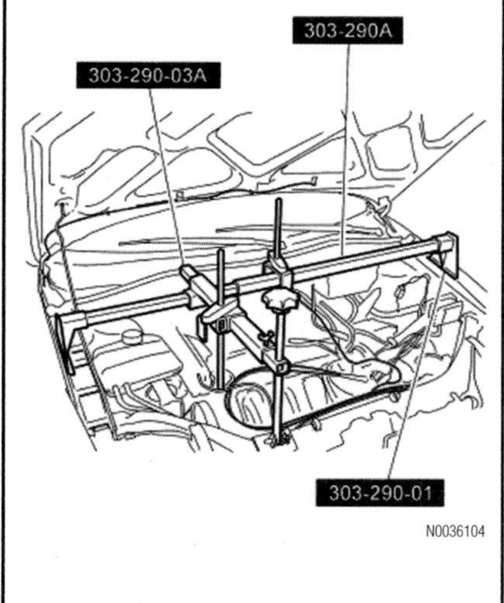

Fig. 15 Install the Engine Support Bar and Adapters as shown

a. Disconnect the shift cable from the retaining bracket by pulling the abutment sleeves rearward then lifting the cable upward.

b. Disconnect the selector cable from the retaining bracket by pulling the abutment sleeve rearward, then lifting the cable upward.

17. Remove the bolt and the power steering tube clamp.

18. Disconnect the clutch hydraulic tube and grommet from the retaining bracket.

19. Disconnect the Heated Oxygen Sensor (HO2S) and the catalyst monitor sensor electrical connectors. Remove the upper sensor bracket nut.

20. Remove the 3 upper transmission-to-engine bolts.

21. Remove the front wheels and tires.

22. If transaxle disassembly is necessary, drain the transaxle fluid.

23. Remove the lower HO2S sensor bracket nut.

24. Remove the 2 engine roll restrictor bolts and the engine roll restrictor.

25. Remove and discard the 2 tie-rod end nuts.

26. Using the Tie-Rod End Remover, separate the tie-rod ends from the wheel knuckles.

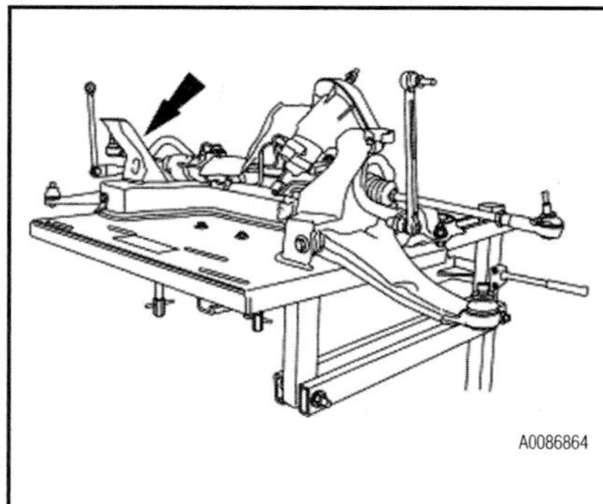

Fig. 17 Lower the subframe assembly from the vehicle

27. Remove and discard the 2 lower control arm bolts and nuts and separate the lower control arms from the wheel knuckles.

28. Remove and discard the 2 stabilizer bar link nuts and separate the stabilizer bar links from the strut.

29. Remove the power steering tube bolt, then disconnect the power steering tubes from the steering gear.

➡Index-mark the subframe to the chassis for reinstallation.

30. Position a suitable lifting device under the subframe. Remove the 6 subframe bolts.

31. Lower the subframe assembly from the vehicle.

32. Disconnect the Vehicle Speed Sensor (VSS) electrical connector.

33. Remove the 2 locknuts and the intermediate shaft center bearing cap. Discard the locknuts and cap.

WARNING

Use a seal protector when removing the halfshaft. Splines on the halfshaft can damage the halfshaft seal. Do not let the halfshafts hang unsupported.

34. Remove the RH halfshaft from the transmission. Position it aside and secure it with mechanic's wire.

35. Using the Halfshaft Remover with the Slide Hammer, remove the LH halfshaft from the transmission. Position it aside and secure it with mechanic's wire.

36. Loosen the starter bolts, but do not remove the starter.

37. Remove the clip, then disconnect the clutch hydraulic tube.

38. Remove the exhaust flexible pipe.

39. Position a suitable jack to the transmission. Secure the transmission to the jack.

40. Remove the 10 transaxle-to-engine bolts.

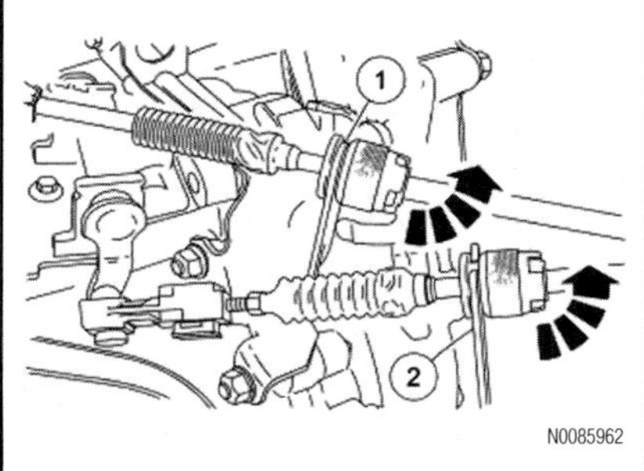

Fig. 16 Remove the gearshift cables from the bracket

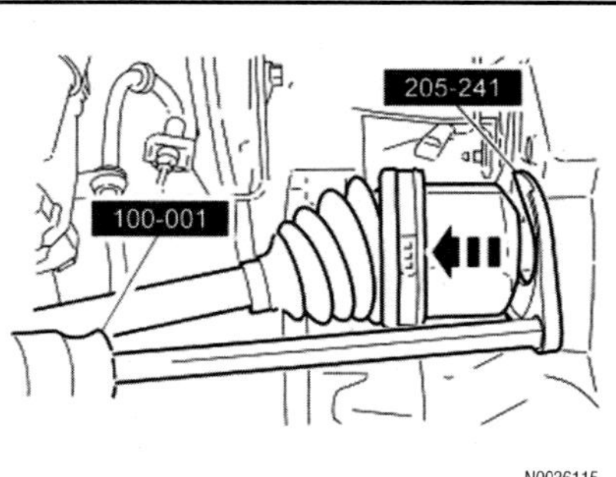

Fig. 18 Using the Halfshaft Remover with the Slide Hammer, remove the LH halfshaft

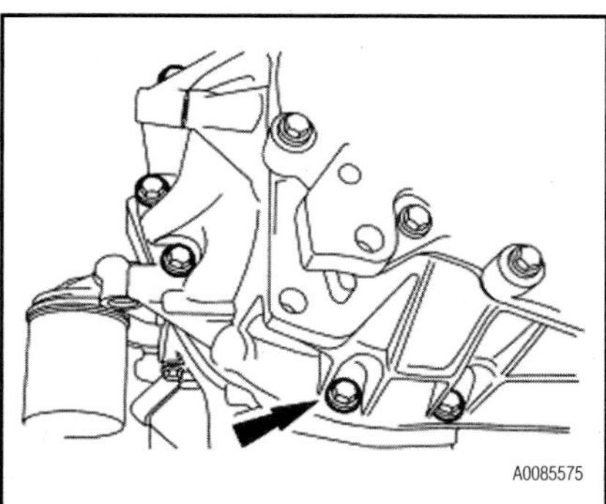

Fig. 19 Remove the 10 transaxle-to-engine bolts

41. Pull the transaxle rearward until the input shaft is clear of the pressure plate, then lower the transaxle from the vehicle.

To install:

42. Position the transaxle to the engine. Install the 10 transaxle-to-engine bolts and tighten to 35 ft. lbs. (47 Nm).
43. Install the exhaust flexible pipe.
44. Connect the clutch hydraulic tube and install the clip.
45. Tighten the starter bolts to 18 ft. lbs. (25 Nm).

➡Install a new halfshaft snap ring.

46. Using a seal protector, install the LH halfshaft into the transaxle.
47. Using a seal protector, install the RH halfshaft into the transaxle.
48. Install the new intermediate shaft center bearing cap and the locknuts. Tighten to 18 ft. lbs. (25 Nm).
49. Connect the VSS electrical connector.

➡Make sure to align the index marks on the subframe to the chassis that were made during removal.

50. Position the subframe into the vehicle, install the 6 subframe bolts.
    a. Tighten the rear subframe bolts to 148 ft. lbs. (200 Nm).
    b. Tighten the front subframe bolts to 85 ft. lbs. (115 Nm).
51. Connect the power steering tubes to the steering gear. Install the power steering tube bolt and tighten to 17 ft. lbs. (23 Nm).
52. Install the 2 new stabilizer bar link nuts and tighten to 37 ft. lbs. (50 Nm).
53. Position the lower control arms into the wheel knuckles. Install the 2 new lower control arm bolts and nuts. Tighten to 35 ft. lbs. (47 Nm).
54. Install the 2 new tie-rod end nuts and tighten to 35 ft. lbs. (47 Nm).
55. Install the engine roll restrictor and the 2 engine roll restrictor bolts. Tighten to 52 ft. lbs. (70 Nm).
56. Position the bracket to the transaxle. Install the lower HO2S sensor bracket nut. Tighten to 18 ft. lbs. (25 Nm).
57. Install the wheels and tires. Tighten the wheel nuts in a star pattern to 100 ft. lbs. (135 Nm).
58. Install the 3 upper transaxle-to-engine bolts and tighten to 35 ft. lbs. (47 Nm).
59. Install the upper sensor bracket nut. Connect the HO2S and the catalyst monitor sensor electrical connectors. Tighten to 18 ft. lbs. (25 Nm).
60. Connect the clutch hydraulic tube and grommet into the retaining bracket.
61. Install the power steering tube clamp bolt.

➡An audible click will be heard when the gearshift cables are correctly seated in the retaining bracket.

62. Install the gearshift cables into the brackets.
63. Connect the gearshift cables to the transaxle.
    a. Press the release button and connect the shift cable to the shift mass.
    b. Press the release button and connect the selector cable to the selector lever.
64. Connect the reverse lamp switch electrical connector.
65. Install the LH transaxle support insulator bracket and the 3 LH transaxle support insulator bracket bolts. Tighten to 59 ft. lbs. (80 Nm).
66. Install the PCM/battery support bracket.
67. Install the LH transaxle support insulator and the 5 LH transaxle support insulator nuts. Install the 3 PCM/battery support bracket bolts.
    a. Tighten the LH transaxle support insulator center nut to 111 ft. lbs. (150 Nm).
    b. Tighten the 4 LH transaxle support insulator outer nuts to 35 ft. lbs. (48 Nm).
68. Install the PCM and the PCM bolt and nut. Tighten to 71 inch lbs. (8 Nm).
69. Connect the PCM electrical connectors.
70. Install the resonator and the 2 resonator bolts and tighten to 97 inch lbs. (11 Nm).
71. Install the intake air hose.
    a. Connect the crankcase ventilation hose.
    b. Connect the booster bleed hose.
    c. Tighten the intake air hose clamps to 35 inch lbs. (4 Nm).

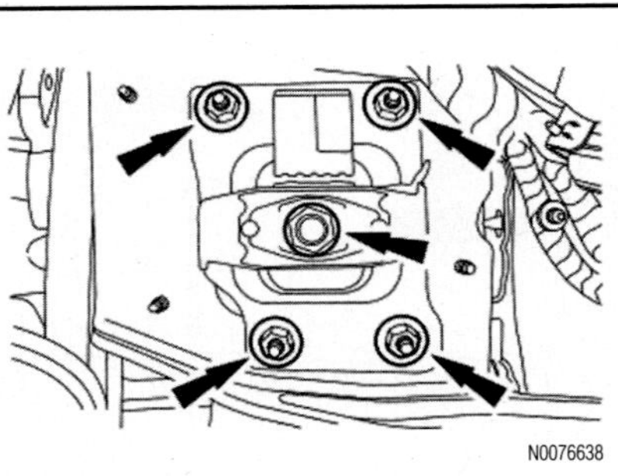

Fig. 20 Install the LH transaxle support insulator and the 5 LH transaxle support insulator nuts

72. Install the battery tray and the 3 battery tray nuts and tighten to 106 inch lbs. (12 Nm). Connect the 2 wiring harness pushpins.
73. Install the battery. Refer to Battery, removal & installation.
74. Install the steering column shaft bolt. Tighten to 21 ft. lbs. (28 Nm).
75. Check and, if necessary, fill the transaxle with the specified fluid. The total fill capacity is 4.0 pts. (1.9L). Apply sealant to the fill plug threads and install the fill plug.
76. Fill and bleed the power steering system.

⁂ WARNING

Brake fluid is harmful to painted and plastic surfaces. If brake fluid is spilled on a painted or plastic surface, wash the affected area immediately with cold water.

77. Fill the brake fluid reservoir to the specified level. Bleed the clutch hydraulic system.
78. Adjust the gearshift cables, as needed.

MANUAL TRANSAXLE FLUID

DRAIN AND REFILL

See Figures 21 and 22.

1. Before servicing the vehicle, refer to the Precautions Section.
2. With the vehicle in NEUTRAL, position it on a hoist.
3. Remove the drain plug and drain the transaxle.

To install:

4. Clean and install the drain plug. Tighten to 26 ft. lbs. (35 Nm).

➡Before removing, clean the area around the filler plug.

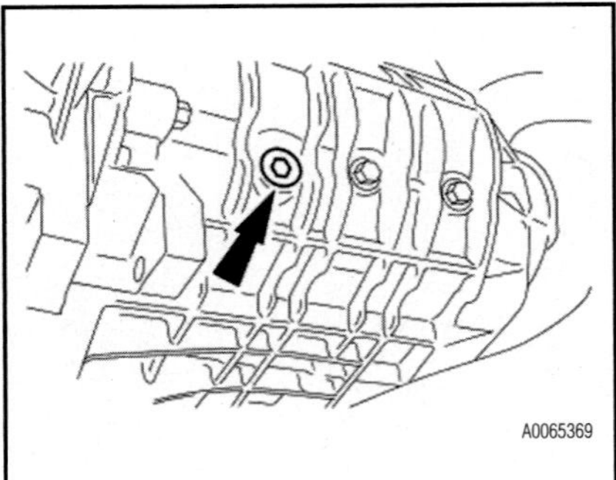

Fig. 21 Filler plug location—manual transaxle

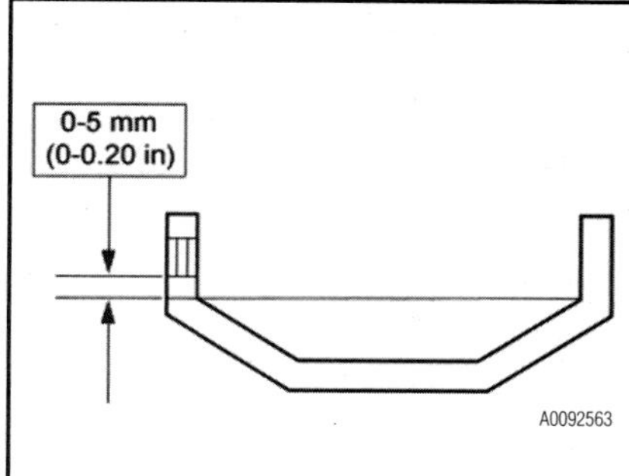

Fig. 22 Correct fluid level indicated from filler plug bore—manual transaxle

5. Remove the fill plug.

6. Using a suitable oil suction gun, fill the transaxle with the proper type of fluid to 0.0–0.2 inch (0.0–5.0mm) below the lower edge of the filler plug bore.

7. Install the fill plug. Tighten to 26 ft. lbs. (35 Nm).

CLUTCH

REMOVAL & INSTALLATION

See Figures 23 and 24.

CAUTION

Do not breathe dust or use compressed air to blow dust from storage containers or friction components. Remove dust using government-approved techniques. Friction component dust may be a cancer and lung disease hazard. Exposure to potentially hazardous components may occur if dusts are created during repair of friction components, such as brake pads and clutch discs. Exposure may also cause irritation to skin, eyes and respiratory tract, and may cause allergic reactions and/or may lead to other chronic health effects. If irritation persists, seek medical attention or advice. Failure to follow these instructions may result in serious personal injury.

1. Before servicing the vehicle, refer to the Precautions Section.

2. Remove the transaxle. Refer to Manual Transaxle Assembly, removal & installation.

3. Loosen the 6 clutch pressure plate-to-flywheel bolts evenly, by 2 turns at a time.

4. Remove the 6 clutch pressure plate-to-flywheel bolts, the clutch disc, and the pressure plate. Discard the pressure plate bolts.

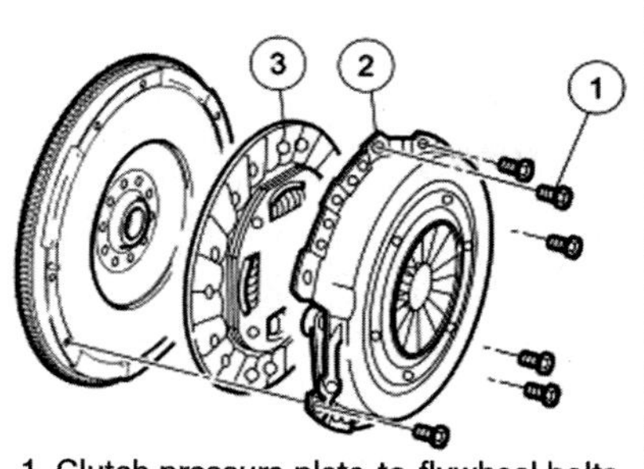

Fig. 23 Exploded view of clutch—manual transaxle

To install:

5. Clean the clutch pressure plate and flywheel with a commercial alcohol-based solvent so surfaces are free from oil film.

➡**Do not use cleaners with a petroleum base. Do not immerse the clutch pressure plate in solvent.**

6. Position the clutch disc on the clutch pressure plate. Using a suitable clutch aligner, centralize the clutch disc to the clutch pressure plate.

7. Using a suitable clutch aligner, position the clutch disc and clutch pressure plate on the flywheel.

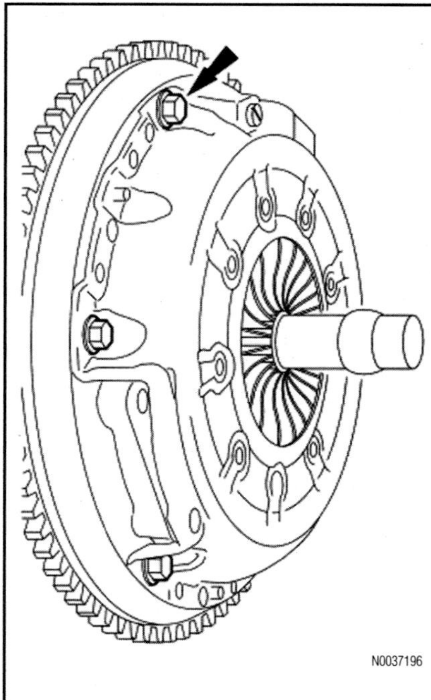

Fig. 24 Clutch aligner shown—manual transaxle

8. Install the 6 new clutch pressure plate-to-flywheel bolts. Tighten the bolts evenly in a star pattern to 21 ft. lbs. (29 Nm).

9. Remove the clutch aligner.

10. Install the transaxle. Refer to Manual Transaxle Assembly, removal & installation.

BLEEDING

See Figure 25.

WARNING

Do not spill brake fluid on painted or plastic surfaces or damage to the surface may occur. If brake fluid is spilled onto a painted or plastic surface, immediately wash the surface with water.

➡**Do not reuse brake fluid.**

1. Before servicing the vehicle, refer to the Precautions Section.

2. With the vehicle in NEUTRAL, position it on a hoist.

3. Remove the brake fluid reservoir cap.

4. Drain the brake fluid reservoir to the MIN mark.

5. Remove the clutch slave cylinder bleeder fitting dust cap.

6. Using the Vacuum Pump Kit, bleed the clutch system as follows:

   a. Fill the reservoir of the Vacuum Pump Kit with approximately 4.1 oz. (120 ml) of brake fluid.

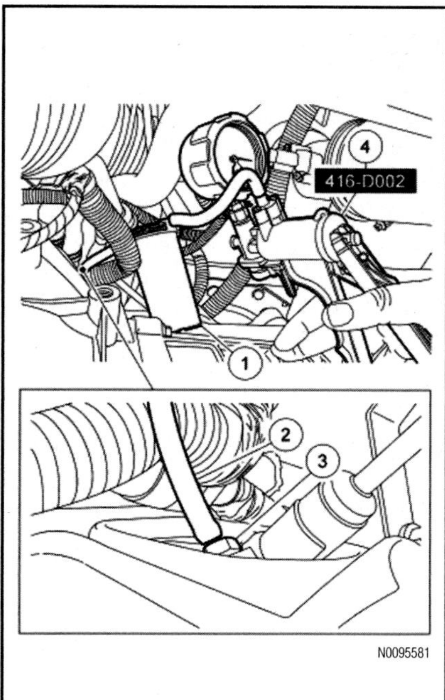

Fig. 25 Using the Vacuum Pump Kit to bleed the clutch system

b. Connect the reservoir hose to the clutch slave cylinder bleeder fitting.

c. Loosen the clutch slave cylinder bleeder fitting.

d. Pump approximately 3.4 oz. (100 ml) of brake fluid into the clutch system.

7. Tighten the clutch slave cylinder bleeder fitting to 15 ft. lbs. (21 Nm).
8. Remove the Vacuum Pump Kit.
9. Install the clutch slave cylinder bleeder fitting dust cap.
10. Check the fluid level in the brake fluid reservoir and add as necessary.
11. Install the brake fluid reservoir cap.

**** WARNING**

Engage the reverse gear carefully.

12. Test the functionality of the clutch control system.

a. Start the engine. After 2 seconds, depress the clutch pedal and carefully engage the reverse gear. If there are abnormal noises, bleed the clutch control system automatically by depressing the clutch pedal 4 or 5 times. During bleeding, full travel of the clutch pedal must be reached.

b. Test the functionality of the clutch control system again after 30 seconds. If there are still abnormal noises, carry out Steps 3 through 12 again.

FLUID FILL PROCEDURE

See Figure 26.

**** CAUTION**

Brake fluid contains polyglycol ethers and polyglycols. Avoid contact with the eyes and wash your hands thoroughly after handling brake fluid. If you do get brake fluid in your eyes, flush your eyes with clean, running water for 15 minutes. If eye irritation persists, or if you have taken brake fluid internally, IMMEDIATELY seek medical assistance.

**** WARNING**

Clean, high quality brake fluid is essential to the safe and proper operation of the clutch and brake system. You should always buy the highest quality brake fluid that is available. If the brake fluid becomes contaminated, drain and flush the system. Never reuse any brake fluid. Any brake fluid that is removed from the system should be discarded. Also, do not allow any brake fluid to come in contact with a painted surface; it will damage the paint.

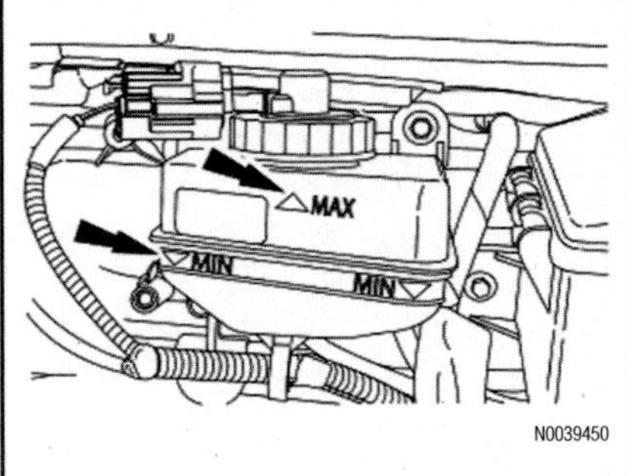

Fig. 26 Fill the fluid level so that it is between the MIN and MAX lines

1. Before servicing the vehicle, refer to the Precautions Section.
2. Fill the fluid level so that it is between the MIN and MAX lines marked on the reservoir.

FRONT HALFSHAFT

REMOVAL & INSTALLATION

Left Side Halfshaft

See Figures 27 through 30.

1. Before servicing the vehicle, refer to the Precautions Section.
2. With the vehicle in NEUTRAL, position it on a hoist.
3. Remove the LH wheel and tire.
4. Remove and discard the wheel hub nut.

**** WARNING**

Do not use a prying device or separator fork between the ball joint and the wheel knuckle. Damage to the ball joint or ball joint seal may result. Only use the pry bar by inserting it into the lower arm body opening.

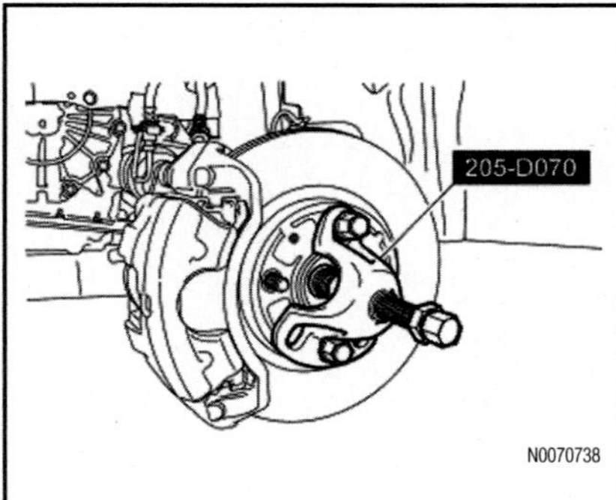

Fig. 27 Using the front wheel hub remover

**** WARNING**

Use care when releasing the lower arm and wheel knuckle into the resting position or damage to the ball joint seal may occur.

5. Remove and discard the ball joint nut and bolt.
6. Insert a pry bar in the lower arm body opening and separate the ball joint from the wheel knuckle.

**** WARNING**

The inner joint must not be bent more than 18 degrees. The outer joint must not be bent more than 45 degrees. Damage to the halfshaft will occur.

7. Using the front wheel hub remover, press out the halfshaft from the wheel hub and detach the LH halfshaft from the wheel hub. Support the halfshaft.
8. Remove the brake hose retainer.
9. Using the slide hammer, the extension from the halfshaft remover and the halfshaft (plate) remover, remove the LH halfshaft from the transaxle.
10. Remove and discard the halfshaft circlip.

To install:

11. Install a new halfshaft circlip.

➡Make sure the snap ring is fully engaged by pulling on the joint housing.

12. Install the LH halfshaft into the transaxle.
13. Using the halfshaft installer, install the LH halfshaft into the wheel hub.
14. Install the brake hose retainer.

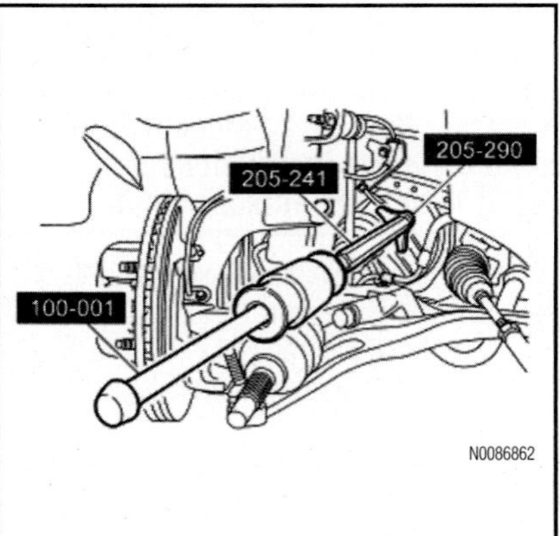

Fig. 28 Using the slide hammer, the extension from the halfshaft remover and the halfshaft (plate) remover, remove the LH halfshaft from the transaxle

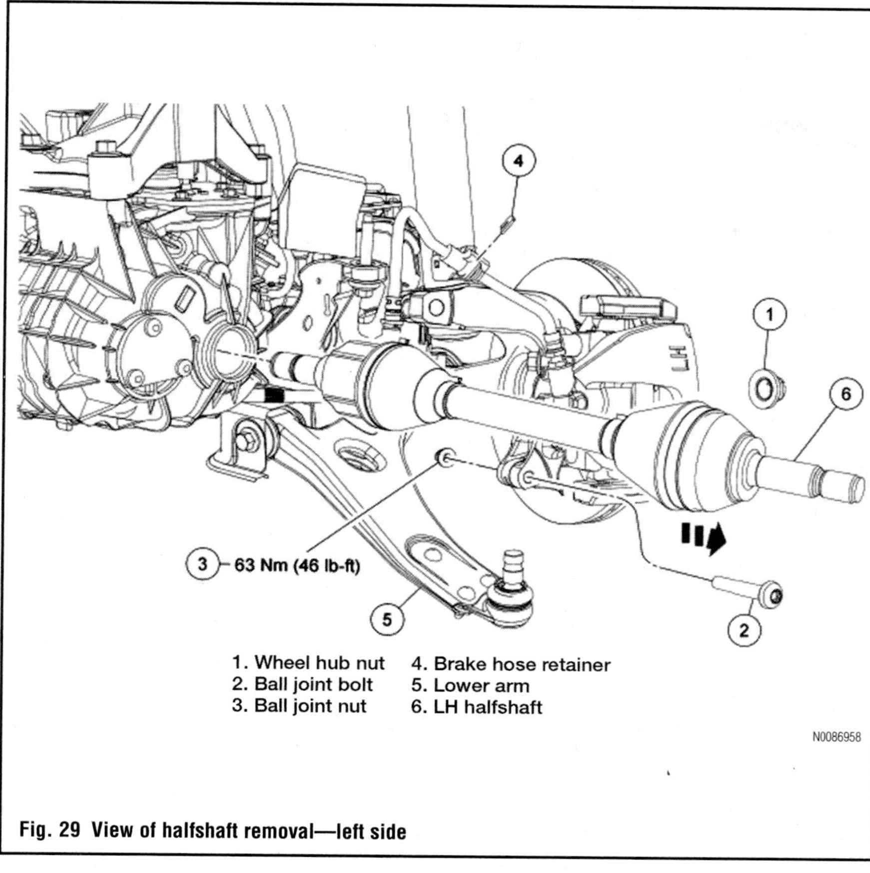

Fig. 29 View of halfshaft removal—left side

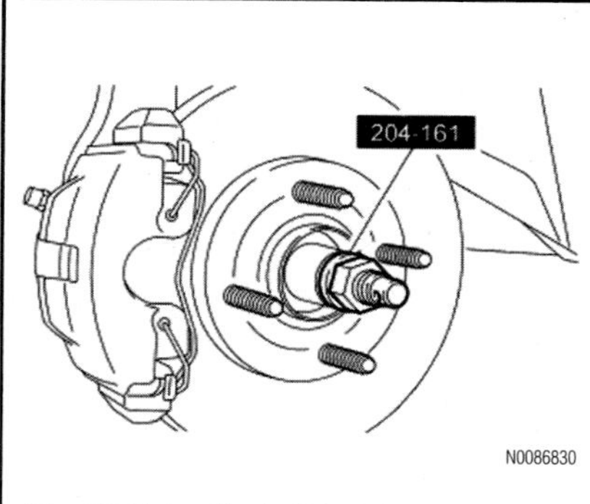

Fig. 30 Using the halfshaft installer, install the LH halfshaft into the wheel hub

WARNING

Make sure the ball joint heat shield is installed on the ball joint stud or damage to the ball joint may occur.

15. Insert the ball joint stud into the wheel knuckle and install a new bolt and nut. Tighten to 46 ft. lbs. (63 Nm).

WARNING

Do not tighten the wheel hub nut with the vehicle on the ground. The nut must be tightened to specification before the vehicle is lowered onto the wheels. Wheel bearing damage will occur if the wheel bearing is loaded with the weight of the vehicle applied.

➡Install and tighten the new wheel hub nut to specification in a continuous rotation. Always install a new wheel hub nut after loosening or when not tightened to specification in a continuous rotation or damage to the components may occur.

16. Apply the brake to keep the halfshaft from rotating.
17. Install a new wheel hub nut. Tighten to 199 ft. lbs. (270 Nm) in a continuous rotation.
18. Install the LH wheel and tire. Tighten the wheel nuts in a star pattern to 100 ft. lbs. (135 Nm).
19. Top off the transmission fluid level.

Right Side Halfshaft

See Figures 31 through 35.

1. Before servicing the vehicle, refer to the Precautions Section.
2. With the vehicle in NEUTRAL, position it on a hoist.
3. Remove the RH wheel and tire.
4. Remove and discard the wheel hub nut.

WARNING

Do not use a prying device or separator fork between the ball joint and the wheel knuckle. Damage to the ball joint or ball joint seal may result. Only use the pry bar by inserting it into the lower arm body opening.

WARNING

Use care when releasing the lower arm and wheel knuckle into the resting position or damage to the ball joint seal may occur.

5. Remove and discard the ball joint nut and bolt.
6. Insert a pry bar in the lower arm body opening and separate the ball joint from the wheel knuckle.

WARNING

The inner joint must not be bent more than 18 degrees. The outer joint must not be bent more than 45 degrees. Damage to the halfshaft will occur.

7. Using the front wheel hub remover, press out the halfshaft from the wheel hub and detach the RH halfshaft from the wheel hub.
8. Support the halfshaft assembly.
9. Remove the brake hose retainer.
10. For automatic transaxle models: remove and discard the retaining strap and 2 nuts.
11. For manual transaxle models: remove and discard the 3 bracket-to-block bolts.
12. Remove the RH halfshaft assembly.

To install:

13. Install the RH halfshaft assembly into the transaxle.
14. For automatic transaxle models:
    a. Install a new retaining strap and 2 nuts on the intermediate shaft bearing.
    b. Install the RH halfshaft assembly into the transaxle.
        - Tighten the lower nut to 44 inch lbs. (5 Nm)
        - Tighten the upper nut to 18 ft. lbs. (25 Nm)
        - Tighten the lower nut to 18 ft. lbs. (25 Nm)
15. For manual transaxle models:
    a. Insert the halfshaft assembly into

205-D070
N0070738

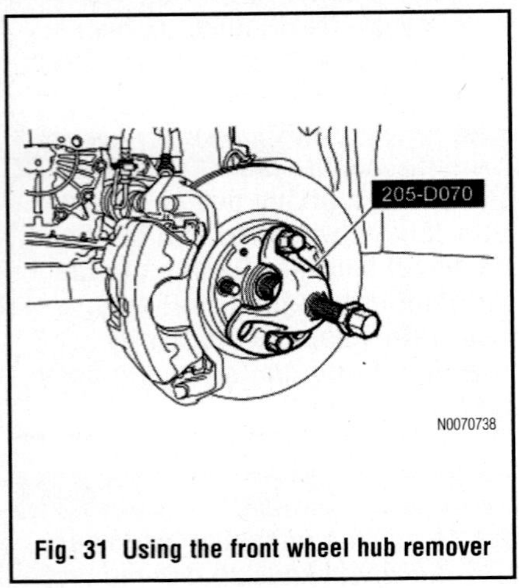

Fig. 31 Using the front wheel hub remover

39
E0000839

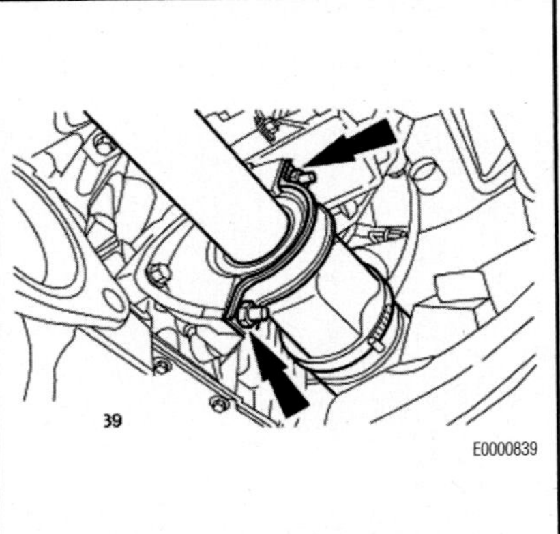

Fig. 32 Remove and discard the retaining strap and 2 nuts—automatic transaxle

N0078507

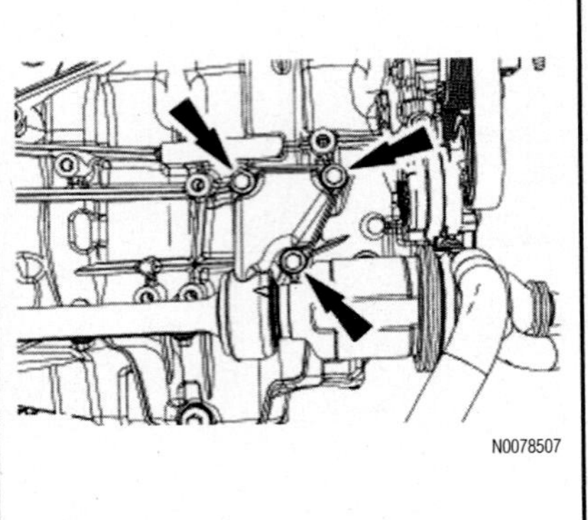

Fig. 33 Remove and discard the 3 bracket-to-block bolts—manual transaxle

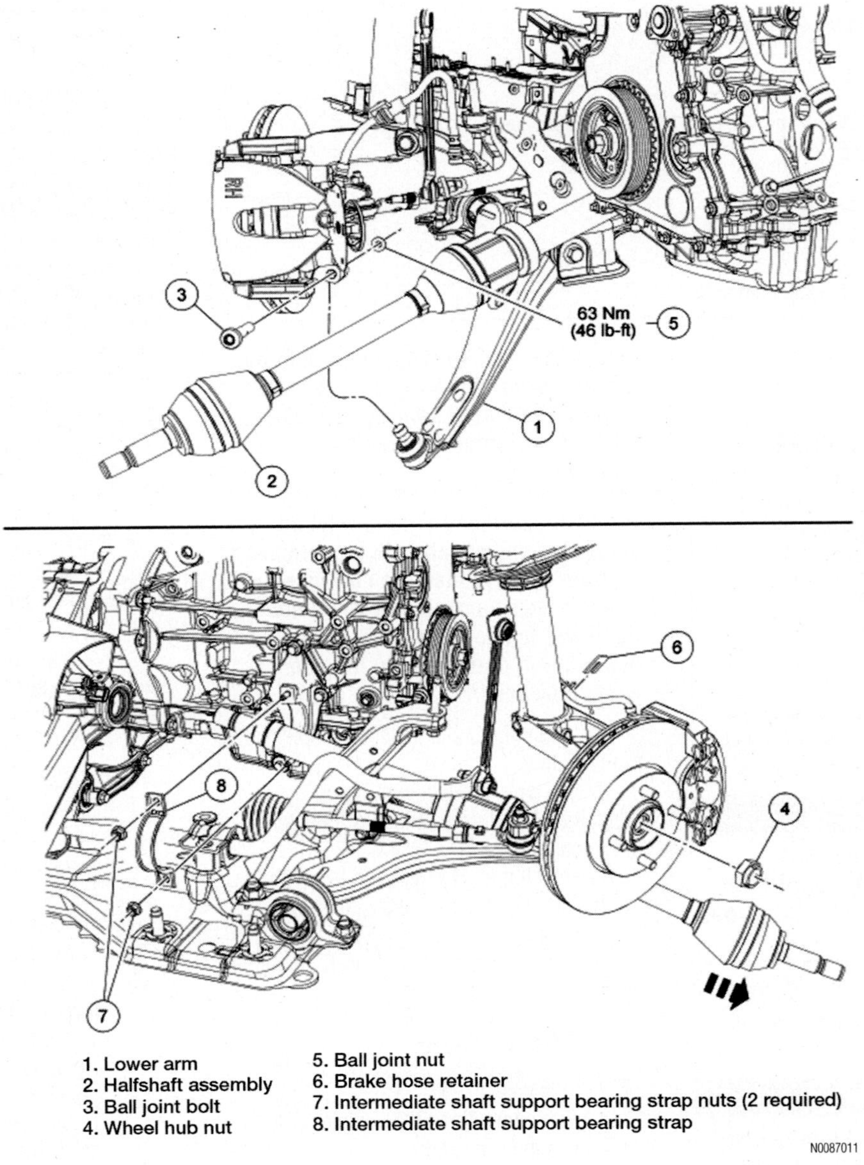

63 Nm
(46 lb-ft)
1
2
3
4
5
6
7
8
1. Lower arm
2. Halfshaft assembly
3. Ball joint bolt
4. Wheel hub nut
5. Ball joint nut
6. Brake hose retainer
7. Intermediate shaft support bearing strap nuts (2 required)
8. Intermediate shaft support bearing strap
N0087011

Fig. 34 View of right side halfshaft removal—automatic shown, manual similar

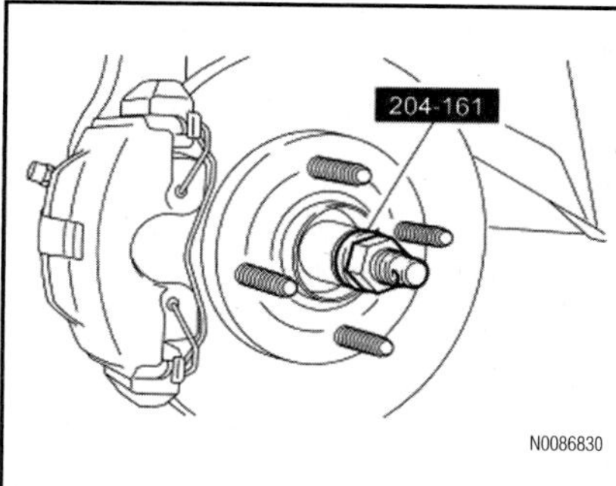

Fig. 35 Using the halfshaft installer, install the RH halfshaft into the wheel hub

the transaxle until the intermediate shaft bearing contacts the rib of the intermediate shaft bracket.

b. Install the 3 new bracket bolts to the engine block. Tighten to 35 ft. lbs. (48 Nm).

16. Using the halfshaft installer, install the RH halfshaft into the wheel hub.

⁂ WARNING

Make sure the ball joint heat shield is installed on the ball joint stud or damage to the ball joint may occur.

17. Insert the ball joint stud into the wheel knuckle and install a new bolt and nut. Tighten to 46 ft. lbs. (63 Nm).

⁂ WARNING

Do not tighten the wheel hub nut with the vehicle on the ground. The nut must be tightened to specification before the vehicle is lowered onto the wheels. Wheel bearing damage will occur if the wheel bearing is loaded with the weight of the vehicle applied.

➡Install and tighten the new wheel hub nut to specification in a continuous rotation. Always install a new wheel hub nut after loosening or when not tightened to specification in a continuous rotation or damage to the components may occur.

18. Apply the brake to keep the halfshaft from rotating.

19. Install a new wheel hub nut. Tighten to 199 ft. lbs. (270 Nm) in a continuous rotation.

20. Install the brake hose retainer.

21. Install the RH wheel and tire. Tighten the wheel nuts in a star pattern to 100 ft. lbs. (135 Nm).

22. Top off the transmission fluid level.

ENGINE COOLING

ENGINE COOLANT

DRAIN & REFILL PROCEDURE

⁂ CAUTION

Always allow the engine to cool before opening the cooling system. Do not unscrew the coolant pressure relief cap when the engine is operating or the cooling system is hot. The cooling system is under pressure; steam and hot liquid can come out forcefully when the cap is loosened slightly. Failure to follow these instructions may result in serious personal injury.

➡The coolant must be recovered in a suitable, clean container for reuse. If the coolant is contaminated, it must be recycled or disposed of correctly. Using contaminated coolant may result in damage to the engine or cooling system components.

⁂ WARNING

The engine cooling system is filled with Motorcraft® Premium Gold Engine Coolant. Mixing coolant types degrades the corrosion protection of Motorcraft® Premium Gold Engine Coolant. Do not mix coolant types. Failure to follow these instructions may result in engine or cooling system damage.

➡If cooling system stop leak pellets are used, Motorcraft® Premium Gold Engine Coolant may darken from yellow to golden tan.

Engine coolant provides boil protection, corrosion protection, freeze protection, and cooling efficiency to the engine and cooling components. In order to obtain these protections, maintain the engine coolant at the correct concentration and fluid level in the degas bottle. To maintain the integrity of the coolant and the cooling system:

- Add Motorcraft® Premium Gold Engine Coolant, or equivalent, meeting Ford specification (yellow color). Do not mix coolant types
- Do not add or mix with any other type of engine coolant. Mixing coolants may degrade the coolant's corrosion protection
- Do not add alcohol, methanol, or brine, or any engine coolants mixed with alcohol or methanol antifreeze. These can cause engine damage from overheating or freezing
- Ford Motor Company does NOT recommend the use of recycled engine coolant in vehicles originally equipped with Motorcraft® Premium Gold Engine Coolant since a Ford-approved recycling process is not yet available

Recommended coolant concentration is 50/50 ethylene glycol to distilled water.

For extremely cold climates (less than -33°F (-36°C):

- It may be necessary to increase the coolant concentration above 50 percent
- NEVER increase the coolant concentration above 60 percent
- Maximum coolant concentration is 60/40 for cold weather areas
- A coolant concentration of 60 percent will provide freeze point protection down to -62°F (-52°C)
- Engine coolant concentration above 60 percent will decrease the overheat protection characteristics of the engine coolant and may damage the engine

For extremely hot climates:

- It is still necessary to maintain the coolant concentration above 40 percent
- NEVER decrease the coolant concentration below 40 percent
- Minimum coolant concentration is 40/60 for warm weather areas
- A coolant concentration of 40 percent will provide freeze point protection down to -11°F (-24°C)
- Engine coolant concentration below 40 percent will decrease the corrosion and freeze protection characteristics of the engine coolant and may damage the engine

Vehicles driven year-round in non-extreme climates should use a 50/50 mixture of engine coolant and distilled water for optimum cooling system and engine protection.

Draining Engine Coolant

See Figure 36.

1. Before servicing the vehicle, refer to the Precautions Section.
2. Release the cooling system pressure by slowly turning the pressure relief cap ¼ of a turn.
3. Remove the pressure relief cap when all the pressure has been released.
4. With the vehicle in NEUTRAL, position it on a hoist.
5. Remove the lower radiator air deflector.
6. Place a suitable container below the radiator drain valve.
7. Open the radiator drain valve and allow the coolant to drain.
8. Close the radiator drain valve.
9. Install the lower radiator air deflector.

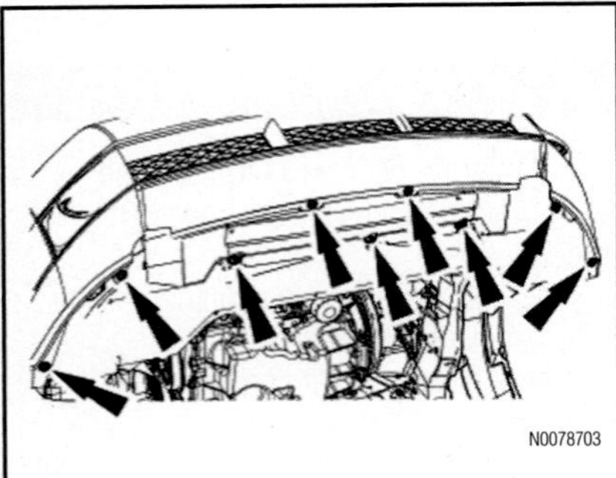

Fig. 36 Removing the lower radiator air deflector

Filling & Bleeding—With Vacuum Cooling System Filler

See Figure 37.

1. Before servicing the vehicle, refer to the Precautions Section.

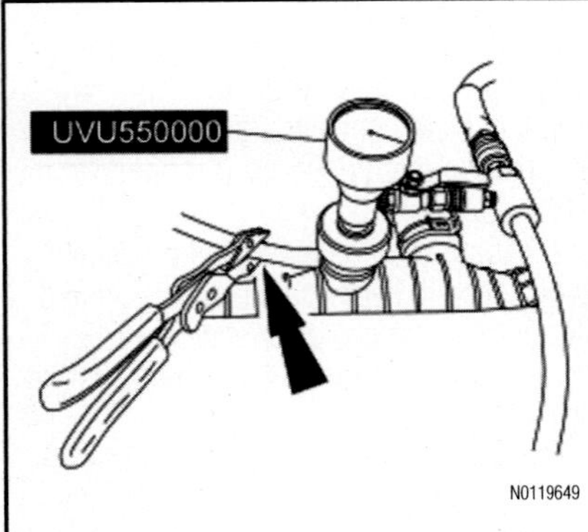

Fig. 37 Vacuum cooling system filler installed

2. Install the vacuum cooling system filler and follow the manufacturer's instructions to fill and bleed the cooling system.

Filling & Bleeding—Without Vacuum Cooling System Filler

1. Before servicing the vehicle, refer to the Precautions Section.
2. Fill the radiator to the top of the fill neck and the coolant expansion tank to the max level mark.
3. Install the pressure relief cap.
4. If the engine overheats or the fluid level in the coolant expansion tank drops below the cold fill line, allow the engine to cool. Once the engine is cool, add coolant to the coolant expansion tank to the cold fill line. Failure to follow these instructions may result in engine damage.
5. Start the engine, run and hold at 2,500 RPM for approximately 8 minutes until the thermostat opens, then for another 3 minutes after the thermostat opens.
6. Increase the engine speed briefly to 4,000 RPM and hold for approximately 5 seconds.
7. If the engine overheats or the fluid level in the coolant expansion tank drops below the cold fill line, allow the engine to cool. Once the engine is cool, add coolant to the coolant expansion tank to the cold fill line. Failure to follow these instructions may result in engine damage.
8. Return the engine speed to 2,500 RPM and hold for another 3 minutes.
9. Shut the engine OFF and allow it to cool.
10. Check the engine for any leaks.
11. Check the coolant level in the coolant expansion tank and fill as necessary.

BLEEDING

Refer to Filling & Bleeding—With or Without Vacuum Cooling System Filler in the Drain & Refill Procedure.

FLUSHING

⁂ CAUTION

Always allow the engine to cool before opening the cooling system. Do not unscrew the coolant pressure relief cap when the engine is operating or the cooling system is hot. The cooling system is under pressure; steam and hot liquid can come out forcefully when the cap is loosened slightly. Failure to follow these instructions may result in serious personal injury.

1. Before servicing the vehicle, refer to the Precautions Section.
2. Drain the cooling system.
3. Remove the thermostat. Refer to Thermostat, removal & installation.
4. Install the water hose connection without the thermostat.

➡If applicable, refer to the cooling system Pro Flush and Fill, or equivalent, operating instructions for specific vehicle hook-up.

5. Use cooling system Pro Flush and Fill, Flush Kit, and Drain Kit, or equivalent, to flush the engine and radiator.
6. Install the thermostat. Refer to Thermostat, removal & installation.
7. Fill the cooling system. Refer to Engine Coolant, Drain & Refill Procedure.

ENGINE FAN

REMOVAL & INSTALLATION

See Figures 36 and 38.

1. Before servicing the vehicle, refer to the Precautions Section.
2. With the vehicle in NEUTRAL, position it on a hoist.
3. Remove the lower radiator air deflector.
4. Disconnect the cooling fan motor and shroud electrical connector and the pin-type retainers.
5. Remove the 2 bolts and remove the cooling fan motor and shroud from the vehicle.

To install:

6. To install, reverse the removal procedure.
7. Tighten the 2 cooling fan motor and shroud bolts to 44 inch lbs. (5 Nm).

RADIATOR

REMOVAL & INSTALLATION

See Figure 38.

1. Before servicing the vehicle, refer to the Precautions Section.
2. With the vehicle in NEUTRAL, position it on a hoist.
3. Drain the cooling system. Refer to Engine Coolant, Drain & Refill Procedure.

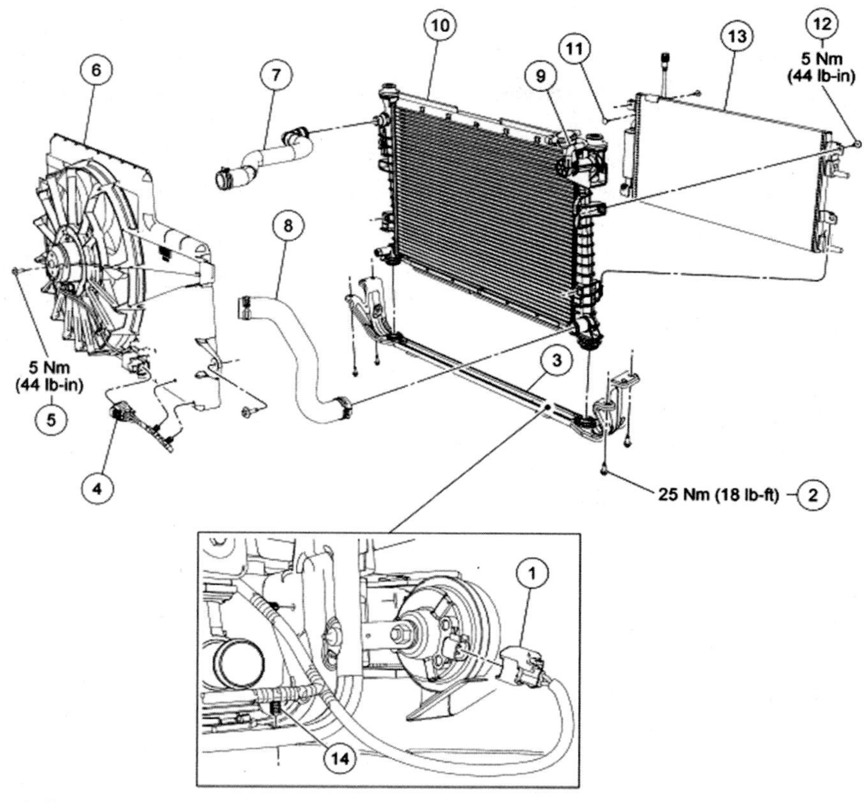

1. Horn assembly electrical connector
2. Lower radiator support bolt (4 required)
3. Lower radiator support
4. Cooling fan motor electrical connector
5. Cooling fan motor and shroud bolt (2 required)
6. Cooling fan motor and shroud
7. Upper radiator hose
8. Lower radiator hose
9. Overflow hose
10. Radiator
11. Transmission oil cooler tube bracket pin-type retainer (if equipped)
12. Condenser core bolt (2 required)
13. Condenser core
14. Pin-type retainer (4 required)

N0077403

Fig. 38 Exploded view of radiator and cooling fan

4. Disconnect the cooling fan motor electrical connector, horn electrical connector and the pin-type retainers.

5. Remove the 2 bolts and the cooling fan motor and shroud from the vehicle.

6. Disconnect the upper radiator and overflow hoses from the radiator.

7. Disconnect the lower radiator hose from the radiator.

8. Position a suitable jackstand below the lower radiator support to support the cooling module.

➡The cooling module will have to be lifted upward to remove the lower radiator support and then positioned back onto the jackstand.

9. Remove the 4 bolts and the lower radiator support.

10. If equipped, remove the transmission oil cooler tube bracket pin-type retainer.

11. Remove the 2 condenser core-to-radiator bolts, separate the condenser core and remove the radiator.

To install:

12. To install, reverse the removal procedure and note the following:
- Tighten the 2 condenser core-to-radiator bolts to 44 inch lbs. (5 Nm)
- Tighten the 4 bolts for the lower radiator support to 18 ft. lbs. (25 Nm)
- Tighten the cooling fan motor and shroud bolts to 44 inch lbs. (5 Nm)

13. Fill and bleed the cooling system. Refer to Engine Coolant, Drain & Refill Procedure.

THERMOSTAT

REMOVAL & INSTALLATION

See Figure 39.

1. Before servicing the vehicle, refer to the Precautions Section.

➡The thermostat and thermostat housing are serviced as an assembly.

2. With the vehicle in NEUTRAL, position it on a hoist.

3. Drain the cooling system. Refer to Engine Coolant, Drain & Refill Procedure.

4. Remove the accessory drive belt. Refer to Accessory Drive Belts, removal & installation.

5. Remove the 2 nuts and position aside the power steering tube.

6. Remove the cooling fan motor and shroud. Refer to Engine Fan, removal & installation.

7. Remove the 2 bolts, the stud bolt and position aside the A/C compressor.

8. Remove the 3 bolts and reposition the thermostat housing to gain access to the hose clamps.

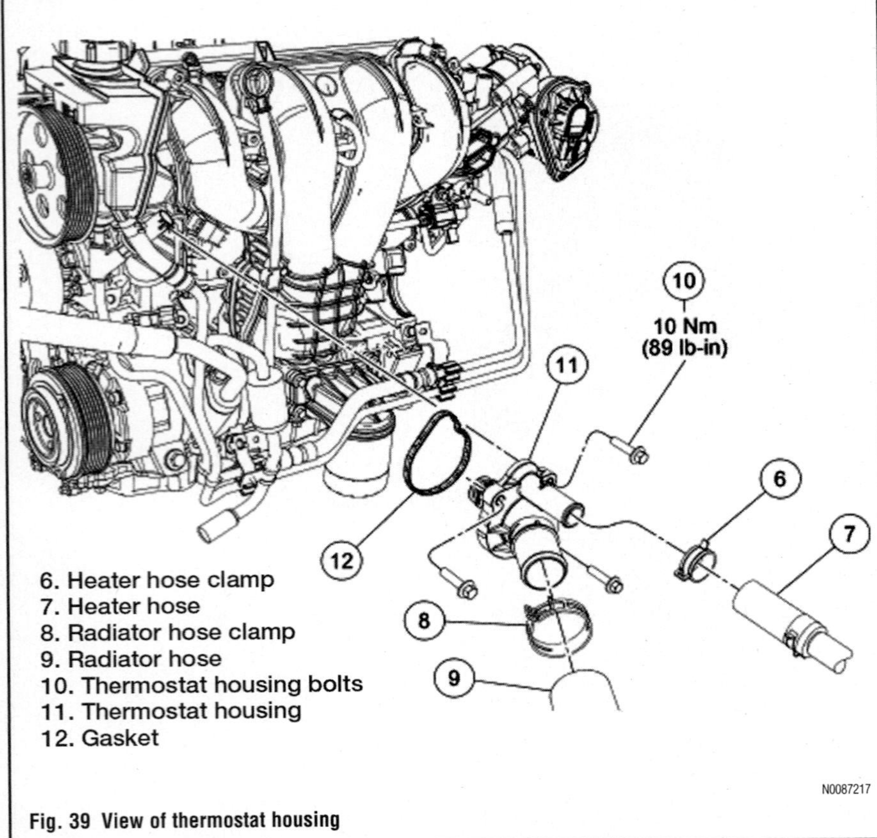

Fig. 39 View of thermostat housing

9. Remove and discard the gasket.
10. Disconnect the radiator and heater hoses from the thermostat housing.

To install:

➡Lubricate the thermostat housing O-ring with clean engine coolant.

11. To install, reverse the removal procedure and note the following:
    - Tighten the bolts on the new thermostat/housing assembly to 89 inch lbs. (10 Nm)
    - Tighten the bolts on the A/C compressor to 18 ft. lbs. (25 Nm)
    - Tighten the nuts on the power steering tube to 89 inch lbs. (10 Nm)
12. Fill and bleed the cooling system. Refer to Engine Coolant, Drain & Refill Procedure.

WATER PUMP

REMOVAL & INSTALLATION

See Figure 40.

1. Before servicing the vehicle, refer to the Precautions Section.
2. With the vehicle in NEUTRAL, position it on a hoist.
3. Remove the 2 bolts and position aside the coolant expansion tank.
4. Loosen the 3 coolant pump pulley bolts.
5. Remove the accessory drive belt. Refer to Accessory Drive Belts, removal & installation.
6. Drain the cooling system. Refer to Engine Coolant, Drain & Refill Procedure.
7. Remove the 3 coolant pump pulley bolts and the pulley.
8. Remove the 3 coolant pump bolts and the coolant pump.

To install:

⁂ WARNING

Make sure the coolant pump is correctly seated to the engine block before installing and tightening the fasteners, or damage to the coolant pump may occur.

9. To install, reverse the removal procedure and note the following:
    - Install a new coolant pump O-ring seal and lubricate with clean engine coolant
    - Tighten the 3 coolant pump bolts to 89 inch lbs. (10 Nm)
    - Tighten the 3 coolant pump pulley bolts to 177 inch lbs. (20 Nm)
    - Tighten the coolant expansion tank bolts to 35 inch lbs. (4 Nm)
10. Fill and bleed the cooling system. For additional information, refer to Cooling System Draining, Filling and Bleeding in this section.

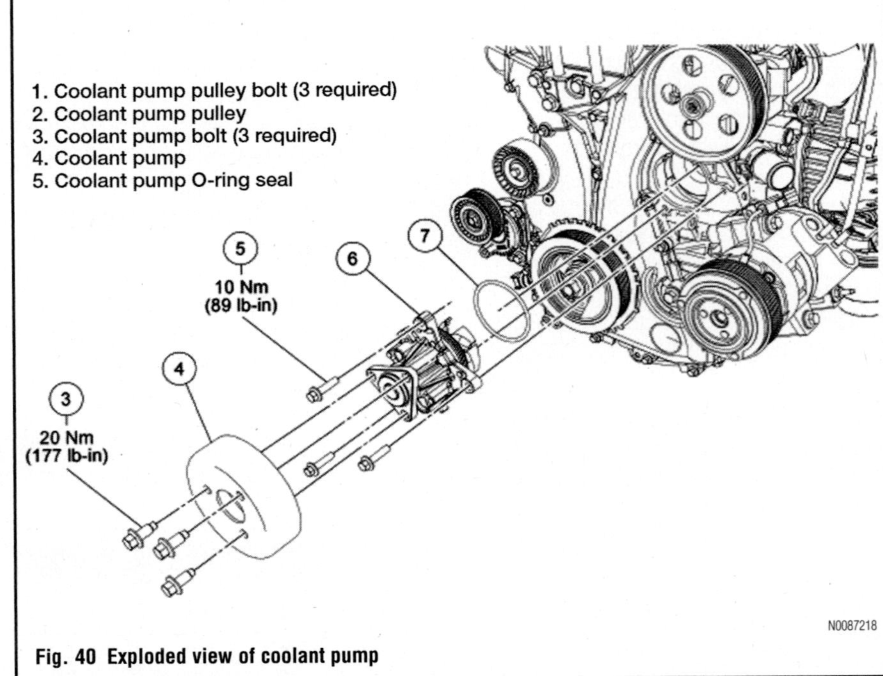

Fig. 40 Exploded view of coolant pump

BATTERY

REMOVAL & INSTALLATION

See Figure 41.

✻✻ CAUTION

Batteries contain sulfuric acid and produce explosive gases. Work in a well-ventilated area. Do not allow the battery to come in contact with flames, sparks or burning substances. Avoid contact with skin, eyes or clothing. Shield eyes when working near the battery to protect against possible splashing of acid solution. In case of acid contact with skin or eyes, flush immediately with water for a minimum of 15 minutes, then get prompt medical attention. If acid is swallowed, call a physician immediately. Failure to follow these instructions may result in serious personal injury.

✻✻ CAUTION

Always lift a plastic-cased battery with a battery carrier or with hands on opposite corners. Excessive pressure on the battery end walls may cause acid to flow through the vent caps, resulting in personal injury and/or damage to the vehicle or battery.

1. Before servicing the vehicle, refer to the Precautions Section.
2. Remove the negative battery cable from the battery, then the positive cable. For additional information, refer to Battery Reconnect/Relearn Procedure.
3. Open the wire harness clamp and remove the harness from the clamp.
4. Thread the wire harness retainer off of the battery hold-down stud.
5. Remove the 2 nuts from the battery clamp and remove the clamp.
6. Remove the battery.

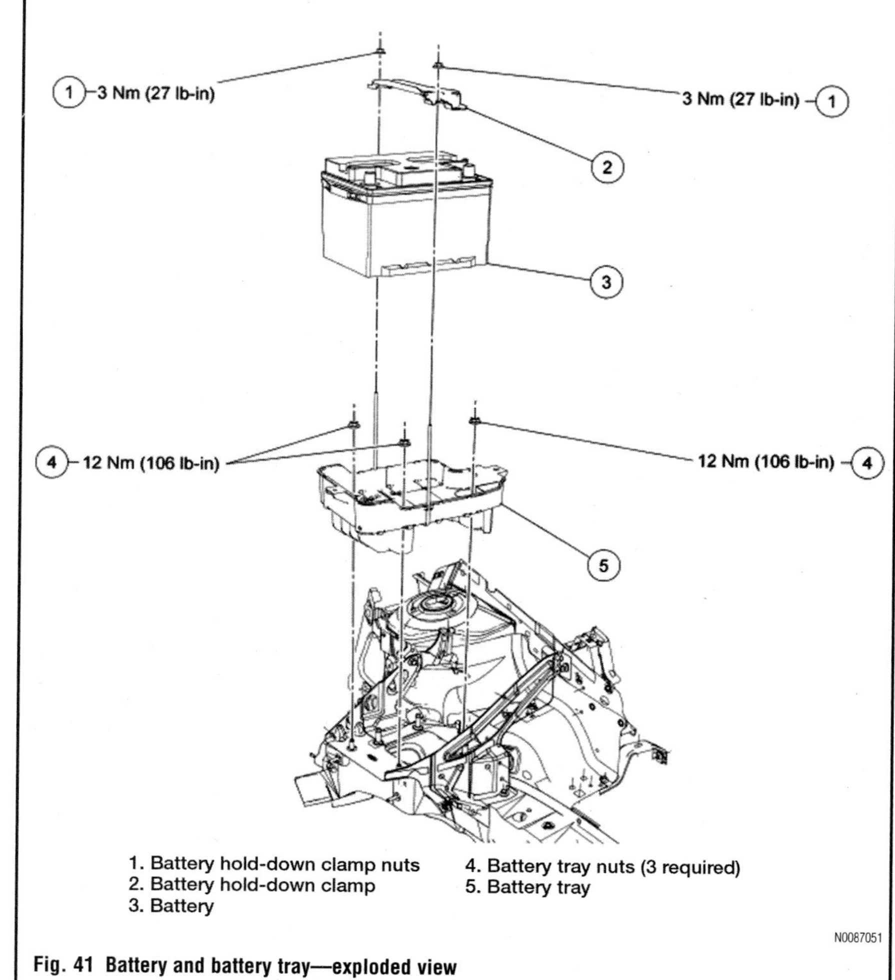

Fig. 41 Battery and battery tray—exploded view

To install:

7. Install the battery.
8. Install the battery hold down clamp and tighten the nuts to 27 inch lbs. (3 Nm).
9. Install the wire harness retainer.
10. Install the wire harness clamp.
11. Connect the positive and then the negative battery terminal, tighten to 80 inch lbs. (9 Nm).
12. Install and close the positive battery terminal cover.
13. Reset electronic systems as necessary. Refer to Battery Reconnect/Relearn Procedure.

BATTERY RECONNECT/RELEARN PROCEDURE

✻✻ CAUTION

Always deplete the backup power supply before repairing or installing any new front or side air bag Supplemental Restraint System (SRS) component and before servicing, removing, installing, adjusting, or striking components near the front or side impact sensors or the Restraints Control Module (RCM). Nearby components include doors, instrument panel, console, door latches, strikers, seats, and hood latches.

1. Before servicing the vehicle, refer to the Precautions Section.
2. To deplete the backup power supply energy, disconnect the battery ground cable and wait at least 1 minute. Be sure to disconnect auxiliary batteries and power supplies (if equipped).

✻✻ CAUTION

Battery posts, terminals and related accessories contain lead and lead components. Wash hands after handling. Failure to follow these instructions may result in serious personal injury.

3. When the battery (or PCM) is disconnected and connected, some abnormal drive symptoms may occur while the vehicle relearns its adaptive strategy. The charging system set point may also vary. The vehicle may need to be driven to relearn its strategy.
4. When the battery is disconnected and connected, the illumination display needs to be calibrated. After the battery is connected, rotate the dimmer switch from the lowest dim position to the full bright, dome ON position.

ALTERNATOR

REMOVAL & INSTALLATION

See Figure 42.

➡The radial arm adapter is a serviceable item. Do not replace the alternator if the radial arm adapter is the only concern.

1. Before servicing the vehicle, refer to the Precautions Section.
2. With the vehicle in NEUTRAL, position it on a hoist.
3. Disconnect the battery. Refer to Battery, removal & installation.
4. Disconnect the alternator electrical connector.

➡Do not remove the RH halfshaft to install a new radial arm adapter. The RH halfshaft only needs to be removed if installing a new alternator.

5. Remove the RH halfshaft. Refer to Front Halfshaft, removal & installation.
6. Remove the 3 bolts and the center support bracket.
7. Remove the 2 screws and the accessory drive splash shield.
8. Rotate the Front End Accessory Drive (FEAD) belt tensioner clockwise and remove the belt from the alternator drive pulley. Position the FEAD belt aside.
9. Release the 2 retainers and remove the lower alternator air duct.
10. Position the protective cover aside, remove the nut and position the alternator B+ terminal aside.
11. Remove the 2 alternator nuts.
12. Remove the 2 alternator studs.
13. Remove the alternator bolt and the alternator.
14. If necessary, remove the bolt and the alternator upper air duct.

To install:

15. If removed, install the alternator upper air duct and the bolt. Tighten to 106 inch lbs. (12 Nm).
16. Install the alternator and alternator bolt. Hand-tighten the bolt. Do not torque the bolt at this time.
17. Install the 2 alternator studs. Tighten to 18 ft. lbs. (24 Nm).

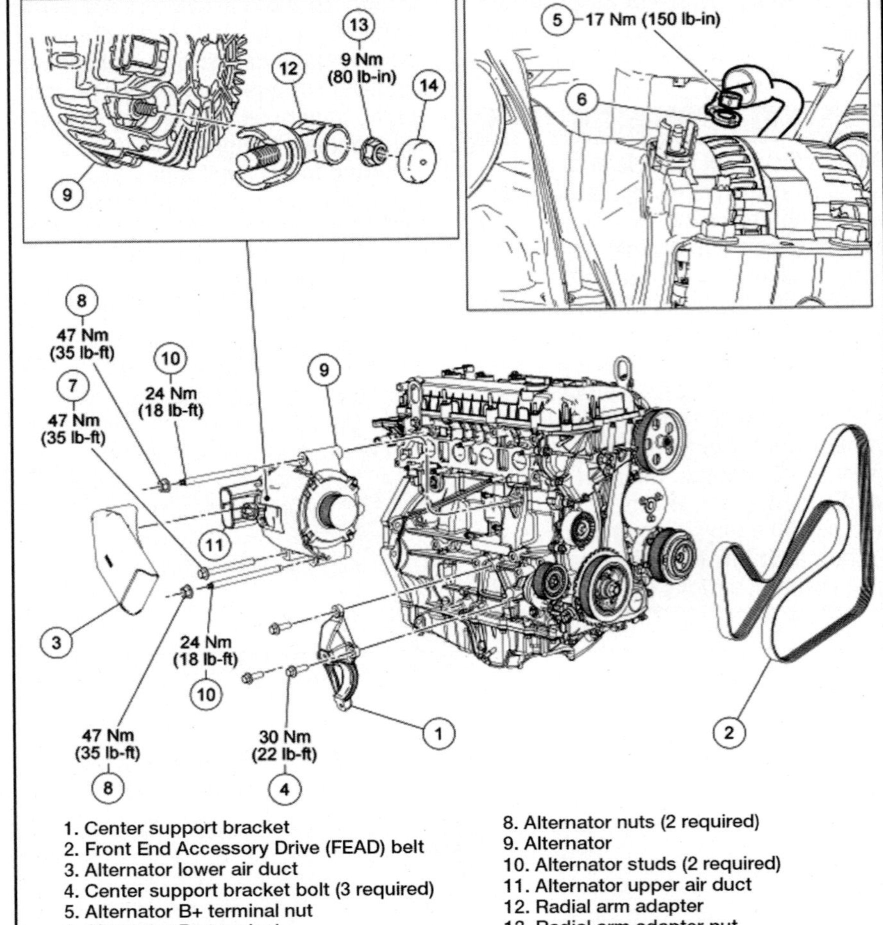

Fig. 42 Expanded view of alternator mounting

18. Install the 2 alternator nuts. Tighten to 35 ft. lbs. (47 Nm).
19. Tighten the alternator bolt. Tighten to 35 ft. lbs. (47 Nm).
20. Position the alternator B+ terminal on the alternator and install the nut. Tighten the nut to 13 ft. lbs. (17 Nm) and position the protective cover on the nut.
21. Install the lower alternator air duct.
22. Rotate the FEAD belt tensioner clockwise and install the FEAD belt.
23. Position the accessory drive splash shield and install the 2 screws. Tighten the screws to 44 inch lbs. (5 Nm).
24. Install the center support bracket and the 3 bolts. Tighten the bolts to 22 ft. lbs. (30 Nm).
25. Install the RH halfshaft. Refer to Front Halfshaft, removal & installation.
26. Connect the alternator electrical connector.
27. Connect the battery. For additional information, refer to Battery, removal & installation.

FIRING ORDER

2.0L Engine firing order: 1–3–4–2

IGNITION COIL

REMOVAL & INSTALLATION

See Figure 43.

1. Before servicing the vehicle, refer to the Precautions Section.
2. Disconnect the ignition coil-on-plug electrical connector.

➡When removing the ignition coil-on-plugs, a slight twisting motion will break the seal and ease removal.

3. Remove the bolt and the ignition coil.

To install:

4. Inspect the coil boots for rips, nicks or tears. Remove and discard any damaged coil boots.
5. To install a new coil boot, slide the new coil boot onto the coil until it is fully seated at the top of the coil.
6. Apply silicone dielectric compound to the inside of the ignition coil boot.
7. Install the ignition coil and tighten the bolt to 89 inch lbs. (10 Nm).
8. Connect the ignition coil-on-plug electrical connector.

IGNITION TIMING

ADJUSTMENT

The ignition timing is controlled by the Powertrain Control Module (PCM). No adjustment is necessary.

SPARK PLUGS

REMOVAL & INSTALLATION

See Figures 43 through 45.

4 - 12 Nm (106 lb-in)

1. Ignition coil-on-plug electrical connector (4 required)
2. Ignition coil-to-valve cover bolt (4 required)
3. Ignition coil (4 required)
4. Spark plug (4 required)
5. Coil boot (4 required)

N0088826

Fig. 43 Engine ignition components—exploded view

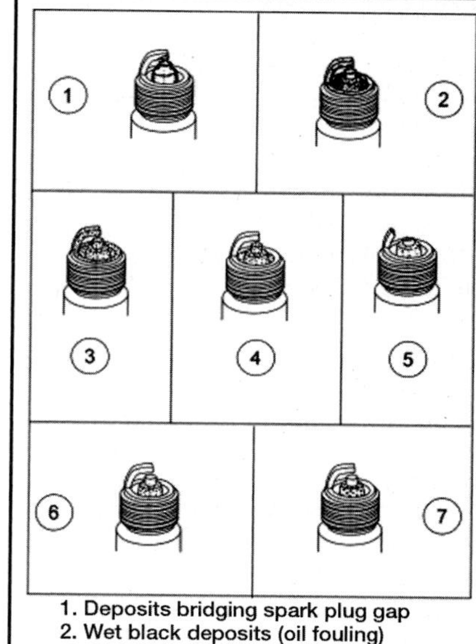

1. Deposits bridging spark plug gap
2. Wet black deposits (oil fouling)
3. Dry black deposits (carbon fouling)
4. Normal spark plug
5. Pre-ignition
6. Overheating
7. Fused spot deposits

DB0020A

Fig. 44 Possible spark plug condition

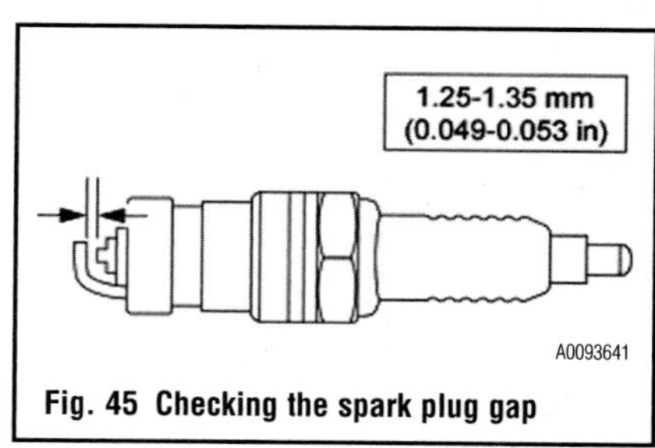

Fig. 45 Checking the spark plug gap

1. Before servicing the vehicle, refer to the Precautions Section.
2. Remove the ignition coil. Refer to Ignition Coil, removal & installation.

⁂ WARNING

Only use hand tools when removing or installing the spark plugs, or damage can occur to the cylinder head or spark plug.

3. Remove foreign material from the spark plug well using compressed air.
4. Remove the spark plug.

To install:

5. Inspect the removed spark plugs.
6. Check and adjust the spark plug gap, as necessary.
7. Install the spark plugs and tighten to 106 inch lbs. (12 Nm).
8. Install the ignition coils. Refer to Ignition Coil, removal & installation.

STARTER

REMOVAL & INSTALLATION

See Figure 46.

⁂ CAUTION

Always disconnect the battery ground cable at the battery before disconnecting the starter motor battery terminal lead. If a tool is shorted at the starter motor battery terminal, the tool can quickly heat enough to cause a skin burn. Failure to follow this instruction may result in serious personal injury.

1. Before servicing the vehicle, refer to the Precautions Section.
2. With the vehicle in NEUTRAL, position it on a hoist.
3. Disconnect the battery ground cable. Refer to Battery, removal & installation.
4. Remove the starter solenoid wire nut.
5. Remove the starter solenoid battery cable nut and the starter motor solenoid wire harness terminal cover.
6. Detach the Engine Oil Pressure (EOP) switch wire harness retainer from the starter stud bolt.
7. Remove the power steering tube bracket nut and position the power steering tube and bracket aside.
8. Remove the upper bolt, the lower stud bolt, and the starter motor.

To install:

9. Install the starter upper bolt and lower stud bolt finger-tight.

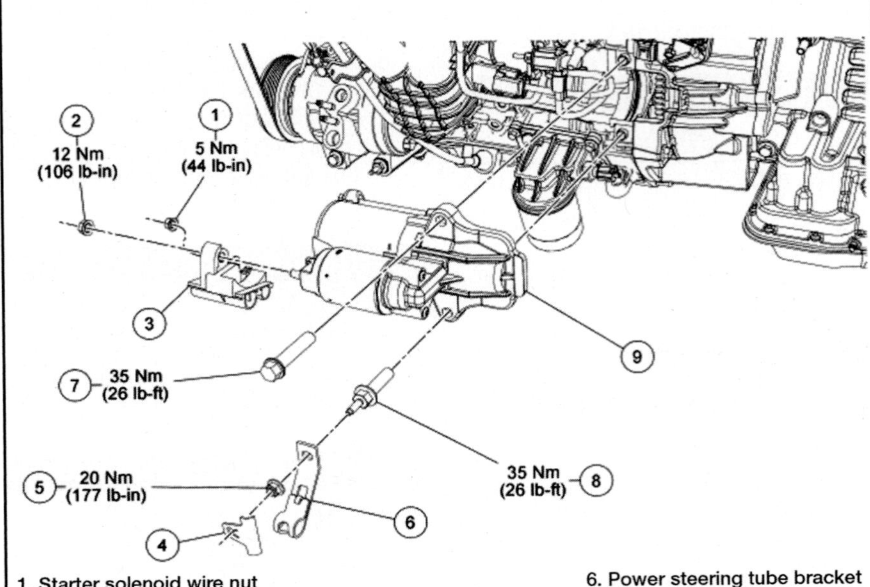

Fig. 46 View of starter motor mounting

10. Tighten the starter upper bolt to 26 ft. lbs. (35 Nm).
11. Tighten the starter lower stud bolt to 26 ft. lbs. (35 Nm).
12. Installation continues in the reverse the removal procedure.
13. Tighten the power steering tube bracket nut to 15 ft. lbs. (20 Nm).
14. Tighten the starter solenoid battery cable nut and the starter motor solenoid wire harness terminal cover to 106 inch lbs. (12 Nm).
15. Tighten the starter solenoid wire nut to 44 inch lbs. (5 Nm).

ENGINE MECHANICAL

➡Disconnecting the negative battery cable may interfere with the functions of the on board computer systems and may require the computer to undergo a relearning process, once the negative battery cable is reconnected.

ACCESSORY DRIVE BELTS

ACCESSORY BELT ROUTING

See Figure 47.

INSPECTION

Inspect the drive belt for signs of glazing or cracking. A glazed belt will be perfectly smooth from slippage, while a good belt will have a slight texture of fabric visible. Cracks will usually start at the inner edge of the belt and run outward. All worn or damaged drive belts should be replaced immediately.

ADJUSTMENT

Accessory belt tension is automatically maintained by a spring-loaded tensioner. No adjustment is necessary.

REMOVAL & INSTALLATION

See Figures 47 and 48.

1. Before servicing the vehicle, refer to the Precautions Section.
2. With the vehicle in NEUTRAL, position it on a hoist.
3. Remove the 2 bolts and the accessory drive belt splash shield.
4. Using the hex feature, rotate the accessory drive belt tensioner clockwise and remove the accessory drive belt.

To install:

5. Rotate the accessory drive belt tensioner clockwise.
6. Route the drive belt.
7. Slowly release the tensioner.
8. Install the splash shield and tighten the 2 mounting bolts to 80 inch lbs. (9 Nm).

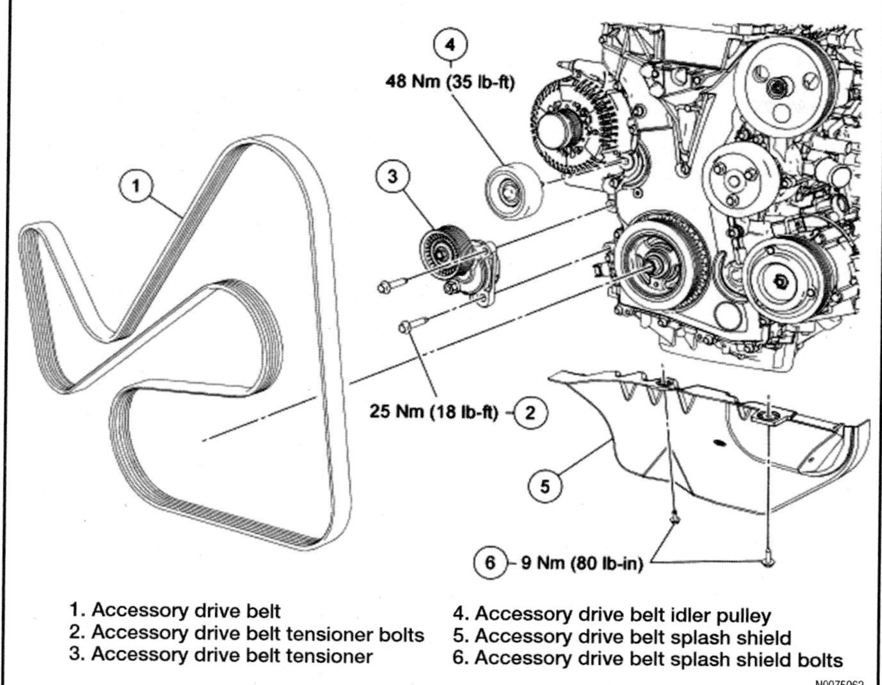

Fig. 47 Accessory drive belt routing

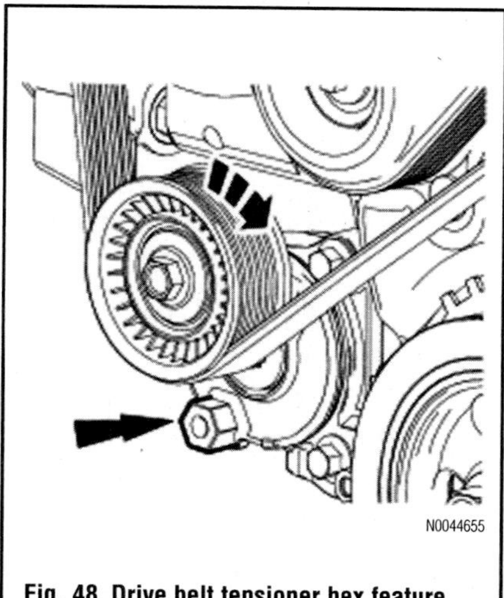

Fig. 48 Drive belt tensioner hex feature shown

AIR CLEANER

REMOVAL & INSTALLATION

See Figure 49.

1. Before servicing the vehicle, refer to the Precautions Section.
2. Disconnect the Mass Air Flow (MAF) sensor electrical connector.
3. Loosen the clamp and separate the Air Cleaner (ACL) outlet pipe from the ACL assembly.
4. Remove the 2 bolts and the ACL assembly.

To install:

5. Install the ACL assembly and tighten the 2 bolts to 80 inch lbs. (9 Nm).
6. Install the ACL outlet pipe and clamp to the ACL assembly. Tighten the clamp to 27 inch lbs. (3 Nm).
7. Connect the MAF sensor electrical connector.

FILTER/ELEMENT REPLACEMENT

See Figure 50.

1. Before servicing the vehicle, refer to the Precautions Section.
2. Disconnect the Mass Air Flow (MAF) sensor electrical connector.
3. Loosen the clamp and separate the Air Cleaner (ACL) outlet pipe from the ACL assembly.
4. Remove the ACL cover.
5. Remove the ACL element.
6. Installation is the reverse of the removal procedure.

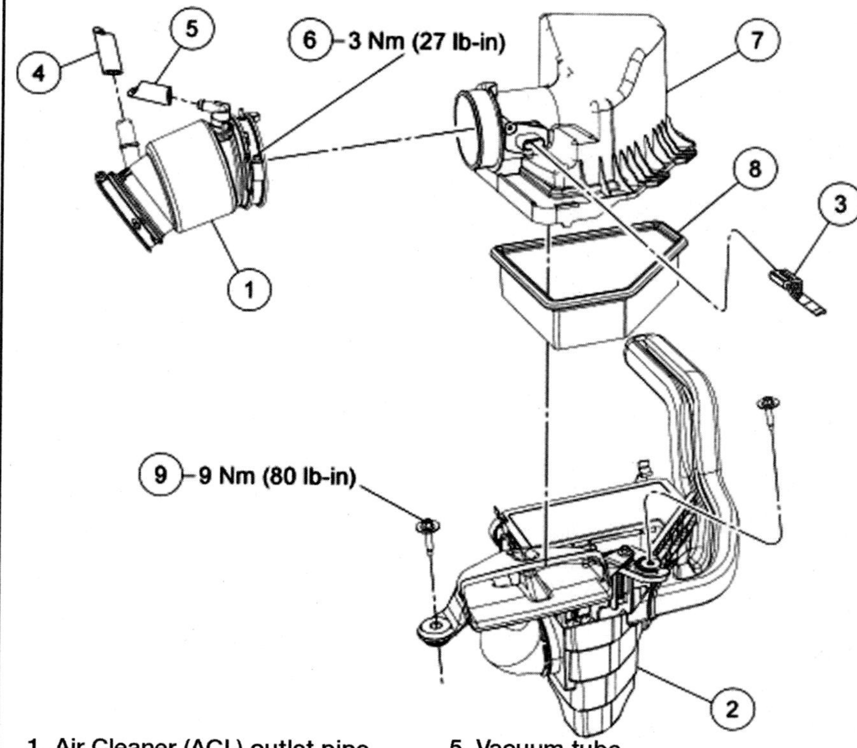

Fig. 49 Intake air system components—exploded view

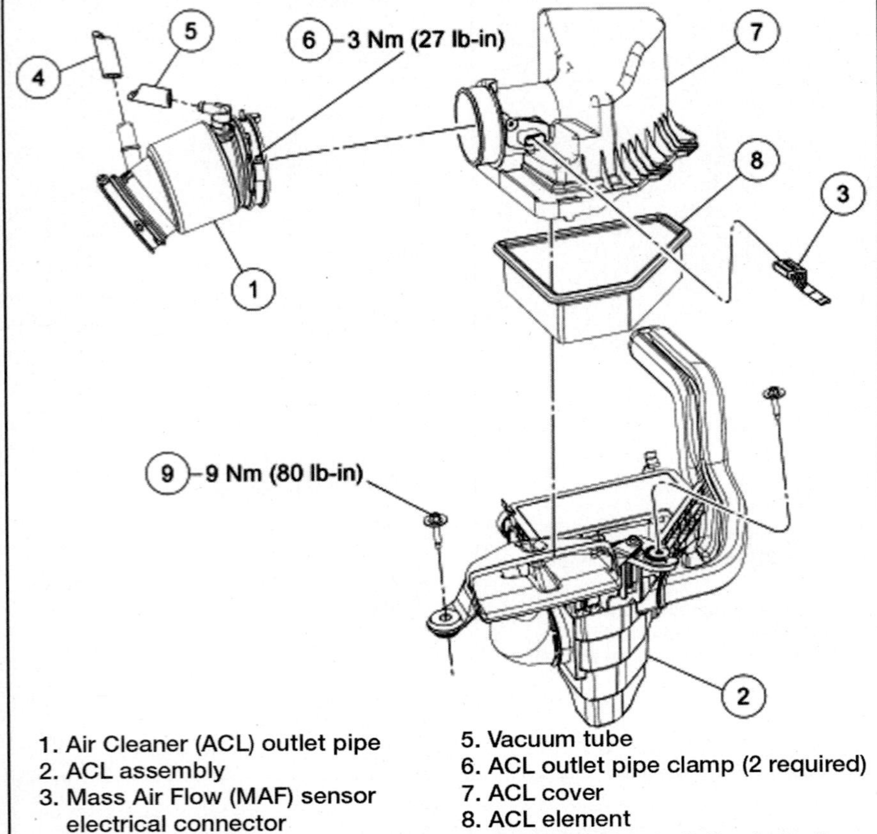

Fig. 50 Intake air system components—exploded view

CAMSHAFT AND VALVE LIFTERS

INSPECTION

Camshaft Bearing Journal Diameter

See Figure 51.

1. Before servicing the vehicle, refer to the Precautions Section.
2. Measure each camshaft journal diameter in 2 directions.
   - Camshaft journal diameter specification: 0.982–0.983 inch

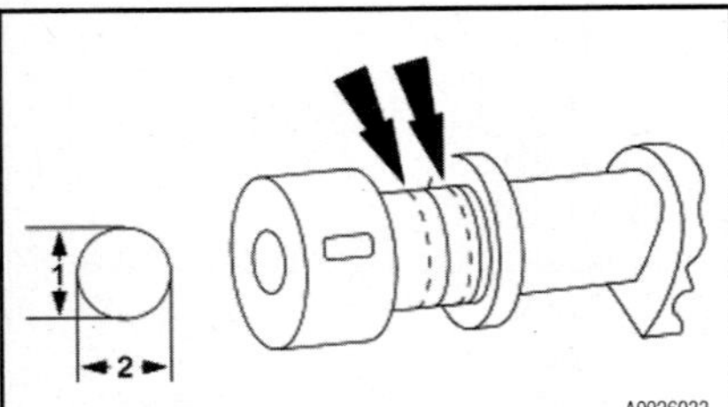

Fig. 51 Measuring camshaft bearing journal diameter

Camshaft End Play

1. Before servicing the vehicle, refer to the Precautions Section.
2. Using the Dial Indicator Gauge with Holding Fixture, measure the camshaft end play.
3. Position the camshaft to the rear of the cylinder head.
4. Zero the Dial Indicator Gauge.
5. Move the camshaft to the front of the cylinder head. Note and record the camshaft end play.
   a. If camshaft end play exceeds specifications, install a new camshaft and recheck end play.
   b. If camshaft end play exceeds specification after camshaft installation, install a new cylinder head.
   - Camshaft end play specification: 0.003–0.009 inch

Camshaft Journal To Bearing Clearance

1. Before servicing the vehicle, refer to the Precautions Section.

➡The camshaft journals must meet specifications before checking camshaft journal clearance.

2. Measure each camshaft bearing in 2 directions.
3. Subtract the camshaft journal diameter from the camshaft bearing diameter to determine bearing oil clearance.
   - Camshaft bearing oil clearance specification: 0.001–0.003 inch

Camshaft Lobe Lift

See Figure 52.

1. Before servicing the vehicle, refer to the Precautions Section.
2. Use the Dial Indicator Gauge with Holding Fixture to measure camshaft intake/exhaust lobe lift.
3. Rotate the camshaft and subtract the lowest Dial Indicator Gauge reading from the highest Dial Indicator Gauge reading to figure the camshaft lobe lift.
   - Camshaft lobe lift specification: Intake 0.324 inch; Exhaust 0.307 inch

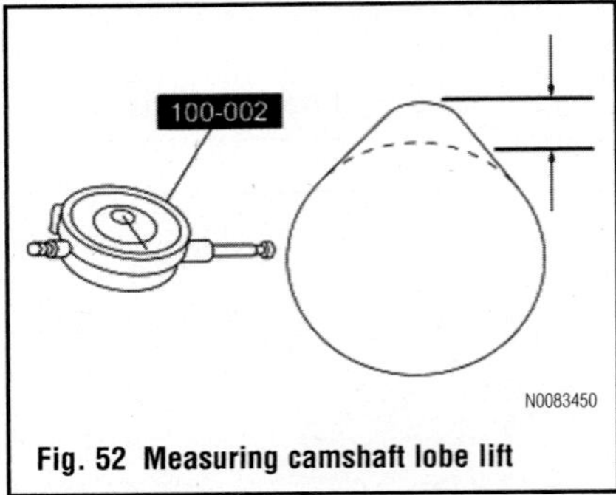

Fig. 52 Measuring camshaft lobe lift

Camshaft Runout

See Figure 53.

1. Before servicing the vehicle, refer to the Precautions Section.

➡Camshaft journals must be within specifications before checking runout.

2. Using the Dial Indicator Gauge with Holding Fixture, measure the camshaft runout.
3. Rotate the camshaft and subtract the lowest Dial Indicator Gauge reading from the highest Dial Indicator Gauge reading.

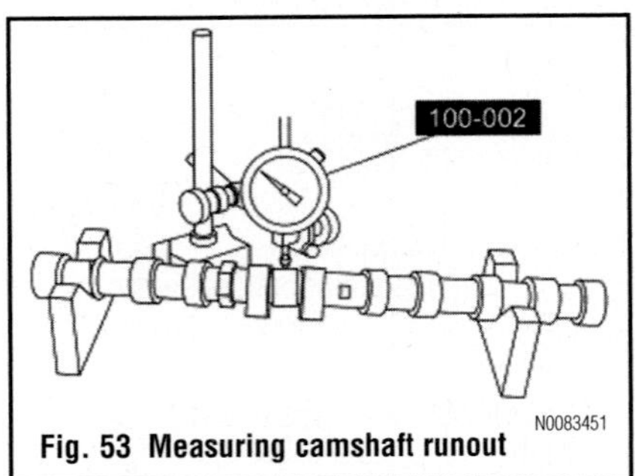

Fig. 53 Measuring camshaft runout

- Camshaft runout specification: 0.0010 inch

Camshaft Surface

See Figure 54.

1. Before servicing the vehicle, refer to the Precautions Section.
2. Inspect camshaft lobes for pitting or damage in the contact area. Minor pitting is acceptable outside the contact area.

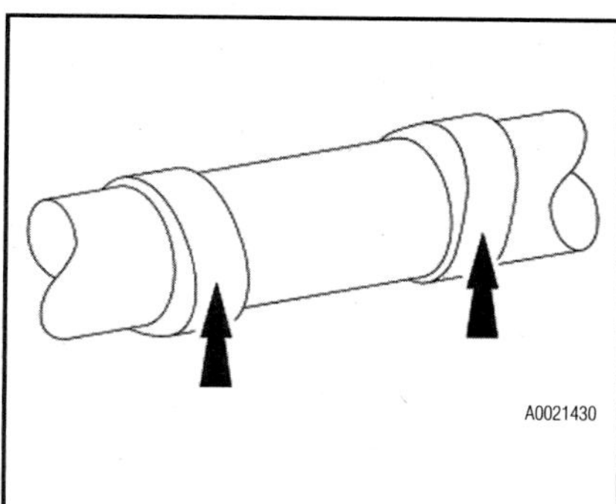

Fig. 54 Camshaft lobe contact area inspection

Valve Clearance Check

Refer to Valve Lash, Adjustment.

REMOVAL & INSTALLATION

See Figures 55 through 61.

✲✲ WARNING

During engine repair procedures, cleanliness is extremely important. Any foreign material (including any material created while cleaning gasket surfaces) that enters the oil passages, coolant passages or the oil pan can cause engine failure.

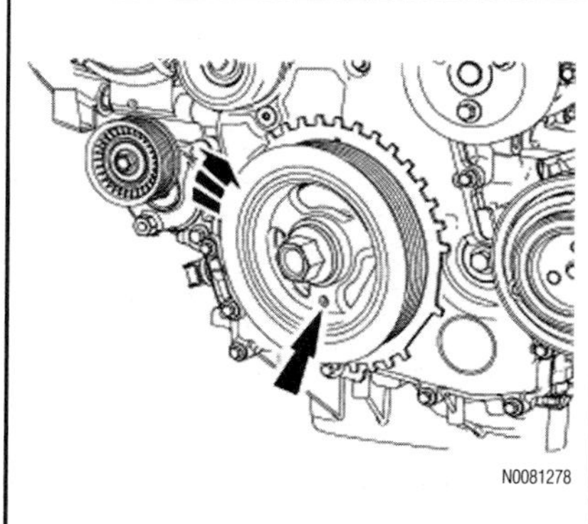

Fig. 55 Turn the crankshaft clockwise to position the No. 1 piston at TDC. The hole in the crankshaft pulley should be in the 6 o'clock position

✲✲ WARNING

Do not rotate the camshafts unless instructed to in this procedure. Rotating the camshafts or crankshaft with timing components loosened or removed can cause serious damage to the valves and pistons.

1. Before servicing the vehicle, refer to the Precautions Section.
2. With the vehicle in NEUTRAL, position it on a hoist.
3. Remove the coolant expansion tank.
4. Remove the RF wheel and tire.
5. Check the valve clearance. Refer to Valve Lash, Adjustment.
6. Remove the accessory drive belt. Refer to Accessory Drive Belts, removal & installation.

✲✲ WARNING

Failure to position the No. 1 piston at Top Dead Center (TDC) can result in damage to the engine. Turn the engine in the normal direction of rotation only.

7. Using the crankshaft pulley bolt, turn the crankshaft clockwise to position the No. 1 piston at TDC. The hole in the crankshaft pulley should be in the 6 o'clock position.

✲✲ WARNING

The Camshaft Alignment Plate is for camshaft alignment only. Using this tool to prevent engine rotation can result in engine damage.

➡The camshaft timing slots are offset. If the Camshaft Alignment Plate cannot be installed, rotate the crankshaft one complete revolution clockwise to correctly position the camshafts.

8. Install the Camshaft Alignment Plate in the slots on the rear of both camshafts.

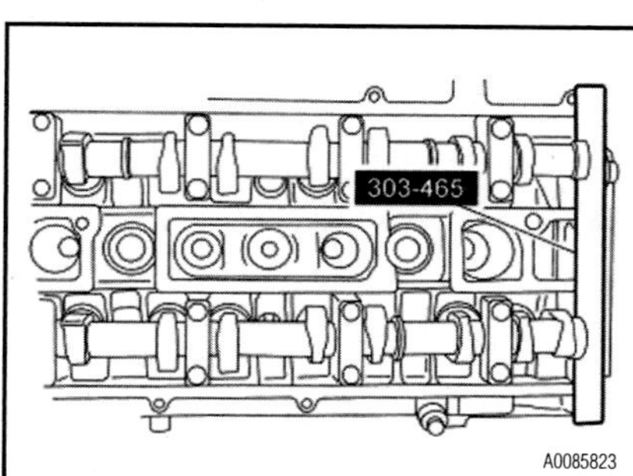

Fig. 56 Install the Camshaft Alignment Plate in the slots on the rear of both camshafts

9. Remove the engine plug bolt.

➡The Crankshaft TDC Timing Peg will contact the crankshaft and prevent it from turning past TDC. However, the crankshaft can still be rotated in the counterclockwise direction. The crankshaft must remain at the TDC position during the camshaft removal and installation.

10. Install the Crankshaft TDC Timing Peg.
11. Install a standard 0.24 inch (6mm) x 0.71 inch (18mm) bolt through the crankshaft pulley and thread it into the front cover.

➡Only hand-tighten the bolt or damage to the front cover can occur.

12. Remove the front cover lower timing hole plug from the engine front cover.

Fig. 57 Remove the engine plug bolt

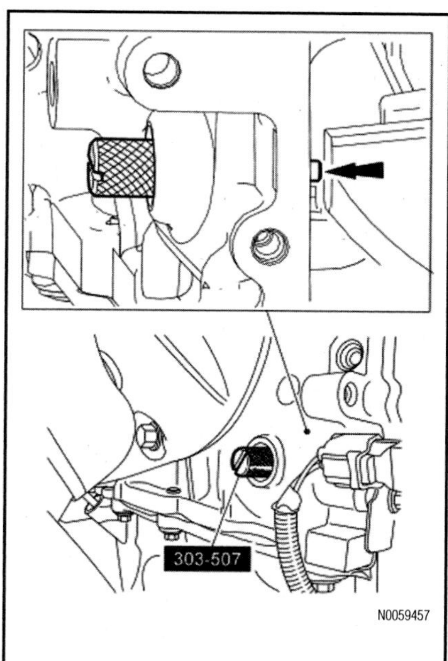

Fig. 58 Install the Crankshaft TDC Timing Peg

13. Remove the front cover upper timing hole plug from the engine front cover.

14. Reposition the Camshaft Alignment Plate to the slot on the rear of the intake camshaft only.

➡**Releasing the ratcheting mechanism in the timing chain tensioner allows the plunger to collapse and create slack in the timing chain. Installing an M6 x 1.18 inch (30mm) bolt into the upper front cover timing hole will hold the tensioner arm in a retracted position and allow enough slack in the timing chain for removal of the exhaust camshaft gear.**

15. Using a small pick tool, unlock the chain tensioner ratchet through the lower front cover timing hole.

a. Using the flats of the camshaft, have an assistant rotate the exhaust camshaft clockwise to collapse the timing chain tensioner plunger.

b. Insert an M6 x 1.18 inch (30mm) bolt into the upper front cover timing hole to hold the tensioner arm in place.

16. Remove the Camshaft Alignment Plate.

17. Using the flats on the camshaft to prevent camshaft rotation, remove the bolt and exhaust camshaft drive gear.

18. Remove the timing chain from the intake camshaft drive gear.

19. Using the flats on the camshaft to prevent camshaft rotation, remove the bolt and intake camshaft drive gear.

20. Mark the position of the camshaft lobes on the No. 1 cylinder for installation reference.

WARNING

Failure to follow the camshaft loosening procedure can result in damage to the camshafts.

➡**Mark the location and orientation of each camshaft bearing cap.**

21. Remove the camshafts from the engine.

a. Loosen the camshaft bearing cap bolts, in sequence, one turn at a time.

b. Repeat the first step until all tension is released from the camshaft bearing caps.

c. Remove the camshaft bearing caps.

d. Remove the camshafts.

To install:

WARNING

Install the camshafts with the alignment slots in the camshafts lined up so the Camshaft Alignment Plate can be installed without rotating the camshafts. Make sure the lobes on the No. 1 cylinder are in the same position as noted in the removal procedure. Rotating the camshafts when the timing chain is removed, or installing the camshafts 180° out of position can cause severe damage to the valves and pistons.

➡**Lubricate the camshaft journals and bearing caps with clean engine oil.**

22. Install the camshafts and bearing caps in their original location and orientation. Tighten the bearing caps in the sequence shown in 3 stages:

- Stage 1: Tighten the camshaft bearing cap bolts one turn at a time until finger-tight
- Stage 2: Tighten to 62 inch lbs. (7 Nm)
- Stage 3: Tighten to 12 ft. lbs. (16 Nm)

23. Install the Camshaft Alignment Plate.

24. Install the intake camshaft drive gear and hand-tighten the bolt.

25. Install the timing chain on the intake camshaft drive gear.

➡**The timing chain must be correctly engaged on the teeth of the crankshaft timing sprocket and the intake camshaft drive gear in order to install the exhaust camshaft drive gear onto the exhaust camshaft.**

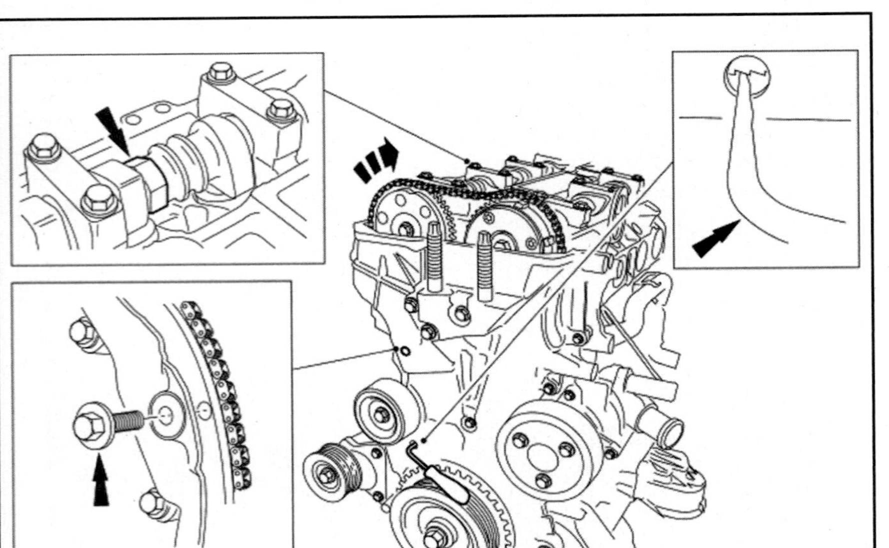

Fig. 59 Using a small pick tool, unlock the chain tensioner ratchet through the lower front cover timing hole

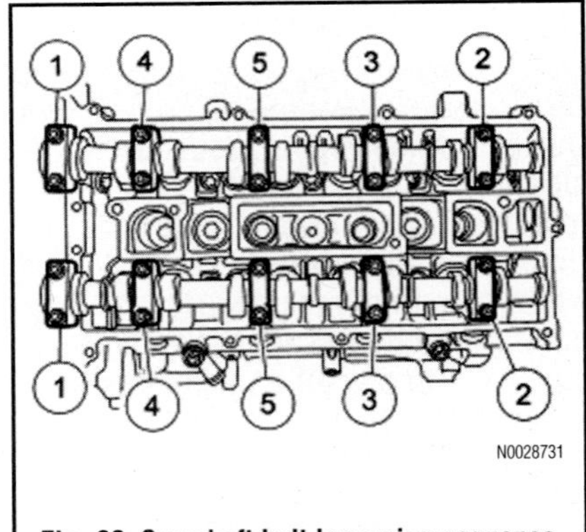

Fig. 60 Camshaft bolt loosening sequence

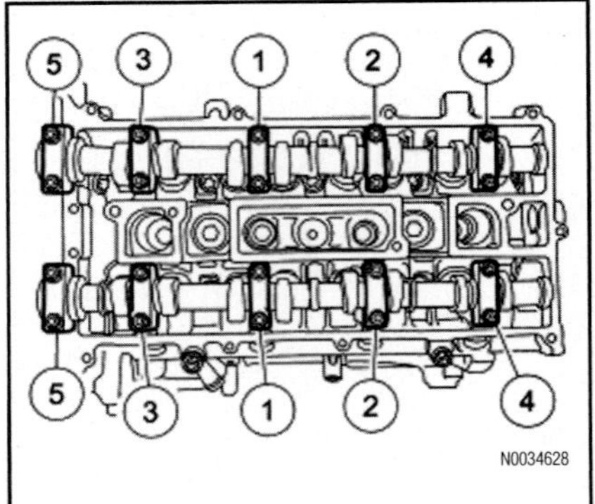

Fig. 61 Camshaft bolt tightening sequence

26. Position the exhaust camshaft drive gear in the timing chain and install the gear and bolt on the exhaust camshaft. Hand-tighten the bolt.

➡**Releasing the tensioner arm will remove the slack from the timing chain release.**

27. Remove the M6 x 1.18 inch (30mm) bolt from the upper front cover timing hole to unlock the tensioner arm.

⁂ WARNING

The Camshaft Alignment Plate is for camshaft alignment only. Using this tool to prevent engine rotation can result in engine damage.

28. Using the flats on the camshafts to prevent camshaft rotation, tighten the camshaft drive gear bolts to 53 ft. lbs. (72 Nm).
29. Remove the Camshaft Alignment Plate.
30. Remove the 0.24 inch (6mm) x 0.71 inch (18mm) bolt from the crankshaft damper.
31. Remove the Crankshaft TDC Timing Peg.
32. Install the front cover upper timing hole plug. Tighten to 89 inch lbs. (10 Nm).
33. Apply silicone gasket and sealant to the threads of the front cover lower timing hole plug. Install the plug and tighten to 106 inch lbs. (12 Nm).
34. Install the engine plug bolt. Tighten to 15 ft. lbs. (20 Nm).
35. Install the accessory drive belt. Refer to Accessory Drive Belts, removal & installation.
36. Install the RF wheel and tire assembly. Tighten the wheel nuts in a star pattern to 100 ft. lbs. (135 Nm).
37. Install the valve cover. Refer to Valve Covers, removal & installation.
38. Install the coolant expansion tank.

CATALYTIC CONVERTER

REMOVAL & INSTALLATION

See Figures 62 through 64.

1. Before servicing the vehicle, refer to the Precautions Section.
2. With the vehicle in NEUTRAL, position it on a hoist.

⁂ WARNING

Do not excessively bend or twist the exhaust flexible pipe. Failure to follow these instructions may cause damage to the flexible pipe.

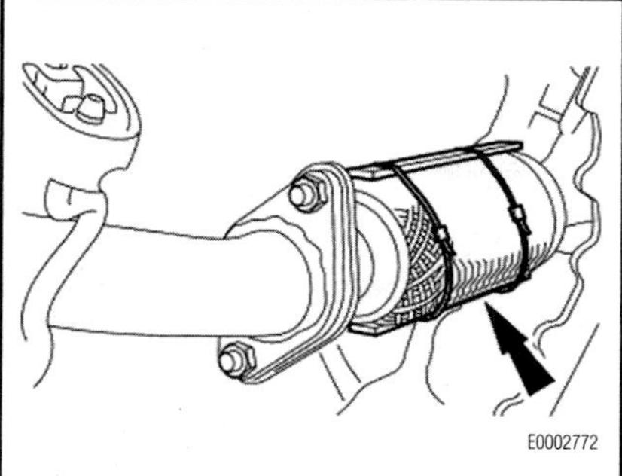

Fig. 62 Support the exhaust flexible pipe with a support wrap or suitable splint

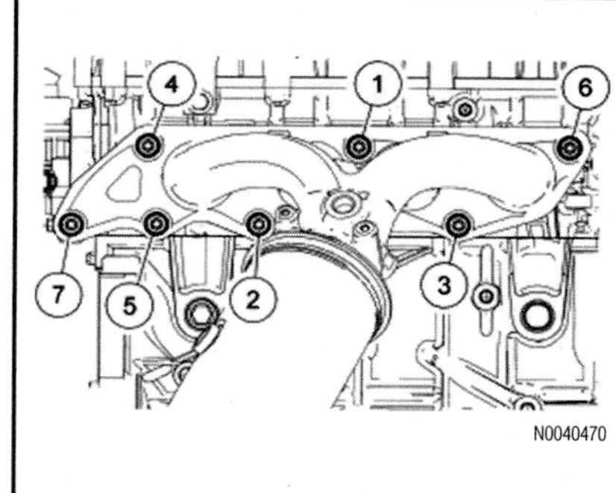

Fig. 63 Exhaust tightening sequence shown

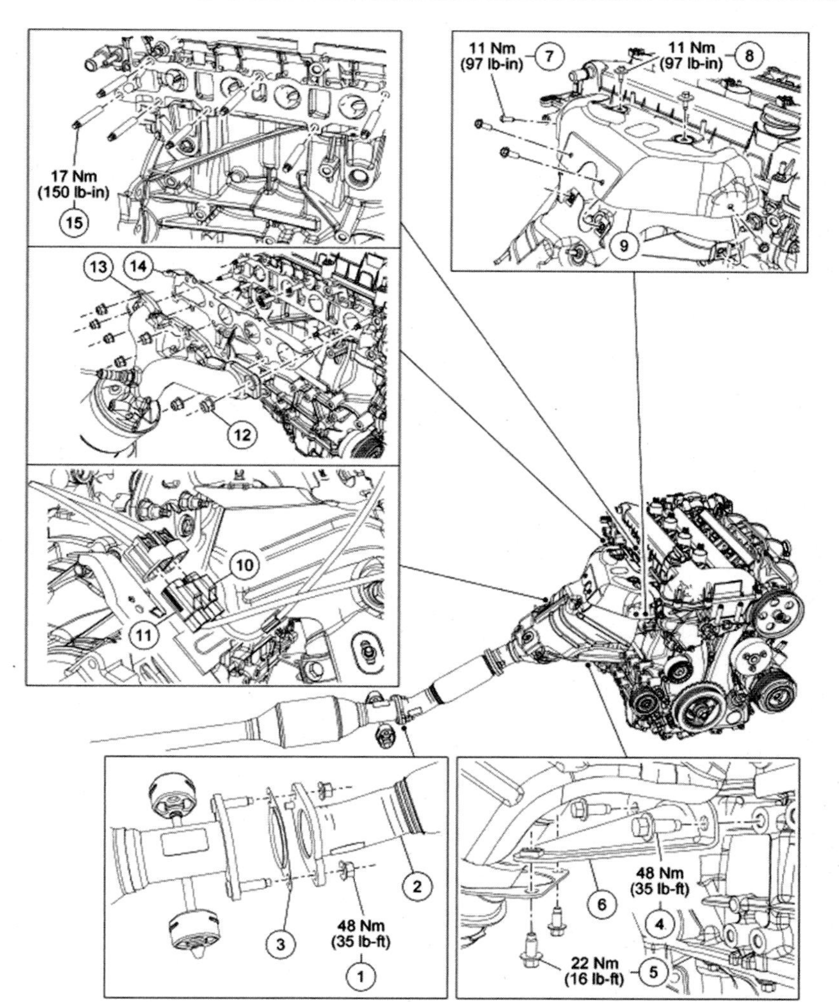

1. Flexpipe-to-muffler and tailpipe assembly nut (2 required)
2. Flexpipe
3. Flexpipe-to-muffler and tailpipe assembly gasket
4. Catalytic converter-to-engine support bracket bolt (2 required)
5. Catalytic converter support bracket bolt (2 required)
6. Catalytic converter support bracket
7. Catalytic converter heat shield bolt (4 required)
8. Catalytic converter heat shield bolt (2 required)
9. Catalytic converter heat shield
10. Heated Oxygen Sensor (HO2S) electrical connector
11. Catalyst Monitor Sensor (CMS) electrical connector
12. Catalytic converter nut (7 required)
13. Catalytic converter
14. Catalytic converter gasket
15. Catalytic converter-to-cylinder head stud (7 required)

N0106082

Fig. 64 Expanded view of catalytic converter and related components

3. Support the exhaust flexible pipe with a support wrap or suitable splint.

4. On a Partial Zero Emissions Vehicle (PZEV): remove the 2 catalytic converter-to-exhaust flexible pipe nuts. Discard the nuts and gasket.

5. On a Non-PZEV: remove the 2 catalytic converter-to-muffler and tailpipe assembly nuts.

Discard the nuts and gasket.

6. Remove the 4 bolts and the catalytic converter-to-engine bracket.

7. Remove the 3 bolts from the lower heat shield.

➡It may be necessary to reposition the engine during catalytic converter removal.

8. Remove the roll restrictor bolt.

9. Disconnect the Catalyst Monitor Sensor (CMS) and Heated Oxygen Sensor (HO2S) electrical connectors.

10. Remove the 6 bolts and the upper heat shield.

11. Remove the 2 retainers and the Evaporative Emission (EVAP) canister purge valve heat shield.

12. Disconnect the EVAP canister purge valve electrical connector.

13. Release the tab and remove the canister purge valve from the bracket, then position aside.

14. Detach the fuel tube from the canister purge valve bracket.

15. Remove the 2 EVAP canister purge valve bracket bolts and position the EVAP canister purge valve bracket aside.

16. Remove and discard the 7 catalytic converter nuts.

17. Remove the bolt and the engine lifting eye.

➡An assistant will be needed to remove the catalytic converter and lower heat shield from the vehicle. Do not let the catalytic converter or the lower heat shield come in contact with the valve cover.

18. Reposition the engine and carefully pull the catalytic converter and heat shield upward. Roll the heat shield toward the RH side of the vehicle and off of the catalytic converter.

19. Remove the catalytic converter from the vehicle. Discard the gasket.

20. Remove and discard the 7 catalytic converter-to-cylinder head studs.

To install:

21. Clean and inspect the catalytic converter flange.

22. Install the 7 new catalytic converter-to-cylinder head studs. Tighten to 13 ft. lbs. (17 Nm).

23. Position the new gasket on the engine.

➡An assistant will be needed to install the catalytic converter and lower heat shield in the vehicle. Do not let the catalytic converter or the lower heat shield come in contact with the valve cover.

24. Reposition the engine and carefully lower the catalytic converter and heat shield downward. Roll the heat shield toward the LH side of the vehicle and onto the catalytic converter.

25. Using 7 new nuts, install the catalytic converter onto the engine.

➡Failure to tighten the catalytic converter manifold nuts to specification a second time may cause the converter to develop an exhaust leak.

26. Tighten the 7 new catalytic converter nuts in 2 stages in the sequence shown.

- Stage 1: Tighten to 41 ft. lbs. (55 Nm)
- Stage 2: Tighten to 41 ft. lbs. (55 Nm)

27. Install the engine lifting eyelet and the bolt. Tighten to 33 ft. lbs. (45 Nm).

28. Reposition the EVAP canister purge valve bracket and install the 2 bolts. Tighten to 53 inch lbs. (6 Nm).

29. Attach the fuel tube to the canister purge valve bracket.

30. Install the canister purge valve on the canister purge valve bracket.

31. Connect the EVAP canister purge valve electrical connector.

32. Install the EVAP canister purge valve heat shield and the 2 retainers.

33. Connect the HO2S and CMS electrical connectors.

34. Install the roll restrictor bolt. Tighten to 52 ft. lbs. (70 Nm).

35. Position the lower heat shield and install the 3 bolts. Tighten to 97 inch lbs. (11 Nm).

36. Install the catalytic converter-to-engine bracket and the 2 bolts. Tighten to 35 ft. lbs. (47 Nm).

37. Install the 2 catalytic converter bracket-to-engine bracket bolts. Tighten to 17 ft. lbs. (23 Nm).

38. On a Non-PZEV: using a new gasket, attach the catalytic converter-to-muffler and tailpipe assembly and install the 2 new nuts. Tighten to 35 ft. lbs. (47 Nm).

39. On a PZEV: using a new gasket, attach the exhaust flexible pipe-to-muffler and tailpipe assembly and install the 2 new nuts. Tighten to 35 ft. lbs. (47 Nm).

40. Remove the exhaust flexible pipe support wrap or suitable splint.

41. Install the upper heat shield and the 6 bolts. Tighten to 97 inch lbs. (11 Nm).

CRANKSHAFT FRONT SEAL

REMOVAL & INSTALLATION

See Figures 65 and 66.

WARNING

Do not loosen or remove the crankshaft pulley bolt without first installing the special tools as instructed in this procedure. The crankshaft pulley and the crankshaft timing sprocket are not keyed to the crankshaft. The crankshaft, the crankshaft sprocket and the pulley are fitted together by friction, using diamond washers between the flange faces on each part. For that reason, the crankshaft sprocket is also unfastened if the pulley bolt is loosened.

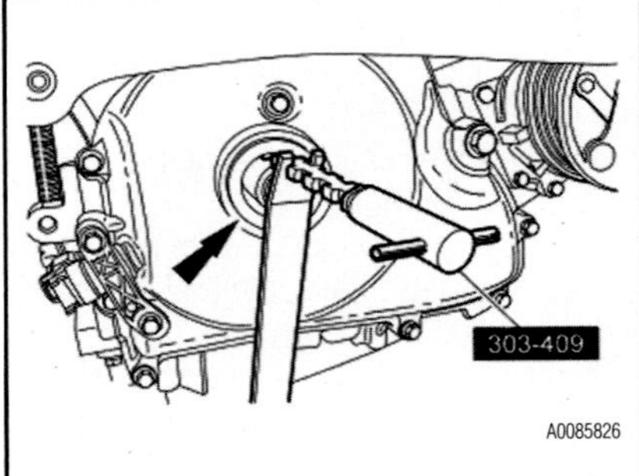

Fig. 65 Using the Oil Seal Remover to remove the crankshaft front oil seal

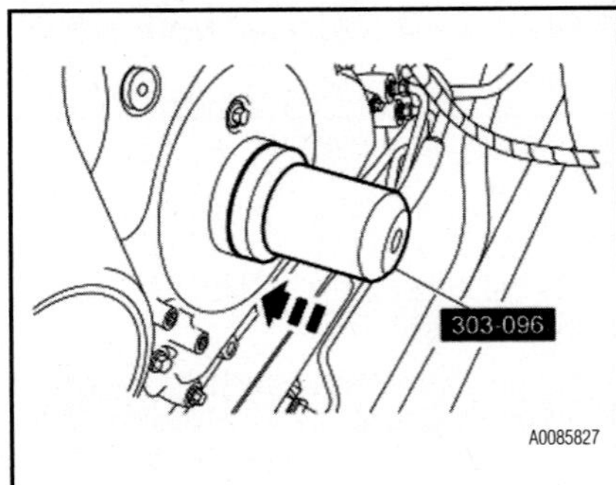

Fig. 66 Using the Oil Seal Remover to remove the crankshaft front oil seal

Before any repair requiring loosening or removal of the crankshaft pulley bolt, the crankshaft and camshafts must be locked in place by the special service tools, otherwise severe engine damage can occur.

⁂ WARNING

During engine repair procedures, cleanliness is extremely important. Any foreign material, including any material created while cleaning gasket surfaces, that enters the oil passages, coolant passages or the oil pan can cause engine failure.

1. Before servicing the vehicle, refer to the Precautions Section.
2. Remove the crankshaft pulley.

➡Use care not to damage the engine front cover or the crankshaft when removing the seal.

3. Using the Oil Seal Remover, remove the crankshaft front oil seal.

To install:

➡Remove the through-bolt from the Camshaft Front Oil Seal Installer.

4. Lubricate the oil seal with clean engine oil.
5. Using the Camshaft Front Oil Seal Installer, install the crankshaft front oil seal.
6. Install the crankshaft pulley.

CYLINDER HEAD

REMOVAL & INSTALLATION

See Figures 67 through 74.

⁂ WARNING

Do not loosen or remove the crankshaft pulley bolt without first installing the special tools as instructed in this procedure. The crankshaft pulley and the crankshaft timing sprocket are not keyed to the crankshaft. The crankshaft, the crankshaft sprocket and the pulley are fitted together by friction, using diamond washers between the flange faces on each part. For that reason, the crankshaft sprocket is also unfastened if the pulley bolt is loosened. Before any repair requiring loosening or removal of the crankshaft pulley bolt, the crankshaft and camshafts must be locked in place by the special service tools, otherwise severe engine damage can occur.

⁂ WARNING

During engine repair procedures, cleanliness is extremely important. Any foreign material, including any material created while cleaning gasket surfaces, that enters the oil passages, coolant passages or the oil pan can cause engine failure.

1. Before servicing the vehicle, refer to the Precautions Section.
2. Release the fuel system pressure. Refer to Relieving Fuel System Pressure.
3. Depower the Supplemental Restraint System (SRS). Refer to Air Bag (Supplemental Restraint System), Disarming The System.
4. Remove the battery tray. Refer to Battery, removal & installation.
5. Drain the cooling system. Refer to Engine Coolant, Drain & Refill Procedure.
6. Check the valve clearance. Refer to Valve Lash, Adjustment.
7. Remove the Alternator. Refer to Alternator, removal & installation.
8. Remove the 2 nuts and disconnect the flex pipe from the muffler and tailpipe assembly. Remove and discard the nuts and gasket.
9. Remove the 2 bolts from the catalytic converter-to-engine support bracket.
10. Remove the 2 bolts and the catalytic converter support bracket.

➡Mark the location of bolts for installation.

11. Remove the 6 bolts and the catalytic converter heat shield.
12. Disconnect the Heated Oxygen Sensor (HO2S) and Catalyst Monitor Sensor (CMS) electrical connectors.
13. Remove and discard the catalytic converter nuts.
14. Position aside the catalytic converter and support with mechanic's wire.
15. Remove and discard the catalytic converter gasket. Refer to Catalytic Converter, removal & installation.
16. Remove the engine oil filter and discard.
17. Remove the fuel rail.
18. Remove the intake manifold. Refer to Intake Manifold, removal & installation.
19. Remove the timing drive components. Refer to Timing Chain & Sprockets, removal & installation.
20. Remove the Camshaft Alignment Plate.

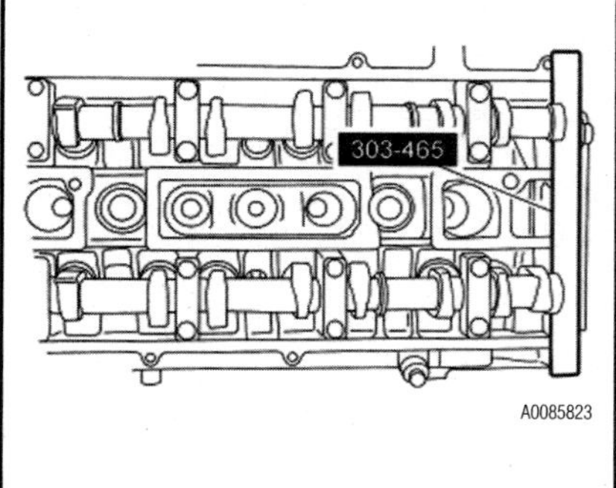

Fig. 67 Remove the Camshaft Alignment Plate

21. Mark the position of the camshaft lobes on the No. 1 cylinder for installation reference.

⁂ WARNING

Failure to follow the camshaft loosening procedure may result in damage to the camshafts.

➡Mark the location and orientation of each camshaft bearing cap.

22. Remove the camshafts from the engine.
    a. Loosen the camshaft bearing cap bolts, in sequence, one turn at a time.
    b. Repeat the first step until all tension is released from the camshaft bearing caps.
    c. Remove the camshaft bearing caps.
    d. Remove the camshafts.

➡If the camshafts and valve tappets are to be reused, mark the location of the valve tappets to make sure they are assembled in their original positions.

23. Remove the valve tappets.

➡The number on the valve tappets only reflects the digits that follow the decimal. For example, a tappet with

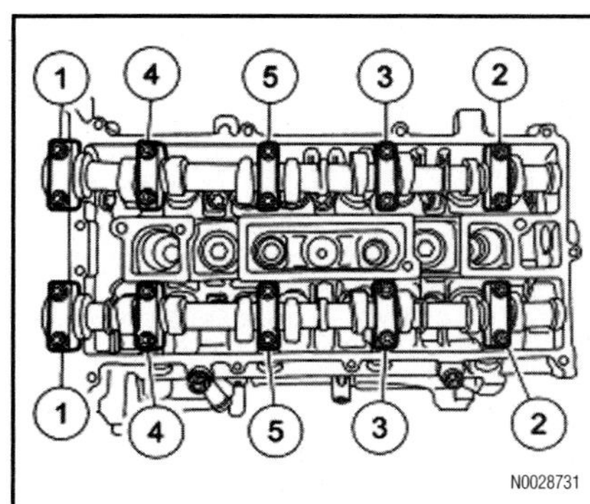

Fig. 68 Loosen the camshaft bearing cap bolts, in sequence, one turn at a time

the number 0.650 has the thickness of 3.650 mm.

24. Inspect the valve tappets.
25. Remove the 3 bolts and position the wiring harness and bracket aside.
26. Disconnect the EGR valve electrical connector.
27. Disconnect the coolant hoses from the coolant bypass.
28. Disconnect the EGR coolant hose.
29. Remove the 7 catalytic converter-to-cylinder head studs and discard.
30. Lower the engine and remove the Engine Support Bar.
31. Remove the 10 bolts and the cylinder head. Discard the bolts.
32. Remove and discard the head gasket.

To install:

WARNING

Do not use metal scrapers, wire brushes, power abrasive discs, or other abrasive means to clean the sealing surfaces. These tools cause scratches and gouges that make leak paths. Use a plastic scraping tool to remove all traces of the head gasket.

33. Clean the cylinder head-to-cylinder block mating surface of both the cylinder head and the cylinder block in the following sequence.
   a. Remove any large deposits of silicone or gasket material with a plastic scraper.
   b. Apply silicone gasket remover, following package directions, and allow to set for several minutes.
   c. Remove the silicone gasket remover with a plastic scraper. A second application of silicone gasket remover may be required if residual traces of silicone or gasket material remain.
   d. Apply metal surface prep, following package directions, to remove any traces of oil or coolant, and to prepare the surfaces to bond with the new gasket. Do not attempt to make the metal shiny. Some staining of the metal surfaces is normal.
34. Clean the cylinder head bolt holes in the cylinder block. Make sure all coolant, oil or other foreign material is removed.
35. Support the cylinder head on a bench with the head gasket side up. Check the cylinder head distortion and the cylinder block distortion.
36. Apply silicone gasket and sealant to the locations shown.
37. Install a new cylinder head gasket.

➡The cylinder head bolts are torque-to-yield and must not be reused. New cylinder head bolts must be installed.

38. Install the cylinder head and the 10 new bolts. Tighten the bolts in the sequence shown in 5 stages.

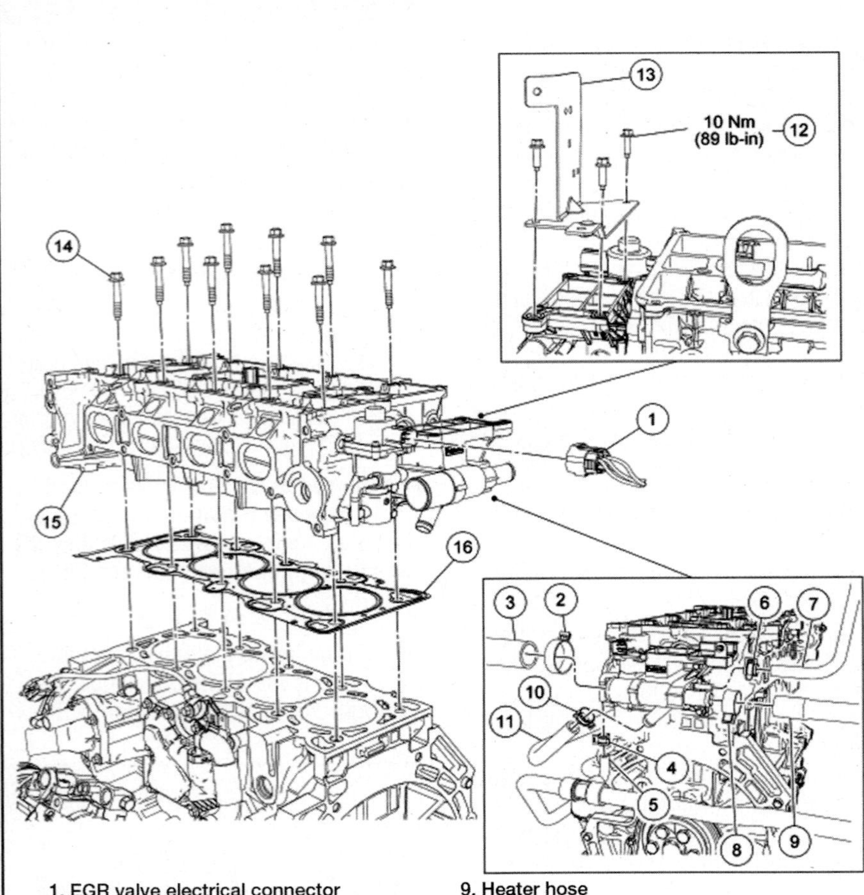

Fig. 69 Cylinder head—exploded view

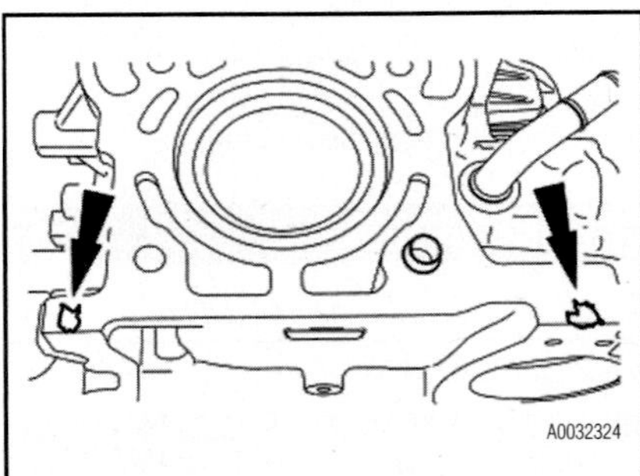

Fig. 70 Apply silicone gasket and sealant to the locations shown

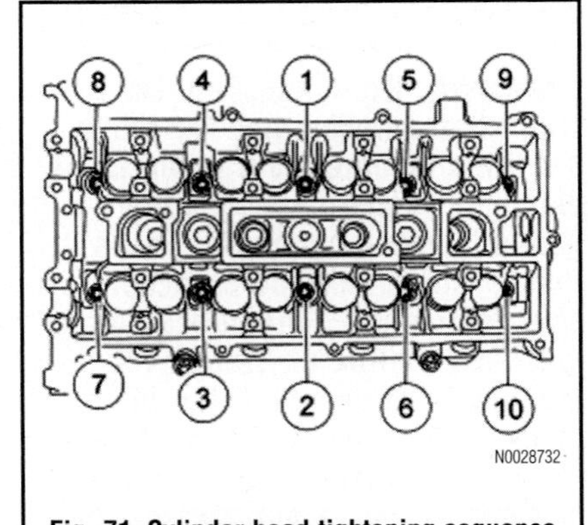

Fig. 71 Cylinder head tightening sequence

- Stage 1: Tighten to 44 inch lbs. (5 Nm)
- Stage 2: Tighten to 11 ft. lbs. (15 Nm)
- Stage 3: Tighten to 33 ft. lbs. (45 Nm)
- Stage 4: Turn 90 degrees
- Stage 5: Turn an additional 90 degrees

39. Install the Engine Support Bar and raise the engine.
40. Install the 7 new catalytic converter-to-cylinder head studs. Tighten to 13 ft. lbs. (17 Nm).
41. Install the EGR coolant hose.
42. Connect the coolant hoses onto the coolant bypass.
43. Connect the EGR valve electrical connector.
44. Position the wire harness bracket and install the 3 bolts. Tighten to 89 inch lbs. (10 Nm).

➡Lubricate the valve tappets with clean engine oil.

45. Install the valve tappets in their original positions.

WARNING

Install the camshafts with the alignment notches in the camshafts lined up so the camshaft alignment plate can be installed. Make sure the lobes on the No. 1 cylinder are in the same position as noted in the removal procedure. Failure to follow this procedure can cause severe damage to the valves and pistons.

46. Lubricate the camshaft journals and bearing caps with clean engine oil.
47. Install the camshafts and bearing caps in their original location and orientation. Tighten the bearing caps in the sequence shown in 3 stages:

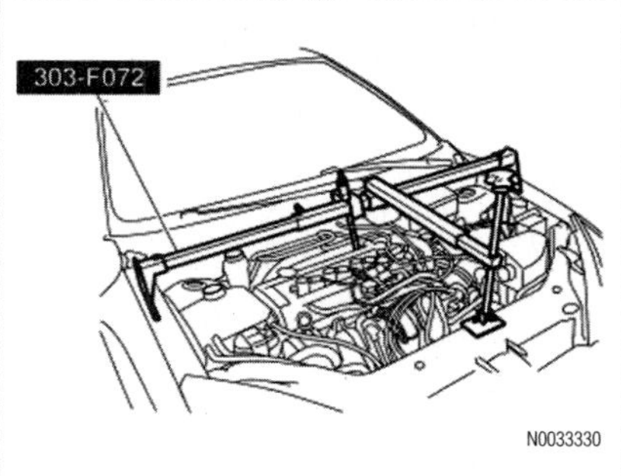

Fig. 72 Install the Engine Support Bar and raise the engine

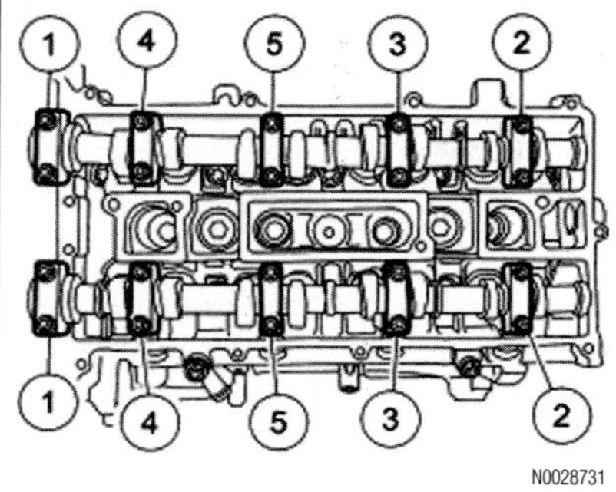

Fig. 73 Camshaft bearing cap bolt tightening sequence

- Stage 1: Tighten the camshaft bearing cap bolts, one turn at a time, until the cam is fully seated
- Stage 2: Tighten to 62 inch lbs. (7 Nm)
- Stage 3: Tighten to 12 ft. lbs. (16 Nm)

48. Install the timing drive components. Refer to Timing Chain & Sprockets, removal & installation.
49. Install the intake manifold. Refer to Intake Manifold, removal & installation.
50. Install the fuel rail.
51. Clean and inspect the catalytic converter flange.

➡Failure to tighten the catalytic converter nuts to specification before installing the converter bracket bolts may cause the converter to develop an exhaust leak.

➡Failure to tighten the catalytic converter nuts to specification a second time may cause the converter to develop an exhaust leak.

52. Using a new gasket and 7 new nuts, install the catalytic converter and tighten in 2 stages in the sequence shown. For additional information, refer to Catalytic Converter, removal & installation.

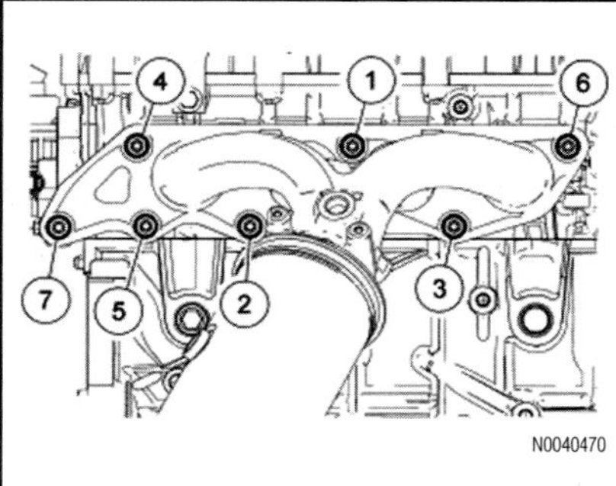

Fig. 74 Catalytic converter nut tightening sequence

- Stage 1: Tighten to 41 ft. lbs. (55 Nm).
- Stage 2: Tighten to 41 ft. lbs. (55 Nm).

53. Connect the HO2S and CMS electrical connectors.
54. Install the catalytic converter heat shield and 6 bolts. Tighten to 97 inch lbs. (11 Nm).
55. Install the catalytic converter support bracket and the 2 bolts. Tighten to 16 ft. lbs. (22 Nm).
56. Install the 2 catalytic converter-to-engine support bracket bolts. Tighten to 35 ft. lbs. (48 Nm).

➡Clean the mating surfaces of the muffler assembly and the flexpipe.

57. Using a new gasket and 2 new nuts, connect the muffler and tailpipe assembly to the flexpipe. Tighten to 35 ft. lbs. (48 Nm).
58. Install the alternator. Refer to Alternator, removal & installation.
59. Install the battery tray. Refer to Battery, removal & installation.
60. Drain the engine oil. Install the drain plug and tighten to 21 ft. lbs. (28 Nm).

➡Lubricate the engine oil filter gasket with clean engine oil prior to installing the oil filter.

61. Install a new engine oil filter. Tighten the oil filter ¾ turn after the oil filter gasket makes contact with the oil filter adapter.
62. Fill the engine with the proper type and amount of clean engine oil.
63. Fill and bleed the cooling system. Refer to Engine Coolant, Drain & Refill Procedure.
64. Repower the SRS. Refer to Air Bag (Supplemental Restraint System), Arming The System.

ENGINE OIL & FILTER

REPLACEMENT

See Figures 75 and 76.

CAUTION

Prolonged and repeated contact with used engine oil may cause skin cancer. Try to avoid direct skin contact with used oil. If skin contact is made, wash thoroughly with soap or hand cleaner as soon as possible. Wear protective clothing, including impervious gloves where practicable. Where there is a risk of eye contact, eye protection should be worn, for example, chemical goggles or face shields; in addition an eye wash facility should be provided.

⁂ CAUTION

Hot oil can scald.

➡Use only engine oil with the American Petroleum Institute (API) Certified For Gasoline Engines "Starburst" symbol. It is highly recommended to use SAE 5W-20 oil.

1. Before servicing the vehicle, refer to the Precautions Section.
2. Before draining the engine oil, check the engine for oil leakage. If any sign of leakage is found, make sure to correct the defective part before proceeding to the following procedure.
3. Drain the engine oil by removing the drain plug.
4. Wipe the drain plug and its mounting surface clean. Reinstall the drain plug with a new gasket, if applicable, and tighten the drain plug to 21 ft. lbs. (28 Nm).
5. Remove the oil filter with an oil filter wrench.

To install:

6. Wipe the oil filter mounting surface clean.

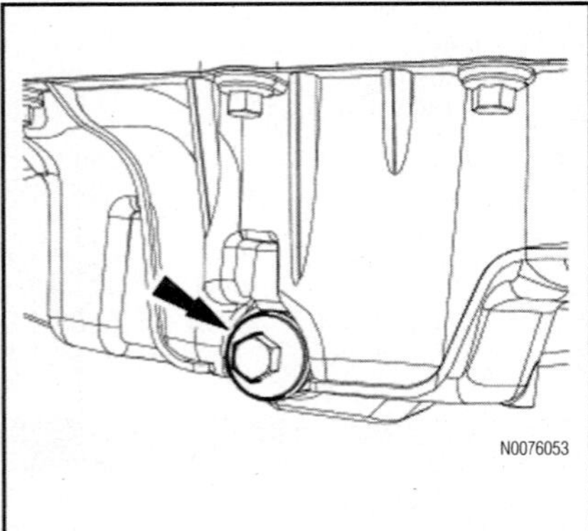

Fig. 75 Engine oil drain plug location

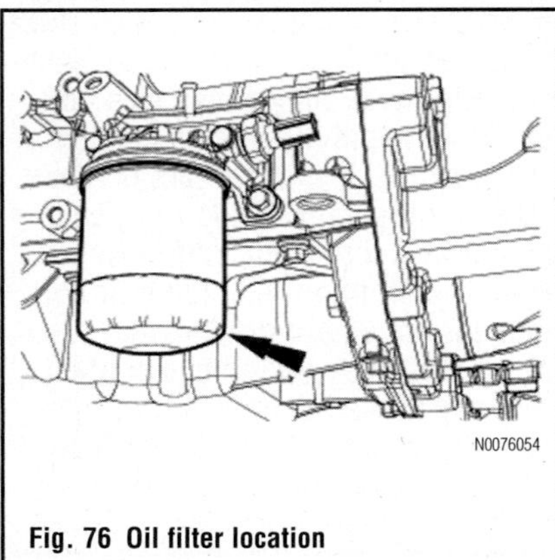

Fig. 76 Oil filter location

➡Lubricate the engine oil filter gasket with clean engine oil prior to installing the oil filter.

7. Install the new oil filter by hand until the filter O-ring touches the filter mounting surface.

➡To tighten the oil filter properly, it is important to accurately identify the position at which the filter O-ring first contacts the mounting surface.

8. Tighten the oil filter ¾ turn from the point of contact with the filter mounting surface.
9. Refill the engine oil to the specified amount.

➡Engine oil capacity is specified below. However, note that the amount of oil required when actually changing the oil may somewhat differ from the data depending on various conditions (temperature, viscosity, etc.)

- Oil pan plus oil filter capacity: About 4.5 quarts (4.3 liters)

10. Check the oil filter and drain plug for oil leakage.
11. Start and run the engine for 3 minutes. After stopping the engine, wait for 5 minutes. Then, confirm that the specified amount of engine oil has been refilled.

EXHAUST MANIFOLD

REMOVAL & INSTALLATION

For more information, refer to Catalytic Converter, Removal & Installation.

INTAKE MANIFOLD

REMOVAL & INSTALLATION

See Figures 77 through 81.

1. Before servicing the vehicle, refer to the Precautions Section.
2. With vehicle in NEUTRAL, position it on a hoist.
3. Remove the Air Cleaner (ACL) outlet pipe. Refer to Air Cleaner, removal & installation.
4. Depower the Supplemental Restraint System (SRS). Refer to Air Bag (Supplemental Restraint System), Disarming The System.
5. Remove the bolt and the front impact severity sensor.
6. Remove the transaxle fluid indicator (automatic transaxle).
7. Remove the lower intake manifold bolt.
8. Remove the oil level indicator and tube.
9. Disconnect the Engine Oil Pressure (EOP) switch electrical connector and detach the wire harness retainer from the starter stud bolt.
10. Disconnect the electronic throttle control electrical connector.
11. Disconnect the fuel vapor return hose.
12. Disconnect the power brake booster vacuum tube.
    a. Depress the quick release locking ring.
    b. Pull the vacuum tube out of the quick release fitting.

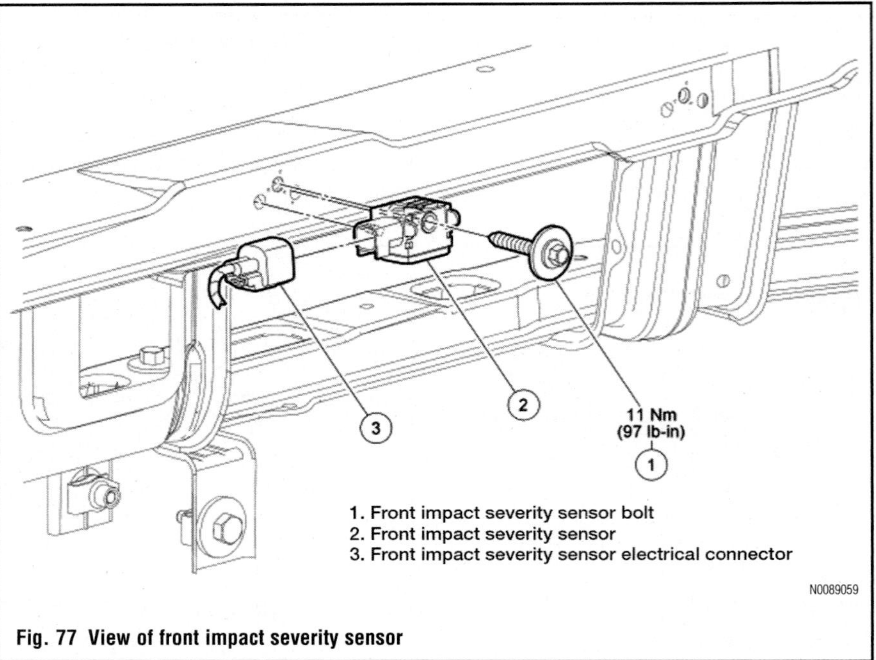

Fig. 77 View of front impact severity sensor

Fig. 78 Remove the lower intake manifold bolt

13. Disconnect the Manifold Absolute Pressure (MAP) sensor electrical connector.

14. Detach and disconnect the Knock Sensor (KS) electrical connector.

15. If equipped, disconnect the swirl control valve solenoid and sensor electrical connectors.

16. Detach all the wiring harness pin-type retainers from the intake manifold.

➡The 2 intake manifold bolts differ in length from rest of the bolts and also retain a crash bracket to the intake manifold. The 2 bolts are equipped with an attachment feature that allows them to be loosened but remain attached to the intake manifold. Do not attempt to remove the 2 bolts or the crash bracket from the intake manifold.

17. Loosen the 2 intake manifold bolts retaining the crash bracket.

18. Remove the remaining 5 intake manifold bolts.

19. Disconnect the PCV hose and remove the intake manifold.

To install:

WARNING

If the engine is repaired or replaced because of upper engine failure,

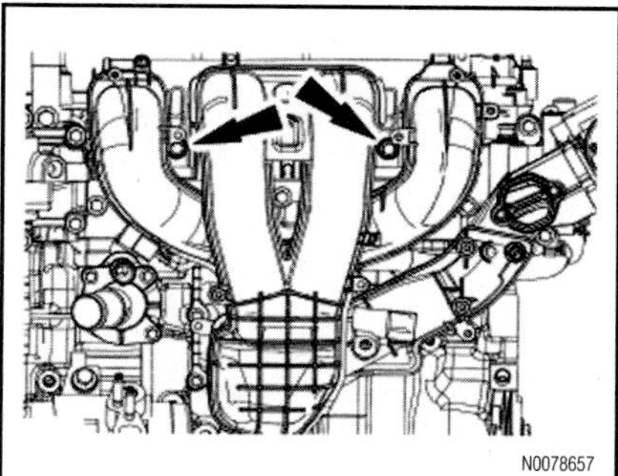

Fig. 79 Loosen the 2 intake manifold bolts retaining the crash bracket

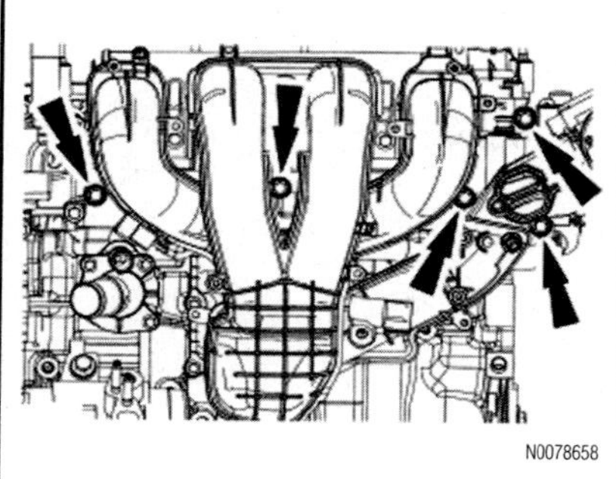

Fig. 80 Remove the remaining 5 intake manifold bolts

typically including valve or piston damage, check the intake manifold for metal debris. If metal debris is found, install a new intake manifold. Failure to follow these instructions can result in engine damage.

20. Inspect and install new intake manifold gaskets, if necessary.

21. Position the intake manifold and connect the PCV hose.

22. Attach the KS to the intake manifold and connect the KS electrical connector.

23. Install the intake manifold and hand-tighten the 2 intake manifold bolts retaining the crash bracket.

24. Install the remaining 5 intake manifold mounting bolts. Tighten all 7 bolts to 13 ft. lbs. (18 Nm).

25. Attach all the wiring harness pin-type retainers to the intake manifold.

26. If equipped, connect the swirl control valve sensor and solenoid electrical connectors.

27. Connect the MAP sensor electrical connector.

28. Connect the power brake booster vacuum tube.

- Push the vacuum tube into the quick release fitting.

29. Connect the fuel vapor return hose.

30. Connect the electronic throttle control electrical connector.

31. Connect the EOP switch electrical connector and attach the wire harness retainer to the starter stud bolt.

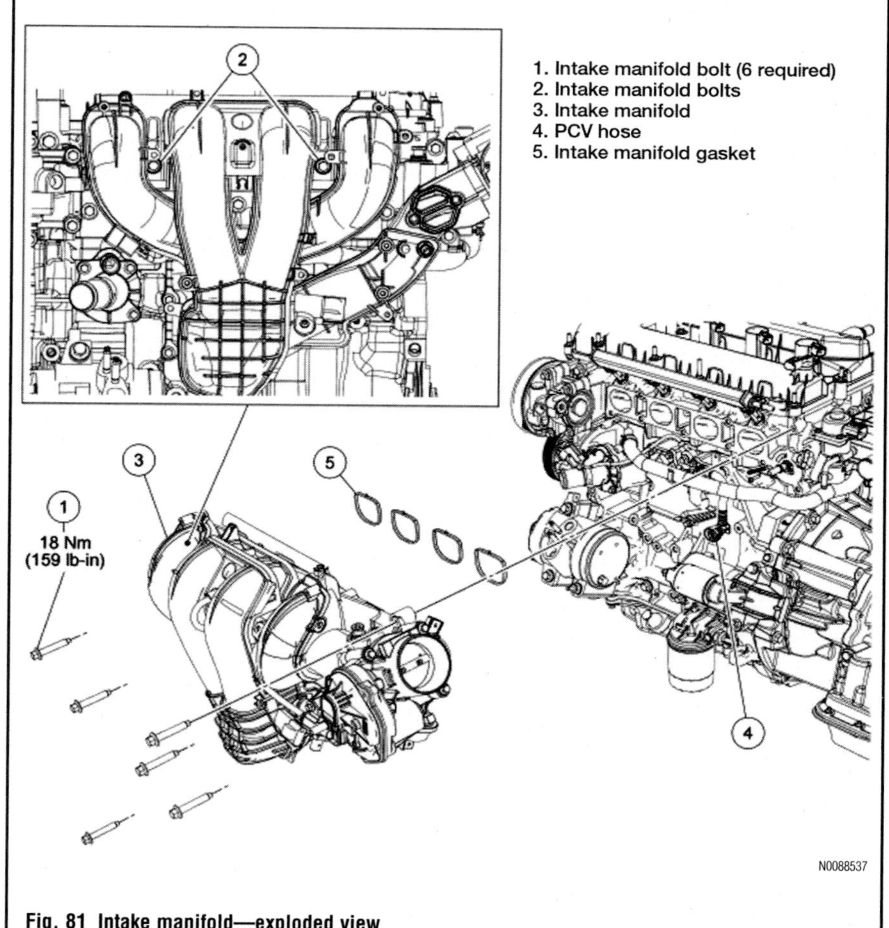

Fig. 81 Intake manifold—exploded view

32. Install the oil level indicator and tube.
33. Install the lower intake manifold bolt. Tighten to 13 ft. lbs. (18 Nm).
34. Install the transaxle fluid indicator (automatic transaxle).

CAUTION

Always tighten the fasteners of the impact sensor to the specified torque. Failure to do so may result in incorrect restraint system operation, which increases the risk of personal injury or death in a crash.

35. Install the front impact severity sensor. Tighten the bolt to 97 inch lbs. (11 Nm).
36. Install the ACL outlet pipe. Refer to Air Cleaner, removal & installation.
37. Power the SRS. Refer to Air Bag (Supplemental Restraint System), Arming The System.

OIL PAN

REMOVAL & INSTALLATION

See Figures 82 through 85.

1. Before servicing the vehicle, refer to the Precautions Section.
2. With the vehicle in NEUTRAL, position it on a hoist.
3. Remove the battery tray. Refer to Battery, removal & installation.
4. Remove the 2 nuts and position the Heated Oxygen Sensor (HO2S) and Catalyst Monitor Sensor (CMS) wire connector bracket aside.

WARNING

To prevent damage to the transmission, do not loosen the transmission-to-engine bolts more than 0.19 inch (5mm).

5. Loosen the upper bellhousing-to-engine bolt and stud bolt 0.19 inch (5mm).
6. Remove the oil level indicator and tube.
7. Loosen the 2 (automatic transaxle) or 3 (manual transaxle) LH bellhousing-to-engine bolts 0.19 inch (5mm).
8. Loosen the RH engine-to-bellhousing bolt and stud bolt 0.19 inch (5mm).
9. Remove the 2 bellhousing-to-oil pan bolts.
10. Remove the 2 oil pan-to-bellhousing bolts.
11. Slide the transaxle rearward 0.19 inch (5mm).
12. Remove the 2 bolts and the accessory drive belt splash shield.

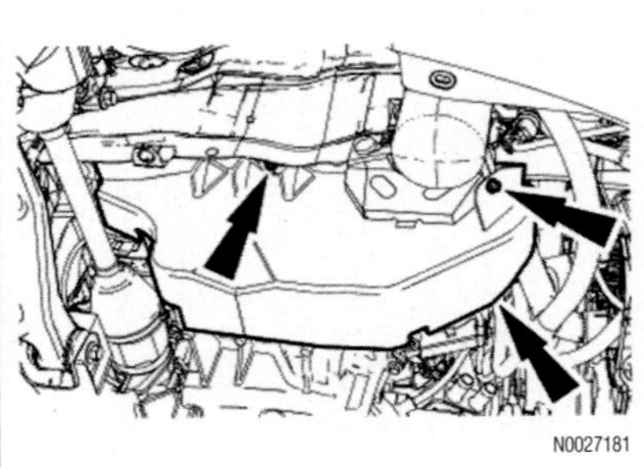

Fig. 82 View of accessory drive belt splash shield

13. Drain the engine oil. Install the drain plug and tighten to 21 ft. lbs. (28 Nm).
14. Remove the 4 engine front cover-to-oil pan bolts.
15. Remove the 13 bolts and the oil pan.

To install:

WARNING

Do not use metal scrapers, wire brushes, power abrasive discs or other abrasive means to clean the sealing surfaces. These tools cause scratches and gouges, which make leak paths. Use a plastic scraping tool to remove traces of sealant.

16. Clean and inspect all mating surfaces.

➡If the oil pan is not secured within 10 minutes of sealant application, the sealant must be removed and the sealing area cleaned with metal surface prep. Allow to dry until there is no sign of wetness, or 10 minutes, whichever is longer. Failure to follow this procedure can cause future oil leakage.

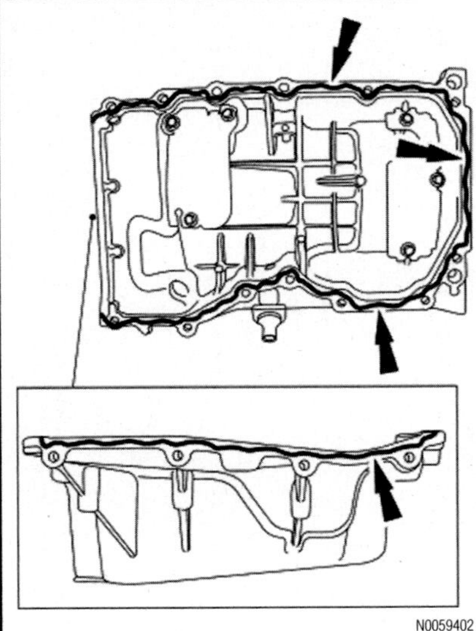

Fig. 83 Apply a bead of sealant to the areas indicated

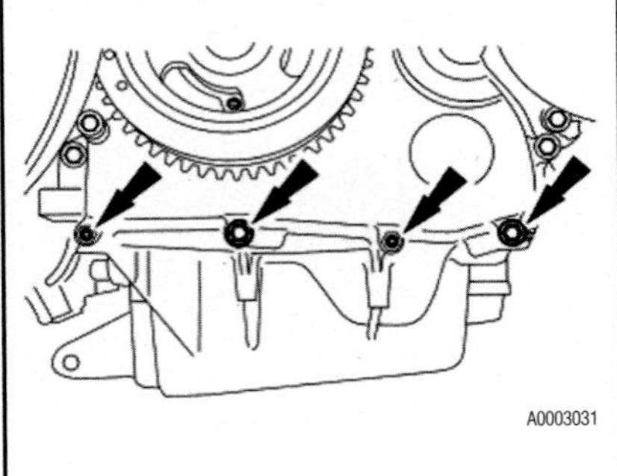

Fig. 84 Install the 4 engine front cover-to-oil pan bolts

17. Apply a 0.09 inch (2.5mm) bead of silicone gasket and sealant to the oil pan-to-engine block and to the oil pan-to-engine front cover mating surface.
18. Position the oil pan onto the engine and install the 13 oil pan bolts finger-tight.

➡The engine front cover-to-oil pan bolts must be tightened first to align the front surface of the oil pan flush with the front surface of the engine block.

19. Install the 4 engine front cover-to-oil pan bolts. Tighten to 89 inch lbs. (10 Nm).
20. Tighten the oil pan bolts in the sequence shown. Tighten to 18 ft. lbs. (25 Nm).
21. Install the accessory drive belt splash shield and the 2 bolts. Tighten to 80 inch lbs. (9 Nm).
22. Alternate tightening the 1 LH bellhousing-to-engine and 1 RH engine-to-bellhousing lower bolts to slide the transaxle and engine together. Tighten to 35 ft. lbs. (48 Nm).
23. Tighten the remaining 1 (automatic transaxle) or 2 (manual transaxle) LH bellhousing-to-engine bolt(s) and the remain-

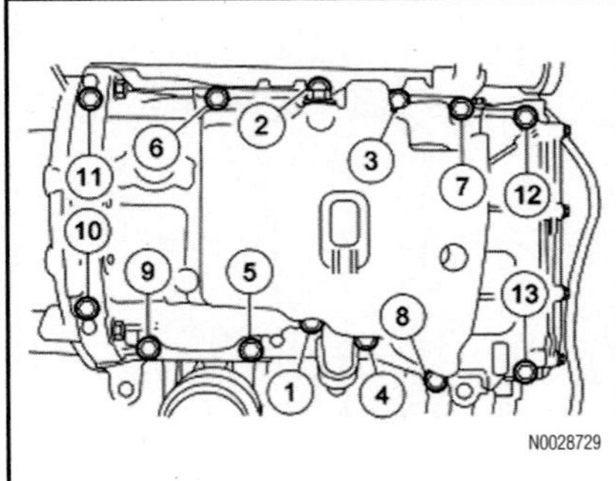

Fig. 85 Tighten the oil pan bolts in the sequence shown

ing rear engine-to-bellhousing stud bolt. Tighten to 35 ft. lbs. (48 Nm).

24. Install the 2 bellhousing-to-oil pan bolts. Tighten to 35 ft. lbs. (48 Nm).

25. Install the 2 oil pan-to-bellhousing bolts. Tighten to 35 ft. lbs. (48 Nm).

26. Install the oil level indicator and tube.

27. Tighten the top bellhousing-to-engine bolt and stud bolt. Tighten to 35 ft. lbs. (48 Nm).

28. Position the HO2S and CMS wire connector bracket and install the 2 nuts. Tighten to 18 ft. lbs. (25 Nm).

29. Install the battery tray. Refer to Battery, removal & installation.

30. Fill the engine with the proper type and amount of clean engine oil.

OIL PUMP

REMOVAL & INSTALLATION

See Figures 86 through 91.

1. Before servicing the vehicle, refer to the Precautions Section.
2. With the engine in NEUTRAL, position it on a hoist.
3. Remove the engine front cover. Refer to Timing Chain Front Cover, removal & installation.
4. Remove the oil level indicator and tube.
5. Drain the engine oil, then install the drain plug and tighten to 21 ft. lbs. (28 Nm).
6. Remove the 2 oil pan-to-bellhousing bolts.
7. Remove the 2 bellhousing-to-oil pan bolts.
8. Remove the 13 bolts and the oil pan.

➡Discard the gasket and clean and inspect the gasket mating surfaces.

9. Remove the 2 bolts and the oil pump screen and pickup tube.
10. Remove the oil pump drive chain tensioner.
    a. Release the tension on the tensioner spring.
    b. Remove the tensioner and the 2 shoulder bolts.
11. Remove the chain from the oil pump sprocket.
12. Remove the bolt and oil pump sprocket.
13. Remove the 4 bolts and the oil pump.

To install:

14. Clean the oil pump and cylinder block mating surfaces with metal surface prep.
15. Install the oil pump assembly. Tighten the 4 bolts in the sequence shown in 2 stages:
    - Stage 1: Tighten to 89 inch lbs. (10 Nm)
    - Stage 2: Tighten to 15 ft. lbs. (20 Nm)
16. Install the oil pump sprocket and bolt. Tighten to 18 ft. lbs. (25 Nm).
17. Install the chain onto the oil pump sprocket.
18. Install the oil pump drive chain tensioner shoulder bolt. Tighten to 89 inch lbs. (10 Nm).
19. Install the oil pump chain tensioner and bolt. Hook the tensioner spring around the shoulder bolt. Tighten to 89 inch lbs. (10 Nm).
20. Install the oil pump screen and pickup tube and the 2 bolts. Tighten to 89 inch lbs. (10 Nm).

⁂ WARNING

Do not use metal scrapers, wire brushes, power abrasive discs or other abrasive means to clean the sealing surfaces. These tools cause scratches and gouges, which make leak paths. Use a plastic scraping tool to remove traces to sealant.

21. Clean all mating surfaces with metal surface prep.

➡If the oil pan is not secured within 10 minutes of sealant application, the sealant must be removed and the sealing area cleaned with metal surface prep. Allow to dry until there is no sign of wetness, or 10 minutes, whichever is longer. Failure to follow this procedure can cause future oil leakage.

22. Apply a 0.09 inch (2.5mm) bead of sealant gasket and sealant to the oil pan. Position the oil pan onto the engine and install the 2 rear oil pan bolts finger-tight.
23. Using a suitable straight edge, align

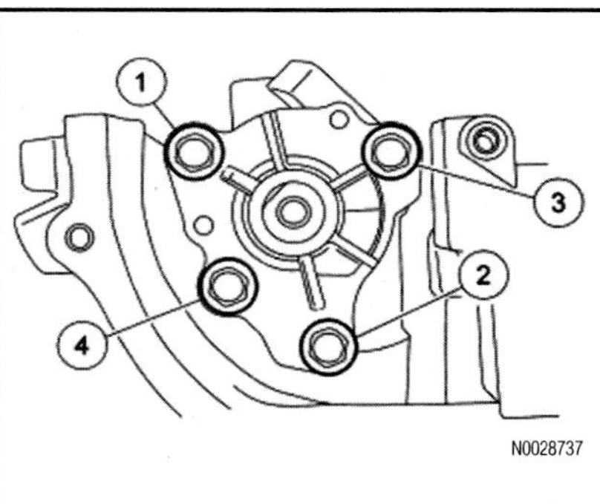

Fig. 87 Oil pump assembly bolt tightening sequence

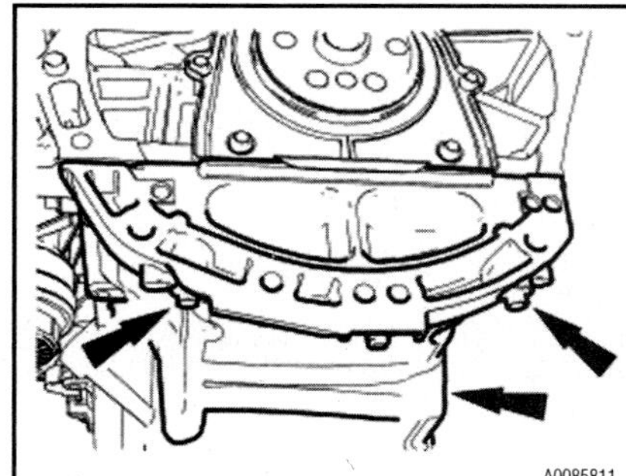

Fig. 89 Position the oil pan onto the engine and install the 2 rear oil pan bolts finger-tight

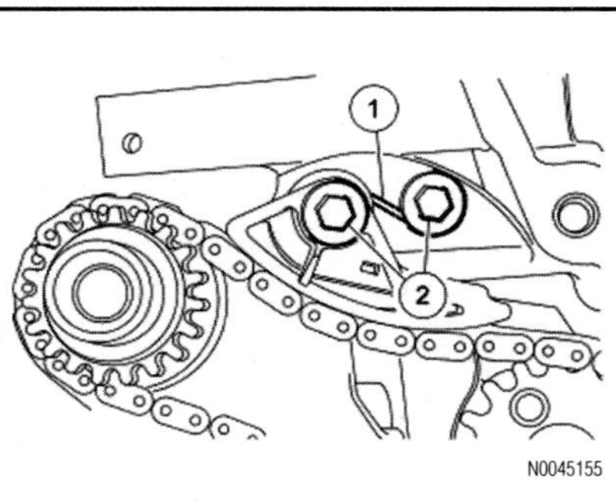

Fig. 86 Remove the oil pump drive chain tensioner

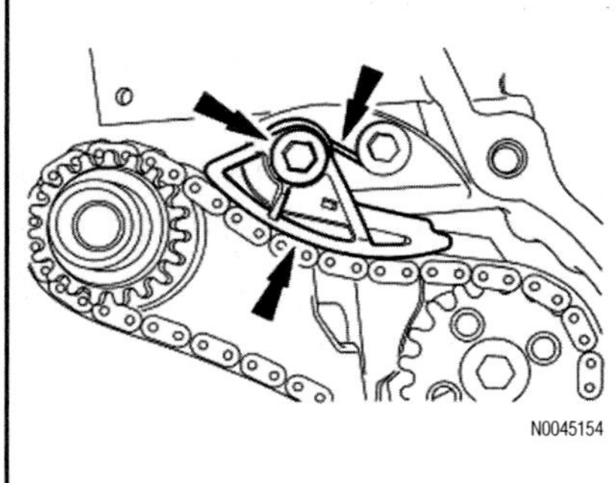

Fig. 88 Install the oil pump chain tensioner and bolt

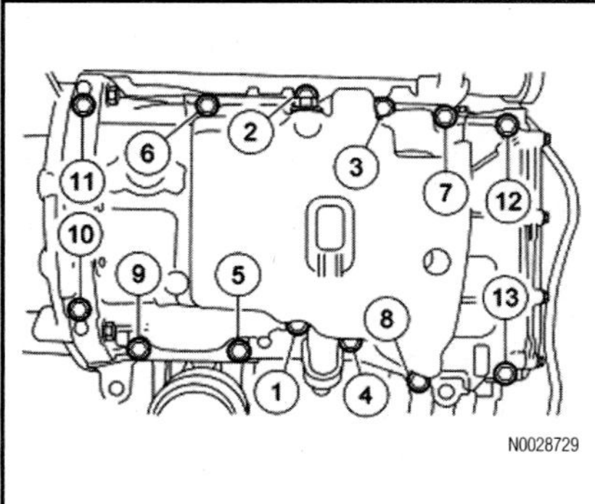

Fig. 90 Oil pan bolt tightening sequence

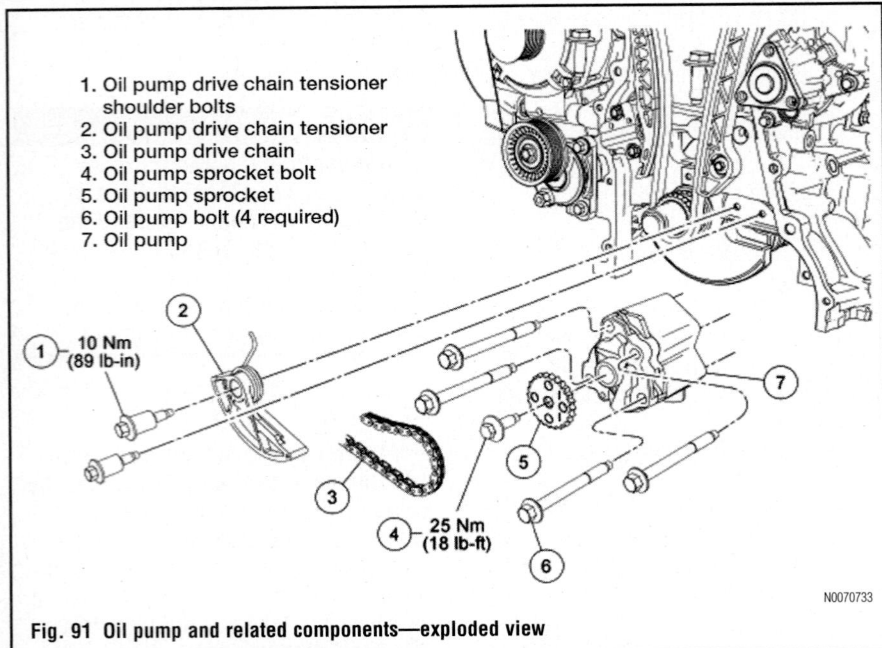

Fig. 91 Oil pump and related components—exploded view

The piston compression upper and lower ring should be installed with the paint mark on the outside diameter circumference of the ring to be positioned on the right side of the ring gap. The lower compression ring can also be installed with the undercut side downward.

REAR MAIN SEAL

REMOVAL & INSTALLATION

See Figures 94 through 99.

1. Before servicing the vehicle, refer to the Precautions Section.
2. With the vehicle in NEUTRAL, position it on a hoist.
3. Remove the flywheel or flexplate.
4. Drain the engine oil. Install the drain plug and tighten to 21 ft. lbs. (28 Nm).
5. Remove the oil level indicator and tube.

the front surface of the oil pan flush with the front surface of the engine block.

24. Install the remaining oil pan bolts. Tighten in sequence to 18 ft. lbs. (25 Nm).
25. Install the 2 bellhousing-to-oil pan bolts. Tighten to 35 ft. lbs. (48 Nm).
26. Install the 4 oil pan-to-bellhousing bolts. Tighten to 35 ft. lbs. (48 Nm).
27. Install the oil level indicator and tube.
28. Install the engine front cover. Refer to Timing Chain Front Cover, removal & installation.
29. Fill the engine with the proper type and amount of clean engine oil.

PISTON AND RING

POSITIONING

See Figures 92 and 93.

The arrow on the top of the piston points towards the front of the engine.

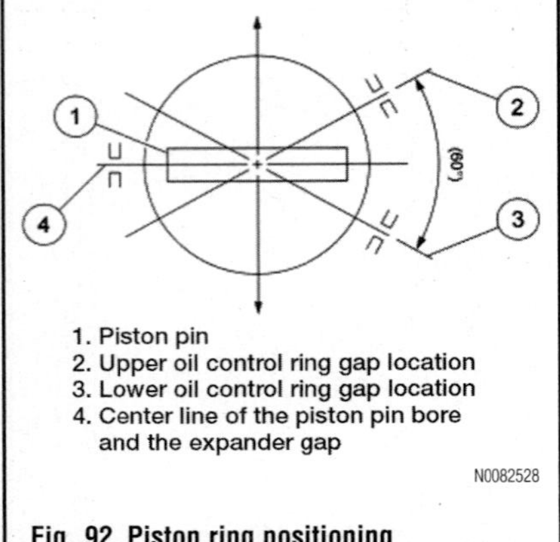

Fig. 92 Piston ring positioning

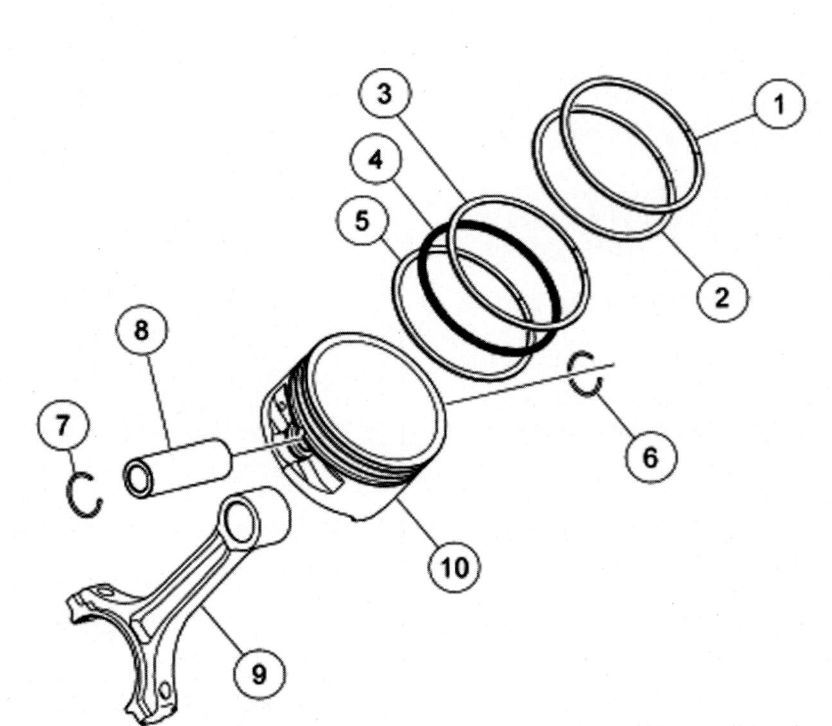

Fig. 93 Piston and ring assembly—exploded view

WARNING

If the oil pan is not removed, damage to the rear oil seal retainer joint can occur.

6. Remove the 17 bolts and the oil pan.
7. Remove the 6 bolts and the crankshaft rear seal with retainer plate.

To install:

8. Using the Crankshaft Rear Main Oil Seal Installer, position the crankshaft rear oil seal with retainer plate onto the crankshaft.

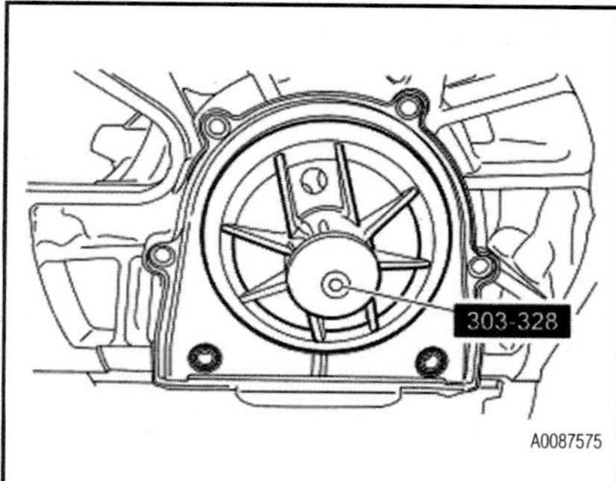

Fig. 94 Using the Crankshaft Rear Main Oil Seal Installer

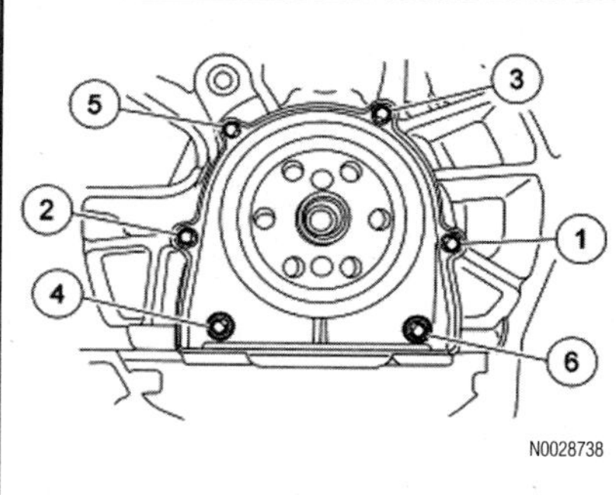

Fig. 95 Crankshaft rear seal with retainer plate bolt tightening sequence

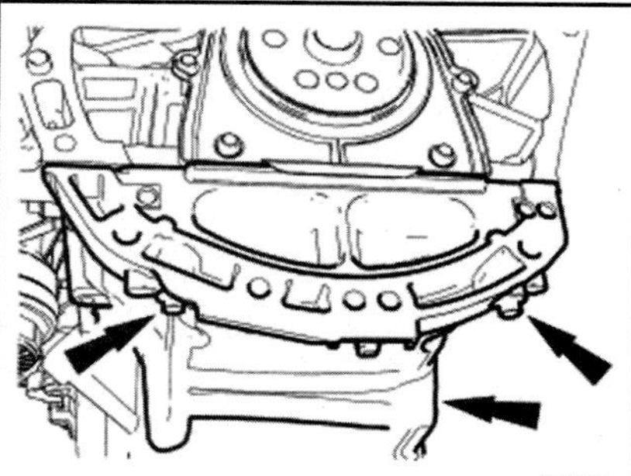

Fig. 96 Position the oil pan onto the engine and install the 2 rear oil pan bolts finger-tight

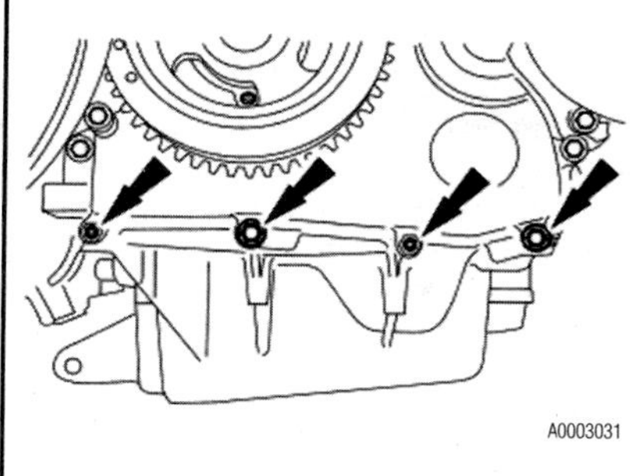

Fig. 97 Install the 4 engine front cover-to-oil pan bolts

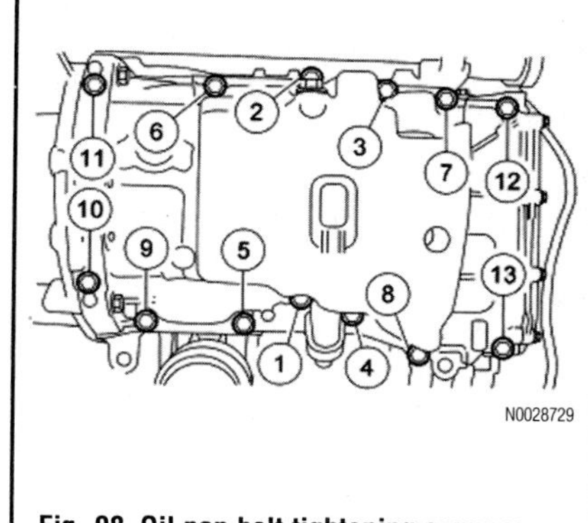

Fig. 98 Oil pan bolt tightening sequence

9. Install the crankshaft rear seal with retainer plate and 6 bolts. Tighten in sequence to 89 inch lbs. (10 Nm).

WARNING

Do not use metal scrapers, wire brushes, power abrasive discs or other abrasive means to clean the sealing surfaces. These tools cause scratches and gouges, which make leak paths. Use a plastic scraping tool to remove traces of sealant.

10. Clean and inspect all the oil pan, cylinder block, and front cover flange mating surfaces.

➡If not secured within 4 minutes, the sealant must be removed and the sealing area cleaned. To clean the sealing area, use silicone gasket remover and

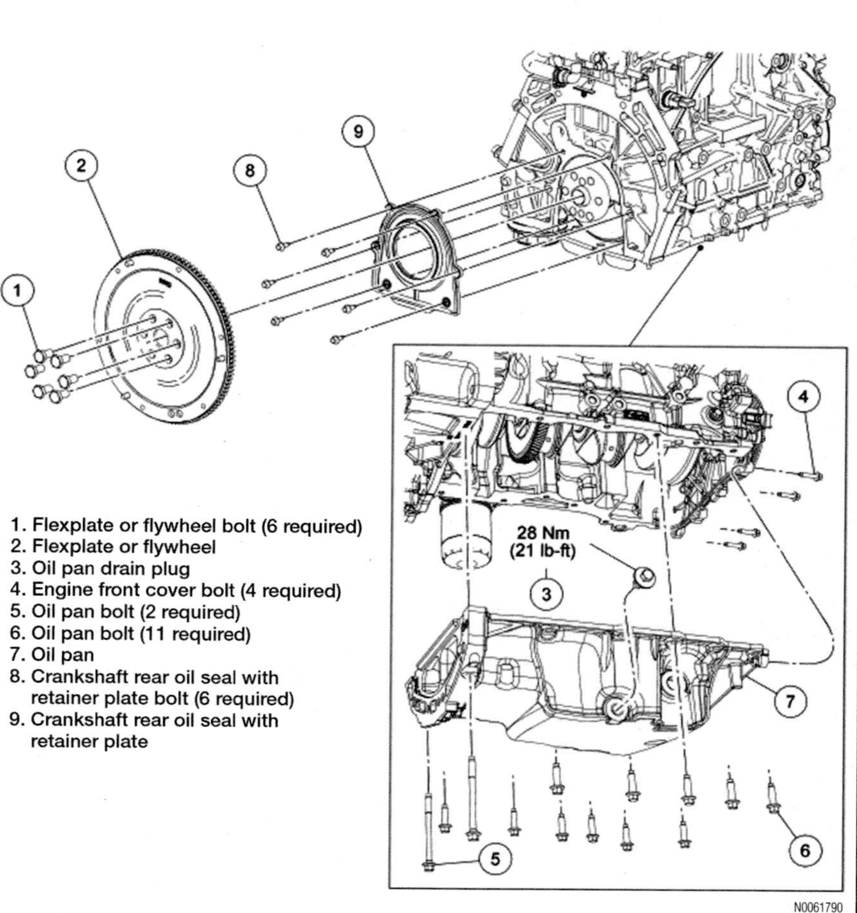

Fig. 99 Exploded view of crankshaft rear seal and related components

metal surface prep. Follow the directions on the packaging. Failure to follow this procedure can cause future oil leakage.

➡**The oil pan must be installed and the bolts tightened within 4 minutes of applying the silicone gasket and sealant.**

11. Apply a 0.09 inch (2.5mm) bead of silicone gasket and sealant to the oil pan.
12. Install the oil pan and the 2 bolts finger-tight.
13. Install the 4 front cover-to-oil pan bolts. Tighten to 89 inch lbs. (10 Nm).
14. Install the remaining oil pan bolts. Tighten in sequence to 18 ft. lbs. (25 Nm).
15. Install the oil level indicator and tube.
16. Install the flywheel or flexplate.
17. Fill the engine with the proper type and amount of clean engine oil.

TIMING CHAIN FRONT COVER

REMOVAL & INSTALLATION

See Figures 100 through 106.

WARNING

Do not loosen or remove the crankshaft pulley bolt without first installing the special tools as instructed in this procedure. The crankshaft pulley and the crankshaft timing sprocket are not keyed to the crankshaft. The crankshaft, the crankshaft sprocket and the pulley are fitted together by friction, using diamond washers between the flange faces on each part. For that reason, the crankshaft sprocket is also unfastened if the pulley bolt is loosened. Before any repair requiring loosening or removal of the crankshaft pulley bolt, the crankshaft and camshafts must be locked in place by the special service tools, otherwise severe engine damage can occur.

WARNING

During engine repair procedures, cleanliness is extremely important. Any foreign material, including any material created while cleaning gasket surfaces, that enters the oil passages, coolant passages or the oil pan can cause engine failure.

1. Before servicing the vehicle, refer to the Precautions Section.
2. With the vehicle in NEUTRAL, position it on a hoist.
3. Depower the Supplemental Restraint System (SRS). Refer to Air Bag (Supplemental Restraint System), Disarming The System.
4. Loosen the 3 coolant pump pulley bolts.
5. Remove the crankshaft pulley.
6. Disconnect the Crankshaft Position (CKP) sensor electrical connector. Detach the 2 wiring harness retainers from the engine front cover.
7. Remove the 2 bolts and the CKP sensor.

WARNING

Use care not to damage the engine front cover or the crankshaft when removing the seal.

8. Using the Oil Seal Remover, remove the crankshaft front oil seal.

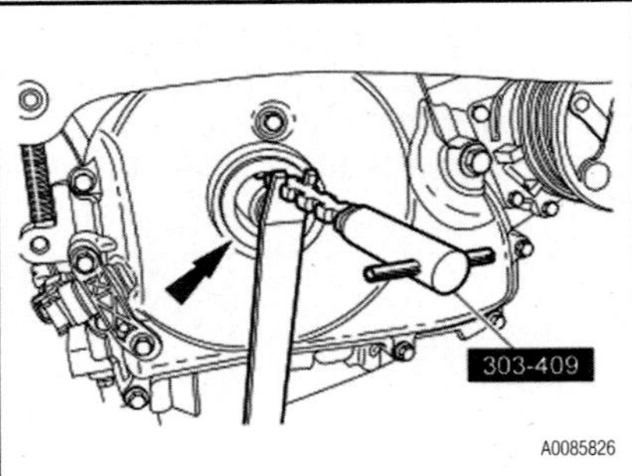

Fig. 100 Using the Oil Seal Remover to remove the crankshaft front oil seal

9. Remove the 3 bolts and the coolant pump pulley.
10. Remove the coolant expansion tank.
11. Remove the power steering pump. Refer to Power Steering Pump, removal & installation.
12. Remove the engine mount.
13. Slightly raise the engine for access to the accessory drive idler pulley.
14. Remove the accessory drive idler pulley.
15. Remove the bolts and the engine front cover.

To install:

WARNING

Do not use metal scrapers, wire brushes, power abrasive disks or other abrasive means to clean sealing surfaces. These tools cause scratches and gouges which make leak paths.

16. Clean and inspect the mounting surfaces of the engine and the front cover.

➡**The engine front cover must be installed and the bolts tightened within 4 minutes of applying the silicone gasket and sealant.**

17. Apply a 0.09 (2.5mm) bead of silicone gasket and sealant to the cylinder head and oil pan joint areas. Apply a 0.09 (2.5mm) bead of silicone gasket and sealant to the front cover.

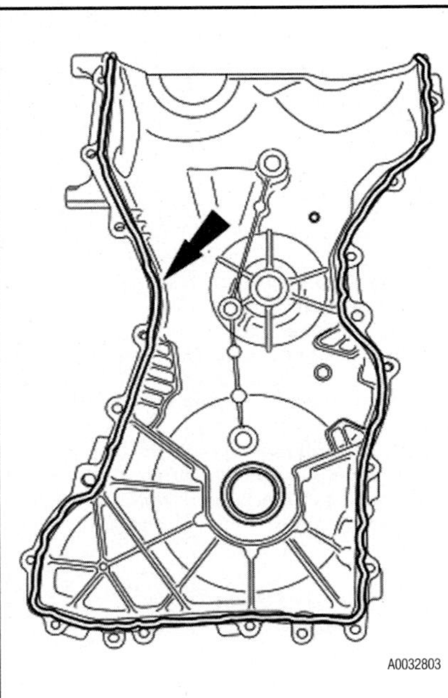

Fig. 101 Apply a bead of silicone gasket sealant in the area shown

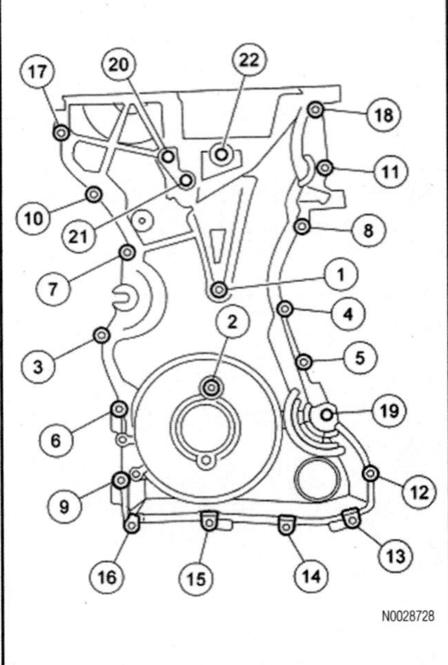

Fig. 102 Engine front cover bolt tightening sequence

18. Install the engine front cover. Tighten the bolts in sequence, to the following specifications:

a. Tighten the 8mm bolts to 89 inch lbs. (10 Nm).

b. Tighten the 13mm bolts to 35 ft. lbs. (48 Nm).

19. Install the accessory drive idler pulley.

20. Lower the engine to the installed position.

21. Install the engine mount.

22. Install the power steering pump.

23. Install the coolant expansion tank.

24. Install the coolant pump pulley and the 3 bolts. Do not tighten at this time.

➡Remove the through-bolt from the Camshaft Front Oil Seal Installer.

25. Lubricate the oil seal with clean engine oil.

26. Using the Camshaft Front Oil Seal Installer, install the crankshaft front oil seal.

27. Install the crankshaft pulley.

✲✲ WARNING

Only hand-tighten the crankshaft pulley holding bolt or damage to the front cover can occur.

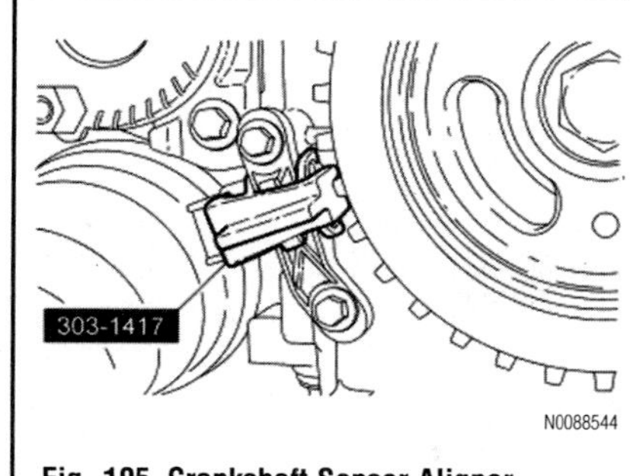

Fig. 105 Crankshaft Sensor Aligner installed

28. Install a standard 6mm x 18mm bolt through the crankshaft pulley and thread it into the front cover.

29. Install the CKP sensor and the 2 bolts. Do not tighten the bolts at this time.

30. Using the Crankshaft Sensor Aligner, adjust the CKP sensor. Tighten the 2 bolts to 62 inch lbs. (7 Nm).

31. Connect the CKP sensor electrical connector. Attach the 2 wiring harness retainers to the engine front cover.

32. Remove the 6mm x 18mm bolt from the crankshaft pulley.

33. Tighten the coolant pump pulley bolts. Tighten to 15 ft. lbs. (20 Nm).

34. Repower the SRS. Refer to Air Bag (Supplemental Restraint System), Arming The System.

35. Fill the power steering system with the proper type and amount of fluid.

TIMING CHAIN & SPROCKETS

REMOVAL & INSTALLATION

See Figures 107 through 110.

✲✲ WARNING

Do not loosen or remove the crankshaft pulley bolt without first installing the special tools as instructed in this procedure. The crankshaft pulley and the crankshaft timing sprocket are not keyed to the crankshaft. The crankshaft, the crankshaft sprocket and the pulley are fitted together by friction, using diamond washers between the flange faces on each part. For that reason, the crankshaft sprocket is also unfastened if the pulley bolt is loosened. Before any repair requiring loosening or removal of the crankshaft pulley bolt, the crankshaft and camshafts must be locked in place by the special service tools, otherwise severe engine damage can occur.

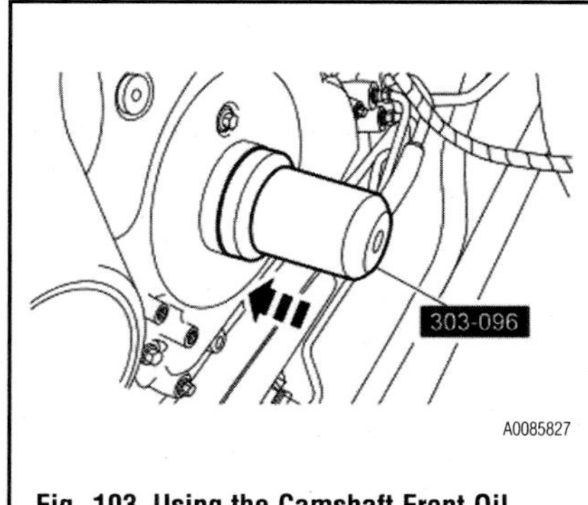

Fig. 103 Using the Camshaft Front Oil Seal Installer

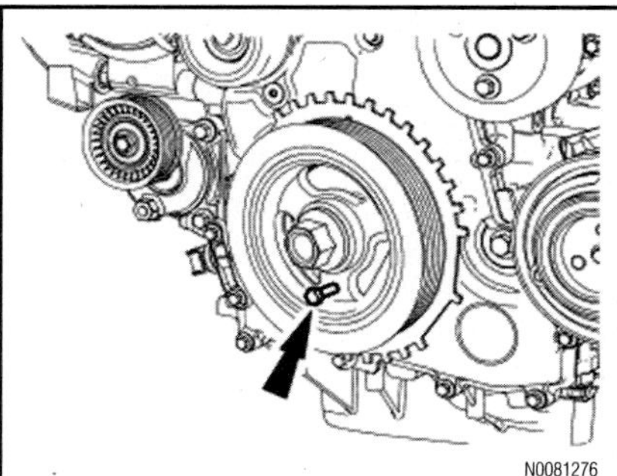

Fig. 104 Install a standard 6mm x 18mm bolt through the crankshaft pulley and thread it into the front cover

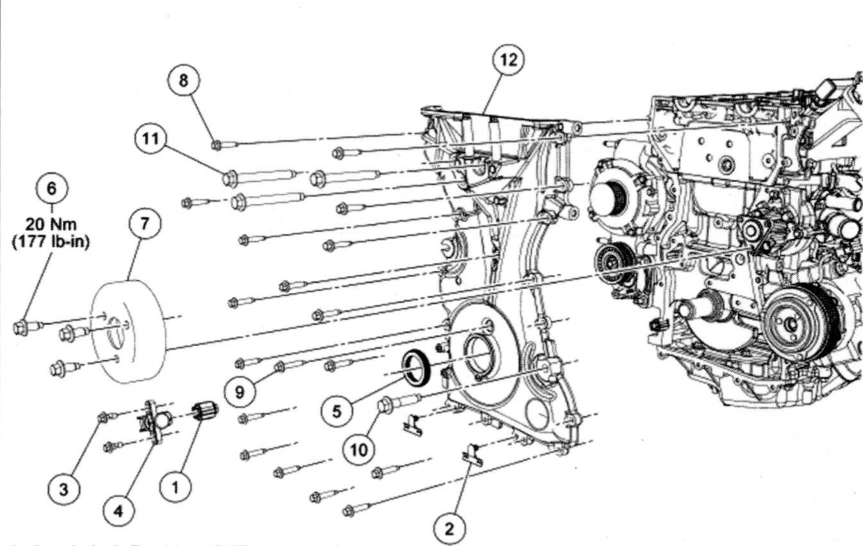

Fig. 106 Exploded view of engine front cover and related components

**** WARNING**

During engine repair procedures, cleanliness is extremely important. Any foreign material, including any material created while cleaning gasket surfaces, that enters the oil passages, coolant passages or the oil pan can cause engine failure.

1. Before servicing the vehicle, refer to the Precautions Section.
2. With the vehicle in NEUTRAL, position it on a hoist.
3. Remove the engine front cover. Refer to Timing Chain Front Cover, removal & installation.
4. Compress the timing chain tensioner in the following sequence.
   a. Using a small pick, release and hold the ratchet mechanism.
   b. While holding the ratchet mechanism in the released position, compress the tensioner by pushing the timing chain arm toward the tensioner.
   c. Insert a paper clip, or equivalent, into the hole to retain the tensioner.
5. Remove the 2 bolts and the timing chain tensioner.

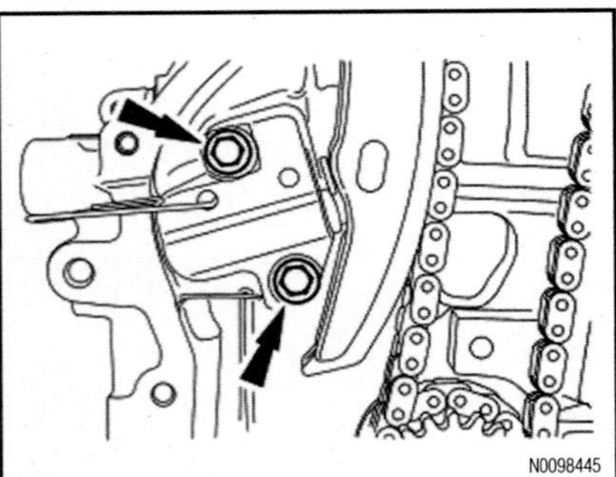

Fig. 107 With paper clip in hole to retain tensioner, remove bolts and timing chain tensioner

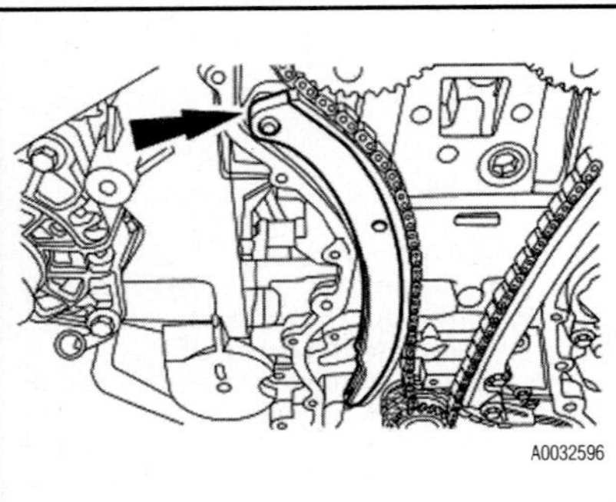

Fig. 108 Remove the RH timing chain guide

6. Remove the RH timing chain guide.
7. Remove the timing chain.
8. Remove the bolts and the LH timing chain guide.

**** WARNING**

Do not rely on the Camshaft Alignment Plate to prevent camshaft rotation. Damage to the tool or the camshaft can occur.

9. Remove the bolts and the camshaft drive gears. Use the flats on the camshaft to prevent camshaft rotation.

To install:

10. Install the camshaft drive gears and the bolts. Do not tighten the bolts at this time.
11. Install the LH timing chain guide and bolts. Tighten to 89 inch lbs. (10 Nm).
12. Install the timing chain.
13. Install the RH timing chain guide.

➡If the timing chain tensioner plunger and ratchet assembly are not pinned in the compressed position, follow the next 4 steps.

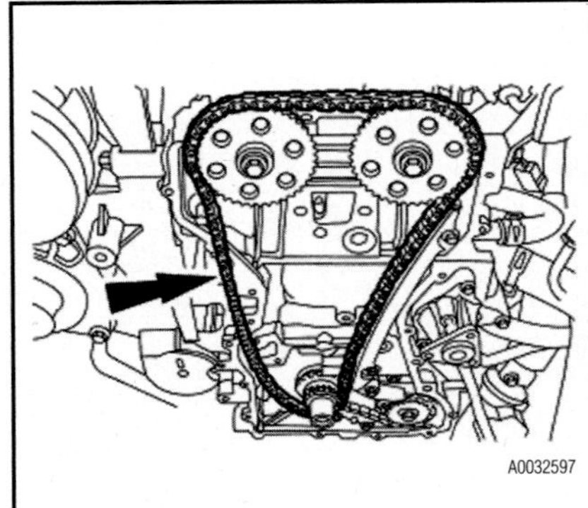

Fig. 109 Remove the timing chain

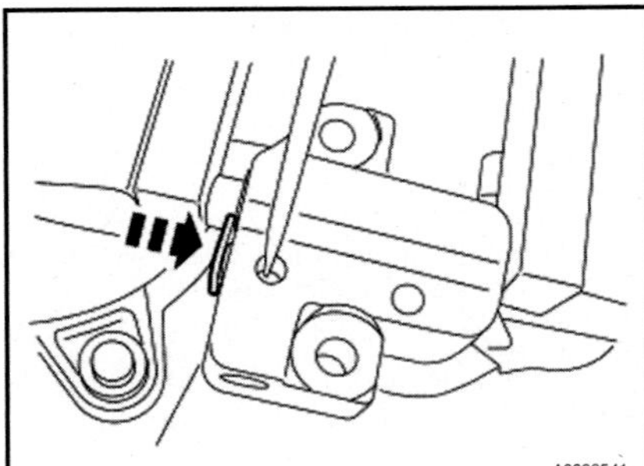

Fig. 110 While holding the ratchet mechanism, push the ratchet arm back into the tensioner housing

**** WARNING**

Do not compress the ratchet assembly. This will damage the ratchet assembly.

14. Using the edge of a vise, compress the timing chain tensioner plunger.
15. Using a small pick, push back and hold the ratchet mechanism.
16. While holding the ratchet mechanism, push the ratchet arm back into the tensioner housing.
17. Install a paper clip into the hole in the tensioner housing to hold the ratchet assembly and the plunger in during installation.
18. Install the timing chain tensioner and the 2 bolts. Tighten to 89 inch lbs. (10 Nm).
19. Remove the paper clip to release the piston.

**** WARNING**

The Camshaft Alignment Plate is for camshaft alignment only. Using this tool to prevent engine rotation can result in engine damage.

20. Using the flats on the camshafts to prevent camshaft rotation, tighten the camshaft drive gear bolts. Tighten to 53 ft. lbs. (72 Nm).
21. Install the front cover. Refer to Timing Chain Front Cover, removal & installation.

VALVE COVERS

REMOVAL & INSTALLATION

See Figures 111 through 113.

**** WARNING**

During engine repair procedures, cleanliness is extremely important. Any foreign material, including any material created while cleaning gasket surfaces, that enters the oil passages, coolant passages or the oil pan can cause engine failure.

1. Before servicing the vehicle, refer to the Precautions Section.
2. Disconnect the Camshaft Position (CMP) sensor electrical connector.
3. Disconnect the 4 ignition coil-on-plug electrical connectors.
4. Remove the 4 ignition coil-to-valve cover bolts and the ignition coils.
5. Lift up the connector boot and disconnect the Cylinder Head Temperature (CHT) sensor electrical connector.
6. Disconnect the crankcase breather tube from the valve cover.

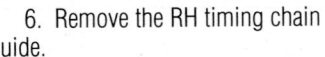

7. Detach all of the wiring harness retainers from the valve cover stud bolts.

8. Disconnect the alternator B+ wire harness retainer from the valve cover stud bolt.

9. Disconnect the alternator electrical connector.

10. Remove the radio interference capacitor bracket bolt.

11. Remove the radio interference capacitor ground bolt and position the bracket aside.

12. Remove the 14 valve cover retainers, the valve cover and gasket.

13. Discard the valve cover gasket.

To install:

WARNING

Do not use metal scrapers, wire brushes, power abrasive discs or other abrasive means to clean the sealing surfaces. These tools cause scratches and gouges which make leak paths.

14. Clean and inspect the sealing surfaces.

15. Apply silicone gasket and sealant to the locations shown.

➡The valve cover must be secured within 4 minutes of silicone gasket application. If the valve cover is not secured within 4 minutes, the sealant must be removed and the sealing area cleaned with metal surface prep.

16. Install the valve cover, a new gasket, and the 14 retainers. Tighten in sequence to 89 inch lbs. (10 Nm).

17. Position the radio interference capacitor bracket and install the bolt. Tighten to 89 inch lbs. (10 Nm).

18. Install the radio interference capacitor ground bolt. Tighten to 89 inch lbs. (10 Nm).

19. Connect the alternator electrical connector.

20. Connect the alternator B+ wire harness retainer to the valve cover stud bolt.

21. Attach all of the wiring harness retainers to the valve cover stud bolts.

22. Connect the crankcase breather tube on the valve cover.

23. Connect the CHT sensor electrical connector and install the connector boot.

24. Install the ignition coils and the 4 ignition coil-to-valve cover bolts. Tighten to 89 inch lbs. (10 Nm).

25. Connect the 4 ignition coil-on-plug electrical connectors.

26. Connect the CMP sensor electrical connector.

VALVE LASH

ADJUSTMENT

See Figures 114 through 116.

1. Before servicing the vehicle, refer to the Precautions Section.

2. Remove the valve cover. Refer to Valve Cover, removal & installation.

3. Remove the 2 bolts and accessory drive belt splash shield.

➡Turn the engine clockwise only, and use the crankshaft bolt only.

➡Measure each valve's clearance at base circle, with the lobe pointed away from the tappet, before removing the camshafts. Failure to measure all clearances prior to removing the camshafts will necessitate repeated removal and installation and wasted labor time.

4. Use a feeler gauge to measure each valve's clearance and record its location.

a. Intake valve specifications:

- Nominal clearance: 0.0095 inch (0.25mm)

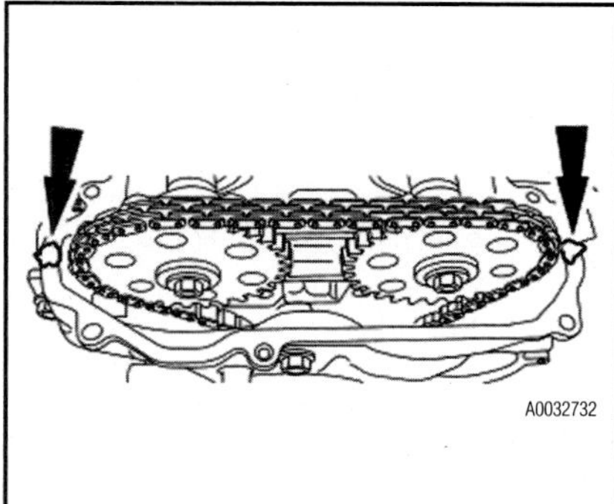

Fig. 111 Apply silicone gasket and sealant to the locations shown

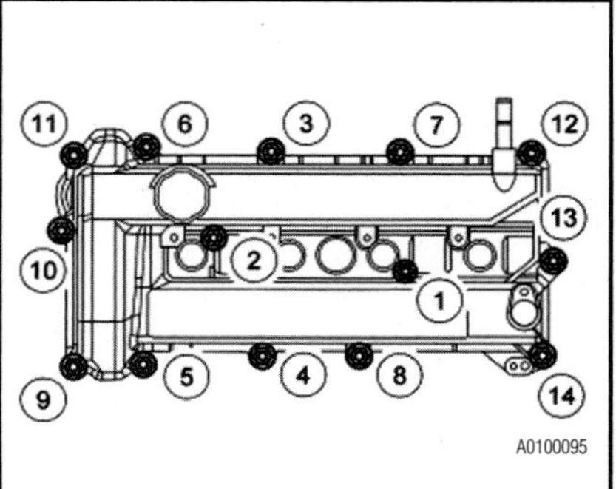

Fig. 112 Valve cover retainer tightening sequence

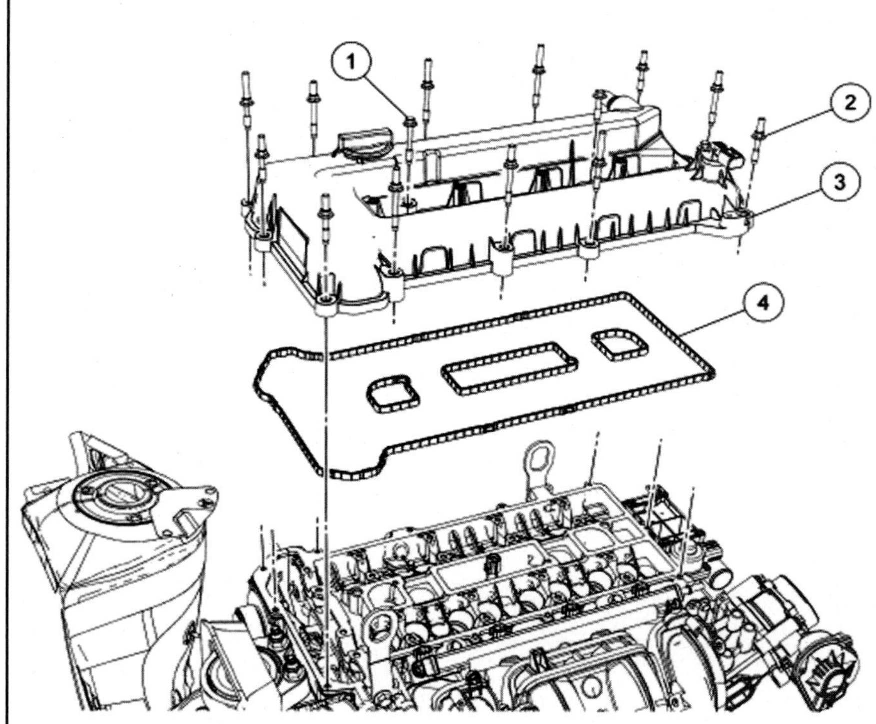

Fig. 113 Valve cover components—exploded view

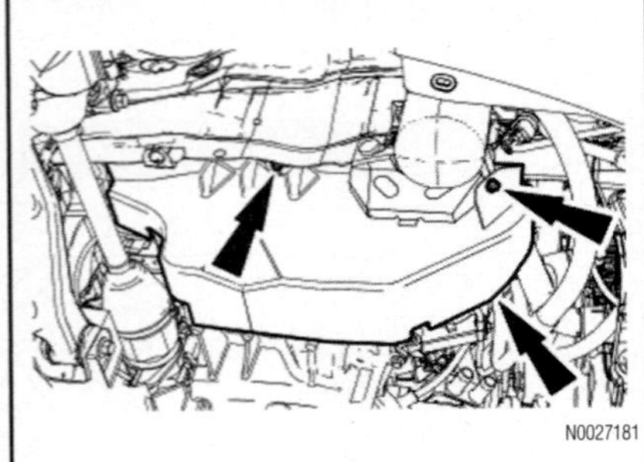

Fig. 114 Remove the accessory drive belt splash shield

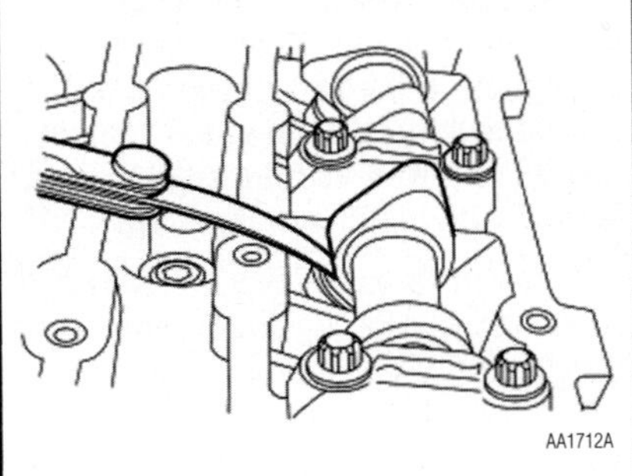

Fig. 115 Use a feeler gauge to measure valve clearance

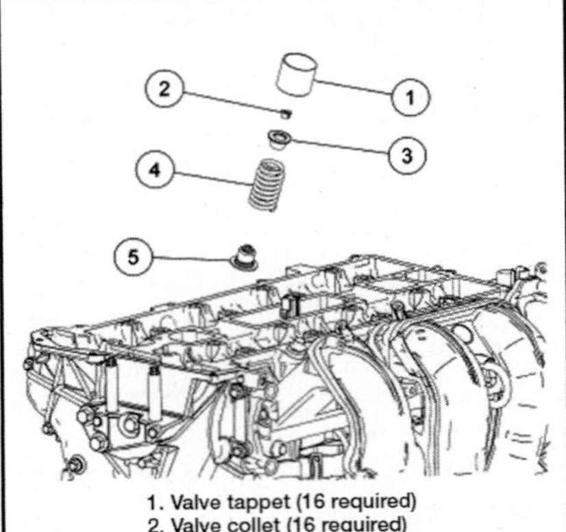

Fig. 116 Use a feeler gauge to measure valve clearance

- Acceptable installed clearance: 0.008–0.011 inch (0.22–0.28mm)

b. Exhaust valve specifications:

- Nominal clearance: 0.0115 inch (0.030mm)
- Acceptable installed clearance: 0.010–0.013 inch (0.27–0.33mm)

➡The number on the valve tappet only reflects the digits that follow the decimal. For example, a tappet with the number 0.650 has the thickness of 3.650mm.

5. Select tappets using this formula: tappet thickness = measured clearance + the existing tappet thickness - nominal clearance. Select the closest tappet size to the ideal tappet thickness available and mark the installation location.
6. If any tappets do not measure within specifications, install new tappets in these locations.
7. Install the 2 bolts and accessory drive belt splash shield. Tighten to 80 inch lbs. (9 Nm).

ENGINE PERFORMANCE & EMISSION CONTROLS

CAMSHAFT POSITION (CMP) SENSOR

LOCATION

See Figure 117.

REMOVAL & INSTALLATION

See Figure 117.

1. Before servicing the vehicle, refer to the Precautions Section.
2. Disconnect the Camshaft Position (CMP) sensor electrical connector.
3. Remove the bolt and the CMP sensor.

To install:

4. Lubricate the O-ring with clean engine oil.
5. Install the CMP sensor into position. Tighten the bolt to 62 inch lbs. (7 Nm).
6. Connect the CMP sensor electrical connector.

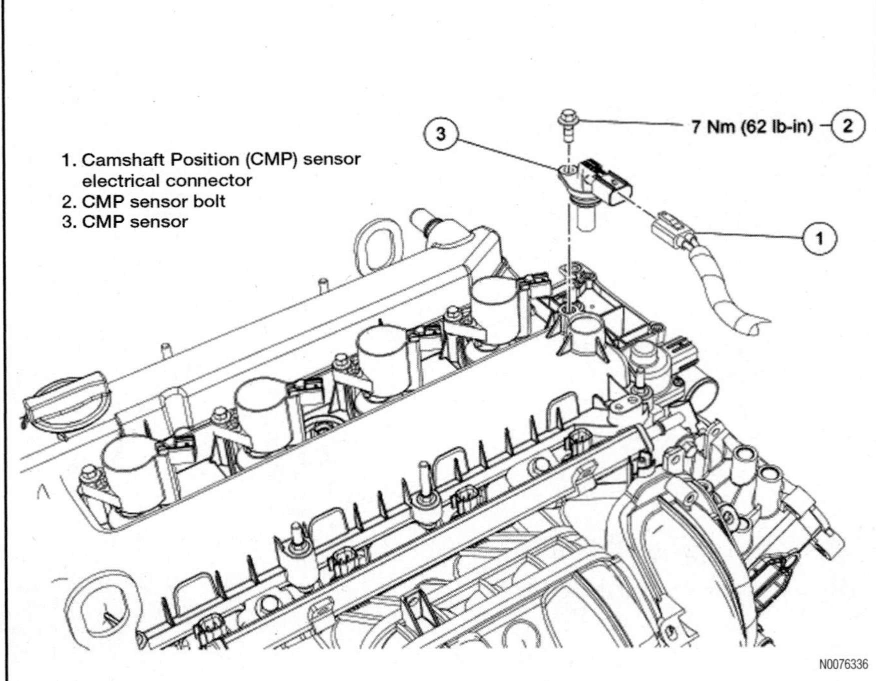

Fig. 117 Camshaft Position (CMP) sensor location

CRANKSHAFT POSITION (CKP) SENSOR

LOCATION

See Figure 118.

REMOVAL & INSTALLATION

See Figures 119 through 124.

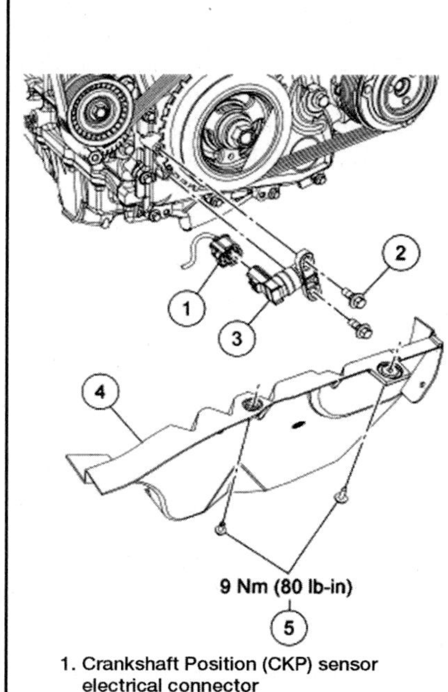

Fig. 118 Crankshaft Position (CKP) sensor location

1. Before servicing the vehicle, refer to the Precautions Section.
2. With the vehicle in NEUTRAL, position it on a hoist.
3. Remove the 2 bolts and the accessory drive belt splash shield.
4. Disconnect the Crankshaft Position (CKP) sensor electrical connector.
5. Turn the crankshaft clockwise until the hole in the crankshaft pulley is in the 3 o'clock position.

➡The cylinder block plug is located on the exhaust side of the engine block near the CKP sensor.

6. Remove the cylinder block plug.

➡When the crankshaft contacts the Crankshaft TDC Timing Peg, the No. 1 cylinder will be at Top Dead Center (TDC).

7. Install the crankshaft TDC Timing Peg.
8. Turn the crankshaft clockwise until the crankshaft contacts the Crankshaft TDC Timing Peg.
9. Remove the CKP sensor retaining bolts and the sensor.

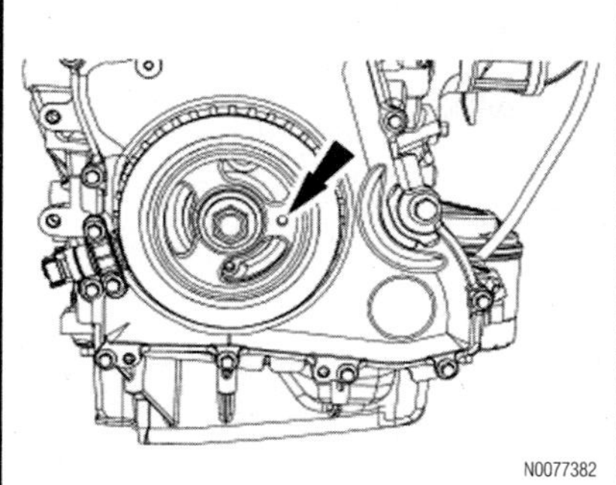

Fig. 119 Turn the crankshaft clockwise until the hole in the crankshaft pulley is in the 3 o'clock position

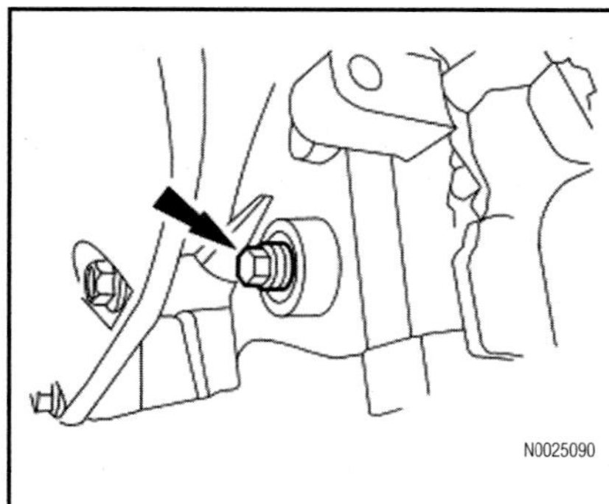

Fig. 120 Remove the cylinder block plug

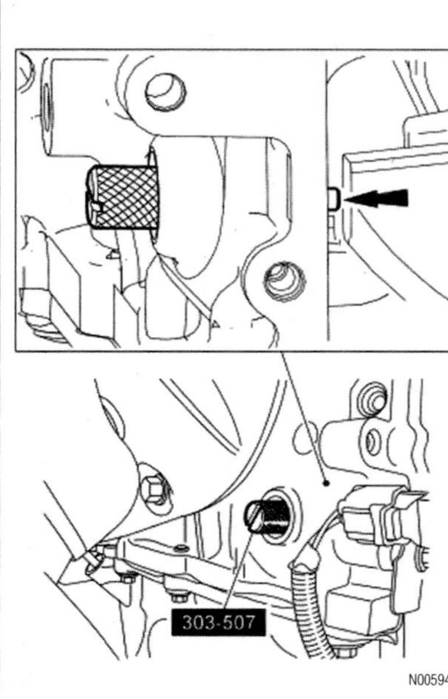

Fig. 121 View of crankshaft TDC Timing Peg installed

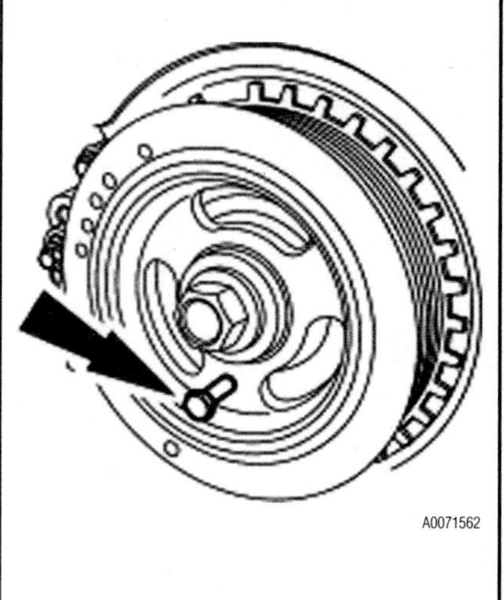

Fig. 122 Install a standard bolt into the crankshaft pulley

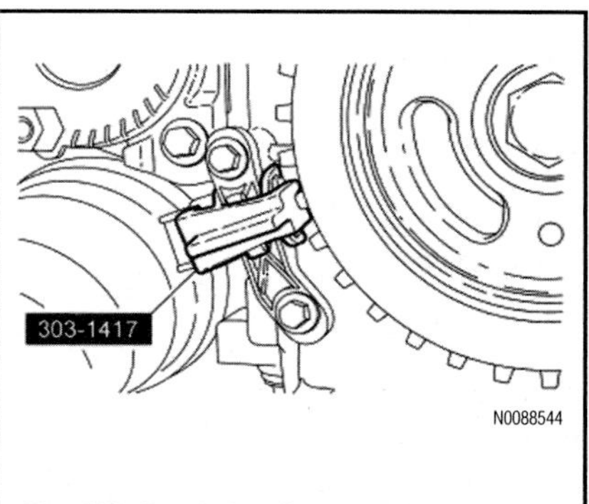

Fig. 123 Crankshaft Sensor Aligner installed

⁂ WARNING

Only hand-tighten the bolt through the crankshaft pulley or damage to the front cover can occur.

10. Install a 6mm x 18mm standard bolt into the crankshaft pulley.

To install:

11. Install the CKP sensor, but do not tighten the 2 bolts at this time.
12. Using the Crankshaft Sensor Aligner, adjust the CKP sensor. Tighten the 2 CKP sensor bolts to 62 inch lbs. (7 Nm).
13. Connect the CKP sensor electrical connector.
14. Remove the 6mm x 18mm bolt from the crankshaft pulley.
15. Remove the Crankshaft TDC Timing Peg.
16. Install the cylinder block plug. Tighten to 15 ft. lbs. (20 Nm).

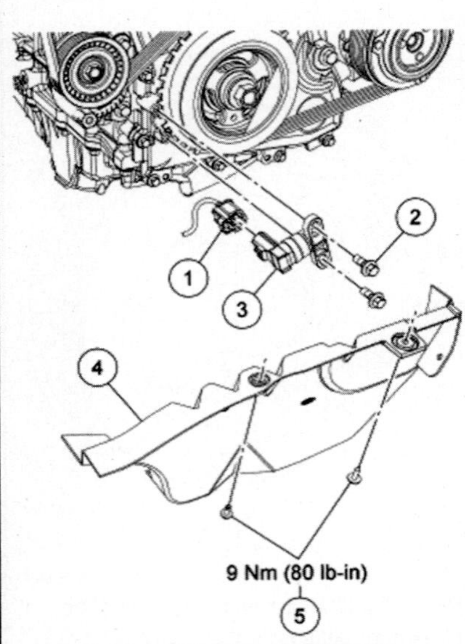

Fig. 124 Crankshaft Position (CKP) sensor location

17. Install the accessory drive belt splash shield and the 2 bolts. Tighten to 80 inch lbs. (9 Nm).

CYLINDER HEAD TEMPERATURE (CHT) SENSOR

LOCATION

See Figure 125.

REMOVAL & INSTALLATION

See Figure 125.

1. Before servicing the vehicle, refer to the Precautions Section.

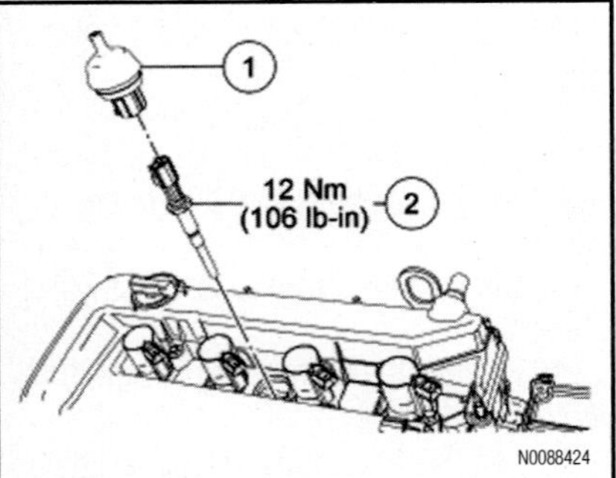

Fig. 125 Cylinder Head Temperature (CHT) sensor (2) and electrical connector (1) location

2. Pull back the Cylinder Head Temperature (CHT) sensor cover and disconnect the electrical connector.
3. Remove the CHT sensor.
4. Installation is the reverse of the removal procedure.
   - Tighten the CHT sensor to 106 inch lbs. (12 Nm).

HEATED OXYGEN (HO2S) SENSOR

LOCATION

See Figure 126.

REMOVAL & INSTALLATION

See Figure 126.

➡For installation and removal of the Catalyst Monitor Sensor (CMS), follow the same procedure used for the Heated Oxygen Sensor (HO2S).

1. Before servicing the vehicle, refer to the Precautions Section.
2. Disconnect the electrical connector and detach the wiring retainer.

➡If necessary, lubricate the sensor threads with penetrating and lock lubricant to assist in removal.

3. Using the Exhaust Gas Oxygen Sensor Socket, remove the HO2S.

To install:

WARNING

Make sure that the sensor wiring is routed away from hot surfaces and sharp edges or damage to the wiring may occur.

4. Apply a light coat of anti-seize lubricant to the threads of the HO2S.
5. Install the HO2S and tighten to 35 ft. lbs. (48 Nm).
6. Connect the electrical connector. Make sure that the electrical connector locking tab is engaged.

KNOCK SENSOR (KS)

LOCATION

See Figure 127.

REMOVAL & INSTALLATION

See Figure 127.

1. Before servicing the vehicle, refer to the Precautions Section.
2. Remove the intake manifold. Refer to Intake Manifold, removal & installation.

➡The Knock Sensor (KS) must not touch the crankcase vent oil separator.

3. Remove the bolt and the KS.
4. To install, reverse the removal procedure. Tighten the KS to 15 ft. lbs. (20 Nm).

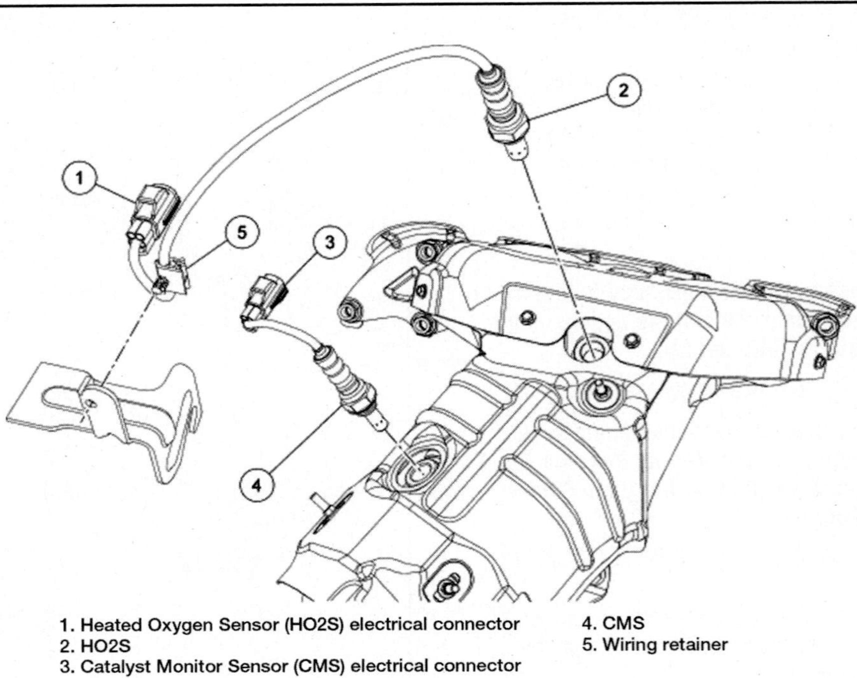

Fig. 126 Heated Oxygen (HO2S) sensor and Catalyst Monitor Sensor (CMS) location

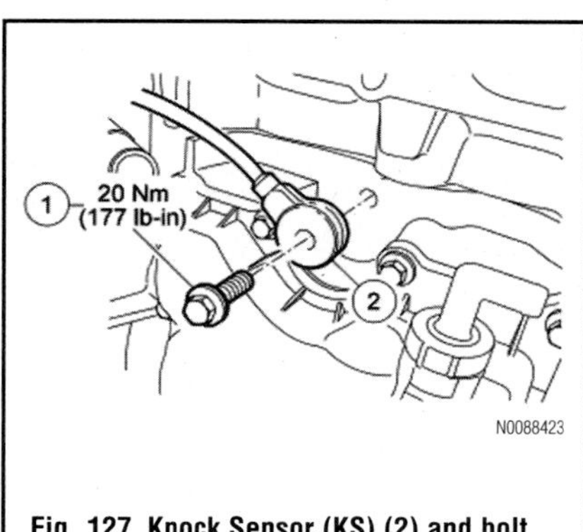

Fig. 127 Knock Sensor (KS) (2) and bolt (1) location

MASS AIR FLOW (MAF) SENSOR

LOCATION

See Figure 128.

REMOVAL & INSTALLATION

See Figure 128.

1. Before servicing the vehicle, refer to the Precautions Section.
2. Disconnect the Mass Air Flow (MAF) sensor electrical connector.
3. Remove the MAF sensor retaining screws.
4. Remove the MAF sensor.
5. Installation is the reverse of the removal procedure.

POWERTRAIN CONTROL MODULE (PCM)

LOCATION

See Figure 129.

The Powertrain Control Module (PCM) is located in the engine compartment above the transaxle.

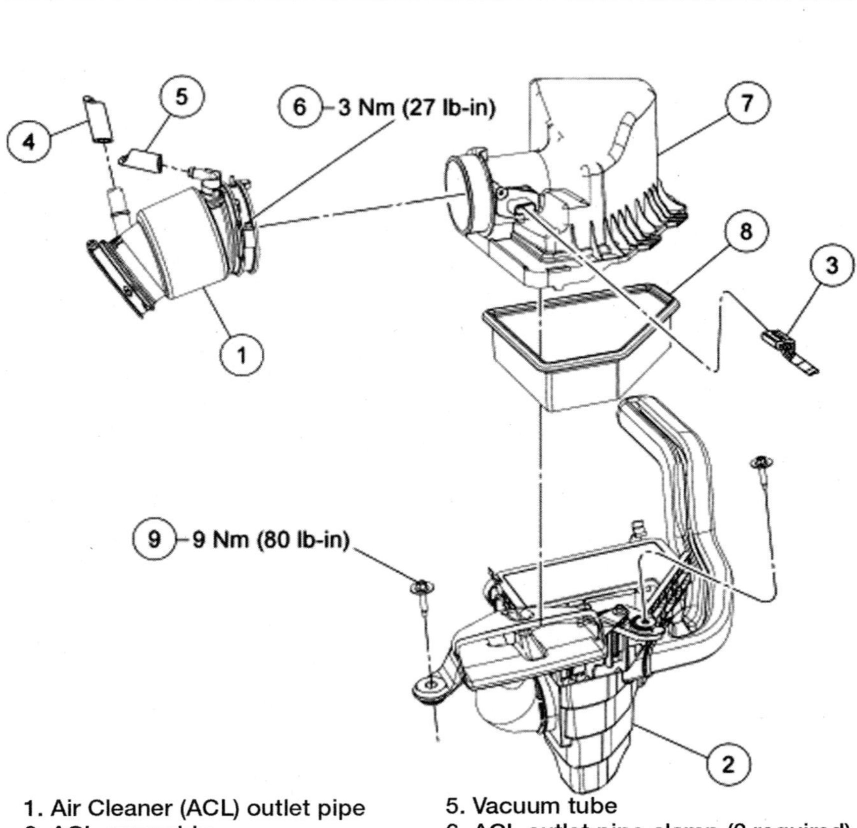

Fig. 128 Air Cleaner (ACL) assembly with Mass Air Flow (MAF) sensor and related components location

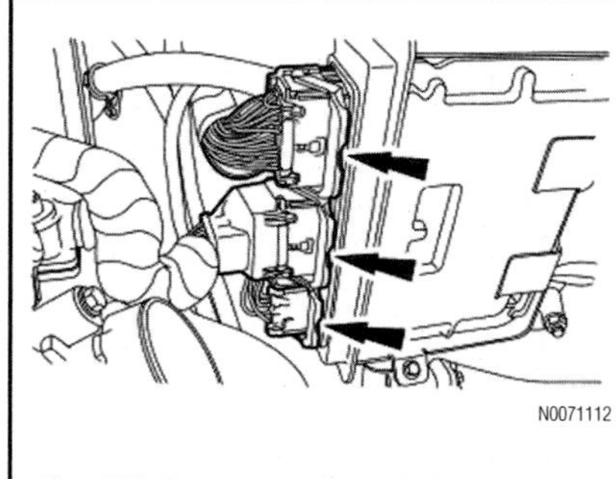

Fig. 129 Powertrain Control Module (PCM) location

REMOVAL & INSTALLATION

See Figure 129.

➡PCM installation DOES NOT require new keys or programming of keys, only a Parameter Reset of the Passive Anti-Theft System (PATS).

1. Before servicing the vehicle, refer to the Precautions Section.
2. Retrieve the module configuration. Carry out the module configuration retrieval steps of the Programmable Module Installation (PMI) procedure.
3. Remove the Air Cleaner (ACL) outlet pipe and the ACL assembly. Refer to Air Cleaner, removal & installation.
4. Disconnect the 3 PCM electrical connectors.
5. Remove the 2 bolts and the PCM.

To install:

6. Install the PCM and the 2 bolts. Tighten to 71 inch lbs. (8 Nm).
7. Connect the 3 PCM electrical connectors.
8. Install the ACL outlet pipe and the air cleaner assembly.
9. Restore the module configuration. Carry out the module configuration restore steps of the Programmable Module Installation (PMI) procedure.
10. Reprogram the PATS. Carry out the Parameter Reset procedure.

PARAMETER RESET PROCEDURE

➡A minimum of 2 Passive Anti-Theft System (PATS) keys must be programmed into the Instrument Cluster (IC) to complete this procedure and allow the vehicle to start.

1. Before servicing the vehicle, refer to the Precautions Section.
2. Turn the key from the OFF position to the ON position.
3. From the scan tool, follow the on-screen instructions to ENTER SECURITY ACCESS.

4. From the scan tool, select: Parameter Reset and follow the on-screen instructions.

➡**If the IC or the IC and the PCM were replaced, updated or reconfigured, follow Steps 5–10. All vehicle keys are erased during the parameter reset procedure. Verify at least 2 vehicle keys are available prior to carrying out the PATS parameter reset. If only the PCM was replaced, go to Step 10.**

5. From the scan tool, select: Ignition Key Code Erase and follow the on-screen instructions.
6. Turn the key to the OFF position and disconnect the scan tool.
7. Turn the key to the ON position for 6 seconds.
8. Turn the key to the OFF position and remove the key.
9. Insert the second PATS key into the ignition lock cylinder and turn the key to the ON position for 6 seconds.
10. Both keys now start the vehicle.

PROGRAMMABLE MODULE INSTALLATION (PMI) PROCEDURE

When Original Module Is Available

➡**Following module installation, some modules require a separate procedure be carried out. For instructions, refer to the specific module removal and installation procedures.**

1. Before servicing the vehicle, refer to the Precautions Section.
2. Connect the Integrated Diagnostic System (IDS) and identify the vehicle as normal.
3. From the Toolbox icon, select Module Programming and press the check mark.
4. Select Programmable Module Installation.
5. Select the module that is being replaced.
6. Follow the on-screen instructions, turn the ignition key to the OFF position, and press the check mark.
7. Install the new module and press the check mark.
8. Follow the on-screen instructions, turn the ignition key to the ON position, and press the check mark.
9. The IDS downloads the data into the new module and displays Module Configuration Complete.
10. Test module for correct operation.

When Original Module Is NOT Available

➡**Following module installation, some modules require a separate procedure be carried out. For instructions, refer to the specific module removal and installation procedures.**

1. Before servicing the vehicle, refer to the Precautions Section.
2. Install the new module.
3. Connect the Integrated Diagnostic System (IDS) and identify the vehicle as normal.
4. From the Toolbox icon, select Module Programming and press the check mark.
5. Select Programmable Module Installation.
6. Select the module that was replaced.
7. Follow the on-screen instructions, turn the ignition key to the OFF position, and press the check mark.
8. Follow the on-screen instructions, turn the ignition key to the ON position, and press the check mark.
9. If the data is not available, the IDS displays a screen stating to contact the As-Built Data Center. Retrieve the data from the technician service publication website at this time and press the check mark.
10. Enter the module data and press the check mark.
11. The IDS downloads the data into the new module and displays Module Configuration Complete.
12. Test module for correct operation.

THROTTLE POSITION SENSOR (TPS)

LOCATION

The Throttle Position (TP) sensor is located on the Throttle Body (TB).

REMOVAL & INSTALLATION

The Throttle Position Sensor (TPS) is integral to the electronic throttle body. Refer to Throttle Body, removal & installation.

VEHICLE SPEED SENSOR (VSS)

LOCATION

See Figure 130.

REMOVAL & INSTALLATION

See Figure 130.

1. Before servicing the vehicle, refer to the Precautions Section.
2. Disconnect the Vehicle Speed Sensor (VSS) electrical connector.
3. Remove the attaching bolt from the VSS and remove the VSS.
4. Installation is the reverse of the removal procedure.

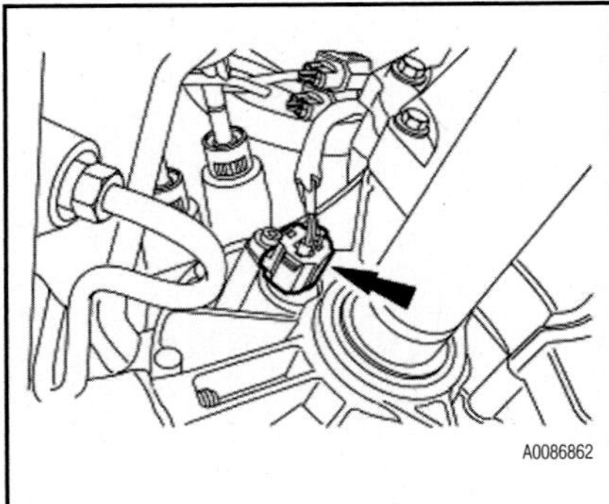

Fig. 130 Vehicle Speed Sensor (VSS) location

FUEL SYSTEM SERVICE PRECAUTIONS

Safety is the most important factor when performing not only fuel system maintenance but any type of maintenance. Failure to conduct maintenance and repairs in a safe manner may result in serious personal injury or death. Maintenance and testing of the vehicle's fuel system components can be accomplished safely and effectively by adhering to the following rules and guidelines.

- To avoid the possibility of fire and personal injury, always disconnect the negative battery cable unless the repair or test procedure requires that battery voltage be applied.
- Always relieve the fuel system pressure prior to disconnecting any fuel system component (injector, fuel rail, pressure regulator, etc.), fitting or fuel line connection. Exercise extreme caution whenever relieving fuel system pressure to avoid exposing skin, face and eyes to fuel spray. Please be advised that fuel under pressure may penetrate the skin or any part of the body that it contacts.
- Always place a shop towel or cloth around the fitting or connection prior to loosening to absorb any excess fuel due to spillage. Ensure that all fuel spillage (should it occur) is quickly removed from engine surfaces. Ensure that all fuel soaked cloths or towels are deposited into a suitable waste container.
- Always keep a dry chemical (Class B) fire extinguisher near the work area.
- Do not allow fuel spray or fuel vapors to come into contact with a spark or open flame.
- Always use a back-up wrench when loosening and tightening fuel line connection fittings. This will prevent unnecessary stress and torsion to fuel line piping.
- Always replace worn fuel fitting O-rings with new Do not substitute fuel hose or equivalent where fuel pipe is installed.

Before servicing the vehicle, make sure to also refer to the precautions in the beginning of this section as well.

RELIEVING FUEL SYSTEM PRESSURE

See Figures 131 and 132.

✲✲ CAUTION

Do not smoke, carry lighted tobacco or have an open flame of any type when working on or near any fuel-related component. Highly flammable mixtures are always present and may be ignited. Failure to follow these instructions may result in serious personal injury.

✲✲ CAUTION

Do not carry personal electronic devices such as cell phones, pagers or audio equipment of any type when working on or near any fuel-related component. Highly flammable mixtures are always present and may be ignited. Failure to follow these instructions may result in serious personal injury.

✲✲ CAUTION

Before working on or disconnecting any of the fuel tubes or fuel system components, relieve the fuel system pressure to prevent accidental spraying of fuel. Fuel in the fuel system remains under high pressure, even when the engine is not running. Failure to follow this instruction may result in serious personal injury.

✲✲ CAUTION

When handling fuel, always observe fuel handling precautions and be prepared in the event of fuel spillage. Spilled fuel may be ignited by hot vehicle components or other ignition sources. Failure to follow these instructions may result in serious personal injury.

1. Before servicing the vehicle, refer to the Precautions Section.
2. Remove the 2 pin-type retainers and the RH A-pillar lower trim panel.
3. Disconnect the Inertia Fuel Shutoff (IFS) switch electrical connector.

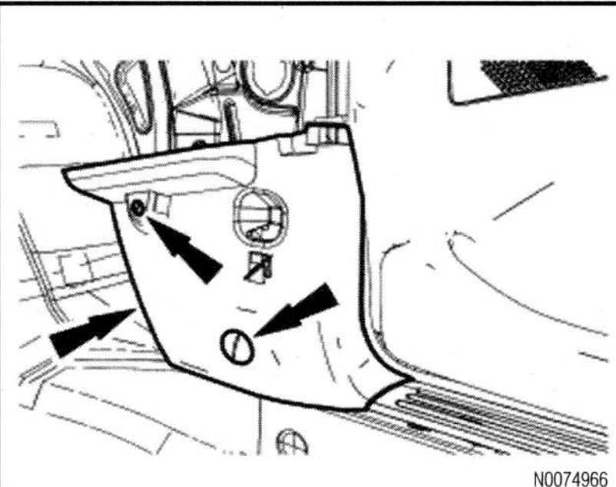

Fig. 131 Remove the 2 pin-type retainers and the RH A-pillar lower trim panel

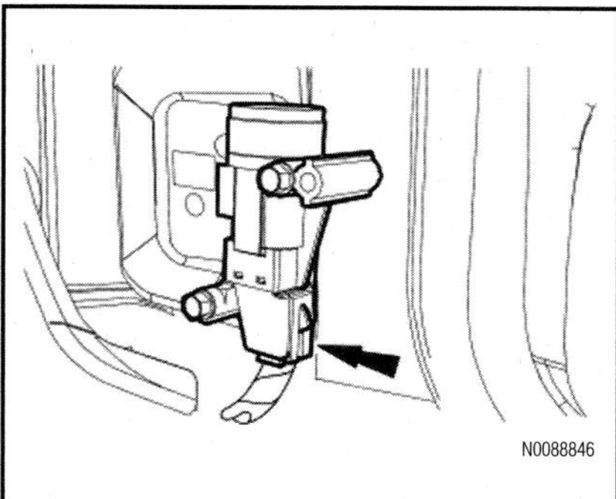

Fig. 132 Disconnect the Inertia Fuel Shutoff (IFS) switch electrical connector

4. Start the engine and allow it to idle until it stalls.
5. After the engine stalls, crank the engine for approximately 5 seconds to make sure the fuel system pressure has been released.
6. Turn the ignition switch to the OFF position.
7. When fuel system service is complete, reconnect the IFS switch electrical connector.

➡It may take more than one key cycle to pressurize the fuel system.

8. Cycle the ignition key and wait 3 seconds to pressurize the fuel system. Check for leaks before starting the engine.
9. Start the vehicle and check the fuel system for leaks.
10. Install the 2 pin-type retainers and the RH A-pillar lower trim panel.

FUEL FILTER

REMOVAL & INSTALLATION

A lifetime fuel filter is serviced as part of the fuel pump module. Refer to Fuel Pump Module, removal & installation.

FUEL INJECTORS

REMOVAL & INSTALLATION

See Figure 133.

✲✲ CAUTION

Do not smoke, carry lighted tobacco or have an open flame of any type when working on or near any fuel-related component. Highly flammable mixtures are always present and may be ignited. Failure to follow these instructions may result in serious personal injury.

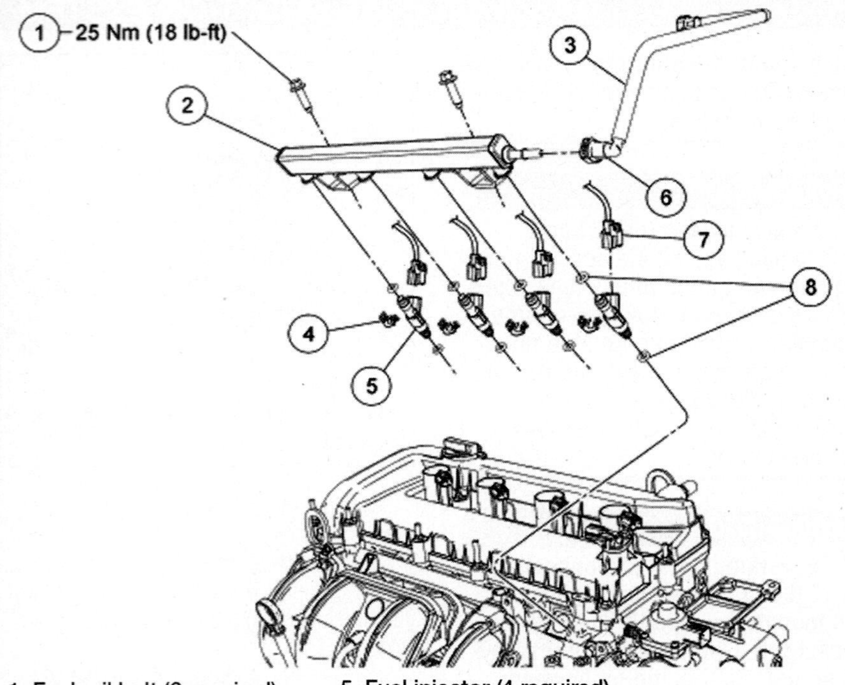

1. Fuel rail bolt (2 required)
2. Fuel rail
3. Fuel tube
4. Fuel injector clip (4 required)
5. Fuel injector (4 required)
6. Fuel tube-to-fuel rail quick connect coupling
7. Fuel injector electrical connector (4 required)
8. Fuel injector O-ring seals (2 required per injector)

N0088801

Fig. 133 Exploded view of fuel rail and injectors

CAUTION

Before working on or disconnecting any of the fuel tubes or fuel system components, relieve the fuel system pressure to prevent accidental spraying of fuel. Fuel in the fuel system remains under high pressure, even when the engine is not running. Failure to follow this instruction may result in serious personal injury.

CAUTION

Clean all fuel residue from the engine compartment. If not removed, fuel residue may ignite when the engine is returned to operation. Failure to follow this instruction may result in serious personal injury.

CAUTION

Do not carry personal electronic devices such as cell phones, pagers or audio equipment of any type when working on or near any fuel-related component. Highly flammable mixtures are always present and may be ignited. Failure to follow these instructions may result in serious personal injury.

CAUTION

Always disconnect the battery ground cable at the battery when working on a fuel-related component. Highly flammable mixtures are always present and may be ignited. Failure to follow these instructions may result in serious personal injury.

➡The fuel injectors are serviced with the fuel rail.

1. Before servicing the vehicle, refer to the Precautions Section.
2. Release the fuel system pressure. Refer to Relieving Fuel System Pressure.
3. Disconnect the battery ground cable. For additional information, refer to Battery, removal & installation.
4. Disconnect the fuel tube-to-fuel rail quick connect coupling.
5. Disconnect the 4 fuel injector electrical connectors.
6. Remove the 2 bolts and the fuel rail and injectors.
7. Remove the fuel injector retaining clips and the fuel injectors. Remove and discard the O-ring seals.

To install:

➡Use O-ring seals that are made of special fuel resistant material. Use of ordinary O-rings can cause the fuel system to leak. Do not reuse the O-ring seals.

8. Install new O-ring seals and lubricate them with clean engine oil.
9. To install, reverse the removal procedure.
   - Tighten the fuel rail bolts to 18 ft. lbs. (25 Nm).

FUEL PUMP MODULE

REMOVAL & INSTALLATION

See Figure 134.

CAUTION

Do not smoke, carry lighted tobacco or have an open flame of any type when working on or near any fuel-related component. Highly flammable mixtures are always present and may be ignited. Failure to follow these instructions may result in serious personal injury.

CAUTION

Before working on or disconnecting any of the fuel tubes or fuel system components, relieve the fuel system pressure to prevent accidental spraying of fuel. Fuel in the fuel system remains under high pressure, even when the engine is not running. Failure to follow this instruction may result in serious personal injury.

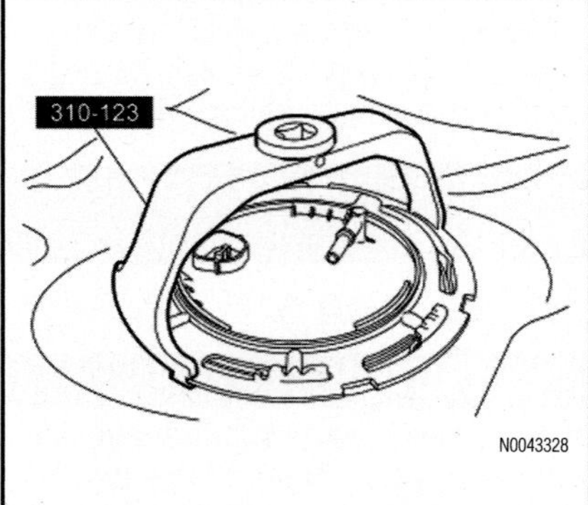

N0043328

Fig. 134 Special tool, lock ring wrench, shown installed

⁂ CAUTION

Clean all fuel residue from the engine compartment. If not removed, fuel residue may ignite when the engine is returned to operation. Failure to follow this instruction may result in serious personal injury.

⁂ CAUTION

Do not carry personal electronic devices such as cell phones, pagers or audio equipment of any type when working on or near any fuel-related component. Highly flammable mixtures are always present and may be ignited. Failure to follow these instructions may result in serious personal injury.

⁂ CAUTION

Always disconnect the battery ground cable at the battery when working on a fuel-related component. Highly flammable mixtures are always present and may be ignited. Failure to follow these instructions may result in serious personal injury.

1. Before servicing the vehicle, refer to the Precautions Section.
2. Remove the fuel tank. Refer to Fuel Tank, removal & installation.

➡Clean the Fuel Pump (FP) module connections, couplings, flange surfaces and the immediate surrounding area of any dirt or foreign material.

3. Disconnect the fuel supply tube-to-FP module quick connect coupling.

⁂ WARNING

Carefully install the lock ring wrench to avoid damaging the FP module when removing the lock ring.

4. Using the lock ring wrench, rotate the lock ring counterclockwise and remove the FP module lock ring.

⁂ WARNING

The FP module must be handled carefully to avoid damage to the float arm.

➡The FP module will have residual fuel remaining internally, drain into a suitable container.

5. Remove the FP module from the fuel tank.
6. Remove and discard the FP module O-ring seal.

To install:

7. Inspect the mating surfaces of the FP module flange and the fuel tank O-ring seal contact surfaces. Do not polish or adjust the O-ring seal contact area of the fuel tank flange or the fuel tank. Install a new FP module or fuel tank if the O-ring seal contact area is bent, scratched or corroded.
8. Apply clean engine oil to the new O-ring seal.
9. To install, reverse the removal procedure.
   - Lubricate the fuel tube quick connect coupling with clean engine oil. Align the fuel tube and the quick connect coupling and press together until an audible click is heard and then pull on the fittings to make sure they are fully engaged
   - Start the engine and check for leaks

FUEL TANK

DRAINING

⁂ CAUTION

Do not smoke, carry lighted tobacco or have an open flame of any type when working on or near any fuel-related component. Highly flammable mixtures are always present and may be ignited. Failure to follow these instructions may result in serious personal injury.

⁂ CAUTION

Before working on or disconnecting any of the fuel tubes or fuel system components, relieve the fuel system pressure to prevent accidental spraying of fuel. Fuel in the fuel system remains under high pressure, even when the engine is not running. Failure to follow this instruction may result in serious personal injury.

⁂ CAUTION

Clean all fuel residue from the engine compartment. If not removed, fuel residue may ignite when the engine is returned to operation. Failure to follow this instruction may result in serious personal injury.

⁂ CAUTION

Do not carry personal electronic devices such as cell phones, pagers or audio equipment of any type when working on or near any fuel-related component. Highly flammable mixtures are always present and may be ignited. Failure to follow these instructions may result in serious personal injury.

⁂ CAUTION

Always disconnect the battery ground cable at the battery when working on a fuel-related component. Highly flammable mixtures are always present and may be ignited. Failure to follow these instructions may result in serious personal injury.

⁂ CAUTION

Remove the fuel filler cap slowly. The fuel system may be under pressure. If the fuel filler cap is venting vapor or if you hear a hissing sound, wait until it stops before completely removing the fuel filler cap. Otherwise, fuel may spray out. Failure to follow these instructions may result in serious personal injury.

1. Before servicing the vehicle, refer to the Precautions Section.
2. Disconnect the battery ground cable. For additional information, refer to Battery, removal & installation.
3. Carefully turn the fuel tank filler cap counterclockwise approximately 1/4 turn until the threads disengage and position aside.

➡The safety valve is located at the inlet of the fuel tank.

4. Insert a suitable drain tube into the fuel tank filler pipe until it enters the fuel tank inlet, opening the safety valve.
5. Attach the special tool, Fuel Storage Tanker, to the drain tube and remove as much fuel as possible from the fuel tank.

REMOVAL & INSTALLATION

See Figure 135.

1. Before servicing the vehicle, refer to the Precautions Section.
2. With the vehicle in NEUTRAL, position it on a hoist.
3. Release the fuel system pressure. Refer to Relieving Fuel System Pressure.
4. Disconnect the battery ground cable.

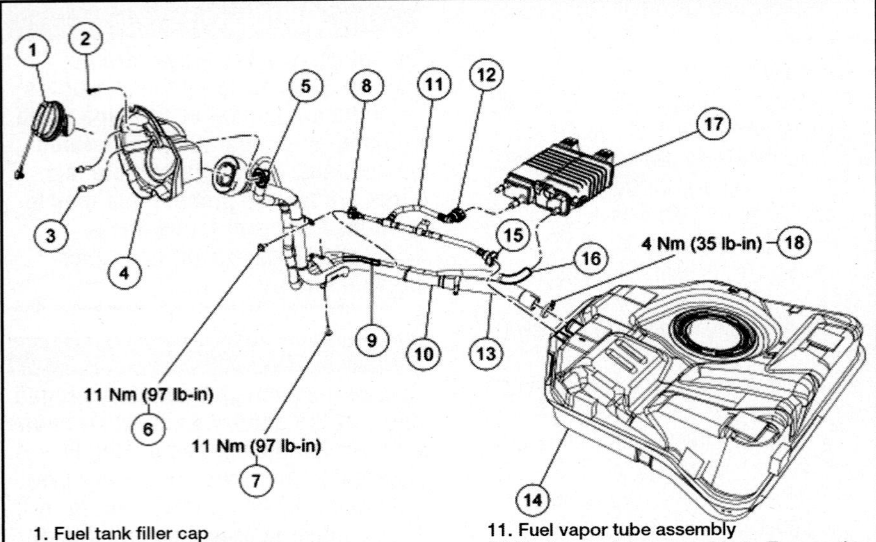

Fig. 135 Fuel tank and filler pipe—exploded view

For additional information, refer to Battery, removal & installation.

5. Drain the fuel tank. Refer to Fuel Tank, removal & installation.
6. Clean the Fuel Pump (FP) module connections, couplings, flange surface and the immediate surrounding area of any dirt or foreign material.
7. Disconnect the FP module electrical connector.
8. Remove the 2 nuts and position the fuel tank heat shield aside.
9. Index-mark the fuel tank filler pipe hose clamp for correct installation.

➡Some residual fuel may remain in the fuel tank filler pipe after draining the fuel tank. Carefully drain any remaining fuel into a suitable container.

10. Release the clamp and remove the fuel tank filler pipe hose from the fuel tank.
11. Disconnect the fuel vapor tube assembly-to-fuel tank quick connect coupling.
12. Disconnect the fuel supply tube-to-fuel tube quick connect coupling.
13. Install a suitable lifting device under the fuel tank.
14. Remove the bolt and the fuel tank straps.
15. Partially lower the RH side of the fuel tank, allowing it to clear the heat shield, then lower completely and remove.

To install:

16. To install, reverse the removal procedure and note the following:
    - Tighten the fuel tank filler pipe hose clamp to 35 inch lbs. (4 Nm).
    - Tighten the fuel tank strap bolts to 18 ft. lbs. (25 Nm).
    - Pressurize the fuel system and check for leakage.

IDLE SPEED

ADJUSTMENT

The idle speed is controlled by the Powertrain Control Module (PCM).

THROTTLE BODY

REMOVAL & INSTALLATION

See Figures 136 and 137.

1. Before servicing the vehicle, refer to the Precautions Section.
2. Remove the Air Cleaner (ACL) outlet pipe. For additional information, refer to Air Cleaner, removal & installation.

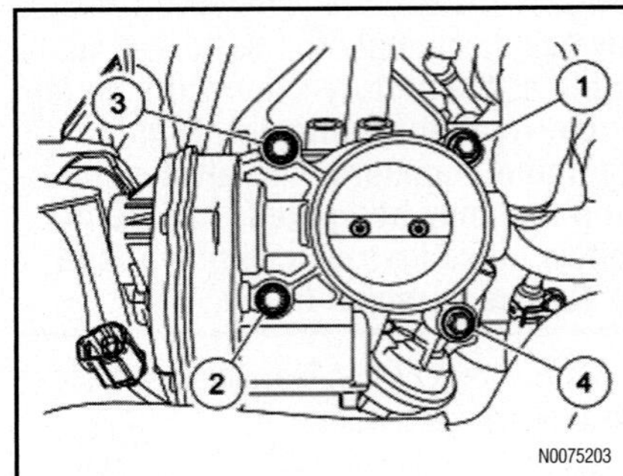

Fig. 136 Throttle body bolt tightening sequence

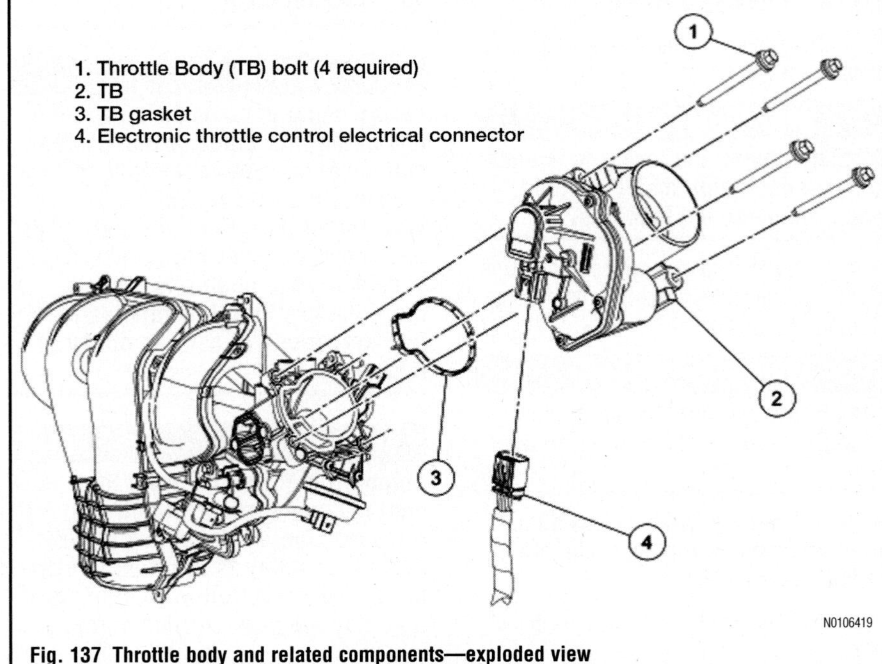

Fig. 137 Throttle body and related components—exploded view

3. Disconnect the electronic throttle control electrical connector.

4. Remove the 4 bolts and the Throttle Body (TB).

To install:

5. To install, reverse the removal procedure and note the following:

- Inspect the TB gasket and install new as necessary.
- Tighten the throttle body retaining bolts in sequence to 89 inch lbs. (10 Nm).

HEATING & AIR CONDITIONING SYSTEM

BLOWER MOTOR

REMOVAL & INSTALLATION

See Figure 138.

1. Before servicing the vehicle, refer to the Precautions Section.
2. Disconnect the blower motor electrical connector and detach the wire harness from the blower motor.
3. Remove the 3 blower motor screws.
4. Remove the blower motor.
5. To install, reverse the removal procedure.

HEATER CORE

REMOVAL & INSTALLATION

See Figures 139 and 140.

➡If a heater core leak is suspected, the heater core should be leak tested before it is removed from the vehicle.

➡It is not necessary to install new heater core inlet and outlet tubes when installing a new heater core unless there is evidence of damage to the heater core tubes. The new O-ring seals supplied with the heater core service kit must be installed any time the heater core tubes are detached from the heater core.

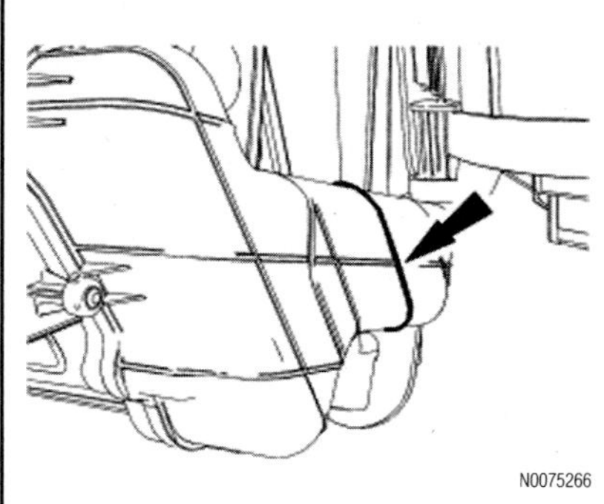

Fig. 139 Cut the heater core tube cover along the rib as shown

1. Before servicing the vehicle, refer to the Precautions Section.
2. Drain the engine coolant. For additional information, refer to Engine Coolant, Drain & Refill Procedure.
3. Remove the 3 glove compartment screws and the glove compartment.
4. Using a suitable utility knife, carefully cut the heater core tube cover along the rib.
5. Detach the climate control wire harness connector from the heater core tube cover.
6. Remove the 2 heater core tube cover screws.
7. Remove the cut portion of the heater core tube cover.

➡Before disconnecting the heater core tube connections, position a suitable drain pan to catch any residual coolant that may drain from the heater core or heater core tubes when disconnected.

8. Remove the 2 heater core tube connection clips and disconnect the 2 heater core tubes from the heater core. Discard the O-ring seals.
9. Detach and remove the heater core access door.

➡The heater core must be carefully manipulated to clear the blower motor housing while being removed.

10. Remove the heater core.

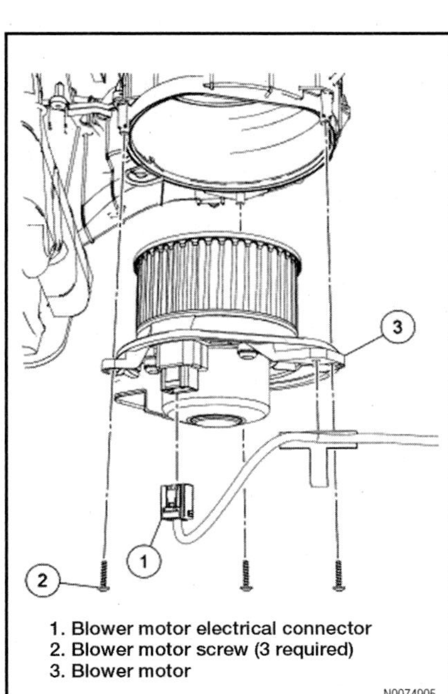

Fig. 138 Blower motor removal

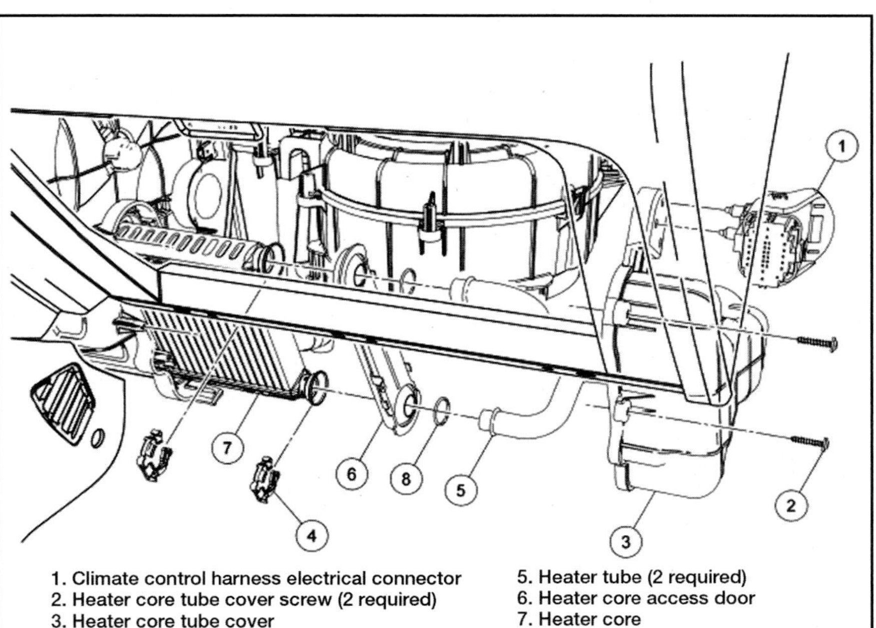

Fig. 140 Heater core removal

To install:

11. To install, reverse the removal procedure and note the following:
    - Be sure that the new O-rings are installed, and the heater core tubes are fully seated into the heater core before installing the heater core tube connection clips.
    - Apply a suitable black duct-type tape over the cut in the heater core tube cover.
    - Tighten the 3 glove compartment screws to 89 inch lbs. (10 Nm).
    - Fill and bleed the engine cooling system. Refer to Engine Coolant, Drain & Refill Procedure.
    - Run the engine and check for coolant leakage.

STEERING

POWER STEERING GEAR

REMOVAL & INSTALLATION

See Figures 141 through 143.

➡Steering fasteners are critical parts because they affect performance of vital components and systems and their failure may result in major service expense. New parts must be installed with the same part numbers or equivalent part, if replacement is necessary. Do not use a replacement part of lesser quality or substitute design. Torque values must be used as specified during reassembly for correct retention of these parts.

⁂ WARNING

While repairing the power steering system, care should be taken to prevent the entry of foreign material or failure of the power steering components may result.

1. Before servicing the vehicle, refer to the Precautions Section.
2. Using a suitable holding device, hold the steering wheel in the straight-ahead position.

⁂ WARNING

Do not allow the steering column to rotate while the steering column shaft is disconnected or damage to the clockspring may result. If there is evidence that the steering column has rotated, the clockspring must be removed and re-centered. For additional information, refer to Clockspring Centering.

3. Remove the upper steering column shaft-to-lower steering column shaft bolt. Discard the bolt.
4. Remove the wheels and tires.

➡Leave the outer tie-rod end nuts in place to protect the ball studs from damage.

5. Using the hex-holding feature to prevent turning of the stud while loosening the nut, loosen the 2 outer tie-rod end nuts.

➡Protect the ball joint seal to prevent damage.

6. Using the Tie-Rod End Remover, separate the outer tie-rod ends from the wheel knuckles.
7. Remove and discard the outer tie-rod end nuts.
8. Using the hex-holding feature to prevent turning of the stud while removing the nut, remove the 2 stabilizer bar link upper nuts.
9. Disconnect the stabilizer bar links from the struts. Discard the nuts.
10. Remove the engine support insulator-to-transaxle bracket bolt.
11. Remove the steering line-to-steering gear retainer bolt and the retainer.
12. Remove the bolt, rotate the steering line clamp plate and disconnect the pressure and return lines from the steering gear. Discard the O-ring seals.
13. Using a suitable jack, support the subframe.
14. Remove the 2 upper and 4 lower subframe bolts.

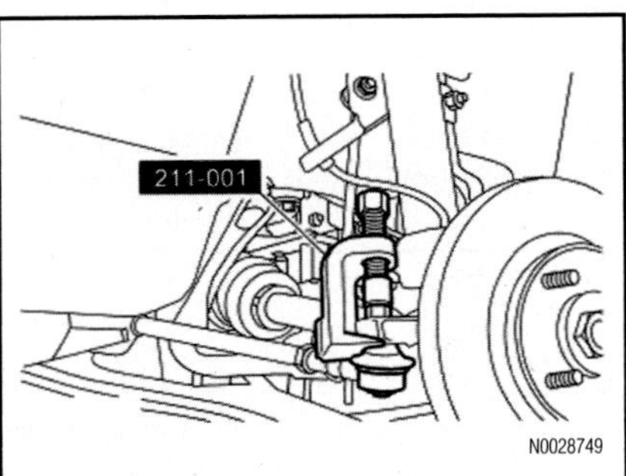

Fig. 141 Using the Tie-Rod End Remover, separate the outer tie-rod ends from the wheel knuckles

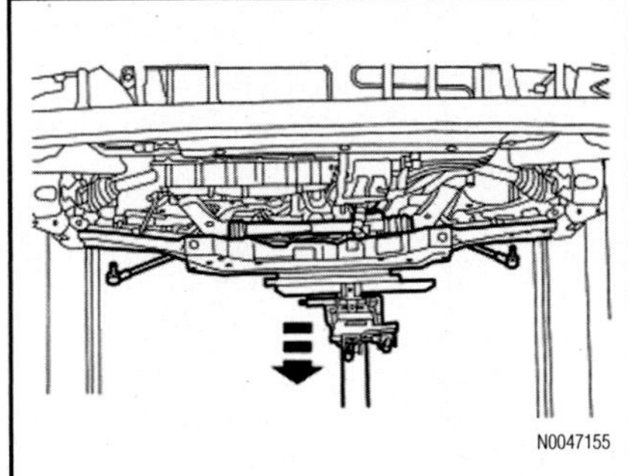

Fig. 142 Using a suitable jack, support and lower the subframe

➡It is not necessary to separate the lower ball joints from the wheel knuckle when lowering the subframe.

15. Lower the subframe.
16. Pull out on the dash seal tabs and push the dash seal upward to detach it from the steering gear. Position the dash seal aside.
17. Remove the bolt and disconnect the lower steering column shaft from the steering gear. Discard the bolt.
18. Remove the 2 steering gear bolts and the steering gear. Discard the bolts.

To install:

➡New O-ring seals must be installed any time the pressure and return lines are disconnected from the steering gear or a fluid leak may occur.

19. Install new O-ring seals on the pressure and return lines.
20. Position the steering gear and install 2 new steering gear bolts. Tighten to 47 ft. lbs. (63 Nm).

⁂ CAUTION

Install a new steering column shaft bolt. Reuse could result in bolt failure and loss of vehicle control. Failure to follow this instruction may result in serious injury to vehicle occupant(s).

21. Connect the lower steering column shaft to the steering gear and install the new bolt. Tighten to 21 ft. lbs. (28 Nm).
22. Center the dash seal on the steering gear and pull down to attach it to the steering gear.

⁂ WARNING

While tightening the subframe bolts, make sure the front subframe does not move. Misalignment of the sub-

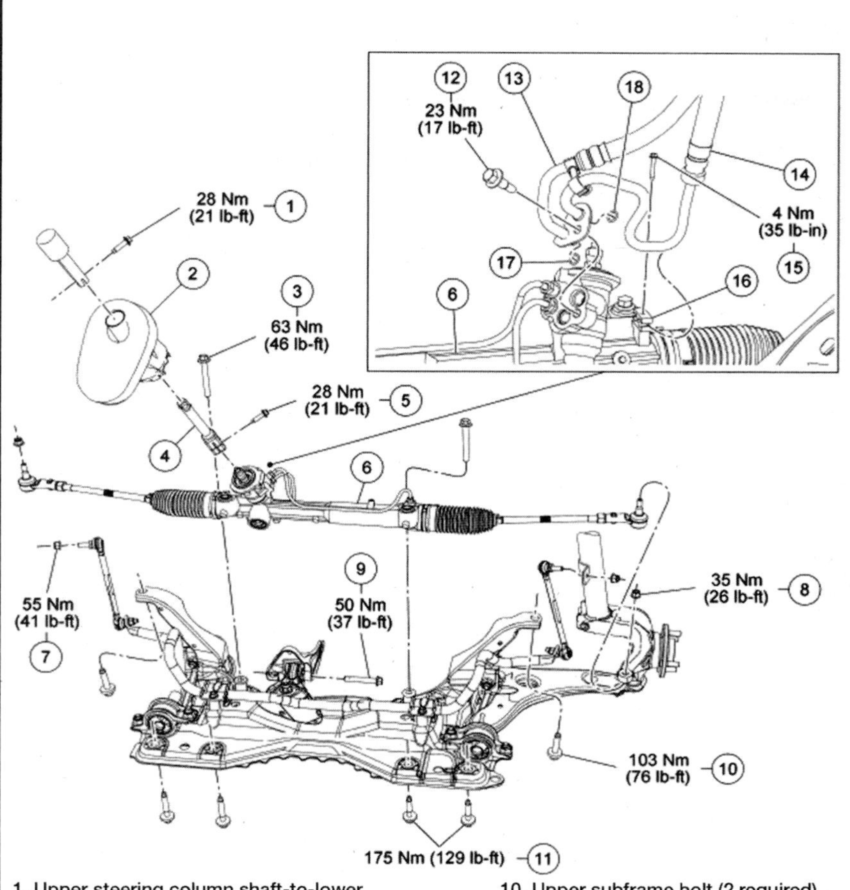

1. Upper steering column shaft-to-lower steering column shaft bolt
2. Dash seal
3. Steering gear bolt (2 required)
4. Lower steering column shaft
5. Lower steering column shaft-to-steering gear bolt
6. Steering gear
7. Stabilizer bar link upper nut (2 required)
8. Outer tie-rod end nut
9. Transaxle roll restrictor bolt
10. Upper subframe bolt (2 required)
11. Lower subframe bolts (4 required)
12. Steering line clamp plate bolt
13. Return line
14. Pressure line
15. Steering line-to-steering gear bolt
16. Steering line-to-steering gear retainer
17. O-ring seal
18. O-ring seal

N0093697

Fig. 143 Steering gear and related components—exploded view

frame during bolt installation may damage the bolts and/or subframe.

23. Using a suitable jack, raise the front subframe and loosely install the 2 upper and 4 lower subframe bolts.
    a. Tighten the 4 lower subframe bolts to 129 ft. lbs. (175 Nm).
    b. Tighten the 2 upper subframe bolts to 76 ft. lbs. (103 Nm).
24. Install the pressure and return lines to the power steering gear, rotate the steering line clamp plate and install the bolt. Tighten to 17 ft. lbs. (23 Nm).
25. Position the steering line retainer and install the steering line-to-steering gear bolt. Tighten to 35 inch lbs. (4 Nm).
26. Install the transaxle roll restrictor bolt. Tighten to 37 ft. lbs. (50 Nm).
27. Connect the stabilizer bar links to the struts and install 2 new nuts. Tighten to 41 ft. lbs. (55 Nm).

CAUTION

Do not reuse a tie rod-to-wheel knuckle nut. This can result in nut failure and loss of steering control. Failure to follow this instruction may result in serious injury to vehicle occupant(s).

28. Install 2 new outer tie-rod end nuts. Tighten to 26 ft. lbs. (35 Nm).
29. Install the wheel and tire assemblies. Tighten the wheel nuts in a star pattern to 100 ft. lbs. (135 Nm).

CAUTION

Install a new steering column shaft bolt. Reuse could result in bolt failure and loss of vehicle control. Failure to follow this instruction may result in serious injury to vehicle occupant(s).

30. Connect the upper steering column shaft to the lower steering column shaft and install the new bolt. Tighten to 21 ft. lbs. (28 Nm).
31. Fill the power steering system with the proper type and amount of fluid.
32. Check and, if necessary, adjust the front toe.

POWER STEERING PUMP

REMOVAL & INSTALLATION

See Figures 144 through 146.

WARNING

While repairing the power steering system, care should be taken to prevent the entry of foreign material or failure of the power steering components may occur.

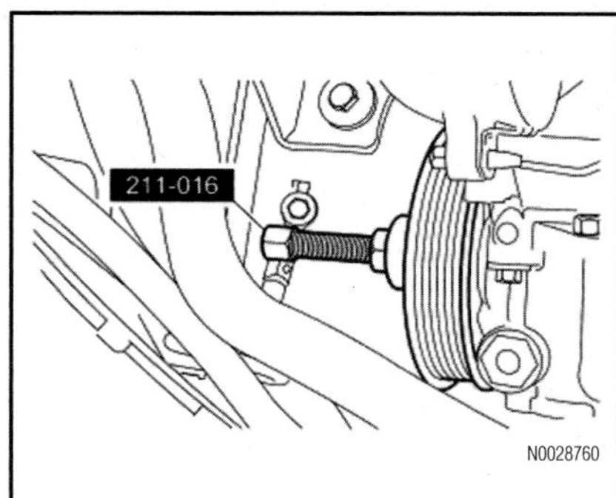

Fig. 144 Using the Power Steering Pump Pulley Remover

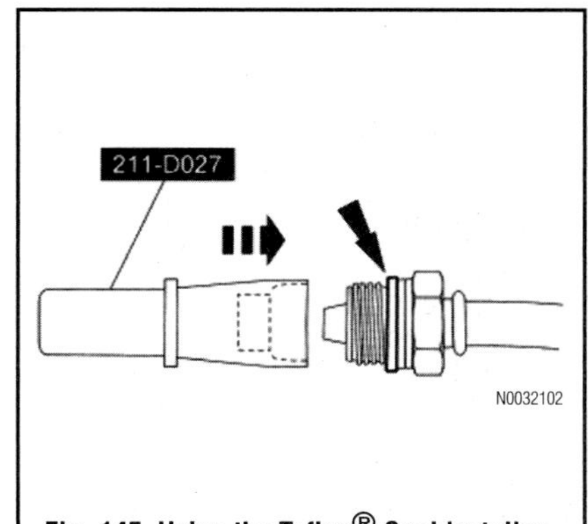

Fig. 145 Using the Teflon® Seal Installer Set

⁂ WARNING

Do not allow power steering fluid to contact the accessory drive belt or damage to the belt may occur.

1. Before servicing the vehicle, refer to the Precautions Section.
2. With a suitable suction device, remove the power steering fluid from the fluid reservoir.
3. With the vehicle in NEUTRAL, position it on a hoist.
4. Remove the 2 bolts and the accessory drive belt splash shield.
5. Rotate the accessory drive belt tensioner clockwise and position the accessory drive belt away from the power steering pump pulley.
6. Remove the 2 engine coolant expansion tank bolts, carefully pull the reservoir up and off the locating pin and position it aside.
7. Using the Power Steering Pump Pulley Remover, remove the power steering pump pulley.
8. Disconnect the pressure line fitting from the power steering pump. Position the pressure line aside.
9. Release the clamp and disconnect the return hose from the power steering pump.
10. Remove the 4 bolts and the power steering pump and fluid reservoir.
11. Remove the Teflon® seal from the power steering pressure line fitting. Discard the Teflon® seal.

➡Use a slight twisting motion when removing the reservoir and carefully pull it away from the pump on the same axis as the reservoir outlet tube to avoid damaging the reservoir.

➡Whenever the fluid reservoir is separated from the pump, new O-ring

seal(s) must be installed or a fluid leak may occur.

12. If necessary, remove the power steering fluid reservoir from the power steering pump and discard the O-ring seal(s).

To install:

13. Using the Teflon® Seal Installer Set, install a new Teflon® seal on the pressure line fitting.
14. If removed, install the power steering fluid reservoir with a new O-ring seal.
15. Install the 4 bolts and the power steering pump and fluid reservoir. Tighten to 18 ft. lbs. (25 Nm).
16. Connect the return hose and install the clamp to the power steering pump.
17. Connect the pressure line fitting to the power steering pump. Tighten to 55 ft. lbs. (75 Nm).

➡Make sure the pulley is flush with the end of the power steering pump shaft.

18. Using the Power Steering Pump Pulley Installer, install the power steering pump pulley.
19. Position the engine coolant reservoir onto the locating pin and install the 2 bolts. Tighten to 35 inch lbs. (4 Nm).
20. Rotate the tensioner clockwise and position the accessory drive belt on the power steering pump pulley.
21. Position the accessory drive belt splash shield and install the 2 bolts. Tighten to 80 inch lbs. (9 Nm).
22. Fill and bleed the power steering system with the proper type and amount of fluid. Refer to Power Steering Pump, Bleeding and Fluid Fill Procedure.

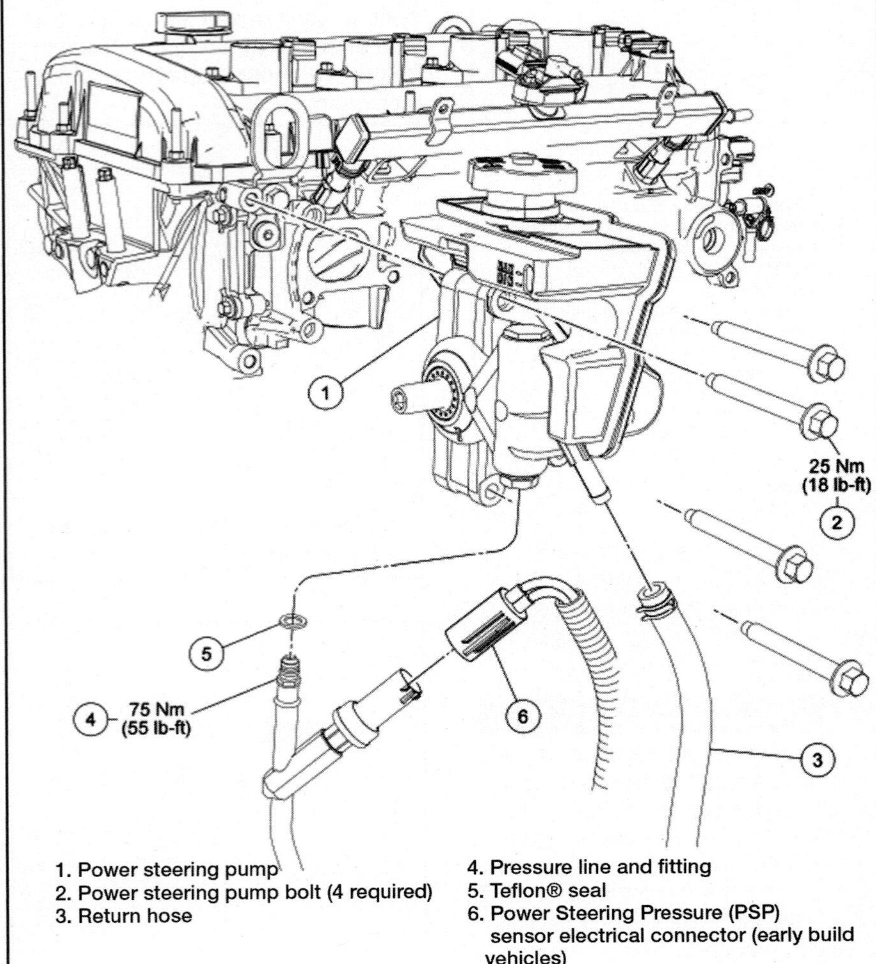

Fig. 146 View of power steering pump and related components

BLEEDING

See Figure 147.

⁂ WARNING

If the air is not purged from the power steering system correctly, premature power steering pump failure may result. The condition may occur on pre-delivery vehicles with evidence of aerated fluid or on vehicles that have had steering component repairs.

➡A whine heard from the power steering pump can be caused by air in the system. The power steering purge procedure must be carried out prior to any component repair for which power steering noise complaints are accompanied by evidence of aerated fluid.

1. Before servicing the vehicle, refer to the Precautions Section.

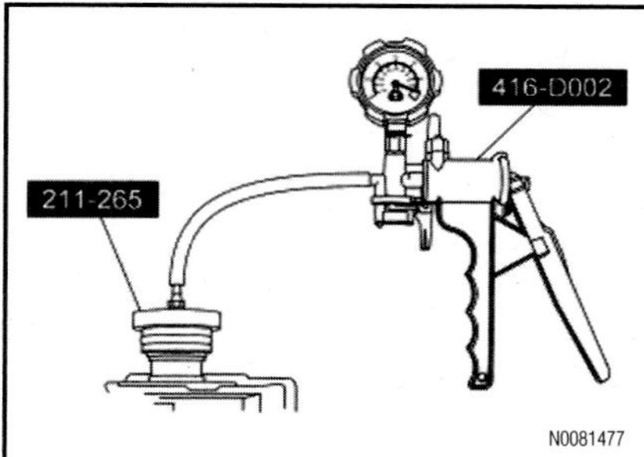

Fig. 147 Power Steering Evacuation Cap and Vacuum Pump Kit installed to vehicle

2. Remove the power steering reservoir cap. Check the fluid.
3. Raise the front wheels off the floor.
4. Tightly insert the Power Steering Evacuation Cap into the reservoir and connect the Vacuum Pump Kit.
5. Start the engine.
6. Using the Vacuum Pump Kit, apply vacuum and maintain the maximum vacuum of 20–25 inches Hg (68–85 kPa).
7. If the Vacuum Pump Kit does not maintain vacuum, check the power steering system for leaks before proceeding.
8. If equipped with Hydro-Boost®, apply the brake pedal 4 times.

WARNING

Do not hold the steering wheel against the stops for an extended amount of time. Damage to the power steering pump may occur.

9. Cycle the steering wheel fully from stop-to-stop 10 times.
10. Stop the engine.
11. Release the vacuum and remove the Vacuum Pump Kit and the Power Steering Evacuation Cap.

➡Do not overfill the reservoir.

12. Fill the reservoir as needed with the specified fluid.
13. Repeat steps 5–12
14. Install the reservoir cap.
15. Visually inspect the power steering system for leaks.

FLUID FILL PROCEDURE

See Figure 148.

WARNING

If the air is not purged from the power steering system correctly, premature power steering pump failure may result. The condition can occur on pre-delivery vehicles with evidence of aerated fluid or on vehicles that have had steering component repairs.

1. Before servicing the vehicle, refer to the Precautions Section.
2. Remove the power steering fluid reservoir cap.
3. Install the Power Steering Evacuation Cap, Power Steering Fill Adapter Manifold, and Vacuum Pump Kit.

➡The Power Steering Fill Adapter Manifold control valves are in the OPEN position when the points of the handles face the center of the Power Steering Fill Adapter Manifold.

Close the Power Steering Fill Adapter Manifold control valve (fluid side).

4. Open the Power Steering Fill Adapter Manifold control valve (vacuum side).
5. Using the Vacuum Pump Kit, apply 20–25 inches Hg (68–85 kPa) of vacuum to the power steering system.
6. Observe the Vacuum Pump Kit gauge for 30 seconds.
7. If the Vacuum Pump Kit gauge reading drops more than 0.88 inch Hg (3 kPa), correct any leaks in the power steering system or the Power Steering Evacuation Cap, Power Steering Fill Adapter Manifold, and Vacuum Pump Kit before proceeding.

➡The Vacuum Pump Kit gauge reading will drop slightly during this next step.

8. Slowly open the Power Steering Fill Adapter Manifold control valve (fluid side) until power steering fluid completely fills the hose and then close the control valve.
9. Using the Vacuum Pump Kit, apply 20–25 inches Hg (68–85 kPa) of vacuum to the power steering system.
10. Close the Power Steering Fill Adapter Manifold control valve (vacuum side).
11. Slowly open the Power Steering Fill Adapter Manifold control valve (fluid side).
12. Once power steering fluid enters the fluid reservoir and reaches the minimum fluid level indicator line on the reservoir, close the Power Steering Fill Adapter Manifold control valve (fluid side).
13. Remove the Power Steering Evacuation Cap, Power Steering Fill Adapter Manifold, and Vacuum Pump Kit.
14. Install the reservoir cap.

WARNING

Do not hold the steering wheel against the stops for an extended amount of time. Damage to the power steering pump may occur.

➡There will be a slight drop in the power steering fluid level in the reservoir when the engine is started.

15. Start the engine and turn the steering wheel from stop-to-stop.
16. Turn the ignition switch to the OFF position.

➡Do not overfill the reservoir.

17. Remove the reservoir cap and fill the reservoir with the specified fluid.
18. Install the reservoir cap.

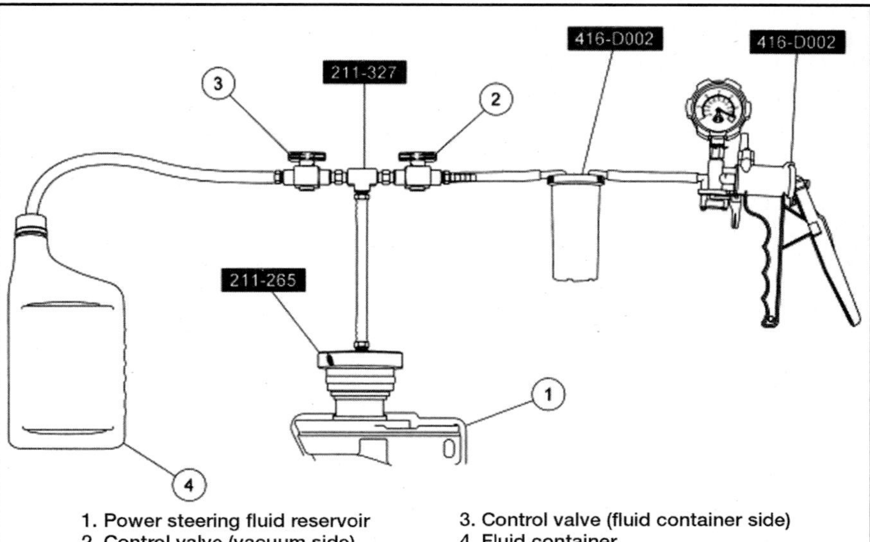

Fig. 148 Install the Power Steering Evacuation Cap, Power Steering Fill Adapter Manifold, and Vacuum Pump Kit

CONTROL LINKS

REMOVAL & INSTALLATION

⁂ WARNING

Suspension fasteners are critical parts because they affect performance of vital components and systems and their failure may result in major service expense. New parts must be installed with the same part numbers or equivalent part, if replacement is necessary. Do not use a replacement part of lesser quality or substitute design. Torque values must be used as specified during reassembly to make sure correct retention of these parts.

⁂ WARNING

Do not use power tools to remove or install the stabilizer bar link nuts or damage to the stabilizer bar link ball joints or boots may occur.

⁂ WARNING

Do not hold the stabilizer bar link boot with any tool or damage to the boot may occur.

⁂ WARNING

Use the internal or external hex-holding feature to prevent the ball and stud from turning while removing or installing the stabilizer bar link nuts. The link boot seal must not be allowed to twist while tightening the link nuts or damage to the boot seal will occur.

➡The stabilizer bar links are designed with low friction ball joints that have a low breakaway torque.

1. Before servicing the vehicle, refer to the Precautions Section.
2. Remove the wheel and tire assembly.
3. Remove and discard the stabilizer bar link lower nuts and detach the stabilizer bar links from the stabilizer bar.

To install:

4. Attach the stabilizer bar links to the stabilizer bar and install the new nuts. Tighten to 47 ft. lbs. (63 Nm).
5. Install the wheel and tire assembly. Tighten the wheel nuts in a star pattern to 100 ft. lbs. (135 Nm).

LOWER BALL JOINT

REMOVAL & INSTALLATION

The lower ball joint is integral to the lower control arm. Refer to Lower Control Arm, removal & installation.

LOWER CONTROL ARM

REMOVAL AND & INSTALLATION

See Figure 149.

⁂ WARNING

Suspension fasteners are critical parts because they affect performance of vital components and systems and their failure may result in major service expense. New parts must be installed with the same part numbers or equivalent part, if replacement is necessary. Do not use a replacement part of lesser quality or substitute design. Torque values must be used as specified during reassembly to make sure correct retention of these parts.

1. Before servicing the vehicle, refer to the Precautions Section.
2. Remove the wheel and tire.

⁂ WARNING

Do not use a prying device or separator fork between the ball joint and the wheel knuckle. Damage to the ball joint or ball joint seal may result. Only use the pry bar by inserting it into the lower control arm body opening.

⁂ WARNING

Use care when releasing the lower arm and wheel knuckle into the resting position or damage to the ball joint seal may occur.

3. Remove and discard the ball joint nut and bolt. Insert a pry bar in the lower arm body opening, separate the lower arm from the wheel knuckle and remove the ball joint heat shield.
4. Remove the lower arm bushing bracket nuts, bolts and the bracket. Discard the nuts and bolts.

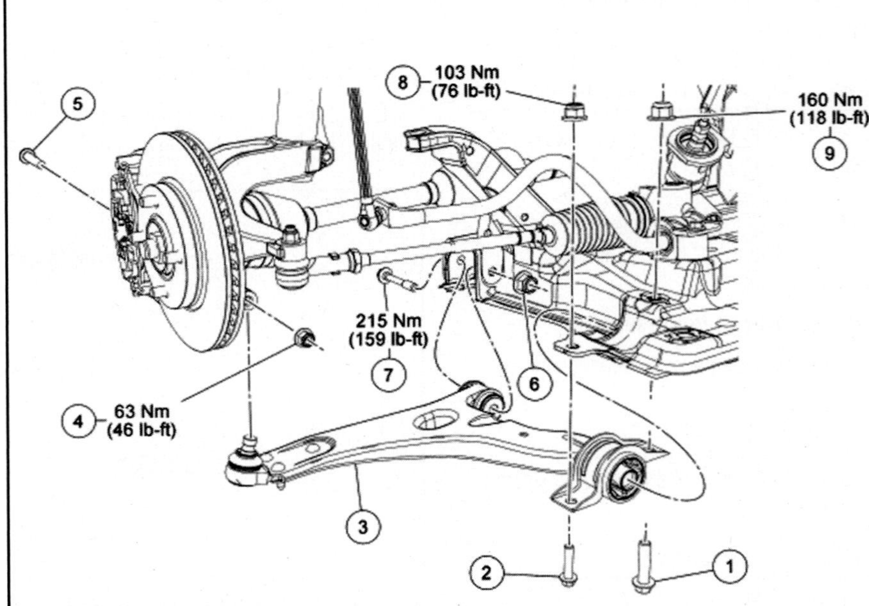

Fig. 149 Lower control arm and related components—exploded view

5. Remove and discard the lower arm forward nut and bolt and remove the lower arm.

To install:

WARNING

To prevent incorrect clamp load or component damage, install the fasteners in their original orientation. Install the lower arm bushing clamp bolts with their heads facing down.

➡Do not tighten the nuts and bolts at this time.

6. Position the lower arm and loosely install the new forward nut and bolt and the 2 new bracket nuts and bolts.
7. Make sure the ball joint heat shield is installed on the ball joint stud or damage to the ball joint may occur.
8. Insert the ball joint stud into the wheel knuckle and install the new ball joint bolt and nut. Tighten to 47 ft. lbs. (63 Nm).
9. Install the wheel and tire assemblies. Tighten the wheel nuts in a star pattern to 100 ft. lbs. (135 Nm).
10. Lower the hoist so the weight of the vehicle is resting on the wheels and tires.
11. Tighten the lower arm forward bolt to 159 ft. lbs. (215 Nm).
12. Tighten the lower arm inboard bracket nut to 118 ft. lbs. (160 Nm).
13. Tighten the lower arm outboard bracket nut to 76 ft. lbs. (103 Nm).
14. Check and, if necessary, align the front end.

STABILIZER BAR

REMOVAL & INSTALLATION

See Figures 150 through 154.

WARNING

Suspension fasteners are critical parts because they affect performance of vital components and systems and their failure may result in major service expense. New parts must be installed with the same part numbers or equivalent part, if replacement is necessary. Do not use a replacement part of lesser quality or substitute design. Torque values must be used as specified during reassembly to make sure correct retention of these parts.

WARNING

Do not use power tools to remove or install the stabilizer bar link nuts or damage to the stabilizer bar link ball joints or boots may occur.

WARNING

Do not hold the stabilizer bar link boot with any tool or damage to the boot may occur.

WARNING

Use the internal or external hex-holding feature to prevent the ball and stud from turning while removing or installing the stabilizer bar link nuts. The link boot seal must not be allowed to twist while tightening the link nuts or damage to the boot seal will occur.

➡The stabilizer bar links are designed with low friction ball joints that have a low breakaway torque.

1. Before servicing the vehicle, refer to the Precautions Section.
2. Remove the wheel and tire.
3. Loosen the tie-rod end nuts.
4. Using the Tie-Rod End Remover, detach the tie-rod ends from the wheel knuckles. Discard the tie-rod end nuts.

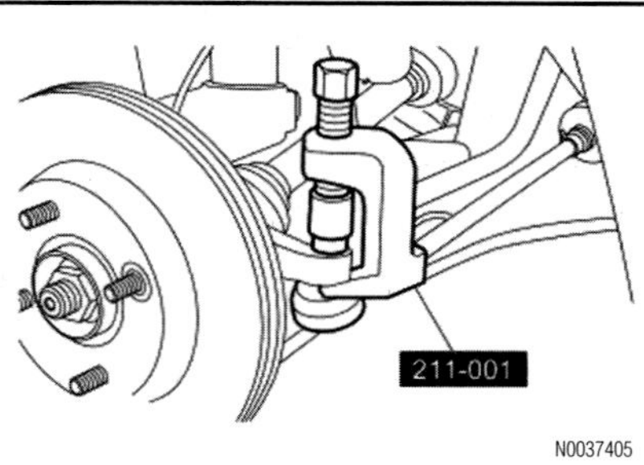

Fig. 150 Using the Tie-Rod End Remover, detach the tie-rod ends from the wheel knuckle

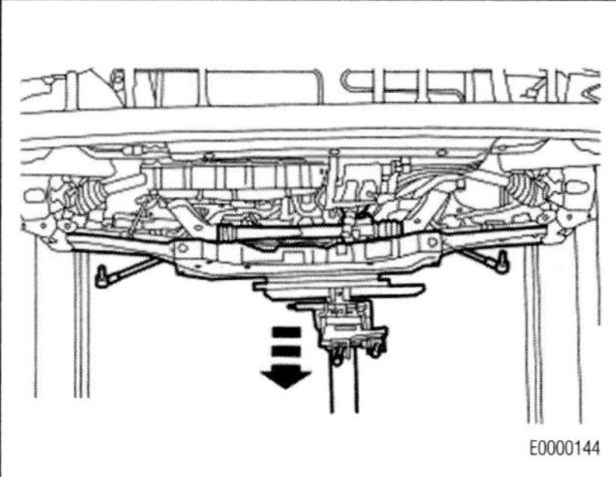

Fig. 151 Using a suitable transmission jack, support and then lower the subframe

5. Remove and discard the stabilizer bar link lower nuts and detach the stabilizer bar links from the stabilizer bar.
6. Using a suitable transmission jack, support the subframe.
7. Index-mark the subframe position.
8. Remove the 4 subframe front bolts and 2 subframe rear bolts.

WARNING

The power steering lines are attached to the steering gear. Failure to use caution when lowering the subframe may result in steering line damage.

9. Lower the subframe to gain access to the stabilizer bar.
10. Remove the stabilizer bar bracket bolts and brackets. Discard the bolts.
11. Remove the stabilizer bar bushings.
12. Remove the stabilizer bar.

To install:

13. Install the stabilizer bar into position.

WARNING

The stabilizer bar bushings must be positioned correctly on the flats of the stabilizer bar or damage to the bushings may occur.

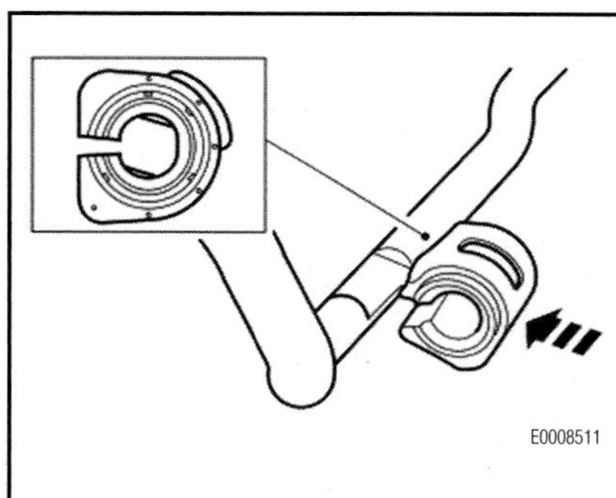

Fig. 152 Install the stabilizer bar bushings as shown

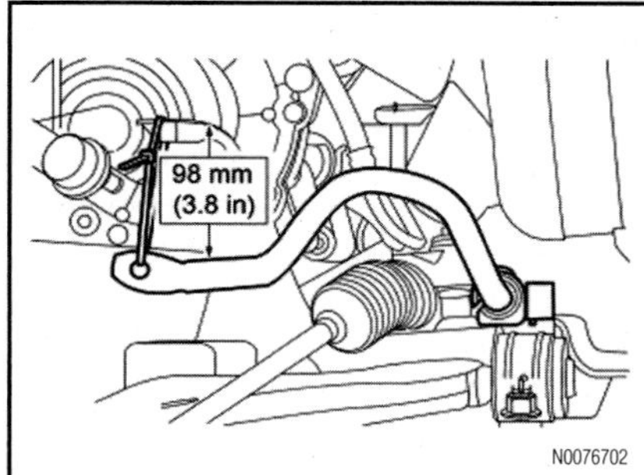

Fig. 153 Position the stabilizer bar and set it to the specification shown using mechanic's wire

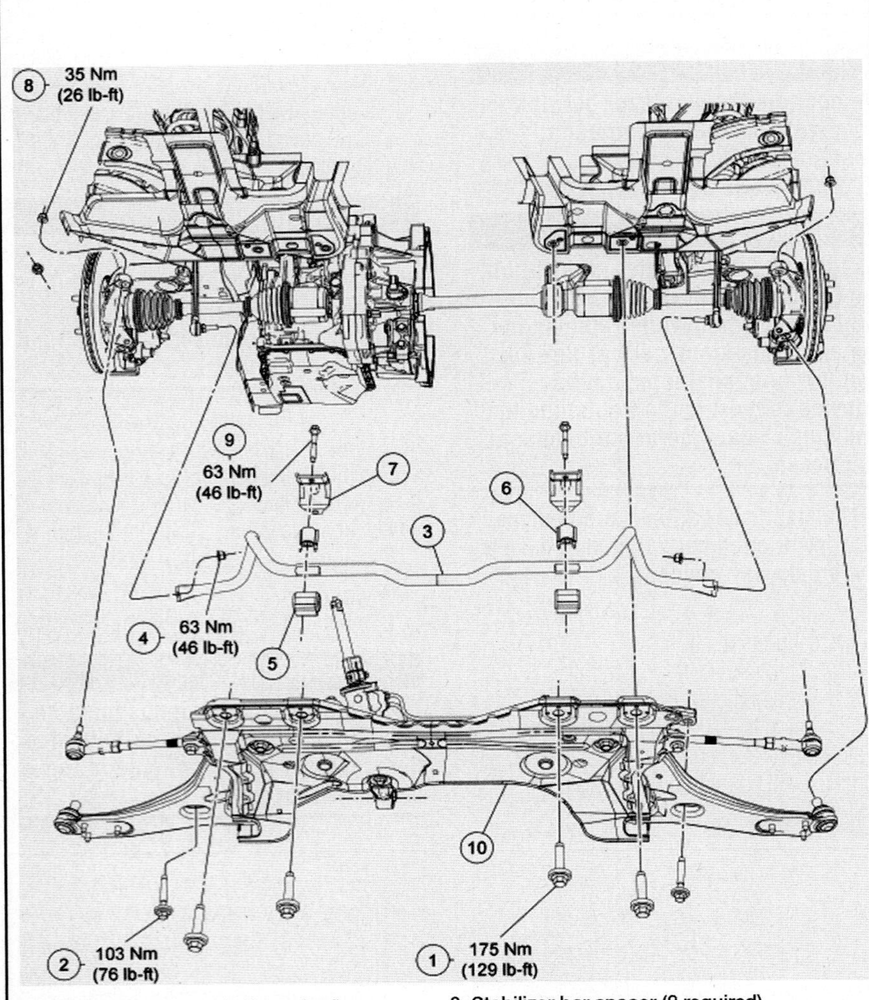

Fig. 154 Stabilizer bar and related components—exploded view

WARNING

Do not apply any type of lubricant to the stabilizer bar or bushings or damage to the bushings may occur.

14. Install the stabilizer bar bushings.
15. Position the stabilizer bar with the bushings against the spacer and set it to the specification listed using tie straps or mechanic's wire.
16. Position the stabilizer bar brackets and install the new bolts. Tighten to 47 ft. lbs. (63 Nm).
17. Remove the stabilizer bar supports.

➡Do not fully tighten the subframe bolts at this time.

18. Using the index marks made during removal, install the subframe bolts. Tighten the bolts until snug.

➡While tightening the subframe bolts, make sure the subframe does not move.

19. Tighten the 4 subframe front bolts to 129 ft. lbs. (175 Nm).
20. Tighten the 2 subframe rear bolts to 76 ft. lbs. (103 Nm).
21. Lower and remove the transmission jack.
22. Attach the stabilizer bar links to the stabilizer bar and install the new nuts. Tighten to 47 ft. lbs. (63 Nm).

➡Install new tie-rod end nuts. Failure to follow this instruction may result in incorrect clamp load.

23. Attach the tie-rod ends to the wheel knuckles and install the new nuts. Tighten to 26 ft. lbs. (35 Nm).
24. Install the wheel and tire assemblies. Tighten the wheel nuts in a star pattern to 100 ft. lbs. (135 Nm).

STEERING KNUCKLE

REMOVAL & INSTALLATION

See Figures 155 through 158.

WARNING

Suspension fasteners are critical parts because they affect performance of vital components and systems and their failure may result in major service expense. New parts must be installed with the same part numbers or equivalent part, if replacement is necessary. Do not use a replacement part of lesser quality or substitute design. Torque values must be used as specified during reassembly to make sure correct retention of these parts.

1. Before servicing the vehicle, refer to the Precautions Section.
2. Loosen the 3 strut upper nuts 5 turns.
3. Remove the wheel and tire.
4. Remove and discard the wheel hub nut.
5. Remove the brake hose retainer.

WARNING

Do not allow the brake caliper to hang from the brake hose or damage to the hose can occur.

6. Remove the 2 brake caliper guide pin bolts and position the caliper assembly aside. Support the caliper assembly using mechanic's wire.
7. Remove the brake disc.
8. If equipped with ABS, remove the wheel speed sensor bolt and position the sensor aside.

WARNING

Leave the tie-rod end nut in place or damage to the tie-rod end may occur.

9. Loosen the tie-rod end nut.

10. Using the Tie-Rod End Remover, detach the tie-rod end from the wheel knuckle. Remove and discard the tie-rod end nut.

WARNING

Do not use a prying device or separator fork between the ball joint and the wheel knuckle. Damage to the ball joint or ball joint seal may result. Only use the pry bar by inserting it into the lower arm body opening.

WARNING

Use care when releasing the lower arm and wheel knuckle into the resting position or damage to the ball joint seal may occur.

11. Remove and discard the ball joint nut and bolt.

12. Insert a pry bar in the lower arm body opening and separate the ball joint from the wheel knuckle.

WARNING

The inner joint must not be bent more than 18 degrees. The outer joint must not be bent more than 45 degrees. Damage to the halfshaft will occur.

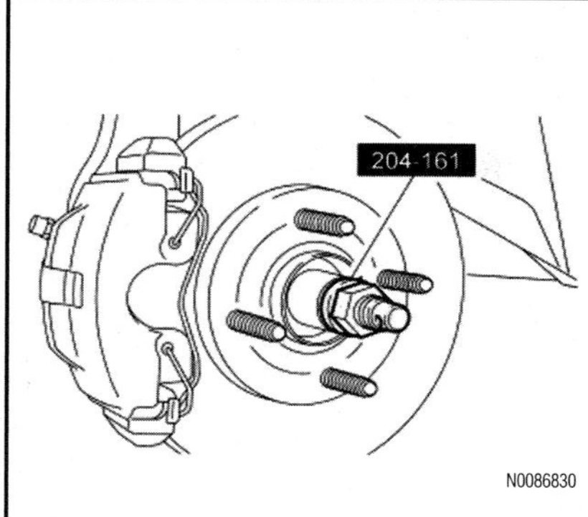

Fig. 157 Using the Halfshaft Installer, install the halfshaft into the wheel hub

13. Using the Front Wheel Hub Remover, press out the halfshaft from the wheel hub and detach the halfshaft from the wheel hub. Support the halfshaft.

14. Remove and discard the wheel knuckle-to-strut bolt.

15. Remove the wheel knuckle.

To install:

16. Position the wheel knuckle and install a new wheel knuckle-to-strut bolt. Tighten to 111 ft. lbs. (150 Nm).

17. Insert the halfshaft into the wheel hub.

WARNING

Make sure the ball joint heat shield is installed on the ball joint stud or damage to the ball joint may occur.

18. Insert the ball joint stud into the wheel knuckle and install a new bolt and nut. Tighten to 47 ft. lbs. (63 Nm).

19. Attach the tie-rod end to the wheel knuckle and install a new nut. Tighten to 26 ft. lbs. (35 Nm).

20. If equipped with ABS, position the wheel speed sensor and install the bolt. Tighten to 80 inch lbs. (9 Nm).

21. Install the brake disc.

22. Position the caliper assembly and install the 2 brake caliper guide pin bolts. Tighten to 20 ft. lbs. (27 Nm).

23. Install the brake hose retainer.

24. Tighten the 3 strut upper nuts to 26 ft. lbs. (35 Nm).

25. Using the Halfshaft Installer, install the halfshaft into the wheel hub.

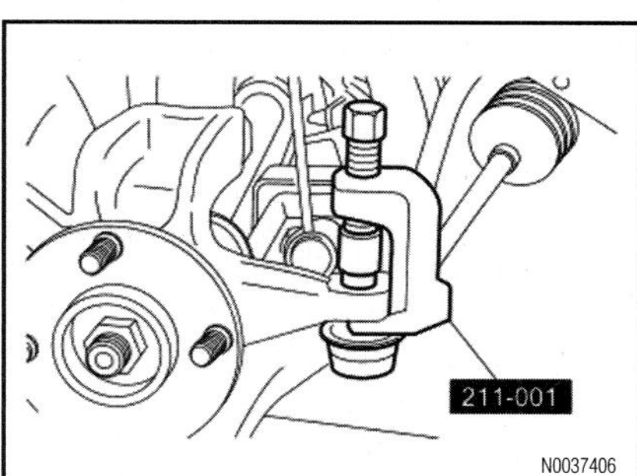

Fig. 155 Using the Tie-Rod End Remover, detach the tie-rod end from the wheel knuckle

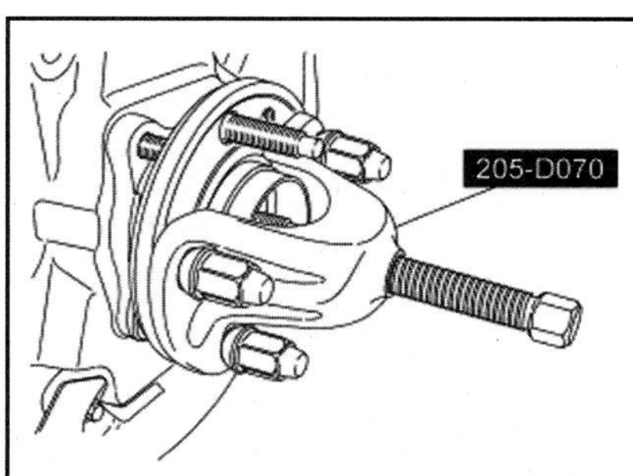

Fig. 156 Using the Front Wheel Hub Remover, press out the halfshaft from the wheel hub

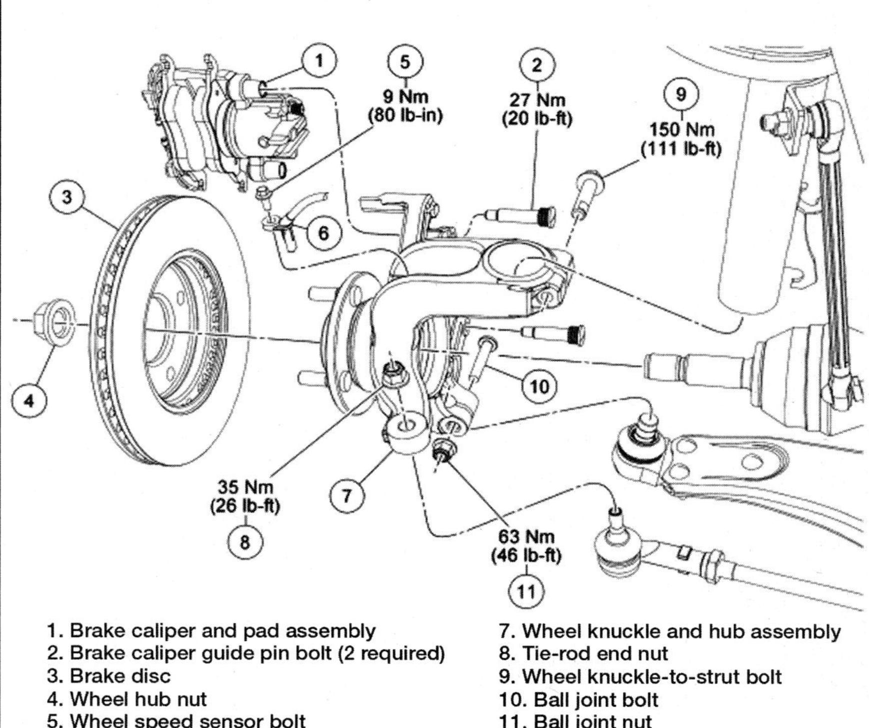

Fig. 158 Steering knuckle and related components—exploded view

⁂ WARNING

Do not tighten the wheel hub nut with the vehicle on the ground. The nut must be tightened to specification before the vehicle is lowered onto the wheels. Wheel bearing damage will occur if the wheel bearing is loaded with the weight of the vehicle applied.

⁂ WARNING

Install and tighten the new wheel hub nut to specification in a continuous rotation. Always install a new wheel hub nut after loosening or when not tightened to specification in a continuous rotation or damage to the component may occur.

➡Apply the brake to keep the halfshaft from rotating.

26. Install the new wheel hub nut. Tighten to 199 ft. lbs. (270 Nm) in a continuous rotation.

27. Install the wheel and tire assemblies. Tighten the wheel nuts in a star pattern to 100 ft. lbs. (135 Nm).

STRUT & SPRING ASSEMBLY

REMOVAL & INSTALLATION

See Figure 159.

NOTICE: Suspension fasteners are critical parts because they affect performance of vital components and systems and their failure may result in major service expense. New parts must be installed with the same part numbers or equivalent part, if replacement is necessary. Do not use a replacement part of lesser quality or substitute design. Torque values must be used as specified during reassembly to make sure correct retention of these parts.

1. Before servicing the vehicle, refer to the Precautions Section.
2. Remove the wheel and tire.
3. Detach the brake hose from the support bracket.
4. Remove the stabilizer bar link upper nut and detach the link from the strut. Discard the nut.
5. Remove and discard the wheel knuckle-to-strut bolt.
6. Detach the wheel knuckle from the strut and spring assembly. Support the halfshaft using mechanic's wire.

⁂ WARNING

Support the strut and spring assembly to prevent damage.

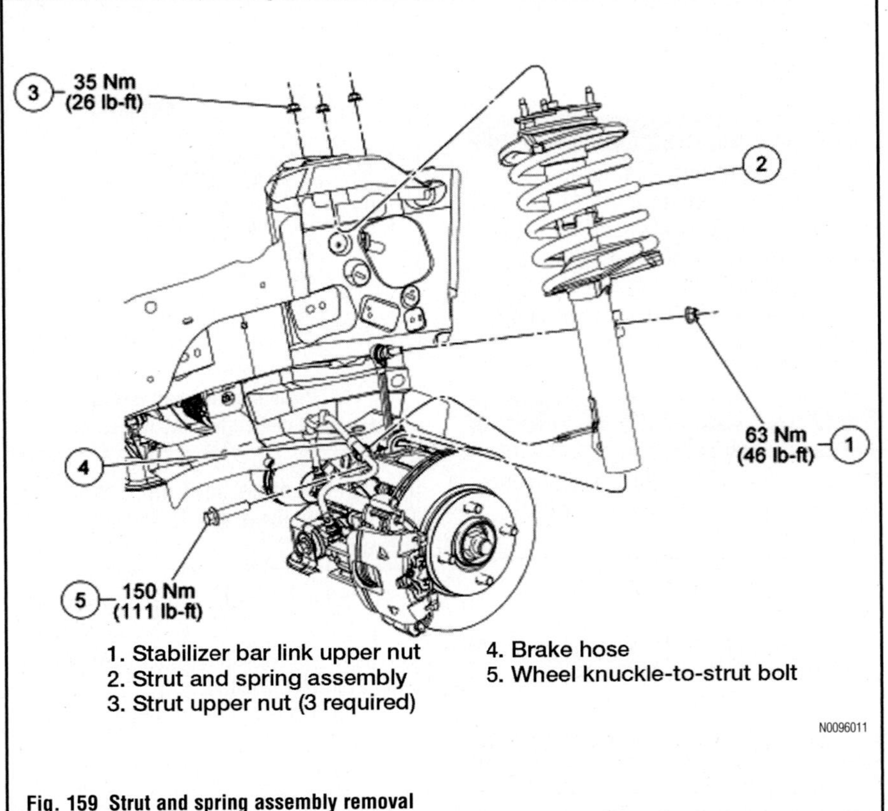

Fig. 159 Strut and spring assembly removal

7. Remove and discard the strut upper nuts.
8. Remove the strut and spring assembly.
9. To install, reverse the removal procedure and note the following:
   - Tighten the new upper strut nuts to 26 ft. lbs. (35 Nm)
   - Tighten the new the wheel knuckle-to-strut bolt to 111 ft. lbs. (150 Nm)
   - Tighten the new stabilizer bar link upper nut to 47 ft. lbs. (63 Nm)
   - Check and, if necessary, align the front end

OVERHAUL

See Figures 160 and 161.

⁂ WARNING

Suspension fasteners are critical parts because they affect performance of vital components and systems and their failure can result in major service expense. A new part with the same part number must be installed if installation is necessary. Do not use a new part of lesser quality or substitute design. Torque values must be used as specified during reassembly to make sure of correct retention of these parts.

1. Before servicing the vehicle, refer to the Precautions Section.
2. Remove the strut and spring assembly. Refer to Strut & Spring Assembly, removal & installation.

⁂ CAUTION

Keep all body parts clear of shock absorbers or strut rods. Shock absorbers or struts can extend unassisted. Failure to follow this instruction may result in serious personal injury.

3. Using a suitable coil spring compressor, compress the spring.

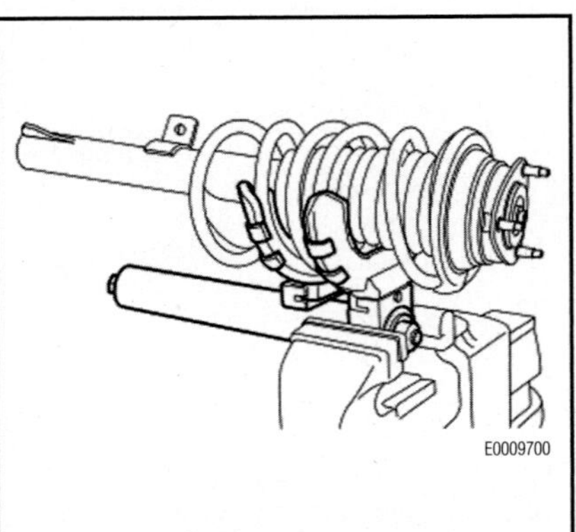

Fig. 160 Coil spring compressor installed

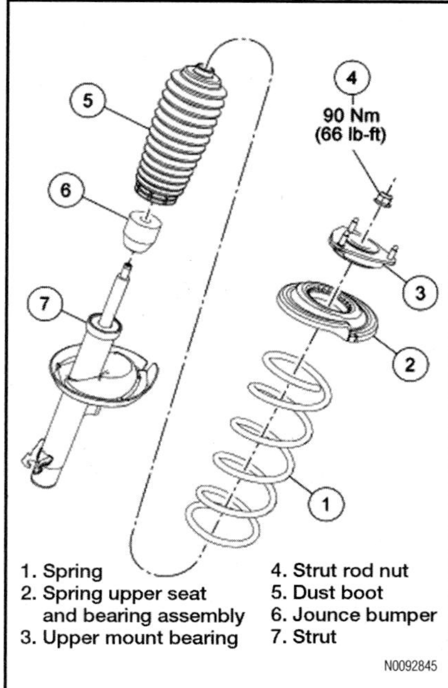

Fig. 161 Strut and spring assembly—exploded view

➡Use the hex-holding feature to prevent the strut rod from rotating while removing the nut.

4. Carefully remove and discard the strut rod nut.
5. Remove the upper mount, spring upper seat, and dust boot.
6. Remove the strut and jounce bumper.
7. Carefully remove the spring from the spring compressor.
8. To assemble, reverse the disassembly procedure and note the following:
   - Make sure the upper mount is correctly seated before assembly or damage to the upper mount may occur
   - Make sure the spring is installed with the flat surface facing up and with the spring end correctly positioned against the spring seat (color code at the bottom). This is to prevent spring seat damage and incorrect spring position
   - Tighten the strut rod nut to 66 ft. lbs. (90 Nm)

WHEEL HUB & BEARINGS

REMOVAL & INSTALLATION

See Figures 162 through 167.

1. Before servicing the vehicle, refer to the Precautions Section.
2. Remove the wheel knuckle. Refer to Steering Knuckle, removal & installation.
3. Remove the circlip from the wheel knuckle.

➡After the wheel hub is removed from the knuckle, the wheel bearing must be discarded. The bearing inner ring will remain in the wheel knuckle.

4. Using the Bearing Puller, Adapter Handle, and Wheel Hub Bearing Cup Installer, remove the wheel hub and outer bearing race.

⁂ WARNING

The Bearing Puller and Bushing Remover/Installer must be used to prevent damage to the hub. If the hub is damaged, a new hub must be installed.

⁂ WARNING

Do not use heat to remove the bearing inner ring or damage to the bearing may occur.

5. Using the Bearing Puller and Bushing Remover/Installer, remove the bearing inner ring from the wheel hub.
6. To aid in removal of the bearing outer ring, install the bearing cage onto the inner ring and install the assembly into the wheel knuckle.
7. Using the Wheel Hub Bearing Cup Installer, Wheel Speed Sensor Ring Installer and the Adapter Handle, remove the bearing outer ring from the wheel knuckle.

To install:

⁂ WARNING

To prevent wheel speed sensor ring damage, make sure that the sensor ring is clean. Make sure that the sensor ring does not make contact with metal surfaces and avoid any impact on the sensor ring.

➡Make sure the wheel bearing is installed into the wheel knuckle with the wheel speed sensor ring, colored

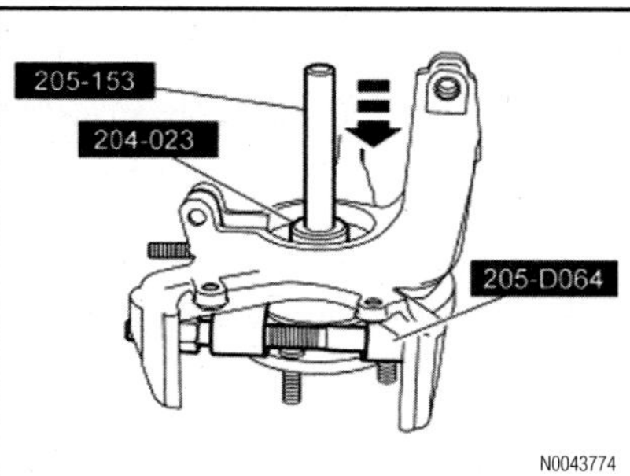

Fig. 162 Using the Bearing Puller, Adapter Handle, and Wheel Hub Bearing Cup Installer, remove the wheel hub and outer bearing race

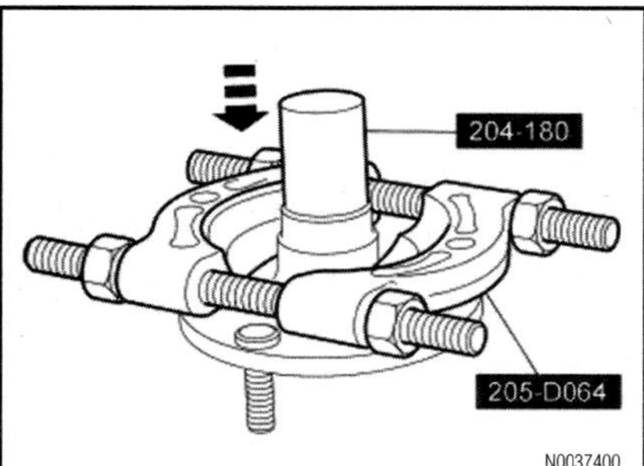

Fig. 163 Using the Bearing Puller and Bushing Remover/Installer, remove the bearing inner ring from the wheel hub

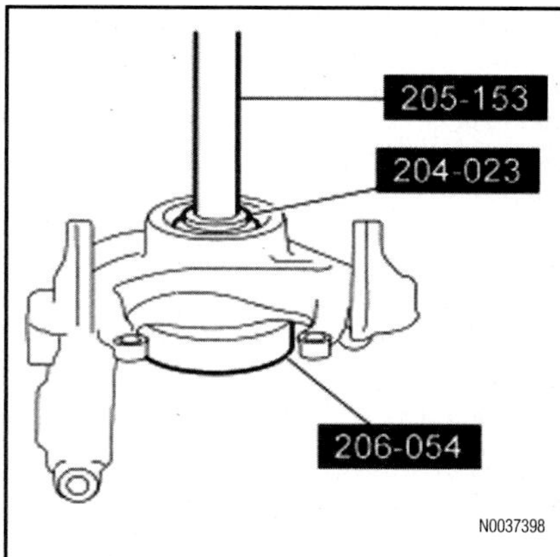

Fig. 164 Using the Wheel Hub Bearing Cup Installer, Wheel Speed Sensor Ring Installer and the Adapter Handle, remove the bearing outer ring from the wheel knuckle

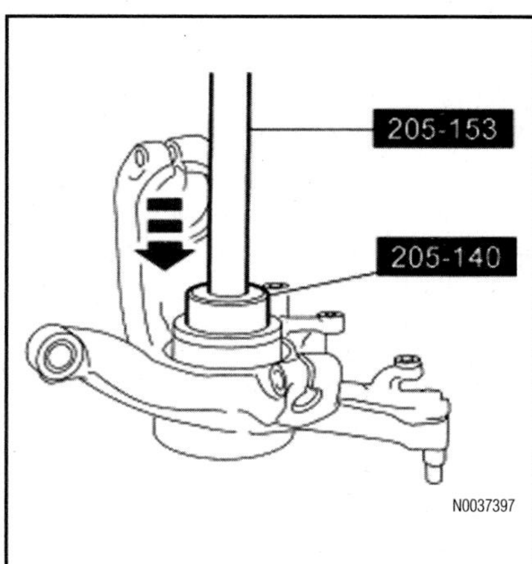

Fig. 165 Using the Drive Pinion Bearing Cup Installer and Adapter Handle, install the new wheel bearing to the wheel knuckle

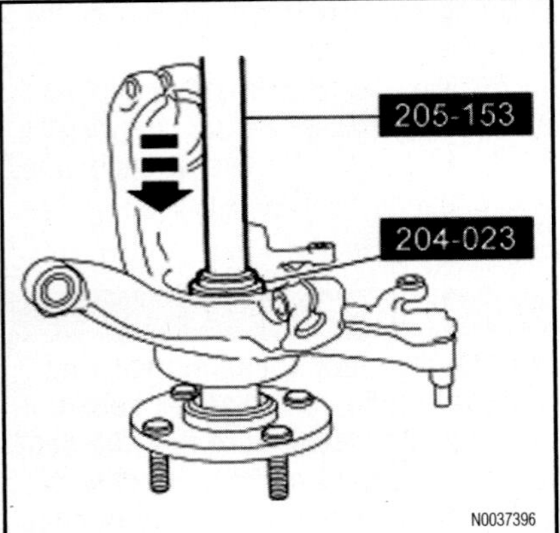

Fig. 166 Using the Wheel Hub Bearing Cup Installer and Adapter Handle, install the wheel hub into the wheel knuckle

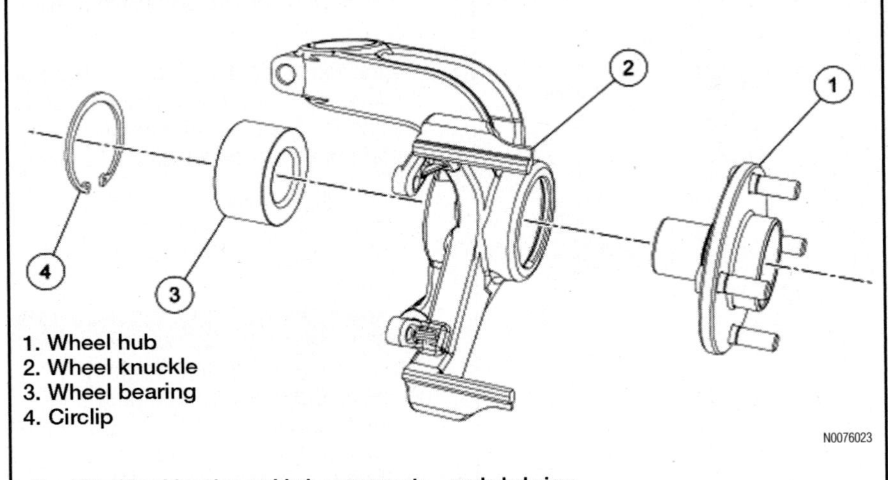

Fig. 167 Wheel bearing and hub components—exploded view

black, at the wheel speed sensor end of the wheel knuckle.

8. Using the Drive Pinion Bearing Cup Installer and Adapter Handle, install the new wheel bearing to the wheel knuckle.
9. Using the Wheel Hub Bearing Cup Installer and Adapter Handle, install the wheel hub into the wheel knuckle.

WARNING

Make sure the circlip does not cover the wheel speed sensor or damage to the sensor may occur.

10. Install the circlip into the wheel knuckle.
11. Install the wheel knuckle. Refer to Steering Knuckle, removal & installation.

ADJUSTMENT

The bearings on the front and rear wheels are a one piece cartridge design and cannot be adjusted. If wheel bearing play is excessive, check the wheel hub retainer nut for proper torque. If the torque is correct, replacement of the wheel bearing is required.

SUSPENSION

REAR SUSPENSION

COIL SPRING

REMOVAL & INSTALLATION

See Figure 168.

WARNING

Suspension fasteners are critical parts because they affect performance of vital components and systems and their failure may result in major service expense. New parts must be installed with the same part numbers or equivalent part, if replacement is necessary. Do not use a replacement part of lesser quality or substitute design. Torque values must be used as specified during reassembly to make sure correct retention of these parts.

1. Before servicing the vehicle, refer to the Precautions Section.
2. Remove the wheel and tire.
3. Remove the stabilizer bar nut and bushings, stabilizer bar links and spacers on both sides of the stabilizer bar. Discard the nuts and bushings.
4. Using a suitable jack, raise the rear lower arm 1.25 inches (32mm).

CAUTION

The coil spring is under extreme load. Care must be taken at all times when removing or installing a loaded spring. Failure to follow this instruction may result in serious personal injury.

5. Remove the rearward lower arm outboard bolt. Discard the bolt.
6. Lower the rear lower arm and remove the jack.
7. Position the stabilizer bar aside.
8. Lower the rear lower control arm and remove the spring.

To install:

9. Inspect the spring upper and lower seats and, if necessary, install new.

➡Make sure the upper spring seat is installed, and the spring ends butt correctly against the upper and lower spring seats.

10. Install the upper spring seat onto the spring.
11. Position the stabilizer bar aside.
12. Position the spring into the upper spring mount and position the lower arm.

WARNING

Make sure the spring butts against the rear lower arm spring stop and is visible through the drain hole or spring and spring seat damage may occur.

13. If necessary, rotate the spring clockwise until the spring-end butts against the rear lower arm spring stop.

➡Do not tighten the rearward lower arm outboard bolt at this time.

14. Using a suitable jack, raise the rear lower arm and install the new rearward lower arm outboard bolt. Tighten until snug.
15. Position the stabilizer bar links and spacers and install the new nut and bushings. Tighten to 11 ft. lbs. (15 Nm).
16. Install the wheel and tire assemblies. Tighten the wheel nuts in a star pattern to 100 ft. lbs. (135 Nm).
17. Lower the vehicle until the weight of the vehicle is resting on the wheels and tires.
18. Tighten the rearward lower arm outboard bolt to 85 ft. lbs. (115 Nm).

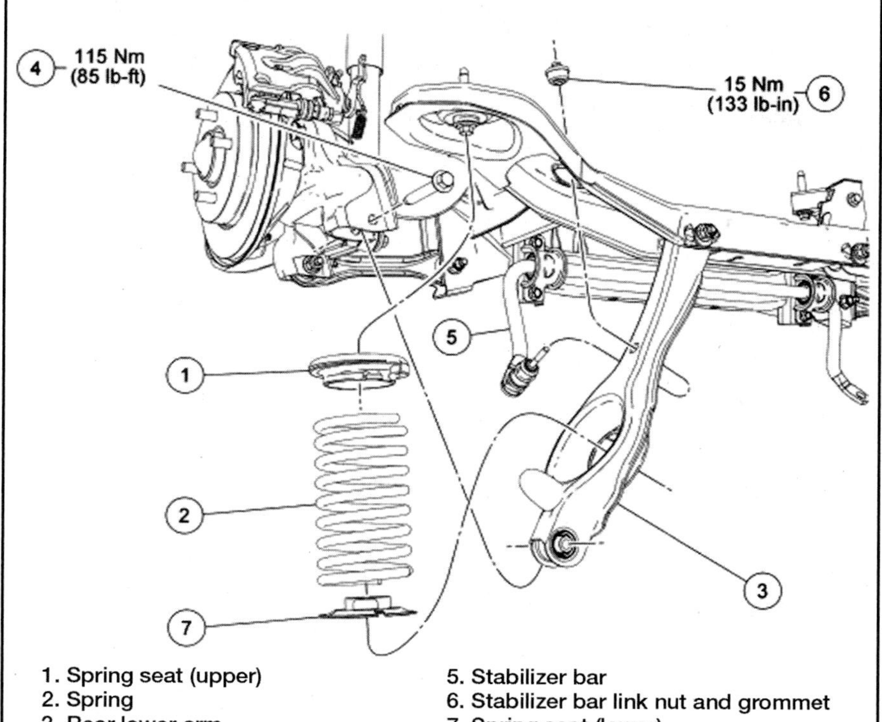

Fig. 168 Rear spring and related components—exploded view

LOWER CONTROL ARM

REMOVAL & INSTALLATION

Lower Arm—Front

See Figure 169.

**** WARNING**

Suspension fasteners are critical parts because they affect performance of vital components and systems and their failure may result in major service expense. New parts must be installed with the same part numbers or equivalent part, if replacement is necessary. Do not use a replacement part of lesser quality or substitute design. Torque values must be used as specified during reassembly to make sure correct retention of these parts.

1. Before servicing the vehicle, refer to the Precautions Section.
2. Remove the wheel and tire.
3. Remove and discard the forward lower arm inboard bolt.
4. Remove the forward lower arm outboard bolt and the forward lower arm. Discard the bolt.

To install:

➡The forward lower arm is marked FRONT. Make a note of the position of the front lower arm to aid installation.

5. Position the front lower arm and loosely install the new lower arm outboard bolt. Do not tighten the bolt at this time.
6. Loosely install the new forward lower arm inboard bolt. Do not tighten the bolt at this time.
7. Install the wheel and tire assemblies. Tighten the wheel nuts in a star pattern to 100 ft. lbs. (135 Nm).
8. Lower the vehicle until the weight of the vehicle is resting on the wheels and tires.
9. Tighten the forward lower arm inboard bolt to 85 ft. lbs. (115 Nm).
10. Tighten the forward lower arm outboard bolt to 85 ft. lbs. (115 Nm).

Lower Arm—Rear

See Figures 170 and 171.

**** WARNING**

Suspension fasteners are critical parts because they affect performance of vital components and systems and their failure may result in major service expense. New parts must be installed with the same part numbers or equivalent part, if replacement is necessary. Do not use a replacement part of lesser quality or substitute design. Torque values must be used as specified during reassembly to make sure correct retention of these parts.

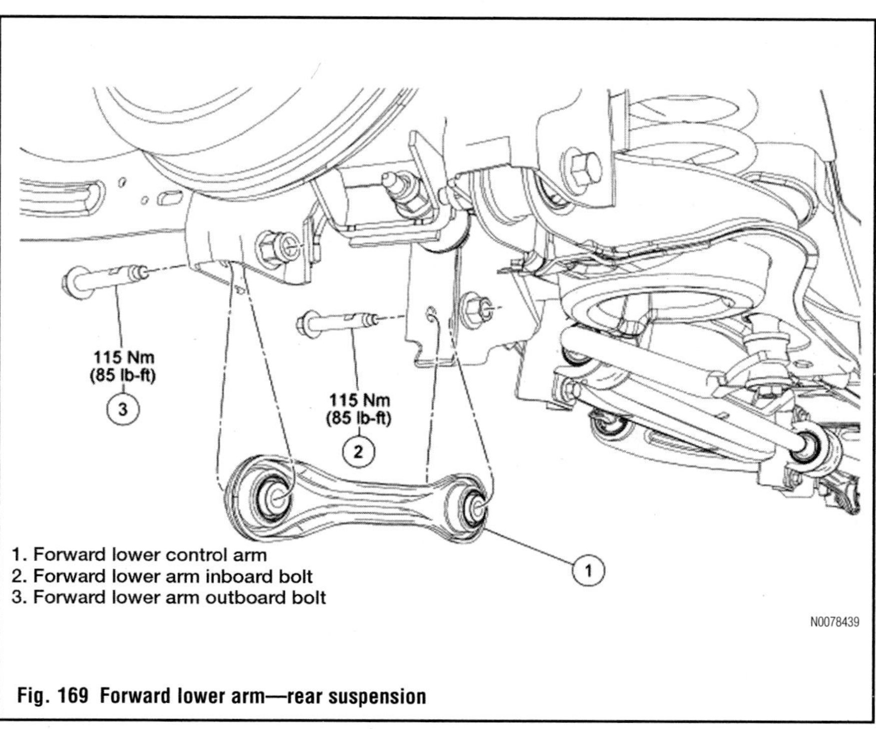

Fig. 169 Forward lower arm—rear suspension

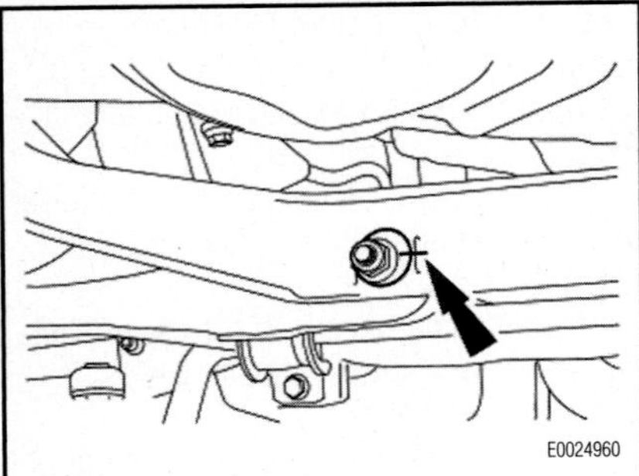

Fig. 170 Mark the position of the rearward lower arm adjustment cam to the cross-member

1. Before servicing the vehicle, refer to the Precautions Section.
2. Mark the position of the rearward lower arm adjustment cam to the cross-member.
3. Remove the spring. Refer to Coil Spring, removal & installation.
4. Remove the rearward lower arm-to-crossmember nut, cam adjuster, cam bolt and the lower arm. Discard the rearward lower arm-to-crossmember nut.

To install:

➡Align the mark on the rearward lower arm adjustment cam to the mark on the crossmember.

➡Do not fully tighten the rearward lower arm-to-crossmember nut at this time.

5. Position the rearward lower arm and install the cam bolt, cam adjuster and new nut. Tighten the nut until snug.
6. Install the spring. Refer to Coil Spring, removal & installation.

➡Final tightening of the rearward lower arm-to-crossmember nut should be carried out with the suspension at curb height.

7. Tighten the rearward lower arm-to-crossmember nut to 66 ft. lbs. (90 Nm).
8. Check and, if necessary, adjust the rear toe.

SHOCK ABSORBERS

REMOVAL & INSTALLATION

See Figures 172 through 174.

WARNING

Suspension fasteners are critical parts because they affect performance of vital components and systems and their failure may result in major service expense. New parts must be installed with the same part numbers or equivalent part, if replacement is necessary. Do not use a replacement part of lesser quality or substitute design. Torque values must be used as specified during reassembly to make sure correct retention of these parts.

1. Before servicing the vehicle, refer to the Precautions Section.
2. Remove the luggage compartment side trim panel to access the shock absorber upper nut.

WARNING

Use the hex-holding feature to prevent the shock rod from turning while removing the nut or damage to the shock absorber may occur.

3. Remove and discard the shock absorber upper nut.
4. Remove the wheel and tire.
5. Remove the shock absorber lower bolt and the shock absorber. Discard the bolt.

To install:

6. Inspect the upper mount and install a new one if necessary.
7. Position the shock absorber and loosely install the new shock absorber lower bolt. Do not tighten the bolt at this time.

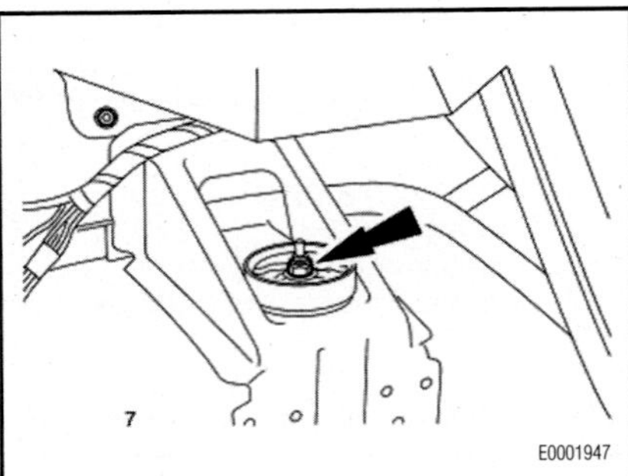

Fig. 172 Remove the luggage compartment side trim panel to access the shock absorber upper nut

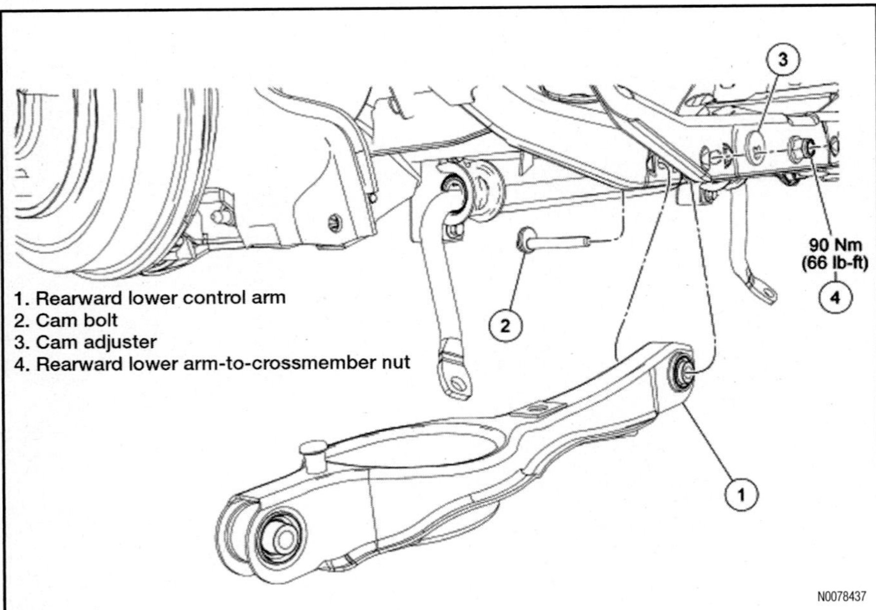

Fig. 171 Rearward lower control arm—rear suspension

Fig. 173 View of shock absorber—rear suspension

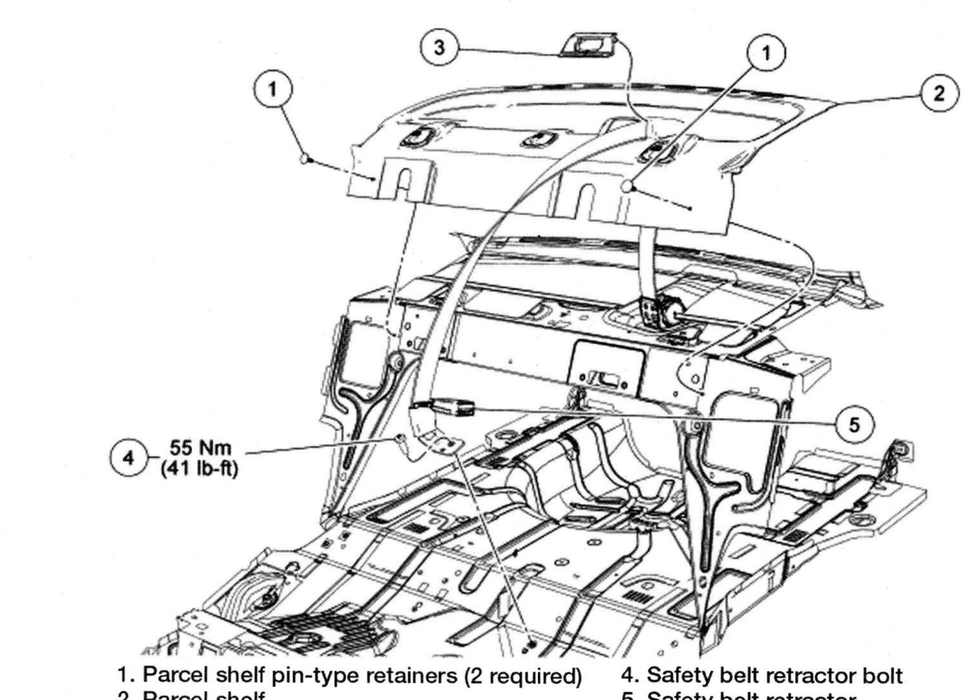

Fig. 174 Exploded view of the parcel shelf support panel

8. Install the wheel and tire assemblies. Tighten the wheel nuts in a star pattern to 100 ft. lbs. (135 Nm).
9. Lower the vehicle until the weight of the vehicle is resting on the wheels and tires.
10. Tighten the shock absorber lower bolt to 76 ft. lbs. (103 Nm).

WARNING

Use the hex-holding feature to prevent the shock rod from turning while installing the nut or damage to the shock absorber may occur.

11. Install the new shock absorber upper nut. Tighten to 15 ft. lbs. (20 Nm).
12. Install the parcel shelf support panel.

TESTING

The easiest test of the shock absorber is to simply push down on one corner of the unladen vehicle and release it. Observe the motion of the body as it is released. In most cases, it will come up beyond its original rest position, dip back below it, and settle quickly to rest. This shows that the damper is controlling the spring action. Any tendency to excessive pitch (up-and-down) motion or failure to return to rest within 2–3 cycles, is a sign of poor function within the shock absorber.

Oil-filled shocks may have a light film of oil around the seal, resulting from normal breathing and air exchange. This should NOT be taken as a sign of failure, but any sign of thick or running oil indicates failure. Gas-filled shocks may also show some film at the shaft; if the gas has leaked out, the shock will have almost no resistance to motion.

While each shock absorber can be replaced individually, it is recommended that they be changed as a pair (both front or both rear) to maintain equal response on both sides of the vehicle. If one side has failed, its mate may also be weak.

1. Before servicing the vehicle, refer to the Precautions Section.
2. Check the rubber parts for damage or deterioration.
3. Check the spring for correct height, deformation, deterioration, or damage.
4. Check the shock absorber for abnormal resistance or unusual sounds.
5. Check for oil seepage around seals.
6. Replace as needed.

STABILIZER BAR

REMOVAL & INSTALLATION

See Figures 175 and 176.

WARNING

Suspension fasteners are critical parts because they affect performance of vital components and systems and their failure may result in major service expense. New parts must be installed with the same part numbers or equivalent part, if replacement is necessary. Do not use a replacement part of lesser quality or substitute design. Torque values must be used as specified during reassembly to make sure correct retention of these parts.

➡This procedure must be carried out with the suspension at or near curb height.

1. Before servicing the vehicle, refer to the Precautions Section.
2. With the vehicle in NEUTRAL, position it on a hoist.
3. Remove the stabilizer bar link nut and bushings, stabilizer bar links and link spacers. Discard the nut and bushings.

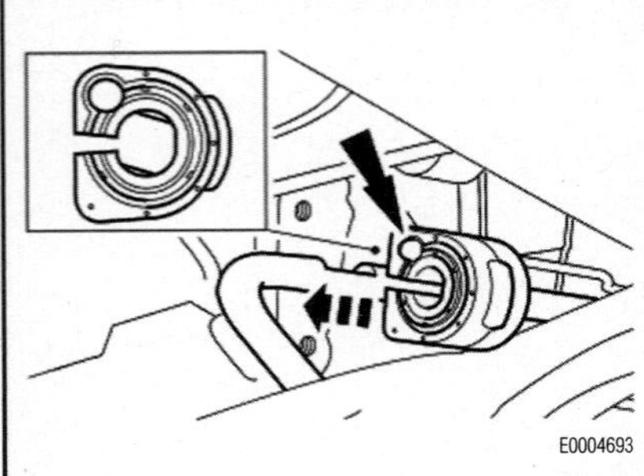

Fig. 175 Correct installation of stabilizer bushings—rear suspension

4. Remove and discard the stabilizer bar bracket bolts and remove the stabilizer bar brackets and stabilizer bar.

To install:

5. Inspect and, if necessary, install new stabilizer bar bushings.

⁂ WARNING

Do not use any lubrication on the stabilizer bar or the bushings or damage to the bushings may occur.

⁂ WARNING

To prevent bushing damage and incorrect stabilizer bar operation, the stabilizer bar bushings must be located correctly on the stabilizer bar. The protrusion on both bushings must be facing the LH side of the vehicle for correct installation.

6. If necessary, install the bushings onto the stabilizer bar.

➡Apply water to the brackets to aid in installation.

7. Position the stabilizer bar and brackets and install the new bolts. Tighten to 41 ft. lbs. (55 Nm).
8. Position the stabilizer bar links and spacers and install the new nut and bushings. Tighten to 11 ft. lbs. (15 Nm).

UPPER CONTROL ARM

REMOVAL & INSTALLATION

See Figure 177.

⁂ WARNING

Suspension fasteners are critical parts because they affect performance of vital components and systems and their failure may result in major service expense. New parts must be installed with the same part numbers or equivalent part, if replacement is necessary. Do not use a replacement part of lesser quality or substitute design. Torque values must be used as specified during reassembly to make sure correct retention of these parts.

1. Before servicing the vehicle, refer to the Precautions Section.
2. Remove the wheel and tire.
3. Remove and discard the shock absorber lower bolt.

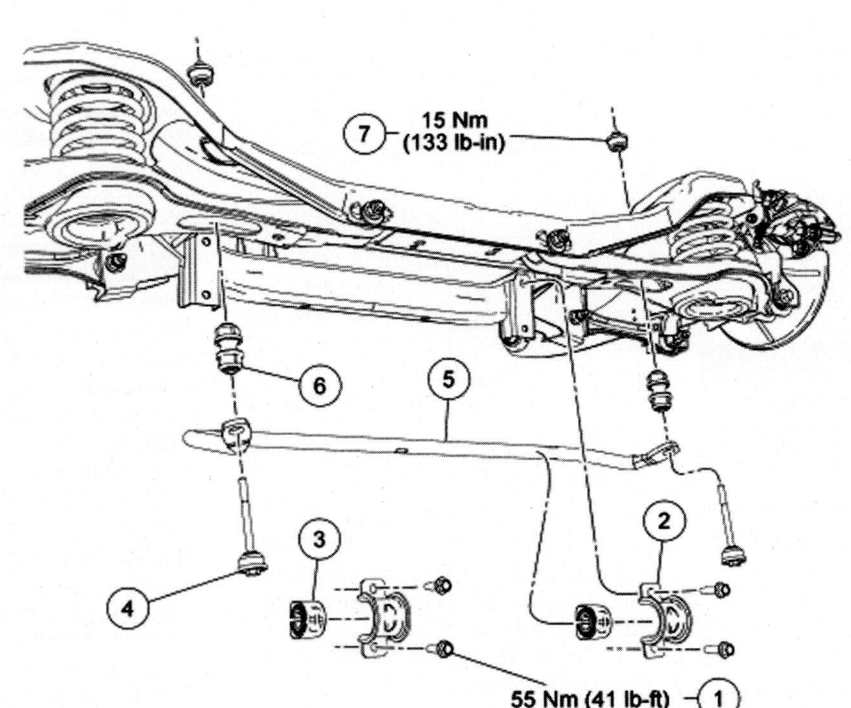

Fig. 176 Expanded view of rear stabilizer bar

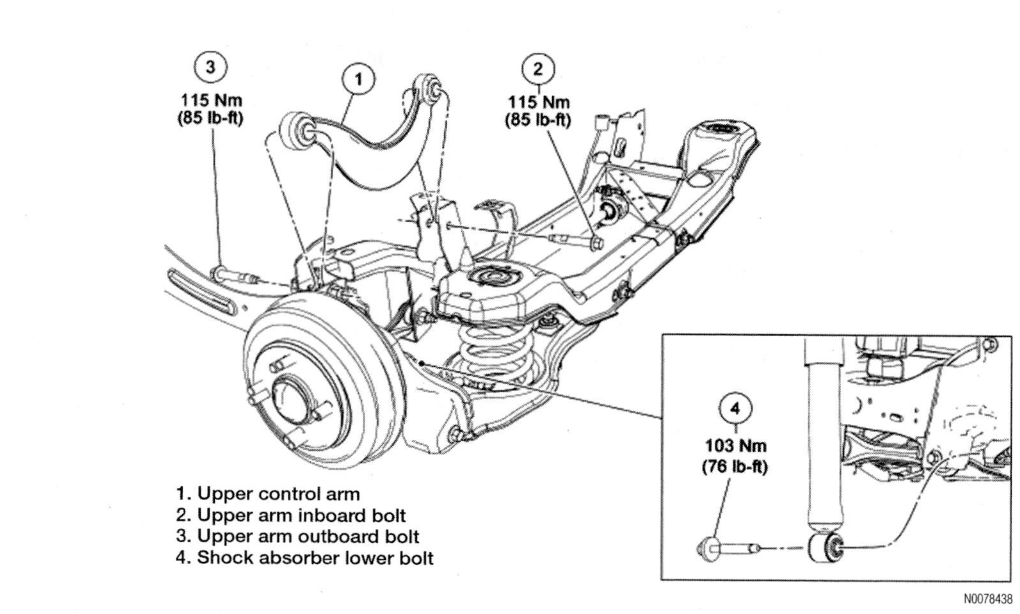

Fig. 177 Upper control arm and related components—rear suspension

4. Remove and discard the upper arm inboard bolt.

➡Note the position of the upper arm to aid installation.

5. Position the shock absorber as necessary to remove the upper arm.
6. Remove the upper arm outboard bolt and the upper arm. Discard the bolt.

To install:

7. Position the shock absorber as necessary to install the upper arm.
8. Position the upper arm and loosely install the new upper arm outboard bolt. Do not tighten the bolt at this time.
9. Loosely install the new upper arm inboard bolt. Do not tighten the bolt at this time.
10. Loosely install the new shock absorber lower bolt. Do not tighten the bolt at this time.
11. Install the wheel and tire assemblies. Tighten the wheel nuts in a star pattern to 100 ft. lbs. (135 Nm).
12. Lower the vehicle until the weight of the vehicle is resting on the wheels and tires.
13. Tighten the upper arm inboard bolt to 85 ft. lbs. (115 Nm).
14. Tighten the upper arm outboard bolt to 85 ft. lbs. (115 Nm).
15. Tighten the shock absorber lower bolt to 76 ft. lbs. (103 Nm).

WHEEL BEARINGS

REMOVAL & INSTALLATION

See Figures 178 through 183.

1. Before servicing the vehicle, refer to the Precautions Section.

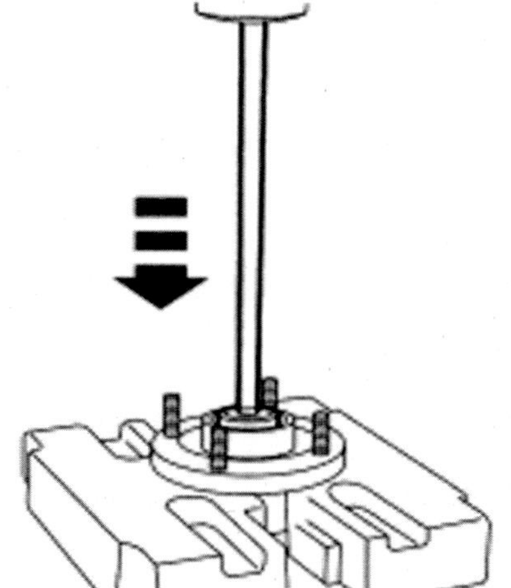

Fig. 178 Using a press and suitable adapters, remove the wheel bearing

2. Remove the brake drum.
Refer to Brake Drum, removal & installation.
3. Remove and discard the wheel speed sensor ring.
4. If equipped, remove and discard the water seal carrier.

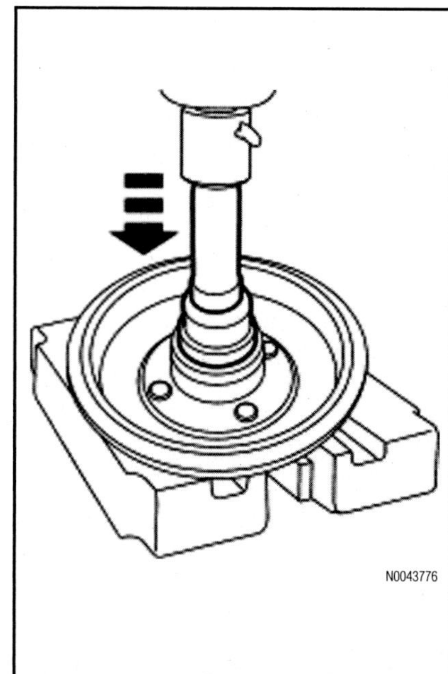

Fig. 179 Using a press and suitable adapters, install a new wheel bearing

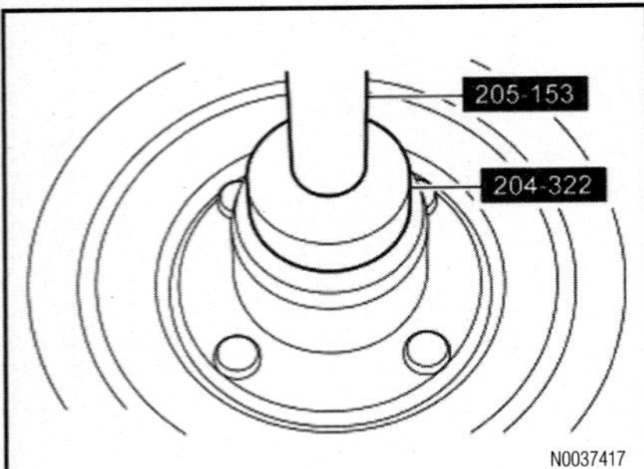

Fig. 180 Using a suitable press, Water Seal Carrier Installer and Adapter Handle, install a new water seal carrier

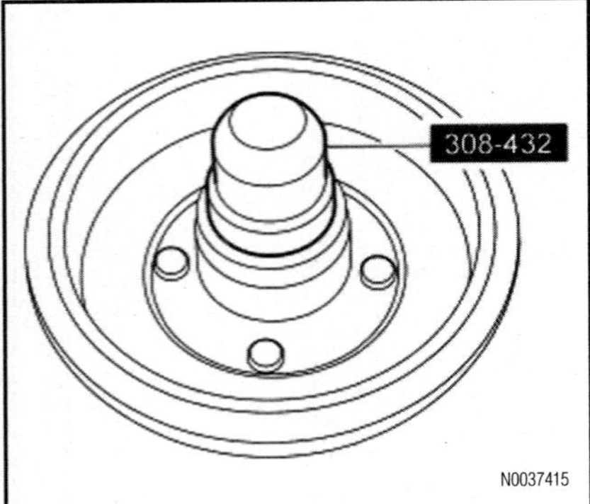

Fig. 181 Using the PTO Dust Flange Installer, install a new wheel speed sensor ring

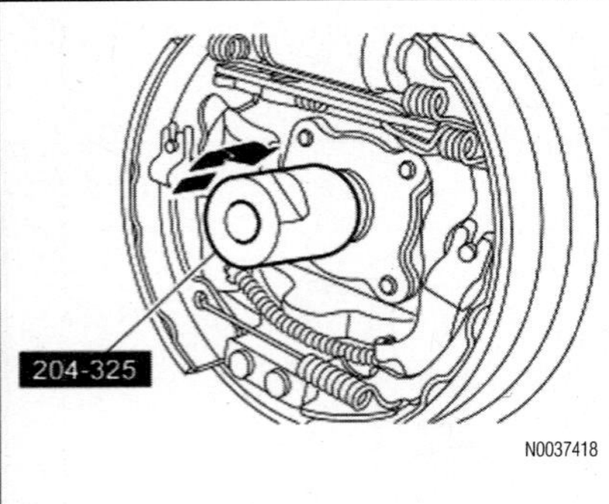

Fig. 182 Using the Seal Installer, install the new water seal and protective cap

5. Remove and discard the water seal carrier.
6. Remove the snap ring.
7. Using a press and suitable dapters, remove the wheel bearing.
8. Remove the water seal from the wheel spindle. Discard the water seal.

To install:

WARNING

Support the brake drum on the wheel mounting face and not on the wheel nut studs or damage to the wheel studs may occur.

9. Using a press and suitable adapters, install a new wheel bearing.
10. Install the snap ring.
11. Using a suitable press, Water Seal Carrier Installer and Adapter Handle, install a new water seal carrier.

WARNING

Avoid impact on the wheel speed sensor ring and any contact between the sensor ring and a magnetic surface or damage to the sensor ring may occur. Make sure the wheel speed sensor ring is clean or sensor failure may occur.

12. Using the PTO Dust Flange Installer, install a new wheel speed sensor ring.
13. Using emery cloth, or other suitable material, remove any pitting or corrosion from the leading edge of the wheel spindle seal running surface.
14. Using the Seal Installer, install the new water seal and protective cap. Tighten the Seal Installer to 62 inch lbs. (7 Nm).
15. Remove and discard the protective cap.
16. Install the brake drum. Refer to Brake Drum, removal & installation.

ADJUSTMENT

The bearings on the front and rear wheels are a one piece cartridge design and cannot be adjusted. If wheel bearing play is excessive, check the wheel hub retainer nut for proper torque. If the torque is correct, replacement of the wheel bearing is required.

WHEEL KNUCKLE

REMOVAL & INSTALLATION

See Figure 184.

WARNING

Suspension fasteners are critical parts because they affect performance of vital components and systems and their failure may result in major service expense. New parts must be installed with the same part numbers or equivalent part, if replacement is necessary. Do not use a replacement part of lesser quality or substitute design. Torque values must be used as specified during reassembly to make sure correct retention of these parts.

1. Before servicing the vehicle, refer to the Precautions Section.
2. Remove the brake drum. Refer to Brake Drum, removal & installation.
3. Remove the wheel speed sensor bolt and disconnect the sensor.
4. Disconnect the wheel speed sensor harness clip from the trailing arm and position the harness and sensor aside.
5. Disconnect the brake tube fitting and remove the clip.
6. Disconnect the parking brake cable.
7. Remove the 4 wheel spindle bolts, spindle and the rear brake assembly. Discard the bolts.
8. Remove the bolt and disconnect the parking brake cable from the trailing arm.
9. Remove and discard the 2 trailing arm bolts.
10. Remove and discard the shock absorber lower bolt.
11. Remove and discard the forward lower arm outboard bolt.
12. Remove and discard the rearward lower arm outboard bolt.
13. Remove and discard the upper arm outboard bolt and remove the wheel knuckle and trailing arm assembly.

To install:

14. Position the wheel knuckle and trailing arm assembly and loosely install the new upper arm outboard bolt. Do not tighten the bolt at this time.
15. Loosely install the new rearward lower arm outboard bolt. Do not tighten the bolt at this time.
16. Loosely install the new forward lower arm outboard bolt. Do not tighten the bolt at this time.
17. Loosely install the new shock absorber lower bolt. Do not tighten the bolt at this time.
18. Loosely install the 2 new trailing arm bolts. Do not tighten the bolt at this time.
19. Connect the parking brake cable to the trailing arm and install the bolt. Tighten to 115 inch lbs. (13 Nm).
20. Connect the brake tube fitting and install the clip. Tighten to 11 ft. lbs. (15 Nm).
21. Position the wheel speed sensor and install the bolt. Tighten to 80 inch lbs. (9 Nm).
22. Position the wheel speed sensor harness and connect the harness to the trailing arm clip.
23. Position the rear brake assembly and install the new wheel spindle and 4 bolts. Tighten to 76 ft. lbs. (103 Nm).
24. Install the brake drum. Refer to Brake Drum, removal & installation.

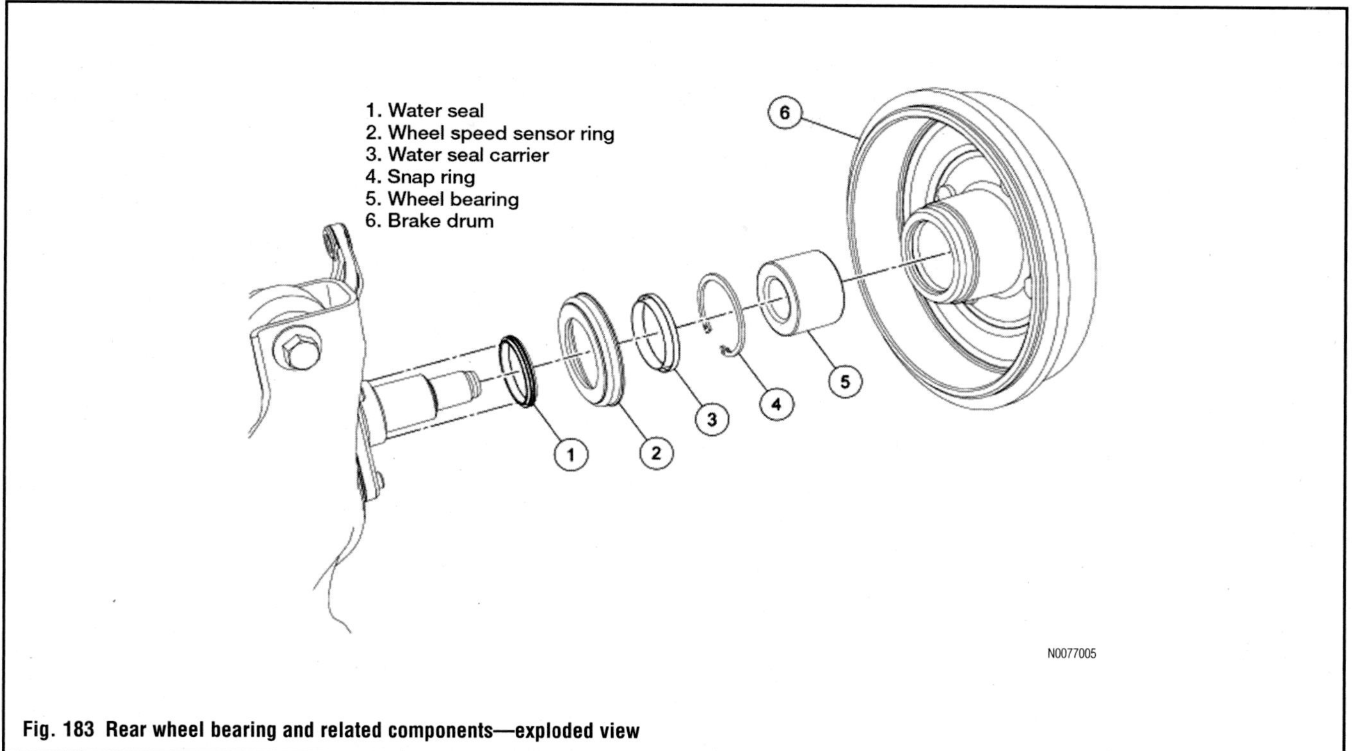

Fig. 183 Rear wheel bearing and related components—exploded view

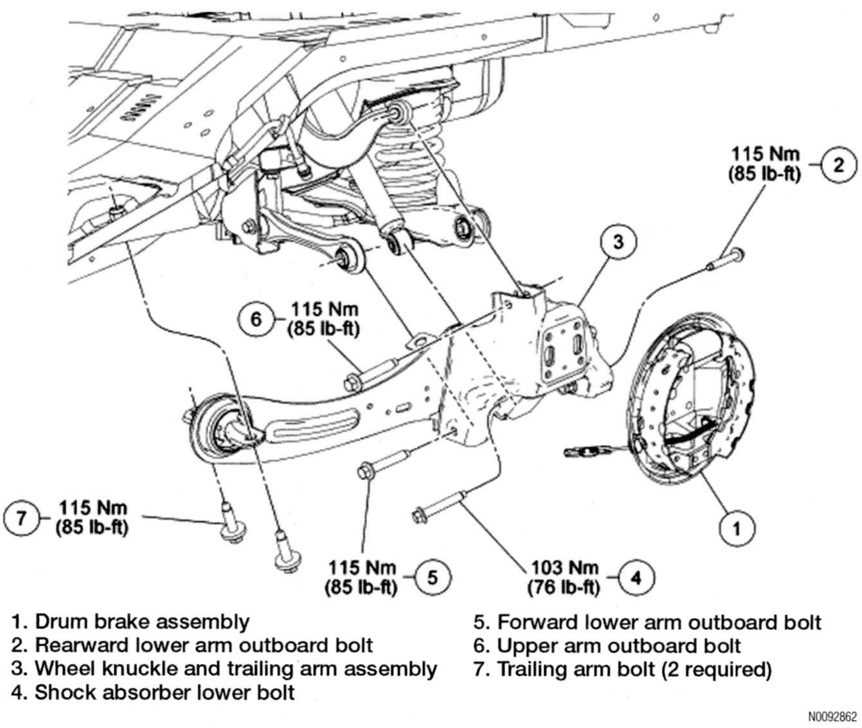

115 Nm (85 lb-ft) 2

3

6 115 Nm (85 lb-ft)

7 115 Nm (85 lb-ft)

115 Nm (85 lb-ft) 5

103 Nm (76 lb-ft) 4

1

1. Drum brake assembly
2. Rearward lower arm outboard bolt
3. Wheel knuckle and trailing arm assembly
4. Shock absorber lower bolt
5. Forward lower arm outboard bolt
6. Upper arm outboard bolt
7. Trailing arm bolt (2 required)

N0092862

Fig. 184 Exploded view of wheel knuckle and trailing arm assembly—rear suspension

25. Install the wheel and tire assemblies. Tighten the wheel nuts in a star pattern to 100 ft. lbs. (135 Nm).

26. Lower the vehicle until the weight of the vehicle is resting on the wheels and tires.

27. Tighten the 2 trailing arm bolts to 85 ft. lbs. (115 Nm).

28. Tighten the shock absorber lower bolt to 76 ft. lbs. (103 Nm).

29. Tighten the forward lower arm outboard bolt to 85 ft. lbs. (115 Nm).

30. Tighten the rearward lower arm outboard bolt to 85 ft. lbs. (115 Nm).

31. Tighten the upper arm outboard bolt to 85 ft. lbs. (115 Nm).

32. Bleed the brake wheel cylinder. For additional information, refer to Bleeding The Brake System under the Brakes section.

33. Check and, if necessary, adjust the rear toe.

FORD, LINCOLN AND MERCURY

12

Fusion • Milan • MKZ

BRAKES 12-12

ANTI-LOCK BRAKE SYSTEM (ABS).......................... 12-12
General Information................. 12-12
Precautions......................... 12-12
Speed Sensors........................ 12-12
Removal & Installation........ 12-12

BLEEDING THE BRAKE SYSTEM 12-15
Bleeding Procedure................. 12-15
Front Brake Caliper Bleeding.......................... 12-16
Hydraulic Control Unit (HCU) Bleeding................ 12-16
Master Cylinder Bleeding ... 12-16
Pressure Bleeding Procedure........................ 12-15
Rear Brake Caliper Bleeding.......................... 12-16

FRONT DISC BRAKES........ 12-17
Brake Caliper.......................... 12-17
Removal & Installation........ 12-17
Disc Brake Pads...................... 12-18
Removal & Installation........ 12-18

PARKING BRAKE............. 12-22
Parking Brake Cables.............. 12-22
Adjustment 12-22

REAR DISC BRAKES 12-19
Brake Caliper........................... 12-19
Removal & Installation........ 12-19
Disc Brake Pads...................... 12-21
Removal & Installation........ 12-21

CHASSIS ELECTRICAL 12-22

AIR BAG (SUPPLEMENTAL RESTRAINT SYSTEM) 12-22
General Information................. 12-22
Arming the System 12-24
Clockspring Centering........ 12-25
Disarming the System......... 12-23
Service Precautions 12-22

DRIVE TRAIN 12-25

Automatic Transmission Fluid... 12-25
Drain and Refill.................. 12-25
Clutch.................................... 12-28
Bleeding 12-28
Removal & Installation........ 12-28
Front Halfshaft........................ 12-30
Removal & Installation........ 12-30
Manual Transaxle Assembly 12-26
Removal & Installation........ 12-26
Manual Transaxle Fluid 12-27
Drain and Refill.................. 12-27
Rear Axle Stub Shaft Bearing and Seal............................... 12-33
Removal & Installation........ 12-33
Rear Halfshaft......................... 12-33
Removal & Installation........ 12-33
Transfer Case Assembly - Power Transfer Unit (PTU) 12-29
Removal & Installation........ 12-29

ENGINE COOLING 12-35

Engine Coolant........................ 12-35
Bleeding 12-37
Drain & Refill Procedure..... 12-35
Flushing............................. 12-36
Engine Fan 12-38
Removal & Installation........ 12-38
Radiator.................................. 12-41
Removal & Installation........ 12-41
Thermostat 12-42
Removal & Installation........ 12-42

ENGINE ELECTRICAL 12-44

BATTERY SYSTEM............ 12-44
Battery................................... 12-44
Removal & Installation........ 12-44

CHARGING SYSTEM 12-45
Alternator 12-45
Removal & Installation........ 12-45

HYBRID SYSTEM 12-48
Alternating Current Powerpoint........................... 12-48
Removal & Installation........ 12-48
Battery Energy Control Module (BECM)................................ 12-53
Removal & Installation........ 12-53
Battery Pack Sensor Module (BPSM)................................ 12-53
Removal & Installation........ 12-53
Buffer Zone............................. 12-48
Direct Current/Alternating Current Inverter..................... 12-49
Removal & Installation........ 12-49
Direct Current/Direct Current Converter............................. 12-50
Removal & Installation........ 12-50
Disarming the High Voltage Traction Battery..................... 12-49
High Voltage Bussed Electrical Center.................... 12-54
Removal & Installation........ 12-54
High Voltage Cables................ 12-54
Removal & Installation........ 12-54
High Voltage Low Current Fuse.................................... 12-56
Removal & Installation........ 12-56
High Voltage Traction Battery.................................. 12-56
Removal & Installation........ 12-56
Removal & Installation........ 12-56
High Voltage Traction Battery Cooling Fan 12-57
Removal & Installation........ 12-57
High Voltage Traction Battery Cooling Inlet Duct..... 12-57
Removal & Installation........ 12-57
High Voltage Traction Battery Cooling Outlet Duct... 12-58
Removal & Installation........ 12-58
High Voltage Traction Battery Inlet Air Temperature Sensor 12-58
Removal & Installation........ 12-58
Precautions 12-48

IGNITION SYSTEM 12-60
Firing Order............................ 12-60
Ignition Coil 12-60
Removal & Installation........ 12-60
Spark Plugs............................. 12-62
Removal & Installation........ 12-62

STARTING SYSTEM 12-65
Starter 12-65
Removal & Installation........ 12-65

ENGINE MECHANICAL......12-66

Accessory Drive Belts 12-66
Accessory Belt Routing.......12-66
Removal & Installation........12-66
Air Cleaner 12-69
Removal & Installation........12-69
Camshaft and Valve Lifters......12-69
Removal & Installation........12-69
Catalytic Converter..................12-82
Removal & Installation........12-82
Crankshaft Front Seal..............12-84
Removal & Installation........12-84
Cylinder Head 12-88
Removal & Installation........12-88
Exhaust Manifold 12-98
Removal & Installation........12-98
Intake Manifold 12-101
Removal & Installation......12-101
Oil Pan 12-109
Removal & Installation......12-109
Oil Pump..............................12-117
Removal & Installation......12-117
Piston and Ring....................12-121
Positioning 12-121
Rear Main Seal.....................12-122
Removal & Installation......12-122
Timing Chain & Sprockets....12-124
Removal & Installation......12-124
Valve Covers 12-129
Removal & Installation......12-129

ENGINE PERFORMANCE & EMISSION CONTROLS....12-139

Camshaft Position (CMP) Sensor 12-139
Removal & Installation......12-139
Crankshaft Position (CKP) Sensor 12-139
Removal & Installation......12-139
Heated Oxygen (HO2S) Sensor 12-142
Removal & Installation......12-142
Knock Sensor (KS)................12-143
Removal & Installation......12-143
Manifold Absolute Pressure (MAP) Sensor 12-144
Removal & Installation......12-144
Mass Air Flow (MAF) Sensor 12-145
Removal & Installation......12-145
Vehicle Speed Sensor (VSS).12-146
Removal & Installation......12-146

FUEL........................12-146

GASOLINE FUEL INJECTION SYSTEM.....................12-146
Fuel Injectors 12-147
Removal & Installation......12-147
Fuel System Service Precautions 12-146
Fuel Tank..............................12-151
Draining...........................12-151
Removal & Installation......12-153
Relieving Fuel System Pressure.............................12-146
Throttle Body.........................12-154
Removal & Installation......12-154

HEATING & AIR CONDITIONING SYSTEM.....................12-156

Blower Motor 12-156
Removal & Installation......12-156
Heater Core 12-156
Removal & Installation......12-156

PRECAUTIONS...............12-12

SPECIFICATIONS AND MAINTENANCE CHARTS.....12-3

Brake Specifications.................12-8
Camshaft Specifications...........12-5
Capacities 12-4
Crankshaft and Connecting Rod Specifications 12-6
Engine and Vehicle Identification 12-3
Engine Tune-Up Specifications 12-3
Fluid Specifications..................12-4
General Engine Specifications 12-3
Piston and Ring Specifications 12-6
Scheduled Maintenance Intervals............................12-9-11
Tire, Wheel and Ball Joint Specifications 12-8
Torque Specifications...............12-7
Valve Specifications 12-5
Wheel Alignment......................12-8

STEERING 12-157

Power Steering Gear.............12-157
Removal & Installation......12-157
Power Steering Pump............12-163
Bleeding 12-164
Fluid Fill Procedure 12-165
Removal & Installation......12-163

SUSPENSION...............12-166

FRONT SUSPENSION.......12-166
Lower Control Arm................12-166
Removal & Installation......................12-166
Stabilizer Bar.........................12-168
Removal & Installation......12-168
Steering (Wheel) Knuckle......12-170
Removal & Installation......12-170
Strut & Spring Assembly 12-171
Removal & Installation......12-171
Upper Control Arm................12-171
Removal & Installation......12-171
Wheel Bearings.....................12-173
Removal & Installation......12-173
REAR SUSPENSION 12-174
Coil Spring............................12-174
Removal & Installation......12-174
Lower Control Arm................12-175
Removal & Installation......12-175
Stabilizer Bar.........................12-175
Removal & Installation......12-175
Toe Link 12-176
Removal & Installation......12-176
Upper Control Arm.........12-177,178
Removal & Installation...............12-177,178
Wheel Bearings.....................12-180
Removal & Installation......12-180
Wheel Spindle.......................12-181
Removal & Installation......12-181

SPECIFICATIONS AND MAINTENANCE CHARTS

ENGINE AND VEHICLE IDENTIFICATION

Engine						
Code ①	Liters (cc)	Cu. In.	Cyl.	Fuel Sys.	Engine Type	Eng. Mfg.
3	2.5 (2500)	153	4	MFI	Hybrid	Ford
A	2.5 (2500)	153	4	MFI	Gas	Ford
G	3.0 (3000)	182	6	MFI	Gas	Ford
C	3.5 (3500)	214	6	MFI	Gas	Ford

Model Year	
Code ②	Year
A	2010
B	2011

① 8th position of VIN

② 10th position of VIN

25759_FUSI_C0001

GENERAL ENGINE SPECIFICATIONS

All measurements are given in inches.

Year	Model	Engine Displacement Liters	Engine ID/VIN	Fuel System Type	Net Horsepower @ rpm	Net Torque @ rpm (ft. lbs.)	Bore x Stroke (in.)	Com-pression Ratio	Oil Pressure @ rpm
2010	Fusion, Milan & MKZ	2.5	3	MFI	175@6000	172@4500	3.50x3.94	NA	NA
		2.5	A	MFI	175@6000	172@4500	3.50x3.94	NA	NA
		3.0	G	MFI	240@6550	223@4300	3.50x3.94	10.3:1	25@1500
		3.5	C	MFI	263@6250	249@4500	3.64x3.41	10.3:1	NA
2011	Fusion, Milan & MKZ	2.5	3	MFI	175@6000	172@4500	3.50x3.94	12.5:1	29-39@2000
		2.5	A	MFI	175@6000	172@4500	3.50x3.94	9.7:1	29-39@2000
		3.0	G	MFI	240@6550	223@4300	3.50x3.94	9.7:1	29-39@2000
		3.5	C	MFI	263@6250	249@4500	3.64x3.41	10.3:1	30@1500

NA: Not Available

25759_FUSI_C0002

ENGINE TUNE-UP SPECIFICATIONS

Year	Engine Displacement Liters	Engine ID/VIN	Spark Plug Gap (in.)	Ignition Timing (deg.)		Fuel Pump (psi)	Idle Speed (rpm)		Valve Clearance (inch)	
				MT	AT		MT	AT	Intake	Exhaust
2010	2.5	3	NA	NA	NA	55-58	NA	NA	0.008-0.011	0.010-0.013
	2.5	A	0.049-0.053	NA	NA	55-58	NA	NA	0.008-0.011	0.010-0.013
	3.0	G	0.045-0.049	NA	NA	55-58	NA	NA	NA	NA
	3.5	C	0.051-0.057	NA	NA	64-67	NA	NA	0.006-0.01	0.014-0.018
2011	2.5	3	NA	NA	NA	55-58	NA	NA	0.008-0.011	0.010-0.013
	2.5	A	0.049-0.053	NA	NA	55-58	NA	NA	0.008-0.011	0.010-0.013
	3.0	G	0.045-0.049	NA	NA	55-58	NA	NA	NA	NA
	3.5	C	0.051-0.057	NA	NA	64-67	NA	NA	0.006-0.01	0.014-0.018

NA: Not Available

25759_FUSI_C0003

CAPACITIES

Year	Model	Engine Displacement Liters	Engine ID/VIN	Engine Oil with Filter (qts.)	Transmission/axle (pts.) Auto.	Transmission/axle (pts.) Manual	Drive Axle (pts.) Front	Drive Axle (pts.) Rear	Transfer Case (pts.)	Fuel Tank (gal.)	Cooling System (qts.)
2010	Fusion, Milan & MKZ	2.5	3	5.3	5.8	NA	NA	NA	1.12	①	9.5
		2.5	A	5.3	18.0	NA	NA	NA	1.12	①	8.6
		3.0	G	NA	18.0	NA	NA	NA	1.12	①	9.7
		3.5	C	5.5	18.0	NA	NA	NA	1.12	①	10.0
2011	Fusion, Milan & MKZ	2.5	3	5.3	5.8	NA	NA	NA	1.12	①	9.5
		2.5	A	5.3	18.0	NA	NA	NA	1.12	①	8.6
		3.0	G	NA	18.0	NA	NA	NA	1.12	①	9.7
		3.5	C	5.5	18.0	NA	NA	NA	1.12	①	10.0

NOTE: All capacities are approximate. Add fluid gradually and ensure a proper fluid level is obtained.

① AWD vehicles: 16.5 gallons
FWD vehicles: 17.5 gallons

25759_FUSI_C0004

FLUID SPECIFICATIONS

Year	Model	Engine Disp. Liters	Engine ID/VIN	Engine Oil	Auto. Trans.	Drive Axle Front	Drive Axle Rear	Transfer Case	Power Steering Fluid	Brake Master Cylinder	Cooling System
2010	Fusion, Milan & MKZ	2.5	3	①	②	NA	NA	②	③	DOT 3	⑤
		2.5	A	④	②	NA	NA	②	③	DOT 3	⑤
		3.0	G	④	②	NA	NA	②	③	DOT 3	⑤
		3.5	C	④	②	NA	NA	②	③	DOT 3	⑤
2011	Fusion, Milan & MKZ	2.5	3	①	②	NA	NA	③	③	DOT 3	⑤
		2.5	A	④	②	NA	NA	②	③	DOT 3	⑤
		3.0	G	④	②	NA	NA	②	③	DOT 3	⑤
		3.5	C	④	②	NA	NA	②	③	DOT 3	⑤

DOT: Department Of Transpotation

① Motorcraft Premium Gold Engine Oil with Bittering Agent

② Motorcraft MERCON LV Automatic Transmission Fluid

④ Motorcraft SAE 5W-20 Premium Synthetic Blend Motor Oil

③ MERCON V Automatic Transmission Fluid

⑤ Motorcraft Specialty Green Engine Coolant

25759_FUSI_C0005

VALVE SPECIFICATIONS

Year	Engine Displacement Liters	Engine ID/VIN	Seat Angle (deg.)	Face Angle (deg.)	Spring Test Pressure (lbs. @ in.)	Spring Free-Length (in.)	Spring Installed Height (in.)	Stem-to-Guide Clearance (in.)		Stem Diameter (in.)	
								Intake	Exhaust	Intake	Exhaust
2010	2.5	3	NA	NA	NA	NA	NA	NA	NA	NA	NA
	2.5	A	NA	NA	NA	NA	NA	NA	NA	NA	NA
	3.0	G	44.75	45.5	575@1.27	1.990	1.680	0.0007-0.0027	0.0017-0.0370	0.2350-0.2358	0.2343-0.2350
	3.5	C	NA	NA	NA	NA	NA	NA	NA	NA	NA
2011	2.5	3	45	45	NA	1.768	1.492	0.0001	0.0001	0.2153-0.2159	0.2151-0.2157
	2.5	A	45	45	NA	1.768	1.492	0.00010	0.00011	0.2153-0.2159	0.2151-0.2157
	3.0	G	44.75	45.5	575@1.27	1.989	1.677	0.0007-0.0027	0.0017-0.0370	0.2350-0.2358	0.2343-0.2350
	3.5	C	44.5-45.5	44.5-45.5	114.7@1.06	1.889	1.450	0.0008-0.0027	0.0013-0.0320	0.21557-0.2164	0.2151-0.2159

NA: Not Available

25759_FUSI_C0006

CAMSHAFT SPECIFICATIONS

All measurements in inches unless noted

Year	Engine Displacement Liters	Engine Code/VIN	Journal Diameter	Brg. Oil Clearance	Shaft End-play	Runout	Journal Bore	Lobe Height	
								Intake	Exhaust
2010	2.5	3	0.982-0.983	0.001-0.003	NA	0.001	NA	0.324	0.3070
	2.5	A	0.982-0.983	0.001-0.003	NA	0.001	NA	0.324	0.3070
	3.0	G	1.060-1.061	0.001-0.0029	0.009	NA	1.062-1.063	0.20	
	3.5	C	①	②	0.0012-0.0066	0.0015	③	0.38	0.38
2011	2.5	3	0.982-0.983	0.001-0.003	NA	0.001	NA	0.324	0.3070
	2.5	A	0.982-0.983	0.001-0.003	NA	0.001	NA	0.324	0.3070
	3.0	G	1.060-1.061	0.001-0.0029	0.009	NA	1.062-1.063	0.20	
	3.5	C	①	②	0.0012-0.0066	0.0015	③	0.38	0.38

N/A: Not Available

① Inside Diameter-1st journal: 1.221-1.222
Inside diameter-intermediate journals: 1.023-1.024

② 1st journal: 0.0029
Intermediate journals: 0.0029

③ 1st journal: 1.221-1.222
Intermediate journals: 1.023-1.024

25759_FUSI_C0007

CRANKSHAFT AND CONNECTING ROD SPECIFICATIONS

All measurements are given in inches.

	Engine		Crankshaft				Connecting Rod		
Year	Displacement Liters	Engine ID/VIN	Main Brg. Journal Dia.	Main Brg. Oil Clearance	Shaft End-play	Thrust on No.	Journal Diameter	Oil Clearance	Side Clearance
2010	2.5	3	2.0460-2.0470	0.0006-0.0015	0.0080-0.0160	NA	2.0463-2.0473	NA	NA
	2.5	A	2.0460-2.0470	0.0006-0.0015	0.0080-0.0180	NA	2.046-2.0470	NA	0.076-0.120
	3	G	2.4670-2.4790	0.0009 0.0018	0.0030-0.0100	NA	1.9670-1.9680	NA	NA
	3.5	C	2.6570	0.0010-0.0016	0.0039-0.1140	NA	2.2040-2.2050	NA	NA
2011	2.5	3	2.0460-2.0470	0.0006-0.0015	0.0080-0.0160	NA	2.0463-2.0473	NA	NA
	2.5	A	2.0460-2.0470	0.0006-0.0015	0.0080-0.0180	NA	2.046-2.0470	NA	0.076-0.120
	3	G	2.4670-2.4790	0.0009 0.0018	0.0030-0.0100	NA	1.9670-1.9680	NA	NA
	3.5	C	2.6570	0.0010-0.0016	0.0039-0.1140	NA	2.2040-2.2050	NA	NA

NA: Not Available

25759_FUSI_C0008

PISTON AND RING SPECIFICATIONS

All measurements are given in inches.

	Engine			Ring Gap			Ring Side Clearance		
Year	Displacement Liters	Engine ID/VIN	Piston Clearance	Top Compression	Bottom Compression	Oil Control	Top Compression	Bottom Compression	Oil Control
2010	2.5	3	NA	NA	NA	NA	NA	NA	NA
	2.5	A	NA	NA	NA	NA	NA	NA	NA
	3.0	G	0.001-0.0025	0.0039-0.0098	0.0106-0.0165	0.0059-0.0255	0.0484-0.0494	0.0602-0.0612	0.0996-0.1005
	3.5	C	NA	NA	NA	NA	NA	NA	NA
2011	2.5	3	0.0009-0.0017	NA	NA	NA	0.0473-0.0474	0.0473-0.0474	0.0984-0.0985
	2.5	A	0.0009-0.0017	NA	NA	NA	0.0473-0.0474	0.0473-0.0474	0.0984-0.0985
	3.0	G	0.001-0.0025	0.0039-0.0097	0.0106-0.0165	0.0059-0.0255	0.0484-0.0494	0.0602-0.0612	0.0996-0.1005
	3.5	C	0.0003-0.0017	0.0059-0.0098	0.0118-0.0216	0.0059-0.0177	0.0484-0.0492	0.0602-0.0610	0.0996-0.1003

NA: Not Available

25759_FUSI_C0009

TORQUE SPECIFICATIONS

All readings in ft. lbs.

Year	Engine Disp. Liters	Engine ID/VIN	Cylinder Head Bolts	Main Bearing Bolts	Rod Bearing Bolts	Crankshaft Damper Bolts	Flywheel Bolts	Manifold Intake	Manifold Exhaust	Spark Plugs	Oil Pan Drain Plug
2010	2.5	3	⑦	⑧	NA	⑨	⑩	13	NA	NA	21
	2.5	A	⑪	⑧	NA	⑨	⑩	13	⑫	9	21
	3.0	G	①	②	NA	③	59	④	9	11	19
	3.5	C	⑤	7	NA	③	59	7	⑥	11	NA
2011	2.5	3	⑦	⑧	NA	⑨	⑩	13	NA	NA	21
	2.5	A	⑪	⑧	NA	⑨	⑩	13	⑫	9	21
	3.0	G	①	②	NA	③	59	④	9	11	19
	3.5	C	⑤	7	NA	③	59	7	⑥	11	NA

NA: Not Available

① Stage 1: Tighten to 30 ft. lbs. (40 Nm)
Stage 2: Tighen 90 degrees
Stage 3: Loosen one full turn
Stage 4: Tighten to 30 ft. lbs. (40 Nm)
Stage 5: Tighten to 90 degrees
Stage 6: Tighten 90 degrees

② Stage 1: Tighten to 7 ft. lbs. (10 Nm)
Stage 2: Individually loosen and then tighten each cam bearing cap to 7 ft. lbs. (10 Nm)

③ Stage 1: Tighten to 89 ft. lbs. (120 Nm)
Stage: 2 Loosen one full turn
Stage 3: Tighten to 37 ft. lbs. (50 Nm)
Stage 4: Tighten an additional 90 degrees

④ Stage 1: 7 ft. lbs. (10 Nm)
Stage 2 (Upper only): Tighten an additional 45 degrees

⑤ Stage 1: Tighten to 15 ft lbs. (20 Nm)
Stage 2: Tighten to 26 ft. lbs. (35 Nm)
Stage 3: Tighen 90 degrees
Stage 4: Tighten 90 degrees
Stage 5: Tighten 90 degrees

⑥ Studs: 9 ft. lbs. (12 Nm)
Stage 1: 15 ft. lbs. (20 Nm)
Stage 2: 18 ft. lbs. (25 Nm)

⑦ Stage 1: Tighten to 4 ft. lbs. (5 Nm)
Stage 2: Tighen to 11 ft. lbs. (15 Nm)
Stage 3: Tighten to 33 ft. lbs. (45 Nm)
Stage 4: Turn 90 degrees
Stage 5: Turn an additional 90 degrees

⑧ Stage 1: Tighten the camshaft bearin cap bolts one turn at a time until finger tight
Stage 2: Tighten to 5 Ft lbs. (7 Nm)
Stage 3: Tighten to 12 ft. lbs. (16 Nm)

⑨ Stage 1: Tighten to 74 ft. lbs. (100 Nm)
Stage 2: Tighten an additional 90 degrees

⑩ Stage 1: Tighten to 37 ft. lbs. (50 Nm)
Stage 2: Tighten to 59 ft. lbs. (80 Nm)
Stage 3: Tighten to 83 ft. lbs. (112 Nm)

⑪ Stage 1: 5 ft. lbs. (7 Nm)
Stage 2: Tighen to 11 ft. lbs. (15 Nm)
Stage 3: Tighten to 33 ft. lbs. (45 Nm)
Stage 4: Turn 90 degrees
Stage 5: Turn an additional 90 degrees

⑫ Stage 1: Tighten to 35 ft. lbs. (48 Nm)
Stage2: Tighten to 35 ft. lbs. (48 Nm)

25759_FUSI_C0010

WHEEL ALIGNMENT

Year	Model		Caster Range (+/-Deg.)	Caster Preferred Setting (Deg.)	Camber Range (+/-Deg.)	Camber Preferred Setting (Deg.)	Toe-in (in.)
2010	Fusion, Milan & MKZ	LF	-0.75	-1.25	-0.75	-0.03	NA
		RF	-0.75	-1.25	-0.75	-0.03	NA
		LR	NA	NA	0.75	-1.25	NA
		RR	NA	NA	0.75	-1.25	NA
2011	Fusion, Milan & MKZ	LF	1	3.75	-0.75	-0.03	NA
		RF	1	4.25	-0.75	-0.03	NA
		LR	NA	NA	0.75	-1.25	NA
		RR	NA	NA	0.75	-1.25	NA

25759_FUSI_C0011

TIRE, WHEEL AND BALL JOINT SPECIFICATIONS

Year	Model	OEM Tires Standard	OEM Tires Optional	Tire Pressures (psi) Front	Tire Pressures (psi) Rear	Wheel Size	Ball Joint Inspection	Lug Nut (ft. lbs.)
2010	Fusion, Milan & MKZ	①	①	①	①	①	lower: 0-0.016 upper: 0-0.008	100
2011	Fusion, Milan & MKZ	①	①	①	①	①	lower: 0-0.016 upper: 0-0.008	100

OEM: Original Equipment Manufacturer

PSI: Pounds Per Square Inch

NA: Information not available

① See Safety Certification Label on driver door jamb

25759_FUSI_C0012

BRAKE SPECIFICATIONS

All measurements in inches unless noted

Year	Model		Brake Disc Original Thickness	Brake Disc Minimum Thickness	Brake Disc Max. Runout	Brake Drum Diameter Original Inside Diameter	Brake Drum Diameter Max. Wear Limit	Brake Drum Diameter Maximum Machine Diamter	Minimum Pad/Lining Thickness Front	Minimum Pad/Lining Thickness Rear	Brake Caliper Bracket Bolts (ft. lbs.)	Brake Caliper Mounting Bolts (ft. lbs.)
2010	Fusion, Milan & MKZ	F	NA	0.905	NA	NA	NA	NA	0.118	0.118	20	66
		R	NA	0.314	NA	NA	NA	NA	0.118	0.118	19	52
2011	Fusion, Milan & MKZ	F	NA	0.905	NA	NA	NA	NA	0.118	0.118	20	66
		R	NA	0.314	NA	NA	NA	NA	0.118	0.118	19	52

F: Front

R: Rear

NA: Information not available

25759_FUSI_C0013

SCHEDULED MAINTENANCE INTERVALS

2010 Ford Fusion, Mercury Milan, Lincoln MKZ - Normal

		VEHICLE MILEAGE INTERVAL (x1000)														
Service Item	**Service Action**	**7.5**	**15**	**22.5**	**30**	**37.5**	**45**	**52.5**	**60**	**67.5**	**75**	**85.5**	**90**	**97.5**	**105**	**122.5**
Engine oil & filter	Replace	✓	✓	✓	✓	✓	✓	✓	✓	✓	✓	✓	✓	✓	✓	✓
Spark plugs	Replace												✓			
Engine coolant	Replace														✓	
Drive belt(s)	Replace															
Cabin air filter	Replace		✓		✓		✓		✓		✓		✓		✓	
Climate-controlled seat filter (if equipped)	Replace				✓				✓				✓			
Engine air filter	Replace				✓				✓				✓			
Manual transmission fluid	Replace															
Cooling system and hoses	Inspect		✓		✓		✓		✓		✓		✓		√	
Brake system (Pads/shoes/rotors/drums, brake lines and hoses, and parking brake system)	Inspect		✓		✓		✓		✓		✓		✓		✓	
Inspect wheels and related components for abnomal noise, wear, looseness or drag	Inspect	✓	✓	✓	✓	✓	✓	✓	✓	✓	✓	✓	✓	✓	✓	✓
Battery performance	Inspect	✓	✓	✓	✓	✓	✓	✓	✓	✓	✓	✓	✓	✓	✓	✓
Engine air filter	Inspect	✓	✓	✓	✓	✓	✓	✓	✓	✓	✓	✓	✓	✓	✓	✓
Drive belt(s)	Inspect	✓	✓	✓	✓	✓	✓	✓	✓	✓	✓	✓	✓	✓	✓	✓
Exhaust system (Leaks, damage, loose parts and foreign material)	Inspect		✓		✓		✓		✓		✓		✓		✓	
Horn, exterior lamps, turn signals and hazard warning light operation	Inspect	✓	✓	✓	✓	✓	✓	✓	✓	✓	✓	✓	✓	✓	✓	✓
Oil and fluid leaks	Inspect	✓	✓	✓	✓	✓	✓	✓	✓	✓	✓	✓	✓	✓	✓	✓
Radiator, coolers, heater and airconditioning hoses	Inspect	✓	✓	✓	✓	✓	✓	✓	✓	✓	✓	✓	✓	✓	✓	✓
Shocks struts and other suspension components for leaks and damage	Inspect	✓	✓	✓	✓	✓	✓	✓	✓	✓	✓	✓	✓	✓	✓	✓
Windshield for cracks, chips and pitting	Inspect	✓	✓	✓	✓	✓	✓	✓	✓	✓	✓	✓	✓	✓	✓	✓
Windshield wiper spray and wiper operation	Inspect	✓	✓	✓	✓	✓	✓	✓	✓	✓	✓	✓	✓	✓	✓	✓
Halfshaft & U-joints	Inspect		✓		✓		✓		✓		✓		✓		✓	
Steering linkage, ball joints, suspension and tie-rod ends, lubricate if equipped with greases fittings	Inspect/ Lubricate															
Fluid levels (all)	Top off	✓	✓	✓	✓	✓	✓	✓	✓	✓	✓	✓	✓	✓	✓	✓
Rotate tires, inspect tread wear, measure tread depth and check pressure	Service	✓	✓	✓	✓	✓	✓	✓	✓	✓	✓	✓	✓	✓	✓	✓

Oil change service intervals should be completed as indicated by the message center (Can be up to 1 year or 10,000 miles)

If the message center is prematurely reset or is inoperative, perform the oil change interval at 6 months or 5,000 miles from your last oil change.

25759_FUSI_C0014

SCHEDULED MAINTENANCE INTERVALS

2011 Ford Fusion, Mercury Milan, Lincoln MKZ - Normal

Service Item	Service Action	1	2	3	4	5	6	7	8	9	10	11	12	13	14	15
Drive belt(s)	Inspect	✓	✓	✓	✓	✓	✓	✓	✓	✓	✓	✓	✓	✓	✓	✓
Cabin air filter	Inspect	✓	✓	✓	✓	✓	✓	✓	✓	✓	✓	✓	✓	✓	✓	✓
Engine oil & filter	Replace	✓	✓	✓	✓	✓	✓	✓	✓	✓	✓	✓	✓	✓	✓	✓
Rotate tires, inspect tread	Inspect/R	✓	✓	✓	✓	✓	✓	✓	✓	✓	✓	✓	✓	✓	✓	✓
Inspect wheels and related	Inspect	✓	✓	✓	✓	✓	✓	✓	✓	✓	✓	✓	✓	✓	✓	✓
Fluid levels (all)	Top off	✓	✓	✓	✓	✓	✓	✓	✓	✓	✓	✓	✓	✓	✓	✓
Brake system	Inspect	✓	✓	✓	✓	✓	✓	✓	✓	✓	✓	✓	✓	✓	✓	✓
Cooling system, hoses,	Inspect	✓	✓	✓	✓	✓	✓	✓	✓	✓	✓	✓	✓	✓	✓	✓
Exhaust system (Leaks, damage, loose parts and	Inspect	✓	✓	✓	✓	✓	✓	✓	✓	✓	✓	✓	✓	✓	✓	✓
Halfshaft boots	Inspect	✓	✓	✓	✓	✓	✓	✓	✓	✓	✓	✓	✓	✓	✓	✓
Steering linkage, ball joints, suspension, tie-rod ends, driveshaft and u-joints: lubricate if equipped with grease fittings	Inspect / Lubricate	✓	✓	✓	✓	✓	✓	✓	✓	✓	✓	✓	✓	✓	✓	✓
Battery performance	Inspect	✓	✓	✓	✓	✓	✓	✓	✓	✓	✓	✓	✓	✓	✓	✓
Horn, exterior lamps, turn	Inspect	✓	✓	✓	✓	✓	✓	✓	✓	✓	✓	✓	✓	✓	✓	✓
Radiator, coolers, heater	Inspect	✓	✓	✓	✓	✓	✓	✓	✓	✓	✓	✓	✓	✓	✓	✓
Windshield wiper spray and wiper operation	Inspect	✓	✓	✓	✓	✓	✓	✓	✓	✓	✓	✓	✓	✓	✓	✓
Windshield for cracks, chips and pitting	Inspect	✓	✓	✓	✓	✓	✓	✓	✓	✓	✓	✓	✓	✓	✓	✓
Suspension components	Inspect	✓	✓	✓	✓	✓	✓	✓	✓	✓	✓	✓	✓	✓	✓	✓
Cabin air filter (If equipped)	Replace		✓		✓		✓		✓		✓		✓		✓	
Spark plugs	Replace										✓					
Drive belt	Replace															✓
Engine coolant	Replace										✓					✓
Engine air filter	Replace			✓			✓			✓			✓			✓
Engine air filter	Inspect	✓	✓	✓	✓	✓	✓	✓	✓	✓	✓	✓	✓	✓	✓	✓
Climate-controlled seat	Replace			✓			✓			✓			✓			✓
Automatic transaxle fluid	Replace															✓

Oil change service intervals should be completed as indicated by the message center (Can be up to 1 year or 10,000 miles)

If the message center is prematurely reset or is inoperative, perform the oil change interval at 6 months or 5,000 miles from your last oil change.

25759_FUSI_C0015

SCHEDULED MAINTENANCE INTERVALS

2011 Ford Fusion, Mercury Milan, Lincoln MKZ - Severe

Service Item	Service Action	1	2	3	4	5	6	7	8	9	10	11	12	13	14	15
Engine oil & filter	Replace	✓	✓	✓	✓	✓	✓	✓	✓	✓	✓	✓	✓	✓	✓	✓
Automatic transaxle fluid	Replace			✓			✓			✓			✓			✓
Battery performance	Inspect	✓	✓	✓	✓	✓	✓	✓	✓	✓	✓	✓	✓	✓	✓	✓
Brake system (Pads/shoes/rotors/drums, brake lines and hoses, and parking brake system)	Inspect	✓	✓	✓	✓	✓	✓	✓	✓	✓	✓	✓	✓	✓	✓	✓
Cabin air filter (If equipped)	Inspect, Service	✓	✓	✓	✓	✓	✓	✓	✓	✓	✓	✓	✓	✓	✓	✓
Climate-controlled seat filter (if equipped)	Replace			✓			✓			✓			✓			✓
Cooling system, hoses, clamps & coolant strength	Inspect	✓	✓	✓	✓	✓	✓	✓	✓	✓	✓	✓	✓	✓	✓	✓
Drive belt	Inspect	✓	✓	✓	✓	✓	✓	✓	✓	✓	✓	✓	✓	✓	✓	✓
Drive belt	Replace	✓	✓	✓	✓	✓	✓	✓	✓	✓	✓	✓	✓	✓	✓	✓
Engine air filter	Inspect, Service	✓	✓	✓	✓	✓	✓	✓	✓	✓	✓	✓	✓	✓	✓	✓
Engine coolant	Replace										✓					✓
Exhaust system (Leaks, damage, loose parts and foreign material)	Inspect	✓	✓	✓	✓	✓	✓	✓	✓	✓	✓	✓	✓	✓	✓	✓
Fluid levels (all)	Top off	✓	✓	✓	✓	✓	✓	✓	✓	✓	✓	✓	✓	✓	✓	✓
Halfshaft & U-joints	Inspect	✓	✓	✓	✓	✓	✓	✓	✓	✓	✓	✓	✓	✓	✓	✓
Horn, exterior lamps, turn signals and hazard warning light operation	Inspect	✓	✓	✓	✓	✓	✓	✓	✓	✓	✓	✓	✓	✓	✓	✓
Inspect wheels and related components for abnomal noise, wear, looseness or drag	Inspect	✓	✓	✓	✓	✓	✓	✓	✓	✓	✓	✓	✓	✓	✓	✓
Oil and fluid leaks	Inspect	✓	✓	✓	✓	✓	✓	✓	✓	✓	✓	✓	✓	✓	✓	✓
Radiator, coolers, heater and air conditioning hoses	Inspect	✓	✓	✓	✓	✓	✓	✓	✓	✓	✓	✓	✓	✓	✓	✓
Rotate tires, inspect tread wear, measure tread depth and check pressure	Inspect/ Rotate	✓	✓	✓	✓	✓	✓	✓	✓	✓	✓	✓	✓	✓	✓	✓
Shocks struts and other suspension components for leaks and damage	Inspect	✓	✓	✓	✓	✓	✓	✓	✓	✓	✓	✓	✓	✓	✓	✓
Spark plugs	Replace						✓						✓			
Steering linkage, ball joints, suspension and tie-rod ends, lubricate if equipped with greases fittings	Inspect/ Lubricate	✓	✓	✓	✓	✓	✓	✓	✓	✓	✓	✓	✓	✓	✓	✓
Windshield for cracks, chips and pitting	Inspect	✓	✓	✓	✓	✓	✓	✓	✓	✓	✓	✓	✓	✓	✓	✓
Windshield wiper spray and wiper operation	Inspect	✓	✓	✓	✓	✓	✓	✓	✓	✓	✓	✓	✓	✓	✓	✓

Oil change service intervals should be completed as indicated by the message center (Can be up to 1 year or 10,000 miles)

If the message center is prematurely reset or is inoperative, perform the oil change interval at 6 months or 5,000 miles from your last oil change.

25759_FUSI_C0016

PRECAUTIONS

Before servicing any vehicle, please be sure to read all of the following precautions, which deal with personal safety, prevention of component damage, and important points to take into consideration when servicing a motor vehicle:

- Never open, service or drain the radiator or cooling system when the engine is hot; serious burns can occur from the steam and hot coolant.
- Observe all applicable safety precautions when working around fuel. Whenever servicing the fuel system, always work in a well-ventilated area. Do not allow fuel spray or vapors to come in contact with a spark, open flame, or excessive heat (a hot drop light, for example). Keep a dry chemical fire extinguisher near the work area. Always keep fuel in a container specifically designed for fuel storage; also, always properly seal fuel containers to avoid the possibility of fire or explosion. Refer to the additional fuel system precautions later in this section.
- Fuel injection systems often remain pressurized, even after the engine has been turned **OFF**. The fuel system pressure must be relieved before disconnecting any fuel lines. Failure to do so may result in fire and/or personal injury.
- Brake fluid often contains polyglycol ethers and polyglycols. Avoid contact with the eyes and wash your hands thoroughly after handling brake fluid. If you do get brake fluid in your eyes, flush your eyes with clean, running water for 15 minutes. If eye irritation persists, or if you have taken brake fluid internally, IMMEDIATELY seek medical assistance.
- The EPA warns that prolonged contact with used engine oil may cause a number of skin disorders, including cancer. You should make every effort to minimize your exposure to used engine oil. Protective gloves should be worn when changing oil. Wash your hands and any other exposed skin areas as soon as possible after exposure to used engine oil. Soap and water, or waterless hand cleaner should be used.
- All new vehicles are now equipped with an air bag system, often referred to as a Supplemental Restraint System (SRS) or Supplemental Inflatable Restraint (SIR) system. The system must be disabled before performing service on or around system components, steering column, instrument panel components, wiring and sensors. Failure to follow safety and disabling procedures could result in accidental air bag deployment, possible personal injury and unnecessary system repairs.
- Always wear safety goggles when working with, or around, the air bag system. When carrying a non-deployed air bag, be sure the bag and trim cover are pointed away from your body. When placing a non-deployed air bag on a work surface, always face the bag and trim cover upward, away from the surface. This will reduce the motion of the module if it is accidentally deployed. Refer to the additional air bag system precautions later in this section.
- Clean, high quality brake fluid from a sealed container is essential to the safe and proper operation of the brake system. You should always buy the correct type of brake fluid for your vehicle. If the brake fluid becomes contaminated, completely flush the system with new fluid. Never reuse any brake fluid. Any brake fluid that is removed from the system should be discarded. Also, do not allow any brake fluid to come in contact with a painted surface; it will damage the paint.
- Never operate the engine without the proper amount and type of engine oil; doing so WILL result in severe engine damage.
- Timing belt maintenance is extremely important. Many models utilize an interference-type, non-freewheeling engine. If the timing belt breaks, the valves in the cylinder head may strike the pistons, causing potentially serious (also time-consuming and expensive) engine damage. Refer to the maintenance interval charts for the recommended replacement interval for the timing belt, and to the timing belt section for belt replacement and inspection.
- Disconnecting the negative battery cable on some vehicles may interfere with the functions of the on-board computer system(s) and may require the computer to undergo a relearning process once the negative battery cable is reconnected.
- When servicing drum brakes, only disassemble and assemble one side at a time, leaving the remaining side intact for reference.
- Only an MVAC-trained, EPA-certified automotive technician should service the air conditioning system or its components.

BRAKES

ANTI-LOCK BRAKE SYSTEM (ABS)

GENERAL INFORMATION

PRECAUTIONS

- Certain components within the ABS system are not intended to be serviced or repaired individually.
- Do not use rubber hoses or other parts not specifically specified for and ABS system. When using repair kits, replace all parts included in the kit. Partial or incorrect repair may lead to functional problems and require the replacement of components.
- Lubricate rubber parts with clean, fresh brake fluid to ease assembly. Do not use shop air to clean parts; damage to rubber components may result.
- Use only DOT 3 brake fluid from an unopened container.
- If any hydraulic component or line is removed or replaced, it may be necessary to bleed the entire system.
- A clean repair area is essential. Always clean the reservoir and cap thoroughly before removing the cap. The slightest amount of dirt in the fluid may plug an orifice and impair the system function. Perform repairs after components have been thoroughly cleaned; use only denatured alcohol to clean components. Do not allow ABS components to come into contact with any substance containing mineral oil; this includes used shop rags.
- The Anti-Lock control unit is a microprocessor similar to other computer units in the vehicle. Ensure that the ignition switch is **OFF** before removing or installing controller harnesses. Avoid static electricity discharge at or near the controller.
- If any arc welding is to be done on the vehicle, the control unit should be unplugged before welding operations begin.

SPEED SENSORS

REMOVAL & INSTALLATION

Front

See Figure 1.

1. With the vehicle in NEUTRAL, position it on a hoist.
2. Remove the fender splash shield.
3. Disconnect the wheel speed sensor electrical connector.

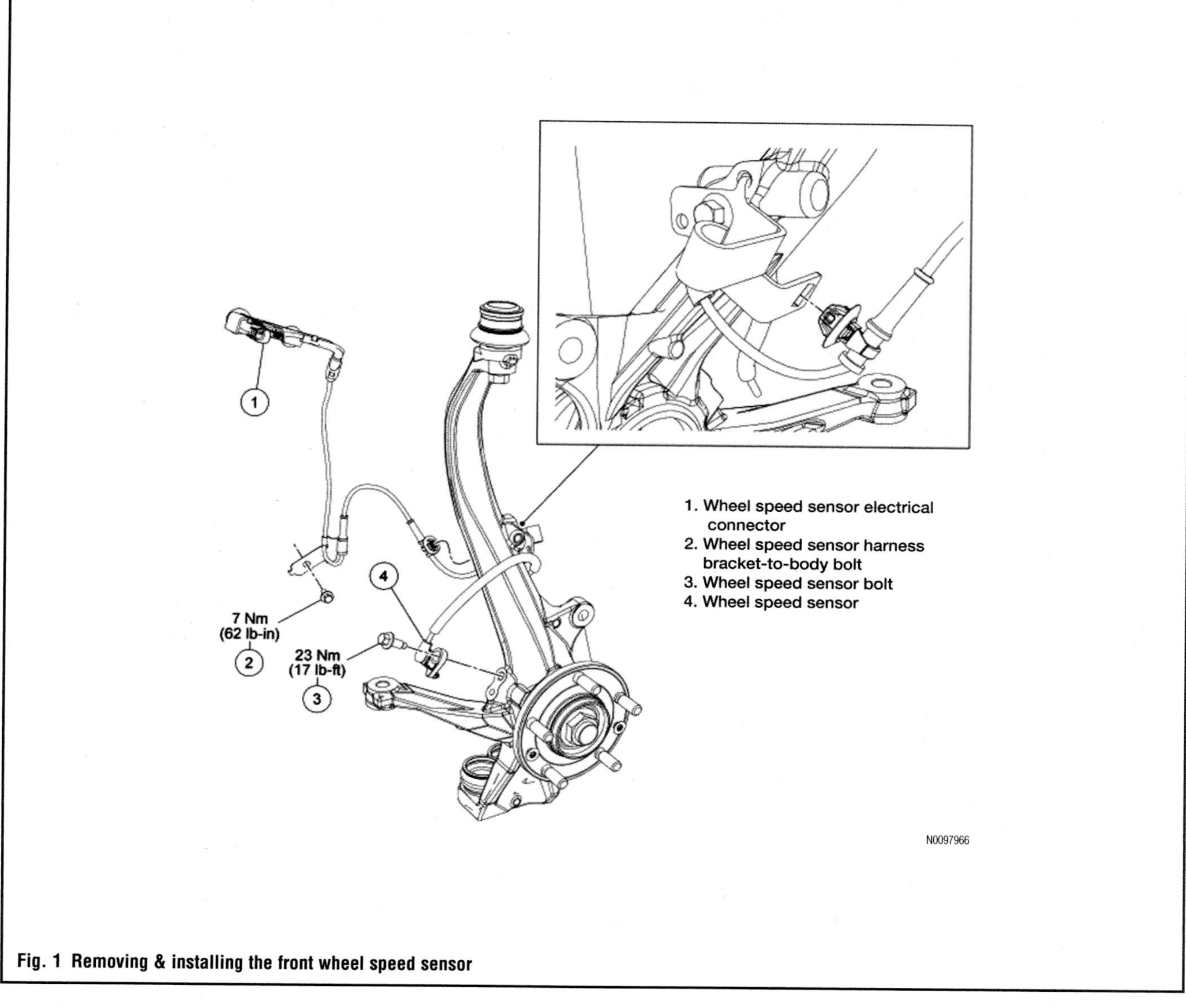

Fig. 1 Removing & installing the front wheel speed sensor

4. Remove the wheel speed sensor harness bracket-to-body bolt.
5. Detach the wheel speed sensor harness from the wheel knuckle bracket.
6. Remove the wheel speed sensor bolt and the wheel speed sensor.

To install:

To install, reverse the removal procedure. Tighten the wheel speed sensor bolt and sensor to 17 ft. lbs. (23 Nm). Tighten the wheel speed sensor harness bracket to body bolt to 62 inch lbs. (7 Nm).

Rear AWD

See Figure 2.

1. Remove the rear seat bolster.
2. Disconnect the wheel speed sensor electrical connector.
3. With the vehicle in NEUTRAL, position it on a hoist.
4. Using a suitable tool, disconnect the grommet from the body.
5. Remove the wheel speed sensor harness nut and bolt.
6. Remove the wheel speed sensor bolt and the wheel speed sensor.

To install:

To install, reverse the removal procedure. Tighten the wheel speed sensor bolt and sensor to 17 ft. lbs. (23 Nm). Tighten the wheel speed sensor harness nut and bolt to 17 ft. lbs. (23 Nm).

Rear FWD

See Figure 3.

1. Remove the rear seat bolster.
2. Disconnect the wheel speed sensor electrical connector.
3. With the vehicle in NEUTRAL, position it on a hoist.
4. Using a suitable tool, disconnect the grommet from the body.

➡It is not necessary to remove the harness routing brackets.

5. Disconnect the wheel speed sensor harness from the brackets.
6. Remove the wheel speed sensor wire bolt and the wheel speed sensor.

To install:

To install, reverse the removal procedure. Tighten the wheel speed sensor to 17 ft. lbs. (23 Nm).

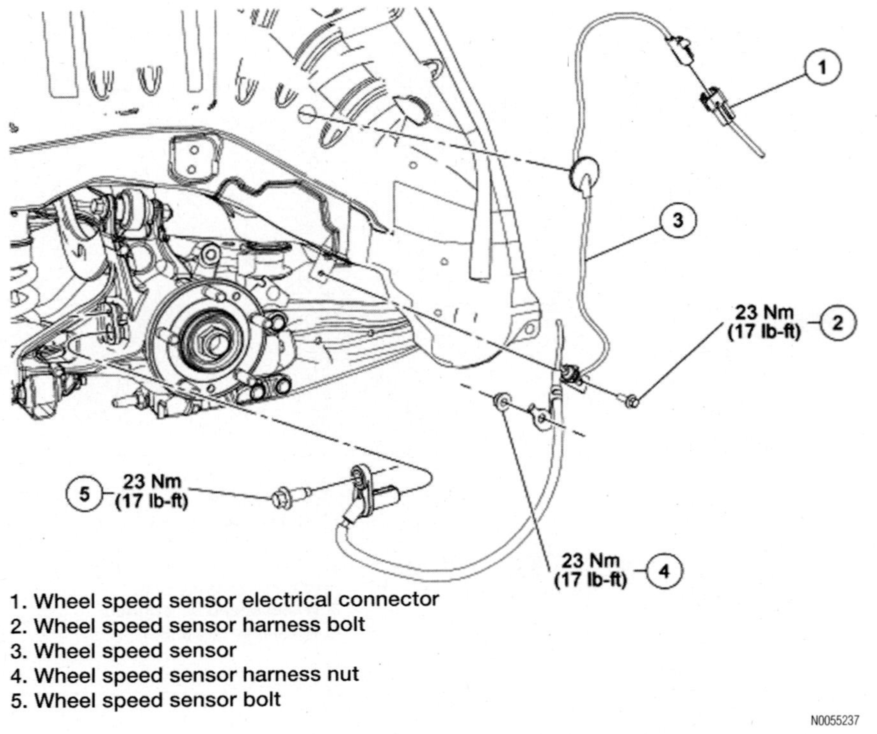

Fig. 2 Removing & installing the rear wheel speed sensor—AWD

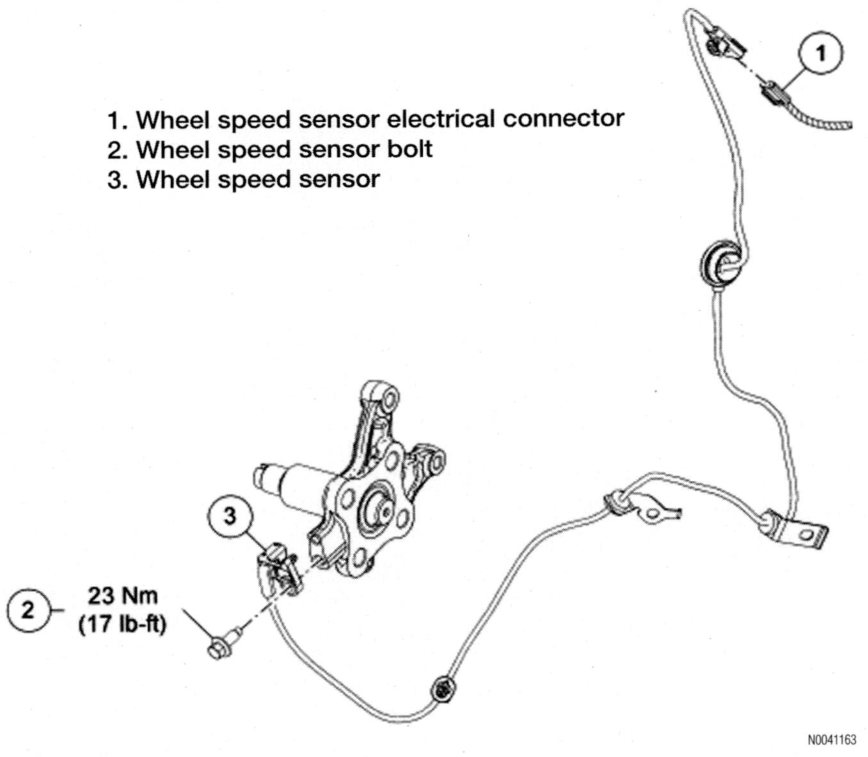

Fig. 3 Removing & installing the rear wheel speed sensor —FWD

BLEEDING PROCEDURE

WARNING

Do not use any fluid other than clean brake fluid meeting manufacturer's specification. Additionally, do not use brake fluid that has been previously drained. Following these instructions will help prevent system contamination, brake component damage and the risk of serious personal injury.

WARNING

Carefully read cautionary information on product label. For additional information, consult the product Material Safety Data Sheet (MSDS) if available. Failure to follow these instructions may result in serious personal injury.

WARNING

Do not allow the brake master cylinder to run dry during the bleeding operation. Master cylinder may be damaged if operated without fluid, resulting in degraded braking performance. Failure to follow this instruction may result in serious personal injury.

➡Do not spill brake fluid on painted or plastic surfaces or damage to the surface may occur. If brake fluid is spilled onto a painted or plastic surface, immediately wash the surface with water.

➡Due to the complexity of the fluid path within the hydraulic system, it is necessary to pressure bleed the system.

➡When any part of the hydraulic system has been disconnected for repair or installation of new components, air can get into the system and cause spongy brake pedal action. This requires bleeding of the hydraulic system after it has been correctly connected.

➡Due to the complexity of the fluid path within the rear integral parking brake calipers, it is necessary to press and release the parking brake during the bleed procedure.

➡The Hydraulic Control Unit (HCU) bleeding procedure must be carried out if the HCU or any components upstream of the HCU are installed new.

PRESSURE BLEEDING PROCEDURE

All vehicles

1. Clean all the dirt from around the brake fluid reservoir cap and remove the cap. Fill the brake master cylinder reservoir with clean, specified brake fluid.

➡Master cylinder pressure bleeder adapter tools are available from various manufacturers of pressure bleeding equipment. Follow the instructions of the manufacturer when installing the adapter.

2. Install the bleeder adapter to the brake master cylinder reservoir and attach the bleeder tank hose to the fitting on the adapter.

➡Make sure the bleeder tank contains enough specified brake fluid to complete the bleeding operation.

3. Open the valve on the bleeder tank.
   a. Apply 30-50 psi (207-345 kPa) to the brake system.
4. Remove the RH rear bleeder cap and place a box-end wrench on the bleeder screw. Attach a rubber drain tube to the RH rear bleeder screw and submerge the free end of the tube in a container partially filled with clean, specified brake fluid.
5. Loosen the RH rear bleeder screw. Leave open until clear, bubble-free brake fluid flows, then tighten the RH rear bleeder screw.
   a. Press and release the parking brake 5 times.
   b. Repeat until clear, bubble-free fluid comes out.
6. Tighten the RH rear bleeder screw. Remove the rubber hose and install the bleeder screw cap.
7. Repeat Steps 4 through 6 for the LH rear brake caliper.
8. Remove the RH front bleeder cap and place a box-end wrench on the bleeder screw. Attach a rubber drain tube to the RH front bleeder screw and submerge the free end of the tube in a container partially filled with clean, specified brake fluid.
9. Loosen the RH front bleeder screw. Leave open until clear, bubble-free brake fluid flows, then tighten the RH front bleeder screw.
10. Tighten the LH rear bleeder screw. Remove the rubber hose and install the bleeder screw cap.
11. Repeat Steps 8 through 10 for the LH front brake caliper.
12. Close the bleeder tank valve and release the pressure. Remove the tank hose from the adapter and remove the adapter. Fill the reservoir with clean, specified brake fluid and install the reservoir cap.

Hybrid vehicles

➡On hybrid vehicles, the brake booster push rod has an elongated slot that attaches to the brake pedal with a clevis pin. The elongated slot allows for a small amount of pedal travel (free play) to occur without the brake pedal applying pressure on the booster push rod. When performing a bleed procedure, it is important to push the pedal through the air gap, so that the clevis pin is contacting the brake booster push rod. Except when required by the scan tool, the ignition key must remain off during the bleed procedure to allow minimal force required to push through the gap.

13. With the ignition off, press the brake pedal through the gap to seat the clevis pin against the brake booster push rod and then confirm the pedal is firm.
   a. If the brake pedal is spongy (soft), repeat the Pressure Bleeding procedure to remove any remaining air from the system.

Non-hybrid vehicles

14. Apply the brakes several times to verify correct brake operation.
   a. If the brake pedal is spongy (soft), repeat the Pressure Bleeding procedure to remove any remaining air from the system.

FRONT BRAKE CALIPER BLEEDING

➡It is not necessary to do a complete brake system bleed if only the brake caliper was disconnected or installed new.

1. Remove the brake caliper bleeder screw cap and place a box-end wrench on the bleeder screw. Attach a rubber drain hose to the bleeder screw and submerge the free end of the hose in a container partially filled with clean, specified brake fluid.

➡On hybrid vehicles, the brake booster push rod has an elongated slot that attaches to the brake pedal with a

clevis pin. The elongated slot allows for a small amount of pedal travel (free play) to occur without the brake pedal applying pressure on the booster push rod. When performing a bleed procedure, it is important to push the pedal through the air gap, so that the clevis pin is contacting the brake booster push rod. Except when required by the scan tool, the ignition key must remain off during the bleed procedure to allow minimal force required to push through the gap.

2. Have an assistant pump the brake pedal at least 2 times and then hold firm pressure on the brake pedal.
3. Loosen the bleeder screw until a stream of brake fluid comes out. While the assistant maintains pressure on the brake pedal, tighten the bleeder screw.
   a. Repeat until clear, bubble-free fluid comes out.
   b. Refill the brake master cylinder reservoir as necessary.
4. Tighten the bleeder screw. Remove the rubber hose and install the bleeder screw cap.

HYDRAULIC CONTROL UNIT (HCU) BLEEDING

All vehicles

1. Use the Pressure Bleeding procedure to bleed the system.
2. Connect the scan tool and follow the ABS Hydraulic Control Unit (HCU) bleeding instructions.
3. Repeat the Pressure Bleeding procedure to bleed the system.

Hybrid vehicles

4. Following the scan tool instructions, carry out the Multi-Calibration Routine.

MASTER CYLINDER BLEEDING

WARNING

Do not allow the brake master cylinder to run dry during the bleeding operation. Master cylinder may be damaged if operated without fluid, resulting in degraded braking performance. Failure to follow this instruction may result in serious personal injury.

➡Do not spill brake fluid on painted or plastic surfaces or damage to the surface may occur. If brake fluid is spilled onto a painted or plastic surface, immediately wash the surface with water.

➡When any part of the hydraulic system is disconnected for repair or installation of new components, air can enter the system and cause spongy brake pedal action. This requires bleeding of the hydraulic system after it is correctly connected.

➡When a new brake master cylinder has been installed, or the system is emptied or partially emptied, it should be primed to prevent air from entering the system.

1. Disconnect the brake tubes from the master cylinder.
2. Install short brake tubes onto the primary and secondary ports with the ends submerged in the brake master cylinder reservoir.
3. Fill the brake master cylinder reservoir with clean, specified brake fluid.

➡On hybrid vehicles, the brake booster push rod has an elongated slot that attaches to the brake pedal with a clevis pin. The elongated slot allows for a small amount of pedal travel (free play) to occur without the brake pedal applying pressure on the booster push rod. When performing a bleed procedure, it is important to push the pedal through the air gap, so that the clevis pin is contacting the brake booster push rod. Except when required by the scan tool, the ignition key must remain off during the bleed procedure to allow minimal force required to push through the gap.

4. Have an assistant slowly pump the brake pedal until clear fluid flows from the brake tubes, without air bubbles.
5. Remove the short brake tubes and install the master cylinder brake tubes.
   a. Tighten to specifications. (NOT AVAIL)
6. Bleed the brake system.

REAR BRAKE CALIPER BLEEDING

See Figure 4.

➡When any part of the hydraulic system is disconnected for repair or installation of new components, air can get into the system and cause spongy brake pedal action. This requires bleeding of the hydraulic system after it is correctly connected. The hydraulic system can be bled manually or with pressure bleeding equipment.

➡Due to the complexity of the fluid path within the rear integral parking brake calipers, it may be necessary to follow this procedure when new calipers are installed.

➡This procedure is necessary only when installing a new rear brake caliper. To bleed the brake system, refer to PRESSURE BLEEDING.

1. Remove the wheel and tire.
2. Remove the 2 brake caliper guide pin bolts and position the brake caliper aside.
3. Remove the outer brake pad.

➡Place a shop towel between the caliper and the brake disc.

4. Install the brake caliper using the 2 guide pin bolts.
   a. Tighten to specifications.
5. Slowly apply the brake pedal to extend the brake caliper piston outward.
6. Remove the 2 guide pin bolts and position the brake caliper aside.
7. Remove the brake caliper bleeder screw cap and place a box-end wrench on the bleeder screw. Attach a rubber drain hose to the bleeder screw and submerge the free end of the hose in a container partially filled with clean, specified brake fluid.
8. Loosen the brake caliper bleeder screw.
9. Using the Rear Caliper Piston Adjuster, fully retract the brake caliper piston and tighten the bleeder screw to specifications.
10. Repeat Steps 4 through 9 until clear, bubble free fluid comes out.
    a. Refill the brake master cylinder reservoir as necessary.
    b. Remove the rubber hose and install the bleeder screw cap.
11. Remove the 2 guide pin bolts and the shop towel.
12. Install the outer brake pad.
13. Position the brake caliper and install the 2 guide pin bolts.
    a. Tighten to specifications.
14. Install the wheel and tire.

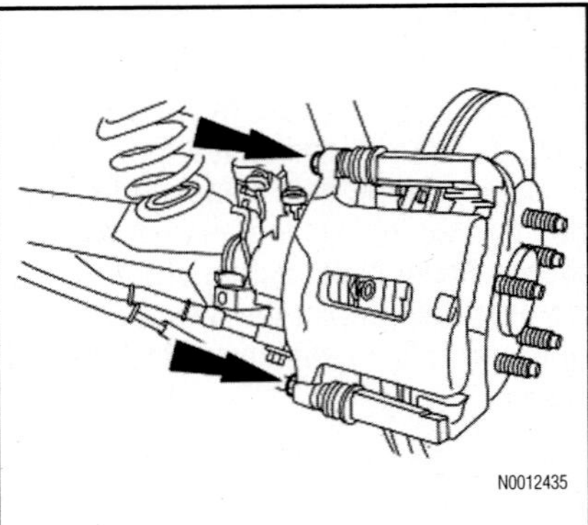

Fig. 4 Identifying the brake caliper guide pin bolts

CAUTION

Dust and dirt accumulating on brake parts during normal use may contain asbestos fibers from production or aftermarket brake linings. Breathing excessive concentrations of asbestos fibers can cause serious bodily harm. Exercise care when servicing brake parts. Do not sand or grind brake lining unless equipment used is designed to contain the dust residue. Do not clean brake parts with compressed air or by dry brushing. Cleaning should be done by dampening the brake components with a fine mist of water, then wiping the brake components clean with a dampened cloth. Dispose of cloth and all residue containing asbestos fibers in an impermeable container with the appropriate label. Follow practices prescribed by the Occupational Safety and Health Administration (OSHA) and the Environmental Protection Agency (EPA) for the handling, processing, and disposing of dust or debris that may contain asbestos fibers.

WARNING

Do not use any fluid other than clean brake fluid meeting manufacturer's specification. Additionally, do not use brake fluid that has been previously drained. Following these instructions will help prevent system contamination, brake component damage and the risk of serious personal injury.

WARNING

Carefully read cautionary information on product label. For additional information, consult the product Material Safety Data Sheet (MSDS) if available. Failure to follow these instructions may result in serious personal injury.

➡Do not spill brake fluid on painted or plastic surfaces or damage to the surface may occur. If brake fluid is spilled onto a painted or plastic surface, immediately wash the surface with water.

BRAKE CALIPER

REMOVAL & INSTALLATION

See Figure 5.

➡The brake caliper and anchor plate are serviced together as a kit.

1. Remove the brake pads.
2. Remove the brake caliper flow bolt and position the hose aside.
    a. Discard the 2 copper washers.
3. Remove the 2 brake caliper anchor plate bolts.

➡The caliper guide pin boots must be seated correctly on the anchor plate or the guide pins may become contaminated.

4. Inspect the guide pin boots and make sure they are seated on the anchor plate correctly. The boot has a lip that fits under the edge of the anchor plate extension.

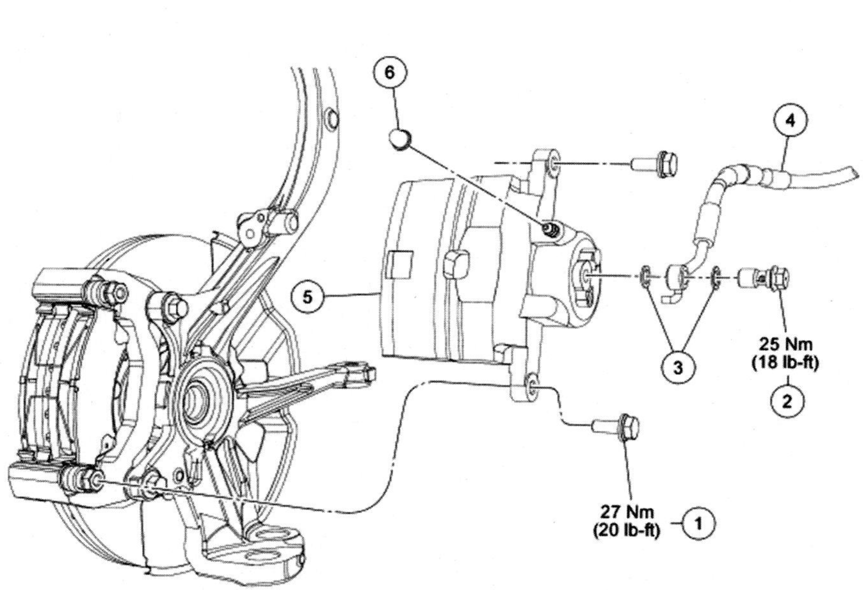

Fig. 5 Removing & installing the front brake caliper

To install:

➡During installation, make sure that the brake caliper hose does not become twisted.

5. To install, reverse the removal procedure.
6. Tighten the brake caliper anchor plate bolts to 66 ft. lbs. (90 Nm).
7. Install new copper washers.
8. Tighten the brake caliper flow bolt to 18 ft. lbs. (25 Nm).
9. Bleed the brake caliper.

DISC BRAKE PADS

REMOVAL & INSTALLATION

See Figures 6 through 9.

1. Always install new brake shoes or pads at both ends of an axle to reduce the possibility of brakes pulling vehicle to one side. Failure to follow this instruction may result in uneven braking and serious personal injury.

➡Do not spill brake fluid on painted or plastic surfaces or damage to the surface may occur. If brake fluid is spilled onto a painted or plastic surface, immediately wash the surface with water.

2. Check the brake fluid level in the brake master cylinder reservoir.
   a. If required, remove the fluid until the brake master cylinder reservoir is half full.
3. Remove the wheel and tire.

➡Do not pry in the caliper sight hole to retract the pistons as this can damage the pistons and boots.

➡Do not allow the brake caliper to hang from the brake hose or damage to the hose can occur.

4. Remove the 2 brake caliper guide pin bolts and position the caliper aside.
   a. Support the caliper using mechanic's wire.
5. Remove the 2 brake pad retraction springs.
6. Remove the brake pads, brake pad shims and stainless steel shims.
   a. Inspect the brake pads and shims for wear or contamination.
7. Remove the brake pad slides.
8. Remove the 4 brake pad slide clips.

To install:

9. Install the 4 brake pad slide clips.

➡Protect the piston and boots when pushing the caliper piston into the caliper piston bores or damage to components may occur.

➡Make sure that the caliper guide pin boots are fully seated or damage to the caliper guide pin boots can occur.

10. If installing new brake pads, using a C-clamp and a worn brake, compress the disc brake caliper pistons into the caliper.

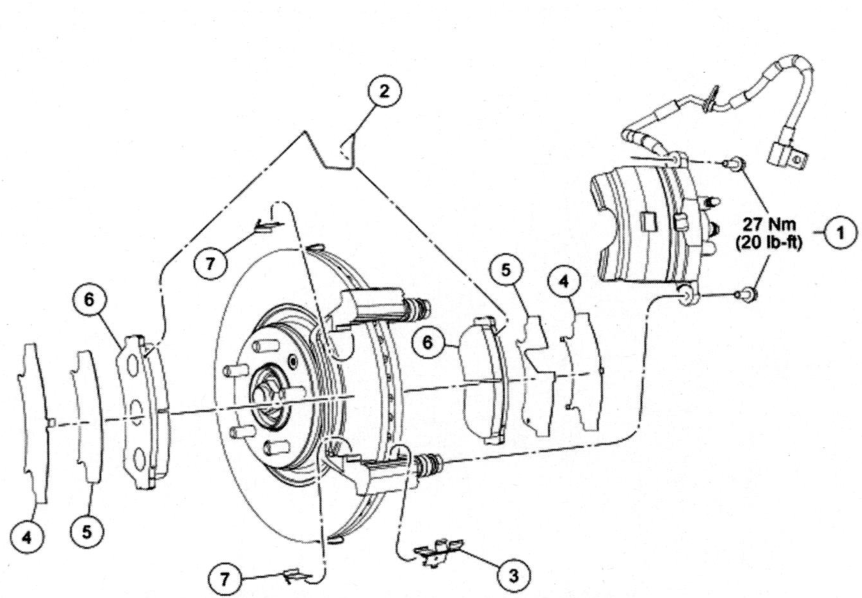

1. Brake caliper guide pin bolts (2 required)
2. Brake pad retraction spring (2 required)
3. Brake pad slide (2 required)
4. Stainless steel shims (2 required)
5. Brake pad shims (2 required)
6. Brake pads (2 required)
7. Brake pad slide clips (4 required)

N0054385

Fig. 6 Exploded view of front brake pads and related components

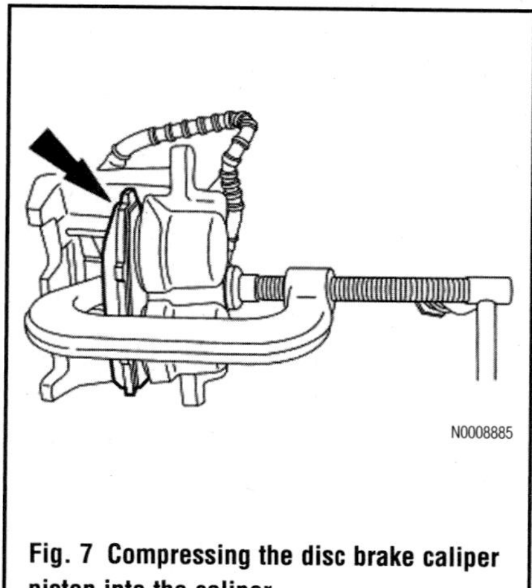

Fig. 7 Compressing the disc brake caliper piston into the caliper

11. Install the brake pad slides.
12. Apply grease that is supplied to the pad backing plate and shims in the areas indicated.
 a. Apply grease to the back of the brake pad.
 b. Apply grease to the inner piston side stainless steel shim.
 c. Apply grease to the outer stainless steel shim.

➡LH inboard shim shown.

➡The cut shim is directional and used on the inboard pad only. The cut is positioned toward the leading side. Correct installation can be verified if the shim hole is positioned on the bottom side.

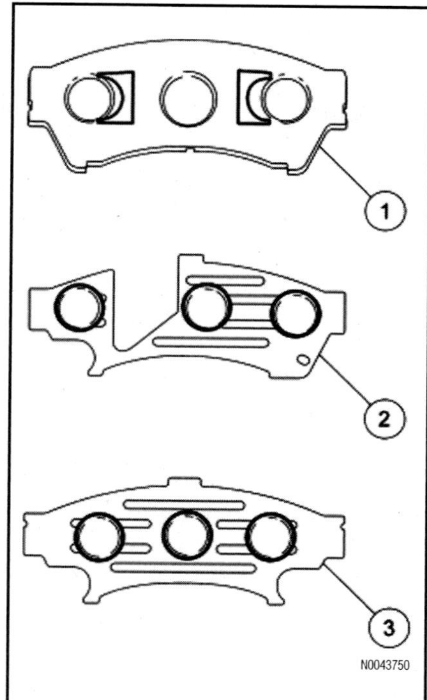

Fig. 8 Applying grease to the pad backing plate and shims

13. Install the brake pad shims and the stainless steel shims to the brake pads.
14. Install the 2 brake pad retraction springs.

➡The caliper guide pin boots must be seated correctly on the anchor plate or the guide pins may become contaminated.

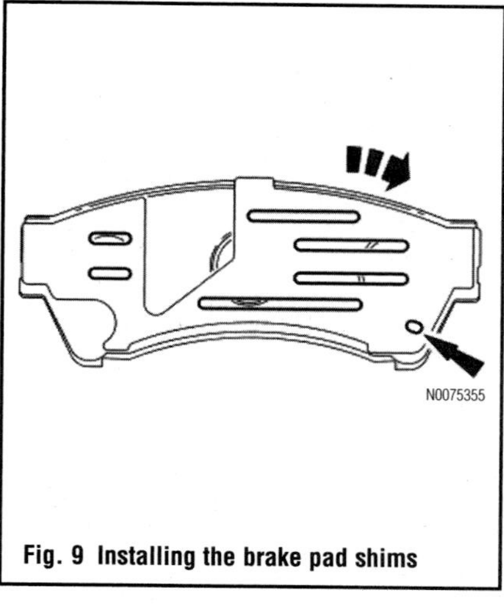

Fig. 9 Installing the brake pad shims

15. Inspect the guide pin boots and make sure they are seated on the anchor plate correctly. The boot has a lip that fits under the edge of the anchor plate extension.

➡Make sure that the brake caliper hose does not become twisted.

16. Position the brake caliper and install the 2 guide pin bolts.
 a. Tighten to 20 ft. lbs. (27 Nm).
17. Fill the brake master cylinder reservoir with clean, specified brake fluid.
18. Install the wheel and tire.
 a. Apply brakes several times to verify correct brake operation.

BRAKES — REAR DISC BRAKES

CAUTION

Dust and dirt accumulating on brake parts during normal use may contain asbestos fibers from production or aftermarket brake linings. Breathing excessive concentrations of asbestos fibers can cause serious bodily harm. Exercise care when servicing brake parts. Do not sand or grind brake lining unless equipment used is designed to contain the dust residue. Do not clean brake parts with compressed air or by dry brushing. Cleaning should be done by dampening the brake components with a fine mist of water, then wiping the brake components clean with a dampened cloth. Dispose of cloth and all residue containing asbestos fibers in an impermeable container with the appropriate label. Follow practices prescribed by the Occupational Safety and Health Administration (OSHA) and the Environmental Protection Agency (EPA) for the handling, processing, and disposing of dust or debris that may contain asbestos fibers.

BRAKE CALIPER

REMOVAL & INSTALLATION

See Figures 10 and 11.

WARNING

Do not use any fluid other than clean brake fluid meeting manufacturer's specification. Additionally, do not use brake fluid that has been previously drained. Following these instructions will help prevent system contamination, brake component damage and the risk of serious personal injury.

WARNING

Carefully read cautionary information on product label. For additional information, consult the product Material Safety Data Sheet (MSDS) if available. Failure to follow these instructions may result in serious personal injury.

➡Do not spill brake fluid on painted or plastic surfaces or damage to the surface may occur. If brake fluid is spilled onto a painted or plastic surface, immediately wash the surface with water.

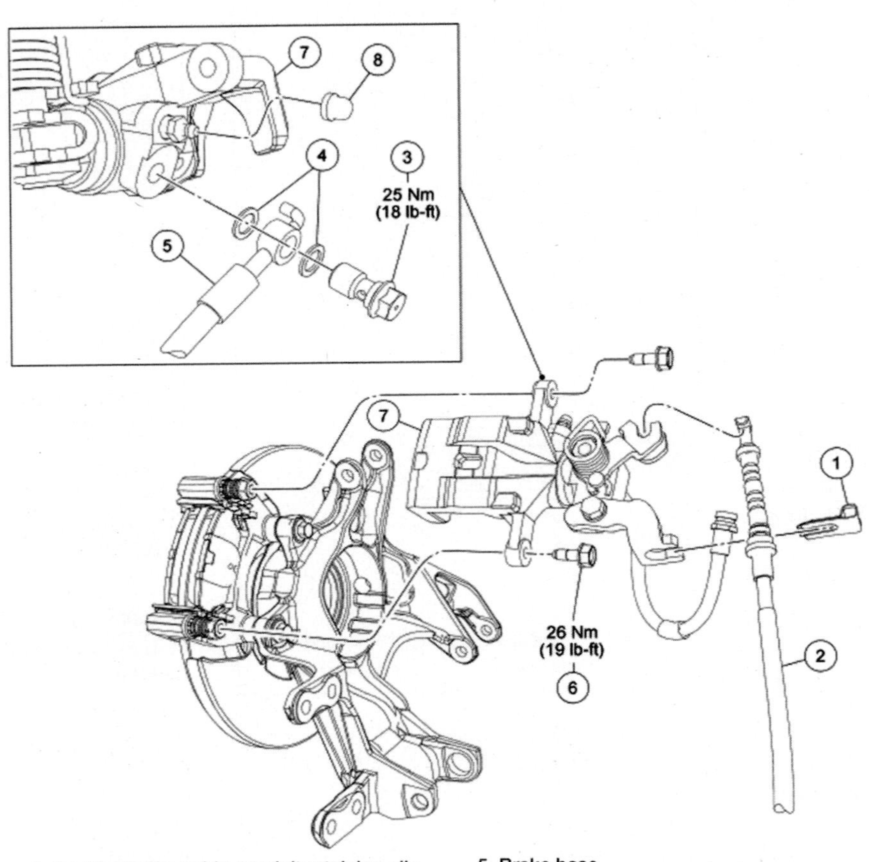

Fig. 10 Identifying the rear brake caliper and related components (FWD shown, AWD similar)

1. Remove the wheel and tire.
2. Disconnect the parking brake cable from the brake caliper.
    a. Pull back the parking brake lever.
    b. Disconnect the cable from the parking brake lever.
    c. Remove the cable conduit retaining clip.
    d. Disconnect the cable from the brake caliper.
3. Remove the brake caliper flow bolt and position the brake hose aside.
    a. Discard the 2 copper washers.
4. Remove the 2 brake caliper guide pin bolts and the brake caliper.
    a. If a leaking or damaged caliper piston boot is found; install a new disc brake caliper.

To install:

5. Position the notch in the caliper piston so that it will correctly align with the pin on the backside of the inboard brake pad.

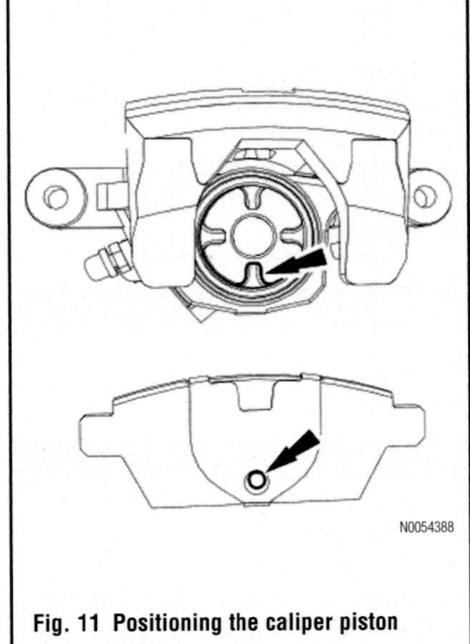

Fig. 11 Positioning the caliper piston

➡Make sure that the brake caliper hose is not twisted.

6. Position the brake caliper onto the anchor plate.
7. Install the 2 brake caliper guide pin bolts.
    a. To install, tighten to 19 ft. lbs. (26 Nm).
8. Using 2 new copper washers, position the brake hose and install the brake caliper flow bolt.
    a. Tighten to 18 ft. lbs. (25 Nm).
9. Install the parking brake cable to the brake caliper.
    a. Pull back the parking brake lever.
    b. Connect the cable to the parking brake lever.

c. Install the cable conduit retaining clip.

10. Bleed the brake caliper.

11. Cycle the park brake several times to verify normal operation.

DISC BRAKE PADS

REMOVAL & INSTALLATION

See Figures 11 and 12.

⁂ WARNING

Always install new brake shoes or pads at both ends of an axle to reduce the possibility of brakes pulling vehicle to one side. Failure to follow this instruction may result in uneven braking and serious personal injury.

➡Do not spill brake fluid on painted or plastic surfaces or damage to the surface may occur. If brake fluid is spilled onto a painted or plastic surface, immediately wash the surface with water.

1. Check the brake fluid level in the brake master cylinder reservoir.
   a. If required, remove the fluid until the brake master cylinder reservoir is 1/2 full.
2. Remove the wheel and tire.
3. Disconnect the parking brake cable from the brake caliper.
   a. Pull back the parking brake lever.
   b. Disconnect the cable from the parking brake lever.
   c. Remove the cable conduit retaining clip.
   d. Disconnect the cable from the brake caliper.

➡Do not pry in the caliper sight hole to retract the pistons, as this can damage the pistons and boots.

➡Do not allow the brake caliper to hang from the brake hose or damage to the hose can occur.

4. Remove the 2 brake caliper guide pin bolts and position the caliper aside.
   a. Support the caliper using mechanic's wire.
5. Remove the 2 brake pads, shims and retraction clips. Inspect the brake pads and shims for wear, damage or contamination.
   a. Discard the slide clips.
   b. Inspect the brake pads for wear and contamination.

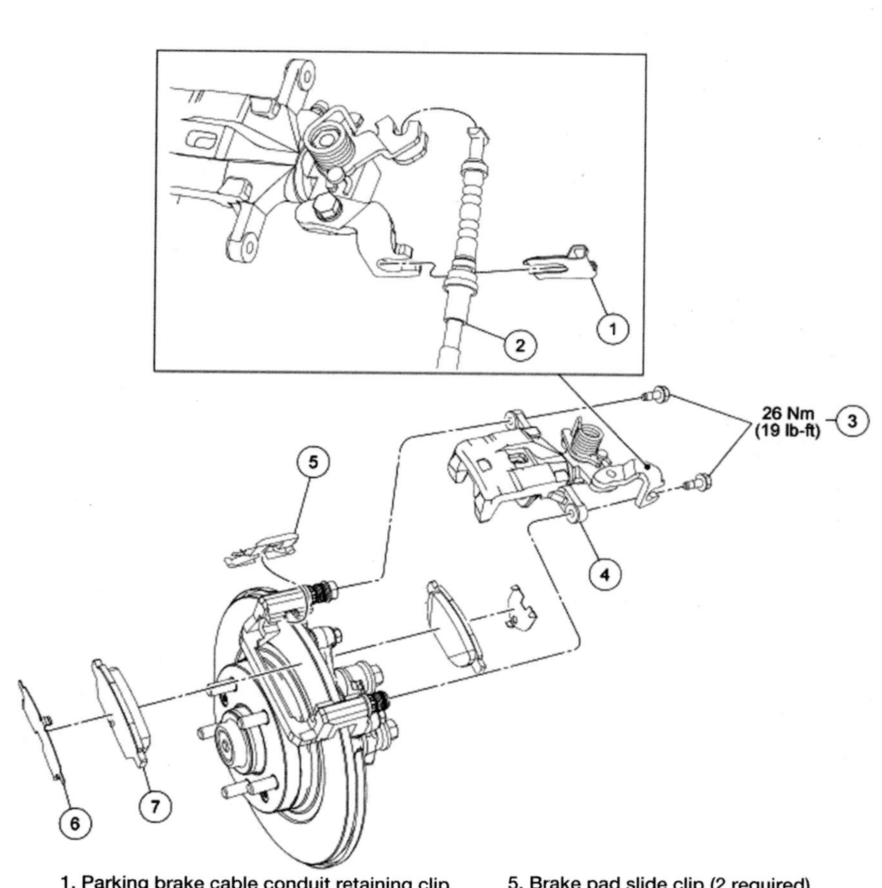

Fig. 12 Identifying the rear brake pads and related components (FWD shown, AWD similar)

To install:

➡Make sure the caliper piston boot is clean and free of foreign material.

6. Using the Rear Brake Caliper Piston Adjuster Adapter, compress the brake caliper piston into the brake caliper bore.
7. Position the notch in the caliper piston so that it will correctly align with the pin on the backside of the inboard brake pad.

➡If installing new brake pads, install all new hardware as supplied with the brake pad kit.

8. Install the shims and slide clips to the brake caliper anchor plate.
9. Apply equal amounts of lubricant (supplied with brake pad kit) to all brake pad-to-caliper anchor plate contact points and install brake pads.

➡Make sure that the brake caliper hose is not twisted.

10. Position the brake caliper on the anchor plate and install the 2 bolts.
    a. Tighten to 19 ft. lbs. (26 Nm).
11. Install the parking brake cable to the brake caliper.
    a. Pull back the parking brake lever.
    b. Connect the cable to the parking brake lever.
    c. Install the cable conduit retaining clip.
12. Install the wheel and tire.
13. Fill the brake master cylinder reservoir with clean, specified brake fluid.
14. Cycle the park brake several times to verify normal operation.
    a. Apply brakes several times to verify correct brake operation.

BRAKES — PARKING BRAKE

PARKING BRAKE CABLES

ADJUSTMENT

See Figure 13.

➡Do not pry at the floor console rear access panel with a screwdriver or damage to the panel may occur.

1. Remove the floor console rear access panel.
2. With the vehicle in NEUTRAL, position it on a hoist.

➡The dimension will vary depending on the amount of cable stretch. New cables require cycling the parking brake control 5-10 times to remove the cable slack.

3. Adjust the parking brake adjustment nut.
4. Verify correct operation of the parking brake system.
    a. At 2 clicks of the parking brake control; slight drag at the rear wheels should be present.
    b. At 5 clicks of the parking brake control; no movement at the rear wheels should be present.
5. Install the floor console rear access panel.

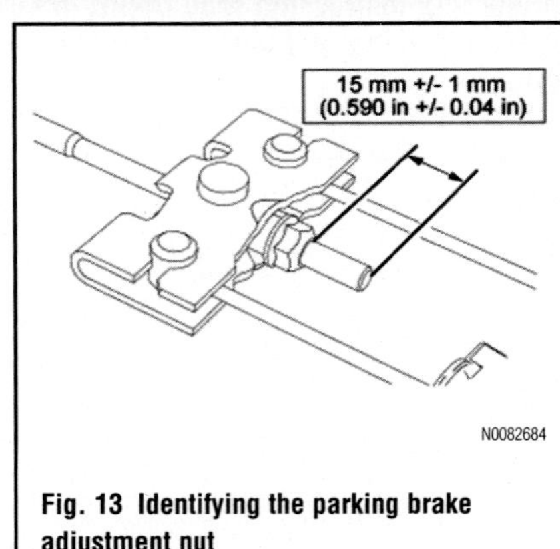

Fig. 13 Identifying the parking brake adjustment nut

CHASSIS ELECTRICAL — AIR BAG (SUPPLEMENTAL RESTRAINT SYSTEM)

GENERAL INFORMATION

⁂ CAUTION

These vehicles are equipped with an air bag system. The system must be disarmed before performing service on, or around, system components, the steering column, instrument panel components, wiring and sensors. Failure to follow the safety precautions and the disarming procedure could result in accidental air bag deployment, possible injury and unnecessary system repairs.

SERVICE PRECAUTIONS

Disconnect and isolate the battery negative cable before beginning any airbag system component diagnosis, testing, removal, or installation procedures. Allow system capacitor to discharge for two minutes before beginning any component service. This will disable the airbag system. Failure to disable the airbag system may result in accidental airbag deployment, personal injury, or death.

Do not place an intact undeployed airbag face down on a solid surface. The airbag will propel into the air if accidentally deployed and may result in personal injury or death.

When carrying or handling an undeployed airbag, the trim side (face) of the airbag should be pointing away from the body to minimize possibility of injury if accidental deployment occurs. Failure to do this may result in personal injury or death.

Replace airbag system components with OEM replacement parts. Substitute parts may appear interchangeable, but internal differences may result in inferior occupant protection. Failure to do so may result in occupant personal injury or death.

Wear safety glasses, rubber gloves, and long sleeved clothing when cleaning powder residue from vehicle after an airbag deployment. Powder residue emitted from a deployed airbag can cause skin irritation. Flush affected area with cool water if irritation is experienced. If nasal or throat irritation is experienced, exit the vehicle for fresh air until the irritation ceases. If irritation continues, see a physician.

Do not use a replacement airbag that is not in the original packaging. This may result in improper deployment, personal injury, or death.

The factory installed fasteners, screws and bolts used to fasten airbag components have a special coating and are specifically designed for the airbag system. Do not use substitute fasteners. Use only original equipment fasteners listed in the parts catalog when fastener replacement is required.

During, and following, any child restraint anchor service, due to impact event or vehicle repair, carefully inspect all mounting hardware, tether straps, and anchors for proper installation, operation, or damage. If a child restraint anchor is found damaged in any way, the anchor must be replaced. Failure to do this may result in personal injury or death.

Deployed and non-deployed airbags may or may not have live pyrotechnic material within the airbag inflator.

Do not dispose of driver/passenger/curtain airbags or seat belt tensioners unless you are sure of complete deployment. Refer to the Hazardous Substance Control System for proper disposal.

Dispose of deployed airbags and tensioners consistent with state, provincial, local, and federal regulations.

After any airbag component testing or service, do not connect the battery negative cable. Personal injury or death may result if the system test is not performed first.

If the vehicle is equipped with the Occupant Classification System (OCS), do not connect the battery negative cable before performing the OCS Verification Test using the scan tool and the appropriate diagnostic information. Personal injury or death may result if the system test is not performed properly.

Never replace both the Occupant Restraint Controller (ORC) and the Occupant Classification Module (OCM) at the same time. If both require replacement, replace one, then perform the Airbag System test before replacing the other.

Both the ORC and the OCM store Occupant Classification System (OCS) calibration data, which they transfer to one another when one of them is replaced. If both are replaced at the same time, an irreversible fault will be set in both modules and the OCS may malfunction and cause personal injury or death.

If equipped with OCS, the Seat Weight Sensor is a sensitive, calibrated unit and must be handled carefully. Do not drop or handle roughly. If dropped or damaged, replace with another sensor. Failure to do so may result in occupant injury or death.

If equipped with OCS, the front passenger seat must be handled carefully as well. When removing the seat, be careful when setting on floor not to drop. If dropped, the sensor may be inoperative, could result in occupant injury, or possibly death.

If equipped with OCS, when the passenger front seat is on the floor, no one should sit in the front passenger seat. This uneven force may damage the sensing ability of the seat weight sensors. If sat on and damaged, the sensor may be inoperative, could result in occupant injury, or possibly death.

DISARMING THE SYSTEM

See Figures 14 through 18.

**** WARNING**

Always wear eye protection when servicing a vehicle. Failure to follow this instruction may result in serious personal injury.

**** WARNING**

To reduce the risk of accidental deployment, do not use any memory saver devices. Failure to follow this instruction may result in serious personal injury or death.

**** WARNING**

Never probe the electrical connectors on air bag, Safety Canopy® or side air curtain modules. Failure to follow this instruction may result in the accidental deployment of these modules, which increases the risk of serious personal injury or death.

**** WARNING**

Never disassemble or tamper with safety belt buckle/retractor pretensioners or adaptive load limiting retractors or probe the electrical connectors. Failure to follow this instruction may result in the accidental deployment of the safety belt pretensioners or adaptive load limiting retractors which increases the risk of serious personal injury or death.

**** WARNING**

The air bag warning indicator illuminates when the correct Restraints Control Module (RCM) fuse is removed and the ignition is ON.

**** WARNING**

The Supplemental Restraint System (SRS) must be fully operational and free of faults before releasing the vehicle to the customer.

All vehicles

1. Turn all vehicle accessories OFF.
2. Turn the ignition OFF.
3. At the Smart Junction Box (SJB), located below the LH side of the instrument panel, remove the cover and the RCM fuse 32 (10A) from the SJB . For additional information, refer to the Wiring Diagrams.
4. Turn the ignition ON and monitor the air bag warning indicator for at least 30 seconds. The air bag warning indicator will remain lit continuously (no flashing) if the correct RCM fuse has been removed. If the air bag warning indicator does not remain lit continuously, remove the correct RCM fuse before proceeding.
5. Turn the ignition OFF.

**** WARNING**

Always deplete the backup power supply before repairing or installing any new front or side air bag supplemental restraint system (SRS) component and before servicing, removing, installing, adjusting or striking components near the front or side impact sensors or the restraints control module (RCM). Nearby components include doors, instrument panel, console, door latches, strikers, seats and hood latches.

6. To deplete the backup power supply energy, disconnect the battery ground cable and wait at least 1 minute. Be sure to disconnect auxiliary batteries and power supplies (if equipped).
   a. Failure to follow these instructions may result in serious personal injury or death in the event of an accidental deployment.
   b. Disconnect the battery ground cable and wait at least one minute. For additional information, refer to Battery, Mounting and Cables.
7. Remove the driver air bag module.

Fusion and Milan Hybrid

8. Remove the steering column opening trim panel.
   a. Remove the 2 screws.
   b. Pull downward to release the retainers and remove the steering column opening panel.
9. Disconnect the knee air bag module electrical connector.

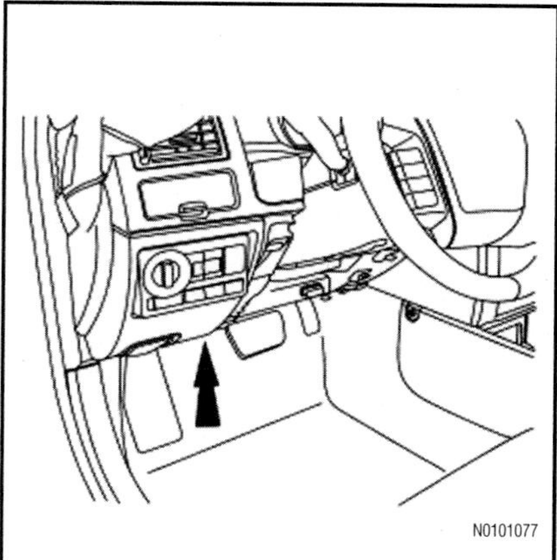

Fig. 14 Locating the knee air bag module electrical connector

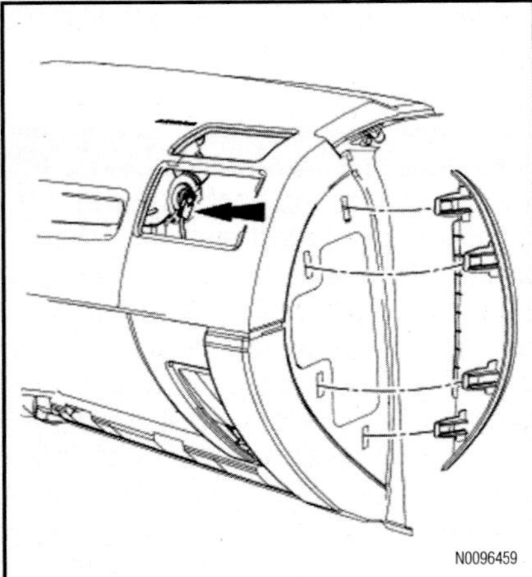

Fig. 15 Locating the RH passenger air bag module electrical connector

All vehicles

10. Disconnect the glove compartment damper and lower the glove compartment.

➡**RH HVAC register omitted for clarity.**

11. Remove the RH instrument panel side finish panel to access the RH passenger air bag module electrical connector.
12. Through the glove compartment opening, access the LH passenger air bag electrical connector.

➡**Do not pull the electrical connectors out by the Connector Position Assurance (CPA) clip. Damage to the clip can occur.**

13. Using an appropriate tool, lift up and release the Connector Position Assurance (CPA) clips and disconnect the 2 electrical connectors.
14. From under the rear of the passenger seat, slide and disengage the passenger seat side air bag module electrical connector locking clip, and then release the tab and disconnect the passenger seat side air bag module electrical connector.

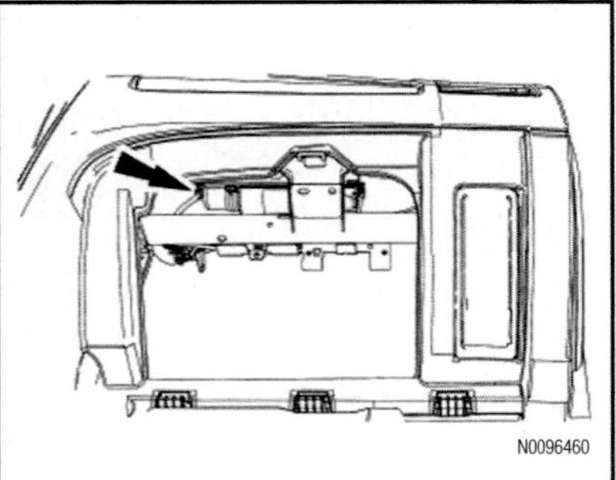

Fig. 16 Locating the LH passenger air bag electrical connector

Fig. 17 Identifying the LH side air curtain module electrical connector

15. Remove the RH C-pillar trim cover retainer cap.
16. Remove the retainer and RH C-pillar trim cover.
17. Disconnect the RH side air curtain module electrical connector.
18. Remove the LH C-pillar trim cover retainer cap.
19. Remove the retainer and LH C-pillar trim cover.
20. Disconnect the LH side air curtain module electrical connector.
21. From under the rear of the driver seat, slide and disengage the driver seat side air bag module electrical connector locking clip, and then release the tab and disconnect the driver seat side air bag module electrical connector.
22. Install RCM fuse 32 (10A) in the SJB .
23. Connect the battery ground cable.

ARMING THE SYSTEM

**** WARNING**

Always wear eye protection when servicing a vehicle. Failure to follow this instruction may result in serious personal injury.

**** WARNING**

To reduce the risk of accidental deployment, do not use any memory saver devices. Failure to follow this instruction may result in serious personal injury or death.

**** WARNING**

Never probe the electrical connectors on air bag, Safety Canopy® or side air curtain modules. Failure to follow this instruction may result in the accidental deployment of these modules, which increases the risk of serious personal injury or death.

**** WARNING**

Never disassemble or tamper with safety belt buckle/retractor pretensioners or adaptive load limiting retractors or probe the electrical connectors. Failure to follow this instruction may result in the accidental deployment of the safety belt pretensioners or adaptive load limiting retractors which increases the risk of serious personal injury or death.

**** WARNING**

The air bag warning indicator illuminates when the correct Restraints Control Module (RCM) fuse is removed and the ignition is ON.

**** WARNING**

The Supplemental Restraint System (SRS) must be fully operational and free of faults before releasing the vehicle to the customer.

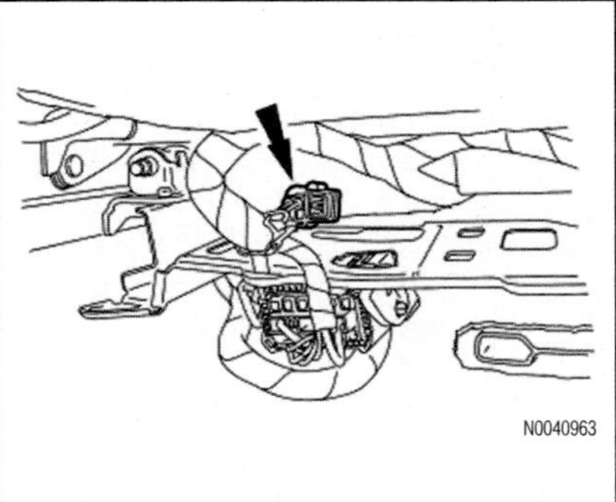

Fig. 18 Disconnecting the driver seat side air bag module electrical connector

All vehicles

1. Remove RCM fuse 32 (10A) from the SJB .
2. Disconnect the battery ground cable and wait at least one minute.
3. Connect the driver seat side air bag module electrical connector and then slide and engage the seat side air bag electrical connector locking clip.
4. Connect the LH side air curtain module electrical connector.
5. Install the LH C-pillar trim cover and retainer.
6. Install the LH C-pillar trim cover retainer cap.

7. Connect the RH side air curtain module electrical connector.
8. Install the RH C-pillar trim cover and retainer.
9. Install the RH C-pillar trim cover retainer cap.
10. Connect the passenger seat side air bag module electrical connector and slide and engage the seat side air bag electrical connector locking clip.

➡The Connector Position Assurance (CPA) clip must be in the released position before installing the electrical connector. Failure to have the CPA clip in the released position may break the tabs on the clip causing DTCs to set in the Restraints Control Module (RCM).

11. Through the RH instrument panel side finish panel opening, connect the RH passenger air bag module electrical connector and push in to seat the CPA clip.
a. Verify that the clip is fully seated.
12. Install the RH instrument panel side finish panel.

➡The Connector Position Assurance (CPA) clip must be in the released position before installing the electrical connector. Failure to have the CPA clip in the released position may break the tabs on the clip causing DTCs to set in the Restraints Control Module (RCM).

13. Through the glove compartment opening, connect the LH passenger air bag electrical connector and push in to seat the CPA clip.
a. Verify that the clip is fully seated.
14. Attach the glove compartment damper cable.

Fusion and Milan Hybrid

15. Connect the knee air bag module electrical connector.
16. Install the steering column opening trim panel and 2 screws.

All vehicles

17. Install the driver air bag module. For additional information, refer to Driver Air Bag Module.
18. Turn the ignition from OFF to ON.
19. Install RCM fuse 32 (10A) in the SJB and close the cover.

⁂ WARNING

Make sure no one is in the vehicle and there is nothing blocking or placed in front of any air bag module when the battery is connected. Failure to follow these instructions may result in serious personal injury in the event of an accidental deployment.

20. Connect the battery ground cable.
21. Prove out the SRS as follows: Turn the ignition from ON to OFF. Wait 10 seconds, then turn the ignition ON and monitor the air bag warning indicator with the air bag modules installed. The air bag warning indicator will light continuously for approximately 6 seconds and then turn off. If an air bag SRS fault is detected, the air bag warning indicator will: - fail to light. - remain lit continuously. - flash. The flashing might not occur until approximately 30 seconds after the ignition has been turned from the OFF to the ON position. This is the time required to complete testing of the SRS . If the air bag warning indicator is inoperative and a SRS fault exists, a chime will sound in a pattern of 5 sets of 5 beeps. If this occurs, the air bag warning indicator and any SRS fault discovered must be diagnosed and repaired. Clear all RCM and OCSM CMDTCs .

CLOCKSPRING CENTERING

Starting with the clockspring inner rotor in the 12 o'clock position, rotate the inner rotor clockwise through approximately 2.25 turns to center the clockspring.

➡The clockspring inner rotor must be in the 12 o'clock position to be correctly centered.

DRIVE TRAIN

AUTOMATIC TRANSMISSION FLUID

DRAIN AND REFILL

6F35

➡In order to completely clean the torque converter, this procedure needs to be carried out 3 times.

1. With the vehicle in NEUTRAL, position it on a hoist.

➡If an internal problem is suspected, drain the transmission fluid through a paper filter. A small amount of metal or friction particles may be found from normal wear. If an excessive amount of metal or friction material is present, the transaxle will need to be overhauled.

2. Remove the transmission fluid drain plug and allow the transmission fluid to drain.
3. Install the transmission fluid drain plug.
a. Tighten to 9 ft. lbs. (12 Nm).
4. Fill the transaxle with clean transmission fluid.
5. Start the engine and let it run for 3 minutes. Move the range selector lever into each gear position. Repeat Steps 2, 3, 4 and 5 two more times. After the transmission fluid has been changed a total of 3 times, check the transmission fluid level for a final time, making sure that the transmission fluid is at the correct level.

Aisin AW21

➡The use of any fluid other than what is recommended for this transmission will cause transmission damage.

1. With the vehicle in NEUTRAL, position it on a hoist.
2. Remove the transmission fluid drain plug and allow the transmission fluid to drain.
3. Install the transmission fluid drain plug.
a. Tighten to 35 ft. lbs. (47 Nm).
4. Remove the transmission fluid fill plug.
5. Fill the transaxle with approximately 4 qt (3.7L) of clean transmission fluid.
6. Install the transmission fluid fill plug.
a. Tighten to 29 ft. lbs. (39 Nm).
7. With the transaxle in (P) PARK, the vehicle should be on a level surface, the engine at idle (680-780 rpm), foot pressed on the brake, move the selector lever through each gear and allow engagement of each gear. Place the selector lever back in the PARK position.
8. Wipe the transmission fluid level indicator cap and remove the fluid level indicator.
9. Wipe the transmission fluid level indicator with a clean cloth.

➡In order to get an accurate transmission fluid level reading, the vehicle should be on a level surface, the engine at idle (680-780 rpm) for 5 minutes and the transmission fluid

temperature should be at least 140°F-158°F (60°C-70°C) using the scan tool.

10. If transmission fluid needs to be added, add transmission fluid in 1/2 pint (0.25L) increments through the transmission fluid fill plug located on the top of the transaxle near the transmission fluid level indicator. Do not overfill the transmission fluid. Install the transmission fluid level indicator back in the transmission fluid filler tube until it is fully seated, then remove the indicator. The transmission fluid level should be at the upper-most mark on the transmission fluid level indicator. Only fill to the upper-most mark on the transmission fluid indicator. Do not overfill. Damage to the transaxle will occur.

➡The correct transmission fluid level at normal operating temperature of 140°F-158°F (60°C-70°C) is between the top 2 marks on the transmission fluid level Indicator.

11. Fill the transaxle to the correct transmission fluid level.

➡The correct transmission fluid level at cool operating temperature of 59°F-77°F (15°C-25°C), is at the bottom mark on the transmission fluid level indicator.

12. If the Transmission Fluid Temperature (TFT) is low, fill the transaxle with transmission fluid to the cold range on the transmission fluid level Indicator. Recheck the transmission fluid level when the transaxle has reached the normal operating temperature.

MANUAL TRANSAXLE ASSEMBLY

REMOVAL & INSTALLATION

See Figures 19 through 26.

1. With the vehicle in NEUTRAL, position it on a hoist.
2. Remove the battery tray.
3. Remove the Air Cleaner (ACL) assembly.
4. Disconnect the shift cables from the transaxle shift control lever, using a suitable tool to lightly pry them off the transaxle shift control lever.

➡Carefully pry the retainer on the shift cables. Do not damage the shift cable retainers. Using a small screwdriver push from the back.

5. Disconnect the shift cables from the transaxle bracket.

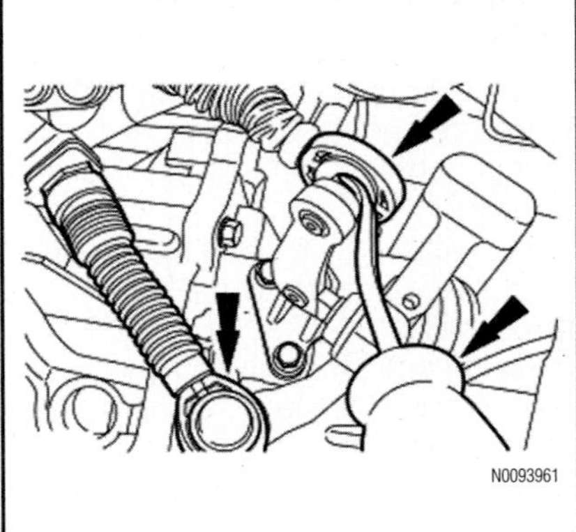

Fig. 19 Disconnecting the shift cables from the transaxle shift control lever

6. Install the Engine Support Bar.
7. Detach the wire harness from the transaxle.
8. Remove the 3 upper transaxle-to-engine bolts.

➡If one or both of the mount studs are removed or come out, do not reinstall the old stud(s). Install a new stud(s). Make sure the studs are properly seated in the case, even if they were not replaced.

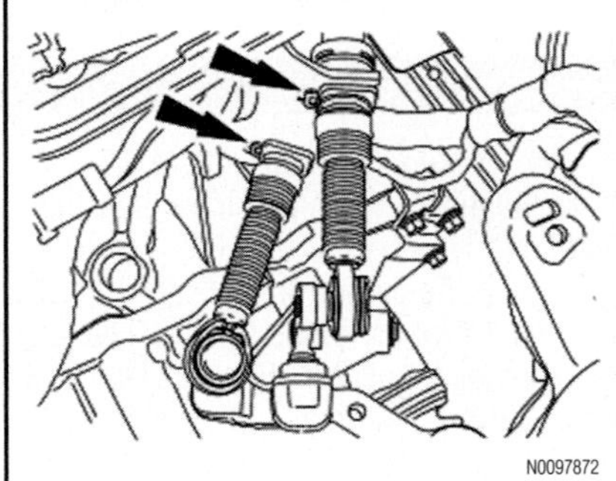

Fig. 20 Disconnecting the shift cables from the transaxle bracket

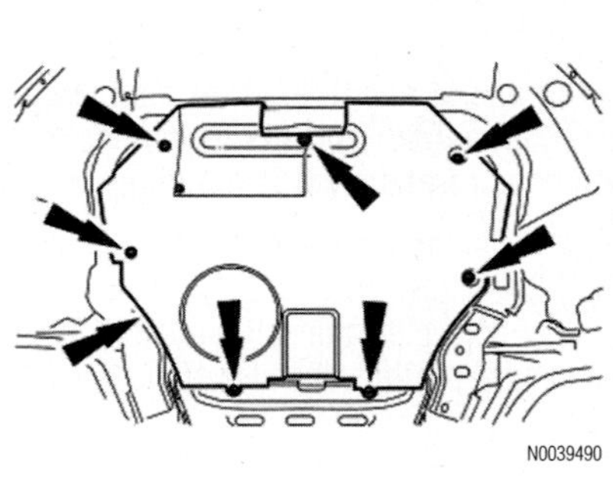

Fig. 21 Removing the splash shield

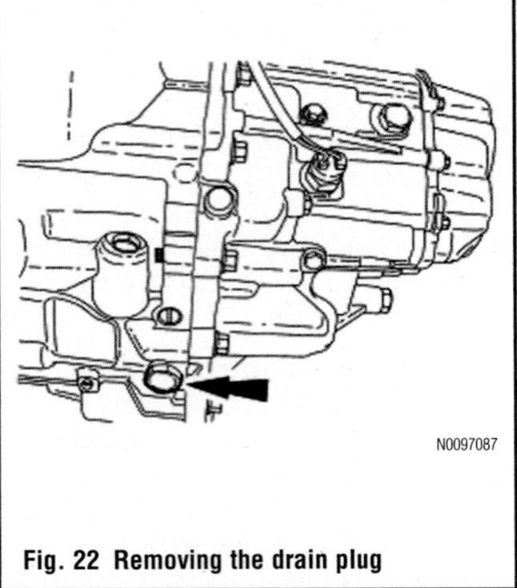

Fig. 22 Removing the drain plug

9. Remove the transaxle rear support insulator nuts and the transaxle rear support insulator bolt.
10. Remove the 7 bolts and the splash shield.
11. Remove the drain plug and drain the transaxle.
12. Once fluid has drained, install the drain plug.
    a. Tighten to 36 ft. lbs. (49 Nm).
13. Remove the 2 clutch tube hydraulic line bracket bolts.

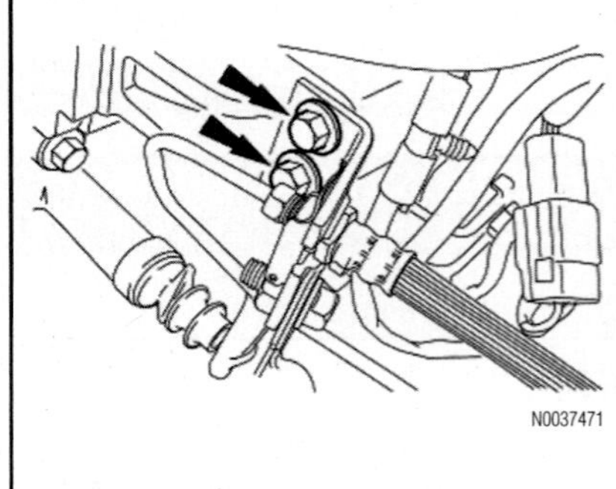

Fig. 23 Removing the clutch tube hydraulic line bracket bolts

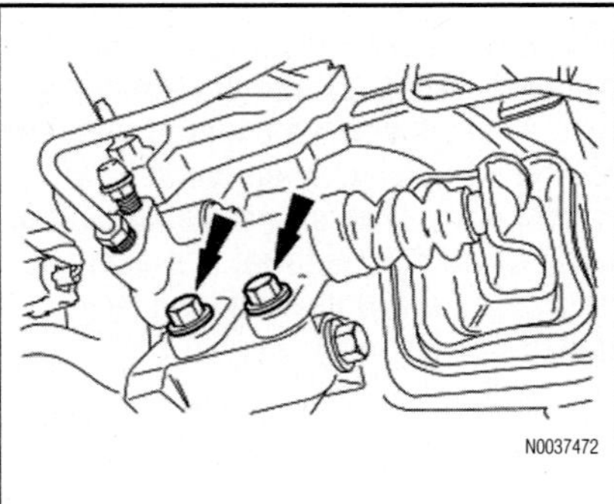

Fig. 24 Removing the clutch slave cylinder bolts

14. Remove the 2 bolts and position the clutch slave cylinder aside.
15. Disconnect the reverse lamp switch electrical connector.
16. Remove the starter motor.
17. Remove the engine roll restrictor and bracket.
  a. Remove the roll restrictor-to-subframe though bolt.
  b. Remove the roll restrictor bracket through bolt.
  c. Remove the roll restrictor.
18. Remove the roll restrictor bracket bolts.
  a. Remove the roll restrictor bracket.
19. Disconnect the Vehicle Speed Sensor (VSS) electrical connector.
20. Remove the front subframe.
21. Remove the LH halfshaft and RH intermediate shaft from the transaxle.
22. Install a Transmission Jack. Secure the transaxle to the Transmission Jack with a safety strap.
23. Remove the clutch housing-to-oil pan bolt.

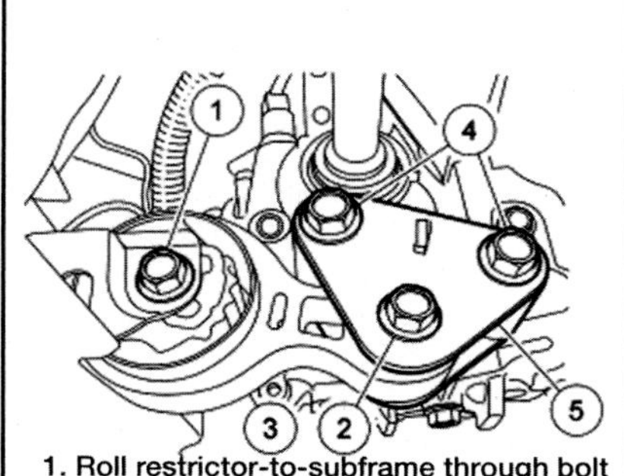

Fig. 25 Removing the engine roll restrictor and bracket

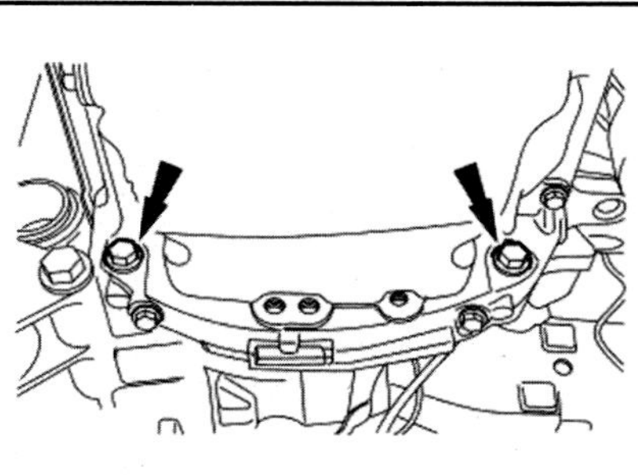

Fig. 26 Removing the 2 oil pan to clutch housing bolts

24. Remove the 2 oil pan-to-clutch housing bolts.
25. Remove the remaining 4 transaxle-to-engine bolts.
26. Move the transaxle away from the engine and lower it from the vehicle.

To install:

➡Wipe off excess grease. The splines should have a thin film of grease only. Excess grease can contaminate the clutch facing and affect clutch function.

27. Apply a very small amount of grease on the input shaft splines.
28. Secure the transaxle to the Transmission Jack with a safety strap. Raise and position the transaxle to the engine.
29. Install the clutch housing-to-oil pan bolt.
  a. Tighten to 35 ft. lbs. (48 Nm).
30. Install the 2 oil pan-to-clutch housing bolts.
  a. Tighten to 35 ft. lbs. (48 Nm).
31. Install the 4 lower transaxle-to-engine bolts.
  a. Tighten to 35 ft. lbs. (48 Nm).
32. Install the 2 transmission lower mount nuts and bolt to the transaxle. Do not tighten the fasteners at this time.
33. Position the clutch slave cylinder to the clutch release arm and install the bolts.
  a. Tighten to 15 ft. lbs. (20 Nm).
34. Install the clutch tube hydraulic line bracket bolts.
  a. Tighten to 16 ft. lbs. (22 Nm).
35. Install the starter motor.
36. Install the LH halfshaft.
37. Install the intermediate shaft and RH halfshaft.
38. Install the front subframe.
39. Install the roll restrictor bracket and roll restrictor.
  a. Install the roll restrictor bracket and bolts. Tighten to 66 ft. lbs. (90 Nm).
  b. Install the roll restrictor and the roll restrictor bracket through bolt. Tighten to 66 ft. lbs. (90 Nm).
  c. Install the roll restrictor-to-subframe through bolt. Tighten to 66 ft. lbs. (90 Nm).
40. Connect the reverse lamp switch electrical connector.
41. Connect the Vehicle Speed Sensor (VSS) electrical connector.

➡If one or both of the mount studs were removed or came out, do not reinstall the old stud(s). Install a new stud(s). Make sure they are properly seated in the case.

42. Tighten the transaxle rear support insulator nuts and bolt to specification.
  a. Tighten to 59 ft. lbs. (80 Nm).
43. Install the 3 upper transaxle-to-engine bolts.
  a. Tighten to 35 ft. lbs. (48 Nm).
44. Attach the wire harness to the transaxle.
45. Remove the Engine Support Bar.
46. Install the gearshift and shift cables onto the transaxle bracket and gearshift control assembly. Make sure the cables are engaged in the shift bracket and fully installed on the gearshift control assembly.
47. Install the battery tray and battery.
48. Install the Air Cleaner (ACL) assembly.
49. Install the splash shield and the 7 bolts.
  a. Tighten to 7 ft. lbs. (9 Nm).
50. Check the vehicle for normal operation.

MANUAL TRANSAXLE FLUID

DRAIN AND REFILL

See Figure 27.

1. With the vehicle in NEUTRAL, position it on a hoist.
2. Remove the drain plug and drain the fluid.
3. Install a new washer and the drain plug.
  a. Tighten to 36 ft. lbs. (49 Nm).

➡Prior to removal, clean the area of the fill plug.

4. Remove the fill plug.

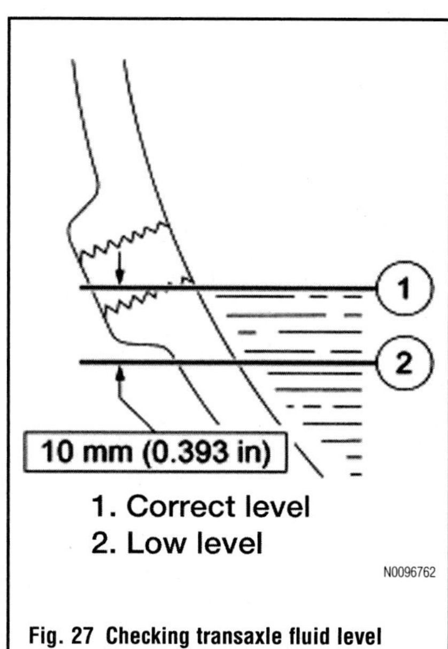

Fig. 27 Checking transaxle fluid level

➡Do not overfill the transaxle. This may result in increased operating temperature or cause transaxle fluid to be forced out of the case.

5. Fill the transaxle with the recommended fluid.
6. Install a new washer and fill plug.
   a. Tighten to 36 ft. lbs. (49 Nm).

CLUTCH

REMOVAL & INSTALLATION

See Figures 28 through 31.

1. Remove the transaxle.
2. Inspect the clutch pressure plate.
   a. Check the diaphragm spring fingers for discoloration, scoring, bent or broken segments.
   b. Using the Dial Indicator Gauge with Holding Fixture, rotate the flywheel and check for spring ends that are higher or lower than the rest.
   c. The specification is 0.023 inch (0.6 mm) maximum.
3. Using the Flywheel Holding Tool, lock the flywheel to the engine.

➡Loosen each bolt, one turn at a time in a star pattern, until spring tension is released.

4. Using a suitable clutch disc aligner, remove the bolts, the clutch pressure plate and the clutch disc.

➡Do not immerse the clutch pressure plate in solvent.

5. Using a suitable cleaning solution, clean the clutch pressure plate.
6. Inspect the clutch pressure plate surface for burn marks, scores, flatness, ridges or cracks.
   a. Maximum clearance for flatness check is 0.011 inch (0.3 mm).

➡If the clutch disc is saturated with oil, inspect the rear engine crankshaft seal or transmission input shaft seal for leakage. If leakage is found, install a new seal prior to clutch disc installation.

➡Use an emery cloth to remove minor imperfections in the clutch disc lining surface.

7. Inspect the clutch disc for the following:
   a. Oil or grease saturation
   b. Worn or loose facings
   c. Warpage or loose rivets at the hub
   d. Wear or rust on the splines
   e. Install a new clutch disc if any of these conditions are present.
8. Check the clutch disc runout.
9. If necessary, conduct a Flywheel Runout Check.

Clutch release bearing and clutch release fork

10. Remove the clutch release bearing.
11. Inspect the clutch release bearing for wear or damage.
    a. Rotate the bearing while applying pressure in the axial direction. If the bearing feels rough, sticks or has excessive resistance, install a new bearing.
12. Inspect the release bearing guide tube for wear or damage.
    a. Slide the release bearing on the guide tube. Check for roughness or sticking.
13. Remove the clutch release fork. Inspect the fork for wear or damage.

To install:

Clutch release bearing and clutch release fork

14. Install the clutch release fork.
15. Check for roughness or sticking. If the bearing feels rough, sticks or has excessive resistance, install a new bearing. Slide the release bearing on the guide tube.
16. Install the clutch release bearing.

Clutch disc and clutch pressure plate

17. Apply a very small amount of grease in the clutch disc hub. Wipe off excess grease to avoid contaminating the clutch disc and affecting clutch function.
18. Using a suitable clutch disc aligner, position the clutch disc on the flywheel.
19. Position the clutch pressure plate on the flywheel and to the dowels. Install the 6 clutch pressure plate bolts.
    a. Tighten the bolts one turn at a time in a star pattern. Tighten to 21 ft. lbs. (29 Nm).
20. Apply a small amount of grease to:
    - clutch release fork fingers
    - clutch release fork spring
    - guide tube
    - clutch slave cylinder end that contacts the release fork

➡Apply a very small amount of grease to the transmission input shaft end and on the splines.

21. Install the transaxle.

BLEEDING

See Figure 32.

⁂ WARNING

Carefully read cautionary information on product label. For EMERGENCY

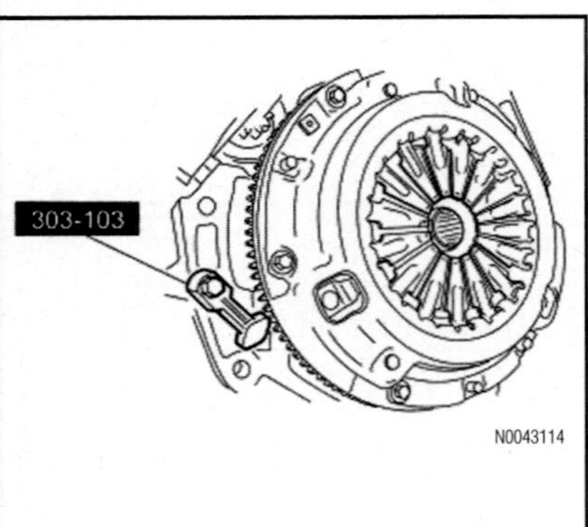

Fig. 28 Locking the flywheel to the engine

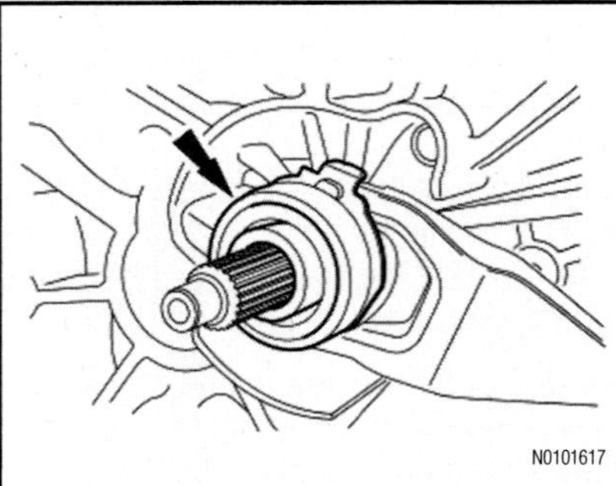

Fig. 29 Removing the clutch release bearing

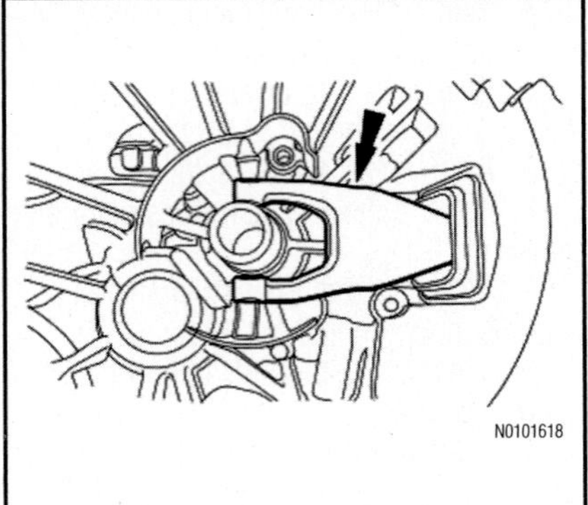

Fig. 30 Removing the clutch release fork

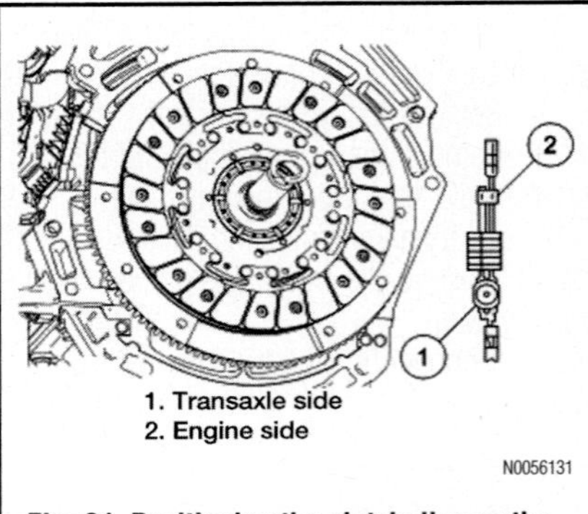

Fig. 31 Positioning the clutch disc on the flywheel

MEDICAL INFORMATION seek medical advice. For additional information, consult the product Material Safety Data Sheet (MSDS) if available. Failure to follow these instructions may result in serious personal injury.

➡Brake fluid is harmful to painted and plastic surfaces. If brake fluid is spilled onto a painted or plastic surface, immediately wash it with cold water.

➡When any part of the hydraulic system has been disconnected for repair or new installation, air may get into the system and cause spongy brake pedal action. This requires bleeding of the hydraulic system after it has been correctly connected. The hydraulic system can be bled manually or with pressure bleeding equipment.

➡Make sure the brake fluid reservoir is to the MAX mark before bleeding the clutch system. Do not allow the fluid level to drop below 0.236 inch (6 mm) of the MAX mark.

1. Attach a rubber drain hose to the bleeder screw and submerge the free end of the hose in a container partially filled with clean brake fluid.
2. Press the clutch pedal slowly to the floor.
3. With the clutch pedal held to the floor, loosen the bleeder screw until fluid and air are expelled from the system.
4. With the clutch pedal held to the floor, tighten the bleeder screw.

➡The clutch hydraulic system fluid is separated from the brake system fluid by a separate reservoir within the brake reservoir. Do not allow the clutch hydraulic system fluid level in the reservoir to fall more than 0.236 inch (6 mm) below the MAX mark during the bleeding operation or fluid supply to the clutch release system will be starved, allowing air to enter the clutch master cylinder. Keep the brake master cylinder reservoir filled with clean, specified brake fluid. Never reuse the brake fluid that has been drained from the hydraulic system.

5. Repeat Steps 2 through 4 until no air bubbles appear in the fluid.
6. Tighten the bleeder screw.
   a. Tighten to 5 ft. lbs. (7 Nm).
7. Fill the brake reservoir.
8. Check system for normal operation.

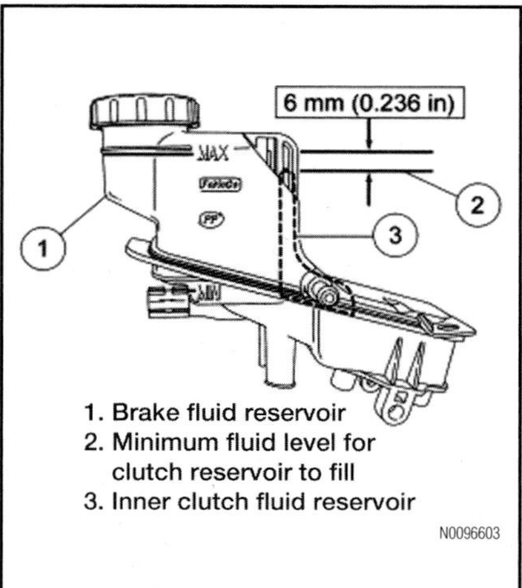

Fig. 32 Bleeding the clutch master cylinder

TRANSFER CASE ASSEMBLY - POWER TRANSFER UNIT (PTU)

REMOVAL & INSTALLATION

See Figures 33 through 36.

➡3.5L with AW21 transmission shown, 3.0L with 6F35 transmission similar.

1. With the vehicle in NEUTRAL, position it on a hoist.
2. Remove the driveshaft.
3. Remove the RH catalytic converter.
4. Remove the 2 Power Transfer Unit (PTU)-to-support bracket bolts, then remove

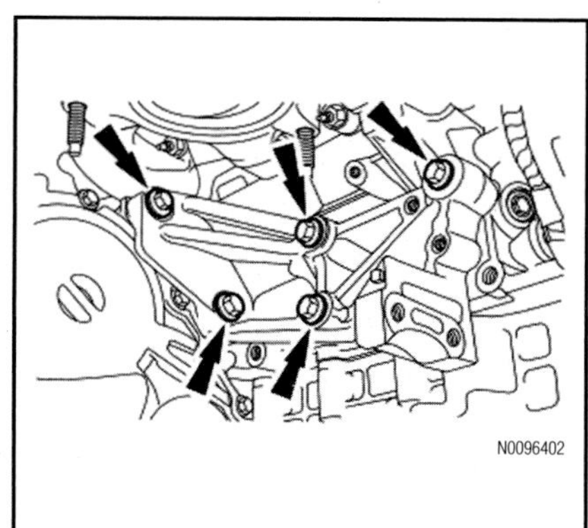

Fig. 34 Removing the PTU support bracket

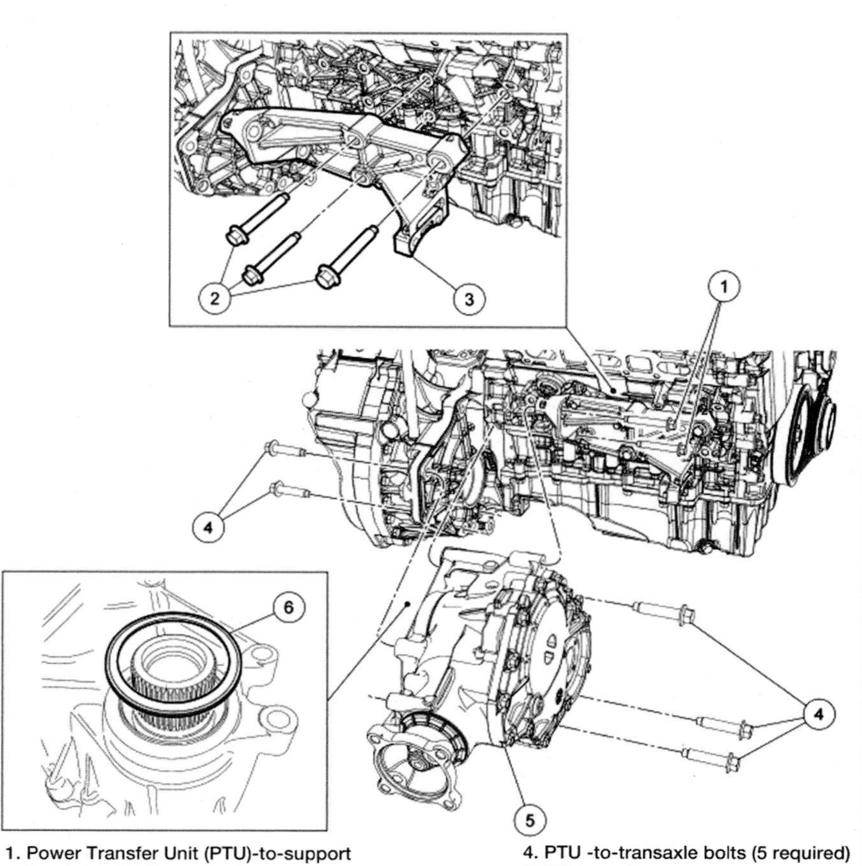

Fig. 33 Exploded view of the PTU

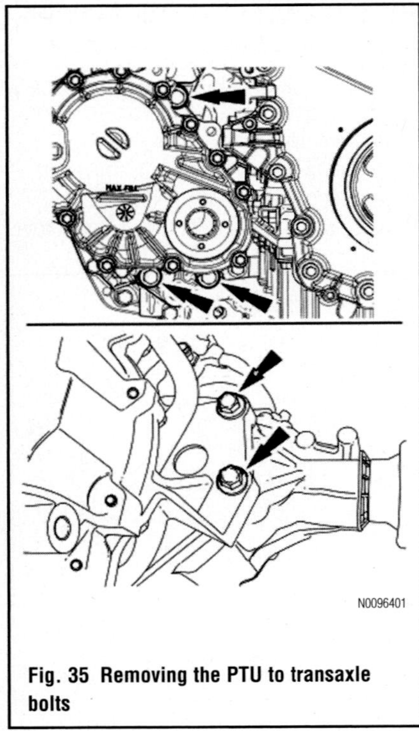

Fig. 35 Removing the PTU to transaxle bolts

the 3 PTU support bracket bolts and the PTU support bracket.

5. Remove the 5 PTU -to-transaxle bolts.

6. Separate the PTU from the transaxle. Remove the PTU from the vehicle.

➡A new compression seal must be installed whenever the PTU is removed from the vehicle.

7. Using a suitable tool, remove the compression seal and discard.

To install:

➡A new compression seal must be installed whenever the Power Transfer Unit (PTU) is removed from the vehicle.

8. Using a suitable tool, install the new compression seal.

➡A new PTU intermediate shaft seal and deflector must be installed whenever the intermediate shaft or PTU is removed from the vehicle.

9. Position the PTU to the transaxle. Install the 5 PTU -to-transaxle bolts.
   a. Tighten to 66 ft. lbs. (90 Nm).

10. Position the PTU support bracket into place and install the 5 PTU support bracket bolts.
   a. Tighten the bolts to the PTU to 35 ft. lbs. (48 Nm).

11. Tighten the bolts to the engine to 35 ft. lbs. (48 Nm).

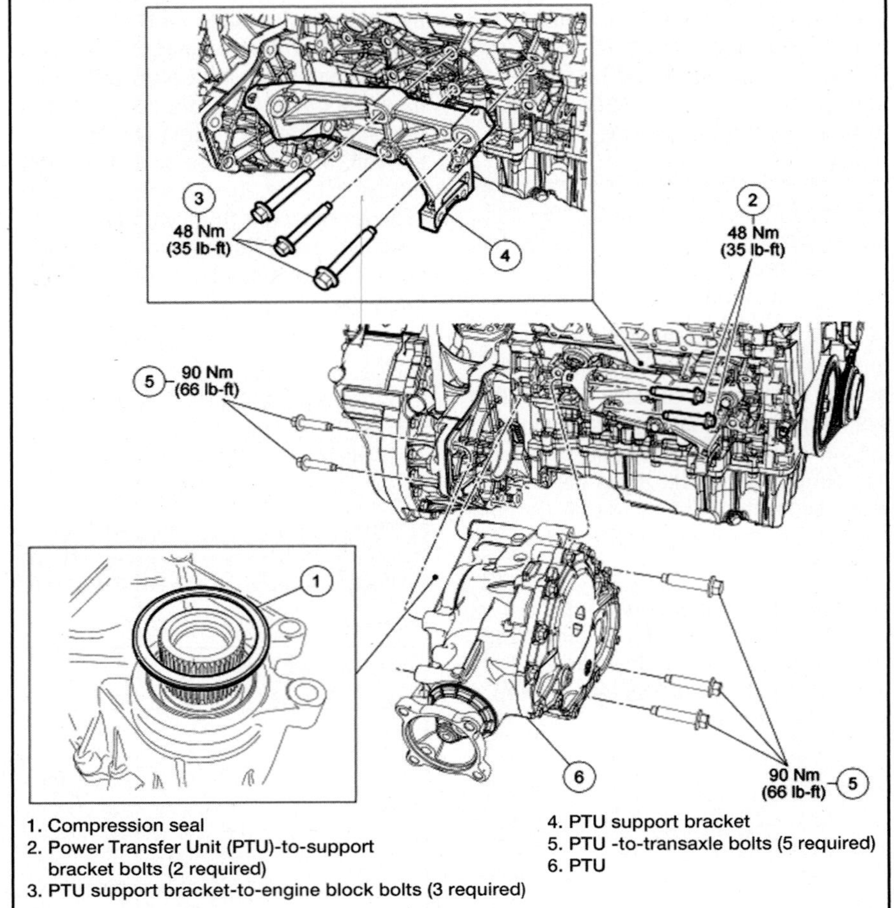

Fig. 36 Installing the PTU

12. Install the driveshaft.

13. Install the RH catalytic converter.

14. Top off transmission and/or PTU fluid as necessary.

FRONT HALFSHAFT

REMOVAL & INSTALLATION

See Figures 37 through 43.

➡Suspension fasteners are critical parts because they affect performance of vital components and systems and their failure may result in major service expense. New parts must be installed with the same part numbers or equivalent part, if replacement is necessary. Do not use a replacement part of lesser quality or substitute design. Torque values must be used as specified during reassembly to make sure of correct retention of these parts.

➡LH halfshaft shown, RH similar.

RH and LH halfshafts

1. Remove the wheel and tire.

➡Apply the brake to keep the halfshaft from rotating.

2. Remove and discard the wheel hub nut.

3. Remove wheel speed sensor harness bracket-to-wheel knuckle bolt.

4. Remove the wheel speed sensor bolt and position the wheel speed sensor aside.

5. Remove the brake flexible hose bracket-to-wheel knuckle bolt.

WARNING

Do not breathe dust or use compressed air to blow dust from storage containers or friction components. Remove dust using government-approved techniques. Friction component dust may be a cancer and lung disease hazard. Exposure to potentially hazardous components may occur if dusts are created during repair of friction components, such as brake pads and clutch discs. Expo-

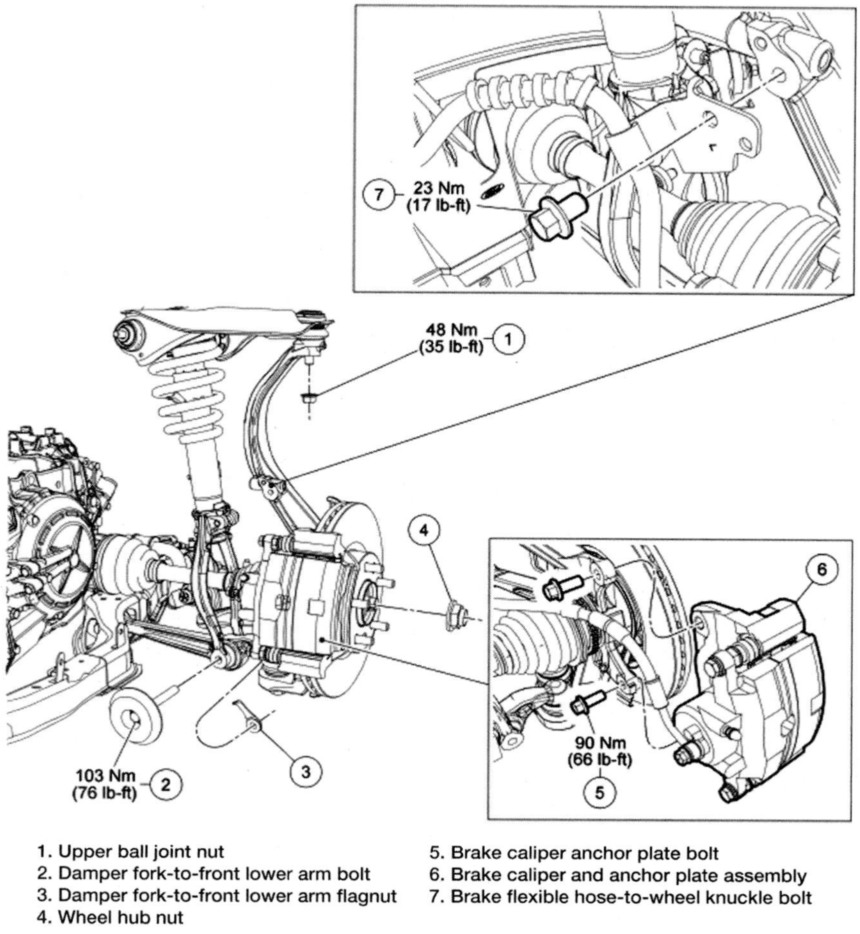

23 Nm
(17 lb-ft)
7
48 Nm
(35 lb-ft)
1
4
6
103 Nm
(76 lb-ft)
2
3
90 Nm
(66 lb-ft)
5
1. Upper ball joint nut
2. Damper fork-to-front lower arm bolt
3. Damper fork-to-front lower arm flagnut
4. Wheel hub nut
5. Brake caliper anchor plate bolt
6. Brake caliper and anchor plate assembly
7. Brake flexible hose-to-wheel knuckle bolt
N0109892

Fig. 37 Exploded view of the LH halfshaft—1 of 2

sure may also cause irritation to skin, eyes and respiratory tract, and may cause allergic reactions and/or may lead to other chronic health effects. If irritation persists, seek medical attention or advice. Failure to follow these instructions may result in serious personal injury.

➡Do not allow the brake caliper to hang from the brake hose or damage to the hose can occur.

6. Remove the 2 brake caliper anchor plate bolts and position the caliper and anchor plate assembly aside.
   a. Support the caliper using mechanic's wire.
7. Remove and discard the upper ball joint nut.
8. Using the Steering Arm Remover, separate the upper ball joint from the wheel knuckle.

8
8. LH/RH halfshaft
N0109893

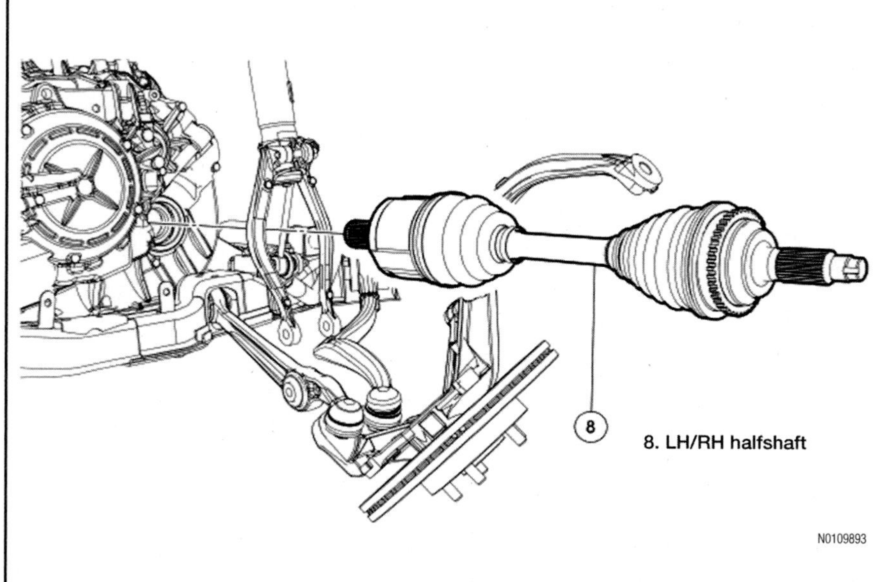

Fig. 38 Exploded view of the LH halfshaft—2 OF 2

9. Remove and discard the damper fork-to-front lower arm bolt and flagnut.

10. Using the Front Wheel Hub Remover, separate the halfshaft from the wheel hub.

11. Remove the pin-type retainers and position the splash shield aside.

RH halfshaft

12. Use a brass drift to strike the RH halfshaft in the indicated area and separate the RH halfshaft from the intermediate shaft.

LH halfshaft

13. Using the Halfshaft Remover and Slide Hammer, separate the halfshaft from the transmission.

RH and LH halfshafts

14. Position the damper fork and halfshaft forward of the front lower arm and remove the halfshaft.

15. Remove and discard the stub shaft circlip (LH) or the intermediate shaft circlip (RH).

To install:

RH and LH halfshafts

➡Make sure to install the correct circlip for each application. Failure to use the correct diameter circlip may result in shaft removal concerns or shaft damage during vehicle operation.

16. Install a new circlip.

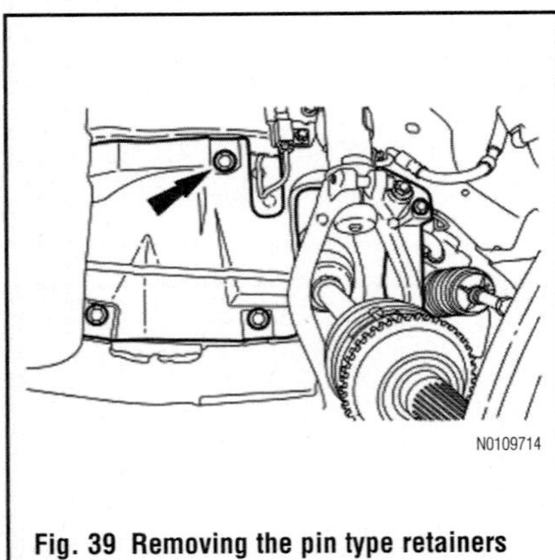

Fig. 39 Removing the pin type retainers

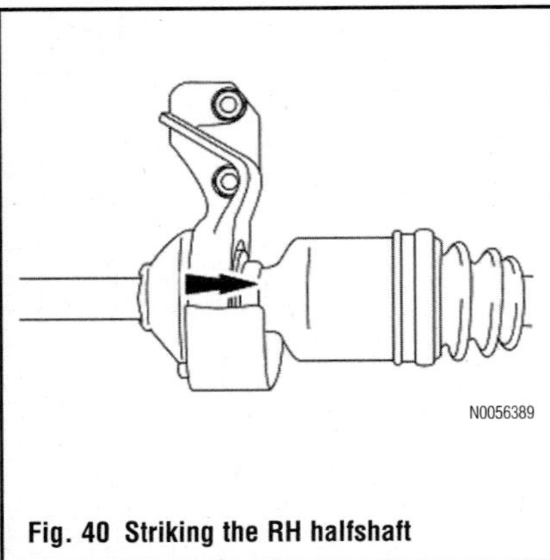

Fig. 40 Striking the RH halfshaft

LH halfshaft

17. Install the Differential Oil Seal Protector.

➡The sharp edges on the stub shaft splines can slice or puncture the oil seal. Use care when inserting the stub shaft into the transmission or damage to the seal may occur.

18. Push the stub shaft into the transmission so the circlip locks into the differential side gear.

a. After insertion, pull the halfshaft inner end to make sure the circlip is locked.

RH halfshaft

19. Align the splines on the RH halfshaft with the intermediate shaft and push the stub shaft in until the circlip locks the shafts together.

a. After insertion, pull the halfshaft inner end to make sure the circlip is locked.

RH and LH halfshafts

20. Position the damper fork and install a new damper fork-to-front lower arm bolt and flagnut.

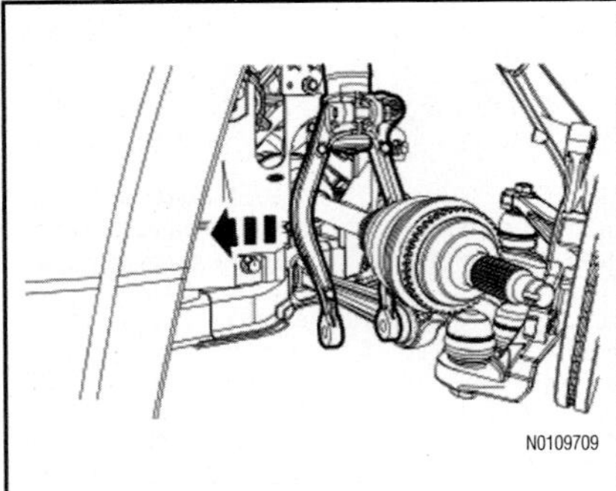

Fig. 41 Positioning the damper fork and halfshaft

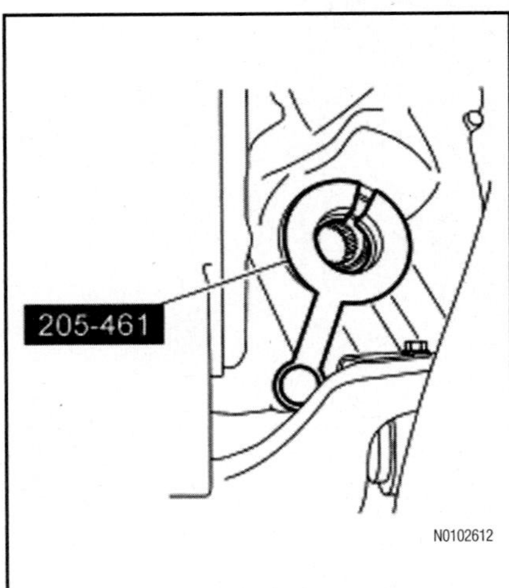

Fig. 42 Installing the differential oil seal protector

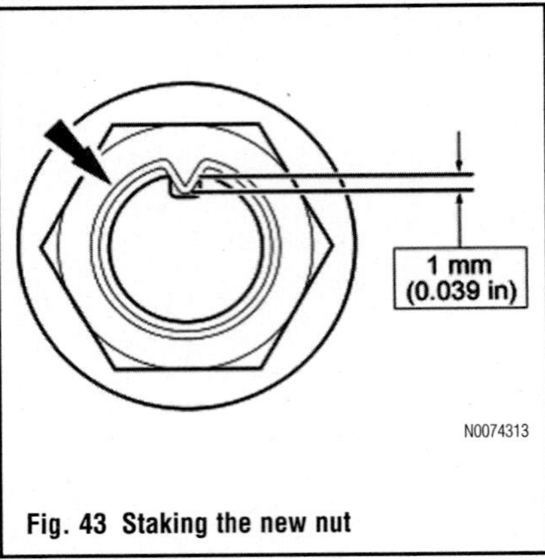

Fig. 43 Staking the new nut

a. Tighten to 76 ft. lbs. (103 Nm).

21. Position the splash shield and install the pin-type retainers.

22. Insert the halfshaft into the wheel hub.

23. Insert the upper ball joint into the wheel knuckle and install a new nut.

a. Tighten to 35 ft. lbs. (48 Nm).

24. Position the brake caliper and anchor plate assembly and install the 2 bolts.

a. Tighten to 66 ft. lbs. (90 Nm).

25. Position the brake flexible hose bracket and install the bolt.

a. Tighten to 17 ft. lbs. (23 Nm).

26. Position the wheel speed sensor and install the bolt.

a. Tighten to 17 ft. lbs. (23 Nm).

27. Position the wheel speed sensor harness bracket and install the bolt.

a. Tighten to 17 ft. lbs. (23 Nm).

28. Using the Halfshaft Installer, seat the halfshaft into the wheel hub.

➡Do not tighten the front wheel hub nut with the vehicle on the ground. The nut must be tightened to specification before the vehicle is lowered onto the wheels. Wheel bearing damage will occur if the wheel bearing is loaded with the weight of the vehicle applied.

➡Apply the brake to keep the halfshaft from rotating.

29. Install a new front wheel hub nut.

a. Tighten to 185 ft. lbs. (255 Nm).

30. Stake the new nut in line with the keyway to a recommended minimum depth of 0.039 inch (1 mm) below the keyway diameter to engage the locking feature.

31. Install the wheel and tire.

REAR AXLE STUB SHAFT BEARING AND SEAL

REMOVAL & INSTALLATION

See Figure 44.

➡**The Rear Drive Unit (RDU) does not have stub shaft pilot bearings. It has stub shaft seals only.**

1. Remove the halfshaft.
2. Using the Torque Converter Fluid Seal Remover and Slide Hammer, remove the stub shaft seal.

To install:

➡**Lubricate the new stub shaft seal with grease.**

3. Using the Front Axle Oil Seal Installer and Adapter Handle, install the stub shaft pilot bearing housing seal.
4. Install the halfshaft assembly.

REAR HALFSHAFT

REMOVAL & INSTALLATION

See Figures 45 through 47.

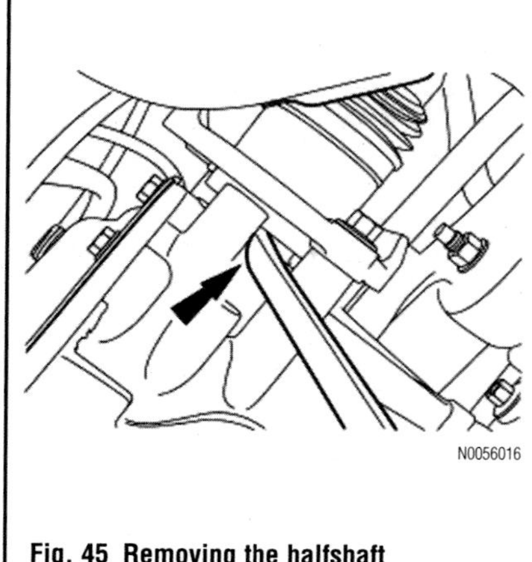

Fig. 45 Removing the halfshaft

1. Remove the wheel and tire.
2. Remove and discard the wheel hub nut.
3. Remove the bolt and position the ABS wheel speed sensor aside.
4. Remove the shock absorber lower bolt and flagnut.
5. Support the lower arm.
6. Remove the upper arm nut and bolt.
7. Remove the 4 toe link bracket nuts.
8. Using the Front Hub Remover, separate the halfshaft from the wheel hub.

➡**Do not damage the oil seal protector when removing the axle halfshaft from the differential.**

9. Using a suitable pry bar, remove the halfshaft.
10. Remove and discard the circlip from the stub shaft.

To install:

➡**Make sure to install the correct circlip for each application. Failure to use the correct diameter circlip may result in shaft removal concerns or shaft separation during vehicle operation.**

11. Install a new circlip on the stub shaft.
12. Using the Axle Seal Protector, install the halfshaft into the differential.
    a. Make sure the circlip locks in the side gear.
13. Using the Halfshaft Installer, install the halfshaft into the hub assembly.
14. Install the upper arm bolt and nut.

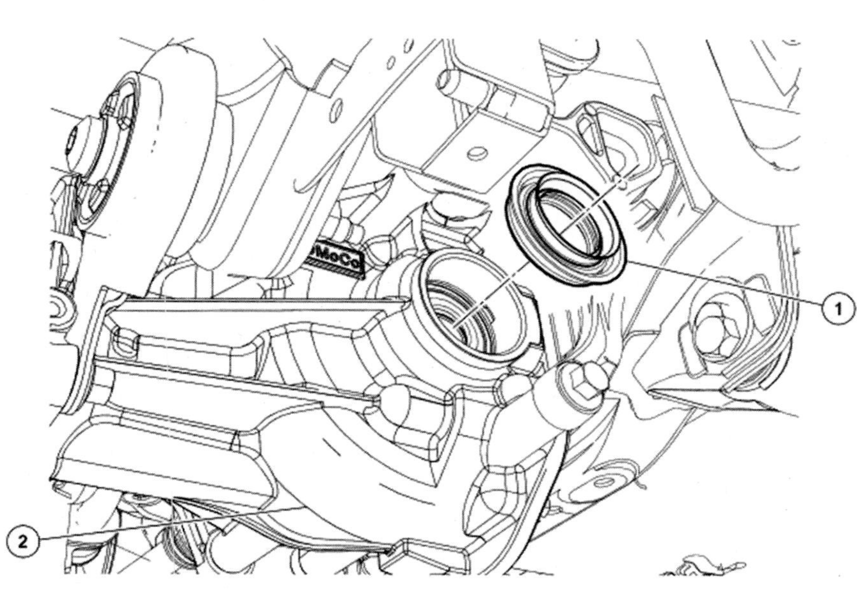

Fig. 44 Removing & installing the rear stub shaft seal

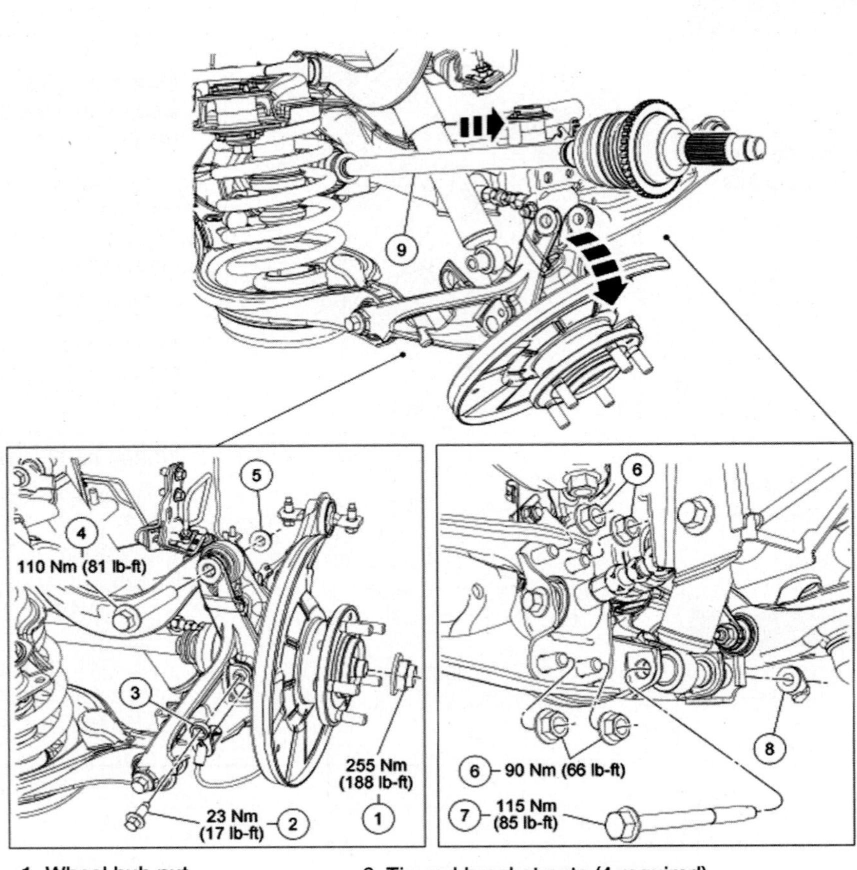

1. Wheel hub nut
2. ABS wheel speed sensor bolt
3. ABS wheel speed sensor
4. Upper arm bolt
5. Upper arm nut
6. Tie-rod bracket nuts (4 required)
7. Lower shock absorber bolt
8. Shock absorber lower flagnut (with 17-in wheel)
8. Shock absorber lower flagnut (with 16-in wheel)
9. Halfshaft assembly

N0082739

Fig. 46 Removing and installing the rear halfshaft

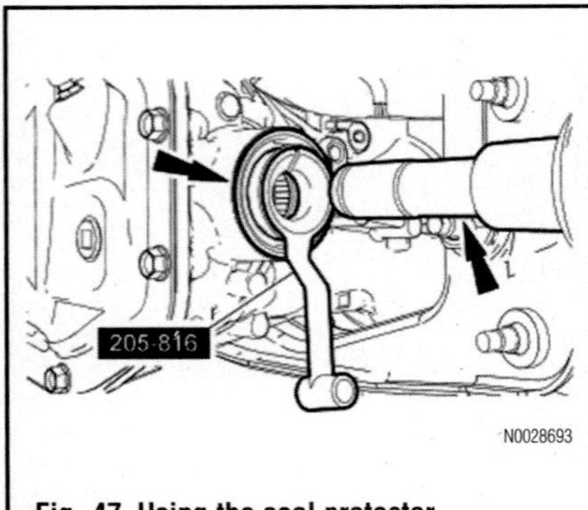

Fig. 47 Using the seal protector

a. Tighten to 81 ft. lbs. (110 Nm).

➡Do not tighten the rear wheel hub nut with the vehicle on the ground. The nut must be tightened to specification before the vehicle is lowered to the ground. Wheel bearing damage will occur if the wheel bearing is loaded with the weight of the vehicle applied.

15. Install the new wheel hub nut.
    a. To install, tighten to 188 ft. lbs. (255 Nm).
16. Stake the new nut in line with the keyway to a recommended minimum depth of 0.039 inch (1 mm) below the keyway diameter to engage the locking feature.
17. Install the 4 rear toe link bracket nuts.
    a. Tighten to 66 ft. lbs. (90 Nm).
18. Install the shock absorber lower bolt and flagnut.
    a. Tighten to 85 ft. lbs. (115 Nm).
19. Position the ABS wheel speed sensor and install the bolt.
    a. Tighten to 17 ft. lbs. (23 Nm).
20. Fill the axle with the specified quantity of the specified lubricant.
21. Install the wheel and tire.

ENGINE COOLING

ENGINE COOLANT

DRAIN & REFILL PROCEDURE

Draining

WARNING

Always allow the engine to cool before opening the cooling system. Do not unscrew the coolant pressure relief cap when the engine is operating or the cooling system is hot. The cooling system is under pressure; steam and hot liquid can come out forcefully when the cap is loosened slightly. Failure to follow these instructions may result in serious personal injury.

➡The coolant must be recovered in a suitable, clean container for reuse. If the coolant is contaminated, it must be recycled or disposed of correctly. Using contaminated coolant may result in damage to the engine or cooling system components.

➡Early build vehicle (built before July 6, 2009) cooling systems are filled with Motorcraft® Premium Gold Engine Coolant. Late build vehicle (built on or after July 6, 2009) cooling systems are filled with Motorcraft® Specialty Green Engine Coolant. Mixing coolant types degrades the corrosion protection of the coolant. Do not mix coolant types. Failure to follow these instructions may result in engine or cooling system damage.

➡Do not allow genuine Mazda® Extended Life Coolant and Motorcraft® products to be exposed to ANY LIGHT for more than a day or two. Extended light exposure causes these products to degrade.

➡Stop-leak style pellets/products must not be used as an additive in this engine cooling system. The addition of stop-leak style pellets/products can clog or damage the cooling system, resulting in degraded cooling system performance and/or failure.

➡Less than 80% of coolant capacity can be recovered with the engine in the vehicle. Dirty, rusty or contaminated coolant requires replacement.

1. With the vehicle in NEUTRAL, position it on a hoist.
2. Release the pressure in the cooling system by slowly turning the pressure relief cap one-half turn counterclockwise. When the pressure is released, remove the pressure relief cap.
3. Place a suitable container below the radiator draincock.
    a. Open the draincock and allow to drain.
    b. Close the draincock after draining.

Filling and Bleeding with RADIATOR REFILLER

➡Early build vehicle (built before July 6, 2009) cooling systems are filled with Motorcraft® Premium Gold Engine Coolant. Late build vehicle (built on or after July 6, 2009) cooling systems are filled with Motorcraft® Specialty Green Engine Coolant. Mixing coolant types degrades the corrosion protection of the coolant. Do not mix coolant types. Failure to follow these instructions may result in engine or cooling system damage.

➡Genuine Mazda® Extended Life Coolant and Motorcraft® Specialty Green Engine Coolant are very sensitive to light. Do NOT allow these products to be exposed to ANY LIGHT for more than a day or two. Extended light exposure causes these products to degrade.

4. Install the RADIATOR REFILLER and follow the manufacturer's instructions to fill and bleed the cooling system.
    a. Recommended coolant concentration is 50/50 ethylene glycol to distilled water.
    b. Maximum coolant concentration is 60/40 for cold weather areas.
    c. Minimum coolant concentration is 40/60 for warm weather areas.

Filling and Bleeding without RADIATOR REFILLER

➡Engine coolant provides freeze protection, boil protection, cooling efficiency and corrosion protection to the engine and cooling components. In order to obtain these protections, the engine coolant must be maintained at the correct concentration and fluid level in the degas bottle. To maintain the integrity of the coolant and the cooling system:

➡Genuine Mazda® Extended Life Coolant and Motorcraft® Specialty Green Engine Coolant are very sensitive to light. Do NOT allow these products to be exposed to ANY LIGHT for more than a day or two. Extended light exposure causes these products to degrade.

5. Add the correct coolant type to the engine cooling system. Early build vehicle (built before July 6, 2009) cooling systems are filled with Motorcraft® Premium Gold Engine Coolant. Late build vehicle (built on or after July 6, 2009) cooling systems are filled with Motorcraft® Specialty Green Engine Coolant. Mixing different coolant types degrades the corrosion protection of the original coolant. Do not mix any type of coolants.
    a. Do not add alcohol, methanol or brine, or any engine coolants mixed with alcohol or methanol antifreeze. These can cause engine damage from overheating or freezing.
6. Ford Motor Company does NOT recommend the use of recycled engine coolant in vehicles.
7. Used engine coolant should be disposed of in an appropriate manner. Follow the community's regulations and standards for recycling and disposing of automotive fluids.

➡Stop-leak style pellets/products must not be used as an additive in this engine cooling system. The addition of stop-leak style pellets/products can clog or damage the cooling system, resulting in degraded cooling system performance and/or failure.

2.5L engine

8. Open the degas bottle cap and the bleed valve on the back of the engine coolant outlet.

3.0L engine

9. Open the degas bottle cap and the bleed valve on the top of the coolant pump housing.

2.5L and 3.0L engines

➡Make sure the coolant flows from the radiator through the upper radiator hose and fills the engine. When full, coolant should flow from the bleed hole.

10. Fill the degas bottle to the MAX fill line.
    a. Recommended coolant concentration is 50/50 ethylene glycol to distilled water.
    b. Maximum coolant concentration is 60/40 for cold weather areas.
    c. Minimum coolant concentration is 40/60 for warm weather areas.

11. Close the degas bottle cap and the bleed valve.

➡If the engine overheats or the fluid level drops below the minimum fill line, shut off the engine and add fluid to the degas bottle maximum fill line once the engine cools. Failure to follow these instructions may result in damage to the engine.

12. Start the engine and let it idle for 10 minutes (3.0L), 30 minutes (2.5L) or until the engine reaches normal operating temperature.
13. Allow the engine to cool and repeat Step 3 if necessary.
14. Start the engine and turn the heater to the MAX position.

➡If the engine overheats or the fluid level drops below the minimum fill line, shut off the engine and add fluid to the degas bottle maximum fill line once the engine cools. Failure to follow these instructions may result in damage to the engine.

15. Run the engine at 2,500 rpm for 10 minutes.
16. Repeat Step 8 if necessary.

⁂ WARNING

Always allow the engine to cool before opening the cooling system. Do not unscrew the coolant pressure relief cap when the engine is operating or the cooling system is hot. The cooling system is under pressure; steam and hot liquid can come out forcefully when the cap is loosened slightly. Failure to follow these instructions may result in serious personal injury.

17. Check the engine coolant level in degas bottle and fill as necessary.

3.5L engine

18. Open the degas bottle cap and fill the degas bottle to the MAX fill line.
    a. Recommended coolant concentration is 50/50 ethylene glycol to distilled water.
    b. Maximum coolant concentration is 60/40 for cold weather areas.
    c. Minimum coolant concentration is 40/60 for warm weather areas.
19. Close the degas bottle cap.

BLEEDING

➡If the engine overheats or the fluid level drops below the minimum fill line, shut off the engine and add fluid to the degas bottle maximum fill line once the engine cools. Failure to follow these instructions may result in damage to the engine.

➡Start the engine and let idle for 10 minutes or until the engine reaches normal operating temperature.

1. Repeat Step 13 if necessary.
2. Start the engine and turn the heater to the MAX position.

➡If the engine overheats or the fluid level drops below the minimum fill line, shut off the engine and add fluid to the degas bottle maximum fill line once the engine cools. Failure to follow these instructions may result in damage to the engine.

3. Idle engine until the fan turns on, indicating the thermostat is fully open.
    a. Increase engine speed to 2,500 rpm for 30 seconds.
    b. Idle engine for 2 minutes.
    c. Repeat Steps 1 and 2 five times.
4. Repeat Step 16 if necessary.

⁂ WARNING

Always allow the engine to cool before opening the cooling system. Do not unscrew the coolant pressure relief cap when the engine is operating or the cooling system is hot. The cooling system is under pressure; steam and hot liquid can come out forcefully when the cap is loosened slightly. Failure to follow these instructions may result in serious personal injury.

5. Check the engine coolant level in the degas bottle and fill as necessary.

Hybrid

Draining

⁂ WARNING

Always allow the engine to cool before opening the cooling system. Do not unscrew the coolant pressure relief cap when the engine is operating or the cooling system is hot. The cooling system is under pressure; steam and hot liquid can come out forcefully when the cap is loosened slightly. Failure to follow these instructions may result in serious personal injury.

➡The coolant must be recovered in a suitable, clean container for reuse. If the coolant is contaminated, it must be recycled or disposed of correctly. Using contaminated coolant may result in damage to the engine or cooling system components.

➡Early build vehicle (built before July 6, 2009) cooling systems are filled with Motorcraft® Premium Gold Engine Coolant. Late build vehicle (built on or after July 6, 2009) cooling systems are filled with Motorcraft® Specialty Green Engine Coolant. Mixing coolant types degrades the corrosion protection of the coolant. Do not mix coolant types. Failure to follow these instructions may result in engine or cooling system damage.

➡Genuine Mazda® Extended Life Coolant and Motorcraft® Specialty Green Engine Coolant are very sensitive to light. Do NOT allow these products to be exposed to ANY LIGHT for more than a day or two. Extended light exposure causes these products to degrade.

➡Less than 80% of coolant capacity can be recovered with the engine in the vehicle. Dirty, rusty or contaminated coolant requires replacement.

1. Release the pressure in the cooling system by slowly turning the pressure relief cap one-half turn counterclockwise. When the pressure is released, remove the pressure relief cap.
2. Place a suitable container below the radiator draincock.
    a. Open the draincock and allow to drain.
    b. Close the draincock after draining.

Filling and Bleeding with RADIATOR REFILLER

➡Early build vehicle (built before July 6, 2009) cooling systems are filled with Motorcraft® Premium Gold Engine Coolant. Late build vehicle (built on or after July 6, 2009) cooling systems are filled with Motorcraft® Specialty Green Engine Coolant. Mixing coolant types degrades the corrosion protection of the coolant. Do not mix coolant types. Failure to follow these instructions may result in engine or cooling system damage.

➡Genuine Mazda® Extended Life Coolant and Motorcraft® Specialty Green Engine Coolant are very sensitive to light. Do NOT allow these products to be exposed to ANY LIGHT for more than a day or two. Extended light exposure causes these products to degrade.

3. Install the RADIATOR REFILLER and follow the manufacturer's instructions to fill and bleed the cooling system.

a. Recommended coolant concentration is 50/50 ethylene glycol to distilled water.

b. Maximum coolant concentration is 60/40 for cold weather areas.

c. Minimum coolant concentration is 40/60 for warm weather areas.

Filling and Bleeding without RADIATOR REFILLER

➡Engine coolant provides freeze protection, boil protection, cooling efficiency and corrosion protection to the engine and cooling components. In order to obtain these protections, the engine coolant must be maintained at the correct concentration and fluid level in the degas bottle. To maintain the integrity of the coolant and the cooling system:

➡Genuine Mazda® Extended Life Coolant and Motorcraft® Specialty Green Engine Coolant are very sensitive to light. Do NOT allow these products to be exposed to ANY LIGHT for more than a day or two. Extended light exposure causes these products to degrade.

4. Add the correct coolant type to the engine cooling system. Early build vehicle (built before July 6, 2009) cooling systems are filled with Motorcraft® Premium Gold Engine Coolant. Late build vehicle (built on or after July 6, 2009) cooling systems are filled with Motorcraft® Specialty Green Engine Coolant. Mixing different coolant types degrades the corrosion protection of the original coolant. Do not mix any type of coolants.

a. Do not add alcohol, methanol, brine or any engine coolants mixed with alcohol or methanol antifreeze. These can cause engine damage from overheating or freezing.

b. Ford Motor Company does NOT recommend the use of recycled engine coolant in vehicles.

c. Used engine coolant should be disposed of in an appropriate manner. Follow your community's regulations and standards for recycling and disposing of automotive fluids.

d. Open the degas bottle cap and the bleed valve on the top of the engine coolant outlet.

➡Make sure the coolant flows from the radiator through the upper radiator hose and fills the engine.

5. Fill the degas bottle to the COLD FILL RANGE line.

a. Recommended coolant concentration is 50/50 ethylene glycol to distilled water.

b. Maximum coolant concentration is 60/40 for cold weather areas.

c. Minimum coolant concentration is 40/60 for warm weather areas.

6. Close the degas bottle cap and the bleed valve.

➡If the engine overheats or the fluid level drops below the minimum fill line, shut off the engine and add fluid to the degas bottle to the cold fill range line once the engine cools. Failure to follow these instructions may result in damage to the engine.

7. Start the engine and let it idle for 30 minutes or until the engine reaches normal operating temperature.

8. Turn the heater to the MAX position

➡If the engine overheats or the fluid level drops below the minimum fill line, shut off the engine and add fluid to the degas bottle to the cold fill range line once the engine cools. Failure to follow these instructions may result in damage to the engine.

9. Start the engine and run at 2,500 to 3,000 rpm for 30 seconds. Let idle at 1,000 rpm for 1 minute. Repeat this 7 or 8 times or 10 minutes.

10. Repeat Step 6 if necessary.

WARNING

Always allow the engine to cool before opening the cooling system. Do not unscrew the coolant pressure relief cap when the engine is operating or the cooling system is hot. The cooling system is under pressure; steam and hot liquid can come out forcefully when the cap is loosened slightly. Failure to follow these instructions may result in serious personal injury.

11. Check the engine coolant level in degas bottle and fill as necessary.

FLUSHING

1. To remove rust, sludge and other foreign material from the cooling system, use cooling system flush that is safe for use with aluminum radiators. For additional information, refer to Specifications in this section. This cleaning restores cooling system efficiency and helps prevent overheating. A pulsating or reversed direction of flushing water will loosen sediment more quickly than a steady flow in the normal coolant flow direction. In severe cases where cleaning solvents will not clean the cooling system efficiently, it will be necessary to use the pressure flushing method using cooling system flusher. Dispose of old coolant and flushing water contaminated with antifreeze and cleaning chemicals in accordance with local, state or federal laws.

2. Remove the radiator.

➡Radiator internal pressure must not exceed 20 psi (138 kPa). Damage to the radiator can result.

3. Backflush the radiator with the radiator in an upside-down position with a high-pressure hose in the lower hose location and backflush.

➡On 2.5L engines, the thermostat and housing are serviced as an assembly.

4. Remove the thermostat.

5. Backflush the engine. Position the high-pressure water hose into the engine through the engine return and backflush the engine.

Hybrid

➡Dispose of old coolant and flushing water contaminated with antifreeze and cleaning chemicals in accordance with local, state or federal laws.

1. To remove rust, sludge and other foreign material from the cooling system, use cooling system flush that is safe for use with aluminum radiators. For additional information, refer to Specifications in this section. This cleaning restores cooling system efficiency and helps prevent overheating. A pulsating or reversed direction of flushing water will loosen sediment more quickly than a steady flow in the normal coolant flow direction. In severe cases where cleaning solvents will not clean the cooling system efficiently, it will be necessary to use the pressure flushing method using cooling system flusher. Dispose of old coolant and flushing water contaminated with antifreeze and cleaning chemicals in accordance with local, state or federal laws.

2. Remove the radiator.

➡Radiator internal pressure must not exceed 20 psi (138 kPa). Damage to the radiator can result.

3. Backflush the radiator with the radiator in an upside-down position and a high-pressure hose in the lower hose location.

➡Thermostat and housing are serviced as an assembly.

4. Remove the thermostat housing.
5. Position a high-pressure water hose into the engine through the engine return and backflush the engine.

ENGINE FAN

REMOVAL & INSTALLATION

2.5L & 3.0L Engines

See Figures 48 and 49.

1. Detach all the wiring harness retainers from the cooling fan and shroud.
2. If equipped, detach the 2 block heater wiring retainers from the cooling fan motor and shroud.
3. Remove the splash shield.
4. Drain the cooling system.
5. Detach the RH lower radiator hose pin-type retainer from the cooling fan motor and shroud.
6. If equipped, detach the 2 transmission cooler tube retainers from the cooling fan motor and shroud.
7. If equipped, detach the LH lower radiator hose pin-type retainer from the cooling fan motor and shroud.
8. Disconnect the upper radiator hose from the radiator.

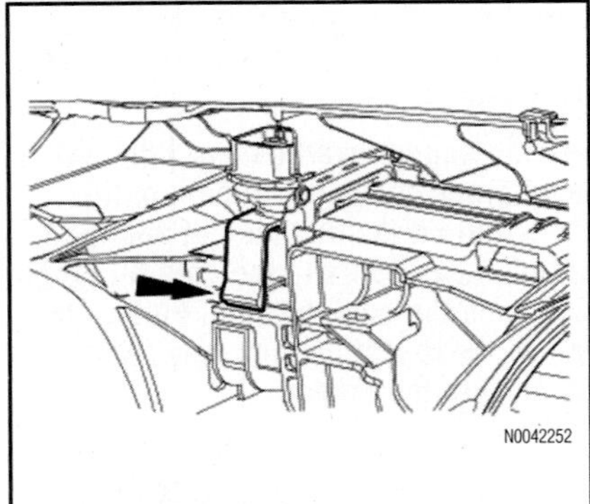

Fig. 49 Releasing the tabs

9. Disconnect the cooling fan electrical connector.
   a. Detach the pin-type retainer.

➡LH shown, RH similar.

10. Release the 2 tabs and remove the cooling fan motor and shroud.

To install:

11. To install, reverse the removal procedure.
12. Fill and bleed the cooling system.

3.5L Engine

See Figures 50 and 51.

1. With vehicle in NEUTRAL, position it on a hoist.
2. Remove the splash shield.
3. Drain the cooling system.
4. Detach the lower radiator hose pin-type retainer from the RH side of the cooling fan motor and shroud.

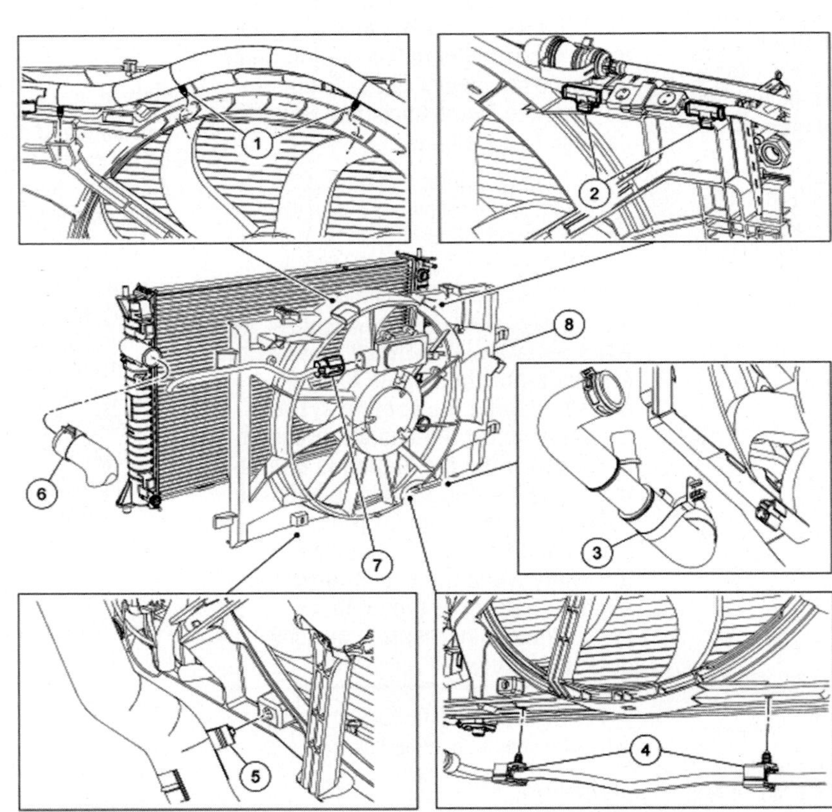

Fig. 48 Removing and installing the cooling fan motor & shroud

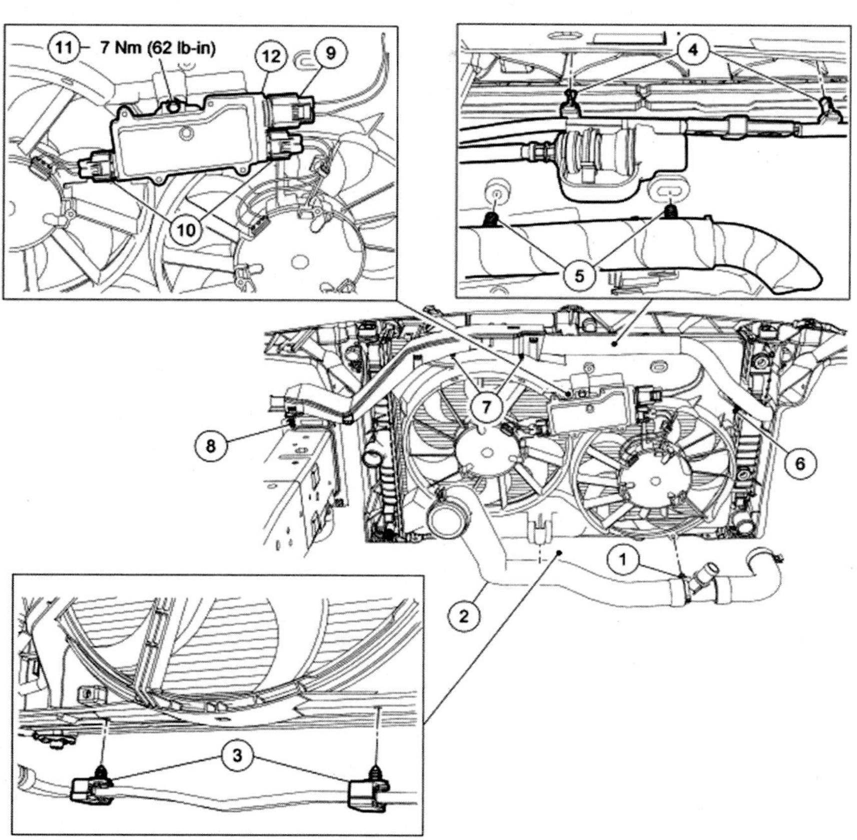

1. RH lower radiator hose pin-type retainer
2. Lower radiator hose
3. Transmission fluid cooler tube retaining clips
4. Block heater retainers
5. Wire harness retainers
6. Wire harness retainer
7. Wire harness shield retainers
8. Wire harness shield retainer
9. Cooling fan module electrical connector
10. Cooling fan module electrical connectors
11. Cooling fan module bolt
12. Cooling fan module

N0096621

Fig. 50 Removing and installing the cooling fan motor and shroud—1 of 2

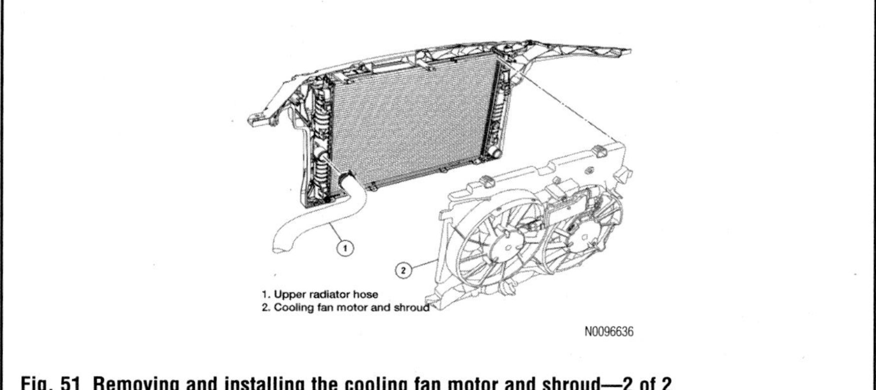

Fig. 51 Removing and installing the cooling fan motor and shroud—2 of 2

5. Detach the lower radiator hose from the LH side of the cooling fan motor and shroud.
6. Detach the transmission cooler tube retaining clips from the cooling fan motor and shroud.
7. Remove the Air Cleaner (ACL) and inlet air resonator.
8. If equipped, detach the 2 block heater wiring retainers from the cooling fan motor and shroud.
9. Disconnect the 3 cooling fan module electrical connectors.
10. Remove the bolt and the cooling fan module.

a. To install, tighten to 62 inch lbs. (7 Nm).

11. Detach the 5 pin-type retainers from the cooling fan and shroud.

12. Detach the wiring harness pin-type retainer from the frame rail.

13. Disconnect the upper radiator hose from the radiator.

➡LH shown, RH similar.

14. Release the 2 tabs and remove the cooling fan motor and shroud.

To install:

15. To install, reverse the removal procedure.

16. Fill and bleed the cooling system.

2.5L Hybrid Engine

See Figures 53 and 54.

1. With the vehicle in NEUTRAL, position it on a hoist.
2. If equipped, detach the 2 block heater wiring retainers from the cooling fan motor and shroud.
3. Remove the splash shield.
4. Detach the lower radiator hose pin-type retainer from the cooling fan motor and shroud.
5. Remove the battery tray.
6. Remove the 2 bolts and position the auxiliary relay box aside.
7. Detach all the wiring harness retainers from the cooling fan and shroud.
8. Disconnect the Evaporative Emission (EVAP) canister purge valve electrical connector.
9. Disconnect the cooling fan electrical connector.

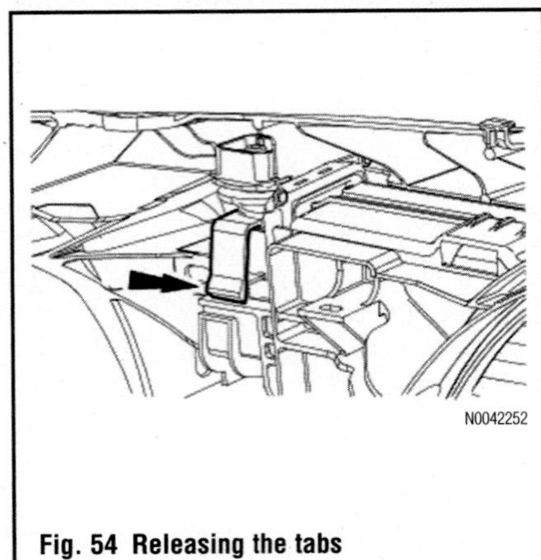

Fig. 54 Releasing the tabs

➡LH shown, RH similar.

10. Release the 2 tabs and remove the cooling fan motor and shroud.

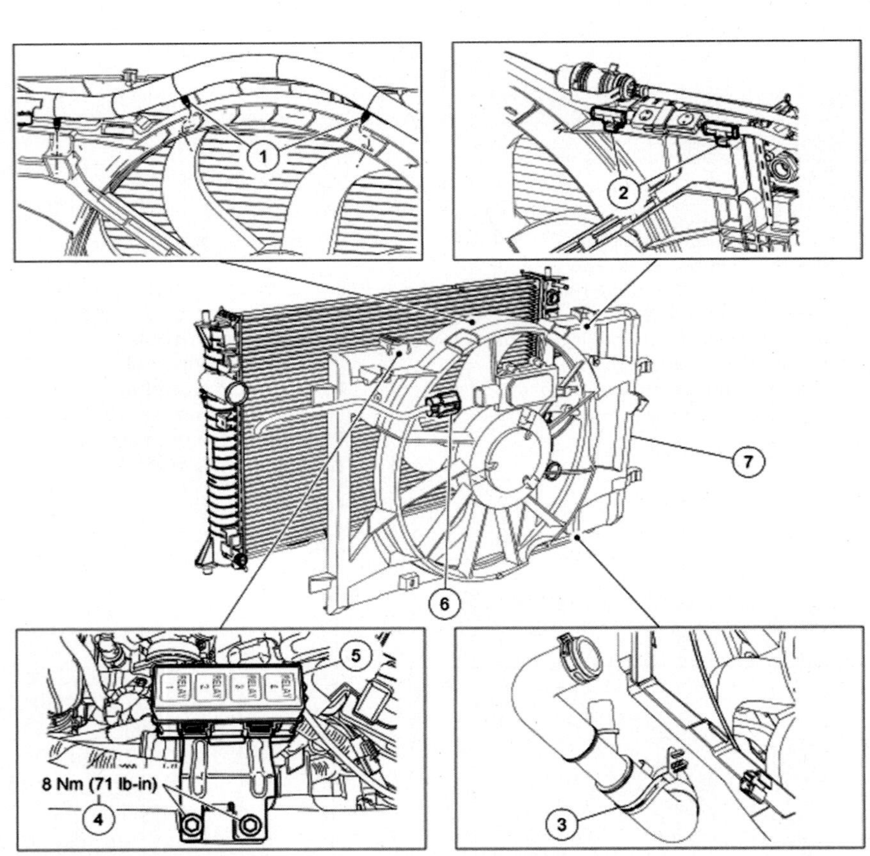

Fig. 53 Removing and installing the cooling fan motor and shroud

To install:

To install, reverse the removal procedure. Tighten the auxiliary relay box bolts to 71 inch lbs. (8 Nm).

RADIATOR

REMOVAL & INSTALLATION

2.5L & 3.0L Engines

See Figure 55.

1. Drain the cooling system.
2. Remove the cooling fan motor and shroud.
3. Disconnect the radiator-to-degas bottle hose from the radiator.
4. If equipped, disconnect the 2 transmission cooling tubes from the radiator.
5. Disconnect the lower radiator hose from the radiator.
6. Remove the 2 bolts from the upper radiator support brackets and position the radiator towards the engine and remove the 2 upper radiator support brackets from the radiator.
7. Remove the A/C condenser-to-radiator pin-type retainer.
8. Squeeze the tabs and separate the A/C condenser from the radiator.
9. Remove the radiator.

To install:

10. To install, reverse the removal procedure.
11. If equipped, disconnect the transmission cooling tubes to 22 ft. lbs. (30 Nm).
12. Tighten the upper radiator support brackets to 89 inch lbs. (10 Nm).
13. Fill and bleed the cooling system.

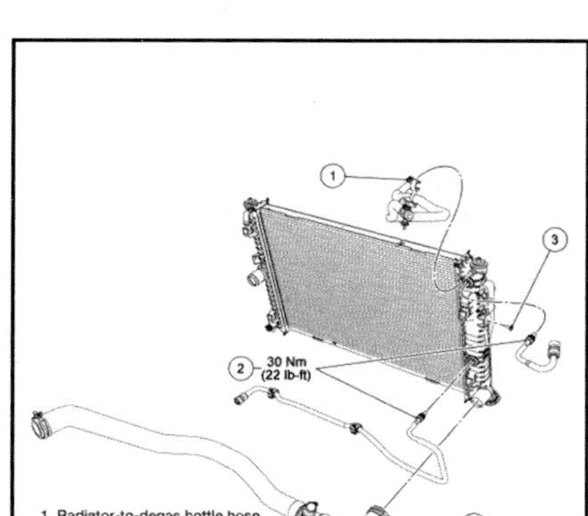

Fig. 55 Exploded view of the radiator and related components

3.5L Engine

See Figures 56 through 58.

1. Drain the cooling system.
2. Remove the cooling fan motor and shroud.
3. Detach the power steering hose retainer from the radiator.
4. Detach the coolant hose retainer from the radiator.
5. Disconnect the radiator-to-degas bottle hose from the radiator.
6. Disconnect the 2 transmission cooling tubes from the radiator.
7. Disconnect the lower radiator hose from the radiator.
8. Remove the 2 bolts from the upper radiator support brackets and position the radiator towards the engine and remove the 2 upper radiator support brackets from the radiator.
9. Remove the A/C condenser-to-radiator pin-type retainer.

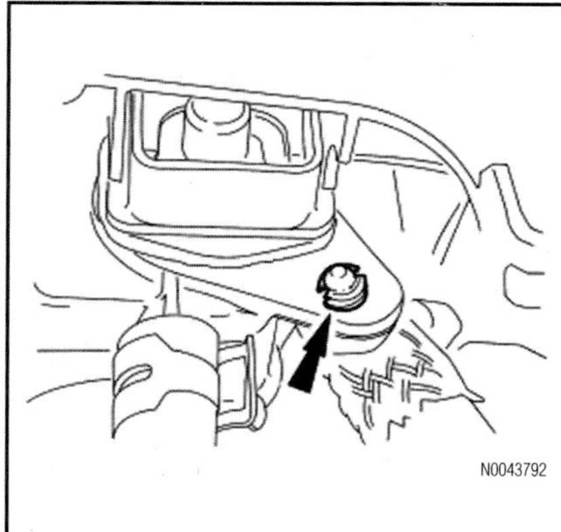

Fig. 56 Detaching the power steering hose retainer from the radiator

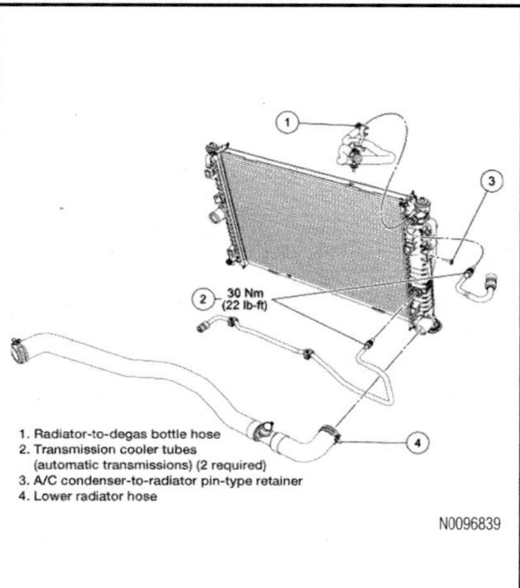

Fig. 57 Exploded view of the radiator and related components—1 of 2

10. Squeeze the tabs and separate the A/C condenser from the radiator.
11. Remove the radiator.

To install:

12. To install, reverse the removal procedure.
13. Tighten the upper radiator support brackets to 89 inch lbs. (10 Nm).
14. Tighten the transmission cooling tubes to 22 ft. lbs. (30 Nm).
15. Fill and bleed the cooling system.

2.5L Hybrid

See Figures 59 and 60.

1. Drain the cooling system.
2. Remove the cooling fan motor and shroud.
3. Disconnect the upper radiator hose from the radiator.
4. Disconnect the radiator-to-degas bottle hose from the radiator.
5. Disconnect the lower radiator hose from the radiator.
6. Remove the A/C tubes retainer bolt.
7. Remove the 2 bolts from the upper radiator support brackets and position the radiator towards the engine and remove the 2 upper radiator support bracket from the radiator.
8. Remove the A/C condenser-to-radiator pin-type retainer.
9. Squeeze the tabs and separate the A/C condenser from the radiator.
10. Remove the radiator.

To install:

11. To install, reverse the removal procedure and note the following steps.
12. Tighten the upper radiator support brackets to 89 inch lbs. (10 Nm).
13. Remove the A/C tube retainer bolt to 62 inch lbs. (7 Nm).
14. Fill and bleed the cooling system.

THERMOSTAT

REMOVAL & INSTALLATION

3.0L Engine

See Figure 61.

1. With the vehicle in NEUTRAL, position it on a hoist.
2. Drain the cooling system.
3. Disconnect the positive battery cable.
4. Disconnect the lower radiator hose from the thermostat housing.

➡Early build vehicle (built before July 6, 2009) cooling systems are filled with Motorcraft® Premium Gold Engine

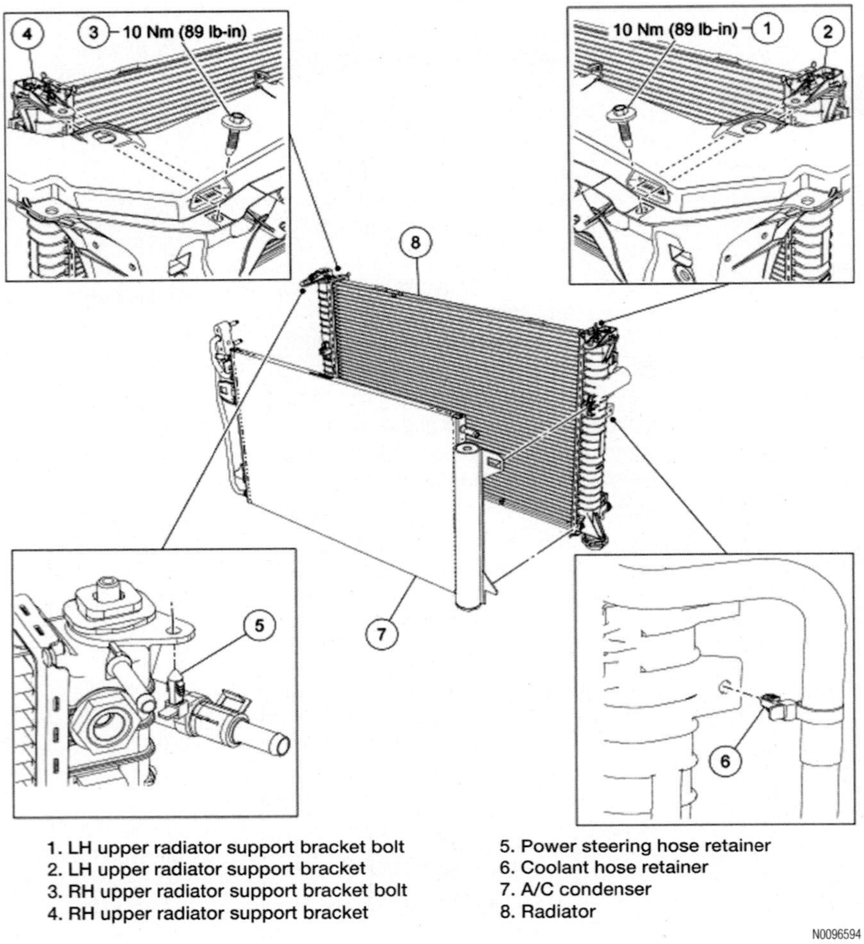

10 Nm (89 lb-in)
10 Nm (89 lb-in)
1. LH upper radiator support bracket bolt
2. LH upper radiator support bracket
3. RH upper radiator support bracket bolt
4. RH upper radiator support bracket
5. Power steering hose retainer
6. Coolant hose retainer
7. A/C condenser
8. Radiator
N0096594

Fig. 58 Exploded view of the radiator and related components—2 of 2

1. Upper radiator hose clamp
2. Upper radiator hose
3. Radiator-to-degas bottle hose clamp
4. Radiator-to-degas bottle hose
5. Lower radiator hose clamp
6. Lower radiator hose
7. A/C condenser-to-radiator pin-type retainer
N0096252

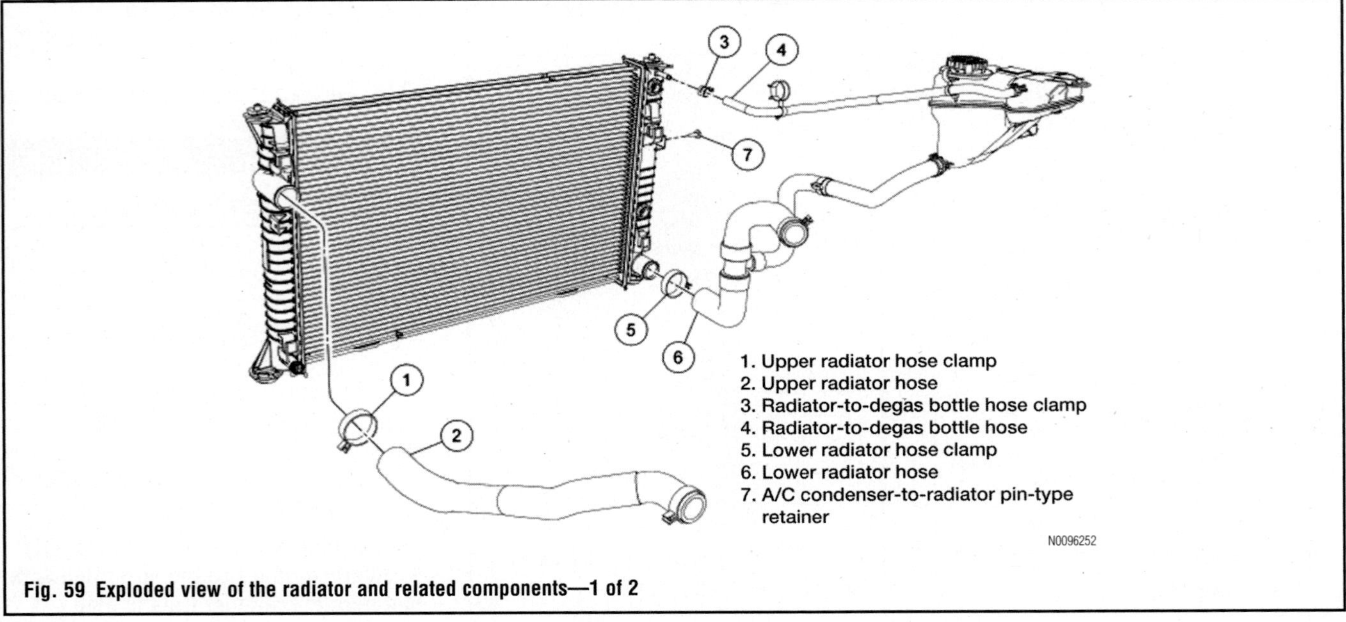

Fig. 59 Exploded view of the radiator and related components—1 of 2

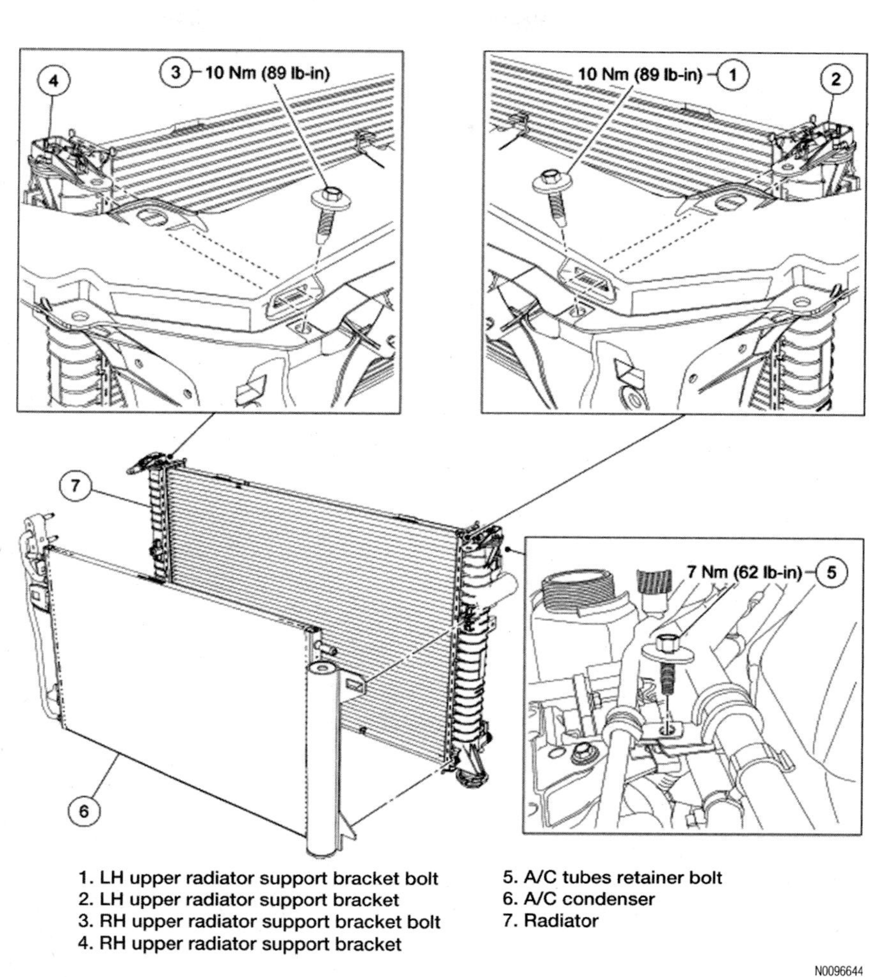

Fig. 60 Exploded view of the radiator and related components—2 of 2

Coolant. Late build vehicle (built on or after July 6, 2009) cooling systems are filled with Motorcraft® Specialty Green Engine Coolant. Mixing coolant types degrades the corrosion protection of the coolant. Do not mix coolant types. Failure to follow these instructions may result in engine or cooling system damage.

➡Genuine Mazda® Extended Life Coolant and Motorcraft® Specialty Green Engine Coolant are very sensitive to light. Do NOT allow these products to be exposed to ANY LIGHT for more than a day or two. Extended light exposure causes these products to degrade.

➡To install, lubricate the thermostat housing O-ring seal with clean engine coolant.

5. Remove the 2 bolts, thermostat housing cover, O-ring seal and thermostat.

To install:

6. To install, reverse the removal procedure.
7. Clean and inspect the O-ring seal. Install a new seal if necessary.
8. Tighten the thermostat housing cover to 89 inch lbs. (10 Nm).
9. Fill and bleed the cooling system.

3.5L Engine

See Figure 62.

1. Drain the cooling system.
2. Remove the air cleaner and outlet pipe.
3. Disconnect the lower radiator hose from the thermostat housing cover and position it aside.
4. Remove the 2 bolts, thermostat housing cover, O-ring seal and thermostat.
    a. Clean and inspect the O-ring seal. Install a new seal if necessary.

➡Early build vehicle (built before July 6, 2009) cooling systems are filled with Motorcraft® Premium Gold Engine Coolant. Late build vehicle (built on or after July 6, 2009) cooling systems are filled with Motorcraft® Specialty Green Engine Coolant. Mixing coolant types

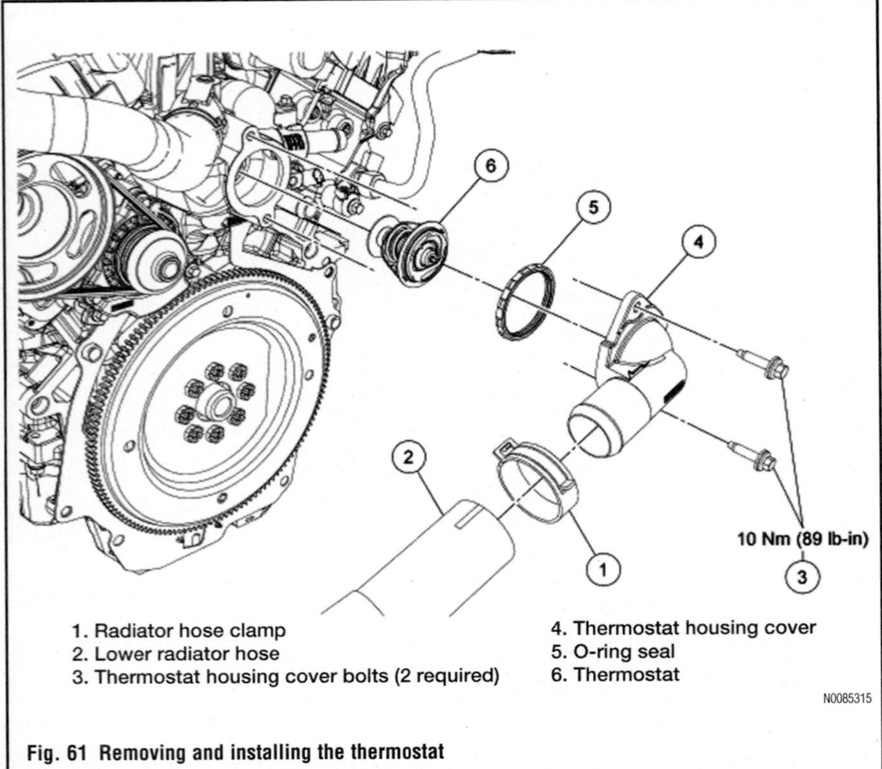

Fig. 61 Removing and installing the thermostat

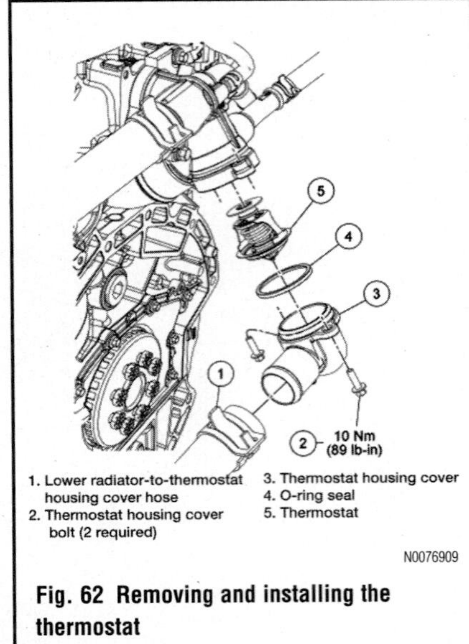

Fig. 62 Removing and installing the thermostat

degrades the corrosion protection of the coolant. Do not mix coolant types. Failure to follow these instructions may result in engine or cooling system damage.

➡Genuine Mazda® Extended Life Coolant and Motorcraft® Specialty Green Engine Coolant are very sensitive to light. Do NOT allow these products to be exposed to ANY LIGHT for more than a day or two. Extended light exposure causes these products to degrade.

➡Lubricate the thermostat O-ring seal with clean engine coolant.

To install:

5. To install, reverse the removal procedure.
6. Tighten the thermostat housing to 89 inch lbs. (10 Nm).
7. Fill and bleed the cooling system.

ENGINE ELECTRICAL

BATTERY SYSTEM

BATTERY

REMOVAL & INSTALLATION

✱✱ WARNING

Batteries contain sulfuric acid and produce explosive gases. Work in a well-ventilated area. Do not allow the battery to come in contact with flames, sparks or burning substances. Avoid contact with skin, eyes or clothing. Shield eyes when working near the battery to protect against possible splashing of acid solution. In case of acid contact with skin or eyes, flush immediately with water for a minimum of 15 minutes, then get prompt medical attention. If acid is swallowed, call a physician immediately. Failure to follow these instructions may result in serious personal injury.

✱✱ WARNING

Always deplete the backup power supply before repairing or installing any new front or side air bag supplemental restraint system (SRS) component and before servicing, removing, installing, adjusting or striking components near the front or side impact sensors or the restraints control module (RCM). Nearby components include doors, instrument panel, console, door latches, strikers, seats and hood latches.

✱✱ WARNING

To deplete the backup power supply energy, disconnect the battery ground cable and wait at least 1 minute. Be sure to disconnect auxiliary batteries and power supplies (if equipped).

✱✱ WARNING

Failure to follow these instructions may result in serious personal injury or death in the event of an accidental deployment.

✱✱ WARNING

Always lift a plastic-cased battery with a battery carrier or with hands on opposite corners. Excessive pressure on the battery end walls may cause acid to flow through the vent caps, resulting in personal injury and/or damage to the vehicle or battery.

➡When the battery (or PCM) is disconnected and connected, some abnormal drive symptoms may occur while the vehicle relearns its adaptive strategy. The charging system set point may also vary. The vehicle may need to be driven to relearn its strategy.

1. Disconnect the battery.
   a. On hybrid vehicles, remove the Air Cleaner (ACL) assembly.

➡When disconnecting the battery ground cable to interrupt power to the vehicle electrical system, disconnect the battery ground cable only. It is not necessary to disconnect the positive battery cable.

   b. Disconnect the battery ground terminal.
   c. Disconnect the positive battery terminal.
2. Remove the bolt and the battery hold-down bracket.
3. If equipped, remove the battery heat shield.
4. Remove the battery.

To install:

5. To install, reverse the removal procedure.
6. Tighten the battery hold down bracket to 89 inch lbs. (10 Nm).
7. Connect the battery ground terminal to 62 inch lbs. (7 Nm).
8. Connect the battery positive terminal to 62 inch lbs. (7 Nm).

ENGINE ELECTRICAL

CHARGING SYSTEM

ALTERNATOR

REMOVAL & INSTALLATION

2.5L Engine

See Figure 63.

➡Do not allow any metal object to come in contact with the generator housing and internal diode cooling fins. A short circuit may result and burn out the diodes. Failure to follow this instruction may result in component damage.

➡The radial arm adapter is a serviceable item. Do not replace the generator if the radial arm adapter is the only concern.

1. With the vehicle in NEUTRAL, position it on a hoist.
2. Disconnect the battery.
3. Remove the 4 RH lower splash shield screws.
4. Remove the 6 pushpins and the RH lower splash shield.
5. Rotate the Front End Accessory Drive (FEAD) belt tensioner clockwise and position the accessory drive belt aside.
6. Working from the top of the vehicle, press the locking tab to release the generator lower air duct from the generator and remove the lower air duct.
7. Remove the battery harness locator from the lower generator stud bolt.
8. Remove the lower generator bolt.
9. Remove the 2 generator stud nuts.
10. Position the generator B+ protective cover aside and remove the generator B+ terminal nut.
11. Position the generator B+ cable aside.
12. Disconnect the generator electrical connector.
13. Remove the 2 generator studs and remove the generator.

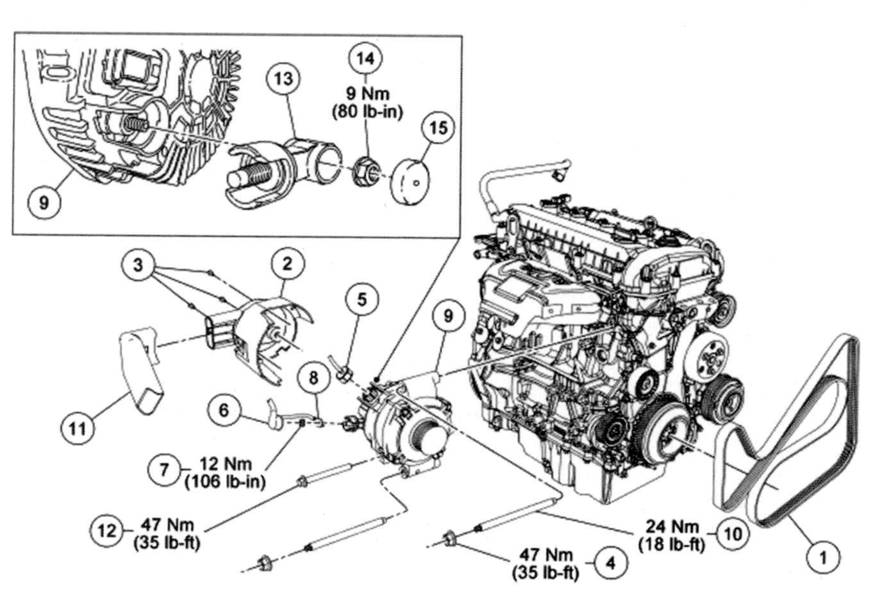

1. Front End Accessory Drive (FEAD) belt
2. Generator upper air duct
3. Generator upper air duct screws (3 required)
4. Generator stud nut (2 required)
5. Generator electrical connector
6. B+ protective cover
7. Generator B+ terminal nut
8. Generator B+ cable
9. Generator
10. Generator stud (2 required)
11. Generator lower air duct
12. Generator bolt
13. Radial arm adapter
14. Radial arm adapter nut
15. Radial arm adapter cap

N0110616

Fig. 63 Exploded view of the generator and related components—2.5L engine

14. Remove the 3 screws and the generator upper air duct.

To install:

15. Position the generator upper air duct and install the 3 screws.
    a. Tighten to 35 inch lbs. (4 Nm).
16. Working from the top of the vehicle, position the generator and install the generator upper stud hand-tight.
17. Install the generator lower stud hand-tight.
18. Install the generator B+ cable and install the generator B+ terminal nut.
    a. Tighten to 9 ft. lbs. (12 Nm).
19. Connect the generator electrical connector.
20. Position the generator B+ protective cover on the B+ terminal.
21. Working from under the vehicle, install the lower generator bolt hand-tight.
22. Working from the top of the vehicle, tighten the 2 generator studs to 18 ft. lbs. (24 Nm).
23. Tighten the 2 generator stud nuts to 35 ft. lbs. (47 Nm).
24. Tighten the generator bolt to 35 ft. lbs. (47 Nm).
25. Push the lower air duct onto the upper air duct until the locking tab is engaged.
26. Position the RH lower splash shield and install the 6 pushpins.
27. Position the RH wheel splash shield and install the 4 screws.
    a. Tighten to 71 inch lbs. (8 Nm).
28. Position the harness locator on the generator stud.
29. Connect the battery.
30. Rotate the FEAD belt tensioner clockwise and position the accessory drive belt on the pulley.

3.0L Engine

See Figure 64.

1. Remove the A/C compressor.
2. Disconnect the battery.
3. Position the generator protective cover aside, remove the nut and position the generator B+ terminal aside.
4. Disconnect the generator electrical connector.
5. Remove the 3 bolts and the generator.

To install:

6. To install, reverse the removal procedure.
7. Tighten the generator bolts to 35 ft. lbs. (47 Nm).
8. Tighten the generator B+ terminal nut to 9 ft. lbs. (12 Nm).

3.5L Engine

See Figure 65.

➡The radial arm adapter is a serviceable item. Do not replace the generator if the radial arm adapter is the only concern.

1. Remove the A/C compressor.
2. Disconnect the battery.
3. Position the generator protective cover aside, remove the nut and position the generator B+ terminal aside.
   To install, tighten to 106 inch lbs. (12 Nm).
4. Disconnect the generator electrical connector.
5. Detach the pin-type retainer and wiring harness.
6. Remove the oil filter.
7. Lubricate the oil filter seal with clean engine oil before installation.
8. Position the engine wiring harness aside.
9. Remove the generator stud nut.
10. Remove the generator bolt and the generator.

To install:

11. To install, reverse the removal procedure.
12. Tighten the generator stud nut to 35 ft. lbs. (47 Nm).
13. Tighten the generator B+ terminal nut to 9 ft. lbs. (12 Nm).

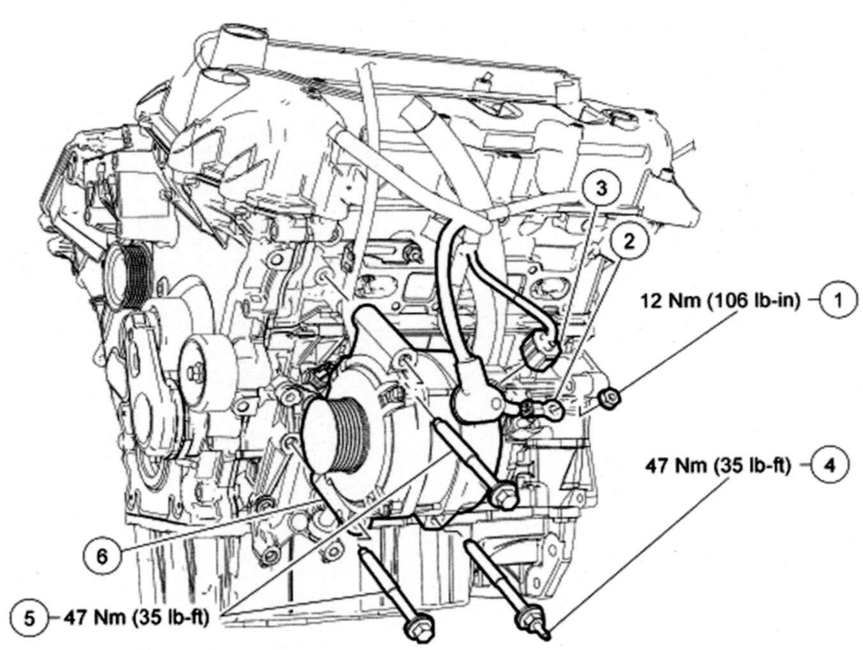

1. Generator B+ terminal nut
2. Generator B+ terminal
3. Generator electrical connector
4. Generator stud bolt
5. Generator bolts (2 required)
6. Generator

N0087755

Fig. 64 Removing and installing the generator—3.0L engine

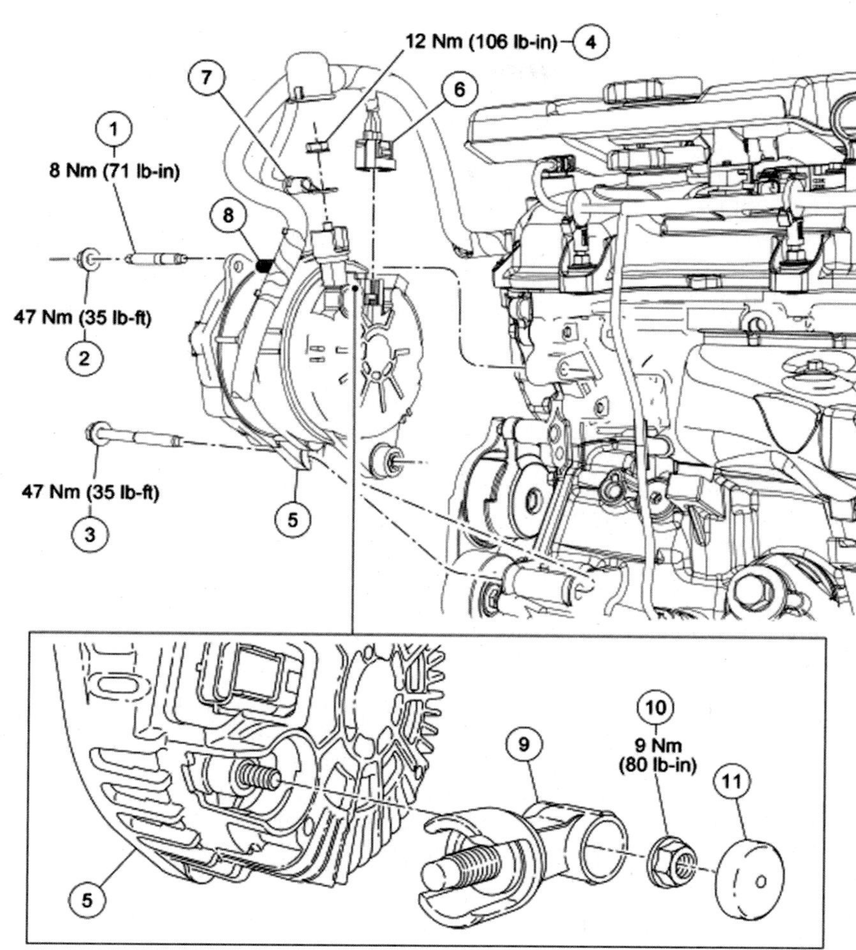

1. Generator stud
2. Generator stud nut
3. Generator bolt
4. Generator B+ terminal nut
5. Generator
6. Generator electrical connector
7. Generator B+ terminal
8. Pin-type retainer, wiring harness
9. Radial arm adapter
10. Radial arm adapter nut
11. Radial arm adapter cap

N0109862

Fig. 65 Exploded view of the generator—3.5L engine

PRECAUTIONS

Before working on any part of the Hybrid high voltage system, observe the following precautions:

**** CAUTION**

The nominal high voltage traction battery voltage is 275 volts DC. The buffer zone must be set up and insulated rubber gloves and a face shield must be worn. Failure to follow these instructions may result in severe injury or death.

**** CAUTION**

The high voltage traction battery and charging system contains high voltage components and wiring. High voltage insulated safety gloves and a face shield must be worn when carrying out any diagnostics on this vehicle. Failure to follow these instructions may result in severe personal injury or death.

**** CAUTION**

Before carrying out any removal and installation procedures of the high voltage traction battery system, the high voltage traction battery must be Disarmed. Failure to follow these instructions may result in severe personal injury or death.

**** CAUTION**

The rubber insulating gloves that are to be worn while working on the high voltage system should be of the appropriate safety and protection rating for use on the high voltage system. They must be inspected before use and must always be worn in conjunction with the leather outer gloves. Any hole in the rubber insulating glove is a potential entry point for high voltage. Failure to follow these instructions may result in severe personal injury or death.

➡The high voltage insulated safety gloves must be re-certified every 6 months to remain within Occupational Safety and Health Administration (OSHA) guidelines:

- Roll the glove up from the open end until the lower portion of the glove begins to balloon from the resulting air pressure. If the glove leaks any air, it must not be used.
- The gloves should not be used if they exhibit any signs of wear and tear.
- The leather gloves must always be worn over the rubber insulating gloves in order to protect them.
- The rubber insulating gloves must be class "00" and meet all of the American Society for Testing and Materials (ASTM) standards

**** CAUTION**

High voltage insulated safety gloves and a face shield must be worn when working with high voltage cables. The ignition switch must be OFF for a minimum of 5 minutes before removing high voltage cables. Failure to follow these instructions may result in severe personal injury or death.

**** CAUTION**

Establish a buffer zone before servicing the high voltage system. The buffer zone is required only when working with the high voltage system. See the text for buffer zone establishment. Failure to follow these instructions may result in severe personal injury or death. Do not allow any unauthorized personnel into the buffer zone during repairs involving the high voltage system. Only personnel trained for repair on the high voltage system are to be permitted in the buffer zone.

**** CAUTION**

Disarm the high voltage traction battery (HVTB) before working on the high voltage system. See the text for the Disarming procedure. Failure to follow these instructions may result in severe personal injury or death.

ALTERNATING CURRENT POWERPOINT

REMOVAL & INSTALLATION

See Figures 66 and 67.

1. Disconnect the 12-volt battery.

➡Make sure that the rear of the floor console is lifted away from the floor as specified. Failure to follow this procedure will result in damage to the floor console and the tabs at the top of the floor console end cover.

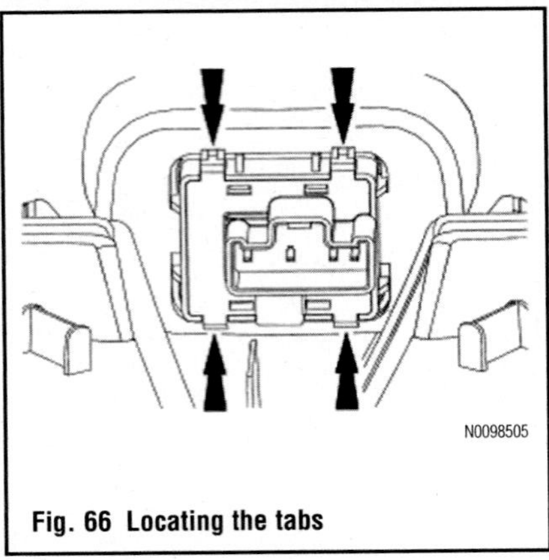

Fig. 66 Locating the tabs

2. Remove the floor console rear screws and lift the floor console about 0.984 inch (25 mm) away from the floor.
3. Remove the floor console end cover by pulling the cover away at the bottom and rotating out. Lower the cover 0.275-0.511 inch (7-13 mm) to clear the tabs on the top of the floor console end cover.
4. Disconnect the electrical connector and remove the AC power point by depressing the 4 tabs as shown.

To install:

5. To install, reverse the removal procedure.

BUFFER ZONE

1. Before servicing the vehicle, refer to the Precautions Section.

**** CAUTION**

Before proceeding, read and observe all of the High Voltage System Precautions.

2. Establish a buffer zone around the vehicle:
   a. Position the vehicle in the repair bay.
   b. Position 4 orange cones at the corners of the vehicle to mark off a 3 ft. (1 m) perimeter around the vehicle.
   c. Do not allow any unauthorized personnel into the buffer zone during repairs involving the high voltage system. Only personnel trained for repair on the high voltage system are to be permitted in the buffer zone.

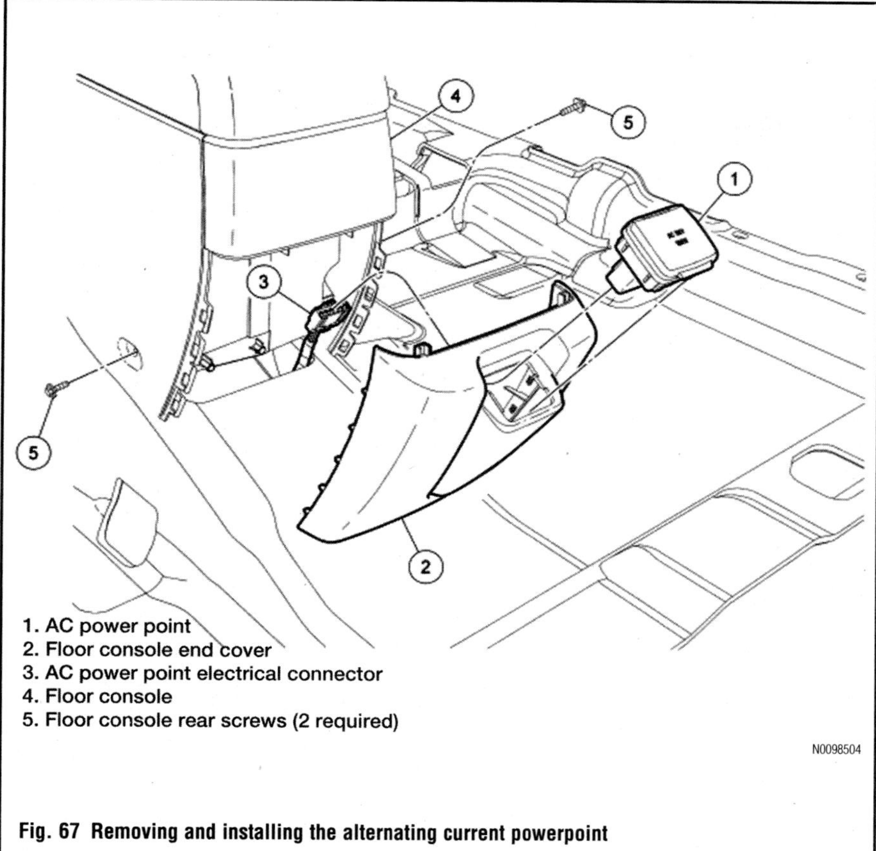

Fig. 67 Removing and installing the alternating current powerpoint

DISARMING THE HIGH VOLTAGE TRACTION BATTERY

See Figures 68 through 70.

WARNING

Never install the service disconnect plug with the high-voltage bussed electrical center (BEC) cover removed. Always install the cover prior to connecting the service disconnect plug. The high-voltage BEC cover prevents inadvertent contact with the high voltage which is present at several points under the cover. Failure to follow these instructions may result in serious personal injury or death.

1. Turn the ignition off.
2. Remove the 4 pin-type retainers and the trunk front cover.

➡If the center safety belt retractor locks and the safety belt webbing prevents the 60 percent backrest from lowering, raise the backrest upward to release the safety belt retractor and belt webbing.

3. Fold the LH backrest down.

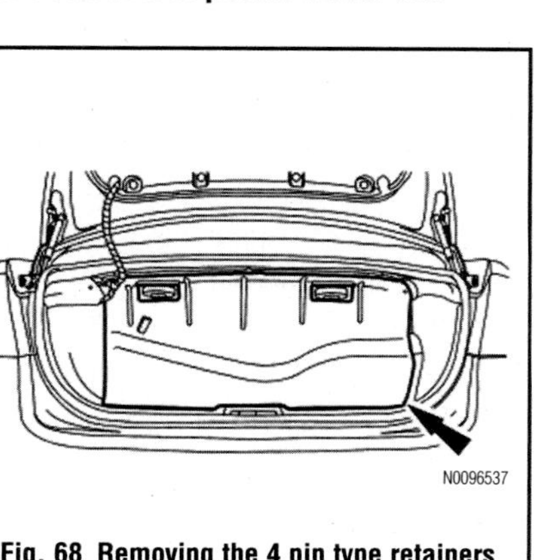

Fig. 68 Removing the 4 pin type retainers

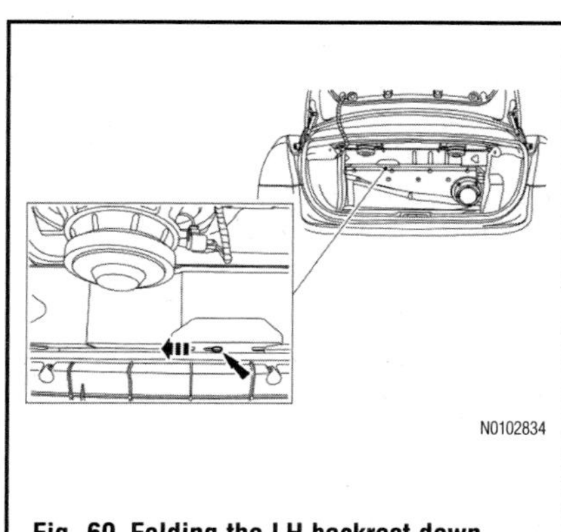

Fig. 69 Folding the LH backrest down

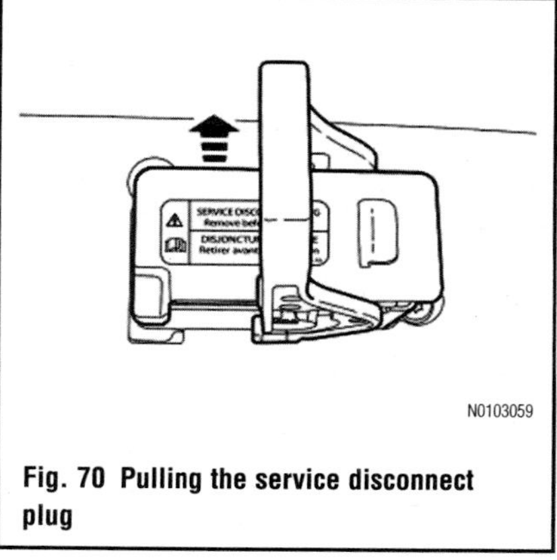

Fig. 70 Pulling the service disconnect plug

a. Between the High Voltage Traction Battery (HVTB) and the sheet metal, locate the seat backrest latch release lever.
b. Push the release lever toward the outboard side of the vehicle and fold the backrest down.

4. Slide the handle of the service disconnect plug toward the LH side of the vehicle.
5. Rotate the handle upward.
6. Pull the service disconnect plug out and away from the HVTB . Be sure to store the plug in a place where it cannot be accidentally re-installed while the vehicle is being serviced.
7. Wait 5 minutes after the service disconnect plug is removed before continuing service. This allows any residual voltage in the high-voltage system to dissipate.

To install:

8. To install, reverse the removal procedure.

DIRECT CURRENT/ ALTERNATING CURRENT INVERTER

REMOVAL & INSTALLATION

See Figure 71.

1. Disconnect the 12-volt battery.
2. Remove 4 pin-type retainers and the front trunk cover.

➡If the center safety belt retractor locks and the safety belt webbing prevents the 60 percent backrest from lowering, raise the backrest upward to release the safety belt retractor and belt webbing.

3. Fold the RH backrest down.

a. Between the High Voltage Traction Battery (HVTB) and the sheet metal, locate the seat backrest latch release lever.

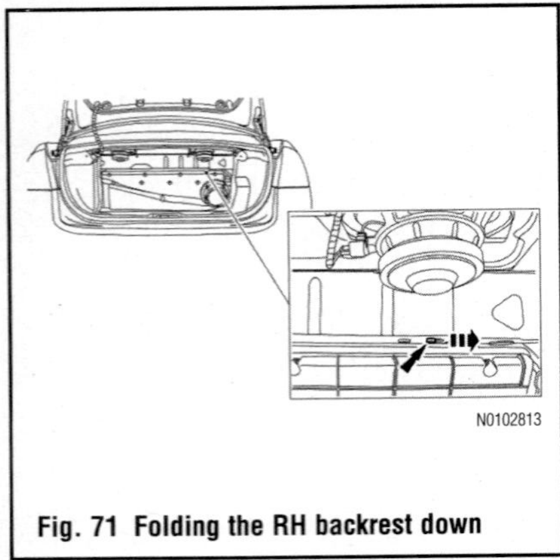

Fig. 71 Folding the RH backrest down

b. Push the release lever toward the outboard side of the vehicle and fold the backrest down.

4. Remove the RH rear seat bolster.
5. Disconnect the 2 electrical connectors at the DC/AC inverter.
6. Remove the 3 nuts and the DC/AC inverter.

To install:

7. To install, reverse the removal procedure.
8. Tighten the DC/AC inverter nuts to 80 inch lbs. (9 Nm).

DIRECT CURRENT/DIRECT CURRENT CONVERTER

REMOVAL & INSTALLATION

See Figure 72.

⁂ WARNING

To prevent the risk of high-voltage shock, always follow precisely all warnings and service instructions, including instructions to depower the system. The high-voltage hybrid system utilizes approximately 300 volts DC, provided through high-voltage cables to its components and modules. The high-voltage cables and wiring are identified by orange harness tape or orange wire covering. All high-voltage components are marked with high-voltage warning labels with a high-voltage symbol. Failure to follow these instructions may result in serious personal injury or death.

1. Depower the High Voltage Traction Battery (HVTB).
2. Disconnect the 12-volt battery.
3. Remove the A/C tube bracket bolt and the 3 DC to DC Converter Control Module (DC/DC) top bracket bolts. Remove the bracket.

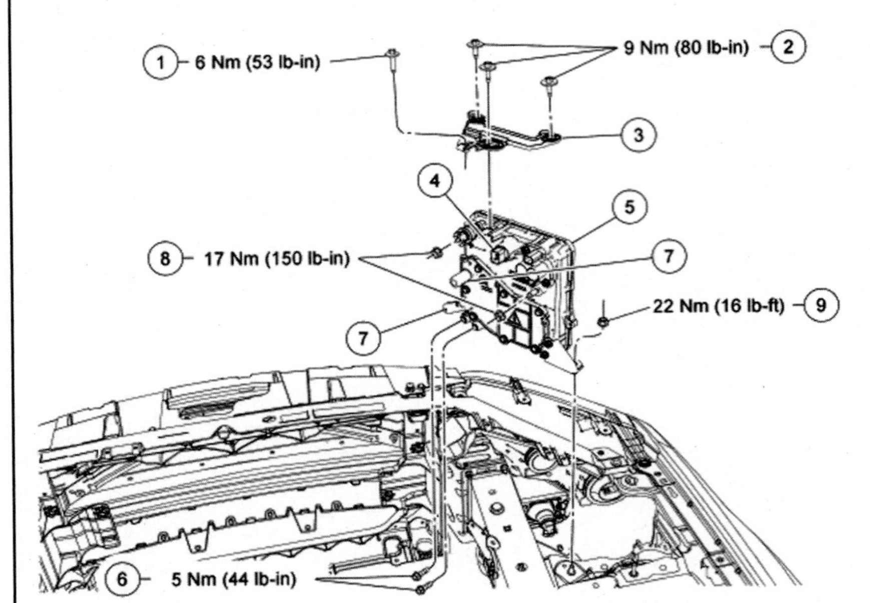

Fig. 72 Exploded view of the direct current/direct current (DC/DC) converter

➡Failure to disconnect high-voltage cable connectors as instructed may result in damage to the connectors.

4. Disconnect the DC/DC high-voltage and interlock connector as follows:
   a. Press the locking tab on the white interlock connector and partially disconnect the connector from the DC/DC .
   b. Press the locking tab on the orange high-voltage connector and fully disconnect both connectors from the DC/DC .
5. Disconnect the DC/DC low-voltage connector.

⁂ WARNING

Always tighten the DC/DC converter low-voltage battery cable fasteners to specification. Loose connections may result in electrical arcing, which increases both the risk of fires and serious personal injury.

6. Remove the 2 DC/DC low-voltage battery cable nuts and position the low-voltage battery cables aside.
7. Clamp the Motor Electronics Cooling System (MECS) hoses to prevent coolant from leaking from the hoses during the repair.
8. Loosen the hose clamps and remove the MECS hoses from the DC/DC .
9. Remove the DC/DC lower RH bracket nut.
10. Detach the wire harness from the lower LH side of the DC/DC .

➡Do not remove the DC to DC Converter Control Module (DC/DC) LH lower bracket from the vehicle rail, as this may degrade the vehicle ground attachment and DC/DC alignment.

➡If a new DC/DC is being installed, the new DC/DC will come with a new LH lower bracket attached. Remove the LH lower bracket from the new DC/DC and discard. Whenever possible, reuse the LH lower bracket which has been left attached to the vehicle. If the new bracket is being installed, make sure the surfaces between the bracket and side rails are clean and free of grease, dirt and debris.

11. Remove the 2 lower LH DC/DC bracket bolts and remove the DC/DC .

To install:

12. To install, reverse the removal procedure.
13. Tighten the lower LH DC/DC bracket bolts to 44 inch lbs. (5 Nm).

14. Tighten the DC/DC lower RH bracket nut to 16 ft. lbs. (22 Nm).

15. Tighten the 2 DC/DC low-voltage battery cable nuts to 12 ft. lbs. (17 Nm).

16. Refill the MECS after installation. Bleed any air from the system.

DIRECT CURRENT/DIRECT CURRENT CONVERTER

REMOVAL & INSTALLATION

See Figure 73.

WARNING

To prevent the risk of high-voltage shock, always follow precisely all warnings and service instructions, including instructions to depower the system. The high-voltage hybrid system utilizes approximately 300 volts DC, provided through high-voltage cables to its components and modules. The high-voltage cables and wiring are identified by orange harness tape or orange wire covering. All high-voltage components are marked with high-voltage warning labels with a high-voltage symbol. Failure to follow these instructions may result in serious personal injury or death.

1. Depower the High Voltage Traction Battery (HVTB).
2. Disconnect the 12-volt battery.
3. Remove the A/C tube bracket bolt and the 3 DC to DC Converter Control Module (DC/DC) top bracket bolts. Remove the bracket.

➡Failure to disconnect high-voltage cable connectors as instructed may result in damage to the connectors.

4. Disconnect the DC/DC high-voltage and interlock connector as follows:
   a. Press the locking tab on the white interlock connector and partially disconnect the connector from the DC/DC .
   b. Press the locking tab on the orange high-voltage connector and fully disconnect both connectors from the DC/DC .
5. Disconnect the DC/DC low-voltage connector.

WARNING

Always tighten the DC/DC converter low-voltage battery cable fasteners to specification. Loose connections may result in electrical arcing, which increases both the risk of fires and serious personal injury.

6. Remove the 2 DC/DC low-voltage battery cable nuts and position the low-voltage battery cables aside.
7. Clamp the Motor Electronics Cooling System (MECS) hoses to prevent coolant from leaking from the hoses during the repair.
8. Loosen the hose clamps and remove the MECS hoses from the DC/DC .
9. Remove the DC/DC lower RH bracket nut.
10. Detach the wire harness from the lower LH side of the DC/DC .

➡Do not remove the DC to DC Converter Control Module (DC/DC) LH lower bracket from the vehicle rail, as this may degrade the vehicle ground attachment and DC/DC alignment.

➡If a new DC/DC is being installed, the new DC/DC will come with a new LH lower bracket attached. Remove the LH lower bracket from the new DC/DC and discard. Whenever possible, reuse the LH lower bracket which has been left attached to the vehicle. If the new bracket is being installed, make sure the surfaces between the bracket and side rails are clean and free of grease, dirt and debris.

11. Remove the 2 lower LH DC/DC bracket bolts and remove the DC/DC .

To install:

12. To install, reverse the removal procedure.
13. Tighten the lower LH DC/DC bracket bolts to 44 inch lbs. (5 Nm).
14. Tighten the DC/DC lower RH bracket nut to 16 ft. lbs. (22 Nm).
15. Refill the MECS after installation. Bleed any air from the system.
16. Tighten the 2 DC/DC low-voltage battery cable nuts to 12 ft. lbs. (17 Nm).
17. Tighten the AC tube bracket bolts to 53 inch lbs. (6 Nm).
18. Tighten the 3 DC/DC top bracket bolts to 80 inch lbs. (9 Nm).

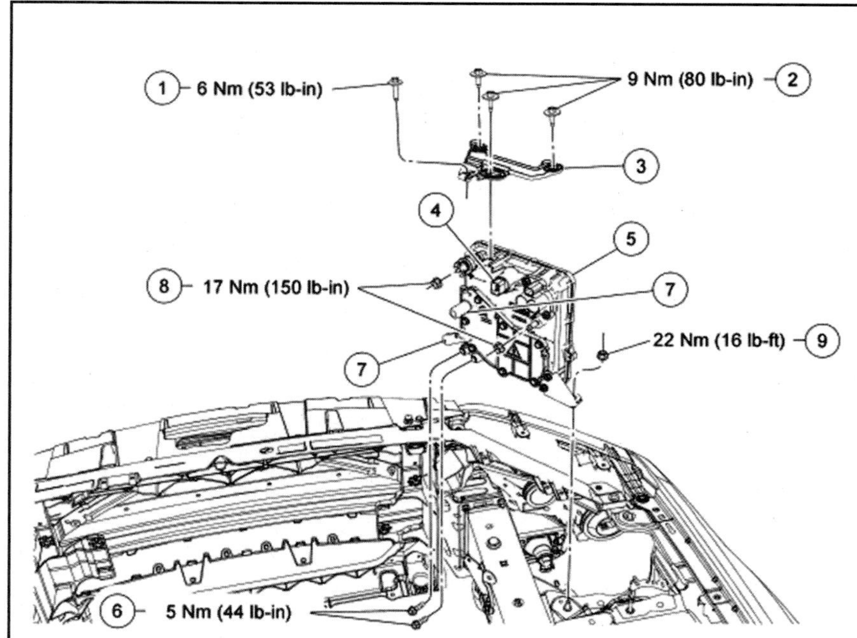

1. A/C tube bracket bolt
2. DC to DC Converter Control Module (DC/DC) top bracket bolts (3 required)
3. DC/DC top bracket
4. DC/DC low-voltage electrical connector
5. DC/DC assembly
6. DC/DC lower LH bracket bolts (2 required)
7. DC/DC coolant inlet/ outlet tubes
8. DC/DC low-voltage battery cable nuts (2 required)
9. DC/DC lower RH bracket nut

N0102830

Fig. 73 Removing and installing the direct current/direct current converter

HIGH VOLTAGE TRACTION BATTERY

REMOVAL AND INSTALLATION

See Figures 74 and 75.

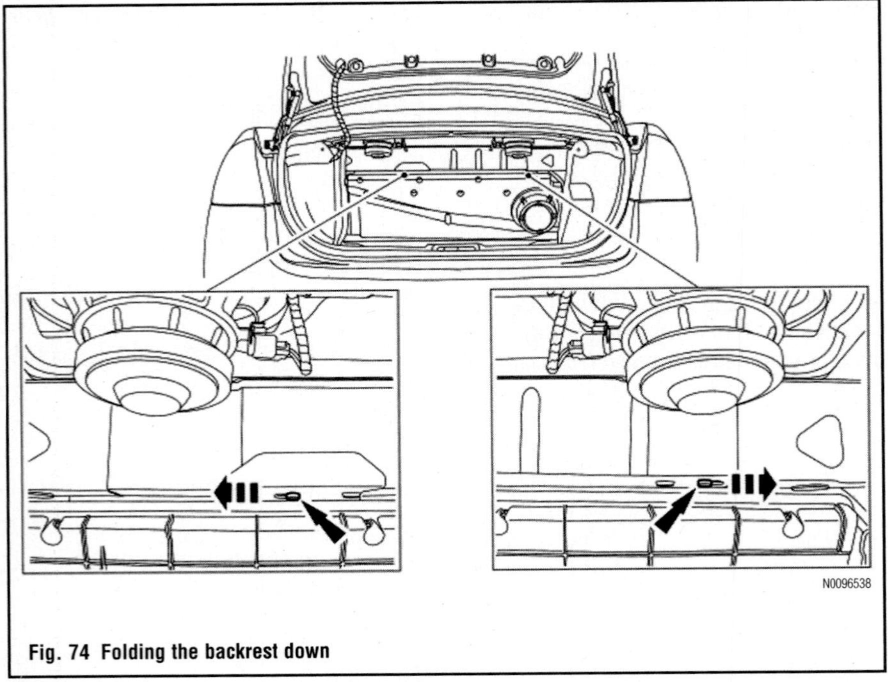

Fig. 74 Folding the backrest down

⁂ WARNING

To prevent the risk of high-voltage shock, always follow precisely all warnings and service instructions, including instructions to depower the system. The high-voltage hybrid system utilizes approximately 300 volts DC, provided through high-voltage cables to its components and modules. The high-voltage cables and wiring are identified by orange harness tape or orange wire covering. All high-voltage components are marked with high-voltage warning labels with a high-voltage symbol. Failure to follow these instructions may result in serious personal injury or death.

1. Depower the High Voltage Traction Battery (HVTB).
2. Fold the RH backrest down.
3. Between the HVTB and the sheet metal, locate the seat backrest latch release lever.
4. Push the release lever toward the outboard side of the vehicle and fold the backrest down.
5. Remove the RH rear seat bolster.
6. Disconnect the cooling fan jumper harness electrical connector, then remove the wiring connector pushpin from the HVTB handle bracket.
7. Remove the HVTB cooling inlet duct.
8. Disconnect the 50-pin connector at the Battery Energy Control Module (BECM).
9. Remove the ground strap-to-chassis bolt and position the ground strap aside.
10. Remove the 2 plastic bumpers from the back of the rear seat back by releasing the 2 pushpins.

➡The attaching bolts have a conductive coating on them and are serrated under the head flange. These features ground the HVTB to the vehicle, which is required for electro-magnetic compatibility. If a bolt(s) is lost or damaged, a new identical bolt(s) must be installed.

11. Remove the 4 HVTB mounting bolts from the trunk area that secure the HVTB to the brackets.

➡The attaching bolts have a conductive coating on them and are serrated under the head flange. These features ground the HVTB to the vehicle, which is required for electro-magnetic compatibility. If a bolt(s) is lost or damaged, a new identical bolt(s) must be installed.

12. From each rear door opening, remove the 2 HVTB mounting bolts (total of 4 bolts) that secure the HVTB to the brackets.

➡Lay a fender cover or other protective material over the seat backs to reduce the possibility of damage when removing the battery.

➡Make certain the High Voltage Traction Battery (HVTB) does not mar or damage the interior panels or seating during removal. There is very little clearance on each side.

13. With the help of an assistant inside the vehicle, grasp the handles on each side

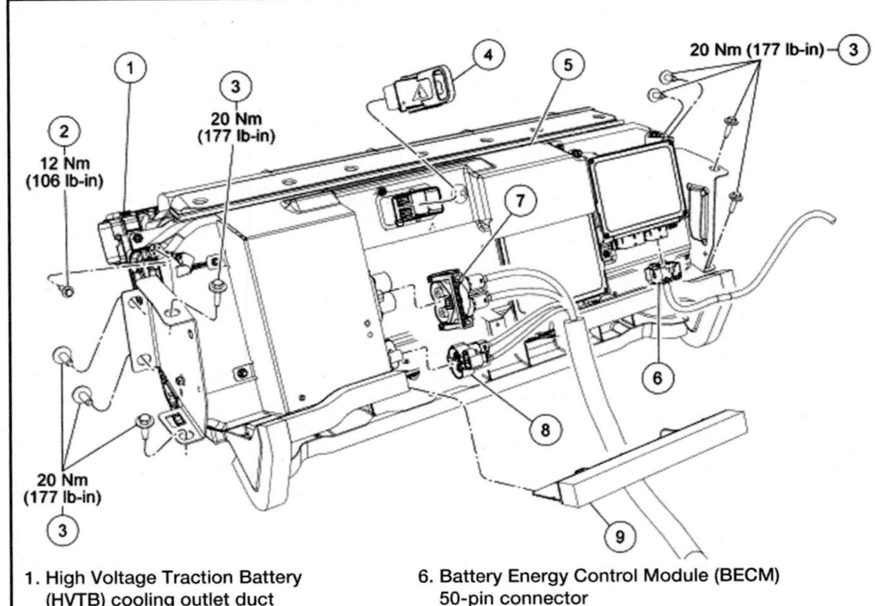

Fig. 75 Removing and installing the high voltage traction battery

of the battery and slide the battery forward and out of the vehicle.

To install:

14. To install, reverse the removal procedure.
15. Tighten the HVTB mounting bolts to 15 ft. lbs. (20 Nm).
16. Tighten the HVTB mounting bolts to 15 ft. lbs. (20 Nm).
17. Tighten the ground strap to chassis bolt to 9 ft. lbs. (12 Nm).

BATTERY ENERGY CONTROL MODULE (BECM)

REMOVAL & INSTALLATION

See Figure 76.

1. Retrieve the module configuration. Carry out the module configuration retrieval steps of the Programmable Module Installation (PMI) procedure.
2. Remove the 4 pin-type retainers and the trunk front cover.

➡If the center safety belt retractor locks and the safety belt webbing prevents the 60 percent backrest from lowering, raise the backrest upward to release the safety belt retractor and belt webbing.

3. Fold the LH backrest down.
4. Between the High Voltage Traction Battery (HVTB) and the sheet metal, locate the seat backrest latch release lever.
5. Push the release lever toward the outboard side of the vehicle and fold the backrest down.
6. Release the locking levers and disconnect the 2 electrical connectors at the Battery Energy Control Module (BECM).
7. Remove the 4 nuts and the BECM .

To install:

8. To install, reverse the removal procedure.
9. When installing a new BECM , carry out the steps necessary to complete Programmable Module Installation (PMI).
10. Tighten the 4 BECM nuts to 80 inch lbs. (9 Nm).

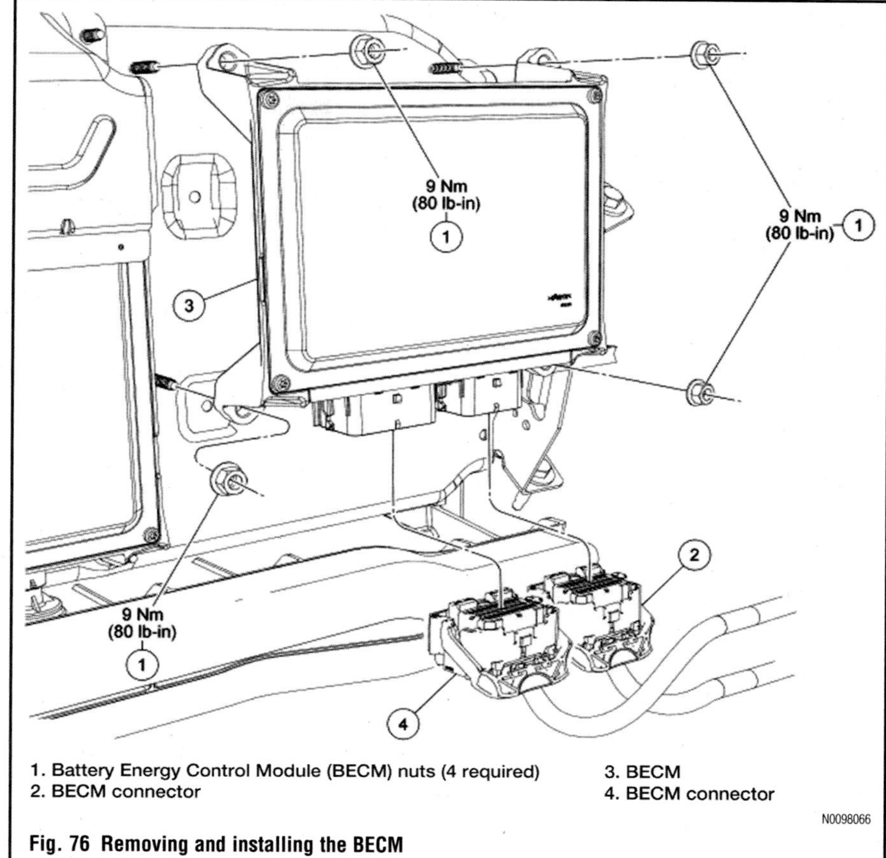

1. Battery Energy Control Module (BECM) nuts (4 required)
2. BECM connector
3. BECM
4. BECM connector

N0098066

Fig. 76 Removing and installing the BECM

BATTERY PACK SENSOR MODULE (BPSM)

REMOVAL & INSTALLATION

See Figure 77.

1. Depower the High Voltage Traction Battery (HVTB).
2. Fold the RH backrest down.

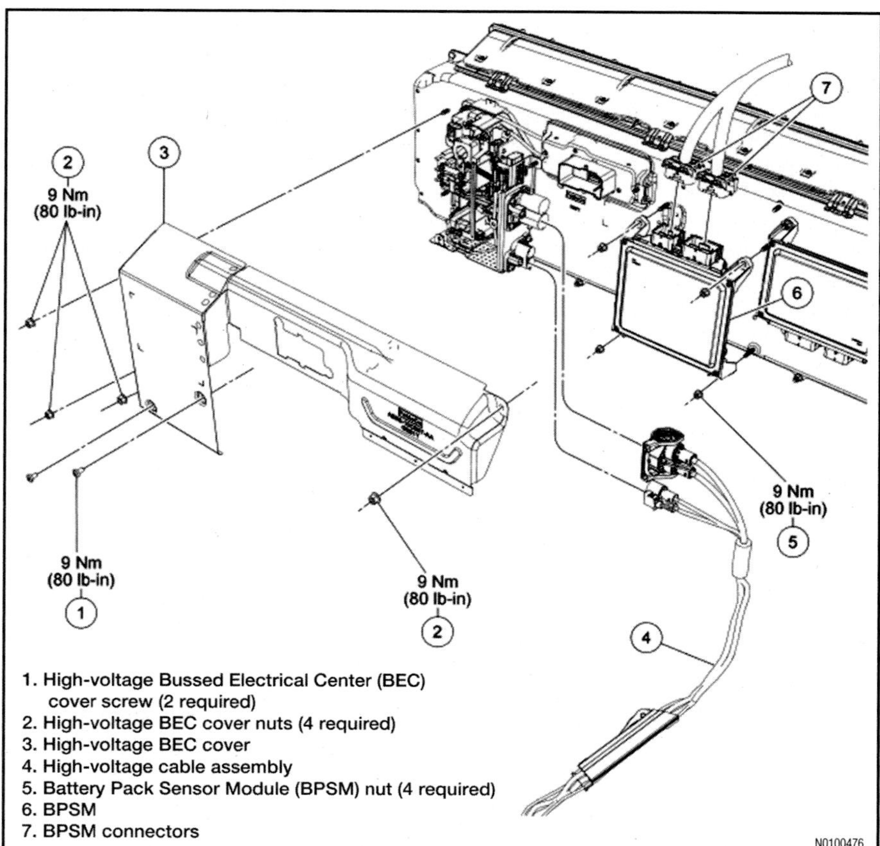

1. High-voltage Bussed Electrical Center (BEC) cover screw (2 required)
2. High-voltage BEC cover nuts (4 required)
3. High-voltage BEC cover
4. High-voltage cable assembly
5. Battery Pack Sensor Module (BPSM) nut (4 required)
6. BPSM
7. BPSM connectors

N0100476

Fig. 77 Removing and installing the BPSM

a. Between the HVTB and the sheet metal, locate the seat backrest latch release lever.

b. Push the release lever toward the outboard side of the vehicle and fold the backrest down.

3. Remove the 4 high-voltage Bussed Electrical Center (BEC) cover nuts, the 2 high-voltage BEC cover screws and the high-voltage BEC cover.

4. Release the locking levers and disconnect the 2 connectors at the Battery Pack Sensor Module (BPSM).

5. Remove the 4 nuts and the BPSM .

To install:

6. To install, reverse the removal procedure.

7. Tighten the BPSM nuts to 80 inch lbs. (9 Nm).

HIGH VOLTAGE BUSSED ELECTRICAL CENTER

REMOVAL & INSTALLATION

See Figures 78 and 79.

1. Depower the High Voltage Traction Battery (HVTB).

2. Fold the RH backrest down.

a. Between the HVTB and the sheet metal, locate the seat backrest latch release lever.

b. Push the release lever toward the outboard side of the vehicle and fold the backrest down.

3. Remove the high-voltage cable connector and bracket.

4. Release the locking tabs and disconnect the 3 connectors.

5. Remove the 2 HVTB cable nuts and detach the cables from the high-voltage Bussed Electrical Center (BEC).

6. Remove the nut at the upper LH corner and remove the high-voltage BEC.

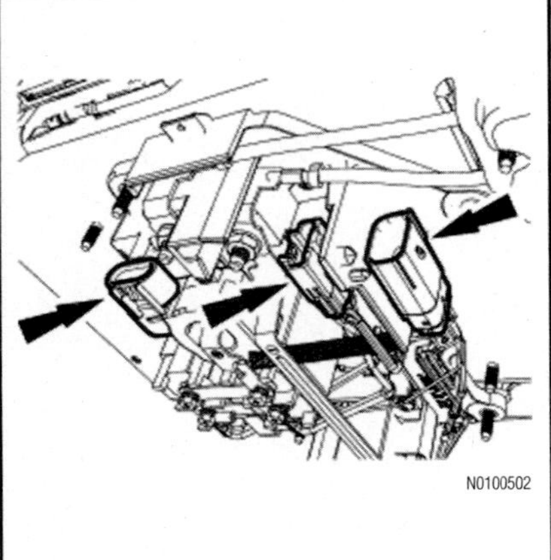

Fig. 78 Disconnecting the connectors

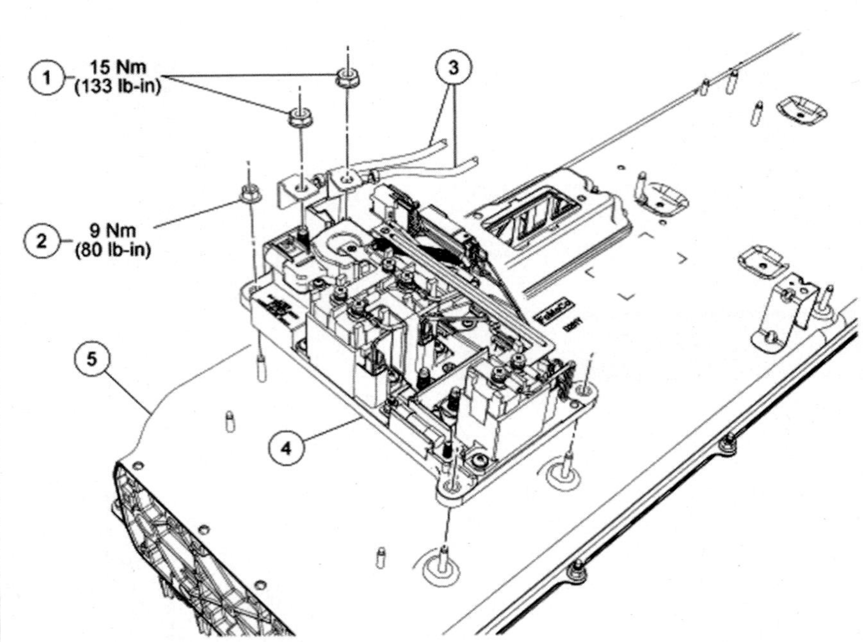

Fig. 79 Removing and installing the high voltage bussed electrical center

To install:

7. To install, reverse the removal procedure.

8. Tighten the high voltage BEC to 80 inch lbs. (9 Nm).

9. Tighten the high voltage BEC nuts to 11 ft. lbs. (15 Nm).

HIGH VOLTAGE CABLES

REMOVAL & INSTALLATION

See Figures 80 and 81.

1. Discharge the A/C system.

2. Disconnect the 12-volt battery.

3. Depower the High Voltage Traction Battery (HVTB).

4. Fold the RH backrest down.

a. Between the HVTB and the sheet metal, locate the seat backrest latch release lever.

b. Push the release lever toward the outboard side of the vehicle and fold the backrest down.

5. Remove the RH rear seat bolster.

➡Failure to disconnect high-voltage cable connectors as instructed may result in damage to the connectors.

➡DC to DC Converter Control Module (DC/DC) connector shown, high-voltage/low-current connector at high-voltage Bussed Electrical Center (BEC) similar.

6. Release the locking lever and locking tabs and disconnect the interlock connector and the 2 high voltage cables at the high-voltage BEC.

a. Press the locking clip on the white interlock connector and disengage the white connector before releasing the locking clip on the orange portion of the high-voltage connector. The white

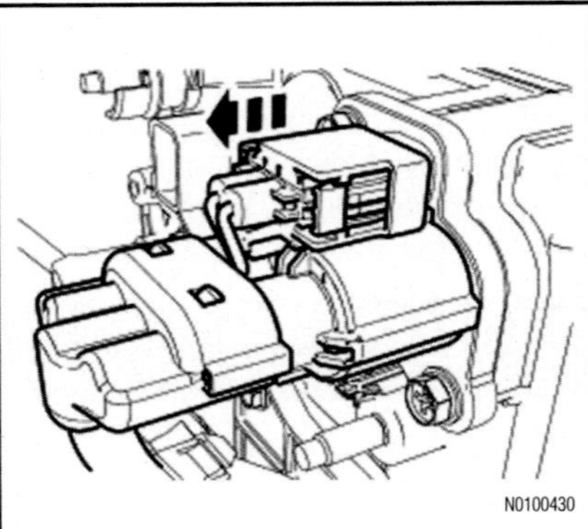

Fig. 80 Disconnecting the interlock connector and 2 high voltage cables at the high voltage BEC

interlock connector will not come completely apart until the orange portion is released.

7. Remove the HVTB cooling inlet duct plate.

8. Remove the pushpin that retains the high-voltage cables to the bracket on the HVTB case.

9. Remove the passenger side front seat.

10. Remove the front door scuff plate trim panel.

11. Remove the rear door scuff plate trim panel.

12. Remove the lower B-pillar trim panel.

13. Slide the lower B-pillar trim panel down to disengage it from the upper B-pillar trim panel.

14. Remove the rear seat cushion.

15. Remove the high-voltage cable shield retaining screw.

16. Partially raise the LR seat back and pull the high-voltage cables out from under the rear seat backrest, then position both rear seat backrests in the upright position.

➡The high-voltage cables are routed under the passenger side rear carpet.

17. Disconnect the high-voltage cable from the DC/AC inverter and remove the 5 retaining clips. Position the cable aside.

➡Make sure that the rear of the floor console is lifted away from the floor as specified. Failure to follow this procedure will result in damage to the floor console and the tabs at the top of the floor console end cover.

18. Remove the floor console end cover in the following sequence.

a. Remove the floor console rear screws.

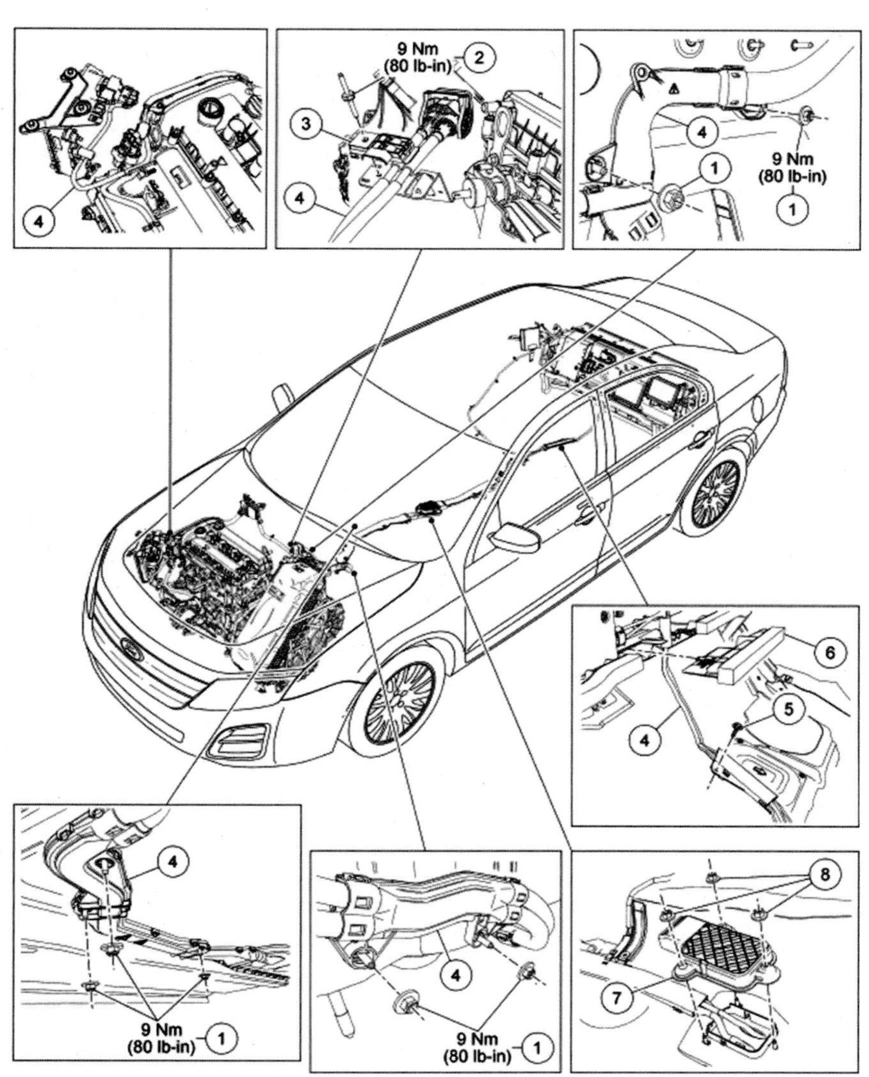

1. High-voltage cable shield nuts (7 required)
2. High-voltage cable strain relief bolt
3. High-voltage cable strain relief clamp
4. High-voltage cable assembly
5. High-voltage cable shield screw
6. High Voltage Traction Battery (HVTB) cooling inlet duct plate
7. High-voltage cable floor pan grommet cover
8. High-voltage cable floor pan grommet nuts (3 required)

N0098583

Fig. 81 Identifying the high voltage cables and related components

b. Lift the floor console about 0.984 inch (25 mm) away from the floor.

c. Remove the floor console end cover by pulling the cover away at the bottom and rotating out. Lower the cover 0.275-0.511 inch (7-13 mm) to clear the tabs on the top of the floor console end cover.

19. Disconnect the AC power point connector.

20. Release the 2 pushpins that hold the high-voltage cables to the floor pan and pull the high-voltage cable out from underneath the carpet and floor console.

21. Remove the 3 nuts at the floor pan grommet cover.

22. With the vehicle in NEUTRAL, position it on a hoist.

23. Remove the 5 nuts that retain the high-voltage cable shield to the floor pan and remove the cables from the studs.

24. Remove the 2 nuts that retain the high-voltage cable shield to the bulkhead and remove the cables from the studs.

25. Remove the pushpin that retains the high-voltage harness to the bulkhead.

26. Push the high-voltage cables through the opening of the vehicle floor pan.

27. Remove the engine cover.

28. Remove the high-voltage cable strain relief bolt and remove the strain relief clamp from the bracket.

29. Disconnect the high-voltage electrical connector from the transmission and position the cable aside.

30. Using a screwdriver or other suitable tool, release the clip that locks the high-voltage junction block to the bracket by pushing the tool between the high-voltage junction block and the bracket from the LH side. Remove the cable from the retainer on the bulkhead and position the cable aside.

31. Lift the high-voltage cables from the 2 studs on the front of the engine and disengage the pushpin at the intake manifold.

➡Failure to disconnect high-voltage cable connectors as instructed may result in damage to the connectors.

➡DC/DC connector shown, high-voltage/low-current connector at Air Conditioning Compressor Module (ACCM) similar.

32. Release the clips and locking tabs and disconnect the interlock connector and the high-voltage cable connector at the ACCM .

a. Press the locking clip on the white interlock connector and disengage the white connector before releasing the locking clip on the orange portion of the high-voltage connector. The white interlock connector will not come completely apart until the orange portion is released.

➡Failure to disconnect high-voltage cable connectors as instructed may result in damage to the connectors.

33. Release the clips and locking tabs and disconnect the interlock connector and the high-voltage cable connector at the DC/DC.

34. Press the locking clip on the white interlock connector and disengage the white connector before releasing the locking clip on the orange portion of the high-voltage connector. The white interlock connector will not come completely apart until the orange portion is released.

35. Remove the A/C evaporator inlet fitting nut from the low side and disconnect the fitting nut. Discard the gasket seal.

36. Remove the A/C compressor manifold and suction tube fitting nut (low side) and disconnect the fitting. Remove the tube and discard the gasket seal.

37. Wrap mechanic's wire around the Hydraulic Control Unit (HCU) motor from above and support the HCU .

38. Remove the 3 bolts that retain the HCU bracket to the frame.

39. An assistant is needed to help feed the cable down through the engine compartment and remove the high-voltage cable assembly from the bottom of the vehicle.

To install:

40. To install, reverse removal procedure.

41. Tighten the HCU bracket to frame bolts to 17 ft. lbs. (23 Nm).

42. Tighten the A/C compressor manifold and suction tube fitting nut to 11 ft. lbs. (15 Nm).

43. Tighten the A/C evaporator inlet fitting nut to 11 ft. lbs. (15 Nm).

44. Tighten the high-voltage cable strain relief bolt to 80 inch lbs. (9 Nm).

45. Tighten the 2 nuts that retain the high-voltage cable shield to the bulkhead 80inch lbs. (9 Nm).

46. Tighten the 5 nuts that retain the high-voltage cable shield to the floor pan to 80 inch lbs. (9 Nm).

HIGH VOLTAGE LOW CURRENT FUSE

REMOVAL & INSTALLATION

See Figure 82.

1. Depower the High Voltage Traction Battery (HVTB).

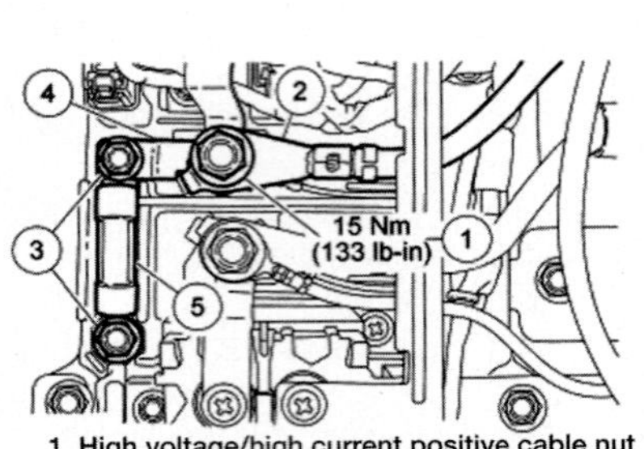

Fig. 82 Removing and installing the high voltage/high current fuse

2. Fold the RH backrest down.

a. Between the HVTB and the sheet metal, locate the seat backrest latch release lever.

b. Push the release lever toward the outboard side of the vehicle and fold the backrest down.

3. Remove the 4 nuts, 2 bolts and the high-voltage BEC cover.

4. Remove the high-voltage/high-current fuse.

a. Remove the high-voltage/high-current positive cable nut.

b. Position the high-voltage/high-current positive cable aside.

c. Remove the 2 high-voltage/low-current fuse nuts on each end of the fuse.

d. Remove the high-voltage/low-current circuit bus bar.

e. Remove the high-voltage/low-current fuse (40A).

To install:

5. To install, reverse the removal procedure.

6. Tighten the 2 high voltage/low current fuse nuts to 35 inch lbs. (4 Nm).

7. Tighten the high voltage/high current positive cable nut to 11 ft. lbs. (15 Nm).

8. Tighten the 4 nuts, 2 bolts and the high voltage BEC cover to 80 inch lbs. (9 Nm).

HIGH VOLTAGE TRACTION BATTERY

REMOVAL & INSTALLATION

See Figure 83.

1. Depower the High Voltage Traction Battery (HVTB).

2. Fold the RH backrest down.

a. Between the HVTB and the sheet

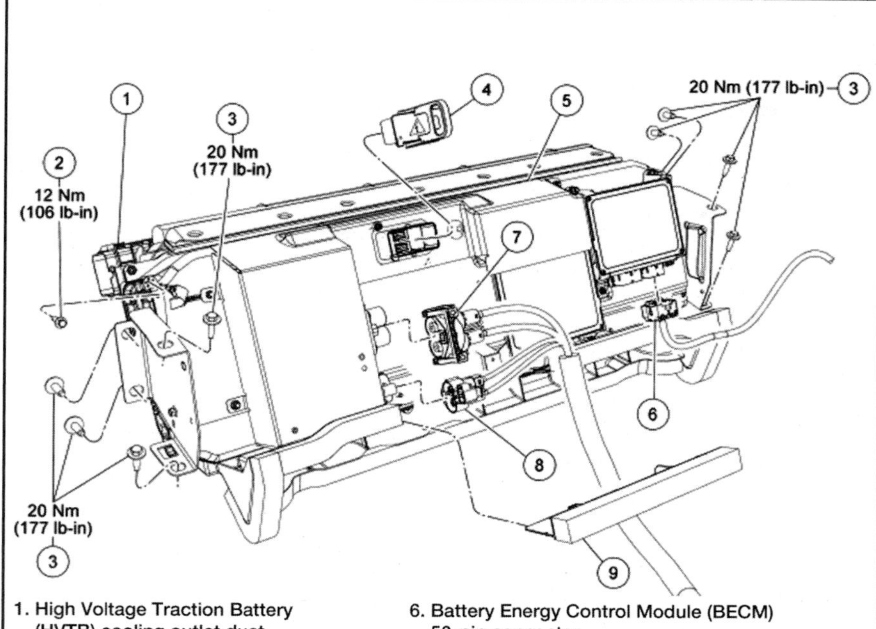

Fig. 83 Removing and installing the high voltage traction battery

metal, locate the seat backrest latch release lever.

b. Push the release lever toward the outboard side of the vehicle and fold the backrest down.

3. Remove the RH rear seat bolster.

4. Disconnect the cooling fan jumper harness electrical connector, then remove the wiring connector pushpin from the HVTB handle bracket.

5. Remove the HVTB cooling inlet duct.

6. Disconnect the 50-pin connector at the Battery Energy Control Module (BECM).

7. Remove the ground strap-to-chassis bolt and position the ground strap aside.

8. Remove the 2 plastic bumpers from the back of the rear seat back by releasing the 2 pushpins.

➡The attaching bolts have a conductive coating on them and are serrated under the head flange. These features ground the HVTB to the vehicle, which is required for electro-magnetic compatibility. If a bolt(s) is lost or damaged, a new identical bolt(s) must be installed.

9. Remove the 4 HVTB mounting bolts from the trunk area that secure the HVTB to the brackets.

➡The attaching bolts have a conductive coating on them and are serrated under the head flange. These features ground the HVTB to the vehicle, which is required for electro-magnetic compatibility. If a bolt(s) is lost or damaged, a new identical bolt(s) must be installed.

10. From each rear door opening, remove the 2 HVTB mounting bolts (total of 4 bolts) that secure the HVTB to the brackets.

➡Lay a fender cover or other protective material over the seat backs to reduce the possibility of damage when removing the battery.

➡Make certain the High Voltage Traction Battery (HVTB) does not mar or damage the interior panels or seating during removal. There is very little clearance on each side.

11. With the help of an assistant inside the vehicle, grasp the handles on each side of the battery and slide the battery forward and out of the vehicle.

To install:

12. To install, reverse the removal procedure.

13. Tighten the HVTB mounting bolts to 15 ft. lbs. (20 Nm).

14. Tighten the HVTB mounting trunk area securing bolts to 15 ft. lbs. (20 Nm).

15. Tighten the ground strap-to-chassis bolt to 9 ft. lbs. (12 Nm).

HIGH VOLTAGE TRACTION BATTERY COOLING FAN

REMOVAL & INSTALLATION

See Figure 84.

1. Open the trunk, remove the 4 pin-type retainers and the front trunk cover.

2. Release the locking tab and separate the High Voltage Traction Battery (HVTB) cooling fan connector.

3. Remove the 4 HVTB cooling fan screws.

4. Remove the HVTB cooling fan.

To install:

5. To install, add a small amount of instant gel adhesive to the HVTB cooling fan screws and reverse the removal procedure.

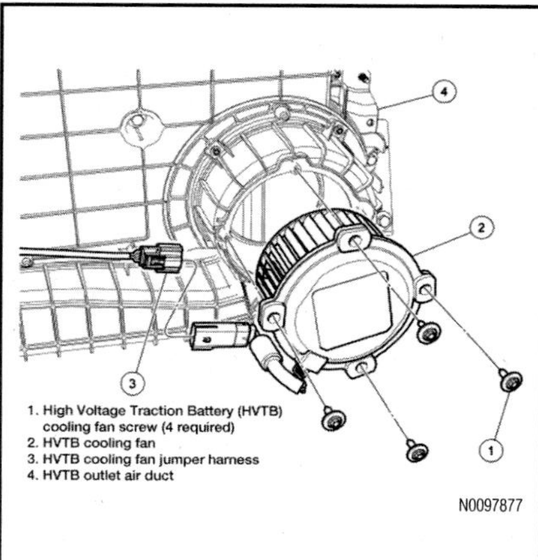

Fig. 84 Removing and installing the high voltage traction battery cooling fan

HIGH VOLTAGE TRACTION BATTERY COOLING INLET DUCT

REMOVAL & INSTALLATION

See Figure 85.

1. Depower the High Voltage Traction Battery (HVTB).

2. Fold the RH backrest down.

a. Between the HVTB and the sheet metal, locate the seat backrest latch release lever.

b. Push the release lever toward the outboard side of the vehicle and fold the backrest down.

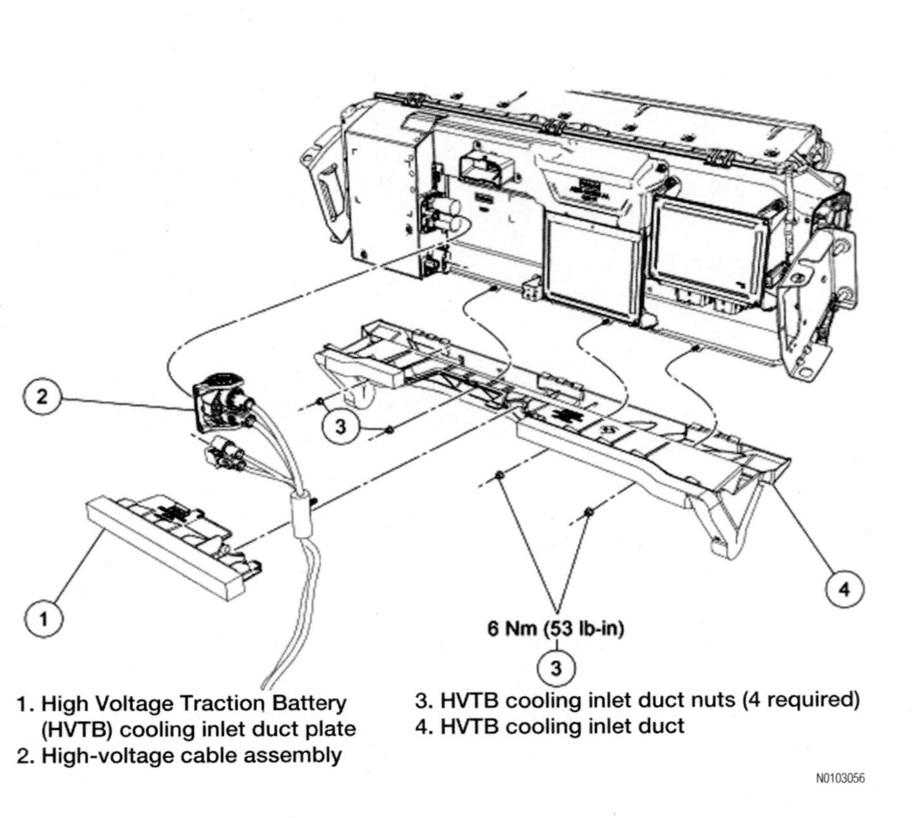

Fig. 85 Removing and installing the high voltage traction battery cooling inlet duct

3. Pull loose and remove the cooling inlet duct plate in front of the high-voltage cables.

➡Failure to disconnect high-voltage cable connectors as instructed may result in damage to the connectors.

4. Disconnect the high-voltage/high-current, high-voltage/low-current and interlock connectors.
   a. Press the locking clip on the white interlock connector and disengage the white connector before releasing the locking clip on the orange portion of the high-voltage/low-current connector. The white interlock connector will not come completely apart until the orange portion is released.
5. Remove the 4 HVTB cooling inlet duct nuts and the inlet duct.

To install:

6. To install, reverse the removal procedure.
7. Tighten the HVTB cooling inlet duct nuts to 53 inch lbs. (6 Nm).

HIGH VOLTAGE TRACTION BATTERY COOLING OUTLET DUCT

REMOVAL & INSTALLATION

See Figure 86.

1. Remove the High Voltage Traction Battery (HVTB) cooling fan.

➡If the center safety belt retractor locks and the safety belt webbing prevents the 60 percent backrest from lowering, raise the backrest upward to release the safety belt retractor and belt webbing.

2. Fold the LH backrest down.
   a. Between the HVTB and the sheet metal, locate the seat backrest latch release lever.
   b. Push the release lever toward the outboard side of the vehicle and fold the backrest down
3. Release the locking tab and disconnect the HVTB cooling fan jumper harness. Remove the clips holding the harness to the HVTB mounting bracket and HVTB case.
4. Release the clips that hold the HVTB cooling fan jumper harness to the HVTB cooling outlet duct and remove the harness from the duct.
5. Remove the 6 bolts and 3 nuts and remove the HVTB cooling outlet duct.

To install:

6. To install, reverse the removal procedure.

HIGH VOLTAGE TRACTION BATTERY INLET AIR TEMPERATURE SENSOR

REMOVAL & INSTALLATION

See Figure 87.

1. Remove the 4 pin-type retainers and the trunk front cover.

➡If the center safety belt retractor locks and the safety belt webbing prevents the 60 percent backrest from lowering, raise the backrest upward to

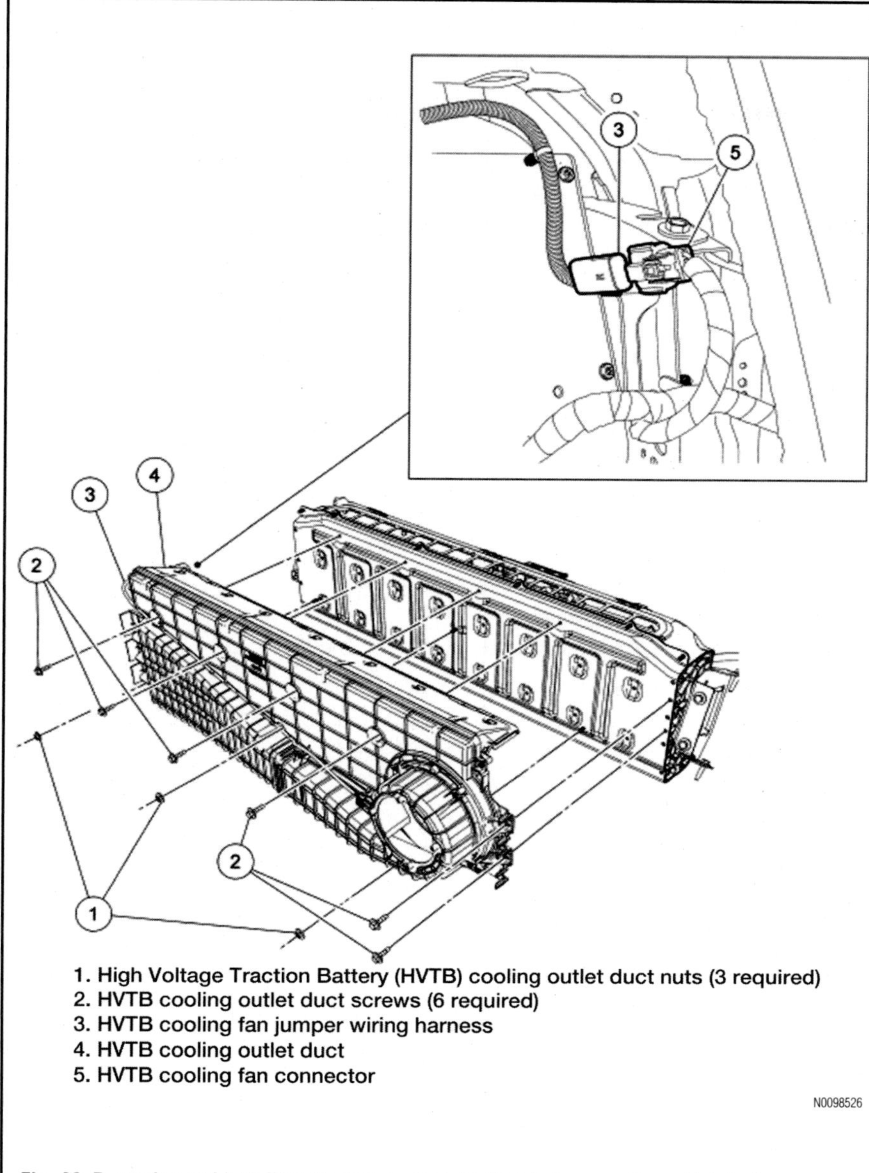

1. High Voltage Traction Battery (HVTB) cooling outlet duct nuts (3 required)
2. HVTB cooling outlet duct screws (6 required)
3. HVTB cooling fan jumper wiring harness
4. HVTB cooling outlet duct
5. HVTB cooling fan connector

N0098526

Fig. 86 Removing and installing the high voltage traction battery cooling outlet duct

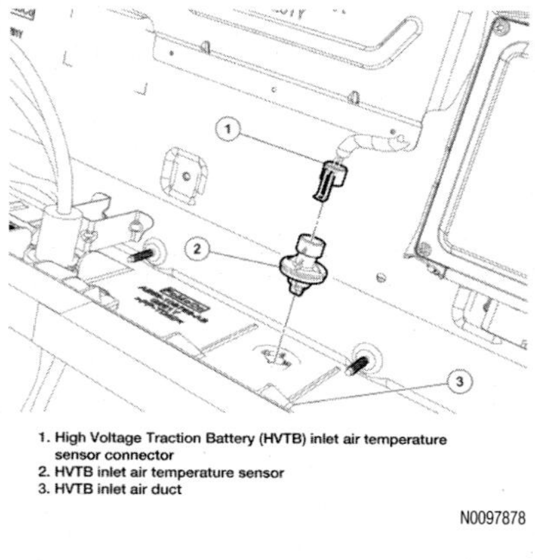

1. High Voltage Traction Battery (HVTB) inlet air temperature sensor connector
2. HVTB inlet air temperature sensor
3. HVTB inlet air duct

N0097878

Fig. 87 Removing and installing the high voltage battery inlet air temperature sensor

release the safety belt retractor and belt webbing.

2. Fold the LH backrest down.
   a. Between the High Voltage Traction Battery (HVTB) and the sheet metal, locate the seat backrest latch release lever.
   b. Push the release lever toward the outboard side of the vehicle and fold the backrest down.
3. Release the locking tab and remove the connector from the HVTB inlet air temperature sensor.
4. Remove the HVTB inlet air temperature sensor.
5. Turn the sensor counterclockwise to unlock and release it from the plenum.

To install:

6. To install, reverse the removal procedure.

FIRING ORDER

The 2.5L engine firing order is 1-3-4-2.
The 3.0L engine firing order is 1–4-2-5-3-6.

IGNITION COIL

REMOVAL & INSTALLATION

2.5L Engine

See Figures 88 and 89.

1. Disconnect the 4 ignition coil-on-plug electrical connectors.

➡When removing the ignition coil-on-plugs, a slight twisting motion will break the seal and ease removal.

2. Remove the 4 bolts and the ignition coil-on-plugs.
3. Inspect the ignition coil-on-plug boots for rips, nicks or tears. Remove and discard any damaged ignition coil-on-plug boots.
    a. To install, slide the new coil-on-boot onto the coil until fully seated at the top of the coil.

To install:

4. To install, reverse the removal procedure.
5. Apply a small amount of dielectric grease to the inside of the ignition coil-on-plug boots before attaching to the spark plugs.
6. Tighten the ignition coil on plug bolts to 89 inch lbs. (10 Nm).

3.0L Engine

See Figures 90 and 91.

RH side

➡The upper intake manifold must be removed to access the RH ignition coil-on-plugs only.

1. Remove the upper intake manifold.

Both sides

2. Disconnect the 6 ignition coil-on-plug electrical connectors.

➡When removing the ignition coil-on-plugs, a slight twisting motion will break the seal and ease removal.

3. Remove the 6 bolts and the 6 ignition coil-on-plugs.

To install:

4. To install, reverse the removal procedure.
5. Apply a small amount of dielectric grease to the inside of the ignition coil-on-plug boots before attaching to the spark plugs.
6. Tighten the ignition coil on plug bolts to 62 inch lbs. (7 Nm).

3.5L Engine

See Figures 92 and 93.

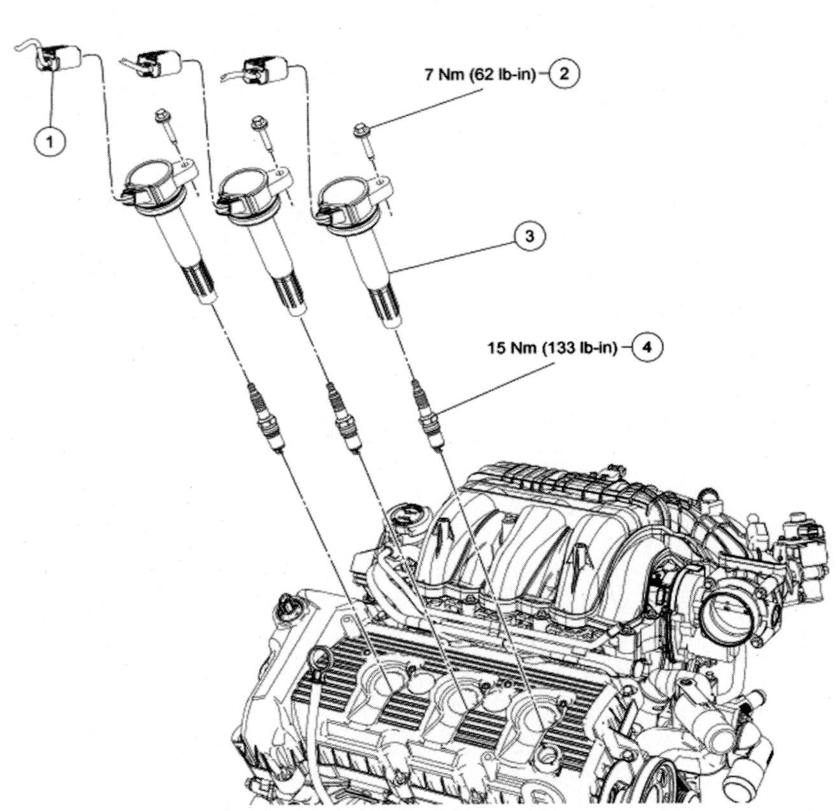

Fig. 88 Exploded view of the engine ignition components—LH side

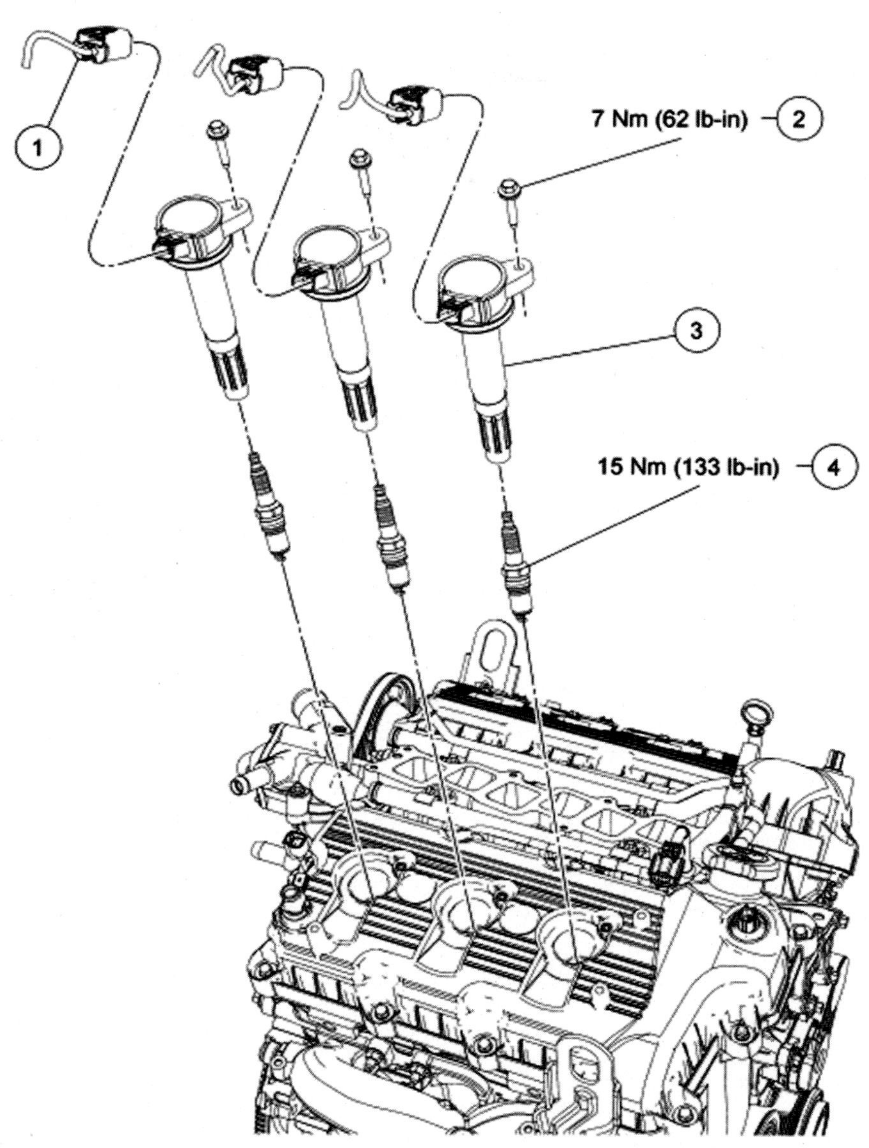

Fig. 89 Exploded view of the engine ignition components—RH side

LH side

1. Disconnect the crankcase ventilation tube-to-valve cover quick connect coupling and position aside.

RH side

➡The upper intake manifold must be removed to access the RH ignition coil-on-plugs.

2. Remove the upper intake manifold.

Both sides

3. Disconnect the 6 ignition coil-on-plug electrical connectors.

➡When removing the ignition coil-on-plugs, a slight twisting motion will break the seal and ease removal.

4. Remove the 6 bolts and the 6 ignition coil-on-plugs.
   a. Inspect the coil seals for rips, nicks or tears. Remove and discard any damaged coil seals.
   b. To install, slide the new coil seal onto the coil until it is fully seated at the top of the coil.

To install:

5. To install, reverse the removal procedure.

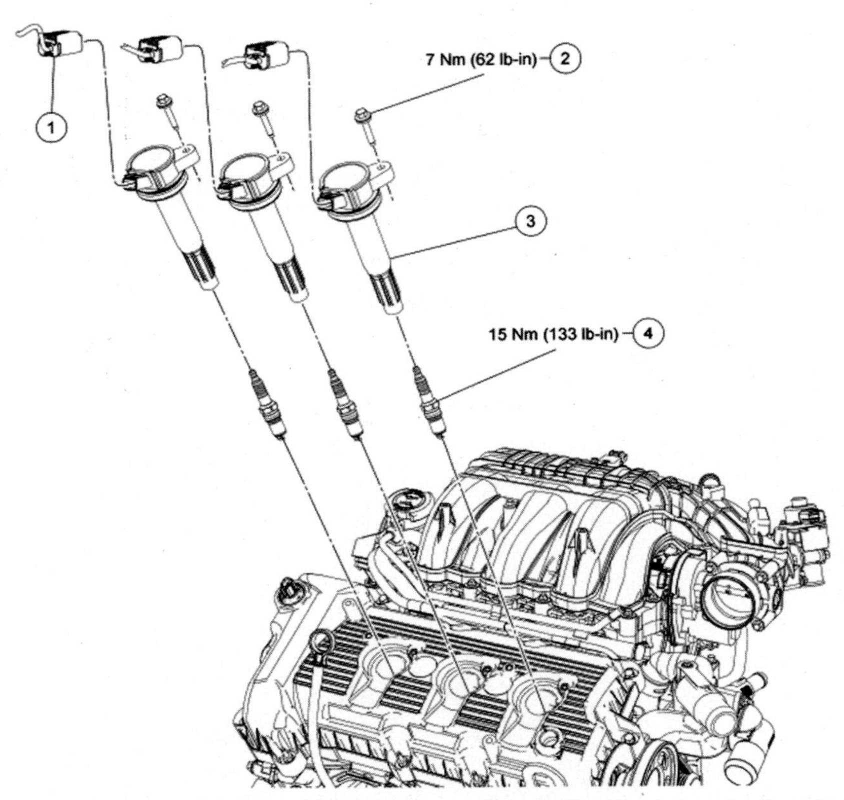

Fig. 90 Exploded view of the engine ignition components—LH side

6. Apply a small amount of dielectric grease to the inside of the ignition coil-on-plug boots before attaching to the spark plugs.
7. Tighten the ignition coil on plug bolts to 62 inch lbs. (7 Nm).

SPARK PLUGS

REMOVAL & INSTALLATION

2.5L Engine

1. Remove the 4 ignition coil-on-plugs.

➡Only use hand tools when removing or installing the spark plugs, or damage can occur to the cylinder head or spark plug.

➡Use compressed air to remove any foreign material in the spark plug well before removing the spark plugs.

2. Remove the 4 spark plugs.
3. Inspect the 4 spark plugs.

To install:

4. To install, reverse the removal procedure.
5. Adjust the spark plug gap as necessary.
6. Tighten the spark plugs to 9 ft. lbs. (12 Nm).

3.0L Engine

1. Remove the 6 ignition coil-on-plugs.

➡Only use hand tools when removing or installing the spark plugs, or damage can occur to the cylinder head or spark plug.

➡Use compressed air to remove any foreign material in the spark plug well before removing the spark plugs.

2. Remove the 6 spark plugs.
3. Inspect the 6 spark plugs.

To install:

4. To install, reverse the removal procedure.
5. Adjust the spark plug gap as necessary.
6. Tighten the spark plugs to 11 ft. lbs. (15 Nm).

3.5L Engine

1. Remove the 6 ignition coil-on-plugs.

➡Only use hand tools when removing or installing the spark plugs, or damage can occur to the cylinder head or spark plug.

➡Use compressed air to remove any foreign material in the spark plug well before removing the spark plugs.

2. Remove the 6 spark plugs.
3. Inspect the 6 spark plugs.

To install:

4. To install, reverse the removal procedure.
5. Adjust the spark plug gap as necessary.
6. Tighten the spark plugs to 11 ft. lbs. (15 Nm).

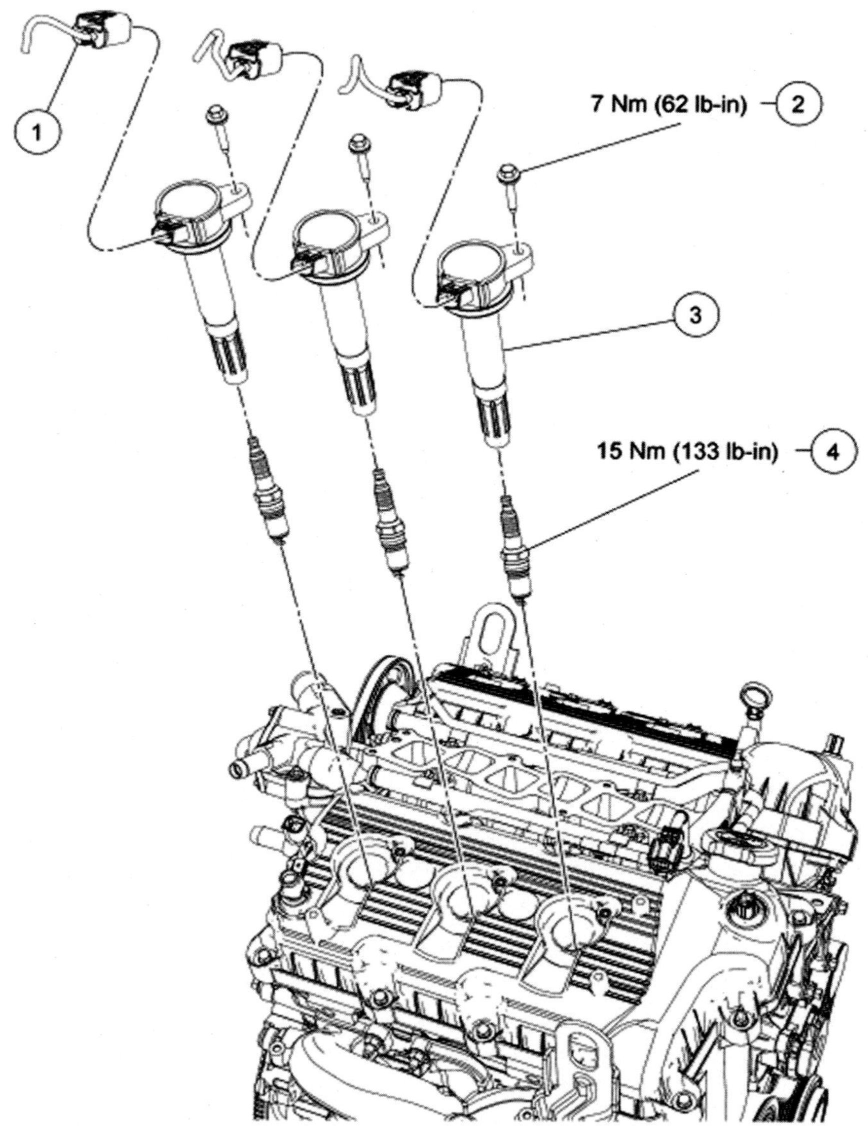

1. RH ignition coil-on-plug electrical connector (3 required)
2. RH ignition coil-on-plug bolt (3 required)
3. RH ignition coil-on-plug (3 required)
4. Spark plug (3 required)

N0095917

Fig. 91 Exploded view of the engine ignition components—RH side

7 Nm
(62 lb-in)
3
4
2
1
6
5
15 Nm
(133 lb-in)

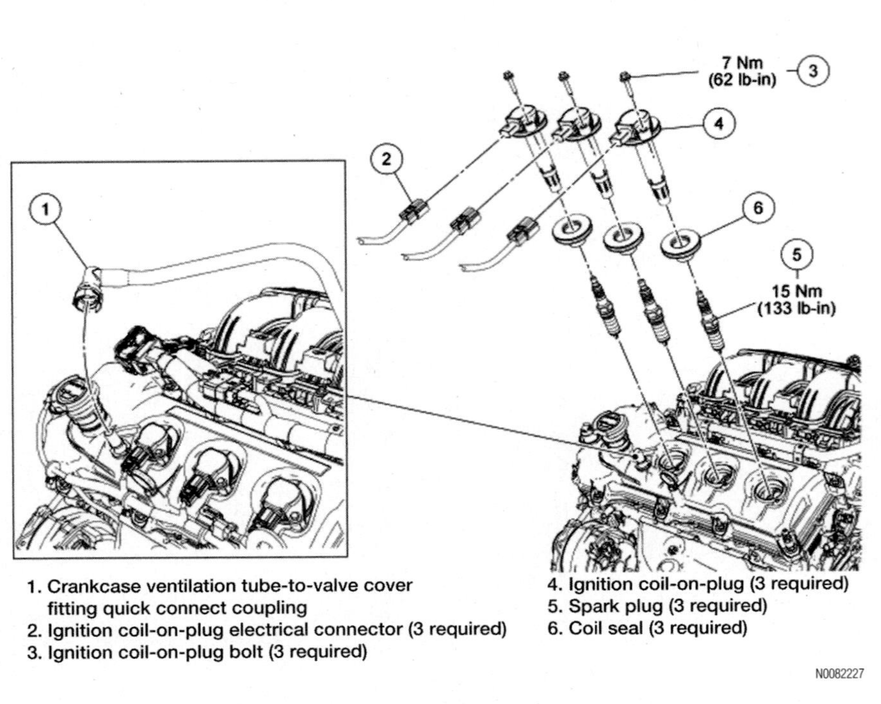

1. Crankcase ventilation tube-to-valve cover fitting quick connect coupling
2. Ignition coil-on-plug electrical connector (3 required)
3. Ignition coil-on-plug bolt (3 required)
4. Ignition coil-on-plug (3 required)
5. Spark plug (3 required)
6. Coil seal (3 required)

N0082227

Fig. 92 Exploded view of the engine ignition components—LH side

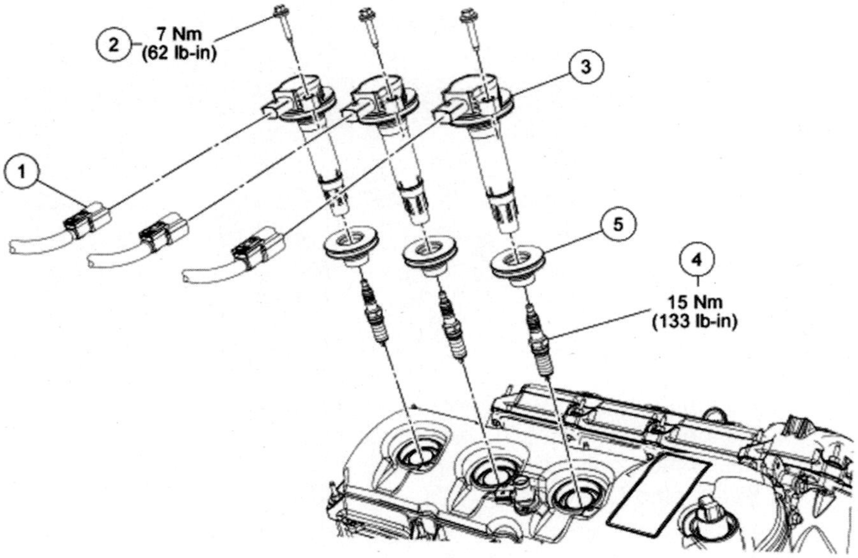

2
7 Nm
(62 lb-in)
3
1
5
4
15 Nm
(133 lb-in)

1. Ignition coil-on-plug electrical connector (3 required)
2. Ignition coil-on-plug bolt (3 required)
3. Ignition coil-on-plug (3 required)
4. Spark plug (3 required)
5. Coil seal (3 required)

N0081451

Fig. 93 Exploded view of the engine ignition components—RH side

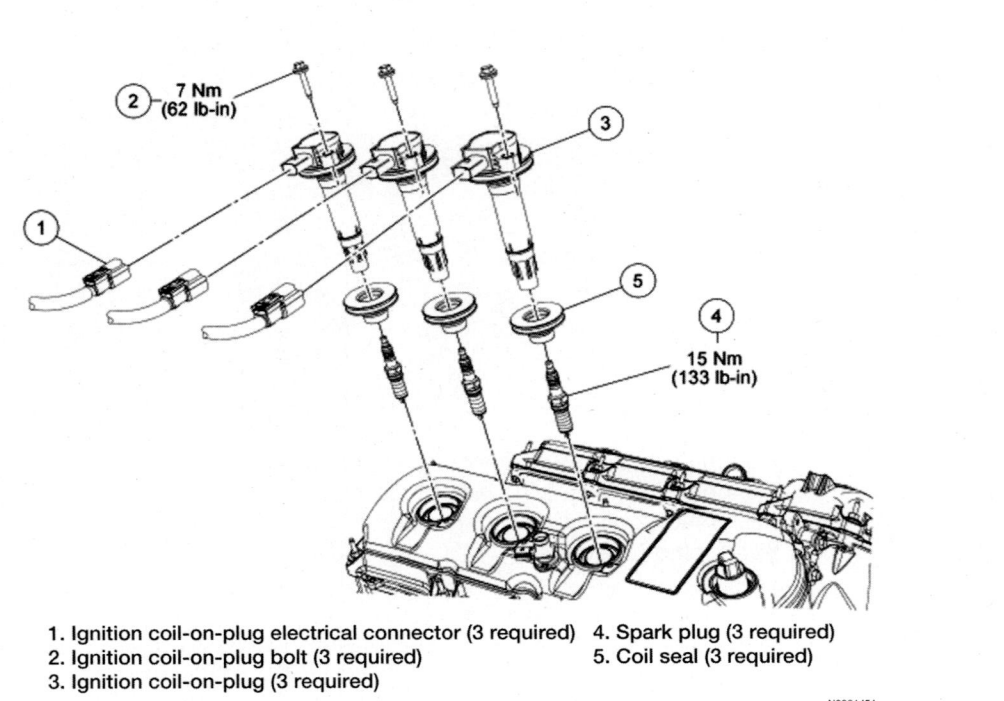

STARTER

REMOVAL & INSTALLATION

2.5L Engine

⁂ WARNING

Always disconnect the battery ground cable at the battery before disconnecting the starter motor battery terminal lead. If a tool is shorted at the starter motor battery terminal, the tool can quickly heat enough to cause a skin burn. Failure to follow this instruction may result in serious personal injury.

1. With the vehicle in NEUTRAL, position it on a hoist.
2. Disconnect the battery ground cable.
3. If equipped, remove the 7 screws and the underbody cover.
4. Remove the starter motor solenoid wire nut and position the wire aside.
5. Position the starter motor solenoid battery cable terminal cover aside.
6. Remove the starter motor solenoid battery cable nut and position the cable aside.
7. Remove the ground wire nut from the starter motor stud bolt and position the ground wire aside.
8. Remove the starter motor bolt, stud bolt and the starter motor.

To install:

9. To install, reverse the removal procedure.
10. Tighten the starter motor bolt and stud bolt to 18 ft. lbs. (25 Nm).
11. Tighten the starter motor solenoid battery cable nut to 9 ft. lbs. (12 Nm).
12. Tighten the starter motor solenoid wire nut to 44 inch lbs. (5 Nm).

3.0L Engine

See Figure 94.

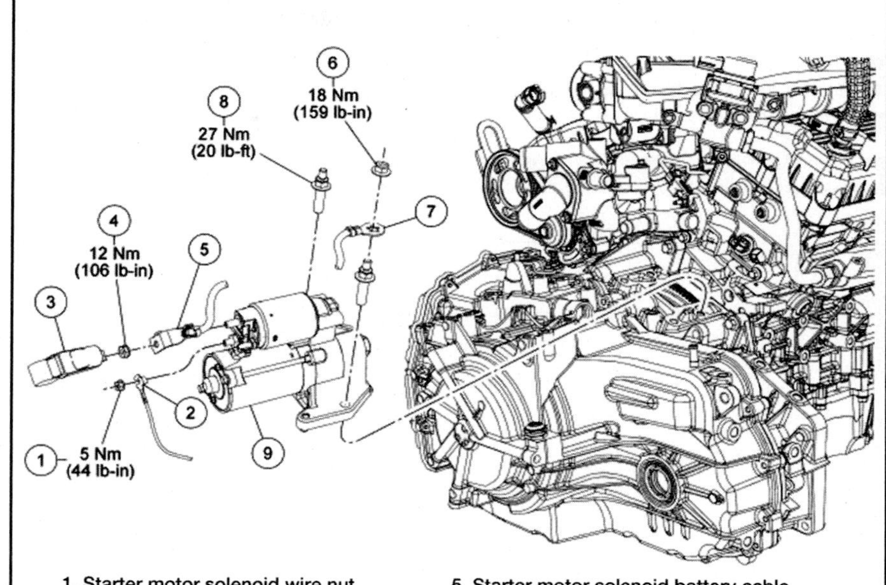

Fig. 94 Removing and installing the starter motor

⁂ WARNING

Always disconnect the battery ground cable at the battery before disconnecting the starter motor battery terminal lead. If a tool is shorted at the starter motor battery terminal, the tool can quickly heat enough to cause a skin burn. Failure to follow this instruction may result in serious personal injury.

1. Remove the battery tray.
2. Remove the starter motor solenoid wire nut and position the wire aside.
3. Position the starter motor solenoid terminal battery cable cover aside.
4. Remove the starter motor solenoid battery cable nut and position aside the cable.
5. Remove the ground wire nut from the starter motor stud bolt and position the ground wire aside.
6. Remove the 2 starter motor stud bolts and the starter motor.

To install:

7. To install, reverse the removal procedure.
8. Tighten the starter motor stud bolts to 20 ft. lbs. (27 Nm).
9. Tighten the starter motor solenoid battery cable nut to 9 ft. lbs. (12 Nm).
10. Tighten the starter motor solenoid wire nut to 44 inch lbs. (5 Nm).

ENGINE MECHANICAL

➡Disconnecting the negative battery cable may interfere with the functions of the on board computer systems and may require the computer to undergo a relearning process, once the negative battery cable is reconnected.

ACCESSORY DRIVE BELTS

ACCESSORY BELT ROUTING

See Figures 95 through 100.

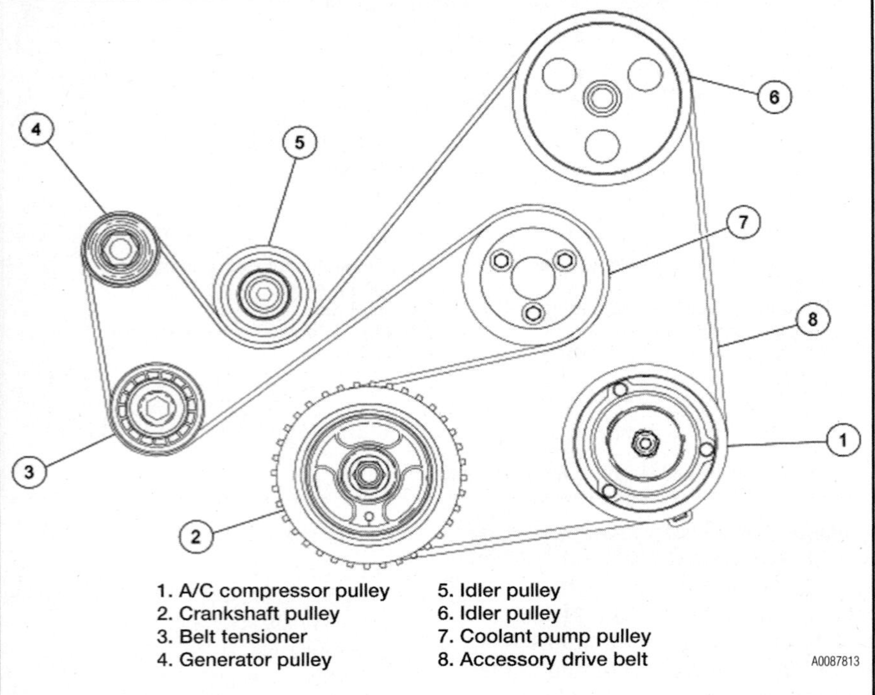

Fig. 95 Accessory drive belt routing—2.5L engine

REMOVAL & INSTALLATION

2.5L Engine

See Figure 101.

1. With the vehicle in NEUTRAL, position it on a hoist
2. Remove the 4 screws and position the RH fender splash shield aside.
3. Remove the 6 pin-type retainers and the RH splash shield.

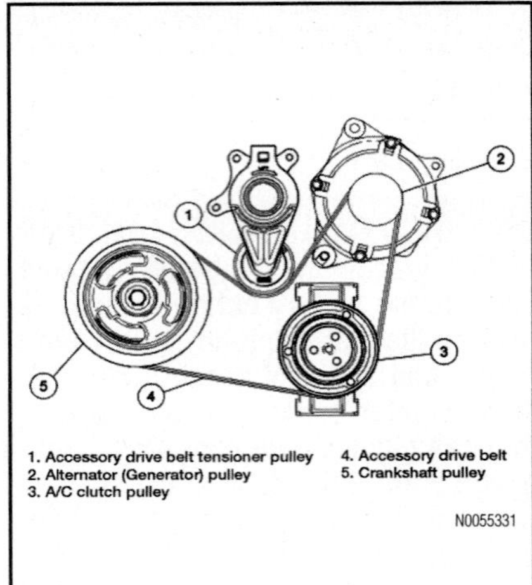

Fig. 98 Accessory drive belt routing—3.5L engine

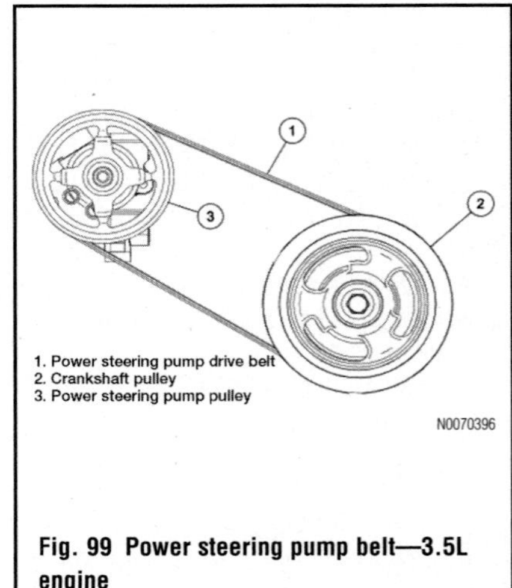

Fig. 99 Power steering pump belt—3.5L engine

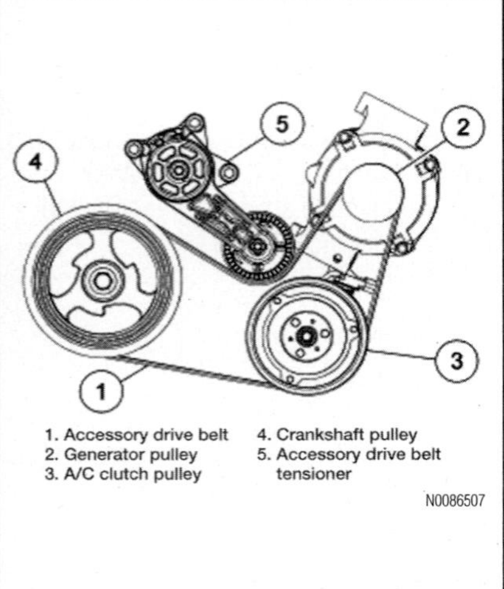

Fig. 96 Accessory drive belt routing—3.0L engine

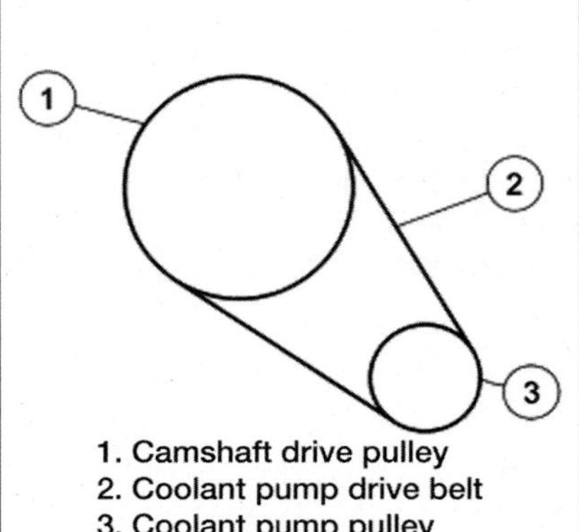

Fig. 97 Coolant pump drive belt—3.0L engine

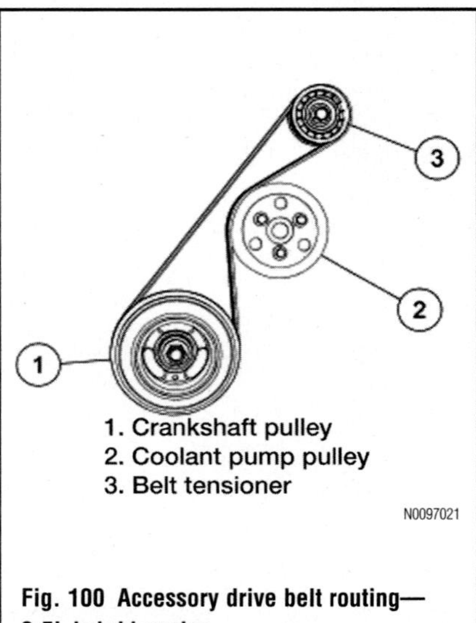

Fig. 100 Accessory drive belt routing—2.5L hybrid engine

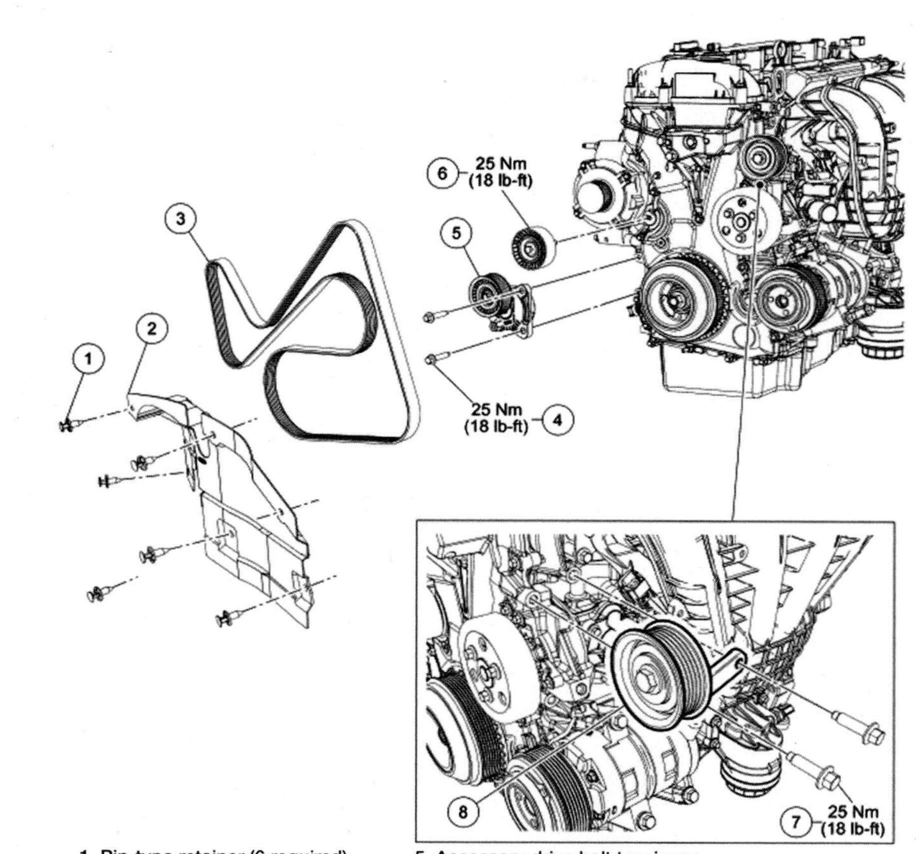

Fig. 101 Front End Accessory Drive (FEAD) exploded view—2.5L engine

4. Using the hex feature, rotate the accessory drive belt tensioner clockwise and remove the accessory drive belt from the coolant pump pulley.

5. Remove the accessory drive belt from the engine.

To install:

6. To install, reverse the removal procedure.

3.0L Engine

See Figure 102.

1. With the vehicle in NEUTRAL, position it on a hoist.

2. Remove the 4 screws and position the RH fender splash shield aside.

3. Remove the 6 pin-type retainers and the RH splash shield.

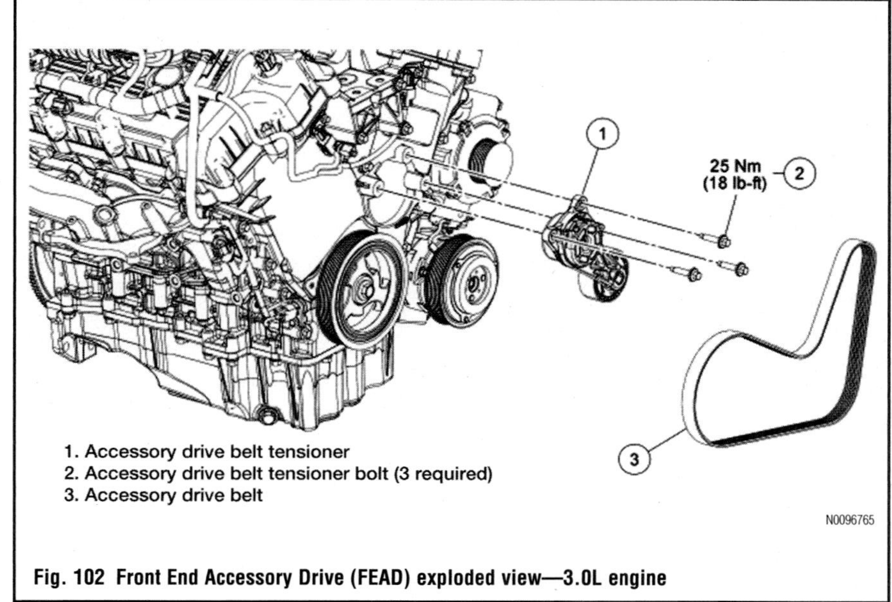

Fig. 102 Front End Accessory Drive (FEAD) exploded view—3.0L engine

4. Rotate the accessory drive belt tensioner counterclockwise and remove the accessory drive belt.

To install:

5. To install, reverse the removal procedure.

3.5L Engine

See Figure 103.

➡Under no circumstances should the accessory drive belt, tensioner or pulleys be lubricated as potential damage to the belt material and tensioner damping mechanism will occur. Do not apply any fluids or belt dressing to the accessory drive belt or pulleys.

1. With the vehicle in NEUTRAL, position it on a hoist.
2. Working from the top of the vehicle, rotate the accessory drive belt tensioner clockwise and remove the accessory drive belt from the generator pulley.
3. Remove the 4 screws and position the RH fender splash shield aside.
4. Remove the 6 pin-type retainers and the RH splash shield.
5. Working from under the vehicle, remove the accessory drive belt.

To install:

6. Working from under the vehicle, position the accessory drive belt on all pulleys, with the exception of the generator pulley.

➡After installation, make sure the accessory drive belt is correctly seated on all pulleys.

7. Working from the top of the vehicle, rotate the accessory drive belt tensioner clockwise and install the accessory drive belt on the generator pulley.
8. Install the RH splash shield and the 6 pin-type retainers.
9. Position the RH fender splash shield and install the 4 screws.

2.5L Hybrid Engine

See Figure 104.

1. With the vehicle in NEUTRAL, position it on a hoist.
2. Remove the 4 screws and position the RH fender splash shield aside.
3. Remove the 6 pin-type retainers and the RH splash shield.
4. Remove the A/C hose retainer bracket bolt.
5. Rotate the accessory drive belt tensioner counterclockwise and remove the accessory drive belt.

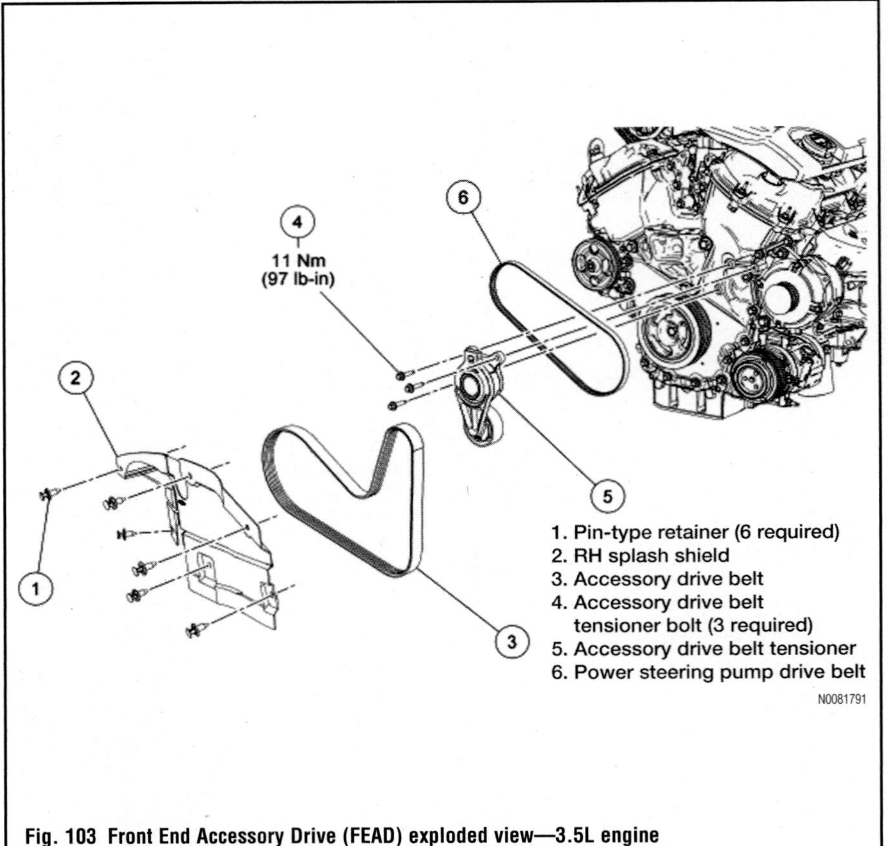

Fig. 103 Front End Accessory Drive (FEAD) exploded view—3.5L engine

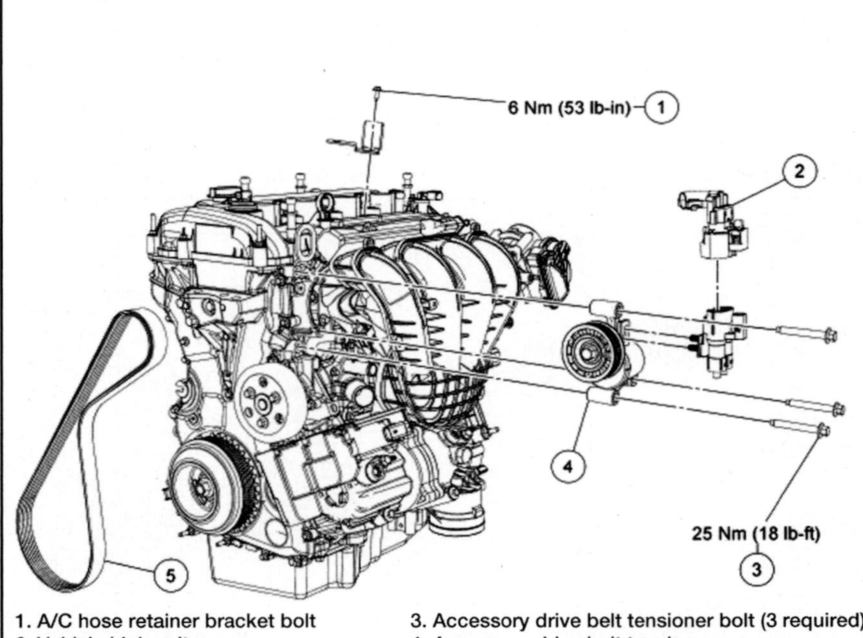

Fig. 104 Front End Accessory Drive (FEAD) exploded view—2.5L hybrid engine

To install:

6. To install, reverse the removal procedure.
7. Tighten the A/C hose retainer bracket bolt to 53 inch lbs. (6 Nm).

AIR CLEANER

REMOVAL & INSTALLATION

2.5L Engine

1. Disconnect the Mass Air Flow (MAF) sensor electrical connector.
2. Loosen the clamp and disconnect the Air Cleaner (ACL) outlet pipe from the ACL housing cover.

➡No tools are needed to remove the ACL assembly. Removal should be carried out using hands only.

3. Separate the 3 ACL feet from the rubber grommets and the ACL inlet pipe and remove the ACL assembly.

➡Make sure that the 3 ACL feet are seated into the rubber grommets under the ACL assembly.

➡The ACL outlet pipe should be securely sealed to prevent unmetered air from entering the engine.

To install:

4. To install, reverse the removal procedure.
5. Tighten the ACL outlet pipe clamp to 35 inch lbs. (4 Nm).

3.0L Engine

1. Disconnect the Mass Air Flow (MAF) sensor electrical connector.
2. Loosen the clamp and disconnect the Air Cleaner (ACL) outlet pipe-to- ACL housing cover.

➡No tools are needed to remove the ACL assembly. Removal should be carried out using hands only.

3. Separate the 3 ACL feet from the rubber grommets and the ACL inlet pipe and remove the ACL assembly.

➡Make sure that the 3 ACL feet are seated into the rubber grommets under the ACL assembly.

➡The ACL outlet pipe should be securely sealed to prevent unmetered air from entering the engine.

To install:

4. To install, reverse the removal procedure.
5. Tighten the ACL outlet pipe to ACL housing cover clamp to 35 inch lbs. (4 Nm).

3.5L Engine

1. Disconnect the Mass Air Flow (MAF) sensor electrical connector and release the wiring harness pin-type retainer from the Air Cleaner (ACL) housing.
2. Loosen the clamp and disconnect the ACL outlet pipe from the ACL housing cover.
3. Remove the ACL housing bolt.
4. Remove the 2 ACL inlet pipe bolts.

➡No tools are needed to remove the ACL assembly. Removal should be carried out using hands only.

5. Separate the 2 ACL feet from the rubber grommets and remove the ACL and the ACL inlet pipe as an assembly.

➡Make sure that the 2 ACL feet are seated into the rubber grommets under the ACL assembly.

➡The ACL outlet pipe should be securely sealed to prevent unmetered air from entering the engine.

To install:

6. To install, reverse the removal procedure.
7. Tighten the 2 ACL inlet pipe bolts to 35 inch lbs. (4 Nm).
8. Tighten the ACL housing bolt to 35 inch lbs. (4 Nm).
9. Tighten the ACL outlet pipe clamp to 35 inch lbs. (4 Nm).

2.5L Hybrid Engine

1. With the vehicle in NEUTRAL, position it on a hoist.
2. Remove the LH fender splash shield.
3. Disconnect the Mass Air Flow (MAF) sensor electrical connector.
4. Loosen the clamp and disconnect the Air Cleaner (ACL) outlet pipe from the ACL assembly.
5. Remove the 3 nuts, release the ACL intake pipe and remove the ACL assembly.

To install:

6. To install, reverse the removal procedure.
7. Tighten the ACL intake pipe nuts to 11 ft. lbs. (15 Nm).
8. Tighten the ACL outlet pipe clamp to 35 inch lbs. (4 Nm).

CAMSHAFT AND VALVE LIFTERS

REMOVAL & INSTALLATION

2.5L Engine

See Figures 105 through 112.

➡During engine repair procedures, cleanliness is extremely important. Any foreign material, including any material created while cleaning gasket surfaces, that enters the oil passages, coolant passages or the oil pan can cause engine failure.

➡Do not rotate the camshafts or crankshaft unless instructed to do so in this procedure. Rotating the camshafts or crankshaft with timing components loosened or removed can cause serious damage to the valves or pistons.

1. With the vehicle in NEUTRAL, position it on a hoist.
2. Remove the accessory drive belt.
3. Remove the front RH wheel and tire.
4. If equipped, remove the 7 screws and the underbody cover.
5. Remove the Variable Camshaft Timing (VCT) solenoid.
6. Check the valve clearance.

➡Turn the engine clockwise only, and only use the crankshaft bolt.

➡Before removing the camshafts, measure the clearance of each valve at base circle, with the lobe pointed away from the tappet. Failure to measure all clearances prior to removing the camshafts will necessitate repeated removal and installation and wasted labor time.

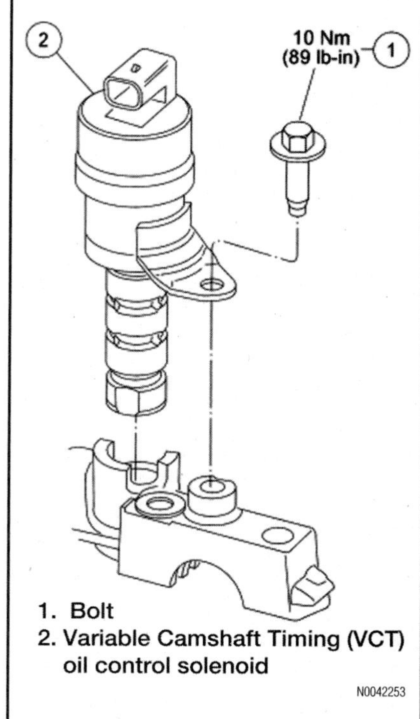

Fig. 105 Removing the VCT solenoid

a. Use a feeler gauge to measure the clearance of each valve and record its location.

➡The number on the valve tappet only reflects the digits that follow the decimal. For example, a tappet with the number 0.650 has the thickness of 3.650 mm.

➡The nominal clearance is:

- intake: 0.0095 inch (0.25 mm)
- exhaust: 0.0115 inch (0.30 mm)

➡The acceptable clearances after being fully installed are:

- intake: 0.008-0.011 inch (0.22-0.28 mm)
- exhaust: 0.010-0.013 inch (0.27-0.33 mm)

b. Select tappets using this formula: ideal tappet thickness = measured clearance + the existing tappet thickness - nominal clearance. Select the closest tappet size to the ideal tappet thickness available and mark the installation location.

c. If any tappets do not measure within specifications, install new tappets in these locations

➡Failure to position the No. 1 piston at Top Dead Center (TDC) can result in damage to the engine. Turn the engine in the normal direction of rotation only.

7. Using the crankshaft pulley bolt, turn the crankshaft clockwise to position the No. 1 piston at Top Dead Center (TDC).

a. The hole in the crankshaft pulley should be in the 6 o'clock position.

➡The Camshaft Alignment Plate is for camshaft alignment only. Using this tool to prevent engine rotation can result in engine damage.

➡The camshaft timing slots are offset. If the Camshaft Alignment Plate cannot be installed, rotate the crankshaft one complete revolution clockwise to correctly position the camshafts.

8. Install the Camshaft Alignment Plate in the slots on the rear of both camshafts.

9. Remove the engine plug bolt.

➡The Crankshaft TDC Timing Peg will contact the crankshaft and prevent it from turning past TDC. However, the crankshaft can still be rotated in the counterclockwise direction. The crankshaft must remain at the TDC position during the camshaft removal and installation.

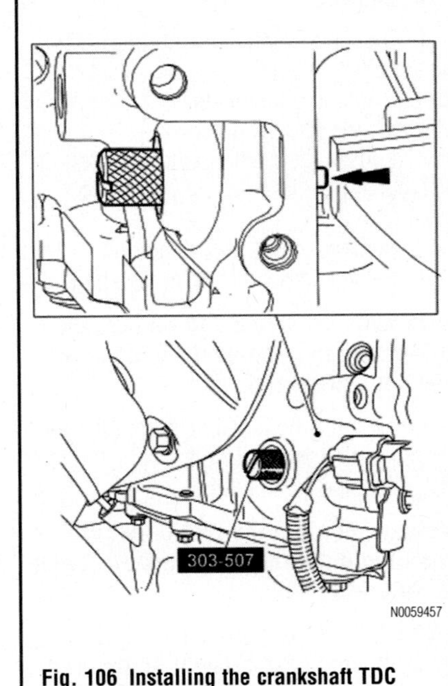

Fig. 106 Installing the crankshaft TDC timing peg

10. Install the Crankshaft TDC Timing Peg.

➡Only hand-tighten the bolt or damage to the front cover can occur.

11. Install a standard 6 mm x 18 mm bolt through the crankshaft pulley and thread it into the front cover.

12. Remove the lower timing hole plug from the engine front cover.

13. Remove the upper timing hole plug from the engine front cover.

14. Reposition the Camshaft Alignment Plate to the slot on the rear of the intake camshaft only.

➡Releasing the ratcheting mechanism in the timing chain tensioner allows the plunger to collapse and create slack in the timing chain. Installing the M6 x 30 mm bolt into the upper front cover timing hole will lock the tensioner arm in a retracted position and allow enough slack in the timing chain for removal of the exhaust camshaft gear.

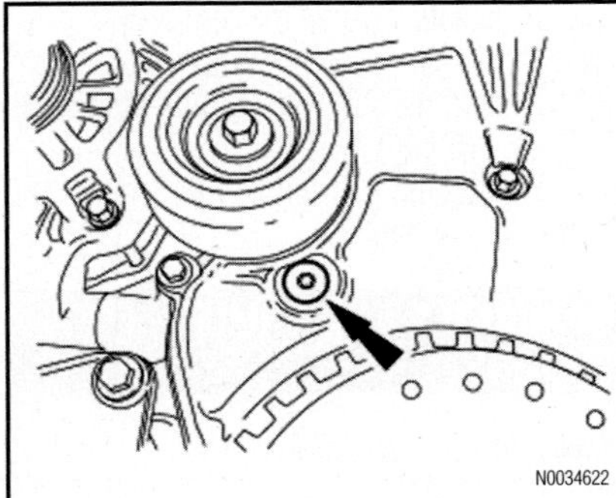

Fig. 107 Removing the lower timing hole plug

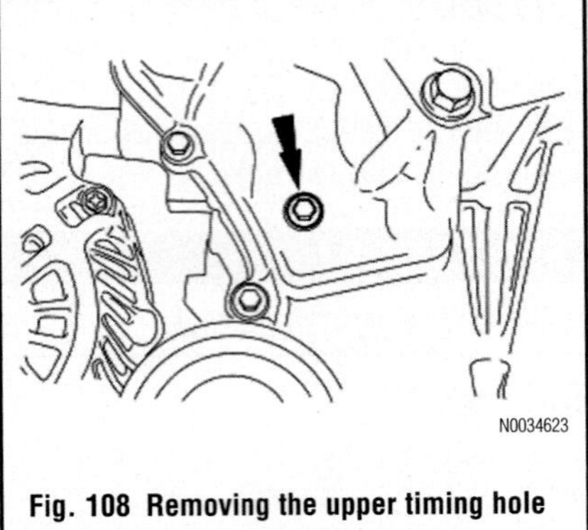

Fig. 108 Removing the upper timing hole plug

15. Using a small pick tool, release the timing chain tensioner ratchet through the lower front cover timing hole.

a. Have an assistant rotate the exhaust camshaft clockwise (using the flats of the camshaft) to collapse the timing chain tensioner plunger.

b. Insert the M6 x 30 mm bolt into the upper front cover timing hole to hold the tensioner arm in the retracted position.

16. Using the flats on the camshaft to prevent camshaft rotation, remove the bolt and the exhaust camshaft drive gear.

17. Remove the Camshaft Alignment Plate.

18. Remove the timing chain from the intake camshaft drive gear.

19. Mark the position of the camshaft lobes on the No. 1 cylinder for installation reference.

➡Failure to follow the camshaft loosening procedure can result in damage to the camshafts.

➡Mark the location and orientation of each camshaft bearing cap.

20. Remove the camshafts from the engine.

a. Loosen the camshaft bearing cap bolts, in the sequence shown, one turn at a time until all tension is released from the camshaft bearing caps.

b. Remove the bolts and the camshaft bearing caps.

c. Remove the camshafts.

21. If removal of the camshaft phaser and sprocket is necessary, mark the sprocket and camshaft for reference during installation.

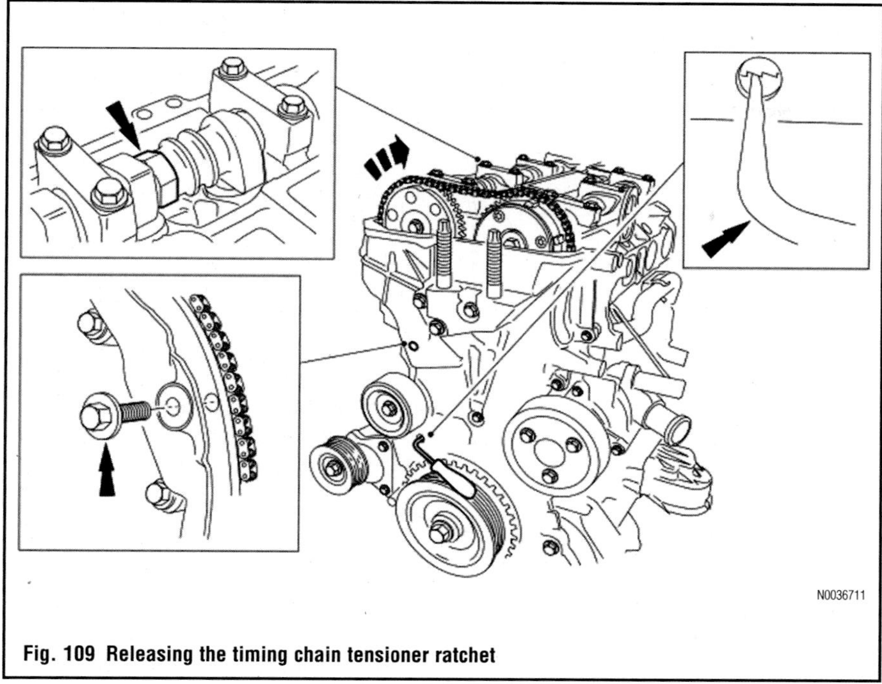

Fig. 109 Releasing the timing chain tensioner ratchet

Fig. 110 Removing the bolt and exhaust camshaft drive gear

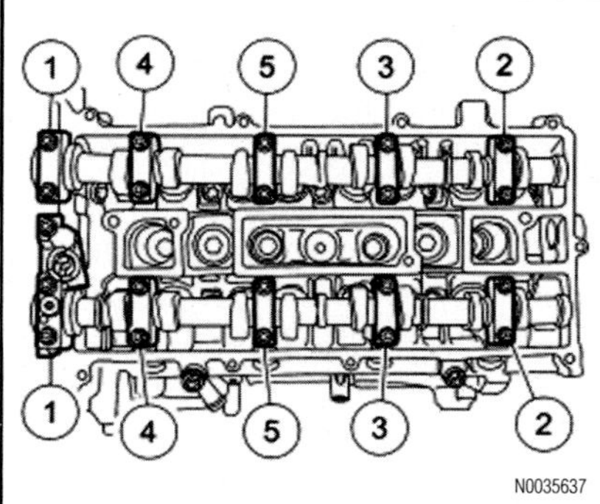

Fig. 111 Loosening the camshaft bearing cap bolts in sequence

a. If necessary, place the camshaft in a soft-jawed vise. Remove the bolt and the camshaft phaser and sprocket.

To install:

➡If new parts are installed, transfer the reference marks made during disassembly to the new parts.

22. If necessary, position the camshaft in a soft-jawed vise and install the camshaft phaser and sprocket and the bolt.

a. Align the reference marks on the camshaft phaser and sprocket and the camshaft. Tighten the bolt to 53 ft. lbs. (72 Nm).

➡Install the camshafts with the alignment slots in the camshafts lined up so the Camshaft Alignment Plate can be installed without rotating the camshafts. Make sure the lobes on the No. 1 cylinder are in the same position as noted in the removal procedure. Rotating the camshafts when the timing chain is removed, or installing the camshafts 180 degrees out of position can cause severe damage to the valves and pistons.

➡Lubricate the camshaft journals and bearing caps with clean engine oil.

23. Install the camshafts and bearing caps in their original locations and orientation. Tighten the bearing caps in the sequence shown in 3 stages:

a. Stage 1: Tighten the camshaft bearing cap bolts until finger-tight.

b. Stage 2: Tighten to 62 inch lbs. (7 Nm).

c. Stage 3: Tighten to 142 inch lbs. (16 Nm).

24. Install the Camshaft Alignment Plate.

25. Install the timing chain on the intake camshaft drive gear.

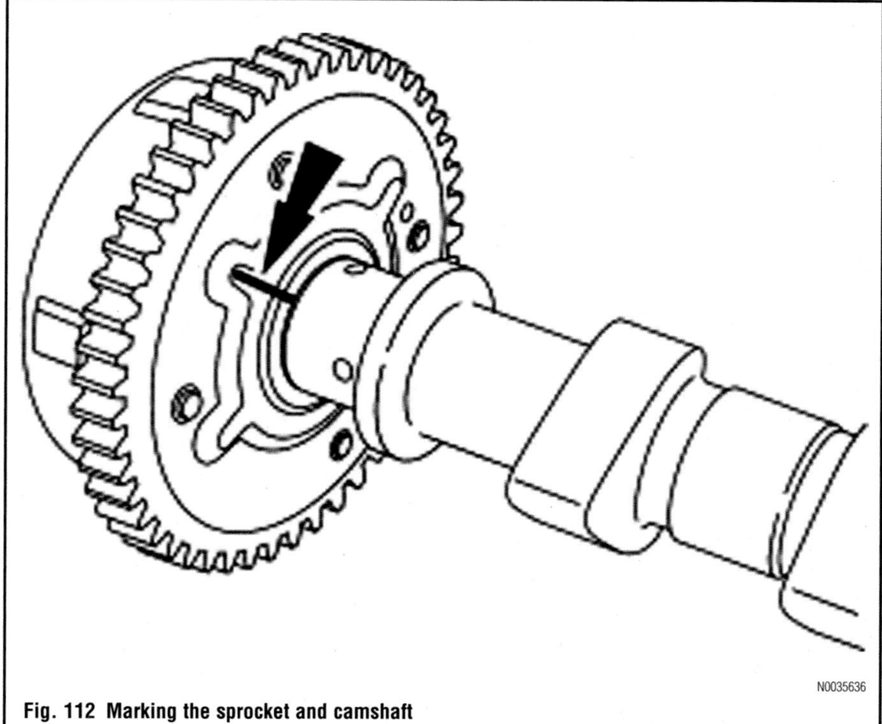

Fig. 112 Marking the sprocket and camshaft

➡The timing chain must be correctly engaged on the teeth of the crankshaft timing sprocket and the intake camshaft drive gear in order to install the exhaust camshaft drive gear onto the exhaust camshaft.

26. Position the exhaust camshaft drive gear in the timing chain and install the gear and bolt on the exhaust camshaft.
27. Hand-tighten the bolt.

➡Releasing the tensioner arm will remove the slack from the timing chain.

28. Remove the M6 x 30 mm bolt from the upper front cover timing hole to release the tensioner arm.

➡The Camshaft Alignment Plate is for camshaft alignment only. Using this tool to prevent engine rotation can result in engine damage.

29. Using the flats on the camshaft to prevent camshaft rotation, tighten the exhaust camshaft drive gear bolt to 53 ft. lbs. (72 Nm).
30. Remove the Camshaft Alignment Plate.
31. Remove the 6 mm x 18 mm bolt.
32. Remove the Crankshaft TDC Timing Peg.
33. Install the upper timing hole plug in the engine front cover. Tighten to 89 inch lbs. (10 Nm).
34. Apply silicone gasket and sealant to the threads of the lower timing hole plug.
   a. Install the lower timing hole plug in the engine front cover. Tighten to 9 ft. lbs. (12 N).
35. Install the engine plug bolt. Tighten to 15 ft. lbs. (20 Nm).
36. If equipped, install the underbody cover and the 7 screws.
37. Install the front RH wheel and tire.
38. Install the accessory drive belt.
39. Install the VCT solenoid.

2.5L Hybrid Engine

See Figures 113 through 120.

➡During engine repair procedures, cleanliness is extremely important. Any foreign material (including any material created while cleaning gasket surfaces) that enters the oil passages, coolant passages or the oil pan can cause engine failure.

➡Do not rotate the camshafts unless instructed to in this procedure. Rotating the camshafts or crankshaft with timing components loosened or removed can cause serious damage to the valves and pistons.

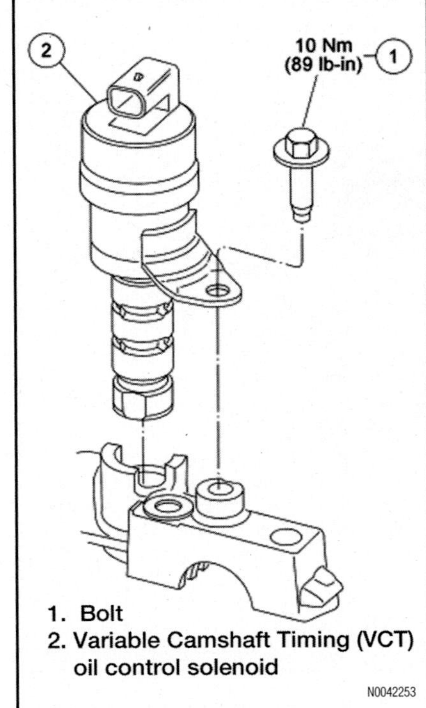

Fig. 113 Removing the VCT solenoid

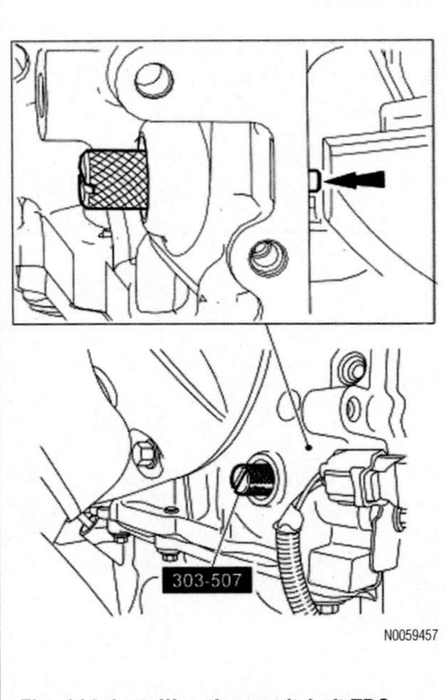

Fig. 114 Installing the crankshaft TDC timing peg

1. With the vehicle in NEUTRAL, position it on a hoist.
2. Remove the degas bottle.
3. Remove the Variable Camshaft Timing (VCT) oil control solenoid.
4. Check the valve clearance.
   a. Remove the valve cover.
   b. Remove the 4 screws and position the RH fender splash shield aside.
   c. Remove the 6 pin-type retainers and the RH splash shield.

➡Turn the engine clockwise only, and only use the crankshaft bolt.

➡Before removing the camshafts, measure the clearance of each valve at base circle, with the lobe pointed away from the tappet. Failure to measure all clearances prior to removing the camshafts will necessitate repeated removal and installation and wasted labor time.

   d. Use a feeler gauge to measure the clearance of each valve and record its location.

➡The number on the valve tappet only reflects the digits that follow the decimal. For example, a tappet with the number 0.650 has the thickness of 3.650 mm.

➡The nominal clearance is:

- intake: 0.25 mm (0.0095 in)
- exhaust: 0.30 mm (0.0115 in)

   e. The acceptable clearances after being fully installed are:
   - intake: 0.22-0.28 mm (0.008-0.011 in)
   - exhaust: 0.27-0.33 mm (0.010-0.013 in)

   f. Select tappets using this formula: tappet thickness = measured clearance + the existing tappet thickness - nominal clearance.
   g. Select the closest tappet size to the ideal tappet thickness available and mark the installation location.
   h. If any tappets do not measure within specifications, install new tappets in these locations.
5. Remove the accessory drive belt.

➡Failure to position the No. 1 piston at Top Dead Center (TDC) can result in damage to the engine. Turn the engine in the normal direction of rotation only.

6. Using the crankshaft pulley bolt, turn the crankshaft clockwise to position the No. 1 piston at Top Dead Center (TDC).
7. The hole in the crankshaft pulley should be in the 6 o'clock position.

➡The Camshaft Alignment Plate 303-465 is for camshaft alignment only. Using this tool to prevent engine rotation can result in engine damage.

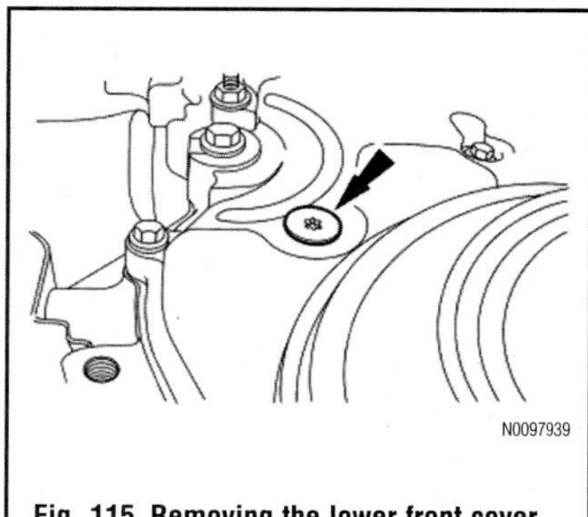

Fig. 115 Removing the lower front cover timing hole plug

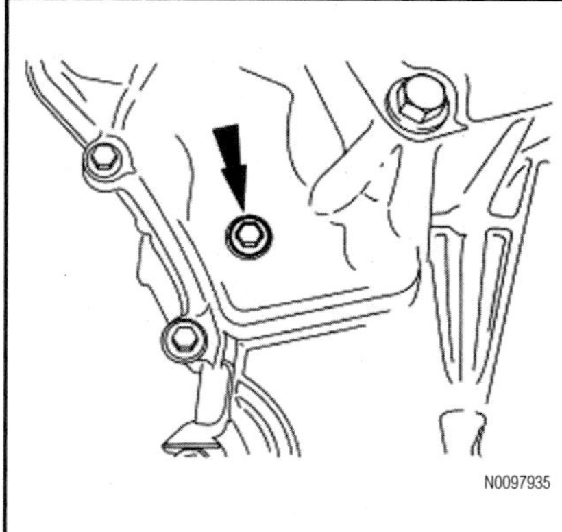

Fig. 116 Removing the upper front cover timing hole plug

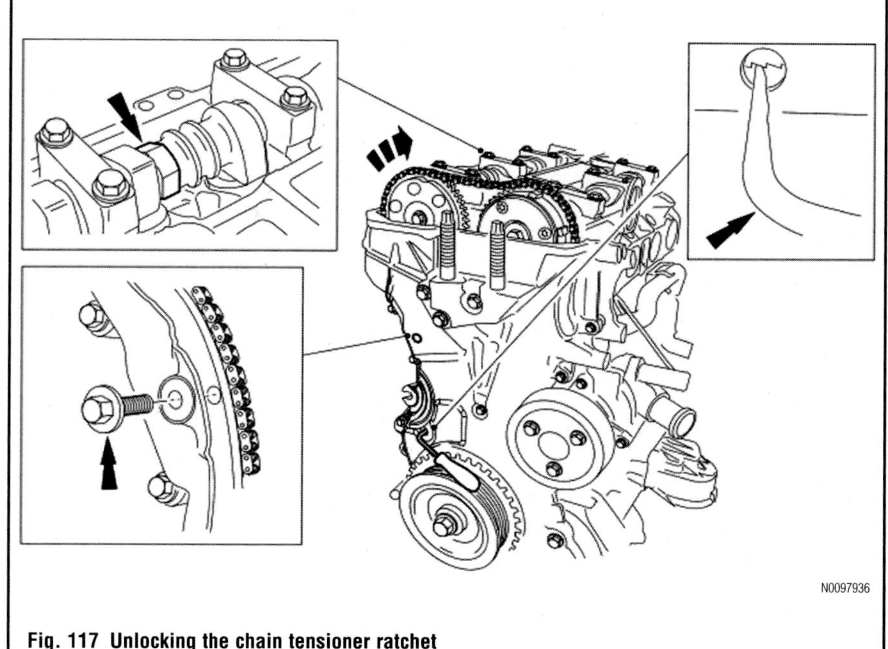

Fig. 117 Unlocking the chain tensioner ratchet

➡The camshaft timing slots are offset. If the Camshaft Alignment Plate cannot be installed, rotate the crankshaft one complete revolution clockwise to correctly position the camshafts.

8. Install the Camshaft Alignment Plate in the slots on the rear of both camshafts.
9. Remove the engine plug bolt.
10. Install the Crankshaft TDC Timing Peg.

➡Only hand-tighten the bolt or damage to the front cover can occur.

11. Install a standard 6 mm x 18 mm bolt through the crankshaft pulley and thread it into the front cover.
12. Remove the lower front cover timing hole plug from the engine front cover.
13. Remove the upper front cover timing hole plug from the engine front cover.
14. Reposition the Camshaft Alignment Plate to the slot on the rear of the intake camshaft only.

➡Releasing the ratcheting mechanism in the timing chain tensioner allows the plunger to collapse and create slack in the timing chain. Installing an M6 x 30 mm (1.18 in) bolt into the upper front cover timing hole will hold the tensioner arm in a retracted position and allow enough slack in the timing chain for removal of the exhaust camshaft gear.

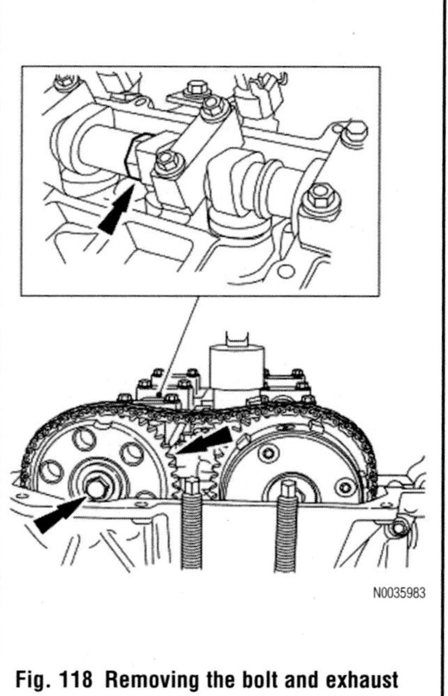

Fig. 118 Removing the bolt and exhaust camshaft drive gear

15. Using a small pick tool, unlock the chain tensioner ratchet through the lower front cover timing hole.
    a. Using the flats of the camshaft, have an assistant rotate the exhaust camshaft clockwise to collapse the timing chain tensioner plunger.
    b. Insert an M6 x 30 mm (1.18 in) bolt into the upper front cover timing hole to hold the tensioner arm in the retracted position.
16. Remove the Camshaft Alignment Plate.
17. Using the flats on the camshaft to prevent camshaft rotation, remove the bolt and exhaust camshaft drive gear.
18. Remove the timing chain from the camshaft phaser and sprocket.
19. Mark the position of the camshaft lobes on the No. 1 cylinder for installation reference.

➡Failure to follow the camshaft loosening procedure can result in damage to the camshafts.

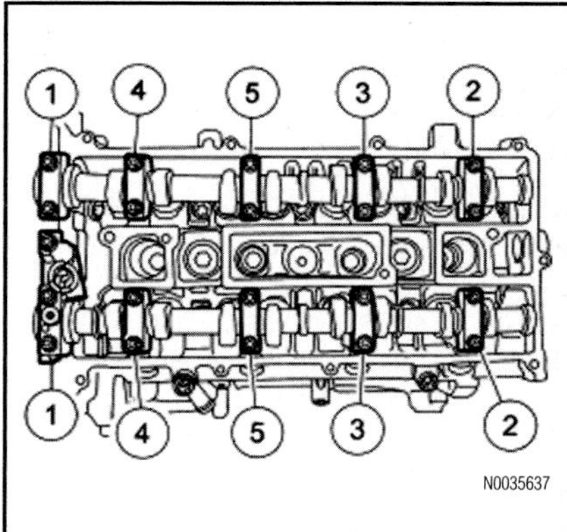

Fig. 119 Identifying camshaft bearing cap bolt loosening sequence

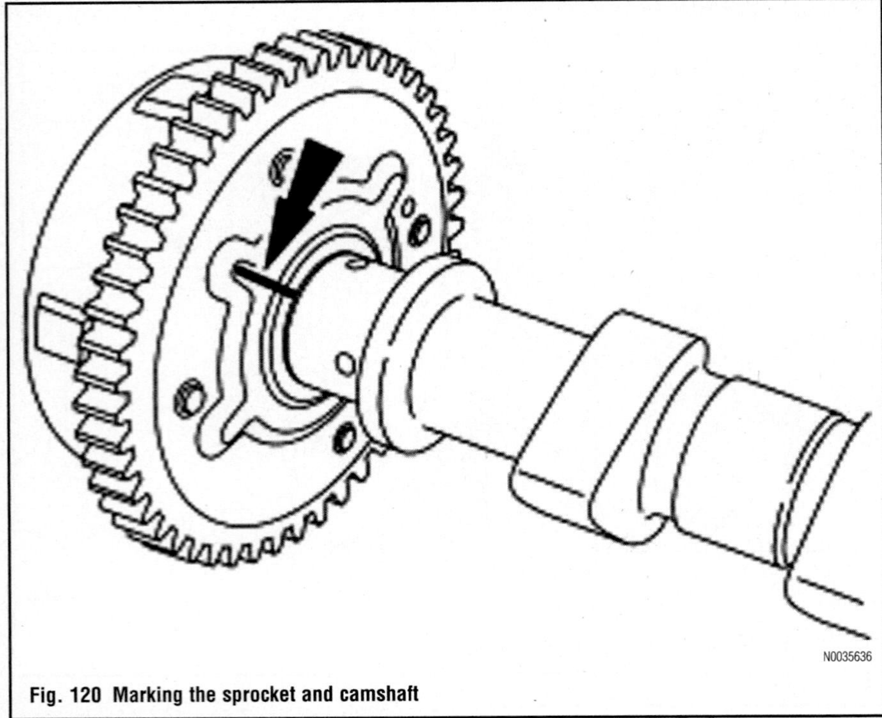

Fig. 120 Marking the sprocket and camshaft

➡Mark the location and orientation of each camshaft bearing cap.

20. Remove the camshafts from the engine.
   a. Loosen the camshaft bearing cap bolts, in sequence, one turn at a time until all tension is released from the camshaft bearing caps.
   b. Remove the bolts and the camshaft bearing caps.
   c. Remove the camshafts.
21. If removal of the camshaft phaser and sprocket is necessary, mark the sprocket and camshaft for reference during installation.
   a. If necessary, place the camshaft in a soft-jawed vise. Remove the bolt and the camshaft phaser and sprocket.

To install:

➡If new parts are installed, transfer the reference marks made during disassembly to the new parts.

22. If necessary, position the camshaft in a soft-jawed vise and install the camshaft phaser and sprocket and the bolt.
   a. Align the reference marks on the camshaft phaser and sprocket and the camshaft. Tighten the bolt to 53 ft. lbs. (72 Nm).

➡Install the camshafts with the alignment slots in the camshafts lined up so the Camshaft Alignment Plate can be installed without rotating the camshafts. Make sure the lobes on the No. 1 cylinder are in the same position as noted in the removal procedure. Rotating the camshafts when the timing chain is removed, or installing the camshafts 180 degrees out of position can cause severe damage to the valves and pistons.

➡Lubricate the camshaft journals and bearing caps with clean engine oil.

23. Install the camshafts and bearing caps in their original location and orientation. Tighten the bearing caps in the sequence shown in 3 stages:
   a. Stage 1: Tighten the camshaft bearing cap bolts one turn at a time, until finger-tight.
   b. Stage 2: Tighten to 63 inch lbs. (7 Nm).
   c. Stage 3: Tighten to 12 ft. lbs. (16 Nm).
24. Install the Camshaft Alignment Plate.
25. Install the timing chain on the camshaft phaser and sprocket.

➡The timing chain must be correctly engaged on the teeth of the crankshaft timing sprocket and the intake camshaft drive gear in order to install the exhaust camshaft drive gear onto the exhaust camshaft.

26. Position the exhaust camshaft drive gear in the timing chain and install the gear and bolt on the exhaust camshaft.
   a. Hand-tighten the bolt.

➡Releasing the tensioner arm will remove the slack from the timing chain.

27. Remove the M6 x 30 mm bolt from the upper front cover timing hole to release the tensioner arm.

➡The Camshaft Alignment Plate 303-465 is for camshaft alignment only. Using this tool to prevent engine rotation can result in engine damage.

28. Using the flats on the camshaft to prevent camshaft rotation, tighten the bolt. Tighten to 53 ft. lbs. (72 Nm).
29. Remove the Camshaft Alignment Plate.
30. Remove the 6 mm x 18 mm bolt.
31. Remove the Crankshaft TDC Timing Peg.
32. Install the upper front cover timing hole plug. Tighten to 89 inch lbs. (10 Nm).
33. Apply silicone gasket and sealant to the threads of the lower front cover timing hole plug.
34. Install the plug and tighten to 9 ft. lbs. (12 Nm).
35. Install the engine plug bolt. Tighten to 15 ft. lbs. (20 Nm).
36. Install the accessory drive belt.
37. Install the VCT oil control solenoid.
38. Install the valve cover.
39. Install the degas bottle.

3.0L Engine

LH Side

See Figures 121 through 132.

1. Remove the coolant pump belt.
2. Remove the timing drive components.

➡Failure to use the correct special tools, assembled as shown in the illustration, will result in damage to the coolant pump pulley and/or special tools.

3. Using the Water Pump Pulley Plate, Water Pump Shaft Protector and the Crankshaft Vibration Damper Remover, remove the coolant pump pulley.

➡Do not scratch the camshaft sealing surface while removing the camshaft oil seal. If scratched, camshaft oil seal leakage may occur.

4. Using the Oil Seal Remover, remove and discard the camshaft oil seal.
5. Remove the 2 bolts and the camshaft oil seal retainer.
   a. Discard the press-in-place gasket.

Fig. 121 Removing the coolant pump pulley

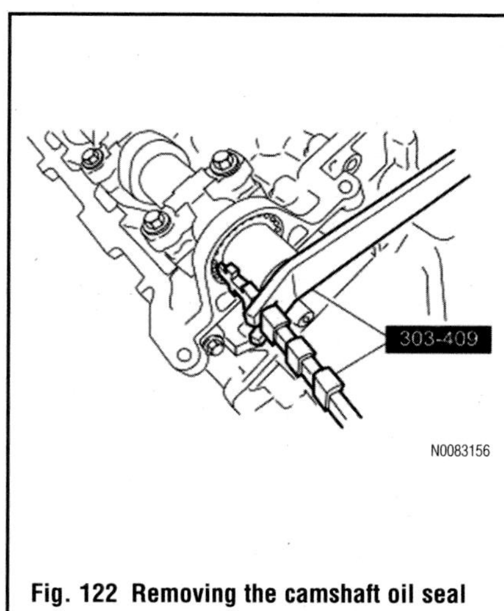

Fig. 122 Removing the camshaft oil seal

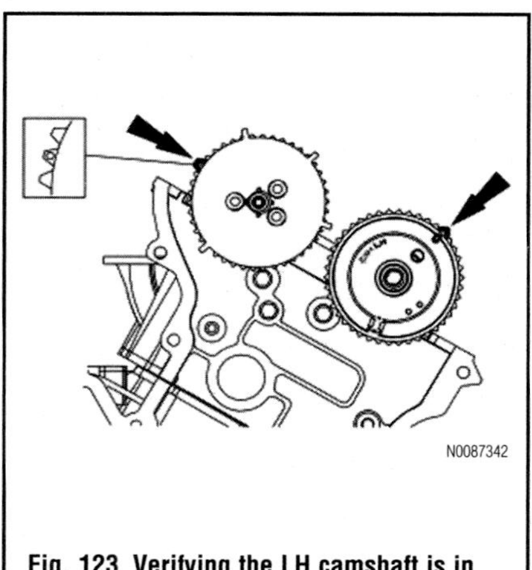

Fig. 123 Verifying the LH camshaft is in the neutral position

➡The camshafts must be in the neutral position before removing the bearing caps or damage to the engine may occur.

6. Verify the LH camshafts are in the neutral position.

➡Do not allow the camshaft to rotate from the neutral position while removing the camshaft phaser and sprocket or damage to the engine may occur.

➡Install a 3/8-in ratchet and extension into the D-slot on the rear of the intake camshaft to hold the camshaft in place for removal of the camshaft phaser and sprocket bolts.

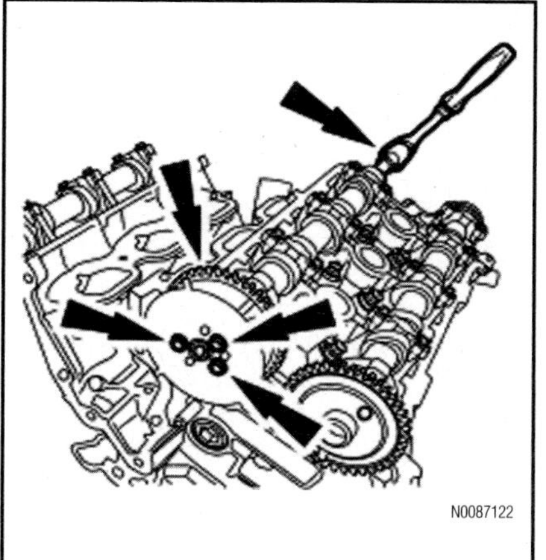

Fig. 124 Removing the 3 bolts and the LH camshaft phaser and sprocket

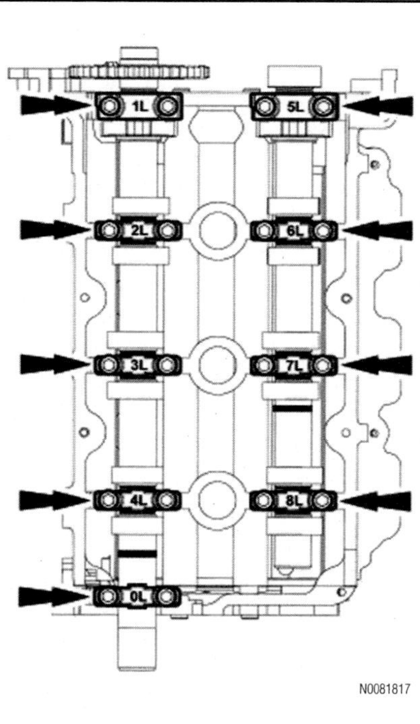

Fig. 125 Marking the camshaft bearing cap position and orientation

7. Remove the 3 bolts and the LH camshaft phaser and sprocket.

➡Cylinder head camshaft bearing caps must be assembled in their original positions. Some engines have factory markings on the camshaft bearing caps (as shown in illustration). Engines that do not have the factory markings must be marked for correct position and orientation prior to removal. Failure to install the camshaft bearing caps in their original positions may result in severe engine damage.

8. If necessary, mark the camshaft bearing cap position and orientation.

➡After loosening all of the camshaft bearing cap bolts, remove the camshaft bearing thrust caps (1L and 5L) first, or damage to the thrust caps may occur.

➡Make sure the camshaft bearing caps are marked as instructed in the previous step.

9. Loosen the bolts evenly in the sequence shown.
   a. Remove the camshaft bearing thrust caps (1L and 5L).
   b. Remove the remaining camshaft bearing caps.

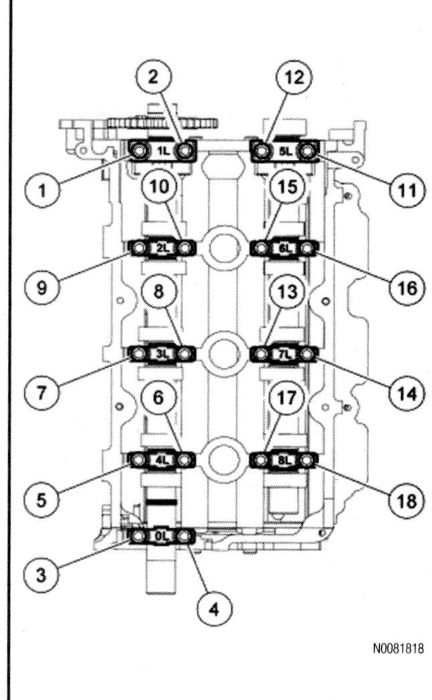

Fig. 126 Identifying the bolt loosening sequence

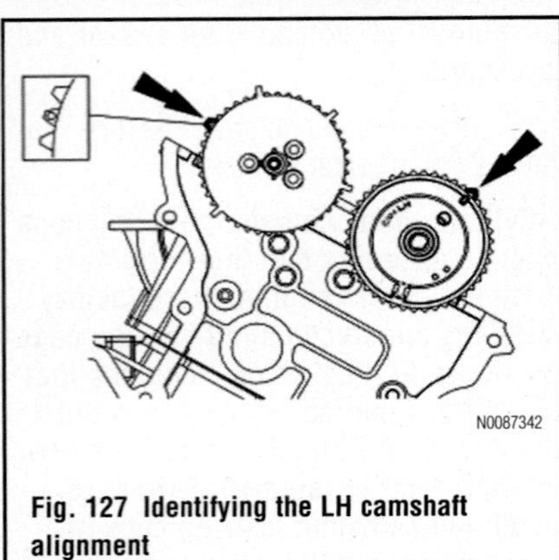

Fig. 127 Identifying the LH camshaft alignment

c. Remove the camshafts from the cylinder head.

To install:

10. Position the camshaft phaser and sprocket onto the intake camshaft.
  a. Install the 3 bolts finger-tight.
11. Lubricate the LH camshafts with clean engine oil and carefully position the camshafts onto the cylinder head.
  a. Align the LH camshafts.

➡Cylinder head camshaft journal caps and cylinder heads are numbered to verify that they are assembled in their original positions. If not reassembled in their original positions, severe engine damage may occur.

➡Do not install the camshaft journal thrust caps until all of the camshaft bearing caps have been installed or damage to the thrust caps can occur.

12. Lubricate the bearing surfaces of the LH camshaft bearing caps with clean engine oil and install the bearing caps.
  a. Loosely install the bolts.
13. Lubricate the bearing surfaces of the LH camshaft bearing thrust caps with clean engine oil and install the bearing thrust caps.
  a. Loosely install the bolts.

➡Make sure to tighten the camshaft bearing cap bolts in sequence in 2 stages.

14. Tighten the LH camshaft bearing cap bolts in the sequence shown in 2 stages.
  a. Stage 1: Tighten to 89 inch lbs. (10 Nm).
  b. Stage 2: Individually loosen and then tighten each camshaft bearing cap to 89 inch lbs. (10 Nm).

➡Do not allow the camshaft to rotate from the neutral position while tightening the camshaft phaser and sprocket bolts or damage to the engine may occur.

➡Install a 3/8-in ratchet and extension into the D-slot on the rear of the intake camshaft to hold the camshaft in place for tightening of the camshaft phaser and sprocket bolts.

15. Tighten the 3 LH camshaft phaser and sprocket bolts to 13 ft. lbs. (18 Nm).

➡Clean the sealing surfaces with metal surface prep before installing a new press-in-place gasket.

16. Install the camshaft oil seal retainer and the 2 bolts. Tighten to 89 inch lbs. (10 Nm).

➡Lubricate the camshaft oil seal with clean engine oil.

17. Using the Camshaft Oil Seal Installer, Camshaft Oil Seal Protector and the Power Steering Pump Pulley Installer, install the camshaft oil seal.

➡Failure to use the correct special tools, will result in damage to the coolant pump pulley and/or special tools.

18. Install the Camshaft Pulley Installer in the camshaft as shown in the illustration.
  a. Adjust the collar on the Camshaft Pulley Installer screw to get the best thread engagement in the rear of the camshaft.

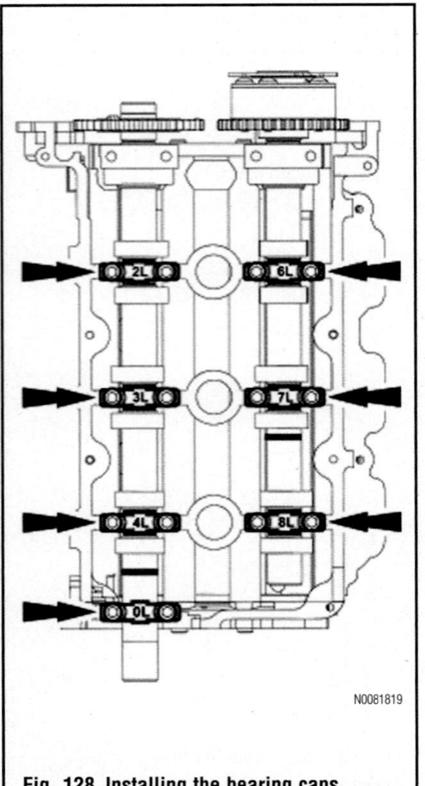

Fig. 128 Installing the bearing caps

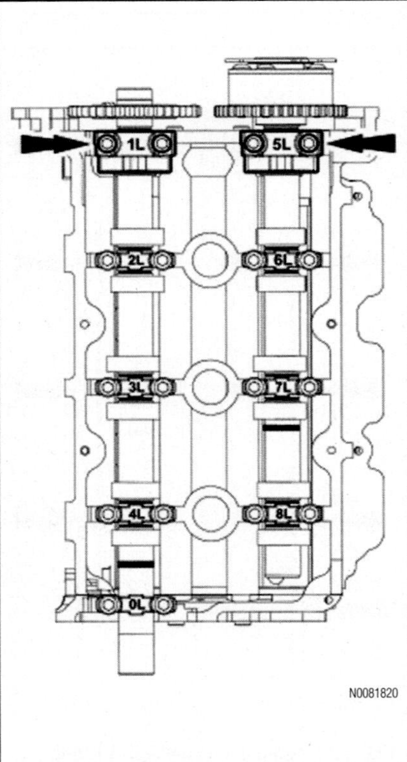

Fig. 129 Installing the bearing thrust caps

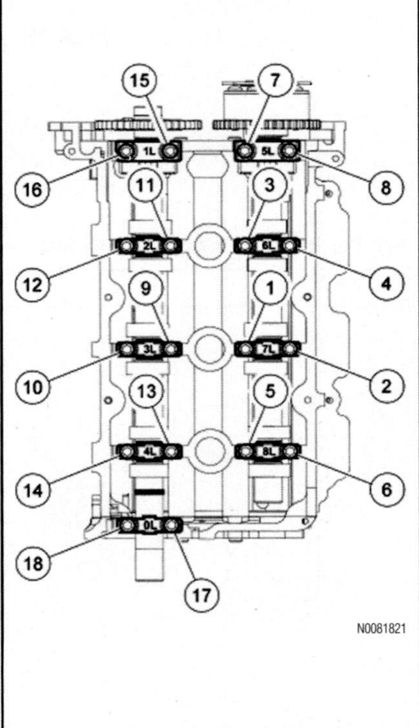

Fig. 130 Identifying the bearing cap bolt tightening sequence

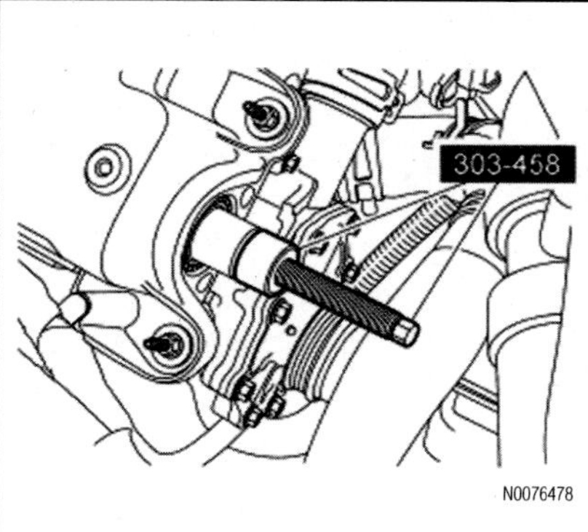

Fig. 131 Installing the camshaft pulley installer in the camshaft

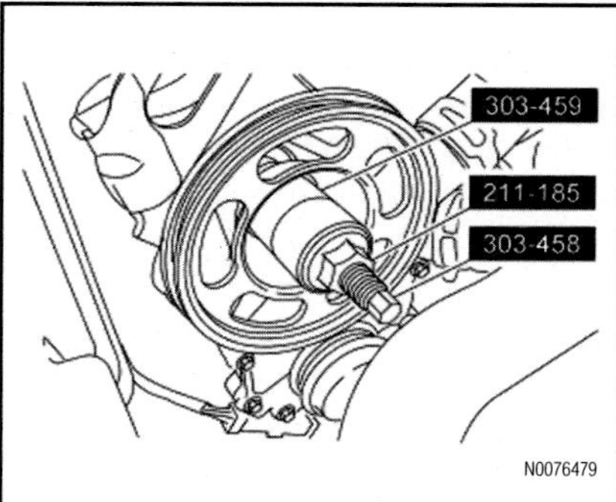

Fig. 132 Installing a new service coolant pump pulley

➡Failure to use the correct special tools, will result in damage to the coolant pump pulley and/or special tools.

➡Only the roller collared nut from the Power Steering Pump Pulley Installer (211-185) is used on Camshaft Pulley Installer (303-458).

19. Position the coolant pump pulley over the previously installed Camshaft Pulley Installer and on the end of the camshaft. Install the Camshaft Pulley Installer, Power Steering Pump Pulley Installer and the Water Pump Pulley Spacer.
    a. Using the Camshaft Pulley Installer, Power Steering Pump Pulley Installer and the Water Pump Pulley Spacer, install a new service coolant pump pulley flush with the end of the camshaft.
20. Install the timing drive components.
21. Install the coolant pump belt.

RH Side

See Figures 133 through 139.

1. Remove the timing drive components.

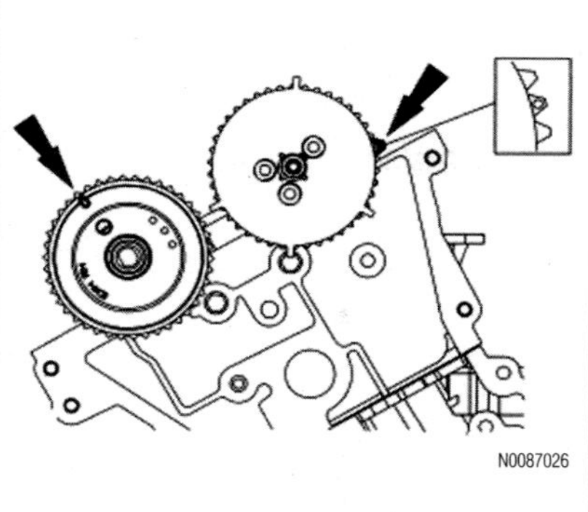

Fig. 133 Verifying the RH camshafts are in the neutral position

➡The camshafts must be in the neutral position before removing the bearing caps or damage to the engine may occur.

2. Verify the RH camshafts are in the neutral position.

➡Do not allow the camshaft to rotate from the neutral position while removing the camshaft phaser and sprocket or damage to the engine may occur.

➡Install a 3/8-in ratchet and extension into the D-slot on the rear of the intake camshaft to hold the camshaft in place for removal of the camshaft phaser and sprocket bolts.

3. Remove the 3 bolts and the RH camshaft phaser and sprocket.

➡Cylinder head camshaft bearing caps must be assembled in their original positions. Some engines have factory markings on the camshaft bearing caps. Engines that do not have the factory markings must be marked for correct position and orientation prior to removal. Failure to install the camshaft bearing caps in their original positions may result in severe engine damage.

4. If necessary, mark the camshaft bearing cap position and orientation.

➡After loosening all of the camshaft bearing cap bolts, remove the camshaft bearing thrust caps (5R and 1R) first, or damage to the thrust caps may occur.

➡Make sure the camshaft bearing caps are marked as instructed in the previous step.

5. Loosen the bolts evenly in the sequence shown.
    a. Remove the camshaft bearing thrust caps (5R and 1R).
    b. Remove the remaining camshaft bearing caps.
    c. Remove the camshafts from the cylinder head.

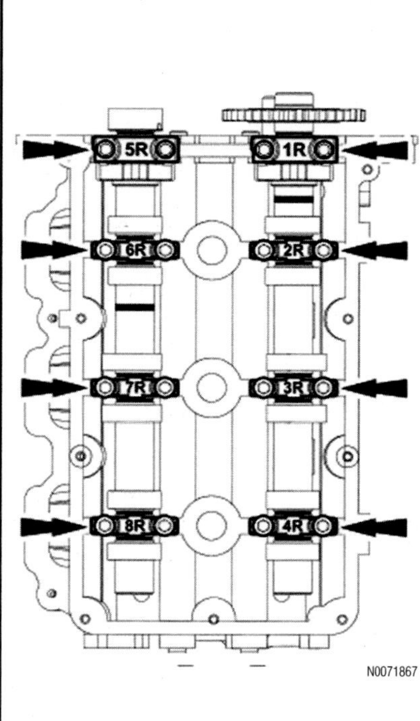

Fig. 134 Marking the camshaft bearing cap position and orientation

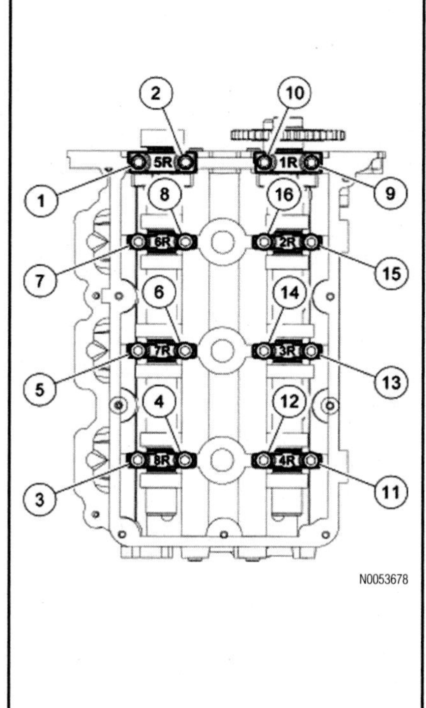

Fig. 135 Identifying the bolt loosening sequence

To install:

6. Position the RH camshaft phaser and sprocket onto the intake camshaft.
   a. Install the 3 bolts finger-tight.
7. Lubricate the RH camshafts with clean engine oil and carefully position the camshafts onto the cylinder head.
8. Align the RH camshafts as shown.

➡Cylinder head camshaft journal caps and cylinder heads are numbered to verify that they are assembled in their original positions. If not reassembled in their original positions, severe engine damage may occur.

➡Do not install the camshaft journal thrust caps until all of the camshaft bearing caps have been installed or damage to the thrust caps can occur.

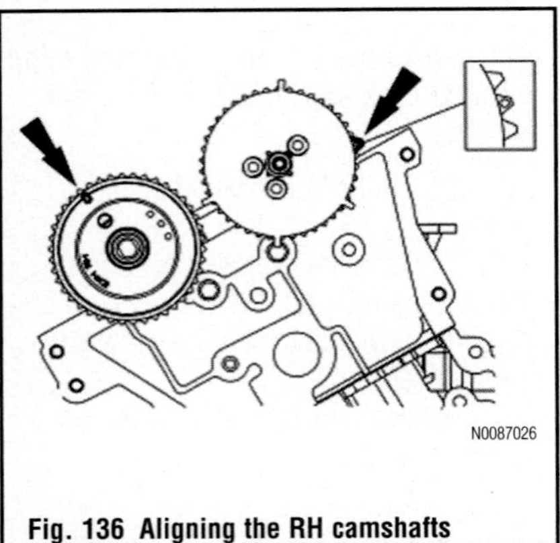

Fig. 136 Aligning the RH camshafts

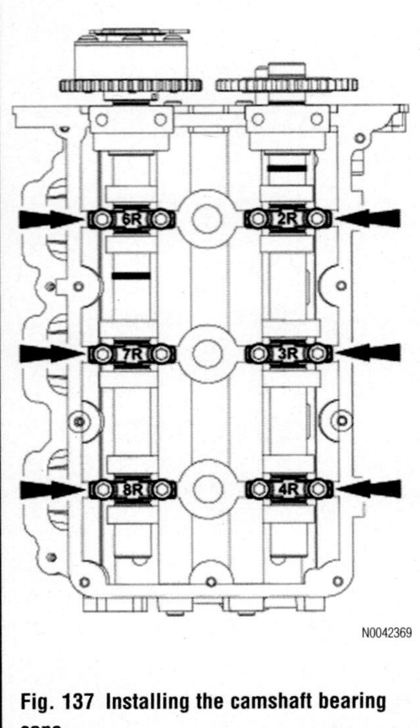

Fig. 137 Installing the camshaft bearing caps

➡Lubricate the bearing surfaces of the RH camshaft bearing caps with clean engine oil.

9. Install the camshaft bearing caps.
   a. Loosely install the bolts.

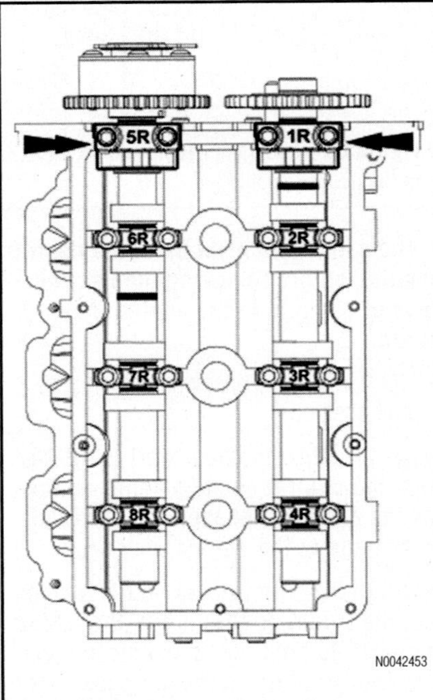

Fig. 138 Installing the camshaft bearing thrust caps

Fig. 139 Identifying the camshaft bearing cap bolt tightening sequence

➡Lubricate the bearing surfaces of the RH camshaft bearing thrust caps with clean engine oil.

10. Install the camshaft bearing thrust caps.
    a. Loosely install the bolts.

➡Make sure to tighten the camshaft bearing cap bolts in sequence in 2 stages.

11. Tighten the RH camshaft bearing cap bolts in the sequence shown in 2 stages.
    a. Stage 1: Tighten to 89 inch lbs. (10 Nm).
    b. Stage 2: Individually loosen and then tighten each camshaft bearing cap to 89 inch lbs. (10 Nm).

➡Do not allow the camshaft to rotate from the neutral position while tightening the camshaft phaser and sprocket bolts or damage to the engine may occur.

➡Install a 3/8-in ratchet and extension into the D-slot on the rear of the intake camshaft to hold the camshaft in place for tightening of the camshaft phaser and sprocket bolts.

12. Tighten the 3 RH camshaft phaser and sprocket bolts to 13 ft. lbs. (18 Nm).
13. Install the timing drive components.

3.5L Engine

See Figures 140 through 158.

➡During engine repair procedures, cleanliness is extremely important. Any foreign material, including any material created while cleaning gasket surfaces, that enters the oil passages, coolant passages or the oil pan can cause engine failure.

All camshafts

1. Remove the engine front cover.

Engines equipped with early build RH timing chain guides

2. Rotate the crankshaft clockwise and align the timing marks on the Variable Camshaft Timing (VCT) assemblies as shown.

Engines equipped with late build/replacement RH timing chain guides

3. Rotate the crankshaft clockwise and align the timing marks on the VCT assemblies as shown.

All vehicles

➡The Camshaft Holding Tool will hold the camshafts in the Top Dead Center (TDC) position.

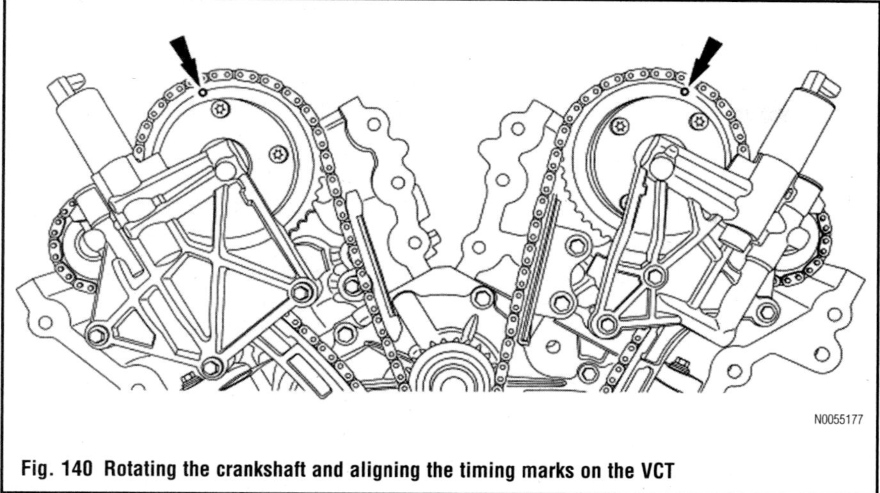

Fig. 140 Rotating the crankshaft and aligning the timing marks on the VCT

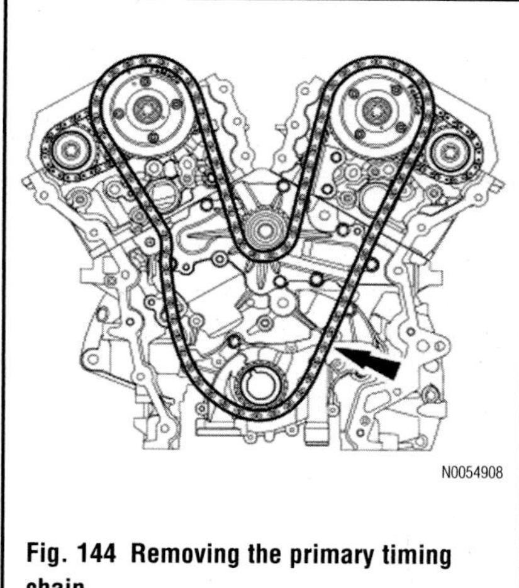

Fig. 144 Removing the primary timing chain

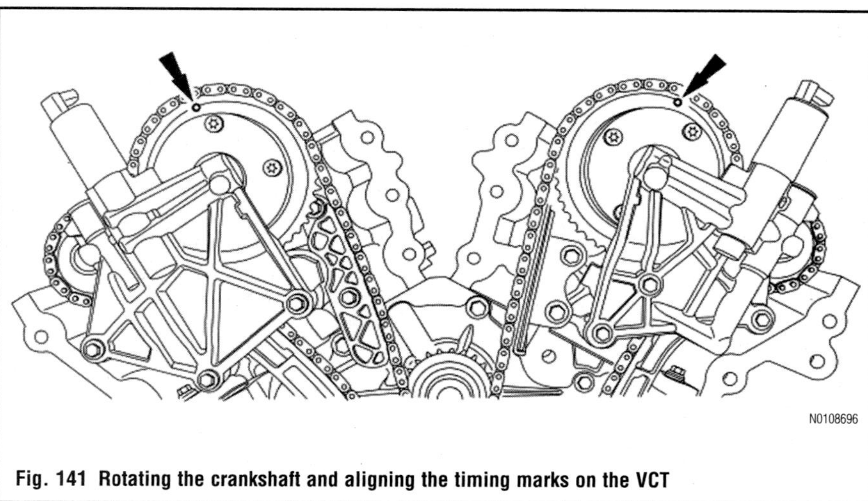

Fig. 141 Rotating the crankshaft and aligning the timing marks on the VCT

4. Install the Camshaft Holding Tool onto the flats of the LH camshafts.

➡The Camshaft Holding Tool will hold the camshafts in the TDC position.

5. Install the Camshaft Holding Tool onto the flats of the RH camshafts.
6. Remove the 3 bolts and the RH VCT housing.
7. Remove the 3 bolts and the LH VCT housing.
8. Remove the 2 bolts and the primary timing chain tensioner.
9. Remove the primary timing chain tensioner arm.
10. Remove the 2 bolts and the lower LH primary timing chain guide.
11. Remove the primary timing chain.

LH camshafts

12. Compress the LH secondary timing chain tensioner and install a suitable lock-pin to retain the tensioner in the collapsed position.

➡The VCT bolt and the exhaust camshaft bolt must be discarded and new ones installed. However, the exhaust camshaft washer is reusable.

13. Remove and discard the LH VCT assembly bolt and the LH exhaust camshaft sprocket bolt.
    a. Remove the LH VCT assembly, secondary timing chain and the LH exhaust camshaft sprocket as an assembly.

➡When the Camshaft Holding Tool is removed, valve spring pressure will rotate the LH camshafts approximately 3 degrees to a neutral position.

14. Remove the Camshaft Holding Tool from the LH camshafts.

➡The camshafts must remain in the neutral position during removal or engine damage may occur.

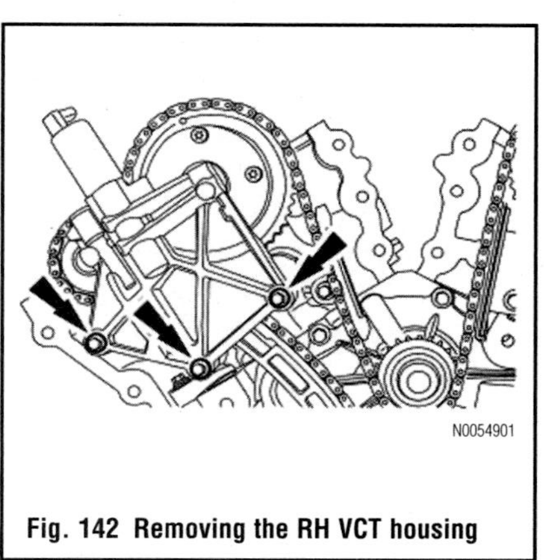

Fig. 142 Removing the RH VCT housing

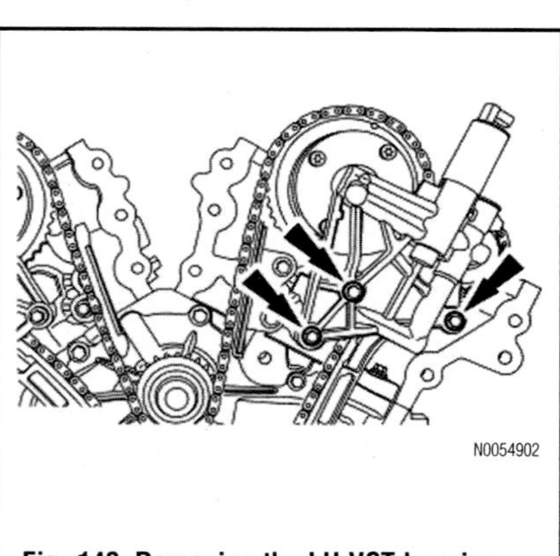

Fig. 143 Removing the LH VCT housing

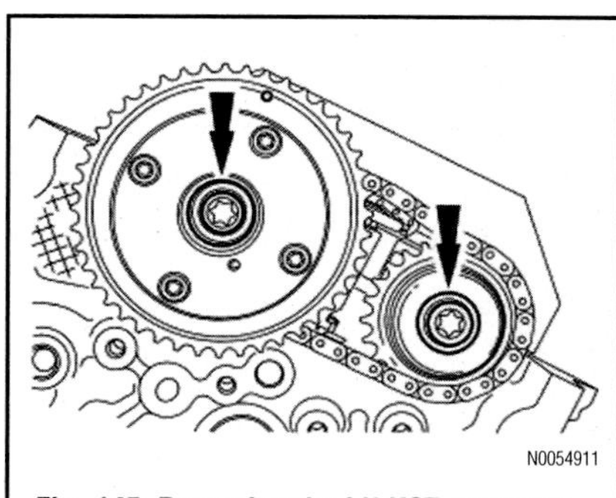

Fig. 145 Removing the LH VCT assembly, secondary timing chain and the LH exhaust camshaft sprocket

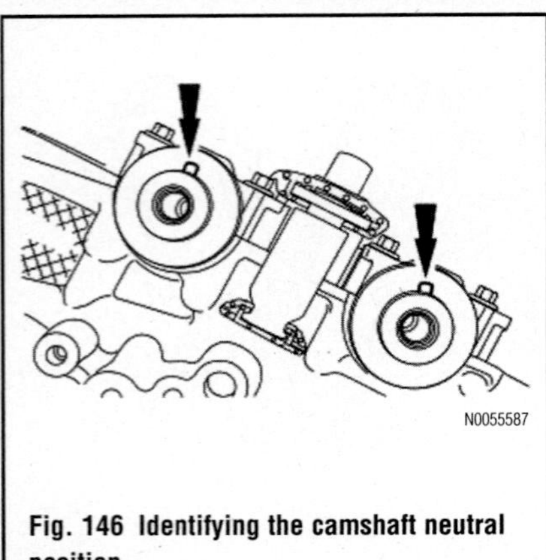

Fig. 146 Identifying the camshaft neutral position

15. Verify the LH camshafts are in the neutral position.

➡**Cylinder head camshaft bearing caps are numbered to verify that they are assembled in their original positions.**

16. Remove the bolts and the LH camshaft bearing caps.
17. Remove the LH camshafts.

RH camshafts

18. Compress the RH secondary timing chain tensioner and install a suitable lock-pin to retain the tensioner in the collapsed position.

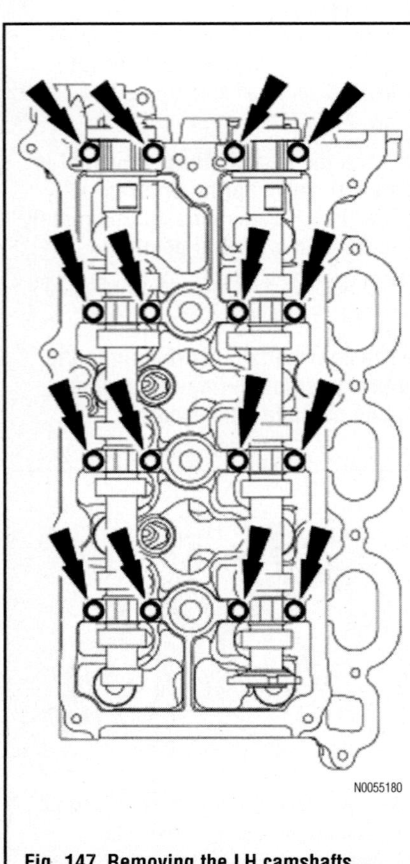

Fig. 147 Removing the LH camshafts

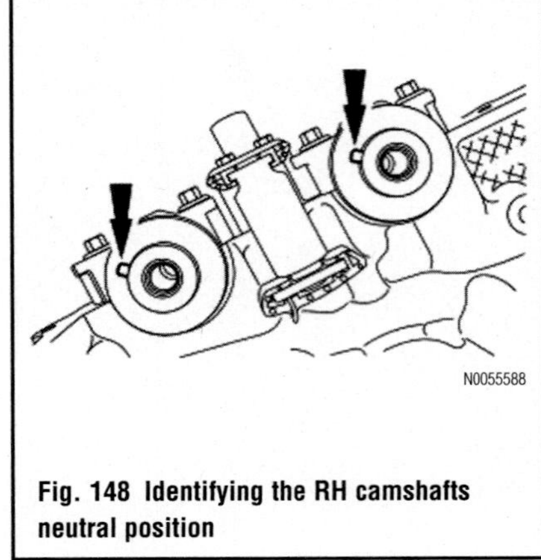

Fig. 148 Identifying the RH camshafts neutral position

➡**The VCT bolt and the exhaust camshaft bolt must be discarded and new ones installed. However, the exhaust camshaft washer is reusable.**

19. Remove and discard the RH VCT assembly bolt and the RH exhaust camshaft sprocket bolt.
20. Remove the RH VCT assembly, secondary timing chain and the RH exhaust camshaft sprocket as an assembly.
21. Remove the Camshaft Holding Tool from the RH camshafts.

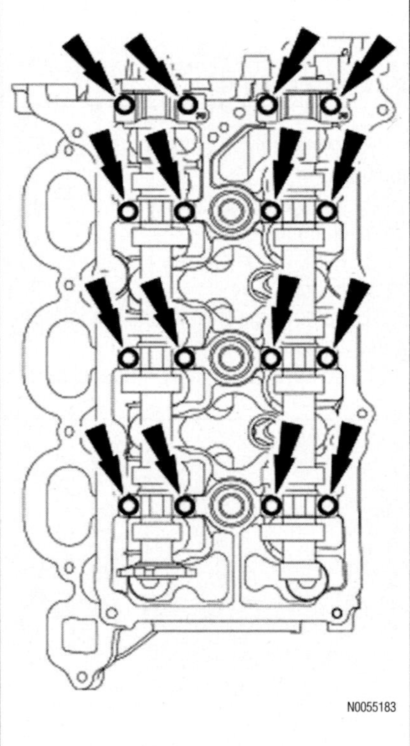

Fig. 149 Removing the RH camshafts

➡**The camshafts must remain in the neutral position during removal or engine damage may occur.**

22. Rotate the RH camshafts counterclockwise to the neutral position.

➡**Cylinder head camshaft bearing caps are numbered to verify that they are assembled in their original positions.**

23. Remove the bolts and the RH camshaft bearing caps.
24. Remove the RH camshafts.

To install:

All camshafts

➡**On early build engines, the timing chain rides on the inner side of the RH timing chain guide. Late build engines are equipped with a different design RH timing chain guide that requires the timing chain to ride on the outer side of the RH timing chain guide. For service, all replacement RH timing chain guides will be the late build design.**

➡**The crankshaft must remain in the freewheeling position (crankshaft dowel pin at 9 o'clock) until after the camshafts are installed and the valve clearance is checked/adjusted. Do not turn the crankshaft until instructed to do so. Failure to follow this process will result in severe engine damage.**

25. Rotate the crankshaft counterclockwise until the crankshaft dowel pin is in the 9 o'clock position.

LH camshafts

➡**The camshafts must remain in the neutral position during installation or engine damage may occur.**

➡**Coat the camshafts with clean engine oil prior to installation.**

26. Position the camshafts onto the LH cylinder head in the neutral position.

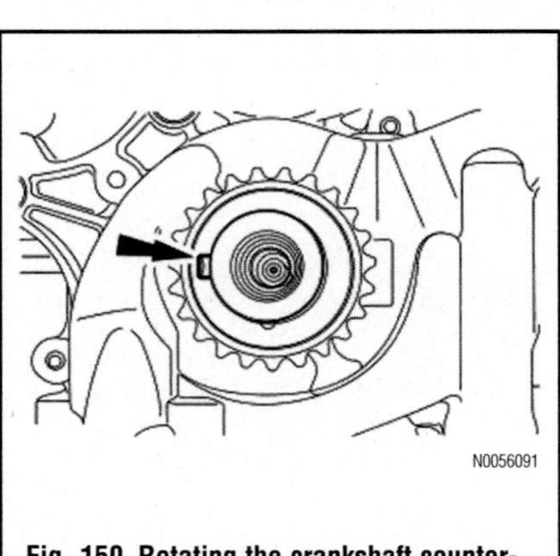

Fig. 150 Rotating the crankshaft counterclockwise to the 9 o'clock position

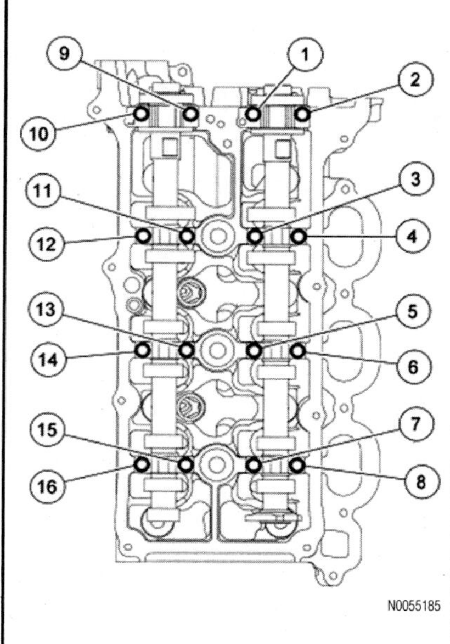

Fig. 151 Identifying the camshaft cap bolt installation sequence

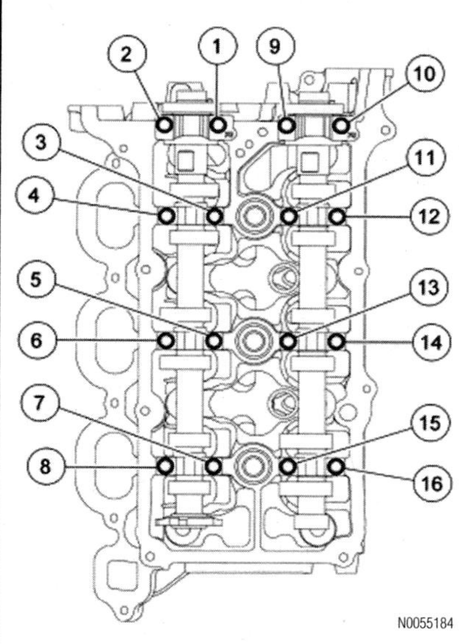

Fig. 152 Identifying the camshaft cap bolt installation sequence

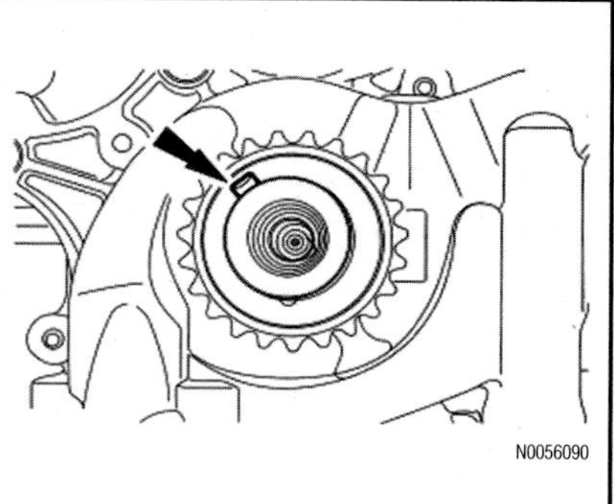

Fig. 153 Rotating the crankshaft to the 11 o'clock position

➡Cylinder head camshaft bearing caps are numbered to verify that they are assembled in their original positions.

27. Install the 8 camshaft caps and the 16 bolts.
    a. Tighten in the sequence shown to 89 inch lbs. (10 Nm).

RH camshafts

➡The camshafts must remain in the neutral position during installation or engine damage may occur.

➡Coat the camshafts with clean engine oil prior to installation.

28. Position the camshafts onto the RH cylinder head in the neutral position.

➡Cylinder head camshaft bearing caps are numbered to verify that they are assembled in their original positions.

29. Install the 8 camshaft caps and the 16 bolts.
    a. Tighten in the sequence shown to 89 inch lbs. (10 Nm).

All camshafts

➡If any components are installed new, the engine valve clearance must be checked/adjusted or engine damage can occur.

➡Use a camshaft sprocket bolt to turn the camshafts.

30. Using a feeler gauge, confirm that the valve tappet clearances are within specification. If valve tappet clearances are not within specification, the clearance must be adjusted by installing new valve tappet(s) of the correct size.

LH camshafts

➡Use a camshaft sprocket bolt to turn the camshafts.

31. Rotate the LH camshafts to the Top Dead Center (TDC) position and install the Camshaft Holding Tool on the flats of the camshafts.
32. Assemble the LH Variable Camshaft Timing (VCT) assembly, the LH exhaust camshaft sprocket and the LH secondary timing chain.
    a. Align the colored links with the timing marks.
33. Position the LH secondary timing assembly onto the camshafts.
34. Install 2 new bolts and the original washer. Tighten in 4 stages.
    a. Stage 1: Tighten to 30 ft. lbs. (40 Nm).
    b. Stage 2: Loosen one full turn.
    c. Stage 3: Tighten to 89 inch lbs. (10 Nm).
    d. Stage 4: Tighten 90 degrees.
35. Remove the lockpin from the LH secondary timing chain tensioner.

RH camshafts

➡Use a camshaft sprocket bolt to turn the camshafts.

36. Rotate the RH camshafts to the TDC position and install the Camshaft Holding Tool on the flats of the camshafts.
37. Assemble the RH VCT assembly, the RH exhaust camshaft sprocket and the RH secondary timing chain.
    a. Align the colored links with the timing marks.
38. Position the RH secondary timing assembly onto the camshafts.
39. Install 2 new bolts and the original washer. Tighten in 4 stages.
    a. Stage 1: Tighten to 30 ft. lbs. (40 Nm).
    b. Stage 2: Loosen one full turn.
    c. Stage 3: Tighten to 89 inch lbs. (10 Nm).
    d. Stage 4: Tighten 90 degrees.
40. Remove the lockpin from the RH secondary timing chain tensioner.

All camshafts

41. Rotate the crankshaft clockwise 60 degrees to the TDC position (crankshaft dowel pin at 11 o'clock).
42. Install the primary timing chain with the colored links aligned with the timing marks on the VCT assemblies and the crankshaft sprocket.

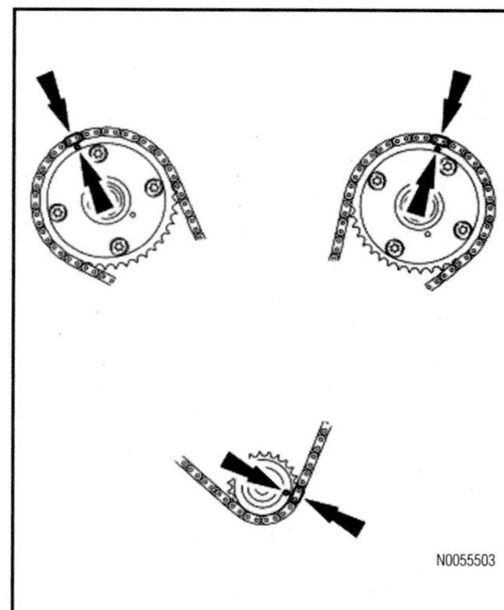

Fig. 154 Installing the primary timing chain on the VCT assemblies and the crankshaft sprocket

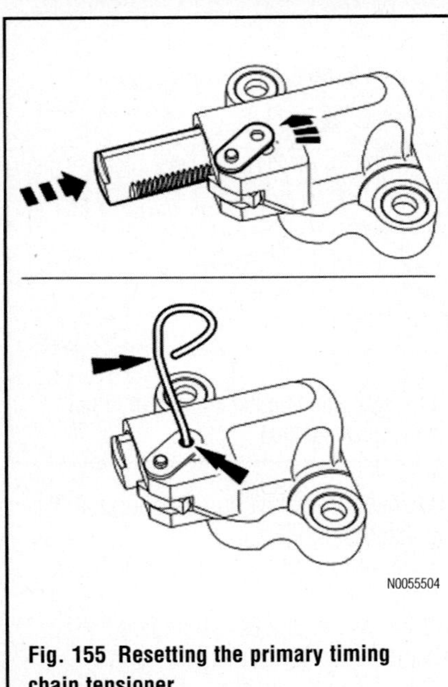

Fig. 155 Resetting the primary timing chain tensioner

43. Install the lower LH primary timing chain guide and the 2 bolts.
   a. Tighten to 89 inch lbs. (10 Nm).
44. Install the primary timing chain tensioner arm.
45. Reset the primary timing chain tensioner.
   a. Rotate the lever counterclockwise.
   b. Using a soft-jawed vise, compress the plunger.
   c. Align the hole in the lever with the hole in the tensioner housing.
   d. Install a suitable lockpin.

➡It may be necessary to rotate the crankshaft slightly to remove slack from the timing chain and install the tensioner.

Fig. 156 Checking alignment of timing marks

Fig. 157 Identifying the LH VCT housing bolt installation sequence

46. Install the primary tensioner and the 2 bolts.
   a. Tighten to 89 inch lbs. (10 Nm).
   b. Remove the lockpin.
47. As a post-check, verify correct alignment of all timing marks.
48. Inspect the VCT housing seals for damage and replace as necessary.

➡Make sure the dowels on the Variable Camshaft Timing (VCT) housing are fully engaged in the cylinder head prior to tightening the bolts. Failure to follow this process will result in severe engine damage.

49. Install the LH VCT housing and the 3 bolts.
   a. Tighten in the sequence shown to 89 inch lbs. (10 Nm).

➡Make sure the dowels on the Variable Camshaft Timing (VCT) housing are fully engaged in the cylinder head prior to tightening the bolts. Failure to follow this process will result in severe engine damage.

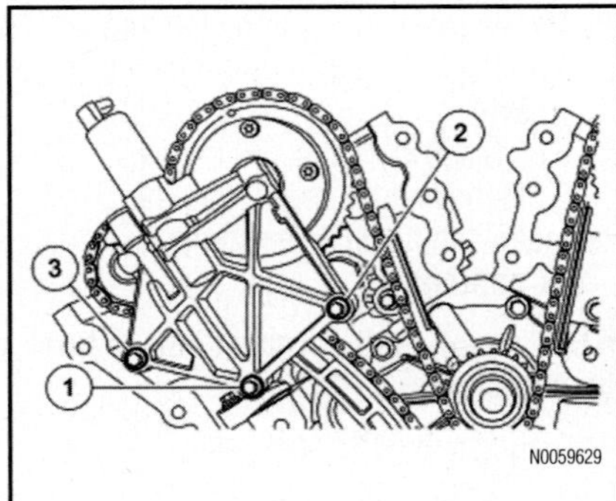

Fig. 158 Identifying the RH VCT housing bolt tightening sequence

50. Install the RH VCT housing and the 3 bolts.
   a. Tighten in the sequence shown to 89 inch lbs. (10 Nm).
51. Install the engine front cover.

CATALYTIC CONVERTER

REMOVAL & INSTALLATION

3.0L Engine

LH Side

1. With the vehicle in NEUTRAL, position it on a hoist.
2. Remove the oil level indicator and tube.
3. Disconnect the Heated Oxygen Sensor (HO2S) and the Catalyst Monitor Sensor (CMS) electrical connectors.
4. Remove the 2 LH catalytic converter-to-exhaust flexible pipe nuts.
   a. Discard the gasket and the 2 nuts.
5. Remove the 4 bolts and the LH catalytic converter manifold shield.
6. Remove the 2 LH catalytic converter manifold shield bracket bolts and the shield bracket.
7. Remove the 2 LH catalytic converter manifold bracket bolts and bracket.
8. Remove the 6 nuts and the LH catalytic converter manifold.
   a. Discard the 6 LH catalytic converter manifold nuts and the gasket.
9. Remove and discard the 6 LH catalytic converter manifold studs.
10. Clean and inspect the catalytic converter manifold.

To install:

11. Install the 6 new LH catalytic converter manifold studs.
   a. Tighten to 97 inch lbs. (11 Nm).
12. Position a new LH catalytic converter manifold gasket on the studs.
13. Position the LH catalytic converter manifold and finger-tighten the 6 new nuts.
14. Install a new gasket and finger-tighten 2 new nuts at the LH catalytic converter-to-exhaust flexible pipe.

➡Failure to tighten the catalytic converter manifold nuts to specification before installing the converter bracket bolts will cause the converter to develop an exhaust leak.

➡Failure to tighten the catalytic converter manifold nuts to specification a second time will cause the converter to develop an exhaust leak.

➡Make sure to tighten the nuts in the sequence shown in 2 stages.

15. Position the LH catalytic converter manifold and tighten the 6 new nuts in the sequence shown, in 2 stages.
   a. Stage 1: Tighten to 15 ft. lbs. (20 Nm).
   b. Stage 2: Tighten to 15 ft. lbs. (20 Nm).
16. Install the shield bracket and the 2 LH catalytic converter manifold shield bracket bolts.
   a. Tighten to 15 ft. lbs. (20 Nm).
17. Install the LH catalytic converter manifold bracket and 2 bolts.
   a. To install, tighten to 15 ft. lbs. (20 Nm).
18. Position the LH catalytic converter manifold shield and install the 4 bolts.
   a. Tighten to 89 inch lbs. (10 Nm).
19. Tighten the 2 new LH catalytic converter-to-exhaust flexible pipe nuts.
   a. Tighten to 30 ft. lbs. (40 Nm).
20. Connect the HO2S and the CMS electrical connectors.
21. Install the oil level indicator and tube.

RH Side

➡Always install new fasteners and gaskets as indicated. Clean flange faces prior to new gasket installation to make sure of proper sealing.

1. With the vehicle in NEUTRAL, position it on a hoist.
2. Remove the exhaust flexible pipe.
3. Remove the intermediate shaft.
4. Remove the Heated Oxygen Sensor (HO2S) and Catalyst Monitor Sensor (CMS).
5. Remove the roll restrictor bolt and rotate the engine forward.
6. Remove the 5 bolts and position aside the catalytic converter manifold shield.
7. Remove the bolt, 2 nuts and the heat shield brackets.
8. Remove the 3 nuts and the RH catalytic converter.
   a. Discard the 3 RH catalytic converter nuts and gasket.
9. Remove and discard the 3 RH catalytic converter-to-manifold studs.

➡Prior to Installation, Inspect the HO2S and the CMS wiring harness for damage.

To install:

10. To install, reverse the removal procedure.
11. Install a new gasket, nuts and studs as indicated.
12. Tighten the 3 RH catalytic converter to manifold studs to 18 ft. lbs. (25 Nm).
13. Tighten the 3 RH catalytic converter nuts to 30 ft. lbs. (40 Nm).
14. Tighten the 2 heat shield bracket nuts 15 ft. lbs. (20 Nm).
15. Tighten the 5 catalytic converter manifold shield bolt 89 inch lbs. (10 Nm).
16. Tighten the roll restrictor bolt to 66 ft. lbs. (90 Nm).

3.5L Engine

LH Side

➡Always install new fasteners and gaskets as indicated. Clean flange faces prior to new gasket installation to make sure of proper sealing.

1. With the vehicle in NEUTRAL, position it on a hoist.
2. Disconnect the Catalyst Monitor Sensor (CMS) electrical connector.
3. Remove the exhaust Y-pipe.
4. Remove the 2 catalytic converter support bracket-to-transmission bolts.
5. Remove the 4 nuts and the LH catalytic converter.
   a. Discard the 4 LH catalytic converter-to-exhaust manifold nuts and gasket.

To install:

6. To install, reverse the removal procedure.
7. Install a new gasket, nuts and studs as indicated.
8. Tighten the catalytic converter to exhaust manifold nuts to 30 ft. lbs. (40 Nm).
9. Tighten the 2 catalytic converter support bracket to transmission bolts to 35 ft. lbs. (48 Nm).

RH Side

All vehicles

➡Always install new fasteners and gaskets as indicated. Clean flange faces prior to new gasket installation to make sure of proper sealing.

1. With the vehicle in NEUTRAL, position it on a hoist.
2. Remove the exhaust Y-pipe.

All-Wheel Drive (AWD) vehicles

3. Remove the intermediate shaft.

All vehicles

4. Remove the 2 bolts and the power steering gear shield.
5. Remove the roll restrictor bolt and rotate the engine forward.
6. Disconnect the Catalyst Monitor Sensor (CMS) electrical connector.
7. Remove the 2 bracket-to-RH catalytic converter bolts.
8. Remove the 4 nuts and the RH catalytic converter.
   a. Discard the 4 RH catalytic converter-to-exhaust manifold nuts and gasket.

➡Prior to Installation, Inspect the CMS wiring harness for damage.

To install:

9. To install, reverse the removal procedure.
10. Install a new gasket, nuts and studs as indicated.
11. Tighten the catalytic converter to exhaust manifold nuts to 30 ft. lbs. (40 Nm).
12. Tighten the 2 bracket to RH catalytic converter bolts to 15 ft. lbs. (20 Nm).
13. Tighten the roll restrictor bolt to 66 ft. lbs. (90 Nm).
14. Tighten the 2 power steering shield bolts to 11 ft. lbs. (15 Nm).

Manifold, Hybrid

See Figure 159.

➡Always install new fasteners and gaskets as indicated. Clean flange faces prior to new gasket installation to make sure of proper sealing.

1. With the vehicle in NEUTRAL, position it on a hoist.
2. Disconnect the Heated Oxygen Sensor (HO2S) and the Catalyst Monitor Sensor (CMS) electrical connectors.
3. Remove the 2 catalytic converter manifold-to-exhaust flexible pipe nuts.
   a. Discard the gasket and the 2 nuts.
4. Remove the 6 catalytic converter manifold shield bolts and the heat shield.
5. Remove the 2 catalytic converter manifold shield bracket bolts and the bracket.
6. Loosen the 2 catalytic converter manifold bracket bolts.
7. Remove the 7 catalytic converter manifold nuts and remove the converter from the vehicle.
   a. Discard the 7 nuts and the gasket.
8. Remove and discard the 7 catalytic converter manifold studs.
9. Clean and inspect the catalytic converter manifold.

To install:

10. Install the 7 new catalytic converter manifold studs. Tighten to 13 ft. lbs. (17 Nm).
11. Position a new catalytic converter manifold gasket on the studs.

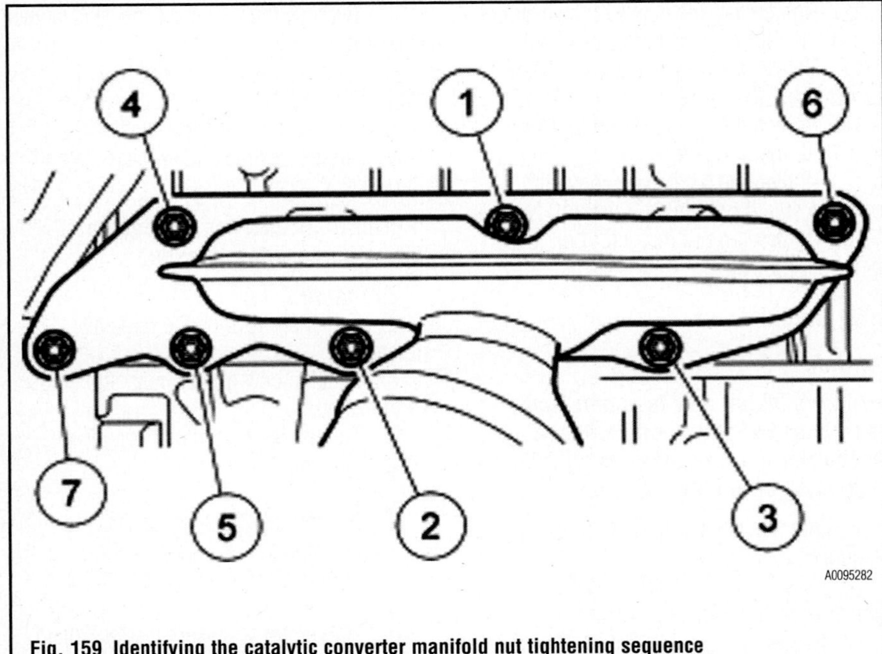

Fig. 159 Identifying the catalytic converter manifold nut tightening sequence

➡Failure to tighten the catalytic converter manifold nuts to specification before installing the converter bracket bolts will cause the converter to develop an exhaust leak.

➡Failure to tighten the catalytic converter manifold nuts to specification a second time will cause the converter to develop an exhaust leak.

➡Make sure to tighten the nuts in the following sequence in 2 stages.

12. Position the catalytic converter manifold and tighten the 7 new nuts in the sequence shown, in 2 stages.
    a. Stage 1: Tighten to 41 ft. lbs. (55 Nm).
    b. Stage 2: Tighten to 41 ft. lbs. (55 Nm).
13. Tighten the 2 catalytic converter manifold bracket bolts. Tighten to 15 ft. lbs. (20 Nm).
14. Install the 2 catalytic converter manifold shield bracket bolts and the bracket. Tighten to 15 ft. lbs. (20 Nm).
15. Position the catalytic converter manifold shield and install the 6 heat shield bolts. Tighten to 89 inch lbs. (10 Nm).
16. Install the exhaust flexible pipe to the catalytic converter.
17. Install a new gasket and nuts. Tighten to 30 ft. lbs. (40 Nm).
18. Connect the HO2S and the CMS electrical connectors.

CRANKSHAFT FRONT SEAL

REMOVAL & INSTALLATION

2.5L Engine

See Figures 160 through 162.

➡Do not loosen or remove the crankshaft pulley bolt without first installing the special tools as instructed in this procedure. The crankshaft pulley and the crankshaft timing sprocket are not keyed to the crankshaft. The crankshaft, the crankshaft sprocket and the pulley are fitted together by friction, using diamond washers between the flange faces on each part. For that reason, the crankshaft sprocket is also unfastened if the pulley bolt is loosened. Before any repair requiring loosening or removal of the crankshaft pulley bolt, the crankshaft and camshafts must be locked in place by the special service tools, otherwise severe engine damage can occur.

➡During engine repair procedures, cleanliness is extremely important. Any foreign material, including any material created while cleaning gasket surfaces, that enters the oil passages, coolant passages or the oil pan can cause engine failure.

1. Remove the crankshaft pulley.
    a. With the vehicle in NEUTRAL, position it on a hoist.
    b. Remove the front RH wheel and tire.
    c. If equipped, remove the 7 screws and the underbody cover.

➡Use care not to damage the engine front cover or the crankshaft when removing the seal.

2. Remove the accessory drive belt.
3. Remove the valve cover.

➡Failure to position the No. 1 piston at Top Dead Center (TDC) can result in damage to the engine. Turn the engine in the normal direction of rotation only.

    a. Using the crankshaft pulley bolt, turn the crankshaft clockwise to position the No. 1 piston at Top Dead Center (TDC).
    b. The hole in the crankshaft pulley should be in the 6 o'clock position.

➡The Camshaft Alignment Plate is for camshaft alignment only. Using this tool to prevent engine rotation can result in engine damage.

➡The camshaft timing slots are offset. If the Camshaft Alignment Plate cannot be installed, rotate the crankshaft one complete revolution clockwise to correctly position the camshafts.

    c. Install the Camshaft Alignment Plate in the slots on the rear of both camshafts.
    d. Remove the engine plug bolt.

➡The Crankshaft TDC Timing Peg will contact the crankshaft and prevent it

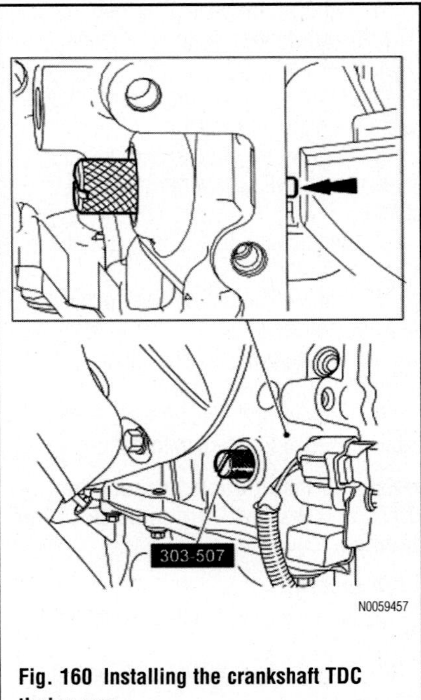

Fig. 160 Installing the crankshaft TDC timing peg

from turning past TDC . However, the crankshaft can still be rotated in the counterclockwise direction. The crankshaft must remain at the TDC position during the crankshaft pulley removal and installation.

e. Install the Crankshaft TDC Timing Peg.

➡**The crankshaft must remain in the Top Dead Center (TDC) position during removal of the pulley bolt or damage to the engine can occur. Therefore, the crankshaft pulley must be held in place with the Crankshaft Damper Holding Tool and the bolt should be removed using an air impact wrench (1/2-in drive minimum).**

➡**The crankshaft sprocket diamond washer may come off with the crankshaft pulley. The diamond washer must be replaced, remove and discard the diamond washer. If the diamond washer is not installed, engine damage may occur.**

f. Using the Crankshaft Damper Holding Tool and an air impact wrench, remove the crankshaft pulley.
g. Remove and discard the crankshaft pulley bolt and washer.
h. Remove the crankshaft pulley.
i. Remove the diamond washer and discard.
4. Using the Oil Seal Remover, remove the crankshaft front oil seal.

To install:

➡**Remove the through bolt from the Camshaft Front Oil Seal Installer.**

➡**Lubricate the oil seal with clean engine oil.**

5. Using the Camshaft Front Oil Seal Installer, install the crankshaft front oil seal.
6. Install the crankshaft pulley.

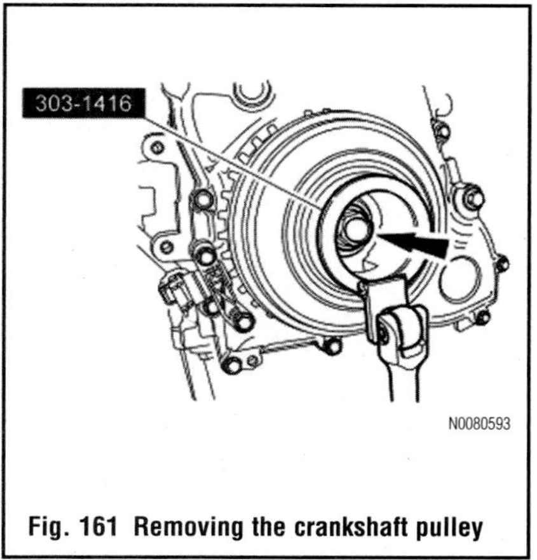

Fig. 161 Removing the crankshaft pulley

a. Install a new diamond washer.

➡**Do not install the crankshaft pulley bolt at this time.**

➡**Apply clean engine oil on the seal area before installing.**

b. Position the crankshaft pulley onto the crankshaft with the hole in the pulley at the 6 o'clock position.

➡**Only hand-tighten the 6 mm bolt or damage to the front cover can occur.**

➡**This step will correctly align the crankshaft pulley to the crankshaft.**

c. Install a standard 6 mm x 18 mm bolt through the crankshaft pulley and thread it into the front cover.

➡**The crankshaft must remain in the Top Dead Center (TDC) position during installation of the pulley bolt or damage to the engine can occur. Therefore, the crankshaft pulley must be held in place with the Crankshaft Damper Holding Tool and the bolt should be installed using hand tools only.**

➡**Do not reuse the crankshaft pulley bolt.**

d. Install a new crankshaft pulley bolt. Using the Crankshaft Damper Holding Tool to hold the crankshaft pulley in place, tighten the crankshaft pulley bolt in 2 stages:

- Stage 1: Tighten to 74 ft. lbs. (100 Nm)
- Stage 2: Tighten an additional 90 degrees (one-fourth turn)

e. Remove the 6 mm x 18 mm bolt.
f. Remove the Crankshaft TDC Timing Peg.
g. Remove the Camshaft Alignment Plate.

➡**Only turn the engine in the normal direction of rotation.**

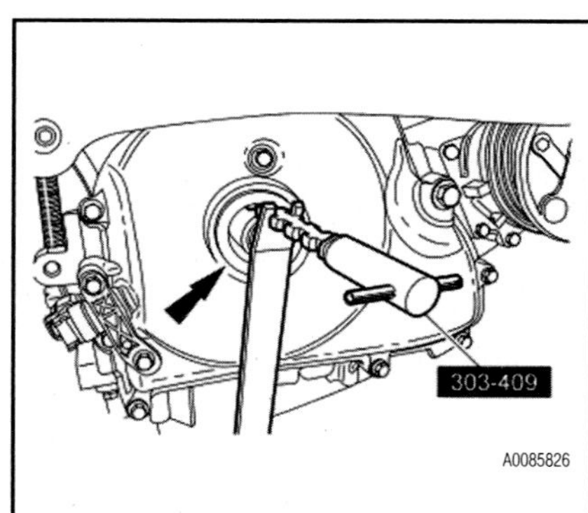

Fig. 162 Removing the crankshaft front oil seal

h. Turn the crankshaft clockwise one and three-fourths turns.
i. Install the Crankshaft TDC Timing Peg.

➡**Only turn the engine in the normal direction of rotation.**

j. Turn the crankshaft clockwise until the crankshaft contacts the Crankshaft TDC Timing Peg.

➡**Only hand-tighten the bolt or damage to the front cover can occur.**

k. Using the 6 mm x 18 mm bolt, check the position of the crankshaft pulley.
l. If it is not possible to install the bolt, the engine valve timing must be corrected by repeating this procedure.
m. Install the Camshaft Alignment Plate to check the position of the camshafts.
n. If it is not possible to install the Camshaft Alignment Plate, the engine valve timing must be corrected by repeating this procedure.
o. Remove the Camshaft Alignment Plate.
p. Remove the 6 mm x 18 mm bolt.
q. Remove the Crankshaft TDC Timing Peg.
r. Install the engine plug bolt. To install, tighten to 15 ft. lbs. (20 Nm).
s. If equipped, install the underbody cover and the 7 screws.
t. Install the accessory drive belt.
u. Install the valve cover.
v. Using the scan tool, perform the Misfire Monitor Neutral Profile Correction procedure, following the on-screen instructions.

2.5L Hybrid Engine

See Figure 163.

➡**Do not loosen or remove the crankshaft pulley bolt without first installing the special tools as instructed in this procedure. The crankshaft pulley and the crankshaft timing sprocket are not keyed to the crankshaft. The crankshaft, the crankshaft sprocket and the pulley are fitted together by friction, using diamond washers between the flange faces on each part. For that reason, the crankshaft sprocket is also unfastened if the pulley bolt is loosened. Before any repair requiring loosening or removal of the crankshaft pulley bolt, the crankshaft and camshafts must be locked in place by the special service tools or severe engine damage can occur.**

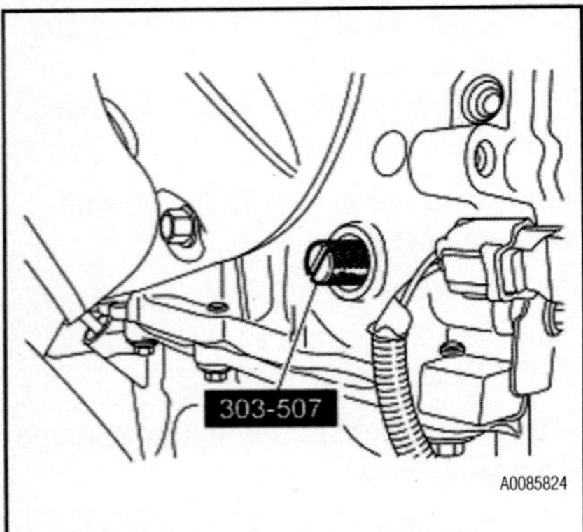

Fig. 163 Installing the crankshaft TDC timing peg

➡During engine repair procedures, cleanliness is extremely important. Any foreign material (including any material created while cleaning gasket surfaces) that enters the oil passages, coolant passages or the oil pan can cause engine failure.

1. Remove the crankshaft pulley.
   a. With the vehicle in NEUTRAL, position it on a hoist.
   b. Remove the RF wheel and tire.
   c. Remove the accessory drive belt.
   d. Remove the valve cover.

➡Failure to position the No. 1 piston at Top Dead Center (TDC) can result in damage to the engine. Turn the engine in the normal direction of rotation only.

   e. Using the crankshaft pulley bolt, turn the crankshaft clockwise to position the No. 1 piston at Top Dead Center (TDC).
   f. The hole in the crankshaft pulley should be in the 6 o'clock position.

➡The Camshaft Alignment Plate is for camshaft alignment only. Using this tool to prevent engine rotation can result in engine damage.

➡The camshaft timing slots are offset. If the Camshaft Alignment Plate cannot be installed, rotate the crankshaft one complete revolution clockwise to correctly position the camshafts.

   g. Install the Camshaft Alignment Plate in the slots on the rear of both camshafts.
   h. Remove the engine plug bolt.

➡The Crankshaft TDC Timing Peg will contact the crankshaft and prevent it from turning past TDC . However, the crankshaft can still be rotated in the counterclockwise direction. The crankshaft must remain at the TDC position during the crankshaft pulley removal and installation.

   i. Install the Crankshaft TDC Timing Peg.

➡The crankshaft must remain in the Top Dead Center (TDC) position during removal of the pulley bolt or damage to the engine can occur. Therefore, the crankshaft pulley must be held in place with the Crankshaft Damper Holding Tool, and the bolt should be removed using an air impact wrench (1/2-in drive minimum).

➡The crankshaft sprocket diamond washer may come off with the crankshaft pulley. The diamond washer must be replaced. Remove and discard the diamond washer. If the diamond washer is not installed, engine damage may occur.

   j. Use the Crankshaft Damper Holding Tool and a suitable 1/2-in drive hand tool to hold the crankshaft pulley. Use an air impact wrench to remove the crankshaft pulley bolt.
   k. Remove and discard the crankshaft pulley bolt and washer.
   l. Remove the crankshaft pulley.
   m. Remove the diamond washer and discard.

➡Use care not to damage the engine front cover or the crankshaft when removing the seal.

2. Using the Oil Seal Remover, remove the crankshaft front seal.

To install:

➡Remove the through bolt from the Camshaft Front Oil Seal Installer.

➡Lubricate the oil seal with clean engine oil.

3. Using the Camshaft Front Oil Seal Installer, install the crankshaft front oil seal.
4. Install the crankshaft pulley.
   a. Install a new diamond washer.

➡Do not install the crankshaft pulley bolt at this time.

➡Apply clean engine oil on the seal area before installing.

   b. Position the crankshaft pulley onto the crankshaft with the hole in the pulley at the 6 o'clock position.

➡Only hand-tighten the 6 mm x 18 mm bolt or damage to the front cover can occur.

➡This step will correctly align the crankshaft pulley to the crankshaft.

   c. Install a 6 mm x 18 mm bolt through the crankshaft pulley and thread it into the front cover.

➡The crankshaft must remain in the TDC position during installation of the pulley bolt or damage to the engine can occur. Therefore, the crankshaft pulley must be held in place with the Crankshaft Damper Holding Tool and the bolt should be installed using hand tools only.

➡Do not reuse the crankshaft pulley bolt.

   d. Install a new crankshaft pulley bolt. Use the Crankshaft Damper Holding Tool and a suitable 1/2-in drive hand tool to hold the crankshaft pulley, tighten the crankshaft pulley bolt in 2 stages:
      - Stage 1: Tighten to 74 ft. lbs. (100 Nm).
      - Stage 2: Tighten an additional 90 degrees
   e. Remove the 6 mm x 18 mm bolt.
   f. Remove the Crankshaft TDC Timing Peg.
   g. Remove the Camshaft Alignment Plate.

➡Only turn the engine in the normal direction of rotation.

   h. Turn the crankshaft clockwise one and three-fourths turns.
   i. Install the Crankshaft TDC Timing Peg.

➡Only turn the engine in the normal direction of rotation.

   j. Turn the crankshaft clockwise until the crankshaft contacts the Crankshaft TDC Timing Peg.
   k. Only hand-tighten the bolt or damage to the front cover can occur.
   l. Using the 6 mm x 18 mm bolt, check the position of the crankshaft pulley.
   m. If it is not possible to install the bolt, the engine valve timing must be corrected by repeating this procedure.
   n. Install the Camshaft Alignment Plate to check the position of the camshafts.
   o. If it is not possible to install the Camshaft Alignment Plate, the engine valve timing must be corrected by repeating this procedure.
   p. Remove the Camshaft Alignment Plate.
   q. Remove the 6 mm x 18 mm bolt.

r. Remove the Crankshaft TDC Timing Peg.
s. Install the engine plug bolt.
t. Tighten to 15 ft. lbs. (20 Nm).
u. Install the accessory drive belt.
v. Install the RF wheel and tire.
w. Install the valve cover.

3.0L Engine

See Figures 164 through 166.

➡**With the vehicle in NEUTRAL, position it on a hoist.**

1. Remove the crankshaft pulley.
   a. Remove the accessory drive belt.
   b. Remove the crankshaft pulley bolt and washer.
   c. Discard the crankshaft pulley bolt.
   d. Using the 3 Jaw Puller, remove the crankshaft pulley.
2. Using the Oil Seal Remover, remove and discard the crankshaft front seal.

To install:

➡**Clean all sealing surfaces with metal surface prep.**

3. Apply clean engine oil to the seal lip and seal bore before installing the seal.
4. Using the Front Cover Oil Seal Installer and the Crankshaft Vibration Damper Installer, install a new crankshaft front seal.

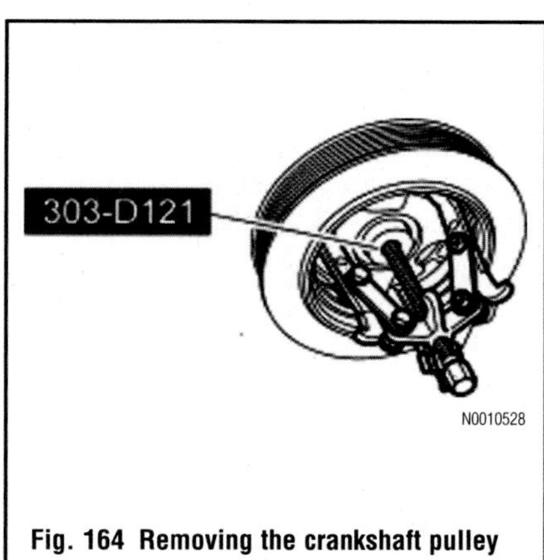

Fig. 164 Removing the crankshaft pulley

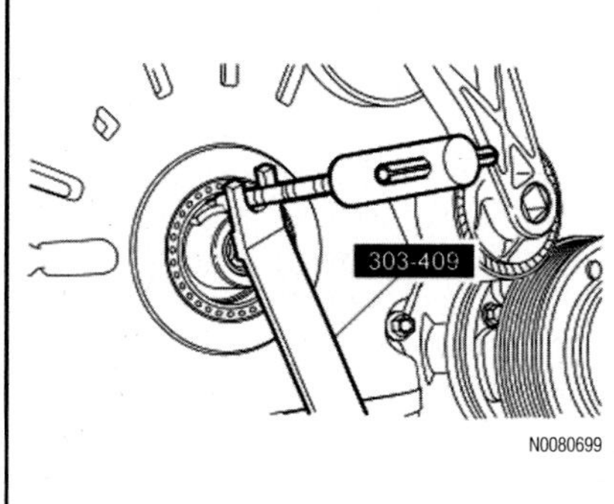

Fig. 165 Removing the crankshaft front seal

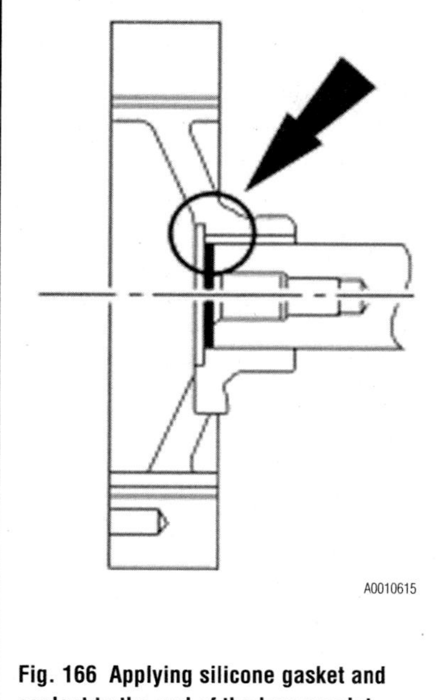

Fig. 166 Applying silicone gasket and sealant to the end of the keyway slot

5. Install the crankshaft pulley.
   a. Lubricate the crankshaft front seal inner lip with clean engine oil.

➡**Clean the keyway and slot using metal surface prep before applying silicone gasket and sealant.**

➡**The crankshaft pulley must be installed and the bolt tightened within 4 minutes of applying the silicone gasket and sealant.**

   b. Apply silicone gasket and sealant to the end of the keyway slot.

➡**Lubricate the outside diameter sealing surface with clean engine oil.**

   c. Using the Crankshaft Vibration Damper Installer, install the crankshaft pulley.
   d. Install the bolt and washer. Tighten the bolt in 4 stages:
      - Stage 1: Tighten to 89 ft. lbs. (120 Nm)
      - Stage 2: Loosen one full turn
      - Stage 3: Tighten to 37 ft. lbs. (50 Nm)
      - Stage 4: Tighten an additional 90 degrees
   e. Install the accessory drive belt.

3.5L Engine

See Figures 167 and 168.

1. With the vehicle in NEUTRAL, position it on a hoist.

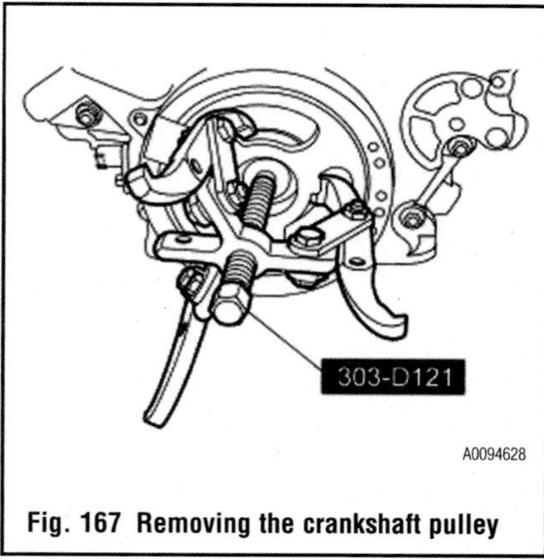

Fig. 167 Removing the crankshaft pulley

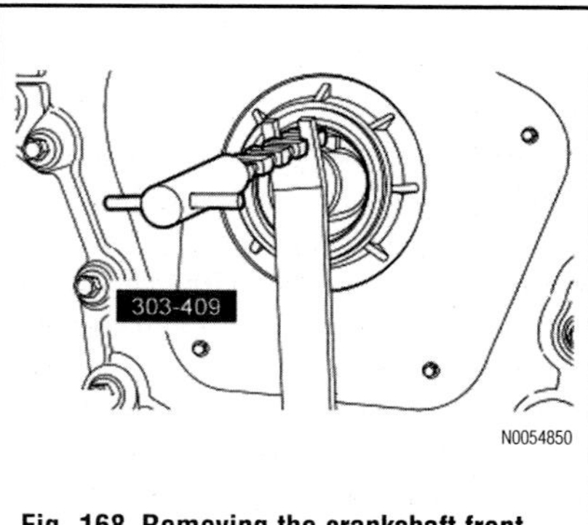

Fig. 168 Removing the crankshaft front seal

2. Remove the crankshaft pulley.
   a. Remove the accessory drive belt and the power steering belt.
   b. Using the Strap Wrench, remove the crankshaft pulley bolt and washer.
   c. Discard the bolt.
   d. Using the 3 Jaw Puller, remove the crankshaft pulley.
3. Using the Oil Seal Remover, remove and discard the crankshaft front seal.
   a. Clean all sealing surfaces with metal surface prep.

To install:

➡**Apply clean engine oil to the crankshaft front seal bore in the engine front cover.**

4. Using the Front Crankshaft Seal Installer and Crankshaft Vibration Damper Installer, install a new crankshaft front seal.
5. Install the crankshaft pulley.
   a. Lubricate the crankshaft front seal inner lip with clean engine oil.

➡**Lubricate the outside diameter sealing surfaces with clean engine oil.**

   b. Using the Front Cover Oil Seal Installer and Crankshaft Vibration Damper Installer, install the crankshaft pulley.

c. Using the Strap Wrench, install the crankshaft pulley washer and new bolt and tighten in 4 stages.

- Stage 1: Tighten to 89 ft. lbs. (120 Nm)
- Stage 2: Loosen one full turn
- Stage 3: Tighten to 37 ft. lbs. (50 Nm)
- Stage 4: Tighten an additional 90 degrees

d. Install the accessory drive belt and the power steering belt.

CYLINDER HEAD

REMOVAL & INSTALLATION

2.5L Engine

See Figures 169 through 171.

NOTICE: Do not loosen or remove the crankshaft pulley bolt without first installing the special tools as instructed in this procedure. The crankshaft pulley and the crankshaft timing sprocket are not keyed to the crankshaft. The crankshaft, the crankshaft sprocket and the pulley are fitted together by friction, using diamond washers between the flange faces on each part. For that reason, the crankshaft sprocket is also unfastened if the pulley bolt is loosened. Before any repair requiring loosening or removal of the crankshaft pulley bolt, the crankshaft and camshafts must be locked in place by the special service tools, otherwise severe engine damage can occur.

➡During engine repair procedures, cleanliness is extremely important. Any foreign material, including any material created while cleaning gasket surfaces, that enters the oil passages, coolant passages or the oil pan can cause engine failure.

1. With the vehicle in NEUTRAL, position it on a hoist.
2. Release the fuel system pressure.
3. Check the valve clearance.
4. Drain the engine cooling system.
5. Disconnect the degas bottle-to-radiator hose from the degas bottle.
6. Remove the nut and bolt and position the degas bottle to access the lower degas bottle hose.
7. Disconnect the lower degas bottle hose and remove the degas bottle.
8. Remove the generator.
9. Remove the fuel supply rail.
10. Remove the intake manifold.
11. Remove the exhaust manifold.
12. Remove the bolt and the engine mount damper from the engine mount bracket.
13. Remove the bolt and the ground wire from the engine mount bracket.
14. Remove the engine mount bracket bolt.
15. Install the Engine Lifting Brackets and a suitable length of chain to the threaded hole in the LH side of the engine block.
16. Using the Engine Support Bar and Engine Lifting Brackets, lift the engine 25 mm (0.98 in).
17. Remove the nut, 2 bolts and the engine mount.
18. Lower the engine 25 mm (0.98 in).
19. Remove the 2 nuts and the engine mount bracket.
20. Remove the timing drive components.
21. Remove the Camshaft Alignment Plate.
22. Mark the position of the camshaft lobes on the No. 1 cylinder for installation reference.
23. Remove the bolt and the Variable Camshaft Timing (VCT) solenoid.

➡Failure to follow the camshaft loosening procedure can result in damage to the camshafts.

➡Mark the location and orientation of each camshaft bearing cap.

24. Remove the camshafts from the engine.
    a. Loosen the camshaft bearing cap bolts, in the sequence shown, one turn at a time until all tension is released from the camshaft bearing caps.
    b. Remove the bolts and the camshaft bearing caps.
    c. Remove the camshafts.

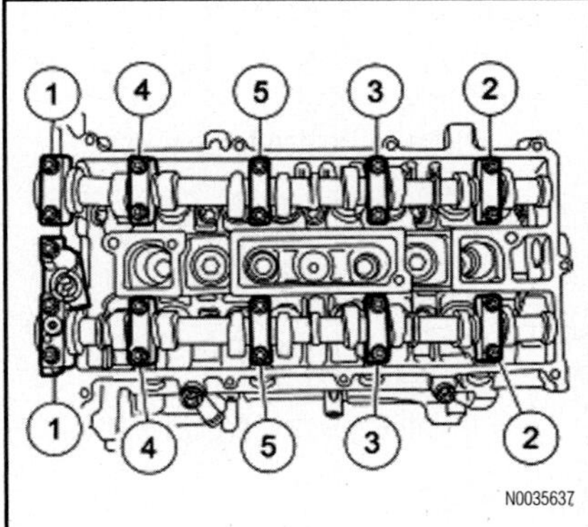

Fig. 169 Identifying the camshaft bearing cap bolt removal sequence

➡If the camshafts and valve tappets are to be reused, mark the location of the valve tappets to make sure they are assembled in their original positions.

➡The number on the valve tappets only reflects the digits that follow the decimal. For example, a tappet with the number 0.650 has the thickness of 3.650 mm.

25. Remove and inspect the valve tappets.
26. Disconnect the upper radiator hose, coolant bypass hose and heater hose from the engine coolant outlet.
27. Disconnect the EGR valve electrical connector.
28. Disconnect the coolant hose from the EGR valve.
29. Remove the 10 bolts and the cylinder head.
    a. Discard the bolts.
    b. Discard the cylinder head gasket.

To install:

➡Do not use metal scrapers, wire brushes, power abrasive discs or other abrasive means to clean the sealing surfaces. These tools cause scratches and gouges that make leak paths. Use a plastic scraping tool to remove all traces of the head gasket.

➡Observe all warnings or cautions and follow all application directions contained on the packaging of the silicone gasket remover and the metal surface prep.

➡If there is no residual gasket material present, metal surface prep can be used to clean and prepare the surfaces.

c. Clean the cylinder head-to-cylinder block mating surface of both the cylinder head and the cylinder block in the following sequence.

d. Remove any large deposits of silicone or gasket material with a plastic scraper.

e. Apply silicone gasket remover, following package directions, and allow to set for several minutes.

f. Remove the silicone gasket remover with a plastic scraper. A second application of silicone gasket remover may be required if residual traces of silicone or gasket material remain.

g. Apply metal surface prep, following package directions, to remove any traces of oil or coolant, and to prepare the surfaces to bond with the new gasket. Do not attempt to make the metal shiny.

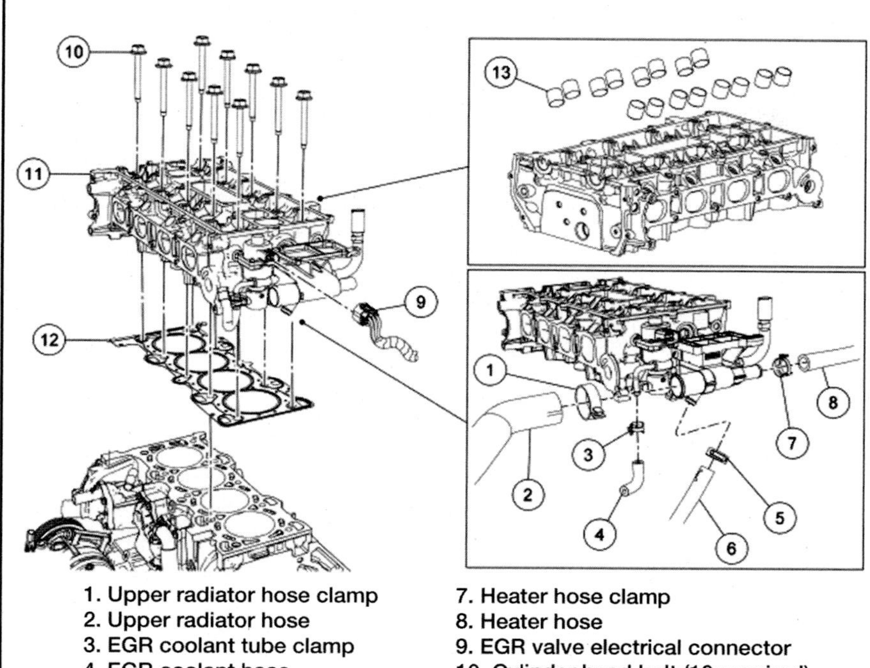

Fig. 170 Exploded view of the cylinder head

Some staining of the metal surfaces is normal.

30. Clean the cylinder head bolt holes in the cylinder block. Make sure all coolant, oil or other foreign material is removed.

31. Support the cylinder head on a bench with the head gasket side up. Check the cylinder head distortion and the cylinder block distortion.

32. Apply silicone gasket and sealant to the locations shown.

33. Install a new cylinder head gasket.

➡The cylinder head bolts are a torque-to-yield design and must not be reused. New cylinder head bolts must be installed.

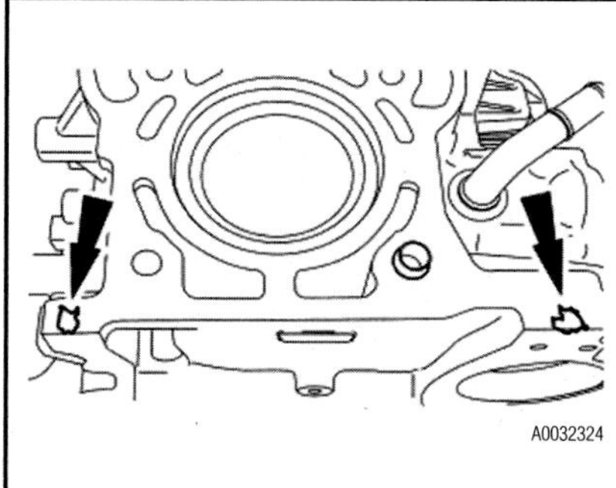

Fig. 171 Applying silicone gasket and sealant

➡Lubricate the bolts with clean engine oil prior to installation.

34. Install the cylinder head and 10 new bolts. Tighten the bolts in the sequence shown in 5 stages:
   a. Stage 1: Tighten to 62 inch lbs. (7 Nm).
   b. Stage 2: Tighten to 11 ft. lbs. (15 Nm).
   c. Stage 3: Tighten to 33 ft. lbs. (45 Nm).
   d. Stage 4: Turn 90 degrees.
   e. Stage 5: Turn an additional 90 degrees.

35. Connect the coolant hose to the EGR valve.

36. Connect the EGR valve electrical connector.

37. Connect the upper radiator hose, coolant bypass hose and heater hose to the engine coolant outlet.

➡Coat the valve tappets with clean engine oil prior to installation.

38. Install the valve tappets.

➡Install the camshafts with the alignment slots in the camshafts lined up so the Camshaft Alignment Plate can be installed without rotating the camshafts. Make sure the lobes on the No. 1 cylinder are in the same position as noted in the removal procedure. Rotating the camshafts when the timing chain is removed, or installing the camshafts 180 degrees out of position can cause severe damage to the valves and pistons.

➡Lubricate the camshaft journals and bearing caps with clean engine oil.

39. Install the camshafts and bearing caps in their original locations and orientation. Tighten the bearing caps in the sequence shown in 3 stages:
   a. Stages 1: Tighten the camshaft bearing cap bolts until finger-tight.
   b. Stages 2: Tighten to 62 inch lbs. (7 Nm).
   c. Stages 3: Tighten to 12 ft. lbs. (16 Nm).

40. Install the Camshaft Alignment Plate.

41. Install the VCT solenoid and bolt.
   a. Tighten to 89 inch lbs. (10 Nm).

42. Install the timing drive components.

43. Install the engine mount bracket and the 2 nuts.
   a. Tighten to 76 ft. lbs. (103 Nm).

44. Using the Engine Support Bar and Engine Lifting Brackets, lift the engine 25 mm (0.98 in).

45. Install the engine mount, nut and 2 bolts.
   a. Tighten to 41 ft. lbs. (55 Nm).

46. Lower the engine 25 mm (0.98 in).

47. Install the engine mount bracket bolt.
   a. Tighten to 85 ft. lbs. (115 Nm).

48. Install the ground wire-to-engine mount bracket and bolt.
   a. Tighten to 89 inch lbs. (10 Nm).

49. Install the engine mount damper and the bolt.
   a. Tighten to 17 ft. lbs. (23 Nm).

50. Install the exhaust manifold.

51. Install the intake manifold.

52. Install the fuel supply rail.

53. Install the generator.

54. Connect the lower degas bottle hose to the degas bottle.

55. Install the degas bottle and the nut and bolt.
   a. Tighten to 80 inch lbs. (9 Nm).

56. Connect the degas bottle-to-radiator hose.

57. Fill and bleed the engine cooling system.

58. Using a new gasket, install the coolant outlet and bolts.
   a. Tighten to 89 inch lbs. (10 Nm).

2.5L Hybrid Engine

See Figures 172 through 174.

➡Do not loosen or remove the crankshaft pulley bolt without first installing the special tools as instructed in this procedure. The crankshaft pulley and the crankshaft timing sprocket are not keyed to the crankshaft. The crankshaft, the crankshaft sprocket and the pulley are fitted together by friction, using diamond washers between the flange faces on each part. For that reason, the crankshaft sprocket is also unfastened if the pulley bolt is loosened. Before any repair requiring loosening or removal of the crankshaft pulley bolt, the crankshaft and camshafts must be locked in place by the special service tools or severe engine damage can occur.

➡During engine repair procedures, cleanliness is extremely important. Any foreign material (including any material created while cleaning gasket surfaces) that enters the oil passages, coolant passages or the oil pan can cause engine failure.

1. With the vehicle in NEUTRAL, position it on a hoist.
2. Release the fuel system pressure.
3. Drain the engine cooling system.
4. Remove the intake manifold.
5. Remove the Variable Camshaft Timing (VCT) oil control solenoid.
6. Remove the timing drive components.
7. Remove the Camshaft Alignment Plate.
8. Mark the position of the camshaft lobes on the No. 1 cylinder for installation reference.

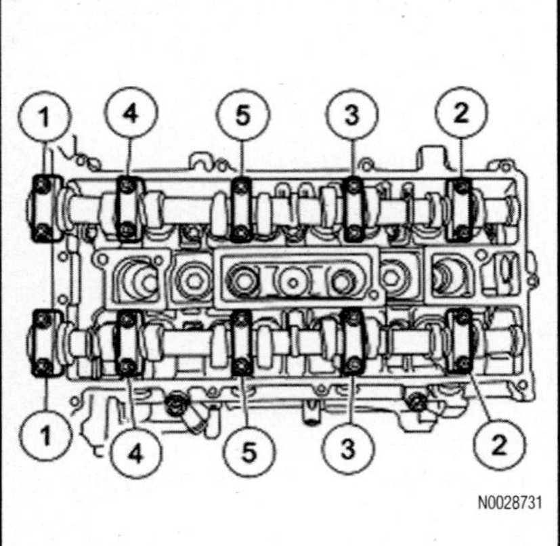

Fig. 172 Identifying the camshaft bearing cap bolt removal sequence

➡Failure to follow the camshaft loosening procedure can result in damage to the camshafts.

➡Mark the location and orientation of each camshaft bearing cap.

9. Remove the camshafts from the engine.
    a. Loosen the camshaft bearing cap bolts, in sequence, one turn at a time until all tension is released from the camshaft bearing caps.
    b. Remove the bolts and the camshaft bearing caps.
    c. Remove the camshafts.

➡If the camshafts and valve tappets are to be reused, mark the location of the valve tappets to make sure they are assembled in their original positions.

10. Remove the valve tappets.
11. Inspect the valve tappets.
12. Remove the catalytic converter.
13. Disconnect the EGR valve electrical connector.
14. Disconnect the upper radiator hose, coolant bypass hose, EGR coolant hose, heater hose and coolant vent hose from the engine coolant outlet and the EGR valve.
15. Remove the bolts and the cylinder head.
16. Discard the bolts and the cylinder head gasket.

To install:

➡Do not use metal scrapers, wire brushes, power abrasive discs or other abrasive means to clean the sealing surfaces. These tools cause scratches and gouges that make leak paths. Use

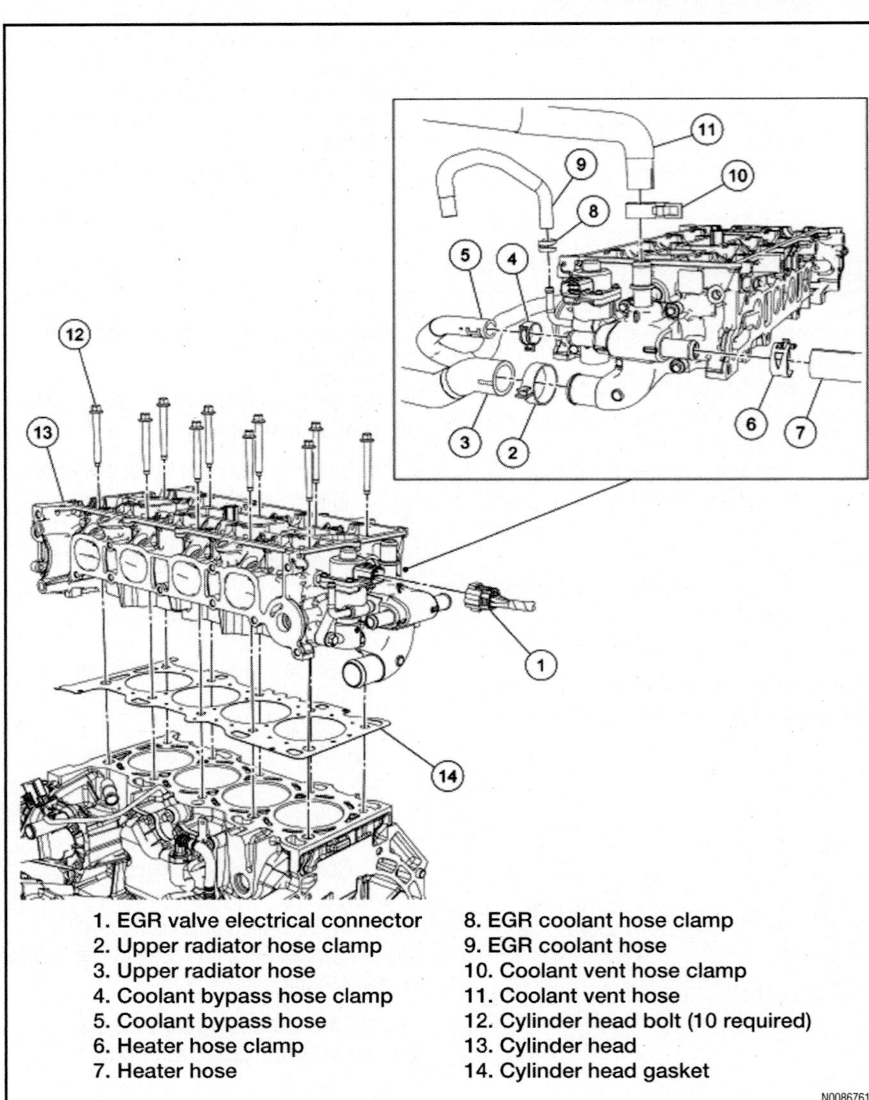

Fig. 173 Exploded view of the cylinder head

a plastic scraping tool to remove all traces of the head gasket.

➡Observe all warnings or cautions and follow all application directions contained on the packaging of the silicone gasket remover and the metal surface prep.

➡If there is no residual gasket material present, metal surface prep can be used to clean and prepare the surfaces.

17. Clean the cylinder head-to-cylinder block mating surface of both the cylinder head and the cylinder block in the following sequence.
    a. Remove any large deposits of silicone or gasket material with a plastic scraper.
    b. Apply silicone gasket remover, following package directions, and allow to set for several minutes.
    c. Remove the silicone gasket remover with a plastic scraper. A second application of silicone gasket remover may be required if residual traces of silicone or gasket material remain.
    d. Apply metal surface prep, following package directions, to remove any traces of oil or coolant, and to prepare the surfaces to bond with the new gasket. Do not attempt to make the metal shiny. Some staining of the metal surfaces is normal.
18. Support the cylinder head on a bench with the head gasket side up. Check the cylinder head distortion and the cylinder block distortion.
19. Clean the cylinder head bolt holes in the cylinder block. Make sure all coolant, oil or other foreign material is removed.
20. Apply silicone gasket and sealant to the locations shown.
21. Install a new cylinder head gasket.

➡The cylinder head bolts are torque-to-yield and must not be reused. New cylinder head bolts must be installed.

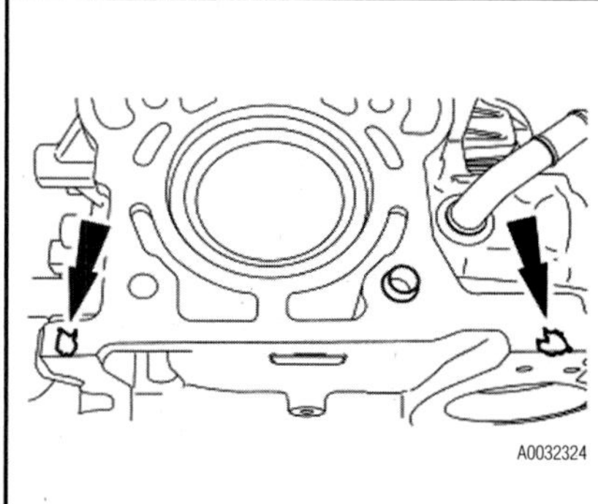

Fig. 174 Applying silicone gasket and sealant

22. Install the cylinder head and 10 new bolts. Tighten the bolts in the sequence shown in the following 5 stages:
    a. Stage 1: Tighten to 44 inch lbs. (5 Nm).
    b. Stage 2: Tighten to 11 ft. lbs. (15 Nm).
    c. Stage 3: Tighten to 33 ft. lbs. (45 Nm).
    d. Stage 4: Turn 90 degrees.
    e. Stage 5: Turn an additional 90 degrees.
23. Connect the upper radiator hose, coolant bypass hose, EGR coolant hose, heater hose and coolant vent hose to the engine coolant outlet and the EGR valve.
24. Connect the EGR valve electrical connector.
25. Install the catalytic converter.

➡Lubricate the valve tappets with clean engine oil.

26. Install the valve tappets in their original positions.

➡Install the camshafts with the alignment notches in the camshafts lined up so the camshaft alignment plate can be installed. Make sure the lobes on the No. 1 cylinder are in the same position as noted in the removal procedure. Failure to follow this procedure can cause severe damage to the valves and pistons.

➡Lubricate the camshaft journals and bearing caps with clean engine oil.

27. Install the camshafts and bearing caps in their original location and orientation. Tighten the bearing caps in the sequence shown in 3 stages:
    a. Stage 1: Tighten the camshaft bearing cap bolts, one turn at a time, until finger-tight.
    b. Stage 2: Tighten the bolts to 62 inch lbs. (7 Nm).
    c. Stage 3: Tighten the bolts to 12 ft. lbs. (16 Nm).
28. Install the Camshaft Alignment Plate.
29. Install the timing drive components.
30. Install the VCT oil control solenoid.
31. Install the intake manifold.
32. Fill and bleed the engine cooling system.

3.0L Engine

LH Side

See Figures 175 through 177.

➡During engine repair procedures, cleanliness is extremely important. Any foreign material (including any material created while cleaning gasket surfaces) that enters the oil passages, coolant passages or the oil pan may cause engine failure.

1. With the vehicle in NEUTRAL, position it on a hoist.
2. Remove the lower intake manifold.
3. Remove the coolant pump housing.
4. Remove the LH camshafts.

➡The camshaft roller followers must be installed in their original positions. If not reassembled in their original positions, severe engine damage may occur.

5. Remove the camshaft roller followers.

➡The hydraulic lash adjusters must be installed in their original positions. If not reassembled in their original positions, severe engine damage may occur.

6. Remove the hydraulic lash adjusters.
7. Remove the LH catalytic converter.
8. Remove the oil level indicator.
9. Remove the stud bolt and then remove the oil level indicator tube.
    a. Remove and discard the O-ring seal.

➡New cylinder head bolts must be installed. They are a torque-to-yield design and cannot be reused.

10. Remove the bolts in the sequence shown.

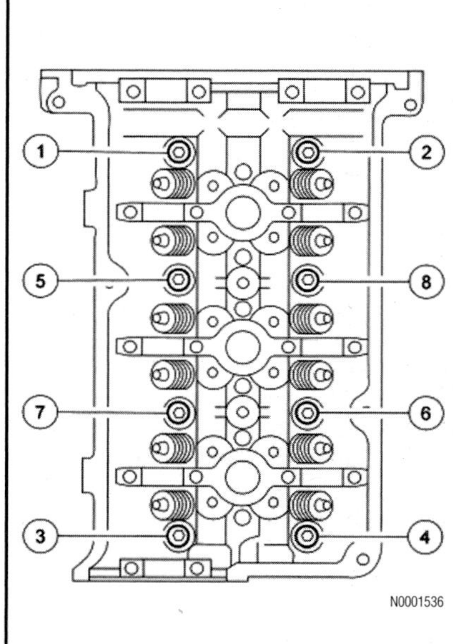

Fig. 175 Identifying the cylinder head bolt removal sequence

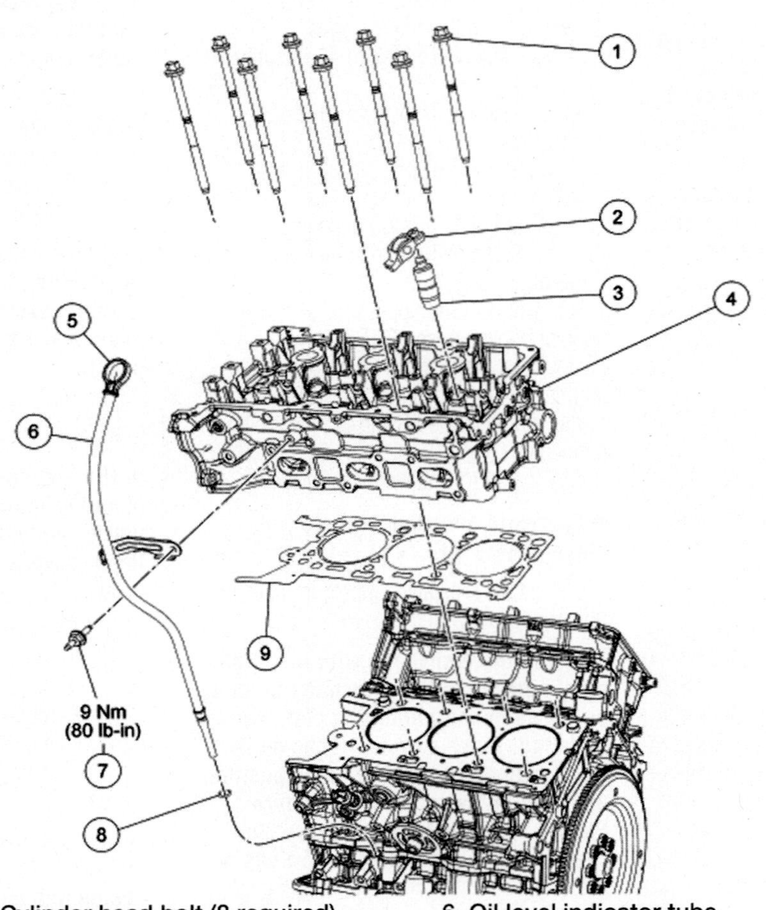

1. Cylinder head bolt (8 required)
2. Camshaft roller follower (12 required)
3. Hydraulic lash adjuster (12 required)
4. Cylinder head
5. Oil level indicator
6. Oil level indicator tube
7. Oil level indicator tube stud bolt
8. Oil level indicator tube O-ring
9. Cylinder head gasket

N0098591

Fig. 176 Exploded view of the LH cylinder head

11. Support the cylinder head on a bench with the head gasket side up. Check the cylinder head distortion and the cylinder block distortion.

To install:

➡Do not use metal scrapers, wire brushes, power abrasive discs or other abrasive means to clean the sealing surfaces. These tools cause scratches and gouges which make leak paths.

12. Use a plastic scraping tool to remove all traces of the head gasket.
    a. Clean all surfaces with metal surface prep.
13. Position a new gasket and the cylinder head.

➡New cylinder head bolts must be installed. They are a torque-to-yield design and cannot be reused.

14. Install the bolts and tighten in 6 stages in the sequence shown.
    a. Stage 1: Tighten to 30 ft. lbs. (40 Nm).
    b. Stage 2: Tighten 90 degrees.
    c. Stage 3: Loosen one full turn.
    d. Stage 4: Tighten to 30 ft. lbs. (40 Nm).
    e. Stage 5: Tighten 90 degrees.
    f. Stage 6: Tighten 90 degrees.

➡Installation of the oil level indicator may require the assistance of a second technician to align the tube with the orifice.

➡Install a new O-ring seal and lubricate with clean engine oil.

15. Install the oil level indicator tube and install the stud bolt.
    a. To install, tighten to 80 inch lbs. (9 Nm).
16. Install the oil level indicator.
17. Install the LH catalytic converter.

➡The hydraulic lash adjusters must be installed in their original positions. If not reassembled in their original positions, severe engine damage may occur.

18. Install the hydraulic lash adjusters.
    a. Lubricate the hydraulic lash adjusters with clean engine oil.

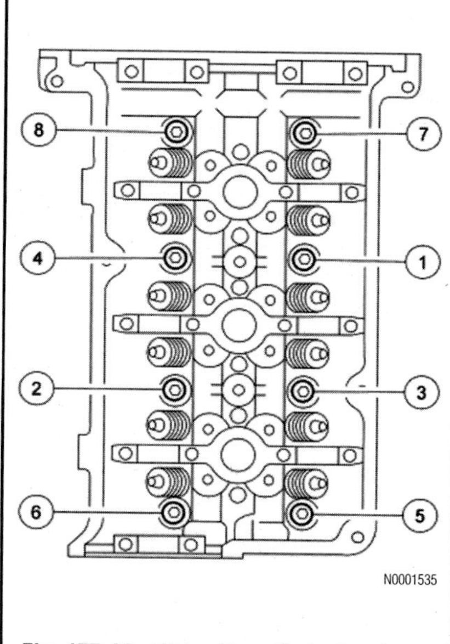

Fig. 177 Identifying the cylinder head installation sequence

➡The camshaft roller followers must be installed in their original positions. If not reassembled in their original positions, severe engine damage may occur.

19. Install the camshaft roller followers.
    a. Lubricate the camshaft roller followers with clean engine oil.
20. Install the camshafts.
21. Install the coolant pump housing.
22. Install the lower intake manifold.

RH Side

See Figures 178 and 179.

➡During engine repair procedures, cleanliness is extremely important. Any foreign material (including any material created while cleaning gasket surfaces) that enters the oil passages, coolant passages or the oil pan may cause engine failure.

1. With the vehicle in NEUTRAL, position it on a hoist.
2. Remove the lower intake manifold.
3. Remove the coolant pump housing.
4. Remove the RH camshafts.

➡The camshaft roller followers must be installed in their original positions. If not reassembled in their original positions, severe engine damage may occur.

5. Remove the camshaft roller followers.

➡The hydraulic lash adjusters must be installed in their original positions. If not reassembled in their original positions, severe engine damage may occur.

6. Remove the hydraulic lash adjusters.
7. Remove the RH exhaust manifold.

➡New cylinder head bolts must be installed. They are a torque-to-yield design and cannot be reused.

8. Remove the bolts in the sequence shown.
    a. Remove the cylinder head.
    b. Discard the bolts and gasket.
9. Support the cylinder head on a bench with the head gasket side up. Check the cylinder head distortion and the cylinder block distortion.

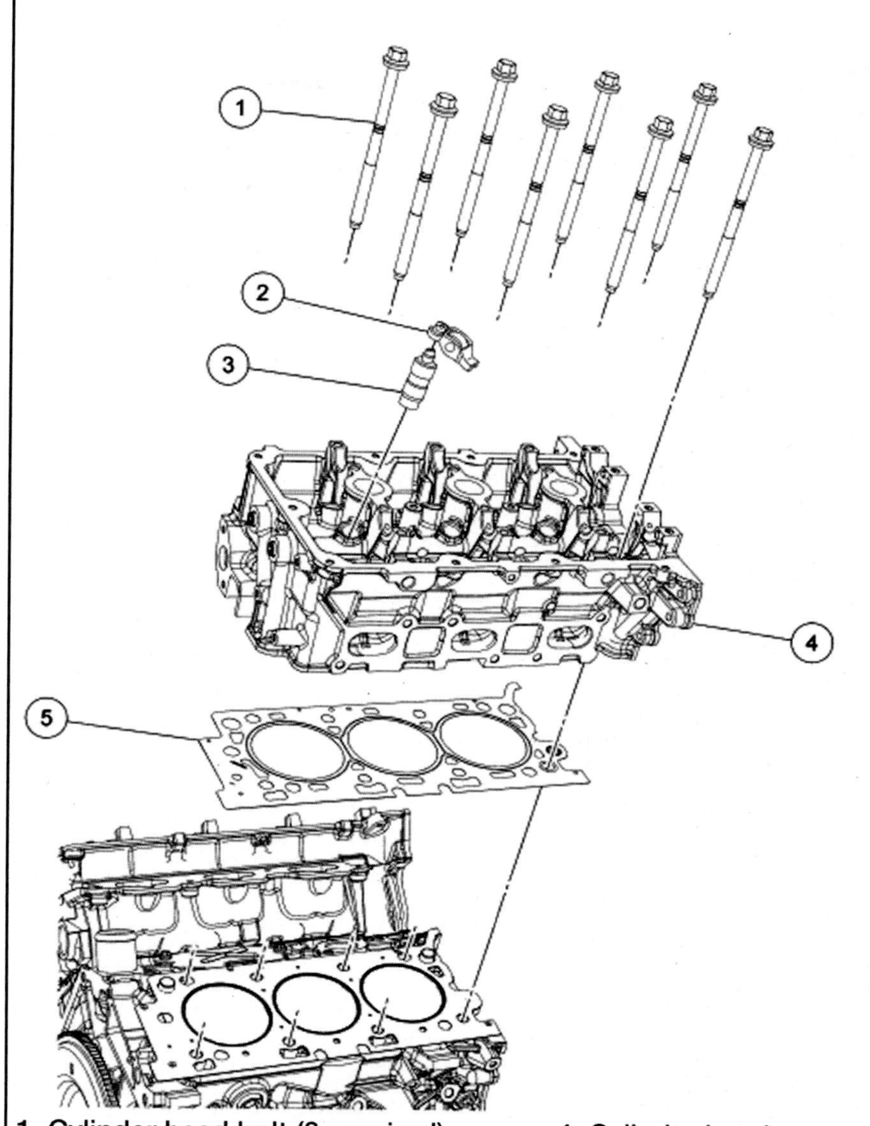

Fig. 178 Exploded view of the RH cylinder head

To install:

➡Do not use metal scrapers, wire brushes, power abrasive discs or other abrasive means to clean the sealing surfaces. These tools cause scratches and gouges which make leak paths.

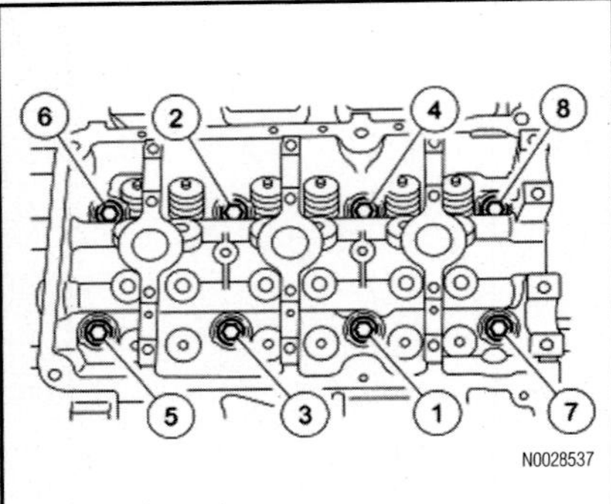

Fig. 179 Identifying the cylinder head bolt installation sequence

10. Use a plastic scraping tool to remove all traces of the head gasket.
   a. Clean all surfaces with metal surface prep.
11. Position a new gasket and the cylinder head.

➡New cylinder head bolts must be installed. They are a torque-to-yield design and cannot be reused.

12. Install the bolts and tighten in 6 stages in the sequence shown.
   a. Stage 1: Tighten to 30 ft. lbs. (40 Nm).
   b. Stage 2: Tighten 90 degrees.
   c. Stage 3: Loosen one full turn.
   d. Stage 4: Tighten to 30 ft. lbs. (40 Nm).
   e. Stage 5: Tighten 90 degrees.
   f. Stage 6: Tighten 90 degrees.
13. Install the RH exhaust manifold.

➡The hydraulic lash adjusters must be installed in their original positions. If not reassembled in their original positions, severe engine damage may occur.

14. Install the hydraulic lash adjusters.
15. Lubricate the hydraulic lash adjusters with clean engine oil.

➡The camshaft roller followers must be installed in their original positions. If not reassembled in their original positions, severe engine damage may occur.

16. Install the camshaft roller followers.
17. Lubricate the camshaft roller followers with clean engine oil.
18. Install the RH camshafts.
19. Install the coolant pump housing.
20. Install the lower intake manifold.

3.5L Engine

LH Side

See Figures 180 through 183.

NOTICE: During engine repair procedures, cleanliness is extremely important. Any foreign material, including any material created while cleaning gasket surfaces that enters the oil passages, coolant passages or the oil pan, can cause engine failure.

All vehicles

1. Remove the LH camshafts.
2. If equipped, remove the heat shield and disconnect the block heater electrical connector.
   a. Remove the block heater wiring harness from the engine.
3. Disconnect the A/C compressor electrical connector.
4. Remove the nut and disconnect the generator B+ cable.
5. Disconnect the generator electrical connector.
6. Detach the wiring harness retainer from the generator.
7. Remove the nut, bolt and the generator.
8. Detach the wiring harness pin-type retainer.
9. Disconnect the 6 fuel injector electrical connectors.
10. Disconnect the Cylinder Head Temperature (CHT) sensor electrical connector.
11. Disconnect the LH Camshaft Position (CMP) sensor electrical connector.
12. Disconnect the LH Heated Oxygen Sensor (HO2S) electrical connector.
13. Disconnect the LH Catalyst Monitor Sensor (CMS) electrical connector.
14. Remove the wiring harness retainer bolt from the rear of the LH cylinder head.
15. Remove the 2 LH catalytic converter bracket bolts.
16. Remove the 4 nuts and the LH catalytic converter.
   a. Discard the nuts and the gasket.
17. Remove the 3 bolts and the LH exhaust manifold heat shield.
18. Remove the 6 nuts and the LH exhaust manifold.
19. Discard the nuts and the exhaust manifold gasket.
20. Clean and inspect the LH exhaust manifold.
21. Remove and discard the 6 LH exhaust manifold studs.
22. Remove the LH cylinder block drain plug.
   a. Allow coolant to drain from the cylinder block.

All-Wheel Drive (AWD) vehicles

23. Remove the 2 RH catalytic converter bracket bolts.

All vehicles

24. Remove the 4 nuts and the RH catalytic converter.
   a. Discard the nuts and the gasket.
25. Remove the RH cylinder block drain plug or, if equipped, the block heater.
   a. Allow coolant to drain from the cylinder block.
26. Remove the 4 bolts and the fuel rail and injectors as an assembly.
27. Disconnect the coolant bypass hose from the thermostat housing.
28. Remove the 2 thermostat housing-to-lower intake manifold bolts.
29. Remove the thermostat housing and discard the gasket and O-ring seal.

➡If the engine is repaired or replaced because of upper engine failure, typically including valve or piston damage, check the intake manifold for metal debris. If metal debris is found, install a new intake manifold. Failure to follow these instructions can result in engine damage.

30. Remove the 10 bolts and the lower intake manifold.
   a. Discard the gaskets.
31. Remove the bolt and the LH CMP sensor.
32. Remove the 2 bolts and the upper LH primary timing chain guide.
33. Remove the 2 bolts and the LH secondary timing chain tensioner.

➡If the components are to be reinstalled, they must be installed in the same positions. Mark the components for installation into their original locations.

34. Remove the valve tappets from the cylinder head.
35. Remove and discard the M6 bolt.

➡Place clean shop towels over exposed engine cavities. Carefully

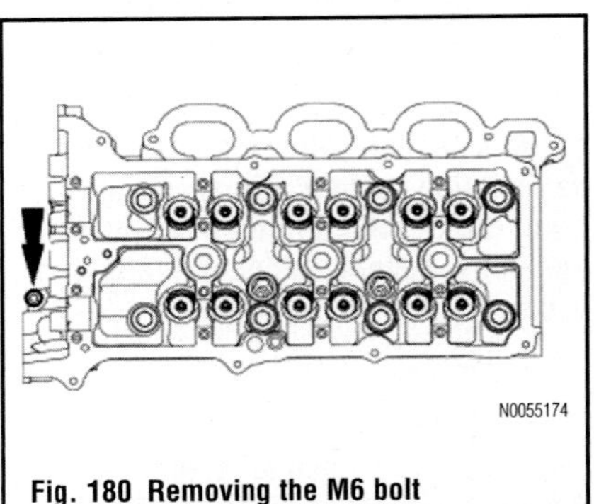

Fig. 180 Removing the M6 bolt

remove the towels so foreign material is not dropped into the engine. Any foreign material (including any material created while cleaning gasket surfaces) that enters the oil passages or the oil pan, may cause engine failure.

➡Aluminum surfaces are soft and may be scratched easily. Never place the cylinder head gasket surface, unprotected, on a bench surface.

➡The cylinder head bolts must be discarded and new bolts must be installed. They are a tighten-to-yield design and cannot be reused.

36. Remove and discard the 8 bolts from the cylinder head.
    a. Remove the cylinder head.
    b. Discard the cylinder head gasket.

➡Do not use metal scrapers, wire brushes, power abrasive discs or other abrasive means to clean the sealing surfaces. These tools cause scratches and gouges that make leak paths. Use a plastic scraping tool to remove all traces of the head gasket.

➡Observe all warnings or cautions and follow all application directions contained on the packaging of the silicone gasket remover and the metal surface prep.

➡If there is no residual gasket material present, metal surface prep can be used to clean and prepare the surfaces.

37. Clean the cylinder head-to-cylinder block mating surfaces of both the cylinder heads and the cylinder block in the following sequence.
38. Remove any large deposits of silicone or gasket material with a plastic scraper.
39. Apply silicone gasket remover, following package directions, and allow to set for several minutes.
40. Remove the silicone gasket remover with a plastic scraper. A second application of silicone gasket remover may be required if residual traces of silicone or gasket material remain.
41. Apply metal surface prep, following package directions, to remove any remaining traces of oil or coolant and to prepare the surfaces to bond with the new gasket. Do not attempt to make the metal shiny. Some staining of the metal surfaces is normal.
42. Support the cylinder head on a bench with the head gasket side up. Check the cylinder head distortion and the cylinder block distortion.

To install:

➡During engine repair procedures, cleanliness is extremely important. Any foreign material, including any material created while cleaning gasket surfaces that enters the oil passages, coolant passages or the oil pan, can cause engine failure.

All vehicles

43. Install a new gasket, the LH cylinder head and 8 new bolts. Tighten in the sequence shown in 5 stages:
    a. Stage 1: Tighten to 15 Nm (20 Nm).
    b. Stage 2: Tighten to 26 ft. lbs. (35 Nm).
    c. Stage 3: Tighten 90 degrees.
    d. Stage 4: Tighten 90 degrees.
    e. Stage 5: Tighten 90 degrees.
44. Install the new M6 bolt.
    a. Tighten to 89 inch lbs. (10 Nm).

➡The valve tappets must be installed in their original positions.

➡Coat the valve tappets with clean engine oil prior to installation.

45. Install the valve tappets.
46. Install the LH secondary timing chain tensioner and the 2 bolts.
    a. Tighten to 89 inch lbs. (10 Nm).
47. Install the upper LH primary timing chain guide and the 2 bolts.
    a. Tighten to 89 inch lbs. (10 Nm).
48. Install LH Camshaft Position (CMP) sensor and the bolt.
    a. Tighten to 89 inch lbs. (10 Nm).

➡If the engine is repaired or replaced because of upper engine failure, typically including valve or piston damage, check the intake manifold for metal debris. If metal debris is found, install a new intake manifold. Failure to follow these instructions can result in engine damage.

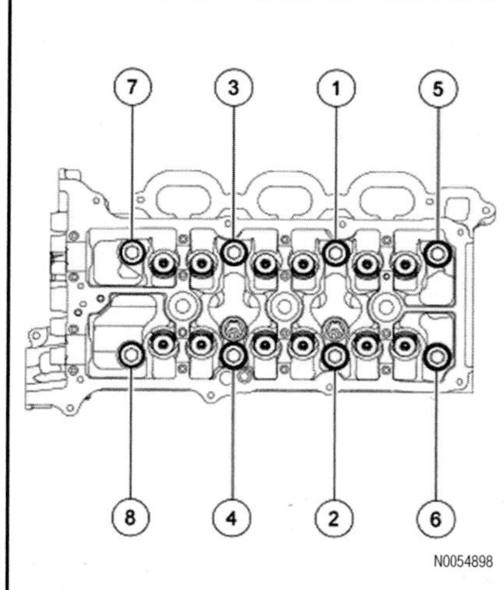

Fig. 181 Identifying the cylinder head bolt tightening sequence

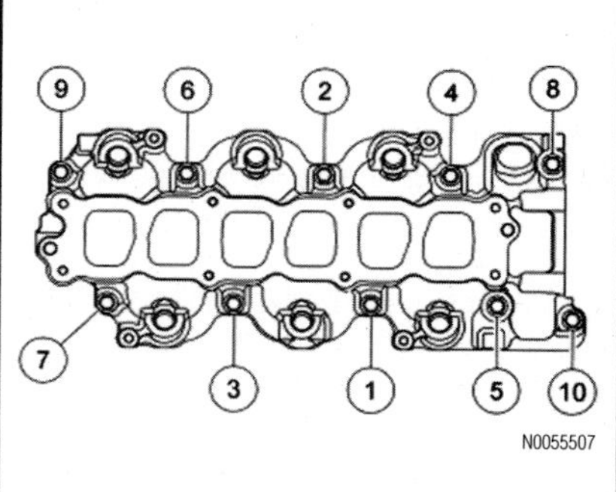

Fig. 182 Identifying the lower intake manifold bolt installation sequence

49. Using new gaskets, install the lower intake manifold and the 10 bolts.
    a. Tighten in the sequence shown to 89 inch lbs. (10 Nm).
50. Using a new gasket and O-ring seal, install the thermostat housing and the 2 bolts.
    a. Tighten to 89 inch lbs. (10 Nm).
51. Connect the coolant bypass hose to the thermostat housing.

➡Use O-ring seals that are made of special fuel-resistant material. The use of ordinary O-rings can cause the fuel system to leak. Do not reuse the O-ring seals.

➡The upper and lower O-ring seals are not interchangeable.

52. Install new fuel injector O-ring seals.
    a. Remove the retaining clips and separate the fuel injectors from the fuel rail.
    b. Remove and discard the O-ring seals.
    c. Install new O-ring seals and lubricate with clean engine oil.
    d. Install the fuel injectors and the retaining clips onto the fuel rail.
53. Install the fuel rail and injectors as an assembly and install the 4 bolts.
    a. Tighten to 89 inch lbs. (10 Nm).
54. Install the RH cylinder block drain plug or, if equipped, the block heater.
    a. Tighten to 30 ft. lbs. (40 Nm).

All-Wheel Drive (AWD) vehicles

➡Do not tighten the 4 catalytic converter nuts at this time.

55. Using a new gasket, install the RH catalytic converter and 4 new nuts.

56. Install the 2 RH catalytic converter bracket bolts.
 a. Tighten the 4 catalytic converter nuts to 30 ft. lbs. (40 Nm).
 b. Tighten the 2 catalytic converter brackets to 15 ft. lbs. (20 Nm).

Front Wheel Drive (FWD) vehicles

57. Using a new gasket, install the RH catalytic converter and 4 new nuts.
 a. Tighten to 30 ft. lbs. (40 Nm).

All vehicles

58. Install the LH cylinder block drain plug.
 a. Tighten to 15 ft. lbs. (20 Nm) plus an additional 180 degrees.
59. Install 6 new LH exhaust manifold studs.
 a. Tighten to 9 ft. lbs. (12 Nm).

➡Failure to tighten the exhaust manifold nuts to specification a second time will cause the exhaust manifold to develop an exhaust leak.

60. Using a new gasket, install the LH exhaust manifold and 6 new nuts. Tighten in 2 stages in the sequence shown:
 a. Stage 1: Tighten to 15 ft. lbs. (20 Nm).
 b. Stage 2: Tighten to 18 ft. lbs. (25 Nm).
61. Install the LH exhaust manifold heat shield and the 3 bolts.
 a. Tighten to 89 inch lbs. (10 Nm).
62. Using a new gasket, install the LH catalytic converter and 4 new nuts.
 a. Tighten to 30 ft. lbs. (40 Nm).
63. Install the 2 LH catalytic converter bracket bolts.
 a. Tighten to 15 ft. lbs. (20 Nm).
64. Install the wiring harness retainer bolt on the rear of the LH cylinder head.
 a. Tighten to 89 inch lbs. (10 Nm).
65. Connect the LH Catalyst Monitor Sensor (CMS) sensor electrical connector.
66. Connect the LH Heated Oxygen Sensor (HO2S) electrical connector.

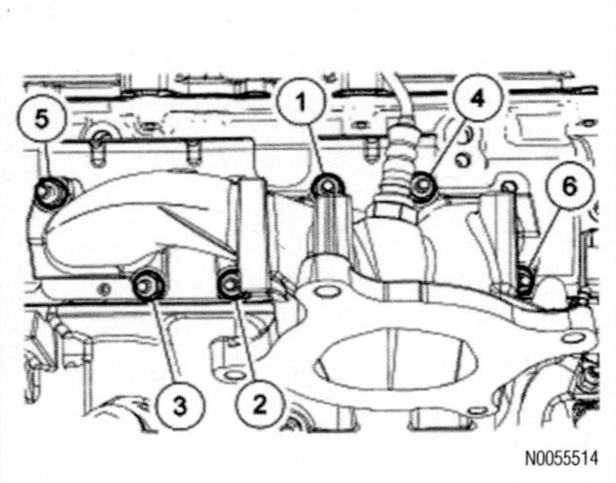

Fig. 183 Identifying the LH exhaust manifold nut tightening sequence

67. Connect the LH CMP sensor electrical connector.
68. Connect the Cylinder Head Temperature (CHT) sensor electrical connector.
69. Connect the 6 fuel injector electrical connectors.
70. Attach the wiring harness pin-type retainer.
71. Install the generator, the bolt and the nut.
 a. Tighten to 35 ft. lbs. (48 Nm).
72. Attach the wiring harness retainer to the generator.
73. Connect the generator electrical connector.
74. Connect the generator B+ cable and install the nut.
 a. Tighten to 9 ft. lbs. (12 Nm).
75. Connect the A/C compressor electrical connector.
76. If equipped, install the block heater wiring harness onto the engine.
77. Connect the block heater electrical connector and install the heat shield.
78. Install the LH camshafts.

RH Side

See Figures 184 through 187.

➡During engine repair procedures, cleanliness is extremely important. Any foreign material, including any material created while cleaning gasket surfaces that enters the oil passages, coolant passages or the oil pan, can cause engine failure.

➡On early build engines, the timing chain rides on the inner side of the RH timing chain guide. Late build engines are equipped with a different design RH timing chain guide that requires the timing chain to ride on the outer side of the RH timing chain guide. For service, all replacement RH timing chain guides will be the late build design.

All vehicles

1. Remove the RH camshafts.
2. If equipped, remove the heat shield and disconnect the block heater electrical connector.
 a. Remove the block heater wiring harness from the engine.
3. Disconnect the RH Heated Oxygen Sensor (HO2S) electrical connector.
4. Disconnect the RH Camshaft Position (CMP) sensor electrical connector.
5. Remove the bolt and the Power Steering Pressure (PSP) tube and bracket assembly.
6. Disconnect the 6 fuel injector electrical connectors.
7. Disconnect the Cylinder Head Temperature (CHT) sensor electrical connector.
8. Disconnect the LH Catalyst Monitor Sensor (CMS) sensor electrical connector.
9. Remove the 2 LH catalytic converter bracket bolts.
10. Remove the 4 nuts (3 shown) and the LH catalytic converter.
 a. Discard the nuts and the gasket.
11. Remove the LH cylinder block drain plug.
 a. Allow coolant to drain from the cylinder block.

All-Wheel Drive (AWD) vehicles

12. Remove the 2 RH catalytic converter bracket bolts.

All vehicles

13. Remove the 4 nuts and the RH catalytic converter.
 a. Discard the nuts and the gasket.
14. Remove the RH cylinder block drain plug or, if equipped, the block heater.
 a. Allow coolant to drain from the cylinder block.
15. Remove the 3 bolts and the RH exhaust manifold heat shield.
16. Remove the 6 nuts and the RH exhaust manifold.
 a. Discard the nuts and exhaust manifold gaskets.
17. Clean and inspect the RH exhaust manifold.
18. Remove and discard the 6 RH exhaust manifold studs.

Engines equipped with early build RH timing chain guides

19. Remove the 2 bolts and the RH primary timing chain guide.

Engines equipped with late build/replacement RH timing chain guides

20. Remove the 2 bolts and the RH primary timing chain guide.

All vehicles

21. Remove the 2 bolts and the RH secondary timing chain tensioner.
22. Remove the 2 bolts and the engine lifting eye.

➡Index-mark the location of the bracket on the cylinder head for installation.

23. Remove the bolt and the upper intake manifold support bracket.
24. Remove the bolt and the RH CMP sensor.
25. Remove the 4 bolts and the fuel rail and injectors as an assembly.
26. Disconnect the coolant bypass hose from the thermostat housing.
27. Remove the 2 thermostat housing-to-lower intake manifold bolts.

28. Remove the thermostat housing and discard the gasket and O-ring seal.

➡If the engine is repaired or replaced because of upper engine failure, typically including valve or piston damage, check the intake manifold for metal debris. If metal debris is found, install a new intake manifold. Failure to follow these instructions can result in engine damage.

29. Remove the 10 bolts and the lower intake manifold.
   a. Discard the gaskets.
30. Disconnect and remove the CHT sensor jumper harness.

➡If the components are to be reinstalled, they must be installed in the same positions. Mark the components for installation into their original locations.

31. Remove the valve tappets from the cylinder head.
32. Remove and discard the M6 bolt.

➡Place clean shop towels over exposed engine cavities. Carefully remove the towels so foreign material is not dropped into the engine. Any foreign material (including any material created while cleaning gasket surfaces) that enters the oil passages or the oil pan, may cause engine failure.

➡Aluminum surfaces are soft and may be scratched easily. Never place the cylinder head gasket surface, unprotected, on a bench surface.

➡The cylinder head bolts must be discarded and new bolts must be installed. They are a tighten-to-yield design and cannot be reused.

33. Remove and discard the 8 bolts from the cylinder head.
   a. Remove the cylinder head.
   b. Discard the cylinder head gasket.

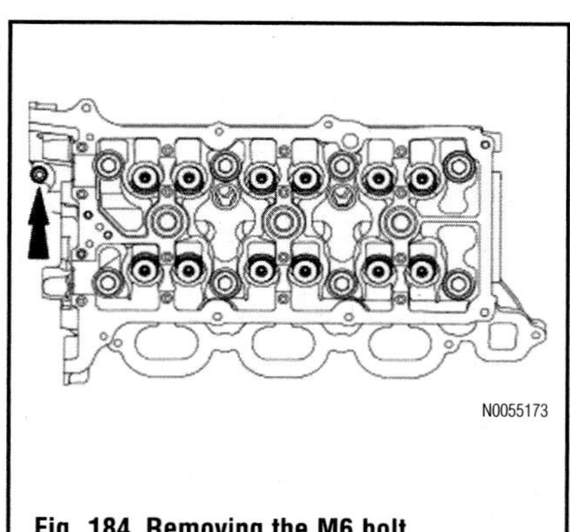

Fig. 184 Removing the M6 bolt

➡Do not use metal scrapers, wire brushes, power abrasive discs or other abrasive means to clean the sealing surfaces. These tools cause scratches and gouges that make leak paths. Use a plastic scraping tool to remove all traces of the head gasket.

➡Observe all warnings or cautions and follow all application directions contained on the packaging of the silicone gasket remover and the metal surface prep.

➡If there is no residual gasket material present, metal surface prep can be used to clean and prepare the surfaces.

34. Clean the cylinder head-to-cylinder block mating surfaces of both the cylinder heads and the cylinder block in the following sequence.
35. Remove any large deposits of silicone or gasket material with a plastic scraper.
36. Apply silicone gasket remover, following package directions, and allow to set for several minutes.
37. Remove the silicone gasket remover with a plastic scraper. A second application of silicone gasket remover may be required if residual traces of silicone or gasket material remain.
38. Apply metal surface prep, following package directions, to remove any remaining traces of oil or coolant and to prepare the surfaces to bond with the new gasket. Do not attempt to make the metal shiny. Some staining of the metal surfaces is normal.
39. Support the cylinder head on a bench with the head gasket side up. Check the cylinder head distortion and the cylinder block distortion.

To install:

➡During engine repair procedures, cleanliness is extremely important. Any foreign material, including any material created while cleaning gasket surfaces that enters the oil passages, coolant passages or the oil pan, can cause engine failure.

➡On early build engines, the timing chain rides on the inner side of the RH timing chain guide. Late build engines are equipped with a different design RH timing chain guide that requires the timing chain to ride on the outer side of the RH timing chain guide. For service, all replacement RH timing chain guides will be the late build design.

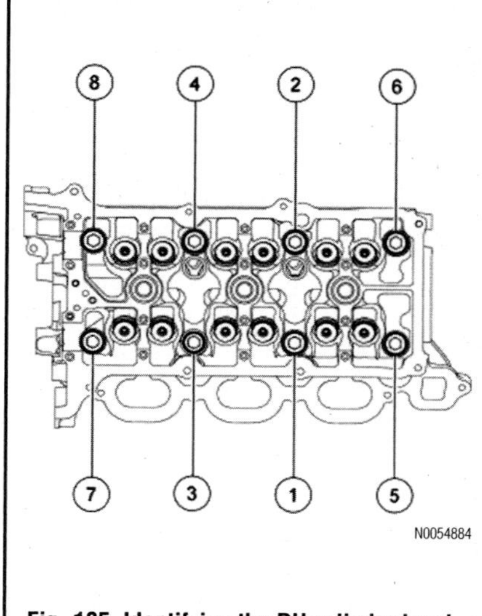

Fig. 185 Identifying the RH cylinder head bolt tightening sequence

All vehicles

40. Install a new gasket, the RH cylinder head and 8 new bolts. Tighten in the sequence shown in 5 stages:
   a. Stage 1: Tighten to 177 inch lbs. (20 Nm).
   b. Stage 2: Tighten to 26 ft. lbs. (35 Nm).
   c. Stage 3: Tighten 90 degrees.
   d. Stage 4: Tighten 90 degrees.
   e. Stage 5: Tighten 90 degrees.
41. Install the new M6 bolt.
   a. Tighten to 89 inch lbs. (10 Nm).

➡The valve tappets must be installed in their original positions.

➡Coat the valve tappets with clean engine oil prior to installation.

42. Install the valve tappets.
43. Install and connect the Cylinder Head Temperature (CHT) sensor jumper harness.

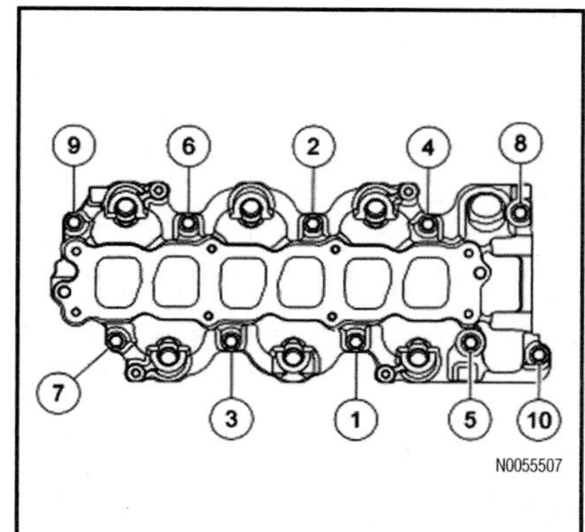

Fig. 186 Installing the lower intake manifold bolts in sequence

➡If the engine is repaired or replaced because of upper engine failure, typically including valve or piston damage, check the intake manifold for metal debris. If metal debris is found, install a new intake manifold. Failure to follow these instructions can result in engine damage.

44. Using new gaskets, install the lower intake manifold and the 10 bolts.
    a. Tighten in the sequence shown to 89 inch lbs. (10 Nm).
45. Using a new gasket and O-ring seal, install the thermostat housing and the 2 bolts.
    a. Tighten to 89 inch lbs. (10 Nm).
46. Connect the coolant bypass hose to the thermostat housing.

➡Use O-ring seals that are made of special fuel-resistant material. The use of ordinary O-rings can cause the fuel system to leak. Do not reuse the O-ring seals.

➡The upper and lower O-ring seals are not interchangeable.

47. Install new fuel injector O-ring seals.
    a. Remove the retaining clips and separate the fuel injectors from the fuel rail.
    b. Remove and discard the O-ring seals.
    c. Install new O-ring seals and lubricate with clean engine oil.
    d. Install the fuel injectors and the retaining clips onto the fuel rail.
48. Install the fuel rail and injectors as an assembly and install the 4 bolts.
    a. Tighten to 89 inch lbs. (10 Nm).
49. Install the RH Camshaft Position (CMP) sensor and the bolt.
    a. Tighten to 89 inch lbs. (10 Nm).

➡Align the bracket with the index mark made during removal.

50. Install the upper intake manifold support bracket and the bolt.
    a. Tighten to 89 inch lbs. (10 Nm).
51. Install the engine lifting eye and the 2 bolts.
    a. Tighten to 18 ft. lbs. (24 Nm).
52. Install the RH secondary timing chain tensioner and the 2 bolts.
    a. Tighten to 89 inch lbs. (10 Nm).

Engines equipped with late build/replacement RH timing chain guides

53. Install the RH primary timing chain guide and the 2 bolts.
    a. Tighten to 89 inch lbs. (10 Nm).

Engines equipped with early build RH timing chain guides

54. Install the RH primary timing chain guide and the 2 bolts.
    a. Tighten to 89 inch lbs. (10 Nm).

All vehicles

55. Install 6 new RH exhaust manifold studs.
    a. Tighten to 9 ft. lbs. (12 Nm).

➡Failure to tighten the exhaust manifold nuts to specification a second time will cause the exhaust manifold to develop an exhaust leak.

56. Using a new gasket, install the RH exhaust manifold and 6 new nuts. Tighten in 2 stages in the sequence shown:
    a. Stage 1: Tighten to 15 ft. lbs. (20 Nm).
    b. Stage 2: Tighten to 18 ft. lbs. (25 Nm).
57. Install the RH exhaust manifold heat shield and the 3 bolts.
    a. Tighten to 89 inch lbs. (10 Nm).
58. Install the RH cylinder block drain plug or, if equipped, the block heater.
    a. Tighten to 30 ft. lbs. (40 Nm).

All-Wheel Drive (AWD) vehicles

➡Do not tighten the 4 catalytic converter nuts at this time.

59. Using a new gasket, install the RH catalytic converter and 4 new nuts.
60. Install the 2 RH catalytic converter bracket bolts.
    a. Tighten the 4 catalytic converter nuts to 30 ft. lbs. (40 Nm).
61. Tighten the 2 catalytic converter brackets to 15 ft. lbs. (20 Nm).

Front Wheel Drive (FWD) vehicles

62. Using a new gasket, install the RH catalytic converter and 4 new nuts.
    a. Tighten to 30 ft. lbs. (40 Nm).

All vehicles

63. Install the LH cylinder block drain plug.

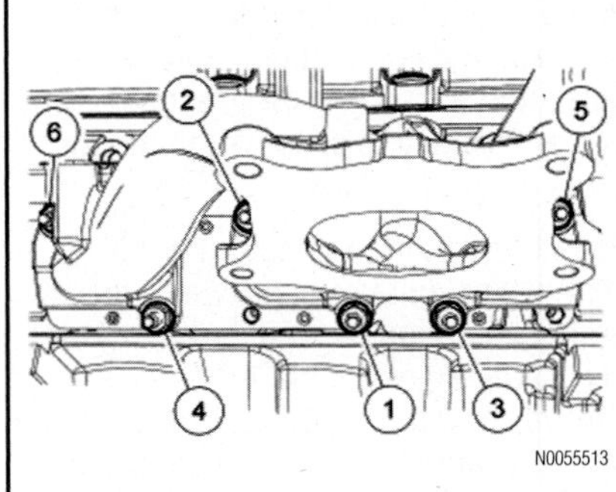

Fig. 187 Identifying the RH exhaust manifold nut tightening sequence

    a. Tighten to 15 ft. lbs. (20 Nm) plus an additional 180 degrees.
64. Using a new gasket, install the LH catalytic converter and 4 new nuts.
    a. Tighten to 30 ft. lbs. (40 Nm).
65. Install the 2 LH catalytic converter bracket bolts.
    a. Tighten to 15 ft. lbs. (20 Nm).
66. Connect the LH Catalyst Monitor Sensor (CMS) sensor electrical connector.
67. Connect the CHT sensor electrical connector.
68. Connect the 6 fuel injector electrical connectors.
69. Install the Power Steering Pressure (PSP) tube bracket and bolt.
    a. Tighten to 89 inch lbs. (10 Nm).
70. Connect the RH CMP sensor electrical connector.
71. Connect the RH HO2S electrical connector.
72. If equipped, install the block heater wiring harness onto the engine.
    a. Connect the block heater electrical connector and install the heat shield.
73. Install the RH camshafts.

EXHAUST MANIFOLD

REMOVAL & INSTALLATION

2.5L Engine

See Figures 188 and 189.

1. With the vehicle in NEUTRAL, position it on a hoist.
2. Remove the exhaust flexible pipe.
3. Disconnect the Heated Oxygen Sensor (HO2S) electrical connector.
4. Remove the 4 exhaust manifold heat shield bolts and the heat shield.
5. If equipped, detach the block heater wire harness retainer from the exhaust manifold stud.
6. Remove and discard the 7 exhaust manifold nuts.
7. Remove the exhaust manifold and discard the exhaust manifold gasket.
8. Remove and discard the 7 cylinder head studs.
9. Clean and inspect the exhaust manifold.

To install:

10. Install the 7 new cylinder head studs.
    a. Tighten to 13 ft. lbs. (17 Nm).

➡Failure to tighten the catalytic converter nuts to specification before installing the converter bracket bolts will cause the converter to develop an exhaust leak.

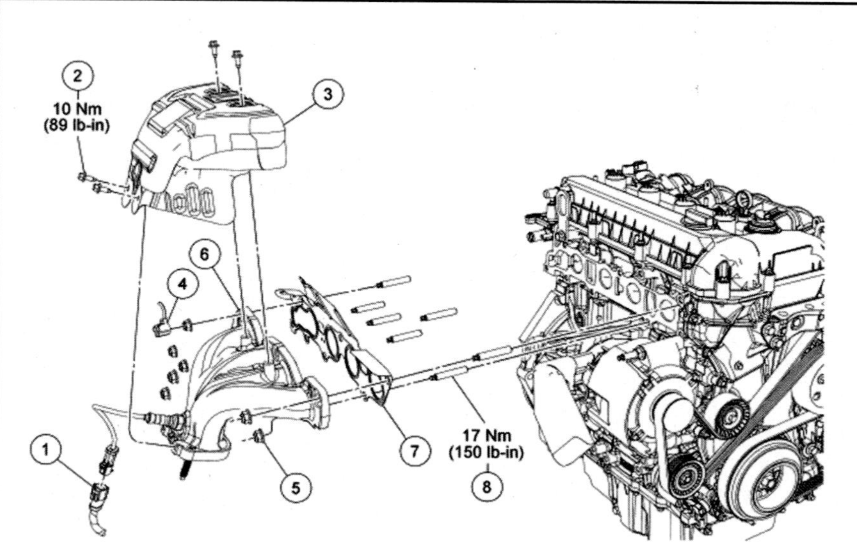

Fig. 188 Exploded view of the exhaust manifold

➡Failure to tighten the catalytic converter nuts to specification a second time will cause the converter to develop an exhaust leak.

11. Install a new exhaust manifold gasket, the exhaust manifold and 7 new nuts in the sequence shown in 2 stages:
   a. Stage 1: Tighten to 35 ft. lbs. (48 Nm).
   b. Stage 2: Tighten to 35 ft. lbs. (48 Nm).
12. If equipped, attach the block heater wire harness retainer to the exhaust manifold stud.
13. Install the exhaust manifold heat shield and the 4 bolts.
   a. Tighten to 89 inch lbs. (10 Nm).

Fig. 189 Identifying the exhaust manifold nut tightening sequence

14. Connect the HO2S electrical connector.
15. Install the exhaust flexible pipe.

3.0L Engine

RH Side

See Figures 190 and 191.

1. With the vehicle in NEUTRAL, position it on a hoist.
2. Remove the EGR tube.
3. Remove the RH catalytic converter.

➡The heat shield that was unbolted from the exhaust manifold during removal of the RH catalytic converter cannot be removed from the vehicle until the Power Transfer Unit (PTU) bracket is removed.

4. Remove the 5 bolts and the PTU bracket.
5. Remove the catalytic converter heat shield from the vehicle.
6. Remove the 6 nuts and the RH exhaust manifold.
   a. Discard the gasket and nuts.

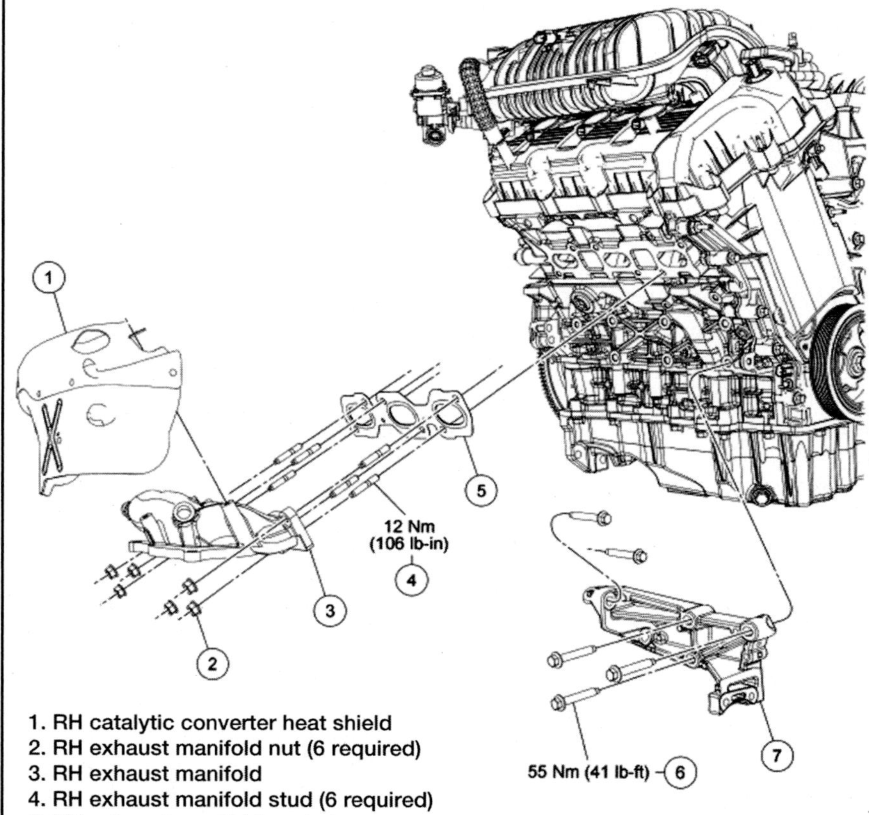

Fig. 190 Exploded view of the RH exhaust manifold and related components

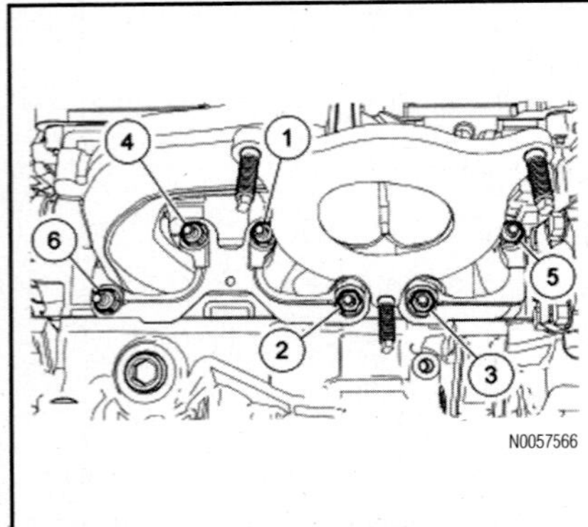

Fig. 191 Identifying the RH exhaust manifold nut tightening sequence

7. Clean and inspect the RH exhaust manifold.

8. Remove and discard the 6 RH exhaust manifold studs.

➡Do not use metal scrapers, wire brushes, power abrasive discs or other abrasive means to clean the sealing surfaces. These may cause scratches and gouges resulting in leak paths. Use a plastic scraper to clean the sealing surfaces.

9. Clean the exhaust manifold mating surface of the cylinder head with metal surface prep. Follow the directions on the packaging.

To install:

10. Install 6 new RH exhaust manifold studs.

a. Tighten to 9 ft. lbs. (12 Nm).

➡The catalytic converter heat shield must be positioned up into the engine compartment prior to installing the PTU bracket.

11. Position the catalytic converter heat shield into the engine compartment.

12. Install the PTU bracket and the 5 bolts.

a. Tighten to 41 inch lbs. (55 Nm).

13. Install a new gasket, the RH exhaust manifold and 6 new nuts.

a. Tighten to 15 ft. lbs. (20 Nm) in the sequence shown.

14. Install the RH catalytic converter.

15. Install the EGR tube.

3.5L Engine

LH Side

See Figures 192 and 193.

1. Remove the LH catalytic converter.

2. Remove the LH Heated Oxygen Sensor (HO2S).

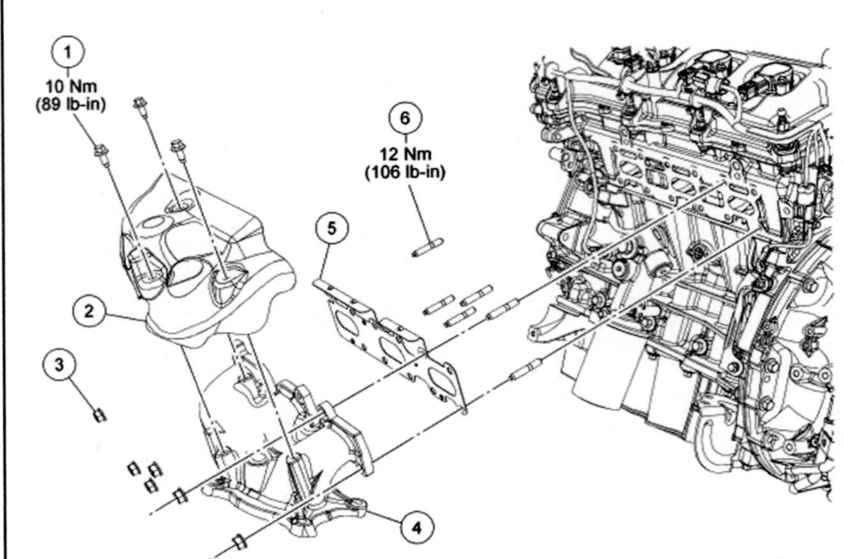

Fig. 192 Exploded view of the LH exhaust manifold and related components

3. Remove the 3 bolts and the LH exhaust manifold heat shield.

4. Remove the 6 nuts and the LH exhaust manifold.

a. Discard the nuts and gasket.

5. Clean and inspect the LH exhaust manifold.

6. Remove and discard the 6 LH exhaust manifold studs.

➡Do not use metal scrapers, wire brushes, power abrasive discs or other abrasive means to clean the sealing surfaces. These may cause scratches and gouges resulting in leak paths. Use a plastic scraper to clean the sealing surfaces.

7. Clean the exhaust manifold mating surface of the cylinder head with metal surface prep. Follow the directions on the packaging.

To install:

8. Install 6 new LH exhaust manifold studs.

a. Tighten to 9 ft. lbs. (12 Nm).

➡Failure to tighten the exhaust manifold nuts to specification a second time will cause the exhaust manifold to develop an exhaust leak.

9. Using a new gasket, install the LH exhaust manifold and 6 new nuts. Tighten in 2 stages in the sequence shown:

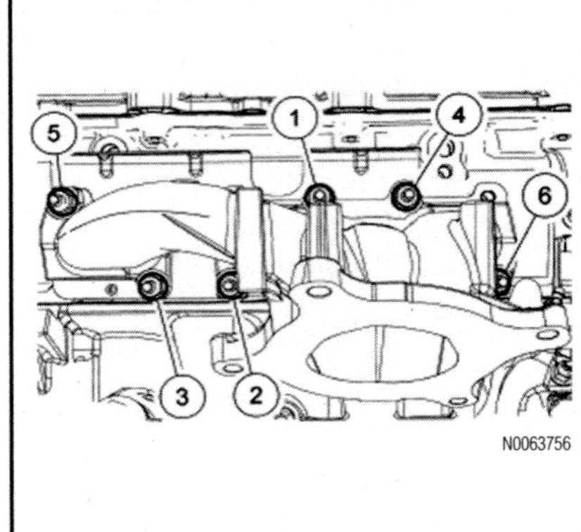

Fig. 193 Identifying the LH exhaust manifold nut tightening sequence

a. Stage 1: Tighten to 15 ft. lbs. (20 Nm).

b. Stage 2: Tighten to 18 ft. lbs. (25 Nm).

10. Install the LH exhaust manifold heat shield and the 3 bolts.

a. Tighten to 89 inch lbs. (10 Nm).

11. Install the LH HO2S.

12. Install the LH catalytic converter.

RH Side

See Figures 194 and 195.

1. Remove the RH catalytic converter.

2. Disconnect the RH Heated Oxygen Sensor (HO2S) electrical connector.

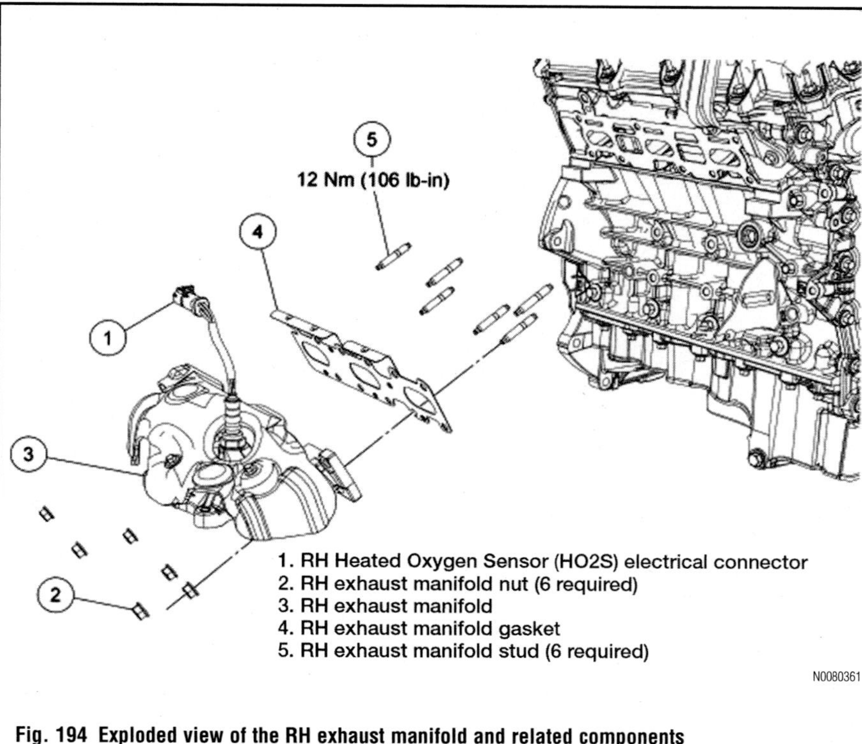

Fig. 194 Exploded view of the RH exhaust manifold and related components

3. Remove the 6 nuts and the RH exhaust manifold.
    a. Discard the nuts and gasket.
4. Clean and inspect the RH exhaust manifold.
5. Remove and discard the 6 RH exhaust manifold studs.

➡Do not use metal scrapers, wire brushes, power abrasive discs or other abrasive means to clean the sealing surfaces. These may cause scratches and gouges resulting in leak paths. Use a plastic scraper to clean the sealing surfaces.

6. Clean the exhaust manifold mating surface of the cylinder head with metal surface prep. Follow the directions on the packaging.

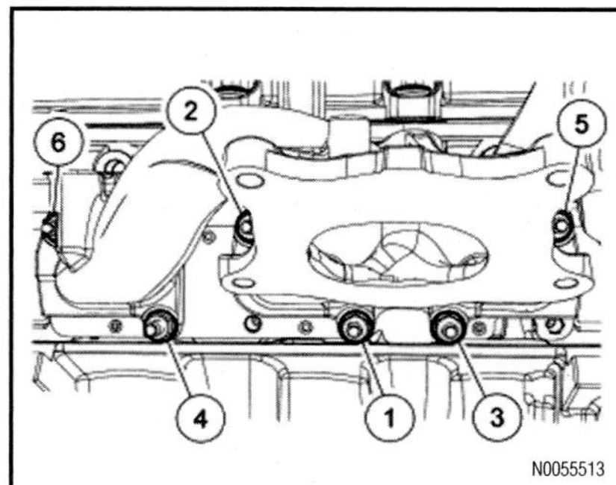

Fig. 195 Identifying the RH exhaust manifold nut tightening sequence

To install:

7. Install 6 new RH exhaust manifold studs.
8. Tighten to 9 ft. lbs. (12 Nm).

➡Failure to tighten the exhaust manifold nuts to specification a second time will cause the exhaust manifold to develop an exhaust leak.

9. Using a new gasket, install the RH exhaust manifold and 6 new nuts. Tighten in 2 stages in the sequence shown:
    a. Stage 1: Tighten to 15 ft. lbs. (20 Nm).
    b. Stage 2: Tighten to 18 ft. lbs. (25 Nm).
10. Connect the RH HO2S electrical connector.
11. Install the RH catalytic converter.

INTAKE MANIFOLD

REMOVAL & INSTALLATION

2.5L Engine

See Figures 196 and 197.

1. With vehicle in NEUTRAL, position it on a hoist
2. Remove the Air Cleaner (ACL) outlet pipe
3. Disconnect the vacuum supply hose.
4. Depress the quick connect locking ring.
5. Pull the vacuum hose out of the quick connect fitting.

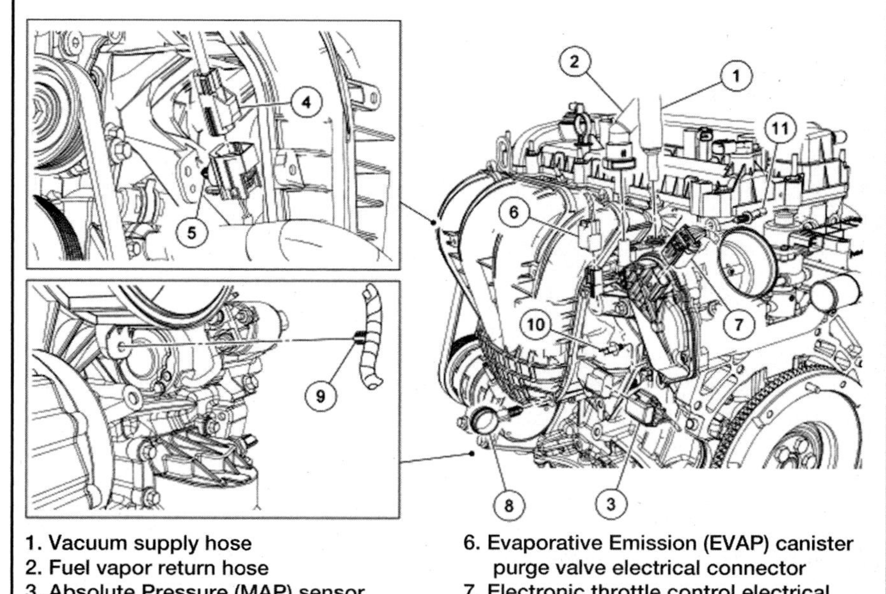

Fig. 196 Removing and installing the intake manifold—1 of 2

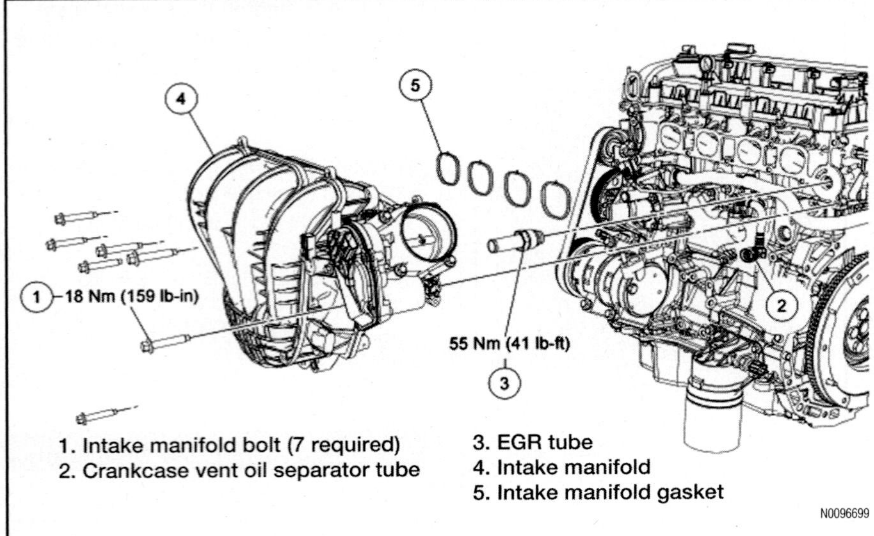

Fig. 197 Removing and installing the intake manifold—2 of 2

6. Disconnect the fuel vapor return hose from the intake manifold.
7. Disconnect the Manifold Absolute Pressure (MAP) electrical connector.
8. Disconnect the Evaporative Emission (EVAP) canister purge valve electrical connector.
9. Disconnect the electronic throttle control electrical connector.
10. Disconnect the Knock Sensor (KS) electrical connector.
11. Detach the wire harness pin-type retainer.
12. Detach the heater hose pin-type retainer.
13. Detach the A/C compressor wiring harness retainer.
14. Detach the 2 wiring harness pin-type retainers from the intake manifold and position the wiring harness aside.
15. If equipped, remove the 7 screws and the underbody cover.
16. Remove the intake manifold lower bolt.
17. Remove the 6 bolts and position the intake manifold aside to access the crankcase vent oil separator tube and the EGR tube.
18. Remove the EGR tube.
19. Squeeze the 2 crankcase vent oil separator tube tabs and disconnect the tube from the intake manifold.
20. Remove the intake manifold.

➡If the engine is repaired or replaced because of upper engine failure, typically including valve or piston damage, check the intake manifold for metal debris. If metal debris is found, install a new intake manifold. Failure to follow these instructions can result in engine damage.

To install:

21. To install, reverse the removal procedure.
22. Inspect and install new intake manifold gaskets if necessary.
23. Tighten the EGR tube to 41 ft. lbs. (55 Nm).
24. Tighten the intake manifold bolts to 13 ft. lbs. (18 Nm).
25. Tighten the lower intake manifold bolts to 13 ft. lbs. (18 Nm).

2.5L Hybrid Engine

See Figures 198 through 200.

1. With vehicle in NEUTRAL, position it on a hoist.

➡Before removing the high voltage cables, the vehicle electrical system must be completely shut down for at least 5 minutes to allow for the high voltage capacitors to discharge.

2. Depower the vehicle high voltage electrical system.

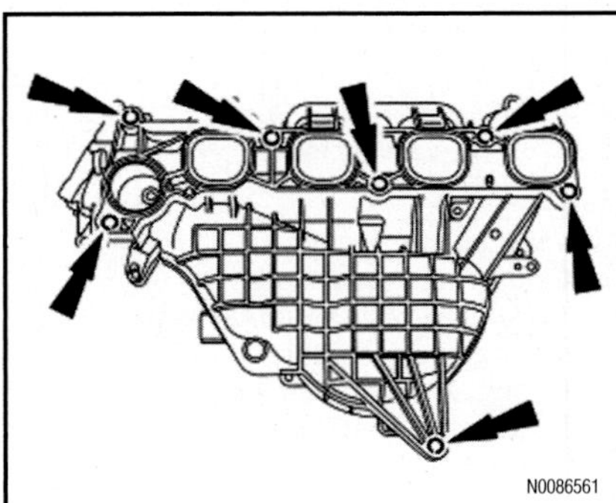

Fig. 198 Location of the intake manifold bolts

3. Remove the fuel rail.
4. Remove the Throttle Body (TB).
5. Remove the accessory drive belt tensioner.
6. Disconnect the Engine Oil Pressure (EOP) switch electrical connector.
7. Disconnect the Manifold Absolute Pressure (MAP) sensor electrical connector.
8. Disconnect the Evaporative Emission (EVAP) canister purge valve electrical connector.
9. Disconnect the EVAP tube-to- EVAP canister purge valve quick connect coupling and the vacuum tube from the intake manifold.
10. Detach the 3 wiring retainers from the intake manifold near the throttle body mounting area.
11. Disconnect the auxiliary coolant pump electrical connector and detach the 2 wiring retainers.
12. Detach the lower radiator hose retainer from the intake manifold.
13. Detach the engine wiring harness retainer and the vehicle high voltage electrical system wire retainer from the intake manifold.
14. Disconnect the Knock Sensor (KS) electrical connector and detach the retainer from the intake manifold.
15. Remove the cooling fan motor and shroud.
16. Remove the 3 A/C compressor bolts and position the compressor aside.

➡The cylinder head side of the intake manifold is showing the location of the 7 bolts.

17. Remove the 7 bolts and position the intake manifold aside to access the PCV hose connector.
18. Squeeze the 2 PCV hose connector tabs and disconnect the PCV hose from the intake manifold.
19. Remove the intake manifold and gaskets.

➡If the engine is repaired or replaced because of upper engine failure, typically including valve or piston damage, check the intake manifold for metal debris. If metal debris is found, install a new intake manifold. Failure to follow these instructions can result in engine damage.

To install:

20. To install, reverse the removal procedure.
21. Inspect and install new intake manifold gaskets if necessary.
22. Tighten the intake manifold bolts to 13 ft. lbs. (18 ft. lbs.)

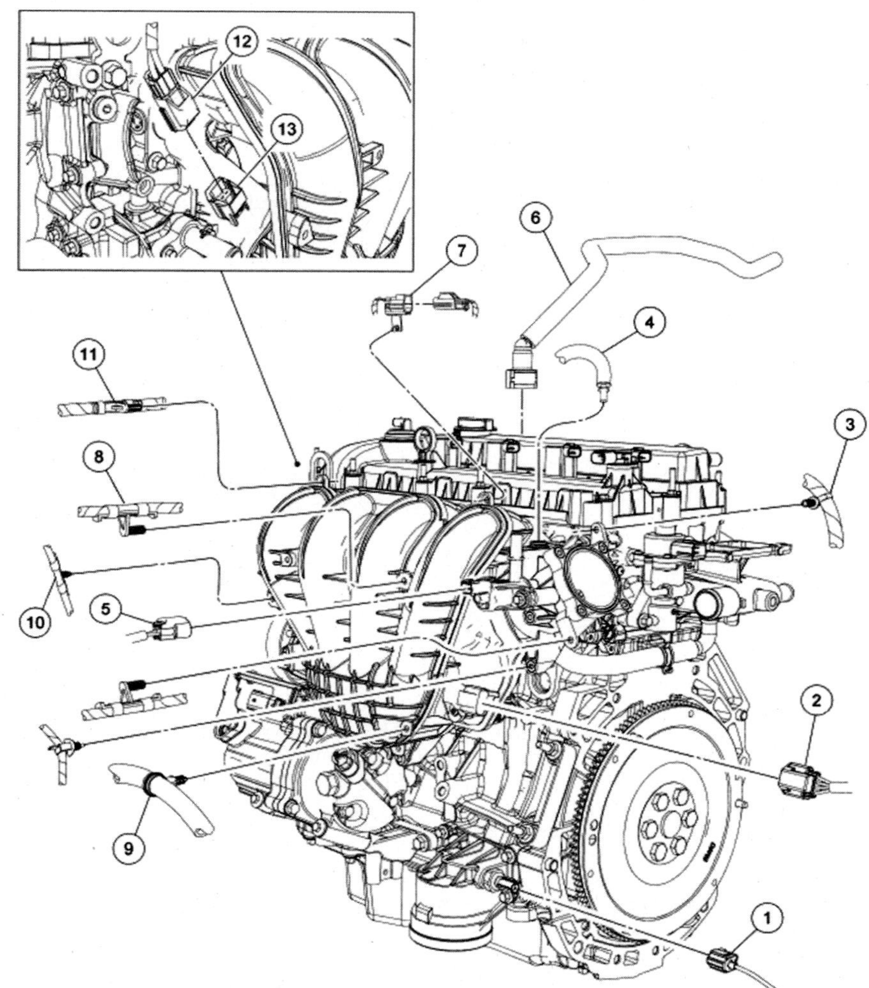

1. Engine Oil Pressure (EOP) switch electrical connector
2. Manifold Absolute Pressure (MAP) sensor electrical connector
3. Wiring harness retainer (3 required)
4. Vacuum tube
5. Evaporative Emission (EVAP) canister purge valve electrical connector
6. EVAP tube-to- EVAP canister purge valve quick connect coupling
7. Auxiliary coolant pump electrical connector
8. Auxiliary coolant pump wiring retainers (2 required)
9. Lower radiator hose retainer
10. Engine wiring harness retainer
11. Vehicle high voltage electrical system wire retainer
12. Knock Sensor (KS) electrical connector
13. KS electrical connector

N0098190

Fig. 199 Removing and installing the intake manifold—1 of 2

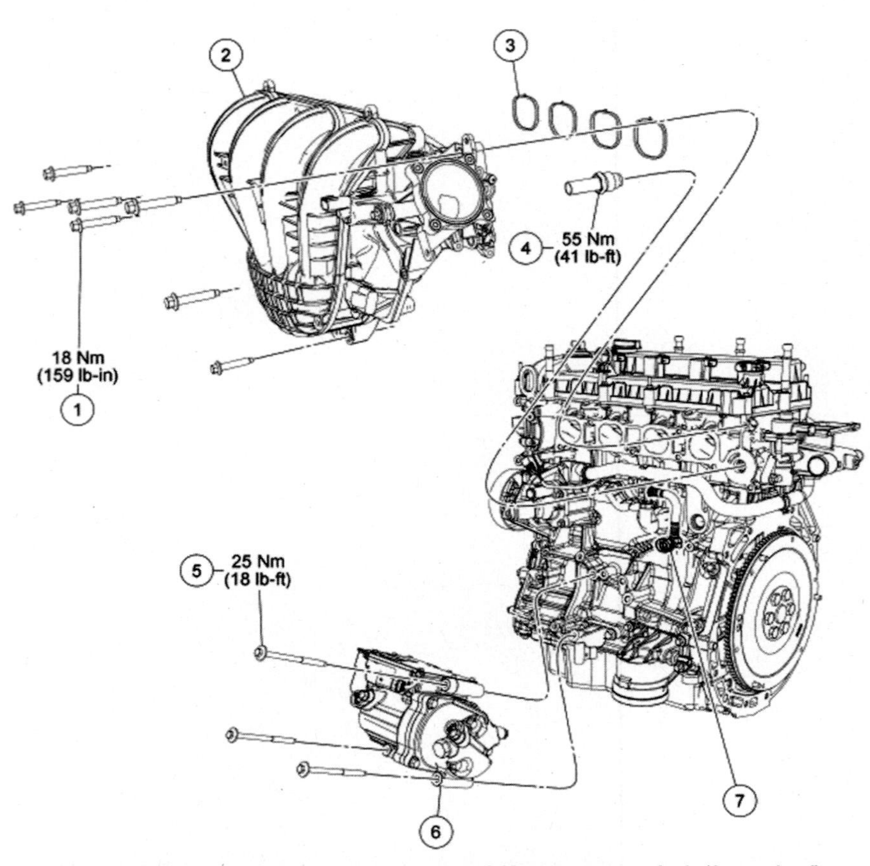

Fig. 200 Removing and installing the intake manifold—2 of 2

23. Tighten the A/C compressor bolts to 18 ft. lbs. (25 Nm).

3.0L Engine

Lower

See Figures 201 and 202.

WARNING

Do not smoke, carry lighted tobacco or have an open flame of any type when working on or near any fuel-related component. Highly flammable mixtures are always present and may be ignited. Failure to follow these instructions may result in serious personal injury.

WARNING

Before working on or disconnecting any of the fuel tubes or fuel system components, relieve the fuel system pressure to prevent accidental spraying of fuel. Fuel in the fuel system remains under high pressure, even when the engine is not running. Failure to follow this instruction may result in serious personal injury.

1. Release the fuel system pressure.
2. Disconnect the battery ground cable.
3. Remove the fuel rail.
4. Remove the 8 lower intake manifold bolts and the lower intake manifold.
5. Remove and discard the gaskets.

To install:

➡If the engine is repaired or replaced because of upper engine failure, typically including valve or piston damage, check the intake manifold for metal debris. If metal debris is found, install a new intake manifold. Failure to follow these instructions can result in engine damage.

➡Clean and inspect all sealing surfaces. Install new gaskets.

6. Position the lower intake manifold and install the 8 bolts.
   a. Tighten in the sequence shown to 89 inch lbs. (10 Nm).
7. Install the fuel rail.
8. Connect the battery ground cable.

Upper

See Figures 205 through 207.

1. Remove the Air Cleaner (ACL) outlet pipe.
2. Remove the battery.
3. Remove the EGR tube fitting from the EGR valve.
4. Disconnect the electronic throttle control electrical connector.
5. Disconnect the Evaporative Emission

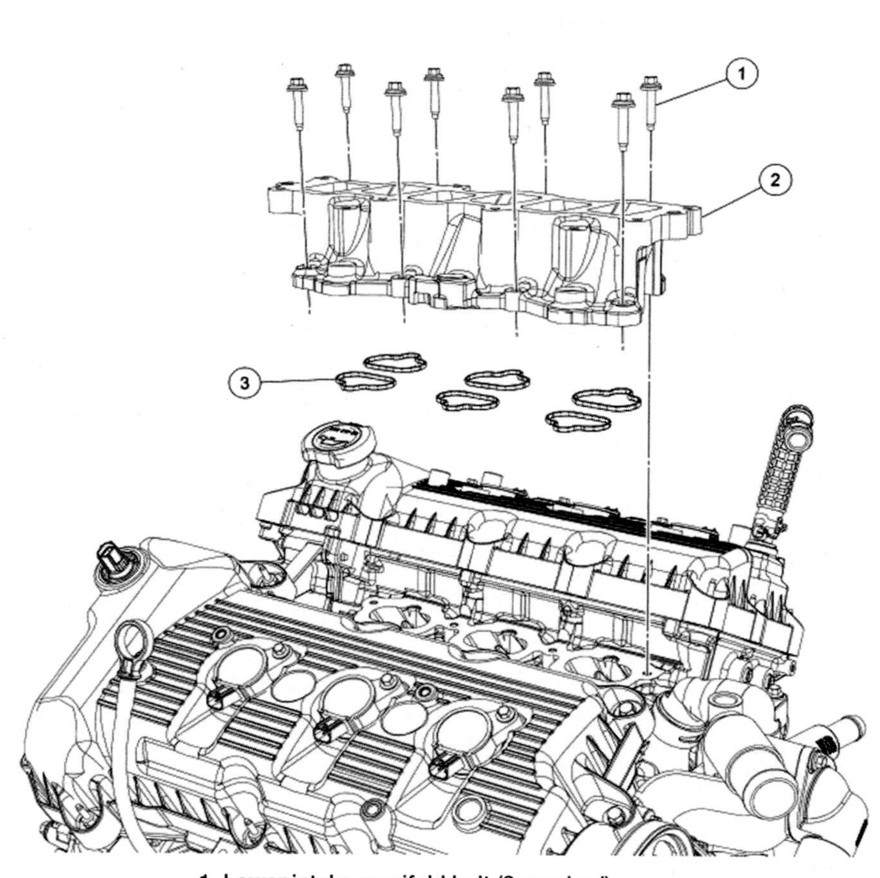

Fig. 201 Exploded view of the lower intake manifold

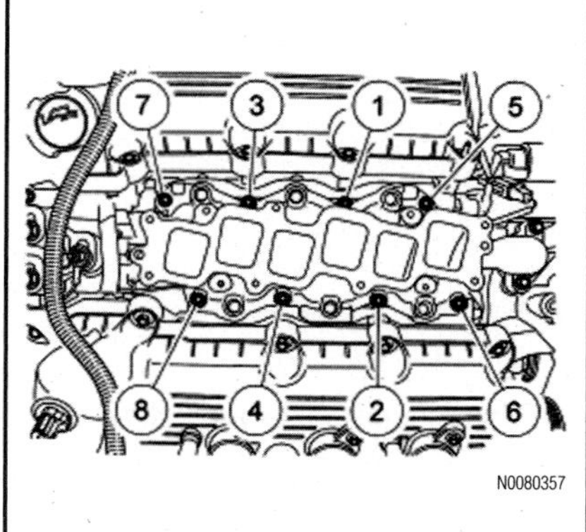

Fig. 202 Identifying the lower intake manifold bolt tightening sequence

(EVAP) canister purge valve electrical connector.

6. Disconnect the EGR valve electrical connector and detach the wiring retainer.

7. Disconnect the EVAP tube-to- EVAP canister purge valve quick connect coupling and the brake booster vacuum tube from the upper intake manifold.

8. Detach the fuel tube and EVAP tube-to- EVAP canister purge valve tube retainer from the upper intake manifold.

9. Detach the engine control wiring harness retainer from the upper intake manifold.

10. Disconnect the PCV tube from the upper intake manifold.

11. Disconnect the Manifold Absolute Pressure (MAP) sensor electrical connector and detach the wiring retainer.

12. Remove the 2 upper intake manifold support bracket bolts from the upper intake manifold.

13. Remove the 7 bolts and the upper intake manifold.

a. Remove and discard the gaskets.

To install:

➡If the engine is repaired or replaced because of upper engine failure, typically including valve or piston damage, check the intake manifold for metal debris. If metal debris is found, install a new intake manifold. Failure to fol-

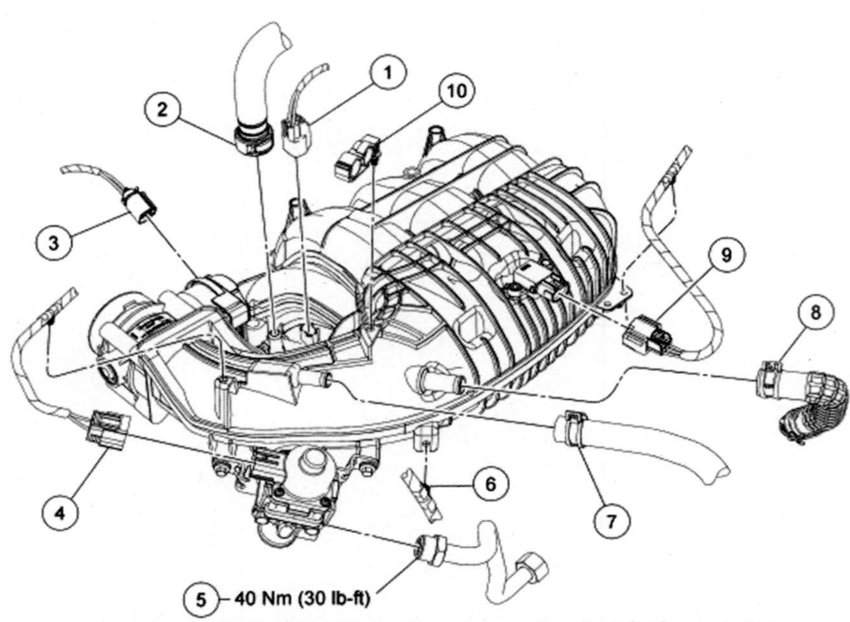

1. Evaporative Emission (EVAP) canister purge valve electrical connector
2. EVAP tube-to- EVAP canister purge valve quick connect coupling
3. Electronic throttle control electrical connector
4. EGR valve electrical connector
5. EGR tube fitting
6. Engine control wiring harness retainer
7. Brake booster vacuum tube
8. PCV tube
9. Manifold Absolute Pressure (MAP) sensor electrical connector
10. Fuel tube and EVAP tube-to- EVAP canister purge valve tube retainer

N0096590

Fig. 203 Removing and installing the upper intake manifold—1 of 2

low these instructions can result in engine damage.

14. Clean and inspect all of the sealing surfaces of the upper intake manifold.

➡Install new upper intake manifold gaskets.

15. Position the upper intake manifold and install the 7 bolts.
    a. Tighten the bolts in 2 stages in the sequence shown.
    b. Stage 1: Tighten to 89 inch lbs. (10 Nm).
    c. Stage 2: Tighten an additional 45 degrees.
16. Install the 2 upper intake manifold support bracket bolts.
    a. Tighten to 89 inch lbs. (10 Nm).
    b. Connect the MAP sensor electrical connector and attach the wiring retainer.
17. Connect the PCV tube to the upper intake manifold.
18. Attach the engine control wiring harness retainer to the upper intake manifold.
19. Connect the EVAP tube-to- EVAP canister purge valve quick connect coupling and the brake booster vacuum tube to the upper intake manifold.
20. Attach the fuel tube and EVAP tube-to- EVAP canister purge valve tube retainer to the upper intake manifold.
21. Connect the EGR valve electrical connector and attach the wiring retainer.
22. Connect the EVAP canister purge valve electrical connector.
23. Connect the electronic throttle control electrical connector.
24. Install the EGR tube fitting to the EGR valve.
    a. Tighten to 30 ft. lbs. (40 Nm).
25. Install the battery.
26. Install the ACL outlet pipe.

3.5L Engine

Lower

See Figures 206 and 207.

➡During engine repair procedures, cleanliness is extremely important. Any foreign material, including any material created while cleaning gasket surfaces that enters the oil passages, coolant passages or the oil pan, can cause engine failure.

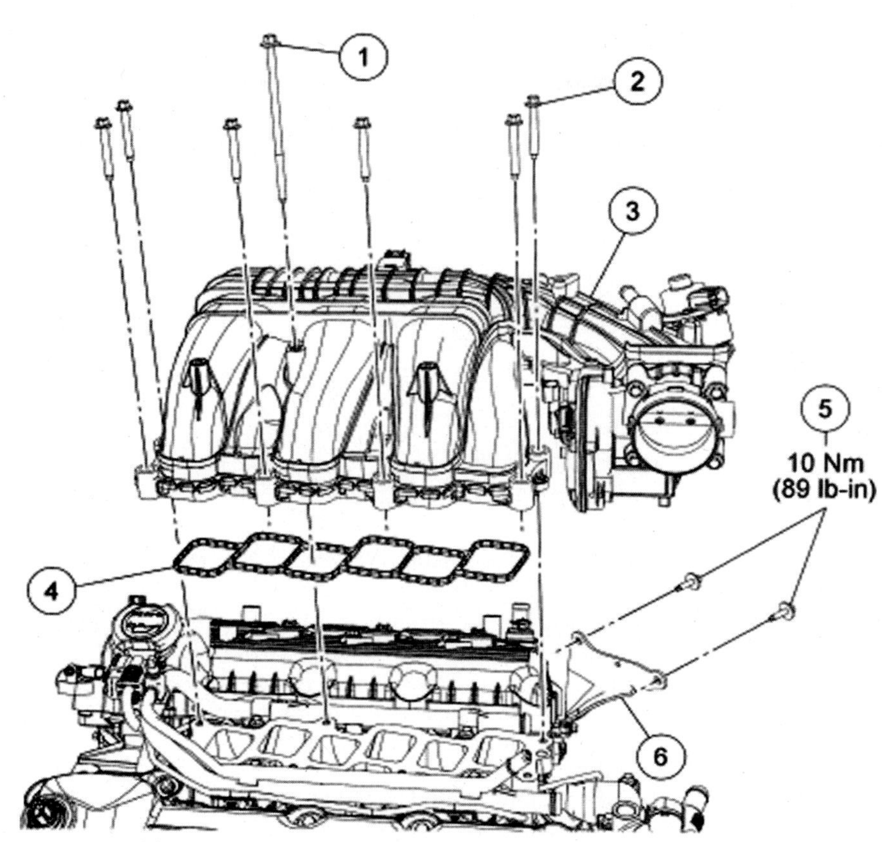

Fig. 204 Removing and installing the upper intake manifold—2 of 2

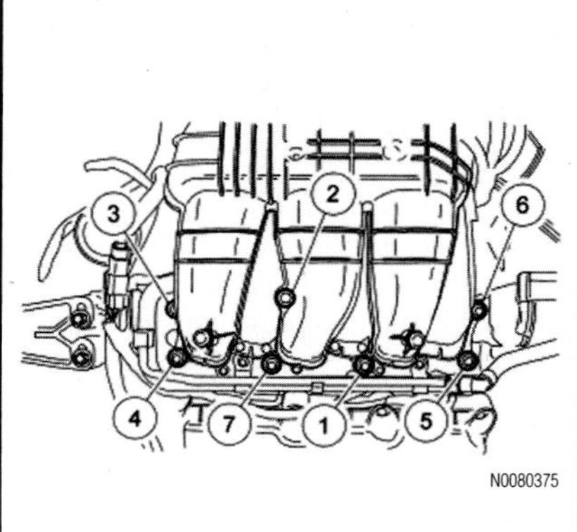

Fig. 205 Identifying the upper intake manifold bolt tightening sequence

1. With the vehicle in NEUTRAL, position it on a hoist.
2. Remove the fuel rail.
3. Drain the cooling system.
4. Remove the 2 thermostat housing-to-lower intake manifold bolts.
5. Remove the 10 bolts and the lower intake manifold.
6. Remove and discard the intake manifold and thermostat housing gaskets.
7. Clean and inspect all sealing surfaces.

To install:

➡If the engine is repaired or replaced because of upper engine failure, typically including valve or piston damage, check the intake manifold for metal debris. If metal debris is found, install a new intake manifold. Failure to follow these instructions can result in engine damage.

8. Using new intake manifold and thermostat housing gaskets, install the lower intake manifold and the 10 bolts.
   a. Tighten in the sequence shown to 89 inch lbs. (10 Nm).
9. Install the 2 thermostat housing-to-lower intake manifold bolts.
   a. Tighten to 89 inch lbs. (10 Nm).
10. Install the fuel rail.
11. Fill and bleed the cooling system.

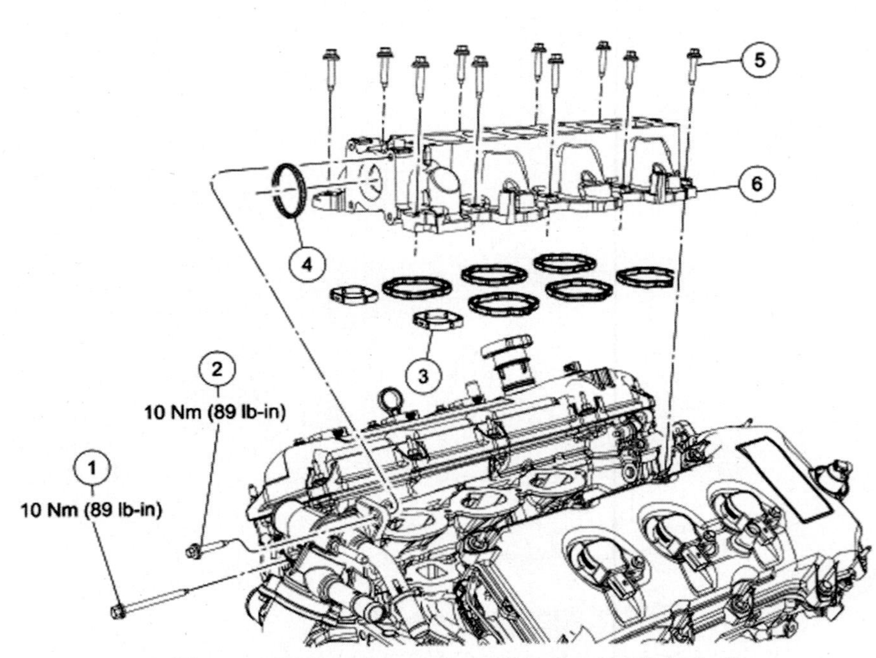

Fig. 206 Removing and installing the lower intake manifold

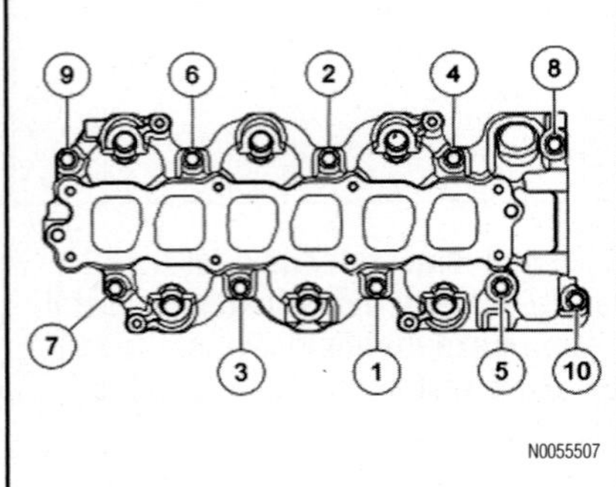

Fig. 207 Identifying the lower intake manifold bolt tightening sequence

Upper

See Figures 208 through 209.

1. Remove the Air Cleaner (ACL) outlet pipe.
2. Disconnect the Throttle Body (TB) electrical connector.
3. Disconnect the Evaporative Emission (EVAP) tube from the intake manifold.
4. Disconnect the brake booster vacuum hose from the intake manifold.
5. Disconnect the PCV tube from the PCV valve.
6. Detach all the wiring harness retainers from the upper intake manifold.
7. If equipped, detach the cylinder block heater wiring harness retainer from the upper intake manifold.
8. Remove the upper intake manifold support bracket bolt.
9. Remove the 6 bolts and the upper intake manifold.
   a. Remove and discard the gaskets.
10. Clean and inspect all of the sealing surfaces of the upper and lower intake manifold.

To install:

➡If the engine is repaired or replaced because of upper engine failure, typically including valve or piston damage, check the intake manifold for metal debris. If metal debris is found, install a new intake manifold. Failure to follow these instructions can result in engine damage.

11. Using new gaskets, install the upper intake manifold and the 6 bolts.
    a. Tighten in the sequence shown to 89 inch lbs. (10 Nm).
12. Install the upper intake manifold support bracket bolt.
    a. Tighten to 89 inch lbs. (10 Nm).
13. If equipped, attach the cylinder block heater wiring harness retainer to the upper intake manifold.
14. Attach all the wiring harness retainers to the upper intake manifold.
15. Connect the PCV tube to the PCV valve.
16. Connect the brake booster vacuum hose to the intake manifold.
17. Connect the EVAP tube to the intake manifold.
18. Connect the TB electrical connector.
19. Install the ACL outlet pipe.

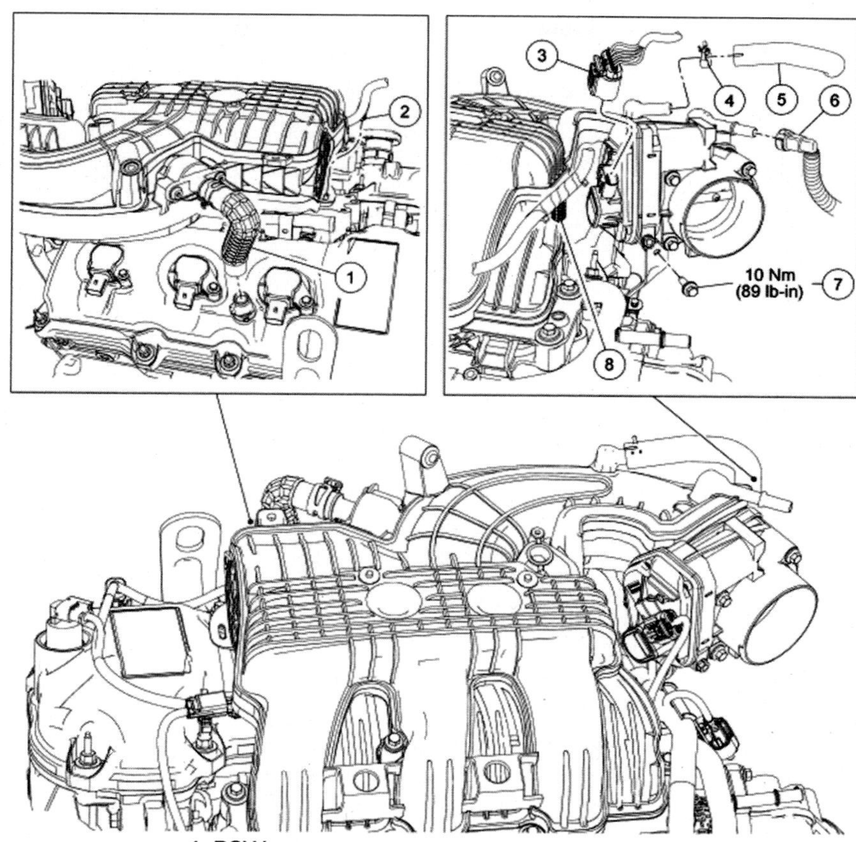

1. PCV hose
2. Block heater wiring harness retainer
3. Throttle Body (TB) electrical connector
4. Brake booster-to-intake manifold vacuum hose clamp
5. Brake booster-to-intake manifold vacuum hose
6. Evaporative Emission (EVAP)-to-intake manifold tube
7. Upper intake manifold support bracket bolt
8. Engine control wiring harness retainer

N0082317

Fig. 208 Removing and installing the upper intake manifold—1 of 2

OIL PAN

REMOVAL & INSTALLATION

2.5L Engine

See Figures 211 and 212.

All vehicles

1. With the vehicle in NEUTRAL, position it on a hoist.
2. Remove the Air Cleaner (ACL).

Automatic transmission

3. Remove the battery tray.

All vehicles

➡To prevent damage to the transmission, do not loosen the transmission-to-engine bolts more than 5 mm (0.19 in).

4. Loosen the 3 upper transaxle-to-engine bolts 5 mm (0.19 in).
5. If equipped, remove the 7 screws and the underbody cover.
6. Loosen the 1 (automatic transmission) or 2 (manual transmission) LH bellhousing-to-engine bolt(s) 5 mm (0.19 in).
7. Loosen the RH engine-to-bellhousing bolt and stud bolt 5 mm (0.19 in).
8. Remove the 2 oil pan-to-bellhousing bolts.
9. Remove the bellhousing-to-oil pan bolt.
10. Slide the transmission rearward 5 mm (0.19 in).
11. Drain the engine oil.
12. Install the drain plug.
    a. To install, tighten to 21 ft. lbs. (28 Nm).
13. Remove the 3 engine front cover-to-oil pan bolts and the stud bolt.
14. Remove the 13 bolts and the oil pan.

To install:

All vehicles

➡Do not use metal scrapers, wire brushes, power abrasive discs or other abrasive means to clean the sealing surfaces. These tools cause scratches

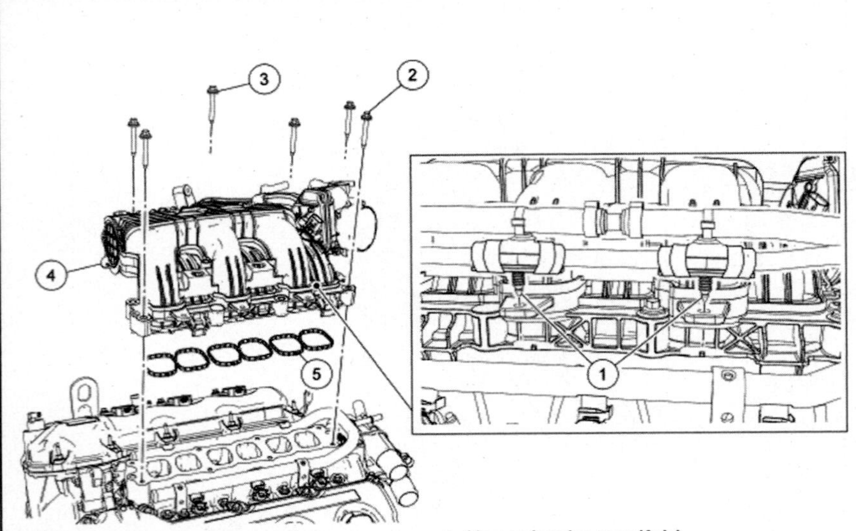

Fig. 209 Removing and installing the upper intake manifold—2 of 2

and gouges, which make leak paths. Use a plastic scraping tool to remove traces of sealant.

15. Clean and inspect all mating surfaces.

➡If the oil pan is not secured within 10 minutes of sealant application, the sealant must be removed and the sealing area cleaned with metal surface prep. Allow to dry until there is no sign of wetness, or 10 minutes, whichever is longer. Failure to follow these instructions can cause future oil leakage.

16. Apply a 2.5 mm (0.09 in) bead of silicone gasket and sealant to the oil pan-to-engine block and to the oil pan-to-engine front cover mating surface.
17. Position the oil pan onto the engine and install the oil pan bolts finger-tight.
18. Install the 3 engine front cover-to-oil pan bolts and the stud bolt.

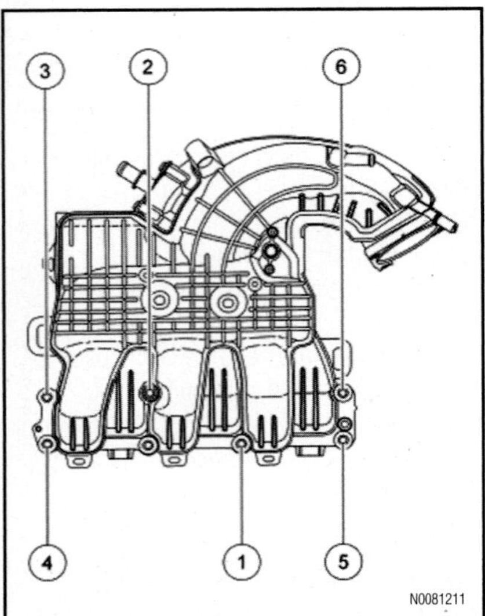

Fig. 210 Identifying the upper intake manifold bolt tightening sequence

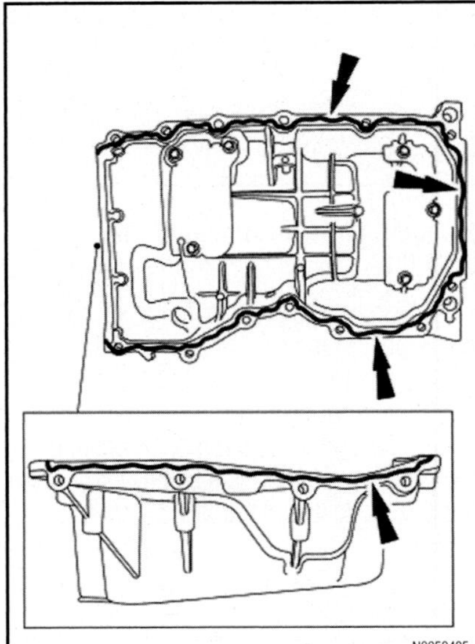

Fig. 211 Applying silicone gasket and sealant to the oil pan to engine block and front cover mating surface

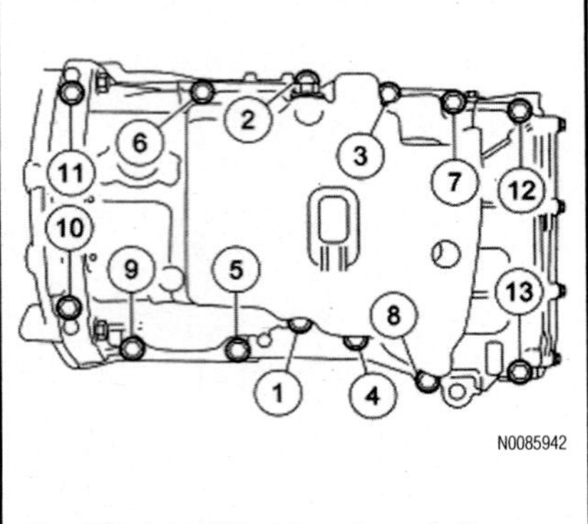

Fig. 212 Identifying the oil pan bolt tightening sequence

a. Tighten to 89 inch lbs. (10 Nm).
19. Tighten the oil pan bolts in the sequence shown.
a. Tighten to 18 ft. lbs. (25 Nm).
20. Alternate tightening the 1 LH and 1 RH lower bolts to slide the transmission and engine together.
a. Tighten to 35 ft. lbs. (48 Nm).
21. Tighten the remaining LH bolt (manual transmission) and RH stud bolt.
a. Tighten to 35 ft. lbs. (48 Nm).
22. Install the bellhousing-to-oil pan bolt.
a. Tighten to 35 ft. lbs. (48 Nm).
23. Install the 2 oil pan-to-bellhousing bolts.
a. Tighten to 35 ft. lbs. (48 Nm).
24. If equipped, install the underbody cover and the 7 screws.
25. Tighten the 3 top bellhousing-to-engine bolts.
a. Tighten to 35 ft. lbs. (48 Nm).

Automatic transmission

26. Install the battery tray.

All vehicles

27. Install the ACL assembly.
28. Fill the engine with clean engine oil.

2.5L Hybrid Engine

See Figures 213 through 215.

1. With the vehicle in NEUTRAL, position it on a hoist.
2. Drain the engine oil, then install the drain plug.
a. Tighten to 21 ft. lbs. (28 Nm).
3. Remove the engine front cover.
4. Remove the 4 oil pan-to-bellhousing bolts.
5. Remove the 13 bolts and the oil pan.

To install:

➡Do not use metal scrapers, wire brushes, power abrasive discs or other abrasive means to clean the sealing

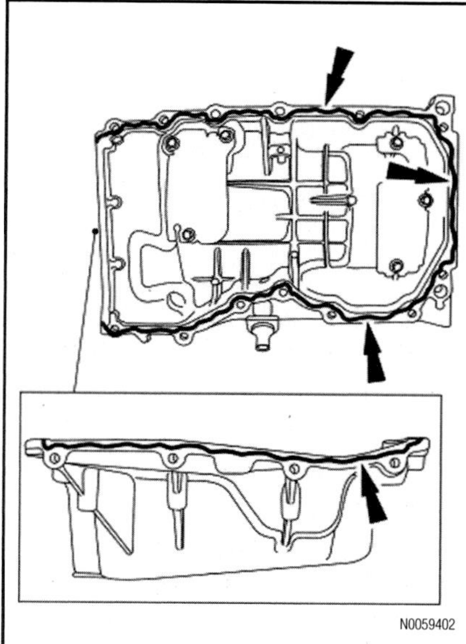

Fig. 213 Applying silicone gasket and sealant to the oil pan

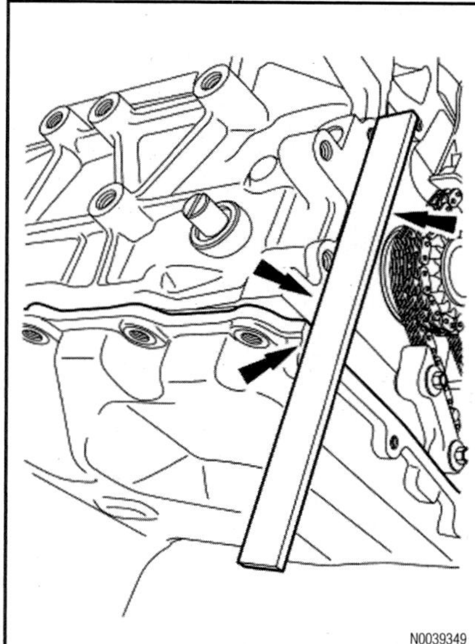

Fig. 214 Aligning the front surface of the oil pan flush with the front surface of the engine block

surfaces. These tools cause scratches and gouges, which make leak paths. Use a plastic scraping tool to remove traces of sealant.

6. Clean and inspect all mating surfaces.

➡If the oil pan is not secured within 4 minutes of sealant application, the sealant must be removed and the sealing area cleaned with metal surface

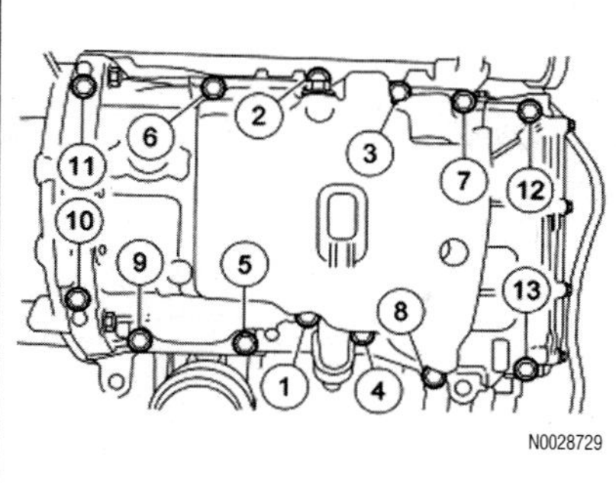

Fig. 215 Identifying the oil pan bolt tightening sequence

prep. Allow to dry until there is no sign of wetness, or 4 minutes, whichever is longer. Failure to follow this procedure can cause future oil leakage.

7. Apply a 2.5 mm (0.09 in) bead of silicone gasket and sealant to the oil pan.
8. Position the oil pan and install the 2 rear oil pan bolts finger-tight.
9. Using a suitable straightedge, align the front surface of the oil pan flush with the front surface of the engine block.
10. Install the remaining oil pan bolts.
   a. Tighten in the sequence shown to 18 ft. lbs. (25 Nm).
11. Install the 4 oil pan-to-bellhousing bolts.
   a. Tighten to 35 ft. lbs. (48 Nm).
12. Install the engine front cover.
13. Fill the engine with clean engine oil.

3.0L Engine

See Figures 216 through 218.

➡During engine repair procedures, cleanliness is extremely important. Any foreign material (including any material created while cleaning gasket surfaces) that enters the oil passages, coolant passages or the oil pan may cause engine failure.

1. With the vehicle in NEUTRAL, position it on a hoist.
2. Remove the exhaust Y-pipe.
3. Drain the engine oil and install the drain plug.
   a. Tighten to 19 ft. lbs. (26 Nm).
4. Remove and discard the oil filter.
5. Remove the access cover.
6. Remove the 2 oil pan-to-transaxle bolts.
7. Remove the 15 bolts and the oil pan.
   a. Remove and discard the oil pan gasket.

Fig. 216 Removing the access cover

To install:

➡Do not use metal scrapers, wire brushes, power abrasive discs or other abrasive means to clean the sealing surfaces. These tools cause scratches and gouges which make leak paths.

8. Use a plastic scraping tool to remove all traces of the oil pan gasket.
9. Clean all sealing surfaces with metal surface prep and install a new oil pan gasket.

➡The oil pan must be installed and the bolts tightened within 4 minutes of sealant application.

10. Apply a 10 mm (0.40 in) diameter dot of silicone sealant to the areas indicated.
11. Position the oil pan and loosely install the bolts.
   a. Install the 2 oil pan-to-transaxle bolts.
   b. Tighten to 30 ft. lbs. (40 Nm).
12. Tighten the oil pan-to-engine bolts in the sequence shown to 18 ft. lbs. (25 Nm).
13. Install the access cover.

➡Lubricate the engine oil filter gasket with clean engine oil prior to installing.

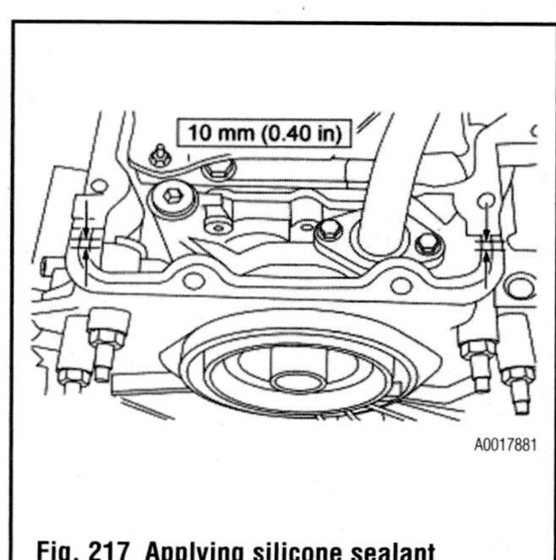

Fig. 217 Applying silicone sealant

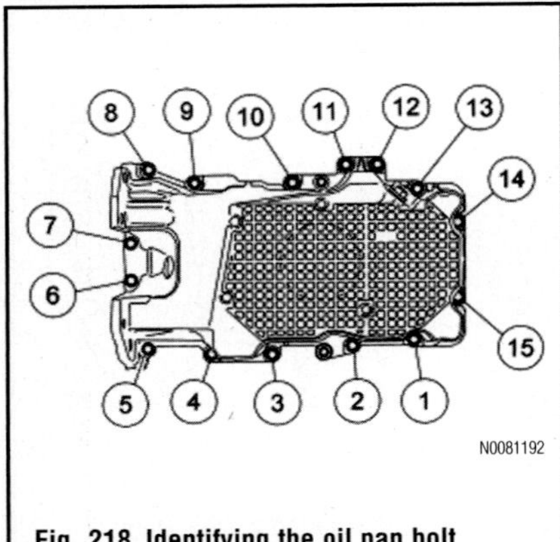

Fig. 218 Identifying the oil pan bolt tightening sequence

14. Install a new oil filter.
    a. Tighten to 44 inch lbs. (5 Nm) and then rotate an additional 180 degrees.
15. Install the exhaust Y-pipe.
16. Fill the engine with clean engine oil.

3.5L Engine

See Figures 219 through 238.

➡During engine repair procedures, cleanliness is extremely important. Any foreign material, including any material created while cleaning gasket surfaces that enters the oil passages, coolant passages or the oil pan, may cause engine failure.

➡Early build engines have 11 fastener valve covers, late built engines have 9 fastener valve covers. Do not attempt to install bolts in the 2 empty late build valve cover holes or damage to the valve cover will occur.

All vehicles

1. Remove the engine from the vehicle.
2. Remove the 8 bolts and the flywheel.
3. Remove the crankshaft sensor ring.

➡Install the engine stand bolts into the cylinder block only. Do not install the bolts into the oil pan.

4. Mount the engine on a suitable engine stand.
5. If equipped, detach the block heater wiring harness retainer from the upper intake manifold.
6. If equipped, remove the heat shield and disconnect the block heater electrical connector.
7. If equipped, detach the block heater wiring harness retainer from the power steering reservoir hose and the Power Steering Pressure (PSP) hose.
8. Remove the block heater wiring harness from the engine.

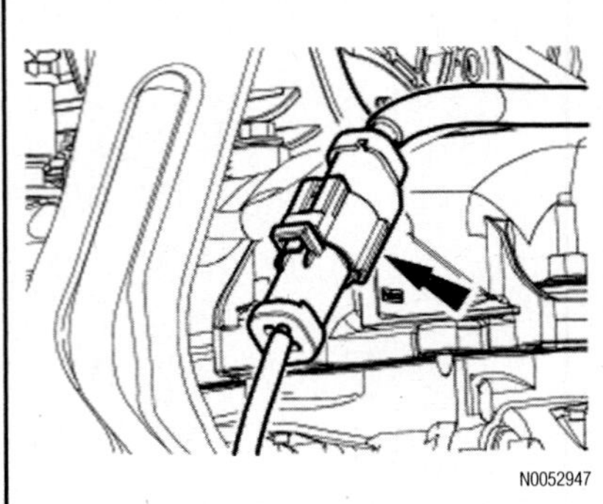

Fig. 219 Disconnecting the RH Catalyst Monitor Sensor (CMS) sensor electrical connector

9. Disconnect the PCV hose from the PCV valve.
10. Disconnect the Throttle Body (TB) electrical connector.
11. Detach the wiring harness retainers from the upper intake manifold.
12. Remove the upper intake manifold support bracket bolt.

➡If the engine is repaired or replaced because of upper engine failure, typically including valve or piston damage, check the intake manifold for metal debris. If metal debris is found, install a new intake manifold. Failure to follow these instructions can result in engine damage.

13. Remove the 6 bolts and the upper intake manifold.
    a. Discard the gaskets.
14. Disconnect the PSP switch electrical connector.

Front Wheel Drive (FWD) vehicles

15. Disconnect the RH Catalyst Monitor Sensor (CMS) sensor electrical connector.

All vehicles

16. Disconnect the RH Variable Camshaft Timing (VCT) solenoid electrical connector.
17. Disconnect the 3 RH coil-on-plug electrical connectors.
18. Detach all of the wiring harness retainers from the RH valve cover and stud bolts.
19. Disconnect the LH CMS sensor electrical connector.
20. Disconnect the LH VCT solenoid electrical connector.
21. Disconnect the 3 LH coil-on-plug electrical connectors.
22. Detach all of the wiring harness retainers from the LH valve cover and stud bolts.

➡The A/C compressor must remain bolted to the cylinder block prior to installing the oil pan.

23. Remove the A/C compressor nut and stud.
24. Detach the PSP hose retainer from the engine lifting eye.
25. Remove the PSP hose bracket nut.
26. Remove the 3 bolts and position the power steering pump aside.
27. Remove the 3 bolts and the accessory drive belt tensioner.
28. Remove the 4 nuts and the LH catalytic converter.
    a. Discard the nuts and the gasket.

FWD vehicles

29. Remove the 4 nuts and the RH catalytic converter.
    a. Discard the nuts and the gasket.

All vehicles

30. Remove the RH cylinder block drain plug or, if equipped, the block heater.
31. Allow coolant to drain from the cylinder block.
32. Remove the LH cylinder block drain plug.
    a. Allow coolant to drain from the cylinder block.
33. Remove the 6 bolts and the 6 coil-on-plugs.
34. Remove the 2 nuts and the wiring harness retaining bracket.

Early build vehicles

35. Loosen the 11 stud bolts and remove the LH valve cover.
    a. Discard the gasket.
36. Loosen the bolt, the 10 stud bolts and remove the RH valve cover.
    a. Discard the gasket.

Late build vehicles

37. Loosen the 9 stud bolts and remove the LH valve cover.
    a. Discard the gasket.
38. Loosen the 9 stud bolts and remove the RH valve cover.
    a. Discard the gasket.

All vehicles

➡VCT solenoid seal removal shown, spark plug tube seal removal similar.

39. Inspect the VCT solenoid seals and the spark plug tube seals. Remove any damaged seals.
40. Using the VCT Spark Plug Tube Seal Remover and Handle, remove the seal(s).
41. Using the Strap Wrench, remove the crankshaft pulley bolt and washer.
    a. Discard the bolt.
42. Using the 3 Jaw Puller, remove the crankshaft pulley.
43. Using the Oil Seal Remover, remove and discard the crankshaft front seal.

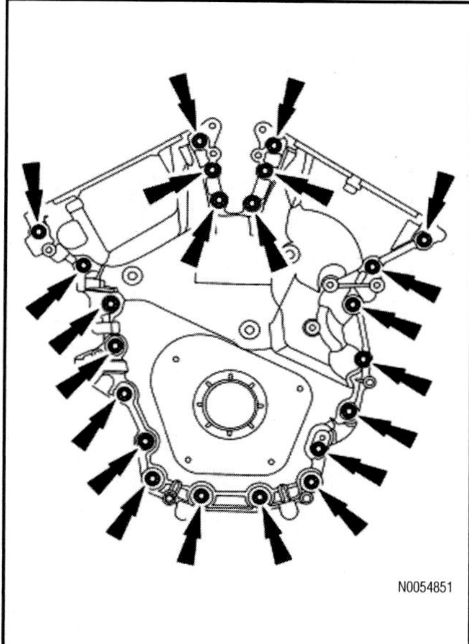

Fig. 220 Identifying the engine front cover bolts

44. Remove the 2 bolts and the engine mount bracket.

➡Only use hand tools to remove the studs.

45. Remove the 2 engine mount studs.
46. Remove the 3 bolts and the engine mount bracket.
47. Remove the 22 engine front cover bolts.
48. Install 6 of the engine front cover bolts (finger-tight) into the 6 threaded holes in the engine front cover in the following sequence.
    a. Tighten the bolts one turn at a time in a crisscross pattern until the engine front cover-to-cylinder block seal is released.
    b. Remove the engine front cover.
49. Remove the 16 oil pan bolts.
50. Install 2 of the oil pan bolts (finger-tight) into the 2 threaded holes in the oil pan.
    a. Alternately tighten the 2 bolts one turn at a time until the oil pan-to-cylinder block seal is released.
    b. Remove the oil pan.

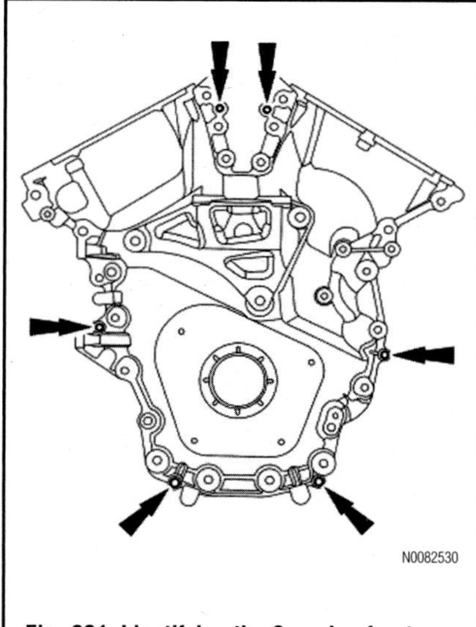

Fig. 221 Identifying the 6 engine front cover bolt tightening sequence

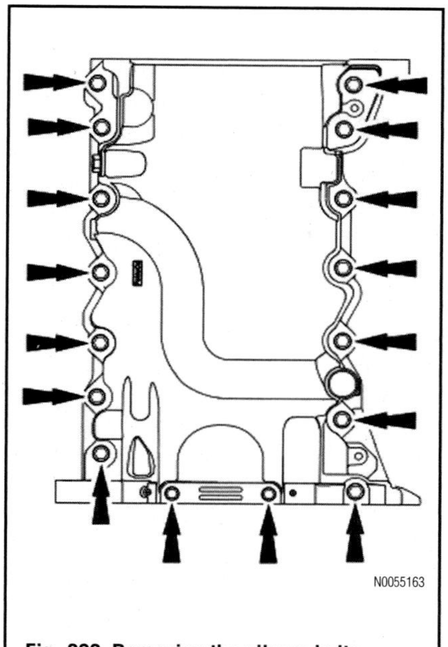

Fig. 222 Removing the oil pan bolts

➡Only use a 3M Roloc® Bristle Disk to clean the engine front cover and oil pan. Do not use metal scrapers, wire brushes or any other power abrasive disk to clean the crankshaft rear seal retainer plate. These tools cause scratches and gouges that make leak paths.

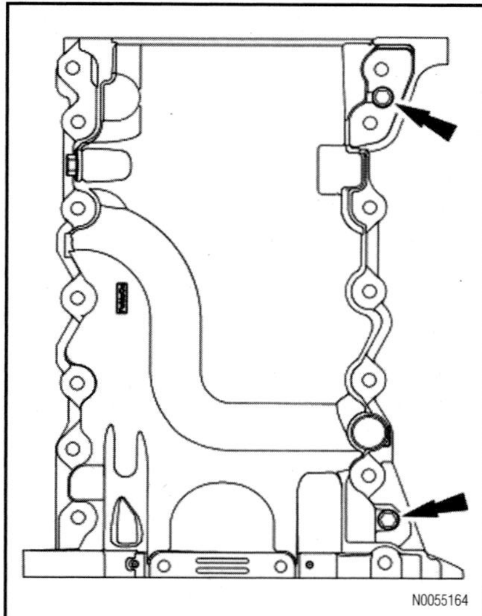

Fig. 223 Installing 2 of the oil pan bolts into the threaded holes in the oil pan

51. Clean the engine front cover and oil pan using a 3M Roloc® Bristle Disk in a suitable tool turning at the recommended speed of 15,000 rpm.
52. Thoroughly wash the engine front cover and oil pan to remove any foreign material, including any abrasive particles created during the cleaning process.

➡Place clean, lint-free shop towels over exposed engine cavities. Carefully remove the towels so foreign material is not dropped into the engine. Any foreign material (including any material created while cleaning gasket surfaces) that enters the oil passages or the oil pan, can cause engine failure.

➡Do not use wire brushes, power abrasive discs or 3M Roloc® Bristle Disk (2-in white, part number 07528) to clean the sealing surfaces. These tools cause scratches and gouges that make leak paths. They also cause contamination that will cause premature engine failure. Remove all traces of the gasket.

53. Clean all engine sealing surfaces of the cylinder block in the following sequence.
    a. Remove any large deposits of silicone or gasket material.
    b. Apply silicone gasket remover and allow to set for several minutes.
    c. Remove the silicone gasket remover. A second application of silicone gasket remover may be required if residual traces of silicone or gasket material remain.
    d. Apply metal surface prep to remove any remaining traces of oil or coolant and to prepare the surfaces to bond. Do not attempt to make the metal shiny. Some staining of the metal surfaces is normal.
    e. Make sure the 2 locating dowel pins are seated correctly in the cylinder block.

To install:

➡During engine repair procedures, cleanliness is extremely important. Any foreign material, including any material created while cleaning gasket surfaces that enters the oil passages, coolant passages or the oil pan, can cause engine failure.

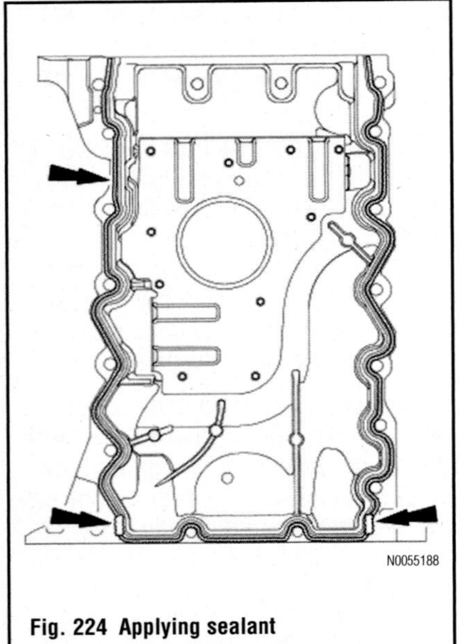

Fig. 224 Applying sealant

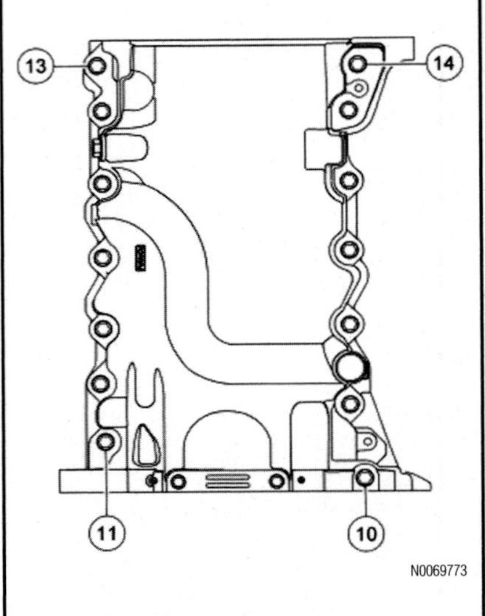

Fig. 225 Installing oil pan bolts 10, 11, 13 and 14

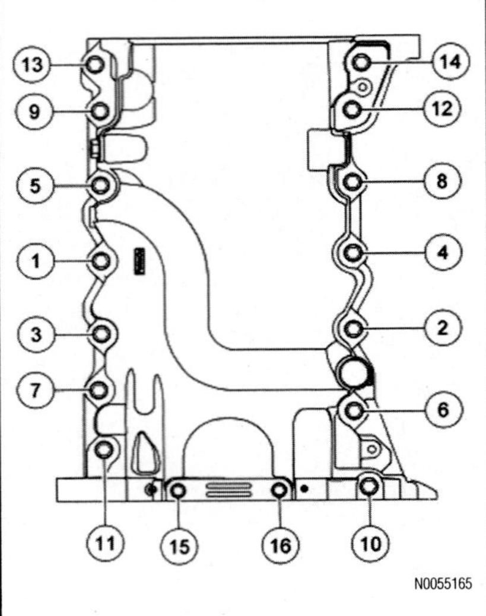

Fig. 227 Identifying the large (1-14) and small (15 and 16) oil pan bolts

➡Early build engines have 11 fastener valve covers, late built engines have 9 fastener valve covers. Do not attempt to install bolts in the 2 empty late build valve cover holes or damage to the valve cover will occur.

All vehicles

➡Failure to use Motorcraft High Performance Engine RTV Silicone may cause the engine oil to foam excessively and result in serious engine damage.

➡The oil pan and the 4 specified bolts must be installed and the oil pan aligned to the cylinder block and A/C compressor within 4 minutes of sealant application. Final tightening of the oil pan bolts must be carried out within 60 minutes of sealant application.

54. Apply a 3 mm (0.11 in) bead of Motorcraft High Performance Engine RTV Silicone to the sealing surface of the oil pan.
   a. Apply a 5.5 mm (0.21 in) bead of Motorcraft High Performance Engine RTV Silicone to the 2 crankshaft seal retainer plate-to-cylinder block joint areas on the sealing surface of the oil pan.

➡The oil pan and the 4 specified bolts must be installed within 4 minutes of the start of sealant application.

55. Install the oil pan and bolts 10, 11, 13 and 14.
   a. Tighten the bolts in the sequence shown to 27 inch lbs. (3 Nm).
   b. Loosen the bolts 180 degrees.
56. Align the oil pan to the cylinder block and A/C compressor.
   a. Position the oil pan so the mounting boss is against the A/C compressor and using a straightedge, align the oil pan flush with the rear of the cylinder block at the 2 areas shown.
57. Tighten bolts 10, 11, 13 and 14 in the sequence shown, to 27 inch lbs. (3 Nm).
58. Install the remaining oil pan bolts. Tighten all the oil pan bolts in the sequence shown.
   a. Tighten the large bolts (1-14) to 18 ft. lbs. (24 Nm).
   b. Tighten the small bolts (15 and 16) to 89 inch lbs. (10 Nm).
59. Install the A/C compressor mounting stud and nut.
   a. Tighten the stud to 80 inch lbs. (9 Nm) and the nut to 18 ft. lbs. (25 Nm).
60. Install the Alignment Pins.

➡Failure to use Motorcraft High Performance Engine RTV Silicone may cause the engine oil to foam excessively and result in serious engine damage.

➡The engine front cover and bolts 17, 18, 19 and 20 must be installed within

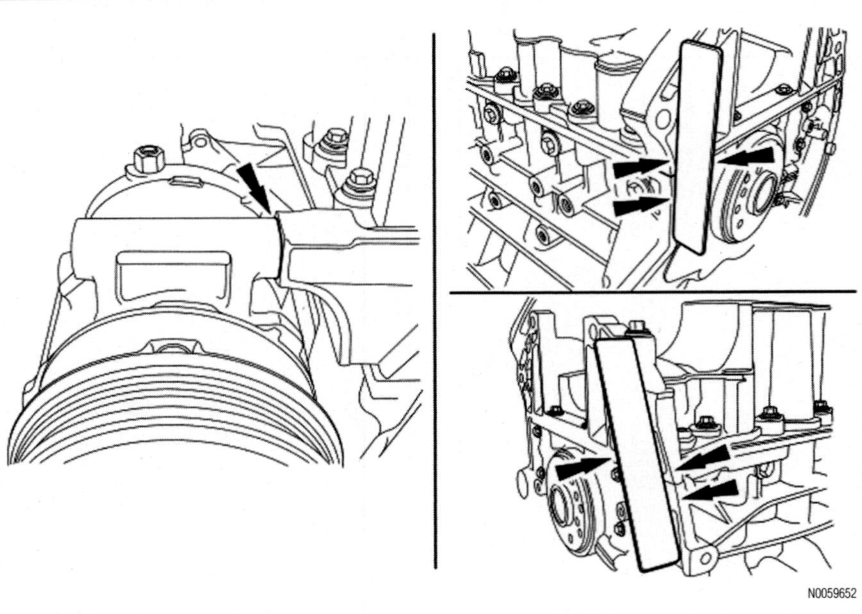

Fig. 226 Aligning the oil pan to the cylinder block and A/C compressor

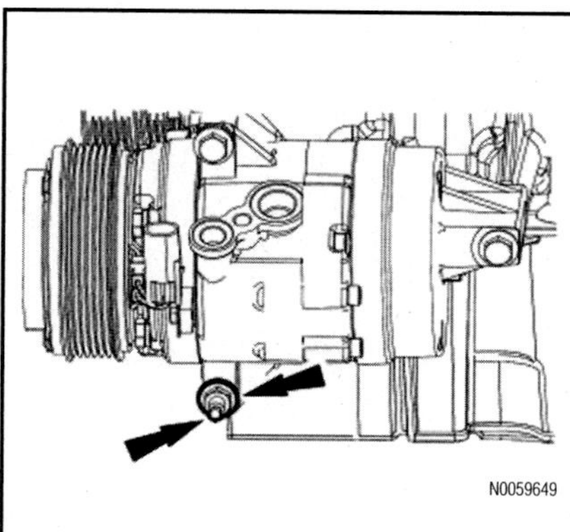

Fig. 228 Installing the A/C compressor mounting stud and nut

4 minutes of the initial sealant application. The remainder of the engine front cover bolts and the engine mount bracket bolts must be installed and tightened within 35 minutes of the initial sealant application. If the time limits are exceeded, the sealant must be removed, the sealing area cleaned and sealant reapplied. To clean the sealing area, use silicone gasket remover and metal surface prep. Failure to follow this procedure can cause future oil leakage.

61. Apply a 3.0 mm (0.11 in) bead of Motorcraft High Performance Engine RTV Silicone to the engine front cover sealing surfaces including the 3 engine mount bracket bosses.
62. Apply a 5.5 mm (0.21 in) bead of Motorcraft High Performance Engine RTV Silicone to the oil pan-to-cylinder block joint and the cylinder head-to-cylinder block joint areas of the engine front cover in 5 places as indicated.

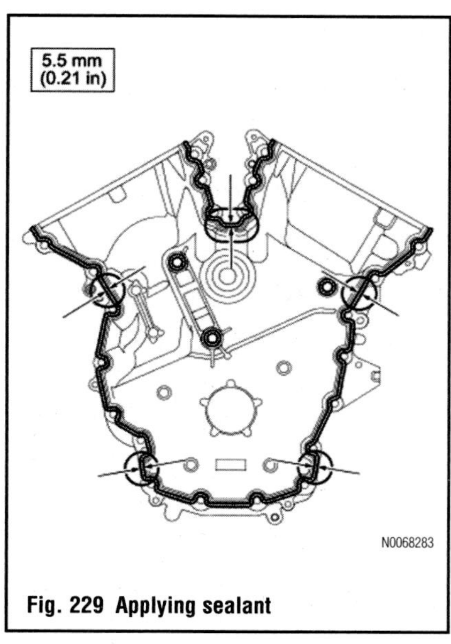

Fig. 229 Applying sealant

➡Make sure the 2 locating dowel pins are seated correctly in the cylinder block.

63. Install the engine front cover and bolts 17, 18, 19 and 20.
 a. Tighten in sequence to 27 inch lbs. (3 Nm).
64. Remove the Alignment Pins.

➡Do not tighten the bolt at this time.

65. Install the engine mount bracket and the 3 bolts.

➡Do not expose the Motorcraft High Performance Engine RTV Silicone to engine oil for at least 90 minutes after installing the engine front cover. Failure to follow this instruction may cause oil leakage.

66. Install the remaining engine front cover bolts. Tighten all the engine front cover bolts and engine mount bracket bolts in the sequence shown in 2 stages:
 a. Stage 1: Tighten bolts 1 thru 22 to 89 inch lbs. (10 Nm). and bolts 23, 24 and 25 to 133 inch lbs. (15 Nm).
 b. Stage 2: Tighten bolts 1 thru 22 to 18 ft. lbs. (24 Nm) and bolts 23, 24 and 25 to 55 ft. lbs. (75 Nm).

➡The thread sealer on the engine mount studs (including new engine mount studs if applicable) must be cleaned off with a wire brush and new Threadlock and Sealer applied prior to installing the engine mount studs. Failure to follow this procedure may result in damage to the engine mount studs or engine.

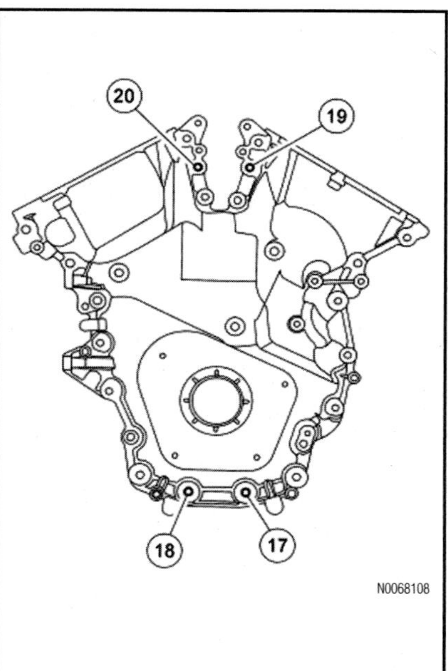

Fig. 230 Identifying the engine front cover bolt 17-20 tightening sequence

67. Install the engine mount studs in the following sequence.
 a. Clean the front cover engine mount stud holes with pressurized air to remove any foreign material.
 b. Clean all the thread sealer from the engine mount studs (old and new studs).
 c. Apply new Threadlock and Sealer to the engine mount stud threads.
 d. Install the 2 engine mount studs.
 e. Tighten to 15 ft. lbs. (20 Nm).
68. Install the engine mount bracket and the 2 bolts.
 a. Tighten to 18 ft. lbs. (24 Nm).

➡Apply clean engine oil to the crankshaft front seal bore in the engine front cover.

69. Using the Front Crankshaft Seal Installer and Crankshaft Vibration Damper Installer, install a new crankshaft front seal.

➡Lubricate the outside diameter sealing surfaces with clean engine oil.

70. Using the Front Cover Oil Seal Installer and Crankshaft Vibration Damper Installer, install the crankshaft pulley.
71. Using the Strap Wrench, install the crankshaft pulley washer and new bolt and tighten in 4 stages.
 a. Stage 1: Tighten to 89 ft. lbs. (120 Nm).
 b. Stage 2: Loosen one full turn.
 c. Stage 3: Tighten to 37 ft. lbs. (50 Nm).
 d. Stage 4: Tighten an additional 90 degrees.

➡Installation of new seals is only required if damaged seals were removed during disassembly of the engine.

72. Using the VCT Spark Plug Tube Seal Installer and Handle, install new VCT solenoid and/or spark plug tube seals.

➡Failure to use Motorcraft High Performance Engine RTV Silicone may cause the engine oil to foam excessively and result in serious engine damage.

73. If the valve cover is not installed and the fasteners tightened within 4 minutes, the sealant must be removed and the sealing area cleaned. To clean the sealing area, use silicone gasket remover and metal surface prep. Failure to follow this procedure can cause future oil leakage.
74. Apply an 8 mm (0.31 in) bead of Motorcraft High Performance Engine RTV

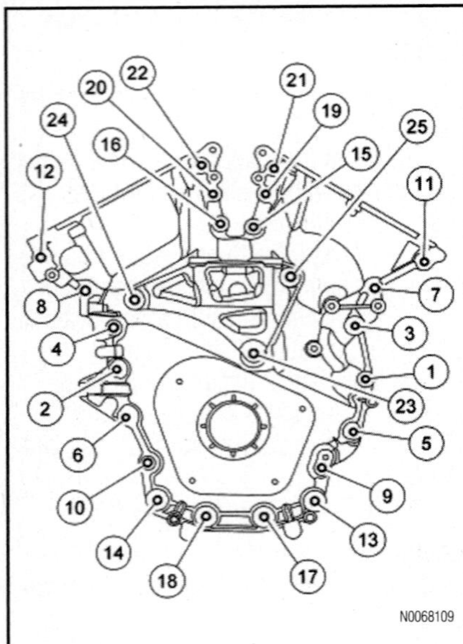

Fig. 231 Installing the remaining engine front cover bolts

Silicone to the engine front cover-to-RH cylinder head joints.

Early build vehicles

75. Using a new gasket, install the RH valve cover, bolt and the 10 stud bolts.

a. Tighten in the sequence shown to 89 inch lbs. (10 Nm).

Late build vehicles

76. Using a new gasket, install the RH valve cover and tighten the 9 stud bolts.

a. Tighten in the sequence shown to 89 inch lbs. (10 Nm).

All vehicles

➡Failure to use Motorcraft High Performance Engine RTV Silicone may cause the engine oil to foam excessively and result in serious engine damage.

➡If the valve cover is not installed and the fasteners tightened within 4 minutes, the sealant must be removed and the sealing area cleaned. To clean the sealing area, use silicone gasket remover and metal surface prep. Failure to follow this procedure can cause future oil leakage.

77. Apply an 8 mm (0.31 in) bead of Motorcraft High Performance Engine RTV Silicone to the engine front cover-to-LH cylinder head joints.

Early build vehicles

78. Using a new gasket, install the LH valve cover and 11 stud bolts.

a. Tighten in the sequence shown to 89 inch lbs. (10 Nm).

Late build vehicles

79. Using a new gasket, install the LH valve cover and tighten the 9 stud bolts.

a. Tighten in the sequence shown to 89 inch lbs. (10 Nm).

All vehicles

80. Install the wiring harness retaining bracket and the 2 nuts.

a. Tighten to 35 inch lbs. (4 Nm).

81. Install the 6 coil-on-plug assemblies and the 6 bolts.

a. Tighten to 62 inch lbs. (7 Nm).

82. Install the LH cylinder block drain plug.

a. Tighten to 15 ft. lbs. (20 Nm) plus an additional 180 degrees.

83. Install the RH cylinder block drain plug or, if equipped, the block heater.

a. Tighten to 40 Nm (30 lb-ft).

Front Wheel Drive (FWD) vehicles

84. Using a new gasket, install the RH catalytic converter and 4 new nuts.

a. Tighten to 30 ft. lbs. (40 Nm).

All vehicles

85. Using a new gasket, install the LH catalytic converter and 4 new nuts.

a. Tighten to 30 ft. lbs. (40 Nm).

86. Install the accessory drive belt tensioner and the 3 bolts.

a. Tighten to 8 ft. lbs. (11 Nm).

87. Install the power steering pump and the 3 bolts.

a. Tighten to 18 ft. lbs. (25 Nm).

88. Install the Power Steering Pressure (PSP) hose bracket and nut.

a. Tighten to 80 inch lbs. (9 Nm).

89. Attach the PSP hose retainer to the engine lifting eye.

90. Attach all of the wiring harness retainers to the LH valve cover and stud bolts.

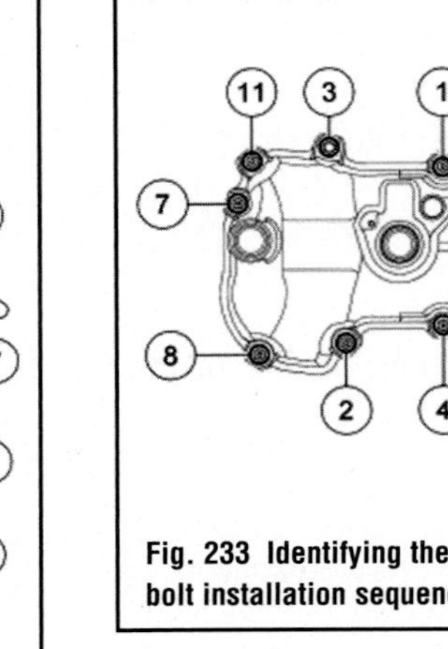

Fig. 233 Identifying the RH valve cover bolt installation sequence

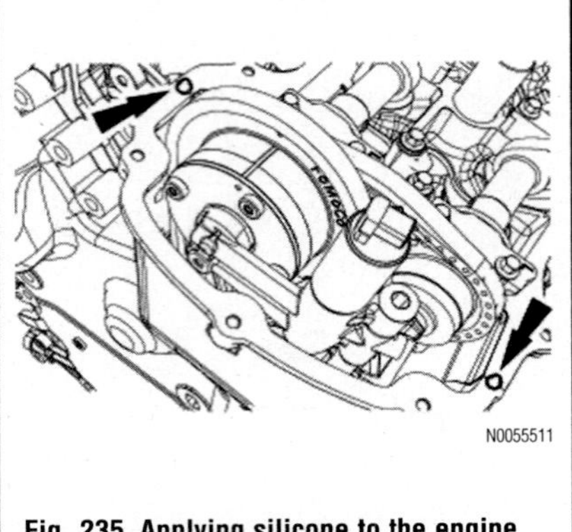

Fig. 235 Applying silicone to the engine front cover to LH cylinder head joints

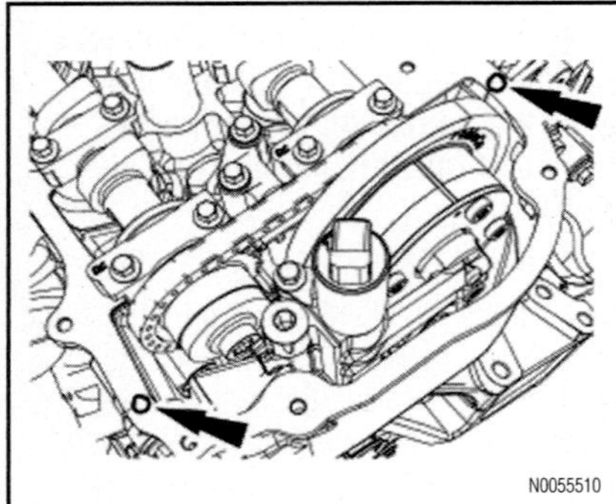

Fig. 232 Applying silicone to the engine front cover to RH cylinder head joints

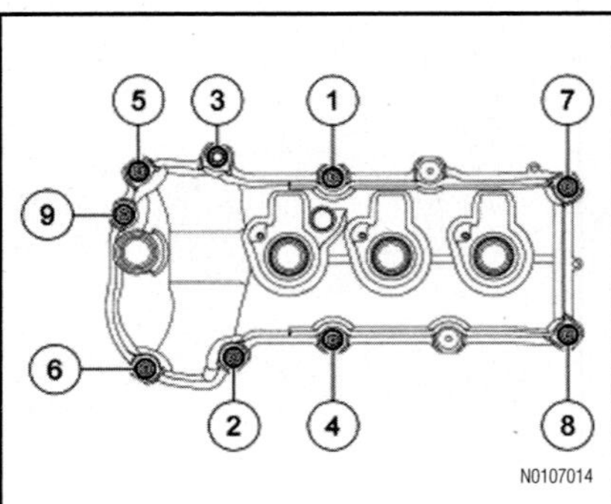

Fig. 234 Identifying the RH valve cover stud bolt tightening sequence

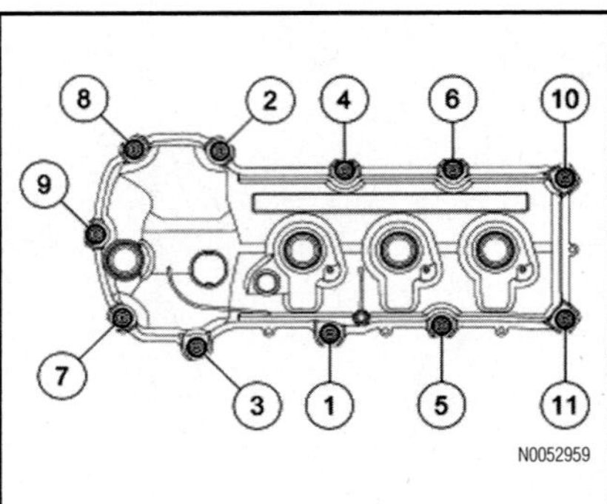

Fig. 236 Identifying the LH valve cover stud bolt tightening sequence

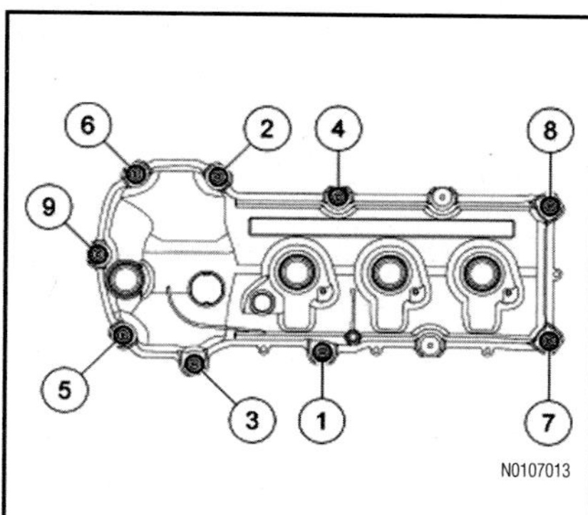

Fig. 237 Identifying the LH valve cover stud bolt tightening sequence

91. Connect the LH camshaft VCT solenoid electrical connector.
92. Connect the 3 LH coil-on-plug electrical connectors.
93. Connect the LH Catalyst Monitor Sensor (CMS) electrical connector.
94. Attach all of the wiring harness retainers to the RH valve cover and stud bolts.
95. Connect the 3 RH coil-on-plug electrical connectors.
96. Connect the RH VCT solenoid electrical connector.

FWD vehicles

97. Connect the RH CMS electrical connector.

All vehicles

98. Connect the PSP switch electrical connector.

➡If the engine is repaired or replaced because of upper engine failure, typically including valve or piston damage, check the intake manifold for metal debris. If metal debris is found, install a new intake manifold. Failure to follow these instructions can result in engine damage.

99. Using new gaskets, install the upper intake manifold and the 6 bolts.
    a. Tighten in the sequence shown to 89 inch lbs. (10 Nm).
100. Install the upper intake manifold support bracket bolt.
    a. Tighten to 89 inch lbs. (10 Nm).
101. Attach the wiring harness retainers to the upper intake manifold.
102. Connect the Throttle Body (TB) electrical connector.
103. Connect the PCV hose to the PCV valve.
104. If equipped, position the block heater wiring harness onto the engine.
105. Attach the block heater wiring harness retainer to the power steering reservoir hose and the PSP hose.
106. If equipped, connect the block heater electrical connector and install the heat shield.
107. If equipped, attach the block heater wiring harness retainer to the upper intake manifold.
108. Using the Heavy Duty Floor Crane and Spreader Bar, remove the engine from the stand.
109. Install the crankshaft sensor ring.
110. Install the flexplate and the 8 bolts.
    a. Tighten to 59 ft. lbs. (80 Nm).
111. Install the engine in the vehicle.

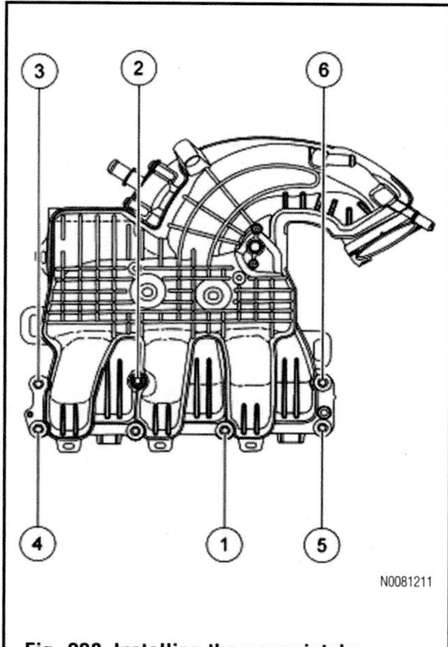

Fig. 238 Installing the upper intake manifold bolts in sequence

OIL PUMP

REMOVAL & INSTALLATION

2.5L Engine

See Figures 239 through 243.

1. With the engine in NEUTRAL, position it on a hoist.
2. Remove the engine front cover.
3. Drain the engine oil, then install the drain plug.
    a. To install, tighten to 21 ft. lbs. (28 Nm).
4. Remove the 3 oil pan-to-bellhousing bolts.
5. Remove the 13 bolts and the oil pan.

➡Discard the gasket and clean and inspect the gasket mating surfaces.

6. Remove the 2 bolts and the oil pump screen and pickup tube.
7. Remove the oil pump drive chain tensioner.
    a. Release the tension on the tensioner spring.
    b. Remove the tensioner and the 2 shoulder bolts.
8. Remove the chain from the oil pump sprocket.
9. Remove the bolt and oil pump sprocket.
10. Remove the 4 bolts and the oil pump.

To install:

➡Clean the oil pump and cylinder block mating surfaces with metal surface prep.

11. Install the oil pump assembly. Tighten the 4 bolts in the sequence shown in 2 stages:
    a. Stage 1: Tighten to 89 inch lbs. (10 Nm).
    b. Stage 2: Tighten to 15 ft. lbs. (20 Nm).
12. Install the oil pump sprocket and bolt.
    a. Tighten to 18 ft. lbs. (25 Nm).
13. Install the chain onto the oil pump sprocket.

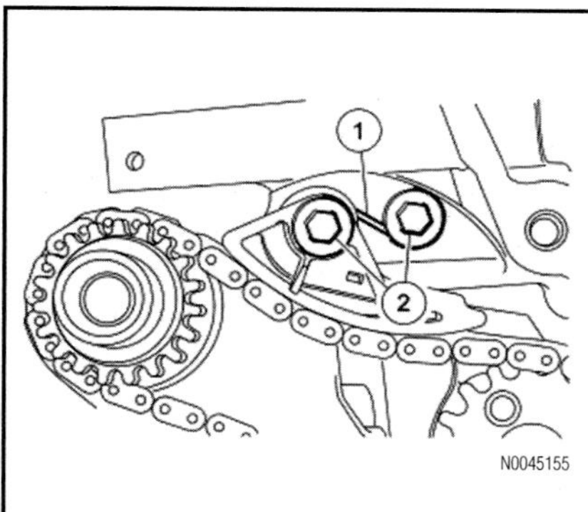

Fig. 239 Removing the oil pump drive chain tensioner spring (1) and shoulder bolts (2)

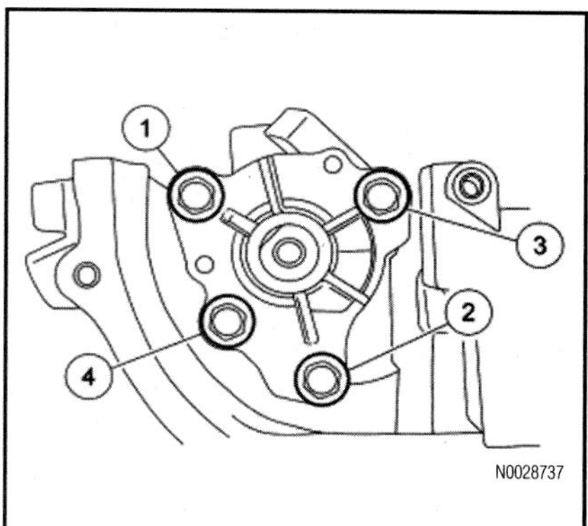

Fig. 240 Installing the oil pump bolts in sequence

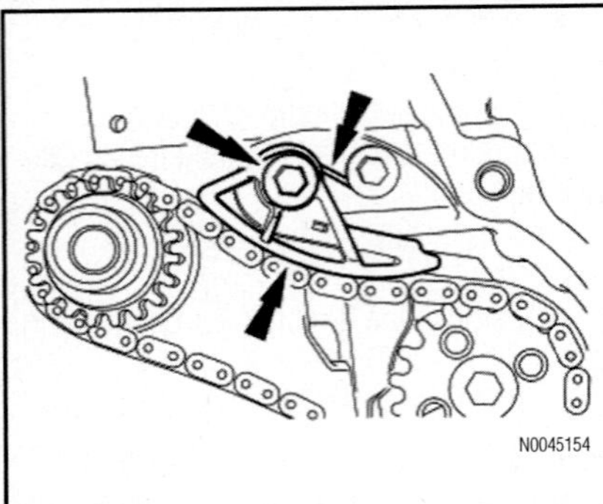

Fig. 241 Hooking the tensioner spring around the shoulder bolt

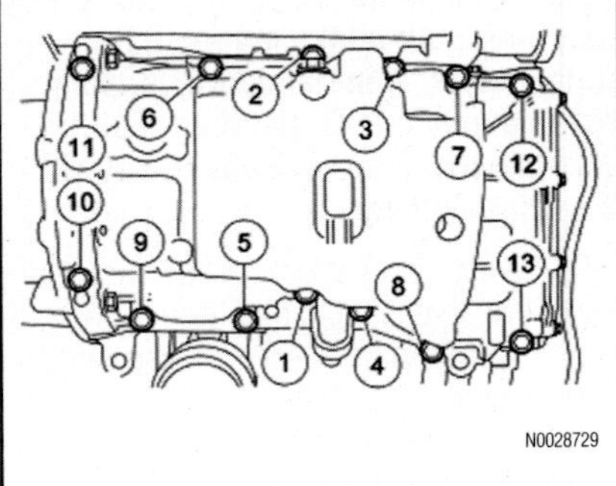

Fig. 243 Identifying the oil pan bolt tightening surface

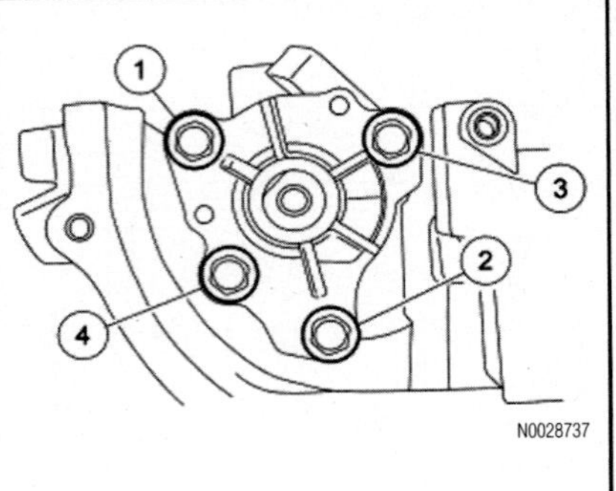

Fig. 245 Identifying the oil pump bolt tightening sequence

14. Install the oil pump drive chain tensioner shoulder bolt.
    a. Tighten to 89 inch lbs. (10 Nm).
15. Install the oil pump chain tensioner and bolt. Hook the tensioner spring around the shoulder bolt.
    a. Tighten to 89 inch lbs. (10 Nm).
16. Install the oil pump screen and pickup tube and the 2 bolts.
    a. Tighten to 89 inch lbs. (10 Nm).

➡Do not use metal scrapers, wire brushes, power abrasive discs or other abrasive means to clean the sealing surfaces. These tools cause scratches and gouges, which make leak paths. Use a plastic scraping tool to remove traces to sealant.

17. Clean all mating surfaces with metal surface prep.

➡If the oil pan is not secured within 10 minutes of sealant application, the sealant must be removed and the sealing area cleaned with metal surface prep. Allow to dry until there is no sign of wetness, or 10 minutes, whichever is longer. Failure to follow these instructions can cause future oil leakage.

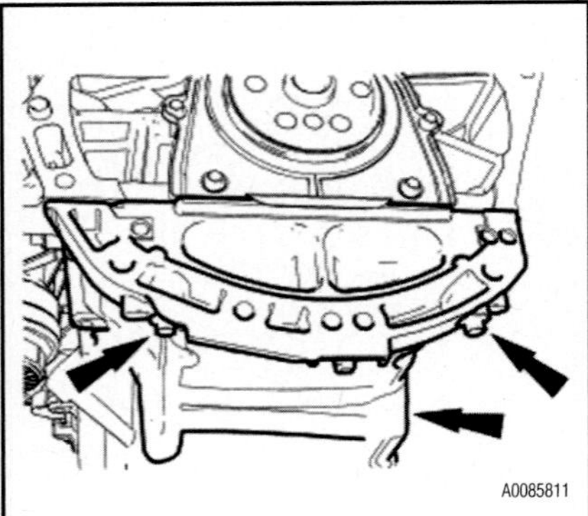

Fig. 242 Applying silicone gasket and sealant to the oil pan

18. Apply a 2.5 mm (0.09 in) bead of silicone gasket and sealant to the oil pan.
    a. Position the oil pan onto the engine and install the 2 rear oil pan bolts finger-tight.
19. Using a suitable straight edge, align the front surface of the oil pan flush with the front surface of the engine block.
20. Install the remaining oil pan bolts.
    a. Tighten in the sequence shown to 18 ft. lbs. (25 Nm).
21. Install the 3 oil pan-to-bellhousing bolts.
    a. Tighten to 35 ft. lbs. (48 Nm).
22. Install the engine front cover.
23. Fill the engine with clean engine oil.

2.5L Hybrid Engine

See Figures 244 through 247.

1. With the engine in NEUTRAL, position it on a hoist.
2. Remove the engine front cover.
3. Drain the engine oil, then install the drain plug.
    a. To install, tighten to 21 ft. lbs. (28 Nm).
4. Remove the 4 oil pan-to-bellhousing bolts.
5. Remove the 13 bolts and the oil pan.

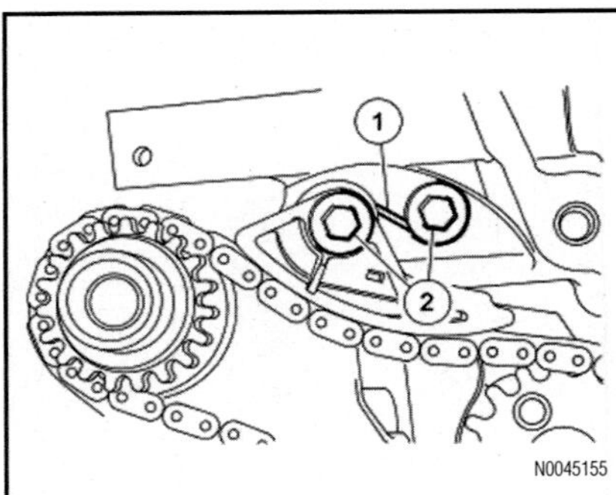

Fig. 244 Removing the oil pump drive chain tensioner spring (1) and shoulder bolts (2)

➡Discard the gasket and clean and inspect the gasket mating surfaces.

6. Remove the 2 bolts and the oil pump screen and pickup tube.
7. Remove the oil pump drive chain tensioner.
    a. Release the tension on the tensioner spring.
    b. Remove the 2 shoulder bolts and the tensioner.
8. Remove the chain from the oil pump sprocket.
9. Remove the bolt and oil pump sprocket.
10. Remove the 4 bolts and the oil pump.

To install:

➡Clean the oil pump and cylinder block mating surfaces with metal surface prep.

11. Install the oil pump assembly. Tighten the 4 bolts in the sequence shown in 2 stages:
    a. Stage 1: Tighten to 89 inch lbs. (10 Nm).
    b. Stage 2: Tighten to 15 ft. lbs. (20 Nm).
12. Install the oil pump sprocket and bolt.
    a. Tighten to 18 ft. lbs. (25 Nm).
13. Install the chain onto the oil pump sprocket.
14. Install the oil pump drive chain tensioner shoulder bolt.
    a. Tighten to 89 inch lbs. (10 Nm).
15. Install the oil pump drive chain tensioner and bolt. Hook the tensioner spring around the shoulder bolt.
    a. Tighten to 89 inch lbs. (10 Nm).
16. Install the oil pump screen and pickup tube and the 2 bolts.
    a. Tighten to 89 inch lbs. (10 Nm).

➡Do not use metal scrapers, wire brushes, power abrasive discs or other

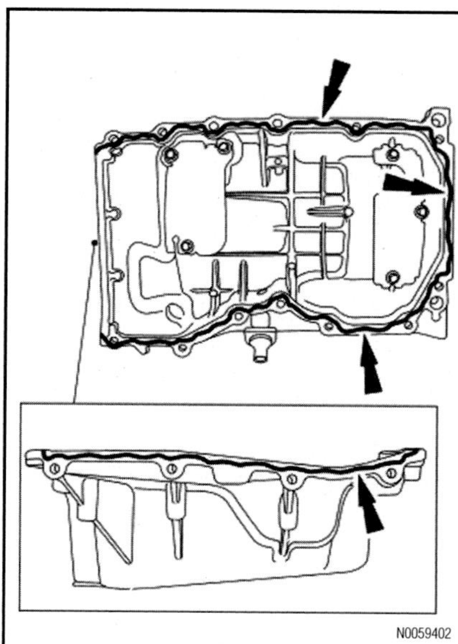

Fig. 246 Applying sealant gasket and sealant to the oil pan

abrasive means to clean the sealing surfaces. These tools cause scratches and gouges, which make leak paths. Use a plastic scraping tool to remove traces to sealant.

17. Clean all mating surfaces with metal surface prep.

➡If the oil pan is not secured within 4 minutes of sealant application, the sealant must be removed and the sealing area cleaned with metal surface prep. Allow to dry until there is no sign of wetness, or 4 minutes, whichever is longer. Failure to follow this procedure can cause future oil leakage.

18. Apply a 2.5 mm (0.09 in) bead of sealant gasket and sealant to the oil pan.
19. Position the oil pan onto the engine and install the 2 rear oil pan bolts finger-tight.

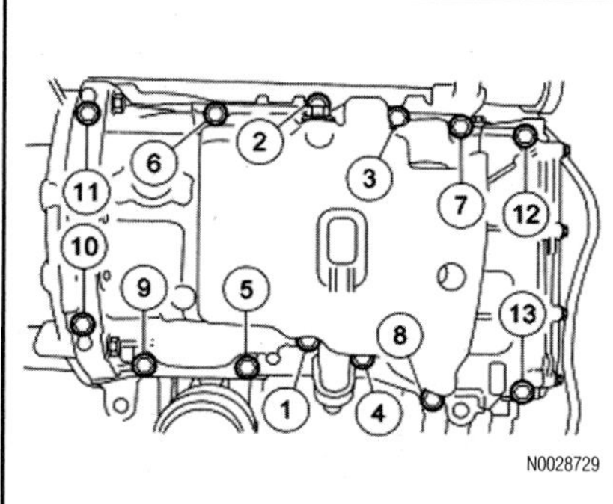

Fig. 247 Identifying the oil pan bolt tightening sequence

20. Using a suitable straight edge, align the front surface of the oil pan flush with the front surface of the engine block.
21. Install the remaining oil pan bolts.
   a. Tighten in the sequence shown to 18 ft. lbs. (25 Nm).
22. Install the 4 oil pan-to-bellhousing bolts.
   a. Tighten to 35 ft. lbs. (48 Nm).
23. Install the engine front cover.
24. Fill the engine with clean engine oil.

3.0L Engine

See Figures 248 and 249.

➡During engine repair procedures, cleanliness is extremely important. Any foreign material (including any material created while cleaning gasket surfaces) that enters the oil passages, coolant passages or the oil pan may cause engine failure.

1. With the vehicle in NEUTRAL, position it on a hoist.
2. Remove the timing drive components.
3. Remove the oil pump screen and pickup tube.
4. Remove the bolts in the sequence shown.

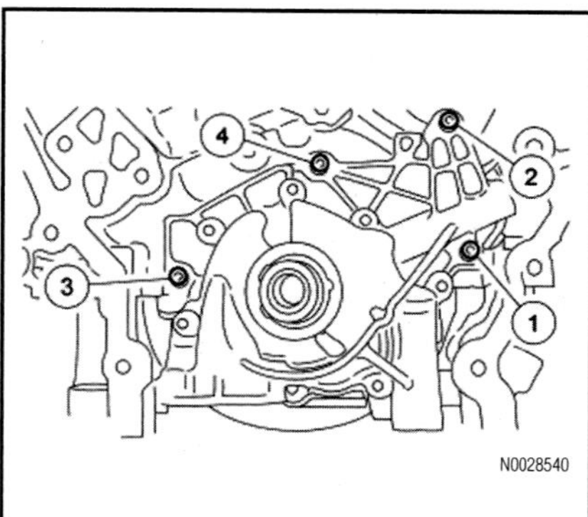

Fig. 248 Identifying the bolt removal sequence

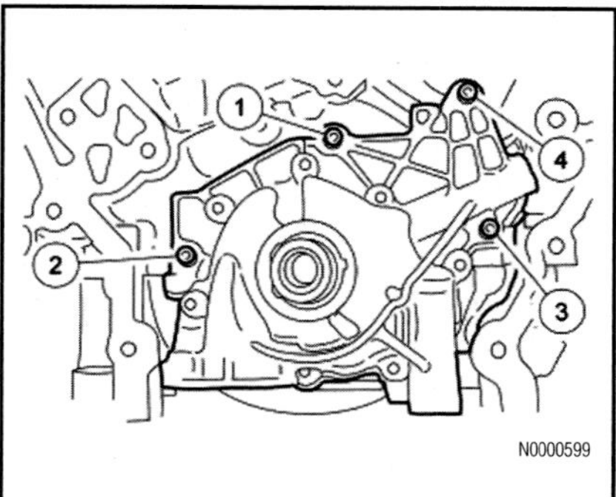

Fig. 249 Identifying the bolt tightening sequence

To install:

5. Position the oil pump and install the bolts.
   a. Tighten in the sequence shown to 89 inch lbs. (10 Nm).
6. Install the oil pump screen and pickup tube.
7. Install the timing drive components.

3.5L Engine

See Figures 250 through 257.

➡During engine repair procedures, cleanliness is extremely important. Any foreign material, including any material created while cleaning gasket surfaces, that enters the oil passages, coolant passages or the oil pan can cause engine failure.

➡On early build engines, the timing chain rides on the inner side of the RH timing chain guide. Late build engines are equipped with a different design RH timing chain guide that requires the timing chain to ride on the outer side of the RH timing chain guide. For service, all replacement RH timing chain guides will be the late build design.

All vehicles

1. Remove the engine front cover.

Engines equipped with early build RH timing chain guides

2. Rotate the crankshaft clockwise and align the timing marks on the Variable Camshaft Timing (VCT) assemblies.

Engines equipped with late build/replacement RH timing chain guides

3. Rotate the crankshaft clockwise and align the timing marks on the VCT assemblies.

All vehicles

➡The Camshaft Holding Tool will hold the camshafts in the Top Dead Center (TDC) position.

4. Install the Camshaft Holding Tool onto the flats of the LH camshafts.

➡The Camshaft Holding Tool will hold the camshafts in the TDC position.

5. Install the Camshaft Holding Tool onto the flats of the RH camshafts.
6. Remove the 3 bolts and the RH VCT housing.
7. Remove the 3 bolts and the LH VCT housing.
8. Remove the 2 bolts and the primary timing chain tensioner.
9. Remove the primary timing chain tensioner arm.

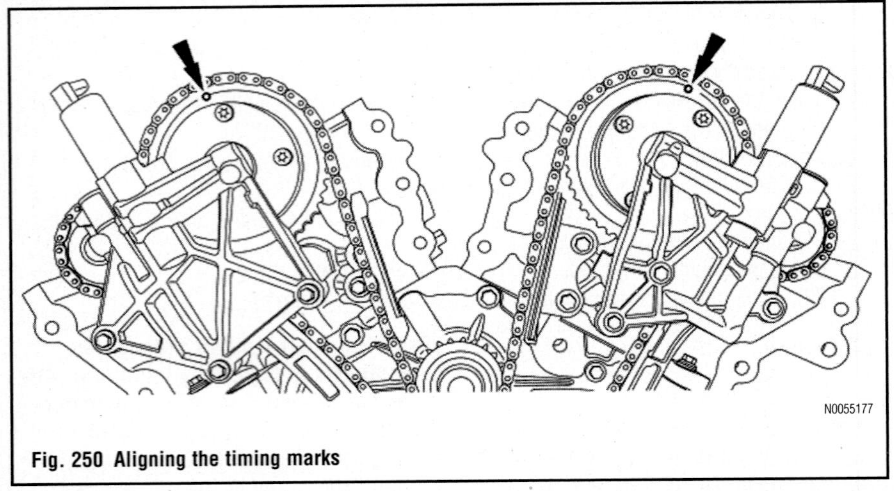

Fig. 250 Aligning the timing marks

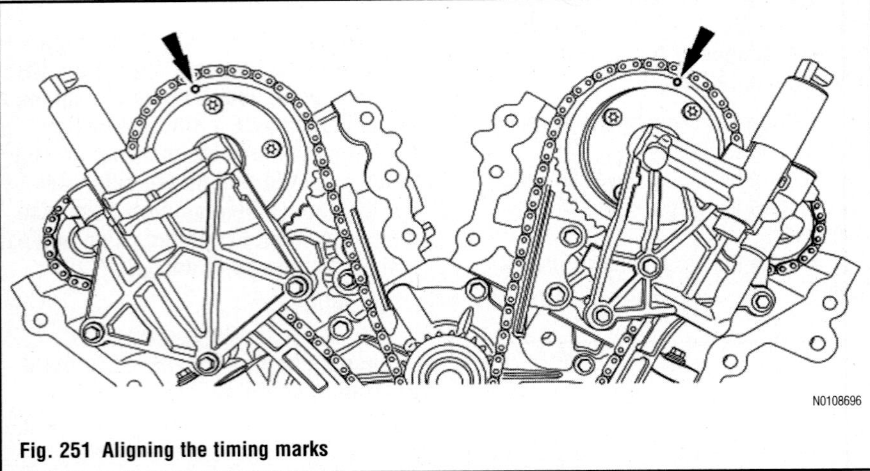

Fig. 251 Aligning the timing marks

10. Remove the 2 bolts and the lower LH primary timing chain guide.
11. Remove the primary timing chain.
12. Remove the crankshaft timing chain sprocket.
13. Remove the 2 oil pump screen and pickup tube bolts.
14. Remove the 3 oil pump bolts.
15. Rotate the oil pump clockwise and separate the oil pump from the oil pump screen and pickup tube.
  a. Remove the oil pump.
  b. Discard the oil pump screen and pickup tube O-ring seal.

To install:

➡During engine repair procedures, cleanliness is extremely important. Any foreign material, including any material created while cleaning gasket surfaces that enters the oil passages, coolant passages or the oil pan, can cause engine failure.

➡Install a new oil pump screen and pickup tube O-ring seal prior to installing the oil pump.

16. Position the oil pump onto the crankshaft and rotate counterclockwise to position the pump onto the oil pump screen and pickup tube.
  a. Install the 3 bolts and tighten to 89 inch lbs. (10 Nm).
17. Install the 2 oil pump screen and pickup tube bolts.
  a. Tighten to 89 inch lbs. (10 Nm).
18. Install the crankshaft timing chain sprocket.
19. Install the primary timing chain with the colored links aligned with the timing marks on the VCT assemblies and the crankshaft sprocket.
20. Install the LH primary timing chain guide and the 2 bolts.
  a. Tighten to 89 inch lbs. (10 Nm).
21. Install the primary timing chain tensioner arm.
22. Reset the primary timing chain tensioner.
  a. Rotate the lever counterclockwise.
  b. Using a soft-jawed vise, compress the plunger.

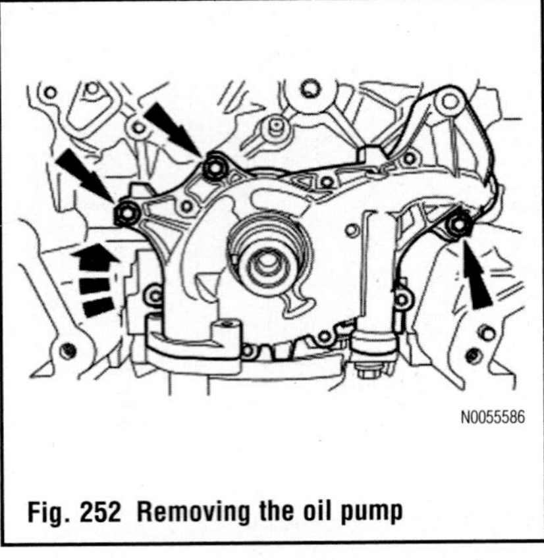

Fig. 252 Removing the oil pump

  c. Align the hole in the lever with the hole in the tensioner housing.
  d. Install a suitable lockpin.

➡It may be necessary to rotate the crankshaft slightly to remove slack from the timing chain and install the tensioner.

23. Install the primary tensioner and the 2 bolts.
  a. Tighten to 89 inch lbs. (10 Nm).
  b. Remove the lockpin.
24. As a post-check, verify correct alignment of all timing marks.
25. Install new VCT housing seals.

➡Make sure the dowels on the Variable Camshaft Timing (VCT) housing are fully engaged in the cylinder head prior to tightening the bolts. Failure to follow this process will result in severe engine damage.

Fig. 253 Resetting the primary timing chain tensioner

Fig. 254 Verifying alignment of all timing marks

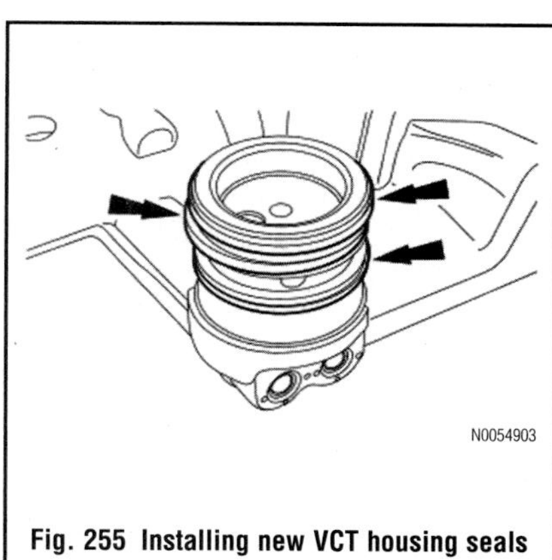

Fig. 255 Installing new VCT housing seals

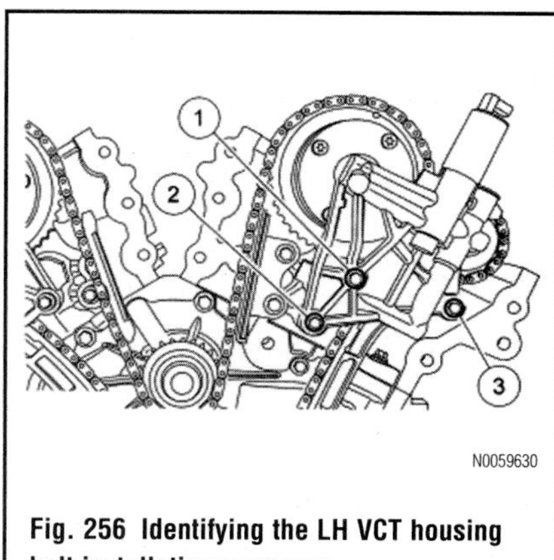

Fig. 256 Identifying the LH VCT housing bolt installation sequence

26. Install the LH VCT housing and the 3 bolts.
   a. Tighten in the sequence shown to 89 inch lbs. (10 Nm).

➡**Make sure the dowels on the Variable Camshaft Timing (VCT) housing are fully engaged in the cylinder head prior to tightening the bolts. Failure to follow this process will result in severe engine damage.**

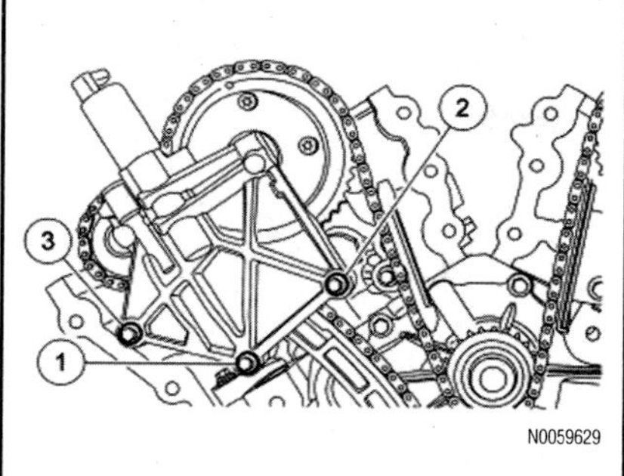

Fig. 257 Identifying the RH VCT housing bolt installation sequence

27. Install the RH VCT housing and the 3 bolts.
   a. Tighten in the sequence shown to 10 Nm (89 lb-in).
28. Install the engine front cover.

PISTON AND RING

POSITIONING

2.5L Engines

See Figure 258.

➡**The arrow on the top of the piston points towards the front of the engine.**

1. Align the piston-to-connecting rod orientation marks, and position the connecting rod in the piston.
2. Lubricate the piston pin and pin bore with clean engine oil.
3. Install the piston pin in the piston and connecting rod assembly.
4. Install the piston pin retaining clips in the piston.
5. Lubricate the piston and the new piston rings with clean engine oil.

➡**The piston compression upper and lower ring should be installed with the paint mark on the outside diameter circumference of the ring to be positioned on the right side of the ring gap. The lower compression ring can also be installed with the undercut side downward.**

➡**The upper and lower compression ring gaps are not controlled for installation.**

6. Install the piston rings onto the piston as shown.
   - Piston pin
   - Upper oil control ring gap location
   - Lower oil control ring gap location

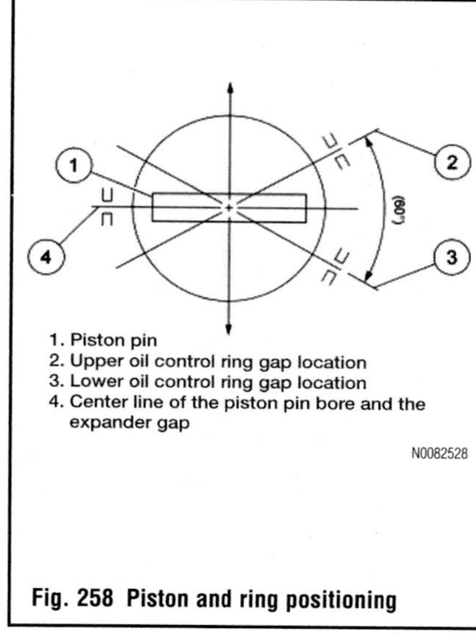

Fig. 258 Piston and ring positioning

   - Center line of the piston pin bore and the expander gap

3.0L Engine

See Figure 259.

1. Align the piston-to-connecting rod orientation marks and position the connecting rod in the piston.
2. Lubricate the piston pin and pin bore with clean engine oil.
3. Install the piston pin in the piston and connecting rod assembly.
4. Install the piston pin retaining clips in the piston.
5. Lubricate the piston and the new piston rings with clean engine oil.

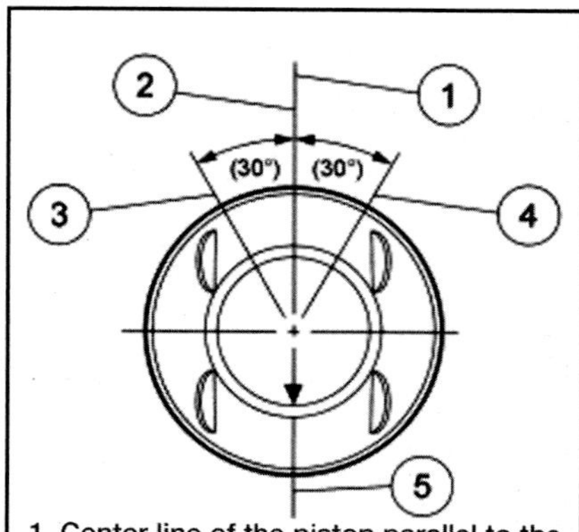

Fig. 259 Piston and ring positioning

➡The piston compression lower ring should be installed with the "O" mark on the ring face pointing up toward the top of the piston.

➡When installing the piston oil control spacer, orient the gap such that the cut ends are pointed toward the top of the piston.

6. Install the piston rings onto the piston as shown.
   - Center line of the piston parallel to the wrist pin bore
   - Upper compression ring gap location
   - Upper oil control segment ring gap location
   - Lower oil control segment ring gap location
   - Expander ring and lower compression ring gap location

3.5L Engine

See Figure 260.

1. Align the piston-to-connecting rod orientation marks and position the connecting rod in the piston.
2. Lubricate the piston pin and pin bore with clean engine oil.
3. Install the piston pin in the piston and connecting rod assembly.
4. Install the new piston pin retaining clips in the piston.
5. The piston pin retaining clip gap orientation must be toward the top or dome of piston.
6. Lubricate the piston and the new piston rings with clean engine oil.

➡The piston compression upper and lower ring should be installed with the "O" mark on the ring face pointing up toward the top of the piston.

7. Install the piston rings onto the piston as shown.
   - Center line of the piston parallel to the wrist pin bore
   - Upper compression ring gap location
   - Upper oil control segment ring gap location
   - Lower oil control segment ring gap location
   - Expander ring and lower compression ring gap location

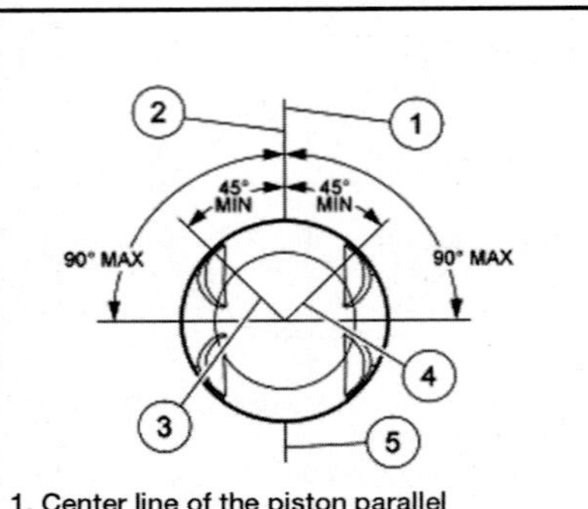

Fig. 260 Piston and ring positioning

REAR MAIN SEAL

REMOVAL & INSTALLATION

2.5L Engine

See Figures 261 through 263.

1. With the vehicle in NEUTRAL, position it on a hoist.
2. Remove the flexplate or flywheel.
3. Drain the engine oil.
   a. Install the drain plug.
   b. Tighten to 21 ft. lbs. (28 Nm).

➡If the oil pan is not removed, damage to the rear oil seal retainer joint can occur.

4. Remove the 16 bolts, stud bolt and the oil pan.
5. Remove the 6 bolts and the crankshaft rear oil seal with retainer plate.

To install:

6. Using the Crankshaft Rear Main Oil Seal Installer, position the crankshaft rear oil seal with retainer plate onto the crankshaft.
7. Install the crankshaft rear oil seal with retainer plate and bolts.
   a. To install, tighten in the sequence shown to 89 inch lbs. (10 Nm).

➡Do not use metal scrapers, wire brushes, power abrasive discs or other abrasive means to clean the sealing surfaces. These tools cause scratches and gouges, which make leak paths. Use a plastic scraping tool to remove traces of sealant.

8. Clean and inspect all the oil pan, engine front cover and cylinder block mating surfaces.

➡If the oil pan is not secured within 4 minutes of sealant application, the sealant must be removed and the sealing area cleaned with metal surface prep. Allow to dry until there is no sign of wetness, or 4 minutes, whichever is longer. Failure to follow these instructions can cause future oil leakage.

9. NOTE: The oil pan must be installed and the bolts tightened within 4 minutes of applying the silicone gasket and sealant.
10. Apply a 2.5 mm (0.09 in) bead of silicone gasket and sealant to the oil pan. Install the oil pan. Install the 2 oil pan bolts finger-tight.

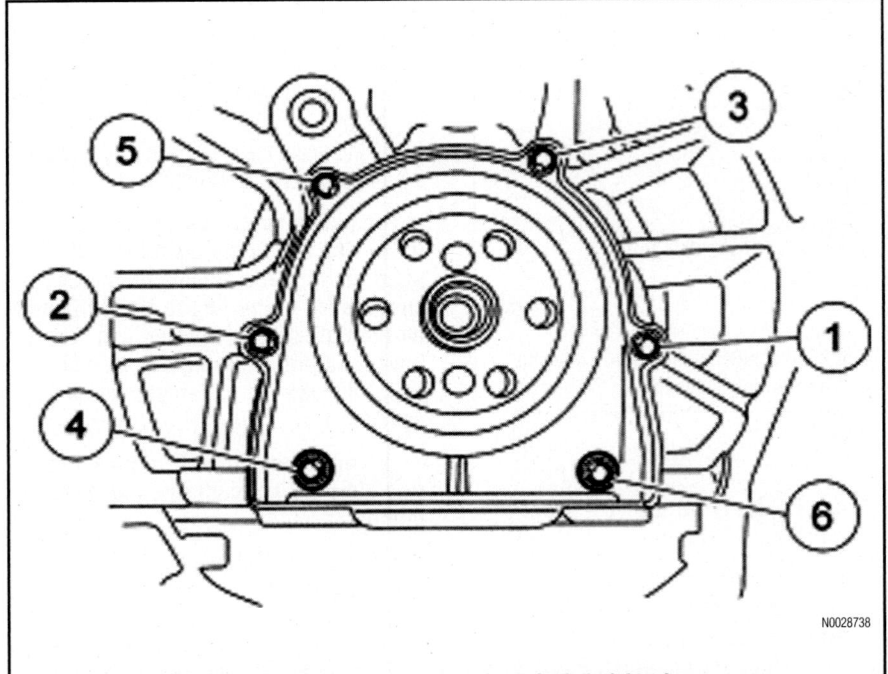

Fig. 261 Identifying the crankshaft rear oil seal retainer plat bolt tightening sequence

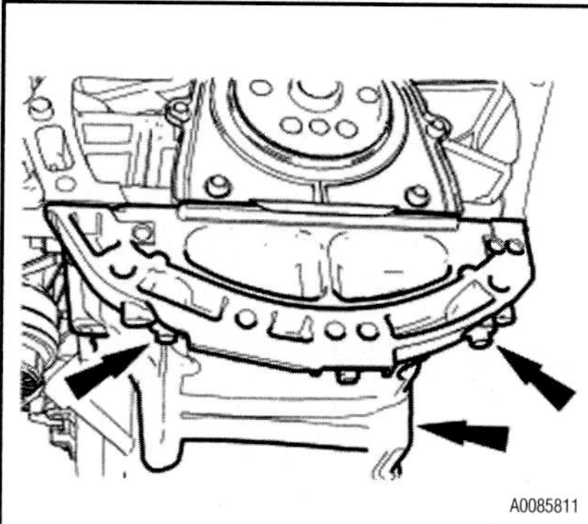
Fig. 262 Applying silicone gasket and sealant

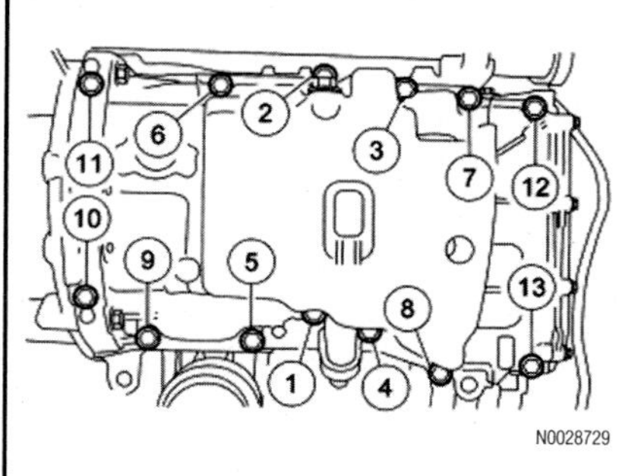

Fig. 263 Identifying the oil pan bolt tightening sequence

11. Install the 3 bolts and the stud bolt.
    a. To install, tighten to 89 inch lbs. (10 Nm).
12. Install the remaining oil pan bolts and tighten the oil pan bolts in the sequence shown to 15 ft. lbs. (20 Nm).
13. Install the flexplate or flywheel.
14. Fill the engine with clean engine oil.

2.5L Hybrid Engine

See Figures 264 through 266.

1. With the vehicle in NEUTRAL, position it on a hoist.
2. Remove the flywheel.
3. Drain the engine oil.
    a. Install the drain plug.
    b. Tighten to 21 ft. lbs. (28 Nm).

➡If the oil pan is not removed, damage to the rear oil seal retainer joint can occur.

4. Remove the 17 bolts and the oil pan.
5. Remove the 6 bolts and the crankshaft rear oil seal with retainer plate.

To install:

6. Using the Crankshaft Rear Main Oil Seal Installer, position the crankshaft rear oil seal with retainer plate onto the crankshaft.
7. Install the crankshaft rear oil seal with retainer plate and bolts.
    a. Tighten in the sequence shown to 89 inch lbs. (10 Nm).

➡Do not use metal scrapers, wire brushes, power abrasive discs or other abrasive means to clean the sealing surfaces. These tools cause scratches and gouges, which make leak paths. Use a plastic scraping tool and metal surface cleaner to remove traces of sealant.

8. Clean and inspect all the oil pan and cylinder block mating surfaces.

➡If the oil pan is not secured within 4 minutes of sealant application, the sealant must be removed and the sealing area cleaned with metal surface prep. Allow to dry until there is no sign of wetness, or 4 minutes, whichever is longer. Failure to follow this procedure can cause future oil leakage.

➡The oil pan must be installed and the bolts tightened within 4 minutes of applying the silicone gasket and sealant.

9. Apply a 2.5 mm (0.09 in) bead of silicone gasket and sealant to the oil pan.
10. Install the oil pan. Install the 2 oil pan bolts finger-tight.
11. Install the 4 bolts.
    a. Tighten to 89 inch lbs. (10 Nm).
12. Install the remaining oil pan bolts and tighten the oil pan bolts in the sequence shown to 18 ft. lbs. (25 Nm).

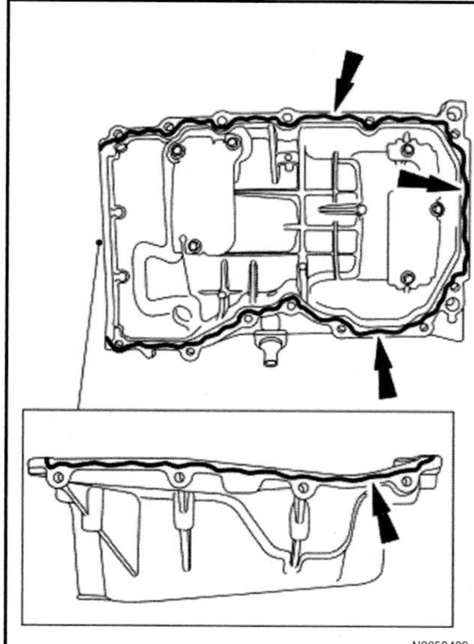
Fig. 264 Applying silicone gasket and sealant

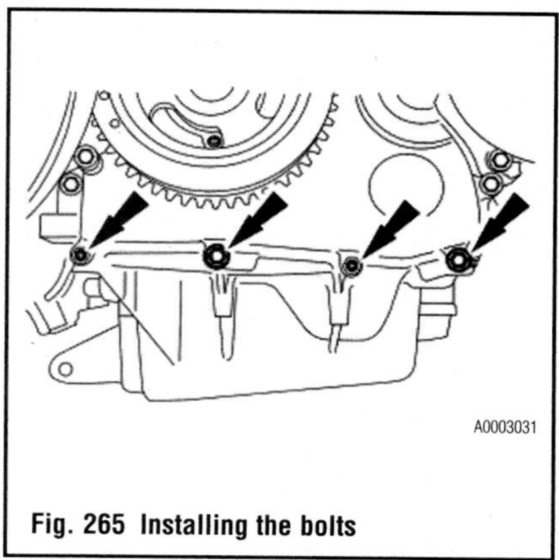
Fig. 265 Installing the bolts

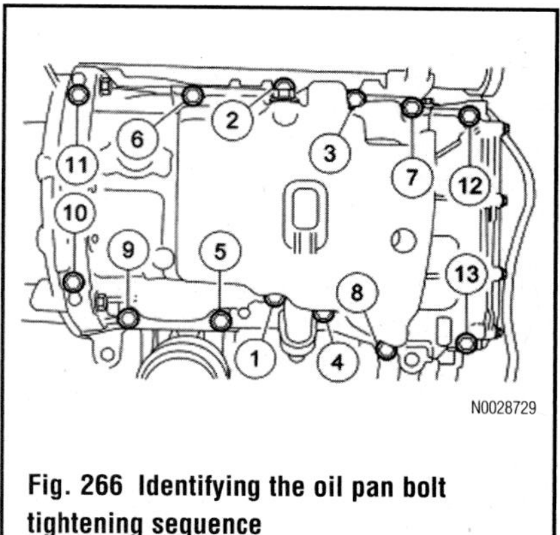

Fig. 266 Identifying the oil pan bolt tightening sequence

13. Install the flywheel.
14. Fill the engine with clean engine oil.

3.0L Engine

See Figure 267.

1. With the vehicle in NEUTRAL, position it on a hoist.
2. Remove the flexplate.
3. Using the Slide Hammer and the Crankshaft Rear Oil Seal Remover, remove and discard the crankshaft rear oil seal.

To install:

➡Clean all sealing surfaces with metal surface prep.

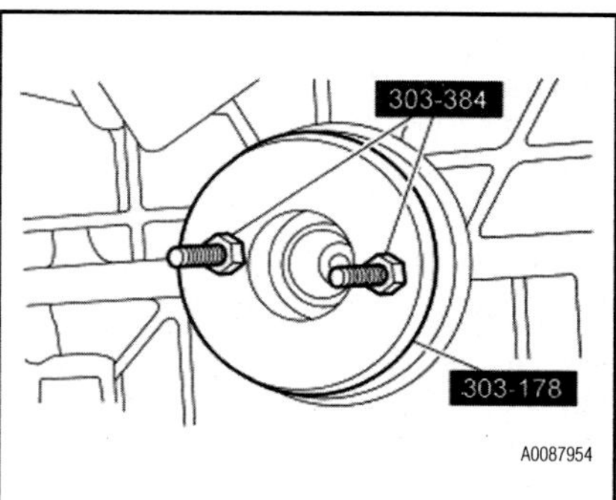

Fig. 267 Installing the crankshaft rear oil seal

➡**Apply clean engine oil to the seal lip and seal bore before installing the seal.**

4. Using the Crankshaft Rear Main Oil Seal Installer Bolts and the Crankshaft Rear Main Oil Seal Installer, install the crankshaft rear oil seal.
5. Install the flexplate.

3.5L Engine

See Figures 268 and 269.

1. With the vehicle in NEUTRAL, position it on a hoist.
2. Remove the flexplate.
3. Remove the crankshaft sensor ring.
4. Using the Crankshaft Rear Oil Seal Remover and Slide Hammer, remove and discard the crankshaft rear seal.
   a. Clean all sealing surfaces with metal surface prep.

To install:

➡**Lubricate the seal lips and bore with clean engine oil prior to installation.**

5. Position the Rear Main Seal Installer onto the end of the crankshaft and slide a new crankshaft rear seal onto the tool.
6. Using the Rear Main Seal Installer and Handle, install the new crankshaft rear seal.
7. Install the crankshaft sensor ring.
8. Install the flexplate.
9. Using the scan tool, perform the Misfire Monitor Neutral Profile Correction procedure, following the on-screen instructions.

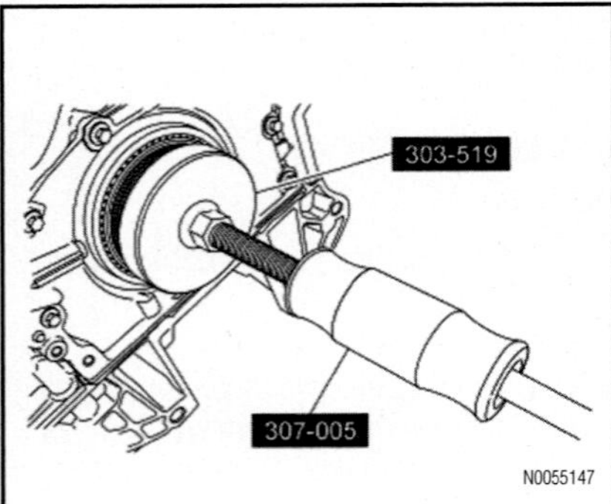

Fig. 268 Removing the crankshaft rear seal

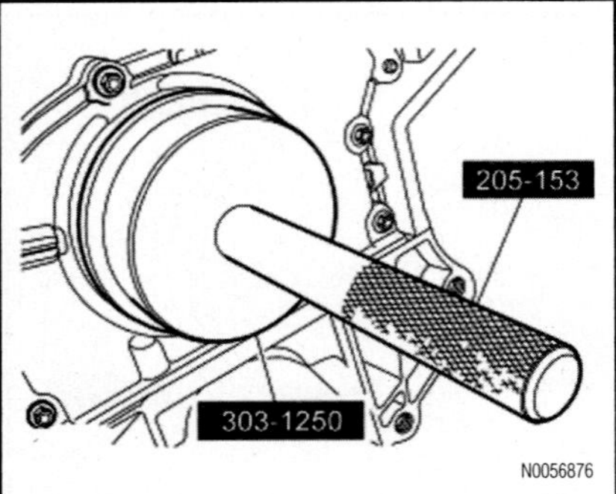

Fig. 269 Installing a new crankshaft rear seal

TIMING CHAIN & SPROCKETS

REMOVAL & INSTALLATION

2.5L Engines

See Figures 270 through 276.

➡**Do not loosen or remove the crankshaft pulley bolt without first installing the special tools as instructed in this procedure. The crankshaft pulley and the crankshaft timing sprocket are not keyed to the crankshaft. The crankshaft, the crankshaft sprocket and the pulley are fitted together by friction, using diamond washers between the flange faces on each part. For that reason, the crankshaft sprocket is also unfastened if the pulley bolt is loosened. Before any repair requiring loosening or removal of the crankshaft pulley bolt, the crankshaft and camshafts must be locked in place by the special service tools, otherwise severe engine damage can occur.**

➡**During engine repair procedures, cleanliness is extremely important. Any foreign material, including any material created while cleaning gasket surfaces, that enters the oil passages, coolant passages or the oil pan can cause engine failure.**

1. With the vehicle in NEUTRAL, position it on a hoist.
2. Remove the engine front cover.
3. Compress the timing chain tensioner in the following sequence.

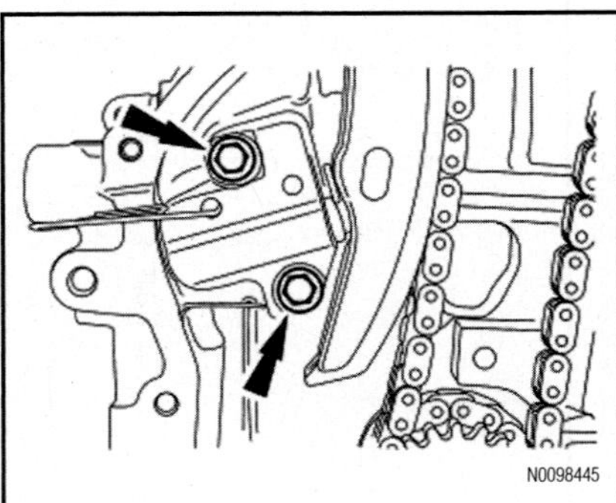

Fig. 270 Removing the timing chain tensioner

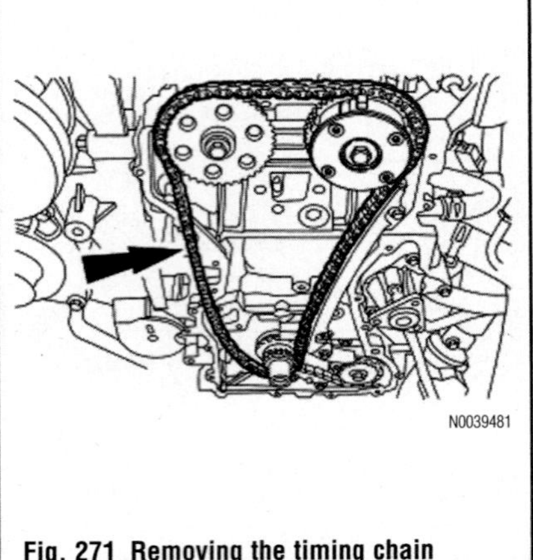

Fig. 271 Removing the timing chain

   a. Using a small pick, release and hold the ratchet mechanism.
   b. While holding the ratchet mechanism in the released position, compress the tensioner by pushing the timing chain arm toward the tensioner.
   c. Insert a paper clip into the hole to retain the tensioner.
4. Remove the 2 bolts and timing chain tensioner.
5. Remove the timing chain tensioner arm.
6. Remove the timing chain.
7. Remove the 2 bolts and the timing chain guide.

➡**The Camshaft Alignment Plate is for camshaft alignment only. Using this tool to prevent engine rotation can result in engine damage.**

8. Using the flats on the camshaft to prevent camshaft rotation, remove the bolt and the exhaust camshaft sprocket.

➡**The Camshaft Alignment Plate is for camshaft alignment only. Using this tool to prevent engine rotation can result in engine damage.**

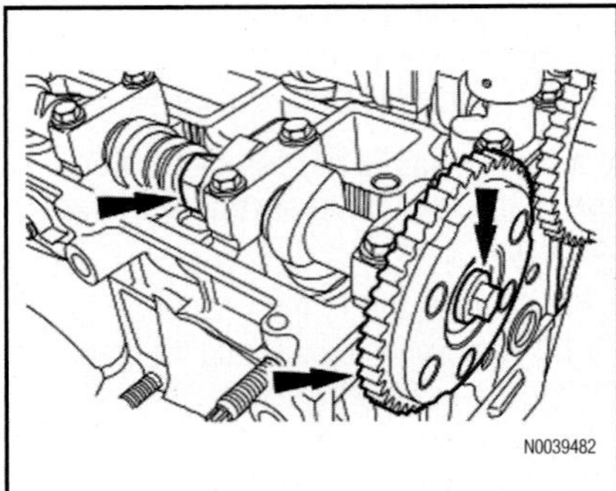

Fig. 272 Removing the bolts and exhaust camshaft sprocket

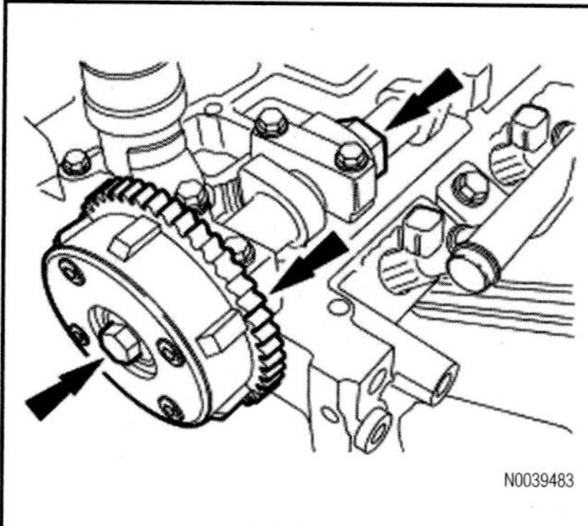

Fig. 273 Removing the bolt and camshaft phaser and sprocket

9. Using the flats on the camshaft to prevent camshaft rotation, remove the bolt and the camshaft phaser and sprocket.

To install:

10. Install the camshaft sprockets and the bolts. Do not tighten the bolts at this time.
11. Install the timing chain guide and the 2 bolts.
    a. To install, tighten to 89 inch lbs. (10 Nm).
12. Install the timing chain.
13. Install the timing chain tensioner arm.

➡If the timing chain tensioner plunger and ratchet assembly are not pinned in the compressed position, follow the next 4 steps.

➡Do not compress the ratchet assembly. This will damage the ratchet assembly.

14. Using the edge of a vise, compress the timing chain tensioner plunger.
15. Using a small pick, push back and hold the ratchet mechanism.
16. While holding the ratchet mechanism, push the ratchet arm back into the tensioner housing.

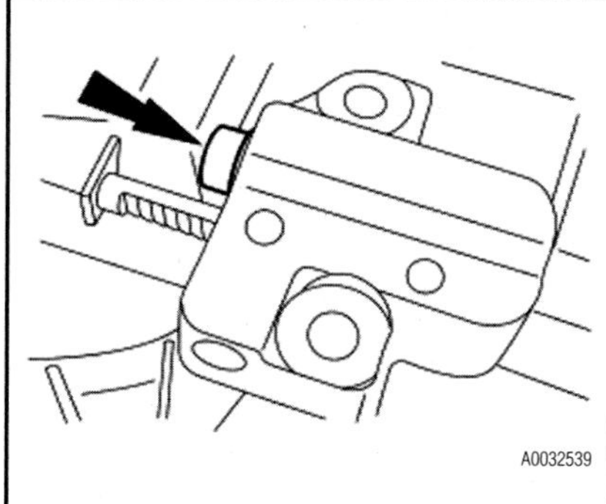

Fig. 274 Identifying the timing chain tensioner plunger

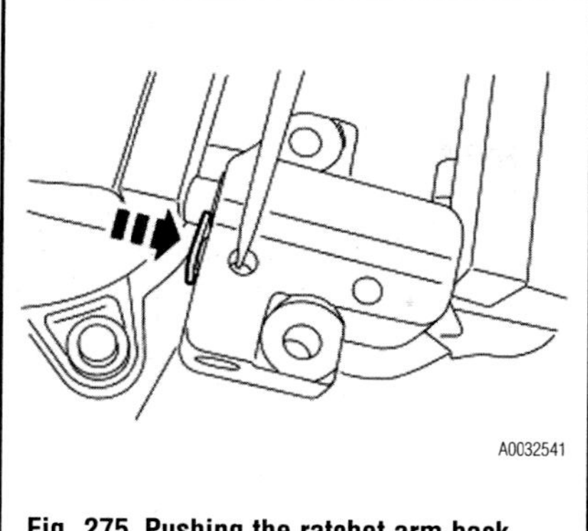

Fig. 275 Pushing the ratchet arm back into the tensioner housing

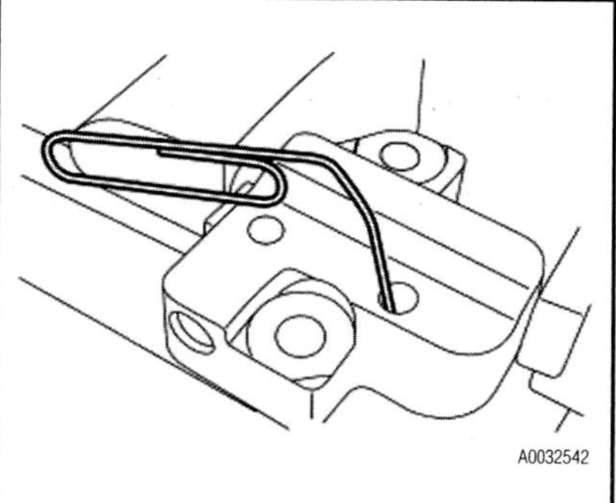

Fig. 276 Installing a paper clip to hold the ratchet assembly and plunger

17. Install a paper clip into the hole in the tensioner housing to hold the ratchet assembly and the plunger in during installation.
18. Install the timing chain tensioner and the 2 bolts. Remove the paper clip to release the piston.
    a. Tighten to 89 inch lbs. (10 Nm).

➡The Camshaft Alignment Plate is for camshaft alignment only. Using this tool to prevent engine rotation can result in engine damage.

19. Using the flats on the camshafts to prevent camshaft rotation, tighten the bolts.
    a. Tighten to 53 ft. lbs. (72 Nm).
20. Install the engine front cover

3.0L Engine

See Figures 277 through 283.

➡During engine repair procedures, cleanliness is extremely important. Any foreign material (including any material created while cleaning gasket surfaces) that enters the oil passages, coolant passages or the oil pan may cause engine failure.

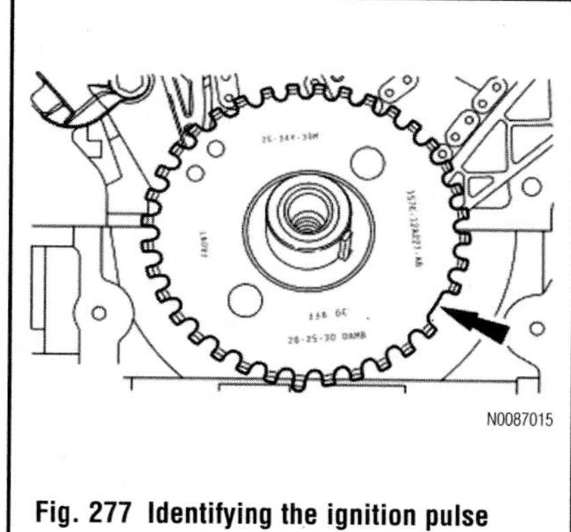

Fig. 277 Identifying the ignition pulse wheel

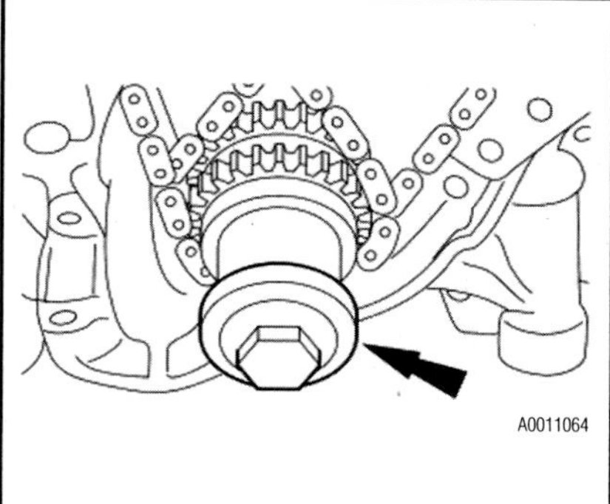

Fig. 278 Installing the crankshaft pulley bolt and washer

➡Failure to verify correct timing drive component alignment will result in severe engine damage.

1. Remove the engine front cover.
2. Remove the LH and RH spark plugs.

➡This pulse wheel is used in several different engines. Install the pulse wheel with the keyway in the slot stamped "30RFF" (orange in color).

3. Remove the ignition pulse wheel.
4. Install the crankshaft pulley bolt and washer.
5. Rotate the crankshaft clockwise to position the crankshaft keyway in the 11 o'clock position and position the camshafts in the correct position. This will position the No. 1 cylinder at Top Dead Center (TDC).
    a. Verify that the camshafts are correctly located. If not, rotate the crankshaft one additional turn and recheck.
6. Rotate the crankshaft clockwise 120 degrees to the 3 o'clock position to position the RH camshafts in the neutral position.
7. Verify that the RH camshafts are in the neutral position.
8. Remove the RH timing chain tensioner arm.
    a. Remove the 2 bolts.

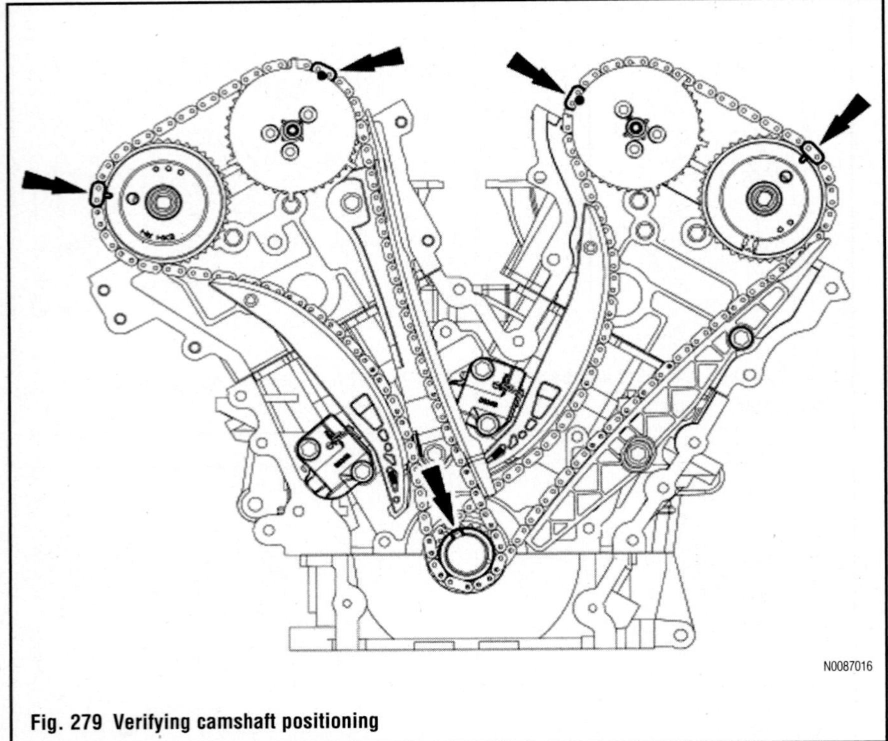

Fig. 279 Verifying camshaft positioning

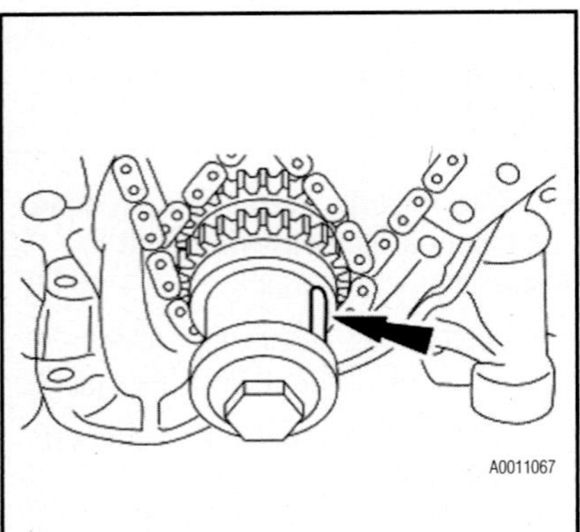

Fig. 280 Positioning the RH camshafts in the neutral position

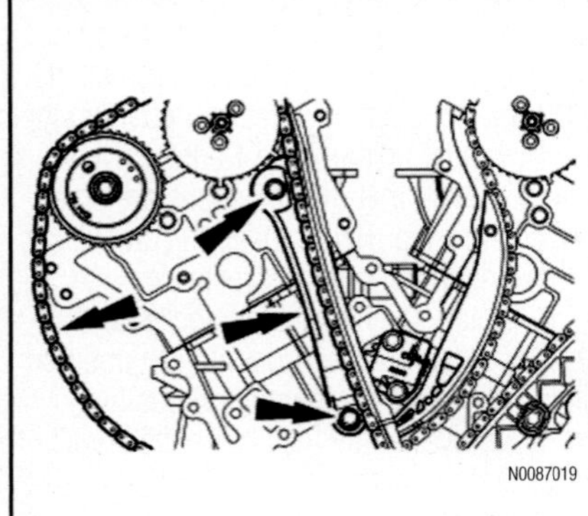

Fig. 281 Removing the timing chain guide

b. Remove the tensioner.

c. Remove the tensioner arm.

9. Remove the 2 bolts and the RH timing chain guide.

a. Remove the RH timing chain from the engine.

10. Rotate the crankcase clockwise 600 degrees (one and two-third turns) to position the crankcase keyway in the 11 o'clock position. This will position the LH camshafts in the neutral position.

11. Verify the LH camshafts are in the neutral position.

12. Remove the LH timing chain and tensioner arm.

a. Remove the 2 bolts.

b. Remove the tensioner.

c. Remove the tensioner arm.

13. Remove the 2 bolts and the LH timing chain guide.

a. Remove the LH timing chain from the engine.

14. Remove the crankshaft pulley bolt and the crankshaft sprocket.

To install:

➡Failure to verify correct timing drive component alignment will result in severe engine damage.

15. Install the crankshaft sprocket with the timing mark facing out. The timing mark on the LH and RH timing chains will be aligned to this mark during assembly.

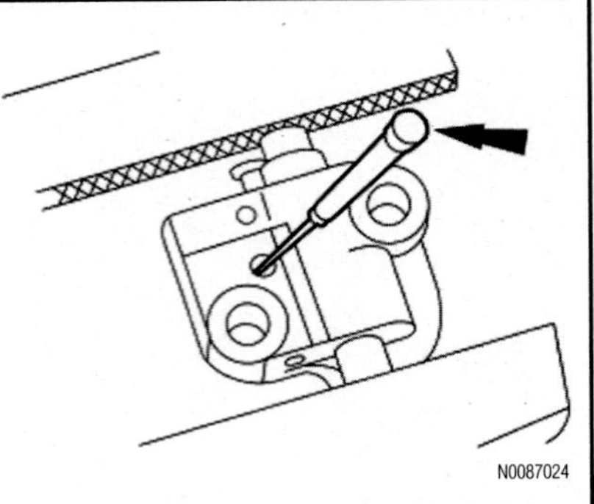

Fig. 282 Holding chain tensioner ratchet lock mechanism with a pick

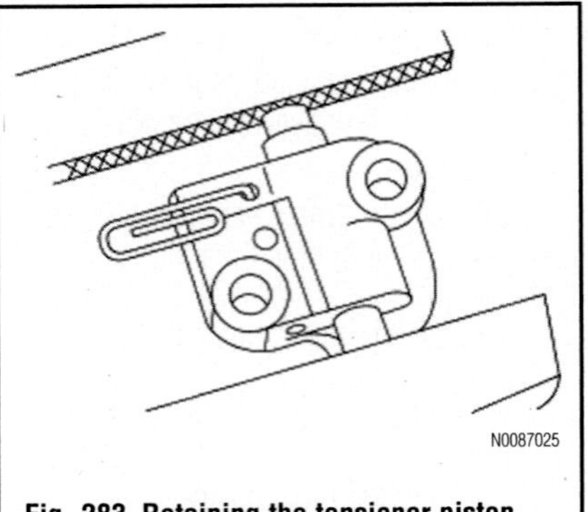

Fig. 283 Retaining the tensioner piston with a paper clip

16. Position the chain tensioner in a soft-jawed vise.

17. Hold the chain tensioner ratchet lock mechanism away from the ratchet stem with a small pick.

➡During tensioner compression, do not release the ratchet stem until the tensioner piston is fully bottomed in its bore or damage to the ratchet stem will result.

18. Slowly compress the timing chain tensioner.

19. Retain the tensioner piston with a 1.5 mm (0.06 in) diameter wire or paper clip.

20. If timing marks in the timing chains are not evident, use a permanent-type marker to mark the crankshaft and camshaft timing marks on the LH and RH timing chains.

a. Mark any link to use as the crankshaft timing mark.

b. Starting with the crankshaft timing mark, count 29 links and mark the link.

c. Continue counting to link 42 and mark the link.

21. Position the LH timing chain and guide and install the bolts.

a. Tighten to 18 ft. lbs. (25 Nm).

b. Align the marks on the timing chain with the marks on the camshaft and crankshaft sprockets.

22. Install the LH timing chain tensioner arm and the LH timing chain tensioner.
   a. Install the tensioner arm.
   b. Position the tensioner.
   c. Install the bolts.
   d. Tighten to 18 ft. lbs. (25 Nm).
23. Install the crankshaft pulley bolt and rotate the crankshaft clockwise 120 degrees until the crankshaft keyway is in the 3 o'clock position.
24. Verify that the RH camshafts are correctly positioned.
25. Install the RH timing chain and chain guide and install the bolts.
   a. Tighten to 18 ft. lbs. (25 Nm).
   b. Align the marks on the timing chain with the marks on the camshaft and crankshaft sprockets.
26. Install the RH timing chain tensioner and tensioner arm.
   a. Install the tensioner arm.
   b. Position the tensioner.
   c. Install the bolts.
   d. Tighten to 18 ft. lbs. (25 Nm).
27. Remove the LH and RH timing chain tensioner piston retaining wires.
28. Rotate the crankshaft counterclockwise 120 degrees to TDC .

➡Failure to verify correct timing drive component alignment will result in severe engine damage.

29. Verify the timing with the following steps.
   a. There should be 12 chain links between the camshaft timing marks.
   b. There should be 27 chain links between the camshaft and the crankshaft timing marks.
   c. There should be 30 chain links between the camshaft and the crankshaft timing marks.
30. Remove the crankshaft pulley bolt and washer.

➡This pulse wheel is used in several different engines. Install the pulse wheel with the keyway in the slot stamped "30RFF" only (orange in color).

31. Install the ignition pulse wheel.
32. Install the LH and RH spark plugs.
33. Install the engine front cover.

3.5L Engine

See Figures 284 through 293.

➡During engine repair procedures, cleanliness is extremely important. Any foreign material, including any material created while cleaning gasket surfaces, that enters the oil passages, coolant passages or the oil pan can cause engine failure.

➡On early build engines, the timing chain rides on the inner side of the RH timing chain guide. Late build engines are equipped with a different design RH timing chain guide that requires the timing chain to ride on the outer side of the RH timing chain guide. For service, all replacement RH timing chain guides will be the late build design.

All vehicles

1. Remove the engine front cover.
2. Rotate the crankshaft clockwise and align the timing marks on the VCT assemblies.

➡The Camshaft Holding Tool will hold the camshafts in the Top Dead Center (TDC) position.

3. Install the Camshaft Holding Tool onto the flats of the LH camshafts.

➡The Camshaft Holding Tool will hold the camshafts in the TDC position.

4. Install the Camshaft Holding Tool onto the flats of the RH camshafts.
5. Remove the 3 bolts and the RH VCT housing.

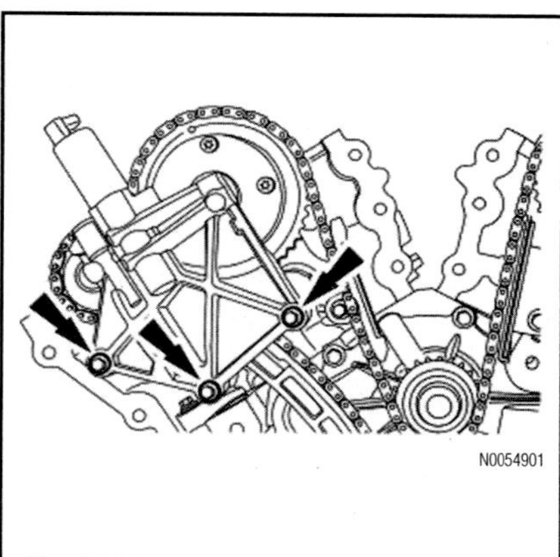

Fig. 284 Removing the RH VCT housing

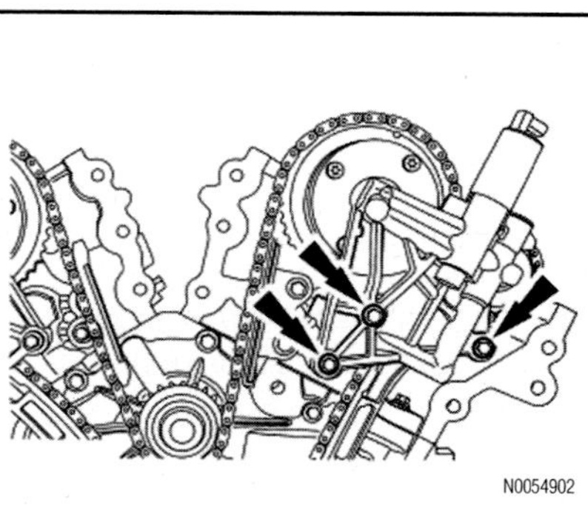

Fig. 285 Removing the LH VCT housing

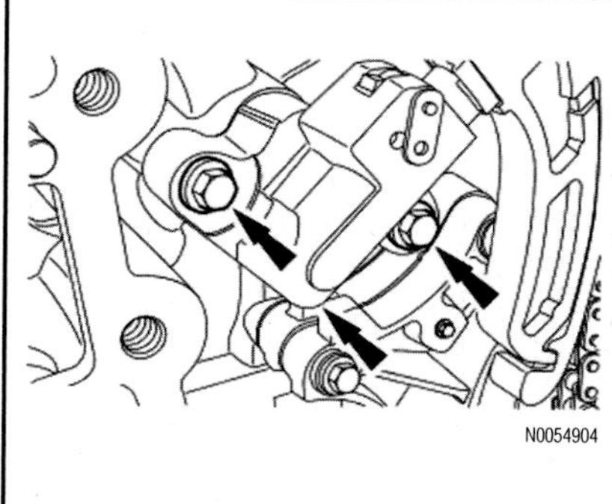

Fig. 286 Removing the primary chain tensioner

6. Remove the 3 bolts and the LH VCT housing.
7. Remove the 2 bolts and the primary timing chain tensioner.
8. Remove the primary timing chain tensioner arm.
9. Remove the 2 bolts and the lower LH primary timing chain guide.
10. Remove the primary timing chain.
11. Remove the crankshaft timing chain sprocket.
12. Remove the 2 bolts and the upper LH primary timing chain guide.

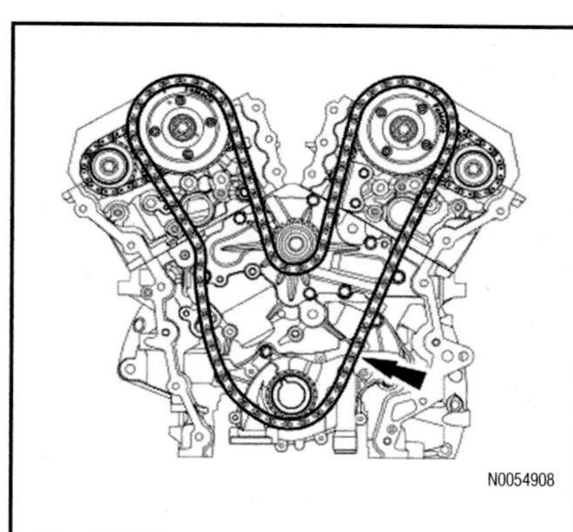

Fig. 287 Removing the primary timing chain

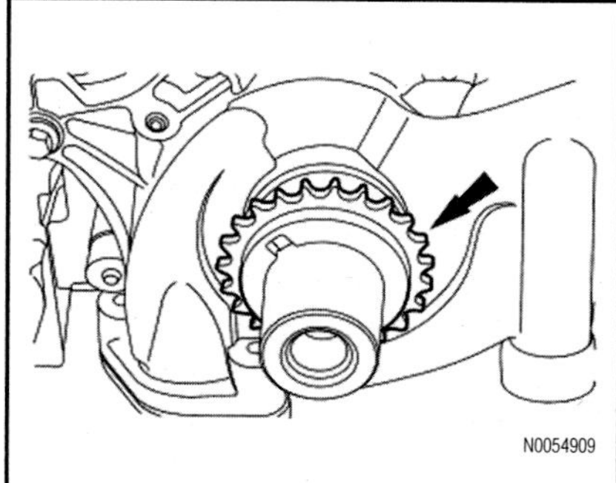

Fig. 288 Removing the crankshaft timing chain sprocket

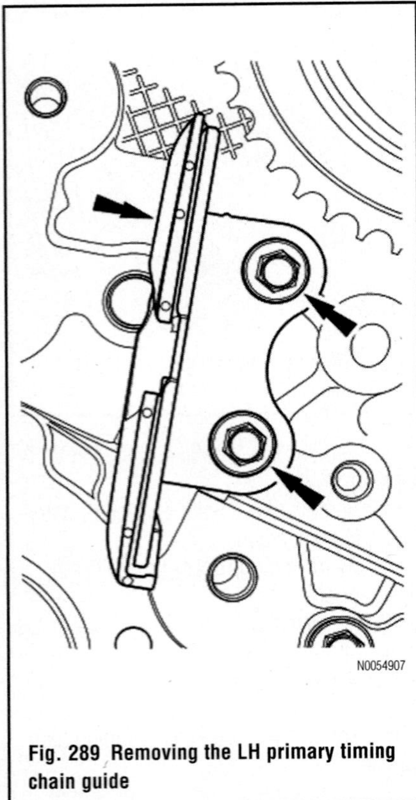

Fig. 289 Removing the LH primary timing chain guide

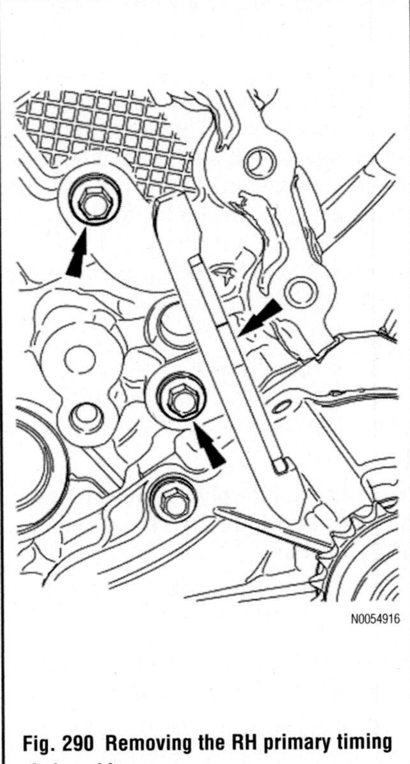

Fig. 290 Removing the RH primary timing chain guide

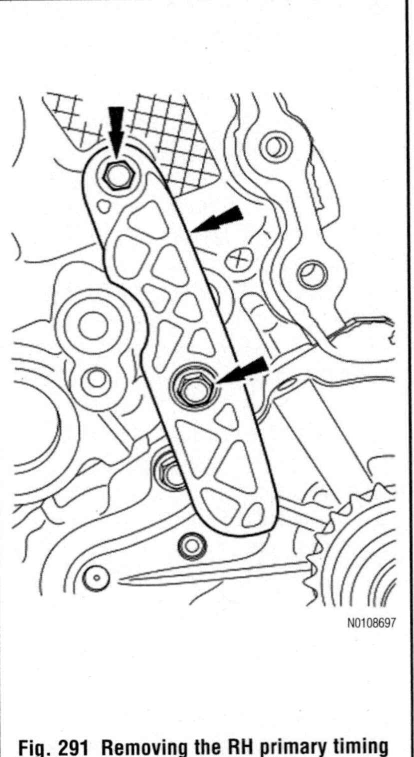

Fig. 291 Removing the RH primary timing chain guide

13. Compress the LH secondary timing chain tensioner and install a suitable lockpin to retain the tensioner in the collapsed position.

➡The VCT bolt and the exhaust camshaft bolt must be discarded and new ones installed. However, the exhaust camshaft washer is reusable.

14. Remove and discard the LH VCT assembly bolt and the LH exhaust camshaft sprocket bolt.
15. Remove the LH VCT assembly, secondary timing chain and the LH exhaust camshaft sprocket as an assembly.

➡It is necessary to tilt the Camshaft Holding Tool toward the rear of the engine to access the rearmost secondary timing chain tensioner bolt.

16. Remove the 2 bolts and the LH secondary timing chain tensioner.
17. Compress the RH secondary timing chain tensioner and install a suitable lockpin to retain the tensioner in the collapsed position.

➡The VCT bolt and the exhaust camshaft bolt must be discarded and new ones installed. However, the exhaust camshaft washer is reusable.

18. Remove and discard the RH VCT assembly bolt and the RH exhaust camshaft sprocket bolt.
19. Remove the RH VCT assembly, secondary timing chain and the RH exhaust camshaft sprocket as an assembly.

➡It is necessary to tilt the Camshaft Holding Tool toward the rear of the engine to access the rearmost secondary timing chain tensioner bolt.

20. Remove the 2 bolts and the RH secondary timing chain tensioner.

Engines equipped with early build RH timing chain guides

21. Remove the 2 bolts and the RH primary timing chain guide.

Engines equipped with late build/replacement RH timing chain guides

22. Remove the 2 bolts and the RH primary timing chain guide.

To install:

➡During engine repair procedures, cleanliness is extremely important. Any foreign material, including any material created while cleaning gasket surfaces, that enters the oil passages, coolant passages or the oil pan can cause engine failure.

Engines equipped with late build/ replacement RH timing chain guides

23. Install the RH primary timing chain guide and the 2 bolts.
    a. Tighten to 89 inch lbs. (10 Nm).

Engines equipped with early build RH timing chain guides

24. Install the RH primary timing chain guide and the 2 bolts.
    a. Tighten to 89 inch lbs. (10 Nm).

All vehicles

➡It is necessary to tilt the Camshaft Holding Tool toward the rear of the engine to access the rearmost secondary timing chain tensioner bolt.

25. Install the RH secondary timing chain tensioner and the 2 bolts.
    a. Tighten to 89 inch lbs. (10 Nm).
26. Assemble the RH Variable Camshaft Timing (VCT) assembly, the RH exhaust camshaft sprocket and the RH secondary timing chain.
    a. Align the colored links with the timing marks.
27. Position the RH secondary timing assembly onto the camshafts.
28. Install 2 new bolts and the original washer. Tighten in 4 stages.
    a. Stage 1: Tighten to 30 ft. lbs. (40 Nm).
    b. Stage 2: Loosen one full turn.
    c. Stage 3: Tighten to 89 inch lbs. (10 Nm).
    d. Stage 4: Tighten 90 degrees.
29. Remove the lockpin from the RH secondary timing chain tensioner.

➡It is necessary to tilt the Camshaft Holding Tool toward the rear of the engine to access the rearmost secondary timing chain tensioner bolt.

30. Install the LH secondary timing chain tensioner and the 2 bolts.
    a. Tighten to 89 inch lbs. (10 Nm).
31. Assemble the LH VCT assembly, the LH exhaust camshaft sprocket and the LH secondary timing chain.
    a. Align the colored links with the timing marks.
32. Position the LH secondary timing assembly onto the camshafts.
33. Install 2 new bolts and the original washer. Tighten in 4 stages.
    a. Stage 1: Tighten to 30 ft. lbs. (40 Nm).
    b. Stage 2: Loosen one full turn.
    c. Stage 3: Tighten to 89 inch lbs. (10 Nm).
    d. Stage 4: Tighten 90 degrees.
34. Remove the lockpin from the LH secondary timing chain tensioner.
35. Install the crankshaft timing chain sprocket.
36. Install the primary timing chain with the colored links aligned with the timing marks on the VCT assemblies and the crankshaft sprocket.
37. Install the upper LH primary timing chain guide and the 2 bolts.
    a. Tighten to 89 inch lbs. (10 Nm).
38. Install the lower LH primary timing chain guide and the 2 bolts.
    a. Tighten to 89 inch lbs. (10 Nm).
39. Install the primary timing chain tensioner arm.
40. Reset the primary timing chain tensioner.
    a. Rotate the lever counterclockwise.
    b. Using a soft-jawed vise, compress the plunger.
    c. Align the hole in the lever with the hole in the tensioner housing.
    d. Install a suitable lockpin.

➡It may be necessary to rotate the crankshaft slightly to remove slack from the timing chain and install the tensioner.

41. Install the primary tensioner and the 2 bolts.
    a. Tighten to 89 inch lbs. (10 Nm).
42. Remove the lockpin.
43. As a post-check, verify correct alignment of all timing marks.
44. Inspect the VCT housing seals for damage and replace as necessary.

➡Make sure the dowels on the Variable Camshaft Timing (VCT) housing are fully engaged in the cylinder head prior to tightening the bolts. Failure to follow this process will result in severe engine damage.

45. Install the LH VCT housing and the 3 bolts.
    a. Tighten in the sequence shown to 89 inch lbs. (10 Nm).

➡Make sure the dowels on the Variable Camshaft Timing (VCT) housing are fully engaged in the cylinder head prior to tightening the bolts. Failure to follow this process will result in severe engine damage.

46. Install the RH VCT housing and the 3 bolts.
    a. Tighten in the sequence shown to 89 inch lbs. (10 Nm).
47. Install the engine front cover.

VALVE COVERS

REMOVAL & INSTALLATION

2.5L Engine

See Figures 294 through 297.

Fig. 292 Identifying the LH VCT housing bolt tightening sequence

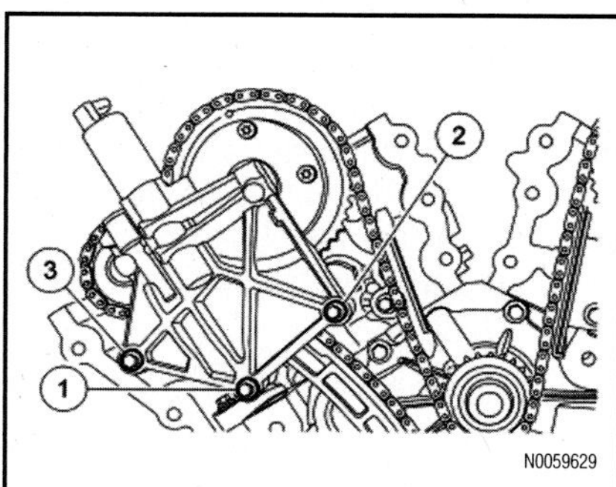

Fig. 293 Identifying the RH VCT housing bolt tightening sequence

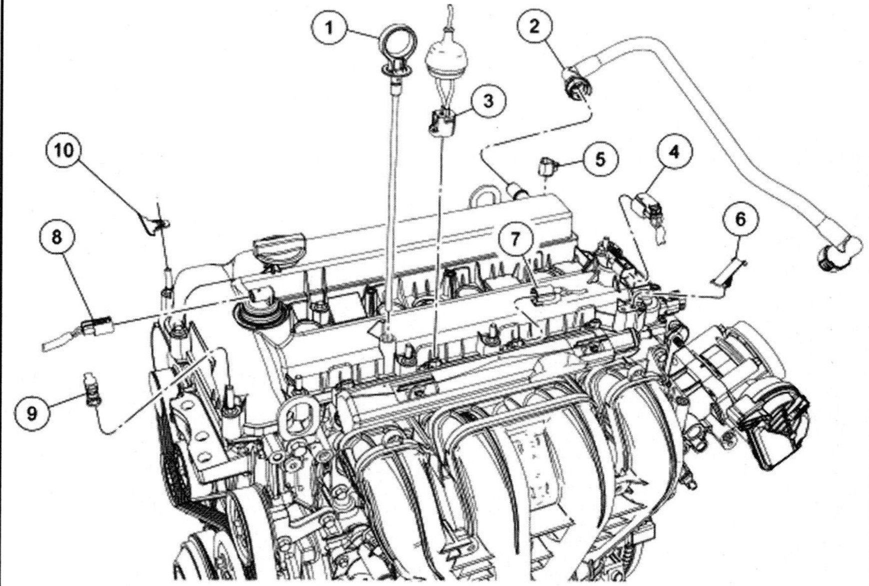

Fig. 294 Exploded view of the valve covers and related components—1 of 2

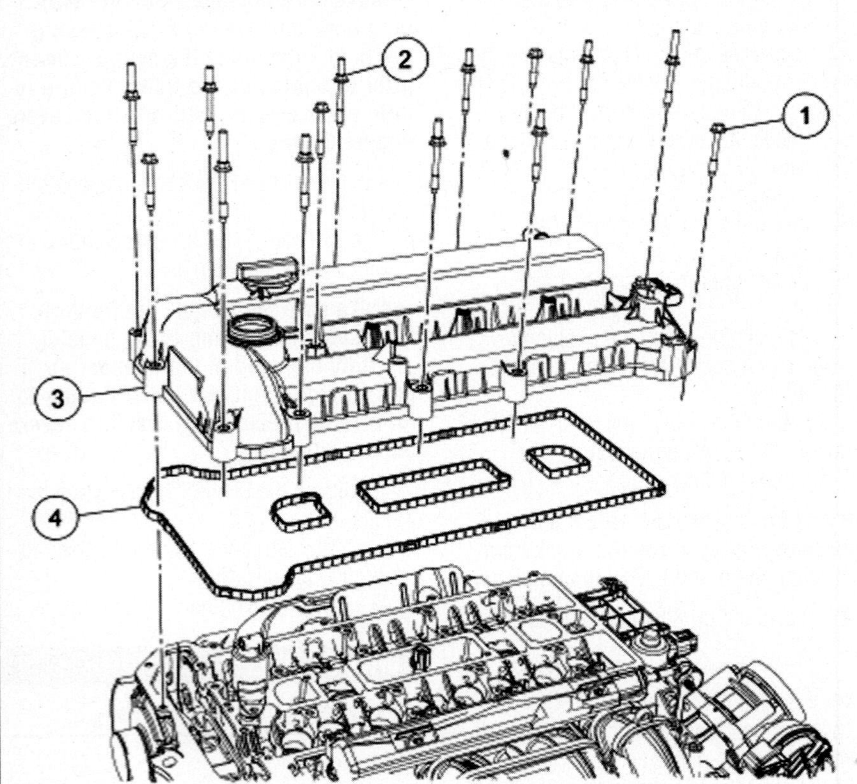

Fig. 295 Exploded view of the valve covers and related components—2 of 2

➡During engine repair procedures, cleanliness is extremely important. Any foreign material, including any material created while cleaning gasket surfaces, that enters the oil passages, coolant passages or the oil pan can cause engine failure.

1. Remove the oil level indicator.
2. Remove the ignition coil-on-plugs.
3. Disconnect the crankcase vent hose.
4. Disconnect the Cylinder Head Temperature (CHT) sensor electrical connector.
5. Disconnect the Camshaft Position (CMP) sensor electrical connector.
6. Disconnect the radio capacitor electrical connector.
7. Disconnect the Variable Camshaft Timing (VCT) solenoid electrical connector.
8. Detach all of the wiring harness retainers from the valve cover studs and position the harness aside.
9. Remove the 14 valve cover retainers and the valve cover.
   a. Discard the gasket.

To install:

➡Do not use metal scrapers, wire brushes, power abrasive discs or other abrasive means to clean the sealing surfaces. These tools cause scratches and gouges which make leak paths.

10. Clean and inspect the sealing surfaces.

➡The valve cover must be secured within 4 minutes of silicone gasket application. If the valve cover is not secured within 4 minutes, the sealant must be removed and the sealing area cleaned with metal surface prep.

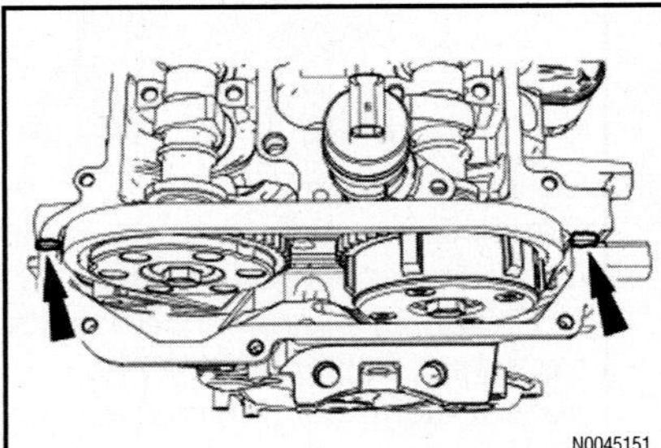

Fig. 296 Applying silicone gasket and sealant

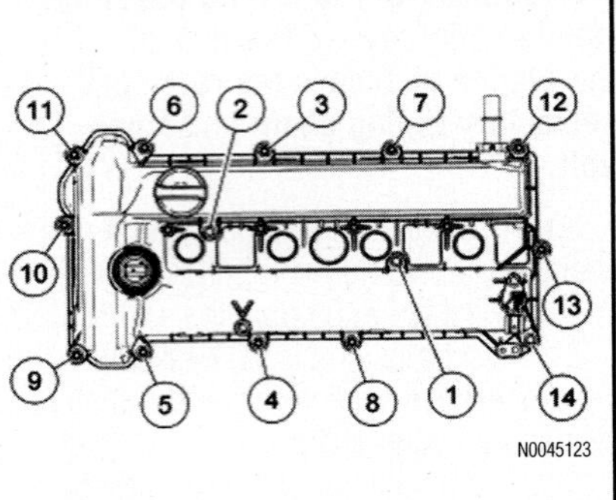

Fig. 297 Identifying the valve cover tightening sequence

11. Apply silicone gasket and sealant to the locations shown.
12. Install the valve cover, new gasket and retainers.
    a. Tighten in the sequence shown to 89 inch lbs. (10 Nm).
13. Position the wiring harness and attach all of the wiring harness retainers to the valve cover studs.
14. Connect the VCT solenoid electrical connector.
15. Connect the radio capacitor electrical connector.
16. Connect the CMP sensor electrical connector.
17. Connect the CHT sensor electrical connector.
18. Connect the crankcase vent hose.
19. Install the ignition coil-on-plugs.

➡Make sure the notch on the oil level indicator is aligned with the V-shaped boss on the valve cover and fully engaged into the valve cover.

20. Install the oil level indicator.

2.5L Hybrid Engine

See Figures 298 through 301.

➡During engine repair procedures, cleanliness is extremely important. Any foreign material (including any material created while cleaning gasket surfaces) that enters the oil passages, coolant passages or the oil pan can cause engine failure.

1. With the vehicle in NEUTRAL, position it on a hoist.
2. Remove the ignition coil-on-plugs.
3. Disconnect the crankcase vent hose from the valve cover.
4. Detach the 2 block heater wiring har-

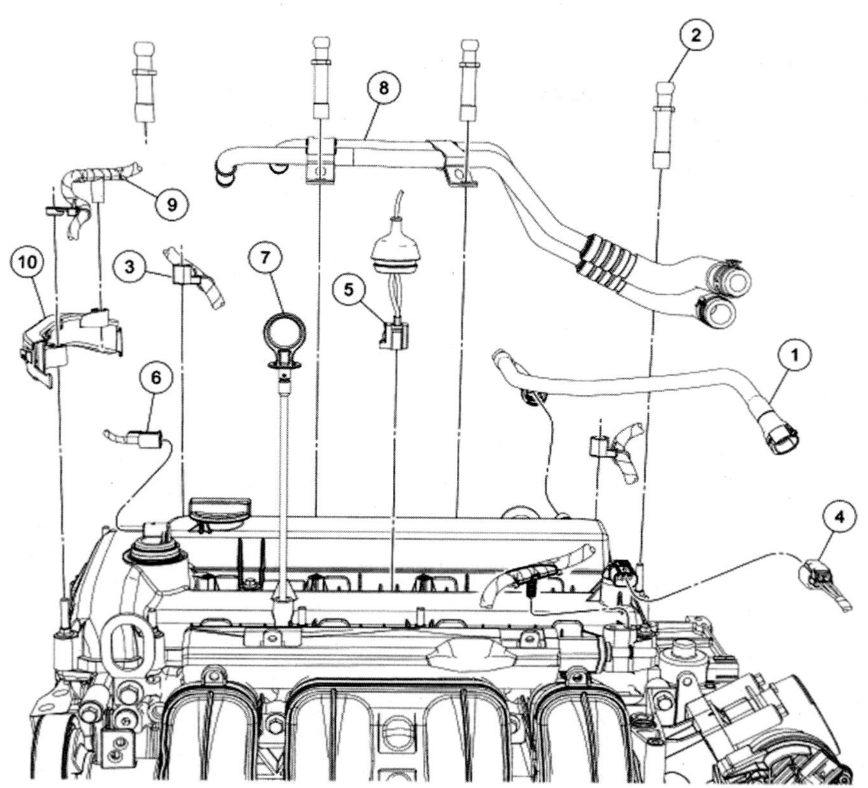

Fig. 298 Exploded view of the valve cover—1 of 2

ness retainers (if equipped) and the 2 high voltage wiring harness retainers from the valve cover studs.

5. Remove the 4 engine cover studs.
6. Position the heater tube assembly off the valve cover stud bolts.
7. Detach the 3 wire harness retainers from the valve cover and stud bolts.
8. Disconnect the Camshaft Position (CMP) sensor electrical connector.
9. Disconnect the Cylinder Head Temperature (CHT) sensor electrical connector.
10. Disconnect the Variable Camshaft Timing (VCT) solenoid electrical connector.
11. Remove the oil level indicator.
12. Remove the 14 valve cover retainers, the valve cover and gasket.

To install:

➡Do not use metal scrapers, wire brushes, power abrasive discs or other abrasive means to clean the sealing surfaces. These tools cause scratches and gouges which make leak paths.

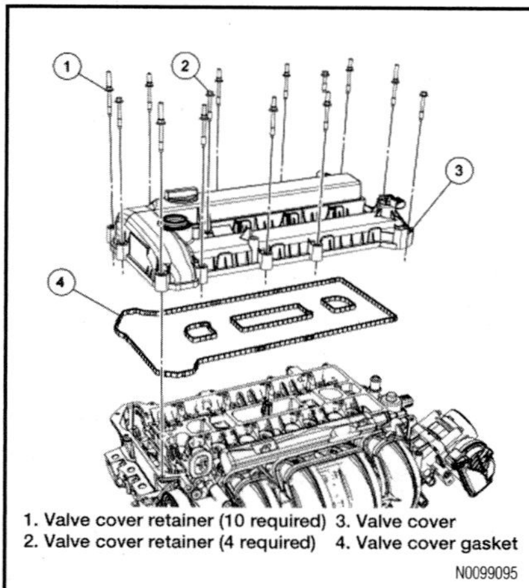

Fig. 299 Exploded view of the valve cover—2 of 2

13. Clean and inspect the sealing surfaces.

➡The valve cover must be secured within 4 minutes of silicone gasket application. If the valve cover is not secured within 4 minutes, the sealant must be removed and the sealing area cleaned with metal surface prep.

14. Apply silicone gasket and sealant to the locations shown.

➡Clean and inspect the gasket. Install a new gasket, if necessary.

15. Install the valve cover, gasket and retainers.
    a. Tighten in the sequence shown to 89 inch lbs. (10 Nm).
16. Install the oil level indicator.
17. Connect the VCT solenoid electrical connector.
18. Connect the CHT sensor electrical connector.

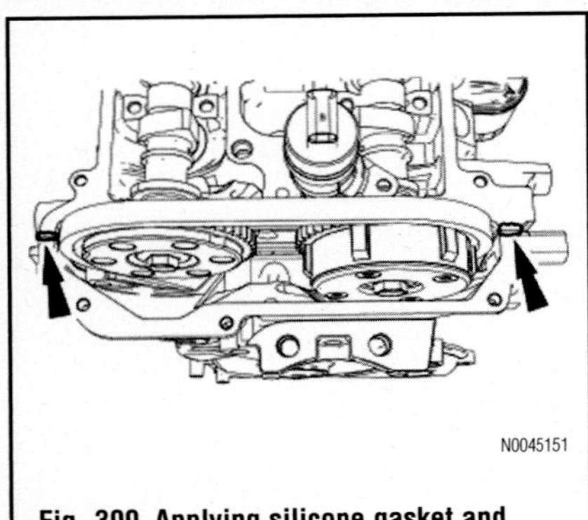

Fig. 300 Applying silicone gasket and sealant

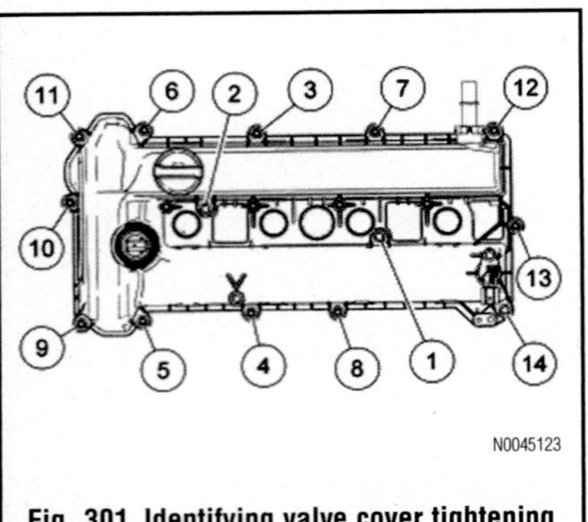

Fig. 301 Identifying valve cover tightening sequence

19. Connect the CMP sensor electrical connector.

20. Attach the 3 wire harness retainers to the valve cover stud bolts.

21. Position the heater tube assembly on the valve cover stud bolts.

22. Install the 4 engine cover studs.

23. Attach the 2 block heater wiring harness retainers (if equipped) and the 2 high voltage wiring harness retainers to the valve cover studs.

24. Connect the crankcase vent hose to the valve cover.

25. Install the ignition coil-on-plugs.

3.0L Engine

LH Side

See Figures 302 through 305.

➡During engine repair procedures, cleanliness is extremely important. Any foreign material (including any material created while cleaning gasket surfaces) that enters the oil passages, coolant passages or the oil pan may cause engine failure.

1. Remove the LH ignition coil-on-plugs.
2. Detach the 3 wiring retainers from the valve cover.

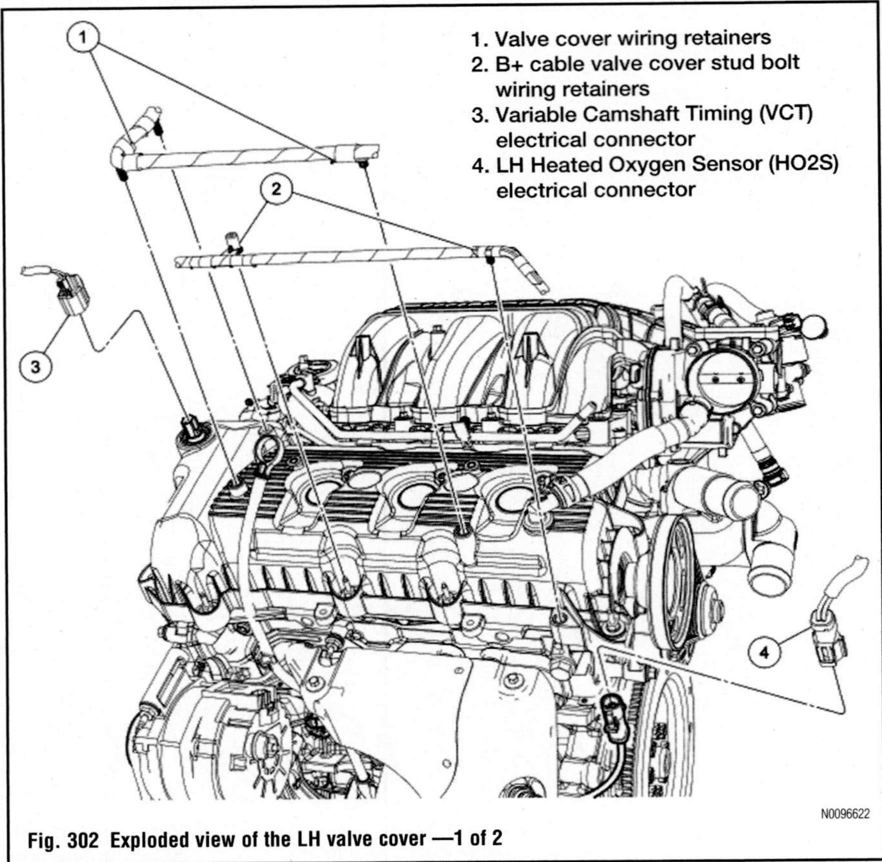

Fig. 302 Exploded view of the LH valve cover —1 of 2

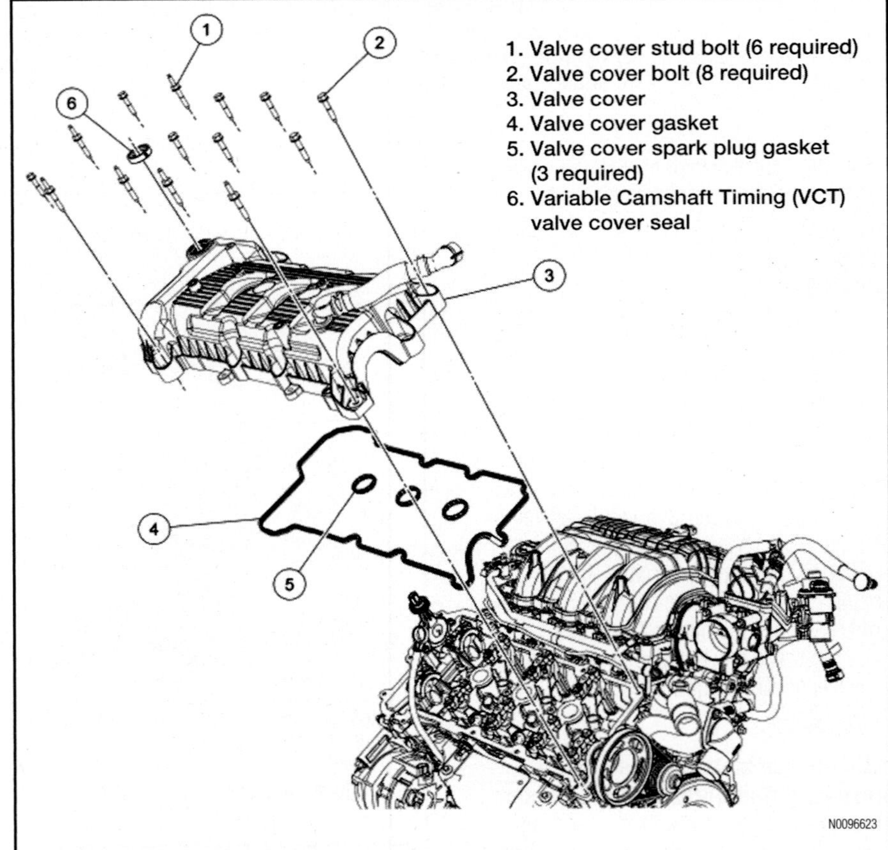

Fig. 303 Exploded view of the LH valve cover —2 of 2

3. Detach the wiring retainer from the valve cover stud bolt and 1 retainer from the valve cover.

4. Disconnect the Variable Camshaft Timing (VCT) electrical connector.

5. Disconnect the Heated Oxygen Sensor (HO2S) electrical connector.

➡Inspect the crankcase ventilation tube and valve cover sealing area. If either a new valve cover or crankcase ventilation tube is required, both components must be installed new.

6. Remove the 9 bolts, 5 stud bolts and the valve cover.

a. Remove and discard the gasket.

To install:

➡If the valve cover is not secured within 4 minutes, the sealant must be removed and the sealing area cleaned with metal surface prep. Failure to follow this procedure can cause future oil leakage.

7. Apply a bead of silicone gasket and sealant in 2 places where the engine front cover meets the cylinder head and the 2 places where the camshaft oil seal retainer meets the cylinder head.

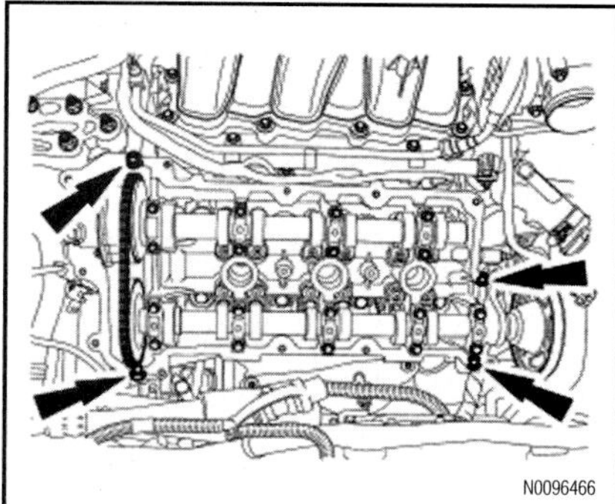

Fig. 304 Applying silicone gasket and sealant

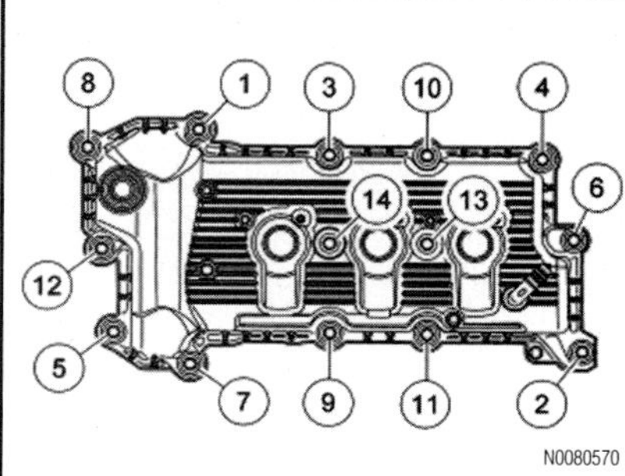

Fig. 305 Identifying valve cover tightening sequence

8. Position the valve cover and install the bolts and stud bolts.

a. Tighten in the sequence shown to 89 inch lbs. (10 Nm).

9. Position the wire harness and connect the HO2S electrical connector.

10. Connect the VCT electrical connector.

11. Attach the wiring retainer to the valve cover stud bolt and attach the pin-type wiring retainer to the valve cover.

12. Attach the 3 wiring retainers to the valve cover.

13. Install the LH ignition coil-on-plugs.

RH Side

See Figures 306 through 309.

➡During engine repair procedures, cleanliness is extremely important. Any foreign material (including any material created while cleaning gasket surfaces) that enters the oil passages, coolant passages or the oil pan may cause engine failure.

1. Remove the RH ignition coil-on-plugs.

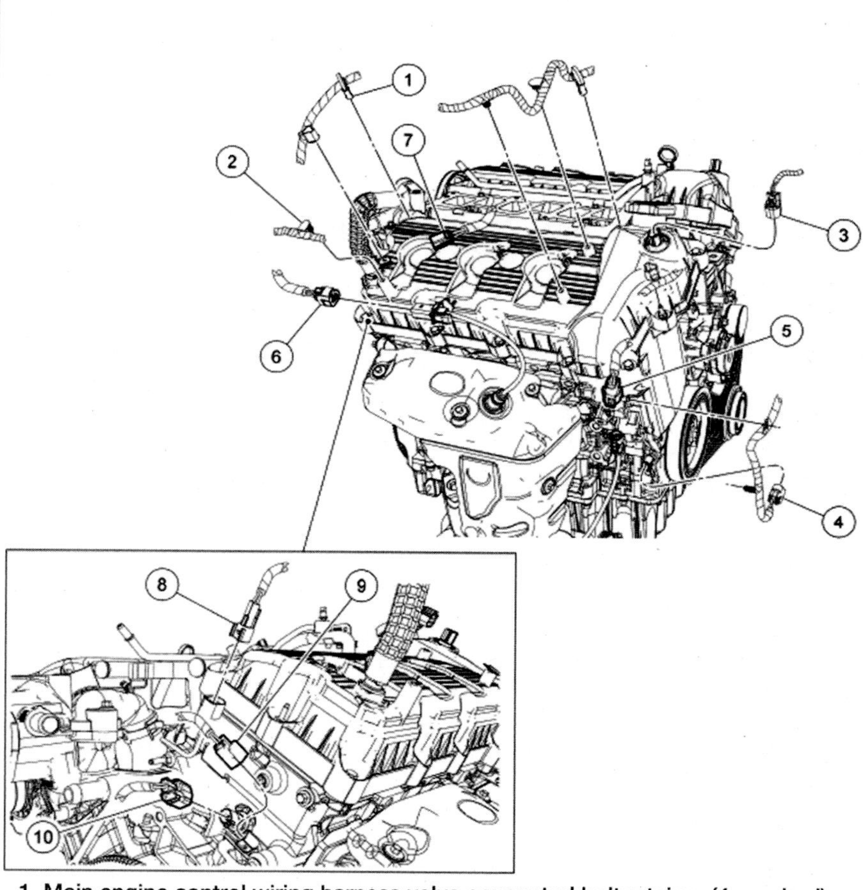

1. Main engine control wiring harness valve cover stud bolt retainer (4 required)
2. Main engine control wiring harness valve cover retainer (3 required)
3. Variable Camshaft Timing (VCT) electrical connector
4. Crankshaft Position (CKP) electrical connector and wiring harness retainer
w5. Catalyst Monitor Sensor (CMS) electrical connector
6. Heated Oxygen Sensor (HO2S) electrical connector
7. Heated PCV electrical connector
8. Cylinder head Knock Sensor (KS) electrical connector
9. Cylinder block KS electrical connector
10. Cylinder Head Temperature (CHT) electrical connector

N0096666

Fig. 306 Exploded view of the RH valve cover —1 of 2

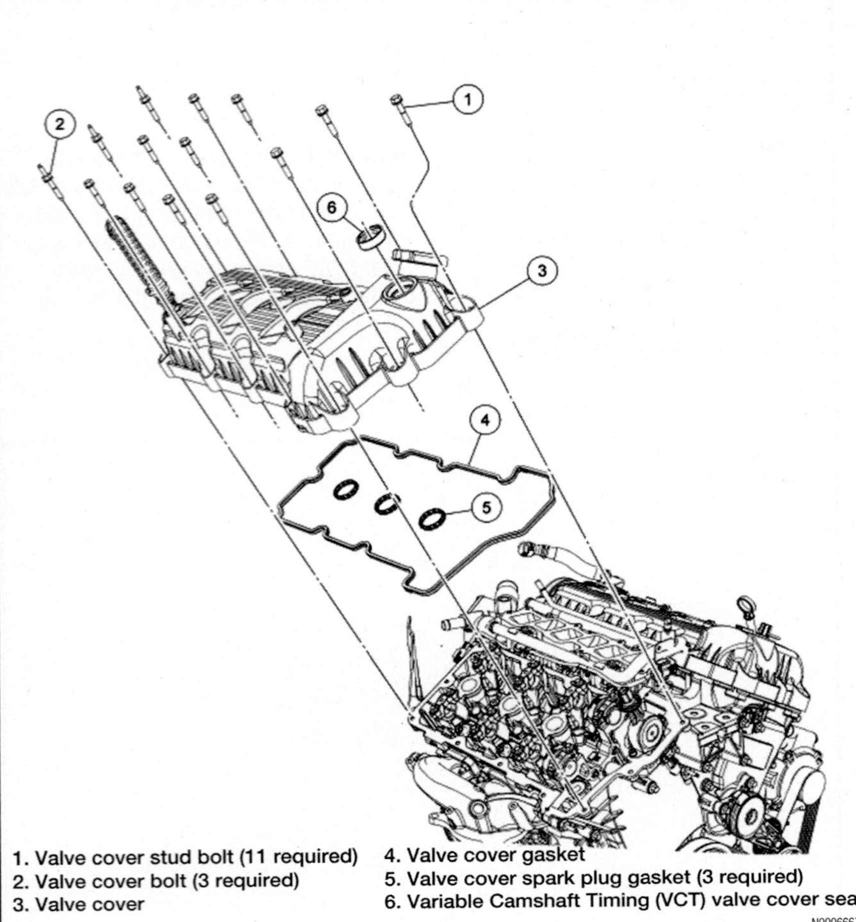

Fig. 307 Exploded view of the RH valve cover —2 of 2

2. Detach the 3 main engine control wiring harness retainers from the valve cover and 4 retainers from the valve cover stud bolts.
3. Disconnect the Variable Camshaft Timing (VCT) electrical connector.
4. Disconnect the Heated Oxygen Sensor (HO2S) electrical connector.
5. Disconnect the Crankshaft Position (CKP) electrical connector and detach the 2 wiring harness retainers.
6. Disconnect the Catalyst Monitor Sensor (CMS) electrical connector.
7. Disconnect the heated PCV electrical connector.
8. Disconnect the Cylinder Head Temperature (CHT) sensor electrical connector and the cylinder head and cylinder block Knock Sensor (KS) electrical connectors.
9. Remove the 11 bolts, 3 stud bolts and the valve cover.
    a. Remove and discard the gasket.

To install:

10. Clean the valve cover, cylinder head and front cover sealing surfaces with metal surface prep and install a new valve cover and spark plug cavity gaskets.

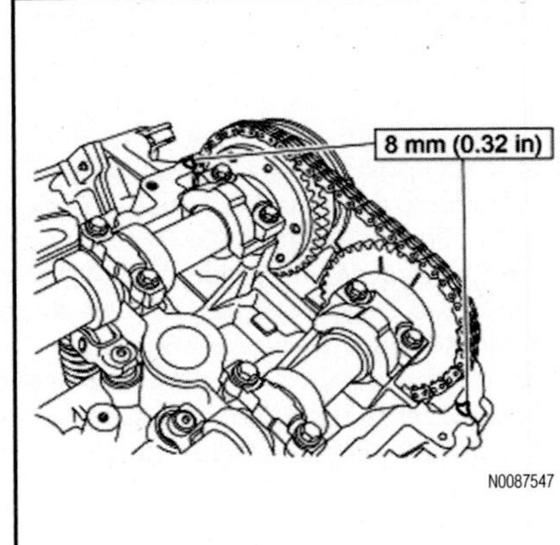

Fig. 308 Applying silicone gasket and sealant

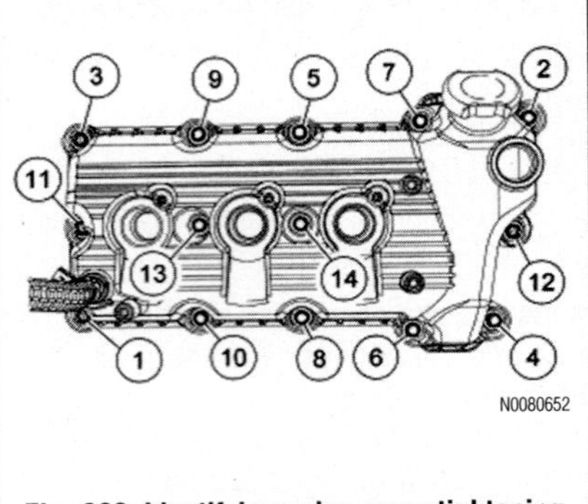

Fig. 309 Identifying valve cover tightening sequence

➡The valve cover must be installed and the bolts and stud bolts tightened within 4 minutes of sealant application.

11. Apply an 8 mm (0.31 in) dot of silicone gasket sealant to the front cover-to-cylinder head joints.
12. Position the valve cover and install the bolts and stud bolts.
    a. Tighten in the sequence shown to 89 inch lbs. (10 Nm).
13. Connect the CHT sensor electrical connector and the cylinder head and cylinder block KS electrical connectors.
14. Connect the heated PCV electrical connector.
15. Connect the CMS electrical connector.
16. Connect the CKP electrical connector and attach the wiring harness retainer.
17. Connect the HO2S electrical connector.
18. Connect the VCT electrical connector.
19. Attach the 3 main engine control wiring harness retainers to the valve cover and the 4 retainers to the valve cover stud bolts.
20. Install the RH ignition coil-on-plugs.

3.5L Engine

LH Side

See Figures 310 through 314.

1. During engine repair procedures, cleanliness is extremely important. Any foreign material, including any material created while cleaning gasket surfaces that enters the oil passages, coolant passages or the oil pan, may cause engine failure.

➡Early build engines have 11 fastener valve covers, late built engines have 9 fastener valve covers. Do not attempt to install bolts in the 2 empty late build valve cover holes or damage to the valve cover will occur.

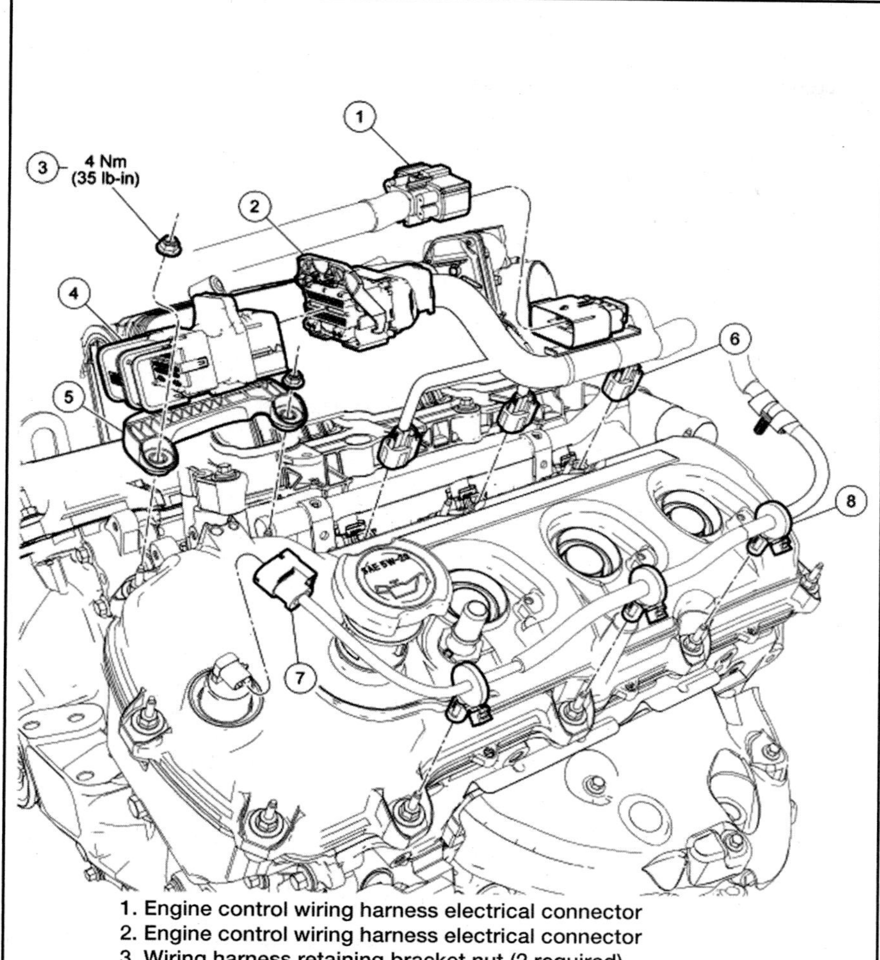

Fig. 310 Exploded view of the LH valve cover —1 of 2 (Early build, late build similar)

All vehicles

2. Remove the Air Cleaner (ACL) outlet pipe.
3. Remove the LH ignition coils.
4. Remove the oil level indicator.
5. Disconnect the LH Variable Camshaft Timing (VCT) solenoid electrical connector.
6. Detach the 2 wiring harness retainers.
7. Disconnect the 2 engine control wiring harness electrical connectors.
8. Remove the 2 nuts and the wiring harness retaining bracket.
9. Detach all of the wiring harness retainers from the valve cover and the stud bolts.
10. Disconnect the 3 LH fuel injector electrical connectors.

Early build vehicles

11. Loosen the 11 stud bolts and remove the LH valve cover.
    a. Discard the gasket.

Late build vehicles

12. Loosen the 9 stud bolts and remove the LH valve cover.
    a. Discard the gasket.

All vehicles

➡VCT solenoid seal removal shown, spark plug tube seal removal similar.

13. Inspect the VCT solenoid seals and the spark plug tube seals. Remove any damaged seals.
14. Using the VCT Spark Plug Tube Seal Remover and Handle, remove the seal(s).
15. Clean the valve cover, cylinder head and engine front cover sealing surfaces with metal surface prep.

To install:

All vehicles

➡Installation of new seals is only required if damaged seals were removed during disassembly of the engine.

➡Spark plug tube seal installation shown, VCT solenoid seal installation similar.

16. Using the VCT Spark Plug Tube Seal Installer and Handle, install new VCT solenoid and/or spark plug tube seals.

➡Failure to use Motorcraft High Performance Engine RTV Silicone may cause the engine oil to foam excessively and result in serious engine damage.

➡If the valve cover is not installed and the fasteners tightened within 4 minutes, the sealant must be removed and the sealing area cleaned. To clean the sealing area, use silicone gasket remover and metal surface prep. Failure to follow this procedure can cause future oil leakage.

17. Apply an 8 mm (0.31 in) bead of Motorcraft High Performance Engine RTV Silicone to the engine front cover-to-LH cylinder head joints.

Late build vehicles

18. Using a new gasket, install the LH valve cover and tighten the 9 stud bolts.
    a. Tighten in the sequence shown to 89 inch lbs. (10 Nm).

Early build vehicles

19. Using a new gasket, install the LH valve cover and 11 stud bolts.
    a. Tighten in the sequence shown to 89 inch lbs. (10 Nm).

All vehicles

20. Connect the 3 LH fuel injector electrical connectors.
21. Attach all of the wiring harness retainers to the valve cover and the stud bolts.
22. Install the wiring harness retaining bracket and the 2 nuts.
    a. Tighten to 35 inch lbs. (4 Nm).
23. Connect the 2 engine control wiring harness electrical connectors.
24. Attach the 2 wiring harness retainers.

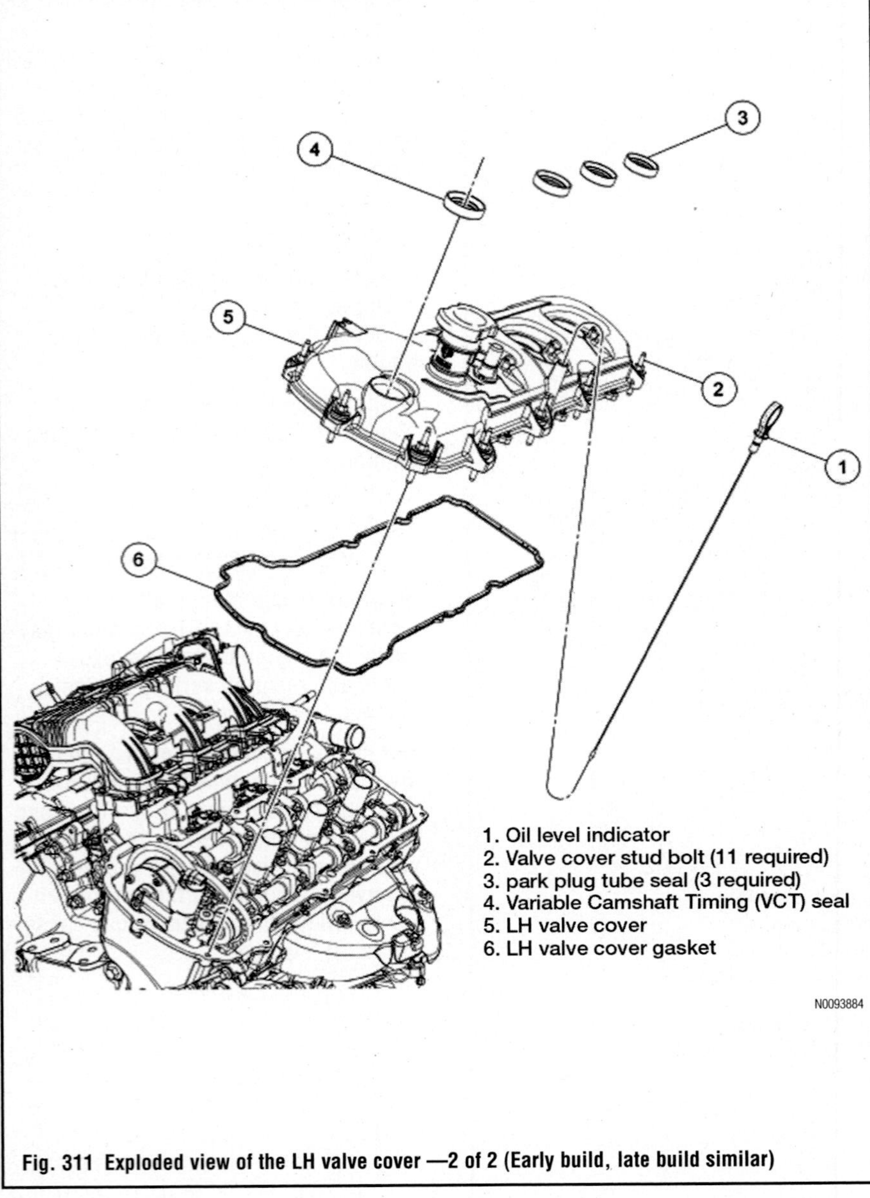

Fig. 311 Exploded view of the LH valve cover —2 of 2 (Early build, late build similar)

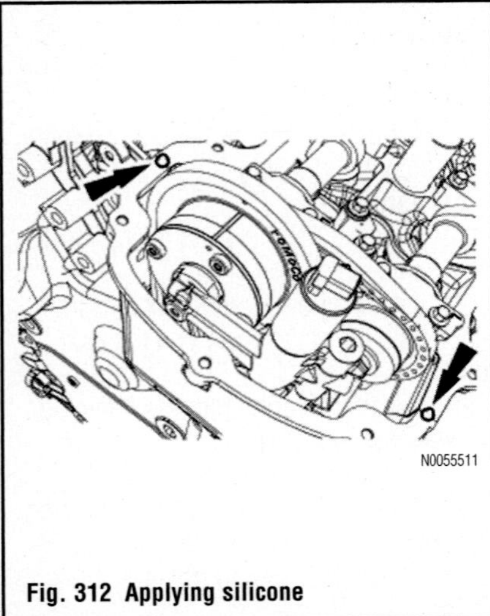

Fig. 312 Applying silicone

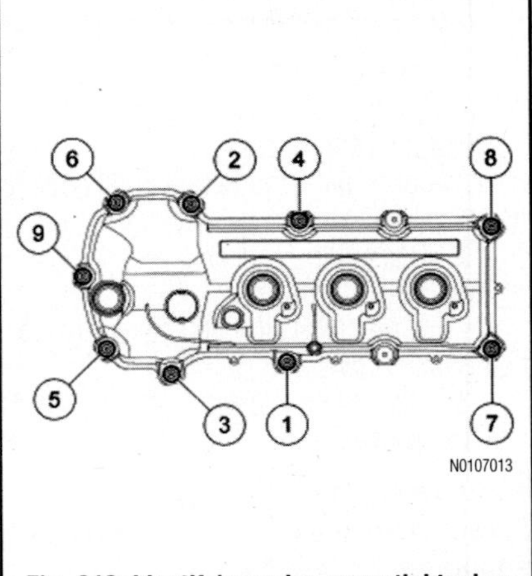

Fig. 313 Identifying valve cover tightening sequence

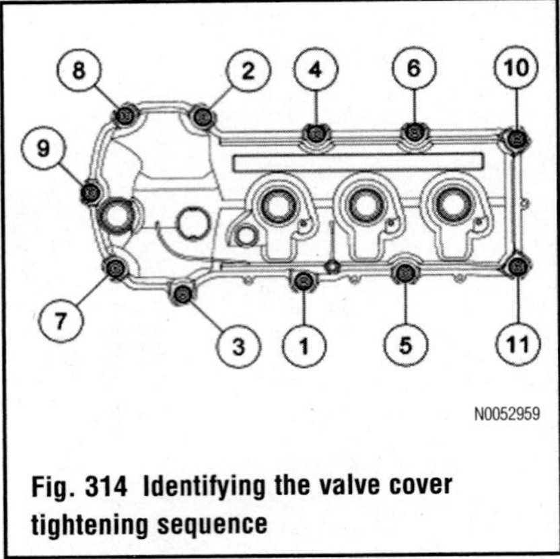

Fig. 314 Identifying the valve cover tightening sequence

25. Connect the LH VCT solenoid electrical connector.
26. Install the oil level indicator.
27. Install the LH ignition coils.
28. Install the ACL outlet pipe.

RH Side

See Figures 315 through 320.

➡During engine repair procedures, cleanliness is extremely important. Any foreign material, including any material created while cleaning gasket surfaces that enters the oil passages, coolant passages or the oil pan, may cause engine failure.

➡Early build engines have 11 fastener valve covers, late built engines have 9 fastener valve covers. Do not attempt to install bolts in the 2 empty late build valve cover holes or damage to the valve cover will occur.

All vehicles

1. Remove the RH ignition coils.
2. Remove the power steering fluid reservoir.
3. Disconnect the Power Steering Pressure (PSP) switch electrical connector.
4. Disconnect the RH Catalyst Monitor Sensor (CMS) electrical connector and retainer.
5. Remove the PSP hose bracket nut from the valve cover stud bolt and position the bracket aside.
6. Disconnect the RH Heated Oxygen Sensor (HO2S) electrical connector.
7. Disconnect the RH Variable Camshaft Timing (VCT) electrical connector.
8. Disconnect the 3 RH fuel injector electrical connectors.
9. Detach all of the wiring harness retainers from the valve cover and the stud bolts.
10. Remove the A/C tube retaining clamp bolt.

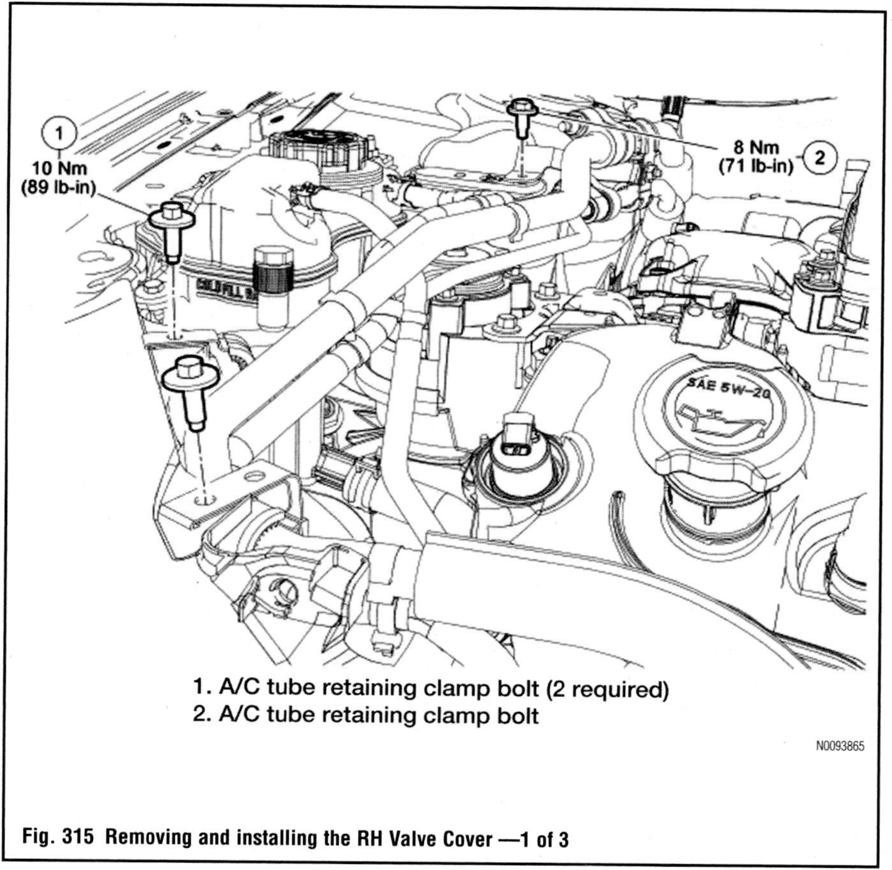

Fig. 315 Removing and installing the RH Valve Cover —1 of 3

11. Remove the 2 A/C tube retaining clamp bolts.

Early build vehicles

➡It is necessary to reposition the A/C tubes to remove the valve cover.

12. Loosen the bolt, the 10 stud bolts and remove the RH valve cover.
    a. Discard the gasket.

Late build vehicles

➡It is necessary to reposition the A/C tubes to remove the valve cover.

13. Loosen the 9 stud bolts and remove the RH valve cover.
    a. Discard the gasket.

All vehicles

➡VCT solenoid seal removal shown, spark plug tube seal removal similar.

14. Inspect the VCT solenoid seals and the spark plug tube seals. Remove any damaged seals.
15. Using the VCT Spark Plug Tube Seal Remover and Handle, remove the seal(s).
16. Clean the valve cover, cylinder head and engine front cover sealing surfaces with metal surface prep.

To install:

All vehicles

➡Installation of new seals is only required if damaged seals were removed during disassembly of the engine.

➡Spark plug tube seal installation shown, VCT solenoid seal installation similar.

17. Using the VCT Spark Plug Tube Seal Installer and Handle, install new VCT solenoid and/or spark plug tube seals.

➡Failure to use Motorcraft High Performance Engine RTV Silicone may cause the engine oil to foam excessively and result in serious engine damage.

➡If the valve cover is not installed and the fasteners tightened within 4 minutes, the sealant must be removed and the sealing area cleaned. To clean the sealing area, use silicone gasket remover and metal surface prep. Failure to follow this procedure can cause future oil leakage.

18. Apply an 8 mm (0.31 in) bead of Motorcraft High Performance Engine RTV

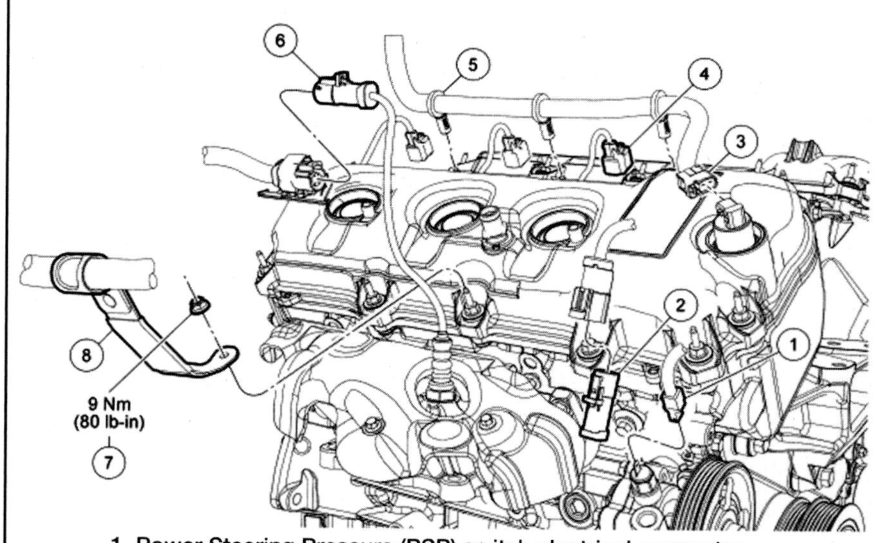

Fig. 316 Removing and installing the RH valve cover —2 of 3

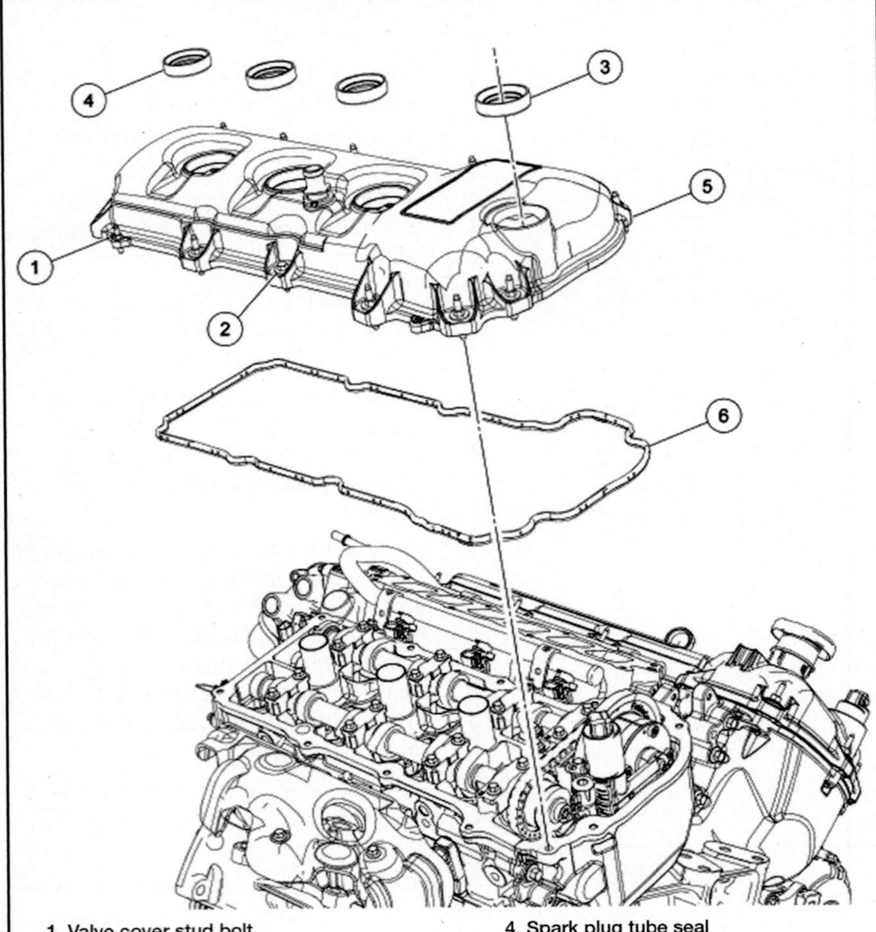

Fig. 317 Removing and installing the RH valve cover —1 of 3 (early build shown, late build similar)

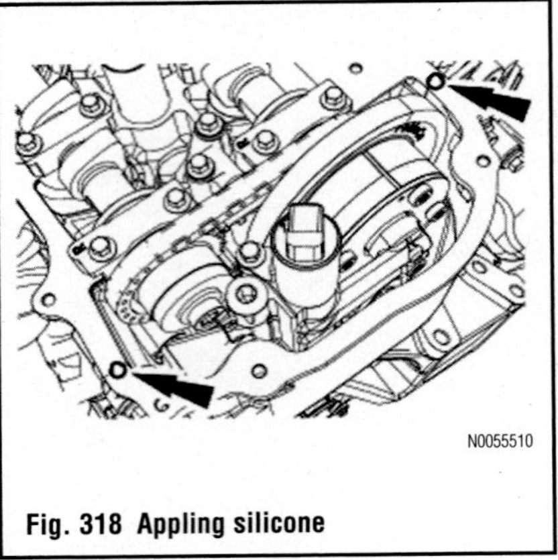

Fig. 318 Appling silicone

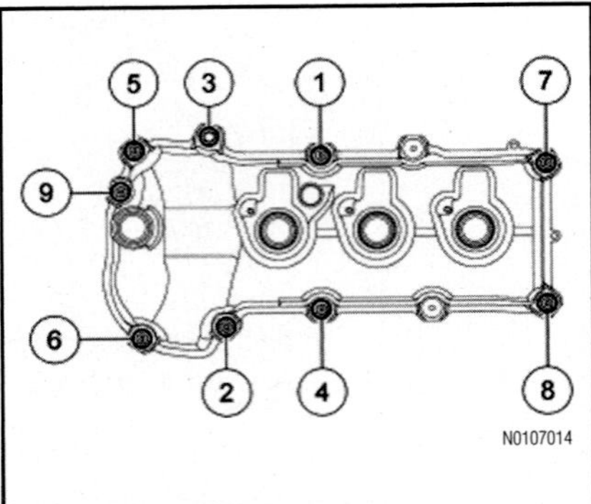

Fig. 319 Identifying the valve cover tightening sequence

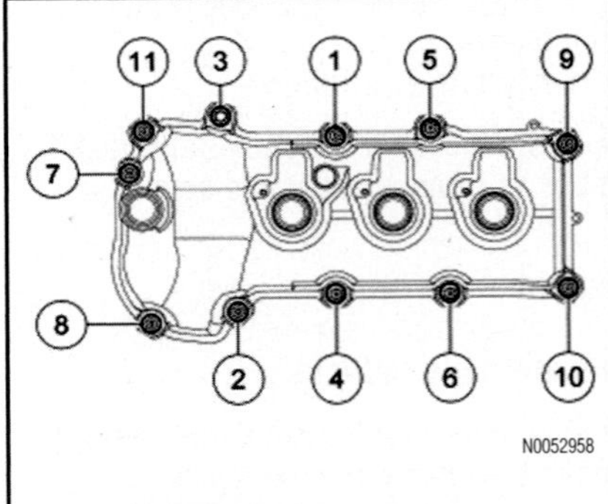

Fig. 320 Identifying the valve cover tightening sequence

Silicone to the engine front cover-to-RH cylinder head joints.

Late build vehicles

19. Using a new gasket, install the RH valve cover and tighten the 9 stud bolts.
    a. Tighten in the sequence shown to 89 inch lbs. (10 Nm).

Early build vehicles

20. Using a new gasket, install the RH valve cover, bolt and the 10 stud bolts.
    a. Tighten in the sequence shown to 89 inch lbs. (10 Nm).

All vehicles

21. Position the A/C tubes and install the 2 retaining clamp bolts.
    a. Tighten to 89 inch lbs. (10 Nm).
22. Install the A/C tube retaining clamp bolt.
    a. Tighten to 71 inch lbs. (8 Nm).
23. Attach all of the wiring harness retainers to the valve cover and the stud bolts.
24. Connect the 3 LH fuel injector electrical connectors.
25. Connect the LH VCT electrical connector.
26. Connect the RH HO2S electrical connector.
27. Install the PSP hose bracket and nut.
    a. Tighten to 80 inch lbs. (9 Nm).
28. Connect the RH CMS electrical connector and retainer.
29. Connect the PSP switch electrical connector.
30. Install the power steering fluid reservoir.
31. Install the RH ignition coils.

ENGINE PERFORMANCE & EMISSION CONTROLS

CAMSHAFT POSITION (CMP) SENSOR

REMOVAL & INSTALLATION

2.5L Engine

See Figure 321.

1. Disconnect the Camshaft Position (CMP) sensor electrical connector.
2. Remove the bolt and the CMP .

To install:

➡Lubricate the CMP O-ring seal with clean engine oil.

3. To install, reverse the removal procedure.
4. Tighten the CMP to 62 inch lbs. (7 Nm).

3.0L Engine

See Figure 322.

1. Disconnect the Camshaft Position (CMP) electrical connector.
2. Remove the bolt and the CMP sensor.

To install:

➡Lubricate the CMP O-ring seal with clean engine oil.

3. To install, reverse the removal procedure.
4. Tighten the CMP sensor to 89 inch lbs. (10 Nm).

3.5L Engine

See Figure 323.

1. Remove the Air Cleaner (ACL) outlet pipe.
2. Disconnect the Camshaft Position (CMP) sensor electrical connector.
3. Remove the bolt and the CMP sensor.

To install:

➡Lubricate the CMP sensor O-ring seal with clean engine oil.

4. To install, reverse the removal procedure.
5. Tighten the CMP sensor to 89 inch lbs. (10 Nm).

CRANKSHAFT POSITION (CKP) SENSOR

REMOVAL & INSTALLATION

2.5L Engines

See Figures 324 through 326.

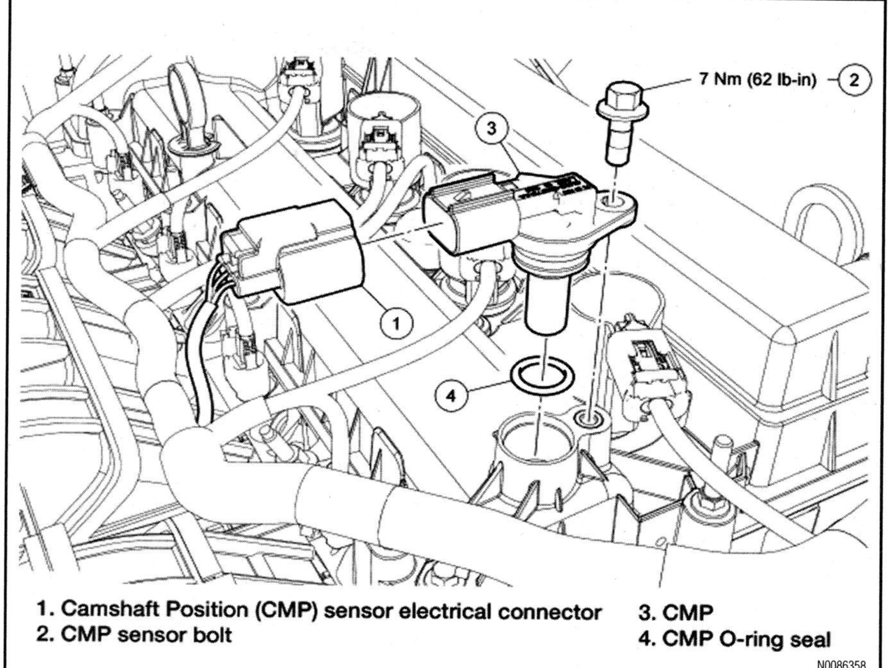

Fig. 321 Removing and installing the CMP sensor

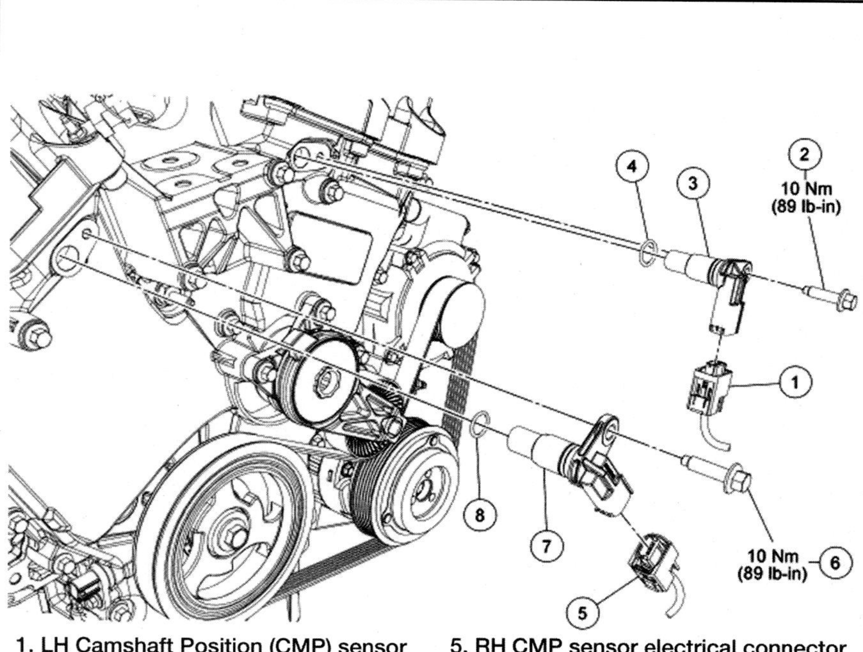

Fig. 322 Removing and installing the CMP sensor

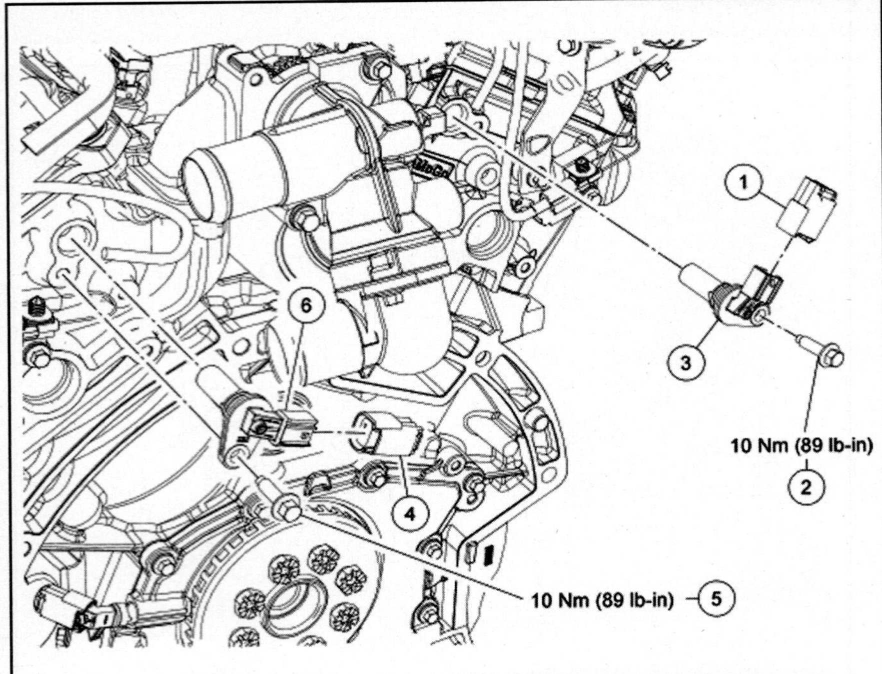

Fig. 323 Removing and installing the CMP sensor

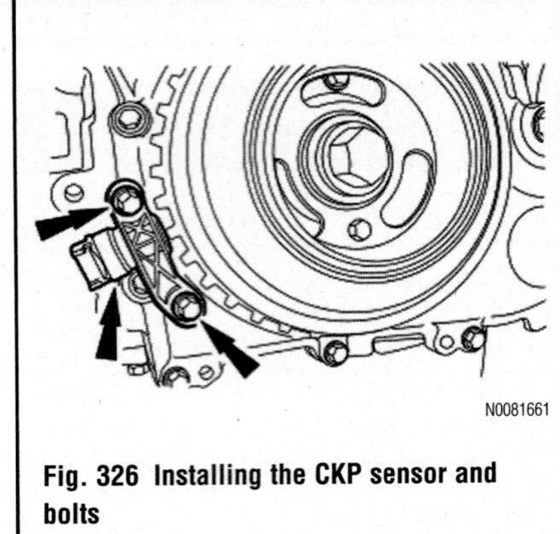

Fig. 326 Installing the CKP sensor and bolts

1. With the vehicle in NEUTRAL, position it on a hoist.
2. Remove the 4 screws and position the RH fender splash shield aside.
3. Remove the 6 pin-type retainers and the RH splash shield.
4. Turn the crankshaft clockwise until the hole in the crankshaft pulley is in the 3 o'clock position.
5. Remove the cylinder block plug.

➡When the crankshaft contacts the Crankshaft TDC Timing Peg, the No. 1 cylinder will be at Top Dead Center (TDC).

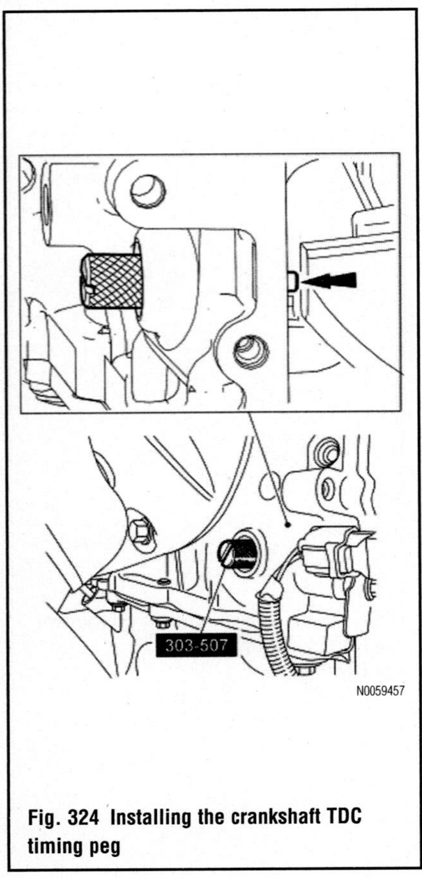

Fig. 324 Installing the crankshaft TDC timing peg

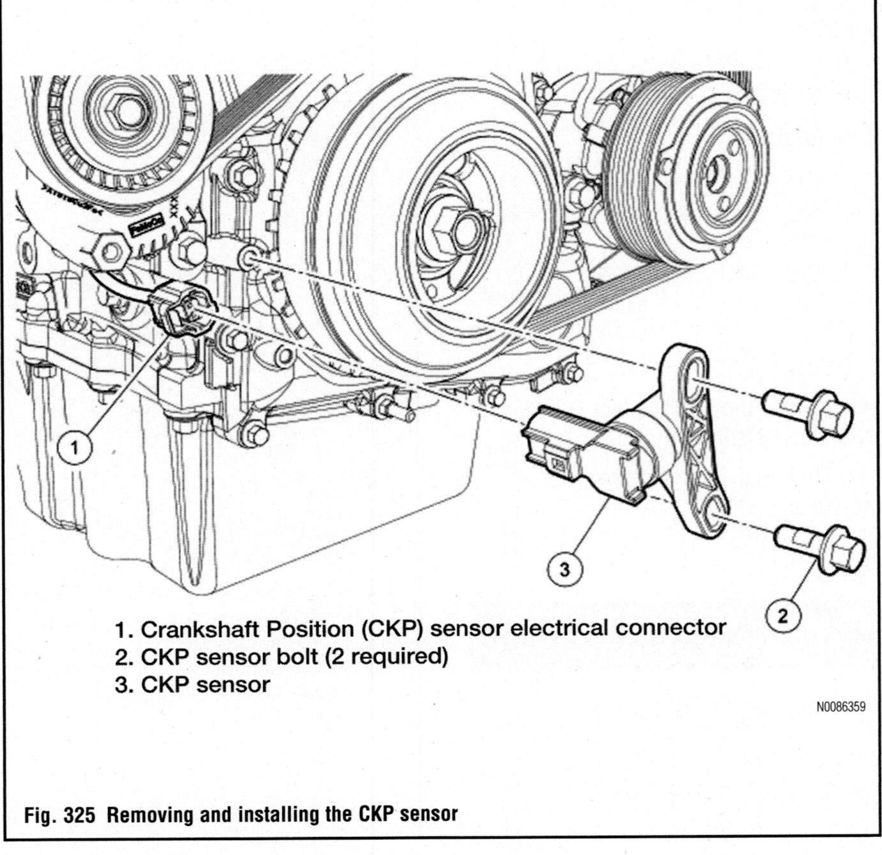

Fig. 325 Removing and installing the CKP sensor

6. Install the Crankshaft TDC Timing Peg and turn the crankshaft clockwise until the crankshaft contacts the Crankshaft TDC Timing Peg.
7. Disconnect the Crankshaft Position (CKP) sensor electrical connector.
8. Remove the bolts and discard the CKP sensor.

To install:

➡Only hand-tighten the bolt or damage to the front cover can occur.

9. Install a 6 mm (0.23 in) x 18 mm (0.7 in) standard bolt in the crankshaft pulley.
10. Install the CKP sensor and the 2 bolts.
    a. Do not tighten the bolts at this time.
11. Adjust the CKP sensor with the Crankshaft Sensor Aligner.
    a. Tighten the 2 CKP bolts to 62 inch lbs. (7 Nm).
12. Connect the CKP sensor electrical connector.
13. Remove the 6 mm (0.23 in) bolt from the crankshaft pulley.
14. Install the cylinder block plug.
    a. Tighten to 15 ft. lbs. (20 Nm).
15. Install the 6 pin-type retainers and the RH splash shield.
16. Install the 4 screws and position the RH fender splash shield aside.
17. Using the scan tool, perform the Misfire Monitor Neutral Profile Correction procedure following the on-screen instructions.

3.0L Engine

See Figure 327.

1. With the vehicle in NEUTRAL, position it on a hoist.
2. Disconnect the Crankshaft Position (CKP) sensor electrical connector.
3. Remove the bolt and the CKP .
4. Inspect the O-ring seal and install new as necessary.

To install:

➡Lubricate the CKP O-ring seal with clean engine oil.

5. To install, reverse the removal procedure.
6. Tighten the CKP to 89 inch lbs. (10 Nm).
7. Using the scan tool, perform the Misfire Monitor Neutral Profile Correction procedure following the on-screen instructions.

3.5L Engine

See Figure 328.

1. With the vehicle in NEUTRAL, position it on a hoist.
2. Remove the LH catalytic converter.
3. Remove the bolt, nut and the heat shield.
    a. To install, tighten to 10 Nm (89 lb-in).
4. Remove the rubber grommet cover.
5. Disconnect the Crankshaft Position (CKP) sensor electrical connector.
6. Remove the bolt and the CKP sensor.

To install:

7. To install, reverse the removal procedure.
8. Tighten the CKP sensor to 89 inch lbs. (10 Nm).
9. Tighten the heat shield to 89 inch lbs. (10 Nm).

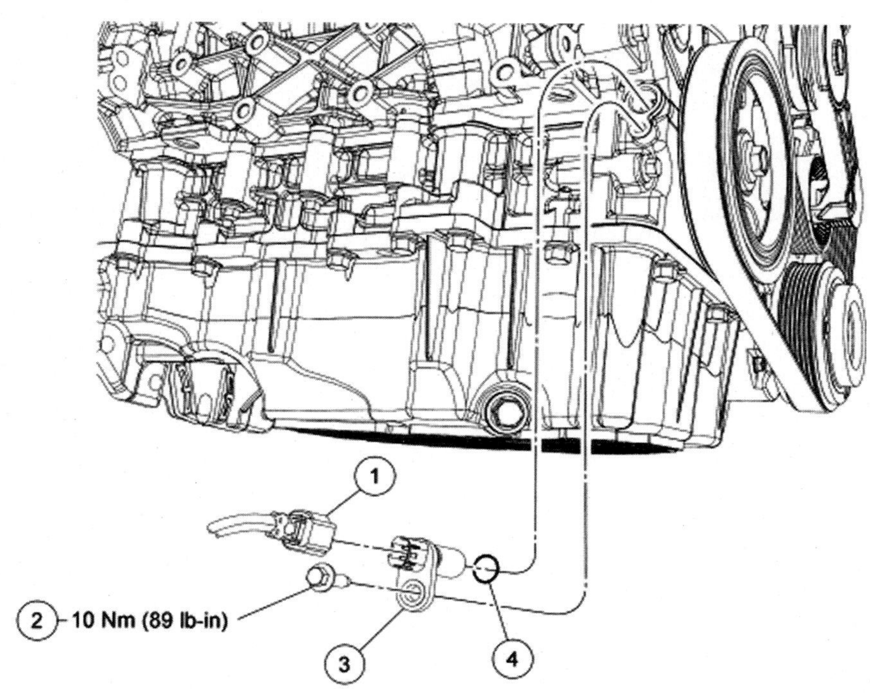

Fig. 327 Removing and installing the CKP sensor

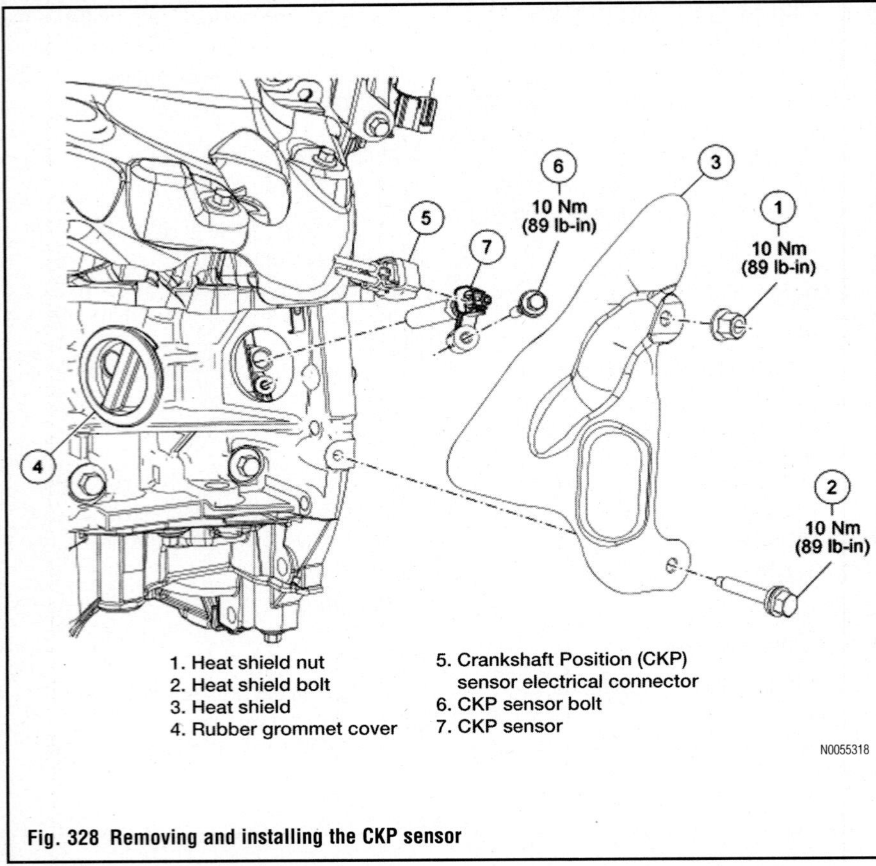

Fig. 328 Removing and installing the CKP sensor

10. Using the scan tool, perform the Misfire Monitor Neutral Profile Correction procedure following the on-screen instructions.

HEATED OXYGEN (HO2S) SENSOR

REMOVAL & INSTALLATION

2.5L Engine

See Figures 329 and 330.

1. Disconnect the Heated Oxygen Sensor (HO2S) electrical connector.

➡**If necessary, lubricate the sensor threads with penetrating and lock lubricant to assist in removal.**

2. Using the Exhaust Gas Oxygen Sensor Socket, remove the HO2S.

To install:

➡**Apply a light coat of anti-seize lubricant to the threads of the HO2S.**

3. To install, reverse the removal procedure.
4. To install, tighten to 35 ft. lbs. (48 Nm).

3.0L Engine

See Figure 331.

Rear sensor

1. With the vehicle in NEUTRAL, position it on a hoist.

Both sensors

2. Disconnect the Heated Oxygen Sensor (HO2S) electrical connector.

➡**If necessary, lubricate the sensor threads with penetrating and lock lubricant to assist in removal.**

3. Using the Exhaust Gas Oxygen Sensor Socket, remove the HO2S.

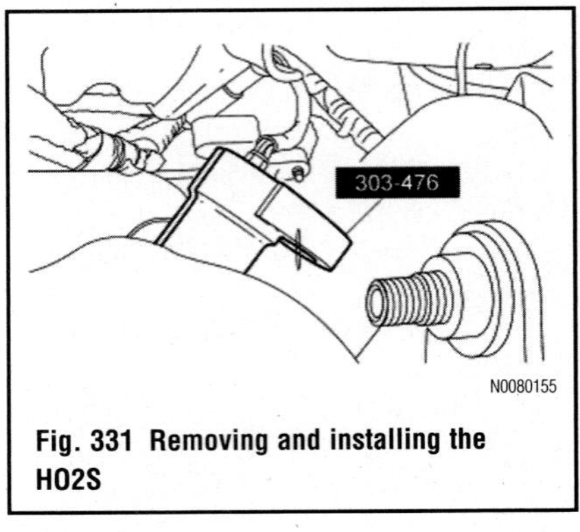

Fig. 331 Removing and installing the HO2S

To install:

➡**Apply a light coat of anti-seize lubricant to the threads of the HO2S.**

4. To install, reverse the removal procedure.
5. Tighten the HO2S to 35 ft. lbs. (48 Nm).

3.5L Engine

See Figure 332.

RH sensor

1. Remove the PCV hose.

Both sensors

2. Disconnect the Heated Oxygen Sensor (HO2S) electrical connector.

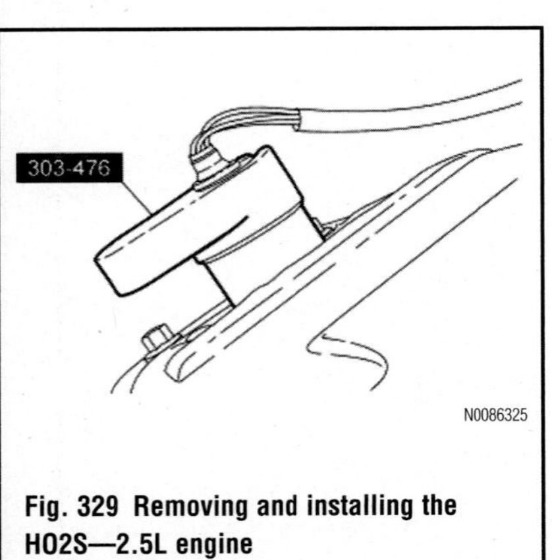

Fig. 329 Removing and installing the HO2S—2.5L engine

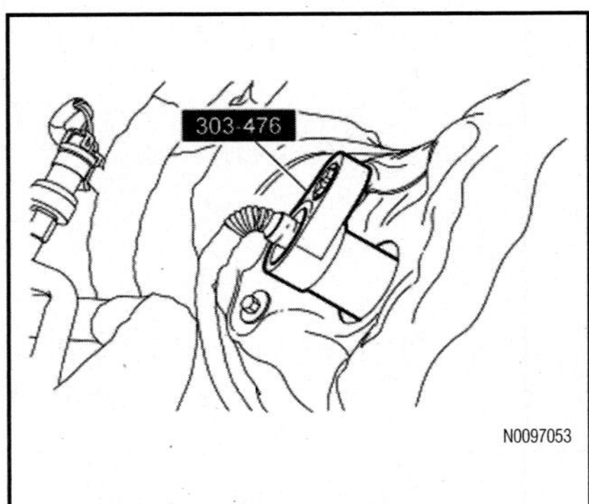

Fig. 330 Removing and installing the HO2S—2.5L hybrid engine

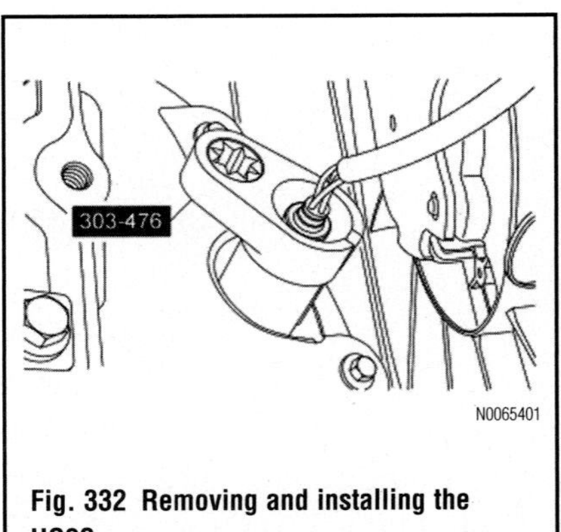

Fig. 332 Removing and installing the HO2S

➡If necessary, lubricate the sensor threads with penetrating and lock lubricant to assist in removal.

3. Using the Exhaust Gas Oxygen Sensor Socket, remove the HO2S.

To install:

➡Apply a light coat of anti-seize lubricant to the threads of the HO2S.

4. To install, reverse the removal procedure.
5. Tighten the HO2S to 35 ft. lbs. (48 Nm).

KNOCK SENSOR (KS)

REMOVAL & INSTALLATION

2.5L Engines

See Figure 333.

1. With the vehicle in NEUTRAL, position it on a hoist.
2. Remove the intake manifold.
3. Remove the bolt and the Knock Sensor (KS).

➡The KS must not touch the crankcase vent oil separator.

To install:

4. To install, reverse the removal procedure.
5. Tighten the KS to 15 ft. lbs. (20 Nm).

3.0L Engine

See Figures 334 and 335.

Cylinder head-mounted

1. Disconnect the Knock Sensor (KS) electrical connector.
2. Remove the bolt and the KS .

Engine block-mounted

3. Remove the lower intake manifold.
4. Disconnect the KS electrical connector.
5. Remove the bolt and the KS .

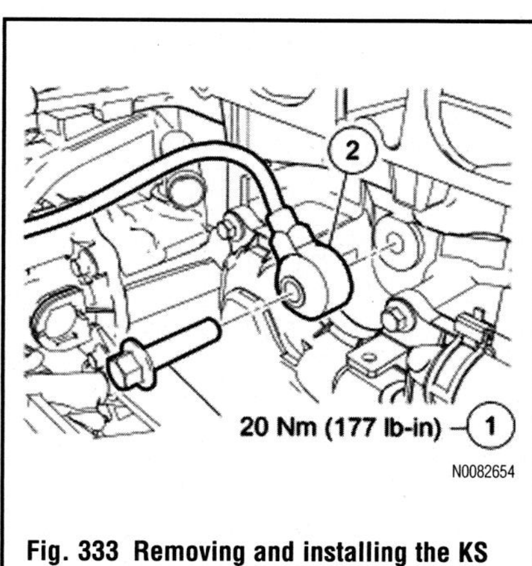

Fig. 333 Removing and installing the KS

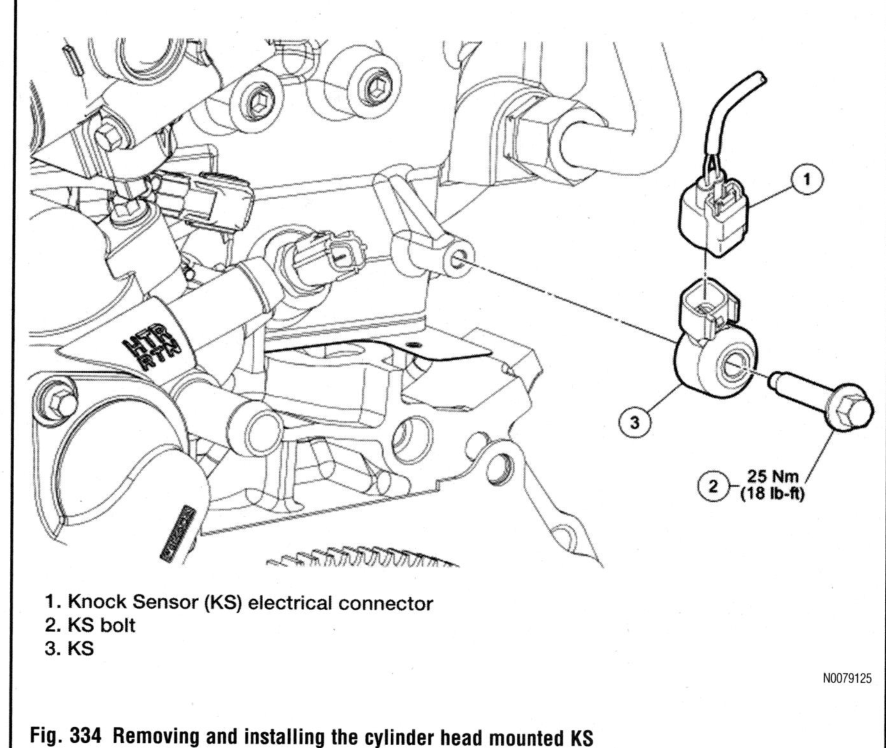

Fig. 334 Removing and installing the cylinder head mounted KS

To install:

Engine block-mounted

6. Install the KS and the bolt.
   a. To install, tighten to 18 ft. lbs. (25 Nm).
7. Connect the KS electrical connector.
8. Install the lower intake manifold.

Cylinder head-mounted

9. Install the KS and the bolt.
   a. To install, tighten to 18 ft. lbs. (25 Nm).
10. Connect the KS electrical connector.

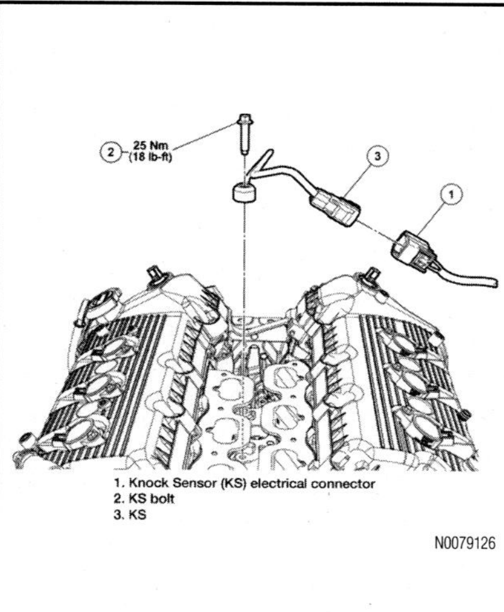

Fig. 335 Removing and installing the cylinder block mounted KS

3.5L Engine

See Figure 336.

➡Early build vehicle (built before July 6, 2009) cooling systems are filled with Motorcraft® Premium Gold Engine Coolant. Late build vehicle (built on or after July 6, 2009) cooling systems are filled with Motorcraft® Specialty Green Engine Coolant. Mixing coolant types degrades the corrosion protection of the coolant. Do not mix coolant types. Failure to follow these instructions may result in engine or cooling system damage.

1. Remove the thermostat housing.
2. Remove the lower intake manifold.
3. Remove the coolant tube.
   a. Discard the O-ring seal.
4. Disconnect the Knock Sensor (KS) electrical connector.

➡Only use hand tools when removing or installing the Knock Sensor (KS) or damage to the KS can occur.

5. Remove the 2 bolts and the KS .

To install:

6. To install, reverse the removal procedure.
   a. Lubricate the new O-ring seal with clean engine coolant.
7. Tighten the KS to 15 ft. lbs. (20 Nm).

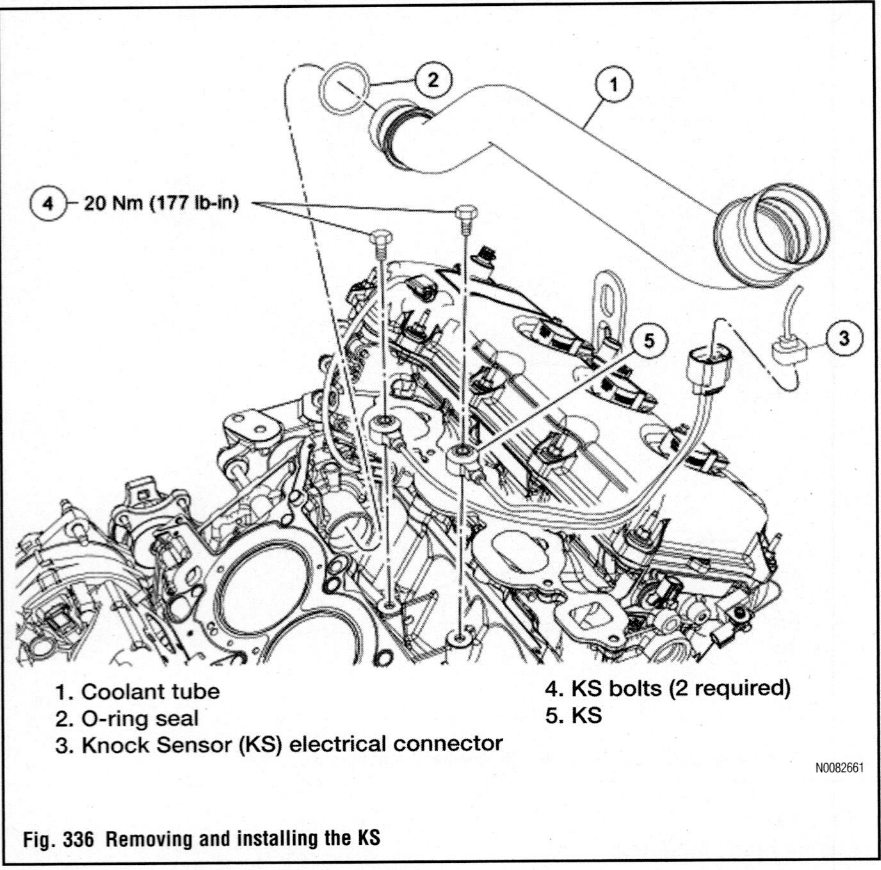

Fig. 336 Removing and installing the KS

MANIFOLD ABSOLUTE PRESSURE (MAP) SENSOR

REMOVAL & INSTALLATION

2.5L Engines

See Figure 337.

1. Disconnect the Manifold Absolute Pressure (MAP) sensor electrical connector.
2. Remove the screw and the MAP sensor.

To install:

➡Lubricate the MAP sensor O-ring seal with clean engine oil.

3. To install, reverse the removal procedure.
4. Tighten the MAP sensor to 27 inch lbs. (3 Nm).

3.0L Engine

See Figure 338.

1. Disconnect the Manifold Absolute Pressure (MAP) sensor electrical connector.
2. Remove the bolt and the MAP sensor.
    a. To install, tighten to 53 inch lbs. (6 Nm).
    b. When installing the sensor, if the bolt fails to hold specified torque, relocate the sensor and retain, using the auxiliary bolt hole in the intake manifold.

To install:

➡Clean and inspect the sealing surface.

3. To install, reverse the removal procedure.

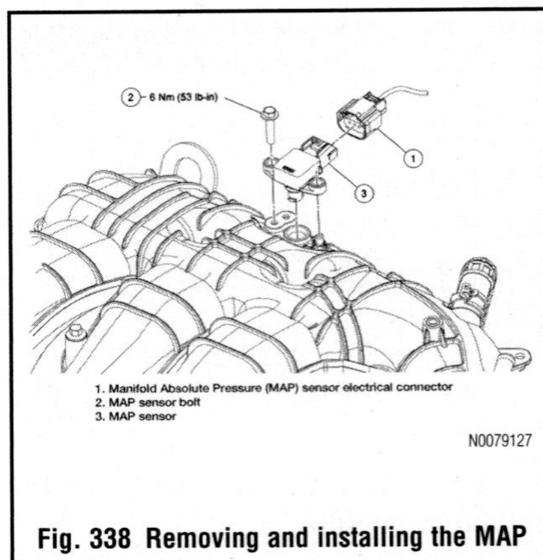

Fig. 338 Removing and installing the MAP sensor

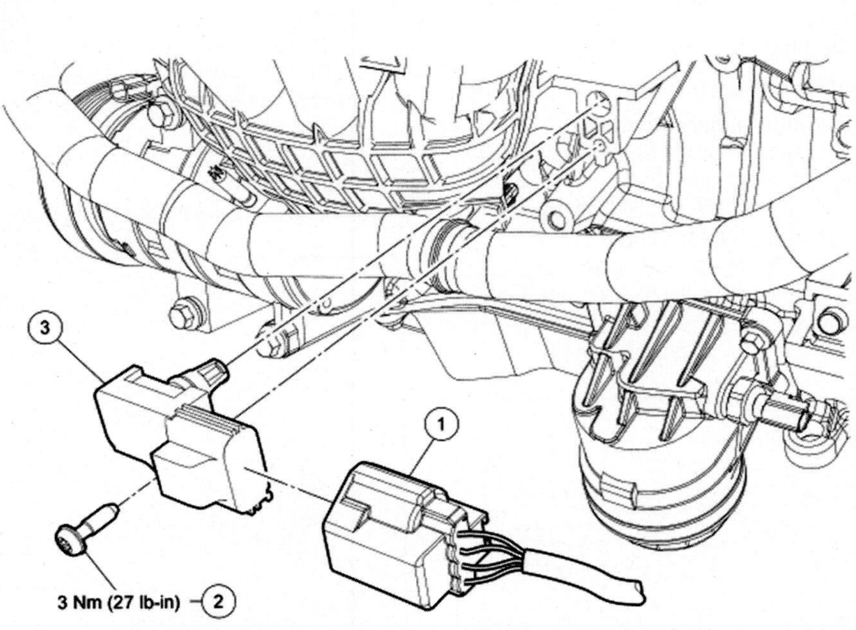

Fig. 337 Removing and installing the MAP sensor

MASS AIR FLOW (MAF) SENSOR

REMOVAL & INSTALLATION

2.5L Engine

See Figure 339.

1. Disconnect the Mass Air Flow (MAF) sensor electrical connector.
2. Remove the 2 screws and the MAF sensor.

To install:

3. To install, reverse the removal procedure.
4. Tighten the MAF sensor to 89 inch lbs. (10 Nm).

2.5L Hybrid Engine

See Figure 340.

1. Remove the Air Cleaner (ACL) outlet pipe.
2. Disconnect the Mass Air Flow (MAF) sensor electrical connector.
3. Remove the 2 screws and the MAF sensor.

To install:

4. To install, reverse the removal procedure.
5. Tighten the MAF sensor to 89 inch lbs. (10 Nm).

3.0L Engine

See Figure 341.

1. Disconnect the Mass Air Flow (MAF) sensor electrical connector.
2. Remove the 2 screws and the MAF sensor.

To install:

3. To install, reverse the removal procedure.
4. Tighten the MAF sensor to 18 inch lbs. (2 Nm).

3.5L Engine

See Figure 342.

1. Disconnect the Mass Air Flow (MAF) sensor electrical connector.
2. Remove the 2 screws and the MAF sensor.

To install:

3. To install, reverse the removal procedure.
4. Tighten the MAF sensor to 18 inch lbs. (2 Nm).

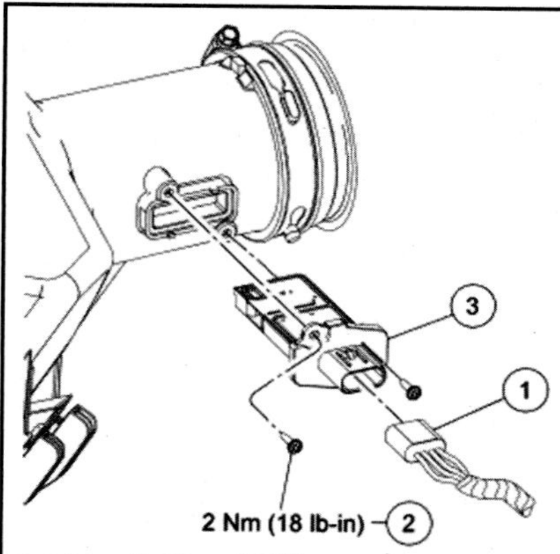

Fig. 342 Removing and installing the MAF sensor

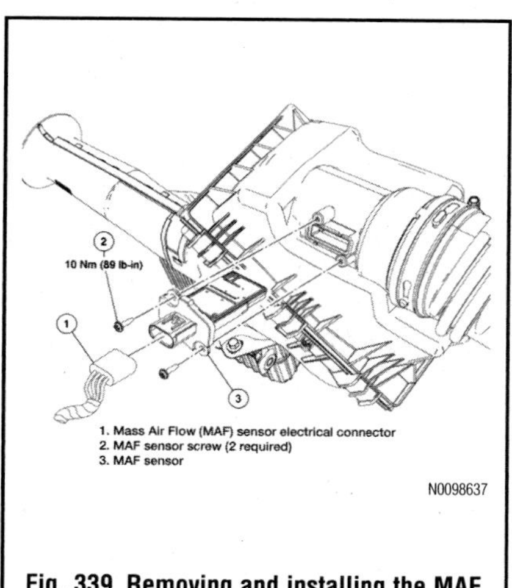

Fig. 339 Removing and installing the MAF sensor

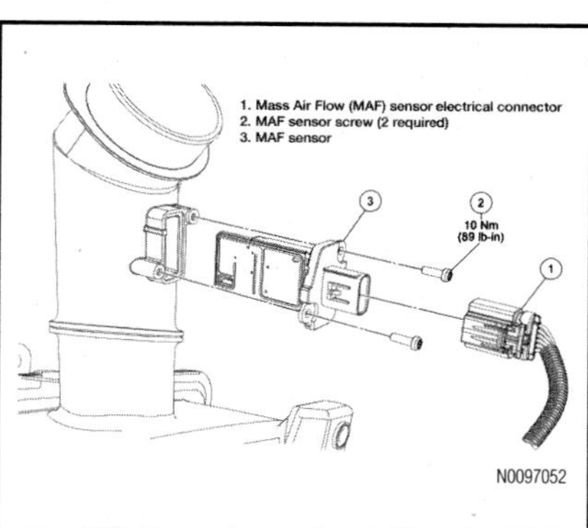

Fig. 340 Removing and installing the MAF sensor

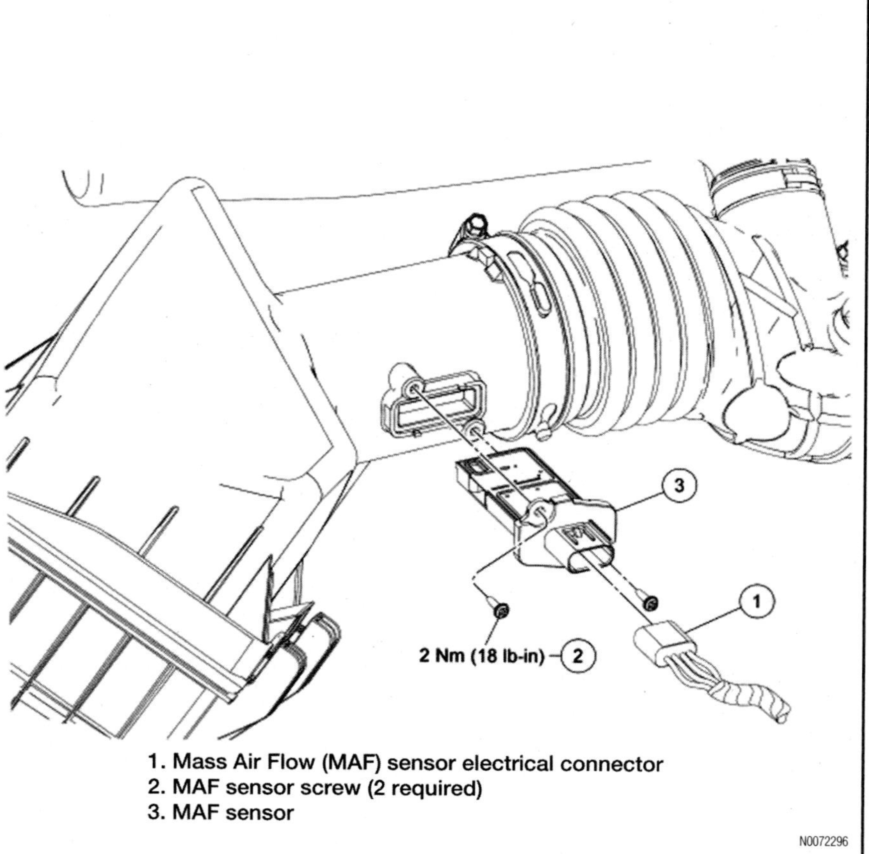

Fig. 341 Removing and installing the MAF sensor

VEHICLE SPEED SENSOR (VSS)

REMOVAL & INSTALLATION

See Figure 343.

1. With the vehicle in NEUTRAL, position it on a hoist.
2. Disconnect the Vehicle Speed Sensor (VSS) electrical connector.
3. Remove the VSS bolt.
4. Remove the VSS.
    a. Discard the O-ring.

To install:

5. To install, reverse the removal procedure.
6. Apply clean manual transaxle fluid to a new O-ring and install it on the VSS.
7. Tighten the VSS bolt to 80 inch lbs. (9 Nm).

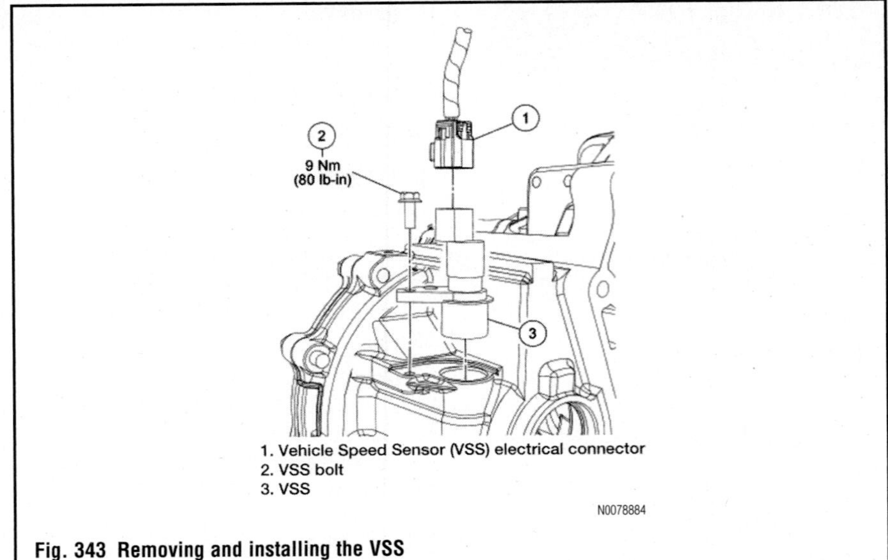

Fig. 343 Removing and installing the VSS

FUEL — GASOLINE FUEL INJECTION SYSTEM

FUEL SYSTEM SERVICE PRECAUTIONS

Safety is the most important factor when performing not only fuel system maintenance but any type of maintenance. Failure to conduct maintenance and repairs in a safe manner may result in serious personal injury or death. Maintenance and testing of the vehicle's fuel system components can be accomplished safely and effectively by adhering to the following rules and guidelines.

- To avoid the possibility of fire and personal injury, always disconnect the negative battery cable unless the repair or test procedure requires that battery voltage be applied.
- Always relieve the fuel system pressure prior to disconnecting any fuel system component (injector, fuel rail, pressure regulator, etc.), fitting or fuel line connection. Exercise extreme caution whenever relieving fuel system pressure to avoid exposing skin, face and eyes to fuel spray. Please be advised that fuel under pressure may penetrate the skin or any part of the body that it contacts.
- Always place a shop towel or cloth around the fitting or connection prior to loosening to absorb any excess fuel due to spillage. Ensure that all fuel spillage (should it occur) is quickly removed from engine surfaces. Ensure that all fuel soaked cloths or towels are deposited into a suitable waste container.
- Always keep a dry chemical (Class B) fire extinguisher near the work area.
- Do not allow fuel spray or fuel vapors to come into contact with a spark or open flame.
- Always use a back-up wrench when loosening and tightening fuel line connection fittings. This will prevent unnecessary stress and torsion to fuel line piping.
- Always replace worn fuel fitting O-rings with new Do not substitute fuel hose or equivalent where fuel pipe is installed.

Before servicing the vehicle, make sure to also refer to the precautions in the beginning of this section as well.

RELIEVING FUEL SYSTEM PRESSURE

**** WARNING**

Do not smoke, carry lighted tobacco or have an open flame of any type when working on or near any fuel-related component. Highly flammable mixtures are always present and may be ignited. Failure to follow these instructions may result in serious personal injury.

**** WARNING**

Do not carry personal electronic devices such as cell phones, pagers or audio equipment of any type when working on or near any fuel-related component. Highly flammable mixtures are always present and may be ignited. Failure to follow these instructions may result in serious personal injury.

**** WARNING**

Before working on or disconnecting any of the fuel tubes or fuel system components, relieve the fuel system pressure to prevent accidental spraying of fuel. Fuel in the fuel system remains under high pressure, even when the engine is not running. Failure to follow this instruction may result in serious personal injury.

2.5L and 3.0L engines

1. Position aside the LR quarter panel luggage compartment trim.
2. Disconnect the Fuel Pump (FP) control module electrical connector.

3.5L engines

3. Remove the RF door scuff plate.
4. Disconnect the Inertia Fuel Shutoff (IFS) switch.

All engines

5. Start the engine and allow it to idle until it stalls.
6. After the engine stalls, crank the engine for approximately 5 seconds to make sure the fuel system pressure has been released.
7. Turn the ignition switch to the OFF position.

2.5L and 3.0L engines

8. When fuel system service is complete, reconnect the FP control module electrical connector.

9. Position the LR quarter panel luggage compartment trim.

3.5L engines

10. When fuel system service is complete, reconnect the IFS switch electrical connector.

11. Install the RF door scuff plate.

All engines

➡It may take more than one key cycle to pressurize the fuel system.

12. Cycle the ignition key and wait 3 seconds to pressurize the fuel system.

➡Carry out a Key ON Engine OFF (KOEO) visual inspection for fuel leaks prior to starting the engine.

13. Start the vehicle and check the fuel system for leaks.

FUEL INJECTORS

REMOVAL & INSTALLATION

2.5L Engines

See Figures 344 and 345.

⁂ WARNING

Do not smoke, carry lighted tobacco or have an open flame of any type when working on or near any fuel-related component. Highly flammable mixtures are always present and may be ignited. Failure to follow these instructions may result in serious personal injury.

⁂ WARNING

Before working on or disconnecting any of the fuel tubes or fuel system components, relieve the fuel system pressure to prevent accidental spraying of fuel. Fuel in the fuel system remains under high pressure, even when the engine is not running. Failure to follow this instruction may result in serious personal injury.

⁂ WARNING

Clean all fuel residue from the engine compartment. If not removed, fuel residue may ignite when the engine is returned to operation. Failure to follow this instruction may result in serious personal injury.

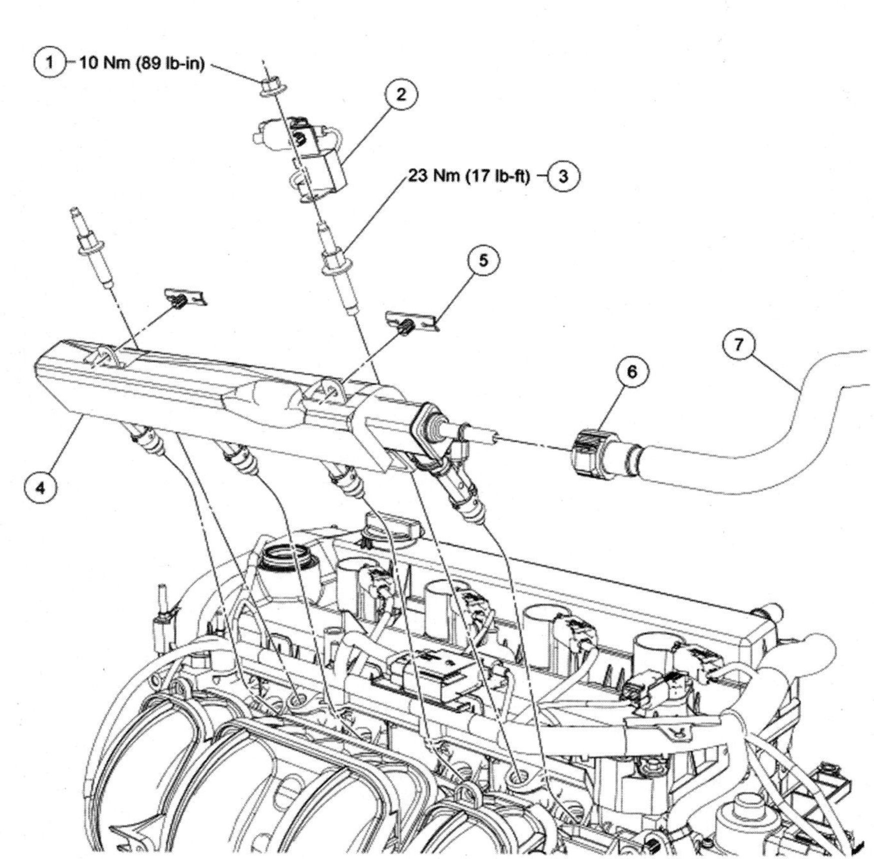

1. Radio capacitor nut
2. Radio capacitor
3. Fuel rail stud bolt (2 required)
4. Fuel rail
5. Wire harness pin-type retainer (2 required)
6. Fuel supply tube-to-fuel rail quick connect coupling
7. Fuel supply tube

N0095913

Fig. 344 Exploded view of fuel rail

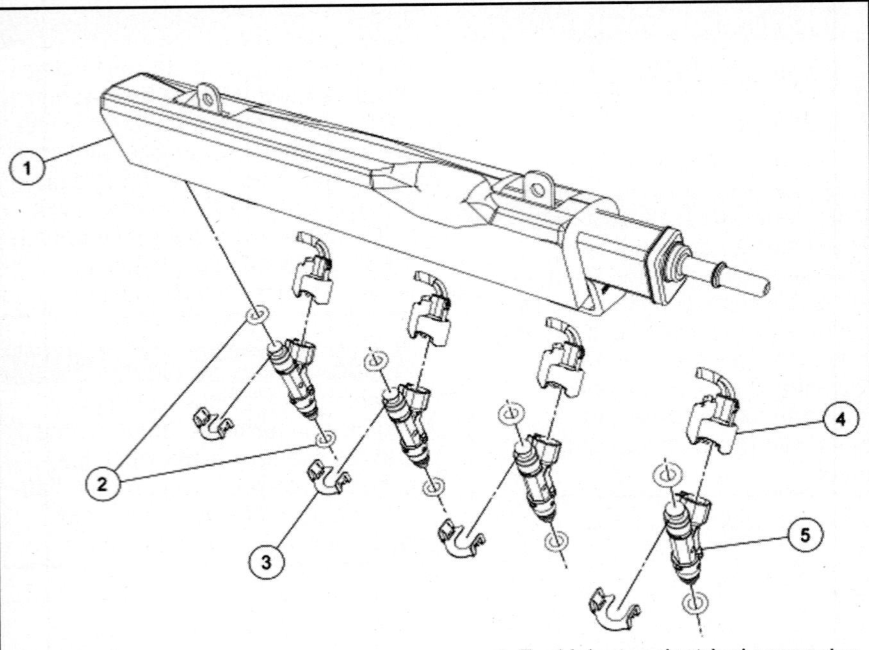

Fig. 345 Exploded view of fuel injectors

⁂ WARNING

Always disconnect the battery ground cable at the battery when working on an evaporative emission (EVAP) system or fuel-related component. Highly flammable mixtures are always present and may be ignited. Failure to follow these instructions may result in serious personal injury.

1. Release the fuel system pressure.
2. Disconnect the battery ground cable.
3. Disconnect the fuel tube-to-fuel rail quick connect coupling.
4. Detach the 2 wire harness pin-type retainers from the fuel rail.
5. Disconnect the 4 fuel injector electrical connectors.
6. Remove the nut and position the radio capacitor aside.
7. Remove the 2 fuel rail stud bolts.
8. Remove the fuel rail and fuel injectors as an assembly.
9. Remove the 4 fuel injector retainer clips and the fuel injectors.
10. Remove and discard the 8 fuel injector O-ring seals.

To install:

➡Use O-ring seals that are made of special fuel-resistant material. Use of ordinary O-ring seals can cause the fuel system to leak. Do not reuse the O-ring seals.

➡Install new fuel injector O-ring seals and lubricate them with clean engine oil.

➡Make sure the fuel rail retainer clips snap back into place.

11. Install the 4 fuel injectors and the retainer clips into the fuel rail.
12. Install the fuel rail and fuel injectors as an assembly.
13. Install the 2 fuel rail stud bolts.
    a. Tighten to 17 ft. lbs. (23 Nm).
14. Position the radio capacitor and install the nut.
    a. Tighten to 89 inch lbs. (10 Nm).
15. Connect the 4 fuel injector electrical connectors.
16. Attach the 2 wire harness pin-type retainers.
17. Connect the fuel tube-to-fuel rail quick connect coupling.
18. Connect the battery ground cable.

3.0L Engine

See Figures 346 and 347.

⁂ WARNING

Do not smoke, carry lighted tobacco or have an open flame of any type when working on or near any fuel-related component. Highly flammable mixtures are always present and may be ignited. Failure to follow these instructions may result in serious personal injury.

⁂ WARNING

Before working on or disconnecting any of the fuel tubes or fuel system components, relieve the fuel system pressure to prevent accidental spraying of fuel. Fuel in the fuel system remains under high pressure, even when the engine is not running. Failure to follow this instruction may result in serious personal injury.

⁂ WARNING

Clean all fuel residue from the engine compartment. If not removed, fuel residue may ignite when the engine is returned to operation. Failure to follow this instruction may result in serious personal injury.

⁂ WARNING

Always disconnect the battery ground cable at the battery when working on an evaporative emission (EVAP) system or fuel-related component. Highly flammable mixtures are always present and may be ignited. Failure to follow these instructions may result in serious personal injury.

1. Release the fuel system pressure.
2. Disconnect the battery ground cable.
3. Remove the upper intake manifold.
4. Disconnect the fuel tube-to-fuel rail quick connect coupling.
5. Release the 5 fuel charging wire harness pin-type retainers from the fuel rail.
6. Release the engine wire harness pin-type retainer from the fuel rail.
7. Disconnect the 6 fuel injector electrical connectors.
8. Remove the 4 fuel rail bolts.
9. Remove the fuel rail and injectors as an assembly.
10. Remove the 6 fuel injector clips and the 6 fuel injectors.

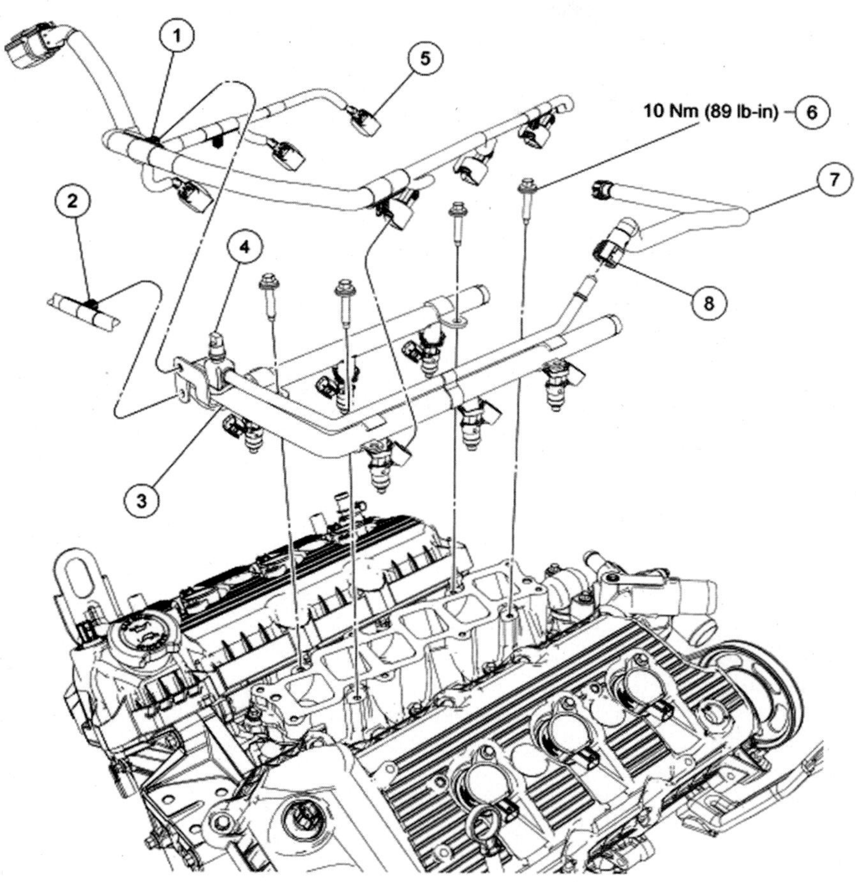

Fig. 346 Exploded view of the fuel rail (early build shown, late build similar)

11. Remove and discard the 12 fuel injector O-ring seals.

To install:

➡**Use O-ring seals that are made of special fuel-resistant material. The use of ordinary O-ring seals can cause the fuel system to leak. Do not reuse the O-ring seals.**

➡**Install new fuel injector O-ring seals and lubricate them with clean engine oil.**

12. Install the 6 fuel injectors and the 6 fuel injector clips into the fuel rail.
13. Install the fuel rail and fuel injectors as an assembly.
14. Install the 4 fuel rail bolts.
    a. Tighten to 89 inch lbs. (10 Nm).
15. Connect the 6 fuel injector electrical connectors.
16. Attach the engine wire harness pin-retainer to the fuel rail.
17. Attach the 5 fuel charging wire harness pin-retainers to the fuel rail.
18. Connect the fuel tube-to-fuel rail quick connect coupling.
19. Install the upper intake manifold.
20. Connect the battery ground cable.

3.5L Engine

See Figure 348.

WARNING

Do not smoke, carry lighted tobacco or have an open flame of any type when working on or near any fuel-related component. Highly flammable mixtures are always present and may be ignited. Failure to follow these instructions may result in serious personal injury.

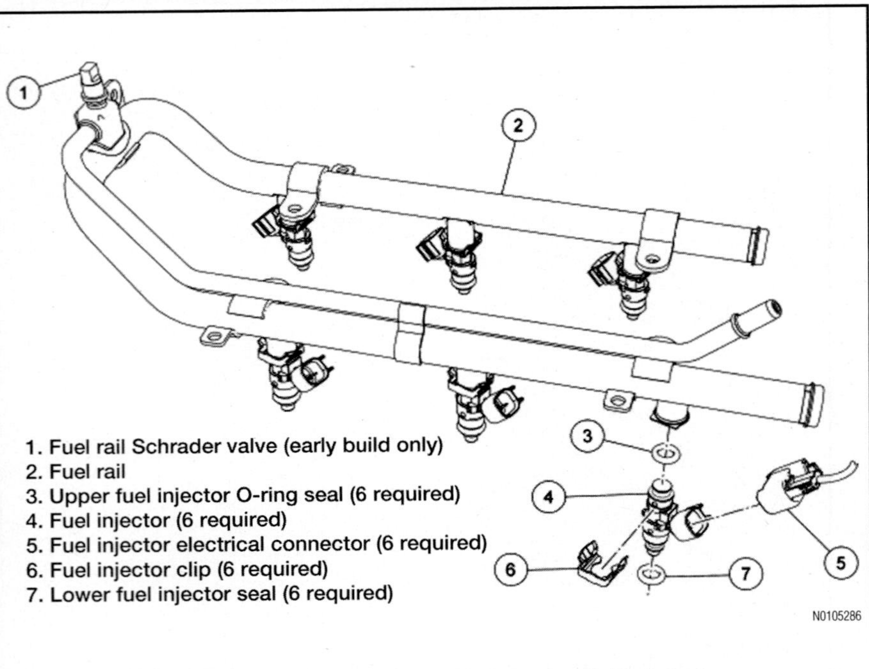

Fig. 347 Exploded view of fuel injectors (early build shown, late build similar)

⁂ WARNING

Before working on or disconnecting any of the fuel tubes or fuel system components, relieve the fuel system pressure to prevent accidental spraying of fuel. Fuel in the fuel system remains under high pressure, even when the engine is not running. Failure to follow this instruction may result in serious personal injury.

⁂ WARNING

Clean all fuel residue from the engine compartment. If not removed, fuel residue may ignite when the engine is returned to operation. Failure to follow this instruction may result in serious personal injury.

⁂ WARNING

Always disconnect the battery ground cable at the battery when working on an evaporative emission (EVAP) system or fuel-related component. Highly flammable mixtures are always present and may be ignited. Failure to follow these instructions may result in serious personal injury.

1. Release the fuel system pressure.
2. Disconnect the battery ground cable.
3. Remove the upper intake manifold.
4. Disconnect the fuel tube-to-fuel rail spring lock coupling.
5. Disconnect the 6 fuel injector electrical connectors.
6. Remove the 4 fuel rail bolts.
7. Remove the fuel rail and injectors as an assembly.
8. Remove the 6 fuel injector clips and the 6 fuel injectors.
9. Remove and discard the 12 fuel injector O-ring seals.

To install:

➡Use O-ring seals that are made of special fuel-resistant material. The use of ordinary O-ring seals can cause the fuel system to leak. Do not reuse the O-ring seals.

➡The upper and lower fuel injector O-ring seals are similar in appearance, but are not interchangeable.

➡Install new fuel injector O-ring seals and lubricate them with clean engine oil.

10. Install the 6 fuel injectors and the 6 fuel injector clips into the fuel rail.

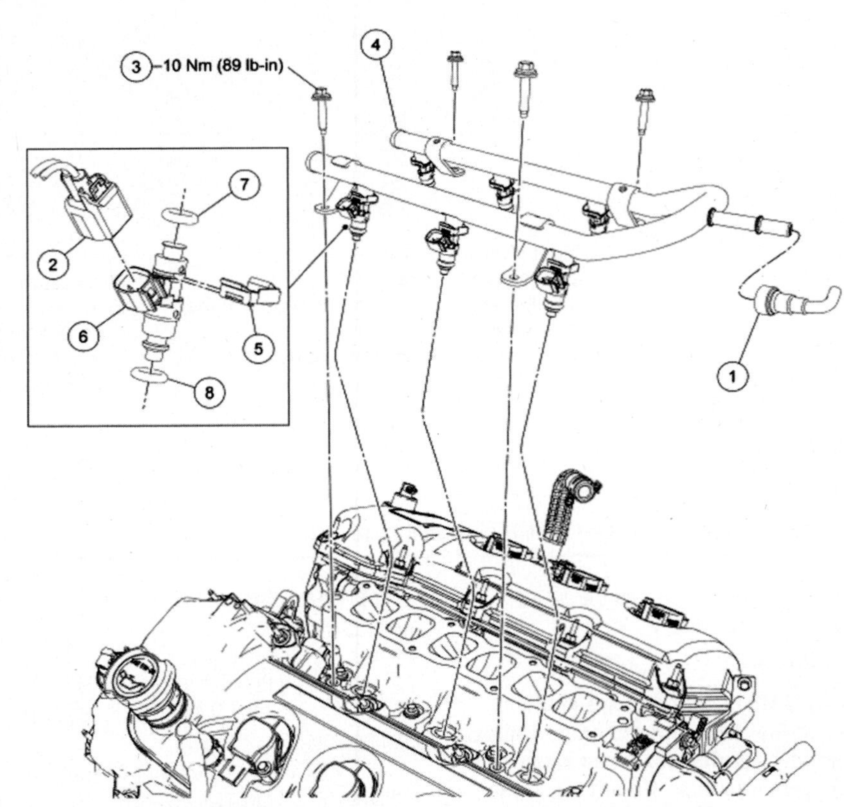

Fig. 348 Exploded view of fuel rail and fuel injector

11. Install the fuel rail and fuel injectors as an assembly.
12. Install the 4 fuel rail bolts.
    a. Tighten to 89 inch lbs. (10 Nm).
13. Connect the 6 fuel injector electrical connectors.
14. Connect the fuel tube-to-fuel rail spring lock coupling.
15. Install the upper intake manifold.
16. Connect the battery ground cable.

FUEL TANK

DRAINING

2.5L Engines

⁂ WARNING

Do not smoke, carry lighted tobacco or have an open flame of any type when working on or near any fuel-related component. Highly flammable mixtures are always present and may be ignited. Failure to follow these instructions may result in serious personal injury.

⁂ WARNING

Do not carry personal electronic devices such as cell phones, pagers or audio equipment of any type when working on or near any fuel-related component. Highly flammable mixtures are always present and may be ignited. Failure to follow these instructions may result in serious personal injury.

⁂ WARNING

When handling fuel, always observe fuel handling precautions and be prepared in the event of fuel spillage. Spilled fuel may be ignited by hot vehicle components or other ignition sources. Failure to follow these instructions may result in serious personal injury.

⁂ WARNING

Always disconnect the battery ground cable at the battery when working on an evaporative emission (EVAP) system or fuel-related component. Highly flammable mixtures are always present and may be ignited. Failure to follow these instructions may result in serious personal injury.

➡For vehicles with an inaccurate or inoperable fuel gauge, follow the instructions for draining a fuel tank with more than three-fourths of a tank of fuel.

All vehicles

1. Release the fuel system pressure.
2. Disconnect the battery ground cable.

Vehicles with more than three-fourths of a tank of fuel.

➡The supplemental refueling adapter is located in the luggage compartment.

3. Install the supplemental refueling adapter and a length of semi-rigid fuel drain tube into the Easy Fuel TM(capless) fuel tank filler pipe until the tube enters the fuel tank.

➡This step will remove approximately one-fourth tank of the fuel from a completely full fuel tank and the majority of any residual fuel in the fuel tank filler pipe, lowering the fuel level below the Fuel Pump (FP) module mounting flange.

4. Attach the Fuel Storage Tanker to the fuel drain tube and remove one-fourth (approximately 4 gallons) of fuel from the tank.

All vehicles

5. Remove the rear seat lower cushion.
6. Remove the 4 screws and the FP module access cover.

➡Clean the FP module connections, couplings, flange surfaces and the immediate surrounding area of any dirt or foreign material.

7. Disconnect the FP module electrical connector.

➡Place absorbent toweling in the immediate surrounding area in case of fuel spillage.

8. Disconnect the fuel tube-to- FP module quick connect coupling.

➡Make sure to install a new FP module O-ring seal.

9. Install the Fuel Tank Sender Unit Wrench, remove the FP module lock ring.
    a. Discard the FP module O-ring seal.

➡The Fuel Pump (FP) module must be handled carefully to avoid damage to the float arm.

10. Position the FP module aside and insert the tube from the Fuel Storage Tanker into the FP module aperture and drain as much fuel from the fuel tank as possible.

3.0L Engine

AWD Vehicles

⁂ WARNING

Do not smoke, carry lighted tobacco or have an open flame of any type when working on or near any fuel-related component. Highly flammable mixtures are always present and may be ignited. Failure to follow these instructions may result in serious personal injury.

⁂ WARNING

Do not carry personal electronic devices such as cell phones, pagers or audio equipment of any type when working on or near any fuel-related component. Highly flammable mixtures are always present and may be ignited. Failure to follow these instructions may result in serious personal injury.

⁂ WARNING

When handling fuel, always observe fuel handling precautions and be prepared in the event of fuel spillage. Spilled fuel may be ignited by hot vehicle components or other ignition sources. Failure to follow these instructions may result in serious personal injury.

⁂ WARNING

Always disconnect the battery ground cable at the battery when working on an evaporative emission (EVAP) system or fuel-related component. Highly flammable mixtures are always present and may be ignited. Failure to follow these instructions may result in serious personal injury.

➡For vehicles with an inaccurate or inoperable fuel gauge, follow the instructions for draining a fuel tank with more than three-fourths of a tank of fuel.

All vehicles

1. Release the fuel system pressure.
2. Disconnect the battery ground cable.

Vehicles with more than one-half of a tank of fuel

➡The Easy Fuel TM(capless) fuel tank filler pipe on 3.0L vehicles have an anti-siphon grate that will not allow a

fuel drain tube to penetrate the fuel tank and requires the following steps to drain the fuel.

3. With the vehicle in NEUTRAL, position it on a hoist.

➡Index-mark the fuel tank filler pipe hose and the clamp prior to removal for correct installation.

4. Release the clamp and disconnect the hose from the fuel tank filler pipe.
   a. To install, tighten to 35 inch lbs. (4 Nm).
5. Insert a semi-rigid fuel drain tube into the fuel tank filler pipe hose until it enters the fuel tank.

➡This step is to remove approximately one-half tank of the fuel from a completely full fuel tank, lowering the fuel level below the Fuel Pump (FP) module mounting flange.

6. Attach the Fuel Storage Tanker to the fuel drain tube and remove one-half (approximately 9 gallons) of fuel from the tank.

All vehicles

7. Remove the rear seat lower cushion.
8. Remove the 3 screws and the FP module access cover.

➡Clean the FP module connections, couplings, flange surfaces and the immediate surrounding area of any dirt or foreign material.

9. Disconnect the FP module electrical connector.

➡Place absorbent toweling in the immediate surrounding area in case of fuel spillage.

10. Disconnect the fuel tube-to- FP module quick connect coupling.

➡Make sure to install a new FP module O-ring seal.

11. Install the Fuel Tank Sender Unit Wrench and remove the FP module lock ring.
   a. Discard the FP module O-ring seal.

➡The Fuel Pump (FP) module must be handled carefully to avoid damage to the float arm.

12. Position the FP module aside and insert the tube from the Fuel Storage Tanker into the FP module aperture and drain as much fuel from the fuel tank as possible.
13. Remove the 3 screws and the fuel level sensor access cover.

➡Clean the fuel level sensor electrical connector, flange surface and the immediate surrounding area of any dirt or foreign material.

14. Disconnect the fuel level sensor electrical connector.

➡Place absorbent toweling in the immediate surrounding area in case of fuel spillage.

15. Release the lock tab and rotate the fuel level sensor counterclockwise approximately one-fourth turn, lift and position aside.
16. Insert the tube from the Fuel Storage Tanker into the fuel level sensor aperture and drain the remainder of the fuel from the fuel tank.

FWD Vehicles

⁂ WARNING

Do not smoke, carry lighted tobacco or have an open flame of any type when working on or near any fuel-related component. Highly flammable mixtures are always present and may be ignited. Failure to follow these instructions may result in serious personal injury.

⁂ WARNING

Do not carry personal electronic devices such as cell phones, pagers or audio equipment of any type when working on or near any fuel-related component. Highly flammable mixtures are always present and may be ignited. Failure to follow these instructions may result in serious personal injury.

⁂ WARNING

When handling fuel, always observe fuel handling precautions and be prepared in the event of fuel spillage. Spilled fuel may be ignited by hot vehicle components or other ignition sources. Failure to follow these instructions may result in serious personal injury.

⁂ WARNING

Always disconnect the battery ground cable at the battery when working on an evaporative emission (EVAP) system or fuel-related component. Highly flammable mixtures are always present and may be ignited. Failure to follow these instructions may result in serious personal injury.

➡For vehicles with an inaccurate or inoperable fuel gauge, follow the instructions for draining a fuel tank with more than three-fourths of a tank of fuel.

All vehicles

1. Release the fuel system pressure.
2. Disconnect the battery ground cable.

Vehicles with more than three-fourths of a tank of fuel

➡The Easy Fuel TM(capless) fuel tank filler pipe on 3.0L vehicles have an anti-siphon grate that will not allow a fuel drain tube to penetrate the fuel tank and requires the following steps to drain the fuel.

3. With the vehicle in NEUTRAL, position it on a hoist.

➡Index-mark the fuel tank filler pipe hose and the clamp prior to removal for correct installation.

4. Release the clamp and disconnect the hose from the fuel tank filler pipe.
   a. To install, tighten to 35 inch lbs. (4 Nm).
5. Insert a semi-rigid fuel drain tube into the fuel tank filler pipe hose until it enters the fuel tank.

➡This step is to remove approximately one-fourth tank of the fuel from a completely full fuel tank, lowering the fuel level below the Fuel Pump (FP) module mounting flange.

6. Attach the Fuel Storage Tanker to the fuel drain tube and remove one-fourth (approximately 4 gallons) of fuel from the tank.

All vehicles

7. Remove the rear seat lower cushion.
8. Remove the 4 screws and the FP module access cover.

➡Clean the FP module connections, couplings, flange surfaces and the immediate surrounding area of any dirt or foreign material.

9. Disconnect the FP module electrical connector.

➡Place absorbent toweling in the immediate surrounding area in case of fuel spillage.

10. Disconnect the fuel tube-to- FP module quick connect coupling.

➡Make sure to install a new FP module O-ring seal.

11. Install the Fuel Tank Sender Unit Wrench and remove the FP module lock ring.

a. Discard the FP module O-ring seal.

➡**The Fuel Pump (FP) module must be handled carefully to avoid damage to the float arm.**

12. Position the FP module aside and insert the tube from the Fuel Storage Tanker into the FP module aperture and drain as much fuel from the fuel tank as possible.

3.5L Engine

**** WARNING**

Do not smoke, carry lighted tobacco or have an open flame of any type when working on or near any fuel-related component. Highly flammable mixtures are always present and may be ignited. Failure to follow these instructions may result in serious personal injury.

**** WARNING**

Do not carry personal electronic devices such as cell phones, pagers or audio equipment of any type when working on or near any fuel-related component. Highly flammable mixtures are always present and may be ignited. Failure to follow these instructions may result in serious personal injury.

**** WARNING**

When handling fuel, always observe fuel handling precautions and be prepared in the event of fuel spillage. Spilled fuel may be ignited by hot vehicle components or other ignition sources. Failure to follow these instructions may result in serious personal injury.

**** WARNING**

Always disconnect the battery ground cable at the battery when working on an evaporative emission (EVAP) system or fuel-related component. Highly flammable mixtures are always present and may be ignited. Failure to follow these instructions may result in serious personal injury.

➡**For (Front Wheel Drive (FWD)) vehicles with an inaccurate or inoperable fuel gauge, follow the instructions for draining a fuel tank with more than three-fourths of a tank of fuel.**

➡**For (All-Wheel Drive (AWD)) vehicles with an inaccurate or inoperable fuel gauge, follow the instructions for draining a fuel tank with more than one-half of a tank of fuel.**

All vehicles

1. Release the fuel system pressure.
2. Disconnect the battery ground cable.
3. Remove the rear seat lower cushion. For additional information, refer to Seating.

Front Wheel Drive (FWD) vehicles with more than three-fourths tank of fuel

➡**The supplemental refueling adapter is located in the luggage compartment.**

4. Install the supplemental refueling adapter and a length of semi-rigid fuel drain tube into the Easy Fuel TM(capless) fuel tank filler pipe until the tube enters the fuel tank.

➡**This step will remove approximately one-fourth tank of the fuel from a completely full fuel tank and the majority of any residual fuel in the fuel tank filler pipe, lowering the fuel level below the Fuel Pump (FP) module mounting flange.**

5. Attach the Fuel Storage Tanker to the fuel drain tube and remove one-fourth (approximately 4 gallons) of fuel from the tank.

All-Wheel Drive (AWD) vehicles with more than one-half tank of fuel

➡**The supplemental refueling adapter is located in the luggage compartment.**

6. Install the supplemental refueling adapter and a length of semi-rigid fuel drain tube into the Easy Fuel TM(capless) fuel tank filler pipe until the tube enters the fuel tank.

➡**This step is to remove approximately one-half tank of the fuel from a completely full fuel tank, lowering the fuel level below the FP module mounting flange.**

7. Attach the Fuel Storage Tanker to the fuel drain tube and remove one-half (approximately 9 gallons) of fuel from the tank.

FWD vehicles

8. Remove the 4 screws and the FP module access cover.

AWD vehicles

9. Remove the 3 screws and the FP module access cover.

All vehicles

➡**Clean the FP module connections, couplings, flange surfaces and the immediate surrounding area of any dirt or foreign material.**

10. Disconnect the FP module electrical connector.

➡**Place absorbent toweling in the immediate surrounding area in case of fuel spillage.**

11. Disconnect the fuel tube-to- FP module quick connect coupling.

➡**Make sure to install a new FP module O-ring seal.**

12. Install the Fuel Tank Sender Unit Wrench, remove the FP module lock ring.
    a. Discard the FP module O-ring seal.

➡**The Fuel Pump (FP) module must be handled carefully to avoid damage to the float arm.**

13. Position the FP module aside and insert the tube from the fuel storage tanker into the FP module aperture and drain as much fuel from the fuel tank as possible.

AWD vehicles

14. Remove the 3 screws and the fuel level sensor access cover.

➡**Clean the fuel level sensor electrical connector, flange surface and the immediate surrounding area of any dirt or foreign material.**

15. Disconnect the fuel level sensor electrical connector.

➡**Place absorbent toweling in the immediate surrounding area in case of fuel spillage.**

16. Release the lock tab and rotate the fuel level sensor counterclockwise approximately one-fourth turn, lift and position aside.
17. Insert the tube from the Fuel Storage Tanker into the fuel level sensor aperture and drain the remainder of the fuel from the fuel tank.

REMOVAL & INSTALLATION

AWD Vehicles

**** WARNING**

Do not smoke, carry lighted tobacco or have an open flame of any type when working on or near any fuel-related component. Highly flammable mixtures are always present and may be ignited. Failure to follow these instructions may result in serious personal injury.

⁂ WARNING

Do not carry personal electronic devices such as cell phones, pagers or audio equipment of any type when working on or near any fuel-related component. Highly flammable mixtures are always present and may be ignited. Failure to follow these instructions may result in serious personal injury.

⁂ WARNING

When handling fuel, always observe fuel handling precautions and be prepared in the event of fuel spillage. Spilled fuel may be ignited by hot vehicle components or other ignition sources. Failure to follow these instructions may result in serious personal injury.

⁂ WARNING

Before working on or disconnecting any of the fuel tubes or fuel system components, relieve the fuel system pressure to prevent accidental spraying of fuel. Fuel in the fuel system remains under high pressure, even when the engine is not running. Failure to follow this instruction may result in serious personal injury.

⁂ WARNING

Always disconnect the battery ground cable at the battery when working on an evaporative emission (EVAP) system or fuel-related component. Highly flammable mixtures are always present and may be ignited. Failure to follow these instructions may result in serious personal injury.

1. With the vehicle in NEUTRAL, position it on a hoist.
2. Drain the fuel tank.
3. Remove the muffler and tailpipe.
4. Remove the driveshaft.
5. Install the Powertrain Lift under the fuel tank.
6. Remove the 4 bolts and the 2 fuel tank straps.
7. Partially lower the fuel tank enough to access the fuel tank filler pipe hose clamp.

➡Some residual fuel may remain in the fuel tank filler pipe after draining the fuel tank. Carefully drain any remaining fuel into a suitable container.

8. Release the clamp and disconnect the fuel tank filler pipe hose from the fuel tank.
9. Disconnect the fuel vapor tube assembly-to-fuel tank quick connect coupling.
10. Carefully lower and remove the fuel tank from the vehicle.

To install:

11. To install, reverse the removal procedure.
12. Tighten the fuel tank filler pipe hose to 35 inch lbs. (4 Nm).
13. Tighten the fuel tank straps to 30 ft. lbs. (40 Nm).

FWD Vehicles

⁂ WARNING

Do not smoke, carry lighted tobacco or have an open flame of any type when working on or near any fuel-related component. Highly flammable mixtures are always present and may be ignited. Failure to follow these instructions may result in serious personal injury.

⁂ WARNING

Do not carry personal electronic devices such as cell phones, pagers or audio equipment of any type when working on or near any fuel-related component. Highly flammable mixtures are always present and may be ignited. Failure to follow these instructions may result in serious personal injury.

⁂ WARNING

When handling fuel, always observe fuel handling precautions and be prepared in the event of fuel spillage. Spilled fuel may be ignited by hot vehicle components or other ignition sources. Failure to follow these instructions may result in serious personal injury.

⁂ WARNING

Before working on or disconnecting any of the fuel tubes or fuel system components, relieve the fuel system pressure to prevent accidental spraying of fuel. Fuel in the fuel system remains under high pressure, even when the engine is not running. Failure to follow this instruction may result in serious personal injury.

⁂ WARNING

Always disconnect the battery ground cable at the battery when working on an evaporative emission (EVAP) system or fuel-related component. Highly flammable mixtures are always present and may be ignited. Failure to follow these instructions may result in serious personal injury.

1. With the vehicle in NEUTRAL, position it on a hoist.
2. Drain the fuel tank.
3. Remove the muffler and tailpipe.

➡Some residual fuel may remain in the fuel tank filler pipe after draining the fuel tank. Carefully drain any remaining fuel into a suitable container.

4. Release the clamp and disconnect the fuel tank filler pipe hose from the fuel tank.
5. Disconnect the fuel vapor tube assembly-to-fuel tank quick connect coupling.
6. Remove the 4 nuts, 2 clips and release the heat shield from the fuel tank.
7. Install the Powertrain Lift under the fuel tank.
8. Remove the 4 bolts and the 2 fuel tank straps.
9. Carefully lower and remove the fuel tank from the vehicle.

To install:

10. To install, reverse the removal procedure.
11. Tighten the fuel tank straps to 30 ft. lbs. (40 Nm).
12. Tighten the fuel tank filler pipe hose to 35 inch lbs. (4 Nm).

THROTTLE BODY

REMOVAL & INSTALLATION

2.5L Engines

See Figure 349.

1. Remove the Air Cleaner (ACL) outlet pipe.
2. Disconnect the electronic throttle control electrical connector.
3. Remove the 4 bolts and the Throttle Body (TB).
   a. Discard the TB gasket.

To install:

➡Install a new TB gasket.

4. To install, reverse the removal procedure.

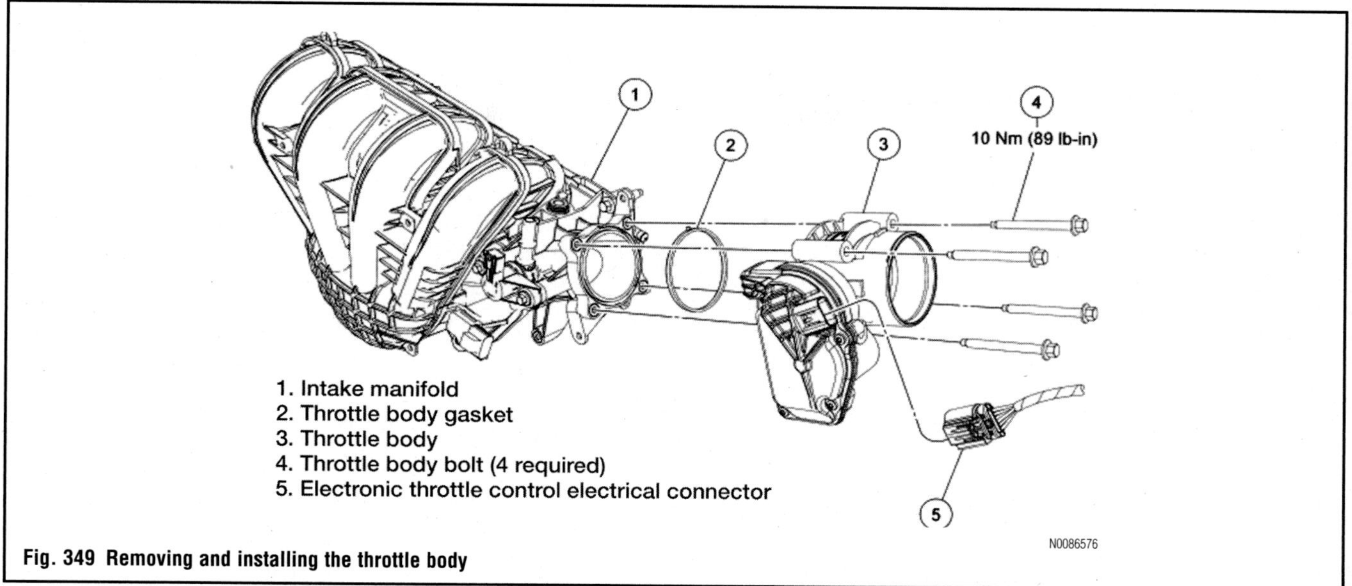

Fig. 349 Removing and installing the throttle body

5. Tighten the TB to 89 inch lbs. (10 Nm).

3.0L Engine

See Figure 350.

1. Remove the Air Cleaner (ACL) outlet pipe.
2. Disconnect the electronic throttle control electrical connector.
3. Remove the 4 bolts and the Throttle Body (TB).
   a. Discard the TB gasket.

To install:

➡Install a new TB gasket.

4. To install, reverse the removal procedure.
5. Tighten the throttle body to 89 inch lbs. (10 Nm).

3.5L Engine

See Figure 351.

1. Remove the Air Cleaner (ACL) outlet pipe.
2. Disconnect the electronic throttle control electrical connector.
3. Remove the 4 bolts and the Throttle Body (TB).
4. Discard the TB gasket.

To install:

➡Install a new TB gasket.

5. To install, reverse the removal procedure.
6. Tighten the throttle body to 89 inch lbs. (10 Nm).

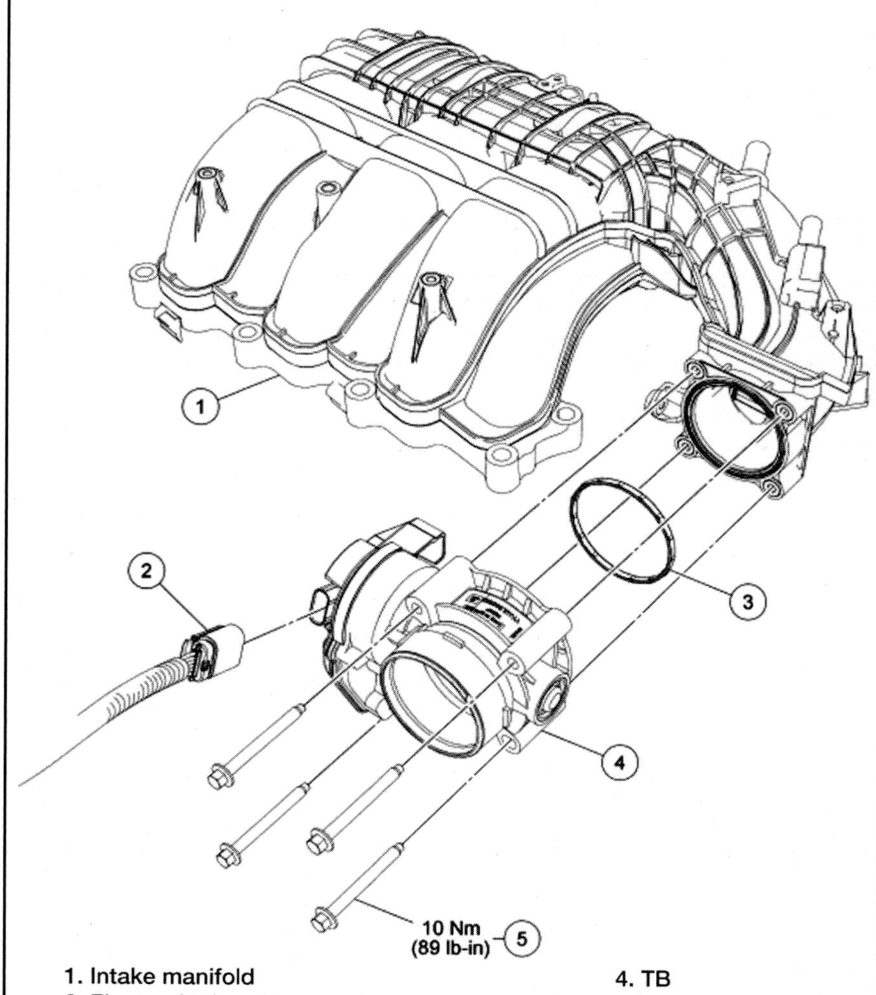

Fig. 350 Removing and installing the throttle body

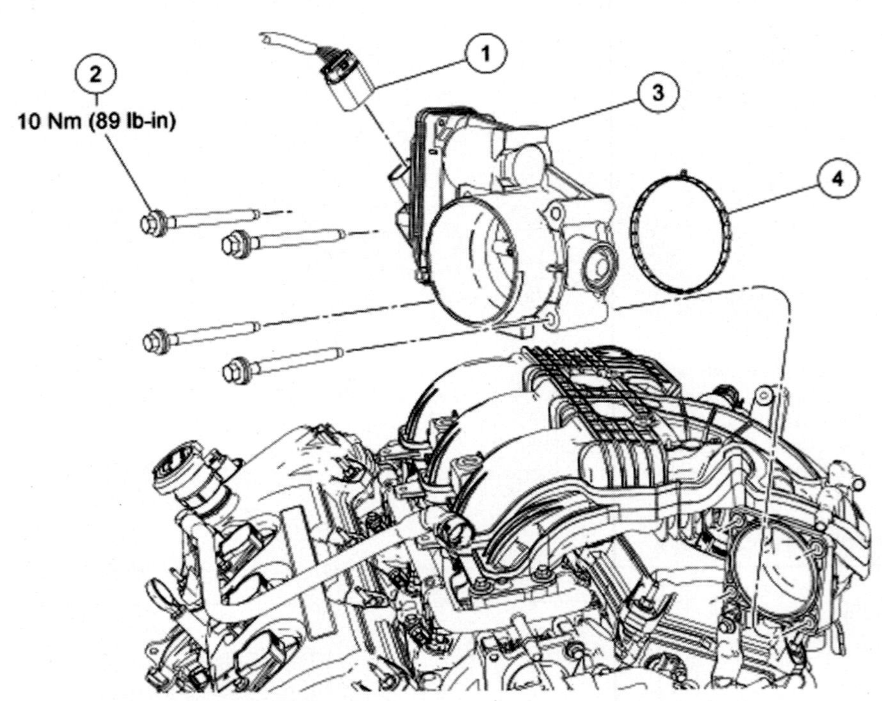

Fig. 351 Removing and installing the throttle body

HEATING & AIR CONDITIONING SYSTEM

BLOWER MOTOR

REMOVAL & INSTALLATION

See Figure 352.

MKZ vehicles

1. Remove the RH lower instrument panel insulator.

All vehicles

2. Disconnect the blower motor electrical connector.
3. Remove the 3 blower motor screws.
4. Remove the blower motor.

To install:

5. To install, reverse the removal procedure.

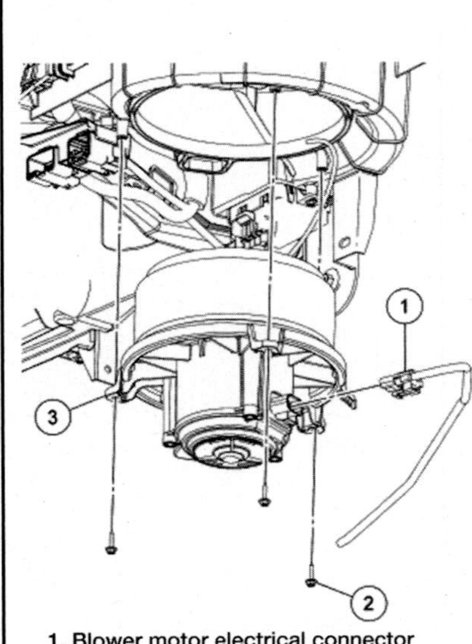

Fig. 352 Removing and installing the blower motor

HEATER CORE

REMOVAL & INSTALLATION

See Figure 353.

➡Motorcraft® Electric A/C Compressor Oil only must be used as a refrigerant system lubricant for hybrid vehicles. Addition of any oil other than Motorcraft® Electric A/C Compressor Oil to the hybrid vehicle refrigerant system will damage the electric Air Conditioning (A/C) compressor and contaminate the refrigerant system.

➡Use only the Air Conditioning (A/C) refrigerant compressor oil specified for this vehicle configuration. Use of any A/C refrigerant compressor oil other than what is specified will contaminate and damage the A/C system.

3.5L vehicles

1. Remove the lower cowl panel grille.

All vehicles

2. Recover the refrigerant.
3. Drain the engine coolant.
4. Remove the instrument panel.
5. Disconnect the A/C pressure transducer electrical connector and detach the wire harness from the Thermostatic Expansion Valve (TXV) stud.
6. Remove the TXV fitting nut and disconnect the fitting.
   a. Discard the gasket seals.
7. Release the 2 heater hoses clamps and disconnect the hoses from the heater core.
8. Remove the 6 heater core and evaporator core housing nuts.

9. Remove the heater core and evaporator core housing.

➡Motorcraft® Electric A/C Compressor Oil only must be used as a refrigerant system lubricant for hybrid vehicles. Addition of any oil other than Motorcraft® Electric A/C Compressor Oil to the hybrid vehicle refrigerant system will damage the electric Air Conditioning (A/C) compressor and contaminate the refrigerant system.

To install:

10. To install, reverse the removal procedure.
   a. Install new gasket seals.
11. Tighten the heater core and evaporator core housing nuts to 80 inch lbs. (9 Nm).
12. Tighten the TXV fitting nut to 11 ft. lbs. (15 Nm).
13. Add the correct amount of clean PAG oil (non-hybrid) or electric A/C compressor oil (hybrid) to the refrigerant system.
14. Fill the engine coolant level.
15. Evacuate, leak test and charge the refrigerant system.

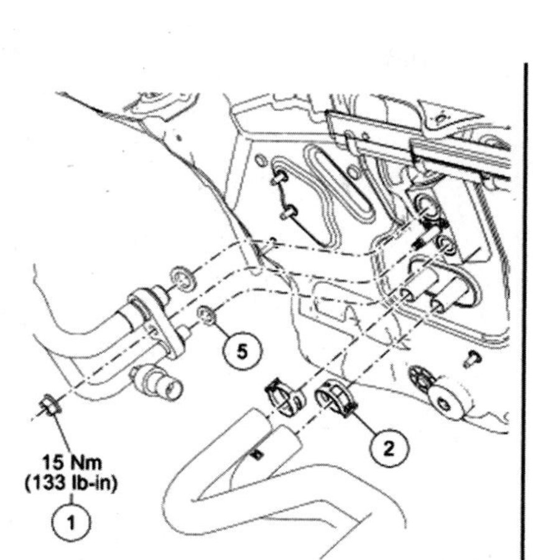

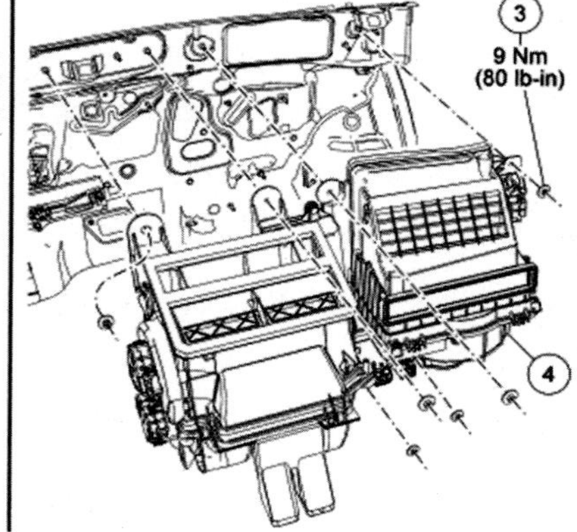

1. Thermostatic Expansion Valve (TXV) fitting nut
2. Heater hose clamp (2 required)
3. Heater core and evaporator core housing nuts
4. Heater core and evaporator core housing
5. Gasket seal (2 pieces from kit required)

N0082859

Fig. 353 Removing and installing the heater core and housing

STEERING

POWER STEERING GEAR

REMOVAL & INSTALLATION

2.5L Hybrid Engine & 3.0L AWD Engine

See Figures 354 and 355.

➡Use a steering wheel holding device.

1. Using a suitable holding device, hold the steering wheel in the straight-ahead position.
2. Remove the 2 lower steering column shaft joint cover nuts and the cover.

➡Do not allow the steering column to rotate while the steering column shaft is disconnected from the steering gear or damage to the clockspring may occur. If there is evidence that the steering column has rotated, the clockspring must be removed and recentered.

3. Remove the bolt and disconnect the steering column shaft from the steering gear.
   a. Discard the bolt.

➡Remove the steering gear/dash seal or damage to the seal may occur.

4. Pulling upward, remove the steering gear/dash seal.
5. Remove the wheels and tires.
6. If equipped, remove the 7 screws and the underbody cover.
7. Remove the 4 screws from each side and position the RH and LH fender splash shields aside.
8. Remove the 6 pin-type retainers from the LH and RH splash shield.
9. Remove the 2 outer tie-rod end cotter pins and nuts.
   a. Discard the cotter pins.

➡Do not use a hammer to separate the outer tie-rod end from the wheel knuckle or damage to the wheel knuckle may result.

10. Using the Ball Joint Separator, separate the outer tie-rod ends from the wheel knuckles.
11. Remove the exhaust flexible pipe.
12. Remove the engine roll restrictor bolt.
13. Disconnect the 2 Electronic Power Assist Steering (EPAS) jumper harness electrical connectors and detach the 3 wiring harness retainers.
14. Remove the bolt and position the ground wire aside.
15. Remove the 2 (one on each side) lower stabilizer bar link nuts and separate the links from the stabilizer bar.
16. Remove the 2 damper fork-to-front lower arm bolts and flagnuts.
17. Position the Powertrain Lift Table under the subframe.
18. Remove the 2 rear mounting nuts and washers from the front subframe.
19. Remove the 4 bolts and the subframe support bracket.
20. Remove the 2 front mounting nuts and washers from the front subframe.
21. Lower the subframe to gain access to the steering gear.
22. Remove the 2 bolts and the EPAS connector shield.
23. Disconnect the 2 EPAS electrical connectors and the wiring retainer.
24. Remove the 3 bolts and the steering gear.

To install:

25. Position the steering gear and install the 3 bolts.
   a. Tighten to 79 ft. lbs. (107 Nm).
26. Connect the 2 EPAS electrical connectors and the wiring retainer.
27. Position the EPAS connector shield and install the 2 bolts.
   a. Tighten to 11 ft. lbs. (15 Nm).

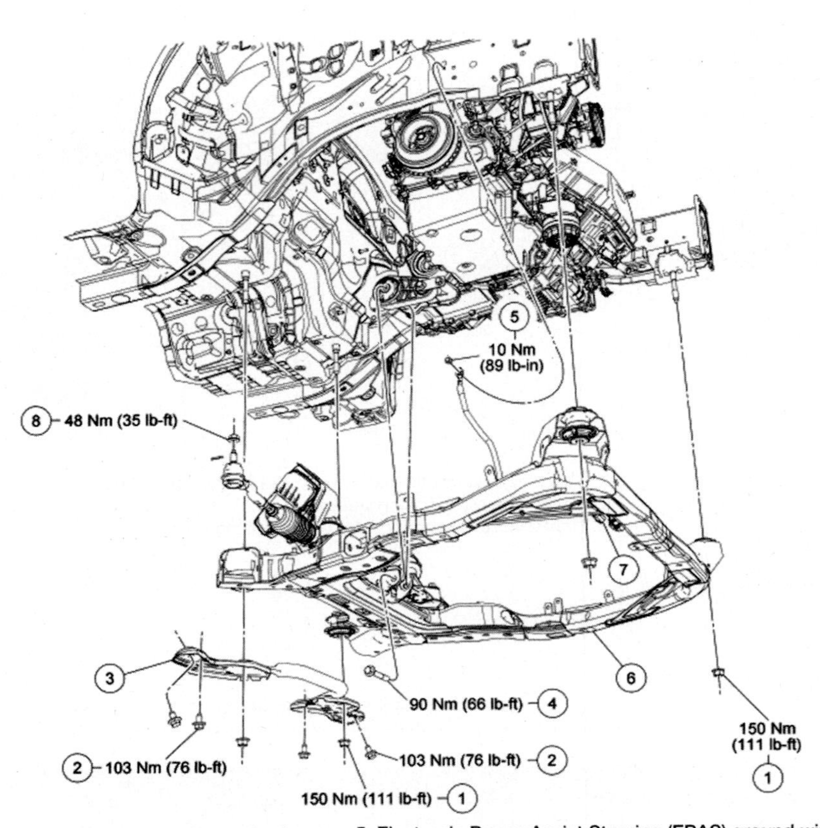

1. Front subframe nuts (4 required)
2. Front subframe support bracket bolts
3. Subframe support bracket
4. Roll restrictor bolt
5. Electronic Power Assist Steering (EPAS) ground wire
6. Front subframe
7. EPAS jumper harness connector (2 required)
8. Tie-rod end nut (2 required)

N0096632

Fig. 354 Removing and installing the power steering gear—1 of 2

28. Raise the subframe.

29. Install the 2 front subframe nuts and washers.

a. Tighten to 111 ft. lbs. (150 Nm).

30. Install the subframe support bracket, 4 rear subframe bolts and 2 rear subframe nuts.

a. To install, tighten the bolts and nuts in 2 stages.

b. Stage 1: Tighten the nuts to 111 ft. lbs. (150 Nm).

c. Stage 2: Tighten the bolts to 76 ft. lbs. (103 Nm).

31. Install the 2 damper fork-to-front lower arm bolts and flagnuts.

a. Tighten to 76 ft. lbs. (103 Nm).

32. Connect the stabilizer bar links and install the 2 nuts.

a. Tighten to 31 ft. lbs. (42 Nm).

33. Position the ground wire and install the bolt.

a. Tighten to 89 inch lbs. (10 Nm).

34. Connect the 2 EPAS jumper harness electrical connectors and attach the 3 wiring harness retainers.

35. Install the engine roll restrictor bolt.

a. Tighten to 66 ft. lbs. (90 Nm).

36. Install the exhaust flexible pipe.

37. Position the 2 outer tie-rod ends and install the nuts.

a. Tighten to 35 ft. lbs. (48 Nm).

38. Install 2 new cotter pins.

39. Install the LH and RH splash shield and the 6 pin-type retainers.

40. Install the RH and LH fender splash shields and the 4 screws from each side.

41. If equipped, install the underbody cover and the 7 screws.

➡The steering gear/dash seal must be fully seated in the steering gear valve tower groove before the retaining clips are fully engaged into the body. If the steering gear/dash seal is not seated to the steering gear valve tower groove and the clips are not fully engaged to the body, water and foreign material may enter the passenger compartment, and damage the vehicle interior.

42. Applying hand force to the center of the seal, install the steering gear/dash seal onto the steering gear valve tower until the seal is fully seated in the valve tower groove.

43. Install the steering gear/dash seal until the retaining clips are fully engaged into the body.

➡Do not allow the steering column to rotate while the steering column shaft is disconnected from the steering gear or damage to the clockspring may occur. If there is evidence that the steering column has rotated, the clockspring must be removed and recentered.

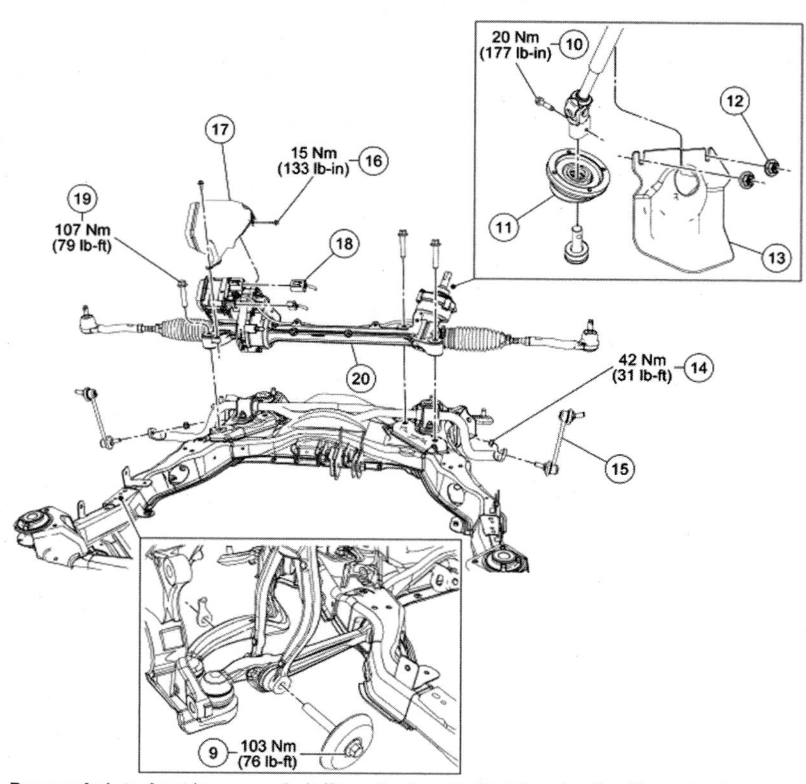

9. Damper fork-to-front lower arm bolt (2 required)
10. Steering column shaft-to-steering gear bolt
11. Steering gear/dash seal
12. Lower steering column shaft joint cover nuts
13. Lower steering column shaft joint cover
14. Lower stabilizer bar link nut (2 required)
15. Stabilizer bar link (2 required)
16. EPAS connector shield bolt (2 required)
17. EPAS connector shield
18. EPAS electrical connectors (part of 3F720)
19. Steering gear bolt (3 required)
20. Steering gear

N0097929

Fig. 355 Removing and installing the power steering gear—2 of 2

44. With the locator on the input shaft correctly aligned, connect the steering column shaft to the steering gear and install the new bolt.
    a. Tighten to 15 ft. lbs. (20 Nm).
45. Install the lower steering column shaft joint cover and the 2 nuts.

2.5L Non-Hybrid Engine & 3.0L FWD Engine

See Figures 356 and 357.

All vehicles

➡Use a steering wheel holding device.

1. Using a suitable holding device, hold the steering wheel in the straight-ahead position.
2. Remove the 2 lower steering column shaft joint cover nuts and the cover.

➡Do not allow the steering column to rotate while the steering column shaft is disconnected from the steering gear or damage to the clockspring may occur. If there is evidence that the steering column has rotated, the clockspring must be removed and recentered.

3. Remove the bolt and disconnect the steering column shaft from the steering gear.
    a. Discard the bolt.

➡Remove the steering gear/dash seal or damage to the seal may occur.

4. Pulling upward, remove the steering gear/dash seal.
5. Remove the wheels and tires.
6. If equipped, remove the 7 screws and the underbody cover.
7. Remove the 4 screws from each side and position the RH and LH fender splash shields aside.
8. Remove the 6 pin-type retainers from the LH and RH splash shields.
9. Remove the 2 outer tie-rod end cotter pins and nuts.

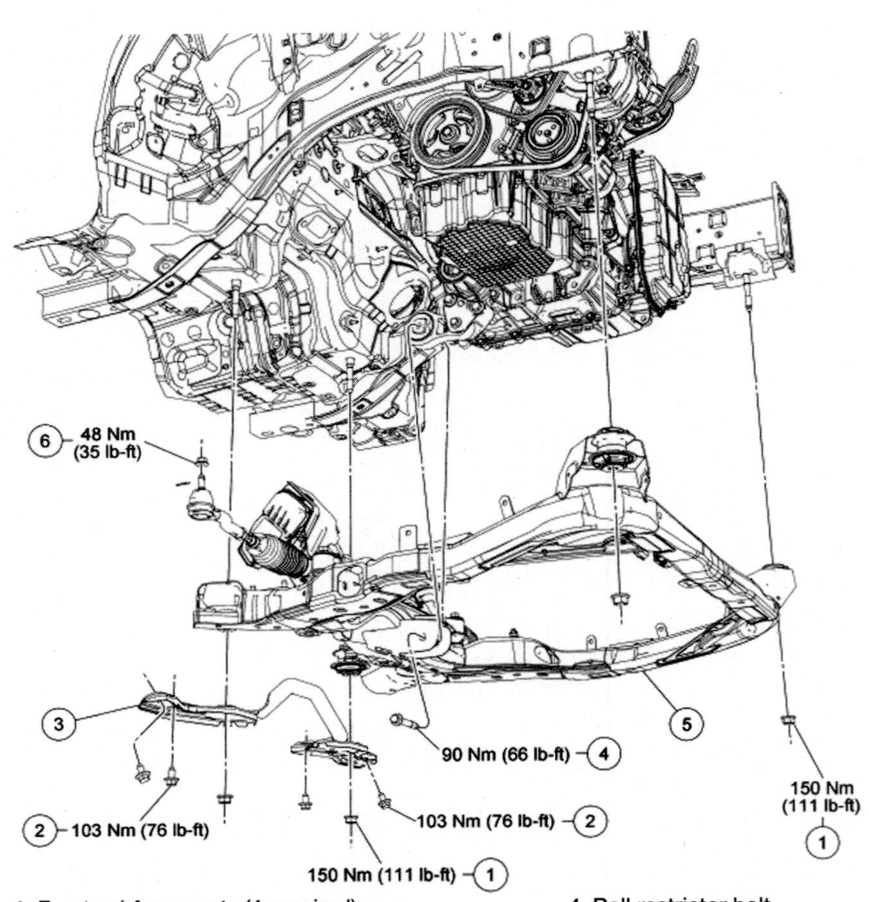

Fig. 356 Removing and installing the power steering gear—1 of 2

a. Discard the cotter pins.

➡Do not use a hammer to separate the outer tie-rod end from the wheel knuckle or damage to the wheel knuckle may result.

10. Using the Ball Joint Separator, separate the outer tie-rod ends from the knuckle.

Vehicles equipped with 2.5L engines

11. Remove the 2 bolts, 2 nuts and the exhaust bracket with U-clamp.

Vehicles equipped with 3.0L engines

12. Remove the exhaust flexible pipe.

All vehicles

13. Remove the 2 bolts and the Electronic Power Assist Steering (EPAS) connector shield.

14. Disconnect the 2 EPAS electrical connectors and the wiring retainer.

15. Remove the engine roll restrictor bolt.

16. Support the rear of the subframe with a suitable jack, remove the 4 rear subframe bolts and 2 rear subframe nuts and the subframe support bracket.

17. Loosen the 2 front subframe nuts.

18. Using the jack, lower the rear of the front subframe 76.2 mm (3 in).

19. Remove the 3 steering gear bolts.

20. Remove the steering gear from the LH side of the vehicle.

To install:

All vehicles

21. From the LH side of the vehicle, install the steering gear.

22. Install the 3 steering gear bolts.
  a. Tighten to 79 ft. lbs. (107 Nm).

23. Using the jack, raise the rear of the front subframe.

24. Tighten the 2 front subframe nuts.
  a. Tighten to 111 ft. lbs. (150 Nm).

25. Install the subframe support bracket, the 4 rear subframe bolts and the 2 rear subframe nuts.
  a. To install, tighten the bolts and nuts in 2 stages.
  b. Stage 1: Tighten the nuts to 111 ft. lbs. (150 Nm).
  c. Stage 2: Tighten the bolts to 76 ft. lbs. (103 Nm).

26. Install the engine roll restrictor bolt.
  a. Tighten to 66 ft. lbs. (90 Nm).

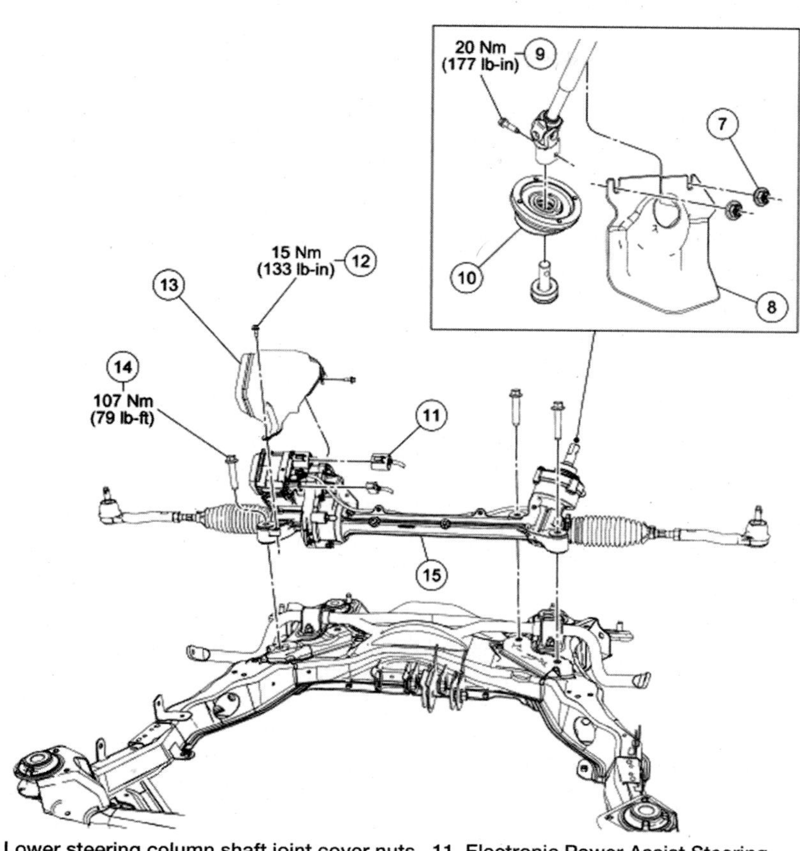

7. Lower steering column shaft joint cover nuts
8. Lower steering column shaft joint cover
9. Steering column shaft-to-steering gear bolt
10. Steering gear/dash seal
11. Electronic Power Assist Steering (EPAS) electrical connector (2 required)
12. EPAS connector shield bolt (2 required)
13. EPAS connector shield
14. Steering gear bolt (3 required)
15. Steering gear

N0097932

Fig. 357 Removing and installing the power steering gear—2 of 2

27. Connect the 2 EPAS electrical connectors and the wiring retainer.

28. Install the EPAS connector shield and the 2 bolts.

a. Tighten to 11 ft. lbs. (15 Nm).

Vehicles equipped with 3.0L engines

29. Install the exhaust flexible pipe.

Vehicles equipped with 2.5L engines

30. Install the 2 bolts, 2 nuts and the exhaust bracket with U-clamp.

a. Tighten to 22 ft. lbs. (30 Nm).

All vehicles

31. Position the outer tie-rod ends and install the 2 nuts.

a. Tighten to 35 ft. lbs. (48 Nm).

32. Install 2 new cotter pins.

33. Install the LH and RH splash shield and the 6 pin-type retainers.

34. Install the RH and LH fender splash shields and the 4 screws from each side.

35. If equipped, install the underbody splash shield and bolts.

a. Tighten to 62 inch lbs. (7 Nm).

➡The steering gear/dash seal must be fully seated in the steering gear valve tower groove before the retaining clips are fully engaged into the body. If the steering gear/dash seal is not seated to the steering gear valve tower groove and the clips are not fully engaged to the body, water and foreign material may enter the passenger compartment and damage the vehicle interior.

36. Applying hand force to the center of the seal, install the steering gear/dash seal onto the steering gear valve tower until the seal is fully seated in the valve tower groove.

37. Install the steering gear/dash seal until the retaining clips are fully engaged into the body.

➡Do not allow the steering column to rotate while the steering column shaft is disconnected from the steering gear or damage to the clockspring may occur. If there is evidence that the steering column has rotated, the clockspring must be removed and recentered.

38. With the locator on the input shaft properly aligned, connect the steering

column shaft to the steering gear and install the new bolt.

a. Tighten to 15 ft. lbs. (20 Nm).

39. Install the lower steering column shaft joint cover and the 2 nuts.

3.5L Engine

See Figure 358.

➡When repairing the power steering system, care should be taken to prevent the entry of foreign material or failure of the power steering components may result.

➡Use a steering wheel holding device.

1. Using a suitable holding device, hold the steering wheel in the straight-ahead position.
2. Remove the wheels and tires.
3. Remove the 2 lower steering column shaft joint cover nuts and the cover.

➡Make sure to correctly index-mark the steering gear-to-steering column shaft position or unequal right-to-left turns may occur, causing tire contact with the body and/or clockspring damage.

4. Index-mark the steering column shaft-to-steering gear position for reference during installation.

➡Do not allow the steering column to rotate while the steering column shaft is disconnected from the steering gear or damage to the clockspring may occur. If there is evidence that the steering column has rotated, the clock-

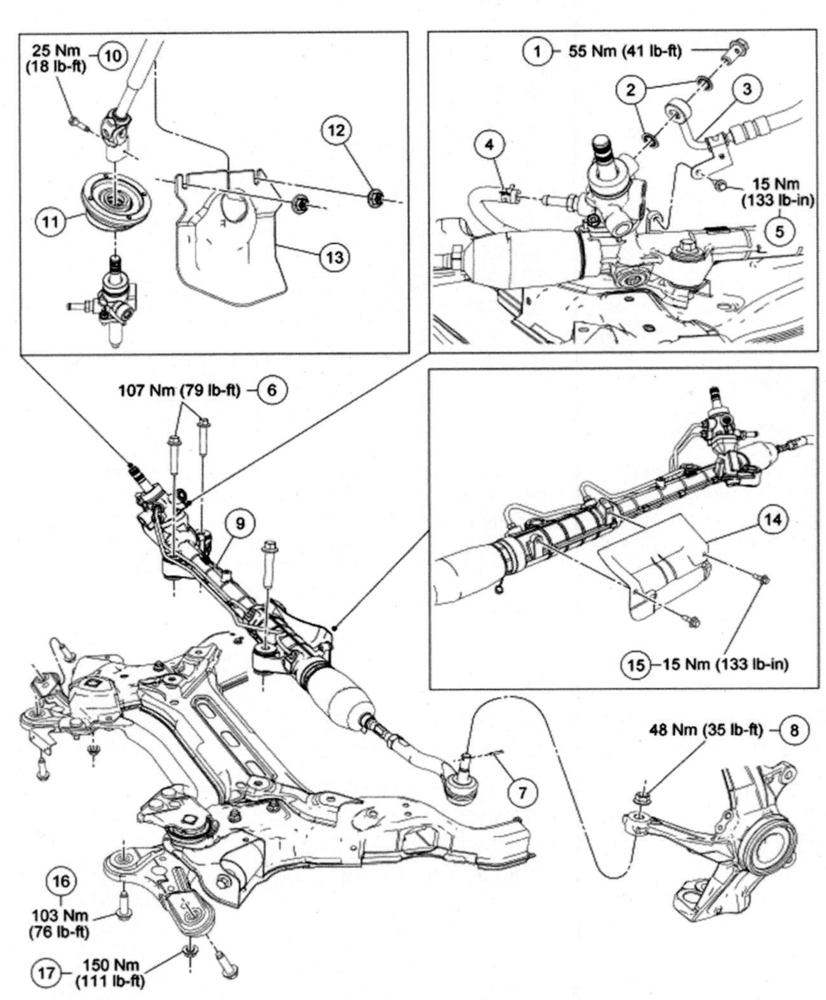

1. Pressure line-to-steering gear banjo bolt
2. Power steering pressure line seals
3. Power steering pressure line
4. Steering gear-to-fluid cooler return hose
5. Pressure line bracket-to-steering gear bolt
6. Steering gear bolts (3 required)
7. Cotter pin (2 required)
8. Outer tie-rod end nut (2 required)
9. Steering gear
10. Steering column shaft-to-steering gear bolt
11. Steering gear/dash seal
12. Lower steering column shaft joint cover nuts
13. Lower steering column shaft joint cover
14. Steering gear heat shield
15. Steering gear heat shield bolt (2 required)
16. Subframe bolt (4 required)
17. Subframe nut (2 required)

N0080038

Fig. 358 Removing and installing the power steering gear

spring must be removed and recentered.

5. Remove the bolt and disconnect the steering column shaft from the steering gear.
   a. Discard the bolt.

➡Remove the steering gear/dash seal or damage to the seal may occur.

6. Pulling upward, remove the steering gear/dash seal.
7. Remove the battery and battery tray.

➡Battery mounting bracket removed for clarity.

8. Disconnect the electrical connectors from the PCM.
9. Detach the wiring harness retainer from the PCM bracket and position the harness aside.
10. Remove the pressure line-to-steering gear banjo bolt.
    a. Discard the bolt and 2 seals.
11. Remove the pressure line bracket-to-steering gear bolt.
12. If equipped, remove the 7 screws and the underbody cover.
13. Remove the 4 screws from each side and position the RH and LH fender splash shield aside.
14. Remove the 6 pin-type retainers from the LH and RH splash shield.
15. Remove the 2 outer tie-rod end cotter pins and nuts.
    a. Discard the cotter pins.

➡Do not use a hammer to separate the outer tie-rod end from the wheel knuckle or damage to the wheel knuckle may result.

16. Using the Ball Joint Separator, separate the outer tie-rod ends from the knuckle.

➡Always install new fasteners and gaskets. Clean flange faces prior to new gasket installation to make sure of proper sealing.

17. Remove and discard the 2 catalytic converter-to-exhaust flexible pipe nuts and separate the exhaust flexible pipe.
18. Remove the 2 bolts and the steering gear heat shield.
19. Support the rear of the subframe with a suitable jack and remove the 4 rear subframe bolts and 2 rear subframe nuts.
20. Lower the rear of the front subframe 76.2 mm (3 in) with the support of the jack.
21. Remove the pressure line bracket-to-steering gear bolt.
22. Release the clamp and disconnect the steering gear-to-fluid cooler return hose.
23. Remove the 3 steering gear bolts.
24. Remove the steering gear from the LH side of the vehicle.

To install:

25. From the LH side of the vehicle, install the steering gear.
    a. Install the 3 steering gear bolts.
    b. Tighten to 79 ft. lbs. (107 Nm).
26. Release the clamp and connect the steering gear-to-fluid cooler return hose.
27. Using a suitable jack, raise the rear of the front subframe.
28. Install the subframe support bracket, 4 rear subframe bolts and 2 rear subframe nuts.
    a. To install, tighten the bolts and nuts in 2 stages.
    b. Stage 1: Tighten the nuts to 111 ft. lbs. (150 Nm).
    c. Stage 2: Tighten the bolts to 76 ft. lbs. (103 Nm).
29. Install the steering gear heat shield and the 2 bolts.
    a. Tighten to 11 ft. lbs. (15 Nm).

➡Always install new fasteners and gaskets. Clean flange faces prior to new gasket installation to make sure of proper sealing.

30. Position the exhaust flexible pipe and install 2 new catalytic converter-to-exhaust flexible pipe nuts.
    a. Tighten to 30 ft. lbs. (40 Nm).
31. Install the 2 outer tie-rod end nuts.
    a. Tighten to 35 ft. lbs. (48 Nm).
32. Install 2 new cotter pins.
33. Install the LH and RH splash shield and the 6 pin-type retainers.
34. Install the RH and LH fender splash shield and the 4 screws from each side.
35. If equipped, install the underbody splash shield and bolts.
    a. Tighten to 62 inch lbs. (7 Nm).
36. Install the pressure line bracket-to-steering gear bolt.
    a. Tighten to 11 ft. lbs. (15 Nm).

➡New banjo bolts and new seals must be installed any time the power steering pressure line is disconnected from the power steering pump and/or the steering gear or a fluid leak may occur.

37. Install the new pressure line-to-steering gear banjo bolt.
    a. Install 2 new seals.
    b. Tighten to 41 ft. lbs. (55 Nm).
38. Connect the electrical connectors to the PCM.
39. Attach the wiring harness retainer to the PCM bracket.
40. Install the battery tray and battery.

➡The steering gear/dash seal must be fully seated in the steering gear valve tower groove before the retaining clips are fully engaged into the body. If the steering gear/dash seal is not seated to the steering gear valve tower groove and the clips are not fully engaged to the body, water and foreign material may enter the passenger compartment and damage the vehicle interior.

41. Applying hand force to the center of the seal, install the steering gear/dash seal onto the steering gear valve tower until the seal is fully seated in the valve tower groove.
42. Install the steering gear/dash seal until the retaining clips are fully engaged into the body.

➡Do not allow the steering column to rotate while the steering column shaft is disconnected from the steering gear or damage to the clockspring may occur. If there is evidence that the steering column has rotated, the clockspring must be removed and recentered.

➡Make sure to correctly align the index marks when installing the steering gear-to-steering column shaft or unequal right-to-left turns may occur, causing tire contact with the body and/or clockspring damage.

43. With the index marks properly aligned, connect the steering column shaft to the steering gear and install the new bolt.
    a. Tighten to 18 ft. lbs. (25 Nm).
44. Install the lower steering column shaft joint cover and the 2 nuts.
45. Fill the power steering system.
46. Check and, if necessary, adjust the front toe.

POWER STEERING PUMP

REMOVAL & INSTALLATION

3.5L Engine

See Figure 359.

➡When repairing the power steering system, care should be taken to prevent the entry of foreign material or failure of the power steering components may result.

1. Remove the power steering fluid reservoir.
2. Remove the power steering pump belt.
3. Disconnect the Power Steering Pressure (PSP) switch electrical connector.

4. If equipped, detach the engine block heater electrical harness from the power steering pressure line.

5. Remove the pressure line-to-power steering pump banjo bolt and disconnect the line from the power steering pump.

a. Discard the bolt and 2 seals.

6. Remove the 3 bolts and the power steering pump.

To install:

➡A new banjo bolt and new seals must be installed any time the power steering pressure line is disconnected from the power steering pump or a fluid leak may occur.

7. To install, reverse the removal procedure.

8. Tighten the power steering pump to 18 ft. lbs. (24 Nm).

9. Tighten the pressure line to power steering pump banjo bolt to 35 ft. lbs. (48 Nm).

10. Fill the power steering system.

BLEEDING

➡If the air is not purged from the power steering system correctly, premature power steering pump failure may result. The condition may occur on pre-delivery vehicles with evidence of aerated fluid or on vehicles that have had steering component repairs.

➡A whine heard from the power steering pump can be caused by air in the system. The power steering purge procedure must be carried out prior to any component repair for which power steering noise complaints are accompanied by evidence of aerated fluid.

1. Remove the power steering reservoir cap. Check the fluid.

2. Raise the front wheels off the floor.

3. Tightly insert the Power Steering Evacuation Cap into the reservoir and connect the Vacuum Pump Kit.

4. Start the engine.

5. Using the Vacuum Pump Kit, apply vacuum and maintain the maximum vacuum of 68-85 kPa (20-25 in-Hg).

6. If the Vacuum Pump Kit does not maintain vacuum, check the power steering system for leaks before proceeding.

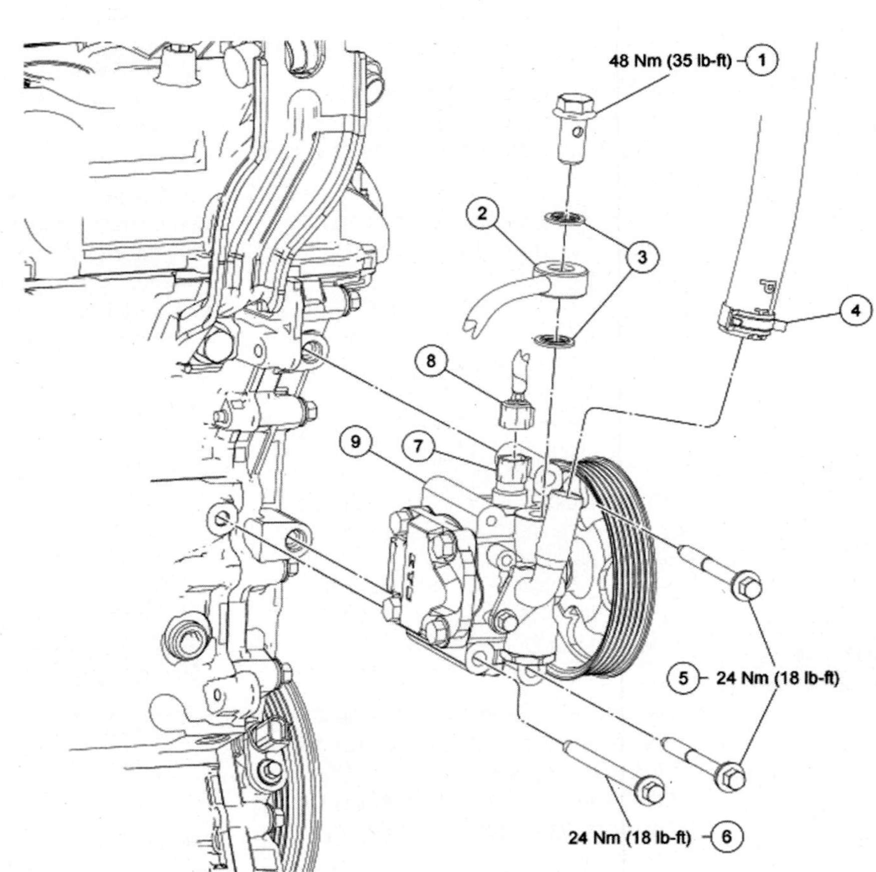

Fig. 359 Removing and installing the power steering pump

7. If equipped with Hydro-Boost®, apply the brake pedal 4 times.

➡Do not hold the steering wheel against the stops for an extended amount of time. Damage to the power steering pump may occur.

8. Cycle the steering wheel fully from stop-to-stop 10 times.
9. Stop the engine.
10. Release the vacuum and remove the Vacuum Pump Kit and the Power Steering Evacuation Cap.

➡Do not overfill the reservoir.

11. Fill the reservoir as needed with the specified fluid.
12. Start the engine.
13. Install the Power Steering Evacuation Cap and the Vacuum Pump Kit. Apply and maintain the maximum vacuum of 68-85 kPa (20-25 in-Hg).

➡Do not hold the steering wheel against the stops for an extended amount of time. Damage to the power steering pump may occur.

14. Cycle the steering wheel fully from stop-to-stop 10 times.
15. Stop the engine, release the vacuum and remove the Vacuum Pump Kit and the Power Steering Evacuation Cap.

➡Do not overfill the reservoir.

16. Fill the reservoir as needed with the specified fluid and install the reservoir cap.
17. Visually inspect the power steering system for leaks.

FLUID FILL PROCEDURE

See Figure 360.

➡If the air is not purged from the power steering system correctly, premature power steering pump failure may result. The condition can occur on pre-delivery vehicles with evidence of aerated fluid or on vehicles that have had steering component repairs.

1. Remove the power steering fluid reservoir cap.
2. Install the Power Steering Evacuation Cap, Power Steering Fill Adapter Manifold and Vacuum Pump Kit.

➡The Power Steering Fill Adapter Manifold control valves are in the OPEN position when the points of the handles face the center of the Power Steering Fill Adapter Manifold.

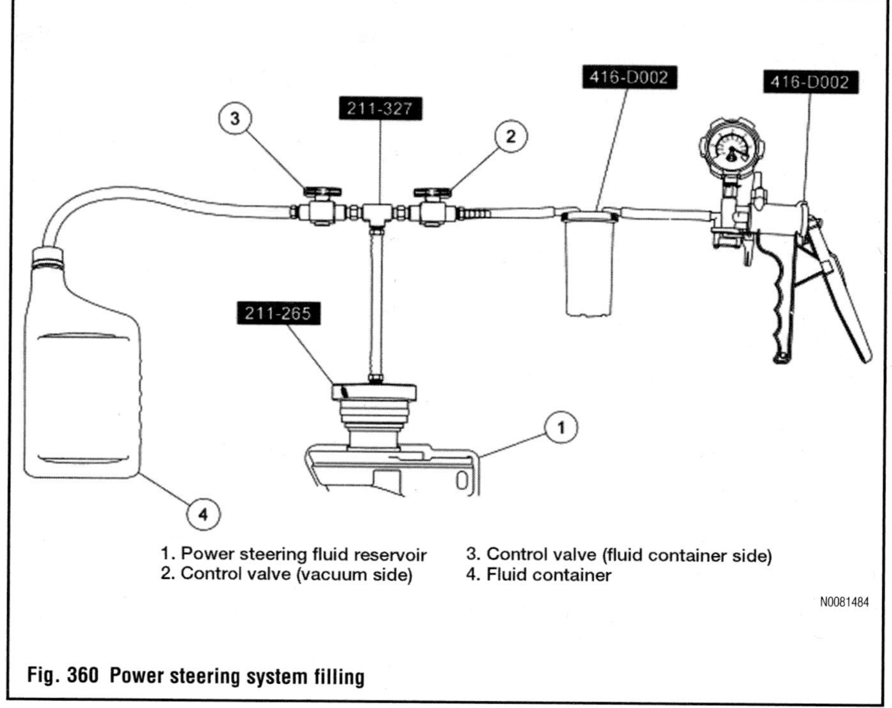

Fig. 360 Power steering system filling

3. Close the Power Steering Fill Adapter Manifold control valve (fluid side).
4. Open the Power Steering Fill Adapter Manifold control valve (vacuum side).
5. Using the Vacuum Pump Kit, apply 68-85 kPa (20-25 in-Hg) of vacuum to the power steering system.
6. Observe the Vacuum Pump Kit gauge for 30 seconds.
7. If the Vacuum Pump Kit gauge reading drops more than 3 kPa (0.88 in-Hg), correct any leaks in the power steering system or the Power Steering Evacuation Cap, Power Steering Fill Adapter Manifold and Vacuum Pump Kit before proceeding.

➡The Vacuum Pump Kit gauge reading will drop slightly during this step.

8. Slowly open the Power Steering Fill Adapter Manifold control valve (fluid side) until power steering fluid completely fills the hose and then close the control valve.
9. Using the Vacuum Pump Kit, apply 68-85 kPa (20-25 in-Hg) of vacuum to the power steering system.
10. Close the Power Steering Fill Adapter Manifold control valve (vacuum side).
11. Slowly open the Power Steering Fill Adapter Manifold control valve (fluid side).
12. Once power steering fluid enters the fluid reservoir and reaches the minimum fluid level indicator line on the reservoir, close the Power Steering Fill Adapter Manifold control valve (fluid side).
13. Remove the Power Steering Evacuation Cap, Power Steering Fill Adapter Manifold and Vacuum Pump Kit.
14. Install the reservoir cap.

➡Do not hold the steering wheel against the stops for an extended amount of time. Damage to the power steering pump may occur.

➡There will be a slight drop in the power steering fluid level in the reservoir when the engine is started.

15. Start the engine and turn the steering wheel from stop-to-stop.
16. Turn the ignition switch to the OFF position.

➡Do not overfill the reservoir.

17. Remove the reservoir cap and fill the reservoir with the specified fluid.
18. Install the reservoir cap.

LOWER CONTROL ARM

REMOVAL & INSTALLATION

Front

See Figure 361.

➡Suspension fasteners are critical parts because they affect performance of vital components and systems and their failure may result in major service expense. New parts must be installed with the same part numbers or equivalent part, if replacement is necessary. Do not use a replacement part of lesser quality or substitute design. Torque values must be used as specified during reassembly to make sure of correct retention of these parts.

1. With the vehicle in NEUTRAL, position it on a hoist.
2. Using a suitable jack, support the front wheel knuckle at the rear lower ball joint.
3. Remove the front lower arm-to-subframe bolt.
    a. Discard the bolt.
    b. To install, tighten the new bolt to 81 ft. lbs. (110 Nm), then tighten an additional 90 degrees with the suspension at the bushing fastener tightening position.
4. Remove the damper fork-to-lower arm bolt flagnut and damper.
    a. Discard the bolt and flagnut.
    b. To install, tighten the new bolt and flagnut to 76 ft. lbs. (103 Nm) with the suspension at the bushing fastener tightening position.
5. Remove and discard the front lower ball joint nut.
    a. To install, tighten the new nut to 148 ft. lbs. (200 Nm).

➡When the lower ball joint is separated from the wheel knuckle, the lower arm may strike the outer Constant Velocity (CV) joint boot with enough force to damage the boot clamp. This will result in a loss of grease from the outer CV joint. Place a block of wood, or similar item, between the lower arm and the outer CV joint to prevent the lower arm from striking the outer CV joint.

➡Once pressure is applied to the ball joint with the Ball Joint Separator and Adapter, it may be necessary to tap the wheel knuckle at the ball joint area to separate the ball joint from the wheel knuckle.

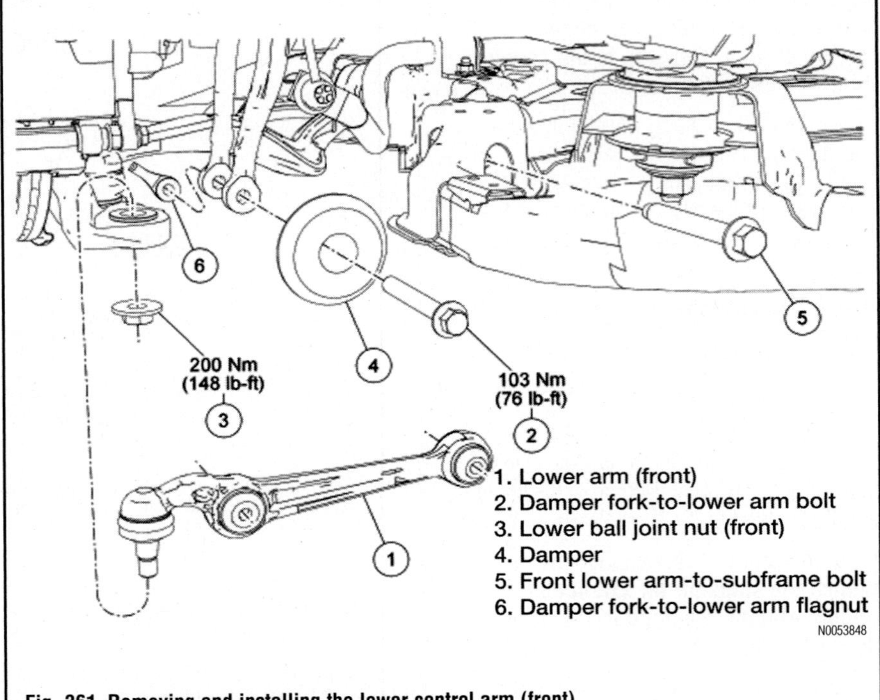

Fig. 361 Removing and installing the lower control arm (front)

6. Using the Ball Joint Separator and Adapter, separate the front lower ball joint from the wheel knuckle and remove the front lower arm.

➡Before tightening any suspension bushing fasteners, the suspension must be at the bushing fastener tightening position. Use a suitable jack to raise the suspension until the distance between the center of the hub and the lip of the fender is equal to 402 mm (15.83 in). This will prevent incorrect clamp load and bushing damage.

To install:

7. To install, reverse the removal procedure.

Rear

See Figures 362 and 363.

➡Suspension fasteners are critical parts because they affect performance of vital components and systems and their failure may result in major service expense. New parts must be installed with the same part numbers or equivalent part, if replacement is necessary. Do not use a replacement part of lesser quality or substitute design. Torque values must be used as specified during reassembly to make sure of correct retention of these parts.

➡Do not allow the steering column to rotate while the steering column shaft is disconnected or damage to the clockspring may result. If there is evidence that the lower shaft has rotated, the clockspring must be removed and recentered. For additional information, refer to Supplemental Restraint System.

➡Use a steering wheel holding device.

1. Using a suitable holding device, hold the steering wheel in the straight-ahead position.
2. Remove the 2 lower steering column shaft joint cover nuts and cover.

➡Do not allow the steering column shaft to rotate while it is disconnected from the gear or damage to the clockspring can occur. If there is evidence that the steering column shaft has rotated, the clockspring must be removed and recentered.

➡If equipped with Hydraulic Power Assist Steering (HPAS), index-mark the steering column shaft position to the steering gear for reference during installation.

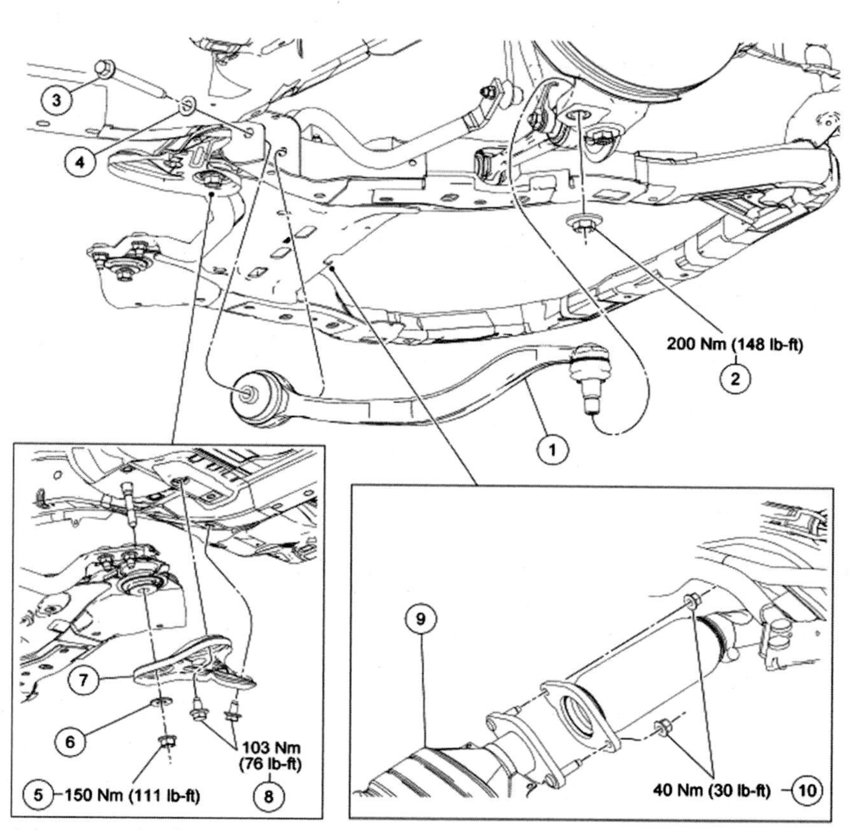

Fig. 362 Removing and installing the lower control arm (rear)—1 of 2

3. Remove the bolt and disconnect the steering column shaft from the steering gear.
   a. To install on HPAS vehicles, align the index marks and tighten to 18 ft. lbs. (25 Nm).
   b. To install on Electronic Power Assist Steering (EPAS) vehicles, tighten to 15 ft. lbs. (20 Nm).

➡Remove the steering column shaft-to-dash seal or damage to the seal can occur.

➡When installing, make sure that the dash seal is correctly positioned on the steering gear and the retaining clips are fully engaged into the body or damage to the steering gear can result.

4. Remove the steering column shaft-to-dash seal.
5. Remove the wheel and tire.
6. Remove the 8 screws and position the LH and RH splash shields aside.
7. Remove the 6 pin-type retainers and the RH splash shield.
8. Remove the 6 pin-type retainers and the LH splash shield.
9. If equipped, remove the 7 screws and the underbody cover shield.
   a. To install, tighten 62 inch lbs. (7 Nm).
10. Remove and discard the 2 catalytic converter manifold-to-exhaust flexible pipe nuts and separate the exhaust flexible pipe.
   a. To install, tighten the new nuts to 30 ft. lbs. (40 Nm).
11. Using 2 suitable jack stands, support the rear of the subframe assembly.
12. Remove and discard the 4 subframe bracket-to-body bolts, the 2 subframe bracket-to-subframe nuts and washers. Lower the rear of the subframe.
   a. To install, tighten the new bolts to 76 ft. lbs. (103 Nm).
   b. To install, tighten the new nuts to 111 ft. lbs (150 Nm).
13. Remove and discard the rear lower ball joint nut.
   a. To install, tighten the new nut to 148 ft. lbs. (200 Nm).

➡When the lower ball joint is separated from the wheel knuckle, the lower arm may strike the outer Constant Velocity (CV) joint boot with enough force to damage the boot clamp. This will result in a loss of grease from the outer CV joint. Place a block of wood, or similar item,

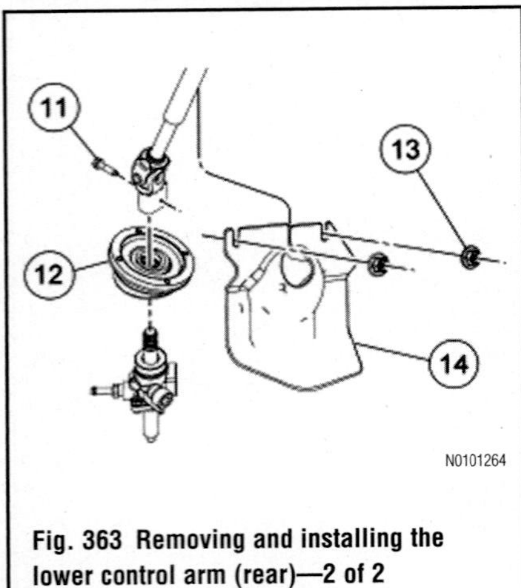

Fig. 363 Removing and installing the lower control arm (rear)—2 of 2

between the lower arm and the outer CV joint to prevent the lower arm from striking the outer CV joint.

➡Once pressure is applied to the ball joint with the Ball Joint Separator and Adapter, it may be necessary to tap the wheel knuckle at the ball joint area to separate the ball joint from the wheel knuckle.

14. Using the Ball Joint Separator and Adapter, separate the rear lower ball joint from the wheel knuckle.
15. Remove the rear lower arm-to-subframe bolt and washer and remove the rear lower arm.
    a. Discard the bolt and washer.
    b. To install, tighten the new bolt to 48 ft. lbs. (65 Nm), then tighten an additional 90 degrees.

➡Before tightening any suspension bushing fasteners, the suspension must be at the bushing fastener tightening position. Use a suitable jack to raise the suspension until the distance between the center of the hub and the lip of the fender is equal to 402 mm (15.83 in). This will prevent incorrect clamp load and bushing damage.

To install:

16. To install, reverse the removal procedure.

STABILIZER BAR

REMOVAL & INSTALLATION

See Figures 364 through 366.

➡Suspension fasteners are critical parts because they affect performance of vital components and systems and their failure may result in major service expense. New parts must be

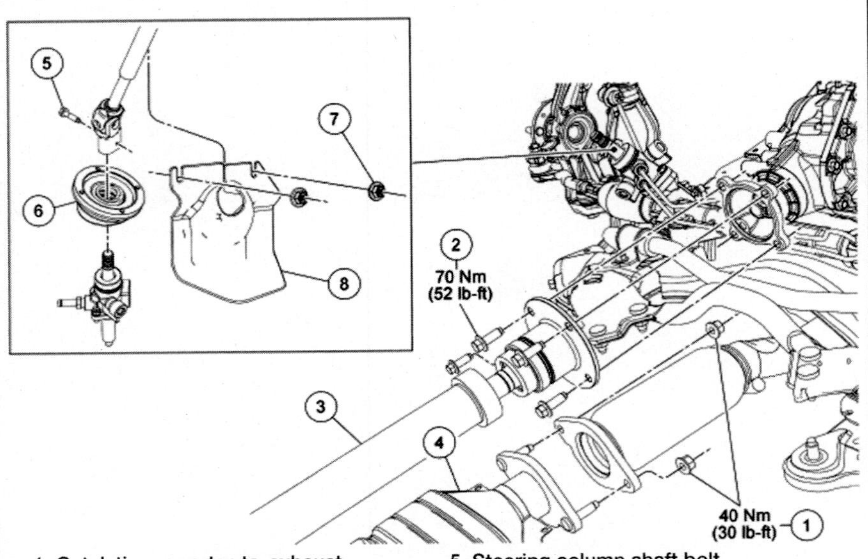

Fig. 364 Removing and installing the stabilizer bar—1 of 3

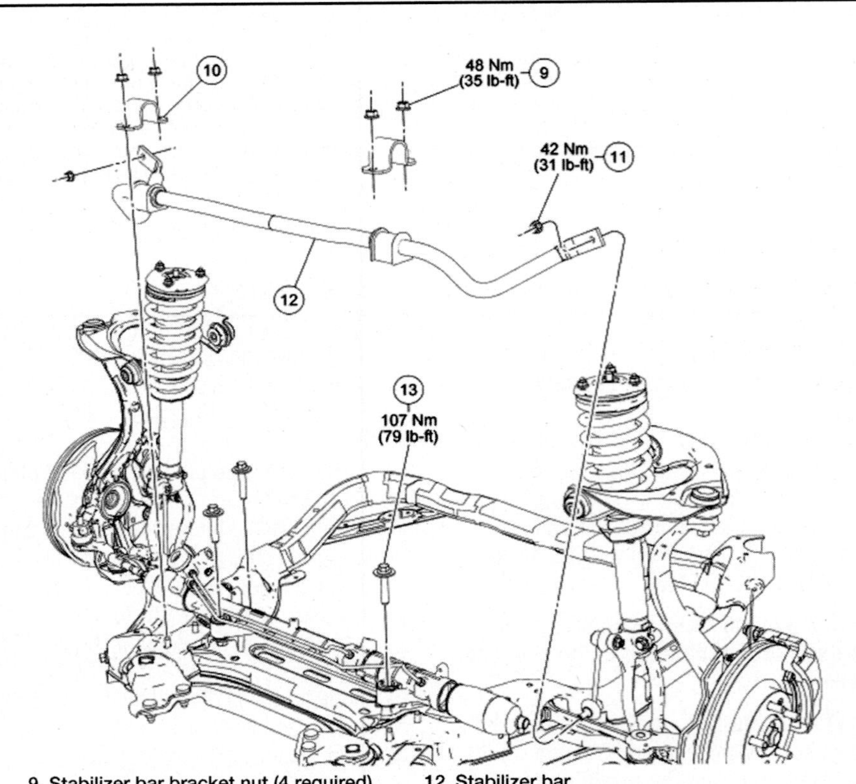

Fig. 365 Removing and installing the stabilizer bar—2 of 3

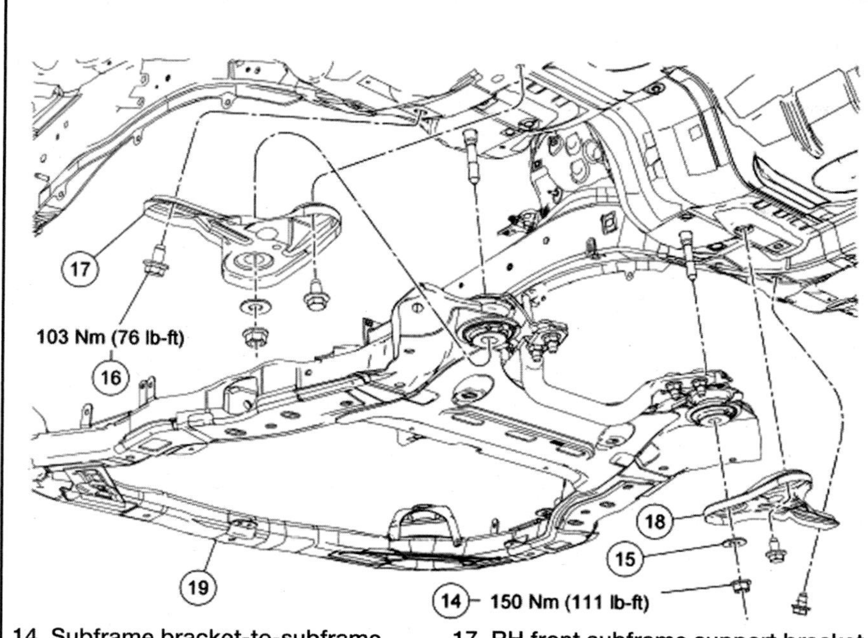

Fig. 366 Removing and installing the stabilizer bar—3 of 3

installed with the same part numbers or equivalent part, if replacement is necessary. Do not use a replacement part of lesser quality or substitute design. Torque values must be used as specified during reassembly to make sure of correct retention of these parts.

All vehicles

➡Do not allow the steering column to rotate while the steering column shaft is disconnected or damage to the clockspring may result. If there is evidence that the lower shaft has rotated, the clockspring must be removed and recentered.

➡Use a steering wheel holding device.

1. Using a suitable holding device, hold the steering wheel in the straight-ahead position.
2. Remove the 2 lower steering column shaft joint cover nuts and cover.

➡Do not allow the steering column shaft to rotate while it is disconnected from the gear or damage to the clockspring can occur. If there is evidence that the steering column shaft has rotated, the clockspring must be removed and recentered.

➡If equipped with Hydraulic Power Assist Steering (HPAS), index-mark the steering column shaft position to the steering gear for reference during installation.

3. Remove the bolt and disconnect the steering column shaft from the steering gear.
   a. To install on HPAS vehicles, align the index marks, tighten to 18 ft. lbs. (25 Nm).
   b. To install on Electronic Power Assist Steering (EPAS) vehicles, tighten to 15 ft. lbs. (20 Nm).

➡Remove the steering column shaft-to-dash seal or damage to the seal can occur.

➡When installing, make sure that the dash seal is correctly positioned on the steering gear and the retaining clips are fully engaged into the body or damage to the steering gear can result.

4. Remove the steering column shaft-to-dash seal.
5. Remove the wheel and tire.
6. Remove the 8 screws and position the LH and RH splash shields aside.
7. Remove the 6 pin-type retainers and the RH splash shield.
8. Remove the 6 pin-type retainers and the LH splash shield.
9. If equipped, remove the 7 screws and the underbody cover shield.
   a. To install, tighten 62 inch lbs. (7 Nm).
10. Remove and discard the 2 tie-rod end cotter pins and nuts.
   a. To install, tighten the new nuts to 35 ft. lbs. (48 Nm) and install new cotter pins.

➡Do not use a hammer to separate the tie-rod end from the wheel knuckle or damage to the wheel knuckle can result.

11. Using the Tie-Rod End Remover, separate the tie-rod ends from the wheel knuckles.

➡Use the hex-holding feature to prevent the ball stud from turning while removing or installing the stabilizer bar link nuts.

12. Remove and discard the 2 stabilizer bar link lower nuts and disconnect both stabilizer bar links from the stabilizer bar.
   a. To install, tighten the new nuts to 31 ft. lbs. (42 Nm).
13. Remove and discard the 2 catalytic converter-to-exhaust flexible pipe nuts and separate the exhaust flexible pipe.
   a. To install, tighten the new nuts to 30 ft. lbs. (40 Nm).

All-Wheel Drive (AWD) vehicles

14. Index-mark the rear driveshaft-to-Power Transfer Unit (PTU).
15. Remove and discard the 4 bolts and position the driveshaft aside.
   a. To install, tighten the new bolts to 52 ft. lbs. (70 Nm).

All vehicles

16. Using 2 suitable jackstands, support the rear of the subframe assembly.
17. Remove and discard the 4 subframe bracket-to-body bolts, the 2 subframe bracket-to-subframe nuts and lower the rear of the subframe.
   a. To install, tighten the new bolts to 76 ft. lbs. (103 Nm).
   b. To install, tighten the new nuts to 111 ft. lbs. (150 Nm).
18. Remove the RH steering gear-to-subframe bolt.
   a. To install, tighten to 79 ft. lbs. (107 Nm).
19. Remove the 2 LH steering gear-to-subframe bolts and position the steering gear to access the stabilizer bar LH bracket front nut.
   a. To install, tighten to 79 ft. lbs. (107 Nm).

20. Remove and discard the 4 stabilizer bar bracket nuts and remove the 2 stabilizer bar brackets.

a. To install, tighten the new bracket nuts to 35 ft. lbs. (48 Nm).

21. Remove the 2 stabilizer bar bushings.

22. Remove the stabilizer bar through the LH wheel opening.

➡**Before tightening the stabilizer bar bracket nuts, the suspension must be at the bushing fastener tightening position. Use a suitable jack to raise the suspension until the distance between the center of the hub and the lip of the fender is equal to 402 mm (15.83 in). This will prevent incorrect clamp load and bushing damage.**

To install:

23. To install, reverse the removal procedure.

STEERING (WHEEL) KNUCKLE

REMOVAL & INSTALLATION

See Figure 367.

➡**Suspension fasteners are critical parts because they affect performance of vital components and systems and their failure may result in major service expense. New parts must be installed with the same part numbers or equivalent part, if replacement is necessary. Do not use a replacement part of lesser quality or substitute design. Torque values must be used as specified during reassembly to make sure of correct retention of these parts.**

1. Remove the wheel and tire.

a. If equipped, remove the wheel speed sensor bolt.

2. If equipped, remove the wheel speed sensor harness bolt and position the wheel speed sensor aside.

3. Remove the brake flexible hose bracket-to-wheel knuckle bolt and position the hose and bracket aside.

➡**Apply the brake to keep the halfshaft from rotating.**

4. Remove and discard the wheel hub nut.

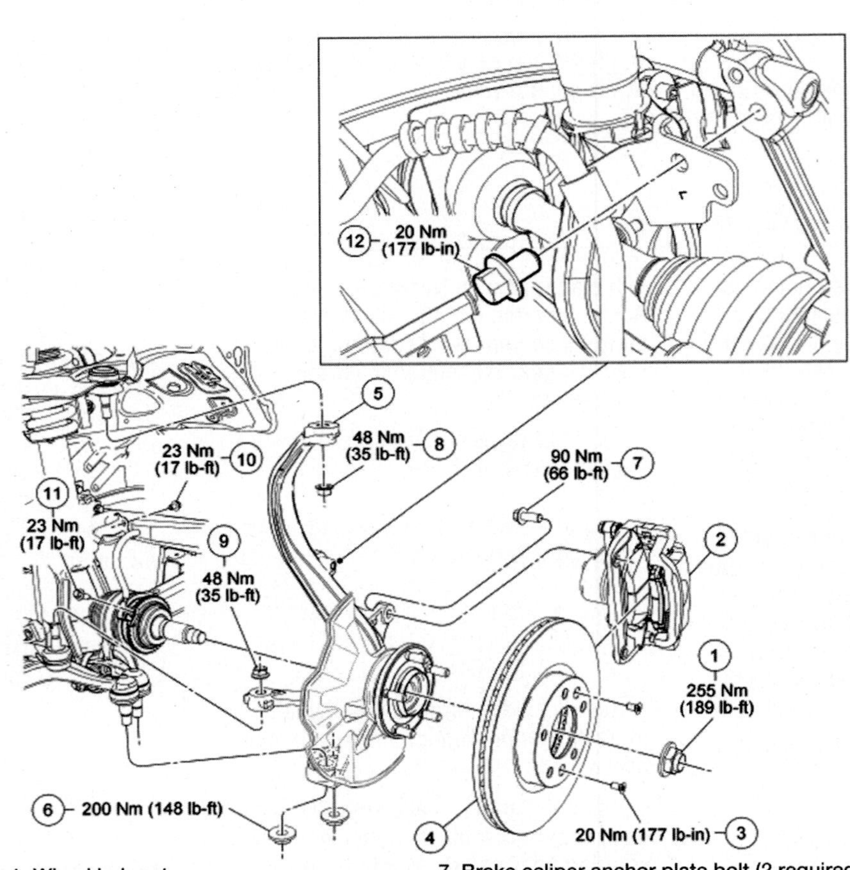

Fig. 367 Removing and installing the wheel knuckle

➡Do not allow the caliper and anchor plate assembly to hang from the brake hose or damage to the hose can occur.

5. Remove the bolts and position the caliper and anchor plate assembly aside.
   a. Support the caliper and anchor plate assembly using mechanic's wire.
6. Remove the 2 brake disc bolts and the brake disc.
7. Using the Front Hub Remover, separate the halfshaft from the wheel hub.
8. Remove and discard the upper ball joint nut.
9. Using the Steering Arm Remover, separate the upper ball joint from the wheel knuckle.
10. Remove and discard the tie-rod end cotter pin and nut.

➡Do not use a hammer to separate the tie-rod end from the wheel knuckle or damage to the wheel knuckle can result.

11. Using the Tie-Rod End Remover, separate the tie-rod end from the wheel knuckle.
12. Remove and discard the 2 lower ball joint nuts.

➡When the lower ball joint is separated from the wheel knuckle, the lower arm may strike the outer Constant Velocity (CV) joint boot with enough force to damage the boot clamp. This will result in a loss of grease from the outer CV joint. Place a block of wood, or similar item, between the lower arm and the outer CV joint to prevent the lower arm from striking the outer CV joint.

➡Once pressure is applied to the ball joint with the Ball Joint Separator and Adapter, it may be necessary to tap the wheel knuckle at the ball joint area to separate the ball joint from the wheel knuckle.

13. Using the Ball Joint Separator and Adapter, separate the 2 lower ball joints from the wheel knuckle and remove the wheel knuckle.

To install:

14. Position the wheel knuckle and install the 2 new lower ball joint nuts.
   a. Tighten to 148 ft. lbs. (200 Nm).
15. Position the tie-rod end and install the new nut and cotter pin.
   a. Tighten to 35 ft. lbs. (48 Nm).
16. Position the upper ball joint and install the new nut.
   a. Tighten to 35 ft. lbs. (48 Nm).
17. If equipped, position the wheel speed sensor and install the bolt.
   a. Tighten to 17 ft. lbs. (23 Nm).
18. If equipped, install the wheel speed sensor harness bolt.
   a. Tighten to 17 ft. lbs. (23 Nm).
19. Position the brake flexible hose bracket and install the bolt.
   a. Tighten to 15 ft. lbs. (20 Nm).
20. Position the brake caliper and anchor plate assembly and install the 2 bolts.
   a. Tighten to 66 ft. lbs. (90 Nm).
21. Install the brake disc and the 2 brake disc bolts.
   a. Tighten to 15 ft. lbs. (20 Nm).
22. Using the Halfshaft Installer, install the halfshaft into the wheel hub.

➡Do not tighten the halfshaft nut with the vehicle on the ground. The nut must be tightened to specification before the vehicle is lowered onto the wheels. Wheel bearing damage will occur if the wheel bearing is loaded with the weight of the vehicle applied.

➡Apply the brake to keep the halfshaft from rotating.

23. Install the wheel hub nut.
   a. Tighten to 189 ft. lbs. (255 Nm).
24. Stack the new nut in line with the keyway to a recommended depth of 1 mm (0.039 in) below the keyway diameter to engage the locking feature.

STRUT & SPRING ASSEMBLY

REMOVAL & INSTALLATION

See Figure 368.

➡Suspension fasteners are critical parts because they affect performance of vital components and systems and their failure may result in major service expense. New parts must be installed with the same part numbers or equivalent part, if replacement is necessary. Do not use a replacement part of lesser quality or substitute design. Torque values must be used as specified during reassembly to make sure of correct retention of these parts.

1. Remove and discard the 3 shock absorber upper mount nuts.
2. Remove the wheel and tire.
3. Remove the wheel speed sensor bolt.
4. Remove the wheel speed sensor harness bolt and position the wheel speed sensor aside.
5. Using a suitable jack, support the wheel knuckle at the lower ball joints.

➡Use the hex-holding feature to prevent the ball stud from turning while removing or installing the stabilizer bar link nut.

6. Remove and discard the stabilizer bar link upper nut.
7. Remove the damper fork-to-front lower arm bolt, flagnut and damper.
   a. Discard the bolt and flagnut.
8. Remove and discard the shock absorber-to-damper fork bolt and separate the damper fork from the shock absorber and spring assembly.
9. Lower the wheel knuckle and remove the shock absorber and spring assembly.

To install:

➡Before tightening any suspension bushing fasteners, the suspension must be at the bushing fastener tightening position. Use a suitable jack to raise the suspension until the distance between the center of the hub and the lip of the fender is equal to 402 mm (15.83 in). This will prevent incorrect clamp load and bushing damage.

10. To install, reverse the removal procedure.
11. Tighten the shock absorber and spring damper bolt to 35 ft. lbs. (48 Nm).
12. Tighten the new flagnut to 76 ft. lbs. (103 Nm) with the suspension at the bushing fastener tightening position.
13. Tighten the new stabilizer bar link upper nut to 31 ft. lbs. (42 Nm).
14. Tighten the wheel speed sensor harness bolt and sensor to 17 ft. lbs. (23 Nm).
15. Tighten the shock absorber upper mounting nuts to 22 ft. lbs. (30 Nm).

UPPER CONTROL ARM

REMOVAL & INSTALLATION

See Figure 369.

➡Suspension fasteners are critical parts because they affect performance of vital components and systems and their failure may result in major service expense. New parts must be installed with the same part numbers or equivalent part, if replacement is necessary. Do not use a replacement part of lesser quality or substitute design. Torque values must be used as specified during reassembly to make sure of correct retention of these parts.

1. Remove and discard the 3 shock absorber upper mount nuts.
2. Remove the wheel and tire.
3. Remove the wheel speed sensor bolt.

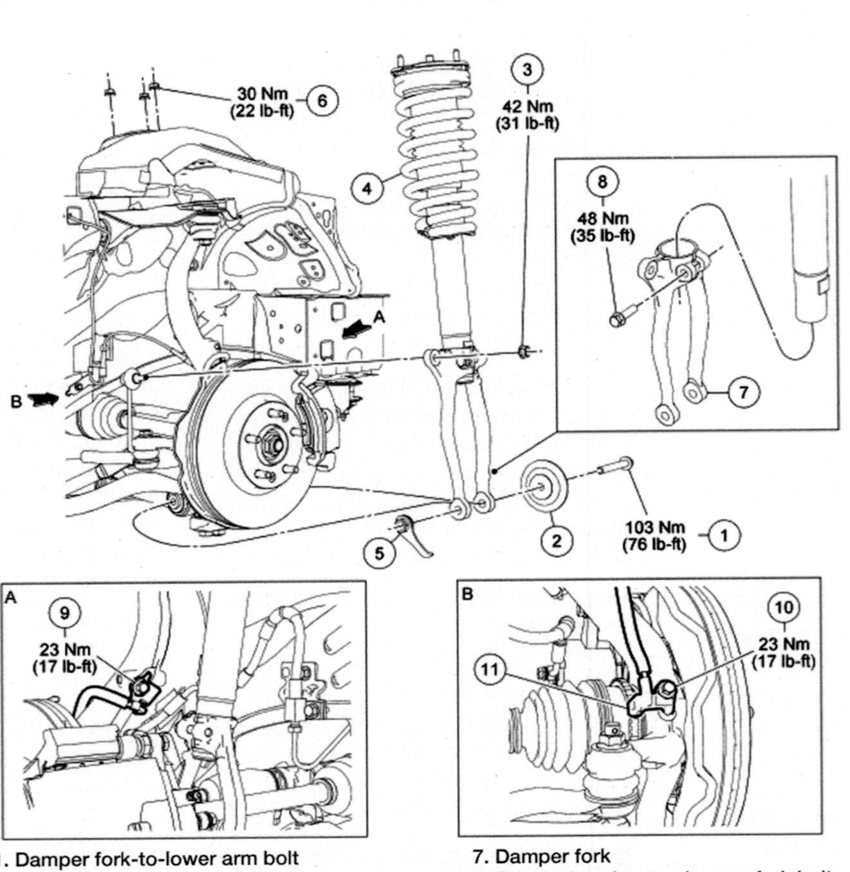

1. Damper fork-to-lower arm bolt
2. Damper
3. Stabilizer bar link upper nut
4. Shock absorber and spring assembly
5. Damper fork-to-lower arm flagnut
6. Shock absorber upper mount nut (3 required)
7. Damper fork
8. Shock absorber-to-damper fork bolt
9. Wheel speed sensor harness bolt
10. Wheel speed sensor bolt
11. Wheel speed sensor

N0097047

Fig. 368 Removing and installing the shock and spring assembly

4. Remove the wheel speed sensor harness bolt and position the wheel speed sensor aside.
5. Remove and discard the upper ball joint nut.
6. Using the Steering Arm Remover, separate the upper ball joint from the wheel knuckle.
7. Position the shock absorber and spring assembly toward the wheel knuckle to access the upper arm-to-body bolts.
8. Remove the 2 upper arm-to-body bolts and the upper arm.
9. Discard the bolts.

To install:

➡Do not tighten the upper arm-to-body bolts at this time.

10. Position the upper arm and install the 2 new upper arm-to-body bolts.
11. Set the upper arm bushing fastener tightening position by aligning the hole in the upper arm with the hole in the body bracket and inserting a 6.35 mm (0.25 in) drill bit through both holes.
    a. Tighten the upper arm-to-body bolts to 41 ft. lbs. (55 Nm) and remove the drill bit.
12. Position the shock and spring assembly and install the 3 new shock upper mount nuts.
    a. Tighten to 22 ft. lbs. (30 Nm).
13. Position the upper ball joint and install a new nut.
    a. Tighten to 35 ft. lbs. (48 Nm).
14. Position the wheel speed sensor harness and install the bolt.
    a. Tighten to 17 ft. lbs. (23 N).
15. Position the wheel speed sensor and install the bolt.
    a. Tighten to 17 ft. lbs. (23 Nm).
16. Install the wheel and tire.
17. Check and, if necessary, align the front end.

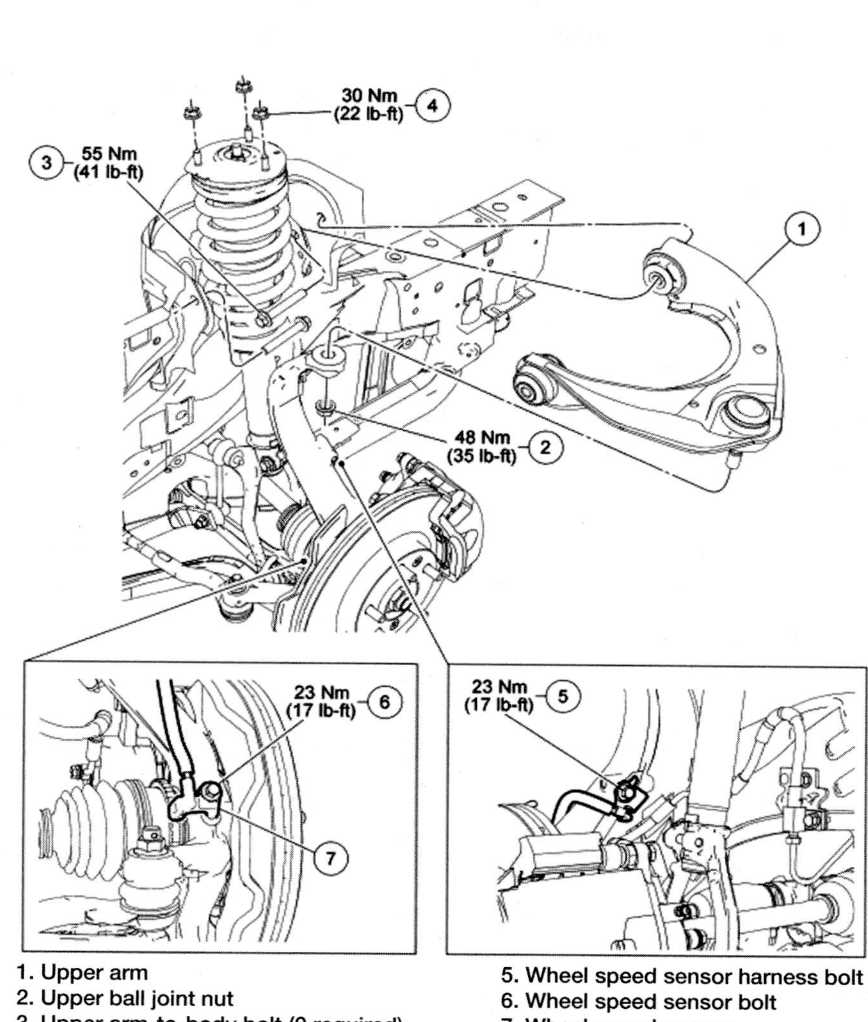

Fig. 369 Removing and installing the upper control arm

WHEEL BEARINGS

REMOVAL & INSTALLATION

See Figure 370.

➡If removing the wheel hub, a new wheel bearing must be installed.

1. Remove the wheel knuckle.
2. Using the Step Plate, press the wheel hub from the wheel bearing.

➡This step may not be necessary if the inner wheel bearing race remains on the wheel hub after removing the wheel hub.

3. If necessary, using the Drive Pinion Bearing Cone Remover, press the inner wheel bearing race from the wheel hub.
4. Remove the snap ring.
5. Using the Wheel Hub Cup Remover/Installer, press the wheel bearing from the wheel knuckle.

To install:

6. Using the Wheel Hub Bearing Cup Installer, press the wheel bearing into the wheel knuckle.
7. Install the snap ring.
8. Using the Step Plate and Wheel Hub Bearing Cup Installer, press the wheel hub into the wheel bearing.
9. Install the wheel knuckle.

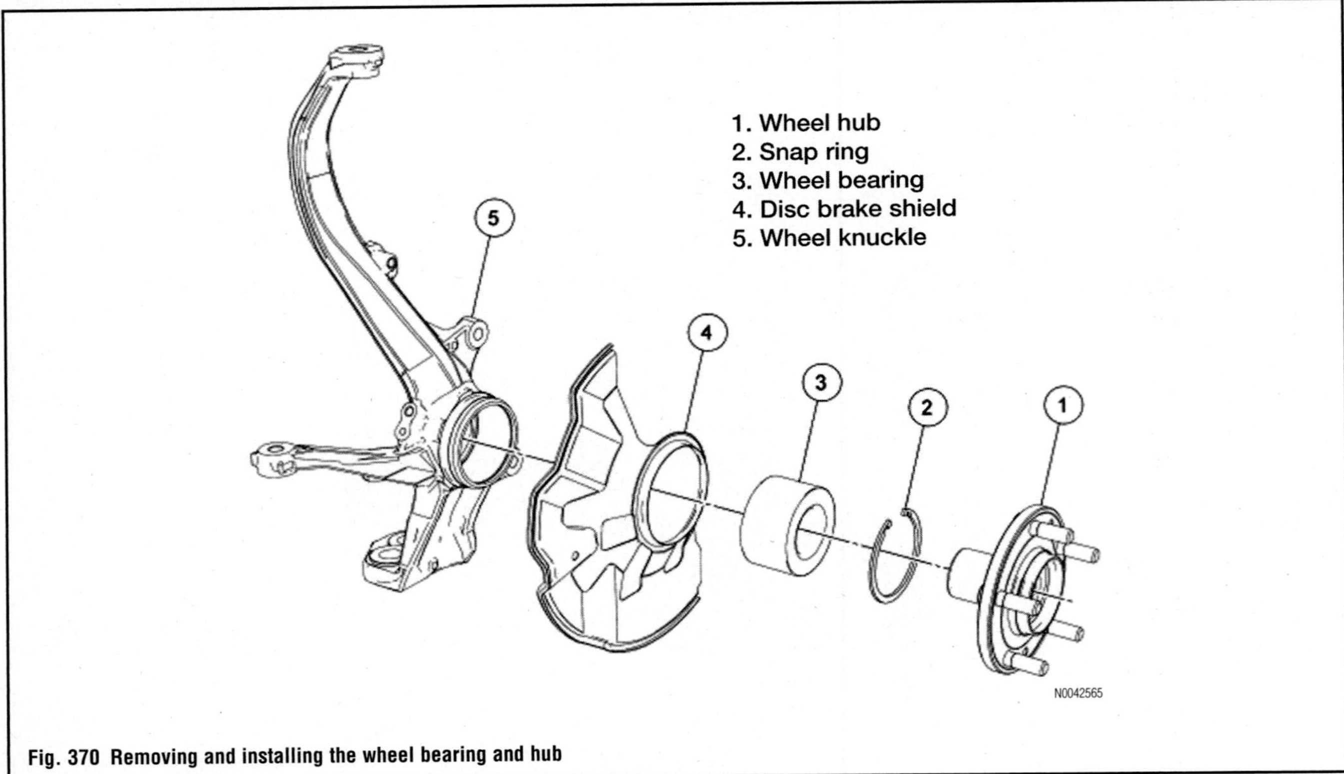

Fig. 370 Removing and installing the wheel bearing and hub

SUSPENSION

REAR SUSPENSION

COIL SPRING

REMOVAL & INSTALLATION

See Figure 371.

➡The coil spring is coated with long-term corrosion protective paint. Do not damage the paint during component servicing or spring damage may occur.

➡Suspension fasteners are critical parts because they affect performance of vital components and systems and their failure may result in major service expense. New parts must be installed with the same part numbers or equivalent part, if replacement is necessary. Do not use a replacement part of lesser quality or substitute design. Torque values must be used as specified during reassembly to make sure of correct retention of these parts.

1. Remove the wheel and tire.

➡Do not fully tighten the cam adjuster nut until the rear alignment has been checked and, if necessary, adjusted.

2. Index-mark the cam bolt and cam adjuster and then loosen the cam adjuster nut.
3. Remove and discard the stabilizer bar link lower bolt.

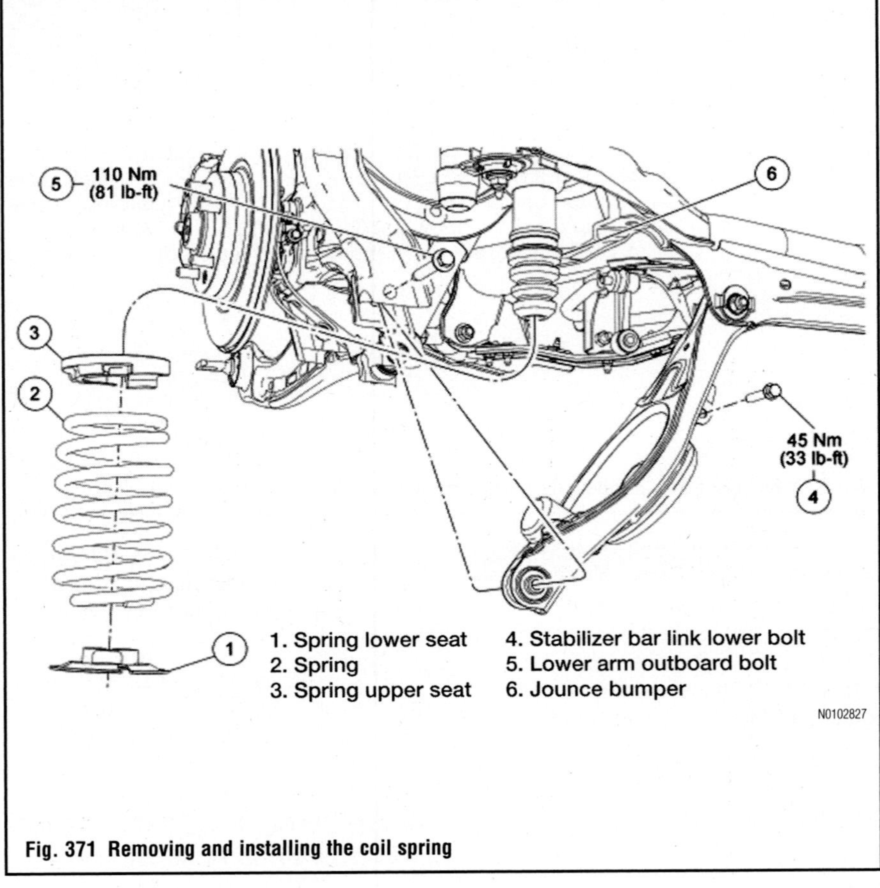

Fig. 371 Removing and installing the coil spring

4. Using a suitable jack, support the lower arm.

⁂ WARNING

The coil spring is under extreme load. Care must be taken at all times when removing or installing a loaded spring. Failure to follow this instruction may result in serious personal injury.

5. Remove and discard the lower arm outboard bolt.
6. Lower the lower arm and remove the spring.
7. Inspect the spring upper and lower seats and install new seats as necessary.

To install:

8. Inspect and if necessary, install a new jounce bumper.
9. Lubricate the top of the new jounce bumper with grease.
10. Position the spring upper seat onto the spring with the end of the spring 0-10 mm (0-0.39 in) from the step on the seat.
11. If removed, position the spring lower seat into the lower arm aligning the recess in the seat with the projection on the lower arm.
12. Position the spring onto the lower arm with the end of the spring 0-10 mm (0-0.39 in) from the step on the spring seat.

➡Do not tighten the bolt at this time.

13. Using the jack, raise the lower arm and install a new lower arm outboard bolt.

➡Before tightening any suspension bushing fasteners, the suspension must be at the bushing fastener tightening position. This will prevent incorrect clamp load and bushing damage.

14. Using the jack, raise the suspension until the distance between the center of the hub and the lip of the fender is equal to 395 mm (15.55 in).
    a. Tighten the lower arm outboard bolt to 81 ft. lbs. (110 Nm).
15. Install a new stabilizer bar link lower bolt.
    a. Tighten to 33 ft. lbs. (45 Nm).
16. Align the index mark on the cam bolt and cam adjuster with the index mark on the lower arm and tighten the cam adjuster nut to 74 ft. lbs. (101 Nm).
17. Check and, if necessary, align the rear end.

LOWER CONTROL ARM

REMOVAL & INSTALLATION

See Figure 372.

➡Suspension fasteners are critical parts because they affect performance of vital components and systems and their failure may result in major service expense. New parts must be installed with the same part numbers or equivalent part, if replacement is necessary. Do not use a replacement part of lesser quality or substitute design. Torque values must be used as specified during reassembly to make sure of correct retention of these parts.

1. Remove the spring.
2. Remove the cam adjuster nut, cam adjuster, cam bolt and the lower arm.
    a. Discard the nut.
    b. To install, tighten the new nut to 74 ft. lbs. (101 Nm) with the suspension at the bushing fastener tightening position.

➡Before tightening any suspension bushing fasteners, the suspension must be at the bushing fastener tightening position. Use a suitable jack to raise the suspension until the distance between the center of the hub and the lip of the fender is equal to 395 mm (15.55 in). This will prevent incorrect clamp load and bushing damage.

➡Do not fully tighten the cam adjuster nut until the rear alignment has been checked and, if necessary, adjusted.

➡Install the cam bolt and the cam adjuster with the cam facing upward.

To install:

3. To install, reverse the removal procedure.

STABILIZER BAR

REMOVAL & INSTALLATION

See Figures 373 and 374.

➡Suspension fasteners are critical parts because they affect performance of vital components and systems and their failure may result in major service expense. New parts must be installed with the same part numbers or equivalent part, if replacement is necessary. Do not use a replacement part of lesser quality or substitute design. Torque values must be used as specified during reassembly to make sure of correct retention of these parts.

All-Wheel Drive (AWD) vehicles

1. Remove the rear halfshafts.
2. Remove the RH side spring.

Front Wheel Drive (FWD) vehicles

3. With the vehicle in NEUTRAL, position it on a hoist.

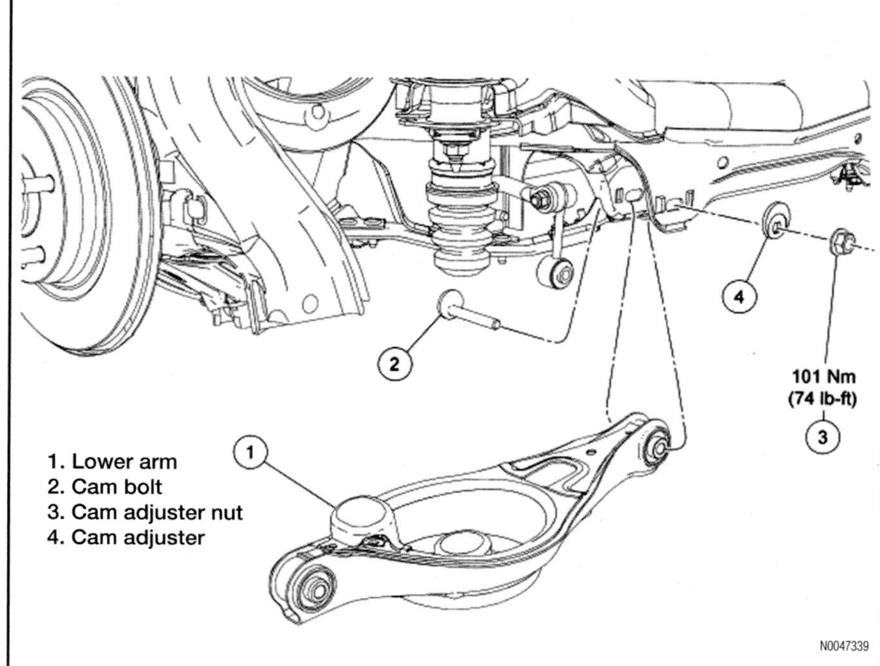

Fig. 372 Removing and installing the lower control arm (Front Wheel Drive (FWD) shown, All-Wheel Drive (AWD) similar)

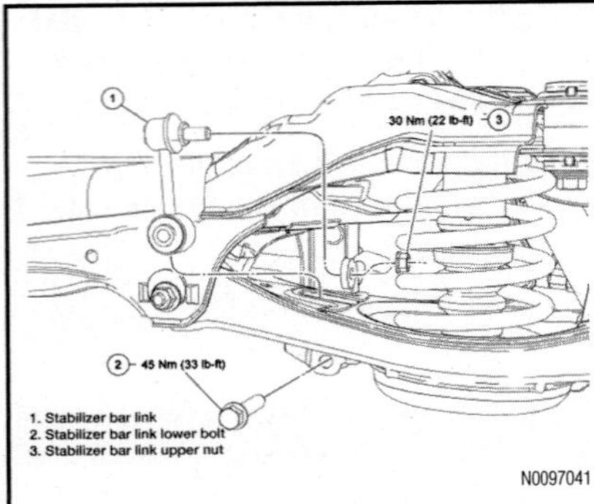

Fig. 373 Removing and installing the stabilizer bar and link (Front Wheel Drive (FWD) shown, All-Wheel Drive (AWD) similar)—1 of 2

All vehicles

4. Remove and discard the 2 stabilizer bar link upper nuts.
   a. To install, tighten the new nuts to 22 ft. lbs. (30 Nm).
5. Remove the 2 stabilizer bar link lower bolts and the stabilizer bar links.
   a. Discard the bolts.
   b. To install, tighten the new bolts to 33 ft. lbs. (45 Nm) with the suspension at the bushing fastener tightening position.
6. Remove and discard the stabilizer bar bracket nuts.
   a. To install, tighten the new nuts to 30 ft. lbs. (40 Nm) with the suspension at the bushing fastener tightening position.
7. Remove the stabilizer bar bracket bolts and the brackets.
   a. Discard the bolts.
   b. To install, tighten the new bolts to 30 ft. lbs. (40 Nm) with the suspension at the bushing fastener tightening position.

FWD vehicles

8. Remove the stabilizer bar.

AWD vehicles

➡Be careful not to contact the fuel lines or wiring harness when removing and installing the stabilizer bar or damage to the wiring harness or fuel lines may occur.

9. Remove the stabilizer bar from the RH side of the vehicle.

All vehicles

10. Inspect the stabilizer bar bushings and install a new bushing(s), if necessary.

➡Before tightening any suspension bushing fasteners, the suspension must be at the bushing fastener tightening position. This will prevent incorrect clamp load and bushing damage.

To install:

11. To install, reverse the removal procedure.

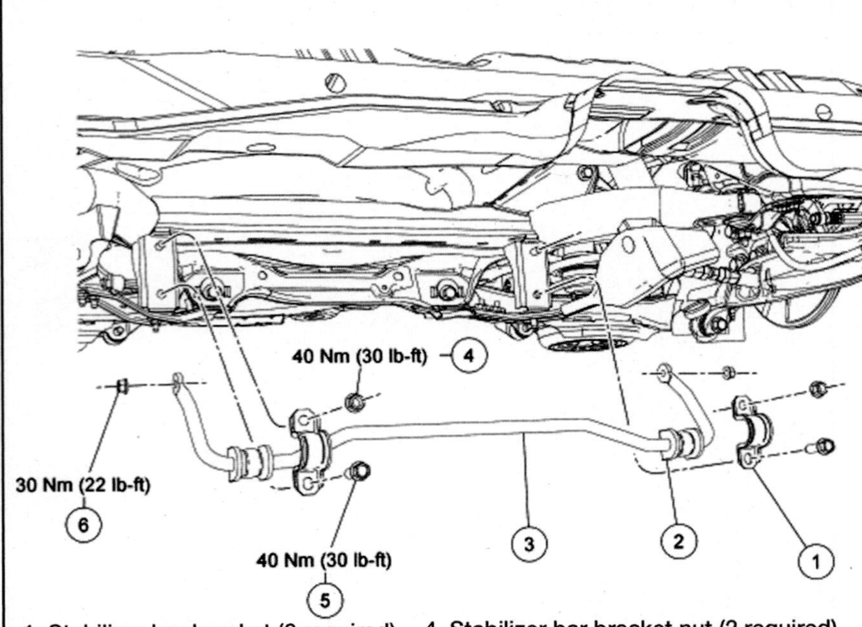

Fig. 374 Removing and installing the stabilizer bar and link (Front Wheel Drive (FWD) shown, All-Wheel Drive (AWD) similar)—2 of 2

TOE LINK

REMOVAL & INSTALLATION

See Figures 375 and 376.

➡Suspension fasteners are critical parts because they affect performance of vital components and systems and their failure may result in major service expense. New parts must be installed with the same part numbers or equivalent part, if replacement is necessary. Do not use a replacement part of lesser quality or substitute design. Torque values must be used as specified during reassembly to make sure of correct retention of these parts.

All vehicles

1. Remove the wheel and tire.

Front Wheel Drive (FWD) vehicles

2. Remove the toe link shield bolt.
   a. To install, tighten to 71 inch lbs. (8 Nm).
3. Remove the pushpin and the shield.

All vehicles

4. Remove and discard the toe link inboard nut and bolt.
   a. To install, tighten the new nut to 81 ft. lbs. (110 Nm) with the suspension at the bushing fastener tightening position.

All-Wheel Drive (AWD) vehicles

5. Remove and discard the toe link outboard nut and bolt and remove the toe link.
   a. To install, tighten the new nut to 66 ft. lbs. (90 Nm) with the suspension at the bushing fastener tightening position.

FWD vehicles

6. Remove the toe link outboard bolt and remove the toe link.
   a. To install, tighten the new bolt to 81 ft. lbs. (110 Nm) with the suspension at the bushing fastener tightening position.

All vehicles

➡Before tightening any suspension bushing fasteners, the suspension must be at the bushing fastener tightening position. Use a suitable jack to raise the suspension until the distance between the center of the hub and the lip of the fender is equal to 395 mm (15.55 in). This will prevent incorrect clamp load and bushing damage.

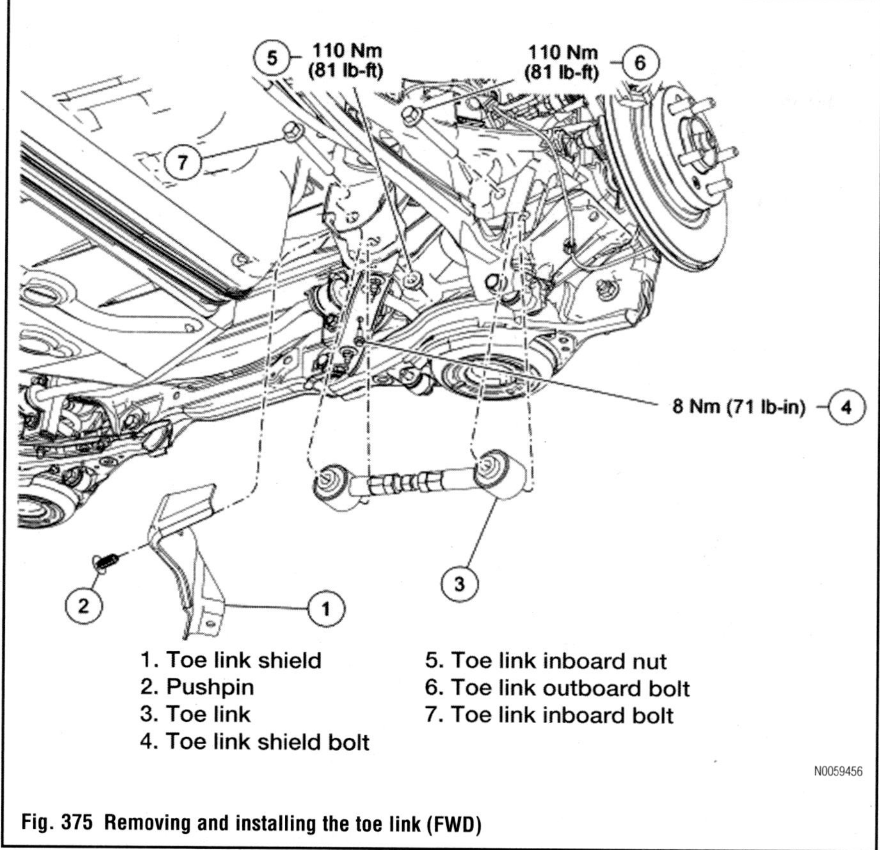

Fig. 375 Removing and installing the toe link (FWD)

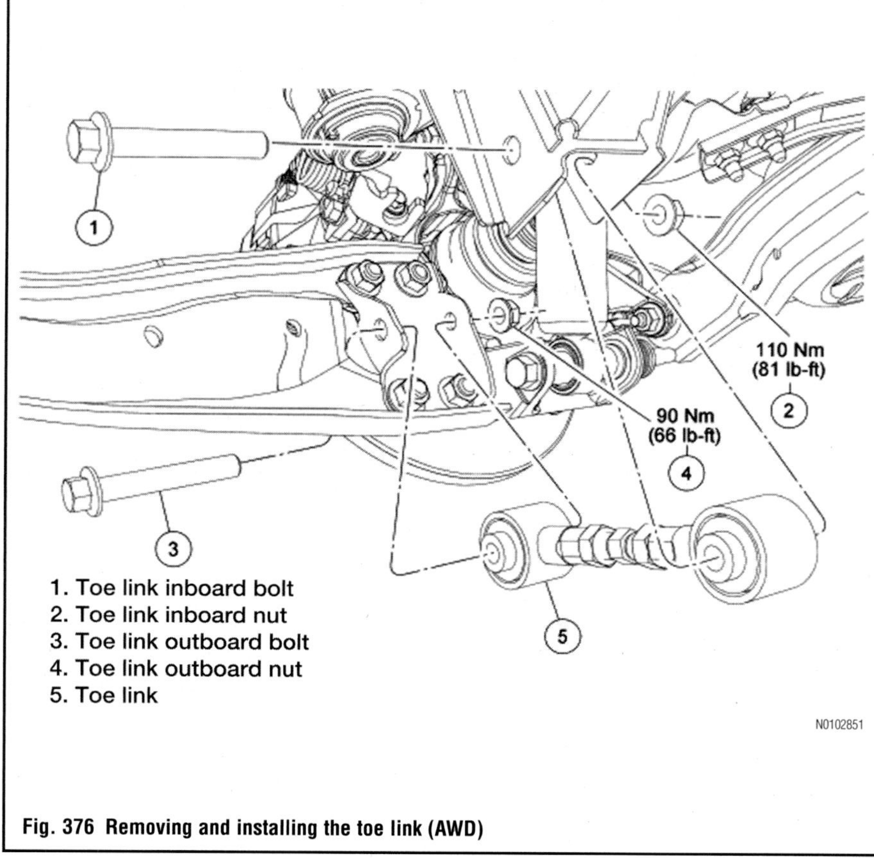

Fig. 376 Removing and installing the toe link (AWD)

To install:

7. To install, reverse the removal procedure.
8. Check and, if necessary, adjust the rear toe.

UPPER CONTROL ARM

REMOVAL & INSTALLATION

See Figures 377 and 378.

➡Suspension fasteners are critical parts because they affect performance of vital components and systems and their failure may result in major service expense. New parts must be installed with the same part numbers or equivalent part, if replacement is necessary. Do not use a replacement part of lesser quality or substitute design. Torque values must be used as specified during reassembly to make sure of correct retention of these parts.

All-Wheel Drive (AWD) vehicles

1. Remove the wheel and tire.

All vehicles

2. Remove the parking brake cable bracket bolt and position the parking brake cable aside.
   a. To install, tighten to 89 inch lbs. (10 Nm).

Front Wheel Drive (FWD) vehicles

3. Remove the wheel spindle.
4. If equipped, detach the wheel speed sensor harness from the trailing arm.
5. Using a suitable jack, support the trailing arm.

WARNING

The coil spring is under extreme load. Care must be taken at all times when removing or installing a loaded spring. Failure to follow this instruction may result in serious personal injury.

6. Remove and discard the lower arm outboard bolt.
   a. To install, tighten the new bolt to 76 ft. lbs. (103 Nm) with the suspension at the bushing fastener tightening position.
7. Remove and discard the upper arm outboard bolt.
   a. To install, tighten the new bolt to 81 ft. lbs. (110 Nm) with the suspension at the bushing fastener tightening position.
8. Carefully lower the trailing arm and remove the jack.
9. Remove and discard the shock absorber lower bolt and flagnut.

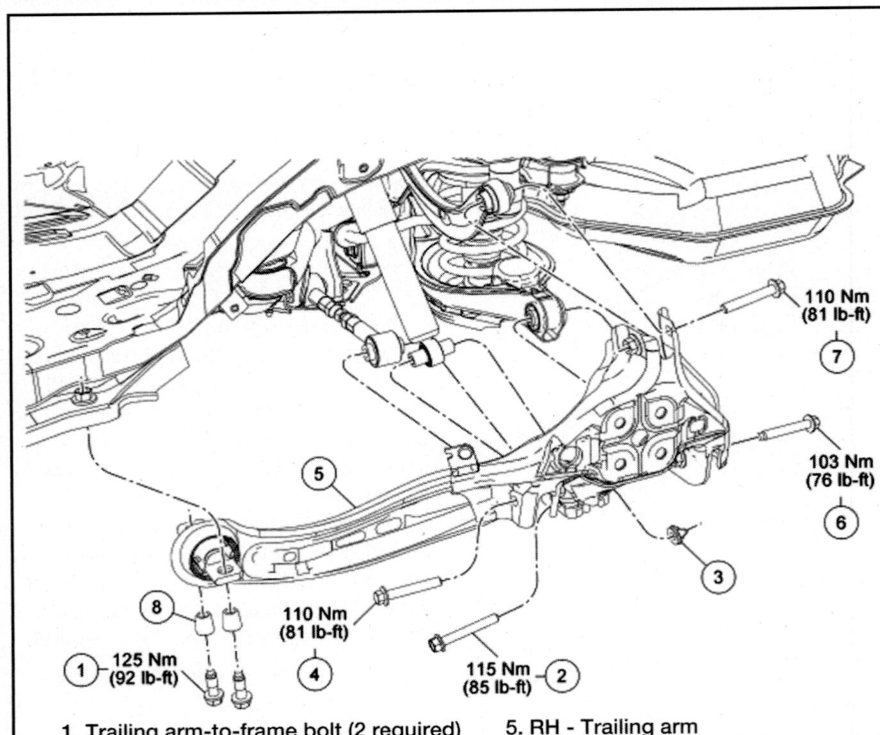

Fig. 377 Removing and installing the trailing arm (FWD)

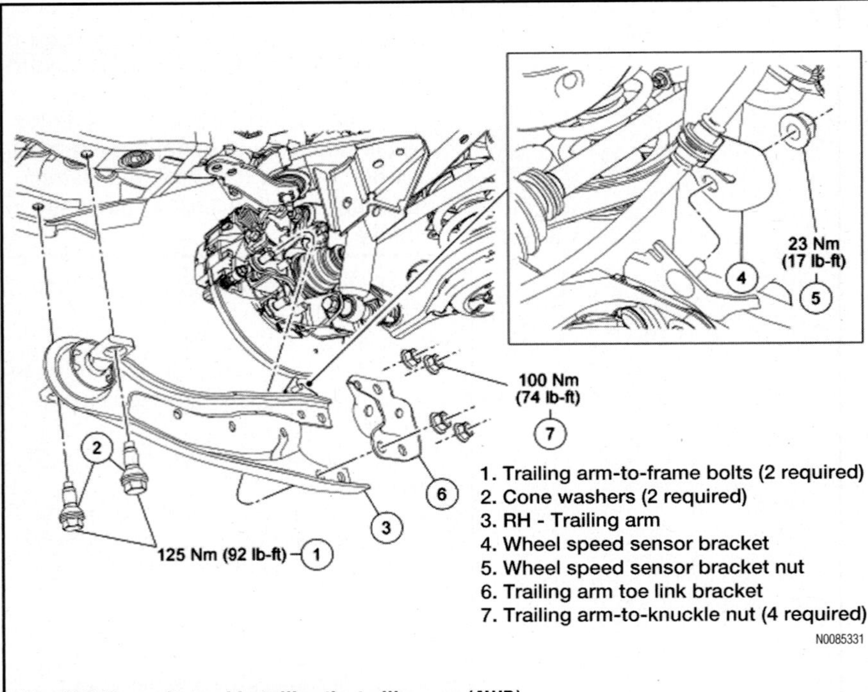

Fig. 378 Removing and installing the trailing arm (AWD)

a. To install, tighten the new bolt and flagnut to 85 ft. lbs. (115 Nm) with the suspension at the bushing fastener tightening position.

10. Remove and discard the toe link outboard bolt.

a. To install, tighten the new bolt to 81 ft. lbs. (110 Nm) with the suspension at the bushing fastener tightening position.

AWD vehicles

11. Remove the wheel speed sensor harness bracket nut and position aside the bracket.

a. To install, tighten to 17 ft. lbs. (23 Nm).

12. Remove the toe link.

13. Remove the 4 trailing arm-to-wheel knuckle nuts and the trailing arm toe link bracket.

a. Discard the nuts.

b. To install, tighten the new nuts to 74 ft. lbs. (100 Nm).

All vehicles

14. Remove the 2 trailing arm-to-frame bolts, cone washers and the trailing arm.

a. Discard the bolts.

b. To install, tighten the new bolts to 92 ft. lbs. (125 Nm).

➡Before tightening any suspension bushing fasteners, the suspension must be at the bushing fastener tightening position. Use a suitable jack to raise the suspension until the distance between the center of the hub and the lip of the fender is equal to 395 mm (15.55 in). This will prevent incorrect clamp load and bushing damage.

To install:

15. To install, reverse the removal procedure.

16. Check and, if necessary, align the rear end.

UPPER CONTROL ARM

REMOVAL & INSTALLATION

See Figures 379 and 380.

➡Suspension fasteners are critical parts because they affect performance of vital components and systems and their failure may result in major service expense. New parts must be installed with the same part numbers or equivalent part, if replacement is necessary. Do not use a replacement part of lesser quality or substitute design. Torque values must be used as specified during reassembly to make sure of correct retention of these parts.

All vehicles

1. Remove the wheel and tire.
2. Using a suitable jack, support the trailing arm.

➡**Do not fully tighten the shock absorber lower nut until the suspension is at the bushing fastener tightening position. This will prevent incorrect clamp load and bushing damage.**

3. Remove and discard the shock absorber lower bolt and flagnut.
    a. To install, tighten the new bolt and flagnut to 66 ft. lbs. (90 Nm), All-Wheel Drive (AWD) vehicles.
    b. To install, tighten the new bolt and flagnut to 85 ft. lbs. (115 Nm), Front Wheel Drive (FWD) vehicles.

Front Wheel Drive (FWD) vehicles

4. Remove and discard the upper arm outboard bolt.
    a. To install, tighten the new bolt to 81 ft. lbs. (110 Nm) with the suspension at the bushing fastener tightening position.

All-Wheel Drive (AWD) vehicles

5. Remove and discard the upper arm outboard bolt and nut.
    a. To install, tighten the new nut and bolt to 81 ft. lbs. (110 Nm) with the suspension at the bushing fastener tightening position.

All vehicles

6. Carefully lower the trailing arm and remove the jack.

➡**Position the shock absorber as necessary to remove the upper arm.**

➡**When tightening the upper arm inboard bolt, the suspension must be at the bushing fastener tightening position.**

7. Remove and discard the upper arm inboard bolt and remove the upper arm.
    a. To install, tighten the new bolt to 74 ft. lbs. (100 Nm) and then rotate an additional 90 degrees.

➡**Before tightening any suspension bushing fasteners, the suspension must be at the bushing fastener tightening position. Use a suitable jack to raise the suspension until the distance between the center of the hub and the lip of the fender is equal to 395 mm (15.55 in). This will prevent incorrect clamp load and bushing damage.**

To install:

    b. To install, reverse the removal procedure.

8. Check and, if necessary, adjust the rear camber.

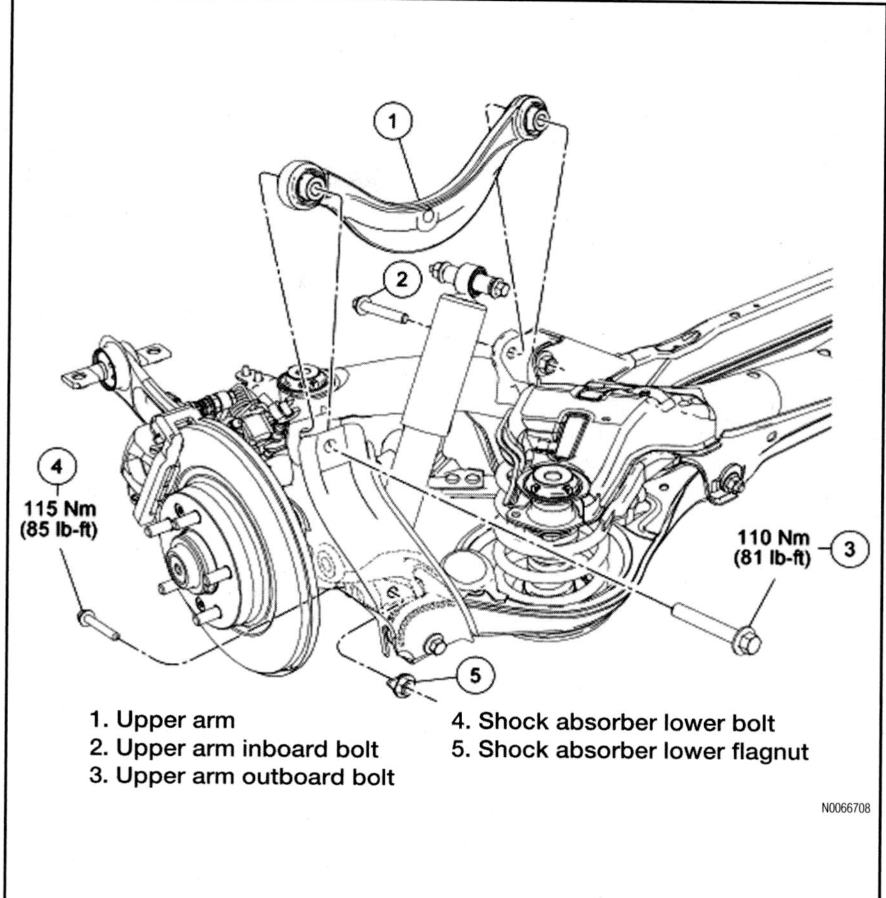

Fig. 379 Removing and installing the upper control arm—1 of 2

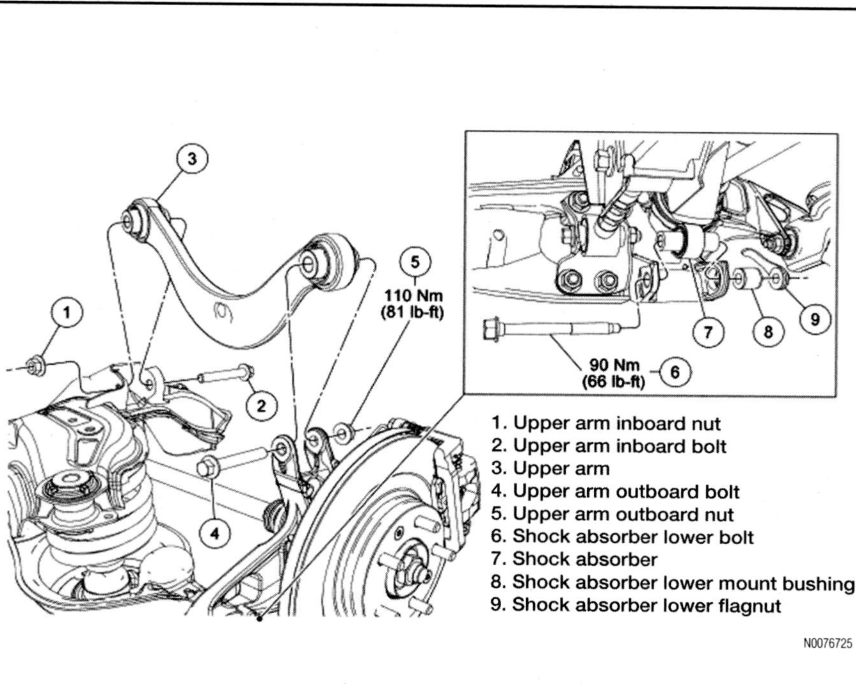

Fig. 380 Removing and installing the upper control arm—2 of 2

WHEEL BEARINGS

REMOVAL & INSTALLATION

See Figures 381 and 382.

➡Suspension fasteners are critical parts because they affect performance of vital components and systems and their failure may result in major service expense. New parts must be installed with the same part numbers or equivalent part, if replacement is necessary. Do not use a replacement part of lesser quality or substitute design. Torque values must be used as specified during reassembly to make sure of correct retention of these parts.

Front Wheel Drive (FWD) vehicles

1. Remove the wheel and tire.
2. Remove the wheel speed sensor bolt and position the sensor aside.
3. Disconnect the parking brake cable from the brake caliper in the following sequence.
4. Remove the clip.
5. Disconnect the parking brake cable from the brake caliper.

➡Do not allow the brake caliper and anchor plate assembly to hang from the brake hose or damage to the hose can occur.

6. Remove the anchor plate bolts and position the brake caliper and anchor plate assembly aside.
   a. Support the brake caliper and anchor plate assembly using mechanic's wire.
7. Remove the 2 brake disc bolts and the brake disc.
   a. Remove and discard the grease cap.
8. Remove and discard the wheel hub nut and remove the wheel hub and bearing assembly.

All-Wheel Drive (AWD) vehicles

9. Remove the wheel knuckle.
10. Using the Step Plate, press the wheel hub from the wheel bearing.

➡This step may be necessary if the inner wheel bearing race remains in the wheel knuckle after removing the wheel hub.

11. Install the Drive Pinion Bearing Cone Remover, position in a suitable press and press the inner wheel bearing race from the wheel hub.

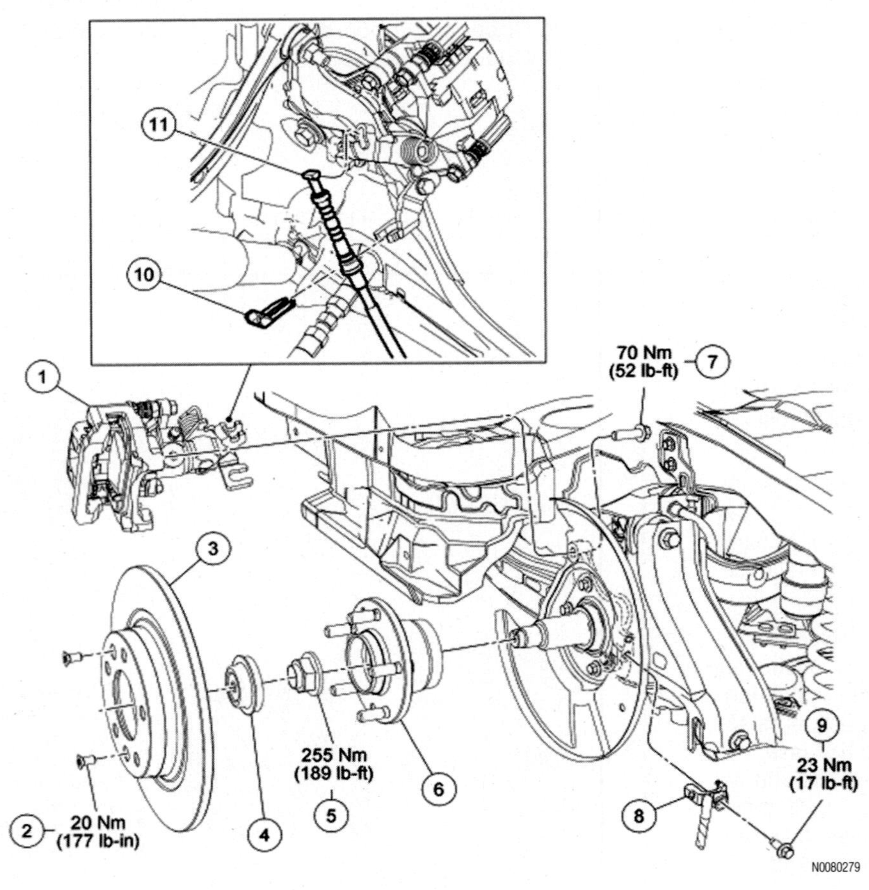

Fig. 381 Removing and installing the wheel bearing and hub—FWD

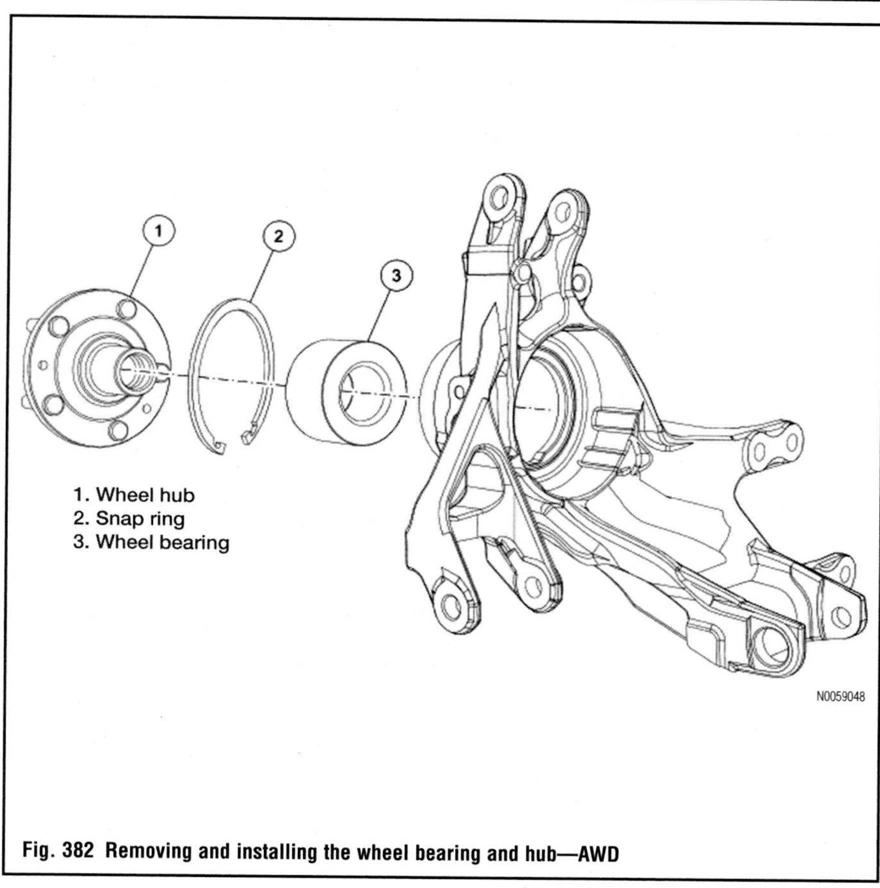

Fig. 382 Removing and installing the wheel bearing and hub—AWD

12. Remove the snap ring.
13. Using the Wheel Bearing Cup Remover/Installer, press the outer wheel bearing race from the wheel knuckle.

To install:

AWD vehicles

14. Using the Wheel Bearing Cup Installer, press the wheel bearing into the wheel knuckle.
15. Using the Wheel Bearing Cup Installer and Step Plate, press the wheel hub into the wheel bearing.
16. Install the wheel knuckle.

FWD vehicles

17. Position the wheel speed sensor and install the bolt.
    a. Tighten to 17 ft. lbs. (23 Nm).
18. Install the brake disc and the 2 brake disc bolts.
    a. Tighten to 15 ft. lbs. (20 Nm).
19. Position the brake caliper and install the brake caliper anchor plate bolts.
    a. Tighten to 52 ft. lbs. (70 Nm).

➡Do not tighten the rear wheel hub nut with the vehicle on the ground. The nut must be tightened to specification before the vehicle is lowered onto the wheels. Wheel bearing damage will occur if the bearing is loaded with the weight of the vehicle applied.

20. Install the new wheel hub and bearing and a new wheel hub nut.
    a. While applying the brakes to keep the halfshaft from rotating, tighten to 189 ft. lbs. (255 Nm).
21. Connect the parking brake cable to the brake caliper in the following sequence.
22. Install the clip.
23. Connect the parking brake cable to the brake caliper.
24. Install the wheel and tire

WHEEL SPINDLE

REMOVAL & INSTALLATION

See Figure 383.

➡Suspension fasteners are critical parts because they affect performance of vital components and systems and their failure may result in major service expense. New parts must be installed with the same part numbers

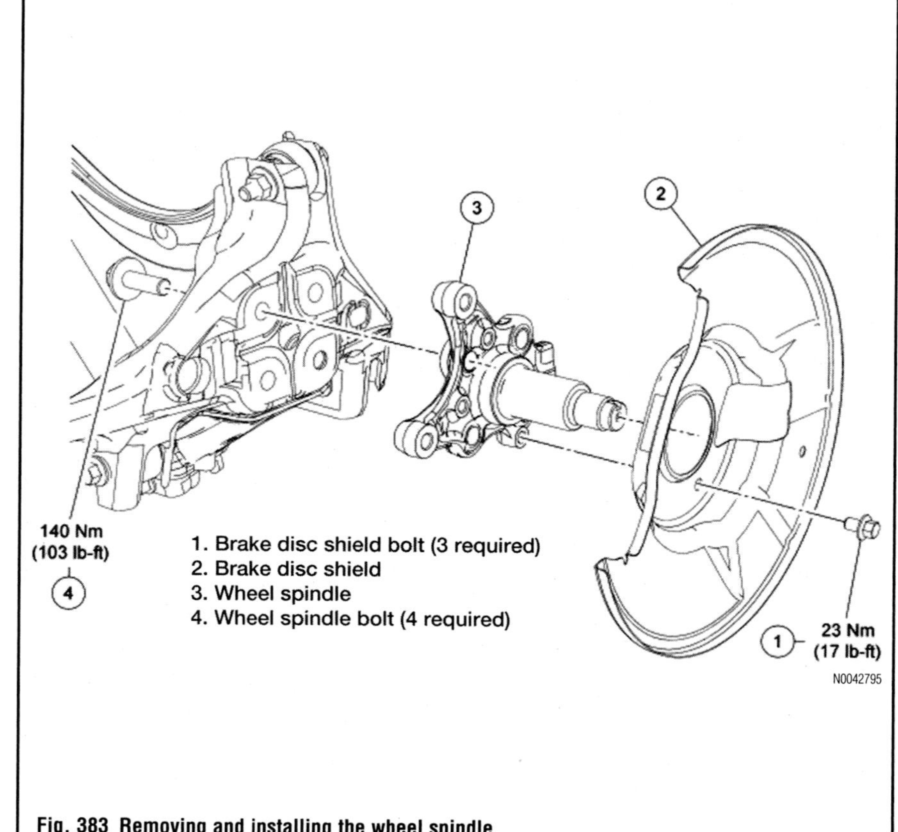

Fig. 383 Removing and installing the wheel spindle

or equivalent part, if replacement is necessary. Do not use a replacement part of lesser quality or substitute design. Torque values must be used as specified during reassembly to make sure of correct retention of these parts.

1. Remove the wheel bearing and wheel hub assembly.
2. Remove the 3 brake disc shield bolts and remove the brake disc shield.
    a. To install, tighten to 17 ft. lbs. (23 Nm).
3. Remove and discard the 4 wheel spindle bolts and remove the wheel spindle.
    a. To install, tighten the new bolts to 103 ft. lbs. (140 Nm).

To install:

4. To install, reverse the removal procedure.

LINCOLN

MKS

13

BRAKES 13-12

ANTI-LOCK BRAKE SYSTEM (ABS)..........................13-12
General Information.................13-12
Precautions.........................13-12
Speed Sensors........................13-12
Removal & Installation........13-12
BLEEDING THE BRAKE SYSTEM 13-14
Bleeding Procedure.................13-14
Bleeding Procedure 13-14
Bleeding the ABS System ...13-15
Master Cylinder Bleeding ...13-14
FRONT DISC BRAKES........13-15
Brake Caliper..........................13-15
Removal & Installation........13-15
Disc Brake Pads......................13-15
Removal & Installation........13-15
PARKING BRAKE..............13-17
Parking Brake Cables.............13-17
Adjustment 13-17
REAR DISC BRAKES 13-16
Brake Caliper..........................13-16
Removal & Installation........13-16
Disc Brake Pads......................13-16
Removal & Installation........13-16

CHASSIS ELECTRICAL 13-17

AIR BAG (SUPPLEMENTAL RESTRAINT SYSTEM) 13-17
General Information.................13-17
Arming the System 13-17
Clockspring Centering........13-18
Disarming the System.........13-17
Service Precautions............13-17

DRIVE TRAIN 13-19

Automatic Transaxle Fluid.......13-19
Drain and Refill...................13-19
Front Halfshaft.........................13-22
Removal & Installation........13-22
Power Transfer Unit (PTU).......13-20
Removal & Installation........13-20
Rear Axle Fluid........................13-26
Drain & Refill......................13-26
Rear Axle Housing...................13-26
Removal & Installation........13-26
Rear Axle Stub Shaft Seal........13-27
Removal & Installation........13-27
Rear Differential Housing Cover 13-27
Removal & Installation........13-27
Rear Driveshaft........................13-29
Removal & Installation........13-29
Rear Halfshaft..........................13-30
Removal & Installation........13-30
Rear Pinion Seal.....................13-32
Removal & Installation........13-32

ENGINE COOLING...........13-33

Engine Coolant........................13-33
Draining, Filling and Bleeding Procedure..........13-33
Flushing.............................13-33
Engine Fan 13-34
Removal & Installation........13-34
Radiator..................................13-36
Removal & Installation........13-36
Thermostat 13-37
Removal & Installation........13-37
Water Pump (Coolant Pump)....13-38
Removal & Installation........13-38

ENGINE ELECTRICAL.......13-41

BATTERY SYSTEM............13-41
Battery....................................13-41
Battery Reconnect/Relearn Procedure.........................13-41
Removal & Installation........13-41
CHARGING SYSTEM 13-42
Alternator 13-42
Removal & Installation........13-42
IGNITION SYSTEM 13-43
Firing Order.............................13-43
Ignition Coil 13-43
Removal & Installation........13-43
Spark Plugs.............................13-44
Removal & Installation........13-44
STARTING SYSTEM 13-46
Starter 13-46
Removal & Installation........13-46

ENGINE MECHANICAL......13-47

Accessory Drive Belts 13-47
Accessory Belt Routing.......13-47
Adjustment 13-47
Inspection 13-47
Removal & Installation........13-47
Air Cleaner 13-49
Removal & Installation........13-49
Catalytic Converter..................13-50
Removal & Installation........13-50
Crankshaft Front Seal..............13-52
Removal & Installation........13-52
Cylinder Head 13-52
Removal & Installation........13-52
Exhaust Manifold 13-60
Removal & Installation........13-60
Intake Manifold 13-63
Removal & Installation........13-63
Oil Pan 13-68
Removal & Installation........13-68
Oil Pump.................................13-77
Removal & Installation........13-77
Piston and Ring.......................13-77
Positioning 13-77
Rear Main Seal........................13-77
Removal & Installation........13-77
Timing Chain & Sprockets......13-83
Removal & Installation........13-83
Timing Chain Front Cover.......13-78
Removal & Installation........13-78
Turbocharger 13-86
Removal & Installation........13-86
Valve Covers 13-92
Removal & Installation........13-92

ENGINE PERFORMANCE & EMISSION CONTROLS 13-97

Camshaft Position (CMP) Sensor 13-97
Location..............................13-97
Removal & Installation........13-97
Crankshaft Position (CKP) Sensor 13-97
Location..............................13-97
Removal & Installation........13-97

Heated Oxygen (HO2S) Sensor 13-98
Location 13-98
Removal & Installation 13-98
Intake Air Temperature (IAT) Sensor 13-98
Location 13-98
Removal & Installation 13-98
Knock Sensor (KS) 13-99
Location 13-99
Removal & Installation 13-99
Manifold Absolute Pressure (MAP) Sensor 13-100
Location 13-100
Removal & Installation 13-100
Powertrain Control Module (PCM) 13-100
Location 13-100
Passive Anti-Theft System (PATS) Parameter Reset Procedure 13-101
Programmable Module Installation (PMI) Procedure Using Integrated Diagnostic System (IDS) 13-101
Removal & Installation 13-100
Throttle Position Sensor (TPS) 13-102
Location 13-102
Removal & Installation 13-102

FUEL 13-103

GASOLINE FUEL INJECTION SYSTEM 13-103
Fuel Injectors 13-103
Removal & Installation 13-103
Fuel Pump 13-106
Removal & Installation 13-106
Fuel System Service Precautions 13-103
Fuel Tank 13-109
Draining 13-109
Removal & Installation 13-111
Relieving Fuel System Pressure 13-103
Throttle Body 13-111
Removal & Installation 13-111

HEATING & AIR CONDITIONING SYSTEM 13-114
Blower Motor 13-114
Removal & Installation 13-114
Heater Core 13-115
Removal & Installation 13-115

PRECAUTIONS 13-12

SPECIFICATIONS AND MAINTENANCE CHARTS 13-3
Brake Specifications 13-7
Camshaft Specifications 13-5
Capacities 13-4
Crankshaft and Connecting Rod Specifications 13-5
Engine and Vehicle Identification 13-3
Engine Tune-Up Specifications 13-3
Fluid Specifications 13-4
General Engine Specifications 13-3
Piston and Ring Specifications 13-6
Scheduled Maintenance Intervals 13-8
Tire, Wheel and Ball Joint Specifications 13-7
Torque Specifications 13-6
Valve Specifications 13-4
Wheel Alignment 13-6

STEERING 13-117
Power Steering Gear 13-117
Removal & Installation 13-117
Power Steering Pump 13-118
Fluid Fill Procedure 13-121
Power Steering System Flushing 13-120
Power Steering System Purging 13-121
Removal & Installation 13-118

SUSPENSION 13-122

FRONT SUSPENSION 13-122
Control Links 13-122
Removal & Installation 13-122
Lower Control Arm 13-122
Control Arm Bushing Replacement 13-123
Removal & Installation 13-122
Stabilizer Bar 13-123
Removal & Installation 13-123
Steering Knuckle 13-124
Removal & Installation 13-124
Strut & Spring Assembly 13-125
Removal & Installation 13-125
Wheel Bearings 13-127
Removal & Installation 13-127

REAR SUSPENSION 13-127
Coil Spring 13-127
Removal & Installation 13-127
Control Links 13-128
Removal & Installation 13-128
Lower Control Arm 13-128
Removal & Installation 13-128
Shock Absorber 13-128
Removal & Installation 13-128
Stabilizer Bar 13-129
Removal & Installation 13-129
Steering Knuckle 13-129
Removal & Installation 13-129
Toe Link 13-131
Removal & Installation 13-131
Trailing Arm 13-132
Removal & Installation 13-132
Upper Control Arm 13-133
Removal & Installation 13-133
Wheel Bearings 13-134
Removal & Installation 13-134

SPECIFICATIONS AND MAINTENANCE CHARTS

ENGINE AND VEHICLE IDENTIFICATION

Engine						
Code ①	Liters (cc)	Cu. In.	Cyl.	Fuel Sys.	Engine Type	Eng. Mfg.
T	3.5	214	V6	Direct Inj.	DOHC	Ford
R	3.7	226	V6	Direct Inj.	DOHC	Ford

Model Year	
Code ②	Year
A	2010
B	2011

① 8th position of VIN

② 10th position of VIN

25759_LMKS_C0001

GENERAL ENGINE SPECIFICATIONS

All measurements are given in inches.

Year	Model	Engine Displacement Liters	Engine ID/VIN	Fuel System Type	Net Horsepower @ rpm	Net Torque @ rpm (ft. lbs.)	Bore x Stroke (in.)	Com-pression Ratio	Oil Pressure @ rpm
2010	MKS	3.5	T	Dir Inj	355@5700	350@3500	3.64x3.41	10:01	30@1500
		3.7	R	Dir Inj	273@6250	270@4250	3.76x3.41	10.3:1	30@1500
2011	MKS	3.5	T	Dir Inj	355@5700	350@3500	3.64x3.41	10:01	30@1500
		3.7	R	Dir Inj	273@6250	270@4250	3.76x3.41	10.3:1	30@1500

25759_LMKS_C0002

ENGINE TUNE-UP SPECIFICATIONS

Year	Engine Displacement Liters	Engine ID/VIN	Spark Plug Gap (in.)	Ignition Timing (deg.)		Fuel Pump (psi)	Idle Speed (rpm)		Valve Clearance (in.)	
				MT	AT		MT	AT	Intake	Exhaust
2010	3.5	T	0.35	NA	NA	65	NA	①	0.006-0.010	0.014-0.018
	3.7	R	0.51-0.57	NA	NA	65	NA	①	0.006-0.010	0.014-0.018
2011	3.5	T	0.35	NA	NA	65	NA	①	0.006-0.010	0.014-0.018
	3.7	R	0.51-0.57	NA	NA	65	NA	①	0.006-0.010	0.014-0.018

NA Not Applicable

① Idle speed is computer controlled and is not adjustable.

25759_LMKS_C0003

CAPACITIES

Year	Model	Engine Displacement Liters	Engine ID/VIN	Engine Oil with Filter (qts.)	Transmission/axle (pts.) Auto.	Transmission/axle (pts.) Manual	Drive Axle (pts.) Front	Drive Axle (pts.) Rear	Transfer Case (pts.)	Fuel Tank (gal.)	Cooling System (qts.)
2010	MKS	3.5	T	6.0	①	NA	NA	2.43	1.125	19.0	11.0
		3.7	R	5.5	①	NA	NA	2.43	1.125	19.0	11.0
2011	MKS	3.5	T	6.0	①	NA	NA	2.43	1.125	19.0	11.0
		3.7	R	5.5	①	NA	NA	2.43	1.125	19.0	11.0

NOTE: All capacities are approximate. Add fluid gradually and ensure a proper fluid level is obtained.

① Transaxle Overhaul: 13.0 pts., Transaxle Drain and Refill: 9.0 pts.

25759_LMKS_C0004

FLUID SPECIFICATIONS

Year	Model	Engine Disp. Liters	Engine Oil	Manual Trans.	Auto. Trans.	Drive Axle Rear	Transfer Case	Power Steering Fluid	Brake Master Cylinder	Cooling System
2010	MKS	3.5	5W-20	NA	①	80W-90	75W-140	②	③	④
		3.7	5W-20	NA	①	80W-90	75W-140	②	③	④
2011	MKS	3.5	5W-20	NA	①	80W-90	75W-140	②	③	④
		3.7	5W-20	NA	①	80W-90	75W-140	②	③	④

DOT: Department Of Transpotation

① Motorcraft® MERCON® LV

② Motorcraft® MERCON® V

③ DOT 3 or equivalent

④ Motorcraft® Specialty Green Engine Coolant

25759_LMKS_C0005

VALVE SPECIFICATIONS

Year	Engine Displacement Liters	Engine ID/VIN	Seat Angle (deg.)	Face Angle (deg.)	Spring Test Pressure (lbs. @ in.)	Spring Free-Length (in.)	Spring Installed Height (in.)	Stem-to-Guide Clearance (in.) Intake	Stem-to-Guide Clearance (in.) Exhaust	Stem Diameter (in.) Intake	Stem Diameter (in.) Exhaust
2010	3.5	T	44.5-45.5	44.5-45.5	60 lb @ 1.45	2.170	1.450	0.0008-0.0027	0.0013-0.0320	0.2157-0.2164	0.2151-0.2159
	3.7	R	44.5-45.5	44.5-45.5	53 lb @ 1.45	1.900	1.450	0.0008-0.0027	0.0013-0.0320	0.2157-0.2164	0.2151-0.2159
2011	3.5	T	44.5-45.5	44.5-45.5	60 lb @ 1.45	1.900	1.450	0.0008-0.0027	0.0013-0.0320	0.2157-0.2164	0.2151-0.2159
	3.7	R	44.5-45.5	44.5-45.5	53 lb @ 1.45	1.900	1.450	0.0008-0.0027	0.0013-0.0320	0.2157-0.2164	0.2151-0.2159

25759_LMKS_C0006

CAMSHAFT SPECIFICATIONS

All measurements in inches unless noted

Year	Engine Displacement Liters	Engine Code/VIN	Journal Diameter	Brg. Oil Clearance	Shaft End-play	Runout	Journal Bore	Lobe Height	
								Intake	Exhaust
2010	3.5	T	①	②	0.0012-0.0066	0.0015	③	0.35	0.36
	3.7	R	①	②	0.0012-0.0066	0.0015	③	0.38	0.38
2011	3.5	T	①	②	0.0012-0.0066	0.0015	③	0.35	0.36
	3.7	R	①	②	0.0012-0.0066	0.0015	③	0.38	0.38

① Journal Diameter 1st: 1.2202-1.2209, Journal Diameter Intermediate: 1.021-1.022

② Journal Bearing Clearance 1st: 0.0027, Journal Bearing Clearance Intermediate: 0.0029

③ Journal Bore Diameter 1st: 1.221-1.222, Journal Bore Diameter Intermediate: 1.023-1.024

25759_LMKS_C0007

CRANKSHAFT AND CONNECTING ROD SPECIFICATIONS

All measurements are given in inches.

Year	Engine Displacement Liters	Engine ID/VIN	Crankshaft				Connecting Rod		
			Main Brg. Journal Dia.	Main Brg. Oil Clearance	Shaft End-play	Thrust on No.	Journal Diameter	Oil Clearance	Side Clearance
2010	3.5	T	2.6570	0.0010-0.0016	0.0039-0.0114	4	2.204-2.205	0.0007-0.0021	0.0068-0.0167
	3.7	R	2.6570	0.0010-0.0016	0.0020-0.0114	4	2.204-2.205	0.0007-0.0021	0.0068-0.0167
2011	3.5	T	2.6570	0.0010-0.0016	0.0039-0.0114	4	2.204-2.205	0.0007-0.0021	0.0068-0.0167
	3.7	R	2.6570	0.0010-0.0016	0.0020-0.0114	4	2.204-2.205	0.0007-0.0021	0.0068-0.0167

25759_LMKS_C0008

PISTON AND RING SPECIFICATIONS

All measurements are given in inches.

Year	Engine Displacement Liters	Engine ID/VIN	Piston Clearance	Ring Gap Top Compression	Ring Gap Bottom Compression	Ring Gap Oil Control	Ring Side Clearance Top Compression	Ring Side Clearance Bottom Compression	Ring Side Clearance Oil Control
2010	3.5	T	0.0003-0.0017	0.0067-0.0106	0.0118-0.0216	0.0059-0.0177	0.0015-0.0031	0.0015-0.0031	NS
	3.7	R	0.0003-0.0017	0.0067-0.0106	0.0118-0.0216	0.0059-0.0177	0.0015-0.0031	0.0015-0.0031	NS
2011	3.5	T	0.0003-0.0017	0.0067-0.0106	0.0118-0.0216	0.0059-0.0177	0.0015-0.0031	0.0015-0.0031	NS
	3.7	R	0.0003-0.0017	0.0067-0.0106	0.0118-0.0216	0.0059-0.0177	0.0015-0.0031	0.0015-0.0031	NS

25759_LMKS_C0009

TORQUE SPECIFICATIONS

All readings in ft. lbs.

Year	Engine Disp. Liters	Engine ID/VIN	Cylinder Head Bolts	Main Bearing Bolts	Rod Bearing Bolts	Crankshaft Damper Bolts	Flywheel Bolts	Manifold Intake	Manifold Exhaust	Spark Plugs	Oil Pan Drain Plug
2010	3.5	T	①	②	③	④	59	7	⑤	11	20
	3.7	R	①	②	③	④	59	7	⑥	11	20
2011	3.5	T	①	②	③	④	59	7	⑤	11	20
	3.7	R	①	②	③	④	59	7	⑥	11	20

① Step 1: 15 ft. lbs.
Step 2: 26 ft. lbs.
Step 3: Plus 90 degrees
Step 4: Plus 90 degrees
Step 5: Plus 90 degrees
M6 Bolt: 89 inch lbs.

② Vertical bolts: 44 ft. lbs. plus 90 degrees
Side bolts: 33 ft. lbs. plus 90 degrees

③ Step 1: 17 ft. lbs.
Step 2: 32 ft. lbs.
Step 3: Plus 90 degrees

④ Step 1: Tighten to 89 ft. lbs.
Step 2: Loosen one full turn
Step 3: Tighten to 37 ft. lbs.
Step 4: Plus 90 degrees

⑤ Step 1: 11 ft. lbs.
Step 2: 15 ft. lbs.

⑥ Step 1: 15 ft. lbs.
Step 2: 18 ft. lbs.

25759_LMKS_C0010

WHEEL ALIGNMENT

Year	Model		Caster Range (+/-Deg.)	Caster Preferred Setting (Deg.)	Camber Range (+/-Deg.)	Camber Preferred Setting (Deg.)	Toe (Deg.)
2010	MKS	F	0.75	LH: 3.10, RH: 3.30	0.75	LH: -0.40, RH: -0.60	0.10 ± 0.10
		R	NA	NA	0.75	-1.00	0.12 ± 0.20
2011	MKS	F	0.75	LH: 3.20, RH: 3.40	0.75	LH: -0.40, RH: -0.60	NS
		R	NA	NA	0.75	-1.00	0.12 ± 0.20

25759_LMKS_C0011

TIRE, WHEEL AND BALL JOINT SPECIFICATIONS

Year	Model	Engine	OEM Tires Standard	OEM Tires Optional	Tire Pressures (psi) Front	Tire Pressures (psi) Rear	Wheel Size	Ball Joint Inspection	Lug Nut (ft. lbs.)
2010	MKS	3.5L	P255/45R19	NS	①	①	8	NS	100
		3.7L	P235/55R18	NS	①	①	7.5	NS	100
2011	MKS	3.5L	P255/45R19	NS	①	①	8	NS	100
		3.7L	P235/55R18	NS	①	①	7.5	NS	100

OEM: Original Equipment Manufacturer

PSI: Pounds Per Square Inch

NA: Information not available

① See Safety Certification Label on driver door jamb

25759_LMKS_C0012

BRAKE SPECIFICATIONS

All measurements in inches unless noted

Year	Model		Brake Disc Original Thickness	Brake Disc Minimum Thickness	Brake Disc Max. Runout	Brake Drum Diameter Original Inside Diameter	Brake Drum Diameter Max. Wear Limit	Brake Drum Diameter Maximum Machine Diamter	Minimum Pad/Lining Thickness Front	Minimum Pad/Lining Thickness Rear	Brake Caliper Bracket Bolts (ft. lbs.)	Brake Caliper Mounting Bolts (ft. lbs.)
2010	MKS	F	NS	1.122	NS	NA	NA	NA	0.118	0.118	111	53
		R	NS	0.394	NS	NA	NA	NA	0.118	0.118	76	24
2011	MKS	F	NS	1.122	NS	NA	NA	NA	0.118	0.118	111	53
		R	NS	0.394	NS	NA	NA	NA	0.118	0.118	76	24

F: Front

R: Rear

NA: Information not available

25759_LMKS_C0013

SCHEDULED MAINTENANCE INTERVALS

2010 Lincoln MKS - Normal

TO BE SERVICED	TYPE OF SERVICE	VEHICLE MILEAGE INTERVAL (x1000)												
		7.5	15	22.5	30	37.5	45	52.5	60	67.5	75	82.5	90	97.5
Engine oil & filter	Replace	✓	✓	✓	✓	✓	✓	✓	✓	✓	✓	✓	✓	✓
Rotate and inspect tires	Service	✓	✓	✓	✓	✓	✓	✓	✓	✓	✓	✓	✓	✓
Inspect wheels and related components for abnomal noise, wear, looseness or drag	Inspect	✓	✓	✓	✓	✓	✓	✓	✓	✓	✓	✓	✓	✓
Fluid levels (all)	Top off	✓	✓	✓	✓	✓	✓	✓	✓	✓	✓	✓	✓	✓
Exhaust system (Leaks, damage, loose parts and foreign material)	Inspect		✓		✓		✓		✓		✓		✓	
Cabin air filter	Replace		✓		✓		✓		✓		✓		✓	
Cooling system and hoses	Inspect		✓		✓		✓		✓		✓		✓	
Brake system (Pads/shoes/rotors/drums, brake lines and hoses, and parking brake system)	Inspect		✓		✓		✓		✓		✓		✓	
Halfshaft & U-joints	Inspect		✓		✓		✓		✓		✓		✓	
Climate-controlled seat filter (if equipped)	Replace				✓				✓				✓	
Engine air filter	Inspect	✓	✓	✓	✓	✓	✓	✓	✓	✓	✓	✓	✓	✓
Engine air filter	Replace				✓				✓				✓	
Spark plugs	Replace												✓	
Drive belt(s)	Inspect	✓	✓	✓	✓	✓	✓	✓	✓	✓	✓	✓	✓	✓
Shocks struts and other suspension components for leaks and damage	Inspect	✓	✓	✓	✓	✓	✓	✓	✓	✓	✓	✓	✓	✓
Oil and fluid leaks	Inspect	✓	✓	✓	✓	✓	✓	✓	✓	✓	✓	✓	✓	✓
Windshield for cracks, chips and pitting	Inspect	✓	✓	✓	✓	✓	✓	✓	✓	✓	✓	✓	✓	✓
Windshield wiper spray and wiper operation	Inspect	✓	✓	✓	✓	✓	✓	✓	✓	✓	✓	✓	✓	✓
Radiator, coolers, heater and airconditioning hoses	Inspect	✓	✓	✓	✓	✓	✓	✓	✓	✓	✓	✓	✓	✓
Horn, exterior lamps, turn signals and hazard warning light operation	Inspect	✓	✓	✓	✓	✓	✓	✓	✓	✓	✓	✓	✓	✓
Battery performance	Inspect	✓	✓	✓	✓	✓	✓	✓	✓	✓	✓	✓	✓	✓
Drive belt(s)	Replace	Every 150,000 miles												
Engine coolant	Replace	At 6 years or 105,000 miles; then every 3 years or 45,000 miles												
Automatic transmisison fluid	Replace	Every 150,000 miles												
Rear differential fluid	Replace	Every 150,000 miles												
Steering linkage, ball joints, suspension and tie-rod ends, lubricate if equipped with greases fittings	Inspect/ Lubricate	✓	✓	✓	✓	✓	✓	✓	✓	✓	✓	✓	✓	✓

25759_LMKS_C0014

SCHEDULED MAINTENANCE INTERVALS

2010 Lincoln MKS - Severe

TO BE SERVICED	TYPE OF SERVICE	VEHICLE MILEAGE INTERVAL (x1000)											
		5	10	15	20	25	30	35	40	45	50	55	60
Battery performance	Inspect	✓	✓	✓	✓	✓	✓	✓	✓	✓	✓	✓	✓
Halfshaft boots	Inspect	✓	✓	✓	✓	✓	✓	✓	✓	✓	✓	✓	✓
Horn, exterior lamps, turn signals and hazard warning light operation	Inspect	✓	✓	✓	✓	✓	✓	✓	✓	✓	✓	✓	✓
Inspect wheels and related components for abnomal noise, wear, looseness or drag	Inspect	✓	✓	✓	✓	✓	✓	✓	✓	✓	✓	✓	✓
Shocks struts and other suspension components for leaks and damage	Inspect	✓	✓	✓	✓	✓	✓	✓	✓	✓	✓	✓	✓
Oil and fluid leaks	Inspect	✓	✓	✓	✓	✓	✓	✓	✓	✓	✓	✓	✓
Radiator, coolers, heater and airconditioning hoses	Inspect	✓	✓	✓	✓	✓	✓	✓	✓	✓	✓	✓	✓
Rotate and inspect tires	Service	✓	✓	✓	✓	✓	✓	✓	✓	✓	✓	✓	✓
Spark plugs	Replace												✓
Automatic transmission fluid	Replace						✓						✓
Windshield wiper spray and wiper operation	Inspect	✓	✓	✓	✓	✓	✓	✓	✓	✓	✓	✓	✓
Windshield for cracks, chips and pitting	Inspect	✓	✓	✓	✓	✓	✓	✓	✓	✓	✓	✓	✓
Exhaust system (Leaks, damage, loose parts and foreign material)	Inspect	✓	✓	✓	✓	✓	✓	✓	✓	✓	✓	✓	✓
Engine oil and filter	Replace	✓	✓	✓	✓	✓	✓	✓	✓	✓	✓	✓	✓
Fluid levels (all)	Top off	✓	✓	✓	✓	✓	✓	✓	✓	✓	✓	✓	✓
Air filter	Inspect	✓	✓	✓	✓	✓	✓	✓	✓	✓	✓	✓	✓
Air filter	Replace						✓						✓
Drive belt(s)	Inspect	✓	✓	✓	✓	✓	✓	✓	✓	✓	✓	✓	✓
Cooling system & hoses	Inspect	✓	✓	✓	✓	✓	✓	✓	✓	✓	✓	✓	✓
Climate-controlled seat filter (if equipped)	Replace						✓						✓
Brake system (Inspect brake pads/shoes/rotors/drums, brake lines and hoses, and parking brake system)	Inspect	✓	✓	✓	✓	✓	✓	✓	✓	✓	✓	✓	✓
Engine coolant	Replace	At 6 years or 105,000 miles; then every 3 years or 45,000 miles											
Drive belt(s)	Replace	every 150,000 miles											
Cabin air filter (If equipped)	Inspect/	✓	✓	✓	✓	✓	✓	✓	✓	✓	✓	✓	✓
Steering linkage, ball joints, suspension and tie-rod ends, lubricate if equipped with greases fittings	Inspect/ Lubricate	✓	✓	✓	✓	✓	✓	✓	✓	✓	✓	✓	✓
Rear differential fluid	Replace	every 150,000 miles											

For extensive idling and or low speed driving, change engine oil and filter every 5,000 miles, 6 months or 200 hours of engine operation.

25759_LMKS_C0015

SCHEDULED MAINTENANCE INTERVALS

2011 Lincoln MKS - Normal

Service Item	Service Action	1	2	3	4	5	6	7	8	9	10	11	12	13	14	15
Auto transmisison fluid	Replace															✓
Spark plugs	Replace										✓					
Engine coolant	Replace										✓					✓
Accessory drive belt	Replace															✓
Engine air filter	Replace			✓			✓			✓			✓			✓
Radiator, coolers, heater and air conditioning hoses	Inspect	✓	✓	✓	✓	✓	✓	✓	✓	✓	✓	✓	✓	✓	✓	✓
Brake system (Pads/shoes/rotors/drums, brake lines and hoses, and parking brake system)	Inspect	✓	✓	✓	✓	✓	✓	✓	✓	✓	✓	✓	✓	✓	✓	✓
Inspect wheels and related components for abnomal noise, wear, looseness or drag	Inspect	✓	✓	✓	✓	✓	✓	✓	✓	✓	✓	✓	✓	✓	✓	✓
Battery performance	Inspect	✓	✓	✓	✓	✓	✓	✓	✓	✓	✓	✓	✓	✓	✓	✓
Windshield for cracks, chips and pitting	Inspect	✓	✓	✓	✓	✓	✓	✓	✓	✓	✓	✓	✓	✓	✓	✓
Windshield wiper spray and wiper operation	Inspect	✓	✓	✓	✓	✓	✓	✓	✓	✓	✓	✓	✓	✓	✓	✓
Oil and fluid leaks	Inspect	✓	✓	✓	✓	✓	✓	✓	✓	✓	✓	✓	✓	✓	✓	✓
Shocks struts and other suspension components for leaks and damage	Inspect	✓	✓	✓	✓	✓	✓	✓	✓	✓	✓	✓	✓	✓	✓	✓
Exhaust system (Leaks, damage, loose parts and foreign material)	Inspect					✓	✓	✓	✓	✓	✓	✓	✓	✓	✓	✓
Horn, exterior lamps, turn signals and hazard warning light operation	Inspect	✓	✓	✓	✓	✓	✓	✓	✓	✓	✓	✓	✓	✓	✓	✓
Cooling system, hoses, clamps & coolant strength	Inspect					✓	✓	✓	✓	✓	✓	✓	✓	✓	✓	✓
Engine air filter	Inspect	✓	✓	✓	✓	✓	✓	✓	✓	✓	✓	✓	✓	✓	✓	✓
Accessory drive belt	Inspect	✓	✓	✓	✓	✓	✓	✓	✓	✓	✓	✓	✓	✓	✓	✓
Halfshaft boots	Inspect					✓	✓	✓	✓	✓	✓	✓	✓	✓	✓	✓
Cabin air filter	Inspect/ Service		✓		✓		✓		✓		✓		✓		✓	✓
Steering linkage, ball joints, suspension and tie-rod ends, lubricate if equipped with greases fittings	Inspect/ Lubricate	✓	✓	✓	✓	✓	✓	✓	✓	✓	✓	✓	✓	✓	✓	✓
Fluid levels (all)	Top off	✓	✓	✓	✓	✓	✓	✓	✓	✓	✓	✓	✓	✓	✓	✓
Rotate tires, inspect tread wear, measure tread depth and check pressure	Inspect/ Rotate	✓	✓	✓	✓	✓	✓	✓	✓	✓	✓	✓	✓	✓	✓	✓
Rear differential fluid	Replace															✓

Oil change service intervals should be completed as indicated by the message center (Can be up to 1 year or 10,000 miles) If the message center is prematurely reset or is inoperative, perform the oil change interval at 6 months or 5,000 miles from your last oil change.

25759_LMKS_C0016

SCHEDULED MAINTENANCE INTERVALS

2011 Lincoln MKS - Severe

Service Item	Service Action	1	2	3	4	5	6	7	8	9	10	11	12	13	14	15
Accessory drive belt	Replace															✓
Spark plugs	Replace						✓						✓			
Engine coolant	Replace										✓					
Automatic transmisison fluid	Replace			✓			✓			✓			✓			✓
Battery performance	Inspect	✓	✓	✓	✓	✓	✓	✓	✓	✓	✓	✓	✓	✓	✓	✓
Cooling system, hoses, clamps & coolant strength	Inspect	✓	✓	✓	✓	✓	✓	✓	✓	✓	✓	✓	✓	✓	✓	✓
Brake system (Pads/shoes/rotors/drums, brake lines and hoses, and parking brake system)	Inspect	✓	✓	✓	✓	✓	✓	✓	✓	✓	✓	✓	✓	✓	✓	✓
Inspect wheels and related components for abnomal noise, wear, looseness or drag	Inspect	✓	✓	✓	✓	✓	✓	✓	✓	✓	✓	✓	✓	✓	✓	✓
Radiator, coolers, heater and air conditioning hoses	Inspect	✓	✓	✓	✓	✓	✓	✓	✓	✓	✓	✓	✓	✓	✓	✓
Fluid levels (all)	Inspect	✓	✓	✓	✓	✓	✓	✓	✓	✓	✓	✓	✓	✓	✓	✓
Exhaust system (Leaks, damage, loose parts and foreign material)	Inspect	✓	✓	✓	✓	✓	✓	✓	✓	✓	✓	✓	✓	✓	✓	✓
Horn, exterior lamps, turn signals and hazard warning light operation	Inspect	✓	✓	✓	✓	✓	✓	✓	✓	✓	✓	✓	✓	✓	✓	✓
Oil and fluid leaks	Inspect	✓	✓	✓	✓	✓	✓	✓	✓	✓	✓	✓	✓	✓	✓	✓
Shocks struts and other suspension components for leaks and damage	Inspect	✓	✓	✓	✓	✓	✓	✓	✓	✓	✓	✓	✓	✓	✓	✓
Windshield for cracks, chips and pitting	Inspect	✓	✓	✓	✓	✓	✓	✓	✓	✓	✓	✓	✓	✓	✓	✓
Windshield wiper spray and wiper operation	Inspect	✓	✓	✓	✓	✓	✓	✓	✓	✓	✓	✓	✓	✓	✓	✓
Accessory drive belt	Inspect	✓	✓	✓	✓	✓	✓	✓	✓	✓	✓	✓	✓	✓	✓	✓
Halfshaft boots	Inspect	✓	✓	✓	✓	✓	✓	✓	✓	✓	✓	✓	✓	✓	✓	✓
Steering linkage, ball joints, suspension and tie-rod ends, lubricate if equipped with greases fittings	Inspect/ Lubricate	✓	✓	✓	✓	✓	✓	✓	✓	✓	✓	✓	✓	✓	✓	✓
Engine air filter	Inspect/ Service	✓	✓	✓	✓	✓	✓	✓	✓	✓	✓	✓	✓	✓	✓	✓
Cabin air filter	Inspect/ Service	✓	✓	✓	✓	✓			✓	✓	✓	✓	✓	✓	✓	✓
Rotate tires, inspect tread wear, measure tread depth and check pressure	Rotate/ Inspect	✓	✓	✓	✓	✓	✓	✓	✓	✓	✓	✓	✓	✓	✓	✓
Rear differential fluid	Replace															✓

For extensive idling and or low speed driving, change engine oil and filter every 5,000 miles, 6 months or 200 hours of engine operation.

For commercial use or extensive idling, change spark plugs at 60,000 miles.

25759_LMKS_C0017

PRECAUTIONS

Before servicing any vehicle, please be sure to read all of the following precautions, which deal with personal safety, prevention of component damage, and important points to take into consideration when servicing a motor vehicle:

- Never open, service or drain the radiator or cooling system when the engine is hot; serious burns can occur from the steam and hot coolant.
- Observe all applicable safety precautions when working around fuel. Whenever servicing the fuel system, always work in a well-ventilated area. Do not allow fuel spray or vapors to come in contact with a spark, open flame, or excessive heat (a hot drop light, for example). Keep a dry chemical fire extinguisher near the work area. Always keep fuel in a container specifically designed for fuel storage; also, always properly seal fuel containers to avoid the possibility of fire or explosion. Refer to the additional fuel system precautions later in this section.
- Fuel injection systems often remain pressurized, even after the engine has been turned **OFF**. The fuel system pressure must be relieved before disconnecting any fuel lines. Failure to do so may result in fire and/or personal injury.
- Brake fluid often contains polyglycol ethers and polyglycols. Avoid contact with the eyes and wash your hands thoroughly after handling brake fluid. If you do get brake fluid in your eyes, flush your eyes with clean, running water for 15 minutes. If eye irritation persists, or if you have taken brake fluid internally, IMMEDIATELY seek medical assistance.
- The EPA warns that prolonged contact with used engine oil may cause a number of skin disorders, including cancer. You should make every effort to minimize your exposure to used engine oil. Protective gloves should be worn when changing oil. Wash your hands and any other exposed skin areas as soon as possible after exposure to used engine oil. Soap and water, or waterless hand cleaner should be used.
- All new vehicles are now equipped with an air bag system, often referred to as a Supplemental Restraint System (SRS) or Supplemental Inflatable Restraint (SIR) system. The system must be disabled before performing service on or around system components, steering column, instrument panel components, wiring and sensors. Failure to follow safety and disabling procedures could result in accidental air bag deployment, possible personal injury and unnecessary system repairs.
- Always wear safety goggles when working with, or around, the air bag system. When carrying a non-deployed air bag, be sure the bag and trim cover are pointed away from your body. When placing a non-deployed air bag on a work surface, always face the bag and trim cover upward, away from the surface. This will reduce the motion of the module if it is accidentally deployed. Refer to the additional air bag system precautions later in this section.
- Clean, high quality brake fluid from a sealed container is essential to the safe and proper operation of the brake system. You should always buy the correct type of brake fluid for your vehicle. If the brake fluid becomes contaminated, completely flush the system with new fluid. Never reuse any brake fluid. Any brake fluid that is removed from the system should be discarded. Also, do not allow any brake fluid to come in contact with a painted surface; it will damage the paint.
- Never operate the engine without the proper amount and type of engine oil; doing so WILL result in severe engine damage.
- Timing belt maintenance is extremely important. Many models utilize an interference-type, non-freewheeling engine. If the timing belt breaks, the valves in the cylinder head may strike the pistons, causing potentially serious (also time-consuming and expensive) engine damage. Refer to the maintenance interval charts for the recommended replacement interval for the timing belt, and to the timing belt section for belt replacement and inspection.
- Disconnecting the negative battery cable on some vehicles may interfere with the functions of the on-board computer system(s) and may require the computer to undergo a relearning process once the negative battery cable is reconnected.
- When servicing drum brakes, only disassemble and assemble one side at a time, leaving the remaining side intact for reference.
- Only an MVAC-trained, EPA-certified automotive technician should service the air conditioning system or its components.

BRAKES

ANTI-LOCK BRAKE SYSTEM (ABS)

GENERAL INFORMATION

PRECAUTIONS

- Certain components within the ABS system are not intended to be serviced or repaired individually.
- Do not use rubber hoses or other parts not specifically specified for and ABS system. When using repair kits, replace all parts included in the kit. Partial or incorrect repair may lead to functional problems and require the replacement of components.
- Lubricate rubber parts with clean, fresh brake fluid to ease assembly. Do not use shop air to clean parts; damage to rubber components may result.
- Use only DOT 3 brake fluid from an unopened container.
- If any hydraulic component or line is removed or replaced, it may be necessary to bleed the entire system.
- A clean repair area is essential. Always clean the reservoir and cap thoroughly before removing the cap. The slightest amount of dirt in the fluid may plug an orifice and impair the system function. Perform repairs after components have been thoroughly cleaned; use only denatured alcohol to clean components. Do not allow ABS components to come into contact with any substance containing mineral oil; this includes used shop rags.
- The Anti-Lock control unit is a microprocessor similar to other computer units in the vehicle. Ensure that the ignition switch is **OFF** before removing or installing controller harnesses. Avoid static electricity discharge at or near the controller.
- If any arc welding is to be done on the vehicle, the control unit should be unplugged before welding operations begin.

SPEED SENSORS

REMOVAL & INSTALLATION

Front

See Figure 1.

1. Before servicing the vehicle, refer to the Precautions Section.
2. Remove the wheel and tire.
3. Disconnect the wheel speed sensor electrical connector.
4. Remove the 2 scrivets and position aside the fender splash shield.
5. Remove the wheel speed sensor harness pin-type retainer.

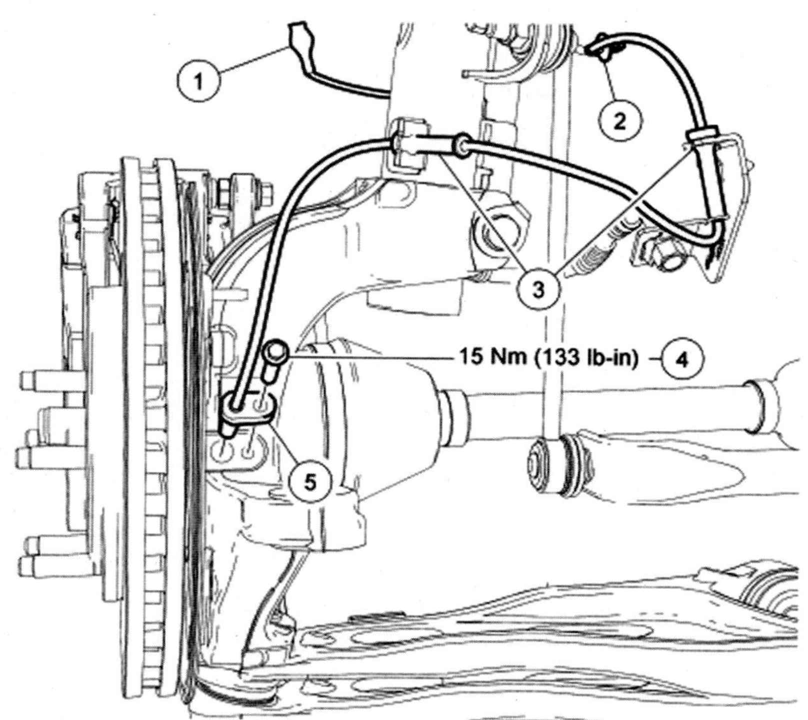

Fig. 1 Front wheel speed sensor

6. Remove the 2 wheel speed sensor harness retainers.
7. Remove the bolt and the wheel speed sensor.

To install:

8. To install, reverse the removal procedure. To install, tighten the bolt to 11 ft. lbs. (15 Nm).

Rear

See Figure 2.

1. Before servicing the vehicle, refer to the Precautions Section.
2. With the vehicle in NEUTRAL, position it on a hoist.
3. Disconnect the wheel speed sensor electrical connector.
4. Detach the 2 wheel speed sensor pin-type retainers.
5. Detach the 2 wheel speed sensor harness retainers.
6. Remove the wheel speed sensor bolt.
7. Remove the wheel speed sensor.

To install:

8. To install, reverse the removal procedure. To install, tighten the bolt to 11 ft. lbs. (15 Nm).

**** WARNING**

Make sure to correctly route and secure the wheel speed sensor harness in the rear subframe assembly or damage to the harness may occur.

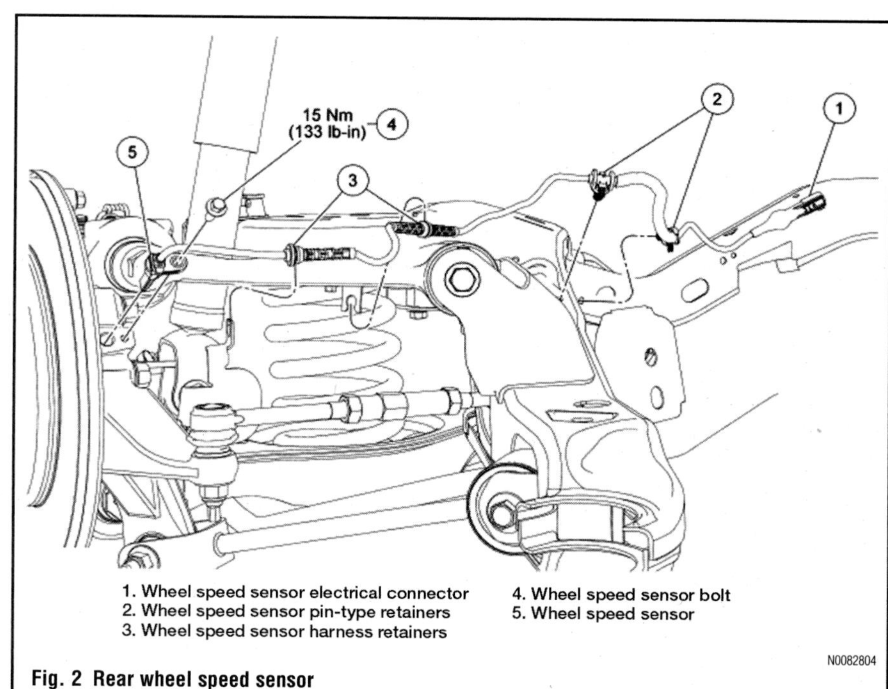

Fig. 2 Rear wheel speed sensor

BLEEDING PROCEDURE

BLEEDING PROCEDURE

Pressure Bleeding

CAUTION

Do not allow the brake master cylinder to run dry during the bleeding operation. Master cylinder may be damaged if operated without fluid, resulting in degraded braking performance. Failure to follow this instruction may result in serious personal injury.

➡Pressure bleeding the brake system is preferred to manual bleeding.

➡The Hydraulic Control Unit (HCU) bleeding procedure must be carried out if the HCU or any components upstream of the HCU are installed new.

1. Before servicing the vehicle, refer to the Precautions Section.
2. Clean all the dirt from around the brake fluid reservoir cap and remove the cap. Fill the brake master cylinder reservoir with clean, specified brake fluid.
3. Install the bleeder adapter to the brake master cylinder reservoir and attach the bleeder tank hose to the fitting on the adapter. Master cylinder pressure bleeder adapter tools are available from various manufacturers of pressure bleeding equipment. Follow the instructions of the manufacturer when installing the adapter.
4. Open the valve on the bleeder tank. Make sure the bleeder tank contains enough specified brake fluid to complete the bleeding operation. Apply 30–50 psi (207–345 kPa) to the brake system.
5. Remove the right-hand rear bleeder cap and place a box-end wrench on the bleeder screw. Attach a rubber drain tube to the right-hand rear bleeder screw and submerge the free end of the tube in a container partially filled with clean, specified brake fluid.

➡Due to the complexity of the fluid path within the rear integral parking brake calipers, it is necessary to press and release the parking brake during the bleed procedure.

6. Loosen the right-hand rear bleeder screw. Leave open until clear, bubble-free brake fluid flows, then tighten the right-hand rear bleeder screw.
7. For rear brake calipers, press and release the parking brake 5 times. Repeat until clear, bubble-free fluid comes out.
8. Tighten the right-hand rear bleeder screw to specification. Remove the rubber hose and install the bleeder screw cap.
9. Repeat the above 3 steps for the left-hand rear brake caliper.
10. Continue bleeding the front of the system, going in order from the right-hand front brake caliper and then to the left-hand front brake caliper. Tighten the front brake caliper bleeder screws to specification.
11. Close the bleeder tank valve and release the pressure. Remove the tank hose from the adapter and remove the adapter. Fill the reservoir with clean, specified brake fluid and install the reservoir cap.

Manual Bleeding

CAUTION

Do not allow the brake master cylinder to run dry during the bleeding operation. Master cylinder may be damaged if operated without fluid, resulting in degraded braking performance. Failure to follow this instruction may result in serious personal injury.

➡Pressure bleeding the brake system is preferred to manual bleeding.

➡The HCU bleeding procedure must be carried out if the HCU or any components upstream of the HCU are installed new.

1. Before servicing the vehicle, refer to the Precautions Section.
2. Clean all the dirt from around the brake fluid reservoir cap and remove the cap. Fill the brake master cylinder reservoir with clean, specified brake fluid.
3. Remove the right-hand rear bleeder cap and place a box-end wrench on the bleeder screw. Attach a rubber drain tube to the right-hand rear bleeder screw and submerge the free end of the tube in a container partially filled with clean, specified brake fluid.
4. Have an assistant hold firm pressure on the brake pedal.

➡Due to the complexity of the fluid path within the rear integral parking brake calipers, it is necessary to press and release the parking brake during the bleed procedure.

5. Loosen the right-hand rear bleeder screw until a stream of brake fluid comes out. While the assistant maintains pressure on the brake pedal, tighten the right-hand rear bleeder screw.
6. Press and release the parking brake 5 times. Repeat until clear, bubble-free fluid comes out.
7. Refill the brake master cylinder reservoir as necessary.
8. Tighten the right-hand rear bleeder screw to specification.
9. Remove the rubber hose and install the bleeder screw cap.
10. Repeat the above steps for the left-hand rear brake caliper.
11. Remove the right-hand front bleeder cap and place a box-end wrench on the bleeder screw. Attach a rubber drain tube to the right-hand front bleeder screw and submerge the free end of the tube in a container partially filled with clean, specified brake fluid.
12. Have an assistant hold firm pressure on the brake pedal.
13. Loosen the right-hand front bleeder screw until a stream of brake fluid comes out. While the assistant maintains pressure on the brake pedal, tighten the right-hand front bleeder screw. Repeat until clear, bubble-free fluid comes out.
14. Refill the brake master cylinder reservoir as necessary.
15. Tighten the right-hand front bleeder screw to specification.
16. Remove the rubber hose and install the bleeder screw cap.
17. Repeat the above steps for the left-hand front brake caliper bleeder screw.

MASTER CYLINDER BLEEDING

CAUTION

Do not allow the brake master cylinder to run dry during the bleeding operation. Master cylinder may be damaged if operated without fluid, resulting in degraded braking performance. Failure to follow this instruction may result in serious personal injury.

➡When a new brake master cylinder has been installed or the system has been emptied, or partially emptied, it should be primed to prevent air from entering the system.

1. Before servicing the vehicle, refer to the Precautions Section.
2. Disconnect the brake tubes from the master cylinder.

3. Install short brake tubes onto the primary and secondary ports with the ends submerged in the brake master cylinder reservoir.

4. Fill the brake master cylinder reservoir with clean, specified brake fluid.

5. Have an assistant pump the brake pedal until clear fluid flows from the brake tubes without air bubbles.

6. Remove the short brake tubes, and install the master cylinder brake tubes.

7. Bleed the brake system. For additional information, refer to Brake Bleeding Procedure in this section.

BLEEDING THE ABS SYSTEM

➡Pressure bleeding the brake system is preferred to manual bleeding.

1. Before servicing the vehicle, refer to the Precautions Section.

2. Follow the pressure bleeding or manual bleeding procedure steps to bleed the system.

3. Connect the scan tool and follow the ABS Service Bleed instructions.

4. Repeat the pressure bleeding or manual bleeding procedure steps to bleed the system.

⁂ CAUTION

Dust and dirt accumulating on brake parts during normal use may contain asbestos fibers from production or aftermarket brake linings. Breathing excessive concentrations of asbestos fibers can cause serious bodily harm. Exercise care when servicing brake parts. Do not sand or grind brake lining unless equipment used is designed to contain the dust residue. Do not clean brake parts with compressed air or by dry brushing. Cleaning should be done by dampening the brake components with a fine mist of water, then wiping the brake components clean with a dampened cloth. Dispose of cloth and all residue containing asbestos fibers in an impermeable container with the appropriate label. Follow practices prescribed by the Occupational Safety and Health Administration (OSHA) and the Environmental Protection Agency (EPA) for the handling, processing, and disposing of dust or debris that may contain asbestos fibers.

BRAKE CALIPER

REMOVAL & INSTALLATION

See Figure 3.

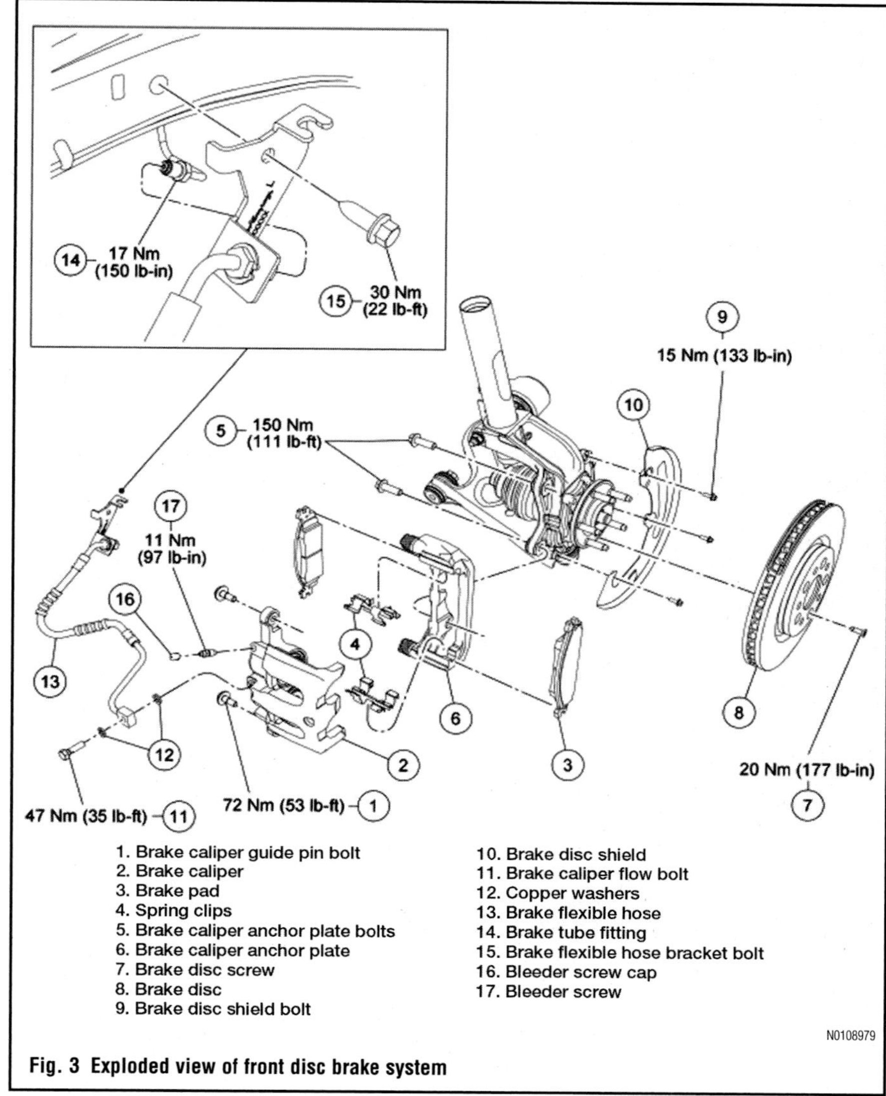

Fig. 3 Exploded view of front disc brake system

1. Before servicing the vehicle, refer to the Precautions Section.

2. Remove the brake pads.

3. Remove the brake caliper flow bolt and position the brake hose aside.

4. Discard the copper washers.

5. Remove the brake caliper.

To install:

6. Position the brake hose and install the brake caliper flow bolt.

7. Install new copper washers. Tighten to 35 ft. lbs. (47 Nm).

8. Install the brake pads.

9. Bleed the brake caliper.

DISC BRAKE PADS

REMOVAL & INSTALLATION

1. Before servicing the vehicle, refer to the Precautions Section.

2. Check the brake fluid level in the brake master cylinder reservoir. If required, remove the fluid until the brake master cylinder reservoir is half full.

3. Remove the wheel and tire.

4. Using a C-clamp, compress the pistons into the caliper housing.

⁂ WARNING

Do not allow the brake caliper to hang from the brake hose or damage to the hose may occur.

5. Remove the 2 brake caliper guide pin bolts and position the caliper aside.
6. Support the caliper using mechanic's wire.
7. Remove the 2 brake pads and spring clips from the brake caliper anchor plate.
8. Discard the spring clips.

To install:

9. If installing new brake pads, make sure to install all new hardware and lubricant supplied with the brake pad kit. Refer to the brake pad instruction sheet when applying lubricant.
10. Install the new spring clips and brake pads to the brake caliper anchor plate.
11. Apply equal amounts of specified lubricant to the brake caliper-to-brake pad contact points.
12. Make sure the caliper pin boots are correctly seated to prevent corrosion to the guide pins.
13. Position the brake caliper onto the brake caliper anchor plate and install the 2 brake caliper guide pin bolts. Tighten to 53 ft. lbs. (72 Nm). Make sure that the brake hose is not twisted when the caliper is positioned on the anchor plate.
14. Install the wheel and tire.
15. If necessary, fill the brake master cylinder reservoir with clean, specified brake fluid.
16. Apply brakes several times to verify correct brake operation.

BRAKES

REAR DISC BRAKES

⁂ CAUTION

Dust and dirt accumulating on brake parts during normal use may contain asbestos fibers from production or aftermarket brake linings. Breathing excessive concentrations of asbestos fibers can cause serious bodily harm. Exercise care when servicing brake parts. Do not sand or grind brake lining unless equipment used is designed to contain the dust residue. Do not clean brake parts with compressed air or by dry brushing. Cleaning should be done by dampening the brake components with a fine mist of water, then wiping the brake components clean with a dampened cloth. Dispose of cloth and all residue containing asbestos fibers in an impermeable container with the appropriate label. Follow practices prescribed by the Occupational Safety and Health Administration (OSHA) and the Environmental Protection Agency (EPA) for the handling, processing, and disposing of dust or debris that may contain asbestos fibers.

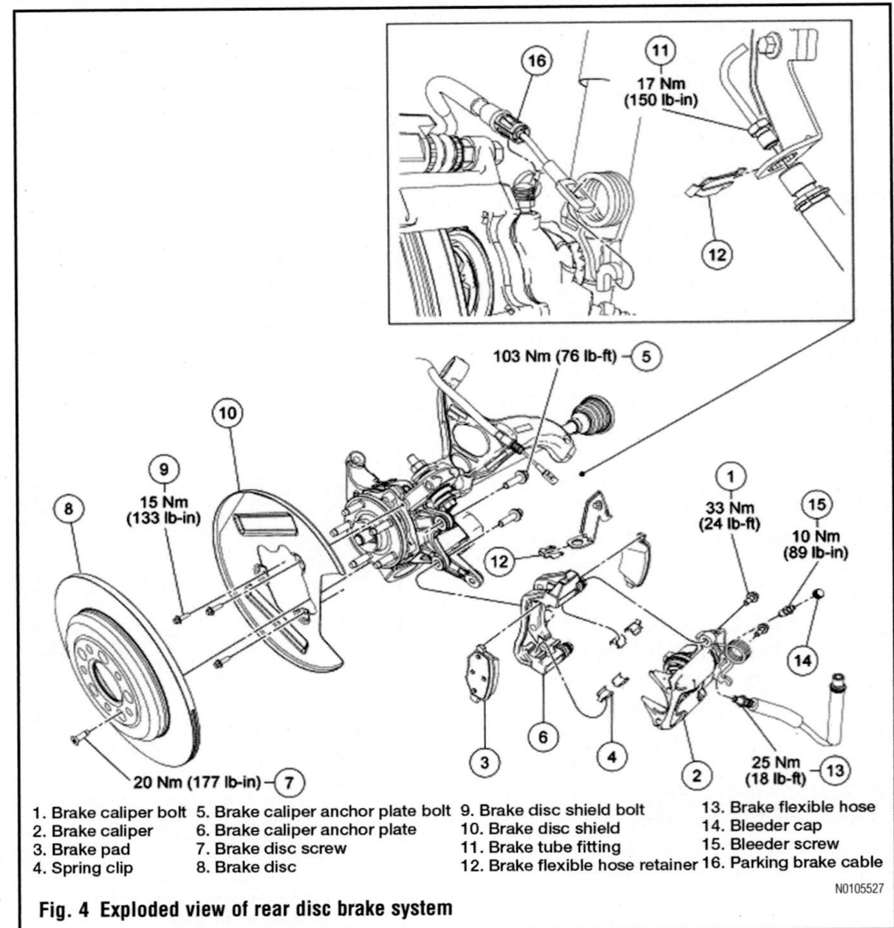

Fig. 4 Exploded view of rear disc brake system

BRAKE CALIPER

REMOVAL & INSTALLATION

See Figure 4.

1. Before servicing the vehicle, refer to the Precautions Section.
2. Release the parking brake cable tension.
3. Disconnect the parking brake cable from the subframe bracket and the caliper.
4. Position the parking brake cable aside.
5. Remove the brake flexible hose.
6. Remove and discard the brake pads.

To install:

7. Install the brake pads.
8. Install the flexible hose. Make sure that the hose does not become twisted. Verify correct installation of the brake flexible hose protective sleeve and tie strap.
9. Connect the parking brake cable.
10. Bleed the caliper.

DISC BRAKE PADS

REMOVAL & INSTALLATION

See Figure 5.

1. Before servicing the vehicle, refer to the Precautions Section.
2. Check the brake fluid level in the brake fluid reservoir. If required, remove fluid until the brake master cylinder reservoir is half full.
3. Remove the wheel and tire.
4. Remove the brake caliper bolts.

⁂ WARNING

Care must be taken when servicing rear brake components without disconnecting the parking brake cable from the brake caliper lever. Carefully position the caliper aside using

a suitable support or damage to the parking brake cable end fittings may occur.

5. Using hand force and a rocking motion, separate the brake caliper from the anchor plate. Position the brake caliper aside.
6. Support the caliper with mechanic's wire. Do not allow the caliper to hang from the brake hose or damage to the hose may occur.
7. Remove and discard the 2 brake pads and spring clips from the brake caliper anchor plate. When the brake pads are separated from the brake caliper, new brake pads must be installed to prevent brake noise and shudder. The brake pads are one-time use only.
8. Inspect the brake caliper anchor plate assembly.
9. Check the guide pins and boots for binding or damage. Do not remove the anchor plate guide pins. The guide pins are press fit to the brake caliper anchor plate. If the guide pins are damaged, a new anchor plate must be installed.
10. Install a new brake caliper anchor plate if it is worn or damaged.

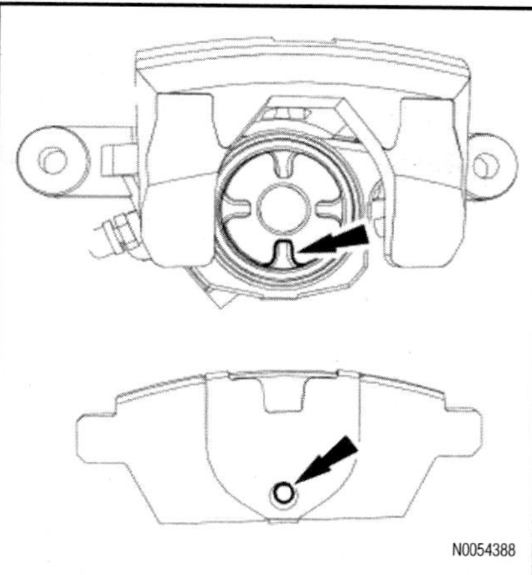

Fig. 5 Position the notch in the caliper piston so that it will correctly align with the pin on the backside of the inboard brake pad

To install:

CAUTION

Always install new brake shoes or pads at both ends of an axle to reduce the possibility of brakes pulling vehicle to one side. Failure to follow this instruction may result in uneven braking and serious personal injury.

11. Using the Rear Caliper Piston Adjuster or equivalent tool, rotate the caliper piston clockwise to compress the piston into its cylinder. A moderate to heavy force toward the caliper piston must be applied. If sufficient force is not applied, the internal park brake mechanism clutch cone will not engage and the piston will not compress.
12. Clean the residual adhesive from the brake caliper fingers and piston using specified brake parts cleaner.
13. Position the notch in the caliper piston so that it will correctly align with the pin on the backside of the inboard brake pad.
14. Install the new spring clips and brake pads to the brake caliper anchor plate. Do not allow grease, oil, brake fluid or other contaminants to contact the pad lining material. Do not install contaminated pads.
15. Position the brake caliper and install the 2 bolts. Tighten to 24 ft. lbs. (33 Nm). Make sure that the brake hose does not become twisted.
16. If necessary, fill the brake fluid reservoir with clean, specified brake fluid.
17. Apply brakes several times to verify correct brake operation.
18. Install the wheel and tire.

BRAKES — PARKING BRAKE

PARKING BRAKE CABLES

ADJUSTMENT

The parking brake cable tension is self-adjusting inside the parking brake control.

CHASSIS ELECTRICAL — AIR BAG (SUPPLEMENTAL RESTRAINT SYSTEM)

GENERAL INFORMATION

CAUTION

These vehicles are equipped with an air bag system. The system must be disarmed before performing service on, or around, system components, the steering column, instrument panel components, wiring and sensors. Failure to follow the safety precautions and the disarming procedure could result in accidental air bag deployment, possible injury and unnecessary system repairs.

SERVICE PRECAUTIONS

Disconnect and isolate the battery negative cable before beginning any airbag system component diagnosis, testing, removal, or installation procedures. Allow system capacitor to discharge for two minutes before beginning any component service. This will disable the airbag system. Failure to disable the airbag system may result in accidental airbag deployment, personal injury, or death.

Do not place an intact undeployed airbag face down on a solid surface. The airbag will propel into the air if accidentally deployed and may result in personal injury or death.

When carrying or handling an undeployed airbag, the trim side (face) of the airbag should be pointing away from the body to minimize possibility of injury if accidental deployment occurs. Failure to do this may result in personal injury or death.

Replace airbag system components with OEM replacement parts. Substitute parts may appear interchangeable, but internal differences may result in inferior occupant protection. Failure to do so may result in occupant personal injury or death.

Wear safety glasses, rubber gloves, and long sleeved clothing when cleaning powder residue from vehicle after an airbag deployment. Powder residue emitted from a deployed airbag can cause skin irritation. Flush affected area with cool water if irritation is experienced. If nasal or throat irritation is experienced, exit the vehicle for fresh air until the irritation ceases. If irritation continues, see a physician.

Do not use a replacement airbag that is not in the original packaging. This may result in improper deployment, personal injury, or death.

The factory installed fasteners, screws and bolts used to fasten airbag components have a special coating and are specifically designed for the airbag system. Do not use substitute fasteners. Use only original equipment fasteners listed in the parts catalog when fastener replacement is required.

During, and following, any child restraint anchor service, due to impact event or vehicle repair, carefully inspect all mounting hardware, tether straps, and anchors for proper installation, operation, or damage. If a child restraint anchor is found damaged in any way, the anchor must be replaced. Failure to do this may result in personal injury or death.

Deployed and non-deployed airbags may or may not have live pyrotechnic material within the airbag inflator.

Do not dispose of driver/passenger/curtain airbags or seat belt tensioners unless you are sure of complete deployment. Refer to the Hazardous Substance Control System for proper disposal.

Dispose of deployed airbags and tensioners consistent with state, provincial, local, and federal regulations.

After any airbag component testing or service, do not connect the battery negative cable. Personal injury or death may result if the system test is not performed first.

If the vehicle is equipped with the Occupant Classification System (OCS), do not connect the battery negative cable before performing the OCS Verification Test using the scan tool and the appropriate diagnostic information. Personal injury or death may result if the system test is not performed properly.

Never replace both the Occupant Restraint Controller (ORC) and the Occupant Classification Module (OCM) at the same time. If both require replacement, replace one, then perform the Airbag System test before replacing the other.

Both the ORC and the OCM store Occupant Classification System (OCS) calibration data, which they transfer to one another when one of them is replaced. If both are replaced at the same time, an irreversible fault will be set in both modules and the OCS may malfunction and cause personal injury or death.

If equipped with OCS, the Seat Weight Sensor is a sensitive, calibrated unit and must be handled carefully. Do not drop or handle roughly. If dropped or damaged, replace with another sensor. Failure to do so may result in occupant injury or death.

If equipped with OCS, the front passenger seat must be handled carefully as well. When removing the seat, be careful when setting on floor not to drop. If dropped, the sensor may be inoperative, could result in occupant injury, or possibly death.

If equipped with OCS, when the passenger front seat is on the floor, no one should sit in the front passenger seat. This uneven force may damage the sensing ability of the seat weight sensors. If sat on and damaged, the sensor may be inoperative, could result in occupant injury, or possibly death.

Never probe the electrical connectors on air bag, Safety Canopy® or side air curtain modules. Failure to follow this instruction may result in the accidental deployment of these modules.

Do not handle, move or change the original horizontal mounting position of the restraints control module (RCM) while the RCM is connected and the ignition switch is ON. Failure to follow this instruction may result in the accidental deployment of the Safety Canopy®.

To reduce the risk of accidental deployment, do not use any memory saver devices.

DISARMING THE SYSTEM

➡The air bag warning indicator illuminates when the correct Restraints Control Module (RCM) fuse is removed and the ignition is ON.

➡The Supplemental Restraint System (SRS) must be fully operational and free of faults before releasing the vehicle to the customer.

1. Before servicing the vehicle, refer to the Precautions Section.
2. Turn all vehicle accessories OFF.
3. Turn the ignition OFF.
4. At the Smart Junction Box (SJB), located below the left-hand side of the instrument panel, remove the cover and RCM fuse 32 (10A) from the SJB. For additional information, refer to the Wiring Diagrams.
5. Turn the ignition ON and monitor the air bag warning indicator for at least 30 seconds. The air bag warning indicator will flash once, then remain illuminated continuously (no flashing) if the correct RCM fuse has been removed. If the air bag warning indicator does not remain illuminated continuously, remove the correct RCM fuse before proceeding.
6. Turn the ignition OFF.
7. Disconnect the battery ground cable and wait at least one minute.

ARMING THE SYSTEM

Vehicles With Keyed Ignition (Ignition Switch)

1. Before servicing the vehicle, refer to the Precautions Section.
2. Turn the ignition from OFF to ON.
3. Install RCM fuse 32 (10A) to the SJB and close the cover.

⁂ CAUTION

Make sure no one is in the vehicle and there is nothing blocking or placed in front of any air bag module when the battery is connected. Failure to follow these instructions may result in serious personal injury in the event of an accidental deployment.

4. Connect the battery ground cable.
5. Prove out the SRS as follows:
    a. Turn the ignition from ON to OFF.
    b. Wait 10 seconds, then turn the ignition back to ON and monitor the air bag warning indicator with the air bag modules installed. The air bag warning indicator will illuminate continuously for approximately 6 seconds and then turn off. If a SRS fault is present, the air bag warning indicator will: - fail to light. - remain lit continuously. - flash. The flashing might not occur until approximately 30 seconds after the ignition has been turned from OFF to the ON position. This is the time required for the RCM to complete the testing of the SRS . If the air bag warning indicator is inoperative and a SRS fault exists, a chime will sound in a pattern of 5 sets of 5 beeps. If this occurs, the air bag warning indicator and any SRS fault discovered must be diagnosed and repaired. Clear all continuous DTCs from the RCM and Occupant Classification System Module (OCSM) using a scan tool.

Vehicles With Keyless Ignition (Push-Button Start System)

See Figure 6.

1. Before servicing the vehicle, refer to the Precautions Section.
2. Install RCM fuse 32 (10A) to the SJB and install the cover.
3. Remove Battery Junction Box (BJB) relay 63.
4. Install a 20A fused jumper wire in BJB relay 63 cavities as shown.

⁂ CAUTION

Make sure no one is in the vehicle and there is nothing blocking or placed in front of any air bag module when the battery is connected. Failure to follow these instructions may

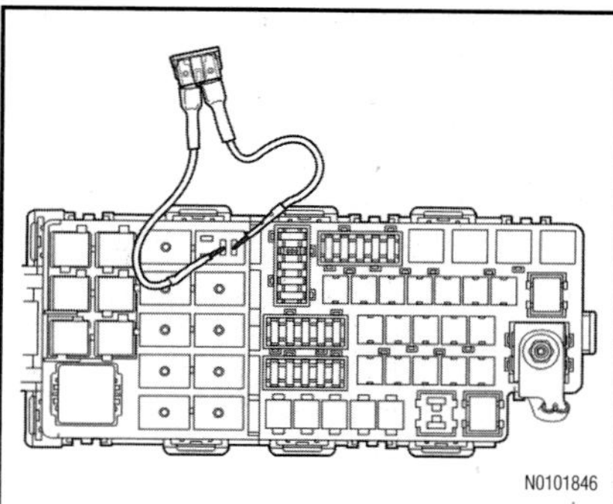

Fig. 6 Install a 20A fused jumper wire in BJB relay 63 cavities as shown

result in serious personal injury in the event of an accidental deployment.

5. Connect the battery ground cable.
6. Prove out the SRS as follows: Turn the ignition from ON to OFF. Wait 10 seconds, then turn the ignition ON and monitor the air bag warning indicator with the air bag modules installed. The air bag warning indicator will light continuously for approximately 6 seconds and then turn off. If an air bag SRS fault is detected, the air bag warning indicator will: - fail to light. - remain lit continuously. - flash. The flashing might not occur until approximately 30 seconds after the ignition has been turned from the OFF to the ON position. This is the time required to complete testing of the SRS. If the air bag warning indicator is inoperative and a SRS fault exists, a chime will sound in a pattern of 5 sets of 5 beeps. If this occurs, the air bag warning indicator and any SRS fault discovered must be diagnosed and repaired. Clear all RCM and OCSM CMDTCs.
7. Disconnect the battery ground cable.
8. Remove the fused jumper wire from the BJB.
9. Install BJB relay 63 and cover.
10. Connect the battery ground cable.
11. Clear all CMDTCs from the RCM and OCSM.

CLOCKSPRING CENTERING

CAUTION

If the clockspring is not correctly centralized, it may fail prematurely. If in doubt, repeat the centralizing procedure. Failure to follow these instructions may increase the risk of serious personal injury or death in a crash.

WARNING

Do not over-rotate the clockspring inner rotor. The internal ribbon wire is connected to the clockspring rotor. The internal ribbon wire acts as a stop and can be broken from its internal connection. Failure to follow this instruction may result in component damage and/or system failure.

WARNING

If installing a new clockspring, do not remove the clockspring anti-rotation key until the steering wheel is installed. If the anti-rotation key has been removed before installing the steering wheel, the clockspring must be centered. Failure to follow this instruction may result in component damage and/or system failure.

1. Before servicing the vehicle, refer to the Precautions Section.
2. Depower (disarm) the SRS.
3. Install the clockspring and 2 screws.
4. Connect the clockspring electrical connector.
5. If equipped, install the steering wheel angle sensor and 2 screws, and connect the electrical connector.
6. If a new clockspring was installed and the anti-rotation key has not been removed, proceed to Step 8, otherwise proceed to Step 6.
7. If a new clockspring was installed and the anti-rotation key has been removed before the steering wheel is installed or the same clockspring is being installed, rotate the clockspring inner rotor counterclockwise and carefully feel for the ribbon wire to run out of length with slight resistance. Stop rotating the clockspring inner rotor at this point.
8. Starting with the clockspring inner rotor in the 12 o'clock position, rotate the inner rotor clockwise through 2 revolutions to center the clockspring. The clockspring inner rotor must be in the 12 o'clock position to be correctly centered.

WARNING

To prevent damage to the clockspring, make sure the road wheels are in the straight-ahead position.

9. Install the steering wheel.
10. If a new clockspring was installed, remove the anti-rotation key.
11. Install the driver air bag module.
12. Repower (arm) the SRS .

DRIVE TRAIN

AUTOMATIC TRANSAXLE FLUID

DRAIN AND REFILL

3.5L Engine

See Figures 7 through 9.

1. Before servicing the vehicle, refer to the Precautions Section.
2. With the vehicle in NEUTRAL, position it on a hoist.
3. Remove the transmission fluid drain plug and allow the transmission fluid to drain. If an internal problem is suspected, drain the transmission fluid through a paper filter. A small amount of metal or friction particles may be found from normal wear. If an excessive amount of metal or friction material is present, the transaxle will need to be overhauled.

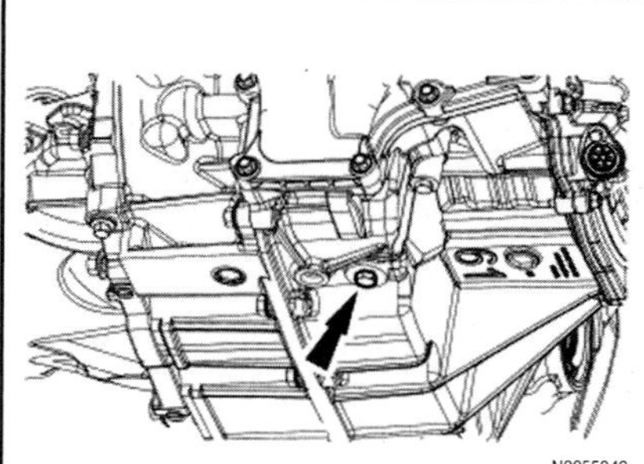

Fig. 7 Remove the transmission fluid drain plug

4. Install the transmission fluid drain plug. Tighten to 80 inch lbs. (9 Nm).
5. Clean the area around the clamp that connects the Air Cleaner (ACL) to the ACL outlet pipe.
6. If equipped, remove the bolt cover.
7. Remove the ACL from the ACL bracket and the ACL outlet hose. Do not disconnect the Intake Air Temperature (IAT) sensor electrical connector.
   a. Remove the wiring harness retainer from the ACL by pulling it up.
   b. Remove the 2 ACL bolts.
   c. Loosen the clamp.
   d. Pull up on the ACL to remove it from the 2 rubber grommets and position it aside with the IAT sensor electrical connector still connected.

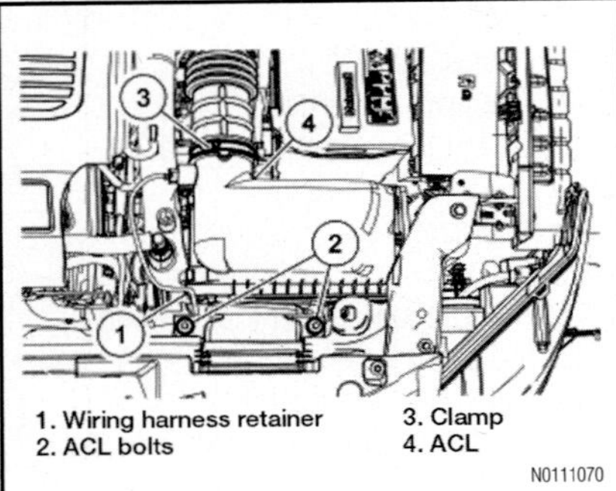

Fig. 8 Remove the ACL from the ACL bracket and the ACL outlet hose

8. With the IAT sensor connected, rotate the ACL 90 degrees to access the transmission fluid level indicator. Install the ACL in the outlet pipe and tighten the clamp. Tighten to 44 inch lbs. (5 Nm).

9. Remove the transmission fluid level indicator. If the transaxle was removed and disassembled, fill the transaxle with 6.5 qt. (6.2L) of clean transmission fluid. If the main control cover was removed for in-vehicle repair, fill the transaxle with 4.5 qt. (4.3L) of clean transmission fluid.

10. Start the engine and let it run for 3 minutes. Move the range selector lever into each gear position and allow engagement for a minimum of ten seconds. Check the transmission fluid level by installing and removing the transmission fluid level indicator. When installing the transmission fluid level indicator, be sure it is seated and rotate it clockwise to the locked position. Adjust the transmission fluid level.

11. Turn the engine off, loosen the clamp and remove the ACL assembly from the ACL outlet pipe and position it aside with the IAT sensor electrical connector connected.

12. Install the ACL .

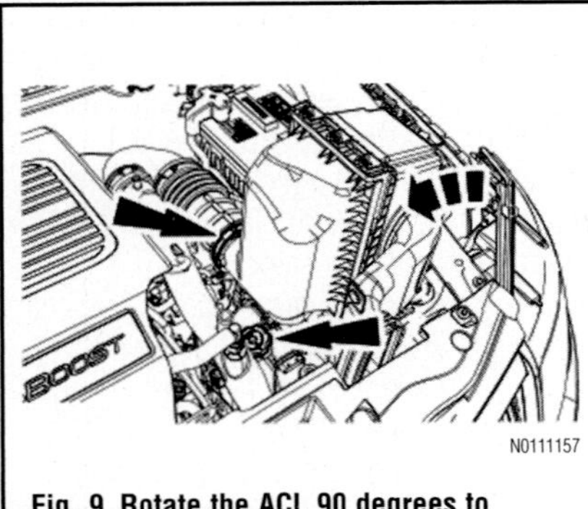

Fig. 9 Rotate the ACL 90 degrees to access the transmission fluid level indicator

a. Position the ACL assembly in the ACL outlet pipe and push down to install it in the 2 rubber grommets.

b. Tighten the clamp to 44 inch lbs. (5 Nm).

c. Install the 2 ACL bolts and tighten to 44 inch lbs. (5 Nm).

d. Install the wiring harness retainer on the ACL .

13. If equipped, install the bolt cover.

3.7L Engine

See Figure 10.

1. Before servicing the vehicle, refer to the Precautions Section.

2. With the vehicle in NEUTRAL, position it on a hoist.

3. Remove the transmission fluid drain plug and allow the transmission fluid to drain. If an internal problem is suspected, drain the transmission fluid through a paper filter. A small amount of metal or friction particles may be found from normal wear. If an excessive amount of metal or friction material is present, the transaxle will need to be overhauled.

4. Install the transmission fluid drain plug. Tighten to 80 inch lbs. (9 Nm).

5. Remove the transmission fluid level indicator. If the transaxle was removed and disassembled, fill the transaxle with 6.5 qt. (6.2L) of clean transmission fluid. If the main control cover was removed for in-vehicle repair, fill the transaxle with 4.5 qt. (4.3L) of clean transmission fluid.

6. Start the engine and let it run for 3 minutes. Move the range selector lever into each gear position and allow engagement for a minimum of ten seconds. Check the transmission fluid level by installing and removing the transmission fluid level indicator. When installing the transmission fluid level indicator, be sure it is seated and rotate it clockwise to the locked position. Adjust the transmission fluid level.

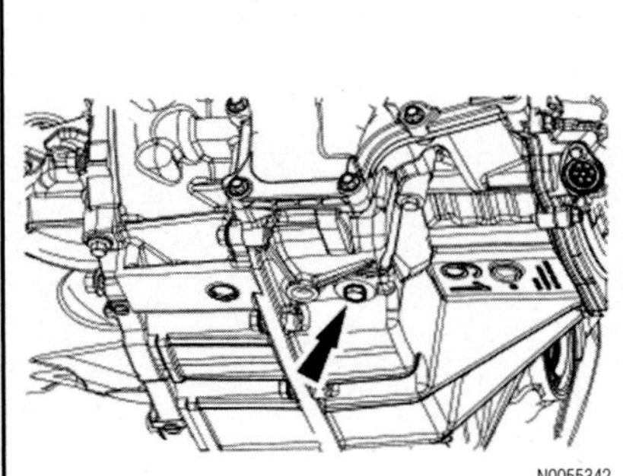

Fig. 10 Remove the transmission fluid drain plug

POWER TRANSFER UNIT (PTU)

REMOVAL & INSTALLATION

3.5L Engine

See Figure 11.

1. Before servicing the vehicle, refer to the Precautions Section.

2. With the vehicle in NEUTRAL, position it on a hoist.

3. Using a suitable holding device, hold the steering wheel in the straight-ahead position.

4. Remove the 4 retainers and the underbody shield.

5. Remove the right-hand halfshaft.

6. Remove the right-hand catalytic converter.

7. Remove the 4 driveshaft-to-output flange bolts, and disconnect the driveshaft from the output flange. Position the driveshaft aside. To maintain the initial driveshaft balance, matchmark the driveshaft flange and the output flange.

8. Remove the bolt and disconnect the steering column shaft from the steering gear. Discard the bolt. Do not allow the intermediate shaft to rotate while it is disconnected from the gear or damage to the clockspring may occur. If there is evidence that the intermediate shaft has rotated, the clockspring must be removed and recentered.

9. Remove the bolt and disconnect the 2 Electronic Power Assist Steering (EPAS) electrical connectors and the wiring retainer.

10. Remove the 3 bolts and the right-hand turbocharger lower bracket.

11. Remove the 3 bolts and the Power Transfer Unit (PTU) support bracket.

12. Position the rear engine roll restrictor aside in the following sequence:

a. Remove the 2 engine roll restrictor-to-transaxle bolts.

b. Loosen the rear engine roll restrictor bolt and pivot the roll restrictor downward.

13. Remove the front engine roll restrictor bolt and position the engine roll restrictor aside.

14. Position a jackstand under the rear of the subframe.

15. Remove the subframe bracket-to-body bolts.

16. Remove the rear subframe bolts and the subframe brackets. Discard the bolts.

17. Position a jackstand under the front roll restrictor bracket and raise the engine far enough to allow the PTU to be removed.

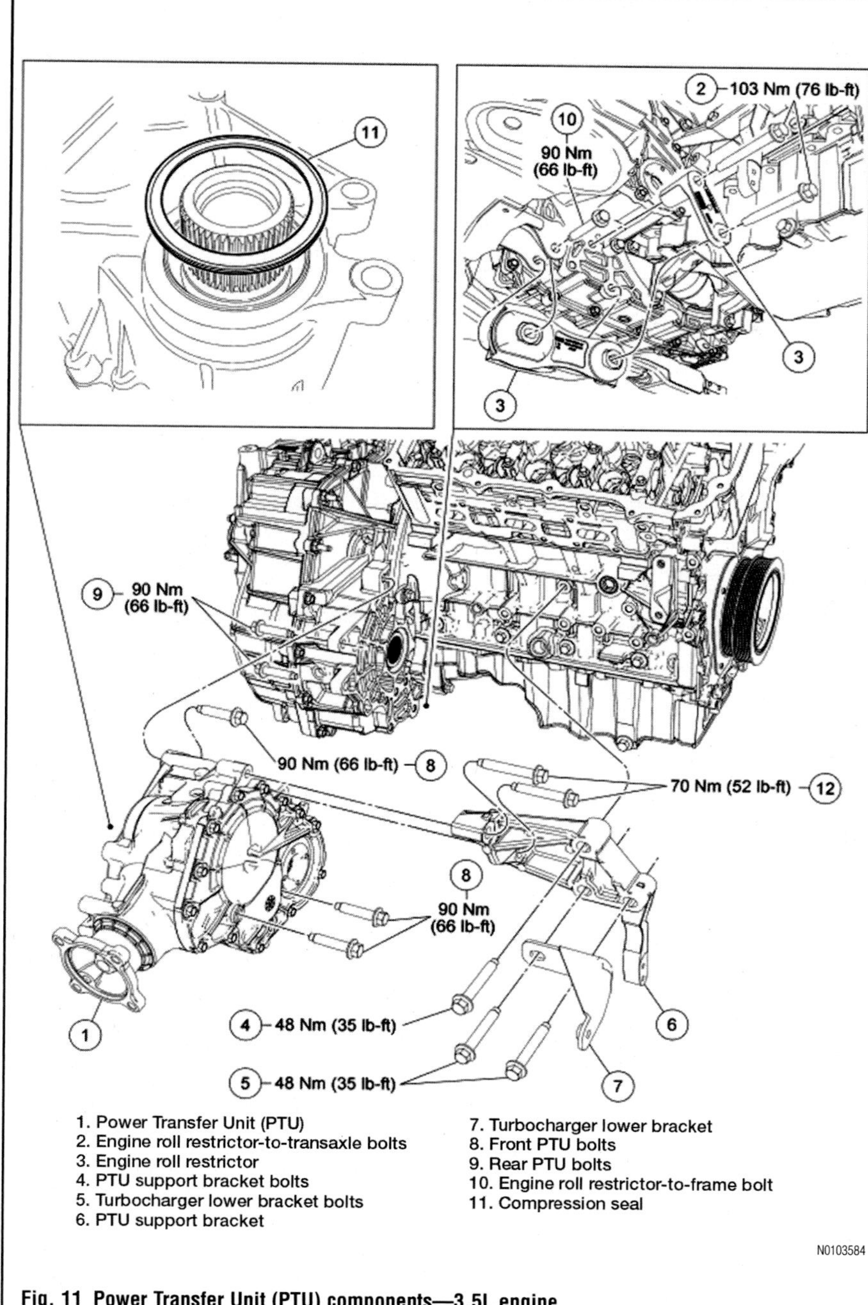

Fig. 11 Power Transfer Unit (PTU) components—3.5L engine

18. Remove the 5 PTU bolts. Pull the PTU outward to separate it from the transaxle. Rotate the output flange upward, then turn it and remove the PTU from the vehicle. Position a drain pan under the vehicle.

19. Using a small screwdriver, remove and discard the compression seal.

To install:

20. Using a suitable tool, install the new compression seal.

21. Position the PTU and install the 5 bolts. Tighten to 66 ft. lbs. (90 Nm).

22. Lower the engine and remove the jackstand from the front of the roll restrictor.

23. Using the jackstand, raise the subframe into the installed position.

24. Position the subframe brackets and loosely install the 4 bolts.

25. Install the 2 rear subframe bolts. Tighten to 111 ft. lbs. (150 Nm).

26. Tighten the 4 subframe bracket-to-body bolts to 41 ft. lbs. (55 Nm).

27. Remove the jackstand from the subframe.

28. Position the front engine roll restrictor to the bracket and install the bolt. Tighten the front engine roll restrictor bolt to 66 ft. lbs. (90 Nm).

29. Position the rear engine roll restrictor to the transaxle and install the 2 bolts.
   a. Tighten the engine roll restrictor-to-transaxle bolts to 76 ft. lbs. (103 Nm).
   b. Tighten the rear engine roll restrictor bolt to 66 ft. lbs. (90 Nm).

30. Position the PTU support bracket in place and install the 3 bolts.
   a. Tighten the 2 bolts to 52 ft. lbs. (70 Nm).
   b. Tighten the 1 bolt to 35 ft. lbs. (48 Nm).

31. Install the right-hand turbocharger lower bracket and the 3 bolts.
   a. Tighten the bolt to 14 ft. lbs. (19 Nm).
   b. Tighten the 2 bolts to 35 ft. lbs. (48 Nm).

32. Connect the 2 Electronic Power Assist Steering (EPAS) electrical connectors, attach the wiring retainer and install the bolt. Tighten to 80 inch lbs. (9 Nm).

33. Install the steering intermediate shaft onto the steering gear and install a new bolt. Tighten to 15 ft. lbs. (20 Nm). Do not allow the intermediate shaft to rotate while it is disconnected from the gear or damage to the clockspring may occur. If there is evidence that the intermediate shaft has rotated, the clockspring must be removed and recentered.

34. Align the matchmarks and install the 4 driveshaft-to-output flange bolts. Tighten to 52 ft. lbs. (70 Nm).

35. Install the right-hand catalytic converter.

36. Install the right-hand front halfshaft.

37. Install the underbody shield and the 4 retainers.

38. Remove the locking device from the steering wheel.

3.7L Engine

See Figure 12.

1. Before servicing the vehicle, refer to the Precautions Section.

2. With the vehicle in NEUTRAL, position it on a hoist.

3. Remove the right-hand halfshaft.

4. Remove the right-hand catalytic converter.

5. Remove the 4 driveshaft-to-output flange bolts, then disconnect the driveshaft from the output flange. Position the driveshaft aside. To maintain the initial driveshaft balance, matchmark the driveshaft flange and the output flange.

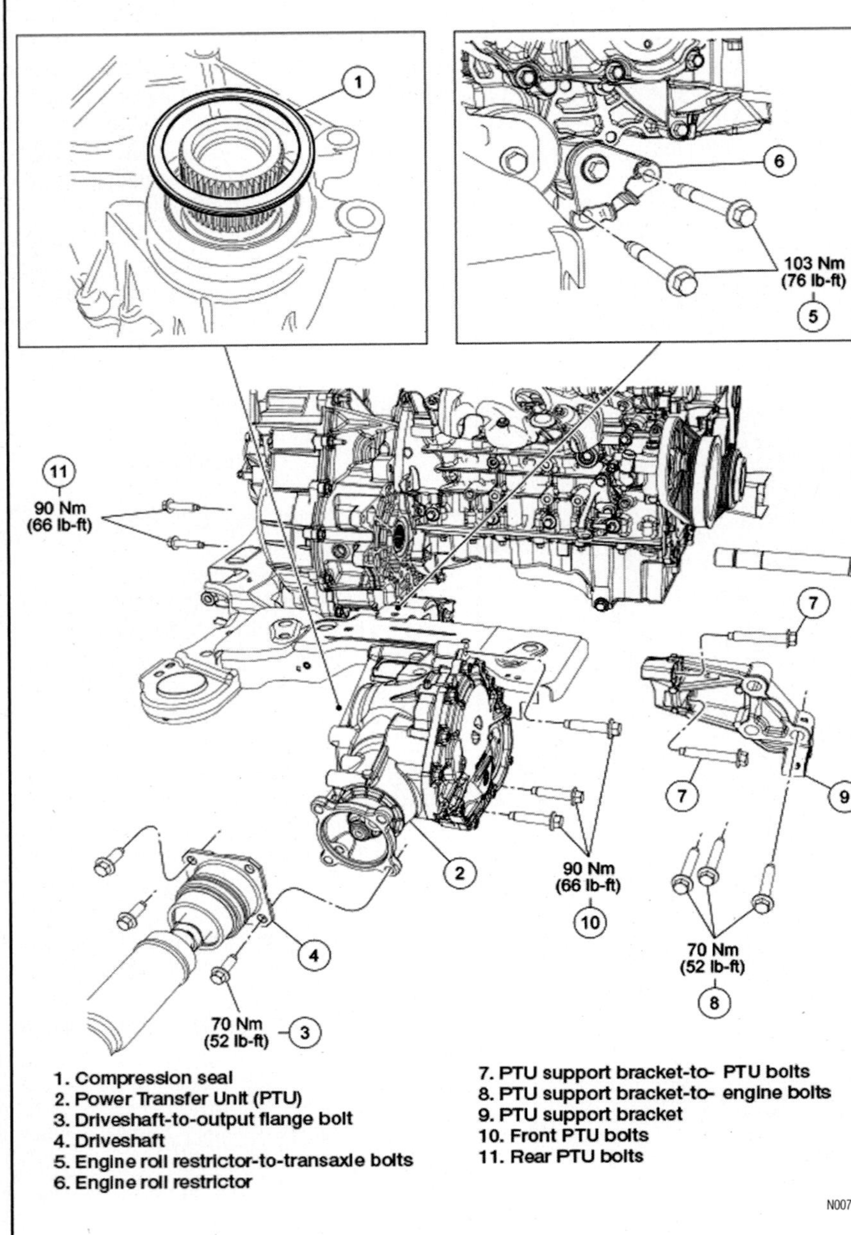

Fig. 12 Power Transfer Unit (PTU) components—3.7L engine

6. Remove the 5 Power Transfer Unit (PTU) support bracket bolts and the support bracket.
7. Position the engine roll restrictor aside.
    a. Remove the 2 engine roll restrictor-to-transaxle bolts.
    b. Loosen the rear engine roll restrictor bolt and pivot the roll restrictor downward.
8. Remove the 5 PTU bolts. Pull the PTU outward and separate it from the transaxle. Rotate the output flange upward, then turn it and remove the PTU from the vehicle. Position a drain pan under the vehicle.
9. Using a small screwdriver, remove and discard the compression seal.

To install:

10. Using a suitable tool, install the new compression seal.
11. Position the PTU and install the 5 bolts. Tighten to 66 ft. lbs. (90 Nm).
12. Position the PTU support bracket in place and install the 3 PTU support bracket-to-engine bolts. Tighten to 52 ft. lbs. (70 Nm).
13. Install the 2 PTU support bracket-to-PTU bolts. Tighten to 52 ft. lbs. (70 Nm).
14. Position the engine roll restrictor to the transaxle and install the 2 bolts.
    a. Tighten the engine roll restrictor-to-transaxle bolts to 76 ft. lbs. (103 Nm).
    b. Tighten the rear engine roll restrictor bolt to 66 ft. lbs. (90 Nm).
15. Align the matchmarks and install the 4 driveshaft-to-output flange bolts. Tighten to 52 ft. lbs. (70 Nm).
16. Install the right-hand catalytic converter.
17. Install the right-hand front halfshaft.
18. Top off fluids as necessary.

FRONT HALFSHAFT

REMOVAL & INSTALLATION

Right-Hand Halfshaft

3.5L Engines

See Figures 13 through 17.

1. Before servicing the vehicle, refer to the Precautions Section.
2. With the vehicle in NEUTRAL, position it on a hoist.
3. Remove the wheel and tire.
4. Apply the brake to keep the halfshaft from rotating, and remove the wheel hub nut. Do not discard at this time.
5. For All-Wheel Drive (AWD) vehicles, Remove the right-hand brake disc.
6. Remove the bolt from the brake hose bracket.

**** WARNING**

Suspension fasteners are critical parts because they affect performance of vital components and systems and their failure may result in major service expense. New parts must be installed with the same part number or equivalent part, if replacement is necessary. Do not use a replacement part of lesser quality or substitute design. Torque values must be used as specified during reassembly to make sure of correct retention of these parts.

**** WARNING**

Use care when releasing the lower arm and knuckle into the resting position or damage to the ball joint seal or Constant Velocity (CV) boot may occur.

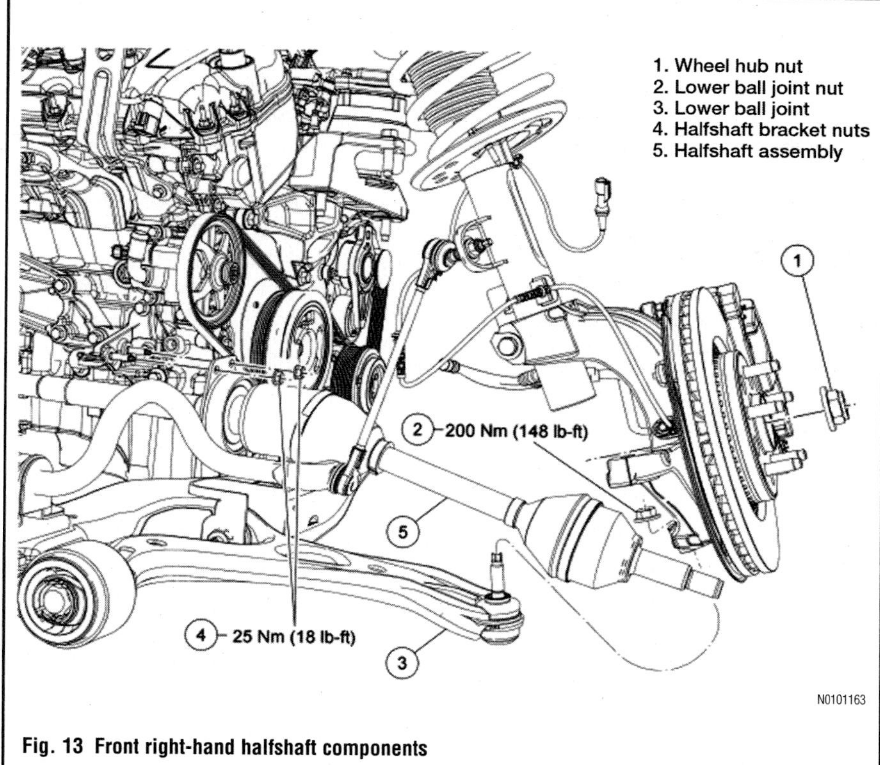

Fig. 13 Front right-hand halfshaft components

7. Remove and discard the lower ball joint nut. Use the hex-holding feature to prevent the stud from turning while removing the nut.
   a. Separate the lower ball joint from the wheel knuckle.
8. Using the Front Wheel Hub Remover or equivalent tool, separate the halfshaft from the wheel hub.
9. Pull the wheel knuckle outboard and rotate it toward the rear of the vehicle. Secure the wheel knuckle assembly.
10. Remove the 2 lower scrivets from the rubber shield and position the shield aside.
11. Separate the halfshaft from the intermediate shaft and remove the halfshaft.

To install:

WARNING

A new Power Transfer Unit (PTU) shaft seal must be installed whenever the intermediate shaft is removed or damage to the components can occur.

12. For AWD vehicles, install a new intermediate shaft seal and deflector.
13. Install the halfshaft to the intermediate shaft.
14. Rotate the wheel knuckle into position and insert the halfshaft into the wheel hub.

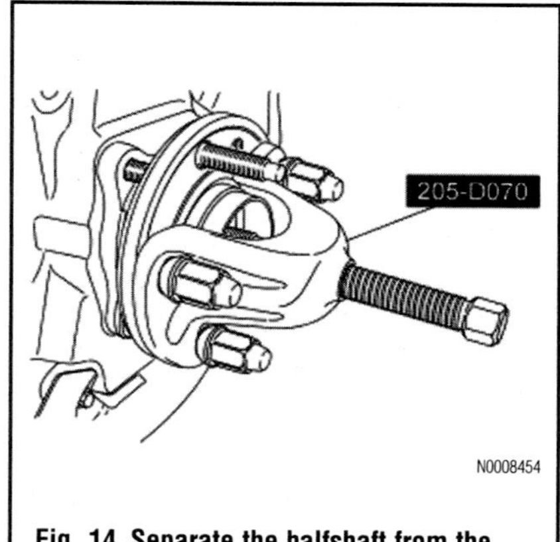

Fig. 14 Separate the halfshaft from the wheel hub

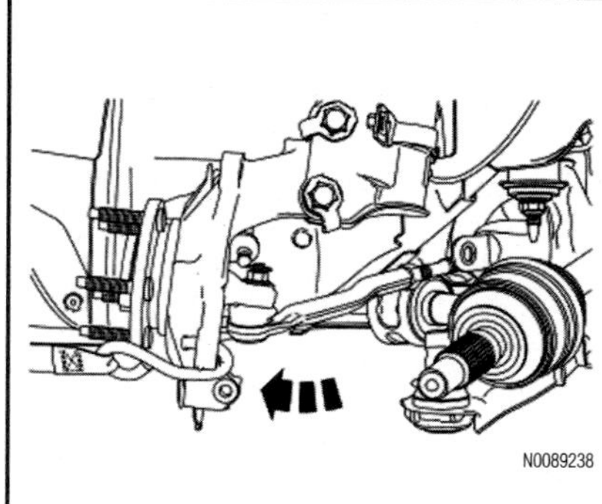

Fig. 15 Pull the wheel knuckle outboard and rotate it toward the rear of the vehicle

15. Position the lower ball joint into the wheel knuckle and install the new nut. Tighten to 148 ft. lbs. (200 Nm).
16. Position the brake hose bracket and install the bolt. Tighten to 22 ft. lbs. (30 Nm).
17. Install the 2 scrivets in the rubber shield.
18. For AWD vehicles, install the right-hand brake disc.

WARNING

Do not tighten the front wheel hub nut with the vehicle on the ground. The nut must be tightened to specification before the vehicle is lowered onto the wheels. Wheel bearing damage will occur if the wheel bearing is loaded with the weight of the vehicle applied.

19. Using the previously removed wheel hub nut, seat the halfshaft. Apply the brake to keep the halfshaft from rotating.
   a. Tighten to 258 ft. lbs. (350 Nm).
   b. Remove and discard the wheel hub nut.

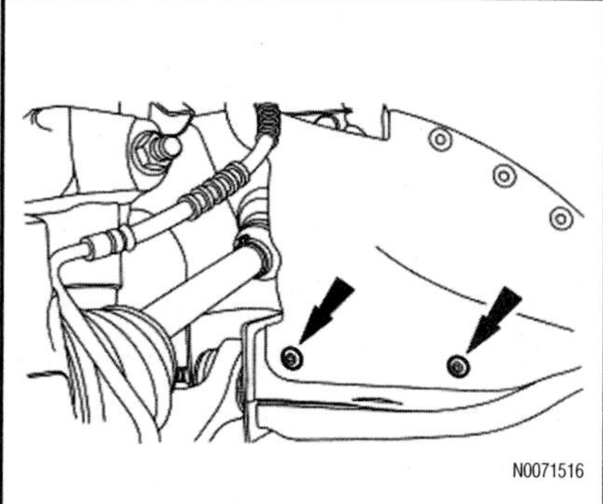

Fig. 16 Remove the 2 lower scrivets from the rubber shield and position the shield aside

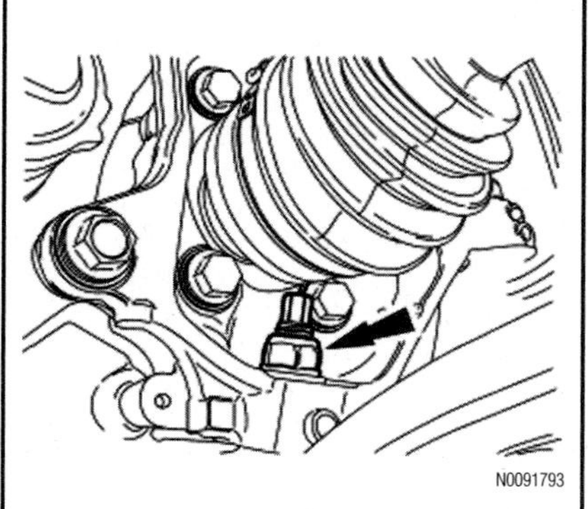

Fig. 17 Position the lower ball joint into the wheel knuckle and install the new nut

⁂ WARNING

The wheel hub nut contains a one-time locking chemical that is activated by the heat created when it is tightened. Install and tighten the new wheel hub nut to specification within 5 minutes of starting it on the threads. Always install a new wheel hub nut after loosening or when not tightened within the specified time or damage to the components can occur.

20. Apply the brake to keep the halfshaft from rotating, and install a new wheel hub nut. Tighten to 258 ft. lbs. (350 Nm).
21. Install the wheel and tire.
22. Lower the vehicle.

3.7L Engines

See Figures 18 through 20.

1. Before servicing the vehicle, refer to the Precautions Section.
2. With the vehicle in NEUTRAL, position it on a hoist.
3. Remove the wheel and tire.
4. Apply the brake to keep the halfshaft from rotating, and remove the wheel hub nut. Do not discard at this time.
5. For All-Wheel Drive (AWD) vehicles, Remove the right-hand brake disc.
6. Remove the bolt from the brake hose bracket.

⁂ WARNING

Suspension fasteners are critical parts because they affect performance of vital components and systems and their failure may result in major service expense. New parts must be installed with the same part number or equivalent part, if replacement is necessary. Do not use a replacement part of lesser quality or substitute design. Torque values must be used as specified during reassembly to make sure of correct retention of these parts.

⁂ WARNING

Use care when releasing the lower arm and knuckle into the resting position or damage to the ball joint seal or Constant Velocity (CV) boot may occur.

7. Remove and discard the lower ball joint nut. Use the hex-holding feature to prevent the stud from turning while removing the nut.
   a. Separate the lower ball joint from the wheel knuckle.
8. Using the Front Wheel Hub Remover or equivalent tool, separate the halfshaft from the wheel hub.
9. Pull the wheel knuckle outboard and rotate it toward the rear of the vehicle. Secure the wheel knuckle assembly.
10. Remove the 2 lower scrivets from the rubber shield and position the shield aside.
11. Remove the 2 halfshaft bracket nuts.
12. Remove the intermediate and halfshaft assembly.
   a. Inspect the intermediate shaft for pitting or damage in the seal contact area. Replace if necessary.
13. Inspect the halfshaft hub for wear or damage and install a new halfshaft, if necessary.
   a. Inspect the differential seal surface.
   b. Inspect the halfshaft bushing surface. If this surface is damaged, inspect the halfshaft bushing for damage.
   c. Inspect the differential side gear splines.

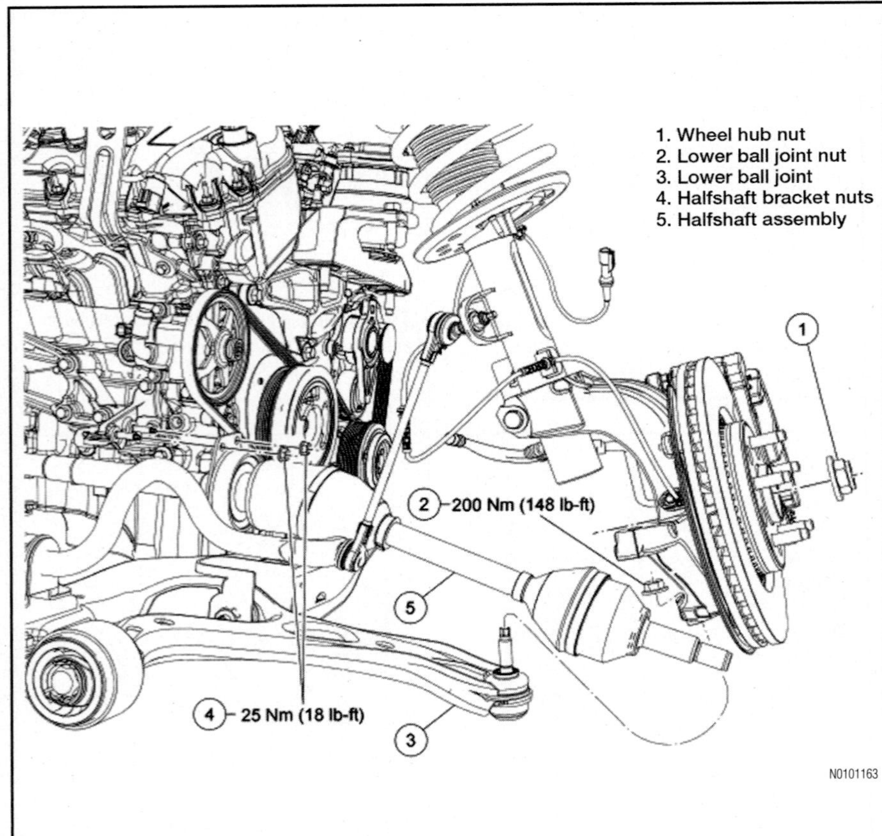

Fig. 18 Front right-hand halfshaft components

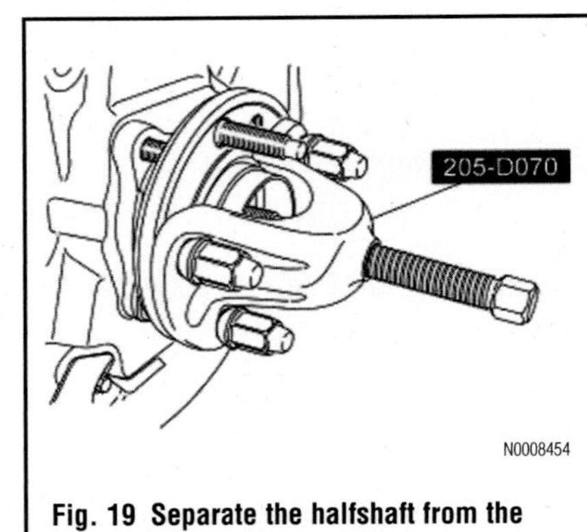

Fig. 19 Separate the halfshaft from the wheel hub

Fig. 20 Remove the 2 lower scrivets from the rubber shield and position the shield aside

To install:

14. For AWD vehicles, install a new intermediate shaft seal and deflector.

⁂ WARNING

A new Power Transfer Unit (PTU) shaft seal must be installed whenever the intermediate shaft is removed or damage to the components can occur.

15. Install the halfshaft to the intermediate shaft.
16. Install the intermediate and halfshaft assembly and the 2 halfshaft bracket nuts. Tighten to 18 ft. lbs. (25 Nm).
17. Rotate the wheel knuckle into position and insert the halfshaft into the wheel hub.
18. Position the lower ball joint into the wheel knuckle and install the new nut. Tighten to 148 ft. lbs. (200 Nm).
19. Position the brake hose bracket and install the bolt. Tighten to 22 ft. lbs. (30 Nm).
20. Install the 2 scrivets in the rubber shield.
21. For AWD vehicles, install the right-hand brake disc.

⁂ WARNING

Do not tighten the front wheel hub nut with the vehicle on the ground. The nut must be tightened to specification before the vehicle is lowered onto the wheels. Wheel bearing damage will occur if the wheel bearing is loaded with the weight of the vehicle applied.

22. Using the previously removed wheel hub nut, seat the halfshaft. Apply the brake to keep the halfshaft from rotating.
    a. Tighten to 258 ft. lbs. (350 Nm).
    b. Remove and discard the wheel hub nut.

⁂ WARNING

The wheel hub nut contains a one-time locking chemical that is activated by the heat created when it is tightened. Install and tighten the new wheel hub nut to specification within 5 minutes of starting it on the threads. Always install a new wheel hub nut after loosening or when not tightened within the specified time or damage to the components can occur.

23. Apply the brake to keep the halfshaft from rotating, and install a new wheel hub nut. Tighten to 258 ft. lbs. (350 Nm).
24. Install the wheel and tire.
25. Lower the vehicle.

Left-Hand Halfshaft

See Figures 21 through 23.

1. Before servicing the vehicle, refer to the Precautions Section.
2. With the vehicle in NEUTRAL, position it on a hoist.
3. Remove the wheel and tire.
4. Apply the brake to keep the halfshaft from rotating, and remove the wheel hub nut. Do not discard at this time.

⁂ WARNING

Use care when releasing the lower arm and knuckle into the resting position or damage to the ball joint seal or Constant Velocity (CV) boot may occur.

➡Use the hex-holding feature to prevent the stud from turning while removing the nut.

5. Remove and discard the lower ball joint nut. Separate the ball joint from the wheel knuckle.
6. Using the Front Wheel Hub Remover or equivalent tool, separate the halfshaft from the wheel hub.
7. Pull the wheel knuckle outboard and rotate it toward the rear of the vehicle.

⁂ WARNING

The sharp edges on the stub shaft splines can slice or puncture the oil seal. Use care when inserting the stub shaft into the transmission or damage to the component may occur.

8. Using the Slide Hammer (SST 100-001) and Halfshaft Remover (SST 205-832) or equivalent tools, remove the halfshaft from the transmission.
9. Remove and discard the circlip from the stub shaft.
10. Inspect the halfshaft hub for wear or damage and install a new halfshaft, if necessary.
    a. Inspect the differential seal surface.
    b. Inspect the halfshaft bushing surface. If this surface is damaged, inspect the halfshaft bushing for damage.
    c. Inspect the differential side gear splines.

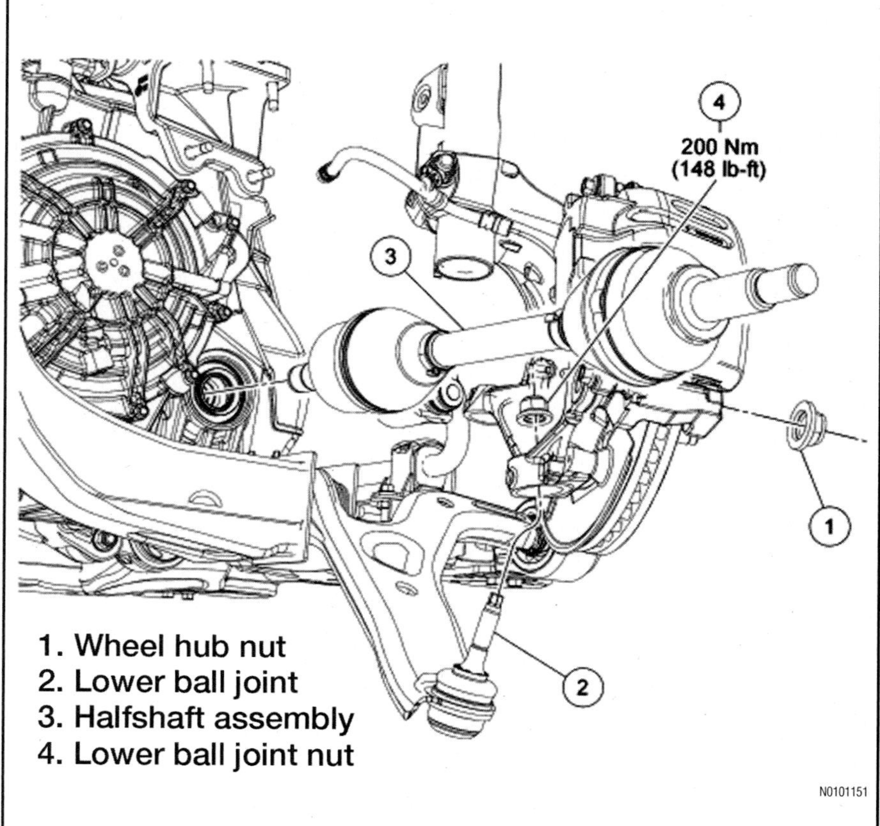

Fig. 21 Front left-hand halfshaft components

To install:

⁂ WARNING

The circlips are unique in size and shape for each shaft. Make sure to use the specified circlip for the application or vehicle damage may occur.

11. Install the correct new circlip on the inboard stub shaft.
12. Push the stub shaft into the transmission so the circlip locks into the differential side gear. After insertion, pull the halfshaft inner end to make sure the circlip is locked.
13. Rotate the wheel knuckle into position and insert the halfshaft into the wheel hub.
14. Position the lower ball joint into the wheel knuckle and install the new nut. Tighten the new nut to 148 ft. lbs. (200 Nm).

⁂ WARNING

Do not tighten the wheel hub nut with the vehicle on the ground. The nut must be tightened to specification before the vehicle is lowered onto the wheels. Wheel bearing damage will occur if the wheel bearing is loaded with the weight of the vehicle applied.

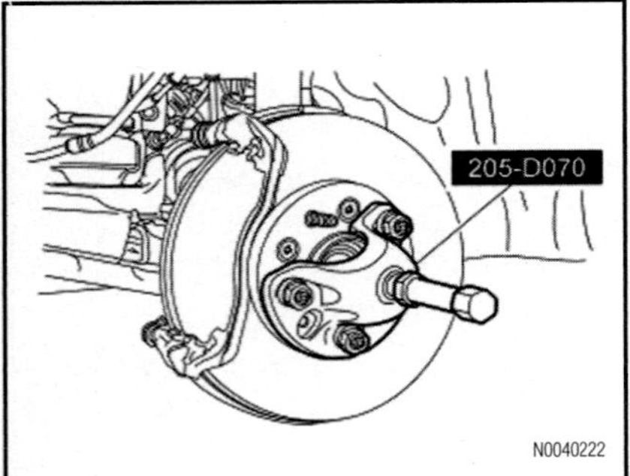

Fig. 22 Separate the halfshaft from the wheel hub

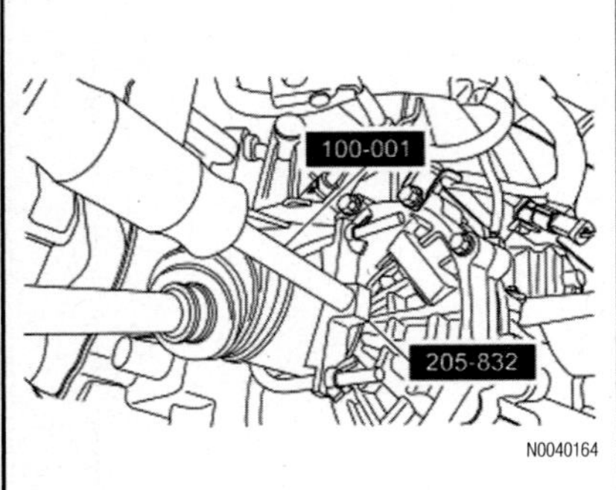

Fig. 23 Remove the halfshaft from the transmission

15. Using the previously removed wheel hub nut, seat the halfshaft. Apply the brake to keep the halfshaft from rotating.
    a. Tighten to 258 ft. lbs. (350 Nm).
    b. Remove and discard the wheel hub nut.

⁂ WARNING

The wheel hub nut contains a one-time locking chemical that is activated by the heat created when it is tightened. Install and tighten the new wheel hub nut to specification within 5 minutes of starting it on the threads. Always install a new wheel hub nut after loosening or when not tightened within the specified time or damage to the components can occur.

16. Apply the brake to keep the halfshaft from rotating, and install a new wheel hub nut. Tighten to 258 ft. lbs. (350 Nm).
17. Install the front wheel and tire.
18. Lower the vehicle.

Intermediate Shaft—3.5L Engines

See Figure 24.

1. Before servicing the vehicle, refer to the Precautions Section.

⁂ WARNING

The intermediate shaft seal in the Power Transfer Unit (PTU) must be replaced whenever the intermediate shaft is removed or a leak may occur.

2. Remove the right front halfshaft assembly.
3. Remove the 2 intermediate shaft support bracket bolts and the intermediate shaft.
4. Remove and discard the circlip from the outboard end of the intermediate shaft.

To install:

5. Install a new 1.181 in. (30 mm) circlip on the outboard end of the intermediate shaft.
6. Install a new intermediate shaft seal in the Power Transfer Unit (PTU).
7. Position the intermediate shaft in the PTU and engage the intermediate shaft splines with the PTU gears.
8. Install the 2 intermediate shaft support bracket bolts. Tighten to 30 ft. lbs. (40 Nm).
9. Install the right halfshaft.

REAR AXLE FLUID

DRAIN & REFILL

See Rear Differential Housing Cover Removal & Installation.

REAR AXLE HOUSING

REMOVAL & INSTALLATION

See Figures 25 and 26.

1. Before servicing the vehicle, refer to the Precautions Section.
2. Remove the driveshaft assembly.
3. Remove the rear halfshafts.
4. Remove the stabilizer bar.
5. Position a suitable transmission

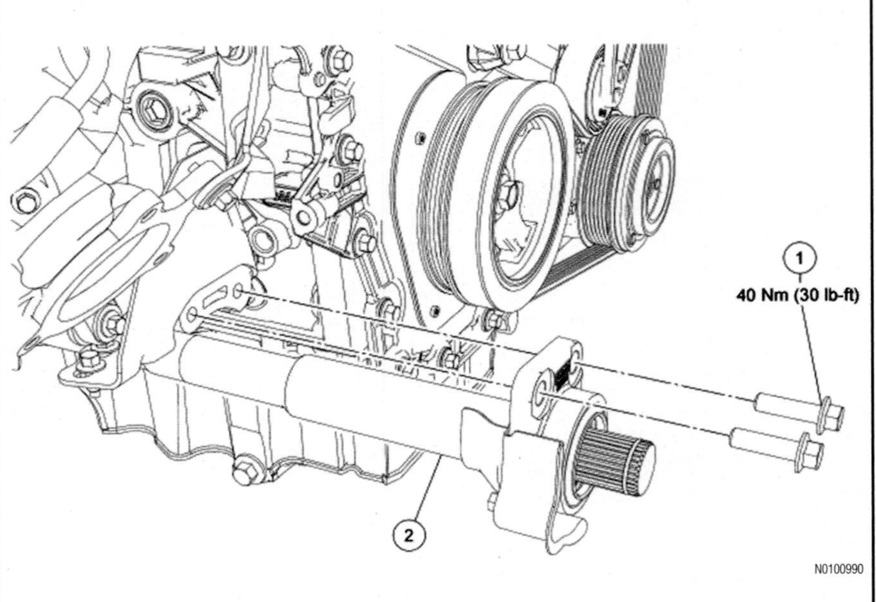

Fig. 24 Intermediate shaft support bracket bolts (1) and intermediate shaft assembly (2)

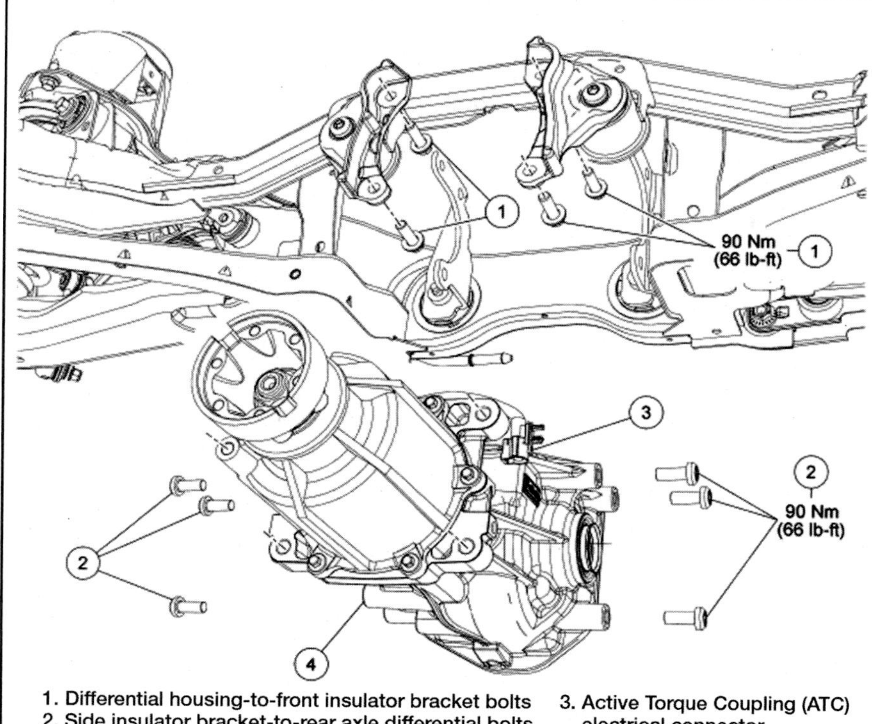

Fig. 25 Rear axle assembly

hydraulic jack to the axle housing. Securely strap the jack to the housing.

6. Remove the 4 differential housing-to-front insulator bracket bolts.
7. Remove the 6 side insulator bracket-to-rear axle differential bolts.
8. Lower the axle to gain clearance to the Active Torque Coupling (ATC) electrical connector and disconnect the connector.
9. Remove the axle assembly.

To install:

10. If replacing the axle assembly, the 4X4 control module will need to be reconfigured with the new Active Torque Coupling (ATC) bar code information. If the new bar code information does not match the existing 4X4 control module information, driveline damage or driveability concerns can occur. The ATC bar code can be found etched on the ATC wire harness connector of the new axle assembly. Record the bar code identification number from the new axle assemblies wire harness connector.
11. Position the axle housing on a suitable transmission hydraulic jack. Securely strap the jack to the housing.
12. Raise the axle and connect the ATC electrical connector.
13. Install the 6 side insulator bracket-to-rear axle differential bolts. Tighten to 66 ft. lbs. (90 Nm).
14. Install the 4 differential housing-to-front insulator bracket bolts. Tighten to 66 ft. lbs. (90 Nm).

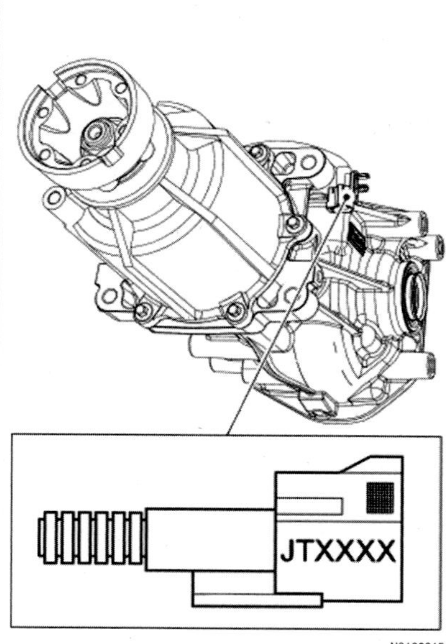

Fig. 26 Record the bar code identification number from the new axle assemblies wire harness connector

15. Install the stabilizer bar.
16. Install the rear halfshafts.
17. Install the driveshaft assembly.
18. Using the scan tool, program the 4-digit bar code information retrieved from the new axle assembly harness connector into the 4X4 control module using the ATC Bar Code Entry service function. The scan tool will verify that the numbers entered are valid and display a message if the information is not correct.

REAR AXLE STUB SHAFT SEAL

REMOVAL & INSTALLATION

See Figures 27 through 29.

➡The Rear Drive Unit (RDU) does not have stub shaft pilot bearings. It has stub shaft seals only.

1. Before servicing the vehicle, refer to the Precautions Section.
2. Remove the halfshaft assembly.
3. Using the Torque Converter Fluid Seal Remover (SST 307-309) and Slide Hammer (SST 100-001), or equivalent tools, remove the stub shaft seal.

To install:

4. Lubricate the new stub shaft seal with grease.
5. Using the Front Axle Oil Seal Installer (SST 205-350) and Handle (SST 205-153) or equivalent tools, install the stub shaft pilot bearing housing seal.
6. Install the halfshaft assembly.

REAR DIFFERENTIAL HOUSING COVER

REMOVAL & INSTALLATION

See Figures 30 and 31.

1. Before servicing the vehicle, refer to the Precautions Section.
2. With the vehicle in NEUTRAL, position it on a hoist.
3. If equipped, remove the exhaust insulator located near the differential housing cover using soapy water.
4. Remove the 10 bolts and the rear differential housing cover.
5. Drain the differential fluid from the housing into a suitable drain pan.

To install:

6. Make sure the machined surfaces on the rear axle housing and the differential housing cover are clean and free of oil before installing the new silicone sealant.

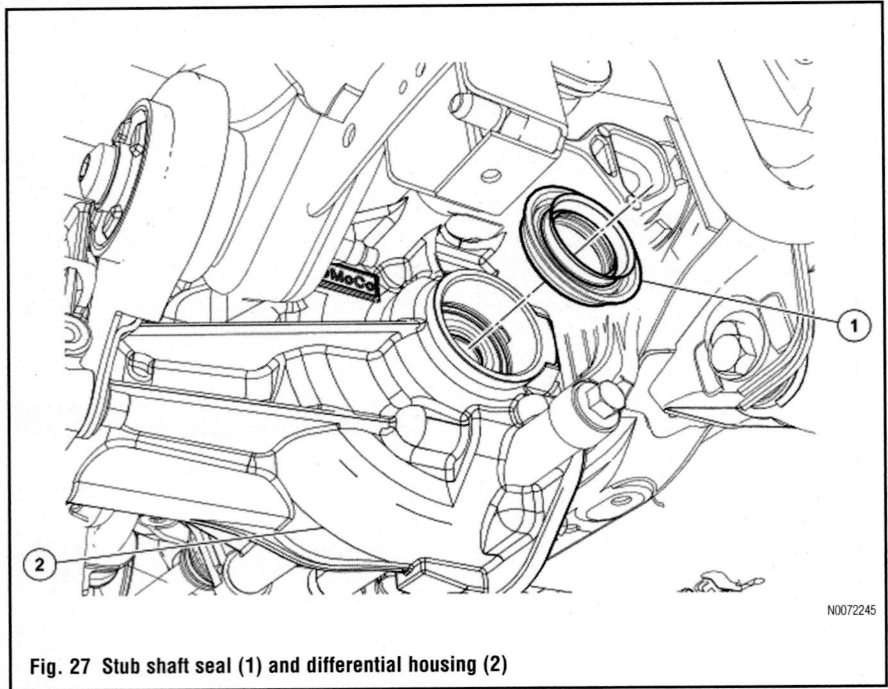

Fig. 27 Stub shaft seal (1) and differential housing (2)

The inside of the rear axle must be covered when cleaning the machined surface to prevent contamination.

7. Clean the gasket mating surfaces of the differential housing and the differential housing cover.

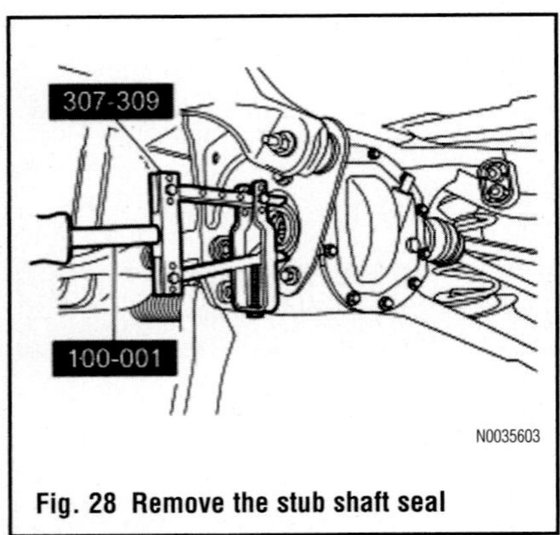

Fig. 28 Remove the stub shaft seal

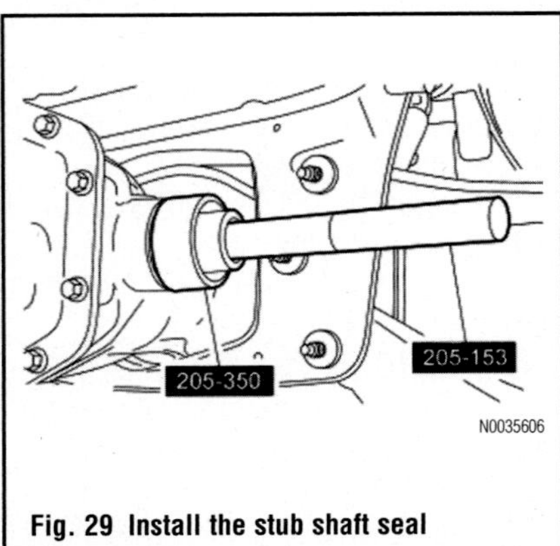

Fig. 29 Install the stub shaft seal

8. Apply a new continuous bead of clear silicone rubber as shown in the illustration. The differential housing cover must be installed within 15 minutes of application of the silicone, or new silicone must be applied. If possible, allow one hour before filling with lubricant to make sure the silicone has correctly cured.

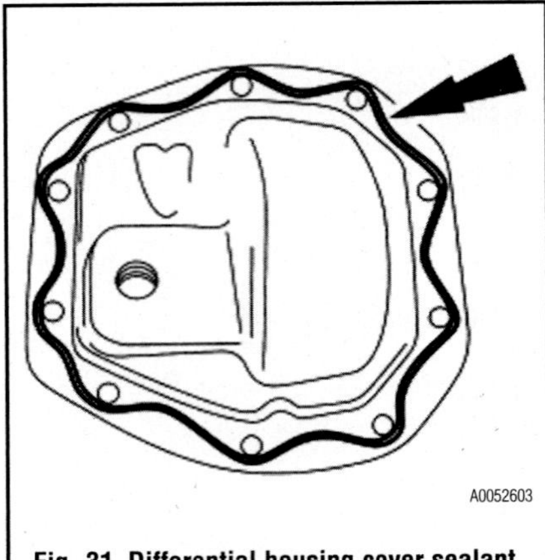

Fig. 31 Differential housing cover sealant application

9. Install the differential housing cover and the 10 bolts. Tighten to 17 ft. lbs. (23 Nm).

10. Remove the filler plug and fill the rear axle with 2.43 pt (1.15L) of rear axle

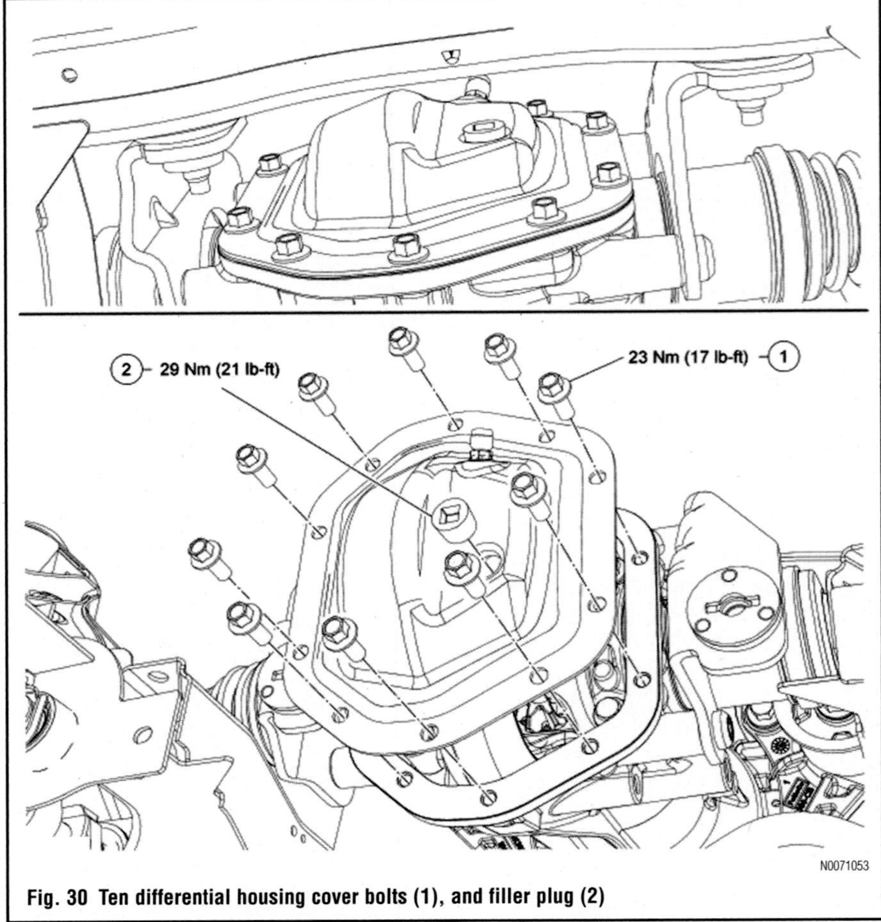

Fig. 30 Ten differential housing cover bolts (1), and filler plug (2)

lubricant, 0.118–0.196 in. (3–5 mm) below the bottom of the filler hole.

11. Install the filler plug and tighten to 21 ft. lbs. (29 Nm).

12. If equipped, install the exhaust insulator located near the differential housing cover.

REAR DRIVESHAFT

REMOVAL & INSTALLATION

See Figures 32 through 35.

1. Before servicing the vehicle, refer to the Precautions Section.
2. With the vehicle in NEUTRAL, position it on a hoist.
3. Remove the muffler and tailpipe.
4. Remove the 4 exhaust support brace bolts and the exhaust brace.

➡**Matchmark both driveshaft flanges.**

5. Remove and discard the 3 Rear Drive Unit (RDU) pinion flange bolt and washer assemblies. Do not reuse the bolt and washer assemblies for the rear Constant Velocity (CV) joint flange. Install new assemblies or damage to the vehicle may occur.
6. Separate the driveshaft CV flange from the RDU flange using a flat-blade screwdriver in the area shown.
7. Remove and discard the 4 Power Transfer Unit (PTU) flange bolts. Do not reuse the Constant Velocity (CV) joint bolts. Install new bolts or damage to the vehicle may occur.
8. Using a suitable prybar as shown, separate the driveshaft flange from the PTU flange.
9. With the help of an assistant, remove the 2 outer center bearing bracket bolts and the driveshaft.
10. If necessary, remove the 2 inner center bearing bolts and remove the bracket.

To install:

11. To install, reverse the removal procedure, noting the following:

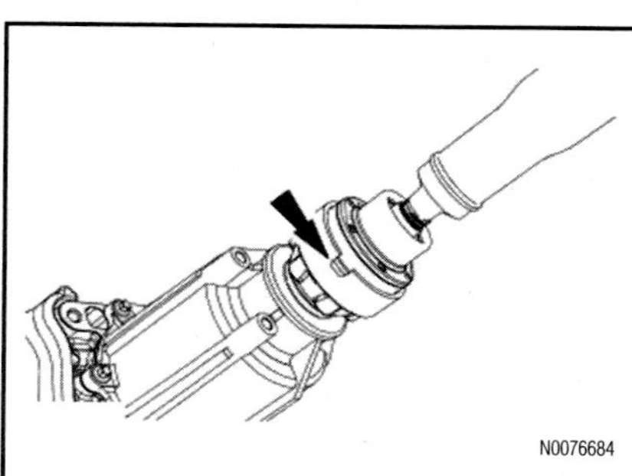

Fig. 33 Separate the driveshaft CV flange from the RDU flange using a flat-blade screwdriver in the area shown

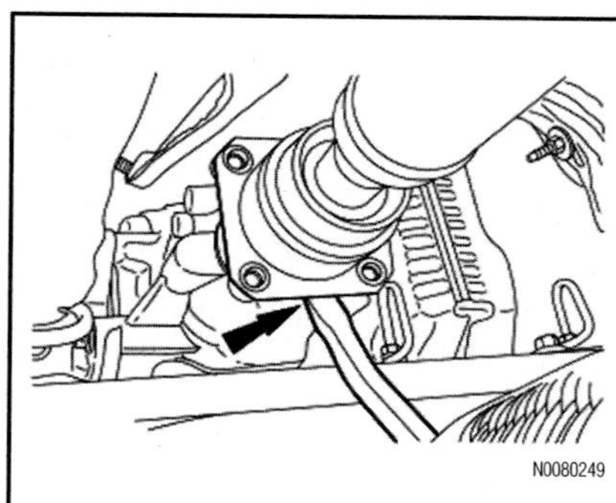

Fig. 34 Separate the driveshaft flange from the PTU flange

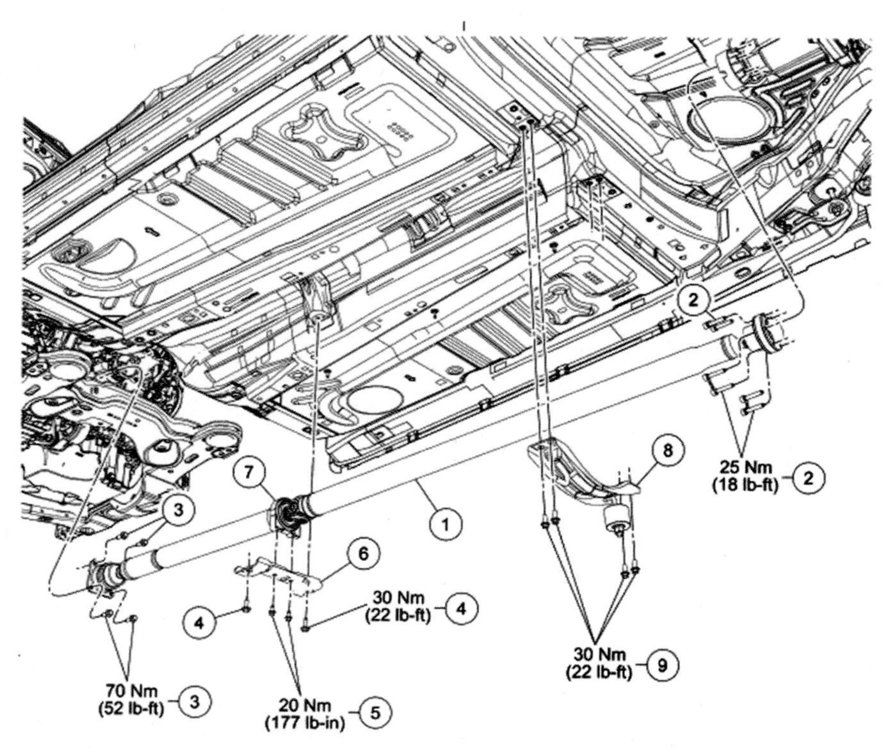

Fig. 32 Driveshaft components

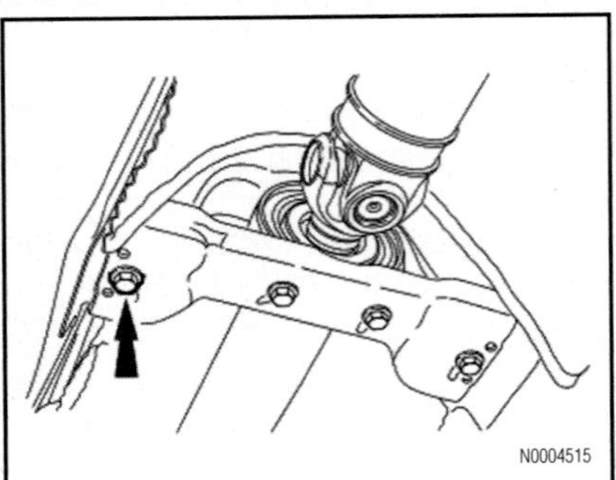

Fig. 35 Remove the 2 outer center bearing bracket bolts and the driveshaft

a. Align the matchmarks on the driveshaft flanges.

b. Do not reuse the bolt and washer assemblies for the rear Constant Velocity (CV) joint flange. Install new assemblies.

c. Do not reuse the Constant Velocity (CV) joint bolts. Install new bolts.

d. Tighten the 2 inner center bearing bolts to 15 ft. lbs. (20 Nm), if removed.

e. Tighten the 2 outer center bearing bracket bolts to 22 ft. lbs. (30 Nm).

f. Tighten the 4 Power Transfer Unit (PTU) flange bolts to 52 ft. lbs. (70 Nm).

g. Tighten the 3 Rear Drive Unit (RDU) pinion flange bolt and washer assemblies to 18 ft. lbs. (25 Nm).

h. Tighten the 4 exhaust support brace bolts to 22 ft. lbs. (30 Nm).

12. If driveshaft vibration is encountered after installation, re-index the driveshaft.

REAR HALFSHAFT

REMOVAL & INSTALLATION

See Figures 36 through 39.

⁂ WARNING

Suspension fasteners are critical parts because they affect performance of vital components and systems and their failure may result in major service expense. New parts must be installed with the same part numbers or equivalent part, if replacement is necessary. Do not use a replacement part of lesser quality or substitute design. Torque values must be used as specified during reassembly to make sure of correct retention of these parts.

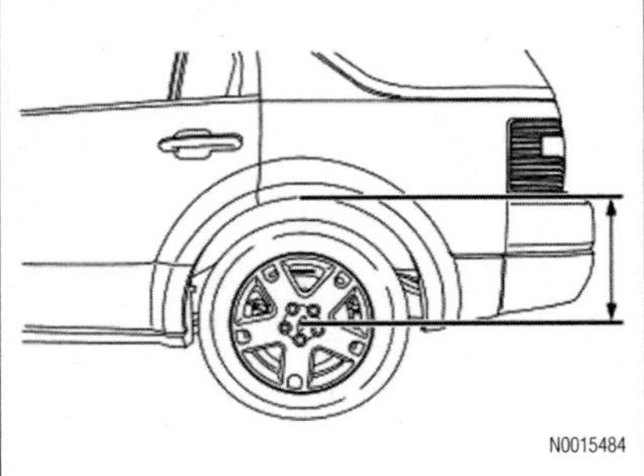

Fig. 36 Measure the distance from the center of the wheel hub to the lip of the fender

➡Before servicing the vehicle, refer to the Precautions Section.

1. Measure the distance from the center of the wheel hub to the lip of the fender with the vehicle in a level, static ground position (curb height).
2. Remove the wheel and tire.
3. Remove the wheel hub nut. Do not discard at this time.
4. Remove and discard the 2 brake caliper anchor plate bolts and position the

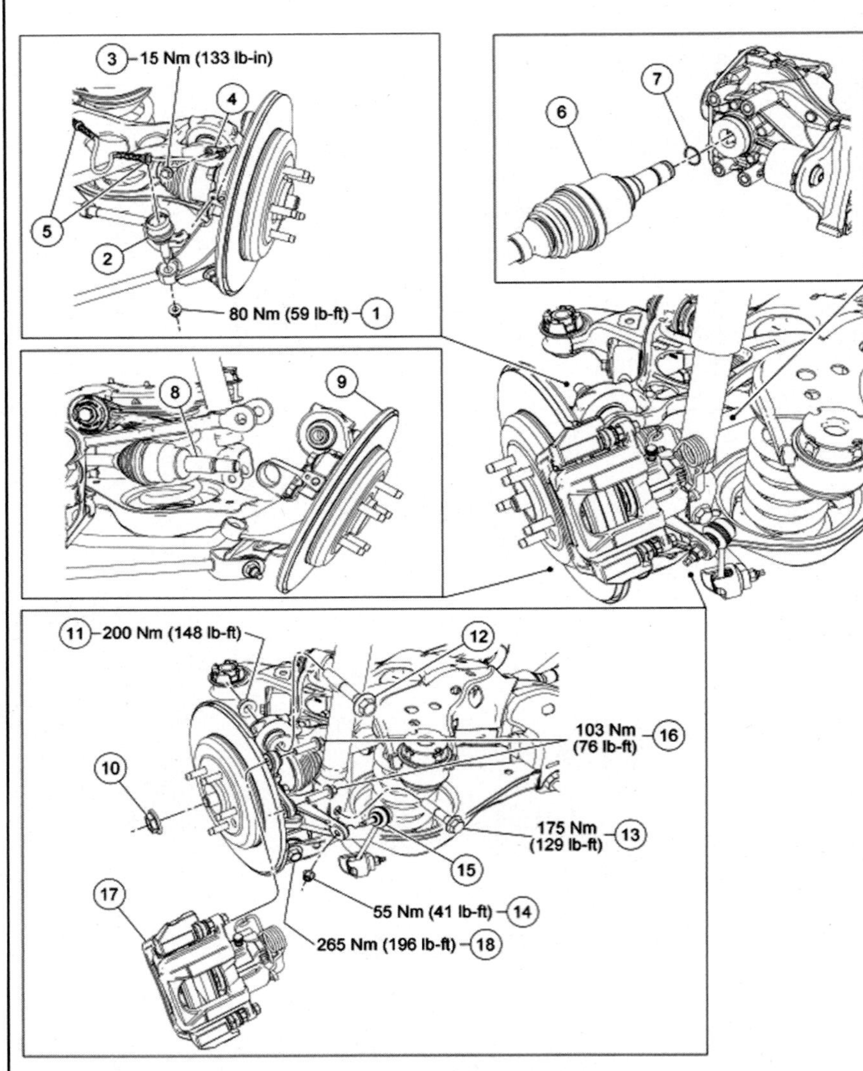

Fig. 37 Rear halfshafts and related components

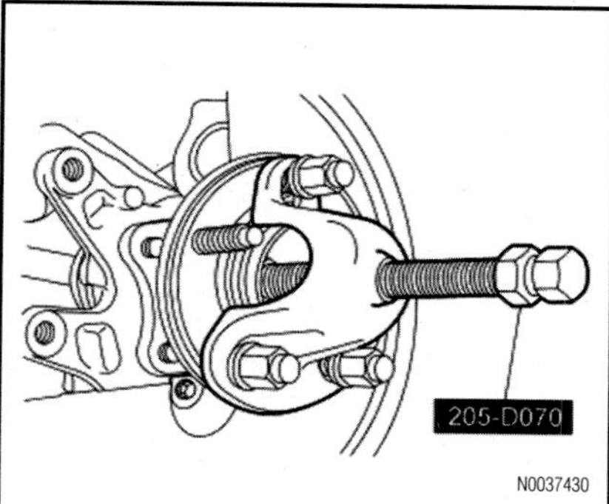

Fig. 38 Separate the halfshaft outer CV joint from the hub bearing

brake caliper and anchor plate assembly aside.

a. Support the brake caliper and anchor plate assembly using mechanic's wire. Do not allow the caliper to hang from the brake hose or damage to the hose can occur.

5. Use the hex-holding feature to prevent the stabilizer bar link stud from turning, remove and discard the stabilizer bar link upper nut, and disconnect the link.
6. Remove and discard the toe link-to-wheel knuckle nut and disconnect the link.
7. Remove the wheel speed sensor bolt. Disconnect the wheel speed sensor harness retainers and position the sensor and harness aside.
8. Position a screw-type jackstand under the lower arm.
9. Remove and discard the upper arm-to-wheel knuckle nut and bolt and disconnect the knuckle from the upper arm.
10. Remove and discard the shock absorber lower bolt and disconnect the shock absorber from the knuckle bracket.

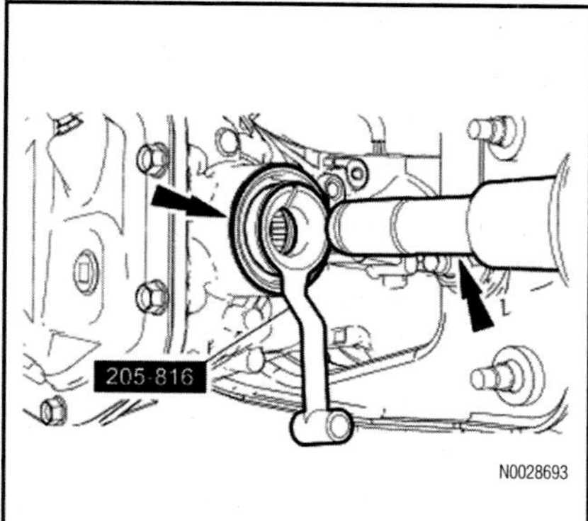

Fig. 39 Install the halfshaft inner CV joint into the differential

11. Loosen, but do not remove the lower arm-to-wheel knuckle bolt.
12. Using the Front Hub Remover or equivalent tool, separate the halfshaft outer CV joint from the hub bearing.
13. Swing the wheel knuckle outward and remove the halfshaft outer CV joint from the hub bearing.
14. Using a suitable pry bar, remove the halfshaft inner CV joint from the differential. Do not damage the oil seal when removing the axle halfshaft from the differential.
15. Remove the halfshaft from the vehicle.
16. Remove and discard the circlip from the halfshaft.

To install:

17. Before tightening suspension bushing fasteners, use a jackstand to raise the rear suspension until the distance between the center of the hub and the lip of the fender is equal to the measurement taken in the removal procedure (curb height).

⁂ WARNING

The circlips are unique in size and shape for each shaft. Make sure to use the specified circlip for the application or vehicle damage may occur.

18. Install a new circlip on the halfshaft.
19. Using the Axle Seal Protector (SST 205-816) or equivalent tool, install the halfshaft inner CV joint into the differential. Make sure the circlip locks in the side gear.
20. Swing the wheel knuckle inward and install the halfshaft outer CV joint through the hub bearing.
21. Position the wheel knuckle to the upper arm and loosely install a new nut and bolt.
22. Position the shock absorber and loosely install a new bolt.
23. Position the wheel speed sensor harness in the retainers and install the sensor and bolt. Tighten to 11 ft. lbs. (15 Nm).
24. Position the toe link and loosely install a new toe link-to-wheel knuckle nut.
25. Position a suitable jackstand under the lower control arm at the shock and spring assembly attachment point and raise the rear suspension until the distance between the center of the hub and the lip of the fender is equal to the measurement taken in Step 1 of the procedure (curb height).
26. A slotted upper arm allows for the rear suspension camber to be adjusted by pushing inward or pulling outward on the wheel knuckle while tightening the upper arm-to-wheel knuckle nut. With the wheel knuckle pushed inward for maximum negative camber, tighten the upper arm-to-wheel knuckle nut to 148 ft. lbs. (200 Nm).
27. Tighten the lower arm-to-wheel knuckle bolt to 196 ft. lbs. (265 Nm).
28. Tighten the shock absorber lower bolt to 129 ft. lbs. (175 Nm).
29. Tighten the toe link-to-wheel knuckle nut to 59 ft. lbs. (80 Nm).
30. Use the hex-holding feature to prevent the stabilizer bar link stud from turning, connect the stabilizer bar link, and install a new stabilizer bar link upper nut. Tighten to 41 ft. lbs. (55 Nm).
31. Position the brake caliper and anchor plate assembly and install the 2 bolts. Tighten to 76 ft. lbs. (103 Nm).

⁂ WARNING

Do not tighten the wheel hub nut with the vehicle on the ground. The nut must be tightened to specification before the vehicle is lowered onto the wheels. Wheel bearing damage will occur if the wheel bearing is loaded with the weight of the vehicle applied.

32. Apply the brake to keep the halfshaft from rotating, and use the previously removed hub nut to seat the halfshaft.
    a. Tighten to 258 ft. lbs. (350 Nm).
    b. Remove and discard the hub nut.

⁂ WARNING

The wheel hub nut contains a one-time locking chemical that is activated by the heat created when it is tightened. Install and tighten the new wheel hub nut to specification within 5 minutes of starting it on the threads. Always install a new wheel hub nut after loosening or when not tightened within the specified time or damage to the components can occur.

33. Apply the brake to keep the halfshaft from rotating, and install a new hub nut. Tighten to 258 ft. lbs. (350 Nm).
34. Install the wheel and tire.
35. Check the rear toe and adjust if necessary.

REAR PINION SEAL

REMOVAL & INSTALLATION

See Figures 40 through 42.

1. Before servicing the vehicle, refer to the Precautions Section.
2. Remove the driveshaft.
3. Using the Drive Pinion Flange Holding Fixture (SST 205-126) or equivalent tool, hold the pinion flange and remove the nut. Discard the nut.
4. Matchmark the location of the pinion to the yoke.
5. Using the 2 Jaw Puller (SST 205-D072) or equivalent tool, remove the pinion flange.
6. Using the Torque Converter Fluid Seal Remover and Slide Hammer or equivalent tools, remove the seal.

To install:

7. Make sure that the mating surface is clean before installing the new seal.

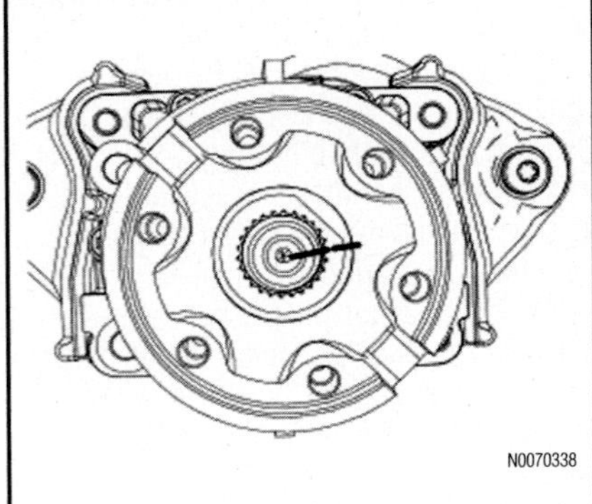

Fig. 41 Matchmark the location of the pinion to the yoke

8. Using the Pinion Seal Replacer or equivalent tool, install the seal.
9. Lubricate the pinion flange with grease.
10. Align the matchmarks and position the pinion flange.

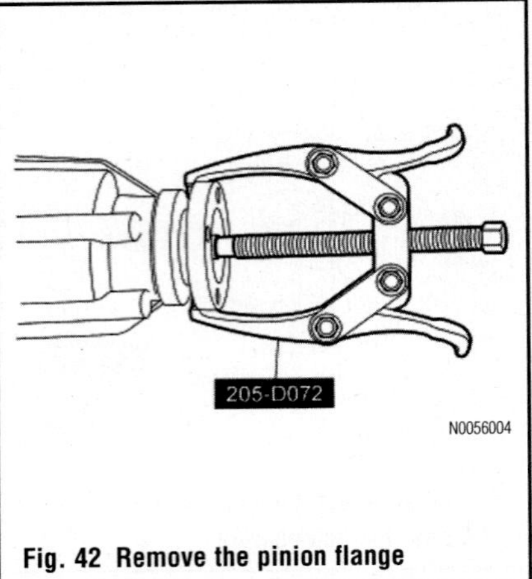

Fig. 42 Remove the pinion flange

11. Using the Drive Pinion Flange Holding Fixture or equivalent tool, install the new pinion nut. Tighten to 180 ft. lbs. (244 Nm).
12. Install the driveshaft.

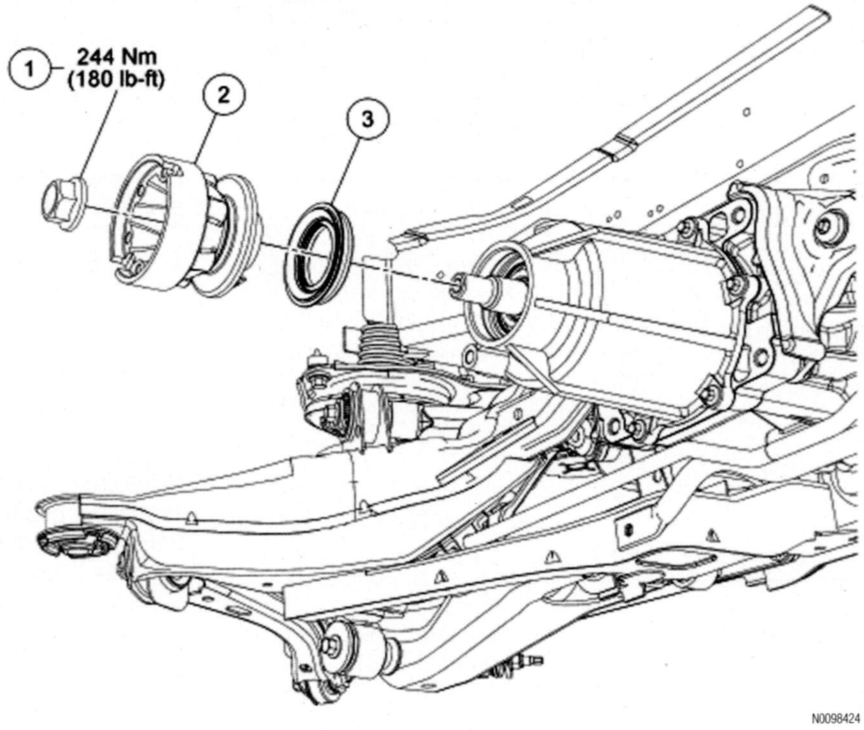

1 244 Nm (180 lb-ft)
2
3
N0098424

Fig. 40 Pinion nut (1), pinion flange (2), and pinion seal (3)

ENGINE COOLING

ENGINE COOLANT

DRAINING, FILLING AND BLEEDING PROCEDURE

CAUTION

Always allow the engine to cool before opening the cooling system. Do not unscrew the coolant pressure relief cap when the engine is operating or the cooling system is hot. The cooling system is under pressure; steam and hot liquid can come out forcefully when the cap is loosened slightly. Failure to follow these instructions may result in serious personal injury.

WARNING

The coolant must be recovered in a suitable, clean container for reuse. If the coolant is contaminated it must be recycled or disposed of correctly. Using contaminated coolant may result in damage to the engine or cooling system components.

WARNING

The engine cooling system is filled with Motorcraft® Specialty Green Engine Coolant. Mixing coolant types degrades the corrosion protection of Motorcraft® Specialty Green Engine Coolant. Motorcraft® Specialty Green Engine Coolant is very sensitive to light. Do NOT allow this product to be exposed to ANY LIGHT for more than a day or two. Extended light exposure causes this product to degrade.

WARNING

Stop-leak style pellets/products must not be used as an additive in this engine cooling system. The addition of stop-leak style pellets/products may clog or damage the cooling system, resulting in degraded cooling system performance and/or failure.

WARNING

Less than 80% of coolant capacity can be recovered with the engine in the vehicle. Dirty, rusty or contaminated coolant requires replacement.

1. Before servicing the vehicle, refer to the Precautions Section.
2. With the vehicle in NEUTRAL, position it on a hoist.
3. Release the pressure in the cooling system by slowly turning the pressure relief cap one-half to one turn counterclockwise to the first stop on the filler neck. When the pressure has been released, remove the pressure relief cap.
4. Remove the 5 bolts, 7 pin-type retainers and the front splash shield.
5. Place a suitable container below the radiator draincock. Open the radiator draincock and drain the coolant.
6. Close the radiator draincock.
7. Install the front splash shield, 7 pin-type retainers and the 5 bolts, when the cooling system or engine service is finished.
8. Install a radiator refiller and follow the manufacturer's instructions to fill and bleed the cooling system. For filling and bleeding without a radiator refiller, proceed as follows:

WARNING

Add Motorcraft® Specialty Green Engine Coolant to the cooling system. Do not add alcohol, methanol or brine, or any engine coolants mixed with alcohol or methanol antifreeze. These can cause engine damage from overheating or freezing. Ford Motor Company does NOT recommend the use of recycled engine coolant in vehicles.

9. Open the degas bottle cap and fill the degas bottle to 0.984 in. (25 mm) above the top of the COLD FILL RANGE.

➡Recommended coolant concentration is 50/50 ethylene glycol to distilled water. Maximum coolant concentration is 60/40 for cold weather areas. Minimum coolant concentration is 40/60 for warm weather areas.

10. Close the degas bottle cap.
11. Turn the HVAC system to OFF.
12. Run the engine at 3,500 rpm for 30 seconds. If the engine overheats or the fluid level drops below the top of the COLD FILL RANGE, shut off the engine and add fluid to 0.984 in. (25 mm) above the top of the COLD FILL RANGE once the engine cools.
13. Turn the engine off for 1 minute to purge any large air pockets.
14. Start the engine and let idle until the engine reaches normal operating temperature and the thermostat is fully open. A fully open thermostat can be verified by the radiator fan cycling on at least once.
15. Run the engine at 3,500 rpm for 30 seconds.
16. Run the engine at idle for 30 seconds. If the engine overheats or the fluid level drops below the top of the COLD FILL RANGE, shut off the engine and add fluid to 0.984 in. (25 mm) above the top of the COLD FILL RANGE once the engine cools.
17. Turn the engine off for 1 minute.
18. Repeat the above 3 steps a total of 10 times to remove any remaining air trapped in the system.
19. Check the engine coolant level in the degas bottle and fill to 0.984 in. (25 mm) above the top of the COLD FILL RANGE when warm or to the top of the COLD FILL RANGE line when cold.
20. Install the degas bottle cap to at least one audible "click."

FLUSHING

CAUTION

Always allow the engine to cool before opening the cooling system. Do not unscrew the coolant pressure relief cap when the engine is operating or the cooling system is hot. The cooling system is under pressure; steam and hot liquid can come out forcefully when the cap is loosened slightly. Failure to follow these instructions may result in serious personal injury.

WARNING

To remove rust, sludge and other foreign material from the cooling system, use cooling system flush that is safe for use with aluminum radiators. This cleaning restores cooling system efficiency and helps prevent overheating. A pulsating or reversed direction of flushing water will loosen sediment more quickly than a steady flow in the normal coolant flow direction. In severe cases where cleaning solvents will not clean the cooling system efficiently, it will be necessary to use the pressure flushing method using cooling system flusher. Dispose of old coolant and flushing water contaminated with antifreeze and cleaning chemicals in accordance with local, state or federal laws.

1. Before servicing the vehicle, refer to the Precautions Section.

2. Add premium cooling system flush to the cooling system and follow the directions on the package.

3. Drain the cooling system. Refer to Draining, Filling & Bleeding Procedure.

4. Remove the radiator. Refer to Radiator Removal & Installation.

WARNING

Radiator internal pressure must not exceed 20 psi (138 kPa). Damage to the radiator can result.

5. Backflush the radiator with the radiator in an upside-down position with a high-pressure hose in the lower hose location and backflush.

6. Remove the thermostat. Refer to Thermostat Removal & Installation.

7. Backflush the engine. Position the high-pressure water hose into the engine through the engine return and backflush the engine.

8. Install the thermostat.

9. Install the radiator.

10. Fill the cooling system.

ENGINE FAN

REMOVAL & INSTALLATION

3.5L Engine

See Figures 43 through 45.

1. Before servicing the vehicle, refer to the Precautions Section.

2. With the vehicle in NEUTRAL, position it on a hoist.

3. Remove the 4 retainers and the underbody shield.

4. Drain the cooling system. Refer to Draining, Filling & Bleeding Procedure.

5. Working from below, disconnect the left-hand CAC tube from the CAC adapter.

6. Remove the lower bolt from the CAC adapter.

7. Detach the lower radiator hose retainer from the cooling fan and shroud.

8. Disconnect the lower radiator hose from the radiator.

9. Remove the Air Cleaner (ACL) assembly and ACL outlet pipe.

10. Remove the right-hand CAC.

11. Remove the upper bolt and the CAC adapter. Inspect and install a new CAC adapter gasket, if necessary.

12. Disconnect the crankcase vent tube quick connect coupling and remove the crankcase vent tube.

13. Disconnect and remove the lower radiator hose from the thermostat housing.

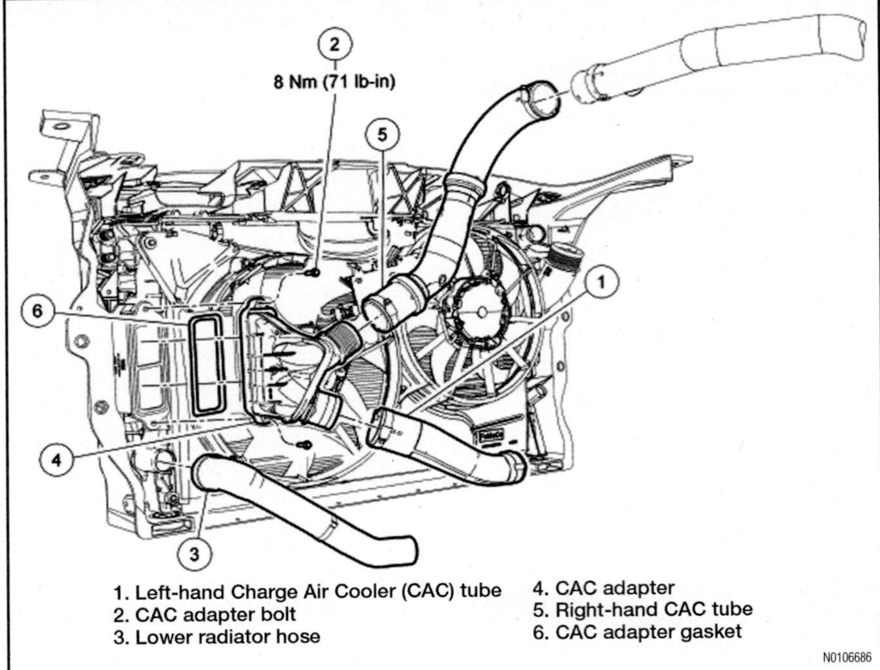

Fig. 43 Cooling fan and motor components 1—3.5L engine

14. Detach the hood release cable retainer from the shroud.

15. If equipped, detach the block heater wiring harness retainers from the engine wiring harness.

16. Detach all the wiring harness retainers from the cooling fan and shroud and radiator grill support.

17. Disconnect the cooling fan motor electrical connector.

18. Disconnect the left-hand Heated Oxygen Sensor (HO2S) electrical connector.

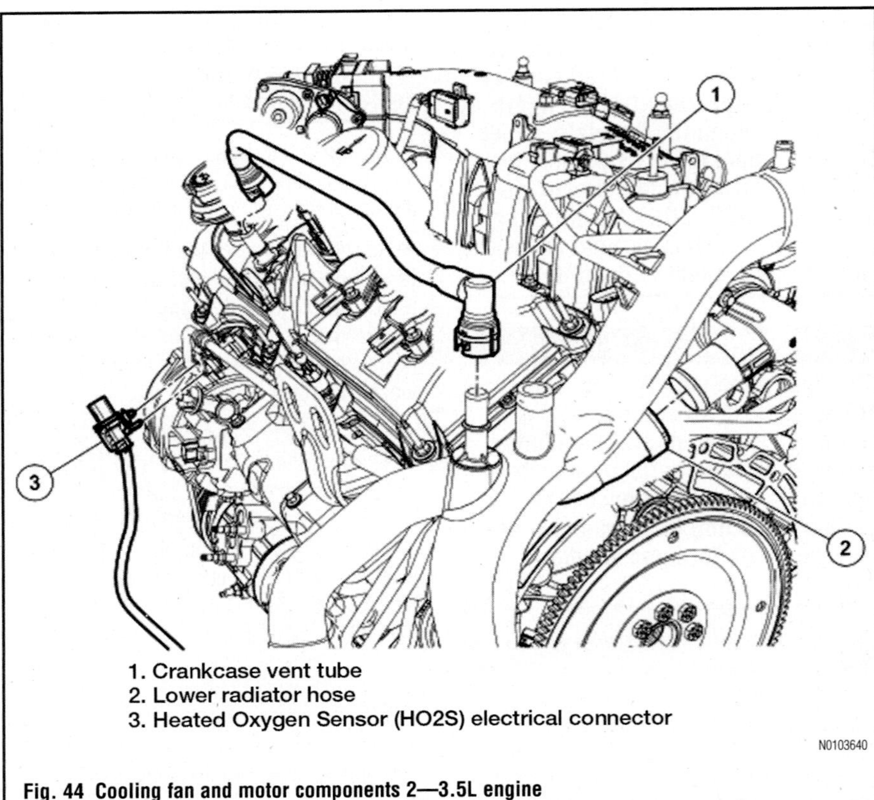

Fig. 44 Cooling fan and motor components 2—3.5L engine

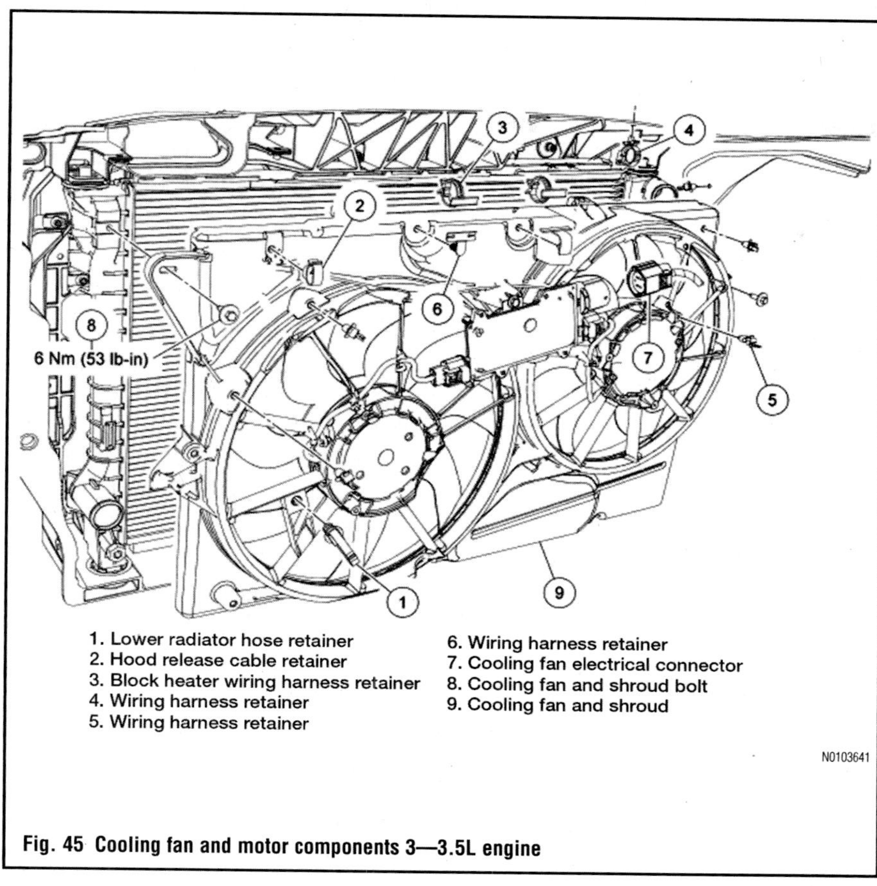

Fig. 45 Cooling fan and motor components 3—3.5L engine

Detach the HO2S connector retainer from the bracket.

19. Remove the 2 bolts and the cooling fan motor and shroud.

To install:

20. Install the cooling fan motor and shroud and the 2 bolts. Tighten to 53 inch lbs. (6 Nm).

21. Connect the left-hand Heated Oxygen Sensor (HO2S) electrical connector. Attach the HO2S connector retainer to the bracket.

22. Connect the cooling fan motor electrical connector.

23. Attach all the wiring harness retainers to the cooling fan and shroud and radiator grill support.

24. If equipped, attach the block heater wiring harness retainers to the engine wiring harness.

25. Attach the hood release cable retainer to the shroud.

26. Install and connect the lower radiator to the thermostat housing.

27. Install the crankcase vent tube quick connect coupling.

28. Install the gasket, the CAC adapter and the upper bolt. Do not tighten the bolt at this time.

29. Install the lower bolt for the CAC adapter. Tighten to 71 inch lbs. (8 Nm).

30. Tighten the upper CAC adapter bolt. Tighten to 71 inch lbs. (8 Nm).

31. Align the marks for the right-hand CAC tube. Install the right-hand CAC tube. Tighten to 44 inch lbs. (5 Nm).

32. Install the ACL outlet pipe and ACL assembly.

33. Connect the lower radiator hose to the radiator.

34. Attach the lower radiator hose retainer to the cooling fan and shroud.

35. Connect the left-hand CAC tube to the CAC adapter. Align the marks for the left-hand CAC tube. Tighten to 44 inch lbs. (5 Nm).

36. Fill and bleed the cooling system. Refer to Draining, Filling & Bleeding Procedure.

37. Install the underbody shield and the 4 retainers.

3.7L Engine

See Figure 46.

1. Before servicing the vehicle, refer to the Precautions Section.

2. With the vehicle in NEUTRAL, position it on a hoist.

3. Remove the Air Cleaner (ACL) assembly.

4. If equipped, detach the block heater

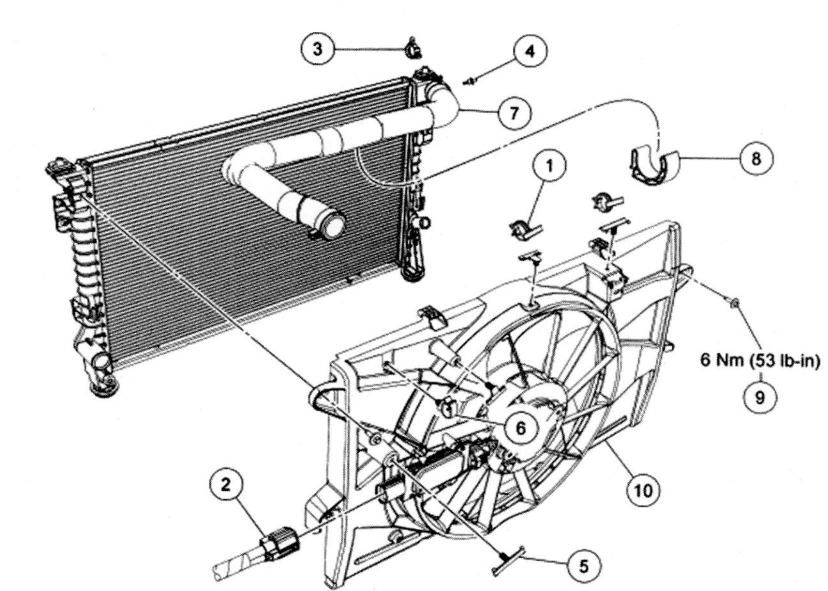

Fig. 46 Cooling fan and motor components—3.7L engine

wiring harness retainers from the engine wiring harness.

5. Disconnect the cooling fan motor electrical connector and detach the all the wiring harness retainers from the shroud.

6. Detach the 2 wiring harness retainers from the radiator support.

7. Detach the hood release cable retainer from the cooling fan motor and shroud.

8. Detach the upper radiator hose from the cooling fan motor and shroud.

9. Release the tab through the access hole and remove the upper radiator hose support.

10. Remove the 2 bolts and the cooling fan motor and shroud.

To install:

11. To install, reverse the removal procedure, noting the following:

a. Tighten the cooling fan motor and shroud bolts to 53 inch lbs. (6 Nm).

RADIATOR

REMOVAL & INSTALLATION

3.5L Engine

See Figures 47 through 50.

1. Before servicing the vehicle, refer to the Precautions Section.

2. Remove the cooling fan motor and shroud. Refer to Engine Fan Removal & Installation.

3. Remove the front bumper cover.

4. Disconnect the Turbocharger Boost Pressure (TCBP)/Charge Air Cooler Temperature (CACT) sensor electrical connector.

5. Remove the CAC outlet pipe. Matchmark the Charge Air Cooler (CAC) outlet pipe position for reference during installation.

6. Disconnect the upper radiator hose and lower degas bottle hose from the radiator.

7. Detach the 4 radiator grill air deflector pin-type retainers and remove the right-hand and left-hand radiator grill air deflectors.

8. Remove the 2 A/C condenser bolts from the CAC and separate the A/C condenser from the CAC .

9. Lift the tabs and remove the radiator support brackets and position the radiator toward the engine.

10. Remove the 2 bolts and separate the CAC from the radiator.

11. Remove the radiator.

To install:

12. To install, reverse the removal procedure, noting the following:

a. Make sure the bottom radiator

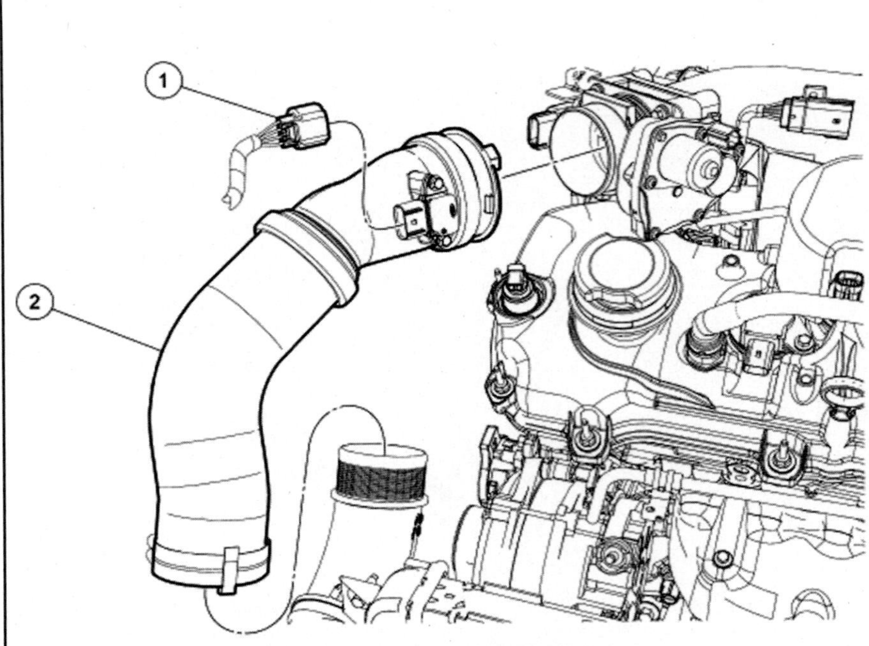

Fig. 47 Radiator components 1—3.5L engine

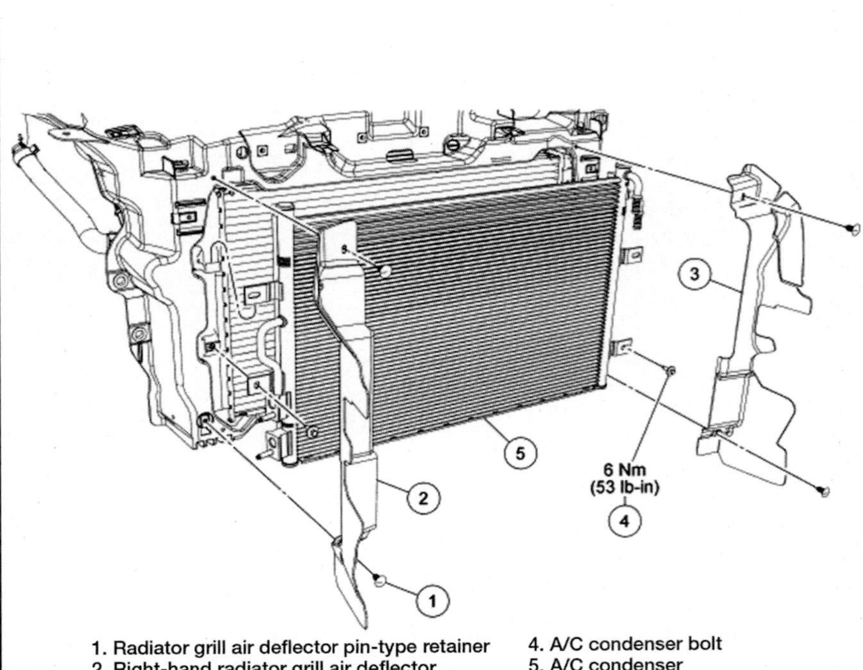

Fig. 48 Radiator components 2—3.5L engine

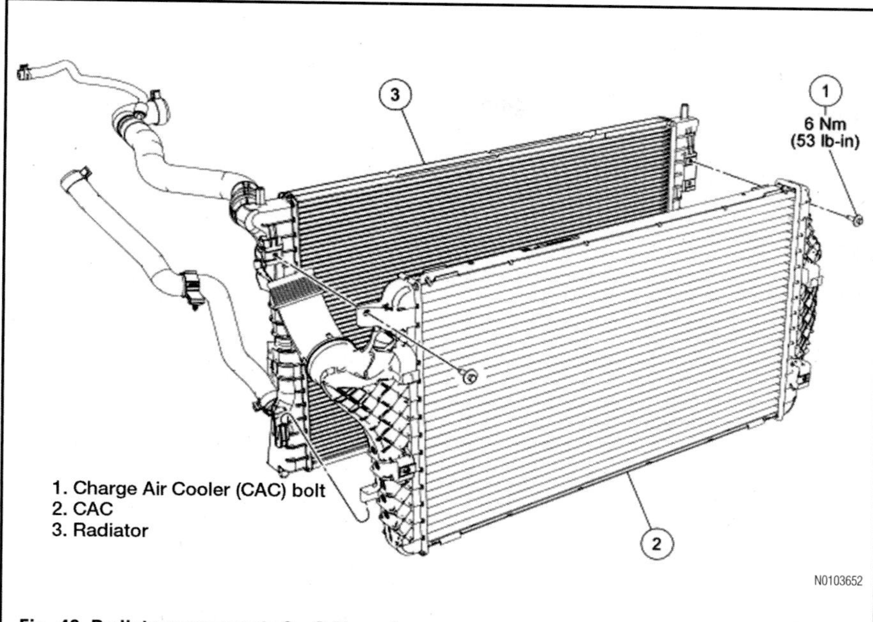

Fig. 49 Radiator components 3—3.5L engine

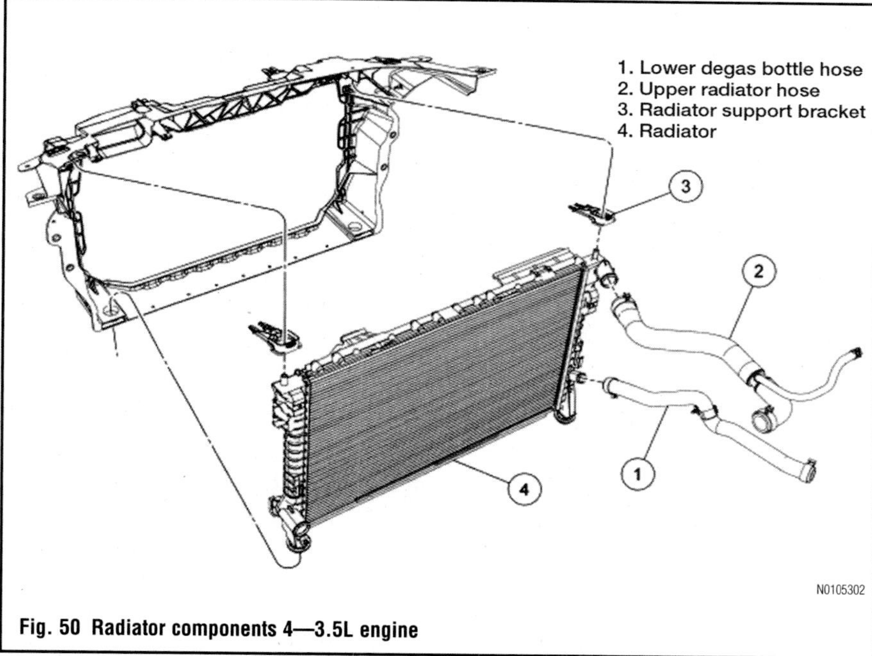

Fig. 50 Radiator components 4—3.5L engine

insulators are in place when installing the radiator.

b. Tighten the CAC bolts to 53 inch lbs. (6 Nm).

c. Tighten the A/C condenser bolts to 53 inch lbs. (6 Nm).

d. Tighten the CAC outlet pipe bolts to 44 inch lbs. (5 Nm).

3.7L Engine

See Figures 51 and 52.

1. Before servicing the vehicle, refer to the Precautions Section.

2. Drain the cooling system. Refer to Draining, Filling & Bleeding Procedure.

3. Remove the cooling fan motor and shroud. Refer to Engine Fan Removal & Installation.

4. Remove the front bumper cover.

5. Disconnect the upper radiator hose and lower degas bottle hose from the radiator.

6. Disconnect the lower radiator hose from the radiator.

7. Lift the tabs and remove the radiator support brackets and position the radiator toward the engine.

8. Remove the 2 A/C condenser bolts from the radiator and separate the condenser from the radiator.

NOTE: Make sure the bottom radiator insulators are in place when installing the radiator.

9. Remove the radiator.

To install:

10. To install, reverse the removal procedure, noting the following:

a. Make sure the bottom radiator insulators are in place when installing the radiator.

b. Tighten the A/C condenser bolts to 53 inch lbs. (6 Nm).

c. Fill and bleed the cooling system. Refer to Draining, Filling & Bleeding Procedure.

THERMOSTAT

REMOVAL & INSTALLATION

Thermostat Housing

See Figures 53 and 54.

1. Before servicing the vehicle, refer to the Precautions Section.

2. Drain the cooling system. Refer to Draining, Filling & Bleeding Procedure.

3. Remove the engine Air Cleaner (ACL) outlet pipe.

4. For 3.5L vehicles, remove the thermostat housing as follows:

a. Disconnect the lower radiator hose from the thermostat housing.

b. Remove the 2 bolts and the thermostat housing.

c. Remove the O-ring seal. Clean and inspect the O-ring seal. Install a new seal if necessary.

5. For 3.7L vehicles, remove the thermostat housing as follows:

a. Disconnect the 5 coolant hoses from the thermostat housing and position them aside.

b. Remove the 3 thermostat housing bolts.

c. Separate the thermostat housing from the coolant tube and remove the thermostat housing. Do not pull the other end of the coolant tube out of the engine block when separating the thermostat housing.

d. Remove and discard the O-ring seals.

To install:

6. To install, reverse the removal procedure, noting the following:

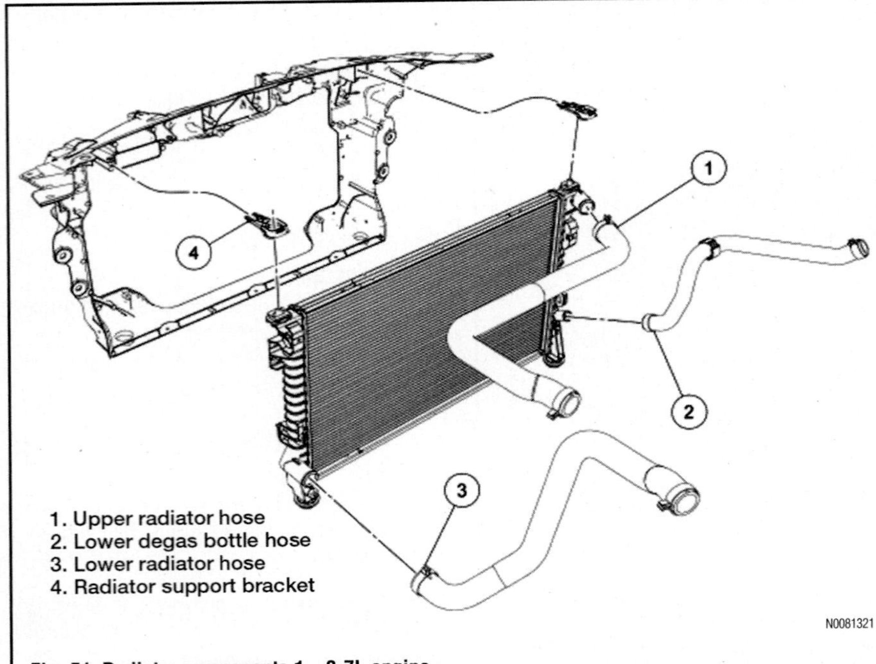

Fig. 51 Radiator components 1—3.7L engine

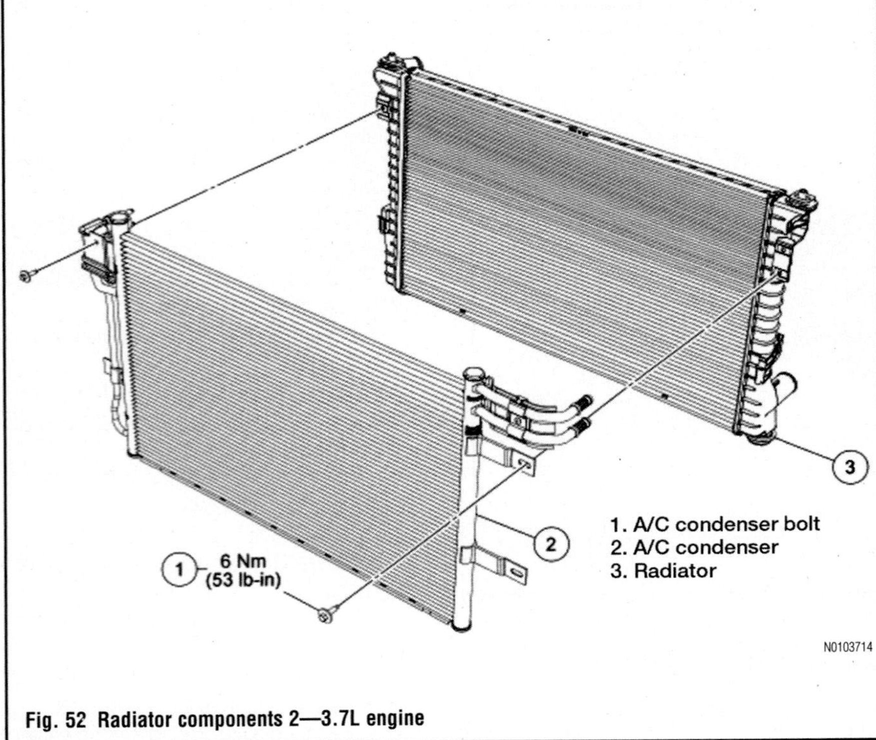

Fig. 52 Radiator components 2—3.7L engine

WARNING

Genuine Motorcraft® Specialty Green Engine Coolant is very sensitive to light. Do NOT allow this product to be exposed to ANY LIGHT for more than a day or two. Extended light exposure causes this product to degrade.

a. Lubricate the new O-ring seal with clean engine coolant.

b. For 3.5L vehicles, clean the bolts and apply Thread Sealant with PTFE before installing the thermostat housing bolts.

c. Tighten the thermostat housing bolts to 89 inch lbs. (10 Nm).

d. Fill and bleed the cooling system. Refer to Draining, Filling & Bleeding Procedure.

Thermostat

See Figure 55.

1. Before servicing the vehicle, refer to the Precautions Section.
2. Drain the cooling system. Refer to Draining, Filling & Bleeding Procedure.
3. Remove the engine Air Cleaner (ACL) outlet pipe.
4. Remove the 2 bolts and position aside the thermostat housing.
5. Remove the O-ring seal and thermostat. Clean and inspect the O-ring seal. Install a new seal if necessary.

To install:

6. To install, reverse the removal procedure, noting the following:

WARNING

Genuine Motorcraft® Specialty Green Engine Coolant is very sensitive to light. Do NOT allow this product to be exposed to ANY LIGHT for more than a day or two. Extended light exposure causes this product to degrade.

a. Lubricate the thermostat O-ring seal with clean engine coolant.

b. For 3.5L vehicles, clean the bolts and apply Thread Sealant with PTFE before installing the thermostat housing bolts.

c. Tighten the thermostat housing bolts to 89 inch lbs. (10 Nm).

d. Fill and bleed the cooling system. Refer to Draining, Filling & Bleeding Procedure.

WATER PUMP (COOLANT PUMP)

REMOVAL & INSTALLATION

See Figures 56 through 58.

WARNING

During engine repair procedures, cleanliness is extremely important. Any foreign material, including any material created while cleaning gasket surfaces, that enters the oil passages, coolant passages or the oil pan may cause engine failure.

➡On early build engines, the timing chain rides on the inner side of the right-hand timing chain guide. Late build engines are equipped with a different design right-hand timing chain guide that requires the timing chain to

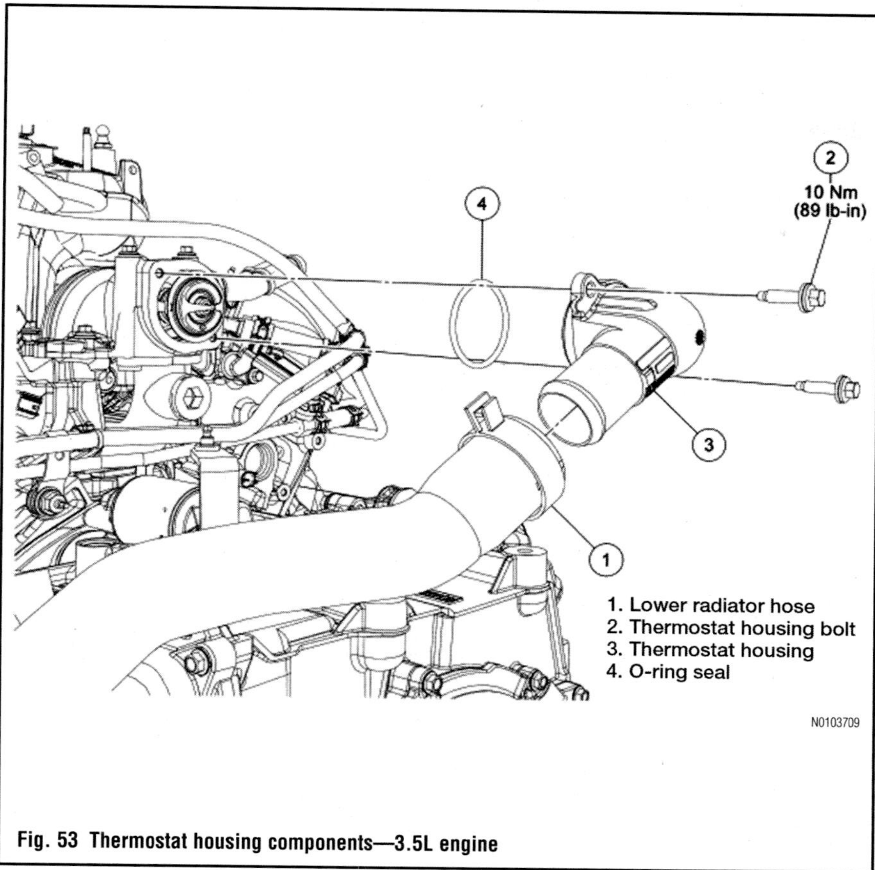

Fig. 53 Thermostat housing components—3.5L engine

ride on the outer side of the right-hand timing chain guide. For service, all replacement right-hand timing chain guides will be the late build design.

1. Before servicing the vehicle, refer to the Precautions Section.
2. With the vehicle in NEUTRAL, position it on a hoist.
3. Drain the cooling system. Refer to Draining, Filling & Bleeding Procedure.
4. Remove the engine front cover.
5. Remove and discard the engine oil filter.
6. Remove the right-hand and left-hand VCT housing. Refer to Timing Chain Removal & Installation in the Engine Mechanical section.
7. Remove the primary timing chain tensioner, tensioner arm, lower left-hand primary timing chain guide, and primary timing chain. Refer to Timing Chain Removal & Installation in the Engine Mechanical section.
8. Remove the 2 bolts and the upper left-hand primary timing chain guide. Refer to Timing Chain Removal & Installation in the Engine Mechanical section.
9. For engines equipped with early build right-hand timing chain guides:
    a. Remove the right-hand primary timing chain guide lower bolt.

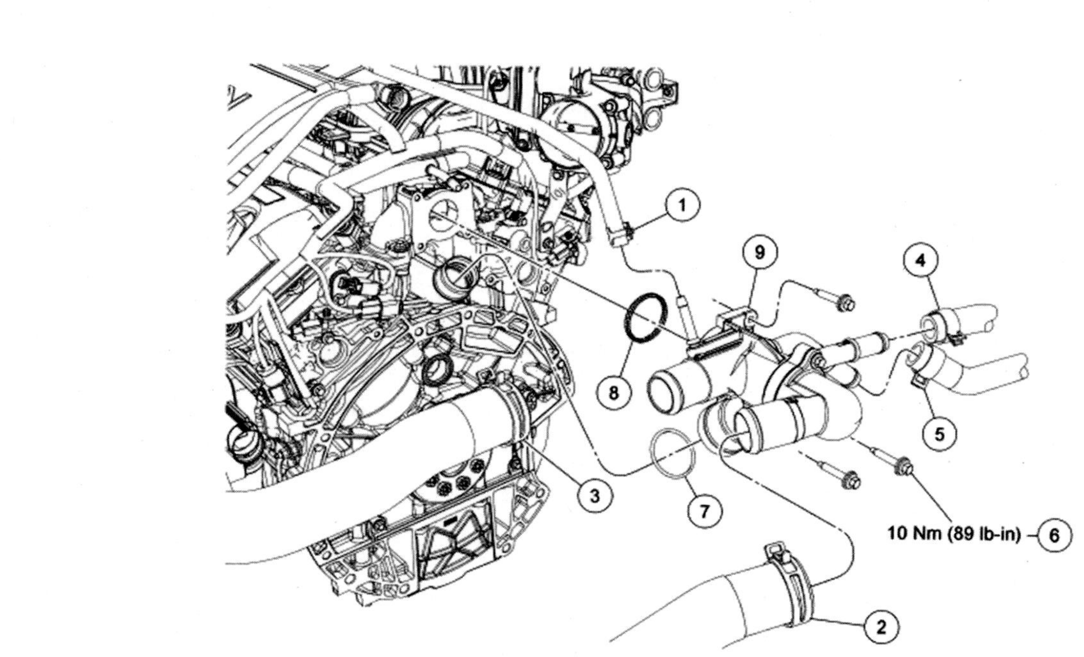

Fig. 54 Thermostat housing components—3.7L engine

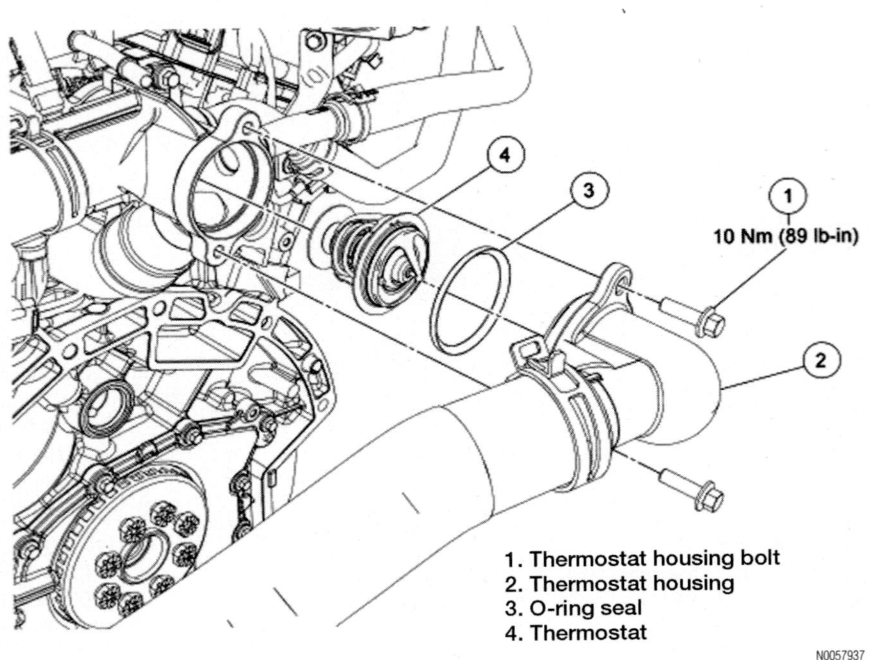

Fig. 55 Thermostat components—3.7L engine shown, 3.5L engines similar

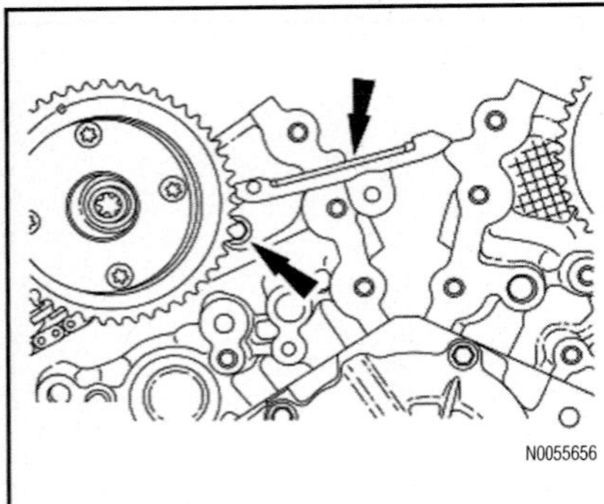

Fig. 56 Rotate the right-hand primary timing chain guide and tighten the bolt

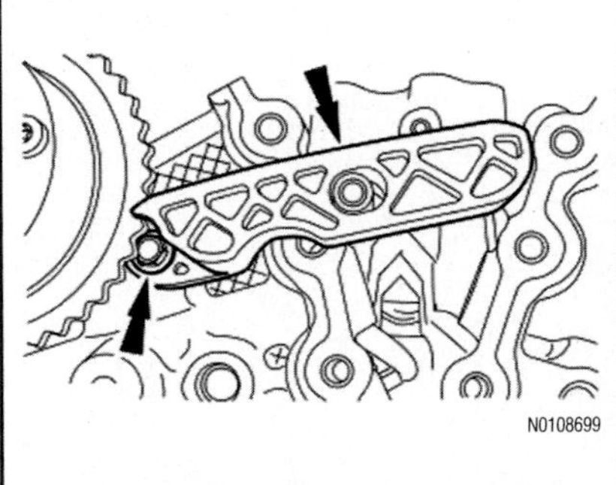

Fig. 57 Remove the right-hand primary timing chain guide lower bolt

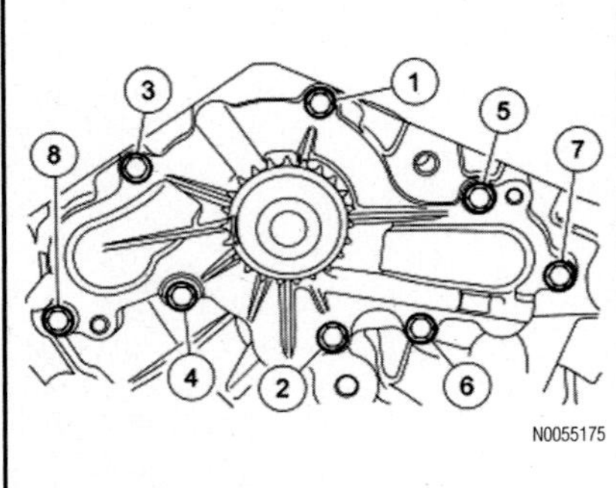

Fig. 58 Remove the 8 bolts and the coolant pump

➡The right-hand primary timing chain guide must be repositioned to allow the coolant pump to be removed.

10. Loosen the right-hand primary timing chain guide upper bolt. Rotate the guide and tighten the bolt.
11. For engines equipped with late build/replacement right-hand timing chain guides:
    a. Remove the right-hand primary timing chain guide lower bolt.
    b. Loosen the right-hand primary timing chain guide upper bolt. Rotate the guide and tighten the bolt. The right-hand primary timing chain guide must be repositioned to allow the coolant pump to be removed.
12. Place clean lint-free shop towels in the oil pan opening to prevent coolant from entering the oil pan during coolant pump removal.
13. Remove the 8 bolts and the coolant pump.

To install:

14. Clean and inspect all sealing surfaces.
15. Install the coolant pump and the 8 bolts. Tighten in the sequence shown to 89 inch lbs. (10 Nm).
16. Remove all of the shop towels from the oil pan opening.
17. Remove the oil pan drain plug and allow any accumulated coolant to drain. Any coolant that has accumulated in the oil pan must be drained from the pan and any residual coolant cleaned from the front of the engine and oil pan. Failure to remove all traces of the coolant can result in oil contamination and severe engine damage.
    a. Remove any residual coolant from the front of the engine and the oil pan using regulated, compressed air and clean, lint-free shop towels.

b. Install the oil pan drain plug and tighten to 20 ft. lbs. (27 Nm).

18. For engines equipped with late build/replacement right-hand timing chain guides:

a. Loosen the right-hand primary timing chain guide upper bolt. Position the right-hand primary timing chain guide and install the lower bolt. Tighten the 2 bolts to 89 inch lbs. (10 Nm).

19. For engines equipped with early build right-hand timing chain guides:

a. Loosen the right-hand primary timing chain guide upper bolt. Position the right-hand primary timing chain guide and install the lower bolt. Tighten the 2 bolts to 89 inch lbs. (10 Nm).

20. Install the primary timing chain tensioner, tensioner arm, upper and lower left-hand primary timing chain guide, and primary timing chain. Reset the tensioner. Verify timing mark alignment. Refer to Timing Chain Removal & Installation in the Engine Mechanical section.

21. Install the right-hand and left-hand VCT housing and inspect the seals. Refer to Timing Chain Removal & Installation in the Engine Mechanical section.

22. Lubricate the engine oil filter gasket with clean engine oil prior to installing the oil filter. Install a new engine oil filter. Tighten to 44 inch lbs. (5 Nm) and rotate an additional 180 degrees.

23. Install the engine front cover.

24. Fill and bleed the cooling system. Refer to Draining, Filling & Bleeding Procedure.

ENGINE ELECTRICAL

BATTERY

REMOVAL & INSTALLATION

CAUTION

Batteries contain sulfuric acid and produce explosive gases. Work in a well-ventilated area. Do not allow the battery to come in contact with flames, sparks or burning substances. Avoid contact with skin, eyes or clothing. Shield eyes when working near the battery to protect against possible splashing of acid solution. In case of acid contact with skin or eyes, flush immediately with water for a minimum of 15 minutes, then get prompt medical attention. If acid is swallowed, call a physician immediately. Always lift a plastic-cased battery with a battery carrier or with hands on opposite corners. Excessive pressure on the battery end walls may cause acid to flow through the vent caps, resulting in personal injury and/or damage to the vehicle or battery. Battery posts, terminals and related accessories contain lead and lead components. Wash hands after handling.

1. Before servicing the vehicle, refer to the Precautions Section.
2. Disconnect the negative battery cable. When disconnecting the battery ground cable to interrupt power to the vehicle electrical system, disconnect the battery ground cable only. It is not necessary to disconnect the positive battery cable.
3. Disconnect the positive battery cable.
4. Remove the 2 nuts and the battery hold-down clamp.
5. Remove the battery.
6. To remove the battery tray:

a. Remove the Air Cleaner (ACL) assembly.

b. Disconnect the wiring harness fastener from the battery tray.

c. Remove the 3 bolts and 1 nut from the battery tray.

d. Disconnect the Battery Junction Box (BJB) fastener and remove the battery tray.

To install:

7. To install, reverse the removal procedure, noting the following:

a. If removed, tighten the battery tray bolts and nut to 11 ft. lbs. (15 Nm).

b. Tighten the battery hold-down clamp nuts to 27 inch lbs. (3 Nm).

c. Connect battery cables and tighten to 44 inch lbs. (5 Nm).

d. Refer to Battery Reconnect/Relearn Procedures.

BATTERY RECONNECT/RELEARN PROCEDURE

When the battery (or PCM) is disconnected and connected, some abnormal drive symptoms may occur while the vehicle relearns its adaptive strategy. The charging system set point may also vary. The vehicle may need to be driven to relearn its strategy.

When the battery is disconnected and connected, the illumination display needs to be calibrated. After the battery is connected, rotate the dimmer switch from the lowest dim position to the full bright, dome ON position.

ALTERNATOR

REMOVAL & INSTALLATION

See Figure 59.

➡The radial arm adapter is a serviceable item. Do not replace the alternator if the radial arm adapter is the only concern.

1. Before servicing the vehicle, refer to the Precautions Section.
2. Disconnect the battery.
3. Remove the engine cover.
4. For 3.5L engines, remove A/C compressor.
5. For 3.7L engines, position the upper radiator hose aside and remove the radiator hose support cradle. Rotate the accessory drive belt tensioner and remove the accessory drive belt from the alternator.
6. Position the alternator protective cover aside, remove the B+ nut and position the B+ terminal aside.
7. Disconnect the alternator electrical connector and position the harness aside.
8. Remove the upper alternator nut and loosen the lower alternator bolt completely. Leave the bolt in the alternator.
9. Remove the upper alternator stud.
10. Remove the alternator.

To install:

11. Position the alternator and install the lower alternator bolt. Hand-tighten the bolt at this time.
12. Install the upper alternator stud and nut. Tighten the alternator stud to 71 inch lbs. (8 Nm). Tighten the alternator nut to 35 ft. lbs. (47 Nm).
13. Tighten the lower alternator bolt to 35 ft. lbs. (47 Nm).
14. Connect the alternator electrical connector and install the B+ nut. Tighten to 13 ft. lbs. (17 Nm).
15. For 3.5L engines, install the A/C compressor.

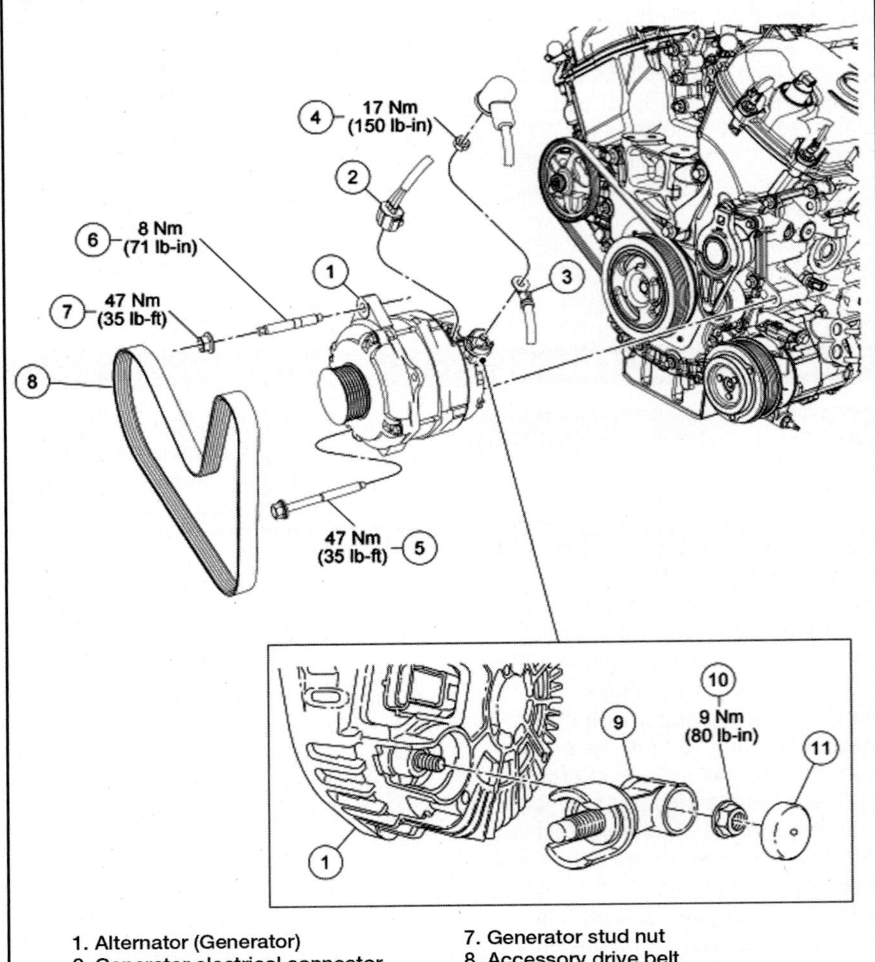

Fig. 59 Alternator (Generator) components

16. For 3.7L engines, rotate the accessory drive belt tensioner and install the accessory drive belt on the alternator. Install the upper radiator hose support cradle and reposition the upper radiator hose into the cradle.
17. Install the engine cover.
18. Connect the battery cable.

FIRING ORDER

Firing order: 1–4–2–5–3–6

IGNITION COIL

REMOVAL & INSTALLATION

3.5L Engines

See Figures 60 and 61.

1. Before servicing the vehicle, refer to the Precautions Section.
2. Disconnect the negative battery cable.
3. For the left-hand side, disconnect the crankcase ventilation tube-to-valve cover fitting quick connect coupling. Remove the fuel injection pump noise insulator shield.
4. Disconnect the 6 ignition coil-on-plug electrical connectors.
5. Remove the 6 bolts and the 6 ignition coil-on-plugs. When removing the ignition coil-on-plugs, a slight twisting motion will break the seal and ease removal.
6. Inspect the coil seals for rips, nicks or tears. Remove and discard any damaged coil seals.

To install:

7. To install, reverse the removal procedure, noting the following:
   a. Apply a small amount of dielectric grease to the inside of the ignition coil-on-plug boots before attaching to the spark plugs.
   b. Slide the new coil seal onto the coil until it is fully seated at the top of the coil.
   c. Install the ignition coil-on-plugs and bolts. Tighten to 62 inch lbs. (7 Nm).

3.7L Engines

See Figures 62 and 63.

1. Before servicing the vehicle, refer to the Precautions Section.
2. Disconnect the negative battery cable.
3. For the left-hand side, disconnect the crankcase ventilation tube-to-valve cover fitting quick connect coupling and position aside.
4. For the right-hand side, Remove the upper intake manifold.
5. Disconnect the 6 ignition coil-on-plug electrical connectors.
6. Remove the 6 bolts and the 6 ignition coil-on-plugs. When removing the ignition coil-on-plugs, a slight twisting motion will break the seal and ease removal.
7. Inspect the coil seals for rips, nicks or tears. Remove and discard any damaged coil seals.

To install:

8. To install, reverse the removal procedure, noting the following:
   a. Apply a small amount of dielectric grease to the inside of the

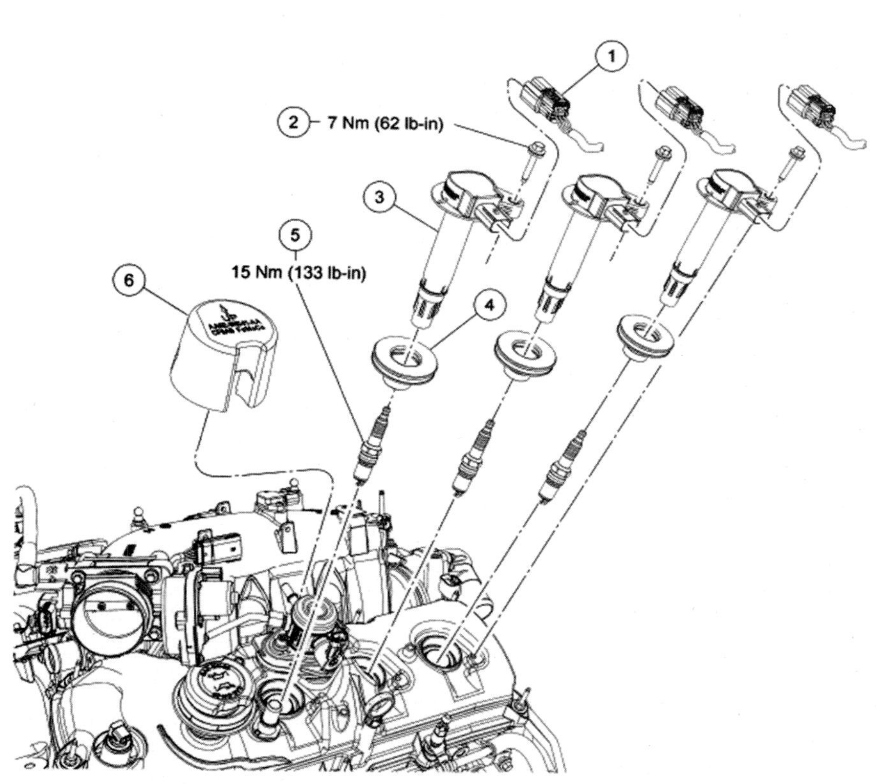

Fig. 60 Left-hand ignition coil components—3.5L engine

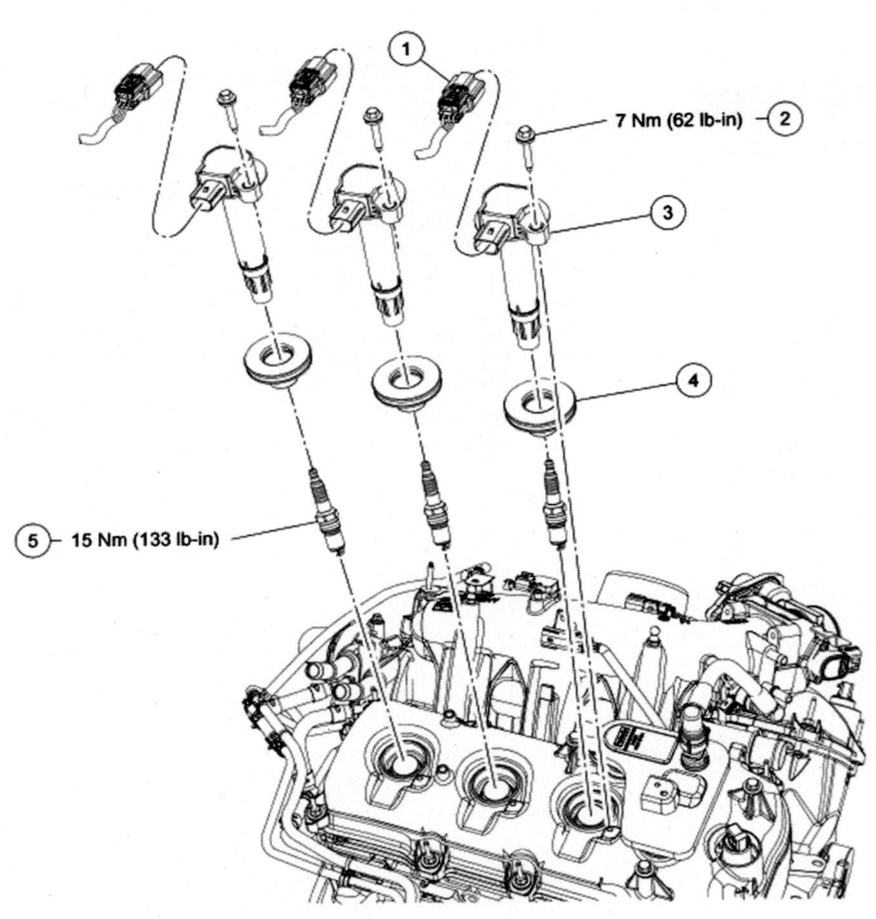

Fig. 61 Right-hand ignition coil components—3.5L engine

ignition coil-on-plug boots before attaching to the spark plugs.

b. Slide the new coil seal onto the coil until it is fully seated at the top of the coil.

c. Install the ignition coil-on-plugs and bolts. Tighten to 62 inch lbs. (7 Nm).

SPARK PLUGS

REMOVAL & INSTALLATION

1. Before servicing the vehicle, refer to the Precautions Section.
2. Disconnect the negative battery cable.
3. Remove the 6 ignition coil-on-plugs. Refer to Ignition Coil Removal & Installation.

WARNING

Only use hand tools when removing or installing the spark plugs, or damage may occur to the cylinder head or spark plug.

4. Use compressed air to remove any foreign material in the spark plug well before removing the spark plugs.
5. Remove the 6 spark plugs.
6. Inspect the 6 spark plugs.

To install:

7. To install, reverse the removal procedure. Tighten to 11 ft. lbs. (15 Nm).
8. Adjust the spark plug gap as necessary:
   - 3.5L Engine: 0.035 in. (0.889 mm)
   - 3.7L Engine: 0.051–0.057 in. (1.29–1.45 mm)

7 Nm
(62 lb-in)
3
4
2
1
6
5
15 Nm
(133 lb-in)
N0082690

1. Crankcase ventilation tube-to-valve cover fitting quick connect coupling
2. Ignition coil-on-plug electrical connector
3. Ignition coil-on-plug bolt
4. Ignition coil-on-plug
5. Spark plug
6. Coil seal

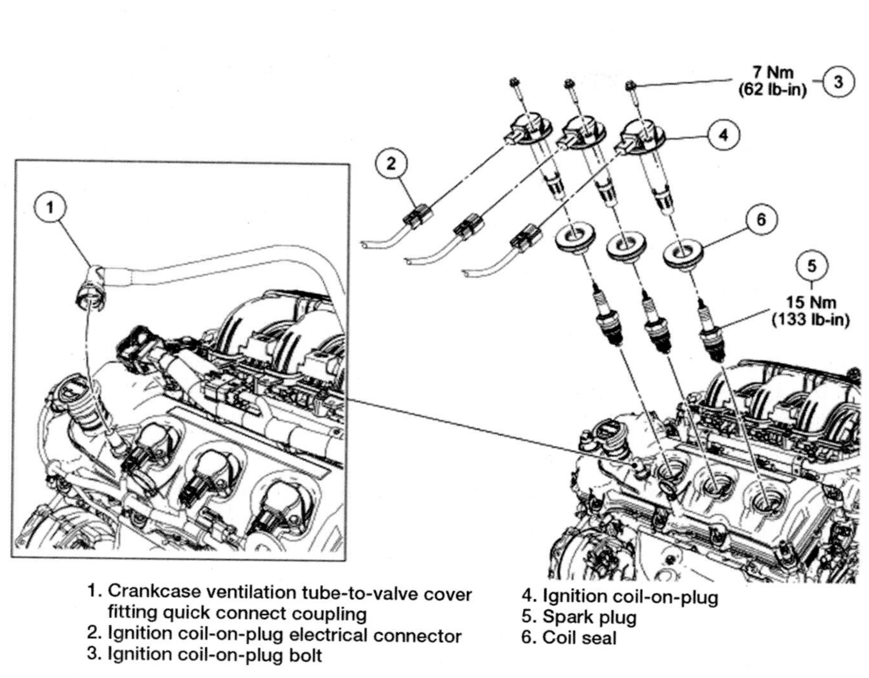

Fig. 62 Left-hand ignition coil components—3.7L engine

2
7 Nm
(62 lb-in)
3
1
5
4
15 Nm
(133 lb-in)
N0082691

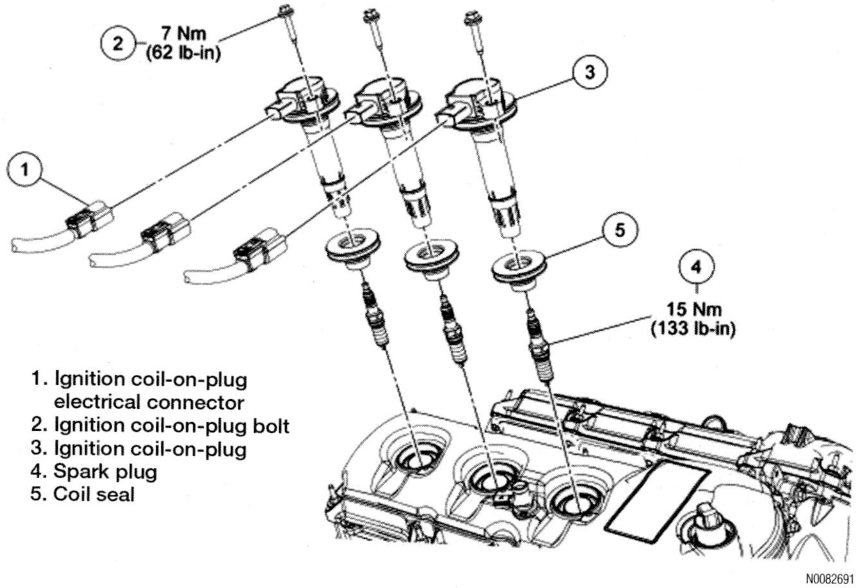

1. Ignition coil-on-plug electrical connector
2. Ignition coil-on-plug bolt
3. Ignition coil-on-plug
4. Spark plug
5. Coil seal

Fig. 63 Right-hand ignition coil components—3.7L engine

STARTER

REMOVAL & INSTALLATION

See Figures 64 and 65.

CAUTION

Always disconnect the battery ground cable at the battery before disconnecting the starter motor battery terminal lead. If a tool is shorted at the starter motor battery terminal, the tool can quickly heat enough to cause a skin burn. Failure to follow this instruction may result in serious personal injury.

1. Before servicing the vehicle, refer to the Precautions Section.
2. Disconnect the battery ground cable.
3. Remove the Air Cleaner (ACL) outlet pipe and ACL assembly.
4. Disconnect the transmission shift cable and adjustment lock from the transmission manual control lever.
5. Disconnect the transmission shift cable rotating slide snap and position aside the transmission cable.

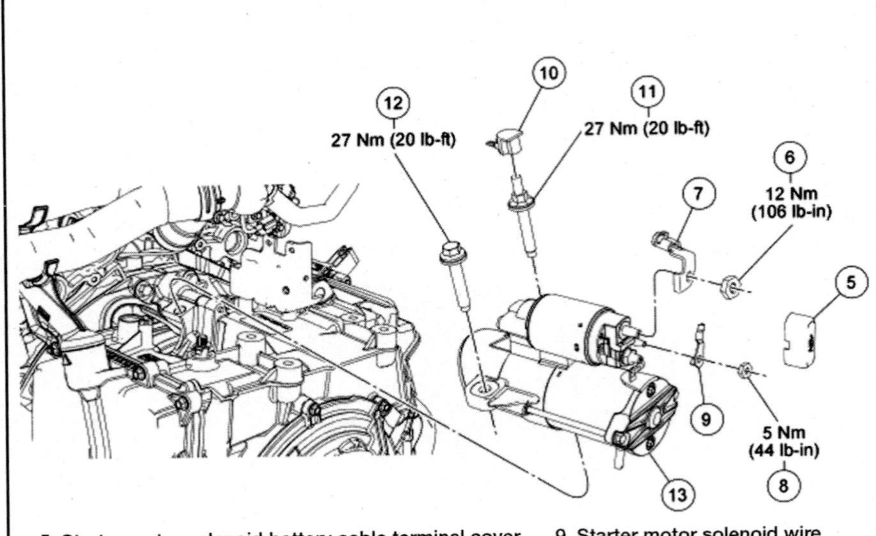

Fig. 65 Starter motor components 2

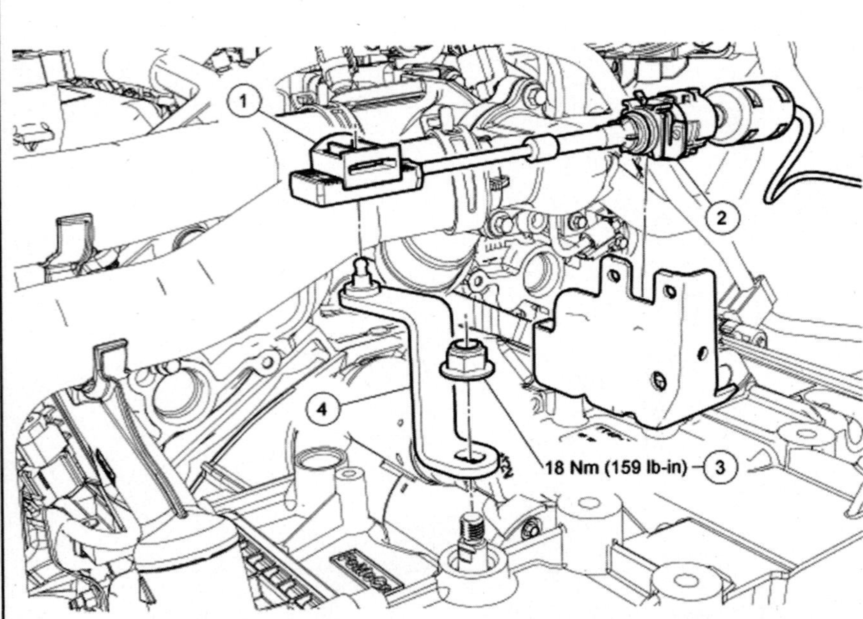

Fig. 64 Starter motor components 1

6. Remove the nut and the transmission manual control lever.
7. Remove the starter motor terminal cover.
8. Remove the starter motor solenoid battery cable nut.
9. Remove the starter motor solenoid wire nut.
10. Disconnect the wiring harness retainer from the starter motor stud bolt.
11. Remove the starter motor stud bolt, bolt and the starter motor.

To install:

12. To install, reverse the removal procedure, noting the following:
    a. Tighten the starter motor stud bolt to 20 ft. lbs. (27 Nm).
    b. Tighten the starter motor solenoid wire nut to 44 inch lbs. (5 Nm).
    c. Tighten the starter motor solenoid battery cable nut to 106 inch lbs. (12 Nm).
    d. Tighten the transmission manual control lever nut to 13 ft. lbs. (18 Nm).

ENGINE MECHANICAL

➡**Disconnecting the negative battery cable may interfere with the functions of the on board computer systems and may require the computer to undergo a relearning process, once the negative battery cable is reconnected.**

ACCESSORY DRIVE BELTS

ACCESSORY BELT ROUTING

See Figures 66 and 67.

Refer to the accompanying illustrations.

INSPECTION

Automatic tensioners are calibrated to provide the correct amount of tension to the belt for a given accessory drive system. Unless a spring or damping band within the tensioner assembly breaks or some other mechanical part of the tensioner fails, there is no need to check the tensioner for correct tension.

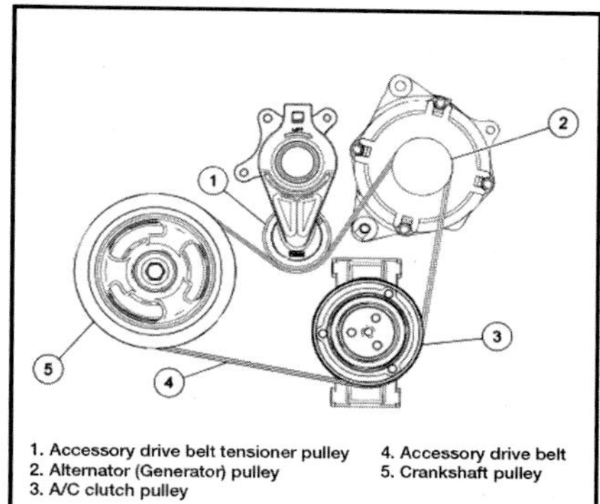

Fig. 66 Front End Accessory Drive (FEAD) Belt Routing

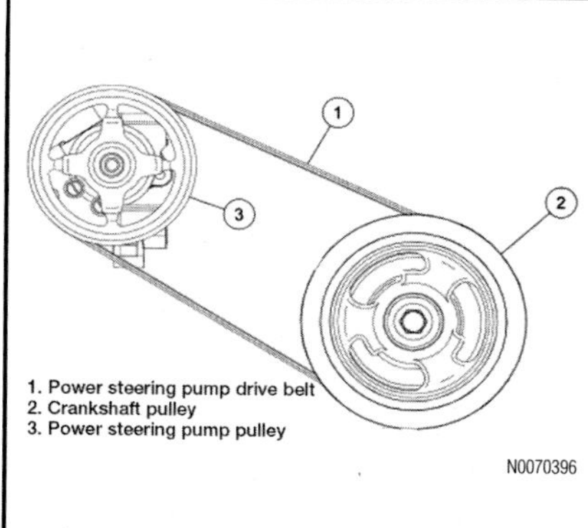

Fig. 67 Power Steering Pump Belt Routing—Vehicles with Hydraulic Power Assist Steering (HPAS)

ADJUSTMENT

The automatic belt tensioner maintains correct belt tension and compensates for component wear and changes in system load.

REMOVAL & INSTALLATION

Accessory Drive Belt

3.5L Engines

See Figure 68.

⁂ WARNING

Under no circumstances should the accessory drive belt, tensioner or pulleys be lubricated, as potential damage to the belt material and tensioner damping mechanism will occur. Do not apply any fluids or belt dressing to the accessory drive belt or pulleys.

1. Before servicing the vehicle, refer to the Precautions Section.
2. Disconnect the negative battery cable.
3. With the vehicle in NEUTRAL, position it on a hoist.
4. Remove the right-hand front wheel and tire.
5. Remove the 7 pin-type retainers and the right-hand splash shield.
6. Working from under the vehicle, rotate the accessory drive belt tensioner clockwise and remove the accessory drive belt.
7. If tensioner removal is required, remove the 3 bolts and the accessory drive belt tensioner.

To install:

8. If tensioner was removed, install the tensioner and tighten the bolts to 97 inch lbs. (11 Nm).
9. Working from under the vehicle, position the accessory drive belt on all pulleys with the exception of the crankshaft pulley.
10. Rotate the accessory drive belt tensioner clockwise and install the accessory drive belt on the crankshaft pulley. After installation, make sure the accessory drive belt is correctly seated on all pulleys.
11. Install the right-hand splash shield and the 7 pin-type retainers.
12. Install the right-hand front wheel and tire.

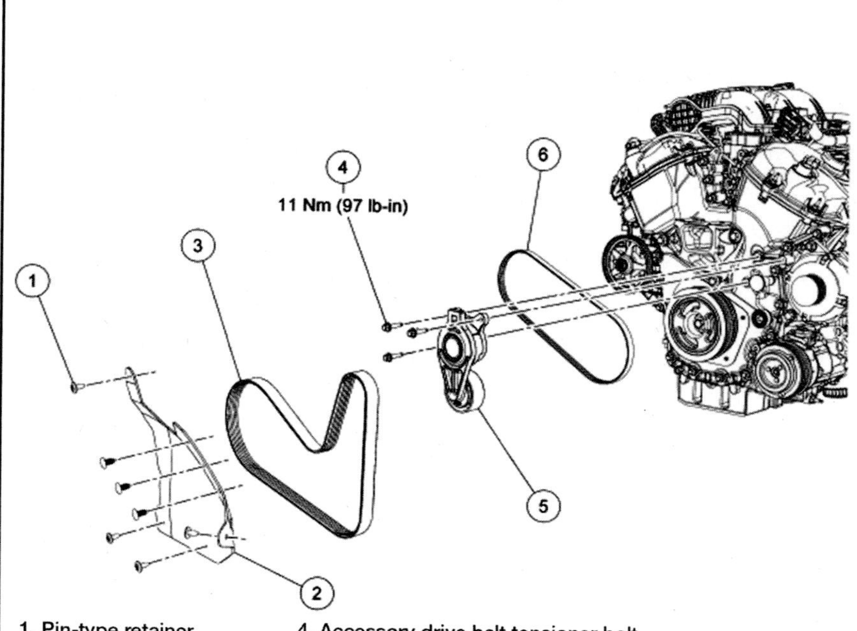

Fig. 68 Front End Accessory Drive (FEAD) Belt—Exploded view

3.7L Engines

See Figure 69.

⁂ WARNING

Under no circumstances should the accessory drive belt, tensioner or pulleys be lubricated, as potential damage to the belt material and tensioner damping mechanism will occur. Do not apply any fluids or belt dressing to the accessory drive belt or pulleys.

1. Before servicing the vehicle, refer to the Precautions Section.
2. Disconnect the negative battery cable.
3. With the vehicle in NEUTRAL, position it on a hoist.
4. Working from the top of the vehicle, rotate the accessory drive belt tensioner clockwise and remove the accessory drive belt from the alternator (generator) pulley.
5. Remove the 7 pin-type retainers and the right-hand splash shield.
6. Working from under the vehicle, remove the accessory drive belt.
7. If tensioner removal is required, remove the 3 bolts and the accessory drive belt tensioner.

To install:

8. If tensioner was removed, install the tensioner and tighten the bolts to 97 inch lbs. (11 Nm).
9. Working from under the vehicle, position the accessory drive belt on all pulleys, with the exception of the alternator pulley.
10. Working from the top of the vehicle, rotate the accessory drive belt tensioner clockwise and install the accessory drive belt on the alternator pulley. After installation, make sure the accessory drive belt is correctly seated on all pulleys.
11. Install the right-hand splash shield and the 7 pin-type retainers.

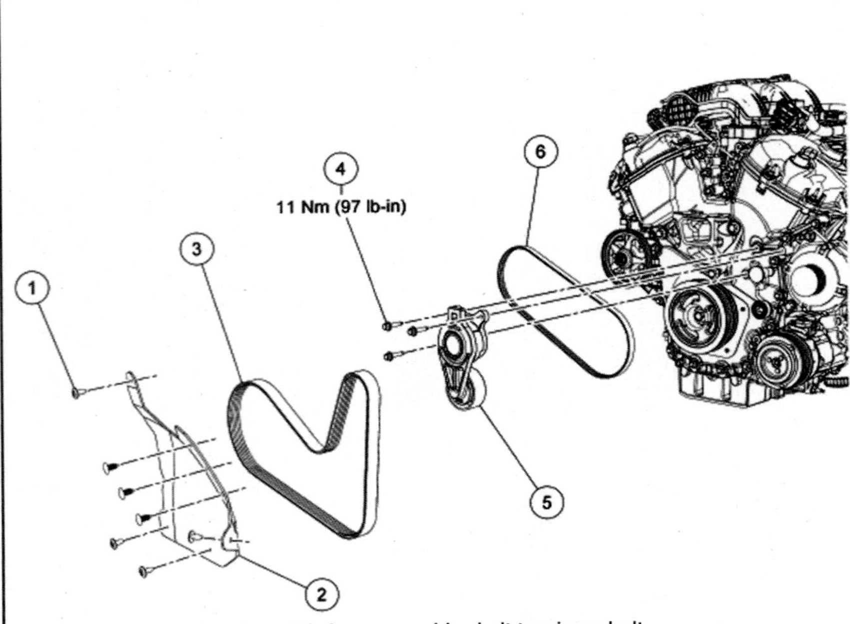

Fig. 69 Front End Accessory Drive (FEAD) Belt—Exploded view

Power Steering Pump Belt

See Figures 70 and 71.

1. Before servicing the vehicle, refer to the Precautions Section.
2. Working from the top of the vehicle, rotate the accessory drive belt tensioner clockwise and remove the accessory drive belt from the alternator (generator) pulley.
3. Remove the right front wheel and tire.
4. Remove the 7 pin-type retainers and the right-hand splash shield.
5. Position the accessory drive belt off the crankshaft pulley.

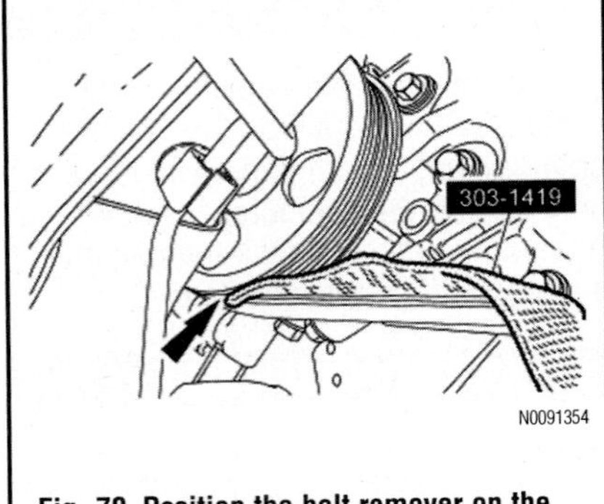

Fig. 70 Position the belt remover on the power steering pump pulley belt

6. Position the Stretchy Belt Remover (SST 303-1419) or equivalent tool on the power steering pump pulley belt as shown.
7. Turn the crankshaft clockwise and feed the belt remover evenly on the power steering pump pulley. Feed the belt remover onto the power steering pump pulley approximately 90 degrees.
8. Remove the power steering pump belt.
   a. Fold the belt remover under the inside of the power steering pump belt as shown.
   b. In one quick motion, firmly pull the belt remover out of the right-hand fender well, removing the coolant pump belt.

To install:

9. Install the power steering drive belt on the crankshaft pulley.
10. Position the power steering drive belt around the Stretchy Belt Installer (SST 303-1252/2) or equivalent tool and the power steering pump pulley.
   a. Make sure the belt is engaged with the power steering pump pulley and rotate the crankshaft clockwise to install the power steering drive belt.

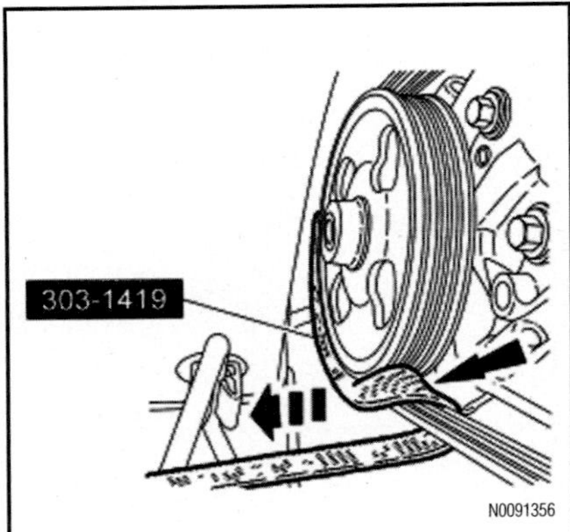

Fig. 71 Fold the belt remover under the power steering pump belt, and pull out to remove the coolant pump belt

b. After installation, make sure the power steering drive belt is correctly seated on the crankshaft and power steering pump pulleys.

11. Position the accessory drive belt on the crankshaft pulley.

12. Working from the top of the vehicle, rotate the accessory drive belt tensioner clockwise and install the accessory drive belt.

a. After installation, make sure the accessory drive belt is correctly seated on all pulleys.

13. Install the right-hand splash shield.

14. Install the right front tire and wheel.

AIR CLEANER

REMOVAL & INSTALLATION

3.5L Engines

See Figure 72.

⁂ WARNING

Whenever turbocharger air intake system components are removed, always cover open ports to protect from debris. It is important that no foreign material enter the system. The turbocharger compressor vanes are susceptible to damage from even small particles. All components should be inspected and cleaned, if necessary, prior to installation or reassembly.

1. Before servicing the vehicle, refer to the Precautions Section.
2. Disconnect the Intake Air Temperature 2 (IAT2) sensor electrical connector.
3. Release the IAT2 sensor wiring harness pin-type retainer from the Air Cleaner (ACL) cover.
4. Loosen the clamp and disconnect the ACL outlet pipe from the ACL .
5. If equipped, remove the bolt cover.
6. Remove the 2 bolts from the ACL assembly. No tools are required to remove the ACL assembly. Removal should be carried out using hands only.
7. Separate the 2 ACL feet from the rubber grommets and remove the ACL assembly.

➡Make sure that the 2 ACL feet are seated into the rubber grommets under the ACL assembly. The ACL outlet pipe should be securely sealed to prevent unmetered air from entering the engine. Utilize the alignment features to make sure the ACL outlet tube is seated within 2 mm of the stops.

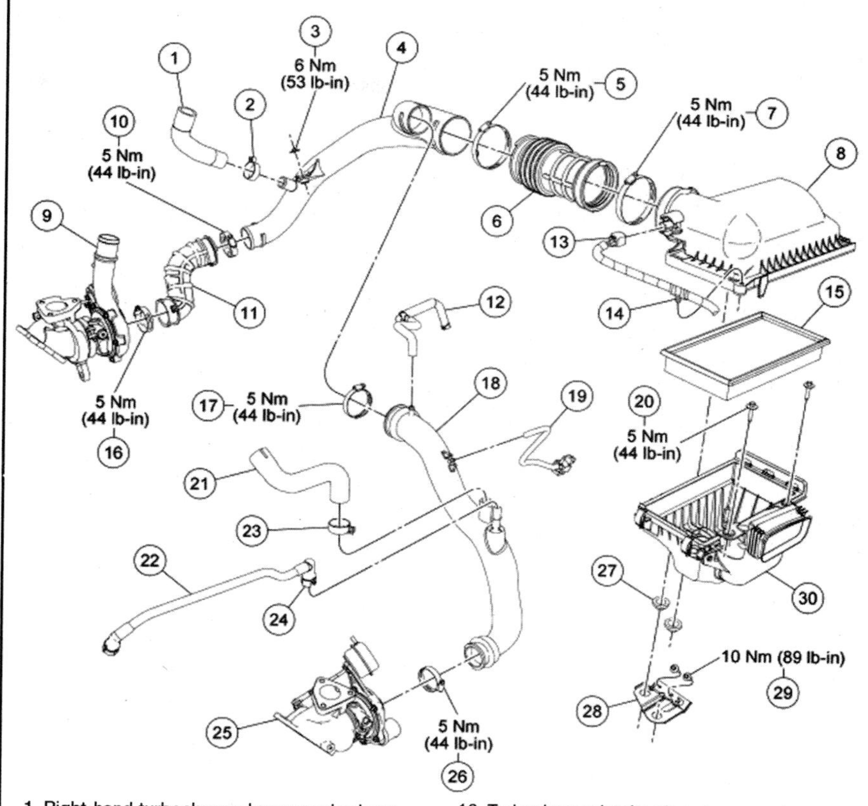

1. Right-hand turbocharger bypass valve hose
2. Turbocharger bypass valve hose clamp
3. Right-hand turbocharger intake tube nut
4. Right-hand turbocharger intake tube
5. Air Cleaner (ACL) outlet pipe clamp
6. ACL outlet pipe
7. ACL outlet pipe clamp
8. ACL cover
9. Right-hand turbocharger
10. Turbocharger intake pipe clamp
11. Right-hand turbocharger intake pipe
12. Power brake booster aspirator hose
13. Intake Air Temperature (IAT) sensor connector
14. IAT sensor wiring harness pin-type retainer
15. ACL element
16. Turbocharger intake pipe clamp
17. Turbocharger intake tube clamp
18. Left-hand turbocharger intake tube
19. Turbocharger wastegate regulating valve hose
20. ACL assembly bolt
21. Left-hand turbocharger bypass valve hose
22. Crankcase ventilation tube
23. Turbocharger bypass valve hose clamp
24. Crankcase ventilation tube quick connect
25. Left-hand turbocharger
26. Turbocharger intake tube clamp
27. ACL insulator
28. ACL bracket
29. ACL bracket bolt
30. ACL tray

N0103527

Fig. 72 Gasoline Turbocharged Direct Injection (GTDI) ACL Assembly—3.5L engines

To install:

8. To install, reverse the removal procedure, noting the following:

a. Tighten the ACL assembly bolts to 44 inch lbs. (5 Nm).

b. Tighten the ACL outlet pipe clamp to 44 inch lbs. (5 Nm).

3.7L Engines

See Figure 73.

1. Before servicing the vehicle, refer to the Precautions Section.
2. Disconnect the Mass Air Flow (MAF) sensor electrical connector.
3. Loosen the clamp and disconnect the Air Cleaner (ACL) outlet pipe from the ACL .
4. Remove the 2 bolts from the ACL assembly. No tools are required to remove the ACL assembly. Removal should be carried out using hands only.
5. Separate the 2 ACL feet from the rubber grommets and remove the ACL assembly.

➡Make sure that the 2 ACL feet are seated into the rubber grommets under the ACL assembly. The ACL outlet pipe should be securely sealed to prevent unmetered air from entering the engine.

To install:

6. To install, reverse the removal procedure, noting the following:

a. Tighten the ACL assembly bolts to 44 inch lbs. (5 Nm).

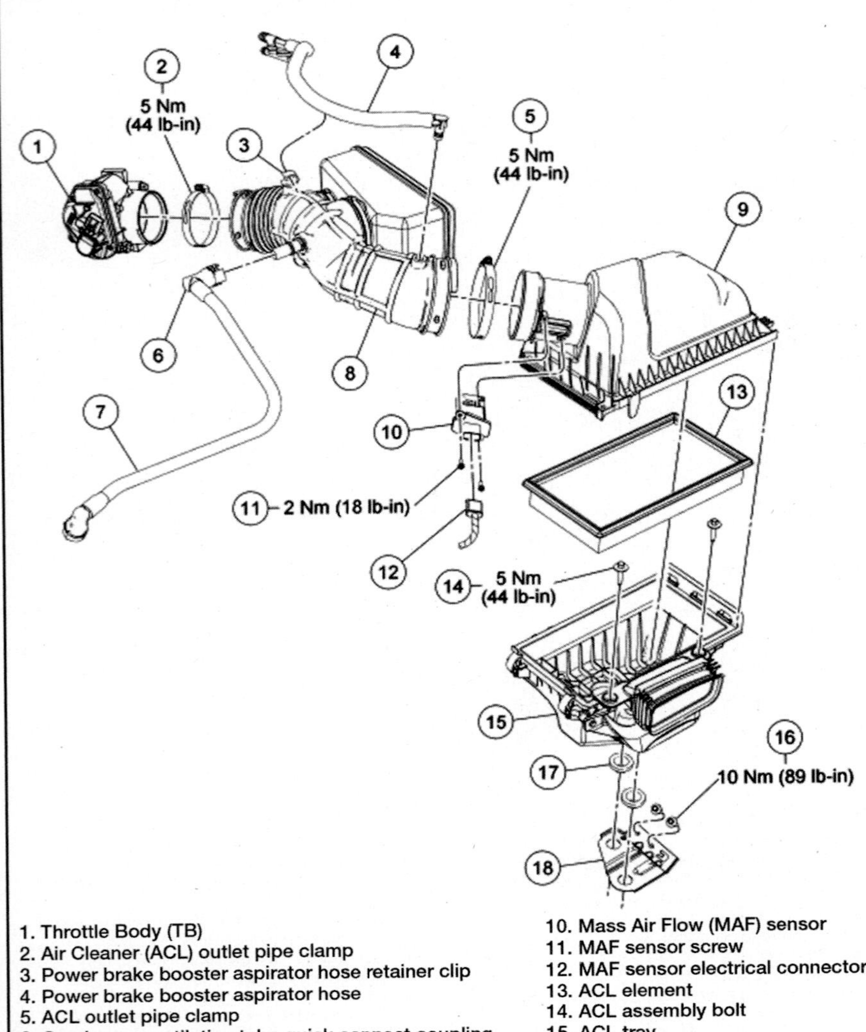

Fig. 73 Air Cleaner (ACL) Assembly—3.7L engines

b. Tighten the ACL outlet pipe clamp to 44 inch lbs. (5 Nm).

CATALYTIC CONVERTER

REMOVAL & INSTALLATION

3.5L Engines

Left-Hand

See Figure 74.

➡Always install new fasteners and gaskets. Clean flange faces prior to new gasket installation to make sure of correct sealing.

1. Before servicing the vehicle, refer to the Precautions Section.
2. With the vehicle in NEUTRAL, position it on a hoist.
3. Remove the left-hand Heated Oxygen Sensor (HO2S).
4. Remove the left-hand exhaust flexible pipe:
   a. Remove the 4 retainers and the underbody shield.
   b. Remove the 2 left-hand exhaust flexible pipe-to-left-hand catalytic converter nuts. Discard the nuts.
   c. Remove the 2 left-hand exhaust flexible pipe-to-underbody catalytic converter nuts. Discard the nuts.
   d. Separate the left-hand exhaust flexible pipe from the left-hand and underbody catalytic converters.
   e. Remove the left-hand exhaust flexible pipe. Discard the gasket.
5. Disconnect the left-hand Catalyst Monitor Sensor (CMS) electrical connector.
6. Remove the 3 left-hand catalytic converter-to-turbocharger nuts and the catalytic converter. Discard the nuts and gasket.
7. Inspect the left-hand turbocharger-to-catalytic converter studs for damage. If damaged, or if a stud comes out when removing the nut, replace the stud.

To install:

8. To install, reverse the removal procedure, noting the following:
   a. Install a new gasket and nuts.
   b. Tighten the turbocharger-to-catalytic converter studs to 18 ft. lbs. (25 Nm).
   c. Tighten the catalytic converter-to-turbocharger nuts to 30 ft. lbs. (40 Nm).
   d. Tighten the exhaust flexible pipe-to-underbody catalytic converter nuts to 30 ft. lbs. (40 Nm).
   e. Make sure the left-hand exhaust flexible pipe is straight and is approximately 25 mm (0.984 in) from all components.
   f. Alternately tighten the 2 exhaust flexible pipe-to-left-hand catalytic converter nuts to 30 ft. lbs. (40 Nm).

Right-Hand

See Figure 74.

➡Always install new fasteners and gaskets. Clean flange faces prior to new gasket installation to make sure of correct sealing.

1. Before servicing the vehicle, refer to the Precautions Section.
2. With the vehicle in NEUTRAL, position it on a hoist.
3. Remove the right-hand front wheel and tire.
4. Disconnect the right-hand Heated Oxygen Sensor (HO2S) electrical connector.
5. Detach the HO2S electrical connector retainer from the bracket.
6. Remove the left-hand exhaust flexible pipe:
   a. Remove the 4 retainers and the underbody shield.
   b. Remove the 2 left-hand exhaust flexible pipe-to-left-hand catalytic converter nuts. Discard the nuts.
   c. Remove the 2 left-hand exhaust flexible pipe-to-underbody catalytic converter nuts. Discard the nuts.
   d. Separate the left-hand exhaust flexible pipe from the left-hand and underbody catalytic converters.

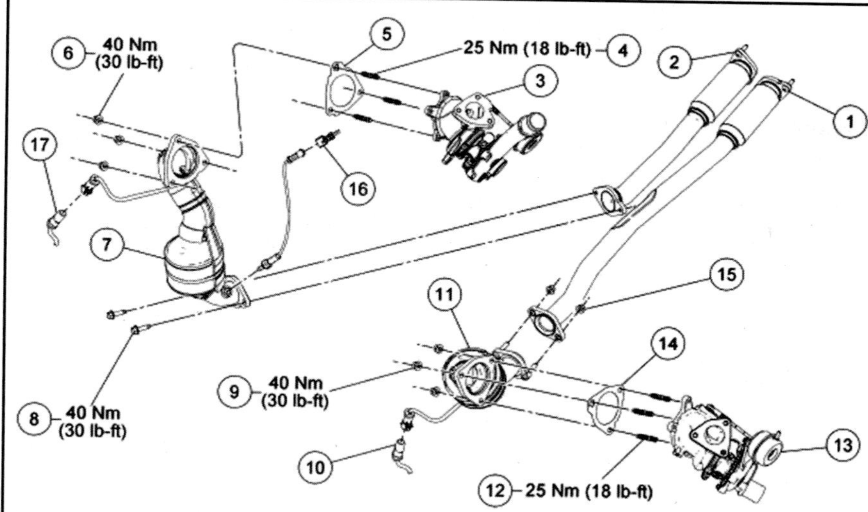

1. Left-hand exhaust flexible pipe
2. Right-hand exhaust flexible pipe
3. Right-hand turbocharger
4. Right-hand turbocharger-to-catalytic converter stud
5. Gasket
6. Right-hand catalytic converter-to-turbocharger nut
7. Right-hand catalytic converter
8. Right-hand exhaust flexible pipe-to-right-hand catalytic converter bolt
9. Left-hand catalytic converter-to-turbocharger nut
10. Left-hand Catalyst Monitor Sensor (CMS) electrical connector
11. Left-hand catalytic converter
12. Left-hand turbocharger-to-catalytic converter stud
13. Left-hand turbocharger
14. Gasket
15. Left-hand exhaust flexible pipe-to-left-hand catalytic converter nut
16. Right-hand CMS sensor electrical connector
17. Right-hand Heated Oxygen Sensor (HO2S) electrical connector (with retainer)

Fig. 74 Catalytic Converters and Exhaust Flexible Pipes—3.5L engines

e. Remove the left-hand exhaust flexible pipe. Discard the gasket.

7. Remove the right-hand exhaust flexible pipes:

a. Remove the 2 right-hand exhaust flexible pipe-to-underbody catalytic converter nuts. Discard the nuts.

b. Remove the 2 right-hand exhaust flexible pipe-to-right-hand catalytic converter bolts. Discard the bolts.

c. Separate the right-hand exhaust flexible pipe from the right-hand and underbody catalytic converters.

d. Remove the right-hand exhaust flexible pipe. Discard the gaskets.

8. Disconnect the right-hand Catalyst Monitor Sensor (CMS) electrical connector.

9. Remove the 3 right-hand catalytic converter-to-turbocharger nuts and the converter. Discard the nuts and gasket.

10. Inspect the right-hand turbocharger-to-catalytic converter studs for damage. If damaged or if a stud comes out when removing the nut, replace the stud.

To install:

11. To install, reverse the removal procedure, noting the following:

a. Prior to installation, inspect the HO2S and the CMS wiring harness for damage.

b. Install new gaskets and nuts.

c. Tighten the turbocharger-to-catalytic converter studs to 18 ft. lbs. (25 Nm).

d. Tighten the catalytic converter-to-turbocharger nuts to 30 ft. lbs. (40 Nm).

e. Tighten the exhaust flexible pipe-to-underbody catalytic converter nuts to 30 ft. lbs. (40 Nm).

f. Tighten the exhaust flexible pipe-to-right-hand catalytic converter bolts to 30 ft. lbs. (40 Nm).

3.7L Engines

Left-Hand

See Figure 75.

➡Always install new fasteners and gaskets. Clean flange faces prior to new gasket installation to make sure of correct sealing.

1. Before servicing the vehicle, refer to the Precautions Section.

2. With the vehicle in NEUTRAL, position it on a hoist.

3. Disconnect the left-hand Catalyst Monitor Sensor (CMS) electrical connector.

4. Remove the exhaust Y-pipe:

a. Remove the 2 exhaust Y-pipe-to-muffler and tail pipe flange nuts. Discard the nuts and gasket.

b. Remove the 2 exhaust Y-pipe-to-left-hand catalytic converter nuts, the 2 exhaust Y-pipe-to-right-hand catalytic converter nuts and the Y-pipe. Discard the nuts and gaskets.

5. Remove the 2 catalytic converter support bracket-to-transmission bolts.

6. Remove the 4 nuts and the left-hand catalytic converter. Discard the nuts and gasket.

7. Inspect the exhaust manifold studs for damage.

8. If damaged, replace the stud, or if stud comes out when removing the nut, replace the stud.

To install:

9. To install, reverse the removal procedure, noting the following:

a. Install new gaskets and nuts.

b. Tighten the exhaust manifold studs to 18 ft. lbs. (25 Nm).

c. Tighten the catalytic converter nuts to 30 ft. lbs. (40 Nm).

d. Tighten the catalytic converter support bracket-to-transmission bolts to 35 ft. lbs. (48 Nm).

e. Tighten the exhaust Y-pipe-to-left-hand catalytic converter nuts to 30 ft. lbs. (40 Nm).

f. Alternately tighten the 2 exhaust Y-pipe-to-right-hand catalytic converter nuts to 30 ft. lbs. (40 Nm).

g. Tighten the exhaust Y-pipe-to-muffler and tail pipe flange nuts to 30 ft. lbs. (40 Nm).

Right-Hand

See Figure 76.

➡Always install new fasteners and gaskets. Clean flange faces prior to new gasket installation to make sure of correct sealing.

1. Before servicing the vehicle, refer to the Precautions Section.

2. With the vehicle in NEUTRAL, position it on a hoist.

3. Remove the exhaust Y-pipe:

a. Remove the 2 exhaust Y-pipe-to-muffler and tail pipe flange nuts. Discard the nuts and gasket.

b. Remove the 2 exhaust Y-pipe-to-left-hand catalytic converter nuts, the 2 exhaust Y-pipe-to-right-hand catalytic converter nuts and the Y-pipe. Discard the nuts and gaskets.

4. Remove the right-hand Catalyst Monitor Sensor (CMS).

5. Remove the 2 bracket-to-right-hand catalytic converter bolts.

6. Remove the 4 nuts and the right-hand

catalytic converter. Discard the nuts and gasket.

7. Inspect the exhaust manifold studs for damage. If damaged, replace the stud, or if stud comes out when removing the nut, replace the stud.

To install:

8. To install, reverse the removal procedure, noting the following:

a. Install new gaskets and nuts.

b. Tighten the exhaust manifold studs to 18 ft. lbs. (25 Nm).

c. Tighten the catalytic converter nuts to 30 ft. lbs. (40 Nm).

d. Tighten the 2 bracket-to-right-hand catalytic converter bolts to 15 ft. lbs. (20 Nm).

e. Tighten the exhaust Y-pipe-to-left-hand catalytic converter nuts to 30 ft. lbs. (40 Nm).

f. Alternately tighten the 2 exhaust Y-pipe-to-right-hand catalytic converter nuts to 30 ft. lbs. (40 Nm).

g. Tighten the exhaust Y-pipe-to-muffler and tail pipe flange nuts to 30 ft. lbs. (40 Nm).

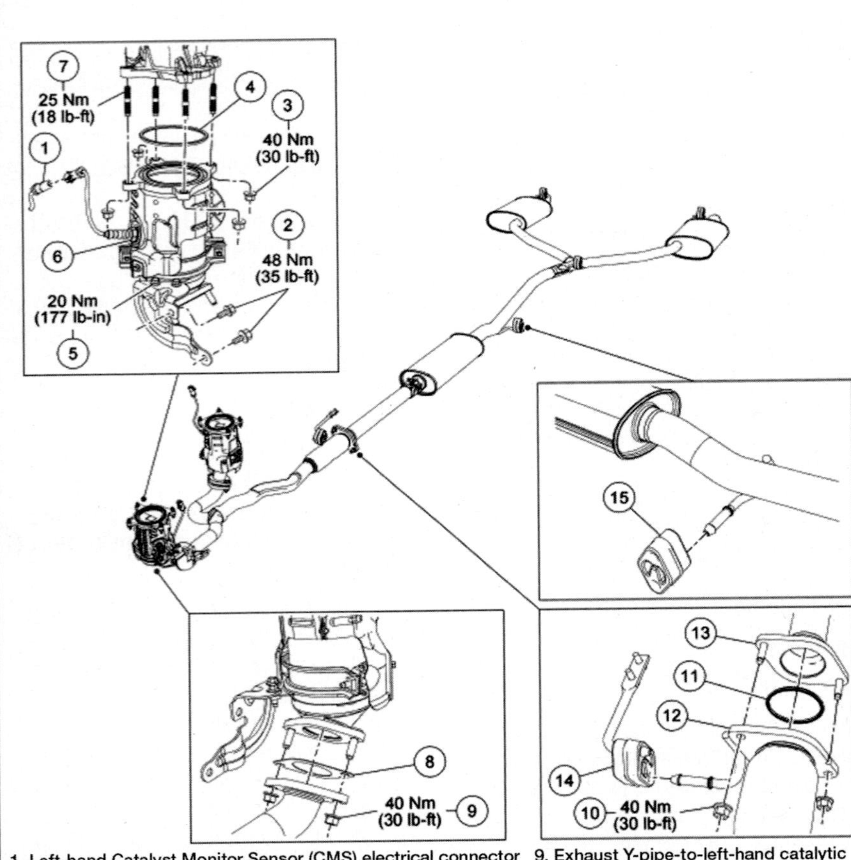

Fig. 75 Left-Hand Catalytic Converters and Exhaust Flexible Pipes—3.7L engines

CRANKSHAFT FRONT SEAL

REMOVAL & INSTALLATION

See Figures 77 and 78.

1. With the vehicle in NEUTRAL, position it on a hoist.

2. Remove the crankshaft pulley:

a. Remove the accessory drive belt.

b. For 3.7L engines, remove the power steering belt.

c. Using the Strap Wrench (SST 303-D055) or equivalent tool, remove the crankshaft pulley bolt and washer. Discard the bolt.

d. Using the 3 Jaw Puller (SST 303-D121) or equivalent tool, remove the crankshaft pulley.

3. Using the Oil Seal Remover (SST 303-409) or equivalent tool, remove and discard the crankshaft front seal.

a. Clean all sealing surfaces with metal surface prep.

To install:

4. Apply clean engine oil to the crankshaft front seal bore in the engine front cover.

5. Using the Front Crankshaft Seal Installer and Crankshaft Vibration Damper Installer (SST 303-1251, 303-102) or equivalent tools, install a new crankshaft front seal.

6. Install the crankshaft pulley:

a. Lubricate the crankshaft front seal inner lip with clean engine oil.

b. Lubricate the outside diameter sealing surfaces with clean engine oil.

c. Using the Crankshaft Vibration Damper Replacer and Front Cover Oil Seal Installer (SST 303-102, 303-335) or equivalent tools, install the crankshaft pulley.

d. Using the Strap Wrench or equivalent tool, install the crankshaft pulley washer and new bolt and tighten in 4 stages:

- Stage 1: Tighten to 89 ft. lbs. (120 Nm)
- Stage 2: Loosen one full turn
- Stage 3: Tighten to 37 ft. lbs. (50 Nm)
- Stage 4: Tighten an additional 90 degrees

e. Install the accessory drive belt.

f. For 3.7L engines, install the power steering belt.

CYLINDER HEAD

REMOVAL & INSTALLATION

3.5L Engines

Left-Hand

See Figures 79 through 81.

⁂ WARNING

During engine repair procedures, cleanliness is extremely important. Any foreign material may cause engine failure.

⁂ WARNING

Whenever turbocharger air intake system components are removed,

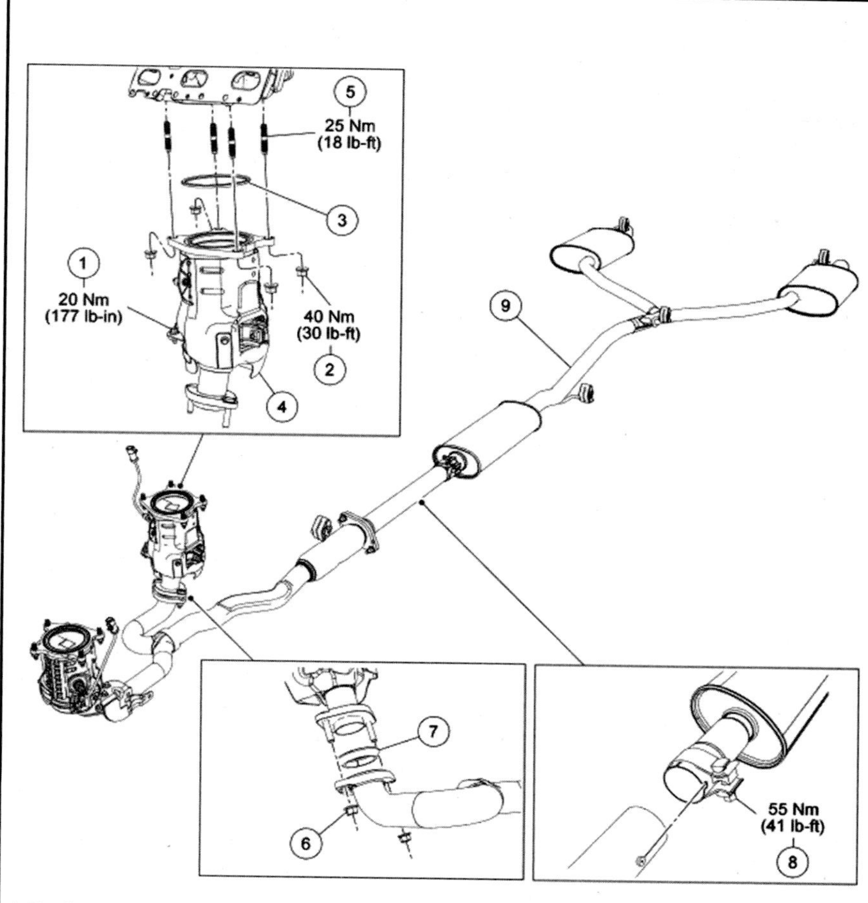

1. Bracket-to-right-hand catalytic converter bolt
2. Right-hand catalytic converter-to-exhaust manifold nut
3. Gasket
4. Right-hand catalytic converter
5. Right-hand catalytic converter-to-exhaust manifold stud
6. Exhaust Y-pipe-to-right-hand catalytic converter nut
7. Gasket
8. Torca® clamp
9. Muffler and tailpipe assembly

N0105874

Fig. 76 Right-Hand Catalytic Converters and Exhaust Flexible Pipes—3.7L engines

always cover open ports to protect from debris. The turbocharger compressor vanes are susceptible to damage from even small particles. All components should be inspected and cleaned, if necessary, prior to installation or reassembly.

➡On early build engines, the timing chain rides on the inner side of the right-hand timing chain guide. Late build engines are equipped with a different design right-hand timing chain guide that requires the timing chain to ride on the outer side of the right-hand timing chain guide. For service, all replacement right-hand timing chain guides will be the late build design.

1. Remove the fuel rails.
2. Remove the left-hand camshafts.
3. Disconnect the left-hand Camshaft Position (CMP) sensor electrical connector; remove the bolt and the left-hand CMP sensor.

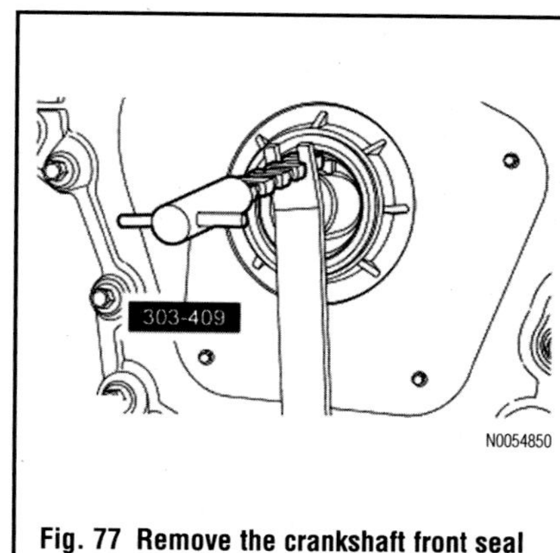

Fig. 77 Remove the crankshaft front seal

4. Detach the wiring harness retainer from the rear of the left-hand cylinder head.
5. Remove the coolant tube bracket-to-cylinder head nut.
6. Disconnect the alternator (generator) B+ cable and electrical connector, and remove the alternator and alternator stud.
7. Remove the 3 bolts and the left-hand exhaust manifold heat shield.
8. Disconnect the turbocharger wastegate regulating valve hose from the left-hand turbocharger assembly.
9. Remove the 2 bolts and the left-hand turbocharger oil return tube from the turbocharger. Remove and discard the gasket.
10. Remove the left-hand oil supply tube secondary latch.
11. Using the Spring Lock Coupling Disconnect Tool, remove the left-hand oil supply tube from the quick connect fitting. Inspect and if necessary, replace the quick connect fitting.
12. Remove the 2 coolant tube banjo bolts and the left-hand turbocharger coolant tubes and sealing washers. Discard the sealing washers.
13. Remove the left-hand turbocharger oil supply tube banjo bolt; discard the sealing washer and the oil supply tube filter.
14. Remove the 2 bolts and the lower left-hand turbocharger-to-cylinder block bracket.
15. Remove the 2 bolts and the upper left-hand turbocharger bracket-to-cylinder block bracket.
16. Remove the 8 left-hand exhaust manifold nuts and the exhaust manifold and turbocharger assembly. Discard the exhaust manifold gasket and nuts. Clean and inspect the left-hand exhaust manifold. Remove and discard the 8 left-hand exhaust manifold studs.

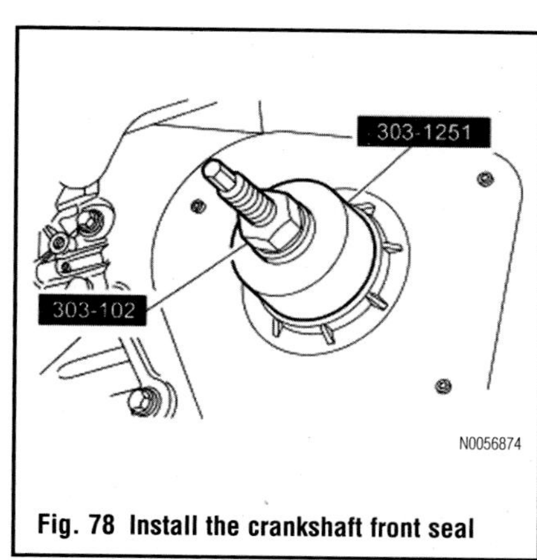

Fig. 78 Install the crankshaft front seal

⁂ WARNING

Do not use metal scrapers, wire brushes, power abrasive discs or other abrasive means to clean the sealing surfaces. These may cause scratches and gouges resulting in leak paths. Use a plastic scraper to clean the sealing surfaces.

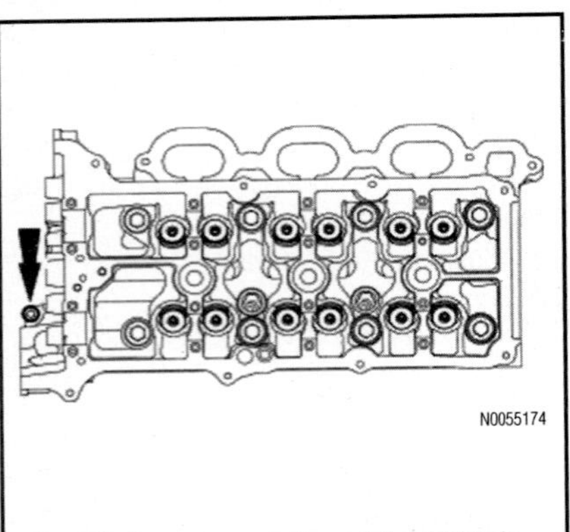

Fig. 79 Remove and discard the M6 bolt

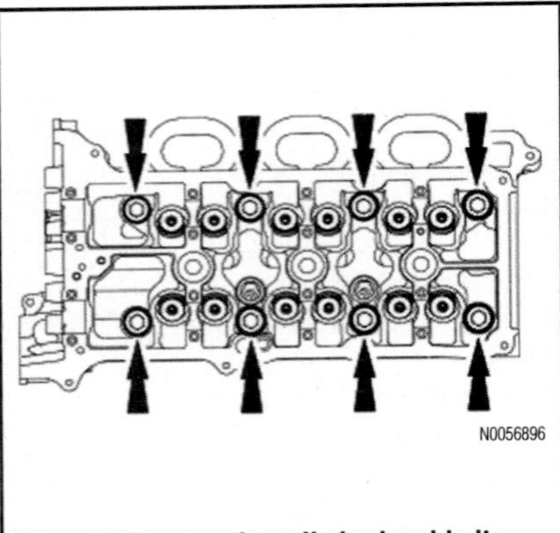

Fig. 80 Remove the cylinder head bolts

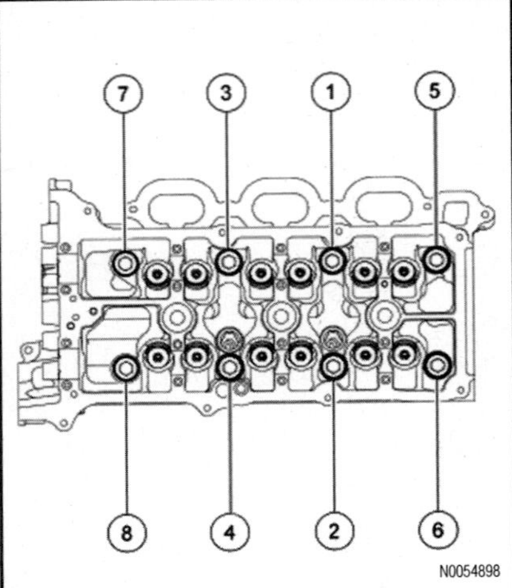

Fig. 81 Cylinder head bolt tightening sequence

17. Clean the exhaust manifold mating surface of the cylinder head with metal surface prep. Follow the directions on the packaging.
18. Remove the left-hand cylinder block drain plug. Allow coolant to drain from the cylinder block.
19. If equipped, remove the heat shield and disconnect the block heater electrical connector. Remove the block heater wiring harness from the engine.
20. Remove the right-hand cylinder block drain plug or, if equipped, the block heater. Allow coolant to drain from the cylinder block.
21. Remove the 2 bolts and the upper left-hand primary timing chain guide.
22. Remove the 2 bolts and the left-hand secondary timing chain tensioner.
23. Remove the valve tappets from the cylinder head. If the components are to be reinstalled, they must be installed in the same positions. Mark the components for installation into their original locations.
24. Inspect the valve tappets.
25. Remove and discard the M6 bolt.

⁂ WARNING

Place clean, lint-free shop towels over exposed engine cavities. Carefully remove the towels so foreign material is not dropped into the engine. Any foreign material (including any material created while cleaning gasket surfaces) that enters the oil passages or the oil pan, may cause engine failure.

⁂ WARNING

Aluminum surfaces are soft and may be scratched easily. Never place the cylinder head gasket surface, unprotected, on a bench surface.

26. Remove and discard the 8 bolts from the cylinder head.
    a. Remove the cylinder head.
    b. Discard the cylinder head gasket.

⁂ WARNING

Do not use metal scrapers, wire brushes, power abrasive discs or other abrasive means to clean the sealing surfaces. These tools cause scratches and gouges that make leak paths. Use a plastic scraping tool to remove all traces of the head gasket.

⁂ WARNING

Observe all warnings or cautions and follow all application directions contained on the packaging of the silicone gasket remover and the metal surface prep.

➡If there is no residual gasket material present, metal surface prep can be used to clean and prepare the surfaces.

27. Clean the cylinder head-to-cylinder block mating surfaces of both the cylinder heads and the cylinder block in the following sequence.
    a. Remove any large deposits of silicone or gasket material with a plastic scraper.
    b. Apply silicone gasket remover, following package directions, and allow to set for several minutes.
    c. Remove the silicone gasket remover with a plastic scraper. A second application of silicone gasket remover may be required if residual traces of silicone or gasket material remain.
    d. Apply metal surface prep, following package directions, to remove any remaining traces of oil or coolant and to prepare the surfaces to bond with the new gasket. Do not attempt to make the metal shiny. Some staining of the metal surfaces is normal.
28. Support the cylinder head on a bench with the head gasket side up. Check the cylinder head distortion and the cylinder block distortion.

To install:

29. Install a new gasket, the left-hand cylinder head and 8 new bolts. Tighten in the sequence shown in 5 stages:
    a. Stage 1: Tighten to 15 ft. lbs. (20 Nm).
    b. Stage 2: Tighten to 26 ft. lbs. (35 Nm).
    c. Stage 3: Tighten 90 degrees.
    d. Stage 4: Tighten 90 degrees.
    e. Stage 5: Tighten 90 degrees.
30. Install the cylinder head M6 bolt. Tighten to 89 inch lbs. (10 Nm).
31. Coat the valve tappets with clean engine oil prior to installation. Install the valve tappets. The valve tappets must be installed in their original positions.
32. Install the left-hand secondary timing chain tensioner and the 2 bolts. Tighten to 89 inch lbs. (10 Nm).
33. Install the upper left-hand primary timing chain guide and the 2 bolts. Tighten to 89 inch lbs. (10 Nm).
34. Install the right-hand cylinder block drain plug or, if equipped, the block heater. Tighten to 30 ft. lbs. (40 Nm).
35. If equipped, install the block heater wiring harness onto the engine.

a. Connect the block heater electrical connector and install the heat shield.

36. Install the left-hand cylinder block drain plug. Tighten to 15 ft. lbs. (20 Nm) plus an additional 180 degrees.

37. Install 8 new left-hand exhaust manifold studs. Tighten to 106 inch lbs. (12 Nm).

38. Install a new gasket, left-hand exhaust manifold and turbocharger assembly and 8 new nuts. Tighten the nuts in 2 stages in the sequence shown in the Exhaust Manifold Removal & Installation procedure.

39. Install the upper turbocharger bracket-to-cylinder block and the 2 bolts. Do not tighten the bolts at this time.

40. Install the lower turbocharger-to-cylinder block bracket and the 2 bolts. Do not tighten the bolts at this time.

41. The next 4 steps must be performed in order or damage to the turbocharger may occur:

a. Tighten the upper turbocharger bracket-to-turbocharger bolt. Tighten to 14 ft. lbs. (19 Nm).

b. Tighten the upper turbocharger bracket-to-cylinder block bolt. Tighten to 18 ft. lbs. (25 Nm).

c. Tighten the lower turbocharger bracket-to-turbocharger bolt. Tighten to 14 ft. lbs. (19 Nm).

d. Tighten the lower turbocharger bracket-to-cylinder block bolt. Tighten to 97 inch lbs. (11 Nm).

42. Install the oil supply tube filter, washer and bolt.

a. Install the oil supply tube filter in the oil supply tube block.

b. Slide the new washer onto the oil supply tube block.

c. Install the banjo bolt into the oil supply tube block.

43. Install the left-hand turbocharger oil supply tube and banjo bolt. Tighten the bolt to 26 ft. lbs. (35 Nm).

44. Using 2 new sealing washers, install the 2 left-hand turbocharger coolant tubes and the banjo bolts. Tighten to 27 ft. lbs. (37 Nm).

45. If necessary, install the left-hand cylinder head turbocharger oil supply quick connect fitting. Tighten to 12 ft. lbs. (16 Nm).

46. Install the left-hand oil supply tube into the quick connect fitting. Listen for audible click.

47. Install the left-hand oil supply tube secondary latch.

48. Install a new gasket, turbocharger oil return tube and the 2 bolts. Tighten to 89 inch lbs. (10 Nm).

49. Connect the turbocharger wastegate regulating valve hose to the left-hand turbocharger assembly. Make sure the turbocharger wastegate regulating valve hose does not contact the exhaust manifold heat shield.

50. Install the left-hand exhaust manifold heat shield and the 3 bolts. Tighten to 10 ft. lbs. (14 Nm).

51. Install the stud, alternator and the nut and bolt. Tighten the stud to 71 inch lbs. (8 Nm), and the nut and bolt to 35 ft. lbs. (47 Nm). Connect the alternator electrical connector. Connect the alternator B+ cable and install the nut. Tighten to 13 ft. lbs. (17 Nm).

52. Install the left-hand coolant tube bracket-to-cylinder head nut. Tighten to 89 inch lbs. (10 Nm).

53. Attach the pin-type wire harness retainer to the rear of left-hand cylinder head.

54. Install the left-hand Camshaft Position (CMP) sensor and the bolt. Tighten to 89 inch lbs. (10 Nm). Connect the CMP sensor electrical connector.

55. Install the left-hand camshafts.

56. Install the fuel rails.

Right-Hand

See Figures 82 through 84.

WARNING

During engine repair procedures, cleanliness is extremely important. Any foreign material, including any material created while cleaning gasket surfaces that enters the oil passages, coolant passages or the oil pan, may cause engine failure.

WARNING

Whenever turbocharger air intake system components are removed, always cover open ports to protect from debris. The turbocharger compressor vanes are susceptible to damage from even small particles. All components should be inspected and cleaned, if necessary, prior to installation or reassembly.

➡On early build engines, the timing chain rides on the inner side of the right-hand timing chain guide. Late build engines are equipped with a different design right-hand timing chain guide that requires the timing chain to ride on the outer side of the right-hand timing chain guide. For service, all replacement right-hand timing chain guides will be the late build design.

1. Remove the fuel rails.

2. Remove the right-hand camshafts.

3. Disconnect the right-hand Camshaft Position (CMP) sensor electrical connector.

4. Remove the bolt and the right-hand CMP sensor.

5. Remove the bolt and the ground wire.

6. Remove the bolt and the radio capacitor from the right-hand cylinder head.

7. Disconnect the Cylinder Head Temperature (CHT) sensor electrical connector from the rear of the right-hand cylinder head.

8. Remove the 5 bolts and the 2 upper right-hand exhaust manifold heat shields.

9. Disconnect the turbocharger wastegate regulating valve hose from the right-hand turbocharger assembly.

10. Remove the 2 bolts and the turbocharger oil return tube from the right-hand turbocharger. Remove and discard the gasket.

11. Remove the oil supply tube secondary latch.

12. Using the Spring Lock Coupling Disconnect Tool, remove the right-hand oil supply tube from the quick connect fitting. Inspect and if necessary, replace the quick connect fitting.

13. Remove the 2 coolant tube banjo bolts and the right-hand turbocharger coolant tubes and sealing washers. Discard the sealing washers.

14. Remove the coolant tube bracket-to-cylinder head bolt.

15. Remove the 3 bolts and the upper turbocharger-to-cylinder block bracket.

16. Remove the 3 exhaust manifold-to-turbocharger bolts and the turbocharger assembly. Discard the gasket and bolts.

17. Remove the right-hand turbocharger oil supply tube banjo bolt; discard the sealing washer and the oil supply tube filter.

18. Remove the 8 nuts and the right-hand exhaust manifold. Discard the nuts and exhaust manifold gaskets. Clean and inspect the right-hand exhaust manifold. Remove and discard the 8 right-hand exhaust manifold studs.

WARNING

Do not use metal scrapers, wire brushes, power abrasive discs or other abrasive means to clean the sealing surfaces. These may cause scratches and gouges resulting in leak paths. Use a plastic scraper to clean the sealing surfaces.

19. Clean the exhaust manifold mating surface of the cylinder head with metal

surface prep. Follow the directions on the packaging.

20. Remove the left-hand cylinder block drain plug. Allow coolant to drain from the cylinder block.

21. If equipped, remove the heat shield and disconnect the block heater electrical connector. Remove the block heater wiring harness from the engine.

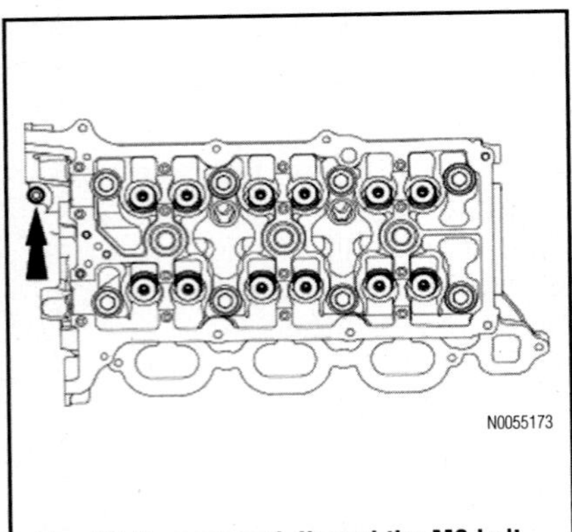

Fig. 82 Remove and discard the M6 bolt

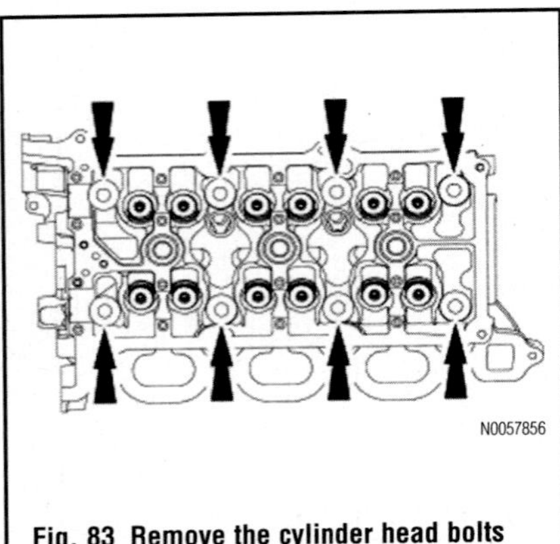

Fig. 83 Remove the cylinder head bolts

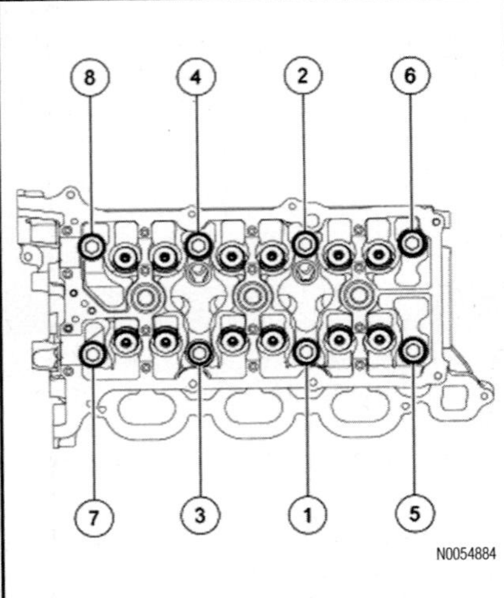

Fig. 84 Cylinder head bolt tightening sequence

22. Remove the right-hand cylinder block drain plug or, if equipped, the block heater. Allow coolant to drain from the cylinder block.

23. Remove the 2 bolts and the right-hand primary timing chain guide.

24. Remove the bolts and the right-hand secondary timing chain tensioner.

25. Remove the 2 bolts and the right-hand engine lifting eye.

26. Remove the valve tappets from the cylinder head. If the components are to be reinstalled, they must be installed in the same positions. Mark the components for installation into their original locations.

27. Inspect the valve tappets.

28. Remove and discard the M6 bolt.

WARNING

Place clean, lint-free shop towels over exposed engine cavities. Carefully remove the towels so foreign material is not dropped into the engine. Aluminum surfaces are soft and may be scratched easily. Never place the cylinder head gasket surface, unprotected, on a bench surface.

29. Remove and discard the 8 bolts from the cylinder head.

a. Remove the cylinder head.

b. Discard the cylinder head gasket.

WARNING

Do not use metal scrapers, wire brushes, power abrasive discs or other abrasive means to clean the sealing surfaces. These tools cause scratches and gouges that make leak paths. Use a plastic scraping tool to remove all traces of the head gasket.

WARNING

Observe all warnings or cautions and follow all application directions contained on the packaging of the silicone gasket remover and the metal surface prep.

➡If there is no residual gasket material present, metal surface prep can be used to clean and prepare the surfaces.

30. Clean the cylinder head-to-cylinder block mating surfaces of both the cylinder heads and the cylinder block in the following sequence:

a. Remove any large deposits of silicone or gasket material with a plastic scraper.

b. Apply silicone gasket remover, following package directions, and allow to set for several minutes.

c. Remove the silicone gasket remover with a plastic scraper. A second application of silicone gasket remover may be required if residual traces of silicone or gasket material remain.

d. Apply metal surface prep, following package directions, to remove any remaining traces of oil or coolant and to prepare the surfaces to bond with the new gasket. Do not attempt to make the metal shiny. Some staining of the metal surfaces is normal.

31. Support the cylinder head on a bench with the head gasket side up. Check the cylinder head distortion and the cylinder block distortion.

To install:

32. Install a new gasket, the right-hand cylinder head and 8 new bolts. Tighten in the sequence shown in 5 stages:

a. Stage 1: Tighten to 15 ft. lbs. (20 Nm).

b. Stage 2: Tighten to 26 ft. lbs. (35 Nm).

c. Stage 3: Tighten 90 degrees.

d. Stage 4: Tighten 90 degrees.

e. Stage 5: Tighten 90 degrees.

33. Install the cylinder head M6 bolt. Tighten to 89 inch lbs. (10 Nm).

34. Coat the valve tappets with clean engine oil prior to installation. Install the valve tappets. The valve tappets must be installed in their original positions.

35. Install the right-hand engine lifting eye and the 2 bolts. Tighten to 18 ft. lbs. (24 Nm).

36. Install the right-hand secondary timing chain tensioner and the 2 bolts. Tighten to 89 inch lbs. (10 Nm).

37. Install the right-hand primary timing chain guide and the 2 bolts. Tighten to 89 inch lbs. (10 Nm).

38. Install the right-hand cylinder block drain plug or, if equipped, the block heater. Tighten to 30 ft. lbs. (40 Nm).

39. If equipped, install the block heater wiring harness onto the engine. Connect the block heater electrical connector and install the heat shield.

40. Install the left-hand cylinder block drain plug. Tighten to 15 ft. lbs. (20 Nm) plus an additional 180 degrees.

41. Install 8 new right-hand exhaust manifold studs. Tighten to 106 inch lbs. (12 Nm). Install a new gasket, right-hand exhaust manifold and 8 new nuts. Tighten in 2 stages in the sequence shown in the

Exhaust Manifold Removal & Installation procedure.

42. Install the oil supply tube filter, washer and bolt. Install a new oil supply tube filter in the oil supply tube block, slide the new washer onto the oil supply tube block, and install the banjo bolt into the oil supply tube block.

43. Install the right-hand turbocharger oil supply tube. Tighten the bolt to 26 ft. lbs. (35 Nm).

44. Install a new gasket, the turbocharger and the 3 new exhaust manifold-to-turbocharger bolts. Tighten to 33 ft. lbs. (45 Nm).

45. Install the upper turbocharger-to-cylinder block bracket and the 3 bolts and position the bracket as far clockwise as possible and tighten the bolts in the following sequence:

a. Tighten the lower bolt to 19 ft. lbs. (26 Nm).

b. Tighten the upper bolt to 19 ft. lbs. (26 Nm).

c. Tighten the turbocharger bolt to 14 ft. lbs. (19 Nm).

46. Using 2 new sealing washers, install the 2 right-hand turbocharger coolant tubes and banjo bolts. Tighten to 27 ft. lbs. (37 Nm).

47. Install the coolant tube bracket-to-cylinder head bolt. Tighten to 89 inch lbs. (10 Nm).

48. If necessary, install the right-hand cylinder head turbocharger oil supply quick connect fitting. Tighten to 12 ft. lbs. (16 Nm).

49. Install the right-hand oil supply tube into the quick connect fitting. Listen for audible click

50. Install the oil supply tube secondary latch.

51. Install a new gasket and the right-hand turbocharger oil return tube and the 2 bolts. Tighten to 89 inch lbs. (10 Nm).

52. Connect the turbocharger wastegate regulating valve hose to the right-hand turbocharger assembly. Make sure the turbocharger wastegate regulating valve hose does not contact the exhaust manifold heat shield.

53. Install the 2 upper right-hand exhaust manifold heat shield and the 5 bolts. Make sure the heat shield does not contact the wastegate arm. Tighten to 10 ft. lbs. (14 Nm).

54. Connect the Cylinder Head Temperature (CHT) sensor electrical connector to the rear of the right-hand cylinder head.

55. Install the radio capacitor and bolt to the right-hand cylinder head. Tighten to 89 inch lbs. (10 Nm).

56. Install the ground wire and the bolt. Tighten to 89 inch lbs. (10 Nm).

57. Install the right-hand Camshaft Position (CMP) sensor and the bolt. Tighten to 89 inch lbs. (10 Nm).

58. Connect the right-hand CMP sensor electrical connector.

59. Install the right-hand camshafts.

60. Install the fuel rails.

3.7L Engines

Left-Hand

See Figures 85 through 87.

✱✱ WARNING

During engine repair procedures, cleanliness is extremely important. Any foreign material, including any material created while cleaning gasket surfaces that enters the oil passages, coolant passages or the oil pan, may cause engine failure.

1. Remove the left-hand camshafts.

2. Disconnect the 6 fuel injector electrical connectors.

3. Disconnect the Cylinder Head Temperature (CHT) sensor electrical connector.

4. Disconnect the left-hand Camshaft Position (CMP) sensor electrical connector, remove the bolt and the left-hand CMP sensor.

5. Disconnect the left-hand Heated Oxygen Sensor (HO2S) electrical connector.

6. Disconnect the left-hand Catalyst Monitor Sensor (CMS) electrical connector.

7. Detach the wiring harness retainer from the rear of the left-hand cylinder head.

8. Disconnect the alternator (generator) B+ cable and electrical connector, and remove the alternator and alternator stud.

9. Disconnect the Engine Oil Pressure (EOP) switch electrical connector and the wiring harness pin-type retainer. Remove the wiring harness from the engine.

10. Remove the 2 left-hand catalytic converter bracket bolts. Remove the 4 nuts and the left-hand catalytic converter. Discard the nuts and the gasket.

11. Remove the 3 bolts and the left-hand exhaust manifold heat shield.

12. Remove the 6 nuts and the left-hand exhaust manifold. Discard the nuts and the exhaust manifold gasket. Clean and inspect the left-hand exhaust manifold. Remove and discard the 6 left-hand exhaust manifold studs.

13. Remove the left-hand cylinder block drain plug. Allow coolant to drain from the cylinder block.

14. Remove the 4 nuts and the right-hand catalytic converter. Discard the nuts and gasket.

15. If equipped, remove the heat shield and disconnect the block heater electrical connector. Remove the block heater wiring harness from the engine.

16. Remove the right-hand cylinder block drain plug or, if equipped, the block heater. Allow coolant to drain from the cylinder block.

17. Remove the coolant bypass hose from the thermostat housing.

18. Remove the 4 bolts and the fuel rail and injectors as an assembly.

19. Remove the 3 thermostat housing-to-lower intake manifold bolts. Remove the thermostat housing and discard the gasket and O-ring seal.

20. Remove the 10 bolts and the lower intake manifold. Discard the gaskets. If the engine is repaired or replaced because of upper engine failure, typically including valve or piston damage, check the intake manifold for metal debris. If metal debris is found, install a new intake manifold.

21. Remove the 2 bolts and the upper left-hand primary timing chain guide.

22. Remove the 2 bolts and the left-hand secondary timing chain tensioner.

23. Remove the valve tappets from the cylinder head. If the components are to be reinstalled, they must be installed in the same positions. Mark the components for installation into their original locations.

24. Inspect the valve tappets.

25. Remove and discard the M6 bolt.

✱✱ WARNING

Place clean, lint-free shop towels over exposed engine cavities. Carefully remove the towels so foreign material is not dropped into the engine. Aluminum surfaces are soft and may be scratched easily. Never place the cylinder head gasket surface, unprotected, on a bench surface.

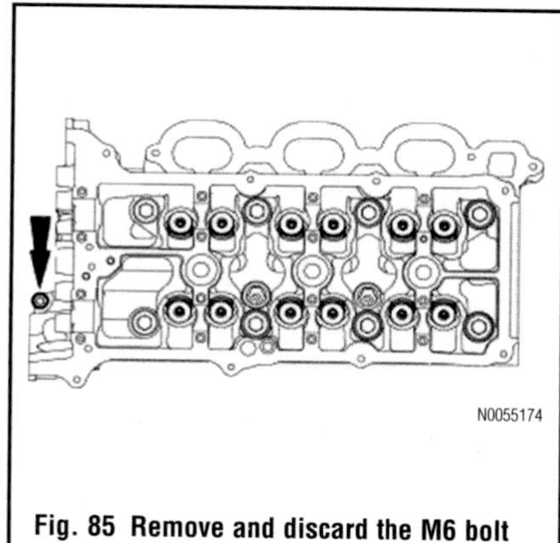

Fig. 85 Remove and discard the M6 bolt

26. Remove and discard the 8 bolts from the cylinder head.
    a. Remove the cylinder head.
    b. Discard the cylinder head gasket.

⁂ WARNING

Do not use metal scrapers, wire brushes, power abrasive discs or other abrasive means to clean the sealing surfaces. These tools cause scratches and gouges that make leak paths. Use a plastic scraping tool to remove all traces of the head gasket.

⁂ WARNING

Observe all warnings or cautions and follow all application directions contained on the packaging of the silicone gasket remover and the metal surface prep.

➡If there is no residual gasket material present, metal surface prep can be used to clean and prepare the surfaces.

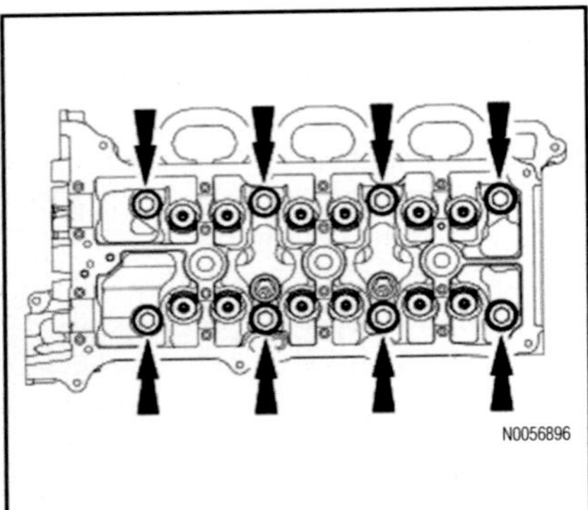

Fig. 86 Remove the cylinder head bolts

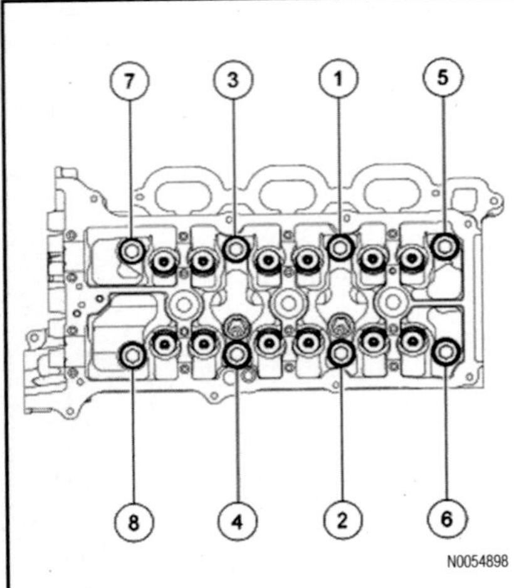

Fig. 87 Cylinder head bolt tightening sequence

27. Clean the cylinder head-to-cylinder block mating surfaces of both the cylinder heads and the cylinder block in the following sequence:
    a. Remove any large deposits of silicone or gasket material with a plastic scraper.
    b. Apply silicone gasket remover, following package directions, and allow to set for several minutes.
    c. Remove the silicone gasket remover with a plastic scraper. A second application of silicone gasket remover may be required if residual traces of silicone or gasket material remain.
    d. Apply metal surface prep, following package directions, to remove any remaining traces of oil or coolant and to prepare the surfaces to bond with the new gasket. Do not attempt to make the metal shiny. Some staining of the metal surfaces is normal.
28. Support the cylinder head on a bench with the head gasket side up. Check the cylinder head distortion and the cylinder block distortion.

To install:

29. Install a new gasket, the left-hand cylinder head and 8 new bolts. Tighten in the sequence shown in 5 stages:
    a. Stage 1: Tighten to 15 ft. lbs. (20 Nm).
    b. Stage 2: Tighten to 26 ft. lbs. (35 Nm).
    c. Stage 3: Tighten 90 degrees.
    d. Stage 4: Tighten 90 degrees.
    e. Stage 5: Tighten 90 degrees.
30. Install the M6 bolt. Tighten to 89 inch lbs. (10 Nm).
31. Coat the valve tappets with clean engine oil prior to installation. Install the valve tappets. The valve tappets must be installed in their original positions.
32. Install the left-hand secondary timing chain tensioner and the 2 bolts. Tighten to 89 inch lbs. (10 Nm).
33. Install the upper left-hand primary timing chain guide and the 2 bolts. Tighten to 89 inch lbs. (10 Nm).
34. Using new gaskets, install the lower intake manifold and the 10 bolts. Tighten in the sequence shown in the Intake Manifold Removal & Installation procedure to 89 inch lbs. (10 Nm).
35. Using a new gasket and O-ring seal, install the thermostat housing and the 3 bolts. Tighten to 89 inch lbs. (10 Nm).
36. Install new fuel injector O-ring seals. Use O-ring seals that are made of special fuel-resistant material. Do not reuse the O-ring seals. The upper and lower O-ring seals are not interchangeable.
    a. Remove the retaining clips and separate the fuel injectors from the fuel rail.
    b. Remove and discard the O-ring seals.
    c. Install new O-ring seals and lubricate with clean engine oil.
    d. Install the fuel injectors and the retaining clips onto the fuel rail.
37. Install the fuel rail and injectors as an assembly and install the 4 bolts. Tighten to 89 inch lbs. (10 Nm).
38. Install the coolant bypass hose to the thermostat housing.
39. Install the right-hand cylinder block drain plug or, if equipped, the block heater. Tighten to 30 ft. lbs. (40 Nm).
40. If equipped, install the block heater wiring harness onto the engine. Connect the block heater electrical connector and install the heat shield.
41. Using a new gasket, install the right-hand catalytic converter and 4 new nuts. Tighten to 30 ft. lbs. (40 Nm).
42. Install the left-hand cylinder block drain plug. Tighten to 15 ft. lbs. (20 Nm) plus an additional 180 degrees.
43. Install 6 new left-hand exhaust manifold studs. Tighten to 106 inch lbs. (12 Nm). Using a new gasket, install the left-hand exhaust manifold and 6 new nuts. Tighten in 2 stages in the sequence shown in the Exhaust Manifold Removal & Installation procedure.
44. Install the left-hand exhaust manifold heat shield and the 3 bolts. Tighten to 89 inch lbs. (10 Nm).
45. Using a new gasket, install the left-hand catalytic converter and 4 new nuts. Tighten to 30 ft. lbs. (40 Nm). Install the left-hand catalytic converter bracket bolts. Tighten to 15 ft. lbs. (20 Nm).
46. Attach the Engine Oil Pressure (EOP) switch wiring harness pin-type retainer.
47. Install the stud, alternator and the nut and bolt. Tighten the stud to 106 inch lbs. (12 Nm); tighten the nut and bolt to 35 ft. lbs. (48 Nm). Connect the alternator electrical connector. Connect the alternator B+ cable and install the nut. Tighten to 13 ft. lbs. (17 Nm).
48. Attach the pin-type wire harness retainer to the rear of left-hand cylinder head.
49. Connect the left-hand Catalyst Monitor Sensor (CMS) electrical connector.
50. Connect the left-hand Heated Oxygen Sensor (HO2S) electrical connector.
51. Install the left-hand Camshaft Position (CMP) sensor and the bolt. Tighten to

89 inch lbs. (10 Nm). Connect the left-hand CMP sensor electrical connector.

52. Connect the Cylinder Head Temperature (CHT) sensor electrical connector.

53. Connect the 6 fuel injector electrical connectors.

54. Install the left-hand camshafts.

Right-Hand

See Figures 88 through 90.

⁂ WARNING

During engine repair procedures, cleanliness is extremely important. Any foreign material, including any material created while cleaning gasket surfaces that enters the oil passages, coolant passages or the oil pan, may cause engine failure.

➡On early build engines, the timing chain rides on the inner side of the right-hand timing chain guide. Late build engines are equipped with a different design right-hand timing chain guide that requires the timing chain to ride on the outer side of the right-hand timing chain guide. For service, all replacement right-hand timing chain guides will be the late build design.

1. Remove the right-hand camshafts.
2. Disconnect the right-hand Heated Oxygen Sensor (HO2S) electrical connector.
3. Disconnect the right-hand Camshaft Position (CMP) sensor electrical connector. Remove the bolt and the right-hand CMP sensor.
4. Remove the bolt and the Power Steering Pressure (PSP) tube bracket from the right-hand cylinder head.
5. Remove the bolt and the ground wire.
6. Disconnect the 6 fuel injector electrical connectors.
7. Disconnect the Cylinder Head Temperature (CHT) sensor electrical connector.
8. Disconnect the left-hand Catalyst Monitor Sensor (CMS) electrical connector.
9. Remove the 2 left-hand catalytic converter bracket bolts. Remove the 4 nuts and the left-hand catalytic converter. Discard the nuts and the gasket.
10. Remove the left-hand cylinder block drain plug. Allow coolant to drain from the cylinder block.
11. Remove the 4 nuts and the right-hand catalytic converter. Discard the nuts and gasket.
12. If equipped, remove the heat shield and disconnect the block heater electrical connector.
    a. Remove the block heater wiring harness from the engine.
13. Remove the right-hand cylinder block drain plug or, if equipped, the block heater. Allow coolant to drain from the cylinder block.
14. Remove the 3 bolts and the right-hand exhaust manifold heat shield.
15. Remove the 6 nuts and the right-hand exhaust manifold. Discard the nuts and exhaust manifold gaskets. Clean and inspect the right-hand exhaust manifold. Remove and discard the 6 right-hand exhaust manifold studs.
16. Remove the 2 bolts and the right-hand primary timing chain guide.
17. Remove the bolts and the right-hand secondary timing chain tensioner.
18. Remove the 2 bolts and the engine lifting eye.
19. Remove the bolt and the upper intake manifold support bracket. Matchmark the location of the bracket on the cylinder head for installation.
20. Remove the coolant bypass hose from the thermostat housing.
21. Remove the 4 bolts and the fuel rail and injectors as an assembly.
22. Remove the 3 thermostat housing-to-lower intake manifold bolts.
23. Remove the thermostat housing and discard the gasket and O-ring seal.
24. Remove the 10 bolts and the lower intake manifold. Discard the gaskets. If the engine is repaired or replaced because of upper engine failure, typically including valve or piston damage, check the intake manifold for metal debris. If metal debris if found, install a new intake manifold.
25. Disconnect and remove the CHT sensor jumper harness.
26. Remove the valve tappets from the cylinder head. If the components are to be reinstalled, they must be installed in the same positions. Mark the components for installation into their original locations.
27. Inspect the valve tappets.
28. Remove and discard the M6 bolt.

⁂ WARNING

Place clean, lint-free shop towels over exposed engine cavities. Carefully remove the towels so foreign material is not dropped into the engine. Aluminum surfaces are soft and may be scratched easily. Never place the cylinder head gasket surface, unprotected, on a bench surface.

29. Remove and discard the 8 bolts from the cylinder head.
    a. Remove the cylinder head.
    b. Discard the cylinder head gasket.

⁂ WARNING

Do not use metal scrapers, wire brushes, power abrasive discs or other abrasive means to clean the sealing surfaces. These tools cause scratches and gouges that make leak paths. Use a plastic scraping tool to remove all traces of the head gasket.

⁂ WARNING

Observe all warnings or cautions and follow all application directions contained on the packaging of the silicone gasket remover and the metal surface prep.

➡If there is no residual gasket material present, metal surface prep can be used to clean and prepare the surfaces.

30. Clean the cylinder head-to-cylinder block mating surfaces of both the cylinder heads and the cylinder block in the following sequence.
    a. Remove any large deposits of silicone or gasket material with a plastic scraper.

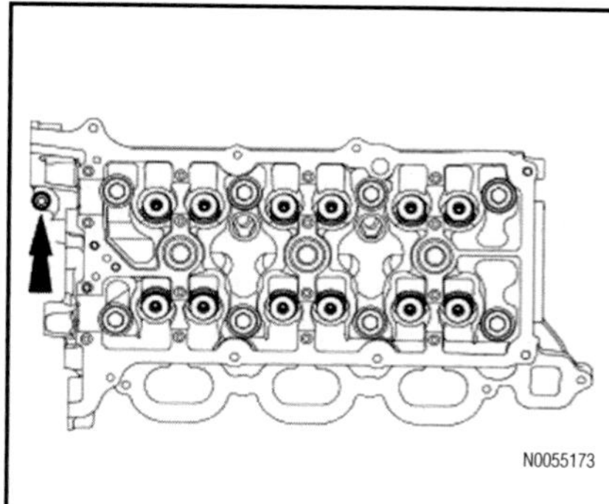

Fig. 88 Remove and discard the M6 bolt

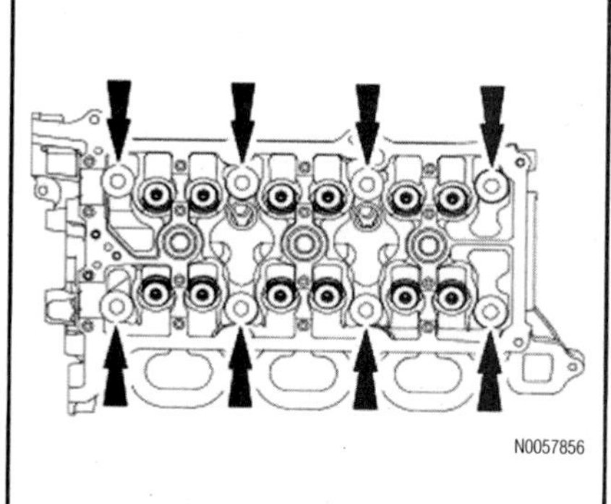

Fig. 89 Remove the cylinder head bolts

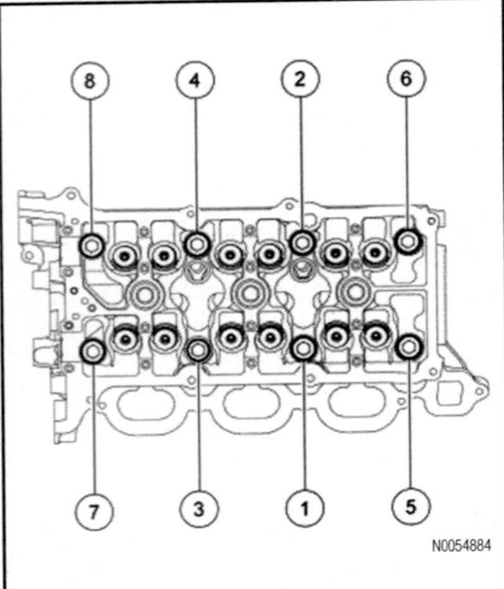

Fig. 90 Cylinder head bolt tightening sequence

b. Apply silicone gasket remover, following package directions, and allow to set for several minutes.

c. Remove the silicone gasket remover with a plastic scraper. A second application of silicone gasket remover may be required if residual traces of silicone or gasket material remain.

d. Apply metal surface prep, following package directions, to remove any remaining traces of oil or coolant and to prepare the surfaces to bond with the new gasket. Do not attempt to make the metal shiny. Some staining of the metal surfaces is normal.

e. Support the cylinder head on a bench with the head gasket side up. Check the cylinder head distortion and the cylinder block distortion.

To install:

31. Install a new gasket, the right-hand cylinder head and 8 new bolts. Tighten in the sequence shown in 5 stages:

a. Stage 1: Tighten to 15 ft. lbs. (20 Nm).

b. Stage 2: Tighten to 26 ft. lbs. (35 Nm).

c. Stage 3: Tighten 90 degrees.

d. Stage 4: Tighten 90 degrees.

e. Stage 5: Tighten 90 degrees.

32. Install the M6 bolt. Tighten to 89 inch lbs. (10 Nm).

33. Coat the valve tappets with clean engine oil prior to installation. Install the valve tappets. The valve tappets must be installed in their original positions.

34. Install and connect the Cylinder Head Temperature (CHT) sensor jumper harness.

35. Using new gaskets, install the lower intake manifold and the 10 bolts. Tighten in the sequence shown in the Intake Manifold Removal & Installation procedure to 89 inch lbs. (10 Nm).

36. Using a new gasket and O-ring seal, install the thermostat housing and the 3 bolts. Tighten to 89 inch lbs. (10 Nm).

37. Install new fuel injector O-ring seals. Use O-ring seals that are made of special fuel-resistant material. Do not reuse the O-ring seals. The upper and lower O-ring seals are not interchangeable.

a. Remove the retaining clips and separate the fuel injectors from the fuel rail.

b. Remove and discard the O-ring seals.

c. Install new O-ring seals and lubricate with clean engine oil.

d. Install the fuel injectors and the retaining clips onto the fuel rail.

38. Install the fuel rail and injectors as an assembly and install the 4 bolts. Tighten to 89 inch lbs. (10 Nm).

39. Install the coolant bypass hose to the thermostat housing.

40. Install the upper intake manifold support bracket and the bolt. Align the bracket with the matchmarks made during removal. Tighten to 89 inch lbs. (10 Nm).

41. Install the engine lifting eye and the 2 bolts. Tighten to 18 ft. lbs. (24 Nm).

42. Install the right-hand secondary timing chain tensioner and the 2 bolts. Tighten to 89 inch lbs. (10 Nm).

43. Install the right-hand primary timing chain guide and the 2 bolts. Tighten to 89 inch lbs. (10 Nm).

44. Install 6 new right-hand exhaust manifold studs. Tighten to 106 inch lbs. (12 Nm). Using a new gasket, install the right-hand exhaust manifold and 6 new nuts. Tighten in 2 stages in the sequence shown in the Exhaust Manifold Removal & Installation procedure.

45. Install the right-hand exhaust manifold heat shield and the 3 bolts. Tighten to 89 inch lbs. (10 Nm).

46. Install the right-hand cylinder block drain plug or, if equipped, the block heater. Tighten to 30 ft. lbs. (40 Nm).

47. If equipped, install the block heater wiring harness onto the engine. Connect the block heater electrical connector and install the heat shield.

48. Using a new gasket, install the right-hand catalytic converter and 4 new nuts. Tighten to 30 ft. lbs. (40 Nm).

49. Install the left-hand cylinder block drain plug. Tighten to 15 ft. lbs. (20 Nm) plus an additional 180 degrees.

50. Using a new gasket, install the left-hand catalytic converter and 4 new nuts. Tighten to 40 Nm (30 lb-ft). Install the 2 left-hand catalytic converter bracket bolts. Tighten to 15 ft. lbs. (20 Nm).

51. Connect the left-hand Catalyst Monitor Sensor (CMS) electrical connector.

52. Connect the CHT sensor electrical connector.

53. Connect the 6 fuel injector electrical connectors.

54. Install the ground wire and the bolt. Tighten to 89 inch lbs. (10 Nm).

55. Install the Power Steering Pressure (PSP) tube bracket and the bolt to the right-hand cylinder head. Tighten to 89 inch lbs. (10 Nm).

56. Install the right-hand Camshaft Position (CMP) sensor and tighten the bolt to 89 inch lbs. (10 Nm). Connect the CMP sensor electrical connector.

57. Connect the right-hand Heated Oxygen Sensor (HO2S) electrical connector.

58. Install the right-hand camshafts.

EXHAUST MANIFOLD

REMOVAL & INSTALLATION

3.5L Engines

Left-Hand

See Figures 91 and 92.

WARNING

Whenever turbocharger air intake system components are removed, always cover open ports to protect from debris. It is important that no foreign material enter the system. The turbocharger compressor vanes are susceptible to damage from even small particles. All components should be inspected and cleaned, if necessary, prior to installation or reassembly.

1. Before servicing the vehicle, refer to the Precautions Section.

2. Remove the 2 top left-hand exhaust manifold heat shield bolts.

3. Remove the left-hand catalytic converter.

4. Remove the bottom bolt and the left-hand exhaust manifold heat shield.

5. Remove the 2 bolts and the left-hand upper turbocharger bracket.

6. Loosen the 2 bolts for the left-hand lower turbocharger bracket.

7. Remove the 3 left-hand turbocharger-to-exhaust manifold bolts. Discard the gasket.

8. Remove the 5 top left-hand exhaust manifold nuts. Discard the nuts.

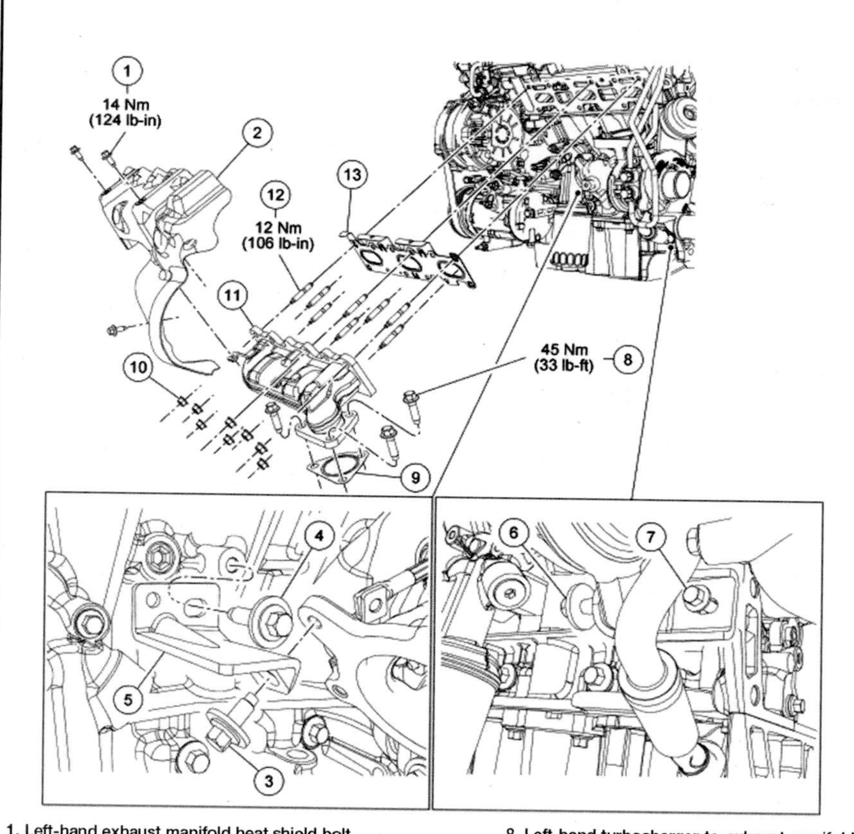

Fig. 91 Left-Hand Exhaust Manifold—3.5L engines

9. Remove the 3 bottom nuts and the left-hand exhaust manifold. Discard the nuts and gasket.

10. Clean and inspect the left-hand exhaust manifold.

11. Remove and discard the 8 left-hand exhaust manifold studs.

12. Clean the exhaust manifold mating surface of the cylinder head with metal surface prep. Follow the directions on the packaging. Do not use metal scrapers, wire brushes, power abrasive discs or other abrasive means to clean the sealing surfaces. Use a plastic scraper to clean the sealing surfaces.

To install:

13. Install 8 new left-hand exhaust manifold studs. Tighten to 106 inch lbs. (12 Nm).

14. Install a new gasket, left-hand exhaust manifold and 8 new nuts. Tighten in 2 stages in the sequence shown. Failure to tighten the exhaust manifold nuts to specification a second time will cause the exhaust manifold to develop an exhaust leak:

- Stage 1: Tighten to 11 ft. lbs. (15 Nm)
- Stage 2: Tighten to 15 ft. lbs. (20 Nm)

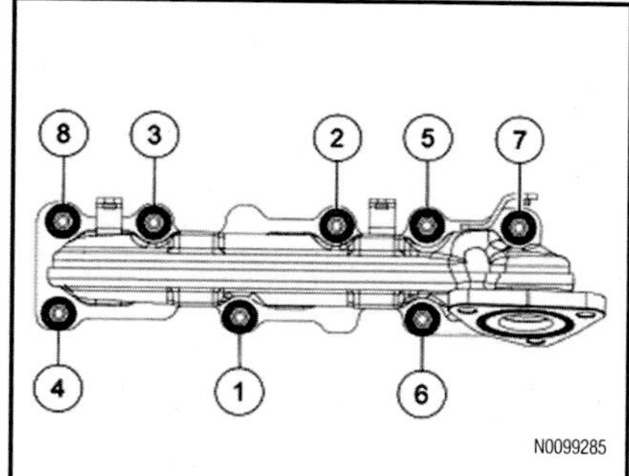

Fig. 92 Left-hand exhaust manifold nut tightening sequence—3.5L engines

15. Install a new gasket and the 3 turbocharger-to-exhaust manifold bolts. Tighten to 33 ft. lbs. (45 Nm).

16. Install the upper turbocharger bracket and the 2 bolts. Do not tighten the bolts at this time.

⁂ WARNING

The next 4 steps must be performed in order or damage to the turbocharger may occur.

17. Tighten the upper turbocharger bracket-to-turbocharger bolt. Tighten to 14 ft. lbs. (19 Nm).

18. Tighten the upper turbocharger bracket-to-cylinder block bolt. Tighten to 18 ft. lbs. (25 Nm).

19. Tighten the lower turbocharger bracket-to-turbocharger bolt. Tighten to 14 ft. lbs. (19 Nm).

20. Tighten the lower turbocharger bracket-to-cylinder block bolt. Tighten to 97 inch lbs. (11 Nm).

21. Install the left-hand exhaust manifold heat shield and the bottom bolt. Do not tighten the bolt at this time.

22. Install the left-hand catalytic converter.

23. Install the 2 top left-hand exhaust manifold heat shield bolts. Tighten to 10 ft. lbs. (14 Nm).

24. Tighten the left-hand exhaust manifold heat shield bottom bolt. Tighten to 10 ft. lbs. (14 Nm).

Right-Hand

See Figures 93 and 94.

⁂ WARNING

Whenever turbocharger air intake system components are removed, always cover open ports to protect from debris. It is important that no foreign material enter the system. The turbocharger compressor vanes are susceptible to damage from even small particles. All components should be inspected and cleaned, if necessary, prior to installation or reassembly.

1. Before servicing the vehicle, refer to the Precautions Section.

2. Remove the right-hand turbocharger.

3. Remove the 8 nuts and the right-hand exhaust manifold. Discard the nuts and exhaust manifold gasket.

4. Clean and inspect the right-hand exhaust manifold.

5. Remove and discard the 8 right-hand exhaust manifold studs.

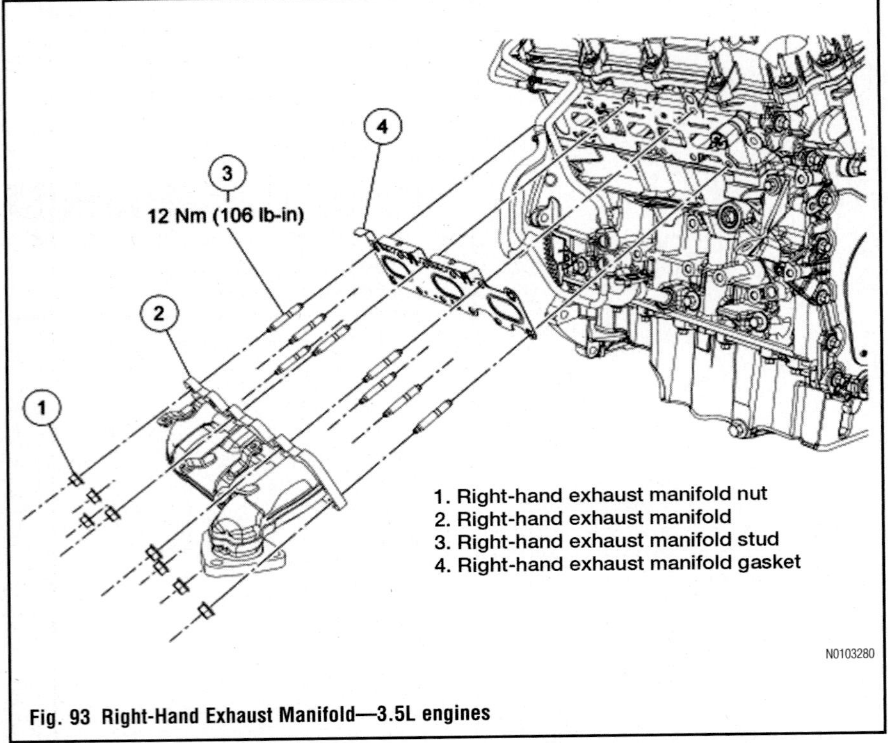

Fig. 93 Right-Hand Exhaust Manifold—3.5L engines

6. Clean the exhaust manifold mating surface of the cylinder head with metal surface prep. Follow the directions on the packaging. Do not use metal scrapers, wire brushes, power abrasive discs or other abrasive means to clean the sealing surfaces. Use a plastic scraper to clean the sealing surfaces.

To install:

7. Install 8 new right-hand exhaust manifold studs. Tighten to 106 inch lbs. (12 Nm).
8. Install a new gasket, right-hand exhaust manifold and 8 new nuts. Tighten in 2 stages in the sequence shown. Failure to tighten the exhaust manifold nuts to specification a second time will cause the exhaust manifold to develop an exhaust leak:

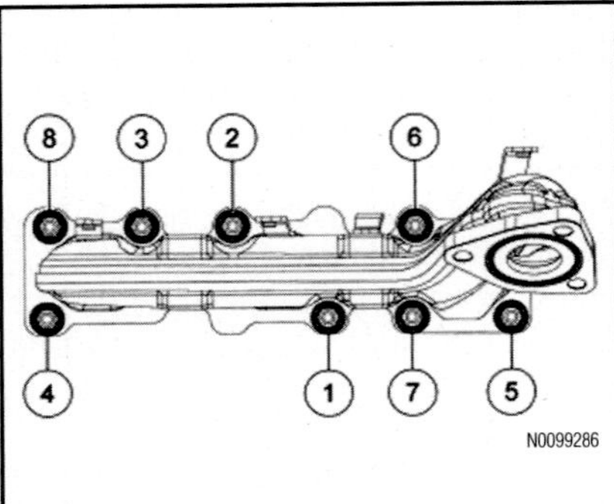

Fig. 94 Right-hand exhaust manifold nut tightening sequence—3.5L engines

- Stage 1: Tighten to 11 ft. lbs. (15 Nm)
- Stage 2: Tighten to 15 ft. lbs. (20 Nm)

9. Install the right-hand turbocharger.

3.7L Engines

Left-Hand

See Figures 95 and 96.

1. Before servicing the vehicle, refer to the Precautions Section.
2. Remove the left-hand catalytic converter.
3. Remove the left-hand Heated Oxygen Sensor (HO2S).
4. Remove the 3 bolts and the left-hand exhaust manifold heat shield.
5. Remove the 6 nuts and the left-hand exhaust manifold. Discard the nuts and gasket.
6. Clean and inspect the left-hand exhaust manifold.
7. Remove and discard the 6 left-hand exhaust manifold studs.
8. Clean the exhaust manifold mating surface of the cylinder head with metal surface prep. Follow the directions on the packaging. Do not use metal scrapers, wire brushes, power abrasive discs or other abrasive means to clean the sealing surfaces. Use a plastic scraper to clean the sealing surfaces.

To install:

9. Install 6 new left-hand exhaust manifold studs. Tighten to 106 inch lbs. (12 Nm).
10. Using a new gasket, install the left-hand exhaust manifold and 6 new nuts.

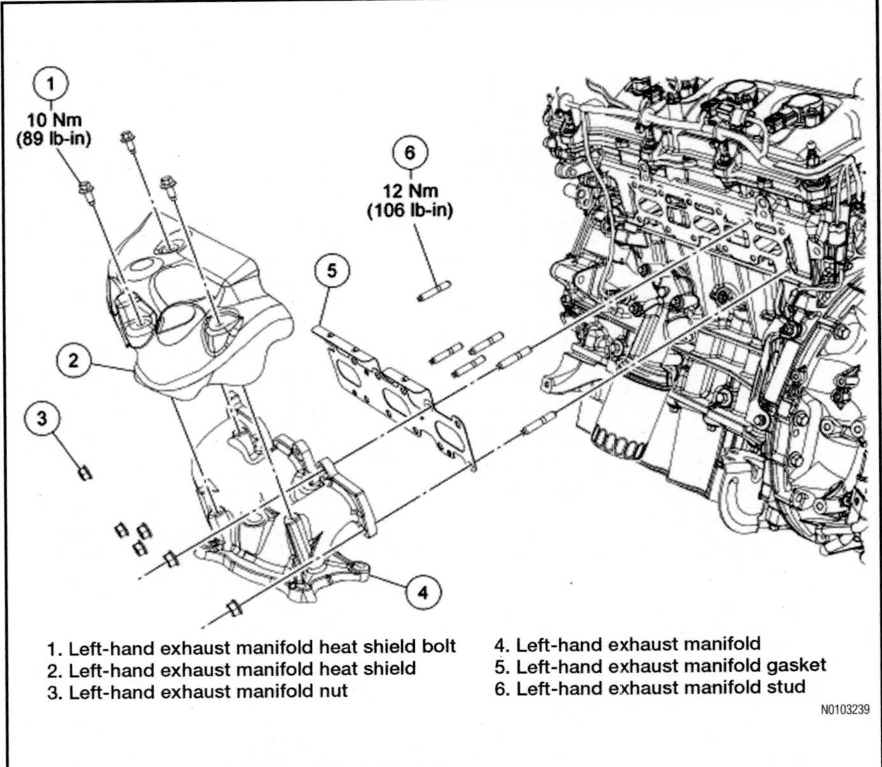

Fig. 95 Left-Hand Exhaust Manifold—3.7L engines

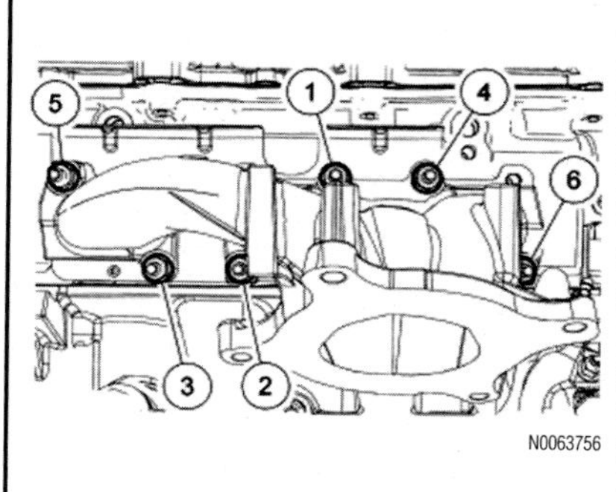

Fig. 96 Left-hand exhaust manifold nut tightening sequence—3.7L engines

Tighten in 2 stages in the sequence shown. Failure to tighten the exhaust manifold nuts to specification a second time will cause the exhaust manifold to develop an exhaust leak:

- Stage 1: Tighten to 15 ft. lbs. (20 Nm)
- Stage 2: Tighten to 18 ft. lbs. (25 Nm)

11. Install the left-hand exhaust manifold heat shield and the 3 bolts. Tighten to 89 inch lbs. (10 Nm).
12. Install the left-hand HO2S.
13. Install the left-hand catalytic converter.

Right-Hand

See Figures 97 and 98.

1. Before servicing the vehicle, refer to the Precautions Section.
2. Remove the right-hand catalytic converter.
3. Disconnect the right-hand Heated Oxygen Sensor (HO2S) electrical connector.
4. Remove the 6 nuts and the right-hand exhaust manifold. Discard the nuts and gasket.
5. Clean and inspect the right-hand exhaust manifold.
6. Remove and discard the 6 right-hand exhaust manifold studs.
7. Clean the exhaust manifold mating surface of the cylinder head with metal surface prep. Follow the directions on the packaging.

To install:

8. Install 6 new right-hand exhaust manifold studs. Tighten to 106 inch lbs. (12 Nm).
9. Using a new gasket, install the right-hand exhaust manifold and 6 new nuts. Tighten in 2 stages in the sequence shown. Failure to tighten the exhaust manifold nuts to specification a second time will cause the exhaust manifold to develop an exhaust leak:

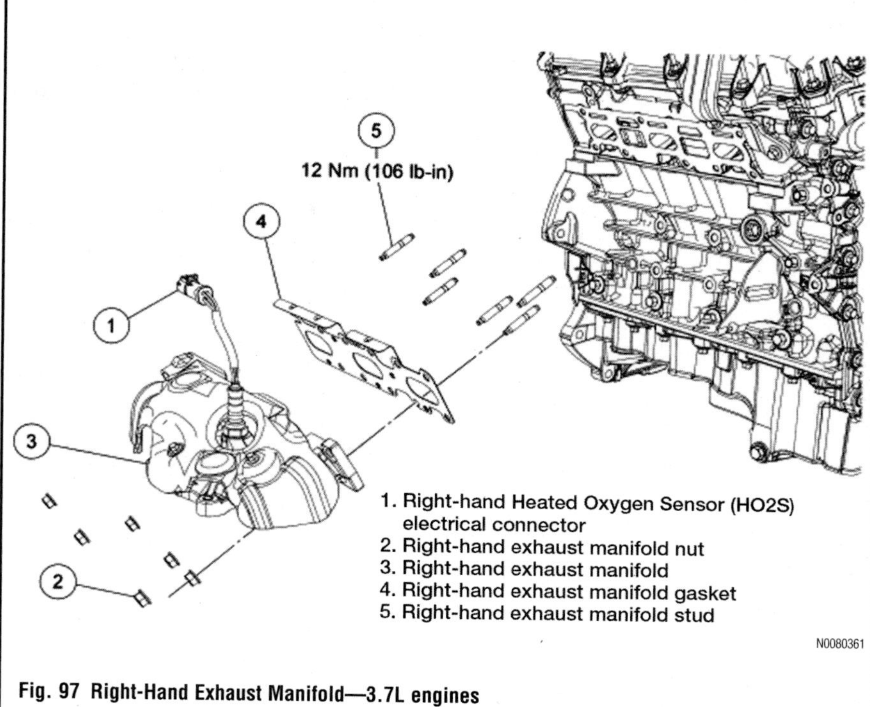

Fig. 97 Right-Hand Exhaust Manifold—3.7L engines

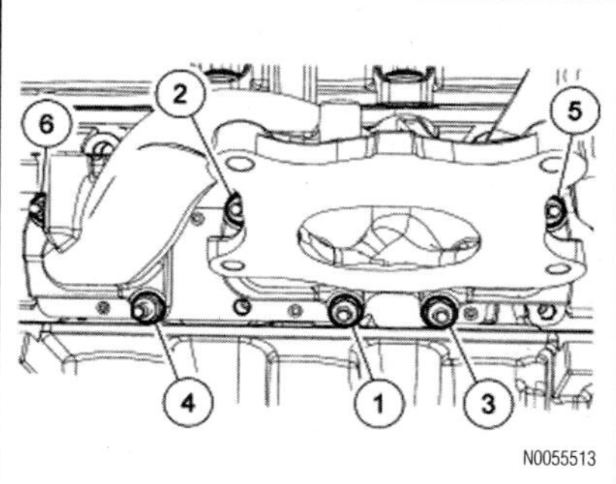

Fig. 98 Right-hand exhaust manifold nut tightening sequence—3.7L engines

- Stage 1: Tighten to 15 ft. lbs. (20 Nm)
- Stage 2: Tighten to 18 ft. lbs. (25 Nm)

10. Connect the right-hand HO2S electrical connector.
11. Install the right-hand catalytic converter.

INTAKE MANIFOLD

REMOVAL & INSTALLATION

3.5L Engines

See Figures 99 through 104.

WARNING

During engine repair procedures, cleanliness is extremely important. Any foreign material, including any material created while cleaning gasket surfaces that enters the oil passages, coolant passages or the oil pan, may cause engine failure.

WARNING

Whenever turbocharger air intake system components are removed, always cover open ports to protect from debris. It is important that no foreign material enter the system. The turbocharger compressor vanes are susceptible to damage from even small particles. All components should be inspected and cleaned, if necessary, prior to installation or reassembly.

1. Before servicing the vehicle, refer to the Precautions Section.
2. Drain the cooling system.
3. Remove the Air Cleaner (ACL) outlet pipe.
4. Disconnect the left-hand turbocharger bypass valve electrical connector.
5. Disconnect the left-hand turbocharger bypass valve hose from the right-hand Charge Air Cooler (CAC) tube.
6. Disconnect the turbocharger wastegate regulating valve hose from the right-hand CAC tube.
7. Disconnect the right-hand turbocharger bypass valve electrical connector.

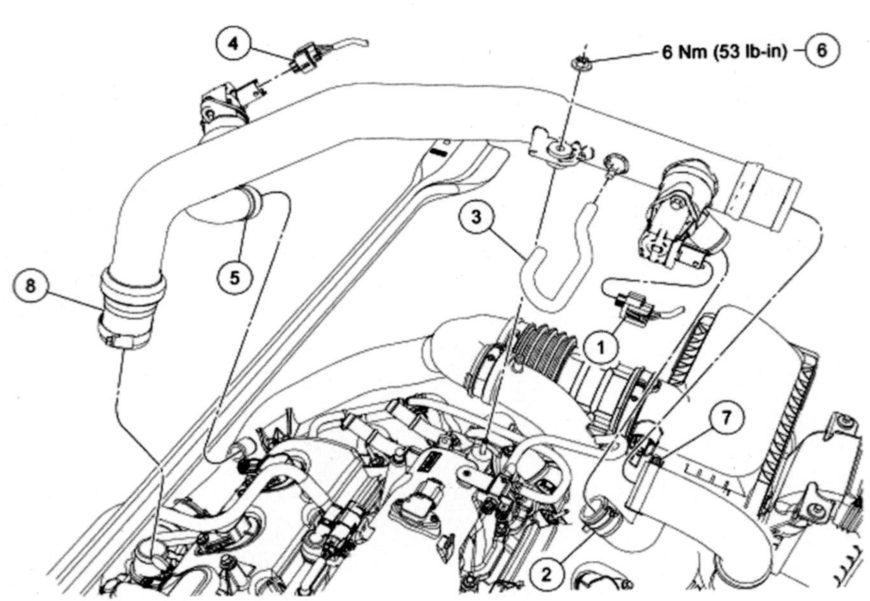

Fig. 99 Intake manifold components 1—3.5L engines

8. Disconnect the right-hand turbocharger bypass valve hose from the right-hand turbocharger intake tube.
9. Remove the right-hand CAC tube nut from the intake manifold.
10. Loosen the clamp and remove the right-hand CAC tube.
11. Loosen the clamp and remove the right-hand CAC tube from the right-hand turbocharger.
12. Loosen the clamp and position CAC outlet pipe-to-throttle body aside.
13. Disconnect the Throttle Position (TP) sensor and electronic TB electrical connectors.
14. Disconnect the quick connect coupling Evaporative Emission (EVAP) tube from the intake manifold. For additional information, refer to Fuel System — General Information.
15. Detach the EVAP purge valve from the intake manifold.
16. Disconnect the brake booster vacuum hose from the intake manifold.
17. Remove the fuel tube-to-engine front cover bracket bolt and position the fuel tube aside.
18. Disconnect the PCV tube quick connect coupling from the intake manifold.
19. If equipped, disconnect the heated PCV valve electrical connector from the intake manifold.
20. Detach and disconnect the 2 fuel injector wiring harness electrical connectors.
21. Disconnect the Manifold Absolute Pressure (MAP)/Intake Air Temperature 2 (IAT2) sensor electrical connector.
22. Disconnect the 2 hoses from the turbocharger wastegate regulating valve. Mark the location of each hose for installation.
23. Disconnect the turbocharger wastegate regulating valve electrical connector.
24. Detach the 2 wire harness-to-intake manifold retainers.
25. Detach the 2 wire harness retainer from the left-hand valve cover stud bolt.
26. Detach the 2 wire harness retainer from the left-hand valve cover.
27. Disconnect the 2 coolant heater hoses from the intake manifold.
28. Disconnect the 2 turbocharger coolant hoses from the intake manifold.
29. Disconnect the lower radiator hose from the thermostat housing.
30. Remove the bolt and ground wire from the engine front cover.
31. Disconnect the upper radiator hose at the intake manifold and position the hose aside.
32. Remove the 12 bolts and the intake manifold.
   a. Note the routing of the 2 fuel rail wiring harnesses for installation.
   b. Remove and discard the intake manifold, coolant crossover and thermostat housing gaskets.
   c. Clean and inspect all sealing surfaces.

To install:

⁂ WARNING

If the engine is repaired or replaced because of upper engine failure, typically including valve or piston damage, check the intake manifold for metal debris. If metal debris is found, install a new intake manifold. Failure to follow these instructions can result in engine damage.

➡Make sure the fuel rail wiring harnesses are routed correctly.

➡Installing the 2 long bolts first will aid in installing the intake manifold.

33. Using new intake manifold, coolant crossover and thermostat housing gaskets, install the intake manifold and the 12 bolts. Tighten in the sequence shown to 89 inch lbs. (10 Nm).

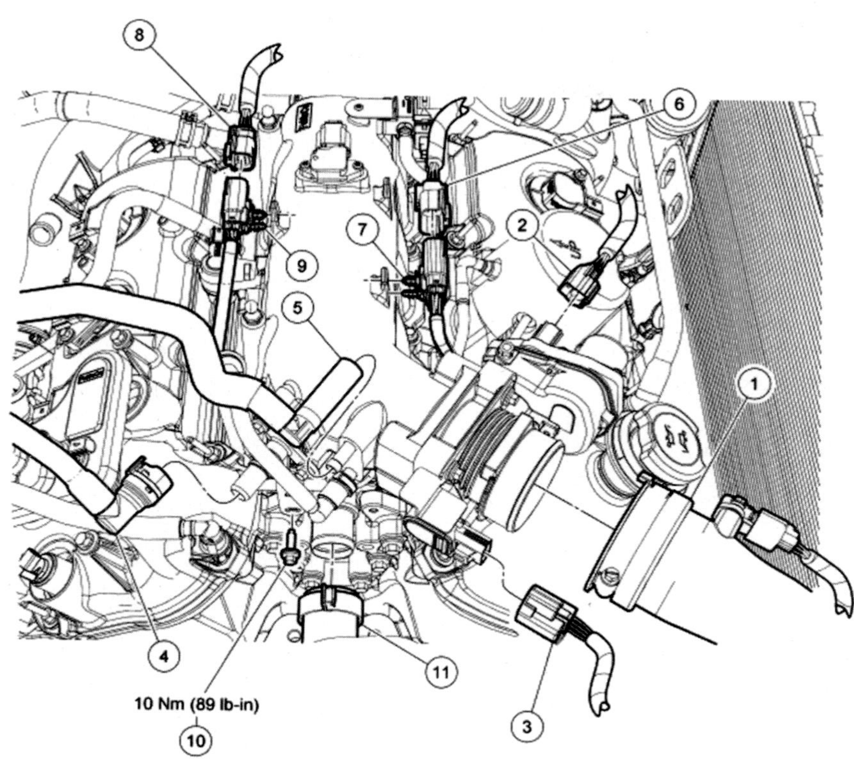

Fig. 100 Intake manifold components 2—3.5L engines

34. Connect the upper radiator hose to the intake manifold.

35. Install the ground wire and bolt to the engine front cover. Tighten to 89 inch lbs. (10 Nm).

36. Connect the lower radiator hose to the thermostat housing.

37. Connect the 2 turbocharger coolant hoses from the intake manifold.

38. Connect the 2 coolant heater hoses from the intake manifold.

39. Attach the 2 wire harness retainers to the left-hand valve cover.

40. Attach the 2 wire harness retainers to the left-hand valve cover stud bolt.

41. Attach the 2 wire harness-to-intake manifold retainers.

42. Connect the turbocharger wastegate regulating valve electrical connector.

43. Connect the 2 hoses to the turbocharger wastegate regulating valve.

44. Connect the MAP/IAT2 sensor electrical connector.

45. Connect and attach the 2 fuel injector wiring harness electrical connectors.

46. If equipped, connect the heated PCV valve electrical connector.

47. Connect the PCV tube quick connect coupling to the intake manifold.

48. Position the fuel tube and install the fuel tube-to-engine front cover bracket bolt. Tighten to 89 inch lbs. (10 Nm).

49. Connect the brake vacuum tube to the intake manifold.

50. Attach the EVAP purge valve to the intake manifold.

51. Connect the quick connect coupling EVAP tube to the intake manifold.

52. Connect the throttle position sensor and electronic throttle body electrical connectors.

53. Position CAC outlet pipe on the throttle body and tighten the clamp. Align the matchmarks. Tighten to 44 inch lbs. (5 Nm).

54. Install the right-hand CAC tube to the right-hand turbocharger and tighten the clamp. Align the matchmarks. Tighten to 44 inch lbs. (5 Nm).

55. Install the right-hand CAC tube and tighten the clamp. Align the matchmarks. Tighten to 44 inch lbs. (5 Nm).

56. Install the right-hand CAC tube and the right-hand CAC tube nut to the intake manifold. The compression limiter bushing may fall out of the mounting bracket grommet on the Charge Air Cooler (CAC) tube during service. Make sure the bushing is in place when reinstalling the tube or damage to the tube may occur. Tighten to 53 inch lbs. (6 Nm).

57. Connect the right-hand turbocharger bypass valve hose to the right-hand turbocharger intake tube.

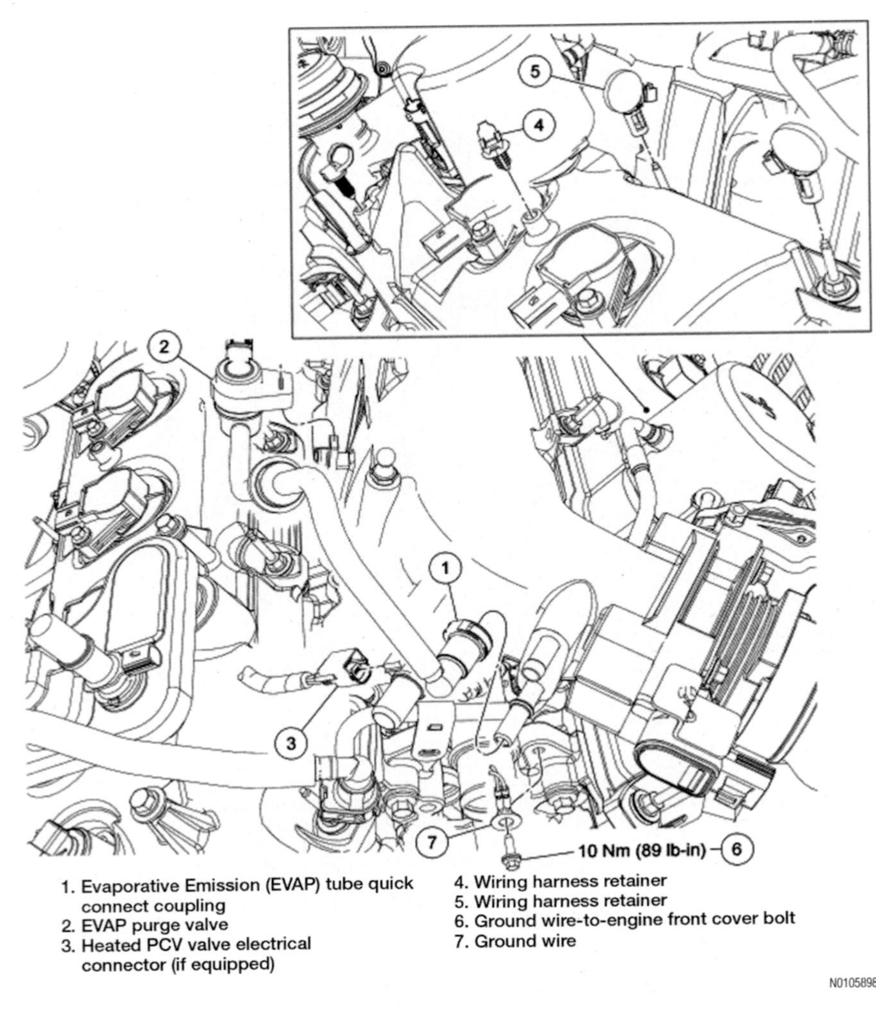

Fig. 101 Intake manifold components 3—3.5L engines

58. Connect the right-hand turbocharger bypass valve electrical connector.
59. Connect the turbocharger wastegate regulating valve hose to the right-hand CAC tube.
60. Connect the left-hand turbocharger bypass valve electrical connector and the turbocharger bypass valve hose.
61. Install the ACL outlet pipe.
62. Fill and bleed the cooling system.

3.7L Engines

Lower Intake Manifold

See Figures 105 and 106.

1. Before servicing the vehicle, refer to the Precautions Section.

WARNING

During engine repair procedures, cleanliness is extremely important. Any foreign material, including any material created while cleaning gasket surfaces that enters the oil passages, coolant passages or the oil pan, may cause engine failure.

2. Remove the fuel rail.
3. Drain the cooling system.
4. Remove the 3 thermostat housing-to-lower intake manifold bolts.
5. Remove the 10 bolts and the lower intake manifold.
    a. Remove and discard the intake manifold and thermostat housing gaskets.
    b. Clean and inspect all sealing surfaces.

To install:

WARNING

If the engine is repaired or replaced because of upper engine failure, typically including valve or piston damage, check the intake manifold for metal debris. If metal debris if found, install a new intake manifold. Failure to follow these instructions can result in engine damage.

6. Using new intake manifold and thermostat housing gaskets, install the lower intake manifold and the 10 bolts. Tighten in the sequence shown to 89 inch lbs. (10 Nm).
7. Install the 3 thermostat housing-to-lower intake manifold bolts. Tighten to 89 inch lbs. (10 Nm).
8. Install the fuel rail.
9. Fill and bleed the cooling system.

Upper Intake Manifold

See Figures 107 through 109.

1. Before servicing the vehicle, refer to the Precautions Section.

WARNING

During engine repair procedures, cleanliness is extremely important.

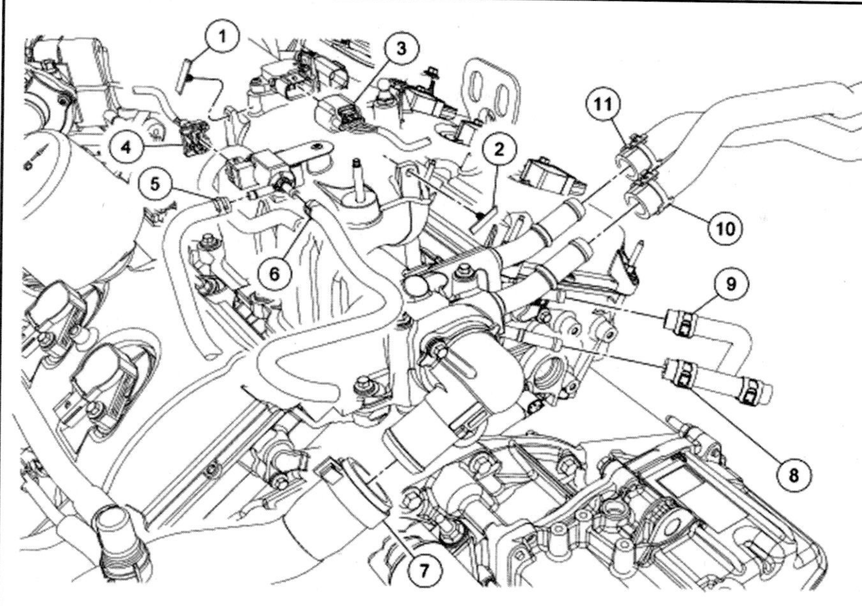

1. Wiring harness pin-type retainer
2. Wiring harness pin-type retainer
3. Manifold Absolute Pressure (MAP)/Intake Air Temperature 2 (IAT2) sensor electrical connector
4. Turbocharger wastegate regulating valve electrical connector
5. Turbocharger wastegate regulating valve hose
6. Turbocharger wastegate regulating valve hose
7. Lower radiator hose
8. Turbocharger coolant inlet hose
9. Turbocharger coolant outlet hose
10. Coolant heater hose
11. Coolant heater hose

N0105899

Fig. 102 Intake manifold components 4—3.5L engines

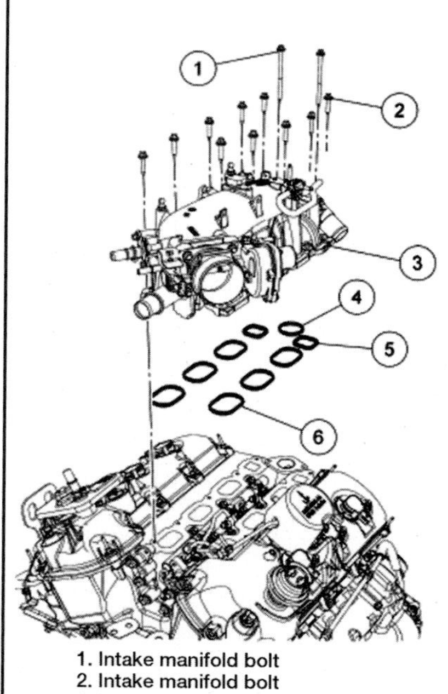

1. Intake manifold bolt
2. Intake manifold bolt
3. Intake manifold
4. Coolant by-pass tube gasket
5. Coolant crossover gasket
6. Intake manifold gasket

N0103471

Fig. 103 Intake manifold components 5—3.5L engines

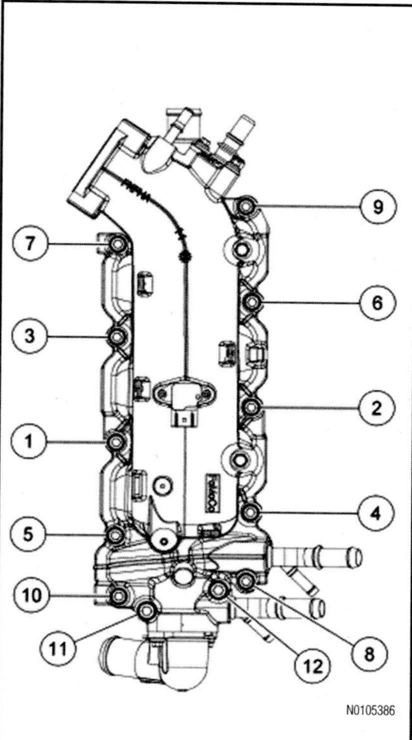

Fig. 104 Intake manifold bolt tightening sequence—3.5L engines

Any foreign material, including any material created while cleaning gasket surfaces that enters the oil passages, coolant passages or the oil pan, may cause engine failure.

2. Remove the Air Cleaner (ACL) outlet pipe.
3. Disconnect the throttle body electrical connector.
4. Disconnect the Evaporative Emission (EVAP) tube from the intake manifold.
5. Detach the EVAP tube pin-type retainer from the upper intake manifold.
6. Disconnect the brake booster vacuum hose from the intake manifold.
7. Disconnect the PCV tube from the PCV valve.

Detach the wiring harness retainers from the upper intake manifold.

8. Remove the upper intake manifold support bracket bolt.
9. Remove the fuel tube bracket bolt.
10. Remove the 6 bolts and the upper intake manifold.
    a. Remove and discard the gaskets.
    b. Clean and inspect all of the sealing surfaces of the upper and lower intake manifold.

To install:

**** WARNING**

If the engine is repaired or replaced because of upper engine failure, typically including valve or piston damage, check the intake manifold for metal debris. If metal debris is found, install a new intake manifold. Failure to follow these instructions can result in engine damage.

11. Using new gaskets, install the upper intake manifold and the 6 bolts. Tighten in the sequence shown to 89 inch lbs. (10 Nm).
12. Install the fuel tube bracket bolt. Tighten to 53 inch lbs. (6 Nm).
13. Install the upper intake manifold support bracket bolt. Tighten to 89 inch lbs. (10 Nm).
14. Attach the wiring harness retainers to the upper intake manifold.
15. Connect the PCV tube to the PCV valve.
16. Connect the brake booster vacuum hose to the intake manifold.
17. Connect the EVAP tube to the intake manifold.
18. Attach the EVAP tube pin-type retainer to the upper intake manifold.
19. Connect the TB electrical connector.

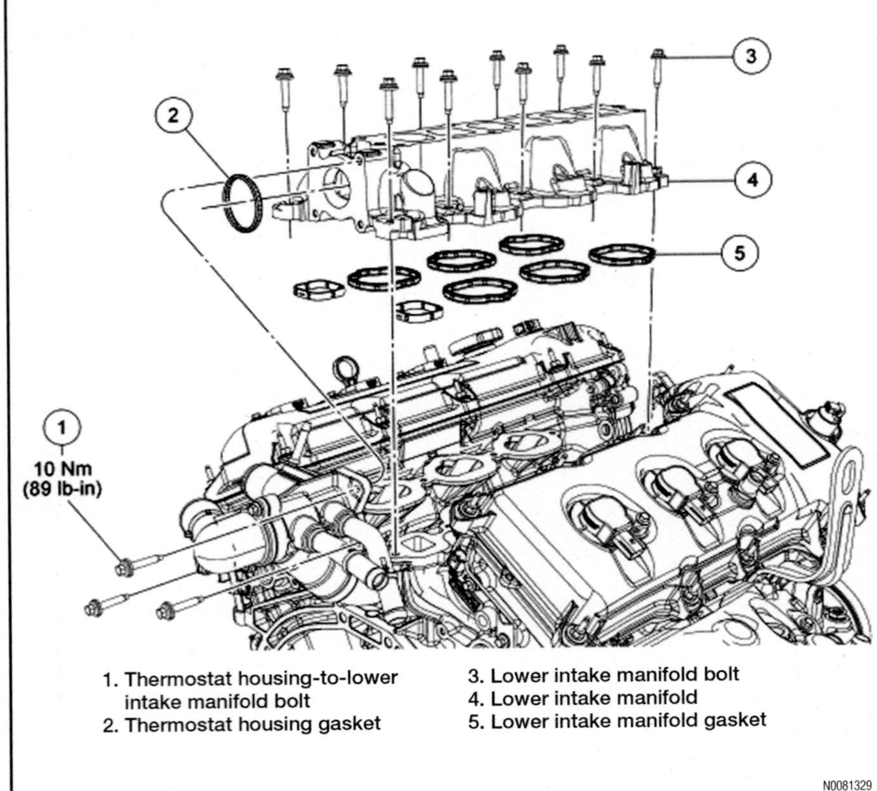

Fig. 105 Lower intake manifold components—3.7L engines

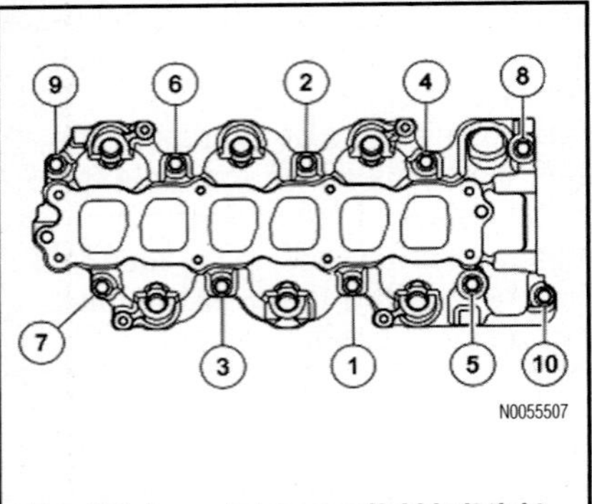

Fig. 106 Lower intake manifold bolt tightening sequence—3.7L engines

20. Install the ACL outlet pipe.

OIL PAN

REMOVAL & INSTALLATION

3.5L Engines

See Figures 110 through 115.

WARNING

During engine repair procedures, cleanliness is extremely important. Any foreign material, including any material created while cleaning gasket surfaces that enters the oil passages, coolant passages or the oil pan, may cause engine failure.

WARNING

Whenever turbocharger air intake system components are removed, always cover open ports to protect from debris. It is important that no foreign material enter the system. The turbocharger compressor vanes are susceptible to damage from even small particles. All components should be inspected and cleaned, if necessary, prior to installation or reassembly.

1. Before servicing the vehicle, refer to the Precautions Section.
2. Remove the engine from the vehicle.
3. Remove the 8 bolts and the flywheel.
4. Remove the crankshaft sensor ring.
5. Mount the engine on an engine stand. Install the engine stand bolts into the cylinder block only. Do not install the bolts into the oil pan.
6. Remove the nut and the A/C tube from the compressor. Discard the O-ring seal and gasket seal.
7. Remove the left-hand cylinder block drain plug. Allow coolant to drain from the cylinder block.
8. If equipped, remove the heat shield and disconnect the block heater electrical connector. Detach all of the engine block heater harness retainers and remove the harness.
9. Remove the right-hand cylinder block drain plug or, if equipped, the block heater. Allow coolant to drain from the cylinder block.
10. Disconnect the brake vacuum tube from the intake manifold.
11. Disconnect the 2 quick connect couplings and remove the PCV tube.
12. If equipped, disconnect the 2 heated PCV electrical connectors.
13. Disconnect the left-hand turbocharger bypass valve electrical connector.
14. Remove the turbocharger wastegate regulating valve hoses from the right-hand CAC tube and turbocharger wastegate regulating valve. Matchmark the hoses for installation.
15. Loosen the clamp and remove the left-hand turbocharger intake tube from the left-hand turbocharger.
16. Remove the 2 bolts and the left-hand turbocharger oil return tube from the turbocharger. Remove and discard the gasket.
17. Remove the left-hand turbocharger oil return tube from the oil pan. Discard the 2 O-ring seals.
18. Disconnect the right-hand turbocharger bypass valve electrical connector.
19. Loosen the clamp and remove the right-hand CAC tube from the right-hand turbocharger.
20. Loosen the clamp and remove the right-hand turbocharger intake pipe from the right-hand turbocharger.
21. Remove the nut from the right-hand valve cover stud bolt for the right-hand turbocharger intake tube.
22. Remove the right-hand CAC tube nut from the intake manifold and remove the right-hand CAC tube and turbocharger intake tube as an assembly.
23. Remove the noise insulator shield for the fuel injection pump and disconnect the electrical connector.
24. Disconnect the Throttle Position (TP) and electronic throttle body electrical connectors.
25. Disconnect the left-hand Variable Camshaft Timing (VCT) solenoid electrical connector.
26. Disconnect the Engine Oil Pressure (EOP) electrical connector.
27. Detach the wiring harness retainer from the block.

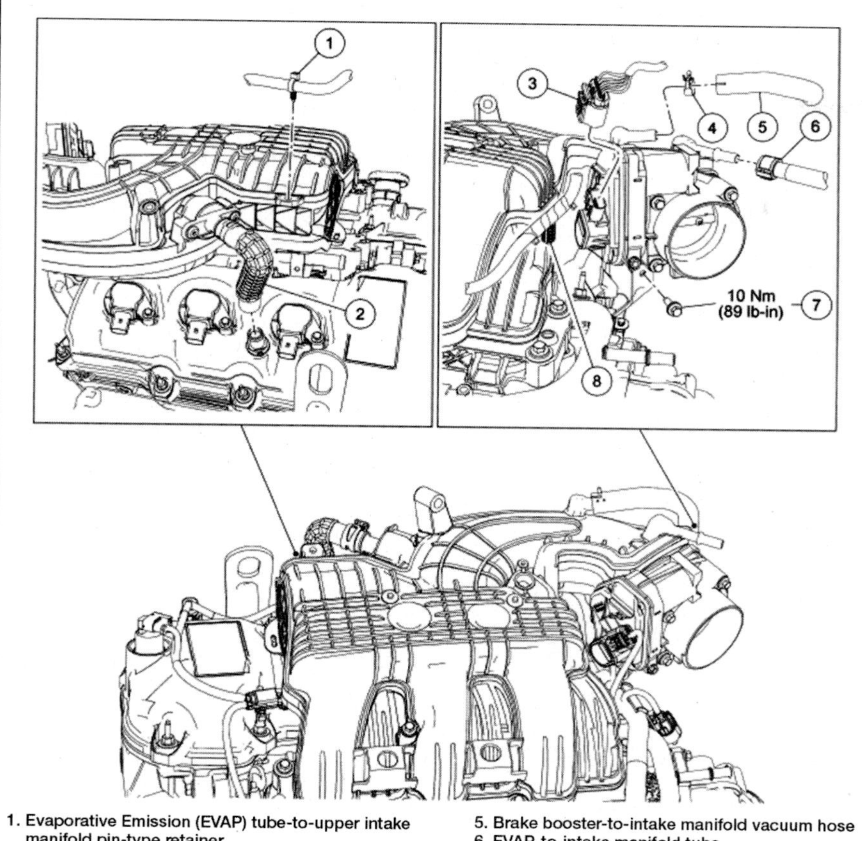

1. Evaporative Emission (EVAP) tube-to-upper intake manifold pin-type retainer
2. PCV hose
3. Throttle body electrical connector
4. Brake booster-to-intake manifold vacuum hose clamp
5. Brake booster-to-intake manifold vacuum hose
6. EVAP-to-intake manifold tube
7. Upper intake manifold support bracket bolt
8. Engine control wiring harness retainer

N0081328

Fig. 107 Upper intake manifold components 1—3.7L engines

28. Disconnect the 3 left-hand ignition coil-on-plug electrical connectors.
29. Remove the lower radiator hose from the thermostat housing.
30. Remove the engine cover mounting stud from the left-hand valve cover stud bolt.
31. Detach all the wiring harness retainers from the left-hand valve cover and stud bolts.
32. Remove the nut and the oil supply tube bracket from the left-hand valve cover stud bolt.
33. Remove the oil level indicator.
34. Detach and disconnect the 2 fuel injector wiring harness electrical connectors.
35. Disconnect the Manifold Absolute Pressure (MAP)/Intake Air Temperature 2 (IAT2) sensor electrical connector.
36. Disconnect the turbocharger wastegate regulating valve electrical connector.
37. Detach the 2 wire harness-to-intake manifold retainers.
38. Remove the fuel tube-to-engine front cover bracket bolt and position the fuel tube aside.
39. Disconnect the 2 turbocharger coolant hoses from the intake manifold.

WARNING

If the engine is repaired or replaced because of upper engine failure, typically including valve or piston damage, check the intake manifold for metal debris. If metal debris is found, install a new intake manifold. Failure to follow these instructions can result in engine damage.

40. Remove the 12 bolts and the intake manifold.
    a. Note the routing of the 2 fuel rail wiring harnesses for installation.
    b. Remove and discard the intake manifold, coolant crossover and thermostat housing gaskets.
    c. Clean and inspect all sealing surfaces.
41. Disconnect the right-hand VCT solenoid electrical connector and detach the 2 wiring harness retainers.
42. Disconnect the 3 right-hand ignition coil-on-plug electrical connectors.
43. Detach all the wiring harness retainers from the right-hand valve cover and stud bolts.
44. For early build vehicles, remove the nut for the high pressure fuel tube.
45. For late build vehicles, remove the high pressure fuel tube bolt from the left-hand cylinder head.
46. Remove the high pressure fuel tube flare nut from the fuel injection pump. Remove the 2 high pressure fuel tube flare nuts from the fuel rails.
    a. To release the fuel pressure in the high pressure fuel tube, wrap the flare nuts with a shop towel to absorb any residual fuel pressure during the loosening of the flare nuts.
    b. Remove the high pressure fuel tube assembly.
47. Remove the 2 bolts and the fuel injection pump.
48. Remove the fuel injection pump mounting plate.
49. Remove the fuel injection pump roller tappet. Inspect the fuel injection pump roller tappet.
50. Remove the 3 bolts and the 3 left-hand ignition coil-on-plugs.
51. Remove the 3 bolts and the 3 right-hand ignition coil-on-plugs.
52. Loosen the 10 stud bolts and remove the left-hand valve cover. Discard the gasket.
53. Loosen the 11 stud bolts and remove the right-hand valve cover. Discard the gasket.
54. Inspect the VCT solenoid seals and the spark plug tube seals. Install new seals if damaged.
    a. Using the VCT Spark Plug Tube Seal Remover and Handle, remove the seal(s).
55. Rotate the accessory drive belt tensioner clockwise and remove the accessory drive belt.
56. Remove the 3 bolts and the accessory drive belt tensioner.
57. Using the Strap Wrench, remove the crankshaft pulley bolt and washer. Discard the bolt.
58. Using the 3 Jaw Puller, remove the crankshaft pulley.
59. Using the Oil Seal Remover, remove and discard the crankshaft front seal.
60. Remove the stud bolt and Heated Oxygen Sensor (HO2S) connector bracket from the engine front cover.
61. Remove the 2 engine mount studs. Only use hand tools to remove the studs.

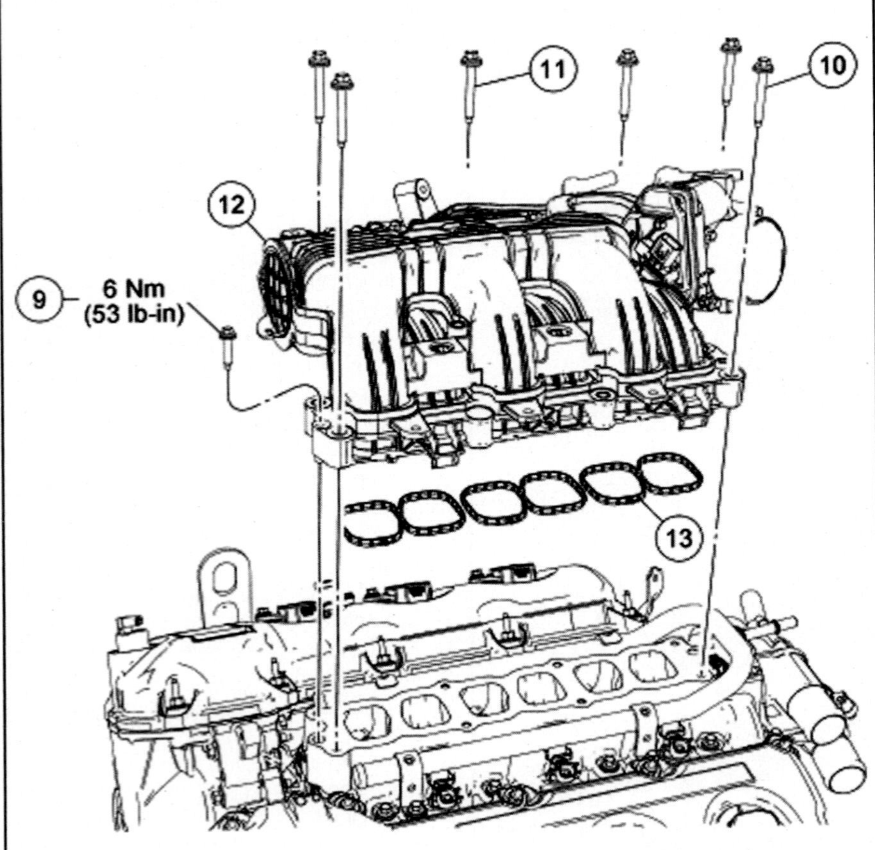

Fig. 108 Upper intake manifold components 2—3.7L engines

62. Remove the 3 bolts and the engine mount bracket.
63. Remove the 22 engine front cover bolts.
64. Install 6 of the engine front cover bolts (finger-tight) into the 6 threaded holes in the engine front cover.
   a. Tighten the bolts one turn at a time in a crisscross pattern until the engine front cover-to-cylinder block seal is released.
   b. Remove the engine front cover.
65. Clean the engine front cover using a 3M® Roloc® Bristle Disk (2-in white, part

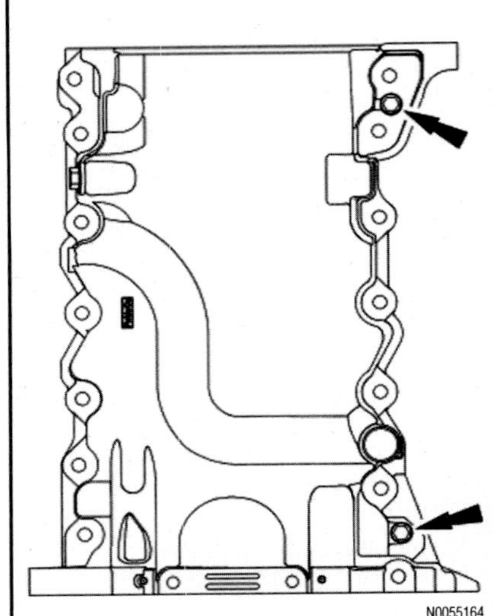

Fig. 111 Alternately tighten the 2 bolts one turn at a time until the seal is released

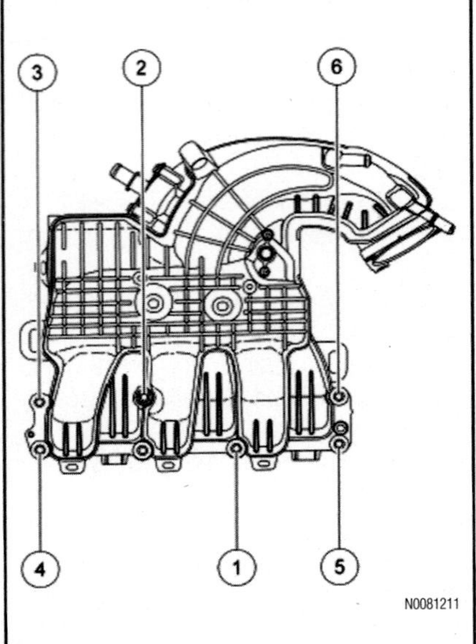

Fig. 109 Upper intake manifold bolt tightening sequence—3.7L engines

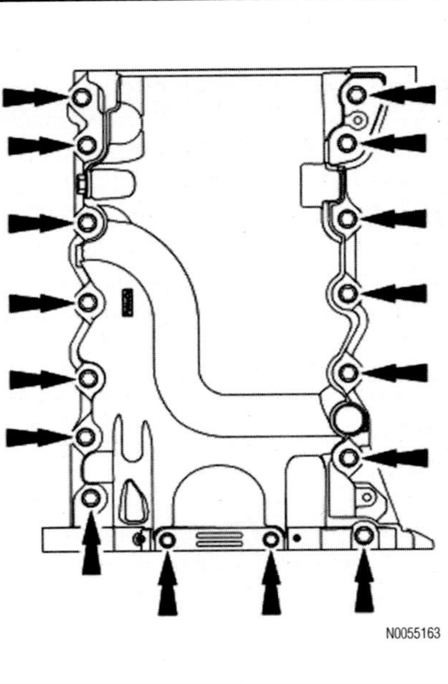

Fig. 110 Remove the 16 oil pan bolts

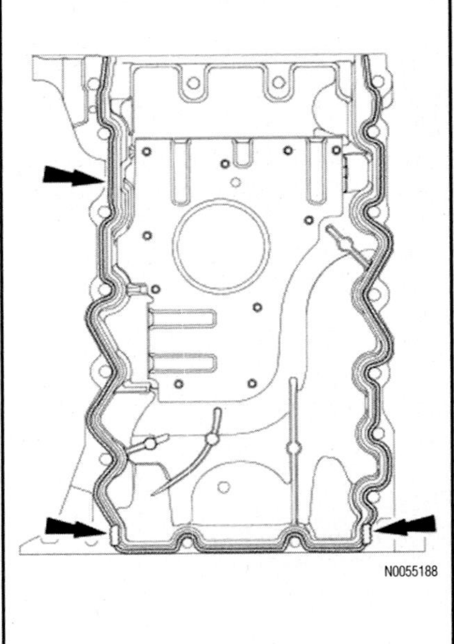

Fig. 112 Oil pan sealant application

number 07528) in a suitable tool turning at the recommended speed of 15,000 rpm.

a. Only use a 3M® Roloc® Bristle Disk to clean the engine front cover. Do not use metal scrapers, wire brushes or any other power abrasive disk to clean the engine front cover. These tools cause scratches and gouges that make leak paths.

b. Thoroughly wash the engine front cover to remove any foreign material, including any abrasive particles created during the cleaning process.

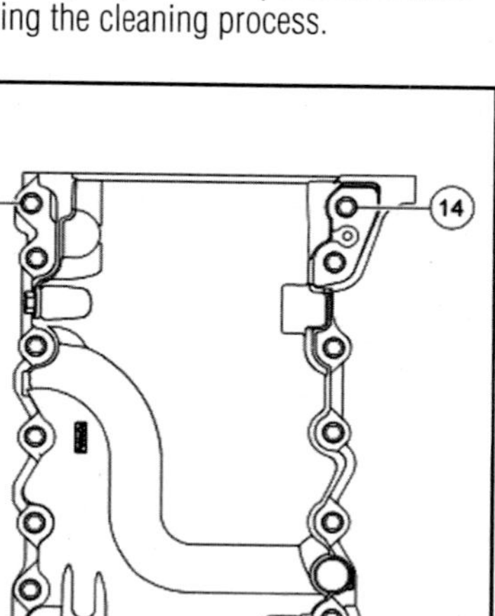

Fig. 113 Oil pan bolts 10, 11, 13 and 14 tightening sequence

66. Remove the A/C compressor nut, bracket and the stud. The A/C compressor must remain bolted to the cylinder block prior to installing the oil pan.

67. Remove the 16 oil pan bolts.

68. Install 2 of the oil pan bolts (finger-tight) into the 2 threaded holes in the oil pan.

a. Alternately tighten the 2 bolts one turn at a time until the oil pan-to-cylinder block seal is released.

b. Remove the oil pan.

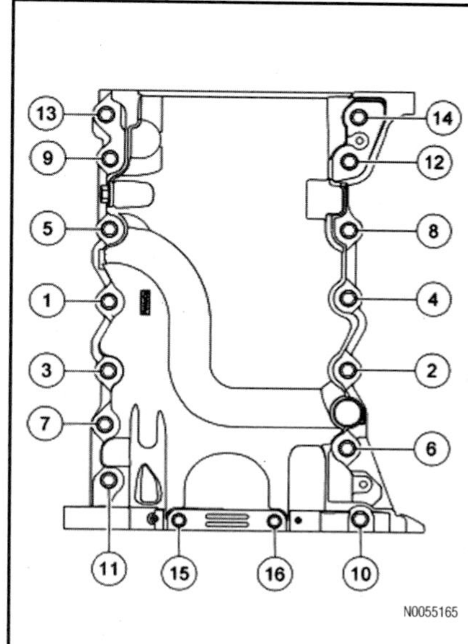

Fig. 115 Oil pan bolts tightening sequence

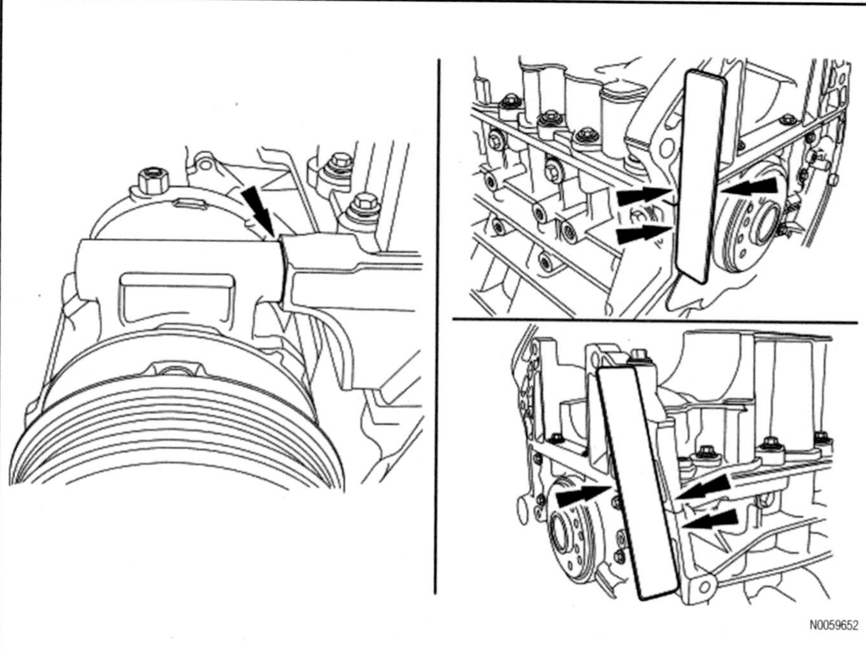

Fig. 114 Align the oil pan to the cylinder block and A/C compressor

69. Clean the engine front cover and oil pan using a 3M® Roloc® Bristle Disk (2-in white, part number 07528) in a suitable tool turning at the recommended speed of 15,000 rpm.

a. Thoroughly wash the engine front cover and oil pan to remove any foreign material, including any abrasive particles created during the cleaning process.

70. Place clean, lint-free shop towels over exposed engine cavities. Carefully remove the towels so foreign material is not dropped into the engine. Any foreign material (including any material created while cleaning gasket surfaces) that enters the oil passages or the oil pan, may cause engine failure.

WARNING

Do not use wire brushes, power abrasive discs or 3M® Roloc® Bristle Disk (2-in white, part number 07528) to clean the sealing surfaces. These tools cause scratches and gouges that make leak paths. They also cause contamination that will cause premature engine failure. Remove all traces of the gasket.

71. Clean the sealing surfaces of the cylinder block in the following sequence.

a. Remove any large deposits of silicone or gasket material.

b. Apply silicone gasket remover and allow to set for several minutes.

c. Remove the silicone gasket remover. A second application of silicone gasket remover may be required if residual traces of silicone or gasket material remain.

d. Apply metal surface prep to remove any remaining traces of oil or coolant and to prepare the surfaces to bond. Do not attempt to make the metal shiny. Some staining of the metal surfaces is normal.

e. Make sure the 2 locating dowel pins are seated correctly in the cylinder block.

To install:

72. Apply a 0.11 in. (3 mm) bead of Motorcraft® High Performance Engine RTV Silicone to the sealing surface of the oil pan. Failure to use Motorcraft® High Performance Engine RTV Silicone may cause the engine oil to foam excessively and result in serious engine damage.

73. Apply a 0.21 in. (5.5 mm) bead of Motorcraft® High Performance Engine RTV Silicone to the 2 crankshaft seal retainer plate-to-cylinder block joint areas on the sealing surface of the oil pan.

a. The oil pan and the 4 specified bolts must be installed and the oil pan aligned to the cylinder block and A/C compressor within 4 minutes of sealant application. Final tightening of the oil pan bolts must be carried out within 60 minutes of sealant application.

74. Install the oil pan and bolts 10, 11, 13 and 14.

a. Tighten in the sequence shown to 27 inch lbs. (3 Nm).

b. Loosen the bolts 180 degrees.

75. Align the oil pan to the cylinder block and A/C compressor.

a. Position the oil pan so the mounting boss is against the A/C compressor and using a straightedge, align the oil pan flush with the rear of the cylinder block at the 2 areas shown.

76. Tighten bolts 10, 11, 13 and 14 in the sequence shown above to 27 inch lbs. (3 Nm).

77. Install the remaining oil pan bolts. Tighten all the oil pan bolts in the sequence shown.

a. Tighten the large bolts (1–14) to 15 ft. lbs. (20 Nm).

b. Tighten the small bolts (15 and 16) to 89 inch lbs. (10 Nm).

78. Install the A/C compressor mounting stud, bracket and nut. Tighten the stud to 80 inch lbs. (9 Nm). and the nut to 18 ft. lbs. (25 Nm).

79. Install the Alignment Pins.

80. Apply a 0.11 in. (3 mm) bead of Motorcraft® High Performance Engine RTV Silicone to the engine front cover sealing surfaces including the 3 engine mount bracket bosses.

81. Apply a 0.21 in. (5.5 mm) bead of Motorcraft® High Performance Engine RTV Silicone to the oil pan-to-cylinder block joint and the cylinder head-to-cylinder block joint areas of the engine front cover in 5 places indicated in the Timing Chain Front Cover Removal & Installation procedure.

82. Install the engine front cover and bolts 17, 18, 19 and 20 as shown in the Timing Chain Front Cover Removal & Installation procedure.

83. Remove the Alignment Pins.

84. Install the engine mount bracket and the 3 bolts. Do not tighten the bolts at this time.

85. Install the remaining engine front cover bolts. Tighten all of the engine front cover bolts and engine mount bracket bolts in 2 stages in the sequence shown in the Timing Chain Front Cover Removal & Installation procedure.

86. Install the engine mount studs in the following sequence:

a. The thread sealer on the engine mount studs (including new engine mount studs if applicable) must be cleaned off with a wire brush and new Threadlock and Sealer applied prior to installing the engine mount studs.

b. Clean the front cover engine mount stud holes with pressurized air to remove any foreign material.

c. Clean all the thread sealer from the engine mount studs (old and new studs).

d. Apply new Threadlock and Sealer to the engine mount stud threads.

e. Install the 2 engine mount studs. Tighten to 15 ft. lbs. (20 Nm).

87. Install the stud bolt and Heated Oxygen Sensor (HO2S) connector bracket to the engine front cover. Tighten to 89 inch lbs. (10 Nm).

88. Using the Crankshaft Vibration Damper Installer and Front Crankshaft Seal Installer, install a new crankshaft front seal. Apply clean engine oil to the crankshaft front seal bore in the engine front cover.

➡Lubricate the outside diameter sealing surfaces with clean engine oil.

89. Using the Crankshaft Vibration Damper Installer and Front Cover Oil Seal Installer, install the crankshaft pulley.

90. Using the Strap Wrench, install the crankshaft pulley washer and new bolt and tighten in 4 stages.

a. Stage 1: Tighten to 89 ft. lbs. (120 Nm).

b. Stage 2: Loosen one full turn.

c. Stage 3: Tighten to 37 ft. lbs. (50 Nm).

d. Stage 4: Tighten an additional 90 degrees.

91. Install the accessory drive belt tensioner and the 3 bolts. Tighten to 97 inch lbs. (11 Nm).

92. Rotate the accessory drive belt tensioner clockwise and install the accessory drive belt.

➡Installation of new seals is only required if damaged seals were removed during disassembly of the engine.

93. Using the VCT Spark Plug Tube Seal Installer and Handle, install new VCT solenoid and/or spark plug tube seals.

94. Apply an 0.31 in (8 mm) bead of Motorcraft® High Performance Engine RTV Silicone to the engine front cover-to-right-hand cylinder head joints.

⁂ WARNING

If the valve cover is not installed and the fasteners tightened within 4 minutes, the sealant must be removed and the sealing area cleaned. To clean the sealing area, use silicone gasket remover and metal surface prep. Failure to follow this procedure can cause future oil leakage.

95. Using new gaskets, install the valve covers and tighten the bolts in the sequence shown in the Valve Cover Removal & Installation procedure to 89 inch lbs. (10 Nm).

96. Apply an 0.31 in (8 mm) bead of Motorcraft® High Performance Engine RTV Silicone to the engine front cover-to-left-hand cylinder head joints. If the valve cover is not installed and the fasteners tightened within 4 minutes, the sealant must be removed and the sealing area cleaned. To clean the sealing area, use silicone gasket remover and metal surface prep. Failure to follow this procedure can cause future oil leakage.

97. Install the ignition coil-on-plugs and bolts. Tighten to 62 inch lbs. (7 Nm).

98. Using the crankshaft pulley bolt, turn the crankshaft until the fuel injection pump cam lobe is at BDC. The cam lobe for the fuel injection pump must be at Bottom Dead Center (BDC) for the fuel injection pump installation.

99. Install the fuel injection pump roller tappet. Apply clean engine oil to the fuel injection pump mounting pedestal bore.

100. Inspect the fuel injection pump mounting plate-to-valve cover gasket and replace if necessary. Apply clean engine oil to the fuel injection pump mounting plate seal.

101. Inspect the 2 fuel injection pump mounting plate O-ring seals and replace if necessary. Apply clean engine oil to the fuel injection pump mounting plate O-ring seals.

102. Install the fuel injection pump on the fuel injection pump mounting plate. Apply clean engine oil to the fuel injection pump O-ring seal.

103. Install the fuel injection pump and the 2 bolts. Start the fuel injection pump bolts by hand then simultaneously tighten to specifications.

a. Tighten to 89 inch lbs. (10 Nm).

b. Tighten an additional 45 degrees.

104. Connect the high-pressure fuel tube flare nut to the fuel injection pump. Connect the 2 high-pressure fuel tube flare nuts to the fuel rails. Tighten to 22 ft. lbs. (30 Nm).

105. For late build vehicles, install the bolt for the high pressure fuel tube to the

left-hand cylinder head. Tighten to 53 inch lbs. (6 Nm).

106. For early build vehicles, install the nut for the high pressure fuel tube to the left-hand valve cover stud bolt. Tighten to 53 inch lbs. (6 Nm).

107. Attach all of the wiring harness retainers to the right-hand valve cover and stud bolts.

108. Connect the 3 right-hand ignition coil-on-plug electrical connectors.

109. Connect the right-hand VCT solenoid electrical connector and attach the 2 wiring harness retainers.

✲✲ WARNING

If the engine is repaired or replaced because of upper engine failure, typically including valve or piston damage, check the intake manifold for metal debris. If metal debris is found, install a new intake manifold. Failure to follow these instructions can result in engine damage.

✲✲ WARNING

Make sure the fuel rail wiring harnesses are routed correctly.

110. Using new intake manifold, coolant crossover and thermostat housing gaskets, install the intake manifold and the 12 bolts. Installing the 2 long bolts first will aid in installing the intake manifold. Tighten in the sequence shown in the Intake Manifold Removal & Installation procedure to 89 inch lbs. (10 Nm).

111. Connect the 2 turbocharger coolant hoses to the intake manifold.

112. Position the fuel tube and install the fuel tube-to-engine front cover bracket bolt. Tighten to 89 inch lbs. (10 Nm).

113. Attach the 2 wire harness-to-intake manifold retainers.

114. Connect the turbocharger wastegate regulating valve electrical connector.

115. Connect the Manifold Absolute Pressure (MAP)/Intake Air Temperature 2 (IAT2) sensor electrical connector.

116. Connect and attach the 2 fuel injector wiring harness electrical connectors.

117. Install the oil level indicator.

118. Install the oil supply tube bracket on the left-hand valve cover stud bolt and install the nut. Tighten to 71 inch lbs. (8 Nm).

119. Attach all of the wiring harness retainers to the left-hand valve cover and stud bolts.

120. Install the engine cover mounting stud to the left-hand valve cover stud bolt. Tighten to 53 inch lbs. (6 Nm).

121. Install the lower radiator hose to the thermostat housing.

122. Connect the 3 left-hand ignition coil-on-plug electrical connectors.

123. Connect the Engine Oil Pressure (EOP) electrical connector. Attach the wiring harness retainer to the block.

124. Connect the left-hand VCT solenoid electrical connector.

125. Connect the Throttle Position (TP) and electronic throttle body electrical connectors.

126. Connect the electrical connector and install the noise insulator shield for the fuel injection pump.

127. Install the right-hand Charge Air Cooler (CAC) tube and turbocharger intake tube as an assembly and install the right-hand CAC tube nut to the intake manifold. The compression limiter bushing may fall out of the mounting bracket grommet on the Charge Air Cooler (CAC) tube during service. Make sure the bushing is in place when reinstalling the tube or damage to the tube may occur. Tighten to 53 inch lbs. (6 Nm).

128. Install the nut to the right-hand valve cover stud bolt for the right-hand turbocharger intake tube. The compression limiter bushing may fall out of the mounting bracket grommet on the turbocharger intake tube during service. Make sure the bushing is in place when reinstalling the tube or damage to the tube may occur. Tighten to 53 inch lbs. (6 Nm).

129. Install the right-hand turbocharger intake pipe to the right-hand turbocharger and tighten the clamp. Align the matchmarks. Tighten to 44 inch lbs. (5 Nm).

130. Install the right-hand CAC tube to the right-hand turbocharger and tighten the clamp. Align the matchmarks. Tighten to 44 inch lbs. (5 Nm).

131. Connect the right-hand turbocharger bypass valve electrical connector.

132. Using 2 new O-ring seals, install the left-hand turbocharger oil return tube in the oil pan. Lubricate the oil pan bore with clean engine oil.

133. Install a new gasket, turbocharger oil return tube and the 2 bolts. Tighten to 89 inch lbs. (10 Nm).

134. Install the turbocharger intake tube to the left-hand turbocharger and tighten the clamp. Align the matchmarks. Tighten to 44 inch lbs. (5 Nm).

135. Install the 2 turbocharger wastegate regulating valve hoses to the turbocharger wastegate regulating valve and to the right-hand CAC tube.

136. Connect the left-hand turbocharger bypass valve electrical connector.

137. If equipped, connect the 2 heated PCV electrical connectors.

138. Install the PCV tube and connect the 2 quick connect couplings.

139. Connect the brake vacuum tube to the intake manifold.

140. Install the left-hand cylinder block drain plug. Tighten to 15 ft. lbs. (20 Nm) plus an additional 180 degrees.

141. Install the right-hand cylinder block drain plug or, if equipped, the block heater. Tighten to 30 ft. lbs. (40 Nm).

142. If equipped, connect the block heater electrical connector and install the heat shield. Attach all the engine block heater wiring harness retainers.

143. Using a new O-ring seal and gasket seal, connect the A/C tube to the compressor and install the nut. Tighten to 11 ft. lbs. (15 Nm).

144. Using the Heavy Duty Floor Crane and Spreader Bar, remove the engine from the stand.

145. Install the crankshaft sensor ring.

146. Install the flexplate and the 8 bolts. Tighten to 59 ft. lbs. (80 Nm).

147. Install the engine in the vehicle.

3.7L Engines

See Figures 116 through 121.

✲✲ WARNING

During engine repair procedures, cleanliness is extremely important. Any foreign material, including any material created while cleaning gasket surfaces that enters the oil passages, coolant passages or the oil pan, may cause engine failure.

✲✲ WARNING

Early build engines have 11 fastener valve covers, late build engines have 9 fastener valve covers. Do not attempt to install bolts in the 2 empty late build valve cover holes or damage to the valve cover will occur.

1. Remove the engine from the vehicle.
2. Remove the 8 bolts and the flywheel.
3. Remove the crankshaft sensor ring.
4. Mount the engine on a suitable engine stand. Install the engine stand bolts into the cylinder block only. Do not install the bolts into the oil pan.
5. If equipped, remove the heat shield and disconnect the block heater electrical connector.
6. Detach all of the engine block heater harness retainers and remove the harness.

7. Disconnect the PCV hose from the PCV valve.
8. Disconnect the throttle body electrical connector.
9. Detach the wiring harness retainers from the upper intake manifold.
10. Remove the upper intake manifold support bracket bolt.
11. Remove the fuel tube bracket bolt from the upper intake manifold.

⁂ WARNING

If the engine is repaired or replaced because of upper engine failure, typically including valve or piston damage, check the intake manifold for metal debris. If metal debris is found, install a new intake manifold. Failure to follow these instructions can result in engine damage.

12. Remove the 6 bolts and the upper intake manifold. Discard the gaskets.
13. Disconnect the Power Steering Pressure (PSP) switch electrical connector.
14. For Front Wheel Drive (FWD) vehicles, disconnect the right-hand Catalyst Monitor Sensor (CMS) electrical connector.
15. Disconnect the right-hand Variable Camshaft Timing (VCT) solenoid electrical connector.
16. Disconnect the 3 right-hand coil-on-plug electrical connectors.
17. Disconnect the right-hand Heated Oxygen Sensor (HO2S) electrical connector.
18. Detach all of the wiring harness retainers from the right-hand valve cover and stud bolts.
19. Disconnect the left-hand CMS electrical connector.
20. Disconnect the left-hand VCT solenoid electrical connector.
21. Disconnect the 3 left-hand coil-on-plug electrical connectors.
22. Detach all of the wiring harness retainers from the left-hand valve cover and stud bolts.
23. Remove the 6 bolts and the 6 coil-on-plugs.
24. Remove the A/C compressor nut and stud. The A/C compressor must remain bolted to the cylinder block prior to installing the oil pan.
25. Remove the PSP tube bracket-to-power steering pump bolt.
26. Remove the nut and the PSP tube bracket from the right-hand valve cover stud bolt.
27. Remove the 3 bolts and position aside the power steering pump.
28. Remove the 3 bolts and the accessory drive belt tensioner.
29. Remove the 4 nuts and the left-hand catalytic converter. Discard the nuts and the gasket.
30. For Front Wheel Drive (FWD) vehicles, remove the 4 nuts and the right-hand catalytic converter. Discard the nuts and the gasket.
31. Remove the right-hand cylinder block drain plug or, if equipped, the block heater. Allow coolant to drain from the cylinder block.
32. Remove the left-hand cylinder block drain plug. Allow coolant to drain from the cylinder block.
33. Remove the engine cover stud from the left-hand valve cover stud bolt.
34. For early build vehicles, loosen the 11 stud bolts and remove the left-hand valve cover. Discard the gasket.
35. Loosen the bolt, the 10 stud bolts and remove the right-hand valve cover. Discard the gasket.
36. For late build vehicles, loosen the 9 stud bolts and remove the left-hand valve cover. Discard the gasket.
37. Loosen the 9 stud bolts and remove the right-hand valve cover. Discard the gasket.
38. Using the VCT Spark Plug Tube Seal Remover and Handle, remove the seal(s). Inspect the VCT solenoid seals and the spark plug tube seals. Remove any damaged seals.
39. Using the Strap Wrench, remove the crankshaft pulley bolt and washer. Discard the bolt.
40. Using the 3 Jaw Puller, remove the crankshaft pulley.
41. Using the Oil Seal Remover, remove and discard the crankshaft front seal.
42. Remove the 2 bolts and the engine mount bracket.
43. Remove the 2 engine mount studs. Only use hand tools to remove the studs.
44. Remove the 3 bolts and the engine mount bracket.
45. Remove the 22 engine front cover bolts.
46. Install 6 of the engine front cover bolts (finger tight) into the 6 threaded holes in the engine front cover.
    a. Tighten the bolts one turn at a time in a crisscross pattern until the engine front cover-to-cylinder block seal is released.
    b. Remove the engine front cover.
47. Remove the 16 oil pan bolts.
48. Install 2 of the oil pan bolts (finger tight) into the 2 threaded holes in the oil pan.
    a. Alternately tighten the 2 bolts one turn at a time until the oil pan-to-cylinder block seal is released.
    b. Remove the oil pan.

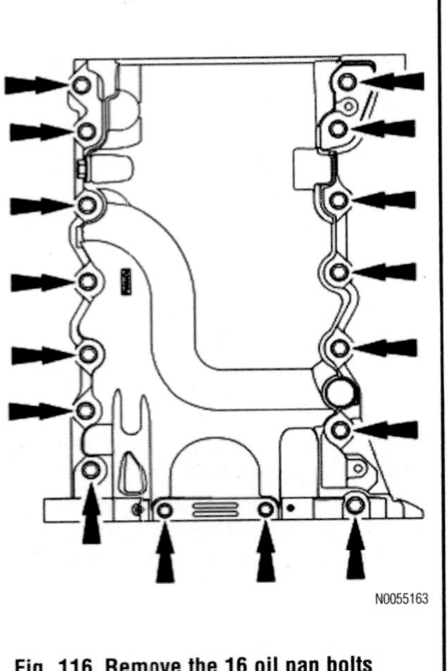

Fig. 116 Remove the 16 oil pan bolts

49. Clean the engine front cover and oil pan using a 3M® Roloc® Bristle Disk (2-in white, part number 07528) in a suitable tool turning at the recommended speed of 15,000 rpm. Only use a 3M® Roloc® Bristle Disk to clean the engine front cover and oil pan. Do not use metal scrapers, wire brushes or any other power abrasive disk to clean the engine front cover. These tools cause scratches and gouges that make leak paths.
    a. Thoroughly wash the engine front cover and oil pan to remove any foreign material, including any abrasive particles created during the cleaning process.

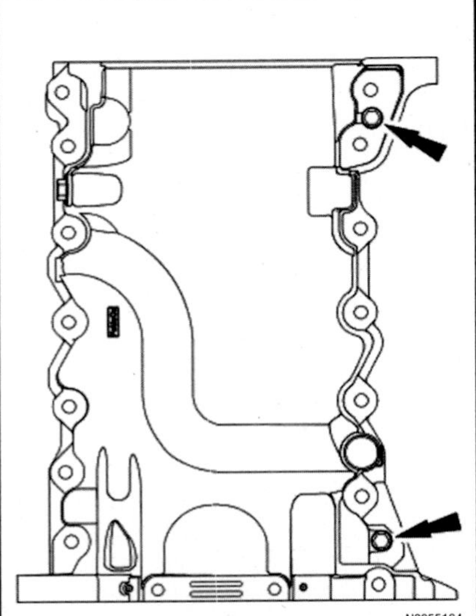

Fig. 117 Alternately tighten the 2 bolts one turn at a time until the seal is released

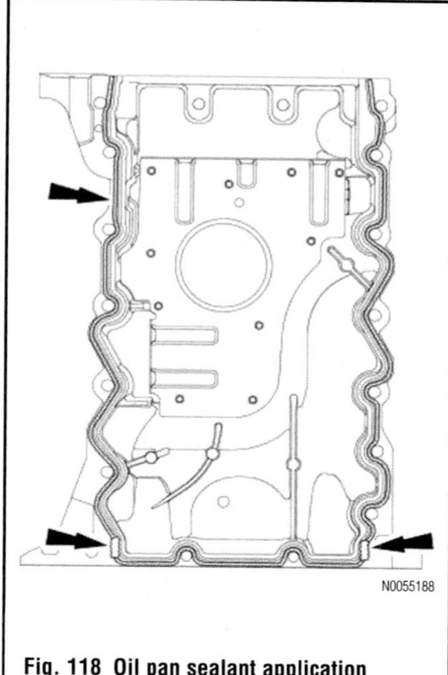

Fig. 118 Oil pan sealant application

50. Place clean, lint-free shop towels over exposed engine cavities. Carefully remove the towels so foreign material is not dropped into the engine. Any foreign material (including any material created while cleaning gasket surfaces) that enters the oil passages or the oil pan, may cause engine failure.

WARNING

Do not use wire brushes, power abrasive discs or 3M® Roloc® Bristle Disk (2-in white, part number 07528) to clean the sealing surfaces. These tools cause scratches and gouges that make leak paths. They also cause contamination that will cause premature engine failure. Remove all traces of the gasket.

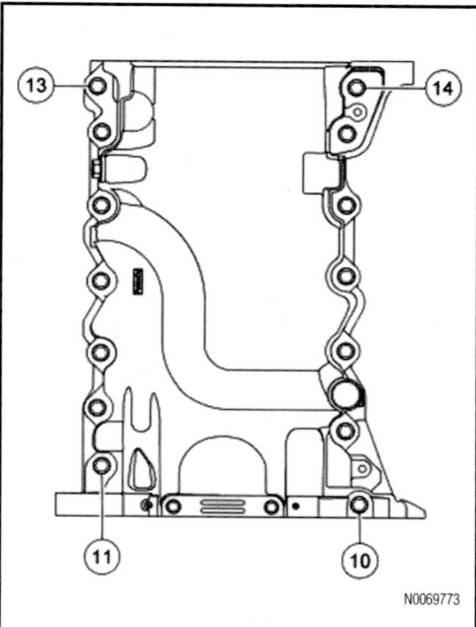

Fig. 119 Oil pan bolts 10, 11, 13 and 14 tightening sequence

51. Clean the sealing surfaces of the cylinder block in the following sequence.
   a. Remove any large deposits of silicone or gasket material.
   b. Apply silicone gasket remover and allow to set for several minutes.
   c. Remove the silicone gasket remover. A second application of silicone gasket remover may be required if residual traces of silicone or gasket material remain.
   d. Apply metal surface prep to remove any remaining traces of oil or coolant and to prepare the surfaces to bond. Do not attempt to make the metal shiny. Some staining of the metal surfaces is normal.
   e. Make sure the 2 locating dowel pins are seated correctly in the cylinder block.

To install:

WARNING

Failure to use Motorcraft® High Performance Engine RTV Silicone may cause the engine oil to foam excessively and result in serious engine damage.

52. Apply a 0.11 in. (3 mm) bead of Motorcraft® High Performance Engine RTV Silicone to the sealing surface of the oil pan.

53. Apply a 0.21 in. (5.5 mm) bead of Motorcraft® High Performance Engine RTV Silicone to the 2 crankshaft seal retainer plate-to-cylinder block joint areas on the sealing surface of the oil pan.

WARNING

The oil pan and the 4 specified bolts must be installed and the oil pan aligned to the cylinder block and A/C compressor within 4 minutes of sealant application. Final tightening of the oil pan bolts must be carried out within 60 minutes of sealant application.

54. Install the oil pan and bolts 10, 11, 13 and 14.
   a. Tighten in the sequence shown to 27 inch lbs. (3 Nm).
   b. Loosen the bolts 180 degrees.

WARNING

The oil pan and the 4 specified bolts must be installed within 4 minutes of the start of sealant application.

55. Position the oil pan so the mounting boss is against the A/C compressor and using a straightedge, align the oil pan flush with the rear of the cylinder block at the 2 areas shown. Align the oil pan to the cylinder block and A/C compressor.

56. Tighten bolts 10, 11, 13 and 14 in the sequence shown, to 27 inch lbs. (3 Nm).

57. Install the remaining oil pan bolts. Tighten all the oil pan bolts in the sequence shown.
   a. Tighten the large bolts (1–14) to 15 ft. lbs. (20 Nm).
   b. Tighten the small bolts (15 and 16) to 89 inch lbs. (10 Nm).

58. Install the A/C compressor mounting stud and nut. Tighten the stud to 80 inch lbs. (9 Nm) and the nut to 18 ft. lbs. (25 Nm).

59. Install the Alignment Pins.

60. Apply a 0.11 in. (3 mm) bead of Motorcraft® High Performance Engine RTV Silicone to the engine front cover sealing surfaces including the 3 engine mount bracket bosses.

61. Apply a 0.21 in. (5.5 mm) bead of Motorcraft® High Performance Engine RTV Silicone to the oil pan-to-cylinder block joint and the cylinder head-to-cylinder block joint areas of the engine front cover in 5 places indicated in the Timing Chain Front Cover Removal & Installation procedure.

62. Install the engine front cover and bolts 17, 18, 19 and 20 as shown in the Timing Chain Front Cover Removal & Installation procedure.

63. Remove the Alignment Pins.

64. Install the engine mount bracket and the 3 bolts. Do not tighten the bolts at this time.

65. Install the remaining engine front cover bolts. Tighten all of the engine front cover bolts and engine mount bracket bolts in 2 stages in the sequence shown in the Timing Chain Front Cover Removal & Installation procedure.

66. Install the engine mount studs in the following sequence.
   a. Clean the front cover engine mount stud holes with pressurized air to remove any foreign material.
   b. Clean all the thread sealer from the engine mount studs (old and new studs).
   c. Apply new Threadlock and Sealer to the engine mount stud threads.
   d. Install the 2 engine mount studs. Tighten to 15 ft. lbs. (20 Nm).

67. Install the engine mount bracket and the 2 bolts. Tighten to 18 ft. lbs. (24 Nm).

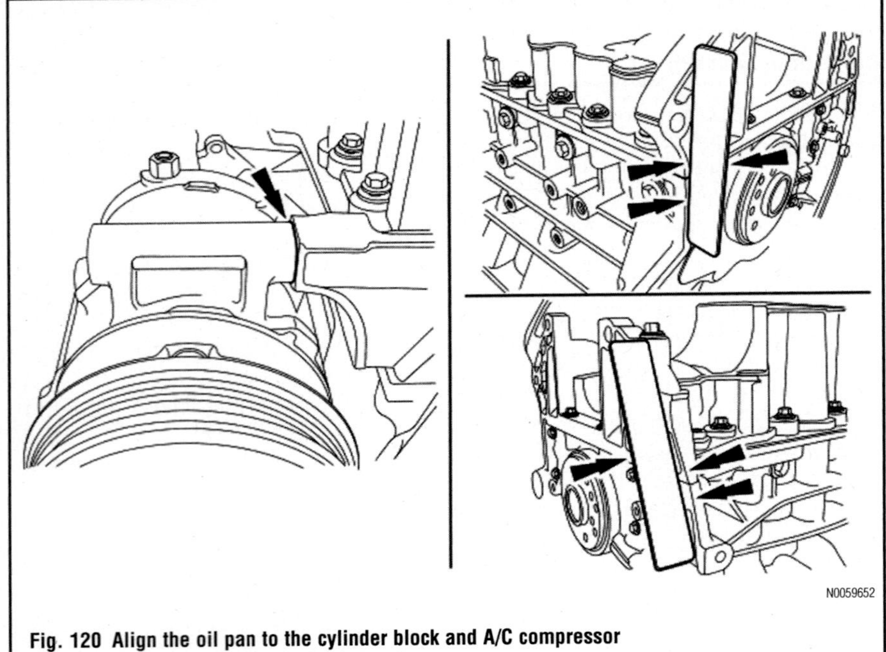

Fig. 120 Align the oil pan to the cylinder block and A/C compressor

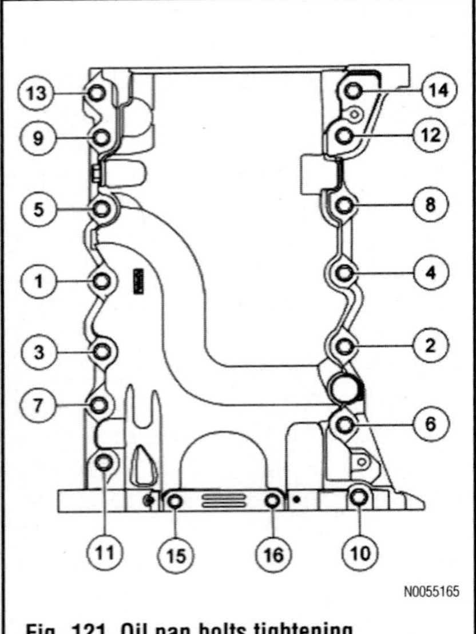

Fig. 121 Oil pan bolts tightening sequence

68. Using the Crankshaft Vibration Damper Installer and Front Crankshaft Seal Installer, install a new crankshaft front seal. Apply clean engine oil to the crankshaft front seal bore in the engine front cover.

69. Using the Crankshaft Vibration Damper Installer and Front Cover Oil Seal Installer, install the crankshaft pulley. Lubricate the outside diameter sealing surfaces with clean engine oil.

70. Using the Strap Wrench, install the crankshaft pulley washer and new bolt and tighten in 4 stages.

a. Stage 1: Tighten to 89 ft. lbs. (120 Nm).

b. Stage 2: Loosen one full turn.

c. Stage 3: Tighten to 37 ft. lbs. (50 Nm).

d. Stage 4: Tighten an additional 90 degrees.

71. Using the VCT Spark Plug Tube Seal Installer and Handle, install new VCT solenoid and/or spark plug tube seals. Installation of new seals is only required if damaged seals were removed during disassembly of the engine.

72. Apply sealant and install the valve covers as shown in the Valve Cover Removal & Installation procedure.

73. Install the engine cover stud to the left-hand valve cover stud bolt. Tighten to 53 inch lbs. (6 Nm).

74. Install the 6 coil-on-plug assemblies and the 6 bolts. Tighten to 62 inch lbs. (7 Nm).

75. Install the left-hand cylinder block drain plug. Tighten to 15 ft. lbs. (20 Nm) plus an additional 180 degrees.

76. Install the right-hand cylinder block drain plug or, if equipped, the block heater. Tighten to 30 ft. lbs. (40 Nm).

77. For Front Wheel Drive (FWD) vehicles, using a new gasket, install the right-hand catalytic converter and 4 new nuts. Tighten to 30 ft. lbs. (40 Nm).

78. Using a new gasket, install the left-hand catalytic converter and 4 new nuts. Tighten to 30 ft. lbs. (40 Nm).

79. Install the accessory drive belt tensioner and the 3 bolts. Tighten to 97 inch lbs. (11 Nm).

80. Install the power steering pump and the 3 bolts. Tighten to 18 ft. lbs. (24 Nm).

81. Install the Power Steering Pressure (PSP) tube bracket bolt. Tighten to 89 inch lbs. (10 Nm).

82. Install the PSP bracket and nut to the right-hand valve cover stud bolt. Tighten to 62 inch lbs. (7 Nm).

83. Attach all of the wiring harness retainers to the left-hand valve cover and stud bolts.

84. Connect the 3 left-hand coil-on-plug electrical connectors.

85. Connect the left-hand camshaft VCT solenoid electrical connector.

86. Connect the left-hand Catalyst Monitor Sensor (CMS) electrical connector.

87. Attach all of the wiring harness retainers to the right-hand valve cover and stud bolts.

88. Connect the right-hand Heated Oxygen Sensor (HO2S) electrical connector.

89. Connect the 3 right-hand coil-on-plug electrical connectors.

90. Connect the right-hand VCT solenoid electrical connector.

91. For Front Wheel Drive (FWD) vehicles, connect the right-hand CMS electrical connector.

92. Connect the PSP switch electrical connector.

WARNING

If the engine is repaired or replaced because of upper engine failure, typically including valve or piston damage, check the intake manifold for metal debris. If metal debris is found, install a new intake manifold.

93. Using new gaskets, install the upper intake manifold and the 6 bolts. Tighten in the sequence shown in the Intake Manifold Removal & Installation procedure to 89 inch lbs. (10 Nm).

94. Install the fuel tube bracket bolt to the upper intake manifold. Tighten to 53 inch lbs. (6 Nm).

95. Install the upper intake manifold support bracket bolt. Tighten to 89 inch lbs. (10 Nm).

96. Attach the wiring harness retainers to the upper intake manifold.

97. Connect the Throttle Body (TB) electrical connector.

98. Connect the PCV hose to the PCV valve.

99. If equipped, connect the block heater electrical connector and install the heat shield.

100. Attach all the engine block heater wiring harness retainer.

101. Using the Heavy Duty Floor Crane and Spreader Bar, remove the engine from the stand.

102. Install the crankshaft sensor ring.

103. Install the flexplate and the 8 bolts. Tighten to 59 ft. lbs. (80 Nm).

104. Install the engine in the vehicle.

OIL PUMP

REMOVAL & INSTALLATION

See Figures 122 and 123.

WARNING

During engine repair procedures, cleanliness is extremely important. Any foreign material, including any material created while cleaning gasket surfaces, that enters the oil passages, coolant passages or the oil pan may cause engine failure.

On early build engines, the timing chain rides on the inner side of the right-hand timing chain guide. Late build engines are equipped with a different design right-hand timing chain guide that requires the timing chain to ride on the outer side of the right-hand timing chain guide. For service, all replacement right-hand timing chain guides will be the late build design.

1. Remove the engine front cover. Refer to Timing Chain Front Cover Removal & Installation.
2. Remove the following components. Refer to Timing Chain Removal & Installation:
   a. Rotate the crankshaft clockwise and align the timing marks on the Variable Camshaft Timing (VCT) assemblies.
   b. Install the Camshaft Holding Tool onto the flats of the left-hand and right-hand camshafts.
   c. Remove the bolts and the right-hand and left-hand VCT housing.
   d. Remove the 2 bolts and the primary timing chain tensioner.
   e. Remove the primary timing chain tensioner arm.
   f. Remove the 2 bolts and the lower left-hand primary timing chain guide.
   g. Remove the primary timing chain.
   h. Remove the crankshaft timing chain sprocket.
3. Remove the 2 bolts and the oil pump screen and pickup tube. Discard the O-ring seal.
4. Remove the 3 bolts and the oil pump.

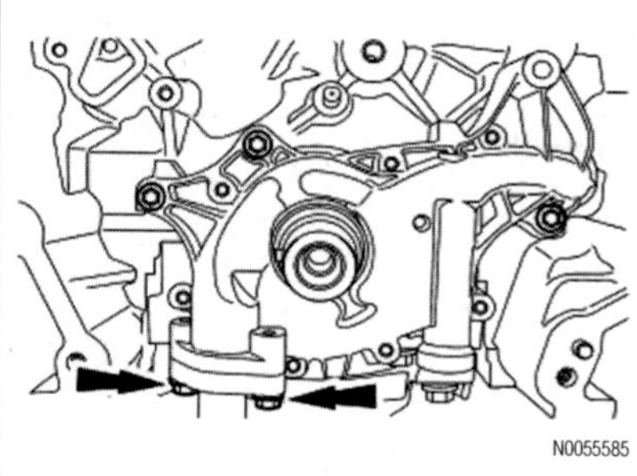

Fig. 122 Remove the 2 bolts and the oil pump screen and pickup tube

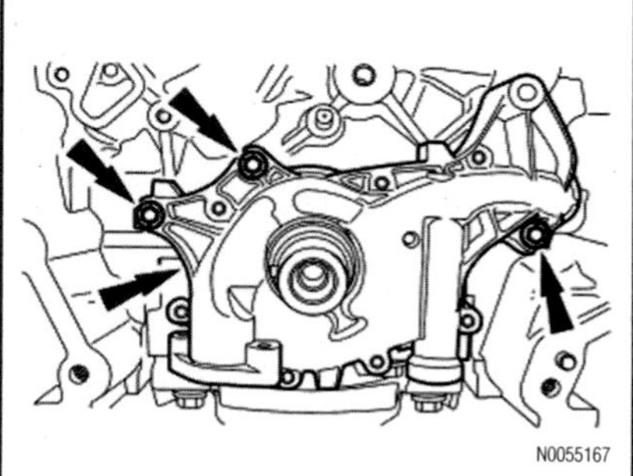

Fig. 123 Remove the 2 bolts and the oil pump screen and pickup tube

To install:

5. Install the oil pump and the 3 bolts. Tighten to 89 inch lbs. (10 Nm).
6. Using a new O-ring seal, install the oil pump screen and pickup tube and the 2 bolts. Tighten to 89 inch lbs. (10 Nm).
7. Install the following components. Refer to Timing Chain Removal & Installation:
   a. Install the crankshaft timing chain sprocket.
   b. Install the primary timing chain with the colored links aligned with the timing marks on the VCT assemblies and the crankshaft sprocket.
   c. Install the left-hand primary timing chain guide and tighten the 2 bolts to 89 inch lbs. (10 Nm).
   d. Install the primary timing chain tensioner arm.
   e. Reset the primary timing chain tensioner.
   f. Install the primary tensioner and tighten the 2 bolts to 89 inch lbs. (10 Nm). Remove the lockpin.
   g. Verify correct alignment of all timing marks.
   h. Inspect the VCT housing seals for damage and replace as necessary. Install the right-hand and left-hand VCT housing and the bolts.
8. Install the engine front cover.

PISTON AND RING

POSITIONING

See Figure 124.

The piston compression upper and lower ring should be installed with the "O" mark on the ring face pointing up toward the top of the piston.

Install the piston rings onto the piston as shown.

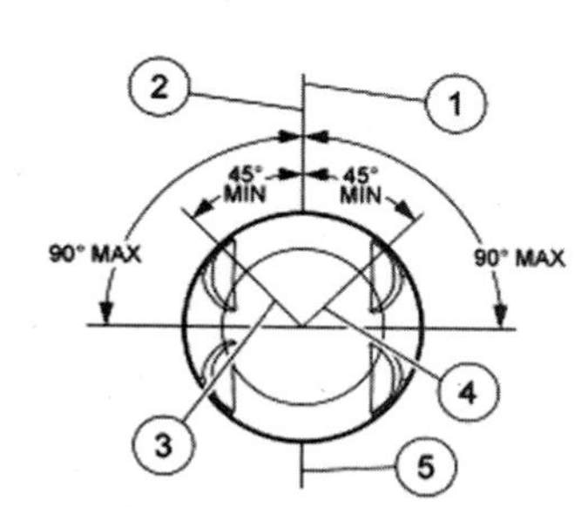

1. Center line of the piston parallel to the wrist pin bore
2. Upper compression ring gap location
3. Upper oil control segment ring gap location
4. Lower oil control segment ring gap location
5. Expander ring and lower compression ring gap location

N0082432

Fig. 124 Piston and ring positioning

REAR MAIN SEAL

REMOVAL & INSTALLATION

See Figures 125 and 126.

1. With the vehicle in NEUTRAL, position it on a hoist.
2. Remove the transaxle.
3. Remove the 8 bolts and the flexplate.
4. Remove the crankshaft sensor ring.
5. Using the Crankshaft Rear Oil Seal Remover and Slide Hammer (SST 303-519, 307-005) or equivalent tools, remove and discard the rear crankshaft seal.
   a. Clean all sealing surfaces with metal surface prep.

To install:

6. Lubricate the seal lips and bore with clean engine oil prior to installation. Position the Rear Main Seal Installer onto the end of the crankshaft and slide a new crankshaft rear seal onto the tool.
7. Using the Rear Main Seal Installer and Handle (SST 303-1250, 205-153) or

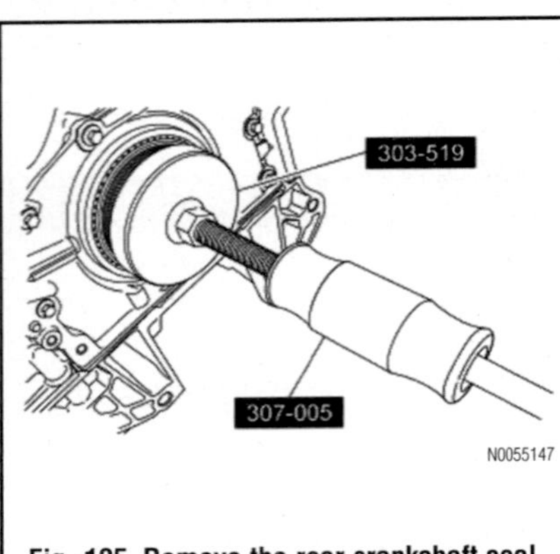

Fig. 125 Remove the rear crankshaft seal

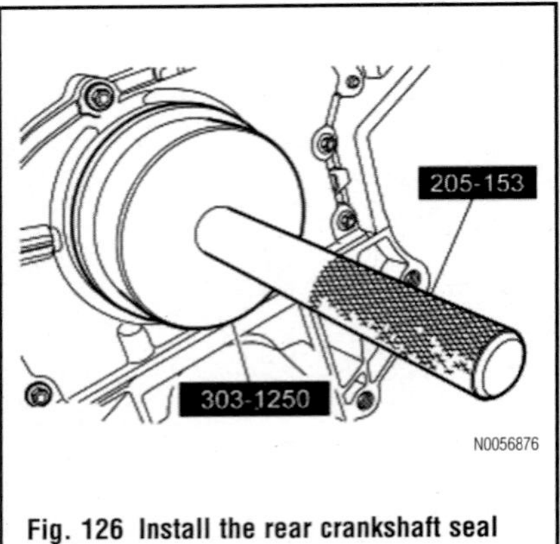

Fig. 126 Install the rear crankshaft seal

equivalent tools, install the new crankshaft rear seal.

8. Install the crankshaft sensor ring.
9. Install the flexplate and the 8 bolts. Tighten to 59 ft. lbs. (80 Nm).
10. Install the transaxle.

TIMING CHAIN FRONT COVER

REMOVAL & INSTALLATION

3.5L Engines

See Figures 127 through 135.

✲✲ WARNING

During engine repair procedures, cleanliness is extremely important. Any foreign material, including any material created while cleaning gasket surfaces, that enters the oil passages, coolant passages or the oil pan may cause engine failure.

➡On early build engines, the timing chain rides on the inner side of the right-hand timing chain guide. Late build engines are equipped with a different design right-hand timing chain guide that requires the timing chain to ride on the outer side of the right-hand timing chain guide. For service, all replacement right-hand timing chain guides will be the late build design.

1. With the vehicle in NEUTRAL, position it on a hoist.
2. Disconnect the left-hand Heated Oxygen Sensor (HO2S) electrical connector.
3. Detach the HO2S connector retainer from the bracket.
4. For late build vehicles, remove the intake manifold.
5. Remove the left-hand and right-hand valve cover.
6. Remove the 4 retainers and the underbody shield.
7. Remove the right-hand inner fender splash shield.
8. Remove the accessory drive belt and tensioner.
9. Loosen the 3 bolts on the rear roll restrictor.
10. Loosen the bolt on each side of the front roll restrictor.
11. Remove the oil pan drain plug and drain the engine oil. Install the drain plug and tighten to 27 Nm (20 lb-ft).
12. Remove the crankshaft bolt and washer. Discard the bolt. Remove the crankshaft pulley, and remove and discard the crankshaft front seal. Refer to Crankshaft Front Seal Removal & Installation.
13. Remove the engine mount.
14. Using only hand tools, remove the 2 engine mount studs.
15. Detach the right-hand Heated Oxygen Sensor (HO2S) electrical connector from the bracket. Remove the stud bolt and the bracket.
16. Using the floor jack, raise the engine slightly.
17. Remove the 2 upper engine mount bracket bolts.
18. Using the floor jack, lower the engine slightly.
19. Loosen the lower engine mount bracket bolt and remove the engine mount bracket and bolt as an assembly.
20. Remove the 22 engine front cover bolts.
21. Install 6 of the engine front cover bolts (finger tight) into the 6 threaded holes in the engine front cover.
    a. Tighten the bolts one turn at a time in a crisscross pattern until the engine front cover-to-cylinder block seal is released.
    b. Remove the engine front cover.

To install:

✲✲ WARNING

Only use a 3M® Roloc® Bristle Disk (2 in white, part number 07528), to clean the engine front cover. Do not use metal scrapers, wire brushes or any other power abrasive disk to clean the engine front cover.

22. Clean the engine front cover using a 3M® Roloc® Bristle Disk in a suitable tool turning at the recommended speed of 15,000 rpm. Thoroughly wash the engine front cover to remove any foreign material, including any abrasive particles created during the cleaning process.

✲✲ WARNING

Place clean, lint free shop towels over exposed engine cavities. Carefully remove the towels so foreign material is not dropped into the engine. Any foreign material (including any material created while cleaning gasket surfaces) that enters the oil passages or the oil pan, may cause engine failure.

23. Clean the sealing surfaces of the cylinder heads, the cylinder block and the oil pan. Refer to Cylinder Head Removal & Installation.

Fig. 127 Loosen the 3 bolts on the rear roll restrictor

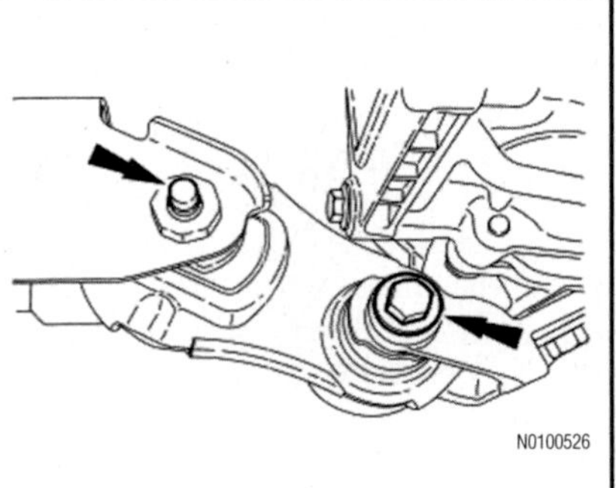

Fig. 128 Loosen the bolt on each side of the front roll restrictor

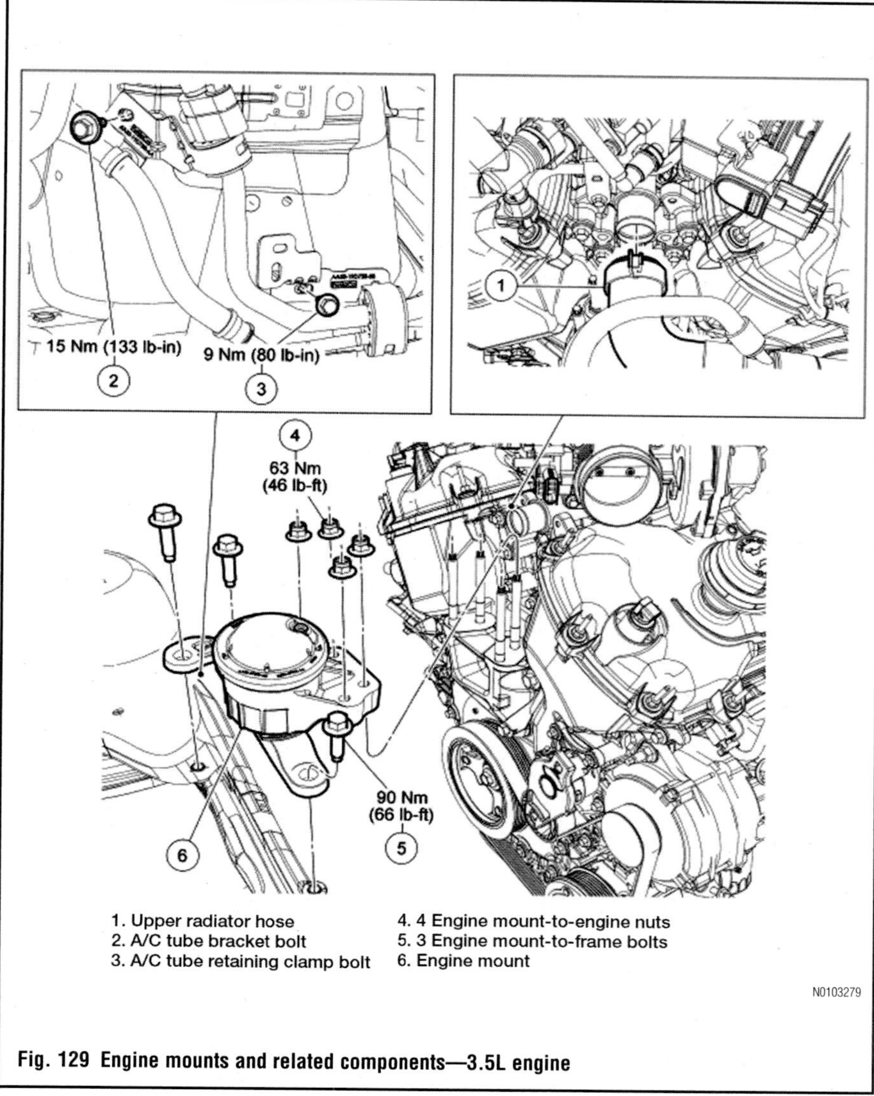

Fig. 129 Engine mounts and related components—3.5L engine

24. Make sure the 2 locating dowel pins are seated correctly in the cylinder block.
25. Install the Alignment Pins.

⁂ WARNING

Failure to use the correct RTV Silicone Sealant (TA-357) may cause the engine oil to foam excessively and result in serious engine damage.

26. Apply a 0.11 in. (3.0 mm) bead of RTV Silicone Sealant (TA-357) to the engine front cover sealing surfaces including the 3 engine mount bracket bosses.
    a. Apply a 0.21 in. (5.5 mm) bead of RTV Silicone Sealant (TA-357) to the oil pan-to-cylinder block joint and the cylinder head-to-cylinder block joint areas of the engine front cover in 5 places as indicated.
27. Install the engine front cover and bolts 17, 18, 19 and 20.

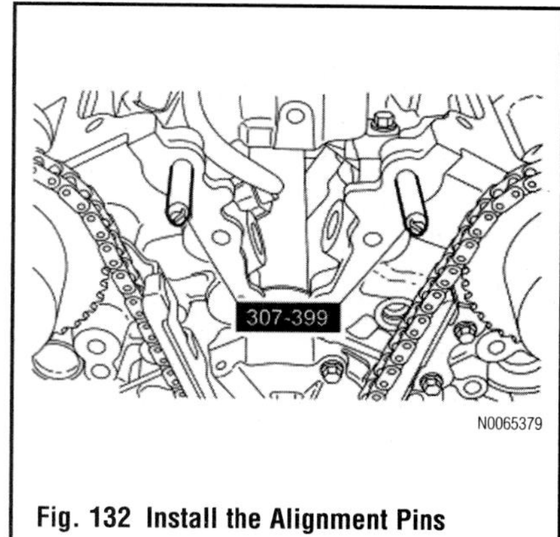

Fig. 132 Install the Alignment Pins

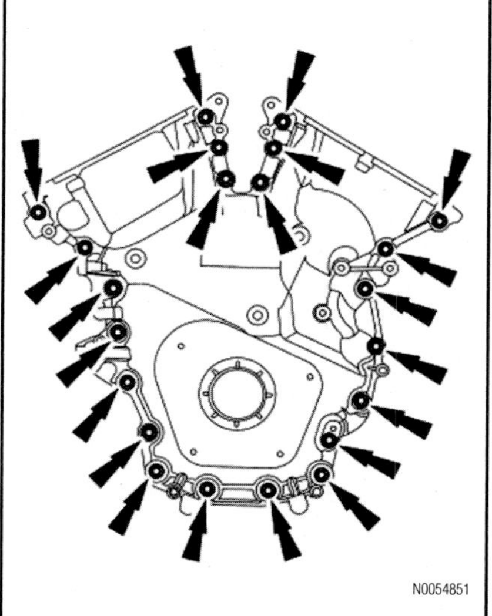

Fig. 130 Remove the 22 engine front cover bolts

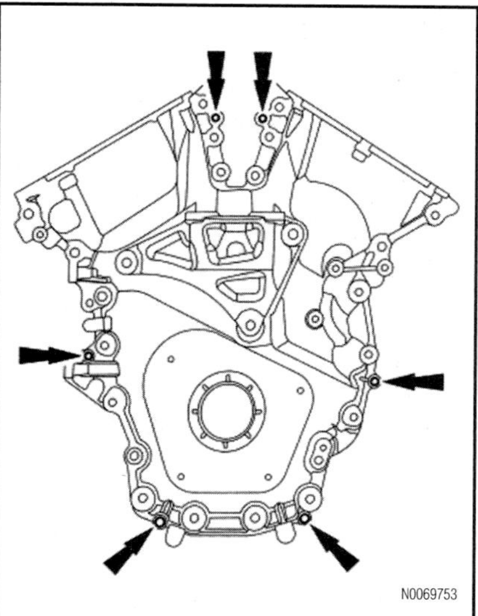

Fig. 131 Install 6 of the engine front cover bolts into the 6 threaded holes in the engine front cover

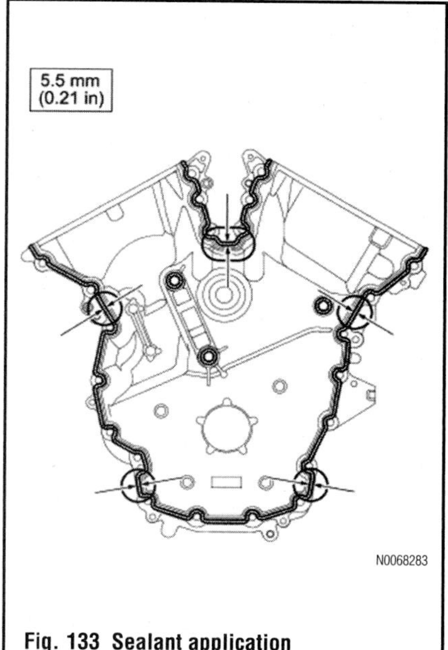

Fig. 133 Sealant application

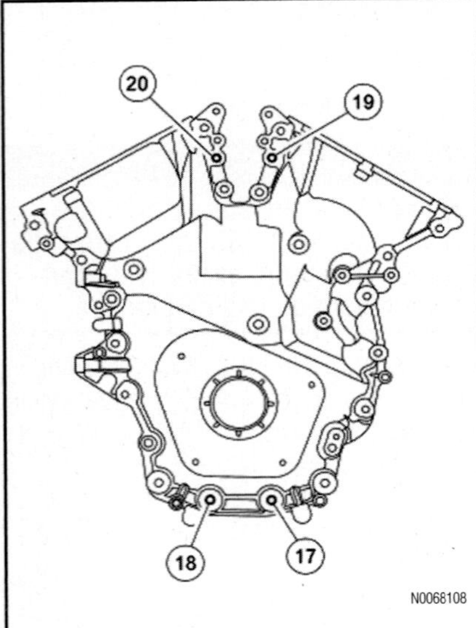

Fig. 134 Tighten bolts 17, 18, 19 and 20 in sequence

a. The engine front cover and bolts 17, 18, 19 and 20 must be installed within 4 minutes of the initial sealant application. The remainder of the engine front cover bolts and the engine mount bracket bolts must be installed and tightened within 35 minutes of the initial sealant application. If the time limits are exceeded, the sealant must be removed, the sealing area cleaned and sealant reapplied. To clean the sealing area, use silicone gasket remover and metal surface prep.

b. Make sure the 2 locating dowel pins are seated correctly in the cylinder block.

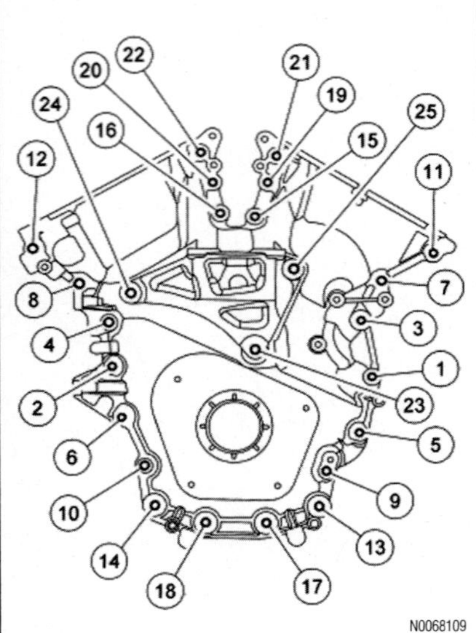

Fig. 135 Engine front cover bolt tightening sequence

c. Tighten in sequence to 27 inch lbs. (3 Nm).

28. Remove the Alignment Pins.

29. Install the engine mount bracket and lower bolt. Do not tighten at this time.

30. Using the floor jack, raise the engine slightly.

31. Install the 2 upper engine mount bracket bolts. Do not tighten at this time.

32. Install the remaining engine front cover bolts. Tighten all of the engine front cover bolts and engine mount bracket bolts in the sequence shown in 2 stages:

a. Stage 1: Tighten bolts 1 thru 22 to 89 inch lbs. (10 Nm) and bolts 23, 24 and 25 to 11 ft. lbs. (15 Nm).

b. Stage 2: Tighten bolts 1 thru 22 to 18 ft. lbs. (24 Nm) and bolts 23, 24 and 25 to 55 ft. lbs. (75 Nm).

c. Do not expose the RTV Silicone Sealant to engine oil for at least 90 minutes after installing the engine front cover. Failure to follow this instruction may cause oil leakage.

33. Install the HO2S connector bracket and stud bolt.

a. Tighten to 89 inch lbs. (10 Nm).

b. Attach the HO2S electrical connector.

WARNING

The thread sealer on the engine mount studs (including new engine mount studs if applicable) must be cleaned off with a wire brush and new Threadlock and Sealer applied prior to installing the engine mount studs. Failure to follow this procedure may result in damage to the engine mount studs or engine.

34. Install the engine mount studs in the following sequence.

a. Clean the front cover engine mount stud holes with pressurized air to remove any foreign material.

b. Clean all the thread sealer from the engine mount studs (old and new studs).

c. Apply new Threadlock and Sealer to the engine mount stud threads.

d. Install the 2 engine mount studs.

e. Tighten to 15 ft. lbs. (20 Nm).

35. Install the engine mount.

36. Install a new crankshaft front seal. Install the crankshaft pulley, crankshaft pulley washer, and new bolt.

37. Tighten the bolt on each side of the front roll restrictor. Tighten to 66 ft. lbs. (90 Nm).

38. Tighten the 3 bolts on the rear roll restrictor. Tighten to 66 ft. lbs. (90 Nm).

39. Install the accessory drive belt tensioner and belt.

40. Install the right-hand inner fender splash shield.

41. Install the underbody shield and the 4 retainers.

42. Install the right-hand and left-hand valve covers.

43. For late build vehicles, install the intake manifold.

44. Connect the left-hand HO2S electrical connector. Attach the HO2S connector retainer to the bracket.

45. Fill the engine with clean engine oil.

3.7L Engines

See Figures 136 through 144.

WARNING

During engine repair procedures, cleanliness is extremely important. Any foreign material, including any material created while cleaning gasket surfaces, that enters the oil passages, coolant passages or the oil pan may cause engine failure.

1. With the vehicle in NEUTRAL, position it on a hoist.
2. Recover the A/C system.
3. Remove the Air Cleaner (ACL) outlet pipe.
4. Remove the front wheels and tires.
5. Remove the accessory drive belt, tensioner and the power steering belt.
6. Remove the degas bottle.
7. Remove the Evaporative Emission (EVAP) canister purge valve.
8. Remove the nut and disconnect the A/C tube. Discard the O-ring seal and gasket seal.
9. Remove the nut and the A/C tube-to-receiver/drier. Discard the O-ring seal and gasket seal.
10. Disconnect the power steering cooler tube and drain the power steering fluid into a suitable container.
11. Remove the right-hand inner fender splash shield.
12. Remove the crankshaft bolt and washer. Discard the bolt. Remove the crankshaft pulley, and remove and discard the crankshaft front seal. Refer to Crankshaft Front Seal Removal & Installation.
13. Remove the 4 Y-pipe-to-catalytic converter nuts. Discard the nuts.
14. Remove the 2 Y-pipe flange nuts.

a. Detach the exhaust hanger and remove the Y-pipe.

b. Discard the gaskets and nuts.

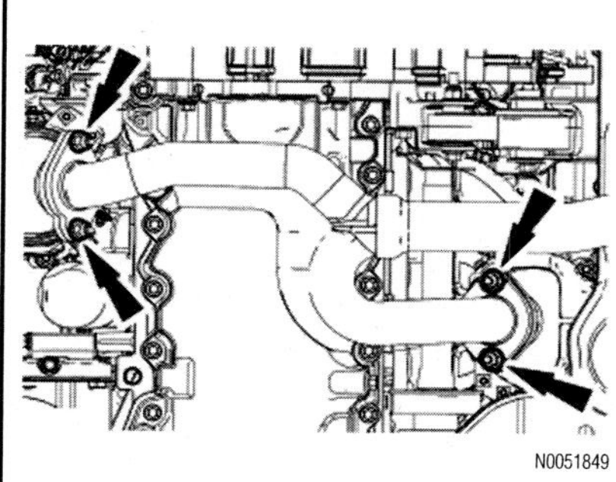
Fig. 136 Remove the 4 Y-pipe-to-catalytic converter nuts

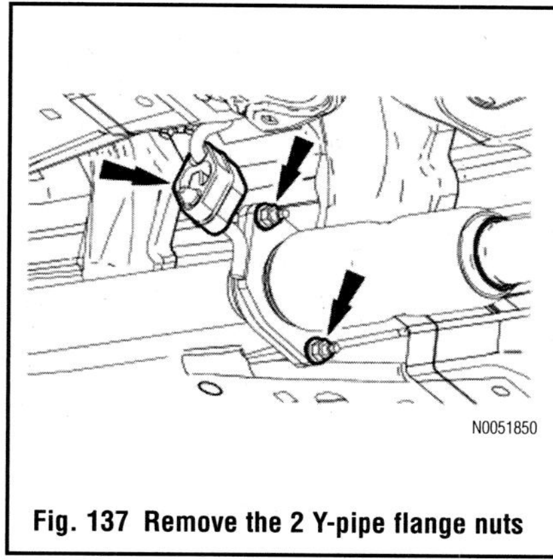
Fig. 137 Remove the 2 Y-pipe flange nuts

15. Remove the drain plug and drain the engine oil. Install the drain plug and tighten to 20 ft. lbs. (27 Nm).
16. Disconnect the hose from the power steering reservoir.
17. Remove the right-hand and left-hand valve covers.
18. Remove the bolt and the ground cable.
19. Disconnect the power steering pressure switch electrical connector.
20. Remove the power steering pressure tube bracket-to-power steering pump bolt.
21. Remove the 3 bolts and position aside the power steering pump.
22. Position a floor jack and the Oil Pan Holding Fixture under the oil pan. The Oil Pan Holding Fixture must be carefully aligned to the mounting bosses on the oil pan.
23. Remove the nut, bolt and engine mount brace.
24. Remove the 4 engine mount nuts.
25. Remove the 3 bolts and the engine mount.
26. Remove the 2 bolts and the engine mount bracket.
27. Using hand tools, remove the 2 engine mount studs.

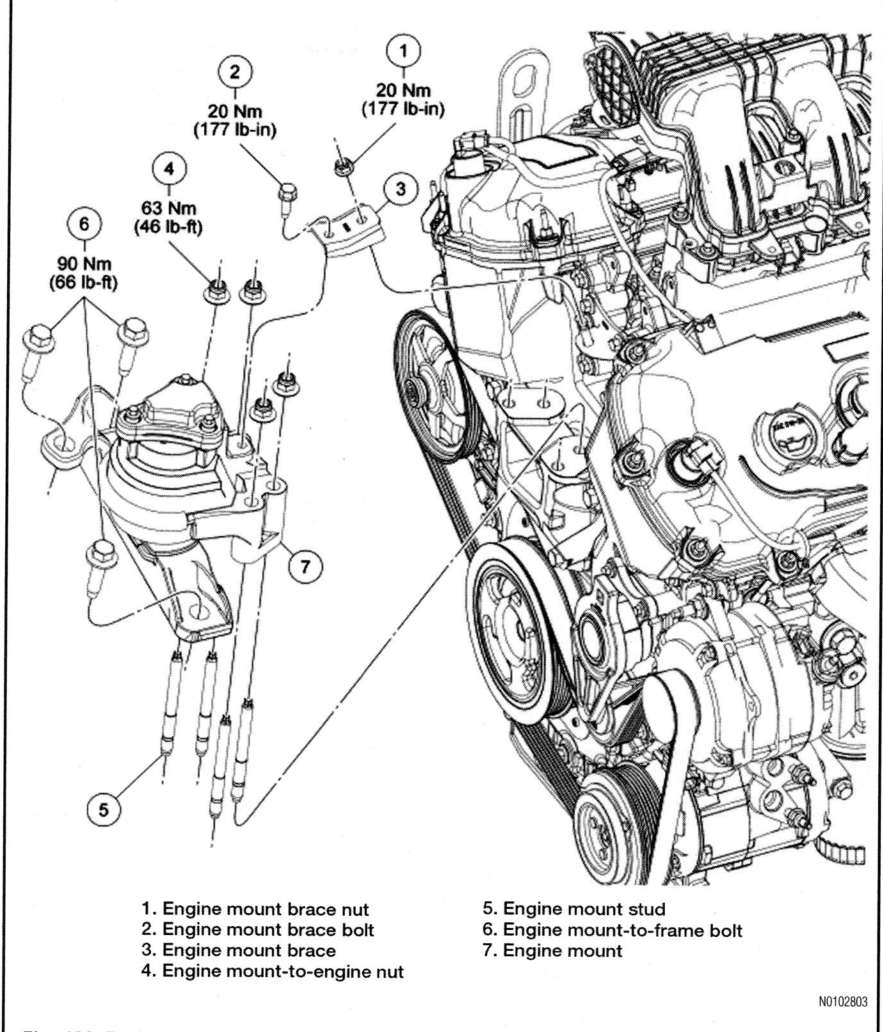

Fig. 138 Engine mounts and related components—3.7L engine

28. Remove the 2 upper engine mount bracket bolts.
29. Loosen the lower engine mount bracket bolt and remove the engine mount bracket and bolt as an assembly.
30. Detach the A/C tube and wiring harness from the retainers.
31. Remove the A/C tube bracket bolt.
32. Remove the A/C tube retaining clamp bolt.
33. Remove the A/C tube-to-evaporator bolt and the 2 A/C tubes. Discard the O-ring seals.
34. Using the floor jack, raise the engine slightly.
35. Remove the 22 engine front cover bolts.
36. Install 6 of the engine front cover bolts (finger tight) into the 6 threaded holes in the engine front cover.
   a. Tighten the bolts one turn at a time in a crisscross pattern until the engine

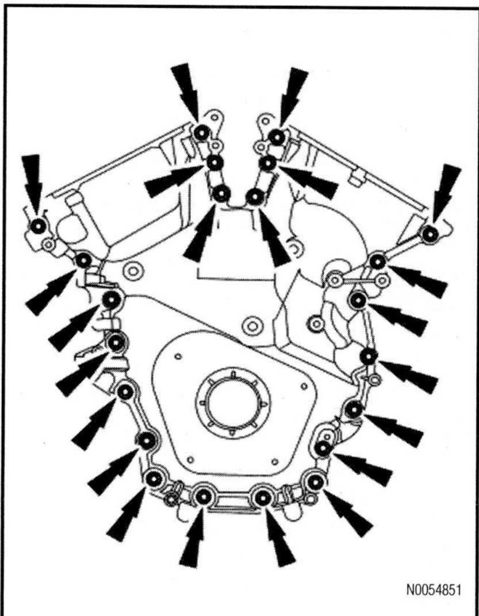
Fig. 139 Remove the 22 engine front cover bolts

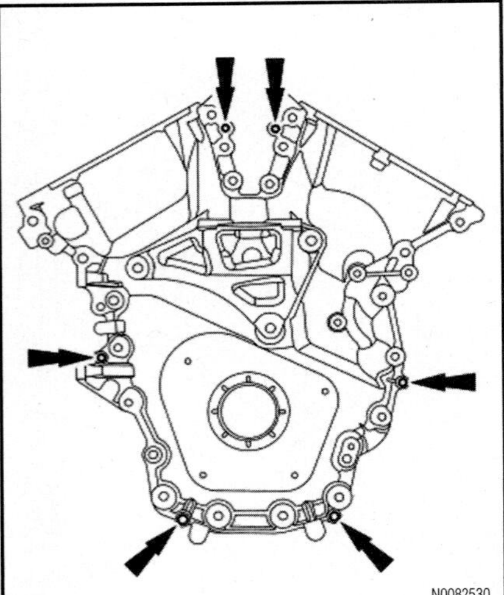

Fig. 140 Install 6 of the engine front cover bolts into the 6 threaded holes in the engine front cover

front cover-to-cylinder block seal is released.

b. Remove the engine front cover.

To install:

⁂ WARNING

Only use a 3M® Roloc® Bristle Disk (2-in white, part number 07528) to clean the engine front cover. Do not use metal scrapers, wire brushes or any other power abrasive disk to clean the engine front cover. These tools cause scratches and gouges that make leak paths.

37. Clean the engine front cover using a 3M® Roloc® Bristle Disk in a suitable tool turning at the recommended speed of 15,000 rpm.

a. Thoroughly wash the engine front cover to remove any foreign material, including any abrasive particles created during the cleaning process.

⁂ WARNING

Place clean, lint-free shop towels over exposed engine cavities. Carefully remove the towels so foreign material is not dropped into the engine. Any foreign material (including any material created while cleaning gasket surfaces) that enters the oil passages or the oil pan may cause engine failure.

38. Clean the sealing surfaces of the cylinder heads, the cylinder block and the oil pan. Refer to Cylinder Head Removal & Installation.

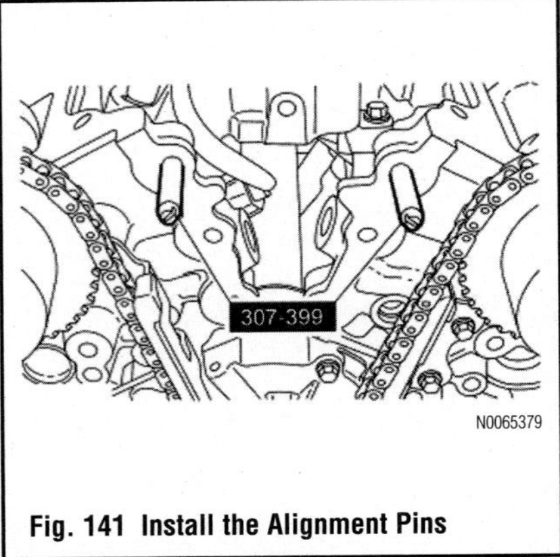

Fig. 141 Install the Alignment Pins

39. Make sure the 2 locating dowel pins are seated correctly in the cylinder block.

40. Install the Alignment Pins.

⁂ WARNING

Failure to use Motorcraft® High Performance Engine RTV Silicone may cause the engine oil to foam excessively and result in serious engine damage.

41. Apply a 0.11 in. (3.0 mm) bead of Motorcraft® High Performance Engine RTV Silicone to the engine front cover sealing surfaces including the 3 engine mount bracket bosses.

a. Apply a 0.21 in. (5.5 mm) bead of Motorcraft® High Performance Engine RTV Silicone to the oil pan-to-cylinder block joint and the cylinder head-to-cylinder block joint areas of the engine front cover in 5 places as indicated.

b. The engine front cover and bolts 17, 18, 19 and 20 must be installed within 4 minutes of the initial sealant application. The remainder of the engine front cover bolts and the engine mount bracket bolts must be installed and tightened within 35 minutes of the initial sealant application. If the time limits are exceeded, the sealant must be removed, the sealing area cleaned and sealant reapplied. To clean the sealing area, use silicone gasket remover and metal surface prep.

42. Install the engine front cover and bolts 17, 18, 19 and 20. Make sure the 2 locating dowel pins are seated correctly in the cylinder block. Tighten in sequence to 27 inch lbs. (3 Nm).

43. Remove the Alignment Pins.

44. Install the engine mount bracket and lower bolt. Do not tighten at this time.

45. Install the 2 upper engine mount bracket bolts. Do not tighten at this time.

46. Install the remaining engine front cover bolts. Tighten all of the engine front cover bolts and engine mount bracket bolts in the sequence shown in 2 stages:

a. Stage 1: Tighten bolts 1 thru 22 to 89 inch lbs. (10 Nm) and bolts 23, 24 and 25 to 11 ft. lbs. (15 Nm).

b. Stage 2: Tighten bolts 1 thru 22 to 18 ft. lbs. (24 Nm) and bolts 23, 24 and 25 to 55 ft. lbs. (75 Nm).

c. Do not expose the Motorcraft® High Performance Engine RTV Silicone to engine oil for at least 90 minutes after installing the engine front cover.

47. Using the floor jack, lower the engine to the installed position.

48. Install the new O-ring seals and the A/C tubes-to-evaporator and the bolt. Tighten to 71 inch lbs. (8 Nm).

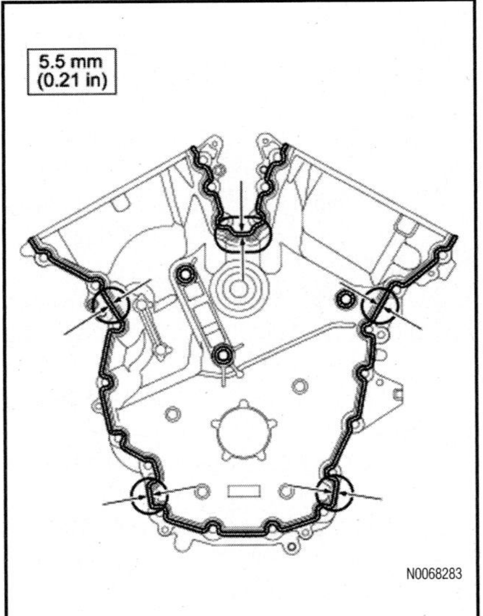

Fig. 142 Sealant application

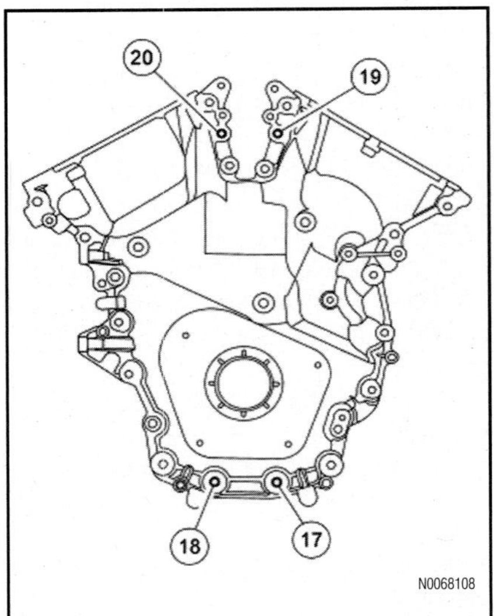

Fig. 143 Tighten bolts 17, 18, 19 and 20 in sequence

49. Install the A/C tube retaining clamp bolt. Tighten to 80 inch lbs. (9 Nm).

50. Install the A/C tube bracket bolt. Tighten to 11 ft. lbs. (15 Nm).

51. Attach the A/C tube and wiring harness to the retainers.

✱✱ WARNING

The thread sealer on the engine mount studs (including new engine mount studs if applicable) must be cleaned off with a wire brush and new Threadlock and Sealer applied prior to installing the engine mount studs. Failure to follow this procedure may result in damage to the engine mount studs or engine.

52. Install the engine mount studs in the following sequence.

a. Clean the front cover engine mount stud holes with pressurized air to remove any foreign material.

b. Clean all the thread sealer from the engine mount studs (old and new studs).

c. Apply new Threadlock and Sealer to the engine mount stud threads.

d. Install the 2 engine mount studs. Tighten to 15 ft. lbs. (20 Nm).

53. Install the engine mount bracket and the 2 bolts. Tighten to 18 ft. lbs. (24 Nm).

54. Install the engine mount and the 3 bolts. Tighten to 66 ft. lbs. (90 Nm).

55. Install the 4 engine mount nuts. Tighten to 46 ft. lbs. (63 Nm).

56. Install the engine mount brace, nut and bolt. Tighten to 15 ft. lbs. (20 Nm).

57. Position the power steering pump and install the 3 bolts. Tighten to 18 ft. lbs. (25 Nm).

58. Install the power steering pressure tube bracket-to-power steering pump bolt. Tighten to 89 inch lbs. (10 Nm).

59. Connect the power steering pressure switch electrical connector.

60. Install the ground cable bolt. Tighten to 106 inch lbs. (12 Nm).

61. Install the right-hand and left-hand valve covers.

62. Connect the hose to the power steering reservoir.

63. Using a new gasket, install the exhaust Y-pipe and install the 2 new nuts.

a. Tighten to 30 ft. lbs. (40 Nm).

b. Attach the exhaust hanger.

64. Install the exhaust Y-pipe assembly and 4 new nuts. Tighten to 30 ft. lbs. (40 Nm).

65. Install a new crankshaft front seal. Install the crankshaft pulley, crankshaft pulley washer, and new bolt.

66. Install the right-hand inner fender splash shield.

67. Connect the power steering cooler tube.

68. Using a new O-ring seal and gasket seal, install the A/C tube and the nut. Tighten to 11 ft. lbs. (15 Nm).

69. Using a new O-ring seal and gasket seal, connect the A/C tube and install the nut. Tighten to 11 ft. lbs. (15 Nm).

70. Install the EVAP canister purge valve.

71. Install the degas bottle.

72. Install the accessory drive belt, tensioner and the power steering belt.

73. Install the front wheels and tires.

74. Install the engine ACL outlet pipe.

75. Fill the engine with clean engine oil.

76. Fill the power steering system.

77. Recharge the A/C system.

TIMING CHAIN & SPROCKETS

REMOVAL & INSTALLATION

See Figures 145 through 163.

✱✱ WARNING

During engine repair procedures, cleanliness is extremely important. Any foreign material, including any material created while cleaning gasket surfaces, that enters the oil passages, coolant passages or the oil pan may cause engine failure.

➡On early build engines, the timing chain rides on the inner side of the right-hand timing chain guide. Late build engines are equipped with a different design right-hand timing chain guide that requires the timing chain to ride on the outer side of the right-hand timing chain guide. For service, all replacement right-hand timing chain guides will be the late build design.

1. Remove the engine front cover. Refer to Timing Chain Front Cover Removal & Installation.

2. Rotate the crankshaft clockwise and align the timing marks on the Variable Camshaft Timing (VCT) assemblies as shown.

3. Install the Camshaft Holding Tool (SST 303-1248) or equivalent tool onto the flats of the left-hand and right-hand camshafts. The tool will hold the camshafts in the Top Dead Center (TDC) position.

4. Remove the 3 bolts and the right-hand VCT housing.

5. Remove the 3 bolts and the left-hand VCT housing.

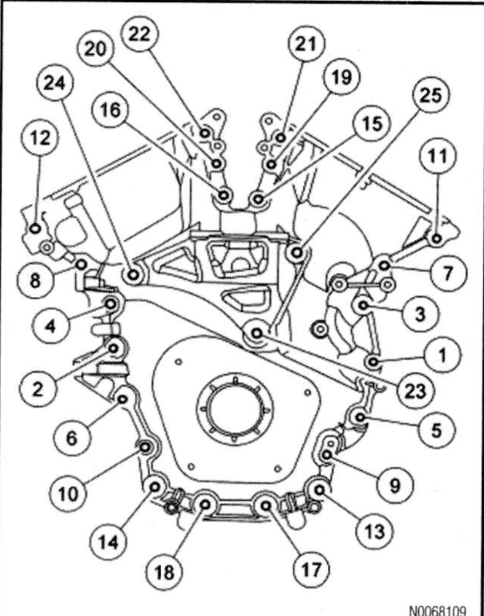

Fig. 144 Engine front cover bolt tightening sequence

Fig. 145 Rotate the crankshaft clockwise and align the timing marks on the VCT assemblies—early build vehicles

Fig. 146 Rotate the crankshaft clockwise and align the timing marks on the VCT assemblies—late build vehicles

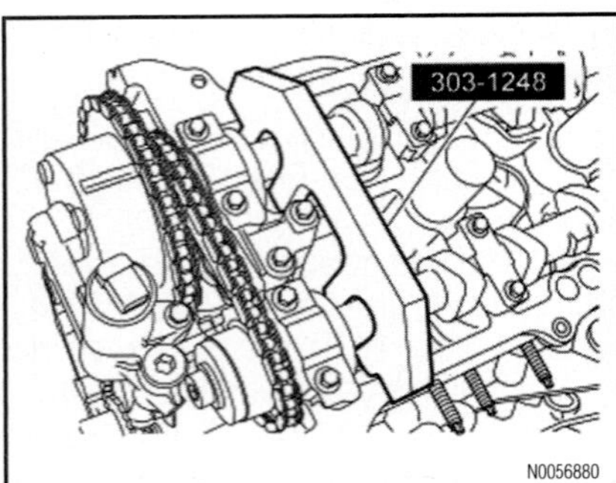

Fig. 147 Install the Camshaft Holding Tool onto the flats of the camshafts—left-hand shown, right-hand similar

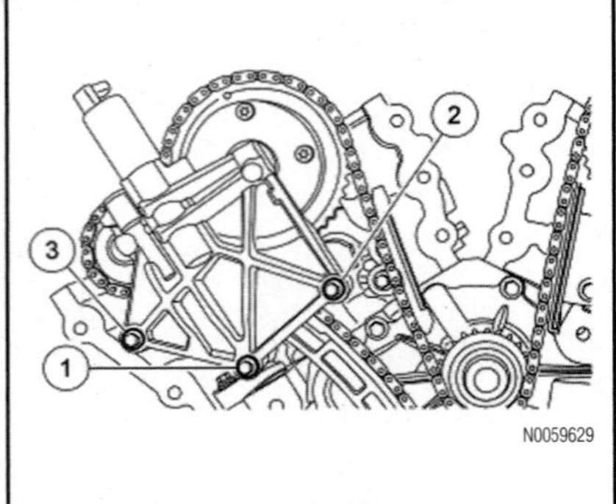

Fig. 148 Right-hand VCT housing bolt installation sequence

6. Remove the 2 bolts and the primary timing chain tensioner.

7. Remove the primary timing chain tensioner arm.

8. Remove the 2 bolts and the lower left-hand primary timing chain guide.

9. Remove the primary timing chain.

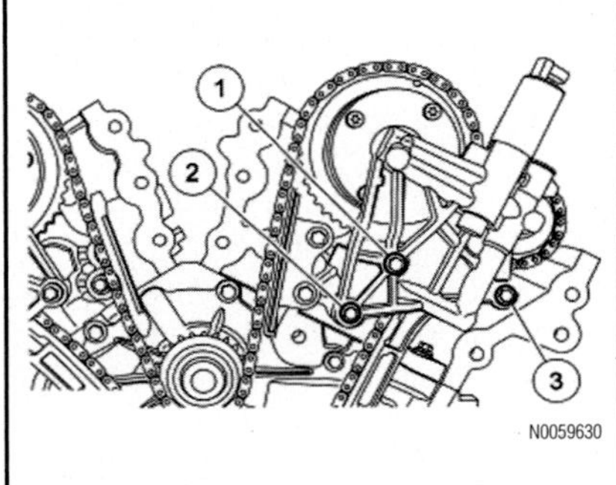

Fig. 149 Left-hand VCT housing bolt installation sequence

10. Remove the crankshaft timing chain sprocket.

11. Remove the 2 bolts and the upper left-hand primary timing chain guide.

12. Compress the left-hand secondary timing chain tensioner and install a suitable lockpin to retain the tensioner in the collapsed position.

13. Remove and discard the left-hand VCT assembly bolt and the left-hand exhaust camshaft sprocket bolt. The VCT bolt and the exhaust camshaft bolt must be discarded and new ones installed. However, the exhaust camshaft washer is reusable.

a. Remove the left-hand VCT assembly, secondary timing chain and the left-hand exhaust camshaft sprocket as an assembly.

14. Remove the 2 bolts and the left-hand secondary timing chain tensioner. It is necessary to tilt the Camshaft Holding Tool toward the rear of the engine to access the rearmost secondary timing chain tensioner bolt.

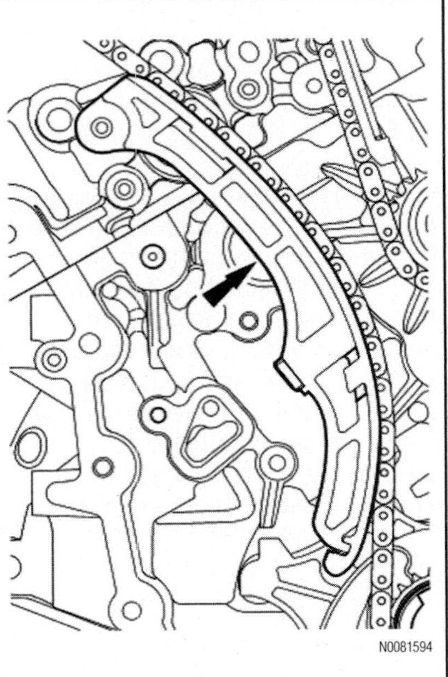
Fig. 150 Remove the primary timing chain tensioner arm

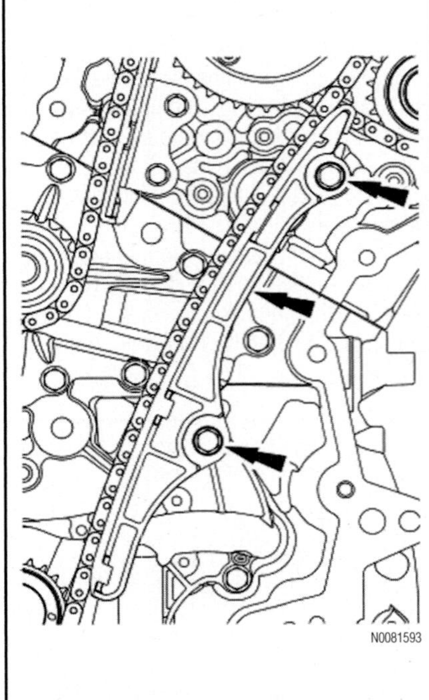
Fig. 151 Remove the 2 bolts and the lower left-hand primary timing chain guide

15. Compress the right-hand secondary timing chain tensioner and install a suitable lockpin to retain the tensioner in the collapsed position.

16. Remove and discard the right-hand VCT assembly bolt and the right-hand exhaust camshaft sprocket bolt. The VCT bolt and the exhaust camshaft bolt must be

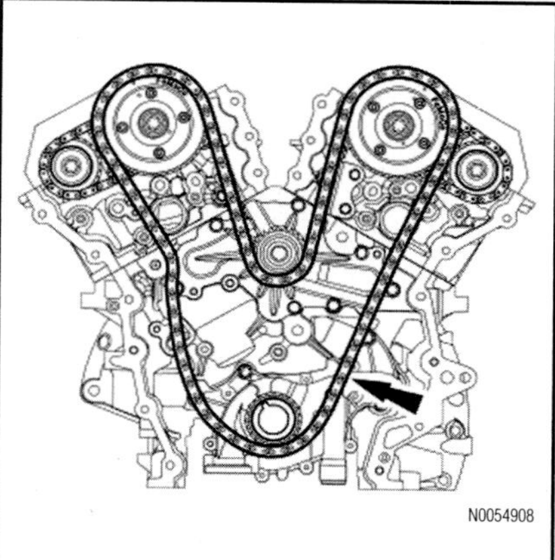
Fig. 152 Remove the primary timing chain

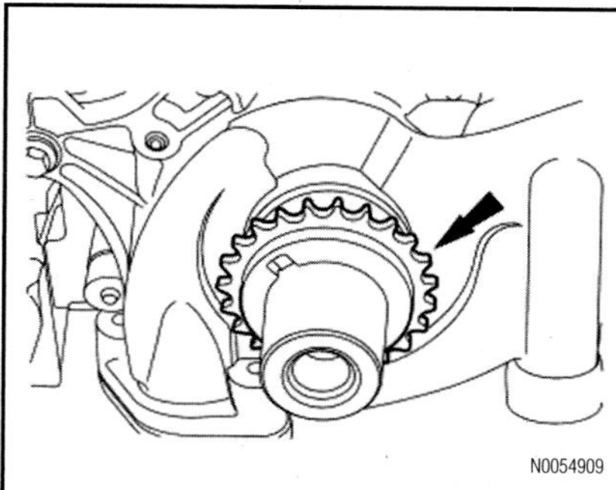
Fig. 153 Remove the crankshaft timing chain sprocket

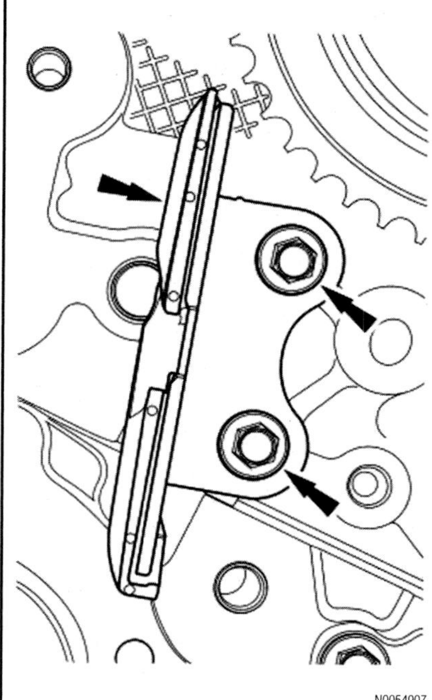
Fig. 154 Remove the 2 bolts and the upper left-hand primary timing chain guide

discarded and new ones installed. However, the exhaust camshaft washer is reusable.

a. Remove the right-hand VCT assembly, secondary timing chain and the right-hand exhaust camshaft sprocket as an assembly.

17. Remove the 2 bolts and the right-hand secondary timing chain tensioner. It is necessary to tilt the Camshaft Holding Tool toward the rear of the engine to access the rearmost secondary timing chain tensioner bolt.

18. Remove the 2 bolts and the right-hand primary timing chain guide.

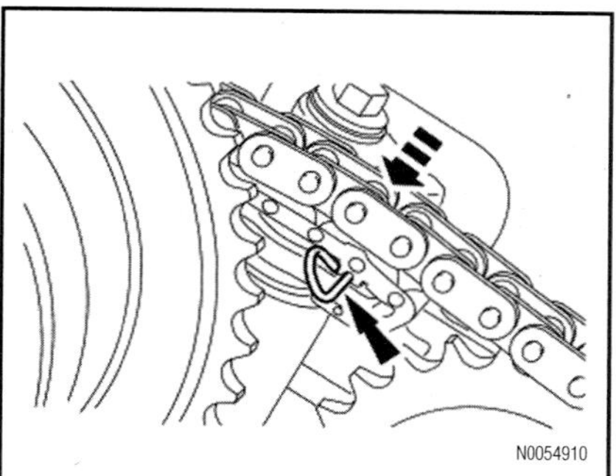
Fig. 155 Install a suitable lockpin to retain the left-hand secondary timing chain tensioner in the collapsed position

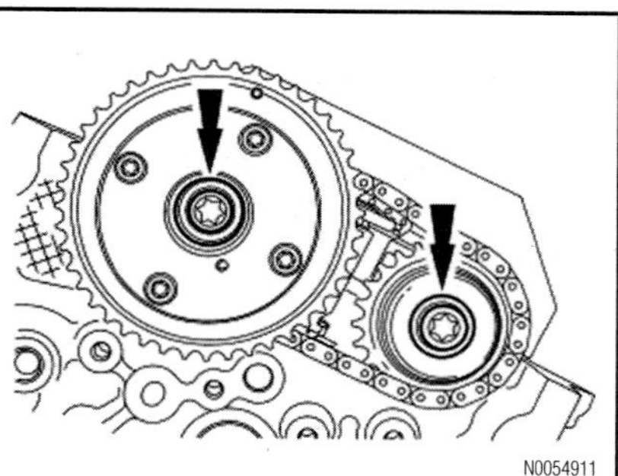
Fig. 156 Remove and discard the left-hand VCT assembly bolt and the left-hand exhaust camshaft sprocket bolt

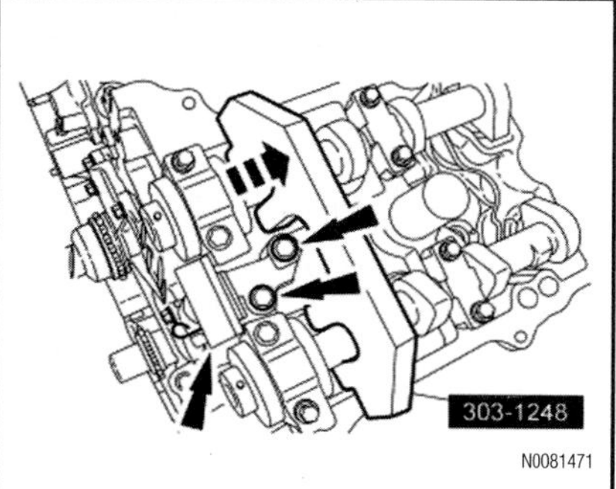

Fig. 157 Remove the 2 bolts and the left-hand secondary timing chain tensioner

To install:

19. Install the right-hand primary timing chain guide and the 2 bolts. Tighten to 89 inch lbs. (10 Nm).

20. Install the right-hand secondary timing chain tensioner and the 2 bolts. Tighten to 89 inch lbs. (10 Nm).

21. Assemble the right-hand VCT assembly, the right-hand exhaust camshaft sprocket and the right-hand secondary timing chain.

a. Align the colored links with the timing marks.

22. Position the right-hand secondary timing assembly onto the camshafts.

23. Install the new VCT bolt and new exhaust camshaft bolt and the original washer. Tighten in 4 stages.

a. Stage 1: Tighten to 30 ft. lbs. (40 Nm).

b. Stage 2: Loosen one full turn.

c. Stage 3: Tighten to 89 inch lbs. (10 Nm).

d. Stage 4: Tighten 90 degrees.

24. Remove the lockpin from the right-hand secondary timing chain tensioner.

25. Install the left-hand secondary timing chain tensioner and the 2 bolts. Tighten to 89 inch lbs. (10 Nm).

26. Assemble the left-hand VCT assembly, the left-hand exhaust camshaft sprocket and the left-hand secondary timing chain.

a. Align the colored links with the timing marks.

27. Position the left-hand secondary timing assembly onto the camshafts.

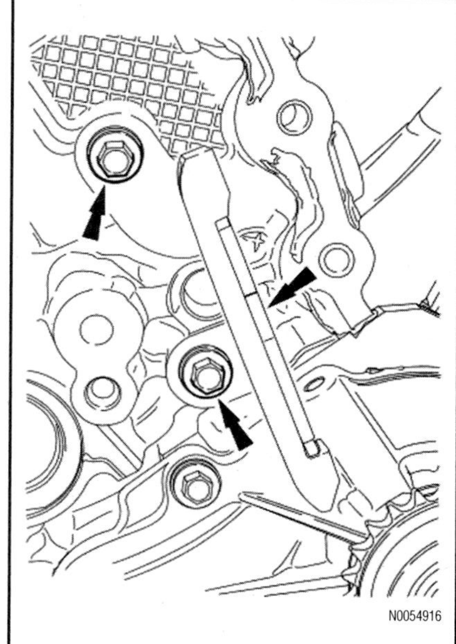
Fig. 158 Remove the 2 bolts and the right-hand primary timing chain guide—Early build vehicles

28. Install the new VCT bolt and new exhaust camshaft bolt and the original washer. Tighten in 4 stages.
   a. Stage 1: Tighten to 30 ft. lbs. (40 Nm).

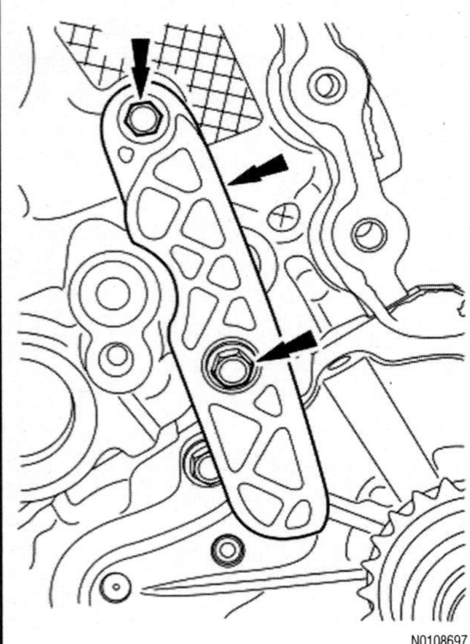

Fig. 159 Remove the 2 bolts and the right-hand primary timing chain guide—Late build vehicles

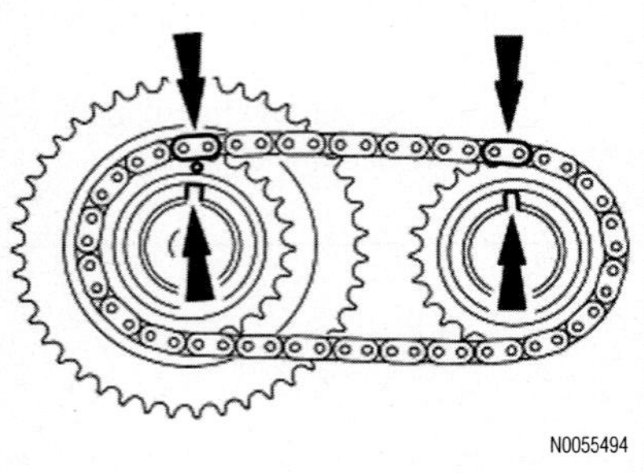

Fig. 160 Align the colored links with the timing marks—right-hand shown, left-hand similar

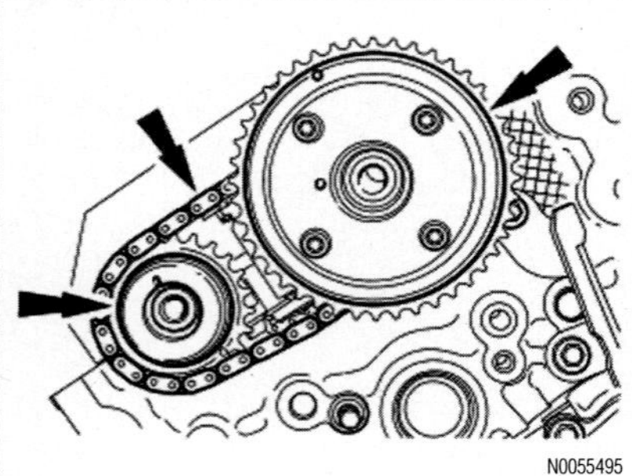

Fig. 161 Position the secondary timing assembly onto the camshafts—right-hand shown, left-hand similar

   b. Stage 2: Loosen one full turn.
   c. Stage 3: Tighten to 89 inch lbs. (10 Nm)
   d. Stage 4: Tighten 90 degrees.
29. Remove the lockpin from the left-hand secondary timing chain tensioner.
30. Install the crankshaft timing chain sprocket.
31. Install the primary timing chain with the colored links aligned with the timing marks on the VCT assemblies and the crankshaft sprocket.
32. Install the upper and lower left-hand primary timing chain guides and tighten the bolts to 89 inch lbs. (10 Nm).
33. Install the primary timing chain tensioner arm.

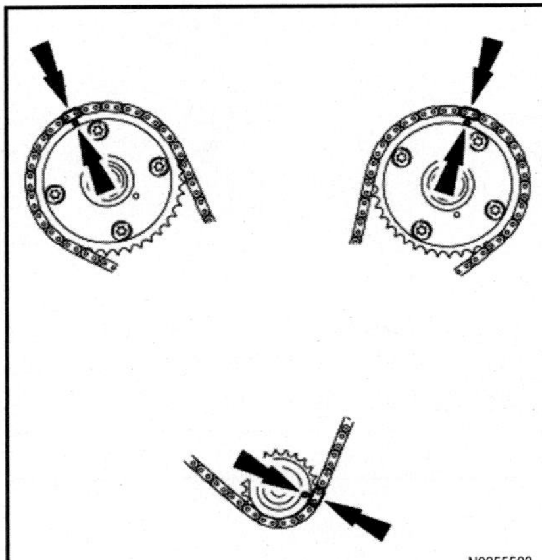

Fig. 162 Install the primary timing chain with the colored links aligned with the timing marks on the VCT assemblies and the crankshaft sprocket

Fig. 163 Reset the primary timing chain tensioner

34. Reset the primary timing chain tensioner.
   a. Rotate the lever counterclockwise.
   b. Using a soft-jawed vise, compress the plunger.
   c. Align the hole in the lever with the hole in the tensioner housing.
   d. Install a suitable lockpin.
35. Install the primary tensioner and the 2 bolts.
   a. Tighten to 89 inch lbs. (10 Nm).
   b. It may be necessary to rotate the crankshaft slightly to remove slack from the timing chain and install the tensioner.
   c. Remove the lockpin.
36. As a post-check, verify correct alignment of all timing marks.
37. Inspect the VCT housing seals for damage and replace as necessary.
38. Install the left-hand and right-hand VCT housing and bolts. Make sure the dowels on the VCT housing are fully engaged in the cylinder head prior to tightening the bolts. Tighten in the sequence shown above to 89 inch lbs. (10 Nm).
39. Install the engine front cover.

TURBOCHARGER

REMOVAL & INSTALLATION

Left-Hand

See Figures 164 through 170.

⁂ WARNING

Whenever turbocharger air intake system components are removed, always cover open ports to protect from debris. It is important that no foreign material enter the system. The turbocharger compressor vanes are susceptible to damage from even small particles. All components should be inspected and cleaned, if necessary, prior to installation or reassembly.

1. With the vehicle in NEUTRAL, position it on a hoist.
2. Remove the Air Cleaner (ACL) assembly.
3. Disconnect the wastegate control valve hose from the left-hand turbocharger assembly.
4. Remove the 2 bolts from the top of the left-hand exhaust manifold heat shield.
5. Loosen the clamp and remove the left-hand turbocharger intake tube from the turbocharger.
6. Remove the left-hand turbocharger oil supply tube bolt and sealing washer.

Discard the sealing washer and oil supply tube filter.

7. Drain the cooling system.

8. Remove the left-hand catalytic converter.

9. Remove the bottom bolt and the left-hand exhaust manifold heat shield.

10. Remove the 2 left-hand oil return tube-to-turbocharger bolts. Remove and discard the gasket.

14 Nm (124 lb-in)

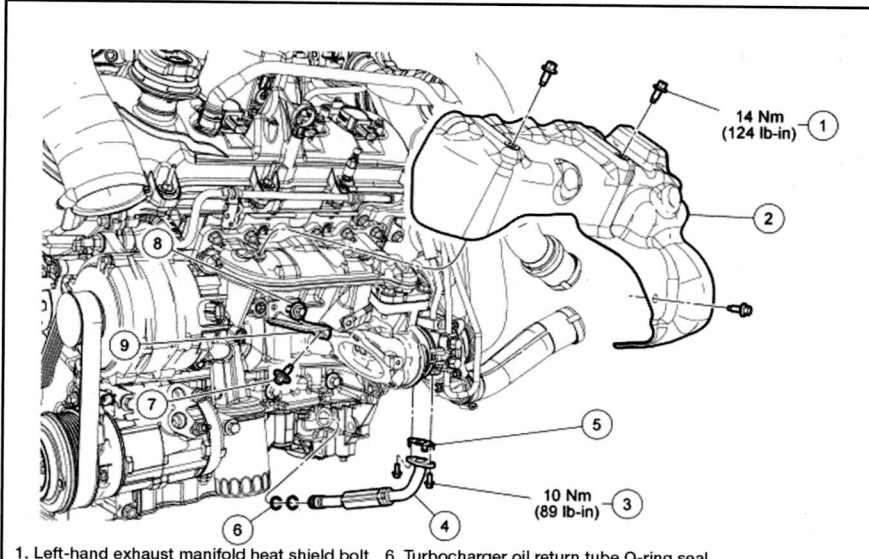

10 Nm (89 lb-in)

1. Left-hand exhaust manifold heat shield bolt
2. Left-hand exhaust manifold heat shield
3. Turbocharger oil return tube bolt
4. Turbocharger oil return tube
5. Turbocharger oil return tube gasket
6. Turbocharger oil return tube O-ring seal
7. Upper left-hand turbocharger bracket-to-turbocharger bolt
8. Upper left-hand turbocharger bracket-to-cylinder block bolt
9. Upper left-hand turbocharger bracket

N0106503

Fig. 164 Left-hand turbocharger components 1

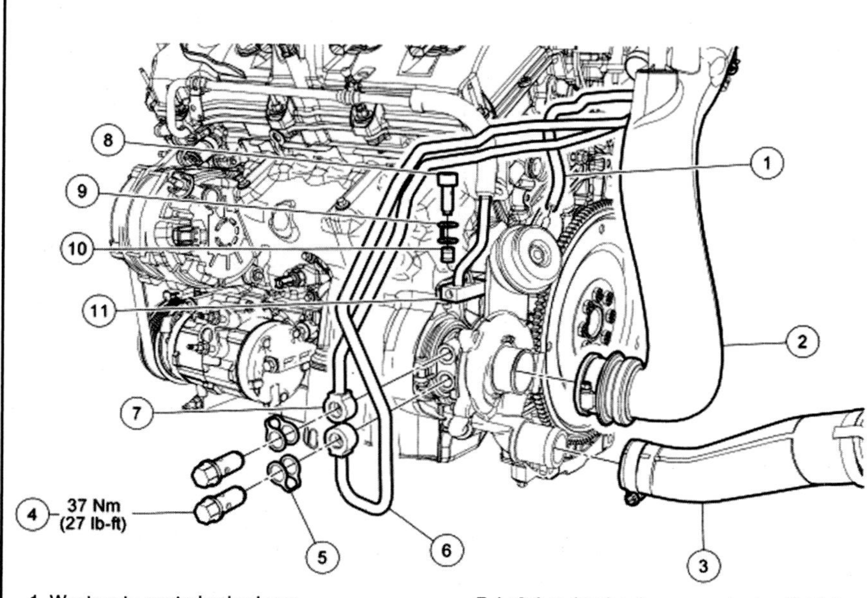

1. Wastegate control valve hose
2. Left-hand turbocharger intake tube
3. Left-hand Charge Air Cooler (CAC) tube
4. Coolant tube banjo bolt
5. Coolant tube sealing washer
6. Left-hand turbocharger coolant inlet tube
7. Left-hand turbocharger coolant outlet tube
8. Oil supply tube bolt
9. Oil supply tube sealing washer
10. Oil supply tube filter
11. Oil supply tube

N0106504

Fig. 165 Left-hand turbocharger components 2

11. Remove the left-hand turbocharger oil return tube from the oil pan. Discard the 2 O-ring seals.

12. Remove the 2 coolant tube banjo bolts and the left-hand turbocharger coolant tubes. Discard the sealing washers.

13. Loosen the clamp and remove the left-hand CAC tube from the left-hand turbocharger.

14. Remove the 3 exhaust manifold-to-left-hand turbocharger bolts. Discard the gasket and bolts.

15. Remove the 2 bolts and the lower left-hand turbocharger-to-cylinder block bracket.

16. Remove the upper left-hand turbocharger bracket-to-turbocharger bolt and the turbocharger assembly.

To install:

WARNING

The upper left-hand turbocharger bracket bolt must be loosened in order to perform the tightening sequence or damage to the turbocharger may occur.

17. Loosen the upper left-hand turbocharger bracket-to-cylinder block bolt.

18. Install a new left-hand exhaust manifold-to-turbocharger gasket.

19. Install the turbocharger assembly and install upper left-hand turbocharger bracket-to-turbocharger bolt. Do not tighten the bolts at this time.

20. Install the lower left-hand turbocharger-to-cylinder block bracket and the 2 bolts. Do not tighten the bolts at this time.

21. Install the 3 new left-hand exhaust manifold-to-turbocharger bolts. Tighten to 33 ft. lbs. (45 Nm).

22. The next 4 steps must be performed in the order written or damage to the turbocharger may occur:

a. Tighten the upper left-hand turbocharger bracket-to-turbocharger bolt to 14 ft. lbs. (19 Nm).

b. Tighten the upper left-hand turbocharger bracket-to-cylinder block bolt to 18 ft. lbs. (25 Nm).

c. Tighten the lower left-hand turbocharger bracket-to-turbocharger bolt to 14 ft. lbs. (19 Nm).

d. Tighten the lower left-hand turbocharger bracket-to-cylinder block bolt to 97 inch lbs. (11 Nm).

23. Install the left-hand CAC tube on the left-hand turbocharger and tighten the clamp. Align the marks for the left-hand CAC tube. Tighten to 44 inch lbs. (5 Nm).

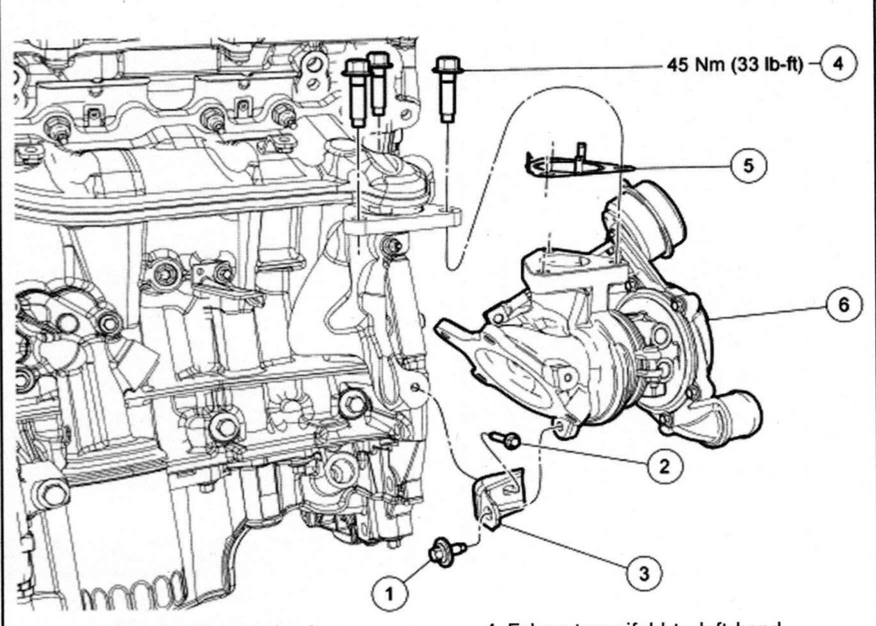

Fig. 166 Left-hand turbocharger components 3

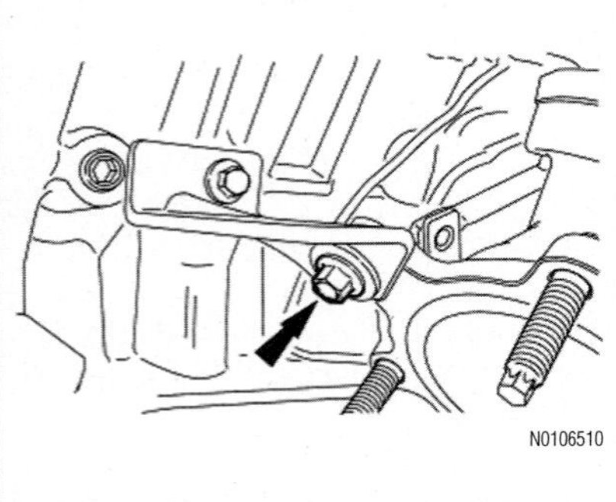

Fig. 167 Upper left-hand turbocharger bracket-to-turbocharger bolt

Fig. 169 Lower left-hand turbocharger bracket-to-turbocharger bolt

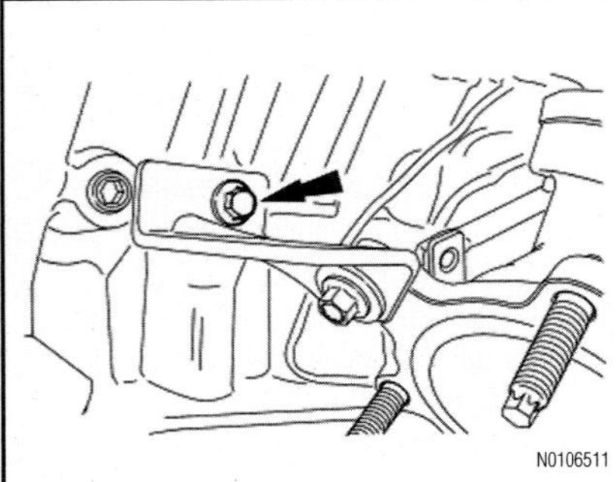

Fig. 168 Upper left-hand turbocharger bracket-to-cylinder block bolt

Fig. 170 Lower left-hand turbocharger bracket-to-cylinder block bolt

24. Using 2 new sealing washers, install the 2 coolant tube banjo bolts. Tighten to 27 ft. lbs. (37 Nm).
25. Lubricate the oil pan bore with clean engine oil. Using 2 new O-ring seals, install the left-hand turbocharger oil return tube to the oil pan.
26. Using a new gasket, install the left-hand turbocharger oil return tube and the 2 bolts. Tighten to 89 inch lbs. (10 Nm).
27. Install left-hand turbocharger intake tube and tighten the clamp. Align the marks for the left-hand turbocharger intake tube. Tighten to 44 inch lbs. (5 Nm).
28. Install the oil supply tube filter, washer and bolt.
    a. Install the new oil supply tube filter in the oil supply tube block.
    b. Slide the new washer onto the oil supply tube block.
    c. Install the bolt into the oil supply tube block.
29. Install the left-hand turbocharger oil supply tube. Tighten to 26 ft. lbs. (35 Nm).

WARNING

Make sure the turbocharger wastegate regulating valve hose does not contact the exhaust manifold heat shield.

30. Connect the wastegate control valve hose to the left-hand turbocharger assembly.
31. Install the left-hand exhaust manifold heat shield and the bottom bolt. Do not tighten the bolts at this time.
32. Install the 2 top left-hand exhaust manifold heat shield bolts. Tighten to 10 ft. lbs. (14 Nm).
33. Tighten the left-hand exhaust manifold heat shield bottom bolt. Tighten to 10 ft. lbs. (14 Nm).
34. Install the left-hand catalytic converter.
35. Fill and bleed the cooling system.
36. Install the ACL assembly.

Right-Hand

See Figures 171 through 179.

WARNING

Whenever turbocharger air intake system components are removed, always cover open ports to protect from debris. It is important that no foreign material enter the system. The turbocharger compressor vanes are susceptible to damage from even small particles. All components should be inspected and cleaned, if

necessary, prior to installation or reassembly.

1. With the vehicle in NEUTRAL, position it on a hoist.
2. Using a suitable holding device, hold the steering wheel in the straight-ahead position.
3. Remove the 4 retainers and the underbody shield.
4. Drain the cooling system.
5. Remove the right-hand catalytic converter. Refer to Catalytic Converter Removal & Installation.
6. Remove the front subframe.
7. Remove the right-hand turbocharger oil supply tube secondary latch.
8. Using a Spring Lock Coupling Disconnect Tool, or equivalent, remove the right-hand turbocharger oil supply tube from the quick connect fitting. Inspect and if necessary, replace the quick connect fitting.
9. Remove the lower right-hand exhaust manifold heat shield bolt.
10. Loosen the clamp and remove the right-hand turbocharger intake pipe from the right-hand turbocharger.
11. Disconnect the turbocharger wastegate regulating valve hose from the right-hand turbocharger assembly.
12. Remove the 3 bolts and the right-hand turbocharger lower bracket.
13. Remove the 2 bolts and the right-hand turbocharger oil return tube from the turbocharger. Remove and discard the gasket.
14. Remove the right-hand turbocharger oil return tube from the cylinder block. Discard the 2 O-ring seals.
15. Remove the 2 coolant tube banjo bolts and the right-hand turbocharger coolant tubes. Discard the sealing washers.
16. Detach the 2 vacuum hose retainers from the strut tower brace.
17. Remove the 4 nuts and the strut tower brace.
18. Disconnect the left-hand turbocharger bypass valve electrical connector and the turbocharger bypass valve hose.
19. Remove the turbocharger wastegate regulating valve hose from the right-hand Charge Air Cooler (CAC) tube.
20. Disconnect the right-hand turbocharger bypass valve electrical connector.
21. Disconnect the right-hand turbocharger bypass valve hose.
22. Remove the right-hand CAC tube nut from the intake manifold.

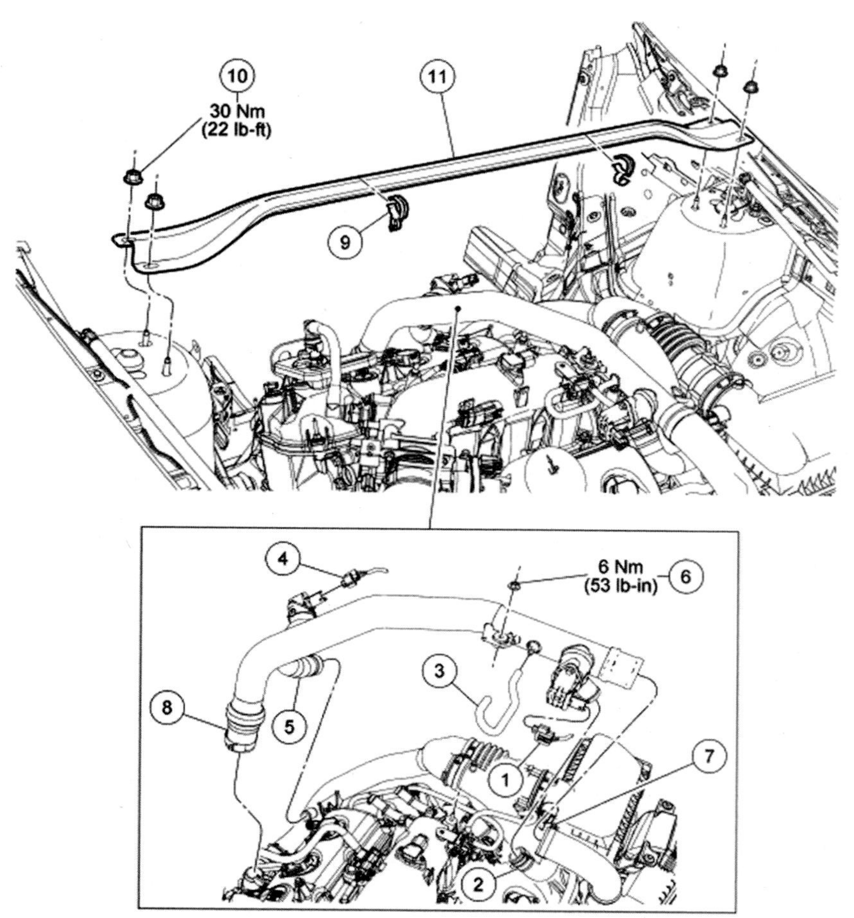

1. Left-hand turbocharger bypass valve electrical connector
2. Left-hand turbocharger bypass valve hose
3. Turbocharger wastegate regulating valve hose
4. Right-hand turbocharger bypass valve electrical connector
5. Right-hand turbocharger bypass valve hose
6. Right-hand Charge Air Cooler (CAC) tube nut
7. Right-hand CAC tube
8. Right-hand CAC tube
9. Brake booster vacuum hose retainer
10. Strut tower brace nut
11. Strut tower brace

N0105578

Fig. 171 Right-hand turbocharger components 1

23. Loosen the clamp and remove the right-hand CAC tube.

24. Loosen the clamp and remove the right-hand CAC tube from the right-hand turbocharger.

25. Remove the 4 bolts and the 2 upper right-hand exhaust manifold heat shields.

26. Remove the 2 bolts and the right-hand engine lifting eye.

27. Remove the 3 right-hand exhaust manifold-to-turbocharger bolts. Discard the gasket.

28. Remove the upper right-hand turbocharger-to-cylinder block bracket bolt and the right-hand turbocharger assembly.

29. Remove the right-hand turbocharger oil supply tube banjo bolt. Discard the sealing washer and oil supply tube filter.

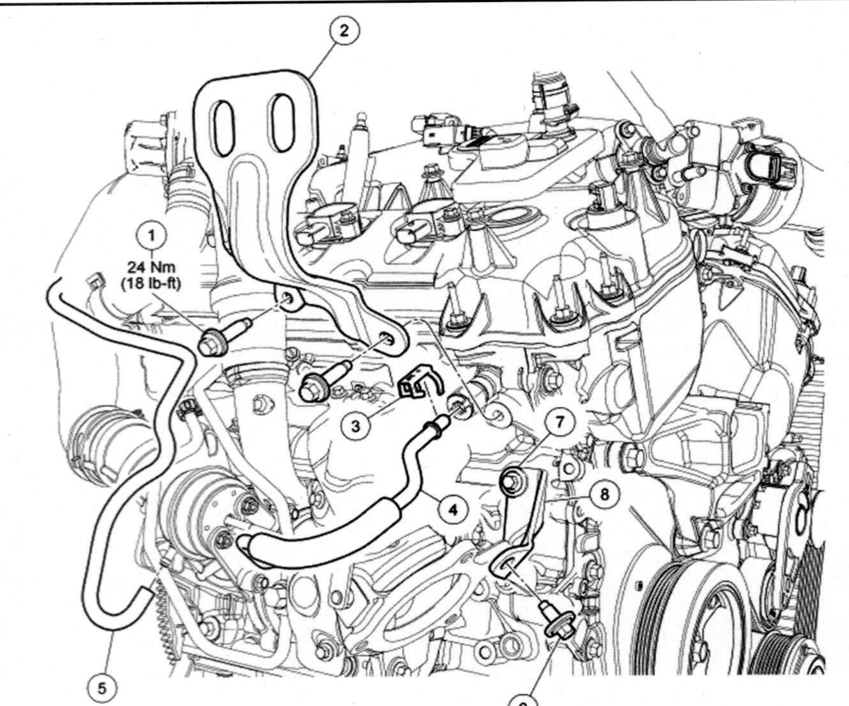

Fig. 172 Right-hand turbocharger components 2

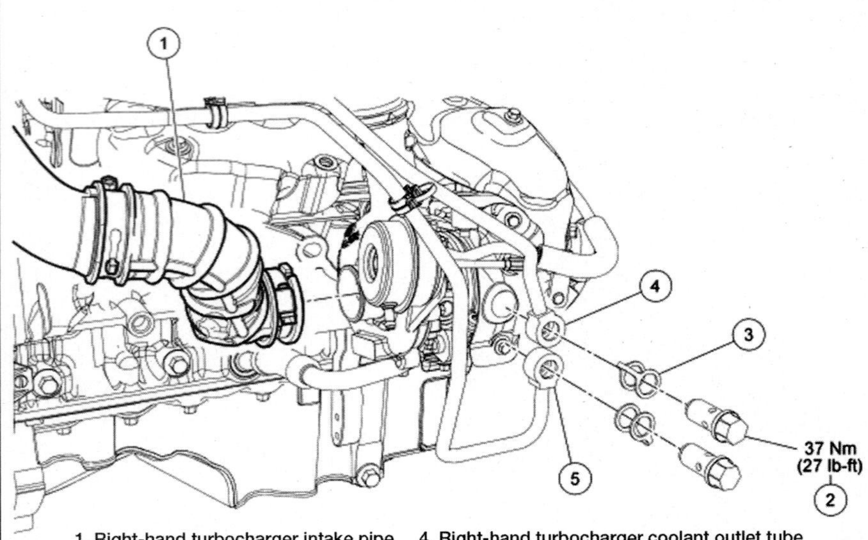

Fig. 173 Right-hand turbocharger components 3

To install:

30. Install the oil supply tube filter, washer and bolt.

   a. Install the new oil supply tube filter in the oil supply tube block.

   b. Slide the new washer onto the oil supply tube block.

   c. Install the bolt into the oil supply tube block.

31. Install the right-hand turbocharger oil supply tube. Tighten the bolt to 26 ft. lbs. (35 Nm).

32. Loosen the 2 bolts for the upper right-hand turbocharger-to-cylinder block bracket.

WARNING

The upper right-hand turbocharger bracket bolts must be loosened in order to perform the tightening sequence or damage to the turbocharger may occur.

33. Install a new right-hand exhaust manifold-to-turbocharger gasket.

34. Install the right-hand turbocharger assembly and the upper right-hand turbocharger-to-cylinder block bracket bolt. Do not tighten the bolts at this time.

35. Install the 3 new right-hand exhaust manifold-to-turbocharger bolts. Tighten to 33 ft. lbs. (45 Nm).

36. Install the right-hand engine lifting eye and the 2 bolts. Tighten to 18 ft. lbs. (24 Nm).

37. Install the 2 upper right-hand exhaust manifold heat shields and the 4 bolts. Tighten to 10 ft. lbs. (14 Nm).

38. Install the right-hand CAC tube to the right-hand turbocharger and tighten the clamp. Align the index marks for the right-hand CAC tube. Tighten to 44 inch lbs. (5 Nm).

39. Install the right-hand CAC and tighten the clamp. Align the index marks for the right-hand CAC tube. Tighten to 44 inch lbs. (5 Nm).

40. Install the right-hand CAC tube and the right-hand CAC tube nut to the intake manifold. Tighten to 53 inch lbs. (6 Nm).

41. Connect the right-hand turbocharger bypass valve hose.

42. Connect the right-hand turbocharger bypass valve electrical connector.

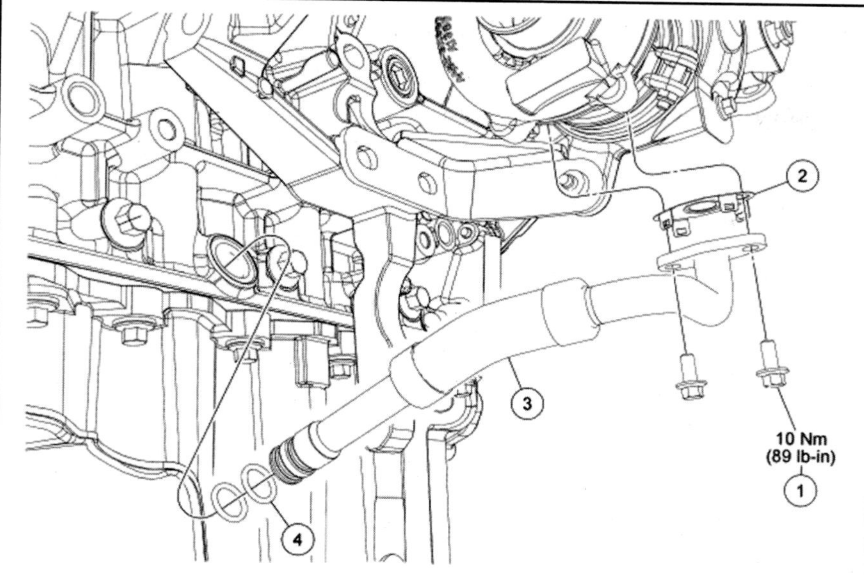

1. Right-hand turbocharger oil return tube bolt
2. Right-hand turbocharger oil return tube
3. Right-hand turbocharger oil return tube gasket
4. Right-hand turbocharger oil return tube O-ring seal

N0106536

Fig. 174 Right-hand turbocharger components 4

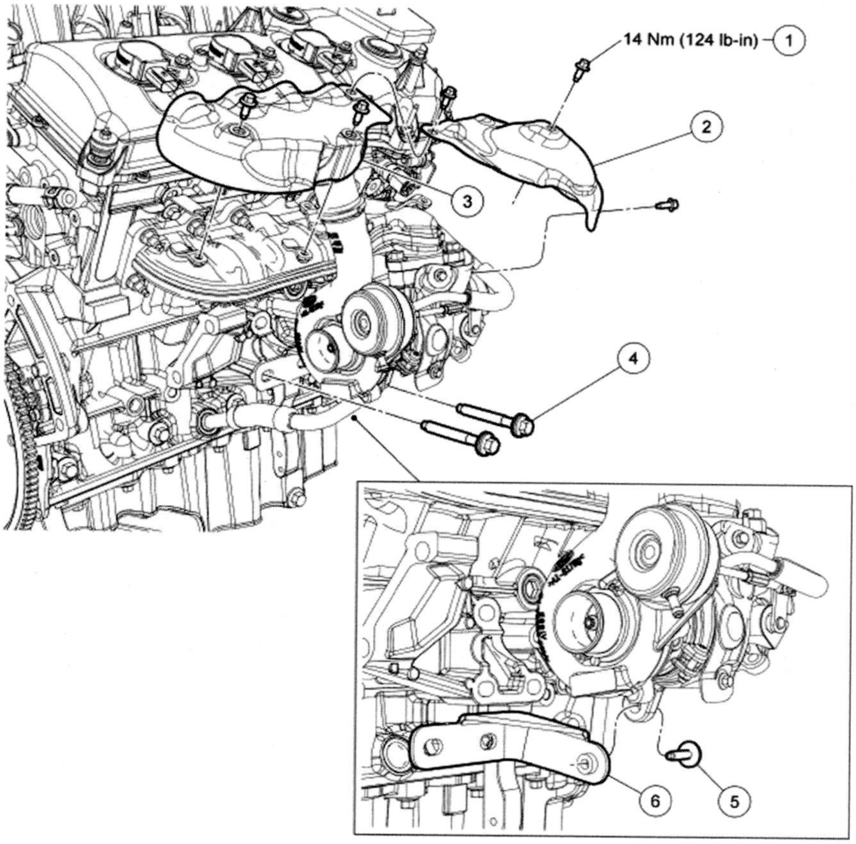

14 Nm (124 lb-in)

1. Right-hand exhaust manifold heat shield bolt
2. Right-hand exhaust manifold heat shield
3. Right-hand exhaust manifold heat shield
4. Lower right-hand turbocharger-to-cylinder block bracket bolt
5. Lower right-hand turbocharger-to-turbocharger bracket bolt
6. Lower right-hand turbocharger bracket

N0106505

Fig. 175 Right-hand turbocharger components 5

43. Install the turbocharger wastegate regulating valve hose to the right-hand CAC tube.

44. Connect the left-hand turbocharger bypass valve electrical connector and the turbocharger bypass valve hose.

45. Install the strut tower brace and the 4 nuts. Tighten to 22 ft. lbs. (30 Nm).

46. Attach the 2 brake booster vacuum hose retainers to the strut tower brace.

47. Position the upper right-hand turbocharger-to-cylinder block bracket as far clockwise as possible and tighten the bolts in the following sequence:
   a. 1: Tighten the lower cylinder block bracket bolt to 19 ft. lbs. (26 Nm).
   b. 2: Tighten the upper cylinder block bracket bolt to 19 ft. lbs. (26 Nm).
   c. 3: Tighten the cylinder block bracket-to-turbocharger bolt to 14 ft. lbs. (19 Nm).

48. Using 2 new sealing washers, install the 2 right-hand turbocharger coolant tube banjo bolts. Tighten to 27 ft. lbs. (37 Nm).

49. Lubricate the cylinder block bore with clean engine oil. Using 2 new O-ring seals, install the right-hand turbocharger oil return tube in the cylinder block.

50. Install a new gasket and install the right-hand turbocharger oil return tube and the 2 bolts. Tighten to 89 inch lbs. (10 Nm).

51. Install the lower right-hand turbocharger bracket and the 3 bolts and tighten in sequence shown:
   a. 1: Tighten the lower right-hand turbocharger bracket-to-turbocharger bolt to 14 ft. lbs. (19 Nm).
   b. 2: Tighten the 2 lower right-hand turbocharger bracket-to-cylinder block bolts to 35 ft. lbs. (48 Nm).

52. Connect the turbocharger wastegate regulating valve hose to the right-hand turbocharger. Make sure the turbocharger wastegate regulating valve hose does not contact the exhaust manifold heat shield.

53. Install the right-hand turbocharger intake pipe to the right-hand turbocharger and tighten the clamp.

54. Align the index marks for the right-hand turbocharger intake pipe. Tighten to 44 inch lbs. (5 Nm).

55. Install the lower right-hand exhaust manifold heat shield bolt. Tighten to 10 ft. lbs. (14 Nm).

56. Install the right-hand turbocharger oil supply tube into the quick connect fitting. Listen for click.

57. Install the right-hand turbocharger oil supply tube secondary latch.

58. Install the front subframe.

59. Install the right-hand catalytic converter.

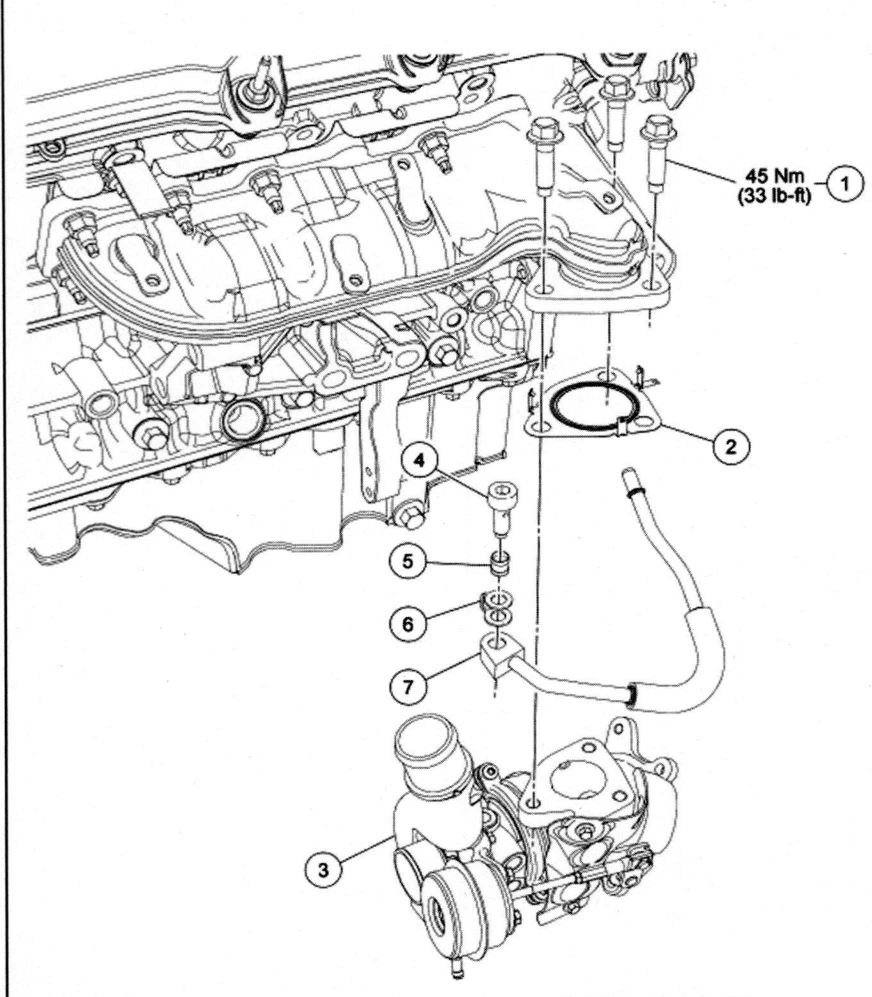

1. Exhaust manifold-to-right-hand turbocharger bolt
2. Right-hand turbocharger-to-exhaust manifold gasket
3. Right-hand turbocharger
4. Oil supply tube bolt
5. Oil supply tube filter
6. Oil supply tube sealing washer
7. Oil supply tube

N0103835

Fig. 176 Right-hand turbocharger components 6

Fig. 177 Upper right-hand turbocharger-to-cylinder block bracket bolts

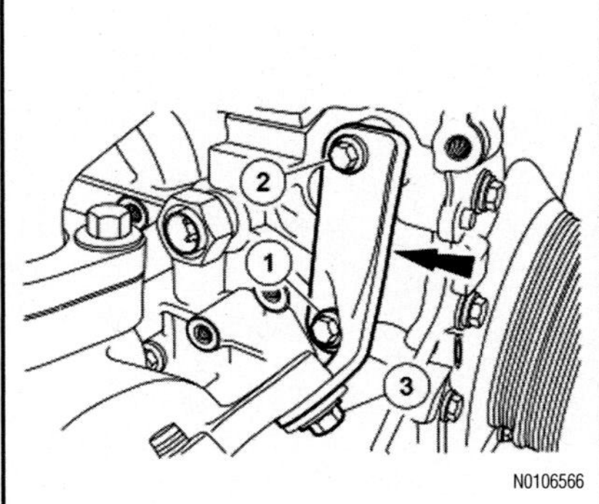

Fig. 178 Upper right-hand turbocharger-to-cylinder block bracket bolt tightening sequence

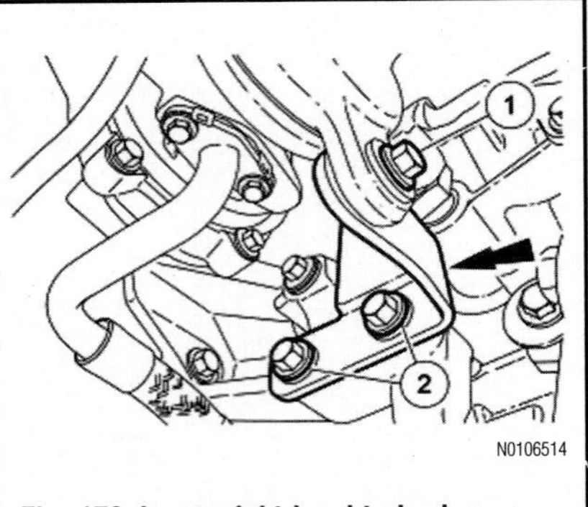

Fig. 179 Lower right-hand turbocharger bolt tightening sequence

60. Fill and bleed the cooling system.
61. Install the underbody shield and the 4 retainers.

VALVE COVERS

REMOVAL & INSTALLATION

3.5L Engines

Left-Hand

See Figures 180 and 181.

⁂ WARNING

During engine repair procedures, cleanliness is extremely important. Any foreign material, including any material created while cleaning gasket surfaces that enters the oil passages, coolant passages or the oil pan, may cause engine failure.

⁂ WARNING

Whenever turbocharger air intake system components are removed, always cover open ports to protect from debris. It is important that no foreign material enter the system. The turbocharger compressor vanes are susceptible to damage from even small particles. All components should be inspected and cleaned, if necessary, prior to installation or reassembly.

1. Release the fuel system pressure.
2. Disconnect the Turbocharger Boost Pressure (TCBP)/Charge Air Cooler Temperature (CACT) sensor electrical connector.
3. Loosen the 2 clamps and remove the Charge Air Cooler (CAC) outlet pipe.
4. Disconnect the 2 quick connect couplings and remove the crankcase vent tube.
5. Remove the fuel injection pump noise insulator shield.

6. Remove the oil level indicator.
7. For early build vehicles:
a. Remove the intake manifold.
b. Remove the nut for the high pressure fuel tube from the left-hand valve cover stud bolt.

➡To release the fuel pressure in the high pressure fuel tubes, wrap the flare nut with a shop towel to absorb any residual fuel pressure during the loosening of the flare nuts.

8. Remove the high pressure fuel tube flare nut from the fuel injection pump. Remove the 2 high pressure fuel tube flare nuts from the fuel rails and remove the high pressure fuel tube assembly.
9. For late build vehicles:
a. Remove the throttle body.
b. Disconnect the left-hand turbocharger bypass valve electrical connector.
c. Disconnect the left-hand turbocharger bypass valve hose from the right-hand CAC tube.
d. Disconnect the turbocharger wastegate regulating valve hose from the right-hand CAC tube.
e. Disconnect the right-hand turbocharger bypass valve electrical connector.
f. Disconnect the right-hand turbocharger bypass valve hose from the right-hand turbocharger intake tube.
g. Remove the right-hand CAC tube nut from the intake manifold.
h. Loosen the clamp and remove the right-hand CAC tube.
i. Loosen the clamp and remove the right-hand CAC tube from the right-hand turbocharger.
10. Remove the fuel injection pump.
11. Disconnect the left-hand Variable Camshaft Timing (VCT) solenoid electrical connector.
12. Remove the engine cover mounting stud from the left-hand valve cover stud bolt.
13. Detach all of the wiring harness retainers from the left-hand valve cover stud bolts.
14. Remove the nut and the oil supply tube bracket from the left-hand valve cover stud bolt.
15. Disconnect the 3 left-hand ignition coil-on-plug electrical connectors.
16. Remove the 3 bolts and the 3 left-hand ignition coil-on-plugs.
17. Loosen the 10 stud bolts and remove the left-hand valve cover. Discard the gasket.
18. Inspect the VCT solenoid seals and the spark plug tube seals. Remove any damaged seals.
19. Clean the valve cover, cylinder head and engine front cover sealing surfaces with metal surface prep.

To install:

20. If necessary, install new VCT solenoid and/or spark plug tube seals. Installation of new seals is only required if damaged seals were removed during disassembly of the engine.

WARNING

Failure to use the correct Motorcraft® High Performance Engine RTV Silicone may cause the engine oil to foam excessively and result in serious engine damage.

21. Apply a 0.31 in. (8 mm) bead of Motorcraft® High Performance Engine RTV Silicone to the engine front cover-to-left-hand cylinder head joints.

WARNING

If the valve cover is not installed and the fasteners tightened within 4 minutes, the sealant must be removed and the sealing area cleaned. To clean the sealing area, use silicone gasket remover and metal surface prep. Failure to follow these instructions can cause future oil leakage.

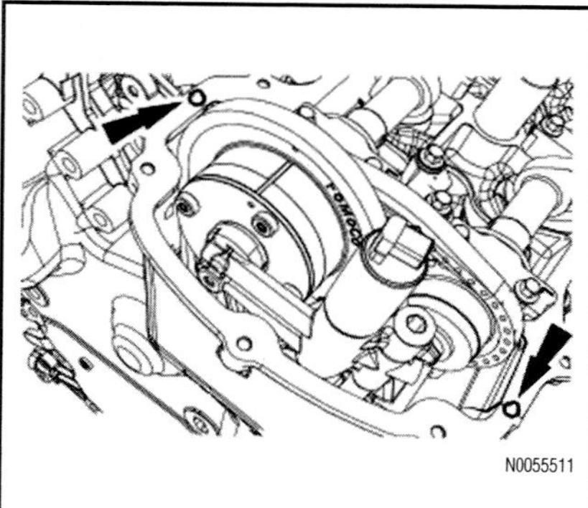

Fig. 180 Sealant application

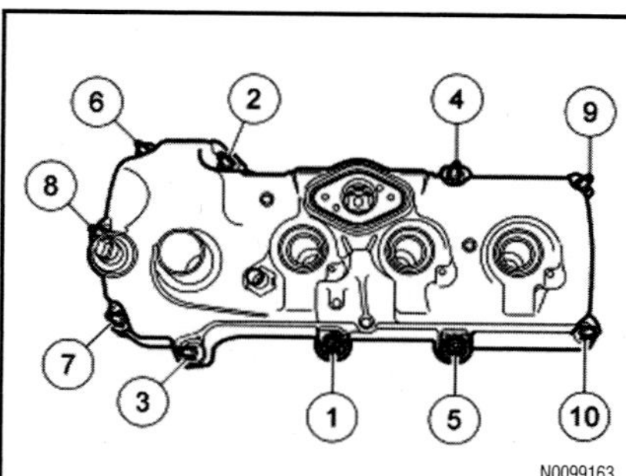

Fig. 181 Left-hand valve cover bolt tightening sequence—3.5L engines

22. Using a new gasket, install the left-hand valve cover and tighten the 10 stud bolts. Tighten in the sequence shown to 89 inch lbs. (10 Nm).
23. Install 3 left-hand ignition coil-on-plugs and the 3 bolts. Tighten to 62 inch lbs. (7 Nm).
24. Connect the 3 left-hand ignition coil-on-plug electrical connectors.
25. Install the oil supply tube bracket on the left-hand valve cover stud bolt and install the nut. Tighten to 71 inch lbs. (8 Nm).
26. Attach all of the wiring harness retainers to the left-hand valve cover and stud bolts.
27. Install the engine cover mounting stud to the left-hand valve cover stud bolt. Tighten to 53 inch lbs. (6 Nm).
28. Connect the left-hand VCT solenoid electrical connector.
29. Install the fuel injection pump.
30. For late build vehicles:
a. Install the right-hand CAC tube to the right-hand turbocharger and tighten the clamp. Align the index marks for the right-hand CAC tube. Tighten to 44 inch lbs. (5 Nm).
b. Install the right-hand CAC tube and tighten the clamp. Align the index marks for the right-hand CAC tube. Tighten to 44 inch lbs. (5 Nm).
c. Install the right-hand CAC tube and the right-hand CAC tube nut to the intake manifold. Tighten to 53 inch lbs. (6 Nm).

WARNING

The compression limiter bushing may fall out of the mounting bracket grommet on the Charge Air Cooler (CAC) tube during service. Make sure the bushing is in place when reinstalling the tube or damage to the tube may occur.

d. Connect the right-hand turbocharger bypass valve hose to the right-hand turbocharger intake tube.
e. Connect the right-hand turbocharger bypass valve electrical connector.
f. Connect the turbocharger wastegate regulating valve hose to the right-hand CAC tube.
g. Connect the left-hand turbocharger bypass valve electrical connector and the turbocharger bypass valve hose.
h. Install the throttle body.
31. For early build vehicles:
a. Connect the high pressure fuel tube flare nut to the fuel injection pump and the 2 high pressure fuel tube flare

nuts to the fuel rails. Tighten to 22 ft. lbs. (30 Nm).

b. Install the nut for the high pressure fuel tube on the left-hand valve cover stud bolt. Tighten to 53 inch lbs. (6 Nm).

c. Install the intake manifold.

32. Install the oil level indicator.
33. Install the fuel injection pump noise insulator shield.
34. Install the crankcase vent tube and connect the 2 quick connect couplings.
35. Install the CAC outlet pipe and tighten the 2 clamps. Align the index marks for the CAC outlet pipe. Tighten to 44 inch lbs. (5 Nm).
36. Connect the TCBP/CACT sensor electrical connector.

Right-Hand

See Figures 182 and 183.

⁂ WARNING

During engine repair procedures, cleanliness is extremely important. Any foreign material, including any material created while cleaning gasket surfaces that enters the oil passages, coolant passages or the oil pan, may cause engine failure.

⁂ WARNING

Whenever turbocharger air intake system components are removed, always cover open ports to protect from debris. It is important that no foreign material enter the system. The turbocharger compressor vanes are susceptible to damage from even small particles. All components should be inspected and cleaned, if necessary, prior to installation or reassembly.

1. Release the fuel system pressure.
2. Disconnect the left-hand turbocharger bypass valve electrical connector.
3. Disconnect the turbocharger bypass valve hose from the right-hand Charge Air Cooler (CAC) tube.
4. Remove the turbocharger wastegate regulating valve hose from the right-hand CAC tube.
5. Disconnect the right-hand turbocharger bypass valve electrical connector.
6. Disconnect the right-hand turbocharger bypass valve hose from the right-hand turbocharger intake tube.
7. Remove the right-hand CAC tube nut from the intake manifold.
8. Loosen the clamp and remove the right-hand CAC tube.
9. Detach the 2 brake booster vacuum hose retainers from the strut tower brace and position aside.
10. Disconnect the fuel supply tube.
11. Remove the fuel tube-to-engine front cover bracket bolt and position the fuel tube aside.
12. Disconnect the right-hand fuel injector wiring harness electrical connector.
13. Disconnect the Evaporative Emission (EVAP) tube quick connect coupling.
14. Disconnect the EVAP valve electrical connector and detach from the intake manifold.
15. Disconnect the quick connect coupling from the intake manifold and remove the EVAP tube assembly.
16. Disconnect the 2 quick connect couplings and remove the PCV tube.
17. If equipped, disconnect the 2 heated PCV electrical connectors.
18. Disconnect the right-hand Variable Camshaft Timing (VCT) solenoid electrical connector and detach the 2 wiring harness retainers.
19. Disconnect the 3 right-hand ignition coil-on-plugs electrical connectors.
20. Detach all of the wiring harness retainers from the right-hand valve cover and stud bolts position aside.
21. Remove the 3 bolts and the 3 right-hand ignition coil-on-plugs.
22. Loosen the clamp and remove the right-hand turbocharger intake tube from the right-hand turbocharger intake pipe.
23. Remove the nut from the right-hand valve cover stud bolt and position the right-hand turbocharger intake tube off the right-hand valve cover stud bolt.
24. Loosen the 11 stud bolts and remove the right-hand valve cover. Discard the gasket.
25. Inspect the VCT solenoid seals and the spark plug tube seals. Remove any damaged seals.
26. Clean the valve cover, cylinder head and engine front cover sealing surfaces with metal surface prep.

To install:

27. If necessary, install new VCT solenoid and/or spark plug tube seals. Installation of new seals is only required if damaged seals were removed during disassembly of the engine.

⁂ WARNING

Failure to use Motorcraft® High Performance Engine RTV Silicone may cause the engine oil to foam excessively and result in serious engine damage.

28. Apply a 0.31 in. (8 mm) bead of Motorcraft® High Performance Engine RTV Silicone to the engine front cover-to-right-hand cylinder head joints.

⁂ WARNING

If the valve cover is not installed and the fasteners tightened within 4 minutes, the sealant must be removed and the sealing area cleaned. To clean the sealing area, use silicone gasket remover and metal surface prep. Failure to follow this procedure can cause future oil leakage.

29. Using a new gasket, install the right-hand valve cover and tighten the 11 stud bolts. Tighten in the sequence shown to 89 inch lbs. (10 Nm).
30. Position the right-hand turbocharger intake tube and install the nut to the right-hand valve cover stud bolt. Tighten to 53 inch lbs. (6 Nm).

⁂ WARNING

The compression limiter bushing may fall out of the mounting bracket grommet on the turbocharger intake tube during service. Make sure the bushing is in place when reinstalling the tube or damage to the tube may occur.

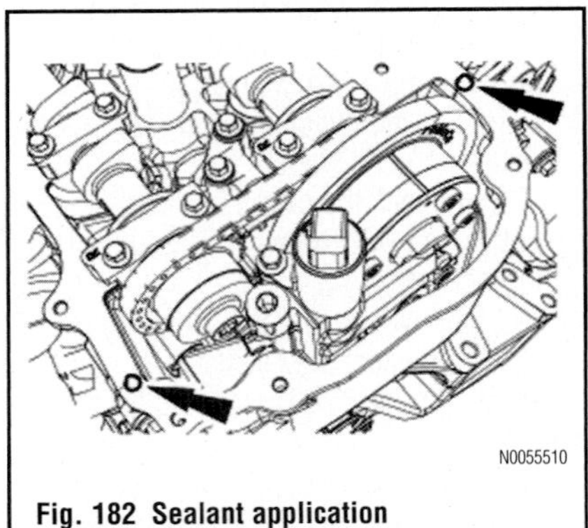

Fig. 182 Sealant application

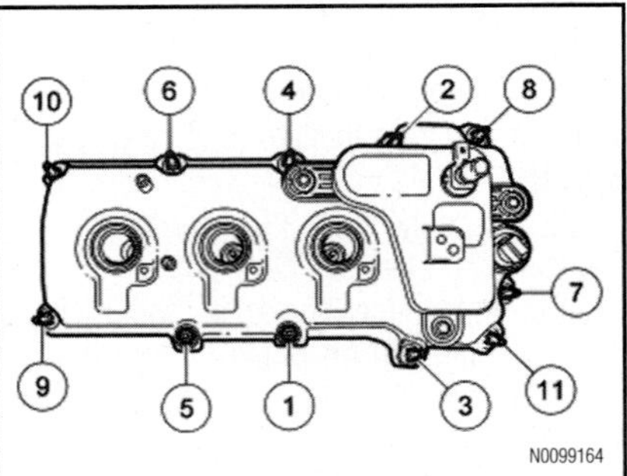

Fig. 183 Right-hand valve cover bolt tightening sequence—3.5L engines

31. Install the right-hand turbocharger intake tube to the right-hand turbocharger intake pipe and tighten the clamp. Align the index marks for the right-hand turbocharger intake tube. Tighten to 44 inch lbs. (5 Nm).

32. Install 3 right-hand ignition coil-on-plugs and the 3 bolts. Tighten to 62 inch lbs. (7 Nm).

33. Attach all of the wiring harness retainers to the right-hand valve cover and stud bolts.

34. Connect the 3 right-hand ignition coil-on-plug electrical connectors.

35. Connect the right-hand VCT solenoid electrical connector and attach the 2 wiring harness retainers.

36. If equipped, connect the 2 heated PCV electrical connectors.

37. Install the PCV tube and connect the 2 quick connect couplings.

38. Install the EVAP tube assembly and connect the quick connect coupling to the intake manifold.

39. Connect the EVAP valve electrical connector and attach to the intake manifold.

40. Connect the EVAP tube quick connect coupling.

41. Connect the right-hand fuel injector wiring harness electrical connector.

42. Position the fuel tube and install the fuel tube-to-engine front cover bracket bolt. Tighten to 10 Nm (89 lb-in).

43. Connect the fuel supply tube.

44. Attach the 2 brake booster vacuum hose retainers to the strut tower brace.

45. Install the right-hand CAC tube to the right-hand turbocharger and tighten the clamp. Align the index marks for the right-hand CAC tube. Tighten to 44 inch lbs. (5 Nm).

46. Install the right-hand CAC tube and tighten the clamp. Align the index marks for the right-hand CAC tube. Tighten to 44 inch lbs. (5 Nm).

47. Install the right-hand CAC tube and turbocharger intake tube as an assembly and install the right-hand CAC tube nut to the intake manifold. Tighten to 53 inch lbs. (6 Nm).

WARNING

The compression limiter bushing may fall out of the mounting bracket grommet on the Charge Air Cooler (CAC) tube during service. Make sure the bushing is in place when reinstalling the tube or damage to the tube may occur.

48. Connect the right-hand turbocharger bypass valve hose to the right-hand turbocharger intake tube.

49. Connect the right-hand turbocharger bypass valve electrical connector.

50. Install the turbocharger wastegate regulating valve hose to the right-hand CAC tube.

51. Connect the turbocharger bypass valve hose to the right-hand CAC tube.

52. Connect the left-hand turbocharger bypass valve electrical connector.

3.7L Engines

Left-Hand

See Figures 184 through 186.

WARNING

During engine repair procedures, cleanliness is extremely important. Any foreign material, including any material created while cleaning gasket surfaces that enters the oil passages, coolant passages or the oil pan, may cause engine failure.

WARNING

Early build engines have 11 fastener valve covers, late build engines have 9 fastener valve covers. Do not attempt to install bolts in the 2 empty late build valve cover holes or damage to the valve cover will occur.

1. Remove the left-hand ignition coils.
2. Remove the oil level indicator.
3. Disconnect the left-hand Variable Camshaft Timing (VCT) solenoid electrical connector.
4. Detach all of the wiring harness retainers from the left-hand valve cover stud bolts.
5. Remove the engine cover stud from the valve cover stud bolt.
6. Disconnect the 3 left-hand fuel injector electrical connectors.
7. For early build vehicles, loosen the 11 stud bolts and remove the left-hand valve cover. Discard the gasket.
8. For late build vehicles, loosen the 9 stud bolts and remove the right-hand valve cover. Discard the gasket.
9. Inspect the VCT solenoid seals and the spark plug tube seals. Remove any damaged seals.
10. Clean the valve cover, cylinder head and engine front cover sealing surfaces with metal surface prep.

To install:

11. If necessary, install new VCT solenoid and/or spark plug tube seals. Installation of new seals is only required if damaged seals were removed during disassembly of the engine.

WARNING

Failure to use the correct Motorcraft® High Performance Engine RTV Silicone may cause the engine oil to foam excessively and result in serious engine damage.

12. Apply a 0.31 in. (8 mm) bead of Motorcraft® High Performance Engine RTV Silicone to the engine front cover-to-left-hand cylinder head joints.

WARNING

If the valve cover is not installed and the fasteners tightened within 4 minutes, the sealant must be removed and the sealing area cleaned. To clean the sealing area, use silicone gasket remover and metal surface prep. Failure to follow this procedure can cause future oil leakage.

13. For late build vehicles, using a new gasket, install the left-hand valve cover and tighten the 9 stud bolts. Tighten in the sequence shown to 89 inch lbs. (10 Nm).
14. For early build vehicles, using a new gasket, install the left-hand valve cover and 11 stud bolts. Tighten in the sequence shown to 89 inch lbs. (10 Nm).
15. Connect the 3 left-hand fuel injector electrical connectors.
16. Install the engine cover stud to the valve cover stud bolt. Tighten to 53 inch lbs. (6 Nm).
17. Attach all of the wiring harness retainers to the left-hand valve cover stud bolts.
18. Connect the left-hand VCT solenoid electrical connector.
19. Install the oil level indicator.
20. Install the left-hand ignition coils.

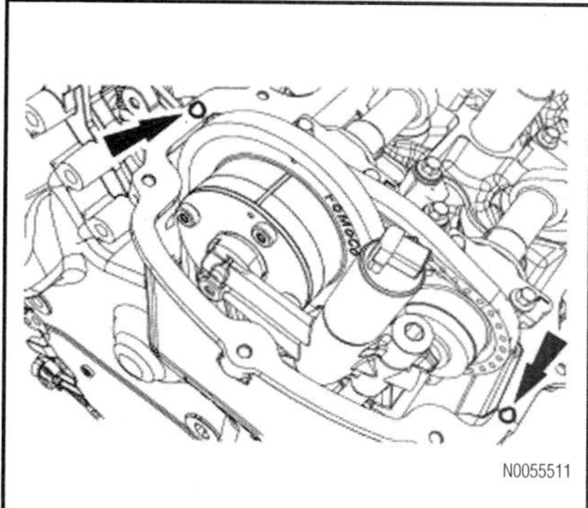

Fig. 184 Sealant application

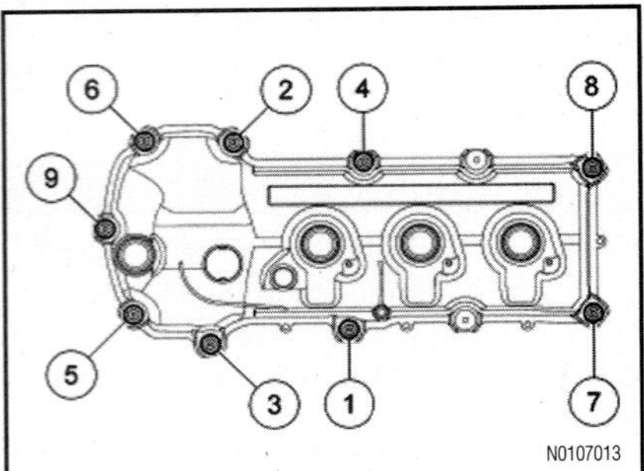

Fig. 185 Left-hand valve cover bolt tightening sequence—3.7L engines—Late build vehicles

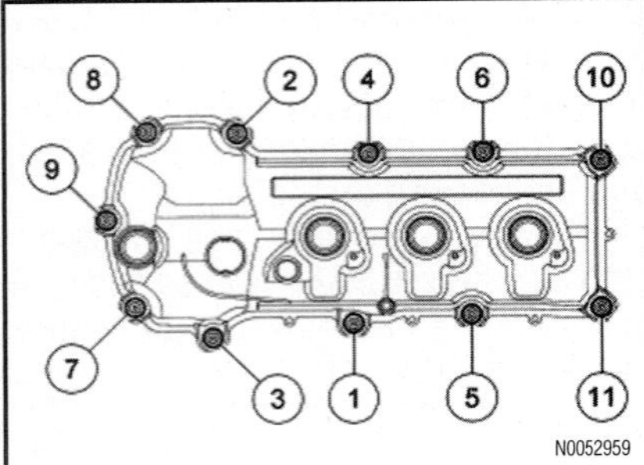

Fig. 186 Left-hand valve cover bolt tightening sequence—3.7L engines—Early build vehicles

Right-Hand

See Figures 187 through 189.

WARNING

During engine repair procedures, cleanliness is extremely important. Any foreign material, including any material created while cleaning gasket surfaces that enters the oil passages, coolant passages or the oil pan, may cause engine failure.

➡Early build engines have 11 fastener valve covers, late build engines have 9 fastener valve covers. Do not attempt to install bolts in the 2 empty late build valve cover holes or damage to the valve cover will occur.

1. Remove the right-hand ignition coils.
2. Detach and disconnect the right-hand Heated Oxygen Sensor (HO2S) electrical connector.
3. Detach and disconnect the right-hand Catalyst Monitor Sensor (CMS) electrical connector.
4. Disconnect the right-hand Variable Camshaft Timing (VCT) solenoid electrical connector.
5. Disconnect the 3 right-hand fuel injector electrical connectors.
6. Detach all of the wiring harness retainers from the right-hand valve cover stud bolts.
7. Remove the nut and the Power Steering Pressure (PSP) tube bracket from the valve cover stud bolt.
8. For early build vehicles, loosen the bolt, the 10 stud bolts and remove the right-hand valve cover. Discard the gasket. It is necessary to reposition the A/C tubes to remove the valve cover.
9. For late build vehicles, loosen the 9 studs bolts and remove the right-hand valve cover. Discard the gasket. It is necessary to reposition the A/C tubes to remove the valve cover.
10. Inspect the VCT solenoid seals and the spark plug tube seals. Remove any damaged seals.
11. Clean the valve cover, cylinder head and engine front cover sealing surfaces with metal surface prep.

To install:

12. If necessary, install new VCT solenoid and/or spark plug tube seals. Installation of new seals is only required if damaged seals were removed during disassembly of the engine.

WARNING

Failure to use Motorcraft® High Performance Engine RTV Silicone may cause the engine oil to foam excessively and result in serious engine damage.

13. Apply a 0.31 in. (8 mm) bead of Motorcraft® High Performance Engine RTV Silicone to the engine front cover-to-right-hand cylinder head joints.

WARNING

If the valve cover is not installed and the fasteners tightened within 4 minutes, the sealant must be removed and the sealing area cleaned. To clean the sealing area, use silicone gasket remover and metal surface prep. Failure to follow this procedure can cause future oil leakage.

14. For late build vehicles, using a new gasket, install the right-hand valve cover and tighten the 9 stud bolts. Tighten in the sequence shown to 89 inch lbs. (10 Nm).
15. For early build vehicles, using a new gasket, install the right-hand valve cover, bolt and the 10 stud bolts.

Tighten in the sequence shown to 89 inch lbs. (10 Nm).

16. Install the PSP tube bracket on the valve cover stud bolt and install the nut. Tighten to 62 inch lbs. (7 Nm).
17. Attach all of the wiring harness retainers to the right-hand valve cover stud bolts.
18. Connect the 3 right-hand fuel injector electrical connectors.
19. Connect the right-hand VCT solenoid electrical connector.
20. Connect the right-hand CMS electrical connector.
21. Connect the right-hand HO2S electrical connector.
22. Install the right-hand ignition coils.

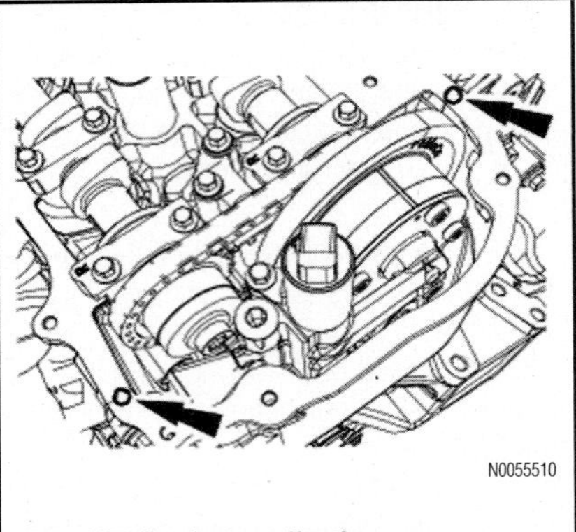

Fig. 187 Sealant application

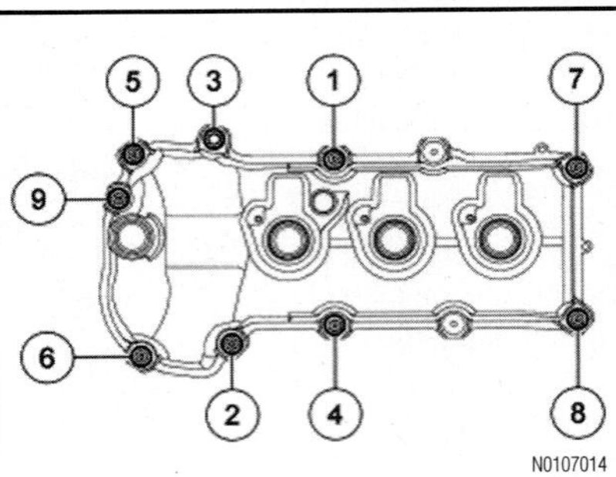

Fig. 188 Right-hand valve cover bolt tightening sequence—3.7L engines—Late build vehicles

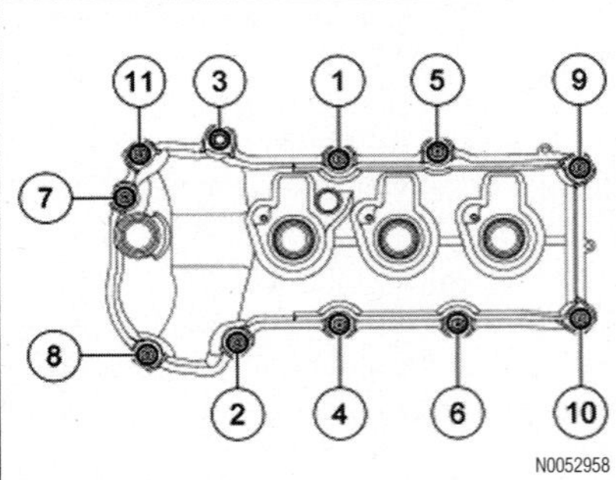

Fig. 189 Right-hand valve cover bolt tightening sequence—3.7L engines—Early build vehicles

ENGINE PERFORMANCE & EMISSION CONTROLS

CAMSHAFT POSITION (CMP) SENSOR

LOCATION

See Figures 190 and 191.

Refer to the accompanying illustrations.

REMOVAL & INSTALLATION

3.5L Engine

1. Remove the Air Cleaner (ACL) outlet pipe and the ACL.
2. Position the right-hand and left-hand turbocharger intake tubes aside.
3. Disconnect the Camshaft Position (CMP) sensor electrical connector.
4. Remove the bolt and the CMP sensor.

To install:

5. To install, reverse the removal procedure, noting the following:
   a. Lubricate the CMP sensor O-ring seal with clean engine oil.
   b. Tighten to 89 inch lbs. (10 Nm).

3.7L Engine

1. Remove the Air Cleaner (ACL) outlet pipe and the ACL.
2. Disconnect the Camshaft Position (CMP) sensor electrical connector.
3. Remove the bolt and the CMP sensor.

To install:

4. To install, reverse the removal procedure, noting the following:
   a. Lubricate the CMP sensor O-ring seal with clean engine oil.
   b. Tighten to 89 inch lbs. (10 Nm).

CRANKSHAFT POSITION (CKP) SENSOR

LOCATION

See Figure 192.

Refer to the accompanying illustration.

REMOVAL & INSTALLATION

1. With the vehicle in NEUTRAL, position it on a hoist.
2. For 3.5L engines, remove the left-hand turbocharger.
3. For 3.7L engines, remove the left-hand catalytic converter.
4. Remove the bolt/nut and the heat shield.
5. Remove the rubber grommet cover.
6. Disconnect the Crankshaft Position (CKP) sensor electrical connector.

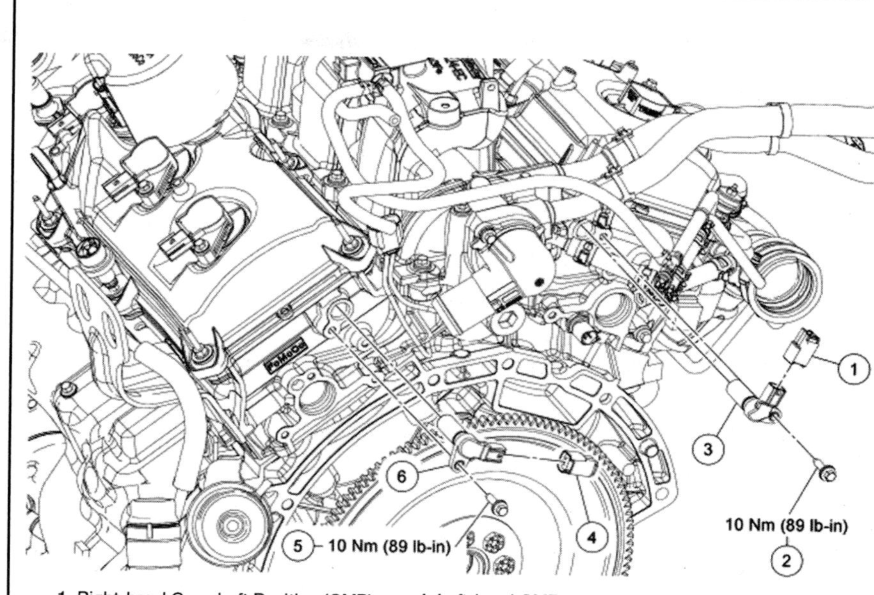

Fig. 190 Camshaft Position (CMP) Sensor—3.5L engines

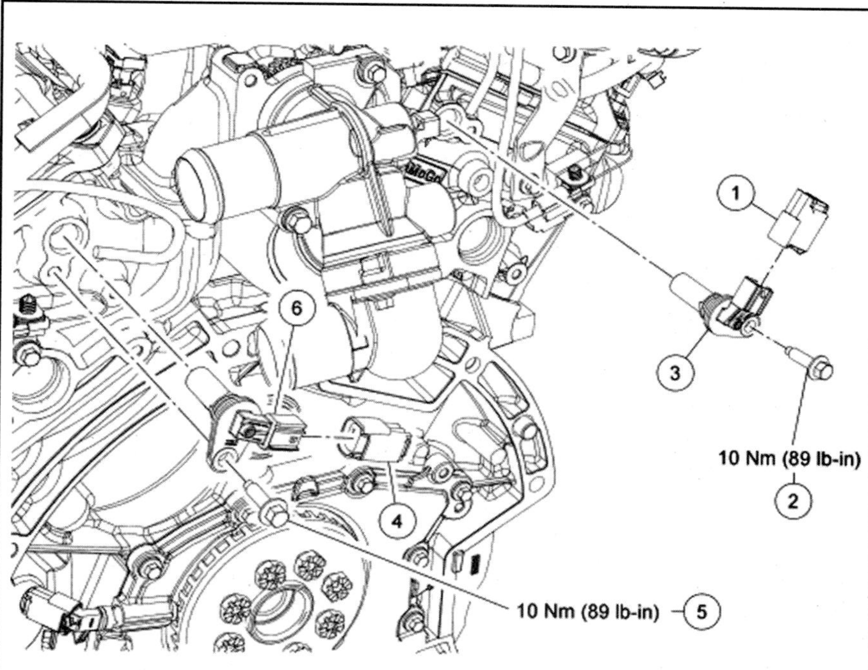

Fig. 191 Camshaft Position (CMP) Sensor—3.7L engines

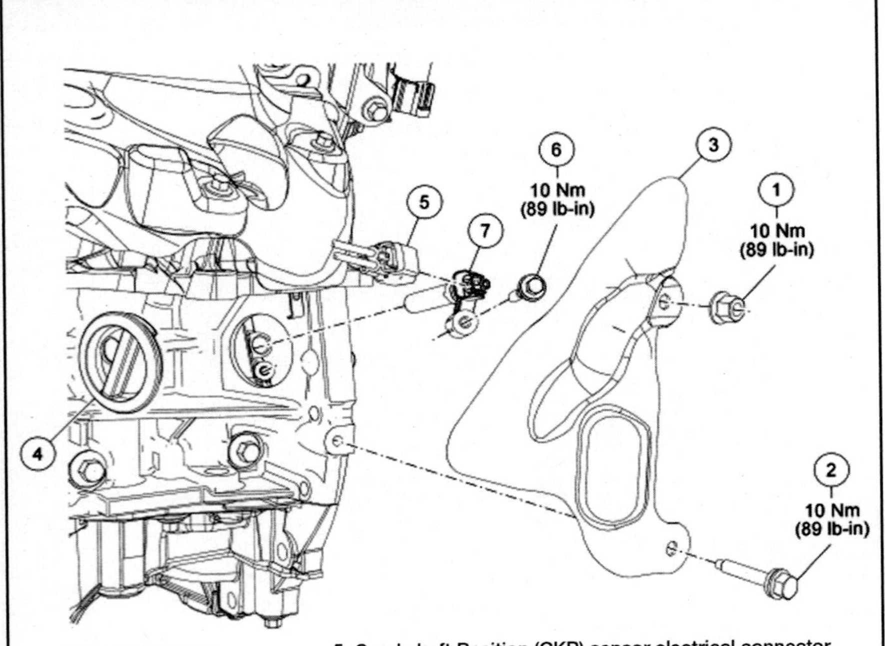

Fig. 192 Crankshaft Position (CKP) Sensor

7. Remove the bolt and the CKP sensor.

To install:

8. To install, reverse the removal procedure, noting the following:
   a. Tighten the sensor mounting bolt to 89 inch lbs. (10 Nm).
   b. Tighten the heat shield bolt/nut to 89 inch lbs. (10 Nm).
   c. Using the scan tool, perform the Misfire Monitor Neutral Profile Correction procedure, following the on-screen instructions.

HEATED OXYGEN (HO2S) SENSOR

LOCATION

See Figures 193 through 195.

REMOVAL & INSTALLATION

1. For all right-hand sensors, with the vehicle in NEUTRAL, position it on a hoist.
2. For all sensors, disconnect the HO2S electrical connector.
   a. For 3.5L engines right-hand sensors, detach the HO2S electrical connector retainer from the bracket.
   b. For 3.5L engines left-hand sensors, remove the 4 retainers and the underbody shield, and detach the HO2S electrical connector retainer from the bracket.
3. For all sensors, lubricate the sensor threads with penetrating and lock lubricant to assist in removal, if necessary.
4. For all sensors, remove the HO2S using the Exhaust Gas Oxygen Sensor Socket.

To install:

5. To install, reverse the removal procedure, noting the following:
   a. Apply a light coat of anti-seize lubricant to the threads of the HO2S.
   b. Tighten the sensor to 35 ft. lbs. (48 Nm).

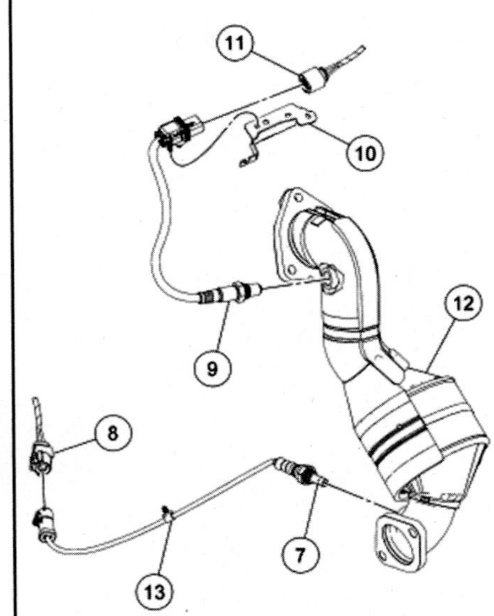

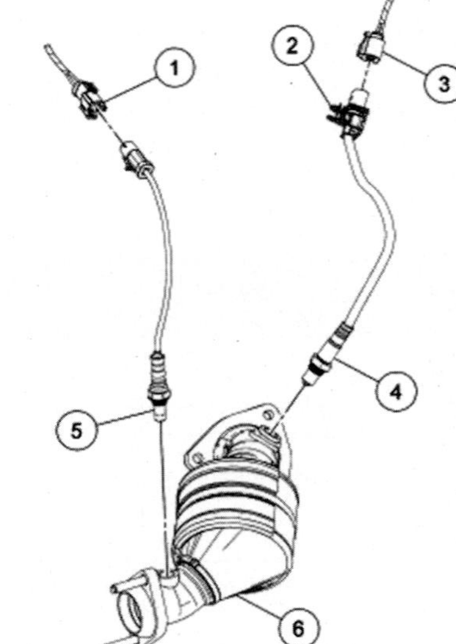

1. Left-hand Catalyst Monitor Sensor (CMS) electrical connector
2. Left-hand Heated Oxygen Sensor (HO2S) electrical connector retainer
3. Left-hand HO2S electrical connector
4. Left-hand HO2S
5. Left-hand CMS
6. Left-hand catalytic converter
7. Right-hand CMS
8. Right-hand CMS electrical connector
9. Right-hand HO2S
10. Right-hand HO2S connector bracket
11. Right-hand HO2S electrical connector
12. Right-hand catalytic converter
13. Right-hand CMS wiring retainer

N0103506

Fig. 193 Heated Oxygen (HO2S) Sensor—3.5L engine

INTAKE AIR TEMPERATURE (IAT) SENSOR

LOCATION

See Figure 196.

Refer to the accompanying illustration.

REMOVAL & INSTALLATION

1. Disconnect the Intake Air Temperature (IAT) sensor electrical connector.
2. Remove the IAT sensor.

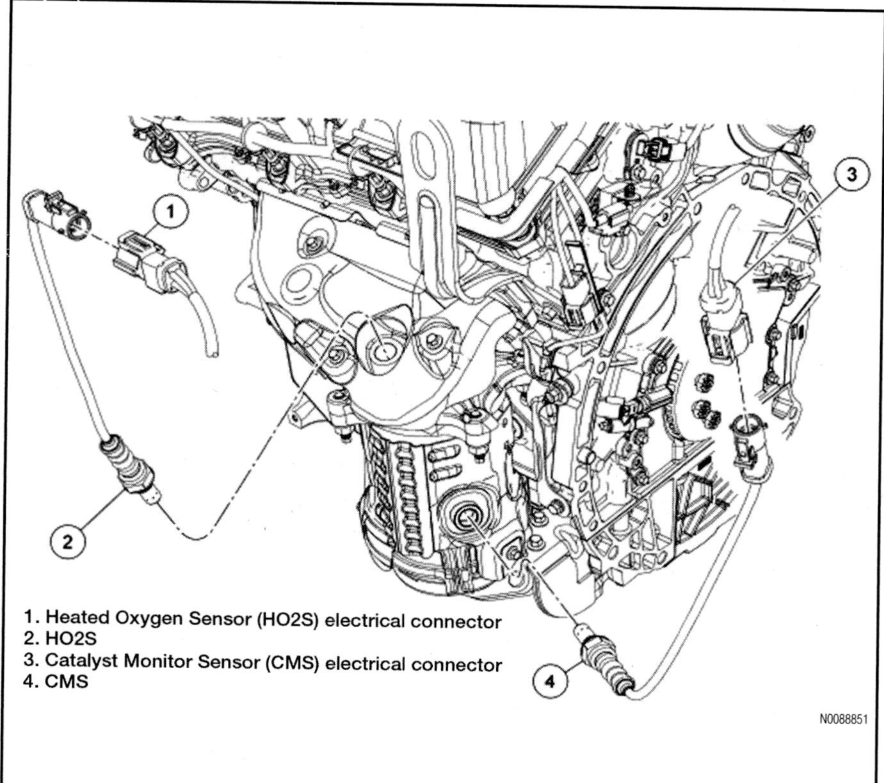

Fig. 194 Left-Hand Heated Oxygen (HO2S) Sensor—3.7L engine

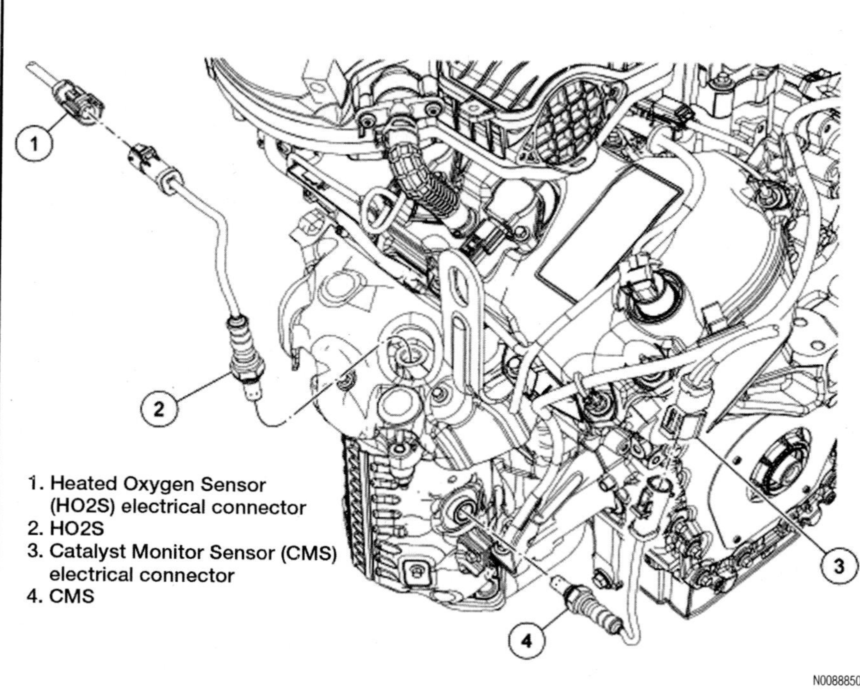

Fig. 195 Right-Hand Heated Oxygen (HO2S) Sensor—3.7L engine

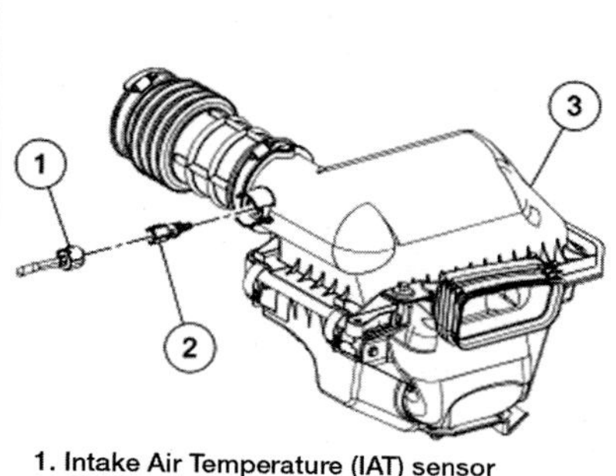

Fig. 196 Intake Air Temperature (IAT) Sensor

3. Lift the tab and turn the IAT sensor counterclockwise to remove.

To install:

4. To install, reverse the removal procedure.
   a. Make sure the IAT sensor tab is fully seated during installation.

KNOCK SENSOR (KS)

LOCATION

See Figures 197 and 198.

Refer to the accompanying illustrations.

REMOVAL & INSTALLATION

3.5L Engine

1. Remove the coolant inlet pipe.
2. Remove the fuel rail.
3. Disconnect the Knock Sensor (KS) electrical connector.
4. Remove the 2 bolts and the KS.

To install:

5. To install, reverse the removal procedure.
   a. Tighten to 15 ft. lbs. (20 Nm).

3.7L Engine

1. Remove the thermostat housing.
2. Remove the lower intake manifold.
3. Remove the coolant tube.
4. Discard the O-ring seal.
5. Disconnect the Knock Sensor (KS) electrical connector.
6. Remove the 2 bolts and the KS.

To install:

7. To install, reverse the removal procedure, noting the following:
   a. Lubricate the new O-ring seal with clean engine coolant.
   b. Tighten to 15 ft. lbs. (20 Nm).

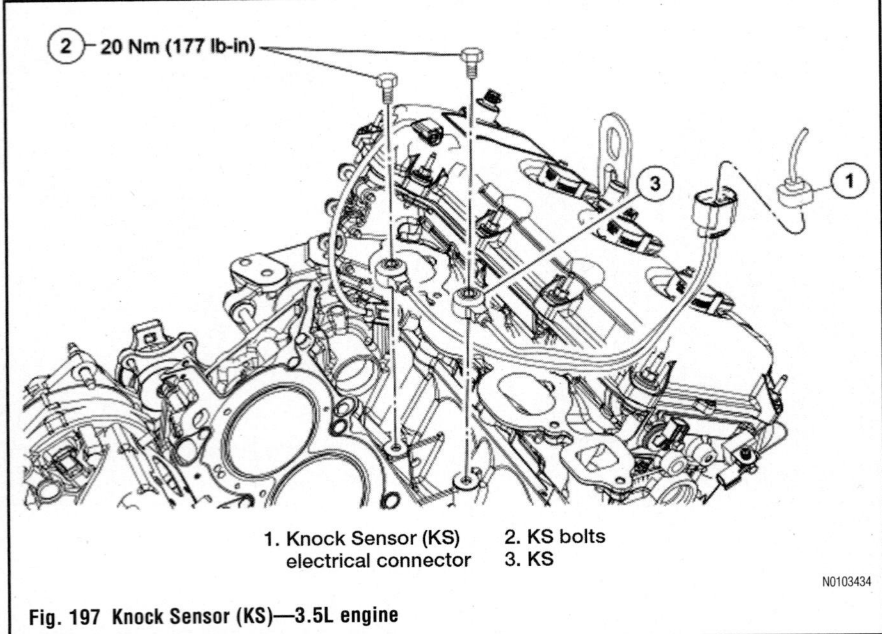

Fig. 197 Knock Sensor (KS)—3.5L engine

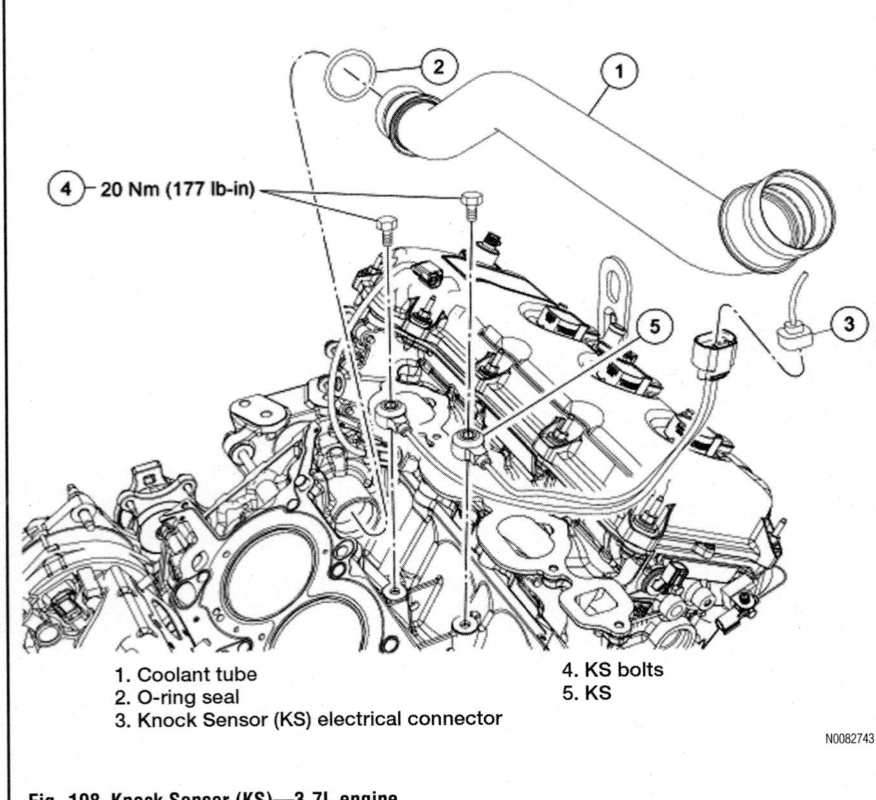

Fig. 198 Knock Sensor (KS)—3.7L engine

MANIFOLD ABSOLUTE PRESSURE (MAP) SENSOR

LOCATION

See Figure 199.

Refer to the accompanying illustration.

REMOVAL & INSTALLATION

➡he Turbocharger Boost Pressure (TCBP)/Charge Air Cooler Temperature (CACT) sensor and the Manifold Absolute Pressure (MAP)/ Intake Air Temperature 2 (IAT2) sensor are not interchangeable.

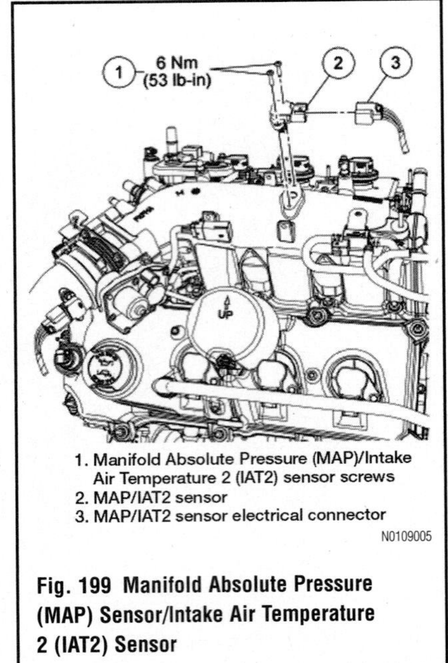

Fig. 199 Manifold Absolute Pressure (MAP) Sensor/Intake Air Temperature 2 (IAT2) Sensor

1. Disconnect the MAP/IAT2 sensor electrical connector.
2. Remove the 2 screws and the MAP/IAT2 sensor.

To install:

3. Lubricate the MAP/IAT2 sensor O-ring seal with clean engine oil.
4. Install the MAP/IAT2 sensor and tighten the 2 screws to 53 inch lbs. (6 Nm).
5. Connect the MAP/IAT2 sensor electrical connector.

POWERTRAIN CONTROL MODULE (PCM)

LOCATION

See Figure 200.

Refer to the accompanying illustration.

REMOVAL & INSTALLATION

➡PCM installation DOES NOT require new keys or programming of keys.

1. Retrieve the module configuration. Carry out the module configuration retrieval steps of the Programmable Module Installation (PMI) procedure, below.
2. Remove the cowl panel grill.
3. Disconnect the 3 PCM electrical connectors.
4. Remove the 2 nuts and the PCM.

To install:

5. Install the PCM and tighten the 2 nuts to 71 inch lbs. (8 Nm).
6. Connect the 3 PCM electrical connectors.
7. Install the cowl panel grill.

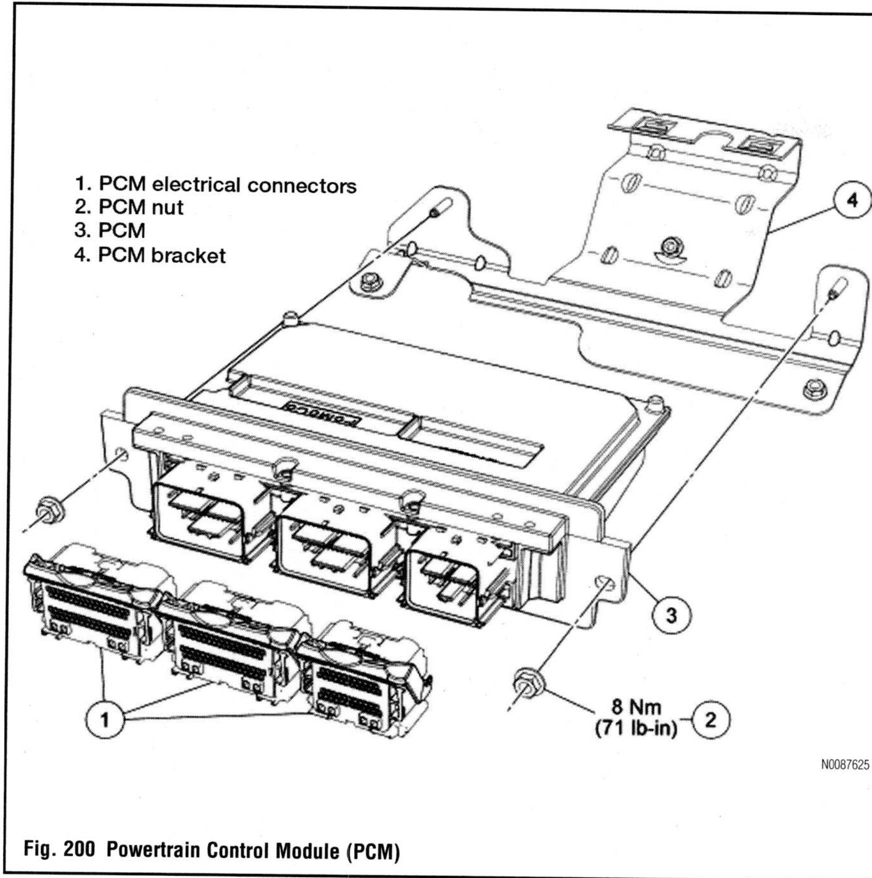

Fig. 200 Powertrain Control Module (PCM)

8. Restore the module configuration. Carry out the module configuration restore steps of the Programmable Module Installation (PMI) procedure, below.
9. Reprogram the Passive Anti-Theft System (PATS). Carry out the Parameter Reset procedure, below.
10. Using the scan tool, perform the Misfire Monitor Neutral Profile Correction procedure, following the on-screen instructions.

PROGRAMMABLE MODULE INSTALLATION (PMI) PROCEDURE USING INTEGRATED DIAGNOSTIC SYSTEM (IDS)

When the Original Module is Available

➡Following module installation, some modules require a separate learning procedure be carried out. For adaptive learning and calibration instructions, refer to the specific module removal and installation procedures.

1. Connect the IDS and identify the vehicle as normal.
2. From the Toolbox icon, select Module Programming and press the check mark.
3. Select Programmable Module Installation.
4. Select the module that is being replaced.
5. Follow the on-screen instructions, turn the ignition key to the OFF position, and press the check mark.
6. Install the new module and press the check mark.
7. Follow the on-screen instructions, turn the ignition key to the ON position, and press the check mark.
8. The IDS downloads the data into the new module and displays Module Configuration Complete.
9. Test module for correct operation.

When the Original Module is NOT Available

➡Following module installation, some modules require a separate learning procedure be carried out. For adaptive learning and calibration instructions, refer to the specific module removal and installation procedures.

1. Install the new module.
2. Connect the IDS and identify the vehicle as normal.
3. From the Toolbox icon, select Module Programming and press the check mark.
4. Select Programmable Module Installation.
5. Select the module that was replaced.
6. Follow the on-screen instructions, turn the ignition key to the OFF position, and press the check mark.
7. Follow the on-screen instructions, turn the ignition key to the ON position, and press the check mark.
8. If the data is not available, the IDS displays a screen stating to contact the As-Built Data Center.
9. Retrieve the data from the technician service publication website at this time and press the check mark.
10. Enter the module data and press the check mark.
11. The IDS downloads the data into the new module and displays Module Configuration Complete.
12. Test module for correct operation.

PASSIVE ANTI-THEFT SYSTEM (PATS) PARAMETER RESET PROCEDURE

Integrated Keyhead Transmitter (IKT)

➡A minimum of 2 Passive Anti-Theft System (PATS) keys must be programmed into the Instrument Panel Cluster (IPC) to complete this procedure and allow the vehicle to start.

1. Turn the key from the OFF position to the ON position.
2. From the scan tool, follow the on-screen instructions to ENTER SECURITY ACCESS.
3. From the scan tool, select: Parameter Reset and follow the on-screen instructions.

➡If the IPC or the IPC and the PCM were replaced, updated or reconfigured, follow Steps 4–9. All vehicle keys are erased during the parameter reset procedure. Verify at least 2 vehicle keys are available prior to carrying out the PATS parameter reset. If only the PCM was replaced, go to Step 9.

4. From the scan tool, select: Ignition Key Code Erase and follow the on-screen instructions.
5. Turn the key to the OFF position and disconnect the scan tool.
6. Turn the key to the ON position for 6 seconds.
7. Turn the key to the OFF position and remove the key.
8. Insert the second PATS key into the ignition lock cylinder and turn the key to the ON position for 6 seconds.
9. Both keys now start the vehicle.

Intelligent Access (IA)

➡If the Remote Function Actuator (RFA) module or the RFA module and the PCM were replaced, updated or reconfigured, follow Steps 1–14. All vehicle keys are erased during the parameter reset procedure. Verify at least 2 vehicle keys are available prior to carrying out the Passive Anti-Theft System (PATS) parameter reset. If only the PCM was replaced, follow Steps 10–12.

➡A minimum of 2 Intelligent Access (IA) keys must be programmed into the RFA module to complete this procedure and allow the vehicle to start.

1. Make sure the ignition is in the OFF mode.
2. From the scan tool, follow the on-screen instructions to ENTER SECURITY ACCESS.
3. Place an IA key in the backup transceiver slot.
4. From the scan tool menu select: Ignition Key Code Erase. Follow the on-screen instructions until the process has been completed and the PATS Functions screen is available again.
5. From the scan tool menu select: Program ignition key. Follow the on-screen instructions until the process has been completed and the PATS Functions screen is available again.
6. Remove the first IA key from the backup transceiver slot and verify the IA key has been programmed by pressing the lock and unlock buttons.
7. Place the second IA key in the backup transceiver slot.
8. From the scan tool menu select: Program ignition key. Follow the on-screen instructions until the process has been completed and the PATS Functions screen is available again.
9. Remove the second IA key from the backup transceiver slot and verify the IA key has been programmed by pressing the lock and unlock buttons.
10. Turn the ignition to the ON mode.
11. From the scan tool, select: Parameter Reset and follow the on-screen instructions.
12. Disconnect the scan tool.
13. The vehicle should now start with both IA keys.
14. Verify the operation of each key by placing one key at a time inside the passenger compartment and start the vehicle (make sure the rest of the keys are out of the vehicle when verifying each key operation).

THROTTLE POSITION SENSOR (TPS)

LOCATION

See Figure 201.

Refer to the accompanying illustration.

REMOVAL & INSTALLATION

1. Remove the Charge Air Cooler (CAC) outlet pipe.

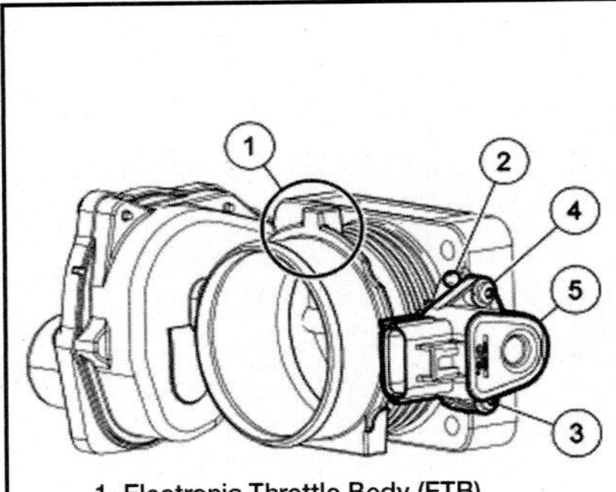

Fig. 201 Throttle Position Sensor (TPS)

2. Disconnect the Throttle Position (TP) sensor electrical connector.

⁂ WARNING

Do not put direct heat on the Throttle Position (TP) sensor or any other plastic parts because heat damage may occur. Damage may also occur if Electronic Throttle Body (ETB) temperature exceeds 248°F (120°C).

➡Do not use power tools.

3. Remove the TP sensor:
   a. Using a suitable heat gun, apply heat to the top of the Electronic Throttle Body (ETB) until the top TP sensor bolt ear reaches approximately 130°F (55°C), this should take no more than 3 minutes using an 1,100-watt heat gun. The heat gun should be about 1 in. (25.4 mm) away from the ETB.
4. Monitor the temperature of the top TP sensor bolt ear on the ETB with a suitable temperature measuring device, such as a digital temperature laser or infrared thermometer, while heating the ETB .
5. Using hand tools, quickly remove the bolt farthest from the heat source first and discard.
6. Using hand tools, remove the remaining bolt and discard.
7. Remove and discard the TP sensor.

To install:

➡When installing the new TP sensor, make sure that the radial locator tab on the TP sensor is aligned with the radial locator hole on the ETB .

➡Do not use power tools.

8. Install the new TP sensor.
   a. Using hand tools, install the 2 new bolts. Tighten to 27 inch lbs. (3 Nm).
9. Connect the TP sensor electrical connector.
10. Install the CAC outlet pipe.

FUEL SYSTEM SERVICE PRECAUTIONS

Safety is the most important factor when performing not only fuel system maintenance but any type of maintenance. Failure to conduct maintenance and repairs in a safe manner may result in serious personal injury or death. Maintenance and testing of the vehicle's fuel system components can be accomplished safely and effectively by adhering to the following rules and guidelines.

- To avoid the possibility of fire and personal injury, always disconnect the negative battery cable unless the repair or test procedure requires that battery voltage be applied.
- Always relieve the fuel system pressure prior to disconnecting any fuel system component (injector, fuel rail, pressure regulator, etc.), fitting or fuel line connection. Exercise extreme caution whenever relieving fuel system pressure to avoid exposing skin, face and eyes to fuel spray. Please be advised that fuel under pressure may penetrate the skin or any part of the body that it contacts.
- Always place a shop towel or cloth around the fitting or connection prior to loosening to absorb any excess fuel due to spillage. Ensure that all fuel spillage (should it occur) is quickly removed from engine surfaces. Ensure that all fuel soaked cloths or towels are deposited into a suitable waste container.
- Always keep a dry chemical (Class B) fire extinguisher near the work area.
- Do not allow fuel spray or fuel vapors to come into contact with a spark or open flame.
- Always use a back-up wrench when loosening and tightening fuel line connection fittings. This will prevent unnecessary stress and torsion to fuel line piping.
- Always replace worn fuel fitting O-rings with new Do not substitute fuel hose or equivalent where fuel pipe is installed.

Before servicing the vehicle, make sure to also refer to the precautions in the beginning of this section as well.

RELIEVING FUEL SYSTEM PRESSURE

➡If applicable, review the procedures for achieving the various ignition states (ignition OFF, ignition in ACCESSORY, ignition ON and ignition START) on vehicles with Intelligent Access with Push Button Start.

➡The Fuel Pump (FP) control module is mounted to the panel behind the rear seat backrest cushion. The FP control module electrical connector can be accessed through the luggage compartment.

1. Disconnect the FP module electrical connector.
2. Start the engine and allow it to idle until it stalls.
3. Turn the ignition to the OFF position.
4. For 3.5L engines:

➡On vehicles equipped with Gasoline Turbocharged Direct Injection (GTDI), it is necessary to release the high pressure system fuel prior to disconnecting a low pressure fuel tube quick connect coupling.

a. To release the fuel pressure in the high pressure fuel tube, wrap the flare nut with a shop towel to absorb any residual fuel pressure during the loosening of the flare nut.

b. Disconnect the high pressure fuel tube-to-fuel injection pump flare nut.

FUEL INJECTORS

REMOVAL & INSTALLATION

3.5L Engine

See Figures 202 through 205.

1. Release the fuel system pressure.
2. Disconnect the battery ground cable.

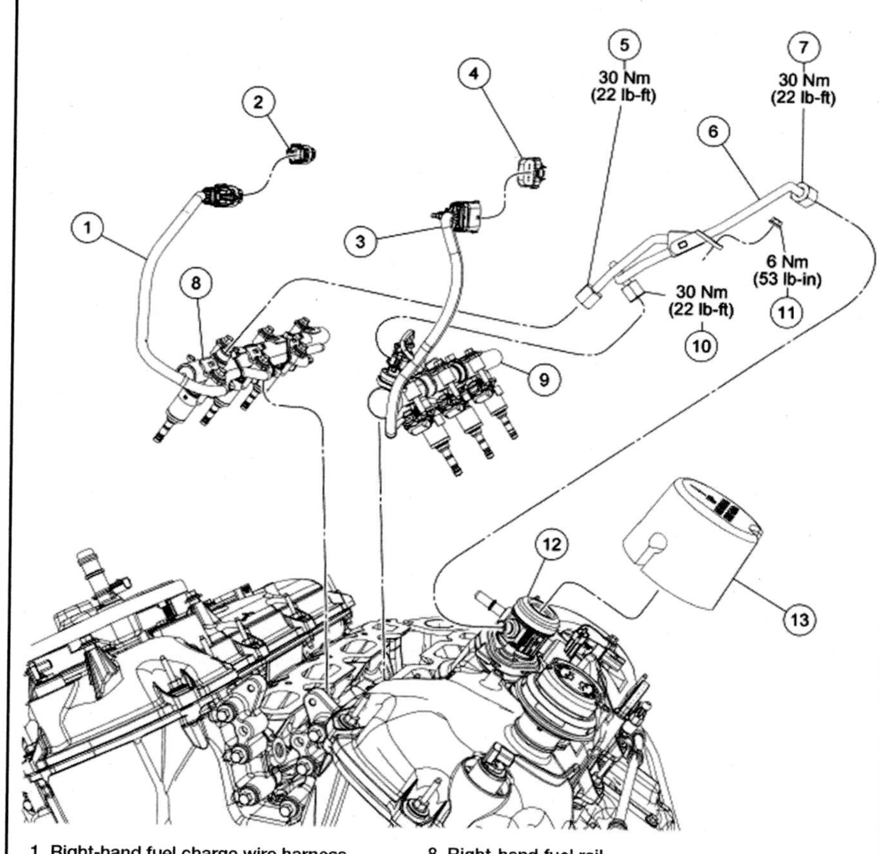

Fig. 202 Gasoline Turbocharged Direct Injection (GTDI) Fuel Rails and High Pressure Fuel Tube—3.5L Engines—Early Build Vehicles

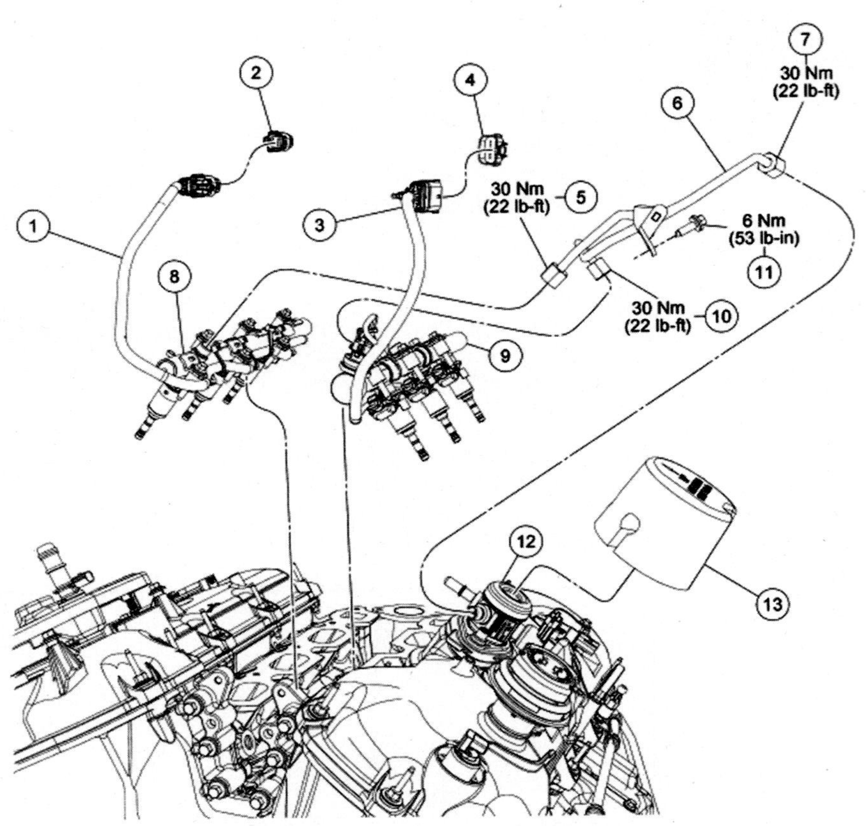

1. Right-hand fuel charge wire harness
2. Engine wire harness connector
3. Left-hand fuel charge wire harness
4. Engine wire harness connector
5. High pressure fuel tube-to-fuel rail flare nut
6. High pressure fuel tube
7. High pressure fuel tube-to-fuel rail flare nut
8. Right-hand fuel rail
9. Left-hand fuel rail
10. High pressure fuel tube-to-fuel injection pump flare nut
11. High pressure fuel tube bolt
12. Fuel injection pump
13. Fuel injection pump noise insulator shield

N0106766

Fig. 203 Gasoline Turbocharged Direct Injection (GTDI) Fuel Rails and High Pressure Fuel Tube—3.5L Engines—Late Build Vehicles

3. Remove the intake manifold.
4. Remove the fuel injection pump noise insulator shield.
5. For early build vehicles, remove the high pressure fuel tube nut.
6. For late build vehicles, remove the high pressure fuel tube bolt.
7. Loosen the 3 flare nuts and remove the high pressure fuel tube. To release the fuel pressure in the high pressure fuel tube, wrap the flare nuts with a shop towel to absorb any residual fuel pressure during the loosening of the flare nuts.
8. Disconnect the Fuel Rail Pressure (FRP) sensor electrical connector.
9. Cut, remove and discard the fuel charge wiring harness tie straps.
   a. It is very important to note the routing of the fuel charge wire harnesses on the fuel rails and matchmark the location of the tie straps prior to removal or damage may occur to the wire harnesses during installation.
   b. Use compressed air and remove any dirt or foreign material from the cylinder head, block and general surrounding area of the fuel rail and injectors.
10. Remove and discard the 6 bolts and remove the left-hand fuel rail.
   a. Pull out the fuel rails in the direction of the fuel injector axis or damage may occur to the fuel injectors.
   b. When removing the fuel rails, the fuel injectors may remain in the fuel rails but normally remain in the cylinder heads and require the use of a Fuel Injector Remover tool to extract.
11. Remove and discard the 6 bolts and remove the right-hand fuel rail.
12. Disconnect the 6 fuel injector electrical connectors and remove the 2 fuel charge wire harnesses.
13. Remove and discard the 6 upper fuel injector O-ring seals.
14. Remove and discard the 6 fuel injector clips.
15. Using the Slide Hammer and the Fuel Injector Remover (SST 307-005, 310-206) or equivalent tools, remove the 6 fuel injectors.

To install:

16. Make sure to thoroughly clean any residual fuel or foreign material from the cylinder head, block and the general surrounding area of the fuel rails and injectors.

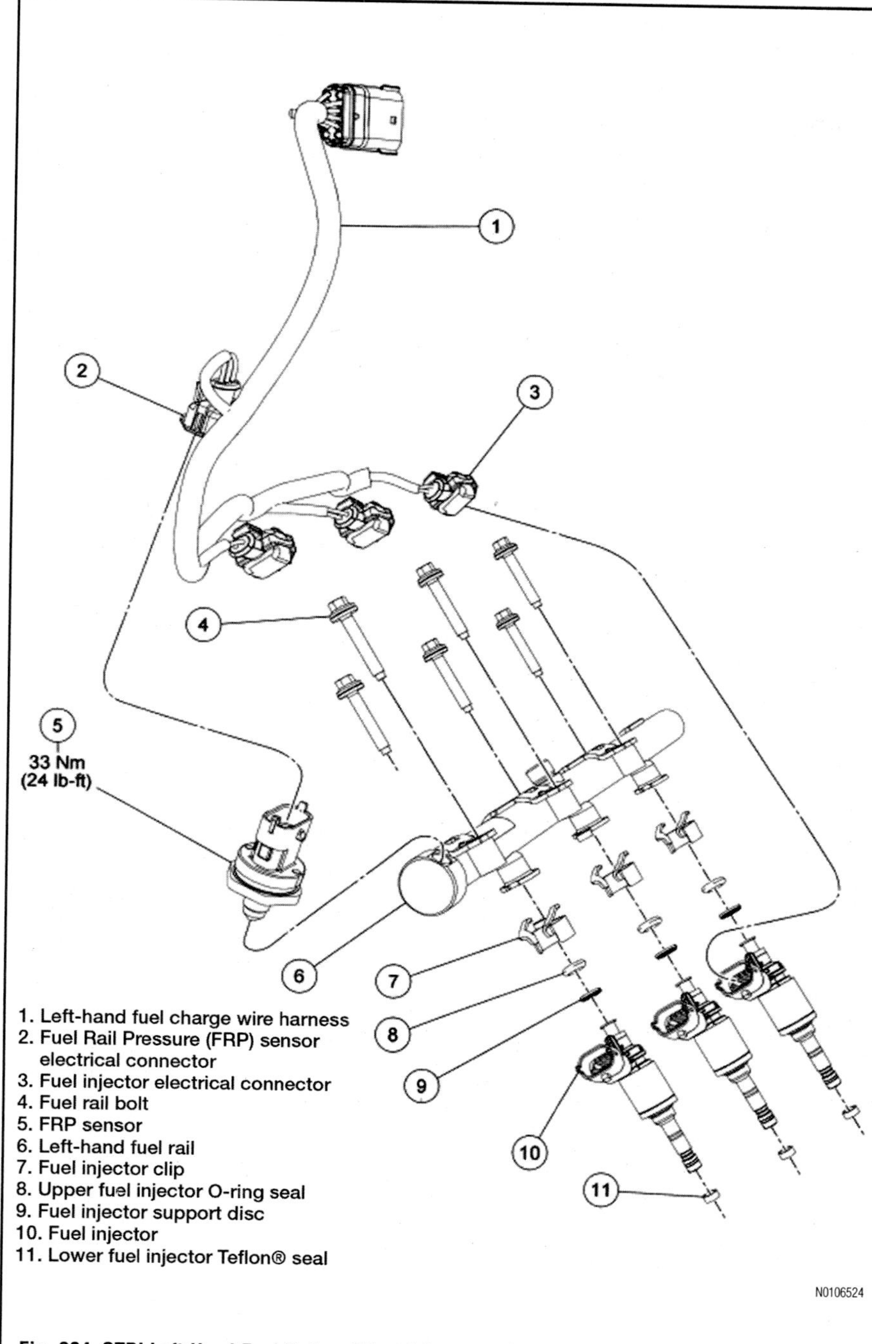

Fig. 204 GTDI Left-Hand Fuel Rail and Fuel Injectors—3.5L Engines

17. Using the Fuel Injector Brush (SST 310-205) or equivalent tool, clean the fuel injector orifices.
18. Pull the lower Teflon® seal away from the injector with narrow tip pliers.
    a. Do not attempt to cut the lower Teflon® seal without first pulling it away from the fuel injector or damage to the injector may occur.
    b. Be very careful when removing the lower Teflon® seals, not to scratch, nick or gouge the fuel injectors.
19. Carefully cut and discard the 6 lower fuel injector Teflon® seals.
20. Install the new lower Teflon® seals on the narrow end of the Arbor (part of the Fuel Injector Seal Installer), then install the Arbor on the fuel injector tips. Do not lubricate the 6 new lower Teflon® fuel injector seals.
21. Using the Pusher Tool (part of the Fuel Injector Seal Installer), slide the Teflon® seals off of the Arbor and into the groove on the fuel injectors.
    a. Once the Teflon® seal is installed on the Arbor, it should immediately be installed onto the fuel injector to avoid excessive expansion of the seal.
22. Place the Adjustment Ring (part of the Fuel Injector Seal Installer) beveled side first, over the fuel injector tip until it bottoms out against the fuel injector and turn 180 degrees.
    a. After one minute, turn the Adjustment Ring back 180 degrees and remove.
23. Install the fuel charge wire harnesses and tie straps to the matchmarked locations on the fuel rails. Start by attaching the first tie strap farthest down the wire harness and continue to the connector end of the harness, leaving ample slack between the fuel injectors. The illustration details the correct fuel charge wire harness routing and tie strap positioning for installation.
24. Connect the FRP sensor electrical connector.
25. Install the 6 new upper fuel injector O-ring seals.
    a. Use fuel injector O-ring seals that are made of special fuel-resistant material. The use of ordinary O-ring seals may cause the fuel system to leak. Do not reuse the O-ring seals.
    b. To install, apply clean engine oil to the 6 new upper fuel injector O-ring seals only. Do not lubricate the lower fuel injector Teflon® seals.
    c. Inspect the fuel injector support disks and replace if necessary.
26. Install the 6 new fuel injector clips.
27. Install the 6 fuel injectors into the fuel rails and connect the 6 electrical connectors.
    a. The anti-rotation device on the fuel injector has to slip into the groove of the fuel rail cup.

WARNING

It is very important to visually inspect the routing of the fuel charge wire harness to make sure that they will not be pinched or damaged between the fuel rail and the cylinder head during installation.

28. Install the 6 new bolts and the right-hand fuel rail assembly. Tighten the bolts in a method that draws the fuel rail evenly to the head, preventing a rocking motion.
    a. Push down on the fuel rail face above the injectors and begin tightening the outer bolts first and then proceed inward.
    b. To install, tighten to 89 inch lbs.(10 Nm).
    c. Tighten an additional 45 degrees.

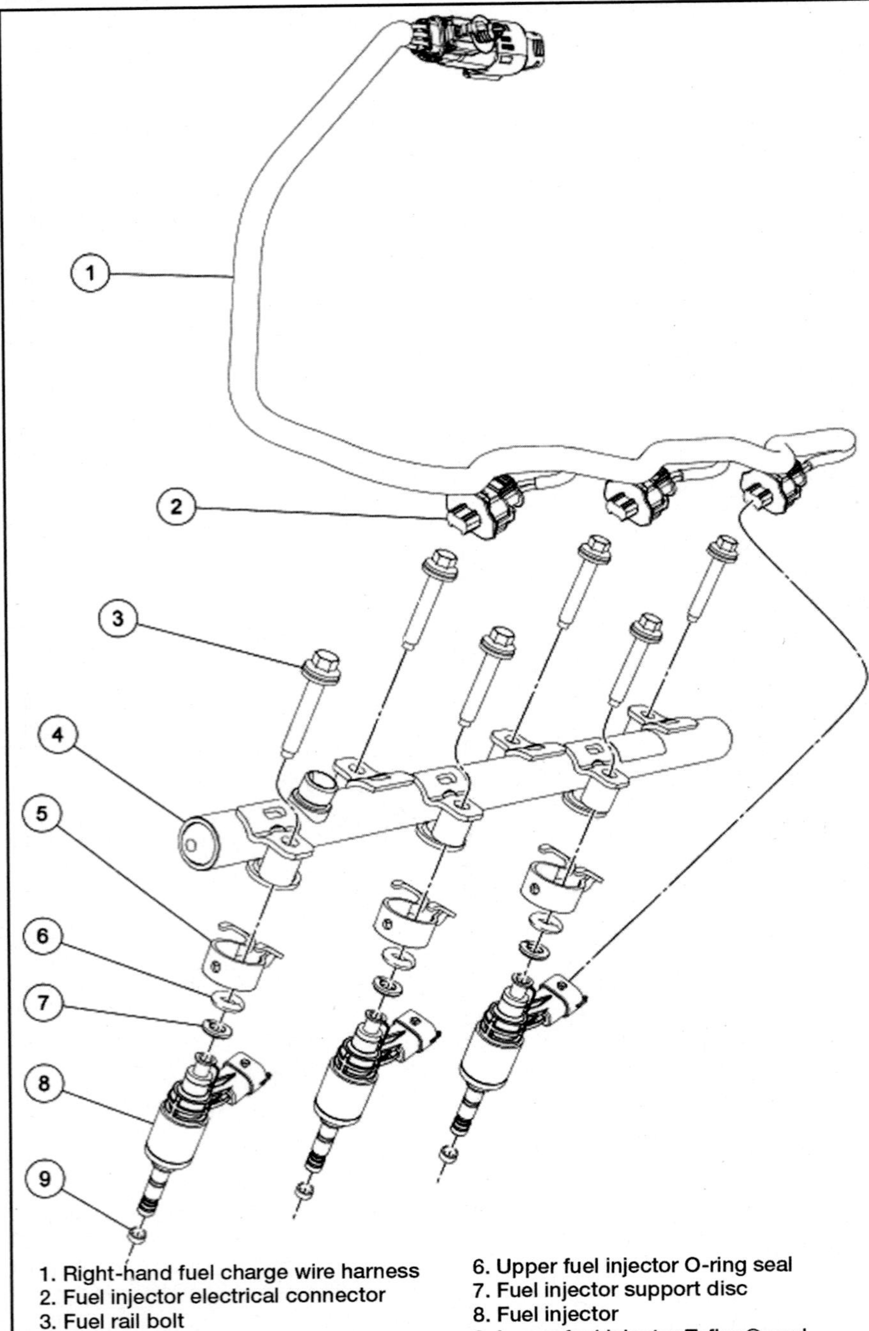

Fig. 205 GTDI Right-Hand Fuel Rail and Fuel Injectors—3.5L Engines

29. Install the 6 new bolts and the left-hand fuel rail assembly. Tighten the bolts in a method that draws the fuel rail evenly to the head, preventing a rocking motion.
    a. Push down on the fuel rail face above the injectors and begin tightening the outer bolts first and proceed inward.
    b. To install, tighten to 89 inch lbs.(10 Nm).
    c. Tighten an additional 45 degrees.
30. Apply clean engine oil to the threads of the 3 high-pressure fuel tube flare nuts. Install the high-pressure fuel tube and tighten the 3 flare nuts. Tighten to 22 ft. lbs. (30 Nm).
31. For early build vehicles, install the high-pressure fuel tube nut. Tighten to 53 inch lbs. (6 Nm).
32. For late build vehicles, install the high-pressure fuel tube bolt. Tighten to 53 inch lbs. (6 Nm).
33. Install the fuel injection pump noise insulator shield.
34. Install the intake manifold.
35. Connect the battery ground cable.

3.7L Engine

See Figure 206.

1. Release the fuel system pressure.
2. Disconnect the battery ground cable.
3. Remove the upper intake manifold.
4. Detach the fuel tube routing clips from the fuel rail.
5. Disconnect the fuel jumper tube-to-fuel rail spring lock coupling.
6. Disconnect the 6 fuel injector electrical connectors.
7. Remove the 4 fuel rail bolts.
8. Remove the fuel rail and injectors as an assembly.
9. Remove the 6 fuel injector clips and the 6 fuel injectors. Remove and discard the 12 fuel injector O-ring seals.

To install:

➡Use O-ring seals that are made of special fuel-resistant material. The use of ordinary O-rings may cause the fuel system to leak. Do not reuse the O-ring seals.

10. Install the new O-ring seals onto the fuel injectors and lubricate them with clean engine oil. The upper and lower fuel injector O-ring seals are similar in appearance, but are not interchangeable.
11. Install the 6 fuel injectors and the 6 fuel injector clips into the fuel rail.
12. Install the fuel rail and fuel injectors as an assembly.
13. Install the 4 fuel rail bolts. Tighten to 89 inch lbs.(10 Nm).
14. Connect the 6 fuel injector electrical connectors.
15. Connect the fuel jumper tube-to-fuel rail spring lock coupling.
16. Attach the fuel tube routing clips to the fuel rail.
17. Install the upper intake manifold.
18. Connect the battery ground cable.

FUEL PUMP

REMOVAL & INSTALLATION

See Figures 207 and 208.

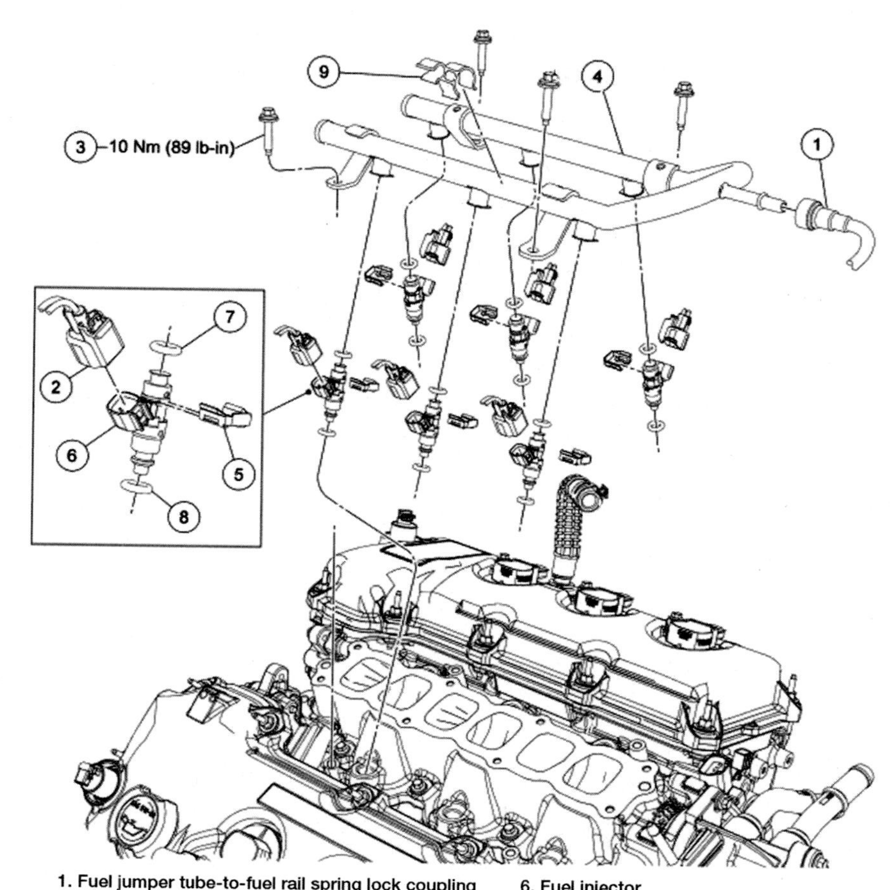

Fig. 206 Fuel Rail and Fuel Injector—3.7L Engines

1. Release the fuel system pressure.
2. Disconnect the battery ground cable.
3. Remove the rear seat lower cushion.
4. Remove the Fuel Pump (FP) module access cover.
5. Clean the FP module connections, couplings, flange surfaces and the immediate surrounding area of any dirt or foreign material.
6. Disconnect the FP module electrical connector.
7. Disconnect the fuel tank wiring harness electrical connector.
8. Disconnect the Fuel Tank Pressure (FTP) sensor electrical connector.
9. Disconnect the fuel tank jumper tube-to- FP module quick connect coupling.
   a. Place absorbent toweling in the immediate surrounding area in case of fuel spillage.
10. Attach the Fuel Storage Tanker tube to the FP module outlet fitting and remove one fourth (approximately 5 gallons) of the fuel from a completely full tank, lowering the fuel level below the FP module mounting flange.
11. For All-Wheel Drive (AWD) vehicles:
    a. Remove the Evaporative Emission (EVAP) canister.
    b. Remove the driveshaft.
    c. Position the Powertrain Lift under the fuel tank.
    d. Loosen the 2 rear fuel tank strap bolts.
    e. Remove the 2 front fuel tank strap bolts.
    f. Partially lower the front of the fuel tank to access the FP module shield nuts.
    g. Install a suitable cap on the FP module port to avoid fuel spillage when lowering the front of the fuel tank.
    h. Remove the 3 nuts and the FP module shield.
    i. Raise the fuel tank into the installed position and reinstall the 2 front fuel tank strap bolts. The fuel tank must be placed back into the installed position prior to FP module removal to avoid fuel spillage.
12. For All Vehicles:
    a. Install the Fuel Tank Sender Unit Wrench, remove the FP module lock ring. Carefully install the Fuel Tank Sender Unit Wrench to avoid damaging the FP module when removing the lock ring.
13. For AWD vehicles:

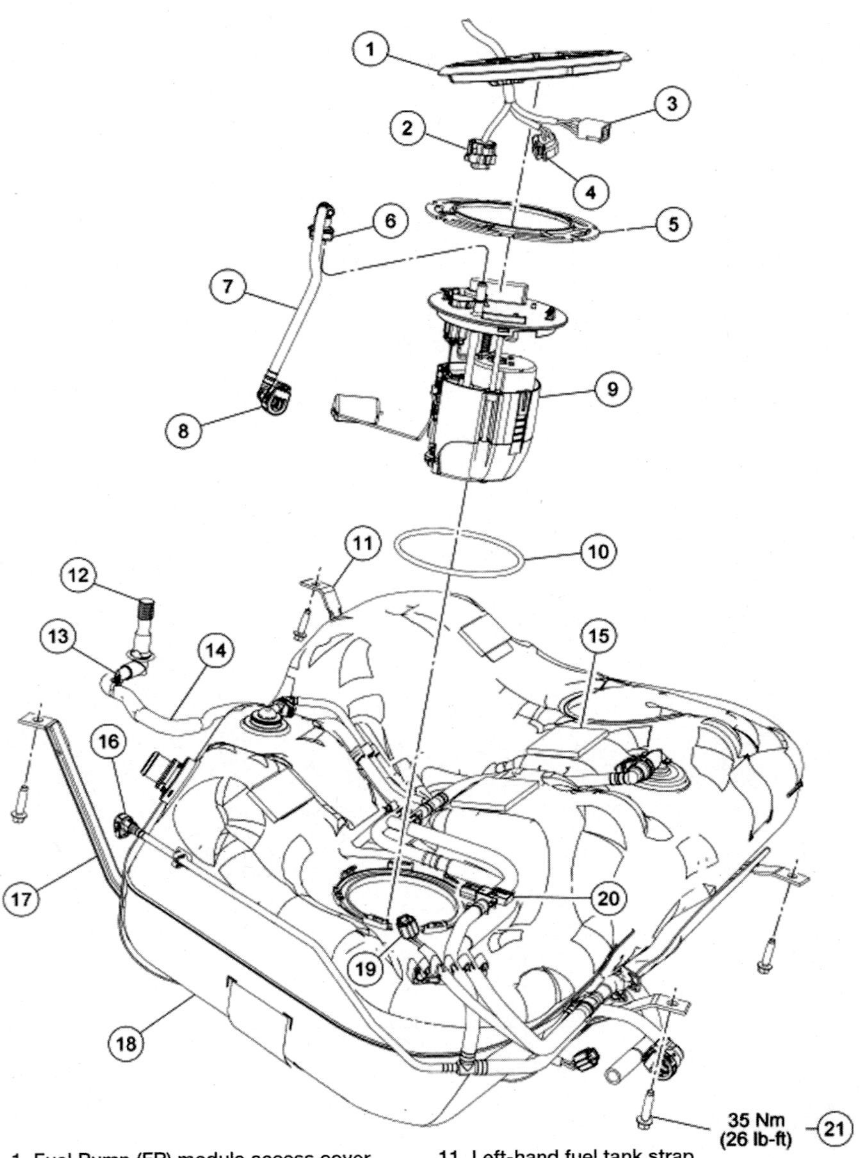
35 Nm
(26 lb-ft)
1. Fuel Pump (FP) module access cover
2. FP module electrical connector
3. Fuel Tank Pressure (FTP) sensor electrical connector
4. Fuel tank jumper wiring harness electrical connector
5. FP module lock ring
6. Fuel tank jumper tube-to-FP module quick connect coupling
7. Fuel tank jumper tube
8. Fuel tank jumper tube-to-fuel tube quick connect coupling
9. FP module
10. FP module O-ring seal
11. Left-hand fuel tank strap
12. Fresh air hose vent cap
13. Fresh air hose pin-type retainer
14. Fresh air hose
15. Isolation pad
16. Fuel vapor tube assembly-to-fuel tank filler pipe recirculation tube quick connect
17. Right-hand fuel tank strap
18. Fuel tank
19. Fuel tank jumper wiring harness electrical connector
20. FTP sensor
21. Fuel tank strap bolt
N0103726

Fig. 207 L-Shaped fuel tank components

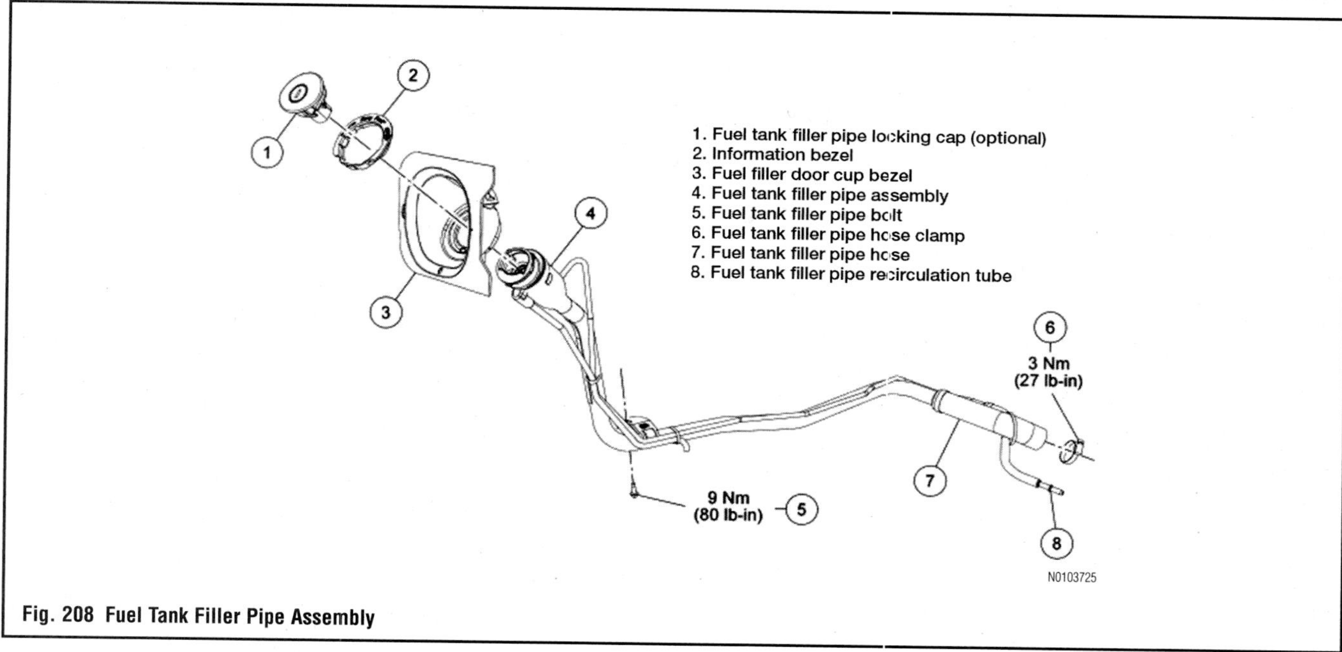

Fig. 208 Fuel Tank Filler Pipe Assembly

⁂ WARNING

The Fuel Pump (FP) module must be handled carefully to avoid damage to the float arm.

a. Carefully lift the FP module out of the fuel tank allowing access and disconnect the FP module internal quick connect coupling.

14. For All Vehicles:

⁂ WARNING

The Fuel Pump (FP) module must be handled carefully to avoid damage to the float arm.

a. Completely remove the FP module from the fuel tank. The FP module will have residual fuel remaining internally, drain into a suitable container.

b. Inspect the surfaces of the FP module flange and fuel tank O-ring seal contact surfaces. Do not polish or adjust the O-ring seal contact area of the fuel tank flange or the fuel tank. Install a new FP module or fuel tank if the O-ring seal contact area is bent, scratched or corroded.

c. Remove and discard the FP module O-ring seal.

To install:

15. To install, reverse the removal procedure, noting the following:

a. Make sure the alignment arrows on the fuel pump module and the fuel tank meet before tightening the FP module lock ring.

b. Tighten the FP lock ring until it meets the stop tabs on the fuel tank.

c. Make sure to install a new FP module O-ring seal.

d. Apply clean engine oil to the O-ring seal.

e. Tighten the FP module shield nuts to 80 inch lbs. (9 Nm).

f. Tighten the 2 front fuel tank strap bolts to 26 ft. lbs. (35 Nm).

g. Tighten the 2 rear fuel tank strap bolts to 26 ft. lbs. (35 Nm).

FUEL TANK

DRAINING

L-Shaped Fuel Tank

1. Release the fuel system pressure.
2. Disconnect the battery ground cable.
3. Remove the rear seat lower cushion. For additional information, refer to Seating.
4. Remove the Fuel Pump (FP) module access cover.
5. Clean the FP module connections, couplings, flange surfaces and the immediate surrounding area of any dirt or foreign material.
6. Disconnect the FP module electrical connector.
7. Disconnect the fuel tank wiring harness electrical connector.
8. Disconnect the Fuel Tank Pressure (FTP) sensor electrical connector.
9. Disconnect the fuel tank jumper tube-to-FP module quick connect coupling.

a. Place absorbent toweling in the immediate surrounding area in case of fuel spillage.

10. Attach the Fuel Storage Tanker tube to the FP module outlet fitting and remove one fourth (approximately 5 gallons) of the fuel from a completely full tank, lowering the fuel level below the FP module flange.
11. Install the Fuel Tank Sender Unit Wrench and remove the FP module lock ring.

⁂ WARNING

Carefully install the Fuel Tank Sender Unit Wrench to avoid damaging the Fuel Pump (FP) module when removing the lock ring.

a. Make sure to install a new FP module O-ring seal.

12. Position the FP module aside, insert the tube from the fuel storage tanker into the FP module aperture and remove as much fuel as possible from the fuel tank.

⁂ WARNING

The Fuel Pump (FP) module must be handled carefully to avoid damage to the float arm and filter.

Saddle Type Fuel Tank

1. Release the fuel system pressure.
2. Disconnect the battery ground cable.

3. Remove the rear seat lower cushion.
4. Remove the Fuel Pump (FP) module access cover.
5. Clean the FP module connections, couplings, flange surfaces and the immediate surrounding area of any dirt or foreign material.
6. Disconnect the FP module electrical connector.
7. Disconnect the fuel tank wiring harness electrical connector.
8. Disconnect the Fuel Tank Pressure (FTP) sensor electrical connector.
9. Disconnect the fuel tank jumper tube-to-FP module quick connect coupling. For additional information, refer to Quick Connect Coupling in this section.
   a. Place absorbent toweling in the immediate surrounding area in case of fuel spillage.
10. Attach the Fuel Storage Tanker tube to the FP module outlet fitting and remove one fourth (approximately 5 gallons) of the fuel from a completely full tank, lowering the fuel level below the fuel level sensor flange.
11. Remove the fuel level sensor access cover.
12. Clean the fuel level sensor connections, couplings, flange surfaces and the immediate surrounding area of any dirt or foreign material.
13. Disconnect the fuel level sensor electrical connector.
14. Install the Fuel Tank Sender Unit Wrench and remove the fuel level sensor lock ring.

WARNING

Carefully install the Fuel Tank Sender Unit Wrench to avoid damaging the fuel level sensor when removing the lock ring.

   a. Place absorbent toweling in the immediate surrounding area in case of fuel spillage.
   b. Make sure to install a new fuel level sensor O-ring seal.
15. Position the fuel level sensor aside, insert the tube from the Fuel Storage Tanker into the fuel level sensor aperture and remove as much of the remaining fuel as possible from the fuel tank.

REMOVAL & INSTALLATION

L-Shaped Fuel Tank

See Figures 209 and 210.

1. With the vehicle in NEUTRAL, position it on a hoist.

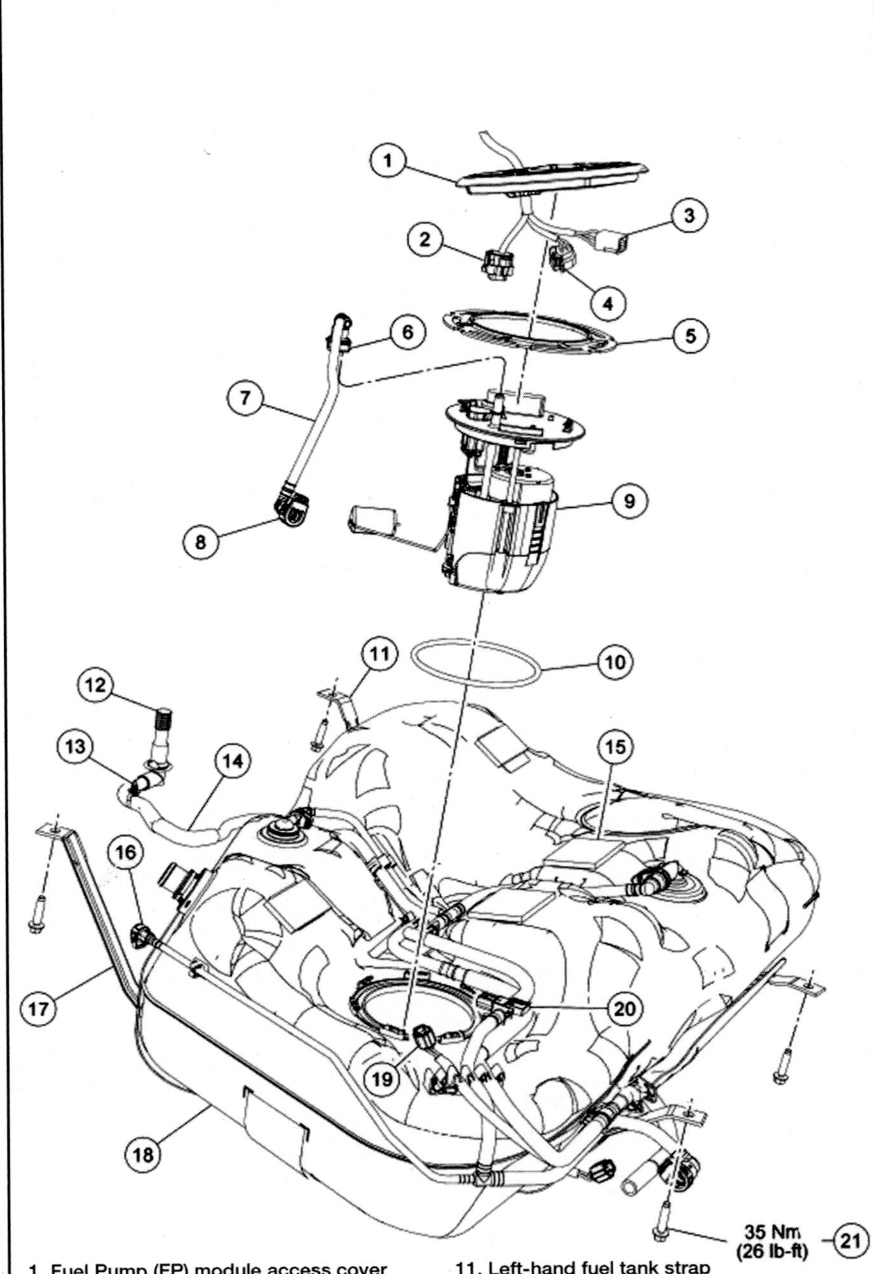

1. Fuel Pump (FP) module access cover
2. FP module electrical connector
3. Fuel Tank Pressure (FTP) sensor electrical connector
4. Fuel tank jumper wiring harness electrical connector
5. FP module lock ring
6. Fuel tank jumper tube-to-FP module quick connect coupling
7. Fuel tank jumper tube
8. Fuel tank jumper tube-to-fuel tube quick connect coupling
9. FP module
10. FP module O-ring seal
11. Left-hand fuel tank strap
12. Fresh air hose vent cap
13. Fresh air hose pin-type retainer
14. Fresh air hose
15. Isolation pad
16. Fuel vapor tube assembly-to-fuel tank filler pipe recirculation tube quick connect
17. Right-hand fuel tank strap
18. Fuel tank
19. Fuel tank jumper wiring harness electrical connector
20. FTP sensor
21. Fuel tank strap bolt

N0103726

Fig. 209 L-Shaped fuel tank components

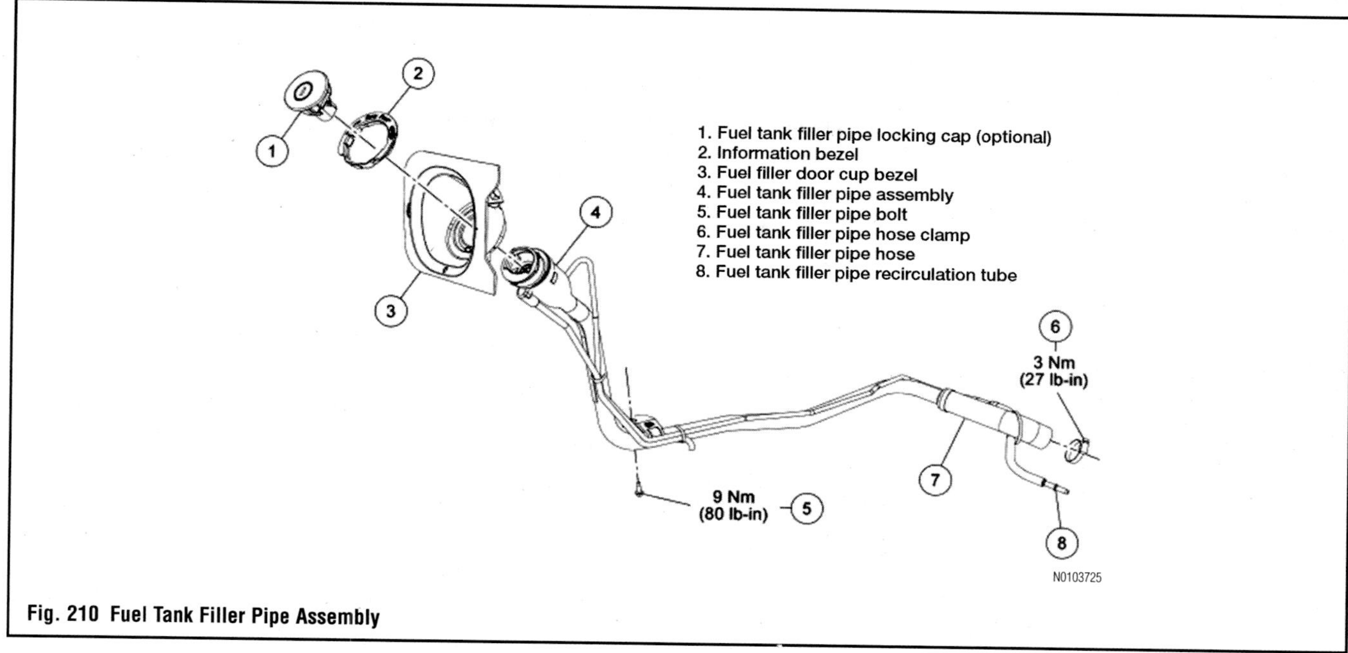

Fig. 210 Fuel Tank Filler Pipe Assembly

2. Drain the fuel tank.
3. Remove the muffler and tail pipe assembly.

⁂ CAUTION

Some residual fuel may remain in the fuel tank filler pipe after draining the fuel tank. Carefully drain any residual fuel into a suitable container.

4. Release the clamp and remove the fuel tank filler pipe hose from the fuel tank.
5. Disconnect the fuel vapor tube assembly-to-fuel tank filler pipe recirculation tube quick connect coupling.
6. Disconnect the fuel tank jumper tube-to-fuel tube quick connect coupling.
7. Release the fresh air hose vent cap and pin-type retainer from the body.
8. Disconnect the EVAP canister vent solenoid electrical connector.
   a. Clean the Evaporative Emission (EVAP) canister vent solenoid electrical connector and the immediate surrounding area of any dirt or foreign material.
9. Disconnect the fresh air hose-to-dust separator fitting.
10. Disconnect the fuel vapor tube assembly-to-EVAP canister quick connect coupling.
11. Position the Powertrain Lift under the fuel tank.
12. Remove the 4 bolts and the 2 fuel tank straps. Do not bend or distort the fuel tank straps.
13. Carefully lower and remove the fuel tank from the vehicle.

To install:

14. To install, reverse the removal procedure.
   a. Tighten the fuel tank straps to 26 ft. lbs. (35 Nm).
   b. Tighten the fuel tank filler pipe hose clamp to 27 inch lbs.(3 Nm).

Saddle Type Fuel Tank

See Figures 211 and 212.

1. With the vehicle in NEUTRAL, position it on a hoist.
2. Remove the muffler and tail pipe.
3. Drain the fuel tank.
4. Remove the driveshaft.
5. Remove the Evaporative Emission (EVAP) canister.

⁂ CAUTION

Some residual fuel may remain in the fuel tank filler pipe after draining the fuel tank. Carefully drain any residual fuel into a suitable container.

6. Release the clamp and remove the fuel tank filler pipe hose from the fuel tank.
7. Disconnect the fuel vapor tube assembly-to-fuel tank filler pipe recirculation tube quick connect coupling.
8. Disconnect the fuel tank jumper tube-to-fuel tube quick connect coupling.
9. Release the fresh air hose vent cap and pin-type retainer from the body.
10. Position the Powertrain Lift under the fuel tank.
11. Loosen the 2 rear fuel tank strap bolts.
12. Remove the 2 front fuel tank strap bolts.
13. Release the 2 straps from the fuel tank and carefully position aside. Do not bend or distort the fuel tank straps.
14. Carefully lower and remove the fuel tank from the vehicle.

To install:

15. To install, reverse the removal procedure, noting the following:
   a. Tighten the 2 front fuel tank strap bolts to 26 ft. lbs. (35 Nm).
   b. Tighten the 2 rear fuel tank strap bolts to 26 ft. lbs. (35 Nm).
   c. Tighten the fuel tank filler pipe hose clamp to 27 inch lbs. (3 Nm).

THROTTLE BODY

REMOVAL & INSTALLATION

3.5L Engine

See Figure 213.

1. Disconnect the Throttle Position (TP) sensor electrical connector.
2. Disconnect the Throttle Actuator Control (TAC) electrical connector.
3. Loosen the clamp and disconnect the Charge Air Cooler (CAC) outlet pipe-to-throttle body.
4. Remove the 4 bolts, the throttle body and the TP sensor shield bracket. Discard the throttle body gasket.

To install:

5. To install, reverse the removal procedure, noting the following:
   a. Install a new throttle body gasket.

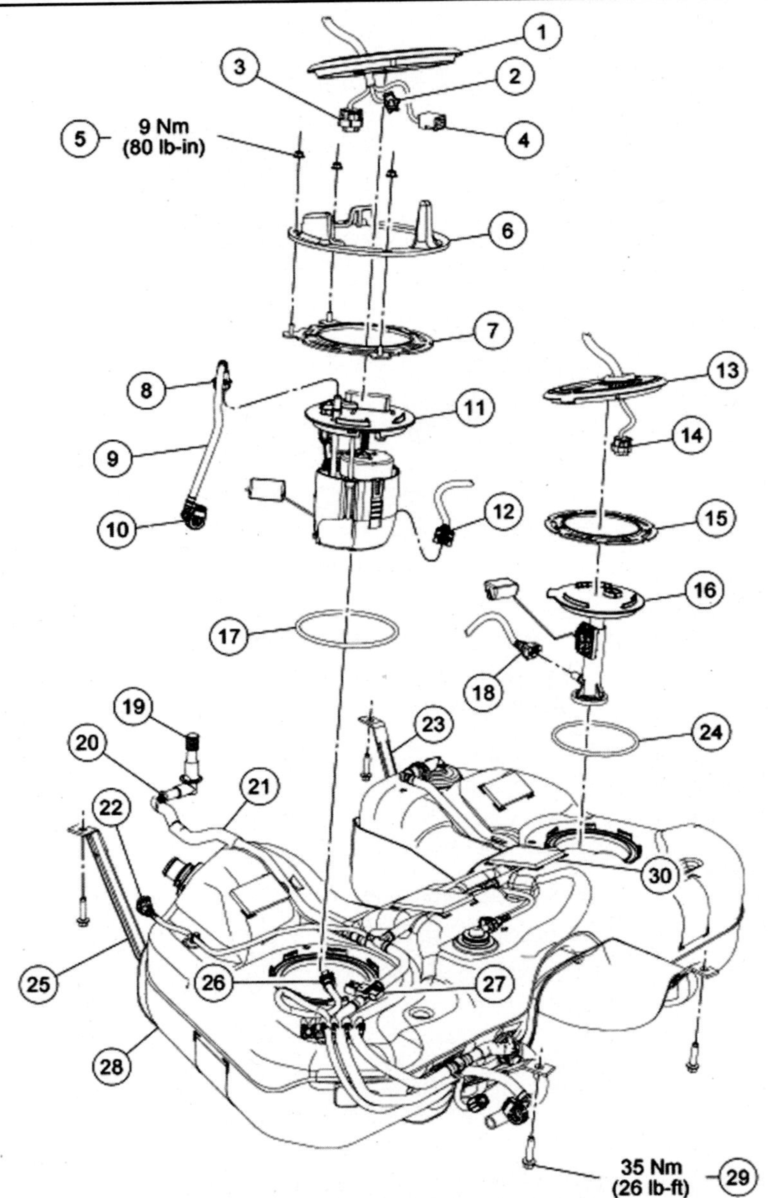

1. Fuel Pump (FP) module access cover
2. Fuel tank jumper wiring harness connector
3. FP module electrical connector
4. Fuel Tank Pressure (FTP) sensor connector
5. FP module shield nut
6. FP module shield
7. FP module lock ring
8. Fuel tank jumper tube-to-FP module quick connect coupling
9. Fuel tank jumper tube
10. Fuel tank jumper tube-to-fuel tube quick connect coupling
11. FP module
12. Internal fuel tube-to-FP module quick connect coupling
13. Fuel level sensor access cover
14. Fuel level sensor connector
15. Fuel level sensor lock ring
16. Fuel level sensor
17. FP module O-ring seal
18. Internal fuel tube-to-FP module quick connect coupling
19. Fresh air hose vent cap
20. Fresh air hose pin-type retainer
21. Fresh air hose
22. Fuel vapor tube assembly-to-fuel tank filler pipe recirculation tube quick connect coupling
23. Left-hand fuel tank strap
24. Fuel level sensor O-ring seal
25. Right-hand fuel tank strap
26. Fuel tank jumper wiring harness electrical connector
27. FTP sensor
28. Fuel tank
29. Fuel tank strap bolt
30. Isolation pad

N0103727

Fig. 211 Saddle type fuel tank components

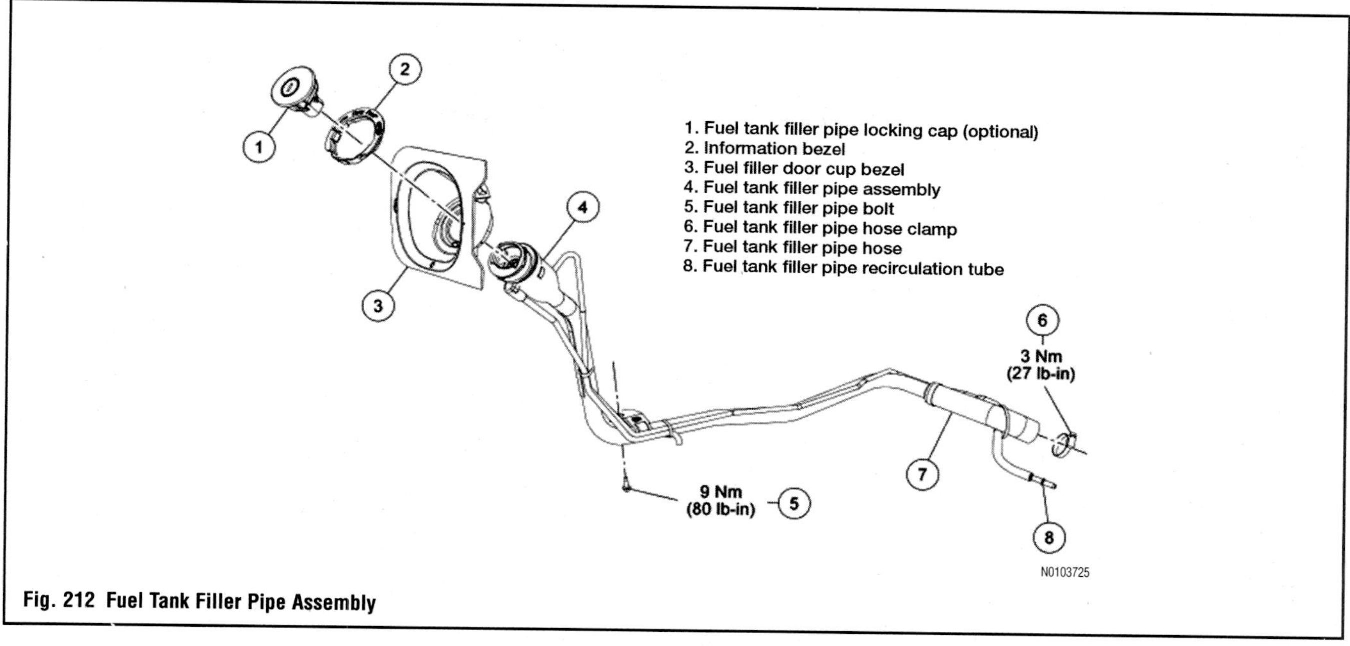

Fig. 212 Fuel Tank Filler Pipe Assembly

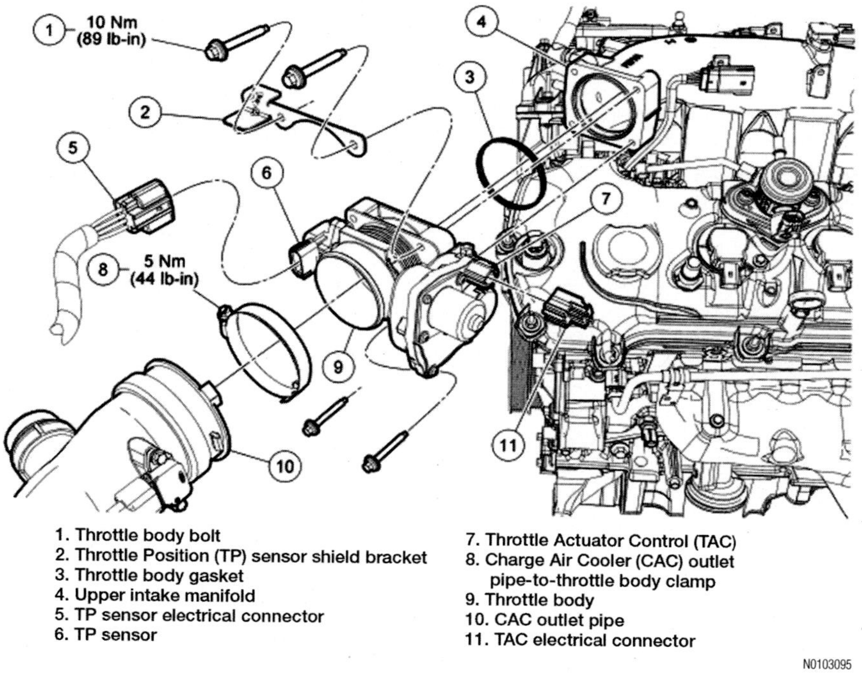

10 Nm (89 lb-in)
5 Nm (44 lb-in)

1. Throttle body bolt
2. Throttle Position (TP) sensor shield bracket
3. Throttle body gasket
4. Upper intake manifold
5. TP sensor electrical connector
6. TP sensor
7. Throttle Actuator Control (TAC)
8. Charge Air Cooler (CAC) outlet pipe-to-throttle body clamp
9. Throttle body
10. CAC outlet pipe
11. TAC electrical connector

N0103095

Fig. 213 Throttle body components—3.5L engines

b. Tighten the throttle body mounting bolts to 89 inch lbs. (10 Nm).

c. Tighten the CAC outlet pipe-to-throttle body clamp to 44 inch lbs. (5 Nm).

3.7L Engine

See Figure 214.

1. Remove the Air Cleaner (ACL) outlet pipe.
2. Disconnect the electronic throttle control electrical connector.
3. Remove the 4 bolts and the throttle body. Discard the gasket.

To install:

4. To install, reverse the removal procedure, noting the following:

a. Install a new throttle body gasket.

b. Tighten the throttle body mounting bolts to 89 inch lbs.(10 Nm).

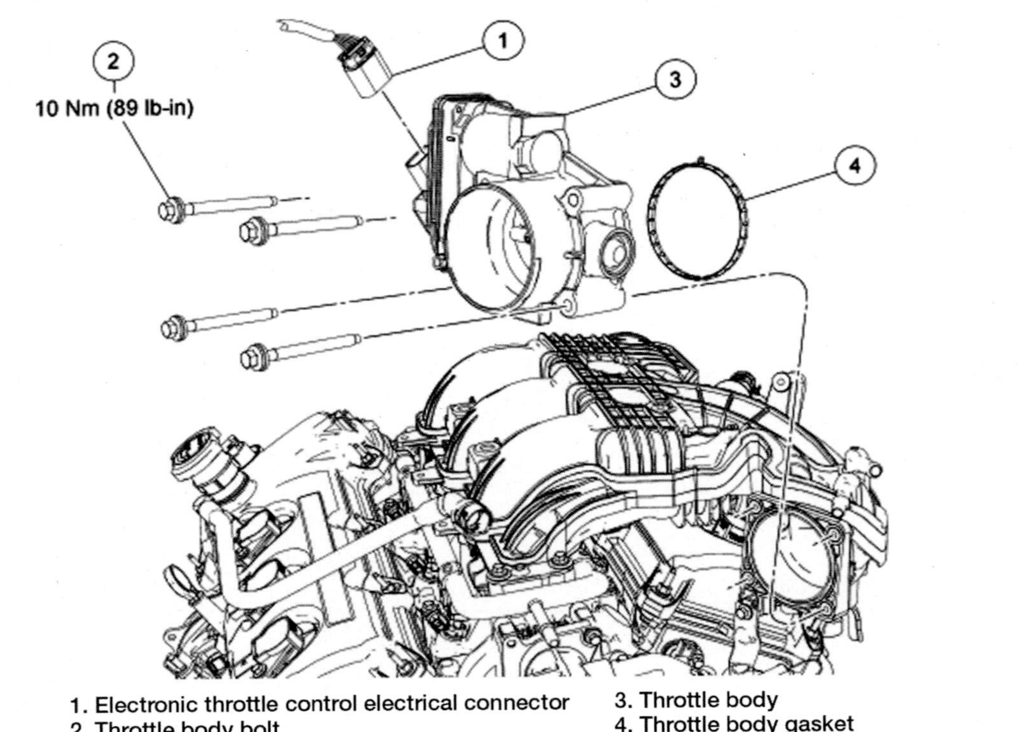

Fig. 214 Throttle body components—3.7L engines

HEATING & AIR CONDITIONING SYSTEM

BLOWER MOTOR

REMOVAL & INSTALLATION

See Figure 215.

⁂ CAUTION

Always deplete the backup power supply before repairing or installing any new front or side air bag supplemental restraint system (SRS) component and before servicing, removing, installing, adjusting or striking components near the front or side impact sensors or the restraints control module (RCM). Nearby components include doors, instrument panel, console, door latches, strikers, seats and hood latches. To deplete the backup power supply energy, disconnect the battery ground cable and wait at least 1 minute. Be sure to disconnect auxiliary batteries and power supplies (if equipped).

1. Remove the 3 right-hand lower instrument panel insulator screws and remove the insulator.
2. Disconnect the blower motor electrical connector.
3. Depress the 2 retaining tabs and detach the blower motor vent tube from the heater core and evaporator core housing.

➡The blower motor vent tube must be completely detached from the heater core and evaporator core

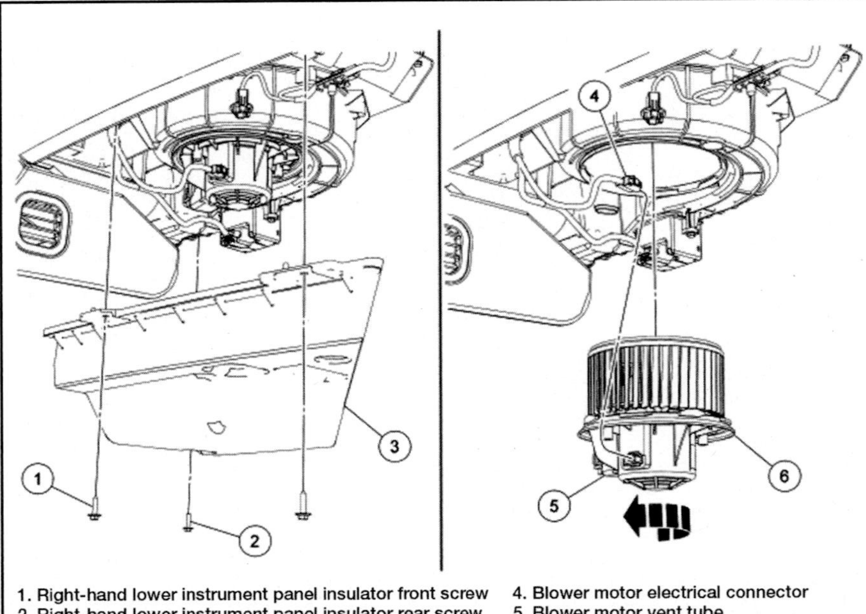

Fig. 215 Blower motor components

housing to allow the blower motor to be rotated.

4. Rotate the blower motor counter-clockwise to detach it from the heater core and evaporator core housing and remove the blower motor.

To install:

5. To install, reverse the removal procedure.

HEATER CORE

REMOVAL & INSTALLATION

See Figures 216 through 219.

CAUTION

Always deplete the backup power supply before repairing or installing any new front or side air bag supplemental restraint system (SRS) component and before servicing, removing, installing, adjusting or striking components near the front or side impact sensors or the restraints control module (RCM). Nearby components include doors, instrument panel, console, door latches, strikers, seats and hood latches. To deplete the backup power supply energy, disconnect the battery ground cable and wait at least 1 minute. Be sure to disconnect auxiliary batteries and power supplies (if equipped).

➡If a heater core leak is suspected, the heater core must be pressure leak tested before it is removed from the vehicle.

1. Remove the heater core and evaporator core housing, as follows:
   a. Remove the instrument panel assembly.
   b. Position the instrument panel with the passenger side supported as shown.
   c. Remove the 3 right-hand lower instrument panel insulator screws and position the insulator aside.
   d. Remove the 2 Remote Function Actuator (RFA) module nuts and position the module aside.
   e. Detach the in-vehicle temperature sensor aspirator from the heater core and evaporator core housing.
   f. Remove the 2 floor duct screws and remove the floor duct.
   g. Remove the 4 Audio Control Module (ACM) screws and the ACM:
   - Disconnect the electrical connectors and antenna connectors
   - Detach the wire harness pin-type retainers

   h. Remove the console duct Y adapter pin-type retainer and the adapter.
   i. Remove the right-hand and left-hand console duct adapters.
   j. Remove the 2 floor duct adapter nuts and the floor duct adapter.
   k. Remove the 2 heater core and evaporator core housing stud-bolts.
   l. Remove the 4 heater core and evaporator core housing bolts.
   m. Disconnect the 3 electrical connectors and detach the wire harness pin-type retainer.
   n. Detach the 4 wire harness pin-type retainers and disconnect the electrical connector.
   o. Disconnect the 3 electrical connectors, detach the wire harness pin-type retainer and detach the instrument panel wire harness from the heater core and evaporator core housing.
   p. Remove the heater core and evaporator core housing.
2. Remove the dash panel seal.
3. Remove the 3 heater core tube support bracket screws and heater core tube support bracket.
4. Remove the 10 plenum chamber screws and separate the heater core and evaporator housing.
5. Remove the heater core.

To install:

6. To install, reverse the removal procedure.
   a. Tighten the heater core and evaporator core housing bolts to 80 inch lbs.(9 Nm).

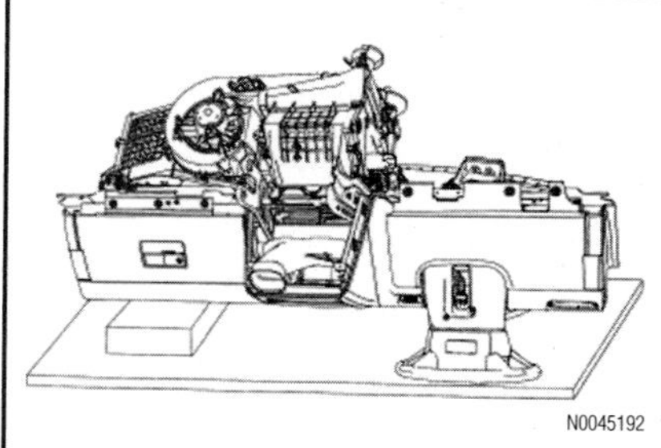

Fig. 216 Instrument panel positioning

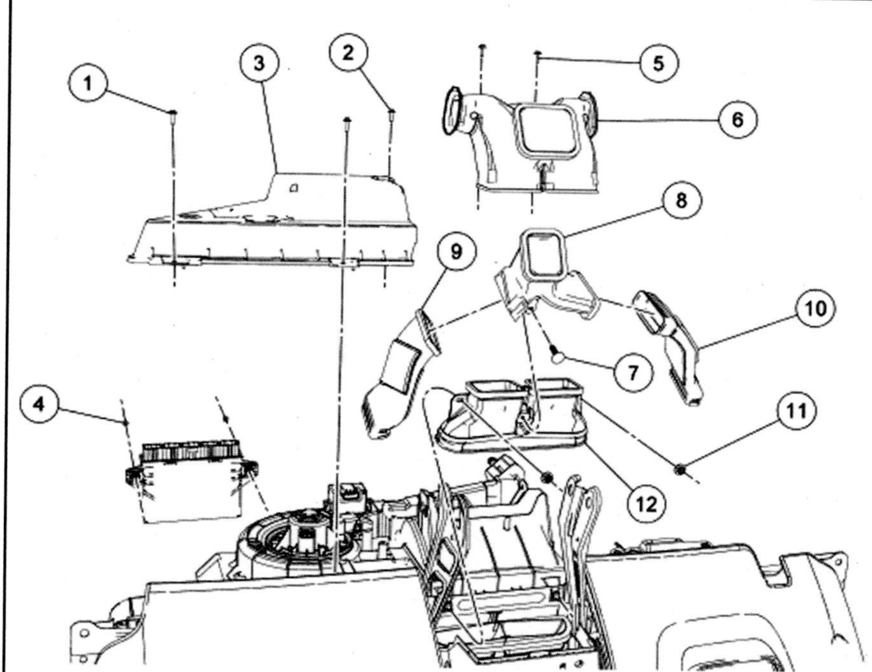

Fig. 217 Heater and evaporator core housing components

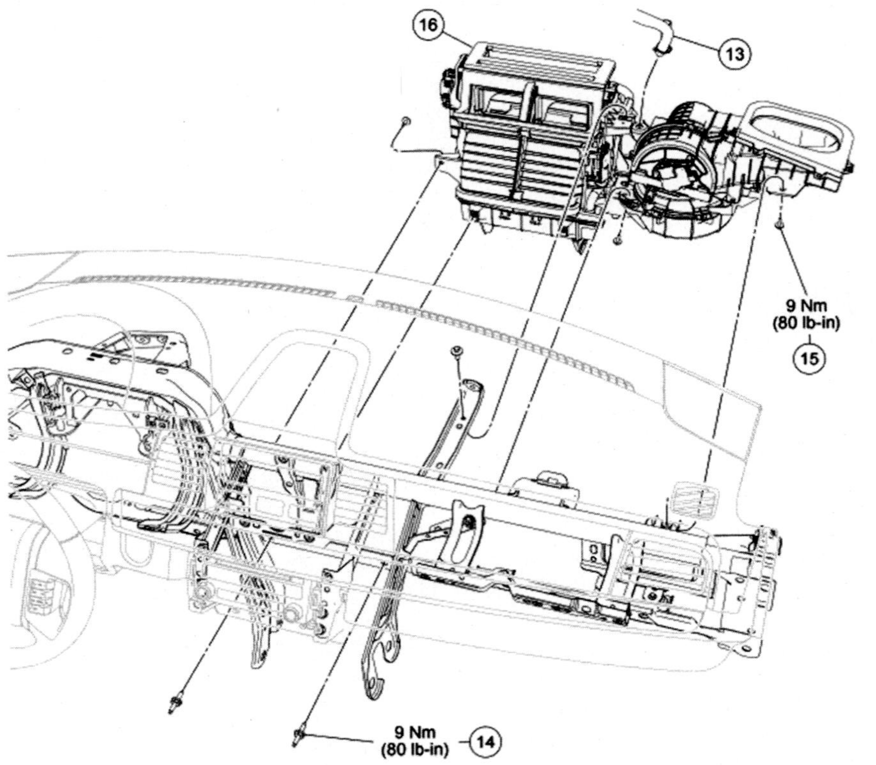

16

13

9 Nm (80 lb-in) 15

9 Nm (80 lb-in) 14

13. In-vehicle temperature sensor aspirator hose assembly
14. Heater core and evaporator core housing stud-bolt
15. Heater core and evaporator core housing bolt
16. Heater core and evaporator core housing

N0091779

Fig. 218 Heater and evaporator core housing

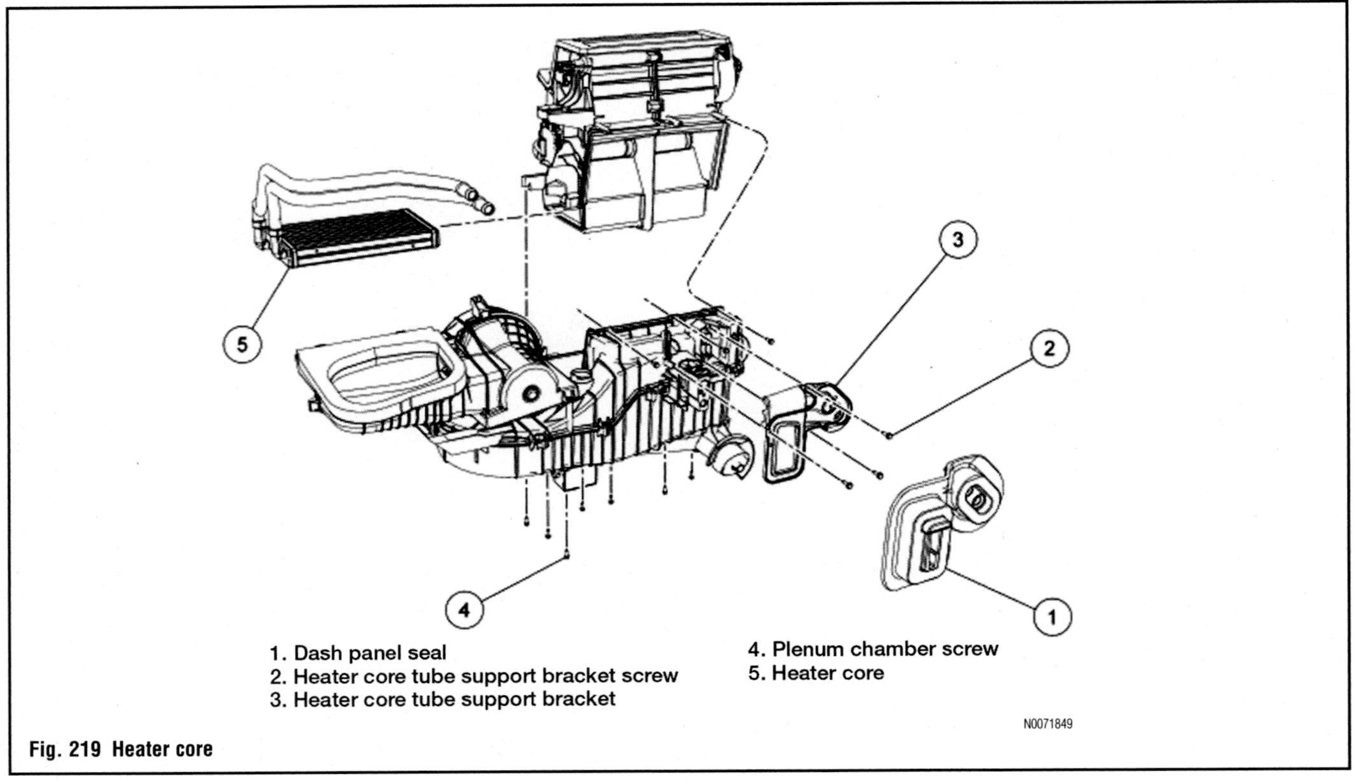

1. Dash panel seal
2. Heater core tube support bracket screw
3. Heater core tube support bracket
4. Plenum chamber screw
5. Heater core

N0071849

Fig. 219 Heater core

STEERING

POWER STEERING GEAR

REMOVAL & INSTALLATION

Electronic Power Assist Steering Gear

See Figures 220 and 221.

1. Using a suitable holding device, hold the steering wheel in the straight-ahead position.
2. Remove the wheels and tires.
3. Remove the bolt and disconnect the steering column shaft from the steering gear. Discard the bolt.
   a. Do not allow the steering column to rotate while the steering column shaft is disconnected from the steering gear or damage to the clockspring may occur. If there is evidence that the steering column has rotated, the clockspring must be removed and recentered.
4. Remove the 2 stabilizer bar link upper nuts. Discard the nuts.
5. Remove the 2 outer tie-rod end nuts and separate the tie-rod ends from the wheel knuckle.
6. Remove the 4 retainers and the underbody shield.
7. Remove the right-hand and left-hand exhaust flexible pipes.
8. Remove the 2 front and rear engine roll restrictor bolts.
9. Position the Powertrain Lift Table under the subframe.
10. Remove the 2 front subframe rearward bolts, the 4 support bracket bolts and the 2 subframe support brackets.
    a. Loosen the 2 front subframe forward bolts.
11. Lower the subframe to gain access to the steering gear.
12. Remove the wiring harness bracket bolt.
13. Disconnect the 2 Electronic Power Assist Steering (EPAS) electrical connectors and the wiring retainer.
14. Remove the 2 steering gear bolts.
    a. Position the stabilizer bar to the full up position.
    b. Remove the steering gear from the right-hand side of the vehicle.

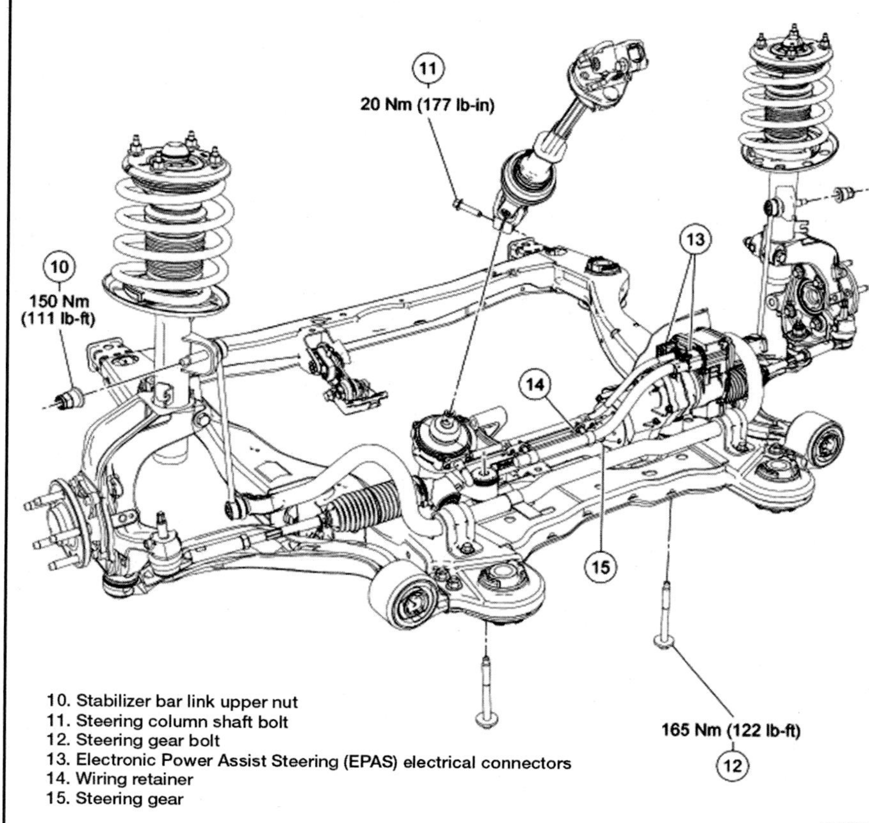

Fig. 220 Electronic power assist steering gear components

To install:

15. Position the steering gear and install the 2 bolts. Tighten to 122 ft. lbs. (165 Nm).
16. Connect the 2 EPAS electrical connectors and the wiring retainer.
17. Position the wiring harness bracket and install the bolt. Tighten to 80 inch lbs. (9 Nm).
18. Raise the subframe.
19. Position the 2 subframe support brackets and install the 4 bolts finger-tight.
20. Install the 2 front subframe rearward bolts.
    a. Tighten the rearward bolts to 111 ft. lbs. (150 Nm).
    b. Tighten the forward bolts to 148 ft. lbs. (200 Nm).
21. Tighten the 4 subframe support bracket bolts to 41 ft. lbs. (55 Nm).
22. Install the 2 front and rear engine roll restrictor bolts. Tighten to 66 ft. lbs. (90 Nm).
23. Install the right-hand and left-hand exhaust flexible pipes.
24. Position the underbody shield and install the 4 retainers.
25. Position the 2 outer tie-rod ends and install the nuts. Tighten to 111 ft. lbs. (150 Nm).
26. Connect the stabilizer bar links and install the 2 nuts. Tighten the new nuts to 111 ft. lbs. (150 Nm).
27. With the locator on the input shaft correctly aligned, connect the steering column shaft to the steering gear and install the new bolt. Tighten to 15 ft. lbs. (20 Nm).
28. Install the wheels and tires.

Hydraulic Power Assist Steering Gear

See Figure 222.

WARNING

When repairing the power steering system, care should be taken to prevent the entry of foreign material or failure of the power steering components may occur.

1. Using a suitable holding device, hold the steering wheel in the straight-ahead position.
2. Remove the wheels and tires.
3. Remove the 2 tie-rod end nuts and disconnect the tie-rod ends from the wheel knuckles. The hex-holding feature can be used to prevent turning of the stud while removing the nut.
4. Remove the pressure line bracket-to-steering gear bolt.

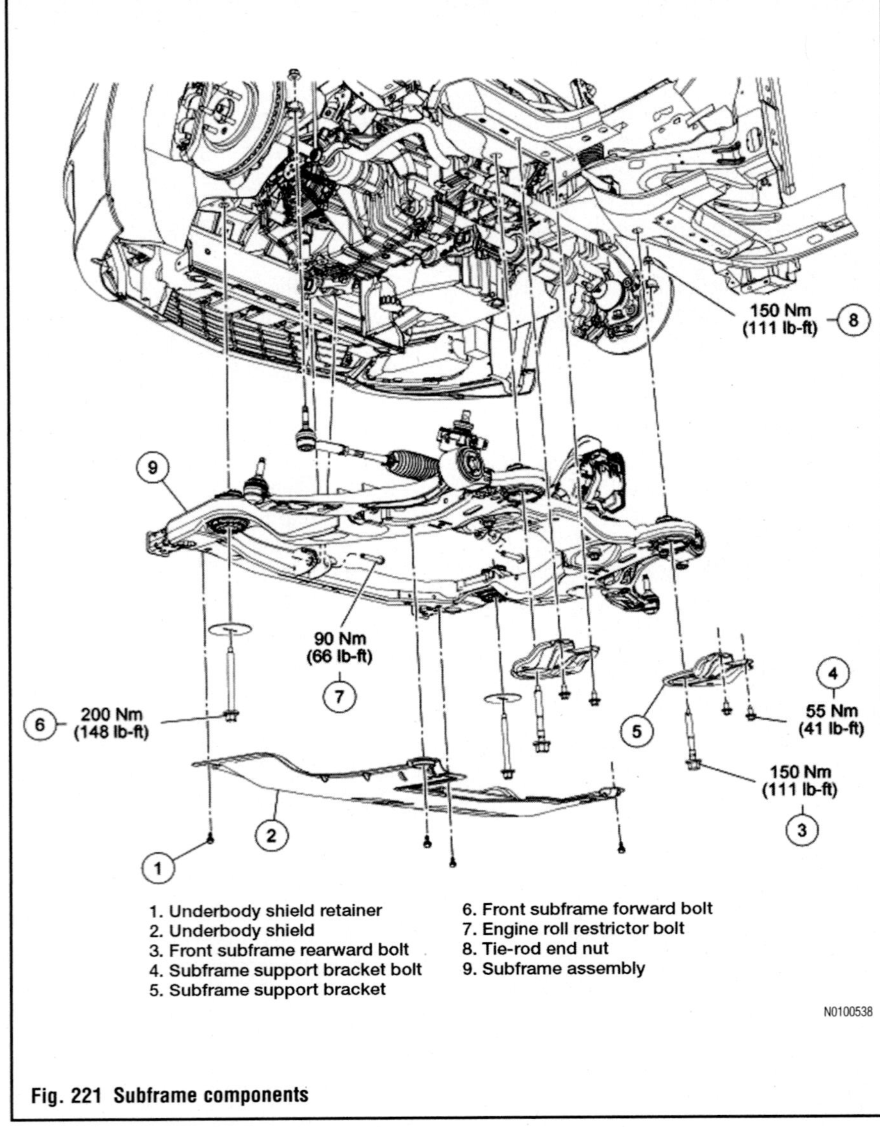

Fig. 221 Subframe components

5. Remove the power steering line clamp plate bolt.
   a. Rotate the clamp plate and disconnect the pressure and return lines from the steering gear.
   b. Discard the 2 O-ring seals.
6. Remove the steering column shaft-to-steering gear bolt and disconnect the shaft from the steering gear. Discard the bolt.
   a. Do not allow the steering column shaft to rotate while the lower shaft is disconnected or damage to the clockspring may result. If there is evidence that the shaft has rotated, the clockspring must be removed and recentered.
7. Remove and discard the stabilizer bar link upper nuts (for AWD vehicles, stabilizer bar bracket bolts). The hex-holding feature can be used to prevent turning of the stud while removing the nut.
   a. Position the stabilizer bar and links upward.
8. If equipped, remove the steering gear heat shield-to-subframe pushpin.
9. Remove and discard the 2 steering gear nuts and bolts.
10. Remove the steering gear from the left side of the vehicle.

To install:

11. To install, reverse the removal procedure, noting the following:
   a. Fill the power steering system.
   b. Whenever the power steering lines are disconnected, new O-ring seals must be installed. Make sure that the O-ring seals are installed in the correct order or a fluid leak may occur.
   c. To install the 2 new steering gear nuts and bolts, tighten in 2 stages:
      - Stage 1: Tighten to 30 ft. lbs. (40 Nm).
      - Stage 2: Tighten an additional 180 degrees.
   d. For AWD vehicles, tighten the stabilizer bar bracket bolts to 41 ft. lbs. (55 Nm).
   e. Tighten the stabilizer bar link upper nuts to 111 ft. lbs. (150 Nm).
   f. Tighten the steering column shaft-to-steering gear bolt to 18 ft. lbs. (25 Nm).
   g. Tighten the power steering line clamp plate bolt to 17 ft. lbs. (23 Nm).
   h. Tighten the pressure line bracket-to-steering gear bolt to 17 ft. lbs. (23 Nm).
   i. Tighten the 2 tie-rod end nuts to 111 ft. lbs. (150 Nm).
   j. Check and the front toe, and adjust if necessary.

POWER STEERING PUMP

REMOVAL & INSTALLATION

See Figures 223 through 226.

1. Before servicing the vehicle, refer to the Precautions Section.
2. With the vehicle in NEUTRAL, position it on a hoist.
3. Using a suitable suction device, siphon the power steering fluid from the power steering fluid reservoir.
4. Remove the 7 pin-type retainers and the right-hand splash shield.
5. Position the Stretchy Belt Remover (SST 303-1419) or equivalent tool on the power steering pump pulley belt as shown.
6. Turn the crankshaft clockwise and feed the belt remover evenly on the power steering pump pulley. Feed the belt remover onto the power steering pump pulley approximately 90 degrees.
7. Remove the power steering pump belt.
   a. Fold the belt remover under the inside of the power steering pump belt as shown.
   b. In one quick motion, firmly pull the belt remover out of the right-hand fender well, removing the coolant pump belt.
8. Release the clamp and disconnect the power steering fluid reservoir-to-pump supply hose from the power steering pump.
   a. Detach the supply hose retainer from the pressure line bracket.
9. Remove the pressure line bracket-to-engine bolt.
10. Remove the 3 power steering pump bolts.
11. Holding the power steering pump

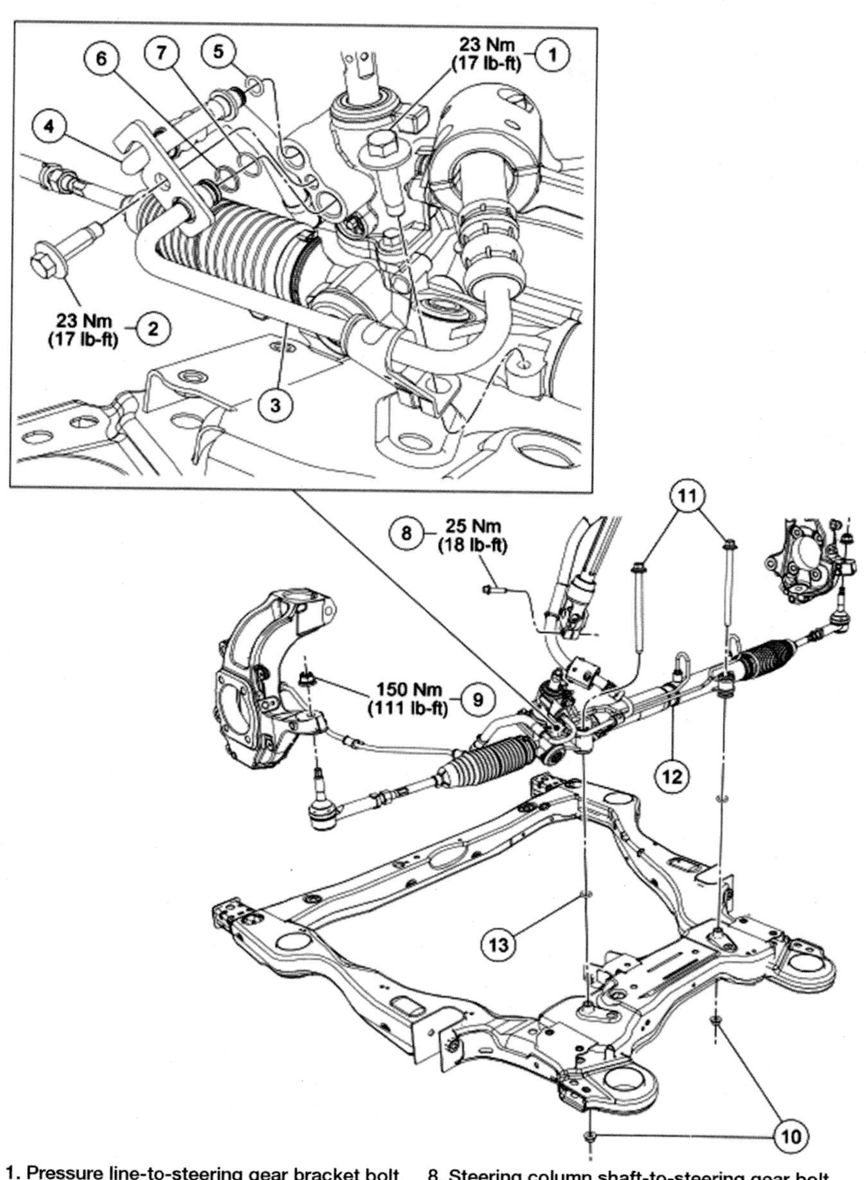

1. Pressure line-to-steering gear bracket bolt
2. Power steering line clamp plate bolt
3. Pressure line
4. Power steering return line
5. Power steering return line O-ring seal
6. Pressure line backup O-ring seal
7. Pressure line primary O-ring seal
8. Steering column shaft-to-steering gear bolt
9. Tie-rod end nut
10. Steering gear nut
11. Steering gear bolts
12. Steering gear
13. Washer

N0109033

Fig. 222 Hydraulic power assist steering gear components

with a punch inserted into a mounting bolt cavity, disconnect the pressure line fitting-to-power steering pump.

To install:

⁂ WARNING

A new Teflon® seal must be installed any time the pressure line is disconnected from the power steering pump or a fluid leak may occur.

12. Using the Teflon® Seal Installer Set, install a new Teflon® seal on the power steering pressure line fitting.

13. Holding the power steering pump with a punch inserted into a mounting cavity, connect the pressure line fitting-to-power steering pump. Tighten to 55 ft. lbs. (75 Nm).

14. Position the power steering pump and install the 3 bolts. Tighten to 18 ft. lbs. (25 Nm).

15. Position the bracket and install the pressure line bracket-to-engine bolt. Tighten to 80 inch lbs. (9 Nm).

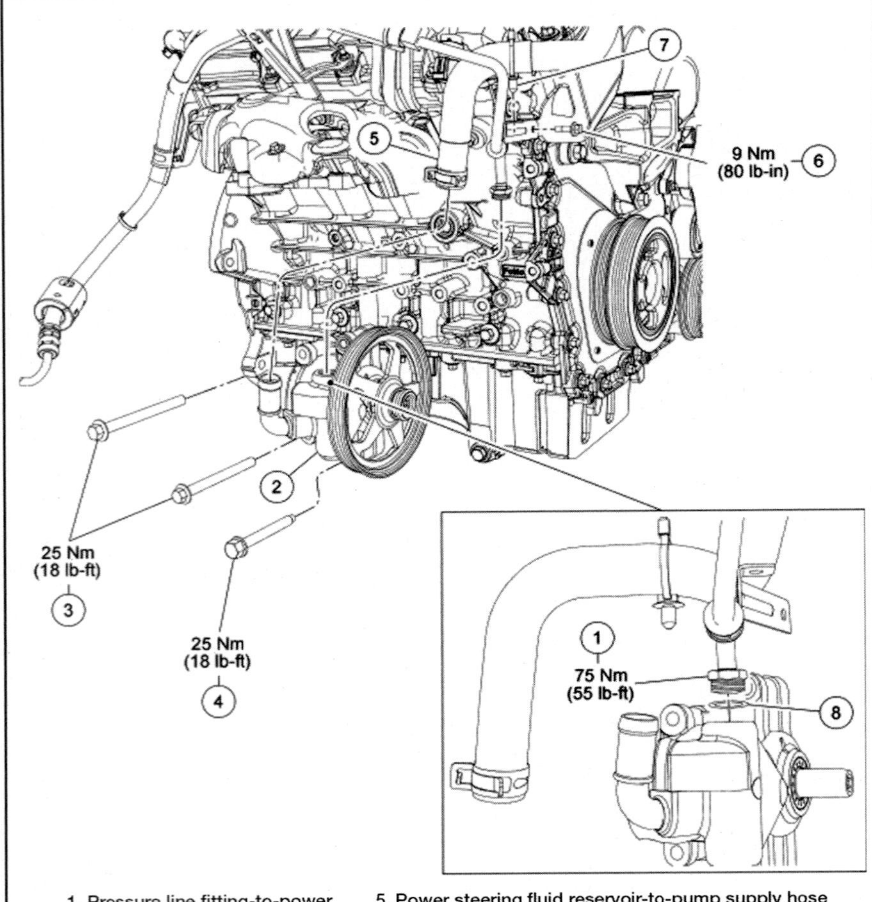

1. Pressure line fitting-to-power steering pump
2. Power steering pump
3. Power steering pump bolts
4. Power steering pump bolt
5. Power steering fluid reservoir-to-pump supply hose
6. Pressure line bracket-to-engine bolt
7. Power steering fluid reservoir-to-pump supply hose retainer
8. Pressure line Teflon® seal

N0103576

Fig. 223 Power steering pump components

Fig. 224 Position the belt remover on the power steering pump pulley belt

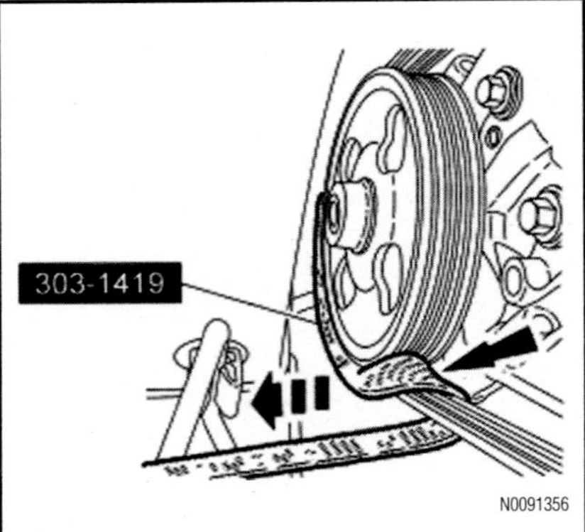

Fig. 225 Fold the belt remover under the power steering pump belt, and pull out to remove the coolant pump belt

16. Release the clamp and connect the power steering fluid cooler-to-pump supply hose.
    a. Attach the supply hose retainer to the pressure line bracket.
17. Install the Stretchy Belt Installer Tool (SST 303-1252/2) or equivalent tool between the power steering pump belt and pulley and turn the crankshaft bolt clockwise. Use the belt installer tool to install the power steering pump belt onto the power steering pump pulley.
18. Install the right-hand inner fender splash shield.
19. Fill the power steering system.

POWER STEERING SYSTEM FLUSHING

⁂ WARNING

Do not mix fluid types. Any mixture or any unapproved fluid may lead to seal deterioration and leaks. A leak may ultimately cause loss of fluid, which may result in a loss of power steering assist.

1. Remove the power steering fluid reservoir cap.
2. Using a suitable suction device, remove the power steering fluid from the reservoir.
3. Release the clamp and disconnect the return hose from the reservoir.
    a. Remove the clamp from the hose and allow the remaining fluid to drain out of the reservoir.
4. Plug the power steering fluid reservoir inlet port.
5. Attach an extension hose to the return hose.

➡Do not reuse the power steering fluid that has been flushed from the power steering system.

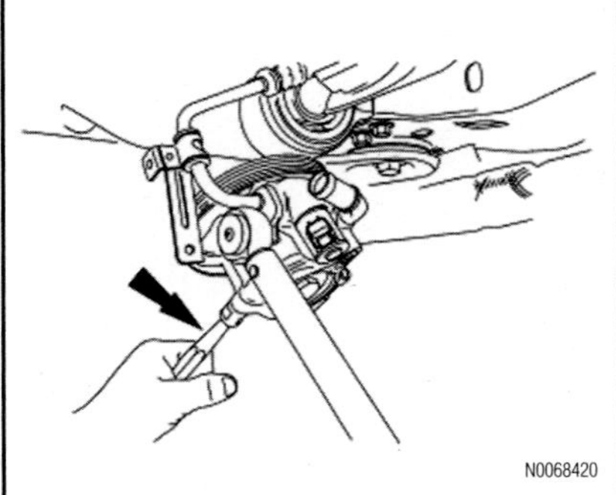

Fig. 226 Holding the power steering pump with a punch inserted into a mounting bolt cavity, disconnect the pressure line fitting-to-power steering pump

6. Place the open end of the extension hose into a suitable container.
7. If equipped with Hydro-Boost®, apply the brake pedal 4 times.
8. Fill the reservoir as needed with the specified fluid. Do not overfill the reservoir.

WARNING

Do not allow the power steering pump to run completely dry of power steering fluid. Damage to the power steering pump may occur.

9. Start the engine while simultaneously turning the steering wheel to lock and then immediately turn the ignition switch to the OFF position.

➡Avoid turning the steering wheel without the engine running as this may cause air to be pulled into the steering gear.

10. Fill the reservoir as needed with the specified fluid. Do not overfill the reservoir.
11. Repeat Steps 8 and 9, turning the steering wheel in the opposite direction each time, until the fluid exiting the power steering fluid return hose is clean and clear of foreign material.
12. Remove the extension hose from the return hose.
13. Remove the plug from the fluid reservoir inlet port.
14. Install the clamp and connect the power steering return hose to the reservoir.

➡It is necessary to correctly fill the power steering system to remove any trapped air and completely fill the power steering system components.

15. If, after correctly filling the power steering system, there is power steering noise accompanied by evidence of aerated fluid and there are no fluid leaks, it may be necessary to purge the power steering system.
16. Fill the power steering system.

POWER STEERING SYSTEM PURGING

See Figure 227.

WARNING

If the air is not purged from the power steering system correctly, premature power steering pump failure may result.

➡A whine heard from the power steering pump can be caused by air in the system. The power steering purge procedure must be carried out prior to any component repair for which power steering noise complaints are accompanied by evidence of aerated fluid.

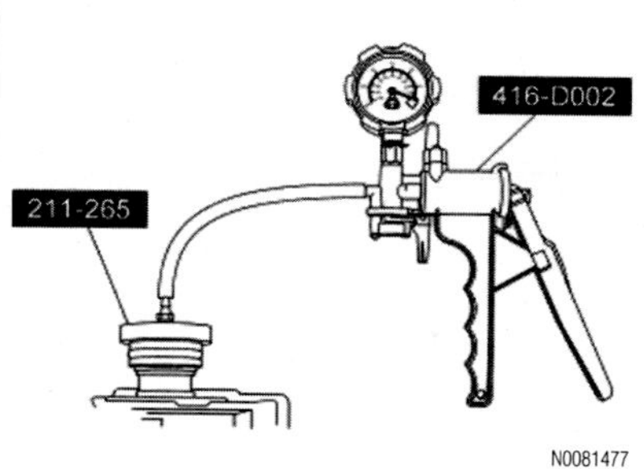

Fig. 227 Tightly insert the Power Steering Evacuation Cap into the reservoir and connect the Vacuum Pump Kit

1. Remove the power steering reservoir cap. Check the fluid.
2. Raise the front wheels off the floor.
3. Tightly insert the Power Steering Evacuation Cap into the reservoir and connect the Vacuum Pump Kit.
4. Start the engine.
5. Using the Vacuum Pump Kit, apply vacuum and maintain the maximum vacuum of 68–85 kPa (20–25 in Hg).
   a. If the Vacuum Pump Kit does not maintain vacuum, check the power steering system for leaks before proceeding.
6. If equipped with Hydro-Boost®, apply the brake pedal 4 times.
7. Cycle the steering wheel fully from stop-to-stop 10 times.

WARNING

Do not hold the steering wheel against the stops for an extended amount of time. Damage to the power steering pump may occur.

8. Stop the engine.
9. Release the vacuum and remove the Vacuum Pump Kit and the Power Steering Evacuation Cap.
10. Fill the reservoir as needed with the specified fluid. Do not overfill the reservoir.
11. Start the engine.
12. Install the Power Steering Evacuation Cap and the Vacuum Pump Kit. Apply and maintain the maximum vacuum of 68–85 kPa (20–25 in Hg).
13. Cycle the steering wheel fully from stop-to-stop 10 times.
14. Stop the engine, release the vacuum and remove the Vacuum Pump Kit and the Power Steering Evacuation Cap.
15. Fill the reservoir as needed with the specified fluid and install the reservoir cap. Do not overfill the reservoir.
16. Visually inspect the power steering system for leaks.

FLUID FILL PROCEDURE

See Figure 228.

WARNING

If the air is not purged from the power steering system correctly, premature power steering pump failure may result.

1. Remove the power steering fluid reservoir cap.
2. Install the Power Steering Evacuation Cap, Power Steering Fill Adapter Manifold and Vacuum Pump Kit as shown in the illustration.

➡The Power Steering Fill Adapter Manifold control valves are in the OPEN position when the points of the handles face the center of the Power Steering Fill Adapter Manifold.

3. Close the Power Steering Fill Adapter Manifold control valve (fluid side).
4. Open the Power Steering Fill Adapter Manifold control valve (vacuum side).
5. Using the Vacuum Pump Kit, apply 68–85 kPa (20–25 in Hg) of vacuum to the power steering system.
6. Observe the Vacuum Pump Kit gauge for 30 seconds.
7. If the Vacuum Pump Kit gauge reading drops more than 3 kPa (0.88 in Hg), correct any leaks in the power steering system or the Power Steering Evacuation Cap, Power Steering Fill Adapter Manifold and Vacuum Pump Kit before proceeding.
8. Slowly open the Power Steering Fill Adapter Manifold control valve (fluid side) until power steering fluid completely fills the hose and then close the control valve. The Vacuum Pump Kit gauge reading will drop slightly during this step.
9. Using the Vacuum Pump Kit, apply 68–85 kPa (20–25 in Hg) of vacuum to the power steering system.
10. Close the Power Steering Fill Adapter Manifold control valve (vacuum side).
11. Slowly open the Power Steering Fill Adapter Manifold control valve (fluid side).
12. Once power steering fluid enters the fluid reservoir and reaches the minimum fluid level indicator line on the reservoir, close the Power Steering Fill Adapter Manifold control valve (fluid side).

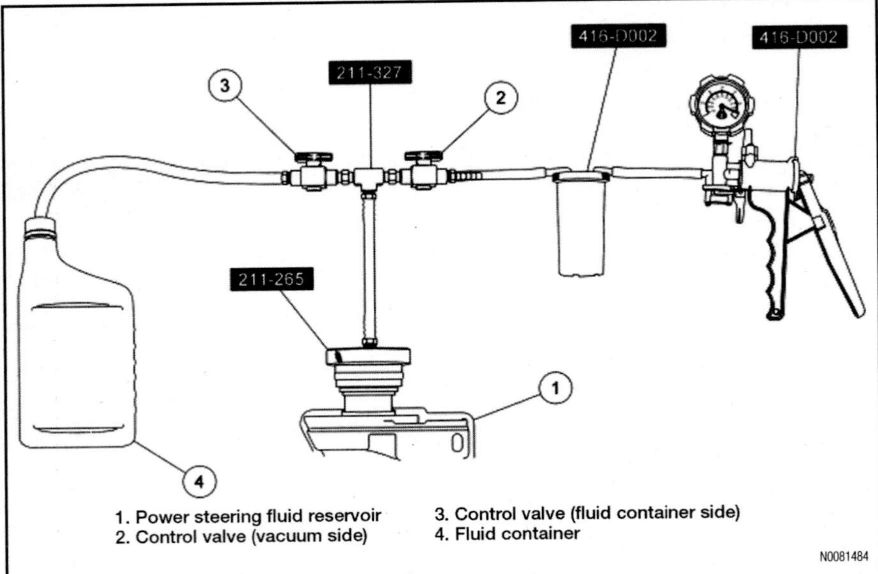

Fig. 228 Power Steering Evacuation Cap, Power Steering Fill Adapter Manifold and Vacuum Pump Kit

13. Remove the Power Steering Evacuation Cap, Power Steering Fill Adapter Manifold and Vacuum Pump Kit.
14. Install the reservoir cap.

WARNING

Do not hold the steering wheel against the stops for an extended amount of time. Damage to the power steering pump may occur.

➡There will be a slight drop in the power steering fluid level in the reservoir when the engine is started.

15. Start the engine and turn the steering wheel from stop-to-stop.
16. Turn the ignition switch to the OFF position.

➡Do not overfill the reservoir.

17. Remove the reservoir cap and fill the reservoir with the specified fluid.
18. Install the reservoir cap.

SUSPENSION

FRONT SUSPENSION

CONTROL LINKS

REMOVAL & INSTALLATION

See Figure 229.

1. With the vehicle in NEUTRAL, position it on a hoist.

WARNING

Do not use power tools to remove the stabilizer bar link nuts. Damage to the stabilizer bar link ball joints or boots may occur.

➡To remove the stabilizer bar link nuts, first loosen the nuts, then use the hex-holding feature to prevent the stabilizer bar link ball joints from turning while removing the stabilizer bar link nuts.

2. Remove and discard the stabilizer bar link lower nut.
3. Remove and discard the stabilizer bar link upper nut.
4. Remove the stabilizer bar link.

To install:

5. To install, reverse the removal procedure, noting the following:

➡To install the nuts, use the hex-holding feature to prevent the stabilizer link ball joints from turning while installing the nuts until snug. Finally, tighten the nuts using a socket and a torque wrench.

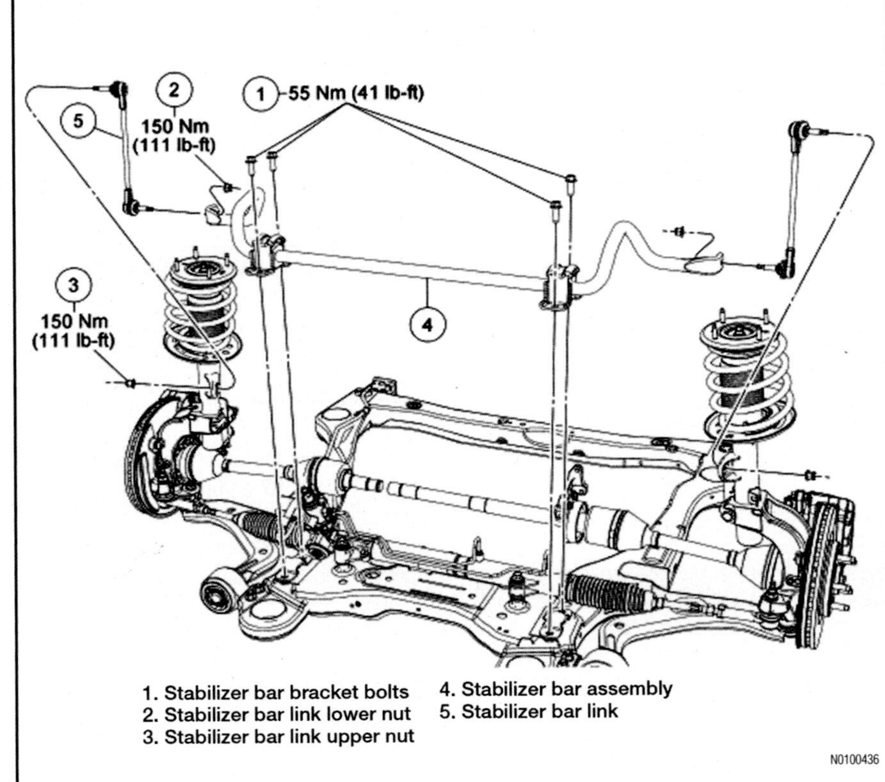

Fig. 229 Front stabilizer bar components

a. Tighten a new stabilizer bar link upper nut to 111 ft. lbs. (150 Nm).
b. Tighten a new stabilizer bar link lower nut to 111 ft. lbs. (150 Nm).

LOWER CONTROL ARM

REMOVAL & INSTALLATION

See Figure 230.

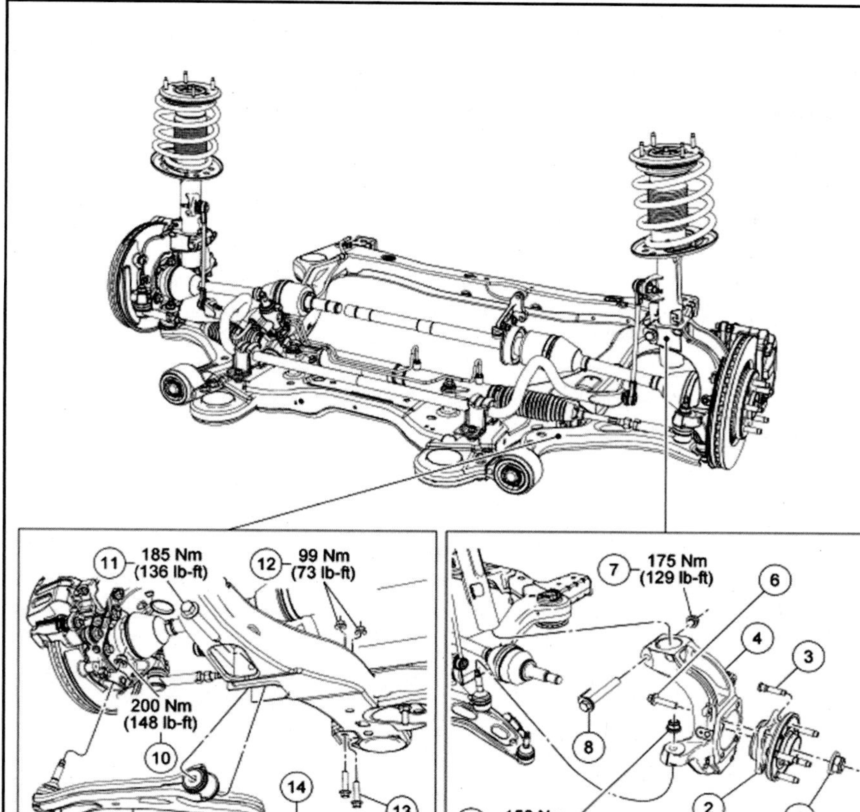

1. Wheel hub nut
2. Wheel bearing and wheel hub
3. Wheel stud
4. Wheel knuckle
5. Tie-rod end nut
6. Wheel bearing and wheel hub bolt
7. Strut-to-wheel knuckle nut
8. Strut-to-wheel knuckle flag bolt
9. Lower control arm
10. Lower ball joint nut
11. Lower arm forward bolt
12. Lower arm rearward nuts
13. Lower arm rearward bolt
14. Lower arm rearward bushing

N0103396

Fig. 230 Front suspension components

1. Remove the wheel and tire.
2. Using a crowfoot wrench, remove and discard the lower ball joint nut. Use the hex-holding feature to prevent the stud from turning while removing the nut.
3. Push the lower arm downward until the ball joint is clear of the wheel knuckle.

⁂ WARNING

Use care when releasing the lower arm and knuckle into the resting position or damage to the ball joint seal may occur.

4. Remove and discard the lower arm forward bolt.
5. Remove and discard the lower arm rearward nuts and bolts.
6. If necessary, remove the lower arm rearward bushing.

To install:

7. To install, reverse the removal procedure, noting the following:
    a. Install the new lower arm rearward bolts from the bottom of the lower arm bushing with the nuts on top.
    b. Tighten new lower arm rearward nuts to 73 ft. lbs. (99 Nm).

⁂ WARNING

The lower arm forward bolt must be tightened with the weight of the vehicle on the wheels and tires or damage to the bushings may occur.

    c. Tighten a new lower arm forward bolt to 136 ft. lbs. (185 Nm).
    d. Tighten the lower ball joint nut to 148 ft. lbs. (200 Nm).

CONTROL ARM BUSHING REPLACEMENT

See Figure 231.

1. Remove the lower arm.
2. Matchmark the bushing-to-lower arm position for reference during the installation procedure.

➡The Drive Pinion Bearing Cone Remover is used to secure the lower arm bushing while separating/installing the bushing from the lower arm.

3. Using the Drive Pinion Bearing Cone Remover (SST 205-D002) or equivalent tool, a suitable press and adapters, remove the lower arm bushing.

To install:

4. Install the Drive Pinion Bearing Cone Remover (SST 205-D002) or equivalent tool onto the lower arm.
5. Transfer the matchmark to the new lower arm bushing.
6. Align the matchmarks, and using the Drive Pinion Bearing Cone Remover, a suitable press and adapters, install a new lower arm bushing.
7. Install the lower arm.

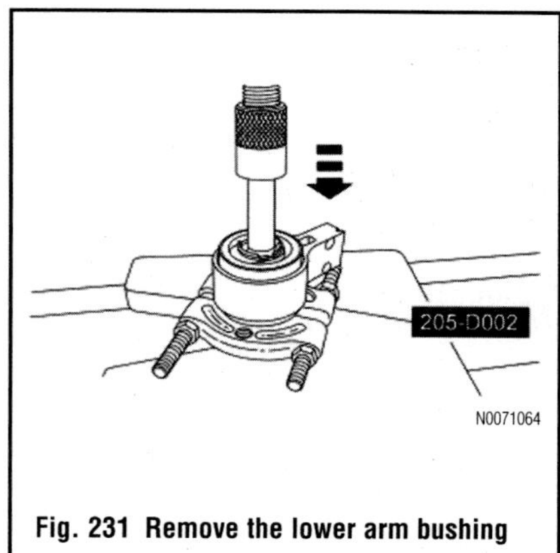

Fig. 231 Remove the lower arm bushing

STABILIZER BAR

REMOVAL & INSTALLATION

See Figures 232 and 233.

1. Make sure the steering wheel is in the unlocked position.

➡The stabilizer bushing and bracket are part of the stabilizer bar assembly. The stabilizer bar will not turn easily in the bushing.

2. With the vehicle in NEUTRAL, position it on a hoist.
3. Disconnect the Heated Oxygen Sensor (HO2S) electrical connector and unclip the connector from the subframe.

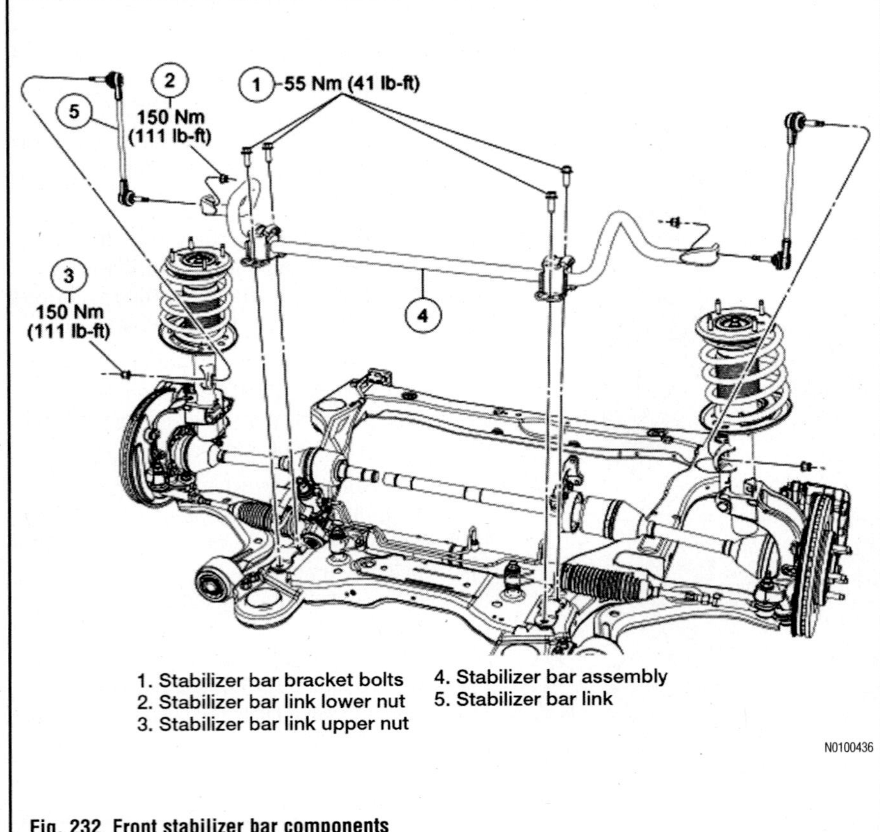

Fig. 232 Front stabilizer bar components

4. For AWD vehicles, remove the exhaust Y-pipe.

WARNING

Do not use power tools to remove the stabilizer bar link nut. Damage to the stabilizer link ball joint or boot may occur.

5. Remove and discard the stabilizer bar link lower nuts. To remove the stabilizer bar link nut, first loosen the nut, then use the hex-holding feature to prevent the ball joint from turning while removing the stabilizer bar link nut.
6. Remove and discard both tie-rod end nuts and separate the tie-rod ends from the knuckles. No special tools are necessary to separate the tie rod from the front knuckle; use a mallet to loosen the joint.
7. Remove and discard the 4 lower arm rearward nuts and bolts.
8. Remove and discard the 2 lower arm forward bolts. Position both lower arms aside.
9. Using a suitable screw-type jackstand, support the rear of the subframe.
10. Remove the 2 steering gear nuts and bolts.
11. Remove and discard the 4 subframe bracket bolts.
12. Remove and discard the subframe forward bolts.
13. Remove and discard the subframe rearward bolts.
14. Lower the rear of the subframe approximately 2 in. (51 mm).
15. Remove and discard the left-hand and right-hand stabilizer bar bracket bolts.
16. Remove the stabilizer bar by guiding it between the subframe and the steering gear toward the right-hand side of the vehicle.

To install:

17. To install, reverse the removal procedure, noting the following:
    a. Install new left-hand and right-hand stabilizer bar bracket bolts and tighten to 41 ft. lbs. (55 Nm).
    b. Install new subframe rearward bolts and tighten:
        - Vehicles with Electronic Power Assist Steering (EPAS): 111 ft. lbs. (150 Nm)
        - Vehicles with Hydraulic Power Assist Steering (HPAS): 130 ft. lbs. (175 Nm)
    c. Install new subframe forward bolts and tighten to 148 ft. lbs. (200 Nm).
    d. Install 4 new subframe bracket bolts and tighten to 41 ft. lbs. (55 Nm).
    e. Install new steering gear nuts and bolts and tighten:
        - Vehicles with EPAS: 122 ft. lbs. (165 Nm)
        - Vehicles with HPAS: 86 ft. lbs. (117 Nm)
    f. Install 2 new lower arm forward bolts and tighten to 136 ft. lbs. (185 Nm).

➡Install the new lower arm rearward bolts from the bottom of the lower arm bushing with the nuts on top.

    g. Install 4 new lower arm rearward nuts and bolts and tighten to 73 ft. lbs. (99 Nm).
    h. Install new tie-rod end nuts and tighten to 111 ft. lbs. (150 Nm).
    i. Install new stabilizer bar link lower nuts and tighten to 111 ft. lbs. (150 Nm).

STEERING KNUCKLE

REMOVAL & INSTALLATION

See Figures 234 and 235.

1. Remove the wheel and tire.
2. Remove the wheel hub nut. Do not discard the wheel hub nut at this time.
3. Remove the brake disc.
4. Remove and discard the tie-rod end nut, then separate the tie rod from the wheel knuckle. No special tools are necessary to separate the tie rod from the front knuckle; use a mallet to loosen the joint.
5. Remove the bolt and the wheel speed sensor from the wheel knuckle. Position the wheel speed sensor aside.
6. Using a crowfoot wrench, remove and discard the lower ball joint nut. Use the hex-holding feature to prevent the stud from turning while removing the nut.
7. Push the lower arm downward until the ball joint is clear of the wheel knuckle.
8. Using the Front Wheel Hub Remover (SST 205-D070) or equivalent tool, press the halfshaft from the wheel bearing and hub. Support the halfshaft in a level position.
    a. Do not allow the halfshaft to move outboard. Overextension of the tripod Constant Velocity (CV) joint may result in separation of internal parts, causing failure of the halfshaft.
9. Remove and discard the strut-to-wheel knuckle nut and flagbolt.
10. Remove the steering knuckle. If necessary, remove the wheel hub and bearing.

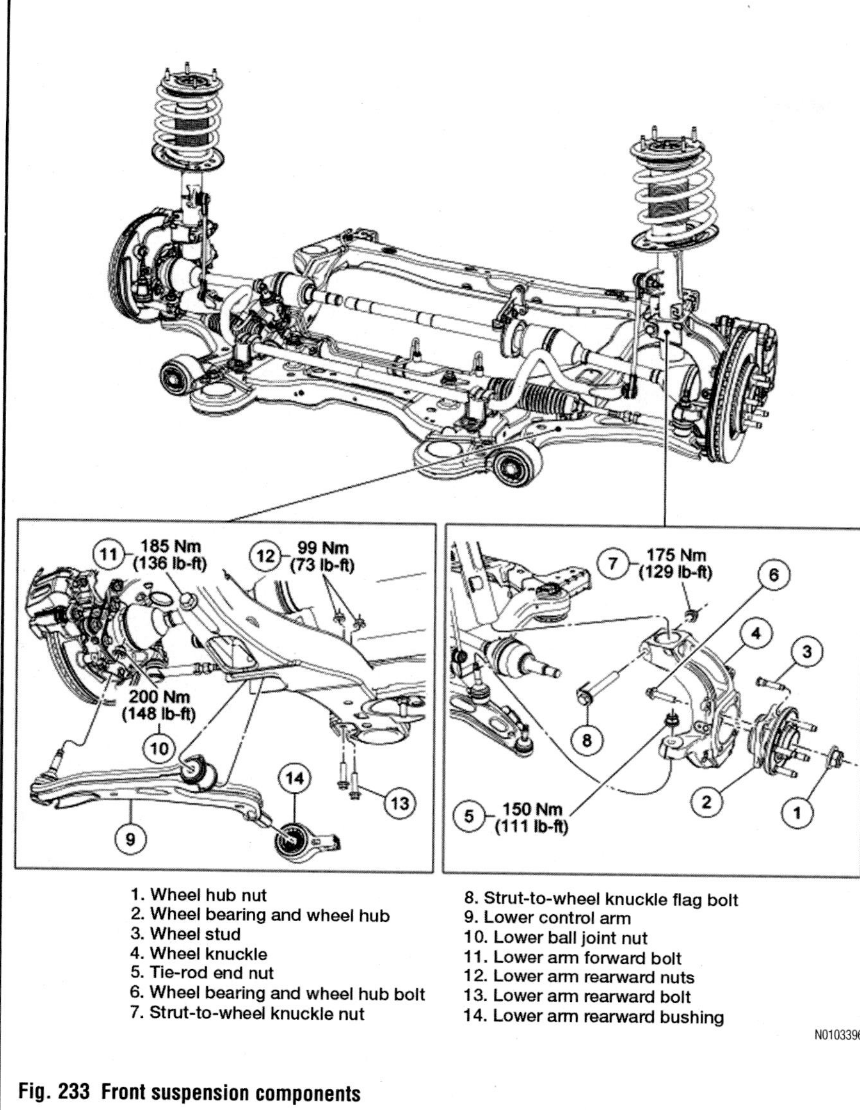

Fig. 233 Front suspension components

To install:

11. Position the wheel knuckle and install a new strut-to-wheel knuckle nut and flagbolt. Tighten to 129 ft. lbs. (175 Nm).

12. While supporting the halfshaft in a level position, install the halfshaft into the wheel bearing and hub.

13. Push the lower arm downward and install the ball joint stud into the wheel knuckle. Use care not to damage the ball joint seal while installing the ball joint stud into the wheel knuckle.

14. Using a crowfoot wrench, install the new lower ball joint nut. Use the hex-holding feature to prevent the stud from turning while installing the nut. Tighten to 148 ft. lbs. (200 Nm).

15. Position the wheel speed sensor and install the bolt. Tighten to 11 ft. lbs. (15 Nm).

16. Position the tie-rod end stud into the wheel knuckle and install a new tie-rod end nut. Tighten to 111 ft. lbs. (150 Nm).

17. Install the brake disc.

WARNING

Do not tighten the front wheel hub nut with the vehicle on the ground. The nut must be tightened to specification before the vehicle is lowered onto the wheels. Wheel bearing damage will occur if the wheel bearing is loaded with the weight of the vehicle applied.

18. Using the previously removed hub nut, seat the halfshaft.

  a. Apply the brake to keep the halfshaft from rotating.

  b. Tighten to 258 ft. lbs. (350 Nm).

  c. Remove and discard the hub nut.

WARNING

The wheel hub nut contains a one-time locking chemical that is activated by the heat created when it is tightened. Install and tighten the new wheel hub nut to specification within 5 minutes of starting it on the threads. Always install a new wheel hub nut after loosening or when not tightened within the specified time or damage to the components can occur.

19. Install a new hub nut. Apply the brake to keep the halfshaft from rotating. Tighten to 258 ft. lbs. (350 Nm).

20. Install the wheel and tire.

STRUT & SPRING ASSEMBLY

REMOVAL & INSTALLATION

See Figures 234 through 236.

1. Make sure the steering wheel is in the unlocked position.
2. Loosen the upper strut mount nuts.
3. Remove the wheel and tire.
4. Remove the wheel hub nut. Do not discard the wheel hub nut at this time.
5. Remove the brake disc.
6. Remove and discard the tie-rod end nut, then separate the tie rod from the wheel knuckle. No special tools are necessary to separate the tie rod from the front knuckle; use a mallet to loosen the joint.
7. Remove and discard the stabilizer bar link upper nut.
8. Detach the wheel speed sensor harness from the strut.
9. Remove the bolt and the wheel speed sensor from the wheel knuckle. Position the wheel speed sensor aside.
10. Using a crowfoot wrench, remove and discard the lower ball joint nut. Use the hex-holding feature to prevent the stud from turning while removing the nut.
11. Push the lower arm downward until the ball joint is clear of the wheel knuckle.
    a. Use care when releasing the lower arm and knuckle into the resting position or damage to the ball joint seal may occur.
12. Using the Front Wheel Hub Remover (SST 205-D070) or equivalent tool, press the halfshaft from the wheel bearing and hub. Support the halfshaft in a level position.
    a. Do not allow the halfshaft to move outboard. Overextension of the tripod Constant Velocity (CV) joint may result in separation of internal parts, causing failure of the halfshaft.

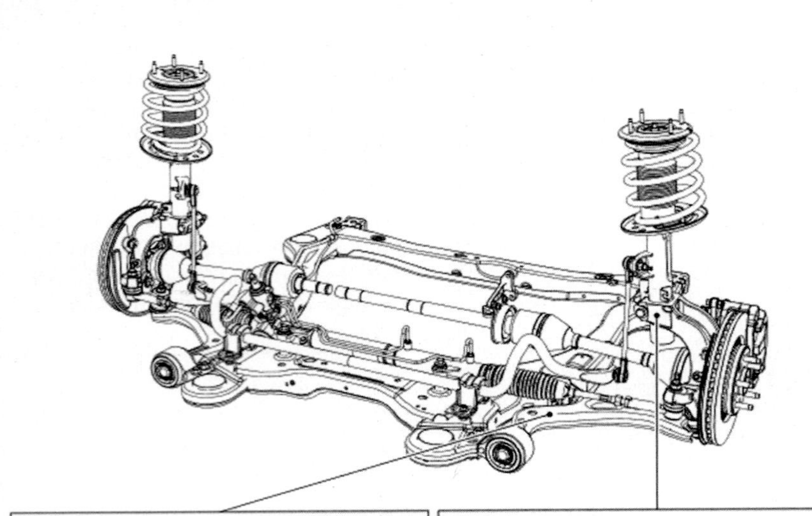

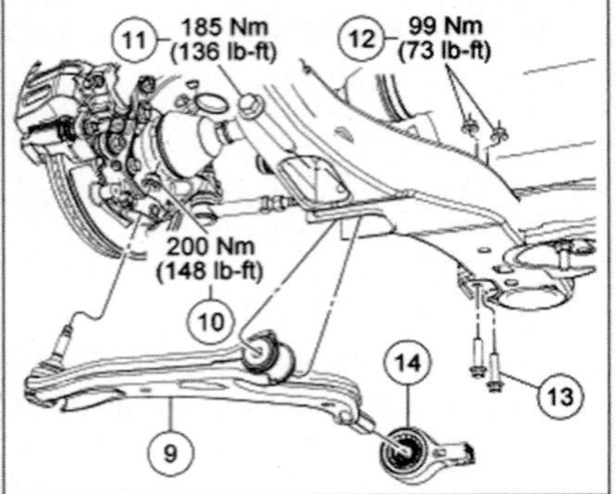

7 175 Nm (129 lb-ft)
6
4
3
8
5 150 Nm (111 lb-ft)
2
1

1. Wheel hub nut
2. Wheel bearing and wheel hub
3. Wheel stud
4. Wheel knuckle
5. Tie-rod end nut
6. Wheel bearing and wheel hub bolt
7. Strut-to-wheel knuckle nut
8. Strut-to-wheel knuckle flag bolt
9. Lower control arm
10. Lower ball joint nut
11. Lower arm forward bolt
12. Lower arm rearward nuts
13. Lower arm rearward bolt
14. Lower arm rearward bushing

N0103396

Fig. 234 Front suspension components

13. Remove and discard the 4 upper strut mount nuts.

14. Remove the wheel knuckle and the strut and spring as an assembly.

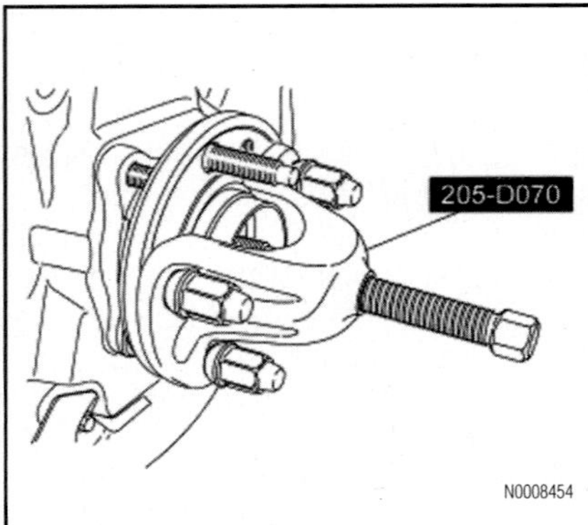

Fig. 235 Remove the halfshaft from the wheel bearing and hub

15. Remove and discard the strut-to-wheel knuckle nut and flagbolt.

16. Separate the strut and spring assembly from the wheel knuckle.

To install:

17. Position the wheel knuckle onto the strut and spring and install a new strut-to-wheel knuckle nut and flagbolt. Tighten the nut to 129 ft. lbs. (175 Nm).

18. Install the wheel knuckle and the strut and spring as an assembly.

19. Loosely install the 4 new upper strut mount nuts.

20. While supporting the halfshaft in a level position, install the halfshaft into the wheel bearing and hub.

21. Push the lower arm downward and install the ball joint stud into the wheel knuckle. Use care not to damage the ball joint seal while installing the ball joint stud into the wheel knuckle.

22. Using a crowfoot wrench, install the new lower ball joint nut. Use the hex-holding feature to prevent the stud from turning while installing the nut. Tighten to 148 ft. lbs. (200 Nm).

23. Position the wheel speed sensor and install the bolt. Tighten to 11 ft. lbs. (15 Nm).

24. Attach the wheel speed sensor harness to the strut.

25. Install the new stabilizer bar link upper nut. Tighten to 111 ft. lbs. (150 Nm).

26. Position the tie-rod end stud into the wheel knuckle and install a new tie-rod end nut. Tighten to 111 ft. lbs. (150 Nm).

27. Install the brake disc.

WARNING

Do not tighten the front wheel hub nut with the vehicle on the ground. The nut must be tightened to specification before the vehicle is lowered onto the wheels. Wheel bearing damage will occur if the wheel bearing is loaded with the weight of the vehicle applied.

28. Using the previously removed hub nut, seat the halfshaft.
  a. Apply the brake to keep the halfshaft from rotating.
  b. Tighten to 258 ft. lbs. (350 Nm).
  c. Remove and discard the hub nut.

29. Install a new hub nut.

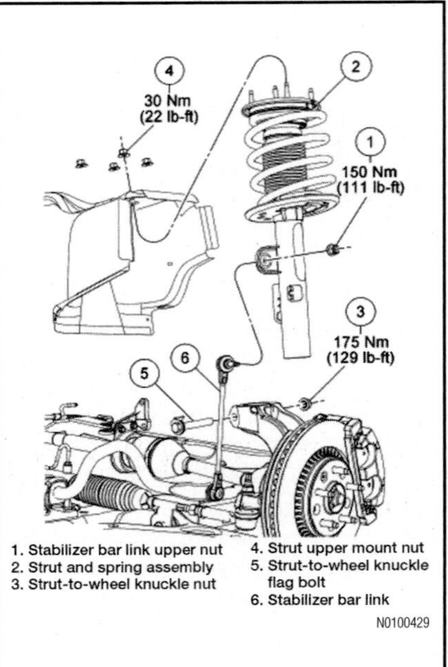

Fig. 236 Front strut and spring assembly components

WARNING

The wheel hub nut contains a one-time locking chemical that is activated by the heat created when it is tightened. Install and tighten the new wheel hub nut to specification within 5 minutes of starting it on the threads. Always install a new wheel hub nut after loosening or when not tightened within the specified time or damage to the components can occur.

a. Apply the brake to keep the half-shaft from rotating.

b. Tighten to 258 ft. lbs. (350 Nm).

30. Install the wheel and tire.

31. Tighten the 4 upper strut mount nuts to 22 ft. lbs. (30 Nm).

WHEEL BEARINGS

REMOVAL & INSTALLATION

See Figure 237.

1. Remove the steering knuckle.
2. Remove and discard the 4 wheel bearing and wheel hub bolts, then separate the wheel bearing and wheel hub from the wheel knuckle.

To install:

3. To install, reverse the removal procedure, noting the following:

a. Using a clean shop towel, clean the wheel hub-to-knuckle mating surfaces.

b. Make sure the wheel hub-to-wheel knuckle mating surfaces are clean and free of any adhesive. Failure to clean the adhesive from both surfaces may cause bearing damage.

c. Clean and inspect the knuckle bearing bore. If the wheel knuckle is cracked, install a new wheel knuckle.

WARNING

The wheel knuckle bore must be clean enough to allow the wheel bearing and wheel hub to seat completely by hand. Do not press or draw the wheel hub and bearing into place or damage to the bearing may occur.

4. Remove and discard the 4 wheel bearing and wheel hub bolts, then separate the wheel bearing and wheel hub from the wheel knuckle.

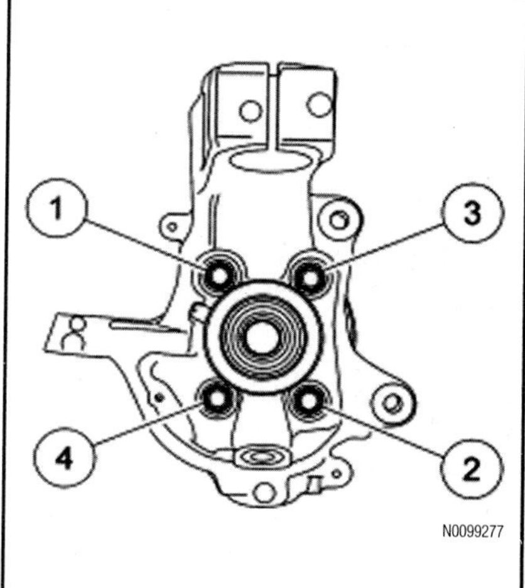

Fig. 237 Wheel hub and bearing bolt tightening sequence

a. Install the wheel bearing and wheel hub to the wheel knuckle and tighten the new bolts to 98 ft. lbs. (133 Nm) in the sequence shown.

b. Lubricate the hub-to-brake disc surface with anti-seize lubricant before installing the brake disc.

SUSPENSION

REAR SUSPENSION

COIL SPRING

REMOVAL & INSTALLATION

See Figures 238 and 239.

1. Measure the distance from the center of the wheel hub to the lip of the fender with the vehicle in a level, static ground position (curb height).
2. Remove the wheel and tire.
3. Remove and discard the 2 stabilizer bar link upper nuts. Use the hex-holding feature to prevent the stabilizer bar link studs from turning while removing the nuts.

Fig. 238 Measure the distance from the center of the wheel hub to the lip of the fender

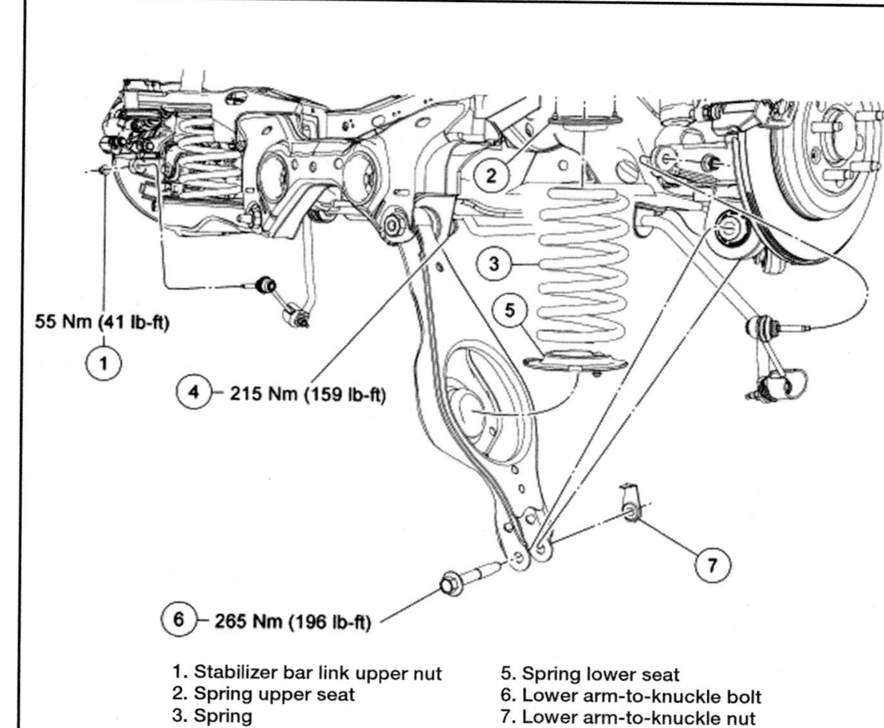

Fig. 239 Rear spring components

a. Position the stabilizer bar away from the lower arm.

4. Using a suitable jackstand, support the lower arm.

5. Loosen the lower arm-to-subframe bolt.

6. Remove and discard the lower arm-to wheel knuckle bolt.

7. Lower the jackstand and remove the spring.

8. Inspect the upper and lower spring seats for damage and, if necessary, install new spring seats.

a. Make sure the lower spring seat is properly positioned in the lower arm.

To install:

9. Before tightening the lower arm bolts, use a jackstand to raise the rear suspension until the distance between the center of the hub and the lip of the fender is equal to the measurement taken in the Removal procedure (curb height).

10. Install the spring and position the jackstand under the lower arm.

11. Raise the jackstand and loosely install a new lower arm-to-wheel knuckle bolt.

12. Position the stabilizer bar and links and install 2 new stabilizer bar link upper nuts. Tighten to 41 ft. lbs. (55 Nm).

13. Using the jackstand, raise the rear suspension until the distance between the center of the hub and the lip of the fender is equal to the measurement taken in the removal procedure (curb height).

14. Tighten the lower arm-to-wheel knuckle bolt to 196 ft. lbs. (265 Nm).

15. Tighten the lower arm-to-subframe bolt to 159 ft. lbs. (215 Nm).

16. Install the wheel and tire.

CONTROL LINKS

REMOVAL & INSTALLATION

See Figure 240.

1. Remove and discard the stabilizer bar link lower nut.

2. Remove the stabilizer bar link upper nut and stabilizer bar link. Discard the nut.

To install:

3. To install, reverse the removal procedure, noting the following:

a. Install a new stabilizer bar link upper nut and tighten to 41 ft. lbs. (55 Nm).

b. Install a new stabilizer bar link lower nut and tighten to 46 ft. lbs. (63 Nm).

LOWER CONTROL ARM

REMOVAL & INSTALLATION

See Figures 241 and 242.

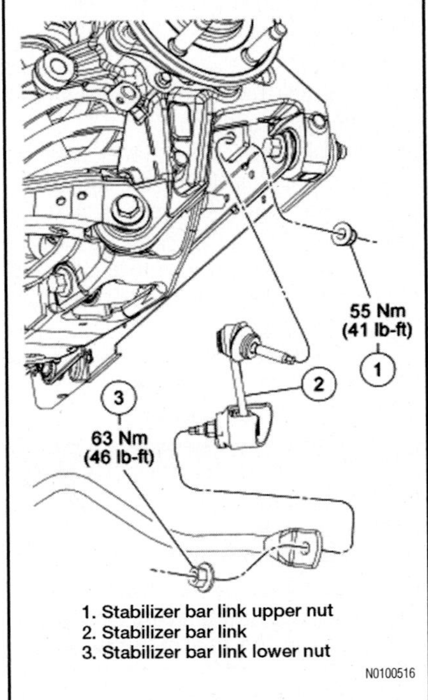

Fig. 240 Rear stabilizer link components

1. Measure the distance from the center of the wheel hub to the lip of the fender with the vehicle in a level, static ground position (curb height).

2. Remove the wheel and tire.

3. Remove both stabilizer bar link upper nuts and disconnect the links from the wheel knuckle. Use the hex-holding feature to prevent the stabilizer bar link stud from turning while removing the nut. Discard the nuts.

4. Position a screw-type jackstand under the lower arm.

5. Remove and discard the lower arm-to-knuckle bolt and nut.

6. Loosen the lower arm inner bolt. Do not remove the lower arm inner bolt at this time.

7. Lower the jackstand and remove the spring.

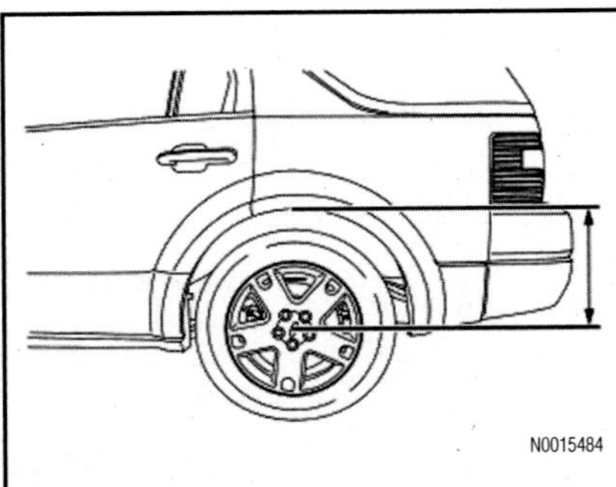

Fig. 241 Measure the distance from the center of the wheel hub to the lip of the fender

8. Remove the lower arm inner bolt and lower arm.

9. Discard the bolt.

To install:

10. Before tightening the lower arm bolts, use a jackstand to raise the rear suspension until the distance between the center of the hub and the lip of the fender is equal to the measurement taken in the Removal procedure (curb height).

11. Position the lower arm and loosely install the new lower arm inner bolt.

12. Install the spring and position the screw-type jackstand under the lower arm.

a. Make sure the lower spring seat is properly positioned in the lower arm.

13. Raise the jackstand and loosely install the new lower arm-to-knuckle bolt and nut. Do not tighten the lower arm nut at this time.

14. Using the jackstand, raise the rear suspension until the distance between the center of the hub and the lip of the fender is equal to the measurement taken in the removal procedure (curb height).

15. Tighten the lower arm-to-subframe bolt to 159 ft. lbs. (215 Nm).

16. Tighten the lower arm-to-knuckle bolt to 196 ft. lbs. (265 Nm).

17. Position the stabilizer bar links and install 2 new stabilizer bar link upper nuts. Tighten to 41 ft. lbs. (55 Nm).

SHOCK ABSORBER

REMOVAL & INSTALLATION

See Figure 243.

1. Pull back the luggage compartment side trim panel to gain access to the shock absorber upper nut.

2. Remove and discard the shock absorber upper mount nut.

3. Remove the wheel and tire.

4. Remove and discard the stabilizer bar link upper nut and disconnect the link from the wheel knuckle. Use the hex-holding feature to prevent the stabilizer bar link stud from turning while removing or installing the nut.

5. Remove and discard the shock absorber lower bolt and remove the shock absorber.

To install:

6. To install, reverse the removal procedure, noting the following:

a. Install a new shock absorber lower bolt and tighten to 129 ft. lbs. (175 Nm).

b. Install a new stabilizer bar link upper nut and tighten to 41 ft. lbs. (55 Nm).

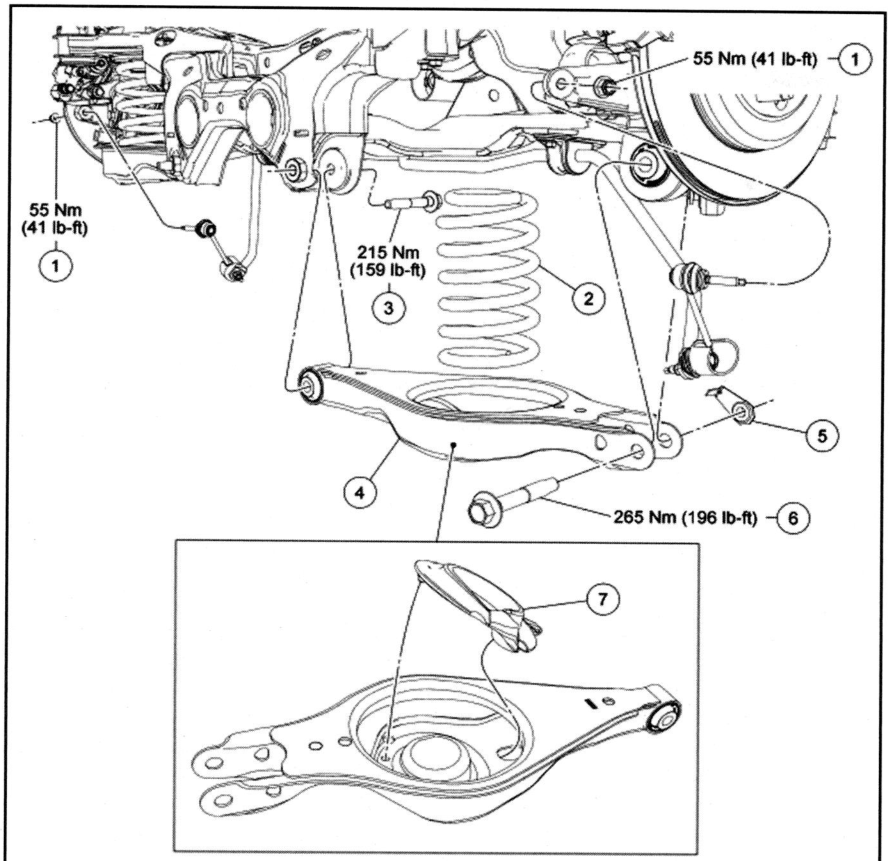

1. Stabilizer bar link upper nuts
2. Spring
3. Lower arm-to-subframe bolt
4. Lower arm
5. Lower arm-to-knuckle nut
6. Lower arm-to-knuckle bolt
7. Spring lower seat

N0087567

Fig. 242 Rear lower arm components

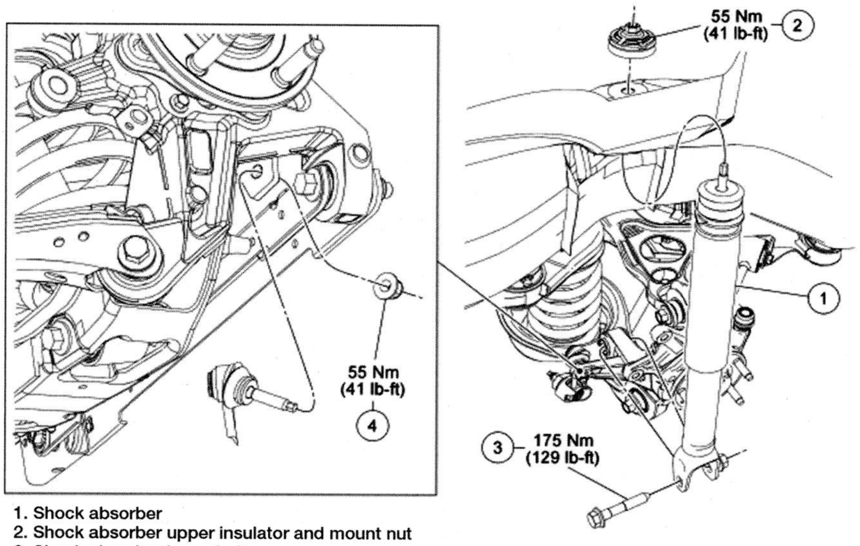

1. Shock absorber
2. Shock absorber upper insulator and mount nut
3. Shock absorber lower bolt
4. Stabilizer bar link upper nut

N0102953

Fig. 243 Rear shock absorber components

c. Install a new shock absorber upper mount nut and tighten to 41 ft. lbs. (55 Nm).

STABILIZER BAR

REMOVAL & INSTALLATION

See Figure 244.

1. With the vehicle in NEUTRAL, position it on a hoist.
2. Support the exhaust system with a suitable jackstand, disconnect the 2 muffler and tail pipe isolators and lower the exhaust approximately 2 in. (50.8 mm).
3. Remove and discard the 2 stabilizer bar link lower nuts.
4. Remove and discard the 4 stabilizer bar bracket bolts.
5. Remove the stabilizer bar.

To install:

6. To install, reverse the removal procedure, noting the following:
    a. Install 4 new stabilizer bar bracket bolts and tighten to 41 ft. lbs. (55 Nm).
    b. Install 2 new stabilizer bar link lower nuts and tighten to 46 ft. lbs. (63 Nm).

STEERING KNUCKLE

REMOVAL & INSTALLATION

AWD Vehicles

See Figures 245 and 246.

1. Measure the distance from the center of the wheel hub to the lip of the fender with the vehicle in a level, static ground position (curb height).
2. Remove the wheel bearing and wheel hub.
3. Using a suitable jackstand, support the lower arm.
4. Remove and discard the trailing arm-to-wheel knuckle nut and bolt.
5. Remove and discard the stabilizer bar link upper nut and disconnect the link. Use the hex-holding feature to prevent the stabilizer bar link stud from turning while removing or installing the nut.
6. Remove and discard the shock absorber lower bolt and disconnect the shock absorber from the knuckle bracket.
7. Remove and discard the toe link-to-knuckle nut.
8. Remove and discard the upper arm-to-wheel knuckle nut and bolt and disconnect the upper arm from the knuckle.
9. Remove and discard the lower arm-to-wheel knuckle nut and bolt.

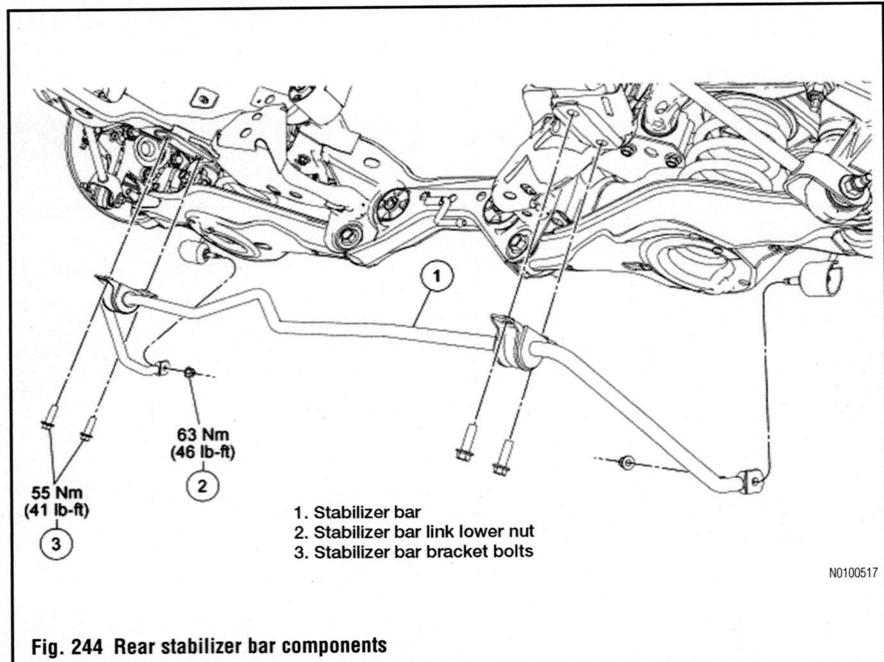

Fig. 244 Rear stabilizer bar components

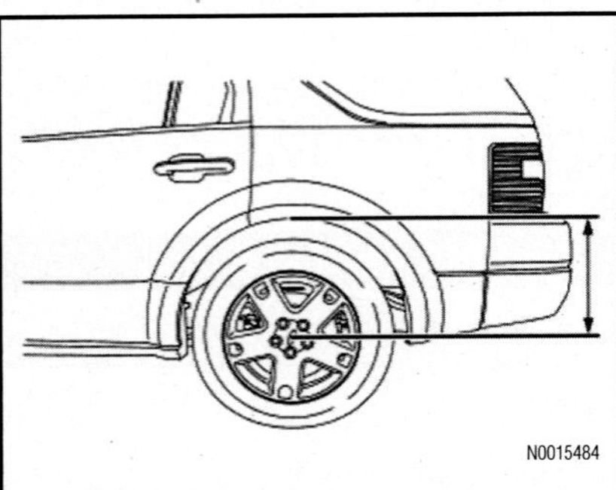

Fig. 245 Measure the distance from the center of the wheel hub to the lip of the fender

10. Lower the jackstand, slide the knuckle off the toe link and remove the knuckle.

11. If necessary, remove the 3 brake disc shield bolts and remove the shield.

To install:

12. Before tightening suspension bushing fasteners, use a jackstand to raise the rear suspension until the distance between the center of the hub and the lip of the fender is equal to the measurement taken in the removal procedure (curb height).

13. If removed, install the brake disc shield. Tighten the 3 bolts to 11 ft. lbs. (15 Nm).

14. Position the wheel knuckle onto the toe link and loosely install a new lower arm-to-wheel knuckle nut and bolt.

15. Loosely install a new toe link-to-knuckle nut.

16. Connect the shock absorber to the knuckle and loosely install a new shock absorber lower bolt.

17. Connect the stabilizer bar link and install a new stabilizer bar link upper nut. Tighten to 41 ft. lbs. (55 Nm).

18. Loosely install a new trailing arm-to-wheel knuckle nut and bolt.

19. Raise the jackstand and loosely install a new upper arm-to-wheel knuckle nut and bolt.

20. Position a suitable jackstand under the lower control arm at the shock and spring assembly attachment point and raise the rear suspension until the distance between the center of the hub and the lip of the fender is equal to the measurement taken in the removal procedure (curb height).

A slotted upper arm allows for the rear suspension camber to be adjusted by pushing inward or pulling outward on the wheel knuckle while tightening the upper arm-to-wheel knuckle nut.

21. With the wheel knuckle pushed inward for maximum negative camber, tighten the upper arm-to-wheel knuckle nut to 148 ft. lbs. (200 Nm). A slotted upper arm allows for the rear suspension camber to be adjusted by pushing inward or pulling outward on the wheel knuckle while tightening the upper arm-to-wheel knuckle nut.

22. Tighten the lower arm-to-wheel knuckle bolt to 196 ft. lbs. (265 Nm).

23. Tighten the shock absorber bolt to 129 ft. lbs. (175 Nm).

24. Tighten the trailing arm-to-wheel knuckle nut to 66 ft. lbs. (90 Nm).

25. Tighten the toe link-to-wheel knuckle nut to 59 ft. lbs. (80 Nm).

26. Install the wheel bearing and wheel hub.

27. Check the rear toe and adjust if necessary.

FWD Vehicles

See Figures 245 and 247.

1. Measure the distance from the center of the wheel hub to the lip of the fender with the vehicle in a level, static ground position (curb height).

2. Remove the brake disc.

3. Using a suitable jackstand, support the lower arm.

4. Remove and discard the trailing arm-to-wheel knuckle nut and bolt.

5. Remove and discard the stabilizer bar link upper nut and disconnect the link. Use the hex-holding feature to prevent the stabilizer bar link stud from turning while removing the nut.

6. Remove and discard the shock absorber lower bolt and disconnect the shock absorber.

7. Remove the wheel speed sensor bolt, disconnect the harness and position the sensor and harness assembly aside.

8. Remove and discard the toe link-to-knuckle nut.

9. Remove and discard the upper arm-to-wheel knuckle nut and bolt and disconnect the upper arm from the knuckle.

10. Remove and discard the lower arm-to-wheel knuckle nut and bolt.

11. Lower the jackstand, slide the knuckle off the toe link and remove the knuckle.

To install:

12. Before tightening any suspension bushing fasteners, use a jackstand to raise the rear suspension until the distance between the center of the hub and the lip of the fender is equal to the measurement taken in the removal procedure (curb height).

13. Position the wheel knuckle onto the toe link and loosely install a new lower arm-to-wheel knuckle nut and bolt.

14. Loosely install a new toe link-to-knuckle nut.

15. Position the wheel speed sensor harness and install the wheel speed sensor and bolt. Tighten to 11 ft. lbs. (15 Nm).

16. Connect the shock absorber to the knuckle and loosely install a new shock absorber lower bolt.

17. Connect the stabilizer bar link and

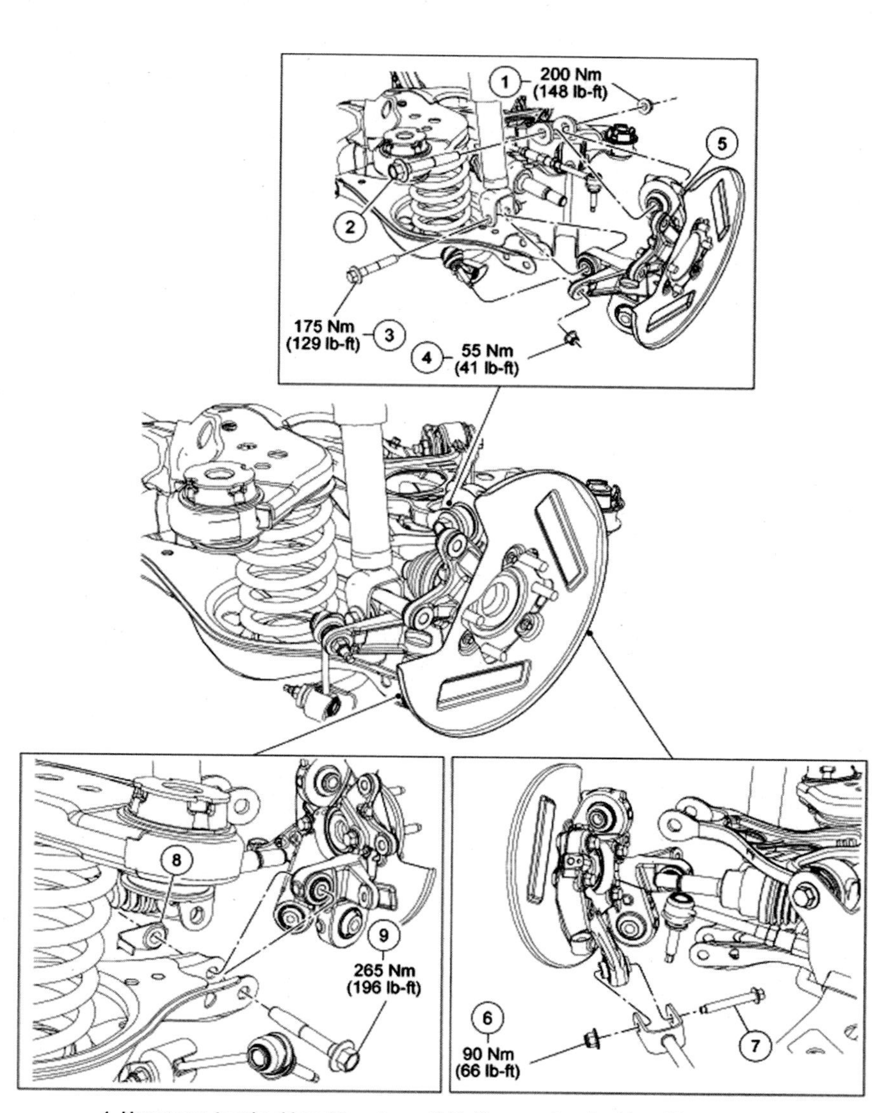

Fig. 246 Rear steering knuckle (wheel knuckle) components—AWD vehicles

install a new stabilizer bar link upper nut. Tighten to 41 ft. lbs. (55 Nm).

18. Loosely install a new trailing arm-to-wheel knuckle nut and bolt.

19. Loosely install a new upper arm-to-wheel knuckle nut and bolt.

20. Position a suitable jackstand under the lower control arm at the shock and spring assembly attachment point and raise the rear suspension until the distance between the center of the hub and the lip of the fender is equal to the measurement taken in the removal procedure (curb height).

21. With the wheel knuckle pushed inward for maximum negative camber, tighten the upper arm-to-wheel knuckle nut to 148 ft. lbs. (200 Nm). A slotted upper arm allows for the rear suspension camber to be adjusted by pushing inward or pulling outward on the wheel knuckle while tightening the upper arm-to-wheel knuckle nut.

22. Tighten the lower arm-to-wheel knuckle bolt to 196 ft. lbs. (265 Nm).

23. Tighten the shock absorber bolt to 129 ft. lbs. (175 Nm).

24. Tighten the trailing arm-to-wheel knuckle nut to 66 ft. lbs. (90 Nm).

25. Tighten the toe link-to-knuckle nut to 59 ft. lbs. (80 Nm).

26. Install the brake disc.

27. Install the wheel and tire.

28. Check the rear toe and adjust if necessary.

TOE LINK

REMOVAL & INSTALLATION

See Figures 248 and 249.

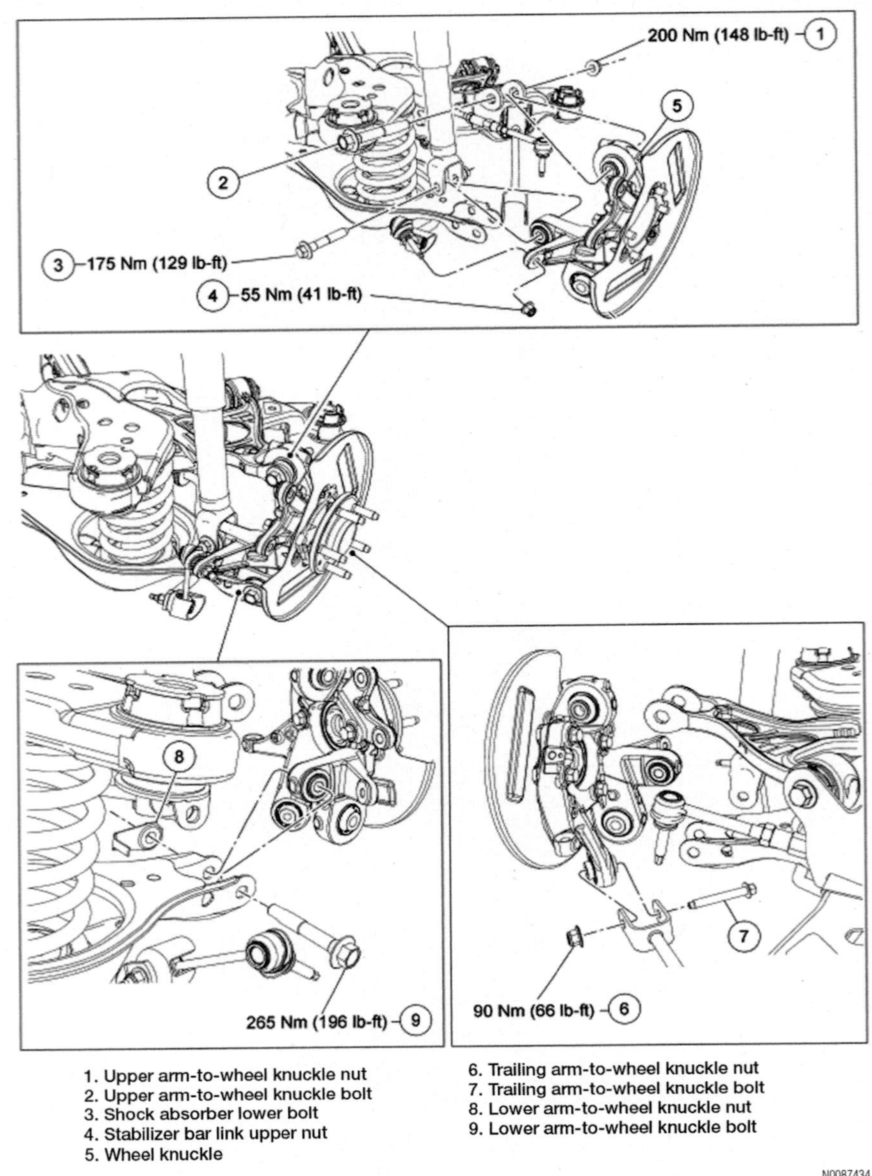

Fig. 247 Rear steering knuckle (wheel knuckle) components—FWD vehicles

Fig. 248 Measure the distance from the center of the wheel hub to the lip of the fender

1. Measure the distance from the center of the wheel hub to the lip of the fender with the vehicle in a level, static ground position (curb height).
2. Remove the wheel and tire.
3. Use a jackstand to raise the rear suspension until the distance between the center of the hub and the lip of the fender is equal to the measurement taken in Step 1 of the procedure (curb height).
4. Remove and discard the toe link-to-wheel knuckle nut.
5. Remove and discard the toe link-to-subframe bolt.

To install:

6. To install, reverse the removal procedure, noting the following:
    a. Install a new toe link-to-subframe bolt and tighten to 52 ft. lbs. (70 Nm).
    b. Install a new toe link-to-wheel knuckle nut and tighten to 59 ft. lbs. (80 Nm).
    c. Check the rear toe and adjust if necessary.

TRAILING ARM

REMOVAL & INSTALLATION

See Figures 248 and 250.

1. Measure the distance from the center of the wheel hub to the lip of the fender with the vehicle in a level, static ground position (curb height).

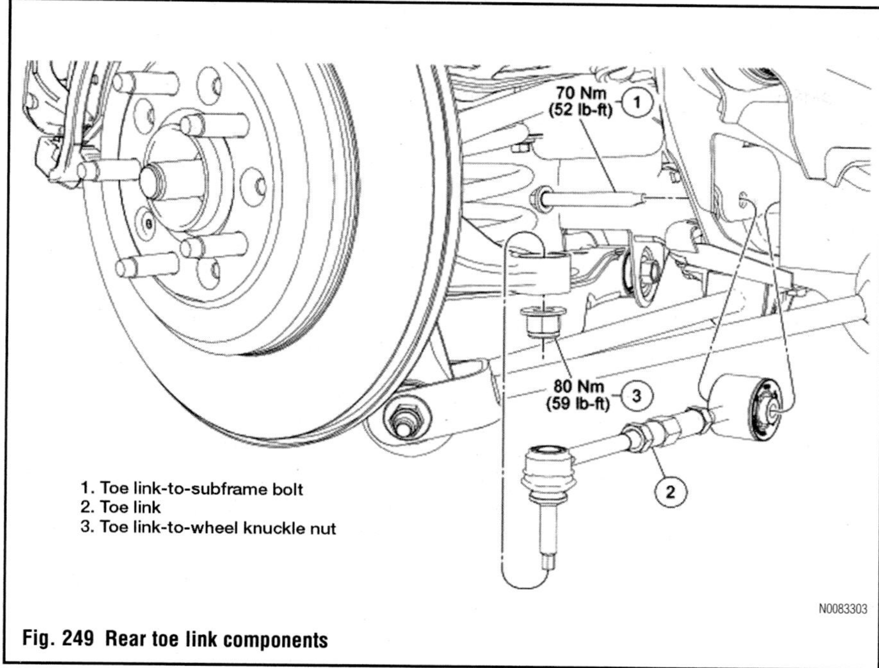

Fig. 249 Rear toe link components

2. Remove the wheel and tire.
3. Use a jackstand to raise the rear suspension until the distance between the center of the hub and the lip of the fender is equal to the measurement taken in Step 1 of the procedure (curb height).
4. Remove and discard the trailing arm-to-knuckle nut and bolt.
5. Remove and discard the trailing arm-to-subframe bolt.

To install:

6. To install, reverse the removal procedure, noting the following:
    a. Install a new trailing arm-to-subframe bolt and tighten to 122 ft. lbs. (165 Nm).
    b. Install a new trailing arm-to-knuckle nut and tighten to 66 ft. lbs. (90 Nm).

UPPER CONTROL ARM

REMOVAL & INSTALLATION

See Figures 248, 251 through 253.

1. Measure the distance from the center of the wheel hub to the lip of the fender with the vehicle in a level, static ground position (curb height).
2. Remove the wheels and tires.
3. Remove left-hand and right-hand parking brake cable bracket bolts.
4. Remove the 4 brake caliper anchor plate bolts and position the left-hand and right-hand brake caliper and anchor plate assemblies aside.
5. Support the brake caliper and anchor plate assemblies using mechanic's wire.
6. Position screw-type jackstands under the left-hand and right-hand wheel knuckles.
7. Remove and discard the upper arm-to-knuckle bolt and nut.
8. Remove and discard the 2 upper arm-to-subframe rearward bolts.
9. Remove and discard the left-hand and right-hand stabilizer bar link upper nuts and disconnect the links from the stabilizer bar. Use the hex-holding feature to prevent the stabilizer bar link stud from turning while removing or installing the nut.
10. Remove and discard the left-hand and right-hand lower shock bolts.
11. Remove and discard the 4 subframe bracket bolts.
12. Remove and discard the 2 subframe forward bolts and remove the 2 subframe brackets.
13. Remove and discard the 2 subframe rearward bolts and lower the subframe enough to allow removal of the upper arm forward bolt.
14. Remove and discard the upper arm-to-subframe forward bolt and nut.
15. Remove the upper arm.
16. If service to the upper arm rearward bushing is required, remove the upper arm bushing bolt and remove the upper arm bushing. Discard the bolt.

To install:

17. Before tightening the shock absorber lower bolts and upper arm nut and bolts, use a jackstand to raise the rear suspension until the distance between the center of the hub and the lip of the fender is equal to the measurement taken in the removal procedure (curb height).
18. If removed, install the upper arm bushing onto the upper arm in the following sequence.
    a. With the upper arm positioned so the top side is facing up and the upper arm bushing is positioned with the TOP OF PART facing up and the ARM TO THIS SIDE arrow is pointing toward the upper arm.
    b. Install the upper arm bushing.

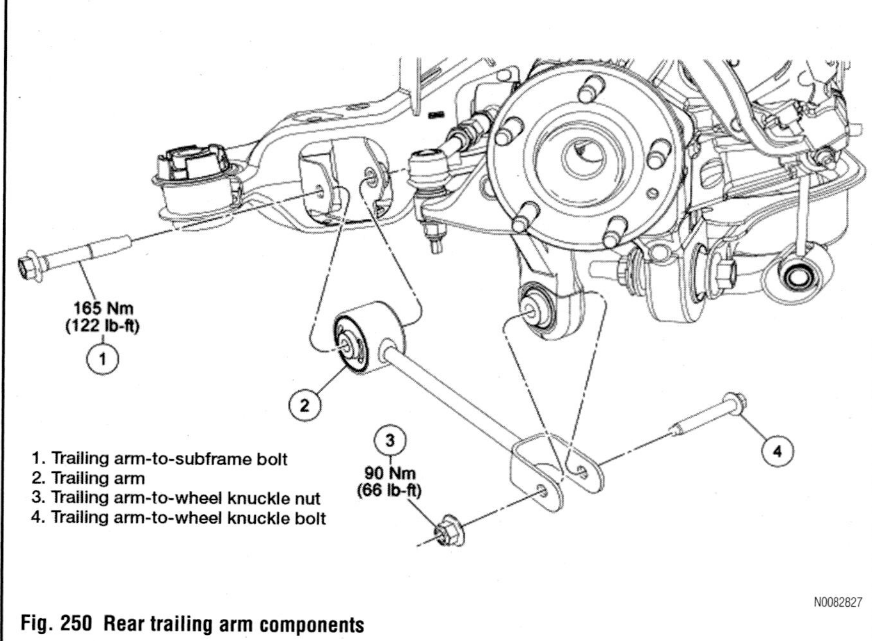

Fig. 250 Rear trailing arm components

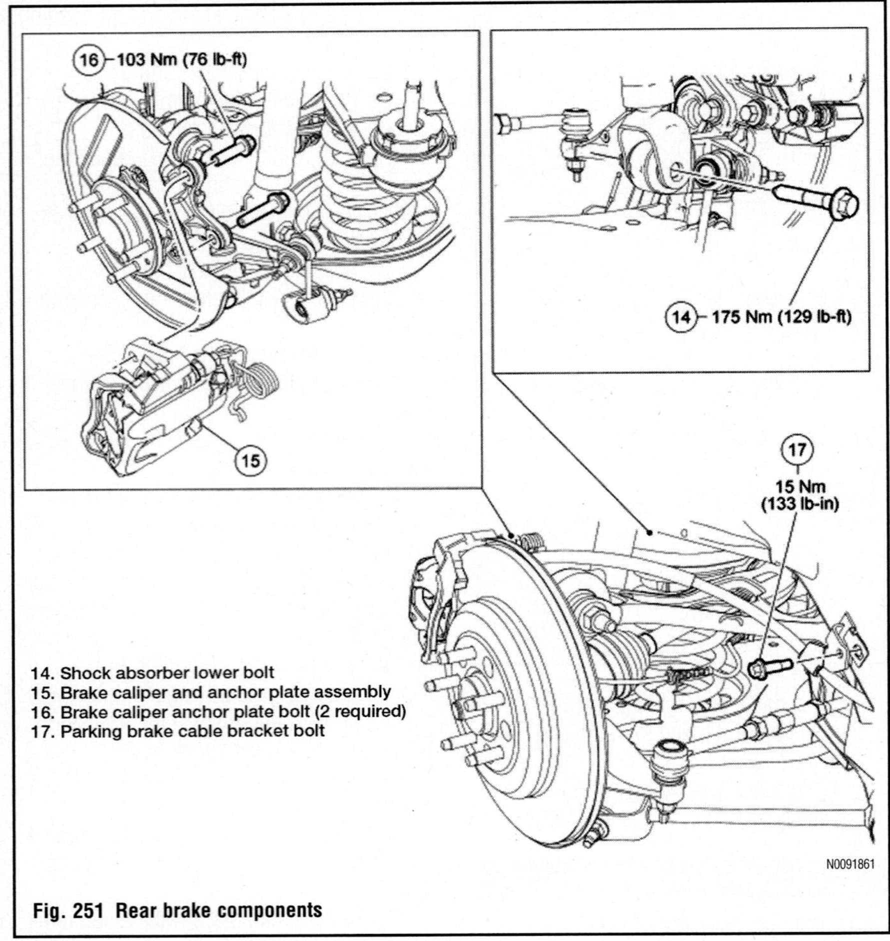

Fig. 251 Rear brake components

c. Install a new upper arm rearward bushing bolt and tighten to 148 ft. lbs. (200 Nm).

19. Position the upper arm and loosely install the new upper arm-to-subframe forward bolt and nut.

20. Raise the subframe and install 2 new subframe rearward bolts. Tighten to 148 ft. lbs. (200 Nm).

21. Position the 2 subframe brackets and install 4 new subframe bracket bolts. Tighten to 41 ft. lbs. (55 Nm).

22. Install 2 new subframe forward bolts. Tighten to 111 ft. lbs. (150 Nm).

23. Loosely install new left-hand and right-hand shock absorber lower bolts.

24. Connect the left-hand and right-hand stabilizer bar links to the stabilizer bar and install the new nuts. Tighten to 41 ft. lbs. (55 Nm).

25. Loosely install 2 new upper arm-to-subframe rearward bolts.

26. Loosely install a new upper arm-to-knuckle bolt and nut.

27. Position the left-hand and right-hand brake caliper and anchor plate assemblies and install the 4 anchor plate bolts. Tighten to 76 ft. lbs. (103 Nm).

28. Install left-hand and right-hand parking brake cable bracket bolts. Tighten to 11 ft. lbs. (15 Nm).

29. Using the screw-type jackstand, raise the rear suspension until the distance between

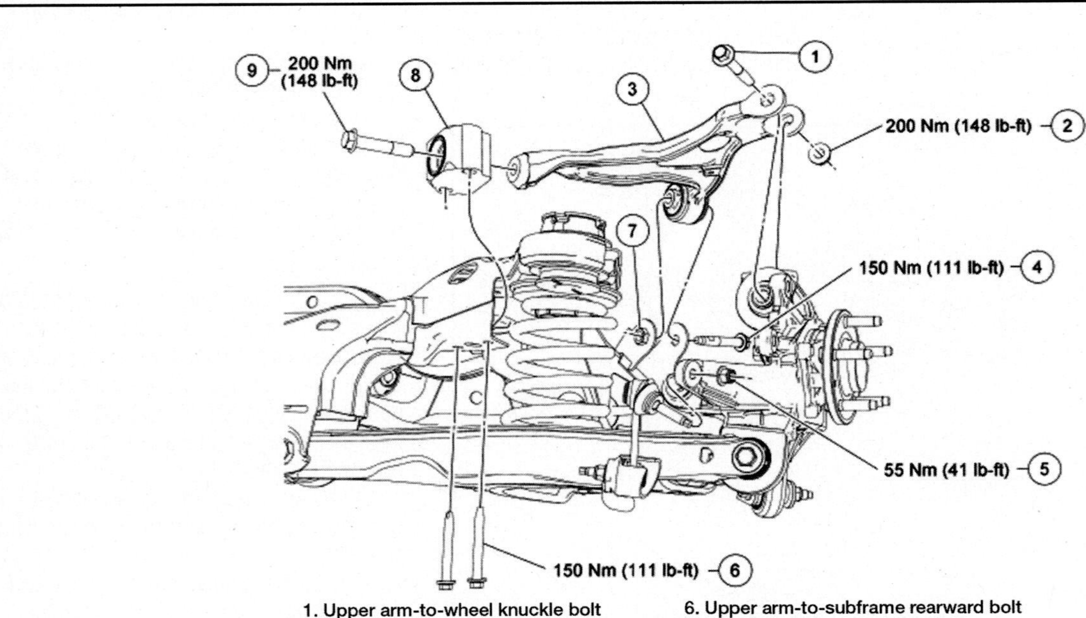

Fig. 252 Rear upper arm components

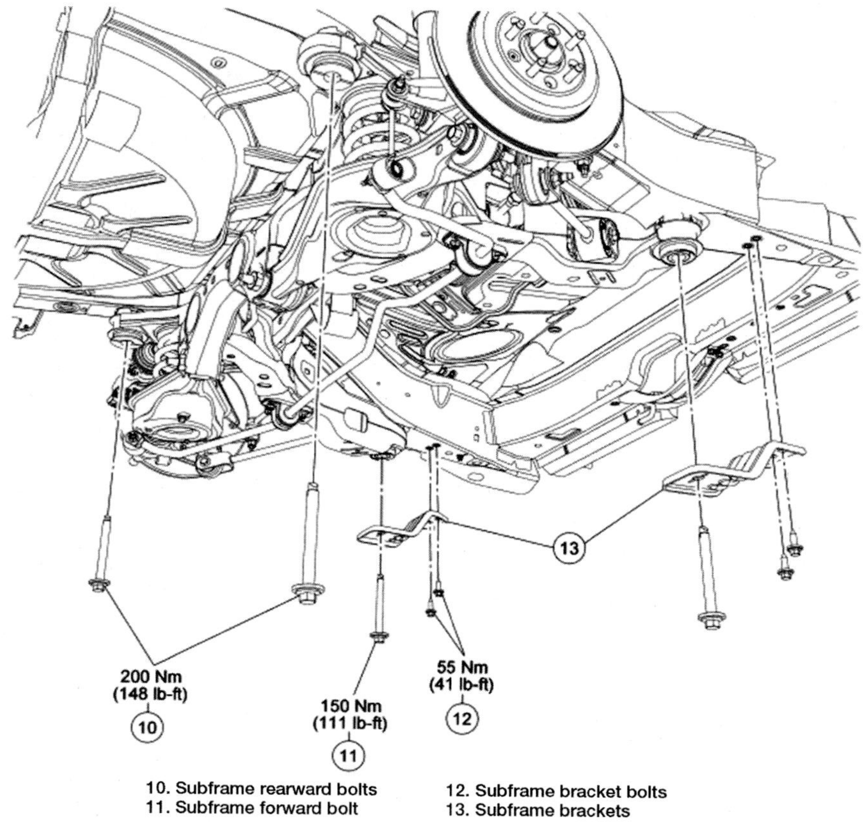

200 Nm (148 lb-ft) 10
150 Nm (111 lb-ft) 11
55 Nm (41 lb-ft) 12
13

10. Subframe rearward bolts
11. Subframe forward bolt
12. Subframe bracket bolts
13. Subframe brackets

N0089355

Fig. 253 Subframe components

the center of the hub and the lip of the fender is equal to the measurement taken in the removal procedure (curb height).

30. Tighten the upper arm-to-subframe forward bolt to 111 ft. lbs. (150 Nm).

31. Tighten the left-hand and right-hand shock absorber lower bolts to 129 ft. lbs. (175 Nm).

32. Tighten the 2 upper arm-to-subframe rearward bolts to 111 ft. lbs. (150 Nm).

33. With the wheel knuckle pushed inward for maximum negative camber, tighten the upper arm-to-wheel knuckle nut to 148 ft. lbs. (200 Nm). A slotted upper arm allows for the rear suspension camber to be adjusted by pushing inward or pulling outward on the wheel knuckle while tightening the upper arm-to-wheel knuckle nut.

34. Remove the 2 jackstands.

35. Install the rear wheels and tires.

36. Check the rear camber and adjust if necessary.

WHEEL BEARINGS

REMOVAL & INSTALLATION

See Figures 254 and 255.

1. Remove the brake disc.
2. Remove the wheel speed sensor bolt and position the sensor aside.
3. For AWD vehicles:
   a. Remove the wheel hub nut. Do not discard the nut at this time.
   b. Using the Front Wheel Hub Remover (SST 205-D070) or equivalent tool, separate the halfshaft from the wheel hub.
4. For all vehicles:

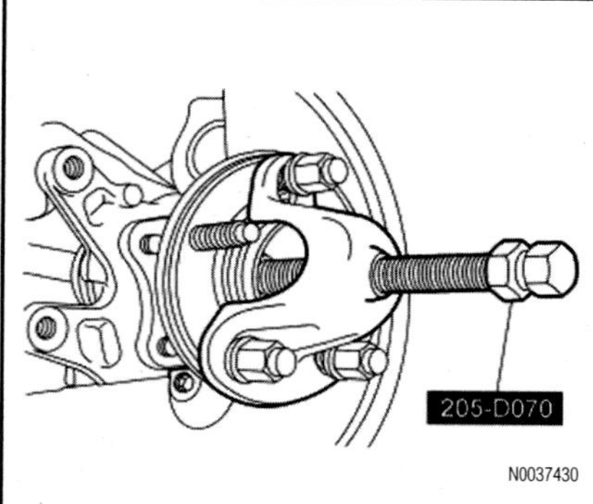

Fig. 254 Separate the halfshaft from the wheel hub

   a. Remove the 4 bolts and the wheel bearing and wheel hub. Discard the bolts.
   b. Using a clean shop towel, clean the wheel knuckle-to-mating surfaces and inspect the knuckle bearing bore. If the wheel knuckle is cracked, install a new wheel knuckle.

To install:

5. For all vehicles:

✲✲ WARNING

The wheel knuckle bore must be clean enough to allow the wheel bearing and wheel hub to seat completely by hand. Do not press or draw the wheel hub and bearing into place or damage to the bearing may occur.

6. Make sure the wheel hub-to-knuckle mating surfaces are clean and free of any adhesive. Failure to clean adhesive from both surfaces may cause bearing damage.
   a. Install the wheel bearing and wheel hub assembly.

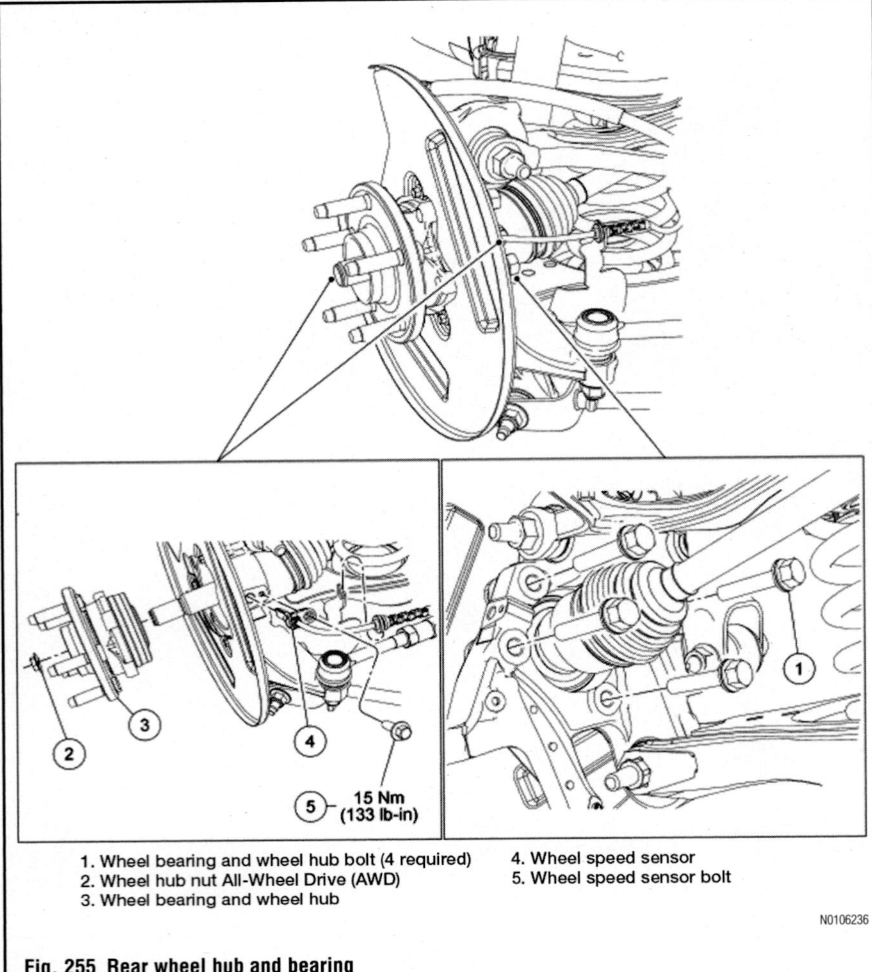

Fig. 255 Rear wheel hub and bearing

b. Install the 4 new wheel bearing and wheel hub bolts. Tighten the bolts to 98 ft. lbs. (133 Nm) in a cross-pattern.

c. Install the brake disc.

d. Position the wheel speed sensor and install the bolt. Tighten to 11 ft. lbs. (15 Nm).

7. For AWD vehicles:

WARNING

Do not tighten the rear wheel hub nut with the vehicle on the ground. The nut must be tightened to specification before the vehicle is lowered to the ground. Wheel bearing damage will occur if the wheel bearing is loaded with the weight of the vehicle applied.

a. Position the halfshaft in the hub and use the previously removed wheel hub nut to seat the halfshaft. Apply the brake to keep the halfshaft from rotating. Tighten the nut to 258 ft. lbs. (350 Nm). Remove and discard the nut.

b. Install a new wheel hub nut. Tighten the nut to 258 ft. lbs. (350 Nm).

c. Install and tighten the new wheel hub nut to specification within 5 minutes of starting it on the threads. Always install a new wheel hub nut after loosening or when not tightening within the specified time or damage to the components may occur.

LINCOLN

MKT

14

BRAKES 14-12

ANTI-LOCK BRAKE SYSTEM (ABS)........................14-12
General Information................14-12
Precautions........................14-12
Speed Sensors........................14-12
Removal & Installation........14-12
BLEEDING THE BRAKE SYSTEM 14-14
Bleeding Procedure................14-14
Bleeding Procedure 14-14
Bleeding the ABS System ...14-15
Master Cylinder Bleeding ...14-14
FRONT DISC BRAKES........14-15
Brake Caliper..........................14-15
Removal & Installation........14-15
Disc Brake Pads......................14-15
Removal & Installation........14-15
PARKING BRAKE..............14-17
Parking Brake Cables.............14-17
Adjustment 14-17
REAR DISC BRAKES 14-16
Brake Caliper..........................14-16
Removal & Installation........14-16
Disc Brake Pads......................14-16
Removal & Installation........14-16

CHASSIS ELECTRICAL 14-17

AIR BAG (SUPPLEMENTAL RESTRAINT SYSTEM) 14-17
General Information................14-17
Arming the System 14-18
Clockspring Centering........14-18
Disarming the System.........14-18
Service Precautions............14-17

DRIVE TRAIN 14-19

Automatic Transaxle Fluid.......14-19
Drain and Refill..................14-19
Front Halfshaft........................14-22
Removal & Installation........14-22
Power Transfer Unit (PTU).......14-20
Removal & Installation........14-20
Rear Axle Fluid.......................14-24
Drain & Refill.....................14-24
Rear Axle Housing..................14-24
Removal & Installation........14-24
Rear Axle Stub Shaft Seal........14-26
Removal & Installation........14-26
Rear Differential Housing Cover 14-26
Removal & Installation........14-26
Rear Driveshaft........................14-27
Removal & Installation........14-27
Rear Halfshaft..........................14-27
Removal & Installation........14-27
Rear Pinion Seal......................14-29
Removal & Installation........14-29

ENGINE COOLING...........14-30

Engine Coolant.......................14-30
Draining, Filling and Bleeding Procedure..........14-30
Flushing.............................14-31
Engine Fan.............................14-31
Removal & Installation........14-31
Radiator..................................14-32
Removal & Installation........14-32
Thermostat.............................14-34
Removal & Installation........14-34
Water Pump (Coolant Pump)....14-36
Removal & Installation........14-36

ENGINE ELECTRICAL.......14-37

BATTERY SYSTEM............14-39
Battery....................................14-39
Battery Reconnect/Relearn Procedure........................14-39
Removal & Installation........14-39
CHARGING SYSTEM 14-39
Alternator 14-39
Removal & Installation........14-39
IGNITION SYSTEM 14-41
Firing Order............................14-41
Ignition Coil 14-41
Removal & Installation........14-41
Spark Plugs............................14-43
Removal & Installation........14-43
STARTING SYSTEM 14-43
Starter 14-43
Removal & Installation........14-43

ENGINE MECHANICAL......14-44

Accessory Drive Belts 14-44
Accessory Belt Routing.......14-44
Adjustment 14-44
Inspection 14-44
Removal & Installation........14-44
Air Cleaner.............................14-46
Removal & Installation........14-46
Catalytic Converter.................14-47
Removal & Installation........14-47
Crankshaft Front Seal.............14-49
Removal & Installation........14-49
Cylinder Head 14-50
Removal & Installation........14-50
Exhaust Manifold 14-57
Removal & Installation........14-57
Intake Manifold 14-60
Removal & Installation........14-60
Oil Pan 14-64
Removal & Installation........14-64
Oil Pump................................14-73
Removal & Installation........14-73
Piston and Ring.......................14-74
Positioning 14-74
Rear Main Seal.......................14-74
Removal & Installation........14-74
Timing Chain & Sprockets......14-80
Removal & Installation........14-80
Timing Chain Front Cover.......14-75
Removal & Installation........14-75
Turbocharger..........................14-83
Removal & Installation........14-83
Valve Covers 14-89
Removal & Installation........14-89

ENGINE PERFORMANCE & EMISSION CONTROLS 14-93

Camshaft Position (CMP) Sensor 14-93
Location.............................14-93
Removal & Installation........14-93
Crankshaft Position (CKP) Sensor 14-93
Location.............................14-93
Removal & Installation........14-93

Heated Oxygen Sensor (HO2S) 14-94
Location 14-94
Removal & Installation 14-94
Intake Air Temperature (IAT) Sensor 14-94
Location 14-94
Removal & Installation 14-94
Knock Sensor (KS) 14-95
Location 14-95
Removal & Installation 14-95
Manifold Absolute Pressure (MAP) Sensor 14-95
Location 14-95
Removal & Installation 14-95
Powertrain Control Module (PCM) 14-96
Location 14-96
Passive Anti-Theft System (PATS) Parameter Reset Procedure 14-98
Programmable Module Installation (PMI) Procedure Using Integrated Diagnostic System (IDS) 14-96
Removal & Installation 14-96
Throttle Position Sensor (TPS) 14-98
Location 14-98
Removal & Installation 14-98

FUEL 14-99

GASOLINE FUEL INJECTION SYSTEM 14-99
Fuel Injectors 14-99
Removal & Installation 14-99
Fuel Pump 14-103
Removal & Installation 14-103
Fuel System Service Precautions 14-99
Relieving Fuel System Pressure 14-99
Throttle Body 14-104
Removal & Installation 14-104

HEATING & AIR CONDITIONING SYSTEM 14-106

Blower Motor 14-106
Removal & Installation 14-106
Heater Core 14-106
Removal & Installation 14-106

PRECAUTIONS 14-12

SPECIFICATIONS AND MAINTENANCE CHARTS 14-3

Brake Specifications 14-7
Camshaft Specifications 14-5
Capacities 14-4
Crankshaft and Connecting Rod Specifications 14-5
Engine and Vehicle Identification 14-3
Engine Tune-Up Specifications 14-3
Fluid Specifications 14-4
General Engine Specifications 14-3
Piston and Ring Specifications 14-5
Scheduled Maintenance Intervals 14-8–11
Tire, Wheel and Ball Joint Specifications 14-7
Torque Specifications 14-5
Valve Specifications 14-4
Wheel Alignment 14-5

STEERING 14-108

Power Steering Gear 14-108
Removal & Installation 14-108
Power Steering Pump 14-109
Fluid Fill Procedure 14-109
Power Steering System Flushing 14-111
Power Steering System Purging 14-112
Removal & Installation 14-112

SUSPENSION 14-113

FRONT SUSPENSION 14-113
Control Links 14-113
Removal & Installation 14-113
Lower Control Arm 14-114
Control Arm Bushing Replacement 14-114
Removal & Installation 14-114
Stabilizer Bar 14-114
Removal & Installation 14-114
Steering Knuckle 14-115
Removal & Installation 14-115
Strut & Spring Assembly 14-116
Removal & Installation 14-116
Wheel Bearings 14-117
Removal & Installation 14-117

REAR SUSPENSION 14-118
Coil Spring 14-118
Removal & Installation 14-118
Control Links 14-118
Removal & Installation 14-118
Lower Control Arm 14-119
Removal & Installation 14-119
Shock Absorber 14-119
Removal & Installation 14-119
Stabilizer Bar 14-119
Removal & Installation 14-119
Steering Knuckle 14-120
Removal & Installation 14-120
Toe Link 14-122
Removal & Installation 14-122
Trailing Arm 14-123
Removal & Installation 14-123
Upper Control Arm 14-123
Removal & Installation 14-123
Wheel Bearings 14-125
Removal & Installation 14-125

SPECIFICATIONS AND MAINTENANCE CHARTS

ENGINE AND VEHICLE IDENTIFICATION

Engine						
Code ①	Liters (cc)	Cu. In.	Cyl.	Fuel Sys.	Engine Type	Eng. Mfg.
T	3.5	214	V6	Direct Inj.	DOHC	Ford
R	3.7	226	V6	Direct Inj.	DOHC	Ford

Model Year	
Code ②	Year
A	2010
B	2011

① 8th position of VIN

② 10th position of VIN

25759_LMKT_C0001

GENERAL ENGINE SPECIFICATIONS

All measurements are given in inches.

Year	Model	Engine Displacement Liters	Engine ID/VIN	Fuel System Type	Net Horsepower @ rpm	Net Torque @ rpm (ft. lbs.)	Bore x Stroke (in.)	Com-pression Ratio	Oil Pressure @ rpm
2010	MKT	3.5	T	Dir Inj	355@5700	350@3500	3.64x3.41	10:01	30@1500
		3.7	R	Dir Inj	273@6250	270@4250	3.76x3.41	10.3:1	30@1500
2011	MKT	3.5	T	Dir Inj	355@5700	350@3500	3.64x3.41	10:01	30@1500
		3.7	R	Dir Inj	273@6250	270@4250	3.76x3.41	10.3:1	30@1500

25759_LMKT_C0002

ENGINE TUNE-UP SPECIFICATIONS

Year	Engine Displacement Liters	Engine ID/VIN	Spark Plug Gap (in.)	Ignition Timing (deg.)		Fuel Pump (psi)	Idle Speed (rpm)		Valve Clearance (in.)	
				MT	AT		MT	AT	Intake	Exhaust
2010	3.5	T	0.35	NA	NA	65	NA	①	0.006-0.010	0.014-0.018
	3.7	R	0.51-0.57	NA	NA	65	NA	①	0.006-0.010	0.014-0.018
2011	3.5	T	0.35	NA	NA	65	NA	①	0.006-0.010	0.014-0.018
	3.7	R	0.51-0.57	NA	NA	65	NA	①	0.006-0.010	0.014-0.018

NA Not Applicable

① Idle speed is computer controlled and is not adjustable.

25759_LMKT_C0003

CAPACITIES

Year	Model	Engine Displacement Liters	Engine ID/VIN	Engine Oil with Filter (qts.)	Transmission (pts.) Auto.	Transmission (pts.) Manual	Drive Axle (pts.) Rear	Transfer Case (pts.)	Fuel Tank (gal.)	Cooling System (qts.)
2010	MKT	3.5	T	6.0	①	NA	2.43	1.125	19.0	11
		3.7	R	5.5	①	NA	2.43	1.125	19.0	11
2011	MKT	3.5	T	6.0	①	NA	2.43	1.125	19.0	11
		3.7	R	5.5	①	NA	2.43	1.125	19.0	11

NOTE: All capacities are approximate. Add fluid gradually and ensure a proper fluid level is obtained.

① Transaxle Overhaul: 13, Transaxle Drain and Refill: 9

25759_LMKT_C0004

FLUID SPECIFICATIONS

Year	Model	Engine Disp. Liters	Engine Oil	Manual Trans.	Auto. Trans.	Drive Axle Rear	Transfer Case	Power Steering Fluid	Brake Master Cylinder	Cooling System
2010	MKT	3.5	5W-20	NA	①	80W-90	75W-140	②	③	④
		3.7	5W-20	NA	①	80W-90	75W-140	②	③	④
2011	MKT	3.5	5W-20	NA	①	80W-90	75W-140	②	③	④
		3.7	5W-20	NA	①	80W-90	75W-140	②	③	④

DOT: Department Of Transpotation

① Motorcraft® MERCON® LV

② Motorcraft® MERCON® V

③ DOT 3 or equivalent

④ Motorcraft® Specialty Green Engine Coolant

25759_LMKT_C0005

VALVE SPECIFICATIONS

Year	Engine Displacement Liters	Engine ID/VIN	Seat Angle (deg.)	Face Angle (deg.)	Spring Test Pressure (lbs. @ in.)	Spring Free-Length (in.)	Spring Installed Height (in.)	Stem-to-Guide Clearance (in.) Intake	Stem-to-Guide Clearance (in.) Exhaust	Stem Diameter (in.) Intake	Stem Diameter (in.) Exhaust
2010	3.5	T	44.5-45.5	44.5-45.5	60 lb @ 1.45	2.170	1.450	0.0008-0.0027	0.0013-0.0320	0.2157-0.2164	0.2151-0.2159
	3.7	R	44.5-45.5	44.5-45.5	53 lb @ 1.45	1.900	1.450	0.0008-0.0027	0.0013-0.0320	0.2157-0.2164	0.2151-0.2159
2011	3.5	T	44.5-45.5	44.5-45.5	60 lb @ 1.45	1.900	1.450	0.0008-0.0027	0.0013-0.0320	0.2157-0.2164	0.2151-0.2159
	3.7	R	44.5-45.5	44.5-45.5	53 lb @ 1.45	1.900	1.450	0.0008-0.0027	0.0013-0.0320	0.2157-0.2164	0.2151-0.2159

25759_LMKT_C0006

CAMSHAFT SPECIFICATIONS

All measurements in inches unless noted

Year	Engine Displacement Liters	Engine Code/VIN	Journal Diameter	Brg. Oil Clearance	Shaft End-play	Runout	Journal Bore	Lobe Height	
								Intake	Exhaust
2010	3.5	T	①	②	0.0012-0.0066	0.0015	③	0.35	0.36
	3.7	R	①	②	0.0012-0.0066	0.0015	③	0.38	0.38
2011	3.5	T	①	②	0.0012-0.0066	0.0015	③	0.35	0.36
	3.7	R	①	②	0.0012-0.0066	0.0015	③	0.38	0.38

① Journal Diameter 1st: 1.2202-1.2209, Journal Diameter Intermediate: 1.021-1.022

② Journal Bearing Clearance 1st: 0.0027, Journal Bearing Clearance Intermediate: 0.0029

③ Journal Bore Diameter 1st: 1.221-1.222, Journal Bore Diameter Intermediate: 1.023-1.024

25759_LMKT_C0007

CRANKSHAFT AND CONNECTING ROD SPECIFICATIONS

All measurements are given in inches.

Year	Engine Displacement Liters	Engine ID/VIN	Crankshaft				Connecting Rod		
			Main Brg. Journal Dia.	Main Brg. Oil Clearance	Shaft End-play	Thrust on No.	Journal Diameter	Oil Clearance	Side Clearance
2010	3.5	T	2.6570	0.0010-0.0016	0.0039-0.0114	4	2.204-2.205	0.0007-0.0021	0.0068-0.0167
	3.7	R	2.6570	0.0010-0.0016	0.0020-0.0114	4	2.204-2.205	0.0007-0.0021	0.0068-0.0167
2011	3.5	T	2.6570	0.0010-0.0016	0.0039-0.0114	4	2.204-2.205	0.0007-0.0021	0.0068-0.0167
	3.7	R	2.6570	0.0010-0.0016	0.0020-0.0114	4	2.204-2.205	0.0007-0.0021	0.0068-0.0167

25759_LMKT_C0008

PISTON AND RING SPECIFICATIONS

All measurements are given in inches.

Year	Engine Displacement Liters	Engine ID/VIN	Piston Clearance	Ring Gap			Ring Side Clearance		
				Top Compression	Bottom Compression	Oil Control	Top Compression	Bottom Compression	Oil Control
2010	3.5	T	0.0003-0.0017	0.0067-0.0106	0.0118-0.0216	0.0059-0.0177	0.0015-0.0031	0.0015-0.0031	NS
	3.7	R	0.0003-0.0017	0.0067-0.0106	0.0118-0.0216	0.0059-0.0177	0.0015-0.0031	0.0015-0.0031	NS
2011	3.5	T	0.0003-0.0017	0.0067-0.0106	0.0118-0.0216	0.0059-0.0177	0.0015-0.0031	0.0015-0.0031	NS
	3.7	R	0.0003-0.0017	0.0067-0.0106	0.0118-0.0216	0.0059-0.0177	0.0015-0.0031	0.0015-0.0031	NS

25759_LMKT_C0009

TORQUE SPECIFICATIONS

All readings in ft. lbs.

Year	Engine Disp. Liters	Engine ID/VIN	Cylinder Head Bolts	Main Bearing Bolts	Rod Bearing Bolts	Crankshaft Damper Bolts	Flywheel Bolts	Manifold Intake	Manifold Exhaust	Spark Plugs	Oil Pan Drain Plug
2010	3.5	T	①	②	③	④	59	7	⑤	11	20
	3.7	R	①	②	③	④	59	7	⑥	11	20
2011	3.5	T	①	②	③	④	59	7	⑤	11	20
	3.7	R	①	②	③	④	59	7	⑥	11	20

① Step 1: 15 ft. lbs.
Step 2: 26 ft. lbs.
Step 3: Plus 90 degrees
Step 4: Plus 90 degrees
Step 5: Plus 90 degrees
M6 Bolt: 89 inch lbs.

② Vertical bolts: 44 ft. lbs. plus 90 degrees
Side bolts: 33 ft. lbs. plus 90 degrees

③ Step 1: 17 ft. lbs.
Step 2: 32 ft. lbs.
Step 3: Plus 90 degrees

④ Step 1: Tighten to 89 ft. lbs.
Step 2: Loosen one full turn
Step 3: Tighten to 37 ft. lbs.
Step 4: Plus 90 degrees

⑤ Step 1: 11 ft. lbs.
Step 2: 15 ft. lbs.

⑥ Step 1: 15 ft. lbs.
Step 2: 18 ft. lbs.

25759_LMKT_C0010

WHEEL ALIGNMENT

Year	Engine		Caster Range (+/-Deg.)	Caster Preferred Setting (Deg.)	Camber Range (+/-Deg.)	Camber Preferred Setting (Deg.)	Toe (Deg.)
2010	3.5L Turbo	F	0.50	LH: 3.10, RH: 3.10	0.75	LH: -0.50, RH: -0.40	0.10 ± 0.20
		R	NA	NA	0.75	-1.00	0.12 ± 0.20
	3.7L	F	0.50	LH: 3.10, RH: 3.10	0.75	-0.40	0.10 ± 0.20
		R	NA	NA	0.75	-0.80	0.12 ± 0.20
2011	3.5L Turbo	F	0.75	LH: 3.30, RH: 3.50	0.75	LH: -0.50, RH: -0.60	0.10 ± 0.20
		R	NA	NA	0.75	-1.00	0.12 ± 0.20
	3.7L	F	0.75	LH: 3.30, RH: 3.50	0.75	LH: -0.40, RH: -0.50	0.10 ± 0.20
		R	NA	NA	0.75	-0.80	0.12 ± 0.20

25759_LMKT_C0011

TIRE, WHEEL AND BALL JOINT SPECIFICATIONS

Year	Model	Engine	OEM Tires Standard	OEM Tires Optional	Tire Pressures (psi) Front	Tire Pressures (psi) Rear	Wheel Size	Ball Joint Inspection	Lug Nut (ft. lbs.)
2010	MKT	3.5L	P255/45R 20	NS	①	①	8	NS	100
		3.7L	P235/55R 19	NS	①	①	7.5	NS	100
2011	MKT	3.5L	P255/45R 20	NS	①	①	8	NS	100
		3.7L	P235/55R 19	NS	①	①	7.5	NS	100

OEM: Original Equipment Manufacturer

PSI: Pounds Per Square Inch

NA: Information not available

① See Safety Certification Label on driver door jamb

25759_LMKT_C0012

BRAKE SPECIFICATIONS

All measurements in inches unless noted

Year	Model		Brake Disc Original Thickness	Brake Disc Minimum Thickness	Brake Disc Max. Runout	Brake Drum Diameter Original Inside Diameter	Brake Drum Diameter Max. Wear Limit	Brake Drum Diameter Maximum Machine Diamter	Minimum Pad/Lining Thickness Front	Minimum Pad/Lining Thickness Rear	Brake Caliper Bracket Bolts (ft. lbs.)	Brake Caliper Mounting Bolts (ft. lbs.)
2010	MKT	F	NS	1.122	NS	NA	NA	NA	0.118	0.118	111	53
		R	NS	0.394	NS	NA	NA	NA	0.118	0.118	76	24
2011	MKT	F	NS	1.122	NS	NA	NA	NA	0.118	0.118	111	53
		R	NS	0.394	NS	NA	NA	NA	0.118	0.118	76	24

F: Front

R: Rear

NA: Information not available

25759_LMKT_C0013

SCHEDULED MAINTENANCE INTERVALS

2010 Lincoln MKT - Normal

		VEHICLE MILEAGE INTERVAL (x1000)												
TO BE SERVICED	TYPE OF SERVICE	7.5	15	22.5	30	37.5	45	52.5	60	67.5	75	82.5	90	97.5
Engine oil & filter	Replace	✓	✓	✓	✓	✓	✓	✓	✓	✓	✓	✓	✓	✓
Rotate and inspect tires	Service	✓	✓	✓	✓	✓	✓	✓	✓	✓	✓	✓	✓	✓
Inspect wheels and related components for abnomal noise, wear, looseness or drag	Inspect	✓	✓	✓	✓	✓	✓	✓	✓	✓	✓	✓	✓	✓
Fluid levels (all)	Top off	✓	✓	✓	✓	✓	✓	✓	✓	✓	✓	✓	✓	✓
Exhaust system (Leaks, damage, loose parts and foreign material)	Inspect		✓		✓		✓		✓		✓		✓	
Cabin air filter	Replace		✓		✓		✓		✓		✓		✓	
Cooling system and hoses	Inspect		✓		✓		✓		✓		✓		✓	
Brake system (Pads/shoes/rotors/drums, brake lines and hoses, and parking brake system)	Inspect		✓		✓		✓		✓		✓		✓	
Halfshaft & U-joints	Inspect		✓		✓		✓		✓		✓		✓	
Climate-controlled seat filter (if equipped)	Replace				✓				✓				✓	
Engine air filter	Inspect	✓	✓	✓	✓	✓	✓	✓	✓	✓	✓	✓	✓	✓
Engine air filter	Replace				✓				✓				✓	
Spark plugs	Replace												✓	
Drive belt(s)	Inspect	✓	✓	✓	✓	✓	✓	✓	✓	✓	✓	✓	✓	✓
Shocks struts and other suspension components for leaks and damage	Inspect	✓	✓	✓	✓	✓	✓	✓	✓	✓	✓	✓	✓	✓
Oil and fluid leaks	Inspect	✓	✓	✓	✓	✓	✓	✓	✓	✓	✓	✓	✓	✓
Windshield for cracks, chips and pitting	Inspect	✓	✓	✓	✓	✓	✓	✓	✓	✓	✓	✓	✓	✓
Windshield wiper spray and wiper operation	Inspect	✓	✓	✓	✓	✓	✓	✓	✓	✓	✓	✓	✓	✓
Radiator, coolers, heater and airconditioning hoses	Inspect	✓	✓	✓	✓	✓	✓	✓	✓	✓	✓	✓	✓	✓
Horn, exterior lamps, turn signals and hazard warning light operation	Inspect	✓	✓	✓	✓	✓	✓	✓	✓	✓	✓	✓	✓	✓
Battery performance	Inspect	✓	✓	✓	✓	✓	✓	✓	✓	✓	✓	✓	✓	✓
Drive belt(s)	Replace	Every 150,000 miles												
Engine coolant	Replace	At 6 years or 105,000 miles; then every 3 years or 45,000 miles												
Automatic transmisison fluid	Replace	Every 150,000 miles												
Rear differential fluid	Replace	Every 150,000 miles												
Steering linkage, ball joints, suspension and tie-rod ends, lubricate if equipped with greases fittings	Inspect/ Lubricate	✓	✓	✓	✓	✓	✓	✓	✓	✓	✓	✓	✓	✓

25759_LMKT_C0014

SCHEDULED MAINTENANCE INTERVALS

2010 Lincoln MKT - Severe

TO BE SERVICED	TYPE OF SERVICE	VEHICLE MILEAGE INTERVAL (x1000)											
		5	10	15	20	25	30	35	40	45	50	55	60
Battery performance	Inspect	✓	✓	✓	✓	✓	✓	✓	✓	✓	✓	✓	✓
Halfshaft boots	Inspect	✓	✓	✓	✓	✓	✓	✓	✓	✓	✓	✓	✓
Horn, exterior lamps, turn signals and hazard warning light operation	Inspect	✓	✓	✓	✓	✓	✓	✓	✓	✓	✓	✓	✓
Inspect wheels and related components for abnomal noise, wear, looseness or drag	Inspect	✓	✓	✓	✓	✓	✓	✓	✓	✓	✓	✓	✓
Shocks struts and other suspension components for leaks and damage	Inspect	✓	✓	✓	✓	✓	✓	✓	✓	✓	✓	✓	✓
Oil and fluid leaks	Inspect	✓	✓	✓	✓	✓	✓	✓	✓	✓	✓	✓	✓
Radiator, coolers, heater and airconditioning hoses	Inspect	✓	✓	✓	✓	✓	✓	✓	✓	✓	✓	✓	✓
Rotate and inspect tires	Service	✓	✓	✓	✓	✓	✓	✓	✓	✓	✓	✓	✓
Spark plugs	Replace												✓
Automatic transmission fluid	Replace						✓						✓
Windshield wiper spray and wiper operation	Inspect	✓	✓	✓	✓	✓	✓	✓	✓	✓	✓	✓	✓
Windshield for cracks, chips and pitting	Inspect	✓	✓	✓	✓	✓	✓	✓	✓	✓	✓	✓	✓
Exhaust system (Leaks, damage, loose parts and foreign material)	Inspect	✓	✓	✓	✓	✓	✓	✓	✓	✓	✓	✓	✓
Engine oil and filter	Replace	✓	✓	✓	✓	✓	✓	✓	✓	✓	✓	✓	✓
Fluid levels (all)	Top off	✓	✓	✓	✓	✓	✓	✓	✓	✓	✓	✓	✓
Air filter	Inspect	✓	✓	✓	✓	✓	✓	✓	✓	✓	✓	✓	✓
Air filter	Replace						✓						✓
Drive belt(s)	Inspect	✓	✓	✓	✓	✓	✓	✓	✓	✓	✓	✓	✓
Cooling system & hoses	Inspect	✓	✓	✓	✓	✓	✓	✓	✓	✓	✓	✓	✓
Climate-controlled seat filter (if equipped)	Replace						✓						✓
Brake system (Inspect brake pads/shoes/rotors/drums, brake lines and hoses, and parking brake system)	Inspect	✓	✓	✓	✓	✓	✓	✓	✓	✓	✓	✓	✓
Engine coolant	Replace	At 6 years or 105,000 miles; then every 3 years or 45,000 miles											
Drive belt(s)	Replace	every 150,000 miles											
Cabin air filter (If equipped)	Inspect/	✓	✓	✓	✓	✓	✓	✓	✓	✓	✓	✓	✓
Steering linkage, ball joints, suspension and tie-rod ends, lubricate if equipped with greases fittings	Inspect/ Lubricate	✓	✓	✓	✓	✓	✓	✓	✓	✓	✓	✓	✓
Rear differential fluid	Replace	every 150,000 miles											

For extensive idling and or low speed driving, change engine oil and filter every 5,000 miles, 6 months or 200 hours of engine operation.

25759_LMKT_C0015

SCHEDULED MAINTENANCE INTERVALS

2011 Lincoln MKT - Normal

Service Item	Service Action	1	2	3	4	5	6	7	8	9	10	11	12	13	14	15
Auto transmisison fluid	Replace															✓
Spark plugs	Replace										✓					
Engine coolant	Replace										✓					✓
Accessory drive belt	Replace															✓
Engine air filter	Replace			✓			✓			✓			✓			✓
Radiator, coolers, heater and air conditioning hoses	Inspect	✓	✓	✓	✓	✓	✓	✓	✓	✓	✓	✓	✓	✓	✓	✓
Brake system (Pads/shoes/rotors/drums, brake lines and hoses, and parking brake system)	Inspect	✓	✓	✓	✓	✓	✓	✓	✓	✓	✓	✓	✓	✓	✓	✓
Inspect wheels and related components for abnomal noise, wear, looseness or drag	Inspect	✓	✓	✓	✓	✓	✓	✓	✓	✓	✓	✓	✓	✓	✓	✓
Battery performance	Inspect	✓	✓	✓	✓	✓	✓	✓	✓	✓	✓	✓	✓	✓	✓	✓
Windshield for cracks, chips and pitting	Inspect	✓	✓	✓	✓	✓	✓	✓	✓	✓	✓	✓	✓	✓	✓	✓
Windshield wiper spray and wiper operation	Inspect	✓	✓	✓	✓	✓	✓	✓	✓	✓	✓	✓	✓	✓	✓	✓
Oil and fluid leaks	Inspect	✓	✓	✓	✓	✓	✓	✓	✓	✓	✓	✓	✓	✓	✓	✓
Shocks struts and other suspension components for leaks and damage	Inspect	✓	✓	✓	✓	✓	✓	✓	✓	✓	✓	✓	✓	✓	✓	✓
Exhaust system (Leaks, damage, loose parts and foreign material)	Inspect					✓	✓	✓	✓	✓	✓	✓	✓	✓	✓	✓
Horn, exterior lamps, turn signals and hazard warning light operation	Inspect	✓	✓	✓	✓	✓	✓	✓	✓	✓	✓	✓	✓	✓	✓	✓
Cooling system, hoses, clamps & coolant strength	Inspect					✓	✓	✓	✓	✓	✓	✓	✓	✓	✓	✓
Engine air filter	Inspect	✓	✓	✓	✓	✓	✓	✓	✓	✓	✓	✓	✓	✓	✓	✓
Accessory drive belt	Inspect	✓	✓	✓	✓	✓	✓	✓	✓	✓	✓	✓	✓	✓	✓	✓
Halfshaft boots	Inspect					✓	✓	✓	✓	✓	✓	✓	✓	✓	✓	✓
Cabin air filter	Inspect/ Service		✓		✓		✓		✓		✓		✓		✓	✓
Steering linkage, ball joints, suspension and tie-rod ends, lubricate if equipped with greases fittings	Inspect/ Lubricate	✓	✓	✓	✓	✓	✓	✓	✓	✓	✓	✓	✓	✓	✓	✓
Fluid levels (all)	Top off	✓	✓	✓	✓	✓	✓	✓	✓	✓	✓	✓	✓	✓	✓	✓
Rotate tires, inspect tread wear, measure tread depth and check pressure	Inspect/ Rotate	✓	✓	✓	✓	✓	✓	✓	✓	✓	✓	✓	✓	✓	✓	✓
Rear differential fluid	Replace															✓

Oil change service intervals should be completed as indicated by the message center (Can be up to 1 year or 10,000 miles) If the message center is prematurely reset or is inoperative, perform the oil change interval at 6 months or 5,000 miles from your last oil change.

25759_LMKT_C0016

SCHEDULED MAINTENANCE INTERVALS

2011 Lincoln MKT - Severe

Service Item	Service Action	1	2	3	4	5	6	7	8	9	10	11	12	13	14	15
Accessory drive belt	Replace															✓
Spark plugs	Replace						✓						✓			
Engine coolant	Replace										✓					
Automatic transmisison fluid	Replace			✓			✓			✓			✓			✓
Battery performance	Inspect	✓	✓	✓	✓	✓	✓	✓	✓	✓	✓	✓	✓	✓	✓	✓
Cooling system, hoses, clamps & coolant strength	Inspect	✓	✓	✓	✓	✓	✓	✓	✓	✓	✓	✓	✓	✓	✓	✓
Brake system (Pads/shoes/rotors/drums, brake lines and hoses, and parking brake system)	Inspect	✓	✓	✓	✓	✓	✓	✓	✓	✓	✓	✓	✓	✓	✓	✓
Inspect wheels and related components for abnomal noise, wear, looseness or drag	Inspect	✓	✓	✓	✓	✓	✓	✓	✓	✓	✓	✓	✓	✓	✓	✓
Radiator, coolers, heater and air conditioning hoses	Inspect	✓	✓	✓	✓	✓	✓	✓	✓	✓	✓	✓	✓	✓	✓	✓
Fluid levels (all)	Inspect	✓	✓	✓	✓	✓	✓	✓	✓	✓	✓	✓	✓	✓	✓	✓
Exhaust system (Leaks, damage, loose parts and foreign material)	Inspect	✓	✓	✓	✓	✓	✓	✓	✓	✓	✓	✓	✓	✓	✓	✓
Horn, exterior lamps, turn signals and hazard warning light operation	Inspect	✓	✓	✓	✓	✓	✓	✓	✓	✓	✓	✓	✓	✓	✓	✓
Oil and fluid leaks	Inspect	✓	✓	✓	✓	✓	✓	✓	✓	✓	✓	✓	✓	✓	✓	✓
Shocks struts and other suspension components for leaks and damage	Inspect	✓	✓	✓	✓	✓	✓	✓	✓	✓	✓	✓	✓	✓	✓	✓
Windshield for cracks, chips and pitting	Inspect	✓	✓	✓	✓	✓	✓	✓	✓	✓	✓	✓	✓	✓	✓	✓
Windshield wiper spray and wiper operation	Inspect	✓	✓	✓	✓	✓	✓	✓	✓	✓	✓	✓	✓	✓	✓	✓
Accessory drive belt	Inspect	✓	✓	✓	✓	✓	✓	✓	✓	✓	✓	✓	✓	✓	✓	✓
Halfshaft boots	Inspect	✓	✓	✓	✓	✓	✓	✓	✓	✓	✓	✓	✓	✓	✓	✓
Steering linkage, ball joints, suspension and tie-rod ends, lubricate if equipped with greases fittings	Inspect/ Lubricate	✓	✓	✓	✓	✓	✓	✓	✓	✓	✓	✓	✓	✓	✓	✓
Engine air filter	Inspect/ Service	✓	✓	✓	✓	✓	✓	✓	✓	✓	✓	✓	✓	✓	✓	✓
Cabin air filter	Inspect/ Service	✓	✓	✓	✓	✓			✓	✓	✓	✓	✓	✓	✓	✓
Rotate tires, inspect tread wear, measure tread depth and check pressure	Rotate/ Inspect	✓	✓	✓	✓	✓	✓	✓	✓	✓	✓	✓	✓	✓	✓	✓
Rear differential fluid	Replace															✓

For extensive idling and or low speed driving, change engine oil and filter every 5,000 miles, 6 months or 200 hours of engine operation.

For commercial use or extensive idling, change spark plugs at 60,000 miles.

25759_LMKT_C0017

PRECAUTIONS

Before servicing any vehicle, please be sure to read all of the following precautions, which deal with personal safety, prevention of component damage, and important points to take into consideration when servicing a motor vehicle:

- Never open, service or drain the radiator or cooling system when the engine is hot; serious burns can occur from the steam and hot coolant.
- Observe all applicable safety precautions when working around fuel. Whenever servicing the fuel system, always work in a well-ventilated area. Do not allow fuel spray or vapors to come in contact with a spark, open flame, or excessive heat (a hot drop light, for example). Keep a dry chemical fire extinguisher near the work area. Always keep fuel in a container specifically designed for fuel storage; also, always properly seal fuel containers to avoid the possibility of fire or explosion. Refer to the additional fuel system precautions later in this section.
- Fuel injection systems often remain pressurized, even after the engine has been turned **OFF**. The fuel system pressure must be relieved before disconnecting any fuel lines. Failure to do so may result in fire and/or personal injury.
- Brake fluid often contains polyglycol ethers and polyglycols. Avoid contact with the eyes and wash your hands thoroughly after handling brake fluid. If you do get brake fluid in your eyes, flush your eyes with clean, running water for 15 minutes. If eye irritation persists, or if you have taken brake fluid internally, IMMEDIATELY seek medical assistance.
- The EPA warns that prolonged contact with used engine oil may cause a number of skin disorders, including cancer. You should make every effort to minimize your exposure to used engine oil. Protective gloves should be worn when changing oil. Wash your hands and any other exposed skin areas as soon as possible after exposure to used engine oil. Soap and water, or waterless hand cleaner should be used.
- All new vehicles are now equipped with an air bag system, often referred to as a Supplemental Restraint System (SRS) or Supplemental Inflatable Restraint (SIR) system. The system must be disabled before performing service on or around system components, steering column, instrument panel components, wiring and sensors. Failure to follow safety and disabling procedures could result in accidental air bag deployment, possible personal injury and unnecessary system repairs.
- Always wear safety goggles when working with, or around, the air bag system. When carrying a non-deployed air bag, be sure the bag and trim cover are pointed away from your body. When placing a non-deployed air bag on a work surface, always face the bag and trim cover upward, away from the surface. This will reduce the motion of the module if it is accidentally deployed. Refer to the additional air bag system precautions later in this section.
- Clean, high quality brake fluid from a sealed container is essential to the safe and proper operation of the brake system. You should always buy the correct type of brake fluid for your vehicle. If the brake fluid becomes contaminated, completely flush the system with new fluid. Never reuse any brake fluid. Any brake fluid that is removed from the system should be discarded. Also, do not allow any brake fluid to come in contact with a painted surface; it will damage the paint.
- Never operate the engine without the proper amount and type of engine oil; doing so WILL result in severe engine damage.
- Timing belt maintenance is extremely important. Many models utilize an interference-type, non-freewheeling engine. If the timing belt breaks, the valves in the cylinder head may strike the pistons, causing potentially serious (also time-consuming and expensive) engine damage. Refer to the maintenance interval charts for the recommended replacement interval for the timing belt, and to the timing belt section for belt replacement and inspection.
- Disconnecting the negative battery cable on some vehicles may interfere with the functions of the on-board computer system(s) and may require the computer to undergo a relearning process once the negative battery cable is reconnected.
- When servicing drum brakes, only disassemble and assemble one side at a time, leaving the remaining side intact for reference.
- Only an MVAC-trained, EPA-certified automotive technician should service the air conditioning system or its components.

BRAKES — ANTI-LOCK BRAKE SYSTEM (ABS)

GENERAL INFORMATION

PRECAUTIONS

- Certain components within the ABS system are not intended to be serviced or repaired individually.
- Do not use rubber hoses or other parts not specifically specified for and ABS system. When using repair kits, replace all parts included in the kit. Partial or incorrect repair may lead to functional problems and require the replacement of components.
- Lubricate rubber parts with clean, fresh brake fluid to ease assembly. Do not use shop air to clean parts; damage to rubber components may result.
- Use only DOT 3 brake fluid from an unopened container.
- If any hydraulic component or line is removed or replaced, it may be necessary to bleed the entire system.
- A clean repair area is essential. Always clean the reservoir and cap thoroughly before removing the cap. The slightest amount of dirt in the fluid may plug an orifice and impair the system function. Perform repairs after components have been thoroughly cleaned; use only denatured alcohol to clean components. Do not allow ABS components to come into contact with any substance containing mineral oil; this includes used shop rags.
- The Anti-Lock control unit is a microprocessor similar to other computer units in the vehicle. Ensure that the ignition switch is **OFF** before removing or installing controller harnesses. Avoid static electricity discharge at or near the controller.
- If any arc welding is to be done on the vehicle, the control unit should be unplugged before welding operations begin.

SPEED SENSORS

REMOVAL & INSTALLATION

Front

See Figure 1.

1. Before servicing the vehicle, refer to the Precautions Section.
2. Remove the wheel and tire.
3. Disconnect the wheel speed sensor electrical connector.
4. Remove the scrivets and position aside the fender splash shield.
5. Remove the wheel speed sensor harness pin-type retainer.

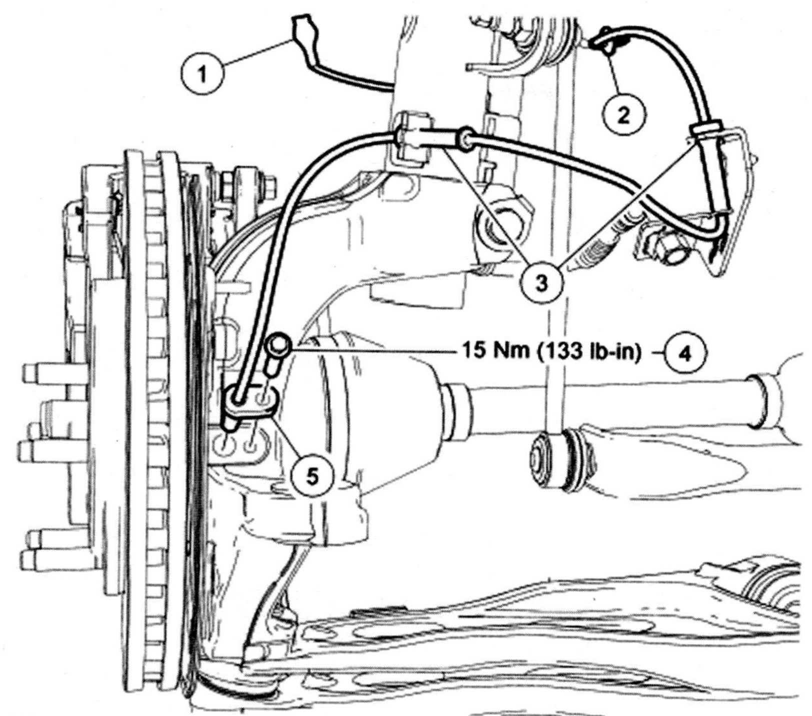

Fig. 1 Front wheel speed sensor

6. Remove the 2 wheel speed sensor harness retainers.
7. Remove the bolt and the wheel speed sensor.

To install:

8. To install, reverse the removal procedure. To install, tighten the bolt to 11 ft. lbs. (15 Nm).

Rear

See Figure 2.

1. Before servicing the vehicle, refer to the Precautions Section.
2. With the vehicle in NEUTRAL, position it on a hoist.
3. Disconnect the wheel speed sensor electrical connector.
4. Detach the 2 wheel speed sensor pin-type retainers.
5. Detach the 2 wheel speed sensor harness retainers.
6. Remove the wheel speed sensor bolt.
7. Remove the wheel speed sensor.

To install:

8. To install, reverse the removal procedure. To install, tighten the bolt to 11 ft. lbs. (15 Nm).

WARNING

Make sure to correctly route and secure the wheel speed sensor harness in the rear subframe assembly or damage to the harness may occur.

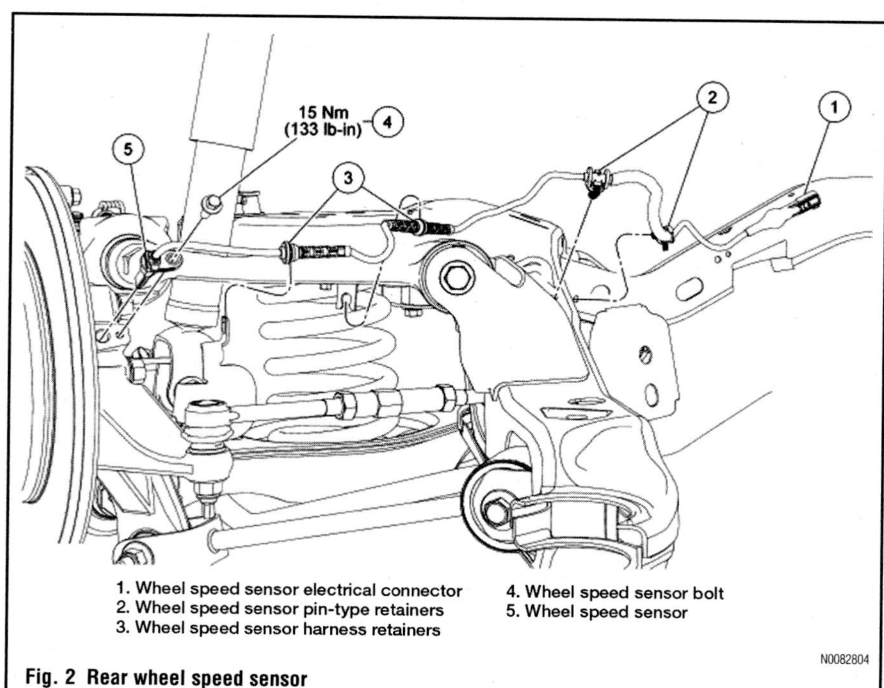

Fig. 2 Rear wheel speed sensor

BLEEDING PROCEDURE

BLEEDING PROCEDURE

Pressure Bleeding

CAUTION

Do not allow the brake master cylinder to run dry during the bleeding operation. Master cylinder may be damaged if operated without fluid, resulting in degraded braking performance. Failure to follow this instruction may result in serious personal injury.

➡Pressure bleeding the brake system is preferred to manual bleeding.

➡The Hydraulic Control Unit (HCU) bleeding procedure must be carried out if the HCU or any components upstream of the HCU are installed new.

1. Before servicing the vehicle, refer to the Precautions Section.
2. Clean all the dirt from around the brake fluid reservoir cap and remove the cap. Fill the brake master cylinder reservoir with clean, specified brake fluid.
3. Install the bleeder adapter to the brake master cylinder reservoir and attach the bleeder tank hose to the fitting on the adapter. Master cylinder pressure bleeder adapter tools are available from various manufacturers of pressure bleeding equipment. Follow the instructions of the manufacturer when installing the adapter.
4. Open the valve on the bleeder tank. Make sure the bleeder tank contains enough specified brake fluid to complete the bleeding operation. Apply 30–50 psi (207–345 kPa) to the brake system.
5. Remove the right-hand rear bleeder cap and place a box-end wrench on the bleeder screw. Attach a rubber drain tube to the right-hand rear bleeder screw and submerge the free end of the tube in a container partially filled with clean, specified brake fluid.

➡Due to the complexity of the fluid path within the rear integral parking brake calipers, it is necessary to press and release the parking brake during the bleed procedure.

6. Loosen the right-hand rear bleeder screw. Leave open until clear, bubble-free brake fluid flows, then tighten the right-hand rear bleeder screw.
7. For rear brake calipers, press and release the parking brake 5 times. Repeat until clear, bubble-free fluid comes out.
8. Tighten the right-hand rear bleeder screw to specification. Remove the rubber hose and install the bleeder screw cap.
9. Repeat the above 3 steps for the left-hand rear brake caliper.
10. Continue bleeding the front of the system, going in order from the right-hand front brake caliper and then to the left-hand front brake caliper. Tighten the front brake caliper bleeder screws to specification.
11. Close the bleeder tank valve and release the pressure. Remove the tank hose from the adapter and remove the adapter. Fill the reservoir with clean, specified brake fluid and install the reservoir cap.

Manual Bleeding

CAUTION

Do not allow the brake master cylinder to run dry during the bleeding operation. Master cylinder may be damaged if operated without fluid, resulting in degraded braking performance. Failure to follow this instruction may result in serious personal injury.

➡Pressure bleeding the brake system is preferred to manual bleeding.

➡The HCU bleeding procedure must be carried out if the HCU or any components upstream of the HCU are installed new.

1. Before servicing the vehicle, refer to the Precautions Section.
2. Clean all the dirt from around the brake fluid reservoir cap and remove the cap. Fill the brake master cylinder reservoir with clean, specified brake fluid.
3. Remove the right-hand rear bleeder cap and place a box-end wrench on the bleeder screw. Attach a rubber drain tube to the right-hand rear bleeder screw and submerge the free end of the tube in a container partially filled with clean, specified brake fluid.
4. Have an assistant hold firm pressure on the brake pedal.

➡Due to the complexity of the fluid path within the rear integral parking brake calipers, it is necessary to press and release the parking brake during the bleed procedure.

5. Loosen the right-hand rear bleeder screw until a stream of brake fluid comes out. While the assistant maintains pressure on the brake pedal, tighten the right-hand rear bleeder screw.
6. Press and release the parking brake 5 times. Repeat until clear, bubble-free fluid comes out.
7. Refill the brake master cylinder reservoir as necessary.
8. Tighten the right-hand rear bleeder screw to specification.
9. Remove the rubber hose and install the bleeder screw cap.
10. Repeat the above steps for the left-hand rear brake caliper.
11. Remove the right-hand front bleeder cap and place a box-end wrench on the bleeder screw. Attach a rubber drain tube to the right-hand front bleeder screw and submerge the free end of the tube in a container partially filled with clean, specified brake fluid.
12. Have an assistant hold firm pressure on the brake pedal.
13. Loosen the right-hand front bleeder screw until a stream of brake fluid comes out. While the assistant maintains pressure on the brake pedal, tighten the right-hand front bleeder screw. Repeat until clear, bubble-free fluid comes out.
14. Refill the brake master cylinder reservoir as necessary.
15. Tighten the right-hand front bleeder screw to specification.
16. Remove the rubber hose and install the bleeder screw cap.
17. Repeat the above steps for the left-hand front brake caliper bleeder screw.

MASTER CYLINDER BLEEDING

CAUTION

Do not allow the brake master cylinder to run dry during the bleeding operation. Master cylinder may be damaged if operated without fluid, resulting in degraded braking performance. Failure to follow this instruction may result in serious personal injury.

➡When a new brake master cylinder has been installed or the system has been emptied, or partially emptied, it should be primed to prevent air from entering the system.

1. Before servicing the vehicle, refer to the Precautions Section.
2. Disconnect the brake tubes from the master cylinder.

3. Install short brake tubes onto the primary and secondary ports with the ends submerged in the brake master cylinder reservoir.
4. Fill the brake master cylinder reservoir with clean, specified brake fluid.
5. Have an assistant pump the brake pedal until clear fluid flows from the brake tubes without air bubbles.
6. Remove the short brake tubes, and install the master cylinder brake tubes.
7. Bleed the brake system. For additional information, refer to Brake Bleeding Procedure in this section.

BLEEDING THE ABS SYSTEM

➡Pressure bleeding the brake system is preferred to manual bleeding.

1. Before servicing the vehicle, refer to the Precautions Section.
2. Follow the pressure bleeding or manual bleeding procedure steps to bleed the system.
3. Connect the scan tool and follow the ABS Service Bleed instructions.
4. Repeat the pressure bleeding or manual bleeding procedure steps to bleed the system.

BRAKES

FRONT DISC BRAKES

CAUTION

Dust and dirt accumulating on brake parts during normal use may contain asbestos fibers from production or aftermarket brake linings. Breathing excessive concentrations of asbestos fibers can cause serious bodily harm. Exercise care when servicing brake parts. Do not sand or grind brake lining unless equipment used is designed to contain the dust residue. Do not clean brake parts with compressed air or by dry brushing. Cleaning should be done by dampening the brake components with a fine mist of water, then wiping the brake components clean with a dampened cloth. Dispose of cloth and all residue containing asbestos fibers in an impermeable container with the appropriate label. Follow practices prescribed by the Occupational Safety and Health Administration (OSHA) and the Environmental Protection Agency (EPA) for the handling, processing, and disposing of dust or debris that may contain asbestos fibers.

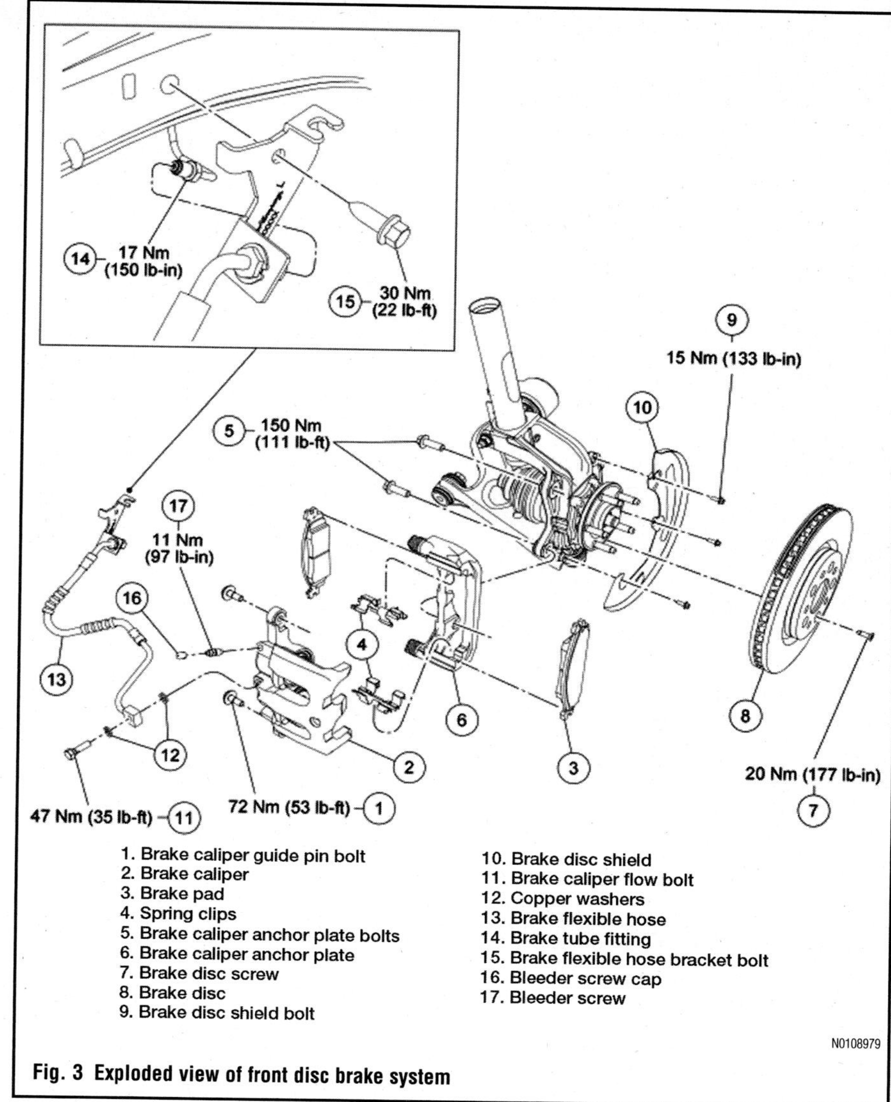

Fig. 3 Exploded view of front disc brake system

BRAKE CALIPER

REMOVAL & INSTALLATION

See Figure 3.

1. Before servicing the vehicle, refer to the Precautions Section.
2. Remove the brake pads.
3. Remove the brake caliper flow bolt and position the brake hose aside.
4. Discard the copper washers.
5. Remove the brake caliper.

To install:

6. Position the brake hose and install the brake caliper flow bolt.
7. Install new copper washers. Tighten to 35 ft. lbs. (47 Nm).
8. Install the brake pads.
9. Bleed the brake caliper.

DISC BRAKE PADS

REMOVAL & INSTALLATION

1. Before servicing the vehicle, refer to the Precautions Section.
2. Check the brake fluid level in the brake master cylinder reservoir. If required, remove the fluid until the brake master cylinder reservoir is half full.
3. Remove the wheel and tire.
4. Using a C-clamp, compress the pistons into the caliper housing.

WARNING

Do not allow the brake caliper to hang from the brake hose or damage to the hose may occur.

5. Remove the 2 brake caliper guide pin bolts and position the caliper aside.

6. Support the caliper using mechanic's wire.

7. Remove the 2 brake pads and spring clips from the brake caliper anchor plate.

8. Discard the spring clips.

To install:

9. If installing new brake pads, make sure to install all new hardware and lubricant supplied with the brake pad kit. Refer to the brake pad instruction sheet when applying lubricant.

10. Install the new spring clips and brake pads to the brake caliper anchor plate.

11. Apply equal amounts of specified lubricant to the brake caliper-to-brake pad contact points.

12. Make sure the caliper pin boots are correctly seated to prevent corrosion to the guide pins.

13. Position the brake caliper onto the brake caliper anchor plate and install the 2 brake caliper guide pin bolts. Tighten to 53 ft. lbs. (72 Nm). Make sure that the brake hose is not twisted when the caliper is positioned on the anchor plate.

14. Install the wheel and tire.

15. If necessary, fill the brake master cylinder reservoir with clean, specified brake fluid.

16. Apply brakes several times to verify correct operation.

BRAKES

REAR DISC BRAKES

⁂ CAUTION

Dust and dirt accumulating on brake parts during normal use may contain asbestos fibers from production or aftermarket brake linings. Breathing excessive concentrations of asbestos fibers can cause serious bodily harm. Exercise care when servicing brake parts. Do not sand or grind brake lining unless equipment used is designed to contain the dust residue. Do not clean brake parts with compressed air or by dry brushing. Cleaning should be done by dampening the brake components with a fine mist of water, then wiping the brake components clean with a dampened cloth. Dispose of cloth and all residue containing asbestos fibers in an impermeable container with the appropriate label. Follow practices prescribed by the Occupational Safety and Health Administration (OSHA) and the Environmental Protection Agency (EPA) for the handling, processing, and disposing of dust or debris that may contain asbestos fibers.

BRAKE CALIPER

REMOVAL & INSTALLATION

See Figure 4.

1. Before servicing the vehicle, refer to the Precautions Section.

2. Release the parking brake cable tension.

3. Disconnect the parking brake cable from the subframe bracket and the caliper. Position the parking brake cable aside.

4. Remove and discard the brake pads.

5. Clean and inspect the disc brake caliper. If leaks or damaged boots are found, install a new disc brake caliper.

6. Disconnect the brake tube fitting from the brake flexible hose.

7. The brake caliper and brake flexible hose are removed as an assembly. Remove the retainer clip from the brake flexible hose.

To install:

8. Install the brake caliper and flexible hose. Make sure that the hose does not become twisted. Tighten the brake tube fitting to 13 ft. lbs. (17 Nm).

9. Install the brake pads.

10. Connect the parking brake cable.

11. Bleed the caliper.

DISC BRAKE PADS

REMOVAL & INSTALLATION

See Figure 5.

1. Before servicing the vehicle, refer to the Precautions Section.

2. Check the brake fluid level in the brake fluid reservoir. If required, remove fluid until the brake master cylinder reservoir is half full.

3. Remove the wheel and tire.

4. Remove the brake caliper bolts.

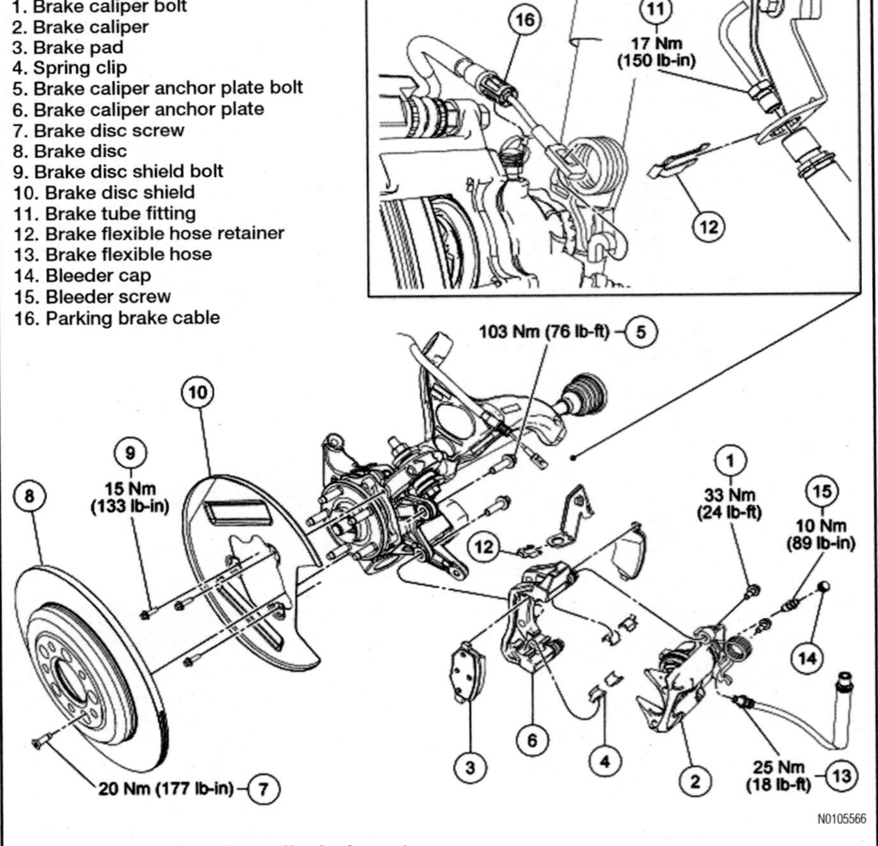

Fig. 4 Exploded view of rear disc brake system

WARNING

Care must be taken when servicing rear brake components without disconnecting the parking brake cable from the brake caliper lever. Carefully position the caliper aside using a suitable support or damage to the parking brake cable end fittings may occur.

5. Using hand force and a rocking motion, separate the brake caliper from the anchor plate. Position the brake caliper aside.
6. Support the caliper with mechanic's wire. Do not allow the caliper to hang from the brake hose or damage to the hose may occur.
7. Remove and discard the 2 brake pads and spring clips from the brake caliper anchor plate. When the brake pads are separated from the brake caliper, new brake pads must be installed to prevent brake noise and shudder. The brake pads are one-time use only.
8. Inspect the brake caliper anchor plate assembly.
9. Check the guide pins and boots for binding or damage. Do not remove the anchor plate guide pins. The guide pins are press fit to the brake caliper anchor plate. If the guide pins are damaged, a new anchor plate must be installed.

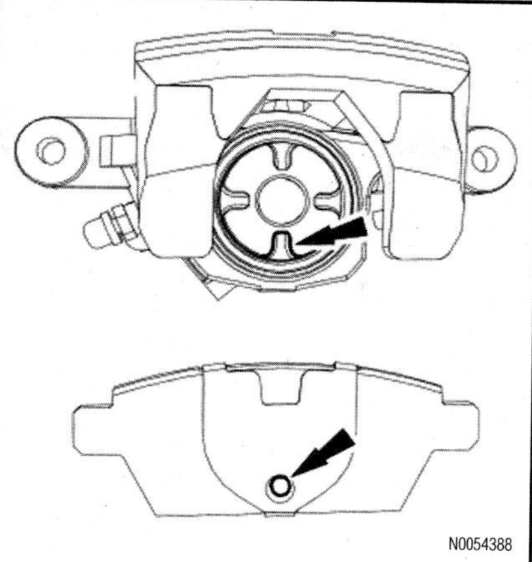

Fig. 5 Position the notch in the caliper piston so that it will correctly align with the pin on the backside of the inboard brake pad

To install:

CAUTION

Always install new brake shoes or pads at both ends of an axle to reduce the possibility of brakes pulling vehicle to one side. Failure to follow this instruction may result in uneven braking and serious personal injury.

10. Install a new brake caliper anchor plate if it is worn or damaged.
11. Using the Rear Caliper Piston Adjuster or equivalent tool, rotate the caliper piston clockwise to compress the piston into its cylinder. A moderate to heavy force toward the caliper piston must be applied. If sufficient force is not applied, the internal park brake mechanism clutch cone will not engage and the piston will not compress.
12. Clean the residual adhesive from the brake caliper fingers and piston using specified brake parts cleaner.
13. Position the notch in the caliper piston so that it will correctly align with the pin on the backside of the inboard brake pad.
14. Install the new spring clips and brake pads to the brake caliper anchor plate. Do not allow grease, oil, brake fluid or other contaminants to contact the pad lining material. Do not install contaminated pads.
15. Position the brake caliper and install the 2 bolts. Tighten to 24 ft. lbs. (33 Nm). Make sure that the brake hose does not become twisted.
16. If necessary, fill the brake fluid reservoir with clean, specified brake fluid.
17. Apply brakes several times to verify correct brake operation.
18. Install the wheel and tire.

BRAKES — PARKING BRAKE

PARKING BRAKE CABLES

ADJUSTMENT

The parking brake cable tension is self-adjusting inside the parking brake control.

CHASSIS ELECTRICAL — AIR BAG (SUPPLEMENTAL RESTRAINT SYSTEM)

GENERAL INFORMATION

CAUTION

These vehicles are equipped with an air bag system. The system must be disarmed before performing service on, or around, system components, the steering column, instrument panel components, wiring and sensors. Failure to follow the safety precautions and the disarming procedure could result in accidental air bag deployment, possible injury and unnecessary system repairs.

SERVICE PRECAUTIONS

Disconnect and isolate the battery negative cable before beginning any airbag system component diagnosis, testing, removal, or installation procedures. Allow system capacitor to discharge for two minutes before beginning any component service. This will disable the airbag system. Failure to disable the airbag system may result in accidental airbag deployment, personal injury, or death.

Do not place an intact undeployed airbag face down on a solid surface. The airbag will propel into the air if accidentally deployed and may result in personal injury or death.

When carrying or handling an undeployed airbag, the trim side (face) of the airbag should be pointing towards the body to minimize possibility of injury if accidental deployment occurs. Failure to do this may result in personal injury or death.

Replace airbag system components with OEM replacement parts. Substitute parts may appear interchangeable, but internal differences may result in inferior occupant protection. Failure to do so may result in occupant personal injury or death.

Wear safety glasses, rubber gloves, and long sleeved clothing when cleaning powder residue from vehicle after an airbag deployment. Powder residue emitted from a deployed airbag can cause skin irritation. Flush affected area with cool water if irritation is experienced. If nasal or throat irritation is experienced, exit the vehicle for fresh air until the irritation ceases. If irritation continues, see a physician.

Do not use a replacement airbag that is not in the original packaging. This may result in improper deployment, personal injury, or death.

The factory installed fasteners, screws and bolts used to fasten airbag components have a special coating and are specifically designed for the airbag system. Do not use substitute fasteners. Use only original equipment fasteners listed in the parts catalog when fastener replacement is required.

During, and following, any child restraint anchor service, due to impact event or vehicle repair, carefully inspect all mounting hardware, tether straps, and anchors for proper installation, operation, or damage. If a child restraint anchor is found damaged in any way, the anchor must be replaced. Failure to do this may result in personal injury or death.

Deployed and non-deployed airbags may or may not have live pyrotechnic material within the airbag inflator.

Do not dispose of driver/passenger/curtain airbags or seat belt tensioners unless you are sure of complete deployment. Refer to the Hazardous Substance Control System for proper disposal.

Dispose of deployed airbags and tensioners consistent with state, provincial, local, and federal regulations.

After any airbag component testing or service, do not connect the battery negative cable. Personal injury or death may result if the system test is not performed first.

If the vehicle is equipped with the Occupant Classification System (OCS), do not connect the battery negative cable before performing the OCS Verification Test using the scan tool and the appropriate diagnostic information. Personal injury or death may result if the system test is not performed properly.

Never replace both the Occupant Restraint Controller (ORC) and the Occupant Classification Module (OCM) at the same time. If both require replacement, replace one, then perform the Airbag System test before replacing the other.

Both the ORC and the OCM store Occupant Classification System (OCS) calibration data, which they transfer to one another when one of them is replaced. If both are replaced at the same time, an irreversible fault will be set in both modules and the OCS may malfunction and cause personal injury or death.

If equipped with OCS, the Seat Weight Sensor is a sensitive, calibrated unit and must be handled carefully. Do not drop or handle roughly. If dropped or damaged, replace with another sensor. Failure to do so may result in occupant injury or death.

If equipped with OCS, the front passenger seat must be handled carefully as well. When removing the seat, be careful when setting on floor not to drop. If dropped, the sensor may be inoperative, could result in occupant injury, or possibly death.

If equipped with OCS, when the passenger front seat is on the floor, no one should sit in the front passenger seat. This uneven force may damage the sensing ability of the seat weight sensors. If sat on and damaged, the sensor may be inoperative, could result in occupant injury, or possibly death.

DISARMING THE SYSTEM

➡The air bag warning indicator illuminates when the correct Restraints Control Module (RCM) fuse is removed and the ignition is ON.

➡The Supplemental Restraint System (SRS) must be fully operational and free of faults before releasing the vehicle to the customer.

1. Before servicing the vehicle, refer to the Precautions Section.
2. Turn all vehicle accessories OFF.
3. Turn the ignition OFF.
4. At the Smart Junction Box (SJB), located below the left-hand side of the instrument panel, remove the cover and RCM fuse 32 (10A) from the SJB. For additional information, refer to the Wiring Diagrams.
5. Turn the ignition ON and monitor the air bag warning indicator for at least 30 seconds. The air bag warning indicator will flash once, then remain illuminated continuously (no flashing) if the correct RCM fuse has been removed. If the air bag warning indicator does not remain illuminated continuously, remove the correct RCM fuse before proceeding.
6. Turn the ignition OFF.
7. Disconnect the battery ground cable and wait at least one minute.

ARMING THE SYSTEM

See Figure 6.

1. Before servicing the vehicle, refer to the Precautions Section.
2. Install RCM fuse 32 (10A) to the SJB and install the cover.
3. Remove Battery Junction Box (BJB) relay 63.
4. Install a 20A fused jumper wire in BJB relay 63 cavities as shown.

CAUTION

Make sure no one is in the vehicle and there is nothing blocking or placed in front of any air bag module when the battery is connected. Failure to follow these instructions may result in serious personal injury in the event of an accidental deployment.

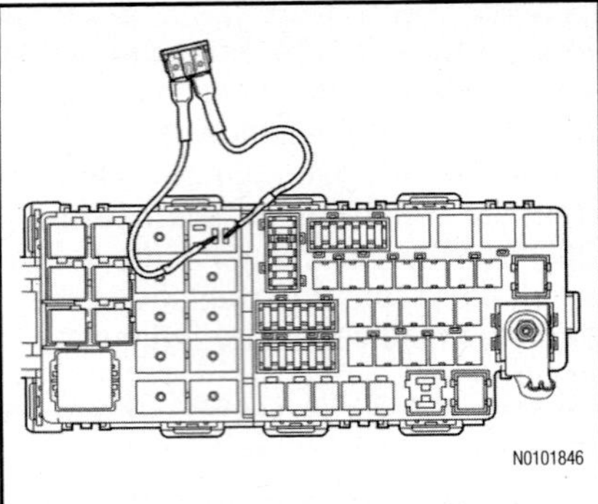

Fig. 6 Install a 20A fused jumper wire in BJB relay 63 cavities as shown

5. Connect the battery ground cable.
6. Prove out the SRS as follows: Turn the ignition from ON to OFF. Wait 10 seconds, then turn the ignition ON and monitor the air bag warning indicator with the air bag modules installed. The air bag warning indicator will illuminate continuously for approximately 6 seconds and then turn off. If an SRS fault is present, the air bag warning indicator will: - fail to light. - remain lit continuously. - flash. The flashing might not occur until approximately 30 seconds after the ignition has been turned from the OFF to the ON position. This is the time required for the RCM to complete the testing of the SRS . If the air bag warning indicator is inoperative and a SRS fault exists, a chime will sound in a pattern of 5 sets of 5 beeps. If this occurs, the air bag warning indicator and any SRS fault discovered must be diagnosed and repaired. Clear all continuous DTCs from the RCM and OCSM.
7. Disconnect the battery ground cable.
8. Remove the fused jumper wire from the BJB .
9. Install BJB relay 63 and cover.
10. Connect the battery ground cable.
11. Clear all CMDTCs from the RCM and OCSM .

CLOCKSPRING CENTERING

CAUTION

If the clockspring is not correctly centralized, it may fail prematurely. If in doubt, repeat the centralizing procedure. Failure to follow these instructions may increase the risk of serious personal injury or death in a crash.

WARNING

Do not over-rotate the clockspring inner rotor. The internal ribbon wire is connected to the clockspring rotor. The internal ribbon wire acts as a

stop and can be broken from its internal connection. Failure to follow this instruction may result in component damage and/or system failure.

⁂ WARNING

If installing a new clockspring, do not remove the clockspring anti-rotation key until the steering wheel is installed. If the anti-rotation key has been removed before installing the steering wheel, the clockspring must be centered. Failure to follow this instruction may result in component damage and/or system failure.

1. Before servicing the vehicle, refer to the Precautions Section.
2. Depower (disarm) the SRS.
3. Install the clockspring and 2 screws.
4. Connect the clockspring electrical connector.
5. If a new clockspring was installed and the anti-rotation key has not been removed, proceed to Step 10, otherwise proceed to Step 7.
6. Rotate the clockspring inner rotor counterclockwise and carefully feel for the ribbon wire to run out of length with slight resistance. Stop rotating the clockspring inner rotor at this point.
7. Starting with the clockspring inner rotor in the 12 o'clock position, rotate the inner rotor clockwise through 2 revolutions to center the clockspring. The clockspring inner rotor must be in the 12 o'clock position to be correctly centered.

⁂ WARNING

To prevent damage to the clockspring, make sure the road wheels are in the straight-ahead position.

8. Install the steering wheel.
9. Install the driver air bag module.
10. Repower (arm) the SRS.

DRIVE TRAIN

AUTOMATIC TRANSAXLE FLUID

DRAIN AND REFILL

3.5L Engine

See Figures 7 through 9.

1. Before servicing the vehicle, refer to the Precautions Section.
2. With the vehicle in NEUTRAL, position it on a hoist.
3. Remove the transmission fluid drain plug and allow the transmission fluid to drain. If an internal problem is suspected, drain the transmission fluid through a paper filter. A small amount of metal or friction particles may be found from normal wear. If an excessive amount of metal or friction material is present, the transaxle will need to be overhauled.
4. Install the transmission fluid drain plug. Tighten to 80 inch lbs. (9 Nm).
5. Clean the area around the clamp that connects the Air Cleaner (ACL) to the ACL outlet pipe.
6. If equipped, remove the bolt cover.

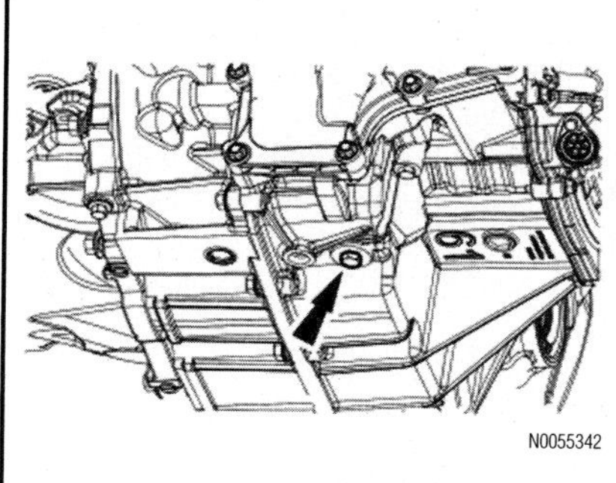

Fig. 7 Remove the transmission fluid drain plug

7. Remove the ACL from the ACL bracket and the ACL outlet hose. Do not disconnect the Intake Air Temperature (IAT) sensor electrical connector.
    a. Remove the wiring harness retainer from the ACL by pulling it up.
    b. Remove the 2 ACL bolts.
    c. Loosen the clamp.
    d. Pull up on the ACL to remove it from the 2 rubber grommets and position it aside with the IAT sensor electrical connector still connected.
8. With the IAT sensor connected, rotate the ACL 90 degrees to access the transmission fluid level indicator. Install the ACL in the outlet pipe and tighten the clamp. Tighten to 44 inch lbs. (5 Nm).
9. Remove the transmission fluid level indicator. If the transaxle was removed and disassembled, fill the transaxle with 6.5 qt. (6.2L) of clean transmission fluid. If the main control cover was removed for in-vehicle repair, fill the transaxle with 4.5 qt. (4.3L) of clean transmission fluid.

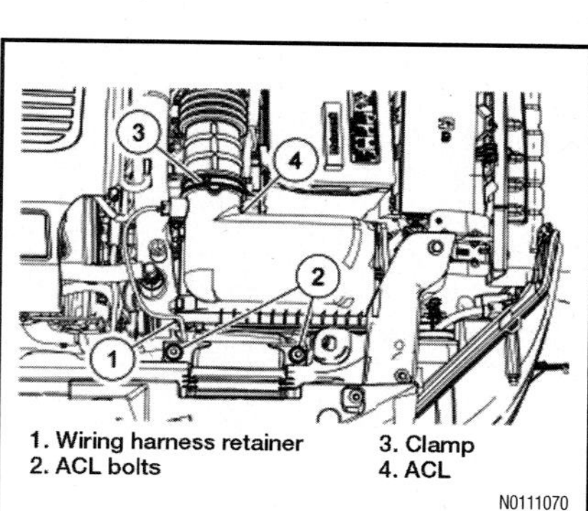

Fig. 8 Remove the ACL from the ACL bracket and the ACL outlet hose

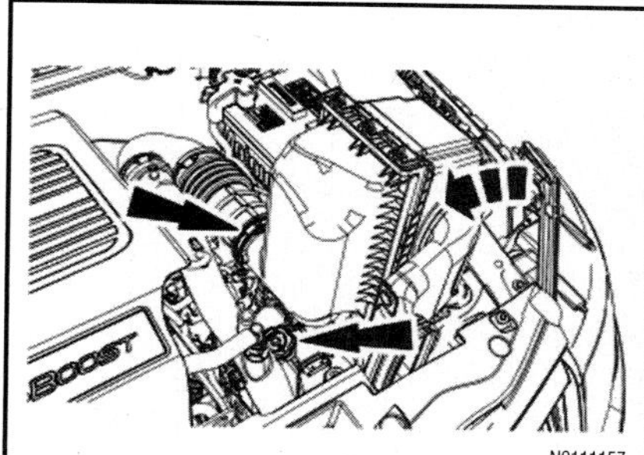

Fig. 9 Rotate the ACL 90 degrees to access the transmission fluid level indicator

10. Start the engine and let it run for 3 minutes. Move the range selector lever into each gear position and allow engagement for a minimum of ten seconds. Check the transmission fluid level by installing and removing the transmission fluid level indicator. When installing the transmission fluid level indicator, be sure it is seated and rotate it clockwise to the locked position. Adjust the transmission fluid level.
11. Turn the engine off, loosen the clamp and remove the ACL assembly from the ACL outlet pipe and position it aside with the IAT sensor electrical connector connected.
12. Install the ACL .
    a. Position the ACL assembly in the ACL outlet pipe and push down to install it in the 2 rubber grommets.
    b. Tighten the clamp to 44 inch lbs. (5 Nm).
    c. Install the 2 ACL bolts and tighten to 44 inch lbs. (5 Nm).
    d. Install the wiring harness retainer on the ACL .
13. If equipped, install the bolt cover.

3.7L Engine

See Figure 10.

1. Before servicing the vehicle, refer to the Precautions Section.
2. With the vehicle in NEUTRAL, position it on a hoist.
3. Remove the transmission fluid drain plug and allow the transmission fluid to drain. If an internal problem is suspected, drain the transmission fluid through a paper filter. A small amount of metal or friction particles may be found from normal wear. If an excessive amount of metal or friction material is present, the transaxle will need to be overhauled.
4. Install the transmission fluid drain plug. Tighten to 80 inch lbs. (9 Nm).
5. Remove the transmission fluid level indicator. If the transaxle was removed and disassembled, fill the transaxle with 6.5 qt. (6.2L) of clean transmission fluid. If the main control cover was removed for in-vehicle repair, fill the transaxle with 4.5 qt. (4.3L) of clean transmission fluid.
6. Start the engine and let it run for 3 minutes. Move the range selector lever into each gear position and allow engagement for a minimum of ten seconds. Check the transmission fluid level by installing and removing the transmission fluid level indicator. When installing the transmission fluid level indicator, be sure it is seated and rotate it clockwise to the locked position. Adjust the transmission fluid level.

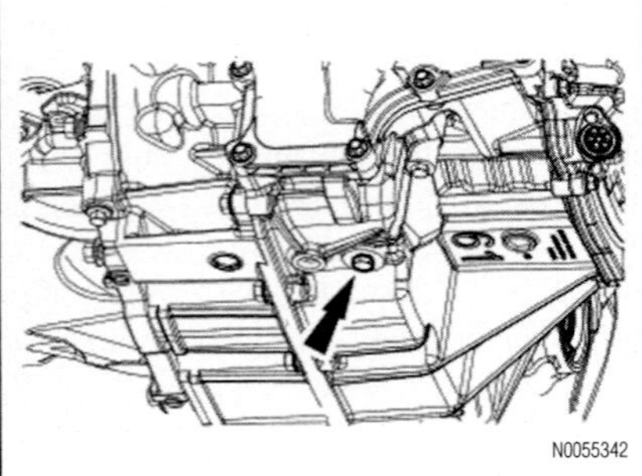

Fig. 10 Remove the transmission fluid drain plug

POWER TRANSFER UNIT (PTU)

REMOVAL & INSTALLATION

3.5L Engine

See Figure 11.

1. Before servicing the vehicle, refer to the Precautions Section.
2. With the vehicle in NEUTRAL, position it on a hoist.
3. Using a suitable holding device, hold the steering wheel in the straight-ahead position.
4. Remove the 4 retainers and the underbody shield.
5. Remove the right-hand halfshaft.
6. Remove the right-hand catalytic converter.
7. Remove the 4 driveshaft-to-output flange bolts, and disconnect the driveshaft from the output flange. Position the driveshaft aside. To maintain the initial driveshaft balance, matchmark the driveshaft flange and the output flange.
8. Remove the bolt and disconnect the steering column shaft from the steering gear. Discard the bolt. Do not allow the intermediate shaft to rotate while it is disconnected from the gear or damage to the clockspring may occur. If there is evidence that the intermediate shaft has rotated, the clockspring must be removed and recentered.
9. Remove the bolt and disconnect the 2 Electronic Power Assist Steering (EPAS) electrical connectors and the wiring retainer.
10. Remove the 3 bolts and the right-hand turbocharger lower bracket.
11. Remove the 3 bolts and the Power Transfer Unit (PTU) support bracket.
12. Position the rear engine roll restrictor aside in the following sequence:
    a. Remove the 2 engine roll restrictor-to-transaxle bolts.
    b. Loosen the rear engine roll restrictor bolt and pivot the roll restrictor downward.
13. Remove the front engine roll restrictor bolt and position the engine roll restrictor aside.
14. Position a jackstand under the rear of the subframe.
15. Remove the subframe bracket-to-body bolts.
16. Remove the rear subframe bolts and the subframe brackets. Discard the bolts.
17. Position a jackstand under the front roll restrictor bracket and raise the engine far enough to allow the PTU to be removed.
18. Remove the 5 PTU bolts. Pull the PTU outward to separate it from the transaxle. Rotate the output flange upward, then turn it and remove the PTU from the vehicle. Position a drain pan under the vehicle.
19. Using a small screwdriver, remove and discard the compression seal.

To install:

20. Using a suitable tool, install the new compression seal.
21. Position the PTU and install the 5 bolts. Tighten to 66 ft. lbs. (90 Nm).
22. Lower the engine and remove the jackstand from the front of the roll restrictor.
23. Using the jackstand, raise the subframe into the installed position.
24. Position the subframe brackets and loosely install the 4 bolts.
25. Install the 2 rear subframe bolts. Tighten to 111 ft. lbs. (150 Nm).
26. Tighten the 4 subframe bracket-to-body bolts to 41 ft. lbs. (55 Nm).
27. Remove the jackstand from the subframe.
28. Position the front engine roll restrictor to the bracket and install the bolt. Tighten the front engine roll restrictor bolt to 66 ft. lbs. (90 Nm).
29. Position the rear engine roll restrictor to the transaxle and install the 2 bolts.
    a. Tighten the engine roll restrictor-to-transaxle bolts to 76 ft. lbs. (103 Nm).
    b. Tighten the rear engine roll restrictor bolt to 66 ft. lbs. (90 Nm).
30. Position the PTU support bracket in place and install the 3 bolts.
    a. Tighten the 2 bolts to 52 ft. lbs. (70 Nm).
    b. Tighten the 1 bolt to 35 ft. lbs. (48 Nm).
31. Install the right-hand turbocharger lower bracket and the 3 bolts.
    a. Tighten the bolt to 14 ft. lbs. (19 Nm).
    b. Tighten the 2 bolts to 35 ft. lbs. (48 Nm).
32. Connect the 2 Electronic Power Assist Steering (EPAS) electrical connectors, attach the wiring retainer and install the bolt. Tighten to 80 inch lbs. (9 Nm).
33. Install the steering intermediate shaft onto the steering gear and install a new bolt. Tighten to 15 ft. lbs. (20 Nm). Do not allow the intermediate shaft to rotate while it is disconnected from the gear or damage to the clockspring may occur. If there is evidence that the intermediate shaft has rotated, the clockspring must be removed and recentered.
34. Align the matchmarks and install the 4 driveshaft-to-output flange bolts. Tighten to 52 ft. lbs. (70 Nm).
35. Install the right-hand catalytic converter.
36. Install the right-hand front halfshaft.
37. Install the underbody shield and the 4 retainers.
38. Remove the locking device from the steering wheel.

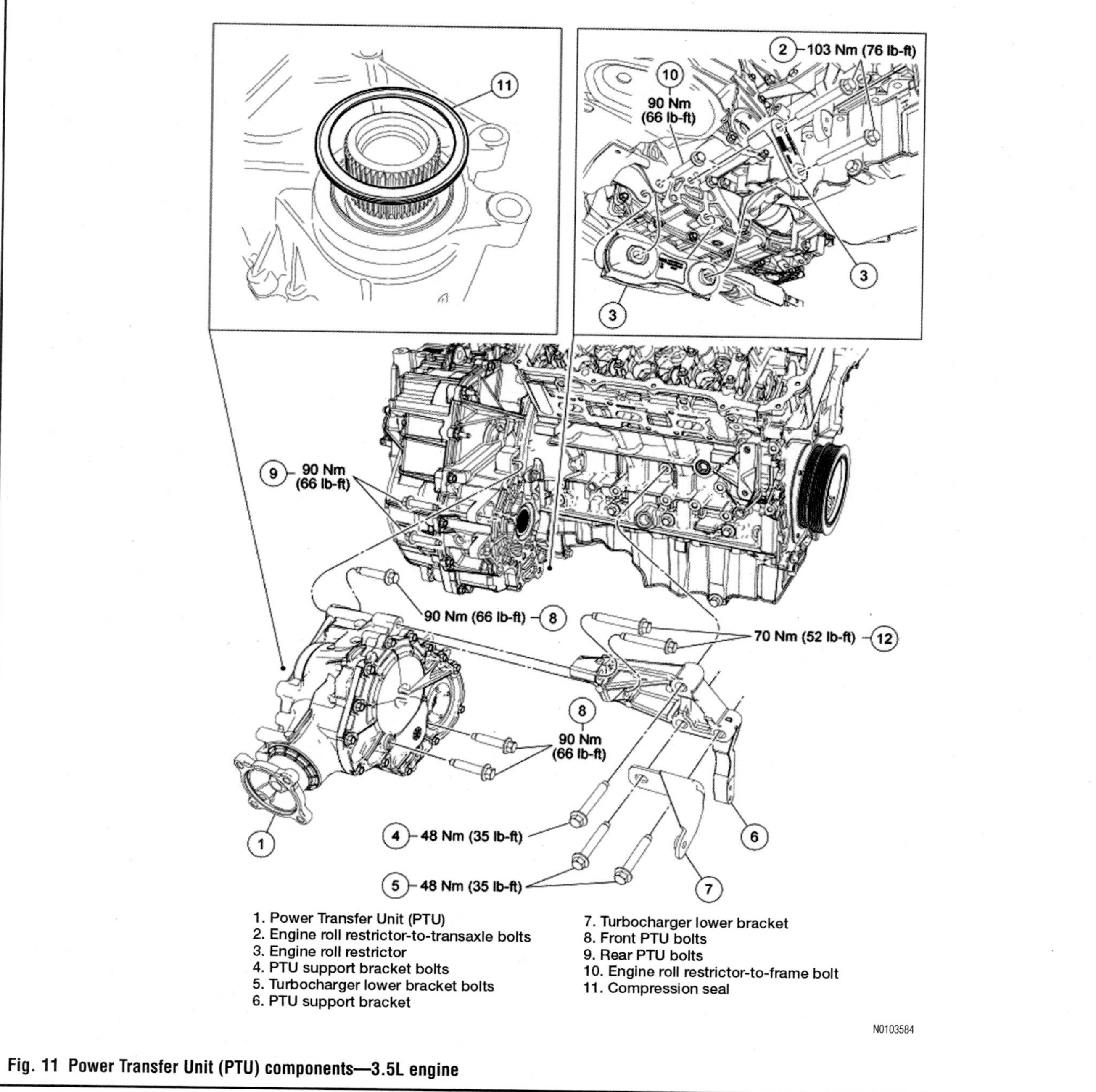

Fig. 11 Power Transfer Unit (PTU) components—3.5L engine

3.7L Engine

See Figure 12.

1. Before servicing the vehicle, refer to the Precautions Section.
2. With the vehicle in NEUTRAL, position it on a hoist.
3. Remove the right-hand halfshaft.
4. Remove the right-hand catalytic converter.
5. Remove the 4 driveshaft-to-output flange bolts, then disconnect the driveshaft from the output flange. Position the driveshaft aside. To maintain the initial driveshaft balance, matchmark the driveshaft flange and the output flange.
6. Remove the 5 Power Transfer Unit (PTU) support bracket bolts and the support bracket.
7. Position the engine roll restrictor aside.
   a. Remove the 2 engine roll restrictor-to-transaxle bolts.
   b. Loosen the rear engine roll restrictor bolt and pivot the roll restrictor downward.
8. Remove the 5 PTU bolts. Pull the PTU outward and separate it from the transaxle. Rotate the output flange upward, then turn it and remove the PTU from the vehicle. Position a drain pan under the vehicle.
9. Using a small screwdriver, remove and discard the compression seal.

To install:

10. Using a suitable tool, install the new compression seal.
11. Position the PTU and install the 5 bolts. Tighten to 66 ft. lbs. (90 Nm).
12. Position the PTU support bracket in place and install the 3 PTU support bracket-to-engine bolts. Tighten to 52 ft. lbs. (70 Nm).

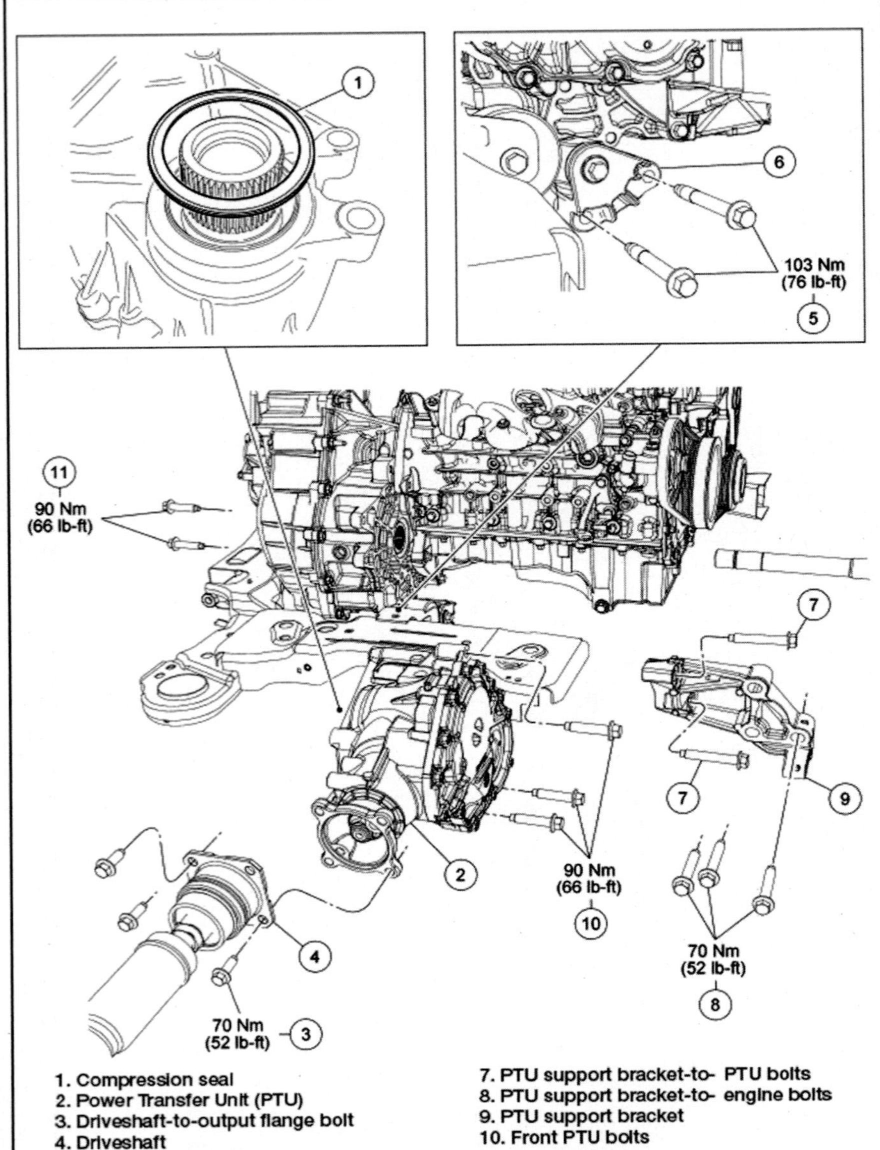

Fig. 12 Power Transfer Unit (PTU) components—3.7L engine

13. Install the 2 PTU support bracket-to-PTU bolts. Tighten to 52 ft. lbs. (70 Nm).
14. Position the engine roll restrictor to the transaxle and install the 2 bolts.
    a. Tighten the engine roll restrictor-to-transaxle bolts to 76 ft. lbs. (103 Nm).
    b. Tighten the rear engine roll restrictor bolt to 66 ft. lbs. (90 Nm).
15. Align the matchmarks and install the 4 driveshaft-to-output flange bolts. Tighten to 52 ft. lbs. (70 Nm).
16. Install the right-hand catalytic converter.
17. Install the right-hand front halfshaft.
18. Top off fluids as necessary.

FRONT HALFSHAFT

REMOVAL & INSTALLATION

Left-Hand Halfshaft

See Figures 13 through 15.

1. Before servicing the vehicle, refer to the Precautions Section.
2. With the vehicle in NEUTRAL, position it on a hoist.
3. Remove the wheel and tire.
4. Apply the brake to keep the halfshaft from rotating, and remove the wheel hub nut. Do not discard at this time.

WARNING

Use care when releasing the lower arm and knuckle into the resting position or damage to the ball joint seal or Constant Velocity (CV) boot may occur.

➡Use the hex-holding feature to prevent the stud from turning while removing the nut.

5. Remove and discard the lower ball joint nut. Separate the ball joint from the wheel knuckle.
6. Using the Front Wheel Hub Remover or equivalent tool, separate the halfshaft from the wheel hub.
7. Pull the wheel knuckle outboard and rotate it toward the rear of the vehicle.

WARNING

The sharp edges on the stub shaft splines can slice or puncture the oil seal. Use care when inserting the stub shaft into the transmission or damage to the component may occur.

8. Using the Slide Hammer (SST 100-001) and Halfshaft Remover (SST 205-832) or equivalent tools, remove the halfshaft from the transmission.
9. Remove and discard the circlip from the stub shaft.
10. Inspect the halfshaft hub for wear or damage and install a new halfshaft, if necessary.
    a. Inspect the differential seal surface.
    b. Inspect the halfshaft bushing surface. If this surface is damaged, inspect the halfshaft bushing for damage.
    c. Inspect the differential side gear splines.

To install:

WARNING

The circlips are unique in size and shape for each shaft. Make sure to use the specified circlip for the application or vehicle damage may occur.

11. Install the correct new circlip on the inboard stub shaft.
12. Push the stub shaft into the transmission so the circlip locks into the differential side gear. After insertion, pull the halfshaft inner end to make sure the circlip is locked.
13. Rotate the wheel knuckle into position and insert the halfshaft into the wheel hub.
14. Position the lower ball joint into the wheel knuckle and install the new nut.

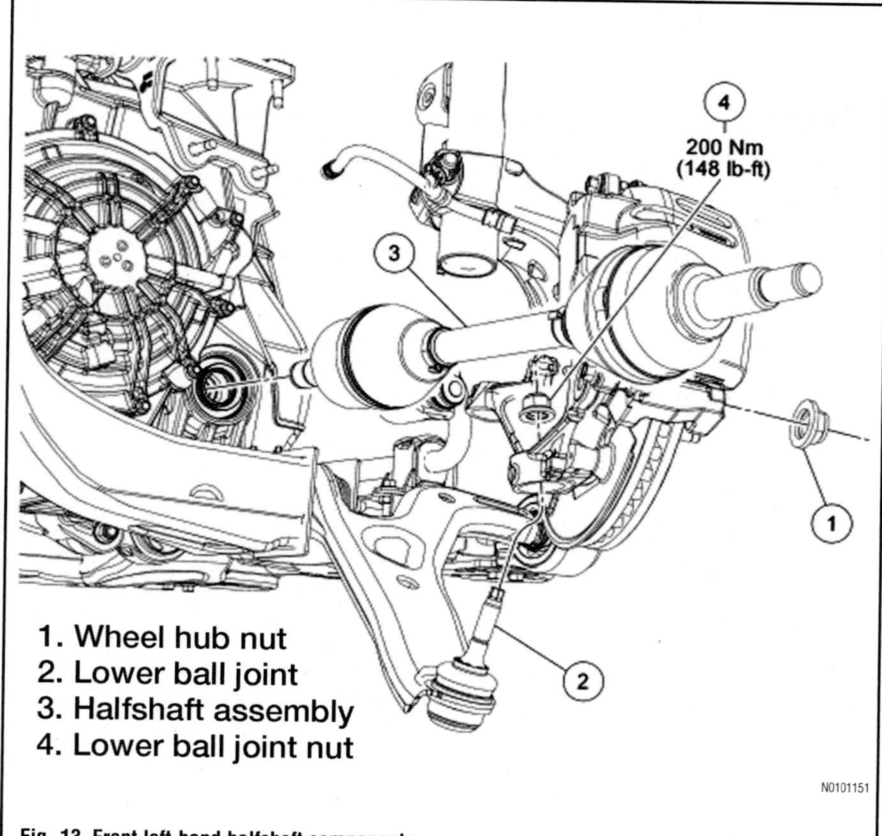

Fig. 13 Front left-hand halfshaft components

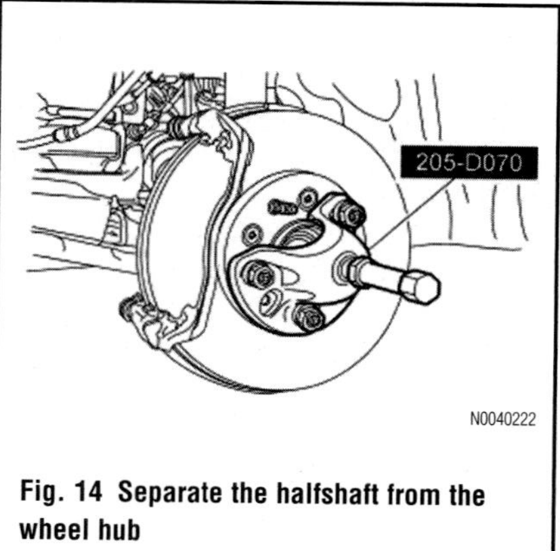

Fig. 14 Separate the halfshaft from the wheel hub

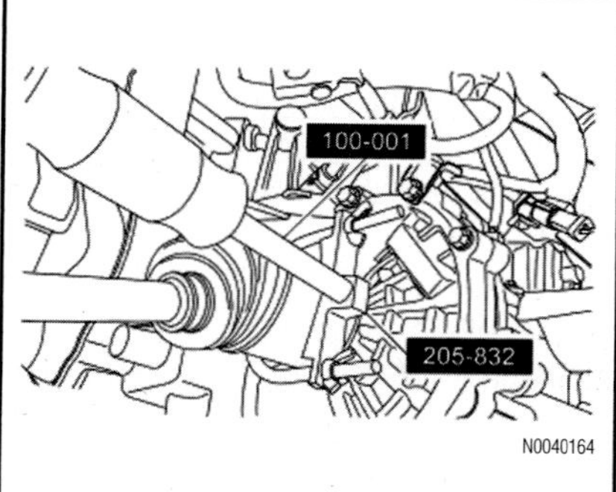

Fig. 15 Remove the halfshaft from the transmission

Tighten the new nut to 148 ft. lbs. (200 Nm).

WARNING

Do not tighten the wheel hub nut with the vehicle on the ground. The nut must be tightened to specification before the vehicle is lowered onto the wheels. Wheel bearing damage will occur if the wheel bearing is loaded with the weight of the vehicle applied.

15. Using the previously removed wheel hub nut, seat the halfshaft. Apply the brake to keep the halfshaft from rotating.
    a. Tighten to 258 ft. lbs. (350 Nm).
    b. Remove and discard the wheel hub nut.

WARNING

The wheel hub nut contains a one-time locking chemical that is activated by the heat created when it is tightened. Install and tighten the new wheel hub nut to specification within 5 minutes of starting it on the threads. Always install a new wheel hub nut after loosening or when not tightened within the specified time or damage to the components can occur.

16. Apply the brake to keep the halfshaft from rotating, and install a new wheel hub nut. Tighten to 258 ft. lbs. (350 Nm).
17. Install the front wheel and tire.
18. Lower the vehicle.

Right-Hand Halfshaft

See Figure 16.

1. Before servicing the vehicle, refer to the Precautions Section.
2. With the vehicle in NEUTRAL, position it on a hoist.
3. Remove the wheel and tire.
4. Apply the brake to keep the halfshaft from rotating, and remove the wheel hub nut. Do not discard at this time.
5. For All-Wheel Drive (AWD) vehicles, Remove the right-hand brake disc.
6. Remove the bolt from the brake hose bracket.

WARNING

Suspension fasteners are critical parts because they affect performance of vital components and systems and their failure may result in major service expense. New parts must be installed with the same part number or equivalent part, if replacement is necessary. Do not use a replacement part of lesser quality or substitute design. Torque values must be used as specified during reassembly to make sure of correct retention of these parts.

WARNING.

Use care when releasing the lower arm and knuckle into the resting position or damage to the ball joint seal or Constant Velocity (CV) boot may occur.

7. Remove and discard the lower ball joint nut. Use the hex-holding feature to prevent the stud from turning while removing the nut.
    a. Separate the lower ball joint from the wheel knuckle.
8. Using the Front Wheel Hub Remover or equivalent tool, separate the halfshaft from the wheel hub.
9. Pull the wheel knuckle outboard and rotate it toward the rear of the vehicle. Secure the wheel knuckle assembly.

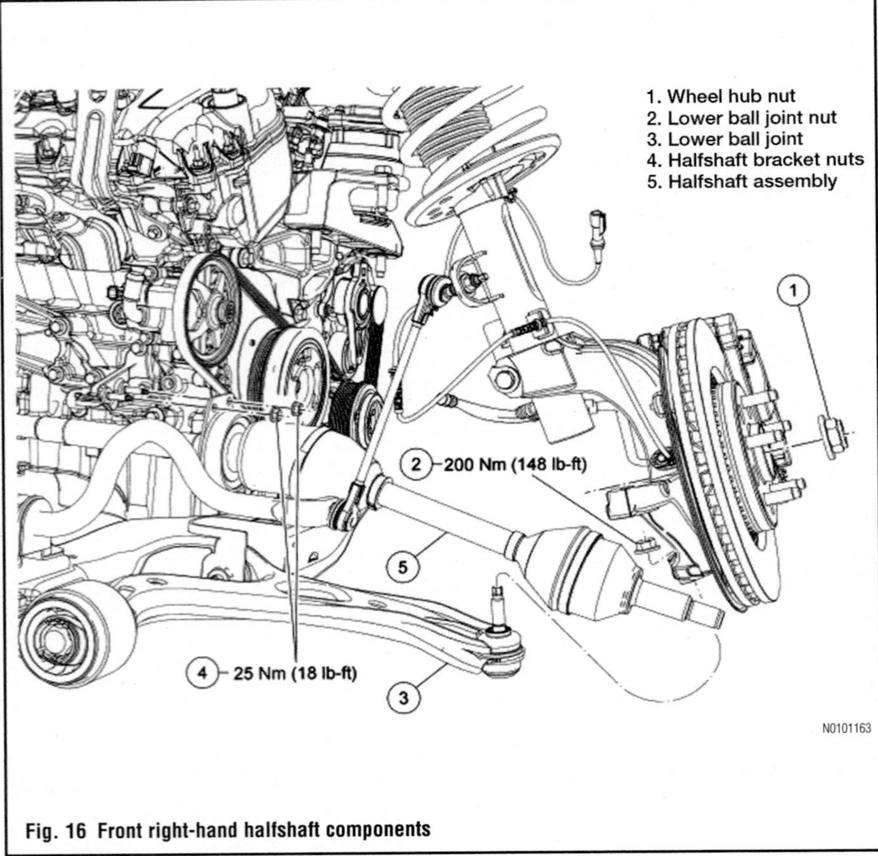

Fig. 16 Front right-hand halfshaft components

10. Remove the 2 lower scrivets from the rubber shield and position the shield aside.

11. For vehicles equipped with 3.5L engines, separate the halfshaft from the intermediate shaft and remove the halfshaft.

12. For vehicles equipped with 3.7L engines, remove the 2 halfshaft bracket nuts, and remove the intermediate and halfshaft assembly.

To install:

⁂ WARNING

A new Power Transfer Unit (PTU) shaft seal must be installed whenever the intermediate shaft is removed or damage to the components can occur.

13. For AWD vehicles, install a new intermediate shaft seal and deflector.

14. For vehicles equipped with 3.5L engines, install the halfshaft to the intermediate shaft.

15. For vehicles equipped with 3.7L engines, install the intermediate and halfshaft assembly and the 2 halfshaft bracket nuts. Tighten to 18 ft. lbs. (25 Nm).

16. Rotate the wheel knuckle into position and insert the halfshaft into the wheel hub.

17. Position the lower ball joint into the wheel knuckle and install the new nut. Tighten to 148 ft. lbs. (200 Nm).

18. Position the brake hose bracket and install the bolt. Tighten to 22 ft. lbs. (30 Nm).

19. Install the 2 scrivets in the rubber shield.

20. For AWD vehicles, install the right-hand brake disc.

⁂ WARNING

Do not tighten the front wheel hub nut with the vehicle on the ground. The nut must be tightened to specification before the vehicle is lowered onto the wheels. Wheel bearing damage will occur if the wheel bearing is loaded with the weight of the vehicle applied.

21. Using the previously removed wheel hub nut, seat the halfshaft. Apply the brake to keep the halfshaft from rotating.

a. Tighten to 258 ft. lbs. (350 Nm).

b. Remove and discard the wheel hub nut.

⁂ WARNING

The wheel hub nut contains a one-time locking chemical that is activated by the heat created when it is tightened. Install and tighten the new wheel hub nut to specification within 5 minutes of starting it on the threads. Always install a new wheel hub nut after loosening or when not tightened within the specified time or damage to the components can occur.

22. Apply the brake to keep the halfshaft from rotating, and install a new wheel hub nut. Tighten to 258 ft. lbs. (350 Nm).

23. Install the wheel and tire.

24. Lower the vehicle.

Intermediate Shaft—3.5L Engines

See Figure 17.

1. Before servicing the vehicle, refer to the Precautions Section.

⁂ WARNING

The intermediate shaft seal in the Power Transfer Unit (PTU) must be replaced whenever the intermediate shaft is removed or a leak may occur.

2. Remove the right front halfshaft assembly.

3. Remove the 2 intermediate shaft support bracket bolts and the intermediate shaft.

4. Remove and discard the circlip from the outboard end of the intermediate shaft.

To install:

5. Install a new 1.181 in. (30 mm) circlip on the outboard end of the intermediate shaft.

6. Install a new intermediate shaft seal in the Power Transfer Unit (PTU).

7. Position the intermediate shaft in the PTU and engage the intermediate shaft splines with the PTU gears.

8. Install the 2 intermediate shaft support bracket bolts. Tighten to 30 ft. lbs. (40 Nm).

9. Install the right halfshaft.

REAR AXLE FLUID

DRAIN & REFILL

See Rear Differential Housing Cover Removal & Installation.

REAR AXLE HOUSING

REMOVAL & INSTALLATION

See Figures 18 and 19.

1. Before servicing the vehicle, refer to the Precautions Section.

2. Remove the driveshaft assembly.

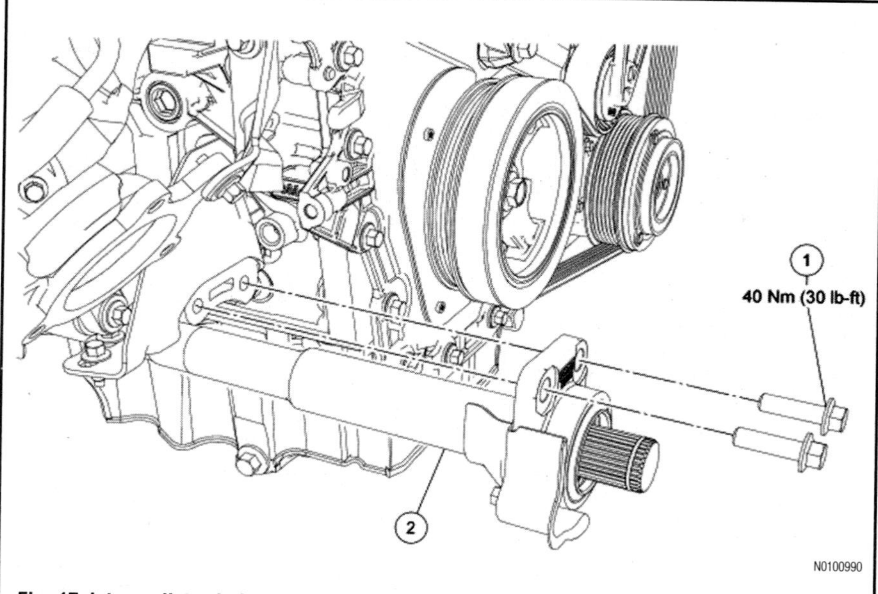

Fig. 17 Intermediate shaft support bracket bolts (1) and intermediate shaft assembly (2)

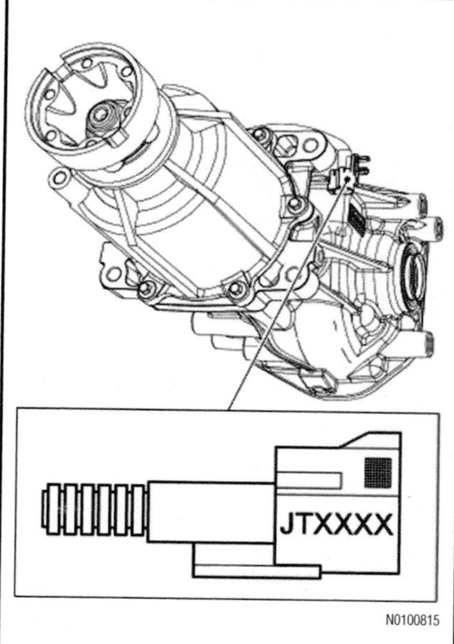

Fig. 19 Record the bar code identification number from the new axle assemblies wire harness connector

3. Remove the rear halfshafts.
4. Remove the stabilizer bar.
5. Position a suitable transmission hydraulic jack to the axle housing. Securely strap the jack to the housing.
6. Remove the 4 differential housing-to-front insulator bracket bolts.
7. Remove the 6 side insulator bracket-to-rear axle differential bolts.
8. Lower the axle to gain clearance to the Active Torque Coupling (ATC) electrical connector and disconnect the connector.
9. Remove the axle assembly.

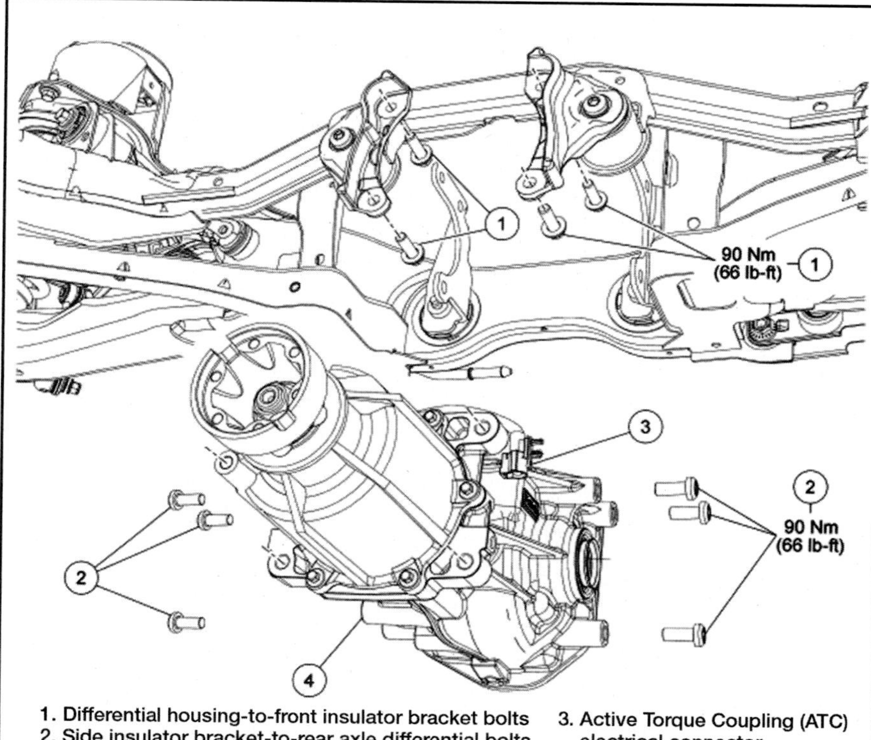

Fig. 18 Rear axle assembly

To install:

10. If replacing the axle assembly, the 4X4 control module will need to be reconfigured with the new Active Torque Coupling (ATC) bar code information. If the new bar code information does not match the existing 4X4 control module information, driveline damage or driveability concerns can occur. The ATC bar code can be found etched on the ATC wire harness connector of the new axle assembly. Record the bar code identification number from the new axle assemblies wire harness connector.
11. Position the axle housing on a suitable transmission hydraulic jack. Securely strap the jack to the housing.
12. Raise the axle and connect the ATC electrical connector.
13. Install the 6 side insulator bracket-to-rear axle differential bolts. Tighten to 66 ft. lbs. (90 Nm).
14. Install the 4 differential housing-to-front insulator bracket bolts. Tighten to 66 ft. lbs. (90 Nm).
15. Install the stabilizer bar.
16. Install the rear halfshafts.
17. Install the driveshaft assembly.
18. Using the scan tool, program the 4-digit bar code information retrieved from the new axle assembly harness connector into the 4X4 control module using the ATC Bar Code Entry service function. The scan tool will verify that the numbers entered are valid and display a message if the information is not correct.

REAR AXLE STUB SHAFT SEAL

REMOVAL & INSTALLATION

See Figures 20 through 22.

➡The Rear Drive Unit (RDU) does not have stub shaft pilot bearings. It has stub shaft seals only.

1. Before servicing the vehicle, refer to the Precautions Section.
2. Remove the halfshaft assembly.
3. Using the Torque Converter Fluid Seal Remover (SST 307-309) and Slide Hammer (SST 100-001), or equivalent tools, remove the stub shaft seal.

To install:

4. Lubricate the new stub shaft seal with grease.
5. Using the Front Axle Oil Seal Installer (SST 205-350) and Handle (SST 205-153) or equivalent tools, install the stub shaft pilot bearing housing seal.
6. Install the halfshaft assembly.

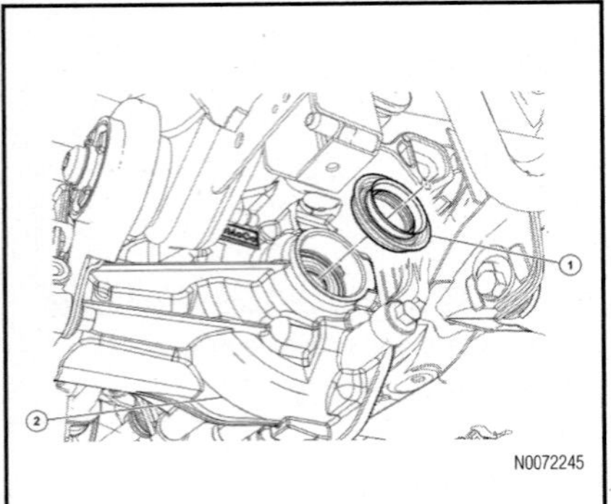

Fig. 20 Stub shaft seal (1) and differential housing (2)

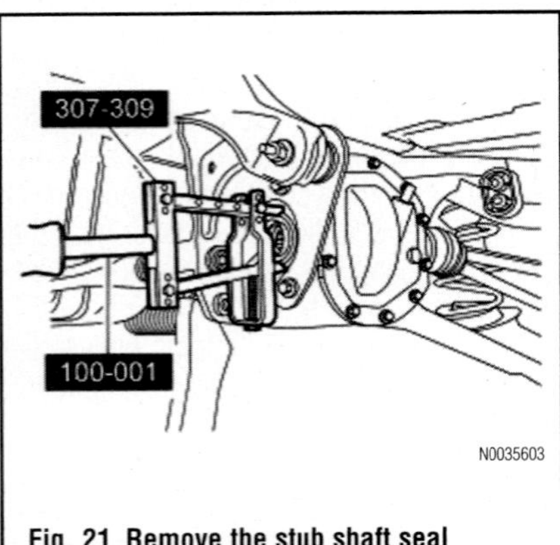

Fig. 21 Remove the stub shaft seal

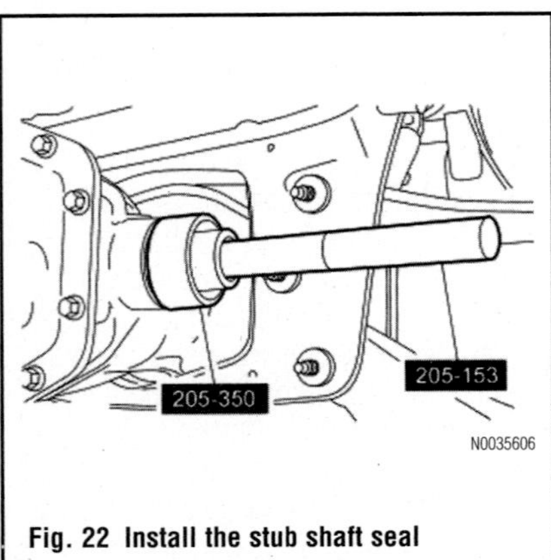

Fig. 22 Install the stub shaft seal

REAR DIFFERENTIAL HOUSING COVER

REMOVAL & INSTALLATION

See Figures 23 and 24.

1. Before servicing the vehicle, refer to the Precautions Section.
2. With the vehicle in NEUTRAL, position it on a hoist.
3. If equipped, remove the exhaust insulator located near the differential housing cover using soapy water.
4. Remove the 10 bolts and the rear differential housing cover.
5. Drain the differential fluid from the housing into a suitable drain pan.

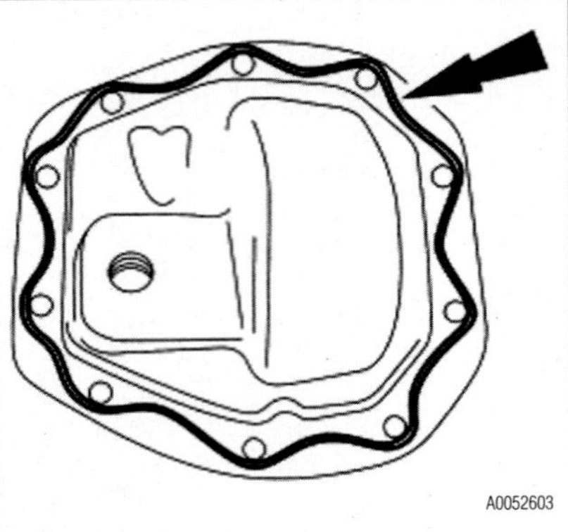

Fig. 24 Differential housing cover sealant application

To install:

6. Make sure the machined surfaces on the rear axle housing and the differential housing cover are clean and free of oil before installing the new silicone sealant. The inside of the rear axle must be covered when cleaning the machined surface to prevent contamination.
7. Clean the gasket mating surfaces of the differential housing and the differential housing cover.

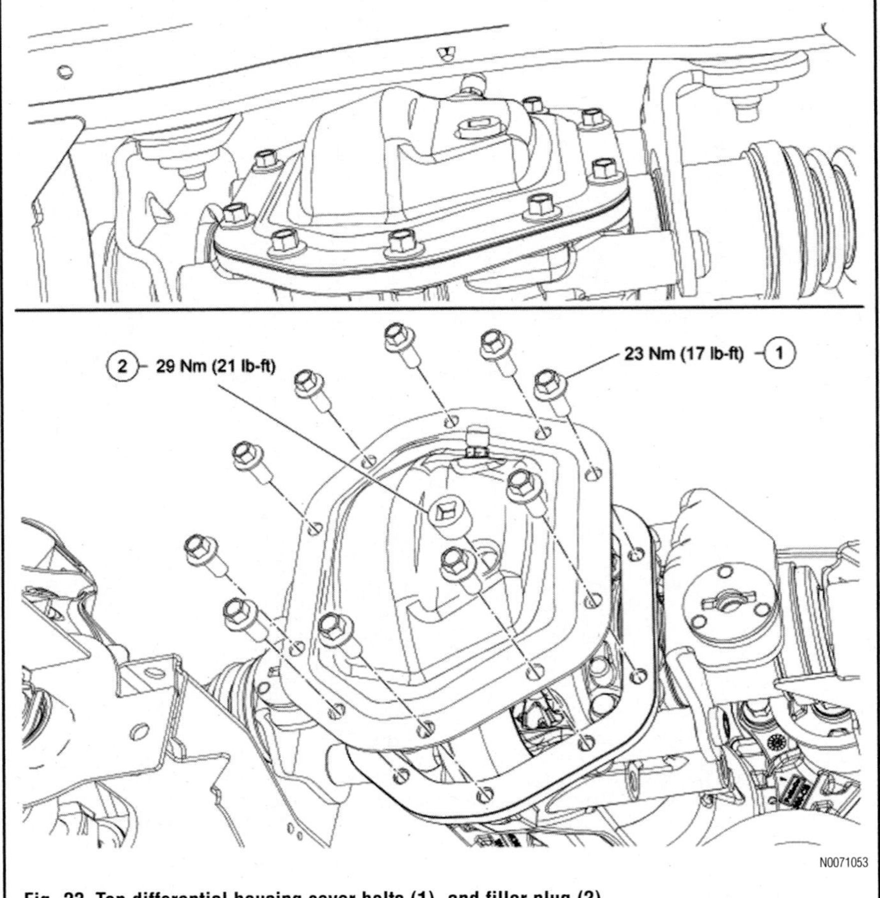

Fig. 23 Ten differential housing cover bolts (1), and filler plug (2)

8. Apply a new continuous bead of clear silicone rubber as shown in the illustration. The differential housing cover must be installed within 15 minutes of application of the silicone, or new silicone must be applied. If possible, allow one hour before filling with lubricant to make sure the silicone has correctly cured.

9. Install the differential housing cover and the 10 bolts. Tighten to 17 ft. lbs. (23 Nm).

10. Remove the filler plug and fill the rear axle with 2.43 pt (1.15L) of rear axle lubricant, 0.118–0.196 in. (3–5 mm) below the bottom of the filler hole.

11. Install the filler plug and tighten to 21 ft. lbs. (29 Nm).

12. If equipped, install the exhaust insulator located near the differential housing cover.

REAR DRIVESHAFT

REMOVAL & INSTALLATION

See Figures 25 through 27.

1. Before servicing the vehicle, refer to the Precautions Section.
2. With the vehicle in NEUTRAL, position it on a hoist.
3. Remove the muffler and tailpipe.
4. Support the driveshaft.
5. Remove the 4 rear center bearing bracket outer bolts.
6. Remove and discard the 3 pinion flange bolt and washer assemblies.
7. Insert a flat-blade screwdriver in the area shown to separate the rear flanges.
8. Remove and discard the 4 Power Transfer Unit (PTU) flange bolts.
9. Using a suitable prybar, separate the front driveshaft flange from the PTU flange
10. Remove the 2 front center bearing bracket outer bolts.
11. With the help of an assistant, remove the driveshaft.
12. If necessary, remove the 4 center bearing bracket inner bolts and remove the 2 brackets.

To install:

13. To install, reverse the removal procedure, noting the following:
    a. Do not reuse the CV joint bolts. Install new bolts.
    b. Do not reuse the bolt and washer assemblies for the rear CV joint flange. Install new assemblies.
    c. Tighten the 4 center bearing bracket inner bolts to 15 ft. lbs. (20 Nm), if removed.
    d. Tighten the 2 front center bearing bracket outer bolts to 22 ft. lbs. (30 Nm).
    e. Tighten the 4 PTU flange bolts to 52 ft. lbs. (70 Nm).
    f. Tighten the 3 pinion flange bolt and washer assemblies to 18 ft. lbs. (25 Nm).
    g. Tighten the 4 rear center bearing bracket outer bolts to 22 ft. lbs. (30 Nm).

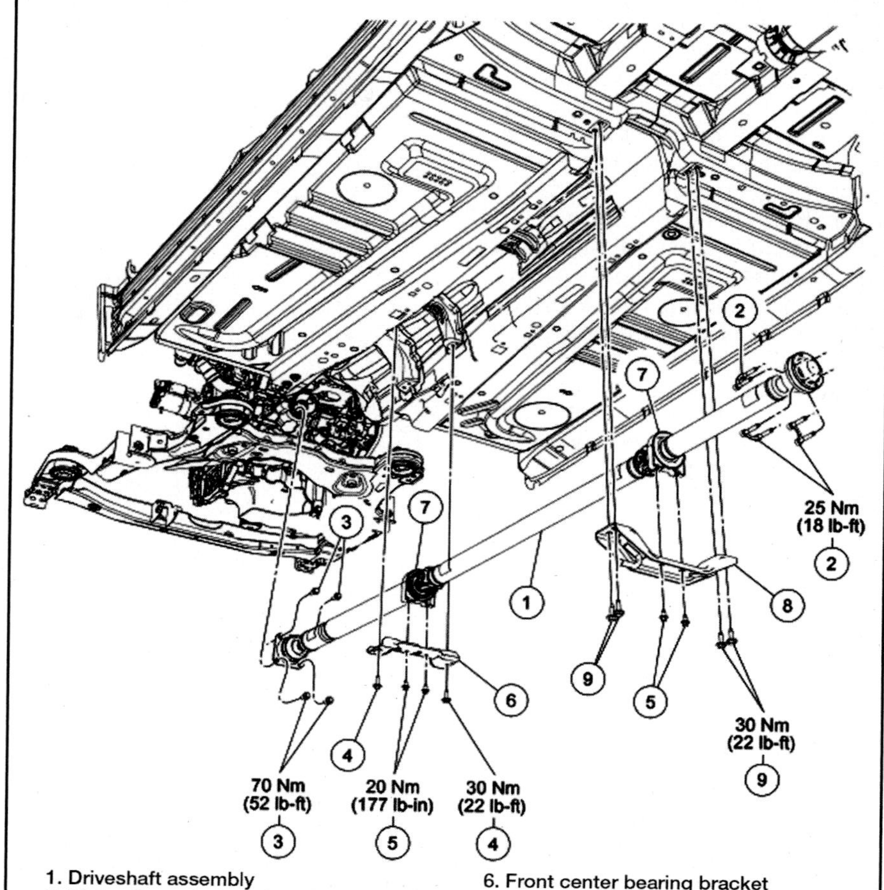

Fig. 25 Driveshaft components

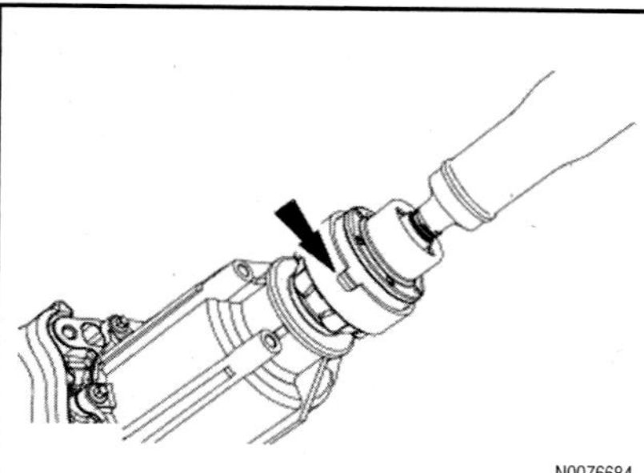

Fig. 26 Insert a flat-blade screwdriver in the area shown to separate the rear flanges

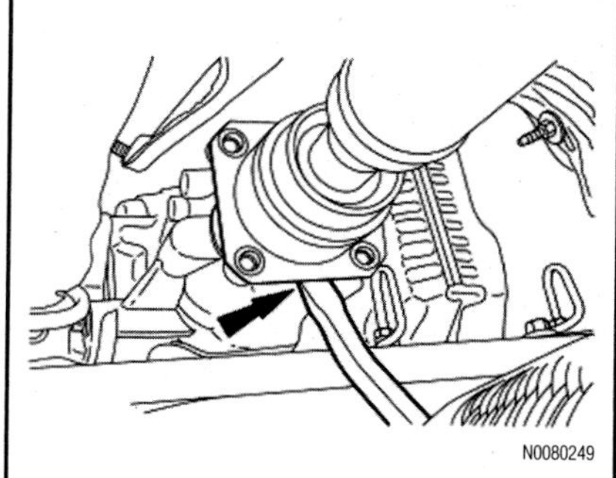

Fig. 27 Separate the driveshaft flange from the PTU flange

14. If driveshaft vibration is encountered after installation, index the driveshaft.

REAR HALFSHAFT

REMOVAL & INSTALLATION

See Figures 28 through 31.

⁂ WARNING

Suspension fasteners are critical parts because they affect performance of vital components and systems and their failure may result in major service expense. New parts must be installed with the same part numbers or equivalent part, if replacement is necessary. Do not use a replacement part of lesser quality or substitute design. Torque values must be used as specified during reassembly to make sure of correct retention of these parts.

➡Before servicing the vehicle, refer to the Precautions Section.

1. Measure the distance from the center of the wheel hub to the lip of the fender with the vehicle in a level, static ground position (curb height).
2. Remove the wheel and tire.
3. Remove the wheel hub nut. Do not discard at this time.
4. Remove and discard the 2 brake caliper anchor plate bolts and position the brake caliper and anchor plate assembly aside.
   a. Support the brake caliper and anchor plate assembly using mechanic's wire. Do not allow the caliper to hang from the brake hose or damage to the hose can occur.
5. Use the hex-holding feature to prevent the stabilizer bar link stud from turning, remove and discard the stabilizer bar link upper nut, and disconnect the link.
6. Remove and discard the toe link-to-wheel knuckle nut and disconnect the link.
7. Remove the wheel speed sensor bolt. Disconnect the wheel speed sensor harness retainers and position the sensor and harness aside.
8. Position a screw-type jackstand under the lower arm.
9. Remove and discard the upper arm-to-wheel knuckle nut and bolt and disconnect the knuckle from the upper arm.
10. Remove and discard the shock absorber lower bolt and disconnect the shock absorber from the knuckle bracket.
11. Loosen, but do not remove the lower arm-to-wheel knuckle bolt.
12. Using the Front Hub Remover or equivalent tool, separate the halfshaft outer CV joint from the hub bearing.
13. Swing the wheel knuckle outward and remove the halfshaft outer CV joint from the hub bearing.
14. Using a suitable pry bar, remove the halfshaft inner CV joint from the differential. Do not damage the oil seal when removing the axle halfshaft from the differential.
15. Remove the halfshaft from the vehicle.
16. Remove and discard the circlip from the halfshaft.

To install:

17. Before tightening suspension bushing fasteners, use a jackstand to raise the rear suspension until the distance between the center of the hub and the lip of the

Fig. 28 Measure the distance from the center of the wheel hub to the lip of the fender

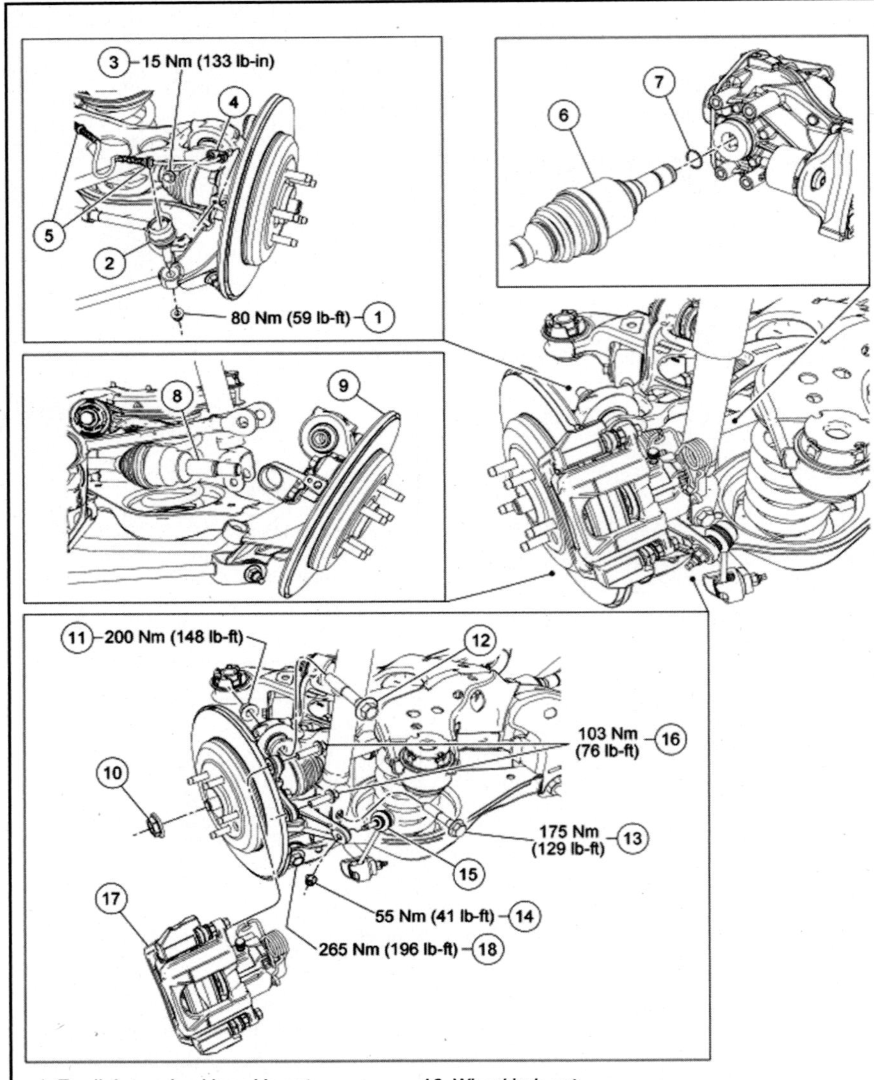

Fig. 29 Rear halfshafts and related components

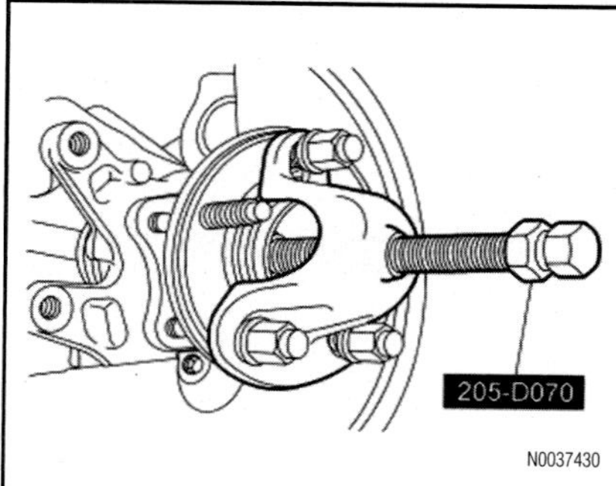

Fig. 30 Separate the halfshaft outer CV joint from the hub bearing

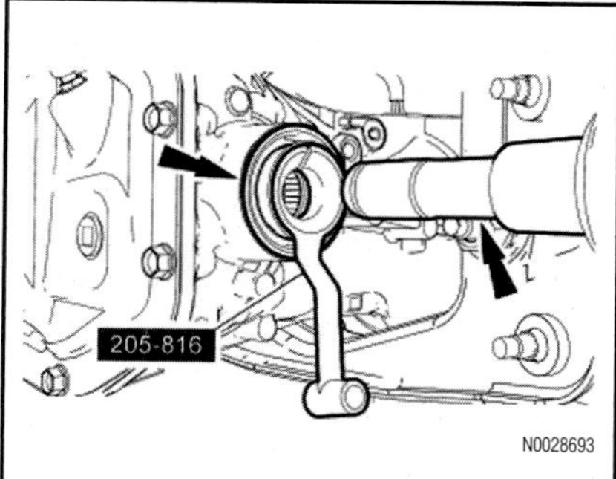

Fig. 31 Install the halfshaft inner CV joint into the differential

fender is equal to the measurement taken in the removal procedure (curb height).

WARNING

The circlips are unique in size and shape for each shaft. Make sure to use the specified circlip for the application or vehicle damage may occur.

18. Install a new circlip on the halfshaft.
19. Using the Axle Seal Protector (SST 205-816) or equivalent tool, install the halfshaft inner CV joint into the differential. Make sure the circlip locks in the side gear.
20. Swing the wheel knuckle inward and install the halfshaft outer CV joint through the hub bearing.
21. Position the wheel knuckle to the upper arm and loosely install a new nut and bolt.
22. Position the shock absorber and loosely install a new bolt.
23. Position the wheel speed sensor harness in the retainers and install the sensor and bolt. Tighten to 11 ft. lbs. (15 Nm).
24. Position the toe link and loosely install a new toe link-to-wheel knuckle nut.
25. Position a suitable jackstand under the lower control arm at the shock and spring assembly attachment point and raise the rear suspension until the distance between the center of the hub and the lip of the fender is equal to the measurement taken in Step 1 of the removal procedure (curb height).
26. A slotted upper arm allows for the rear suspension camber to be adjusted by pushing inward or pulling outward on the wheel knuckle while tightening the upper arm-to-wheel knuckle nut. With the wheel knuckle pushed inward for maximum negative camber, tighten the upper arm-to-wheel knuckle nut to 148 ft. lbs. (200 Nm).
27. Tighten the lower arm-to-wheel knuckle bolt to 196 ft. lbs. (265 Nm).
28. Tighten the shock absorber lower bolt to 129 ft. lbs. (175 Nm).
29. Tighten the toe link-to-wheel knuckle nut to 59 ft. lbs. (80 Nm).
30. Use the hex-holding feature to prevent the stabilizer bar link stud from turning, connect the stabilizer bar link, and install a new stabilizer bar link upper nut. Tighten to 41 ft. lbs. (55 Nm).
31. Position the brake caliper and anchor plate assembly and install the 2 bolts. Tighten to 76 ft. lbs. (103 Nm).

WARNING

Do not tighten the wheel hub nut with the vehicle on the ground. The nut must be tightened to specification before the vehicle is lowered onto the wheels. Wheel bearing damage will occur if the wheel bearing is loaded with the weight of the vehicle applied.

32. Apply the brake to keep the halfshaft from rotating, and use the previously removed hub nut to seat the halfshaft.
    a. Tighten to 258 ft. lbs. (350 Nm).
    b. Remove and discard the hub nut.

WARNING

The wheel hub nut contains a one-time locking chemical that is activated by the heat created when it is tightened. Install and tighten the new wheel hub nut to specification within 5 minutes of starting it on the threads. Always install a new wheel hub nut after loosening or when not tightened within the specified time or damage to the components can occur.

33. Apply the brake to keep the halfshaft from rotating, and install a new hub nut. Tighten to 258 ft. lbs. (350 Nm).
34. Install the wheel and tire.
35. Check the rear toe and adjust if necessary.

REAR PINION SEAL

REMOVAL & INSTALLATION

See Figures 32 through 34.

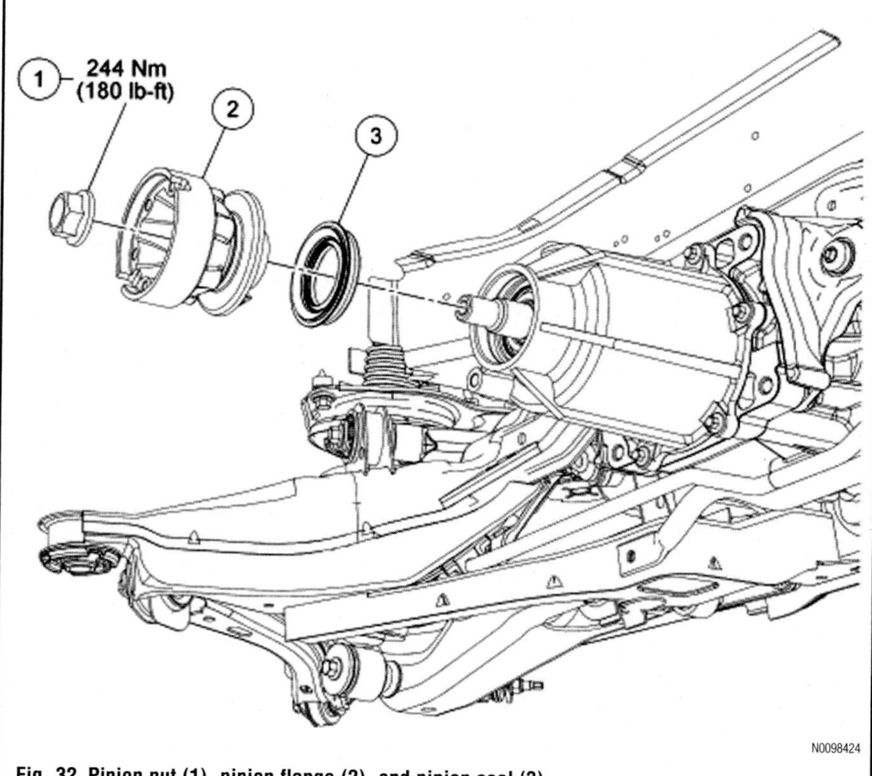

Fig. 32 Pinion nut (1), pinion flange (2), and pinion seal (3)

1. Before servicing the vehicle, refer to the Precautions Section.
2. Remove the driveshaft.
3. Using the Drive Pinion Flange Holding Fixture (SST 205-126) or equivalent tool, hold the pinion flange and remove the nut. Discard the nut.
4. Matchmark the location of the pinion to the yoke.
5. Using the 2 Jaw Puller (SST 205-D072) or equivalent tool, remove the pinion flange.
6. Using the Torque Converter Fluid Seal Remover and Slide Hammer or equivalent tools, remove the seal.

To install:

7. Make sure that the mating surface is clean before installing the new seal.
8. Using the Pinion Seal Replacer or equivalent tool, install the seal.

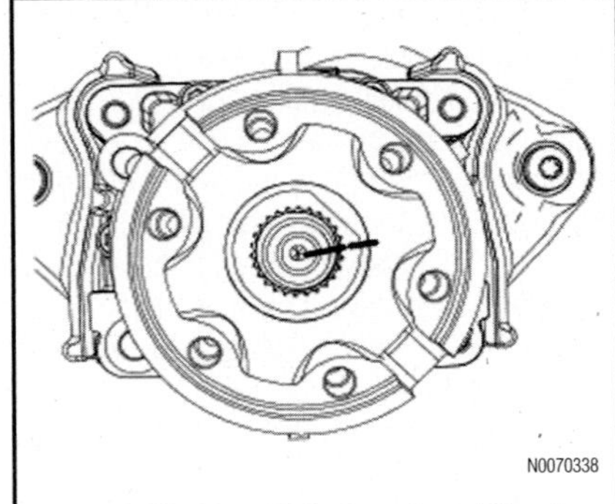

Fig. 33 Matchmark the location of the pinion to the yoke

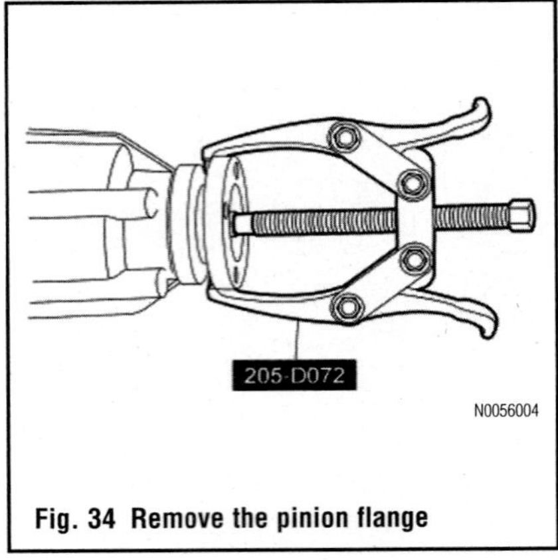

Fig. 34 Remove the pinion flange

9. Lubricate the pinion flange with grease.
10. Align the matchmarks and position the pinion flange.
11. Using the Drive Pinion Flange Holding Fixture or equivalent tool, install the new pinion nut. Tighten to 180 ft. lbs. (244 Nm).
12. Install the driveshaft.

ENGINE COOLING

ENGINE COOLANT

DRAINING, FILLING AND BLEEDING PROCEDURE

Draining

CAUTION

Always allow the engine to cool before opening the cooling system. Do not unscrew the coolant pressure relief cap when the engine is operating or the cooling system is hot. The cooling system is under pressure; steam and hot liquid can come out forcefully when the cap is loosened slightly. Failure to follow these instructions may result in serious personal injury.

WARNING

The coolant must be recovered in a suitable, clean container for reuse. If the coolant is contaminated it must be recycled or disposed of correctly. Using contaminated coolant may result in damage to the engine or cooling system components.

WARNING

The engine cooling system is filled with Motorcraft® Specialty Green Engine Coolant. Mixing coolant types degrades the corrosion protection of Motorcraft® Specialty Green Engine Coolant. Motorcraft® Specialty Green Engine Coolant is very sensitive to light. Do NOT allow this product to be exposed to ANY LIGHT for more than a day or two. Extended light exposure causes this product to degrade.

WARNING

Stop-leak style pellets/products must not be used as an additive in this engine cooling system. The addition of stop-leak style pellets/products may clog or damage the cooling system, resulting in degraded cooling system performance and/or failure.

WARNING

Less than 80% of coolant capacity can be recovered with the engine in the vehicle. Dirty, rusty or contaminated coolant requires replacement.

1. Before servicing the vehicle, refer to the Precautions Section.
2. With the vehicle in NEUTRAL, position it on a hoist.
3. Release the pressure in the cooling system by slowly turning the pressure relief cap one-half to one turn counterclockwise to the first stop on the filler neck. When the pressure has been released, remove the pressure relief cap.
4. Remove the bolts, pin-type retainers, and the front splash shield.
5. Place a suitable container below the radiator draincock. Open the radiator draincock and drain the coolant.
6. Close the radiator draincock.
7. Install the front splash shield when the cooling system or engine service is finished.

Filling & Bleeding

1. If using a radiator refiller, follow the manufacturer's instructions to fill and bleed the cooling system. Radiator refiller must be used whenever the underbody coolant lines and/or rear heater core are drained or removed.

WARNING

Add Motorcraft® Specialty Green Engine Coolant to the cooling system. Do not add alcohol, methanol or brine, or any engine coolants mixed with alcohol or methanol antifreeze. These can cause engine damage from overheating or freezing. Ford Motor Company does NOT recommend the use of recycled engine coolant in vehicles.

2. Fill the degas bottle to 0.984 in. (25 mm) above the top of the COLD FILL RANGE.

➡Recommended coolant concentration is 50/50 ethylene glycol to distilled water. Maximum coolant concentration is 60/40 for cold weather areas. Minimum coolant concentration is 40/60 for warm weather areas.

3. Close the degas bottle cap.
4. Turn the HVAC system to OFF.
5. Run the engine at 3,500 rpm for 30

seconds. If the engine overheats or the fluid level drops below the top of the COLD FILL RANGE, shut off the engine and add fluid to 0.984 in. (25 mm) above the top of the COLD FILL RANGE once the engine cools.

6. Turn the engine off for 1 minute to purge any large air pockets.

7. Start the engine and let idle until the engine reaches normal operating temperature and the thermostat is fully open. A fully open thermostat can be verified by the radiator fan cycling on at least once.

8. Run the engine at 3,500 rpm for 30 seconds.

9. Run the engine at idle for 30 seconds. If the engine overheats or the fluid level drops below the top of the COLD FILL RANGE, shut off the engine and add fluid to 0.984 in. (25 mm) above the top of the COLD FILL RANGE once the engine cools.

10. Turn the engine off for 1 minute.

11. Repeat the above 3 steps a total of 10 times to remove any remaining air trapped in the system.

12. Check the engine coolant level in the degas bottle and fill to 0.984 in. (25 mm) above the top of the COLD FILL RANGE when warm or to the top of the COLD FILL RANGE line when cold.

13. Install the degas bottle cap to at least one audible "click."

FLUSHING

**** CAUTION**

Always allow the engine to cool before opening the cooling system. Do not unscrew the coolant pressure relief cap when the engine is operating or the cooling system is hot. The cooling system is under pressure; steam and hot liquid can come out forcefully when the cap is loosened slightly. Failure to follow these instructions may result in serious personal injury.

**** WARNING**

To remove rust, sludge and other foreign material from the cooling system, use cooling system flush that is safe for use with aluminum radiators. This cleaning restores cooling system efficiency and helps prevent overheating. A pulsating or reversed direction of flushing water will loosen sediment more quickly than a steady flow in the normal coolant flow direction. In severe cases where cleaning solvents will not clean the cooling system efficiently, it will be necessary to use the pressure flushing method using cooling system flusher.

1. Before servicing the vehicle, refer to the Precautions Section.

2. Add premium cooling system flush to the cooling system and follow the directions on the package.

3. Drain the cooling system. Refer to Draining, Filling & Bleeding Procedure.

4. Remove the radiator. Refer to Radiator Removal & Installation.

**** WARNING**

Radiator internal pressure must not exceed 20 psi (138 kPa). Damage to the radiator can result.

5. Backflush the radiator with the radiator in an upside-down position with a high-pressure hose in the lower hose location and backflush.

6. Remove the thermostat. Refer to Thermostat Removal & Installation.

7. Backflush the engine. Position the high-pressure water hose into the engine through the engine return and backflush the engine.

8. Install the thermostat.

9. Install the radiator.

10. Fill the cooling system.

ENGINE FAN

REMOVAL & INSTALLATION

3.5L Engine

See Figures 35 through 37.

1. Before servicing the vehicle, refer to the Precautions Section.

2. With the vehicle in NEUTRAL, position it on a hoist.

3. Remove the 4 retainers and the underbody shield.

4. Drain the cooling system. Refer to Draining, Filling & Bleeding Procedure.

5. Working from below, disconnect the left-hand CAC tube from the CAC adapter.

6. Remove the lower bolt from the CAC adapter.

7. Detach the lower radiator hose retainer from the cooling fan and shroud.

8. Disconnect the lower radiator hose from the radiator.

9. Remove the Air Cleaner (ACL) assembly and ACL outlet pipe.

10. Remove the right-hand CAC.

11. Remove the upper bolt and the CAC adapter. Inspect and install a new CAC adapter gasket, if necessary.

12. Disconnect the crankcase vent tube quick connect coupling and remove the crankcase vent tube.

13. Disconnect and remove the lower radiator hose from the thermostat housing.

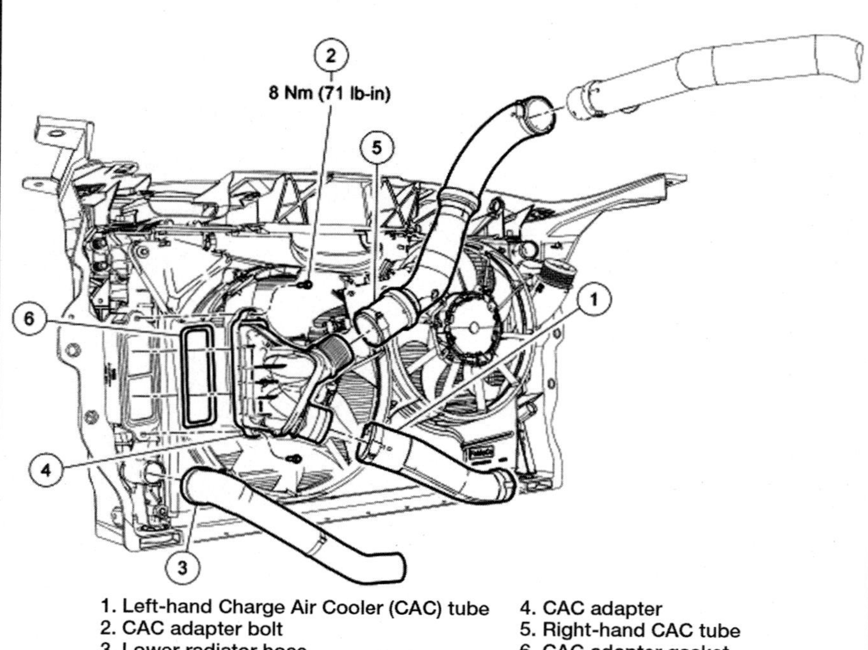

Fig. 35 Cooling fan and motor components 1—3.5L engine

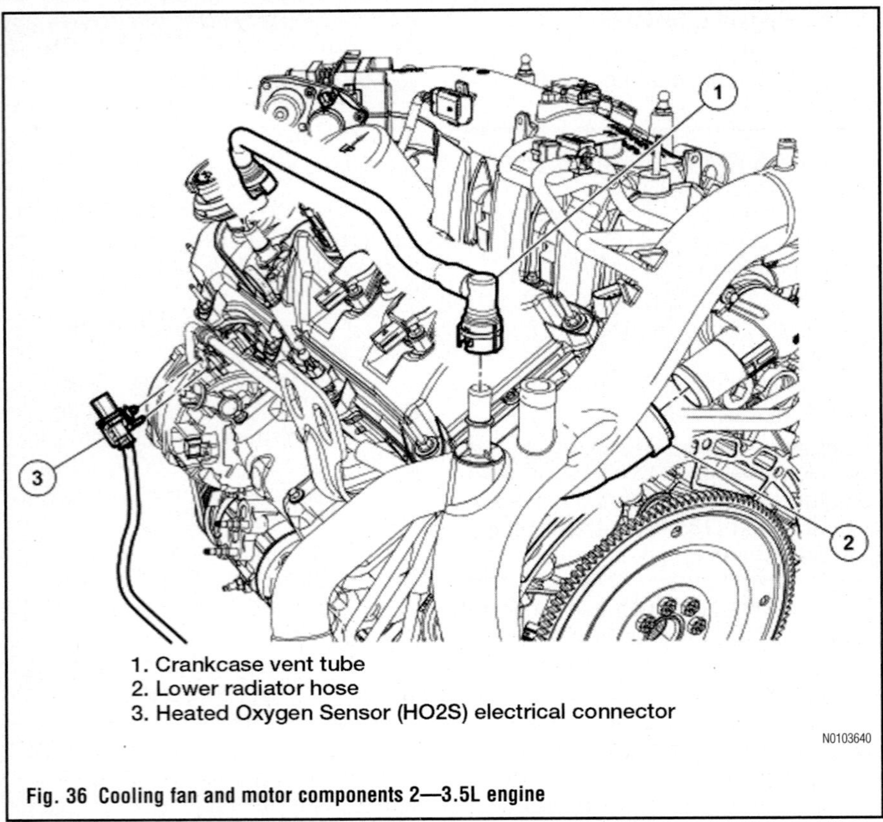

Fig. 36 Cooling fan and motor components 2—3.5L engine

14. Detach the hood release cable retainer from the shroud.

15. If equipped, detach the block heater wiring harness retainers from the engine wiring harness.

16. Detach all the wiring harness retainers from the cooling fan and shroud and radiator grill support.

17. Disconnect the cooling fan motor electrical connector.

18. Disconnect the left-hand Heated Oxygen Sensor (HO2S) electrical connector. Detach the HO2S connector retainer from the bracket.

19. Remove the 2 bolts and the cooling fan motor and shroud.

To install:

20. Install the cooling fan motor and shroud and the 2 bolts. Tighten to 53 inch lbs. (6 Nm).

21. Connect the left-hand Heated Oxygen Sensor (HO2S) electrical connector. Attach the HO2S connector retainer to the bracket.

22. Connect the cooling fan motor electrical connector.

23. Attach all the wiring harness retainers to the cooling fan and shroud and radiator grill support.

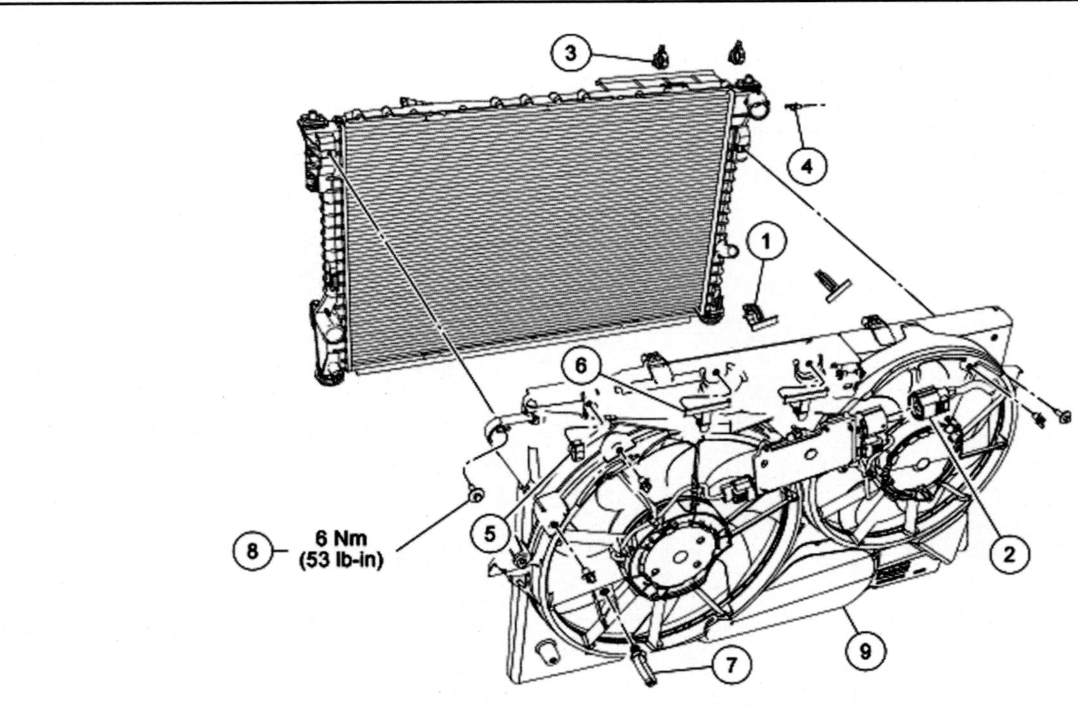

Fig. 37 Cooling fan and motor components 3—3.5L engine

24. If equipped, attach the block heater wiring harness retainers to the engine wiring harness.

25. Attach the hood release cable retainer to the shroud.

26. Install and connect the lower radiator to the thermostat housing.

27. Install the crankcase vent tube quick connect coupling.

28. Install the gasket, the CAC adapter and the upper bolt. Do not tighten the bolt at this time.

29. Install the lower bolt for the CAC adapter. Tighten to 71 inch lbs. (8 Nm).

30. Tighten the upper CAC adapter bolt. Tighten to 71 inch lbs. (8 Nm).

31. Align the marks for the right-hand CAC tube. Install the right-hand CAC tube. Tighten to 44 inch lbs. (5 Nm).

32. Install the ACL outlet pipe and ACL assembly.

33. Connect the lower radiator hose to the radiator.

34. Attach the lower radiator hose retainer to the cooling fan and shroud.

35. Connect the left-hand CAC tube to the CAC adapter. Align the marks for the left-hand CAC tube. Tighten to 44 inch lbs. (5 Nm).

36. Fill and bleed the cooling system. Refer to Draining, Filling & Bleeding Procedure.

37. Install the underbody shield and the 4 retainers.

3.7L Engine

See Figure 38.

1. Before servicing the vehicle, refer to the Precautions Section.

2. With the vehicle in NEUTRAL, position it on a hoist.

3. Remove the Air Cleaner (ACL) assembly.

4. If equipped, detach the block heater wiring harness retainers from the engine wiring harness.

5. Disconnect the cooling fan motor electrical connector and detach the all the wiring harness retainers from the shroud.

6. Detach the wiring harness retainers from the radiator support.

7. Detach the hood release cable retainer from the cooling fan motor and shroud.

8. Detach the upper radiator hose from the cooling fan motor and shroud.

9. Release the tab through the access hole and remove the upper radiator hose support.

10. Remove the 2 bolts and the cooling fan motor and shroud.

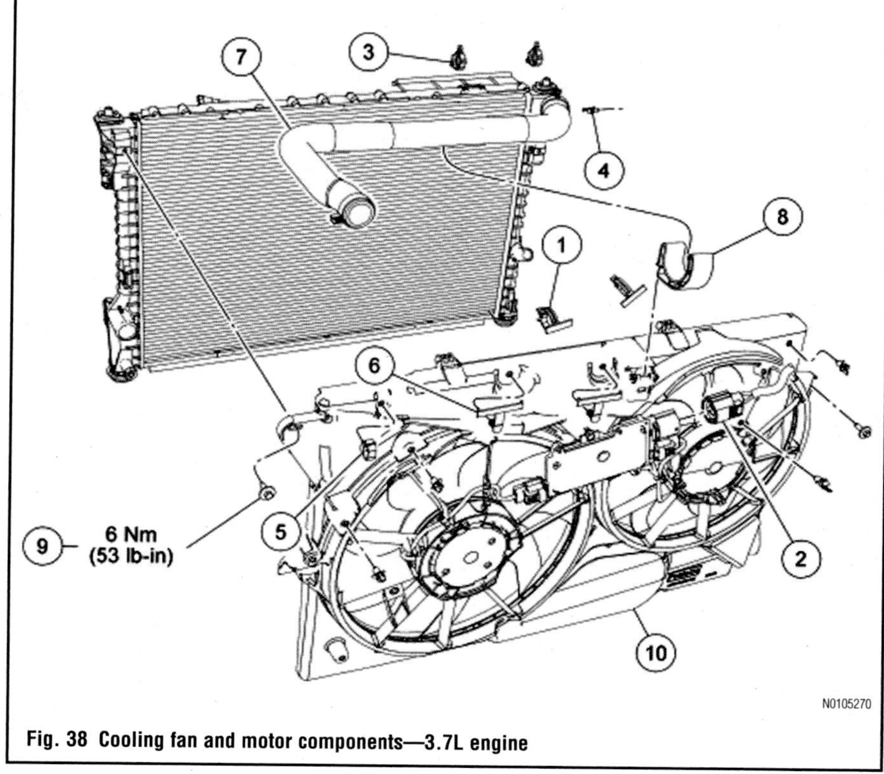

Fig. 38 Cooling fan and motor components—3.7L engine

To install:

11. To install, reverse the removal procedure, noting the following:

a. Tighten the cooling fan motor and shroud bolts to 53 inch lbs. (6 Nm).

RADIATOR

REMOVAL & INSTALLATION

3.5L Engine

See Figures 39 through 42.

1. Before servicing the vehicle, refer to the Precautions Section.

2. Remove the cooling fan motor and shroud. Refer to Engine Fan Removal & Installation.

3. Remove the front bumper cover.

4. Disconnect the Turbocharger Boost Pressure (TCBP)/Charge Air Cooler Temperature (CACT) sensor electrical connector.

5. Remove the CAC outlet pipe. Matchmark the Charge Air Cooler (CAC) outlet pipe position for reference during installation.

6. Disconnect the upper radiator hose and lower degas bottle hose from the radiator.

7. Detach the 4 radiator grill air deflector pin-type retainers and remove the right-hand and left-hand radiator grill air deflectors.

8. Remove the 2 A/C condenser bolts from the CAC and separate the A/C condenser from the CAC .

9. Lift the tabs and remove the radiator support brackets and position the radiator toward the engine.

10. Remove the 2 bolts and separate the CAC from the radiator.

11. Remove the radiator.

To install:

12. To install, reverse the removal procedure, noting the following:

a. Make sure the bottom radiator insulators are in place when installing the radiator.

b. Tighten the CAC bolts to 53 inch lbs. (6 Nm).

c. Tighten the A/C condenser bolts to 53 inch lbs. (6 Nm).

d. Tighten the CAC outlet pipe bolts to 44 inch lbs. (5 Nm).

3.7L Engine

See Figures 43 and 44.

1. Before servicing the vehicle, refer to the Precautions Section.

2. Drain the cooling system. Refer to Draining, Filling & Bleeding Procedure.

3. Remove the cooling fan motor and shroud. Refer to Engine Fan Removal & Installation.

4. Remove the front bumper cover.

5. Disconnect the upper radiator hose and lower degas bottle hose from the radiator.

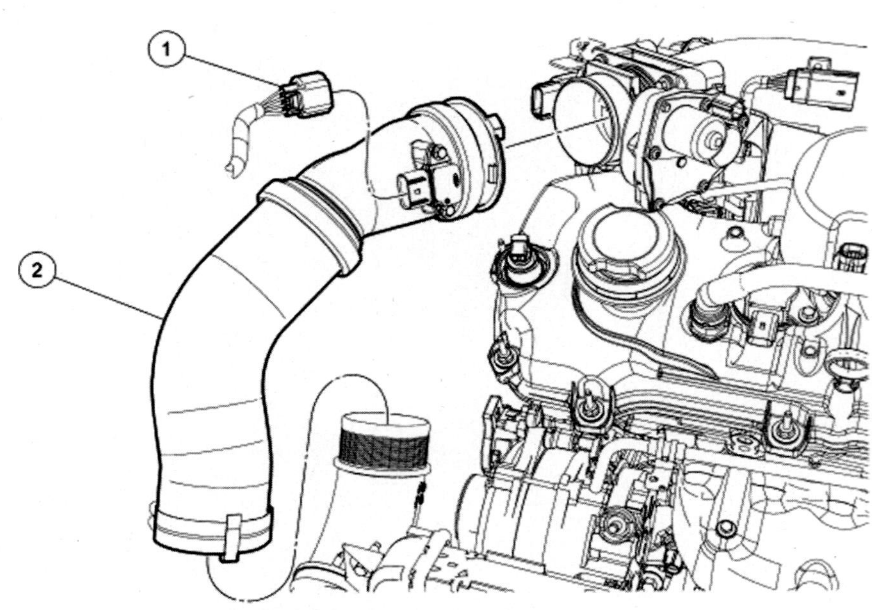

Fig. 39 Radiator components 1—3.5L engine

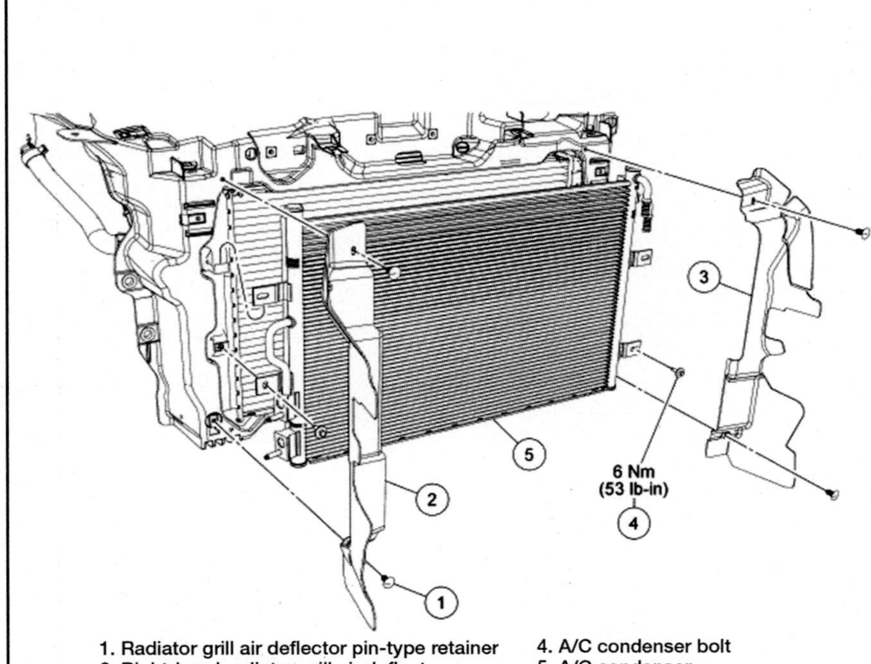

Fig. 40 Radiator components 2—3.5L engine

6. Disconnect the lower radiator hose from the radiator.
7. Lift the tabs and remove the radiator support brackets and position the radiator toward the engine.
8. Remove the 2 A/C condenser bolts from the radiator and separate the condenser from the radiator.

NOTE: Make sure the bottom radiator insulators are in place when installing the radiator.

9. Remove the radiator.

To install:

10. To install, reverse the removal procedure, noting the following:
    a. Make sure the bottom radiator insulators are in place when installing the radiator.
    b. Tighten the A/C condenser bolts to 53 inch lbs. (6 Nm).
    c. Fill and bleed the cooling system. Refer to Draining, Filling & Bleeding Procedure.

THERMOSTAT

REMOVAL & INSTALLATION

Thermostat Housing

See Figures 45 and 46.

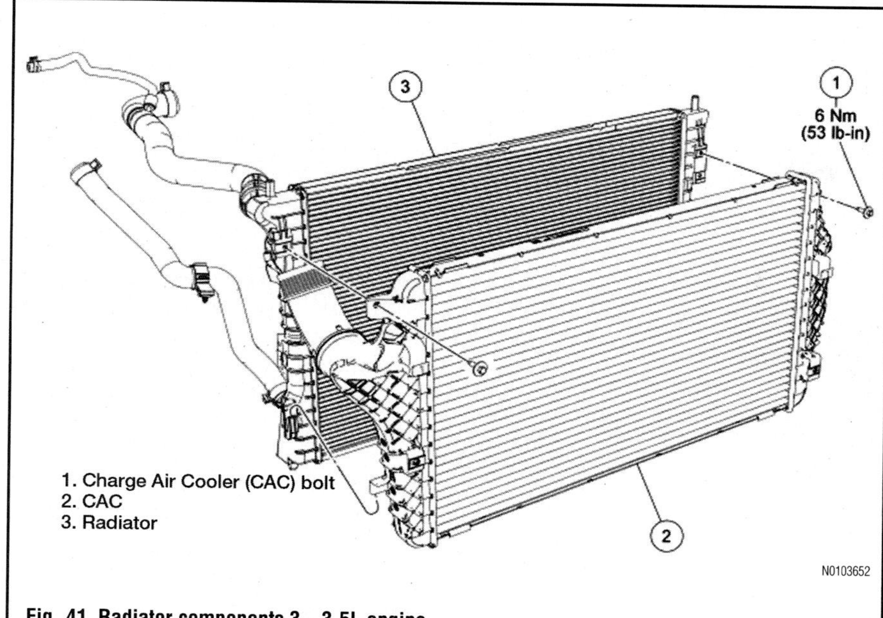

Fig. 41 Radiator components 3—3.5L engine

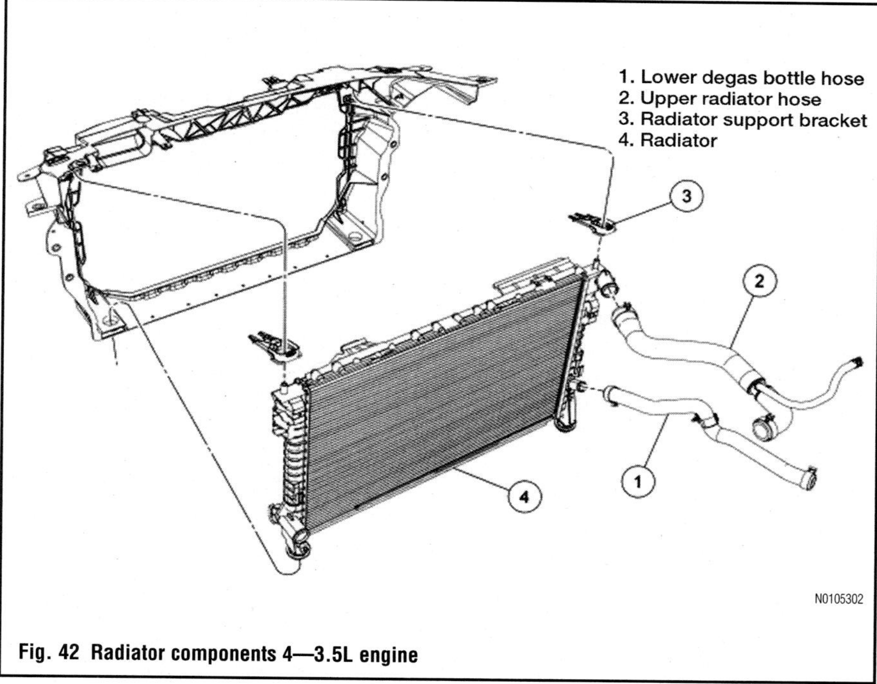

Fig. 42 Radiator components 4—3.5L engine

1. Before servicing the vehicle, refer to the Precautions Section.
2. Drain the cooling system. Refer to Draining, Filling & Bleeding Procedure.
3. Remove the engine Air Cleaner (ACL) outlet pipe.
4. For 3.5L vehicles, remove the thermostat housing as follows:
   a. Disconnect the lower radiator hose from the thermostat housing.
   b. Remove the 2 bolts and the thermostat housing.
   c. Remove the O-ring seal. Clean and inspect the O-ring seal. Install a new seal if necessary.
5. For 3.7L vehicles, remove the thermostat housing as follows:
   a. Disconnect the 5 coolant hoses from the thermostat housing and position them aside.
   b. Remove the 3 thermostat housing bolts.
   c. Separate the thermostat housing from the coolant tube and remove the thermostat housing. Do not pull the other end of the coolant tube out of the engine block when separating the thermostat housing.
   d. Remove and discard the O-ring seals.

To install:

6. To install, reverse the removal procedure, noting the following:

**** WARNING**

Genuine Motorcraft® Specialty Green Engine Coolant is very sensitive to light. Do NOT allow this product to be exposed to ANY LIGHT for more than a day or two. Extended light exposure causes this product to degrade.

   a. Lubricate the new O-ring seal with clean engine coolant.
   b. For 3.5L vehicles, clean the bolts and apply Thread Sealant with PTFE before installing the thermostat housing bolts.
   c. Tighten the thermostat housing bolts to 89 inch lbs. (10 Nm).
   d. Fill and bleed the cooling system. Refer to Draining, Filling & Bleeding Procedure.

Thermostat

See Figure 47.

1. Before servicing the vehicle, refer to the Precautions Section.
2. Drain the cooling system. Refer to Draining, Filling & Bleeding Procedure.
3. Remove the engine Air Cleaner (ACL) outlet pipe.
4. Remove the 2 bolts and position aside the thermostat housing.
5. Remove the O-ring seal and thermostat. Clean and inspect the O-ring seal. Install a new seal if necessary.

To install:

6. To install, reverse the removal procedure, noting the following:

**** WARNING**

Genuine Motorcraft® Specialty Green Engine Coolant is very sensitive to light. Do NOT allow this product to be exposed to ANY LIGHT for more than a day or two. Extended light exposure causes this product to degrade.

   a. Lubricate the thermostat O-ring seal with clean engine coolant.
   b. For 3.5L vehicles, clean the bolts and apply Thread Sealant with PTFE before installing the thermostat housing bolts.
   c. Tighten the thermostat housing bolts to 89 inch lbs. (10 Nm).

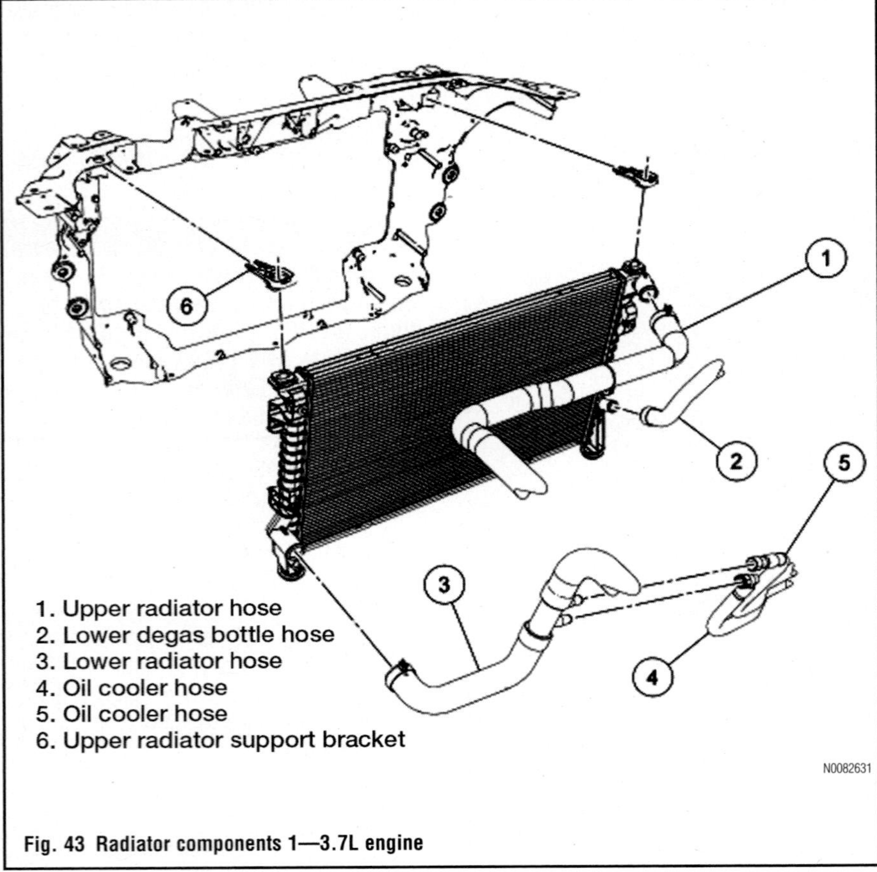

Fig. 43 Radiator components 1—3.7L engine

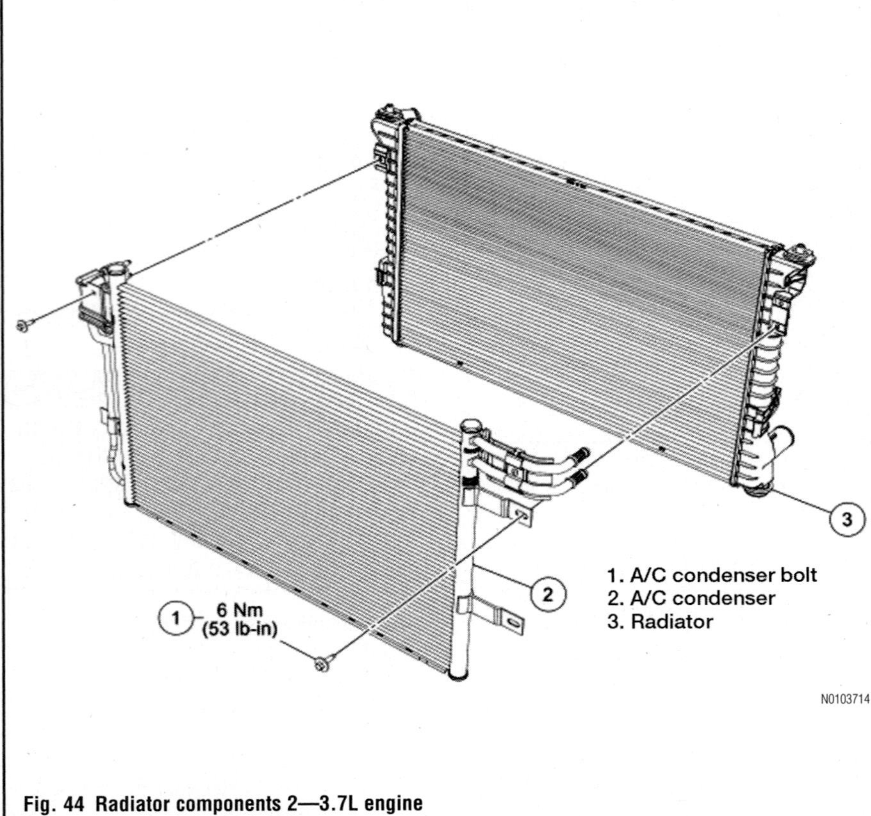

Fig. 44 Radiator components 2—3.7L engine

d. Fill and bleed the cooling system. Refer to Draining, Filling & Bleeding Procedure.

WATER PUMP (COOLANT PUMP)

REMOVAL & INSTALLATION

See Figures 48 through 52.

⁂ WARNING

During engine repair procedures, cleanliness is extremely important. Any foreign material, including any material created while cleaning gasket surfaces, that enters the oil passages, coolant passages or the oil pan may cause engine failure.

➡On early build engines, the timing chain rides on the inner side of the right-hand timing chain guide. Late build engines are equipped with a different design right-hand timing chain guide that requires the timing chain to ride on the outer side of the right-hand timing chain guide. For service, all replacement right-hand timing chain guides will be the late build design.

1. Before servicing the vehicle, refer to the Precautions Section.
2. With the vehicle in NEUTRAL, position it on a hoist.
3. Drain the cooling system. Refer to Draining, Filling & Bleeding Procedure.
4. Remove the engine front cover.
5. Remove and discard the engine oil filter.
6. Remove the right-hand and left-hand VCT housing. Refer to Timing Chain Removal & Installation in the Engine Mechanical section.
7. Remove the primary timing chain tensioner, tensioner arm, lower left-hand primary timing chain guide, and primary timing chain. Refer to Timing Chain Removal & Installation in the Engine Mechanical section.
8. Remove the 2 bolts and the upper left-hand primary timing chain guide. Refer to Timing Chain Removal & Installation in the Engine Mechanical section.
9. For engines equipped with early build right-hand timing chain guides:
    a. Remove the right-hand primary timing chain guide lower bolt.

➡The right-hand primary timing chain guide must be repositioned to allow the coolant pump to be removed.

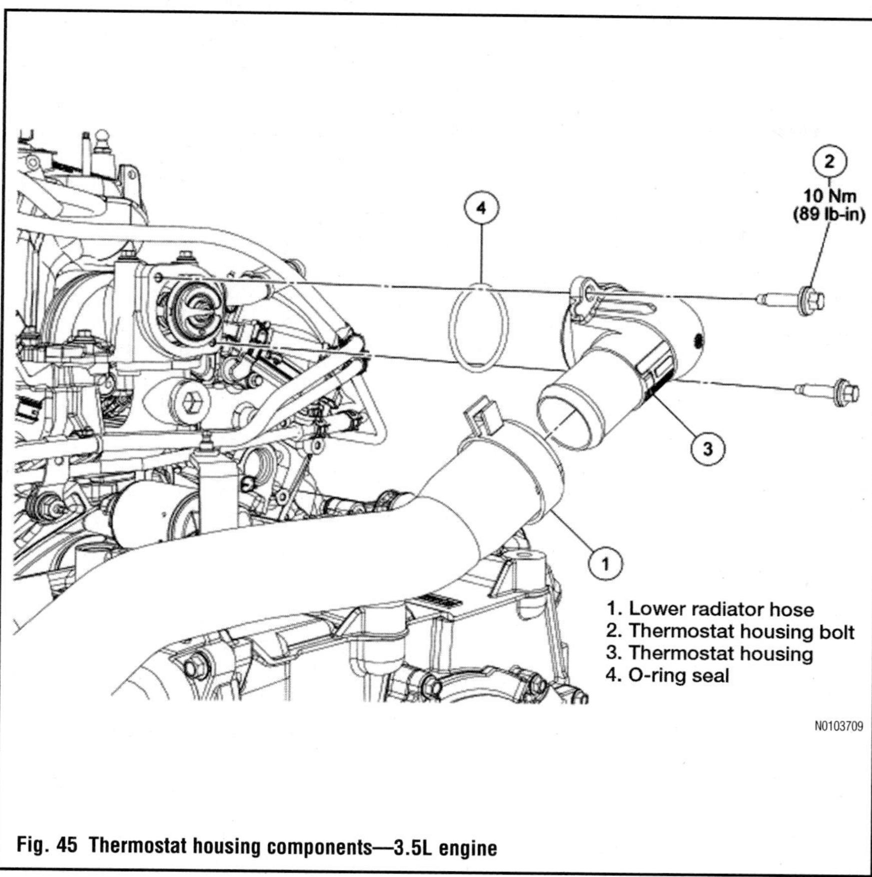

Fig. 45 Thermostat housing components—3.5L engine

10. Loosen the right-hand primary timing chain guide upper bolt. Rotate the guide and tighten the bolt.

11. For engines equipped with late build/replacement right-hand timing chain guides:

 a. Remove the right-hand primary timing chain guide lower bolt.

 b. Loosen the right-hand primary timing chain guide upper bolt. Rotate the guide and tighten the bolt. The right-hand primary timing chain guide must be repositioned to allow the coolant pump to be removed.

12. Place clean lint-free shop towels in the oil pan opening to prevent coolant from entering the oil pan during coolant pump removal.

13. Remove the 8 bolts and the coolant pump.

To install:

14. Clean and inspect all sealing surfaces.

15. Install the coolant pump and the 8 bolts. Tighten in the sequence shown to 89 inch lbs. (10 Nm).

16. Remove all of the shop towels from the oil pan opening.

17. Remove the oil pan drain plug and allow any accumulated coolant to drain. Any

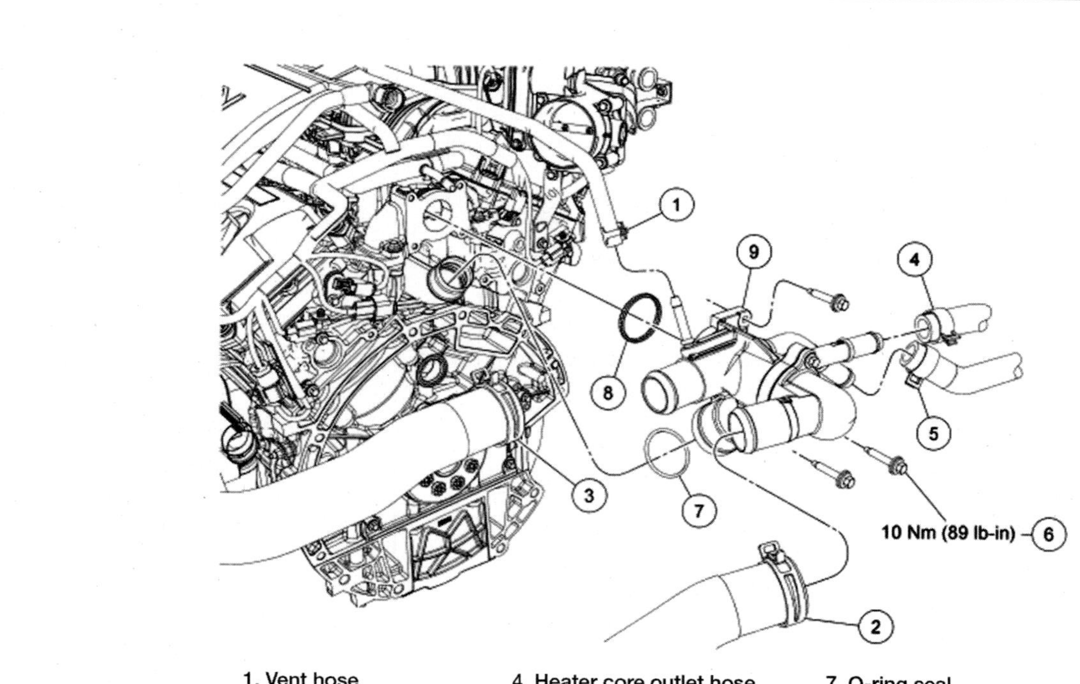

Fig. 46 Thermostat housing components—3.7L engine

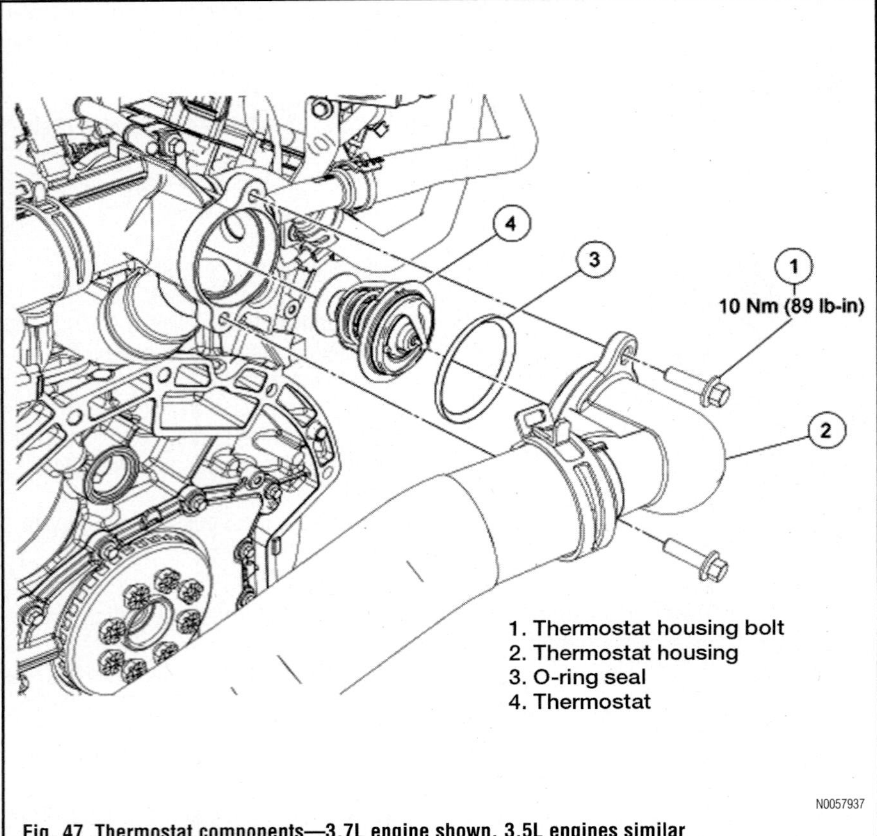

Fig. 47 Thermostat components—3.7L engine shown, 3.5L engines similar

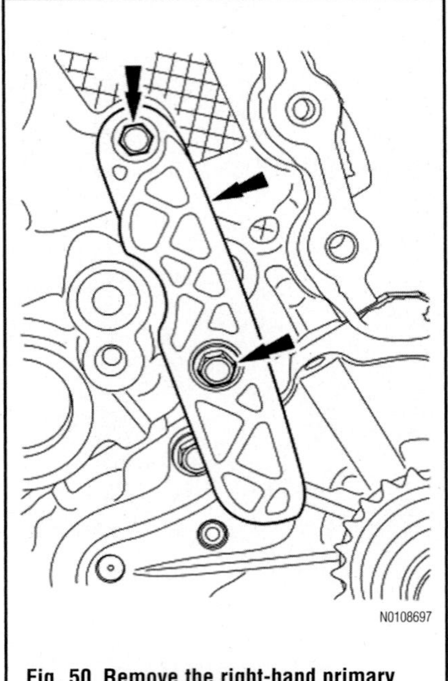

Fig. 50 Remove the right-hand primary timing chain guide lower bolt

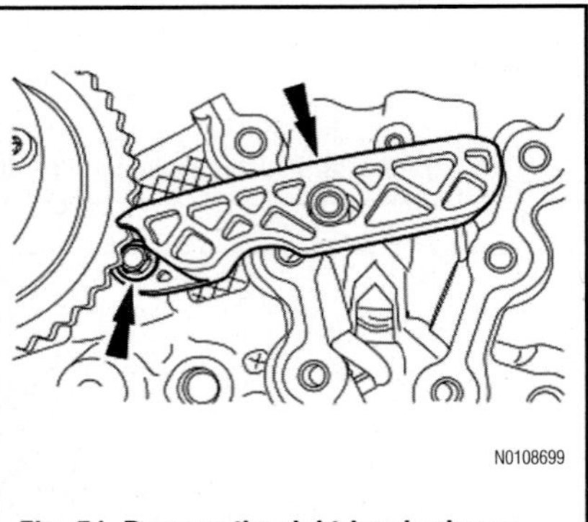

Fig. 51 Remove the right-hand primary timing chain guide lower bolt

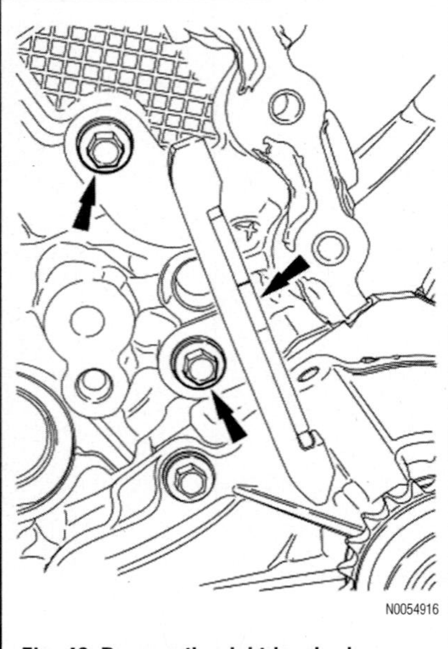

Fig. 48 Remove the right-hand primary timing chain guide lower bolt

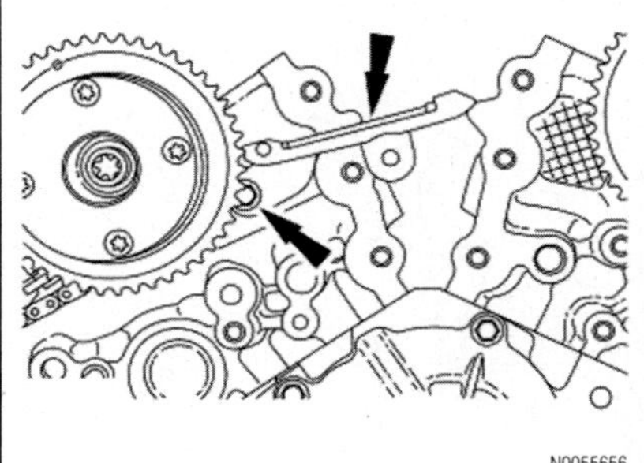

Fig. 49 Rotate the right-hand primary timing chain guide and tighten the bolt

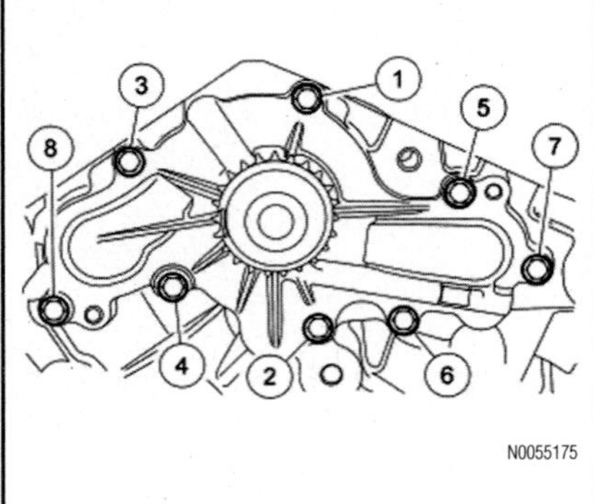

Fig. 52 Remove the 8 bolts and the coolant pump

coolant that has accumulated in the oil pan must be drained from the pan and any residual coolant cleaned from the front of the engine and oil pan. Failure to remove all traces of the coolant can result in oil contamination and severe engine damage.

a. Remove any residual coolant from the front of the engine and the oil pan using regulated, compressed air and clean, lint-free shop towels.

b. Install the oil pan drain plug and tighten to 20 ft. lbs. (27 Nm).

18. For engines equipped with late build/replacement right-hand timing chain guides:

a. Loosen the right-hand primary timing chain guide upper bolt. Position the right-hand primary timing chain guide and install the lower bolt. Tighten the 2 bolts to 89 inch lbs. (10 Nm).

19. For engines equipped with early build right-hand timing chain guides:

a. Loosen the right-hand primary timing chain guide upper bolt. Position the right-hand primary timing chain guide and install the lower bolt. Tighten the 2 bolts to 89 inch lbs. (10 Nm).

20. Install the primary timing chain tensioner, tensioner arm, upper and lower left-hand primary timing chain guide, and primary timing chain. Reset the tensioner. Verify timing mark alignment. Refer to Timing Chain Removal & Installation in the Engine Mechanical section.

21. Install the right-hand and left-hand VCT housing and inspect the seals. Refer to Timing Chain Removal & Installation in the Engine Mechanical section.

22. Lubricate the engine oil filter gasket with clean engine oil prior to installing the oil filter. Install a new engine oil filter. Tighten to 44 inch lbs. (5 Nm) and rotate an additional 180 degrees.

23. Install the engine front cover.

24. Fill and bleed the cooling system. Refer to Draining, Filling & Bleeding Procedure.

ENGINE ELECTRICAL — BATTERY SYSTEM

BATTERY

REMOVAL & INSTALLATION

⁂ CAUTION

Batteries contain sulfuric acid and produce explosive gases. Work in a well-ventilated area. Do not allow the battery to come in contact with flames, sparks or burning substances. Avoid contact with skin, eyes or clothing. Shield eyes when working near the battery to protect against possible splashing of acid solution. In case of acid contact with skin or eyes, flush immediately with water for a minimum of 15 minutes, then get prompt medical attention. If acid is swallowed, call a physician immediately. Always lift a plastic-cased battery with a battery carrier or with hands on opposite corners. Excessive pressure on the battery end walls may cause acid to flow through the vent caps, resulting in personal injury and/or damage to the vehicle or battery. Battery posts, terminals and related accessories contain lead and lead components. Wash hands after handling.

1. Before servicing the vehicle, refer to the Precautions Section.
2. Disconnect the negative battery cable. When disconnecting the battery ground cable to interrupt power to the vehicle electrical system, disconnect the battery ground cable only. It is not necessary to disconnect the positive battery cable.
3. Disconnect the positive battery cable.
4. Remove the 2 nuts and the battery hold-down clamp.
5. Remove the battery.
6. To remove the battery tray:
   a. Remove the Air Cleaner (ACL) assembly.
   b. Disconnect the wiring harness fastener from the battery tray.
   c. Remove the 3 bolts and 1 nut from the battery tray.
   d. Disconnect the Battery Junction Box (BJB) fastener and remove the battery tray.

To install:

7. To install, reverse the removal procedure, noting the following:
   a. If removed, tighten the battery tray bolts and nut to 11 ft. lbs. (15 Nm).
   b. Tighten the battery hold-down clamp nuts to 27 inch lbs. (3 Nm).
   c. Connect battery cables and tighten to 44 inch lbs. (5 Nm).
   d. Refer to Battery Reconnect/Relearn Procedures.

BATTERY RECONNECT/RELEARN PROCEDURE

When the battery (or PCM) is disconnected and connected, some abnormal drive symptoms may occur while the vehicle relearns its adaptive strategy. The charging system set point may also vary. The vehicle may need to be driven to relearn its strategy.

When the battery is disconnected and connected, the illumination display needs to be calibrated. After the battery is connected, rotate the dimmer switch from the lowest dim position to the full bright, dome ON position.

ENGINE ELECTRICAL — CHARGING SYSTEM

ALTERNATOR

REMOVAL & INSTALLATION

See Figure 53.

➡The radial arm adapter is a serviceable item. Do not replace the alternator if the radial arm adapter is the only concern.

1. Before servicing the vehicle, refer to the Precautions Section.
2. Disconnect the battery.
3. Remove the engine cover.
4. For 3.7L engines, position the upper radiator hose aside and remove the radiator hose support cradle. Rotate the accessory drive belt tensioner and remove the accessory drive belt from the alternator.
5. Position the alternator protective cover aside, remove the B+ nut and position the B+ terminal aside.
6. Disconnect the alternator electrical connector and position the harness aside.
7. For 3.5L non-turbocharged engines, remove the cooling fan assembly.
8. For 3.5L and 3.7L non-turbocharged engines, rotate the accessory drive belt tensioner and remove the accessory drive belt from the alternator.
9. For 3.5L engines, remove A/C compressor.
10. Remove the upper alternator nut and stud.
11. Loosen the lower alternator bolt.
12. Remove the alternator.

To install:

13. Install the alternator and hand-tighten the lower generator bolt.
14. Install the upper alternator stud and nut. Tighten the alternator stud to 71 inch lbs. (8 Nm). Tighten the alternator nut to 35 ft. lbs. (47 Nm).
15. Tighten the lower alternator bolt to 35 ft. lbs. (47 Nm).
16. For 3.5L engines, install the A/C compressor.
17. For 3.5L and 3.7L non-turbocharged engines, rotate the accessory drive belt tensioner and install the accessory drive belt on the alternator.
18. For 3.5L non-turbocharged engines, install the cooling fan assembly.
19. Connect the alternator electrical connector.
20. Install the alternator B+ terminal and tighten the B+ terminal nut to 13 ft. lbs. (17 Nm).
21. For 3.7L engines, install the upper radiator support cradle and reposition the upper radiator hose.
22. Install the engine cover.
23. Connect the battery cable.

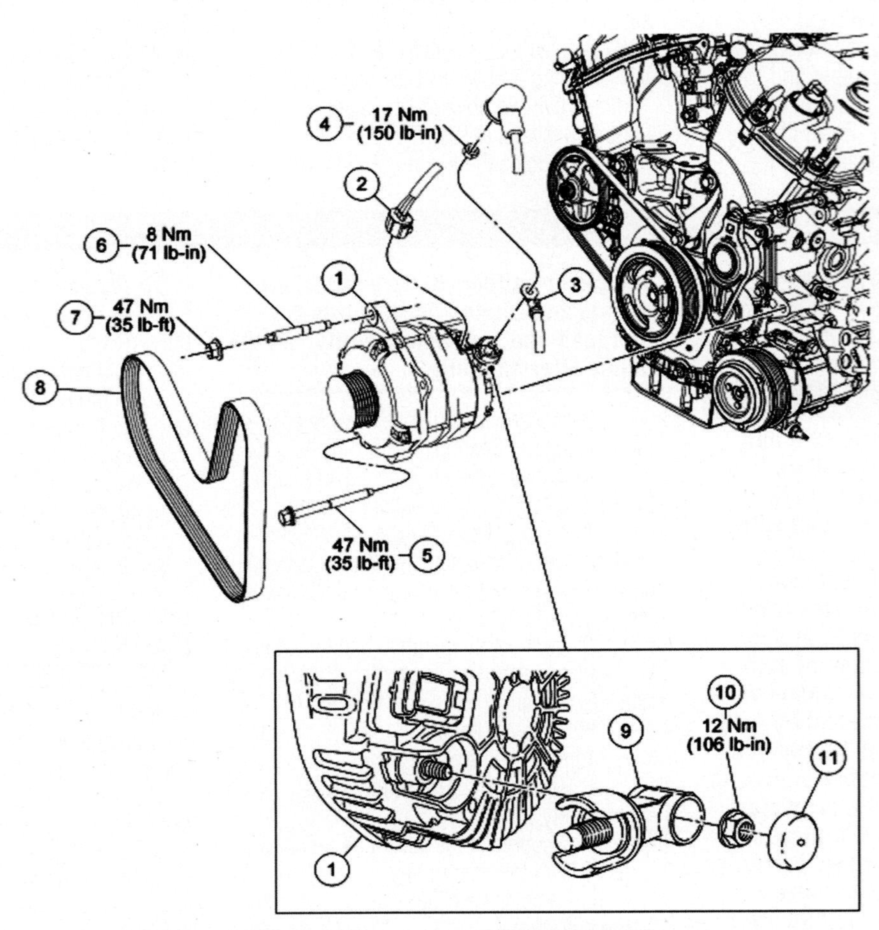

1. Alternator (Generator)
2. Generator electrical connector
3. Generator B+ terminal
4. Generator B+ terminal nut
5. Generator bolt
6. Generator stud
7. Generator nut
8. Accessory drive belt
9. Radial arm adapter
10. Radial arm adapter nut
11. Radial arm adapter cap

N0106886

Fig. 53 Alternator (Generator) components

FIRING ORDER

Firing order: 1–4–2–5–3–6

IGNITION COIL

REMOVAL & INSTALLATION

3.5L Engines

See Figures 54 and 55.

1. Before servicing the vehicle, refer to the Precautions Section.
2. Disconnect the negative battery cable.
3. For the left-hand side, disconnect the crankcase ventilation tube-to-valve cover fitting quick connect coupling. Remove the fuel injection pump noise insulator shield.
4. Disconnect the 6 ignition coil-on-plug electrical connectors.
5. Remove the 6 bolts and the 6 ignition coil-on-plugs. When removing the ignition coil-on-plugs, a slight twisting motion will break the seal and ease removal.
6. Inspect the coil seals for rips, nicks or tears. Remove and discard any damaged coil seals.

To install:

7. To install, reverse the removal procedure, noting the following:
   a. Apply a small amount of dielectric grease to the inside of the ignition coil-on-plug boots before attaching to the spark plugs.
   b. Slide the new coil seal onto the coil until it is fully seated at the top of the coil.
   c. Install the ignition coil-on-plugs and bolts. Tighten to 62 inch lbs. (7 Nm).

3.7L Engines

See Figures 56 and 57.

1. Before servicing the vehicle, refer to the Precautions Section.
2. Disconnect the negative battery cable.
3. For the left-hand side, disconnect the crankcase ventilation tube-to-valve cover fitting quick connect coupling and position aside.
4. For the right-hand side, remove the upper intake manifold.
5. Disconnect the 6 ignition coil-on-plug electrical connectors.
6. Remove the 6 bolts and the 6 ignition coil-on-plugs. When removing the ignition coil-on-plugs, a slight twisting motion will break the seal and ease removal.
7. Inspect the coil seals for rips, nicks or tears. Remove and discard any damaged coil seals.

To install:

8. To install, reverse the removal procedure, noting the following:
   a. Apply a small amount of dielectric grease to the inside of the ignition coil-on-plug boots before attaching to the spark plugs.

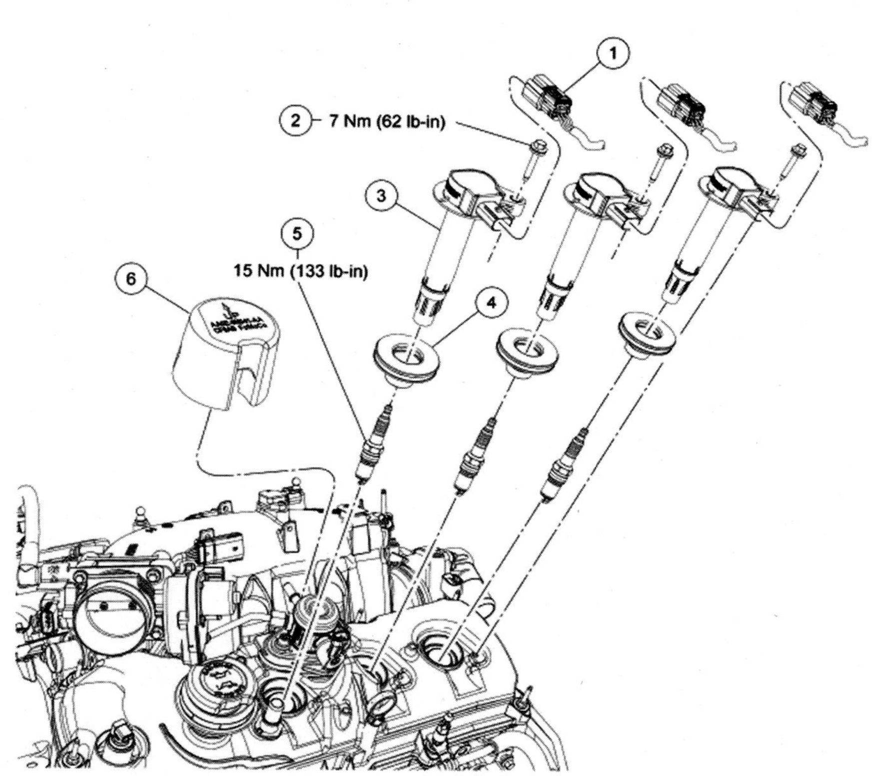

Fig. 54 Left-hand ignition coil components—3.5L engine

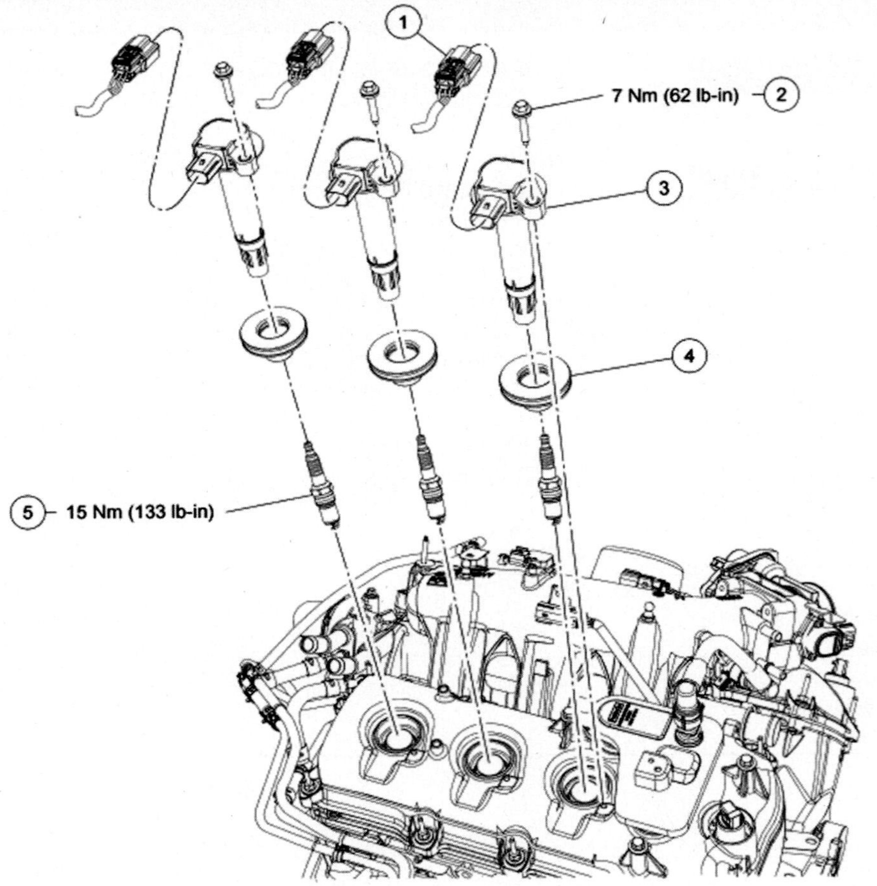

1
7 Nm (62 lb-in)
2
3
4
5
15 Nm (133 lb-in)

1. Ignition coil-on-plug electrical connector
2. Ignition coil-on-plug bolt
3. Ignition coil-on-plug
4. Coil seal
5. Spark plug

N0103162

Fig. 55 Right-hand ignition coil components—3.5L engine

7 Nm
(62 lb-in)
3
4
2
1
6
5
15 Nm
(133 lb-in)

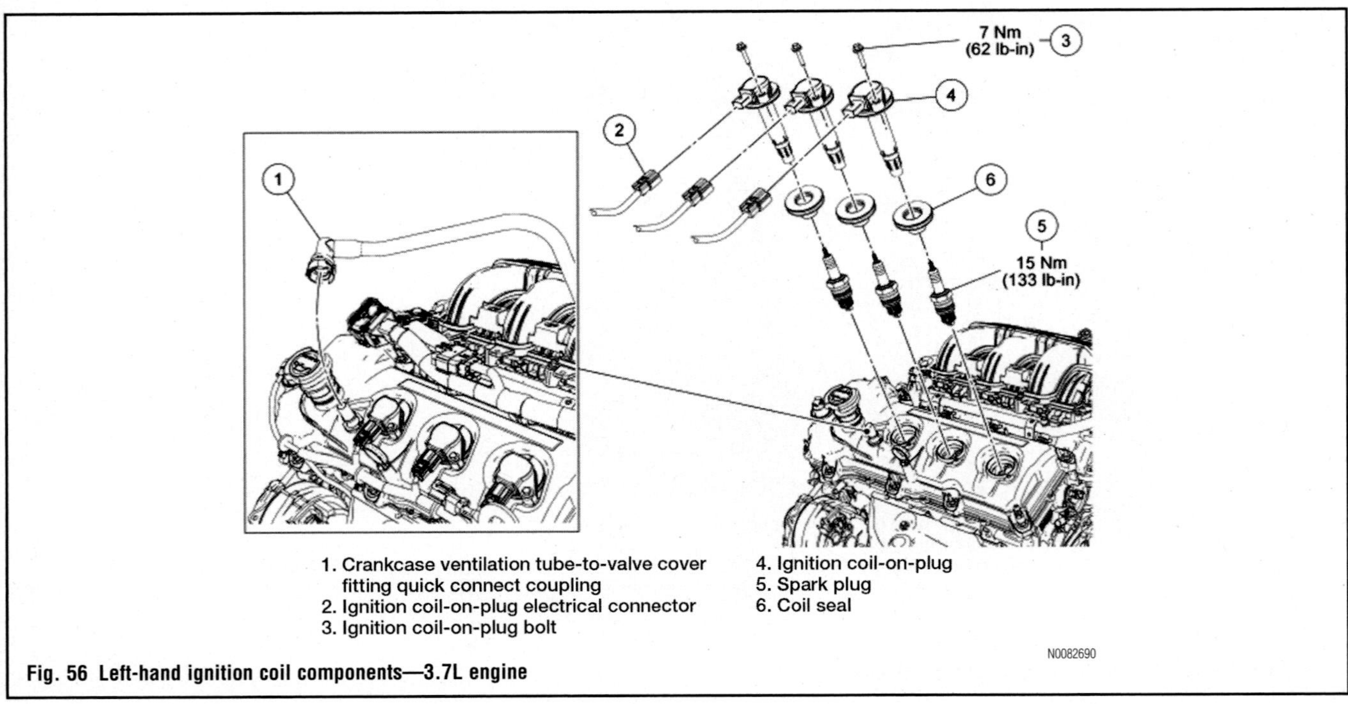

1. Crankcase ventilation tube-to-valve cover fitting quick connect coupling
2. Ignition coil-on-plug electrical connector
3. Ignition coil-on-plug bolt
4. Ignition coil-on-plug
5. Spark plug
6. Coil seal

N0082690

Fig. 56 Left-hand ignition coil components—3.7L engine

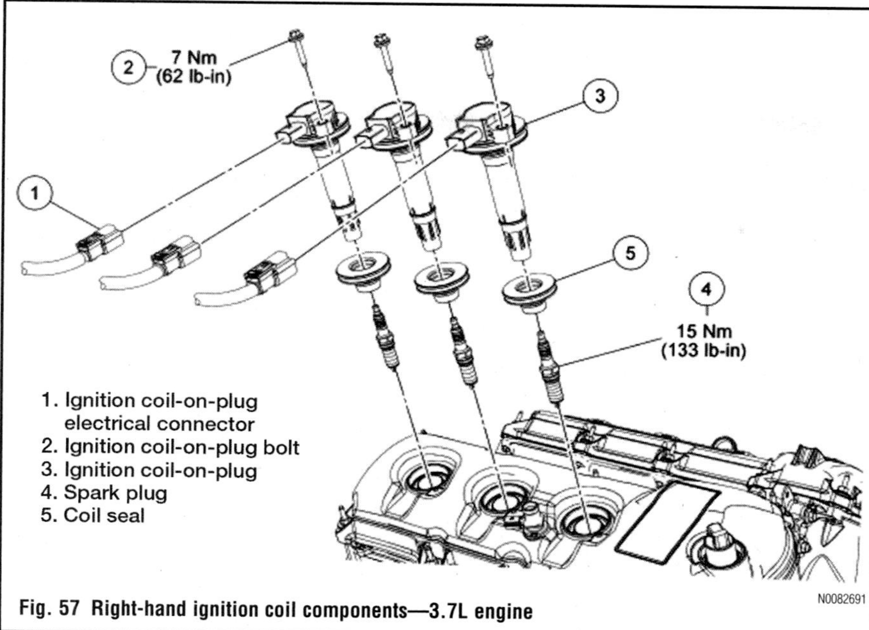

Fig. 57 Right-hand ignition coil components—3.7L engine

b. Slide the new coil seal onto the coil until it is fully seated at the top of the coil.

c. Install the ignition coil-on-plugs and bolts. Tighten to 62 inch lbs. (7 Nm).

SPARK PLUGS

REMOVAL & INSTALLATION

1. Before servicing the vehicle, refer to the Precautions Section.
2. Disconnect the negative battery cable.
3. Remove the 6 ignition coil-on-plugs. Refer to Ignition Coil Removal & Installation.

WARNING

Only use hand tools when removing or installing the spark plugs, or damage may occur to the cylinder head or spark plug.

4. Use compressed air to remove any foreign material in the spark plug well before removing the spark plugs.
5. Remove the 6 spark plugs.
6. Inspect the 6 spark plugs.

To install:

7. To install, reverse the removal procedure. Tighten to 11 ft. lbs. (15 Nm).
8. Adjust the spark plug gap as necessary:
   - 3.5L Engine: 0.032–0.038 in. (0.81–0.97 mm)
   - 3.7L Engine: 0.051–0.057 in. (1.29–1.45 mm)

ENGINE ELECTRICAL

STARTING SYSTEM

STARTER

REMOVAL & INSTALLATION

See Figures 58 and 59.

CAUTION

Always disconnect the battery ground cable at the battery before disconnecting the starter motor battery terminal lead. If a tool is shorted at the starter motor battery terminal, the tool can quickly heat enough to cause a skin burn. Failure to follow this instruction may result in serious personal injury.

1. Before servicing the vehicle, refer to the Precautions Section.
2. Disconnect the battery ground cable.
3. Remove the Air Cleaner (ACL) outlet pipe and ACL assembly.
4. Disconnect the transmission shift cable and adjustment lock from the transmission manual control lever.
5. Disconnect the transmission shift cable rotating slide snap and position aside the transmission cable.
6. Remove the nut and the transmission manual control lever.

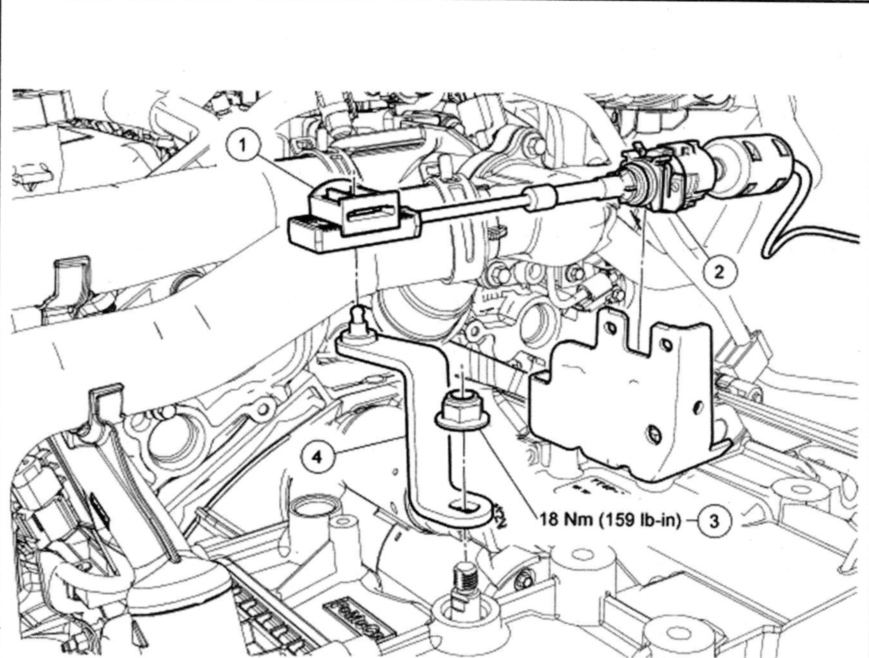

Fig. 58 Starter motor components 1

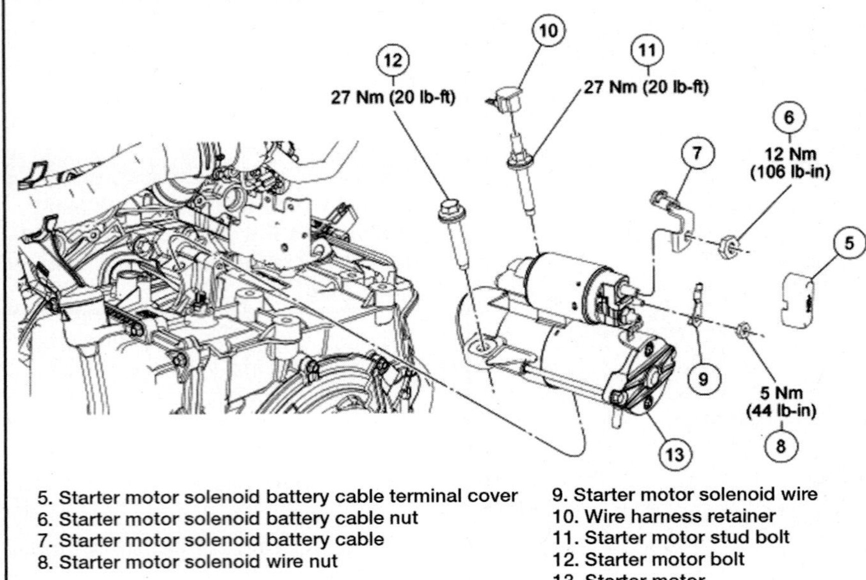

Fig. 59 Starter motor components 2

7. Remove the starter motor terminal cover.
8. Remove the starter motor solenoid battery cable nut.
9. Remove the starter motor solenoid wire nut.
10. Disconnect the wiring harness retainer from the starter motor stud bolt.
11. Remove the starter motor stud bolt, bolt and the starter motor.

To install:

12. To install, reverse the removal procedure, noting the following:
    a. Tighten the starter motor stud bolt to 20 ft. lbs. (27 Nm).
    b. Tighten the starter motor solenoid wire nut to 44 inch lbs. (5 Nm).
    c. Tighten the starter motor solenoid battery cable nut to 106 inch lbs. (12 Nm).
    d. Tighten the transmission manual control lever nut to 13 ft. lbs. (18 Nm).

ENGINE MECHANICAL

➡Disconnecting the negative battery cable may interfere with the functions of the on board computer systems and may require the computer to undergo a relearning process, once the negative battery cable is reconnected.

ACCESSORY DRIVE BELTS

ACCESSORY BELT ROUTING

See Figures 60 and 61.

Refer to the accompanying illustrations.

INSPECTION

Automatic tensioners are calibrated to provide the correct amount of tension to the belt for a given accessory drive system. Unless a spring or damping band within the tensioner assembly breaks or some other mechanical part of the tensioner fails, there is no need to check the tensioner for correct tension.

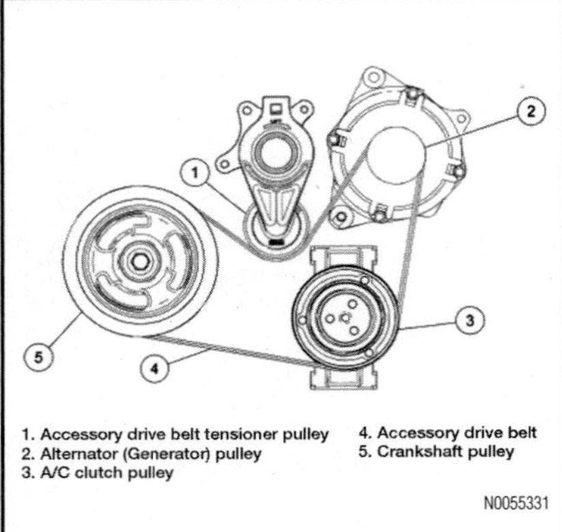

Fig. 60 Front End Accessory Drive (FEAD) Belt Routing

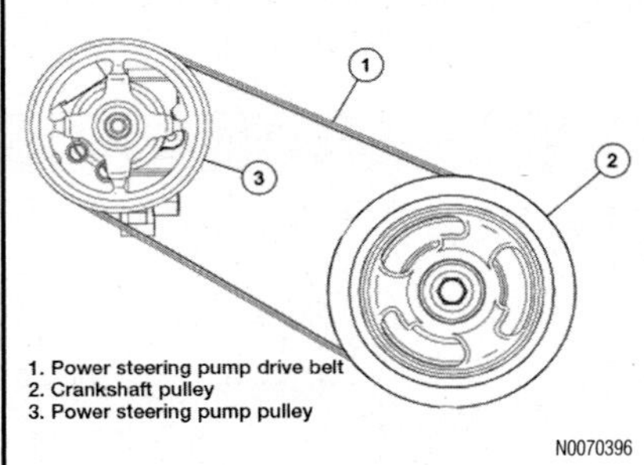

Fig. 61 Power Steering Pump Belt Routing—Vehicles with Hydraulic Power Assist Steering (HPAS)

ADJUSTMENT

The automatic belt tensioner maintains correct belt tension and compensates for component wear and changes in system load.

REMOVAL & INSTALLATION

Accessory Drive Belt

3.5L Engines

See Figure 62.

⁂ WARNING

Under no circumstances should the accessory drive belt, tensioner or pulleys be lubricated, as potential damage to the belt material and tensioner damping mechanism will occur. Do not apply any fluids or belt dressing to the accessory drive belt or pulleys.

1. Before servicing the vehicle, refer to the Precautions Section.
2. Disconnect the negative battery cable.
3. With the vehicle in NEUTRAL, position it on a hoist.
4. Remove the right-hand front wheel and tire.
5. Remove the pin-type retainers and the right-hand splash shield.
6. Working from under the vehicle, rotate the accessory drive belt tensioner clockwise and remove the accessory drive belt.
7. If tensioner removal is required, remove the 3 bolts and the accessory drive belt tensioner.

To install:

8. If tensioner was removed, install the tensioner and tighten the bolts to 97 inch lbs. (11 Nm).
9. Working from under the vehicle, position the accessory drive belt on all pulleys with the exception of the crankshaft pulley.

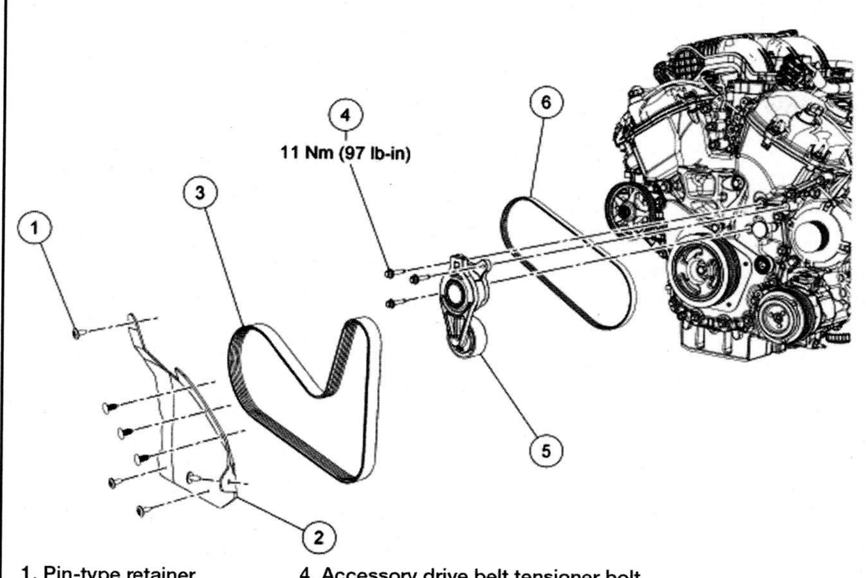

Fig. 62 Front End Accessory Drive (FEAD) Belt—Exploded view

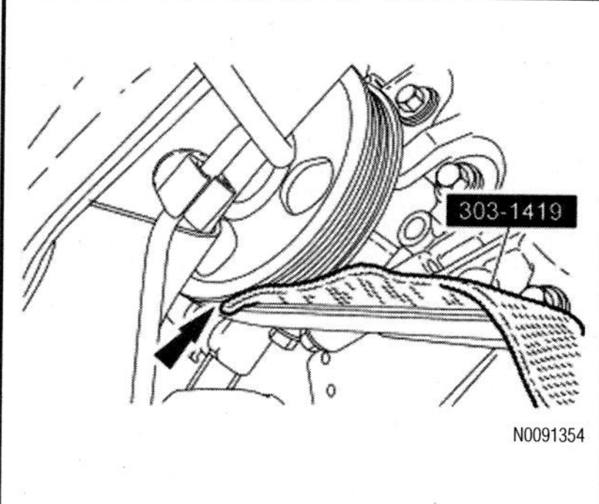

Fig. 63 Position the belt remover on the power steering pump pulley belt

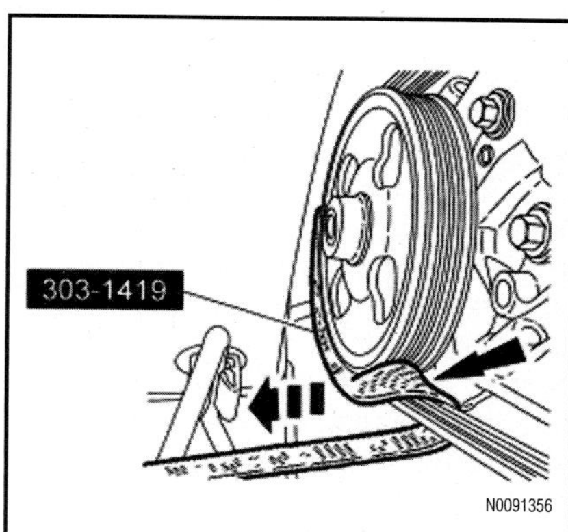

Fig. 64 Fold the belt remover under the power steering pump belt, and pull out to remove the coolant pump belt

10. Rotate the accessory drive belt tensioner clockwise and install the accessory drive belt on the crankshaft pulley. After installation, make sure the accessory drive belt is correctly seated on all pulleys.
11. Install the right-hand splash shield.
12. Install the right-hand front wheel and tire.

3.7L Engines

See Figure 62.

WARNING

Under no circumstances should the accessory drive belt, tensioner or pulleys be lubricated, as potential damage to the belt material and tensioner damping mechanism will occur. Do not apply any fluids or belt dressing to the accessory drive belt or pulleys.

1. Before servicing the vehicle, refer to the Precautions Section.
2. Disconnect the negative battery cable.
3. With the vehicle in NEUTRAL, position it on a hoist.
4. Working from the top of the vehicle, rotate the accessory drive belt tensioner clockwise and remove the accessory drive belt from the alternator (generator) pulley.
5. Remove the pin-type retainers and the right-hand splash shield.
6. Working from under the vehicle, remove the accessory drive belt.
7. If tensioner removal is required, remove the 3 bolts and the accessory drive belt tensioner.

To install:

8. If tensioner was removed, install the tensioner and tighten the bolts to 97 inch lbs. (11 Nm).
9. Working from under the vehicle, position the accessory drive belt on all pulleys, with the exception of the alternator pulley.
10. Working from the top of the vehicle, rotate the accessory drive belt tensioner clockwise and install the accessory drive belt on the alternator pulley. After installation, make sure the accessory drive belt is correctly seated on all pulleys.
11. Install the right-hand splash shield.

Power Steering Pump Belt

See Figures 63 and 64.

1. Before servicing the vehicle, refer to the Precautions Section.
2. Working from the top of the vehicle, rotate the accessory drive belt tensioner clockwise and remove the accessory drive belt from the alternator (generator) pulley.
3. Remove the right front wheel and tire.
4. Remove the pin-type retainers and the right-hand splash shield.
5. Position the accessory drive belt off the crankshaft pulley.
6. Position the Stretchy Belt Remover (SST 303-1419) or equivalent tool on the power steering pump pulley belt as shown.
7. Turn the crankshaft clockwise and feed the belt remover evenly on the power steering pump pulley. Feed the belt remover onto the power steering pump pulley approximately 90 degrees.
8. Remove the power steering pump belt.
   a. Fold the belt remover under the inside of the power steering pump belt as shown.
   b. In one quick motion, firmly pull the belt remover out of the right-hand fender well, removing the coolant pump belt.

To install:

9. Install the power steering drive belt on the crankshaft pulley.
10. Position the power steering drive belt around the Belt Installer or equivalent tool and the power steering pump pulley.
   a. Make sure the belt is engaged with the power steering pump pulley and rotate the crankshaft clockwise to install the power steering drive belt.
   b. After installation, make sure the power steering drive belt is correctly

seated on the crankshaft and power steering pump pulleys.

11. Position the accessory drive belt on the crankshaft pulley.

12. Working from the top of the vehicle, rotate the accessory drive belt tensioner clockwise and install the accessory drive belt.

a. After installation, make sure the accessory drive belt is correctly seated on all pulleys.

13. Install the right-hand splash shield.

14. Install the right front tire and wheel.

AIR CLEANER

REMOVAL & INSTALLATION

3.5L Engines

See Figure 65.

⁂ WARNING

Whenever turbocharger air intake system components are removed, always cover open ports to protect from debris. It is important that no foreign material enter the system. The turbocharger compressor vanes are susceptible to damage from even small particles. All components should be inspected and cleaned, if necessary, prior to installation or reassembly.

1. Before servicing the vehicle, refer to the Precautions Section.

2. Disconnect the Intake Air Temperature 2 (IAT2) sensor electrical connector.

3. Release the IAT2 sensor wiring harness pin-type retainer from the Air Cleaner (ACL) cover.

4. Loosen the clamp and disconnect the ACL outlet pipe from the ACL.

5. If equipped, remove the bolt cover.

6. Remove the 2 bolts from the ACL assembly. No tools are required to remove the ACL assembly. Removal should be carried out using hands only.

7. Separate the 2 ACL feet from the rubber grommets and remove the ACL assembly.

To install:

8. To install, reverse the removal procedure, noting the following:

a. Make sure that the 2 ACL feet are seated into the rubber grommets under the ACL assembly. The ACL outlet pipe should be securely sealed to prevent unmetered air from entering the engine. Utilize the alignment features to make sure the ACL outlet tube is seated within 2 mm of the stops.

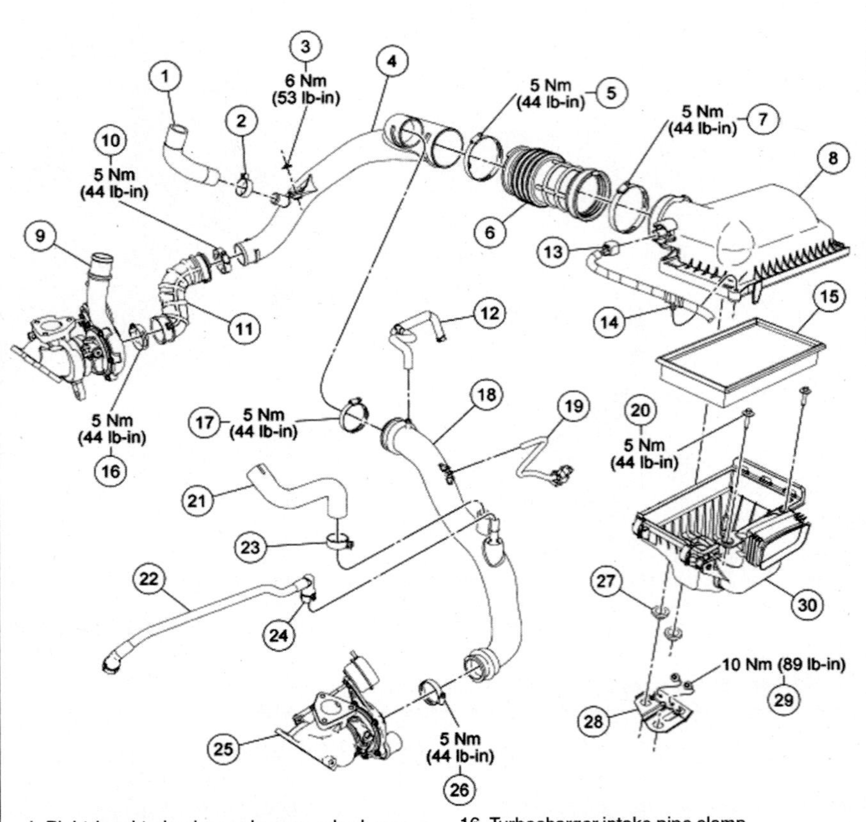

1. Right-hand turbocharger bypass valve hose
2. Turbocharger bypass valve hose clamp
3. Right-hand turbocharger intake tube nut
4. Right-hand turbocharger intake tube
5. Air Cleaner (ACL) outlet pipe clamp
6. ACL outlet pipe
7. ACL outlet pipe clamp
8. ACL cover
9. Right-hand turbocharger
10. Turbocharger intake pipe clamp
11. Right-hand turbocharger intake pipe
12. Power brake booster aspirator hose
13. Intake Air Temperature (IAT) sensor connector
14. IAT sensor wiring harness pin-type retainer
15. ACL element
16. Turbocharger intake pipe clamp
17. Turbocharger intake tube clamp
18. Left-hand turbocharger intake tube
19. Turbocharger wastegate regulating valve hose
20. ACL assembly bolt
21. Left-hand turbocharger bypass valve hose
22. Crankcase ventilation tube
23. Turbocharger bypass valve hose clamp
24. Crankcase ventilation tube quick connect
25. Left-hand turbocharger
26. Turbocharger intake tube clamp
27. ACL insulator
28. ACL bracket
29. ACL bracket bolt
30. ACL tray

Fig. 65 Gasoline Turbocharged Direct Injection (GTDI) ACL Assembly—3.5L engines

b. Tighten the ACL assembly bolts to 44 inch lbs. (5 Nm).

c. Tighten the ACL outlet pipe clamp to 44 inch lbs. (5 Nm).

3.7L Engines

See Figure 66.

1. Before servicing the vehicle, refer to the Precautions Section.

2. Disconnect the Mass Air Flow (MAF) sensor electrical connector.

3. Loosen the clamp and disconnect the Air Cleaner (ACL) outlet pipe from the ACL.

4. Remove the 2 bolts from the ACL assembly. No tools are required to remove the ACL assembly. Removal should be carried out using hands only.

5. Separate the 2 ACL feet from the rubber grommets and remove the ACL assembly.

To install:

6. To install, reverse the removal procedure, noting the following:

a. Make sure that the 2 ACL feet are seated into the rubber grommets under the ACL assembly. The ACL outlet pipe should be securely sealed to prevent unmetered air from entering the engine.

b. Tighten the ACL assembly bolts to 44 inch lbs. (5 Nm).

c. Tighten the ACL outlet pipe clamp to 44 inch lbs. (5 Nm).

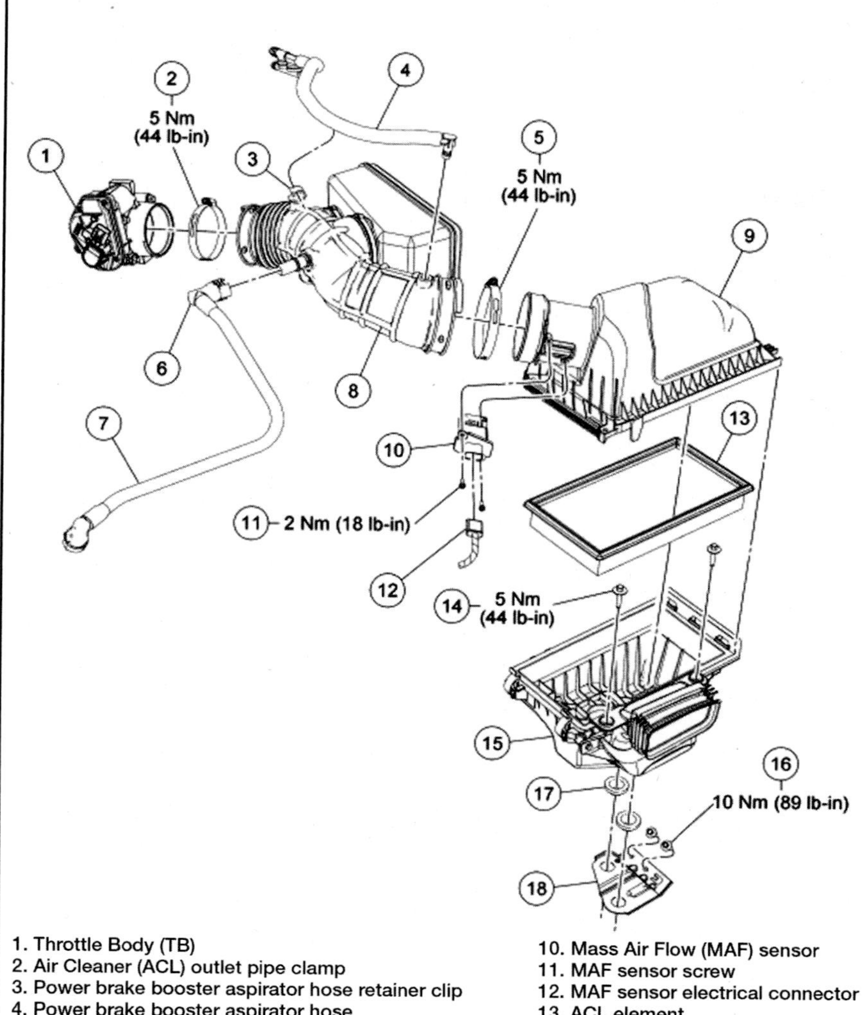

Fig. 66 Air Cleaner (ACL) Assembly—3.7L engines

CATALYTIC CONVERTER

REMOVAL & INSTALLATION

3.5L Engines

Left-Hand

See Figure 67.

➡Always install new fasteners and gaskets. Clean flange faces prior to new gasket installation to make sure of correct sealing.

1. Before servicing the vehicle, refer to the Precautions Section.
2. With the vehicle in NEUTRAL, position it on a hoist.
3. Remove the left-hand Heated Oxygen Sensor (HO2S).
4. Remove the left-hand exhaust flexible pipe:
   a. Remove the 4 retainers and the underbody shield.
   b. Remove the 2 left-hand exhaust flexible pipe-to-left-hand catalytic converter nuts. Discard the nuts.
   c. Remove the 2 left-hand exhaust flexible pipe-to-underbody catalytic converter nuts. Discard the nuts.
   d. Separate the left-hand exhaust flexible pipe from the left-hand and underbody catalytic converters.
   e. Remove the left-hand exhaust flexible pipe. Discard the gasket.
5. Disconnect the left-hand Catalyst Monitor Sensor (CMS) electrical connector.
6. Remove the 3 left-hand catalytic converter-to-turbocharger nuts and the catalytic converter. Discard the nuts and gasket.
7. Inspect the left-hand turbocharger-to-catalytic converter studs for damage. If damaged, or if a stud comes out when removing the nut, replace the stud.

To install:

8. To install, reverse the removal procedure, noting the following:
   a. Install a new gasket and nuts.
   b. Tighten the turbocharger-to-catalytic converter studs to 18 ft. lbs. (25 Nm).
   c. Tighten the catalytic converter-to-turbocharger nuts to 30 ft. lbs. (40 Nm).
   d. Tighten the exhaust flexible pipe-to-underbody catalytic converter nuts to 30 ft. lbs. (40 Nm).
   e. Make sure the left-hand exhaust flexible pipe is straight and is approximately 25 mm (0.984 in) from all components.
   f. Alternately tighten the 2 exhaust flexible pipe-to-left-hand catalytic converter nuts to 30 ft. lbs. (40 Nm).

Right-Hand

See Figure 67.

➡Always install new fasteners and gaskets. Clean flange faces prior to new gasket installation to make sure of correct sealing.

1. Before servicing the vehicle, refer to the Precautions Section.
2. With the vehicle in NEUTRAL, position it on a hoist.
3. Remove the right-hand front wheel and tire.
4. Disconnect the right-hand Heated Oxygen Sensor (HO2S) electrical connector.
5. Detach the HO2S electrical connector retainer from the bracket.
6. Remove the left-hand exhaust flexible pipe:
   a. Remove the 4 retainers and the underbody shield.
   b. Remove the 2 left-hand exhaust flexible pipe-to-left-hand catalytic converter nuts. Discard the nuts.
   c. Remove the 2 left-hand exhaust flexible pipe-to-underbody catalytic converter nuts. Discard the nuts.
   d. Separate the left-hand exhaust flexible pipe from the left-hand and underbody catalytic converters.
   e. Remove the left-hand exhaust flexible pipe. Discard the gasket.

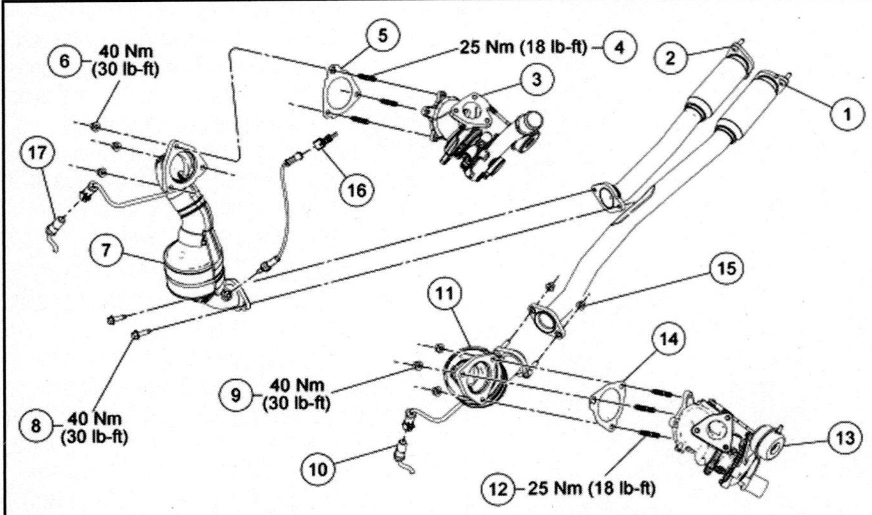

1. Left-hand exhaust flexible pipe
2. Right-hand exhaust flexible pipe
3. Right-hand turbocharger
4. Right-hand turbocharger-to-catalytic converter stud
5. Gasket
6. Right-hand catalytic converter-to-turbocharger nut
7. Right-hand catalytic converter
8. Right-hand exhaust flexible pipe-to-right-hand catalytic converter bolt
9. Left-hand catalytic converter-to-turbocharger nut
10. Left-hand Catalyst Monitor Sensor (CMS) electrical connector
11. Left-hand catalytic converter
12. Left-hand turbocharger-to-catalytic converter stud
13. Left-hand turbocharger
14. Gasket
15. Left-hand exhaust flexible pipe-to-left-hand catalytic converter nut
16. Right-hand CMS sensor electrical connector
17. Right-hand Heated Oxygen Sensor (HO2S) electrical connector (with retainer)

N0105875

Fig. 67 Catalytic Converters and Exhaust Flexible Pipes—3.5L engines

7. Remove the right-hand exhaust flexible pipes:
   a. Remove the 2 right-hand exhaust flexible pipe-to-underbody catalytic converter nuts. Discard the nuts.
   b. Remove the 2 right-hand exhaust flexible pipe-to-right-hand catalytic converter bolts. Discard the bolts.
   c. Separate the right-hand exhaust flexible pipe from the right-hand and underbody catalytic converters.
   d. Remove the right-hand exhaust flexible pipe. Discard the gaskets.
8. Disconnect the right-hand Catalyst Monitor Sensor (CMS) electrical connector.
9. Remove the 3 right-hand catalytic converter-to-turbocharger nuts and the converter. Discard the nuts and gasket.
10. Inspect the right-hand turbocharger-to-catalytic converter studs for damage. If damaged or if a stud comes out when removing the nut, replace the stud.

To install:

11. To install, reverse the removal procedure, noting the following:
   a. Prior to installation, inspect the HO2S and the CMS wiring harness for damage.
   b. Install new gaskets and nuts.
   c. Tighten the turbocharger-to-catalytic converter studs to 18 ft. lbs. (25 Nm).
   d. Tighten the catalytic converter-to-turbocharger nuts to 30 ft. lbs. (40 Nm).
   e. Tighten the exhaust flexible pipe-to-underbody catalytic converter nuts to 30 ft. lbs. (40 Nm).
   f. Tighten the exhaust flexible pipe-to-right-hand catalytic converter bolts to 30 ft. lbs. (40 Nm).

3.7L Engines

Left-Hand

See Figure 68.

➡Always install new fasteners and gaskets. Clean flange faces prior to new gasket installation to make sure of correct sealing.

1. Before servicing the vehicle, refer to the Precautions Section.
2. With the vehicle in NEUTRAL, position it on a hoist.
3. Disconnect the left-hand Catalyst Monitor Sensor (CMS) electrical connector.
4. Remove the exhaust Y-pipe:
   a. Remove the 2 exhaust Y-pipe-to-muffler and tail pipe flange nuts. Discard the nuts and gasket.
   b. Remove the 2 exhaust Y-pipe-to-left-hand catalytic converter nuts, the 2 exhaust Y-pipe-to-right-hand catalytic converter nuts and the Y-pipe. Discard the nuts and gaskets.
5. Remove the 2 catalytic converter support bracket-to-transmission bolts.
6. Remove the 4 nuts and the left-hand catalytic converter. Discard the nuts and gasket.
7. Inspect the exhaust manifold studs for damage.
8. If damaged, replace the stud, or if stud comes out when removing the nut, replace the stud.

To install:

9. To install, reverse the removal procedure, noting the following:
   a. Install new gaskets and nuts.
   b. Tighten the exhaust manifold studs to 18 ft. lbs. (25 Nm).
   c. Tighten the catalytic converter nuts to 30 ft. lbs. (40 Nm).
   d. Tighten the catalytic converter support bracket-to-transmission bolts to 35 ft. lbs. (48 Nm).
   e. Tighten the exhaust Y-pipe-to-left-hand catalytic converter nuts to 30 ft. lbs. (40 Nm).
   f. Alternately tighten the 2 exhaust Y-pipe-to-right-hand catalytic converter nuts to 30 ft. lbs. (40 Nm).
   g. Tighten the exhaust Y-pipe-to-muffler and tail pipe flange nuts to 30 ft. lbs. (40 Nm).

Right-Hand

See Figure 69.

➡Always install new fasteners and gaskets. Clean flange faces prior to new gasket installation to make sure of correct sealing.

1. Before servicing the vehicle, refer to the Precautions Section.
2. With the vehicle in NEUTRAL, position it on a hoist.
3. Remove the exhaust Y-pipe:
   a. Remove the 2 exhaust Y-pipe-to-muffler and tail pipe flange nuts. Discard the nuts and gasket.
   b. Remove the 2 exhaust Y-pipe-to-left-hand catalytic converter nuts, the 2 exhaust Y-pipe-to-right-hand catalytic converter nuts and the Y-pipe. Discard the nuts and gaskets.
4. Remove the right-hand Catalyst Monitor Sensor (CMS).
5. Remove the 2 bracket-to-right-hand catalytic converter bolts.
6. Remove the 4 nuts and the right-hand

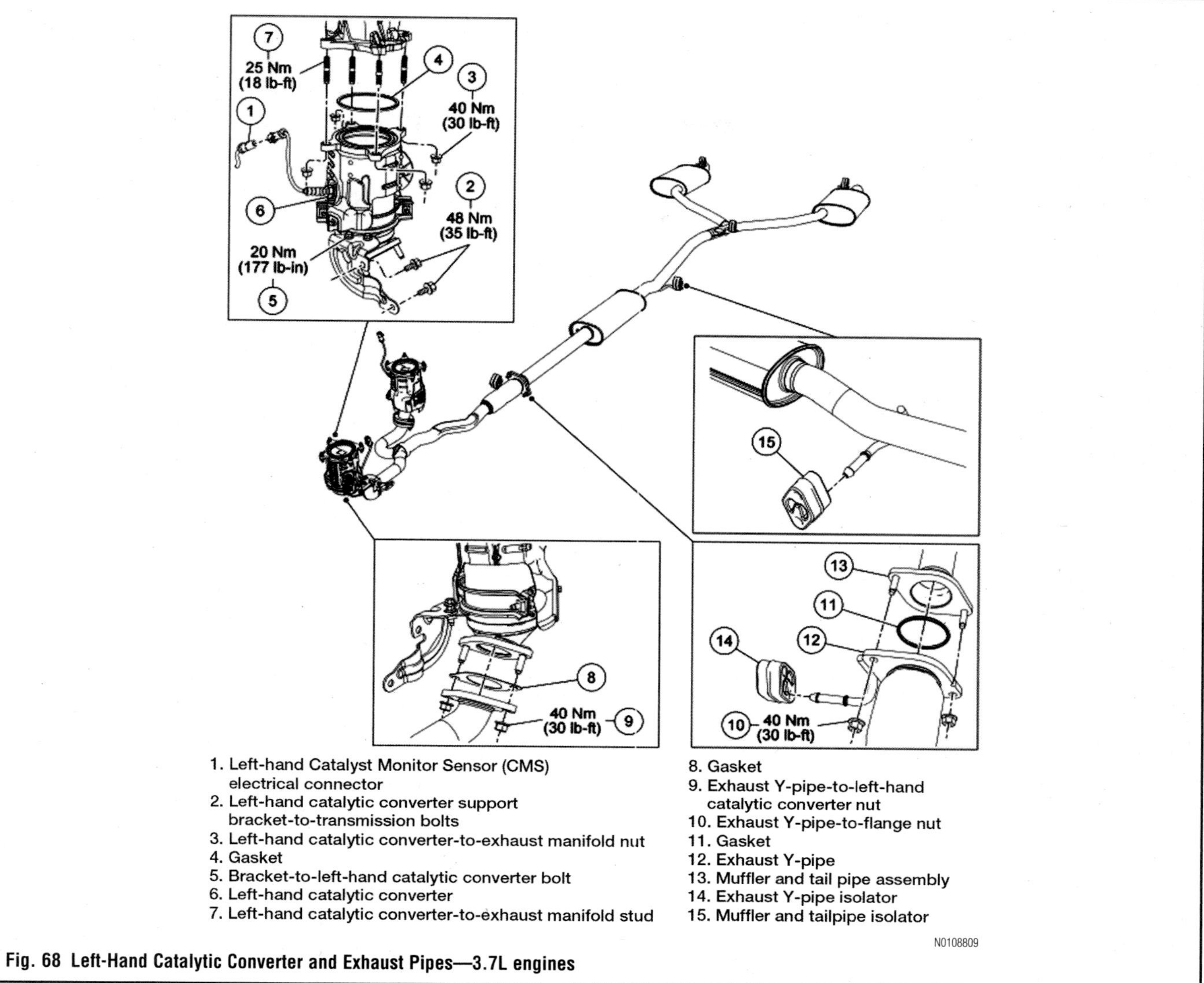

Fig. 68 Left-Hand Catalytic Converter and Exhaust Pipes—3.7L engines

catalytic converter. Discard the nuts and gasket.

7. Inspect the exhaust manifold studs for damage. If damaged, replace the stud, or if stud comes out when removing the nut, replace the stud.

To install:

8. To install, reverse the removal procedure, noting the following:
   a. Install new gaskets and nuts.
   b. Tighten the exhaust manifold studs to 18 ft. lbs. (25 Nm).
   c. Tighten the catalytic converter nuts to 30 ft. lbs. (40 Nm).
   d. Tighten the 2 bracket-to-right-hand catalytic converter bolts to 15 ft. lbs. (20 Nm).
   e. Tighten the exhaust Y-pipe-to-left-hand catalytic converter nuts to 30 ft. lbs. (40 Nm).
   f. Alternately tighten the 2 exhaust Y-pipe-to-right-hand catalytic converter nuts to 30 ft. lbs. (40 Nm).
   g. Tighten the exhaust Y-pipe-to-muffler and tail pipe flange nuts to 30 ft. lbs. (40 Nm).

CRANKSHAFT FRONT SEAL

REMOVAL & INSTALLATION

See Figures 70 and 71.

1. With the vehicle in NEUTRAL, position it on a hoist.
2. Remove the crankshaft pulley:
   a. Remove the accessory drive belt.
   b. For 3.7L engines, remove the power steering belt.
   c. Using the Strap Wrench (SST 303-D055) or equivalent tool, remove the crankshaft pulley bolt and washer. Discard the bolt.
   d. Using the 3 Jaw Puller (SST 303-D121) or equivalent tool, remove the crankshaft pulley.
3. Using the Oil Seal Remover (SST 303-409) or equivalent tool, remove and discard the crankshaft front seal.
   a. Clean all sealing surfaces with metal surface prep.

To install:

4. Apply clean engine oil to the crankshaft front seal bore in the engine front cover.
5. Using the Front Crankshaft Seal Installer and Crankshaft Vibration Damper Installer (SST 303-1251, 303-102) or equivalent tools, install a new crankshaft front seal.
6. Install the crankshaft pulley:
   a. Lubricate the crankshaft front seal inner lip with clean engine oil.
   b. Lubricate the outside diameter sealing surfaces with clean engine oil.

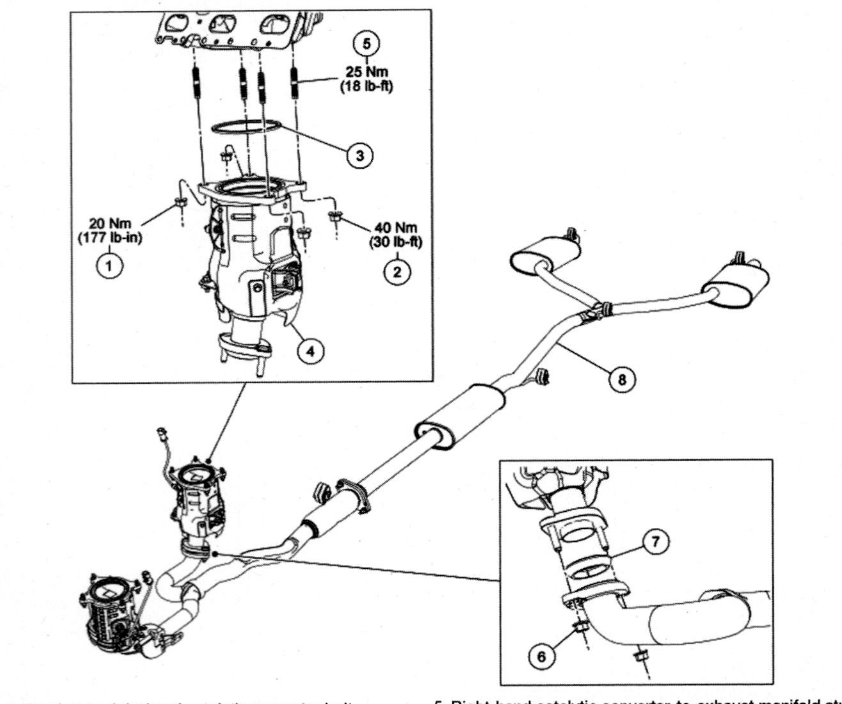

Fig. 69 Right-Hand Catalytic Converter and Exhaust Pipes—3.7L engines

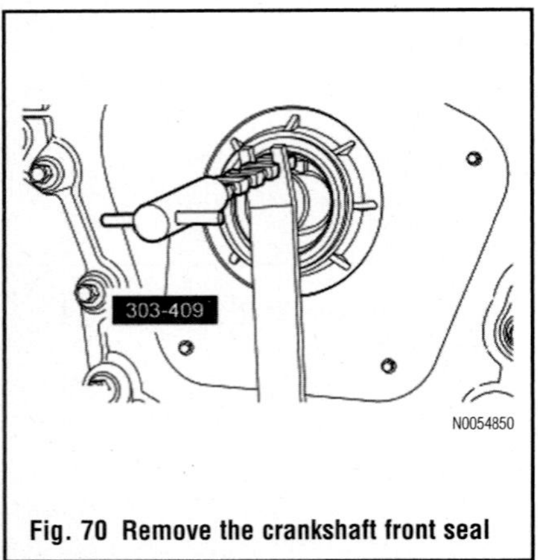

Fig. 70 Remove the crankshaft front seal

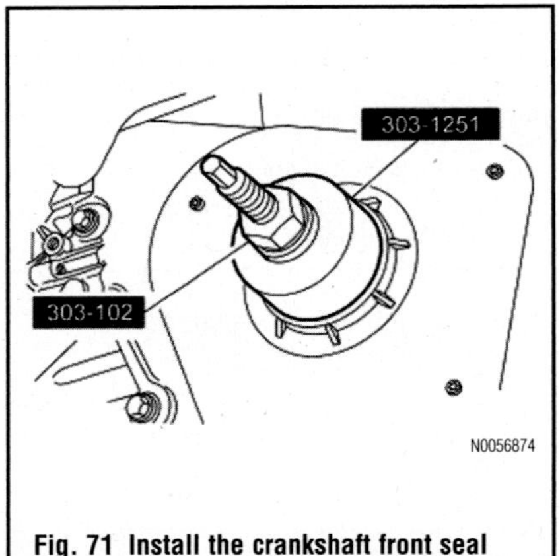

Fig. 71 Install the crankshaft front seal

c. Using the Crankshaft Vibration Damper Replacer and Front Cover Oil Seal Installer (SST 303-102, 303-335) or equivalent tools, install the crankshaft pulley.

d. Using the Strap Wrench or equivalent tool, install the crankshaft pulley washer and new bolt and tighten in 4 stages:

- Stage 1: Tighten to 89 ft. lbs. (120 Nm)
- Stage 2: Loosen one full turn
- Stage 3: Tighten to 37 ft. lbs. (50 Nm)
- Stage 4: Tighten an additional 90 degrees

e. Install the accessory drive belt.

f. For 3.7L engines, install the power steering belt.

CYLINDER HEAD

REMOVAL & INSTALLATION

3.5L Engines

Left-Hand

See Figures 72 through 74.

WARNING

During engine repair procedures, cleanliness is extremely important. Any foreign material may cause engine failure.

WARNING

Whenever turbocharger air intake system components are removed, always cover open ports to protect from debris. The turbocharger compressor vanes are susceptible to damage from even small particles. All components should be inspected and cleaned, if necessary, prior to installation or reassembly.

➡On early build engines, the timing chain rides on the inner side of the right-hand timing chain guide. Late build engines are equipped with a different design right-hand timing chain guide that requires the timing chain to ride on the outer side of the right-hand timing chain guide. For service, all replacement right-hand timing chain guides will be the late build design.

1. Remove the fuel rails.
2. Remove the left-hand camshafts.
3. Disconnect the left-hand Camshaft Position (CMP) sensor electrical connector; remove the bolt and the left-hand CMP sensor.
4. Detach the wiring harness retainer from the rear of the left-hand cylinder head.
5. Remove the coolant tube bracket-to-cylinder head nut.
6. Disconnect the alternator (generator) B+ cable and electrical connector, and remove the alternator and alternator stud.
7. Remove the 3 bolts and the left-hand exhaust manifold heat shield.

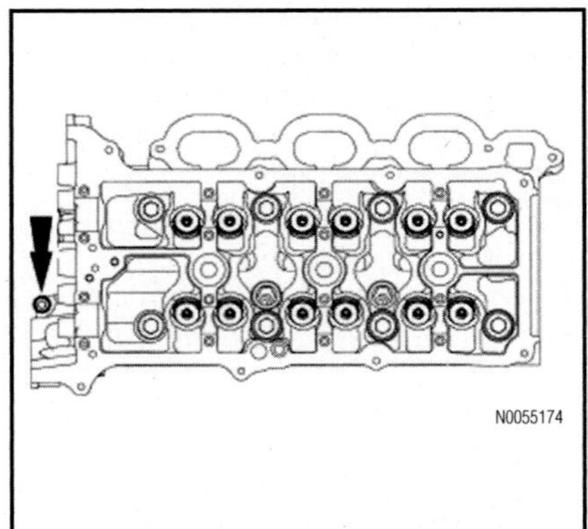

Fig. 72 Remove and discard the M6 bolt

8. Disconnect the turbocharger wastegate regulating valve hose from the left-hand turbocharger assembly.

9. Remove the 2 bolts and the left-hand turbocharger oil return tube from the turbocharger. Remove and discard the gasket.

10. Remove the left-hand oil supply tube secondary latch.

11. Using the Spring Lock Coupling Disconnect Tool, remove the left-hand oil supply tube from the quick connect fitting. Inspect and if necessary, replace the quick connect fitting.

12. Remove the 2 coolant tube banjo bolts and the left-hand turbocharger coolant tubes and sealing washers. Discard the sealing washers.

13. Remove the left-hand turbocharger oil supply tube banjo bolt; discard the sealing washer and the oil supply tube filter.

14. Remove the 2 bolts and the lower left-hand turbocharger-to-cylinder block bracket.

15. Remove the 2 bolts and the upper left-hand turbocharger bracket-to-cylinder block bracket.

16. Remove the 8 left-hand exhaust manifold nuts and the exhaust manifold and turbocharger assembly. Discard the exhaust manifold gasket and nuts. Clean and inspect the left-hand exhaust manifold. Remove and discard the 8 left-hand exhaust manifold studs.

WARNING

Do not use metal scrapers, wire brushes, power abrasive discs or other abrasive means to clean the sealing surfaces. These may cause scratches and gouges resulting in leak paths. Use a plastic scraper to clean the sealing surfaces.

17. Clean the exhaust manifold mating surface of the cylinder head with metal surface prep. Follow the directions on the packaging.

18. Remove the left-hand cylinder block drain plug. Allow coolant to drain from the cylinder block.

19. If equipped, remove the heat shield and disconnect the block heater electrical connector. Remove the block heater wiring harness from the engine.

20. Remove the right-hand cylinder block drain plug or, if equipped, the block heater. Allow coolant to drain from the cylinder block.

21. Remove the 2 bolts and the upper left-hand primary timing chain guide.

22. Remove the 2 bolts and the left-hand secondary timing chain tensioner.

23. Remove the valve tappets from the cylinder head. If the components are to be reinstalled, they must be installed in the same positions. Mark the components for installation into their original locations.

24. Inspect the valve tappets.

25. Remove and discard the M6 bolt.

WARNING

Place clean, lint-free shop towels over exposed engine cavities. Carefully remove the towels so foreign material is not dropped into the engine. Any foreign material (including any material created while cleaning gasket surfaces) that enters the oil passages or the oil pan, may cause engine failure.

WARNING

Aluminum surfaces are soft and may be scratched easily. Never place the cylinder head gasket surface, unprotected, on a bench surface.

26. Remove and discard the 8 bolts from the cylinder head.

a. Remove the cylinder head.

b. Discard the cylinder head gasket.

WARNING

Do not use metal scrapers, wire brushes, power abrasive discs or other abrasive means to clean the sealing surfaces. These tools cause scratches and gouges that make leak paths. Use a plastic scraping tool to remove all traces of the head gasket.

WARNING

Observe all warnings or cautions and follow all application directions contained on the packaging of the silicone gasket remover and the metal surface prep.

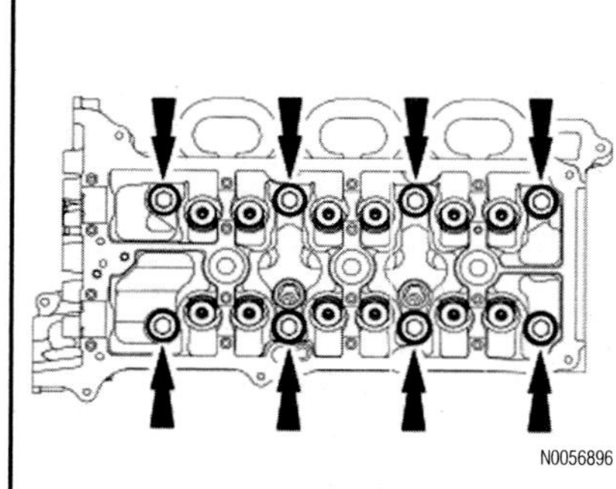

Fig. 73 Remove the cylinder head bolts

➡If there is no residual gasket material present, metal surface prep can be used to clean and prepare the surfaces.

27. Clean the cylinder head-to-cylinder block mating surfaces of both the cylinder heads and the cylinder block in the following sequence.

a. Remove any large deposits of silicone or gasket material with a plastic scraper.

b. Apply silicone gasket remover, following package directions, and allow to set for several minutes.

c. Remove the silicone gasket remover with a plastic scraper. A second application of silicone gasket remover may be required if residual traces of silicone or gasket material remain.

d. Apply metal surface prep, following package directions, to remove any remaining traces of oil or coolant and to prepare the surfaces to bond with the new gasket. Do not attempt to make the metal shiny. Some staining of the metal surfaces is normal.

28. Support the cylinder head on a bench with the head gasket side up. Check the cylinder head distortion and the cylinder block distortion.

To install:

29. Install a new gasket, the left-hand cylinder head and 8 new bolts. Tighten in the sequence shown in 5 stages:

a. Stage 1: Tighten to 15 ft. lbs. (20 Nm).

b. Stage 2: Tighten to 26 ft. lbs. (35 Nm).

c. Stage 3: Tighten 90 degrees.

d. Stage 4: Tighten 90 degrees.

e. Stage 5: Tighten 90 degrees.

30. Install the cylinder head M6 bolt. Tighten to 89 inch lbs. (10 Nm).

31. Coat the valve tappets with clean engine oil prior to installation. Install the valve tappets. The valve tappets must be installed in their original positions.

32. Install the left-hand secondary timing chain tensioner and the 2 bolts. Tighten to 89 inch lbs. (10 Nm).

33. Install the upper left-hand primary timing chain guide and the 2 bolts. Tighten to 89 inch lbs. (10 Nm).

34. Install the right-hand cylinder block drain plug or, if equipped, the block heater. Tighten to 30 ft. lbs. (40 Nm).

35. If equipped, install the block heater wiring harness onto the engine.

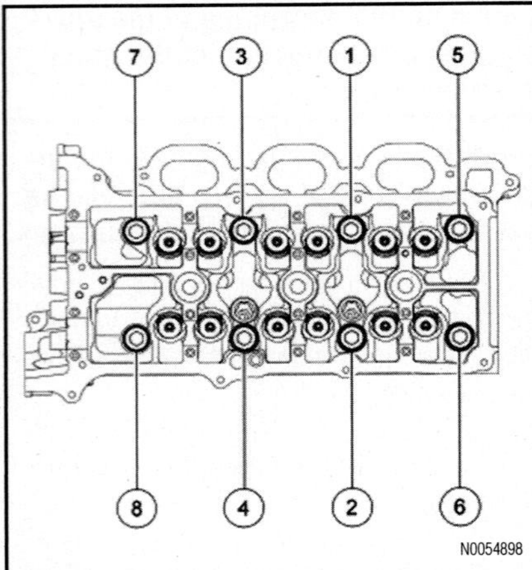

Fig. 74 Cylinder head bolt tightening sequence

a. Connect the block heater electrical connector and install the heat shield.

36. Install the left-hand cylinder block drain plug. Tighten to 15 ft. lbs. (20 Nm) plus an additional 180 degrees.

37. Install 8 new left-hand exhaust manifold studs. Tighten to 106 inch lbs. (12 Nm).

38. Install a new gasket, left-hand exhaust manifold and turbocharger assembly and 8 new nuts. Tighten the nuts in 2 stages in the sequence shown in the Exhaust Manifold Removal & Installation procedure.

39. Install the upper turbocharger bracket-to-cylinder block and the 2 bolts. Do not tighten the bolts at this time.

40. Install the lower turbocharger-to-cylinder block bracket and the 2 bolts. Do not tighten the bolts at this time.

41. The next 4 steps must be performed in order or damage to the turbocharger may occur:

a. Tighten the upper turbocharger bracket-to-turbocharger bolt. Tighten to 14 ft. lbs. (19 Nm).

b. Tighten the upper turbocharger bracket-to-cylinder block bolt. Tighten to 18 ft. lbs. (25 Nm).

c. Tighten the lower turbocharger bracket-to-turbocharger bolt. Tighten to 14 ft. lbs. (19 Nm).

d. Tighten the lower turbocharger bracket-to-cylinder block bolt. Tighten to 97 inch lbs. (11 Nm).

42. Install the oil supply tube filter, washer and bolt.

a. Install the oil supply tube filter in the oil supply tube block.

b. Slide the new washer onto the oil supply tube block.

c. Install the banjo bolt into the oil supply tube block.

43. Install the left-hand turbocharger oil supply tube and banjo bolt. Tighten the bolt to 26 ft. lbs. (35 Nm).

44. Using 2 new sealing washers, install the 2 left-hand turbocharger coolant tubes and the banjo bolts. Tighten to 27 ft. lbs. (37 Nm).

45. If necessary, install the left-hand cylinder head turbocharger oil supply quick connect fitting. Tighten to 12 ft. lbs. (16 Nm).

46. Install the left-hand oil supply tube into the quick connect fitting. Listen for audible click.

47. Install the left-hand oil supply tube secondary latch.

48. Install a new gasket, turbocharger oil return tube and the 2 bolts. Tighten to 89 inch lbs. (10 Nm).

49. Connect the turbocharger wastegate regulating valve hose to the left-hand turbocharger assembly. Make sure the turbocharger wastegate regulating valve hose does not contact the exhaust manifold heat shield.

50. Install the left-hand exhaust manifold heat shield and the 3 bolts. Tighten to 10 ft. lbs. (14 Nm).

51. Install the stud, alternator and the nut and bolt. Tighten the stud to 71 inch lbs. (8 Nm), and the nut and bolt to 35 ft. lbs. (47 Nm). Connect the alternator electrical connector. Connect the alternator B+ cable and install the nut. Tighten to 13 ft. lbs. (17 Nm).

52. Install the left-hand coolant tube bracket-to-cylinder head nut. Tighten to 89 inch lbs. (10 Nm).

53. Attach the pin-type wire harness retainer to the rear of left-hand cylinder head.

54. Install the left-hand Camshaft Position (CMP) sensor and the bolt. Tighten to 89 inch lbs. (10 Nm). Connect the CMP sensor electrical connector.

55. Install the left-hand camshafts.

56. Install the fuel rails.

Right-Hand

See Figures 75 through 77.

⁂ WARNING

During engine repair procedures, cleanliness is extremely important. Any foreign material, including any material created while cleaning gasket surfaces that enters the oil passages, coolant passages or the oil pan, may cause engine failure.

⁂ WARNING

Whenever turbocharger air intake system components are removed, always cover open ports to protect from debris. The turbocharger compressor vanes are susceptible to damage from even small particles. All components should be inspected and cleaned, if necessary, prior to installation or reassembly.

➡On early build engines, the timing chain rides on the inner side of the right-hand timing chain guide. Late build engines are equipped with a different design right-hand timing chain guide that requires the timing chain to ride on the outer side of the right-hand timing chain guide. For service, all replacement right-hand timing chain guides will be the late build design.

1. Remove the fuel rails.
2. Remove the right-hand camshafts.
3. Disconnect the right-hand Camshaft Position (CMP) sensor electrical connector.
4. Remove the bolt and the right-hand CMP sensor.
5. Remove the bolt and the ground wire.
6. Remove the bolt and the radio capacitor from the right-hand cylinder head.
7. Disconnect the Cylinder Head Temperature (CHT) sensor electrical connector from the rear of the right-hand cylinder head.
8. Remove the 5 bolts and the 2 upper right-hand exhaust manifold heat shields.
9. Disconnect the turbocharger wastegate regulating valve hose from the right-hand turbocharger assembly.
10. Remove the 2 bolts and the turbocharger oil return tube from the right-hand turbocharger. Remove and discard the gasket.
11. Remove the oil supply tube secondary latch.
12. Using the Spring Lock Coupling Disconnect Tool, remove the right-hand oil supply tube from the quick connect fitting. Inspect and if necessary, replace the quick connect fitting.
13. Remove the 2 coolant tube banjo bolts and the right-hand turbocharger coolant tubes and sealing washers. Discard the sealing washers.
14. Remove the coolant tube bracket-to-cylinder head bolt.
15. Remove the 3 bolts and the upper turbocharger-to-cylinder block bracket.
16. Remove the 3 exhaust manifold-to-turbocharger bolts and the turbocharger assembly. Discard the gasket and bolts.

17. Remove the right-hand turbocharger oil supply tube banjo bolt; discard the sealing washer and the oil supply tube filter.

18. Remove the 8 nuts and the right-hand exhaust manifold. Discard the nuts and exhaust manifold gaskets. Clean and inspect the right-hand exhaust manifold. Remove and discard the 8 right-hand exhaust manifold studs.

WARNING

Do not use metal scrapers, wire brushes, power abrasive discs or other abrasive means to clean the sealing surfaces. These may cause scratches and gouges resulting in leak paths. Use a plastic scraper to clean the sealing surfaces.

19. Clean the exhaust manifold mating surface of the cylinder head with metal surface prep. Follow the directions on the packaging.

20. Remove the left-hand cylinder block drain plug. Allow coolant to drain from the cylinder block.

21. If equipped, remove the heat shield and disconnect the block heater electrical connector. Remove the block heater wiring harness from the engine.

22. Remove the right-hand cylinder block drain plug or, if equipped, the block heater. Allow coolant to drain from the cylinder block.

23. Remove the 2 bolts and the right-hand primary timing chain guide.

24. Remove the bolts and the right-hand secondary timing chain tensioner.

25. Remove the 2 bolts and the right-hand engine lifting eye.

26. Remove the valve tappets from the cylinder head. If the components are to be reinstalled, they must be installed in the same positions. Mark the components for installation into their original locations.

27. Inspect the valve tappets.

28. Remove and discard the M6 bolt.

WARNING

Place clean, lint-free shop towels over exposed engine cavities. Carefully remove the towels so foreign material is not dropped into the engine. Aluminum surfaces are soft and may be scratched easily. Never place the cylinder head gasket surface, unprotected, on a bench surface.

29. Remove and discard the 8 bolts from the cylinder head.

a. Remove the cylinder head.

b. Discard the cylinder head gasket.

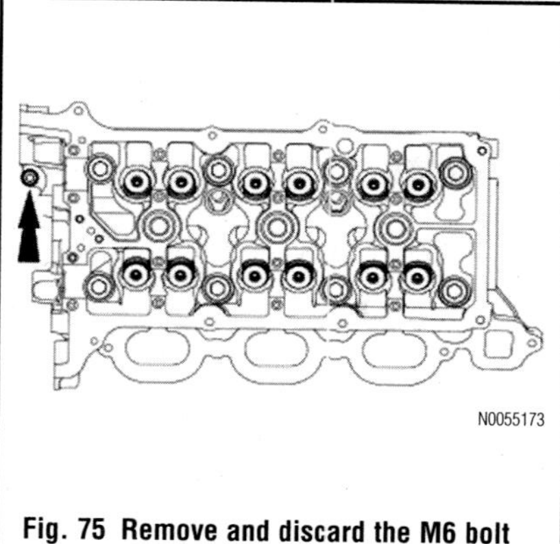

Fig. 75 Remove and discard the M6 bolt

WARNING

Do not use metal scrapers, wire brushes, power abrasive discs or other abrasive means to clean the sealing surfaces. These tools cause scratches and gouges that make leak paths. Use a plastic scraping tool to remove all traces of the head gasket.

WARNING

Observe all warnings or cautions and follow all application directions contained on the packaging of the silicone gasket remover and the metal surface prep.

➡If there is no residual gasket material present, metal surface prep can be used to clean and prepare the surfaces.

30. Clean the cylinder head-to-cylinder block mating surfaces of both the cylinder heads and the cylinder block in the following sequence:

a. Remove any large deposits of silicone or gasket material with a plastic scraper.

b. Apply silicone gasket remover, following package directions, and allow to set for several minutes.

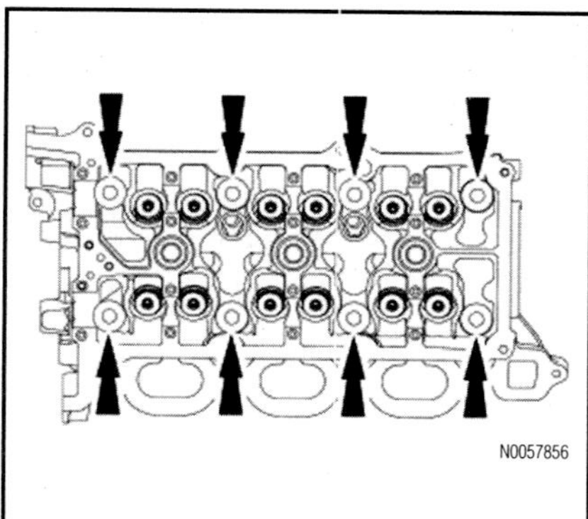

Fig. 76 Remove the cylinder head bolts

c. Remove the silicone gasket remover with a plastic scraper. A second application of silicone gasket remover may be required if residual traces of silicone or gasket material remain.

d. Apply metal surface prep, following package directions, to remove any remaining traces of oil or coolant and to prepare the surfaces to bond with the new gasket. Do not attempt to make the metal shiny. Some staining of the metal surfaces is normal.

31. Support the cylinder head on a bench with the head gasket side up. Check the cylinder head distortion and the cylinder block distortion.

To install:

32. Install a new gasket, the right-hand cylinder head and 8 new bolts. Tighten in the sequence shown in 5 stages:

a. Stage 1: Tighten to 15 ft. lbs. (20 Nm).

b. Stage 2: Tighten to 26 ft. lbs. (35 Nm).

c. Stage 3: Tighten 90 degrees.

d. Stage 4: Tighten 90 degrees.

e. Stage 5: Tighten 90 degrees.

33. Install the cylinder head M6 bolt. Tighten to 89 inch lbs. (10 Nm).

34. Coat the valve tappets with clean engine oil prior to installation. Install the valve tappets. The valve tappets must be installed in their original positions.

35. Install the right-hand engine lifting eye and the 2 bolts. Tighten to 18 ft. lbs. (24 Nm).

36. Install the right-hand secondary timing chain tensioner and the 2 bolts. Tighten to 89 inch lbs. (10 Nm).

37. Install the right-hand primary timing chain guide and the 2 bolts. Tighten to 89 inch lbs. (10 Nm).

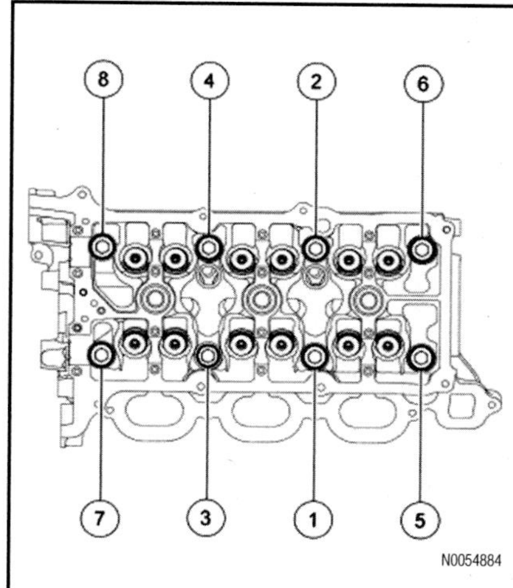

Fig. 77 Cylinder head bolt tightening sequence

38. Install the right-hand cylinder block drain plug or, if equipped, the block heater. Tighten to 30 ft. lbs. (40 Nm).

39. If equipped, install the block heater wiring harness onto the engine. Connect the block heater electrical connector and install the heat shield.

40. Install the left-hand cylinder block drain plug. Tighten to 15 ft. lbs. (20 Nm) plus an additional 180 degrees.

41. Install 8 new right-hand exhaust manifold studs. Tighten to 106 inch lbs. (12 Nm). Install a new gasket, right-hand exhaust manifold and 8 new nuts. Tighten in 2 stages in the sequence shown in the Exhaust Manifold Removal & Installation procedure.

42. Install the oil supply tube filter, washer and bolt. Install a new oil supply tube filter in the oil supply tube block, slide the new washer onto the oil supply tube block, and install the banjo bolt into the oil supply tube block.

43. Install the right-hand turbocharger oil supply tube. Tighten the bolt to 26 ft. lbs. (35 Nm).

44. Install a new gasket, the turbocharger and the 3 new exhaust manifold-to-turbocharger bolts. Tighten to 33 ft. lbs. (45 Nm).

45. Install the upper turbocharger-to-cylinder block bracket and the 3 bolts and position the bracket as far clockwise as possible and tighten the bolts in the following sequence:

a. Tighten the lower bolt to 19 ft. lbs. (26 Nm).

b. Tighten the upper bolt to 19 ft. lbs. (26 Nm).

c. Tighten the turbocharger bolt to 14 ft. lbs. (19 Nm).

46. Using 2 new sealing washers, install the 2 right-hand turbocharger coolant tubes and banjo bolts. Tighten to 27 ft. lbs. (37 Nm).

47. Install the coolant tube bracket-to-cylinder head bolt. Tighten to 89 inch lbs. (10 Nm).

48. If necessary, install the right-hand cylinder head turbocharger oil supply quick connect fitting. Tighten to 12 ft. lbs. (16 Nm).

49. Install the right-hand oil supply tube into the quick connect fitting. Listen for audible click

50. Install the oil supply tube secondary latch.

51. Install a new gasket and the right-hand turbocharger oil return tube and the 2 bolts. Tighten to 89 inch lbs. (10 Nm).

52. Connect the turbocharger wastegate regulating valve hose to the right-hand turbocharger assembly. Make sure the turbocharger wastegate regulating valve hose does not contact the exhaust manifold heat shield.

53. Install the 2 upper right-hand exhaust manifold heat shield and the 5 bolts. Make sure the heat shield does not contact the wastegate arm. Tighten to 10 ft. lbs. (14 Nm).

54. Connect the Cylinder Head Temperature (CHT) sensor electrical connector to the rear of the right-hand cylinder head.

55. Install the radio capacitor and bolt to the right-hand cylinder head. Tighten to 89 inch lbs. (10 Nm).

56. Install the ground wire and the bolt. Tighten to 89 inch lbs. (10 Nm).

57. Install the right-hand Camshaft Position (CMP) sensor and the bolt. Tighten to 89 inch lbs. (10 Nm).

58. Connect the right-hand CMP sensor electrical connector.

59. Install the right-hand camshafts.

60. Install the fuel rails.

3.7L Engines

Left-Hand

See Figures 78 through 80.

⁂ WARNING

During engine repair procedures, cleanliness is extremely important. Any foreign material, including any material created while cleaning gasket surfaces that enters the oil passages, coolant passages or the oil pan, may cause engine failure.

1. Remove the left-hand camshafts.

2. Disconnect the 6 fuel injector electrical connectors.

3. Disconnect the Cylinder Head Temperature (CHT) sensor electrical connector.

4. Disconnect the left-hand Camshaft Position (CMP) sensor electrical connector, remove the bolt and the left-hand CMP sensor.

5. Disconnect the left-hand Heated Oxygen Sensor (HO2S) electrical connector.

6. Disconnect the left-hand Catalyst Monitor Sensor (CMS) electrical connector.

7. Detach the wiring harness retainer from the rear of the left-hand cylinder head.

8. Disconnect the alternator (generator) B+ cable and electrical connector, and remove the alternator and alternator stud.

9. Disconnect the Engine Oil Pressure (EOP) switch electrical connector and the wiring harness pin-type retainer. Remove the wiring harness from the engine.

10. Remove the 2 left-hand catalytic converter bracket bolts. Remove the 4 nuts and the left-hand catalytic converter. Discard the nuts and the gasket.

11. Remove the 3 bolts and the left-hand exhaust manifold heat shield.

12. Remove the 6 nuts and the left-hand exhaust manifold. Discard the nuts and the exhaust manifold gasket. Clean and inspect the left-hand exhaust manifold. Remove and discard the 6 left-hand exhaust manifold studs.

13. Remove the left-hand cylinder block drain plug. Allow coolant to drain from the cylinder block.

14. Remove the 4 nuts and the right-hand catalytic converter. Discard the nuts and gasket.

15. If equipped, remove the heat shield and disconnect the block heater electrical connector. Remove the block heater wiring harness from the engine.

16. Remove the right-hand cylinder block drain plug or, if equipped, the block heater. Allow coolant to drain from the cylinder block.

17. Remove the coolant bypass hose from the thermostat housing.

18. Remove the 4 bolts and the fuel rail and injectors as an assembly.

19. Remove the 3 thermostat housing-to-lower intake manifold bolts. Remove the thermostat housing and discard the gasket and O-ring seal.

20. Remove the 10 bolts and the lower intake manifold. Discard the gaskets. If the engine is repaired or replaced because of upper engine failure, typically including valve or piston damage, check the intake manifold for metal debris. If metal debris is found, install a new intake manifold.

21. Remove the 2 bolts and the upper left-hand primary timing chain guide.

22. Remove the 2 bolts and the left-hand secondary timing chain tensioner.

23. Remove the valve tappets from the cylinder head. If the components are to be reinstalled, they must be installed in the same positions. Mark the components for installation into their original locations.

24. Inspect the valve tappets.

25. Remove and discard the M6 bolt.

⁂ WARNING

Place clean, lint-free shop towels over exposed engine cavities. Carefully remove the towels so foreign material is not dropped into the engine. Aluminum surfaces are soft and may be scratched easily. Never place the cylinder head gasket surface, unprotected, on a bench surface.

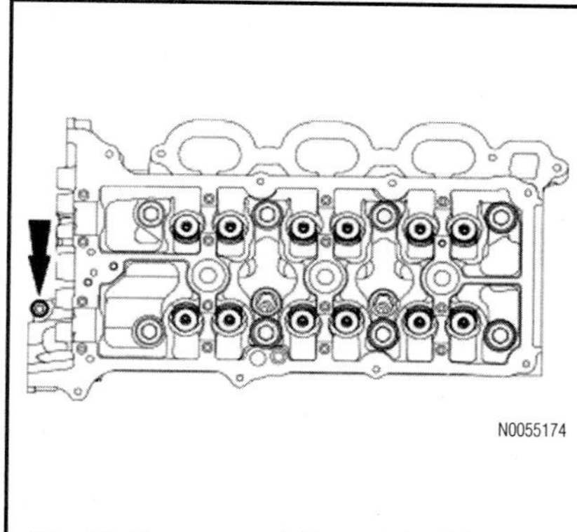

Fig. 78 Remove and discard the M6 bolt

26. Remove and discard the 8 bolts from the cylinder head.
   a. Remove the cylinder head.
   b. Discard the cylinder head gasket.

WARNING

Do not use metal scrapers, wire brushes, power abrasive discs or other abrasive means to clean the sealing surfaces. These tools cause scratches and gouges that make leak paths. Use a plastic scraping tool to remove all traces of the head gasket.

WARNING

Observe all warnings or cautions and follow all application directions contained on the packaging of the silicone gasket remover and the metal surface prep.

➡If there is no residual gasket material present, metal surface prep can be used to clean and prepare the surfaces.

27. Clean the cylinder head-to-cylinder block mating surfaces of both the cylinder heads and the cylinder block in the following sequence:
   a. Remove any large deposits of silicone or gasket material with a plastic scraper.
   b. Apply silicone gasket remover, following package directions, and allow to set for several minutes.
   c. Remove the silicone gasket remover with a plastic scraper. A second application of silicone gasket remover may be required if residual traces of silicone or gasket material remain.
   d. Apply metal surface prep, following package directions, to remove any remaining traces of oil or coolant and to prepare the surfaces to bond with the new gasket. Do not attempt to make the metal shiny. Some staining of the metal surfaces is normal.

28. Support the cylinder head on a bench with the head gasket side up. Check the cylinder head distortion and the cylinder block distortion.

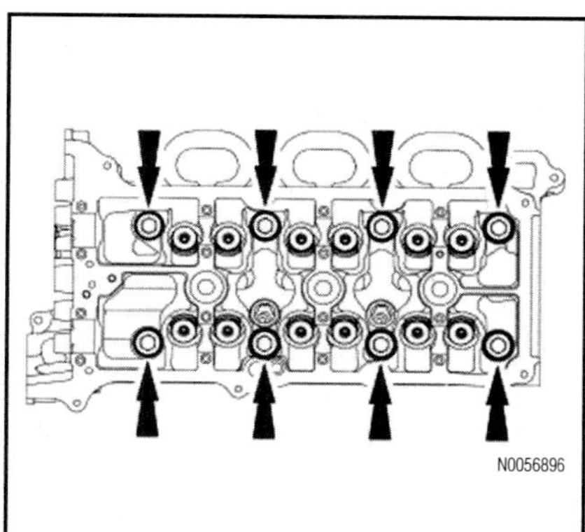

Fig. 79 Remove the cylinder head bolts

To install:

29. Install a new gasket, the left-hand cylinder head and 8 new bolts. Tighten in the sequence shown in 5 stages:
   a. Stage 1: Tighten to 15 ft. lbs. (20 Nm).
   b. Stage 2: Tighten to 26 ft. lbs. (35 Nm).
   c. Stage 3: Tighten 90 degrees.
   d. Stage 4: Tighten 90 degrees.
   e. Stage 5: Tighten 90 degrees.

30. Install the M6 bolt. Tighten to 89 inch lbs. (10 Nm).

31. Coat the valve tappets with clean engine oil prior to installation. Install the valve tappets. The valve tappets must be installed in their original positions.

32. Install the left-hand secondary timing chain tensioner and the 2 bolts. Tighten to 89 inch lbs. (10 Nm).

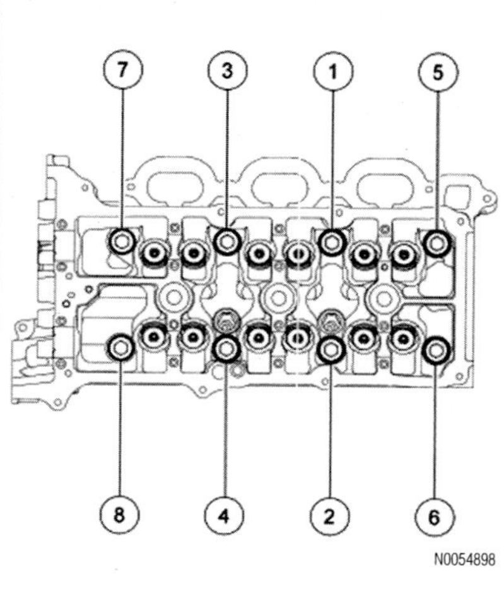

Fig. 80 Cylinder head bolt tightening sequence

33. Install the upper left-hand primary timing chain guide and the 2 bolts. Tighten to 89 inch lbs. (10 Nm).

34. Using new gaskets, install the lower intake manifold and the 10 bolts. Tighten in the sequence shown in the Intake Manifold Removal & Installation procedure to 89 inch lbs. (10 Nm).

35. Using a new gasket and O-ring seal, install the thermostat housing and the 3 bolts. Tighten to 89 inch lbs. (10 Nm).

36. Install new fuel injector O-ring seals. Use O-ring seals that are made of special fuel-resistant material. Do not reuse the O-ring seals. The upper and lower O-ring seals are not interchangeable.
   a. Remove the retaining clips and separate the fuel injectors from the fuel rail.
   b. Remove and discard the O-ring seals.
   c. Install new O-ring seals and lubricate with clean engine oil.
   d. Install the fuel injectors and the retaining clips onto the fuel rail.

37. Install the fuel rail and injectors as an assembly and install the 4 bolts. Tighten to 89 inch lbs. (10 Nm).

38. Install the coolant bypass hose to the thermostat housing.

39. Install the right-hand cylinder block drain plug or, if equipped, the block heater. Tighten to 30 ft. lbs. (40 Nm).

40. If equipped, install the block heater wiring harness onto the engine. Connect the block heater electrical connector and install the heat shield.

41. Using a new gasket, install the right-hand catalytic converter and 4 new nuts. Tighten to 30 ft. lbs. (40 Nm).

42. Install the left-hand cylinder block drain plug. Tighten to 15 ft. lbs. (20 Nm) plus an additional 180 degrees.

43. Install 6 new left-hand exhaust manifold studs. Tighten to 106 inch lbs. (12 Nm). Using a new gasket, install the left-hand exhaust manifold and 6 new nuts. Tighten in 2 stages in the sequence shown in the Exhaust Manifold Removal & Installation procedure.

44. Install the left-hand exhaust manifold heat shield and the 3 bolts. Tighten to 89 inch lbs. (10 Nm).

45. Using a new gasket, install the left-hand catalytic converter and 4 new nuts. Tighten to 30 ft. lbs. (40 Nm). Install the left-hand catalytic converter bracket bolts. Tighten to 15 ft. lbs. (20 Nm).

46. Attach the Engine Oil Pressure (EOP) switch wiring harness pin-type retainer.

47. Install the stud, alternator and the nut and bolt. Tighten the stud to 106 inch

lbs. (12 Nm); tighten the nut and bolt to 35 ft. lbs. (48 Nm). Connect the alternator electrical connector. Connect the alternator B+ cable and install the nut. Tighten to 13 ft. lbs. (17 Nm).

48. Attach the pin-type wire harness retainer to the rear of left-hand cylinder head.

49. Connect the left-hand Catalyst Monitor Sensor (CMS) electrical connector.

50. Connect the left-hand Heated Oxygen Sensor (HO2S) electrical connector.

51. Install the left-hand Camshaft Position (CMP) sensor and the bolt. Tighten to 89 inch lbs. (10 Nm). Connect the left-hand CMP sensor electrical connector.

52. Connect the Cylinder Head Temperature (CHT) sensor electrical connector.

53. Connect the 6 fuel injector electrical connectors.

54. Install the left-hand camshafts.

Right-Hand

See Figures 81 through 83.

WARNING

During engine repair procedures, cleanliness is extremely important. Any foreign material, including any material created while cleaning gasket surfaces that enters the oil passages, coolant passages or the oil pan, may cause engine failure.

➡On early build engines, the timing chain rides on the inner side of the right-hand timing chain guide. Late build engines are equipped with a different design right-hand timing chain guide that requires the timing chain to ride on the outer side of the right-hand timing chain guide. For service, all replacement right-hand timing chain guides will be the late build design.

1. Remove the right-hand camshafts.
2. Disconnect the right-hand Heated Oxygen Sensor (HO2S) electrical connector.
3. Disconnect the right-hand Camshaft Position (CMP) sensor electrical connector. Remove the bolt and the right-hand CMP sensor.
4. Remove the bolt and the Power Steering Pressure (PSP) tube bracket from the right-hand cylinder head.
5. Remove the bolt and the ground wire.
6. Disconnect the 6 fuel injector electrical connectors.
7. Disconnect the Cylinder Head Temperature (CHT) sensor electrical connector.
8. Disconnect the left-hand Catalyst Monitor Sensor (CMS) electrical connector.
9. Remove the 2 left-hand catalytic converter bracket bolts. Remove the 4 nuts and the left-hand catalytic converter. Discard the nuts and the gasket.
10. Remove the left-hand cylinder block drain plug. Allow coolant to drain from the cylinder block.
11. Remove the 4 nuts and the right-hand catalytic converter. Discard the nuts and gasket.
12. If equipped, remove the heat shield and disconnect the block heater electrical connector.
    a. Remove the block heater wiring harness from the engine.
13. Remove the right-hand cylinder block drain plug or, if equipped, the block heater. Allow coolant to drain from the cylinder block.
14. Remove the 3 bolts and the right-hand exhaust manifold heat shield.
15. Remove the 6 nuts and the right-hand exhaust manifold. Discard the nuts and exhaust manifold gaskets. Clean and inspect the right-hand exhaust manifold. Remove and discard the 6 right-hand exhaust manifold studs.
16. Remove the 2 bolts and the right-hand primary timing chain guide.
17. Remove the bolts and the right-hand secondary timing chain tensioner.
18. Remove the 2 bolts and the engine lifting eye.
19. Remove the bolt and the upper intake manifold support bracket. Matchmark the location of the bracket on the cylinder head for installation.
20. Remove the coolant bypass hose from the thermostat housing.
21. Remove the 4 bolts and the fuel rail and injectors as an assembly.
22. Remove the 3 thermostat housing-to-lower intake manifold bolts.
23. Remove the thermostat housing and discard the gasket and O-ring seal.
24. Remove the 10 bolts and the lower intake manifold. Discard the gaskets. If the engine is repaired or replaced because of upper engine failure, typically including valve or piston damage, check the intake manifold for metal debris. If metal debris if found, install a new intake manifold.
25. Disconnect and remove the CHT sensor jumper harness.
26. Remove the valve tappets from the cylinder head. If the components are to be reinstalled, they must be installed in the same positions. Mark the components for installation into their original locations.
27. Inspect the valve tappets.
28. Remove and discard the M6 bolt.

WARNING

Place clean, lint-free shop towels over exposed engine cavities. Carefully remove the towels so foreign material is not dropped into the engine. Aluminum surfaces are soft and may be scratched easily. Never place the cylinder head gasket surface, unprotected, on a bench surface.

29. Remove and discard the 8 bolts from the cylinder head.
    a. Remove the cylinder head.
    b. Discard the cylinder head gasket.

WARNING

Do not use metal scrapers, wire brushes, power abrasive discs or other abrasive means to clean the sealing surfaces. These tools cause scratches and gouges that make leak paths. Use a plastic scraping tool to remove all traces of the head gasket.

WARNING

Observe all warnings or cautions and follow all application directions con-

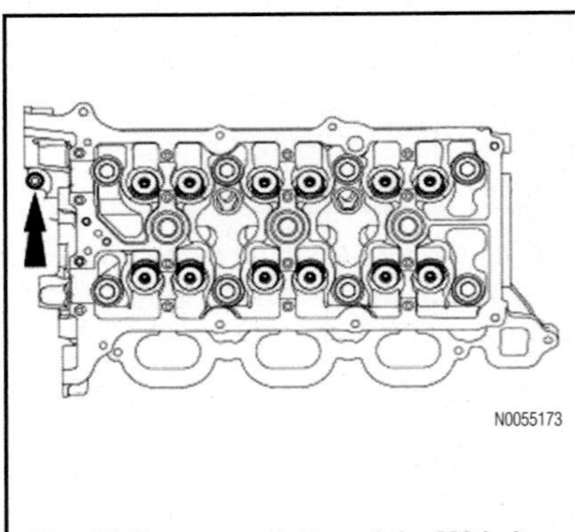

Fig. 81 Remove and discard the M6 bolt

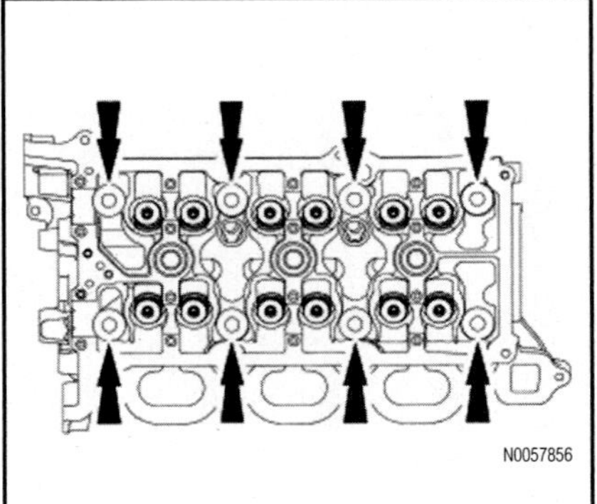

Fig. 82 Remove the cylinder head bolts

tained on the packaging of the silicone gasket remover and the metal surface prep.

➡If there is no residual gasket material present, metal surface prep can be used to clean and prepare the surfaces.

30. Clean the cylinder head-to-cylinder block mating surfaces of both the cylinder heads and the cylinder block in the following sequence.
    a. Remove any large deposits of silicone or gasket material with a plastic scraper.
    b. Apply silicone gasket remover, following package directions, and allow to set for several minutes.
    c. Remove the silicone gasket remover with a plastic scraper. A second application of silicone gasket remover may be required if residual traces of silicone or gasket material remain.
    d. Apply metal surface prep, following package directions, to remove any remaining traces of oil or coolant and to prepare the surfaces to bond with the new gasket. Do not attempt to make the metal shiny. Some staining of the metal surfaces is normal.
    e. Support the cylinder head on a bench with the head gasket side up. Check the cylinder head distortion and the cylinder block distortion.

To install:

31. Install a new gasket, the right-hand cylinder head and 8 new bolts. Tighten in the sequence shown in 5 stages:
    a. Stage 1: Tighten to 15 ft. lbs. (20 Nm).
    b. Stage 2: Tighten to 26 ft. lbs. (35 Nm).
    c. Stage 3: Tighten 90 degrees.
    d. Stage 4: Tighten 90 degrees.
    e. Stage 5: Tighten 90 degrees.
32. Install the M6 bolt. Tighten to 89 inch lbs. (10 Nm).
33. Coat the valve tappets with clean engine oil prior to installation. Install the valve tappets. The valve tappets must be installed in their original positions.
34. Install and connect the Cylinder Head Temperature (CHT) sensor jumper harness.
35. Using new gaskets, install the lower intake manifold and the 10 bolts. Tighten in the sequence shown in the Intake Manifold Removal & Installation procedure to 89 inch lbs. (10 Nm).
36. Using a new gasket and O-ring seal, install the thermostat housing and the 3 bolts. Tighten to 89 inch lbs. (10 Nm).

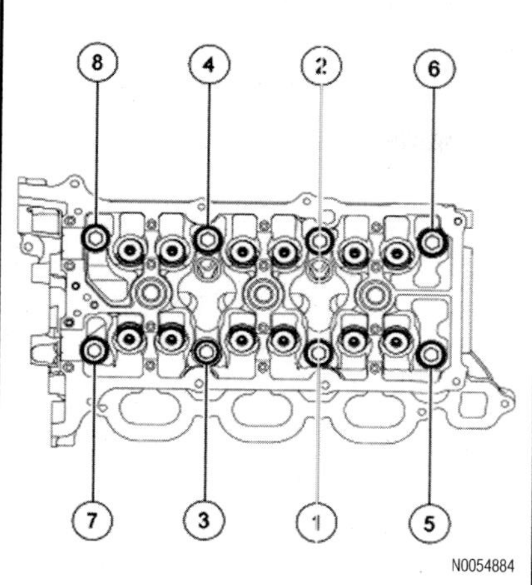

Fig. 83 Cylinder head bolt tightening sequence

37. Install new fuel injector O-ring seals. Use O-ring seals that are made of special fuel-resistant material. Do not reuse the O-ring seals. The upper and lower O-ring seals are not interchangeable.
    a. Remove the retaining clips and separate the fuel injectors from the fuel rail.
    b. Remove and discard the O-ring seals.
    c. Install new O-ring seals and lubricate with clean engine oil.
    d. Install the fuel injectors and the retaining clips onto the fuel rail.
38. Install the fuel rail and injectors as an assembly and install the 4 bolts. Tighten to 89 inch lbs. (10 Nm).
39. Install the coolant bypass hose to the thermostat housing.
40. Install the upper intake manifold support bracket and the bolt. Align the bracket with the matchmarks made during removal. Tighten to 89 inch lbs. (10 Nm).
41. Install the engine lifting eye and the 2 bolts. Tighten to 18 ft. lbs. (24 Nm).
42. Install the right-hand secondary timing chain tensioner and the 2 bolts. Tighten to 89 inch lbs. (10 Nm).
43. Install the right-hand primary timing chain guide and the 2 bolts. Tighten to 89 inch lbs. (10 Nm).
44. Install 6 new right-hand exhaust manifold studs. Tighten to 106 inch lbs. (12 Nm). Using a new gasket, install the right-hand exhaust manifold and 6 new nuts. Tighten in 2 stages in the sequence shown in the Exhaust Manifold Removal & Installation procedure.
45. Install the right-hand exhaust manifold heat shield and the 3 bolts. Tighten to 89 inch lbs. (10 Nm).
46. Install the right-hand cylinder block drain plug or, if equipped, the block heater. Tighten to 30 ft. lbs. (40 Nm).
47. If equipped, install the block heater wiring harness onto the engine. Connect the block heater electrical connector and install the heat shield.
48. Using a new gasket, install the right-hand catalytic converter and 4 new nuts. Tighten to 30 ft. lbs. (40 Nm).
49. Install the left-hand cylinder block drain plug. Tighten to 15 ft. lbs. (20 Nm) plus an additional 180 degrees.
50. Using a new gasket, install the left-hand catalytic converter and 4 new nuts. Tighten to 30 ft. lbs. (40 Nm). Install the 2 left-hand catalytic converter bracket bolts. Tighten to 15 ft. lbs. (20 Nm).
51. Connect the left-hand Catalyst Monitor Sensor (CMS) electrical connector.
52. Connect the CHT sensor electrical connector.
53. Connect the 6 fuel injector electrical connectors.
54. Install the ground wire and the bolt. Tighten to 89 inch lbs. (10 Nm).
55. Install the Power Steering Pressure (PSP) tube bracket and the bolt to the right-hand cylinder head. Tighten to 89 inch lbs. (10 Nm).
56. Install the right-hand Camshaft Position (CMP) sensor and tighten the bolt to 89 inch lbs. (10 Nm). Connect the CMP sensor electrical connector.
57. Connect the right-hand Heated Oxygen Sensor (HO2S) electrical connector.
58. Install the right-hand camshafts.

EXHAUST MANIFOLD

REMOVAL & INSTALLATION

3.5L Engines

Left-Hand

See Figures 84 and 85.

⁂ WARNING

Whenever turbocharger air intake system components are removed, always cover open ports to protect from debris. It is important that no foreign material enter the system. The turbocharger compressor vanes are susceptible to damage from even small particles. All components should be inspected and cleaned, if necessary, prior to installation or reassembly.

1. Before servicing the vehicle, refer to the Precautions Section.

2. Remove the 2 top left-hand exhaust manifold heat shield bolts.

3. Remove the left-hand catalytic converter.

4. Remove the bottom bolt and the left-hand exhaust manifold heat shield.

5. Remove the 2 bolts and the left-hand upper turbocharger bracket.

6. Loosen the 2 bolts for the left-hand lower turbocharger bracket.

7. Remove the 3 left-hand turbocharger-to-exhaust manifold bolts. Discard the gasket.

8. Remove the 5 top left-hand exhaust manifold nuts. Discard the nuts.

9. Remove the 3 bottom nuts and the left-hand exhaust manifold. Discard the nuts and gasket.

10. Clean and inspect the left-hand exhaust manifold.

11. Remove and discard the 8 left-hand exhaust manifold studs.

12. Clean the exhaust manifold mating surface of the cylinder head with metal surface prep. Follow the directions on the packaging. Do not use metal scrapers, wire brushes, power abrasive discs or other abrasive means to clean the sealing surfaces. Use a plastic scraper to clean the sealing surfaces.

To install:

13. Install 8 new left-hand exhaust manifold studs. Tighten to 106 inch lbs. (12 Nm).

14. Install a new gasket, left-hand exhaust manifold and 8 new nuts. Tighten in 2 stages in the sequence shown. Failure to tighten the exhaust manifold nuts to specification a second time will cause the exhaust manifold to develop an exhaust leak:

- Stage 1: Tighten to 11 ft. lbs. (15 Nm)
- Stage 2: Tighten to 15 ft. lbs. (20 Nm)

15. Install a new gasket and the 3 turbocharger-to-exhaust manifold bolts. Tighten to 33 ft. lbs. (45 Nm).

16. Install the upper turbocharger bracket and the 2 bolts. Do not tighten the bolts at this time.

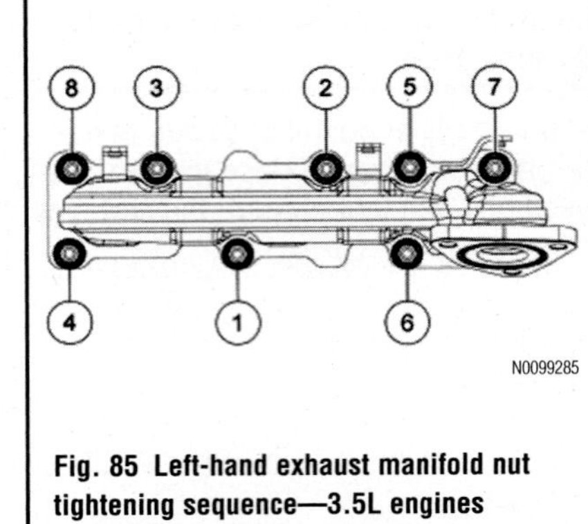

Fig. 85 Left-hand exhaust manifold nut tightening sequence—3.5L engines

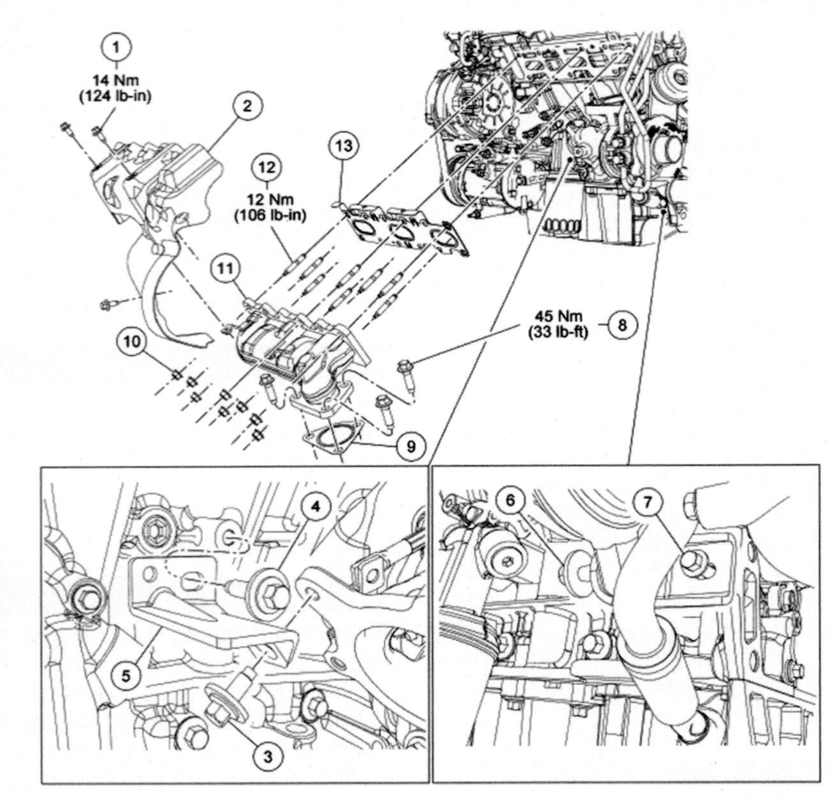

Fig. 84 Left-Hand Exhaust Manifold—3.5L engines

WARNING

The next 4 steps must be performed in order or damage to the turbocharger may occur.

17. Perform the next four steps in following order:

a. Tighten the upper turbocharger bracket-to-turbocharger bolt. Tighten to 14 ft. lbs. (19 Nm).

b. Tighten the upper turbocharger bracket-to-cylinder block bolt. Tighten to 18 ft. lbs. (25 Nm).

c. Tighten the lower turbocharger bracket-to-turbocharger bolt. Tighten to 14 ft. lbs. (19 Nm).

d. Tighten the lower turbocharger bracket-to-cylinder block bolt. Tighten to 97 inch lbs. (11 Nm).

18. Install the left-hand exhaust manifold heat shield and the bottom bolt. Do not tighten the bolt at this time.

19. Install the left-hand catalytic converter.

20. Install the 2 top left-hand exhaust manifold heat shield bolts. Tighten to 10 ft. lbs. (14 Nm).

21. Tighten the left-hand exhaust manifold heat shield bottom bolt. Tighten to 10 ft. lbs. (14 Nm).

Right-Hand

See Figures 86 and 87.

WARNING

Whenever turbocharger air intake system components are removed, always cover open ports to protect from debris. It is important that no foreign material enter the system. The turbocharger compressor vanes are susceptible to damage from even small particles. All components

should be inspected and cleaned, if necessary, prior to installation or reassembly.

1. Before servicing the vehicle, refer to the Precautions Section.
2. Remove the right-hand turbocharger.
3. Remove the 8 nuts and the right-hand exhaust manifold. Discard the nuts and exhaust manifold gasket.
4. Clean and inspect the right-hand exhaust manifold.
5. Remove and discard the 8 right-hand exhaust manifold studs.
6. Clean the exhaust manifold mating surface of the cylinder head with metal surface prep. Follow the directions on the packaging. Do not use metal scrapers, wire brushes, power abrasive discs or other abrasive means to clean the sealing surfaces. Use a plastic scraper to clean the sealing surfaces.

To install:

7. Install 8 new right-hand exhaust manifold studs. Tighten to 106 inch lbs. (12 Nm).
8. Install a new gasket, right-hand exhaust manifold and 8 new nuts. Tighten in 2 stages in the sequence shown. Failure to tighten the exhaust manifold nuts to specification a second time will cause the exhaust manifold to develop an exhaust leak:

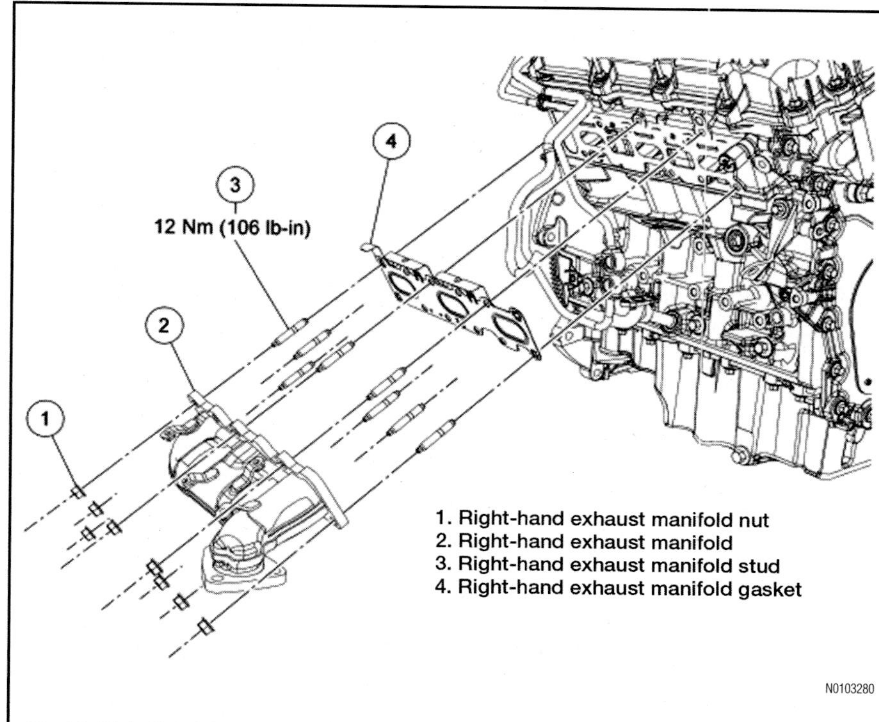

Fig. 86 Right-Hand Exhaust Manifold—3.5L engines

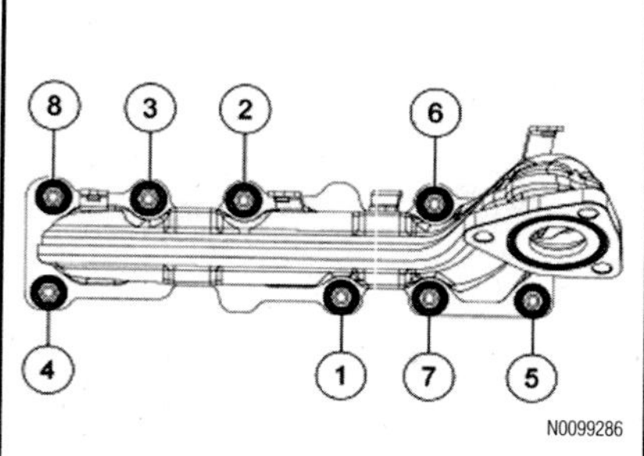

Fig. 87 Right-hand exhaust manifold nut tightening sequence—3.5L engines

- Stage 1: Tighten to 11 ft. lbs. (15 Nm)
- Stage 2: Tighten to 15 ft. lbs. (20 Nm)

9. Install the right-hand turbocharger.

3.7L Engines

Left-Hand

See Figures 88 and 89.

1. Before servicing the vehicle, refer to the Precautions Section.
2. Remove the left-hand catalytic converter.
3. Remove the left-hand Heated Oxygen Sensor (HO2S).
4. Remove the 3 bolts and the left-hand exhaust manifold heat shield.
5. Remove the 6 nuts and the left-hand exhaust manifold. Discard the nuts and gasket.
6. Clean and inspect the left-hand exhaust manifold.
7. Remove and discard the 6 left-hand exhaust manifold studs.
8. Clean the exhaust manifold mating surface of the cylinder head with metal surface prep. Follow the directions on the packaging. Do not use metal scrapers, wire brushes, power abrasive discs or other abrasive means to clean the sealing surfaces. Use a plastic scraper to clean the sealing surfaces.

To install:

9. Install 6 new left-hand exhaust manifold studs. Tighten to 106 inch lbs. (12 Nm).
10. Using a new gasket, install the left-hand exhaust manifold and 6 new nuts. Tighten in 2 stages in the sequence shown. Failure to tighten the exhaust manifold nuts to specification a second time will cause the exhaust manifold to develop an exhaust leak:
    - Stage 1: Tighten to 15 ft. lbs. (20 Nm)
    - Stage 2: Tighten to 18 ft. lbs. (25 Nm)
11. Install the left-hand exhaust manifold heat shield and the 3 bolts. Tighten to 89 inch lbs. (10 Nm).
12. Install the left-hand HO2S.
13. Install the left-hand catalytic converter.

Right-Hand

See Figures 90 and 91.

1. Before servicing the vehicle, refer to the Precautions Section.
2. Remove the right-hand catalytic converter.
3. Disconnect the right-hand Heated Oxygen Sensor (HO2S) electrical connector.
4. Remove the 6 nuts and the right-hand exhaust manifold. Discard the nuts and gasket.
5. Clean and inspect the right-hand exhaust manifold.
6. Remove and discard the 6 right-hand exhaust manifold studs.
7. Clean the exhaust manifold mating surface of the cylinder head with metal surface prep. Follow the directions on the packaging.

To install:

8. Install 6 new right-hand exhaust manifold studs. Tighten to 106 inch lbs. (12 Nm).

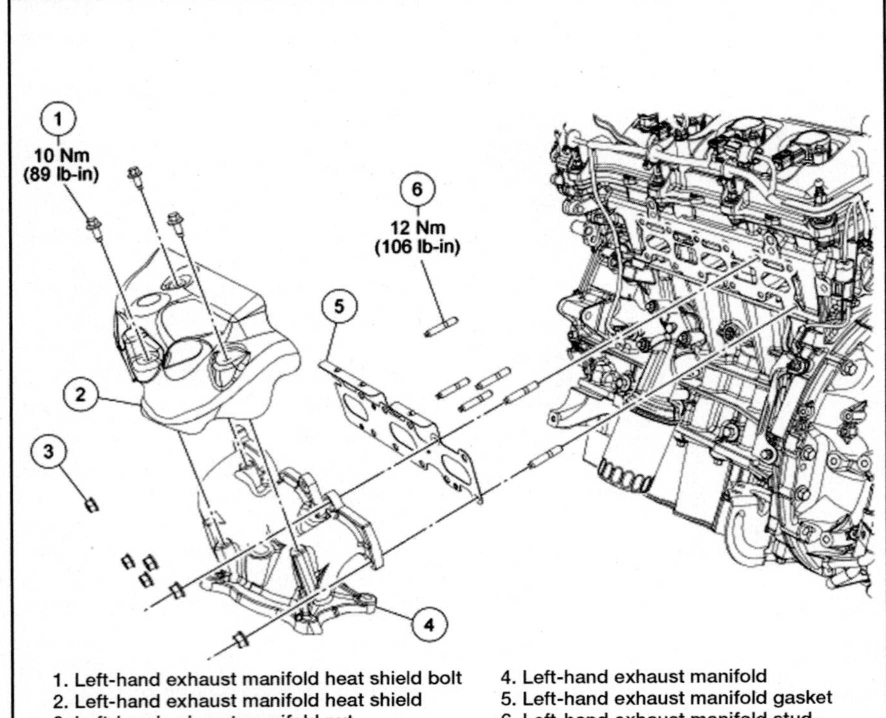

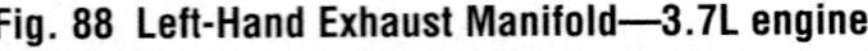

Fig. 88 Left-Hand Exhaust Manifold—3.7L engines

Fig. 89 Left-hand exhaust manifold nut tightening sequence—3.7L engines

9. Using a new gasket, install the right-hand exhaust manifold and 6 new nuts. Tighten in 2 stages in the sequence shown. Failure to tighten the exhaust manifold nuts to specification a second time will cause the exhaust manifold to develop an exhaust leak:
    - Stage 1: Tighten to 15 ft. lbs. (20 Nm)
    - Stage 2: Tighten to 18 ft. lbs. (25 Nm)
10. Connect the right-hand HO2S electrical connector.
11. Install the right-hand catalytic converter.

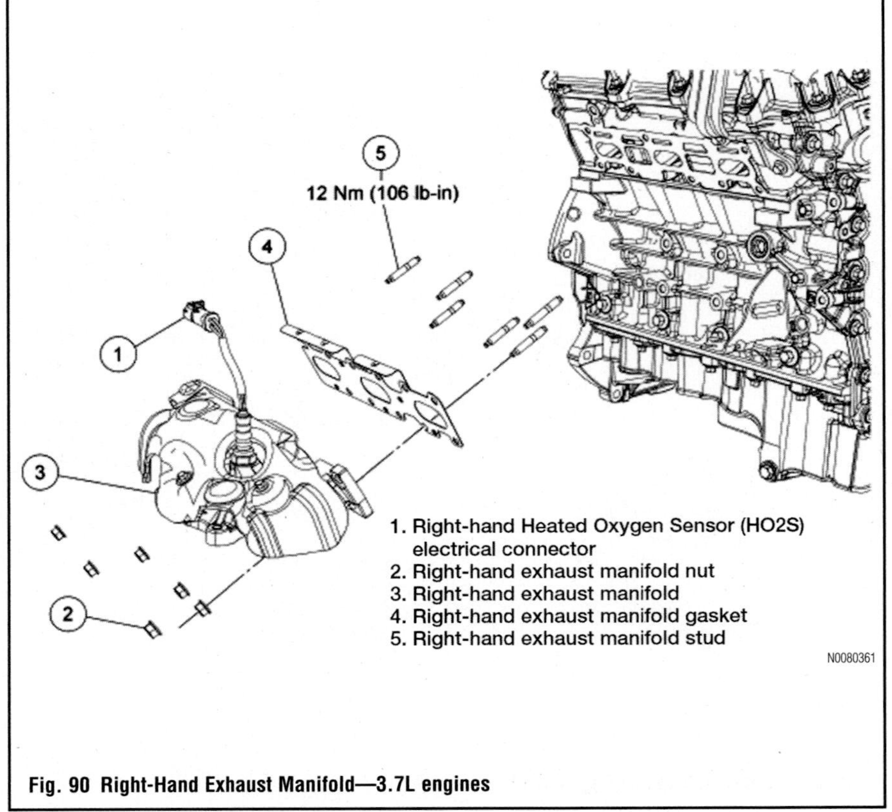

Fig. 90 Right-Hand Exhaust Manifold—3.7L engines

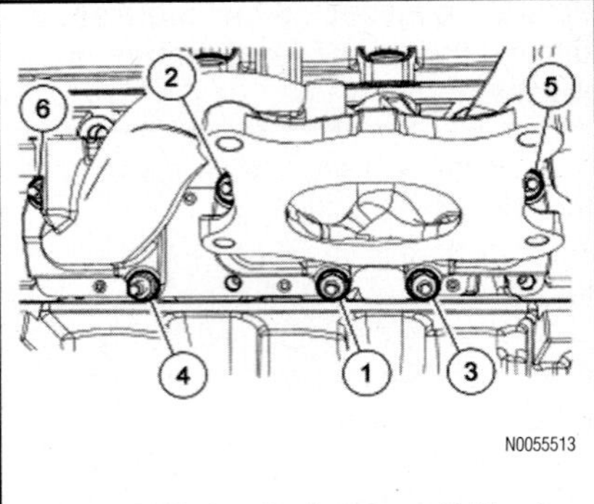

Fig. 91 Right-hand exhaust manifold nut tightening sequence—3.7L engines

INTAKE MANIFOLD

REMOVAL & INSTALLATION

3.5L Engines

See Figures 92 through 97.

WARNING

During engine repair procedures, cleanliness is extremely important. Any foreign material, including any material created while cleaning gasket surfaces that enters the oil passages, coolant passages or the oil pan, may cause engine failure.

WARNING

Whenever turbocharger air intake system components are removed, always cover open ports to protect from debris. It is important that no foreign material enter the system. The turbocharger compressor vanes are susceptible to damage from even small particles. All components should be inspected and cleaned, if necessary, prior to installation or reassembly.

1. Before servicing the vehicle, refer to the Precautions Section.
2. Drain the cooling system.
3. Remove the Air Cleaner (ACL) outlet pipe.
4. Disconnect the left-hand turbocharger bypass valve electrical connector.
5. Disconnect the left-hand turbocharger bypass valve hose from the right-hand Charge Air Cooler (CAC) tube.
6. Disconnect the turbocharger wastegate regulating valve hose from the right-hand CAC tube.
7. Disconnect the right-hand turbocharger bypass valve electrical connector.
8. Disconnect the right-hand turbocharger bypass valve hose from the right-hand turbocharger intake tube.
9. Remove the right-hand CAC tube nut from the intake manifold.
10. Loosen the clamp and remove the right-hand CAC tube.
11. Loosen the clamp and remove the right-hand CAC tube from the right-hand turbocharger.
12. Loosen the clamp and position CAC outlet pipe-to-throttle body aside.
13. Disconnect the Throttle Position (TP) sensor and electronic throttle body electrical connectors.
14. Disconnect the quick connect coupling Evaporative Emission (EVAP) tube from the intake manifold.
15. Detach the EVAP purge valve from the intake manifold.
16. Disconnect the brake booster vacuum hose from the intake manifold.
17. Remove the fuel tube-to-engine front cover bracket bolt and position the fuel tube aside.
18. Disconnect the PCV tube quick connect coupling from the intake manifold.
19. If equipped, disconnect the heated PCV valve electrical connector from the intake manifold.
20. Detach and disconnect the 2 fuel injector wiring harness electrical connectors.
21. Disconnect the Manifold Absolute Pressure (MAP)/Intake Air Temperature 2 (IAT2) sensor electrical connector.
22. Disconnect the 2 hoses from the turbocharger wastegate regulating valve. Mark the location of each hose for installation.
23. Disconnect the turbocharger wastegate regulating valve electrical connector.
24. Detach the 2 wire harness-to-intake manifold retainers.
25. Detach the 2 wire harness retainers from the left-hand valve cover stud bolt.
26. Detach the 2 wire harness retainers from the left-hand valve cover.
27. Disconnect the 2 coolant heater hoses from the intake manifold.
28. Disconnect the 2 turbocharger coolant hoses from the intake manifold.
29. Disconnect the lower radiator hose from the thermostat housing.
30. Remove the bolt and ground wire from the engine front cover.
31. Disconnect the upper radiator hose at the intake manifold and position the hose aside.
32. Remove the 12 bolts and the intake manifold.
   a. Note the routing of the 2 fuel rail wiring harnesses for installation.
   b. Remove and discard the intake manifold, coolant crossover and thermostat housing gaskets.
   c. Clean and inspect all sealing surfaces.

To install:

WARNING

If the engine is repaired or replaced because of upper engine failure, typically including valve or piston damage, check the intake manifold for metal debris. If metal debris is found, install a new intake manifold. Failure to follow these instructions can result in engine damage.

➡Make sure the fuel rail wiring harnesses are routed correctly.

➡Installing the 2 long bolts first will aid in installing the intake manifold.

33. Using new intake manifold, coolant crossover and thermostat housing gaskets, install the intake manifold and the 12 bolts. Tighten in the sequence shown to 89 inch lbs. (10 Nm).
34. Connect the upper radiator hose to the intake manifold.
35. Install the ground wire and bolt to the engine front cover. Tighten to 89 inch lbs. (10 Nm).

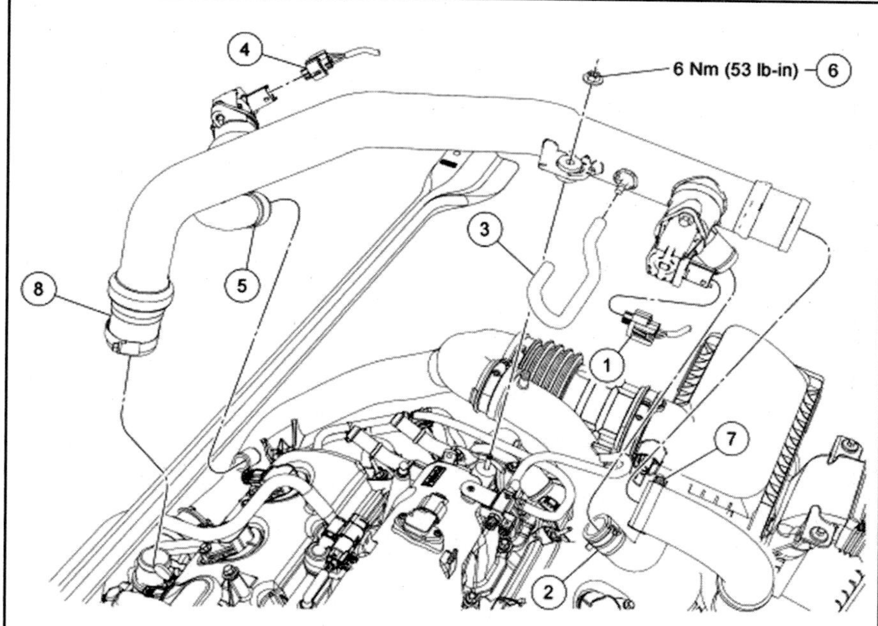

Fig. 92 Intake manifold components 1—3.5L engines

36. Connect the lower radiator hose to the thermostat housing.
37. Connect the 2 turbocharger coolant hoses from the intake manifold.
38. Connect the 2 coolant heater hoses from the intake manifold.
39. Attach the 2 wire harness retainers to the left-hand valve cover.
40. Attach the 2 wire harness retainers to the left-hand valve cover stud bolt.
41. Attach the 2 wire harness-to-intake manifold retainers.
42. Connect the turbocharger wastegate regulating valve electrical connector.
43. Connect the 2 hoses to the turbocharger wastegate regulating valve.
44. Connect the MAP/IAT 2 sensor electrical connector.
45. Connect and attach the 2 fuel injector wiring harness electrical connectors.
46. If equipped, connect the heated PCV valve electrical connector.
47. Connect the PCV tube quick connect coupling to the intake manifold.
48. Position the fuel tube and install the fuel tube-to-engine front cover bracket bolt. Tighten to 89 inch lbs. (10 Nm).
49. Connect the brake vacuum tube to the intake manifold.
50. Attach the EVAP purge valve to the intake manifold.
51. Connect the quick connect coupling EVAP tube to the intake manifold.
52. Connect the throttle position sensor and electronic throttle body electrical connectors.
53. Position CAC outlet pipe on the throttle body and tighten the clamp. Align the matchmarks. Tighten to 44 inch lbs. (5 Nm).
54. Install the right-hand CAC tube to the right-hand turbocharger and tighten the clamp. Align the matchmarks. Tighten to 44 inch lbs. (5 Nm).
55. Install the right-hand CAC tube and tighten the clamp. Align the matchmarks. Tighten to 44 inch lbs. (5 Nm).
56. Install the right-hand CAC tube and the right-hand CAC tube nut to the intake manifold. The compression limiter bushing may fall out of the mounting bracket grommet on the Charge Air Cooler (CAC) tube during service. Make sure the bushing is in place when reinstalling the tube or damage to the tube may occur. Tighten to 53 inch lbs. (6 Nm).
57. Connect the right-hand turbocharger bypass valve hose to the right-hand turbocharger intake tube.
58. Connect the right-hand turbocharger bypass valve electrical connector.
59. Connect the turbocharger wastegate regulating valve hose to the right-hand CAC tube.
60. Connect the left-hand turbocharger bypass valve electrical connector and the turbocharger bypass valve hose.

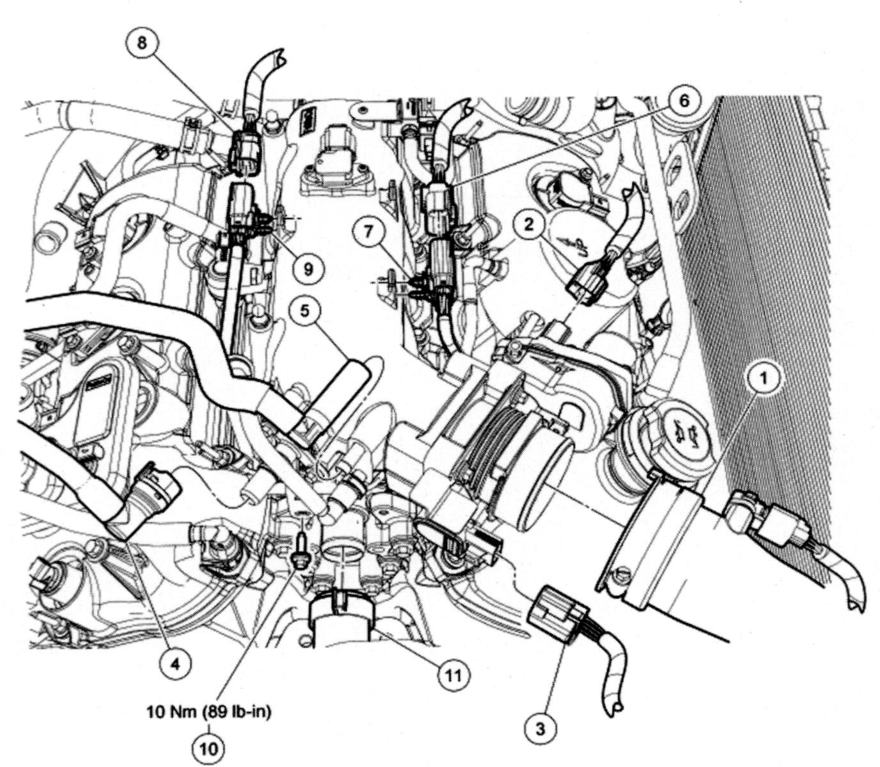

1. Charge Air Cooler (CAC) outlet pipe
2. Electronic Throttle Body (TB) electrical connector
3. Throttle Position (TP) sensor electrical connector
4. PCV tube quick connect coupling
5. Brake booster vacuum hose
6. Fuel injector wiring harness electrical connector
7. Fuel injector wiring harness electrical connector pin-type retainer
8. Fuel injector wiring harness electrical connector
9. Fuel injector wiring harness electrical connector pin-type retainer
10. Fuel tube retainer bolt
11. Upper radiator hose

N0105847

Fig. 93 Intake manifold components 2—3.5L engines

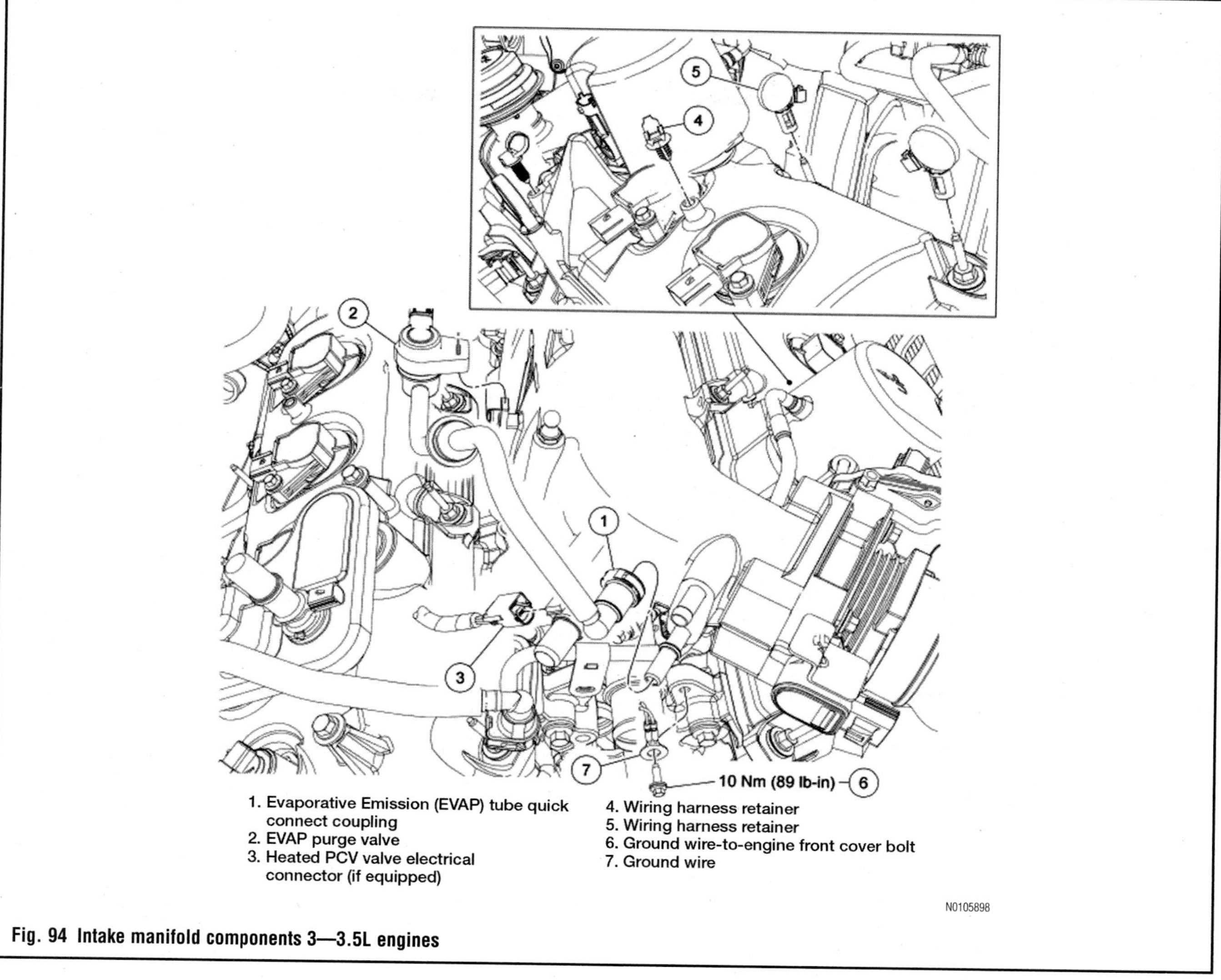

Fig. 94 Intake manifold components 3—3.5L engines

61. Install the ACL outlet pipe.
62. Fill and bleed the cooling system.

3.7L Engines

Lower Intake Manifold

See Figures 98 and 99.

1. Before servicing the vehicle, refer to the Precautions Section.

⁂ WARNING

During engine repair procedures, cleanliness is extremely important. Any foreign material, including any material created while cleaning gasket surfaces that enters the oil passages, coolant passages or the oil pan, may cause engine failure.

2. Remove the fuel rail.
3. Drain the cooling system.
4. Remove the 3 thermostat housing-to-lower intake manifold bolts.
5. Remove the 10 bolts and the lower intake manifold.
   a. Remove and discard the intake manifold and thermostat housing gaskets.
   b. Clean and inspect all sealing surfaces.

To install:

⁂ WARNING

If the engine is repaired or replaced because of upper engine failure, typically including valve or piston damage, check the intake manifold for metal debris. If metal debris if found, install a new intake manifold. Failure to follow these instructions can result in engine damage.

6. Using new intake manifold and thermostat housing gaskets, install the lower intake manifold and the 10 bolts. Tighten in the sequence shown to 89 inch lbs. (10 Nm).
7. Install the 3 thermostat housing-to-lower intake manifold bolts. Tighten to 89 inch lbs. (10 Nm).
8. Install the fuel rail.
9. Fill and bleed the cooling system.

Upper Intake Manifold

See Figures 100 through 102.

1. Before servicing the vehicle, refer to the Precautions Section.

⁂ WARNING

During engine repair procedures, cleanliness is extremely important. Any foreign material, including any material created while cleaning gasket surfaces that enters the oil passages, coolant passages or the oil pan, may cause engine failure.

2. Remove the Air Cleaner (ACL) outlet pipe.
3. Disconnect the throttle body electrical connector.

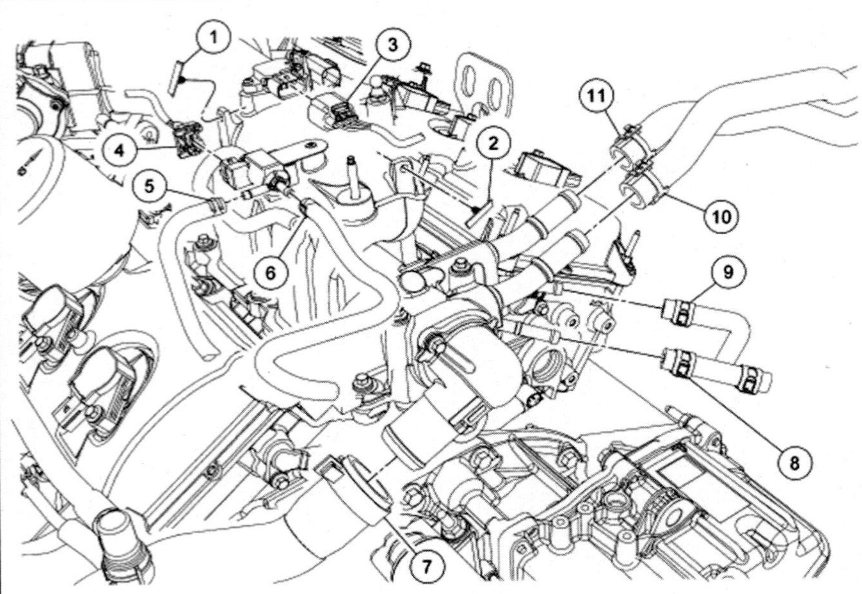

1. Wiring harness pin-type retainer
2. Wiring harness pin-type retainer
3. Manifold Absolute Pressure (MAP)/Intake Air Temperature 2 (IAT2) sensor electrical connector
4. Turbocharger wastegate regulating valve electrical connector
5. Turbocharger wastegate regulating valve hose
6. Turbocharger wastegate regulating valve hose
7. Lower radiator hose
8. Turbocharger coolant inlet hose
9. Turbocharger coolant outlet hose
10. Coolant heater hose
11. Coolant heater hose

Fig. 95 Intake manifold components 4—3.5L engines

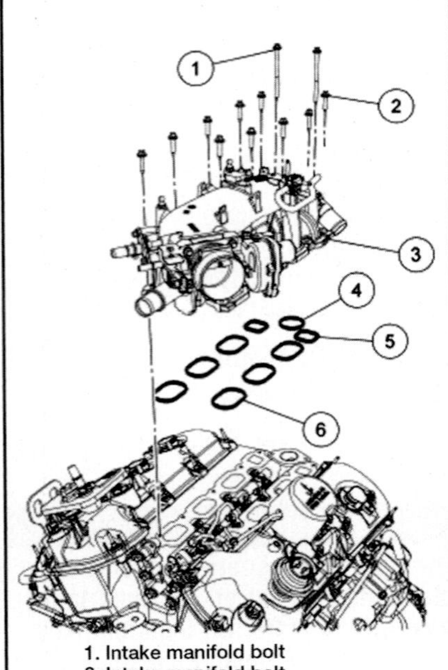

1. Intake manifold bolt
2. Intake manifold bolt
3. Intake manifold
4. Coolant by-pass tube gasket
5. Coolant crossover gasket
6. Intake manifold gasket

Fig. 96 Intake manifold components 5—3.5L engines

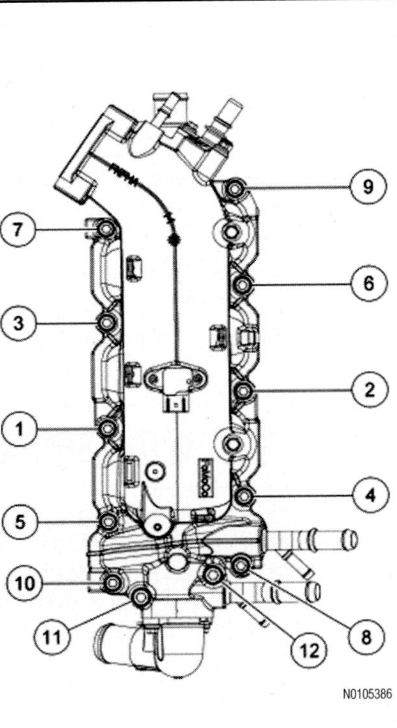

Fig. 97 Intake manifold bolt tightening sequence—3.5L engines

4. Disconnect the Evaporative Emission (EVAP) tube from the intake manifold.
5. Detach the EVAP tube pin-type retainer from the upper intake manifold.
6. Disconnect the brake booster vacuum hose from the intake manifold.
7. Disconnect the PCV tube from the PCV valve.
8. Detach the wiring harness retainers from the upper intake manifold.
9. Remove the upper intake manifold support bracket bolt.
10. Remove the fuel tube bracket bolt.
11. Remove the 6 bolts and the upper intake manifold.
    a. Remove and discard the gaskets.
    b. Clean and inspect all of the sealing surfaces of the upper and lower intake manifold.

To install:

WARNING

If the engine is repaired or replaced because of upper engine failure, typically including valve or piston damage, check the intake manifold for metal debris. If metal debris is found, install a new intake manifold. Failure to follow these instructions can result in engine damage.

12. Using new gaskets, install the upper intake manifold and the 6 bolts. Tighten in the sequence shown to 89 inch lbs. (10 Nm).
13. Install the fuel tube bracket bolt. Tighten to 53 inch lbs. (6 Nm).
14. Install the upper intake manifold support bracket bolt. Tighten to 89 inch lbs. (10 Nm).
15. Attach the wiring harness retainers to the upper intake manifold.
16. Connect the PCV tube to the PCV valve.
17. Connect the brake booster vacuum hose to the intake manifold.
18. Connect the EVAP tube to the intake manifold.
19. Attach the EVAP tube pin-type retainer to the upper intake manifold.
20. Connect the TB electrical connector.
21. Install the ACL outlet pipe.

OIL PAN

REMOVAL & INSTALLATION

3.5L Engines

See Figures 103 through 108.

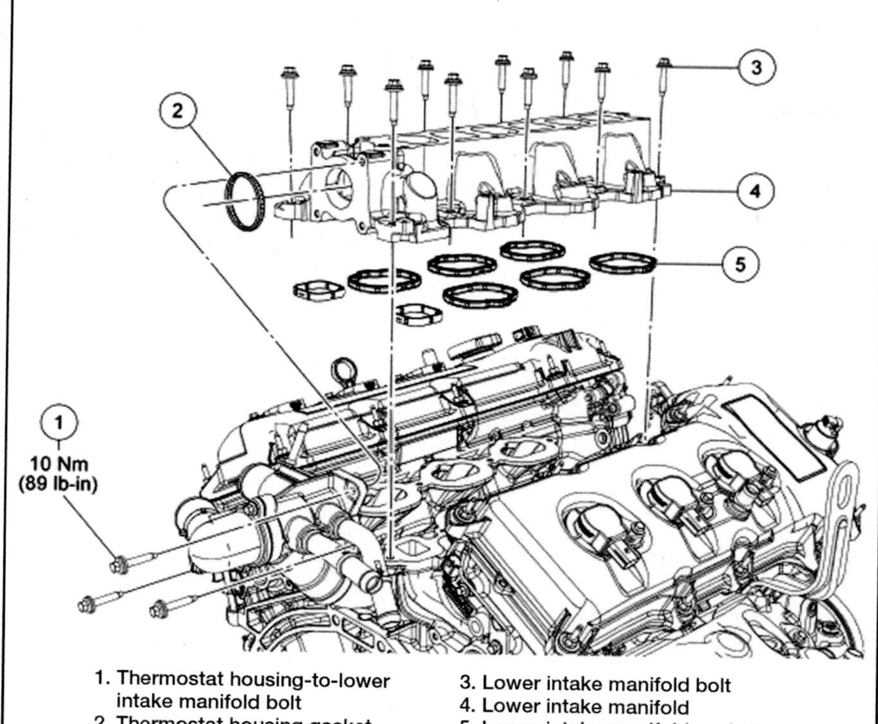

Fig. 98 Lower intake manifold components—3.7L engines

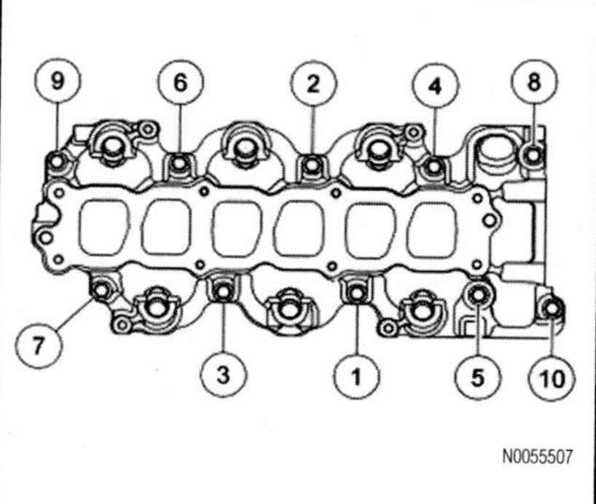

Fig. 99 Lower intake manifold bolt tightening sequence—3.7L engines

⁂ WARNING

During engine repair procedures, cleanliness is extremely important. Any foreign material, including any material created while cleaning gasket surfaces that enters the oil passages, coolant passages or the oil pan, may cause engine failure.

⁂ WARNING

Whenever turbocharger air intake system components are removed, always cover open ports to protect from debris. It is important that no foreign material enter the system. The turbocharger compressor vanes are susceptible to damage from even small particles. All components should be inspected and cleaned, if necessary, prior to installation or reassembly.

1. Before servicing the vehicle, refer to the Precautions Section.
2. Remove the engine from the vehicle.
3. Remove the 8 bolts and the flywheel.
4. Remove the crankshaft sensor ring.
5. Mount the engine on an engine stand. Install the engine stand bolts into the cylinder block only. Do not install the bolts into the oil pan.
6. Remove the nut and the A/C tube from the compressor. Discard the O-ring seal and gasket seal.
7. Remove the left-hand cylinder block drain plug. Allow coolant to drain from the cylinder block.
8. If equipped, remove the heat shield and disconnect the block heater electrical connector. Detach all of the engine block heater harness retainers and remove the harness.
9. Remove the right-hand cylinder block drain plug or, if equipped, the block heater. Allow coolant to drain from the cylinder block.
10. Disconnect the brake vacuum tube from the intake manifold.
11. Disconnect the 2 quick connect couplings and remove the PCV tube.
12. If equipped, disconnect the 2 heated PCV electrical connectors.
13. Disconnect the left-hand turbocharger bypass valve electrical connector.
14. Remove the turbocharger wastegate regulating valve hoses from the right-hand CAC tube and turbocharger wastegate regulating valve. Matchmark the hoses for installation.
15. Loosen the clamp and remove the left-hand turbocharger intake tube from the left-hand turbocharger.
16. Remove the 2 bolts and the left-hand turbocharger oil return tube from the turbocharger. Remove and discard the gasket.
17. Remove the left-hand turbocharger oil return tube from the oil pan. Discard the 2 O-ring seals.
18. Disconnect the right-hand turbocharger bypass valve electrical connector.
19. Loosen the clamp and remove the right-hand CAC tube from the right-hand turbocharger.
20. Loosen the clamp and remove the right-hand turbocharger intake pipe from the right-hand turbocharger.
21. Remove the nut from the right-hand valve cover stud bolt for the right-hand turbocharger intake tube.
22. Remove the right-hand CAC tube nut from the intake manifold and remove the right-hand CAC tube and turbocharger intake tube as an assembly.
23. Remove the noise insulator shield for the fuel injection pump and disconnect the electrical connector.
24. Disconnect the Throttle Position (TP) and electronic throttle body electrical connectors.
25. Disconnect the left-hand Variable Camshaft Timing (VCT) solenoid electrical connector.
26. Disconnect the Engine Oil Pressure (EOP) electrical connector. Detach the wiring harness retainer from the block.
27. Disconnect the 3 left-hand ignition coil-on-plug electrical connectors.
28. Remove the lower radiator hose from the thermostat housing.
29. Remove the engine cover mounting stud from the left-hand valve cover stud bolt.
30. Detach all the wiring harness retainers from the left-hand valve cover and stud bolts.

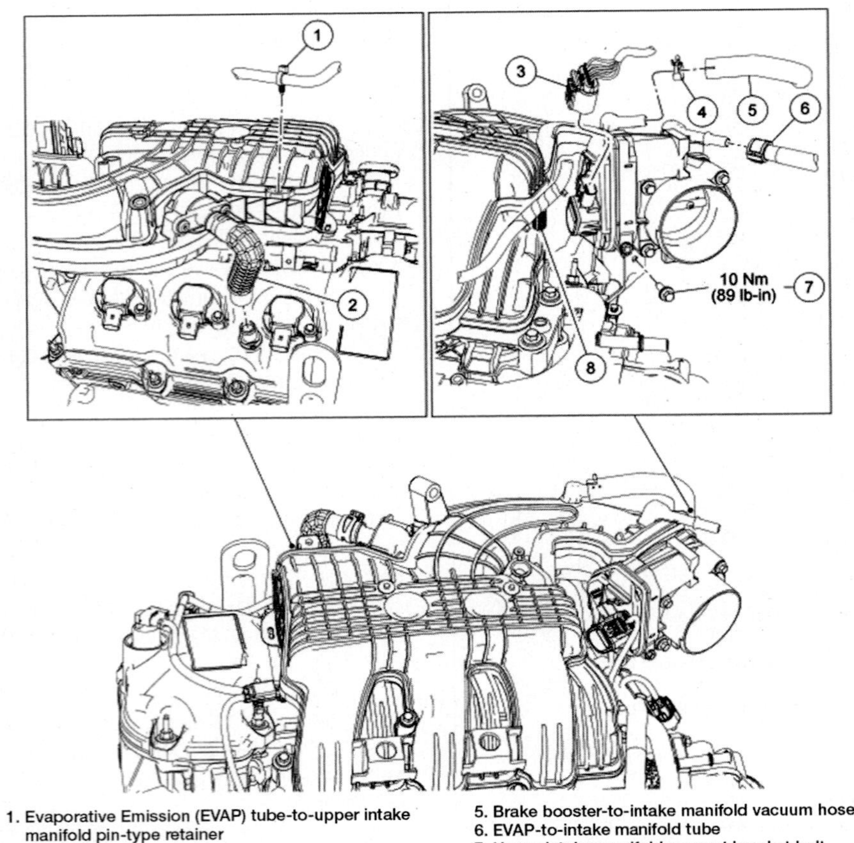

Fig. 100 Upper intake manifold components 1—3.7L engines

31. Remove the nut and the oil supply tube bracket from the left-hand valve cover stud bolt.
32. Remove the oil level indicator.
33. Detach and disconnect the 2 fuel injector wiring harness electrical connectors.
34. Disconnect the Manifold Absolute Pressure (MAP)/Intake Air Temperature 2 (IAT2) sensor electrical connector.
35. Disconnect the turbocharger wastegate regulating valve electrical connector.
36. Detach the 2 wire harness-to-intake manifold retainers.
37. Remove the fuel tube-to-engine front cover bracket bolt and position the fuel tube aside.
38. Disconnect the 2 turbocharger coolant hoses from the intake manifold.

WARNING

If the engine is repaired or replaced because of upper engine failure, typically including valve or piston damage, check the intake manifold for metal debris. If metal debris is found, install a new intake manifold. Failure to follow these instructions can result in engine damage.

39. Remove the 12 bolts and the intake manifold.
    a. Note the routing of the 2 fuel rail wiring harnesses for installation.
    b. Remove and discard the intake manifold, coolant crossover and thermostat housing gaskets.
    c. Clean and inspect all sealing surfaces.
40. Disconnect the right-hand VCT solenoid electrical connector and detach the 2 wiring harness retainers.
41. Disconnect the 3 right-hand ignition coil-on-plug electrical connectors.
42. Detach all the wiring harness retainers from the right-hand valve cover and stud bolts.
43. For early build vehicles, remove the nut for the high pressure fuel tube.
44. For late build vehicles, remove the high pressure fuel tube bolt from the left-hand cylinder head.
45. Remove the high pressure fuel tube flare nut from the fuel injection pump. Remove the 2 high pressure fuel tube flare nuts from the fuel rails.
    a. To release the fuel pressure in the high pressure fuel tube, wrap the flare nuts with a shop towel to absorb any residual fuel pressure during the loosening of the flare nuts.
    b. Remove the high pressure fuel tube assembly.
46. Remove the 2 bolts and the fuel injection pump.
47. Remove the fuel injection pump mounting plate.
48. Remove the fuel injection pump roller tappet. Inspect the fuel injection pump roller tappet.
49. Remove the 3 bolts and the 3 left-hand ignition coil-on-plugs.
50. Remove the 3 bolts and the 3 right-hand ignition coil-on-plugs.
51. Loosen the 10 stud bolts and remove the left-hand valve cover. Discard the gasket.
52. Loosen the 11 stud bolts and remove the right-hand valve cover. Discard the gasket.
53. Inspect the VCT solenoid seals and the spark plug tube seals. Install new seals if damaged.
    a. Using the VCT Spark Plug Tube Seal Remover and Handle, remove the seal(s).
54. Rotate the accessory drive belt tensioner clockwise and remove the accessory drive belt.
55. Remove the 3 bolts and the accessory drive belt tensioner.
56. Using the Strap Wrench, remove the crankshaft pulley bolt and washer. Discard the bolt.
57. Using the 3 Jaw Puller, remove the crankshaft pulley.
58. Using the Oil Seal Remover, remove and discard the crankshaft front seal.
59. Remove the stud bolt and Heated Oxygen Sensor (HO2S) connector bracket from the engine front cover.
60. Remove the 3 bolts and the engine mount bracket.
61. Remove the 22 engine front cover bolts.
62. Install 6 of the engine front cover bolts (finger-tight) into the 6 threaded holes in the engine front cover.
    a. Tighten the bolts one turn at a time in a crisscross pattern until the engine front cover-to-cylinder block seal is released.
    b. Remove the engine front cover.
63. Clean the engine front cover using a 3M® Roloc® Bristle Disk (2-in white, part

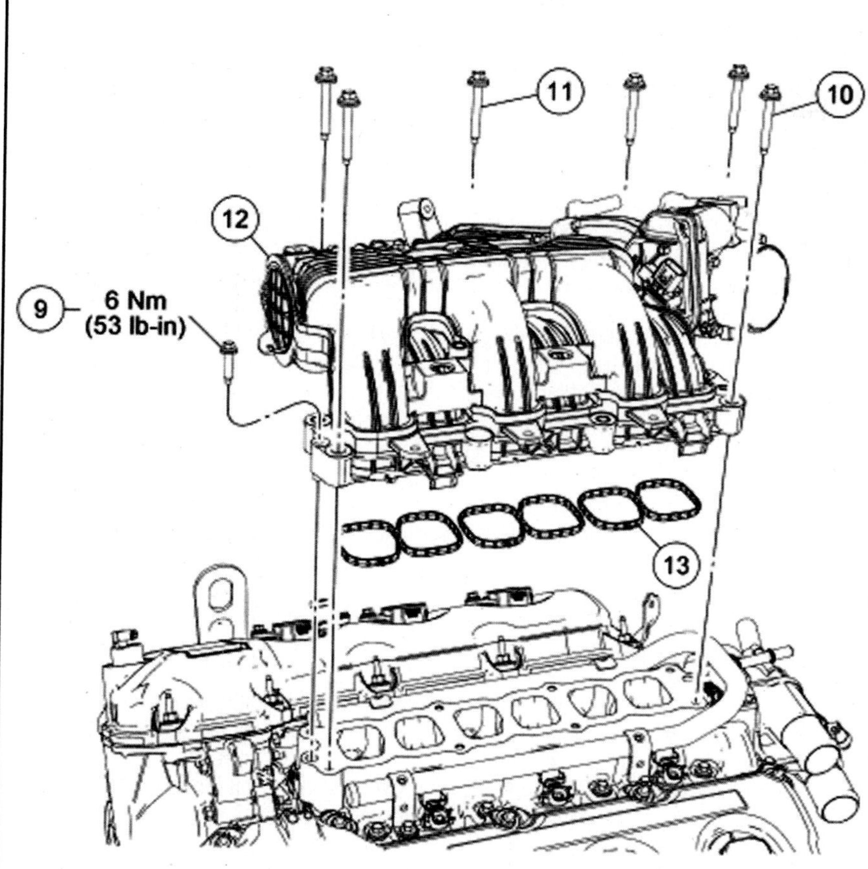

Fig. 101 Upper intake manifold components 2—3.7L engines

number 07528) in a suitable tool turning at the recommended speed of 15,000 rpm.

a. Only use a 3M® Roloc® Bristle Disk to clean the engine front cover. Do not use metal scrapers, wire brushes or any other power abrasive disk to clean the engine front cover. These tools cause scratches and gouges that make leak paths.

b. Thoroughly wash the engine front cover to remove any foreign material, including any abrasive particles created during the cleaning process.

64. Remove the A/C compressor nut, bracket and the stud. The A/C compressor must remain bolted to the cylinder block prior to installing the oil pan.

65. Remove the 16 oil pan bolts.

66. Install 2 of the oil pan bolts (finger-tight) into the 2 threaded holes in the oil pan.

a. Alternately tighten the 2 bolts one turn at a time until the oil pan-to-cylinder block seal is released.

b. Remove the oil pan.

67. Clean the engine front cover and oil pan using a 3M® Roloc® Bristle Disk (2-in white, part number 07528) in a suitable tool turning at the recommended speed of 15,000 rpm.

a. Thoroughly wash the engine front cover and oil pan to remove any foreign material, including any abrasive particles created during the cleaning process.

68. Place clean, lint-free shop towels over exposed engine cavities. Carefully remove the towels so foreign material is not dropped into the engine. Any foreign material (including any material created while

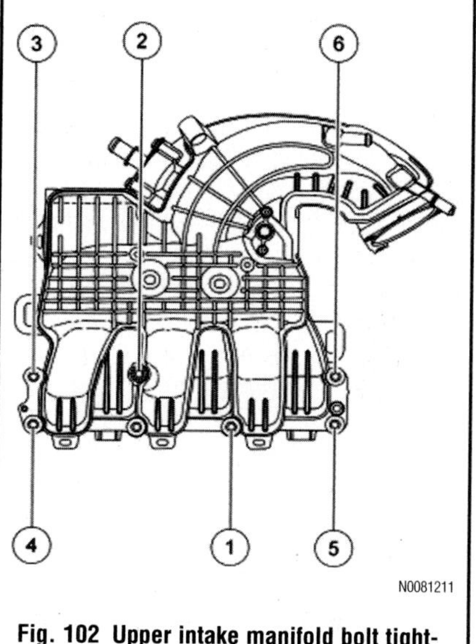

Fig. 102 Upper intake manifold bolt tightening sequence—3.7L engines

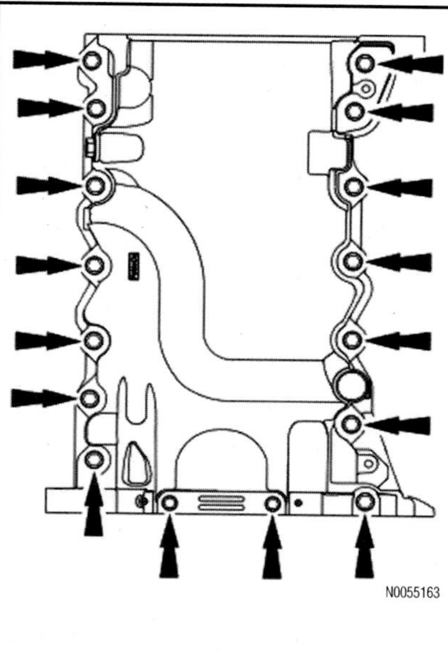

Fig. 103 Remove the 16 oil pan bolts

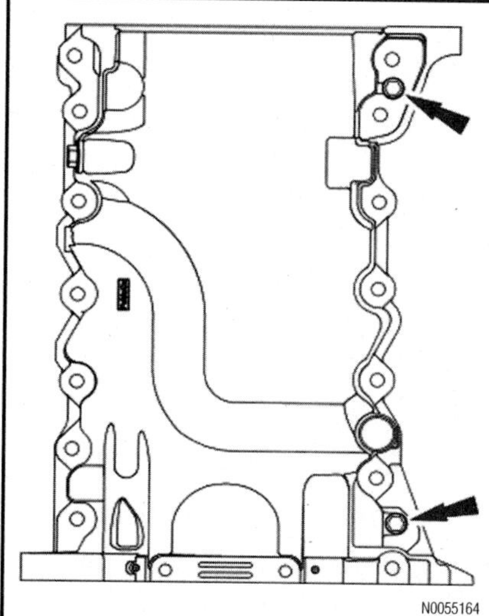

Fig. 104 Alternately tighten the 2 bolts one turn at a time until the seal is released

cleaning gasket surfaces) that enters the oil passages or the oil pan, may cause engine failure.

⁂ WARNING

Do not use wire brushes, power abrasive discs or 3M® Roloc® Bristle Disk (2-in white, part number 07528) to clean the sealing surfaces. These tools cause scratches and gouges that make leak paths. They also cause contamination that will cause premature engine failure. Remove all traces of the gasket.

69. Clean the sealing surfaces of the cylinder block in the following sequence.

a. Remove any large deposits of silicone or gasket material.

b. Apply silicone gasket remover and allow to set for several minutes.

c. Remove the silicone gasket remover. A second application of silicone gasket remover may be required if residual traces of silicone or gasket material remain.

d. Apply metal surface prep to remove any remaining traces of oil or coolant and to prepare the surfaces to bond. Do not attempt to make the metal shiny. Some staining of the metal surfaces is normal.

e. Make sure the 2 locating dowel pins are seated correctly in the cylinder block.

To install:

70. Apply a 0.11 in. (3 mm) bead of Motorcraft® High Performance Engine RTV Silicone to the sealing surface of the oil pan. Failure to use Motorcraft® High Performance Engine RTV Silicone may cause the engine oil to foam excessively and result in serious engine damage.

71. Apply a 0.21 in. (5.5 mm) bead of Motorcraft® High Performance Engine RTV Silicone to the 2 crankshaft seal retainer plate-to-cylinder block joint areas on the sealing surface of the oil pan.

a. The oil pan and the 4 specified bolts must be installed and the oil pan aligned to the cylinder block and A/C compressor within 4 minutes of sealant application. Final tightening of the oil pan bolts must be carried out within 60 minutes of sealant application.

72. Install the oil pan and bolts 10, 11, 13 and 14.

a. Tighten in the sequence shown to 27 inch lbs. (3 Nm).

b. Loosen the bolts 180 degrees.

73. Align the oil pan to the cylinder block and A/C compressor.

a. Position the oil pan so the mounting boss is against the A/C compressor and using a straightedge, align the oil pan flush with the rear of the cylinder block at the 2 areas shown.

74. Tighten bolts 10, 11, 13 and 14 in the sequence shown above to 27 inch lbs. (3 Nm).

75. Install the remaining oil pan bolts. Tighten all the oil pan bolts in the sequence shown.

a. Tighten the large bolts (1–14) to 15 ft. lbs. (20 Nm).

b. Tighten the small bolts (15 and 16) to 89 inch lbs. (10 Nm).

76. Install the A/C compressor mounting stud, bracket and nut. Tighten the stud to 80 inch lbs. (9 Nm). and the nut to 18 ft. lbs. (25 Nm).

77. Install the Alignment Pins.

78. Apply a 0.11 in. (3 mm) bead of Motorcraft® High Performance Engine RTV Silicone to the engine front cover sealing surfaces including the 3 engine mount bracket bosses.

79. Apply a 0.21 in. (5.5 mm) bead of Motorcraft® High Performance Engine RTV Silicone to the oil pan-to-cylinder block joint and the cylinder head-to-cylinder block joint areas of the engine front cover in 5 places indicated in the Timing Chain Front Cover Removal & Installation procedure.

80. Install the engine front cover and bolts 17, 18, 19 and 20 as shown in the Timing Chain Front Cover Removal & Installation procedure.

81. Remove the Alignment Pins.

82. Install the engine mount bracket and the 3 bolts. Do not tighten the bolts at this time.

83. Install the remaining engine front cover bolts. Tighten all of the engine front cover bolts and engine mount bracket bolts in 2 stages in the sequence shown in the Timing Chain Front Cover Removal & Installation procedure.

84. Install the stud bolt and Heated Oxygen Sensor (HO2S) connector bracket to the engine front cover. Tighten to 89 inch lbs. (10 Nm).

85. Using the Crankshaft Vibration Damper Installer and Front Crankshaft Seal Installer, install a new crankshaft front seal. Apply clean engine oil to the crankshaft front seal bore in the engine front cover.

➡Lubricate the outside diameter sealing surfaces with clean engine oil.

86. Using the Crankshaft Vibration Damper Installer and Front Cover Oil Seal Installer, install the crankshaft pulley.

87. Using the Strap Wrench, install the crankshaft pulley washer and new bolt and tighten in 4 stages.

a. Stage 1: Tighten to 89 ft. lbs. (120 Nm).

b. Stage 2: Loosen one full turn.

c. Stage 3: Tighten to 37 ft. lbs. (50 Nm).

d. Stage 4: Tighten an additional 90 degrees.

88. Install the accessory drive belt tensioner and the 3 bolts. Tighten to 97 inch lbs. (11 Nm).

89. Rotate the accessory drive belt tensioner clockwise and install the accessory drive belt.

N0055188

Fig. 105 Oil pan sealant application

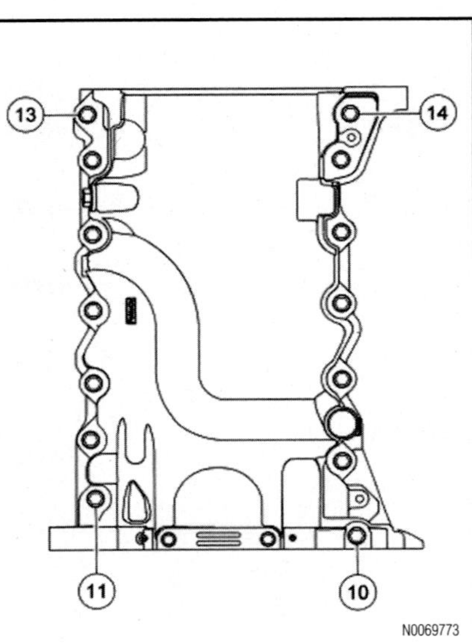

Fig. 106 Oil pan bolts 10, 11, 13 and 14 tightening sequence

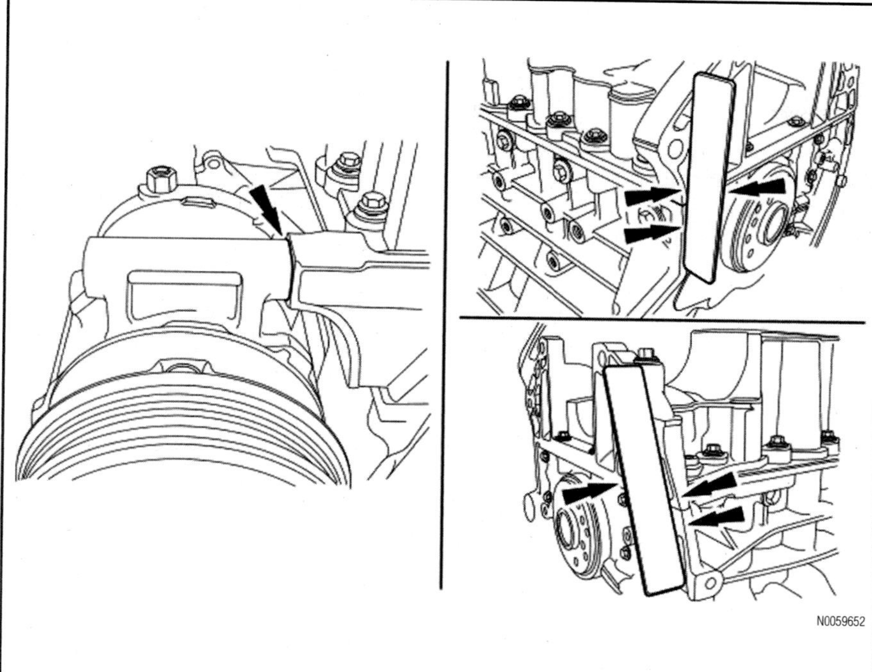

Fig. 107 Align the oil pan to the cylinder block and A/C compressor

➡**Installation of new seals is only required if damaged seals were removed during disassembly of the engine.**

90. Using the VCT Spark Plug Tube Seal Installer and Handle, install new VCT solenoid and/or spark plug tube seals.

91. Apply an 0.31 in (8 mm) bead of Motorcraft® High Performance Engine RTV Silicone to the engine front cover-to-right-hand cylinder head joints.

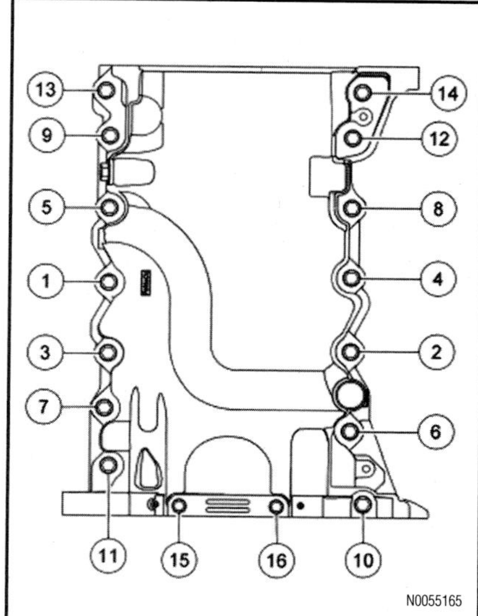

Fig. 108 Oil pan bolts tightening sequence

WARNING

If the valve cover is not installed and the fasteners tightened within 4 minutes, the sealant must be removed and the sealing area cleaned. To clean the sealing area, use silicone gasket remover and metal surface prep. Failure to follow this procedure can cause future oil leakage.

92. Using new gaskets, install the valve covers and tighten the bolts in the sequence shown in the Valve Cover Removal & Installation procedure to 89 inch lbs. (10 Nm).

93. Apply an 0.31 in (8 mm) bead of Motorcraft® High Performance Engine RTV Silicone to the engine front cover-to-left-hand cylinder head joints. If the valve cover is not installed and the fasteners tightened within 4 minutes, the sealant must be removed and the sealing area cleaned. To clean the sealing area, use silicone gasket remover and metal surface prep. Failure to follow this procedure can cause future oil leakage.

94. Install the ignition coil-on-plugs and bolts. Tighten to 62 inch lbs. (7 Nm).

95. Using the crankshaft pulley bolt, turn the crankshaft until the fuel injection pump cam lobe is at BDC. The cam lobe for the fuel injection pump must be at Bottom Dead Center (BDC) for the fuel injection pump installation.

96. Install the fuel injection pump roller tappet. Apply clean engine oil to the fuel injection pump mounting pedestal bore.

97. Inspect the fuel injection pump mounting plate-to-valve cover gasket and replace if necessary. Apply clean engine oil to the fuel injection pump mounting plate seal.

98. Inspect the 2 fuel injection pump mounting plate O-ring seals and replace if necessary. Apply clean engine oil to the fuel injection pump mounting plate O-ring seals.

99. Install the fuel injection pump on the fuel injection pump mounting plate. Apply clean engine oil to the fuel injection pump O-ring seal.

100. Install the fuel injection pump and the 2 bolts. Start the fuel injection pump bolts by hand, and then simultaneously tighten to specifications.

a. Tighten to 89 inch lbs. (10 Nm).

b. Tighten an additional 45 degrees.

101. Connect the high-pressure fuel tube flare nut to the fuel injection pump. Connect the 2 high-pressure fuel tube flare nuts to the fuel rails. Tighten to 22 ft. lbs. (30 Nm).

102. For late build vehicles, install the bolt for the high pressure fuel tube to the left-hand cylinder head. Tighten to 53 inch lbs. (6 Nm).

103. For early build vehicles, install the nut for the high pressure fuel tube to the left-hand valve cover stud bolt. Tighten to 53 inch lbs. (6 Nm).

104. Attach all of the wiring harness retainers to the right-hand valve cover and stud bolts.

105. Connect the 3 right-hand ignition coil-on-plug electrical connectors.

106. Connect the right-hand VCT solenoid electrical connector and attach the 2 wiring harness retainers.

WARNING

If the engine is repaired or replaced because of upper engine failure, typically including valve or piston damage, check the intake manifold for metal debris. If metal debris is found, install a new intake manifold. Failure to follow these instructions can result in engine damage.

WARNING

Make sure the fuel rail wiring harnesses are routed correctly.

107. Using new intake manifold, coolant crossover and thermostat housing gaskets, install the intake manifold and the 12 bolts. Installing the 2 long bolts first will aid in installing the intake manifold. Tighten in the sequence shown in the Intake Manifold

Removal & Installation procedure to 89 inch lbs. (10 Nm).

108. Connect the 2 turbocharger coolant hoses to the intake manifold.

109. Position the fuel tube and install the fuel tube-to-engine front cover bracket bolt. Tighten to 89 inch lbs. (10 Nm).

110. Attach the 2 wire harness-to-intake manifold retainers.

111. Connect the turbocharger wastegate regulating valve electrical connector.

112. Connect the Manifold Absolute Pressure (MAP)/Intake Air Temperature 2 (IAT2) sensor electrical connector.

113. Connect and attach the 2 fuel injector wiring harness electrical connectors.

114. Install the oil level indicator.

115. Install the oil supply tube bracket on the left-hand valve cover stud bolt and install the nut. Tighten to 71 inch lbs. (8 Nm).

116. Attach all of the wiring harness retainers to the left-hand valve cover and stud bolts.

117. Install the engine cover mounting stud to the left-hand valve cover stud bolt. Tighten to 53 inch lbs. (6 Nm).

118. Install the lower radiator hose to the thermostat housing.

119. Connect the 3 left-hand ignition coil-on-plug electrical connectors.

120. Connect the Engine Oil Pressure (EOP) electrical connector. Attach the wiring harness retainer to the block.

121. Connect the left-hand VCT solenoid electrical connector.

122. Connect the Throttle Position (TP) and electronic throttle body electrical connectors.

123. Connect the electrical connector and install the noise insulator shield for the fuel injection pump.

124. Install the right-hand Charge Air Cooler (CAC) tube and turbocharger intake tube as an assembly and install the right-hand CAC tube nut to the intake manifold. The compression limiter bushing may fall out of the mounting bracket grommet on the Charge Air Cooler (CAC) tube during service. Make sure the bushing is in place when reinstalling the tube or damage to the tube may occur. Tighten to 53 inch lbs. (6 Nm).

125. Install the nut to the right-hand valve cover stud bolt for the right-hand turbocharger intake tube. The compression limiter bushing may fall out of the mounting bracket grommet on the turbocharger intake tube during service. Make sure the bushing is in place when reinstalling the tube or damage to the tube may occur. Tighten to 53 inch lbs. (6 Nm).

126. Install the right-hand turbocharger intake pipe to the right-hand turbocharger and tighten the clamp. Align the matchmarks. Tighten to 44 inch lbs. (5 Nm).

127. Install the right-hand CAC tube to the right-hand turbocharger and tighten the clamp. Align the matchmarks. Tighten to 44 inch lbs. (5 Nm).

128. Connect the right-hand turbocharger bypass valve electrical connector.

129. Using 2 new O-ring seals, install the left-hand turbocharger oil return tube in the oil pan. Lubricate the oil pan bore with clean engine oil.

130. Install a new gasket, turbocharger oil return tube and the 2 bolts. Tighten to 89 inch lbs. (10 Nm).

131. Install the turbocharger intake tube to the left-hand turbocharger and tighten the clamp. Align the matchmarks. Tighten to 44 inch lbs. (5 Nm).

132. Install the 2 turbocharger wastegate regulating valve hoses to the turbocharger wastegate regulating valve and to the right-hand CAC tube.

133. Connect the left-hand turbocharger bypass valve electrical connector.

134. If equipped, connect the 2 heated PCV electrical connectors.

135. Install the PCV tube and connect the 2 quick connect couplings.

136. Connect the brake vacuum tube to the intake manifold.

137. Install the left-hand cylinder block drain plug. Tighten to 15 ft. lbs. (20 Nm) plus an additional 180 degrees.

138. Install the right-hand cylinder block drain plug or, if equipped, the block heater. Tighten to 30 ft. lbs. (40 Nm).

139. If equipped, connect the block heater electrical connector and install the heat shield. Attach all the engine block heater wiring harness retainers.

140. Using a new O-ring seal and gasket seal, connect the A/C tube to the compressor and install the nut. Tighten to 11 ft. lbs. (15 Nm).

141. Using the Heavy Duty Floor Crane and Spreader Bar, remove the engine from the stand.

142. Install the crankshaft sensor ring.

143. Install the flexplate and the 8 bolts. Tighten to 59 ft. lbs. (80 Nm).

144. Install the engine in the vehicle.

3.7L Engines

See Figures 109 through 114.

⁂ WARNING

During engine repair procedures, cleanliness is extremely important. Any foreign material, including any material created while cleaning gasket surfaces that enters the oil passages, coolant passages or the oil pan, may cause engine failure.

⁂ WARNING

Early build engines have 11 fastener valve covers, late build engines have 9 fastener valve covers. Do not attempt to install bolts in the 2 empty late build valve cover holes or damage to the valve cover will occur.

1. Remove the engine from the vehicle.
2. Remove the 8 bolts and the flywheel.
3. Remove the crankshaft sensor ring.
4. Mount the engine on a suitable engine stand. Install the engine stand bolts into the cylinder block only. Do not install the bolts into the oil pan.
5. If equipped, remove the heat shield and disconnect the block heater electrical connector.
6. Detach all of the engine block heater harness retainers and remove the harness.
7. Disconnect the PCV hose from the PCV valve.
8. Disconnect the throttle body electrical connector.
9. Detach the wiring harness retainers from the upper intake manifold.
10. Remove the upper intake manifold support bracket bolt.
11. Remove the fuel tube bracket bolt from the upper intake manifold.

⁂ WARNING

If the engine is repaired or replaced because of upper engine failure, typically including valve or piston damage, check the intake manifold for metal debris. If metal debris is found, install a new intake manifold. Failure to follow these instructions can result in engine damage.

12. Remove the 6 bolts and the upper intake manifold. Discard the gaskets.
13. Disconnect the Power Steering Pressure (PSP) switch electrical connector.
14. For Front Wheel Drive (FWD) vehicles, disconnect the right-hand Catalyst Monitor Sensor (CMS) electrical connector.
15. Disconnect the right-hand Variable Camshaft Timing (VCT) solenoid electrical connector.
16. Disconnect the 3 right-hand coil-on-plug electrical connectors.
17. Disconnect the right-hand Heated Oxygen Sensor (HO2S) electrical connector.

18. Detach all of the wiring harness retainers from the right-hand valve cover and stud bolts.

19. Disconnect the left-hand CMS electrical connector.

20. Disconnect the left-hand VCT solenoid electrical connector.

21. Disconnect the 3 left-hand coil-on-plug electrical connectors.

22. Detach all of the wiring harness retainers from the left-hand valve cover and stud bolts.

23. Remove the 6 bolts and the 6 coil-on-plugs.

24. Remove the A/C compressor nut and stud. The A/C compressor must remain bolted to the cylinder block prior to installing the oil pan.

25. Remove the PSP tube bracket-to-power steering pump bolt.

26. Remove the nut and the PSP tube bracket from the right-hand valve cover stud bolt.

27. Remove the 3 bolts and position aside the power steering pump.

28. Remove the 3 bolts and the accessory drive belt tensioner.

29. Remove the 4 nuts and the left-hand catalytic converter. Discard the nuts and the gasket.

30. For Front Wheel Drive (FWD) vehicles, remove the 4 nuts and the right-hand catalytic converter. Discard the nuts and the gasket.

31. Remove the right-hand cylinder block drain plug or, if equipped, the block heater. Allow coolant to drain from the cylinder block.

32. Remove the left-hand cylinder block drain plug. Allow coolant to drain from the cylinder block.

33. Remove the engine cover stud from the left-hand valve cover stud bolt.

34. For early build vehicles, loosen the 11 stud bolts and remove the left-hand valve cover. Discard the gasket.

35. Loosen the bolt, the 10 stud bolts and remove the right-hand valve cover. Discard the gasket.

36. For late build vehicles, loosen the 9 stud bolts and remove the left-hand valve cover. Discard the gasket.

37. Loosen the 9 stud bolts and remove the right-hand valve cover. Discard the gasket.

38. Using the VCT Spark Plug Tube Seal Remover and Handle, remove the seal(s). Inspect the VCT solenoid seals and the spark plug tube seals. Remove any damaged seals.

39. Using the Strap Wrench, remove the crankshaft pulley bolt and washer. Discard the bolt.

40. Using the 3 Jaw Puller, remove the crankshaft pulley.

41. Using the Oil Seal Remover, remove and discard the crankshaft front seal.

42. Remove the 2 bolts and the engine mount bracket.

43. Remove the 2 engine mount studs. Only use hand tools to remove the studs.

44. Remove the 3 bolts and the engine mount bracket.

45. Remove the 22 engine front cover bolts.

46. Install 6 of the engine front cover bolts (finger tight) into the 6 threaded holes in the engine front cover.

a. Tighten the bolts one turn at a time in a crisscross pattern until the engine front cover-to-cylinder block seal is released.

b. Remove the engine front cover.

47. Remove the 16 oil pan bolts.

48. Install 2 of the oil pan bolts (finger tight) into the 2 threaded holes in the oil pan.

a. Alternately tighten the 2 bolts one turn at a time until the oil pan-to-cylinder block seal is released.

b. Remove the oil pan.

49. Clean the engine front cover and oil pan using a 3M® Roloc® Bristle Disk (2-in white, part number 07528) in a suitable tool turning at the recommended speed of 15,000 rpm. Only use a 3M® Roloc® Bristle Disk to clean the engine front cover and oil pan. Do not use metal scrapers, wire brushes or any other power abrasive disk to clean the engine front cover. These tools cause scratches and gouges that make leak paths.

a. Thoroughly wash the engine front cover and oil pan to remove any foreign material, including any abrasive particles created during the cleaning process.

50. Place clean, lint-free shop towels over exposed engine cavities. Carefully remove the towels so foreign material is not dropped into the engine. Any foreign material (including any material created while cleaning gasket surfaces) that enters the oil passages or the oil pan, may cause engine failure.

WARNING

Do not use wire brushes, power abrasive discs or 3M® Roloc® Bristle Disk (2-in white, part number 07528) to clean the sealing surfaces. These tools cause scratches and gouges that make leak paths. They also cause contamination that will cause premature engine failure. Remove all traces of the gasket.

51. Clean the sealing surfaces of the cylinder block in the following sequence.

a. Remove any large deposits of silicone or gasket material.

b. Apply silicone gasket remover and allow to set for several minutes.

c. Remove the silicone gasket remover. A second application of silicone gasket remover may be required if residual traces of silicone or gasket material remain.

d. Apply metal surface prep to remove any remaining traces of oil or coolant and to prepare the surfaces to bond. Do not attempt to make the metal shiny.

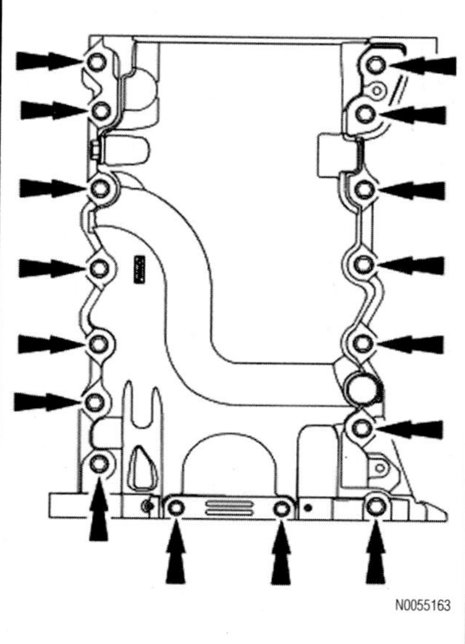

Fig. 109 Remove the 16 oil pan bolts

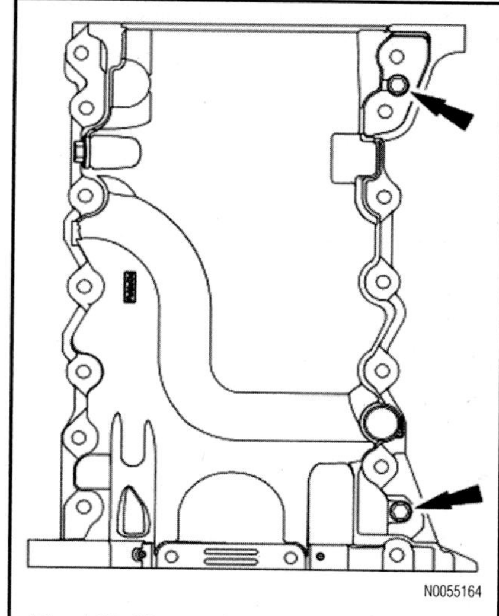

Fig. 110 Alternately tighten the 2 bolts one turn at a time until the seal is released

Some staining of the metal surfaces is normal.

e. Make sure the 2 locating dowel pins are seated correctly in the cylinder block.

To install:

⁂ WARNING

Failure to use Motorcraft® High Performance Engine RTV Silicone may cause the engine oil to foam excessively and result in serious engine damage.

52. Apply a 0.11 in. (3 mm) bead of Motorcraft® High Performance Engine RTV Silicone to the sealing surface of the oil pan.

53. Apply a 0.21 in. (5.5 mm) bead of Motorcraft® High Performance Engine RTV Silicone to the 2 crankshaft seal retainer plate-to-cylinder block joint areas on the sealing surface of the oil pan.

⁂ WARNING

The oil pan and the 4 specified bolts must be installed and the oil pan aligned to the cylinder block and A/C compressor within 4 minutes of sealant application. Final tightening of the oil pan bolts must be carried out within 60 minutes of sealant application.

54. Install the oil pan and bolts 10, 11, 13 and 14.

a. Tighten in the sequence shown to 27 inch lbs. (3 Nm).

b. Loosen the bolts 180 degrees.

⁂ WARNING

The oil pan and the 4 specified bolts must be installed within 4 minutes of the start of sealant application.

55. Position the oil pan so the mounting boss is against the A/C compressor and using a straightedge, align the oil pan flush with the rear of the cylinder block at the 2 areas shown. Align the oil pan to the cylinder block and A/C compressor.

56. Tighten bolts 10, 11, 13 and 14 in the sequence shown, to 27 inch lbs. (3 Nm).

57. Install the remaining oil pan bolts. Tighten all the oil pan bolts in the sequence shown.

a. Tighten the large bolts (1–14) to 15 ft. lbs. (20 Nm).

b. Tighten the small bolts (15 and 16) to 89 inch lbs. (10 Nm).

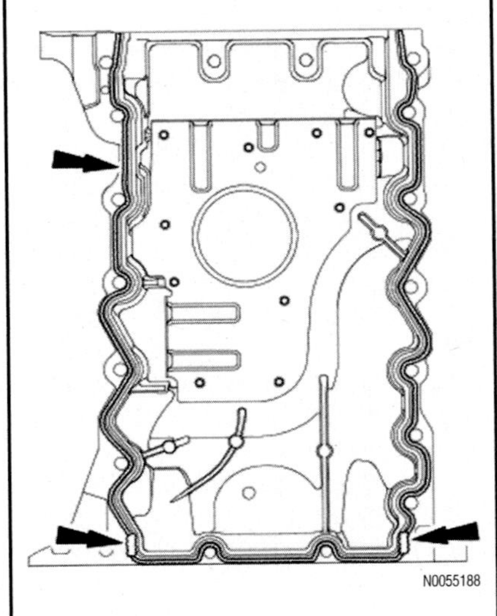

Fig. 111 Oil pan sealant application

58. Install the A/C compressor mounting stud and nut. Tighten the stud to 80 inch lbs. (9 Nm) and the nut to 18 ft. lbs. (25 Nm).

59. Install the Alignment Pins.

60. Apply a 0.11 in. (3 mm) bead of Motorcraft® High Performance Engine RTV Silicone to the engine front cover sealing surfaces including the 3 engine mount bracket bosses.

61. Apply a 0.21 in. (5.5 mm) bead of Motorcraft® High Performance Engine RTV Silicone to the oil pan-to-cylinder block joint and the cylinder head-to-cylinder block joint areas of the engine front cover in 5 places indicated in the Timing Chain Front Cover Removal & Installation procedure.

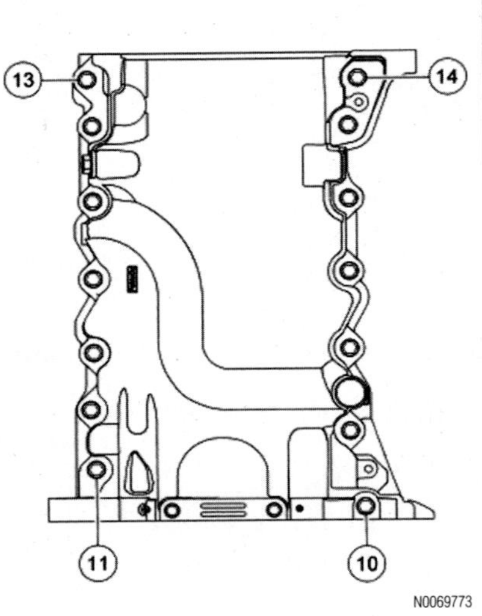

Fig. 112 Oil pan bolts 10, 11, 13 and 14 tightening sequence

62. Install the engine front cover and bolts 17, 18, 19 and 20 as shown in the Timing Chain Front Cover Removal & Installation procedure.

63. Remove the Alignment Pins.

64. Install the engine mount bracket and the 3 bolts. Do not tighten the bolts at this time.

65. Install the remaining engine front cover bolts. Tighten all of the engine front cover bolts and engine mount bracket bolts in 2 stages in the sequence shown in the Timing Chain Front Cover Removal & Installation procedure.

66. Install the engine mount studs in the following sequence.

a. Clean the front cover engine mount stud holes with pressurized air to remove any foreign material.

b. Clean all the thread sealer from the engine mount studs (old and new studs).

c. Apply new Threadlock and Sealer to the engine mount stud threads.

d. Install the 2 engine mount studs. Tighten to 15 ft. lbs. (20 Nm).

67. Install the engine mount bracket and the 2 bolts. Tighten to 18 ft. lbs. (24 Nm).

68. Using the Crankshaft Vibration Damper Installer and Front Crankshaft Seal Installer, install a new crankshaft front seal. Apply clean engine oil to the crankshaft front seal bore in the engine front cover.

69. Using the Crankshaft Vibration Damper Installer and Front Cover Oil Seal Installer, install the crankshaft pulley. Lubricate the outside diameter sealing surfaces with clean engine oil.

70. Using the Strap Wrench, install the crankshaft pulley washer and new bolt and tighten in 4 stages.

a. Stage 1: Tighten to 89 ft. lbs. (120 Nm).

b. Stage 2: Loosen one full turn.

c. Stage 3: Tighten to 37 ft. lbs. (50 Nm).

d. Stage 4: Tighten an additional 90 degrees.

71. Using the VCT Spark Plug Tube Seal Installer and Handle, install new VCT solenoid and/or spark plug tube seals. Installation of new seals is only required if damaged seals were removed during disassembly of the engine.

72. Apply sealant and install the valve covers as shown in the Valve Cover Removal & Installation procedure.

73. Install the engine cover stud to the left-hand valve cover stud bolt. Tighten to 53 inch lbs. (6 Nm).

74. Install the 6 coil-on-plug assemblies

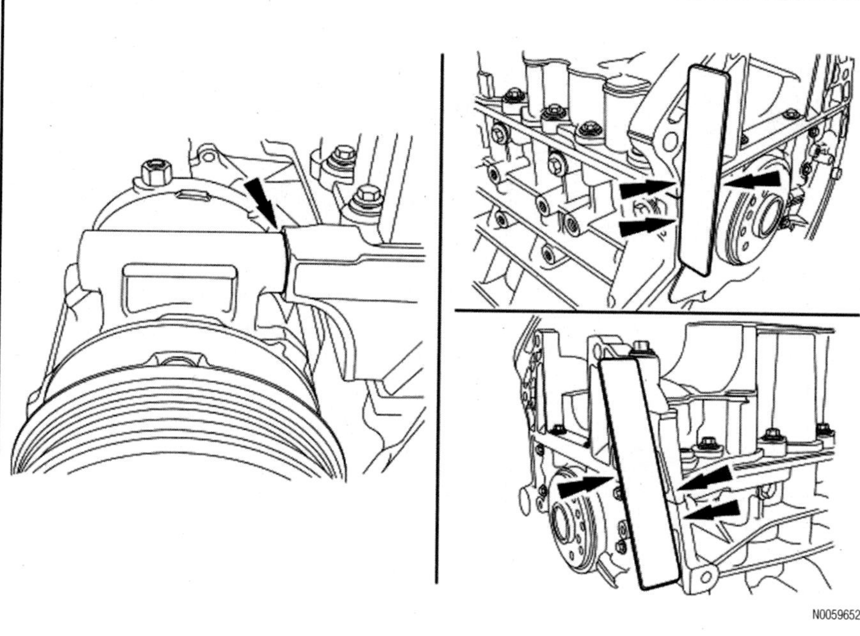

Fig. 113 Align the oil pan to the cylinder block and A/C compressor

and the 6 bolts. Tighten to 62 inch lbs. (7 Nm).

75. Install the left-hand cylinder block drain plug. Tighten to 15 ft. lbs. (20 Nm) plus an additional 180 degrees.

76. Install the right-hand cylinder block drain plug or, if equipped, the block heater. Tighten to 30 ft. lbs. (40 Nm).

77. For Front Wheel Drive (FWD) vehicles, using a new gasket, install the right-hand catalytic converter and 4 new nuts. Tighten to 30 ft. lbs. (40 Nm).

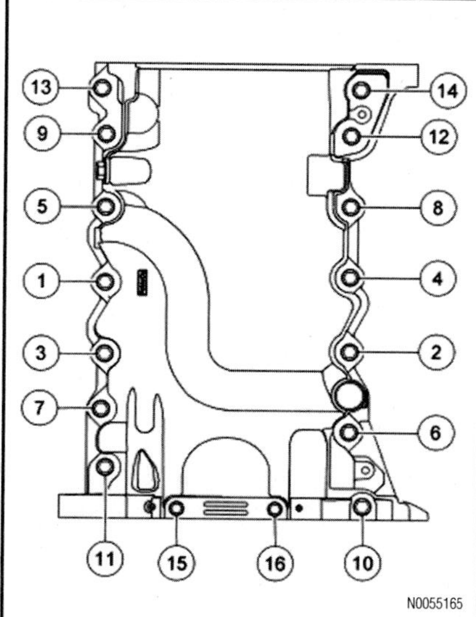

Fig. 114 Oil pan bolts tightening sequence

78. Using a new gasket, install the left-hand catalytic converter and 4 new nuts. Tighten to 30 ft. lbs. (40 Nm).

79. Install the accessory drive belt tensioner and the 3 bolts. Tighten to 97 inch lbs. (11 Nm).

80. Install the power steering pump and the 3 bolts. Tighten to 18 ft. lbs. (24 Nm).

81. Install the Power Steering Pressure (PSP) tube bracket bolt. Tighten to 89 inch lbs. (10 Nm).

82. Install the PSP bracket and nut to the right-hand valve cover stud bolt. Tighten to 62 inch lbs. (7 Nm).

83. Attach all of the wiring harness retainers to the left-hand valve cover and stud bolts.

84. Connect the 3 left-hand coil-on-plug electrical connectors.

85. Connect the left-hand camshaft VCT solenoid electrical connector.

86. Connect the left-hand Catalyst Monitor Sensor (CMS) electrical connector.

87. Attach all of the wiring harness retainers to the right-hand valve cover and stud bolts.

88. Connect the right-hand Heated Oxygen Sensor (HO2S) electrical connector.

89. Connect the 3 right-hand coil-on-plug electrical connectors.

90. Connect the right-hand VCT solenoid electrical connector.

91. For Front Wheel Drive (FWD) vehicles, connect the right-hand CMS electrical connector.

92. Connect the PSP switch electrical connector.

WARNING

If the engine is repaired or replaced because of upper engine failure, typically including valve or piston damage, check the intake manifold for metal debris. If metal debris is found, install a new intake manifold.

93. Using new gaskets, install the upper intake manifold and the 6 bolts. Tighten in the sequence shown in the Intake Manifold Removal & Installation procedure to 89 inch lbs. (10 Nm).

94. Install the fuel tube bracket bolt to the upper intake manifold. Tighten to 53 inch lbs. (6 Nm).

95. Install the upper intake manifold support bracket bolt. Tighten to 89 inch lbs. (10 Nm).

96. Attach the wiring harness retainers to the upper intake manifold.

97. Connect the Throttle Body (TB) electrical connector.

98. Connect the PCV hose to the PCV valve.

99. If equipped, connect the block heater electrical connector and install the heat shield.

100. Attach all the engine block heater wiring harness retainer.

101. Using the Heavy Duty Floor Crane and Spreader Bar, remove the engine from the stand.

102. Install the crankshaft sensor ring.

103. Install the flexplate and the 8 bolts. Tighten to 59 ft. lbs. (80 Nm).

104. Install the engine in the vehicle.

OIL PUMP

REMOVAL & INSTALLATION

See Figures 115 and 116.

WARNING

During engine repair procedures, cleanliness is extremely important. Any foreign material, including any material created while cleaning gasket surfaces, that enters the oil passages, coolant passages or the oil pan may cause engine failure.

➡On early build engines, the timing chain rides on the inner side of the right-hand timing chain guide. Late build engines are equipped with a different design right-hand timing chain guide that requires the timing chain to ride on the outer side of the right-hand

timing chain guide. For service, all replacement right-hand timing chain guides will be the late build design.

1. Remove the engine front cover. Refer to Timing Chain Front Cover Removal & Installation.
2. Remove the following components. Refer to Timing Chain Removal & Installation:
    a. Rotate the crankshaft clockwise and align the timing marks on the Variable Camshaft Timing (VCT) assemblies.
    b. Install the Camshaft Holding Tool onto the flats of the left-hand and right-hand camshafts.
    c. Remove the bolts and the right-hand and left-hand VCT housing.
    d. Remove the 2 bolts and the primary timing chain tensioner.
    e. Remove the primary timing chain tensioner arm.
    f. Remove the 2 bolts and the lower left-hand primary timing chain guide.
    g. Remove the primary timing chain.
    h. Remove the crankshaft timing chain sprocket.
3. Remove the 2 bolts and the oil pump screen and pickup tube. Discard the O-ring seal.
4. Remove the 3 bolts and the oil pump.

To install:

5. Install the oil pump and the 3 bolts. Tighten to 89 inch lbs. (10 Nm).
6. Using a new O-ring seal, install the oil pump screen and pickup tube and the 2 bolts. Tighten to 89 inch lbs. (10 Nm).
7. Install the following components. Refer to Timing Chain Removal & Installation:
    a. Install the crankshaft timing chain sprocket.
    b. Install the primary timing chain with the colored links aligned with the timing marks on the VCT assemblies and the crankshaft sprocket.

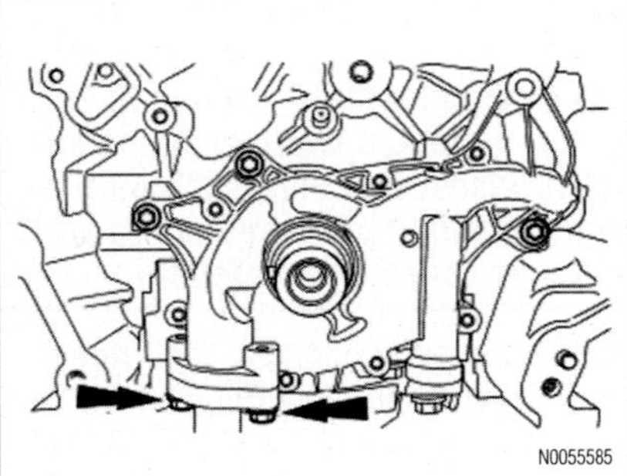

Fig. 115 Remove the 2 bolts and the oil pump screen and pickup tube

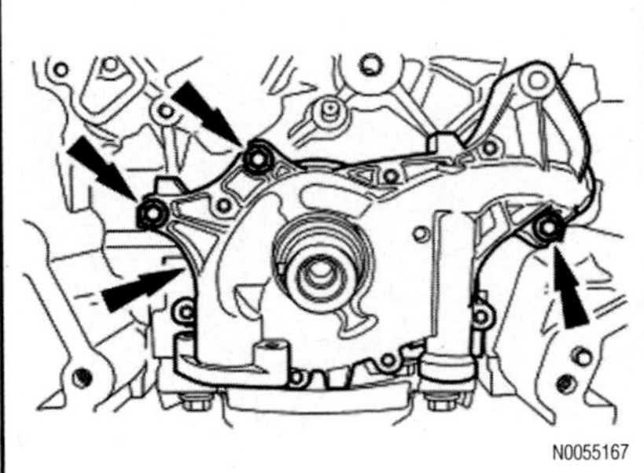

Fig. 116 Remove the 3 bolts and the oil pump

    c. Install the left-hand primary timing chain guide and tighten the 2 bolts to 89 inch lbs. (10 Nm).
    d. Install the primary timing chain tensioner arm.
    e. Reset the primary timing chain tensioner.
    f. Install the primary tensioner and tighten the 2 bolts to 89 inch lbs. (10 Nm). Remove the lockpin.
    g. Verify correct alignment of all timing marks.
    h. Inspect the VCT housing seals for damage and replace as necessary. Install the right-hand and left-hand VCT housing and the bolts.
8. Install the engine front cover.

PISTON AND RING

POSITIONING

See Figure 117.

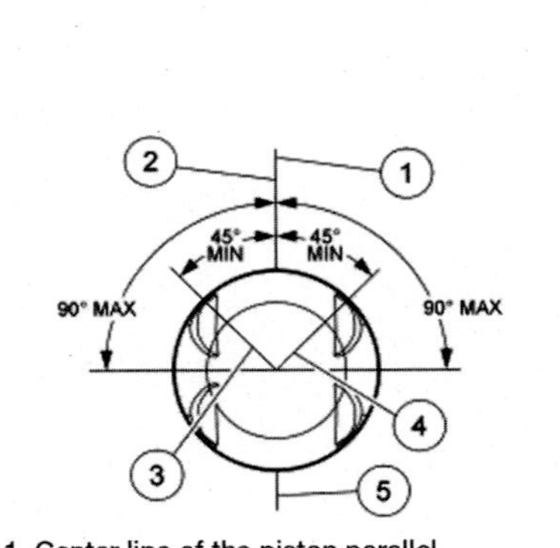

Fig. 117 Piston and ring positioning

The piston compression upper and lower ring should be installed with the "O" mark on the ring face pointing up toward the top of the piston.

Install the piston rings onto the piston as shown.

REAR MAIN SEAL

REMOVAL & INSTALLATION

See Figures 118 and 119.

1. With the vehicle in NEUTRAL, position it on a hoist.
2. Remove the transaxle.
3. Remove the 8 bolts and the flexplate.
4. Remove the crankshaft sensor ring.
5. Using the Crankshaft Rear Oil Seal Remover and Slide Hammer (SST 303-519, 307-005) or equivalent tools, remove and discard the rear crankshaft seal.
    a. Clean all sealing surfaces with metal surface prep.

To install:

6. Lubricate the seal lips and bore with clean engine oil prior to installation. Position the Rear Main Seal Installer onto the end of the crankshaft and slide a new crankshaft rear seal onto the tool.

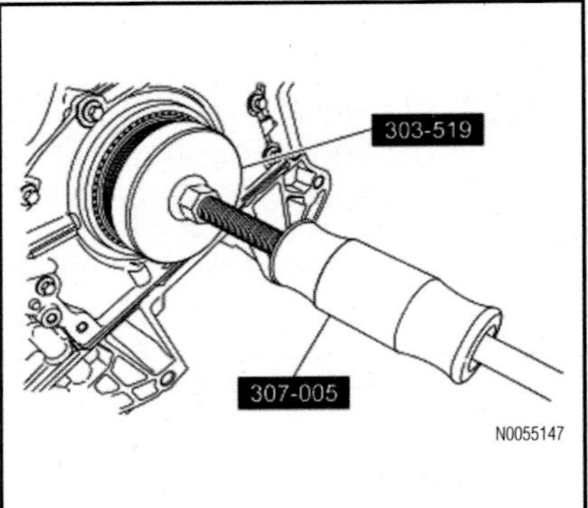

Fig. 118 Remove the rear crankshaft seal

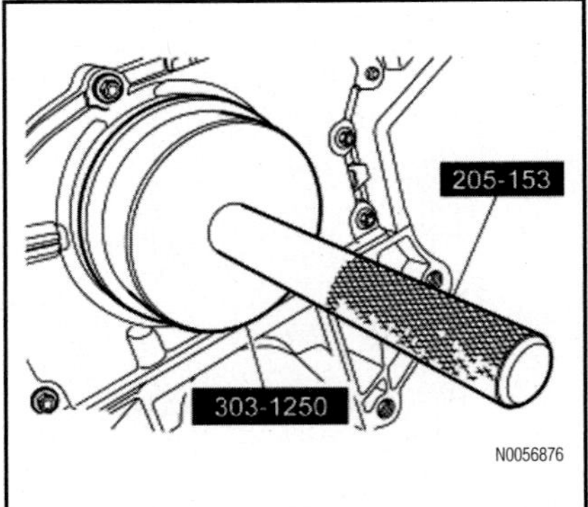

Fig. 119 Install the rear crankshaft seal

7. Using the Rear Main Seal Installer and Handle (SST 303-1250, 205-153) or equivalent tools, install the new crankshaft rear seal.
8. Install the crankshaft sensor ring.
9. Install the flexplate and the 8 bolts. Tighten to 59 ft. lbs. (80 Nm).
10. Install the transaxle.

TIMING CHAIN FRONT COVER

REMOVAL & INSTALLATION

3.5L Engines

See Figures 120 through 126.

**** WARNING**

During engine repair procedures, cleanliness is extremely important. Any foreign material, including any material created while cleaning gasket surfaces, that enters the oil passages, coolant passages or the oil pan may cause engine failure.

➡On early build engines, the timing chain rides on the inner side of the right-hand timing chain guide. Late build engines are equipped with a different design right-hand timing chain guide that requires the timing chain to ride on the outer side of the right-hand timing chain guide. For service, all replacement right-hand timing chain guides will be the late build design.

1. With the vehicle in NEUTRAL, position it on a hoist.
2. Disconnect the left-hand Heated Oxygen Sensor (HO2S) electrical connector.
3. Detach the HO2S connector retainer from the bracket.
4. For late build vehicles, remove the intake manifold.
5. Remove the left-hand and right-hand valve cover.
6. Remove the 4 retainers and the underbody shield.
7. Remove the right-hand inner fender splash shield.
8. Remove the accessory drive belt and tensioner.
9. Loosen the 3 bolts on the rear roll restrictor.
10. Loosen the bolt on each side of the front roll restrictor.
11. Remove the oil pan drain plug and drain the engine oil. Install the drain plug and tighten to 30 ft. lbs. (27 Nm).

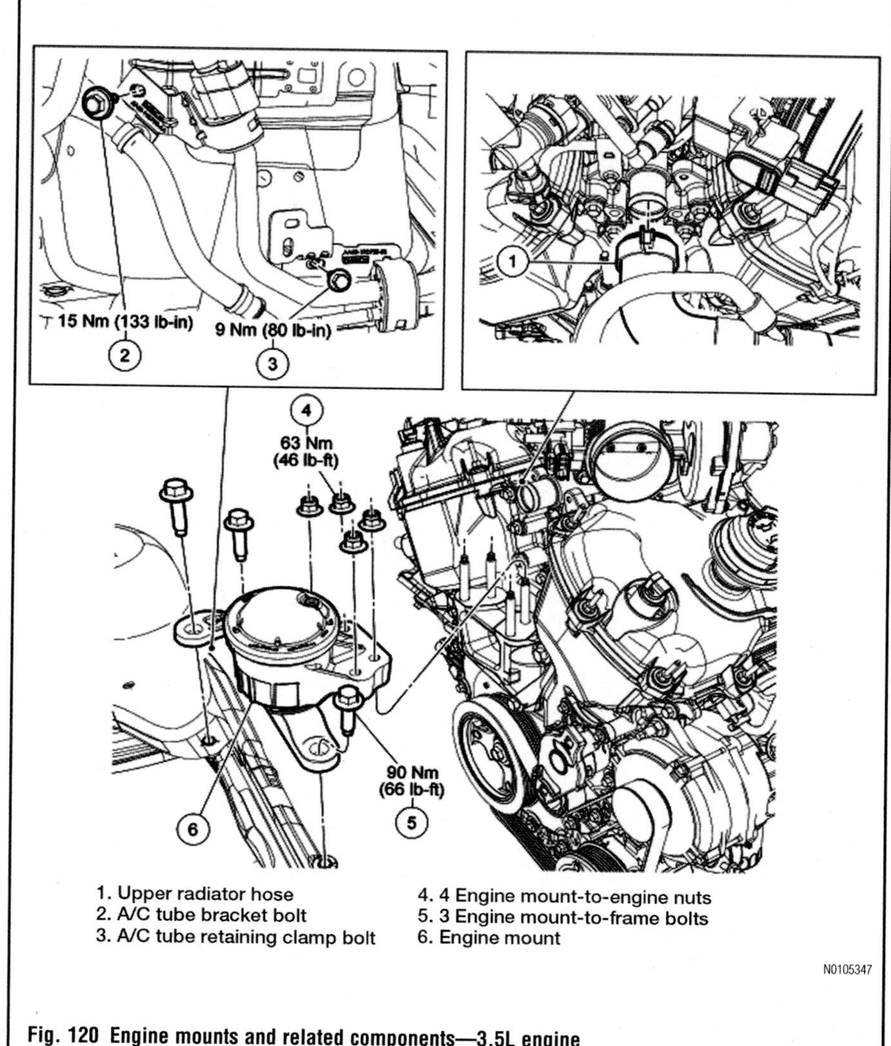

Fig. 120 Engine mounts and related components—3.5L engine

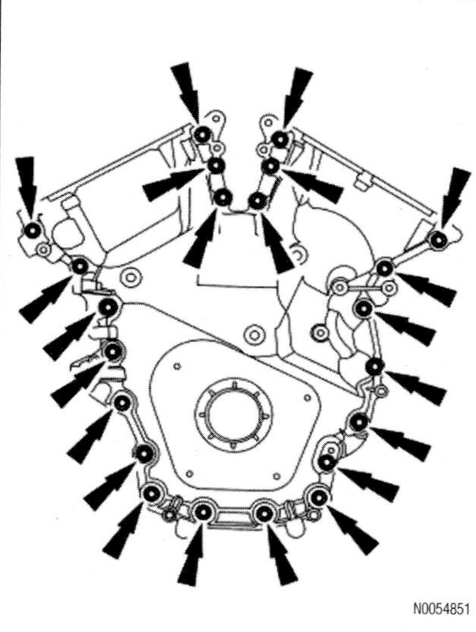

Fig. 121 Remove the 22 engine front cover bolts

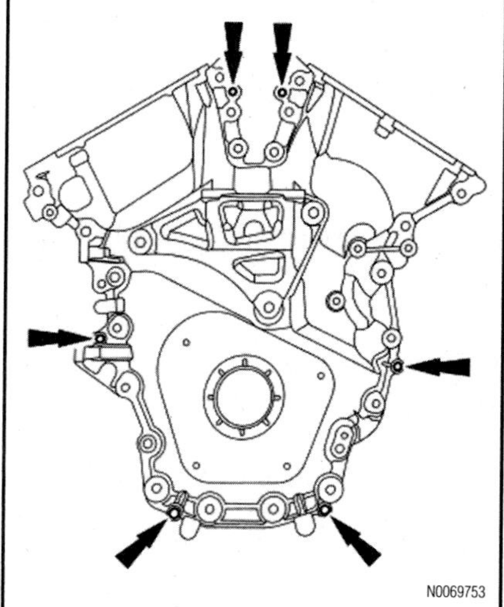

Fig. 122 Install 6 of the engine front cover bolts into the 6 threaded holes in the engine front cover

12. Remove the crankshaft bolt and washer. Discard the bolt. Remove the crankshaft pulley, and remove and discard the crankshaft front seal. Refer to Crankshaft Front Seal Removal & Installation.

13. Remove the engine mount.

14. Detach the right-hand Heated Oxygen Sensor (HO2S) electrical connector from the bracket. Remove the stud bolt and the bracket.

15. Using the floor jack, raise the engine slightly.

16. Remove the 2 upper engine mount bracket bolts.

17. Using the floor jack, lower the engine slightly.

18. Loosen the lower engine mount bracket bolt and remove the engine mount bracket and bolt as an assembly.

19. Remove the 22 engine front cover bolts.

20. Install 6 of the engine front cover bolts (finger tight) into the 6 threaded holes in the engine front cover.

a. Tighten the bolts one turn at a time in a crisscross pattern until the engine front cover-to-cylinder block seal is released.

b. Remove the engine front cover.

To install:

WARNING

Only use a 3M® Roloc® Bristle Disk (2 in white, part number 07528), to clean the engine front cover. Do not use metal scrapers, wire brushes or any other power abrasive disk to clean the engine front cover.

21. Clean the engine front cover using a 3M® Roloc® Bristle Disk in a suitable tool turning at the recommended speed of 15,000 rpm. Thoroughly wash the engine front cover to remove any foreign material, including any abrasive particles created during the cleaning process.

WARNING

Place clean, lint free shop towels over exposed engine cavities. Carefully remove the towels so foreign material is not dropped into the engine. Any foreign material (including any material created while cleaning gasket surfaces) that enters the oil passages or the oil pan, may cause engine failure.

22. Clean the sealing surfaces of the cylinder heads, the cylinder block and the oil pan. Refer to Cylinder Head Removal & Installation.

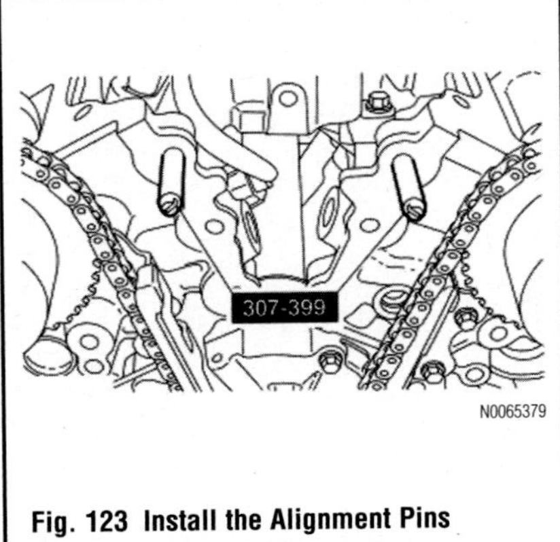

Fig. 123 Install the Alignment Pins

23. Make sure the 2 locating dowel pins are seated correctly in the cylinder block.

24. Install the Alignment Pins.

WARNING

Failure to use the correct RTV Silicone Sealant (TA-357) may cause the engine oil to foam excessively and result in serious engine damage.

25. Apply a 0.11 in. (3.0 mm) bead of RTV Silicone Sealant (TA-357) to the engine front cover sealing surfaces including the 3 engine mount bracket bosses.

a. Apply a 0.21 in. (5.5 mm) bead of RTV Silicone Sealant (TA-357) to the oil pan-to-cylinder block joint and the cylinder head-to-cylinder block joint areas of the engine front cover in 5 places as indicated.

26. Install the engine front cover and bolts 17, 18, 19 and 20.

a. The engine front cover and bolts 17, 18, 19 and 20 must be installed within 4 minutes of the initial sealant application. The remainder of the engine front cover bolts and the engine mount bracket bolts must be installed and tightened within 35 minutes of the initial sealant application. If the time limits are exceeded, the sealant must be removed, the sealing area cleaned and sealant reapplied. To clean the sealing area, use silicone gasket remover and metal surface prep.

b. Make sure the 2 locating dowel pins are seated correctly in the cylinder block.

c. Tighten in sequence to 27 inch lbs. (3 Nm).

27. Remove the Alignment Pins.

28. Install the engine mount bracket and lower bolt. Do not tighten at this time.

29. Using the floor jack, raise the engine slightly.

30. Install the 2 upper engine mount bracket bolts. Do not tighten at this time.

31. Install the remaining engine front cover bolts. Tighten all of the engine front cover bolts and engine mount bracket bolts in the sequence shown in 2 stages:

a. Stage 1: Tighten bolts 1 thru 22 to 89 inch lbs. (10 Nm) and bolts 23, 24 and 25 to 11 ft. lbs. (15 Nm).

b. Stage 2: Tighten bolts 1 thru 22 to 18 ft. lbs. (24 Nm) and bolts 23, 24 and 25 to 55 ft. lbs. (75 Nm).

c. Do not expose the RTV Silicone Sealant to engine oil for at least 90 minutes after installing the engine front

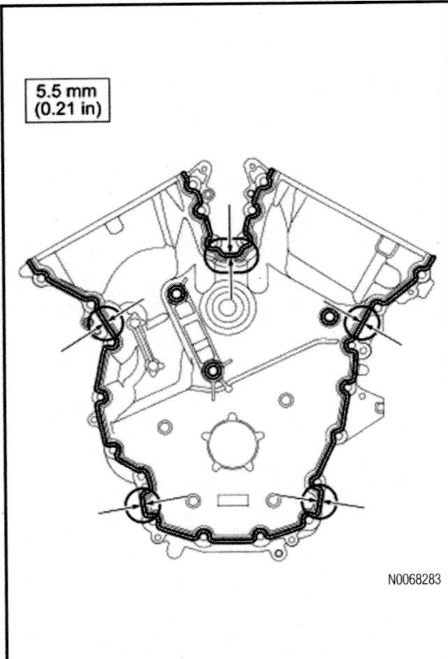

Fig. 124 Sealant application

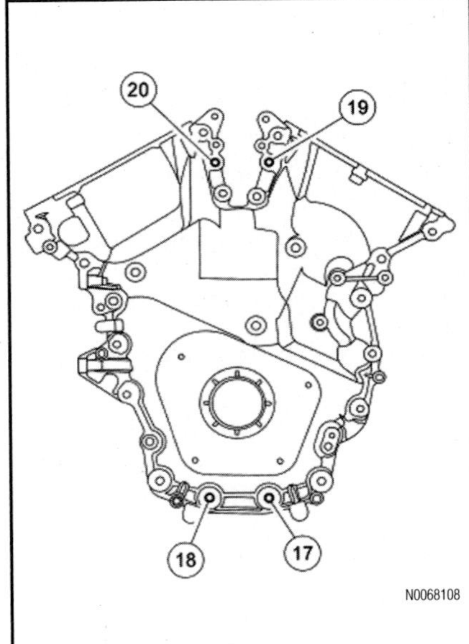

Fig. 125 Tighten bolts 17, 18, 19 and 20 in sequence

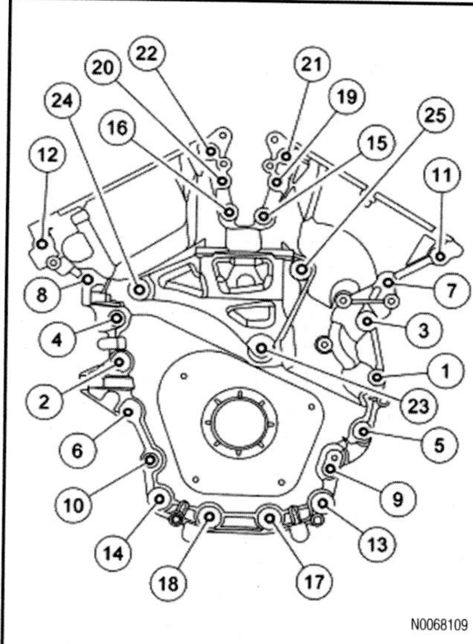

Fig. 126 Engine front cover bolt tightening sequence

cover. Failure to follow this instruction may cause oil leakage.

32. Install the HO2S connector bracket and stud bolt.
    a. Tighten to 89 inch lbs. (10 Nm).
    b. Attach the HO2S electrical connector.

⁂ WARNING

The thread sealer on the engine mount studs (including new engine mount studs if applicable) must be cleaned off with a wire brush and new Threadlock and Sealer applied prior to installing the engine mount studs. Failure to follow this procedure may result in damage to the engine mount studs or engine.

33. Install the engine mount.
34. Install a new crankshaft front seal. Install the crankshaft pulley, crankshaft pulley washer, and new bolt.
35. Tighten the bolt on each side of the front roll restrictor. Tighten to 66 ft. lbs. (90 Nm).
36. Tighten the 3 bolts on the rear roll restrictor. Tighten to 66 ft. lbs. (90 Nm).
37. Install the accessory drive belt tensioner and belt.
38. Install the right-hand inner fender splash shield.
39. Install the underbody shield and the 4 retainers.
40. Install the right-hand and left-hand valve covers.
41. For late build vehicles, install the intake manifold.
42. Connect the left-hand HO2S electrical connector. Attach the HO2S connector retainer to the bracket.
43. Fill the engine with clean engine oil.

3.7L Engines

See Figures 127 through 133.

⁂ WARNING

During engine repair procedures, cleanliness is extremely important. Any foreign material, including any material created while cleaning gasket surfaces, that enters the oil passages, coolant passages or the oil pan may cause engine failure.

1. With the vehicle in NEUTRAL, position it on a hoist.
2. Recover the A/C system.
3. Remove the Air Cleaner (ACL) outlet pipe.
4. Remove the front wheels and tires.
5. Remove the accessory drive belt, tensioner and the power steering belt.
6. Remove the degas bottle.
7. Remove the Evaporative Emission (EVAP) canister purge valve.
8. Remove the nut and disconnect the A/C tube. Discard the O-ring seal and gasket seal.
9. Remove the nut and the A/C tube. Discard the O-ring seal and gasket seal.
10. Remove the nut and disconnect the rear A/C tube. Discard the O-ring seal and gasket seal.
11. Working from under the vehicle, remove the nut and disconnect the rear A/C tube. Discard the O-ring seal and gasket seal.
12. Disconnect the power steering cooler tube and drain the power steering fluid into a suitable container.

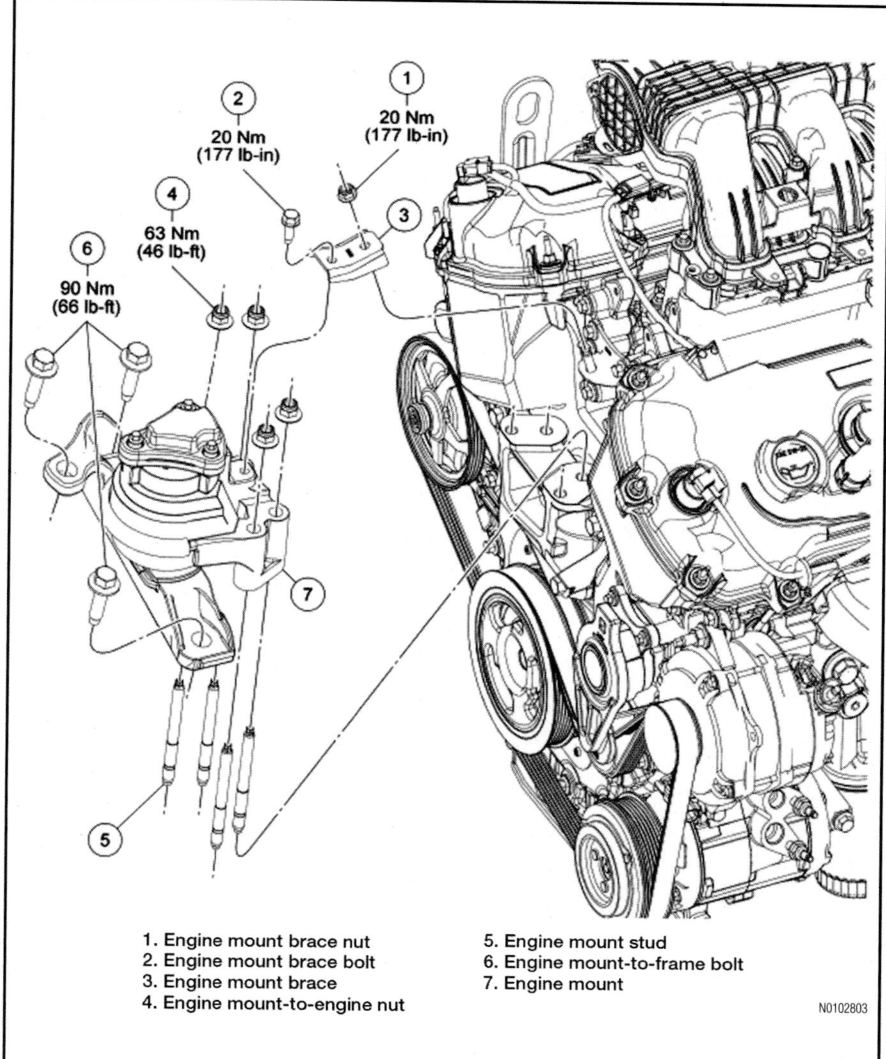

Fig. 127 Engine mounts and related components—3.7L engine

13. Remove the right-hand inner fender splash shield.

14. Remove the crankshaft bolt and washer. Discard the bolt. Remove the crankshaft pulley, and remove and discard the crankshaft front seal. Refer to Crankshaft Front Seal Removal & Installation.

15. Remove the 4 Y-pipe-to-catalytic converter nuts. Discard the nuts.

16. Remove the 2 Y-pipe flange nuts.

a. Detach the exhaust hanger and remove the Y-pipe.

b. Discard the gaskets and nuts.

17. Remove the drain plug and drain the engine oil. Install the drain plug and tighten to 20 ft. lbs. (27 Nm).

18. Disconnect the hose from the power steering reservoir.

19. Remove the right-hand and left-hand valve covers.

20. Remove the bolt and the ground cable.

21. Disconnect the power steering pressure switch electrical connector.

22. Remove the power steering pressure tube bracket-to-power steering pump bolt.

23. Remove the 3 bolts and position aside the power steering pump.

24. Position a floor jack and the Oil Pan Holding Fixture under the oil pan. The Oil Pan Holding Fixture must be carefully aligned to the mounting bosses on the oil pan.

25. Remove the nut, bolt and engine mount brace.

26. Remove the 4 engine mount nuts.

27. Remove the 3 bolts and the engine mount.

N0054851

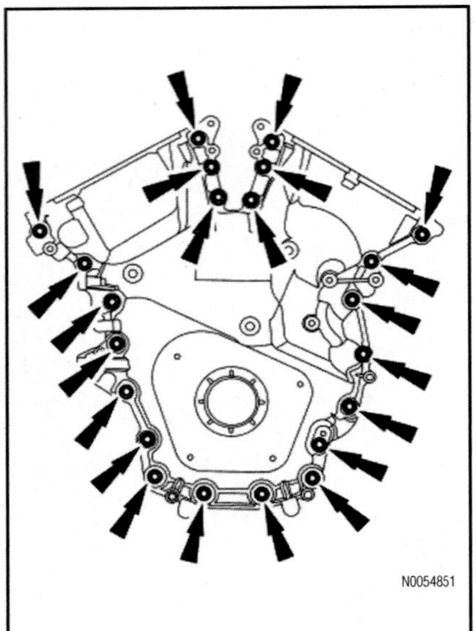

Fig. 128 Remove the 22 engine front cover bolts

28. Remove the 2 bolts and the engine mount bracket.

29. Using hand tools, remove the 2 engine mount studs.

30. Remove the 2 upper engine mount bracket bolts.

31. Loosen the lower engine mount bracket bolt and remove the engine mount bracket and bolt as an assembly.

32. Detach the A/C tube and wiring harness from the retainers.

33. Remove the A/C tube bracket bolt.

34. Remove the A/C tube retaining clamp bolt.

35. Remove the A/C tube-to-evaporator bolt and the 2 A/C tubes. Discard the O-ring seals.

36. Using the floor jack, raise the engine slightly.

37. Remove the 22 engine front cover bolts.

38. Install 6 of the engine front cover bolts (finger tight) into the 6 threaded holes in the engine front cover.

a. Tighten the bolts one turn at a time in a crisscross pattern until the engine front cover-to-cylinder block seal is released.

b. Remove the engine front cover.

To install:

WARNING

Only use a 3M® Roloc® Bristle Disk (2-in white, part number 07528) to clean the engine front cover. Do not use metal scrapers, wire brushes or any other power abrasive disk to clean the engine front cover. These tools cause scratches and gouges that make leak paths.

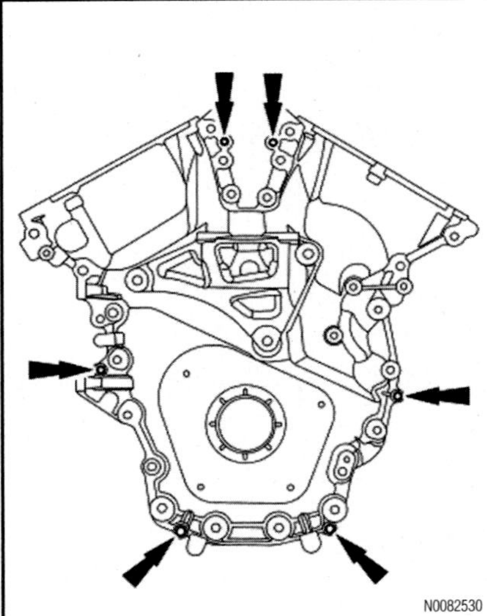

Fig. 129 Install 6 of the engine front cover bolts into the 6 threaded holes in the engine front cover

39. Clean the engine front cover using a 3M® Roloc® Bristle Disk in a suitable tool turning at the recommended speed of 15,000 rpm.

a. Thoroughly wash the engine front cover to remove any foreign material, including any abrasive particles created during the cleaning process.

WARNING

Place clean, lint-free shop towels over exposed engine cavities. Carefully remove the towels so foreign material is not dropped into the engine. Any foreign material (including any material created while cleaning gasket surfaces) that enters the oil passages or the oil pan may cause engine failure.

40. Clean the sealing surfaces of the cylinder heads, the cylinder block and the oil pan. Refer to Cylinder Head Removal & Installation.

41. Make sure the 2 locating dowel pins are seated correctly in the cylinder block.

42. Install the Alignment Pins.

WARNING

Failure to use Motorcraft® High Performance Engine RTV Silicone may cause the engine oil to foam excessively and result in serious engine damage.

43. Apply a 0.11 in. (3.0 mm) bead of Motorcraft® High Performance Engine RTV Silicone to the engine front cover sealing surfaces including the 3 engine mount bracket bosses.

a. Apply a 0.21 in. (5.5 mm) bead of Motorcraft® High Performance Engine RTV Silicone to the oil pan-to-cylinder

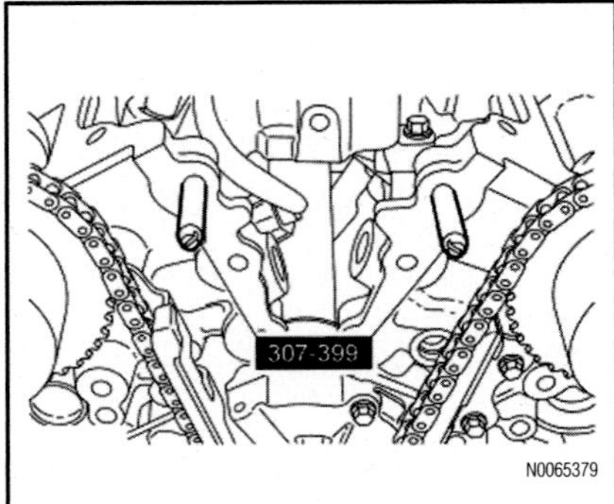

Fig. 130 Install the Alignment Pins

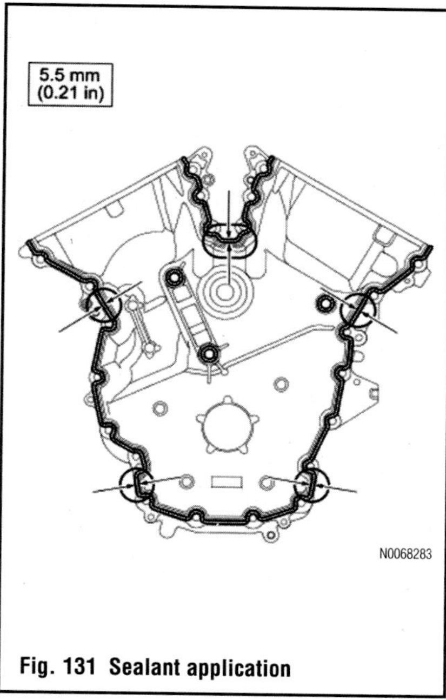

Fig. 131 Sealant application

block joint and the cylinder head-to-cylinder block joint areas of the engine front cover in 5 places as indicated.

b. The engine front cover and bolts 17, 18, 19 and 20 must be installed within 4 minutes of the initial sealant application. The remainder of the engine front cover bolts and the engine mount bracket bolts must be installed and tightened within 35 minutes of the initial sealant application. If the time limits are exceeded, the sealant must be removed, the sealing area cleaned and sealant reapplied. To clean the sealing area, use silicone gasket remover and metal surface prep.

44. Install the engine front cover and bolts 17, 18, 19 and 20. Make sure the 2 locating dowel pins are seated correctly in the cylinder block. Tighten in sequence to 27 inch lbs. (3 Nm).

45. Remove the Alignment Pins.

46. Install the engine mount bracket and lower bolt. Do not tighten at this time.

47. Install the 2 upper engine mount bracket bolts. Do not tighten at this time.

48. Install the remaining engine front cover bolts. Tighten all of the engine front cover bolts and engine mount bracket bolts in the sequence shown in 2 stages:

a. Stage 1: Tighten bolts 1 thru 22 to 89 inch lbs. (10 Nm) and bolts 23, 24 and 25 to 11 ft. lbs. (15 Nm).

b. Stage 2: Tighten bolts 1 thru 22 to 18 ft. lbs. (24 Nm) and bolts 23, 24 and 25 to 55 ft. lbs. (75 Nm).

c. Do not expose the Motorcraft® High Performance Engine RTV Silicone to engine oil for at least 90 minutes after installing the engine front cover.

49. Using the floor jack, lower the engine to the installed position.

50. Install the new O-ring seals and the A/C tubes-to-evaporator and the bolt. Tighten to 71 inch lbs. (8 Nm).

51. Install the A/C tube retaining clamp bolt. Tighten to 80 inch lbs. (9 Nm).

52. Install the A/C tube bracket bolt. Tighten to 11 ft. lbs. (15 Nm).

53. Attach the A/C tube and wiring harness to the retainers.

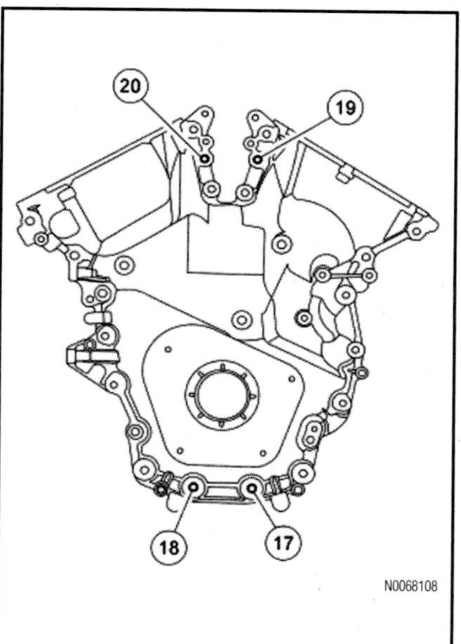

Fig. 132 Tighten bolts 17, 18, 19 and 20 in sequence

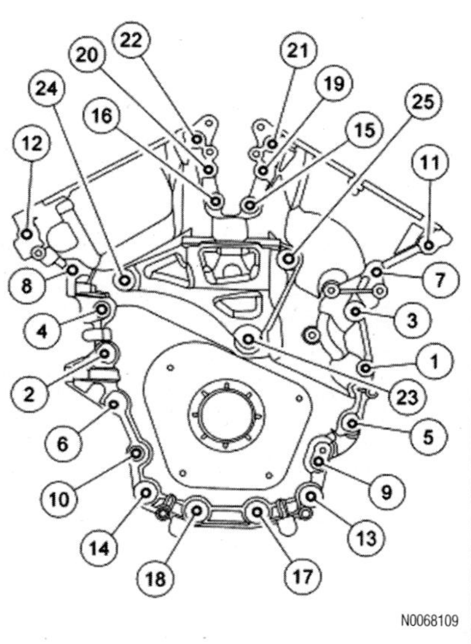

Fig. 133 Engine front cover bolt tightening sequence

WARNING

The thread sealer on the engine mount studs (including new engine mount studs if applicable) must be cleaned off with a wire brush and new Threadlock and Sealer applied prior to installing the engine mount studs. Failure to follow this procedure may result in damage to the engine mount studs or engine.

54. Install the engine mount studs in the following sequence.

a. Clean the front cover engine mount stud holes with pressurized air to remove any foreign material.

b. Clean all the thread sealer from the engine mount studs (old and new studs).

c. Apply new Threadlock and Sealer to the engine mount stud threads.

d. Install the 2 engine mount studs. Tighten to 15 ft. lbs. (20 Nm).

55. Install the engine mount bracket and the 2 bolts. Tighten to 18 ft. lbs. (24 Nm).

56. Install the engine mount and the 3 bolts. Tighten to 66 ft. lbs. (90 Nm).

57. Install the 4 engine mount nuts. Tighten to 46 ft. lbs. (63 Nm).

58. Install the engine mount brace, nut and bolt. Tighten to 15 ft. lbs. (20 Nm).

59. Position the power steering pump and install the 3 bolts. Tighten to 18 ft. lbs. (25 Nm).

60. Install the power steering pressure tube bracket-to-power steering pump bolt. Tighten to 89 inch lbs. (10 Nm).

61. Connect the power steering pressure switch electrical connector.

62. Install the ground cable bolt. Tighten to 106 inch lbs. (12 Nm).

63. Install the right-hand and left-hand valve covers.

64. Connect the hose to the power steering reservoir.

65. Using a new gasket, install the exhaust Y-pipe and install the 2 new nuts.

a. Tighten to 30 ft. lbs. (40 Nm).

b. Attach the exhaust hanger.

66. Install the exhaust Y-pipe assembly and 4 new nuts. Tighten to 30 ft. lbs. (40 Nm).

67. Install a new crankshaft front seal. Install the crankshaft pulley, crankshaft pulley washer, and new bolt.

68. Install the right-hand inner fender splash shield.

69. Connect the power steering cooler tube.

70. Using new O-ring seals and gasket seals, install the A/C tubes and the nuts. Tighten to 11 ft. lbs. (15 Nm).

71. Install the EVAP canister purge valve.
72. Install the degas bottle.
73. Install the accessory drive belt, tensioner and the power steering belt.
74. Install the front wheels and tires.
75. Install the engine ACL outlet pipe.
76. Fill the engine with clean engine oil.
77. Fill the power steering system.
78. Recharge the A/C system.

TIMING CHAIN & SPROCKETS

REMOVAL & INSTALLATION

See Figures 134 through 152.

⁂ WARNING

During engine repair procedures, cleanliness is extremely important. Any foreign material, including any material created while cleaning gasket surfaces, that enters the oil passages, coolant passages or the oil pan may cause engine failure.

➡On early build engines, the timing chain rides on the inner side of the right-hand timing chain guide. Late build engines are equipped with a different design right-hand timing chain guide that requires the timing chain to ride on the outer side of the right-hand timing chain guide. For service, all replacement right-hand timing chain guides will be the late build design.

1. Remove the engine front cover. Refer to Timing Chain Front Cover Removal & Installation.
2. Rotate the crankshaft clockwise and align the timing marks on the Variable Camshaft Timing (VCT) assemblies as shown.
3. Install the Camshaft Holding Tool (SST 303-1248) or equivalent tool onto the flats of the left-hand and right-hand camshafts. The tool will hold the camshafts in the Top Dead Center (TDC) position.
4. Remove the 3 bolts and the right-hand VCT housing.
5. Remove the 3 bolts and the left-hand VCT housing.
6. Remove the 2 bolts and the primary timing chain tensioner.
7. Remove the primary timing chain tensioner arm.
8. Remove the 2 bolts and the lower left-hand primary timing chain guide.
9. Remove the primary timing chain.
10. Remove the crankshaft timing chain sprocket.
11. Remove the 2 bolts and the upper left-hand primary timing chain guide.
12. Compress the left-hand secondary timing chain tensioner and install a suitable lockpin to retain the tensioner in the collapsed position.
13. Remove and discard the left-hand VCT assembly bolt and the left-hand exhaust camshaft sprocket bolt. The VCT bolt and the exhaust camshaft bolt must be discarded and new ones installed. However, the exhaust camshaft washer is reusable.

Fig. 134 Rotate the crankshaft clockwise and align the timing marks on the VCT assemblies—early build vehicles

Fig. 135 Rotate the crankshaft clockwise and align the timing marks on the VCT assemblies—late build vehicles

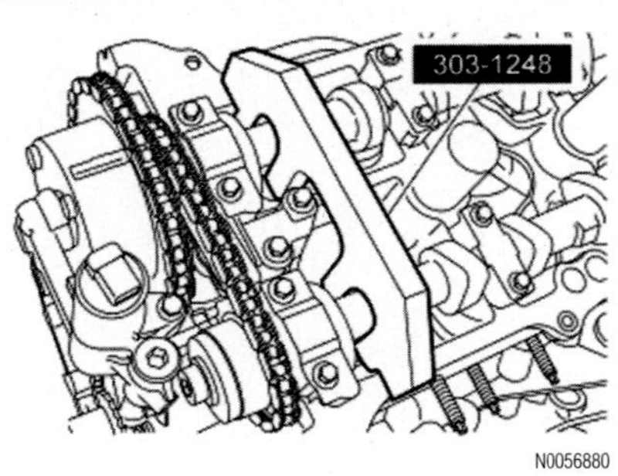

Fig. 136 Install the Camshaft Holding Tool onto the flats of the camshafts—left-hand shown, right-hand similar

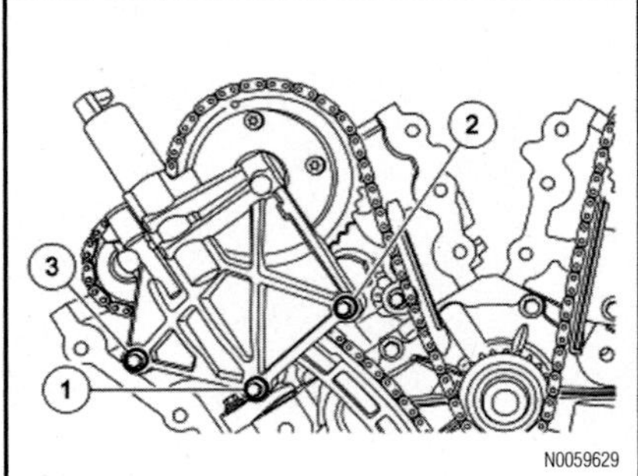

Fig. 137 Right-hand VCT housing bolt installation sequence

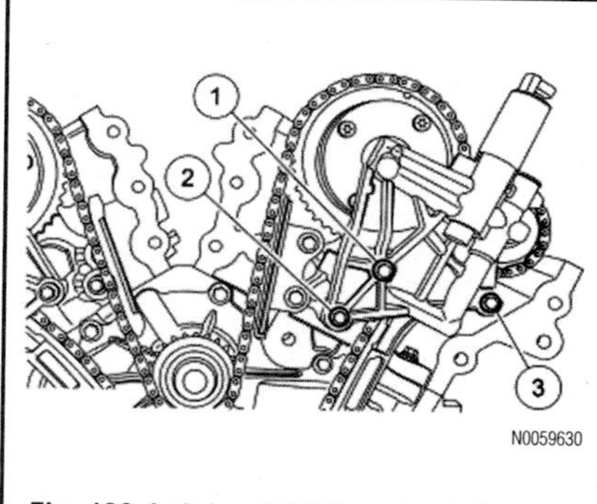

Fig. 138 Left-hand VCT housing bolt installation sequence

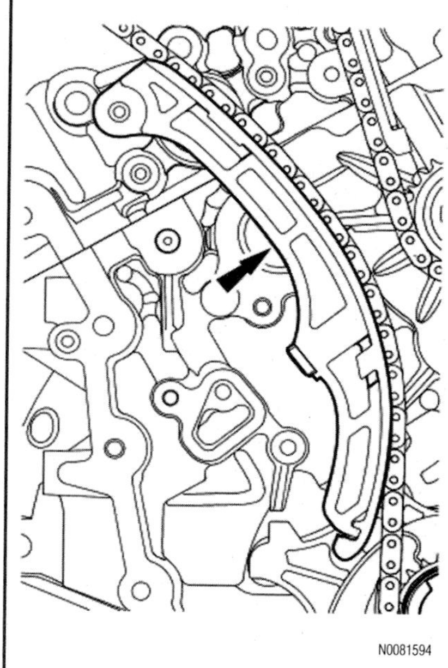

Fig. 139 Remove the primary timing chain tensioner arm

a. Remove the left-hand VCT assembly, secondary timing chain and the left-hand exhaust camshaft sprocket as an assembly.

14. Remove the 2 bolts and the left-hand secondary timing chain tensioner. It is necessary to tilt the Camshaft Holding Tool toward the rear of the engine to access the rearmost secondary timing chain tensioner bolt.

15. Compress the right-hand secondary timing chain tensioner and install a suitable lockpin to retain the tensioner in the collapsed position.

16. Remove and discard the right-hand VCT assembly bolt and the right-hand exhaust camshaft sprocket bolt. The VCT bolt and the exhaust camshaft bolt must be discarded and new ones installed. However, the exhaust camshaft washer is reusable.

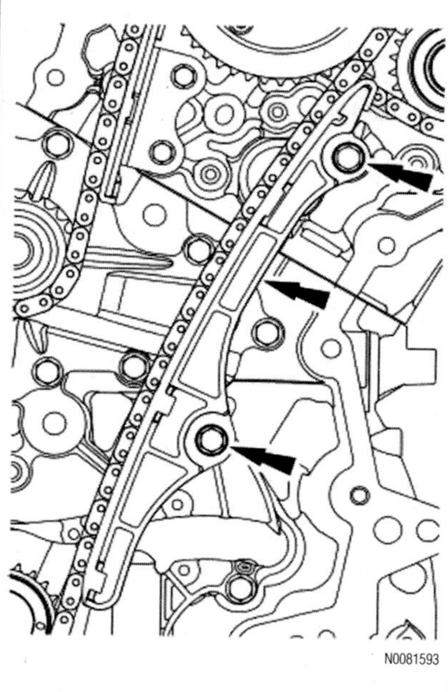

Fig. 140 Remove the 2 bolts and the lower left-hand primary timing chain guide

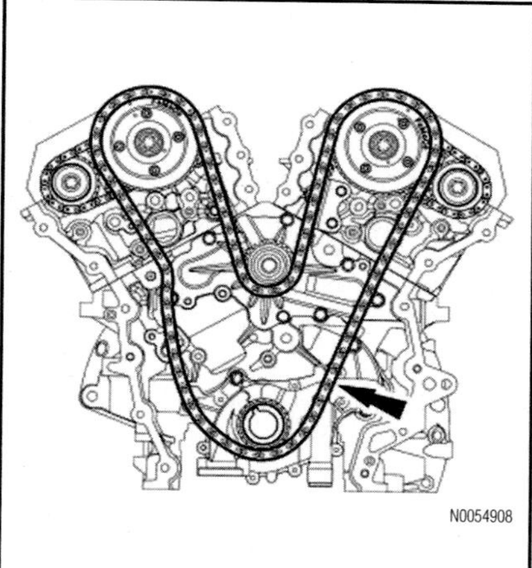

Fig. 141 Remove the primary timing chain

a. Remove the right-hand VCT assembly, secondary timing chain and the right-hand exhaust camshaft sprocket as an assembly.

17. Remove the 2 bolts and the right-hand secondary timing chain tensioner. It is necessary to tilt the Camshaft Holding Tool toward the rear of the engine to access the rearmost secondary timing chain tensioner bolt.

18. Remove the 2 bolts and the right-hand primary timing chain guide.

To install:

19. Install the right-hand primary timing chain guide and the 2 bolts. Tighten to 89 inch lbs. (10 Nm).

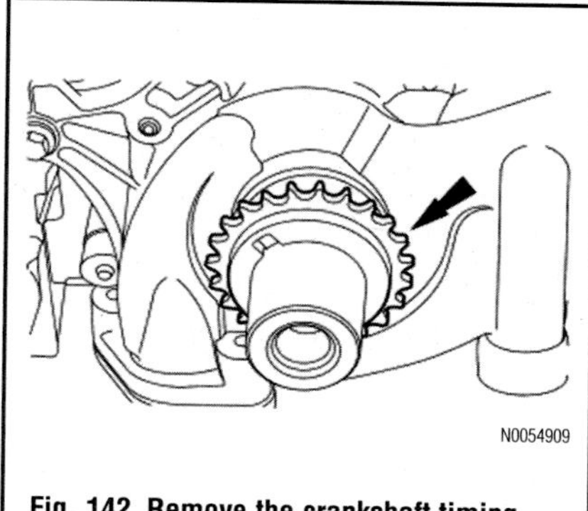

Fig. 142 Remove the crankshaft timing chain sprocket

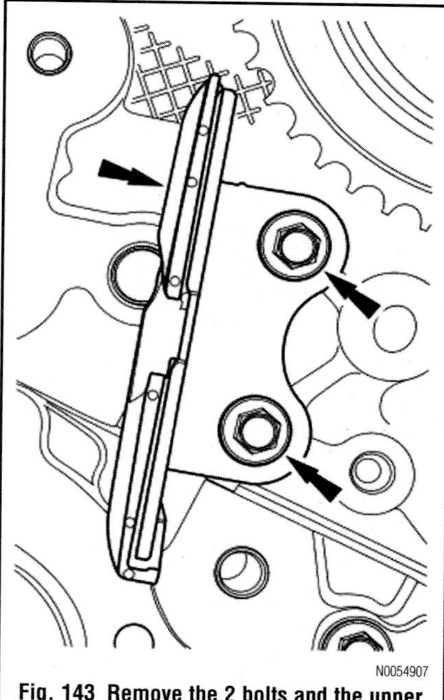

Fig. 143 Remove the 2 bolts and the upper left-hand primary timing chain guide

20. Install the right-hand secondary timing chain tensioner and the 2 bolts. Tighten to 89 inch lbs. (10 Nm).

21. Assemble the right-hand VCT assembly, the right-hand exhaust camshaft sprocket and the right-hand secondary timing chain.

a. Align the colored links with the timing marks.

22. Position the right-hand secondary timing assembly onto the camshafts.

23. Install the new VCT bolt and new exhaust camshaft bolt and the original washer. Tighten in 4 stages.

a. Stage 1: Tighten to 30 ft. lbs. (40 Nm).

b. Stage 2: Loosen one full turn.

c. Stage 3: Tighten to 89 inch lbs. (10 Nm).

d. Stage 4: Tighten 90 degrees.

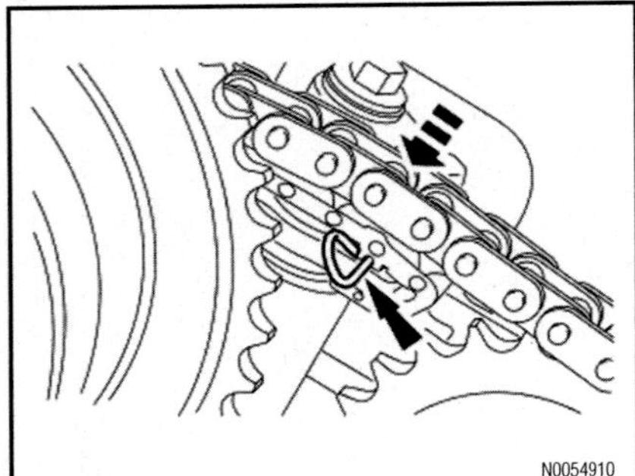

Fig. 144 Install a suitable lockpin to retain the left-hand secondary timing chain tensioner in the collapsed position

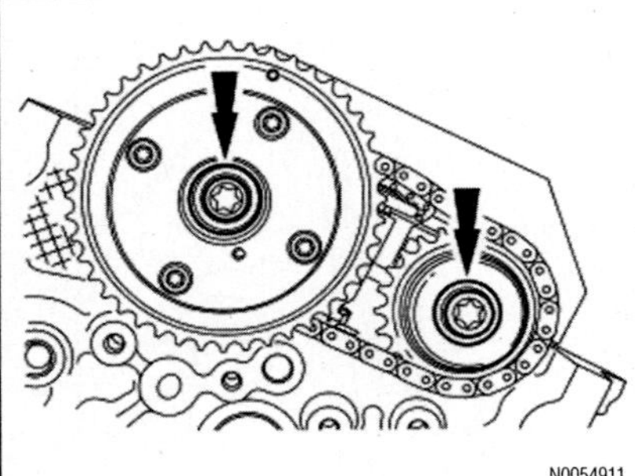

Fig. 145 Remove and discard the left-hand VCT assembly bolt and the left-hand exhaust camshaft sprocket bolt

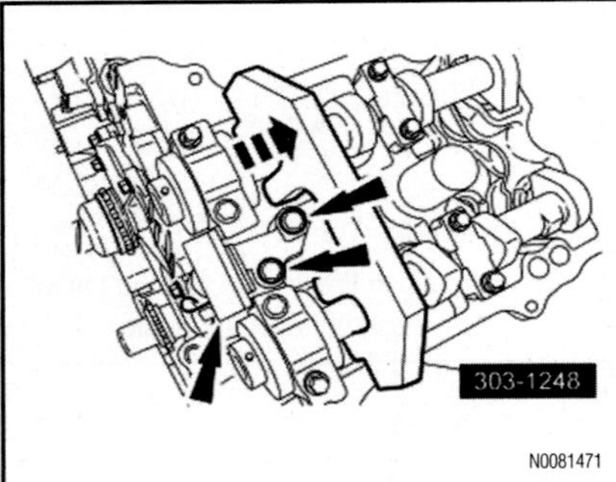

Fig. 146 Remove the 2 bolts and the left-hand secondary timing chain tensioner

24. Remove the lockpin from the right-hand secondary timing chain tensioner.
25. Install the left-hand secondary timing chain tensioner and the 2 bolts. Tighten to 89 inch lbs. (10 Nm).
26. Assemble the left-hand VCT assembly, the left-hand exhaust camshaft sprocket and the left-hand secondary timing chain.
    a. Align the colored links with the timing marks.
27. Position the left-hand secondary timing assembly onto the camshafts.
28. Install the new VCT bolt and new

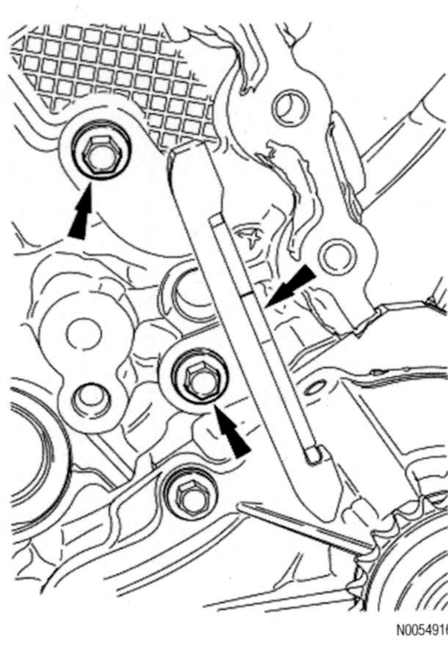

Fig. 147 Remove the 2 bolts and the right-hand primary timing chain guide—Early build vehicles

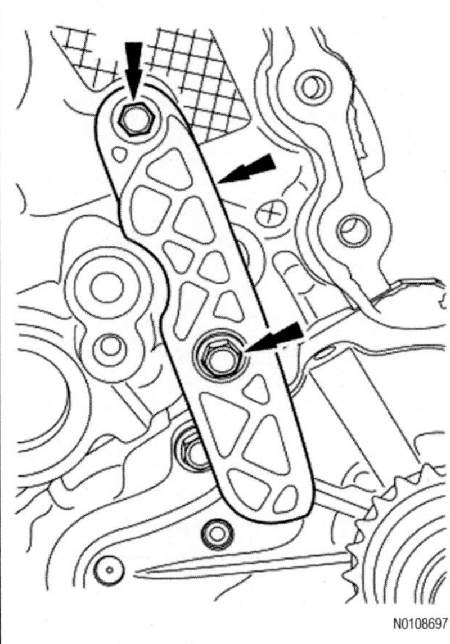

Fig. 148 Remove the 2 bolts and the right-hand primary timing chain guide—Late build vehicles

exhaust camshaft bolt and the original washer. Tighten in 4 stages.
    a. Stage 1: Tighten to 30 ft. lbs. (40 Nm).
    b. Stage 2: Loosen one full turn.
    c. Stage 3: Tighten to 89 inch lbs. (10 Nm)
    d. Stage 4: Tighten 90 degrees.
29. Remove the lockpin from the left-hand secondary timing chain tensioner.

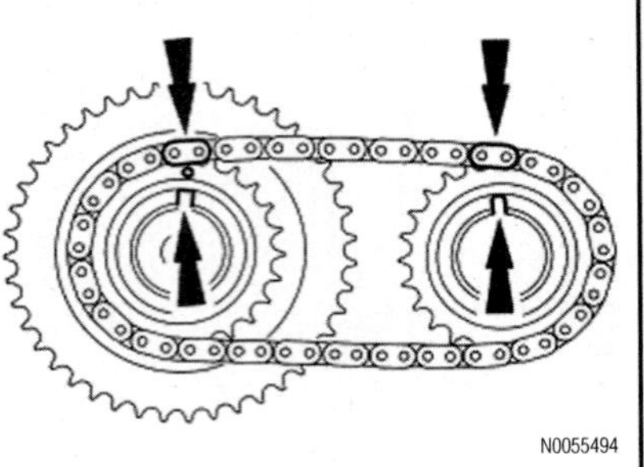

Fig. 149 Align the colored links with the timing marks—right-hand shown, left-hand similar

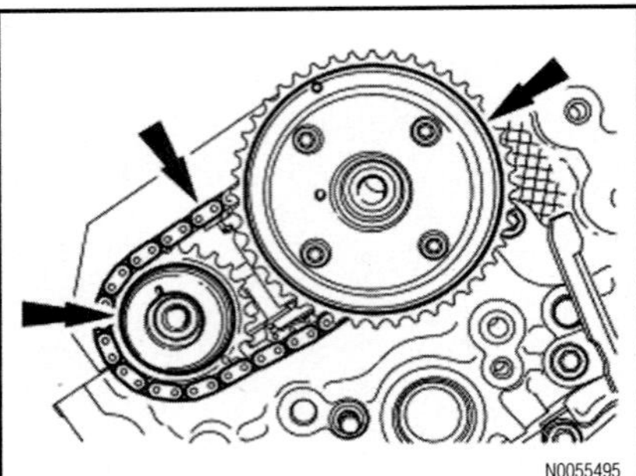

Fig. 150 Position the secondary timing assembly onto the camshafts—right-hand shown, left-hand similar

30. Install the crankshaft timing chain sprocket.
31. Install the primary timing chain with the colored links aligned with the timing marks on the VCT assemblies and the crankshaft sprocket.
32. Install the upper and lower left-hand primary timing chain guides and tighten the bolts to 89 inch lbs. (10 Nm).
33. Install the primary timing chain tensioner arm.
34. Reset the primary timing chain tensioner.
    a. Rotate the lever counterclockwise.
    b. Using a soft-jawed vise, compress the plunger.
    c. Align the hole in the lever with the hole in the tensioner housing.
    d. Install a suitable lockpin.
35. Install the primary tensioner and the 2 bolts.
    a. Tighten to 89 inch lbs. (10 Nm).
    b. It may be necessary to rotate the crankshaft slightly to remove slack from the timing chain and install the tensioner.
    c. Remove the lockpin.
36. As a post-check, verify correct alignment of all timing marks.
37. Inspect the VCT housing seals for damage and replace as necessary.

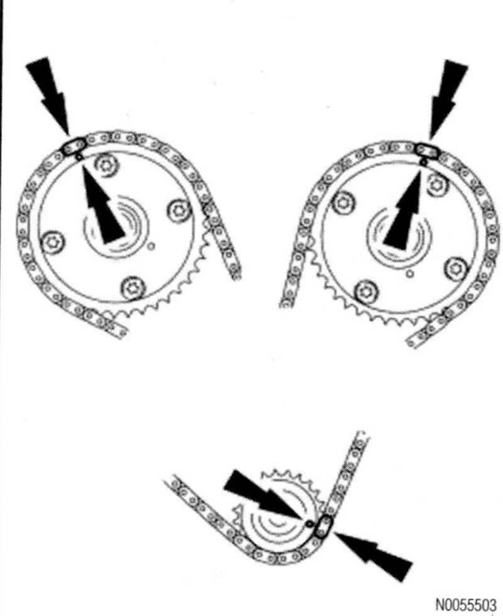

Fig. 151 Install the primary timing chain with the colored links aligned with the timing marks on the VCT assemblies and the crankshaft sprocket

Fig. 152 Reset the primary timing chain tensioner

38. Install the left-hand and right-hand VCT housing and bolts. Make sure the dowels on the VCT housing are fully engaged in the cylinder head prior to tightening the bolts. Tighten in the sequence shown above to 89 inch lbs. (10 Nm).
39. Install the engine front cover.

TURBOCHARGER

REMOVAL & INSTALLATION

Left-Hand

See Figures 153 through 159.

WARNING

Whenever turbocharger air intake system components are removed, always cover open ports to protect from debris. It is important that no foreign material enter the system. The turbocharger compressor vanes are susceptible to damage from even small particles. All components should be inspected and cleaned, if necessary, prior to installation or reassembly.

1. With the vehicle in NEUTRAL, position it on a hoist.
2. Remove the Air Cleaner (ACL) assembly.
3. Disconnect the wastegate control valve hose from the left-hand turbocharger assembly.
4. Remove the 2 bolts from the top of the left-hand exhaust manifold heat shield.
5. Loosen the clamp and remove the left-hand turbocharger intake tube from the turbocharger.
6. Remove the left-hand turbocharger oil supply tube bolt and sealing washer. Discard the sealing washer and oil supply tube filter.
7. Drain the cooling system.
8. Remove the left-hand catalytic converter.
9. Remove the bottom bolt and the left-hand exhaust manifold heat shield.
10. Remove the 2 left-hand oil return tube-to-turbocharger bolts. Remove and discard the gasket.
11. Remove the left-hand turbocharger oil return tube from the oil pan. Discard the 2 O-ring seals.
12. Remove the 2 coolant tube banjo bolts and the left-hand turbocharger coolant tubes. Discard the sealing washers.
13. Loosen the clamp and remove the left-hand CAC tube from the left-hand turbocharger.
14. Remove the 3 exhaust manifold-to-left-hand turbocharger bolts. Discard the gasket and bolts.
15. Remove the 2 bolts and the lower left-hand turbocharger-to-cylinder block bracket.
16. Remove the upper left-hand turbocharger bracket-to-turbocharger bolt and the turbocharger assembly.

To install:

WARNING

The upper left-hand turbocharger bracket bolt must be loosened in order to perform the tightening sequence or damage to the turbocharger may occur.

17. Loosen the upper left-hand turbocharger bracket-to-cylinder block bolt.
18. Install a new left-hand exhaust manifold-to-turbocharger gasket.

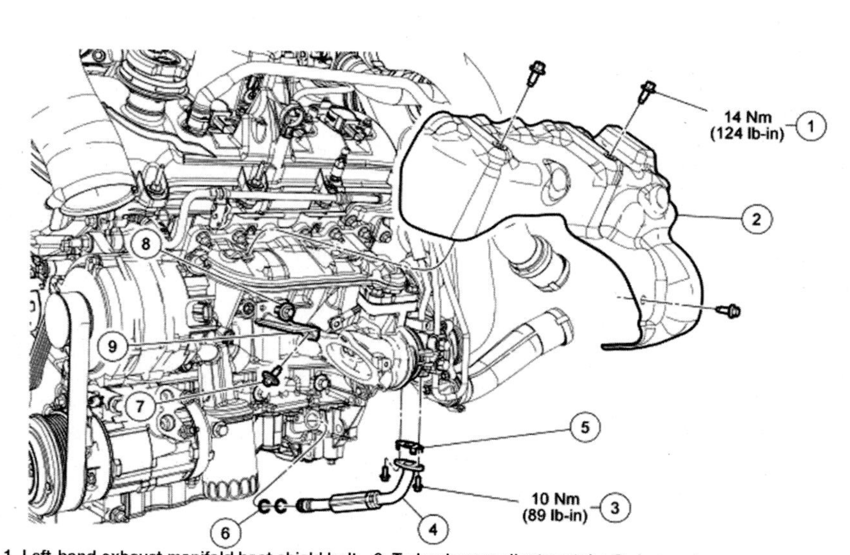

1. Left-hand exhaust manifold heat shield bolt
2. Left-hand exhaust manifold heat shield
3. Turbocharger oil return tube bolt
4. Turbocharger oil return tube
5. Turbocharger oil return tube gasket
6. Turbocharger oil return tube O-ring seal
7. Upper left-hand turbocharger bracket-to-turbocharger bolt
8. Upper left-hand turbocharger bracket-to-cylinder block bolt
9. Upper left-hand turbocharger bracket

N0106503

Fig. 153 Left-hand turbocharger components 1

19. Install the turbocharger assembly and install upper left-hand turbocharger bracket-to-turbocharger bolt. Do not tighten the bolts at this time.

20. Install the lower left-hand turbocharger-to-cylinder block bracket and the 2 bolts. Do not tighten the bolts at this time.

21. Install the 3 new left-hand exhaust manifold-to-turbocharger bolts. Tighten to 33 ft. lbs. (45 Nm).

22. The next 4 steps must be performed in the order written or damage to the turbocharger may occur:

a. Tighten the upper left-hand turbocharger bracket-to-turbocharger bolt to 14 ft. lbs. (19 Nm).

b. Tighten the upper left-hand turbocharger bracket-to-cylinder block bolt to 18 ft. lbs. (25 Nm).

c. Tighten the lower left-hand turbocharger bracket-to-turbocharger bolt to 14 ft. lbs. (19 Nm).

d. Tighten the lower left-hand turbocharger bracket-to-cylinder block bolt to 97 inch lbs. (11 Nm).

23. Install the left-hand CAC tube on the left-hand turbocharger and tighten the clamp. Align the marks for the left-hand CAC tube. Tighten to 44 inch lbs. (5 Nm).

24. Using 2 new sealing washers, install the 2 coolant tube banjo bolts. Tighten to 27 ft. lbs. (37 Nm).

25. Lubricate the oil pan bore with clean engine oil. Using 2 new O-ring seals, install the left-hand turbocharger oil return tube to the oil pan.

26. Using a new gasket, install the left-hand turbocharger oil return tube and the 2 bolts. Tighten to 89 inch lbs. (10 Nm).

27. Install left-hand turbocharger intake tube and tighten the clamp. Align the marks for the left-hand turbocharger intake tube. Tighten to 44 inch lbs. (5 Nm).

28. Install the oil supply tube filter, washer and bolt.

a. Install the new oil supply tube filter in the oil supply tube block.

b. Slide the new washer onto the oil supply tube block.

c. Install the bolt into the oil supply tube block.

29. Install the left-hand turbocharger oil supply tube. Tighten to 26 ft. lbs. (35 Nm).

⁂ WARNING

Make sure the turbocharger wastegate regulating valve hose does not contact the exhaust manifold heat shield.

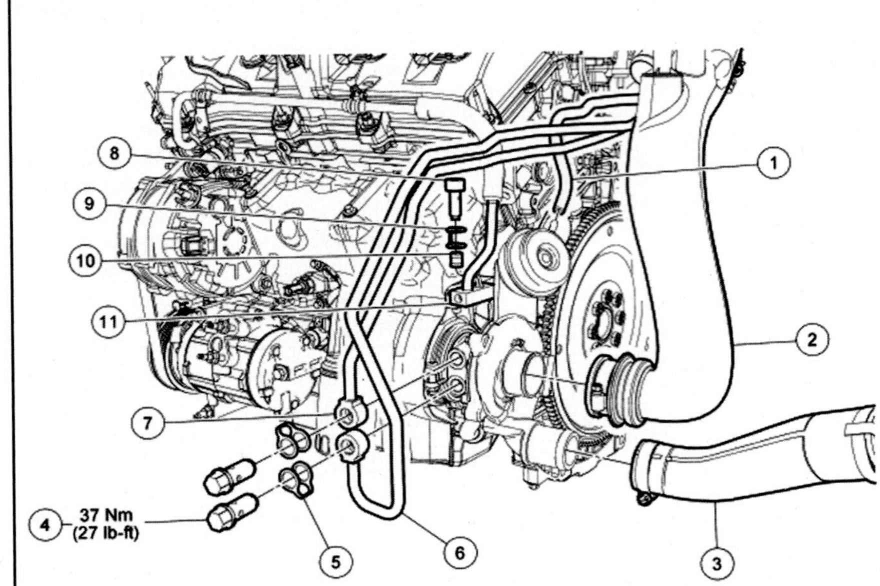

Fig. 154 Left-hand turbocharger components 2

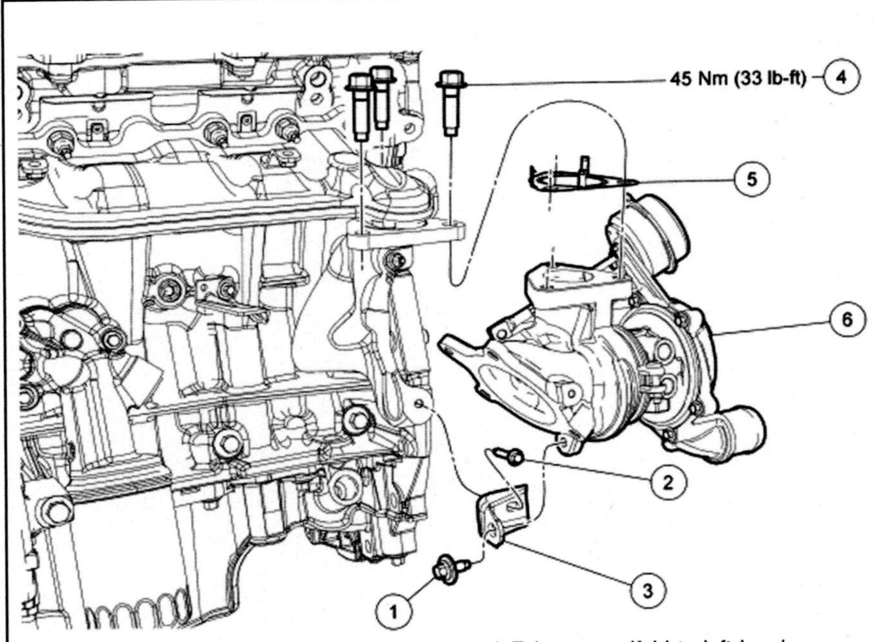

Fig. 155 Left-hand turbocharger components 3

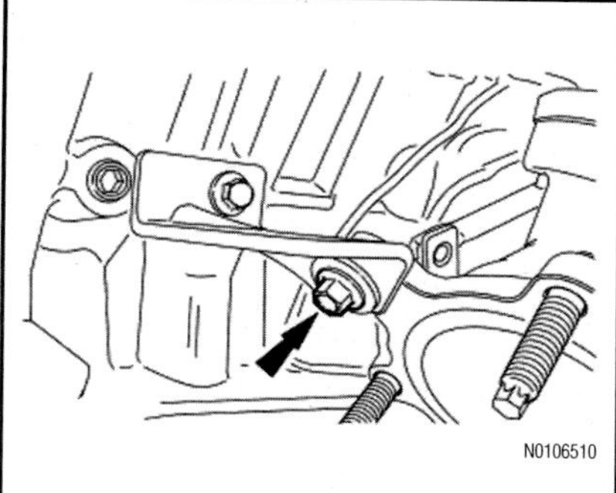

Fig. 156 Upper left-hand turbocharger bracket-to-turbocharger bolt

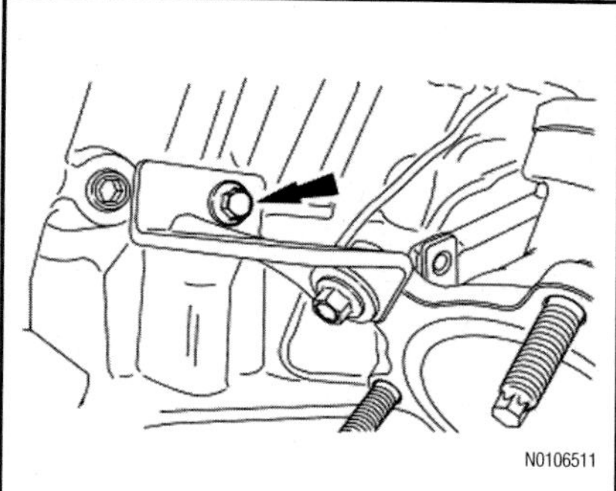

Fig. 157 Upper left-hand turbocharger bracket-to-cylinder block bolt

Fig. 158 Lower left-hand turbocharger bracket-to-turbocharger bolt

30. Connect the wastegate control valve hose to the left-hand turbocharger assembly.
31. Install the left-hand exhaust manifold heat shield and the bottom bolt. Do not tighten the bolts at this time.
32. Install the 2 top left-hand exhaust manifold heat shield bolts. Tighten to 10 ft. lbs. (14 Nm).
33. Tighten the left-hand exhaust manifold heat shield bottom bolt. Tighten to 10 ft. lbs. (14 Nm).
34. Install the left-hand catalytic converter.
35. Fill and bleed the cooling system.
36. Install the ACL assembly.

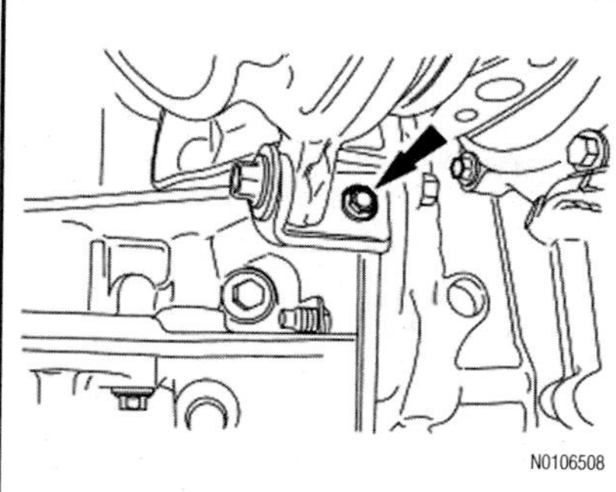

Fig. 159 Lower left-hand turbocharger bracket-to-cylinder block bolt

Right-Hand

See Figures 160 through 168.

WARNING

Whenever turbocharger air intake system components are removed, always cover open ports to protect from debris. It is important that no foreign material enter the system. The turbocharger compressor vanes are susceptible to damage from even small particles. All components should be inspected and cleaned, if necessary, prior to installation or reassembly.

1. With the vehicle in NEUTRAL, position it on a hoist.
2. Using a suitable holding device, hold the steering wheel in the straight-ahead position.
3. Remove the 4 retainers and the underbody shield.
4. Drain the cooling system.
5. Remove the right-hand catalytic converter. Refer to Catalytic Converter Removal & Installation.
6. Remove the front subframe.

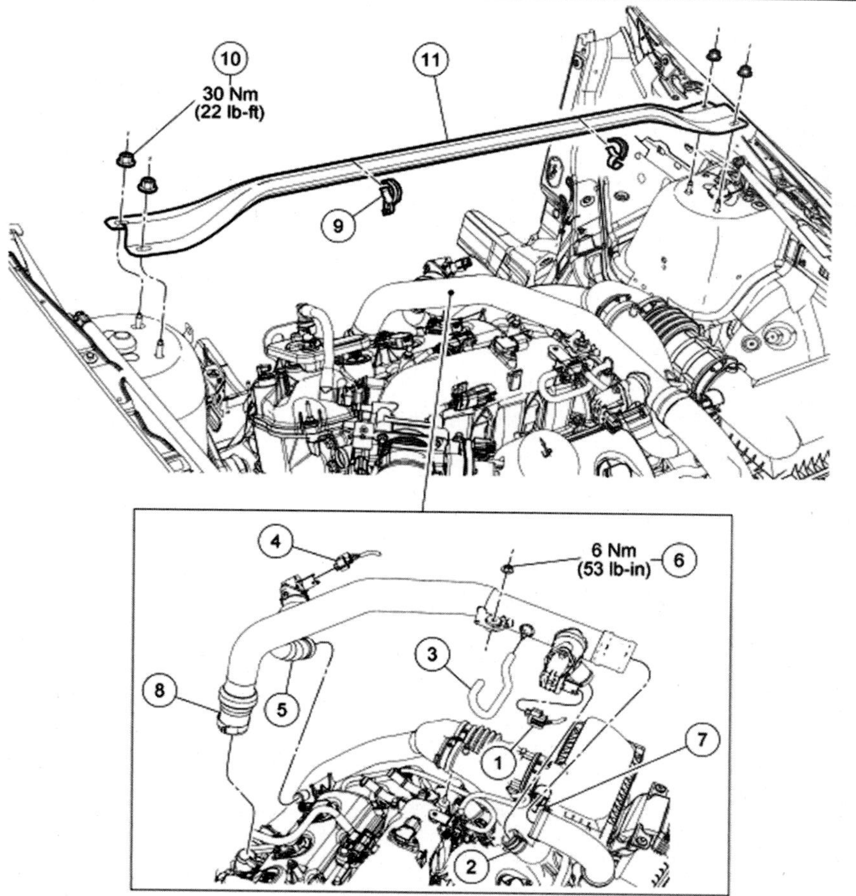

Fig. 160 Right-hand turbocharger components 1

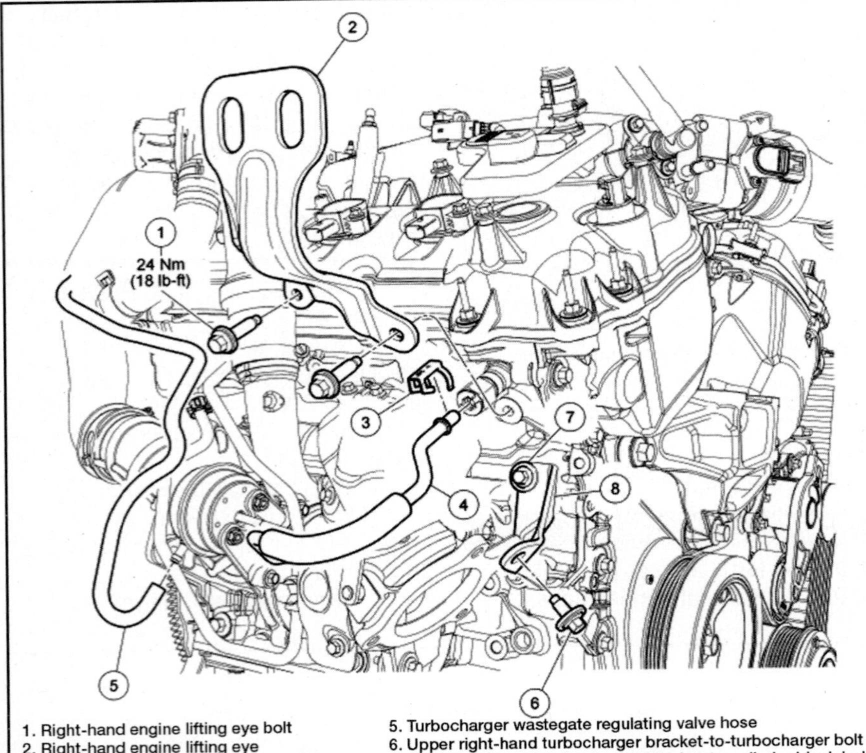

1. Right-hand engine lifting eye bolt
2. Right-hand engine lifting eye
3. Right-hand oil supply tube secondary latch
4. Right-hand oil supply tube
5. Turbocharger wastegate regulating valve hose
6. Upper right-hand turbocharger bracket-to-turbocharger bolt
7. Upper right-hand turbocharger bracket-to-cylinder block bolt
8. Upper right-hand turbocharger-to-cylinder block bracket

Fig. 161 Right-hand turbocharger components 2

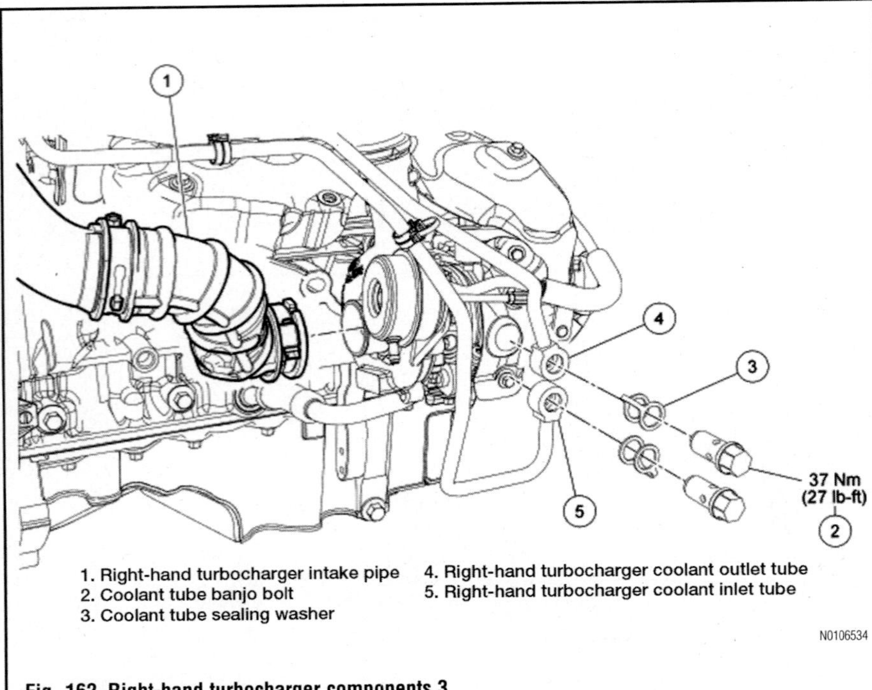

1. Right-hand turbocharger intake pipe
2. Coolant tube banjo bolt
3. Coolant tube sealing washer
4. Right-hand turbocharger coolant outlet tube
5. Right-hand turbocharger coolant inlet tube

Fig. 162 Right-hand turbocharger components 3

7. Remove the right-hand turbocharger oil supply tube secondary latch.
8. Using a Spring Lock Coupling Disconnect Tool, or equivalent, remove the right-hand turbocharger oil supply tube from the quick connect fitting. Inspect and if necessary, replace the quick connect fitting.
9. Remove the lower right-hand exhaust manifold heat shield bolt.
10. Loosen the clamp and remove the right-hand turbocharger intake pipe from the right-hand turbocharger.
11. Disconnect the turbocharger wastegate regulating valve hose from the right-hand turbocharger assembly.
12. Remove the 3 bolts and the right-hand turbocharger lower bracket.
13. Remove the 2 bolts and the right-hand turbocharger oil return tube from the turbocharger. Remove and discard the gasket.
14. Remove the right-hand turbocharger oil return tube from the cylinder block. Discard the 2 O-ring seals.
15. Remove the 2 coolant tube banjo bolts and the right-hand turbocharger coolant tubes. Discard the sealing washers.
16. Detach the 2 vacuum hose retainers from the strut tower brace.
17. Remove the 4 nuts and the strut tower brace.
18. Disconnect the left-hand turbocharger bypass valve electrical connector and the turbocharger bypass valve hose.
19. Remove the turbocharger wastegate regulating valve hose from the right-hand Charge Air Cooler (CAC) tube.
20. Disconnect the right-hand turbocharger bypass valve electrical connector.
21. Disconnect the right-hand turbocharger bypass valve hose.
22. Remove the right-hand CAC tube nut from the intake manifold.
23. Loosen the clamp and remove the right-hand CAC tube.
24. Loosen the clamp and remove the right-hand CAC tube from the right-hand turbocharger.
25. Remove the 4 bolts and the 2 upper right-hand exhaust manifold heat shields.
26. Remove the 2 bolts and the right-hand engine lifting eye.
27. Remove the 3 right-hand exhaust manifold-to-turbocharger bolts. Discard the gasket.
28. Remove the upper right-hand turbocharger-to-cylinder block bracket bolt and the right-hand turbocharger assembly.
29. Remove the right-hand turbocharger oil supply tube banjo bolt. Discard the sealing washer and oil supply tube filter.

To install:

30. Install the oil supply tube filter, washer and bolt.
    a. Install the new oil supply tube filter in the oil supply tube block.
    b. Slide the new washer onto the oil supply tube block.

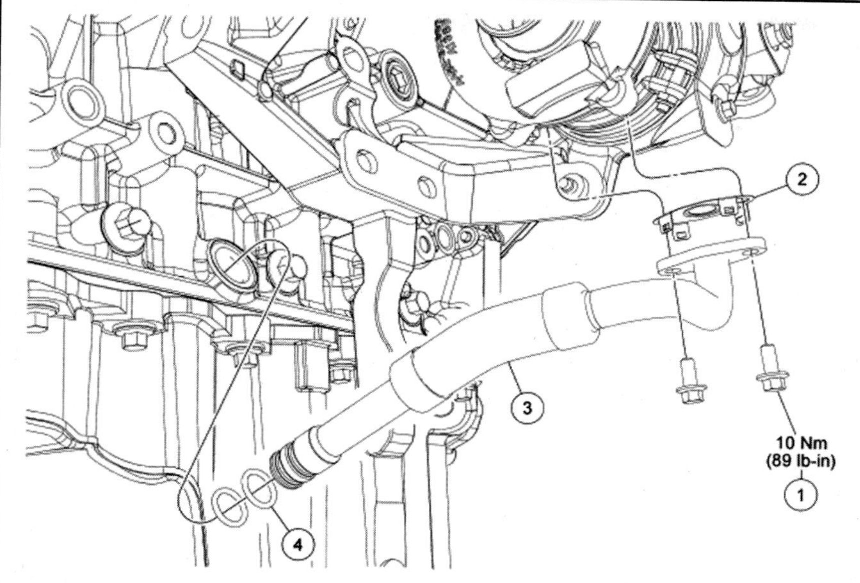

1. Right-hand turbocharger oil return tube bolt
2. Right-hand turbocharger oil return tube
3. Right-hand turbocharger oil return tube gasket
4. Right-hand turbocharger oil return tube O-ring seal

N0106536

Fig. 163 Right-hand turbocharger components 4

1. Right-hand exhaust manifold heat shield bolt
2. Right-hand exhaust manifold heat shield
3. Right-hand exhaust manifold heat shield
4. Lower right-hand turbocharger-to-cylinder block bracket bolt
5. Lower right-hand turbocharger-to-turbocharger bracket bolt
6. Lower right-hand turbocharger bracket

N0106505

Fig. 164 Right-hand turbocharger components 5

c. Install the bolt into the oil supply tube block.

31. Install the right-hand turbocharger oil supply tube. Tighten the bolt to 26 ft. lbs. (35 Nm).

32. Loosen the 2 bolts for the upper right-hand turbocharger-to-cylinder block bracket.

WARNING

The upper right-hand turbocharger bracket bolts must be loosened in order to perform the tightening sequence or damage to the turbocharger may occur.

33. Install a new right-hand exhaust manifold-to-turbocharger gasket.

34. Install the right-hand turbocharger assembly and the upper right-hand turbocharger-to-cylinder block bracket bolt. Do not tighten the bolts at this time.

35. Install the 3 new right-hand exhaust manifold-to-turbocharger bolts. Tighten to 33 ft. lbs. (45 Nm).

36. Install the right-hand engine lifting eye and the 2 bolts. Tighten to 18 ft. lbs. (24 Nm).

37. Install the 2 upper right-hand exhaust manifold heat shields and the 4 bolts. Tighten to 10 ft. lbs. (14 Nm).

38. Install the right-hand CAC tube to the right-hand turbocharger and tighten the clamp. Align the index marks for the right-hand CAC tube. Tighten to 44 inch lbs. (5 Nm).

39. Install the right-hand CAC and tighten the clamp. Align the index marks for the right-hand CAC tube. Tighten to 44 inch lbs. (5 Nm).

40. Install the right-hand CAC tube and the right-hand CAC tube nut to the intake manifold. Tighten to 53 inch lbs. (6 Nm).

41. Connect the right-hand turbocharger bypass valve hose.

42. Connect the right-hand turbocharger bypass valve electrical connector.

43. Install the turbocharger wastegate regulating valve hose to the right-hand CAC tube.

44. Connect the left-hand turbocharger bypass valve electrical connector and the turbocharger bypass valve hose.

45. Install the strut tower brace and the 4 nuts. Tighten to 22 ft. lbs. (30 Nm).

46. Attach the 2 brake booster vacuum hose retainers to the strut tower brace.

47. Position the upper right-hand turbocharger-to-cylinder block bracket as far clockwise as possible and tighten the bolts in the following sequence:

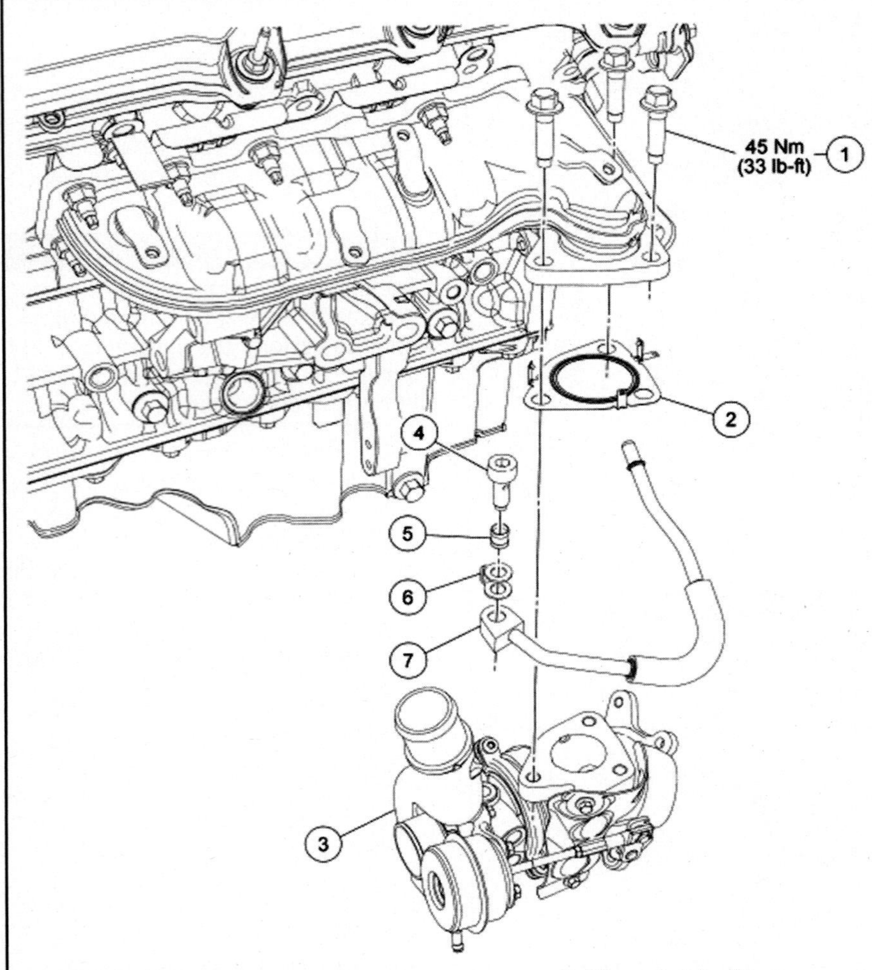

1. Exhaust manifold-to-right-hand turbocharger bolt
2. Right-hand turbocharger-to-exhaust manifold gasket
3. Right-hand turbocharger
4. Oil supply tube bolt
5. Oil supply tube filter
6. Oil supply tube sealing washer
7. Oil supply tube

Fig. 165 Right-hand turbocharger components 6

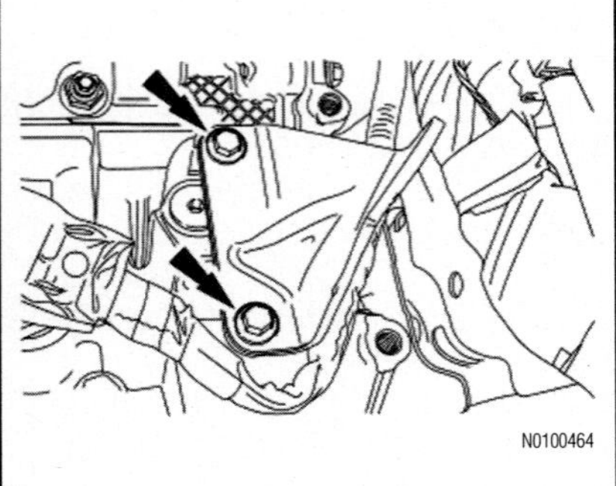

Fig. 166 Upper right-hand turbocharger-to-cylinder block bracket bolts

a. 1: Tighten the lower cylinder block bracket bolt to 19 ft. lbs. (26 Nm).

b. 2: Tighten the upper cylinder block bracket bolt to 19 ft. lbs. (26 Nm).

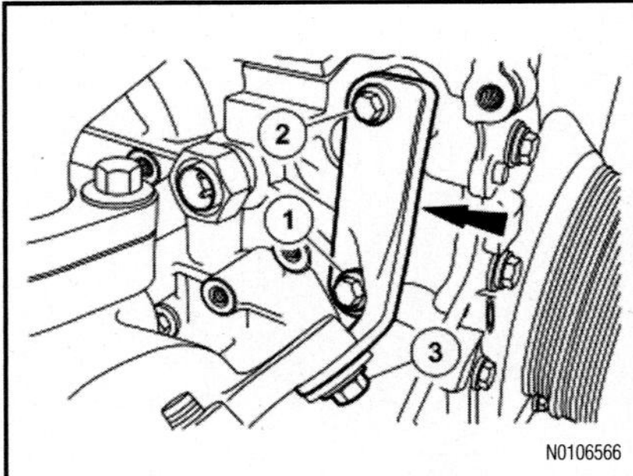

Fig. 167 Upper right-hand turbocharger-to-cylinder block bracket bolt tightening sequence

c. 3: Tighten the cylinder block bracket-to-turbocharger bolt to 14 ft. lbs. (19 Nm).

48. Using 2 new sealing washers, install the 2 right-hand turbocharger coolant tube banjo bolts. Tighten to 27 ft. lbs. (37 Nm).

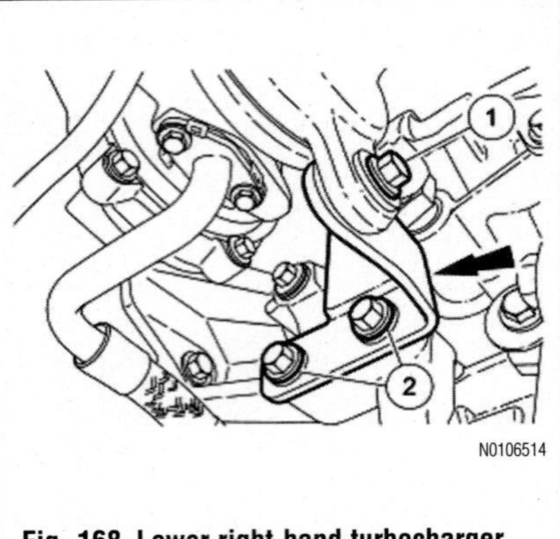

Fig. 168 Lower right-hand turbocharger bolt tightening sequence

49. Lubricate the cylinder block bore with clean engine oil. Using 2 new O-ring seals, install the right-hand turbocharger oil return tube in the cylinder block.

50. Install a new gasket and install the right-hand turbocharger oil return tube and the 2 bolts. Tighten to 89 inch lbs. (10 Nm).

51. Install the lower right-hand turbocharger bracket and the 3 bolts and tighten in sequence shown:

a. 1: Tighten the lower right-hand turbocharger bracket-to-turbocharger bolt to 14 ft. lbs. (19 Nm).

b. 2: Tighten the 2 lower right-hand turbocharger bracket-to-cylinder block bolts to 35 ft. lbs. (48 Nm).

52. Connect the turbocharger wastegate regulating valve hose to the right-hand turbocharger. Make sure the turbocharger wastegate regulating valve hose does not contact the exhaust manifold heat shield.

53. Install the right-hand turbocharger intake pipe to the right-hand turbocharger and tighten the clamp.

54. Align the index marks for the right-hand turbocharger intake pipe. Tighten to 44 inch lbs. (5 Nm).

55. Install the lower right-hand exhaust manifold heat shield bolt. Tighten to 10 ft. lbs. (14 Nm).

56. Install the right-hand turbocharger oil supply tube into the quick connect fitting. Listen for click.

57. Install the right-hand turbocharger oil supply tube secondary latch.

58. Install the front subframe.

59. Install the right-hand catalytic converter.

60. Fill and bleed the cooling system.

61. Install the underbody shield and the 4 retainers.

VALVE COVERS

REMOVAL & INSTALLATION

3.5L Engines

Left-Hand

See Figures 169 and 170.

WARNING

During engine repair procedures, cleanliness is extremely important. Any foreign material, including any material created while cleaning gasket surfaces that enters the oil passages, coolant passages or the oil pan, may cause engine failure.

WARNING

Whenever turbocharger air intake system components are removed, always cover open ports to protect from debris. It is important that no foreign material enter the system. The turbocharger compressor vanes are susceptible to damage from even small particles. All components should be inspected and cleaned, if necessary, prior to installation or reassembly.

1. Release the fuel system pressure.
2. Disconnect the Turbocharger Boost Pressure (TCBP)/Charge Air Cooler Temperature (CACT) sensor electrical connector.
3. Loosen the 2 clamps and remove the Charge Air Cooler (CAC) outlet pipe.
4. Disconnect the 2 quick connect couplings and remove the crankcase vent tube.
5. Remove the fuel injection pump noise insulator shield.
6. Remove the oil level indicator.
7. For early build vehicles:
   a. Remove the intake manifold.
   b. Remove the nut for the high pressure fuel tube from the left-hand valve cover stud bolt.

➡To release the fuel pressure in the high pressure fuel tubes, wrap the flare nut with a shop towel to absorb any residual fuel pressure during the loosening of the flare nuts.

8. Remove the high pressure fuel tube flare nut from the fuel injection pump. Remove the 2 high pressure fuel tube flare nuts from the fuel rails and remove the high pressure fuel tube assembly.
9. For late build vehicles:
   a. Remove the throttle body.
   b. Disconnect the left-hand turbocharger bypass valve electrical connector.
   c. Disconnect the left-hand turbocharger bypass valve hose from the right-hand CAC tube.
   d. Disconnect the turbocharger wastegate regulating valve hose from the right-hand CAC tube.
   e. Disconnect the right-hand turbocharger bypass valve electrical connector.
   f. Disconnect the right-hand turbocharger bypass valve hose from the right-hand turbocharger intake tube.
   g. Remove the right-hand CAC tube nut from the intake manifold.
   h. Loosen the clamp and remove the right-hand CAC tube.
   i. Loosen the clamp and remove the right-hand CAC tube from the right-hand turbocharger.
10. Remove the fuel injection pump.
11. Disconnect the left-hand Variable Camshaft Timing (VCT) solenoid electrical connector.
12. Remove the engine cover mounting stud from the left-hand valve cover stud bolt.
13. Detach all of the wiring harness retainers from the left-hand valve cover stud bolts.
14. Remove the nut and the oil supply tube bracket from the left-hand valve cover stud bolt.
15. Disconnect the 3 left-hand ignition coil-on-plug electrical connectors.
16. Remove the 3 bolts and the 3 left-hand ignition coil-on-plugs.
17. Loosen the 10 stud bolts and remove the left-hand valve cover. Discard the gasket.
18. Inspect the VCT solenoid seals and the spark plug tube seals. Remove any damaged seals.
19. Clean the valve cover, cylinder head and engine front cover sealing surfaces with metal surface prep.

To install:

20. If necessary, install new VCT solenoid and/or spark plug tube seals. Installation of new seals is only required if damaged seals were removed during disassembly of the engine.

WARNING

Failure to use the correct Motorcraft® High Performance Engine RTV Silicone may cause the engine oil to foam excessively and result in serious engine damage.

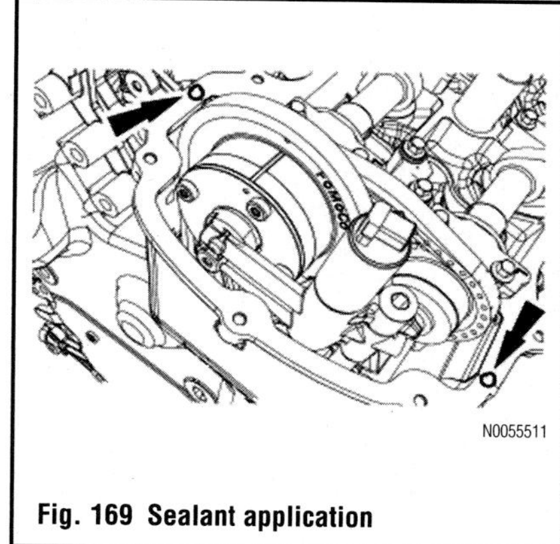

Fig. 169 Sealant application

21. Apply a 0.31 in. (8 mm) bead of Motorcraft® High Performance Engine RTV Silicone to the engine front cover-to-left-hand cylinder head joints.

WARNING

If the valve cover is not installed and the fasteners tightened within 4 minutes, the sealant must be removed and the sealing area cleaned. To clean the sealing area, use silicone gasket remover and metal surface prep. Failure to follow these instructions can cause future oil leakage.

22. Using a new gasket, install the left-hand valve cover and tighten the 10 stud bolts. Tighten in the sequence shown to 89 inch lbs. (10 Nm).
23. Install 3 left-hand ignition coil-on-plugs and the 3 bolts. Tighten to 62 inch lbs. (7 Nm).
24. Connect the 3 left-hand ignition coil-on-plug electrical connectors.
25. Install the oil supply tube bracket on the left-hand valve cover stud bolt and install the nut. Tighten to 71 inch lbs. (8 Nm).
26. Attach all of the wiring harness retainers to the left-hand valve cover and stud bolts.

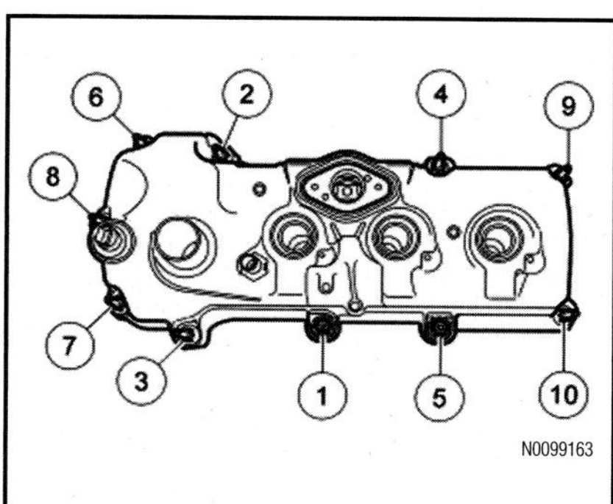

Fig. 170 Left-hand valve cover bolt tightening sequence—3.5L engines

27. Install the engine cover mounting stud to the left-hand valve cover stud bolt. Tighten to 53 inch lbs. (6 Nm).
28. Connect the left-hand VCT solenoid electrical connector.
29. Install the fuel injection pump.
30. For late build vehicles:
    a. Install the right-hand CAC tube to the right-hand turbocharger and tighten the clamp. Align the index marks for the right-hand CAC tube. Tighten to 44 inch lbs. (5 Nm).
    b. Install the right-hand CAC tube and tighten the clamp. Align the index marks for the right-hand CAC tube. Tighten to 44 inch lbs. (5 Nm).
    c. Install the right-hand CAC tube and the right-hand CAC tube nut to the intake manifold. Tighten to 53 inch lbs. (6 Nm).

WARNING

The compression limiter bushing may fall out of the mounting bracket grommet on the Charge Air Cooler (CAC) tube during service. Make sure the bushing is in place when reinstalling the tube or damage to the tube may occur.

    d. Connect the right-hand turbocharger bypass valve hose to the right-hand turbocharger intake tube.
    e. Connect the right-hand turbocharger bypass valve electrical connector.
    f. Connect the turbocharger wastegate regulating valve hose to the right-hand CAC tube.
    g. Connect the left-hand turbocharger bypass valve electrical connector and the turbocharger bypass valve hose.
    h. Install the throttle body.
31. For early build vehicles:
    a. Connect the high pressure fuel tube flare nut to the fuel injection pump and the 2 high pressure fuel tube flare nuts to the fuel rails. Tighten to 22 ft. lbs. (30 Nm).
    b. Install the nut for the high pressure fuel tube on the left-hand valve cover stud bolt. Tighten to 53 inch lbs. (6 Nm).
    c. Install the intake manifold.
32. Install the oil level indicator.
33. Install the fuel injection pump noise insulator shield.
34. Install the crankcase vent tube and connect the 2 quick connect couplings.
35. Install the CAC outlet pipe and tighten the 2 clamps. Align the index marks for the CAC outlet pipe. Tighten to 44 inch lbs. (5 Nm).
36. Connect the TCBP/CACT sensor electrical connector.

Right-Hand

See Figures 171 and 172.

WARNING

During engine repair procedures, cleanliness is extremely important. Any foreign material, including any material created while cleaning gasket surfaces that enters the oil passages, coolant passages or the oil pan, may cause engine failure.

WARNING

Whenever turbocharger air intake system components are removed, always cover open ports to protect from debris. It is important that no foreign material enter the system. The turbocharger compressor vanes are susceptible to damage from even small particles. All components should be inspected and cleaned, if necessary, prior to installation or reassembly.

1. Release the fuel system pressure.
2. Disconnect the left-hand turbocharger bypass valve electrical connector.
3. Disconnect the turbocharger bypass valve hose from the right-hand Charge Air Cooler (CAC) tube.
4. Remove the turbocharger wastegate regulating valve hose from the right-hand CAC tube.
5. Disconnect the right-hand turbocharger bypass valve electrical connector.
6. Disconnect the right-hand turbocharger bypass valve hose from the right-hand turbocharger intake tube.
7. Remove the right-hand CAC tube nut from the intake manifold.
8. Loosen the clamp and remove the right-hand CAC tube.
9. Detach the 2 brake booster vacuum hose retainers from the strut tower brace and position aside.
10. Disconnect the fuel supply tube.
11. Remove the fuel tube-to-engine front cover bracket bolt and position the fuel tube aside.
12. Disconnect the right-hand fuel injector wiring harness electrical connector.
13. Disconnect the Evaporative Emission (EVAP) tube quick connect coupling.
14. Disconnect the EVAP valve electrical connector and detach from the intake manifold.
15. Disconnect the quick connect coupling from the intake manifold and remove the EVAP tube assembly.
16. Disconnect the 2 quick connect couplings and remove the PCV tube.
17. If equipped, disconnect the 2 heated PCV electrical connectors.
18. Disconnect the right-hand Variable Camshaft Timing (VCT) solenoid electrical connector and detach the 2 wiring harness retainers.
19. Disconnect the 3 right-hand ignition coil-on-plugs electrical connectors.
20. Detach all of the wiring harness retainers from the right-hand valve cover and stud bolts position aside.
21. Remove the 3 bolts and the 3 right-hand ignition coil-on-plugs.
22. Loosen the clamp and remove the right-hand turbocharger intake tube from the right-hand turbocharger intake pipe.
23. Remove the nut from the right-hand valve cover stud bolt and position the right-hand turbocharger intake tube off the right-hand valve cover stud bolt.
24. Loosen the 11 stud bolts and remove the right-hand valve cover. Discard the gasket.
25. Inspect the VCT solenoid seals and the spark plug tube seals. Remove any damaged seals.
26. Clean the valve cover, cylinder head and engine front cover sealing surfaces with metal surface prep.

To install:

27. If necessary, install new VCT solenoid and/or spark plug tube seals. Installation of new seals is only required if damaged seals were removed during disassembly of the engine.

WARNING

Failure to use Motorcraft® High Performance Engine RTV Silicone may cause the engine oil to foam excessively and result in serious engine damage.

28. Apply a 0.31 in. (8 mm) bead of Motorcraft® High Performance Engine RTV Silicone to the engine front cover-to-right-hand cylinder head joints.

WARNING

If the valve cover is not installed and the fasteners tightened within 4 minutes, the sealant must be removed and the sealing area cleaned. To clean the sealing area, use silicone gasket remover and metal surface prep. Failure to follow this procedure can cause future oil leakage.

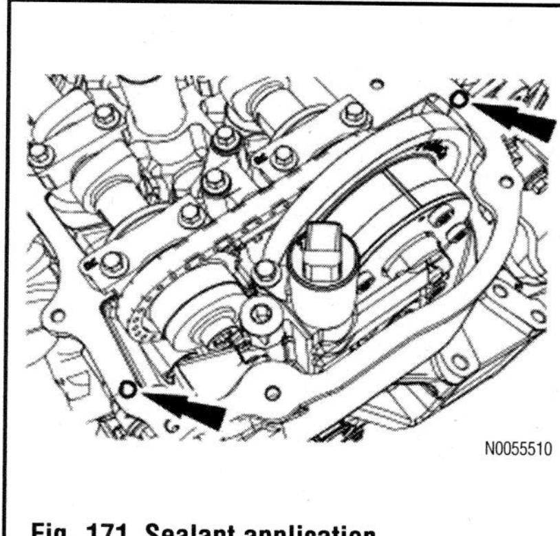

Fig. 171 Sealant application

29. Using a new gasket, install the right-hand valve cover and tighten the 11 stud bolts. Tighten in the sequence shown to 89 inch lbs. (10 Nm).

30. Position the right-hand turbocharger intake tube and install the nut to the right-hand valve cover stud bolt. Tighten to 53 inch lbs. (6 Nm).

WARNING

The compression limiter bushing may fall out of the mounting bracket grommet on the turbocharger intake tube during service. Make sure the bushing is in place when reinstalling the tube or damage to the tube may occur.

31. Install the right-hand turbocharger intake tube to the right-hand turbocharger intake pipe and tighten the clamp. Align the index marks for the right-hand turbocharger intake tube. Tighten to 44 inch lbs. (5 Nm).

32. Install 3 right-hand ignition coil-on-plugs and the 3 bolts. Tighten to 62 inch lbs. (7 Nm).

33. Attach all of the wiring harness retainers to the right-hand valve cover and stud bolts.

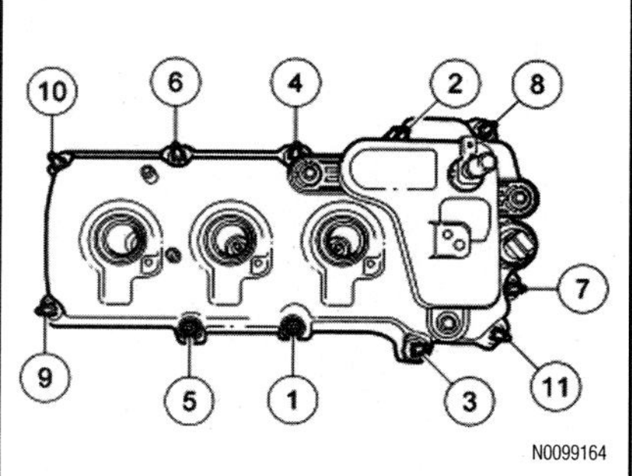

Fig. 172 Right-hand valve cover bolt tightening sequence—3.5L engines

34. Connect the 3 right-hand ignition coil-on-plug electrical connectors.

35. Connect the right-hand VCT solenoid electrical connector and attach the 2 wiring harness retainers.

36. If equipped, connect the 2 heated PCV electrical connectors.

37. Install the PCV tube and connect the 2 quick connect couplings.

38. Install the EVAP tube assembly and connect the quick connect coupling to the intake manifold.

39. Connect the EVAP valve electrical connector and attach to the intake manifold.

40. Connect the EVAP tube quick connect coupling.

41. Connect the right-hand fuel injector wiring harness electrical connector.

42. Position the fuel tube and install the fuel tube-to-engine front cover bracket bolt. Tighten to 89 inch lbs. (10 Nm).

43. Connect the fuel supply tube.

44. Attach the 2 brake booster vacuum hose retainers to the strut tower brace.

45. Install the right-hand CAC tube to the right-hand turbocharger and tighten the clamp. Align the index marks for the right-hand CAC tube. Tighten to 44 inch lbs. (5 Nm).

46. Install the right-hand CAC tube and tighten the clamp. Align the index marks for the right-hand CAC tube. Tighten to 44 inch lbs. (5 Nm).

47. Install the right-hand CAC tube and turbocharger intake tube as an assembly and install the right-hand CAC tube nut to the intake manifold. Tighten to 53 inch lbs. (6 Nm).

WARNING

The compression limiter bushing may fall out of the mounting bracket grommet on the Charge Air Cooler (CAC) tube during service. Make sure the bushing is in place when reinstalling the tube or damage to the tube may occur.

48. Connect the right-hand turbocharger bypass valve hose to the right-hand turbocharger intake tube.

49. Connect the right-hand turbocharger bypass valve electrical connector.

50. Install the turbocharger wastegate regulating valve hose to the right-hand CAC tube.

51. Connect the turbocharger bypass valve hose to the right-hand CAC tube.

52. Connect the left-hand turbocharger bypass valve electrical connector.

3.7L Engines

Left-Hand

See Figures 173 through 175.

WARNING

During engine repair procedures, cleanliness is extremely important. Any foreign material, including any material created while cleaning gasket surfaces that enters the oil passages, coolant passages or the oil pan, may cause engine failure.

WARNING

Early build engines have 11 fastener valve covers, late build engines have 9 fastener valve covers. Do not attempt to install bolts in the 2 empty late build valve cover holes or damage to the valve cover will occur.

1. Remove the left-hand ignition coils.
2. Remove the oil level indicator.
3. Disconnect the left-hand Variable Camshaft Timing (VCT) solenoid electrical connector.
4. Detach all of the wiring harness retainers from the left-hand valve cover stud bolts.
5. Remove the engine cover stud from the valve cover stud bolt.
6. Disconnect the 3 left-hand fuel injector electrical connectors.
7. For early build vehicles, loosen the 11 stud bolts and remove the left-hand valve cover. Discard the gasket.
8. For late build vehicles, loosen the 9 stud bolts and remove the right-hand valve cover. Discard the gasket.
9. Inspect the VCT solenoid seals and the spark plug tube seals. Remove any damaged seals.
10. Clean the valve cover, cylinder head and engine front cover sealing surfaces with metal surface prep.

To install:

11. If necessary, install new VCT solenoid and/or spark plug tube seals. Installation of new seals is only required if damaged seals were removed during disassembly of the engine.

WARNING

Failure to use the correct Motorcraft® High Performance Engine RTV Silicone may cause the engine oil to foam excessively and result in serious engine damage.

12. Apply a 0.31 in. (8 mm) bead of Motorcraft® High Performance Engine RTV

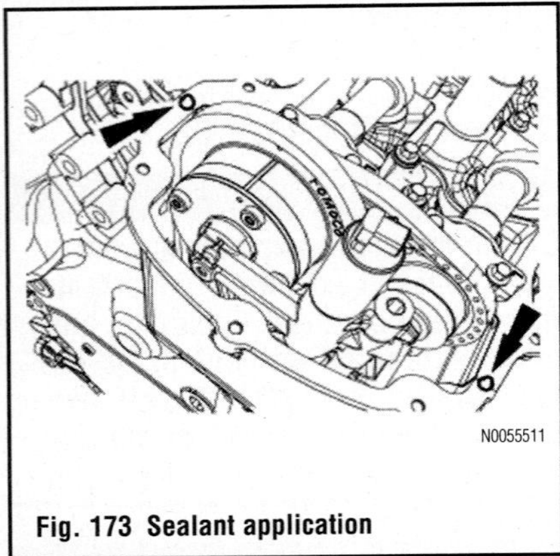

Fig. 173 Sealant application

Silicone to the engine front cover-to-left-hand cylinder head joints.

WARNING

If the valve cover is not installed and the fasteners tightened within 4 minutes, the sealant must be removed and the sealing area cleaned. To clean the sealing area, use silicone gasket remover and metal surface prep. Failure to follow this procedure can cause future oil leakage.

13. For late build vehicles, using a new gasket, install the left-hand valve cover and tighten the 9 stud bolts. Tighten in the sequence shown to 89 inch lbs. (10 Nm).
14. For early build vehicles, using a new gasket, install the left-hand valve cover and 11 stud bolts. Tighten in the sequence shown to 89 inch lbs. (10 Nm).
15. Connect the 3 left-hand fuel injector electrical connectors.
16. Install the engine cover stud to the valve cover stud bolt. Tighten to 53 inch lbs. (6 Nm).
17. Attach all of the wiring harness retainers to the left-hand valve cover stud bolts.
18. Connect the left-hand VCT solenoid electrical connector.
19. Install the oil level indicator.

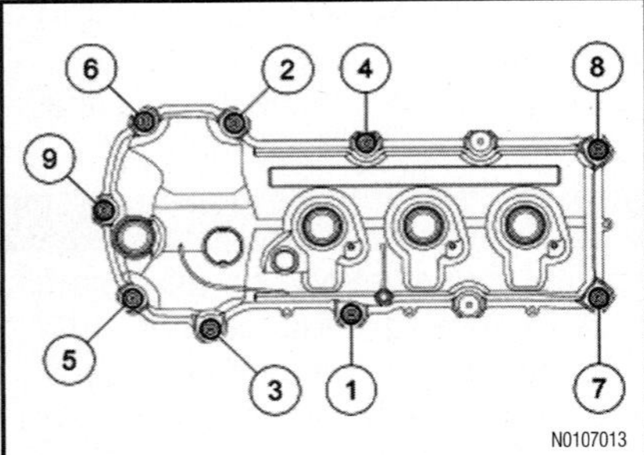

Fig. 174 Left-hand valve cover bolt tightening sequence—3.7L engines—Late build vehicles

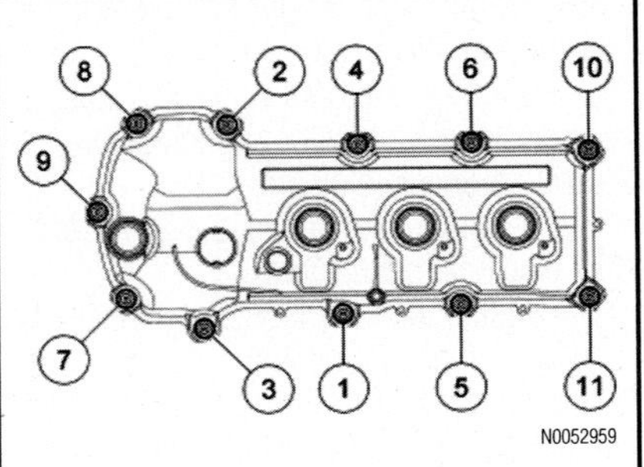

Fig. 175 Left-hand valve cover bolt tightening sequence—3.7L engines—Early build vehicles

20. Install the left-hand ignition coils.

Right-Hand

See Figures 176 through 178.

WARNING

During engine repair procedures, cleanliness is extremely important. Any foreign material, including any material created while cleaning gasket surfaces that enters the oil passages, coolant passages or the oil pan, may cause engine failure.

➡Early build engines have 11 fastener valve covers, late build engines have 9 fastener valve covers. Do not attempt to install bolts in the 2 empty late build valve cover holes or damage to the valve cover will occur.

1. Remove the right-hand ignition coils.
2. Detach and disconnect the right-hand Heated Oxygen Sensor (HO2S) electrical connector.
3. Detach and disconnect the right-hand Catalyst Monitor Sensor (CMS) electrical connector.
4. Disconnect the right-hand Variable Camshaft Timing (VCT) solenoid electrical connector.
5. Disconnect the 3 right-hand fuel injector electrical connectors.
6. Detach all of the wiring harness retainers from the right-hand valve cover stud bolts.
7. Remove the nut and the Power Steering Pressure (PSP) tube bracket from the valve cover stud bolt.
8. For early build vehicles, loosen the bolt, the 10 stud bolts and remove the right-hand valve cover. Discard the gasket. It is necessary to reposition the A/C tubes to remove the valve cover.
9. For late build vehicles, loosen the 9 studs bolts and remove the right-hand valve cover. Discard the gasket. It is necessary to reposition the A/C tubes to remove the valve cover.
10. Inspect the VCT solenoid seals and the spark plug tube seals. Remove any damaged seals.
11. Clean the valve cover, cylinder head and engine front cover sealing surfaces with metal surface prep.

To install:

12. If necessary, install new VCT solenoid and/or spark plug tube seals. Installation of new seals is only required if damaged seals were removed during disassembly of the engine.

WARNING

Failure to use Motorcraft® High Performance Engine RTV Silicone may cause the engine oil to foam excessively and result in serious engine damage.

13. Apply a 0.31 in. (8 mm) bead of Motorcraft® High Performance Engine RTV Silicone to the engine front cover-to-right-hand cylinder head joints.

WARNING

If the valve cover is not installed and the fasteners tightened within 4 minutes, the sealant must be removed and the sealing area cleaned. To clean the sealing area, use silicone gasket remover and metal surface prep. Failure to follow this procedure can cause future oil leakage.

14. For late build vehicles, using a new gasket, install the right-hand valve cover and tighten the 9 stud bolts. Tighten in the sequence shown to 89 inch lbs. (10 Nm).
15. For early build vehicles, using a new gasket, install the right-hand valve cover, bolt and the 10 stud bolts.

Tighten in the sequence shown to 89 inch lbs. (10 Nm).

16. Install the PSP tube bracket on the

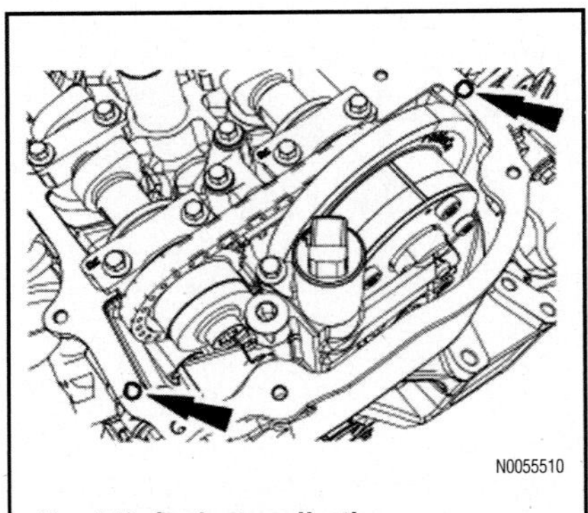

Fig. 176 Sealant application

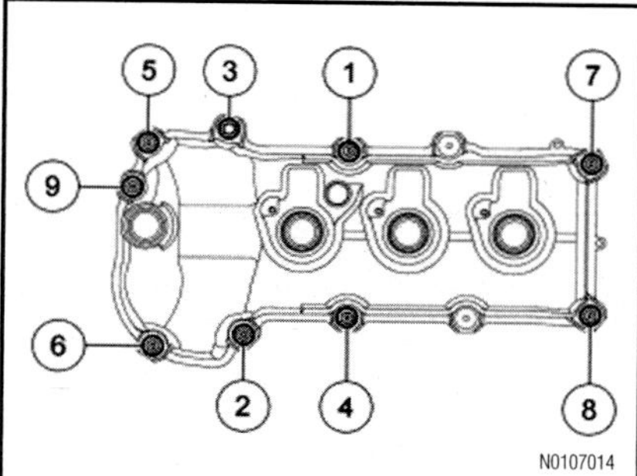

Fig. 177 Right-hand valve cover bolt tightening sequence—3.7L engines—Late build vehicles

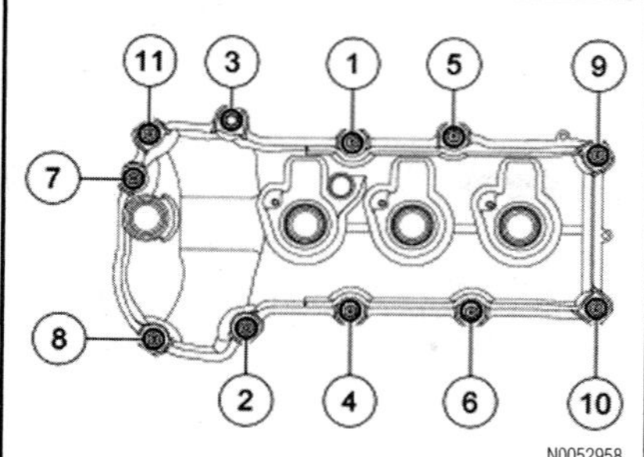

Fig. 178 Right-hand valve cover bolt tightening sequence—3.7L engines—Early build vehicles

valve cover stud bolt and install the nut. Tighten to 62 inch lbs. (7 Nm).

17. Attach all of the wiring harness retainers to the right-hand valve cover stud bolts.

18. Connect the 3 right-hand fuel injector electrical connectors.

19. Connect the right-hand VCT solenoid electrical connector.

20. Connect the right-hand CMS electrical connector.

21. Connect the right-hand HO2S electrical connector.

22. Install the right-hand ignition coils.

ENGINE PERFORMANCE & EMISSION CONTROLS

CAMSHAFT POSITION (CMP) SENSOR

LOCATION

See Figures 179 and 180.

Refer to the accompanying illustrations.

REMOVAL & INSTALLATION

3.5L Engine

1. Remove the Air Cleaner (ACL) outlet pipe and the ACL.
2. Position the right-hand and left-hand turbocharger intake tubes aside.
3. Disconnect the Camshaft Position (CMP) sensor electrical connector.
4. Remove the bolt and the CMP sensor.

To install:

5. To install, reverse the removal procedure, noting the following:
    a. Lubricate the CMP sensor O-ring seal with clean engine oil.
    b. Tighten to 89 inch lbs. (10 Nm).

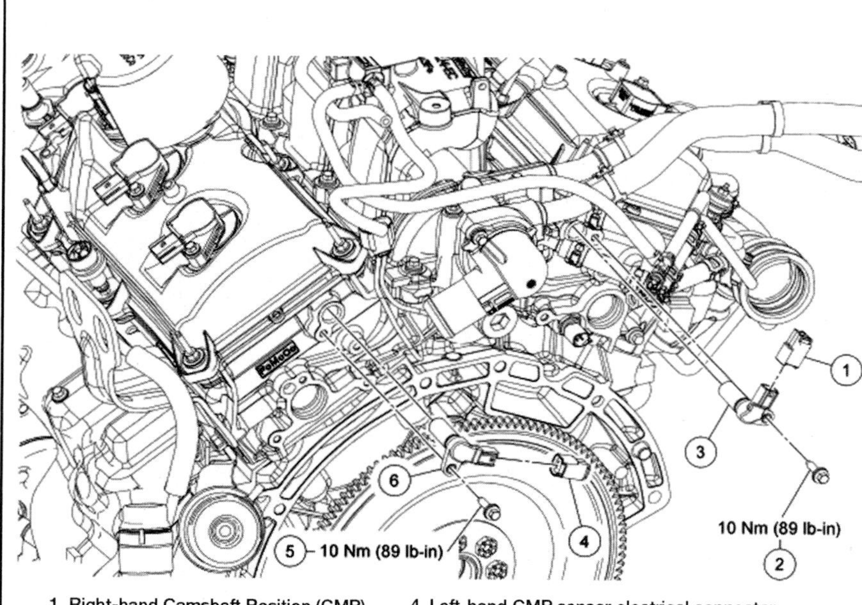

Fig. 179 Camshaft Position (CMP) Sensor—3.5L engines

3.7L Engine

1. Remove the Air Cleaner (ACL) outlet pipe and the ACL.
2. Disconnect the Camshaft Position (CMP) sensor electrical connector.
3. Remove the bolt and the CMP sensor.

To install:

4. To install, reverse the removal procedure, noting the following:
    a. Lubricate the CMP sensor O-ring seal with clean engine oil.
    b. Tighten to 89 inch lbs. (10 Nm).

CRANKSHAFT POSITION (CKP) SENSOR

LOCATION

See Figure 181.

Refer to the accompanying illustration.

REMOVAL & INSTALLATION

1. With the vehicle in NEUTRAL, position it on a hoist.
2. For 3.5L engines, remove the left-hand turbocharger.
3. For 3.7L engines, remove the left-hand catalytic converter.
4. Remove the bolt/nut and the heat shield.
5. Remove the rubber grommet cover.
6. Disconnect the Crankshaft Position (CKP) sensor electrical connector.
7. Remove the bolt and the CKP sensor.

To install:

8. To install, reverse the removal procedure, noting the following:
    a. Tighten the sensor mounting bolt to 89 inch lbs. (10 Nm).
    b. Tighten the heat shield bolt/nut to 89 inch lbs. (10 Nm).

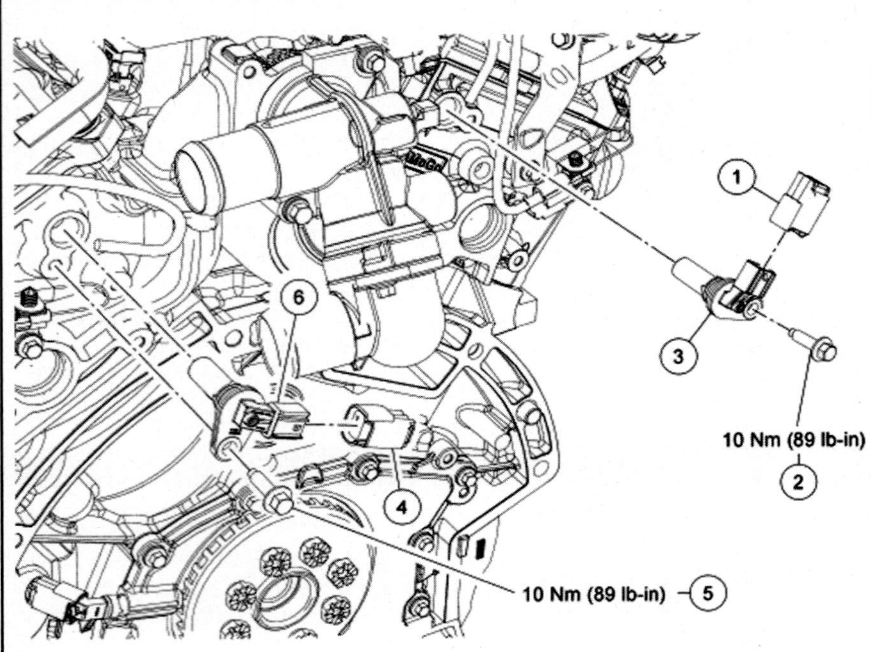

Fig. 180 Camshaft Position (CMP) Sensor—3.7L engines

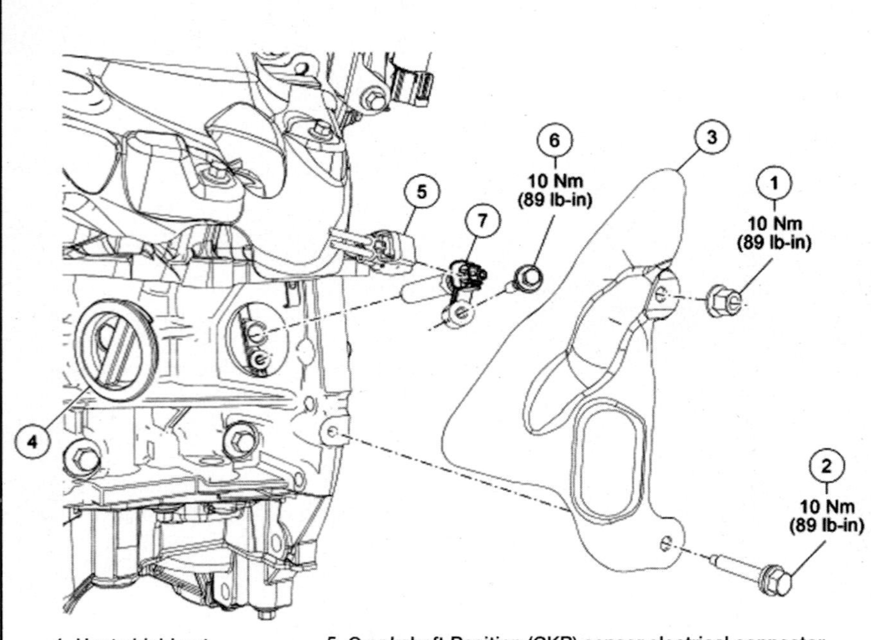

Fig. 181 Crankshaft Position (CKP) Sensor

c. Using the scan tool, perform the Misfire Monitor Neutral Profile Correction procedure, following the on-screen instructions.

HEATED OXYGEN SENSOR (HO2S)

LOCATION

See Figures 182 through 184.

Refer to the accompanying illustrations.

REMOVAL & INSTALLATION

1. For all right-hand sensors, with the vehicle in NEUTRAL, position it on a hoist.
2. Remove the 4 retainers and the underbody shield, if applicable.
3. For all sensors, disconnect the HO2S electrical connector.
    a. For 3.5L engines right-hand sensors, detach the HO2S electrical connector retainer from the bracket.
    b. For 3.5L engines left-hand sensors, remove the 4 retainers and the underbody shield, and detach the HO2S electrical connector retainer from the bracket.
4. For all sensors, lubricate the sensor threads with penetrating and lock lubricant to assist in removal, if necessary.
5. For all sensors, remove the HO2S using the Exhaust Gas Oxygen Sensor Socket.

To install:

6. To install, reverse the removal procedure, noting the following:
    a. Apply a light coat of anti-seize lubricant to the threads of the HO2S.
    b. Tighten the sensor to 35 inch lbs. (48 Nm).

INTAKE AIR TEMPERATURE (IAT) SENSOR

LOCATION

See Figure 185.

Refer to the accompanying illustration.

REMOVAL & INSTALLATION

1. Disconnect the Intake Air Temperature (IAT) sensor electrical connector.
2. Remove the IAT sensor.
3. Lift the tab and turn the IAT sensor counterclockwise to remove.

To install:

4. To install, reverse the removal procedure.
    a. Make sure the IAT sensor tab is fully seated during installation.

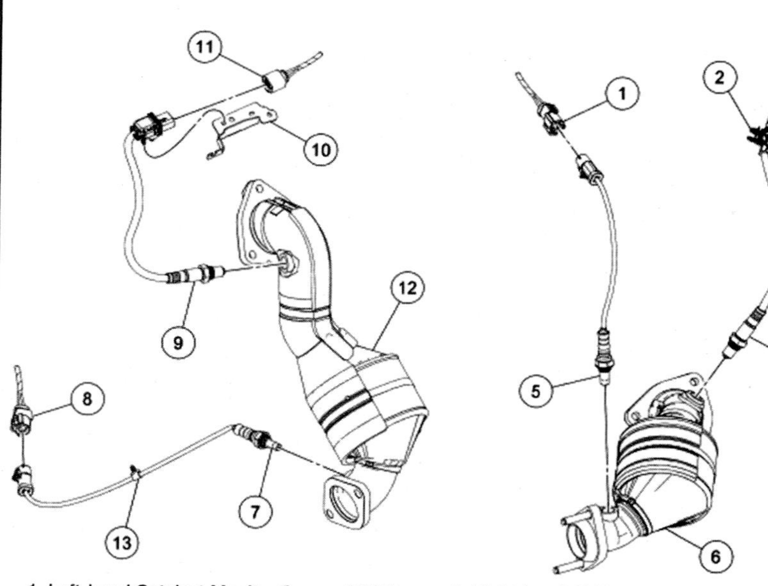

Fig. 182 Heated Oxygen Sensor (HO2S)—3.5L engine

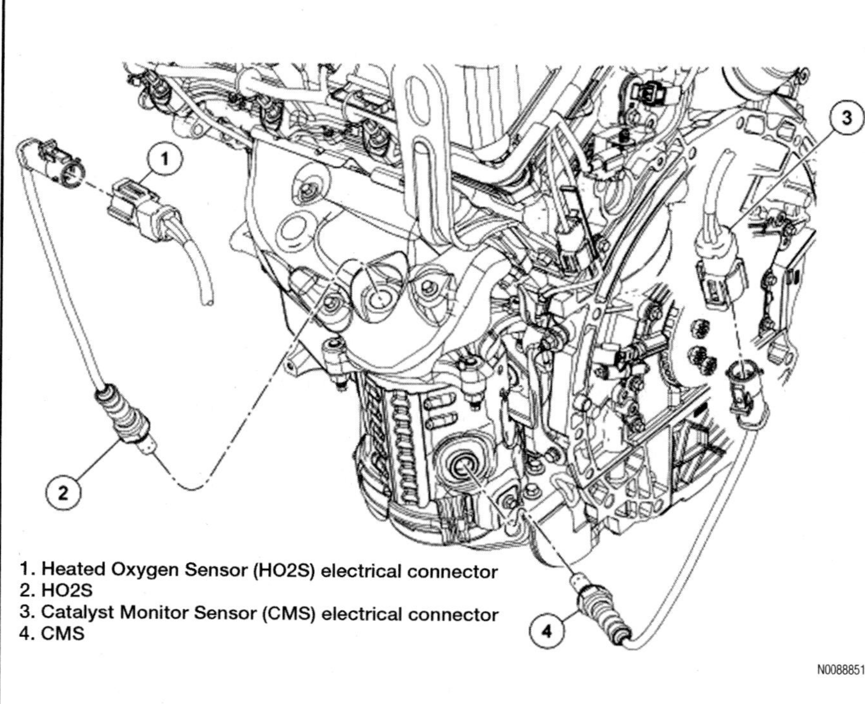

Fig. 183 Left-Hand Heated Oxygen Sensor (HO2S)—3.7L engine

KNOCK SENSOR (KS)

LOCATION

See Figures 186 and 187.

Refer to the accompanying illustrations.

REMOVAL & INSTALLATION

3.5L Engine

1. Remove the coolant inlet pipe.
2. Remove the fuel rail.
3. Disconnect the Knock Sensor (KS) electrical connector.
4. Remove the 2 bolts and the KS.

To install:

5. To install, reverse the removal procedure.
   a. Tighten to 15 ft. lbs. (20 Nm).

3.7L Engine

1. Remove the thermostat housing.
2. Remove the lower intake manifold.
3. Remove the coolant tube.
4. Discard the O-ring seal.
5. Disconnect the Knock Sensor (KS) electrical connector.
6. Remove the 2 bolts and the KS.

To install:

7. To install, reverse the removal procedure, noting the following:
   a. Lubricate the new O-ring seal with clean engine coolant.
   b. Tighten to 15 ft. lbs. (20 Nm).

MANIFOLD ABSOLUTE PRESSURE (MAP) SENSOR

LOCATION

See Figure 188.

Refer to the accompanying illustration.

REMOVAL & INSTALLATION

➡The Turbocharger Boost Pressure (TCBP)/Charge Air Cooler Temperature (CACT) sensor and the Manifold Absolute Pressure (MAP)/ Intake Air Temperature 2 (IAT2) sensor are not interchangeable.

1. Disconnect the MAP/IAT2 sensor electrical connector.
2. Remove the 2 screws and the MAP/IAT2 sensor.

To install:

3. Lubricate the MAP/IAT2 sensor O-ring seal with clean engine oil.
4. Install the MAP/IAT2 sensor and tighten the 2 screws to 53 inch lbs. (6 Nm).

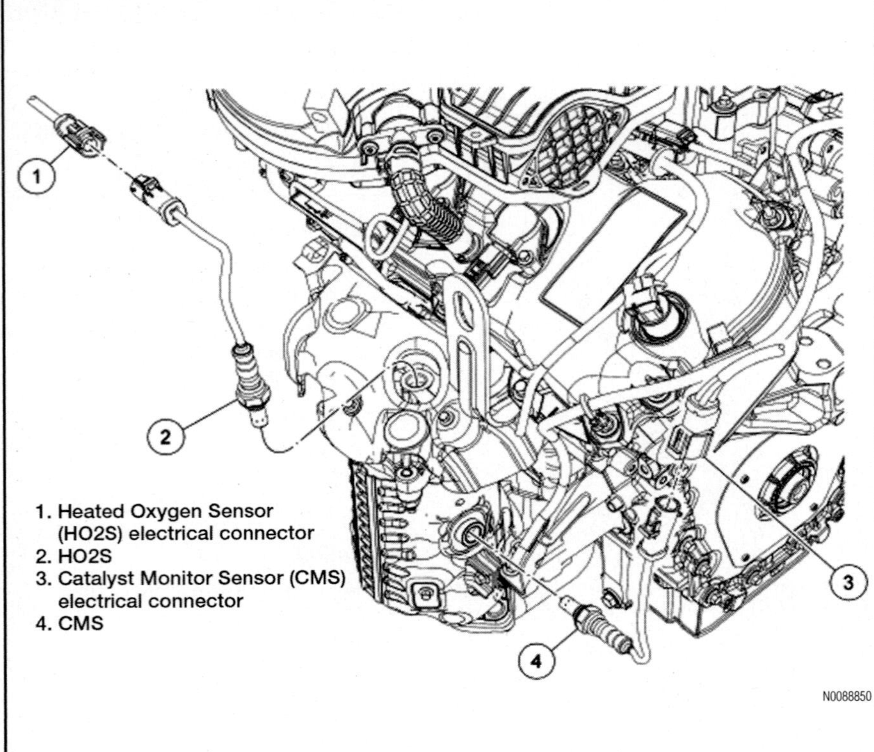

Fig. 184 Right-Hand Heated Oxygen Sensor (HO2S)—3.7L engine

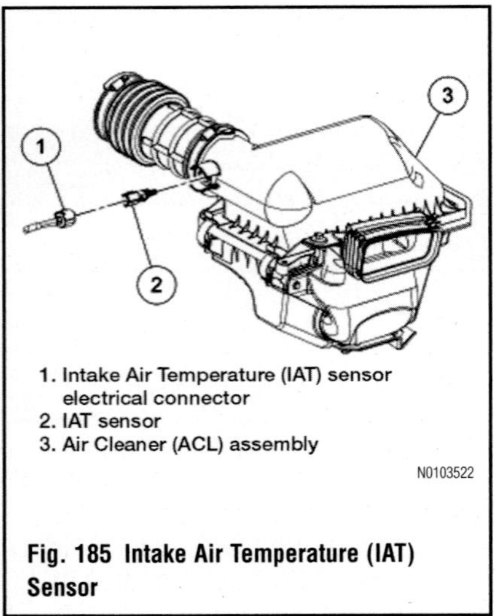

Fig. 185 Intake Air Temperature (IAT) Sensor

5. Connect the MAP/IAT2 sensor electrical connector.

POWERTRAIN CONTROL MODULE (PCM)

LOCATION

See Figure 189.

Refer to the accompanying illustration.

REMOVAL & INSTALLATION

➡PCM installation DOES NOT require new keys or programming of keys.

1. Retrieve the module configuration. Carry out the module configuration retrieval steps of the Programmable Module Installation (PMI) procedure, below.
2. Remove the cowl panel grill.
3. Disconnect the 3 PCM electrical connectors.
4. Remove the 2 nuts and the PCM.

To install:

5. Install the PCM and tighten the 2 nuts to 71 inch lbs. (8 Nm).
6. Connect the 3 PCM electrical connectors.
7. Install the cowl panel grill.
8. Restore the module configuration. Carry out the module configuration restore steps of the Programmable Module Installation (PMI) procedure, below.
9. Reprogram the Passive Anti-Theft System (PATS). Carry out the Parameter Reset procedure, below.
10. Using the scan tool, perform the Misfire Monitor Neutral Profile Correction procedure, following the on-screen instructions.

PROGRAMMABLE MODULE INSTALLATION (PMI) PROCEDURE USING INTEGRATED DIAGNOSTIC SYSTEM (IDS)

When the Original Module is Available

➡Following module installation, some modules require a separate learning procedure be carried out. For adaptive learning and calibration instructions, refer to the specific module removal and installation procedures.

1. Connect the IDS and identify the vehicle as normal.
2. From the Toolbox icon, select Module Programming and press the check mark.

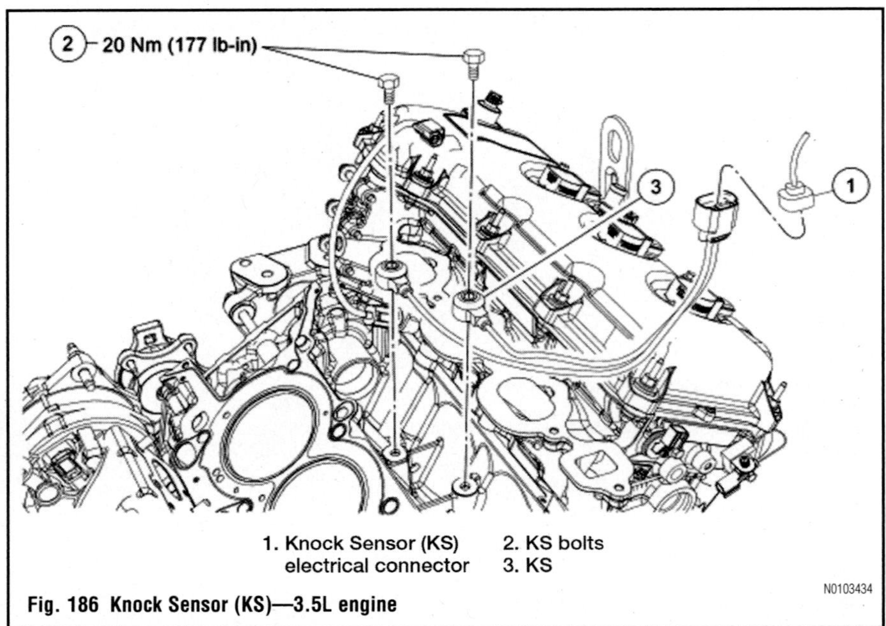

Fig. 186 Knock Sensor (KS)—3.5L engine

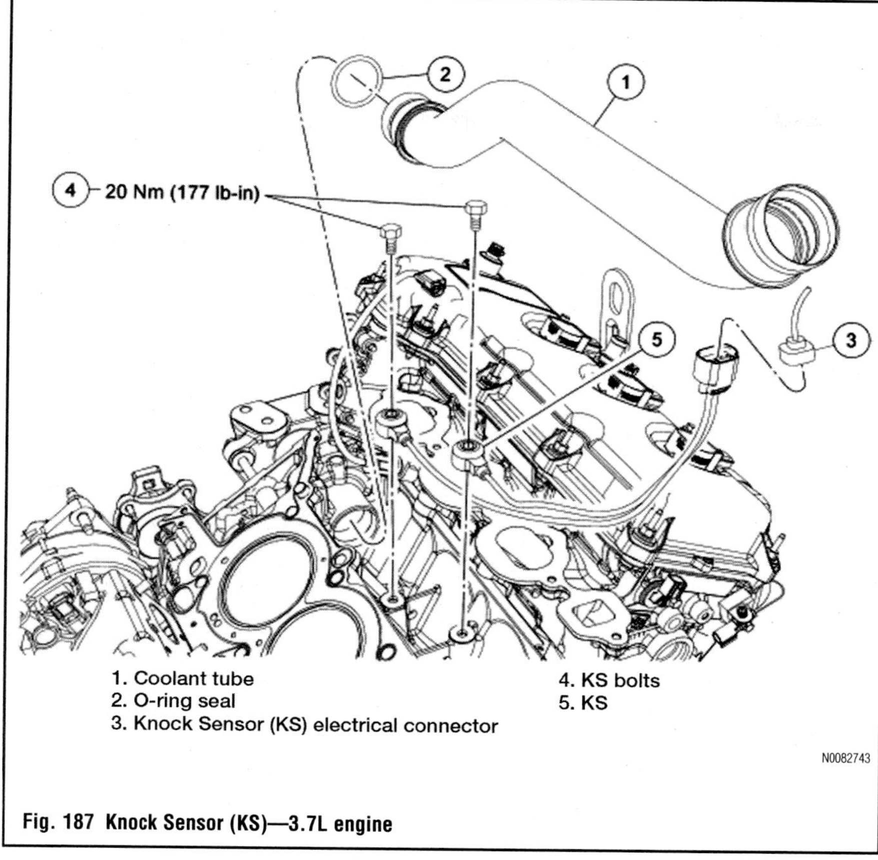

Fig. 187 Knock Sensor (KS)—3.7L engine

3. Select Programmable Module Installation.
4. Select the module that is being replaced.
5. Follow the on-screen instructions, turn the ignition key to the OFF position, and press the check mark.
6. Install the new module and press the check mark.
7. Follow the on-screen instructions, turn the ignition key to the ON position, and press the check mark.
8. The IDS downloads the data into the new module and displays Module Configuration Complete.
9. Test module for correct operation.

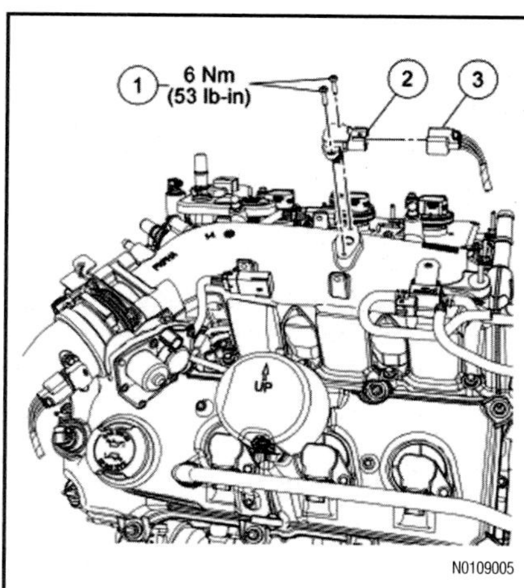

Fig. 188 Manifold Absolute Pressure (MAP) Sensor/Intake Air Temperature 2 (IAT2) Sensor

When the Original Module is NOT Available

➡Following module installation, some modules require a separate learning procedure be carried out. For adaptive learning and calibration instructions, refer to the specific module removal and installation procedures.

1. Install the new module.
2. Connect the IDS and identify the vehicle as normal.
3. From the Toolbox icon, select Module Programming and press the check mark.
4. Select Programmable Module Installation.
5. Select the module that was replaced.
6. Follow the on-screen instructions, turn the ignition key to the OFF position, and press the check mark.
7. Follow the on-screen instructions, turn the ignition key to the ON position, and press the check mark.
8. If the data is not available, the IDS displays a screen stating to contact the As-Built Data Center.
9. Retrieve the data from the technician service publication website at this time and press the check mark.

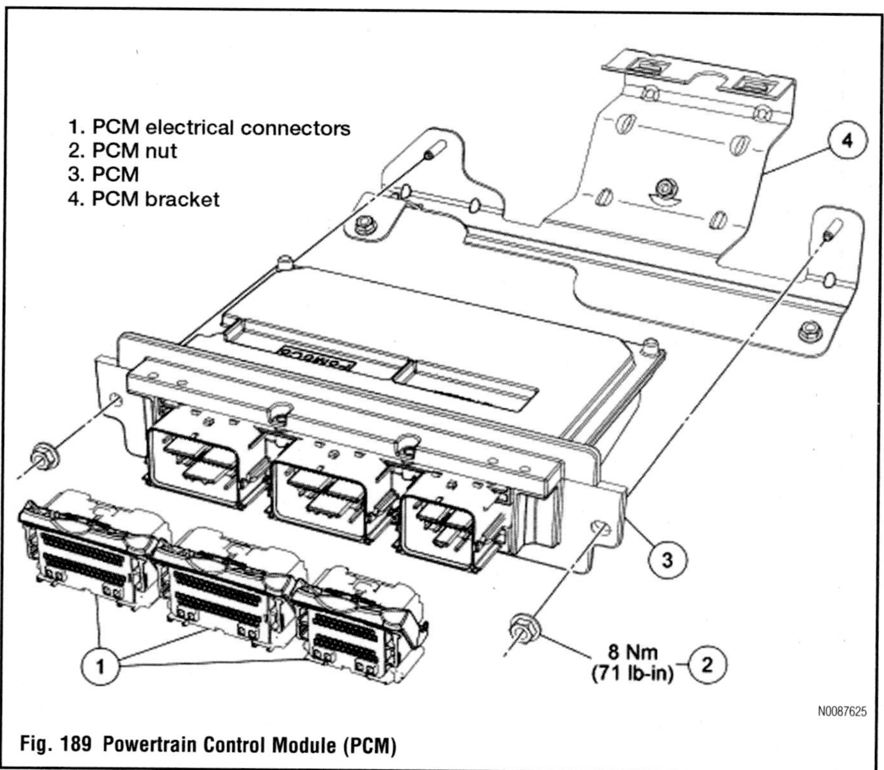

Fig. 189 Powertrain Control Module (PCM)

10. Enter the module data and press the check mark.
11. The IDS downloads the data into the new module and displays Module Configuration Complete.
12. Test module for correct operation.

PASSIVE ANTI-THEFT SYSTEM (PATS) PARAMETER RESET PROCEDURE

Integrated Keyhead Transmitter (IKT)

➡A minimum of 2 Passive Anti-Theft System (PATS) keys must be programmed into the Instrument Panel Cluster (IPC) to complete this procedure and allow the vehicle to start.

1. Turn the key from the OFF position to the ON position.
2. From the scan tool, follow the on-screen instructions to ENTER SECURITY ACCESS.
3. From the scan tool, select: Parameter Reset and follow the on-screen instructions.

➡If the IPC or the IPC and the PCM were replaced, updated or reconfigured, follow Steps 4–9. All vehicle keys are erased during the parameter reset procedure. Verify at least 2 vehicle keys are available prior to carrying out the PATS parameter reset. If only the PCM was replaced, go to Step 9.

4. From the scan tool, select: Ignition Key Code Erase and follow the on-screen instructions.
5. Turn the key to the OFF position and disconnect the scan tool.
6. Turn the key to the ON position for 6 seconds.
7. Turn the key to the OFF position and remove the key.
8. Insert the second PATS key into the ignition lock cylinder and turn the key to the ON position for 6 seconds.
9. Both keys now start the vehicle.

Intelligent Access (IA)

➡If the Remote Function Actuator (RFA) module or the RFA module and the PCM were replaced, updated or reconfigured, follow Steps 1–14. All vehicle keys are erased during the parameter reset procedure. Verify at least 2 vehicle keys are available prior to carrying out the Passive Anti-Theft System (PATS) parameter reset. If only the PCM was replaced, follow Steps 10–12.

➡A minimum of 2 Intelligent Access (IA) keys must be programmed into the RFA module to complete this procedure and allow the vehicle to start.

1. Make sure the ignition is in the OFF mode.
2. From the scan tool, follow the on-screen instructions to ENTER SECURITY ACCESS.
3. Place an IA key in the backup transceiver slot.
4. From the scan tool menu select: Ignition Key Code Erase. Follow the on-screen instructions until the process has been completed and the PATS Functions screen is available again.
5. From the scan tool menu select: Program ignition key. Follow the on-screen instructions until the process has been completed and the PATS Functions screen is available again.
6. Remove the first IA key from the backup transceiver slot and verify the IA key has been programmed by pressing the lock and unlock buttons.
7. Place the second IA key in the backup transceiver slot.
8. From the scan tool menu select: Program ignition key. Follow the on-screen instructions until the process has been completed and the PATS Functions screen is available again.
9. Remove the second IA key from the backup transceiver slot and verify the IA key has been programmed by pressing the lock and unlock buttons.
10. Turn the ignition to the ON mode.
11. From the scan tool, select: Parameter Reset and follow the on-screen instructions.
12. Disconnect the scan tool.
13. The vehicle should now start with both IA keys.
14. Verify the operation of each key by placing one key at a time inside the passenger compartment and start the vehicle (make sure the rest of the keys are out of the vehicle when verifying each key operation).

THROTTLE POSITION SENSOR (TPS)

LOCATION

See Figure 190.

Refer to the accompanying illustration.

REMOVAL & INSTALLATION

1. Remove the Charge Air Cooler (CAC) outlet pipe.
2. Disconnect the Throttle Position (TP) sensor electrical connector.

⁂ WARNING

Do not put direct heat on the Throttle Position (TP) sensor or any other plastic parts because heat damage may occur. Damage may also occur if Electronic Throttle Body (ETB) temperature exceeds 248°F (120°C).

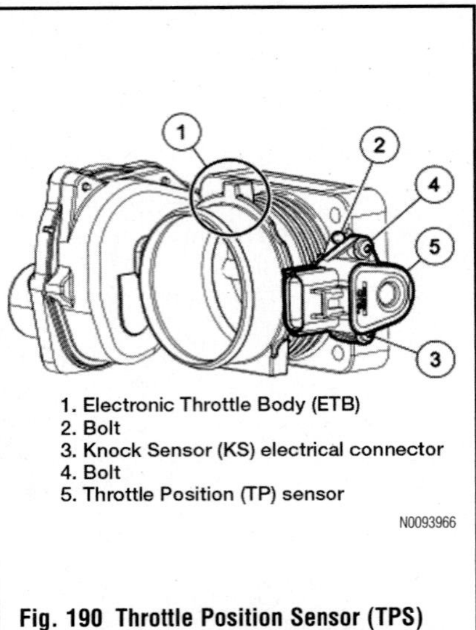

Fig. 190 Throttle Position Sensor (TPS)

➡Do not use power tools.

3. Remove the TP sensor:
   a. Using a suitable heat gun, apply heat to the top of the Electronic Throttle Body (ETB) until the top TP sensor bolt ear reaches approximately 130°F (55°C), this should take no more than 3 minutes using an 1,100-watt heat gun. The heat gun should be about 1 in. (25.4 mm) away from the ETB.
4. Monitor the temperature of the top TP sensor bolt ear on the ETB with a suitable temperature measuring device, such as a digital temperature laser or infrared thermometer, while heating the ETB .
5. Using hand tools, quickly remove the bolt farthest from the heat source first and discard.
6. Using hand tools, remove the remaining bolt and discard.
7. Remove and discard the TP sensor.

To install:

➡When installing the new TP sensor, make sure that the radial locator tab on the TP sensor is aligned with the radial locator hole on the ETB .

➡Do not use power tools.

8. Install the new TP sensor.
   a. Using hand tools, install the 2 new bolts. Tighten to 27 inch lbs. (3 Nm).
9. Connect the TP sensor electrical connector.
10. Install the CAC outlet pipe.

FUEL SYSTEM SERVICE PRECAUTIONS

Safety is the most important factor when performing not only fuel system maintenance but any type of maintenance. Failure to conduct maintenance and repairs in a safe manner may result in serious personal injury or death. Maintenance and testing of the vehicle's fuel system components can be accomplished safely and effectively by adhering to the following rules and guidelines.

- To avoid the possibility of fire and personal injury, always disconnect the negative battery cable unless the repair or test procedure requires that battery voltage be applied.
- Always relieve the fuel system pressure prior to disconnecting any fuel system component (injector, fuel rail, pressure regulator, etc.), fitting or fuel line connection. Exercise extreme caution whenever relieving fuel system pressure to avoid exposing skin, face and eyes to fuel spray. Please be advised that fuel under pressure may penetrate the skin or any part of the body that it contacts.
- Always place a shop towel or cloth around the fitting or connection prior to loosening to absorb any excess fuel due to spillage. Ensure that all fuel spillage (should it occur) is quickly removed from engine surfaces. Ensure that all fuel soaked cloths or towels are deposited into a suitable waste container.
- Always keep a dry chemical (Class B) fire extinguisher near the work area.
- Do not allow fuel spray or fuel vapors to come into contact with a spark or open flame.
- Always use a back-up wrench when loosening and tightening fuel line connection fittings. This will prevent unnecessary stress and torsion to fuel line piping.
- Always replace worn fuel fitting O-rings with new Do not substitute fuel hose or equivalent where fuel pipe is installed.

Before servicing the vehicle, make sure to also refer to the precautions in the beginning of this section as well.

RELIEVING FUEL SYSTEM PRESSURE

➡If applicable, review the procedures for achieving the various ignition states (ignition OFF, ignition in ACCESSORY, ignition ON and ignition START) on vehicles with Intelligent Access with Push Button Start.

➡The Fuel Pump (FP) control module is mounted to the panel behind the rear seat backrest cushion. The FP control module electrical connector can be accessed through the luggage compartment.

1. Disconnect the FP module electrical connector.
2. Start the engine and allow it to idle until it stalls.
3. Turn the ignition to the OFF position.
4. For 3.5L engines:

➡On vehicles equipped with Gasoline Turbocharged Direct Injection (GTDI), it is necessary to release the high pressure system fuel prior to disconnecting a low pressure fuel tube quick connect coupling.

a. To release the fuel pressure in the high pressure fuel tube, wrap the flare nut with a shop towel to absorb any residual fuel pressure during the loosening of the flare nut.

b. Disconnect the high pressure fuel tube-to-fuel injection pump flare nut.

FUEL INJECTORS

REMOVAL & INSTALLATION

3.5L Engine

See Figures 191 through 194.

1. Release the fuel system pressure.
2. Disconnect the battery ground cable.

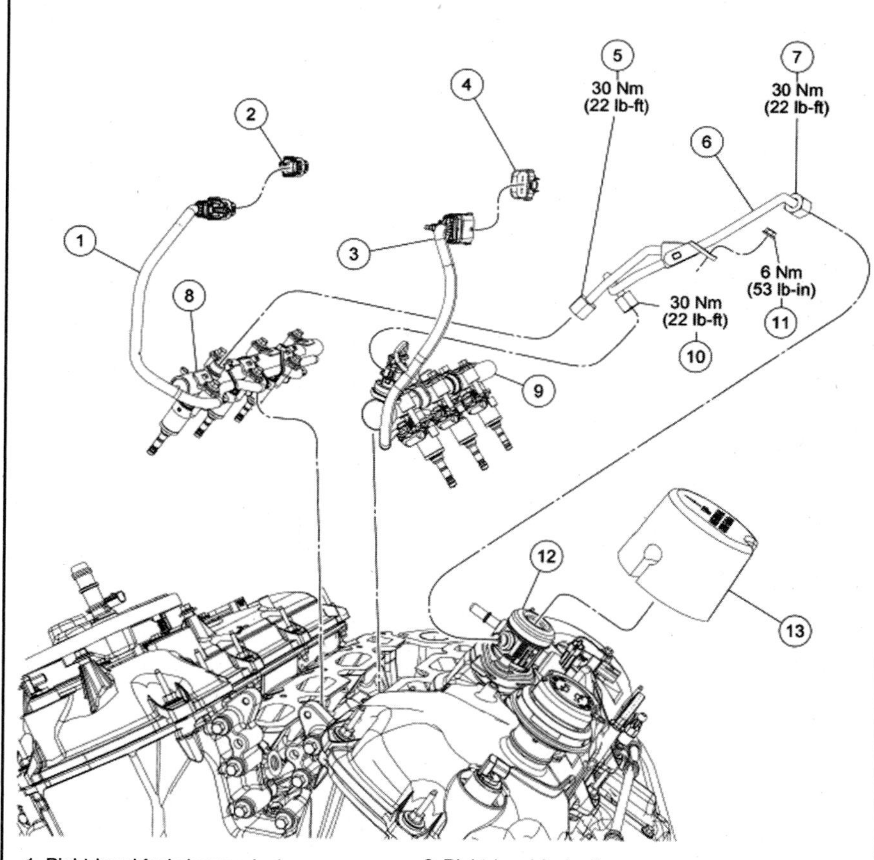

Fig. 191 Gasoline Turbocharged Direct Injection (GTDI) Fuel Rails and High Pressure Fuel Tube—3.5L Engines—Early Build Vehicles

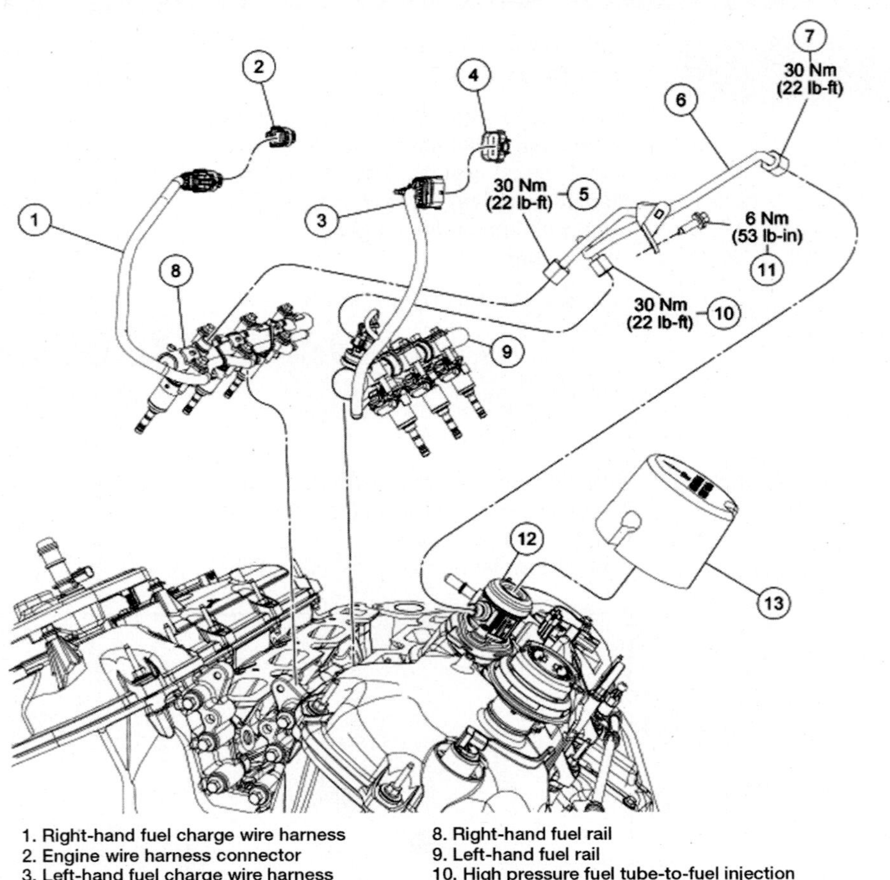

Fig. 192 Gasoline Turbocharged Direct Injection (GTDI) Fuel Rails and High Pressure Fuel Tube—3.5L Engines—Late Build Vehicles

3. Remove the intake manifold.

4. Remove the fuel injection pump noise insulator shield.

5. For early build vehicles, remove the high pressure fuel tube nut.

6. For late build vehicles, remove the high pressure fuel tube bolt.

7. Loosen the 3 flare nuts and remove the high pressure fuel tube. To release the fuel pressure in the high pressure fuel tube, wrap the flare nuts with a shop towel to absorb any residual fuel pressure during the loosening of the flare nuts.

8. Disconnect the Fuel Rail Pressure (FRP) sensor electrical connector.

9. Cut, remove and discard the fuel charge wiring harness tie straps.

a. It is very important to note the routing of the fuel charge wire harnesses on the fuel rails and matchmark the location of the tie straps prior to removal or damage may occur to the wire harnesses during installation.

b. Use compressed air and remove any dirt or foreign material from the cylinder head, block and general surrounding area of the fuel rail and injectors.

10. Remove and discard the 6 bolts and remove the left-hand fuel rail.

a. Pull out the fuel rails in the direction of the fuel injector axis or damage may occur to the fuel injectors.

b. When removing the fuel rails, the fuel injectors may remain in the fuel rails but normally remain in the cylinder heads and require the use of a Fuel Injector Remover tool to extract.

11. Remove and discard the 6 bolts and remove the right-hand fuel rail.

12. Disconnect the 6 fuel injector electrical connectors and remove the 2 fuel charge wire harnesses.

13. Remove and discard the 6 upper fuel injector O-ring seals.

14. Remove and discard the 6 fuel injector clips.

15. Using the Slide Hammer and the Fuel Injector Remover (SST 307-005, 310-206) or equivalent tools, remove the 6 fuel injectors.

To install:

16. Make sure to thoroughly clean any residual fuel or foreign material from the cylinder head, block and the general surrounding area of the fuel rails and injectors.

17. Using the Fuel Injector Brush (SST 310-205) or equivalent tool, clean the fuel injector orifices.

18. Pull the lower Teflon® seal away from the injector with narrow tip pliers.

a. Do not attempt to cut the lower Teflon® seal without first pulling it away

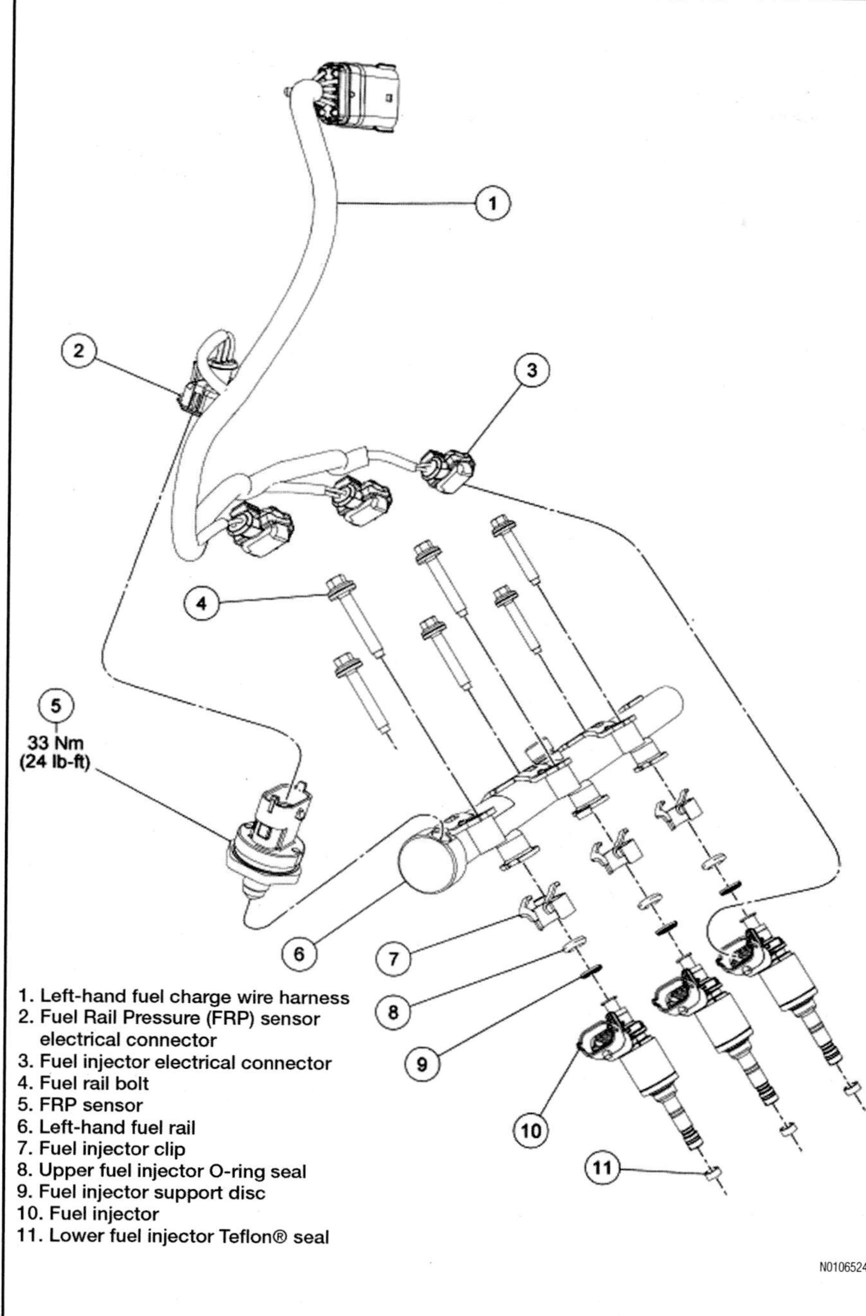

Fig. 193 GTDI Left-Hand Fuel Rail and Fuel Injectors—3.5L Engines

from the fuel injector or damage to the injector may occur.

b. Be very careful when removing the lower Teflon® seals, not to scratch, nick or gouge the fuel injectors.

19. Carefully cut and discard the 6 lower fuel injector Teflon® seals.

20. Install the new lower Teflon® seals on the narrow end of the Arbor (part of the Fuel Injector Seal Installer), then install the Arbor on the fuel injector tips. Do not lubricate the 6 new lower Teflon® fuel injector seals.

21. Using the Pusher Tool (part of the Fuel Injector Seal Installer), slide the Teflon® seals off of the Arbor and into the groove on the fuel injectors.

a. Once the Teflon® seal is installed on the Arbor, it should immediately be installed onto the fuel injector to avoid excessive expansion of the seal.

22. Place the Adjustment Ring (part of the Fuel Injector Seal Installer) beveled side first, over the fuel injector tip until it bottoms out against the fuel injector and turn 180 degrees.

a. After one minute, turn the Adjustment Ring back 180 degrees and remove.

23. Install the fuel charge wire harnesses and tie straps to the matchmarked locations on the fuel rails. Start by attaching the first tie strap farthest down the wire harness and continue to the connector end of the harness, leaving ample slack between the fuel injectors. The illustration details the correct fuel charge wire harness routing and tie strap positioning for installation.

24. Connect the FRP sensor electrical connector.

25. Install the 6 new upper fuel injector O-ring seals.

a. Use fuel injector O-ring seals that are made of special fuel-resistant material. The use of ordinary O-ring seals may cause the fuel system to leak. Do not reuse the O-ring seals.

b. To install, apply clean engine oil to the 6 new upper fuel injector O-ring seals only. Do not lubricate the lower fuel injector Teflon® seals.

c. Inspect the fuel injector support disks and replace if necessary.

26. Install the 6 new fuel injector clips.

27. Install the 6 fuel injectors into the fuel rails and connect the 6 electrical connectors.

a. The anti-rotation device on the fuel injector has to slip into the groove of the fuel rail cup.

WARNING

It is very important to visually inspect the routing of the fuel charge wire harness to make sure that they will not be pinched or damaged between the fuel rail and the cylinder head during installation.

28. Install the 6 new bolts and the right-hand fuel rail assembly. Tighten the bolts in a method that draws the fuel rail evenly to the head, preventing a rocking motion.

a. Push down on the fuel rail face above the injectors and begin tightening the outer bolts first and then proceed inward.

b. To install, tighten to 89 inch lbs.(10 Nm).

c. Tighten an additional 45 degrees.

29. Install the 6 new bolts and the left-hand fuel rail assembly. Tighten the bolts in

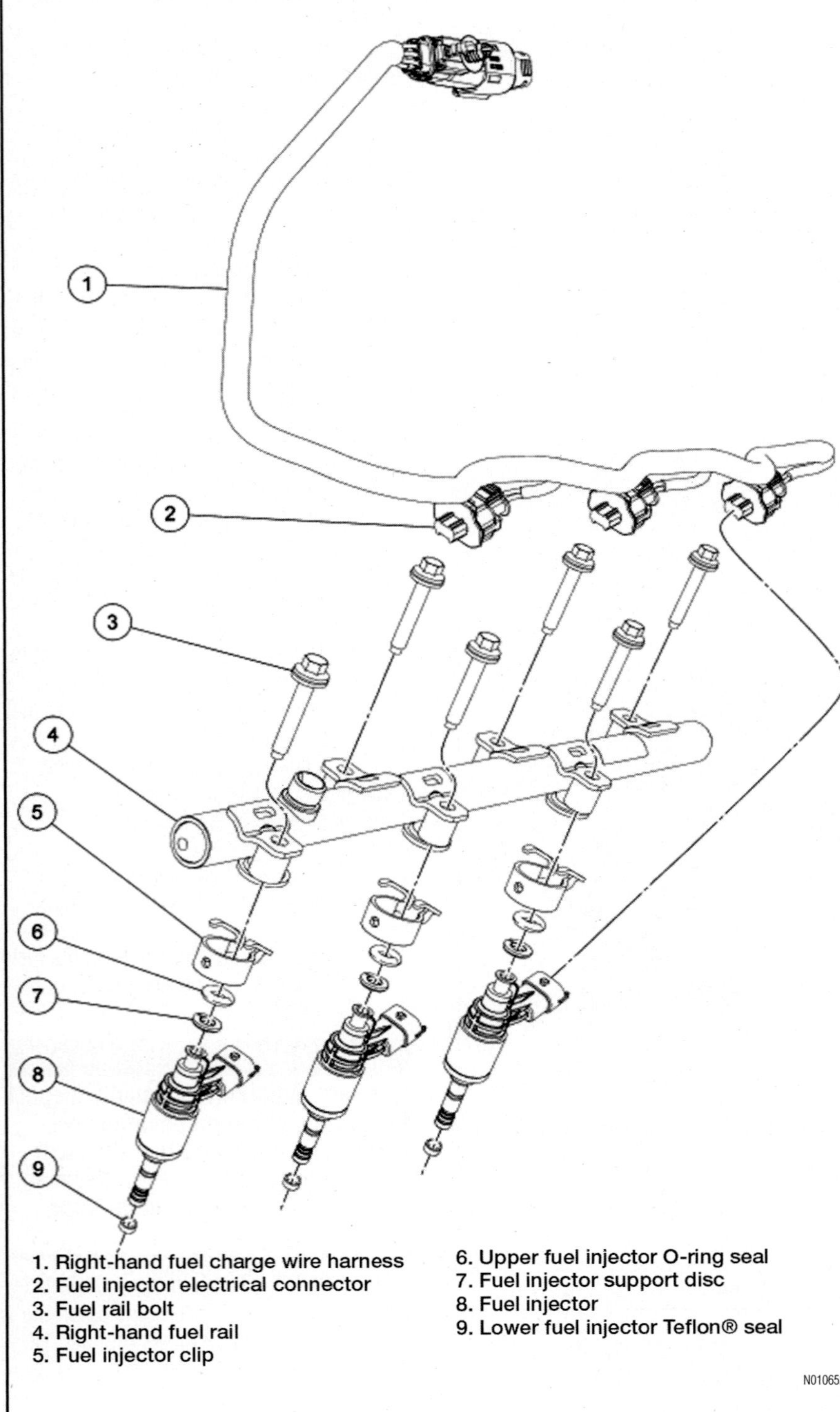

Fig. 194 GTDI Right-Hand Fuel Rail and Fuel Injectors—3.5L Engines

a method that draws the fuel rail evenly to the head, preventing a rocking motion.

a. Push down on the fuel rail face above the injectors and begin tightening the outer bolts first and proceed inward.

b. To install, tighten to 89 inch lbs. (10 Nm).

c. Tighten an additional 45 degrees.

30. Apply clean engine oil to the threads of the 3 high-pressure fuel tube flare nuts. Install the high-pressure fuel tube and tighten the 3 flare nuts. Tighten to 22 ft. lbs. (30 Nm).

31. For early build vehicles, install the high-pressure fuel tube nut. Tighten to 53 inch lbs. (6 Nm).

32. For late build vehicles, install the high-pressure fuel tube bolt. Tighten to 53 inch lbs. (6 Nm).

33. Install the fuel injection pump noise insulator shield.

34. Install the intake manifold.

35. Connect the battery ground cable.

3.7L Engine

See Figure 195.

1. Release the fuel system pressure.
2. Disconnect the battery ground cable.
3. Remove the upper intake manifold.
4. Detach the fuel tube routing clips from the fuel rail.
5. Disconnect the fuel jumper tube-to-fuel rail spring lock coupling.
6. Disconnect the 6 fuel injector electrical connectors.
7. Remove the 4 fuel rail bolts.
8. Remove the fuel rail and injectors as an assembly.
9. Remove the 6 fuel injector clips and the 6 fuel injectors. Remove and discard the 12 fuel injector O-ring seals.

To install:

➡Use O-ring seals that are made of special fuel-resistant material. The use of ordinary O-rings may cause the fuel system to leak. Do not reuse the O-ring seals.

10. Install the new O-ring seals onto the fuel injectors and lubricate them with clean engine oil. The upper and lower fuel injector O-ring seals are similar in appearance, but are not interchangeable.
11. Install the 6 fuel injectors and the 6 fuel injector clips into the fuel rail.
12. Install the fuel rail and fuel injectors as an assembly.
13. Install the 4 fuel rail bolts. Tighten to 89 inch lbs. (10 Nm).
14. Connect the 6 fuel injector electrical connectors.
15. Connect the fuel jumper tube-to-fuel rail spring lock coupling.
16. Attach the fuel tube routing clips to the fuel rail.
17. Install the upper intake manifold.
18. Connect the battery ground cable.

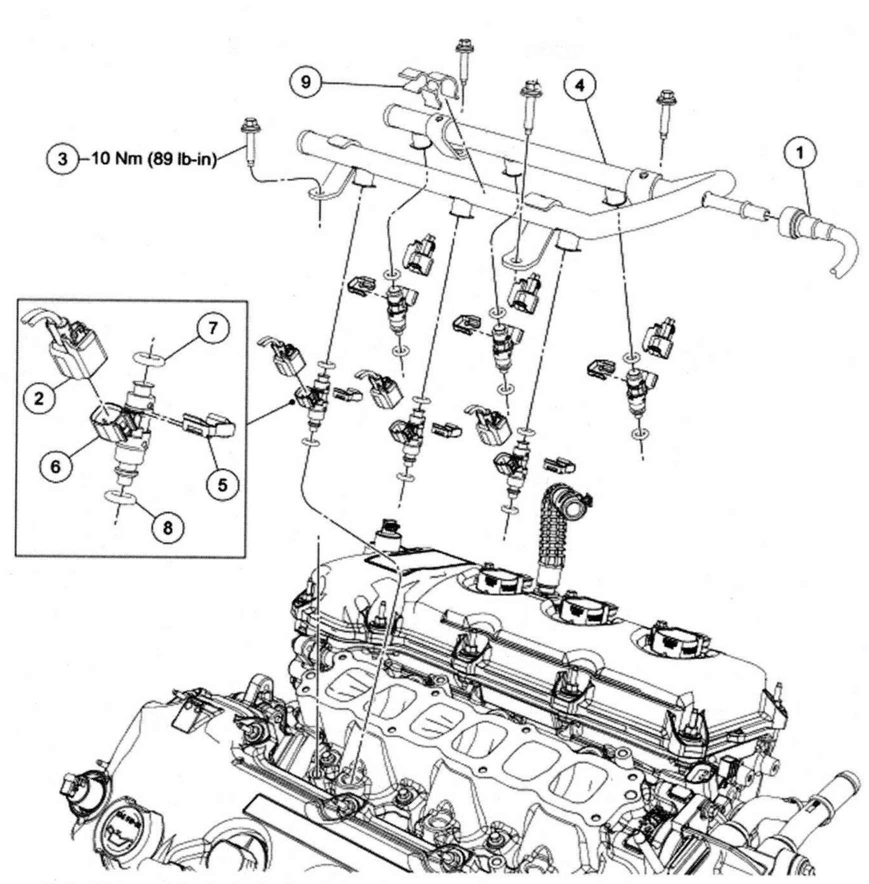

Fig. 195 Fuel Rail and Fuel Injector—3.7L Engines

FUEL PUMP

REMOVAL & INSTALLATION

See Figures 196 and 197.

1. Release the fuel system pressure.
2. Disconnect the battery ground cable.
3. Remove the Fuel Pump (FP) module access cover.
4. Clean the FP module connections, couplings, flange surfaces and the immediate surrounding area of any dirt or foreign material.
5. Disconnect the FP module electrical connector.
6. Disconnect the fuel tank jumper tube-to-FP module quick connect coupling.
   a. Place absorbent toweling in the immediate surrounding area in case of fuel spillage.
7. Attach the Fuel Storage Tanker tube to the FP module outlet fitting and remove approximately one-fourth (approximately 5 gallons) of the fuel from a completely full tank, lowering the fuel level below the FP module mounting flange.
8. Carefully install the Fuel Tank Sender Unit Wrench to avoid damaging the FP module when removing the lock ring.
9. Install the Fuel Tank Sender Unit Wrench; remove the FP module lock ring.

WARNING

The Fuel Pump (FP) module must be handled carefully to avoid damage to the float arm.

10. Carefully lift the FP module out of the fuel tank allowing access and disconnect the internal fuel tube-to-FP module quick connect coupling.
    a. Completely remove the FP module from the fuel tank. The FP module will have residual fuel remaining internally, drain into a suitable container.
    b. Inspect the surfaces of the FP module flange and fuel tank O-ring seal contact surfaces. Do not polish or adjust the

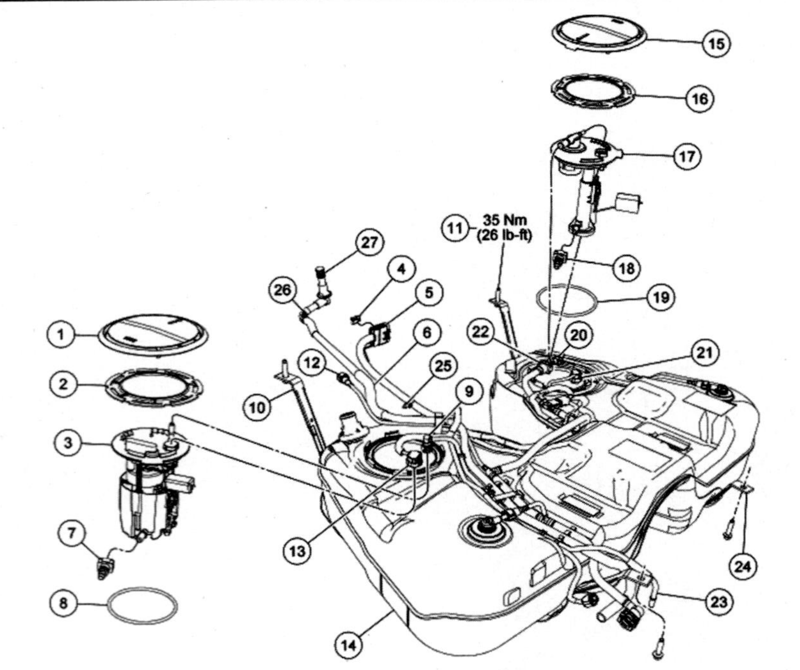

1. Fuel Pump (FP) module access cover
2. FP module lock ring
3. FP module
4. Fuel tank wire harness connector pin-type retainer
5. Fuel tank wire harness electrical connector
6. Evaporative Emission (EVAP) canister fresh air hose
7. Internal fuel tube-to-FP module quick connect coupling
8. FP module O-ring seal
9. Fuel tank jumper tube-to-FP module quick connect coupling
10. Right-hand fuel tank strap
11. Fuel tank strap bolt
12. Fuel vapor tube assembly-to-fuel tank filler pipe recirculation tube quick connect coupling
13. FP module electrical connector
14. Fuel tank
15. Fuel level sensor access cover
16. Fuel level sensor lock ring
17. Fuel level sensor
18. Internal fuel tube-to-fuel level sensor quick connect coupling
19. Fuel level sensor O-ring seal
20. Fuel vapor tube-to-fuel level sensor quick connect coupling
21. Fuel level sensor electrical connector
22. Fuel vapor tube assembly-to-fuel level sensor quick connect coupling
23. Fuel tank jumper tube
24. Left-hand fuel tank strap
25. Fuel tank wire harness pin-type retainer
26. EVAP canister fresh air hose pin-type retain
27. Fresh air hose vent cap

N0105820

Fig. 196 L-Shaped fuel tank components

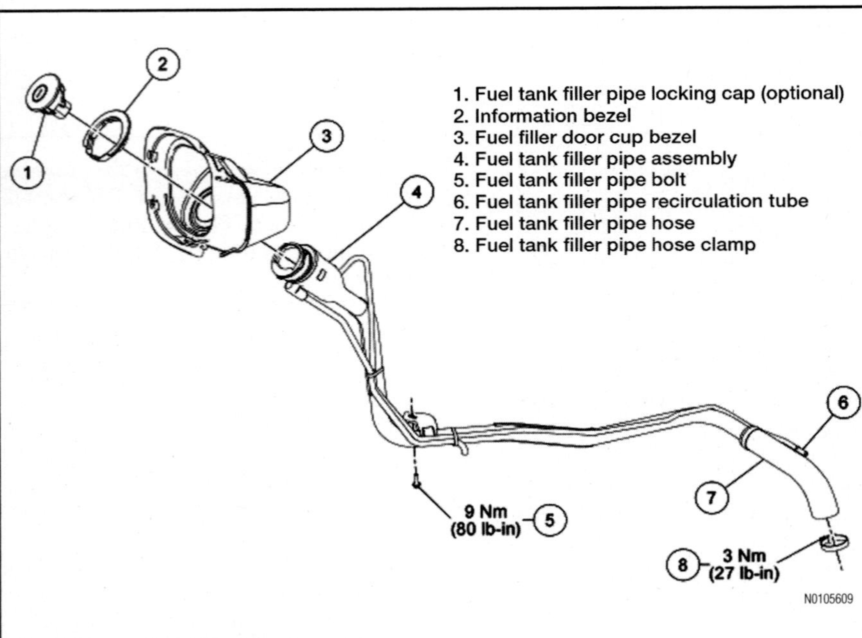

Fig. 197 Fuel Tank Filler Pipe Assembly

O-ring seal contact area of the fuel tank flange or the fuel tank. Install a new FP module or fuel tank if the O-ring seal contact area is bent, scratched or corroded.

c. Remove and discard the FP module O-ring seal.

To install:

11. To install, reverse the removal procedure, noting the following:

a. Make sure the alignment arrows on the fuel pump module and the fuel tank meet before tightening the FP module lock ring.

b. Tighten the FP lock ring until it meets the stop tabs on the fuel tank.

c. Make sure to install a new FP module O-ring seal.

d. Apply clean engine oil to the O-ring seal.

THROTTLE BODY

REMOVAL & INSTALLATION

3.5L Engine

See Figure 198.

1. Disconnect the Throttle Position (TP) sensor electrical connector.
2. Disconnect the Throttle Actuator Control (TAC) electrical connector.
3. Loosen the clamp and disconnect the Charge Air Cooler (CAC) outlet pipe-to-throttle body.
4. Remove the 4 bolts, the throttle body and the TP sensor shield bracket. Discard the throttle body gasket.

To install:

5. To install, reverse the removal procedure, noting the following:

a. Install a new throttle body gasket.

b. Tighten the throttle body mounting bolts to 89 inch lbs. (10 Nm).

c. Tighten the CAC outlet pipe-to-throttle body clamp to 44 inch lbs. (5 Nm).

3.7L Engine

See Figure 199.

1. Remove the Air Cleaner (ACL) outlet pipe.
2. Disconnect the electronic throttle control electrical connector.
3. Remove the 4 bolts and the throttle body. Discard the gasket.

To install:

4. To install, reverse the removal procedure, noting the following:

a. Install a new throttle body gasket.

b. Tighten the throttle body mounting bolts to 89 inch lbs. (10 Nm).

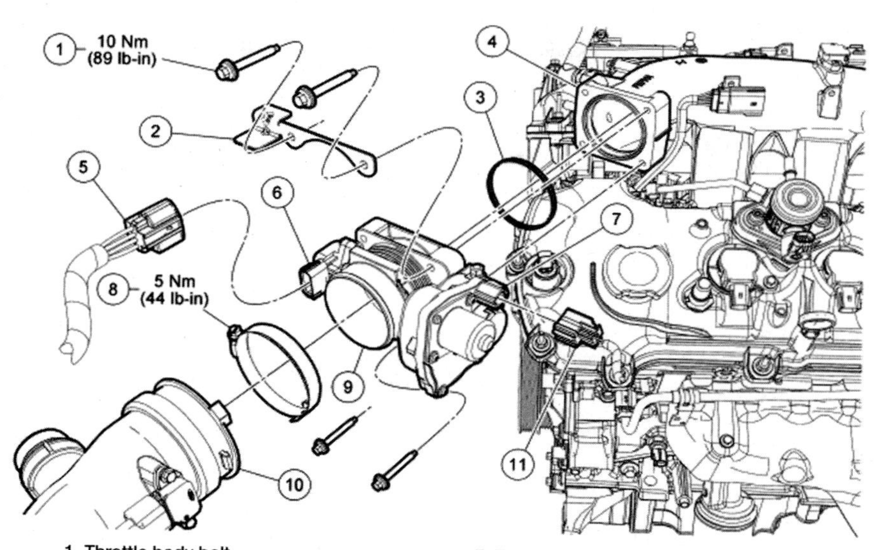

Fig. 198 Throttle body components—3.5L engines

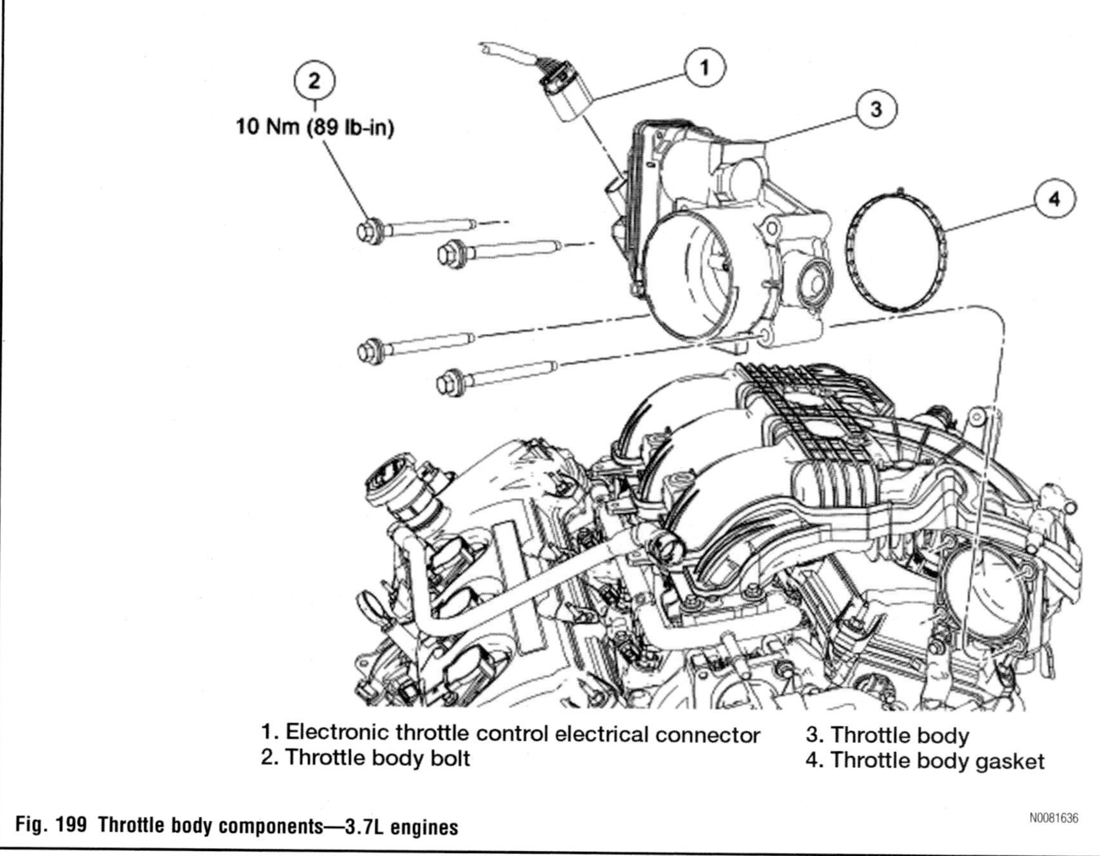

Fig. 199 Throttle body components—3.7L engines

HEATING & AIR CONDITIONING SYSTEM

BLOWER MOTOR

REMOVAL & INSTALLATION

See Figure 200.

✳✳ CAUTION

Always deplete the backup power supply before repairing or installing any new front or side air bag supplemental restraint system (SRS) component and before servicing, removing, installing, adjusting or striking components near the front or side impact sensors or the restraints control module (RCM). Nearby components include doors, instrument panel, console, door latches, strikers, seats and hood latches. To deplete the backup power supply energy, disconnect the battery ground cable and wait at least 1 minute. Be sure to disconnect auxiliary batteries and power supplies (if equipped).

1. Remove the 3 right-hand lower instrument panel insulator screws and remove the insulator.
2. Disconnect the blower motor electrical connector.
3. Depress the 2 retaining tabs and detach the blower motor vent tube from the heater core and evaporator core housing.

➡The blower motor vent tube must be completely detached from the heater core and evaporator core housing to allow the blower motor to be rotated.

4. Rotate the blower motor counterclockwise to detach it from the heater core and evaporator core housing and remove the blower motor.

To install:

5. To install, reverse the removal procedure.

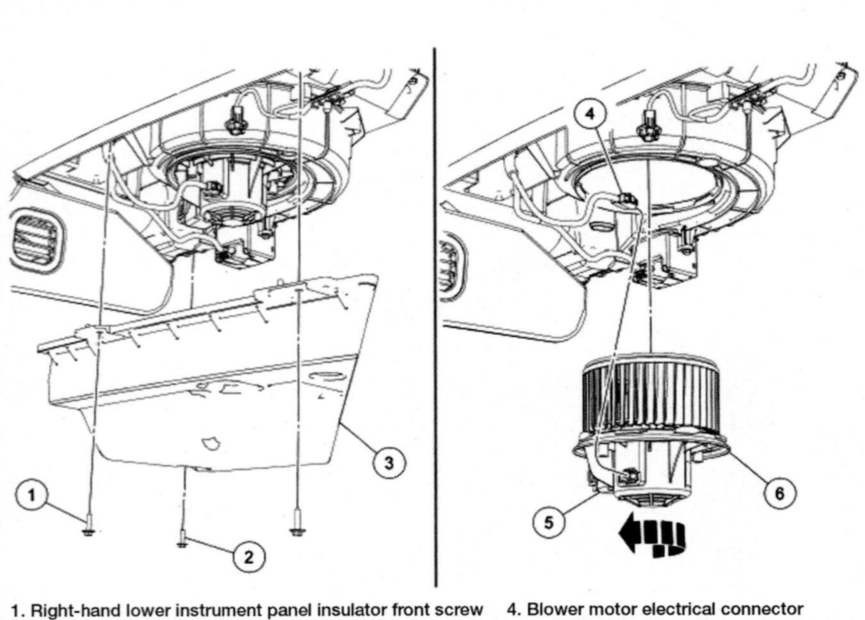

1. Right-hand lower instrument panel insulator front screw
2. Right-hand lower instrument panel insulator rear screw
3. Right-hand lower instrument panel insulator
4. Blower motor electrical connector
5. Blower motor vent tube
6. Blower motor and wheel assembly

N0083884

Fig. 200 Blower motor components

HEATER CORE

REMOVAL & INSTALLATION

See Figures 201 through 204.

✳✳ CAUTION

Always deplete the backup power supply before repairing or installing any new front or side air bag supplemental restraint system (SRS) component and before servicing, removing, installing, adjusting or striking components near the front or side impact sensors or the restraints control module (RCM). Nearby components include doors, instrument panel, console, door latches, strikers, seats and hood latches. To deplete the backup power supply energy, disconnect the battery ground cable and wait at least 1 minute. Be sure to disconnect auxiliary batteries and power supplies (if equipped).

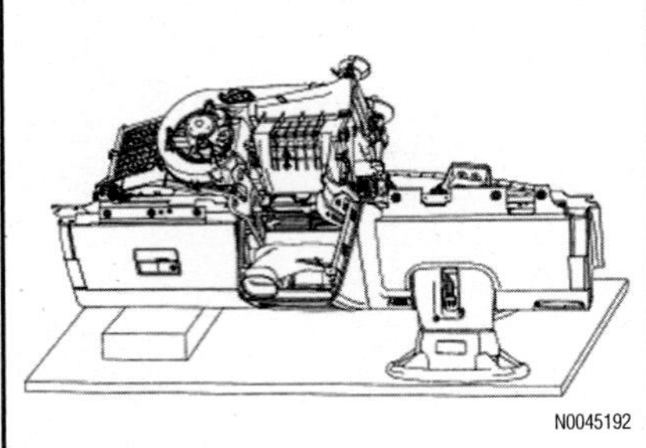

N0045192

Fig. 201 Instrument panel positioning

➡If a heater core leak is suspected, the heater core must be pressure leak tested before it is removed from the vehicle.

1. Remove the heater core and evaporator core housing, as follows:
    a. Remove the instrument panel assembly.
    b. Position the instrument panel with the passenger side supported as shown.
    c. Remove the 3 right-hand lower instrument panel insulator screws and position the insulator aside.
    d. Remove the 2 Remote Function Actuator (RFA) module nuts and position the module aside.

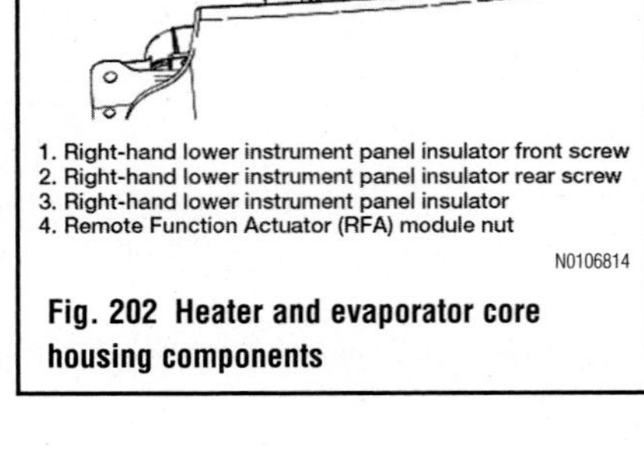

1. Right-hand lower instrument panel insulator front screw
2. Right-hand lower instrument panel insulator rear screw
3. Right-hand lower instrument panel insulator
4. Remote Function Actuator (RFA) module nut

N0106814

Fig. 202 Heater and evaporator core housing components

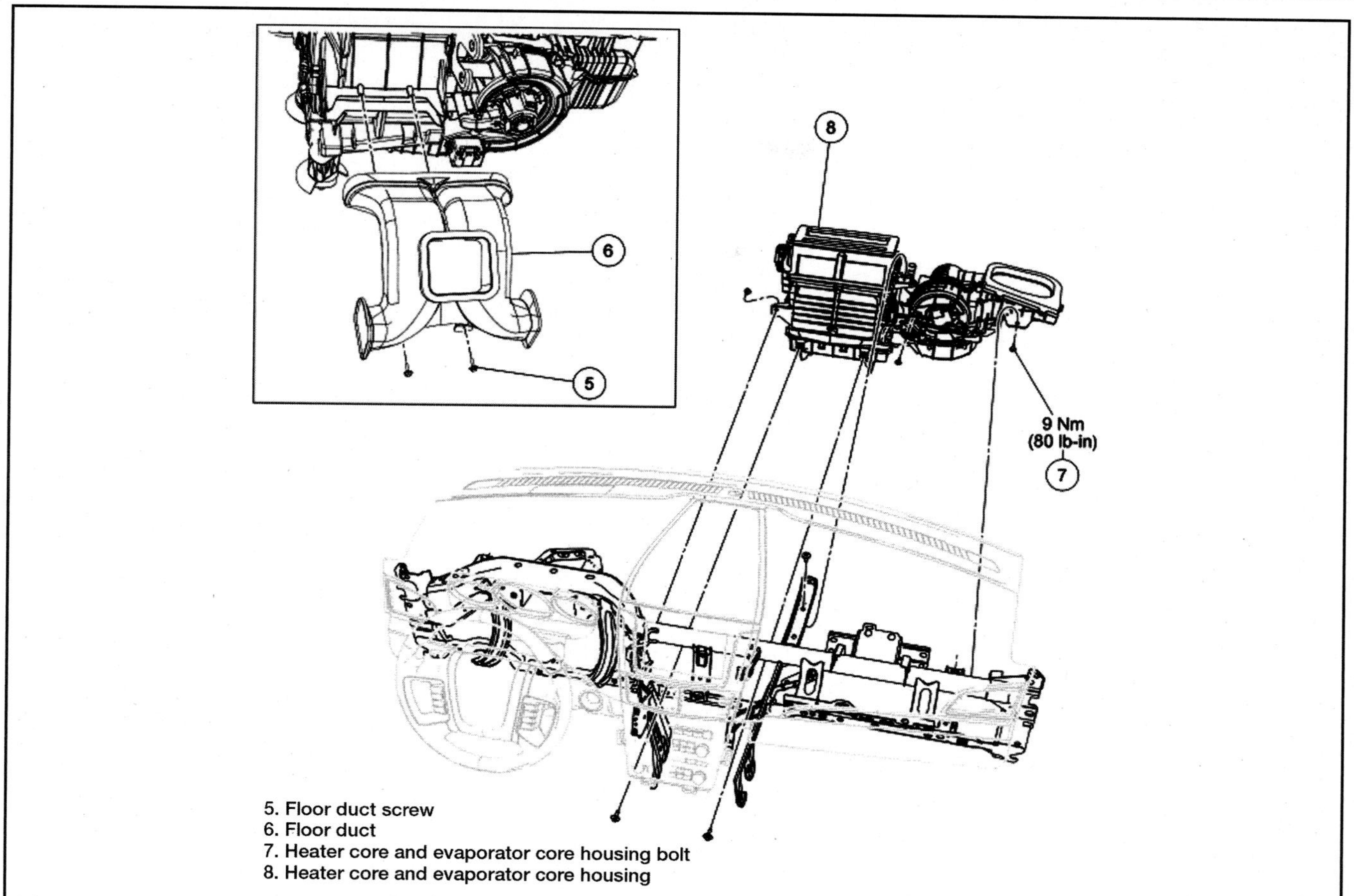

9 Nm (80 lb-in)

5. Floor duct screw
6. Floor duct
7. Heater core and evaporator core housing bolt
8. Heater core and evaporator core housing

N0106815

Fig. 203 Heater and evaporator core housing

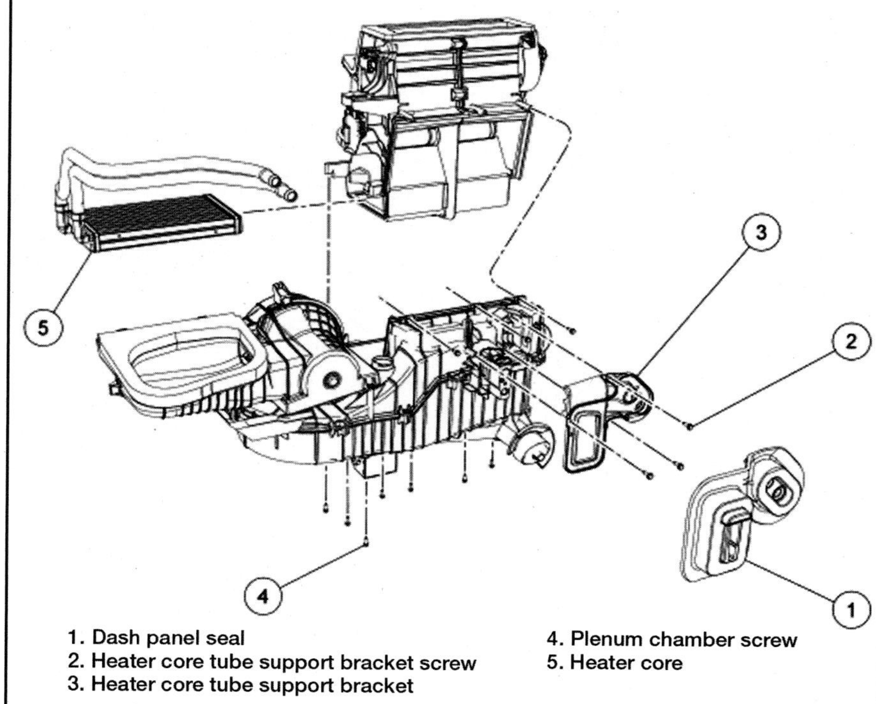

1. Dash panel seal
2. Heater core tube support bracket screw
3. Heater core tube support bracket
4. Plenum chamber screw
5. Heater core

Fig. 204 Heater core

e. Remove the 2 floor duct screws and remove the floor duct.

f. Detach the in-vehicle temperature sensor aspirator from the heater core and evaporator core housing.

g. Remove the 6 heater core and evaporator core housing bolts.

h. Disconnect the 3 electrical connectors and detach the wire harness pin-type retainer.

i. Detach the 4 wire harness pin-type retainers and disconnect the electrical connector.

j. Disconnect the 3 electrical connectors, detach the wire harness pin-type retainer and detach the instrument panel wire harness from the heater core and evaporator core housing.

k. Remove the heater core and evaporator core housing.

To install:

2. To install, reverse the removal procedure.

a. Tighten the heater core and evaporator core housing bolts to 80 inch lbs. (9 Nm).

POWER STEERING GEAR

REMOVAL & INSTALLATION

Electronic Power Assist Steering Gear

See Figures 205 and 206.

1. Using a suitable holding device, hold the steering wheel in the straight-ahead position.
2. Remove the wheels and tires.
3. Remove the bolt and disconnect the steering column shaft from the steering gear. Discard the bolt.
   a. Do not allow the steering column to rotate while the steering column shaft is disconnected from the steering gear or damage to the clockspring may occur. If there is evidence that the steering column has rotated, the clockspring must be removed and recentered.
4. Remove the 2 stabilizer bar link upper nuts. Discard the nuts.
5. Remove the 2 outer tie-rod end nuts and separate the tie-rod ends from the wheel knuckle.
6. Remove the 4 retainers and the underbody shield.
7. Remove the right-hand and left-hand exhaust flexible pipes.
8. Remove the 2 front and rear engine roll restrictor bolts.
9. Position the Powertrain Lift Table under the subframe.
10. Remove the 2 front subframe rearward bolts, the 4 support bracket bolts and the 2 subframe support brackets.
    a. Loosen the 2 front subframe forward bolts.
11. Lower the subframe to gain access to the steering gear.
12. Remove the wiring harness bracket bolt.
13. Disconnect the 2 Electronic Power Assist Steering (EPAS) electrical connectors and the wiring retainer.
14. Remove the 2 steering gear bolts.
    a. Position the stabilizer bar to the full up position.
    b. Remove the steering gear from the right-hand side of the vehicle.

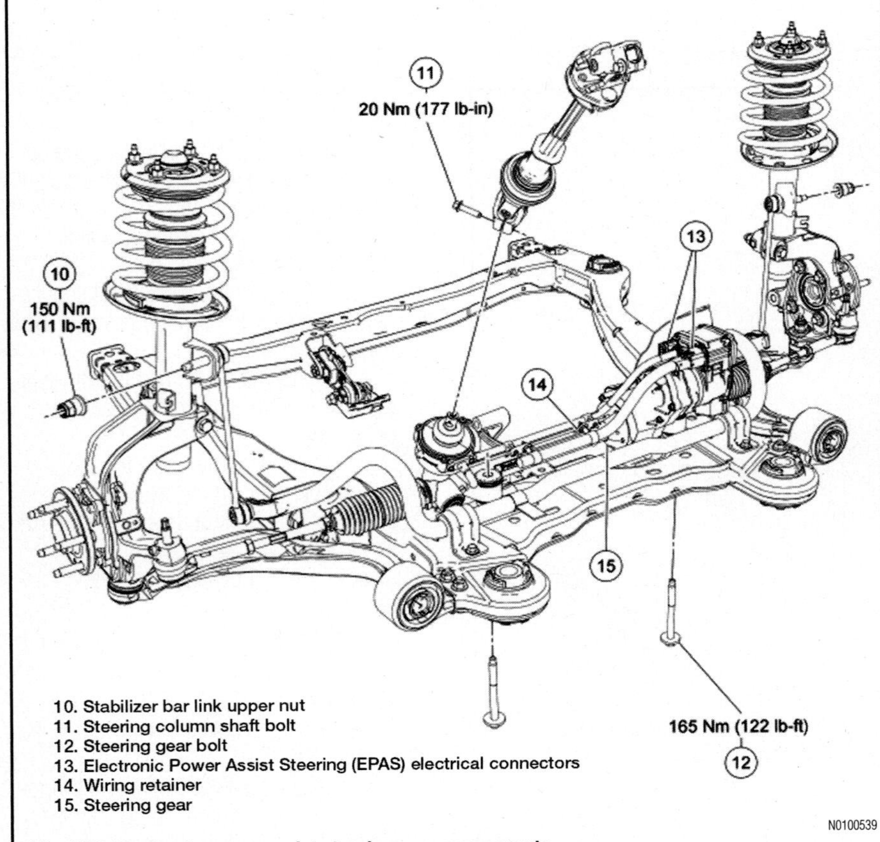

Fig. 205 Electronic power assist steering gear components

To install:

15. Position the steering gear and install the 2 bolts. Tighten to 122 ft. lbs. (165 Nm).
16. Connect the 2 EPAS electrical connectors and the wiring retainer.
17. Position the wiring harness bracket and install the bolt. Tighten to 80 inch lbs. (9 Nm).
18. Raise the subframe.
19. Position the 2 subframe support brackets and install the 4 bolts finger-tight.
20. Install the 2 front subframe rearward bolts.
    a. Tighten the rearward bolts to 111 ft. lbs. (150 Nm).
    b. Tighten the forward bolts to 148 ft. lbs. (200 Nm).
21. Tighten the 4 subframe support bracket bolts to 41 ft. lbs. (55 Nm).
22. Install the 2 front and rear engine roll restrictor bolts. Tighten to 66 ft. lbs. (90 Nm).
23. Install the right-hand and left-hand exhaust flexible pipes.
24. Position the underbody shield and install the 4 retainers.
25. Position the 2 outer tie-rod ends and install the nuts. Tighten to 111 ft. lbs. (150 Nm).
26. Connect the stabilizer bar links and install the 2 nuts. Tighten the new nuts to 111 ft. lbs. (150 Nm).
27. With the locator on the input shaft correctly aligned, connect the steering column shaft to the steering gear and install the new bolt. Tighten to 15 ft. lbs. (20 Nm).
28. Install the wheels and tires.

Hydraulic Power Assist Steering Gear

See Figure 207.

⁂ WARNING

When repairing the power steering system, care should be taken to prevent the entry of foreign material or failure of the power steering components may occur.

1. Using a suitable holding device, hold the steering wheel in the straight-ahead position.
2. Remove the wheels and tires.
3. Remove the 2 tie-rod end nuts and disconnect the tie-rod ends from the wheel knuckles. The hex-holding feature can be used to prevent turning of the stud while removing the nut.
4. Remove the pressure line bracket-to-steering gear bolt.

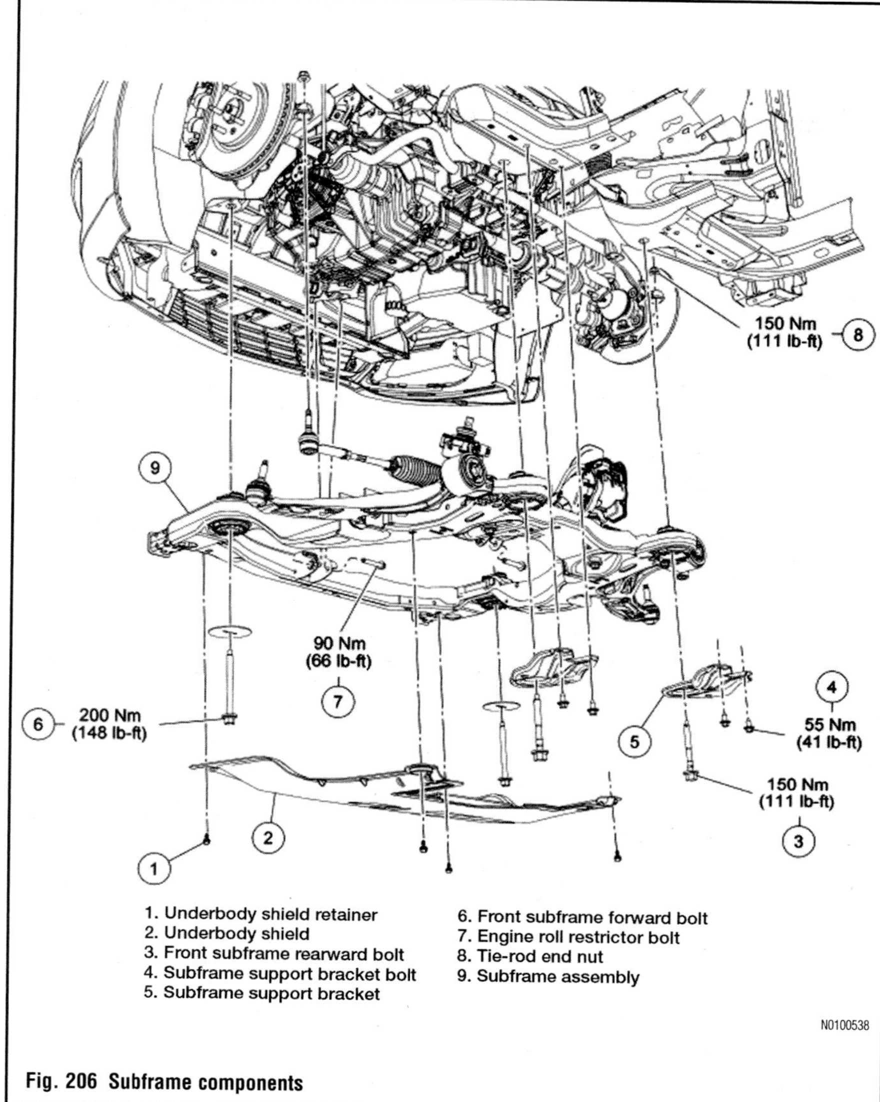

Fig. 206 Subframe components

5. Remove the power steering line clamp plate bolt.
   a. Rotate the clamp plate and disconnect the pressure and return lines from the steering gear.
   b. Discard the 2 O-ring seals.
6. Remove the steering column shaft-to-steering gear bolt and disconnect the shaft from the steering gear. Discard the bolt.
   a. Do not allow the steering column shaft to rotate while the lower shaft is disconnected or damage to the clockspring may result. If there is evidence that the shaft has rotated, the clockspring must be removed and recentered.
7. Remove and discard the stabilizer bar link upper nuts (for AWD vehicles, stabilizer bar bracket bolts). The hex-holding feature can be used to prevent turning of the stud while removing the nut.
   a. Position the stabilizer bar and links upward.
8. If equipped, remove the steering gear heat shield-to-subframe pushpin.
9. Remove and discard the 2 steering gear nuts and bolts.
10. Remove the steering gear from the left side of the vehicle.

To install:

11. To install, reverse the removal procedure, noting the following:
   a. Fill the power steering system.
   b. Whenever the power steering lines are disconnected, new O-ring seals must be installed. Make sure that the O-ring seals are installed in the correct order or a fluid leak may occur.
   c. To install the 2 new steering gear nuts and bolts, tighten in 2 stages:
      - Stage 1: Tighten to 30 ft. lbs. (40 Nm).
      - Stage 2: Tighten an additional 180 degrees.
   d. For AWD vehicles, tighten the stabilizer bar bracket bolts to 41 ft. lbs. (55 Nm).
   e. Tighten the stabilizer bar link upper nuts to 111 ft. lbs. (150 Nm).
   f. Tighten the steering column shaft-to-steering gear bolt to 18 ft. lbs. (25 Nm).
   g. Tighten the power steering line clamp plate bolt to 17 ft. lbs. (23 Nm).
   h. Tighten the pressure line bracket-to-steering gear bolt to 17 ft. lbs. (23 Nm).
   i. Tighten the 2 tie-rod end nuts to 111 ft. lbs. (150 Nm).
   j. Check and the front toe, and adjust if necessary.

POWER STEERING PUMP

REMOVAL & INSTALLATION

See Figures 208 through 211.

1. Before servicing the vehicle, refer to the Precautions Section.
2. With the vehicle in NEUTRAL, position it on a hoist.
3. Using a suitable suction device, siphon the power steering fluid from the power steering fluid reservoir.
4. Remove the 7 pin-type retainers and the right-hand splash shield.
5. Position the Stretchy Belt Remover (SST 303-1419) or equivalent tool on the power steering pump pulley belt as shown.
6. Turn the crankshaft clockwise and feed the belt remover evenly on the power steering pump pulley. Feed the belt remover onto the power steering pump pulley approximately 90 degrees.
7. Remove the power steering pump belt.
   a. Fold the belt remover under the inside of the power steering pump belt as shown.
   b. In one quick motion, firmly pull the belt remover out of the right-hand fender well, removing the coolant pump belt.
8. Release the clamp and disconnect the power steering fluid reservoir-to-pump supply hose from the power steering pump.
   a. Detach the supply hose retainer from the pressure line bracket.
9. Remove the pressure line bracket-to-engine bolt.
10. Remove the 3 power steering pump bolts.
11. Holding the power steering pump with a punch inserted into a mounting bolt cavity, disconnect the pressure line fitting-to-power steering pump.

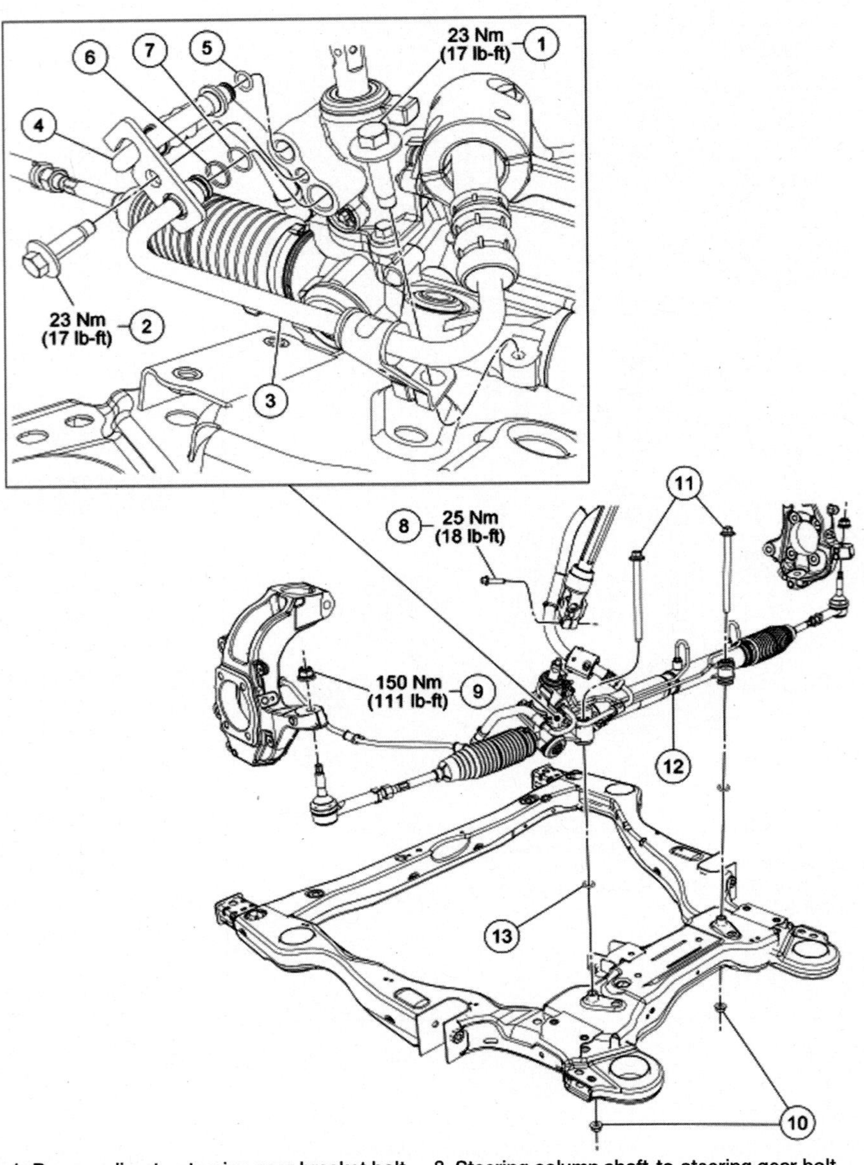

Fig. 207 Hydraulic power assist steering gear components

To install:

⁂ WARNING

A new Teflon® seal must be installed any time the pressure line is disconnected from the power steering pump or a fluid leak may occur.

12. Using the Teflon® Seal Installer Set, install a new Teflon® seal on the power steering pressure line fitting.
13. Holding the power steering pump with a punch inserted into a mounting cavity, connect the pressure line fitting-to-power steering pump. Tighten to 55 ft. lbs. (75 Nm).
14. Position the power steering pump and install the 3 bolts. Tighten to 18 ft. lbs. (25 Nm).
15. Position the bracket and install the pressure line bracket-to-engine bolt. Tighten to 80 inch lbs. (9 Nm).
16. Release the clamp and connect the

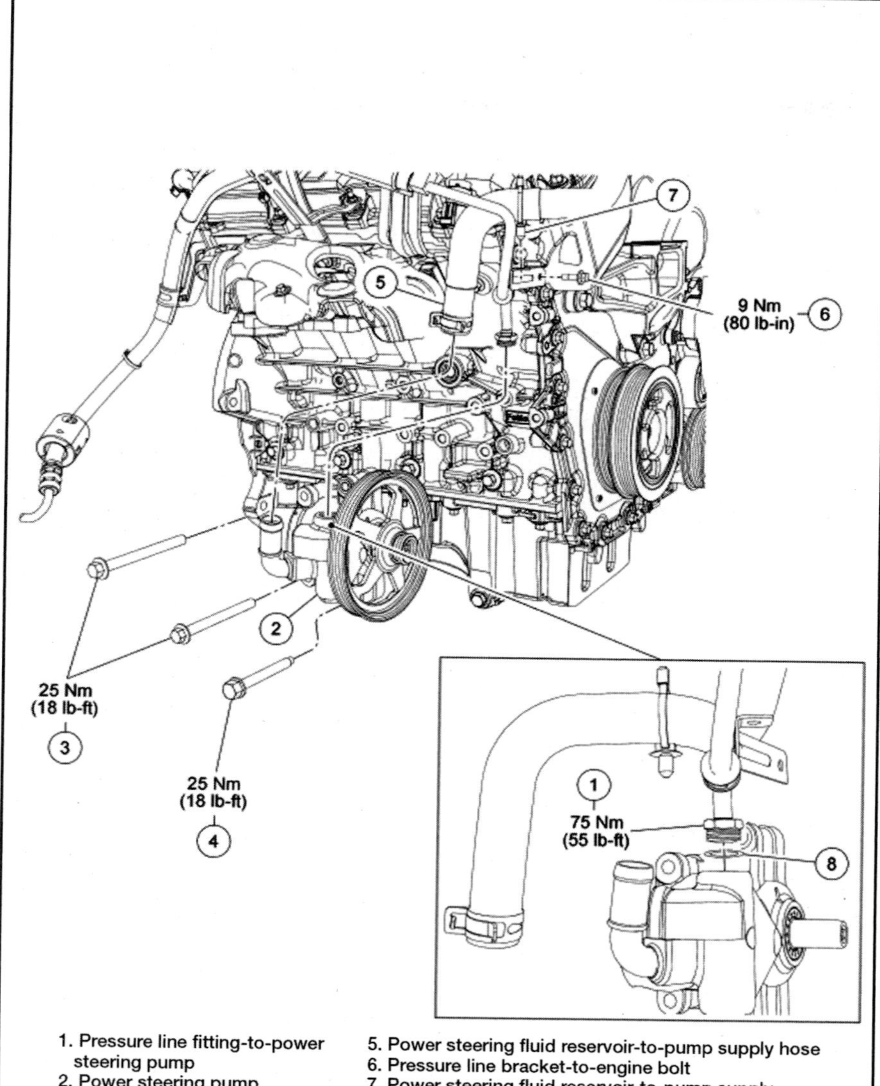

Fig. 208 Power steering pump components

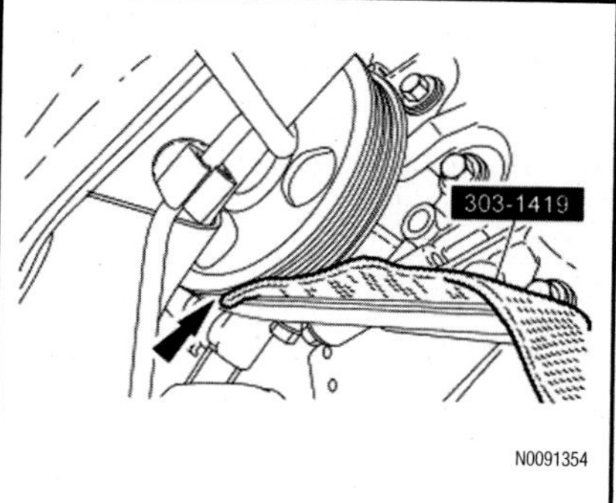

Fig. 209 Position the belt remover on the power steering pump pulley belt

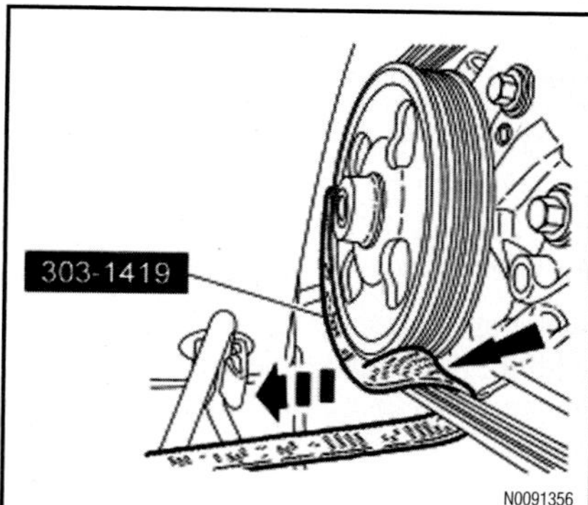

Fig. 210 Fold the belt remover under the power steering pump belt, and pull out to remove the coolant pump belt

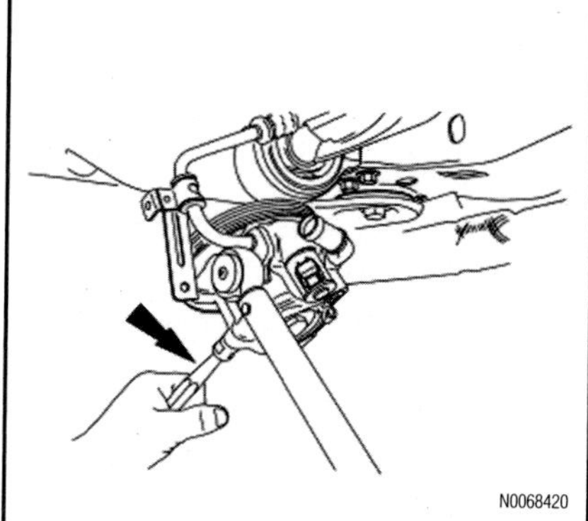

Fig. 211 Holding the power steering pump with a punch inserted into a mounting bolt cavity, disconnect the pressure line fitting-to-power steering pump

power steering fluid cooler-to-pump supply hose.

a. Attach the supply hose retainer to the pressure line bracket.

17. Install the Stretchy Belt Installer Tool (SST 303-1252/2) or equivalent tool between the power steering pump belt and pulley and turn the crankshaft bolt clockwise. Use the belt installer tool to install the power steering pump belt onto the power steering pump pulley.

18. Install the right-hand inner fender splash shield.

19. Fill the power steering system.

POWER STEERING SYSTEM FLUSHING

⁂ WARNING

Do not mix fluid types. Any mixture or any unapproved fluid may lead to seal deterioration and leaks. A leak may ultimately cause loss of fluid, which may result in a loss of power steering assist.

1. Remove the power steering fluid reservoir cap.

2. Using a suitable suction device, remove the power steering fluid from the reservoir.

3. Release the clamp and disconnect the return hose from the reservoir.

a. Remove the clamp from the hose and allow the remaining fluid to drain out of the reservoir.

4. Plug the power steering fluid reservoir inlet port.

5. Attach an extension hose to the return hose.

➡Do not reuse the power steering fluid that has been flushed from the power steering system.

6. Place the open end of the extension hose into a suitable container.
7. If equipped with Hydro-Boost®, apply the brake pedal 4 times.
8. Fill the reservoir as needed with the specified fluid. Do not overfill the reservoir.

⁂ WARNING

Do not allow the power steering pump to run completely dry of power steering fluid. Damage to the power steering pump may occur.

9. Start the engine while simultaneously turning the steering wheel to lock and then immediately turn the ignition switch to the OFF position.

➡Avoid turning the steering wheel without the engine running as this may cause air to be pulled into the steering gear.

10. Fill the reservoir as needed with the specified fluid. Do not overfill the reservoir.
11. Repeat Steps 8 and 9, turning the steering wheel in the opposite direction each time, until the fluid exiting the power steering fluid return hose is clean and clear of foreign material.
12. Remove the extension hose from the return hose.
13. Remove the plug from the fluid reservoir inlet port.
14. Install the clamp and connect the power steering return hose to the reservoir.

➡It is necessary to correctly fill the power steering system to remove any trapped air and completely fill the power steering system components.

15. If, after correctly filling the power steering system, there is power steering noise accompanied by evidence of aerated fluid and there are no fluid leaks, it may be necessary to purge the power steering system.
16. Fill the power steering system.

POWER STEERING SYSTEM PURGING

See Figure 212.

⁂ WARNING

If the air is not purged from the power steering system correctly, premature power steering pump failure may result.

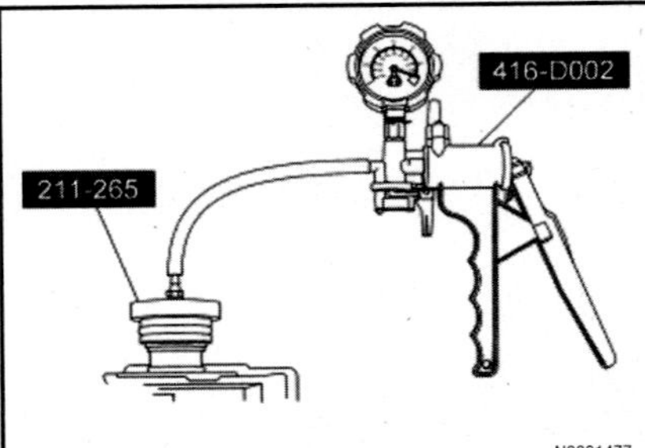

Fig. 212 Tightly insert the Power Steering Evacuation Cap into the reservoir and connect the Vacuum Pump Kit

➡A whine heard from the power steering pump can be caused by air in the system. The power steering purge procedure must be carried out prior to any component repair for which power steering noise complaints are accompanied by evidence of aerated fluid.

1. Remove the power steering reservoir cap. Check the fluid.
2. Raise the front wheels off the floor.
3. Tightly insert the Power Steering Evacuation Cap into the reservoir and connect the Vacuum Pump Kit.
4. Start the engine.
5. Using the Vacuum Pump Kit, apply vacuum and maintain the maximum vacuum of 68–85 kPa (20–25 in Hg).
   a. If the Vacuum Pump Kit does not maintain vacuum, check the power steering system for leaks before proceeding.
6. If equipped with Hydro-Boost®, apply the brake pedal 4 times.
7. Cycle the steering wheel fully from stop-to-stop 10 times.

⁂ WARNING

Do not hold the steering wheel against the stops for an extended amount of time. Damage to the power steering pump may occur.

8. Stop the engine.
9. Release the vacuum and remove the Vacuum Pump Kit and the Power Steering Evacuation Cap.
10. Fill the reservoir as needed with the specified fluid. Do not overfill the reservoir.
11. Start the engine.
12. Install the Power Steering Evacuation Cap and the Vacuum Pump Kit. Apply and maintain the maximum vacuum of 68–85 kPa (20–25 in Hg).
13. Cycle the steering wheel fully from stop-to-stop 10 times.
14. Stop the engine, release the vacuum and remove the Vacuum Pump Kit and the Power Steering Evacuation Cap.
15. Fill the reservoir as needed with the specified fluid and install the reservoir cap. Do not overfill the reservoir.
16. Visually inspect the power steering system for leaks.

FLUID FILL PROCEDURE

See Figure 213.

⁂ WARNING

If the air is not purged from the power steering system correctly, premature power steering pump failure may result.

1. Remove the power steering fluid reservoir cap.
2. Install the Power Steering Evacuation Cap, Power Steering Fill Adapter Manifold and Vacuum Pump Kit as shown in the illustration.

➡The Power Steering Fill Adapter Manifold control valves are in the OPEN position when the points of the handles face the center of the Power Steering Fill Adapter Manifold.

3. Close the Power Steering Fill Adapter Manifold control valve (fluid side).
4. Open the Power Steering Fill Adapter Manifold control valve (vacuum side).
5. Using the Vacuum Pump Kit, apply 68–85 kPa (20–25 in Hg) of vacuum to the power steering system.
6. Observe the Vacuum Pump Kit gauge for 30 seconds.
7. If the Vacuum Pump Kit gauge reading drops more than 3 kPa (0.88 in Hg), correct any leaks in the power steering system or the Power Steering Evacuation Cap, Power Steering Fill Adapter Manifold and Vacuum Pump Kit before proceeding.
8. Slowly open the Power Steering Fill Adapter Manifold control valve (fluid side) until power steering fluid completely fills the hose and then close the control valve. The Vacuum Pump Kit gauge reading will drop slightly during this step.
9. Using the Vacuum Pump Kit, apply 68–85 kPa (20–25 in Hg) of vacuum to the power steering system.
10. Close the Power Steering Fill Adapter Manifold control valve (vacuum side).
11. Slowly open the Power Steering Fill Adapter Manifold control valve (fluid side).
12. Once power steering fluid enters the fluid reservoir and reaches the minimum fluid level indicator line on the reservoir, close the Power Steering Fill Adapter Manifold control valve (fluid side).

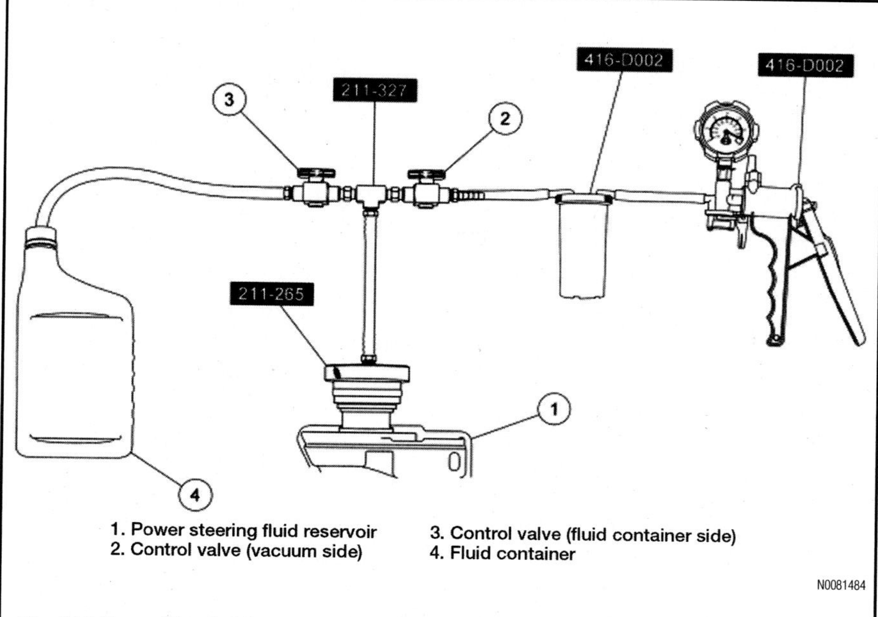

Fig. 213 Power Steering Evacuation Cap, Power Steering Fill Adapter Manifold and Vacuum Pump Kit

13. Remove the Power Steering Evacuation Cap, Power Steering Fill Adapter Manifold and Vacuum Pump Kit.
14. Install the reservoir cap.

WARNING

Do not hold the steering wheel against the stops for an extended amount of time. Damage to the power steering pump may occur.

➡There will be a slight drop in the power steering fluid level in the reservoir when the engine is started.

15. Start the engine and turn the steering wheel from stop-to-stop.
16. Turn the ignition switch to the OFF position.

➡Do not overfill the reservoir.

17. Remove the reservoir cap and fill the reservoir with the specified fluid.
18. Install the reservoir cap.

SUSPENSION

FRONT SUSPENSION

CONTROL LINKS

REMOVAL & INSTALLATION

See Figure 214.

1. With the vehicle in NEUTRAL, position it on a hoist.

WARNING

Do not use power tools to remove the stabilizer bar link nuts. Damage to the stabilizer bar link ball joints or boots may occur.

➡To remove the stabilizer bar link nuts, first loosen the nuts, then use the hex-holding feature to prevent the stabilizer bar link ball joints from turning while removing the stabilizer bar link nuts.

2. Remove and discard the stabilizer bar link lower nut.
3. Remove and discard the stabilizer bar link upper nut.
4. Remove the stabilizer bar link.

To install:

5. To install, reverse the removal procedure, noting the following:

➡To install the nuts, use the hex-holding feature to prevent the stabilizer link ball joints from turning while installing the nuts until snug. Finally, tighten the nuts using a socket and a torque wrench.

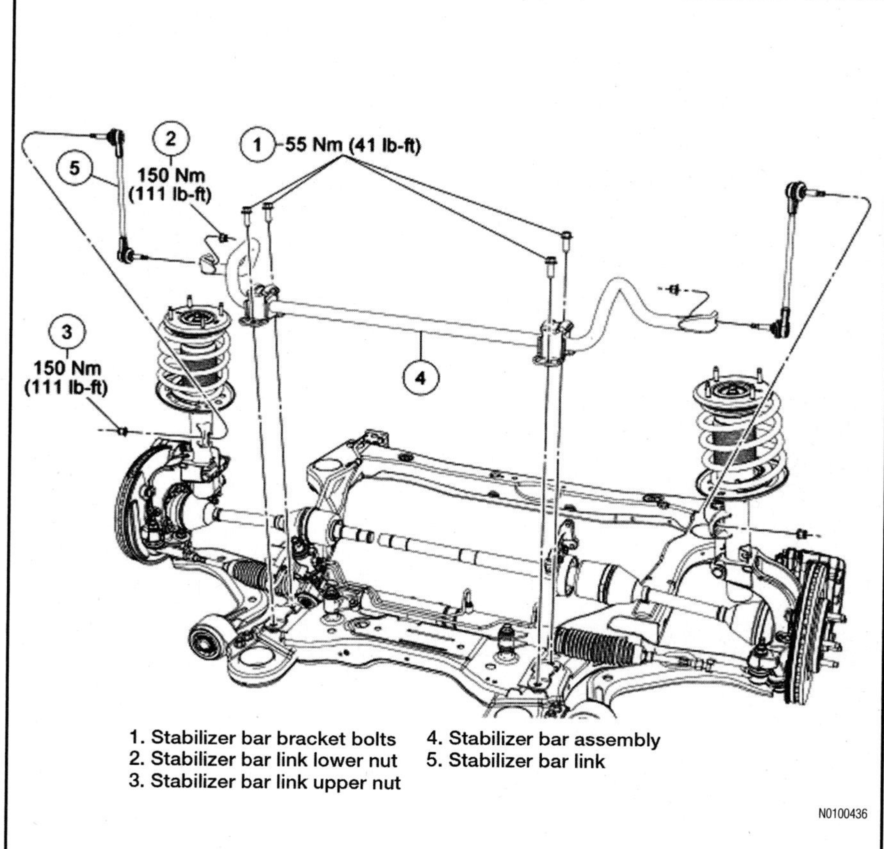

Fig. 214 Front stabilizer bar components

a. Tighten a new stabilizer bar link upper nut to 111 ft. lbs. (150 Nm).

b. Tighten a new stabilizer bar link lower nut to 111 ft. lbs. (150 Nm).

LOWER CONTROL ARM

REMOVAL & INSTALLATION

See Figure 215.

1. Remove the wheel and tire.
2. Using a crowfoot wrench, remove and discard the lower ball joint nut. Use the hex-holding feature to prevent the stud from turning while removing the nut.
3. Push the lower arm downward until the ball joint is clear of the wheel knuckle.

⁂ WARNING

Use care when releasing the lower arm and knuckle into the resting position or damage to the ball joint seal may occur.

4. Remove and discard the lower arm forward bolt.
5. Remove and discard the lower arm rearward nuts and bolts.
6. If necessary, remove the lower arm rearward bushing.

To install:

7. To install, reverse the removal procedure, noting the following:

a. Install the new lower arm rearward bolts from the bottom of the lower arm bushing with the nuts on top.

b. Tighten new lower arm rearward nuts to 73 ft. lbs. (99 Nm).

⁂ WARNING

The lower arm forward bolt must be tightened with the weight of the vehicle on the wheels and tires or damage to the bushings may occur.

c. Tighten a new lower arm forward bolt to 136 ft. lbs. (185 Nm).

d. Tighten the lower ball joint nut to 148 ft. lbs. (200 Nm).

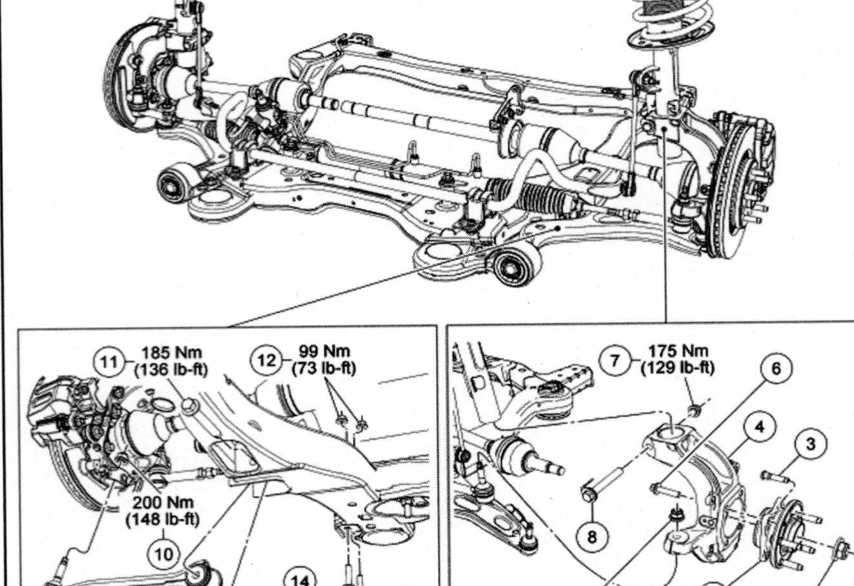

1. Wheel hub nut
2. Wheel bearing and wheel hub
3. Wheel stud
4. Wheel knuckle
5. Tie-rod end nut
6. Wheel bearing and wheel hub bolt
7. Strut-to-wheel knuckle nut
8. Strut-to-wheel knuckle flag bolt
9. Lower control arm
10. Lower ball joint nut
11. Lower arm forward bolt
12. Lower arm rearward nuts
13. Lower arm rearward bolt
14. Lower arm rearward bushing

N0103396

Fig. 215 Front suspension components

CONTROL ARM BUSHING REPLACEMENT

See Figure 216.

1. Remove the lower arm.
2. Matchmark the bushing-to-lower arm position for reference during the installation procedure.

➡The Drive Pinion Bearing Cone Remover is used to secure the lower arm bushing while separating/installing the bushing from the lower arm.

3. Using the Drive Pinion Bearing Cone Remover (SST 205-D002) or equivalent tool, a suitable press and adapters, remove the lower arm bushing.

To install:

4. Install the Drive Pinion Bearing Cone Remover (SST 205-D002) or equivalent tool onto the lower arm.
5. Transfer the matchmark to the new lower arm bushing.
6. Align the matchmarks, and using the Drive Pinion Bearing Cone Remover, a suitable press and adapters, install a new lower arm bushing.
7. Install the lower arm.

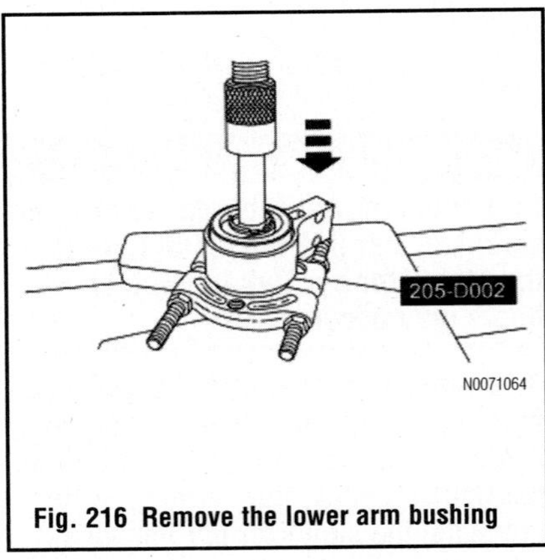

Fig. 216 Remove the lower arm bushing

STABILIZER BAR

REMOVAL & INSTALLATION

See Figures 215 and 217.

1. Make sure the steering wheel is in the unlocked position.

➡The stabilizer bushing and bracket are part of the stabilizer bar assembly. The stabilizer bar will not turn easily in the bushing.

2. With the vehicle in NEUTRAL, position it on a hoist.

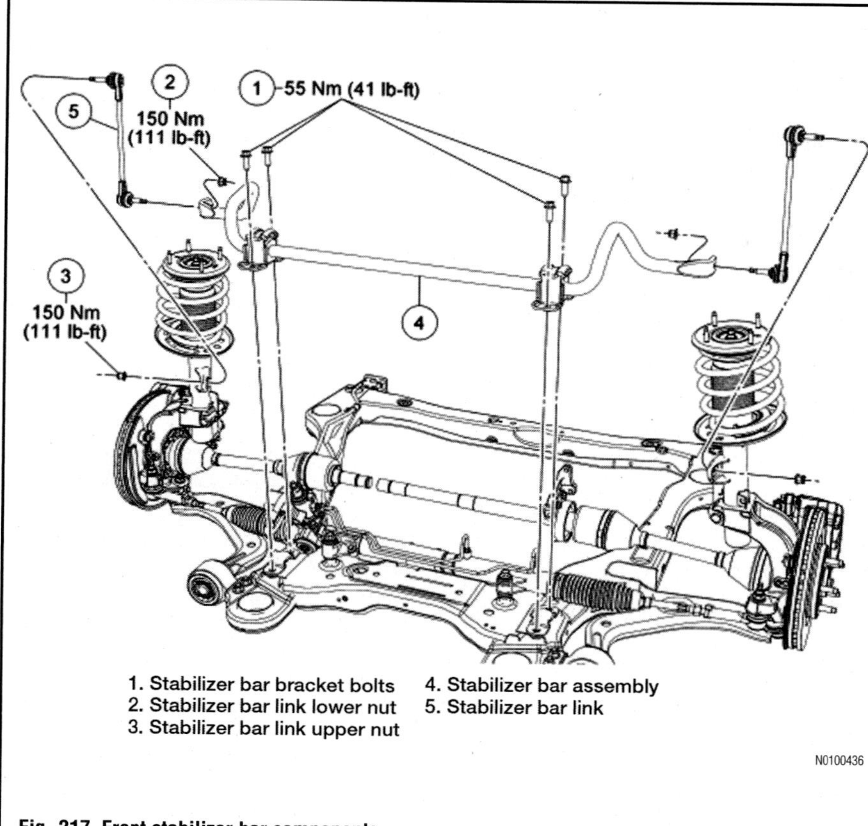

Fig. 217 Front stabilizer bar components

3. Disconnect the Heated Oxygen Sensor (HO2S) electrical connector and unclip the connector from the subframe.
4. For AWD vehicles, remove the exhaust Y-pipe.

⁂ WARNING

Do not use power tools to remove the stabilizer bar link nut. Damage to the stabilizer link ball joint or boot may occur.

5. Remove and discard the stabilizer bar link lower nuts. To remove the stabilizer bar link nut, first loosen the nut, then use the hex-holding feature to prevent the ball joint from turning while removing the stabilizer bar link nut.
6. Remove and discard both tie-rod end nuts and separate the tie-rod ends from the knuckles. No special tools are necessary to separate the tie rod from the front knuckle; use a mallet to loosen the joint.
7. Remove and discard the 4 lower arm rearward nuts and bolts.
8. Remove and discard the 2 lower arm forward bolts. Position both lower arms aside.
9. Using a suitable screw-type jackstand, support the rear of the subframe.
10. Remove the 2 steering gear nuts and bolts.
11. Remove and discard the 4 subframe bracket bolts.
12. Remove and discard the subframe forward bolts.
13. Remove and discard the subframe rearward bolts.
14. Lower the rear of the subframe approximately 2 in. (51 mm).
15. Remove and discard the left-hand and right-hand stabilizer bar bracket bolts.
16. Remove the stabilizer bar by guiding it between the subframe and the steering gear toward the right-hand side of the vehicle.

To install:

17. To install, reverse the removal procedure, noting the following:
    a. Install new left-hand and right-hand stabilizer bar bracket bolts and tighten to 41 ft. lbs. (55 Nm).
    b. Install new subframe rearward bolts and tighten:
       - Vehicles with Electronic Power Assist Steering (EPAS): 111 ft. lbs. (150 Nm)
       - Vehicles with Hydraulic Power Assist Steering (HPAS): 130 ft. lbs. (175 Nm)
    c. Install new subframe forward bolts and tighten to 148 ft. lbs. (200 Nm).
    d. Install 4 new subframe bracket bolts and tighten to 41 ft. lbs. (55 Nm).
    e. Install new steering gear nuts and bolts and tighten:
       - Vehicles with EPAS: 122 ft. lbs. (165 Nm)
       - Vehicles with HPAS: 86 ft. lbs. (117 Nm)
    f. Install 2 new lower arm forward bolts and tighten to 136 ft. lbs. (185 Nm).

➡Install the new lower arm rearward bolts from the bottom of the lower arm bushing with the nuts on top.

    g. Install 4 new lower arm rearward nuts and bolts and tighten to 73 ft. lbs. (99 Nm).
    h. Install new tie-rod end nuts and tighten to 111 ft. lbs. (150 Nm).
    i. Install new stabilizer bar link lower nuts and tighten to 111 ft. lbs. (150 Nm).

STEERING KNUCKLE

REMOVAL & INSTALLATION

See Figures 218 and 219.

1. Remove the wheel and tire.
2. Remove the wheel hub nut. Do not discard the wheel hub nut at this time.
3. Remove the brake disc.
4. Remove and discard the tie-rod end nut, then separate the tie rod from the wheel knuckle. No special tools are necessary to separate the tie rod from the front knuckle; use a mallet to loosen the joint.
5. Remove the bolt and the wheel speed sensor from the wheel knuckle. Position the wheel speed sensor aside.
6. Using a crowfoot wrench, remove and discard the lower ball joint nut. Use the hex-holding feature to prevent the stud from turning while removing the nut.
7. Push the lower arm downward until the ball joint is clear of the wheel knuckle.
8. Using the Front Wheel Hub Remover (SST 205-D070) or equivalent tool, press the halfshaft from the wheel bearing and hub. Support the halfshaft in a level position.
    a. Do not allow the halfshaft to move outboard. Overextension of the tripod Constant Velocity (CV) joint may result in separation of internal parts, causing failure of the halfshaft.
9. Remove and discard the strut-to-wheel knuckle nut and flagbolt.
10. Remove the steering knuckle. If necessary, remove the wheel hub and bearing.

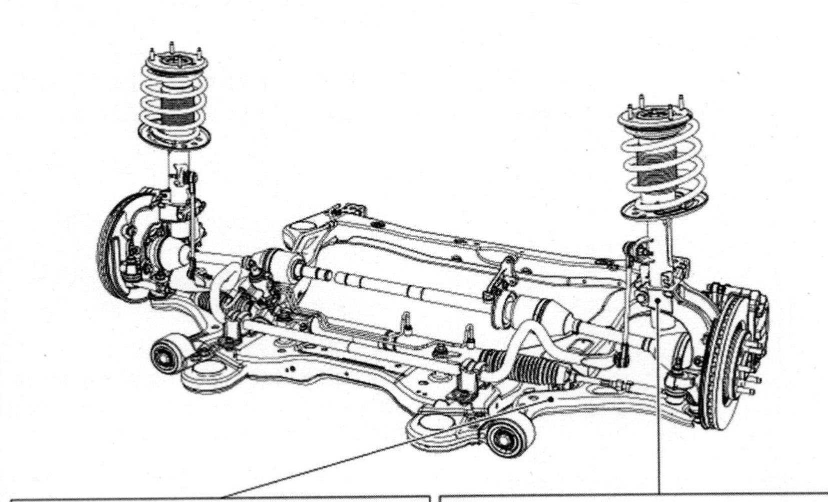

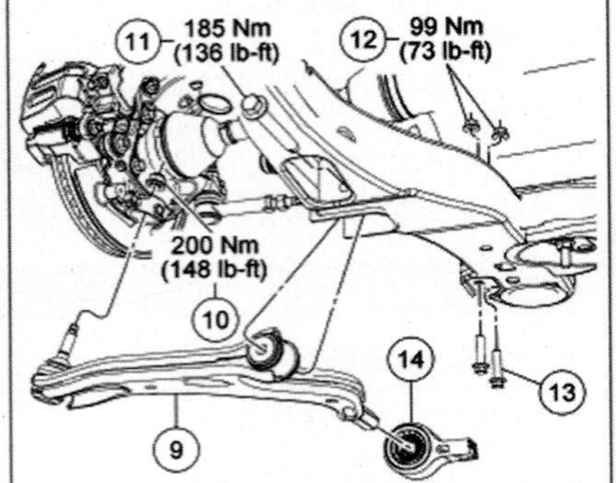

Fig. 218 Front suspension components

To install:

11. Position the wheel knuckle and install a new strut-to-wheel knuckle nut and flagbolt. Tighten to 129 ft. lbs. (175 Nm).

12. While supporting the halfshaft in a level position, install the halfshaft into the wheel bearing and hub.

13. Push the lower arm downward and install the ball joint stud into the wheel knuckle. Use care not to damage the ball joint seal while installing the ball joint stud into the wheel knuckle.

14. Using a crowfoot wrench, install the new lower ball joint nut. Use the hex-holding feature to prevent the stud from turning while installing the nut. Tighten to 148 ft. lbs. (200 Nm).

15. Position the wheel speed sensor and install the bolt. Tighten to 11 ft. lbs. (15 Nm).

16. Position the tie-rod end stud into the wheel knuckle and install a new tie-rod end nut. Tighten to 111 ft. lbs. (150 Nm).

17. Install the brake disc.

⁂ WARNING

Do not tighten the front wheel hub nut with the vehicle on the ground. The nut must be tightened to specification before the vehicle is lowered onto the wheels. Wheel bearing damage will occur if the wheel bearing is loaded with the weight of the vehicle applied.

18. Using the previously removed hub nut, seat the halfshaft.
    a. Apply the brake to keep the halfshaft from rotating.
    b. Tighten to 258 ft. lbs. (350 Nm).
    c. Remove and discard the hub nut.

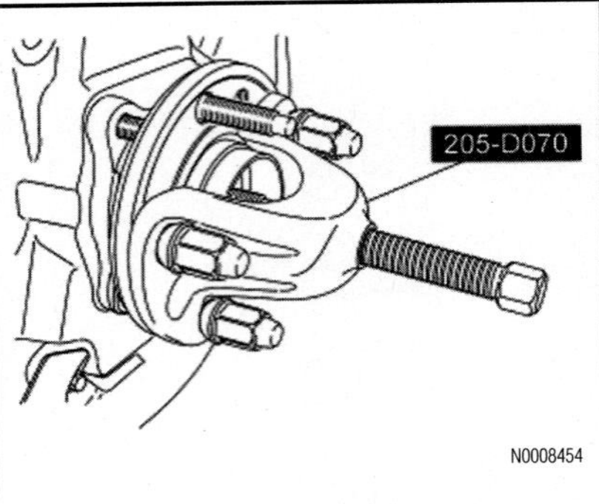

Fig. 219 Remove the halfshaft from the wheel bearing and hub

⁂ WARNING

The wheel hub nut contains a one-time locking chemical that is activated by the heat created when it is tightened. Install and tighten the new wheel hub nut to specification within 5 minutes of starting it on the threads. Always install a new wheel hub nut after loosening or when not tightened within the specified time or damage to the components can occur.

19. Install a new hub nut. Apply the brake to keep the halfshaft from rotating. Tighten to 258 ft. lbs. (350 Nm).

20. Install the wheel and tire.

STRUT & SPRING ASSEMBLY

REMOVAL & INSTALLATION

See Figures 218 through 220.

1. Make sure the steering wheel is in the unlocked position.

2. Loosen the upper strut mount nuts.

3. Remove the wheel and tire.

4. Remove the wheel hub nut. Do not discard the wheel hub nut at this time.

5. Remove the brake disc.

6. Remove and discard the tie-rod end nut and separate the tie rod from the wheel knuckle. No special tools are necessary to separate the tie rod from the front knuckle; use a mallet to loosen the joint.

7. Remove and discard the stabilizer bar link upper nut.

8. Detach the wheel speed sensor harness from the strut.

9. Remove the bolt and the wheel speed sensor from the wheel knuckle. Position the wheel speed sensor aside.

10. Using a crowfoot wrench, remove and discard the lower ball joint nut. Use the

hex-holding feature to prevent the stud from turning while removing the nut.

11. Push the lower arm downward until the ball joint is clear of the wheel knuckle.

a. Use care when releasing the lower arm and knuckle into the resting position or damage to the ball joint seal may occur.

12. Using the Front Wheel Hub Remover (SST 205-D070) or equivalent tool, press the halfshaft from the wheel bearing and hub. Support the halfshaft in a level position.

a. Do not allow the halfshaft to move outboard. Overextension of the tripod Constant Velocity (CV) joint may result in separation of internal parts, causing failure of the halfshaft.

13. Remove and discard the 4 upper strut mount nuts.

14. Remove the wheel knuckle and the strut and spring as an assembly.

15. Remove and discard the strut-to-wheel knuckle nut and flagbolt.

16. Separate the strut and spring assembly from the wheel knuckle.

To install:

17. Position the wheel knuckle onto the strut and spring and install a new strut-to-wheel knuckle nut and flagbolt. Tighten the nut to 129 ft. lbs. (175 Nm).

18. Install the wheel knuckle and the strut and spring as an assembly.

19. Loosely install the 4 new upper strut mount nuts.

20. While supporting the halfshaft in a level position, install the halfshaft into the wheel bearing and hub.

21. Push the lower arm downward and install the ball joint stud into the wheel knuckle. Use care not to damage the ball joint seal while installing the ball joint stud into the wheel knuckle.

22. Using a crowfoot wrench, install the new lower ball joint nut. Use the hex-holding feature to prevent the stud from turning while installing the nut. Tighten to 148 ft. lbs. (200 Nm).

23. Position the wheel speed sensor and install the bolt. Tighten to 11 ft. lbs. (15 Nm).

24. Attach the wheel speed sensor harness to the strut.

25. Install the new stabilizer bar link upper nut. Tighten to 111 ft. lbs. (150 Nm).

26. Position the tie-rod end stud into the wheel knuckle and install a new tie-rod end nut. Tighten to 111 ft. lbs. (150 Nm).

27. Install the brake disc.

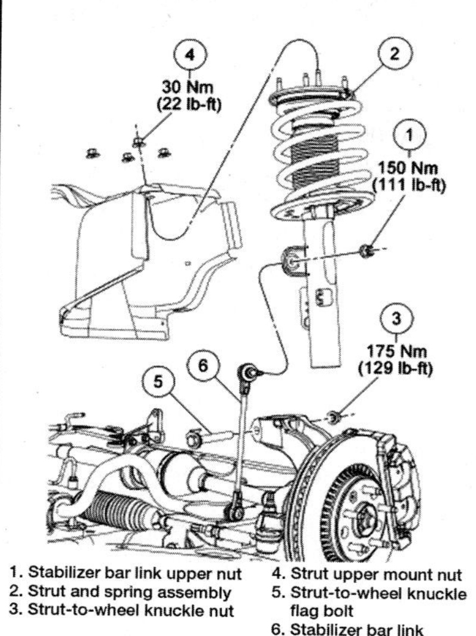

Fig. 220 Front strut and spring assembly components

WARNING

Do not tighten the front wheel hub nut with the vehicle on the ground. The nut must be tightened to specification before the vehicle is lowered onto the wheels. Wheel bearing damage will occur if the wheel bearing is loaded with the weight of the vehicle applied.

28. Using the previously removed hub nut, seat the halfshaft.

a. Apply the brake to keep the halfshaft from rotating.

b. Tighten to 258 ft. lbs. (350 Nm).

c. Remove and discard the hub nut.

29. Install a new hub nut.

WARNING

The wheel hub nut contains a one-time locking chemical that is activated by the heat created when it is tightened. Install and tighten the new wheel hub nut to specification within 5 minutes of starting it on the threads. Always install a new wheel hub nut after loosening or when not tightened within the specified time or damage to the components can occur.

a. Apply the brake to keep the halfshaft from rotating.

b. Tighten to 258 ft. lbs. (350 Nm).

30. Install the wheel and tire.

31. Tighten the 4 upper strut mount nuts to 22 ft. lbs. (30 Nm).

WHEEL BEARINGS

REMOVAL & INSTALLATION

See Figure 221.

1. Remove the steering knuckle.

2. Remove and discard the 4 wheel bearing and wheel hub bolts, then separate the wheel bearing and wheel hub from the wheel knuckle.

To install:

3. To install, reverse the removal procedure, noting the following:

a. Using a clean shop towel, clean the wheel hub-to-knuckle mating surfaces.

b. Make sure the wheel hub-to-wheel knuckle mating surfaces are clean and free of any adhesive. Failure to clean the adhesive from both surfaces may cause bearing damage.

c. Clean and inspect the knuckle bearing bore. If the wheel knuckle is cracked, install a new wheel knuckle.

WARNING

The wheel knuckle bore must be clean enough to allow the wheel bearing and wheel hub to seat completely by hand. Do not press or draw the wheel hub and bearing into place or damage to the bearing may occur.

4. Install the wheel bearing and wheel hub to the wheel knuckle and tighten the new bolts to 98 ft. lbs. (133 Nm) in the sequence shown.

5. Lubricate the hub-to-brake disc surface with anti-seize lubricant before installing the brake disc.

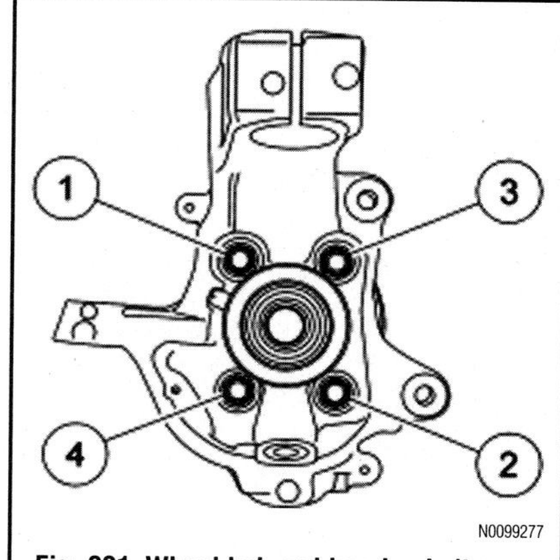

Fig. 221 Wheel hub and bearing bolt tightening sequence

COIL SPRING

REMOVAL & INSTALLATION

See Figures 222 and 223.

1. Measure the distance from the center of the wheel hub to the lip of the fender with the vehicle in a level, static ground position (curb height).
2. Remove the wheel and tire.
3. Remove and discard the 2 stabilizer bar link upper nuts. Position the stabilizer bar away from the lower arm. Use the hex-holding feature to prevent the stabilizer bar link studs from turning while removing the nuts.
4. Using a suitable jackstand, support the lower arm.
5. Loosen the lower arm-to-subframe bolt.
6. Remove and discard the lower arm-to wheel knuckle bolt.
7. Lower the jackstand and remove the spring.
8. Inspect the upper and lower spring seats for damage and, if necessary, install new spring seats.
   a. Make sure the lower spring seat is properly positioned in the lower arm.

To install:

9. Before tightening the lower arm bolts, use a jackstand to raise the rear suspension until the distance between the center of the hub and the lip of the fender is equal to the measurement taken in the Removal procedure (curb height).
10. Install the spring and position the jackstand under the lower arm.
11. Raise the jackstand and loosely install a new lower arm-to-wheel knuckle bolt.
12. Position the stabilizer bar and links and install 2 new stabilizer bar link upper nuts. Tighten to 41 ft. lbs. (55 Nm).

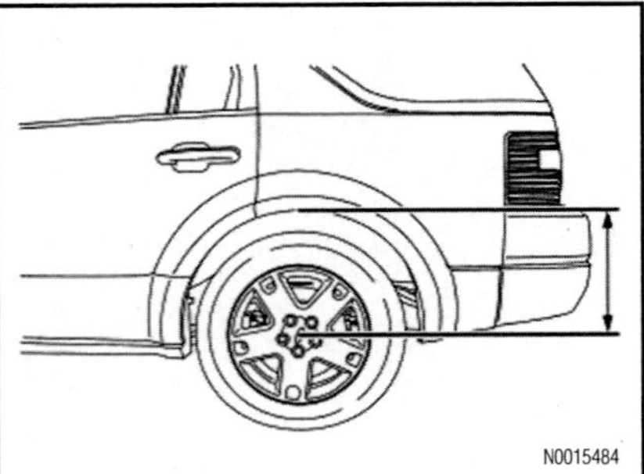

Fig. 222 Measure the distance from the center of the wheel hub to the lip of the fender

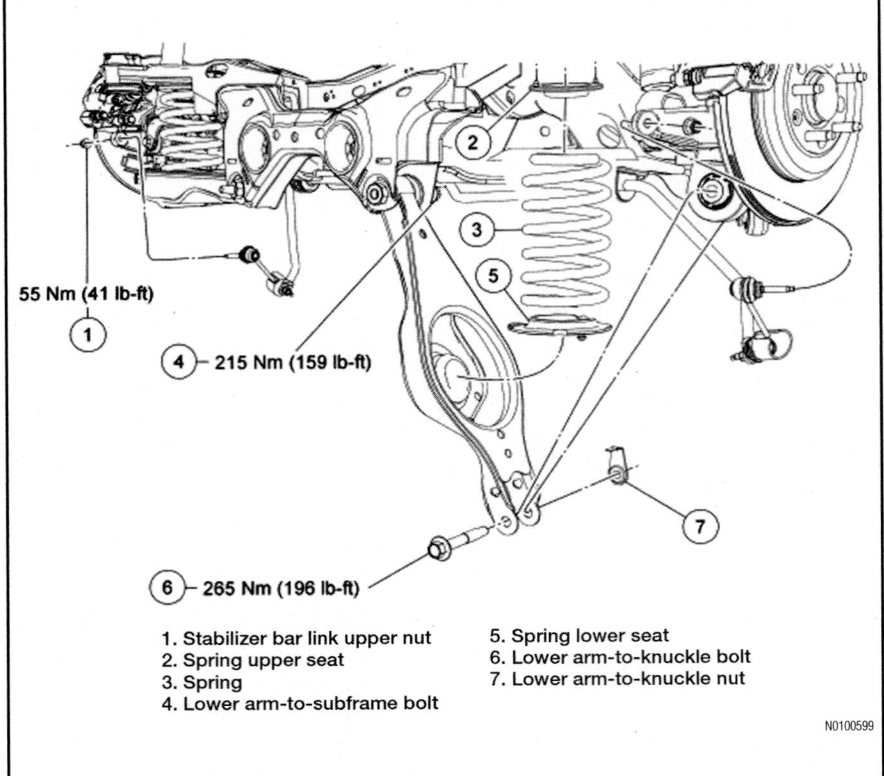

Fig. 223 Rear spring components

13. Using the jackstand, raise the rear suspension until the distance between the center of the hub and the lip of the fender is equal to the measurement taken in the removal procedure (curb height).
14. Tighten the lower arm-to-wheel knuckle bolt to 196 ft. lbs. (265 Nm).
15. Tighten the lower arm-to-subframe bolt to 159 ft. lbs. (215 Nm).
16. Install the wheel and tire.

CONTROL LINKS

REMOVAL & INSTALLATION

See Figure 224.

1. Remove and discard the stabilizer bar link lower nut.
2. Remove the stabilizer bar link upper nut and stabilizer bar link. Discard the nut.

To install:

3. To install, reverse the removal procedure, noting the following:
   a. Install a new stabilizer bar link upper nut and tighten to 41 ft. lbs. (55 Nm).
   b. Install a new stabilizer bar link

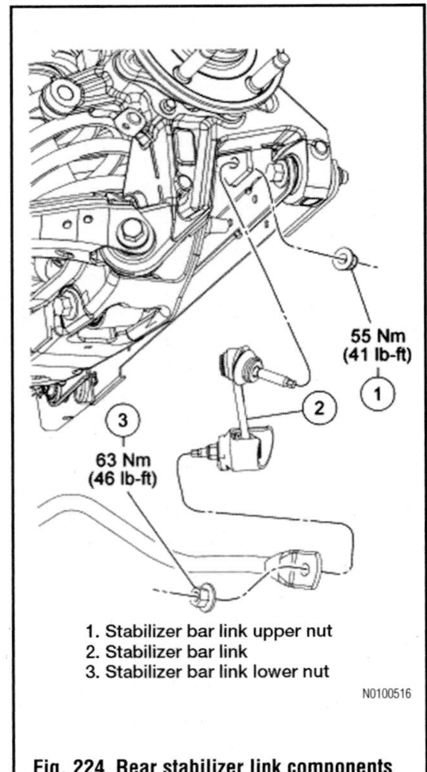

Fig. 224 Rear stabilizer link components

lower nut and tighten to 46 ft. lbs. (63 Nm).

LOWER CONTROL ARM

REMOVAL & INSTALLATION

See Figures 222 and 225.

1. Measure the distance from the center of the wheel hub to the lip of the fender with the vehicle in a level, static ground position (curb height).
2. Remove the wheel and tire.
3. Remove both stabilizer bar link upper nuts and disconnect the links from the wheel knuckle. Use the hex-holding feature to prevent the stabilizer bar link stud from turning while removing the nut. Discard the nuts.
4. Position a screw-type jackstand under the lower arm.
5. Remove and discard the lower arm-to-knuckle bolt and nut.
6. Loosen the lower arm inner bolt. Do not remove the lower arm inner bolt at this time.
7. Lower the jackstand and remove the spring.
8. Remove the lower arm inner bolt and lower arm.
9. Discard the bolt.

To install:

10. Before tightening the lower arm bolts, use a jackstand to raise the rear suspension until the distance between the center of the hub and the lip of the fender is equal to the measurement taken in the Removal procedure (curb height).
11. Position the lower arm and loosely install the new lower arm inner bolt.
12. Install the spring and position the screw-type jackstand under the lower arm.
    a. Make sure the lower spring seat is properly positioned in the lower arm.
13. Raise the jackstand and loosely install the new lower arm-to-knuckle bolt and nut. Do not tighten the lower arm nut at this time.
14. Using the jackstand, raise the rear suspension until the distance between the center of the hub and the lip of the fender is equal to the measurement taken in the removal procedure (curb height).
15. Tighten the lower arm-to-subframe bolt to 159 ft. lbs. (215 Nm).
16. Tighten the lower arm-to-knuckle bolt to 196 ft. lbs. (265 Nm).
17. Position the stabilizer bar links and install 2 new stabilizer bar link upper nuts. Tighten to 41 ft. lbs. (55 Nm).

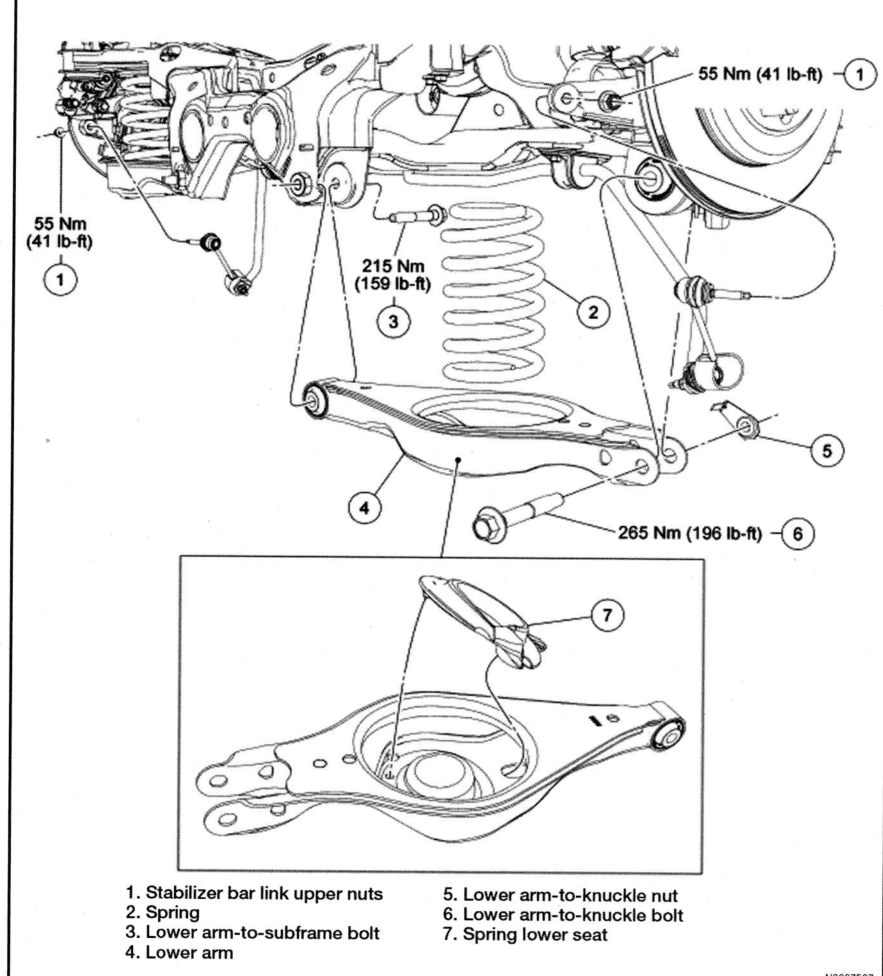

Fig. 225 Rear lower arm components

SHOCK ABSORBER

REMOVAL & INSTALLATION

See Figure 226.

1. Remove the rear quarter trim panel trim insert.
2. Remove and discard the shock absorber upper insulator and nut.
3. Remove the wheel and tire.
4. Remove and discard the stabilizer bar link upper nut and disconnect the link from the wheel knuckle. Use the hex-holding feature to prevent the stabilizer bar link stud from turning while removing or installing the nut.
5. Remove and discard the shock absorber lower bolt and remove the shock absorber.

To install:

6. To install, reverse the removal procedure, noting the following:
    a. Install a new shock absorber lower bolt and tighten to 129 ft. lbs. (175 Nm).
    b. Install a new stabilizer bar link upper nut and tighten to 41 ft. lbs. (55 Nm).
    c. Install a new shock absorber upper insulator and tighten the nut to 41 ft. lbs. (55 Nm).

STABILIZER BAR

REMOVAL & INSTALLATION

See Figure 227.

1. With the vehicle in NEUTRAL, position it on a hoist.
2. Support the exhaust system with a suitable jackstand. Using soapy water, disconnect the 2 muffler and tail pipe isolators and lower the exhaust approximately 2 in. (50.8 mm).
3. Remove and discard the 2 stabilizer bar link lower nuts.

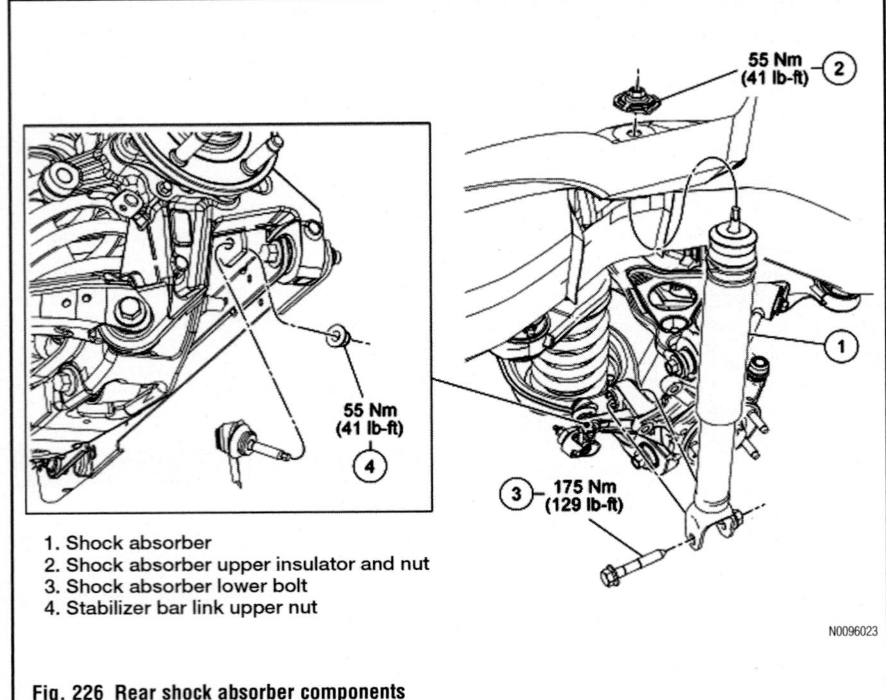

Fig. 226 Rear shock absorber components

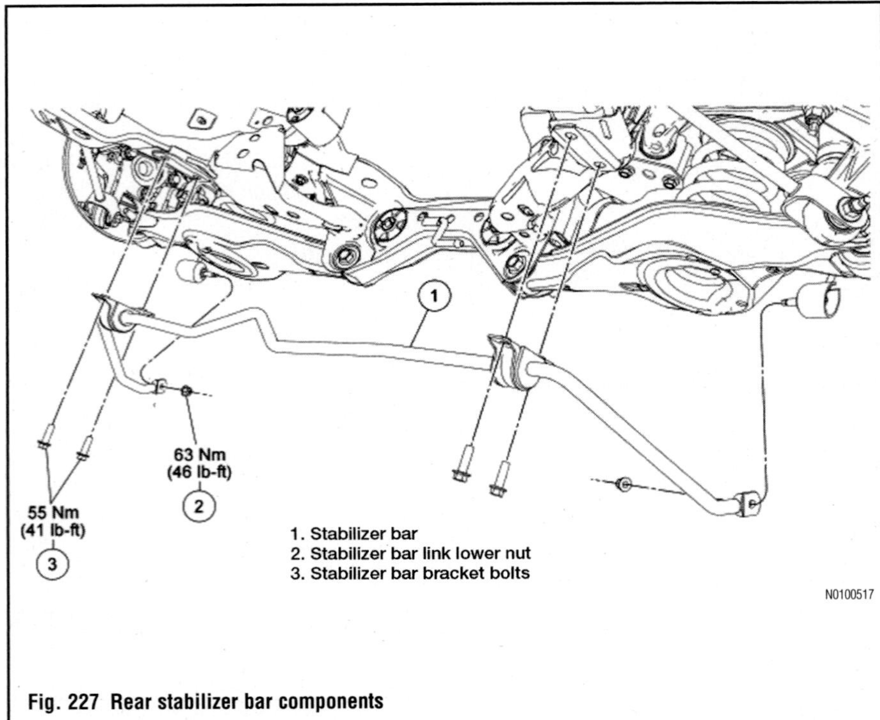

Fig. 227 Rear stabilizer bar components

4. Remove and discard the 4 stabilizer bar bracket bolts.
5. Remove the stabilizer bar.

To install:

6. To install, reverse the removal procedure, noting the following:
    a. Install new stabilizer bar bracket bolts and tighten to 41 ft. lbs. (55 Nm).
    b. Install new stabilizer bar link lower nuts and tighten to 46 ft. lbs. (63 Nm).

STEERING KNUCKLE

REMOVAL & INSTALLATION

AWD Vehicles

See Figures 228 and 229.

1. Measure the distance from the center of the wheel hub to the lip of the fender with the vehicle in a level, static ground position (curb height).
2. Remove the wheel bearing and wheel hub.
3. Using a suitable jackstand, support the lower arm.
4. Remove and discard the trailing arm-to-wheel knuckle nut and bolt.
5. Remove and discard the stabilizer bar link upper nut and disconnect the link. Use the hex-holding feature to prevent the stabilizer bar link stud from turning while removing or installing the nut.
6. Remove and discard the shock absorber lower bolt and disconnect the shock absorber from the knuckle bracket.
7. Remove and discard the toe link-to-knuckle nut.
8. Remove and discard the upper arm-to-wheel knuckle nut and bolt and disconnect the upper arm from the knuckle.
9. Remove and discard the lower arm-to-wheel knuckle nut and bolt.
10. Lower the jackstand, slide the knuckle off the toe link and remove the knuckle.
11. If necessary, remove the 3 brake disc shield bolts and remove the shield.

To install:

12. Before tightening suspension bushing fasteners, use a jackstand to raise the rear suspension until the distance between the center of the hub and the lip of the fender is equal to the measurement taken in the removal procedure (curb height).
13. If removed, install the brake disc shield. Tighten the 3 bolts to 11 ft. lbs. (15 Nm).
14. Position the wheel knuckle onto the toe link and loosely install a new lower arm-to-wheel knuckle nut and bolt.
15. Loosely install a new toe link-to-knuckle nut.

Fig. 228 Measure the distance from the center of the wheel hub to the lip of the fender

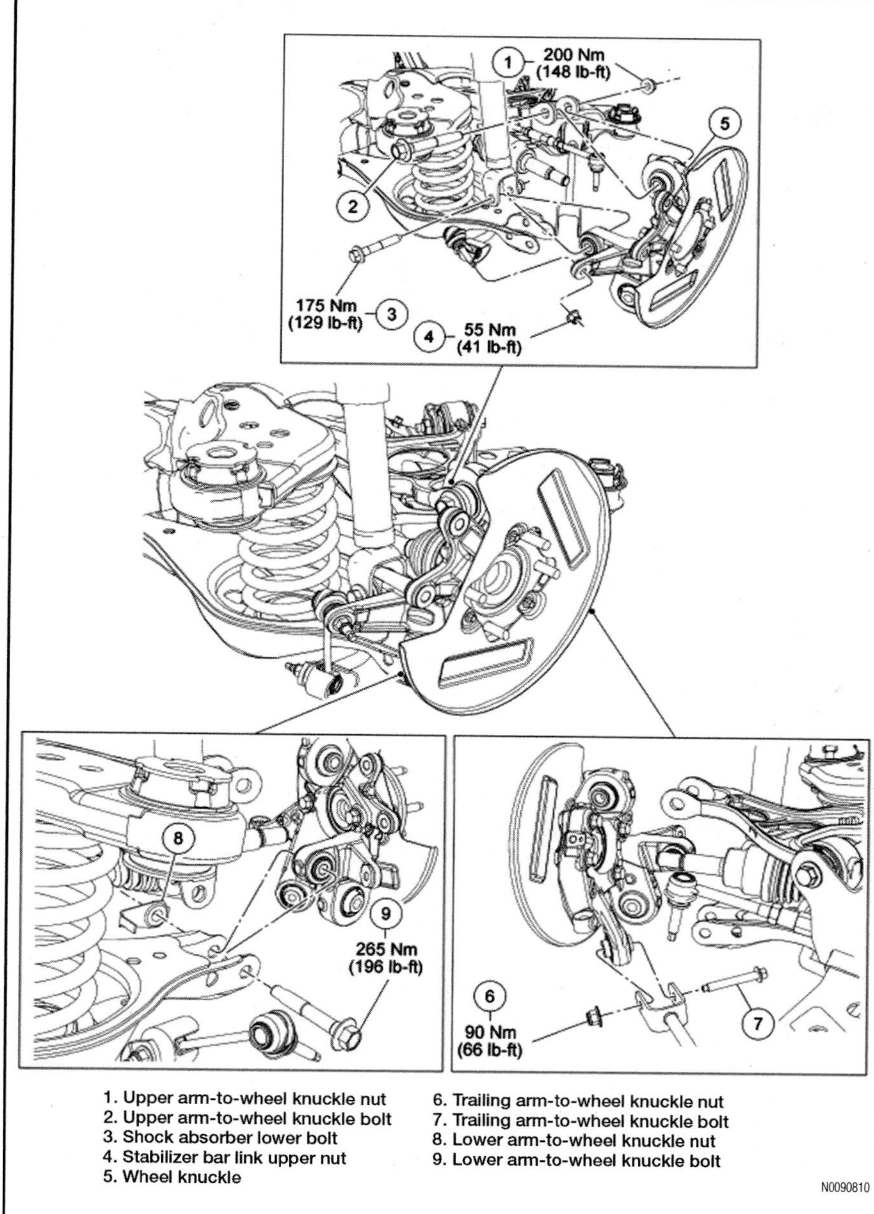

Fig. 229 Rear steering knuckle (wheel knuckle) components—AWD vehicles

16. Connect the shock absorber to the knuckle and loosely install a new shock absorber lower bolt.

17. Connect the stabilizer bar link and install a new stabilizer bar link upper nut. Tighten to 41 ft. lbs. (55 Nm).

18. Loosely install a new trailing arm-to-wheel knuckle nut and bolt.

19. Raise the jackstand and loosely install a new upper arm-to-wheel knuckle nut and bolt.

20. Position a suitable jackstand under the lower control arm at the shock and spring assembly attachment point and raise the rear suspension until the distance between the center of the hub and the lip of the fender is equal to the measurement taken in the removal procedure (curb height).

A slotted upper arm allows for the rear suspension camber to be adjusted by pushing inward or pulling outward on the wheel knuckle while tightening the upper arm-to-wheel knuckle nut.

21. With the wheel knuckle pushed inward for maximum negative camber, tighten the upper arm-to-wheel knuckle nut to 148 ft. lbs. (200 Nm). A slotted upper arm allows for the rear suspension camber to be adjusted by pushing inward or pulling outward on the wheel knuckle while tightening the upper arm-to-wheel knuckle nut.

22. Tighten the lower arm-to-wheel knuckle bolt to 196 ft. lbs. (265 Nm).

23. Tighten the shock absorber bolt to 129 ft. lbs. (175 Nm).

24. Tighten the trailing arm-to-wheel knuckle nut to 66 ft. lbs. (90 Nm).

25. Tighten the toe link-to-wheel knuckle nut to 59 ft. lbs. (80 Nm).

26. Install the wheel bearing and wheel hub.

27. Check the rear toe and adjust if necessary.

FWD Vehicles

See Figures 228 and 230.

1. Measure the distance from the center of the wheel hub to the lip of the fender with the vehicle in a level, static ground position (curb height).
2. Remove the brake disc.
3. Using a suitable jackstand, support the lower arm.
4. Remove and discard the trailing arm-to-wheel knuckle nut and bolt.
5. Remove and discard the stabilizer bar link upper nut and disconnect the link. Use the hex-holding feature to prevent the stabilizer bar link stud from turning while removing the nut.
6. Remove and discard the shock absorber lower bolt and disconnect the shock absorber.
7. Remove the wheel speed sensor bolt, disconnect the harness and position the sensor and harness assembly aside.
8. Remove and discard the toe link-to-knuckle nut.
9. Remove and discard the upper arm-to-wheel knuckle nut and bolt and disconnect the upper arm from the knuckle.
10. Remove and discard the lower arm-to-wheel knuckle nut and bolt.
11. Lower the jackstand, slide the knuckle off the toe link and remove the knuckle.

To install:

12. Before tightening any suspension bushing fasteners, use a jackstand to raise the rear suspension until the distance between the center of the hub and the lip of the fender is equal to the measurement taken in the removal procedure (curb height).
13. Position the wheel knuckle onto the toe link and loosely install a new lower arm-to-wheel knuckle nut and bolt.
14. Loosely install a new toe link-to-knuckle nut.
15. Position the wheel speed sensor harness and install the wheel speed sensor and bolt. Tighten to 11 ft. lbs. (15 Nm).

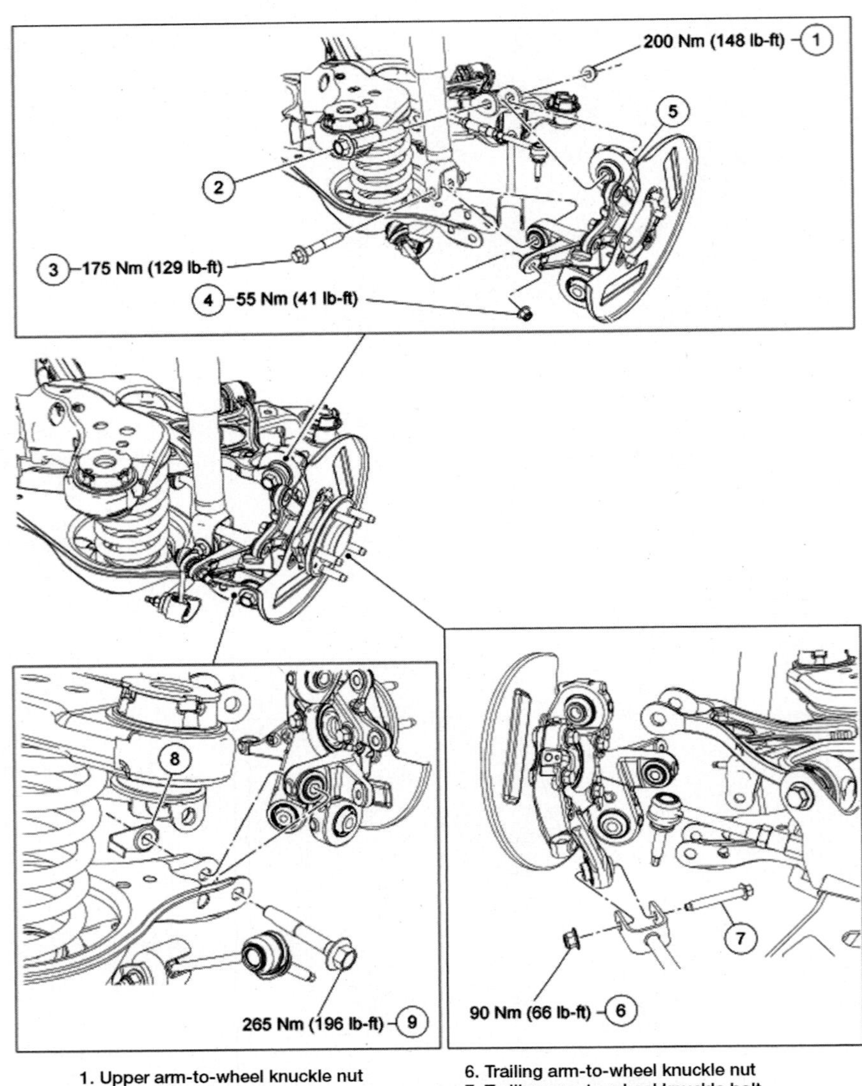

Fig. 230 Rear steering knuckle (wheel knuckle) components—FWD vehicles

16. Connect the shock absorber to the knuckle and loosely install a new shock absorber lower bolt.

17. Connect the stabilizer bar link and install a new stabilizer bar link upper nut. Tighten to 41 ft. lbs. (55 Nm).

18. Loosely install a new trailing arm-to-wheel knuckle nut and bolt.

19. Loosely install a new upper arm-to-wheel knuckle nut and bolt.

20. Position a suitable jackstand under the lower control arm at the shock and spring assembly attachment point and raise the rear suspension until the distance between the center of the hub and the lip of the fender is equal to the measurement taken in the removal procedure (curb height).

21. With the wheel knuckle pushed inward for maximum negative camber, tighten the upper arm-to-wheel knuckle nut to 148 ft. lbs. (200 Nm). A slotted upper arm allows for the rear suspension camber to be adjusted by pushing inward or pulling outward on the wheel knuckle while tightening the upper arm-to-wheel knuckle nut.

22. Tighten the lower arm-to-wheel knuckle bolt to 196 ft. lbs. (265 Nm).

23. Tighten the shock absorber bolt to 129 ft. lbs. (175 Nm).

24. Tighten the trailing arm-to-wheel knuckle nut to 66 ft. lbs. (90 Nm).

25. Tighten the toe link-to-knuckle nut to 59 ft. lbs. (80 Nm).

26. Install the brake disc.

27. Install the wheel and tire.

28. Check the rear toe and adjust if necessary.

TOE LINK

REMOVAL & INSTALLATION

See Figures 231 and 232.

1. Measure the distance from the center of the wheel hub to the lip of the fender with the vehicle in a level, static ground position (curb height).

2. Remove the wheel and tire.

3. Use a jackstand to raise the rear suspension until the distance between the center of the hub and the lip of the fender is equal to the measurement taken in Step 1 of the procedure (curb height).

4. Remove and discard the toe link-to-wheel knuckle nut.

5. Remove and discard the toe link-to-subframe bolt.

To install:

6. To install, reverse the removal procedure, noting the following:

a. Install a new toe link-to-subframe bolt and tighten to 52 ft. lbs. (70 Nm).

b. Install a new toe link-to-wheel knuckle nut and tighten to 59 ft. lbs. (80 Nm).

c. Check the rear toe and adjust if necessary.

TRAILING ARM

REMOVAL & INSTALLATION

See Figures 231 and 233.

1. Measure the distance from the center of the wheel hub to the lip of the fender with the vehicle in a level, static ground position (curb height).

2. Remove the wheel and tire.

3. Use a jackstand to raise the rear suspension until the distance between the center of the hub and the lip of the fender is equal to the measurement taken in Step 1 of the procedure (curb height).

4. Remove and discard the trailing arm-to-knuckle nut and bolt.

5. Remove and discard the trailing arm-to-subframe bolt.

To install:

6. To install, reverse the removal procedure, noting the following:

a. Install a new trailing arm-to-subframe bolt and tighten to 122 ft. lbs. (165 Nm).

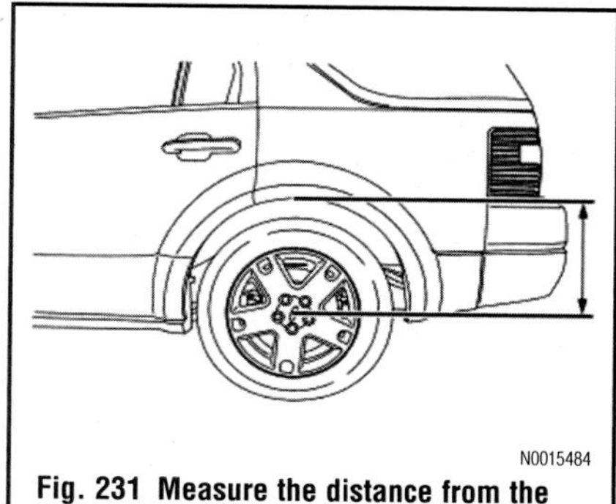

Fig. 231 Measure the distance from the center of the wheel hub to the lip of the fender

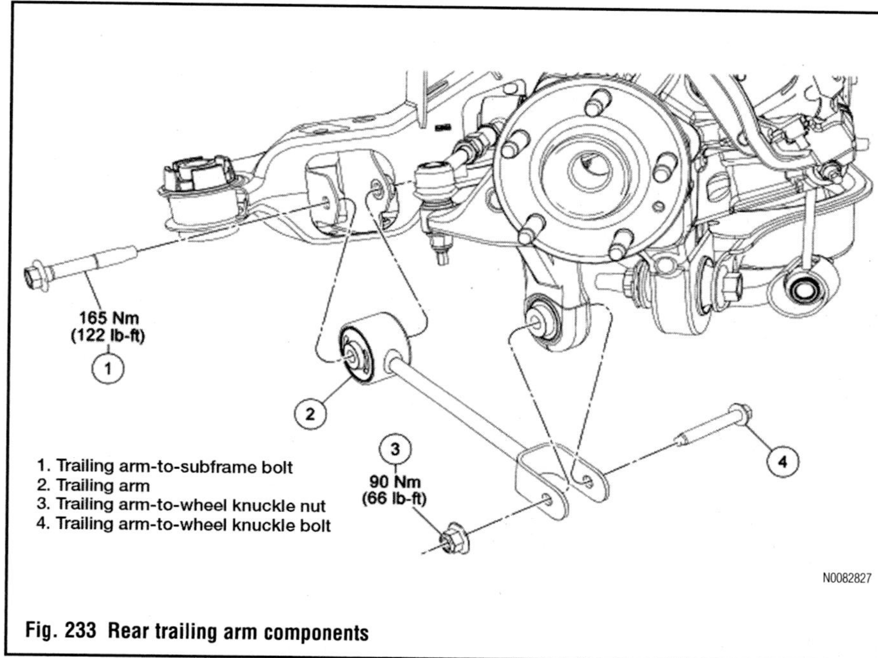

Fig. 233 Rear trailing arm components

70 Nm (52 lb-ft) 1
80 Nm (59 lb-ft) 3
2
1. Toe link-to-subframe bolt
2. Toe link
3. Toe link-to-wheel knuckle nut
N0083303

Fig. 232 Rear toe link components

b. Install a new trailing arm-to-knuckle nut and tighten to 66 ft. lbs. (90 Nm).

UPPER CONTROL ARM

REMOVAL & INSTALLATION

See Figures 231, 234 through 236.

1. Measure the distance from the center of the wheel hub to the lip of the fender with the vehicle in a level, static ground position (curb height).

2. Remove the wheels and tires.

3. Remove left-hand and right-hand parking brake cable bracket bolts.

4. Remove the 4 brake caliper anchor plate bolts and position the left-hand and right-hand brake caliper and anchor plate assemblies aside.

5. Support the brake caliper and anchor plate assemblies using mechanic's wire.

6. Position screw-type jackstands under the left-hand and right-hand wheel knuckles.

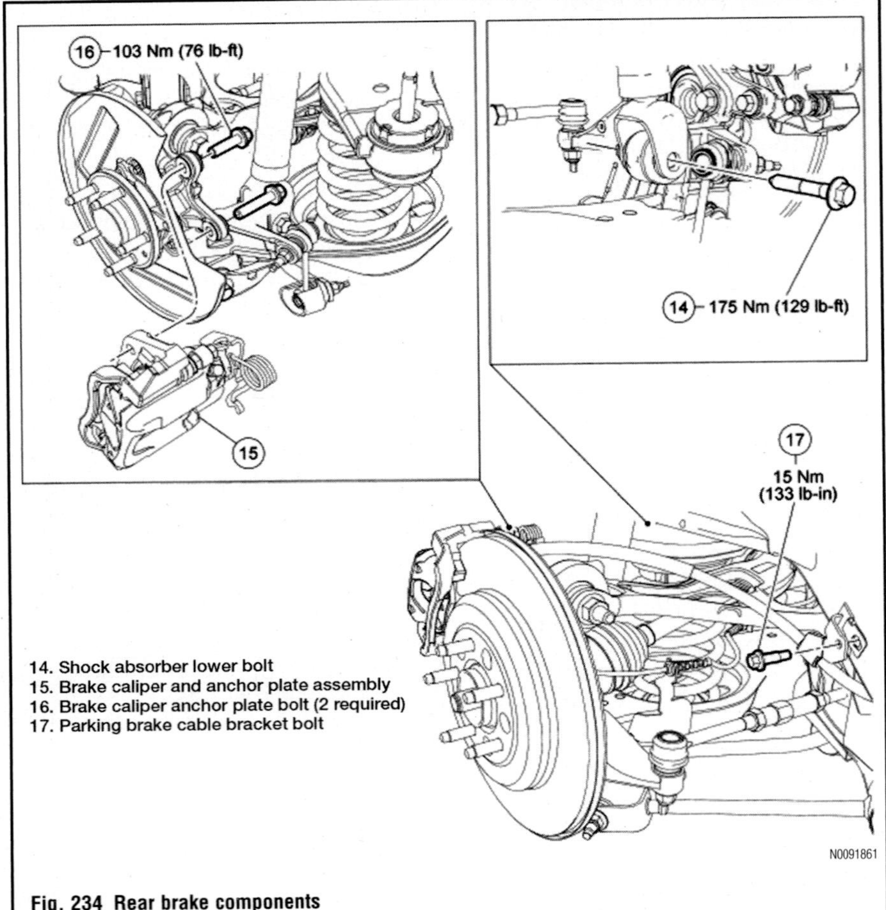

Fig. 234 Rear brake components

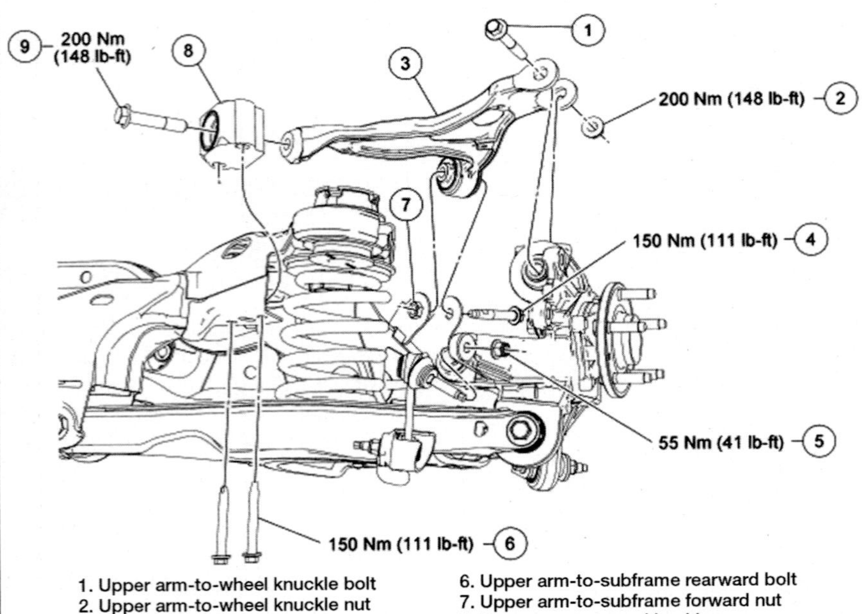

Fig. 235 Rear upper arm components

7. Remove and discard the upper arm-to-knuckle bolt and nut.
8. Remove and discard the 2 upper arm-to-subframe rearward bolts.
9. Remove and discard the left-hand and right-hand stabilizer bar link upper nuts and disconnect the links from the stabilizer bar. Use the hex-holding feature to prevent the stabilizer bar link stud from turning while removing or installing the nut.
10. Remove and discard the left-hand and right-hand lower shock bolts.
11. Remove and discard the 4 subframe bracket bolts.
12. Remove and discard the 2 subframe forward bolts and remove the 2 subframe brackets.
13. Remove and discard the 2 subframe rearward bolts and lower the subframe enough to allow removal of the upper arm forward bolt.
14. Remove and discard the upper arm-to-subframe forward bolt and nut.
15. Remove the upper arm.
16. If service to the upper arm rearward bushing is required, remove the upper arm bushing bolt and remove the upper arm bushing. Discard the bolt.

To install:

17. Before tightening the shock absorber lower bolts and upper arm nut and bolts, use a jackstand to raise the rear suspension until the distance between the center of the hub and the lip of the fender is equal to the measurement taken in the removal procedure (curb height).
18. If removed, install the upper arm bushing onto the upper arm in the following sequence.
    a. With the upper arm positioned so the top side is facing up and the upper arm bushing is positioned with the TOP OF PART facing up and the ARM TO THIS SIDE arrow is pointing toward the upper arm. b. Install the upper arm bushing.
    c. Install a new upper arm rearward bushing bolt and tighten to 148 ft. lbs. (200 Nm).
19. Position the upper arm and loosely install the new upper arm-to-subframe forward bolt and nut.
20. Raise the subframe and install 2 new subframe rearward bolts. Tighten to 148 ft. lbs. (200 Nm).
21. Position the 2 subframe brackets and install 4 new subframe bracket bolts. Tighten to 41 ft. lbs. (55 Nm).
22. Install 2 new subframe forward bolts. Tighten to 111 ft. lbs. (150 Nm).

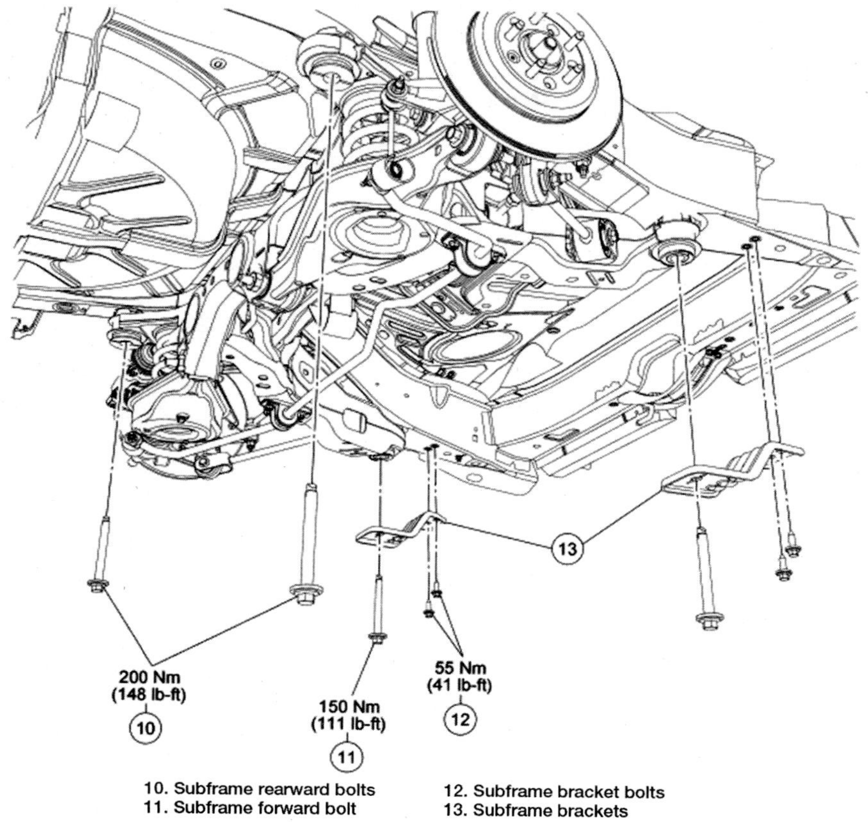

200 Nm (148 lb-ft) (10)
150 Nm (111 lb-ft) (11)
55 Nm (41 lb-ft) (12)
(13)

10. Subframe rearward bolts
11. Subframe forward bolt
12. Subframe bracket bolts
13. Subframe brackets

N0089355

Fig. 236 Subframe components

23. Loosely install new left-hand and right-hand shock absorber lower bolts.

24. Connect the left-hand and right-hand stabilizer bar links to the stabilizer bar and install the new nuts. Tighten to 41 ft. lbs. (55 Nm).

25. Loosely install 2 new upper arm-to-subframe rearward bolts.

26. Loosely install a new upper arm-to-knuckle bolt and nut.

27. Position the left-hand and right-hand brake caliper and anchor plate assemblies and install the 4 anchor plate bolts. Tighten to 76 ft. lbs. (103 Nm).

28. Install left-hand and right-hand parking brake cable bracket bolts. Tighten to 11 ft. lbs. (15 Nm).

29. Using the screw-type jackstand, raise the rear suspension until the distance between the center of the hub and the lip of the fender is equal to the measurement taken in the removal procedure (curb height).

30. Tighten the upper arm-to-subframe forward bolt to 111 ft. lbs. (150 Nm).

31. Tighten the left-hand and right-hand shock absorber lower bolts to 129 ft. lbs. (175 Nm).

32. Tighten the 2 upper arm-to-subframe rearward bolts to 111 ft. lbs. (150 Nm).

33. With the wheel knuckle pushed inward for maximum negative camber, tighten the upper arm-to-wheel knuckle nut to 148 ft. lbs. (200 Nm). A slotted upper arm allows for the rear suspension camber to be adjusted by pushing inward or pulling outward on the wheel knuckle while tightening the upper arm-to-wheel knuckle nut.

34. Remove the 2 jackstands.

35. Install the rear wheels and tires.

36. Check the rear camber and adjust if necessary.

WHEEL BEARINGS

REMOVAL & INSTALLATION

See Figures 237 and 238.

1. Remove the brake disc.
2. Remove the wheel speed sensor bolt and position the sensor aside.
3. For AWD vehicles:
   a. Remove the wheel hub nut. Do not discard the nut at this time.
   b. Using the Front Wheel Hub Remover (SST 205-D070) or equivalent tool, separate the halfshaft from the wheel hub.
4. For all vehicles:
   a. Remove the 4 bolts and the wheel bearing and wheel hub. Discard the bolts.
   b. Using a clean shop towel, clean the wheel knuckle-to-mating surfaces and inspect the knuckle bearing bore. If the wheel knuckle is cracked, install a new wheel knuckle.

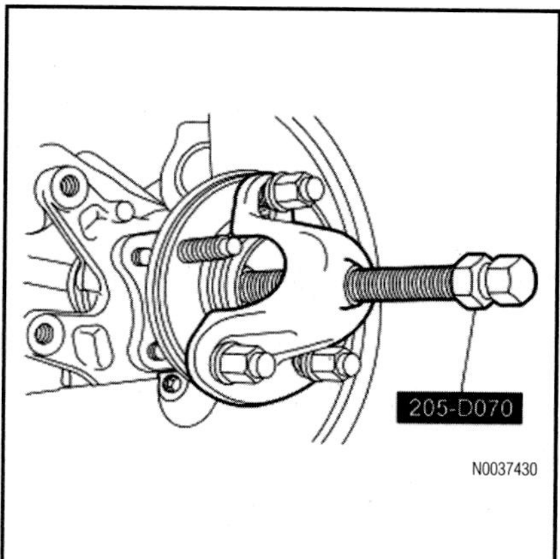

Fig. 237 Separate the halfshaft from the wheel hub

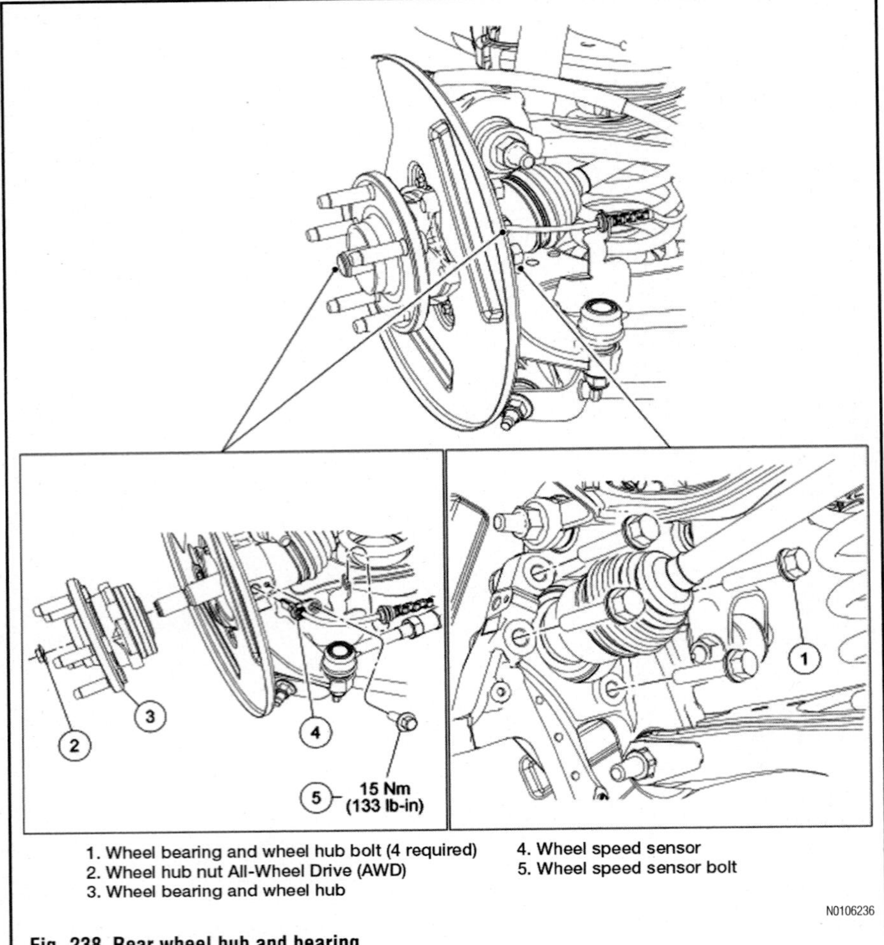

Fig. 238 Rear wheel hub and bearing

To install:

5. For all vehicles:

WARNING

The wheel knuckle bore must be clean enough to allow the wheel bearing and wheel hub to seat completely by hand. Do not press or draw the wheel hub and bearing into place or damage to the bearing may occur.

6. Make sure the wheel hub-to-knuckle mating surfaces are clean and free of any adhesive. Failure to clean adhesive from both surfaces may cause bearing damage.
   a. Install the wheel bearing and wheel hub assembly.
   b. Install the 4 new wheel bearing and wheel hub bolts. Tighten the bolts to 98 ft. lbs. (133 Nm) in a cross-pattern.
   c. Install the brake disc.
   d. Position the wheel speed sensor and install the bolt. Tighten to 11 ft. lbs. (15 Nm).
7. For AWD vehicles:

WARNING

Do not tighten the rear wheel hub nut with the vehicle on the ground. The nut must be tightened to specification before the vehicle is lowered to the ground. Wheel bearing damage will occur if the wheel bearing is loaded with the weight of the vehicle applied.

   a. Position the halfshaft in the hub and use the previously removed wheel hub nut to seat the halfshaft. Apply the brake to keep the halfshaft from rotating. Tighten the nut to 258 ft. lbs. (350 Nm). Remove and discard the nut.
   b. Install a new wheel hub nut. Tighten the nut to 258 ft. lbs. (350 Nm).
   c. Install and tighten the new wheel hub nut to specification within 5 minutes of starting it on the threads. Always install a new wheel hub nut after loosening or when not tightening within the specified time or damage to the components may occur.

FORD

Mustang

15

BRAKES 15-14

ANTI-LOCK BRAKE SYSTEM (ABS).......................... 15-14
General Information................. 15-15
Precautions......................... 15-14
Speed Sensors........................ 15-14
Removal & Installation........ 15-14
BLEEDING THE BRAKE SYSTEM 15-16
Bleeding Procedure................. 15-16
Bleeding the ABS System ... 15-17
Fluid Fill Procedure............ 15-17
FRONT DISC BRAKES 15-18
Brake Caliper.......................... 15-18
Removal & Installation........ 15-18
Disc Brake Pads..................... 15-18
Removal & Installation........ 15-18
PARKING BRAKE............. 15-23
Parking Brake Cables............. 15-23
Adjustment 15-23
REAR DISC BRAKES 15-21
Brake Caliper.......................... 15-21
Removal & Installation........ 15-21
Disc Brake Pads..................... 15-21
Removal & Installation........ 15-21

CHASSIS ELECTRICAL 15-23

AIR BAG (SUPPLEMENTAL RESTRAINT SYSTEM) 15-23
General Information................. 15-23
Arming the System 15-24
Clockspring Centering........ 15-24
Disarming the System......... 15-24
Service Precautions 15-23

DRIVE TRAIN 15-25

Automatic Transmission Fluid. 15-25
Drain and Refill.................. 15-25
Filter Replacement............. 15-25
Fluid Cooler Backflushing .. 15-25
Clutch.................................... 15-33
Bleeding 15-36
Removal & Installation........ 15-33
Front Driveshaft...................... 15-36
Removal & Installation........ 15-36
Manual Transmission Assembly 15-26
Removal & Installation........ 15-26
Manual Transmission Fluid..... 15-32
Drain and Refill.................. 15-32
Rear Axle Fluid........................ 15-37
Drain & Refill...................... 15-37
Rear Axle Housing.................. 15-37
Removal & Installation........ 15-37
Rear Axle Shaft, Bearing & Seal 15-38
Removal & Installation........ 15-38
Rear Driveshaft....................... 15-39
Removal & Installation........ 15-39
Rear Pinion Seal..................... 15-39
Removal & Installation........ 15-39

ENGINE COOLING........... 15-40

Engine Coolant........................ 15-40
Draining, Refill & Bleeding Procedure......................... 15-40
Flushing............................. 15-42
Heater Core Backflushing..................... 15-42
Supercharger Draining, Filling & Bleeding 15-42
Engine Fan 15-43
Removal & Installation........ 15-43
Radiator.................................. 15-44
Removal & Installation........ 15-44
Thermostat 15-45
Removal & Installation........ 15-45
Water Pump 15-48
Removal & Installation........ 15-48

ENGINE ELECTRICAL 15-52

BATTERY SYSTEM............ 15-52
Battery.................................... 15-52
Battery Reconnect/Relearn Procedure......................... 15-52
Removal & Installation........ 15-52
CHARGING SYSTEM 15-54
Alternator 15-54
Removal & Installation........ 15-54
IGNITION SYSTEM 15-58
Firing Order............................ 15-58
Ignition Coil 15-58
Removal & Installation........ 15-58
Ignition Timing........................ 15-61
Adjustment 15-61
Spark Plugs............................ 15-61
Inspection 15-61
Removal & Installation........ 15-61
STARTING SYSTEM 15-63
Starter 15-63
Removal & Installation........ 15-63

ENGINE MECHANICAL...... 15-66

Accessory Drive Belts 15-66
Accessory Belt Routing....... 15-66
Adjustment 15-66
Inspection 15-66
Removal & Installation........ 15-66
Air Cleaner 15-66
Removal & Installation........ 15-66
Camshaft and Valve Lifters...... 15-72
Removal & Installation........ 15-72
Catalytic Converter................. 15-80
Removal & Installation........ 15-80
Crankshaft Front Seal............. 15-82
Removal & Installation........ 15-82
Cylinder Head 15-83
Removal & Installation........ 15-83
Engine Oil & Filter 15-86
Replacement 15-86
Exhaust Manifold 15-86
Removal & Installation........ 15-86
Intake Manifold 15-92
Removal & Installation........ 15-92
Oil Pan 15-98
Removal & Installation........ 15-98
Oil Pump.............................. 15-105
Removal & Installation...... 15-105
Piston and Ring.................... 15-108
Positioning 15-108
Rear Main Seal..................... 15-109
Removal & Installation...... 15-109
Supercharger........................ 15-110
Removal & Installation...... 15-110
Timing Chain & Sprockets.... 15-118
Removal & Installation...... 15-118
Timing Chain Front Cover..... 15-111
Removal & Installation...... 15-111

Valve Covers 15-129
Removal & Installation......15-129

ENGINE PERFORMANCE & EMISSION CONTROLS....15-136

Camshaft Position (CMP) Sensor 15-136
Location....................15-136
Removal & Installation......15-136
Crankshaft Position (CKP) Sensor 15-136
Location....................15-136
Removal & Installation......15-137
Engine Coolant Temperature (ECT) Sensor 15-140
Location....................15-140
Removal & Installation......15-140
Heated Oxygen Sensor (HO2S)....................15-141
Location....................15-141
Removal & Installation......15-141
Intake Air Temperature 2 (IAT2) Sensor....................15-143
Location....................15-143
Removal & Installation......15-143
Knock Sensor (KS)....................15-144
Location....................15-144
Removal & Installation......15-144
Mass Air Flow (MAF) Sensor 15-144
Location....................15-144
Removal & Installation......15-145
Powertrain Control Module (PCM)....................15-145
Location....................15-145
Module Configuration.......15-145
Removal & Installation......15-145
Throttle Position Sensor (TPS) 15-146
Location....................15-146
Removal & Installation......15-146

FUEL....................15-147

GASOLINE FUEL INJECTION SYSTEM....................15-147
Fuel Filter....................15-147
Removal & Installation......15-147
Fuel Injectors 15-148
Removal & Installation......15-148
Fuel Pump....................15-153
Removal & Installation......15-153
Fuel System Service Precautions....................15-147
Fuel Tank....................15-154
Draining....................15-154
Removal & Installation......15-155
Idle Speed 15-156
Adjustment 15-156
Relieving Fuel System Pressure....................15-147
Throttle Body....................15-156
Removal & Installation......15-156

HEATING & AIR CONDITIONING SYSTEM....................15-160

Blower Motor 15-160
Removal & Installation......15-160
Heater Core....................15-160
Removal & Installation......15-160

PRECAUTIONS..............15-14

SPECIFICATIONS AND MAINTENANCE CHARTS.....15-3

Brake Specifications....................15-8
Camshaft Specifications............15-5
Capacities 15-4
Crankshaft and Connecting Rod Specifications 15-6
Engine and Vehicle Identification 15-3
Engine Tune-Up Specifications .15-3
Fluid Specifications....................15-4
General Engine Specifications...15-3
Piston and Ring Specifications...15-6
Scheduled Maintenance Intervals....................15-9–13
Tire, Wheel and Ball Joint Specifications 15-8
Torque Specifications 15-7
Valve Specifications 15-5
Wheel Alignment....................15-8

STEERING 15-165

Power Steering Gear..............15-165
Removal & Installation......15-165
Power Steering Pump............15-168
Bleeding & Flushing.........15-170
Fluid Fill Procedure..........15-171
Purging....................15-171
Removal & Installation......15-168

SUSPENSION...............15-172

FRONT SUSPENSION.......15-172
Coil Spring....................15-172
Removal & Installation......15-172
Control Links 15-173
Removal & Installation......15-173
Lower Control Arm................15-174
Removal & Installation......15-174
Stabilizer Bar....................15-175
Bushings 15-176
Removal & Installation......15-175
Steering Knuckle 15-176
Removal & Installation......15-176
Strut & Spring Assembly 15-177
Removal & Installation......15-177
Wheel Bearing & Hub 15-178
Removal & Installation......15-178

REAR SUSPENSION 15-179
Coil Spring....................15-179
Removal & Installation......15-179
Lateral Bar....................15-180
Removal & Installation......15-180
Lower Control Arm................15-181
Removal & Installation......15-182
Panhard Rod 15-182
Removal & Installation......15-182
Stabilizer Bar....................15-182
Removal & Installation......15-182
Upper Control Arm................15-183
Removal & Installation......15-183

SPECIFICATIONS AND MAINTENANCE CHARTS

ENGINE AND VEHICLE IDENTIFICATION

Engine						
Code ①	Liters (cc)	Cu. In.	Cyl.	Fuel Sys.	Engine Type	Eng. Mfg.
M	3.7		6	EFI	DOHC	Ford
N	4.0		6	EFI	SOHC	Ford
H	4.6		8	EFI	SOHC	Ford
F	5.0		8	EFI	DOHC	Ford
S	5.4		8	EFI	DOHC	Ford

Model Year	
Code ②	Year
A	2010
B	2011

① 8th position of VIN

② 10th position of VIN

25759_MUST_C0001

GENERAL ENGINE SPECIFICATIONS

All measurements are given in inches.

Year	Model	Engine Displacement Liters	Engine ID/VIN	Fuel System Type	Net Horsepower @ rpm	Net Torque @ rpm (ft. lbs.)	Bore x Stroke (in.)	Com-pression Ratio	Oil Pressure @ rpm
2010	Mustang	4.0	N	SFI	210@5300	240@3500	3.95x3.32	9.7:1	15@2000
		4.6	H	SFI	315@4500	325@4250	3.55x3.54	9.8:1	75@2000
		5.4	S	SFI	540@6200	510@4500	3.55x4.16	8.4:1	40-60@2000
2011	Mustang	3.7	M	SFI	305@6500	280@4250	3.75x3.41	10.5:1	30@2000
		5.0	F	SFI	412@6500	390@4250	3.63x3.65	11:01	NA
		5.4	S	SFI	550@6000	510@4500	3.55x4.23	8.4:1	40-60@2000

NA: Not Available

25759_MUST_C0002

ENGINE TUNE-UP SPECIFICATIONS

Year	Engine Displacement Liters (VIN)	Spark Plug Gap (in.)	Ignition Timing (deg.) MT	Ignition Timing (deg.) AT	Fuel Pump (psi)	Idle Speed (rpm) MT	Idle Speed (rpm) AT	Valve Clearance Intake	Valve Clearance Exhaust
2010	4.0 (N)	0.052-0.056	①	①	②	NA	2,000	0.001-0.002	0.001-0.003
	4.6 (H)	0.039-0.043	①	①	②	NA	2,000	0.001-0.003	0.002-0.004
	5.4 (S)	0.041-0.047	①	①	②	NA	2,000	0.0022-0.0009	0.0028-0.0015
2011	3.7 (M)	0.049-0.053	①	①	②	NA	2,000	0.0008-0.0027	0.0013-0.032
	5.0 (F)	0.049 - 0.053	①	①	②	NA	2,000	0.0008-0.0027	0.0018-0.0037
	5.4 (S)	0.041-0.047	①	①	②	NA	2,000	0.0022-0.0009	0.0028-0.0015

NA: Not Available

① 10 degrees Before Top Dead Center (BTDC) and is not adjustable

② Key ON Engine Running (KOER): 27-41 psi
Key On Engine OFF (KOEO): 35-77 psi

25759_MUST_C0003

CAPACITIES

Year	Model	Engine Displacement Liters	Engine ID/VIN	Engine Oil with Filter	Transmission/axle (pts.) Auto.	Transmission/axle (pts.) Manual	Drive Axle (pts.) Front	Drive Axle (pts.) Rear	Transfer Case (pts.)	Fuel Tank (gal.)	Cooling System (qts.)
2010	Mustang	4.0	N	5.0	24	①	NA	3.00	NA	17	16.0
		4.6	H	6.0	24	①	NA	3.00	NA	17	16.0
		5.4	S	6.0	24	①	NA	3.00	NA	17	16.0
2011	Mustang	3.7	M	6.0	26	②	NA	5.25	NA	16	12.4
		5.0	F	8.0	26	②	NA	5.25	NA	16	13.0
		5.4	S	7.4	26	②	NA	5.25	NA	16	16.0

NA: Not Available

NOTE: All capacities are approximate. Add fluid gradually and ensure a proper fluid level is obtained.

① T5OD transmission: 5.6 pints
TR3650 transmission: 6.3 pints
TR6060 transmission: 7.3 pints

② Mt82 transmission: 5.4 pints
TR6060 transmission: 7.3 pints

25759_MUST_C0004

FLUID SPECIFICATIONS

Year	Model	Engine Disp. Liters	Engine Oil	Auto. Trans.	Man. Trans	Drive Axle Front	Drive Axle Rear	Power Steering Fluid	Brake Master Cylinder	Cooling System
2010	Mustang	4.0	5W-20	XT-10-QLVC	XT-5-QM	NE	②	ATF XT-5-QM	DOT 3	③
		4.6	5W-20	XT-10-QLVC	XT-5-QM	NE	②	ATF XT-5-QM	DOT 3	③
		5.4	5W-50 ①	XT-10-QLVC	XT-5-QM	NE	②	ATF XT-5-QM	DOT 3	③
2011	Mustang	3.7	5W-20	XT-10-QLVC	④	NE	②	ATF XT-5-QM	DOT 3	⑤
		5.0	5W-20	XT-10-QLVC	④	NE	②	ATF XT-5-QM	DOT 3	⑤
		5.4	5W-50 ①	XT-10-QLVC	④	NE	②	ATF XT-5-QM	DOT 3	③

NE: Not Equipped

① Synthetic

② 7.5 inch ring gear: 80w-90
8.8 inch ring gear: 75W-140 synthetic

③ Motorcraft® Premium Gold Engine Coolant with Bittering Agent (bittered in US only)

④ Mt82 transmission: XT-M5-QS Full Synthetic Manual Transmission Fluid
TR6060 transmission: XT-5-QM MERCON® V Automatic Transmission Fluid

⑤ Motorcraft® Specialty Orange Engine Coolant □□VC-3-B

25759_MUST_C0005

VALVE SPECIFICATIONS

Year	Engine Displacement Liters	Engine ID/VIN	Seat Angle (deg.)	Face Angle (deg.)	Spring Test Pressure (lbs. @ in.)	Spring Free-Length (in.)	Spring Installed Height (in.)	Stem-to-Guide Clearance (in.) Intake	Stem-to-Guide Clearance (in.) Exhaust	Stem Diameter (in.) Intake	Stem Diameter (in.) Exhaust
2010	4.0	N	45	45	202.84-224.97 @ 1.413-1.445	1.70	1.569-1.609	0.0010-0.0020	0.0010-0.0030	0.274-0.275	0.270-0.274
	4.6	H	44.5-45	45.5	40-118 @ 1.22	2.220	1.660	0.0010-0.0030	0.0020-0.0040	0.235-0.236	0.234-0.235
	5.4	S	45-44.5	45.75-45.25	①	②	③	0.0022-0.0009	0.0028-0.0015	0.2762-0.2754	0.2756-0.2748
2011	3.7	M	44.5-45.5	45.25-45.75	114.7 @ 1.06	1.889	1.450	0.0008-0.0027	0.0013-0.0320	0.2157-0.2164	0.2151-0.2159
	5.0	F	45.5	45.25-45.75	NA	2.020	1.5748	0.0008-0.0027	0.0018-0.0037	0.2368-0.2379	0.2368-0.2379
	5.4	S	45-44.5	45.25-45.75	①	②	③	0.0022-0.0009	0.0028-0.0015	0.2762-0.2754	0.2756-0.2748

NA: Not Available

① Intake: 183 @ 1.2528 inches
Exhaust: 171 @ 1.2528 inches

② Intake: 2.1417 inches
Exhaust: 2.0039 inches

③ Intake: 1.692 inches
Exhaust: 1.555 inches

25759_MUST_C0006

CAMSHAFT SPECIFICATIONS

All measurements in inches unless noted

Year	Engine Displacement Liters	Engine Code/VIN	Journal Diameter	Brg. Oil Clearance	Shaft End-play	Runout	Journal Bore	Lobe Height Intake	Lobe Height Exhaust
2010	4.0	N	1.099-1.101	0.002-0.004	0.003-0.007	0.002	1.102-1.104	0.256	0.256
	4.6	H	1.126-1.127	0.001-0.003	0.001-0.007	0.001	1.128-1.129	0.217	0.2170
	5.4	S	1.0615-1.0605	0.0030-0.0010	0.0011-0.0075	0.0035	1.0635-1.0625	0.24239	0.2597
2011	3.7	M	1.021-1.022	0.0029 0.001-	0.0012-0.0066	0.0015	1.023-1.024	0.390	0.380
	5.0	F	1.1267	0.002	0.0059	0.0016	1.0625-1.0635	0.02348	0.2160
	5.4	S	1.0615-1.0605	0.0030-0.0010	0.0011-0.0075	0.0035	1.0635-1.0625	0.24239	0.2597

25759_MUST_C0007

CRANKSHAFT AND CONNECTING ROD SPECIFICATIONS

All measurements are given in inches.

Year	Engine Displacement Liters	Engine ID/VIN	Crankshaft Main Brg. Journal Dia.	Crankshaft Main Brg. Oil Clearance	Crankshaft Shaft End-play	Connecting Rod Journal Diameter	Connecting Rod Oil Clearance	Connecting Rod Side Clearance
2010	4.0	N	2.243-2.2440	0.0003-0.0024	0.002-0.0126	2.125-2.1260	0.0008-0.0025	0.0036-0.0125
	4.6	H	2.6567-2.6576	0.0009-0.0019	0.0030-0.0148	2.0867-2.0859	0.0009-0.0026	0.0187
	5.4	S	2.6567-2.6577	0.0009-0.0019	0.0020-0.0114	2.0867-2.0859	0.0025-0.0010	0.0012-0.0024
2011	3.7	M	2.6500	0.0010-0.0016	0.0051-0.0120	2.204-2.2050	0.0007-0.0021	0.0068-0.0167
	5.0	F	2.657-2.6580	0.0009-0.0018	0.0110	2.086-2.0870	0.0011-0.0027	0.0128
	5.4	S	2.6567-2.6577	0.0009-0.0019	0.003-0.0148	2.0867-2.0859	0.0025-0.0010	0.0187

25759_MUST_C0008

PISTON AND RING SPECIFICATIONS

All measurements are given in inches.

Year	Engine Displacement Liters	Engine ID/VIN	Piston Clearance	Ring Gap Top Compression	Ring Gap Bottom Compression	Ring Gap Oil Control	Ring Side Clearance Top Compression	Ring Side Clearance Bottom Compression	Ring Side Clearance Oil Control
2010	4.0	N	0.0012-0.0020	0.009-0.0150	0.016-0.025	NA	0.0016-0.0031	0.0012-0.0027	NA
	4.6	H	NA	0.0006-0.0012	0.0098-0.0197	0.0059-0.0256	0.0598-0.0606	0.0598-0.0606	NA
	5.4	S	0.0002-0.0005	0.011-0.021	0.055-0.065	0.0059-0.0256	0.0012-0.0020	0.0012-0.0031	0.1193-0.1201
2011	3.7	M	0.0003-0.0017	0.0067-0.0106	0.0118-0.0216	0.0059-0.0177	0.0015-0.0031	0.0015-0.0031	NA
	5.0	F	NA	0.0059-0.0098	0.0118-0.0216	0.0059-0.0177	0.0019-0.0031	0.0019-0.0028	NA
	5.4	S	0.0002-0.0005	0.011-0.021	0.055-0.065	0.0059-0.0256	0.0012-0.0020	0.0012-0.0031	0.1193-0.1201

25759_MUST_C0009

TORQUE SPECIFICATIONS

All readings in ft. lbs.

Year	Engine Disp. Liters	Engine ID/VIN	Cylinder Head Bolts	Main Bearing Bolts	Rod Bearing Bolts	Crankshaft Damper Bolts	Flywheel Bolts	Manifold Intake	Manifold Exhaust	Spark Plugs	Oil Pan Drain Plug
2010	4.0	N	①	②	③	④	⑤	7	17	13	19
	4.6	H	⑥	⑦	⑧	⑨	59	7	18	13	19
	5.4	S	⑩	⑪	⑫	⑨	59	7	15	13	19
2011	3.7	M	⑬	⑭	⑮	⑨	59	7	18	18	17
	5.0	F	⑯	⑰	⑱	⑲	⑳	㉑	㉒	11	19
	5.4	S	⑩	⑪	⑫	⑨	59	7	15	13	17

NA: Not Available

① First pass: 9 ft. lbs. (12 Nm)
Second pass: 18 ft. lbs. (25 Nm)

② First pass: 26 ft. lbs. (35 Nm)
Second pass: 57 degrees

③ Stage 1: 15 ft. lbs. (20 Nm)
Stage 2: 90 degrees

④ First pass: 41 ft. lbs. (55 Nm)
Second pass: 85 degrees

⑤ Stage 1: 10 ft. lbs. (13 Nm)
Stage 2: 37 ft. lbs. (50 Nm)
Stage 3: Tighten an additional 90 degrees

⑥ Stage 1: Tighten to 30 ft. lbs. (40 Nm)
Stage 2: Tighten an additional 90 degrees
Stage 3: Tighten an additional 90 degrees

⑦ Stage 1: Tighten fasteners 1 through 20 to 7 ft. lbs. (10 Nm)
Stage 2: Tighten fasteners 1 through 10 to 18 ft. lbs. (25 Nm)
Stage 3: Tighten fasteners 11 through 20 to 30 ft. lbs. (40 Nm)
Stage 4: Tighten fasteners 1 through 20 an additional 90 degrees
*Refer to appropriate illustration for bolt references

⑧ Stage 1: Tighten to 32 ft. lbs. (43 Nm)
Stage 2: Tighten an additional 105 degrees

⑨ Stage 1: Tighten to 66 ft. lbs. (90 Nm)
Stage 2: Loosen 360 degrees
Stage 3: Tighten to 37 ft. lbs. (50 Nm).
Stage 4: Tighten an additional 90 degrees

⑩ Stage 1: Tighten to 15 ft. lbs. (20 Nm)
Stage 2: Tighten to 37 ft. lbs. (50 Nm)
Stage 3: Tighten to 59 ft. lbs. (80 Nm)
Stage 4: Tighten an additional 90 degrees
Stage 5: Tighten an additional 90 degrees

⑪ Stage 1: Tighten to 7 ft. lbs. (10 Nm)
Stage 2: Tighten to 30 ft. lbs. (40 Nm)
Stage 3: Tighten an additional 90 degrees

⑫ Stage 1: Tighten to 30 inch lbs (40 Nm)
Stage 2: Tighten an additional 90 degrees

⑬ Stage 1: Tighten to 14 ft. lbs. (20 Nm)
Stage 2: Tighten to 26 ft. lbs. (35 Nm)
Stage 3: Tighten 90 degrees
Stage 4: Tighten 90 degrees
Stage 5: Tighten 45 degrees

⑭ Stage 1: Tighten fasteners 1 through 8 to 44 ft. lbs. (60 Nm)
Stage 2: Tighten fasteners 1 through 8 an additional 90 degrees
*Refer to appropriate illustration for bolt references

⑮ Stage 1: Tighten to 17 ft. lbs. (23 Nm)
Stage 2: Tighten to 32 ft. lbs. (43 Nm)
Stage 3: Tighten an additional 90 degrees

⑯ Stage 1: Tighten to 18 ft. lbs. (25 Nm)
Stage 2: Tighten to 30 ft. lbs. (40 Nm)
Stage 3: Tighten an additional 90 degrees
Stage 4: Tighten an additional 90 degrees

⑰ Stage 1: Tighten fasteners 1 through 20 to 15 ft. lbs. (20 Nm)
Stage 2: Tighten fasteners 1 through 10 to 30 ft. lbs. (40 Nm)
Stage 3: Tighten fasteners 11 through 20 to 48 ft. lbs. (65 Nm)
Stage 4: Tighten fasteners 1 through 20 an additional 90 degrees
*Refer to appropriate illustration for bolt references

⑱ Stage 1: Tighten to 15 ft. lbs. (20 Nm)
Stage 2: Tighten to 28 ft. lbs. (38 Nm)
Stage 3: Tighten an additional 105 degrees

⑲ Stage 1: Tighten to 103 ft. lbs. (140 Nm)
Stage 2: Loosen 360 degrees
Stage 3: Tighten to 74 ft. lbs. (100 Nm).
Stage 4: Tighten an additional 90 degrees

⑳ Stage 1: Tighten to 15 ft. lbs. (20 Nm)
Stage 2: Tighten an additional 60 degrees

㉑ Stage 1: Tighten to 7 ft. lbs. (10 Nm)
Stage 2: Tighten an additional 45 degrees

㉒ Early build: Stage 1: Tighten to 21 ft. lbs. (28 Nm)
Stage 2: Tighten 27 ft. lbs. (37 Nm)
Late build: Stage 1: Tighten to 18 ft. lbs. (24 Nm)
Stage 2: Tighten 24 ft. lbs. (32 Nm)

25759_MUST_C0010

WHEEL ALIGNMENT

Year	Model		Caster Range (+/-Deg.)	Caster Preferred Setting (Deg.)	Camber Range (+/-Deg.)	Camber Preferred Setting (Deg.)	Toe-in (Deg.)
2010	Mustang	L	0° ± 0.75°	7.1° ± 0.75°	0° ± 0.75°	-0.75° ± 0.75°	0.20° ± 0.20° ①
		R	0° ± 0.75°	7.1° ± 0.75°	0° ± 0.75°	-0.75° ± 0.75°	0.20° ± 0.20° ①
2011	Mustang	L	0° ± 0.75°	②	0° ± 0.75°	③	0.20° ± 0.20° ①
		R	0° ± 0.75°	②	0° ± 0.75°	③	0.20° ± 0.20° ①

① Shelby Models: 0.00° ± 0.20°

② All models except Shelby 7.1° ± 0.75° (L and R)
Shelby Models: 7.2° ± 0.75° (L and R)

③ All models except Shelby:-0.75° ± 0.75° (L and R)
Shelby Models: -1.0° ± 0.75° (L and R)

25759_MUST_C0011

TIRE, WHEEL AND BALL JOINT SPECIFICATIONS

Year	Model	OEM Tires Standard	OEM Tires Optional	Tire Pressures (psi) Front	Tire Pressures (psi) Rear	Wheel Size	Ball Joint Inspection	Lug Nut (ft. lbs.)
2010	Mustang	①	①	35	35	①	NA	100
2011	Mustang	①	①	35	35	①	0-0.012 in	100

OEM: Original Equipment Manufacturer

PSI: Pounds Per Square Inch

NA: Information not available

① Refer to the Vehicle Certification (VC) label located on the driver door jamb.

25759_MUST_C0012

BRAKE SPECIFICATIONS

All measurements in inches unless noted

Year	Model		Brake Disc Original Thickness	Brake Disc Minimum Thickness	Brake Disc Max. Runout	Minimum Pad/Lining Thickness Front	Minimum Pad/Lining Thickness Rear	Brake Caliper Bracket Bolts (ft. lbs.)	Brake Caliper Mounting Bolts (ft. lbs.)
2010	Mustang	F	NA	1.118 ①	NA	0.118 ②	—	115	25
		R	NA	0.685	NA	—	0.118	115	25
2011	Mustang	F	NA	1.118 ③	NA	0.118 ④	—	115	25
		R	NA	0.685	NA	—	0.118	115	25

F: Front

R: Rear

NA: Information not available

① For 5.4L engines: 1.181

② For 5.4L engines: 0.071

③ For 4 piston calipers: 0.181

④ For 4 pisotn calipers: 0.071

25759_MUST_C0013

SCHEDULED MAINTENANCE INTERVALS

2010 Ford Mustang, Except Shelby GT500

TO BE SERVICED	TYPE OF SERVICE	VEHICLE MILEAGE INTERVAL (x1000)											
		7.5	15	22.5	30	37.5	45	52.5	60	67.5	75	82.5	90
Engine oil & filter	Replace	✓	✓	✓	✓	✓	✓	✓	✓	✓	✓	✓	✓
Rotate tires	Service/Inspect	✓	✓	✓	✓	✓	✓	✓	✓	✓	✓	✓	✓
Engine coolant strength hoses & clamps	Service/Inspect			✓			✓				✓		
Air cleaner filter	Replace						✓						
Automatic transmission fluid & filter	Replace						✓						
Engine coolant	Replace	Initially at 105,000 miles or 6 years; every 45,000 miles thereafter											
PCV valve	Replace												
Spark plugs	Replace	Replace every 100,000 miles											
Drive belts	Service/Inspect						✓						
Exhaust system & heat shields	Service/Inspect						✓						
Front & rear brakes	Service/Inspect	✓	✓	✓	✓	✓	✓	✓	✓	✓	✓	✓	✓
Fuel filter	Replace			✓			✓				✓		

Special Operating Condition Requirements

During extensive idling and/or low speed driving for long distances, as in heavy commercial use such as delivery, taxi, patrol car or livery:

Lube front lower control arm and steering linkage ball joints with

Zerk fittings (if equipped) every 4,800 km (3,000 miles) or 3 months.

Inspect brake system and check battery electrolyte level (Patrol cars) every 8,000 km (5,000 miles).

Install a new cabin air filter as required.

When operating in dusty conditions such as unpaved or dusty roads:

Install a new engine air filter as required.

Install a new cabin air filter as required.

When operating in off-road conditions:

Change automatic transmission fluid every 48,000 km (30,000 miles).

Install a new cabin air filter as required.

Inspect and lubricate U-joints.

Inspect and lubricate steering linkage ball joints with zerk fittings.

25759_MUST_C0014

SCHEDULED MAINTENANCE INTERVALS

2011 Ford Mustang (Except Shelby GT500) - Normal

Service Item	Service Action	1	2	3	4	5	6	7	8	9	10	11	12	13	14	15
Engine oil & filter	Replace	✓	✓	✓	✓	✓	✓	✓	✓	✓	✓	✓	✓	✓	✓	✓
Spark plugs	Replace										✓					
Engine coolant	Replace										✓					✓
Auto transmission fluid	Replace															✓
Manual transmission fluid	Replace															✓
Cabin air filter	Inspect	✓	✓	✓	✓	✓	✓	✓	✓	✓	✓	✓	✓	✓	✓	✓
Engine air filter	Replace			✓			✓			✓			✓			✓
Engine air filter	Inspect	✓	✓	✓	✓	✓	✓	✓	✓	✓	✓	✓	✓	✓	✓	✓
Drive belt(s)	Replace															✓
Drive belt(s)	Inspect	✓	✓	✓	✓	✓	✓	✓	✓	✓	✓	✓	✓	✓	✓	✓
Cooling system, hoses, clamps & coolant strength	Inspect	✓	✓	✓	✓	✓	✓	✓	✓	✓	✓	✓	✓	✓	✓	✓
Battery performance	Inspect	✓	✓	✓	✓	✓	✓	✓	✓	✓	✓	✓	✓	✓	✓	✓
Exhaust system (Leaks, damage, loose parts and foreign material)	Inspect	✓	✓	✓	✓	✓	✓	✓	✓	✓	✓	✓	✓	✓	✓	✓
Horn, exterior lamps, turn signals and hazard warning light operation	Inspect	✓	✓	✓	✓	✓	✓	✓	✓	✓	✓	✓	✓	✓	✓	✓
Windshield for cracks, chips and pitting	Inspect	✓	✓	✓	✓	✓	✓	✓	✓	✓	✓	✓	✓	✓	✓	✓
Windshield wiper spray and wiper operation	Inspect	✓	✓	✓	✓	✓	✓	✓	✓	✓	✓	✓	✓	✓	✓	✓
Fluid levels (all)	Top off	✓	✓	✓	✓	✓	✓	✓	✓	✓	✓	✓	✓	✓	✓	✓
Brake system (Pads/shoes/rotors/drums, brake lines and hoses, and parking brake system)	Inspect	✓	✓	✓	✓	✓	✓	✓	✓	✓	✓	✓	✓	✓	✓	✓
Inspect wheels and related components for abnomal noise, wear, looseness or drag	Inspect	✓	✓	✓	✓	✓	✓	✓	✓	✓	✓	✓	✓	✓	✓	✓
Cabin air filter	Replace		✓		✓		✓		✓		✓		✓		✓	
Steering linkage, ball joints, suspension, tie-rod ends, driveshaft and u-joints: lubricate if equipped with grease fittings	Inspect / Lubricate	✓	✓	✓	✓	✓	✓	✓	✓	✓	✓	✓	✓	✓	✓	✓
Radiator, coolers, heater and air conditioning hoses	Inspect	✓	✓	✓	✓	✓	✓	✓	✓	✓	✓	✓	✓	✓	✓	✓
Rotate tires, inspect tread wear, measure tread depth and check pressure	Inspect/Rotate	✓	✓	✓	✓	✓	✓	✓	✓	✓	✓	✓	✓	✓	✓	✓
Suspension components for leaks and damage	Inspect	✓	✓	✓	✓	✓	✓	✓	✓	✓	✓	✓	✓	✓	✓	✓
Rear differential fluid	Replace															✓

Oil change service intervals should be completed as indicated by the message center (Can be up to 1 year or 10,000 miles) If the message center is prematurely reset or is inoperative, perform the oil change interval at 6 months or 5,000 miles from your last oil change.

For extensive idling and or low speed driving, change engine oil and filter every 5,000 miles, 6 months or 200 hours of engine operation.

25759_MUST_C0015

SCHEDULED MAINTENANCE INTERVALS

2011 Ford Mustang (Except Shelby GT500) - Severe

Service Item	Service Action	1	2	3	4	5	6	7	8	9	10	11	12	13	14	15
Engine oil & filter	Replace	✓	✓	✓	✓	✓	✓	✓	✓	✓	✓	✓	✓	✓	✓	✓
Spark plugs	Replace						✓						✓			
Engine coolant	Replace										✓					✓
Auto transmission fluid	Replace			✓			✓			✓			✓			✓
Manual transmission fluid	Replace			✓			✓			✓			✓			✓
Engine air filter	Inspect/ Service	✓	✓	✓	✓	✓	✓	✓	✓	✓	✓	✓	✓	✓	✓	✓
Drive belt(s)	Inspect	✓	✓	✓	✓	✓	✓	✓	✓	✓	✓	✓	✓	✓	✓	✓
Drive belt(s)	Replace															✓
Cooling system, hoses, clamps & coolant strength	Inspect	✓	✓	✓	✓	✓	✓	✓	✓	✓	✓	✓	✓	✓	✓	✓
Battery performance	Inspect	✓	✓	✓	✓	✓	✓	✓	✓	✓	✓	✓	✓	✓	✓	✓
Exhaust system (Leaks, damage, loose parts and foreign material)	Inspect	✓	✓	✓	✓	✓	✓	✓	✓	✓	✓	✓	✓	✓	✓	✓
Horn, exterior lamps, turn signals and hazard warning light operation	Inspect	✓	✓	✓	✓	✓	✓	✓	✓	✓	✓	✓	✓	✓	✓	✓
Oil and fluid leaks	Inspect	✓	✓	✓	✓	✓	✓	✓	✓	✓	✓	✓	✓	✓	✓	✓
Shocks struts and other suspension components for leaks and damage	Inspect	✓	✓	✓	✓	✓	✓	✓	✓	✓	✓	✓	✓	✓	✓	✓
Windshield for cracks, chips and pitting	Inspect	✓	✓	✓	✓	✓	✓	✓	✓	✓	✓	✓	✓	✓	✓	✓
Windshield wiper spray and wiper operation	Inspect	✓	✓	✓	✓	✓	✓	✓	✓	✓	✓	✓	✓	✓	✓	✓
Fluid levels (all)	Top off	✓	✓	✓	✓	✓	✓	✓	✓	✓	✓	✓	✓	✓	✓	✓
Brake system (Pads/shoes/rotors/drums, brake lines and hoses, and parking brake system)	Inspect	✓	✓	✓	✓	✓	✓	✓	✓	✓	✓	✓	✓	✓	✓	✓
Inspect wheels and related components for abnomal noise, wear, looseness or drag	Inspect	✓	✓	✓	✓	✓	✓	✓	✓	✓	✓	✓	✓	✓	✓	✓
Cabin air filter	Inspect/ Service	✓	✓	✓	✓	✓	✓	✓	✓	✓	✓	✓	✓	✓	✓	✓
Radiator, coolers, heater and air conditioning hoses	Inspect	✓	✓	✓	✓	✓	✓	✓	✓	✓	✓	✓	✓	✓	✓	✓
Rotate tires, inspect tread wear, measure tread depth and check pressure	Inspect/ Rotate	✓	✓	✓	✓	✓	✓	✓	✓	✓	✓	✓	✓	✓	✓	✓
Steering linkage, ball joints, suspension and tie-rod ends, lubricate if equipped with greases fittings	Inspect/ Lubricate	✓	✓	✓	✓	✓	✓	✓	✓	✓	✓	✓	✓	✓	✓	✓
Rear differential fluid	Replace															✓

Oil change service intervals should be completed as indicated by the message center (Can be up to 1 year or 10,000 miles) If the message center is prematurely reset or is inoperative, perform the oil change interval at 6 months or 5,000 miles from your last oil change.

For extensive idling and or low speed driving, change engine oil and filter every 5,000 miles, 6 months or 200 hours of engine operation.

25759_MUST_C0016

SCHEDULED MAINTENANCE INTERVALS

2010-11 Ford Shelby GT500 - Normal

TO BE SERVICED	TYPE OF SERVICE	VEHICLE MILEAGE INTERVAL (x1000)											
		7.5	15	22.5	30	37.5	45	52.5	60	67.5	75	82.5	90
Engine oil & filter	Service	✓	✓	✓	✓	✓	✓	✓	✓	✓	✓	✓	✓
Spark plugs	Replace	Replace every 105,000 miles											
Engine coolant	Replace	Initially at 105,000 miles or 6 years; every 45,000 miles thereafter											
Fuel filter	Replace				✓				✓				✓
Engine coolant strength hoses & clamps	Inspect		✓		✓		✓		✓		✓		✓
Battery performance	Inspect	✓	✓	✓	✓	✓	✓	✓	✓	✓	✓	✓	✓
Rear differential fluid	Replace	Replace every 150,000 miles											
Cabin air filter	Replace		✓		✓		✓		✓		✓		✓
Engine air filter	Inspect	✓	✓	✓	✓	✓	✓	✓	✓	✓	✓	✓	✓
Engine air filter	Replace				✓				✓				✓
Drive belt	Inspect	✓	✓	✓	✓	✓	✓	✓	✓	✓	✓	✓	✓
Drive belt	Replace												
Tires (Rotate, inspect the tire tread for wear, and adjust air pressure.)	Rotate/ Inspect		✓		✓		✓		✓		✓		✓
Automatic transmisison fluid & filter	Replace	Replace every 150,000 miles											
Brake system (Inspect brake pads, shoes, rotors, drums, brake lines, hoses and parking brake system (adjust parking brake if required).	Inspect		✓		✓		✓		✓		✓		✓
Exhaust system (Leaks, damage, loose parts and foreign material)	Inspect	✓	✓	✓	✓	✓	✓	✓	✓	✓	✓	✓	✓
Horn, exterior lamps, turn signals and hazard warning light operation	Inspect	✓	✓	✓	✓	✓	✓	✓	✓	✓	✓	✓	✓
Oil and fluid leaks	Inspect	✓	✓	✓	✓	✓	✓	✓	✓	✓	✓	✓	✓
Radiator, coolers, heater and airconditioning hoses	Inspect	✓	✓	✓	✓	✓	✓	✓	✓	✓	✓	✓	✓
Shocks struts and other suspension components for leaks and damage	Inspect	✓	✓	✓	✓	✓	✓	✓	✓	✓	✓	✓	✓
Windshield for cracks, chips and pitting	Inspect	✓	✓	✓	✓	✓	✓	✓	✓	✓	✓	✓	✓
Windshield wiper spray and wiper operation	Inspect	✓	✓	✓	✓	✓	✓	✓	✓	✓	✓	✓	✓
Fluid levels (all)	Top off	✓	✓	✓	✓	✓	✓	✓	✓	✓	✓	✓	✓
Steering linkage, suspension, driveshaft U-joints	Inspect/ Lubricate	✓	✓	✓	✓	✓	✓	✓	✓	✓	✓	✓	✓
Inspect wheels and related components for abnomal noise, wear, looseness or drag	Inspect	✓	✓	✓	✓	✓	✓	✓	✓	✓	✓	✓	✓

Use of E85 50% of the time or greater, change engine oil and filter every 5,000 miles or 6 months.

25759_MUST_C0017

SCHEDULED MAINTENANCE INTERVALS

2010-11 Ford Shelby GT500 - Severe

TO BE SERVICED	TYPE OF SERVICE	VEHICLE MILEAGE INTERVAL (x1000)											
		5	10	15	20	25	30	35	40	45	50	55	60
Engine oil & filter	Inspect	✓	✓	✓	✓	✓	✓	✓	✓	✓	✓	✓	✓
Spark plugs	Replace												✓
Engine coolant	Replace	Initially at 105,000 miles or 6 years; every 45,000 miles thereafter											
Fuel filter	Replace			✓			✓			✓			✓
Rear differential fluid	Replace	Replace every 150,000 miles											
Rotate tires, inspect tread wear, measure tread depth and check pressure	Rotate/ Inspect	✓	✓	✓	✓	✓	✓	✓	✓	✓	✓	✓	✓
Cabin air filter	Inspect/ Service	✓	✓	✓	✓	✓	✓	✓	✓	✓	✓	✓	✓
Engine air filter	Replace						✓						✓
Engine air filter	Inspect	✓	✓	✓	✓	✓	✓	✓	✓	✓	✓	✓	✓
Lubricate Drivetrain/ Steering/Suspension grease fittings	Inspect/ Lubricate	✓	✓	✓	✓	✓	✓	✓	✓	✓	✓	✓	✓
Drive belt	Inspect	✓	✓	✓	✓	✓	✓	✓	✓	✓	✓	✓	✓
Drive belt	Replace	Replace every 150,000 miles											
Automatic transmisison fluid	Replace						✓						✓
Battery performance	Inspect	✓	✓	✓	✓	✓	✓	✓	✓	✓	✓	✓	✓
Brake system (Inspect brake pads, shoes, rotors, drums, brake lines, hoses and parking brake system (adjust parking brake if required).	Inspect	✓	✓	✓	✓	✓	✓	✓	✓	✓	✓	✓	✓
Exhaust system (Leaks, damage, loose parts and foreign material)	Inspect	✓	✓	✓	✓	✓	✓	✓	✓	✓	✓	✓	✓
Horn, exterior lamps, turn signals and hazard warning light operation	Inspect	✓	✓	✓	✓	✓	✓	✓	✓	✓	✓	✓	✓
Oil and fluid leaks	Inspect	✓	✓	✓	✓	✓	✓	✓	✓	✓	✓	✓	✓
Shocks struts and other suspension components for leaks and damage	Inspect	✓	✓	✓	✓	✓	✓	✓	✓	✓	✓	✓	✓
Windshield for cracks, chips and pitting	Inspect	✓	✓	✓	✓	✓	✓	✓	✓	✓	✓	✓	✓
Windshield wiper spray and wiper operation	Inspect	✓	✓	✓	✓	✓	✓	✓	✓	✓	✓	✓	✓
Fluid levels (all)	Top off	✓	✓	✓	✓	✓	✓	✓	✓	✓	✓	✓	✓
Radiator, coolers, heater and air conditioning hoses	Inspect	✓	✓	✓	✓	✓	✓	✓	✓	✓	✓	✓	✓
Steering linkage, ball joints, suspension and tie-rod ends, lubricate if equipped with greases fittings	Inspect/ Lubricate	✓	✓	✓	✓	✓	✓	✓	✓	✓	✓	✓	✓

For extensive idling and or low speed driving, change engine oil and filter every 5,000 miles, 6 months or 200 hours of engine operation.

25759_MUST_C0018

PRECAUTIONS

Before servicing any vehicle, please be sure to read all of the following precautions, which deal with personal safety, prevention of component damage, and important points to take into consideration when servicing a motor vehicle:

- Never open, service or drain the radiator or cooling system when the engine is hot; serious burns can occur from the steam and hot coolant.
- Observe all applicable safety precautions when working around fuel. Whenever servicing the fuel system, always work in a well-ventilated area. Do not allow fuel spray or vapors to come in contact with a spark, open flame, or excessive heat (a hot drop light, for example). Keep a dry chemical fire extinguisher near the work area. Always keep fuel in a container specifically designed for fuel storage; also, always properly seal fuel containers to avoid the possibility of fire or explosion. Refer to the additional fuel system precautions later in this section.
- Fuel injection systems often remain pressurized, even after the engine has been turned **OFF**. The fuel system pressure must be relieved before disconnecting any fuel lines. Failure to do so may result in fire and/or personal injury.
- Brake fluid often contains polyglycol ethers and polyglycols. Avoid contact with the eyes and wash your hands thoroughly after handling brake fluid. If you do get brake fluid in your eyes, flush your eyes with clean, running water for 15 minutes. If eye irritation persists, or if you have taken brake fluid internally, IMMEDIATELY seek medical assistance.
- The EPA warns that prolonged contact with used engine oil may cause a number of skin disorders, including cancer. You should make every effort to minimize your exposure to used engine oil. Protective gloves should be worn when changing oil. Wash your hands and any other exposed skin areas as soon as possible after exposure to used engine oil. Soap and water, or waterless hand cleaner should be used.
- All new vehicles are now equipped with an air bag system, often referred to as a Supplemental Restraint System (SRS) or Supplemental Inflatable Restraint (SIR) system. The system must be disabled before performing service on or around system components, steering column, instrument panel components, wiring and sensors. Failure to follow safety and disabling procedures could result in accidental air bag deployment, possible personal injury and unnecessary system repairs.
- Always wear safety goggles when working with, or around, the air bag system. When carrying a non-deployed air bag, be sure the bag and trim cover are pointed away from your body. When placing a non-deployed air bag on a work surface, always face the bag and trim cover upward, away from the surface. This will reduce the motion of the module if it is accidentally deployed. Refer to the additional air bag system precautions later in this section.
- Clean, high quality brake fluid from a sealed container is essential to the safe and proper operation of the brake system. You should always buy the correct type of brake fluid for your vehicle. If the brake fluid becomes contaminated, completely flush the system with new fluid. Never reuse any brake fluid. Any brake fluid that is removed from the system should be discarded. Also, do not allow any brake fluid to come in contact with a painted surface; it will damage the paint.
- Never operate the engine without the proper amount and type of engine oil; doing so WILL result in severe engine damage.
- Timing belt maintenance is extremely important. Many models utilize an interference-type, non-freewheeling engine. If the timing belt breaks, the valves in the cylinder head may strike the pistons, causing potentially serious (also time-consuming and expensive) engine damage. Refer to the maintenance interval charts for the recommended replacement interval for the timing belt, and to the timing belt section for belt replacement and inspection.
- Disconnecting the negative battery cable on some vehicles may interfere with the functions of the on-board computer system(s) and may require the computer to undergo a relearning process once the negative battery cable is reconnected.
- When servicing drum brakes, only disassemble and assemble one side at a time, leaving the remaining side intact for reference.
- Only an MVAC-trained, EPA-certified automotive technician should service the air conditioning system or its components.

BRAKES

ANTI-LOCK BRAKE SYSTEM (ABS)

GENERAL INFORMATION

PRECAUTIONS

- Certain components within the ABS system are not intended to be serviced or repaired individually.
- Do not use rubber hoses or other parts not specifically specified for and ABS system. When using repair kits, replace all parts included in the kit. Partial or incorrect repair may lead to functional problems and require the replacement of components.
- Lubricate rubber parts with clean, fresh brake fluid to ease assembly. Do not use shop air to clean parts; damage to rubber components may result.
- Use only DOT 3 brake fluid from an unopened container.
- If any hydraulic component or line is removed or replaced, it may be necessary to bleed the entire system.
- A clean repair area is essential. Always clean the reservoir and cap thoroughly before removing the cap. The slightest amount of dirt in the fluid may plug an orifice and impair the system function. Perform repairs after components have been thoroughly cleaned; use only denatured alcohol to clean components. Do not allow ABS components to come into contact with any substance containing mineral oil; this includes used shop rags.
- The Anti-Lock control unit is a microprocessor similar to other computer units in the vehicle. Ensure that the ignition switch is **OFF** before removing or installing controller harnesses. Avoid static electricity discharge at or near the controller.
- If any arc welding is to be done on the vehicle, the control unit should be unplugged before welding operations begin.

SPEED SENSORS

REMOVAL & INSTALLATION

Front

See Figure 1.

1. With the vehicle in NEUTRAL, position it on a hoist.
2. Disconnect the wheel speed sensor electrical connector.

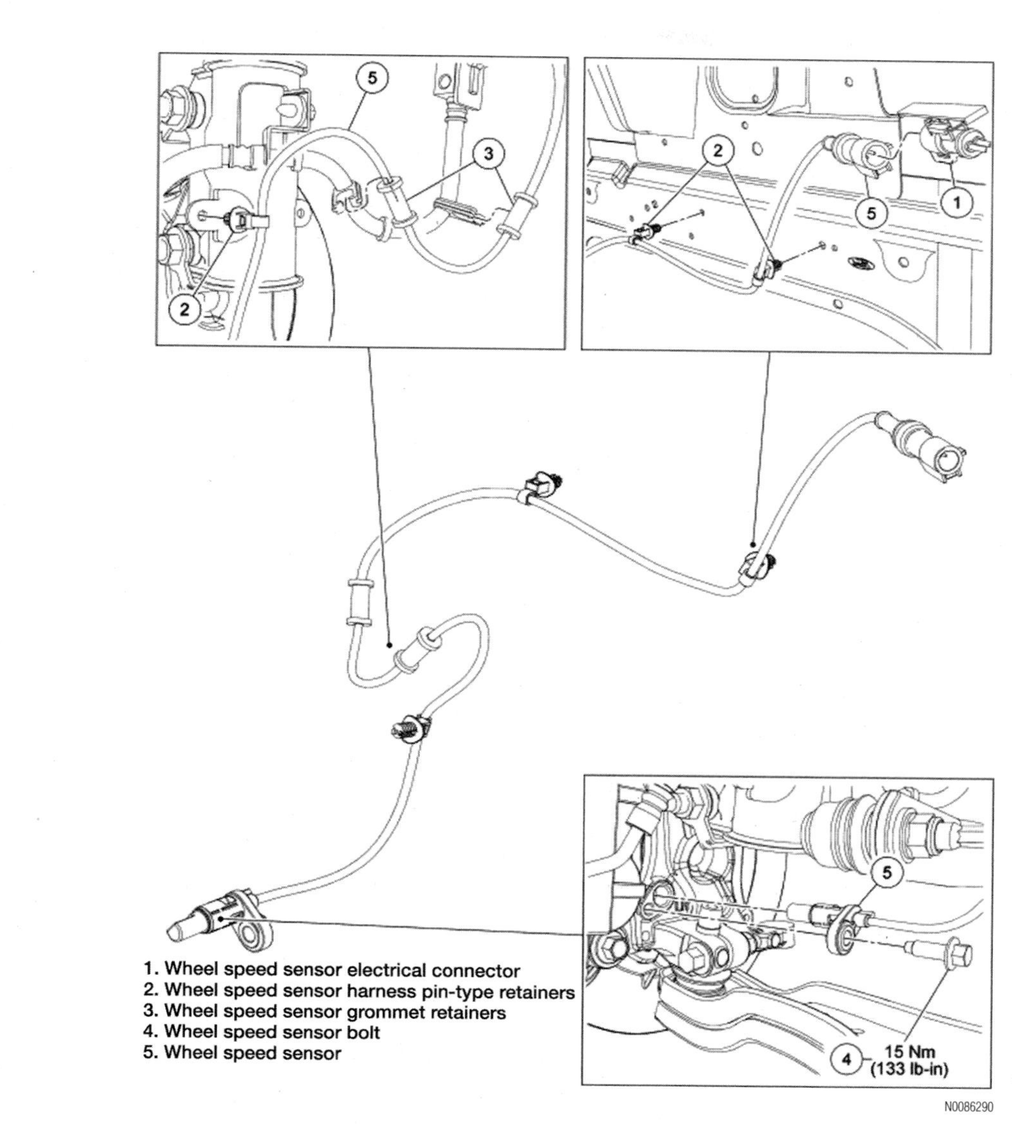

Fig. 1 Exploded view of the front wheel speed sensor

3. Disconnect the 3 wheel speed sensor harness pin-type retainers.
4. Disconnect the 2 wheel speed sensor grommet retainers from the brake hose clips.
5. Remove the wheel speed sensor bolt.
6. Remove the wheel speed sensor and harness assembly.
7. To install, reverse the removal procedure.

Rear

See Figure 2.

1. With the vehicle in NEUTRAL, position it on a hoist.
2. Disconnect the wheel speed sensor electrical connector.
3. Disconnect the 2 wheel speed sensor harness pin-type retainers.
4. Disconnect the wheel speed sensor grommet retainer from the brake hose clip.
5. Remove the wheel speed sensor bolt.
6. Remove the wheel speed sensor and harness assembly.
7. To install, reverse the removal procedure.

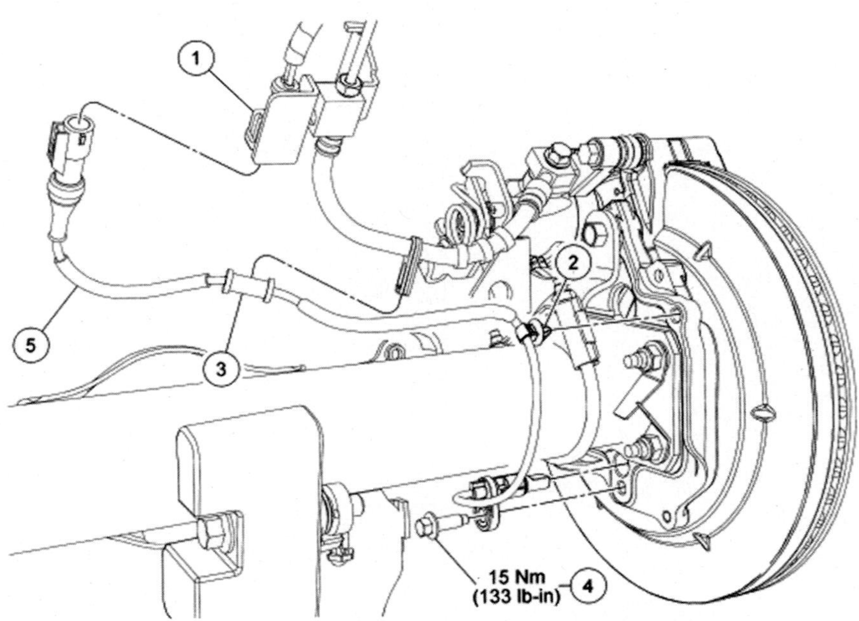

Fig. 2 Exploded view of the rear wheel speed sensor

BLEEDING PROCEDURE

Pressure Bleeding

WARNING

Do not use any fluid other than clean brake fluid meeting manufacturer's specification. Additionally, do not use brake fluid that has been previously drained. Following these instructions will help prevent system contamination, brake component damage and the risk of serious personal injury.

CAUTION

Brake fluid contains polyglycol ethers and polyglycols. Avoid contact with the eyes and wash your hands thoroughly after handling brake fluid. If you do get brake fluid in your eyes, flush your eyes with clean, running water for 15 minutes. If eye irritation persists, or if you have taken brake fluid internally, IMMEDIATELY seek medical assistance.

➡When any part of the hydraulic system has been disconnected for repair or installation of new components, air can get into the system and cause spongy brake pedal action. This requires bleeding of the hydraulic system after it has been correctly connected.

➡The Hydraulic Control Unit (HCU) bleeding procedure must be carried out if the HCU or any components upstream of the HCU are installed new.

➡Pressure bleed the brake system at 30-50 psi.

1. If equipped with a fire suppression system, depower the system, disconnect the negative battery cable and wait one minute.
2. Clean all dirt from and remove the brake master cylinder filler cap. Fill the brake master cylinder reservoir with clean, specified brake fluid.

➡Master cylinder pressure bleeder adapter tools are available from various manufacturers of pressure bleeding equipment. Follow the instructions of the manufacturer when installing the adapter.

3. Install the bleeder adapter to the brake master cylinder reservoir and attach the bleeder tank hose to the fitting on the adapter.
4. Place a box-end wrench on the master cylinder bleeder screw. Attach a rubber drain hose to the bleeder screw and submerge the free end of the hose in a container partially filled with clean, specified brake fluid.

➡Make sure the bleeder tank contains enough clean, specified brake fluid to complete the bleeding operation.

5. Open the valve on the bleeder tank.
6. Apply 30-50 psi to the brake system.
7. Loosen the bleeder screw and leave open until clear, bubble-free brake fluid flows into the container.
8. Remove the brake caliper bleeder screw cap and place a box-end wrench on the bleeder screw. Attach a rubber drain hose to the RH rear brake caliper bleeder screw, and submerge the free end of the hose in a container partially filled with clean, specified brake fluid.
9. Loosen the bleeder screw and leave open until clear, bubble-free brake fluid flows into the container.
10. Remove the rubber hose and install the bleeder screw cap. Tighten the brake caliper bleeder screw to specification.

11. Repeat Steps 5 through 7 for the LH rear, RH front and LH front bleeder screws in this order.

12. Release the bleeder tank pressure and close the bleeder tank valve. Remove the tank hose from the adapter and remove the adapter.

13. Install the reservoir cap.

➡If the brake pedal remains spongy, air may be trapped in the HCU.

14. If the brake pedal remains spongy after pressure bleeding, carry out the ABS HCU bleeding procedure in this section with the scan tool.

15. If equipped with a fire suppression system, repower the system by connecting the negative battery cable.

Manual Bleeding

⁂ WARNING

Do not use any fluid other than clean brake fluid meeting manufacturer's specification. Additionally, do not use brake fluid that has been previously drained. Following these instructions will help prevent system contamination, brake component damage and the risk of serious personal injury.

⁂ CAUTION

Brake fluid contains polyglycol ethers and polyglycols. Avoid contact with the eyes and wash your hands thoroughly after handling brake fluid. If you do get brake fluid in your eyes, flush your eyes with clean, running water for 15 minutes. If eye irritation persists, or if you have taken brake fluid internally, IMMEDIATELY seek medical assistance.

1. If equipped with a fire suppression system, depower the system, disconnect the negative battery cable and wait one minute.

2. Clean all dirt from the brake master cylinder filler cap and remove the filler cap.

3. Fill the brake master cylinder reservoir with clean, specified brake fluid.

4. Place a box-end wrench on the master cylinder bleeder screw. Attach a rubber drain hose to the bleeder screw and submerge the free end of the hose in a container partially filled with clean, specified brake fluid.

5. Loosen the bleeder screw and leave open until clear, bubble-free brake fluid flows into the container.

6. Remove the rubber hose.

7. Remove the brake caliper bleeder screw cap and place a box end wrench on the RH rear bleeder screw. Attach a rubber drain hose to the bleeder screw and submerge the free end of the hose in a container partially filled with clean, specified brake fluid.

8. Have an assistant pump the brake pedal and then hold firm pressure on the brake pedal.

9. Loosen the bleeder screw until a stream of brake fluid comes out. While the assistant maintains pressure on the brake pedal, tighten the bleeder screw.

10. Repeat until clear, bubble-free fluid comes out.

11. Refill the brake master cylinder reservoir as necessary.

12. Tighten the brake caliper bleeder screw to specification.

13. Remove the rubber hose and install the bleeder screw cap.

14. Repeat Steps 7 through 13 for the LH rear, RH front and LH front bleeder screws in this order.

15. If equipped with a fire suppression system, repower the system. Connect the negative battery cable.

BLEEDING THE ABS SYSTEM

⁂ WARNING

Do not use any fluid other than clean brake fluid meeting manufacturer's specification. Additionally, do not use brake fluid that has been previously drained. Following these instructions will help prevent system contamination, brake component damage and the risk of serious personal injury.

⁂ CAUTION

Brake fluid contains polyglycol ethers and polyglycols. Avoid contact with the eyes and wash your hands thoroughly after handling brake fluid. If you do get brake fluid in your eyes, flush your eyes with clean, running water for 15 minutes. If eye irritation persists, or if you have taken brake fluid internally, IMMEDIATELY seek medical assistance.

➡Follow the Pressure Bleeding or Manual Bleeding procedure steps to bleed the system.

1. If equipped with a fire suppression system, depower the system, disconnect the negative battery cable and wait one minute.

2. Connect the scan tool and follow the ABS Service Bleed instructions.

3. Repeat the Pressure Bleeding or Manual Bleeding procedure steps to bleed the system.

4. If equipped with a fire suppression system, repower the system. Connect the negative battery cable.

FLUID FILL PROCEDURE

See Figure 3.

⁂ WARNING

Do not use any fluid other than clean brake fluid meeting manufacturer's specification. Additionally, do not use brake fluid that has been previously drained. Following these instructions will help prevent system contamination, brake component damage and the risk of serious personal injury.

⁂ CAUTION

Brake fluid contains polyglycol ethers and polyglycols. Avoid contact with the eyes and wash your hands thoroughly after handling brake fluid. If you do get brake fluid in your eyes, flush your eyes with clean, running water for 15 minutes. If eye irritation persists, or if you have taken brake fluid internally, IMMEDIATELY seek medical assistance.

1. Clean all dirt from the brake master cylinder filler cap and remove the filler cap.

2. Fill the brake master cylinder reservoir with clean, specified brake fluid.

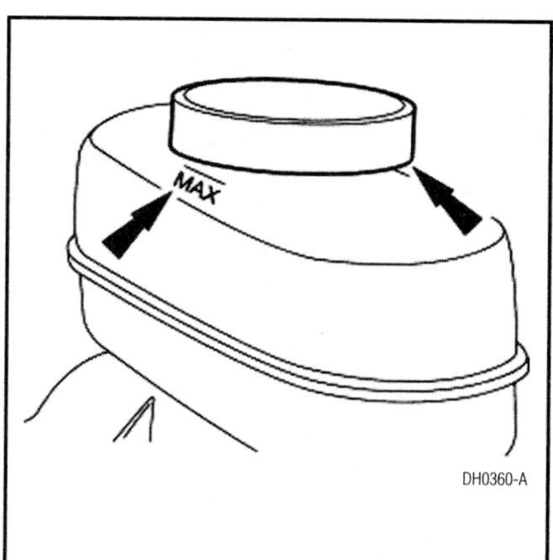

Fig. 3 Filling the brake master cylinder reservoir

CAUTION

Dust and dirt accumulating on brake parts during normal use may contain asbestos fibers from production or aftermarket brake linings. Breathing excessive concentrations of asbestos fibers can cause serious bodily harm. Exercise care when servicing brake parts. Do not sand or grind brake lining unless equipment used is designed to contain the dust residue. Do not clean brake parts with compressed air or by dry brushing. Cleaning should be done by dampening the brake components with a fine mist of water, then wiping the brake components clean with a dampened cloth. Dispose of cloth and all residue containing asbestos fibers in an impermeable container with the appropriate label. Follow practices prescribed by the Occupational Safety and Health Administration (OSHA) and the Environmental Protection Agency (EPA) for the handling, processing, and disposing of dust or debris that may contain asbestos fibers.

CAUTION

Brake fluid contains polyglycol ethers and polyglycols. Avoid contact with the eyes and wash your hands thoroughly after handling brake fluid. If you do get brake fluid in your eyes, flush your eyes with clean, running water for 15 minutes. If eye irritation persists, or if you have taken brake fluid internally, IMMEDIATELY seek medical assistance.

WARNING

Clean, high quality brake fluid is essential to the safe and proper operation of the brake system. You should always buy the highest quality brake fluid that is available. If the brake fluid becomes contaminated, drain and flush the system, then refill the master cylinder with new fluid. Never reuse any brake fluid. Any brake fluid that is removed from the system should be discarded. Also, do not allow any brake fluid to come in contact with a painted surface; it will damage the paint.

BRAKE CALIPER

REMOVAL & INSTALLATION

2 Piston Caliper

See Figure 4.

➡Do not spill brake fluid on painted or plastic surfaces or damage to the surface may occur. If brake fluid is spilled onto a painted or plastic surface, immediately wash the surface with water.

1. Remove the wheel and tire.
2. Remove the brake caliper flow bolt and discard the 2 copper washers.

➡Do not use the caliper sight hole to retract pistons as this may damage the pistons and boots.

3. Remove and discard the 2 brake caliper guide pin bolts and remove the brake caliper.
4. Inspect the brake caliper.
5. If leaks or damaged boots are found, install a new brake caliper.

To install:

6. Position the brake caliper and install 2 new guide pin bolts. Tighten to 25 ft. lbs. (34 Nm).
7. Using 2 new copper washers, position the brake flexible hose on the brake caliper and install the brake caliper flow bolt. Tighten to 41 ft. lbs. (55 Nm)
8. Bleed the brake caliper.
9. Install the wheel and tire.

4 Piston Caliper

See Figure 5.

➡Do not spill brake fluid on painted or plastic surfaces or damage to the surface may occur. If brake fluid is spilled onto a painted or plastic surface, immediately wash the surface with water.

1. Remove the brake pads.
2. Remove the brake caliper flow bolt and discard the 2 copper washers. Upon installation, install new copper washers.

➡Do not remove the bolts securing the 2 caliper halves together. Do not attempt to separate the 2 caliper halves or damage to components may occur.

3. Remove the 2 brake caliper bolts and the brake caliper.
4. To install, reverse the removal procedure. Refer to illustration for torque values.
5. Bleed the brake caliper.

DISC BRAKE PADS

REMOVAL & INSTALLATION

2 Piston

See Figure 6.

WARNING

Always install new brake shoes or pads at both ends of an axle to reduce the possibility of brakes pulling vehicle to one side. Failure to follow this instruction may result in uneven braking and serious personal injury.

➡Do not spill brake fluid on painted or plastic surfaces or damage to the surface may occur. If brake fluid is spilled onto a painted or plastic surface, immediately wash the surface with water.

➡Do not allow grease, oil, brake fluid or other contaminants to contact the pad lining material or damage to components may occur. Do not install contaminated pads.

1. Check the brake fluid level in the brake fluid reservoir. If required, remove fluid until the brake master cylinder reservoir is half full.
2. Remove the wheel and tire.

➡Do not use the caliper sight hole to retract pistons as this may damage the pistons and boots.

➡Do not allow the brake caliper, brake pads and anchor plate assembly to hang from the brake hose or damage to the hose may occur.

3. Remove and discard the 2 brake caliper guide pin bolts and position the brake caliper aside.
4. Support the brake caliper using mechanic's wire.

➡Install new brake pads if they are worn past the specified thickness above the metal backing plates.

5. Remove the brake pads and discard the 4 spring clips.
6. Inspect the brake caliper anchor plate assembly.
7. Check the guide pins and boots for binding or damage.

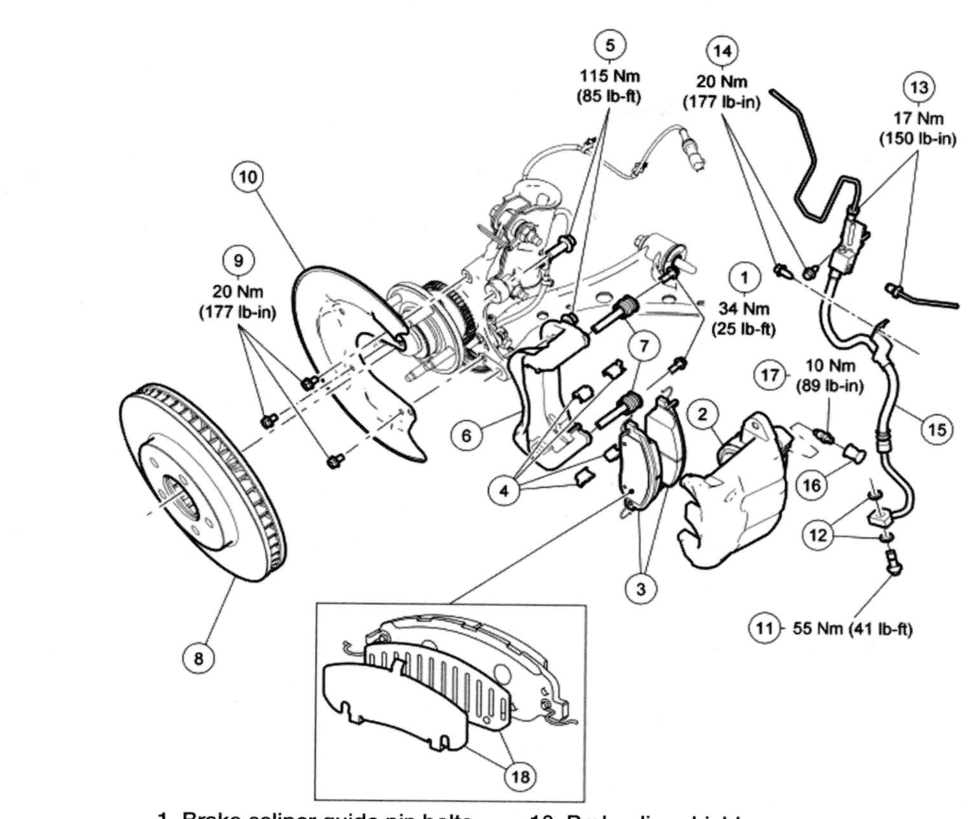

1. Brake caliper guide pin bolts
2. Brake caliper
3. Brake pads kit
4. Spring clips
5. Brake caliper anchor plate bolts
6. Brake caliper anchor plate
7. Guide pins
8. Brake disc
9. Brake disc shield bolts
10. Brake disc shield
11. Brake caliper flow bolt
12. Copper washers
13. Brake tube fittings
14. Brake flexible hose bracket bolts
15. Brake flexible hose
16. Bleeder screw cap
17. Bleeder screw
18. Shims (8 cylinder only)

N0116386

Fig. 4 Exploded view of the 2 piston front caliper

8. Lubricate the guide pins with the specified grease.
9. Install a new brake caliper anchor plate if it is worn or damaged

To install:

➡Protect the piston and boots when pushing the caliper piston into the caliper piston bores or damage to the piston or boots may occur.

10. If installing new brake pads, using a C-clamp and a worn brake pad, compress the brake caliper pistons into the caliper.

➡Install all the hardware supplied with the brake pad kits. For vehicles equipped with an 8 cylinder engine, install the brake pad shims (2 shims for each pad/slotted shim first) and apply a thin coat of the supplied lubricant between the 2 shims.

11. Install 4 new spring clips and the 2 brake pads.
12. Position the brake caliper on the anchor plate and install 2 new guide pin bolts. Tighten to 25 ft. lbs. (34 Nm).
13. If necessary, fill the brake fluid reservoir with clean, specified brake fluid.
14. Apply the brakes several times to verify correct brake operation.

4 Piston

See Figure 7.

⁂ WARNING

Always install new brake shoes or pads at both ends of an axle to reduce the possibility of brakes pulling vehicle to one side. Failure to follow this instruction may result in uneven braking and serious personal injury.

➡Do not allow grease, oil, brake fluid or other contaminants to contact the pad lining material or damage to components may occur. Do not install contaminated pads.

1. Remove the wheel and tire.

➡Install new brake pads if they are worn past the specified thickness above the metal backing plates. Inspect and install new brake pad mounting hardware as necessary.

2. Remove the brake pad mounting pins and spring retainer clip. Remove the brake pads from the caliper assembly.

➡Do not allow the brake caliper to hang from the brake hose or damage to the hose may occur.

➡Protect the piston and boots when pushing the caliper piston

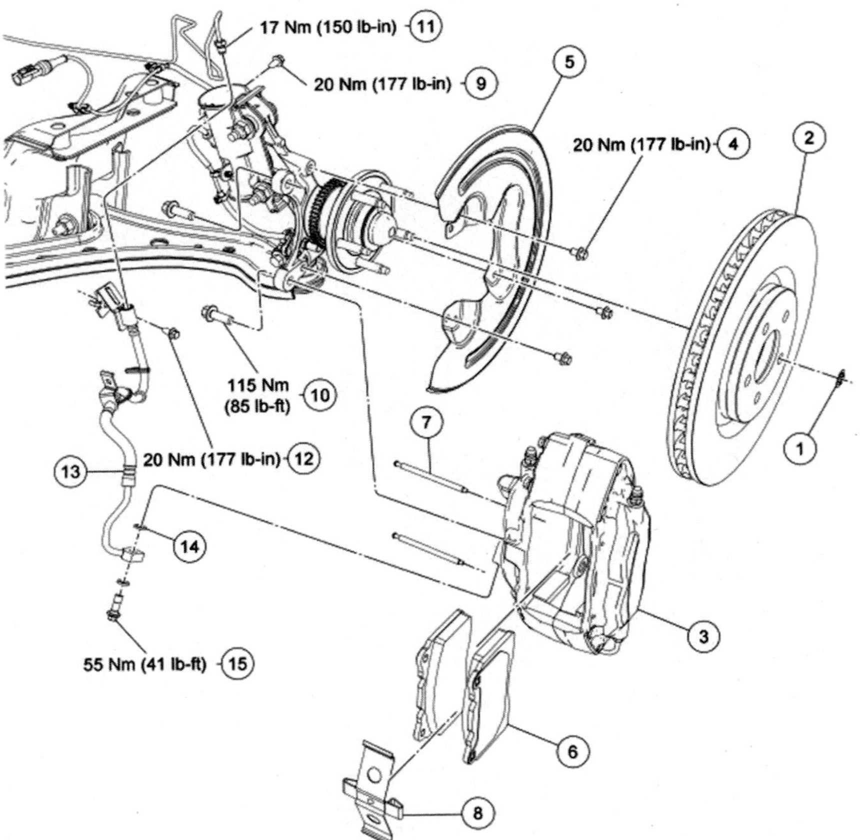

17 Nm (150 lb-in) (11)
20 Nm (177 lb-in) (9)
(5)
20 Nm (177 lb-in) (4)
(2)
115 Nm (85 lb-ft) (10)
(7)
(1)
(13)
20 Nm (177 lb-in) (12)
(14)
(3)
55 Nm (41 lb-ft) (15)
(6)
(8)

1. Retaining nut
2. Brake disc
3. Brake caliper
4. Brake disc shield bolt (3 required)
5. Brake disc shield
6. Brake pad (2 required)
7. Brake pad mounting pin (2 required)
8. Spring retainer clip
9. Brake hose-to-strut bolt
10. Brake caliper bolt (2 required)
11. Brake tube fitting
12. Brake flexible hose bracket bolt
13. Brake flexible hose
14. Copper washer (2 required)
15. Brake caliper flow bolt

N0116391

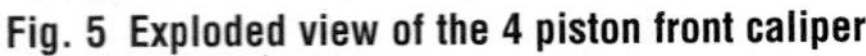

Fig. 5 Exploded view of the 4 piston front caliper

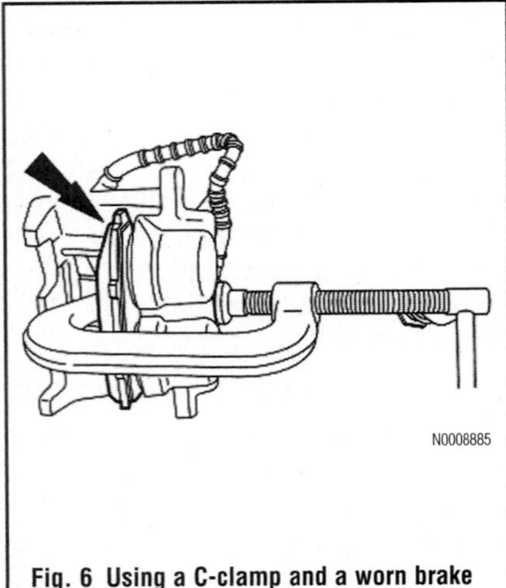

Fig. 6 Using a C-clamp and a worn brake pad, compress the brake caliper pistons into the caliper

Fig. 7 Removing the brake pads

into the caliper piston bores or damage to the piston or boots may occur.

3. If installing new brake pads, remove and discard the 2 brake caliper bolts and position the brake caliper aside.

4. Support the brake caliper using mechanic's wire.

5. Using a C-clamp and a worn brake pad, compress the brake caliper pistons into the caliper. To install, tighten new caliper bolts to 85 ft. lbs. (115 Nm).

6. To install, reverse the removal procedure.

7. Apply the brake pedal several times to verify correct brake operation.

⁂ CAUTION

Dust and dirt accumulating on brake parts during normal use may contain asbestos fibers from production or aftermarket brake linings. Breathing excessive concentrations of asbestos fibers can cause serious bodily harm. Exercise care when servicing brake parts. Do not sand or grind brake lining unless equipment used is designed to contain the dust residue. Do not clean brake parts with compressed air or by dry brushing. Cleaning should be done by dampening the brake components with a fine mist of water, then wiping the brake components clean with a dampened cloth. Dispose of cloth and all residue containing asbestos fibers in an impermeable container with the appropriate label. Follow practices prescribed by the Occupational Safety and Health Administration (OSHA) and the Environmental Protection Agency (EPA) for the handling, processing, and disposing of dust or debris that may contain asbestos fiber.

⁂ WARNING

Clean, high quality brake fluid is essential to the safe and proper operation of the brake system. You should always buy the highest quality brake fluid that is available. If the brake fluid becomes contaminated, drain and flush the system, then refill the master cylinder with new fluid. Never reuse any brake fluid. Any brake fluid that is removed from the system should be discarded. Also, do not allow any brake fluid to come in contact with a painted surface; it will damage the paint.

⁂ CAUTION

Brake fluid contains polyglycol ethers and polyglycols. Avoid contact with the eyes and wash your hands thoroughly after handling brake fluid. If you do get brake fluid in your eyes, flush your eyes with clean, running water for 15 minutes. If eye irritation persists, or if you have taken brake fluid internally, IMMEDIATELY seek medical assistance.

BRAKE CALIPER

REMOVAL & INSTALLATION

See Figure 8.

➡Do not spill brake fluid on painted or plastic surfaces or damage to the surface may occur. If brake fluid is spilled onto a painted or plastic surface, immediately wash the surface with water.

1. Remove the wheel and tire.
2. Remove the retaining clip and the parking brake cable and conduit from the brake caliper.
3. Remove the brake caliper flow bolt and discard the 2 copper washers.
4. Remove the 2 brake caliper guide pin bolts and the brake caliper.
5. Inspect the brake caliper.
6. If leaks or a damaged piston boot are found, install a new brake caliper.

To install:

7. Position the brake caliper and install the 2 brake caliper guide pin bolts until snug.
8. Tighten the RH caliper guide pin bolts in the following sequence:
    a. Tighten the top bolt to 24 ft. lbs. (33 Nm).
    b. Tighten the bottom bolt to 24 ft. lbs. (33 Nm).
9. Tighten the LH caliper guide pin bolts in the following sequence:
    a. Tighten the bottom bolt to 24 ft. lbs. (33 Nm).
    b. Tighten the top bolt to 24 ft. lbs. (33 Nm).
10. Using 2 new copper washers, position the front brake hose on the brake caliper and install the flow bolt. Tighten to 40 ft. lbs. (55 Nm).
11. Connect the parking brake cable and conduit to the brake caliper.
12. Install the retaining clip.
13. Bleed the caliper.
14. Install the wheel and tire.

DISC BRAKE PADS

REMOVAL & INSTALLATION

See Figure 9.

⁂ WARNING

Always install new brake shoes or pads at both ends of an axle to reduce the possibility of brakes pulling vehicle to one side. Failure to follow this instruction may result in uneven braking and serious personal injury.

➡Do not spill brake fluid on painted or plastic surfaces or damage to the surface may occur. If brake fluid is spilled onto a painted or plastic surface, immediately wash the surface with water.

1. Remove the wheel and tire.

➡Care must be used when servicing rear brake components without disconnecting the parking brake cable from the brake caliper lever. Carefully position the caliper aside using a suitable support or damage to the parking brake cable end fittings may occur.

➡Do not use caliper sight hole to retract pistons as this may damage the pistons and boots.

➡Do not allow the caliper to hang from the brake hose or damage to the hose may occur.

2. Remove the 2 brake caliper guide pin bolts and position the brake caliper aside.
3. Support the caliper using mechanic's wire.
4. Remove the brake pads and discard the spring clips.
5. Measure the brake disc thickness.
6. Install a new brake disc if not within specification.
7. Inspect the brake caliper.
8. If leaks or damaged boots are found, install a new brake caliper.
9. Inspect the brake caliper anchor plate assembly.
10. Check the guide pins and boots for binding and damage.
11. Replace worn or damaged pins. Lubricate the pins with the specified grease.
12. Install a new brake caliper anchor plate if it is worn or damaged.

To install:

13. Using the Rear Brake Caliper Piston Adjuster Adapter, compress the brake caliper piston into the brake caliper bore.
14. Position the notch in the caliper piston up and down to align with the alignment pin on the brake pad.

➡Do not allow grease, oil, brake fluid or other contaminants to contact the pad lining material, or damage to components may occur. Do not install contaminated pads.

➡Install all hardware supplied with the pad kit.

15. Install the 2 new spring clips and the brake pads.
16. Position the brake caliper on the

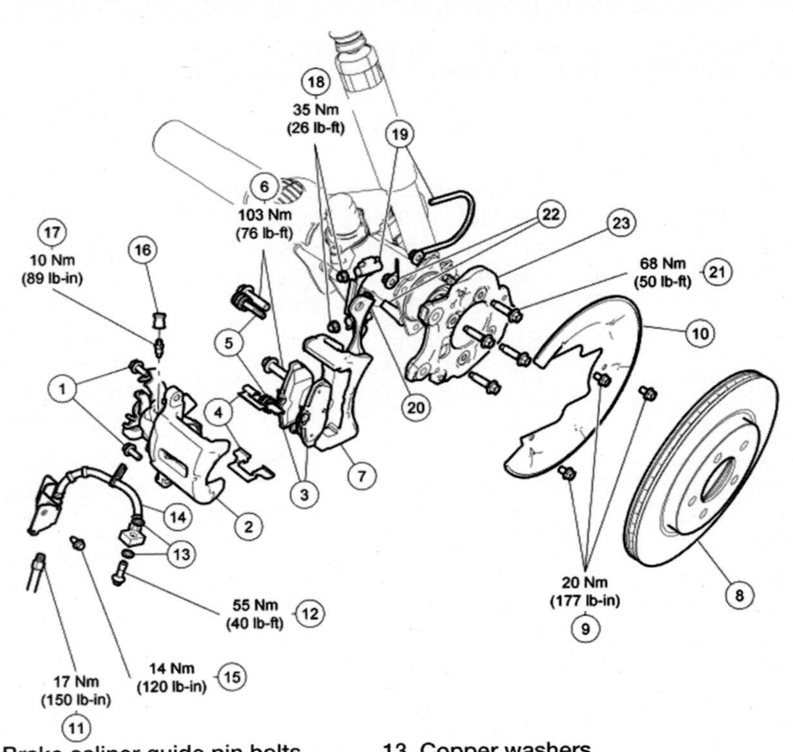

1. Brake caliper guide pin bolts
2. Brake caliper
3. Brake pads (kit)
4. Spring clips
5. Guide pin and boot
6. Brake caliper anchor plate bolt kits
7. Brake caliper anchor plate
8. Brake disc
9. Brake disc shield bolts
10. Brake disc shield
11. Brake tube fitting
12. Brake caliper flow bolt
13. Copper washers
14. Brake flexible hose
15. Brake flexible hose bracket bolt
16. Bleeder screw cap
17. Bleeder screw
18. Anti-moan bracket U-bolt nuts
19. Anti-moan bracket U-bolt and clamp
20. Anti-moan bracket (3.7L and 5.0L only)
21. Brake caliper support bracket bolts
22. Brake caliper support bracket flag nuts
23. Brake caliper support bracket

N0117243

Fig. 8 Exploded view of the rear brake system

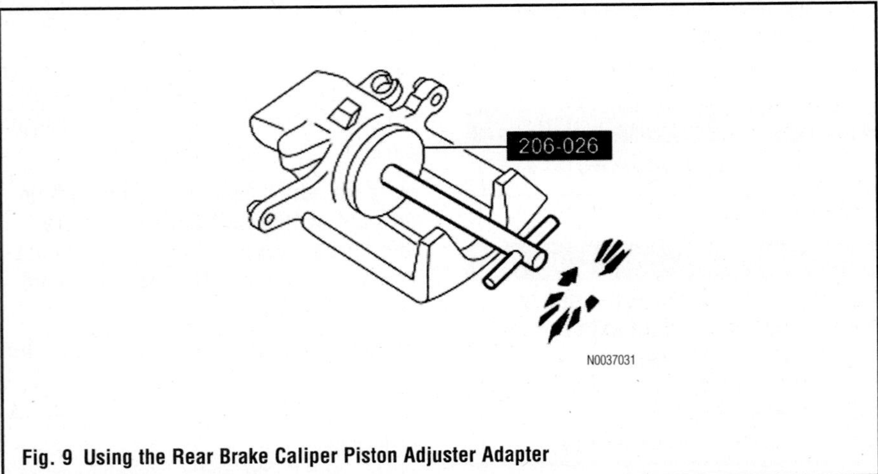

Fig. 9 Using the Rear Brake Caliper Piston Adjuster Adapter

anchor plate and install the 2 brake caliper guide pin bolts until snug.

17. Tighten the RH caliper guide pin bolts in the following sequence:
    a. Tighten the top bolt to 24 ft. lbs. (33 Nm).
    b. Tighten the bottom bolt to 24 ft. lbs. (33 Nm).
18. Tighten the LH caliper guide pin bolts in the following sequence:
    a. Tighten the bottom bolt to 24 ft. lbs. (33 Nm).
    b. Tighten the top bolt to 24 ft. lbs. (33 Nm).
19. Install the wheel and tire.
20. Apply brakes several times to verify correct brake operation.

PARKING BRAKE CABLES

ADJUSTMENT

See Figures 10 and 11.

➡Do not overtighten the parking brake cable adjustment nut. Overtightening will cause the brakes to drag or lock up.

1. Remove the access cover inside the floor console bin.
2. Position the parking brake handle up at the fourth notch to access the adjuster nut.

➡The rod is staked to prevent the removal of the nut.

3. Loosen, but do not remove, the parking brake cable adjuster nut.
4. Apply the tension by tightening the parking brake cable adjustment nut until there is no lash in the system with the handle in the lowered position.

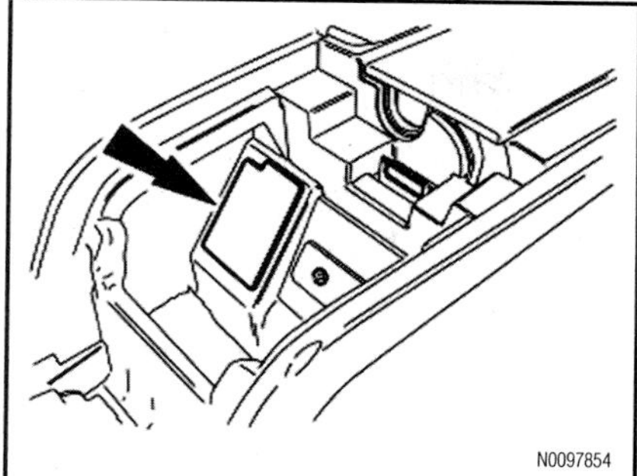

Fig. 10 Remove the access cover inside the floor console bin

5. Cycle the parking brake control 4 times and adjust as necessary.
6. Lower the parking brake handle and install the access cover.
7. Test the parking brake system for proper operation.

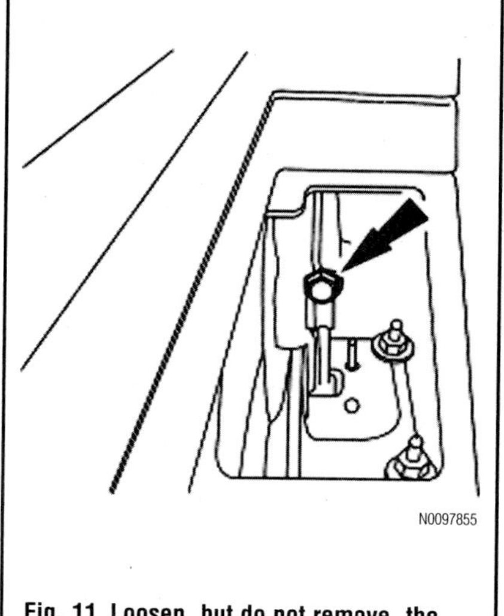

Fig. 11 Loosen, but do not remove, the parking brake cable adjuster nut

AIR BAG (SUPPLEMENTAL RESTRAINT SYSTEM)

GENERAL INFORMATION

⁂ CAUTION

These vehicles are equipped with an air bag system. The system must be disarmed before performing service on, or around, system components, the steering column, instrument panel components, wiring and sensors. Failure to follow the safety precautions and the disarming procedure could result in accidental air bag deployment, possible injury and unnecessary system repairs.

SERVICE PRECAUTIONS

Disconnect and isolate the battery negative cable before beginning any airbag system component diagnosis, testing, removal, or installation procedures. Allow system capacitor to discharge for two minutes before beginning any component service. This will disable the airbag system. Failure to disable the airbag system may result in accidental airbag deployment, personal injury, or death.

Do not place an intact undeployed airbag face down on a solid surface. The airbag will propel into the air if accidentally deployed and may result in personal injury or death.

When carrying or handling an undeployed airbag, the trim side (face) of the airbag should be pointing away from the body to minimize possibility of injury if accidental deployment occurs. Failure to do this may result in personal injury or death.

Replace airbag system components with OEM replacement parts. Substitute parts may appear interchangeable, but internal differences may result in inferior occupant protection. Failure to do so may result in occupant personal injury or death.

Wear safety glasses, rubber gloves, and long sleeved clothing when cleaning powder residue from vehicle after an airbag deployment. Powder residue emitted from a deployed airbag can cause skin irritation. Flush affected area with cool water if irritation is experienced. If nasal or throat irritation is experienced, exit the vehicle for fresh air until the irritation ceases. If irritation continues, see a physician.

Do not use a replacement airbag that is not in the original packaging. This may result in improper deployment, personal injury, or death.

The factory installed fasteners, screws and bolts used to fasten airbag components have a special coating and are specifically designed for the airbag system. Do not use substitute fasteners. Use only original equipment fasteners listed in the parts catalog when fastener replacement is required.

During, and following, any child restraint anchor service, due to impact event or vehicle repair, carefully inspect all mounting hardware, tether straps, and anchors for proper installation, operation, or damage. If a child restraint anchor is found damaged in any way, the anchor must be replaced. Failure to do this may result in personal injury or death.

Deployed and non-deployed airbags may or may not have live pyrotechnic material within the airbag inflator.

Do not dispose of driver/passenger/curtain airbags or seat belt tensioners unless you are sure of complete deployment. Refer to the Hazardous Substance Control System for proper disposal.

Dispose of deployed airbags and tensioners consistent with state, provincial, local, and federal regulations.

After any airbag component testing or service, do not connect the battery negative cable. Personal injury or death may result if the system test is not performed first.

If the vehicle is equipped with the Occupant Classification System (OCS), do not connect the battery negative cable before performing the OCS Verification Test using the scan tool and the appropriate diagnostic information. Personal injury or death may result if the system test is not performed properly.

Never replace both the Occupant Restraint Controller (ORC) and the Occupant Classification Module (OCM) at the same time. If both require replacement, replace one, then perform the Airbag System test before replacing the other.

Both the ORC and the OCM store Occupant Classification System (OCS) calibration data, which they transfer to one another when one of them is replaced. If both are replaced at the same time, an irreversible fault will be set in both modules and the OCS may malfunction and cause personal injury or death.

If equipped with OCS, the Seat Weight Sensor is a sensitive, calibrated unit and must be handled carefully. Do not drop or handle roughly. If dropped or damaged, replace with another sensor. Failure to do so may result in occupant injury or death.

If equipped with OCS, the front passenger seat must be handled carefully as well. When removing the seat, be careful when setting on floor not to drop. If dropped, the sensor may be inoperative, could result in occupant injury, or possibly death.

If equipped with OCS, when the passenger front seat is on the floor, no one should sit in the front passenger seat. This uneven force may damage the sensing ability of the seat weight sensors. If sat on and damaged, the sensor may be inoperative, could result in occupant injury, or possibly death.

DISARMING THE SYSTEM

➡The air bag warning indicator illuminates when the correct Restraints Control Module (RCM) fuse is removed and the ignition is ON.

➡The Supplemental Restraint System (SRS) must be fully operational and free of faults before releasing the vehicle to the customer.

1. Turn all vehicle accessories OFF.
2. Turn the ignition to OFF.
3. At the Smart Junction Box (SJB), located in the RH lower kick panel, remove the cover and the RCM fuse 31 (10A) from the SJB. For additional information, refer to the Wiring Diagrams manual.
4. Turn the ignition ON and monitor the air bag warning indicator for at least 30 seconds. The air bag warning indicator will remain lit continuously (no flashing) if the correct RCM fuse has been removed. If the air bag warning indicator does not remain lit continuously, remove the correct RCM fuse before proceeding.
5. Turn the ignition OFF.

⁂ WARNING

Always deplete the backup power supply before repairing or installing any new front or side air bag supplemental restraint system (SRS) component and before servicing, removing, installing, adjusting or striking components near the front or side impact sensors or the restraints control module (RCM). Nearby components include doors, instrument panel, console, door latches, strikers, seats and hood latches. To deplete the backup power supply energy, disconnect the battery ground cable and wait at least 1 minute. Be sure to disconnect auxiliary batteries and power supplies (if equipped). Failure to follow these instructions may result in serious personal injury or death in the event of an accidental deployment.

6. Disconnect the battery ground cable and wait at least one minute.
7. Remove the driver air bag module.
8. Open and lower the glove compartment door.
9. Disconnect the passenger air bag module electrical connector.
10. Release the locking tab and disconnect the passenger seat side air bag module electrical connector.
11. Release the locking tab and disconnect the driver seat side air bag module electrical connector.
12. Install RCM fuse 31 (10A) to the RCM.
13. Connect the battery ground cable.

ARMING THE SYSTEM

1. Remove RCM fuse 31 (10A) from the SJB.
2. Disconnect the battery ground cable and wait at least one minute.
3. Connect the driver seat side air bag module electrical connector and close the red locking tab.
4. Connect the passenger seat side air bag module electrical connector and close the red locking tab.
5. Connect the passenger air bag module electrical connector.
6. Install the driver air bag module.
7. Turn the ignition from OFF to ON.
8. Install RCM fuse 31 (10A) to the SJB and close the cover.

⁂ WARNING

Make sure no one is in the vehicle and there is nothing blocking or placed in front of any air bag module when the battery is connected. Failure to follow these instructions may result in serious personal injury in the event of an accidental deployment.

9. Connect the battery ground cable.
10. Prove out the SRS as follows:
    a. Turn the ignition from ON to OFF.
    b. Wait 10 seconds, then turn the ignition ON and monitor the air bag warning indicator with the air bag modules installed. The air bag warning indicator will light continuously for approximately 6 seconds and then turn off. If an air bag SRS fault is detected, the air bag warning indicator will: - fail to light. - remain lit continuously. - flash. The flashing might not occur until approximately 30 seconds after the ignition has been turned from the OFF to the ON position. This is the time required to complete testing of the SRS.
    c. If the air bag warning indicator is inoperative and a SRS fault exists, a chime will sound in a pattern of 5 sets of 5 beeps. If this occurs, the air bag warning indicator and any SRS fault discovered must be diagnosed and repaired. Clear all RCM and Occupant Classification System Module (OCSM) Continuous Memory Diagnostic Trouble Codes (CMDTCs).

CLOCKSPRING CENTERING

1. If a new clockspring was installed and the anti-rotation key has been removed before the steering wheel is installed or the same clockspring is being installed, rotate the clockspring inner rotor counterclockwise and carefully feel for the ribbon wire to run out of length with slight resistance.
2. Stop rotating the clockspring inner rotor at this point.
3. Starting with the clockspring inner rotor in the 12 o'clock position, rotate the inner rotor clockwise through 2 revolutions to center the clockspring.
4. The clockspring inner rotor must be in the 12 o'clock position to be correctly centered.

AUTOMATIC TRANSMISSION FLUID

DRAIN AND REFILL

See Figures 12 and 13.

1. With the vehicle in PARK, position it on a hoist. Set the vehicle as close to level as possible.
2. Remove the transmission fluid pan drain plug (large plug) and allow the transmission fluid to drain.
3. Refill:
4. Install the transmission fluid pan drain plug. Tighten to 19 ft. lbs. (26 Nm).
5. Hold the larger transmission fluid pan drain plug with a wrench and remove the small (center) transmission fluid level indicator plug.
6. Install the Transmission Fluid Fill Tool into the transmission fluid pan.

➡Prior to filling the Transporter Fluid Evacuator/Injector with transmission fluid, make sure that the canister is clean.

7. Fill the Transporter Fluid Evacuator/Injector with transmission fluid.
8. Hang the Transporter Fluid Evacuator/Injector under the vehicle, upright and close to the transmission.
9. Connect the Transporter Fluid Evacuator/Injector.
10. Connect the open end of the fluid hose from the Transporter Fluid Evacuator/Injector to the Transmission Fluid Fill Tool at the bottom of the transmission fluid pan.
11. Apply a maximum of 30 psi to the open end of the vacuum/pressure hose from the Rubber Tip Air Nozzle. Transmission fluid will immediately start flowing out of the Transporter Fluid Evacuator/Injector into the transmission fluid pan.
12. Add 2 or 3 quarts of transmission fluid into the transmission fluid pan. Stop the process by releasing the air pressure and removing the Rubber Tip Air Nozzle from the end of the hose.

➡Engine idle speed is approximately 650 rpm.

13. Using the scan tool, start and run the engine until the Transmission Fluid Temperature (TFT) is between 80°-120°F.
14. Inspect the transmission fluid level in the Transporter Fluid Evacuator/Injector. If the fluid drains back into the canister, the transmission is full. If no transmission fluid drains back, more transmission fluid will need to be added.
15. Once the transmission is full, place a hand Vacuum Pump Kit on the open end of the vacuum/pressure hose on the Transporter Fluid Evacuator/Injector and apply vacuum to the system. This will pull out any extra fluid trapped in the system and direct it into the container.
16. Allow the transmission fluid to drain. When the transmission fluid comes out as a thin stream or drip, the transmission fluid is at the correct level.
17. Reinstall the small (center) transmission fluid level indicator plug. Tighten to 7 ft. lbs. (10 Nm).

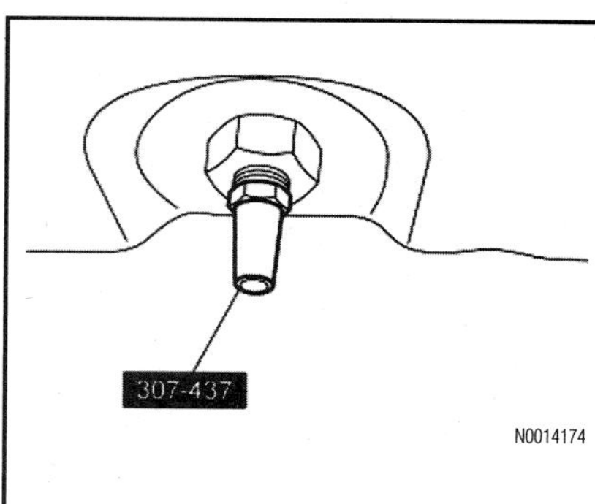

Fig. 12 Install the Transmission Fluid Fill Tool

Fig. 13 Fill the Transporter Fluid Evacuator/Injector with transmission fluid

FLUID COOLER BACKFLUSHING

➡Do not use any supplemental transmission fluid additives or cleaning agents. The use of these products could cause internal transmission components to fail; this will affect the operation of the transmission.

➡Transmission fluid cooler backflushing and cleaning will be performed using the Transmission Heated Cooler Line Flusher or equivalent. Follow the manufacturer's instructions included with the machine. Test the equipment to make sure that a vigorous fluid flow is present before proceeding.

➡If the Transmission Heated Cooler Line Flusher or equivalent is not available, install a new transmission fluid cooler and/or an auxiliary transmission fluid cooler will be required.

1. Check and top off the fluid level of the cooler line flusher with transmission fluid.
2. Allow the transmission fluid in the cooler line flusher 15-30 minutes to heat up to 140°F before using.
3. Install the line adapters into the transmission fluid cooler tubes.
4. Attach the cooler line flusher red line to the transmission fluid cooler pressure tube quick connect fitting.
5. Attach the cooler line flusher blue line to the transmission fluid cooler return tube quick connect fitting.
6. Follow the equipment instructions to purge the transmission fluid cooler tubes and cooler prior to starting the flushing procedure.
7. Allow the transmission fluid cooling system to backflush for 10-15 minutes, then flush the transmission fluid cooler in a normal flow direction for an additional 10-15 minutes.

FILTER REPLACEMENT

See Figures 14 and 15.

➡The use of any transmission fluid other than specified can result in the transmission failing to operate in a normal manner or transmission failure.

1. With the vehicle in NEUTRAL, position it on a hoist.
2. Remove the transmission fluid fill plug transmission fluid level indicator assembly located on the passenger side front portion of the transmission case. Removal of the transmission fluid fill plug will relieve any vacuum that might have built up in the transmission. This will aid in allowing the transmission fluid pan to be easily removed when the bolts are removed.
3. Remove the transmission fluid pan and allow the transmission fluid to drain.
4. Remove the transmission fluid pan gasket.

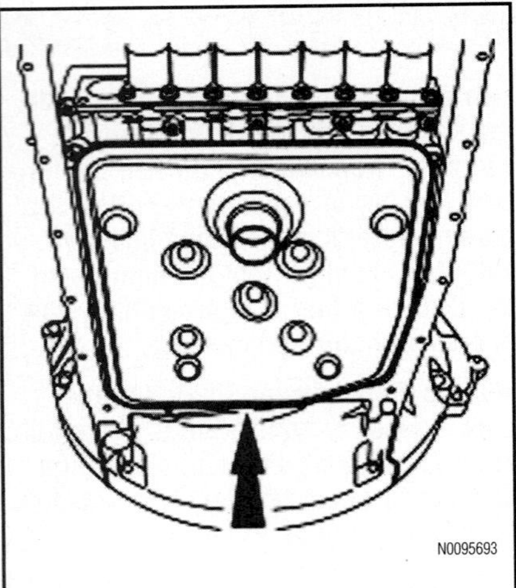

Fig. 14 Remove and discard the transmission fluid filter

➡The transmission fluid filter may be reused if no excessive contamination is indicated.

5. Remove and discard the transmission fluid filter.
6. Clean and inspect the transmission fluid pan and magnet.

To install:

➡If the transmission is being repaired for a contamination-related failure, install a new transmission fluid filter and seal assembly. The transmission fluid filter may be reused if no excessive contamination is indicated.

7. Inspect the transmission case for the transmission fluid filter seal. If the seal is in the case, carefully remove the seal without scratching the case.
8. Make sure that the seal is on the transmission fluid filter and lubricate the seal with automatic transmission fluid.

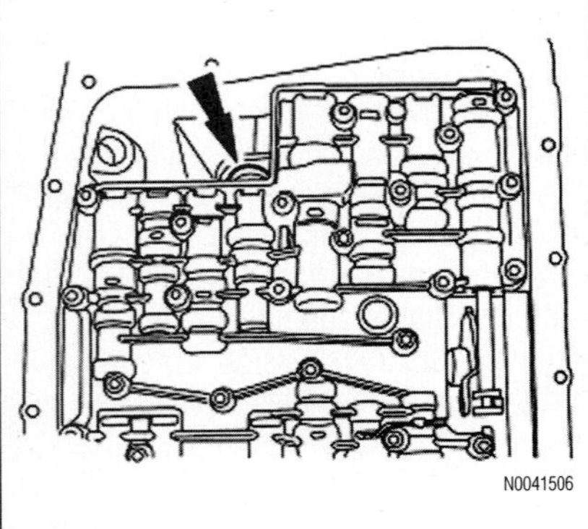

Fig. 15 Locating the transmission fluid filter seal

➡The transmission fluid filter may be reused if no excessive contamination is indicated.

9. If required, install a new transmission fluid filter.
10. Position the magnet in the transmission fluid pan.

➡The transmission fluid pan gasket can be reused if not damaged.

11. Install a new transmission fluid pan gasket if required.
12. Install the transmission fluid pan and tighten the bolts in a crisscross pattern.
13. Tighten to 9 ft. lbs. (12 Nm).
14. Fill and check the transmission fluid.

MANUAL TRANSMISSION ASSEMBLY

REMOVAL & INSTALLATION

Mt82 Getrag Transmission

See Figures 16 through 19.

1. With the vehicle in NEUTRAL, position it on a hoist.
2. Disconnect the battery ground cable.
3. If equipped, remove the 4 nuts and the strut tower cross brace.

➡If the engine appearance cover is not removed it will be damaged when lowering transmission.

4. Remove engine appearance cover.
5. Remove the gearshift lever knob and position the floor console finish panel aside.
6. Turn the gearshift lever knob in a counterclockwise direction.
7. Vehicles equipped with 5.0L:
   a. Using a suitable holding device, hold the steering wheel in the straight-ahead position.
   b. Remove the 2 steering column dash boot bearing nuts.
   c. Remove and discard the RH catalytic converter-to-exhaust manifold nut.
   d. If equipped, remove the 9 screws and the lower air deflector.
   e. Loosen the 2 crossmember brace nuts.
   f. Remove the 6 crossmember brace bolts and remove the crossmember brace.
   g. Disconnect the Catalyst Monitor Sensor (CMS) and the reverse lamp switch electrical connectors.
   h. Disconnect the CMS and the Output Shaft Speed (OSS) sensor electrical connectors.

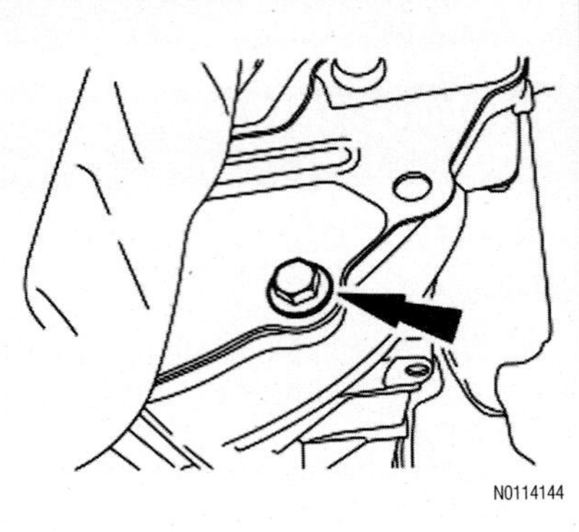

Fig. 16 Remove the 2 engine spacer plate-to-transmission bolts

   i. Remove and discard the 2 LH catalytic converter-to-exhaust manifold nuts.
   j. Remove and discard the RH catalytic converter-to-exhaust manifold nut.
   k. Using a jackstand, support the intermediate pipe and loosen the 2 exhaust (H-pipe) clamps.
   l. Remove the catalytic converter (H-pipe) assembly from the vehicle.
   m. Remove and discard the gaskets.
   n. Remove the 2 engine spacer plate-to-transmission bolts.
8. Vehicles equipped with 3.7L:
   a. Remove the catalytic converter assembly (H-pipe).
   b. Disconnect the OSS sensor and the reverse lamp switch electrical connectors.
9. All vehicles:
10. Remove the driveshaft. For additional information, refer to Driveshaft.
11. Remove the starter motor. For additional information, refer to Starter in Engine Electrical.
12. Remove the 4 subframe cross brace nuts and the subframe cross brace.

➡If transmission disassembly is required, drain the transmission fluid.

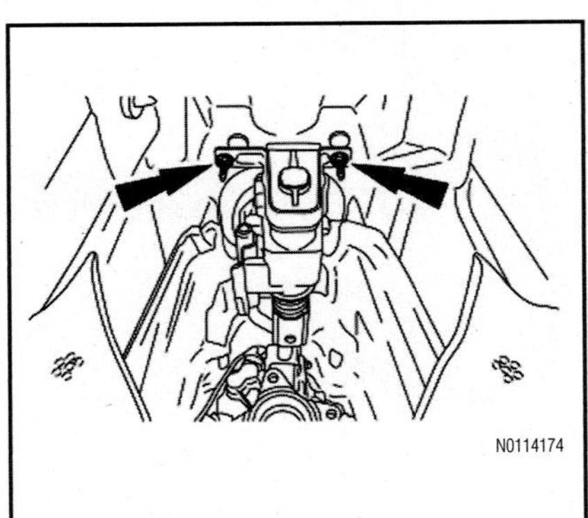

Fig. 17 Remove the 2 gearshift lever nuts

13. Remove the drain plug and drain the transmission fluid. Install the drain plug. Tighten to 26 ft. lbs. (35 Nm).
14. Remove the 2 gearshift lever nuts.
15. Position a transmission jack and support the transmission.
16. Remove the transmission crossmember.
17. Vehicles equipped with 5.0L:

➡Do not allow the steering wheel to rotate while the steering column intermediate shaft is disconnected or damage to the clockspring can result. If there is evidence that the wheel has rotated, remove and recenter the clockspring.

a. Remove and discard the steering column shaft pinch bolt and disconnect the steering column shaft.
b. Using two adjustable jackstands, support the subframe.

➡Mark the bolts and the crossmember for assembly reference.

NOTE: LH shown, RH similar.

c. Remove the 4 rear subframe bolts.
d. Loosen but do not remove the 4 front subframe nuts.
e. Using the adjustable jackstands, lower the subframe 26 mm (1.023 in).

18. All vehicles:
19. Partially lower the transmission.
20. Disconnect wiring harness clips and position the wiring harness aside.
21. If equipped, disconnect the skip shift solenoid.

➡Do not spill brake fluid on painted or plastic surfaces or damage to the surface may occur. If brake fluid is spilled onto a painted or plastic surface, immediately wash the surface with water.

22. Release the clutch hydraulic tube clip and disconnect the clutch hydraulic tube from the clutch slave cylinder connector.
23. Drain the fluid into a suitable container.
24. Vehicles equipped with 3.7L:
a. Remove the 2 engine-to-transmission bolts.
25. All vehicles:
26. Remove the 4 transmission-to-engine bolts and 3 transmission-to-engine stud bolts.
27. Pull the transmission rearward until the input shaft is clear of the pressure plate, then lower the transmission from the vehicle.

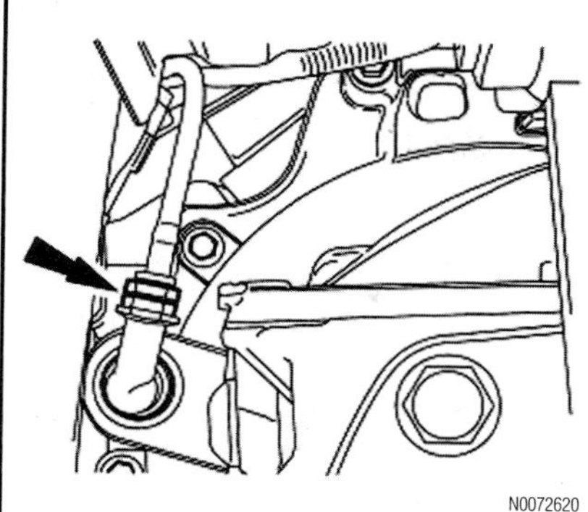

Fig. 18 Disconnect the clutch hydraulic tube from the clutch slave cylinder connector

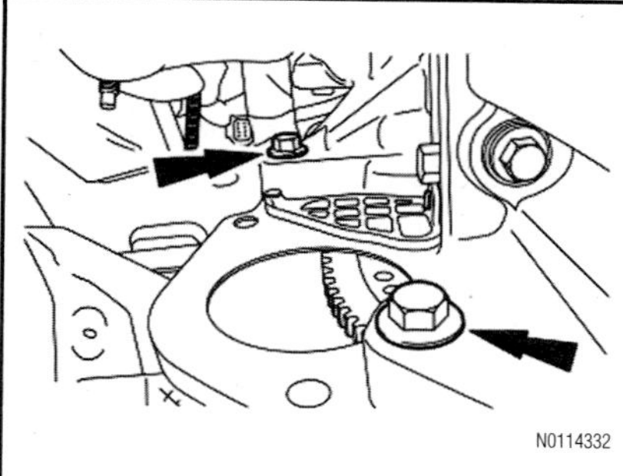

Fig. 19 Remove the 2 engine-to-transmission bolts

To install:

WARNING

Do not breathe dust or use compressed air to blow dust from storage containers or friction components. Remove dust using government-approved techniques. Friction component dust may be a cancer and lung disease hazard. Exposure to potentially hazardous components may occur if dusts are created during repair of friction components, such as brake pads and clutch discs. Exposure may also cause irritation to skin, eyes and respiratory tract, and may cause allergic reactions and/or may lead to other chronic health effects. If irritation persists, seek medical attention or advice. Failure to follow these instructions may result in serious personal injury.

➡Before installing the transmission, clean and lubricate the input shaft with a small amount of grease.

28. Position the transmission to the engine.
29. Install the 4 transmission-to-engine bolts and 3 transmission-to-engine stud bolts. Tighten to 35 ft. lbs. (48 Nm).
30. Vehicles equipped with a 3.7L engine:
a. Install the 2 engine-to-transmission bolts. Tighten to 35 ft. lbs. (48 Nm).
31. All vehicles:
32. Connect the clutch slave cylinder tube to the clutch slave cylinder connector.
33. Attach the clutch hydraulic tube clip.
34. Position the wiring harness and connect the wiring harness clips.
35. If equipped, connect the skip shift solenoid.
36. Partially raise the transmission.
37. Vehicles equipped with a 5.0L engine:
a. Using the adjustable jackstands, raise the subframe to the marked position.
b. Install the 4 rear subframe bolts. Tighten to 85 ft. lbs. (115 Nm).
c. Tighten the 4 front subframe nuts. Tighten to 85 ft. lbs. (115 Nm).
d. Connect the steering column shaft and install the new steering column shaft pinch bolt. Tighten to 35 ft. lbs. (48 Nm).
38. All vehicles
39. Install the transmission crossmember.
40. Install the 2 gearshift lever nuts.
41. Install the starter motor. For additional information, refer to Starter.
42. Install the subframe cross brace and the 4 subframe cross brace nuts. Tighten to 35 ft. lbs. (48 Nm).
43. Install the driveshaft. For additional information, refer to Driveshaft.
44. Vehicles equipped with a 3.7L engine:
a. Connect the Output Shaft Speed (OSS) sensor and the reverse lamp switch electrical connectors.
b. Install the catalytic converter assembly (H-pipe).
c. Vehicles equipped with a 5.0L engine:
d. Install the 2 engine spacer plate-to-transmission bolts. Tighten to 26 ft. lbs. (35 Nm).

➡Prior to installing the catalytic converter (H-pipe) assembly, inspect the Heated Oxygen Sensor (HO2S) and the Catalyst Monitor Sensor (CMS) wiring harness for damage.

e. Using new gaskets, position the catalytic converter (H-pipe) assembly to the vehicle and support with a suitable jackstand.

➡**Tighten the catalytic converter-to-exhaust manifold nuts alternately in increments to maintain torque and to draw the flange evenly making sure correct alignment of the exhaust system.**

f. Install the 2 new LH catalytic converter-to-exhaust manifold nuts. Tighten to 30 ft. lbs. (40 Nm).

➡**Tighten the catalytic converter-to-exhaust manifold nuts alternately in increments to maintain torque and to draw the flange evenly making sure correct alignment of the exhaust system.**

g. Install the 2 new RH catalytic converter-to-exhaust manifold nuts. Tighten to 30 ft. lbs. (40 Nm).

h. Tighten the 2 exhaust (H-pipe) clamps. Tighten to 35 ft. lbs. (48 Nm).

➡**Inspect the CMS and reverse lamp switch wiring harness for damage.**

i. Connect the CMS and the reverse lamp switch electrical connectors.

➡**Inspect the CMS and OSS wiring harness for damage.**

j. Connect the CMS and the OSS sensor electrical connectors.

k. Install the crossmember brace and 6 crossmember brace bolts. Tighten to 35 ft. lbs. (48 Nm).

l. Tighten the 2 crossmember brace nuts. Tighten to 35 ft. lbs. (48 Nm).

m. If equipped, install the lower air deflector and install the 9 screws.

45. All vehicles

➡**The use of any other transmission fluid than specified can result in the transmission failing to operate in a normal manner or transmission failure.**

46. Check, and as necessary, fill the transmission with transmission fluid.

a. Vehicles equipped with a 5.0L engine

b. Install the 2 dash boot bearing nuts.

47. All vehicles:

48. Lightly pull up on the gearshift lever boot to fully seat the gearshift lever boot to the floor pan.

49. Install the floor console finish panel and the gearshift lever knob.

50. Engage anti-rotation tabs of trim boot into holes at top of gearshift lever.

51. Turn the gearshift lever knob in a clockwise direction.

52. If equipped, install the strut tower cross brace and 4 nuts. Tighten to 26 ft. lbs. (35 Nm).

53. Connect the battery ground cable.

➡**Do not spill brake fluid on painted or plastic surfaces or damage to the surface may occur. If brake fluid is spilled onto a painted or plastic surface, immediately wash the surface with water.**

54. Fill the brake and clutch reservoir.

➡**If the input shaft was replaced, use the scan tool to perform the Misfire Monitor Neutral Profile Correction procedure, following the on-screen instructions.**

T50D Transmission

See Figures 20 through 22.

➡**Do not separate the transmission from the clutch housing. Remove the transmission and clutch housing as an assembly.**

1. With the vehicle in NEUTRAL, position it on a hoist.

2. Disconnect the battery ground cable.

➡**Index-mark the driveshaft to the output shaft flange.**

3. Remove the driveshaft. For additional information, refer to Driveshaft.

4. Remove the transmission shift linkage bolt and the gearshift lever bolt. Disconnect the shift linkage from the transmission.

5. Disconnect the wiring harness to the transmission. Disconnect the following:

a. Catalyst Monitor Sensor (CMS) electrical connector.

b. Reverse lamp switch electrical connector.

c. Wiring harness clips.

6. Disconnect the Output Shaft Speed (OSS) sensor electrical connector.

7. Remove the 2 starter motor bolts and position the starter motor aside. Using mechanic's wire, support the starter motor.

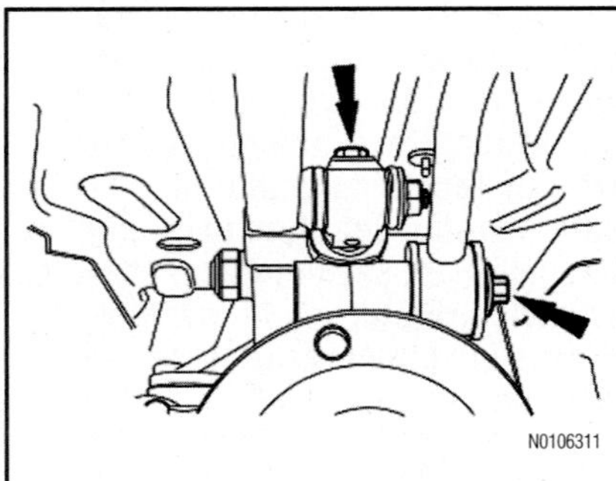

Fig. 20 Remove the transmission shift linkage bolt and the gearshift lever bolt

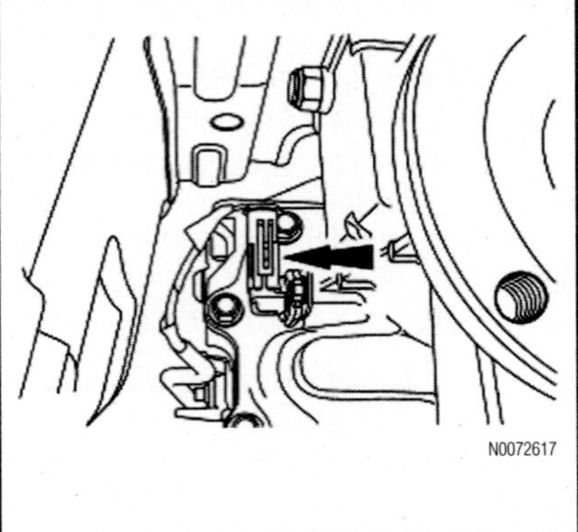

Fig. 21 Disconnect the Output Shaft Speed (OSS) sensor electrical connector

➡**Take note that the hump side of the crossmember goes down.**

8. Remove the crossmember.

9. Release the clutch hydraulic tube clip and separate the connector from the clutch slave cylinder.

10. Loosen the exhaust coupler and disconnect the intermediate pipe from the catalytic converter. Discard the exhaust coupler.

11. Remove the 8 transmission-to-engine bolts and the separator plate bolt.

12. Pull the transmission rearward until the input shaft is clear of the pressure plate, then lower the transmission from the vehicle.

To install:

➡**Before installing the transmission, the input shaft must be cleaned and lubricated with a small amount of grease.**

13. Position the transmission to the engine.

➡**Insert the clutch hydraulic tube into the clutch slave cylinder and install the clip before tightening the transmission-to-engine bolts.**

14. Install the 8 transmission-to-engine bolts and the separator plate bolt. Tighten to 33 ft. lbs. (45 Nm).

15. Install a new exhaust coupler. Connect the intermediate pipe to the catalytic converter. Tighten to 40 ft. lbs. (54 Nm).

➡**The hump side on the crossmember goes down.**

16. Install the transmission crossmember.

➡**Clean the starter motor mounting flange and mating surface of the starter motor to make sure of a proper ground connection.**

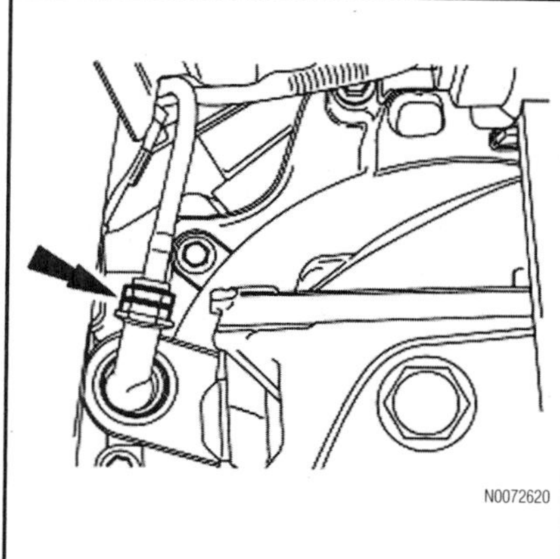
Fig. 22 Release the clutch hydraulic tube clip

17. Install the starter motor and the 2 starter motor bolts. Tighten to 18 ft. lbs. (25 Nm).
18. Connect the Output Shaft Speed (OSS) sensor electrical connector.
19. Connect the wiring harness to the transmission. Connect the following:
    a. Catalyst Monitor Sensor (CMS) electrical connector
    b. Reverse lamp switch electrical connector
    c. Wiring harness clips
20. Connect the shift linkage to the transmission:
    a. Tighten the gearshift lever bolt to 133 inch lbs. (15 Nm).
    b. Tighten the transmission shift linkage bolt to 30 ft. lbs. (40 Nm).

➡Align the index marks made during removal.

21. Install the driveshaft.
22. Check, and as necessary, fill the transmission with transmission fluid. Apply threadlock and sealer to the fill plug threads and install the fill plug.
    a. Total fill capacity is 2.6L (2.8 pt).
    b. Tighten to 159 inch lbs. (18 Nm).
23. Connect the battery ground cable.
24. Fill the brake and clutch reservoir.

TR3650 Transmission

See Figures 23 through 26.

1. With the vehicle in NEUTRAL, position it on a hoist.
2. Disconnect the battery ground cable.
3. Remove the gearshift lever knob and boot.
4. Turn the gearshift lever knob in a counterclockwise direction.
5. Remove the catalytic converter H-pipe. For additional information, refer to Exhaust.

➡Index-mark the driveshaft flange and pinion flange, and the driveshaft flange and output shaft flange.

6. Remove the driveshaft. For additional information, refer to Driveshaft.
7. Remove the 3 starter motor bolts and position the starter motor aside.
8. Remove the 4 subframe cross brace nuts and the subframe cross brace.
9. Disconnect the reverse lamp switch electrical connector. Disconnect the wiring harness from the transmission.
10. Disconnect the Output Shaft Speed (OSS) sensor electrical connector. Disconnect the wiring harness from the transmission.
11. If transmission disassembly is necessary, remove the drain plug and drain the transmission fluid.
12. Position a transmission jack and support the transmission.

➡Take note that the hump side of the crossmember goes up.

13. Remove the transmission crossmember. For additional information, refer Automatic Transmission.
14. Lower the transmission.
15. Remove the 2 rear gearshift lever nuts.

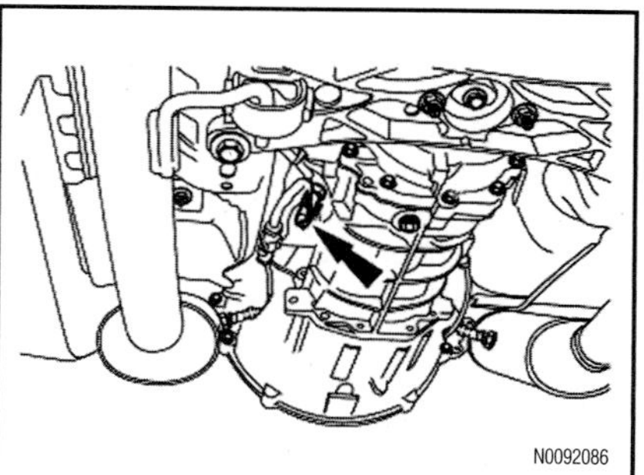
Fig. 23 Locating the reverse lamp switch electrical connector

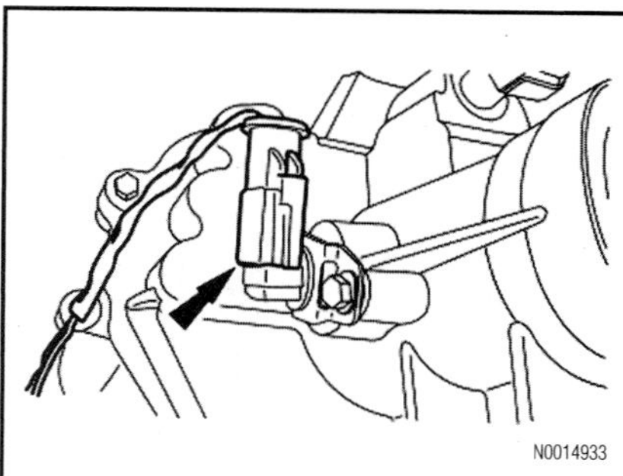
Fig. 24 Disconnect the Output Shaft Speed (OSS) sensor electrical connector

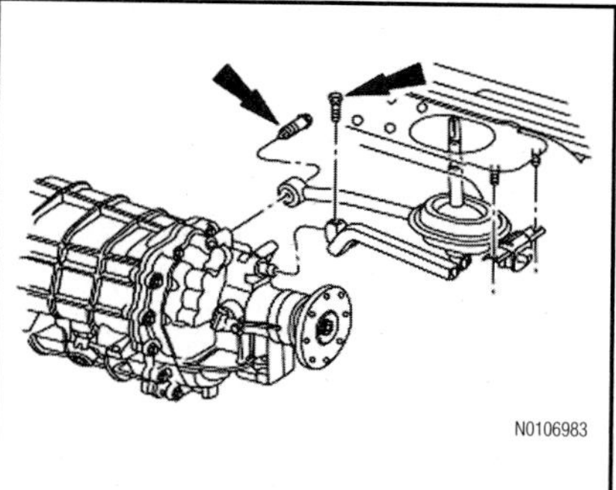
Fig. 25 Remove the gearshift lever assembly bolts and the gearshift assembly

➡Transmission removed for clarity.

Remove the gearshift lever assembly bolts and the gearshift assembly.

16. Detach the wire harness retaining clip from the transmission.

➡Do not spill brake fluid on painted or plastic surfaces or damage to the surface may occur. If brake fluid is spilled onto a painted or plastic surface, immediately wash the surface with water.

17. Release the clutch hydraulic tube clip and separate the connector from the clutch slave cylinder.
18. Remove the 2 spacer plate bolts.
19. Remove the 7 transmission-to-engine bolts.
20. Rotate the transmission 30 degrees counterclockwise. Securely strap the transmission to the transmission jack.
21. Pull the transmission rearward until the input shaft is clear of the pressure plate, then lower the transmission from the vehicle.

To install:

➡Before installing the transmission, the input shaft must be cleaned and lubricated with a small amount of grease.

Position the transmission to the transmission jack at a 30 degree counterclockwise angle and securely strap the transmission to the transmission jack.

22. Position the transmission to the engine. Rotate the transmission clockwise and align the dowels.

➡Insert the clutch hydraulic tube into the clutch slave cylinder and install the clip before tightening the transmission-to-engine bolts.

23. Install the 7 transmission-to-engine bolts. Tighten to 33 ft. lbs. (45 Nm).

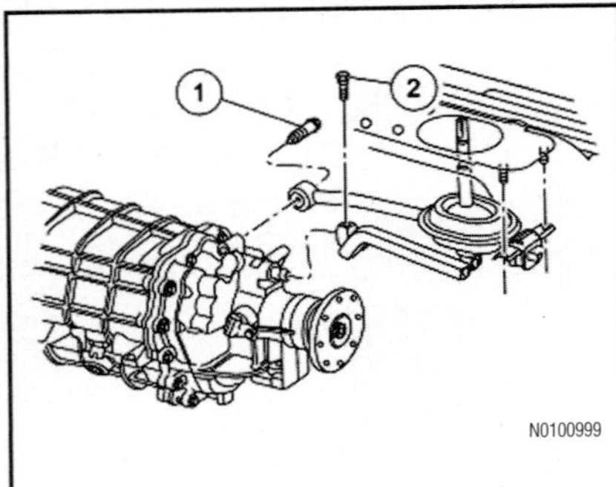

Fig. 26 Install the gearshift lever assembly bolts (1, 2)

24. Install the 2 spacer plate bolts. Tighten to 26 ft. lbs. (35 Nm).
25. Attach the wire harness retainer clip to the transmission.
26. Connect the shift linkage to the transmission and install the gearshift lever assembly bolts.
    a. Tighten to 30 ft. lbs. (40 Nm).
    b. Tighten to 10 ft. lbs. (15 Nm).
27. Install the 2 rear gearshift lever nuts.

➡The hump side of the crossmember goes up.

28. Install the transmission crossmember.
29. Connect the Output Shaft Speed (OSS) sensor electrical connector and attach the wiring harness to the transmission.
30. Install the catalytic converter H-pipe. For additional information, refer to Exhaust.
31. Connect the reverse lamp switch electrical connector and attach the wiring harness to the transmission.
32. Install the subframe cross brace and the 4 subframe cross brace nuts. Tighten to 35 ft. lbs. (48 Nm).
33. Install the starter and the 3 starter motor bolts. Tighten to 18 ft. lbs. (25 Nm).
34. Install the driveshaft. For additional information, refer to Driveshaft.
35. Fill the transmission with transmission fluid as necessary.
36. Install the gearshift lever boot and knob.
37. Turn the gearshift lever knob in a clockwise direction.
38. Connect the battery ground cable.
39. Fill the brake and clutch reservoir. Bleed the clutch hydraulic system.

TR6060

See Figures 27 through 31.

WARNING

Do not breathe dust or use compressed air to blow dust from storage containers or friction components. Remove dust using government-approved techniques. Friction component dust may be a cancer and lung disease hazard. Exposure to potentially hazardous components may occur if dusts are created during repair of friction components, such as brake pads and clutch discs. Exposure may also cause irritation to skin, eyes and respiratory tract, and may cause allergic reactions and/or may lead to other chronic health effects. If irritation persists, seek medical attention or advice. Failure to follow these instructions may result in serious personal injury.

1. With the vehicle in NEUTRAL, position it on a hoist.
2. Disconnect the battery ground cable.
3. If equipped, remove the 4 nuts and the strut tower cross brace.
4. Position the floor console finish panel aside.
5. Remove the 2 upper gearshift lever bolts and the upper gearshift lever.
6. Using a suitable holding device, hold the steering wheel in the straight-ahead position.
7. Remove the 2 steering column dash boot bearing nuts.
8. If equipped, remove the 9 screws and the lower air deflector.
9. Loosen the 2 crossmember brace nuts.
10. Remove the 6 crossmember brace bolts and remove the crossmember brace.
11. Remove the catalytic converter assembly (H-pipe).

➡Index-mark the driveshaft flange and pinion flange, and the driveshaft flange and transmission output shaft flange.

12. Remove the driveshaft. For additional information, refer to Driveshaft.
13. Remove the starter motor. For additional information, refer to Starter.
14. Remove the 4 subframe cross brace nuts and the subframe cross brace.

➡If transmission disassembly is required, drain the transmission fluid.

15. Remove the drain plug and drain the transmission fluid.
16. Clean the drain plug. Apply thread-lock and sealer to the plug threads and install the drain plug. Tighten to 20 ft. lbs. (27 Nm).
17. Remove the 2 gearshift lever nuts.
18. Position a transmission jack and support the transmission.
19. Remove the transmission crossmember.

➡Do not allow the steering wheel to rotate while the steering column intermediate shaft is disconnected or damage to the clockspring can result. If there is evidence that the wheel has rotated, remove and recenter the clockspring.

20. Remove and discard the steering column shaft pinch bolt and disconnect the steering column shaft.
21. Using two adjustable jackstands, support the subframe.

➡Mark the bolts and the crossmember for assembly reference.

22. Remove the 4 rear subframe bolts.
23. Loosen but do not remove the 4 front subframe nuts.
24. Using the adjustable jackstands, lower the subframe 26 mm (1.023 in).
25. Partially lower the transmission.
26. Remove the wiring harness retaining nut.
27. Disconnect the wiring harness from the LH side of the transmission and position the wiring harness aside.
28. Disconnect the reverse lockout solenoid electrical connector.

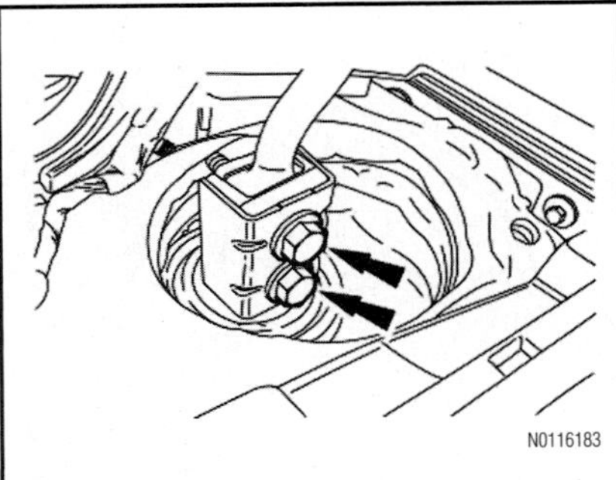

Fig. 27 Remove the 2 upper gearshift lever bolts and the upper gearshift lever

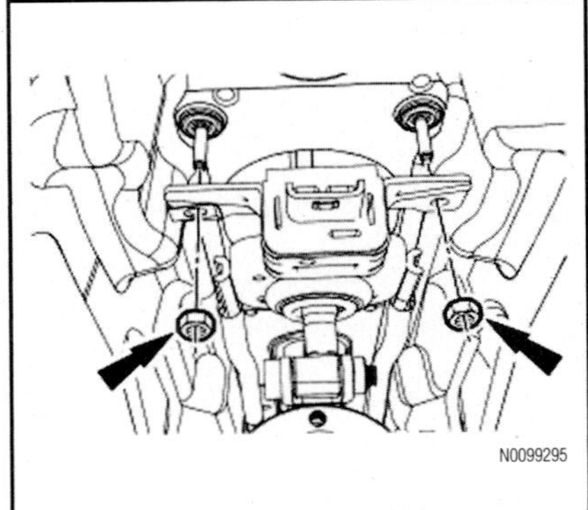

Fig. 28 Remove the 2 gearshift lever nuts

29. Disconnect the 2 wiring harness clips.

30. Disconnect the wiring harness from the RH side of the transmission and position the wiring harness aside.

31. Disconnect the Output Shaft Speed (OSS) sensor electrical connector.

32. Disconnect the reverse lamp switch electrical connector.

33. Disconnect the 2 wiring harness clips.

➡Do not spill brake fluid on painted or plastic surfaces or damage to the surface may occur. If brake fluid is spilled onto a painted or plastic surface, immediately wash the surface with water.

34. Release the clutch hydraulic tube clip and disconnect the clutch hydraulic tube from the clutch slave cylinder connector.

35. Drain the fluid into a suitable container.

36. Remove the 2 engine spacer plate-to-transmission bolts.

WARNING

Secure the assembly to the jack. Avoid any obstructions while lowering and raising the jack. Contact with obstructions may cause the assembly to fall off the jack, which may result in serious personal injury.

37. Remove the 6 transmission-to-engine bolts and the transmission-to-engine stud bolt.

➡Disconnect the wiring harness clip from the top of the transmission before rotating the transmission.

38. Using the transmission jack, rotate the transmission 45 degrees clockwise. Pull the transmission rearward until the input shaft is clear of the pressure plate, then lower the transmission from the vehicle.

39. Disconnect the wiring harness clip from the top of the transmission.

40. If necessary, remove the gearshift lever assembly.

a. Insert a suitable tool into the lower holes to unlock the clips.

b. Rotate the gearshift lever retainers, then remove the retainers.

c. Remove the gearshift lever bolt.

d. Remove the gearshift lever assembly.

To install:

WARNING

Do not breathe dust or use compressed air to blow dust from storage containers or friction components. Remove dust using government-approved techniques. Friction component dust may be a cancer and lung disease hazard. Exposure to potentially hazardous components may occur if dusts are created during repair of friction components, such as brake pads and clutch discs. Exposure may also cause irritation to skin, eyes and respiratory tract, and may cause allergic reactions and/or may lead to other chronic health effects. If irritation persists, seek medical attention or advice. Failure to follow these instructions may result in serious personal injury.

41. If removed, install the gearshift lever assembly.

42. Position the gearshift assembly on the transmission.

43. Install the gearshift assembly bolt. Tighten to 30 ft. lbs. (40 Nm).

44. Position the gearshift lever assembly retainers. Rotate the gearshift lever retainers to lock the clips.

➡Before installing the transmission, clean and lubricate the input shaft with a small amount of grease.

➡When installing the transmission with the gearshift lever attached, position the gear shifter into NEUTRAL position, so that the shifter will not damage the shift boot.

45. Position the transmission at a 45-degree angle, slide the input shaft into the pressure plate and rotate the

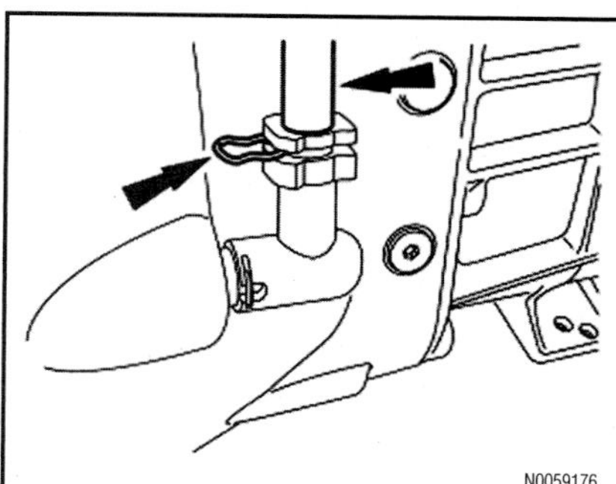

Fig. 29 Disconnect the clutch hydraulic tube from the clutch slave cylinder connector

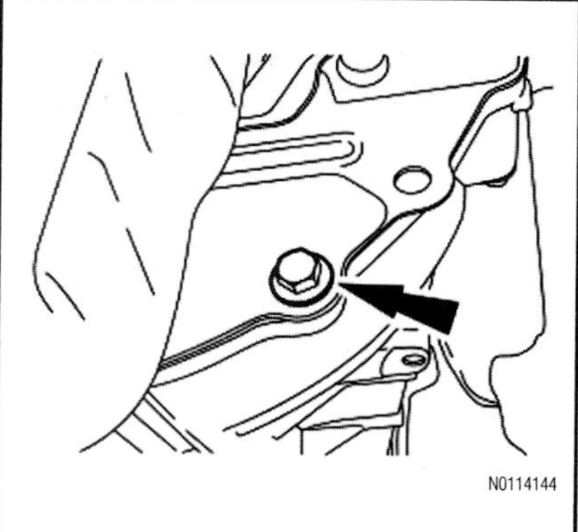

Fig. 30 Remove the 2 engine spacer plate-to-transmission bolts

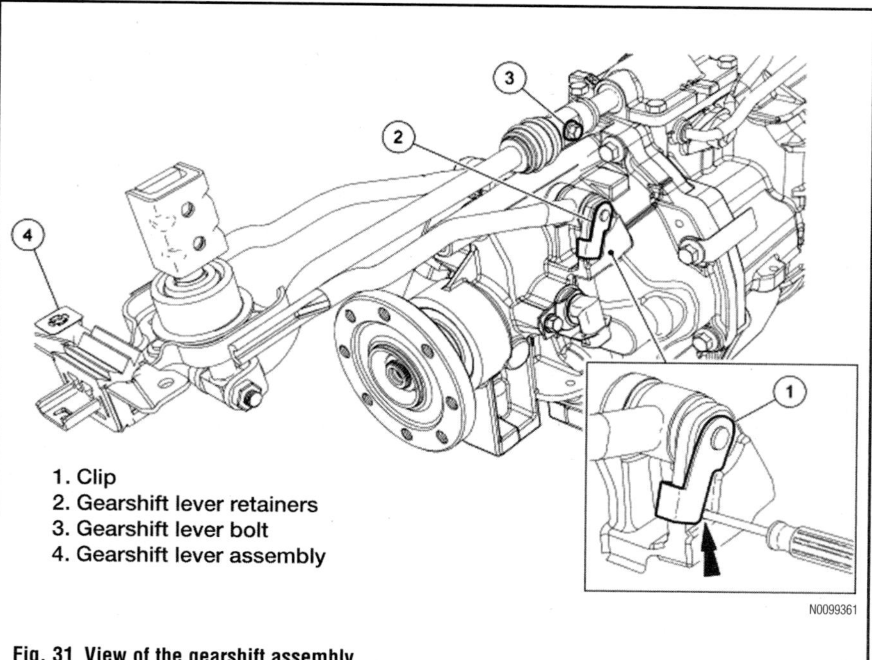

Fig. 31 View of the gearshift assembly

transmission counterclockwise 45 degrees to align with the dowels.

46. Connect the wiring harness clip to the top of the transmission.

47. Install the 6 transmission-to-engine bolts and the transmission-to-engine stud bolt. Tighten to 35 ft. lbs. (48 Nm).

48. Install the 2 engine spacer plate-to-transmission bolts. Tighten to 26 ft. lbs. (35 Nm).

49. Connect the clutch slave cylinder tube to the clutch slave cylinder connector.

50. Attach the clutch hydraulic tube clip.

51. Connect the wiring harness to the RH side of the transmission.

52. Connect the Output Shaft Speed (OSS) sensor electrical connector.

53. Connect the reverse lamp switch electrical connector.

54. Connect the 2 wiring harness clips.

55. Connect the wiring harness to the LH side of the transmission.

56. Connect the reverse lockout solenoid electrical connector.

57. Connect the 2 wiring harness clips.

58. Install the wiring harness retaining nut.

59. Using the adjustable jackstands, raise the subframe to the marked position.

60. Install the 4 rear subframe bolts. Tighten to 85 ft. lbs. (115 Nm).

61. Tighten the 4 front subframe nuts. Tighten to 85 ft. lbs. (115 Nm).

62. Connect the steering column shaft and install the new steering column shaft pinch bolt. Tighten to 35 ft. lbs. (48 Nm).

63. Install the transmission crossmember.

64. Install the 2 gearshift lever nuts.

65. Install the starter motor. For additional information, refer to Starter.

66. Install the subframe cross brace and the 4 subframe cross brace nuts. Tighten to 35 ft. lbs. (48 Nm).

➡Align the index marks on the driveshaft flange and pinion flange, and the driveshaft flange and transmission output shaft flange.

67. Install the driveshaft. For additional information, refer to Driveshaft.

68. Install the catalytic converter assembly (H-pipe).

69. Install the crossmember brace and 6 crossmember brace bolts. Tighten to 35 ft. lbs. (48 Nm).

70. Tighten the 2 crossmember brace nuts to 35 ft. lbs. (48 Nm).

71. If equipped, install the lower air deflector and install the 9 screws.

➡The use of any other transmission fluid than specified can result in the transmission failing to operate in a normal manner or transmission failure.

72. Check, and as necessary, fill the transmission with transmission fluid. Apply threadlock and sealer to the fill plug threads and install the fill plug. Tighten to 18 ft. lbs. (25 Nm).

73. Install the 2 dash boot bearing nuts. Tighten to 80 inch lbs. (9 Nm).

74. Install the upper gearshift lever and the upper gearshift lever bolts. Tighten to 26 ft. lbs. (35 Nm).

75. Install the floor console finish panel.

76. If equipped, install the strut tower cross brace and 4 nuts. Tighten to 26 ft. lbs. (35 Nm).

77. Connect the battery ground cable.

➡Do not spill brake fluid on painted or plastic surfaces or damage to the surface may occur. If brake fluid is spilled onto a painted or plastic surface, immediately wash the surface with water.

78. Fill the brake and clutch reservoir. Bleed the clutch hydraulic system.

MANUAL TRANSMISSION FLUID

DRAIN AND REFILL

Mt82 Getrag Transmission

See Figures 32 and 33.

1. With the vehicle in NEUTRAL, position it on a hoist.

2. Remove the drain plug and drain the fluid.

3. Install the drain plug. Tighten to 26 ft. lbs. (35 Nm).

➡Prior to removal, clean the area around the fill plug.

4. Remove the fill plug.

➡The use of any other transmission fluid than specified can result in the transmission failing to operate in a normal manner or transmission failure.

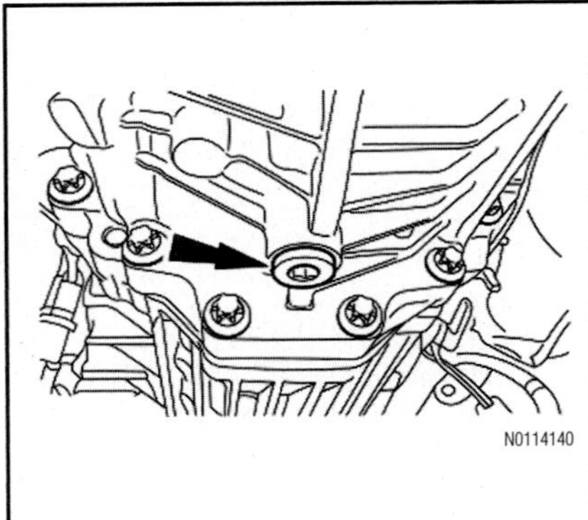

Fig. 32 Remove the drain plug

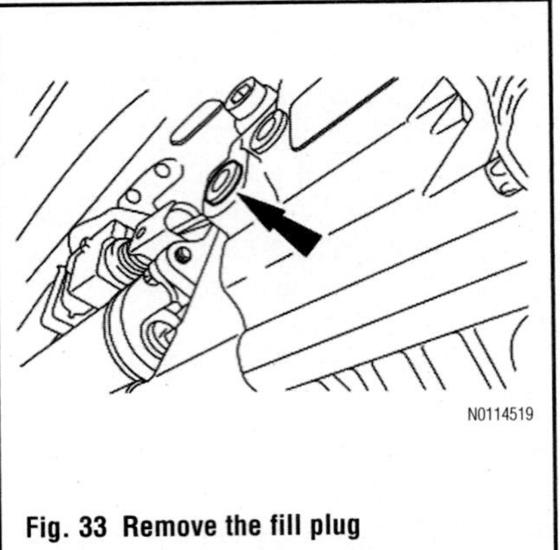

Fig. 33 Remove the fill plug

➡Do not overfill the transmission. This will cause transmission fluid to be forced out of the case.

5. Using a suitable oil suction gun, fill the transmission with the recommended fluid. Transmission capacity is 2.7 quarts.

6. Install the fill plug. Tighten to 26 ft. lbs. (35 Nm).

T50D Transmission

See Figures 34 and 35.

1. With the vehicle in NEUTRAL, position it on a hoist.

➡Drain the transmission while the transmission fluid is warm.

➡Position a drain pan under the transmission.

2. Remove the drain plug and drain the fluid.

3. Clean the drain plug. Apply thread sealant and reinstall. Tighten to 15 ft. lbs. (18 Nm).

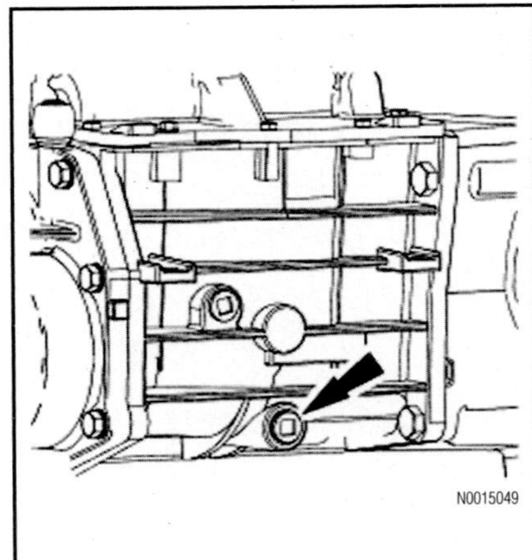

Fig. 34 Remove the drain plug and drain the fluid

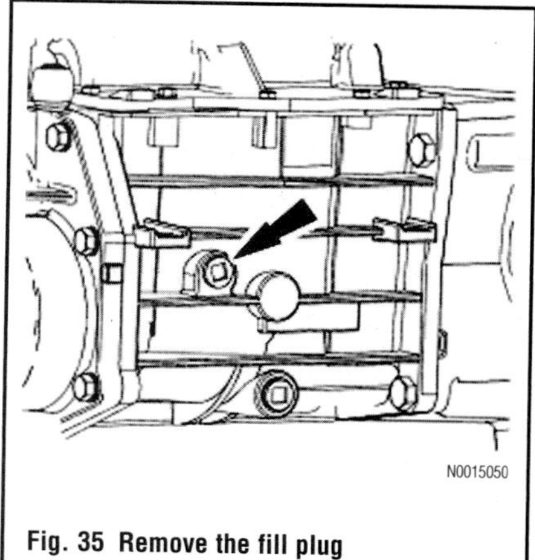

Fig. 35 Remove the fill plug

➡Prior to removal, clean the area around the fill plug.

4. Remove the fill plug.

➡Do not overfill the transmission. This will cause transmission fluid to be forced out of the case.

5. Using an Oil Suction Gun, fill the transmission with the recommended fluid. Transmission capacity is 2.8 quarts.
6. Clean the fill plug. Apply thread sealant and reinstall. Tighten to 15 ft. lbs. (18 Nm).

TR3650 Transmission

See Figures 36 and 37.

1. With the vehicle in NEUTRAL, position it on a hoist.

➡Drain the transmission while the transmission fluid is warm.

➡Position a drain pan under the transmission.

2. Remove the drain plug and drain the transmission fluid.
3. Clean the drain plug. Apply threadlock and sealer and install the drain plug. Tighten to 20 ft. lbs. (27 Nm).

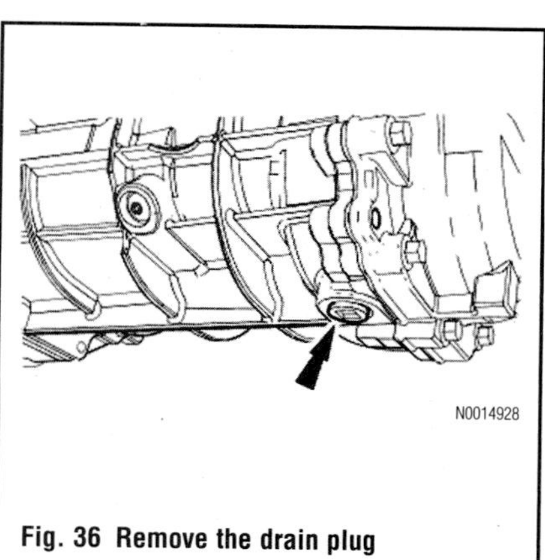

Fig. 36 Remove the drain plug

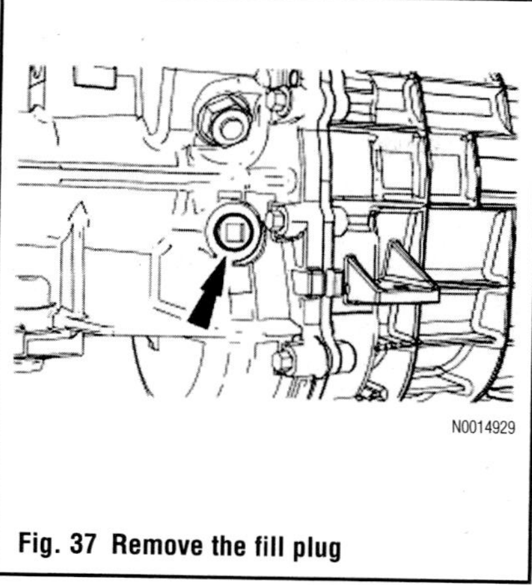

Fig. 37 Remove the fill plug

➡Prior to removal, clean the area around the fill plug.

4. Remove the fill plug.

➡Do not overfill the transmission. This will cause transmission fluid to be forced out of the case.

5. Fill the transmission with the recommended fluid.
6. Make sure the fluid is 0.5 inches below the fill opening for the correct fluid level. Using a tie strap, measure an inch from the end and bend it at a 90-degree angle, place it in the fill opening and check the fluid. Adjust the fluid level as necessary.
7. Apply threadlock and sealer and install the fill plug. Tighten to 18 ft. lbs. (25 Nm).

TR6060 Transmission

See Figures 38 and 39..

1. With the vehicle in NEUTRAL, position it on a hoist.

➡Position a suitable drain pan under the transmission.

2. Remove the drain plug and drain the transmission.
3. Clean the drain plug. Apply threadlock and sealer to the plug threads and install the drain plug. Tighten to 20 ft. lbs. (27 Nm).

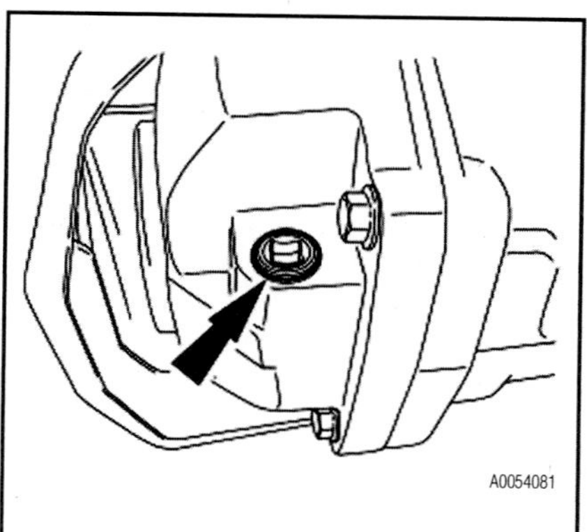

Fig. 38 Remove the drain plug

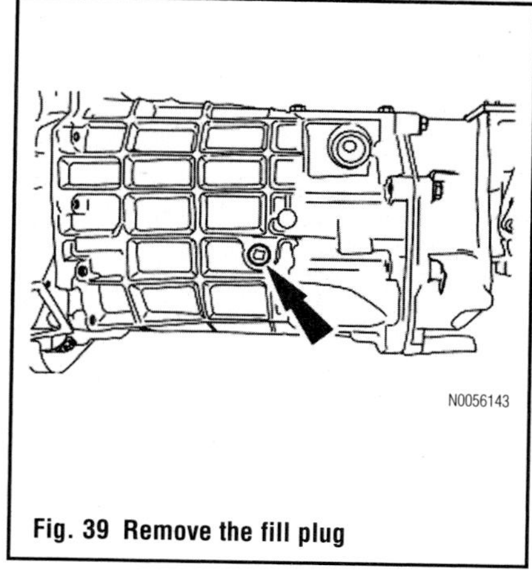

Fig. 39 Remove the fill plug

➡Before removing, clean the area around the fill plug.

4. Remove the fill plug.
5. Using a suitable oil suction gun, fill the transmission to the correct level with the specified fluid.

Transmission capacity is 3.65 quarts.

6. Apply threadlock and sealer to the plug threads and install the fill plug. Tighten to 18 ft. lbs. (25 Nm).

CLUTCH

REMOVAL & INSTALLATION

3.7L Engines

See Figure 40.

WARNING

Do not breathe dust or use compressed air to blow dust from storage containers or friction components. Remove dust using government-approved techniques. Friction component dust may be a cancer and lung disease hazard. Exposure to potentially hazardous components may occur if dusts are created during repair of friction components, such as brake pads and clutch discs. Exposure may also cause irritation to skin, eyes and respiratory tract, and may cause allergic reactions and/or may lead to other chronic health effects. If irritation persists, seek medical attention or advice. Failure to follow these instructions may result in serious personal injury.

1. Remove the transmission. For additional information, refer to Manual Transmission —MT82 Getrag.

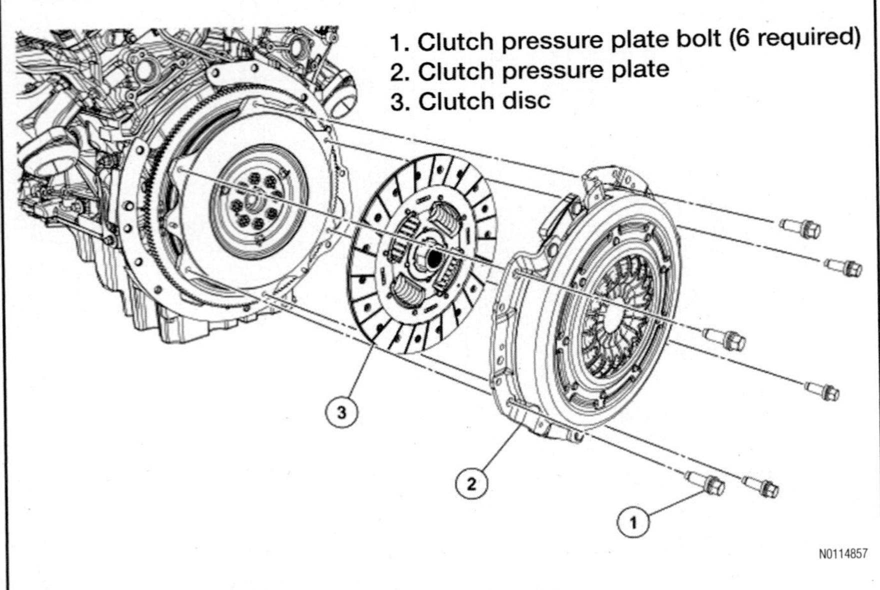

Fig. 40 Exploded view of the clutch assembly—3.7L Engines

➡Loosen the bolts evenly to prevent clutch pressure plate damage.

➡If the parts are to be reused, index-mark the pressure plate to the flywheel.

2. Remove the 6 pressure plate bolts, remove the pressure plate and the clutch disc.
3. Discard the pressure plate bolts.

To install:

➡The dual mass flywheel normally has up to a total of 14 degrees (6.5 ring gear teeth) maximum rotational freeplay between the primary (bolted to crankshaft) and secondary mass (clutch disc face).

4. Inspect the flywheel.

➡If installing the original pressure plate, align it using the index marks made during removal.

➡Always install new pressure plate bolts.

5. Using a suitable clutch aligner, position the clutch disc on the flywheel, install the pressure plate and 6 new pressure plate bolts. Turn the bolts 1-2 turns at a time in a star pattern until the clutch is fully secured.
    a. Tighten the pressure plate bolts in 2 stages in a star pattern.
    b. Stage 1: Tighten to 35 ft. lbs. (47 Nm).
    c. Stage 2: Tighten an additional 60 degrees.

➡Before securing the transmission to the engine, connect the clutch hydraulic tube to the slave cylinder.

Install the transmission.

6. Bleed the clutch hydraulic system.
7. After completing the repairs, use the scan tool to perform the Misfire Monitor Neutral Profile Correction procedure, following the on-screen instructions.

4.0L Engines

See Figure 41.

1. Remove the transmission. For additional information, refer to Manual Transmission - T50D.

➡Loosen the bolts evenly to prevent clutch pressure plate damage.

➡If the parts are to be reused, index-mark the pressure plate to the flywheel.

2. Remove the 6 pressure plate bolts, then remove the pressure plate and the clutch disc.

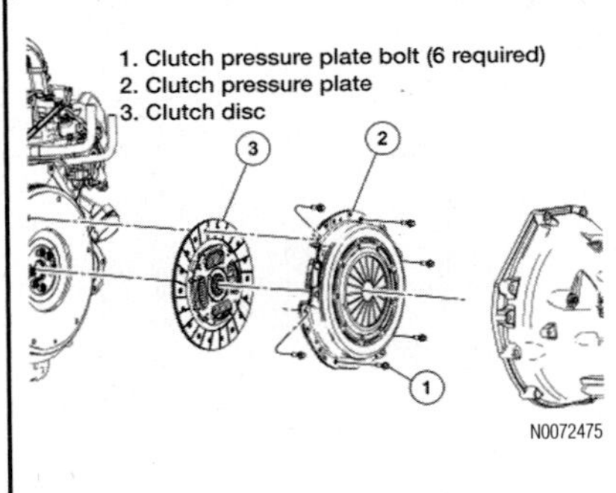

Fig. 41 Exploded view of the clutch assembly—4.0L Engines

3. Discard the pressure plate bolts.

To install:

➡If installing the original pressure plate, align it using the index marks made during removal.

➡Always install new pressure plate bolts.

4. Inspect the flywheel.
5. Using a suitable clutch aligner, position the clutch disc on the flywheel, then install the pressure plate and 6 new pressure plate bolts.
    a. Tighten the bolts in a star pattern.
    b. Tighten to 26 ft. lbs. (35 Nm).

➡Before securing the transmission to the engine, connect the clutch hydraulic tube to the slave cylinder.

6. Install the transmission.
7. Bleed the clutch hydraulic system.

4.6L Engines

See Figure 42.

1. Remove the transmission. For additional information, refer to Manual Transmission —TR3650.

➡Loosen the bolts evenly to prevent damage to the pressure plate.

➡If the pressure plate is to be reused, index-mark the pressure plate to the flywheel.

2. Remove the 6 pressure plate bolts, then remove the pressure plate and the clutch disc.
3. Discard the pressure plate bolts.

To install:

4. Inspect the flywheel.

➡If installing the original pressure plate, align it using the index marks made during removal.

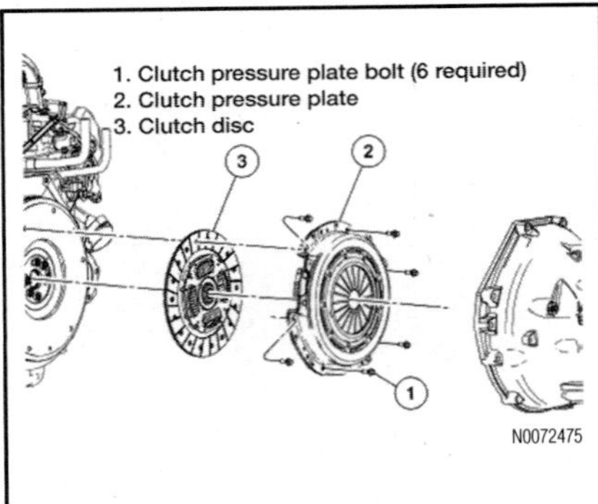

Fig. 42 Exploded view of the clutch assembly—4.6L Engines

➡**Always install new pressure plate bolts.**

5. Using a suitable clutch aligner, position the clutch disc on the flywheel, then install the pressure plate and 6 new pressure plate bolts.
6. Tighten the pressure plate bolts in 2 stages in a star pattern.
   a. Stage 1: Tighten to 33 ft. lbs. (45 Nm).
   b. Stage 2: Tighten an additional 60 degrees.

➡**Before securing the transmission to the engine, connect the clutch hydraulic tube to the slave cylinder.**

Install the transmission.

7. Bleed the clutch hydraulic system.

5.0L Engines

See Figure 43.

WARNING

Do not breathe dust or use compressed air to blow dust from storage containers or friction components. Remove dust using government-approved techniques. Friction component dust may be a cancer and lung disease hazard. Exposure to potentially hazardous components may occur if dusts are created during repair of friction components, such as brake pads and clutch discs. Exposure may also cause irritation to skin, eyes and respiratory tract, and may cause allergic reactions and/or may lead to other chronic health effects. If irritation persists, seek medical attention or advice. Failure to follow these instructions may result in serious personal injury.

1. Remove the transmission. For additional information, refer to Manual Transmission —MT82 Getrag.

➡**Loosen the bolts evenly to prevent clutch pressure plate damage.**

➡**If the parts are to be reused, index-mark the pressure plate to the flywheel.**

2. Remove the 6 pressure plate bolts, remove the pressure plate and the clutch disc. Discard the pressure plate bolts.

To install:

3. Inspect the flywheel.

➡**If installing the original pressure plate, align it using the index marks made during removal.**

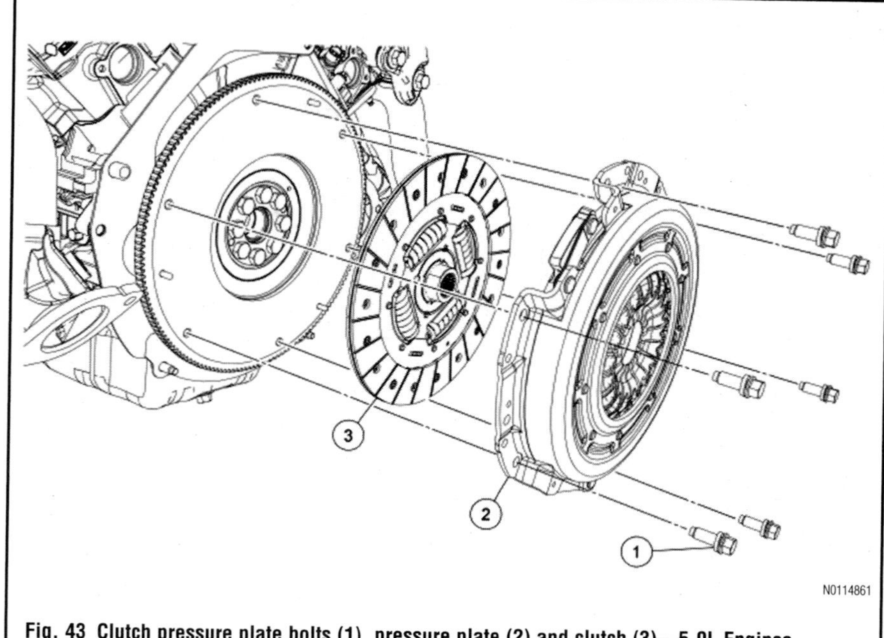

Fig. 43 Clutch pressure plate bolts (1), pressure plate (2) and clutch (3)—5.0L Engines

➡**Always install new pressure plate bolts.**

4. Using a suitable clutch aligner, position the clutch disc on the flywheel, install the pressure plate and 6 new pressure plate bolts. Turn the bolts 1-2 turns at a time in a star pattern until the clutch is fully secured.
5. Tighten the pressure plate bolts in 2 stages in a star pattern.
   a. Stage 1: Tighten to 35 ft. lbs. (47 Nm).
   b. Stage 2: Tighten an additional 60 degrees.

➡**Before securing the transmission to the engine, connect the clutch hydraulic tube to the slave cylinder.**

Install the transmission.

6. Bleed the clutch hydraulic system.
7. If the clutch was replaced, use the scan tool to perform the Misfire Monitor Neutral Profile Correction procedure, following the on-screen instructions.

5.7L Engines

See Figures 44 and 45.

WARNING

Do not breathe dust or use compressed air to blow dust from storage containers or friction components. Remove dust using government-approved techniques. Friction component dust may be a cancer and lung disease hazard. Exposure to potentially hazardous components may occur if dusts are created during repair of friction components, such as brake pads and clutch discs. Exposure may also cause irritation to skin, eyes and respiratory tract, and may cause allergic reactions and/or may lead to other chronic health effects. If irritation persists, seek medical attention or advice. Failure to follow these instructions may result in serious personal injury.

1. Remove the transmission. For additional information, refer to Manual Transmission—TR6060.

➡**If the parts are to be reused, index-mark the clutch disc and plate assembly to the flywheel. Failure to install the clutch disc and plate assembly to the flywheel in the original position may result in a clutch system vibration.**

➡**Loosen the bolts evenly to prevent damage to the clutch disc and plate assembly.**

2. Remove the 6 clutch disc and plate assembly bolts by loosening them 1 turn at a time using the tightening sequence, then remove the clutch disc and plate assembly.
3. Discard the clutch disc and plate assembly bolts.

To install:

4. Inspect the flywheel.

➡**Clutch Aligner 308-599, must be used or clutch damage may occur.**

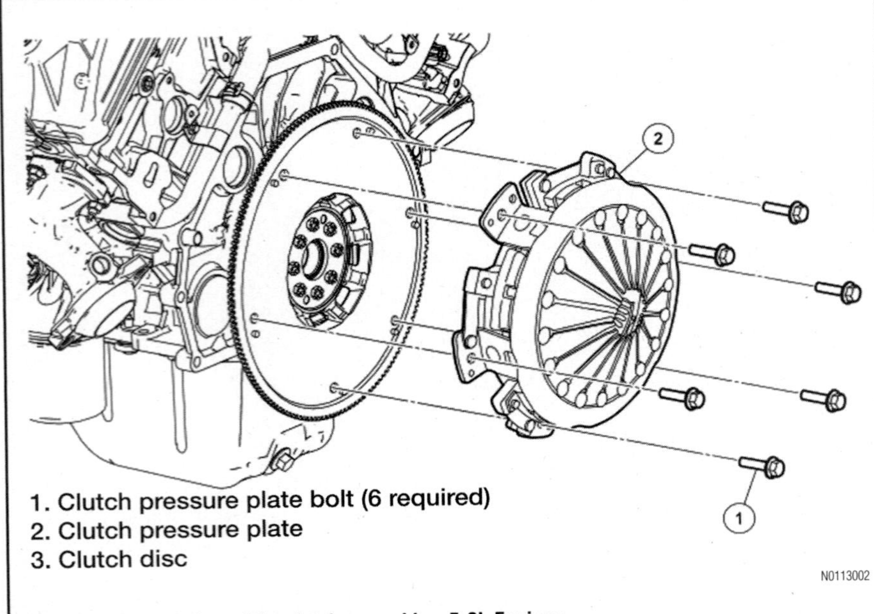

Fig. 44 Exploded view of the clutch assembly—5.0L Engines

5. Using the Clutch Aligner, align the entrapped clutch disc in the pressure plate assembly.

➡**If installing the original clutch disc and plate assembly, align it using the index-marks made during removal or a clutch system vibration can occur.**

➡**Always install new clutch disc and plate assembly bolts.**

6. Using the Clutch Aligner, position the clutch disc and plate assembly on the flywheel using the index-marks made during removal, install the 6 new clutch disc and plate assembly bolts turning them until they contact the clutch housing surface.

7. Turn the bolts 1 turn at a time until the clutch disc and plate assembly is fully secured. Tighten the bolts in 2 stages, in the sequence shown.

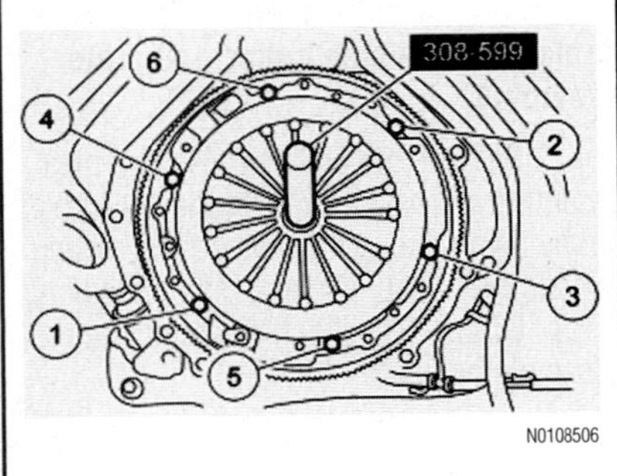

Fig. 45 Clutch tightening sequence and special tool identification

a. Stage 1: Tighten to 35 ft. lbs. (47 Nm).

b. Stage 2: Tighten an additional 60 degrees.

➡**Apply a small amount of PTFE lubricant to the splines of the clutch hub. This will make sure that the clutch will not bind on the transmission input shaft, making sure of correct clutch operation. Using lubricant other than Motorcraft PTFE lubricant may cause clutch chatter.**

➡**Before securing the transmission to the engine, connect the clutch hydraulic line to the slave cylinder.**

8. Install the transmission.
9. Bleed the clutch hydraulic system.
10. After completing the repairs, use the scan tool to perform the Misfire Monitor Neutral Profile Correction procedure, following the on-screen instructions.

BLEEDING

➡**Do not spill brake fluid on painted or plastic surfaces or damage to the surface may occur. If brake fluid is spilled onto a painted or plastic surface, immediately wash the surface with water.**

1. Make sure all hydraulic tubes are correctly seated.
2. Make sure the clutch pedal is in the most upward position.
3. Check the fluid level of the brake/clutch reservoir. Fill the reservoir with the specified fluid to the MAX mark.
4. Using a suitable bleeder kit and a Vacuum Pump Kit, install the rubber stopper in the reservoir opening. Make sure the rubber stopper has a tight fit.
5. Alternate method: use a 1.96 inch rubber stopper with an 0.31 inch pipe inserted through the rubber stopper.
6. Holding the rubber stopper in place, operate the vacuum pump to 15-20 inches of vacuum. Hold the vacuum for one minute, then quickly relieve the vacuum. Remove the special tools.
7. Check the fluid level of the reservoir. Fill the reservoir with the specified fluid to the MAX mark. Install the reservoir cap.
8. Depress and release the clutch pedal 10 to 12 times or until clutch pedal effort is consistent and positive at top of clutch pedal travel.

FRONT DRIVESHAFT

REMOVAL & INSTALLATION

3.7L and 4.0L Engines

See Figure 46.

1. With the vehicle in NEUTRAL, position it on a hoist.
2. Index-mark the driveshaft at both ends to maintain alignment during installation.
3. Remove and discard the 4 driveshaft flange-to-transmission bolts. To install, tighten the new bolts evenly in a cross pattern to 80 ft. lbs. (109 Nm).
4. Remove and discard the 4 driveshaft flange-to-axle bolts. To install, tighten the new bolts evenly in a cross pattern to 76 ft. lbs. (103 Nm).

➡**The driveshaft flanges fit tightly on the flange pilots. Never hammer on the driveshaft or any of its components to disconnect the driveshaft flanges from the flange pilots. Pry only in the area shown, with a suitable tool, to disconnect the driveshaft flanges from the flange pilots.**

5. Using a suitable tool, disconnect the driveshaft flanges from the flange pilots and remove the driveshaft.

➡**If new driveshaft flange bolts are not available, coat the threads of the original bolts with threadlock and sealer.**

➡**The driveshaft flanges fit tightly on the pinion flange pilots. To make sure that the driveshaft flanges seat squarely on the pinion flange pilots, tighten the driveshaft flange bolts evenly in a cross pattern.**

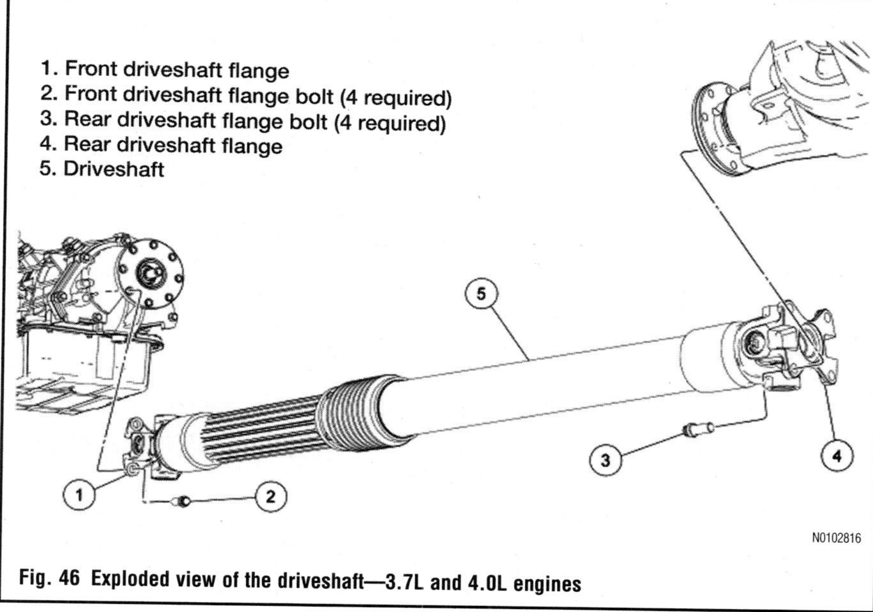

Fig. 46 Exploded view of the driveshaft—3.7L and 4.0L engines

6. To install, reverse the removal procedure.

4.6L, 5.0L & 5.4L Engines

See Figure 47.

1. With the vehicle in NEUTRAL, position it on a hoist.
2. Index-mark the driveshaft at both ends to maintain alignment during installation.
3. Remove and discard the 3 driveshaft CV joint bolt and washer assemblies, then disconnect the CV joint from the pinion flange. To install, tighten the new bolts evenly in a star pattern to 41 ft. lbs. (55 Nm).
4. Support the front and rear ends of the driveshaft.
5. Remove and discard the 4 driveshaft flange bolts. To install, tighten the new bolts evenly in a cross pattern to 76 ft. lbs. (103 Nm).

➡The driveshaft flanges fit tightly on the transmission flange pilot. Never hammer on the driveshaft or any of its components to disconnect the driveshaft flange from the transmission flange pilot. Pry only in the area shown, with a suitable tool, to disconnect the driveshaft flange from the transmission flange pilot.

6. Using a suitable tool as shown, disconnect the driveshaft flange from the transmission flange pilot.

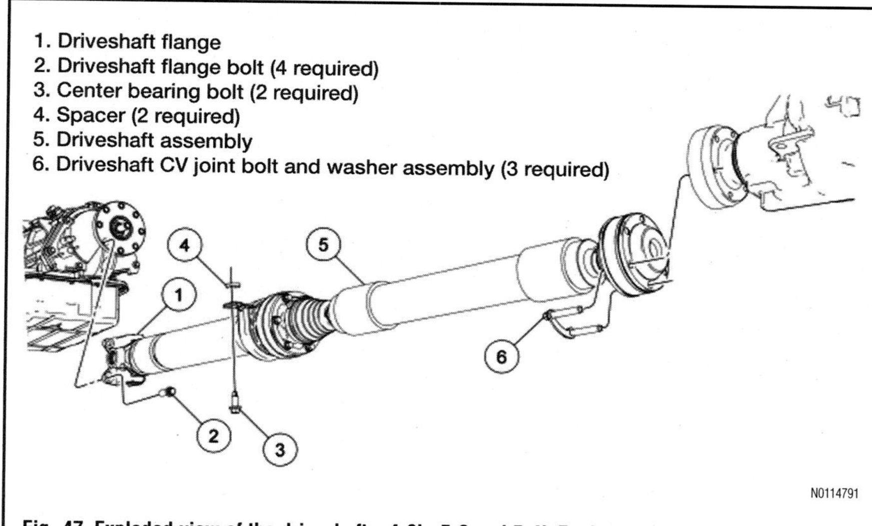

Fig. 47 Exploded view of the driveshaft—4.6L, 5.0 and 5.4L Engines

➡The center bearing spacers must be installed between the body and the center bearing bracket.

7. Remove and discard the 2 center bearing bolts and spacers, then remove the driveshaft.
8. Install the new center bearing bolts finger-tight until after the front and rear flanges are tightened to specifications. To install, tighten the bolts to 35 ft. lbs. (48 Nm).

➡If new driveshaft bolts or center bearing bolts are not available, coat the threads of the original bolts with threadlock and sealer and reuse the original washers and spacers.

➡The driveshaft flanges fit tightly on the transmission output flange pilot. To make sure that the driveshaft flange seats squarely on the transmission output flange, tighten the driveshaft flange bolts evenly in a cross pattern.

9. To install, reverse the removal procedure.

REAR AXLE FLUID

DRAIN & REFILL

➡Service refill capacities are determined by filling the axle to the bottom of the fill hole with the axle at ride height.

1. Remove the axle plug, fill the axle with 5-5.25 pints of axle lubricant and a additional 4.0 oz of friction modifier additive and install the filler plug.
2. Tighten to 22 ft. lbs. (30 Nm).

REAR AXLE HOUSING

REMOVAL & INSTALLATION

See Figure 48.

➡Suspension fasteners are critical parts because they affect performance of vital components and systems and their failure may result in major service expense. New parts must be installed with the same part numbers or equivalent part, if replacement is necessary. Do not use a replacement part of lesser quality or substitute design. Torque values must be used as specified during reassembly to make sure of correct retention of these parts.

1. Mark the rear shock absorber relative to the protective sleeve with the vehicle in a static, level ground position (curb height).

2. Remove the brake discs. For additional information, refer to Rear Disc Brake.
3. Remove the driveshaft. For additional information, refer to Driveshaft.
4. Disconnect the 2 ABS wheel speed sensor electrical connectors.
5. Remove the stabilizer bar. For additional information, refer to Rear Suspension.
6. Remove the panhard rod. For additional information, refer to Rear Suspension.
7. Convertibles:
 a. Remove the rear support braces. For additional information, refer to Rear Suspension.
8. All vehicles:

➡Secure the differential housing to the transmission jack with a suitable strap.

9. Support the differential housing with a suitable transmission jack.
10. Remove and discard the 2 shock absorber lower nuts and bolts.
11. If equipped, disconnect the vent hose clip.
12. Remove and discard the upper arm bushing nut and bolt.
13. Lower the axle slightly and remove the springs.
14. Remove and discard the 2 lower arm nuts and bolts.
15. Disconnect the lower arms from the axle housing.
16. Lower the axle housing from the vehicle.

To install:

17. If installing a new rear axle, install a new upper arm bushing.
18. If installing a new rear axle, If equipped, transfer the mass dampeners. Tighten to 67 ft. lbs. (90 Nm).
19. Using a suitable transmission jack, position the axle housing in the vehicle and install the springs.

➡Tighten the new suspension fasteners while the suspension is at curb height or bushing damage and incorrect clamp load may occur.

20. Using 2 jackstands, raise the rear axle so the mark made on the rear shock absorber during removal lines up with the protective sleeve.
21. Install a new upper arm bushing nut and bolt. Tighten to 129 ft. lbs. (175 Nm).
22. If equipped, connect the vent hose clip.
23. Position the lower arms to the axle housing.
24. Install 2 new lower arm nuts and bolts. Tighten to 129 ft. lbs. (175 Nm).
25. Install 2 new shock absorber bolts and flagnuts. Tighten to 85 ft. lbs (115 Nm).
26. Convertibles: Install the rear support braces.
27. Install the stabilizer bar. For additional information, refer to Rear Suspension.
28. Install the panhard rod. For additional information, refer to Rear Suspension.
29. Connect the 2 ABS wheel speed sensor electrical connectors.
30. Install the driveshaft. For additional information, refer to Driveshaft.
31. Install the rear brake discs. For additional information, refer to Rear Disc Brake.

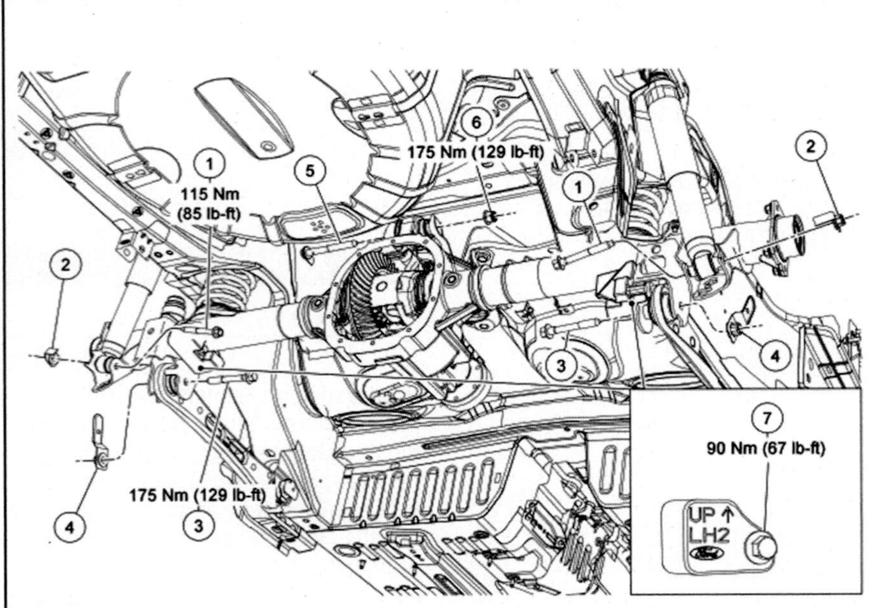

Fig. 48 Exploded view of the rear axle and assembly

REAR AXLE SHAFT, BEARING & SEAL

REMOVAL & INSTALLATION

See Figures 49 through 54.

1. With the vehicle in NEUTRAL, position it on a hoist.
2. Remove the differential housing cover.
3. Remove the rear brake disc. For additional information, refer to Rear Disc Brake.

➡Damage to the rear wheel speed sensor may occur if it is not removed before the axle shaft U-washer.

4. Remove the bolt and position the rear wheel speed sensor aside.
5. Remove the differential pinion shaft.
 a. Remove and discard the differential pinion shaft lock bolt.
 b. Remove the differential pinion shaft.

➡Do not damage the rubber O-ring in the axle shaft grooves.

6. Remove the axle shaft U-washer.
7. Push in on the axle shaft.
8. Remove the U-washer.

➡Do not damage the axle shaft oil seal.

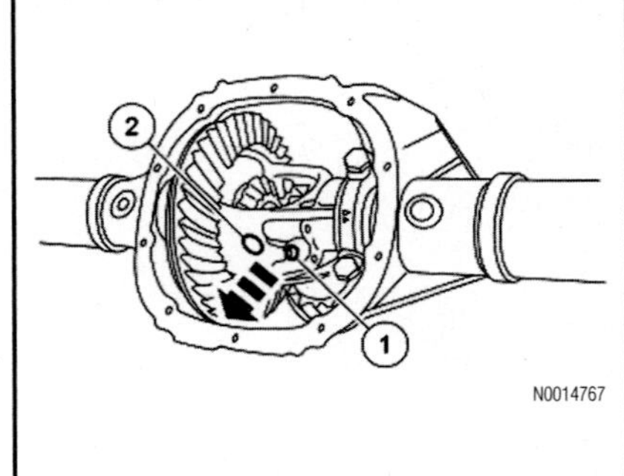

Fig. 49 Remove the differential pinion shaft lock bolt (1) and the o-ring (2)

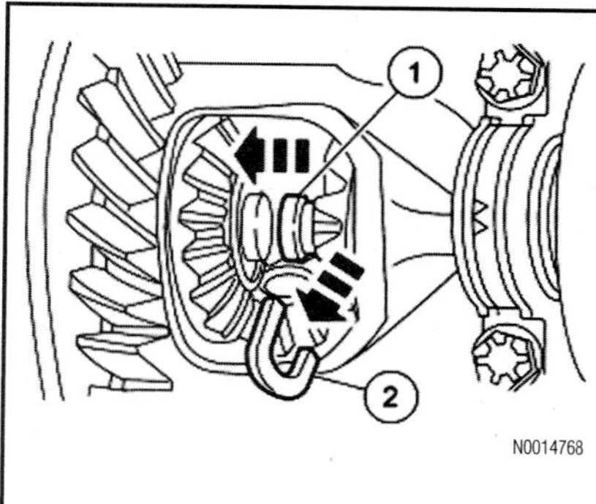

Fig. 50 Push in on the axle shaft (1) and remove the U-washer (2)

9. Remove the axle shaft.

➡If the axle shaft oil seal is leaking, the axle housing vent may be plugged.

10. Using the Slide Hammer and Axle Bearing Remover, remove the rear wheel bearing and axle shaft oil seal.

To install:

11. Lubricate the new rear wheel bearing with the axle lubricant.
12. Using the Axle Shaft Bearing Installer and Adapter, install the new rear wheel bearing.
13. Lubricate the lip of the new axle shaft oil seal with grease.
14. Using the Rear Axle Oil Seal Installer and Adapter, install the new axle shaft oil seal.
15. Lubricate the lip of the axle shaft oil seal with grease.

➡Do not damage the axle shaft oil seal when installing the axle shaft.

16. Install the axle shaft.

➡Do not damage the rubber O-ring in the U-washer groove.

17. Install the axle shaft U-washer.
    a. Position the U-washer on the button end of the axle shaft.
    b. Pull the axle shaft outward.
18. Install the differential pinion shaft.
    a. Align the hole in the differential pinion shaft with the differential case lock bolt hole.
    b. Install a new differential pinion shaft lock bolt. Tighten to 26 ft. lbs. (35 Nm).
19. Position the rear wheel speed sensor and install the bolt. Tighten to 10 ft. lbs. (15 Nm).
20. Install the rear brake disc. For additional information, refer to Rear Disc Brake.
21. Install the differential housing cover.

REAR DRIVESHAFT

REMOVAL & INSTALLATION

Refer to Front Driveshaft.

REAR PINION SEAL

REMOVAL & INSTALLATION

See Figures 55 through 58.

➡This operation disturbs the pinion bearing preload. Install a new pinion nut with the same color as the original if not replacing the collapsible spacer. If a new collapsible spacer is installed, install the pinion nut in the kit or damage to the component may occur.

1. With the vehicle in NEUTRAL, position it on a hoist.
2. Remove the driveshaft. For additional information, refer to Driveshaft.

➡The disc brake calipers must be removed to prevent brake drag during drive pinion bearing preload adjustment.

3. Remove the rear brake disc. For additional information, refer to Rear Disc Brake.

Fig. 51 Exploded view of the axle shaft oil seal (1), wheel bearing (2) and housing (3)

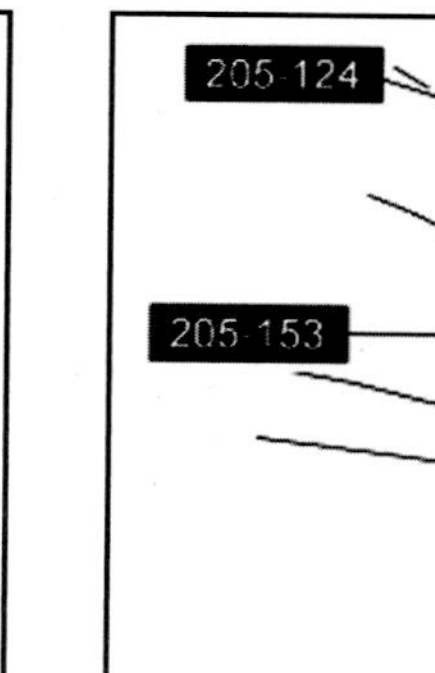

Fig. 53 Using the Axle Shaft Bearing Installer and Adapter

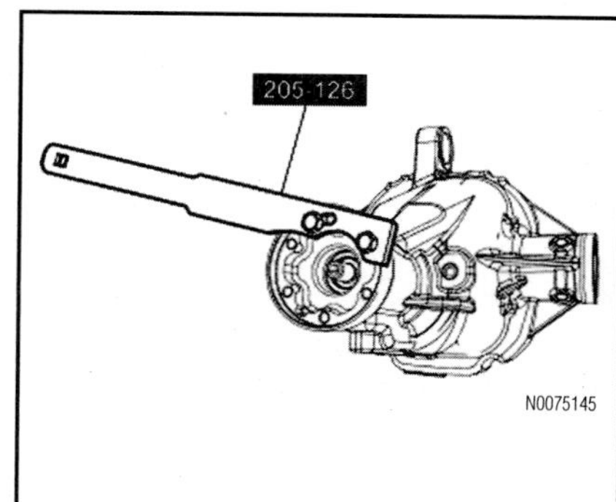

Fig. 55 Using the Drive Pinion Flange Holding Fixture

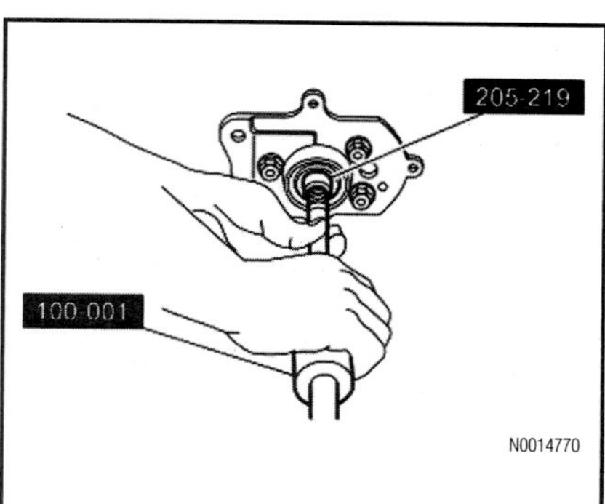

Fig. 52 Using the Slide Hammer and Axle Bearing Remover

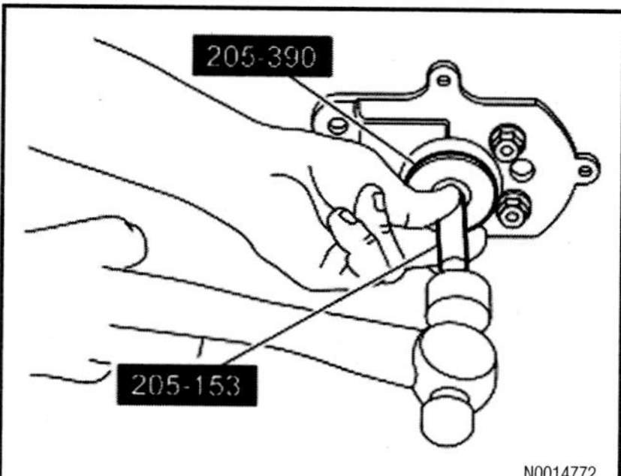

Fig. 54 Using the Rear Axle Oil Seal Installer and Adapter, install the new axle shaft oil seal

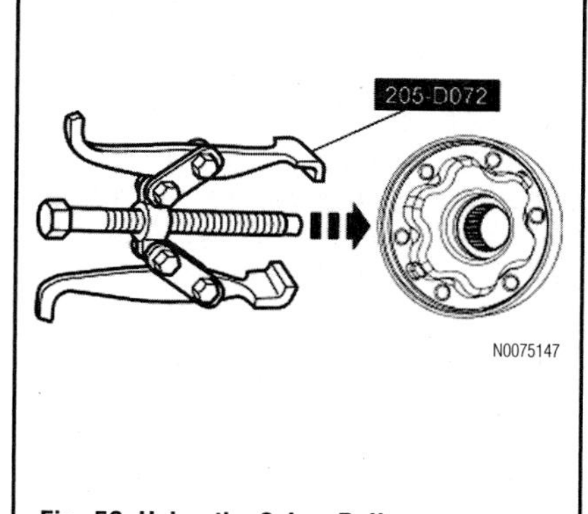

Fig. 56 Using the 2 Jaw Puller

4. Using a torque wrench on the pinion nut, record the torque required to maintain rotation of the pinion gear through several revolutions.
5. Using the Drive Pinion Flange Holding Fixture to hold the pinion flange, remove and discard the pinion nut.
6. Index-mark the pinion flange in relation to the drive pinion stem to make sure of correct alignment during installation.
7. Using the 2 Jaw Puller, remove the pinion flange.
8. Force up on the metal flange of the drive pinion seal. Install gripping pliers and strike with a hammer until the drive pinion seal is removed.

To install:

9. Lubricate the new drive pinion seal with grease.

➡If the new drive pinion seal becomes misaligned during installation, remove the drive pinion seal and install a new drive pinion seal.

10. Using the Drive Pinion Oil Seal Installer, install a new drive pinion seal.
11. Lubricate the pinion flange splines with axle lubricant.

➡Disregard the scribe marks if a new pinion flange is being installed.

12. Align the pinion flange with the drive pinion shaft.
13. Using the Drive Pinion Flange Installer, install the pinion flange.
14. Position the new pinion nut.

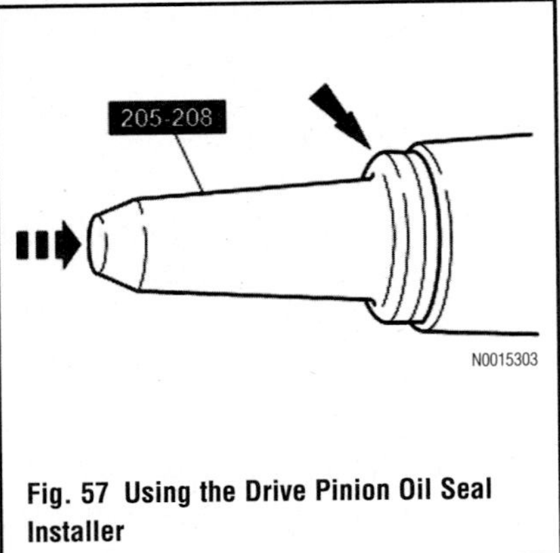

Fig. 57 Using the Drive Pinion Oil Seal Installer

➡Under no circumstances is the pinion nut to be backed off to reduce drive pinion bearing preload. If reduced drive pinion bearing preload is required, a new drive pinion collapsible spacer and pinion nut kit must be installed.

➡Remove the Drive Pinion Flange Holding Fixture while taking drive pinion bearing preload readings with the inch lbs. (Nm) torque wrench.

15. Using the Drive Pinion Flange Holding Fixture to hold the pinion flange, tighten the pinion nut.
16. Rotate the drive pinion occasionally to make sure the drive pinion bearings are seating correctly.
17. Install a inch lbs. (Nm) torque wrench on the pinion nut.

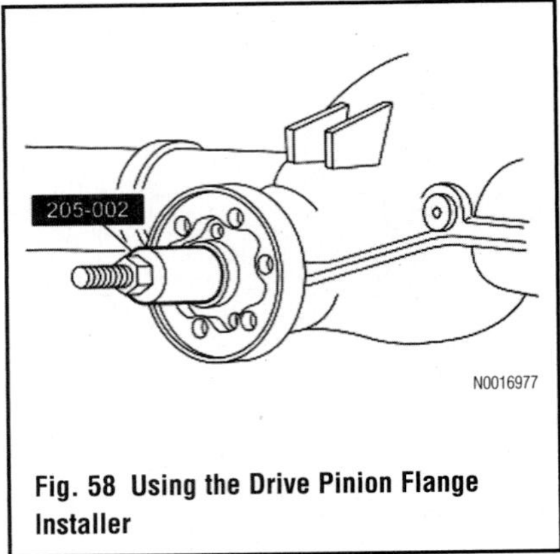

Fig. 58 Using the Drive Pinion Flange Installer

18. Rotating the drive pinion through several revolutions, take frequent drive pinion bearing preload readings until the original recorded drive pinion bearing preload reading is obtained.
19. If the original recorded drive pinion bearing preload is lower than specifications, tighten to the specification. If the drive pinion bearing preload is higher than specification, tighten the pinion nut to the original reading as recorded. For additional information, refer to the Specifications portion of this section.
20. Install the driveshaft. For additional information, refer to Driveshaft.
21. Install the rear brake disc. For additional information, refer to Rear Disc Brake.

ENGINE COOLING

ENGINE COOLANT

DRAINING, REFILL & BLEEDING PROCEDURE

See Figure 59.

⁂ CAUTION

Always allow the engine to cool before opening the cooling system. Do not unscrew the coolant pressure relief cap when the engine is operating or the cooling system is hot. The cooling system is under pressure; steam and hot liquid can come out forcefully when the cap is loosened slightly. Failure to follow these instructions may result in serious personal injury.

Draining

➡The coolant must be recovered in a suitable, clean container for reuse. If the coolant is contaminated, it must be recycled or disposed of correctly. Using contaminated coolant may result in damage to the engine or cooling system components.

➡Less than 80% of coolant capacity can be recovered with the engine in the vehicle. Dirty, rusty or contaminated coolant should be drained and the system filled with new coolant.

➡During normal vehicle operation, Motorcraft Specialty Orange Engine Coolant may change color from orange to pink or light red. As long as the engine coolant is clear and uncontaminated, this color change does not indicate the engine coolant has degraded nor does it require the engine coolant to be drained, the system to be flushed, or the engine coolant to be replaced.

1. With the vehicle in NEUTRAL, position it on a hoist.
2. Release the pressure in the cooling system by slowly turning the pressure relief cap one half turn counterclockwise. When the pressure is released, remove the pressure relief cap.
3. Place a suitable container below the radiator draincock. Open the draincock and drain the engine coolant.
4. Close the radiator draincock when finished.

Filling and Bleeding with a Vacuum Cooling System Filler

➡The engine cooling system is filled with Motorcraft® Specialty Orange Engine Coolant. Always fill the cooling system with the manufacturer's specified coolant. If a non-specified coolant has been used the cooling system must be chemically flushed. Refer to Cooling System Flushing in this section. Failure to follow these instructions may damage the engine or cooling system.

➡**The engine cooling system is filled with Motorcraft® Specialty Orange Engine Coolant. Do not mix cooling types. Mixing coolant types degrades the corrosion protection of Motorcraft® Specialty Orange Engine Coolant.**

➡**Engine coolant provides boil protection, corrosion protection, freeze protection, and cooling efficiency to the engine and cooling components. In order to obtain these protections, maintain the engine coolant at the correct concentration and fluid level in the degas bottle. To maintain the integrity of the coolant and the cooling system:**

- Add Motorcraft® Specialty Orange Engine Coolant or equivalent meeting Ford specification WSS-M97B44-D (orange color).
- Do not add or mix with any other type of engine coolant. Mixing coolants may degrade the coolant's corrosion protection.
- Do not add alcohol, methanol, or brine, or any engine coolants mixed with alcohol or methanol antifreeze. These can cause engine damage from overheating or freezing.
- Ford Motor Company does NOT recommend the use of recycled engine coolant in vehicles originally equipped with Motorcraft® Specialty Orange Engine Coolant since a Ford-approved recycling process is not yet available.

5. Install the vacuum cooling system filler and follow the manufacturer's instructions to fill and bleed the cooling system.

➡**Recommended coolant concentration is 50/50 engine coolant to distilled water.**

➡**For extremely cold climates (less than -34°F:**

a. It may be necessary to increase the coolant concentration above 50%.
b. NEVER increase the coolant concentration above 60%.
c. Maximum coolant concentration is 60/40 for cold weather areas.
d. A coolant concentration of 60% will provide freeze point protection down to -58°F.
e. Engine coolant concentration above 60% will decrease the overheat protection characteristics of the engine coolant and may damage the engine.

6. For extremely hot climates:

a. It is still necessary to maintain the coolant concentration above 40%.

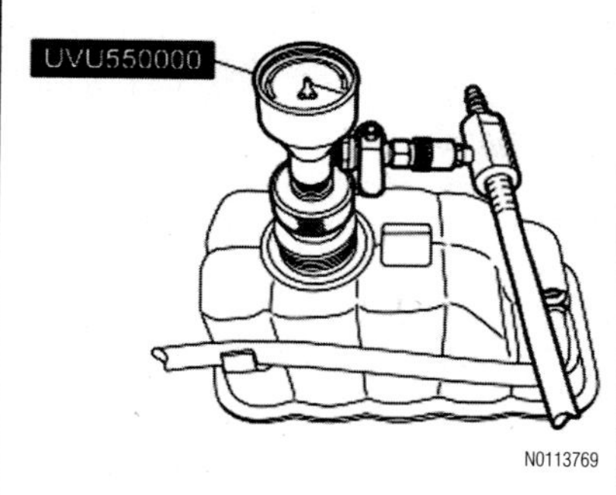

Fig. 59 Filling and Bleeding with a Vacuum Cooling System Filler

b. NEVER decrease the coolant concentration below 40%.
c. Minimum coolant concentration is 40/60 for warm weather areas.
d. A coolant concentration of 40% will provide freeze point protection down to -26°C (-15°F).
e. Engine coolant concentration below 40% will decrease the corrosion and freeze protection characteristics of the engine coolant and may damage the engine.
f. Vehicles driven year-round in non-extreme climates should use a 50/50 mixture of engine coolant and distilled water for optimum cooling system and engine protection.

Filling and Bleeding without a Vacuum Cooling System Filler

➡**The engine cooling system is filled with Motorcraft® Specialty Orange Engine Coolant. Always fill the cooling system with the manufacturer's specified coolant. If a non-specified coolant has been used the cooling system must be chemically flushed. Refer to Cooling System Flushing in this section. Failure to follow these instructions may damage the engine or cooling system.**

➡**The engine cooling system is filled with Motorcraft® Specialty Orange Engine Coolant. Do not mix cooling types. Mixing coolant types degrades the corrosion protection of Motorcraft® Specialty Orange Engine Coolant.**

➡**Engine coolant provides boil protection, corrosion protection, freeze protection and cooling efficiency to the engine and cooling components. In order to obtain these protections, maintain the engine coolant at the correct concentration and fluid level in the degas bottle. To maintain the integrity of the coolant and the cooling system:**

7. Add Motorcraft® Specialty Orange Engine Coolant or equivalent meeting Ford specification WSS-M97B44-D (orange color).

a. Do not add or mix with any other type of engine coolant. Mixing coolants may degrade the coolant's corrosion protection.
b. Do not add alcohol, methanol, or brine, or any engine coolants mixed with alcohol or methanol antifreeze. These can cause engine damage from overheating or freezing.
c. Ford Motor Company does NOT recommend the use of recycled engine coolant in vehicles originally equipped with Motorcraft® Specialty Orange Engine Coolant since a Ford-approved recycling process is not yet available.
d. Fill the radiator through the degas bottle until the coolant level is between the COOLANT FILL LEVEL marks.
e. Recommended coolant concentration is 50/50 engine coolant to distilled water.
f. For extremely cold climates (less than -34°F:
g. It may be necessary to increase the coolant concentration above 50%.

NEVER increase the coolant concentration above 60%.

h. Maximum coolant concentration is 60/40 for cold weather areas.
i. A coolant concentration of 60% will provide freeze point protection down to -58°F.
j. Engine coolant concentration above 60% will decrease the overheat protection characteristics of the engine coolant and may damage the engine.

8. For extremely hot climates:

a. It is still necessary to maintain the coolant concentration above 40%.
b. NEVER decrease the coolant concentration below 40%.
c. Minimum coolant concentration is 40/60 for warm weather areas.
d. A coolant concentration of 40% will provide freeze point protection down to -15°F.
e. Engine coolant concentration below 40% will decrease the corrosion and freeze protection characteristics of the engine coolant and may damage the engine.

9. Vehicles driven year-round in non-extreme climates should use a 50/50 mixture of engine coolant and distilled water for optimum cooling system and engine protection.
10. Select the maximum heater temperature and blower motor speed settings. Position the control to discharge air at A/C vents in instrument panel.

11. Start the engine and allow to idle. While engine is idling, feel for hot air at A/C vents.

➡If the air discharge remains cool and the Engine Coolant Temperature (ECT) gauge does not move, the engine coolant level is low and must be filled. Stop the engine, allow the engine to cool and fill cooling system. Failure to follow these instructions may result in damage to the engine.

12. Start the engine and allow it to idle until normal operating temperature is reached. Hot air should discharge from A/C vents. The Engine Coolant Temperature (ECT) gauge should maintain a stabilized reading in the middle of the NORMAL range. The upper radiator hose should feel hot to the touch.
13. Shut the engine off and allow the engine to cool.
14. Check the engine for coolant leaks.
15. Check the engine coolant level in the degas bottle and fill as necessary.

FLUSHING

CAUTION

Always allow the engine to cool before opening the cooling system. Do not unscrew the coolant pressure relief cap when the engine is operating or the cooling system is hot. The cooling system is under pressure; steam and hot liquid can come out forcefully when the cap is loosened slightly. Failure to follow these instructions may result in serious personal injury.

1. Once pressure is released, remove the pressure relief cap/radiator cap.
2. Drain the cooling system.
3. Remove the coolant thermostat. For additional information, refer to Thermostat in this section.
4. Install the coolant hose connection without the thermostat.

➡Refer to the cooling system flusher manufacturer's operating instructions for specific vehicle hook-up.

5. Using an appropriate cooling system flusher, flush the engine and radiator. Use Motorcraft® Premium Cooling System Flush and follow the directions on the packaging.
6. Install the thermostat.
7. Backflush the heater core. For additional information, refer to Heater Core Backflushing in this section.

Fill and bleed the cooling system.

HEATER CORE BACKFLUSHING

CAUTION

Always allow the engine to cool before opening the cooling system. Do not unscrew the coolant pressure relief cap when the engine is operating or the cooling system is hot. The cooling system is under pressure; steam and hot liquid can come out forcefully when the cap is loosened slightly. Failure to follow these instructions may result in serious personal injury.

1. Once pressure is released, remove the pressure relief cap/radiator cap.
2. Partially drain the cooling system.

➡For additional information, refer to the cooling system flusher manufacturer's operating instructions for particular vehicle hook-up.

3. Use an appropriate cooling system flusher to backflush the heater core. Use Motorcraft® Premium Cooling System Flush or equivalent meeting Ford specification ESR-M14P7-A. Flush with water thoroughly after using VC-1 or equivalent prior to refilling the cooling system.
4. Fill and bleed the cooling system.

SUPERCHARGER DRAINING, FILLING & BLEEDING

CAUTION

Always allow the engine to cool before opening the cooling system. Do not unscrew the coolant pressure relief cap when the engine is operating or the cooling system is hot. The cooling system is under pressure; steam and hot liquid can come out forcefully when the cap is loosened slightly. Failure to follow these instructions may result in serious personal injury.

➡Recover the coolant in a suitable, clean container for reuse. If the coolant is contaminated, recycle or dispose of it correctly. Using contaminated coolant may result in damage to the cooling system components.

➡The Supercharger (SC) cooling system is filled with Motorcraft® Specialty Orange Engine Coolant. Mixing coolant types degrades the corrosion protection of Motorcraft® Specialty Orange Engine Coolant.

➡Dirty, rusty or contaminated coolant requires replacement.

1. With the vehicle in NEUTRAL, position it on a hoist.
2. Remove the 9 bolts and the lower splash shield. Remove the 2 RH and the 2 LH screws securing the bumper and splash shield.
3. Remove the 12 bolts and the front bumper cover lower valance.
4. Disconnect the radiator-to-Charge Air Cooler (CAC) hose from the radiator and allow the coolant to drain in a suitable container.

➡The following steps must be performed after the Supercharger (SC) cooling system service has been completed.

5. Connect the radiator-to- CAC hose to the radiator.
6. Install the front bumper cover lower valance and the 12 bolts.
7. Install the 2 RH and the 2 LH screws.
8. Install the lower splash shield and the 9 bolts.

Filling and Bleeding with a Vacuum Cooling System Refiller

➡Coolant provides freeze protection, boil protection, corrosion protection and cooling efficiency to the cooling system components. In order to obtain these protections, maintain the engine coolant at the correct concentration and fluid level in the degas bottle.

➡The Supercharger (SC) cooling system is filled with Motorcraft® Specialty Orange Engine Coolant. Mixing coolant types degrades the corrosion protection of Motorcraft® Specialty Orange Engine Coolant.

➡When adding coolant, use a 50/50 mixture of coolant and distilled water.

9. To maintain the integrity of the coolant and the cooling system:
    a. Add Motorcraft® Specialty Orange Engine Coolant or equivalent meeting Ford specification WSS-M97B44-D (orange color). Use the same type of coolant that was drained from the cooling system. Do not mix coolant types.
    b. Do not add or mix any other engine coolant. Mixing coolants may degrade the coolant's corrosion protection.
    c. Do not add alcohol, methanol, brine or any coolants mixed with alcohol or methanol antifreeze. These can cause damage from overheating or freezing.
    d. Do not mix with recycled coolant.

Use of such coolants can harm the cooling system components.

Install the vacuum cooling system refiller and follow the manufacturer's instructions to fill and bleed the cooling system.

Filling and Bleeding without a Vacuum Cooling System Refiller

➡Coolant provides freeze protection, boil protection, corrosion protection and cooling efficiency to the cooling system components. In order to obtain these protections, maintain the engine coolant at the correct concentration and fluid level in the degas bottle.

➡The Supercharger (SC) cooling system is filled with Motorcraft® Specialty Orange Engine Coolant. Mixing coolant types degrades the corrosion protection of Motorcraft® Specialty Orange Engine Coolant.

➡When adding coolant, use a 50/50 mixture of coolant and distilled water.

10. To maintain the integrity of the coolant and the cooling system:
    a. Add Motorcraft® Specialty Orange Engine Coolant or equivalent meeting Ford specification WSS-M97B44-D (orange color). Use the same type of coolant that was drained from the cooling system.
    b. Do not mix coolant types.
    c. Do not add or mix any other engine coolant. Mixing coolants may degrade the coolant's corrosion protection.
    d. Do not add alcohol, methanol, brine or any coolants mixed with alcohol or methanol antifreeze. These can cause damage from overheating or freezing.
    e. Do not mix with recycled coolant. Use of such coolants can harm the cooling system components.
11. Fill the degas bottle.
12. Start the engine and allow to run until coolant circulation is observed in the degas bottle. Absence of circulation indicates air is trapped in the system.
13. Turn the engine off.
14. Add coolant as needed.
15. Repeat the above procedure to make sure all entrapped air is released.

ENGINE FAN

REMOVAL & INSTALLATION

3.7L and 5.0L Engines

See Figure 60.

1. Remove the air cleaner and the air cleaner outlet tube.

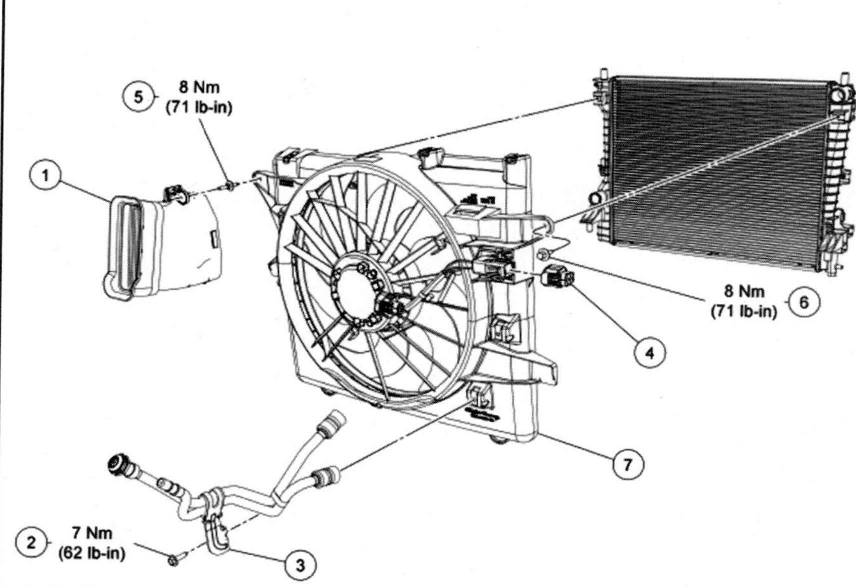

Fig. 60 Clutch pressure plate bolts (1), pressure plate (2) and clutch (3)—3.7L and 5.0L Engines

2. Release the tabs and remove the air cleaner inlet pipe.
3. Remove the 2 bolts and position the degas bottle aside.
4. Disconnect the cooling fan motor and shroud electrical connector.
5. If equipped, remove the transmission cooler tubes bracket bolt.
6. Remove the bolt, the stud bolt and the cooling fan motor and shroud.
7. To install, reverse the removal procedure.

4.0L Engines

See Figure 61.

1. Remove the Air Cleaner (ACL) outlet pipe.
2. Remove the bolt and position aside the power steering reservoir.
3. Detach the lower degas bottle hose from the cooling fan and shroud retaining clip.
4. Remove the 2 bolts and position aside the degas bottle.
5. Disconnect the cooling fan motor and shroud electrical connector.
6. Remove the 2 bolts and the cooling fan motor and shroud.
7. To install, reverse the removal procedure.

4.6L Engines

See Figure 62.

1. Remove the Air Cleaner (ACL) assembly and the ACL outlet tube.
2. Remove the ACL pipe from the cooling fan and shroud stud bolt.
3. Detach the lower degas bottle hose from the cooling fan and shroud retaining clip.
4. Remove the 2 bolts and position aside the degas bottle.
5. Disconnect the cooling fan motor and shroud electrical connector.
6. Remove the bolt, stud bolt and the cooling fan motor and shroud.
7. To install, reverse the removal procedure.

5.4L Engines

See Figure 63.

1. Drain the cooling system. For additional information, refer to Cooling System Draining, Filling and Bleeding in this section.
2. Drain the Supercharger (SC) cooling system.
3. Remove the Air Cleaner (ACL) assembly.
4. Remove the ACL inlet pipe from the cooling fan and shroud stud bolt.

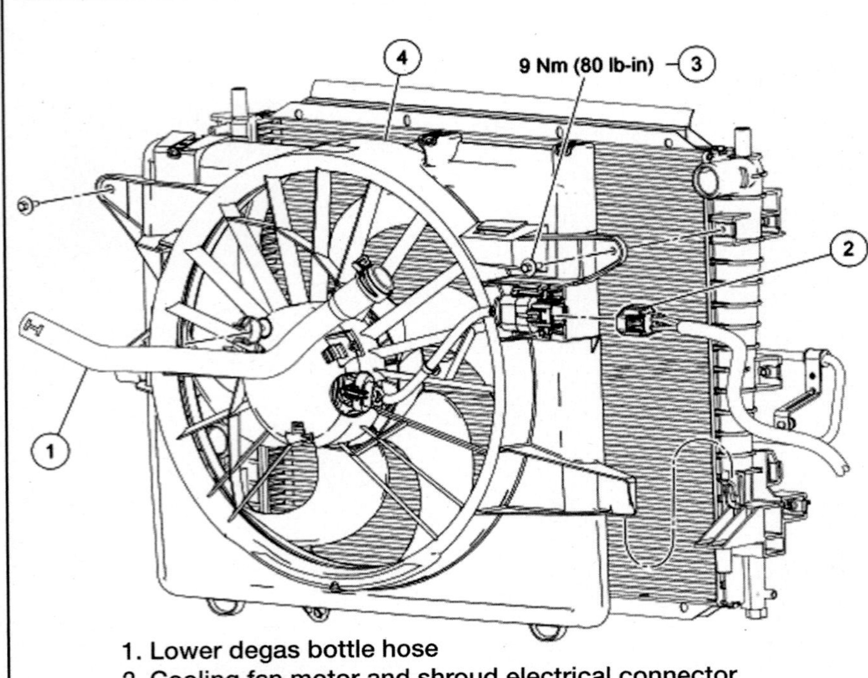

Fig. 61 View of the cooling fan and components—4.0L Engines

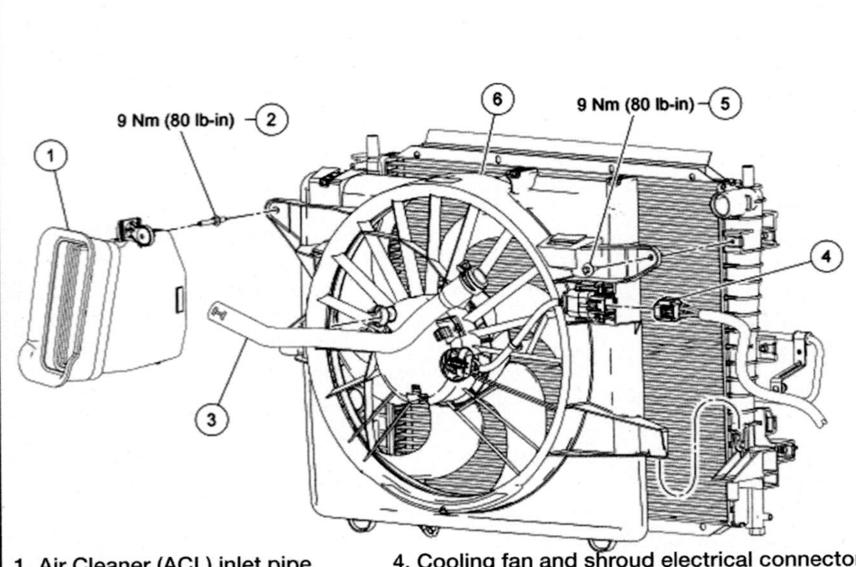

Fig. 62 View of the cooling fan and components—4.6L Engines

5. Disconnect the upper SC degas bottle hose and position it aside.
6. Remove the bolt and position aside the SC degas bottle.
7. Disconnect the upper degas bottle hose and position it aside.
8. Remove the 2 bolts and position aside the degas bottle.
9. Disconnect the cooling fan motor and shroud electrical connector.
10. Remove the bolt and position the charge air cooler aside.
11. Remove the bolt, stud bolt and the cooling fan motor and shroud.
12. To install, reverse the removal procedure.
13. Fill and bleed the cooling system.
14. Fill and bleed the SC cooling system.

RADIATOR

REMOVAL & INSTALLATION

1. Drain the cooling system.
2. Remove the 9 bolts and the lower splash shield.
3. Remove the 2 A/C condenser-to-radiator nuts.
4. To install, make sure the A/C condenser and the power steering tube brackets are installed on the studs.
5. Remove the cooling fan motor and shroud.
6. Remove the 8 pushpins and the radiator air deflector.
7. Vehicles equipped with 3.7L, 4.0L, 4.6L or 5.0L engine:
    a. Release the clamp and disconnect the radiator-to-degas bottle hose from the radiator.
8. All vehicles:
9. Release the clamp and disconnect the upper radiator hose from the radiator.
10. Release the clamp and disconnect the lower radiator hose from the radiator.
11. Remove the 4 bolts and the 2 radiator support brackets.
12. Lift the radiator off the lower radiator support and position the radiator, the A/C condenser and if equipped the transmission fluid cooler assembly toward the engine.
13. Remove the 2 A/C condenser-to-radiator bolts and position the A/C condenser aside.
14. If equipped, remove the 2 transmission fluid cooler bolts and position the transmission fluid cooler aside.
15. Remove the radiator.
16. To install, reverse the removal procedure.
17. Fill and bleed the cooling system.

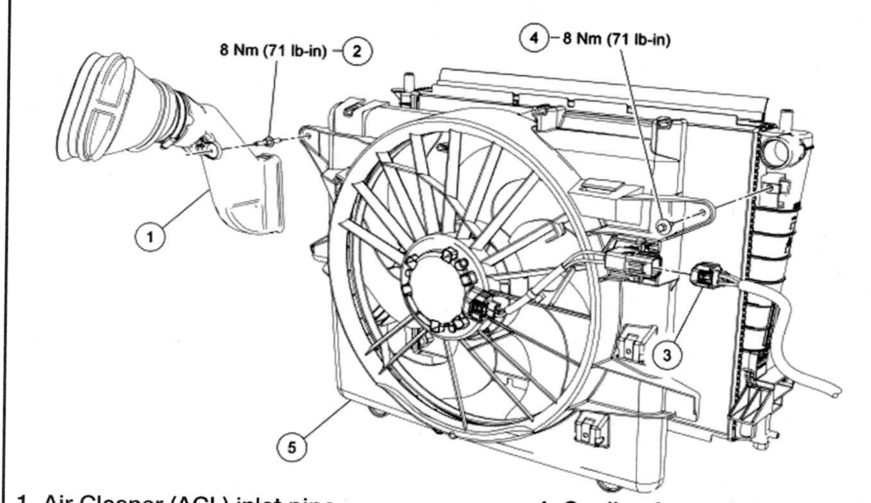

Fig. 63 View of the cooling fan and components—4.6L Engines

For additional information, refer to Cooling System Draining, Filling and Bleeding in this section.

THERMOSTAT

REMOVAL & INSTALLATION

3.7L Engines

Thermostat

See Figure 64.

1. Drain the cooling system.
2. Remove the air cleaner outlet pipe.

➡Cover the accessory drive belts to prevent coolant contamination of the belts.

3. Completely cover the accessory drive belts with waterproof plastic.
4. If installing a new coolant inlet connector, release the clamp and disconnect the lower radiator hose.
5. Remove the bolts and the coolant inlet connector.
6. Remove the thermostat and the thermostat O-ring seal.
7. Discard the O-ring seal.
8. To install, reverse the removal procedure.
9. Use a new O-ring seal and lubricate it with clean engine coolant.
10. Fill and bleed the cooling system.

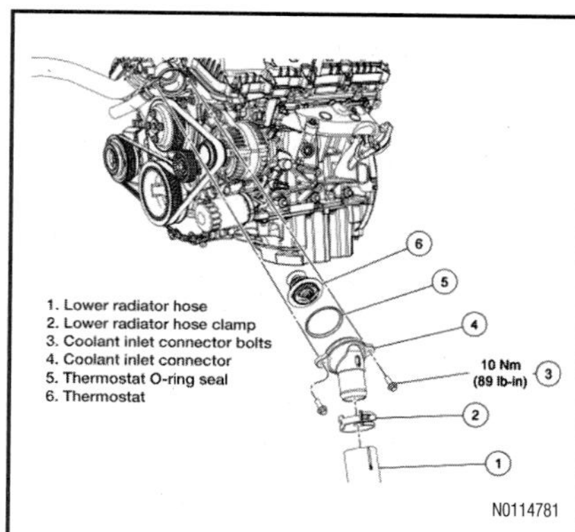

Fig. 64 Exploded view of the thermostat and components—3.7L Engines

Thermostat Housing

See Figure 65.

1. Drain the cooling system.
2. Remove the air cleaner outlet pipe.

➡Cover the accessory drive belts to prevent coolant contamination of the belts.

3. Completely cover the accessory drive belts with waterproof plastic.
4. Release the clamp and disconnect the thermostat housing-to-degas bottle from the thermostat housing.
5. Release the clamp and disconnect the lower radiator hose from the thermostat housing.
6. Release the clamp and disconnect the coolant return hose from the thermostat housing.
7. Release the clamp and disconnect the upper radiator hose from the thermostat housing.
8. Remove the 4 bolts and the thermostat housing.

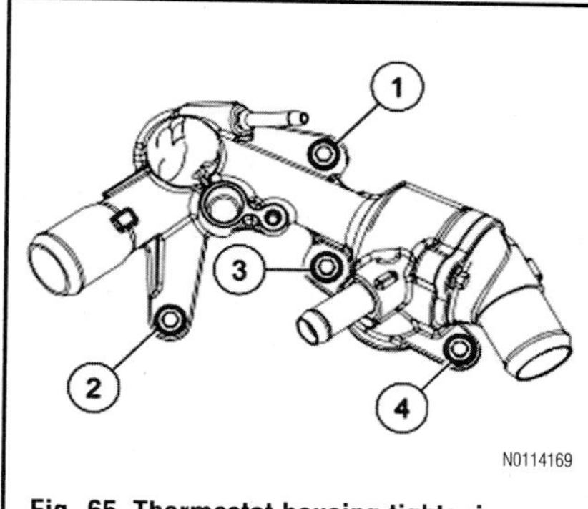

Fig. 65 Thermostat housing tightening sequence

9. Remove and discard the 2 O-ring seals.

To install:

10. Install 2 new O-ring seals and lubricate them with clean engine coolant.
11. Position the thermostat housing and install the bolts finger tight.
12. Tighten the 4 thermostat housing bolts in the sequence shown in 2 stages.
    a. Stage 1: Tighten to 70 inch lbs. (8 Nm).
    b. Stage 2: Tighten an additional 45 degrees.
13. Connect the upper radiator hose to the thermostat housing and position the clamp.
14. Connect the coolant return hose to the thermostat housing and position the clamp.
15. Connect the lower radiator hose to the thermostat housing and position the clamp.
16. Connect the thermostat housing-to-degas bottle to the thermostat housing and position the clamp.
17. Remove the plastic covering the accessory drive belts.
18. Install the air cleaner outlet pipe.
19. Fill and bleed the cooling system.

4.0L Engines

See Figure 66.

1. Drain the cooling system.
2. Remove the Air Cleaner (ACL) outlet pipe.
3. Remove the Throttle Body (TB). For additional information, refer to Fuel System.
4. Remove the 3 upper thermostat housing bolts and position aside the thermostat housing.
5. Discard the thermostat O-ring seal.
6. Remove the thermostat.

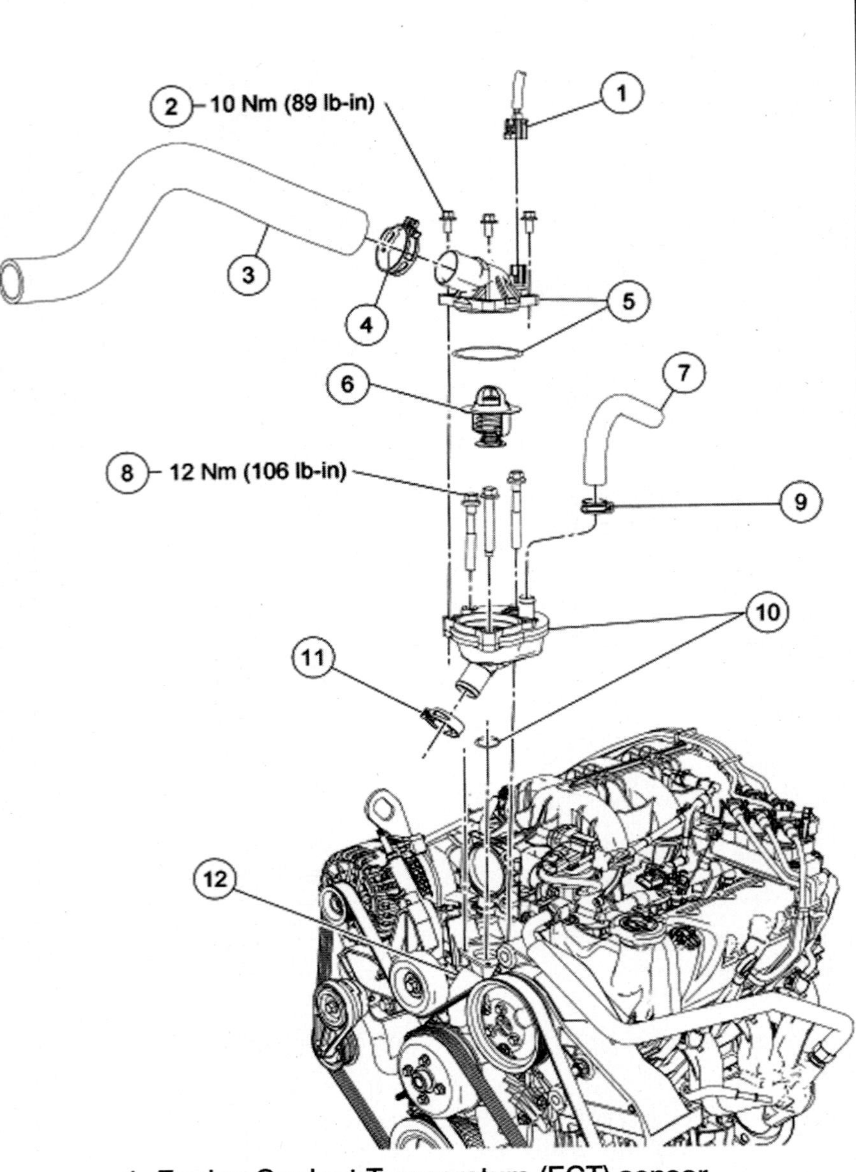

1. Engine Coolant Temperature (ECT) sensor electrical connector
2. Upper thermostat housing bolt (3 required)
3. Upper radiator hose
4. Upper radiator hose clamp
5. Thermostat housing cover and gasket
6. Thermostat
7. Heater inlet hose
8. Lower thermostat housing bolt (3 required)
9. Heater inlet hose clamp
10. Thermostat housing with O-ring seal
11. Bypass hose clamp
12. Bypass hose

N0089465

Fig. 66 Exploded view of the thermostat and components—4.0L Engines

7. To install, reverse the removal procedure.
8. Install a new thermostat O-ring seal and lubricate with clean engine coolant.
9. Fill and bleed the cooling system.

4.6L Engines

See Figure 67.

1. Disconnect the battery ground cable.
2. Drain the engine cooling system.
3. Remove the Air Cleaner (ACL) outlet pipe.
4. Remove the accessory drive belt. For additional information, refer to Accessory Drive.
5. Disconnect the crankcase vent tube from the intake manifold and position it aside.
6. Remove the 2 generator support bracket outer bolts.
7. Remove the 2 lower generator nuts and position the generator and wiring harness forward.
8. Loosen the 2 generator support bracket inner bolts and position aside the generator and wiring harness.

➡The thermostat cover has a slotted flange for the RH bolt.

9. Remove the LH thermostat cover bolt and loosen the RH bolt.
10. Position aside the thermostat cover and hose assembly.
11. Remove the thermostat O-ring seal and the thermostat.
12. Discard the thermostat O-ring seal.

To install:

➡Lubricate the O-ring seal with clean engine coolant.

13. Install the thermostat and a new O-ring seal.
14. Position the thermostat cover slotted flange under the RH bolt and install the LH bolt.
15. Position the generator and wiring harness.
16. Tighten the 2 generator support bracket inner bolts.
17. Install the 2 lower generator nuts.
18. Install the 2 outer generator support bracket bolts.
19. Connect the crankcase vent tube to the intake manifold.
20. Install the accessory drive belt.
21. Install the ACL outlet pipe.
22. Connect the battery ground cable.
23. Fill and bleed the cooling system.

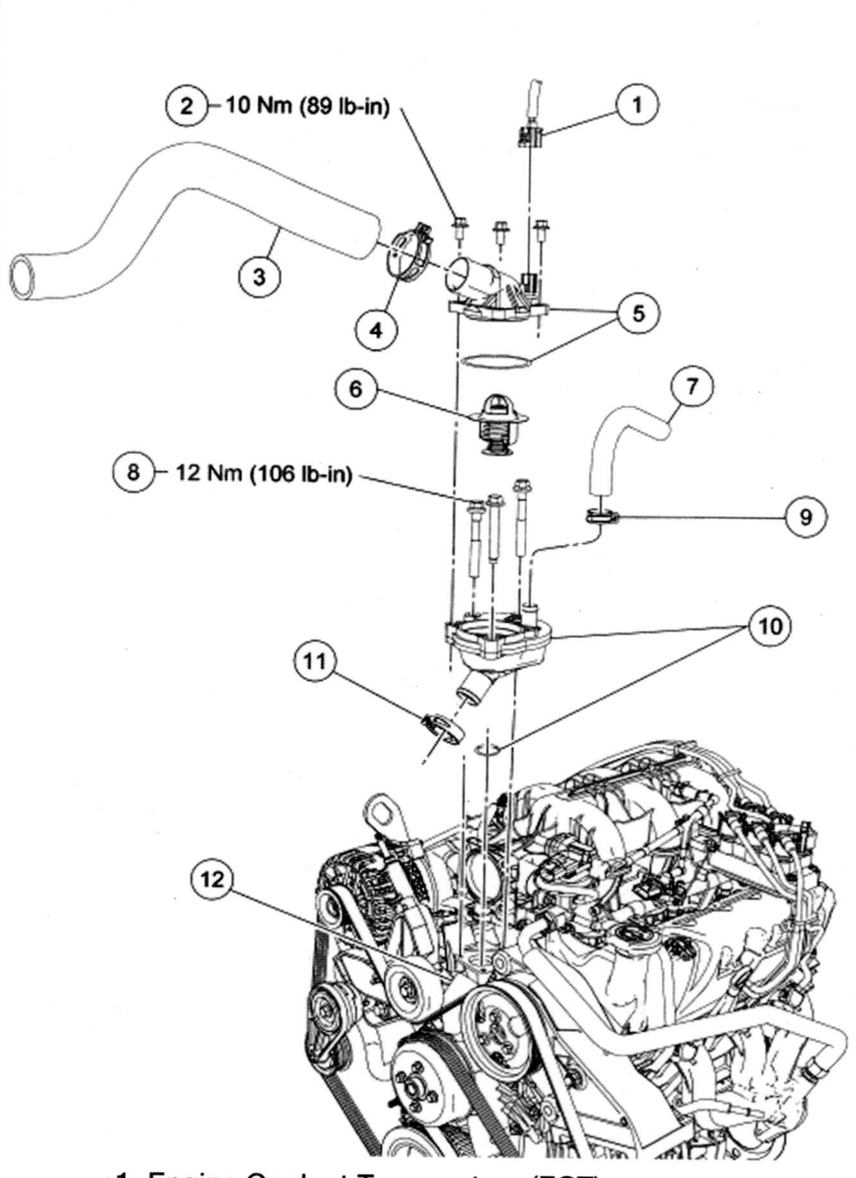

Fig. 67 Exploded view of the thermostat and components—4.6L Engines

5.0L Engines

Thermostat

See Figure 68.

1. Drain the cooling system.
2. Remove the air cleaner outlet pipe.

➡Cover the accessory drive belts to prevent coolant contamination of the belts.

3. Completely cover the accessory drive belts with waterproof plastic.
4. If installing a new coolant inlet connector, release the clamp and disconnect the lower radiator hose.
5. Remove the bolts and the coolant inlet connector.
6. Remove the thermostat and the O-ring seal.
7. Discard the O-ring seal.
8. To install, reverse the removal procedure.
9. Use a new O-ring seal and lubricate it with clean engine coolant.
10. Fill and bleed the cooling system.

Thermostat Housing

See Figure 69.

1. Drain the cooling system.

➡Cover the accessory drive belts to prevent coolant contamination of the belts.

2. Completely cover the accessory drive belts with waterproof plastic.
3. Release the clamp and disconnect the lower radiator hose from the coolant inlet connection.

➡The quick connect coupling illustrated is to show the spring clip release location only. The quick connect coupling on the hose may differ.

4. Pull the upper radiator hose spring clip up until the end of the clip is in the detent on the quick connect coupling and disconnect the upper radiator hose from the upper radiator hose T-connector.
5. To install, push the spring clip in place and connect the upper radiator hose quick connect coupling, making sure the coupling is secure.
6. Remove the thermostat housing bolts.

➡The quick connect coupling illustrated is to show the spring clip release location only. The quick connect coupling on the hose may differ.

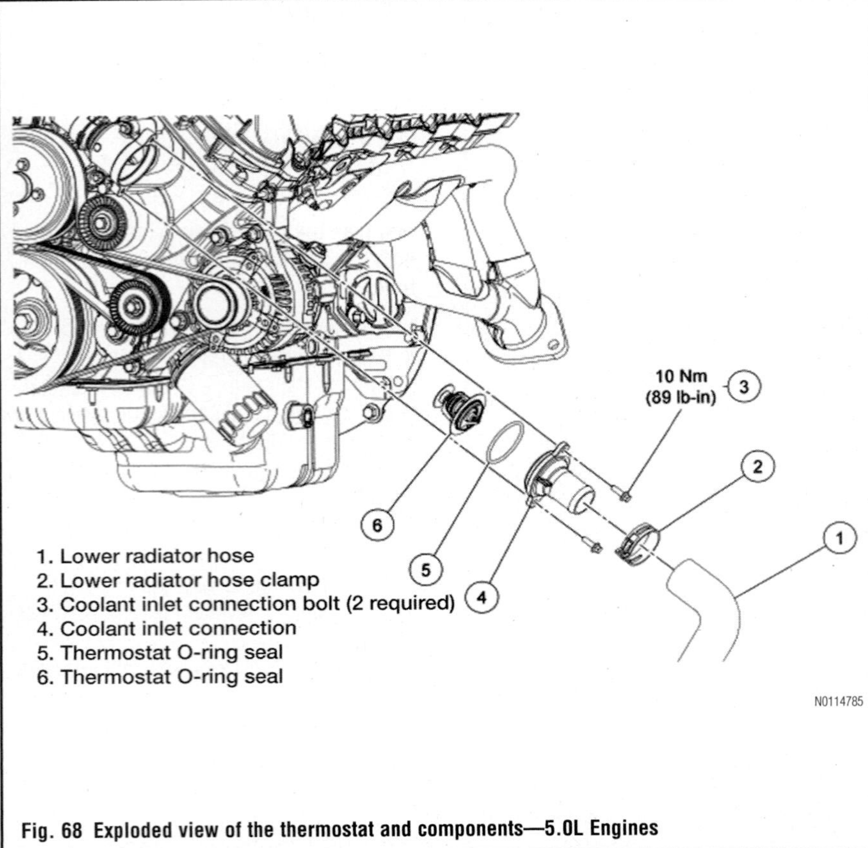

Fig. 68 Exploded view of the thermostat and components—5.0L Engines

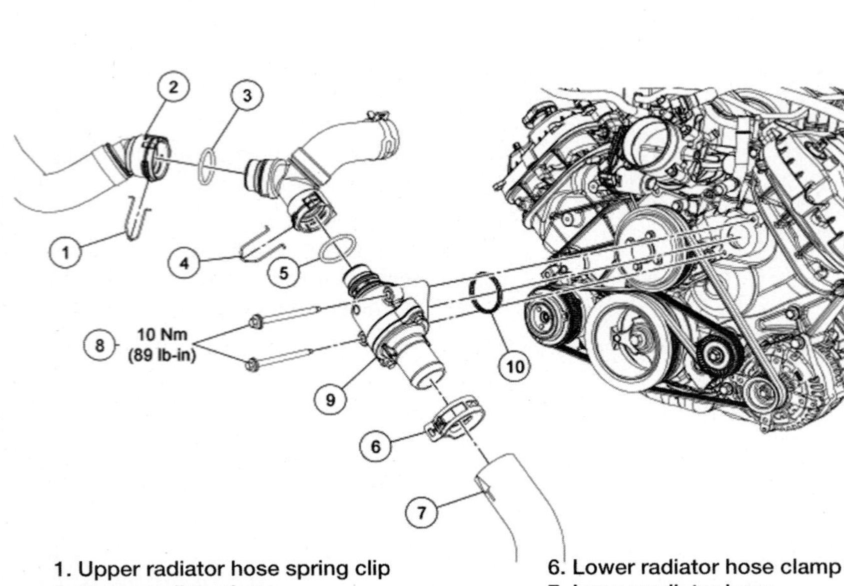

Fig. 69 Exploded view of the thermostat housing—5.0L Engines

7. Pull the upper radiator hose T-connector spring clip up until the end of the clip is in the detent on the quick connect coupling and remove the thermostat housing from the upper radiator hose T-connector.
8. Remove and discard the thermostat housing gasket.
9. To install, align the tab on the thermostat housing with the slot in the upper radiator hose T-connector.
10. To install, push the spring clip in place and connect the thermostat housing to the upper radiator hose T-connector quick connect coupling, making sure the coupling is secure.
11. To install, reverse the removal procedure.
12. Use a new thermostat housing gasket.
13. Fill and bleed the cooling system.

5.4L Engines

See Figure 70.

1. Drain the engine cooling system.
2. Remove the 2 bolts and position aside the thermostat housing cover and hose assembly.
3. Remove the O-ring seal and the thermostat.
4. Discard the O-ring seal.
5. To install, reverse the removal procedure.
6. Lubricate the new O-ring seal with clean engine coolant.
7. Fill and bleed the cooling system.

WATER PUMP

REMOVAL & INSTALLATION

3.7L Engines

See Figures 71 and 72.

1. Remove the air cleaner outlet pipe.
2. Loosen the 4 coolant pump pulley bolts.
3. Remove the accessory drive belt. For additional information, refer to Accessory Drive.

➡Cover the A/C compressor belt to prevent coolant contamination of the belt.

4. Completely cover the A/C compressor belt with waterproof plastic.
5. Remove the thermostat housing. For additional information, refer to Thermostat Housing —3.7L in this section.
6. Remove the 4 bolts and the coolant pump pulley.
7. Remove the 7 bolts and the coolant pump.

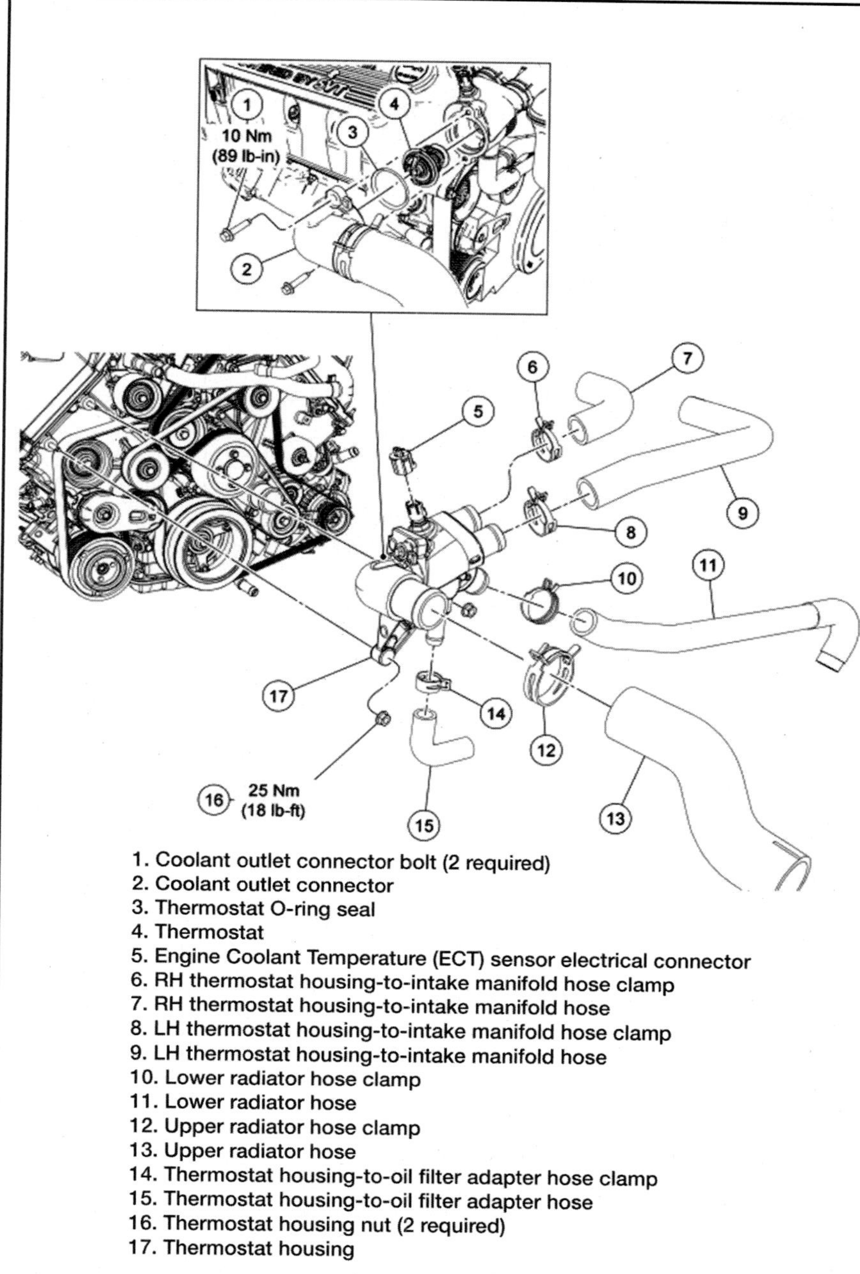

Fig. 70 Exploded view of the thermostat and components—5.4L Engines

8. Remove and discard the gasket and the O-ring seal in the coolant pump.

To install:

Install a new O-ring seal in the coolant pump and lubricate it with clean engine coolant.

Position a new gasket, press the coolant pump over the channel cover plate snout protruding from the engine front cover and install the 7 bolts finger tight.

Tighten the coolant pump bolts in the sequence shown in 2 stages.

Stage 1: Tighten to 89 inch lbs. (10 Nm).

Stage 2: Tighten an additional 45 degrees.

9. Position the coolant pump pulley and install the 4 bolts finger tight.
10. Install the thermostat housing.
11. Remove the plastic from the A/C compressor belt.
12. Install the accessory drive belt.
13. Tighten the 4 coolant pump pulley bolts to 18 ft. lbs. (24 Nm).
14. Install the air cleaner outlet pipe.
15. Fill and bleed the cooling system.

4.0L Engines

See Figure 73.

1. Drain the engine coolant.
2. Remove the Air Cleaner (ACL) outlet pipe.
3. Loosen the 4 coolant pump pulley bolts.
4. Remove the accessory drive belt.
5. Remove the 4 coolant pump pulley bolts and the coolant pump pulley.
6. Disconnect the thermostat housing-to-coolant pump hose.
7. Disconnect the heater hose and position aside.
8. Disconnect the radiator-to-coolant pump hose and position aside.
9. Remove the 12 coolant pump bolts and the coolant pump.
10. Discard the coolant pump gasket.
11. Use metal surface prep and a suitable plastic or wooden scraper to clean the sealing surfaces.
12. To install, reverse the removal procedure.
13. Install a new coolant pump gasket.
14. Fill and bleed the cooling system.

4.6L Engines

See Figure 74.

1. Drain the engine cooling system.
2. Remove the Air Cleaner (ACL) outlet pipe.
3. Loosen the 4 coolant pump pulley bolts.
4. Remove the accessory drive belt. For additional information, refer to Accessory Drive.
5. Remove the 4 coolant pump pulley bolts and the coolant pump pulley.
6. Remove the 4 coolant pump bolts and the coolant pump.
7. Discard the coolant pump O-ring seal.
8. To install, reverse the removal procedure.
9. Install a new coolant pump O-ring seal and lubricate with clean engine coolant.
10. Fill and bleed the cooling system.

5.0L Engines

See Figure 75.

1. Drain the cooling system.
2. Remove the air cleaner outlet pipe.
3. Loosen the 4 coolant pump pulley bolts.

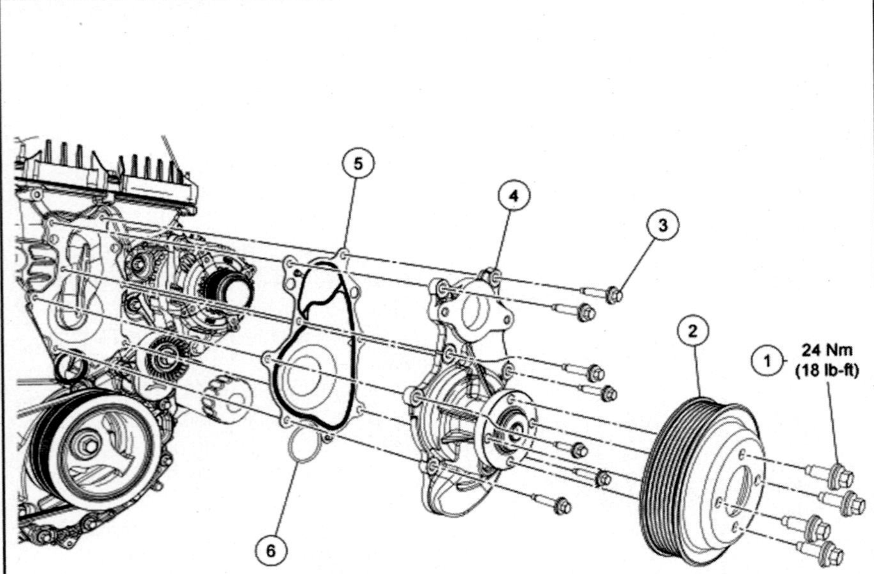

1. Coolant pump pulley bolt (4 required)
2. Coolant pump pulley
3. Coolant pump bolt (7 required)
4. Coolant pump
5. Coolant pump gasket
6. Coolant pump O-ring seal

N0114761

Fig. 71 Exploded view of the water pump and components

4. Remove the accessory drive belt. For additional information, refer to Accessory Drive.

➡Cover the A/C compressor belt to prevent coolant contamination of the belt.

5. Completely cover the A/C compressor belt with waterproof plastic.
6. Remove the thermostat housing. For additional information, refer to Thermostat Housing —5.0L in this section.
7. Remove the bolts and the coolant pump pulley.
8. Disconnect the heater outlet hose from the heater outlet tube.
9. Release the clamp and disconnect the degas bottle-to-engine hose from the heater outlet tube.
10. Remove the 4 bolts and the coolant pump.
11. If a new coolant pump is being installed, remove the bolt and the heater outlet tube.
12. Remove and discard the O-ring seal.

To install:

13. If a new coolant pump is being installed, install a new O-ring seal on the heater outlet tube and lubricate it with clean engine coolant.

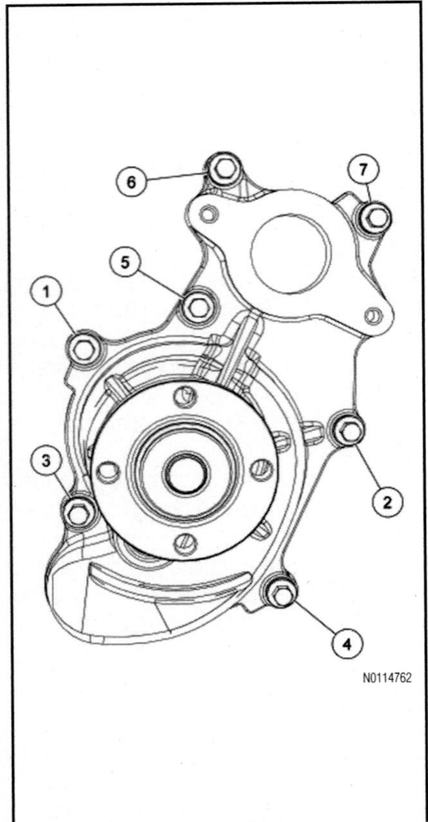

Fig. 72 Water pump tightening sequence

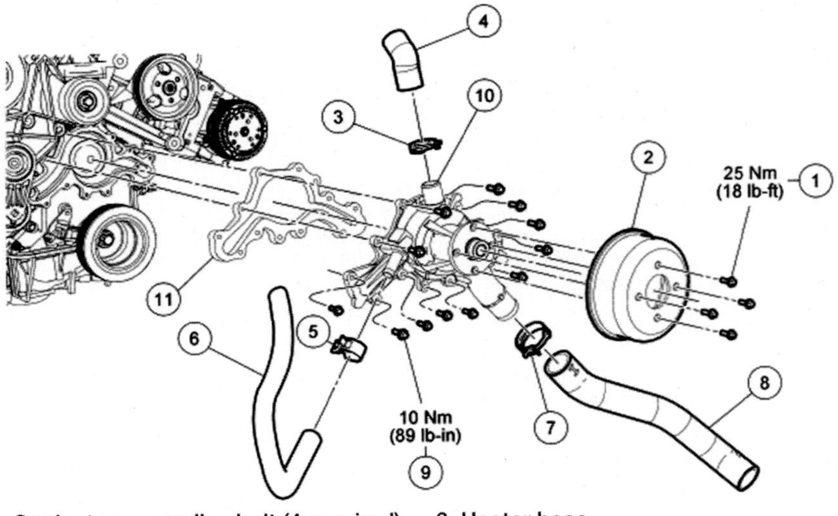

4
10
3
2
25 Nm
(18 lb-ft)
1
11
6
5
8
10 Nm
(89 lb-in)
7
9

1. Coolant pump pulley bolt (4 required)
2. Coolant pump pulley
3. Hose clamp
4. Thermostat housing-to-coolant pump hose
5. Hose clamp
6. Heater hose
7. Hose clamp
8. Radiator-to-coolant pump hose
9. Coolant pump bolt (12 required)
10. Coolant pump
11. Coolant pump gasket

N0073921

Fig. 73 Exploded view of the water pump and components—4.0L Engines

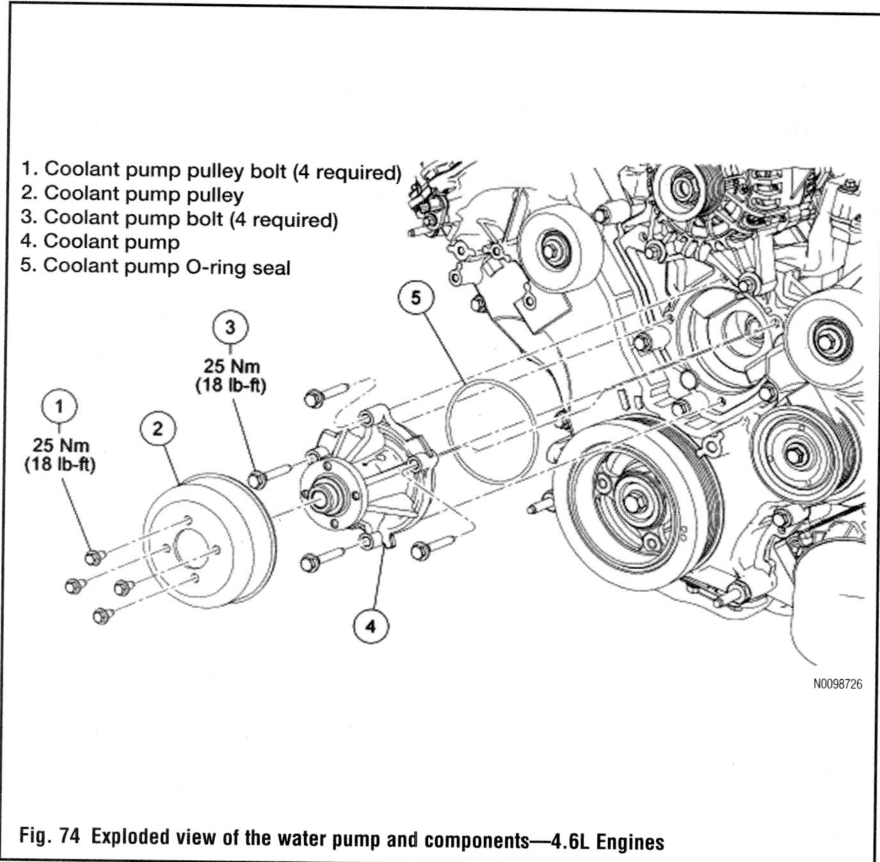

Fig. 74 Exploded view of the water pump and components—4.6L Engines

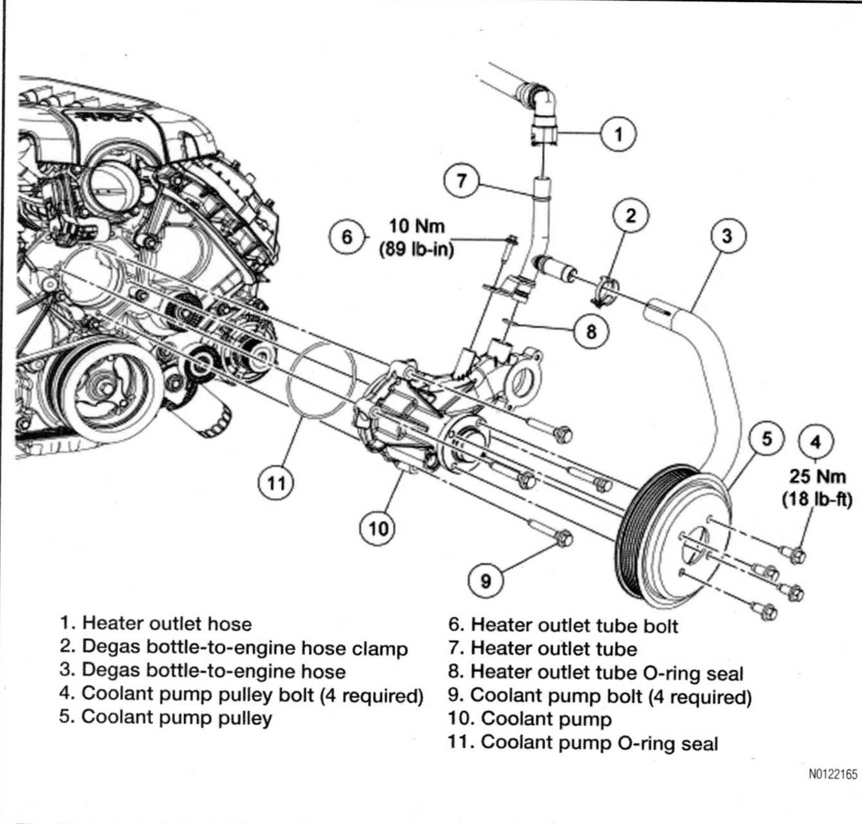

Fig. 75 Exploded view of the water pump and components—5.0L Engines

14. Install the heater outlet tube and the bolt.
15. Inspect the sealing surfaces and clean with metal surface prep. Follow the instructions on the packaging.

➡Align the bolt holes with the bosses prior to insertion of the coolant pump and insert the pump straight into the coolant pump cavity. Do not rotate the coolant pump once installed into the coolant pump cavity or the O-ring seal can be damaged, causing the coolant pump to leak.

➡Install a new O-ring seal and lubricate it with clean engine coolant.

16. Install the coolant pump and the bolts.
17. Tighten the coolant pump bolts in 2 stages.
    a. Stage 1: Tighten to 15 ft. lbs (20 Nm).
    b. Stage 2: Tighten an additional 60 degrees.
18. Connect the degas bottle-to-engine hose to the heater outlet tube and position the clamp.
19. Connect the heater outlet hose to the heater outlet tube.
20. Position the coolant pump pulley and install the bolts finger tight.
21. Install the thermostat housing.
22. Remove the plastic from the A/C compressor belt.
23. Install the accessory drive belt.
24. Tighten the coolant pump pulley bolts in a criss-cross pattern. Tighten to 18 ft. lbs. (25 Nm)
25. Install the air cleaner outlet tube.
26. Fill and bleed the cooling system.

5.4L Engine

See Figure 76.

1. Drain the cooling system.
2. Drain the Supercharger (SC) cooling system.
3. Disconnect the upper intake manifold-to-degas bottle hose, remove the 2 bolts and position the degas bottle aside.
4. Disconnect the Charge Air Cooler (CAC)-to- SC degas bottle hose, remove the bolt and position the SC degas bottle aside.
5. Loosen the 4 coolant pump pulley bolts.
6. Remove the accessory drive belt. For additional information, refer to Accessory Drive.
7. Rotate the SC belt tensioner clockwise and remove the SC belt off the SC.
8. Remove the 4 coolant pump pulley bolts and the coolant pump pulley.

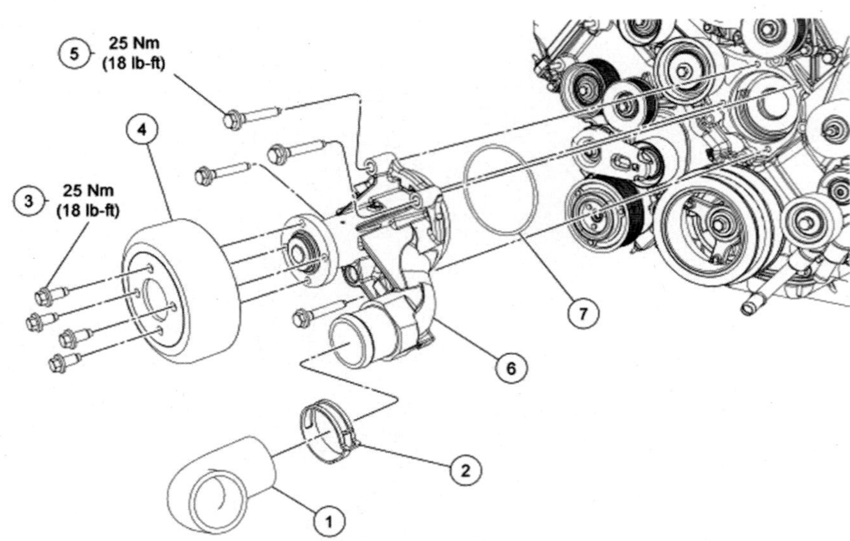

Fig. 76 Exploded view of the water pump and components—5.4L Engines

9. Release the clamp and disconnect the lower radiator hose from the coolant pump.
10. Remove the 4 bolts and the coolant pump.
11. Discard the coolant pump O-ring seal.
12. To install, reverse the removal procedure.
13. Install a new coolant pump O-ring seal and lubricate with clean engine coolant.
14. Fill and bleed the cooling system.
15. Fill and bleed the SC cooling system.

ENGINE ELECTRICAL

BATTERY

REMOVAL & INSTALLATION

See Figure 77.

WARNING

Always lift a plastic-cased battery with a battery carrier or with hands on opposite corners. Excessive pressure on the battery end walls may cause acid to flow through the vent caps, resulting in personal injury and/or damage to the vehicle or battery.

Refer to the illustration to remove the battery.

BATTERY RECONNECT/RELEARN PROCEDURE

WARNING

Batteries contain sulfuric acid and produce explosive gases. Work in a well-ventilated area. Do not allow the battery to come in contact with flames, sparks or burning substances. Avoid contact with skin, eyes or clothing. Shield eyes when working near the battery to protect against possible splashing of acid solution. In case of acid contact with skin or eyes, flush immediately with water for a minimum of 15 minutes, then get prompt medical attention. If acid is swallowed, call a physician immediately. Failure to follow these instructions may result in serious personal injury.

WARNING

Always deplete the backup power supply before repairing or installing any new front or side air bag supplemental restraint system (SRS) component and before servicing, removing, installing, adjusting or striking components near the front or side impact sensors or the restraints control module (RCM). Nearby components include doors, instrument panel, console, door latches, strikers, seats and hood latches.

WARNING

Battery posts, terminals and related accessories contain lead and lead components. Wash hands after handling. Failure to follow these instructions may result in serious personal injury.

1. To deplete the backup power supply energy, disconnect the battery ground cable and wait at least 1 minute. Be sure to disconnect auxiliary batteries and power supplies (if equipped).

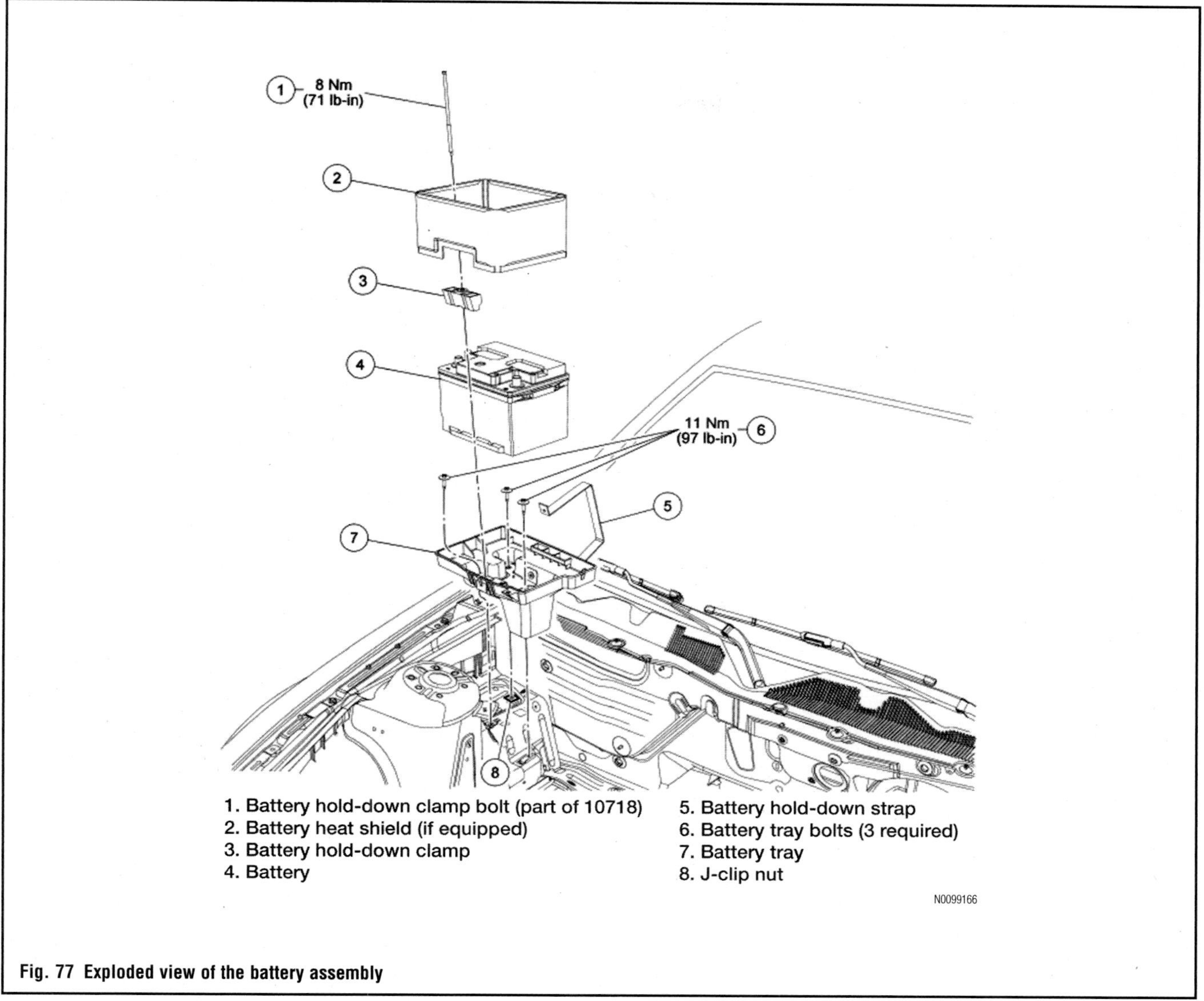

Fig. 77 Exploded view of the battery assembly

Failure to follow these instructions may result in serious personal injury or death in the event of an accidental deployment.

➡When the battery (or PCM) is disconnected and connected, some abnormal drive symptoms may occur while the vehicle relearns its adaptive strategy. The charging system set point may also vary. The vehicle may need to be driven to relearn its strategy.

➡When disconnecting the battery ground cable to interrupt power to the vehicle electrical system, disconnect the battery ground cable only. It is not necessary to disconnect the positive battery cable.

2. Disconnect the battery ground terminal.
3. Disconnect the positive battery terminal.
4. To connect, reverse the disconnect procedure.

ALTERNATOR

REMOVAL & INSTALLATION

3.7L Engines

See Figure 78.

1. Disconnect the battery.
2. Rotate the Front End Accessory Drive (FEAD) belt tensioner counterclockwise and position the FEAD belt aside.
3. Disconnect the generator electrical connector.
4. Position the generator B+ protective boot aside, remove the B+ nut and position the B+ terminal aside.
5. Remove the generator stud nut.
6. Remove the generator bolt and the generator.
7. To install, reverse the removal procedure.
8. Refer to illustration for torque values.

4.0L Engines

See Figure 79.

1. Disconnect the battery.
2. Rotate the Front End Accessory Drive (FEAD) belt tensioner counterclockwise and position the FEAD belt aside.
3. Disconnect the generator electrical connector.

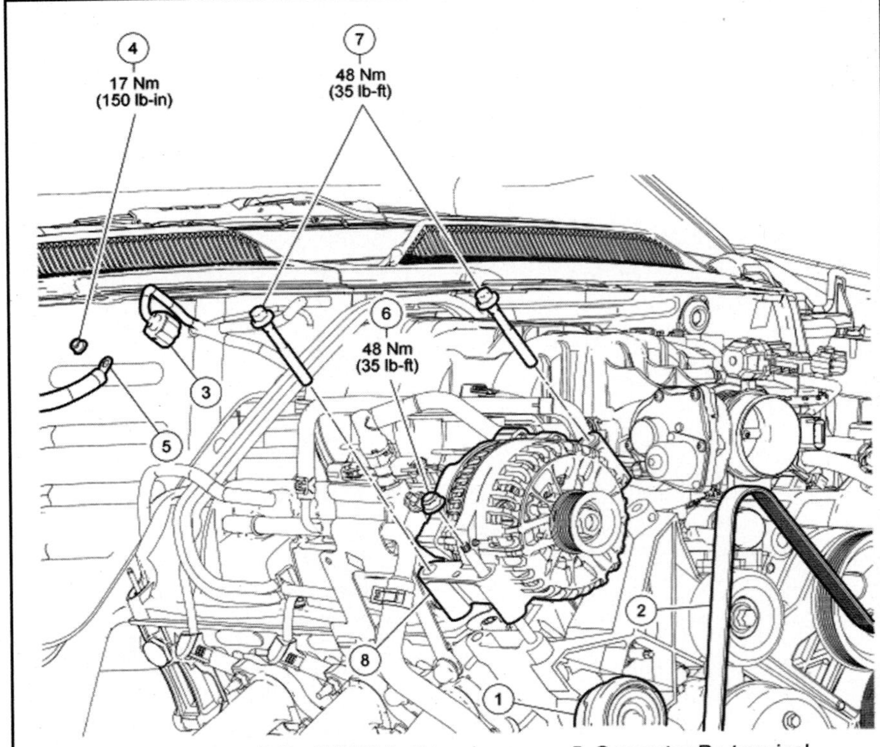

1. Front End Accessory Drive (FEAD) belt tensioner
2. FEAD belt
3. Generator electrical connector
4. Generator B+ terminal nut
5. Generator B+ terminal
6. Generator stud nut
7. Generator bolts (2 required)
8. Generator

N0089585

Fig. 79 View of the alternator—4.0L Engines

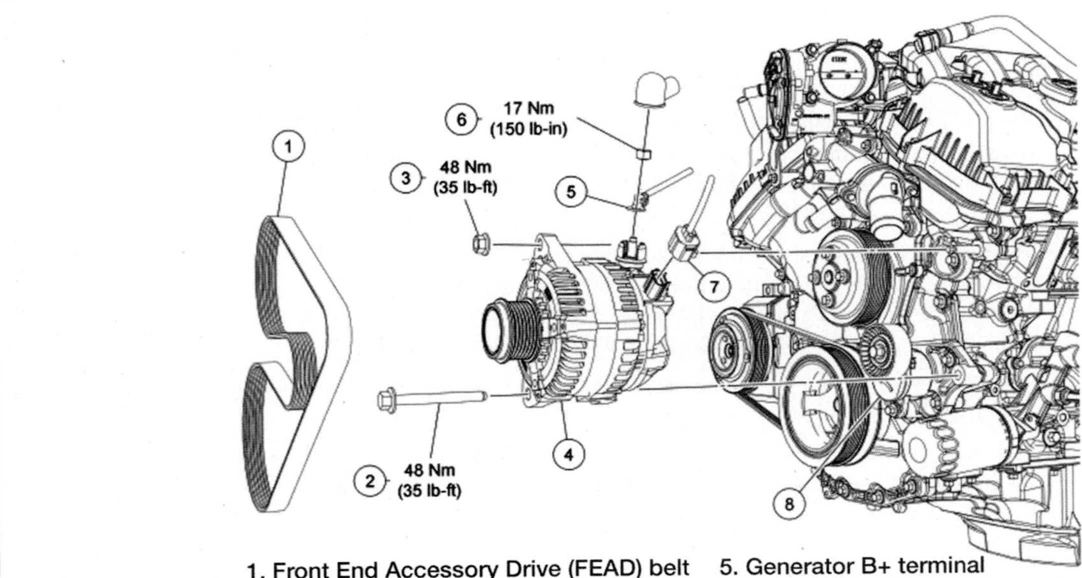

1. Front End Accessory Drive (FEAD) belt
2. Generator bolt
3. Generator stud nut
4. Generator
5. Generator B+ terminal
6. Generator B+ terminal nut
7. Generator electrical connector
8. FEAD belt tensioner

N0116435

Fig. 78 View of the alternator—3.7L Engines

4. Position the generator B+ protective boot aside, remove the nut and position the generator B+ terminal aside.
5. Remove the generator stud nut.
6. Remove the 2 bolts and the generator.
7. To install, reverse the removal procedure.
8. Refer to illustration for torque values.

4.6L Engines

See Figure 80.

1. Disconnect the battery.
2. Press the lock tab, remove the crankcase vent tube from the Air Cleaner (ACL) outlet pipe and position it aside.
3. Loosen the clamps, remove the ACL outlet pipe from the throttle body and remove it from the vehicle.
4. Rotate the Front End Accessory Drive (FEAD) belt tensioner clockwise and position the FEAD belt aside.
5. Remove the generator harness locator.
6. Remove the 2 generator bolts.
7. Remove the 2 outer generator bracket bolts and position the generator aside.
8. Loosen the 2 inner generator bracket bolts.
9. Pull the generator outward.
10. Remove the generator bracket.
11. Disconnect the generator electrical connector.
12. Position the generator B+ protective boot aside, remove the nut and position the generator B+ terminal aside.
13. Remove the generator.
14. To install, reverse the removal procedure.
15. Refer to illustration for torque values.

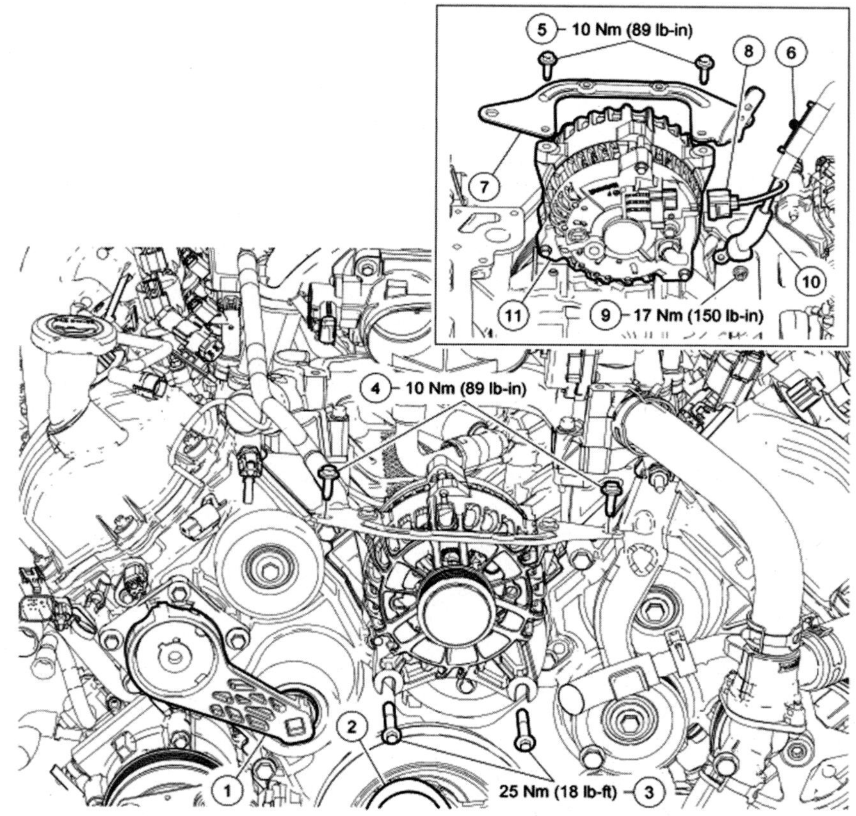

Fig. 80 View of the alternator—4.6L Engines

5.0L Engines

See Figure 81.

1. Disconnect the battery.
2. Remove the Air Cleaner (ACL) outlet pipe and ACL assembly.
3. Remove the ACL inlet pipe from the radiator support.
4. Remove the Front End Accessory Drive (FEAD) belt tensioner. For additional information, refer to Accessory Drive.
5. Position the generator B+ protective boot aside, remove the B+ nut and position the B+ terminal aside.
6. Disconnect the generator electrical connector.
7. Remove the upper generator stud nut.
8. Remove the upper generator stud.
9. Remove the lower generator bolt and the generator.
10. To install, reverse the removal procedure.
11. Refer to illustration for torque values.

5.4L Engines

See Figure 82.

1. With the vehicle in NEUTRAL, position it on a hoist.
2. Disconnect the battery.
3. Rotate the Front End Accessory Drive (FEAD) tensioner clockwise and position the FEAD belt aside.
4. Remove the Air Cleaner (ACL) assembly.
5. Remove the 2 upper generator bolts.
6. Remove the power steering tube bracket nut and position the bracket aside.
7. Remove and discard the 4 stabilizer bracket nuts, then remove the stabilizer bar brackets and position the sway bar aside.
8. Disconnect the generator electrical connector and remove the harness retainer pushpin from the rear of the generator.
9. Position the harness aside.
10. Position the generator B+ protective boot aside, remove the nut and position the generator B+ terminal aside.
11. Remove the lower generator bolt.
12. Remove the generator.
13. To install, reverse the removal procedure.
14. Refer to illustration for torque values.

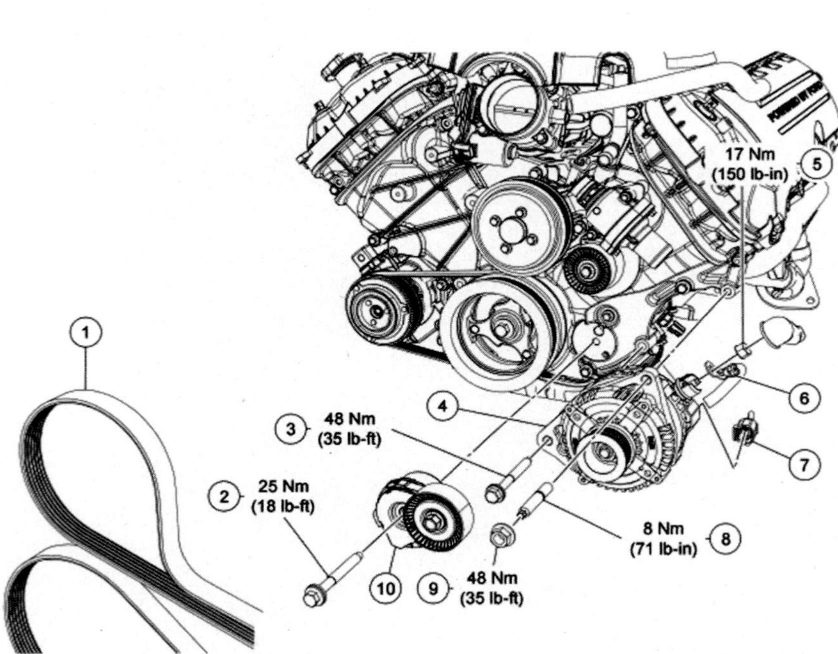

Fig. 81 View of the alternator—5.0L Engines

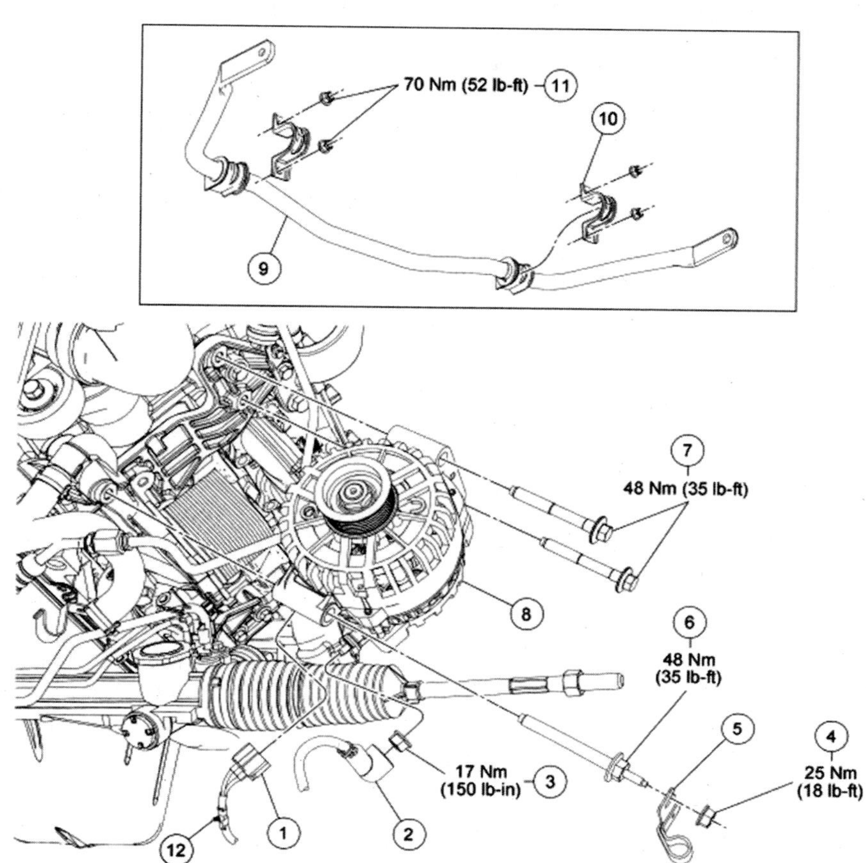

1. Generator electrical connector
2. Generator B+ terminal
3. Generator B+ terminal nut
4. Generator stud nut
5. Power steering fluid line bracket
6. Lower generator bolt
7. Upper generator bolts (2 required)
8. Generator
9. Stabilizer
10. Stabilizer bar bracket
11. Bracket nuts (4 required)
12. Wire harness retainer

N0089586

Fig. 82 View of the alternator—5.4L Engines

FIRING ORDER

See Figures 83 and 84.

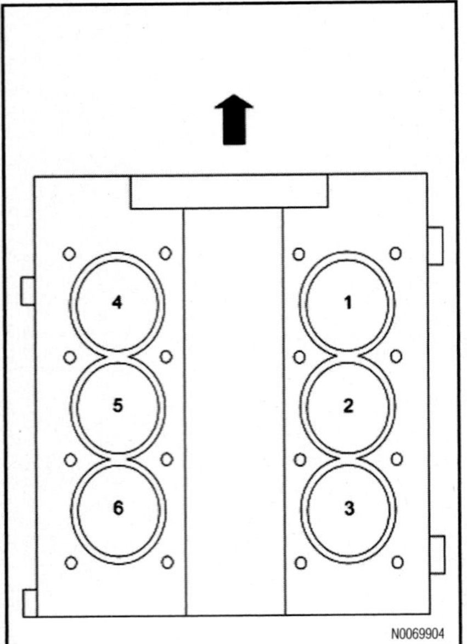

Fig. 83 Engine firing order—6 cylinder engines

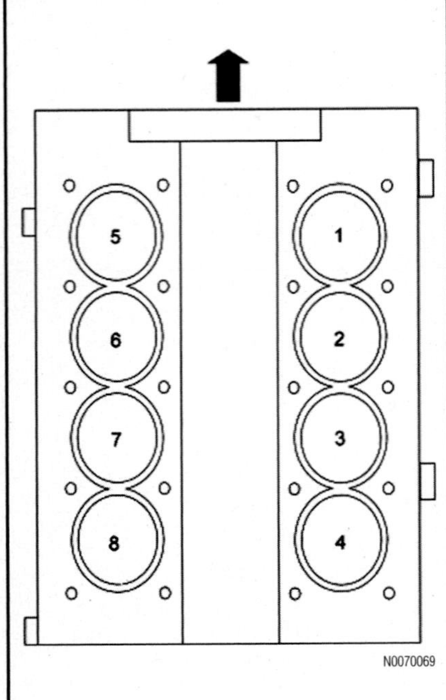

Fig. 84 Engine firing order—8 cylinder engines

IGNITION COIL

REMOVAL & INSTALLATION

3.7L Engines

See Figure 85.

1. LH side: Disconnect the crankcase ventilation tube-to-valve cover fitting quick connect coupling and position aside. For additional information, refer to Engine Performance.
2. RH side:

➡The upper intake manifold must be removed to access the RH ignition coil-on-plugs.

   a. Remove the upper intake manifold. For additional information, refer to Intake Manifold.

3. Both sides:
4. Disconnect the ignition coil-on-plug electrical connector.

➡When removing the ignition coil-on-plug, a slight twisting motion will break the seal and ease removal.

5. Remove the bolt and the ignition coil-on-plug.
6. Inspect the coil seal for rips, nicks or tears. Remove and discard any damaged coil seals.
7. To install, slide the new coil seal onto the coil until it is fully seated at the top of the coil.
8. To install, reverse the removal procedure.
9. Apply a small amount of dielectric grease to the inside of the ignition coil-on-plug boot before attaching to the spark plug.

4.0L Engines

See Figure 86.

1. Disconnect the negative battery cable.
2. Disconnect the electrical connector from the ignition coil.

➡It is important to twist the spark plug wire boots while pulling upward to avoid possible damage to the spark plug wires.

➡Spark plug wires must be connected to the correct ignition coil terminal.

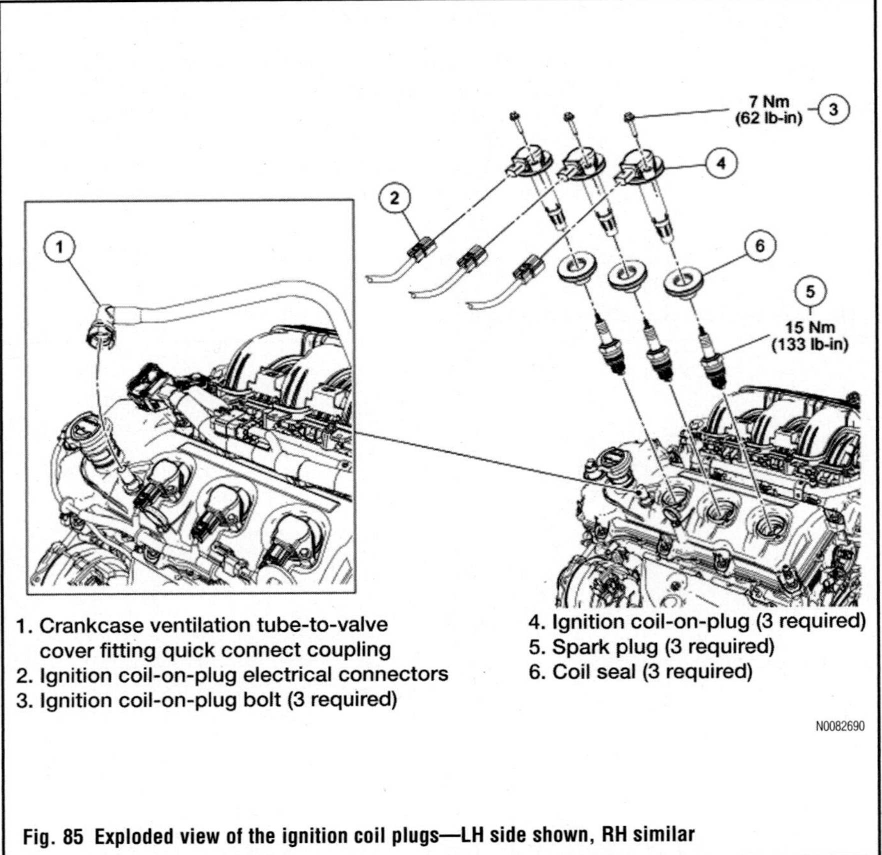

Fig. 85 Exploded view of the ignition coil plugs—LH side shown, RH similar

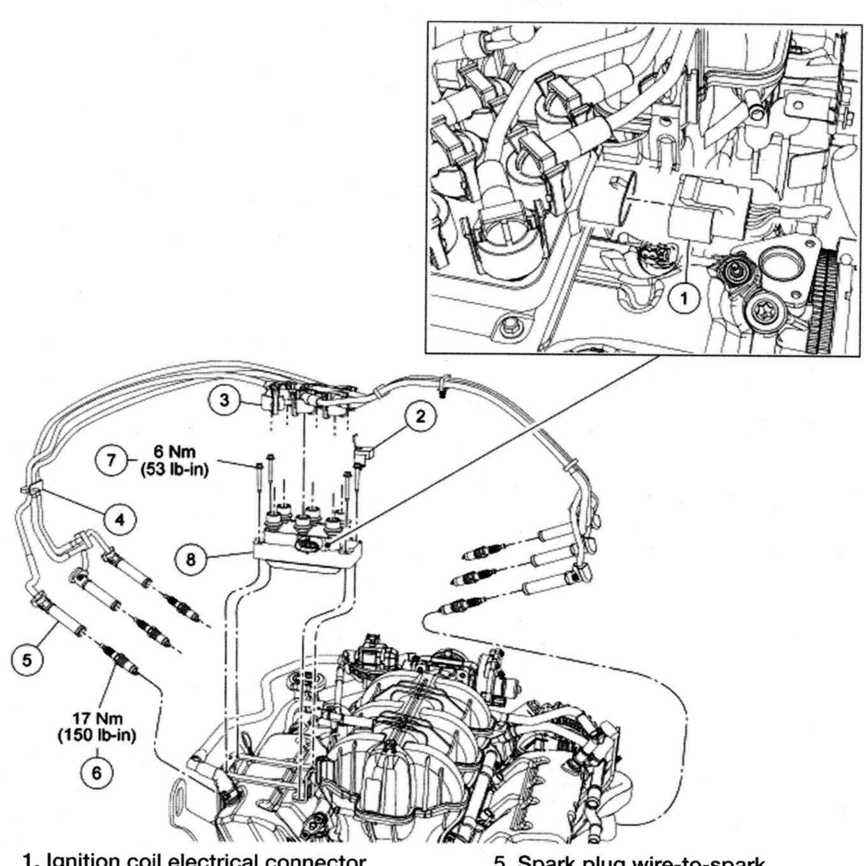

Fig. 86 Exploded view of the ignition coil plugs

3. Disconnect the 6 spark plug wires from the ignition coil.
4. Remove the 4 bolts and the ignition coil.

➡Be sure to reinstall the radio ignition interference capacitor under the correct mounting bolt.

5. To install, reverse the removal procedure.

4.6L Engines

See Figures 87.

1. Disconnect the negative battery cable.
2. Disconnect the 8 ignition coil electrical connectors.
3. Remove the 8 ignition coil bolts.

➡When removing the ignition coils, a slight twisting motion will break the seal and ease removal.

4. Remove the 8 ignition coils.
5. To install, reverse the removal procedure.
6. Apply a light film of brake caliper grease to the inside of the coil boots before installation.

5.0L Engines

See Figures 88 and 89.

1. LH side:
   a. Disconnect the PCV tube-to-valve cover fitting quick connect coupling and position aside.
2. RH side:
   a. For ignition coil-on-plugs on cylinders 3 and 4, disconnect the battery ground cable.
   b. Disconnect the crankcase ventilation tube-to-valve cover fitting quick connect coupling and position aside.
3. Both sides:
4. Remove the ignition coil-on-plug cover.

➡Detach the engine appearance cover and lift to gain access to the ignition coil-on-plug electrical connectors.

5. Disconnect the ignition coil-on-plug electrical connector.

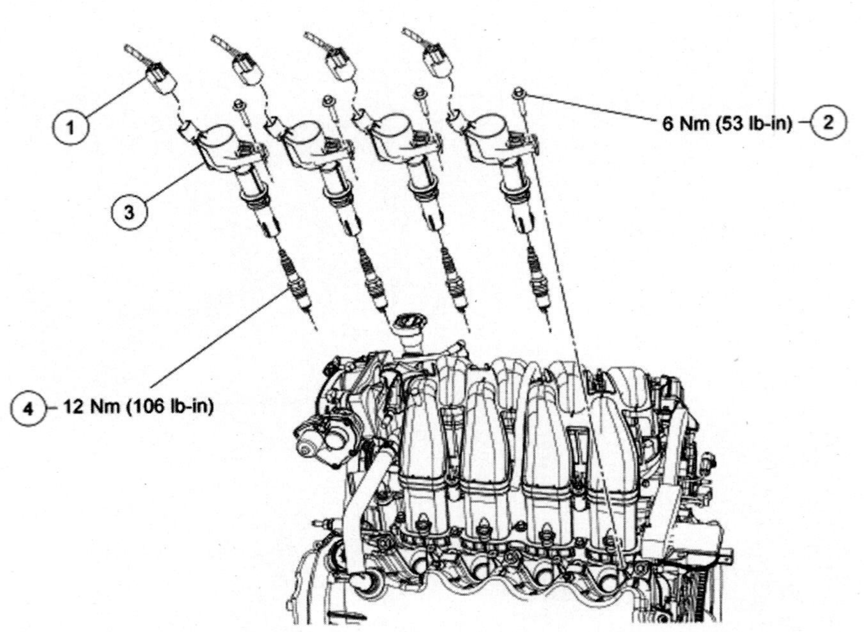

1. Ignition coil-on-plug electrical connector (4 required)
2. Ignition coil-on-plug bolt (4 required)
3. Ignition coil-on-plug (4 required)
4. Spark plug (4 required)

N0099011

Fig. 87 Exploded view of the ignition coil plugs—LH side shown, RH similar

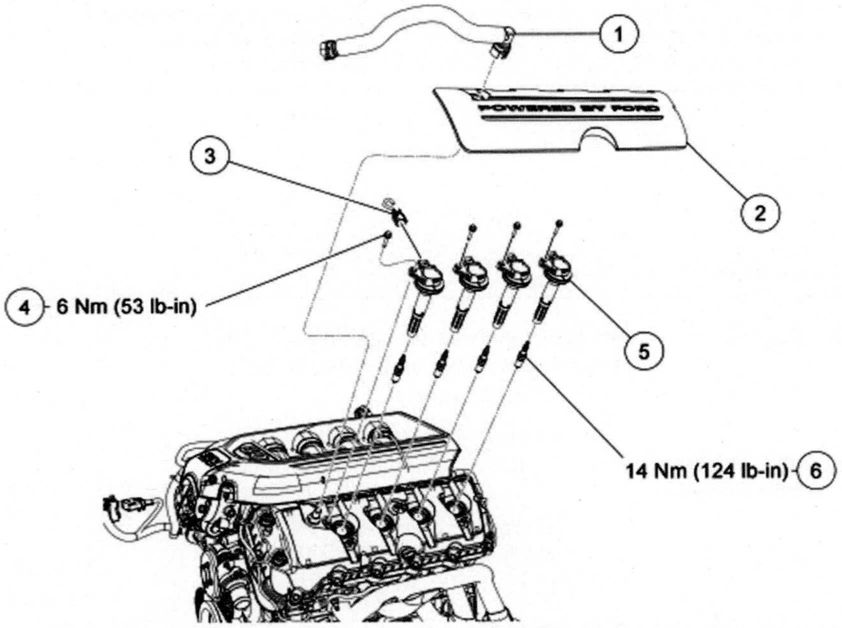

4 - 6 Nm (53 lb-in)

14 Nm (124 lb-in) - 6

1. Crankcase ventilation tube
2. Ignition coil-on-plug cover
3. Ignition coil-on-plug electrical connector (4 required)
4. Ignition coil-on-plug bolt (4 required)
5. Ignition coil-on-plug (4 required)
6. Spark plug (4 required)

N0114160

Fig. 88 Exploded view of the ignition coil plugs—LH side

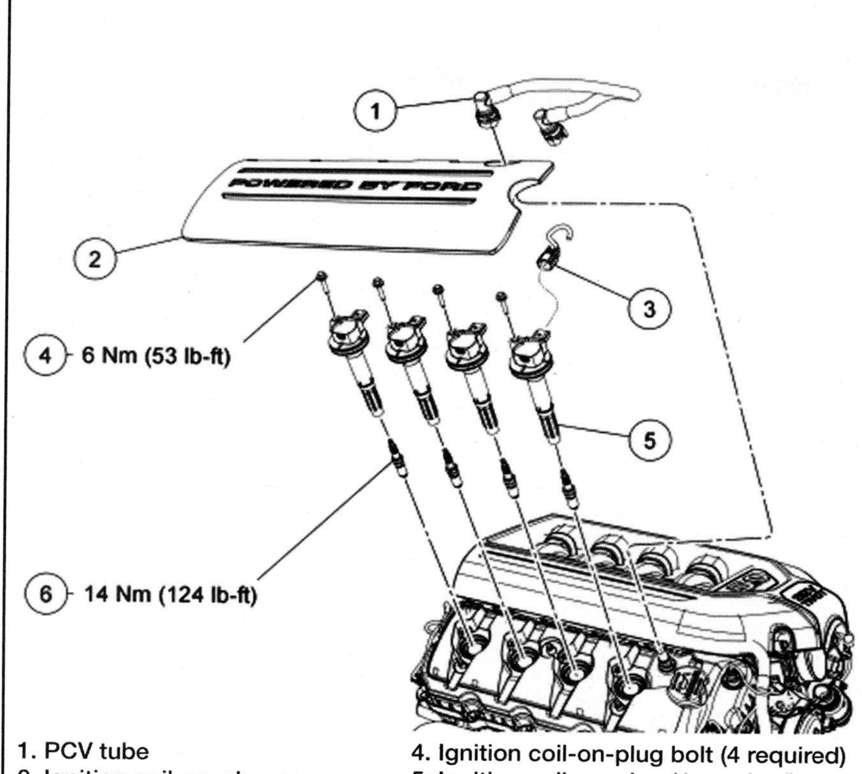

Fig. 89 Exploded view of the ignition coil plugs—RH side

➡When removing the ignition coil-on-plug, a slight twisting motion will break the seal and ease removal.

6. Remove the bolt and the ignition coil-on-plug.
7. Inspect the coil seals for rips, nicks or tears. Remove and discard any damaged coil seals.
8. To install, slide the new coil seal onto the coil until it is fully seated at the top of the coil.
9. To install, reverse the removal procedure.
10. Apply a small amount of dielectric grease to the inside of the ignition coil-on-plug boots before attaching to the spark plugs.

5.4L Engines

See Figures 90 and 91.

1. LH ignition coil-on-plugs:
   a. Remove the Air Cleaner (ACL) outlet pipe.
   b. Remove the 2 bolts and the LH ignition coil-on-plug cover.
   c. Inspect the gasket. Install a new gasket if necessary.
   d. Disconnect the 4 LH ignition coil-on-plug electrical connectors.
   e. Remove the 4 LH ignition coil-on-plugs, using a twisting motion while pulling up on the ignition coil-on-plug.
2. RH ignition coil-on-plugs:
   a. Detach the 2 wire harness retainers from the stud bolts.
   b. Remove the bolt, stud bolt and the RH ignition coil-on-plug cover.
   c. Inspect the gasket. Install a new gasket if necessary.
   d. Disconnect the 4 RH ignition coil-on-plug electrical connectors.
   e. Remove the 4 RH ignition coil-on-plugs, using a twisting motion while pulling up on the ignition coil-on-plug.

➡Verify that the ignition coil-on-plug spring is correctly located inside the ignition coil-on-plug boot and that there is no damage to the tip of the boot.

3. To install, reverse the removal procedure.
4. Apply a light coat of dielectric grease to the inside of the ignition coil-on-plug boots.

IGNITION TIMING

ADJUSTMENT

10 degrees Before Top Dead Center (BTDC) (not adjustable).

SPARK PLUGS

REMOVAL & INSTALLATION

1. Remove the ignition coil-on-plugs.

➡Only use hand tools when removing or installing the spark plugs, or damage may occur to the cylinder head or spark plug.

➡Use compressed air to remove any foreign material from the spark plug well before removing the spark plugs.

➡If an original spark plug is used, make sure it is installed in the same cylinder from which it was taken. New spark plugs can be used in any cylinder.

Remove the spark plugs.

2. To install, tighten to 13 ft. lbs. (18 Nm).
3. Inspect the spark plugs. Install new spark plugs as necessary.
4. Adjust the spark plug gap as necessary.

INSPECTION

1. Inspect the spark plug for a bridged gap.
   a. Check for deposit build-up closing the gap between the electrodes. Deposits are caused by oil or carbon fouling.
   b. Install a new spark plug.
2. Check for oil fouling.
   a. Check for wet, black deposits on the insulator shell bore electrodes, caused by excessive oil entering the combustion chamber through worn rings and pistons, excessive valve-to-guide clearance or worn or loose bearings.
   b. Correct the oil leak concern.
   c. Install a new spark plug.
3. Inspect for carbon fouling. Look for black, dry, fluffy carbon deposits on the insulator tips, exposed shell surfaces and electrodes, caused by a spark plug with an incorrect heat range, dirty air cleaner, too rich a fuel mixture or excessive idling.
   a. Install new spark plugs.
4. Inspect for normal burning.
   a. Check for light tan or gray deposits on the firing tip.

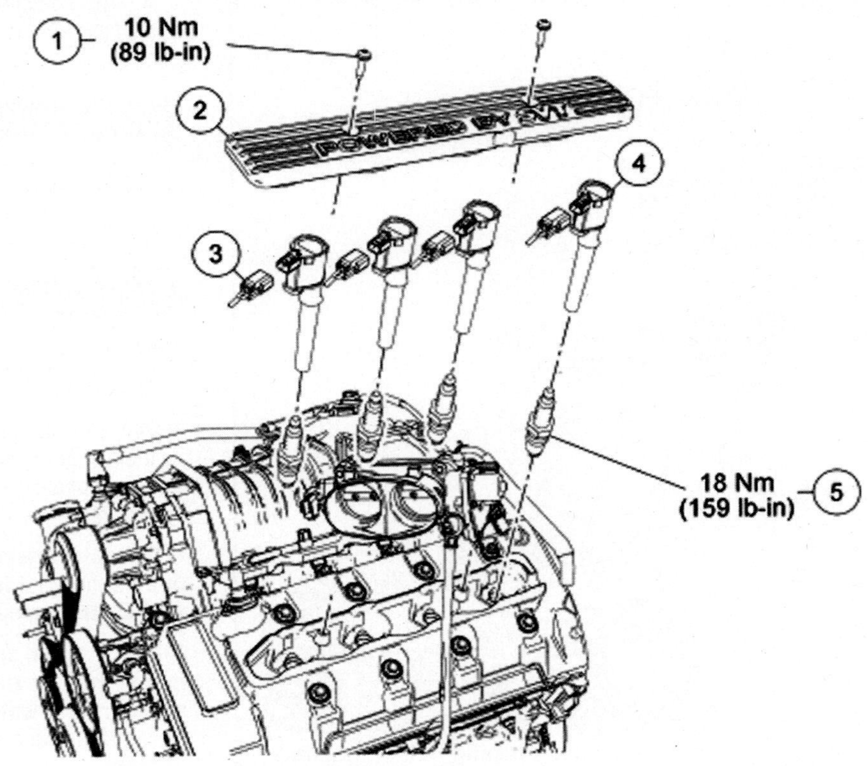

1. Ignition coil-on-plug cover bolt (2 required)
2. Ignition coil-on-plug cover
3. Ignition coil-on-plug electrical connector (4 required)
4. Ignition coil-on-plug (4 required)
5. Spark plug (4 required)

N0084919

Fig. 90 Exploded view of the ignition coil plugs—LH side

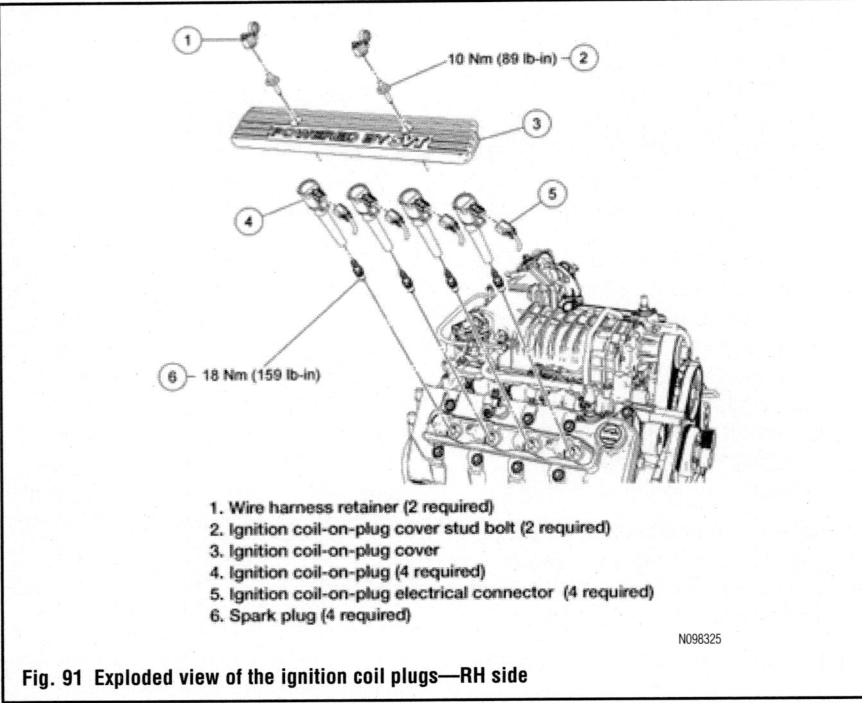

1. Wire harness retainer (2 required)
2. Ignition coil-on-plug cover stud bolt (2 required)
3. Ignition coil-on-plug cover
4. Ignition coil-on-plug (4 required)
5. Ignition coil-on-plug electrical connector (4 required)
6. Spark plug (4 required)

N098325

Fig. 91 Exploded view of the ignition coil plugs—RH side

5. Inspect for pre-ignition, identified by melted electrodes and a possibly damaged insulator. Metallic deposits on the insulator indicate engine damage. This may be caused by incorrect ignition timing, wrong type of fuel or the unauthorized installation of a heli-coil insert in place of the spark plug threads.
    a. Install a new spark plug.
6. Inspect for overheating, identified by white or light gray spots and a bluish-burnt appearance of electrodes. This is caused by engine overheating, wrong type of fuel, loose spark plugs, spark plugs with an incorrect heat range, low fuel pump pressure or incorrect ignition timing.
    a. Install a new spark plug.
7. Inspect for fused deposits, identified by melted or spotty deposits resembling bubbles or blisters. These are caused by sudden acceleration.
    a. Install new spark plugs.

STARTER

REMOVAL & INSTALLATION

3.7L Engines

See Figure 92.

✳✳ WARNING

Always disconnect the battery ground cable at the battery before disconnecting the starter motor battery terminal lead. If a tool is shorted at the starter motor battery terminal, the tool can quickly heat enough to cause a skin burn. Failure to follow this instruction may result in serious personal injury.

1. With the vehicle in NEUTRAL, position it on a hoist.
2. Disconnect the battery ground cable.
3. Remove the starter solenoid terminal cover.
4. Remove the 2 starter solenoid terminal nuts and position aside the wires.
5. If equipped, remove the nut and position the automatic transmission cooler tube bracket aside.
6. Remove the 2 stud bolts and the starter motor.

To install:

➡To make sure of correct starter installation, the upper bolt must be tightened first.

➡Clean the starter motor mounting flange and mating surface of the starter motor to make sure there is a correct ground connection.

7. Position the starter motor and install the 2 stud bolts finger-tight.
8. If equipped, position the automatic transmission cooler tube bracket and install the nut. Tighten to 106 inch lbs. (12 Nm).
9. Install the wires and the 2 starter solenoid terminal nuts.
10. Install the starter solenoid terminal cover.
11. Connect the battery ground cable.
12. Refer to illustration for torque values.

4.0L Engine

See Figure 93.

✳✳ WARNING

Always disconnect the battery ground cable at the battery before disconnecting the starter motor battery terminal lead. If a tool is shorted at the starter motor battery terminal, the tool can quickly heat enough to cause a skin burn. Failure to follow this instruction may result in serious personal injury.

1. With the vehicle in NEUTRAL, position it on a hoist.
2. Disconnect the battery ground cable.
3. Remove the starter solenoid terminal cover.
4. Remove the 2 starter solenoid terminal nuts and position aside the wires.
5. Remove the 2 bolts and the starter motor.

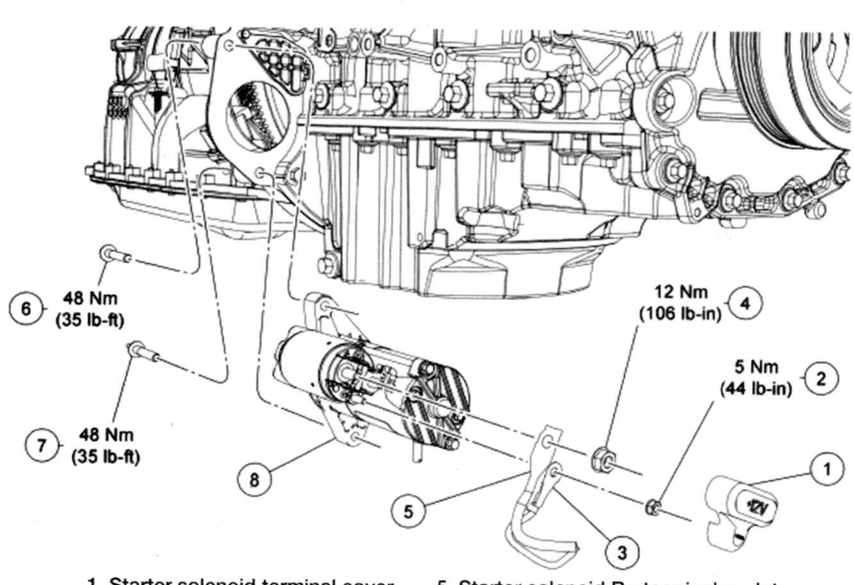

Fig. 92 Exploded view of the starter and components—3.7L Engines

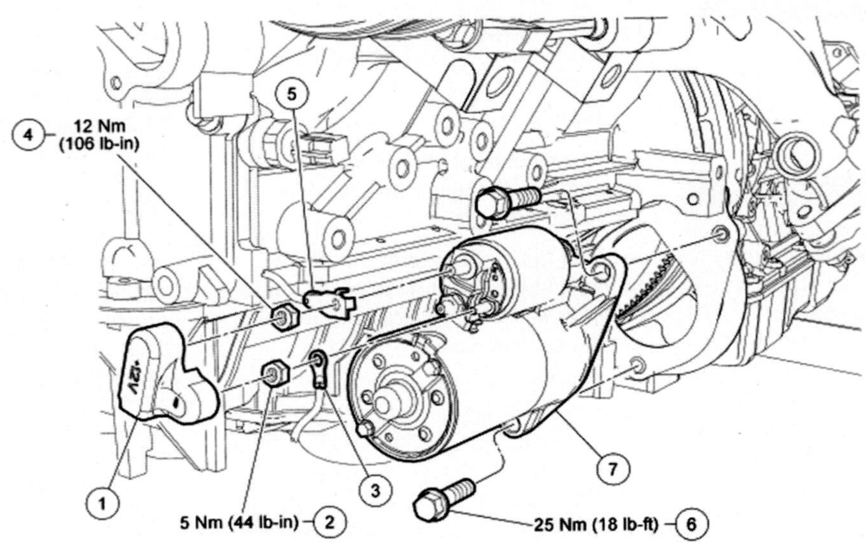

Fig. 93 Exploded view of the starter and components—4.0L Engines

To install:

➡To make sure of correct starter installation, the upper bolt must be tightened first.

➡Clean the starter motor mounting flange and mating surface of the starter motor to make sure there is a correct ground connection.

6. Position the starter motor and install the 2 bolts finger-tight.
7. Install the wires and the 2 starter solenoid terminal nuts.
8. Install the starter solenoid terminal cover.
9. Connect the battery ground cable.
10. Refer to illustration for torque values.

4.6L Engine

See Figure 94.

⁂ WARNING

Always disconnect the battery ground cable at the battery before disconnecting the starter motor battery terminal lead. If a tool is shorted at the starter motor battery terminal, the tool can quickly heat enough to cause a skin burn. Failure to follow this instruction may result in serious personal injury.

1. With the vehicle in NEUTRAL, position it on a hoist.
2. Disconnect the battery ground cable.
3. Remove the starter solenoid terminal cover.
4. Remove the 2 starter solenoid terminal nuts and position aside the wires.
5. Remove the 3 bolts and the starter motor.

To install:

➡To make sure of correct starter installation, the upper bolt must be tightened first.

➡Clean the starter motor mounting flange and mating surface of the starter motor to make sure there is a correct ground connection.

6. Position the starter motor and install the 3 bolts finger-tight.
7. Install the wires and the 2 starter solenoid terminal nuts.
8. Install the starter solenoid terminal cover.
9. Connect the battery ground cable.
10. Refer to illustration for torque values.

5.0L Engine

See Figures 95.

⁂ WARNING

Always disconnect the battery ground cable at the battery before disconnecting the starter motor battery terminal lead. If a tool is shorted at the starter motor battery terminal, the tool can quickly heat enough to cause a skin burn. Failure to follow this instruction may result in serious personal injury.

1. With the vehicle in NEUTRAL, position it on a hoist.
2. Disconnect the battery ground cable.
3. Remove the starter solenoid terminal cover.
4. Remove the 2 starter solenoid terminal nuts and position aside the wires.
5. Remove the 3 bolts and the starter motor.

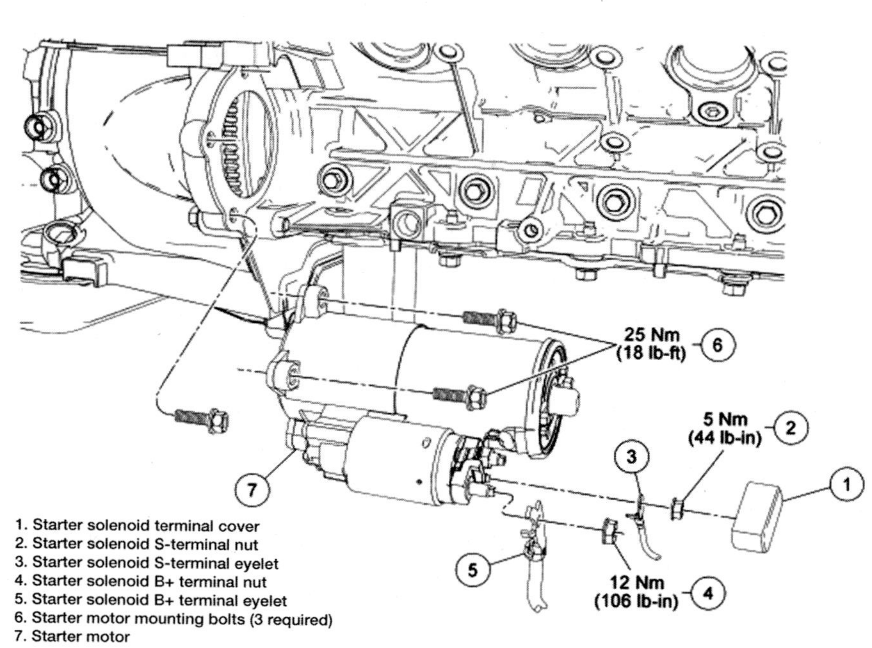

Fig. 94 Exploded view of the starter and components—4.6L Engines

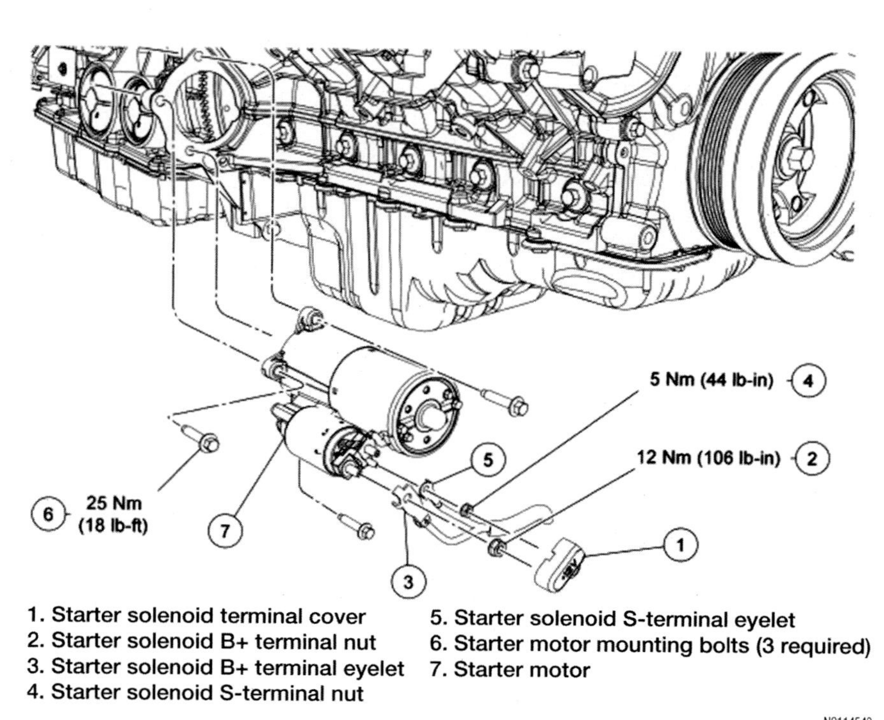

Fig. 95 Exploded view of the starter and components—5.0L Engines

To install:

➡To make sure of correct starter installation, the upper bolt must be tightened first.

➡Clean the starter motor mounting flange and mating surface of the starter motor to make sure there is a correct ground connection.

6. Position the starter motor and install the 3 bolts finger-tight.
7. Install the wires and the 2 starter solenoid terminal nuts.
8. Install the starter solenoid terminal cover.
9. Connect the battery ground cable.
10. Refer to illustration for torque values.

5.4L Engines

See Figure 96.

WARNING

Always disconnect the battery ground cable at the battery before disconnecting the starter motor battery terminal lead. If a tool is shorted at the starter motor battery terminal, the tool can quickly heat enough to cause a skin burn. Failure to follow this instruction may result in serious personal injury.

1. With the vehicle in NEUTRAL, position it on a hoist.
2. Disconnect the battery ground cable.
3. Remove the starter solenoid terminal cover.
4. Remove the 2 starter solenoid terminal nuts and position aside the wires.
5. Remove the 3 bolts and the starter motor.

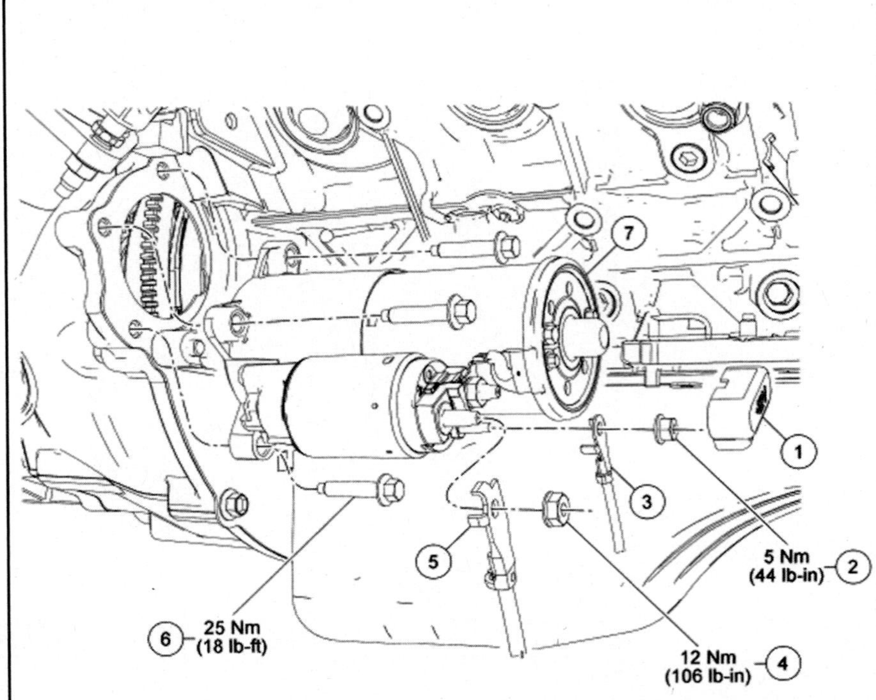

Fig. 96 Exploded view of the starter and components—5.4L Engines

To install:

➡To make sure of correct starter installation, the upper bolt must be tightened first.

➡Clean the starter motor mounting flange and mating surface of the starter motor to make sure there is a correct ground connection.

6. Position the starter motor and install the 3 bolts finger-tight then tighten.
7. Install the wires and the 2 starter solenoid terminal nuts.
8. Install the starter solenoid terminal cover.
9. Connect the battery ground cable.
10. Refer to illustration for torque values.

ENGINE MECHANICAL

➡Disconnecting the negative battery cable may interfere with the functions of the on board computer systems and may require the computer to undergo a relearning process, once the negative battery cable is reconnected.

ACCESSORY DRIVE BELTS

ACCESSORY BELT ROUTING

See Figures 97 through 102.

Refer to the accompanying illustrations.

INSPECTION

Inspect for glazing, cracking, splitting, delaminating and shredding. Replace as necessary.

ADJUSTMENT

Adjustment is not possible or necessary.

REMOVAL & INSTALLATION

1. Rotate the tensioner clockwise and remove the accessory drive belt.

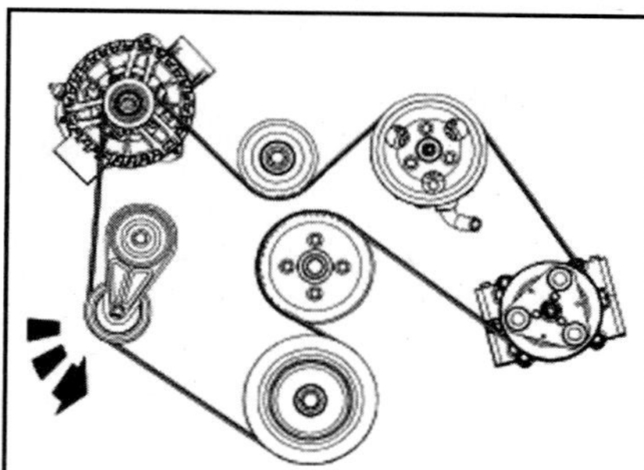

Fig. 98 Accessory belt routing—4.0L Engines

2. For supercharged engines:
   a. Remove the accessory drive belt.
   b. Rotate the Supercharger (SC) belt tensioner clockwise and remove the SC belt from the SC pulley.

➡The SC belt is routed behind the SC belt tensioner.

3. Remove the SC belt tensioner bolt, the tensioner and the SC belt. To install, tighten to 35 ft. lbs. (48 Nm).

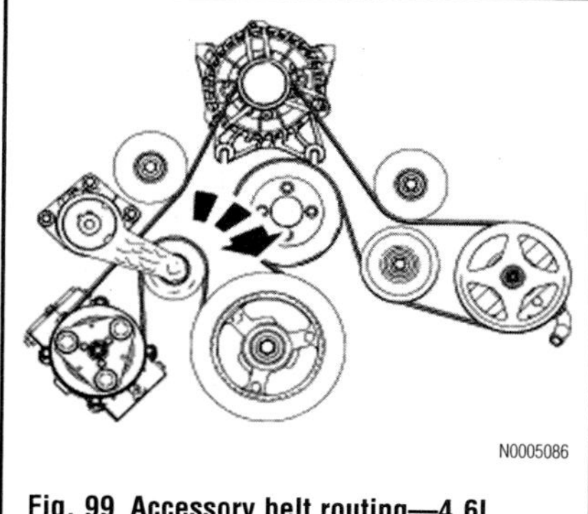

Fig. 99 Accessory belt routing—4.6L Engines

4. To install, reverse the removal procedure.

AIR CLEANER

REMOVAL & INSTALLATION

3.7L Engines

See Figure 103.

Refer to the illustration to remove and install.

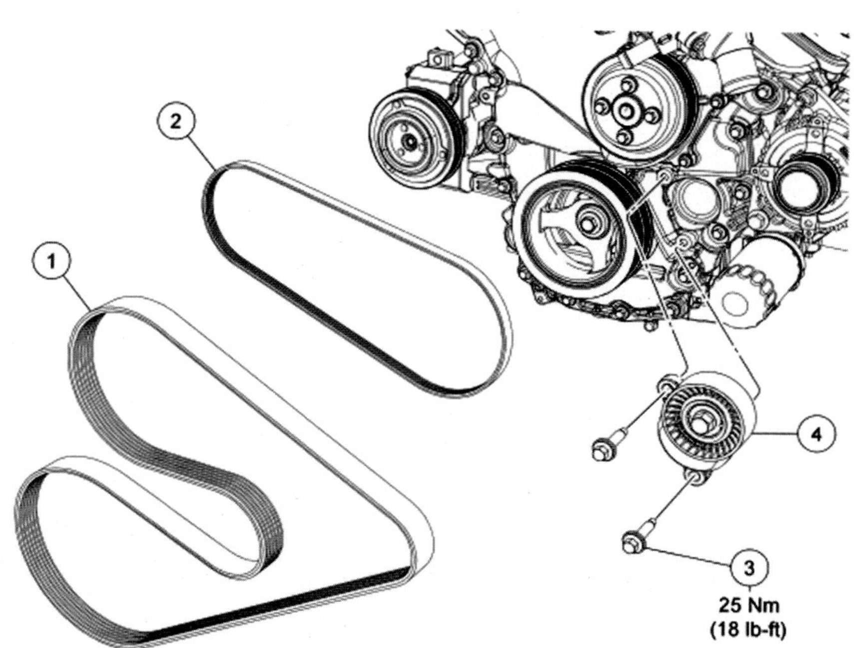

Fig. 97 Accessory belt routing—3.7L Engines

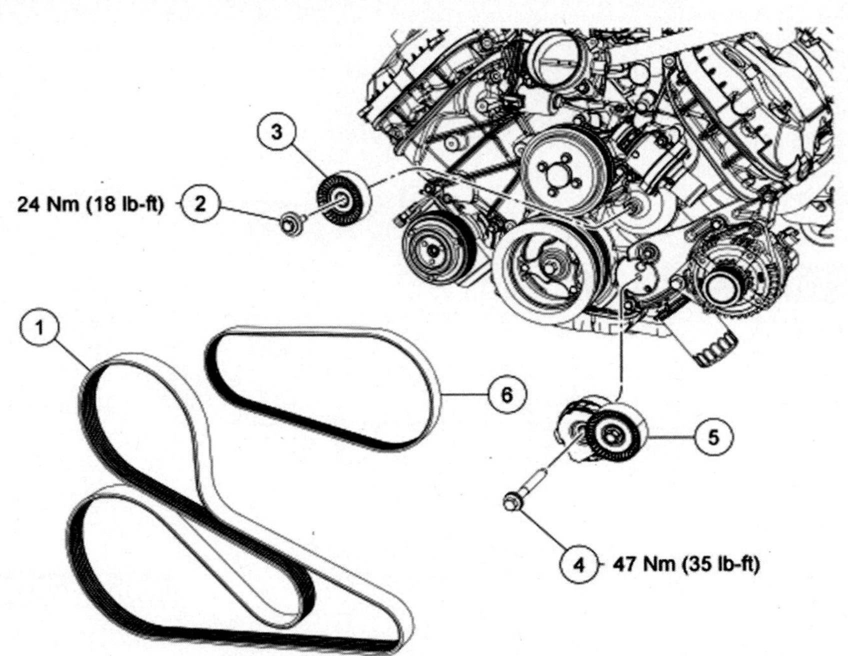

Fig. 100 Accessory belt routing—5.0L Engines

Fig. 101 Accessory belt routing—5.4L Engines

Fig. 102 Accessory belt routing—Supercharged 5.4L Engines

4.0L, 4.6L and 5.4L Engines

See Figures 104 through 106.

1. Disconnect the Mass Air Flow (MAF) electrical connector.
2. Remove the Air Cleaner (ACL) housing bolt.
3. 4.0L SOHC and 4.6L vehicles:
    a. Loosen the clamp and disconnect the ACL outlet pipe-to- ACL housing cover.
4. 5.4L vehicles:
    a. Loosen the clamp and disconnect the ACL outlet pipe-to- ACL housing.
5. All vehicles:

➡Make sure that the 2 rubber grommets are retained to the ACL assembly feet.

6. Release the ACL housing from the ACL inlet pipe and remove the ACL assembly.

➡Make sure that the 2 ACL assembly feet rubber grommets are seated into the locating holes in the fender.

➡The ACL outlet pipe should be securely sealed to prevent unmetered air from entering the engine.

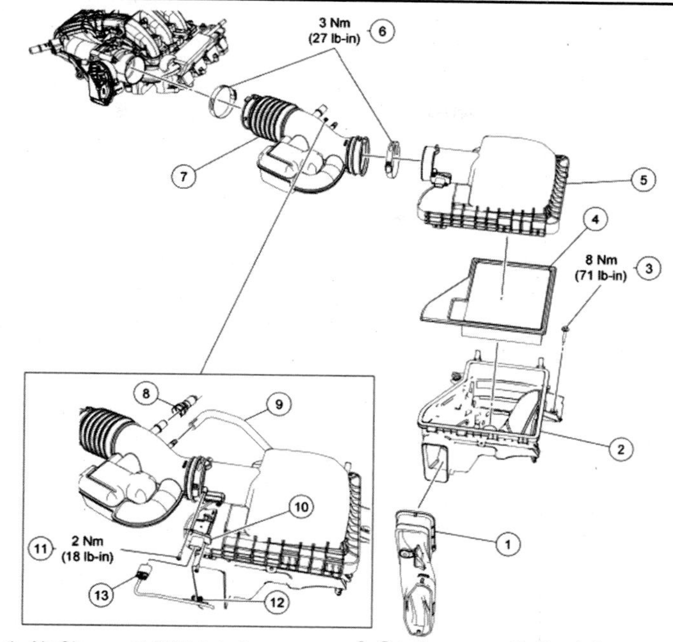

1. Air Cleaner (ACL) inlet pipe
2. ACL housing
3. ACL housing bolt
4. ACL element
5. ACL housing cover
6. ACL outlet pipe clamp (2 required)
7. ACL outlet pipe
8. Crankcase ventilation tube
9. Vacuum hose (if equipped)
10. Mass Air Flow (MAF) sensor
11. MAF sensor screw (2 required)
12. Wiring harness retainer
13. MAF sensor electrical connector

N0113663

Fig. 103 Exploded view of the air cleaner assembly—3.7L Engines

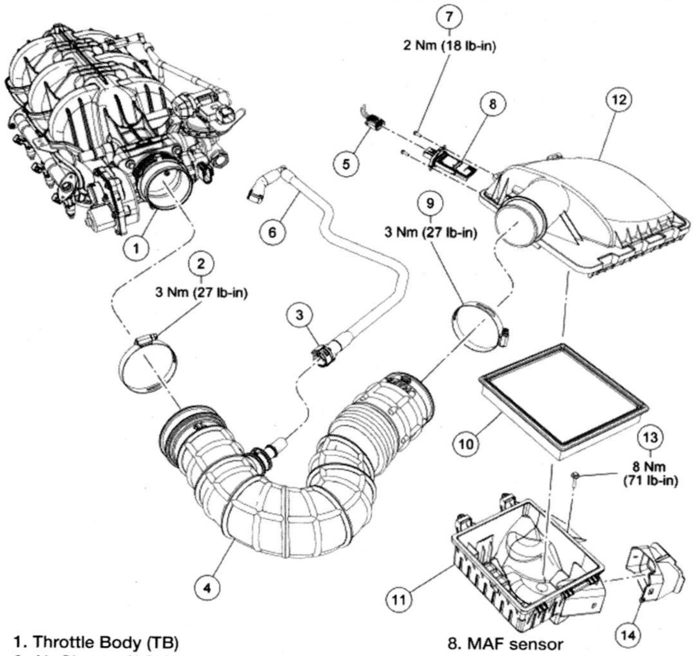

1. Throttle Body (TB)
2. Air Cleaner (ACL) outlet pipe-to- TB clamp
3. Crankcase ventilation tube-to- ACL outlet pipe quick connect coupling (part of 6758)
4. ACL outlet pipe
5. Mass Air Flow (MAF) sensor electrical connector
6. Crankcase ventilation tube
7. MAF sensor screw (2 required)
8. MAF sensor
9. ACL outlet pipe-to- ACL housing cover clamp
10. ACL element
11. ACL housing
12. ACL housing cover
13. ACL housing bolt
14. ACL inlet pipe

N0098301

Fig. 104 Exploded view of the air cleaner assembly—4.0L Engines

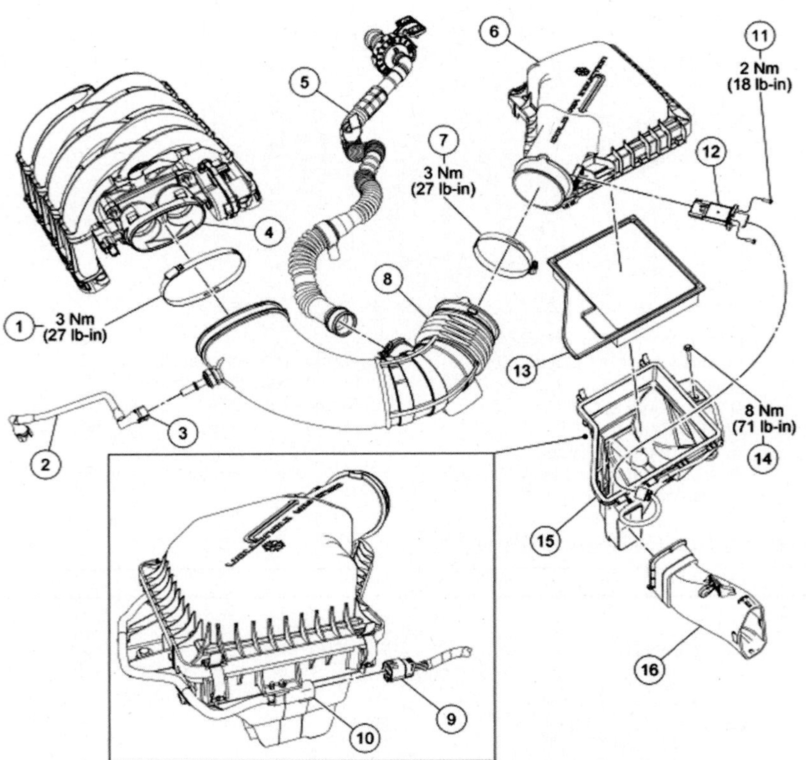

1. Air Cleaner (ACL) outlet pipe-to- Throttle Body (TB) clamp
2. Crankcase ventilation tube
3. Crankcase ventilation tube-to- ACL outlet pipe quick connect coupling (part of 6758)
4. TB
5. Sound enhancement pipe
6. ACL housing cover
7. ACL outlet pipe-to- ACL housing cover clamp
8. ACL outlet pipe
9. Engine wiring harness electrical connector
10. Mass Air Flow (MAF) wiring harness electrical connector
11. MAF sensor screw (2 required)
12. MAF sensor
13. ACL element
14. ACL housing bolt
15. ACL housing
16. ACL inlet pipe

N0098292

Fig. 105 Exploded view of the air cleaner assembly—4.6L Engines

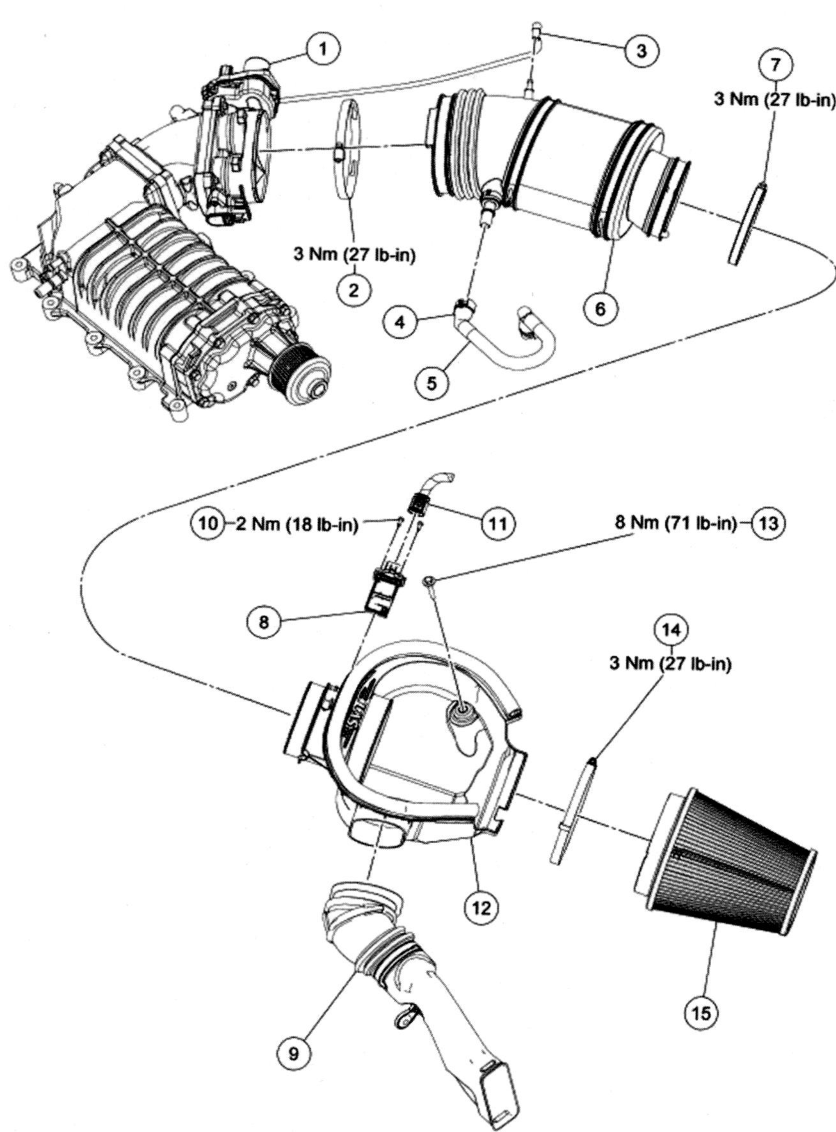

Fig. 106 Exploded view of the air cleaner assembly—5.4L Engines

7. To install, reverse the removal procedure.

5.0L Engines

See Figure 107.

Refer to the illustration to remove and install.

CAMSHAFT AND VALVE LIFTERS

REMOVAL & INSTALLATION

3.7L Engine

See Figures 108 through 116.

➡**During engine repair procedures, cleanliness is extremely important. Any foreign material, including any material created while cleaning gasket surfaces that enters the oil passages, coolant passages or the oil pan, may cause engine failure.**

➡**This procedure is for the LH camshaft, RH procedure is similar.**

1. Remove the engine front cover Refer to Timing Chain Front Cover in this section.
2. Rotate the crankshaft clockwise and align the timing marks on the intake Variable Camshaft Timing (VCT) assemblies as shown.
3. Remove the 3 bolts and the LH valve train oil tube.

➡**The Camshaft Holding Tool will hold the camshafts in the Top Dead Center (TDC) position.**

4. Install the Camshaft Holding Tool onto the flats of the LH camshafts.
5. Remove the 3 bolts and the RH valve train oil tube.

➡**The Camshaft Holding Tool will hold the camshafts in the TDC position.**

6. Install the Camshaft Holding Tool onto the flats of the RH camshafts.
7. Remove the timing chain. Refer to Timing Chain in this section.

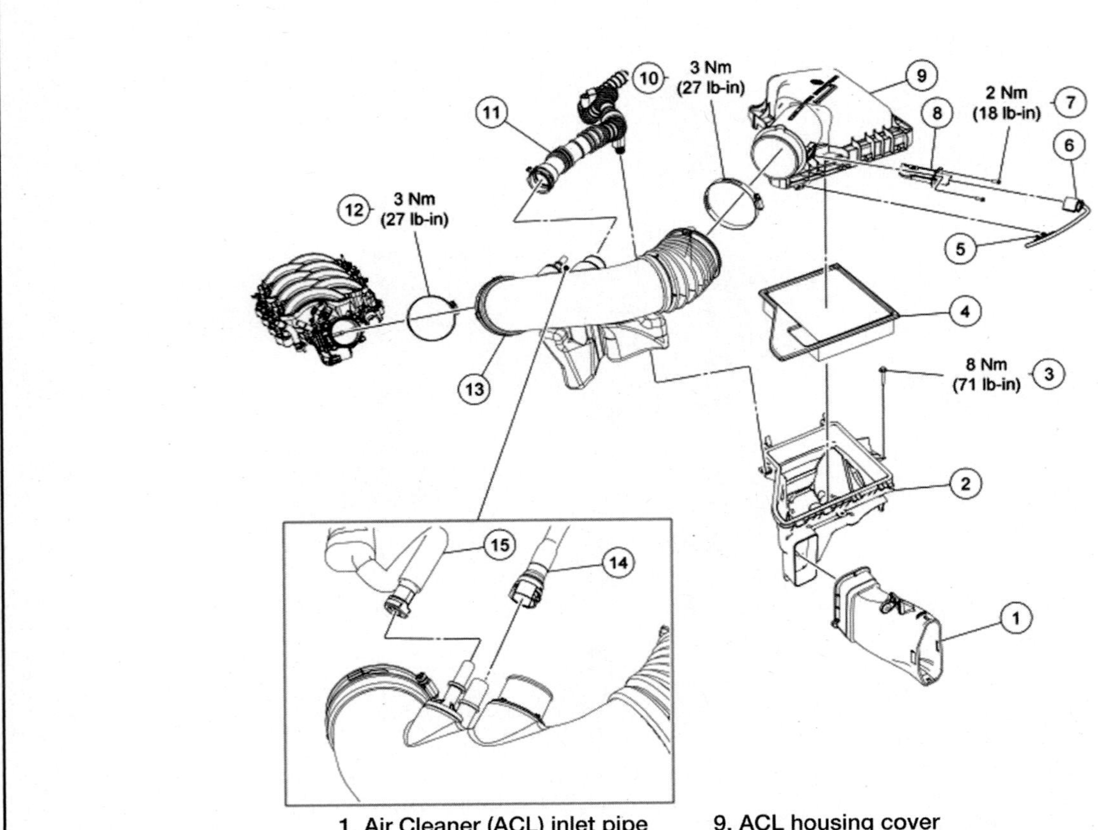

Fig. 107 Exploded view of the air cleaner assembly—5.0L Engines

Fig. 108 Align the timing marks on the intake Variable Camshaft Timing (VCT) assemblies

Fig. 109 Remove the 3 bolts and the LH valve train oil tube

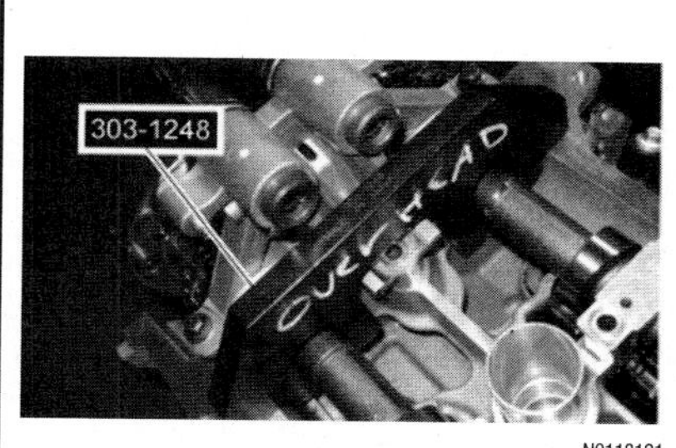

Fig. 110 Install the Camshaft Holding Tool

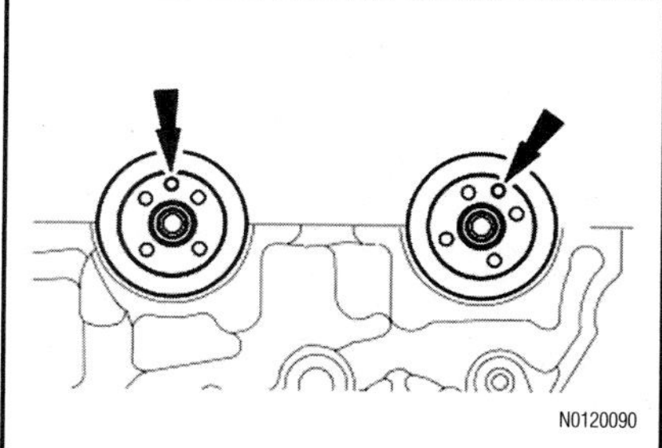

Fig. 111 Position the camshafts onto the LH cylinder head in the neutral position

➡When the Camshaft Holding Tool is removed, valve spring pressure may rotate the LH camshafts approximately 3 degrees to a neutral position.

8. Remove the Camshaft Holding Tool from the LH camshafts.

➡Cylinder head camshaft bearing caps are numbered to verify that they are assembled in their original positions.

➡Mark the exhaust and intake camshafts for installation into their original locations.

9. Remove the 12 bolts, 6 camshaft caps, mega cap and the LH camshafts.

To install:

➡Coat the camshafts with clean engine oil prior to installation.

10. Position the camshafts onto the LH cylinder head in the neutral position as shown.

➡The crankshaft must remain in the freewheeling position (crankshaft dowel pin at 9 o'clock) until after the camshafts are installed and the valve clearance is checked/adjusted. Do not turn the crankshaft until instructed to do so. Failure to follow this process will result in severe engine damage.

11. Rotate the crankshaft counterclockwise until the crankshaft dowel pin is in the 9 o'clock position.

➡The camshaft seal gaps must be at the 12 o'clock position or damage to the engine may occur.

12. Position the 4 camshaft seals gaps as shown.

➡Cylinder head camshaft bearing caps are numbered to verify that they are assembled in their original positions.

13. Install the 6 camshaft caps, mega cap, valve train oil tube and the 15 bolts in the sequence shown. Tighten to 6 ft. lbs. (8 Nm) then additional 45 degrees.

14. Loosen the 4 camshaft caps bolts.

15. Tighten the 4 camshaft caps bolts in the sequence shown. Tighten bolts 8, 9, 10 and 11 to 6 ft. lbs. (8 Nm) then additional 45 degrees.

➡If any components are installed new, the engine valve clearance must be checked/adjusted or engine damage may occur.

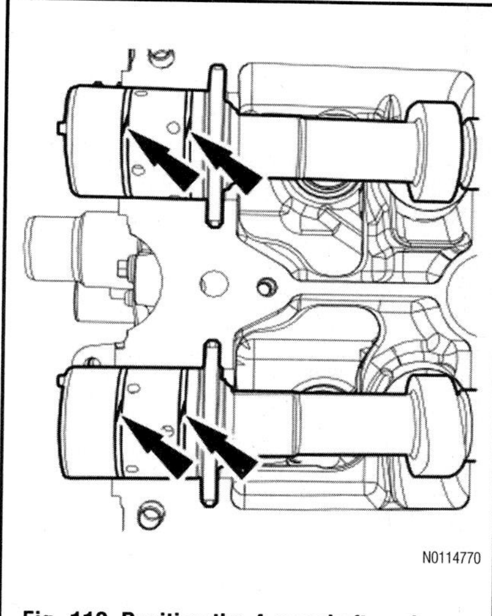

Fig. 112 Position the 4 camshaft seals gaps

➡Use a camshaft sprocket bolt to turn the camshafts.

16. Using a feeler gauge, confirm that the valve tappet clearances are within specification. If valve tappet clearances are not within specification, the clearance must be adjusted by installing new valve tappet(s) of the correct size.

17. Remove the 3 bolts and the LH valve train oil tube.

18. Rotate the LH camshafts to the TDC position as shown.

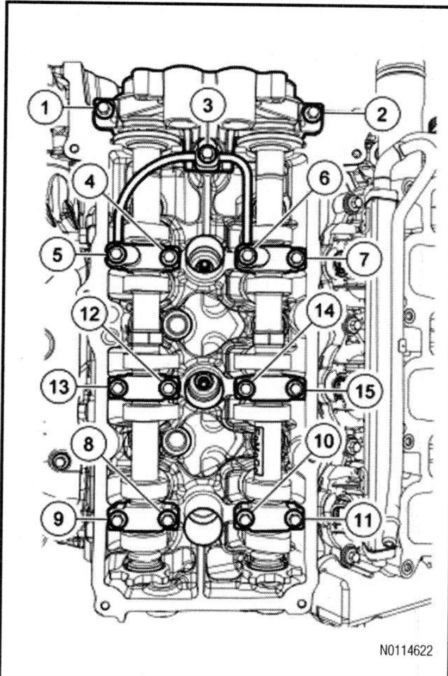

Fig. 113 Tighten 6 camshaft caps, mega cap, valve train oil tube and the 15 bolts in the sequence

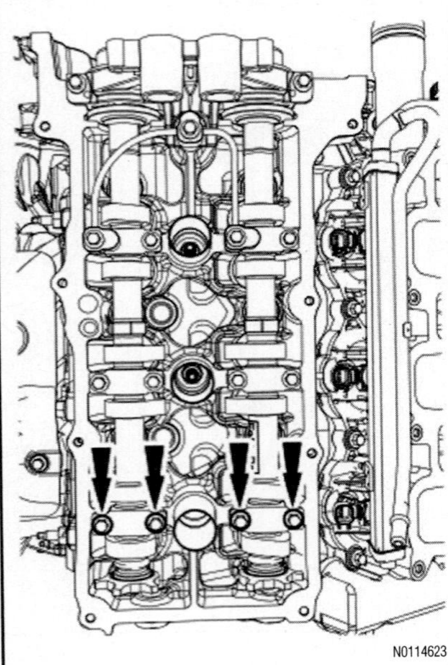

Fig. 114 Loosen the 4 camshaft caps bolts

➡The Camshaft Holding Tool will hold the camshafts in the Top Dead Center (TDC) position.

19. Install the Camshaft Holding Tool onto the flats of the LH camshafts.
20. Install the timing chain.
21. Remove the RH Camshaft Holding Tool.
22. Install the RH valve train oil tube and the 3 bolts and tighten in 2 stages.

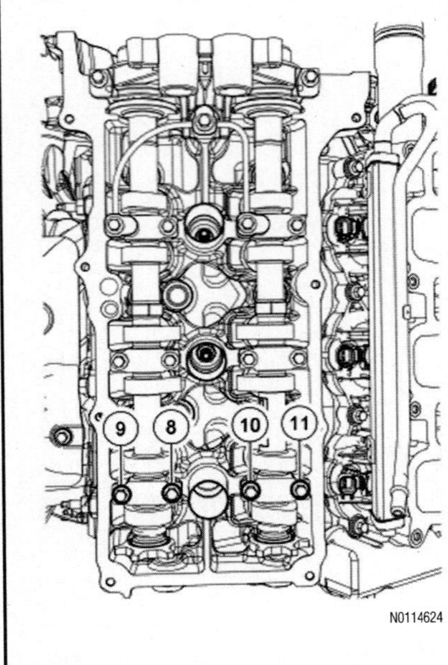

Fig. 115 Tighten the 4 camshaft caps bolts in the sequence

Fig. 116 Rotate the LH camshafts to the TDC position as shown

a. Stage 1: Tighten to 6 ft. lbs. (8 Nm).
b. Stage 2: Tighten an additional 45 degrees.

23. Remove the LH Camshaft Holding Tool.
24. Install the LH valve train oil tube and the 3 bolts and tighten in 2 stages.

a. Stage 1: Tighten to 6 ft. lbs. 8 Nm.
b. Stage 2: Tighten an additional 45 degrees.

25. Install the engine front cover. For additional information, refer to Engine Timing Chain Front Cover in this section.

4.0L Engine

Roller Follower

See Figures 117 and 118.

1. With the vehicle in NEUTRAL, position it on a hoist.
2. Remove the valve covers. For additional information, refer to Valve Cover in this section.
3. Position the piston of the cylinder being repaired at the bottom of the stroke.
4. Install the Valve Spring Compressor Spacer between the valve spring coils to prevent valve stem seal damage.

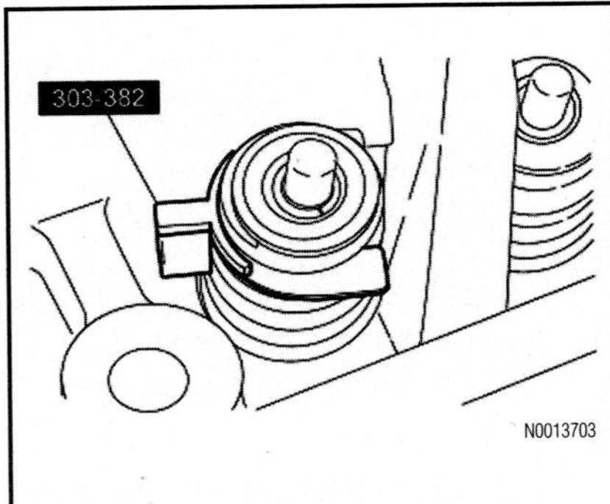

Fig. 117 Install the Valve Spring Compressor Spacer

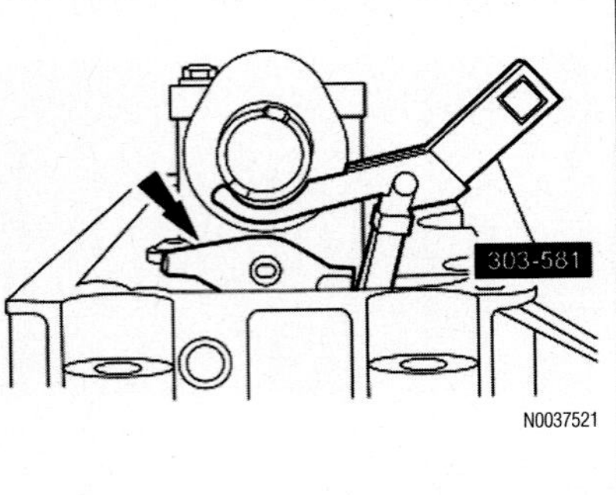

Fig. 118 Using the Valve Spring Compressor, compress the valve springs

5. Using the Valve Spring Compressor, compress the valve springs and remove the camshaft roller followers.

To install:

6. Using the Valve Spring Compressor, compress the valve spring and install the camshaft roller followers.
7. Remove the Valve Spring Compressor from between the valve spring.
8. Install the valve covers.

Camshaft

See Figures 119 through 123.

1. Remove the camshaft roller followers.

➡The RH and LH camshaft timing procedure must be carried out when either camshaft is serviced.

2. Rotate the crankshaft clockwise to position the No. 1 cylinder at Top Dead Center (TDC).

➡Do not rotate the engine counterclockwise. Rotating the engine counterclockwise will result in damage to the damper crank sensor speed wheel and incorrect timing of the engine.

➡The Crankshaft TDC Timing Tool must be installed on the damper and should

Fig. 119 Install the Crankshaft TDC Timing Tool

contact the engine block. This positions the piston at TDC.

3. Install the Crankshaft TDC Timing Tool.

4. RH side:

a. Install the Camshaft Sprocket Holding Tool and Adapter on the rear of the RH cylinder head and tighten the top 2 clamp bolts to 89 inch lbs. (10 Nm).

➡The RH camshaft sprocket is a LH-threaded bolt.

b. Using the Torque Wrench Extension and the Camshaft Sprocket Nut Socket 303-565, loosen the camshaft sprocket bolt.

c. Remove the camshaft sprocket bolt and position the RH camshaft sprocket aside.

5. LH side:

a. Install the Camshaft Sprocket Holding Tool and Adapter on the front of the LH camshaft and tighten the 2 top clamp bolts to 89 inch lbs. (10 Nm).

b. Loosen the camshaft sprocket bolt.

c. Remove the bolt and position the LH camshaft sprocket aside.

6. Both sides:

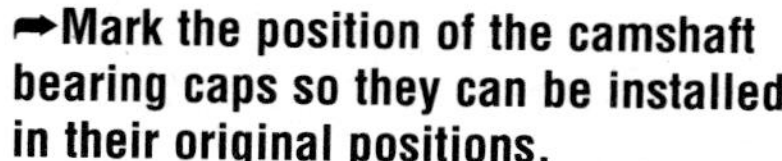

➡Mark the position of the camshaft bearing caps so they can be installed in their original positions.

7. Remove the bolts in the sequence shown and remove the camshaft bearing caps.

8. Remove the camshaft.

To install:

9. Both sides:

➡Lubricate the camshafts with clean engine oil.

10. Install the camshaft.

➡Lubricate the camshaft bearing caps with clean engine oil.

➡The camshaft bearing caps must be installed in their original positions.

➡After installing the bolts, check the camshaft for free rotation.

11. Install the camshaft bearing caps and the bolts.

12. Tighten the bolts in the sequence shown in 2 stages.

a. Stage 1: Tighten to 53 inch lbs. (6 Nm).

b. Stage 2: Tighten to 11 ft. lbs (16 Nm).

13. RH side:

➡The camshaft gear must turn freely on the camshaft. Do not tighten the bolt at this time.

a. Install the RH camshaft sprocket and loosely install the bolt.

14. LH side:

➡The camshaft gear must turn freely on the camshaft. Do not tighten the bolt at this time.

a. Install the LH camshaft sprocket and loosely install the bolt.

15. Both sides:

16. Retime the camshafts. For additional information, refer to Camshaft Timing in this section.

17. Install the camshaft roller followers.

Camshaft Timing

See Figures 124 through 126.

1. Remove the camshaft roller followers. For additional information, refer to Camshaft Roller Follower in this section.

2. Remove the Alternator. For additional information, refer to Engine Electrical.

3. Remove the Engine Coolant Temperature (ECT) sensor. For additional information, refer to Engine Performance.

➡The LH and RH camshafts must be retimed when either camshaft is disturbed.

4. Turn the crankshaft clockwise to position the No. 1 cylinder at Top Dead Center (TDC).

➡Do not rotate the engine counterclockwise. Rotating the engine counterclockwise will result in damage to the damper crank sensor speed wheel and incorrect timing of the engine.

➡The Crankshaft TDC Timing Tool must be installed on the damper and should contact the engine block, this positions the engine at TDC.

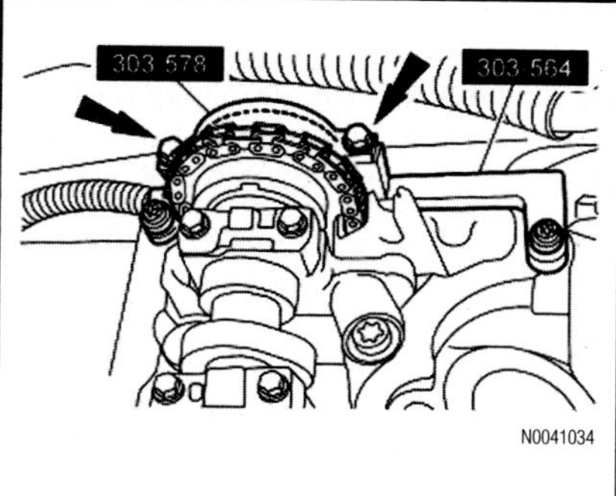

Fig. 120 Install the Camshaft Sprocket Holding Tool and Adapter

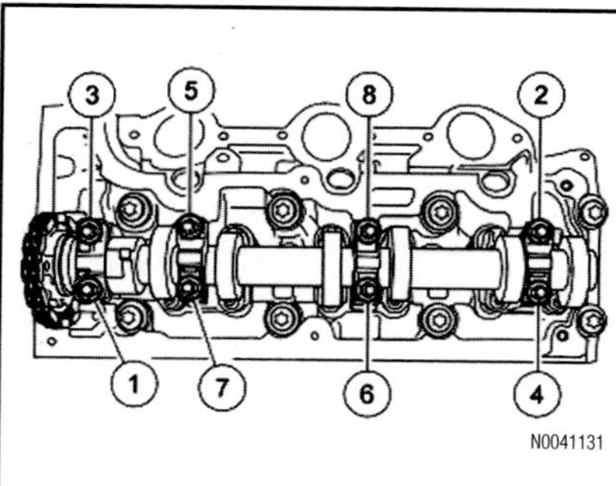

Fig. 122 Remove the bolts in the sequence shown

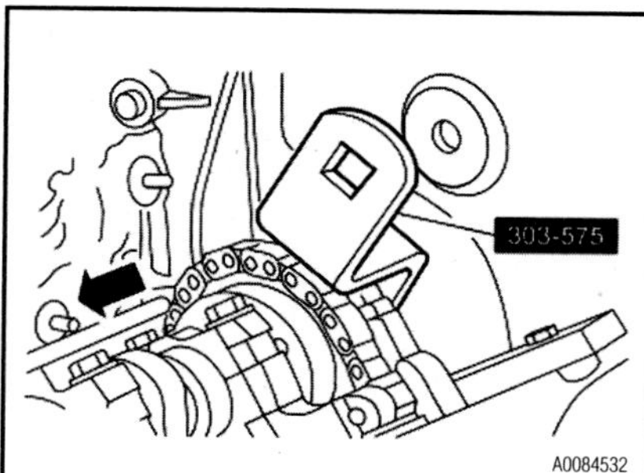

Fig. 121 Using the Torque Wrench Extension and the Camshaft Sprocket Nut Socket 303-565

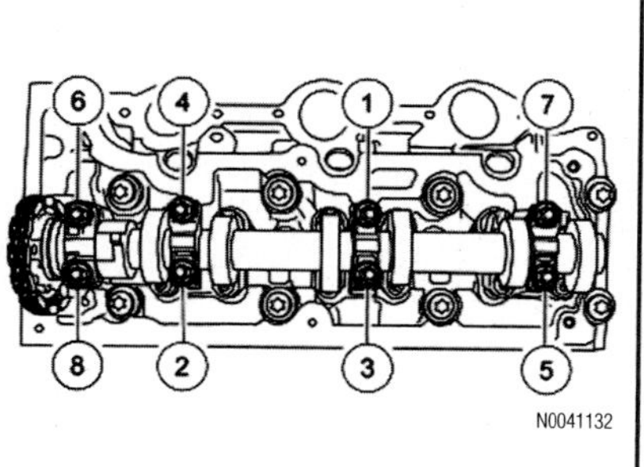

Fig. 123 Tighten the bolts in the sequence shown

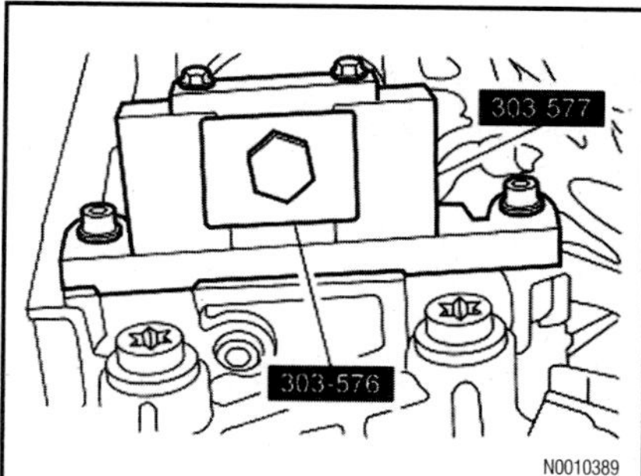

Fig. 124 Correctly fit the Adapter and install the Camshaft Holding Tool and Adapter

5. Install the Crankshaft TDC Timing Tool.

6. Install the Camshaft Sprocket Holding Tool and Adapter to the RH cylinder head and tighten the 2 top clamp bolts. Tighten to 7 ft. lbs. (10 Nm).

➡The RH camshaft sprocket bolt is a LH-threaded bolt.

7. Using the Torque Wrench Extension with the Camshaft Sprocket Nut Socket 303-565, loosen the RH camshaft sprocket bolt.

8. Loosen the top 2 Camshaft Sprocket Holding Tool clamp bolts.

➡The camshaft timing slots are off-center.

9. Position the camshaft timing slots below the centerline of the camshaft to correctly fit the Adapter and install the Camshaft Holding Tool and Adapter on the front of the RH cylinder head.

10. Remove the RH camshaft tensioner. Remove and discard the washer.

11. Install the Timing Chain Tensioner.

➡The RH camshaft sprocket bolt is a LH-threaded bolt.

12. Tighten the bolts.

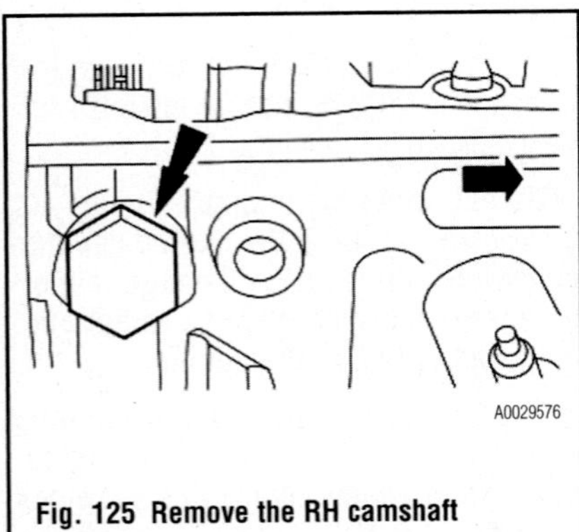

Fig. 125 Remove the RH camshaft tensioner

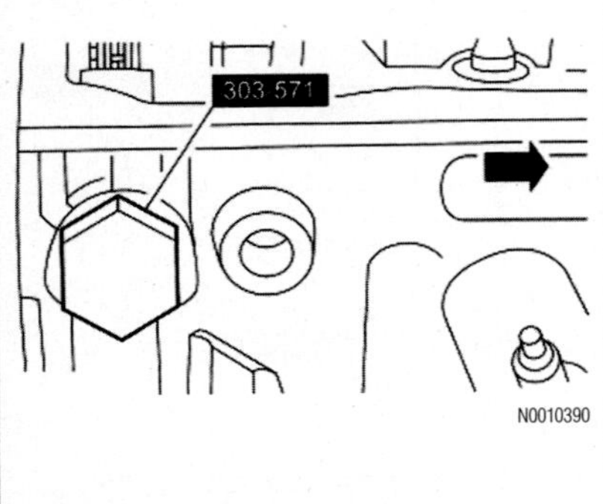

Fig. 126 Install the Timing Chain Tensioner

13. Tighten the Camshaft Sprocket Holding Tool top 2 clamp bolts to 89 inch lbs. (10 Nm).

14. Using the Torque Wrench Extension with the Camshaft Sprocket Nut Socket 303-565, tighten the camshaft bolt.

15. Remove the Timing Chain Tensioner.

➡Install a new washer on the tensioner.

16. Install the RH camshaft tensioner. Tighten to 32 ft. lbs. (44 Nm).

17. Install the Camshaft Sprocket Holding Tool and Adapter on the front of the LH cylinder head and tighten the top 2 clamp bolts. Tighten to 7 ft. lbs. (10 Nm).

18. Loosen the LH camshaft sprocket bolt.

19. Loosen the top 2 clamp bolts on the Camshaft Sprocket Holding Tool to allow the camshaft sprocket to rotate freely.

➡The camshaft timing slots are off-center.

20. Position the camshaft timing slots below the centerline of the camshaft to correctly fit the Adapter, and install the Camshaft Holding Tool and Adapter on the rear of the LH cylinder head.

21. Remove the LH camshaft tensioner.

22. Remove and discard the washer.

23. Install the Timing Chain Tensioner.

24. Tighten the bolts.

a. Tighten the Camshaft Sprocket Holding Tool top 2 clamp bolts to 7 ft. lbs (10 Nm).

b. Tighten the LH camshaft bolt to 63 ft. lbs. (85 Nm).

25. Remove the Timing Chain Tensioner.

➡Install a new washer on the tensioner.

26. Install the LH camshaft tensioner. Tighten to 32 ft. lbs. (44 Nm).

27. Install the ECT sensor. For additional information, refer to Engine Performance.

28. Install the generator. For additional information, refer to Engine Electrical.

29. Install the camshaft roller followers. For additional information, refer to Camshaft Roller Follower in this section.

4.6L Engine

See Figures 127 through 131.

➡This procedure is for the LH camshaft, RH procedure is similar.

➡This procedure must be followed exactly or damage to the valves and pistons will result.

1. Remove the LH valve cover. For additional information, refer to Valve Cover in this section.

➡Damage to the camshaft phaser and sprocket assembly will occur if mishandled or used as a lifting or leveraging device.

➡Only use hand tools to remove the camshaft phaser and sprocket assembly or damage may occur to the camshaft or camshaft phaser and sprocket.

2. Loosen and back off the LH camshaft phaser and sprocket bolt one full turn.

3. Remove the bolt and the LH Camshaft Position (CMP) sensor. Refer to Engine Performance.

4. Rotate the crankshaft clockwise until the No. 5 cylinder camshaft exhaust lobe opens the valve and the 2 intake lobes are in the 3 o'clock position as shown.

5. Remove only the 3 camshaft roller followers shown in the illustration.

➡The camshaft roller followers must be installed in their original locations. Record camshaft roller follower locations. Failure to follow these instructions may result in engine damage.

➡Do not allow the valve keepers to fall off of the valve or the valve may drop into the cylinder. If a valve drops into the cylinder, the cylinder head must be removed. For additional information, refer to Cylinder Head in this section.

➡It may be necessary to push the valve down while compressing the spring.

6. Using the Valve Spring Compressor, remove only the 3 designated camshaft roller followers from the previous step.

➡The crankshaft cannot be moved once set or engine damage may occur.

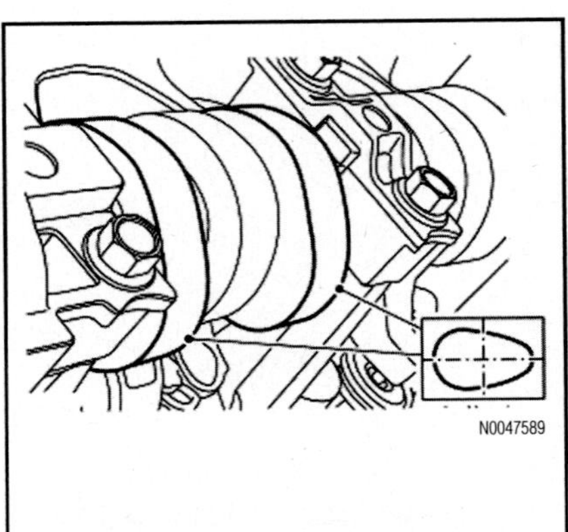

Fig. 127 Rotate the crankshaft clockwise

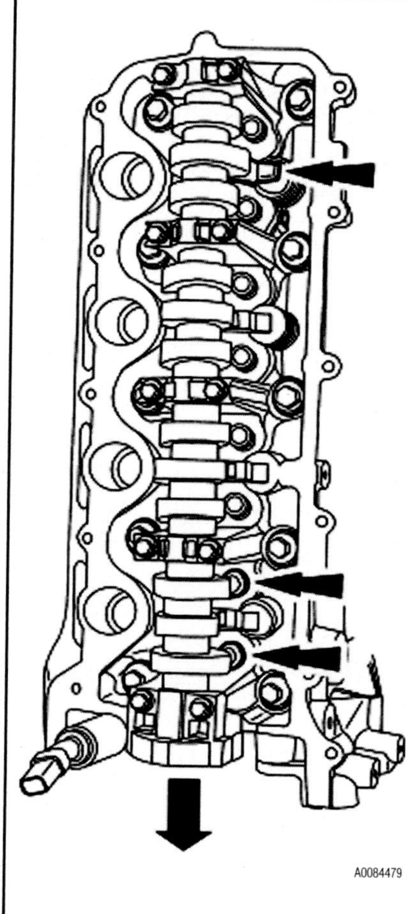

Fig. 128 Remove only the 3 camshaft roller followers shown

7. Rotate the crankshaft a half turn clockwise, as viewed from the front, positioning the No. 5 cylinder camshaft exhaust lobe at the 11 o'clock position as shown.

➡Engine is not freewheeling. Camshaft procedure must be followed exactly or damage to valves and pistons will result.

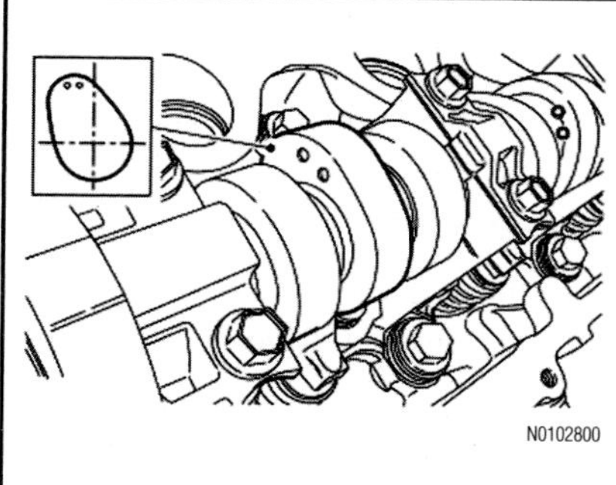

Fig. 129 Rotate the crankshaft a half turn clockwise

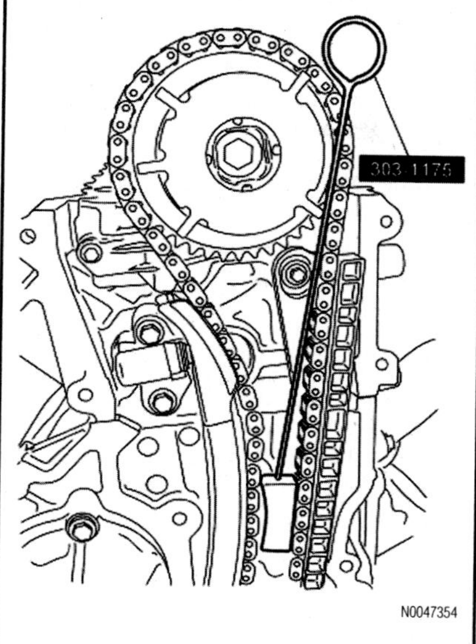

Fig. 130 Install the Timing Chain Locking Tool

➡The Timing Chain Locking Tool must be installed square to the timing chain and the engine block.

➡Engine front cover removed for clarity.

8. Install the Timing Chain Locking Tool in the LH timing chain as shown.

➡Do not remove the Timing Chain Locking Tool at any time during assembly. If the Timing Chain Locking Tool is removed or out of placement, the engine front cover must be removed and the engine must be retimed. For additional information, refer to Timing Chain in this section.

➡The timing chain must be installed in its original position onto the camshaft phaser and sprocket using the scribed marks, or damage to valves and pistons will result.

➡RH shown, LH similar.

9. Scribe a location mark on the timing chain and the camshaft phaser and sprocket assembly.

➡Damage to the camshaft phaser and sprocket assembly will occur if mishandled or used as a lifting or leveraging device.

➡Only use hand tools to remove the camshaft phaser and sprocket bolt or damage may occur to the camshaft or camshaft phaser and sprocket.

➡Do not remove the Timing Chain Locking Tool at any time during assembly. If the Timing Chain Locking Tool is removed or out of placement, the engine front cover must be removed and the engine must be retimed. For additional information, refer to Timing Chain in this section.

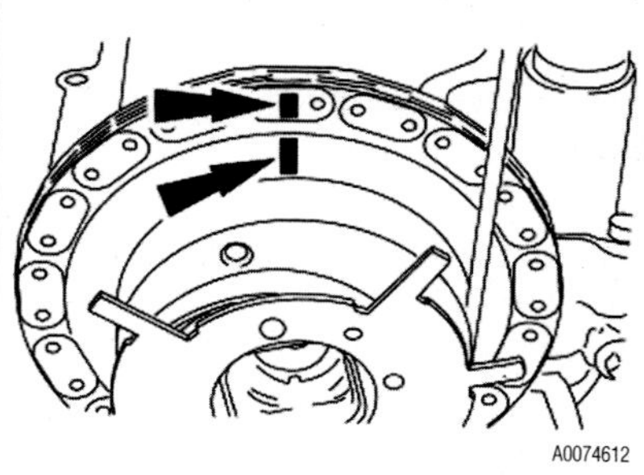

Fig. 131 Scribe a location mark on the timing chain and the camshaft phaser and sprocket assembly

10. Remove the bolt and remove the camshaft phaser and sprocket assembly from camshaft and then from the timing chain.

11. Discard the bolt and washer.

➡If replacement of the camshaft phaser and sprocket is necessary, transfer the scribe mark to the new camshaft phaser and sprocket.

12. Inspect the camshaft phaser and sprocket for damage.

To install:

➡Do not remove the Timing Chain Locking Tool at any time during assembly. If the Timing Chain Locking Tool is removed or out of placement, the engine front cover must be removed and the engine must be retimed. For additional information, refer to Timing Chain Components in this section.

➡The timing chain must be installed in its original position onto the camshaft phaser and sprocket using the scribed marks, or damage to valves and pistons will result.

13. Position the camshaft phaser and sprocket into the timing chain with the timing chain scribe marks in alignment.

➡Do not remove the Timing Chain Locking Tool at any time during assembly. If the Timing Chain Locking Tool is removed or out of placement, the engine front cover must be removed and the engine must be retimed. For additional information, refer to Timing Chain in this section.

➡Damage to the camshaft phaser and sprocket assembly will occur if mishandled or used as a lifting or leveraging device.

➡Only use hand tools to install the camshaft phaser and sprocket bolt or damage may occur to the camshaft or camshaft phaser and sprocket.

14. Position the camshaft phaser and sprocket onto the camshaft. Install a new camshaft phaser and sprocket bolt finger-tight.

➡Engine front cover removed for clarity.

15. Remove the Timing Chain Locking Tool.
16. Rotate the crankshaft a half turn counterclockwise until the No. 5 cylinder camshaft exhaust lobe opens the valve and the 2 intake lobes are in the 3 o'clock position.

➡Do not allow the valve keepers to fall off of the valve or the valve may drop into the cylinder. If a valve drops into the cylinder, the cylinder head must be removed. For additional information, refer to Cylinder Head in this section.

➡It may be necessary to push the valve down while compressing the spring.

17. Using the Valve Spring Compressor, install the 3 originally removed camshaft roller followers.
18. Install the CMP sensor and the bolt.

➡Only use hand tools to install the camshaft phaser and sprocket assembly or damage may occur to the camshaft or camshaft phaser and sprocket.

➡Damage to the camshaft phaser and sprocket assembly will occur if mishandled or used as a lifting or leveraging device.

19. Tighten the camshaft phaser and sprocket bolt in 2 stages:
    a. Stage 1: Tighten to 30 ft. lbs. (40 Nm).
    b. Stage 2: Tighten an additional 90 degrees.
20. Install the LH valve cover.

5.0L Engines

See Figures 132 through 139.

➡This procedure is for the RH camshaft, LH procedure is similar.

➡During engine repair procedures, cleanliness is extremely important. Any foreign material, including any material created while cleaning gasket surfaces, that enters the oil passages, coolant passages or the oil pan, can cause engine failure.

➡If the components are to be reinstalled, they must be installed in their original location. Mark the components for installation into their original location.

1. Remove the engine front cover. For additional information, refer to Front Cover in this section.
2. Remove the RH intake and exhaust Camshaft Position (CMP) sensors. For additional information, refer to Engine Performance.
3. Remove the timing chain. Refer to Timing Chain in this section.
4. Remove the 3 RH intake Variable Camshaft Timing (VCT) assembly bolts and the 3 RH exhaust VCT assembly bolts.
5. Slide the RH VCT assemblies and secondary timing chain forward 0.078 inches.
6. If not already done, depress the RH secondary timing chain tensioner and turn the tensioner 90 degrees.

N0121766

Fig. 132 Remove the 3 RH intake Variable Camshaft Timing (VCT) assembly bolts and the 3 RH exhaust VCT assembly bolts

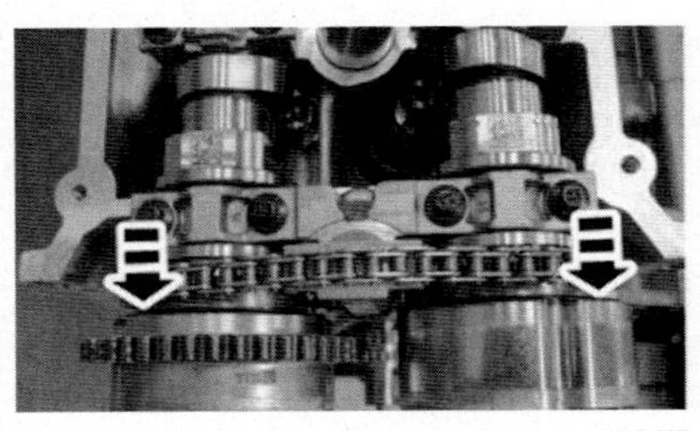
N0121767

Fig. 133 Slide the RH VCT assemblies and secondary timing chain forward 0.078 inches

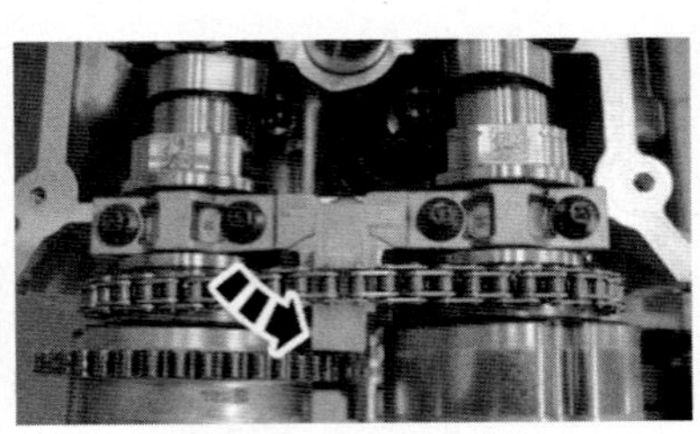
N0121768

Fig. 134 Depress the RH secondary timing chain tensioner and turn the tensioner 90 degrees

N0121769

Fig. 135 Remove the RH VCT assemblies and the RH secondary timing chain

7. If not already done, remove the RH VCT assemblies and the RH secondary timing chain.

➡Intake camshaft shown, exhaust camshaft similar.

8. Remove the VCT system oil filter from the intake and exhaust camshafts.

➡The front camshaft bearing mega cap must be removed first and then the remaining camshaft bearing caps. Failure to follow this direction may result in damage to the engine.

9. Remove the 4 bolts and the RH front camshaft bearing mega cap.
10. Remove the 16 bolts and the 8 camshaft bearing caps.
11. Remove the RH intake and exhaust camshafts.

To install:

➡Lubricate the camshafts with clean engine oil prior to installation.

12. Install the RH intake and exhaust camshafts in the neutral position. Align the D-slots as shown in the illustration.
13. Install the 8 camshaft bearing caps and the 16 bolts. Do not tighten the bolts at this time.

Fig. 136 Remove the VCT system oil filter from the intake and exhaust camshafts

Fig. 137 Align the D-slots as shown

14. Install the RH front camshaft bearing mega cap and the 4 bolts. Do not tighten at this time
15. Tighten the bolts in the sequence shown in 2 stages.
   a. Stage 1: Tighten to 53 inch lbs. (6 Nm)s.
   b. Stage 2: Tighten an additional 45 degrees.
16. Install the VCT system oil filter in the intake and exhaust camshafts.
17. Install the secondary timing chain onto the RH VCT assemblies. Align the colored links on the secondary timing chain with the timing marks on the VCT assemblies as shown in the illustration.
18. The timing mark on the intake VCT assembly should align between the 2 consecutive colored links.
19. The timing mark on the exhaust VCT assembly should align with the single colored link.
20. Install the RH VCT assemblies and the secondary timing chain onto the RH camshafts to a position 2 mm (0.078 in) from fully seated. The timing mark on the exhaust VCT assembly should be in the 1 o'clock position.

➡It may be necessary to rotate the exhaust camshaft slightly (using a wrench on the flats of the camshaft) to seat the VCT assemblies onto the camshafts.

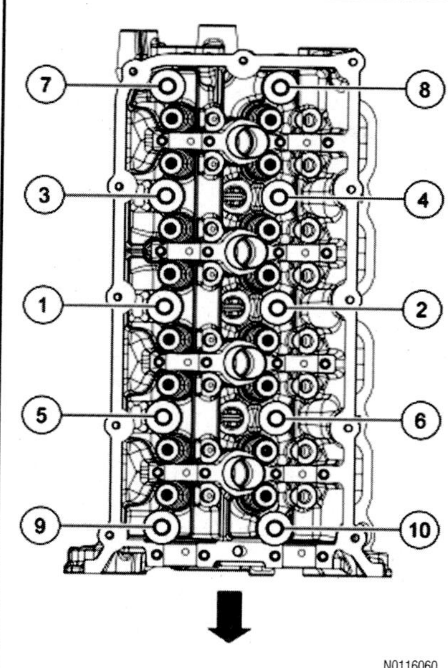

Fig. 138 Tighten the bolts in the sequence shown

21. Rotate the secondary timing chain tensioner 90 degrees so the ramped area is facing forward and fully seat the VCT assemblies onto the camshafts.
22. If the secondary timing chain is not centered over the tensioner, reposition the VCT assemblies until they are fully seated on the camshafts.

➡Use a wrench on the flats of the camshaft to hold the camshafts while tightening the VCT assembly bolts.

23. Install the 3 RH intake VCT assembly bolts and the 3 RH exhaust VCT assembly bolts. Tighten to 11 ft. lbs. (15 Nm) plus an additional 90 degrees.

Fig. 139 Identifying the 2 consecutive colored links (1) and the single colored link (2)

24. To complete the installation, reverse the remaining removal procedure.

5.4L Engine

Roller Follower

See Figure 140.

➡During engine repair procedures, cleanliness is extremely important. Any foreign material, including any material created while cleaning gasket surfaces, that enters the oil passages, coolant passages or the oil pan, can cause engine failure.

➡If servicing both the RH and LH cylinder head camshaft roller followers, the LH valve cover procedure must be completed prior to the RH valve cover procedure.

1. With the vehicle in NEUTRAL, position it on a hoist.

➡If the engine is difficult to rotate while positioning the piston to the bottom of the cylinder, remove the spark plugs.

2. Remove the valve covers. For additional information, refer to Valve Cover in this section.
3. Position the piston of the cylinder being repaired at the bottom of the stroke or position the camshaft lobe at base circle.

➡If the roller followers are to be reinstalled, they must be installed in their original positions. Mark the roller followers for installation into their original locations. Failure to follow these instructions may result in engine damage.

4. Using the Valve Spring Compressor, compress the valve springs and remove the camshaft roller followers.
5. Repeat the previous 2 steps to remove each of the roller followers. Inspect the roller followers.

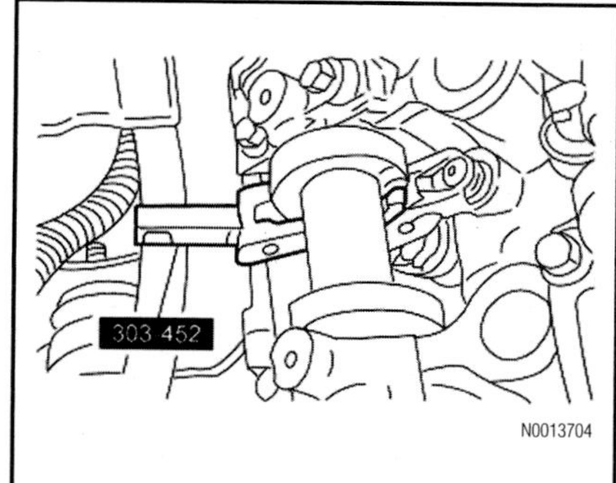

Fig. 140 Install the Valve Spring Compressor Spacer

To install:

6. Lubricate each of the roller followers with clean engine oil prior to installation.
7. Using the Valve Spring Compressor, compress the valve spring and install the camshaft roller followers.
8. Remove the Valve Spring Compressor from between the valve spring.
9. Install the valve covers.

Camshaft

See Figures 141 through 144.

➡This procedure is for the LH camshaft, RH procedure is similar.

1. Remove the timing drive components. For additional information, refer to Timing Chain in this section.
2. Install the Camshaft Holding Tool.
3. Remove the bolt, washer and camshaft drive sprocket.
4. Remove the bolt, washer and camshaft sprocket spacer.
5. Compress the secondary timing chain tensioner and install a lockpin.
6. Remove the timing chain and the 2 camshaft sprockets.
7. Remove the 2 bolts and the secondary timing chain tensioner.

➡The camshaft bearing cap bolts vary in length and head design and must be installed in their original positions. Camshaft bearing caps are not interchangeable and must be installed in their original positions. If not reassembled in their original positions, severe engine damage may occur.

8. Remove the camshaft bearing cap bolts in the sequence shown.
   a. Remove the camshaft bearing caps.
   b. Remove the camshafts.

To install:

➡Lubricate the camshafts with clean engine oil prior to installation.

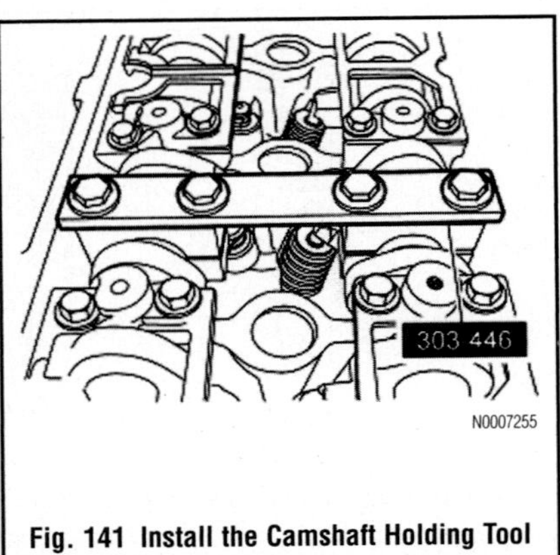

Fig. 141 Install the Camshaft Holding Tool

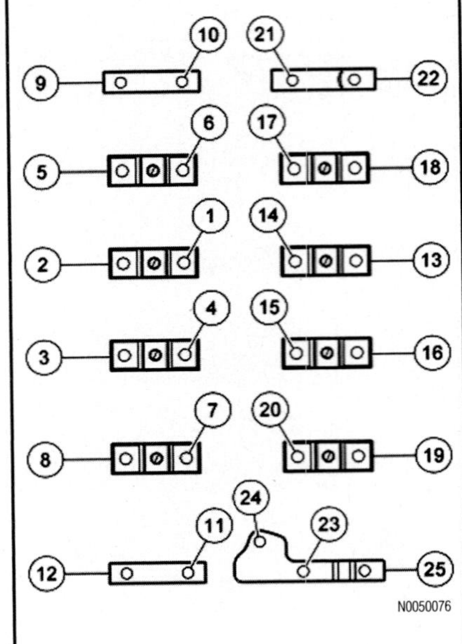

Fig. 142 Remove the camshaft bearing cap bolts in the sequence

Install the camshafts.

➡The camshaft bearing cap bolts vary in length and head design and must be installed in their original positions. Camshaft bearing caps are not interchangeable and must be installed in their original positions. If not reassembled in their original positions, severe engine damage may occur.

➡Lubricate the camshaft bearing cap bearing surfaces with clean engine oil prior to installation.

9. Install the camshaft bearing caps.
10. Install the bearing cap bolts and tighten in the sequence shown above to 7 ft. lbs. (10 Nm).
11. Install the secondary timing chain tensioner and the bolts. Tighten to 7 ft. lbs. (10 Nm).

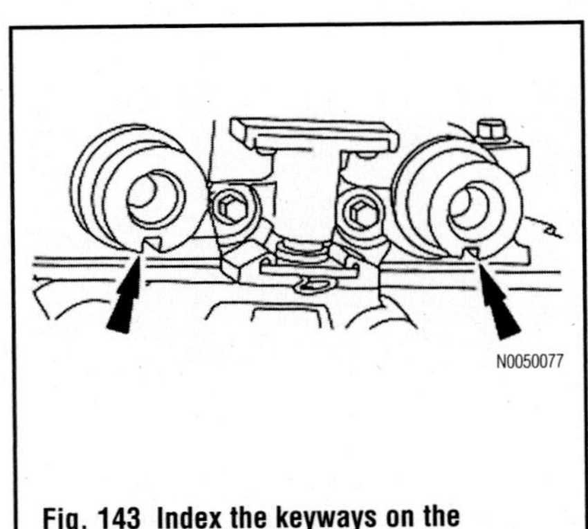

Fig. 143 Index the keyways on the camshafts to the 6 o'clock position

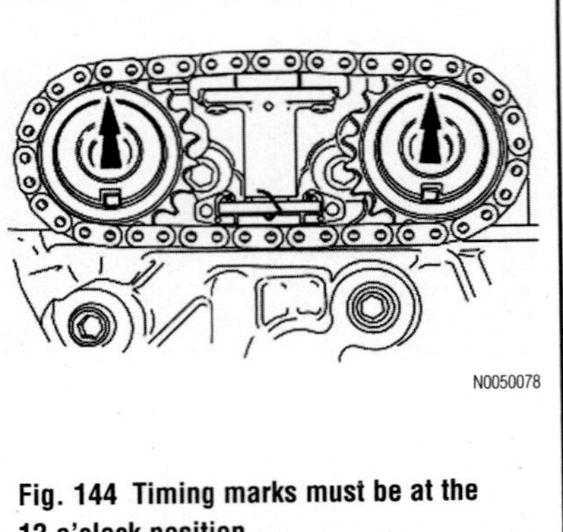

Fig. 144 Timing marks must be at the 12 o'clock position

12. Index the keyways on the camshafts to the 6 o'clock position.

➡Timing marks must be at the 12 o'clock position or damage to the engine may occur.

13. Install the camshaft sprockets and the chain as an assembly.
14. Install the Camshaft Holding Tool.
15. Install the camshaft sprocket spacer, washer and bolt, and hand-tighten the bolt.
16. Install the camshaft drive sprocket, washer and bolt, and hand-tighten the bolt.
17. Tighten the bolts in 2 stages:
    a. Stage 1: Tighten to 30 ft. lbs (40 Nm).
    b. Stage 2: Tighten an additional 90 degrees.
18. Install the timing drive components. For additional information, refer to Timing Chain in this section.

CATALYTIC CONVERTER

REMOVAL & INSTALLATION

3.7L & 5.4L Engines

See Figure 145.

➡Exhaust fasteners are of a torque prevailing design. Use only new fasteners with the same part number as the original. Torque values must be used as specified during reassembly to make sure of correct retention of exhaust components.

1. With the vehicle in NEUTRAL, position it on a hoist.

➡When repairing the exhaust system or removing exhaust components, disconnect all Heated Oxygen Sensor (HO2S) and Catalyst Monitor Sensor (CMS) at the wiring connectors to prevent damage to the sensors and wiring harnesses.

2. Disconnect the RH and LH Heated Oxygen Sensor (HO2S) electrical connectors.

3. Disconnect the RH and LH Catalyst Monitor Sensor (CMS) electrical connectors.

4. Using a jackstand, support the catalytic converter.

5. Loosen the Torca® couplers.

6. Slide the Torca® couplers on to the intermediate pipe and disconnect the intermediate pipe from the catalytic converter assembly.

7. Remove and discard the 2 RH catalytic converter-to-exhaust manifold nuts.

8. Remove and discard the 2 LH catalytic converter-to-exhaust manifold nuts.

9. Remove the jackstand and the catalytic converter.

To install:

➡Prior to installation, inspect the Heated Oxygen Sensor (HO2S) and the Catalyst Monitor Sensor (CMS) wiring harness for damage.

➡Using a Scotch Brite® pad, clean the mating surfaces of the manifold outlet flare and the catalytic converter inlet flare, at the catalytic converter outlet flare and the muffler inlet pipe. Keep foreign materials out of the catalytic converters.

➡Using a jackstand, support the catalytic converter near the rear outlet while positioning the converter into place. Align the manifold studs into the pipe flange. Make sure not to damage the studs or mating surfaces.

➡Hand-tighten all the catalytic converter nuts.

10. Install the catalytic converter and hand tighten the new LH and RH catalytic converter-to-exhaust manifold nuts.

11. Do not tighten the LH and RH catalytic converter-to-exhaust manifold nuts at this time.

➡Similar catalytic converter shown.

➡Make sure that the catalytic converter is inserted into the couplers correctly.

12. Slide the Torca® couplers over catalyst pipes and engage the coupler clip completely over the converter button.

13. Do not tighten the Torca® couplers at this time.

➡Tighten the catalytic converter-to-exhaust manifold nuts alternately in 7 ft. lbs. (10 Nm) increments to maintain torque and draw flange evenly to assure alignment of exhaust system. Tighten the new nuts to 30 ft. lbs (40 Nm).

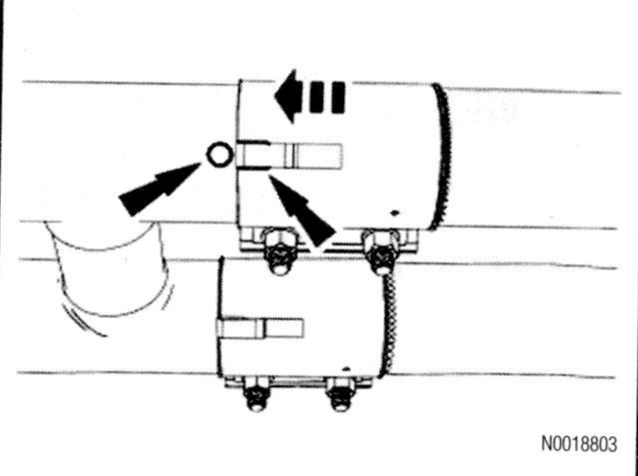

Fig. 145 Slide the Torca® couplers over catalyst pipes and engage the coupler clip

➡Make sure to correctly align the catalytic converter to the exhaust manifold and intermediate pipes before tightening the fasteners.

14. Tighten the 2 LH catalytic converter-to-exhaust manifold nuts. Tighten to 30 ft. lbs (40 Nm).

15. Alternately tighten, in 7 ft. lbs. (10 Nm) increments.

➡Tighten the catalytic converter-to-exhaust manifold nuts alternately in 7 ft. lbs. (10 Nm) increments to maintain torque and draw flange evenly to assure alignment of exhaust system. Tighten the new nuts to 30 ft. lbs (40 Nm).

16. Tighten the 2 RH catalytic converter-to-exhaust manifold nuts. Tighten to 30 ft. lbs (40 Nm).

17. Alternately tighten, in 7 ft. lbs. (10 Nm) increments.

18. Tighten the Torca® couplers. Tighten to 35 ft. lbs. (48 Nm).

19. Connect the RH and LH CMS electrical connectors.

20. Connect the RH and LH HO2S electrical connectors.

4.0L & 4.6L Engines

See Figures 146 and 147.

1. With the vehicle in NEUTRAL, position it on a hoist.

2. Using a jackstand, support the muffler.

3. Loosen the exhaust coupler and disconnect the intermediate pipe from the catalytic converter assembly. Discard the exhaust coupler. To install, tighten to 35 ft. lbs. (48 Nm).

4. Alternately tighten, in 89 inch lbs. (10 Nm) increments.

➡When repairing the exhaust system or removing exhaust components, disconnect all Heated Oxygen Sensor (HO2S) and Catalyst Monitor Sensor (CMS) at the wiring connectors to prevent damage to the sensors and wiring harnesses.

5. Disconnect the RH and LH Heated Oxygen Sensor (HO2S) electrical connectors.

6. Disconnect the RH and LH Catalyst Monitor Sensor (CMS) electrical connectors.

7. Using a jackstand, support the catalytic converter.

➡Hand-tighten all the catalytic converter nuts.

8. Remove and discard the 2 RH catalytic converter-to-exhaust manifold nuts. To install, tighten to 35 ft. lbs. (45 Nm).

9. Remove and discard the 2 LH catalytic converter-to-exhaust manifold nuts. To install, tighten to 35 ft. lbs. (45 Nm).

10. Remove the jackstand and the catalytic converter.

11. Remove and discard the 4 catalytic converter-to-exhaust manifold studs. To install, tighten to 30 ft. lbs. (40 Nm).

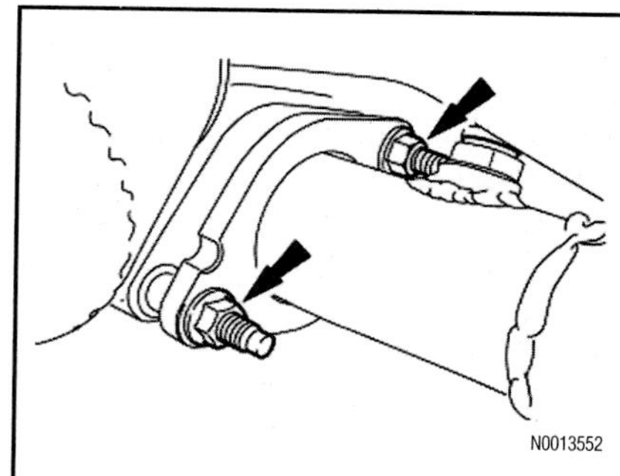

Fig. 146 Remove and discard the 2 RH catalytic converter-to-exhaust manifold nuts

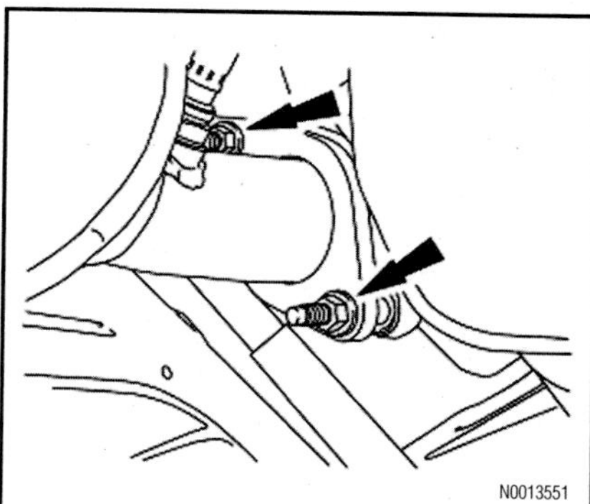

Fig. 147 Remove and discard the 2 LH catalytic converter-to-exhaust manifold nuts

➡Prior to Installation, inspect the Heated Oxygen Sensor (HO2S) and the Catalyst Monitor Sensor (CMS) wiring harness for damage.

➡Using a Scotch Brite® pad, clean the mating surfaces of the manifold outlet flare and the catalytic converter inlet flare, at the catalytic converter outlet flare and the muffler inlet pipe. Keep foreign materials out of the catalytic converters.

➡Using a jackstand, support the catalytic converter near the rear outlet while positioning the converter into place. Align the manifold studs into the pipe flange. Make sure not to damage the studs or mating surfaces.

12. Make sure to correctly align the catalytic converter to the exhaust manifold before installing the fasteners. The catalytic converter is correctly positioned when the hanger rods are centered in the isolators.
13. To install, reverse the removal procedure.
14. Always install new converter-to-manifold nuts, studs and exhaust coupler.

5.0L Engine

See Figure 148.

➡Exhaust fasteners are of a torque prevailing design. Use only new fasteners with the same part number as the original. Torque values must be used as specified during reassembly to make sure of correct retention of exhaust components.

➡Discard the ball clamps and fasteners after removal.

1. With the vehicle in NEUTRAL, position it on a hoist.
2. RH catalytic converter: Remove and discard the RH catalytic converter-to-exhaust manifold nut.

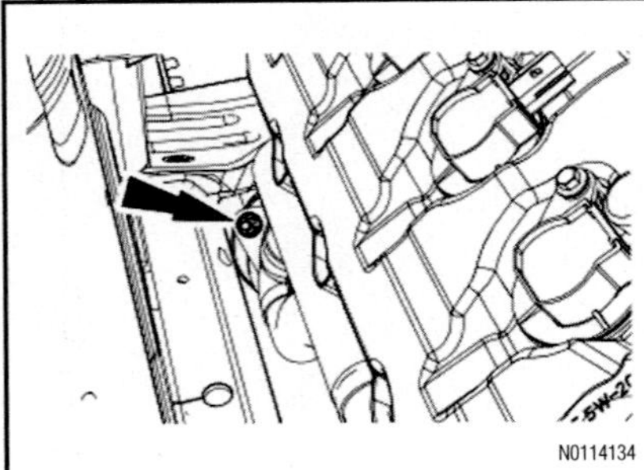

Fig. 148 Remove and discard the RH catalytic converter-to-exhaust manifold nut

3. Using a jackstand, support the catalytic converter.

➡When repairing the exhaust system or removing exhaust components, disconnect the Catalyst Monitor Sensor (CMS) at the wiring connector to prevent damage to the sensor and wiring harness.

4. Disconnect the Catalyst Monitor Sensor (CMS) electrical connector.
5. Loosen the catalytic converter-to-exhaust H-pipe ball clamp.
6. RH catalytic converter:
   a. Remove and discard the RH catalytic converter-to-exhaust manifold nut.
   b. Remove the RH catalytic converter and discard the gasket.
7. LH catalytic converter:
   a. Remove and discard the LH catalytic converter-to-exhaust manifold nuts.
   b. Remove the LH catalytic converter and discard the gasket.
8. All catalytic converters: Remove and discard the ball clamp from the exhaust H-pipe.

To install:

9. Install a new ball clamp on the exhaust H-pipe.
10. LH catalytic converter:

➡Prior to installation, inspect the Catalyst Monitor Sensor (CMS) wiring harness for damage.

➡Using a Scotch Brite® pad, clean the mating surfaces of the manifold outlet flare and the catalytic converter inlet flare, at the catalytic converter outlet flare and the exhaust H-pipe. Keep foreign materials out of the catalytic converters.

➡Hand tighten all the catalytic converter nuts.

   a. Install the LH catalytic converter, gasket and 2 new nuts.
   b. Do not tighten the LH catalytic converter-to-exhaust manifold nuts at this time.
11. RH catalytic converter:

➡Prior to installation, inspect the Catalyst Monitor Sensor (CMS) wiring harness for damage.

➡Using a Scotch Brite® pad, clean the mating surfaces of the manifold outlet flare and the catalytic converter inlet flare, at the catalytic converter outlet flare and the exhaust H-pipe. Keep foreign materials out of the catalytic converters.

➡Hand tighten all the catalytic converter nuts.

   a. Install the RH catalytic converter, gasket and 2 new nuts.
   b. Do not tighten the RH catalytic converter-to-exhaust manifold nuts at this time.
12. All catalytic converters:
13. Using a jackstand, support the exhaust H-pipe.
14. LH catalytic converter:

➡Tighten the LH catalytic converter-to-exhaust manifold nuts alternately in 7 ft. lbs. (10 Nm) increments to maintain torque and draw flange evenly to assure alignment of exhaust system. Tighten the new nuts to 30 ft. lbs (40 Nm).

➡Make sure to correctly align the catalytic converter to the exhaust manifold and exhaust H-pipe before tightening the fasteners.

   a. Tighten the 2 LH catalytic converter-to-exhaust manifold nuts.
   b. Tighten to 30 ft. lbs (40 Nm).
   c. Alternately tighten, in 7 ft. lbs. (10 Nm) increments.
15. Perform the same routine on the RH catalytic converter:
16. All catalytic converters:
17. Tighten the catalytic converter-to-exhaust H-pipe ball clamp. Tighten to 22 ft. lbs. (30 Nm).
18. Connect the Catalyst Monitor Sensor (CMS) electrical connector.

CRANKSHAFT FRONT SEAL

REMOVAL & INSTALLATION

3.7L, 5.0L & 5.4L Engines

See Figures 149 and 150.

1. With the vehicle in NEUTRAL, position it on a hoist.

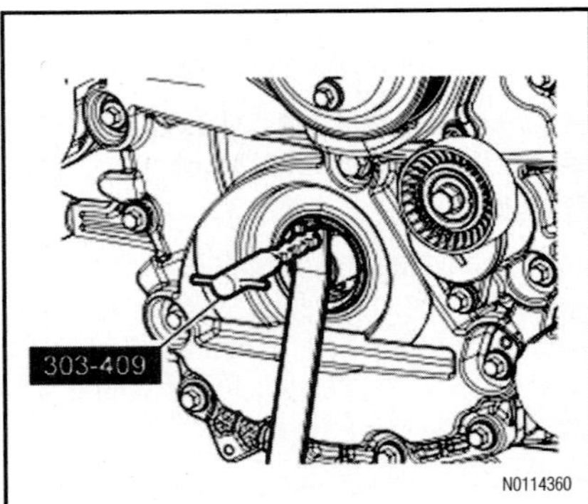

Fig. 149 Using the Oil Seal Remover

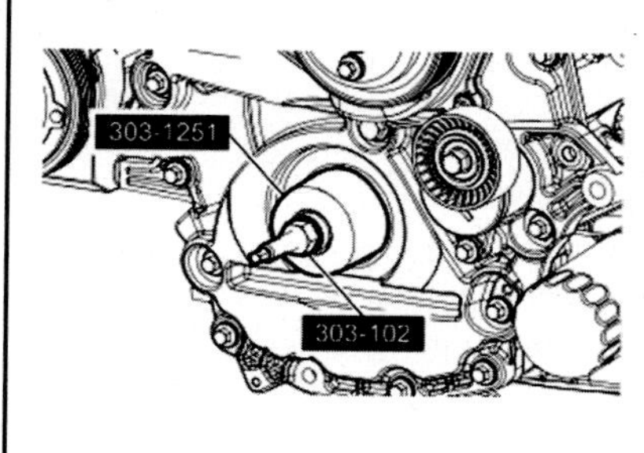

Fig. 150 Using the Front Crankshaft Seal Installer and Crankshaft Vibration Damper Installer

2. Remove the crankshaft pulley. For additional information, refer to Timing Chain in this section.
3. Using the Oil Seal Remover, remove and discard the crankshaft front seal.
4. Clean all sealing surfaces with metal surface prep.

To install:

➡Apply clean engine oil to the crankshaft front seal bore in the engine front cover.

5. Using the Front Crankshaft Seal Installer and Crankshaft Vibration Damper Installer, install a new crankshaft front seal.
6. Install the crankshaft pulley.

4.0L & 4.6L Engines

See Figures 151 and 152.

1. Remove the crankshaft pulley. For additional information, refer to Timing Chain in this section.
2. Using the Crankshaft Front Oil Seal Remover, remove and discard the crankshaft front seal.

To install:

➡Lubricate the new front seal with clean engine oil.

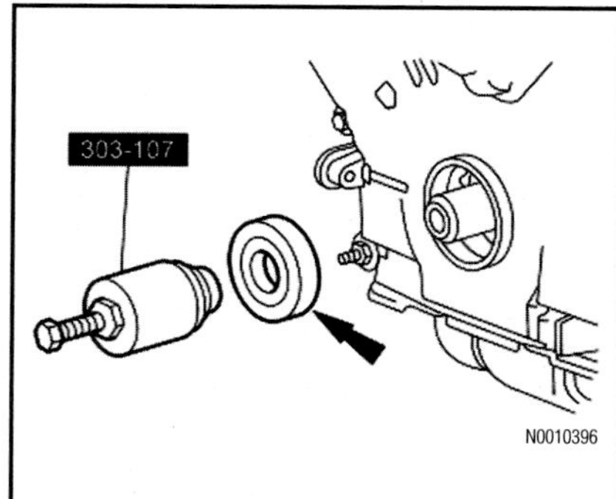

Fig. 151 Using the Crankshaft Front Oil Seal Remover

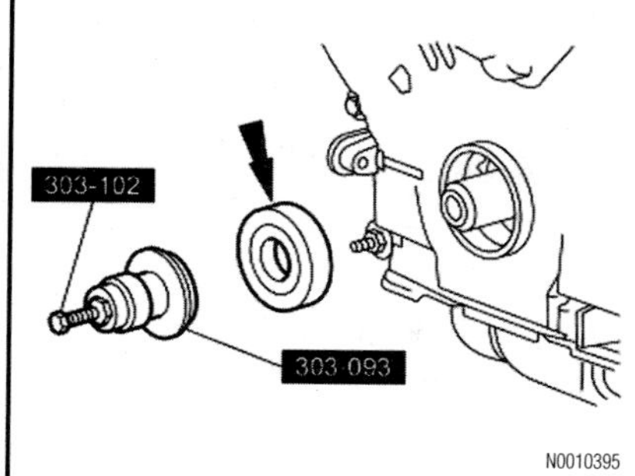

Fig. 152 Using the Front Cover Aligner and Crankshaft Vibration Damper Installer

3. Using the Front Cover Aligner and Crankshaft Vibration Damper Installer, install a new crankshaft front seal.
4. Install the crankshaft pulley.

CYLINDER HEAD

REMOVAL & INSTALLATION

3.7L Engines

See Figures 153 through 155.

WARNING

Do not smoke, carry lighted tobacco or have an open flame of any type when working on or near any fuel-related component. Highly flammable mixtures are always present and may be ignited. Failure to follow these instructions may result in serious personal injury.

WARNING

Before working on or disconnecting any of the fuel tubes or fuel system components, relieve the fuel system pressure to prevent accidental spraying of fuel. Fuel in the fuel system remains under high pressure, even when the engine is not running. Failure to follow this instruction may result in serious personal injury.

WARNING

Do not carry personal electronic devices such as cell phones, pagers or audio equipment of any type when working on or near any fuel-related component. Highly flammable mixtures are always present and may be ignited. Failure to follow these instructions may result in serious personal injury.

WARNING

Always disconnect the battery ground cable at the battery when working on an evaporative emission (EVAP) system or fuel-related component. Highly flammable mixtures are always present and may be ignited. Failure to follow these instructions may result in serious personal injury.

WARNING

Clean all fuel residue from the engine compartment. If not removed, fuel residue may ignite when the engine is returned to operation. Failure to follow this instruction may result in serious personal injury.

➡During engine repair procedures, cleanliness is extremely important. Any foreign material, including any material created while cleaning gasket surfaces that enters the oil passages, coolant passages or the oil pan, may cause engine failure.

➡Release the fuel system pressure. For additional information, refer to Fuel—Gasoline Fuel Injection Systems.

➡This procedure is for the LH cylinder head, RH cylinder head is similar.

1. Disconnect the battery ground cable.
2. Detach and disconnect the RH and LH Heated Oxygen Sensor (HO2S) electrical connectors.
3. Remove and discard the LH and RH catalytic converter-to-exhaust manifold nuts and lower the catalytic converter assembly.
4. Remove the LH camshafts. For additional information, refer to Camshaft in this section.
5. Remove the lower intake manifold. For additional information, refer to Intake Manifold in this section.

➡Do not use power tools to remove the bolt or damage to the LH primary timing chain guide may occur.

6. Remove the bolt and the LH upper primary timing chain guide.
7. Disconnect the 2 LH Camshaft Position (CMP) sensors electrical connectors.
8. Remove the 2 bolts and the 2 LH CMP sensors.
9. Remove the bolt and ground strap from the rear of the LH cylinder head.
10. Detach the wiring harness retainer from the rear of the LH cylinder head.

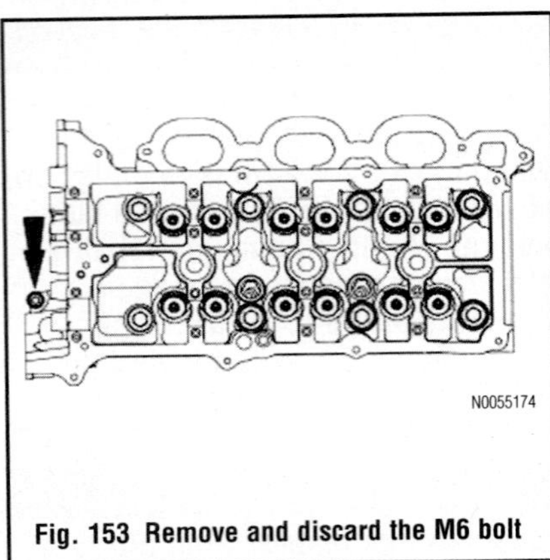

Fig. 153 Remove and discard the M6 bolt

➡If the components are to be reinstalled, they must be installed in the same positions. Mark the components for installation into their original locations.

11. Remove the valve tappets from the cylinder head.
12. Inspect the valve tappets.
13. Remove and discard the M6 bolt.

➡Place clean, lint-free shop towels over exposed engine cavities. Carefully remove the towels so foreign material is not dropped into the engine. Any foreign material (including any material created while cleaning gasket surfaces) that enters the oil passages or the oil pan, may cause engine failure

➡Aluminum surfaces are soft and may be scratched easily. Never place the cylinder head gasket surface, unprotected, on a bench surface.

➡The cylinder head bolts must be discarded and new bolts must be installed. They are a tighten-to-yield design and cannot be reused.

14. Remove and discard the 8 bolts from the cylinder head.

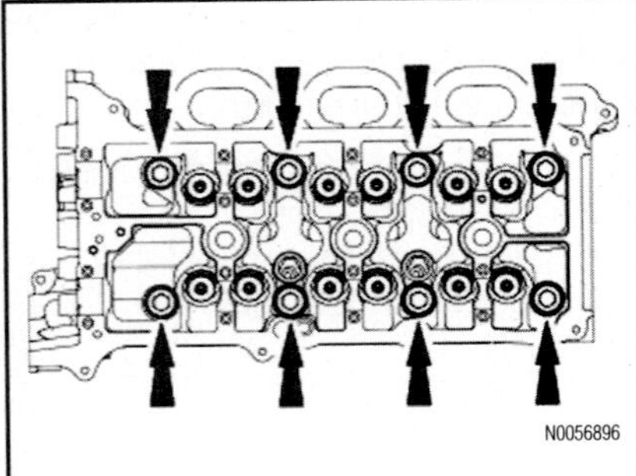

Fig. 154 Remove and discard the 8 bolts from the cylinder head

15. Remove the cylinder head.
16. Discard the cylinder head gasket.

➡Do not use metal scrapers, wire brushes, power abrasive discs or other abrasive means to clean the sealing surfaces. These tools cause scratches and gouges that make leak paths. Use a plastic scraping tool to remove all traces of the head gasket.

➡Observe all warnings or cautions and follow all application directions contained on the packaging of the silicone gasket remover and the metal surface prep.

➡If there is no residual gasket material present, metal surface prep can be used to clean and prepare the surfaces.

17. Clean the cylinder head-to-cylinder block mating surfaces of both the cylinder heads and the cylinder block in the following sequence.
18. Remove any large deposits of silicone or gasket material with a plastic scraper.
19. Apply silicone gasket remover, following package directions, and allow to set for several minutes.
20. Remove the silicone gasket remover with a plastic scraper. A second application of silicone gasket remover may be required if residual traces of silicone or gasket material remain.
21. Apply metal surface prep, following package directions, to remove any remaining traces of oil or coolant and to prepare the surfaces to bond with the new gasket. Do not attempt to make the metal shiny.
22. Some staining of the metal surfaces is normal

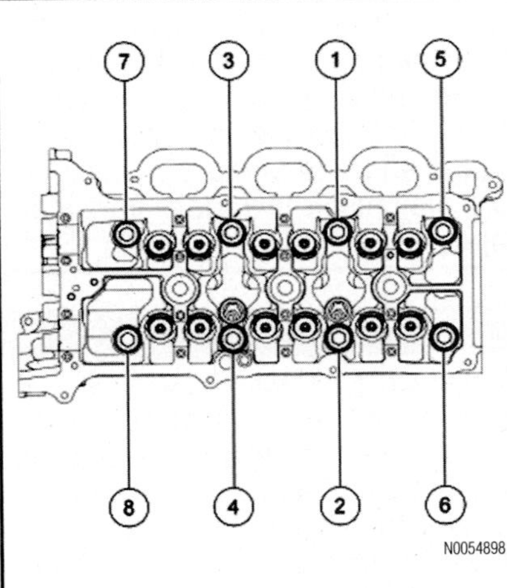

Fig. 155 LH cylinder head tightening sequence

23. Support the cylinder head on a bench with the head gasket side up. Check the cylinder head distortion and the cylinder block distortion.

To install:

➡If the cylinder head is replaced, a new secondary timing chain tensioner will need to be installed.

24. Install a new gasket, the LH cylinder head and 8 new bolts. Tighten in the sequence shown in 5 stages:
    a. Stage 1: Tighten to 14 ft. lbs. (20 Nm).
    b. Stage 2: Tighten to 26 ft. lbs. (35 Nm).
    c. Stage 3: Tighten 90 degrees.
    d. Stage 4: Tighten 90 degrees
    e. Stage 5: Tighten 45 degrees.
25. Install the M6 bolt. Tighten to 7 ft. lbs. (10 Nm).

➡The valve tappets must be installed in their original positions.

➡Coat the valve tappets with clean engine oil prior to installation.

26. Install the valve tappets.
27. To complete installation, reverse the remaining removal procedure.
28. Connect the battery ground cable. For additional information, refer to Battery, Mounting and Cables.

4.0L Engine

See Figures 156 through 160.

➡During engine repair procedures, cleanliness is extremely important. Any foreign material, including any material created while cleaning gasket surfaces that enters the oil passages, coolant passages or the oil pan, can cause engine failure.

1. With the vehicle in NEUTRAL, position it on a hoist.
2. Release the fuel system pressure. For additional information, refer to Fuel—Gasoline Fuel Injection Systems.
3. Drain the engine cooling system. For additional information, refer to Engine Cooling.
4. Remove the intake manifold. For additional information, refer to Intake Manifold in this section.
5. Remove the hydraulic lash adjusters. For additional information, refer to Hydraulic Lash Adjuster in this section.
6. Rotate the accessory drive belt tensioner counterclockwise and remove the accessory drive belt.
7. RH side:

a. Remove the 2 coolant tube bracket bolts.

b. Disconnect the generator electrical connector, remove the nut and detach the B+ terminal.

c. Detach the pin-type retainer.

d. Remove the bolt and the accessory drive belt tensioner.

e. Remove the nut, the 2 bolts and the generator mounting bracket assembly.

f. Disconnect the heater hose from the thermostat housing.

g. Disconnect the upper radiator hose.

h. Position the coolant bypass hose clamp aside.

i. Remove the 3 bolts and the thermostat housing.

j. Disconnect the Engine Coolant Temperature (ECT) sensor electrical connector.

8. LH side:

a. Remove the bolt and the oil level indicator tube.

b. Remove the stud bolt and detach the ground strap.

c. Position the ground strap aside.

d. Remove the bolt and detach the power steering supply hose bracket from the Front End Accessory

e. Drive (FEAD) bracket.

f. Remove the bolt and detach the Power Steering Pressure (PSP) tube bracket from the crossmember.

g. Remove the 3 bolts and the power steering pump pulley.

h. Remove the 3 bolts and position the power steering pump aside.

i. Remove the 3 bolts, the nut and position the FEAD bracket and A/C compressor aside.

j. Remove the bolt and detach the starter motor wiring retainer bracket.

k. Remove the ground strap bolt and detach the wiring harness retainer from the backside of the cylinder head.

9. Both sides:

➡is important to twist the spark plug wire boots while pulling upward to avoid possible damage to the spark plug wires.

10. Using the Spark Plug Wire Remover, disconnect the 6 spark plug wires from the spark plugs.

11. Remove the 4 bolts and the fuel rail and injectors.

12. Separate the 6 fuel injectors from the fuel rail and discard the O-ring seals.

NOTE: LH side shown, RH side similar.

13. Remove the 4 catalytic converter-to-manifold nuts.

14. Discard the nuts.

15. Remove the 12 nuts and the exhaust manifolds and gaskets.

16. Discard the nuts and gaskets.

17. Remove and discard the 12 exhaust manifold studs.

18. RH side:

a. Remove the camshafts.

b. Remove the timing chain.

19. Both sides:

➡To avoid damage to the timing chain cassette, an assistant will be required to help lift the cylinder head from the vehicle.

➡On the RH side, when lifting the cylinder head, be careful to avoid contacting the A/C tube.

➡New cylinder head bolts must be installed. They are a torque-to-yield design and cannot be reused.

20. Remove the cylinder heads.

21. Remove the cylinder head bolts in the sequence shown. Discard all the bolts.

22. Remove and discard the head gaskets.

➡Make sure all coolant residue and foreign material are cleaned from the block surface and cylinder bore. Failure to follow these instructions may result in engine damage.

➡Do not use metal scrapers, wire brushes, power abrasive discs or other abrasive means to clean the sealing surfaces. These tools cause scratches and gouges that make leak paths. Use a plastic scraping tool to remove all traces of the head gasket.

➡Observe all warnings and cautions and follow all application directions contained on the packaging of the silicone gasket remover and the metal surface prep.

➡If there is no residual gasket material present, metal surface prep can be used to clean and prepare the surfaces.

23. Clean the cylinder head-to-cylinder block mating surface of both the cylinder head and the cylinder block in the following sequence.

24. Remove any large deposits of silicone or gasket material with a plastic scraper.

25. Apply silicone gasket remover, following package directions, and allow to set for several minutes.

26. Remove the silicone gasket remover with a plastic scraper. A second application of silicone gasket remover may be required if residual traces of silicone or gasket material remain.

27. Apply metal surface prep, following package directions, to remove any traces of oil or coolant and to prepare the surfaces to bond with the new gasket. Do not attempt to make the metal shiny. Some staining of the metal surfaces is normal.

28. Support the cylinder head on a bench with the head gasket side up. Check the cylinder head distortion and the cylinder block distortion.

To install:

29. Both sides:

30. Clean the cylinder head bolt holes in the cylinder block. Make sure all coolant, oil or other foreign material is removed.

31. Position the cylinder head gaskets on the block.

32. RH side:

➡To avoid damage to the timing chain cassette, an assistant will be required to help position the cylinder head in the vehicle.

a. New cylinder head bolts must be installed. They are a torque-to-yield design and cannot be reused.

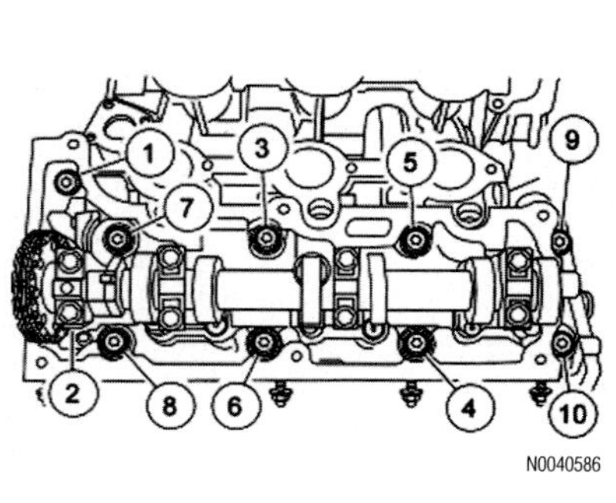

Fig. 156 Cylinder head removal sequence

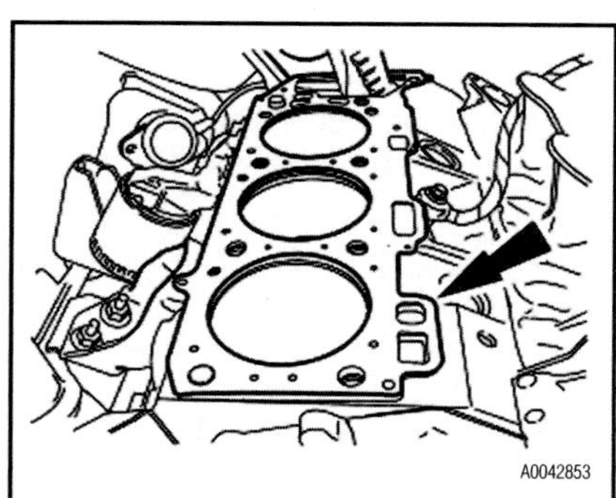

Fig. 157 Position the cylinder head gaskets on the block

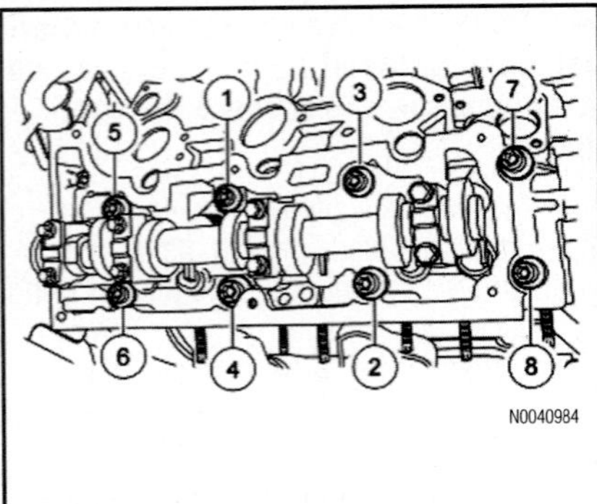

Fig. 158 Cylinder head tightening sequence

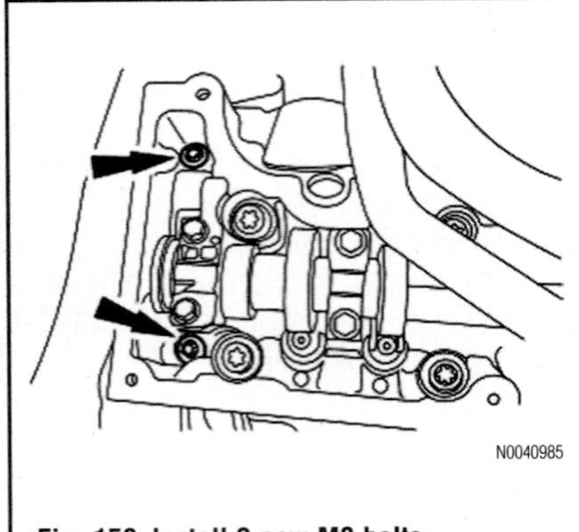

Fig. 159 Install 2 new M8 bolts.

Position the RH cylinder head. Install 8 new M12 bolts and tighten in the sequence shown in 2 stages.

b. Stage 1: Tighten to 9 ft. lbs. (12 Nm).

c. Stage 2: Tighten to 18 ft. lbs. (25 Nm).

d. Install 2 new M8 bolts. Tighten to 24 ft. lbs. (32 Nm).

e. Tighten the 8 M12 bolts in the sequence shown in 2 stages.

f. Stage 1: Tighten 90 degrees.

g. Stage 2: Tighten an additional 90 degrees.

➡The camshaft gear must turn freely on the camshaft. Do not tighten the bolt at this time.

➡The right-hand camshaft sprocket bolt is a left-hand threaded bolt.

h. Remove the rubber band, position the camshaft sprocket and chain. Loosely install the bolt.

i. Install the RH side cassette bolt. Tighten to 9 ft. lbs. (12 Nm).

33. LH side:

➡To avoid damage to the timing chain cassette, an assistant will be required to help position the cylinder head in the vehicle.

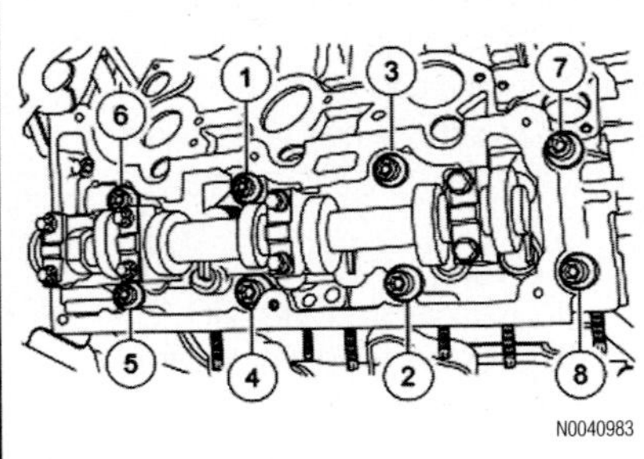

Fig. 160 LH cylinder head tightening sequence

➡New cylinder head bolts must be installed. They are a torque-to-yield design and cannot be reused.

a. Position the LH cylinder head. Install 8 new M12 bolts and tighten in the sequence shown in 2 stages.

b. Stage 1: Tighten to 106 inch lbs. (12 Nm).

c. Stage 2: Tighten to 18 ft. lbs. (25 Nm).

d. Install 2 new M8 bolts. Tighten to 24 ft. lbs. (32 Nm).

e. Tighten the 8 M12 bolts in the sequence shown in 2 stages.

f. Stage 1: Tighten 90 degrees.

g. Stage 2: Tighten an additional 90 degrees.

34. To complete the installation, reverse the remaining removal procedure.

35. Fill and bleed the engine cooling system. For additional information, refer to Engine Cooling.

ENGINE OIL & FILTER

REPLACEMENT

See Figures 161 and 162.

1. Remove the oil cap on top of the engine.

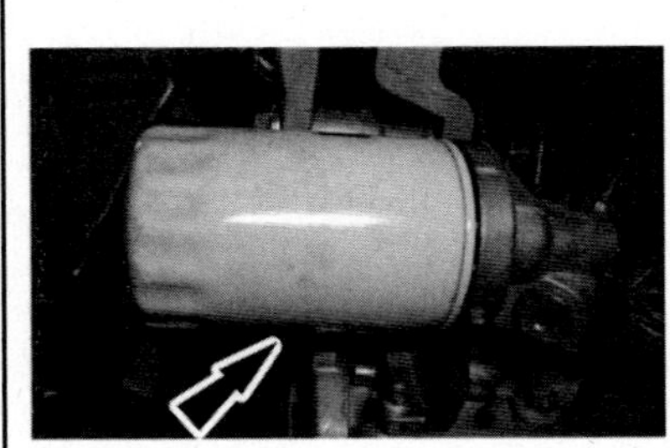

Fig. 161 3.7L Engine oil filter location

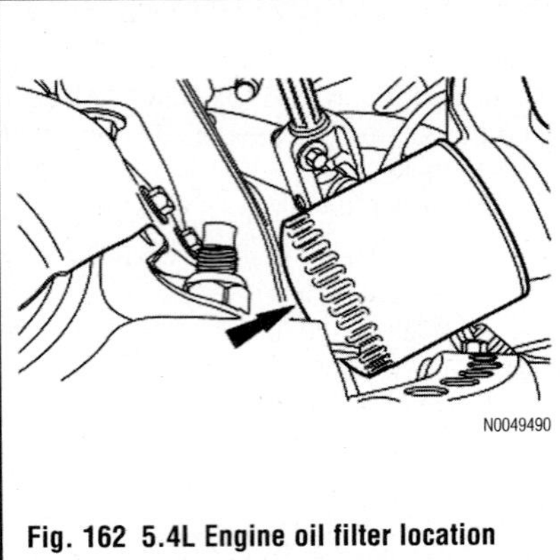

Fig. 162 5.4L Engine oil filter location

2. With the vehicle in NEUTRAL, position it on a hoist.
3. Position a oil receptacle under the vehicle.
4. Remove the oil pan drain plug until all the oil has fully drained. Install the oil pan plug.
5. Remove the oil filter.
6. Lubricate the new oil filter seal with clean engine oil.
7. Install the oil filter.
8. Fill the engine with the recommended oil.
9. Check the dipstick for accurate fill levels.

EXHAUST MANIFOLD

REMOVAL & INSTALLATION

3.7L Engines

LH Exhaust Manifold

See Figure 163.

1. With the vehicle in NEUTRAL, position it on a hoist.
2. If equipped, remove the 4 nuts and the strut tower cross brace.
3. Detach and disconnect the RH and LH Heated Oxygen Sensor (HO2S) electrical connectors.
4. Remove and discard the LH and RH catalytic converter-to-exhaust manifold nuts and lower the catalytic converter assembly.
5. Remove the 2 bolts and the LH exhaust manifold heat shield.
6. Remove the 6 nuts and the LH exhaust manifold.
7. Discard the nuts and gasket.
8. Clean and inspect the LH exhaust manifold.
9. Remove and discard the 6 LH exhaust manifold studs.

➡Do not use metal scrapers, wire brushes, power abrasive discs or other abrasive means to clean the sealing

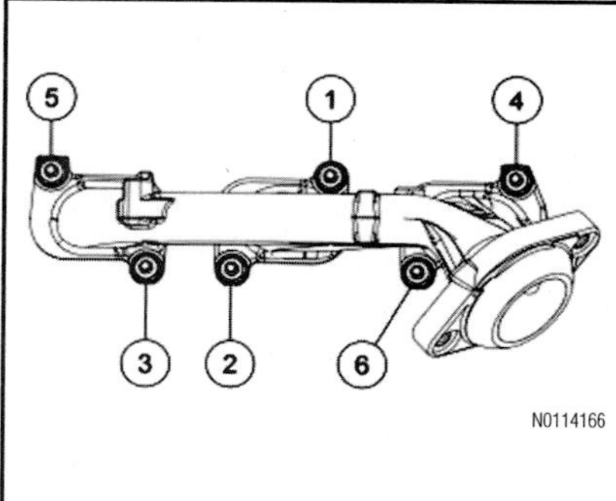

Fig. 163 LH exhaust manifold tightening sequence

surfaces. These may cause scratches and gouges resulting in leak paths. Use a plastic scraper to clean the sealing surfaces.

10. Clean the exhaust manifold mating surface of the cylinder head with metal surface prep. Follow the directions on the packaging.

To install:

11. Install 6 new LH exhaust manifold studs. Tighten to 9 ft. lbs. (12 Nm).

➡Failure to tighten the exhaust manifold nuts to specification a second time will cause the exhaust manifold to develop an exhaust leak.

12. Using a new gasket, install the LH exhaust manifold and 6 new nuts. Tighten in 2 stages in the sequence shown:
    a. Stage 1: Tighten to 14 ft. lbs. (19 Nm).
    b. Stage 2: Tighten to 18 ft. lbs. (25 Nm).
13. Install the LH exhaust manifold heat shield and the 2 bolts.
14. Raise the catalytic converter and install the new LH and RH catalytic converter-to-exhaust manifold nuts. Tighten to 35 ft. lbs. (45 Nm).
15. Connect and attach the RH and LH HO2S electrical connectors.
16. If equipped, install the strut tower cross brace and the 4 nuts (2 shown). Tighten to 26 ft. lbs. (35 Nm)

RH Exhaust Manifold

See Figure 164.

1. With the vehicle in NEUTRAL, position it on a hoist.
2. If equipped, remove the 4 nuts and the strut tower cross brace.
3. Detach and disconnect the RH and LH Heated Oxygen Sensor (HO2S) electrical connectors.
4. Remove and discard the LH and RH catalytic converter-to-exhaust manifold nuts and lower the catalytic converter assembly.
5. Remove the 2 bolts and the RH exhaust manifold heat shield.
6. Remove the heater tube bolt.
7. Remove the 6 nuts and the RH exhaust manifold.
8. Discard the nuts and gasket.
9. Clean and inspect the RH exhaust manifold.
10. Remove and discard the 6 RH exhaust manifold studs.

➡Do not use metal scrapers, wire brushes, power abrasive discs or other abrasive means to clean the sealing surfaces. These may cause scratches and gouges resulting in leak paths. Use a plastic scraper to clean the sealing surfaces.

11. Clean the exhaust manifold mating surface of the cylinder head with metal surface prep. Follow the directions on the packaging.

To install:

12. Install 6 new LH exhaust manifold studs. Tighten to 9 ft. lbs. (12 Nm).

➡Failure to tighten the exhaust manifold nuts to specification a second time will cause the exhaust manifold to develop an exhaust leak.

13. Using a new gasket, install the LH exhaust manifold and 6 new nuts. Tighten in 2 stages in the sequence shown:
    a. Stage 1: Tighten to 14 ft. lbs. (19 Nm).
    b. Stage 2: Tighten to 18 ft. lbs. (25 Nm).
14. Install the heater tube bolt. Tighten to 17 ft. lbs. (23 Nm).
15. Install the LH exhaust manifold heat shield and the 2 bolts.
16. Raise the catalytic converter and install the new LH and RH catalytic converter-to-exhaust manifold nuts. Tighten to 35 ft. lbs. (45 Nm).

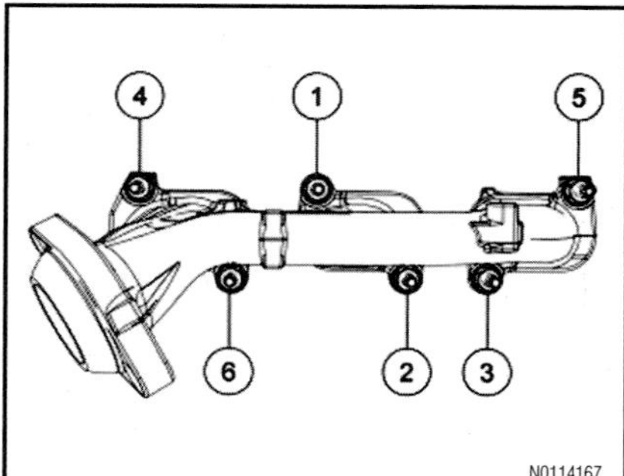

Fig. 164 RH exhaust manifold tightening sequence

17. Connect and attach the RH and LH HO2S electrical connectors.
18. If equipped, install the strut tower cross brace and the 4 nuts (2 shown). Tighten to 26 ft. lbs. (35 Nm)

4.0L Engine

LH Exhaust Manifold

See Figure 165.

1. With the vehicle in NEUTRAL, position it on a hoist.
2. Remove the 2 catalytic converter-to-exhaust manifold nuts.
3. Discard the nuts.
4. Disconnect the EGR system module tube from the exhaust manifold.
5. Remove the 6 nuts, the LH exhaust manifold and the gasket.
6. Discard the nuts and gasket.
7. Clean and inspect the LH exhaust manifold.
8. Remove and discard the 6 LH exhaust manifold studs.

To install:

9. Refer to illustration for torque values.
10. Install the 6 new LH exhaust manifold studs.
11. Install the new LH exhaust manifold gasket, manifold and 6 new nuts.
12. Connect the EGR system module tube to the exhaust manifold.
13. Install the 2 new catalytic converter-to-exhaust manifold nuts.

RH Exhaust Manifold

See Figure 166.

1. With the vehicle in NEUTRAL, position it on a hoist.
2. Remove the 2 catalytic converter-to-exhaust manifold nuts.
3. Discard the nuts.
4. Remove the 6 nuts, the RH exhaust manifold and the gasket.
5. Discard the nuts and gasket.
6. Clean and inspect the RH exhaust manifold.
7. Remove and discard the 6 RH exhaust manifold studs.

To install:

8. Refer to illustration for torque values.
9. Install the 6 new RH exhaust manifold studs.
10. Install the new RH exhaust manifold gasket, manifold and 6 new nuts.
11. Install the 2 new catalytic converter-to-exhaust manifold nuts.

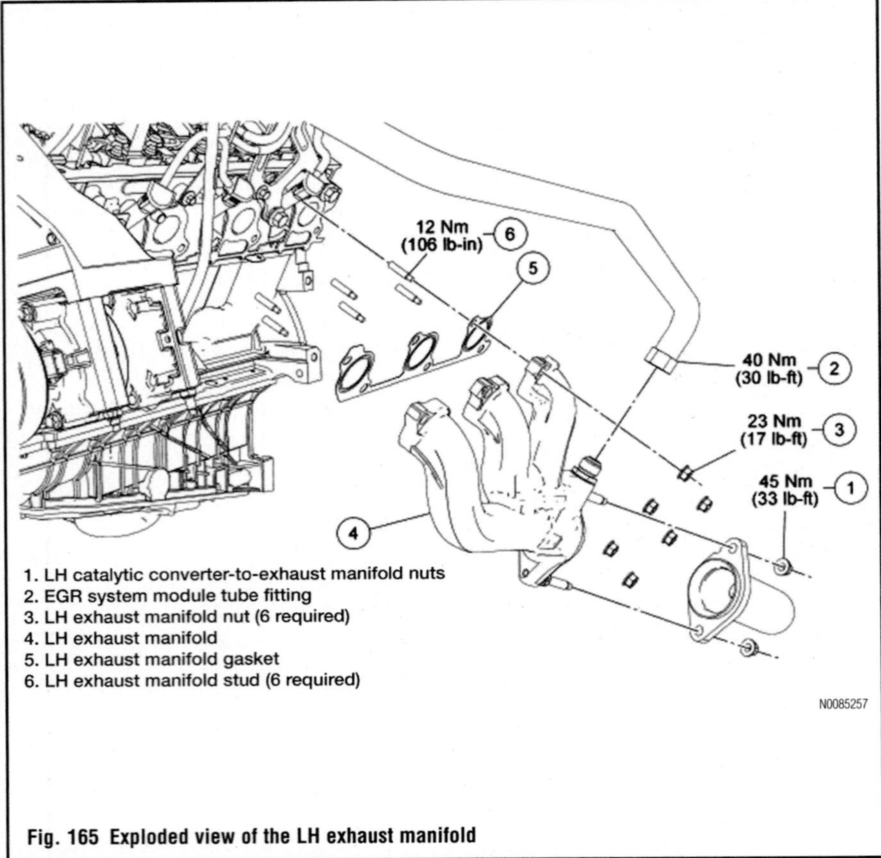

Fig. 165 Exploded view of the LH exhaust manifold

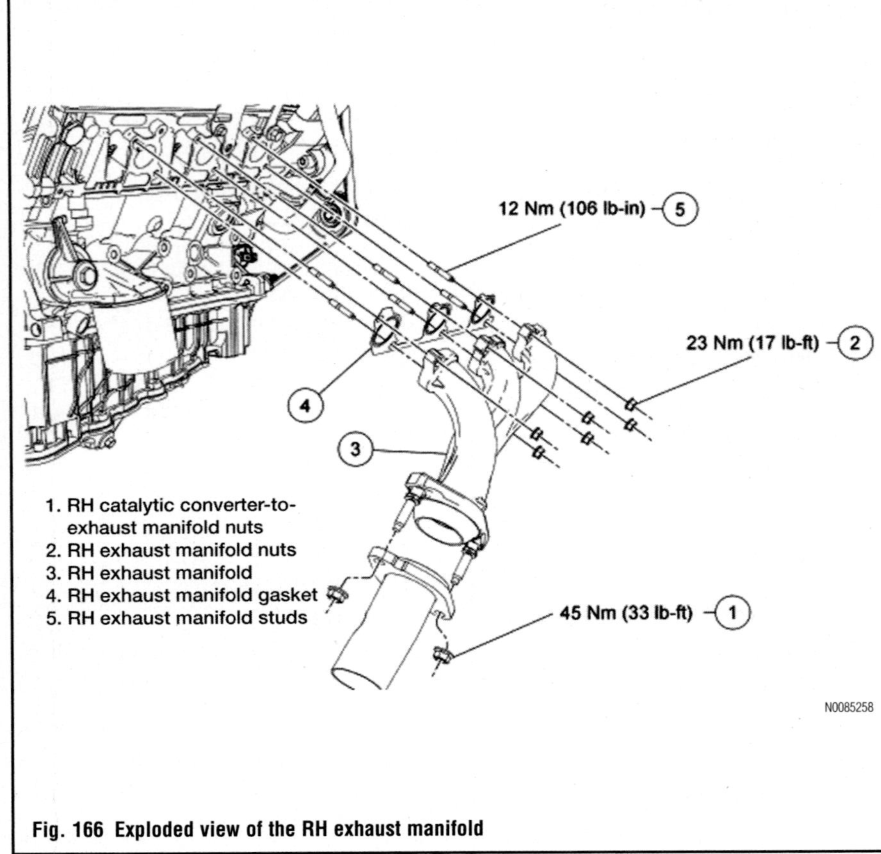

Fig. 166 Exploded view of the RH exhaust manifold

4.6L Engine

LH Exhaust Manifold

See Figure 167.

1. With the vehicle in NEUTRAL, position it on a hoist.
2. Disconnect the battery ground cable.
3. Remove the Air Cleaner (ACL) assembly.
4. Remove the Throttle Body (TB) For additional information, refer to Engine Performance.
5. Disconnect the LH Heated Oxygen Sensor (HO2S) electrical connector and wiring retainer.
6. Remove the 2 RH catalytic converter-to-exhaust manifold nuts.
7. Remove the 2 LH catalytic converter-to-exhaust manifold nuts.
8. Remove the 8 pin-type retainers and the radiator sight shield.
9. Using a suitable belt tensioner release tool, rotate the accessory drive belt tensioner clockwise and position the accessory drive belt aside from the generator pulley.
10. Remove the alternator
11. Install the Engine Lifting Brackets.
12. If equipped, remove the 4 nuts and the strut tower cross brace.
13. Install the Engine Support Bar.
14. Both the RH and LH engine support insulator nuts must be removed to allow the engine to be raised.
15. Remove the RH and LH engine support insulator nuts.
16. Using the Engine Support Bar, raise the engine 1.57 inches.
17. Use a steering wheel holding device (such as Hunter® 28-75-1 or equivalent). Using a suitable holding device, hold the steering wheel in the straight-ahead position.

➡Do not allow the steering wheel to rotate while the steering column intermediate shaft is disconnected or damage to the clockspring can result. If there is evidence that the wheel has rotated, the clockspring must be removed and recentered. For additional information, refer to Supplemental Restraint System.

18. Remove the bolt and disconnect the steering coupling. Discard the bolt.
19. Remove the 4 bolts and the LH engine support insulator bracket.
20. Remove the 8 nuts and the exhaust manifold.
21. Discard the nuts and gaskets.
22. Clean and inspect the LH exhaust manifold.

23. Remove and discard the 8 LH exhaust manifold studs.

➡Do not use metal scrapers, wire brushes, power abrasive discs or other abrasive means to clean the sealing surfaces. These may cause scratches and gouges resulting in leak paths. Use a plastic scraper to clean the sealing surfaces.

24. Clean the sealing surfaces with metal surface prep. Follow the directions on the packaging.

To install:

25. Install 8 new LH exhaust manifold studs. Tighten to 9 ft. lbs. (12 Nm).
26. Install new exhaust manifold gaskets.
27. Install the exhaust manifold and 8 new nuts. Tighten the nuts in the sequence shown to 18 ft. lbs. (25 Nm).
28. Install the LH engine support insulator bracket and the 4 bolts. Tighten to 41 ft. lbs. (55 Nm).

➡Do not allow the steering wheel to rotate while the steering column intermediate shaft is disconnected or damage to the clockspring can result. If there is evidence that the wheel has rotated, the clockspring must be removed and recentered. For additional information, refer to Supplemental Restraint System.

29. Connect the steering coupling and install the new bolt. Tighten to 18 ft. lbs. (25 Nm).
30. Using the Engine Support Bar, lower the engine.
31. If equipped, install the strut tower cross brace and the 4 nuts. Tighten to 26 ft. lbs. (35 Nm).
32. Install the RH and LH engine support insulator nuts. Tighten to 46 ft. lbs. (63 Nm).
33. To complete installation, reverse the remaining removal procedure.

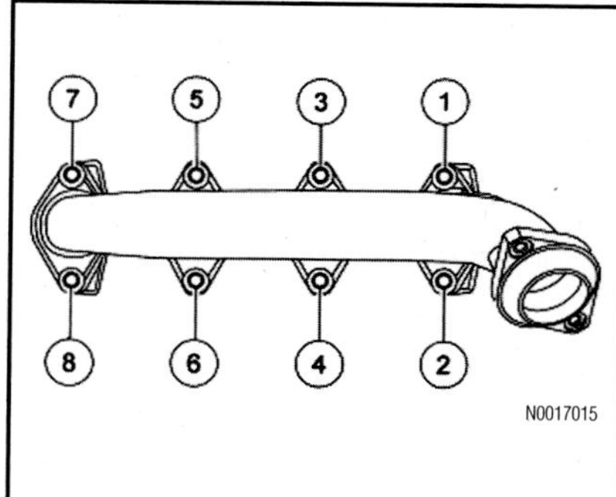

Fig. 167 LH exhaust manifold tightening sequence

RH Exhaust Manifold

See Figure 168.

1. With the vehicle in NEUTRAL, position it on a hoist.
2. Disconnect the battery ground cable.
3. Remove the Air Cleaner (ACL) assembly.
4. Remove the Throttle Body (TB) For additional information, refer to Engine Performance.
5. Disconnect the LH Heated Oxygen Sensor (HO2S) electrical connector and wiring retainer.
6. Remove the 2 RH catalytic converter-to-exhaust manifold nuts.
7. Remove the 2 LH catalytic converter-to-exhaust manifold nuts.
8. Remove the 8 pin-type retainers and the radiator sight shield.
9. Using a suitable belt tensioner release tool, rotate the accessory drive belt tensioner clockwise and position the accessory drive belt aside from the generator pulley.
10. Remove the alternator
11. Install the Engine Lifting Brackets.
12. If equipped, remove the 4 nuts and the strut tower cross brace.
13. Install the Engine Support Bar.
14. Both the RH and LH engine support insulator nuts must be removed to allow the engine to be raised.
15. Remove the RH and LH engine support insulator nuts.
16. Using the Engine Support Bar, raise the engine 1.57 inches.
17. Remove the nut and the ground wire from the stud bolt.
18. If equipped, remove the nut and position aside the transmission cooler tube bracket.
19. Remove the 2 bolts, 2 stud bolts and the RH engine support bracket.
20. Remove the 8 nuts and the exhaust manifold.
21. Discard the nuts and gaskets.
22. Clean and inspect the RH exhaust manifold.
23. Remove and discard the 8 RH exhaust manifold studs.

➡Do not use metal scrapers, wire brushes, power abrasive discs or other abrasive means to clean the sealing surfaces. These may cause scratches and gouges resulting in leak paths. Use a plastic scraper to clean the sealing surfaces.

24. Clean the sealing surfaces with metal surface prep. Follow the directions on the packaging.

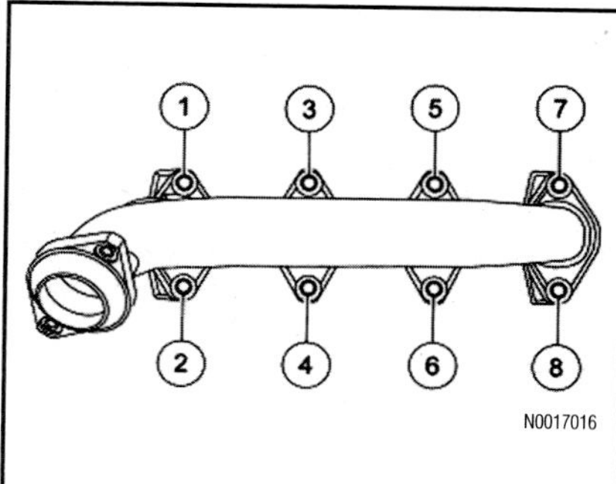

Fig. 168 RH exhaust manifold tightening sequence

To install:

25. Install 8 new RH exhaust manifold studs. Tighten to 9 ft. lbs. (12 Nm).
26. Install new exhaust manifold gaskets.
27. Install the exhaust manifold and 8 new nuts. Tighten the nuts in the sequence shown to 18 ft. lbs. (25 Nm).
28. Install the RH engine support insulator bracket, the 2 bolts and 2 stud bolts. Tighten to 41 ft. lbs. (55 Nm).
29. If equipped, install the transmission cooler tube bracket and nut. Tighten to 18 ft. lbs. (25 Nm).
30. Install the ground wire and nut onto the stud bolt. Tighten to 18 ft. lbs. (25 Nm).
31. Using the Engine Support Bar, lower the engine.
32. If equipped, install the strut tower cross brace and the 4 nuts. Tighten to 26 ft. lbs. (35 Nm).
33. Install the RH and LH engine support insulator nuts. Tighten to 46 ft. lbs. (63 Nm).
34. To complete installation, reverse the remaining removal procedure.

5.0L Engines

LH Exhaust Manifold

See Figure 169.

1. With the vehicle in NEUTRAL, position it on a hoist.
2. Disconnect the battery ground cable.
3. Remove the 2 steering column dash boot nuts.

➡Use a steering wheel holding device (such as Hunter® 28-75-1 or equivalent).

4. Using a suitable holding device, hold the steering wheel in the straight-ahead position.
5. If equipped, remove the 4 nuts and the strut tower cross brace.

➡The engine appearance cover rubber grommets may remain on the cover. If

so, remove the grommets from the cover and install them on the intake manifold before installing the cover.

6. Remove the engine appearance cover.
7. Disconnect the sound enhancement pipe from the Air Cleaner (ACL) outlet pipe and the ACL.
8. Position the sound enhancement pipe aside.
9. Remove the LH catalytic converter. For additional information, refer to Catalytic Converter in this section.
10. Disconnect the LH Heated Oxygen Sensor (HO2S) electrical connector.
11. Remove the bolt and position the steering intermediate shaft aside.
12. Remove the 8 nuts and the LH exhaust manifold.
13. Discard the gasket.
14. Clean and inspect the LH exhaust manifold.
15. Remove and discard the 8 LH exhaust manifold studs.

To install:

➡Do not use metal scrapers, wire brushes, power abrasive discs or other abrasive means to clean the sealing surfaces. These tools cause scratches and gouges which make leak paths. Use a plastic scraper to clean the sealing surfaces.

16. Clean the exhaust manifold mating surface of the cylinder head with metal surface prep. Follow the directions on the packaging.
17. Install 8 new LH exhaust manifold studs. Tighten to 18 ft. lbs. (25 Nm).

➡The tightening specification differs between early build (coarse thread) and late build (fine thread) exhaust manifold nuts.

18. Install new gaskets, the LH exhaust manifold and 8 new nuts.
19. Tighten early build (coarse thread) nuts in the sequence shown in 2 stages.
    a. Stage 1: Tighten to 21 ft. lbs. (28 Nm).
    b. Stage 2: Tighten to 27 ft. lbs. (37 Nm).
20. Tighten late build (fine thread) nuts in the sequence shown in 2 stages.
    a. Stage 1: Tighten to 18 ft. lbs. (25 Nm).
    b. Stage 2: Tighten to 24 ft. lbs. (32 Nm).
21. Position the steering intermediate shaft and install the bolt. Tighten to 35 ft. lbs. (47 Nm).

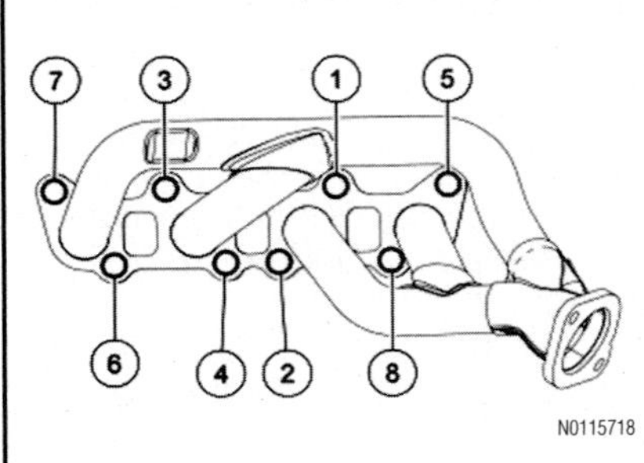

Fig. 169 LH exhaust manifold tightening sequence

22. Connect the LH HO2S electrical connector.
23. Install the LH catalytic converter.
24. Connect the sound enhancement pipe to the ACL outlet pipe and the ACL.

➡The engine appearance cover rubber grommets may remain on the cover. If so, remove the grommets from the cover and install them on the intake manifold before installing the cover.

25. Install the engine appearance cover.
26. If equipped, install the strut tower cross brace and the 4 nuts. Tighten to 26 ft. lbs. (35 Nm).
27. Install the 2 steering column dash boot nuts. Tighten to 80 inch lbs. (9 Nm).
28. Connect the battery ground cable. For additional information, refer to Battery, Mounting and Cables.

RH Exhaust Manifold

See Figure 170.

1. With the vehicle in NEUTRAL, position it on a hoist.
2. Recover the refrigerant.
3. If equipped, remove the 4 nuts and the strut tower cross brace.

➡The engine appearance cover rubber grommets may remain on the cover. If so, remove the grommets from the cover and install them on the intake manifold before installing the cover.

4. Remove the engine appearance cover.
5. Remove the bolt and position the sound enhancement pipe aside.
6. Remove the 8 pin-type retainers and the upper radiator sight shield.
7. Remove the A/C compressor fitting nut and disconnect the fitting.
8. Discard the O-ring seals and gasket seals.
9. Remove the battery tray.
10. Disconnect the RH Heated Oxygen Sensor (HO2S) electrical connector.
11. Install an Engine Lifting Bracket on the rear of the RH cylinder head.

➡The draw screw and bracket from the heavy duty Engine Support Bar (303-F070) must be used with the light duty Engine Support Bar (303-F072). This will provide enough clearance between the draw screw bracket and the cowl.

12. Install the Engine Support Bar.
13. Remove the RH and LH engine support insulator nuts.
14. Using the Engine Support Bar, raise the engine 0.984 inches.
15. Remove the 4 nuts and the front crossmember brace.
16. Remove the RH catalytic converter. For additional information, refer to Catalytic converter.
17. Remove the starter. For additional information, refer to Engine Electrical.
18. Remove the 3 bolts and lower the underbody shield.
19. Remove the transmission fluid cooler tube nut and bracket from the flexplate inspection cover stud bolt.
20. Remove the nut from the RH engine support insulator bracket stud bolt and position the transmission cooler tube clamp aside.
21. Detach the wiring harness retainers from the RH side of the oil pan and the RH engine support insulator bracket stud bolt.
22. Remove the nut and ground strap from the RH engine support insulator bracket.
23. Remove the 2 bolts, the 2 stud bolts and the RH engine support insulator bracket.
24. Remove the 8 nuts and the RH exhaust manifold.
25. Discard the gasket.
26. Clean and inspect the RH exhaust manifold.
27. Remove and discard the 8 RH exhaust manifold studs.

To install:

➡Do not use metal scrapers, wire brushes, power abrasive discs or other abrasive means to clean the sealing surfaces. These tools cause scratches and gouges which make leak paths. Use a plastic scraper to clean the sealing surfaces.

28. Clean the exhaust manifold mating surface of the cylinder head with metal surface prep. Follow the directions on the packaging.
29. Install 8 new RH exhaust manifold studs. Tighten to 18 ft. lbs. (25 Nm).

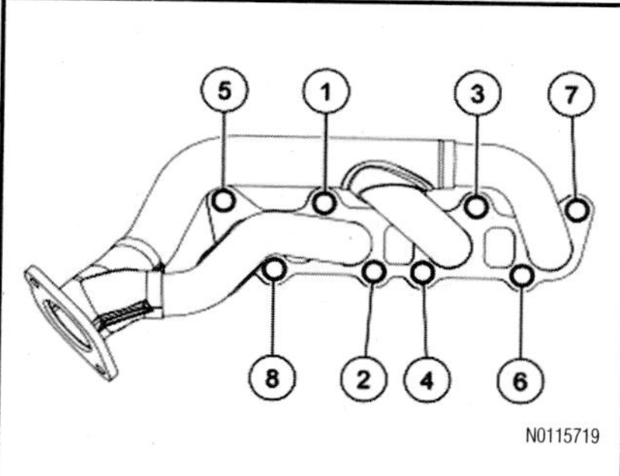

Fig. 170 RH exhaust manifold tightening sequence

➡The tightening specification differs between early build (coarse thread) and late build (fine thread) exhaust manifold nuts.

30. Install new gaskets, the RH exhaust manifold and 8 new nuts.
31. Tighten early build (coarse thread) nuts in the sequence shown in 2 stages.
    a. Stage 1: Tighten to 21 ft. lbs. (28 Nm).
    b. Stage 2: Tighten to 27 ft. lbs. (37 Nm).
32. Tighten late build (fine thread) nuts in the sequence shown in 2 stages.
    a. Stage 1: Tighten to 18 ft. lbs. (25 Nm).
    b. Stage 2: Tighten to 24 ft. lbs. (32 Nm).

➡The engine support insulator bracket must be positioned on the engine support insulator stud. If necessary, adjust the height of the engine using the engine support bar.

33. Install the RH engine support insulator bracket, the 2 bolts and the 2 stud bolts. Tighten to 41 ft. lbs. (55 Nm).
34. Install the ground strap and the nut to the RH engine support insulator bracket. Tighten to 35 ft. lbs. (48 Nm).
35. Attach the wiring harness retainers to the RH side of the oil pan and the RH engine support insulator bracket stud bolt.
36. Install the transmission cooler tube clamp and nut to the RH engine support insulator bracket. Tighten to 35 ft. lbs. (48 Nm).
37. Install the transmission fluid cooler tube bracket and nut to the flexplate inspection cover stud bolt. Tighten to 10 ft. lbs. (13 Nm).
38. Position the underbody shield and install the 3 bolts. Tighten to 89 inch lbs. (10 Nm).
39. Install the starter.
40. Install the RH catalytic converter.
41. Install the front crossmember brace and the 4 nuts (2 shown). Tighten to 35 ft. lbs. (48 Nm).
42. Using the Engine Support Bar, lower the engine onto the engine support insulators.
43. Install the RH and LH engine support insulator nuts. Tighten to 46 ft. lbs. (63 Nm).
44. Connect the RH HO2S electrical connector.
45. Install the battery tray.
46. Using a new O-ring seal and gasket seal, connect the A/C compressor fitting and install the nut. Tighten to 133 inch lbs. (15 Nm).
47. Position the sound enhancement pipe and install the bolt.
48. Install the upper radiator sight shield and the 8 pin-type retainers.

➡The engine appearance cover rubber grommets may remain on the cover. If so, remove the grommets from the cover and install them on the intake manifold before installing the cover.

49. Install the engine appearance cover.
50. If equipped, install the strut tower cross brace and the 4 nuts. Tighten to 26 ft. lbs. (35 Nm).
51. Recharge the A/C system.

5.4L Engine

LH Exhaust Manifold

See Figure 171.

1. With the vehicle in NEUTRAL, position it on a hoist.
2. Remove the Evaporative Emission (EVAP) canister purge valve. For additional information, refer to Engine Performance.
3. Remove the 2 dash boot nuts.
4. Remove the catalytic converter. For additional information, refer to Catalytic converter.
5. Disconnect the LH Heated Oxygen Sensor (HO2S) electrical connector.
6. Remove and discard the engine oil filter.

➡Use a steering wheel holding device (such as Hunter® 28-75-1 or equivalent).

7. Using a suitable holding device, hold the steering wheel in the straight-ahead position.

➡Do not allow the steering wheel to rotate while the steering column intermediate shaft is disconnected or damage to the clockspring can result. If there is evidence that the wheel has rotated, the clockspring must be removed and recentered. For additional information, refer to Supplemental Restraint System.

8. Remove the upper bolt from the intermediate steering shaft and position the intermediate steering shaft aside.
9. Remove the 8 nuts and the LH exhaust manifold.
10. Discard the nuts and gaskets.
11. Clean and inspect the LH exhaust manifold.
12. Remove and discard the 8 LH exhaust manifold studs.

To install:

➡Do not use metal scrapers, wire brushes, power abrasive discs or other abrasive means to clean the sealing surfaces. These tools cause scratches and gouges which make leak paths. Use a plastic scraping tool to remove all traces of old sealant.

13. Clean the exhaust manifold mating surface of the cylinder head with metal surface prep. Follow the directions on the packaging.
14. Install 8 new LH exhaust manifold studs. Tighten to 7 ft. lbs. (12 Nm).
15. Install new gaskets, the LH exhaust manifold and 8 new nuts. Tighten in the sequence shown to 15 ft. lbs. (20 Nm).

➡Do not allow the steering wheel to rotate while the steering column intermediate shaft is disconnected or damage to the clockspring can result. If there is evidence that the wheel has rotated, the clockspring must be removed and recentered. For additional information, refer to Supplemental Restraint System.

16. Install the intermediate steering shaft and the upper bolt. Tighten to 35 ft. lbs. (47 Nm).

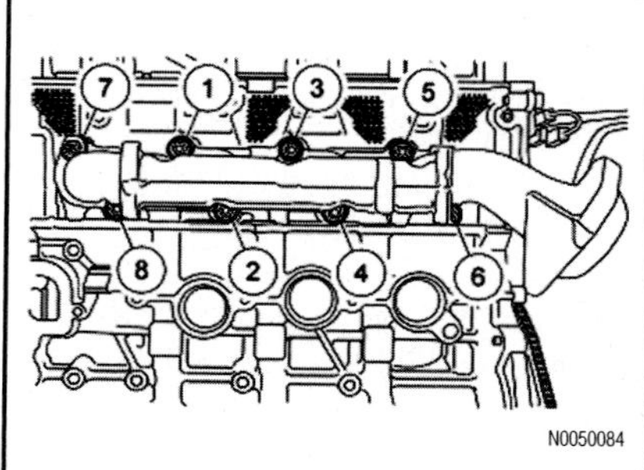

Fig. 171 LH exhaust manifold tightening sequence

17. Install a new engine oil filter.
18. Lubricate the oil filter gasket with clean engine oil and tighten until the seal makes contact.
19. Using an oil filter strap wrench, tighten the filter an additional 270 degrees.
20. Connect the LH HO2S electrical connector.
21. Install the catalytic converter.
22. Install the 2 dash boot nuts.
23. Install the EVAP canister purge valve.

RH Exhaust Manifold

See Figure 172.

1. With the vehicle in NEUTRAL, position it on a hoist.
2. Remove the EGR tube.
3. Remove the catalytic converter. For additional information, refer to Catalytic converter.
4. Rotate the Supercharger (SC) drive belt tensioner clockwise and remove the drive belt from the SC drive pulley.
5. Install the Engine Lifting Bracket.

➡The heavy duty Engine Support Bar (303-F070) must be used with the draw screws from the light duty Engine Support Bar (303-F072). This will provide enough clearance between the SC and the Engine Support Bar, and enough clearance between the draw screw and the vehicle hood.

6. Install the Engine Support Bars.
7. Remove the RH engine support insulator nut.
8. Using the Engine Support Bars, raise the RH side of the engine.
9. Remove the SC drive belt from the A/C compressor pulley.
10. Remove the wiring harness retainers from the A/C compressor stud bolts and position the wiring harness aside.

➡The A/C compressor stud bolts must be loosened to gain access to the RH exhaust manifold nuts.

11. Loosen the A/C compressor stud bolts 0.98 inches.
12. Remove the 8 nuts and the RH exhaust manifold.
13. Discard the nuts and gaskets.
14. Clean and inspect the RH exhaust manifold.
15. Remove and discard the 8 RH exhaust manifold studs.

To install:

➡Do not use metal scrapers, wire brushes, power abrasive discs or other abrasive means to clean the sealing surfaces. These tools cause scratches and gouges which make leak paths. Use a plastic scraping tool to remove all traces of old sealant.

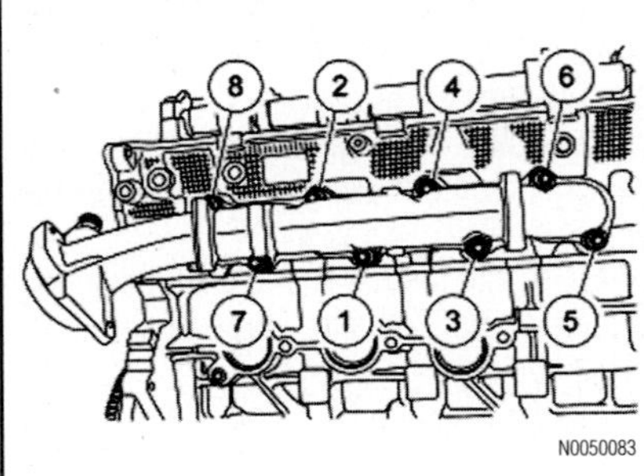

Fig. 172 RH exhaust manifold tightening sequence

16. Clean the exhaust manifold mating surface of the cylinder head with metal surface prep. Follow the directions on the packaging.
17. Install the 8 new RH exhaust manifold-to-cylinder head studs. Tighten to 9 ft. lbs. (12 Nm).
18. Install new gaskets, RH exhaust manifold and 8 new nuts. Tighten in the sequence shown to 15 ft. lbs. (20 Nm).
19. Tighten the A/C compressor stud bolts to 18 ft. lbs. (25 Nm).
20. Install the wiring harness retainers onto the A/C compressor stud bolts.
21. Position the SC drive belt onto the A/C compressor pulley.
22. Using the Engine Support Bars, lower the engine onto the engine support insulator.
23. Install the RH engine support insulator nut. Tighten to 46 ft. lbs. (63 Nm).
24. Rotate the SC drive belt tensioner clockwise and install the drive belt onto the SC drive pulley.
25. Install the catalytic converter.
26. Install the EGR tube.

INTAKE MANIFOLD

REMOVAL & INSTALLATION

3.7L Engine

Upper Intake

See Figures 173 and 174.

1. If equipped, remove the 4 nuts (2 shown) and the strut tower cross brace.
2. If equipped, detach the 2 retainers and remove the engine appearance cover.

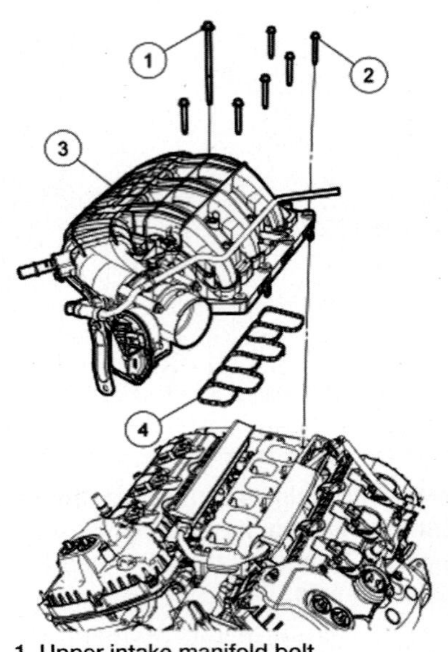

Fig. 173 Exploded view of the upper intake manifold

3. Remove the Air Cleaner (ACL) outlet tube.
4. Disconnect the PCV tube quick connect coupling from the intake manifold.
5. Disconnect the Throttle Body (TB) electrical connector.
6. Detach the TB electrical connector wiring harness pin-type retainer from the TB.
7. Disconnect Evaporative Emission (EVAP) tube from the EVAP canister purge valve.
8. Detach the EVAP hose retainer from the intake manifold.
9. Disconnect the EVAP canister purge valve electrical connector.
10. Detach the EVAP canister purge valve electrical connector wiring harness pin-type retainer.
11. Disconnect the brake booster vacuum hose from the upper intake manifold vacuum tube.
12. Detach the wiring harness pin-type retainer from the rear of the upper intake manifold.
13. Remove the upper intake manifold support bracket bolt from the front of the RH cylinder head.
14. Loosen the 7 bolts and remove the upper intake manifold.

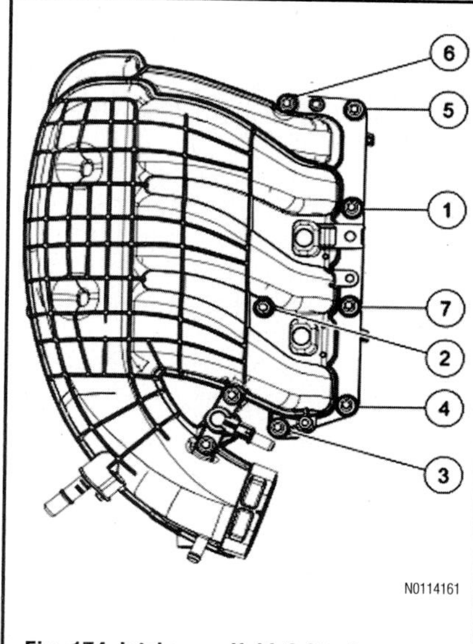

Fig. 174 Intake manifold tightening sequence

15. Remove and discard the gaskets.
16. Clean and inspect all of the sealing surfaces of the upper and lower intake manifold.

To install:

➡If the engine is repaired or replaced because of upper engine failure, typically including valve or piston damage, check the intake manifold for metal debris. If metal debris is found, install a new intake manifold. Failure to follow these instructions can result in engine damage.

17. Using new gaskets, install the upper intake manifold and tighten the 7 bolts in the sequence shown in 2 stages.
    a. Stage 1: Tighten to 7 ft. lbs. (10 Nm).
    b. Stage 2: Tighten an additional 45 degrees.
18. Install the upper intake manifold support bracket bolt to the RH cylinder head. Tighten to 7 ft. lbs. (10 Nm).
19. Attach the wiring harness pin-type retainer to the rear of the upper intake manifold.
20. To complete installation, reverse the remaining removal procedure.
21. If equipped, install the strut tower cross brace and the 4 nuts. Tighten to 26 ft. lbs. (35 Nm).

Lower Intake

See Figures 175 and 176.

✻✻ WARNING

Do not smoke, carry lighted tobacco or have an open flame of any type when working on or near any fuel-related component. Highly flammable mixtures are always present and may be ignited. Failure to follow these instructions may result in serious personal injury.

✻✻ WARNING

Do not carry personal electronic devices such as cell phones, pagers or audio equipment of any type when working on or near any fuel-related component. Highly flammable mixtures are always present and may be ignited. Failure to follow these instructions may result in serious personal injury.

✻✻ WARNING

Always disconnect the battery ground cable at the battery when working on an evaporative emission (EVAP) system or fuel-related component. Highly flammable mixtures are always present and may be ignited. Failure to follow these instructions may result in serious personal injury.

✻✻ WARNING

Clean all fuel residue from the engine compartment. If not removed, fuel residue may ignite when the engine is returned to operation. Failure to follow this instruction may result in serious personal injury.

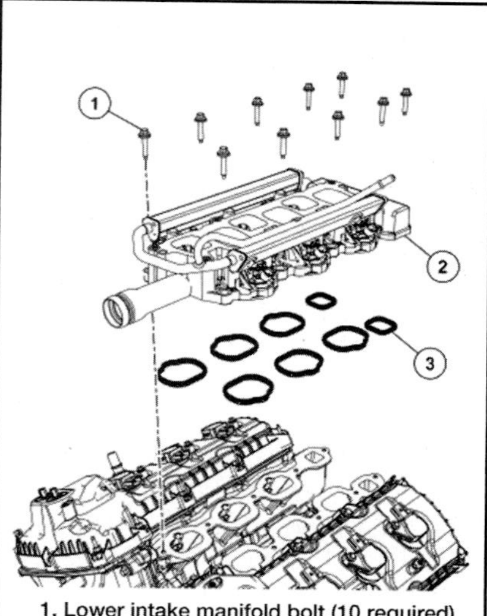

Fig. 175 Exploded view of the lower intake

➡During engine repair procedures, cleanliness is extremely important. Any foreign material, including any material created while cleaning gasket surfaces that enters the oil passages, coolant passages or the oil pan, may cause engine failure.

1. Release the fuel system pressure. For additional information, refer to Fuel System.
2. Disconnect the battery ground cable.
3. Drain the cooling system.
4. Remove the upper intake manifold.
5. Disconnect the fuel tube-to-fuel rail quick connect coupling. For additional information, refer to Fuel System.
6. Remove the LH and RH fuel rail noise insulator shields.
7. Remove the thermostat. Refer to Engine Cooling.
8. Disconnect the heater hose from the rear of the lower intake manifold.
9. Remove the 10 bolts and the lower intake manifold.
10. Remove and discard the lower intake manifold gaskets.
11. Clean and inspect all sealing surfaces.

To install:

➡If the engine is repaired or replaced because of upper engine failure, typically including valve or piston damage, check the intake manifold for metal debris. If metal debris if found, install a new intake manifold. Failure to follow these instructions can result in engine damage.

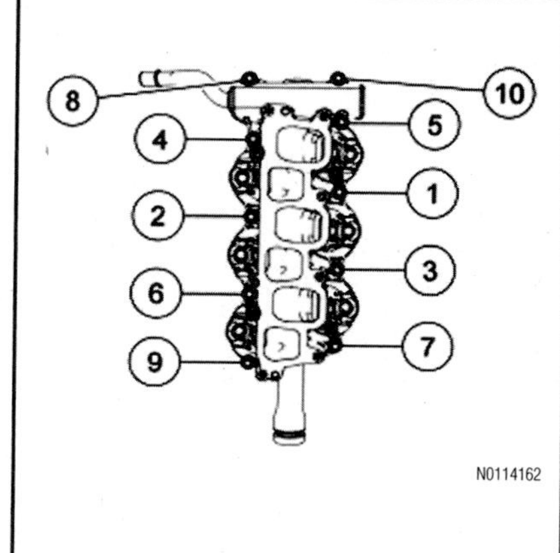

Fig. 176 Lower intake tightening sequence

12. Using new lower intake manifold gaskets, install the lower intake manifold and the 10 bolts and tighten in the sequence shown. Tighten to 7 ft. lbs. (10 Nm).
13. To complete installation, reverse the remaining removal procedure.
14. Connect the battery ground cable.
15. Fill and bleed the cooling system.

4.0L Engine

See Figures 177 and 178.

➡During engine repair procedures, cleanliness is extremely important. Any foreign material, including any material created while cleaning gasket surfaces that enters the oil passages, coolant passages or the oil pan, can cause engine failure.

1. Remove the Air Cleaner (ACL) outlet pipe.
2. Disconnect the radio capacitor electrical connector.
3. Disconnect the RH spark plug wires from the ignition coil.
4. Detach the RH spark plug wire retainer from the intake manifold.
5. Remove the 2 ignition coil bracket upper bolts.
6. Remove the 2 ignition coil lower bolts.
7. Position the ignition coil and bracket assembly aside.
8. Disconnect the EGR system module electrical connector.

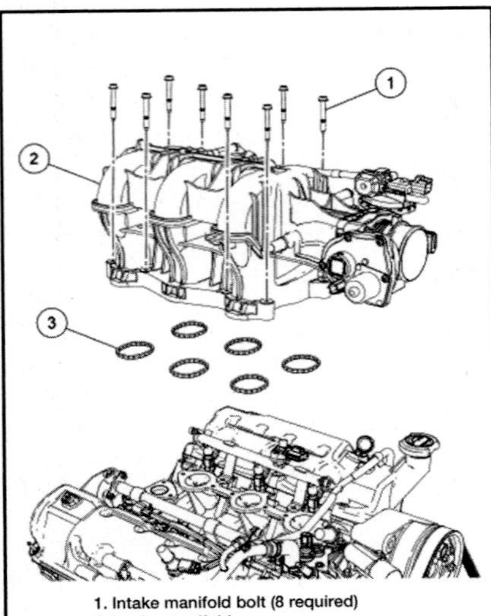

Fig. 177 Exploded view of the intake manifold

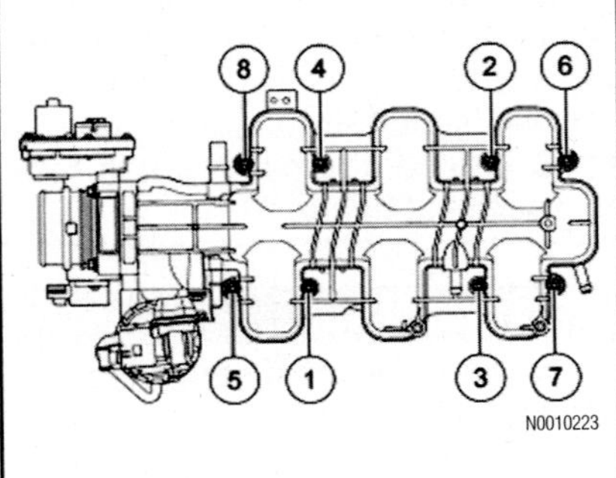

Fig. 178 Intake manifold tightening sequence

9. Disconnect the EGR system module tube from the EGR system module.
10. Disconnect the brake booster vacuum hose from the intake manifold.
11. Disconnect the vacuum tube from the fuel rail pressure and temperature sensor.
12. Disconnect the vapor tube from the intake manifold.
13. Remove the PCV tube.
14. Detach the Knock Sensor (KS) electrical connector retainer from the intake manifold.
15. Disconnect the Throttle Position (TP) sensor and Throttle Body (TB) electrical connectors.
16. Remove the 8 bolts and the intake manifold.

To install:

➡If the engine is repaired or replaced because of upper engine failure, typically including valve or piston damage, check the intake manifold for metal debris. If metal debris is found, install a new intake manifold. Failure to follow these instructions can result in engine damage.

➡Clean and inspect all sealing surfaces. Inspect and install new gaskets as necessary.

17. Position the intake manifold and install the 8 bolts. Tighten in the sequence shown to 7 ft. lbs. (10 Nm).
18. To complete installation, reverse the remaining removal procedure.

4.6L Engine

See Figures 179 and 180.

1. If equipped, remove the 4 nuts and the strut tower cross brace.
2. Release the fuel system pressure.
3. Remove the Air Cleaner (ACL) outlet pipe.
4. Remove the fuel rail and injectors.

For additional information, refer to Fuel System.

5. Disconnect the Evaporative Emission (EVAP) tube from the intake manifold and position the tube aside.
6. Disconnect the PCV tube from the intake manifold, LH valve cover and remove.
7. Disconnect the Throttle Position (TP) sensor and electronic Throttle Body (TB) electrical connectors.
8. Disconnect the Charge Motion Control Valve (CMCV) electrical connector.
9. Detach the wiring retainers from the intake manifold stud bolt and the CMCV bracket and then position the wiring harness aside.
10. Disconnect the vacuum hose from the T-fitting.

➡Do not use metal scrapers, wire brushes, power abrasive discs or other abrasive means to clean the sealing surfaces. These tools cause scratches and gouges which make leak paths. Use a plastic scraping tool to remove all traces of old sealant.

➡Clean and inspect the sealing surfaces with metal surface prep. Follow the directions on the packaging.

11. Remove the 9 bolts, the stud bolt and the intake manifold.
12. Discard the gaskets.

To install:

➡If the engine is repaired or replaced because of upper engine failure, typically including valve or piston damage, check the intake manifold for metal debris. If metal debris is found, install a new intake manifold. Failure to follow these instructions can result in engine damage.

➡Electrical and vacuum harnesses must not restrict movement of the CMCV control rods at rear of the intake manifold. Use extreme care on installation of the intake manifold to prevent any pinching of electrical and vacuum harnesses.

13. Using new intake manifold gaskets, position the intake manifold.
14. Install the 9 intake manifold bolts and stud bolt. Tighten in the sequence shown to 7 ft. lbs. (10 Nm).
15. To complete installation, reverse the remaining removal procedure.
16. If equipped, install the strut tower cross brace and the 4 nuts. Tighten to 26 ft. lbs. (35 Nm).

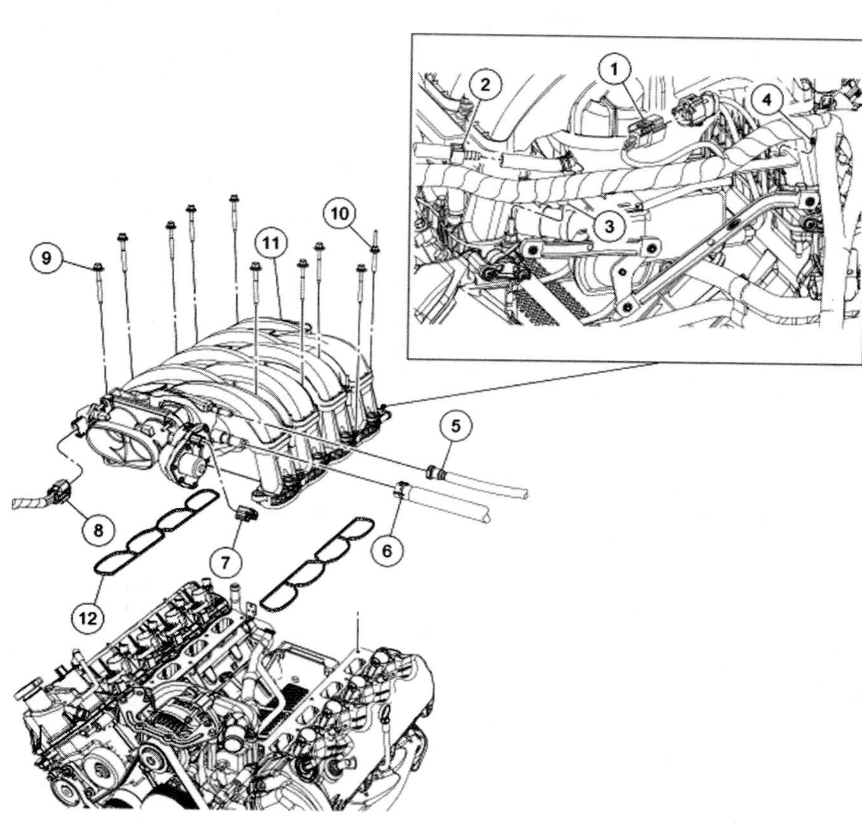

1. Charge Motion Control Valve (CMCV) electrical connector
2. Vacuum hose T-fitting
3. Wiring harness retainer
4. Wiring harness pin-type retainer
5. Evaporative Emission (EVAP) tube
6. PCV tube
7. Electronic Throttle Body (TB) electrical connector
8. Throttle Position (TP) sensor electrical connector
9. Intake manifold bolt (9 required)
10. Intake manifold stud bolt
11. Intake manifold
12. Intake manifold gasket (2 required)

N0101480

Fig. 179 Exploded view of the intake manifold

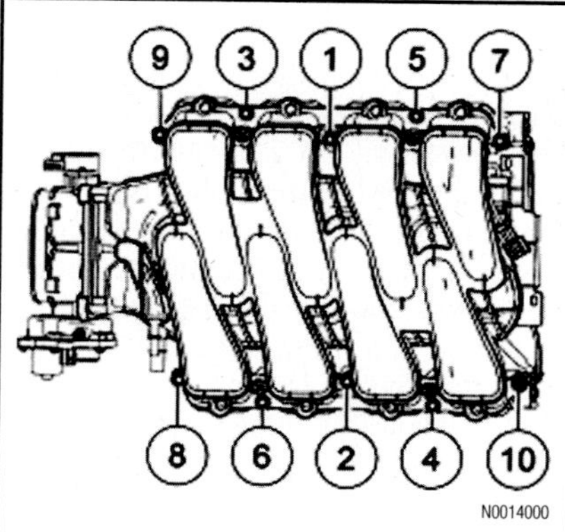

Fig. 180 Intake manifold tightening sequence

5.0L Engine

See Figures 181 and 182.

✲✲ WARNING

Do not smoke, carry lighted tobacco or have an open flame of any type when working on or near any fuel-related component. Highly flammable mixtures are always present and may be ignited. Failure to follow these instructions may result in serious personal injury.

✲✲ WARNING

Before working on or disconnecting any of the fuel tubes or fuel system components, relieve the fuel system pressure to prevent accidental spraying of fuel. Fuel in the fuel system remains under high pressure, even when the engine is not running. Failure to follow this instruction may result in serious personal injury.

1. Release the fuel system pressure.
2. If equipped, remove the 4 nuts and the strut tower cross brace.

➡The engine appearance cover rubber grommets may remain on the cover. If so, remove the grommets from the cover and install them on the intake manifold before installing the cover.

3. Remove the engine appearance cover.
4. Remove the Air Cleaner (ACL) outlet pipe.
5. Disconnect the Throttle Body (TB) electrical connector.
6. Disconnect the Evaporative Emission (EVAP) canister purge valve tube and electrical connector.
7. Remove the crankcase ventilation tube.
8. Disconnect the fuel supply tube. For additional information refer to the quick connect procedure in Fuel System.
9. Disconnect the vacuum tube from the intake manifold.
10. Position the heater hoses aside.
11. Remove the 2 nuts and the LH heater hose support.
12. Position the vacuum tube assembly aside.
13. Remove the 2 nuts and the RH heater hose support.
14. Remove the fuel rail. Refer to Fuel System.
15. Loosen the 6 bolts and remove the intake manifold.
16. Discard the gaskets.

To install:

➡If the engine is repaired or replaced because of upper engine failure, typically including valve or piston damage, check the intake manifold for metal debris. If metal debris if found, install a new intake manifold. Failure to follow these instructions can result in engine damage.

➡Clean the sealing surfaces with metal surface prep. Follow the directions on the packaging. Inspect the mating surfaces.

➡Fuel rail removed from graphic for clarity.

17. Using new gaskets, install the intake manifold.

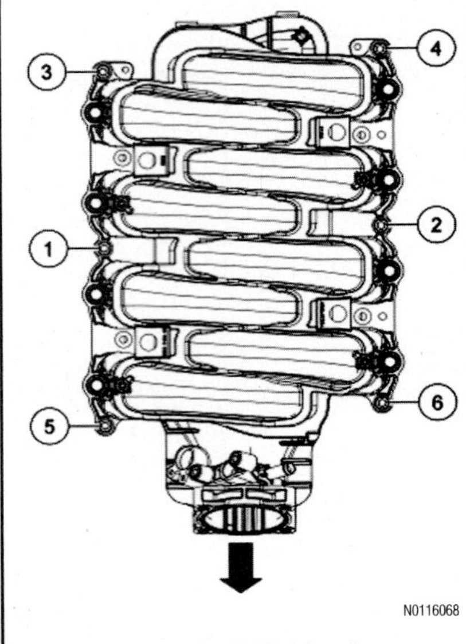

Fig. 182 Intake manifold tightening sequence

18. Tighten the 6 intake manifold bolts in the sequence shown in 2 stages.
    a. Stage 1: Tighten to 7 ft. lbs. (10 Nm).
    b. Stage 2: Tighten an additional 45 degrees.
19. Install the fuel rail.
20. To complete the installation, reverse the remaining removal procedure.

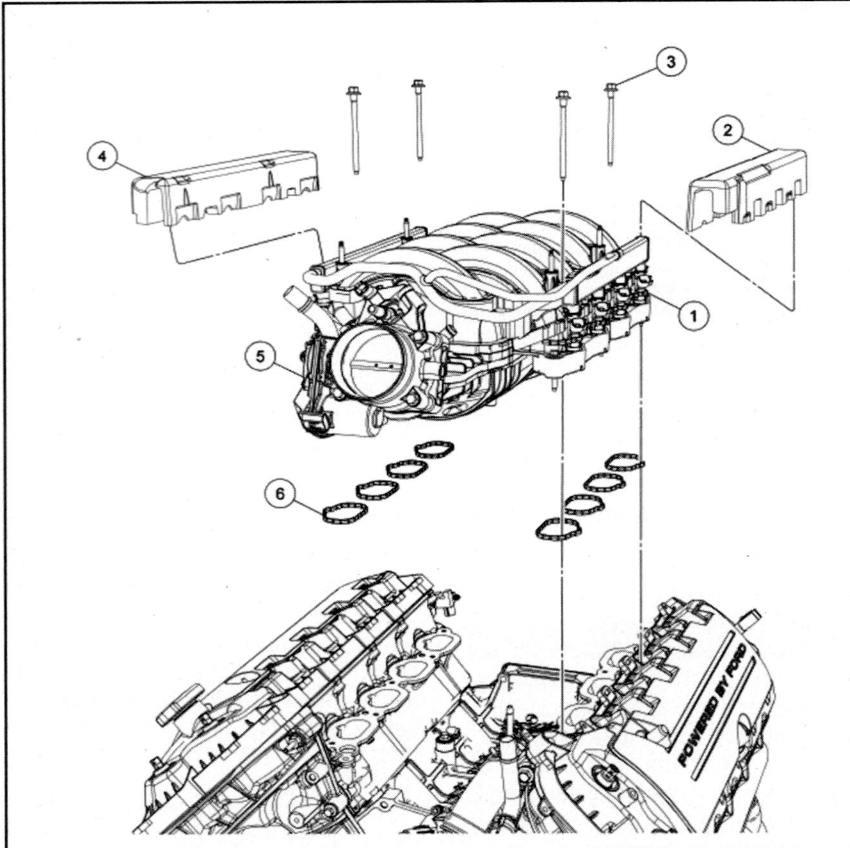

Fig. 181 Exploded view of the intake manifold

5.4L Engine

See Figures 183 through 185.

⁂ WARNING

Do not smoke, carry lighted tobacco or have an open flame of any type when working on or near any fuel-related component. Highly flammable mixtures are always present and may be ignited. Failure to follow these instructions may result in serious personal injury.

⁂ WARNING

Before working on or disconnecting any of the fuel tubes or fuel system components, relieve the fuel system pressure to prevent accidental spraying of fuel. Fuel in the fuel system remains under high pressure, even when the engine is not running. Failure to follow this instruction may result in serious personal injury.

➡During engine repair procedures, cleanliness is extremely important. Any foreign material, including any mater-

ial created while cleaning gasket surfaces that enters the oil passages, coolant passages or the oil pan, can cause engine failure.

1. Release the fuel system pressure.
2. Drain the engine cooling system.
3. Drain the Supercharger (SC) cooling system.
4. Remove the Air Cleaner (ACL) outlet pipe.
5. Disconnect the battery ground cable.
6. Remove the EGR tube.
7. Disconnect the Throttle Position (TP) sensor electrical connector.
8. Remove the 4 bolts and position the Throttle Body (TB) and spacer assembly aside.
9. Disconnect the Intake Air Temperature 2 (IAT2) sensor electrical connector.
10. Disconnect the fuel supply tube. For additional information, refer to Fuel section.
11. Disconnect the 4 LH fuel injector electrical connectors.
12. Remove the 2 bolts and the wiring harness retainer from the rear of the intake manifold.
13. Detach the 2 wiring harness pin-type retainers from the rear of the intake manifold.
14. Disconnect the fuel rail pressure and temperature sensor electrical connector.
15. Disconnect the 4 RH fuel injector electrical connectors.
16. Disconnect the EGR system module electrical connector.
17. Disconnect the crankcase ventilation tube from the RH side of the SC.
18. Disconnect the SC bubbler hose from the rear of the SC.
19. Rotate the SC drive belt tensioner clockwise and remove the drive belt from the SC drive pulley.
20. Disconnect the 2 upper radiator hoses and the 2 coolant vent hoses from the intake manifold.
21. Disconnect the 2 coolant hoses from the Charge Air Cooler (CAC).
22. Disconnect the heater hose located below the rear of the intake manifold.
23. Remove the 14 bolts and the intake manifold assembly.
24. Discard the gaskets.

To install:

➡If the engine is repaired or replaced because of upper engine failure, typically including valve or piston damage, check the intake manifold for metal debris. If metal debris is found, install a new intake manifold. Failure to follow these instructions can result in engine damage.

➡Clean the sealing surfaces with metal surface prep. Follow the directions on the packaging. Inspect the mating surfaces.

25. Using new intake manifold gaskets, position the intake manifold.

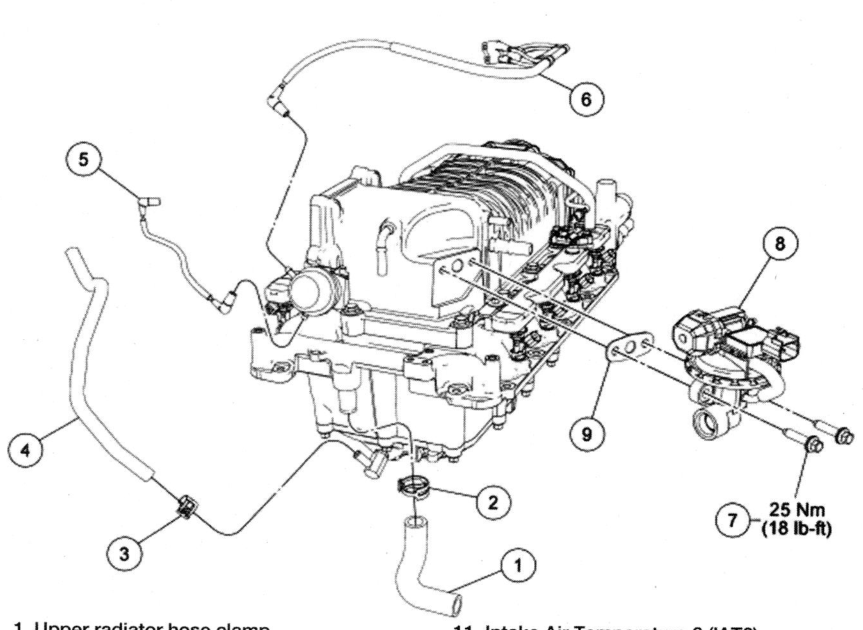

1. Upper radiator hose clamp
2. Upper radiator hose
3. Coolant vent hose clamp
4. Coolant vent hose
5. Upper radiator hose clamp
6. Upper radiator hose
7. Coolant vent hose clamp
8. Coolant vent hose
9. Fuel injector electrical connector (8 required)
10. Throttle Position (TP) sensor electrical connector
11. Intake Air Temperature 2 (IAT2) sensor electrical connector
12. Supercharger (SC) bubbler hose clamp
13. SC bubbler hose
14. EGR system module electrical connector
15. Crankcase ventilation tube
16. Fuel rail pressure and temperature sensor electrical connector
17. Fuel supply tube
18. Throttle Body (TB) spacer bolt (4 required)
19. TB and spacer assembly
20. TB spacer gasket

N0071919

Fig. 183 Exploded view of the intake assembly—1 of 2

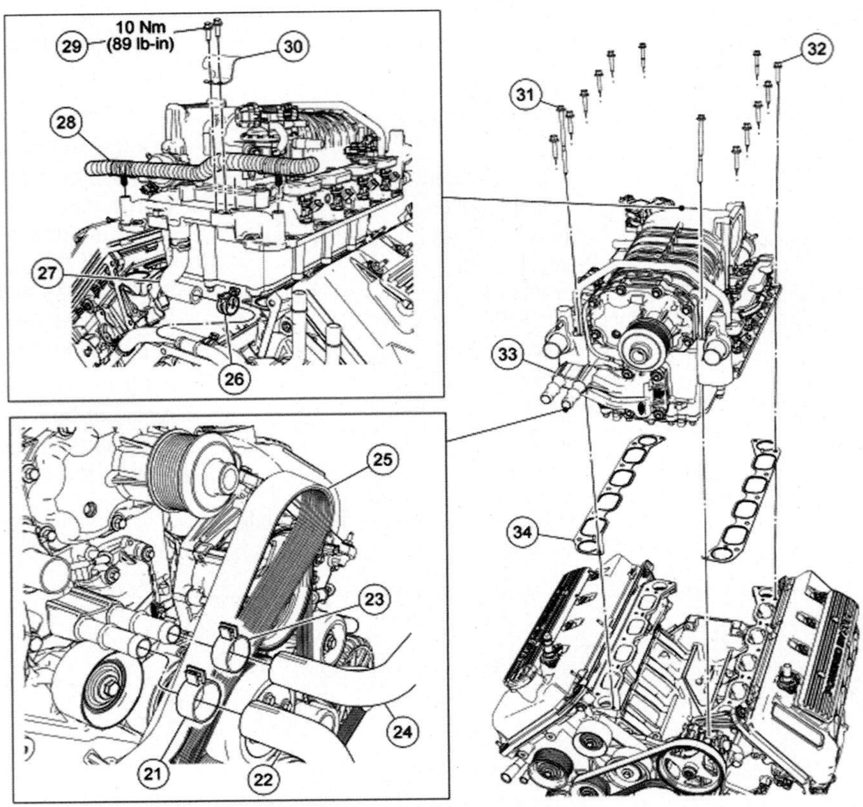

1. Charge Air Cooler (CAC) hose clamp
2. CAC hose
3. CAC hose clamp
4. CAC hose
5. SC drive belt
6. Heater hose clamp
7. Heater hose
8. Wiring harness pin-type retainer (2 required)
9. Wiring harness retainer bolt (2 required)
10. Wiring harness retainer
11. Intake manifold bolt (2 required)
12. Intake manifold bolt (12 required)
13. Intake manifold
14. Intake manifold gasket (2 required)

N0071118

Fig. 184 Exploded view of the intake assembly—2 of 2

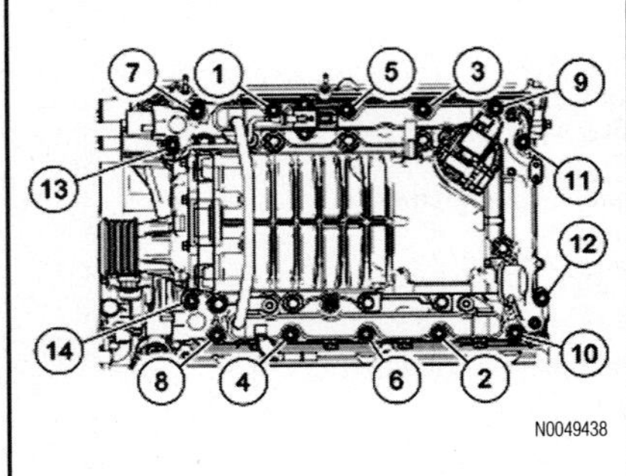

Fig. 185 Intake manifold tightening sequence

26. Install the 14 bolts. Tighten in the sequence shown to 7 ft. lbs. (10 Nm).
27. Connect the heater hose located below the rear of the intake manifold.
28. To complete the installation, reverse the remaining removal procedure. Refer to exploded illustrations for torque values.
29. Connect the battery ground cable.
30. Fill and bleed the SC cooling system.
31. Fill and bleed the engine cooling system.

OIL PAN

REMOVAL & INSTALLATION

3.7L Engine

See Figures 186 through 189.

➡During engine repair procedures, cleanliness is extremely important. Any foreign material, including any material created while cleaning gasket surfaces, that enters the oil passages, coolant passages or the oil pan, may cause engine failure.

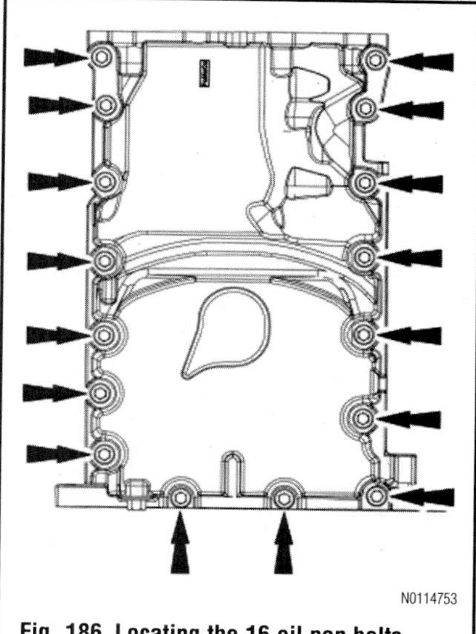

Fig. 186 Locating the 16 oil pan bolts

➡Automatic transmission shown, manual transmission similar.

1. With the vehicle in NEUTRAL, position it on a hoist.
2. Remove the 2 steering column dash boot bearing nuts.

➡Use a steering wheel holding device (such as Hunter® 28-75-1 or equivalent).

3. Using a suitable holding device, hold the steering wheel in the straight-ahead position.
4. If equipped, remove the 4 nuts (2 shown) and the strut tower cross brace.
5. If equipped, detach the 2 retainers and remove the engine appearance cover.
6. Remove the battery tray.
7. Remove the oil level indicator.

➡The ground wire must be remove for access to upper transmission bolt and stud bolts.

8. Remove the bolt and the ground wire from the rear of the engine.
9. Detach the 2 wiring harness retainers (1 shown) from the 2 upper bellhousing-to-engine stud bolts.
10. Loosen the 4 upper bellhousing-to-engine bolts and stud bolts 0.19 inches.
11. Remove the RH and LH engine mount-to-engine bracket mount nuts.
12. Remove the nut from the rear LH valve cover stud bolt and position the generator wiring harness bracket aside.
13. Install the LH engine lift eye.
14. Install the RH front engine lift eye.
15. Remove the 8 pin-type retainers and the radiator sight shield.
16. Remove the 2 bolts and the RH radiator support bracket.

➡Do not position the legs of the Engine Support Bar on the fenders. Instead, position the legs on the body structure near the suspension strut tower. Failure to follow these instructions may result in body damage.

17. Install the Engine Support Bar.
18. Remove the 9 bolts and the lower air deflector.
19. Loosen the 2 nuts for the crossmember brace.
20. Remove the 6 bolts and slide the crossmember brace forward and remove.
21. Remove the 4 nuts and the front crossmember brace.
22. Remove the drain plug and drain the engine oil.
23. Install the drain plug.
24. Remove and discard the engine oil filter.
25. Disconnect the 2 Electronic Power Assist Steering (EPAS) electrical connectors.
26. Detach the 2 EPAS wiring harness pin-type retainers.
27. Remove the steering shaft pinch bolt and disconnect the steering shaft.

➡Mark the position of the 4 subframe nuts and 4 subframe bolts for reference during installation.

➡RH shown, LH similar.

28. Remove the 4 rear subframe bolts.
29. Using an adjustable jackstand, support the subframe.

➡RH shown, LH similar.

30. Remove the 4 front subframe nuts and lower the subframe, using the adjustable jackstand.
31. Loosen the engine-to-bellhousing bolt above the starter motor.
32. Remove the oil pan-to-bellhousing bolt from below the starter motor.
33. Loosen the 2 LH bellhousing-to-engine bolts

➡The automatic transmission has one more bottom bellhousing-to-oil pan bolt than the manual transmission.

34. Remove the 2 LH bellhousing-to-oil pan bolts.
35. Slide the transmission rearward 0.19 inches.
36. Remove the 4 lower engine front cover bolts.
37. Remove the 16 oil pan bolts.

➡The subframe may need to be lowered more for clearance to remove the oil pan.

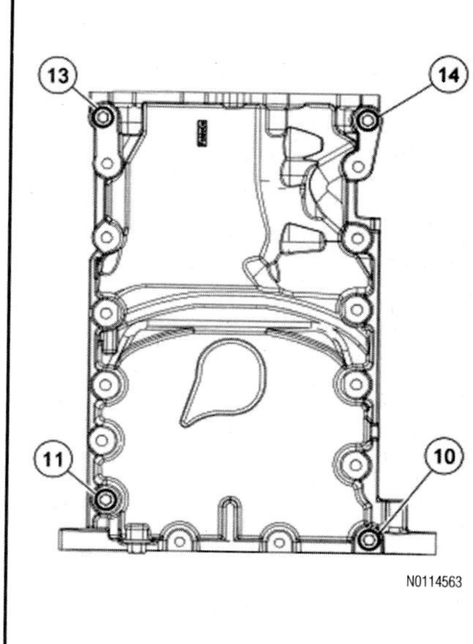

Fig. 187 Identifying oil pan bolts 10, 11, 13 and 14

38. Using a suitable pry tool, locate the 2 pry pads (1 shown) at the LH and RH side of the oil pan and pry the oil pan loose and remove.

➡Only use a 3M(tm) Roloc® Bristle Disk (2-in white, part number 07528) to clean the oil pan. Do not use metal scrapers, wire brushes or any other power abrasive disk to clean. These tools cause scratches and gouges that make leak paths.

39. Clean the engine oil pan using a 3M® Roloc® Bristle Disk (2-in white, part number 07528) in a suitable tool turning at the recommended speed of 15,000 rpm.
40. Thoroughly wash the oil pan to remove any foreign material, including any abrasive particles created during the cleaning process.

➡Do not use wire brushes, power abrasive discs or 3M® Roloc® Bristle Disk (2-in white, part number 07528) to clean the sealing surfaces. These tools cause scratches and gouges that make leak paths. They also cause contamination that causes premature engine failure. Remove all traces of the gasket.

41. Clean the sealing surfaces of the cylinder block and engine front cover in the following sequence.
42. Remove any large deposits of silicone or gasket material.
43. Apply silicone gasket remover and allow to set for several minutes.

44. Remove the silicone gasket remover. A second application of silicone gasket remover may be required if residual traces of silicone or gasket material remain.

45. Apply metal surface prep to remove any remaining traces of oil and to prepare the surfaces to bond.

46. Do not attempt to make the metal shiny. Some staining of the metal surfaces is normal.

To install:

47. Apply a 0.21 inch bead of Motorcraft® High Performance Engine RTV Silicone to the 2 engine front cover-to-cylinder block joint areas on the sealing surface of the oil pan.

➡Failure to use Motorcraft® High Performance Engine RTV Silicone may cause the engine oil to foam excessively and result in serious engine damage.

➡The oil pan and the 4 specified bolts must be installed and the oil pan aligned to the cylinder block within 4 minutes of sealant application. Final tightening of the oil pan bolts must be carried out within 60 minutes of sealant application.

48. Apply a 0.11 inch bead of Motorcraft® High Performance Engine RTV Silicone to the sealing surface of the oil pan-to-engine block and to the oil pan-to-engine front cover mating surface.

49. Apply a 0.21 inch bead of Motorcraft® High Performance Engine RTV Silicone to the 2 crankshaft seal retainer plate-to-cylinder block joint areas on the sealing surface of the oil pan.

➡The oil pan and the 4 specified bolts must be installed within 4 minutes of the start of sealant application.

➡Keep the oil pan as close as possible to the transmission while installing, then slide forward towards the engine front cover to prevent wiping off of the sealant.

50. Install the oil pan and bolts 10, 11, 13 and 14 finger tight.

51. Tighten the 2 LH bellhousing-to-engine bolts. Do not torque at this time.

52. Tighten the RH engine-to-bellhousing bolt. Do not torque at this time.

➡The automatic transmission has one more bottom bellhousing-to-oil pan bolt than the manual transmission.

53. Install and tighten the 2 LH bellhousing-to-oil pan bolts. Do not torque at this time.

54. Install and tighten the RH oil pan-to-bellhousing bolt. Do not torque at this time.

55. Laterally align the oil pan to the block. Make sure the oil pan is flush with the block at these 2 points.

56. Tighten bolts 10, 11, 13 and 14 in the sequence to 27 inch lbs. (3 Nm).

57. Install the 4 lower engine front cover bolts finger tight.

58. Install the remaining oil pan bolts and tighten in the sequence shown.

a. Tighten bolts 1 through 9 and 11 through 14 to 15 ft. lbs, (20 Nm), then rotate an additional 45 degrees.

b. Tighten bolts 15 and 16 to 15 ft. lbs. (20 Nm), then rotate an additional 45 degrees.

c. Tighten bolt 10 to 15 ft. lbs. (20 Nm), then rotate an additional 90 degrees.

59. Tighten the 4 lower engine front cover bolts to 18 ft. lbs. (24 Nm).

60. Using the adjustable jackstand, raise the subframe and install the 4 front subframe nuts finger tight.

61. Align the subframe and install the 4 rear subframe bolts with the reference marks made during removal. Tighten to 85 ft. lbs. (115 Nm).

62. Tighten the 4 front subframe nuts to 85 ft. lbs. (115 Nm).

63. Connect the steering shaft and install the steering shaft pinch bolt. Tighten to 35 ft. lbs. (47 Nm).

64. Connect the 2 EPAS electrical connectors.

65. Attach the 2 EPAS wiring harness pin-type retainers.

66. Tighten the 2 LH bellhousing-to-engine bolts to 35 ft. lbs. (48 Nm).

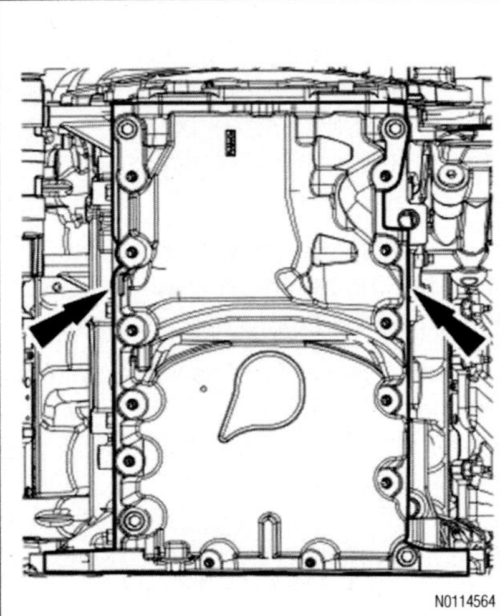

Fig. 188 Locating the flush points

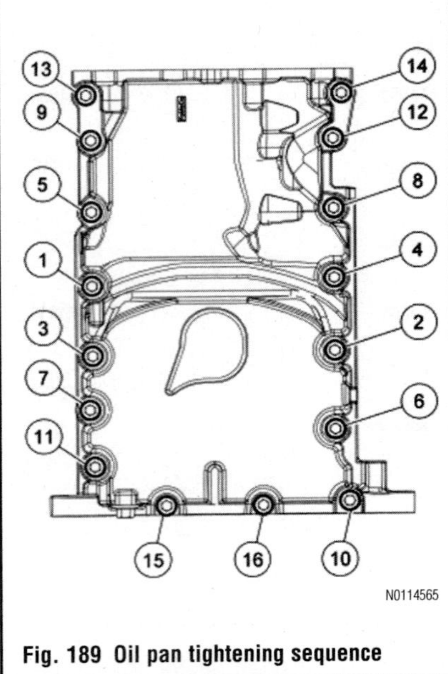

Fig. 189 Oil pan tightening sequence

67. Tighten the RH engine-to-bellhousing bolt to 35 ft. lbs. (48 Nm).

➡The automatic transmission has one more bottom bellhousing-to-oil pan bolt.

68. Tighten the 2 LH bellhousing-to-oil pan bolts to 35 ft. lbs. (48 Nm).

69. Tighten the RH oil pan-to-bellhousing bolt to 35 ft. lbs. (48 Nm).

➡Do not lubricate the engine oil filter gasket.

70. Install a new engine oil filter. Tighten to 44 inch lbs. and then rotate an additional 180 degrees.

71. Install the front crossmember brace and the 4 nuts. Tighten to 35 ft. lbs. (48 Nm).

72. Install the crossmember brace and the 6 bolts. Tighten to 48 ft. lbs. (65 Nm).

73. Tighten the 2 nuts for the crossmember brace to 48 ft. lbs. (65 Nm).

74. Install the lower air deflector and the 9 bolts.

75. Install the RH radiator support bracket and the 2 bolts.

76. Install the radiator sight shield and the 8 pin-type retainers.

77. Position the generator wiring harness bracket on the rear LH valve cover stud bolt and install the nut.

78. Tighten the 4 (2 shown) upper bellhousing-to-engine bolts and stud bolts to 35 ft. lbs. (48 Nm).

79. To complete the installation, reverse the remaining removal procedure.

80. Fill the engine with clean engine oil.

81. Install the battery tray.

4.0L Engine

See Figure 190.

➡During engine repair procedures, cleanliness is extremely important. Any foreign material, including any material created while cleaning gasket surfaces that enters the oil passages, coolant passages or the oil pan, can cause engine failure.

1. With the vehicle in NEUTRAL, position it on a hoist.
2. Remove the bolt and detach the Power Steering Pressure (PSP) tube bracket from the crossmember.
3. Remove the 2 power steering gear bolts and position aside the steering gear. To install tighten to 85 ft. lbs. (115 Nm).
4. Remove the oil drain plug and drain the engine oil.
5. Remove the bolts, the oil pan and the gasket. Discard the gasket.

➡Do not use metal scrapers, wire brushes, power abrasive discs or other abrasive means to clean sealing surfaces. These tools cause scratches and gouges which make leak paths.

6. Clean and inspect the sealing surfaces.

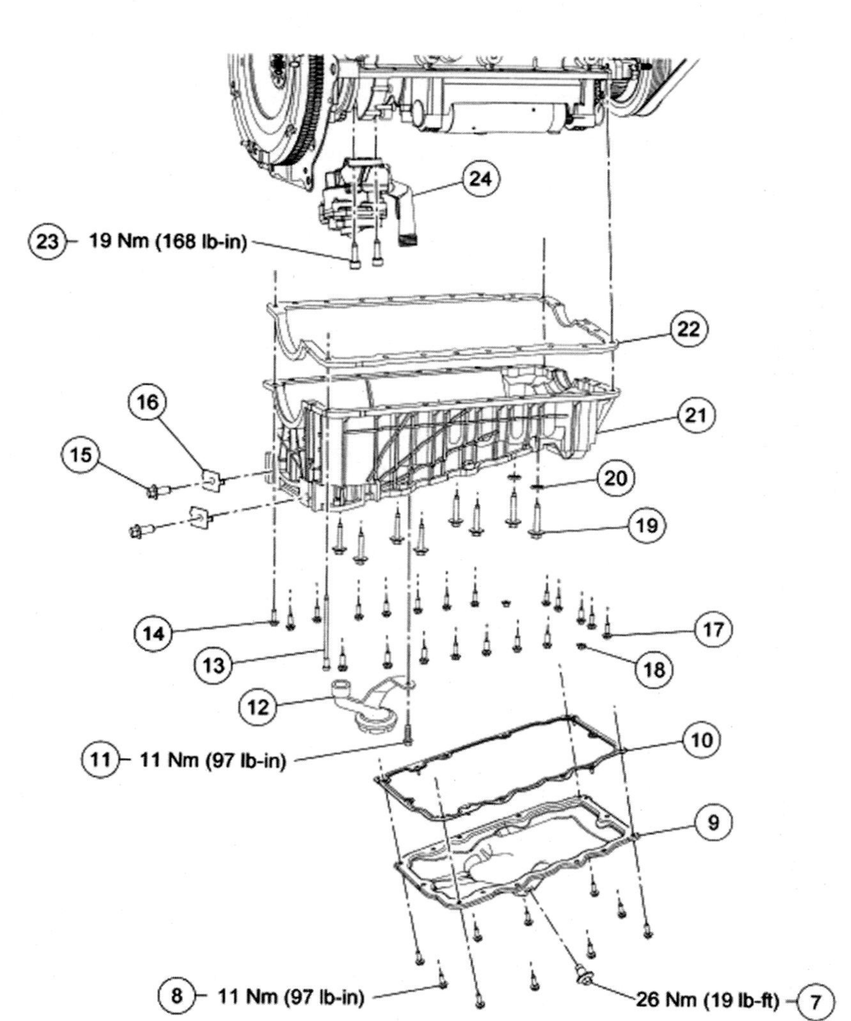

1. Oil pan drain plug
2. Oil pan bolt (10 required)
3. Oil pan
4. Oil pan gasket
5. Oil pump screen and pickup tube bolt
6. Oil pump screen and pickup tube
7. Cylinder block cradle bolt
8. Cylinder block cradle bolt
9. Bell housing-to-cylinder block cradle spacer bolt (2 required)
10. Bell housing-to-cylinder block cradle spacer (2 required)
11. Cylinder block cradle bolt (20 required)
12. Cylinder block cradle nut (2 required)
13. Cylinder block cradle bolt (8 required)
14. Washer (2 required)
15. Cylinder block cradle
16. Cylinder block cradle gasket
17. Oil pump bolt (2 required)
18. Oil pump

N0085242

Fig. 190 Exploded view of the oil pan and components

7. To install, reverse the removal procedure.
8. Fill the engine with clean engine oil.

4.6L Engine

See Figure 191.

1. With the vehicle in NEUTRAL, position it on a hoist.
2. Disconnect the battery ground cable.
3. Drain the engine oil.
4. Remove the Air Cleaner (ACL) assembly.
5. Remove the Throttle Body (TB). For additional information, refer to Fuel System.
6. Remove the 8 pin-type retainers and the radiator sight shield.
7. Rotate the accessory drive belt tensioner clockwise and remove the accessory drive belt from the generator pulley.
8. Remove the alternator. Refer to Alternator in Engine Electrical.
9. Install the Engine Lifting Brackets.
10. If equipped, remove the 4 nuts and the strut tower cross brace.
11. Install the Engine Support Bar.

➡Both the RH and LH engine support insulator nuts must be removed to allow the engine to be raised.

12. Remove the RH and LH engine support insulator nuts.
13. Using the Engine Support Bar, raise the engine 1.57 inches.
14. Position a suitable adjustable jackstand under the subframe.
15. Mark the position of the 4 subframe nuts and 4 subframe bolts for referencing during assembly.
16. Remove the 4 subframe nuts and 4 subframe bolts.
17. Using the adjustable jackstand, lower the subframe 1.96 inches.
18. Detach the 2 pin-type retainers.

➡Be careful when removing the oil pan gasket. It is reusable.

19. Remove the 16 bolts, the oil pan and the gasket.
20. Discard the oil pan gasket.

To install:

➡Do not use metal scrapers, wire brushes, power abrasive discs or other abrasive means to clean the sealing surfaces. These tools cause scratches and gouges, which make leak paths. Use a plastic scraping tool to remove all traces of old sealant.

21. Inspect the oil pan. Clean the mating surface of the oil pan with silicone gasket remover and metal surface prep. Follow the directions on the packaging.

➡If not secured within 4 minutes, the sealant must be removed and the sealing area cleaned. To clean the sealing area, use silicone gasket remover and metal surface prep. Follow the directions on the packaging. Failure to follow this procedure can cause future oil leakage.

22. Apply silicone gasket and sealant at the crankshaft rear seal retainer plate-to-cylinder block sealing surface.

➡If not secured within 4 minutes, the sealant must be removed and the sealing area cleaned. To clean the sealing area, use silicone gasket remover and metal surface prep. Follow the directions on the packaging. Failure to follow this procedure can cause future oil leakage.

23. Apply silicone gasket and sealant at the engine front cover-to-cylinder block sealing surface.
24. Install the new oil pan gasket and the oil pan and loosely install the 16 bolts.
25. Tighten the bolts in 3 stages, in the sequence shown.
    a. Stage 1: Tighten to 18 inch lbs. (2 Nm).
    b. Stage 2: Tighten to 15 ft. lbs. (20 Nm).
    c. Stage 3: Tighten an additional 60 degrees.
26. Attach the 2 pin-type retainers.

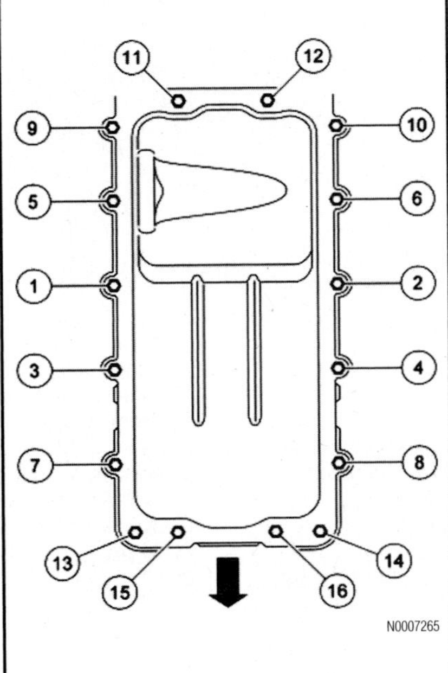

Fig. 191 Oil pan tightening sequence

27. Using the adjustable jackstand, raise the subframe.

➡Do not tighten the subframe nuts and bolts at this time.

28. Install the 4 subframe nuts and 4 subframe bolts.
29. Align the subframe nuts and bolts with the reference marks made during removal.
    a. Tighten nuts to 85 ft. lbs. (115 Nm).
    b. Tighten bolts to 85 ft. lbs. (115 Nm).
30. If equipped, install the 4 nuts and the strut tower cross brace. Tighten to 26 ft. lbs. (35 Nm).
31. Using the Engine Support Bar, lower the engine.
32. Install the RH and LH engine support insulator nuts. Tighten to 46 ft. lbs. (63 Nm).

➡Make sure the B+ cable is positioned close to the generator when the nut is being tightened.

33. Install the alternator.
34. Rotate the accessory drive belt tensioner clockwise and install the accessory drive belt on the generator pulley.
35. Install the radiator sight shield and 8 pin-type retainers.
36. Install the TB.
37. Install the ACL assembly.
38. Fill the crankcase with clean engine oil.
39. Connect the battery ground cable.

5.0L Engine

See Figure 192.

➡During engine repair procedures, cleanliness is extremely important. Any foreign material, including any material created while cleaning gasket surfaces, that enters the oil passages, coolant passages or the oil pan, can cause engine failure.

1. With the vehicle in NEUTRAL, position it on a hoist.
2. Disconnect the battery ground cable.
3. Remove the 2 steering column dash boot nuts.

➡Use a steering wheel holding device (such as Hunter® 28-75-1 or equivalent).

4. Using a suitable holding device, hold the steering wheel in the straight-ahead position.
5. If equipped, remove the 4 nuts and the strut tower cross brace.

➡The engine appearance cover rubber grommets may remain on the cover. If so, remove the grommets from the cover and install them on the intake manifold before installing the cover.

6. Remove the engine appearance cover.
7. Remove the ACL outlet pipe.
8. Remove the bolt and position the sound enhancement pipe aside.
9. Remove the 8 pin-type retainers and the upper radiator sight shield.
10. Install an Engine Lifting Bracket on the rear of the RH cylinder head.

➡It may be necessary to install washers between the Engine Lifting Bracket and the cylinder head to prevent the Engine Lifting Bracket from contacting the valve cover while supporting the engine.

11. Install an Engine Lifting Bracket on the side of the LH cylinder head.

➡The draw screw and bracket from the heavy duty Engine Support Bar (303-F070) must be used with the light duty Engine Support Bar (303-F072). This will provide enough clearance between the draw screw bracket and the cowl.

12. Install the Engine Support Bar.
13. Remove the RH and LH engine support insulator nuts.
14. Using the Engine Support Bar, raise the engine 25 mm (0.984 in).
15. Remove the 9 screws and the lower radiator sight shield.
16. Remove the crossmember brace.
17. Remove the oil pan drain plug and drain the engine oil.
18. Disconnect the oil level sensor electrical connector.
19. Remove the 2 nuts and detach the wiring harness retainers from the LH side of the oil pan and the front oil pan stud bolts.
20. Detach the wiring harness retainers from the RH side of the oil pan and the RH engine support insulator bracket stud bolt.
21. Detach the wiring harness retainers from A/C compressor stud bolt and the RH side of the oil pan.
22. Remove the bolt and position the steering intermediate shaft aside.
23. Remove the 4 nuts and the front crossmember brace.
24. Mark the position of the 4 subframe nuts and 4 subframe bolts for referencing during assembly
25. Position 2 adjustable jackstands under the subframe.
26. Remove the 4 rear subframe bolts.
27. Remove the 4 front subframe nuts.
28. Using the adjustable jackstands, lower the subframe 100 mm (3.937 in).
29. Remove the 3 stud bolts, the 13 bolts and the oil pan.
30. Remove the 3 bolts and the oil pump screen and pickup tube.
31. Remove and discard the O-ring seal.
32. Remove and inspect the oil pan baffle and gasket, replace as necessary.

To install:

➡Do not use metal scrapers, wire brushes, power abrasive discs or other abrasive means to clean the sealing surfaces. These tools cause scratches and gouges, which make leak paths. Use a plastic scraping tool to remove all traces of old sealant.

➡Inspect the oil pan and engine sealing surfaces. Clean the mating surfaces of the engine and oil pan with silicone gasket remover and metal surface prep. Follow the directions on the packaging.

➡If the oil pan is not installed and the fasteners tightened within 5 minutes, the sealant must be removed and the sealing area cleaned. To clean the sealing area, use silicone gasket remover and metal surface prep.
➡Failure to follow this procedure can cause future oil leakage. If this timing cannot be met, tighten fasteners 7, 8, 9 and 10 to 71 inch lbs. within 5 minutes of applying the sealer and final torque all of the fasteners within 1 hour of applying the sealer.

➡If the engine front cover has been removed, it is only necessary to apply sealant to the crankshaft rear seal retainer plate-to-cylinder block sealing surfaces.

33. Apply an 0.31 inch bead of silicone gasket and sealant to the crankshaft rear seal retainer plate-to-cylinder block sealing surfaces and the engine front cover-to-cylinder block sealing surfaces.
34. Position the oil pan baffle and gasket.

➡The 2 oil pump screen and pickup tube-to-oil pump bolts must be tightened prior to tightening the oil pump screen and pickup tube-to-spacer bolt.

35. Using a new O-ring seal, install the oil pump screen and pickup tube and the 3 bolts. Tighten the 2 oil pump screen and pickup tube-to-oil pump bolts in 2 stages.
    a. Stage 1: Tighten to 7 ft. lbs. (10 Nm).
    b. Stage 2: Tighten an additional 45 degrees.
36. Tighten the oil pump screen and pickup tube-to-spacer bolt to 18 ft. lbs. (25 Nm).

➡Fastener locations 7, 13 and 16 are stud bolts.

37. Install the oil pan and tighten the fasteners in sequence in 3 stages.
    a. Stage 1: Tighten to 19 inch lbs. (2 Nm).
    b. Stage 2: Tighten to 7 ft. lbs. (10 Nm).
    c. Stage 3: Tighten an additional 45 degrees.
38. Using the adjustable jackstands, raise the subframe 100 mm (3.937 in).

➡Do not tighten the subframe nuts and bolts at this time.

39. Install the 4 subframe nuts and 4 subframe bolts. Align the subframe nuts and bolts with the reference marks made during removal. Tighten the bolts and nuts to 85 ft. lbs. (115 Nm).
40. Install the front crossmember brace and the 4 nuts. Tighten to 35 ft. lbs. (48 Nm).
41. Position the steering intermediate shaft and install the bolt. Tighten to 35 ft. lbs. (47 Nm).
42. Attach the wiring harness retainers to A/C compressor stud bolts and the RH side of the oil pan.

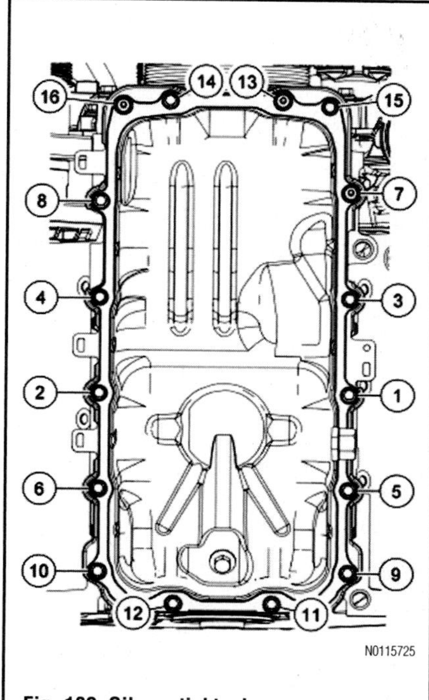

Fig. 192 Oil pan tightening sequence

43. Attach the wiring harness retainers to the RH side of the oil pan and the RH engine support insulator bracket stud bolt.

44. Attach the wiring harness retainers to the LH side of the oil pan and the front oil pan studs.

45. Install the 2 nuts to the front oil pan studs.

46. Connect the oil level sensor electrical connector.

47. Install the crossmember brace.

48. Install the lower radiator sight shield and the 9 screws.

49. Using the Engine Support Bar, lower the engine.

50. Install the RH and LH engine support insulator nuts. Tighten to 46 ft. lbs. (63 Nm).

51. Install the upper radiator sight shield and the 8 pin-type retainers.

52. Position the sound enhancement pipe and install the bolt.

53. Install the ACL outlet pipe.

➡The engine appearance cover rubber grommets may remain on the cover. If so, remove the grommets from the cover and install them on the intake manifold before installing the cover.

54. Install the engine appearance cover.

55. If equipped, install the strut tower cross brace and the 4 nuts. Tighten to 26 ft. lbs. (35 Nm).

56. Install the 2 steering column dash boot nuts.

57. Fill the engine with clean engine oil.

58. Connect the battery ground cable.

5.7L Engine

See Figures 193 and 194.

1. With the vehicle in NEUTRAL, position it on a hoist.

2. Remove the 2 dash boot nuts.

➡Use a steering wheel holding device (such as Hunter® 28-75-1 or equivalent).

3. Using a suitable holding device, hold the steering wheel in the straight-ahead position.

4. Remove the battery and tray.

5. Remove the Air Cleaner (ACL) outlet pipe.

6. Install the Engine Lifting Brackets.

7. Remove the LH and RH engine support insulator nuts.

➡The heavy duty Engine Support Bar (303-F070) must be used with the draw screws from the light duty Engine Support Bar (303-F072). This will provide enough clearance between the Supercharger (SC) and the Engine Support Bar, and enough clearance between the draw screw and the vehicle hood.

8. Install the Engine Support Bars and raise the engine.

9. Drain the engine oil.

10. Remove the 4 nuts and the subframe cross brace.

11. Position a suitable adjustable jackstand under the subframe.

➡Do not allow the steering wheel to rotate while the steering column intermediate shaft is disconnected or damage to the clockspring can result. If there is evidence that the wheel has rotated, the clockspring must be removed and recentered. For additional information, refer to Supplemental Restraint System.

12. Remove the upper bolt from the intermediate steering shaft.

Mark the position of the 4 subframe nuts and 4 subframe bolts for referencing during assembly.

13. Remove the 4 subframe nuts and 4 subframe bolts.

14. Using the adjustable jackstand, lower the subframe 50 mm (1.96 in).

15. Detach the 2 wiring harness retainers from the oil pan.

16. Detach the wiring harness retainer from the oil pan stud bolt.

17. Remove the nut and the wire harness retainer bracket from the oil pan stud bolt.

18. Remove the 14 bolts, 2 stud bolts and the oil pan.

19. Discard the gasket.

To install:

➡Do not use metal scrapers, wire brushes, power abrasive discs or other abrasive means to clean the sealing surfaces. These tools cause scratches and gouges which make leak paths. Use a plastic scraping tool to remove all traces of old sealant.

➡Clean the sealing surfaces with silicone gasket remover and metal surface prep. Follow the directions on the packaging. Failure to follow this procedure can cause future oil leakage.

Clean and inspect the mating surfaces of the engine block and oil pan.

➡If not secured within 4 minutes, the sealant must be removed and the sealing area cleaned. To clean the sealing area, use silicone gasket remover and metal surface prep. Follow the directions on the packaging. Failure to follow this procedure can cause future oil leakage.

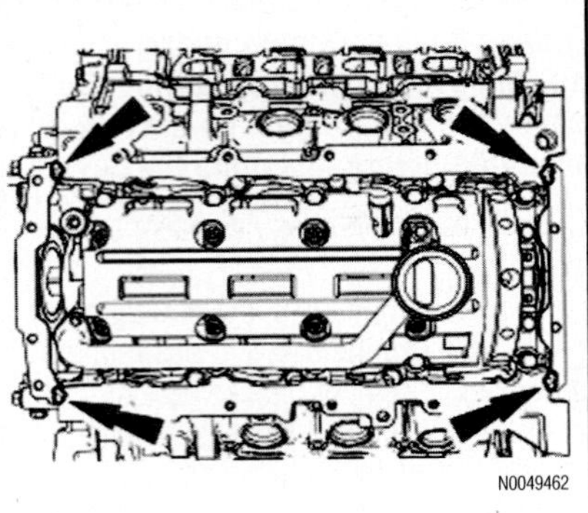

Fig. 193 Locating the front cover-to-cylinder block sealing joints and the crankshaft rear seal retainer plate-to-cylinder block sealing joints

20. Apply silicone gasket and sealant at the engine front cover-to-cylinder block sealing joints and the crankshaft rear seal retainer plate-to-cylinder block sealing joints.

21. Using a new gasket, install the oil pan, 14 bolts and 2 stud bolts. Tighten in the sequence shown to 18 ft. lbs. (25 Nm)

22. Install the wire harness retainer bracket on the oil pan stud bolt and install the nut.

23. Attach the wiring harness retainer to the oil pan stud bolt.

24. Attach the 2 wiring harness retainers to the oil pan.

25. Using the adjustable jackstand, raise the subframe.

26. Install the steering intermediate shaft into the steering coupler.

➡Do not allow the steering wheel to rotate while the steering column intermediate shaft is disconnected or damage to the clockspring can result. If there is evidence that the wheel has rotated, the clockspring must be removed and recentered. For additional information, refer to Supplemental Restraint System.

27. Position the intermediate steering shaft and install the upper bolt. Tighten to 35 ft. lbs. (47 Nm).

➡Do not tighten the subframe nuts and bolts at this time.

28. Install the 4 subframe nuts and 4 subframe bolts.

29. Align the subframe nuts and bolts with the reference marks made during removal.

   a. Tighten the nuts to 85 ft. lbs. (115 Nm).

   b. Tighten the bolts to 85 ft. lbs. (115 Nm).

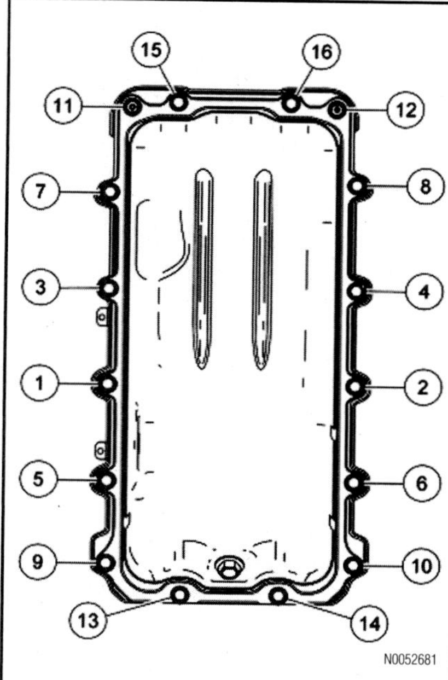

Fig. 194 Oil pan tightening sequence

30. Install the subframe cross brace and the 4 nuts. Tighten to 35 ft. lbs. (48 Nm).
31. Using the Engine Support Bars, lower the engine onto the engine support insulators.
32. Install the LH and RH engine support insulator nuts. Tighten to 46 ft. lbs. (63 Nm).
33. Install the ACL outlet pipe.
34. Install the battery and tray.
35. Fill the engine with clean engine oil.
36. Install the dash boot and the 2 nuts.

OIL PUMP

REMOVAL & INSTALLATION

3.7L Engine

See Figure 195.

1. Remove the timing chain front cover.
2. Remove the oil pan.

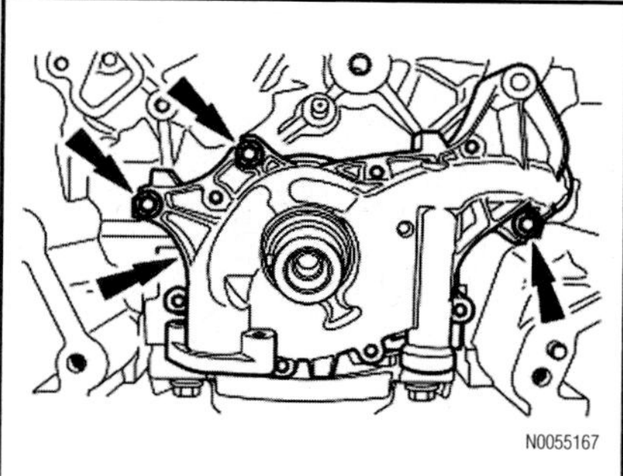

Fig. 195 Remove the 3 bolts and the oil pump

3. Remove the crankshaft timing chain sprocket.
4. Remove the 3 bolts and the oil pump screen and pickup tube. Discard the O-ring seal.
5. Remove the 3 bolts and the oil pump.

To install:

6. Install the oil pump and the 3 bolts. Tighten to 7 ft. lbs. (10 Nm).
7. Using a new O-ring seal, install the oil pump screen and pickup tube and the 3 bolts. Tighten to 7 ft. lbs. (10 Nm).
8. Install the crankshaft timing chain sprocket.
9. To complete the installation, reverse the remaining removal procedure.

4.0L Engine

See Figures 196 through 198.

➡During engine repair procedures, cleanliness is extremely important. Any foreign material, including any material created while cleaning gasket surfaces that enters the oil passages, coolant passages or the oil pan, can cause engine failure.

1. With the vehicle in NEUTRAL, position it on a hoist.
2. Disconnect the battery ground cable.
3. Remove the Throttle Body (TB). For additional information, refer to Fuel System.
4. Remove the Front End Accessory Drive (FEAD) bracket bolt and install the Engine Lifting Bracket.
5. Remove the 8 pin-type retainers and the radiator sight shield.
6. Install the Engine Support Bar.

➡Use a steering wheel holding device (such as Hunter® 28-75-1 or equivalent).

7. Using a suitable holding device, hold the steering wheel in the straight-ahead position.
8. Remove the RH engine mount nut.
9. Remove the LH engine mount nut.
10. Remove the oil pump screen and pickup tube.

➡Do not allow the steering wheel to rotate while the steering column intermediate shaft is disconnected or damage to the clockspring can result. If there is evidence that the wheel has rotated, the clockspring must be removed and recentered. For additional information, refer to Supplemental Restraint System.

11. Remove the bolt and detach the steering column intermediate shaft from the steering gear.
12. Remove the bolt and detach the Power Steering Pressure (PSP) tube bracket from the crossmember.
13. Remove the 2 steering gear-to-crossmember bolts and detach the gear from the crossmember.
14. Remove the starter. For additional information, refer to Engine Electrical.

➡The cylinder block cradle removed for clarity. Note the location of the 2 Torx® head bolts at the rear of the cylinder block cradle.

15. Remove the 2 cylinder block cradle rear Torx® bolts.
16. Remove the 20 bolts and 2 nuts along the outside of the cylinder block cradle.

➡Note the location of the 2 silver-colored bolts that have washer seals. They must be installed in the same position with new washer seals.

17. Remove the 8 cylinder block cradle inner bolts and the 2 washer seals.
18. Discard the washer seals.
19. Using the Engine Support Bar, raise the engine and then remove the lower block cradle.
20. Remove the 2 bolts and the oil pump.

To install:

21. Install the oil pump and tighten the 2 bolts to 14 ft. lbs. (20 Nm).

➡Failure to back off the set screws can result in damage to the cylinder block cradle.

22. Back the set screws off until they are below the cylinder block cradle boss.

➡Do not use metal scrapers, wire brushes, power abrasive discs or other abrasive means to clean the sealing surfaces. These tools cause scratches and gouges which make leak paths. Use a plastic scraping tool to remove all traces of old sealant.

➡Gasket material as well as silicone sealant may be present in the cavities in the main bearing cap. This material must be removed completely prior to assembly.

23. Clean the gasket mating surfaces, making sure all the sealant is removed from the cavities on the rear main bearing cap. To clean the sealing area, use silicone gasket remover and metal surface prep. Follow the directions on the packaging.

➡If not secured within 4 minutes, the sealant must be removed and the seal-

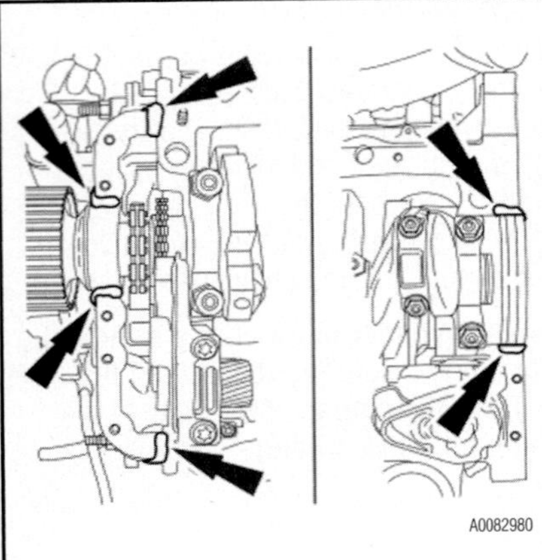

Fig. 196 Apply silicone in the 6 places shown

ing area cleaned. To clean the sealing area, use silicone gasket remover and metal surface prep. Follow the directions on the packaging. Failure to follow this procedure can cause future oil leakage.

24. Apply silicone in the 6 places shown.
25. Position a new gasket and the cylinder block cradle.
26. Install the outer 20 bolts and 2 nuts finger-tight.
27. Install the 2 cylinder block cradle rear Torx® bolts finger-tight.
28. Install the 2 bellhousing-to-cylinder block cradle bolts. Tighten to 35 ft. lbs. (47 Nm).
29. Tighten the outer 20 bolts and 2 nuts. Tighten the nuts to 7 ft. lbs. (10 Nm). Tighten the bolts to 10 ft. lbs. (14 Nm).
30. Tighten the 2 cylinder block cradle rear Torx® bolts. Tighten to 7 ft. lbs (10 Nm).
    a. Tighten the 8 inserts.
    b. Tighten to 27 ft. lbs. (3 Nm).
31. Install the 2 silver-colored bolts and new washer seals finger-tight.

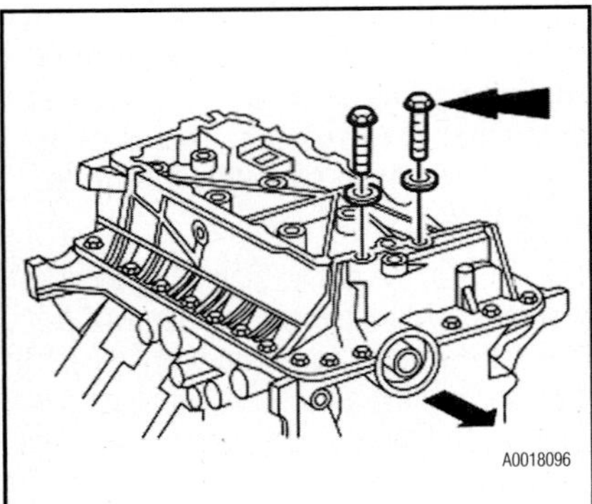

Fig. 197 Install the 2 silver-colored bolts

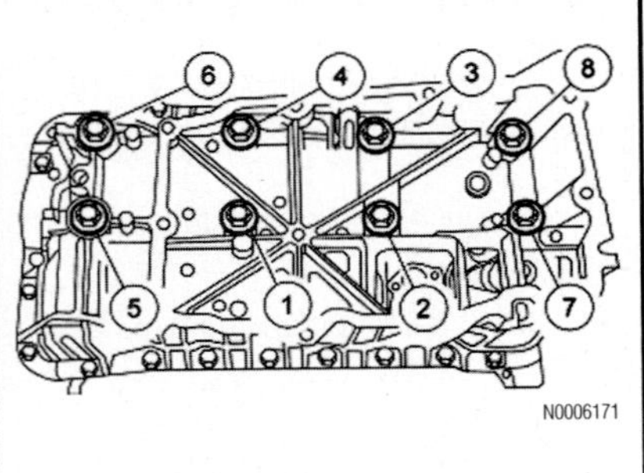

Fig. 198 Tighten the 8 inner bolts in the sequence

32. Install the 6 remaining inner bolts finger-tight.
33. Tighten the 8 inner bolts in the sequence shown in 2 stages.
    a. Stage 1: Tighten to 133 inch lbs. (15 Nm).
    b. Stage 2: Tighten to 25 ft. lbs. (34 Nm).
34. Install the starter.
35. Position the steering gear and install the 2 bolts. Tighten to 85 ft. lbs. (115 Nm).
36. Attach the PSP tube bracket to the crossmember and install the bolt.

➡Do not allow the steering wheel to rotate while the steering column intermediate shaft is disconnected or damage to the clockspring can result. If there is evidence that the wheel has rotated, the clockspring must be removed and recentered. For additional information, refer to Supplemental Restraint System.

37. Attach the steering column intermediate shaft to the steering gear and install the bolt. Tighten to 18 ft. lbs. (25 Nm).
38. Install the oil pump screen and pickup tube.
39. Lower the engine and install the LH and RH engine mount nut. Tighten to 46 ft. lbs. (63 Nm).
40. Remove the Engine Lifting Brackets and install the FEAD bracket bolt. Tighten to 35 ft. lbs. (48 Nm).
41. Position the radiator sight shield and install the 8 pin-type retainers.
42. Install the TB.
43. Connect the battery ground cable.

4.6L Engine

See Figures 199 and 200.

1. Remove the oil pan. Refer to Oil Pan in this section.
2. Remove the timing chain. Refer to Timing Chain and Sprockets in this section.

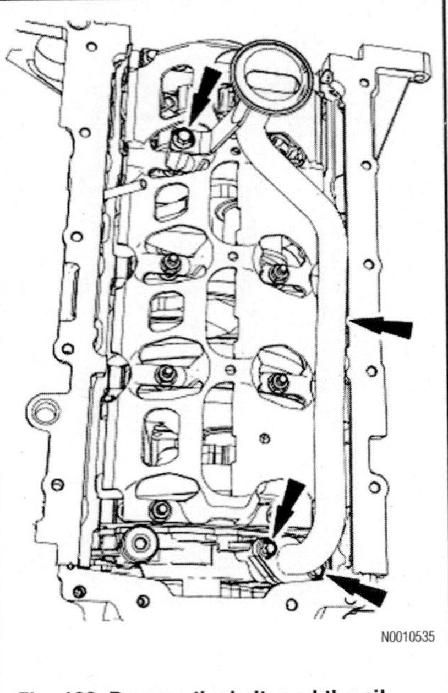

Fig. 199 Remove the bolts and the oil pump screen and pickup tube

3. Remove the bolts and the oil pump screen and pickup tube.
4. Remove the 3 bolts and the oil pump.

To install:

➡Do not use metal scrapers, wire brushes, power abrasive discs or other abrasive means to clean the sealing surfaces. These tools cause scratches and gouges which make leak paths. Use a plastic scraping tool to remove all traces of old sealant.

5. Clean the sealing surfaces with metal surface prep. Follow the directions on the packaging. Inspect the mating surfaces.
6. Position the oil pump and install the bolts. Tighten to 7 ft. lbs. (10 Nm).

➡Make sure the O-ring seal is in place and not damaged. A missing or damaged O-ring seal can cause foam in the

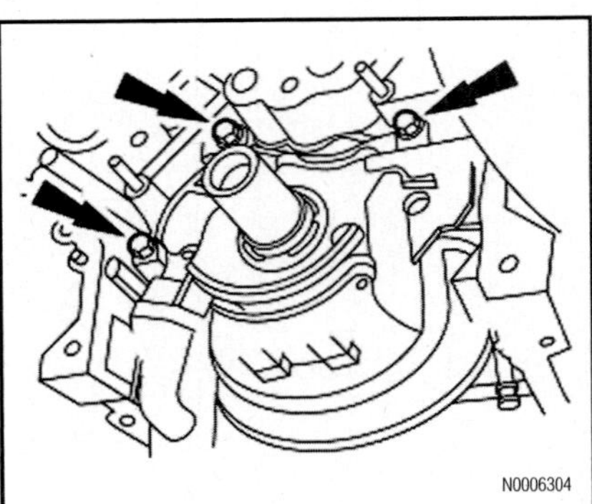

Fig. 200 Remove the 3 bolts and the oil pump

lubrication system, low oil pressure and severe engine damage.

➡**Clean and inspect the mating surfaces and install a new O-ring seal. Lubricate the O-ring seal with clean engine oil prior to installation.**

7. Position the oil pump screen and pickup tube and install the bolts.
8. Tighten the oil pump screen and pickup tube-to-oil pump bolts to 7 ft. lbs. (10 Nm).
9. Tighten the oil pump screen and pickup tube-to-spacer bolt to 18 ft. lbs. (25 Nm).

5.0L Engine

See Figures 201 and 202.

1. Remove the timing chain. Refer to Timing Chain and Sprockets in this section.
2. Remove the crankshaft sprocket.
3. Remove the oil pan. Refer to Oil Pan in this section.
4. Remove the 2 bolts, the 2 stud bolts and the oil pump.

To install:

5. Rotate the inner rotor of the oil pump assembly to align the flats on the crankshaft and slip the oil pump over the crankshaft until seated against the block.
6. Rotate the oil pump until the bolt holes are aligned to the block and install the fasteners.

➡**Oil pump must be held against the cylinder block until all bolts are tightened.**

7. Tighten the fasteners in the sequence shown in 3 stages:
   a. Stage 1: Hand tighten.
   b. Stage 2: Tighten the bolt (1) to 7 ft. lbs. (10 Nm), the stud bolt (2) to 18 ft. lbs. (25 Nm), the bolt (3) to 7 ft. lbs.

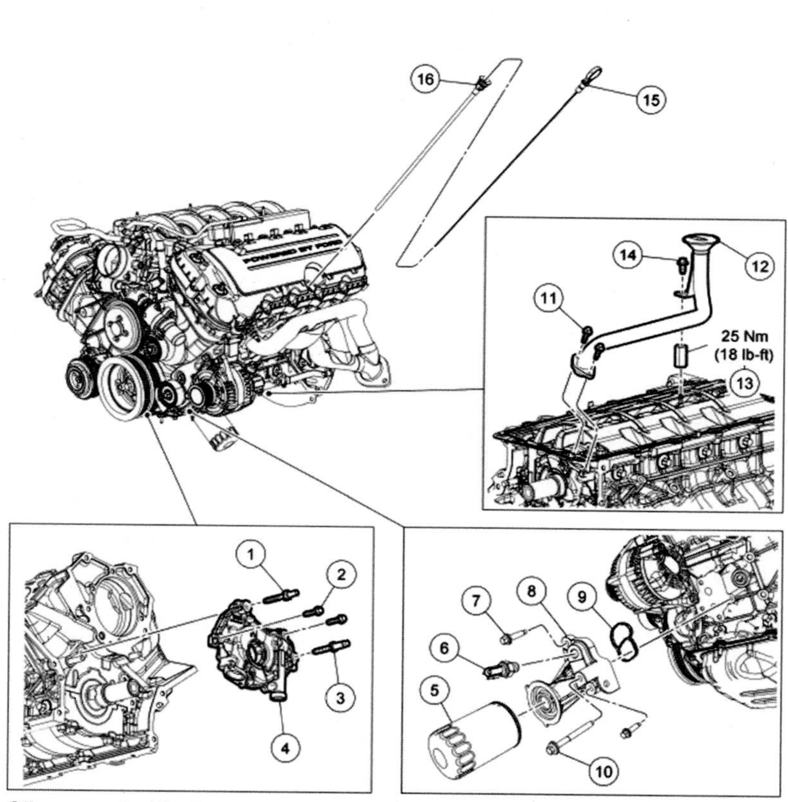

1. Oil pump stud bolt
2. Oil pump bolt (2 required)
3. Oil pump stud bolt
4. Oil pump
5. Oil filter
6. Engine Oil Pressure (EOP) switch
7. Oil filter adapter bolt (2 required)
8. Oil filter adapter
9. Oil filter adapter gasket
10. Oil filter adapter bolt
11. Oil pump screen and pickup tube bolt (2 required)
12. Oil pump screen and pickup tube
13. Oil pump screen and pickup tube spacer
14. Oil pump screen and pickup tube bolt
15. Oil indicator
16. Oil indicator tube

N0115813

Fig. 201 Exploded view of the oil pump and related components

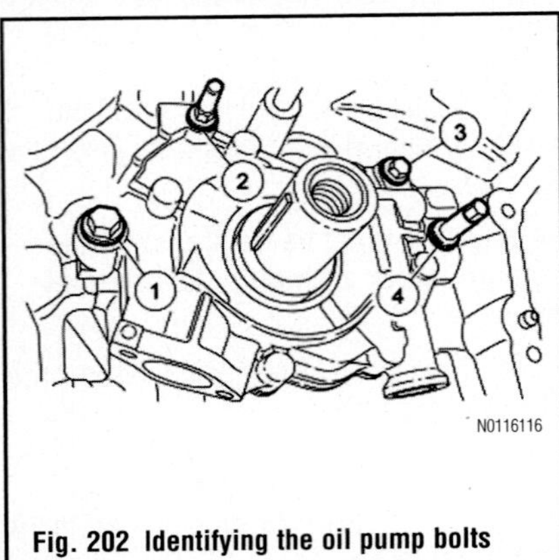

Fig. 202 Identifying the oil pump bolts

(10 Nm) and the stud bolt (4) to 15 ft. lbs. (20 Nm).

c. Stage 3: Tighten the bolt (1) an additional 45 degrees, the stud bolt (2) an additional 75 degrees, the bolt (3) an additional 45 degrees and the stud bolt (4) an additional 60 degrees.

8. Install the oil pan.
9. Install the crankshaft sprocket with the flange facing forward.
10. Install the timing chain. Refer to Timing Chain and Sprockets in this section.

5.4L Engine

See Figures 203 and 204.

➡During engine repair procedures, cleanliness is extremely important. Any foreign material, including any material created while cleaning gasket surfaces that enters the oil passages, coolant passages or the oil pan, can cause engine failure.

1. With the vehicle in NEUTRAL, position it on a hoist.
2. Remove the timing drive components. Refer to Timing Chain and Sprockets in this section.
3. Remove the oil pan. Refer to Oil Pan in this section.
4. Remove the 3 bolts and the oil pump screen and pickup tube assembly. Discard the O-ring seal.

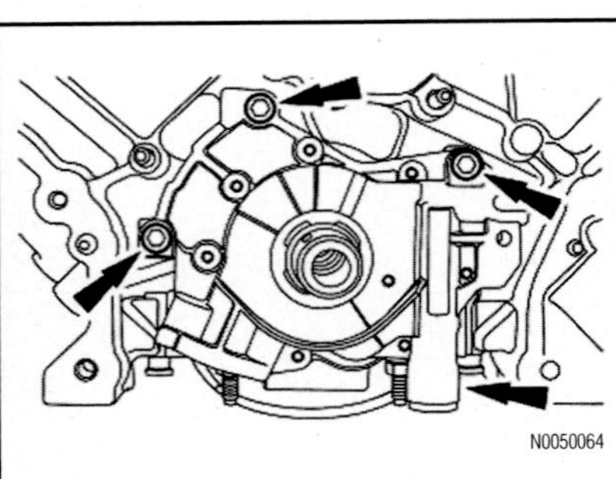

Fig. 203 Locating the oil pump bolts

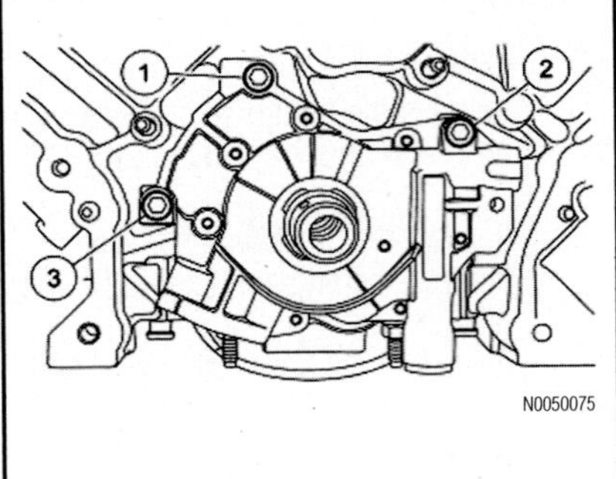

Fig. 204 Oil pump bolt tightening sequence

5. Remove the 3 bolts and the oil pump.

To install:

➡Do not use metal scrapers, wire brushes, power abrasive discs or other abrasive means to clean the sealing surfaces. These tools cause scratches and gouges which make leak paths.

6. Clean the sealing surfaces with metal surface prep. Follow the directions on the packaging.
7. Inspect the mating surfaces.
8. Install the oil pump and 3 bolts. Tighten the bolts in the sequence shown to 89 inch lbs. (10 Nm).
9. Install the oil pump screen and pickup tube.
   a. Clean and inspect the mating surfaces and install a new O-ring. Lubricate the O-ring with clean engine oil prior to installation.
   b. Position the oil pump screen and pickup tube and install the bolts.
   c. Tighten the oil pump screen and pickup tube-to-oil pump bolts to 7 ft. lbs. (10 Nm).
   d. Tighten the oil pump screen and pickup tube-to-spacer bolt to 18 ft. lbs. (25 Nm).
10. Install the timing drive components.
11. Install the oil pan.

PISTON AND RING

POSITIONING

See Figure 205.

Refer to the accompanying illustration.

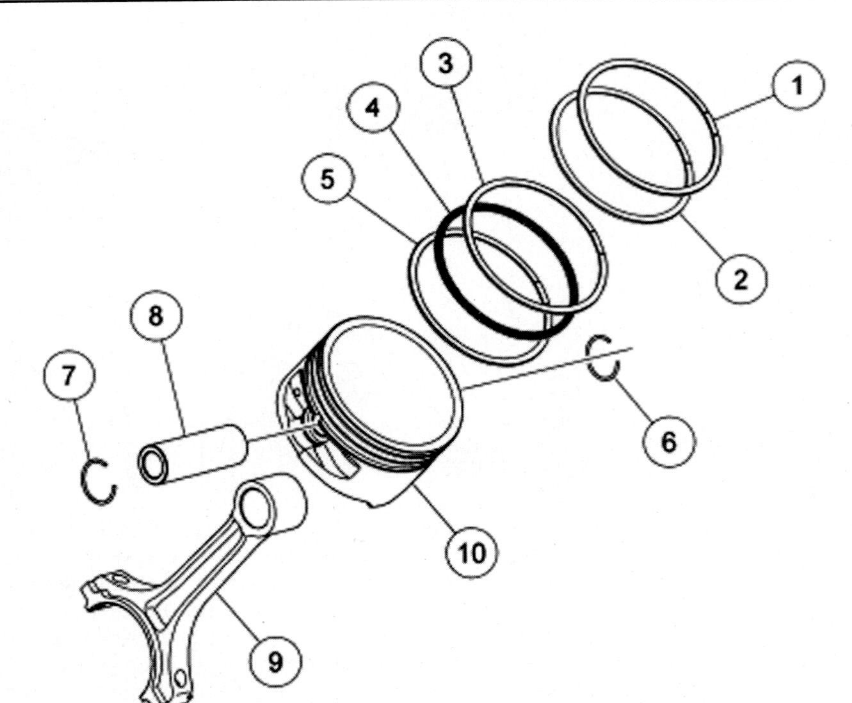

Fig. 205 Exploded view of the piston and ring

REAR MAIN SEAL

REMOVAL & INSTALLATION

3.7L Engine

See Figures 206 and 207.

1. With the vehicle in NEUTRAL, position it on a hoist.
2. Remove the flexplate or flywheel.
3. Remove the crankshaft sensor ring.
4. Using the Crankshaft Rear Oil Seal Remover and Slide Hammer, remove and discard the crankshaft rear seal.
5. Clean all sealing surfaces with metal surface prep.

To install:

➡Lubricate the seal lips and bore with clean engine oil prior to installation.

6. Position the Rear Main Seal Installer onto the end of the crankshaft and slide a new crankshaft rear seal onto the tool.
7. Using the Rear Main Seal Installer and Handle, install the new crankshaft rear seal.
8. Install the crankshaft sensor ring.
9. Install the flexplate or flywheel.

4.0L & 5.0L Engines

See Figures 208 through 211.

1. Remove the flexplate or flywheel.
2. Remove the spacer plate.

➡The original crankshaft rear seal does not have a speedy sleeve. Only a new replacement crankshaft rear seal comes with a speedy sleeve.

➡The crankshaft rear seal may have a metal speedy sleeve. This sleeve must be removed before attempting to remove the seal.

3. If necessary, remove the speedy sleeve using 2 screwdrivers or small pry bars.

➡Avoid scratching or damaging the crankshaft rear seal running surface during removal of the crankshaft rear seal.

4. Using the Oil Seal Remover, remove the crankshaft rear seal.

To install:

➡The new replacement crankshaft rear seal comes with a speedy sleeve. Do not remove the speedy sleeve, it must be installed with the crankshaft rear seal.

Fig. 210 Positioning the crankshaft rear seal with speedy sleeve

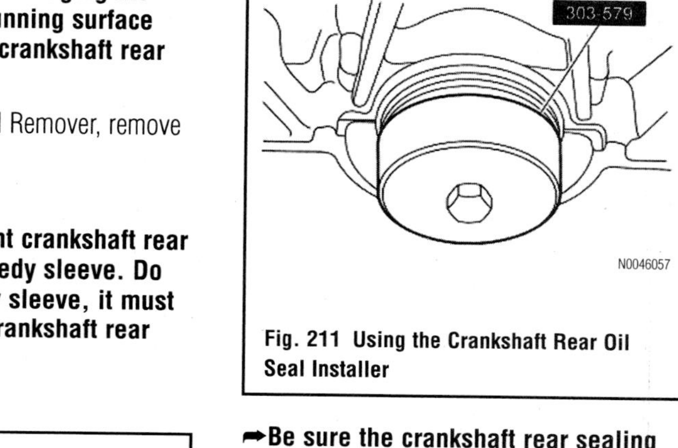

Fig. 211 Using the Crankshaft Rear Oil Seal Installer

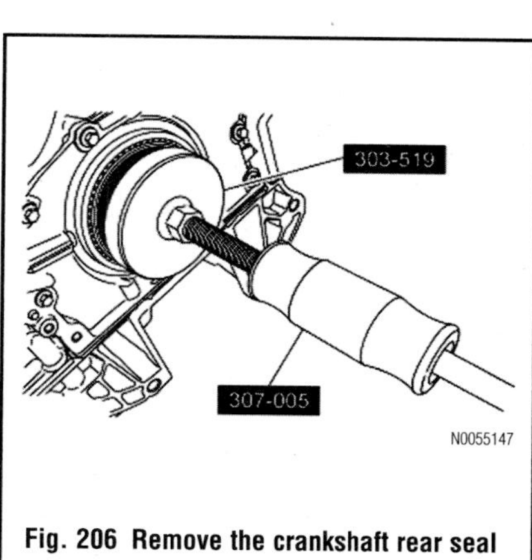

Fig. 206 Remove the crankshaft rear seal

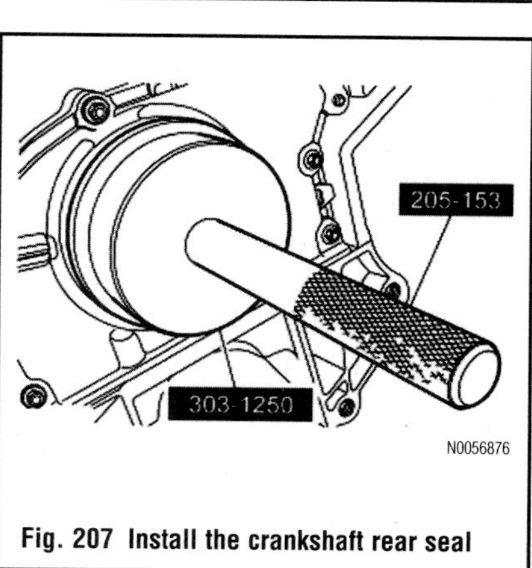

Fig. 207 Install the crankshaft rear seal

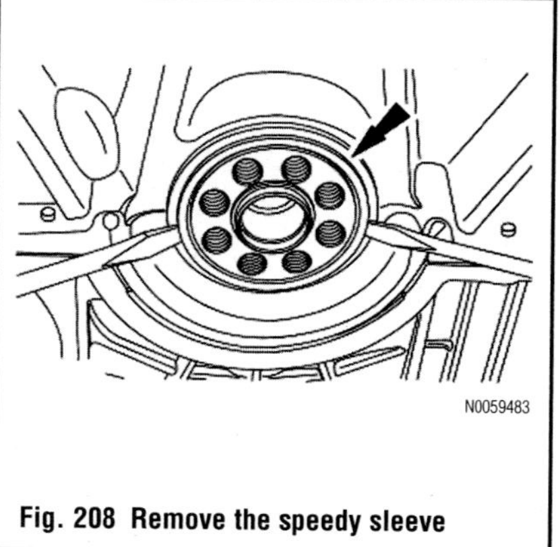

Fig. 208 Remove the speedy sleeve

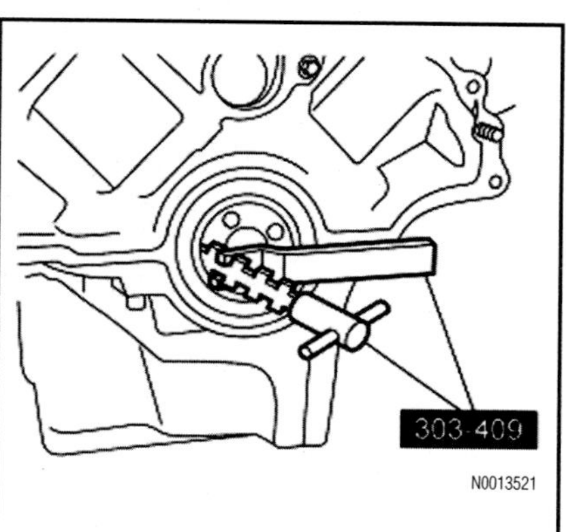

Fig. 209 Using the Oil Seal Remover

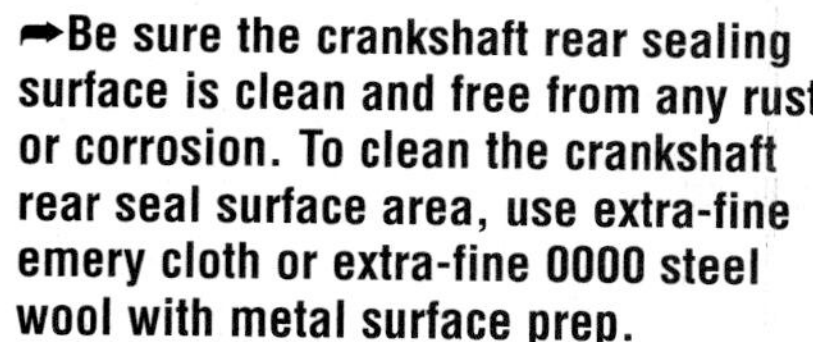

➡Be sure the crankshaft rear sealing surface is clean and free from any rust or corrosion. To clean the crankshaft rear seal surface area, use extra-fine emery cloth or extra-fine 0000 steel wool with metal surface prep.

5. Lubricate the crankshaft rear oil seal with clean engine oil.
6. Install the Crankshaft Rear Oil Seal Screws and Adapter.
7. Position the crankshaft rear seal with speedy sleeve around the Crankshaft Rear Oil Seal Screws and Adapter.
8. Using the Crankshaft Rear Oil Seal Installer, install the crankshaft rear seal with speedy sleeve.
9. Install the flexplate-to-crankshaft spacer.
10. Install the spacer plate.
11. Install the flexplate or flywheel.

4.6L & 5.4L Engines

See Figures 212 through 215.

1. With the vehicle in NEUTRAL, position it on a hoist.
2. Remove the flexplate.
3. Using the Crankshaft Rear Oil Slinger Remover and Slide Hammer, remove the crankshaft oil slinger.

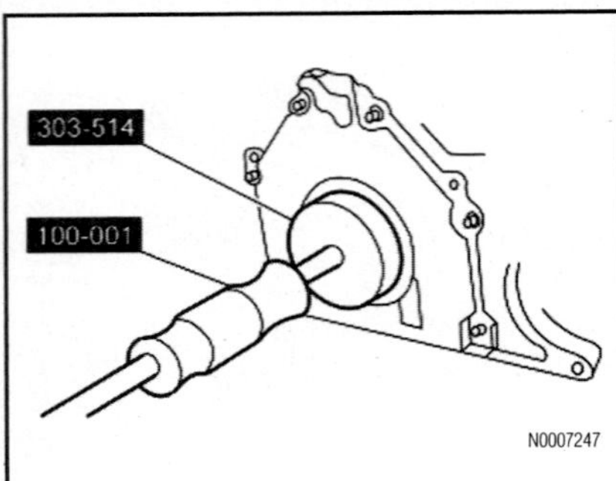

Fig. 212 Remove the crankshaft oil slinger

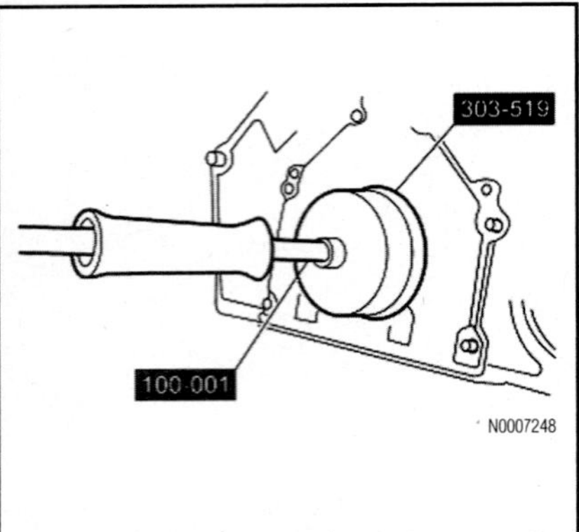

Fig. 213 Remove the crankshaft rear seal

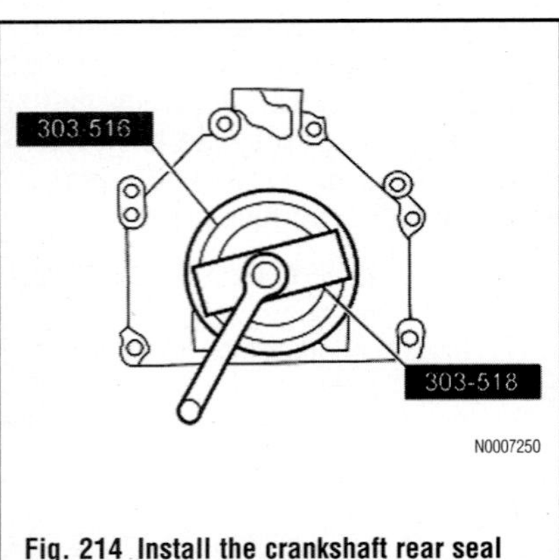

Fig. 214 Install the crankshaft rear seal

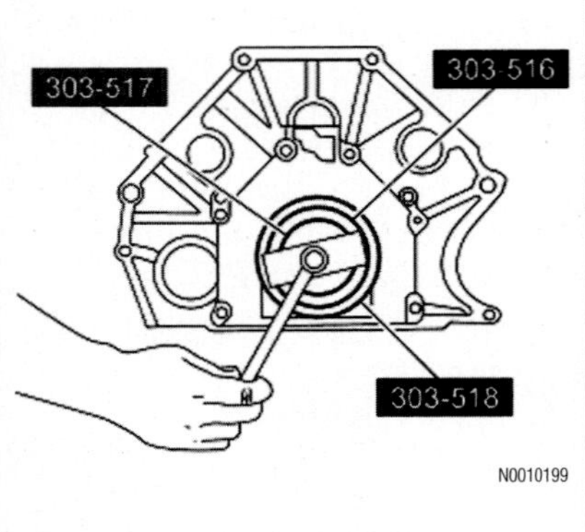

Fig. 215 Install the crankshaft oil slinger

4. Using the Crankshaft Rear Oil Seal Remover and Slide Hammer, remove the crankshaft rear seal.

To install:

➡Lubricate the inner lip of the crankshaft rear seal with engine oil.

5. Using the Crankshaft Rear Oil Seal Installers, install the crankshaft rear seal.
6. Using the Crankshaft Rear Oil Slinger Installer and Crankshaft Rear Oil Seal Installers, install the crankshaft oil slinger.
7. Install the flexplate.

SUPERCHARGER

REMOVAL & INSTALLATION

5.4L Engine

See Figures 216 and 217.

1. Release the fuel system pressure.
2. Disconnect the battery ground cable.
3. Rotate the drive belt tensioner clockwise and detach the drive belt from the Supercharger (SC) pulley.
4. Remove the EGR system module.
5. Remove the fuel rail. For additional information, refer to Fuel System.
6. Disconnect the SC bubbler hose and the SC bypass vacuum actuator vacuum connector.
7. Remove the 10 bolts and the SC.
8. Remove and discard the SC gasket.
9. Cover the lower intake manifold with a shop towel to prevent foreign material from falling into the engine.

To install:

➡Install a new gasket.

10. Position the SC gasket on the lower intake manifold dowels.
11. Position the SC and install the bolts.
12. Tighten the bolts in the sequence shown in 2 stages:

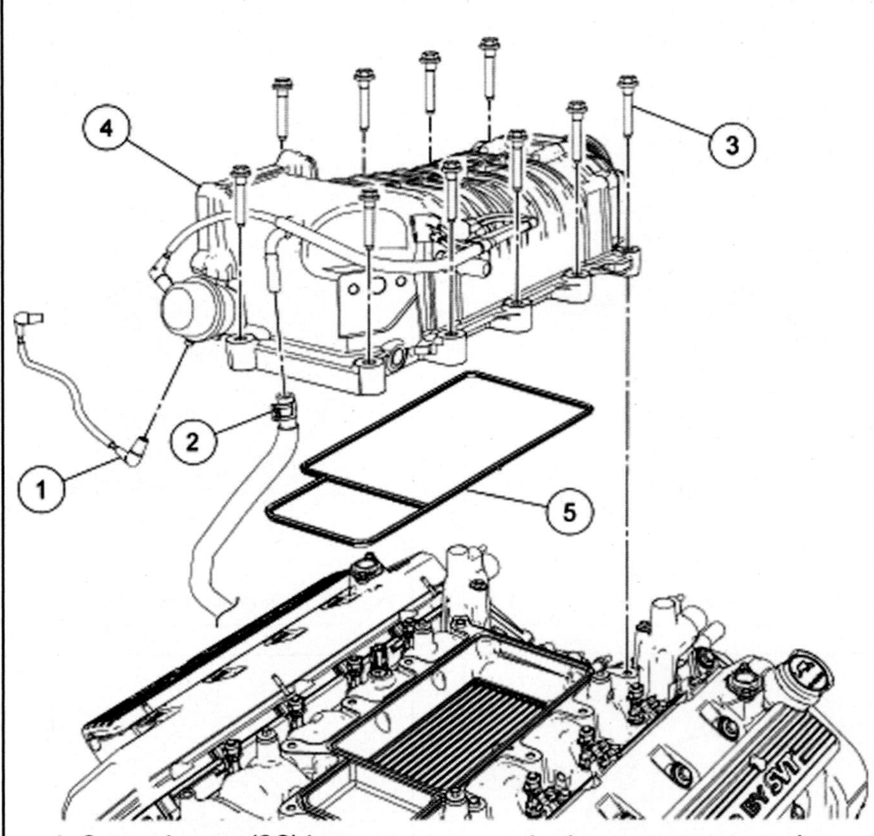

Fig. 216 Exploded view of the supercharger assembly

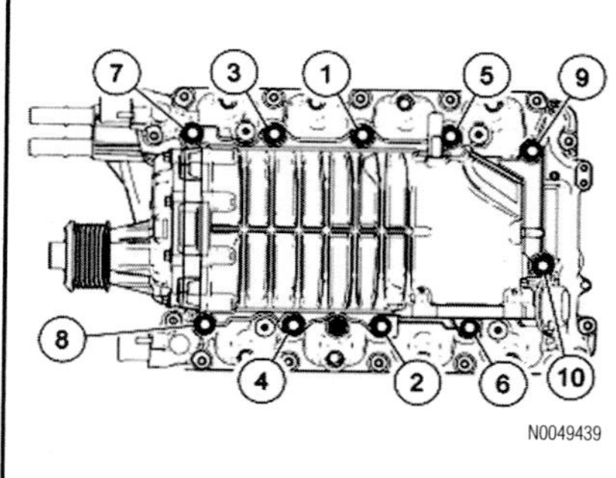

Fig. 217 Supercharger tightening sequence

a. Stage 1: Tighten to 44 inch lbs. (5 Nm).
b. Stage 2: Tighten to 18 ft. lbs. (25 Nm).

13. Connect the SC bubbler hose and the SC bypass vacuum actuator vacuum connector.
14. Install the fuel rail.
15. Install the EGR system module.
16. Rotate the drive belt tensioner clockwise and attach the drive belt to the SC pulley.
17. Connect the battery ground cable.

TIMING CHAIN FRONT COVER

REMOVAL & INSTALLATION

3.7L Engine

See Figures 218 through 223.

➡During engine repair procedures, cleanliness is extremely important. Any foreign material, including any material created while cleaning gasket surfaces that enters the oil passages, coolant passages or the oil pan, may cause engine failure.

1. With the vehicle in NEUTRAL, position it on a hoist.
2. Disconnect the battery ground cable.
3. Remove the LH and RH valve covers. For additional information, refer to Valve Covers in this section.
4. Remove the degas bottle.
5. Remove the drain plug and drain the engine oil.
6. Remove the water pump. For additional information, refer to Engine Cooling.
7. Remove the nut, bolt and position the generator aside.
8. Remove the Alternator stud.
9. Remove the 2 bolts and the accessory drive belt tensioner.
10. Remove the crankshaft front seal. For additional information, refer to Crankshaft Front Seal in this section.

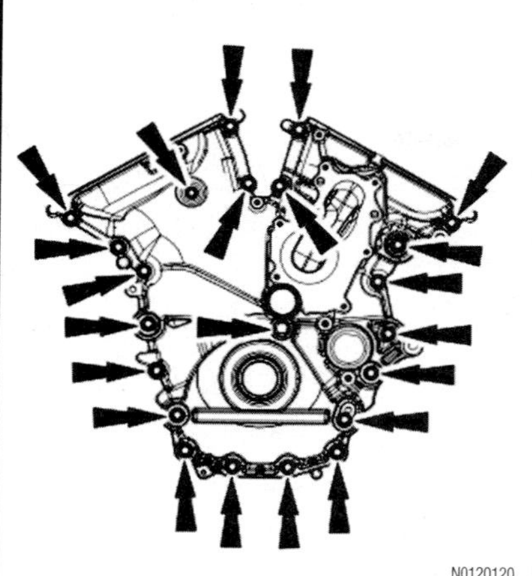

Fig. 218 Locating the 22 engine front cover bolts

11. Remove the 22 engine front cover bolts.
12. Using a suitable pry tool, locate the 7 pry pads shown and pry the engine front cover loose and remove.

➡The front cover radial seal must be replaced.

13. Using the Spindle Bearing Installer and Handle, remove the front cover radial seal from the rear side of the front cover.

To install:

➡Only use a 3M® Roloc® Bristle Disk (2-in white, part number 07528) to clean the engine front cover. Do not use metal scrapers, wire brushes or any other power abrasive disk to clean. These tools cause scratches and gouges that make leak paths.

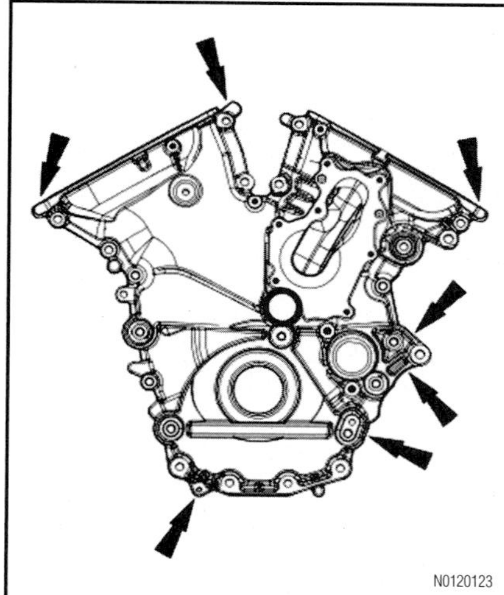

Fig. 219 Locate the 7 pry pads shown

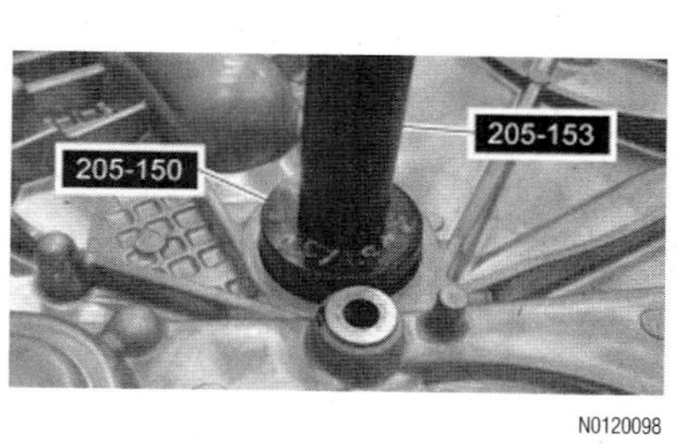

Fig. 220 Using the Spindle Bearing Installer and Handle

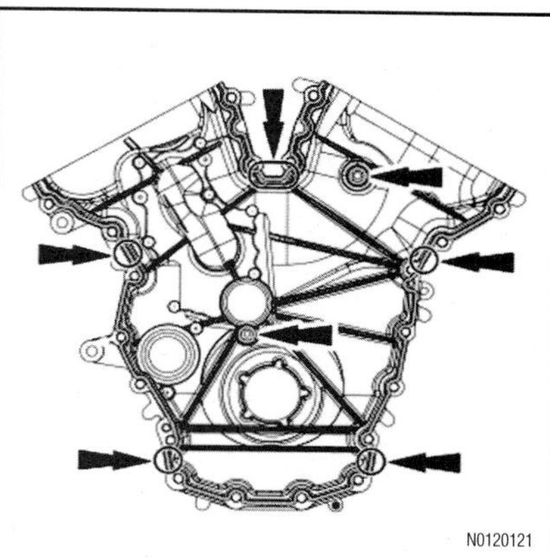

Fig. 221 Locating oil pan-to-cylinder block joint and the cylinder head-to-cylinder block joint areas

14. Clean the engine front cover using a 3M® Roloc® Bristle Disk (2-in white, part number 07528) in a suitable tool turning at the recommended speed of 15,000 rpm.
15. Thoroughly wash the engine front cover to remove any foreign material, including any abrasive particles created during the cleaning process.

➡Place clean, lint-free shop towels over exposed engine cavities. Carefully remove the towels so foreign material is not dropped into the engine. Any foreign material (including any material created while cleaning gasket surfaces) that enters the oil passages or the oil pan may cause engine failure.

➡Do not use wire brushes, power abrasive discs or 3M® Roloc® Bristle Disk (2-in white, part number 07528) to clean the sealing surfaces. These tools cause scratches and gouges that make leak paths.

16. They also cause contamination that causes premature engine failure. Remove all traces of the gasket.

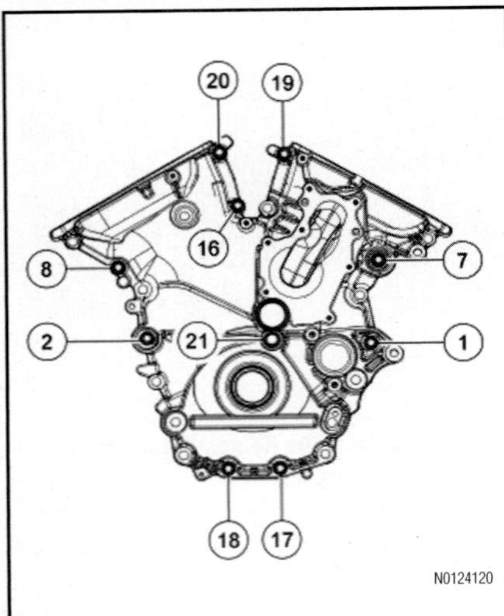

Fig. 222 First pass front cover tightening sequence

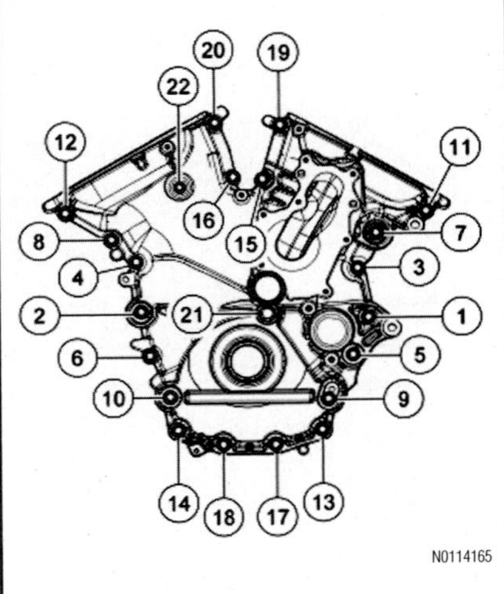

Fig. 223 Second pass front cover tightening sequence

17. Clean the sealing surfaces of the cylinder heads, the cylinder block and the oil pan in the following sequence.
   a. Remove any large deposits of silicone or gasket material.
   b. Apply silicone gasket remover and allow to set for several minutes.
   c. Remove the silicone gasket remover. A second application of silicone gasket remover may be required if residual traces of silicone or gasket material remain.
   d. Apply metal surface prep to remove any remaining traces of oil and to prepare the surfaces to bond. Do not attempt to make the metal shiny. Some staining of the metal surfaces is normal.
   e. Make sure the 2 locating dowel pins are seated correctly in the cylinder block.
18. Using the Spindle Bearing Installer, install the front cover radial seal from the rear side of the front cover.

➡Failure to use Motorcraft® High Performance Engine RTV Silicone may cause the engine oil to foam excessively and result in serious engine damage.

➡The engine front cover and bolts 1, 2, 7, 8, 16, 17, 18, 19, 20 and 21 must be installed within 4 minutes of the initial sealant application. The remainder of the engine front cover bolts and the engine mount bracket bolts must be installed and tightened within 35 minutes of the initial sealant application. If the time limits are exceeded, the sealant must be removed, the sealing area cleaned and sealant reapplied.

To clean the sealing area, use silicone gasket remover and metal surface prep. Failure to follow this procedure can cause future oil leakage.

19. Apply a 0.11 inch bead of Motorcraft® High Performance Engine RTV Silicone to the engine front cover sealing surfaces including the 2 engine front cover bolt bosses.
20. Apply a 0.21 inch bead of Motorcraft® High Performance Engine RTV Silicone to the oil pan-to-cylinder block joint and the cylinder head-to-cylinder block joint areas of the engine front cover in 5 places as indicated.

➡Make sure the 2 locating dowel pins are seated correctly in the cylinder block.

21. Install the engine front cover and bolts 1, 2, 7, 8, 16, 17, 18, 19, 20 and 21. Tighten in sequence to 27 inch lbs. (3 Nm).
22. Install the remaining 12 engine front cover bolts. Tighten all of the engine front cover bolts in the sequence shown in 4 stages:
   a. Stage 1: Tighten bolts 1 through 21 to 7 ft. lbs (10 Nm).
   b. Stage 2: Tighten bolts 1 through 20 to 18 ft. lbs. (24 Nm).
   c. Stage 3: Tighten bolt 21 to 15 ft. lbs. (20 Nm) then an additional 90 degrees.
   d. Stage 4: Tighten bolt 22 to 7 ft. lbs. (10 Nm) then an additional 45 degrees.
23. Install the crankshaft front seal.
24. Install the accessory drive belt tensioner and the 2 bolts.
25. Install the generator stud.
26. Position the generator and install the nut and bolt.
27. Install the coolant pump.
28. Install the degas bottle.
29. Install the LH and RH valve covers.
30. Connect the battery ground cable.

4.0L Engine

See Figures 224 through 226.

➡During engine repair procedures, cleanliness is extremely important. Any foreign material, including any material created while cleaning gasket surfaces that enters the oil passages, coolant passages or the oil pan, can cause engine failure.

1. Drain the cooling system.
2. Remove the crankshaft front oil seal.
3. Disconnect the upper radiator hose.
4. Disconnect the heater hose from the coolant pump.
5. Disconnect the lower radiator hose from the coolant pump.
6. Remove the bolt and the accessory drive belt idler pulley.
7. Disconnect the Crankshaft Position (CKP) sensor and detach the 2 wiring retainers.
8. Remove the 5 engine block cradle-to-engine front cover bolts.

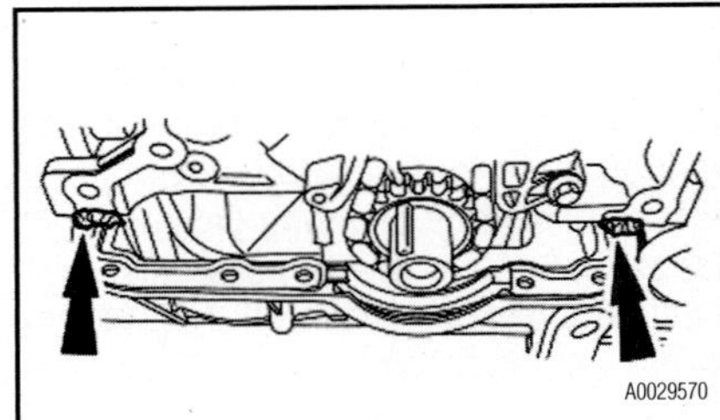

Fig. 224 Locating the oil pan and engine block mating surfaces

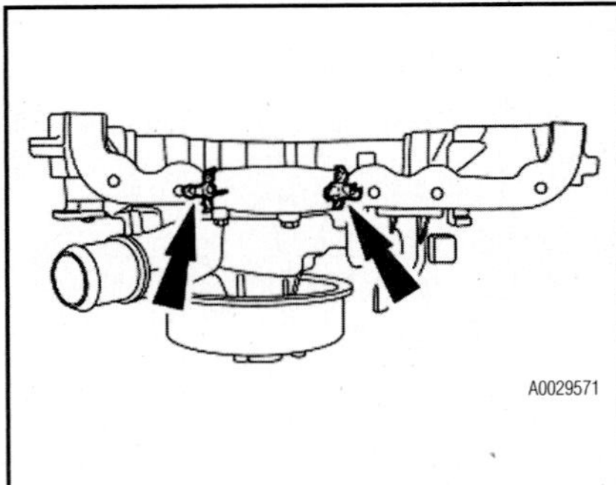

Fig. 225 Apply silicone gasket and sealant to the front cover in 2 places

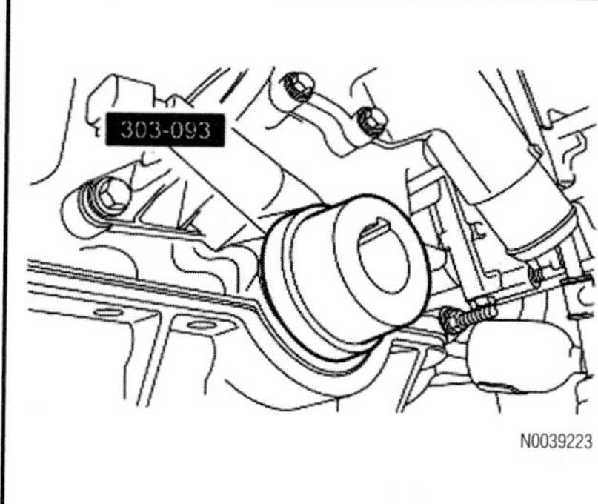

Fig. 226 Use the Front Cover Aligner, align the front cover

9. Remove the 5 bolts and the 5 stud bolts from the engine front cover.

10. Disconnect the coolant bypass hose from the coolant pump and remove the engine front cover.

➡Make sure that any coolant that drains into the front corners of the engine block cradle is removed.

11. Remove the oil pan drain plug and drain the engine oil. Install the drain plug.

To install:

➡Do not use metal scrapers, wire brushes, power abrasive discs or other abrasive means to clean sealing surfaces. These tools cause scratches and gouges which make leak paths.

12. Clean and inspect the gasket mating surfaces. Use silicone gasket remover and metal surface prep and a plastic or wooden scraping tool. Follow the directions on the packaging.

13. Position a new front cover gasket.

➡If not secured within 4 minutes, the sealant must be removed and the sealing area cleaned. To clean the sealing area, use silicone gasket remover and metal surface prep. Follow the directions on the packaging. Failure to follow this procedure can cause future oil leakage.

14. Apply silicone gasket and sealant to the oil pan and engine block mating surfaces.

15. Apply silicone gasket and sealant to the front cover in 2 places.

➡Apply thread sealant to the stud bolts and make sure that the stud bolts are installed in their original positions.

16. Position the front cover and connect the coolant bypass hose to the thermostat housing.

17. Loosely install the 5 bolts and the 5 stud bolts.

18. Use the Front Cover Aligner, align the front cover. Tighten the bolts and stud bolts to 168 inch lbs. (19 Nm).

19. Install the 5 engine block cradle-to-engine front cover bolts. Tighten to 10 ft. lbs. (14 Nm).

20. Connect the CKP sensor and attach the 2 wiring retainers.

21. Install the accessory drive belt idler pulley and the bolt.

22. Connect the lower radiator hose to the coolant pump.

23. Connect the heater hose to the coolant pump.

24. Connect the upper radiator hose.

25. Install the crankshaft front oil seal.

26. Fill the engine with clean engine oil.

27. Fill and bleed the engine cooling system.

4.6L Engine

See Figures 227 through 230.

1. With the vehicle in NEUTRAL, position it on a hoist.

2. Drain the engine oil.

3. Install the drain plug.

4. Remove the engine coolant degas bottle.

5. Remove the RH side idler pulley.

6. Remove the valve covers. For additional information, refer to Valve Cover in this section.

7. Disconnect the upper coolant hose from the engine.

8. Remove the nut and position aside the RH radio ignition interference capacitor.

9. Disconnect the RH Camshaft Position (CMP) sensor electrical connector.

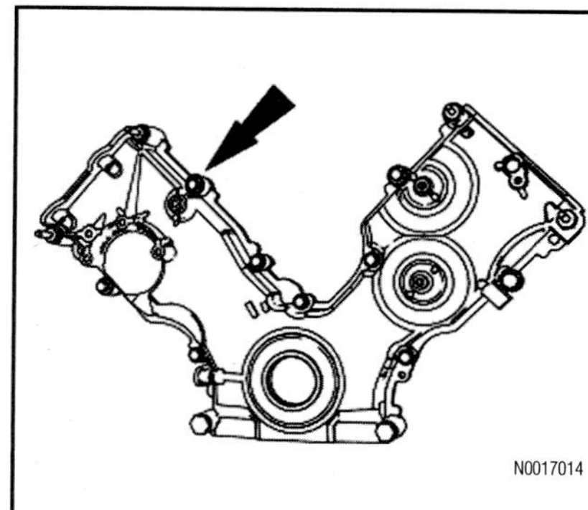

Fig. 227 Locating the front cover bolts

10. Remove the nut and position aside the LH radio ignition interference capacitor.

11. Remove the 4 bolts and the coolant pump pulley.

12. Remove the wiring harness retainer from the power steering stud bolt.

13. Remove the 3 stud bolts and position the power steering pump aside.

14. Support the power steering pump with a length of mechanic's wire.

15. Disconnect the Crankshaft Position (CKP) sensor electrical connector.

16. Remove the crankshaft pulley bolt and washer.

17. Discard the crankshaft pulley bolt.

18. Using the 3 Jaw Puller, remove the crankshaft pulley.

19. Using the Crankshaft Front Oil Seal Remover, remove the crankshaft front oil seal.

20. Remove the 4 front oil pan bolts.

21. Remove the bolts and the stud bolts.

➡Do not use metal scrapers, wire brushes, power abrasive discs or other abrasive means to clean the sealing surfaces. These tools cause scratches and gouges which make leak paths. Use a plastic scraping tool to remove all traces of old sealant.

22. Remove the engine front cover from the front cover to cylinder block dowel.

23. Remove the engine front cover gaskets.

24. Clean the mating surfaces with silicone gasket remover and metal surface prep. Follow the directions on the packaging.

25. Inspect the mating surfaces.

To install:

➡Do not use metal scrapers, wire brushes, power abrasive discs or other abrasive means to clean the sealing surfaces. These tools cause scratches and gouges which make leak paths. Use a plastic scraping tool to remove all traces of old sealant.

➡If the engine front cover is not secured within 4 minutes, the sealant must be removed and the sealing area cleaned. To clean the sealing area, use silicone gasket remover and metal surface prep. Follow the directions on the packaging. Failure to follow this procedure can cause future oil leakage.

➡Make sure that the engine front cover gasket is in place on the engine front cover before installation.

26. Apply a bead of silicone gasket and sealant along the cylinder head-to-cylinder

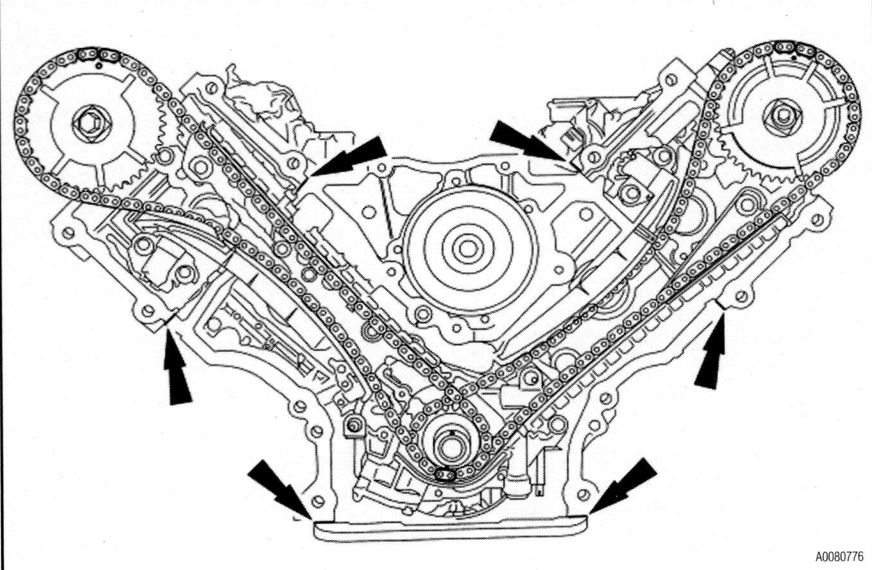

Fig. 228 Locating the cylinder head-to-cylinder block surface and the oil pan-to-cylinder block surfaces

block surface and the oil pan-to-cylinder block surface, at the locations shown.

27. Install a new engine front cover gasket on the engine front cover. Position the engine front cover onto the dowels. Install the fasteners finger-tight.

28. Tighten the engine front cover fasteners in the sequence shown to 18 ft. lbs. (25 Nm).

29. Loosely install the 4 bolts, then tighten the bolts in 2 stages, in the sequence shown.

a. Stage 1: Tighten to 15 ft. lbs. (20 Nm).

b. Stage 2: Tighten an additional 60 degrees.

30. Lubricate the engine front cover and the crankshaft front oil seal inner lip with clean engine oil.

31. Using the Crankshaft Vibration Damper Installer, Crankshaft Front Oil Seal Installer and the Front Cover Oil Seal Installer, install the crankshaft front oil seal.

➡If not secured within 4 minutes, the sealant must be removed and the sealing area cleaned with silicone gasket remover and metal surface prep. Allow to dry until there is no sign of wetness, or 4 minutes, whichever is longer. Failure to follow this procedure can cause future oil leakage.

32. Apply silicone gasket and sealant to the Woodruff key slot in the crankshaft pulley.

33. Using the Crankshaft Vibration Damper Installer, install the crankshaft pulley.

34. Using a new crankshaft pulley bolt, install the bolt and washer and tighten the bolt in 4 stages.

a. Stage 1: Tighten to 66 ft. lbs. (90 Nm).

b. Stage 2: Loosen 360 degrees.

c. Stage 3: Tighten to 37 ft. lbs. (50 Nm).

d. Stage 4: Tighten an additional 90 degrees.

35. Connect the CKP sensor electrical connector.

36. Position the power steering pump assembly and install the stud bolts. Tighten to 18 ft. lbs. (25 Nm).

37. Install the wiring retainer on the power steering stud bolt.

38. Install the LH radio ignition interference capacitor and nut onto the engine front cover stud bolt. Tighten to 18 ft. lbs. (25 Nm).

39. Install the coolant pump pulley and the 4 bolts. Tighten to 18 ft. lbs. (25 Nm).

40. Connect the RH CMP sensor electrical connector.

41. Install the RH radio ignition interference capacitor and the nut. Tighten to 18 ft. lbs. (25 Nm).

42. Connect the upper coolant hose to the engine.

43. Install the valve covers.

44. Install the accessory drive belt tensioner and 3 idler pulleys.

45. Fill the crankcase with clean engine oil.

46. Install the engine coolant degas bottle.

5.0L Engine

See Figures 231 and 232.

1. With the vehicle in NEUTRAL, position it on a hoist.
2. Release the fuel system pressure.
3. Disconnect the battery ground cable.
4. Drain the engine cooling system.
5. Remove the valve covers. For additional information, refer to Valve Covers in this section.
6. Remove the engine coolant degas bottle.
7. Remove the cooling fan motor and shroud.
8. Remove the accessory drive and A/C compressor belts.
9. Disconnect the lower radiator hose from the thermostat housing assembly.
10. Remove the 2 thermostat housing bolts.
11. Release the clamp and position the upper radiator hose T-connector/thermostat housing assembly aside.
12. Remove and discard the thermostat housing O-ring seal.
13. Disconnect the heater hose.
14. Remove the 4 bolts and the coolant pump pulley.
15. Remove the 4 bolts and the coolant pump.
16. Remove and discard the O-ring seal.
17. Disconnect the throttle body and Evaporative Emission (EVAP) purge valve electrical connectors.
18. Detach the 3 wiring harness retainers from the engine front cover and stud bolt.
19. Remove the bolt and the accessory drive belt tensioner.
20. Remove the nut, the bolt and position the generator aside.
21. Remove the crankshaft pulley bolt and washer.
22. Using the 3 Jaw Puller and the crankshaft pulley bolt, remove the crankshaft pulley.
23. Discard the crankshaft pulley bolt.

➡Use care not to damage the engine front cover or the crankshaft when removing the seal.

24. Using the Oil Seal Remover, remove the crankshaft front oil seal.
25. Remove the 3 bolts and lower the underbody shield.
26. Remove the 2 wiring harness retainer nuts from the front oil pan stud bolts.
27. Remove the 2 front oil pan stud bolts and 2 front oil pan bolts.
28. Remove the 13 engine front cover bolts and the 2 stud bolts.

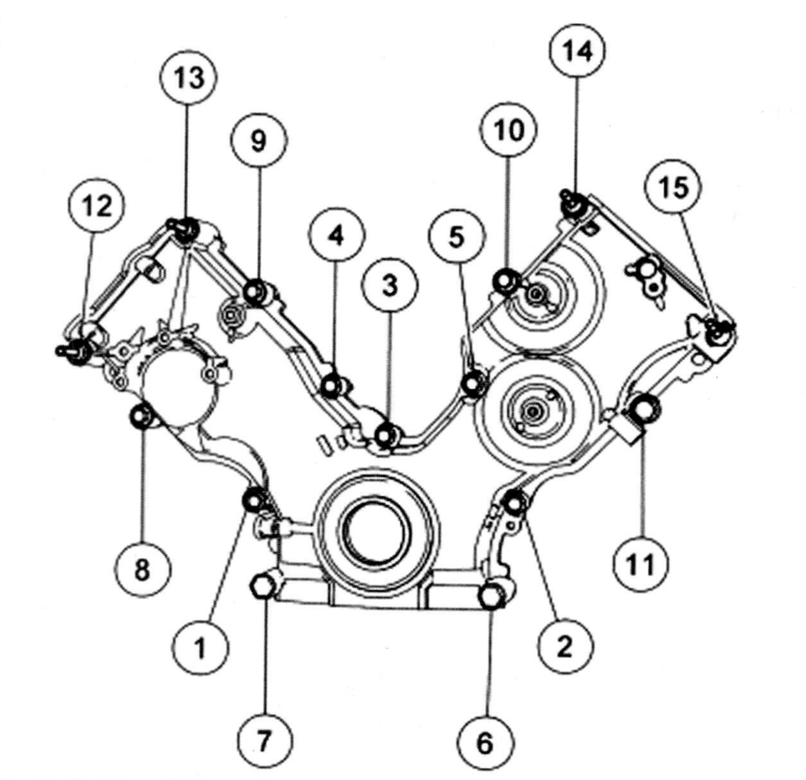

1. Bolt, Hex Flange Head Pilot, M8 x 1.25 x 53
2. Bolt, Hex Flange Head Pilot, M8 x 1.25 x 53
3. Bolt, Hex Flange Head Pilot, M8 x 1.25 x 53
4. Bolt, Hex Flange Head Pilot, M8 x 1.25 x 53
5. Bolt, Hex Flange Head Pilot, M8 x 1.25 x 53
6. Stud, Hex Shoulder Pilot, M8 x 1.25 x 50 - M6 x 1 x 10
7. Stud and Washer, Hex Head Pilot, M8 x 1.25 - M6 x 1 x 86.35
8. Bolt, Hex Flange Head Pilot, M8 x 1.25 x 53
9. Bolt, Hex Flange Head Pilot, M8 x 1.25 x 53
10. Bolt, Hex Flange Head Pilot, M8 x 1.25 x 53
11. Bolt, Hex Flange Head Pilot, M8 x 1.25 x 53
12. Stud, Hex Shoulder Pilot, M8 x 1.25 x 1.25 x 91.1
13. Stud, Hex Shoulder Pilot, M8 x 1.25 x 1.25 x 91.1
14. Stud, Hex Shoulder Pilot, M8 x 1.25 x 1.25 x 91.1
15. Stud, Hex Shoulder Pilot, M8 x 1.25 x 1.25 x 91.1

N0017013

Fig. 229 Front cover tightening sequence

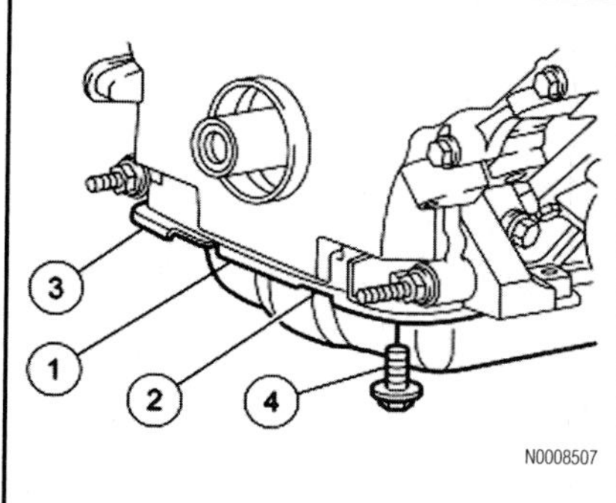

Fig. 230 Loosely install the 4 bolts, then tighten the bolts in 2 stages, in the sequence

Fig. 231 Identifying cylinder head-to-cylinder block joints and the oil pan-to-cylinder block joints

➡Do not use metal scrapers, wire brushes, power abrasive discs or other abrasive means to clean the sealing surfaces. These tools cause scratches and gouges which make leak paths. Use a plastic scraping tool to remove all traces of old sealant.

29. Remove the engine front cover from the front cover to cylinder block dowel.

30. Remove and discard the engine front cover gaskets.

31. Clean the mating surfaces with silicone gasket remover and metal surface prep. Follow the directions on the packaging.

32. Inspect the mating surfaces.

33. Drain the engine oil. Install the drain plug.

To install:

➡The Variable Camshaft Timing (VCT) variable force solenoid pins must be fully depressed to avoid interference with the VCT valve tips when installing the engine front cover. Failure to follow these instructions can result in damage to the engine.

34. Fully depress the VCT variable force solenoid pins.

➡The engine front cover must be installed and all fasteners final tightened within 5 minutes of applying the sealer. If this cannot be accomplished, install the engine front cover and tighten fasteners 6, 7, 8, 9, 10 and 11 to 70 inch lbs. (8 Nm) within 5 minutes of applying the sealer. All of the fasteners must then be final tightened within 1 hour of applying the sealer. If this time limit is exceeded, all sealant must be removed and the sealing area cleaned. To clean the sealing area, use silicone gasket remover and metal surface prep. Follow the directions on the packaging. Failure to follow this procedure can cause future oil leakage.

35. Apply a bead of silicone gasket and sealant to the cylinder head-to-cylinder block joints and the oil pan-to-cylinder block joints as illustrated.

➡Make sure that the engine front cover gaskets are in place on the engine front cover before installation.

Using new gaskets, position the engine front cover onto the dowels.

36. Install the 13 engine front cover bolts, 2 stud bolts and the 4 oil pan-to-engine front cover bolts finger-tight.

➡The engine front cover must be installed and all fasteners final tightened within 5 minutes of applying the sealer. If this cannot be accomplished, install the engine front cover and tighten fasteners 6, 7, 8, 9, 10 and 11 to 71 inch lbs. within 5 minutes of applying the sealer. All of the fasteners must then be final tightened within 1 hour of applying the sealer. If this time limit is exceeded, all sealant must be removed and the sealing area cleaned. To clean the sealing area, use silicone gasket remover and metal surface prep. Follow the directions on the packaging. Failure to follow this procedure can cause future oil leakage.

37. Tighten the bolts in the sequence shown in 2 stages.
   a. Stage 1: Tighten bolts 1-15 to 18 ft. lbs. (25 Nm) and bolts 16-19 to 89 inch lbs. (10 Nm).
   b. Stage 2: Tighten bolts 1-15 an additional 60 degrees and bolts 16-19 an additional 45 degrees.

38. Position the wiring harness and install the 2 wiring harness retainer nuts to the front oil pan stud bolts.

Position the underbody shield and install the 3 bolts.

Tighten to 89 inch lbs. (10 Nm).

➡Lubricate the engine front cover bore and the crankshaft front oil seal inner lip with clean engine oil.

39. Using the Front Crank Seal and Damper Installer and the Front Cover Oil Seal Installer (plate only), install the crankshaft front oil seal.

➡If not secured within 5 minutes, the sealant must be removed and the sealing area cleaned with silicone gasket remover and metal surface prep. Failure to follow this procedure can cause future oil leakage.

40. Apply silicone gasket and sealant to the Woodruff key slot in the crankshaft pulley.

41. Lubricate the crankshaft pulley sealing surface with clean engine oil prior to installation.

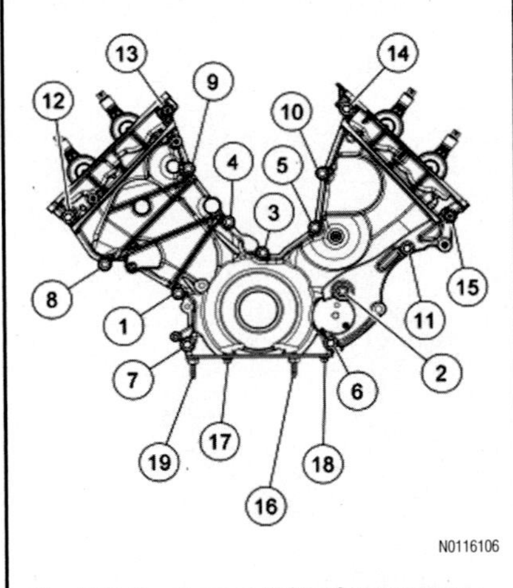

Fig. 232 Front cover tightening sequence

42. Using the Front Crank Seal and Damper Installer and the Front Cover Oil Seal Installer (plate only), install the crankshaft pulley.

43. Using the Strap Wrench, install a new crankshaft pulley bolt and the original washer, tighten the bolt in 4 stages:
   a. Stage 1: Tighten to 103 ft. lbs. (140 Nm).
   b. Stage 2: Loosen 360 degrees.
   c. Stage 3: Tighten to 74 ft. lbs. (100 Nm).
   d. Stage 4: Tighten an additional 90 degrees.

44. Install the alternator, the bolt and the nut. Refer to Engine Electrical.

45. Install the accessory drive belt tensioner and bolt. Tighten to 35 ft. lbs. (48 Nm).

46. Attach the 3 wiring harness retainers to the engine front cover and stud bolt.

47. Connect the throttle body and Evaporative Emission (EVAP) purge valve electrical connectors.

➡Lubricate the new coolant pump O-ring seal with clean engine coolant.

48. Using a new O-ring seal, install the water pump. Refer to Engine Cooling.

49. Connect the heater hose.

➡Lubricate the new thermostat housing O-ring seal with clean engine coolant.

50. Install the thermostat. Refer to Engine Cooling.

51. Connect the lower radiator hose to the thermostat housing assembly.

52. Install the accessory drive and A/C compressor belts.

53. Install the cooling fan motor and shroud. For additional information, refer to Engine Cooling.

54. Install the engine coolant degas bottle. For additional information, refer to Engine Cooling.

55. Install the RH and LH valve covers.

56. Fill the crankcase with clean engine oil.

57. Connect the battery ground cable.

58. Fill and bleed the engine cooling system.

59. After completing the repairs, use the scan tool to perform the Misfire Monitor Neutral Profile Correction procedure following the on-screen instructions.

5.4L Engine

See Figures 233 through 237.

1. With the vehicle in NEUTRAL, position it on a hoist.
2. Release the fuel system pressure.
3. Remove the engine coolant degas bottle.
4. Remove the Supercharger (SC) coolant degas bottle.
5. Remove the valve covers. For additional information, refer to Valve Covers
6. Remove the water pump. Refer to Engine Cooling.
7. Remove the SC drive belt, SC drive belt tensioner and the 3 SC drive belt idler pulleys. For additional information, refer to Accessory Drive.
8. Remove the thermostat housing. For additional information, refer to Engine Cooling.
9. Remove the crankshaft front seal. For additional information, refer to Front Seal in this section.
10. Disconnect the 2 coolant vent hoses from the intake manifold.
11. Disconnect the 2 upper radiator hoses from the intake manifold.
12. Disconnect the coolant hoses from the Charge Air Cooler (CAC).
13. Disconnect the lower radiator hose assembly from the coolant pump, radiator, oil filter adapter and the coolant tube assembly (located above the generator).
14. Remove the lower radiator hose assembly from the vehicle.
15. Disconnect the A/C pressure transducer electrical connector.
16. Disconnect the Crankshaft Position (CKP) sensor electrical connector.
17. Install the Engine Lifting Brackets.

➡The heavy duty Engine Support Bar (303-F070) must be used with the draw screws from the light duty Engine Support Bar (303-F072). This will provide enough clearance between the SC and the Engine Support Bar, and enough

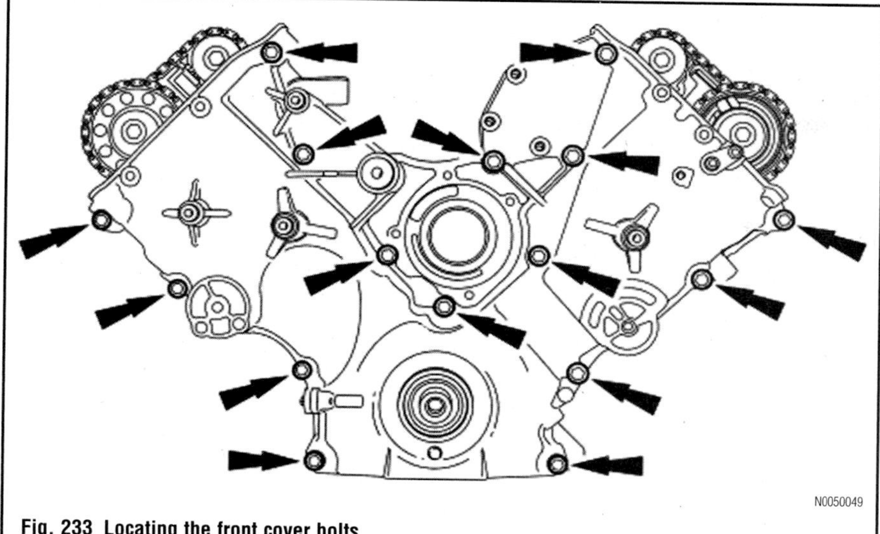

Fig. 233 Locating the front cover bolts

clearance between the draw screw and the vehicle hood.

18. Install the Engine Support Bars.
19. Remove the LH and RH engine support insulator nuts.
20. Using the Engine Support Bars, raise the engine.
21. Remove the 3 bolts and lower the underbody shield.
22. Remove the alternator. Refer to Engine Electrical.
23. Disconnect the coolant hose from the oil filter adapter.

➡If metal or aluminum material is present in the oil cooler, mechanical concerns exist.

24. Remove the 6 bolts and the oil cooler.
25. Discard the gaskets.
26. Inspect the oil cooler.
27. Drain the engine oil. Tighten the drain plug.
28. Remove and discard the engine oil filter.
29. Remove the 3 coolant tube assembly bolts.
30. Disconnect the Engine Oil Pressure (EOP) switch electrical connector and the 2 wiring harness pin-type retainers.
31. Remove the 8 bolts and the oil filter adapter.
32. Discard the gasket.
33. Remove the oil pan-to-engine front cover bolt and the 3 oil pan-to-engine front cover stud bolts.

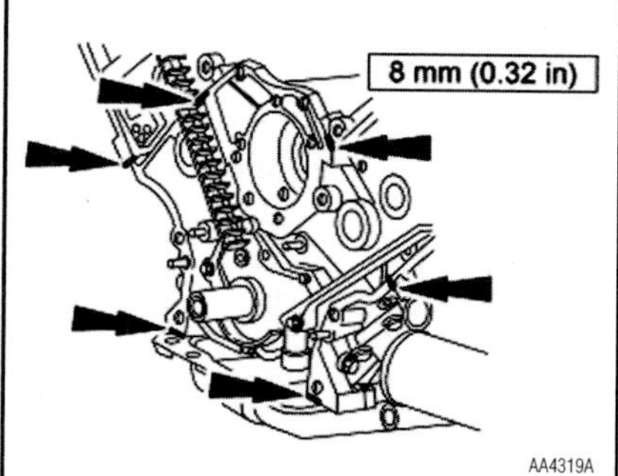

Fig. 234 Locating cylinder head-to-cylinder block joints and the oil pan-to-cylinder block joints

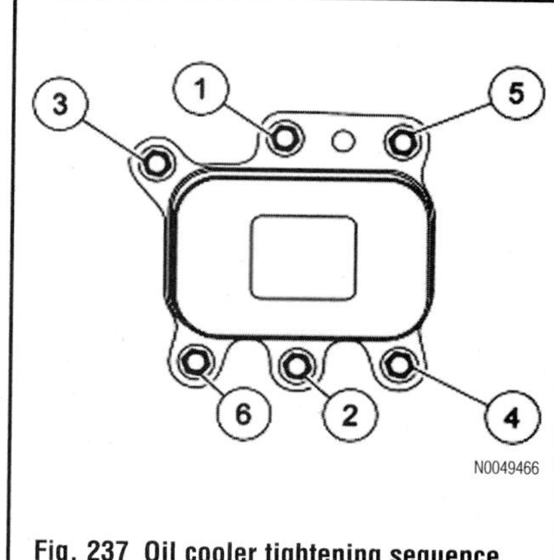

Fig. 237 Oil cooler tightening sequence

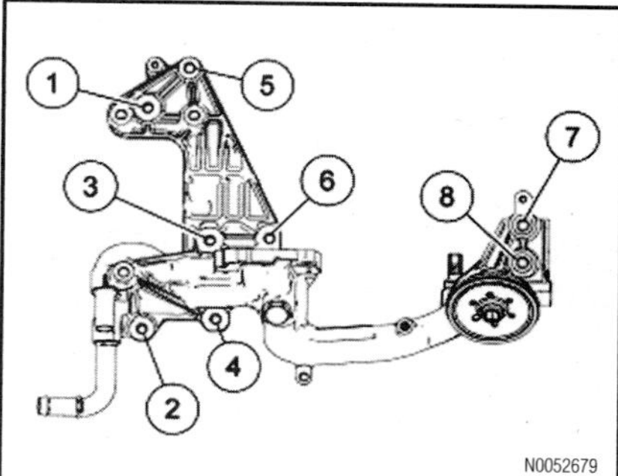

Fig. 236 Oil filter adapter tightening sequence

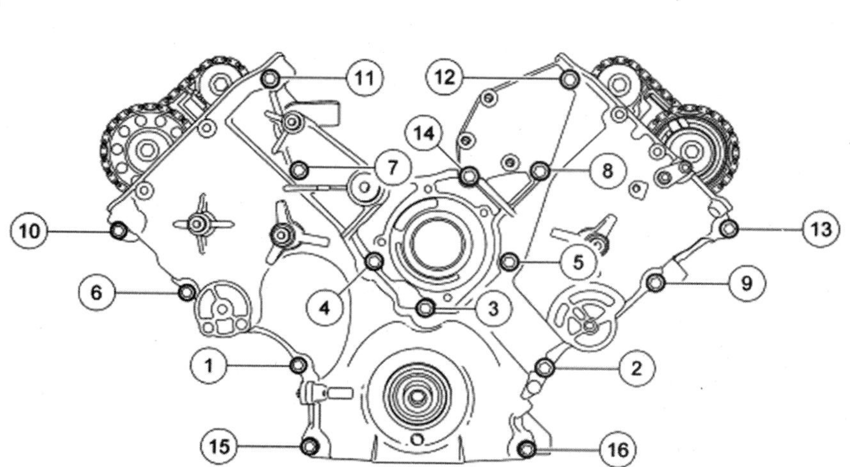

Fig. 235 Front cover tightening sequence

34. Remove the 4 bolts and the coolant pump.

Discard the gasket.

35. Remove the 16 bolts and the engine front cover.

36. Remove and discard the engine front cover gaskets.

➡Do not use metal scrapers, wire brushes, power abrasive discs or other abrasive means to clean the sealing surfaces. These tools cause scratches and gouges which make leak paths. Use a plastic scraping tool to remove all traces of old sealant.

37. Clean the mating surfaces with silicone gasket remover and metal surface prep. Follow the directions on the packaging.

38. Inspect the mating surfaces.

To install:

➡The engine front cover must be installed and all fasteners final tightened within 5 minutes of applying the sealer. If this cannot be accomplished, install the engine front cover and tighten fasteners 6, 7, 8, 9, 10 and 11 to 71 inch lbs. within 5 minutes of applying the sealer. All of the fasteners must then be final tightened within 1 hour of applying the sealer. If this time limit is exceeded, all sealant must be removed and the sealing area cleaned. To clean the sealing area, use silicone gasket remover and metal surface prep.

39. Follow the directions on the packaging. Failure to follow this procedure can cause future oil leakage.

40. Apply a bead of silicone sealer to the cylinder head-to-cylinder block joints and the oil pan-to-cylinder block joints as illustrated.

➡Make sure that the engine front cover gaskets are in place on the engine front cover before installation.

41. Using new gaskets, position the engine front cover onto the dowels and install the 16 bolts. Tighten the bolts in the sequence shown:

a. Bolts 1 through 14 to 18 ft. lbs. (25 Nm).

b. Bolts 15 and 16 to 37 ft. lbs. (50 Nm).

42. Install the oil pan-to-engine front cover bolt and the 3 oil pan-to-engine front cover stud bolts. Tighten to 18 ft. lbs. (25 Nm).

43. Using a new gasket, install the coolant pump and the 4 bolts. Tighten 18 ft. lbs. (25 Nm).

➡Clean and inspect the sealing surfaces with metal surface prep. Follow the directions on the packaging.

44. Using a new gasket, install the oil filter adapter and the 8 bolts.

45. Tighten in the sequence shown:

a. Bolts 1 through 6 to 18 ft. lbs. (25 Nm).

b. Bolts 7 and 8 to 37 ft. lbs. (50 Nm).

46. Connect the EOP switch electrical connector and the 2 wiring harness pin-type retainers.

47. Install the 3 coolant tube assembly bolts. Tighten to 7 ft. lbs. (10 Nm).

48. Install a new engine oil filter in the following sequence.

49. Lubricate the oil filter gasket with clean engine oil and tighten until the seal makes contact.

50. Using an oil filter strap wrench, tighten the filter an additional 270 degrees.

➡Clean the sealing surfaces with metal surface prep. Follow the directions on the packaging. Inspect the mating surfaces.

51. Using new gaskets, install the oil cooler and the 6 bolts. Tighten in the sequence shown to 89 inch lbs. (10 Nm).

52. Connect the coolant hose to the oil filter adapter.

53. Install the alternator. Refer to Engine Electrical.

54. Position the underbody shield and install the 3 bolts.

55. Using the Engine Support Bars, lower the engine onto the engine support insulators.

56. Install the LH and RH engine support insulator nuts. Tighten to 46 ft. lbs. (63 Nm).

57. Connect the CKP sensor electrical connector.

58. Connect the A/C pressure transducer electrical connector.

59. Install the lower radiator hose assembly to the coolant pump, radiator, oil filter adapter and the coolant tube assembly (located above the generator).

60. Connect the coolant hoses from the CAC.

61. Connect the 2 upper radiator hoses to the intake manifold.

62. Connect the 2 coolant vent hoses to the intake manifold.

63. Install the crankshaft front seal. For additional information, refer to Front Seal in this section.

64. Install the thermostat housing. For additional information, refer to Engine Cooling.

65. Install the 3 SC drive belt idler pulleys, SC drive belt and the SC drive belt tensioner. For additional information, refer to Accessory Drive.

66. Install the coolant pump pulley and the 4 bolts.

67. Install the 2 accessory drive belt idler pulleys, the accessory drive belt tensioner and the accessory drive belt. For additional information, refer to Accessory Drive.

68. Tighten the 4 coolant pump pulley bolts to 18 ft. lbs. (25 Nm).

69. Install the valve covers. For additional information, refer to Valve Cover in this section.

70. Install the SC coolant degas bottle. For additional information, refer to Supercharger Cooling.

71. Install the engine coolant degas bottle. For additional information, refer to Engine Cooling.

72. Fill the engine with clean engine oil.

73. Fill and bleed the SC cooling system. For additional information, refer to Supercharger Cooling.

74. Fill and bleed the engine cooling system. For additional information, refer to Engine Cooling.

75. After completing the repairs, use the scan tool to perform the Misfire Monitor Neutral Profile Correction procedure following the on-screen instructions.

TIMING CHAIN & SPROCKETS

REMOVAL & INSTALLATION

3.7L Engine

See Figures 238 through 253.

➡During engine repair procedures, cleanliness is extremely important. Any foreign material, including any material created while cleaning gasket surfaces, that enters the oil passages, coolant passages or the oil pan may cause engine failure.

1. With the vehicle in NEUTRAL, position it on a hoist.

2. Remove the Timing Chain Front Cover. For additional information, refer to Timing Chain Front Cover in this section.

3. Rotate the crankshaft clockwise and align the timing marks on the intake Variable Camshaft Timing (VCT) assemblies as shown.

4. Remove the 3 bolts and the LH valve train oil tube.

5. The Camshaft Holding Tool will hold the camshafts in the Top Dead Center (TDC) position.

6. Install the Camshaft Holding Tool onto the flats of the LH camshafts.

7. Remove the 3 bolts and the RH valve train oil tube.

➡The Camshaft Holding Tool will hold the camshafts in the TDC position.

8. Install the Camshaft Holding Tool onto the flats of the RH camshafts.

➡The following 3 steps are for primary timing chains that the colored links are not visible.

9. Mark the timing chain link that aligns with the timing mark on the LH intake VCT assembly.

10. Mark the timing chain link that aligns with the timing mark on the RH intake VCT assembly.

➡The crankshaft sprocket timing mark should be between the 2 colored links.

11. Mark the 2 timing chain links that align with the timing mark on the crankshaft sprocket as shown.

12. Remove the 2 bolts and the primary timing chain tensioner.

N0117971

Fig. 238 Rotate the crankshaft clockwise and align the timing marks on the intake Variable Camshaft Timing

N0120881

Fig. 239 Mark the 2 timing chain links that align with the timing mark on the crankshaft sprocket

13. Remove the primary timing chain tensioner arm.

14. Remove the 2 bolts and the lower LH primary timing chain guide.

➡Removal of the VCT oil control solenoid will aid in the removal of the primary timing chain.

➡A slight twisting motion will aid in the removal of the VCT oil control solenoid.

➡Keep the VCT oil control solenoid clean of dirt and debris.

15. Remove the bolt and the LH intake VCT oil control solenoid.

➡Removal of the VCT oil control solenoid will aid in the removal of the primary timing chain.

➡A slight twisting motion will aid in the removal of the VCT oil control solenoid.

➡Keep the VCT oil control solenoid clean of dirt and debris.

16. Remove the bolt and the RH intake VCT oil control solenoid.

17. Remove the primary timing chain.

18. Remove the crankshaft timing chain sprocket.

➡Do not use power tools to remove the bolt or damage to the LH primary timing chain guide may occur.

19. Remove the bolt and the upper LH primary timing chain guide.

➡The 2 VCT oil control solenoids are removed for clarity.

➡The Secondary Chain Hold Down is inserted through a hole in the top of the mega cap.

20. Compress the LH secondary timing chain tensioner and install the Secondary Chain Hold Down in the hole on the rear of the secondary timing chain tensioner guide and let it hold against the mega cap to retain the tensioner in the collapsed position.

21. Remove and discard the 2 LH VCT assembly bolts.

22. Remove the 2 LH VCT assemblies and secondary timing chain.

➡The Secondary Chain Hold Down is inserted through a hole in the top of the mega cap.

23. Compress the RH secondary timing chain tensioner and install the Secondary Chain Hold Down in the hole on the rear of the secondary timing chain tensioner guide and let it hold against the mega cap to retain the tensioner in the collapsed position.

24. Remove and discard the 2 RH VCT assembly bolts.

25. Remove the 2 RH VCT assemblies and secondary timing chain.

➡Do not use power tools to remove the bolt or damage to the RH primary timing chain guide may occur.

26. Remove the bolt and the RH primary timing chain guide.

27. Remove the 9 bolts and the channel cover plate. Discard the gasket.

28. Engines with secondary timing chain tensioner removed:

➡The following steps are only for the replacement of the secondary timing chain tensioners. Do not reuse the secondary timing chain tensioners if removed, or damage to the engine may occur.

➡A slight twisting motion will aid in the removal of the VCT oil control solenoid.

➡Keep the VCT oil control solenoid clean of dirt and debris.

29. Remove the LH exhaust VCT oil control solenoid.

30. Remove the LH secondary timing chain tensioner shoe.

31. Remove the LH secondary timing chain tensioner by pushing up from the bottom and remove.

➡A slight twisting motion will aid in the removal of the VCT oil control solenoid.

➡Keep the VCT oil control solenoid clean of dirt and debris.

32. Remove the RH exhaust VCT oil control solenoid.

33. Remove the RH secondary timing chain tensioner shoe.

34. Remove the RH secondary timing chain tensioner by pushing up from the bottom and remove.

To install:

35. Using a new gasket, install the channel cover plate and the 9 bolts. Tighten in the sequence shown in 2 stages:

a. Stage 1: Tighten to 89 inch lbs. (10 Nm).

b. Stage 2: Tighten an additional 45 degrees.

36. Install the RH primary timing chain guide and the bolt. Tighten to 7 ft. lbs. (10 Nm).

37. Engines with secondary timing chain tensioner removed:

➡The following steps are only for the replacement of the secondary timing chain tensioners. Do not reuse the secondary timing chain tensioners if removed or damage to the engine may occur.

➡Apply clean engine oil to the secondary timing chain tensioner O-ring seals and mega cap bore.

➡Do not remove the secondary timing chain tensioner shipping clip, until instructed to do so.

38. Install the RH secondary timing chain tensioner by pushing it down all the way until a snap is heard and the tensioner is seated all the way down the mega cap bore.
39. Install the RH secondary timing chain tensioner shoe.
40. Remove and discard the RH secondary timing chain tensioner shipping clip.
41. Assemble the RH Variable Camshaft Timing (VCT) assembly, the RH exhaust camshaft sprocket and the RH secondary timing chain. Align the colored links with the timing marks.

➡It may be necessary to rotate the camshafts slightly, to install the RH secondary timing assembly.

N0118136

Fig. 240 Remove the bolt and the LH intake VCT oil control solenoid—LH shown, RH is similar

N0118123

Fig. 241 Remove the crankshaft timing chain sprocket

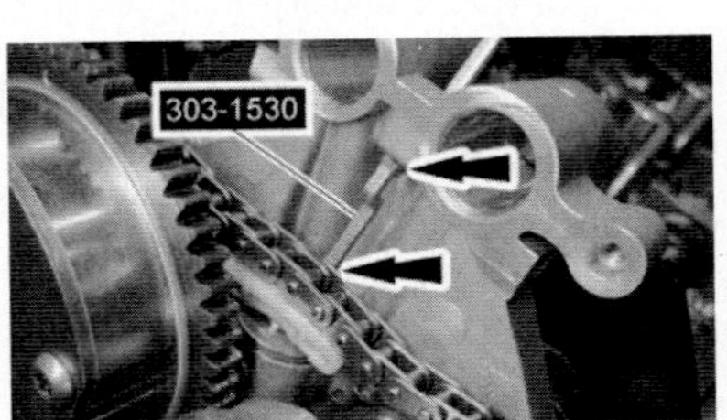

N0118130

Fig. 242 Install the Secondary Chain Hold Down in the hole on the rear of the secondary timing chain tensioner guide—LH shown, RH similar

N0118537

Fig. 243 Remove the 2 LH VCT assemblies and secondary timing chain

N0124121

Fig. 244 Remove the 9 bolts and the channel cover plate

N0124122

Fig. 245 Channel cover plate tightening sequence

N0118676

Fig. 246 Install the RH secondary timing chain tensioner by pushing it down—LH similar

N0118735

Fig. 247 Install the RH secondary timing chain tensioner shoe—LH similar

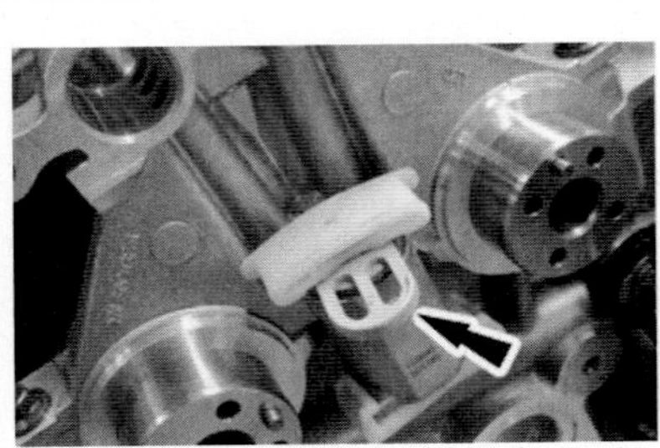

N0118736

Fig. 248 Remove and discard the RH secondary timing chain tensioner shipping clip—LH similar

N0118117

Fig. 249 Align the colored links with the timing marks—RH side

Fig. 250 Aligning the holes in the VCT assemblies with the dowel pins in the camshafts

Fig. 251 Align the colored links with the timing marks—LH side

Position the 2 RH VCT assemblies and secondary timing chain onto the camshafts by aligning the holes in the VCT assemblies with the dowel pins in the camshafts.

42. Install the 2 new RH VCT bolts and tighten in 4 stages.
   a. Stage 1: Tighten to 30 ft. lbs. (40 Nm).
   b. Stage 2: Loosen one full turn.
   c. Stage 3: Tighten to 18 ft. lbs. (25 Nm).
   d. Stage 4: Tighten an additional 180 degrees.
43. Activate the RH secondary timing chain tensioner by pressing down on the secondary tensioner shoe until it bottoms out, let go of the tensioner and it will spring up putting tension on the chain.

➡Do not use excessive force when installing the Variable Camshaft Timing (VCT) oil control solenoid. Damage to the mega cap could cause the cylinder head to be inoperable. If difficult to install the VCT oil control solenoid, inspect the bore and VCT oil control solenoid to ensure there are no burrs, sharp edges or contaminants present on the mating surface. Only clean the external surfaces as necessary.

➡A slight twisting motion will aid in the installation of the VCT oil control solenoid.

➡Keep the VCT oil control solenoid clean of dirt and debris.

44. Install the RH exhaust VCT oil control solenoid. Tighten to 71 inch lbs. (8 Nm) then an additional 20 degrees.

➡Apply clean engine oil to the secondary timing chain tensioner O-ring seals and mega cap bore.

➡Do not remove the secondary timing chain tensioner shipping clip, until instructed to do so.

45. Install the LH secondary timing chain tensioner by pushing it down all the way until a snap is heard and the tensioner is seated all the way down the mega cap bore.
46. Install the LH secondary timing chain tensioner shoe.
47. Remove and discard the LH secondary timing chain tensioner shipping clip.
48. Assemble the 2 LH VCT assemblies and the LH secondary timing chain.
49. Align the colored links with the timing marks.

➡It may be necessary to rotate the camshafts slightly, to install the LH secondary timing assembly.

50. Position the 2 LH VCT assemblies and secondary timing chain onto the camshafts by aligning the holes in the VCT assemblies with the dowel pins in the camshafts.
51. Install the 2 new LH VCT bolts and tighten in 4 stages.
   a. Stage 1: Tighten to 30 ft. lbs. (40 Nm).
   b. Stage 2: Loosen one full turn.
   c. Stage 3: Tighten to 18 ft. lbs. (25 Nm).
   d. Stage 4: Tighten an additional 180 degrees.
52. Activate the LH secondary timing chain tensioner by pressing down on the secondary tensioner shoe until it bottoms out, let go of the tensioner and it will spring up putting tension on the chain.

➡Do not use excessive force when installing the Variable Camshaft Timing (VCT) oil control solenoid. Damage to the mega cap could cause the cylinder head to be inoperable. If difficult to install the VCT oil control solenoid, inspect the bore and VCT oil control solenoid to ensure there are no burrs, sharp edges or contaminants present on the mating surface. Only clean the external surfaces as necessary.

➡A slight twisting motion will aid in the installation of the VCT oil control solenoid.

➡Keep the VCT oil control solenoid clean of dirt and debris.

53. Install the LH exhaust VCT oil control solenoid. Tighten to 71 inch lbs. (8 Nm) then an additional 20 degrees.
54. Engines with secondary timing chain tensioner not removed:
55. Compress the RH secondary timing chain tensioner and install the Secondary Chain Hold Down to retain the tensioner in the collapsed position.
56. Assemble the RH VCT assembly, the RH exhaust camshaft sprocket and the RH secondary timing chain.
57. Align the colored links with the timing marks.

➡It may be necessary to rotate the camshafts slightly, to install the RH secondary timing assembly.

58. Position the 2 RH VCT assemblies and secondary timing chain onto the camshafts by aligning the holes in the VCT assemblies with the dowel pins in the camshafts.
59. Install the 2 new RH VCT bolts and tighten in 4 stages.
   a. Stage 1: Tighten to 30 ft. lbs. (40 Nm).
   b. Stage 2: Loosen one full turn.
   c. Stage 3: Tighten to 18 ft. lbs. (25 Nm).
   d. Stage 4: Tighten an additional 180 degrees.
60. Compress the RH secondary timing chain tensioner and remove the Secondary Chain Hold Down.
61. Make sure the secondary timing chain is centered on the timing chain tensioner guides.
62. Compress the LH secondary timing chain tensioner and install the Secondary Chain Hold Down to retain the tensioner in the collapsed position.
63. Assemble the 2 LH VCT assemblies and the LH secondary timing chain.
64. Align the colored links with the timing marks.

➡It may be necessary to rotate the camshafts slightly, to install the LH secondary timing assembly.

65. Position the 2 LH VCT assemblies

and secondary timing chain onto the camshafts by aligning the holes in the VCT assemblies with the dowel pins in the camshafts.

66. Install the 2 new LH VCT bolts and tighten in 4 stages.
   a. Stage 1: Tighten to 30 ft. lbs. (40 Nm).
   b. Stage 2: Loosen one full turn.
   c. Stage 3: Tighten to 18 ft. lbs. (25 Nm).
   d. Stage 4: Tighten an additional 180 degrees.
67. Compress the LH secondary timing chain tensioner and remove the Secondary Chain Hold Down.
68. Make sure the secondary timing chain is centered on the timing chain tensioner guides.
69. All engines:
70. Install the upper LH primary timing chain guide and the bolt. Tighten to 7 ft. lbs. (10 Nm).
71. Install the crankshaft timing chain sprocket with timing dot mark out.

➡It may be necessary to rotate the camshafts slightly, to align the timing marks.

72. Install the primary timing chain with the colored links aligned with the timing marks on the VCT assemblies and the crankshaft sprocket.
73. Install the lower LH primary timing chain guide and the 2 bolts. Tighten to 7 ft. lbs. (10 Nm).
74. Install the primary timing chain tensioner arm.
75. Reset the primary timing chain tensioner:
   a. Release the ratchet detent.
   b. Using a soft-jawed vise, compress the ratchet plunger.
   c. Align the hole in the ratchet plunger with the hole in the tensioner housing.
   d. Install a suitable lockpin.

➡It may be necessary to rotate the camshafts slightly to remove slack from the timing chain to install the tensioner.

76. Install the primary tensioner and the 2 bolts. Tighten to 7 ft. lbs. (10 Nm).
77. Remove the lockpin.
78. As a post-check, verify correct alignment of all timing marks.
79. There are 48 links in between the RH intake VCT assembly colored link and the LH intake VCT assembly colored link.
80. There is 35 links in between LH intake VCT assembly colored link and the 2 crankshaft sprocket links.

➡Do not use excessive force when installing the Variable Camshaft Timing (VCT) oil control solenoid. Damage to the mega cap could cause the cylinder head to be inoperable. If difficult to install the VCT oil control solenoid, inspect the bore and VCT oil control solenoid to ensure there are no burrs, sharp edges or contaminants present on the mating surface. Only clean the external surfaces as necessary.

➡A slight twisting motion will aid in the installation of the VCT oil control solenoid.

➡Keep the VCT oil control solenoid clean of dirt and debris.

81. Install the LH intake VCT oil control solenoid and the bolt. Tighten to 71 inch lbs. (8 Nm) then an additional 20 degrees.

➡Do not use excessive force when installing the Variable Camshaft Timing (VCT) oil control solenoid. Damage to the mega cap could cause the cylinder head to be inoperable. If difficult to install the VCT oil control solenoid, inspect the bore and VCT oil control solenoid to ensure there are no burrs, sharp edges or contaminants present on the mating surface. Only clean the external surfaces as necessary.

➡A slight twisting motion will aid in the installation of the VCT oil control solenoid.

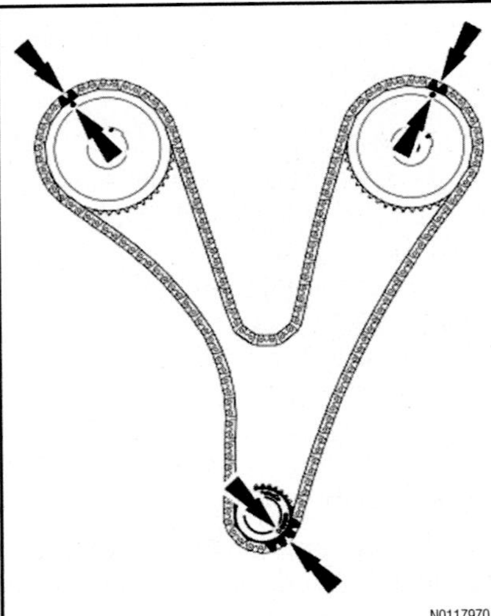

Fig. 252 Install the primary timing chain with the colored links aligned with the timing marks on the VCT

Fig. 253 Resetting the primary timing chain tensioner

➡Keep the VCT oil control solenoid clean of dirt and debris.

82. Install the RH intake VCT oil control solenoid and the bolt. Tighten to 71 inch lbs. (8 Nm) then an additional 20 degrees.
83. Remove the RH Camshaft Holding Tool.
84. Install the RH valve train oil tube and the 3 bolts and tighten in 2 stages.
   a. Stage 1: Tighten to 71 inch lbs. (8 Nm).
   b. Stage 2: Tighten an additional 45 degrees.
85. Remove the LH Camshaft Holding Tool.
86. Install the LH valve train oil tube and the 3 bolts and tighten in 2 stages.
   a. Stage 1: Tighten to 71 inch lbs. (8 Nm).
   b. Stage 2: Tighten an additional 45 degrees.
87. Install the engine front cover. For additional information, refer to Timing Chain Front Cover in this section.

4.0L Engine

See Figures 254 and 255.

1. Release the fuel system pressure. For additional information, refer to Fuel System.
2. Disconnect the battery ground cable.
3. Remove the intake manifold. For additional information, refer to Intake Manifold in this section.

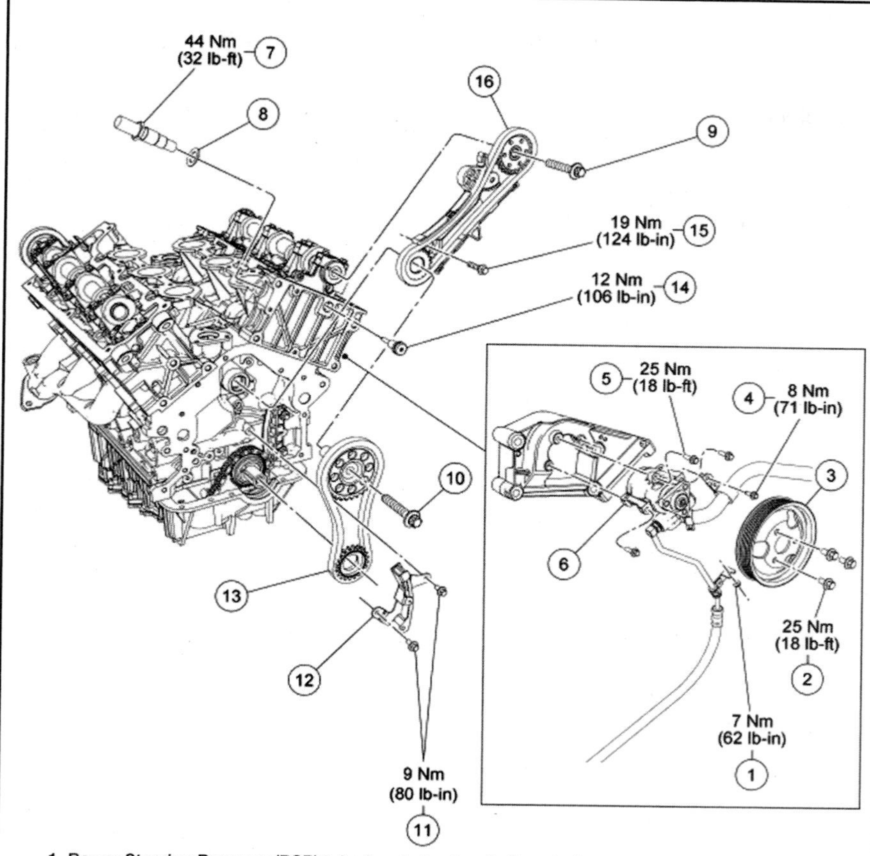

1. Power Steering Pressure (PSP) tube bracket nut
2. Power steering pump pulley bolt (3 required)
3. Power steering pump pulley
4. Suction hose bracket bolt
5. Power steering pump bolt (3 required)
6. Power steering pump
7. Hydraulic chain tensioner
8. LH hydraulic chain tensioner washer
9. Camshaft sprocket bolt
10. Jackshaft sprocket bolt
11. Jackshaft chain tensioner bolts
12. Jackshaft chain tensioner
13. Primary chain and sprocket assembly
14. LH cassette-to-cylinder head bolt
15. LH cassette-to-cylinder block bolt
16. Timing chain and guide assembly

N0085181

Fig. 254 Exploded view of the timing chain assembly

4. Remove the timing chain cover. For additional information, refer to Timing Chain Cover in this section.
5. Remove all of the roller followers. For additional information, refer to Camshaft Roller Follower in this section.

➡The LH and RH camshafts must be retimed when either camshaft is disturbed.

6. Turn the crankshaft clockwise to position the No. 1 cylinder at Top Dead Center (TDC).
7. Remove the LH hydraulic chain tensioner.
8. Remove and discard the washer.
9. Remove the LH camshaft sprocket bolt.
10. Install the Camshaft Sprocket Holding Tool and Adapter and tighten to 7 ft. lbs (10 Nm).
11. Remove the LH camshaft sprocket bolt.
12. Using the Crankshaft Holding Tool, prevent the crankshaft from turning, remove the jackshaft sprocket bolt.
13. Remove the 2 bolts and the primary chain tensioner.
14. Remove the primary chain and sprockets as an assembly.
15. Remove the suction hose bracket bolt.
16. Remove the Power Steering Pressure (PSP) tube bracket nut.
17. Remove the 3 bolts and the power steering pump pulley.
18. Remove the 3 bolts and position the power steering pump aside.
19. Remove the LH cassette upper bolt.
20. Remove the LH cassette lower bolt and the LH cassette.

To install:

➡The camshaft chain sprockets must be oriented correctly.

21. Position the LH cassette.
22. Install the LH cassette lower bolt. Tighten to 9 ft. lbs. (12 Nm).
23. Install the LH cassette upper bolt. Tighten to 14 ft. lbs. (19 Nm).
24. Position the power steering pump and install the 3 bolts. Tighten to 18 ft. lbs. (25 Nm).
25. Install the power steering pump pulley and the 3 bolts. Tighten to 18 ft. lbs. (25 Nm).
26. Install the PSP tube bracket nut. Tighten to 62 inch lbs. (7 Nm).
27. Install the suction hose bracket bolt. Tighten to 71 inch lbs. (8 Nm).
28. Install the primary chain and sprockets as an assembly.
29. Install the jackshaft chain tensioner and the 2 bolts. Tighten to 80 inch lbs. (9 Nm).
30. Using the Crankshaft Holding Tool, prevent the crankshaft from turning, tighten the jackshaft sprocket bolt in 2 stages.
    a. Stage 1: Tighten to 33 ft. lbs. (45 Nm).
    b. Stage 2: Tighten an additional 90 degrees.
31. Loosely install the camshaft sprocket bolt.
32. Install the engine front cover. For additional information, refer to Timing Chain Front Cover in this section.

➡The LH and RH camshafts must be retimed when either camshaft is disturbed.

➡The LH hydraulic chain tensioner will be installed during camshaft timing.

33. Retime the LH and RH camshafts. For additional information, refer to Camshaft Timing in this section.
34. Install the camshaft roller followers. For additional information, refer to Camshaft Roller Follower in this section.

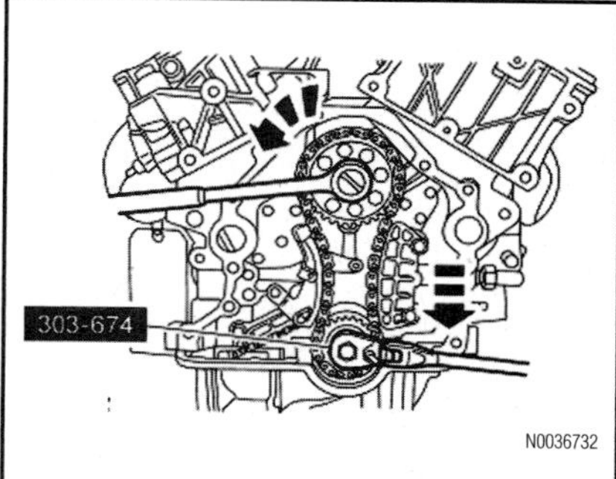

N0036732

Fig. 255 Using the Crankshaft Holding Tool

35. Install the intake manifold. For additional information, refer to Intake Manifold in this section.
36. Connect the battery ground cable. For additional information, refer to Battery, Mounting and Cables.
37. Fill and bleed the engine cooling system. For additional information, refer to Engine Cooling.

4.6L Engine

See Figures 256 through 266.

1. Remove the engine front cover. For additional information, refer to Timing Chain Cover in this section.
2. Remove the crankshaft sensor ring from the crankshaft.
3. Position the crankshaft keyway at the 12 o'clock position.

➡If the camshaft lobes are not exactly positioned as shown, the crankshaft will require one full additional rotation to 12 o'clock.

4. The No. 1 cylinder must be coming up on the exhaust stroke with the crankshaft keyway at the 12 o'clock position. Verify by noting the position of the 2 intake lobes and the exhaust lobe on the No. 1 cylinder.

➡If the components are to be reinstalled, they must be installed in their original positions. Mark the components for installation into their original locations. Failure to follow these instructions may result in engine damage.

5. Remove only the 3 roller followers shown in the illustration from the RH cylinder head.

➡Do not allow the valve keepers to fall off the valve or the valve may drop into the cylinder. If a valve drops into the cylinder, the cylinder head must be removed. For additional information, refer to Cylinder Head in this section.

➡It may be necessary to push the valve down while compressing the spring.

6. Using the Valve Spring Compressor, remove the 3 roller followers designated in the previous step from the RH cylinder head. Refer to Camshafts in this sections.

➡If the components are to be reinstalled, they must be installed in their original positions. Mark the components for installation into their original locations. Failure to follow these instructions may result in engine damage.

7. Remove only the 3 roller followers shown in the illustration from the LH cylinder head.

➡Do not allow the valve keepers to fall off the valve or the valve may drop into the cylinder. If a valve drops into the cylinder, the cylinder head must be removed. For additional information, refer to Cylinder Head in this section.

➡It may be necessary to push the valve down while compressing the spring.

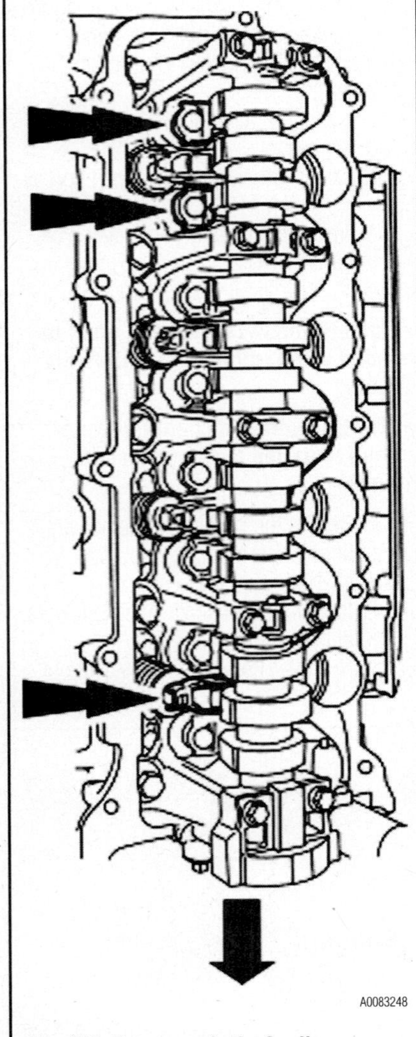

Fig. 256 Remove only the 3 roller followers shown

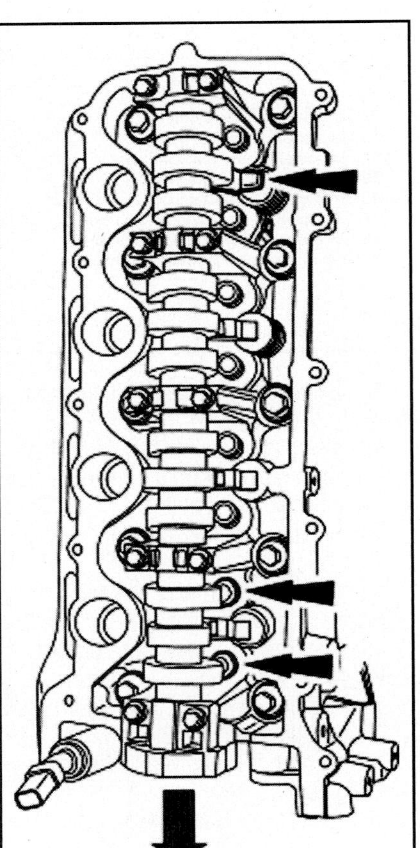

Fig. 257 Remove only the 3 roller followers shown—LH cylinder head

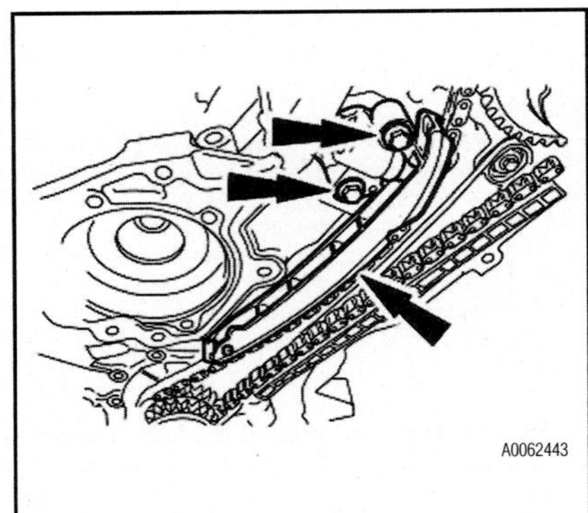

Fig. 258 Remove the bolts, the LH timing chain tensioner and tensioner arm

Fig. 259 Remove the bolts, the RH timing chain tensioner and tensioner arm

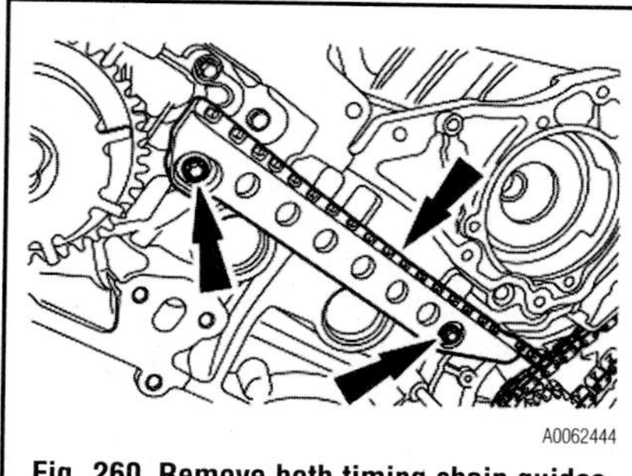

Fig. 260 Remove both timing chain guides

A0029147

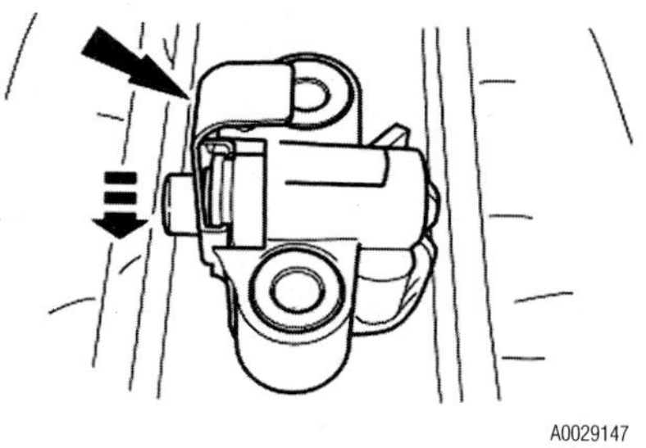

Fig. 261 Install a retaining clip on the tensioner

8. Using the Valve Spring Compressor, remove the 3 roller followers designated in the previous step from the LH cylinder head.

➡**The crankshaft cannot be moved past the 6 o'clock position once set or engine damage may occur.**

9. Rotate the crankshaft clockwise and position the crankshaft keyway at the 6 o'clock position.
10. Remove the bolts, the LH timing chain tensioner and tensioner arm.
11. Remove the bolts, the RH timing chain tensioner and tensioner arm.
12. Remove the RH and LH timing chains and the crankshaft sprocket.
13. Remove the RH timing chain from the camshaft sprocket.
14. Remove the RH timing chain from the crankshaft sprocket.
15. Remove the LH timing chain from the camshaft sprocket.
16. Remove the LH timing chain and crankshaft sprocket.
17. Remove the LH and RH timing chain guides.
18. Remove the bolts.
19. Remove both timing chain guides.

➡**Damage to the camshaft phaser sprocket assembly will occur if mishandled or used as a lifting or leveraging device.**

➡**Only use hand tools to remove the camshaft phaser sprocket assembly or damage may occur to the camshaft or camshaft phaser unit.**

20. Using the Cam Phaser Locking Tool, remove the bolt and the RH camshaft phaser sprocket assembly.
21. Discard the camshaft phaser sprocket bolt.

➡**Damage to the camshaft phaser sprocket assembly will occur if mishandled or used as a lifting or leveraging device.**

➡**Only use hand tools to remove the camshaft phaser sprocket assembly or damage may occur to the camshaft or camshaft phaser unit.**

22. Remove the camshafts. Refer to Camshafts in this section.
23. Remove all of the remaining roller followers from the cylinder heads.

To install:

24. Install the LH and RH camshafts. Refer to Camshafts in this section.

➡**If one or both of the tensioner mounting bolts are loosened or removed, the tensioner-sealing bead must be inspected for seal integrity. If cracks, tears, separation from the tensioner body or permanent compression of the seal bead is observed, install a new tensioner or engine damage may occur.**

25. Inspect the RH and LH timing chain tensioners.
26. Install new tensioners as necessary.

➡**Timing chain procedures must be followed exactly or damage to valves and pistons will result.**

27. Compress the tensioner plunger, using a vise.

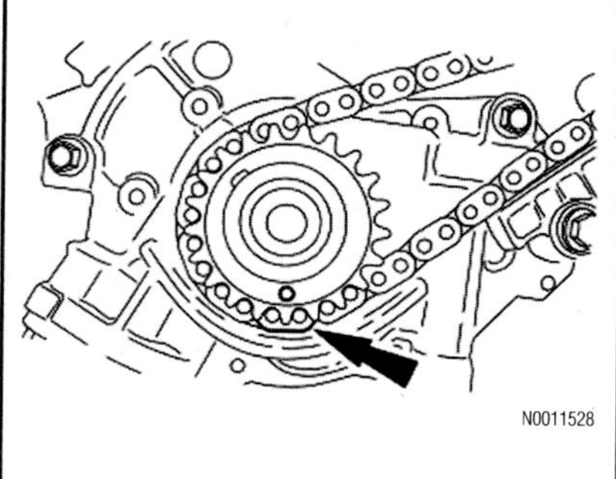

Fig. 262 Position the lower end of the LH (inner) timing chain

28. Install a retaining clip on the tensioner to hold the plunger in during installation.
29. Remove the tensioner from the vise.
30. If the colored links are not visible, mark one link on one end and one link on the other end and use as timing marks.
31. Install the 4 bolts and the LH and RH timing chain guides. Tighten to 7 ft. lbs. (10 Nm).
32. Position the lower end of the LH (inner) timing chain on the crankshaft sprocket, aligning the timing mark on the outer flange of the crankshaft sprocket with the single colored (marked) link on the chain.

➡**Make sure the upper half of the timing chain is below the tensioner arm dowel.**

33. Position the LH timing chain on the camshaft sprocket. Make sure the camshaft sprocket timing mark is aligned with the colored (marked) chain link.

➡**The LH timing chain tensioner arm has a bump near the dowel hole for identification.**

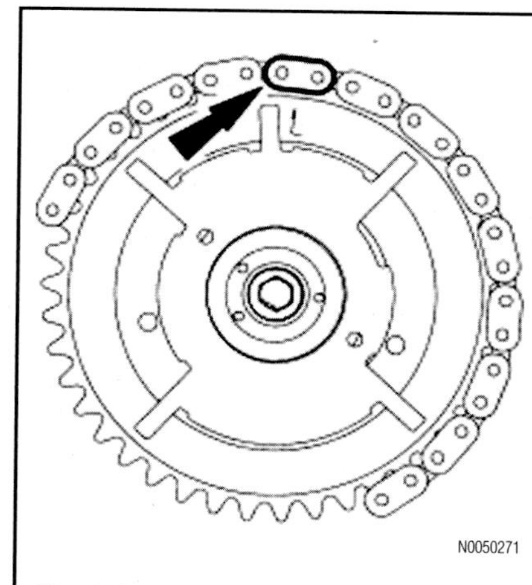

Fig. 263 Position the LH timing chain on the camshaft sprocket

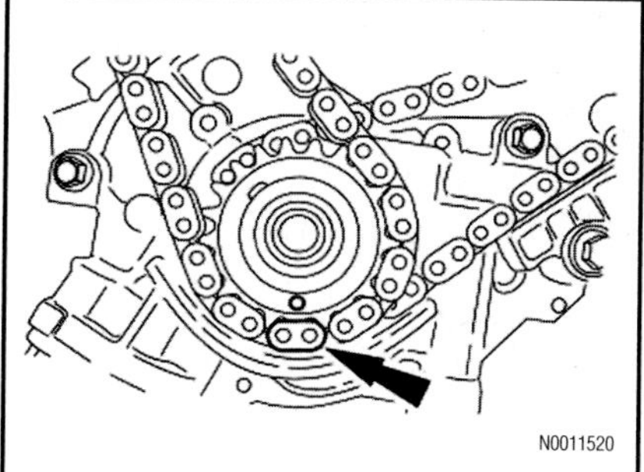

Fig. 264 Position the lower end of the RH (outer) timing chain on the crankshaft sprocket

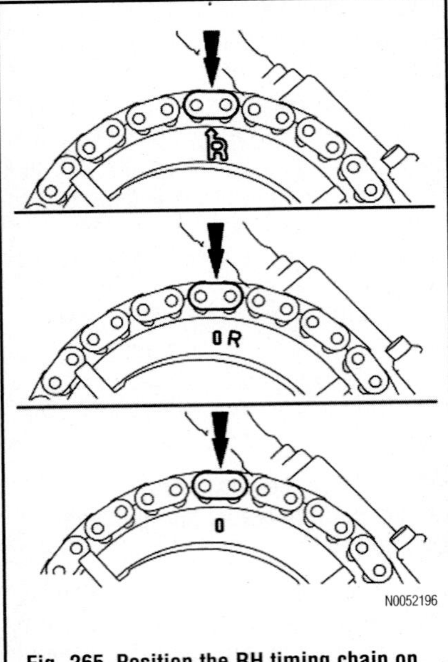

Fig. 265 Position the RH timing chain on the camshaft sprocket

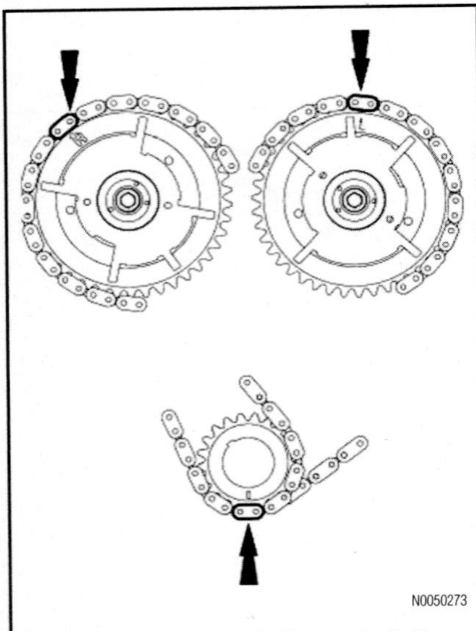

Fig. 266 Verify correct alignment of all timing marks

34. Position the LH timing chain tensioner arm on the dowel pin and install the LH timing chain tensioner and bolts. Tighten to 18 ft. lbs. (25 Nm).

35. Remove the retaining clip from the LH timing chain tensioner.

36. Position the lower end of the RH (outer) timing chain on the crankshaft sprocket, aligning the timing mark on the sprocket with the single colored (marked) chain link.

➡The camshaft phaser and sprocket will be stamped with one of the illustrated timing marks for the RH camshaft.

➡The lower half of the timing chain must be positioned above the tensioner arm dowel.

37. Position the RH timing chain on the camshaft sprocket. Make sure the camshaft sprocket timing mark is aligned with the colored (marked) chain link.

38. Position the RH timing chain tensioner arm on the dowel pin and install the RH timing chain tensioner and bolts. Tighten to 18 ft. lbs. (25 Nm).

39. Remove the retaining clip from the RH timing chain tensioner.

➡The RH and LH camshaft phaser sprockets are similar. Refer to the single timing mark to identify the RH camshaft phaser sprocket and the L timing mark to identify the LH camshaft phaser sprocket.

40. As a post-check, verify correct alignment of all timing marks. Make sure the timing marks on the sprockets correspond to the above note.

41. Install the crankshaft sensor ring on the crankshaft.

➡It is necessary to rotate the engine to position the camshaft lobes at base circle to install the roller followers.

42. Using the Valve Spring Compressor, install all of the camshaft roller followers.

43. Lubricate the roller followers with clean engine oil prior to installation.

44. Install the engine front cover. For additional information, refer to Timing Chain Front Cover in this section.

5.0L Engines

See Figures 267 through 269.

➡During engine repair procedures, cleanliness is extremely important. Any foreign material, including any material created while cleaning gasket surfaces, that enters the oil passages, coolant passages or the oil pan, can cause engine failure.

1. Remove the engine front cover.

2. Using the crankshaft holding tool, rotate the crankshaft clockwise until the keyway is at the 12 o'clock position.

3. Verify the data matrix on the camshafts is facing up, if not, rotate the crankshaft clockwise one revolution.

4. Remove the 2 bolts and the RH primary timing chain tensioner.

➡It may be necessary to rotate the crankshaft slightly to provide enough slack in the chain to remove the RH timing chain tensioner arm. Return the crankshaft keyway to the 12 o'clock position after removing the RH timing chain tensioner arm.

5. Remove the RH timing chain tensioner arm.

NOTE: It may be necessary to rotate the crankshaft slightly to provide enough slack in the chain to remove the RH timing chain guide. Return the crankshaft keyway to the 12 o'clock position after removing the RH timing chain guide.

6. Remove the bolt and the RH timing chain guide.

7. Remove the RH primary timing chain.

8. Remove the 3 RH intake Variable Camshaft Timing (VCT) assembly bolts and the 3 RH exhaust VCT assembly bolts. Refer to Camshafts in this section.

9. Slide the RH VCT assemblies and secondary timing chain forward 0.078 inches. Refer to Camshafts in this section.

10. Depress the RH secondary timing chain tensioner and turn the tensioner 90 degrees.

11. Remove the RH VCT assemblies and the RH secondary timing chain.

12. Using the crankshaft holding tool, rotate the crankshaft counterclockwise until

Fig. 267 Push back and hold the ratchet mechanism, then push the ratchet arm back into the tensioner housing

Fig. 268 Install a suitable pin into the hole of the tensioner housing

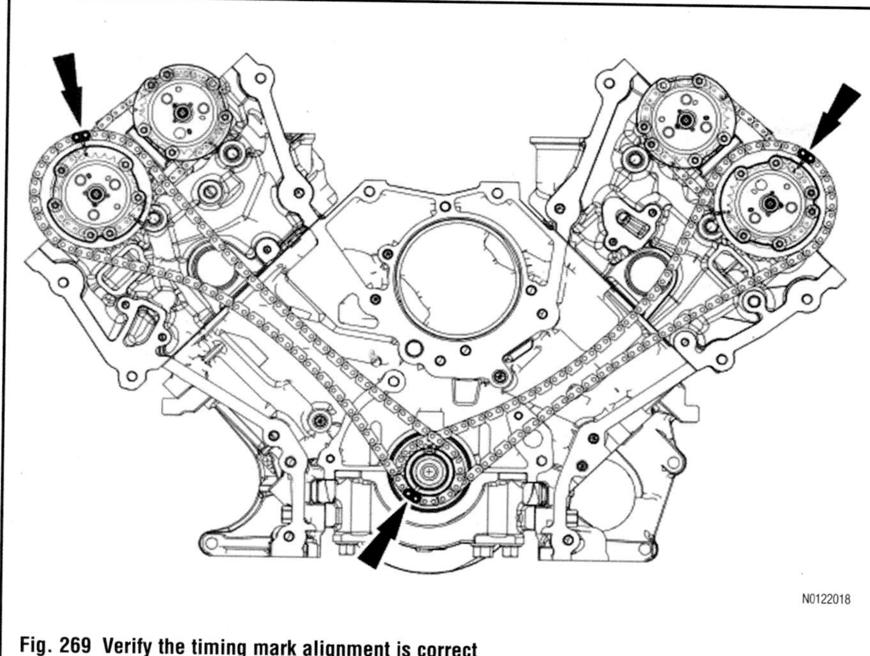

Fig. 269 Verify the timing mark alignment is correct

the crankshaft keyway is at the 9 o'clock position.

13. Remove the 2 bolts and the LH primary timing chain tensioner.

➡It may be necessary to rotate the crankshaft slightly to provide enough slack in the chain to remove the LH timing chain tensioner arm. Return the crankshaft keyway to the 9 o'clock position after removing the LH timing chain tensioner arm.

14. Remove the LH timing chain tensioner arm.

➡It may be necessary to rotate the crankshaft slightly to provide enough slack in the chain to remove the LH timing chain guide. Return the crankshaft keyway to the 9 o'clock position after removing the LH timing chain guide.

15. Remove the bolt and the LH timing chain guide.
16. Remove the LH primary timing chain.
17. Remove the 3 LH intake Variable Camshaft Timing (VCT) assembly bolts and the 3 LH exhaust VCT assembly bolts. Refer to Camshafts in this section.
18. Slide the LH VCT assemblies and secondary timing chain forward 2 mm (0.078 in). Refer to Camshafts in this section.
19. Depress the LH secondary timing chain tensioner and turn the tensioner 90 degrees.
20. Remove the LH VCT assemblies and the LH secondary timing chain.
21. Remove the crankshaft sprocket.

To install:

22. Install the crankshaft sprocket with the flange facing forward.
23. Install the secondary timing chain onto the LH VCT assemblies. Align the colored links on the secondary timing chain with the timing marks on the VCT assemblies as shown in the illustration.
24. The timing mark on the intake VCT assembly should align between the 2 consecutive colored links. The timing mark on the exhaust VCT assembly should align with the single colored link. Refer to Camshafts in this section.
25. Install the LH VCT assemblies and the secondary timing chain onto the LH camshafts to a position 0.078 inches from fully seated. The timing mark on the exhaust VCT assembly should be in the 11 o'clock position. Refer to Camshafts in this section.

➡It may be necessary to rotate the exhaust camshaft slightly (using a wrench on the flats of the camshaft) to seat the VCT assemblies onto the camshafts.

26. Rotate the secondary timing chain tensioner 90 degrees so the ramped area is facing forward and fully seat the VCT assemblies onto the camshafts.
27. If the secondary timing chain is not centered over the tensioner, reposition the VCT assemblies until they are fully seated on the camshafts.

➡Use a wrench on the flats of the camshaft to hold the camshafts while tightening the VCT assembly bolts.

28. Install the 3 LH intake VCT assembly bolts and the 3 LH exhaust VCT assembly bolts. Tighten to 11 ft. lbs. (15 Nm) plus an additional 90 degrees.
29. Install the LH primary timing chain.
30. Align the colored link on the timing chain with the timing mark on the LH VCT assembly.
31. Align the remaining colored link on the timing chain with the timing mark on the crankshaft sprocket.

➡It may be necessary to rotate the crankshaft slightly to provide enough slack in the chain to install the LH timing chain guide. Return the crankshaft keyway to the 9 o'clock position after installing the LH timing chain guide.

32. Install the LH timing chain guide and bolt. Tighten to 89 inch. lbs. (10 Nm).

➡It may be necessary to rotate the crankshaft slightly to provide enough slack in the chain to install the LH timing chain tensioner arm. Return the crankshaft keyway to the 9 o'clock position after installing the LH timing chain tensioner arm.

33. Install the LH timing chain tensioner arm.

➡Complete the following 3 steps on both the LH and RH primary timing chain tensioners.

➡Do not compress the ratchet assembly or damage to the tensioner will occur.

34. Compress the primary timing chain tensioner plunger, using an edge of a vise.
35. Using a small screwdriver or pick, push back and hold the ratchet mechanism, then push the ratchet arm back into the tensioner housing.
36. Install a suitable pin into the hole of the tensioner housing to hold the ratchet assembly and plunger in place during installation.
37. Install the LH primary timing chain tensioner and 2 bolts. Tighten to 89 inch lbs. (10 Nm).
38. Remove the holding pin from the tensioner.
39. Using the crankshaft holding tool, rotate the crankshaft clockwise until the crankshaft keyway is at the 12 o'clock position.
40. Install the secondary timing chain onto the RH VCT assemblies. Align the colored links on the secondary timing chain with the timing marks on the VCT assemblies. Refer to Camshafts in this section.
41. The timing mark on the intake VCT assembly should align between the 2 consecutive colored links.

42. The timing mark on the exhaust VCT assembly should align with the single colored link. Refer to Camshafts in this section.

43. Install the RH VCT assemblies and the secondary timing chain onto the RH camshafts to a position 2 mm (0.078 in) from fully seated. The timing mark on the exhaust VCT assembly should be in the 1 o'clock position. Refer to Camshafts in this section.

➡It may be necessary to rotate the exhaust camshaft slightly (using a wrench on the flats of the camshaft) to seat the VCT assemblies onto the camshafts.

44. Rotate the secondary timing chain tensioner 90 degrees so the ramped area is facing forward and fully seat the VCT assemblies onto the camshafts.

45. If the secondary timing chain is not centered over the tensioner, reposition the VCT assemblies until they are fully seated on the camshafts.

➡Use a wrench on the flats of the camshaft to hold the camshafts while tightening the VCT assembly bolts.

46. Install the 3 RH intake VCT assembly bolts and the 3 RH exhaust VCT assembly bolts. Tighten to 11 ft. lbs. (15 Nm) plus an additional 90 degrees. Refer to Camshafts in this section.

47. Install the RH primary timing chain.

48. Align the colored link on the timing chain with the timing mark on the RH VCT assembly.

49. Align the remaining colored link on the timing chain with the timing mark on the crankshaft sprocket.

➡It may be necessary to rotate the crankshaft slightly to provide enough slack in the chain to install the RH timing chain guide. Return the crankshaft keyway to the 12 o'clock position after installing the RH timing chain guide.

50. Install the RH timing chain guide and bolt. Tighten to 7 ft. lbs. (10 Nm).

➡It may be necessary to rotate the crankshaft slightly to provide enough slack in the chain to install the RH timing chain tensioner arm. Return the crankshaft keyway to the 12 o'clock position after installing the RH timing chain tensioner arm.

51. Install the RH timing chain tensioner arm.

52. Install the RH primary timing chain tensioner and 2 bolts. Tighten to 7 ft. lbs. (10 Nm).

53. Remove the holding pin from the tensioner.

54. With the crankshaft keyway still at the 12 o'clock position, verify the timing mark alignment is correct.

55. Install the engine front cover.

5.4L Engine

See Figures 270 through 275.

➡During engine repair procedures, cleanliness is extremely important. Any foreign material, including any material created while cleaning gasket surfaces, that enters the oil passages, coolant passages or the oil pan, can cause engine failure.

1. Remove the camshaft roller followers. For additional information, refer to Camshaft Roller Follower in this section.
2. Remove the engine front cover. For additional information, refer to Timing Chain Cover in this section.
3. Remove the crankshaft sensor ring.
4. Remove the crankshaft washer.
5. Remove the 2 bolts and the RH primary timing chain tensioner.
6. Remove the RH primary timing chain tensioner arm.
7. Remove the RH primary timing chain.
8. Remove the 2 bolts and the RH primary timing chain guide.
9. Remove the 2 bolts and the LH primary timing chain tensioner.
10. Remove the LH primary timing chain tensioner arm.
11. Remove the LH primary timing chain.
12. Remove the 2 bolts and the LH primary timing chain guide.
13. Remove the crankshaft sprocket.

To install:

➡Do not compress the ratchet assembly. This will damage the ratchet assembly.

NOTE: LH shown, RH similar.

14. Compress each tensioner plunger, using an edge of a vise.
15. Using a small screwdriver or pick, push back and hold the ratchet mechanism.
16. While holding the ratchet mechanism, push the ratchet arm back into the tensioner housing.
17. Install a suitable pin into the hole of each tensioner housing to hold the ratchet

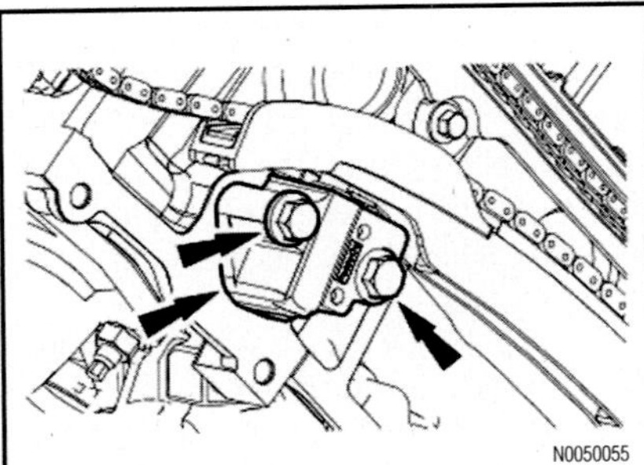

Fig. 270 Remove the 2 bolts and the RH primary timing chain tensioner—LH similar

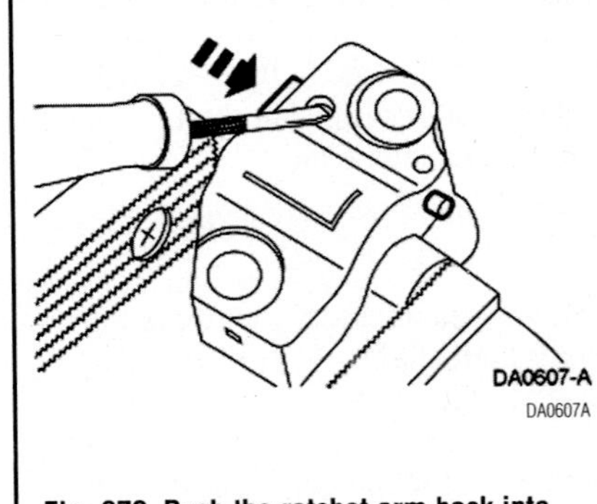

Fig. 272 Push the ratchet arm back into the tensioner housing

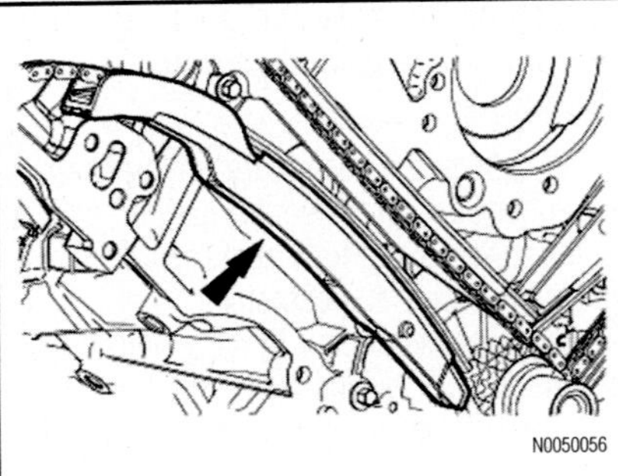

Fig. 271 Remove the RH primary timing chain tensioner arm—LH similar

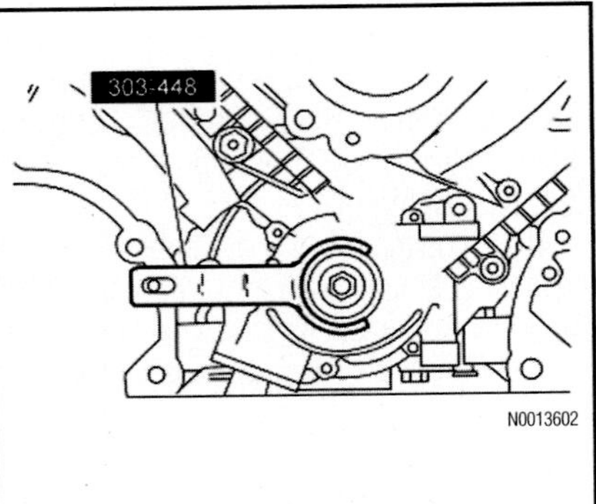

Fig. 273 Using the Crankshaft Holding Tool

assembly and plunger in place during installation.

18. Remove the tensioner from the vise.

19. If the colored links are not visible, mark one link on one end and 2 links on the other end, and use as timing marks.

20. Using the Crankshaft Holding Tool, position the crankshaft.

21. Install the crankshaft sprocket with the flange facing forward.

22. Install the LH primary timing chain guide and the 2 bolts. Tighten to 7 ft. lbs. (10 Nm).

23. Position the camshaft sprocket timing marks as shown.

24. Position the LH (inner) timing chain onto the crankshaft sprocket, aligning the one colored link on the timing chain with the slot on the crankshaft sprocket.

25. Install the LH timing chain on the camshaft sprocket, aligning the 2 colored links with the timing mark on the sprocket.

26. Install the LH primary timing chain tensioner arm.

27. Install the LH primary timing chain tensioner and the 2 bolts. Tighten to 18 ft. lbs. (25 Nm).

28. Remove the pin from the tensioner.

29. Install the RH primary timing chain guide and the 2 bolts. Tighten to 7 ft. lbs. (10 Nm).

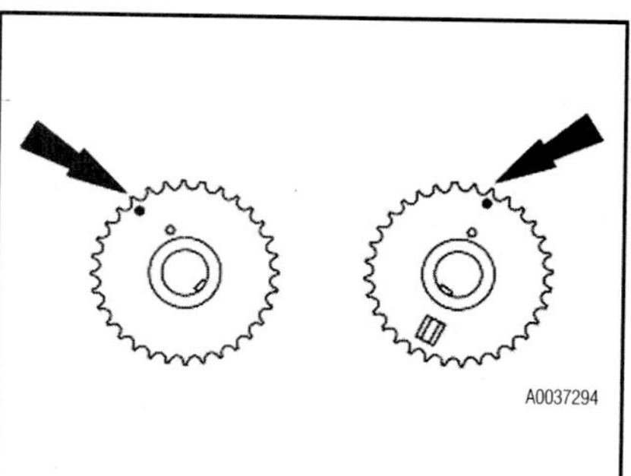

Fig. 274 Position the camshaft sprocket timing marks

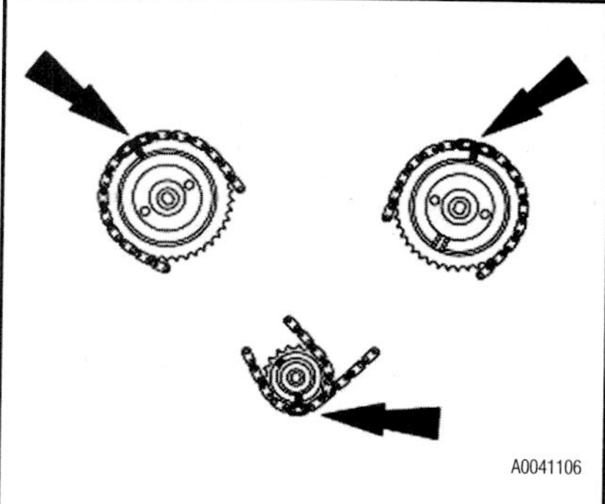

Fig. 275 Timing chain and sprocket orientation

30. Position the RH (outer) timing chain on the crankshaft sprocket, aligning the colored link with the timing marks on the sprocket.

31. Install the RH timing chain on the camshaft sprocket, aligning the 2 colored links with the timing mark on the sprocket.

32. Install the RH primary timing chain tensioner arm.

33. Install the RH primary timing chain tensioner and the 2 bolts. Tighten to 18 ft. lbs. (25 Nm).

34. Remove the pin from the tensioner.

35. As a post-check, verify correct alignment of all timing marks. Make sure that the colored links are lined up with the marks on the crankshaft sprocket and the camshaft sprockets.

36. Install the crankshaft washer.

37. Install the crankshaft sensor ring.

38. Install the engine front cover.

39. Install the camshaft roller followers.

VALVE COVERS

REMOVAL & INSTALLATION

3.7L Engine

LH Valve Cover

See Figures 276 through 279.

➡During engine repair procedures, cleanliness is extremely important. Any foreign material, including any material created while cleaning gasket surfaces that enters the oil passages, coolant passages or the oil pan, may cause engine failure.

1. If equipped, remove the 4 nuts and the strut tower cross brace.

2. If equipped, detach the 2 retainers and remove the engine appearance cover.

3. Remove the Air Cleaner (ACL) outlet tube.

4. Disconnect the crankcase ventilation tube quick connect coupling from the LH valve cover.

5. Remove the oil level indicator.

6. Detach the fuel supply tube and Evaporative Emission (EVAP) tube retainer from the LH valve cover.

7. Remove the LH ignition coils. For additional information, refer to Engine Electrical.

8. Disconnect the 2 LH Variable Camshaft Timing (VCT) solenoid electrical connectors.

9. Disconnect the Engine Oil Pressure (EOP) switch electrical connector.

10. Detach the EOP switch wiring harness retainer from the cylinder head.

11. Detach all of the wiring harness retainers from the LH valve cover and stud bolts.

12. Remove the nut and the LH valve cover stud bolt wiring harness bracket.

➡While removing the valve cover do not apply excessive force to the Variable Camshaft Timing (VCT) oil control solenoid or damage may occur.

➡If the Variable Camshaft Timing (VCT) oil control solenoid sticks to the VCT seal, carefully wiggle the valve

Fig. 276 Using the Differential Bearing Cone Installer and Handle

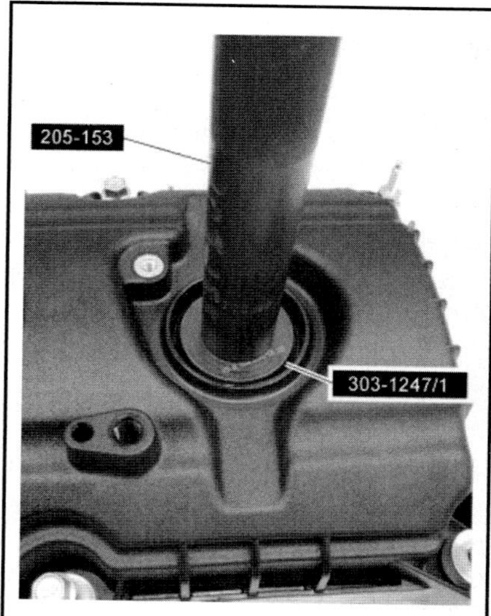

Fig. 277 Using the VCT Spark Plug Tube Seal Remover and Handle

Fig. 278 Application points

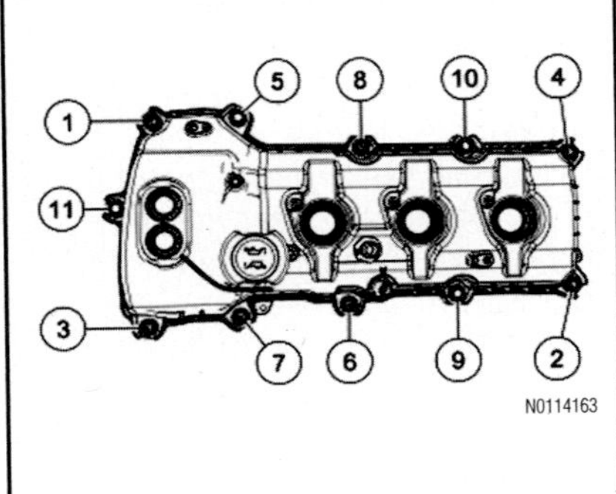

Fig. 279 LH valve cover tightening sequence

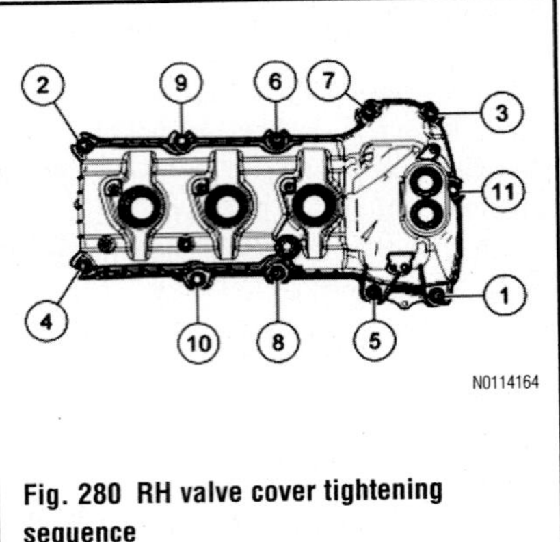

Fig. 280 RH valve cover tightening sequence

cover until the bond breaks free or damage to the VCT seal and VCT oil control solenoid may occur.

➡The plastic electrical connector on the VCT oil control solenoid will rotate approximately 12 degrees inside the steel housing, which is normal.

13. Loosen the 7 stud bolts, 4 bolts and remove the LH valve cover.
14. Discard the gasket.
15. Inspect the 2 VCT solenoid seals. Remove any damaged seals.
16. Using the Differential Bearing Cone Installer and Handle, remove the seal(s).
17. Inspect the spark plug tube seals. Remove any damaged seals.
18. Using the VCT Spark Plug Tube Seal Remover and Handle, remove the seal(s).
19. Clean the valve cover, cylinder head and engine front cover sealing surfaces with metal surface prep.

To install:

➡Installation of new seals is only required if damaged seals were removed.

20. Using the VCT Spark Plug Tube Seal Installer and Handle, install new spark plug tube seals.

➡Installation of new seals is only required if damaged seals were removed.

21. Using the Differential Bearing Cone Installer and Handle, install new VCT solenoid seal(s).

➡Failure to use the correct Motorcraft® High Performance Engine RTV Silicone may cause the engine oil to foam excessively and result in serious engine damage.

➡If the valve cover is not installed and the fasteners tightened within 4 minutes, the sealant must be removed and the sealing area cleaned. To clean the sealing area, use silicone gasket remover and metal surface prep. Failure to follow this procedure can cause future oil leakage.

22. Apply an 8 mm (0.31 in) bead of Motorcraft® High Performance Engine RTV Silicone to the engine front cover-to-LH cylinder head joints.
23. Using a new gasket, install the LH valve cover and tighten the 4 bolts and 7 stud bolts in the sequence shown. Tighten to 7 ft. lbs. (10 Nm).
24. Ensure the VCT seals in the valve cover are below the top of the VCT oil control solenoid electrical connector or the VCT seal may leak oil.
25. Install the wiring harness bracket on the LH valve cover stud bolt and install the nut.
26. Attach all of the wiring harness retainers to the LH valve cover and stud bolts.
27. Connect the EOP switch electrical connector.
28. Attach the EOP switch wiring harness retainer to the cylinder head.
29. Connect the 2 LH VCT solenoid electrical connectors.
30. Install the LH ignition coils.
31. Attach the fuel supply tube and EVAP tube retainer to the LH valve cover.
32. Install the oil level indicator.
33. Connect the crankcase ventilation tube quick connect coupling to the LH valve cover.
34. Install the ACL outlet tube.
35. If equipped, install the engine appearance cover.
36. If equipped, install the strut tower cross brace and the 4 nuts. Tighten to 26 ft. lbs. (35 Nm).

RH Valve Cover

See Figure 280.

➡During engine repair procedures, cleanliness is extremely important. Any foreign material, including any material created while cleaning gasket surfaces that enters the oil passages, coolant passages or the oil pan, may cause engine failure.

1. Remove the RH ignition coils. For additional information, refer to Engine Electrical.
2. Disconnect the PCV tube quick connect coupling from the RH valve cover.
3. Disconnect the 2 RH Variable Camshaft Timing (VCT) solenoid electrical connectors.
4. Detach all of the wiring harness retainers from the RH valve cover and stud bolts.
5. Remove the heater tube bolt.
6. Detach the heater tube retainer from the RH valve cover stud bolt.

➡While removing the valve cover do not apply excessive force to the Variable Camshaft Timing (VCT) oil control solenoid or damage may occur.

➡If the Variable Camshaft Timing (VCT) oil control solenoid sticks to the VCT seal, carefully wiggle the valve cover until the bond breaks free or damage to the VCT seal and VCT oil control solenoid may occur.

➡The plastic electrical connector on the VCT oil control solenoid will rotate approximately 12 degrees inside the steel housing, which is normal.

7. Loosen the 8 stud bolts, 3 bolts and remove the RH valve cover.
8. Discard the gasket.
9. Inspect the 2 VCT solenoid seals. Remove any damaged seals.
10. Using the Differential Bearing Cone Installer and Handle, remove the seal(s).
11. Inspect the spark plug tube seals. Remove any damaged seals.
12. Using the VCT Spark Plug Tube Seal Remover and Handle, remove the seal(s).
13. Clean the valve cover, cylinder head and engine front cover sealing surfaces with metal surface prep.

To install:

➡Installation of new seals is only required if damaged seals were removed.

14. Using the VCT Spark Plug Tube Seal Installer and Handle, install new spark plug tube seals.

➡Installation of new seals is only required if damaged seals were removed.

15. Using the Differential Bearing Cone Installer and Handle, install new VCT solenoid seal(s).

➡Failure to use the correct Motorcraft® High Performance Engine RTV Silicone may cause the engine oil to foam excessively and result in serious engine damage.

➡If the valve cover is not installed and the fasteners tightened within 4 minutes, the sealant must be removed and the sealing area cleaned. To clean the sealing area, use silicone gasket remover and metal surface prep. Failure to follow this procedure can cause future oil leakage.

16. Apply an 0.31 inch bead of Motorcraft® High Performance Engine RTV Silicone to the engine front cover-to-RH cylinder head joints.
17. Using a new gasket, install the RH valve cover and tighten the 3 bolts and 8 stud bolts in the sequence shown. Tighten to 89 inch lbs. (10 Nm).
18. Ensure the VCT seals in the valve cover are below the top of the VCT oil control solenoid electrical connector or the VCT seal may leak oil.
19. Attach the heater tube retainer to the RH valve cover stud bolt. Install the heater tube bolt. Tighten to 17 ft. lbs. (23 Nm).
20. Attach all of the wiring harness retainers to the RH valve cover and stud bolts.
21. Connect the 2 RH VCT solenoid electrical connectors.
22. Connect the PCV tube quick connect coupling to the RH valve cover.
23. Install the RH ignition coils.

4.0L Engine

LH Valve Cover

See Figure 281.

➡During engine repair procedures, cleanliness is extremely important. Any foreign material, including any material created while cleaning gasket surfaces that enters the oil passages, coolant passages or the oil pan, can cause engine failure.

1. Disconnect the radio capacitor electrical connector.
2. Disconnect the 6 spark plug wires from the ignition coil.
3. Remove the 2 upper ignition coil bracket bolts.
4. Remove the 2 lower ignition coil bracket bolts and remove the ignition coil and bracket assembly.
5. Remove the fuel rail supply tube bracket-to-cylinder head bolt.
6. Remove the fuel rail supply tube bracket-to-valve cover bolt.
7. Position the fuel rail supply tube aside.
8. Disconnect the crankcase ventilation tube from the valve cover and position the tube aside.
9. Disconnect the Camshaft Position (CMP) sensor electrical connector.
10. Disconnect the fuel rail pressure and temperature sensor electrical connector.
11. Disconnect the 3 LH fuel injector electrical connectors.
12. Detach the wiring retainer from the valve cover stud bolt and position the wiring harness aside.
13. Detach the spark plug wire retainer from the valve cover stud bolt.
14. Remove the 3 bolts, the 3 stud bolts and the LH valve cover.

To install:

➡Clean the valve cover and cylinder head sealing surfaces with metal surface prep. Inspect and install a new gasket as necessary.

15. Position the LH valve cover and install the 3 bolts and the 3 stud bolts. Tighten in the sequence shown to 7 ft. lbs. (10 Nm).
16. Attach the spark plug wire retainer to the valve cover stud bolt.
17. Position the wiring harness, attach the wiring retainer to the valve cover stud bolt and then connect the 3 LH fuel injector electrical connectors.
18. Connect the fuel rail pressure and temperature sensor electrical connector.
19. Connect the CMP sensor electrical connector.
20. Connect the crankcase ventilation tube to the valve cover.
21. Position the fuel rail supply tube and install the fuel rail supply tube bracket-to-valve cover bolt. Tighten to 53 inch lbs. (6 Nm).
22. Install the fuel rail supply tube bracket-to-cylinder head bolt. Tighten to 7 ft. lbs. (10 Nm).
23. Install the ignition coil and bracket assembly and the lower bolts.
    a. Tighten the M8 bolts to 18 ft. lbs. (24 Nm).
    b. Tighten the M12 bolt to 25 ft. lbs. (34 Nm).
24. Install the upper ignition coil bracket bolts. Tighten to 80 inch lbs. (9 Nm).
25. Connect the 6 spark plug wire to the ignition coil.
26. Connect the radio capacitor electrical connector.

RH Valve Cover

See Figure 282.

➡During engine repair procedures, cleanliness is extremely important. Any foreign material, including any material created while cleaning gasket surfaces that enters the oil passages, coolant passages or the oil pan, can cause engine failure.

1. Remove the PCV tube.
2. Disconnect the PCV valve electrical connector.
3. Detach the heater hose retainer from the valve cover.
4. Remove the wiring harness bracket bolt from the back of the RH cylinder head and detach the bracket from the valve cover stud bolt.

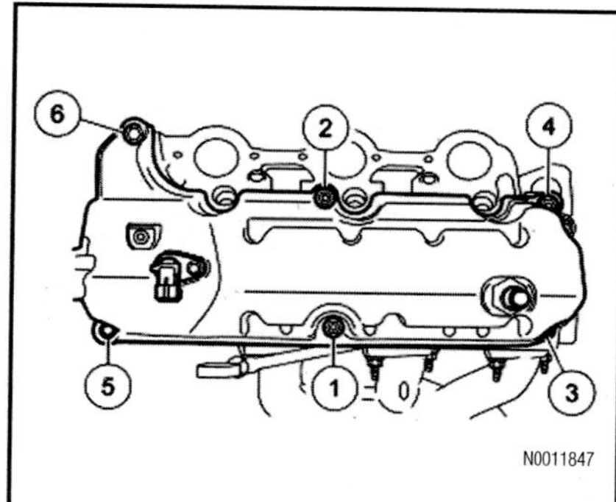

Fig. 281 LH valve tightening sequence

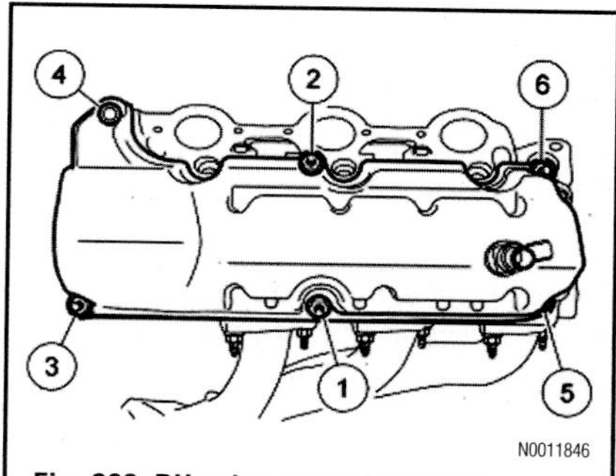

Fig. 282 RH valve cover tightening sequence

5. Detach the engine wiring and spark plug wiring retainers from the 2 valve cover stud bolts.

6. Remove the 2 bolts, the 4 stud bolts and the RH valve cover.

To install:

➡Clean the valve cover and cylinder head sealing surfaces with metal surface prep. Inspect and install a new gasket as necessary.

7. Position the RH valve cover and install the 2 bolts and the 4 stud bolts.

8. Tighten in the sequence shown to 89 inch lbs. (10 Nm).

9. Attach the engine wiring and spark plug wiring retainers to the 2 valve cover stud bolts.

10. Position the wiring harness bracket on the valve cover stud bolt and install the wiring harness bracket bolt to the back of the RH cylinder head. Tighten to 30 ft. lbs. (40 Nm).

11. Attach the heater hose retainer to the valve cover.

12. Connect the PCV valve electrical connector.

13. Install the PCV tube.

4.6L Engine

LH Valve Cover

See Figure 283.

1. Remove the Air Cleaner (ACL) assembly and outlet pipe.

2. Remove the LH ignition coils. For additional information, refer to Engine Electrical.

3. Remove the oil level indicator and tube.

4. Disconnect the Evaporative Emission (EVAP) tube from the intake manifold.

5. Remove the PCV tube.

6. Disconnect the LH Variable Camshaft Timing (VCT) solenoid electrical connector and detach the 2 wiring harness pin-type retainers.

7. Detach the 2 wiring harness retainers from the valve cover stud bolts.

8. Disconnect the LH Camshaft Position (CMP) sensor electrical connector.

9. Remove the 2 nuts and position the power steering reservoir and bracket aside.

➡Do not use metal scrapers, wire brushes, power abrasive discs or other abrasive means to clean the sealing surfaces. These tools cause scratches and gouges which make leak paths. Use a plastic scraping tool to remove all traces of old sealant.

10. Loosen the 10 fasteners and remove the LH valve cover and gasket.

11. Clean the valve cover mating surface of the cylinder head with silicone gasket remover and metal surface prep. Follow the directions on the packaging.

12. Discard the valve cover gasket. Clean the valve cover gasket groove with soap and water or a suitable solvent.

To install:

➡If the valve cover is not secured within 4 minutes, the sealant must be removed and the sealing area cleaned with metal surface prep. Failure to follow this procedure can cause future oil leakage.

13. Apply a bead of silicone gasket and sealant in 2 places where the engine front cover meets the cylinder head.

14. Position the LH valve cover and new gasket on the cylinder head and tighten the bolts in the sequence shown. Tighten to 7 ft. lbs. (10 Nm).

15. Install the power steering reservoir and bracket and the 2 nuts.

16. Connect the LH CMP electrical connector.

17. Attach the 2 wiring harness retainers to the valve cover stud bolts.

18. Connect the LH VCT solenoid electrical connector and attach the 2 wiring harness pin-type retainers.

19. Install the PCV tube.

20. Connect the EVAP tube to the intake manifold.

21. Install the oil level indicator and tube.

22. Install the LH ignition coils.

23. Install the ACL assembly and output pipe.

RH Valve Cover

See Figure 284.

1. Remove the RH ignition coils. For additional information, refer to Engine Electrical.

2. Detach the wiring harness retainer from the engine front cover stud bolt.

3. Disconnect the RH Variable Camshaft Timing (VCT) solenoid electrical connector.

4. Disconnect the PCV tube from the RH valve cover.

5. Detach the 3 wiring harness retainers from the valve cover stud bolts.

➡Do not use metal scrapers, wire brushes, power abrasive discs or other abrasive means to clean the sealing surfaces. These tools cause scratches and gouges which make leak paths. Use a plastic scraping tool to remove all traces of old sealant.

6. Loosen the 9 fasteners and remove the RH valve cover and gasket.

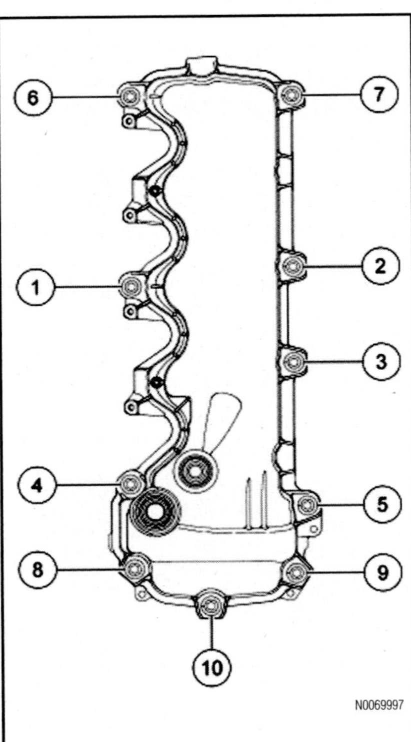

Fig. 283 LH valve cover tightening sequence

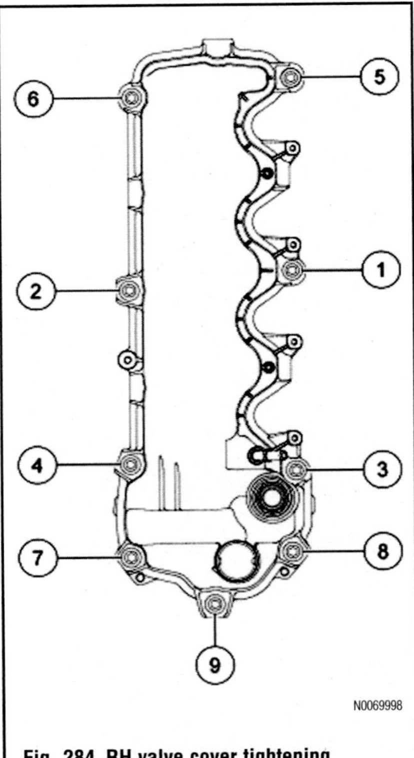

Fig. 284 RH valve cover tightening sequence

7. Clean the valve cover mating surface of the cylinder head with silicone gasket remover and metal surface prep. Follow the directions on the packaging.

8. Discard the valve cover gasket. Clean the valve cover gasket groove with soap and water or a suitable solvent.

To install:

➡If the valve cover is not secured within 4 minutes, the sealant must be removed and the sealing area cleaned with metal surface prep. Failure to follow this procedure can cause future oil leakage.

9. Apply a bead of silicone gasket and sealant in 2 places where the engine front cover meets the cylinder head.

10. Position the RH valve cover and new gasket on the cylinder head and tighten the bolts in the sequence shown. Tighten to Tighten to 7 ft. lbs. (10 Nm).

11. Attach the 3 wiring harness retainers to the valve cover stud bolts.

12. Connect the PCV tube to the RH valve cover.

13. Connect the RH VCT solenoid electrical connector.

14. Attach the wiring harness retainer to the engine front cover stud bolt.

15. Install the RH ignition coils.

5.0L Engine

LH Valve Cover

See Figures 285 through 288.

➡During engine repair procedures, cleanliness is extremely important. Any foreign material, including any material created while cleaning gasket surfaces, that enters the oil passages, coolant passages or the oil pan, can cause engine failure.

1. Release the fuel system pressure.
2. Disconnect the battery ground cable.
3. If equipped, remove the 4 nuts and the strut tower cross brace.

➡engine appearance cover rubber grommets may remain on the cover. If so, remove the grommets from the cover and install them on the intake manifold before installing the cover.

4. Remove the engine appearance cover.
5. Remove the Air Cleaner (ACL) and ACL outlet pipe.
6. Detach the sound enhancement pipe from the inner fender and position aside.
7. Remove the LH ignition coils. For additional information, refer to Engine Electrical.
8. Disconnect the Evaporative Emission (EVAP) canister purge valve tube.
9. Detach the EVAP canister purge valve tube retaining clips from the LH valve cover and the inner fender.
10. Disconnect the 2 LH Variable Camshaft Timing (VCT) variable force solenoid electrical connectors.
11. Detach the 10 wiring harness retainers.
12. Remove the oil level indicator.
13. Disconnect the fuel supply tube.
14. Detach the fuel supply tube retaining clip from the LH valve cover.

➡Do not use metal scrapers, wire brushes, power abrasive discs or other abrasive means to clean the sealing surfaces. These tools cause scratches and gouges which make leak paths. Use a plastic scraping tool to remove all traces of old sealant.

15. Loosen the 14 bolts and remove the LH valve cover and gasket.
16. Clean the valve cover mating surface of the cylinder head with silicone gasket remover and metal surface prep. Follow the directions on the packaging.
17. Discard the valve cover gasket. Clean the valve cover gasket groove with soap and water or a suitable solvent.

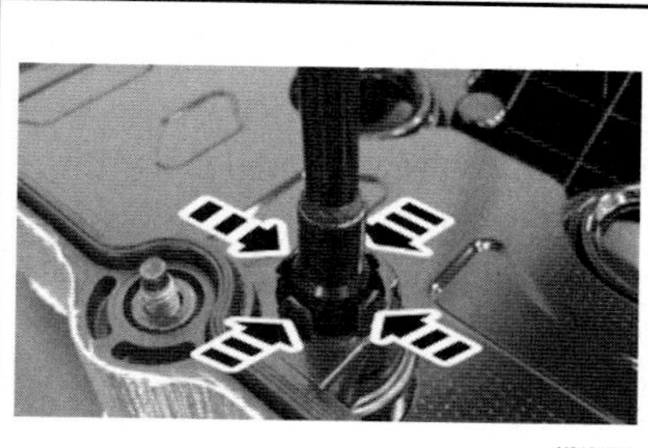

Fig. 285 Depress the 4 tabs and remove the oil level indicator tube

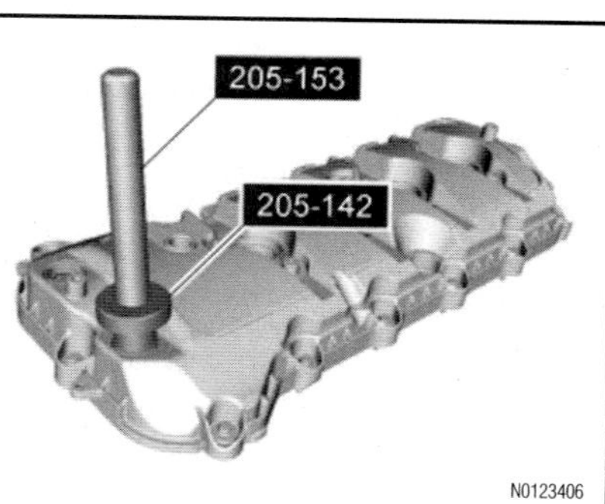

Fig. 286 Using the Differential Bearing Cone Installer and Handle

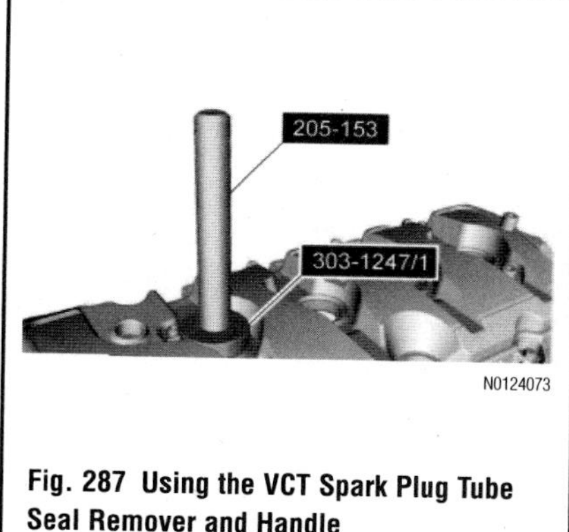

Fig. 287 Using the VCT Spark Plug Tube Seal Remover and Handle

18. If necessary, depress the 4 tabs and remove the oil level indicator tube.
19. Inspect the 2 VCT variable force solenoid seals. Remove any damaged seals.
20. Using the Differential Bearing Cone Installer and Handle, remove the seal(s).
21. Inspect the spark plug tube seals. Remove any damaged seals.
22. Using the VCT Spark Plug Tube Seal Remover and Handle, remove the seal(s).

To install:

➡Installation of new seals is only required if damaged seals were removed.

23. Using the VCT Spark Plug Tube Seal Installer and Handle, install new spark plug tube seals.

➡Installation of new seals is only required if damaged seals were removed.

24. Using the Differential Bearing Cone Installer and Handle, install new VCT variable force solenoid seal(s).

➡If the valve cover is not installed and the fasteners tightened within 5 minutes, the sealant must be removed and the sealing area cleaned. To clean the sealing area, use silicone gasket remover and metal surface prep. Failure to follow this procedure can cause future oil leakage.

25. Apply an 0.31 inch bead of silicone gasket and sealant to the engine front cover-to-LH cylinder head joints.
26. Position the LH valve cover and new gasket on the cylinder head.
27. Tighten the bolts in the sequence shown to 89 inch lbs. (10 Nm).
28. Attach the fuel supply tube retaining clip to the LH valve cover.
29. Connect the fuel supply tube.
30. If necessary, install the oil level indicator tube.

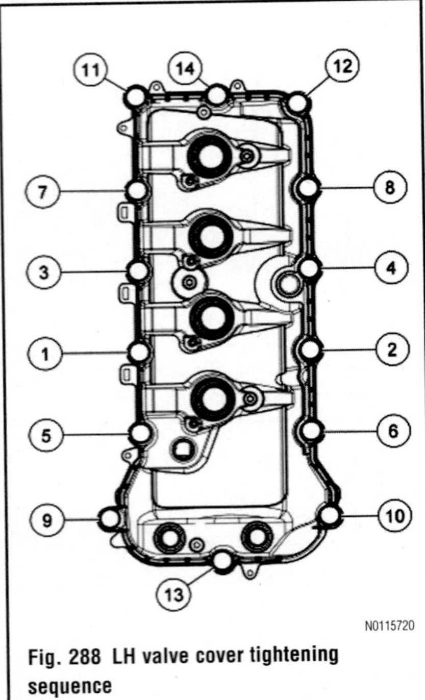

Fig. 288 LH valve cover tightening sequence

31. Push the oil level indicator tube into the valve cover until it clicks into place.

32. Install the oil level indicator.

33. Attach the 10 wiring harness retainers.

34. Connect the 2 LH VCT variable force solenoid electrical connectors.

35. Attach the EVAP canister purge valve tube retaining clips to the LH valve cover and the inner fender.

36. Connect the Evaporative Emission (EVAP) canister purge valve tube.

37. Install the LH ignition coils.

38. Attach the sound enhancement pipe to the inner fender.

39. Install the Air Cleaner (ACL) and ACL outlet pipe.

➡The engine appearance cover rubber grommets may remain on the cover. If so, remove the grommets from the cover and install them on the intake manifold before installing the cover.

40. Install the engine appearance cover.

41. If equipped, install the strut tower cross brace and the 4 nuts. Tighten to 26 ft. lbs. (35 Nm).

42. Connect the battery ground cable.

RH Valve Cover

See Figure 289.

➡During engine repair procedures, cleanliness is extremely important. Any foreign material, including any material created while cleaning gasket surfaces, that enters the oil passages, coolant passages or the oil pan, can cause engine failure.

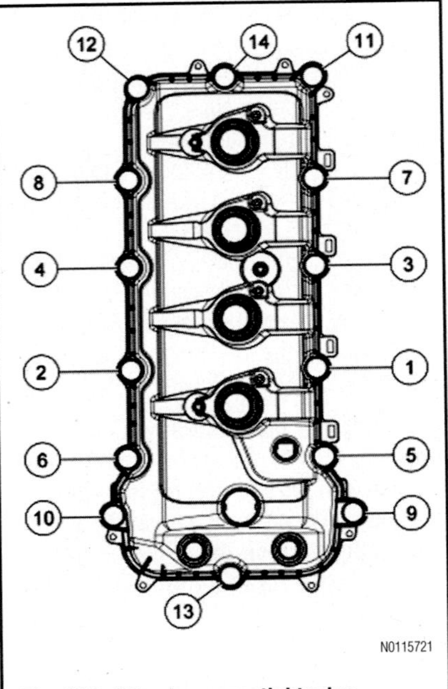

Fig. 289 RH valve cover tightening sequence

1. If equipped, remove the 4 nuts and the strut tower cross brace.

➡The engine appearance cover rubber grommets may remain on the cover. If so, remove the grommets from the cover and install them on the intake manifold before installing the cover.

2. Remove the engine appearance cover.

3. Remove the RH ignition coils. For additional information, refer to Engine Electrical.

4. Disconnect the 2 RH Variable Camshaft Timing (VCT) variable force solenoid electrical connectors.

5. Detach the 9 wiring harness retainers.

➡Do not use metal scrapers, wire brushes, power abrasive discs or other abrasive means to clean the sealing surfaces. These tools cause scratches and gouges which make leak paths. Use a plastic scraping tool to remove all traces of old sealant.

6. Loosen the 14 bolts and remove the RH valve cover and gasket.

7. Clean the valve cover mating surface of the cylinder head with silicone gasket remover and metal surface prep. Follow the directions on the packaging.

8. Discard the valve cover gasket. Clean the valve cover gasket groove with soap and water or a suitable solvent.

9. Inspect the 2 VCT variable force solenoid seals. Remove any damaged seals.

10. Using the Differential Bearing Cone Installer and Handle, remove the seal(s).

11. Inspect the spark plug tube seals. Remove any damaged seals.

12. Using the VCT Spark Plug Tube Seal Remover and Handle, remove the seal(s).

13. Clean the valve cover, cylinder head and engine front cover sealing surfaces with metal surface prep.

To install:

➡Installation of new seals is only required if damaged seals were removed.

14. Using the VCT Spark Plug Tube Seal Installer and Handle, install new spark plug tube seals.

➡Installation of new seals is only required if damaged seals were removed.

15. Using the Differential Bearing Cone Installer and Handle, install new VCT variable force solenoid seal(s).

➡If the valve cover is not installed and the fasteners tightened within 5 minutes, the sealant must be removed and the sealing area cleaned. To clean the sealing area, use silicone gasket remover and metal surface prep. Failure to follow this procedure can cause future oil leakage.

16. Apply an 0.31 inch bead of silicone gasket and sealant to the engine front cover-to-RH cylinder head joints.

17. Position the RH valve cover and new gasket on the cylinder head. Tighten the bolts in the sequence shown to 7 ft. lbs. (10 Nm).

18. Attach the 9 wiring harness retainers.

19. Connect the 2 RH VCT variable force solenoid electrical connectors.

20. Install the RH ignition coils.

➡The engine appearance cover rubber grommets may remain on the cover. If so, remove the grommets from the cover and install them on the intake manifold before installing the cover.

21. Install the engine appearance cover.

22. If equipped, install the strut tower cross brace and the 4 nuts. Tighten to 26 ft. lbs. (35 Nm).

5.4L Engines

LH Valve Cover

See Figures 290 and 291.

1. Release the fuel system pressure.

2. Disconnect the battery ground cable.

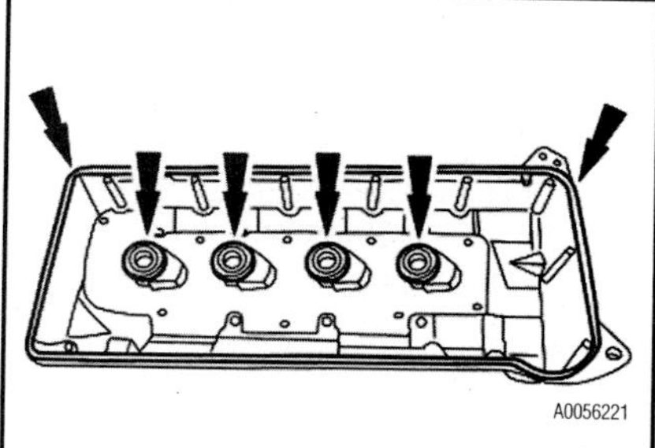

Fig. 290 Make sure the gaskets are correctly seated on the valve cover

3. Remove the power brake booster.
4. Remove the Air Cleaner (ACL) assembly and ACL outlet pipe.
5. Remove the LH ignition coils. For additional information, refer to Engine Electrical.
6. Disconnect the Throttle Position (TP) sensor electrical connector.
7. Disconnect the electronic throttle control electrical connector.
8. Disconnect the brake booster vacuum hose from the Throttle Body (TB) spacer.
9. Disconnect the Evaporative Emission (EVAP) canister purge valve tube from the TB spacer.
10. Disconnect the EVAP purge valve electrical connector.
11. Remove the 4 bolts and the TB and spacer assembly.
12. Discard the gasket.
13. Disconnect the 4 LH fuel injector electrical connectors.
14. Disconnect the fuel supply tube.
15. Remove the nut and the LH radio interference capacitor.
16. Disconnect the Camshaft Position (CMP) sensor electrical connector.
17. Detach the 3 wiring harness retainers from the LH valve cover studs.
18. Remove the bolt and position the oil level indicator tube aside.
19. Remove the 8 bolts, 2 stud bolts and LH valve cover.
20. Remove and discard the gaskets.

➡Do not use metal scrapers, wire brushes, power abrasive discs or other abrasive means to clean the sealing surfaces. These tools cause scratches and gouges which make leak paths. Use a plastic scraping tool to remove all traces of old sealant.

21. Clean the mating surfaces with silicone gasket remover and metal surface prep. Follow the directions on the packaging.
22. Inspect the mating surfaces.

To install:

23. Install new gaskets. Make sure the gaskets are correctly seated on the valve cover.

➡If the valve cover is not secured within 4 minutes, the sealant must be removed and the sealing area cleaned with metal surface prep. Allow to dry until there is no sign of wetness, or 4 minutes, whichever is longer. Failure to follow this procedure can result in future oil leakage.

Apply a bead of silicone gasket and sealant in 2 places where the engine front cover meets the cylinder head.

24. Install the RH valve cover, the 8 bolts and 2 stud bolts. Tighten in the sequence shown to 7 ft. lbs. (10 Nm).
25. Position the oil level indicator tube and install the bolt. Tighten to 7 ft. lbs. (10 Nm).
26. Attach the 3 wiring harness retainers to the LH valve cover studs.
27. Connect the CMP sensor electrical connector.
28. Install the LH radio interference capacitor and nut. Tighten to 7 ft. lbs. (10 Nm).
29. Connect the fuel supply tube.
30. Connect the 4 LH fuel injector electrical connectors.
31. Using a new gasket, install the TB and spacer assembly and the 4 bolts. Tighten to 7 ft. lbs. (10 Nm).
32. Connect the EVAP canister purge valve tube to the TB spacer.
33. Connect the EVAP purge valve electrical connector.
34. Connect the brake booster vacuum hose to the TB spacer.
35. Connect the electronic throttle control electrical connector.
36. Connect the TP sensor electrical connector.
37. Install the LH ignition coils. For additional information, refer to Engine Electrical.
38. Install the ACL assembly and ACL outlet pipe.
39. Install the power brake booster.
40. Connect the battery ground cable.

RH Valve Cover

See Figure 292.

1. Remove the battery and tray.
2. Remove the RH ignition coils. For additional information, refer to Engine Electrical.
3. Remove the crankcase ventilation tube.
4. Disconnect the PCV valve electrical connector.
5. Remove the nut and the RH radio interference capacitor.
6. Disconnect the 4 RH fuel injector electrical connectors.
7. Disconnect the fuel rail pressure and temperature sensor electrical connector.
8. Disconnect the Engine Coolant Temperature (ECT) sensor electrical connector.
9. Detach the 3 wiring harness retainers from the RH valve cover studs.

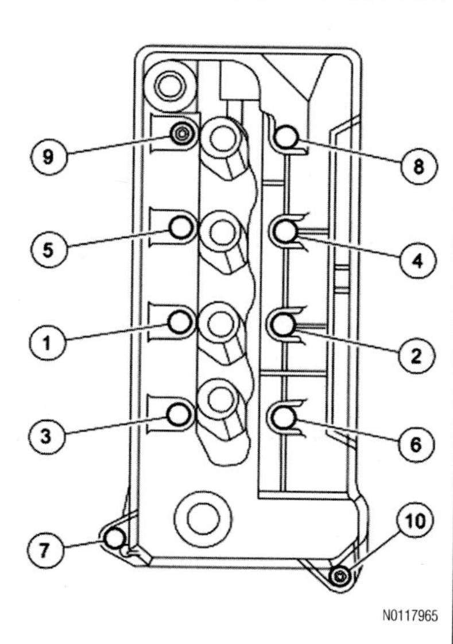

Fig. 291 LH valve cover tightening sequence

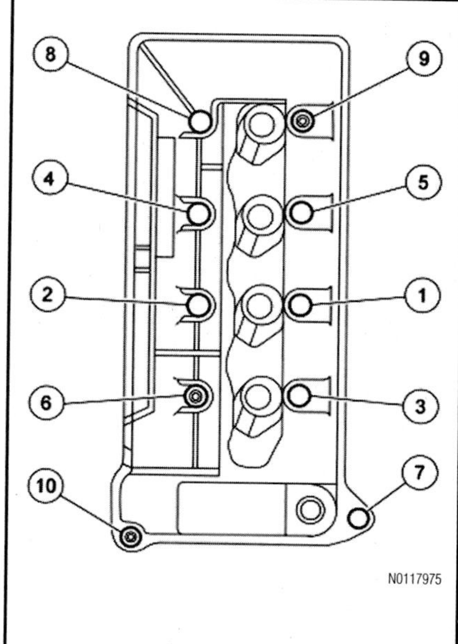

Fig. 292 RH valve cover tightening sequence

10. Detach the wiring harness pin-type retainer from the rear of the intake manifold.
11. Remove the nut and the A/C tube support bracket.
12. Remove the 7 bolts, 3 stud bolts and RH valve cover.
13. Remove and discard the gaskets.

➡Do not use metal scrapers, wire brushes, power abrasive discs or other abrasive means to clean the sealing surfaces. These tools cause scratches and gouges which make leak paths. Use a plastic scraping tool to remove all traces of old sealant.

14. Clean the mating surfaces with silicone gasket remover and metal surface prep. Follow the directions on the packaging.
15. Inspect the mating surfaces.

To install:

16. Install new gaskets. Make sure the gaskets are correctly seated on the valve cover.

➡If the valve cover is not secured within 4 minutes, the sealant must be removed and the sealing area cleaned with metal surface prep. Allow to dry until there is no sign of wetness, or 4 minutes, whichever is longer. Failure to follow this procedure can result in future oil leakage.

17. Apply a bead of silicone gasket and sealant in 2 places where the engine front cover meets the cylinder head.
18. Install the RH valve cover, the 7 bolts and 3 stud bolts.

Tighten in the sequence shown to 89 inch lbs. (10 Nm).

19. Install the A/C tube support bracket and nut. Tighten to 80 inch lbs. (9 Nm).
20. Attach the wiring harness pin-type retainer to the rear of the intake manifold.
21. Attach the 3 wiring harness retainers to the RH valve cover studs.
22. Connect the ECT sensor electrical connector.
23. Connect the fuel rail pressure and temperature sensor electrical connector.
24. Connect the 4 RH fuel injector electrical connectors.
25. Install the RH radio interference capacitor and the nut. Tighten to 89 inch lbs. (10 Nm).
26. Connect the PCV valve electrical connector.
27. Install the crankcase ventilation tube.
28. Install the RH ignition coils.
29. Install the battery and tray.

ENGINE PERFORMANCE & EMISSION CONTROLS

CAMSHAFT POSITION (CMP) SENSOR

LOCATION

See Figures 293 through 297.

Refer to the accompanying illustrations.

REMOVAL & INSTALLATION

4.0L Engine

1. Disconnect the Camshaft Position (CMP) sensor electrical connector.
2. Remove the bolt and the CMP sensor.
3. To install, tighten to 53 inch lbs. (6 Nm).
4. To install, reverse the removal procedure.

4.6L Engine

1. LH side:
2. Remove the Air Cleaner (ACL) outlet pipe.
3. Both sides:
4. Disconnect the Camshaft Position (CMP) sensor electrical connector.
5. Remove the bolt and the CMP sensor.
6. To install, tighten to 7 ft. lbs. (10 Nm).

5.4L Engine

1. Disconnect the Camshaft Position (CMP) sensor electrical connector.
2. Remove the bolt and the CMP sensor.
3. To install, tighten to 7 ft. lbs. (10 Nm).
4. To install, reverse the removal procedure.

CRANKSHAFT POSITION (CKP) SENSOR

LOCATION

See Figures 298 through 302.

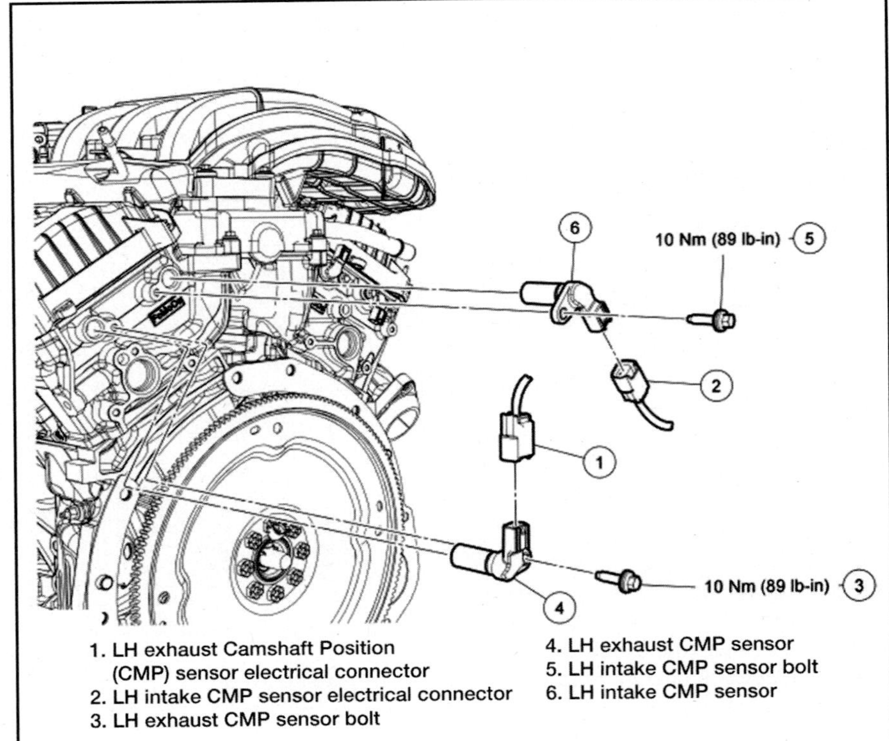

Fig. 293 Camshaft Position (CMP) Sensor location—3.7L Engine

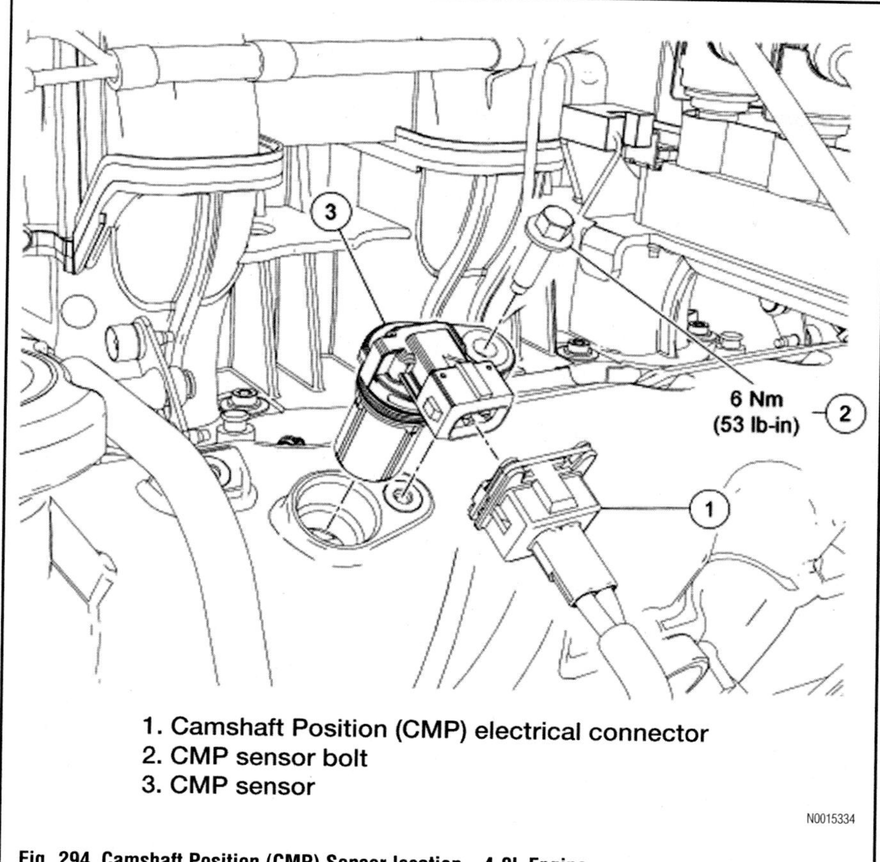

Fig. 294 Camshaft Position (CMP) Sensor location—4.0L Engine

REMOVAL & INSTALLATION

4.0L Engine

1. With the vehicle in NEUTRAL, position it on a hoist.
2. Disconnect the Crankshaft Position (CKP) sensor electrical connector.
3. Remove the 2 bolts and the CKP sensor. To install, tighten to 7 ft. lbs. (10 Nm).
4. To install, reverse the removal procedure.

4.6L & 5.4L Engines

1. With vehicle in NEUTRAL, position it on a hoist.
2. Remove the accessory drive belt. For additional information, refer to Accessory Drive.
3. Detach the wiring harness retainers from the A/C compressor stud bolts.
4. Disconnect the A/C compressor field coil and the Crankshaft Position (CKP) sensor electrical connectors.
5. Remove the stud bolts and position the A/C compressor aside. To install, tighten to 18 ft. lbs. (25 Nm).
6. Remove the CKP sensor bolt and sensor. To install, tighten to 7 ft. lbs. (10 Nm).
7. To install, reverse the removal procedure.

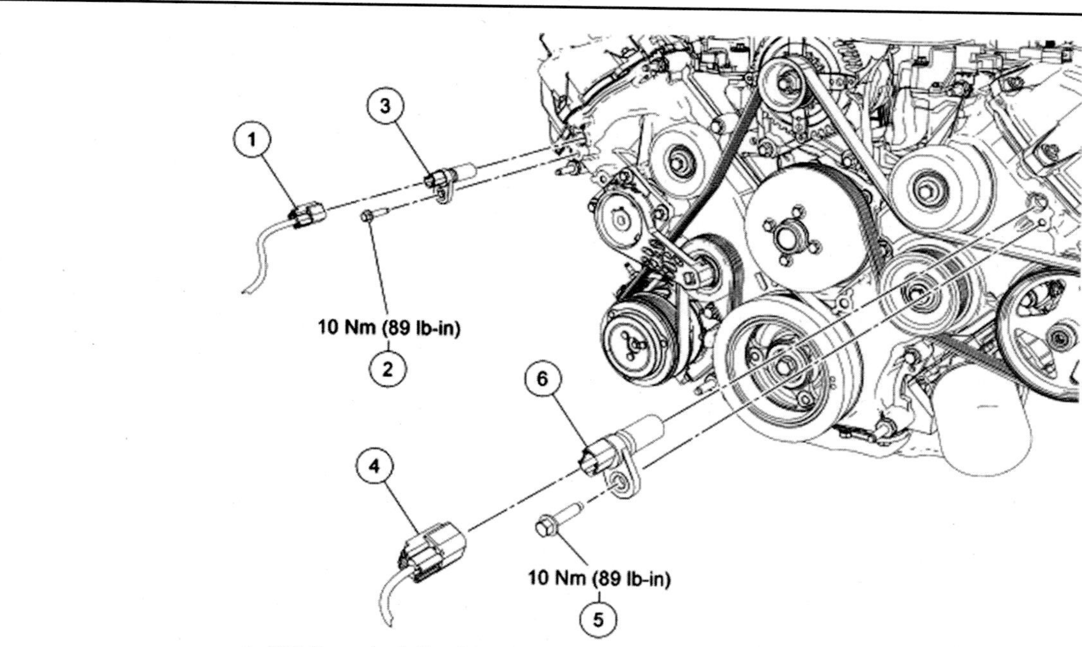

Fig. 295 Camshaft Position (CMP) Sensor location—4.6L Engine

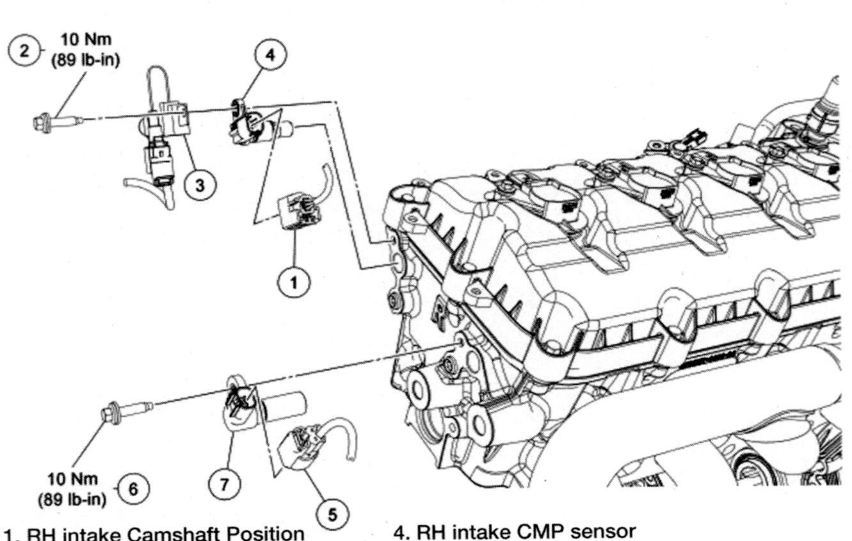

Fig. 296 Camshaft Position (CMP) Sensor location—5.0L Engine

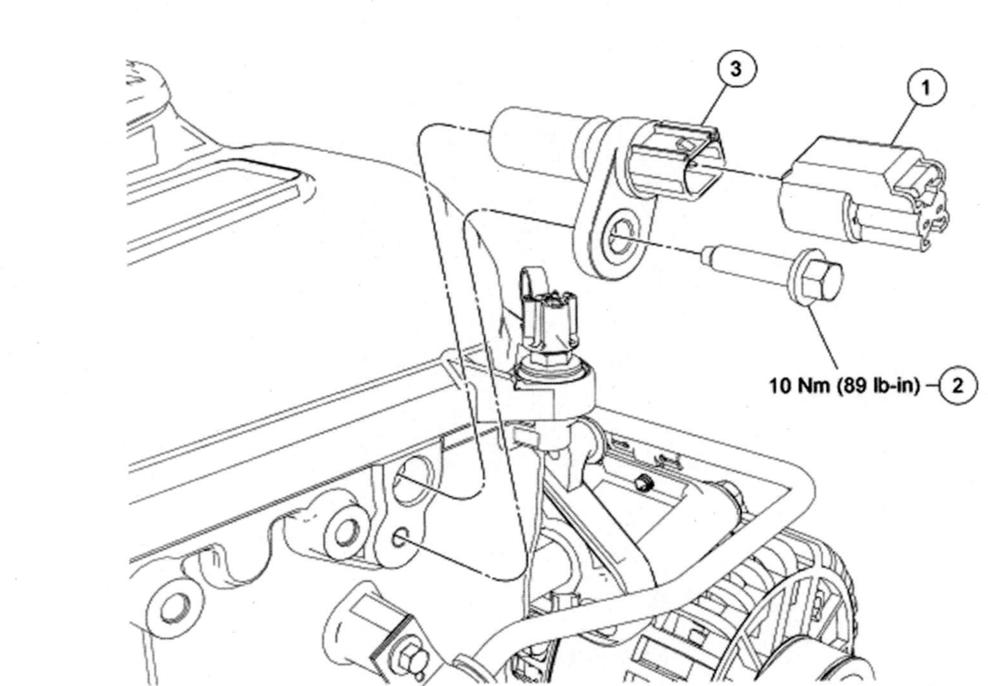

Fig. 297 Camshaft Position (CMP) Sensor location—5.4L Engine

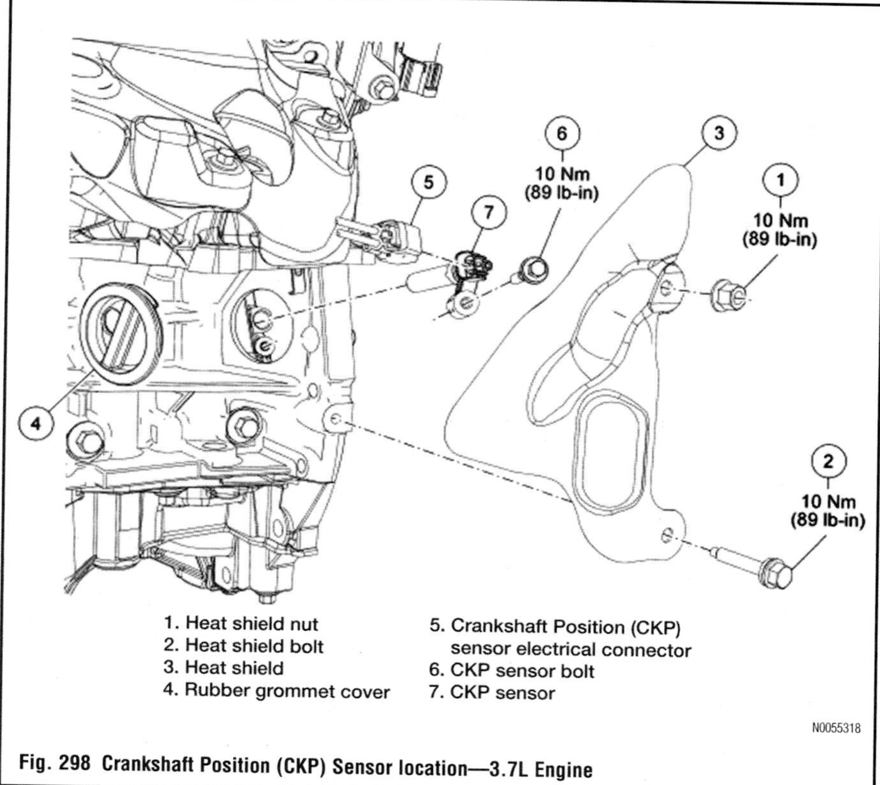

Fig. 298 Crankshaft Position (CKP) Sensor location—3.7L Engine

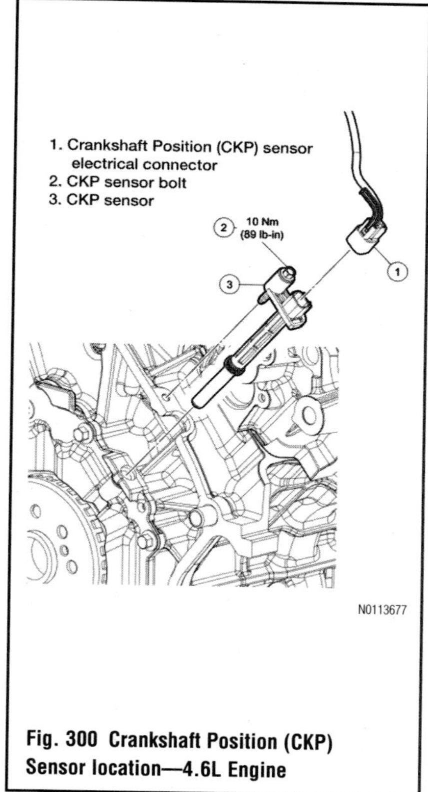

Fig. 300 Crankshaft Position (CKP) Sensor location—4.6L Engine

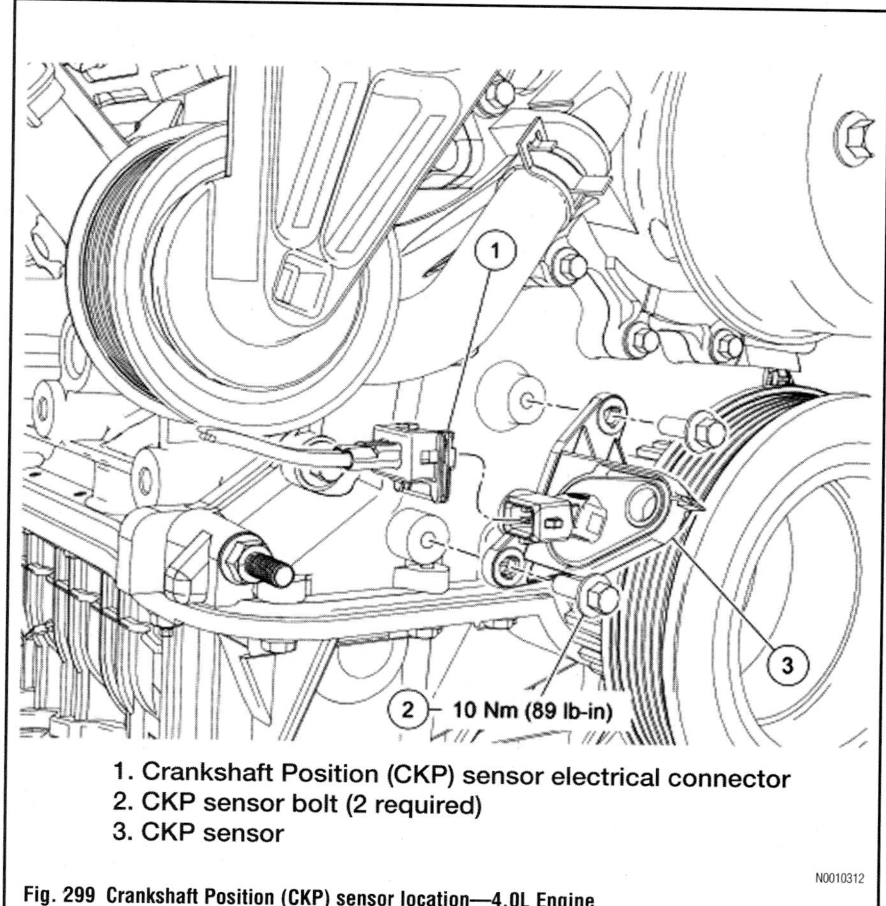

Fig. 299 Crankshaft Position (CKP) sensor location—4.0L Engine

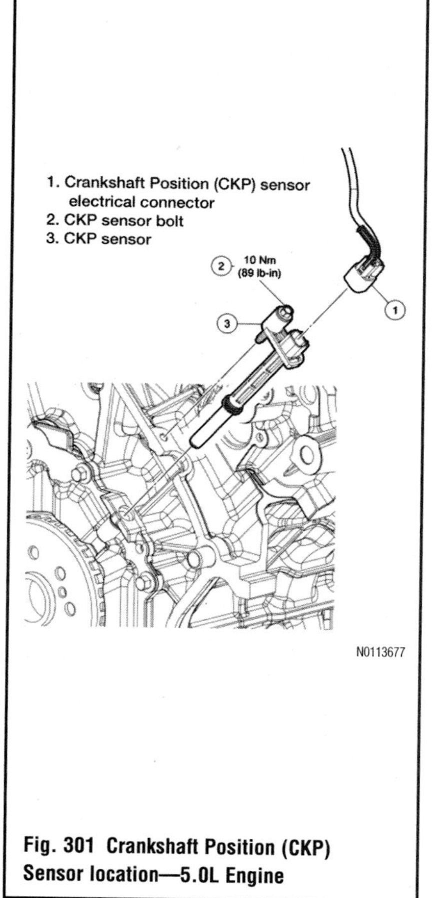

Fig. 301 Crankshaft Position (CKP) Sensor location—5.0L Engine

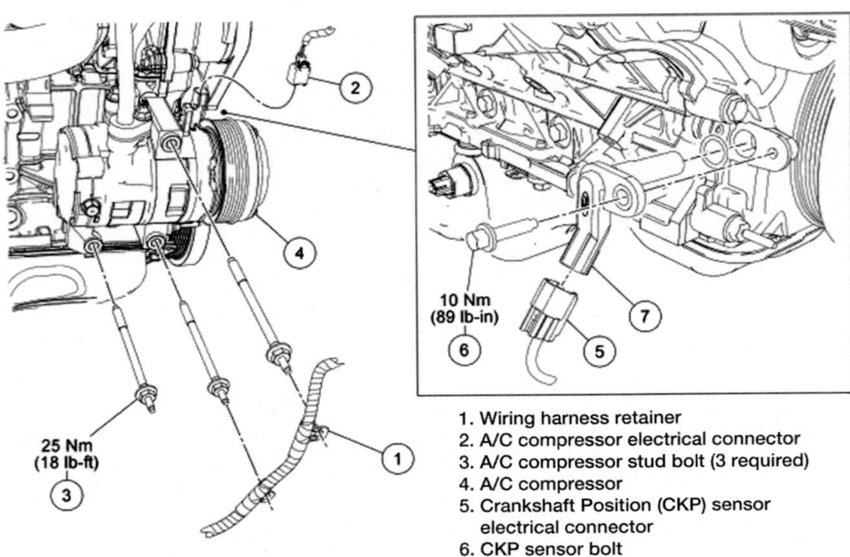

Fig. 302 Crankshaft Position (CKP) Sensor location—5.4L Engine

ENGINE COOLANT TEMPERATURE (ECT) SENSOR

LOCATION

See Figures 303 and 304

REMOVAL & INSTALLATION

4.0L Engine

1. Drain the cooling system.
2. Disconnect the Engine Coolant Temperature (ECT) sensor electrical connector.
3. Remove the retaining clip and the ECT sensor.
4. To install, reverse the removal procedure.
5. Fill and bleed the cooling system.

5.4L Engine

1. Drain the cooling system.
2. Disconnect the Engine Coolant Temperature (ECT) sensor electrical connector.
3. Remove the ECT sensor. To install, tighten to 11 ft. lbs. (15 Nm)
4. To install, reverse the removal procedure.
5. Fill and bleed the cooling system.

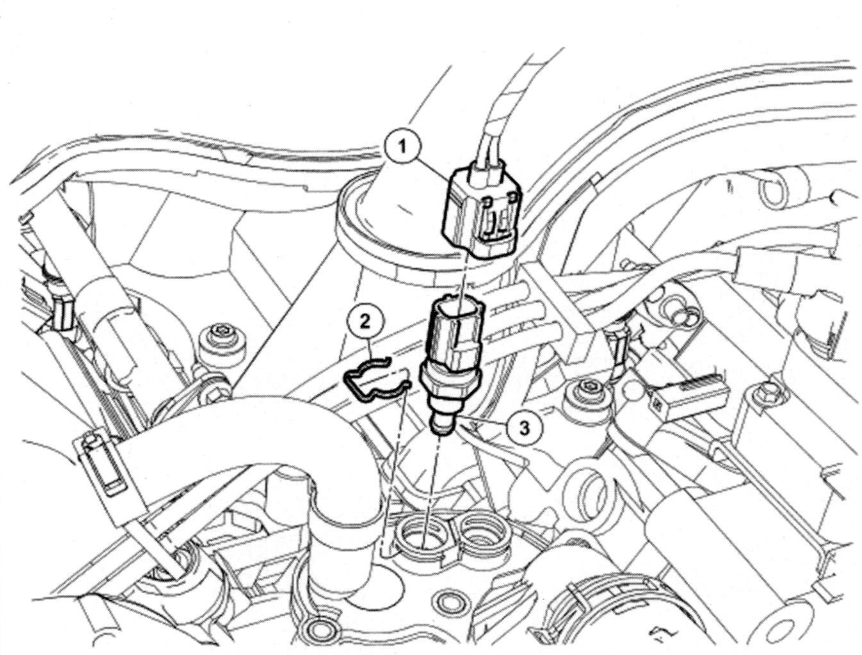

Fig. 303 Engine Coolant Temperature (ECT) sensor location—4.0L Engine

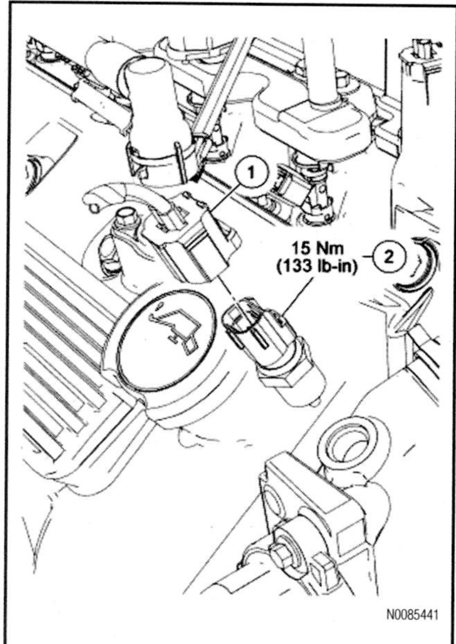

Fig. 304 Engine Coolant Temperature Sensor electrical connector (1) and sensor (2) location—5.4L Engine

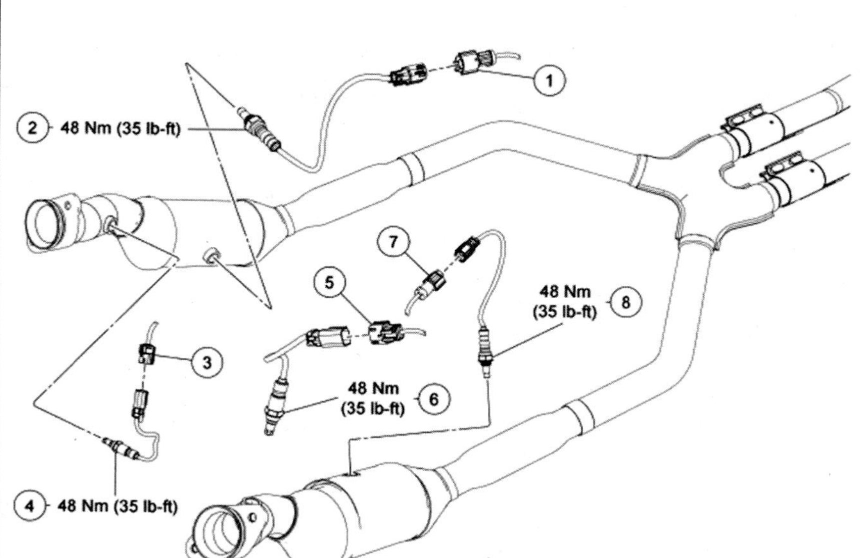

Fig. 305 Heated Oxygen Sensor and Catalyst Monitor Sensor location—3.7L Engine

HEATED OXYGEN SENSOR (HO2S)

LOCATION

See Figures 305 through 309.

REMOVAL & INSTALLATION

3.7L, 4.0L & 4.6L Engines

See Figure 310.

1. With the vehicle in NEUTRAL, position it on a hoist.
2. Disconnect the Heated Oxygen Sensor (HO2S) electrical connector.

➡If necessary, lubricate the HO2S threads with penetrating and lock lubricant to assist in removal.

3. Using the Exhaust Gas Oxygen Sensor Socket, remove the HO2S. To install, tighten to 35 ft. lbs. (48 Nm).
4. To install, reverse the removal procedure.
5. Apply a light coat of anti-seize lubricant to the threads of the HO2S before installing.

5.0L & 5.4L Engines

1. With the vehicle in NEUTRAL, position it on a hoist.
2. RH Heated Oxygen Sensor (HO2S) on 5.0L engine with automatic transmission:
    a. Disconnect the transmission vehicle harness connector by twisting the

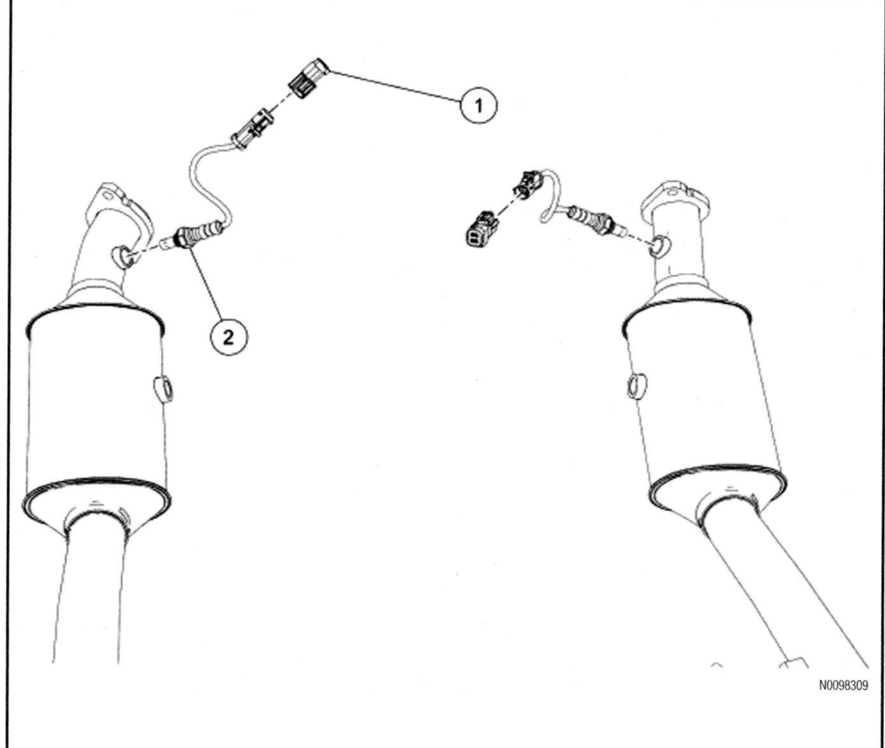

Fig. 306 Heated Oxygen Sensor (HO2S) electrical connector (1) and sensor (2) location—4.0L Engine

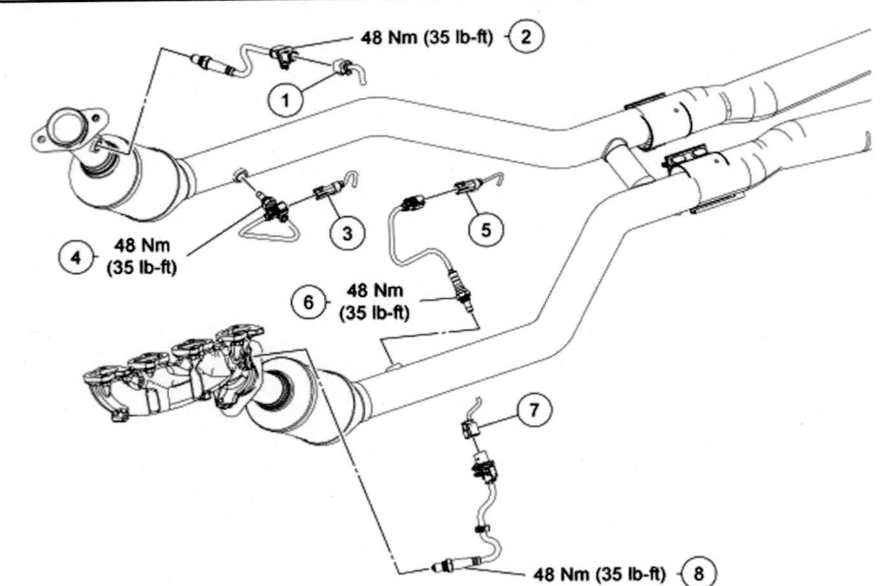

1. RH Heated Oxygen Sensor (HO2S) electrical connector
2. RH HO2S
3. RH Catalyst Monitor Sensor (CMS) electrical connector
4. CMS
5. LH CMS electrical connector
6. LH CMS
7. LH HO2S electrical connector
8. LH HO2S

N0113679

Fig. 307 Heated Oxygen Sensor electrical connector (1) and Sensor (2) location—4.6L Engine

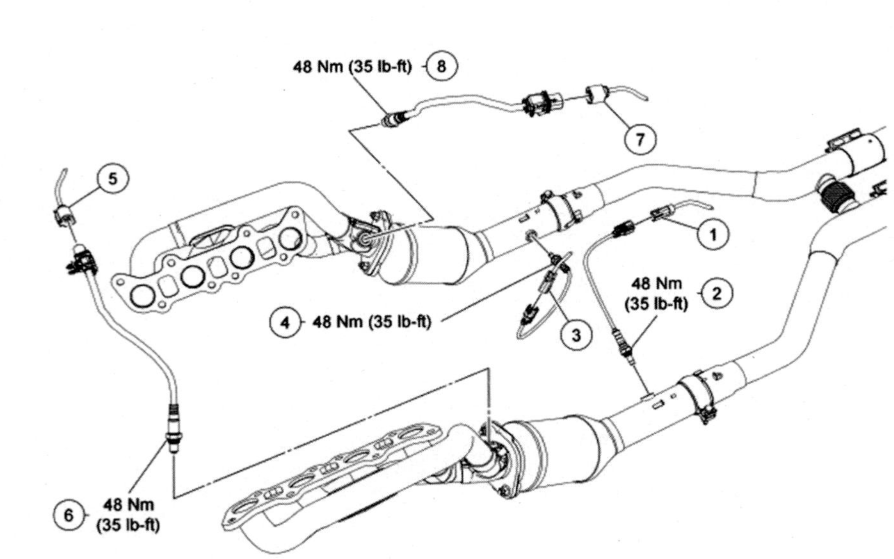

1. LH Catalyst Monitor Sensor (CMS) electrical connector
2. LH CMS
3. RH CMS electrical connector
4. RH CMS
5. LH Heated Oxygen Sensor (HO2S) electrical connector
6. LH HO2S
7. RH HO2S electrical connector
8. RH HO2S

N0113676

Fig. 308 Heated Oxygen Sensor and Catalyst Monitor Sensor—5.0L Engine location

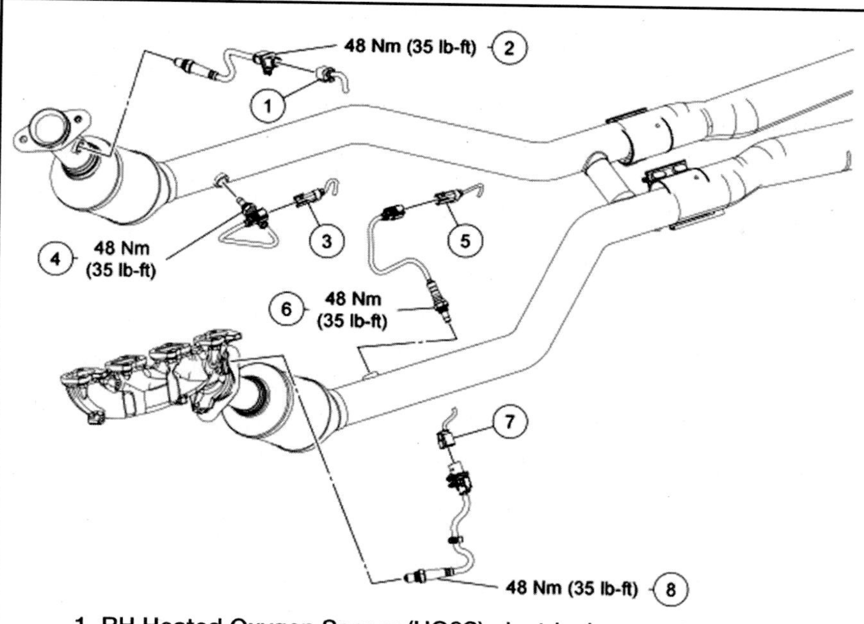

Fig. 309 Heated Oxygen Sensor and Catalyst Monitor Sensor location—5.4L Engine

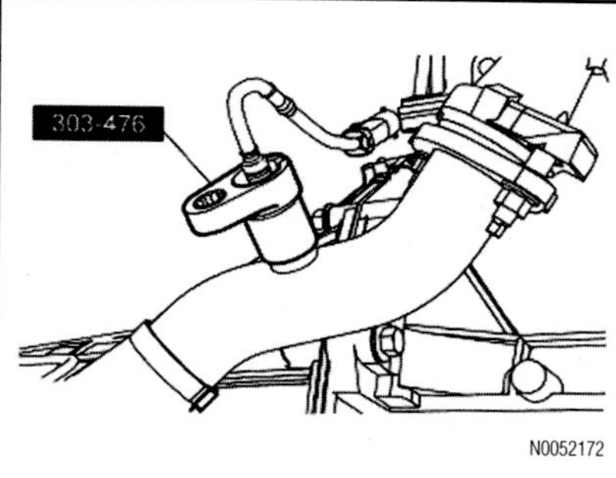

Fig. 310 Using the Exhaust Gas Oxygen Sensor Socket

outer shell and pulling back on the connector.

b. Detach the wiring harness retainer.

c. Detach the 2 wiring harness retainers.

3. RH Heated Oxygen Sensor (HO2S) on 5.0L engine with manual transmission:

a. Disconnect the skip shift solenoid electrical connector.

b. Detach the 2 wiring harness retainers.

4. RH Heated Oxygen Sensor (HO2S) on 5.0L and 5.4L engines:

a. Remove the battery tray. For additional information, refer to Battery, Mounting and Cables.

5. RH Heated Oxygen Sensor (HO2S) on 5.0L engine

a. Pull the wiring harness up toward the rear of the engine to access the Heated Oxygen Sensor (HO2S) electrical connector.

6. All sensors:

a. Detach the pin type retainer and disconnect the Heated Oxygen Sensor (HO2S) electrical connector.

➡If necessary, lubricate the HO2S threads with penetrating and lock lubricant to aid in removal.

b. Using a suitable crowfoot wrench, remove the HO2S.

c. Calculate the correct torque wrench setting for the following torque.

d. To install, use a suitable crowfoot wrench, tighten to 35 ft. lbs. (48 Nm).

7. To install, reverse the removal procedure.

8. Apply a light coat of anti-seize lubricant to the threads of the HO2S before installing.

INTAKE AIR TEMPERATURE 2 (IAT2) SENSOR

LOCATION

See Figure 311.

Refer to the accompanying illustration.

REMOVAL & INSTALLATION

See Figure 312.

1. Disconnect the Intake Air Temperature 2 (IAT2) sensor electrical connector.

2. Remove the IAT2 sensor.

To install:

3. Install the IAT2 sensor. Tighten the IAT2 sensor in 2 stages:

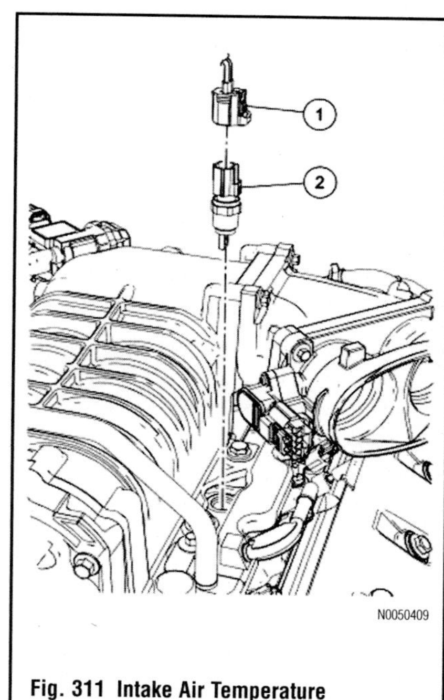

Fig. 311 Intake Air Temperature Sensor—5.4L Engine

Fig. 312 Tighten the IAT2 sensor until it is aligned

a. Stage 1: Tighten the IAT2 sensor to 133 inch lbs. (15 Nm).

➡During Stage 2, do not tighten the IAT2 sensor more than one full turn and do not rotate the IAT2 sensor counterclockwise after tightening.

b. Stage 2: Tighten the IAT2 sensor until it is aligned as shown.

4. Connect the IAT2 sensor electrical connector.

KNOCK SENSOR (KS)

LOCATION

See Figures 313 through 317.

REMOVAL & INSTALLATION

1. Remove the intake manifold. For additional information, refer to Intake Manifold in Engine Mechanical.
2. Disconnect the Knock Sensor (KS) electrical connector. Discard the pin type retainer if equipped.
3. Remove the bolt(s) and the KS.
4. To install, reverse the removal procedure.

MASS AIR FLOW (MAF) SENSOR

LOCATION

The MAF sensor is located on the air cleaner assembly.

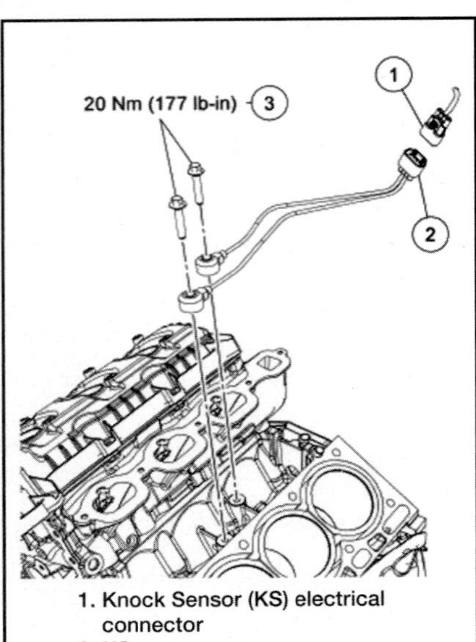

Fig. 313 Knock Sensor (KS) location—3.7L Engine

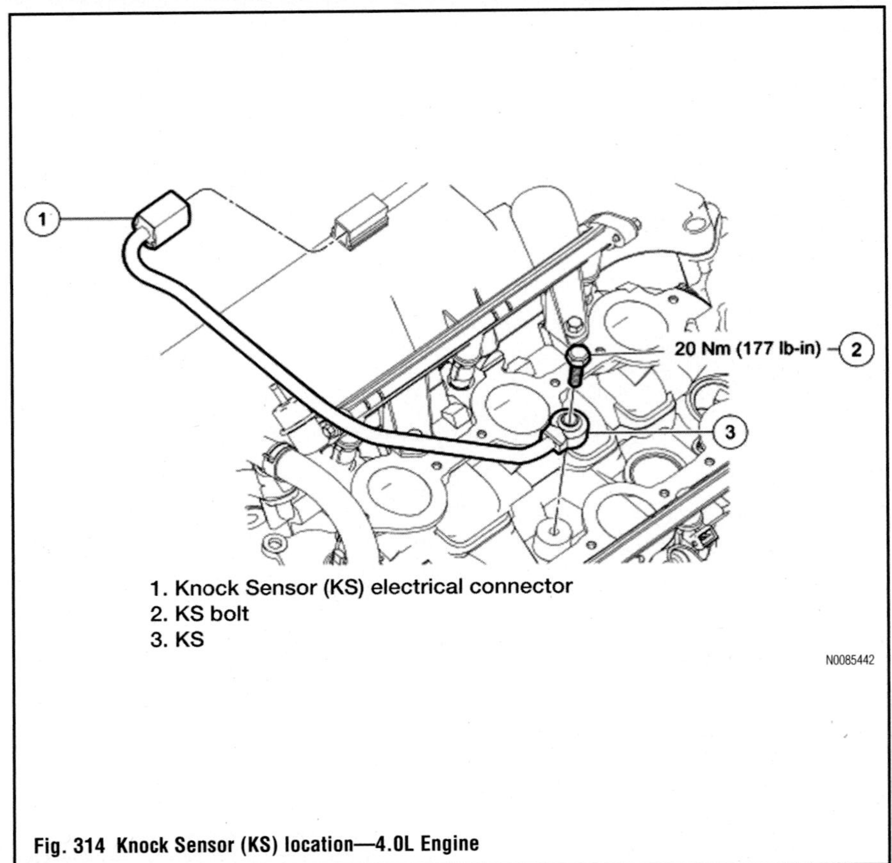

Fig. 314 Knock Sensor (KS) location—4.0L Engine

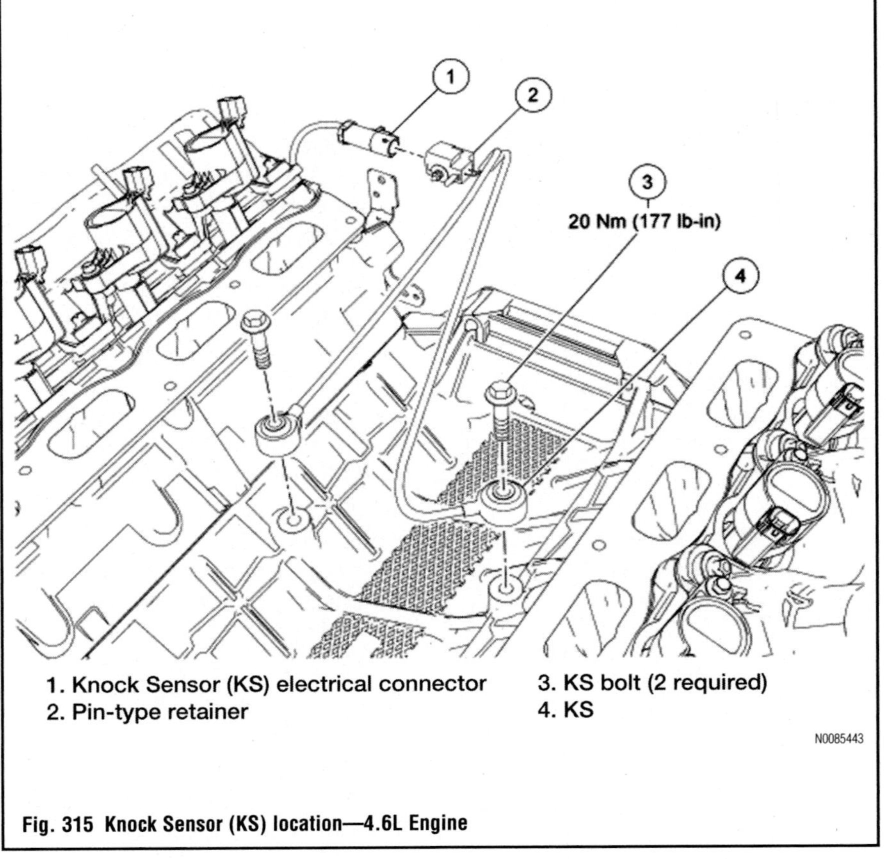

Fig. 315 Knock Sensor (KS) location—4.6L Engine

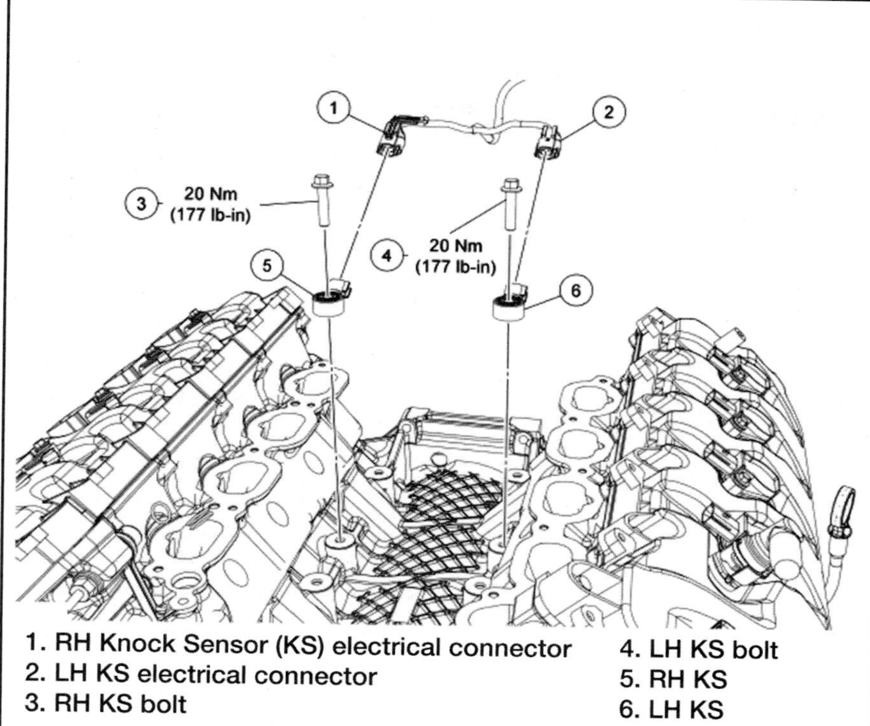

Fig. 316 Knock Sensor (KS) location—5.0L Engine

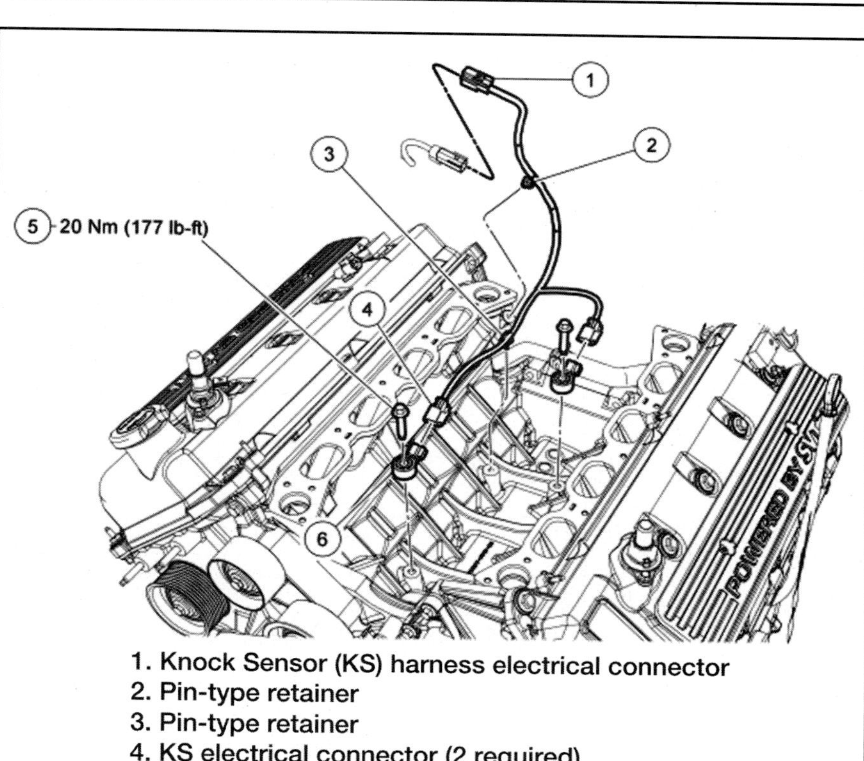

Fig. 317 Knock Sensor (KS) location—5.4L Engine

REMOVAL & INSTALLATION

Refer to Air Cleaner Assembly in Engine Mechanical.

POWERTRAIN CONTROL MODULE (PCM)

LOCATION

See Figure 318.

Refer to the accompanying illustration.

REMOVAL & INSTALLATION

1. Retrieve the module configuration. Carry out the module configuration retrieval steps of the
2. Programmable Module Installation (PMI) procedure.
3. Remove the 8 retainers and the radiator sight shield.
4. Disconnect the 3 PCM electrical connectors.
5. Remove the 2 bolts and the PCM.

To install:

6. Install the PCM and the 2 bolts. Tighten to 71 inch lbs. (8 Nm).
7. Connect the 3 PCM electrical connectors.
8. Install the radiator sight shield and the 8 retainers.
9. Restore the module configuration. Carry out the module configuration restore steps of the Programmable Module Installation (PMI) procedure.
10. After completing the repairs, use the scan tool to perform the Misfire Monitor Neutral Profile Correction procedure, following the on-screen instructions.

MODULE CONFIGURATION

PROGRAMMABLE MODULE INSTALLATION (PMI) USING THE INTEGRATED DIAGNOSTIC SYSTEM (IDS) WHEN THE ORIGINAL MODULE IS AVAILABLE

➡Following module installation, some modules require a separate procedure be carried out. For instructions, refer to the specific module removal and installation procedures.

1. Connect the IDS and identify the vehicle as normal.
2. From the Toolbox icon, select Module Programming and press the check mark.
3. Select Programmable Module Installation.
4. Select the module that is being replaced.

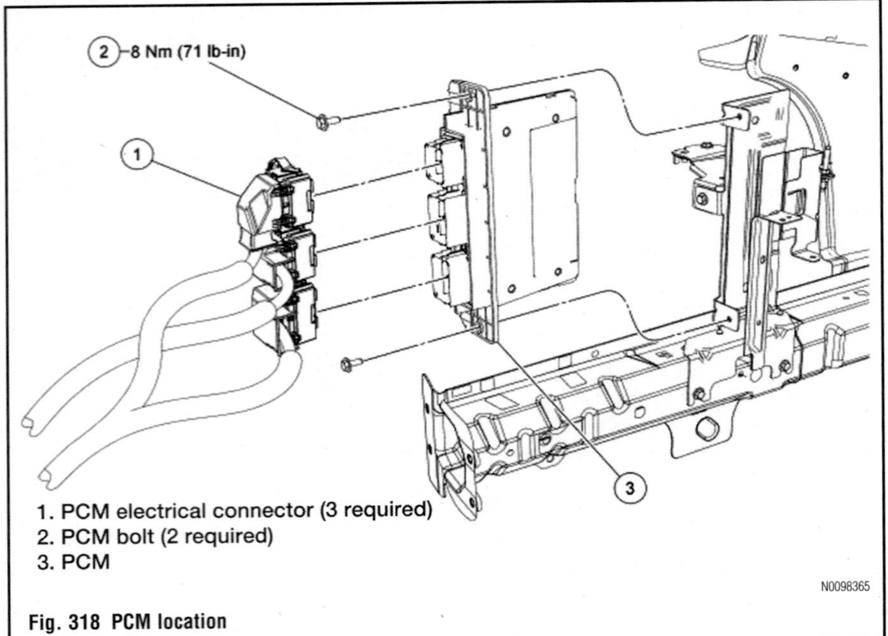

Fig. 318 PCM location

5. Follow the on-screen instructions, turn the ignition key to the OFF position, and press the check mark.
6. Install the new module and press the check mark.
7. Follow the on-screen instructions, turn the ignition key to the ON position, and press the check mark.
8. The IDS downloads the data into the new module and displays Module Configuration Complete.
9. Test module for correct operation.

Programmable Module Installation (PMI) Using the Integrated Diagnostic System (IDS) When the Original Module is NOT Available

➡Following module installation, some modules require a separate procedure be carried out. For instructions, refer to the specific module removal and installation procedures.

10. Install the new module.
11. Connect the IDS and identify the vehicle as normal.
12. From the Toolbox icon, select Module Programming and press the check mark.
13. Select Programmable Module Installation.
14. Select the module that was replaced.
15. Follow the on-screen instructions, turn the ignition key to the OFF position, and press the check mark.
16. Follow the on-screen instructions, turn the ignition key to the ON position, and press the check mark.
17. If the data is not available, the IDS displays a screen stating to contact the As-Built Data Center.
18. Retrieve the data from the technician service publication website at this time and press the check mark.
19. Enter the module data and press the check mark.
20. The IDS downloads the data into the new module and displays Module Configuration Complete.
21. Test module for correct operation.
Bottom of Form

THROTTLE POSITION SENSOR (TPS)

LOCATION

The TPS sensor is located on the throttle body housing.

REMOVAL & INSTALLATION

See Figures 319 and 320.

1. Remove the Air Cleaner (ACL) outlet pipe.
2. Disconnect the TP sensor electrical connector.

➡Do not put direct heat on the Throttle Position (TP) sensor or any other plastic parts because heat damage may occur. Damage may also occur if Electronic Throttle Body (ETB) temperature exceeds 248°F.

➡Do not use power tools.

3. Remove the TP sensor.
    a. Using a suitable heat gun, apply heat to the top of the ETB until the top TP sensor bolt ear reaches approximately 130°F. This should take no more than 3 minutes using an 1,100-watt heat gun. The heat gun should be about 1 inch away from the ETB.
    b. Monitor the temperature of the top TP sensor bolt ear on the ETB with a suitable temperature measuring device, such as a digital temperature laser or infrared thermometer, while heating the ETB.
    c. Using hand tools, quickly remove the bolt farthest from the heat source first and discard.
    d. Using hand tools, remove the remaining bolt and discard.
    e. Remove and discard the TP sensor.

To install:

➡When installing the new TP sensor, make sure that the radial locator tab on the TP sensor is aligned with the radial locator hole on the ETB.

➡Do not use power tools.

4. Install the new TP sensor.
5. Using hand tools, install the 2 new bolts. Tighten to 27 inch lbs. (3 Nm).
6. Connect the TP sensor electrical connector.
7. Install the ACL outlet pipe.

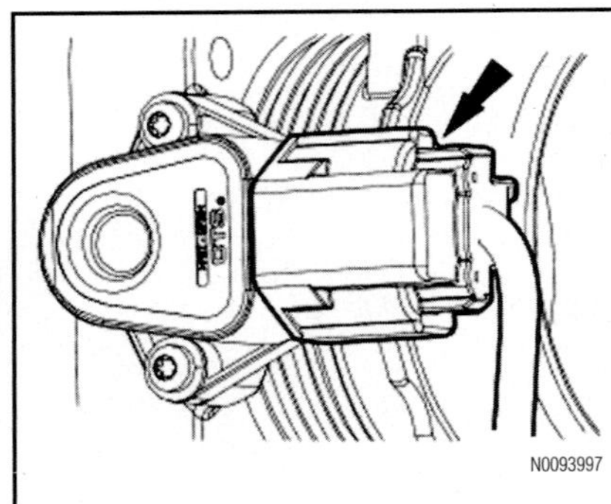

Fig. 319 Disconnect the TP sensor electrical connector

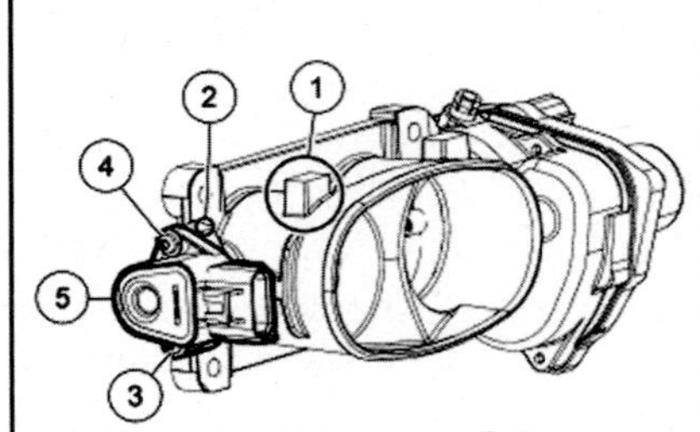

Fig. 320 Removing the TPS

FUEL SYSTEM SERVICE PRECAUTIONS

Safety is the most important factor when performing not only fuel system maintenance but any type of maintenance. Failure to conduct maintenance and repairs in a safe manner may result in serious personal injury or death. Maintenance and testing of the vehicle's fuel system components can be accomplished safely and effectively by adhering to the following rules and guidelines.

- To avoid the possibility of fire and personal injury, always disconnect the negative battery cable unless the repair or test procedure requires that battery voltage be applied.
- Always relieve the fuel system pressure prior to disconnecting any fuel system component (injector, fuel rail, pressure regulator, etc.), fitting or fuel line connection. Exercise extreme caution whenever relieving fuel system pressure to avoid exposing skin, face and eyes to fuel spray. Please be advised that fuel under pressure may penetrate the skin or any part of the body that it contacts.
- Always place a shop towel or cloth around the fitting or connection prior to loosening to absorb any excess fuel due to spillage. Ensure that all fuel spillage (should it occur) is quickly removed from engine surfaces. Ensure that all fuel soaked cloths or towels are deposited into a suitable waste container.
- Always keep a dry chemical (Class B) fire extinguisher near the work area.
- Do not allow fuel spray or fuel vapors to come into contact with a spark or open flame.
- Always use a back-up wrench when loosening and tightening fuel line connection fittings. This will prevent unnecessary stress and torsion to fuel line piping.
- Always replace worn fuel fitting O-rings with new Do not substitute fuel hose or equivalent where fuel pipe is installed.

Before servicing the vehicle, make sure to also refer to the precautions in the beginning of this section as well.

RELIEVING FUEL SYSTEM PRESSURE

See Figure 321.

✲✲ WARNING

Observe all applicable safety precautions when working around fuel. Whenever servicing the fuel system, always work in a well ventilated area. Do not allow fuel spray or vapors to come in contact with a spark or open flame. Keep a dry chemical fire extinguisher near the work area. Always keep fuel in a container specifically designed for fuel storage; also, always properly seal fuel containers to avoid the possibility of fire or explosion.

✲✲ WARNING

Do not smoke, carry lighted tobacco or have an open flame of any type when working on or near any fuel-related component. Highly flammable mixtures are always present and may be ignited. Failure to follow these instructions may result in serious personal injury.

✲✲ WARNING

Do not carry personal electronic devices such as cell phones, pagers or audio equipment of any type when working on or near any fuel-related component. Highly flammable mixtures are always present and may be ignited. Failure to follow these instructions may result in serious personal injury.

✲✲ WARNING

Before working on or disconnecting any of the fuel tubes or fuel system components, relieve the fuel system pressure to prevent accidental spraying of fuel. Fuel in the fuel system remains under high pressure, even when the engine is not running. Failure to follow this instruction may result in serious personal injury.

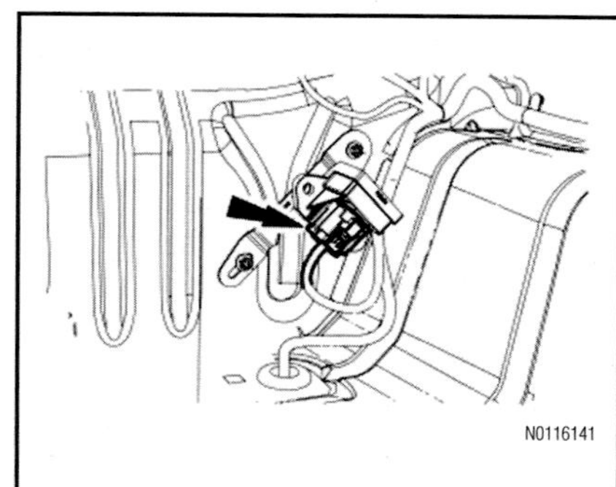

Fig. 321 Locating the Fuel Pump Control Module (FPCM)

➡The Fuel Pump Control Module (FPCM) is located in the spare tire stowage compartment.

1. Disconnect the Fuel Pump Control Module (FPCM) electrical connector(s).
2. Start the engine and allow it to idle until it stalls.
3. After the engine stalls, crank the engine for approximately 10 seconds to make sure the fuel injection supply manifold pressure has been released.
4. Turn the ignition switch to the OFF position.
5. When the fuel system service is complete, connect the FPCM electrical connector(s).

➡It may take more than one key cycle to pressurize the fuel system.

6. Cycle the ignition key and wait 3 seconds to pressurize the fuel system. Check for leaks before starting the engine.
7. Start the vehicle and check the fuel system for leaks.

FUEL FILTER

REMOVAL & INSTALLATION

See Figures 322 and 323.

1. With the vehicle in NEUTRAL, position it on a hoist.
2. Release the fuel system pressure.
3. Disconnect the battery ground cable.
4. Remove the 2 fuel tube bundle shield bolts.
5. Remove the 2 fuel tube bundle shield nuts.
6. Remove the pin-type retainer and the fuel tube bundle shield.

➡Some residual fuel may remain in the fuel tubes and filter. Upon disconnecting or removal, carefully drain into a suitable container.

7. Disconnect the front fuel tube-to-fuel filter quick connect coupling.
8. Disconnect the rear fuel tube-to-fuel filter quick connect coupling.
9. Loosen the bolt and remove the fuel filter from the fuel filter bracket.

➡Make sure the fuel tubes are completely seated and that the quick connect couplings are locked correctly in place. Pull on the tube to make sure it

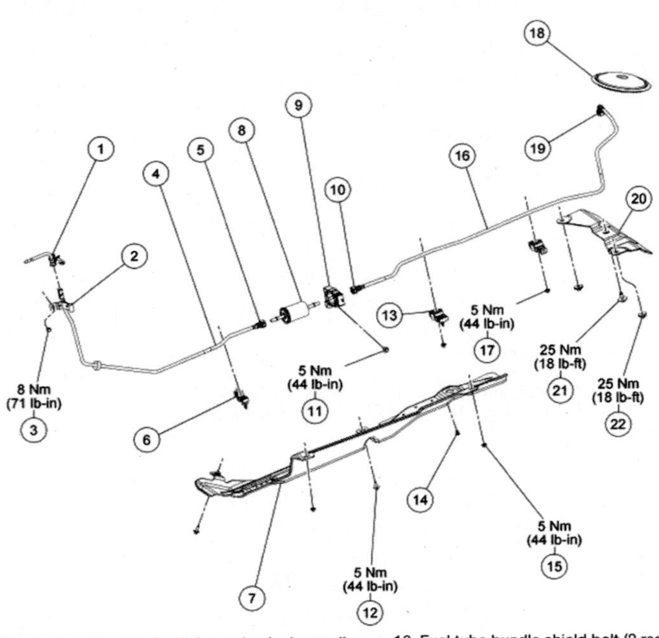

1. Fuel jumper tube-to-front fuel tube spring lock coupling
2. Fuel tube bundle bracket
3. Fuel tube bundle bracket bolt
4. Front fuel tube
5. Front fuel tube-to-fuel filter quick connect coupling
6. Fuel tube bundle pin-type retainer
7. Fuel tube bundle shield
8. Fuel filter
9. Fuel filter bracket
10. Rear fuel tube-to-fuel filter quick connect coupling
11. Fuel filter bracket bolt
12. Fuel tube bundle shield bolt (2 required)
13. Fuel tube bundle retainer (2 required)
14. Fuel tube bundle shield pin-type retainer
15. Fuel tube bundle shield nut (2 required)
16. Rear fuel tube
17. Fuel tube bundle retainer nut (2 required)
18. Fuel Pump (FP) module access cover
19. Rear fuel tube-to- FP module quick connect coupling
20. Fuel tank deflector
21. Fuel tank deflector bolt
22. Fuel tank deflector nut (2 required)

N0098535

Fig. 322 Exploded view of the fuel lines and filter—4.0L, 4.6L and 5.4L Engines—2010 models

is fully seated. Pressurize the system and check for leaks.

10. To install, reverse the removal procedure.

FUEL INJECTORS

REMOVAL & INSTALLATION

3.7L Engines

See Figure 324.

⁂ WARNING

Do not smoke, carry lighted tobacco or have an open flame of any type when working on or near any fuel-related component. Highly flammable mixtures are always present and may be ignited. Failure to follow these instructions may result in serious personal injury.

⁂ WARNING

Before working on or disconnecting any of the fuel tubes or fuel system components, relieve the fuel system pressure to prevent accidental spraying of fuel. Fuel in the fuel system remains under high pressure, even when the engine is not running. Failure to follow this instruction may result in serious personal injury.

⁂ WARNING

Do not carry personal electronic devices such as cell phones, pagers or audio equipment of any type when working on or near any fuel-related component. Highly flammable mixtures are always present and may be ignited. Failure to follow these instructions may result in serious personal injury.

⁂ WARNING

Always disconnect the battery ground cable at the battery when working on an evaporative emission (EVAP) system or fuel-related component. Highly flammable mixtures are always present and may be ignited. Failure to follow these instructions may result in serious personal injury.

⁂ WARNING

Clean all fuel residue from the engine compartment. If not removed, fuel residue may ignite when the engine is returned to operation. Failure to follow this instruction may result in serious personal injury.

1. Release the fuel system pressure.
2. Disconnect the battery ground cable.
3. Remove the upper intake manifold. For additional information, refer to Intake Manifold in Engine Mechanical.
4. Disconnect the fuel tube-to-fuel rail quick connect coupling.
5. Remove the LH and RH fuel rail noise insulator shields.

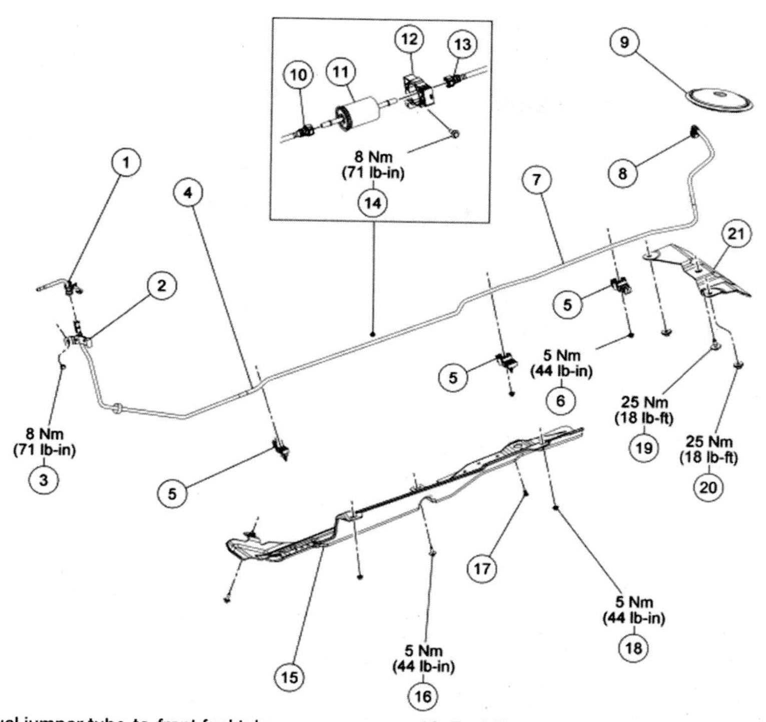

1. Fuel jumper tube-to-front fuel tube spring lock coupling
2. Fuel tube bundle bracket
3. Fuel tube bundle bracket bolt
4. Fuel tube (front fuel tube on 5.4L vehicles)
5. Fuel tube bundle retainer
6. Fuel tube bundle retainer nut (2 required)
7. Fuel tube (rear fuel tube on 5.4L vehicles)
8. Fuel tube-to- FP module quick connect coupling
9. Fuel Pump (FP) module access cover
10. Front fuel tube-to-fuel filter quick connect coupling (5.4L vehicles only)
11. Fuel filter (5.4L vehicles only)
12. Fuel filter bracket (5.4L vehicles only)
13. Rear fuel tube-to-fuel filter quick connect coupling (5.4L vehicles only)
14. Fuel filter bracket bolt (5.4L vehicles only)
15. Fuel tube bundle shield
16. Fuel tube bundle shield bolt (2 required)
17. Fuel tube bundle shield pin-type retainer
18. Fuel tube bundle shield nut (2 required)
19. Fuel tank deflector bolt
20. Fuel tank deflector nut (2 required)
21. Fuel tank deflector

N0116185

Fig. 323 Exploded view of the fuel lines and filter—3.7L, 5.0L and 5.4L Engines—2011 models

6. Disconnect the 6 fuel injector electrical connectors.
7. Remove the 4 fuel rail bolts.
8. Remove the fuel rail and injectors as an assembly.
9. Remove the 6 fuel injector clips and the 6 fuel injectors.
10. Remove and discard the 12 fuel injector O-ring seals.

To install:

➡Use O-ring seals that are made of special fuel-resistant material. The use of ordinary O-rings may cause the fuel system to leak. Do not reuse the O-ring seals.

➡The upper and lower fuel injector O-ring seals are similar in appearance, but are not interchangeable.

11. Install the new O-ring seals onto the fuel injectors and lubricate them with clean engine oil.
12. Install the 6 fuel injectors and the 6 fuel injector clips into the fuel rail.
13. Install the fuel rail and fuel injectors as an assembly.
14. Install the 4 fuel rail bolts.
15. Connect the 6 fuel injector electrical connectors.
16. Install the LH and RH fuel rail noise insulator shields.
17. Connect the fuel tube-to-fuel rail quick connect coupling.
18. Install the upper intake manifold.
19. Connect the battery ground cable.

4.0L Engines

See Figure 325.

⁂ WARNING

Do not smoke, carry lighted tobacco or have an open flame of any type when working on or near any fuel-related component. Highly flammable mixtures are always present and may be ignited. Failure to follow these instructions may result in serious personal injury.

⁂ WARNING

Before working on or disconnecting any of the fuel tubes or fuel system components, relieve the fuel system pressure to prevent accidental spraying of fuel. Fuel in the fuel system remains under high pressure, even when the engine is not running. Failure to follow this instruction may result in serious personal injury.

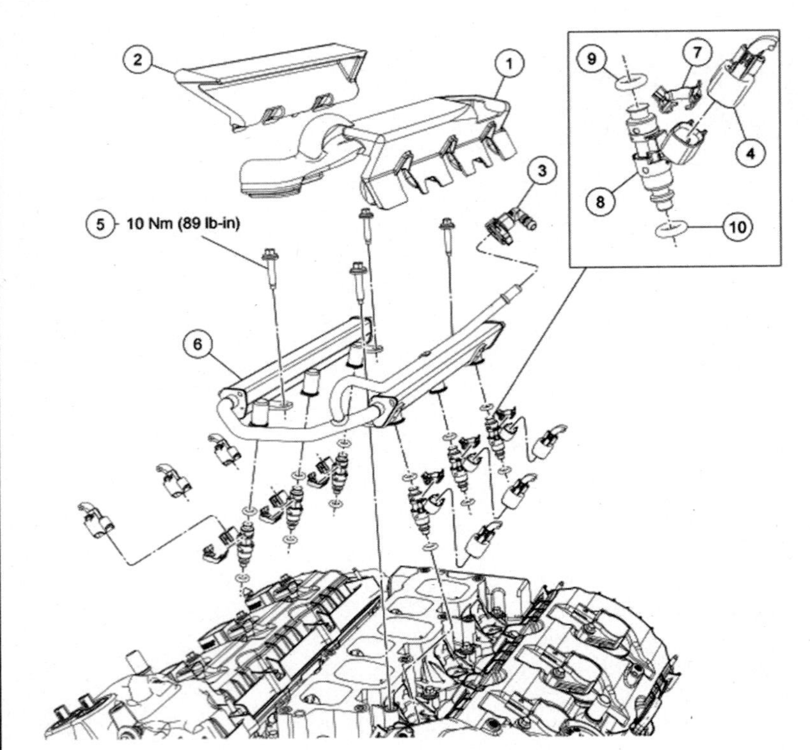

1. LH fuel rail noise insulator shield
2. RH fuel rail noise insulator shield
3. Fuel tube-to-fuel rail quick connect coupling
4. Fuel injector electrical connector (6 required)
5. Fuel rail bolt (4 required)
6. Fuel rail
7. Fuel injector clip (6 required)
8. Fuel injector (6 required)
9. Upper fuel injector O-ring seal (6 required)
10. Lower fuel injector O-ring seal (6 required)

N0114067

Fig. 324 Exploded view of the fuel rail and injector assembly

**** WARNING**

Do not carry personal electronic devices such as cell phones, pagers or audio equipment of any type when working on or near any fuel-related component. Highly flammable mixtures are always present and may be ignited. Failure to follow these instructions may result in serious personal injury.

**** WARNING**

Always disconnect the battery ground cable at the battery when working on an evaporative emission (EVAP) system or fuel-related component. Highly flammable mixtures are always present and may be ignited. Failure to follow these instructions may result in serious personal injury.

**** WARNING**

Clean all fuel residue from the engine compartment. If not removed, fuel residue may ignite when the engine is returned to operation. Failure to follow this instruction may result in serious personal injury.

1. Release the fuel system pressure.
2. Disconnect the battery ground cable.
3. RH side:
   a. Remove the wiring harness retainer from the RH valve cover stud bolt.
   b. Disconnect the 3 fuel injector electrical connectors.
   c. Remove the 2 fuel rail supply tube bolts from the RH side fuel rail.

➡Use O-ring seals that are made of special fuel-resistant material. The use of ordinary O-ring seals may cause the fuel system to leak. Do not reuse the O-ring seals.

   d. Remove and discard the fuel rail supply tube O-ring seal.
   e. Remove the 2 bolts and the RH side fuel rail.
   f. Remove the 3 fuel injectors from the fuel rail.

➡Use O-ring seals that are made of special fuel-resistant material. The use of ordinary O-ring seals may cause the fuel system to leak. Do not reuse the O-ring seals.

   g. Remove and discard the fuel injector O-ring seals.
4. LH side:
   a. Disconnect the fuel rail pressure and temperature sensor electrical connector and vacuum hose.
   b. Disconnect the radio capacitor electrical connector.
   c. Remove the 2 ignition coil bracket upper bolts.
   d. Remove the (M8) ignition coil bracket lower bolt.
   e. Remove the (M12) ignition coil bracket lower bolt.
   f. Position the ignition coil and bracket aside.
   g. Remove the wiring harness retainer from the LH valve cover stud bolt.
   h. Disconnect the 3 fuel injector electrical connectors.
   i. Remove the 2 fuel rail supply tube bolts from the LH side fuel rail.

➡Use O-ring seals that are made of special fuel-resistant material. The use of ordinary O-ring seals may cause the fuel system to leak. Do not reuse the O-ring seals.

   j. Remove and discard the fuel rail supply tube O-ring seal.
   k. Remove the 2 bolts and the LH side fuel rail.
   l. Remove the 3 fuel injectors from the fuel rail.

➡Use O-ring seals that are made of special fuel-resistant material. The use of ordinary O-ring seals may cause the fuel system to leak. Do not reuse the O-ring seals.

   m. Remove and discard the fuel injector O-ring seals.
5. To install reverse the removal procedure. Refer to illustration for torque values.
6. Lubricate the new O-ring seals with clean engine oil prior to installation.

4.6L Engine

See Figure 326.

**** WARNING**

Do not smoke, carry lighted tobacco or have an open flame of any type when working on or near any fuel-

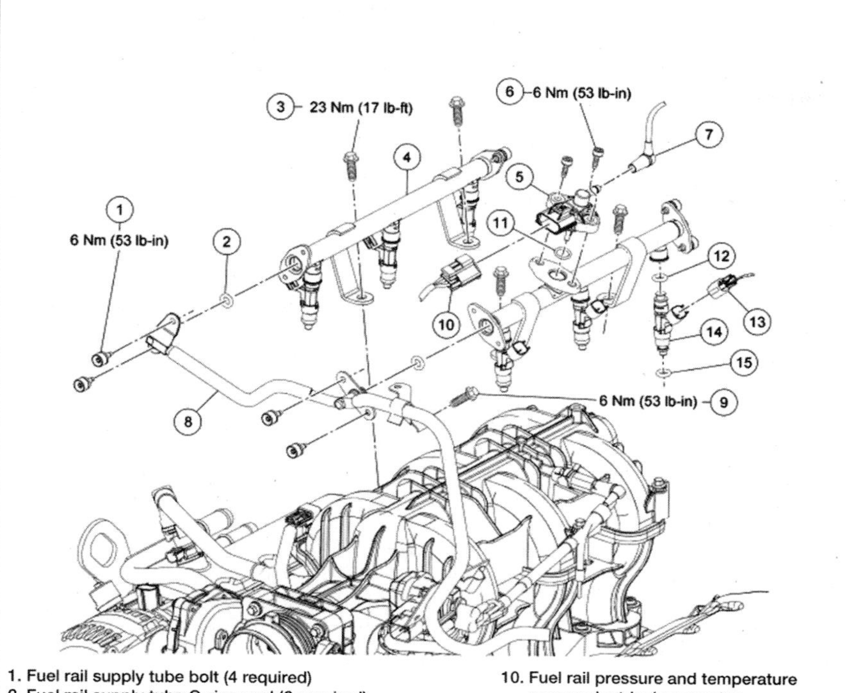

1. Fuel rail supply tube bolt (4 required)
2. Fuel rail supply tube O-ring seal (2 required)
3. Fuel rail bolt (4 required)
4. Fuel rail (2 required)
5. Fuel rail pressure and temperature sensor
6. Fuel rail pressure and temperature sensor bolt (2 required)
7. Fuel rail pressure and temperature sensor vacuum hose
8. Fuel rail supply tube
9. Upper fuel rail supply tube bracket bolt
10. Fuel rail pressure and temperature sensor electrical connector
11. Fuel rail pressure and temperature sensor O-ring seal
12. Upper fuel injector O-ring seal (6 required)
13. Fuel injector electrical connector (6 required)
14. Fuel injector (6 required)
15. Lower fuel injector O-ring seal (6 required)

N0098201

Fig. 325 Exploded view of the fuel rail and injector assembly

related component. Highly flammable mixtures are always present and may be ignited. Failure to follow these instructions may result in serious personal injury.

⁂ WARNING

Before working on or disconnecting any of the fuel tubes or fuel system components, relieve the fuel system pressure to prevent accidental spraying of fuel. Fuel in the fuel system remains under high pressure, even when the engine is not running. Failure to follow this instruction may result in serious personal injury.

⁂ WARNING

Do not carry personal electronic devices such as cell phones, pagers or audio equipment of any type when working on or near any fuel-related component. Highly flammable mixtures are always present and may be ignited. Failure to follow these instructions may result in serious personal injury.

⁂ WARNING

Always disconnect the battery ground cable at the battery when working on an evaporative emission (EVAP) system or fuel-related component. Highly flammable mixtures are always present and may be ignited. Failure to follow these instructions may result in serious personal injury.

⁂ WARNING

Clean all fuel residue from the engine compartment. If not removed, fuel residue may ignite when the engine is returned to operation. Failure to follow this instruction may result in serious personal injury.

1. Release the fuel system pressure.
2. Disconnect the battery ground cable.
3. Disconnect the fuel jumper tube-to-fuel rail spring lock coupling.
4. Disconnect the fuel rail pressure and temperature sensor vacuum hose retainer from the LH fuel rail stud bolt.
5. Disconnect the fuel rail pressure and temperature sensor electrical connector and vacuum hose.
6. Disconnect the 8 fuel injector electrical connectors.
7. Remove the 4 fuel rail stud bolts.
8. Remove the fuel rail and fuel injectors as an assembly from the intake manifold.

➡The fuel injector clip can be reused if it is not damaged during removal. If the clip is reused, the 2 sides of the clip should be squeezed back into shape by placing it between index finger and thumb.

9. Remove the retaining clips and fuel injectors from the fuel rail.

➡Use O-ring seals that are made of special fuel-resistant material. Use of ordinary O-ring seals may cause the fuel system to leak. Do not reuse the O-ring seals.

10. Remove and discard the fuel injector O-ring seals.
11. To install, reverse the removal procedure.
12. Lubricate the new upper and lower fuel injector O-ring seals with clean engine oil prior to installation.

5.0L Engine

See Figure 327.

⁂ WARNING

Do not smoke, carry lighted tobacco or have an open flame of any type when working on or near any fuel-related component. Highly flammable mixtures are always present and may be ignited. Failure to follow these instructions may result in serious personal injury.

⁂ WARNING

Before working on or disconnecting any of the fuel tubes or fuel system components, relieve the fuel system pressure to prevent accidental spraying of fuel. Fuel in the fuel system remains under high pressure, even when the engine is not running. Failure to follow this instruction may result in serious personal injury.

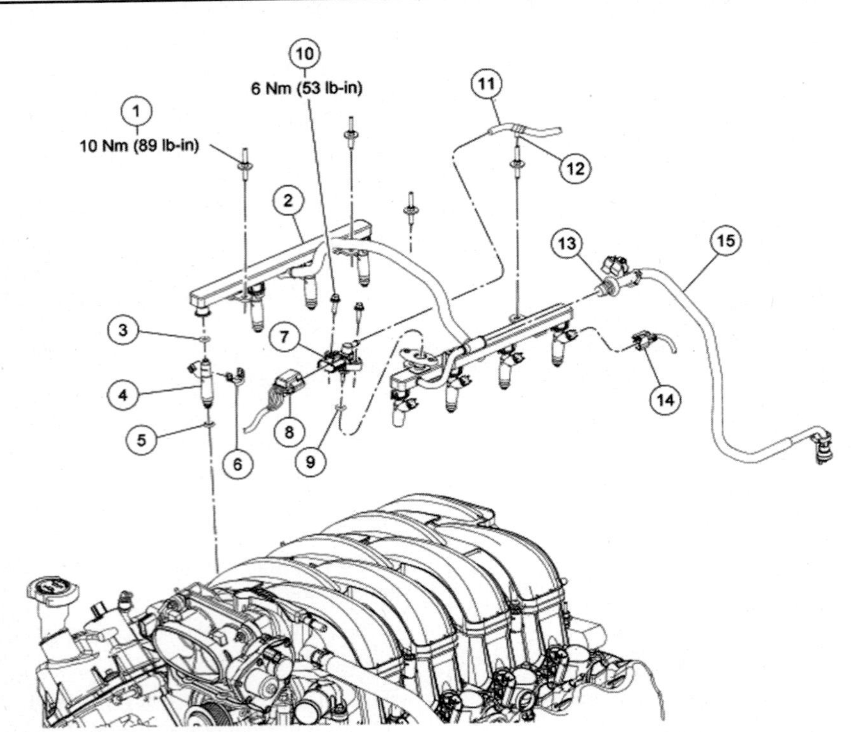

Fig. 326 Exploded view of the fuel rail and injector assembly

⁂ WARNING

Do not carry personal electronic devices such as cell phones, pagers or audio equipment of any type when working on or near any fuel-related component. Highly flammable mixtures are always present and may be ignited. Failure to follow these instructions may result in serious personal injury.

⁂ WARNING

Always disconnect the battery ground cable at the battery when working on an evaporative emission (EVAP) system or fuel-related component. Highly flammable mixtures are always present and may be ignited. Failure to follow these instructions may result in serious personal injury.

⁂ WARNING

Clean all fuel residue from the engine compartment. If not removed, fuel residue may ignite when the engine is returned to operation. Failure to follow this instruction may result in serious personal injury.

1. Release the fuel system pressure.
2. Disconnect the battery ground cable.
3. If equipped, remove the 4 nuts and the strut tower cross brace.
4. Remove the engine appearance cover.
5. Position the heater hoses aside.
6. Remove the 2 nuts and the LH heater hose support.
7. Position the vacuum tube assembly aside.
8. Remove the 2 nuts and the RH heater hose support.
9. Remove the LH and RH fuel rail insulators.
10. Disconnect the 8 fuel injector electrical connectors.
11. Disconnect the fuel supply tube.
12. Remove the 4 fuel rail bolts.
13. Remove the fuel rail and fuel injectors as an assembly from the intake manifold.
14. Remove the retaining clips and fuel injectors from the fuel rail.

➡Do not reuse the O-ring seals. Failure to follow this direction may cause the fuel system to leak.

15. Remove and discard the fuel injector O-ring seals.

To install:

➡Use O-ring seals that are made of special fuel-resistant material. Use of ordinary O-ring seals may cause the fuel system to leak.

16. Install new O-ring seals on the fuel injectors.

➡The fuel injector clip can be reused if it is not damaged during removal. If the clip is reused, the 2 sides of the clip should be squeezed back into shape by placing it between index finger and thumb.

➡Lubricate the upper and lower fuel injector O-ring seals with clean engine oil prior to installation.

17. Install the fuel injectors and retaining clips onto the fuel rail.

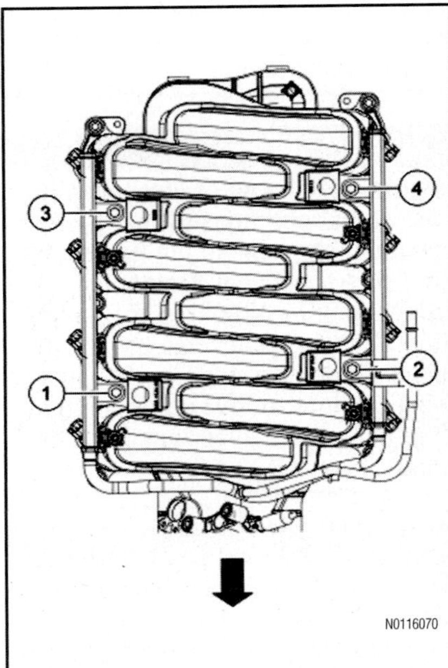

Fig. 327 Fuel rail tightening sequence

18. Install the fuel rail and fuel injectors as an assembly onto the intake manifold.
19. Install the 4 bolts and tighten in the sequence shown in 3 stages.
   a. Stage 1: Hand tighten.
   b. Stage 2: Tighten to 89 inch lbs. (10 Nm).
   c. Stage 3: Tighten an additional 90 degrees.
20. Connect the fuel supply tube.
21. Connect the 8 fuel injector electrical connectors.
22. Install the LH and RH fuel rail insulators.
23. Install the RH heater hose support and the 2 nuts.
24. Install the vacuum tube assembly, the LH heater hose support and the 2 nuts.
25. Position the heater hoses.

➡The engine appearance cover rubber grommets may remain on the cover. If so, remove the grommets from the cover and install them on the intake manifold before installing the cover.

26. Install the engine appearance cover.
27. If equipped, install the strut tower cross brace and the 4 nuts. Tighten to 26 ft. lbs. (35 Nm).
28. Connect the battery ground cable.

5.4L Engine

✻✻ WARNING

Do not smoke, carry lighted tobacco or have an open flame of any type when working on or near any fuel-related component. Highly flammable mixtures are always present and may be ignited. Failure to follow these instructions may result in serious personal injury.

✻✻ WARNING

Before working on or disconnecting any of the fuel tubes or fuel system components, relieve the fuel system pressure to prevent accidental spraying of fuel. Fuel in the fuel system remains under high pressure, even when the engine is not running. Failure to follow this instruction may result in serious personal injury.

✻✻ WARNING

Do not carry personal electronic devices such as cell phones, pagers or audio equipment of any type when working on or near any fuel-related component. Highly flammable mixtures are always present and may be ignited. Failure to follow these instructions may result in serious personal injury.

✻✻ WARNING

Always disconnect the battery ground cable at the battery when working on an evaporative emission (EVAP) system or fuel-related component. Highly flammable mixtures are always present and may be ignited. Failure to follow these instructions may result in serious personal injury.

✻✻ WARNING

Clean all fuel residue from the engine compartment. If not removed, fuel residue may ignite when the engine is returned to operation. Failure to follow this instruction may result in serious personal injury.

1. Release the fuel system pressure.
2. Disconnect the battery ground cable.
3. Remove the Air Cleaner (ACL) outlet pipe.
4. Disconnect the Evaporative Emission (EVAP) canister purge valve vapor tube-to-Throttle Body (TB) spacer quick connect coupling.
5. Disconnect the brake booster-to- TB spacer quick connect coupling.
6. Disconnect the electronic throttle control electrical connector.
7. Disconnect the Throttle Position (TP) sensor electrical connector.
8. Remove the 4 bolts and the TB spacer assembly.
9. Discard the gasket.
10. Disconnect the Intake Air Temperature 2 (IAT2) sensor electrical connector.
11. Disconnect the fuel supply tube-to-fuel rail quick connect coupling.
12. Disconnect the PCV valve-to-Supercharger (SC) tube quick connect coupling and position aside.
13. Disconnect the fuel rail pressure and temperature sensor electrical and vacuum connectors.
14. Disconnect the 8 fuel injector electrical connectors.
15. Remove the 4 fuel rail bolts.
16. Remove the fuel rail and the 8 fuel injectors.

➡The fuel injector clip can be reused if it is not damaged during removal.

17. Remove the fuel injector clips and the fuel injectors.
18. Inspect the fuel injector O-ring seals for damage.
19. To install, reverse the removal procedure.
20. Lubricate the upper and lower fuel injector O-ring seals with clean engine oil prior to installation.
21. Install a new TB spacer-to- SC gasket.

FUEL PUMP

REMOVAL & INSTALLATION

See Figure 328.

✻✻ WARNING

Do not smoke, carry lighted tobacco or have an open flame of any type when working on or near any fuel-related component. Highly flammable mixtures are always present and may be ignited. Failure to follow these instructions may result in serious personal injury.

✻✻ WARNING

Before working on or disconnecting any of the fuel tubes or fuel system components, relieve the fuel system pressure to prevent accidental spraying of fuel. Fuel in the fuel system remains under high pressure, even when the engine is not running. Failure to follow this instruction may result in serious personal injury.

✻✻ WARNING

Do not carry personal electronic devices such as cell phones, pagers or audio equipment of any type when working on or near any fuel-related component. Highly flammable mixtures are always present and may be ignited. Failure to follow these instructions may result in serious personal injury.

✻✻ WARNING

Always disconnect the battery ground cable at the battery when working on an evaporative emission (EVAP) system or fuel-related component. Highly flammable mixtures are always present and may be ignited. Failure to follow these instructions may result in serious personal injury.

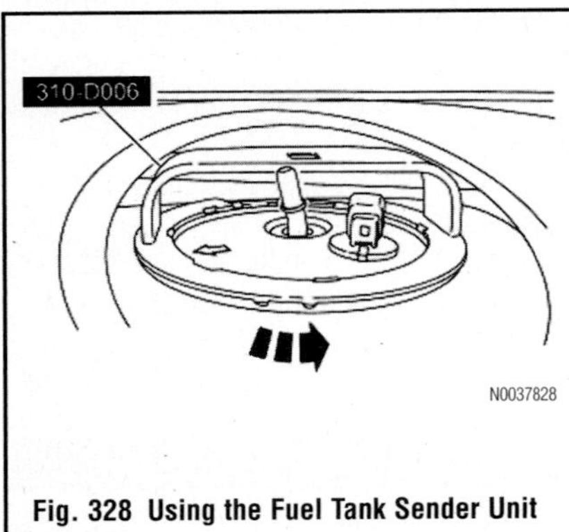

Fig. 328 Using the Fuel Tank Sender Unit Socket

**** WARNING**

Clean all fuel residue from the engine compartment. If not removed, fuel residue may ignite when the engine is returned to operation. Failure to follow this instruction may result in serious personal injury.

1. Release the fuel system pressure.
2. Disconnect the battery ground cable.

➡The supplemental refueling adapter is located in the luggage compartment.

3. Install the supplemental refueling adapter and a length of semi-rigid fuel drain tube into the Easy Fuel® (capless) fuel tank filler pipe until the tube enters the fuel tank.

➡This step will remove approximately one-eighth tank of fuel from a completely full fuel tank and the majority of any residual fuel from the fuel tank filler pipe. Also the fuel in the fuel tank will be below the Fuel Pump (FP) module mounting flange for FP module removal without fuel spillage.

4. Attach the Fuel Storage Tanker to the drain tube and remove one-eighth of the fuel (approximately 2 gallons) from a completely full tank, lowering the fuel below the FP module mounting flange.
5. Remove the rear seat cushion.
6. Remove the FP module access cover and position aside.

➡Clean the FP module connections, couplings, flange surfaces and the immediate surrounding area of any dirt or foreign material.

7. Disconnect the FP module electrical connector.

➡Place absorbent pads in the general work area in case of fuel spillage.

8. Disconnect the rear fuel tube-to- FP module quick connect coupling.

➡Carefully install the Fuel Tank Sender Unit Socket to avoid damaging the FP module when removing the lock ring.

9. Using the Fuel Tank Sender Unit Socket, remove the FP module lock ring.

➡The Fuel Pump (FP) module must be handled carefully to avoid damage to the float arm.

10. Carefully lift the FP module out of the fuel tank allowing access and disconnect the internal fuel tube-to- FP module quick connect coupling.

➡Drain any residual fuel in the FP module into a suitable container.

11. Completely remove the FP module from the fuel tank.

➡Inspect the surfaces of the FP module flange and fuel tank O-ring seal contact surfaces. Do not polish or adjust the O-ring seal contact area of the fuel tank flange or the fuel tank. Install a new FP module or fuel tank if the O-ring seal contact area is bent, scratched or corroded.

➡To install, apply clean engine oil to the O-ring seal.

12. Remove and discard the FP module O-ring seal.

➡Make sure to install a new FP module O-ring seal.

➡Make sure the alignment tabs on the FP module and the slots on the fuel tank meet before tightening the FP module lock ring.

13. To install, reverse the removal procedure.
14. Tighten the FP module lock ring until it meets the stop tabs on the fuel tank.

FUEL TANK

DRAINING

**** WARNING**

Observe all applicable safety precautions when working around fuel. Whenever servicing the fuel system, always work in a well ventilated area. Do not allow fuel spray or vapors to come in contact with a spark or open flame. Keep a dry chemical fire extinguisher near the work area. Always keep fuel in a container specifically designed for fuel storage; also, always properly seal fuel containers to avoid the possibility of fire or explosion.

**** WARNING**

Do not smoke, carry lighted tobacco or have an open flame of any type when working on or near any fuel-related component. Highly flammable mixtures are always present and may be ignited. Failure to follow these instructions may result in serious personal injury.

**** WARNING**

Do not carry personal electronic devices such as cell phones, pagers or audio equipment of any type when working on or near any fuel-related component. Highly flammable mixtures are always present and may be ignited. Failure to follow these instructions may result in serious personal injury.

**** WARNING**

Before working on or disconnecting any of the fuel tubes or fuel system components, relieve the fuel system pressure to prevent accidental spraying of fuel. Fuel in the fuel system remains under high pressure, even when the engine is not running. Failure to follow this instruction may result in serious personal injury.

**** WARNING**

When handling fuel, always observe fuel handling precautions and be prepared in the event of fuel spillage. Spilled fuel may be ignited by hot vehicle components or other ignition sources. Failure to follow these instructions may result in serious personal injury.

**** WARNING**

Always disconnect the battery ground cable at the battery when working on an evaporative emission (EVAP) system or fuel-related component. Highly flammable mixtures are always present and may be ignited. Failure to follow these instructions may result in serious personal injury.

1. Release the fuel system pressure.
2. Disconnect the battery ground cable.

➡The supplemental refueling adapter is located in the luggage compartment.

3. Install the supplemental refueling adapter and a length of semi-rigid fuel drain tube into the Easy Fuel TM(capless) fuel tank filler pipe until the tube enters the fuel tank.

➡This step is to remove approximately one-eighth tank of the fuel from a completely full fuel tank and the majority of any residual fuel in the fuel tank filler pipe, lowering the fuel level below the Fuel Pump (FP) module mounting flange.

4. Attach the Fuel Storage Tanker to the fuel drain tube and remove approximately one-eighth (approximately 2 gallons) of fuel from the tank.
5. Remove the rear seat cushion.
6. Remove the FP module and fuel level sensor access covers and position aside.

➡Clean the FP module connections, couplings, flange surfaces and the immediate surrounding area of any dirt or foreign material.

7. Disconnect the FP module electrical connector.

➡Place absorbent pads in the general work area in case of fuel spillage.

8. Disconnect the rear fuel tube-to- FP module quick connect coupling.

➡Carefully install the Fuel Tank Sender Unit Socket to avoid damage to the Fuel Pump (FP) module when removing the lock ring.

➡When installing the FP module, install a new O-ring seal.

Install the Fuel Tank Sender Unit Socket and remove the FP module lock ring.

➡The Fuel Pump (FP) module must be handled carefully to avoid damage to the float arm.

9. Position the FP module aside. Using the Fuel Storage Tanker, completely drain the remaining fuel from the LH saddle of the fuel tank.

➡Inspect the surfaces of the FP module flange and fuel tank O-ring seal contact surfaces. Do not polish or adjust the O-ring seal contact area of the fuel tank flange or the fuel tank. Install a new FP module or fuel tank if the O-ring seal contact area is bent, scratched or corroded.

➡To install, apply clean engine oil to the O-ring seal.

Remove and discard the FP module O-ring seal.

➡Clean the fuel level sensor connections, flange surfaces and the immediate surrounding area of any dirt or foreign material.

10. Disconnect the fuel level sensor electrical connector.
11. Carefully install the Fuel Tank Sender Unit Socket to avoid damage to the fuel level sensor when removing the lock ring.

➡When installing the fuel level sensor, install a new O-ring seal.

12. Install the Fuel Tank Sender Unit Socket and remove the fuel level sensor lock ring.

➡The fuel level sensor must be handled carefully to avoid damage to the float arm.

Position the fuel level sensor aside. Using the Fuel Storage Tanker, completely drain the RH saddle of the fuel tank.

➡Inspect the surfaces of the fuel level sensor flange and fuel tank O-ring seal contact surfaces. Do not polish or adjust the O-ring seal contact area of the fuel tank flange or the fuel tank. Install a new fuel level sensor or fuel tank if the O-ring seal contact area is bent, scratched or corroded.

➡To install, apply clean engine oil to the O-ring seal.

13. Remove and discard the fuel level sensor O-ring seal.

REMOVAL & INSTALLATION

See Figures 329 and 330.

1. With the vehicle in NEUTRAL, position it on a hoist.

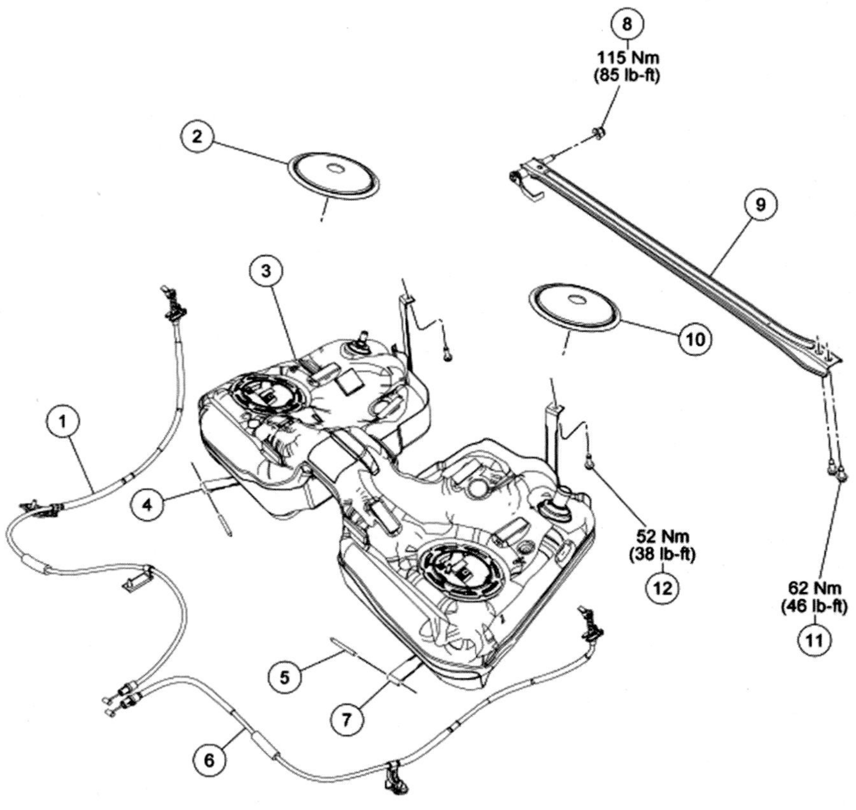

Fig. 329 Exploded view of the fuel tank and related components—3.7L and 5.0L Engines

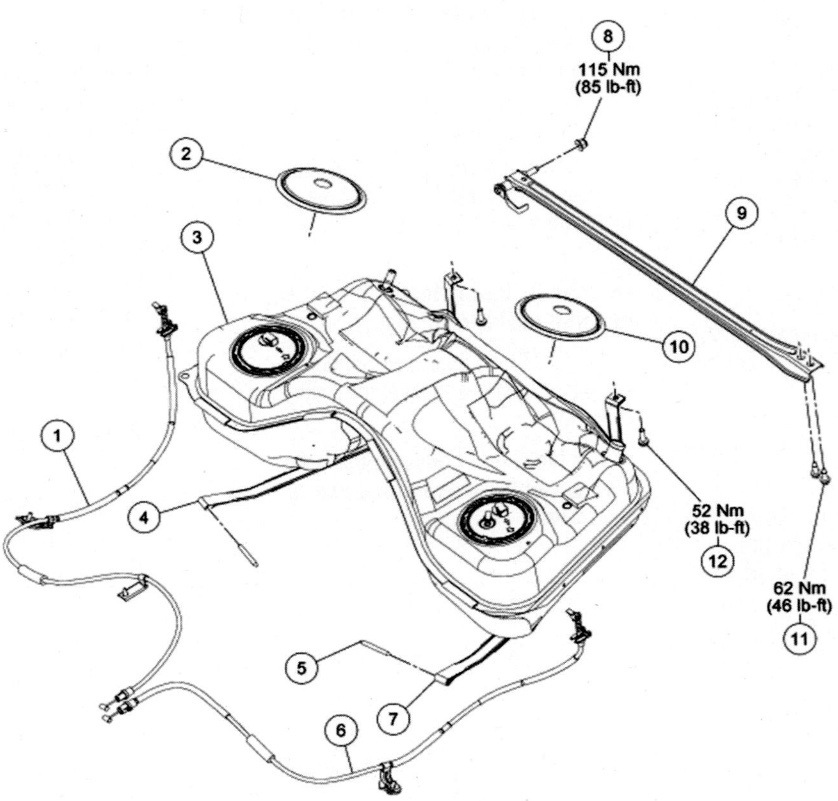

1. Rear parking brake cable (RH)
2. Fuel level sensor access cover
3. Fuel tank
4. Fuel tank strap (RH)
5. Fuel tank strap pin (2 required)
6. Rear parking brake cable (LH)
7. Fuel tank strap (LH)
8. Lateral stiffener bar-to-body mount nut
9. Lateral stiffener bar
10. Fuel Pump (FP) module access cover
11. Lateral stiffener bar-to-body bolt (2 required)
12. Fuel tank strap bolt (2 required)

N0098533

Fig. 330 Exploded view of the fuel tank and related components—4.0L, 4.6L and 5.4L Engines

2. Disconnect the battery ground cable.
3. Drain the fuel tank.
4. If equipped, remove the rear support braces.
5. Remove the exhaust intermediate pipe(s).
6. Remove the driveshaft. For additional information, refer to Driveshaft.
7. Disconnect the fuel vapor tube assembly-to-fuel tank quick connect coupling.

➡Some residual fuel may remain in the fuel tank filler pipe after draining the fuel tank. Carefully drain any residual fuel into a suitable container.

8. Release the clamp and disconnect the fuel tank filler pipe from the fuel tank.
9. Position the Powertrain Lift under the fuel tank.
10. Position the emergency brake cables away from the fuel tank.
11. Remove the 2 bolts, pins and the fuel tank straps. To install, tighten to 38 ft. lbs. (52 Nm).
12. Completely lower and remove the fuel tank from the vehicle.
13. To install, reverse the removal procedure.

IDLE SPEED

ADJUSTMENT

Idle speed adjustment is not necessary or possible.

THROTTLE BODY

REMOVAL & INSTALLATION

3.7L Engine

See Figure 331.

1. If equipped, remove the 4 nuts (2 shown) and the strut tower cross brace. To install, tighten to 26 ft. lbs. (35 Nm).

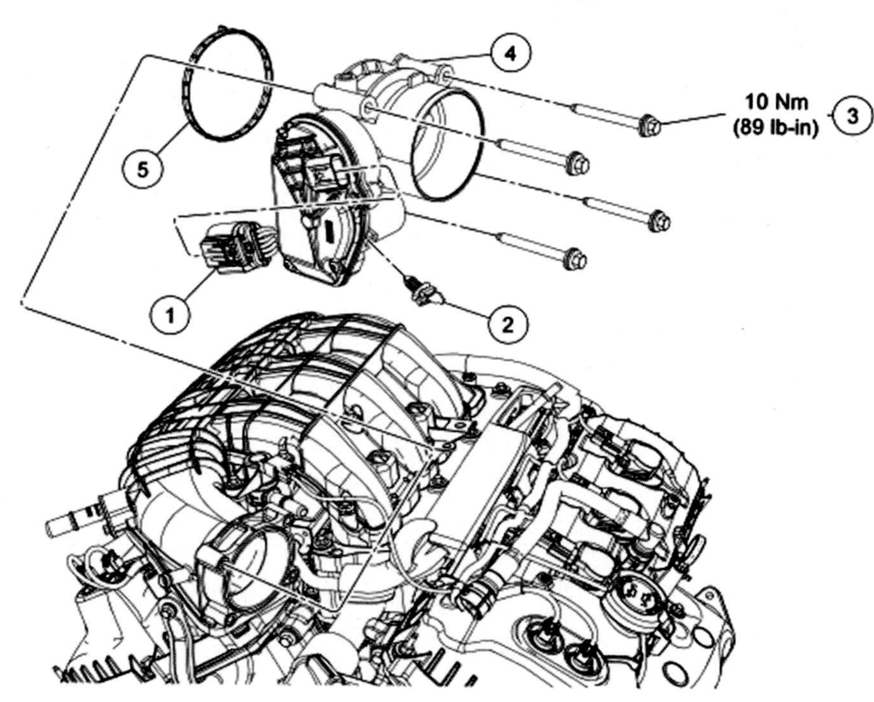

1. Electronic throttle control electrical connector
2. Electronic throttle control electrical connector wiring harness pin-type retainer
3. Throttle Body (TB) bolt (4 required)
4. TB
5. TB gasket

N0115476

Fig. 331 Exploded view of the throttle body

2. If equipped, detach the 2 retainers and remove the engine appearance cover.
3. Remove the engine Air Cleaner (ACL) outlet pipe.
4. Remove the bolt for the intake manifold vacuum tube.
5. Detach the intake manifold vacuum tube pin-type retainer from the Throttle Body (TB).
6. Disconnect the electronic throttle control electrical connector.
7. Detach the electronic throttle control electrical connector wiring harness pin-type retainer.
8. Remove the 4 bolts and the TB.
9. Discard the TB gasket.

➡Install a new TB gasket.

10. To install, reverse the removal procedure. Refer to illustration for torque values.

4.0L Engine

See Figure 332.

1. Remove the Air Cleaner (ACL) outlet pipe.
2. Disconnect the Throttle Position (TP) sensor electrical connector.
3. Disconnect the electronic throttle control electrical connector.

➡Inspect and install a new Throttle Body (TB) gasket as necessary.

4. Remove the 4 bolts and the TB.
5. To install, reverse the removal procedure. Refer to illustration for torque values.

4.6L Engine

See Figure 333.

1. Remove the Air Cleaner (ACL) outlet pipe.
2. Disconnect the Throttle Position (TP) sensor electrical connector.
3. Disconnect the electronic throttle control electrical connector.

➡Discard the Throttle Body (TB) gasket.

4. Remove the 2 stud bolts, 2 nuts and the TB.

➡Install a new TB gasket.

5. To install, reverse the removal procedure.

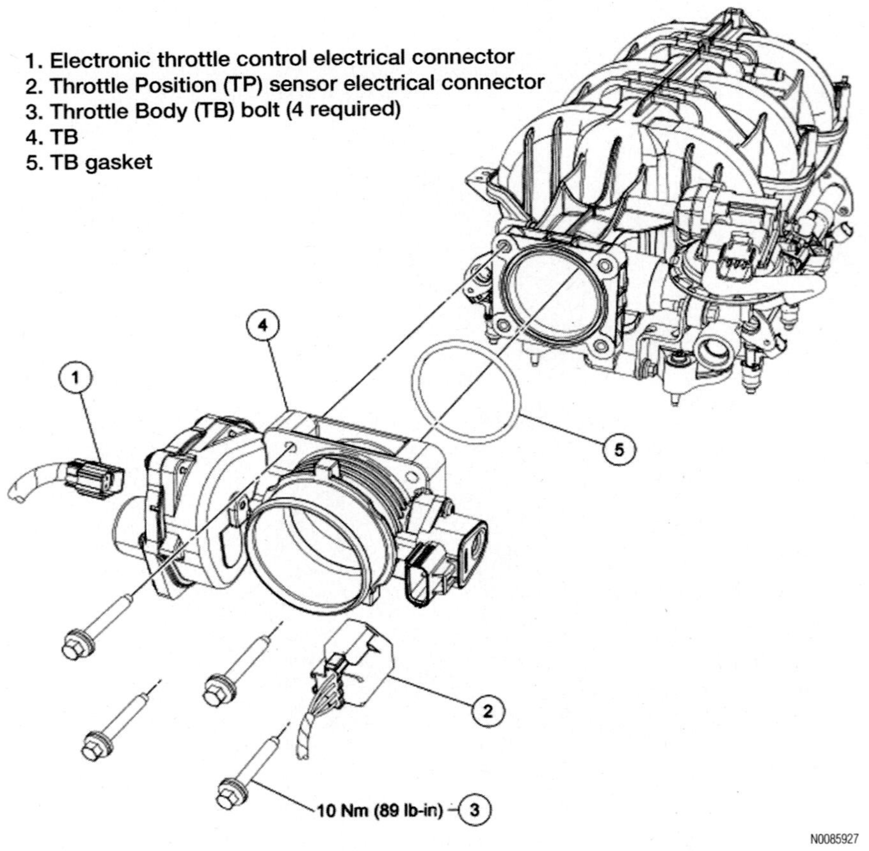

1. Electronic throttle control electrical connector
2. Throttle Position (TP) sensor electrical connector
3. Throttle Body (TB) bolt (4 required)
4. TB
5. TB gasket
10 Nm (89 lb-in)
N0085927

Fig. 332 Exploded view of the throttle body

10 Nm
(89 lb-in)
10 Nm (89 lb-in)
1. Electronic throttle control electrical connector
2. Throttle Position (TP) sensor electrical connector
3. Throttle Body (TB) bolt (2 required)
4. TB nut (2 required)
5. TB
6. TB gasket
N0070934

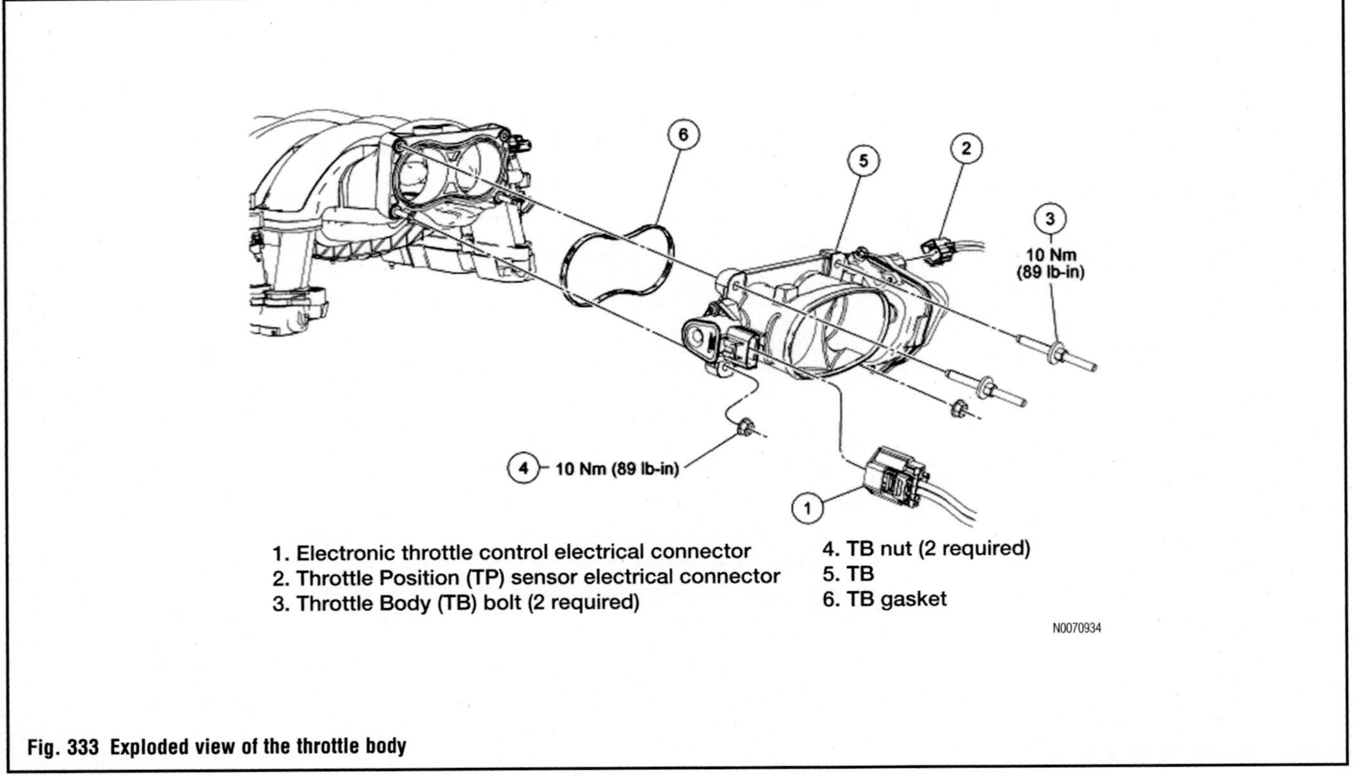

Fig. 333 Exploded view of the throttle body

5.0L Engine

See Figure 334.

1. If equipped, remove the 4 nuts and the strut tower cross brace. To install, tighten to 26 ft. lbs. (35 Nm).

➡The engine appearance cover rubber grommets may remain on the cover. If so, remove the grommets from the cover and install them on the intake manifold before installing the cover.

2. Remove the engine appearance cover.
3. Remove the Air Cleaner (ACL) outlet pipe.
4. Disconnect the electronic throttle control electrical connector.
5. Remove the 4 bolts and the Throttle Body (TB)
6. Discard the gasket.
7. To install, tighten to 7 ft. lbs. (10 Nm) plus an additional 45 degrees.

➡Install a new TB gasket.

8. To install, reverse the removal procedure.

5.4L Engine

See Figure 335.

1. Remove the Air Cleaner (ACL) outlet pipe.
2. Disconnect the Throttle Position (TP) sensor electrical connector.
3. Disconnect the electronic throttle control electrical connector.
4. Remove the 4 bolts and the Throttle Body (TB) and discard the gasket.
5. To install, reverse the removal procedure.
6. Install a new TB gasket.

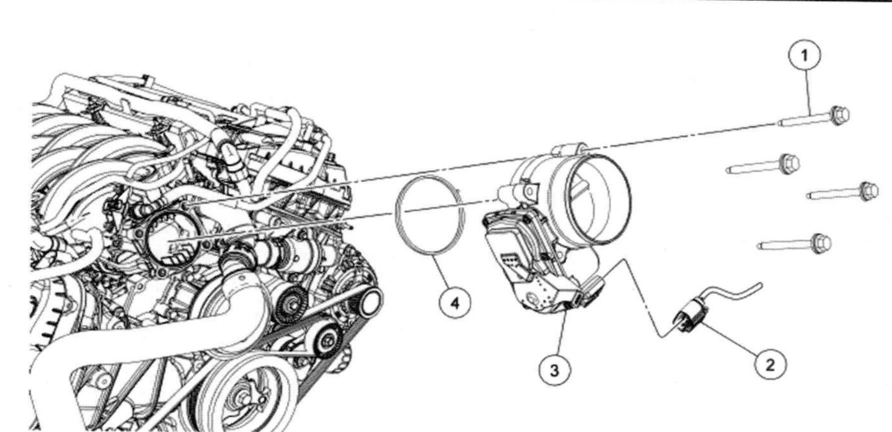

Fig. 334 Exploded view of the throttle body

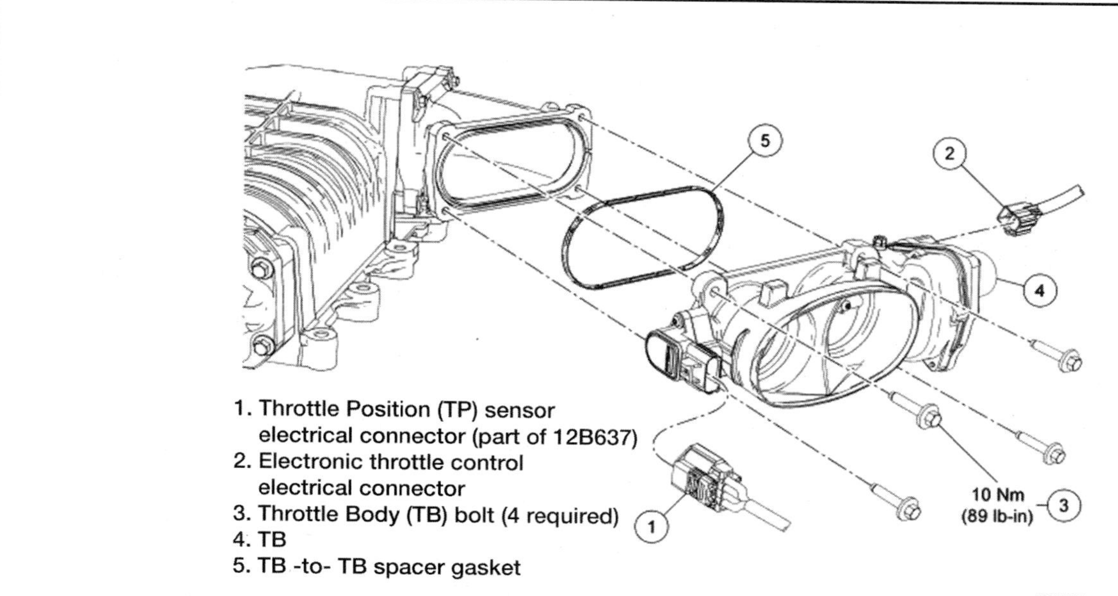

Fig. 335 Exploded view of the throttle body

HEATING & AIR CONDITIONING SYSTEM

BLOWER MOTOR

REMOVAL & INSTALLATION

See Figure 336.

1. Remove the RH lower instrument panel insulator.
2. Disconnect the blower motor speed control electrical connector.
3. Disconnect the blower motor electrical connector.
4. Remove the 3 blower motor screws.
5. Remove the blower motor.
6. To install, reverse the removal procedure.

HEATER CORE

REMOVAL & INSTALLATION

See Figures 337 through 343.

➡The heater core and evaporator core are not individually serviced. They are serviced only with the heater core and evaporator core housing.

➡If a heater core leak is suspected, the heater core must be leak tested before it is removed from the vehicle.

1. 5.4L (4V) vehicles: Release the fuel system pressure.
2. Recover the refrigerant.
3. Drain the engine coolant.
4. Remove the floor console:
   a. Apply the parking brake.
   b. Vehicles with manual transmission:
   c. Place the gearshift lever in the NEUTRAL position.
   d. Remove the gearshift lever knob.
   e. Turn the gearshift lever knob in a counterclockwise direction.
   f. Vehicles with automatic transmission:
   g. Place the selector lever in the NEUTRAL position.

➡When prying on a component, a non-marring tool must be used or damage to the component may occur.

   h. Remove the selector lever bezel.
   i. With a non-marring tool, lift the selector lever bezel upward.
   j. All vehicles
   k. Open the storage compartment door.
   l. Remove the floor console finish panel.
   m. Lift the floor console finish panel upward to release the retaining clips.
   n. Disconnect the traction/hazard/trunk switch electrical connector.
   o. Disconnect the 2 ambient light electrical connectors, if equipped.
   p. Remove the parking brake control handle boot.
   q. Disconnect the power point and audio jack electrical connectors. If equipped, disconnect the Universal Serial Bus (USB) electrical connector.
   r. Release the LH and RH floor console side panels from the instrument panel.
   s. Pull outward on the console side panels to release the retaining clips.

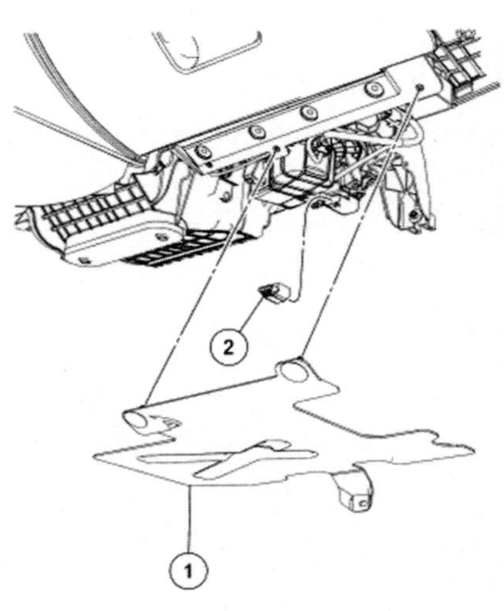

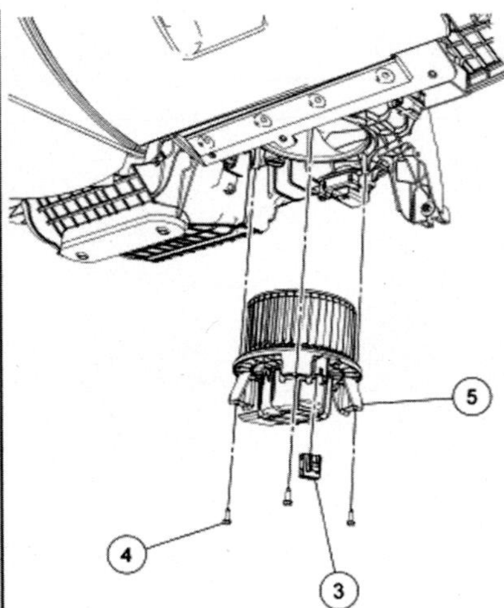

1. RH lower instrument panel insulator
2. Blower motor speed control electrical connector
3. Blower motor electrical connector
4. Blower motor screw (3 required)
5. Blower motor

N0100370

Fig. 336 Locating the blower motor

t. Remove the 2 floor console screws.

u. Remove the storage compartment mat.

v. Remove the 2 floor console nuts.

w. Remove the floor console.

5. Remove the instrument panel:

a. Remove the 2 door scuff plates:

- Remove the front door scuff plate trim panel by lifting straight up on the front and rear edge of the scuff plate trim panel to release the 4 lower retaining clips.
- Disconnect the door scuff plate trim panel electrical connector.
- Remove the door scuff plate trim panel.

b. Remove the 2 A-pillar lower trim panels.

- Remove the 2 sun visor screws and set the sun visor aside.
- Pull outward on the A-pillar trim to release the retaining

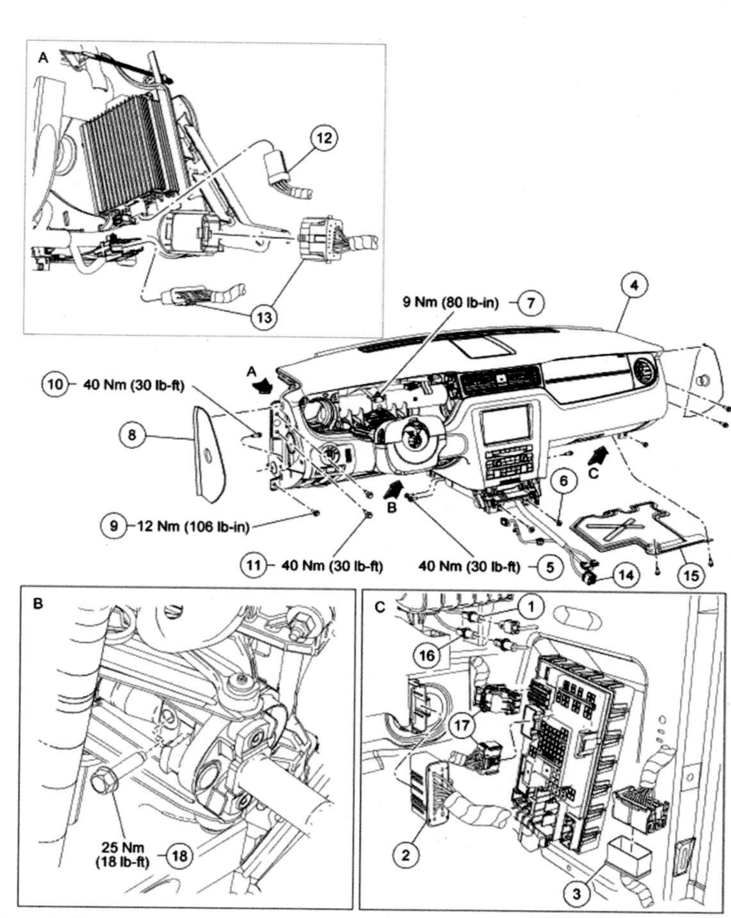

Fig. 337 Exploded view of the instrument panel—1 of 2

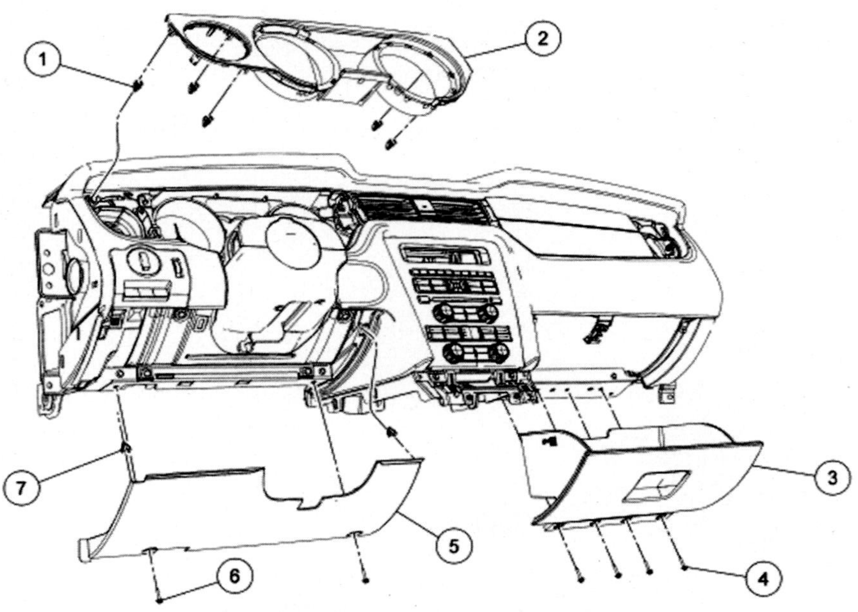

Fig. 338 Exploded view of the instrument panel—2 of 2

clip and the pushpin from the body.

- Pull slightly down and straight back on the A-pillar to unhook the front lower portions of the A-pillar trim panel.

➡To avoid any damage to the A-pillar trim panel, remove any clips from the body and attach them to the A-pillar trim panel.

c. Remove the steering wheel.

➡Do not allow the steering column to rotate while the steering column shaft is disconnected or damage to the clockspring may result. If there is evidence that the steering column shaft has rotated, the clockspring must be removed and recentered. For additional information, refer to Supplemental Restraint System.

d. Remove the instrument cluster:

➡If installing a new Instrument Panel Cluster (IPC), all vehicle keys are erased during the parameter reset procedure. Verify at least 2 of the vehicle keys are available prior to carrying out this procedure.

If installing a new IPC , it is necessary to upload the IPC configuration information to the scan tool.

- Lower the steering column to the lowest position.

➡The IPC finish panel is held in place with retaining clips that are attached to the bezel.

- Pull the IPC finish panel straight out to release the retainers and remove the finish panel.
- Remove the 2 screws and pull the IPC straight out to release the retainers at the bottom of the IPC.
- Disconnect the electrical connector.
- If necessary, push the retainers in from the back of the IPC to assist in releasing them.

e. Remove and discard the steering column shaft bolt. Separate the steering column shaft from the steering column. To install, use a new steering column shaft bolt and tighten to 18 ft. lbs. (25 Nm).

f. Disconnect the 2 instrument panel electrical connectors at the LH lower cowl. If equipped, disconnect the LH audio amplifier.

g. On the LH side, remove the instrument panel side support bolt.

h. If equipped, remove the RH lower instrument panel insulator.

i. On the RH side, disconnect the 2 electrical connectors at the Smart Junction Box (SJB).

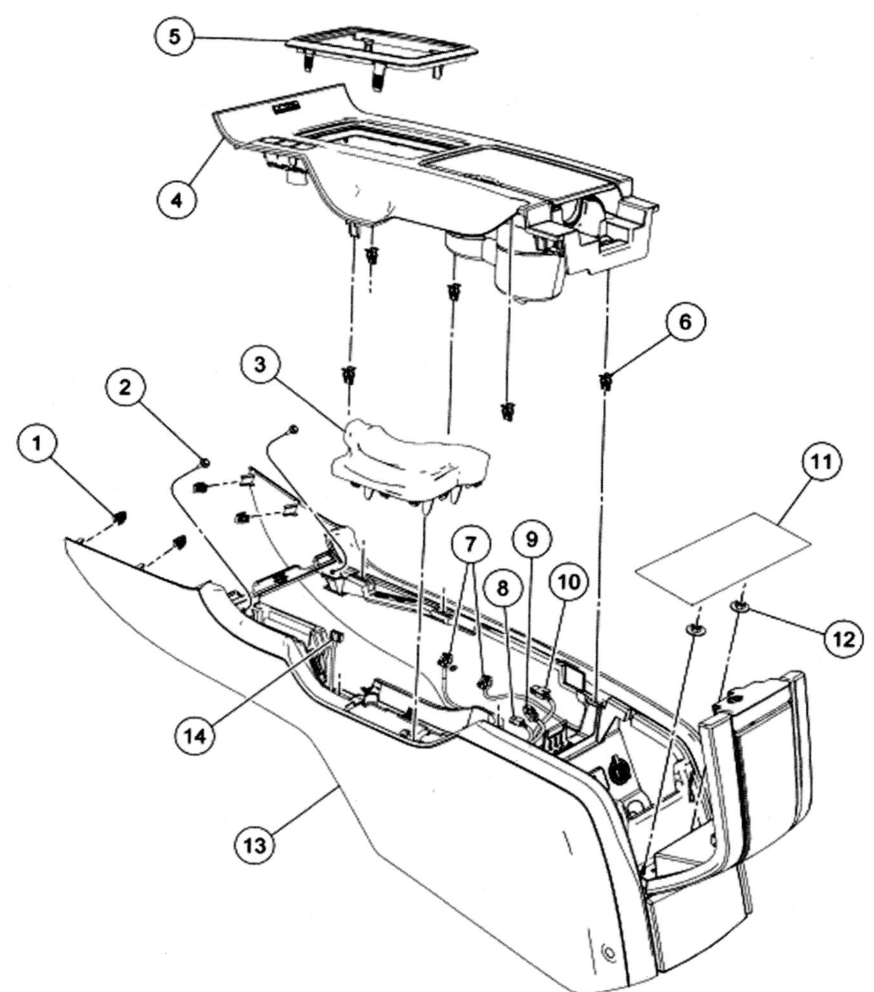

1. Floor console side panel retaining clip (4 required)
2. Floor console screw (2 required)
3. Parking brake control handle boot
4. Floor console finish panel
5. Selector lever bezel
6. Floor console finish panel retaining clip (5 required)
7. Ambient light electrical connectors
8. Universal Serial Bus (USB) electrical connector (if equipped)
9. Audio jack electrical connector
10. Power point electrical connector
11. Storage compartment mat
12. Floor console nut (2 required)
13. Floor console
14. Traction/hazard/trunk switch electrical connector

N0100411

Fig. 339 Exploded view of the floor console

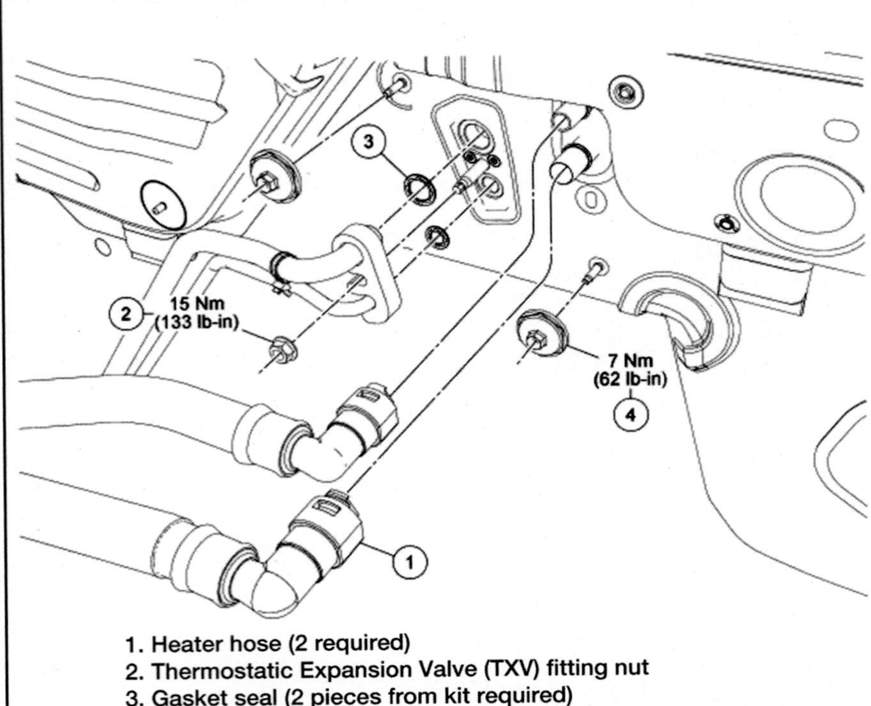

Fig. 340 Heater core and evaporator core housing components—1 of 2

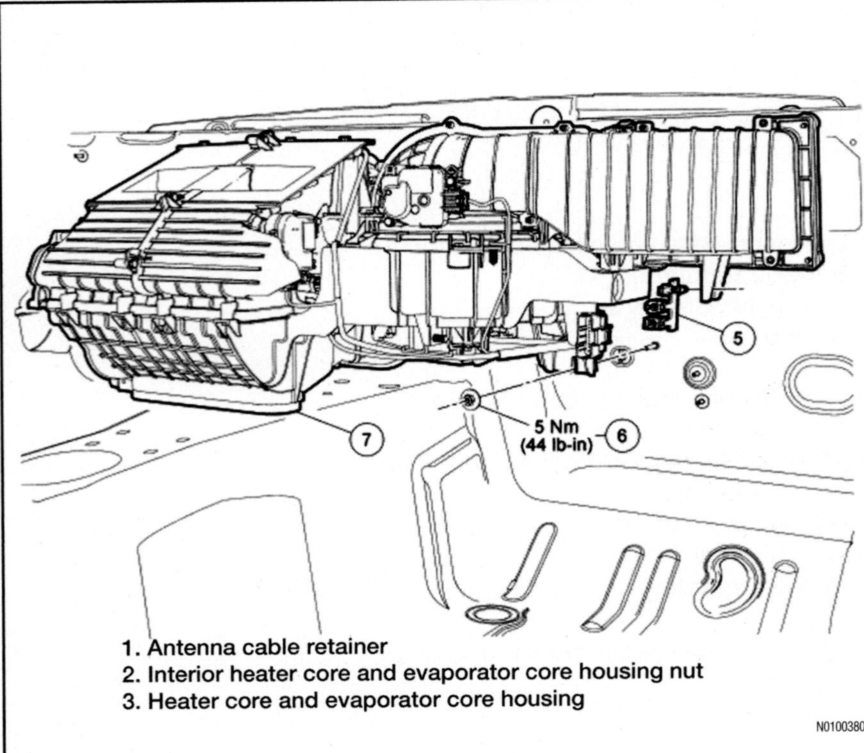

Fig. 341 Heater core and evaporator core housing components—2 of 2

N0098289

Fig. 342 Disconnect the 2 electrical connectors at the Smart Junction Box (SJB)

j. Disconnect the bulkhead electrical connector, near the RH lower side of the SJB.

k. Disconnect the blower motor in-line electrical connector and antenna in-line connector. If equipped, disconnect the satellite radio antenna in-line connector.

l. Remove the 2 instrument panel center support screws.

m. Remove the 3 instrument panel center support bolts.

n. Through the instrument cluster opening, loosen the instrument panel cowl top bracket nut.

o. Remove the 2 instrument panel lower support bolts.

➡When prying on a component, a non-marring tool must be used or damage to the component may occur.

p. Remove the 2 instrument panel side finish panels.

q. With a non-marring tool, lift the instrument panel side finish panels outward.

r. Remove the 4 instrument panel upper support bolts.

s. Disconnect the Restraints Control Module (RCM) small connector.

➡To avoid damaging the instrument panel, the aid of an assistant is required to carry out this step.

➡Make sure that all electrical connectors and wiring are not hindered before removing the instrument panel or damage to the components may occur.

t. Remove the instrument panel.

➡To avoid damaging the instrument panel, the aid of an assistant is required when positioning the instrument panel to the vehicle.

➡Make sure that all electrical connectors and wiring are correctly routed

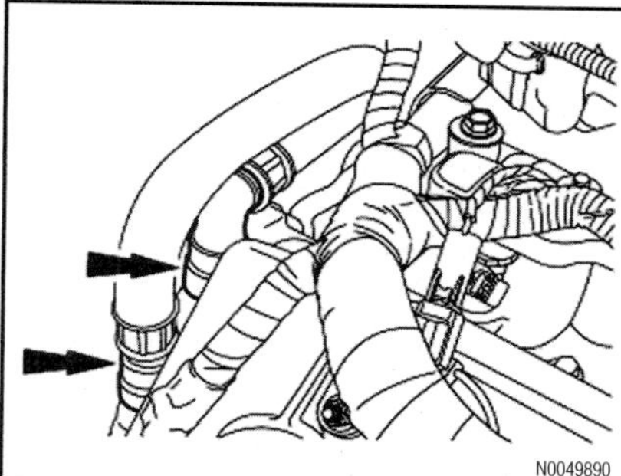

Fig. 343 Disconnect the heater hose fittings at the rear of the RH cylinder head—5.4L Engine

when installing the instrument panel or damage to the components may occur.

6. For 5.4L Engines:
   a. Remove the supercharger. For additional information, refer to Engine Mechanical.
   b. Disconnect the heater hose fittings at the rear of the RH cylinder head and position the heater hoses aside.
7. Disconnect the heater core inlet and outlet hoses at the heater core.
8. Remove the Thermostatic Expansion Valve (TXV) fitting nut and disconnect the fitting.
9. Discard the gasket seals.
10. Remove the 2 exterior heater core and evaporator core housing nuts at the dash panel.
11. Detach the antenna cable retainers from the heater core and evaporator core housing.
12. Remove the interior heater core and evaporator core housing nut.
13. Remove the heater core and evaporator core housing.
14. To install, reverse the removal procedure. Refer to the appropriate illustration for torque values.
15. Install new gasket seals.
16. Add the correct amount of clean PAG oil to the refrigerant system.
17. Fill the engine cooling system.
18. Evacuate, leak test and charge the refrigerant system.

STEERING

POWER STEERING GEAR

REMOVAL & INSTALLATION

2010 Models

See Figure 344.

➡**When repairing the power steering system, care should be taken to prevent the entry of foreign material or failure of the power steering components may result.**

➡**Do not allow the intermediate shaft to rotate while it is disconnected from the steering gear or damage to the clockspring may result. If there is evidence that the intermediate shaft has rotated, the clockspring must be removed and recentered. For additional information, refer to Supplemental Restraint System.**

1. 5.4L engine:
   a. Remove the 4 nuts and the strut tower cross brace.
   b. Remove the Air Cleaner (ACL) outlet pipe.
   c. Install the Engine Lifting Bracket.
   d. Remove the LH engine mount nut. To install, tighten to 46 ft. lbs. (63 Nm).
   e. Install the Engine Support Bar.
   f. Using the Engine Lifting Bracket and Engine Support Bar, raise the LH side of the engine to gain clearance for removal of the power steering pressure line clamp plate bolt and the steering gear mounting bolt.
2. All vehicles:
3. Remove the front wheels and tires.
4. Remove and discard the 2 tie-rod end nuts. Using the Tie-Rod End Remover, disconnect the tie-rod ends from the wheel knuckles. To install, tighten the new nuts to 59 ft. lbs. (80 Nm).

➡**Do not allow the intermediate shaft to rotate while it is disconnected from the steering gear or damage to the clockspring may result. If there is evidence that the intermediate shaft has rotated, the clockspring must be removed and recentered. For additional information, refer to Supplemental Restraint System.**

5. Remove the steering column coupling-to-steering gear bolt and

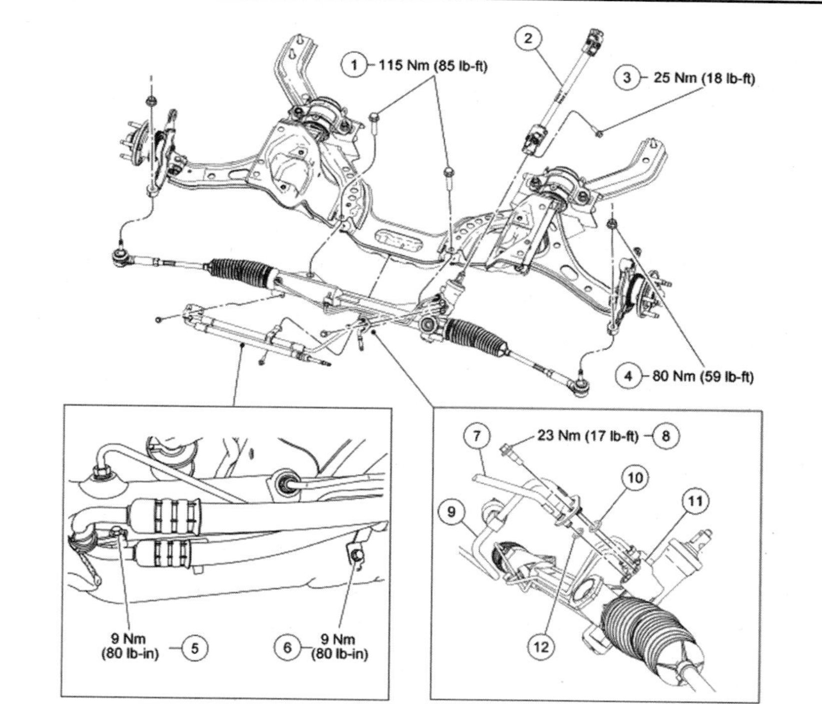

Fig. 344 Exploded view of the power steering gear assembly

disconnect the coupling from the steering gear.

6. Discard the bolt. To install, tighten the new bolt to 18 ft. lbs. (25 Nm).

➡When installing the pressure and return lines to the steering gear, make sure the lines are fully seated into the steering gear prior to installing the clamp plate. Additionally, make sure that the clamp plate surfaces are free of foreign material. DO NOT exceed the specified torque when tightening the clamp plate. Leakage and/or premature failure of the power steering components may occur.

➡New O-ring seals must be installed anytime the power steering lines are disconnected from the steering gear.

7. Remove the power steering line clamp plate bolt, rotate the clamp plate and disconnect the power steering pressure and return lines.
8. Discard the O-ring seals.
9. Remove the pressure line bracket-to-steering gear bolt.
10. Remove the pressure line bracket-to-crossmember bolt.
11. Position the pressure line aside.
12. Remove the 2 bolts and the steering gear.
13. To install, reverse the removal procedure. Refer to illustration for torque values.
14. Fill the power steering system.
15. Check and, if necessary, adjust the front toe.

2011 Models

See Figure 345.

1. If installing a new steering gear, connect the scan tool and upload the module configuration information from the Power Steering Control Module (PSCM).
2. Disconnect the battery ground cable. For additional information, refer to Battery, Mounting and Cables.
3. Vehicles with 5.4L engine:
4. Remove the battery and battery tray.
5. Remove the Air Cleaner (ACL) outlet pipe.
6. Remove the 2 LH cowl vent screen plastic rivets.
7. Lift the cowl screen and remove the ground strap bolt.

Detach the ground strap retainer from the cowl.

8. Disconnect the brake booster vacuum hose quick connect at the engine.
9. Install the Engine Lifting Bracket.
10. Remove the LH engine mount nut.

➡Lift engine approximately 45 mm (1.771 in) from the bottom of the engine mount to the bottom of the engine bracket ensuring that no contact is made with the bulk head or damage to components may occur.

11. Install the Engine Support Bar.
12. Using the Engine Lifting Bracket and Engine Support Bar, raise the LH side of the engine to gain clearance for removal of the LH steering gear mounting bolt.
13. All vehicles:
14. With the vehicle in NEUTRAL, position it on a hoist. Remove the starter
15. Position the wheels to gain access to the steering column shaft coupling-to-steering gear bolt.

➡Do not allow the steering column to rotate while the steering column shaft is disconnected from the steering gear or damage to the clockspring may occur. If there is evidence that the steering column has rotated, the clockspring must be removed and recentered. For additional information, refer to Supplemental Restraint System.

16. Remove the steering column shaft coupling-to-steering gear bolt.
17. Discard the bolt.

➡Use a steering wheel holding device (such as Hunter® 28-75-1 or equivalent).

18. Using a suitable holding device, hold the steering wheel in the straight-ahead position.

➡The steering column shaft coupling will not be completely separated from the steering gear.

Slide the steering column shaft coupling upwards on the steering gear input shaft.

19. Remove the wheels and tires.
20. Remove and discard the 2 tie-rod end nuts.

➡Do not use a hammer to separate the outer tie-rod end from the wheel knuckle or damage to the wheel knuckle may result.

21. Using the Ball Joint Separator, separate the tie-rod ends from the wheel knuckles.
22. Remove the 9 screws and the lower splash shield.
23. If equipped, loosen the 2 crossmember brace nuts.
24. If equipped, remove the 6 crossmember brace bolts and the crossmember brace.
25. Vehicles with automatic transmission: Remove the 2 transmission cooler line bracket nuts and position tubes aside.
26. Remove the 4 rearward subframe crossmember brace nuts and crossmember brace.

➡The ignition must be off when disconnecting Electronic Power Assist Steering (EPAS) electrical connectors. Failure to follow this direction may lead to DTCs being set in the EPAS module that cannot be cleared, and result in the need to install a new EPAS assembly.

27. Release the 2 red Connector Position Assurance (CPA) features and disconnect the 2 Electronic Power Assist Steering (EPAS) electrical connectors.
28. Detach the wiring harness pin-type retainers.

➡If equipped with a 5.4L (4V) engine, it may be necessary to use a pry bar between the LH engine mount and engine bracket, pulling the engine forward slightly to remove LH steering gear bolt

29. Remove the 3 steering gear bolts and the steering gear.
30. Discard the bolts.

To install:

➡Do not allow the steering column to rotate while the steering column shaft is disconnected from the steering gear or damage to the clockspring may occur. If there is evidence that the steering column has rotated, the clockspring must be removed and recentered. For additional information, refer to Supplemental Restraint System.

➡Make sure the steering column coupling is aligned with the locator on the steering gear input shaft and the shaft is fully seated on the steering gear.

Position the steering gear, attach the steering column coupling and install the 3 steering gear bolts.

Tighten to 85 ft. lbs. (115 Nm).

31. To install, reverse the removal procedure. Refer to illustration for torque values.
32. Install the battery and battery tray.
33. Connect the battery ground cable.
34. When installing a new steering gear, it must be configured (using vehicle as-built data or module configuration information retrieved earlier in this procedure).

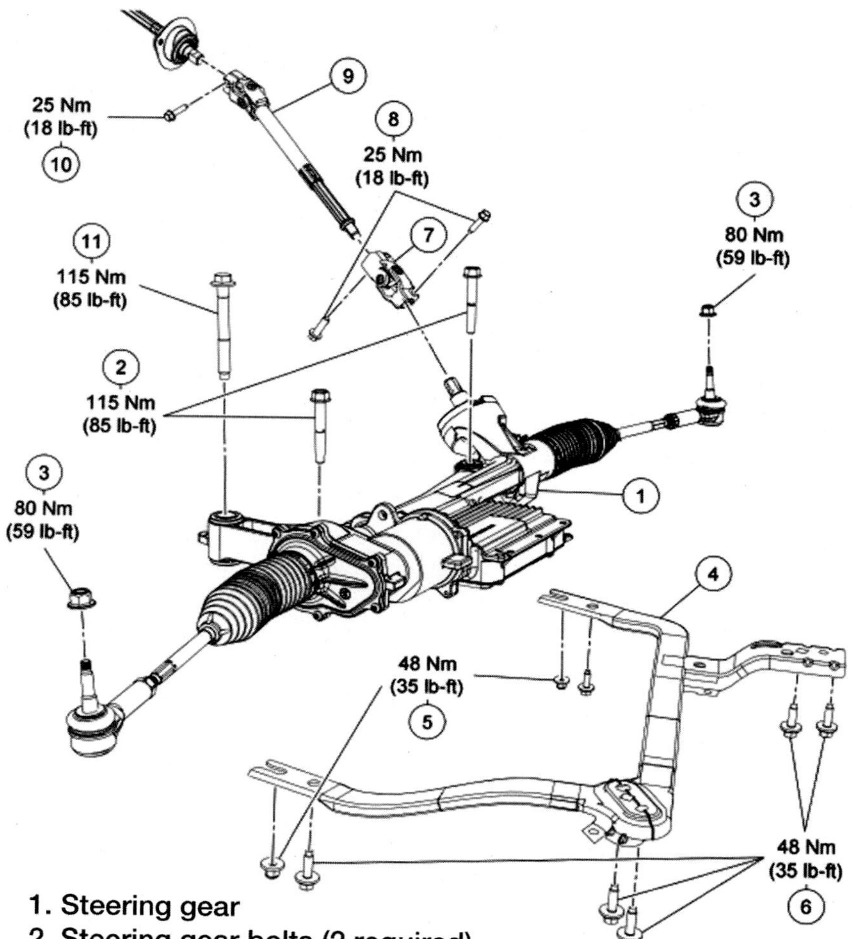

1. Steering gear
2. Steering gear bolts (2 required)
3. Tie-rod end nuts (2 required)
4. Crossmember brace (if equipped)
5. Crossmember brace nuts (if equipped) (2 required)
6. Crossmember brace bolts (if equipped) (6 required)
7. Steering column shaft coupling
8. Steering column shaft coupling bolts (2 required)
9. Lower steering column shaft
10. Lower steering column shaft-to-upper steering column shaft bolt
11. Steering gear bolt

N0112458

Fig. 345 Exploded view of the power steering gear assembly

POWER STEERING PUMP

REMOVAL & INSTALLATION

2010 Models

➡2011 models utilize a Electronic Power Assist Steering (EPAS) system. The EPAS system utilizes a rack-and-pinion type steering gear. Power assist is provided by a motor that is connected to the steering rack by a belt and a pulley and bearing assembly. The steering gear and motor/module are serviced as an assembly. A new steering gear includes inner tie rods, however, the inner and outer tie rods can also be serviced separately.

4.0L Engine

See Figure 346.

➡When repairing the power steering system, care should be taken to prevent the entry of foreign material or failure of the power steering components may result.

1. Remove the Air Cleaner (ACL) outlet pipe.
2. Using a suitable suction device, remove the power steering fluid from the fluid reservoir.
3. Loosen the 3 power steering pump pulley bolts.
4. Rotate the tensioner and remove the accessory drive belt from the power steering pump pulley.
5. Remove the 3 bolts and the power steering pump pulley.
6. Release the clamp and disconnect the power steering pump supply hose from the power steering pump.
7. Remove the pressure line bracket-to-A/C compressor stud nut.
8. Remove the power steering pump supply hose bracket bolt.

➡A new Teflon® seal must be installed.

9. Disconnect the pressure line-to-pump fitting from the power steering pump.
10. Discard the Teflon® seal.
11. Remove the 3 bolts and the power steering pump.

➡For additional information on the accessory drive belt routing, refer to Accessory Drive.

12. To install, reverse the removal procedure. Refer to illustration for torque references.

➡A new Teflon® seal must be installed.

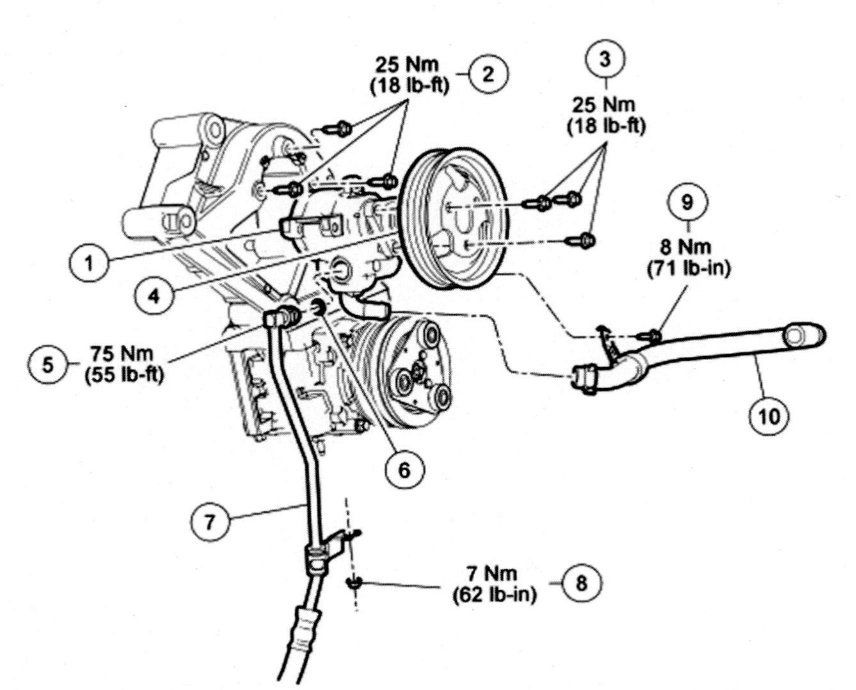

1. Power steering pump
2. Power steering pump bolts (3 required)
3. Power steering pump pulley bolts (3 required)
4. Power steering pump pulley
5. Pressure line-to-pump fitting
6. Teflon® seal
7. Power steering pressure line
8. Pressure line bracket-to-A/C compressor stud nut
9. Power steering pump supply hose bracket bolt
10. Power steering pump supply hose

N0110605

Fig. 346 Exploded view of the power steering pump

13. Using the Teflon® Seal Installer Set, install a new Teflon® seal to the pressure line-to-pump fitting.
14. Fill the power steering system.

4.6L Engine

See Figures 347 and 348.

➡When repairing the power steering system, care should be taken to prevent the entry of foreign material or failure of the power steering components may result.

1. With the vehicle in NEUTRAL, position it on a hoist.
2. Using a suitable suction device, remove the power steering fluid from the fluid reservoir.
3. Remove the Air Cleaner (ACL) outlet pipe.
4. Remove the power steering pump pulley.
   a. Rotate the tensioner and remove the accessory drive belt from the power steering pump pulley.
   b. Using the Power Steering Pump Pulley Remover, remove the pulley.
5. Remove the pressure line bracket-to-pump stud nut.

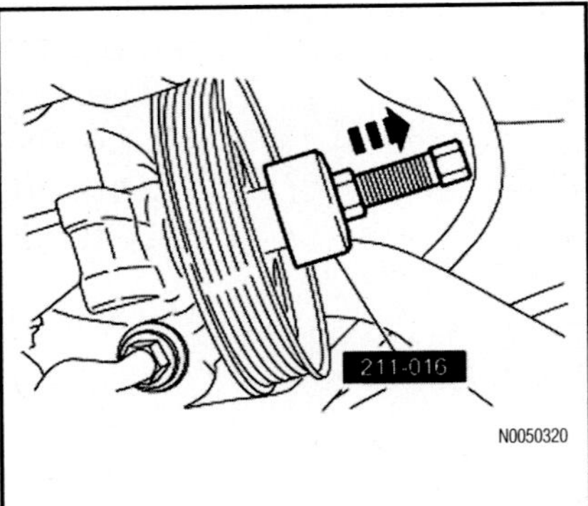

Fig. 347 Using the Power Steering Pump Pulley Remover

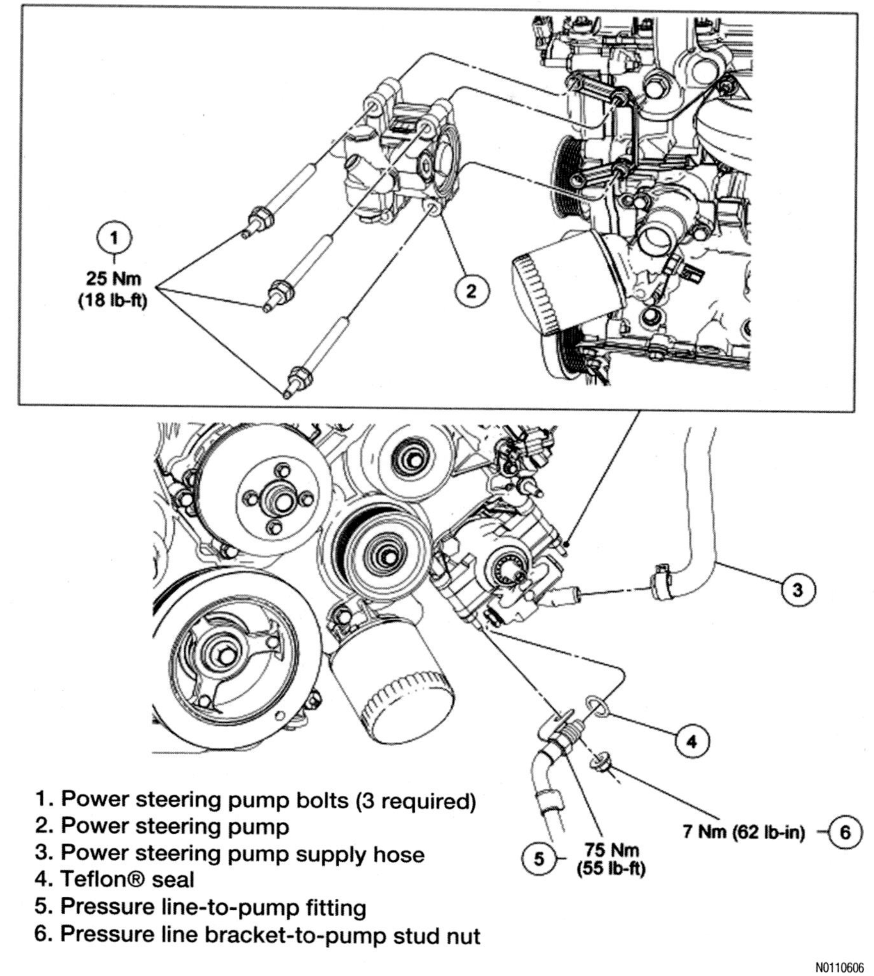

Fig. 348 Exploded view of the power steering pump

6. Release the clamp and disconnect the power steering pump supply hose from the pump.

➡A new Teflon® seal must be installed.

7. Disconnect the pressure line-to-pump fitting.
8. Discard the Teflon® seal.
9. Remove the 3 bolts and the power steering pump.

➡A new Teflon® seal must be installed.

10. To install, reverse the removal procedure. Refer to illustration for torque values.

➡Installation of a new power steering pump pulley is necessary after being removed and installed 2 times or pulley and/or pump failure may occur.

11. Using the Power Steering Pump Pulley Installer, install the pulley.
12. Inspect the pulley for paint marks in the web area near the hub. If there are 2 paint marks, install a new pulley.
13. If there is no paint or one paint mark, use a paint pencil to mark the web area of the pulley near the hub.
14. Rotate the tensioner and install the accessory drive belt to the power steering pump pulley. For additional information on the accessory drive belt routing, refer to Accessory Drive.
15. Using the Teflon® Seal Installer Set, install a new Teflon® seal to the pressure line-to-pump fitting.
16. Fill the power steering system.

5.4L Engine

See Figures 349 and 350.

➡When repairing the power steering system, care should be taken to prevent the entry of foreign material or failure of the power steering components may result.

1. Remove the power steering pump pulley.
   a. Rotate the tensioner and remove

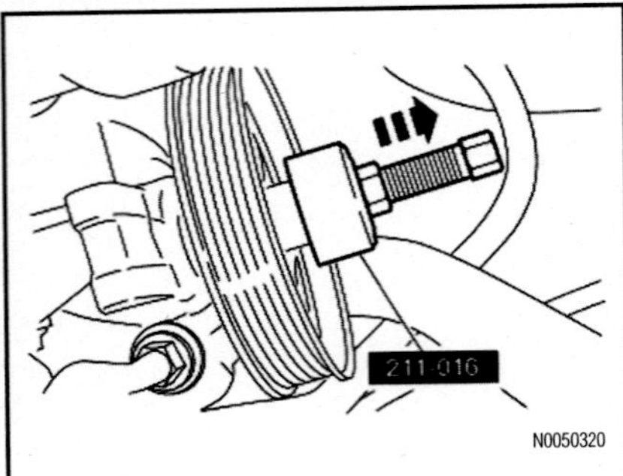

Fig. 349 Using the Power Steering Pump Pulley Remover

the accessory drive belt from the power steering pump pulley.

b. Using the Power Steering Pump Pulley Remover, remove the pulley.

2. Using a suitable suction device, remove the power steering fluid from the fluid reservoir.

➡Make sure to remove the power steering reservoir bolt and separate the reservoir from the bracket or damage to the power steering reservoir may occur.

3. Remove the power steering fluid reservoir bolt and separate the reservoir from the power steering reservoir bracket.

4. Release the clamp and disconnect the power steering pump supply hose from the power steering pump.

5. Position the power steering fluid reservoir aside.

6. Remove the pressure line bracket-to-engine bolt.

➡A new Teflon® seal must be installed.

7. Disconnect the pressure line-to-pump fitting.

8. Discard the Teflon® seal.

9. Remove the 3 bolts and the power steering pump.

10. To install, reverse the removal procedure. Refer to illustration for torque values.

➡Installation of a new power steering pump pulley is necessary after being removed and installed 2 times or pulley and/or pump failure may occur.

11. Using the Power Steering Pump Pulley Installer, install the pulley.

12. Inspect the pulley for paint marks in the web area near the hub. If there are 2 paint marks, install a new pulley.

13. If there is no paint or one paint mark, use a paint pencil to mark the web area of the pulley near the hub.

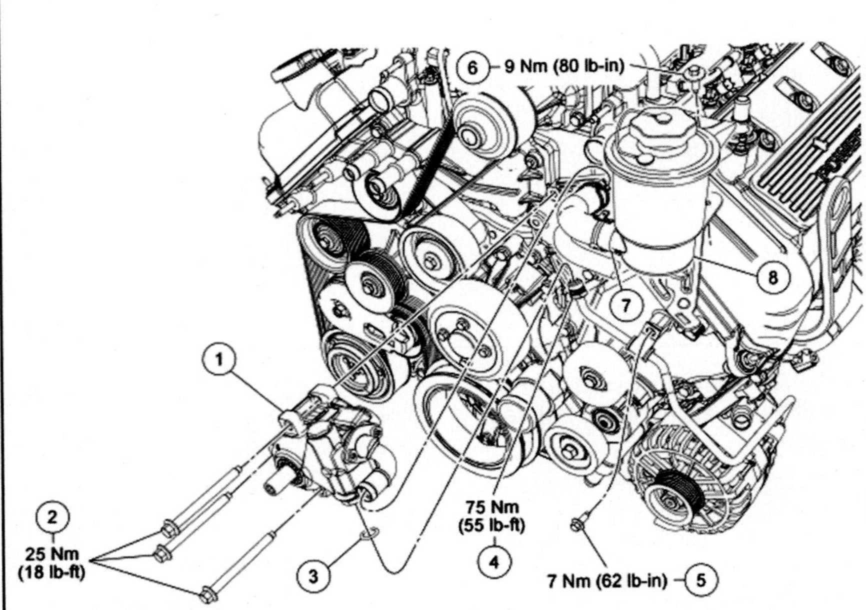

Fig. 350 Exploded view of the power steering pump

14. Rotate the tensioner and install the accessory drive belt to the power steering pump pulley. For additional information on the accessory drive belt routing, refer to Accessory Drive.

➡A new Teflon® seal must be installed.

15. Using the Teflon® Seal Installer Set, install a new Teflon® seal to the pressure line-to-pump fitting.

16. Fill the power steering system.

BLEEDING & FLUSHING

1. Remove the power steering fluid reservoir cap.

2. Using a suitable suction device, remove the power steering fluid from the reservoir.

3. Release the clamp and disconnect the return hose from the reservoir.

a. Remove the clamp from the hose and allow the remaining fluid to drain out of the reservoir.

4. Plug the power steering fluid reservoir inlet port.

5. Attach an extension hose to the return hose.

➡Do not reuse the power steering fluid that has been flushed from the power steering system.

6. Place the open end of the extension hose into a suitable container.

7. If equipped with Hydro-Boost® , apply the brake pedal 4 times.

➡Do not overfill the reservoir.

8. Fill the reservoir as needed with the specified fluid.

➡Do not allow the power steering pump to run completely dry of power steering fluid. Damage to the power steering pump may occur.

9. Start the engine while simultaneously turning the steering wheel to lock and then immediately turn the ignition switch to the OFF position.

➡Avoid turning the steering wheel without the engine running as this may cause air to be pulled into the steering gear.

➡Do not overfill the reservoir.

10. Fill the reservoir as needed with the specified fluid.

11. Repeat Steps 8 and 9, turning the steering wheel in the opposite direction each time, until the fluid exiting the power steering fluid return hose is clean and clear of foreign material.

12. Remove the extension hose from the return hose.
13. Remove the plug from the fluid reservoir inlet port.
14. Install the clamp and connect the power steering return hose to the reservoir.

➡It is necessary to correctly fill the power steering system to remove any trapped air and completely fill the power steering system components.

15. If, after correctly filling the power steering system, there is power steering noise accompanied by evidence of aerated fluid and there are no fluid leaks, it may be necessary to purge the power steering system.
16. Fill the power steering system.

PURGING

See Figure 351.

➡If the air is not purged from the power steering system correctly, power steering pump failure may result. The condition may occur on pre-delivery vehicles with evidence of aerated fluid or on vehicles that have had steering component repairs.

1. If equipped with a fire suppression system, depower the system.

➡A whine heard from the power steering pump can be caused by air in the system. The power steering purge procedure must be carried out prior to any component repair for which power steering noise complaints are accompanied by evidence of aerated fluid.

2. Remove the power steering fluid reservoir cap.
3. Fill the reservoir as needed with the specified fluid.
4. Raise the front wheels off the floor.
5. Tightly insert the Power Steering Evacuation Cap into the reservoir and connect the Vacuum Pump Kit.
6. Start the engine.
7. Using the Vacuum Pump Kit, apply vacuum and maintain the maximum vacuum of 68-85 kPa (20-25 in-Hg).
8. If equipped with Hydro-Boost®, apply the brake pedal twice.

➡Do not hold the steering wheel against the stops for an extended amount of time. Damage to the power steering pump may occur.

9. Cycle the steering wheel fully from stop-to-stop 10 times.
10. Stop the engine.

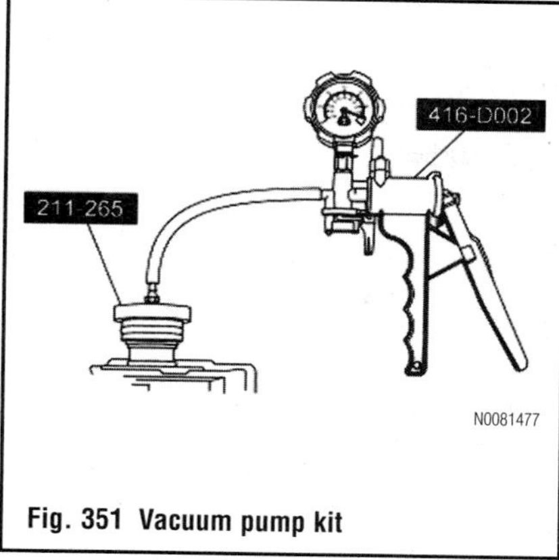

Fig. 351 Vacuum pump kit

11. Release the vacuum and remove the Vacuum Pump Kit.

➡Do not overfill the reservoir.

12. Fill the reservoir as needed.
13. Start the engine.
14. Install the Power Steering Evacuation Cap and the Vacuum Pump Kit. Apply and maintain the maximum vacuum of 68-85 kPa (20-25 in-Hg).

➡Do not hold the steering wheel against the stops for an extended amount of time. Damage to the power steering pump may occur.

15. Cycle the steering wheel fully from stop-to-stop 10 times.
16. Stop the engine, release the vacuum and remove the Vacuum Pump Kit and Power Steering Evacuation Cap.

➡Do not overfill the reservoir.

17. Fill the reservoir as needed and install the reservoir cap.
18. Visually inspect the power steering system for leaks.

FLUID FILL PROCEDURE

See Figure 352.

➡If the air is not purged from the power steering system correctly, premature power steering pump failure may result. The condition can occur on pre-delivery vehicles with evidence of aerated fluid or on vehicles that have had steering component repairs.

1. Remove the power steering fluid reservoir cap.
2. Install the Power Steering Evacuation Cap, Power Steering Fill Adapter Manifold and Vacuum Pump Kit as shown in the illustration.

➡The Power Steering Fill Adapter Manifold control valves are in the OPEN position when the points of the handles face the center of the Power Steering Fill Adapter Manifold.

3. Close the Power Steering Fill Adapter Manifold control valve (fluid side).
4. Open the Power Steering Fill Adapter Manifold control valve (vacuum side).
5. Using the Vacuum Pump Kit, apply 68-85 kPa (20-25 in-Hg) of vacuum to the power steering system.
6. Observe the Vacuum Pump Kit gauge for 30 seconds.
7. If the Vacuum Pump Kit gauge reading drops more than 3 kPa (0.88 in-Hg), correct any leaks in the power steering system or the Power Steering Evacuation Cap, Power Steering Fill Adapter Manifold and Vacuum Pump Kit before proceeding.

➡The Vacuum Pump Kit gauge reading will drop slightly during this step.

8. Slowly open the Power Steering Fill Adapter Manifold control valve (fluid side) until power steering fluid completely fills the hose and then close the control valve.
9. Using the Vacuum Pump Kit, apply 68-85 kPa (20-25 in-Hg) of vacuum to the power steering system.
10. Close the Power Steering Fill Adapter Manifold control valve (vacuum side).
11. Slowly open the Power Steering Fill Adapter Manifold control valve (fluid side).
12. Once power steering fluid enters the fluid reservoir and reaches the minimum fluid level indicator line on the reservoir, close the Power Steering Fill Adapter Manifold control valve (fluid side).
13. Remove the Power Steering Evacuation Cap, Power Steering Fill Adapter Manifold and Vacuum Pump Kit.
14. Install the reservoir cap.

➡Do not hold the steering wheel against the stops for an extended amount of time. Damage to the power steering pump may occur.

➡There will be a slight drop in the power steering fluid level in the reservoir when the engine is started.

Start the engine and turn the steering wheel from stop-to-stop.

Turn the ignition switch to the OFF position.

➡Do not overfill the reservoir.

15. Remove the reservoir cap and fill the reservoir with the specified fluid.
16. Install the reservoir cap.

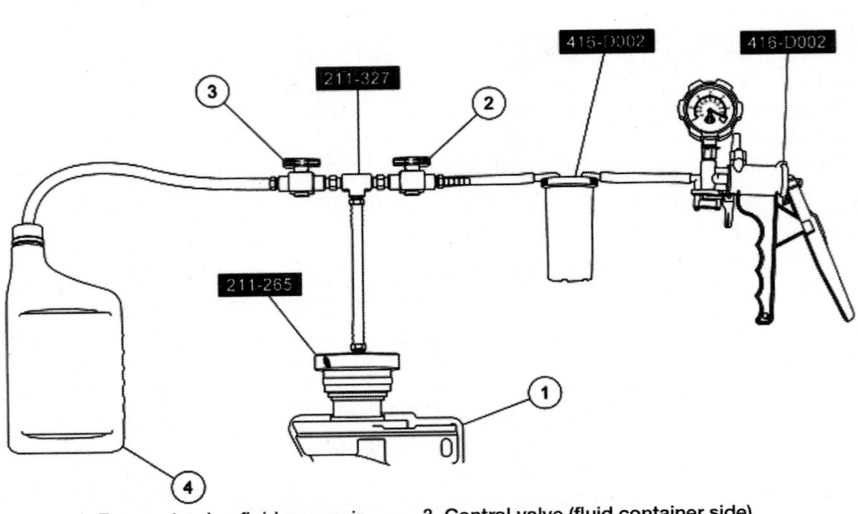

Fig. 352 Fluid filling tools

SUSPENSION

FRONT SUSPENSION

COIL SPRING

REMOVAL & INSTALLATION

See Figures 353 through 355.

⁂ WARNING

Do not apply heat or flame to the shock absorber or strut tube. The shock absorber and strut tube are gas pressurized and could explode if heated. Failure to follow this instruction may result in serious personal injury.

⁂ WARNING

Keep all body parts clear of shock absorbers or strut rods. Shock absorbers or struts can extend unassisted. Failure to follow this instruction may result in serious personal injury.

⁂ WARNING

Do not attempt to disassemble the shock absorber and spring assembly without using a spring compressor. Assemblies are under extreme load. Failure to follow this instruction may result in serious personal injury.

➡Suspension fasteners are critical parts because they affect performance of vital components and systems and their failure may result in major service expense. New parts must be installed with the same part number or equivalent part, if replacement is necessary. Do not use a replacement part of lesser quality or substitute design. Torque values must be used as specified during reassembly to make sure of correct retention of these parts.

1. Remove the strut and spring assembly. For additional information, refer to Strut and Spring Assembly in this section.

➡If installing a new spring, make sure the part number is correct. Refer to the Vehicle Certification (VC) label for the correct spring code.

2. Using a suitable spring compressor, compress the spring until the tension is released from the strut.

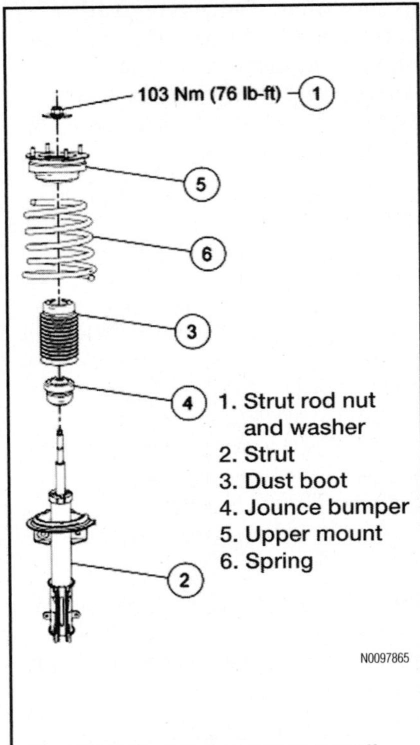

Fig. 353 Exploded view of the front coil spring and strut

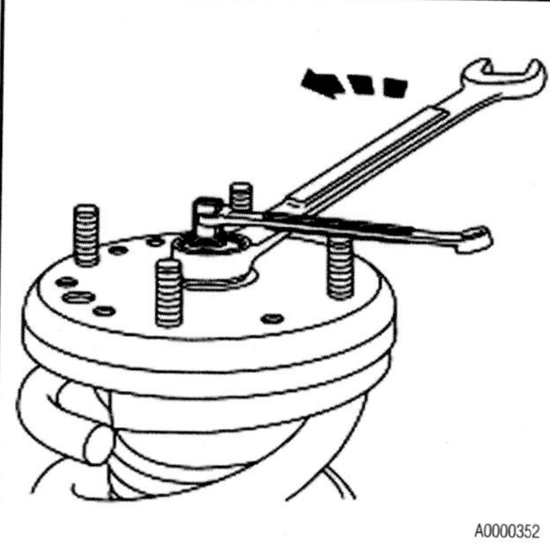

Fig. 354 While holding the strut rod, remove and discard the strut rod nut and washer

3. While holding the strut rod, remove and discard the strut rod nut and washer and remove the strut.

To install, tighten the new nut to 76 ft. lbs. (103 Nm).

4. If necessary, remove the dust boot and jounce bumper.

5. Remove the upper mount assembly.

6. Carefully release the tension on the spring compressor and remove the spring.

7. When installing the spring onto the strut, make sure the spring end is positioned against the seat stop and is resting in the spring seat pocket.

8. To assemble, reverse the disassembly procedure. Refer to illustration for torque values.

9. Align the notch on the upper bearing assembly with the clevis at the bottom of the strut.

Fig. 355 Locating the seat stop and spring seat pocket

CONTROL LINKS

REMOVAL & INSTALLATION

See Figure 356.

➡Suspension fasteners are critical parts because they affect performance of vital components and systems and their failure may result in major service expense. New parts must be installed with the same part number or equivalent part, if replacement is necessary. Do not use a replacement part of lesser quality or substitute design. Torque values must be used as specified during reassembly to make sure of correct retention of these parts.

➡Do not use power tools to remove or install the stabilizer bar link nuts or damage to the link ball joint or boot may occur.

➡Do not hold the stabilizer bar link boot with any tool, as damage to the boot will occur.

➡Inspect and clean all mating surfaces. Make sure the mating surfaces are free of foreign material. Do not use solvents and/or lubricants. Wipe all surfaces with a clean shop towel.

1. With the vehicle in NEUTRAL, position it on a hoist.

➡Use the hex-holding feature to prevent the studs from turning while removing or installing the stabilizer bar link nuts. The boot seal must not be allowed to twist at all while tightening the nuts or damage to the boot seal may occur.

2. Remove and discard the stabilizer bar link lower nut.
3. Disconnect the link from the stabilizer bar.
4. Use the hex-holding feature to prevent the studs from turning while removing or installing the stabilizer bar link nuts. The boot seal must not be allowed to twist at all while tightening the nuts or damage to the boot seal may occur.
5. Remove and discard the stabilizer bar link upper nut.
6. Disconnect the link from the strut.
7. To install, reverse the removal procedure. Refer to illustration for torque values.

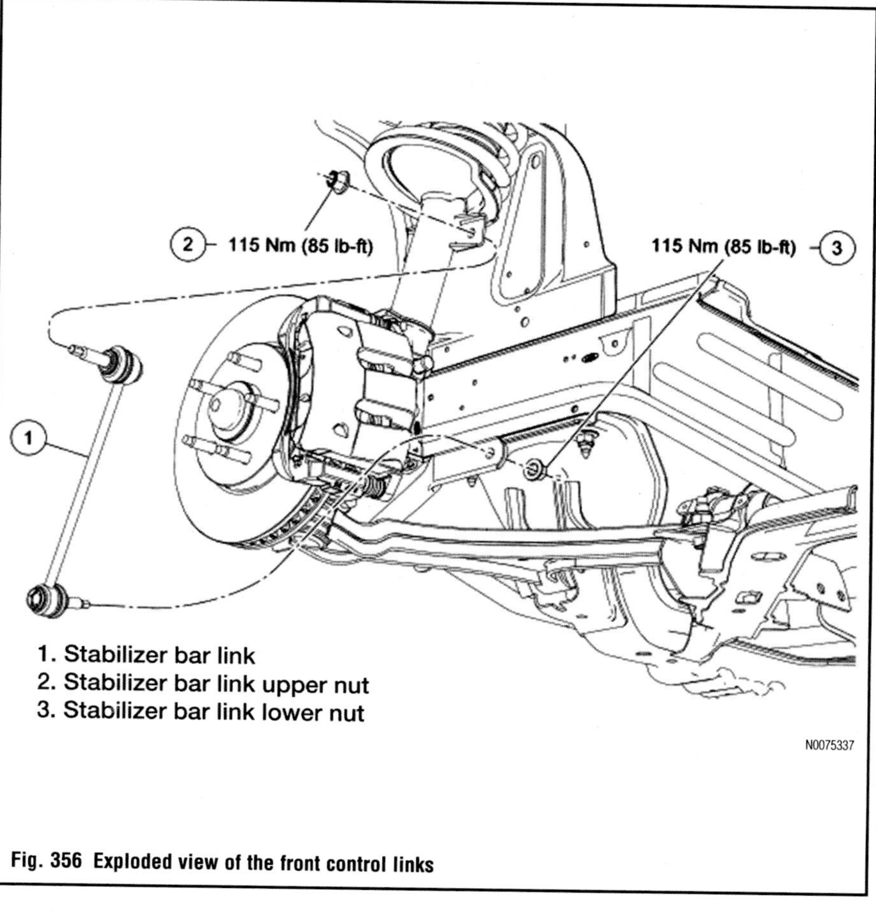

Fig. 356 Exploded view of the front control links

LOWER CONTROL ARM

REMOVAL & INSTALLATION

See Figure 357.

➡Suspension fasteners are critical parts because they affect performance of vital components and systems and their failure may result in major service expense. New parts must be installed with the same part number or equivalent part, if replacement is necessary. Do not use a replacement part of lesser quality or substitute design. Torque values must be used as specified during reassembly to make sure of correct retention of these parts.

1. Remove the wheel and tire.

➡Note the orientation of the lower ball joint nut and bolt. They must be installed using the same orientation or damage to the steering gear bellows boot may occur.

2. Remove and discard the lower ball joint nut and bolt.
3. Separate the lower arm and the wheel spindle.
4. Remove the steering gear bolts. Position the steering gear to gain access to the lower control arm forward bolt.

➡Use care not to damage the steering gear bellows boot while removing the lower arm forward bolt.

5. Remove and discard the lower arm forward bolt.
6. Remove and discard the lower control arm rearward nuts and flag bolts.
7. Remove the lower control arm and bracket assembly.

To install:

➡Refer to illustration for torque values.

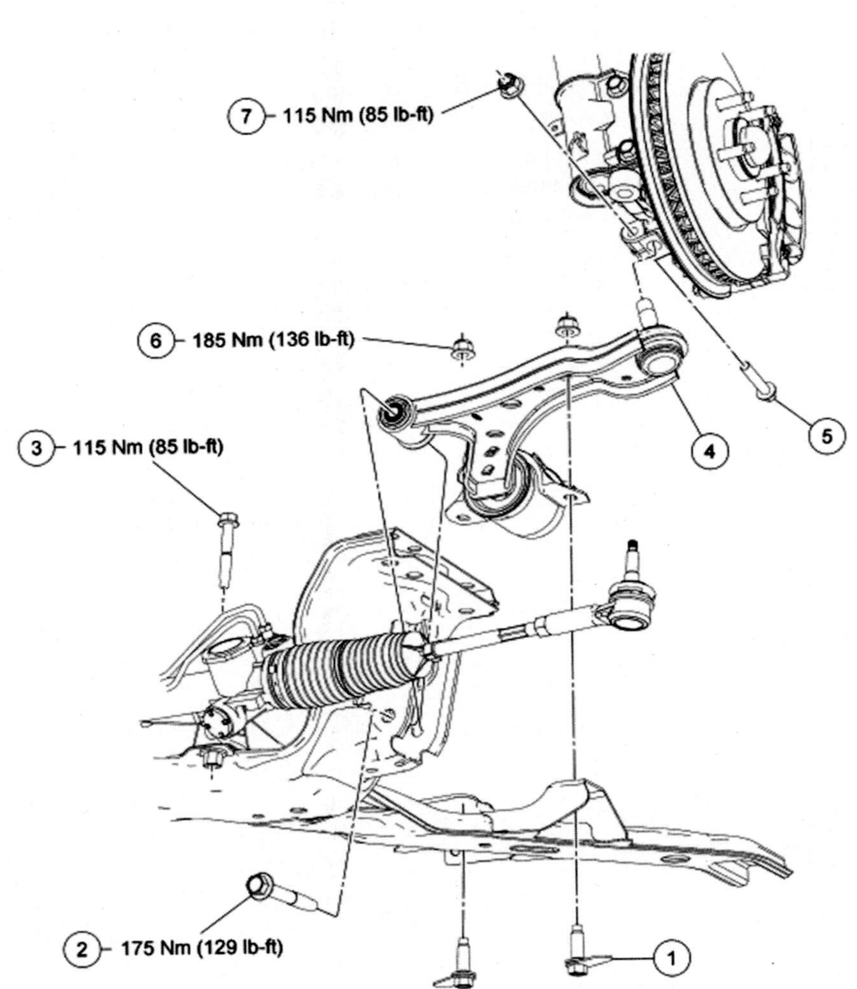

Fig. 357 Exploded view of the front lower control arm

➡To ease installation, the position of the lower control arm nut and flag bolt may be reversed to allow installation of the nut from underneath the vehicle.

Install the lower arm and bracket assembly and the lower arm rearward nuts and flag bolts.

Tighten the new nuts to 136 ft. lbs. (185 Nm).

➡Use care not to damage the steering gear bellows boot while installing the lower arm forward bolt.

➡Do not tighten the lower arm forward bolt at this time.

8. Loosely install the lower arm forward bolt.
9. Position the steering gear and install the steering gear bolts. Tighten to 85 ft. lbs. (115 Nm).

➡The lower ball joint seal must be fully seated against the wheel spindle or damage to the ball joint may occur.

10. Position the lower ball joint into the wheel spindle and install the new lower ball joint nut and bolt.
11. Install the wheel and tire.
12. Lower the vehicle so the weight of the vehicle is resting on the wheel and tires.
13. Tighten the new lower arm forward bolt to 129 ft. lbs. (175 Nm).

STABILIZER BAR

REMOVAL & INSTALLATION

See Figure 358.

➡Suspension fasteners are critical parts because they affect performance of vital components and systems and their failure may result in major service expense. New parts must be installed with the same part number or equivalent part, if replacement is necessary. Do not use a replacement part of lesser quality or substitute design. Torque values must be used as specified during reassembly to make sure of correct retention of these parts.

➡Do not use power tools to remove or install the stabilizer bar link nuts or damage to the link ball joint or boot may occur.

➡Do not hold the stabilizer bar link boot with any tool, as damage to the boot will occur.

➡Inspect and clean all mating surfaces. Make sure the mating surfaces are free of foreign material. Do not use solvents and/or lubricants. Wipe all surfaces with a clean shop towel.

1. With the vehicle in NEUTRAL, position it on a hoist.

➡Use the hex-holding feature to prevent the studs from turning while removing or installing the stabilizer bar link nuts. The boot seal must not be allowed to twist at all while tightening the nut or damage to the boot seal may occur.

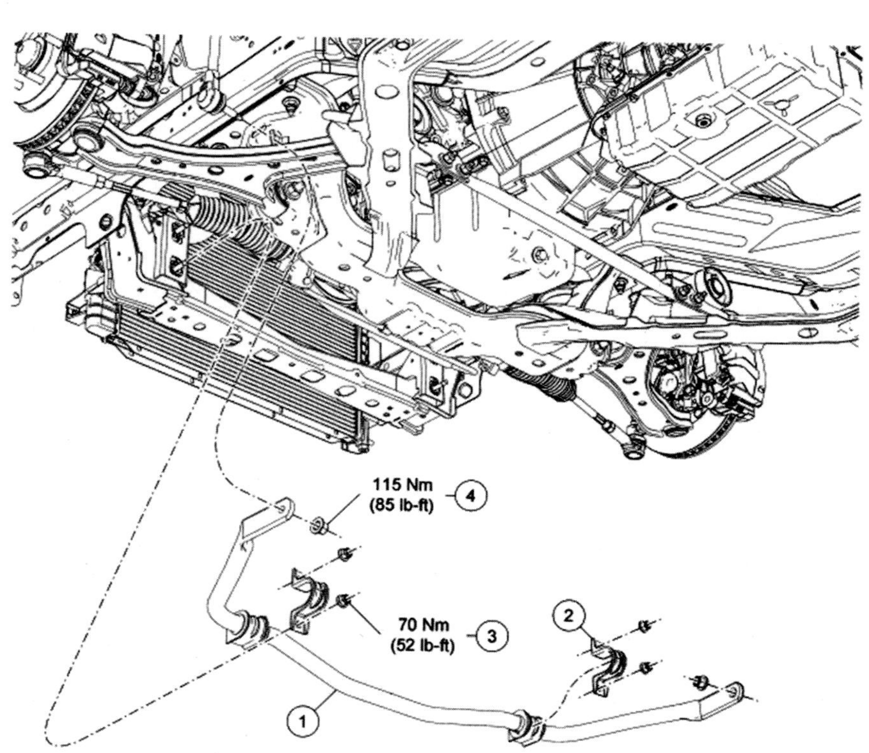

Fig. 358 Exploded view of the stabilizer bar

2. Remove and discard both stabilizer bar link lower nuts.

3. Disconnect both links from the stabilizer bar.

4. Remove and discard the 4 stabilizer bracket nuts, then remove the stabilizer bar brackets and the stabilizer bar.

5. If necessary, remove the stabilizer bar bushings.

➡When installing the stabilizer bar, make sure the stabilizer bar is centered symmetrically between the 2 stabilizer bar brackets. The distance between the stabilizer bar brackets and links should be the same on both sides, as shown in the illustration.

6. To install, reverse the removal procedure. Refer to illustration for torque values.

BUSHINGS

1. Remove the stabilizer bar.

➡To aid removal, apply a light coat of lubricant to the necessary parts of the front stabilizer bar.

2. Remove the stabilizer bar bushing by sliding it off the stabilizer bar.

➡To aid installation, apply a light coat of lubricant to the necessary parts of the front stabilizer bar and the inside diameter of the stabilizer bar bushing.

3. To install, reverse the removal procedure.

STEERING KNUCKLE

REMOVAL & INSTALLATION

See Figure 359.

➡Suspension fasteners are critical parts because they affect performance of vital components and systems and their failure may result in major service expense. New parts must be installed with the same part number or equivalent part, if replacement is necessary. Do not use a replacement part of lesser quality or substitute design.

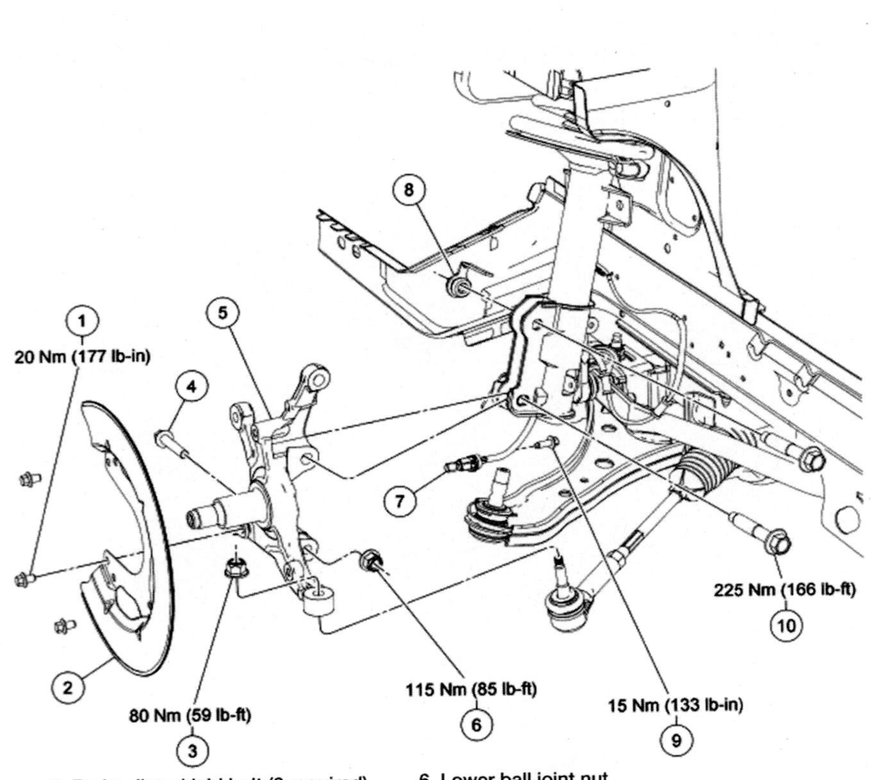

Fig. 359 Exploded view of the steering knuckle

Torque values must be used as specified during reassembly to make sure of correct retention of these parts.

➡Disconnect the Electronic Power Assist Steering (EPAS) steering gear power supply electrical connector or damage to the steering gear internal power relay may occur resulting in steering gear replacement.

➡The ignition must be off when disconnecting Electronic Power Assist Steering (EPAS) electrical connectors. Failure to follow this direction may lead to DTCs being set in the EPAS module that cannot be cleared, and result in the need to install a new EPAS assembly.

1. On 2011 models, release the red Connector Position Assurance (CPA) feature and disconnect the Electronic Power Assist Steering (EPAS) power supply electrical connector.
2. Remove the wheel bearing and hub assembly. For additional information, refer to Wheel Bearing and Wheel Hub in this section.
3. Remove the 3 bolts and the brake disc shield.
4. Remove the wheel speed sensor bolt and position the sensor aside.
5. Remove and discard the tie-rod end nut.

➡Use care not to damage the tie-rod end dust boot when using the Tie-Rod End Remover.

6. Using the Tie-Rod End Remover, disconnect the tie-rod end from the front wheel spindle.
7. Support the front suspension lower arm with a jackstand.
8. Remove and discard the lower ball joint nut and bolt.

➡Use care not to damage the lower ball joint boot while separating the lower control arm and the wheel spindle.

9. Separate the lower control arm and the wheel spindle.
10. If equipped, index-mark the 2 strut-to-spindle cam bolts.

**** WARNING**

Do not apply heat or flame to the shock absorber or strut tube. The shock absorber and strut tube are gas pressurized and could explode if heated. Failure to follow this instruction may result in serious personal injury.

**** WARNING**

Keep all body parts clear of shock absorbers or strut rods. Shock absorbers or struts can extend unassisted. Failure to follow this instruction may result in serious personal injury.

➡If equipped, do not discard the strut-to-spindle cam nuts and bolts.

11. Remove and discard the strut-to-spindle bolts and flagnuts.
12. Remove the wheel spindle.
13. To install, reverse the removal procedure. Refer to illustration for torque values.
14. Check and, if necessary, align the front end.

STRUT & SPRING ASSEMBLY

REMOVAL & INSTALLATION

See Figures 360 and 361.

**** WARNING**

Do not apply heat or flame to the shock absorber or strut tube. The shock absorber and strut tube are gas pressurized and could explode if heated. Failure to follow this instruction may result in serious personal injury.

**** WARNING**

Keep all body parts clear of shock absorbers or strut rods. Shock absorbers or struts can extend unassisted. Failure to follow this instruction may result in serious personal injury.

➡Suspension fasteners are critical parts because they affect performance of vital components and systems and their failure may result in major service expense. New parts must be installed with the same part number or equivalent part, if replacement is necessary. Do not use a replacement part of lesser quality or substitute design. Torque values must be used as specified during reassembly to make sure of correct retention of these parts.

1. Remove and discard the 4 strut upper mount nuts.
2. Remove the wheel and tire.
3. Remove the wheel speed sensor bolt and position the sensor aside.

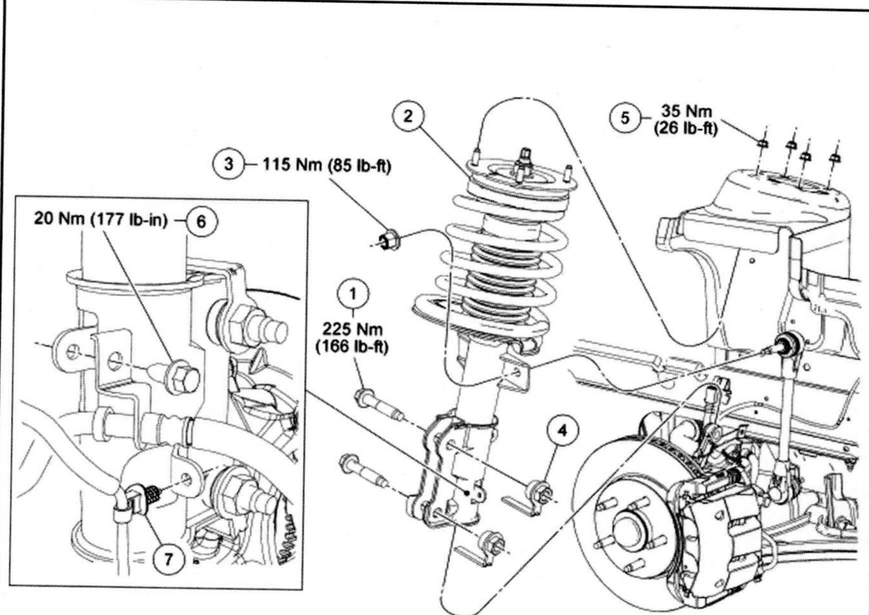

1. Strut-to-wheel spindle bolt (2 required)
2. Strut and spring assembly
3. Stabilizer bar link upper nut
4. Strut-to-wheel spindle flagnut (2 required)
5. Strut upper mount nut (4 required)
6. Brake hose bracket bolt
7. Wheel speed sensor harness retainer

N0097864

Fig. 360 Exploded view of the front strut and spring assembly

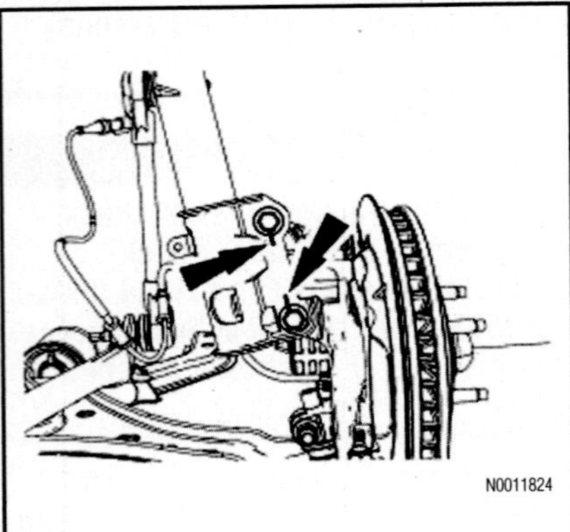

Fig. 361 Index-mark the 2 strut-to-spindle cam bolts

4. Remove the brake hose bracket bolt and disconnect the wheel speed sensor wire from the bracket.

➡Use the hex-holding feature to prevent the studs from turning while removing or installing the stabilizer bar link nuts. The boot seal must not be allowed to twist at all while tightening the nuts or damage to the boot seal may occur.

5. Remove and discard the stabilizer bar link upper nut and disconnect the link from the strut.
6. To install, tighten the new nut to 85 ft. lbs. (115 Nm).
7. Using a suitable jackstand, support the lower control arm.
8. If equipped, index-mark the 2 strut-to-spindle cam bolts.

WARNING

Do not apply heat or flame to the shock absorber or strut tube. The shock absorber and strut tube are gas pressurized and could explode if heated. Failure to follow this instruction may result in serious personal injury.

WARNING

Keep all body parts clear of shock absorbers or strut rods. Shock absorbers or struts can extend unassisted. Failure to follow this instruction may result in serious personal injury.

➡If equipped, do not discard the strut-to-spindle cam nuts and bolts.

9. Remove and discard the strut-to-spindle bolts and flagnuts.

➡Damage to the lower control arm bushings may occur if the lower control arm is not supported.

10. Carefully lower the lower control arm and remove the strut and spring assembly.
11. To install, the notch and the arrow etched into the upper bearing assembly must face the outboard side of the vehicle.
12. If necessary, disassemble the strut and spring assembly. Refer to Coil Spring.
13. To install, reverse the removal procedure. Refer to illustration for torque values.
14. Check and, if necessary, adjust the front end alignment.

WHEEL BEARING & HUB

REMOVAL & INSTALLATION

See Figure 362.

➡Suspension fasteners are critical parts because they affect performance of vital components and systems and their failure may result in major service expense. New parts must be installed with the same part number or equivalent part, if replacement is necessary. Do not use a replacement part of lesser quality or substitute design. Torque values must be used as specified during reassembly to make sure of correct retention of these parts.

1. Remove the wheel and tire.

➡Do not allow the caliper and anchor plate assembly to hang from the brake hose or damage to the hose can occur.

2. Remove the brake anchor plate bolts and position the brake caliper and anchor plate assembly aside.
3. Support the caliper and anchor plate assembly using mechanic's wire.
4. Remove the brake disc.
5. Remove and discard the wheel hub grease cap.

WARNING

The wheel hub nut is a one-time use item and a new wheel hub nut must be installed. Failure to do so may result in hub separation from the vehicle and loss of vehicle control. Failure to follow this instruction may result in serious injury to vehicle occupant(s).

6. Remove and discard the wheel hub nut.
7. Remove the wheel bearing and wheel hub.
8. To install, reverse the removal procedure. Refer to illustration for torque values.

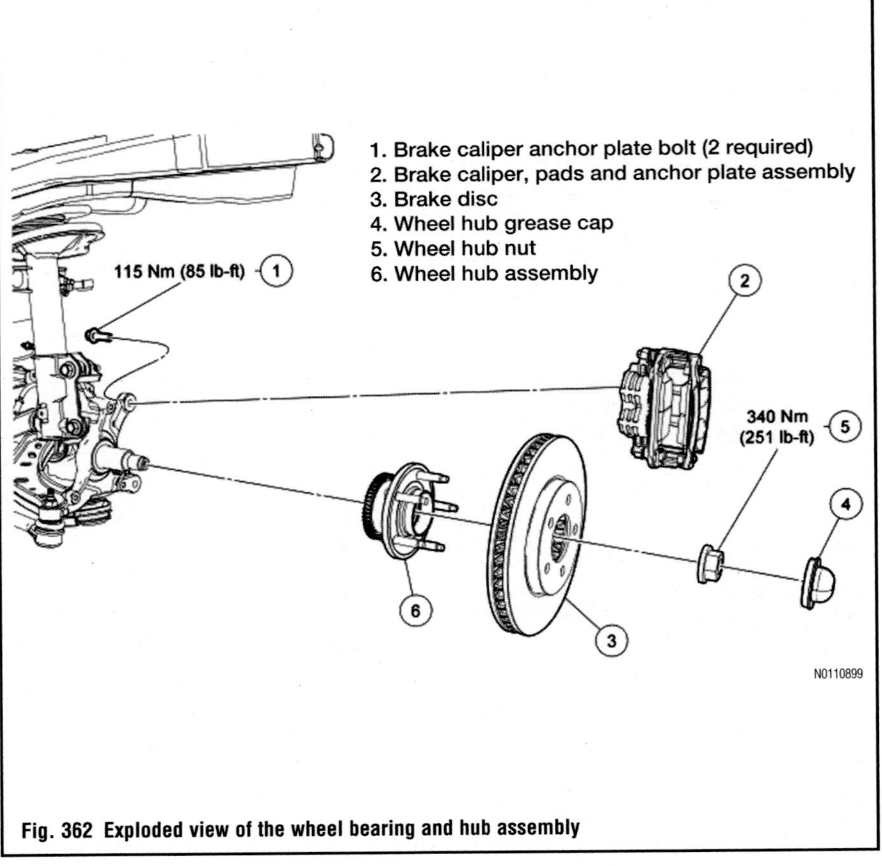

Fig. 362 Exploded view of the wheel bearing and hub assembly

COIL SPRING

REMOVAL & INSTALLATION

See Figures 363 and 364.

➡Suspension fasteners are critical parts because they affect performance of vital components and systems and their failure may result in major service expense. New parts must be installed with the same part numbers or equivalent part, if replacement is necessary. Do not use a replacement part of lesser quality or substitute design. Torque values must be used as specified during reassembly to make sure of correct retention of these parts.

1. To aid in installation, mark the rear shock absorber relative to the protective sleeve with the vehicle in a static, level ground position (curb height).
2. Remove the wheel and tire.
3. Convertible vehicles:
   a. Remove the rear support braces.
4. All vehicles:

➡Do not support the rear axle at the differential housing or damage to the housing may occur.

5. Using 2 suitable jackstands, support the rear axle.
6. Vehicles with a rear stabilizer bar:
   a. Remove and discard both stabilizer bar link bolts and clip nuts.
   b. Position the stabilizer bar to gain access to the shock absorber lower bolt.
7. All vehicles:
8. Remove and discard the shock absorber lower bolt and nut.
9. Remove the brake hose bracket bolt.
10. Lower the rear axle and remove the spring.
11. Inspect the upper and lower spring insulators for wear or damage. Install new insulators if necessary.

To install:

➡Refer to illustration for torque values.

➡The springs are vehicle specific and are marked with a tag indicating the spring code. Make sure the new spring has the same spring code as the one being replaced. If the tag is not on the spring being replaced, look on the vehicle information label located on the driver's door for the spring code and compare that to the new spring code.

12. Position the spring onto the axle with the tag toward the axle assembly.

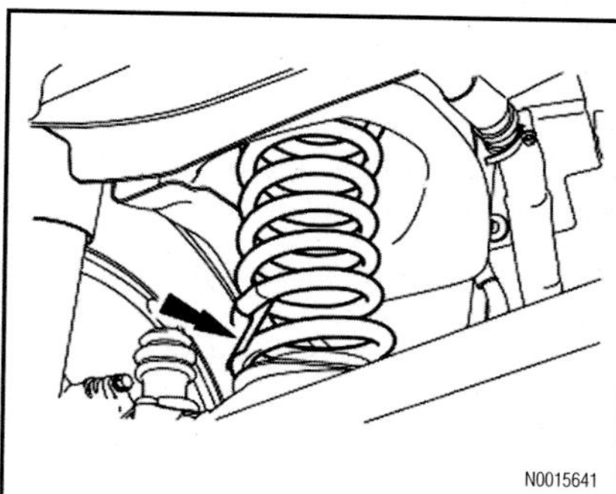

Fig. 364 Position the spring onto the axle with the tag toward the axle assembly

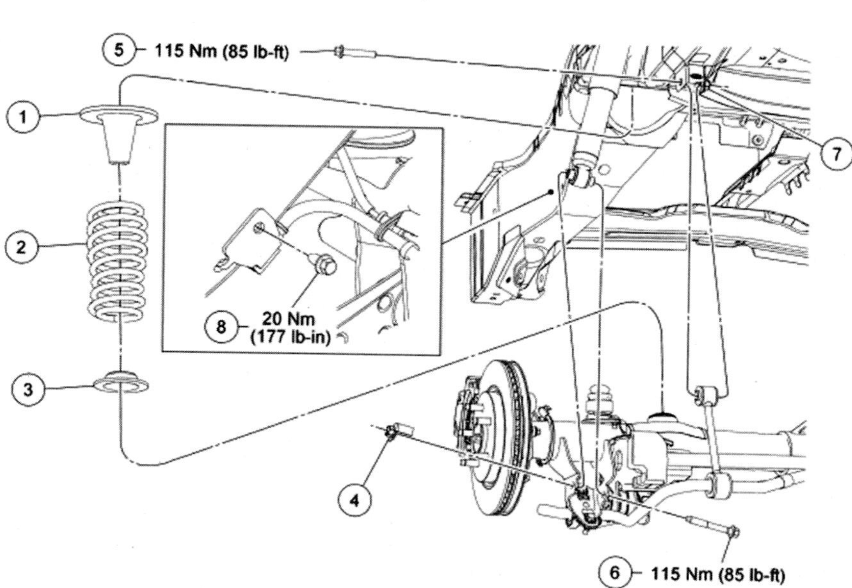

Fig. 363 Exploded view of the rear coil spring

13. Raise the rear axle so the mark made on the rear shock absorber in Removal Step 1 lines up with the protective sleeve.

➡Tighten the shock absorber lower bolt while the suspension is at curb height or bushing damage and incorrect clamp load may occur.

14. Install a new shock absorber lower bolt and nut.
15. Install the brake hose bracket bolt.
16. Convertible vehicles: Install the rear support braces.
17. Vehicles with a rear stabilizer bar:

➡The stabilizer bar is equipped with a tag. This tag indicates the LH side of the stabilizer bar. When installing a new stabilizer bar, make sure the tag is on the LH side of the vehicle or damage to the stabilizer bar may occur.

a. Position the stabilizer bar and links and install new stabilizer bar link bolts and clip nuts.

LATERAL BAR

REMOVA & INSTALLATION

See Figure 365.

➡Suspension fasteners are critical parts because they affect performance of vital components and systems and their failure may result in major service expense. New parts must be installed with the same part numbers or equivalent part, if replacement is necessary. Do not use a replacement part of lesser quality or substitute design. Torque values must be used as specified during reassembly to make sure of correct retention of these parts.

1. Mark the rear shock absorber relative to the protective sleeve with the vehicle in a static, level ground position (curb height).
2. With the vehicle in NEUTRAL, position it on a hoist.

➡Do not support the rear axle at the differential housing or damage to the housing may occur.

3. Using 2 suitable jackstands, support the rear axle.
4. Raise the rear axle so the mark made on the rear shock absorber in Step 1 lines up with the protective sleeve.
5. Remove and discard the RH panhard rod bolt, then remove and discard the lateral stiffener bar-to-body mount nut and flag bolt.
6. Remove and discard the lateral stiffener bar-to-body bolts.
7. Remove the lateral stiffener bar.

➡Tighten the new RH panhard rod bolt while the suspension is at curb height or bushing damage and incorrect clamp load may occur.

8. To install, reverse the removal procedure. Refer to illustration for torque values.

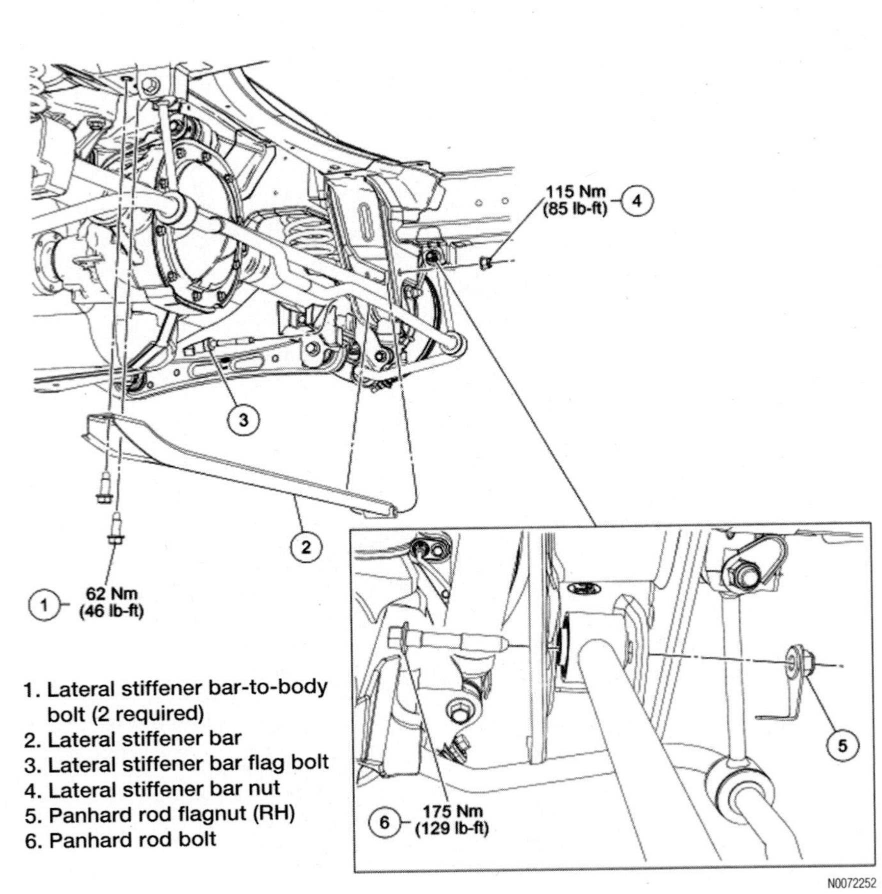

Fig. 365 Exploded view of the lateral stiffener bar

LOWER CONTROL ARM

REMOVAL & INSTALLATION

See Figure 366.

➡Suspension fasteners are critical parts because they affect performance of vital components and systems and their failure may result in major service expense. New parts must be installed with the same part numbers or equivalent part, if replacement is necessary. Do not use a replacement part of lesser quality or substitute design. Torque values must be used as specified during reassembly to make sure of correct retention of these parts.

1. To aid in installation, mark the rear shock absorber relative to the protective sleeve with the vehicle in a static, level ground position (curb height).
2. With the vehicle in NEUTRAL, position it on a hoist.

➡Do not support the rear axle at the differential housing or damage to the housing may occur.

3. Using 2 suitable jackstands, support the rear axle.
4. Raise the rear axle so the mark made on the rear shock absorber in Step 1 lines up with the protective sleeve.
5. Remove the clip and disconnect the parking brake cable from the rear caliper.
6. Remove the parking brake cable bracket bolt.
7. Remove and discard the lower arm front bolt.
8. Remove and discard the lower arm front nut.
9. Rotate the nut clockwise.
10. Remove and discard the nut.
11. Remove and discard the lower arm rear bolt and flagnut and then remove the lower arm.

➡Tighten the lower arm bolts while the suspension is at curb height or bushing damage and incorrect clamp load may occur.

12. To install, reverse the removal procedure. Refer to illustration for torque values.

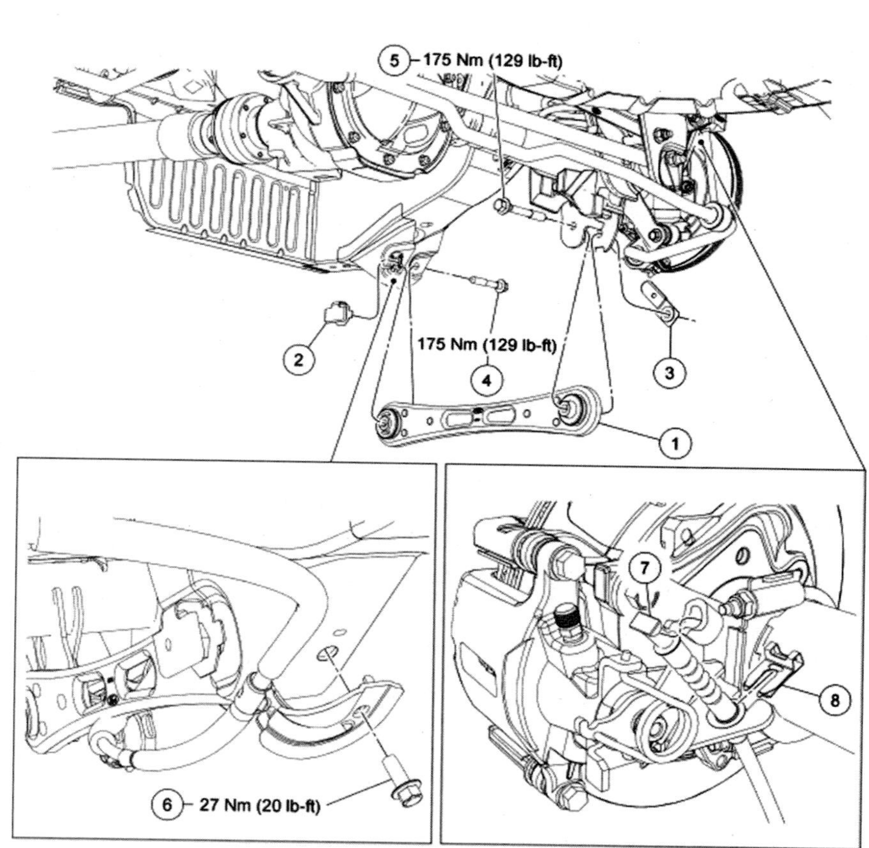

Fig. 366 Exploded view of the rear lower control arm

PANHARD ROD

REMOVAL & INSTALLATION

See Figures 367 and 368.

➡Suspension fasteners are critical parts because they affect performance of vital components and systems and their failure may result in major service expense. New parts must be installed with the same part numbers or equivalent part, if replacement is necessary. Do not use a replacement part of lesser quality or substitute design. Torque values must be used as specified during reassembly to make sure of correct retention of these parts.

1. To aid in installation, mark the rear shock absorber relative to the protective sleeve with the vehicle in a static, level ground position (curb height).
2. With the vehicle in NEUTRAL, position it on a hoist.

➡Do not support the rear axle at the differential housing or damage to the housing may occur.

3. Using 2 suitable jackstands, support the rear axle.

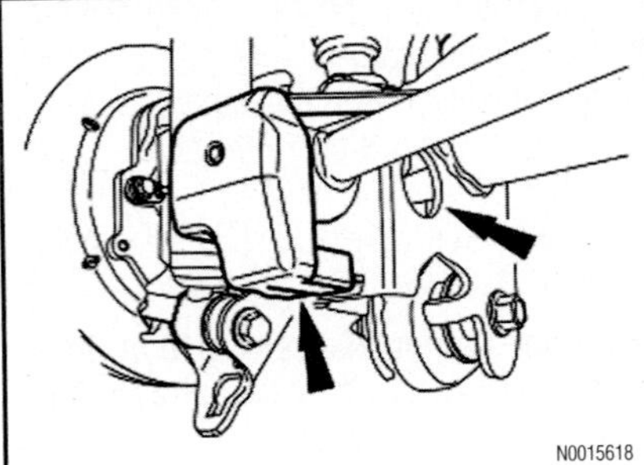

Fig. 368 Depress the tabs of the panhard rod bolt cover retaining clip and remove the cover

4. Raise the rear axle so the mark made on the rear shock absorber in Step 1 lines up with the protective sleeve.
5. Using 2 screwdrivers inserted through the access hole, depress the tabs of the panhard rod bolt cover retaining clip and remove the cover.
6. Remove and discard the panhard rod bolts and flagnuts.

➡Tighten the LH and RH panhard rod bolts with the suspension at curb height or damage may occur.

7. To install, reverse the removal procedure. Refer to illustration for torque values.

STABILIZER BAR

REMOVAL & INSTALLATION

See Figure 369.

➡Suspension fasteners are critical parts because they affect performance of vital components and systems and their failure may result in major service expense. New parts must be installed with the same part numbers or equivalent part, if replacement is necessary. Do not use a replacement part of lesser quality or substitute design. Torque values must be used as specified during reassembly to make sure of correct retention of these parts.

1. With the vehicle in NEUTRAL, position it on a hoist.
2. Remove and discard the stabilizer bar link bolts and clip nuts.
3. Remove the stabilizer bar bracket nuts, studs, brackets and stabilizer bar.
4. Discard the stabilizer bar bracket nuts and studs.
5. If necessary, remove the stabilizer bar bushings and links.

➡The stabilizer bar is equipped with a tag. This tag indicates the LH side of

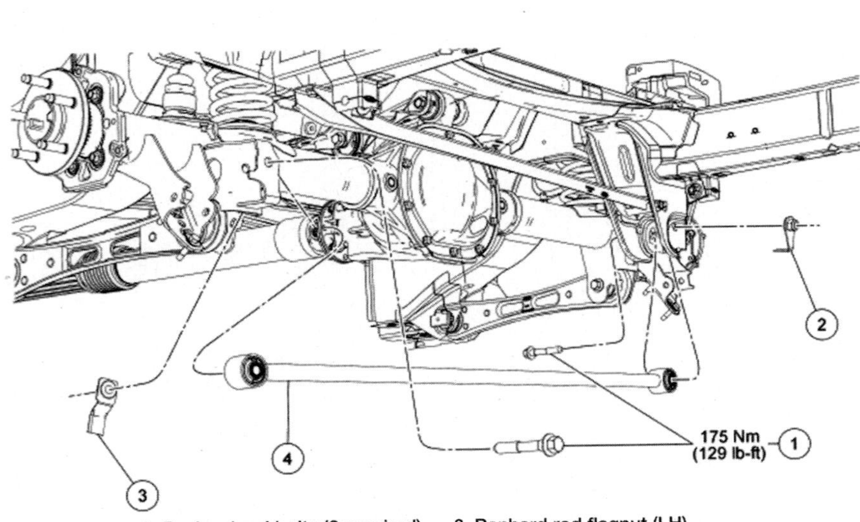

Fig. 367 Exploded view of the panhard rod

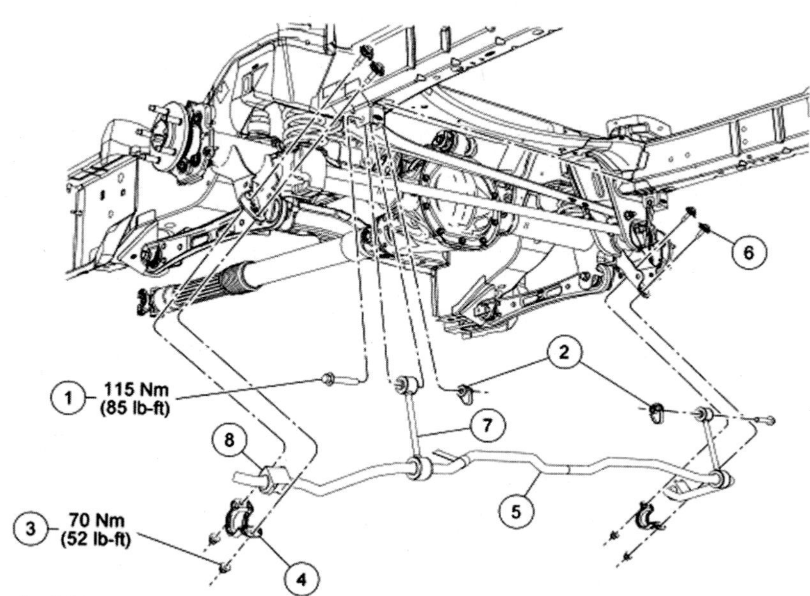

1. Stabilizer bar link bolt (2 required)
2. Stabilizer bar link flagnuts (2 required)
3. Stabilizer bar bracket nut (4 required)
4. Stabilizer bar bracket (2 required)
5. Stabilizer bar
6. Stabilizer bar bracket clip stud
7. Stabilizer bar link (2 required)
8. Stabilizer bar bushing (2 required)

N0072262

Fig. 369 Exploded view of the rear stabilizer bar

the stabilizer bar. When installing a new stabilizer bar, make sure the tag is on the LH side of the vehicle or damage to the stabilizer bar may occur.

➡The stabilizer bar is vehicle specific (convertible and coupe). Make sure the correct stabilizer bar goes on the correct vehicle.

6. Make sure that a new stabilizer bar has the same tag color as the one being replaced. If the stabilizer bar being replaced does not have a tag, it will be necessary to inspect the stabilizer bar link coating color to determine the proper replacement stabilizer bar.
   a. Black-coated stabilizer bar link will require a yellow tag stabilizer bar with the suffix "A" in the part number.
   b. White-coated stabilizer bar link will require a green tag stabilizer bar with the suffix "B" in the part number.
   c. Blue/gray-coated stabilizer bar link will require an orange tag stabilizer bar with the suffix "C" in the part number.
7. To install, reverse the removal procedure. Refer to illustration for torque values.

UPPER CONTROL ARM

REMOVAL & INSTALLATION

See Figure 370.

➡Suspension fasteners are critical parts because they affect performance of vital components and systems and their failure may result in major service expense. New parts must be installed with the same part numbers or equivalent part, if replacement is necessary. Do not use a replacement part of lesser quality or substitute design. Torque values must be used as specified during reassembly to make sure of correct retention of these parts.

➡The upper arm is a 2-piece design and is replaced as an assembly. Do not remove or loosen the nut and bolt that joins the 2 pieces together. The assembly is set at ride height during production, loosening the nut and bolt will disturb this setting.

1. Remove the rear seat cushion.
2. Remove and discard the upper arm bracket forward bolt.
3. To aid in installation, mark the rear shock absorber relative to the protective sleeve with the vehicle in a static, level ground position (curb height).
4. With the vehicle in NEUTRAL, position it on a hoist.
5. Place a safety support under the fuel tank.
6. Remove the rear bolts from the 2 fuel tank support straps and position both straps aside.

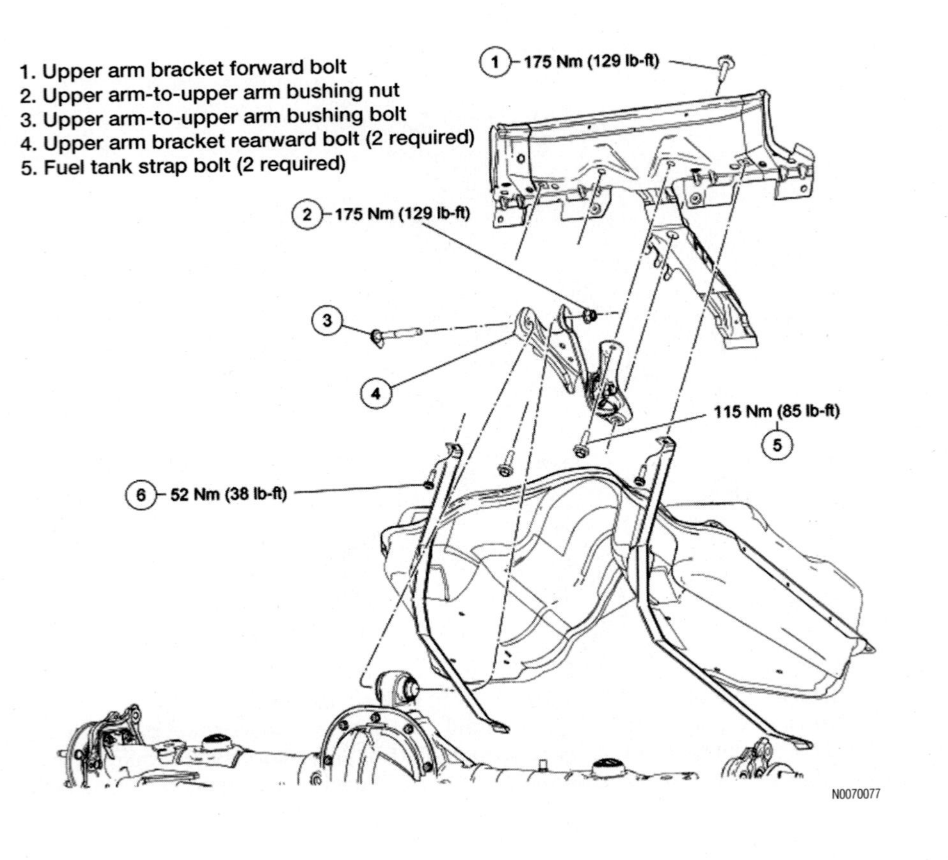

Fig. 370 Exploded view of the rear upper control arm

7. Partially lower the fuel tank to gain access to the upper control arm.
8. Remove and discard the 2 upper arm bracket rearward bolts.
9. Remove and discard the upper arm-to-upper arm bushing flag bolt and nut.
10. Remove the upper arm assembly.
11. Raise the rear axle so the mark made in Step 3 lines up with the protective sleeve.

➡Tighten the upper arm fasteners while the suspension is at curb height or bushing damage and incorrect clamp load may occur.

12. To install, reverse the removal procedure. Refer to illustration for torque values.

FORD

Ranger

16

BRAKES 16-10

ANTI-LOCK BRAKE SYSTEM (ABS) 16-10
General Information 16-10
Precautions 16-10
Speed Sensors 16-10
Removal & Installation 16-10

BLEEDING THE BRAKE SYSTEM 16-13
Bleeding Procedure 16-13
Bleeding Procedure 16-13
Bleeding the ABS System 16-14
Fluid Fill Procedure 16-14

FRONT DISC BRAKES 16-15
Brake Caliper 16-15
Removal & Installation 16-15
Disc Brake Pads 16-15
Removal & Installation 16-15

PARKING BRAKE 16-18
Parking Brake Shoes 16-18
Adjustment 16-19
Removal & Installation 16-18

REAR DISC BRAKES 16-16
Brake Caliper 16-16
Removal & Installation 16-16
Disc Brake Pads 16-16
Removal & Installation 16-16

CHASSIS ELECTRICAL 16-20

AIR BAG (SUPPLEMENTAL RESTRAINT SYSTEM) 16-20
General Information 16-20
Arming the System 16-21
Clockspring Centering 16-21
Disarming the System 16-20
Service Precautions 16-20

DRIVE TRAIN 16-22

Automatic Transmission Fluid ... 16-22
Drain and Refill 16-22
Filter Replacement 16-22
Clutch 16-24
Pilot Bearing 16-25
Removal & Installation 16-24
Front Driveshaft 16-26
Removal & Installation 16-26
Front Halfshaft 16-26
Removal & Installation 16-26
Front Pinion Seal 16-27
Removal & Installation 16-27
Manual Transmission Assembly 16-23
Removal & Installation 16-23
Manual Transmission Fluid 16-24
Drain and Refill 16-24
Rear Axle Fluid 16-28
Drain & Refill 16-28
Rear Axle Housing Cover 16-28
Removal & Installation 16-28
Rear Axle Shaft 16-28
Remove & Installation 16-28
Rear Axle Shaft Bearing & Seal 16-29
Removal & Installation 16-29
Rear Driveshaft 16-30
Removal & Installation 16-30
Rear Pinion Seal 16-31
Removal & Installation 16-31
Transfer Case Assembly 16-25
Draining & Filling 16-25

ENGINE COOLING 16-32

Engine Coolant 16-32
Drain, Refill & Bleeding Procedure 16-32
Flushing 16-34
Engine Fan 16-34
Removal & Installation 16-34
Radiator 16-34
Removal & Installation 16-34
Thermostat 16-35
Removal & Installation 16-35
Water Pump 16-36
Removal & Installation 16-36

ENGINE ELECTRICAL 16-38

BATTERY SYSTEM 16-38
Battery 16-38
Battery Reconnect/Relearn Procedure 16-38
Removal & Installation 16-38

CHARGING SYSTEM 16-39
Alternator 16-39
Removal & Installation 16-39

IGNITION SYSTEM 16-40
Firing Order 16-40
Ignition Coil 16-40
Removal & Installation 16-40
Ignition Timing 16-41
Adjustment 16-41
Spark Plugs 16-41
Inspection 16-41
Removal & Installation 16-41

STARTING SYSTEM 16-43
Starter 16-43
Removal & Installation 16-43

ENGINE MECHANICAL 16-45

Accessory Drive Belts 16-45
Accessory Belt Routing 16-45
Adjustment 16-45
Inspection 16-45
Removal & Installation 16-45
Air Cleaner 16-45
Filter/Element Replacement 16-46
Removal & Installation 16-45
Camshaft and Valve Lifters 16-46
Inspection 16-46
Removal & Installation 16-47
Catalytic Converter 16-50
Removal & Installation 16-50
Crankshaft Front Seal 16-50
Removal & Installation 16-50
Cylinder Head 16-52
Removal & Installation 16-52
Engine Oil & Filter 16-55
Replacement 16-55
Exhaust Manifold 16-55
Removal & Installation 16-55
Intake Manifold 16-56
Removal & Installation 16-56
Oil Pan 16-59
Removal & Installation 16-59
Oil Pump 16-60
Removal & Installation 16-60

Rear Main Seal........................16-62
Removal & Installation........16-62
Timing Chain & Sprockets......16-63
Removal & Installation........16-63
Timing Chain Front Cover.......16-65
Removal & Installation........16-65
Valve Covers..........................16-66
Removal & Installation........16-66

ENGINE PERFORMANCE & EMISSION CONTROLS 16-69

Camshaft Position (CMP) Sensor 16-69
Location..............................16-69
Removal & Installation........16-69
Crankshaft Position (CKP) Sensor 16-69
Location..............................16-69
Removal & Installation........16-69
Electronic Control Module (ECM)..................................16-70
Module Configuration.........16-71
Removal & Installation........16-70
Engine Coolant Temperature (ECT) Sensor 16-71
Location..............................16-71
Removal & Installation........................16-71
Heated Oxygen (HO2S) Sensor 16-71
Location..............................16-71
Removal & Installation........16-71
Knock Sensor (KS)..................16-72
Location..............................16-72
Removal & Installation........16-72
Manifold Absolute Pressure (MAP) Sensor.......................16-72
Location..............................16-72
Removal & Installation........16-72
Throttle Position Sensor (TPS)......................................16-72
Location..............................16-72
Removal & Installation........16-73

FUEL 16-74

GASOLINE FUEL INJECTION SYSTEM 16-74
Fuel Filter..............................16-74
Removal & Installation........16-74
Fuel Injectors.........................16-75
Removal & Installation........16-75
Fuel Pump..............................16-76
Removal & Installation........16-76
Fuel System Service Precautions..........................16-74
Fuel Tank...............................16-76
Draining............................16-76
Removal & Installation........16-76
Idle Speed..............................16-76
Adjustment........................16-76
Relieving Fuel System Pressure..............................16-74
Throttle Body..........................16-76
Removal & Installation........16-76

HEATING & AIR CONDITIONING SYSTEM...16-79

Blower Motor.........................16-79
Removal & Installation........16-79
Heater Core............................16-79
Removal & Installation........16-79

PRECAUTIONS..............16-10

SPECIFICATIONS AND MAINTENANCE CHARTS.....16-3

Brake Specifications.................16-7
Camshaft Specifications............16-5
Capacities...............................16-4
Crankshaft and Connecting Rod Specifications..................16-5
Engine and Vehicle Identification..........................16-3
Engine Tune-Up Specifications.........................16-3
Fluid Specifications..................16-4
General Engine Specifications...16-3
Piston and Ring Specifications.........................16-5
Scheduled Maintenance Intervals................................16-8
Tire, Wheel and Ball Joint Specifications.........................16-7
Torque Specifications................16-6
Valve Specifications..................16-4
Wheel Alignment......................16-6

STEERING...................16-81

Power Steering Gear................16-81
Removal & Installation........16-81
Power Steering Pump.............16-83
Bleeding & Flushing...........16-84
Fluid Fill Procedure............16-85
Purging..............................16-85
Removal & Installation........16-83

SUSPENSION...............16-86

FRONT SUSPENSION 16-86
Coil Spring.............................16-86
Removal & Installation........16-86
Control Links..........................16-86
Removal & Installation........16-86
Lower Ball Joint......................16-86
Removal & Installation........16-86
Lower Control Arm..................16-88
Removal & Installation........16-88
Stabilizer Bar..........................16-89
Removal & Installation........16-89
Steering Knuckle.....................16-90
Removal & Installation........16-90
Torsion Bar.............................16-91
Removal & Installation........16-91
Upper Control Arm.................16-92
Removal & Installation........16-92
Wheel Bearings.......................16-93
Removal & Installation........16-93
REAR SUSPENSION 16-95
Leaf Spring.............................16-95
Removal & Installation........16-95

SPECIFICATIONS AND MAINTENANCE CHARTS

ENGINE AND VEHICLE IDENTIFICATION

Engine						
Code ①	Liters (cc)	Cu. In.	Cyl.	Fuel Sys.	Engine Type	Eng. Mfg.
D	2.3	140	4	EFI	DOHC	Ford
E	4.0	244	6	EFI	SOHC	Ford

Model Year	
Code ②	Year
A	2010
B	2011

① 8th position of VIN

② 10th position of VIN

25759_RANG_C0001

GENERAL ENGINE SPECIFICATIONS

All measurements are given in inches.

Year	Model	Engine Displacement Liters	Engine ID/VIN	Fuel System Type	Net Horsepower @ rpm	Net Torque @ rpm (ft. lbs.)	Bore x Stroke (in.)	Com-pression Ratio	Oil Pressure @ rpm
2010	Ranger	2.3	D	SFI	143@5250	154@3750	8.75x9.4	9.7:1	29-39@2000
		4.0	E	SFI	207@5250	238@3000	3.95x3.32	9.7:1	15@2000
2011	Ranger	2.3	D	SFI	143@5250	154@3750	8.75x9.4	9.7:1	29-39@2000
		4.0	E	SFI	207@5250	238@3000	3.95x3.32	9.7:1	15@2000

25759_RANG_C0002

ENGINE TUNE-UP SPECIFICATIONS

Year	Engine Displacement Liters	Engine ID/VIN	Spark Plug Gap (in.)	Ignition Timing (deg.)		Fuel Pump (psi)	Idle Speed (rpm)		Valve Clearance	
				MT	AT		MT	AT	Intake	Exhaust
2010	2.3	D	0.049-0.053	①	①	60-65	2,000	2,000	NA	NA
	4.0	E	0.049-0.053	①	①	60-65	2,000	2,000	NA	NA
2011	2.3	D	0.049-0.053	①	①	60-65	2,000	2,000	NA	NA
	4.0	E	0.049-0.053	①	①	60-65	2,000	2,000	NA	NA

NA: Not Available

① 10 degrees Before Top Dead Center (BTDC) and is not adjustable

25759_RANG_C0003

CAPACITIES

Year	Model	Engine Displacement Liters	Engine ID/VIN	Engine Oil with Filter	Transmission/axle (pts.) Auto.	Transmission/axle (pts.) Manual	Drive Axle (pts.) Front	Drive Axle (pts.) Rear	Transfer Case (pts.)	Fuel Tank (gal.)	Cooling System (qts.)
2010	Ranger	2.3	D	4.0	20	5.6	NA	5.0	2.5	①	11.0
		4.0	E	6.0	20	5.6	NA	5.0	2.5	①	13-13.5
2011	Ranger	2.3	D	4.0	20	5.6	NA	5.0	2.5	①	11.0
		4.0	E	6.0	20	5.6	NA	5.0	2.5	①	13-13.5

NA: Not Available

NOTE: All capacities are approximate. Add fluid gradually and ensure a proper fluid level is obtained.

① Long Wheel Base: 20.3 gallons

Standard: 17 gallons

SuperCab: 19.5 gallons

25759_RANG_C0004

FLUID SPECIFICATIONS

Year	Model	Engine Displacment Liters	Engine Oil	Auto. Trans.	Drive Axle Front	Drive Axle Rear	Power Steering Fluid	Brake Master Cylinder	Cooling System
2010	Ranger	2.3	5W-20	XT-5-QM	NA	80W-90	XT-5-QM	DOT 3	①
		4.0	5W-30	XT-5-QM	NA	80W-90	XT-5-QM	DOT 3	①
2011	Ranger	2.3	5W-20	XT-5-QM	NA	80W-90	XT-5-QM	DOT 3	①
		4.0	5W-30	XT-5-QM	NA	80W-90	XT-5-QM	DOT 3	①

NA: Not Available

① Motorcraft® Premium Gold Engine Coolant with Bittering Agent

25759_RANG_C0005

VALVE SPECIFICATIONS

Year	Engine Displacement Liters	Engine ID/VIN	Seat Angle (deg.)	Face Angle (deg.)	Spring Test Pressure (lbs. @ in.)	Spring Free-Length (in.)	Spring Installed Height (in.)	Stem-to-Guide Clearance (in.) Intake	Stem-to-Guide Clearance (in.) Exhaust	Stem Diameter (in.) Intake	Stem Diameter (in.) Exhaust
2010	2.3	D	45	45	NA	1.768	1.492	0.0009	0.0011	0.2153-0.2159	0.2151-0.2157
	4.0	E	45	45	NA	1.7	1.569-1.608	0.001-0.002	0.001-0.003	0.274-0.275	0.274
2011	2.3	D	45	45	NA	1.768	1.492	0.0009	0.0011	0.2153-0.2159	0.2151-0.2157
	4.0	E	45	45	NA	1.7	1.569-1.608	0.001-0.002	0.001-0.003	0.274-0.275	0.274

NA: Not Available

25759_RANG_C0006

CAMSHAFT SPECIFICATIONS

All measurements in inches unless noted

Year	Engine Displacement Liters	Engine Code/VIN	Journal Diameter	Brg. Oil Clearance	Shaft End-play	Runout	Journal Bore	Lobe Height	
								Intake	Exhaust
2010	2.3	D	0.982-0.983	0.001-0.003	NA	0.001	1.0625-1.0635	0.324	0.307
	4.0	E	1.099-1.101	0.002-0.004	0.0003-0.007	0.002	1.102-1.104	0.259	0.259
2011	2.3	D	0.982-0.983	0.001-0.003	NA	0.001	1.0625-1.0635	0.324	0.307
	4.0	E	1.099-1.101	0.002-0.004	0.0003-0.007	0.002	1.102-1.104	0.259	0.259

NA: Not Available

25759_RANG_C0007

CRANKSHAFT AND CONNECTING ROD SPECIFICATIONS

All measurements are given in inches.

Year	Engine Displacement Liters	Engine ID/VIN	Crankshaft				Connecting Rod		
			Main Brg. Journal Dia.	Main Brg. Oil Clearance	Shaft End-play	Thrust on No.	Journal Diameter	Oil Clearance	Side Clearance
2010	2.3	D	2.046-2.047	0.0007-0.0018	0.008-0.016	NA	2.087-2.088	0.005-0.014	0.076-0.12
	4.0	E	2.243-2.244	0.0003-0.0024	0.002-0.0126	NA	2.2370-2.2378	0.0008-0.0025	0.0036-0.0106
2011	2.3	D	2.046-2.047	0.0007-0.0018	0.008-0.016	NA	2.087-2.088	0.005-0.014	0.076-0.12
	4.0	E	2.243-2.244	0.0003-0.0024	0.002-0.0126	NA	2.2370-2.2378	0.0008-0.0025	0.0036-0.0106

NA: Not Available

25759_RANG_C0008

PISTON AND RING SPECIFICATIONS

All measurements are given in inches.

Year	Engine Displacement Liters	Engine ID/VIN	Piston Clearance	Ring Gap			Ring Side Clearance		
				Top Compression	Bottom Compression	Oil Control	Top Compression	Bottom Compression	Oil Control
2010	2.3	D	0.0009-0.0017	0.006-0.012	0.012-0.018	0.007-0.027	0.0460-0.0466	0.0471-0.0472	0.093-0.096
	4.0	E	0.0012-0.0023	0.008-0.018	0.018-0.028	NA	0.0645-0.0654	0.0705-0.0713	0.1378-0.1399
2011	2.3	D	0.0009-0.0017	0.006-0.012	0.012-0.018	0.007-0.027	0.0460-0.0466	0.0471-0.0472	0.093-0.096
	4.0	E	0.0012-0.0023	0.008-0.018	0.018-0.028	NA	0.0645-0.0654	0.0705-0.0713	0.1378-0.1399

NA: Not available

25759_RANG_C0009

TORQUE SPECIFICATIONS

All readings in ft. lbs.

Year	Engine Disp. Liters	Engine ID/VIN	Cylinder Head Bolts	Main Bearing Bolts	Rod Bearing Bolts	Crankshaft Damper Bolts	Flywheel Bolts	Manifold Intake	Manifold Exhaust	Spark Plugs	Oil Pan Drain Plug
2010	2.3	D	①	NA	NA	②	③	13	40	9	21
	4.0	E	④	NA	NA	⑤	⑥	7	22	15	19
2011	2.3	D	①	NA	NA	②	③	13	40	9	21
	4.0	E	④	NA	NA	⑤	⑥	7	22	15	19

① Stage 1: Tighten to 44 inch lbs. (5 Nm)
Stage 2: Tighten to 11 ft. lbs. (15 Nm)
Stage 3: Tighten to 33 ft. lbs. (45 Nm)
Stage 4: Tighten an additional 90 degrees
Stage 5: Tighten an additional 90 degrees

② Tighten to 74 ft. lbs. (100 Nm)
Rotate an additional 90 degrees

③ Stage 1: 37 ft. lbs. (50 Nm)
Stage 2: 59 ft. lbs. (80 Nm)
Stage 3: Tighten to 83 ft. lbs. (112 Nm)

④ Stage 1: Tighten to 9 ft. lbs. (12 Nm)
Stage 2: Tighten to 18 ft. lbs. (25 Nm)

⑤ Stage 1: Tighten to 41 ft. lbs. (55 Nm)
Stage 2: Tighten an additional 85 degrees

⑥ Stage 1: Tighten to 10 ft. lbs. (13 Nm)
Stage 2: Tighten to 37 ft. lbs. (50 Nm)
Stage 3: Tighten an additional 90 degrees

25759_RANG_C0010

WHEEL ALIGNMENT

Year	Model		Caster Range (+/-Deg.)	Caster Preferred Setting (Deg.)	Camber Range (+/-Deg.)	Camber Preferred Setting (Deg.)	Toe-in (in.)
2010	Ranger w/ Coil Suspension	LH	0.0° ± 0.70°	3.0° ± 1.0°	-0.2° ± 0.70°	-0.5° ± 0.70°	0.06° ± 0.25°
		RH	0.0° ± 0.70°	3.2° ± 1.0°	-0.2° ± 0.70°	-0.5° ± 0.70°	0.06° ± 0.25°
	Torsion Bar Suspension	LH	-0.5° ± 0.70°	2.8° ± 1.0°	0.0° ± 0.70°	0.0° ± 0.70°	0.12° ± 0.25°
		RH	-0.5° ± 0.70°	3.3° ± 1.0°	0.0° ± 0.70°	0.0° ± 0.70°	0.12° ± 0.25°
	4WD	LH	-0.7° ± 0.70°	2.8° ± 1.0°	0.0° ± 0.70°	0.0° ± 0.70°	0.12° ± 0.25°
		RH	-0.7° ± 0.70°	3.3° ± 1.0°	0.0° ± 0.70°	0.0° ± 0.70°	0.12° ± 0.25°
2011	Ranger w/ Coil Suspension	LH	0.0° ± 0.70°	3.0° ± 1.0°	-0.2° ± 0.70°	-0.5° ± 0.70°	0.06° ± 0.25°
		RH	0.0° ± 0.70°	3.2° ± 1.0°	-0.2° ± 0.70°	-0.5° ± 0.70°	0.06° ± 0.25°
	Torsion Bar Suspension	LH	-0.5° ± 0.70°	2.8° ± 1.0°	0.0° ± 0.70°	0.0° ± 0.70°	0.12° ± 0.25°
		RH	-0.5° ± 0.70°	3.3° ± 1.0°	0.0° ± 0.70°	0.0° ± 0.70°	0.12° ± 0.25°
	4WD	LH	-0.7° ± 0.70°	2.8° ± 1.0°	0.0° ± 0.70°	0.0° ± 0.70°	0.12° ± 0.25°
		RH	-0.7° ± 0.70°	3.3° ± 1.0°	0.0° ± 0.70°	0.0° ± 0.70°	0.12° ± 0.25°

25759_RANG_C0011

TIRE, WHEEL AND BALL JOINT SPECIFICATIONS

Year	Model	OEM Tires		Tire Pressures (psi)		Wheel Size	Ball Joint Inspection	Lug Nut (ft. lbs.)
		Standard	Optional	Front	Rear			
2010	Ranger	NA	NA	NA	NA	NA	NA	100
2011	Ranger	NA	NA	NA	NA	NA	NA	100

OEM: Original Equipment Manufacturer

PSI: Pounds Per Square Inch

NA: Information not available

25759_RANG_C0012

BRAKE SPECIFICATIONS

All measurements in inches unless noted

Year	Model		Brake Disc			Minimum Pad/Lining Thickness		Brake Caliper	
			Original Thickness	Minimum Thickness	Max. Runout	Front	Rear	Bracket Bolts (ft. lbs.)	Mounting Bolts (ft. lbs.)
2010	Ranger	F	NA	0.964	NA	0.118	0.118	27	NA
		R	NA	0.708	NA	0.118	0.118	27	NA
2011	Ranger	F	NA	0.964	NA	0.118	0.118	27	NA
		R	NA	0.708	NA	0.118	0.118	27	NA

F: Front

R: Rear

NA: Information not available

25759_RANG_C0013

SCHEDULED MAINTENANCE INTERVALS

Ford Ranger - Normal

SERVICE ITEM	SERVICE ACTION	VEHICLE MILEAGE INTERVAL (x1000)													
		7.5	15	22.5	30	37.5	45	52.5	60	67.5	75.0	82.5	90.0	97.5	100.5
Engine oil & filter	Replace	✓	✓	✓	✓	✓	✓	✓	✓	✓	✓	✓	✓	✓	✓
Rotate tires, inspect tread wear, measure tread depth and check pressure	Rotate/ Inspect	✓	✓	✓	✓	✓	✓	✓	✓	✓	✓	✓	✓	✓	✓
Inspect wheels & related components for abnormal noise, wear, looseness or drag	Inspect	✓	✓	✓	✓	✓	✓	✓	✓	✓	✓	✓	✓	✓	✓
Fluid levels (all)	Top off	✓	✓	✓	✓	✓	✓	✓	✓	✓	✓	✓	✓	✓	✓
Brake system	Inspect	✓	✓	✓	✓	✓	✓	✓	✓	✓	✓	✓	✓	✓	✓
Cooling system, hoses, clamps & coolant strength	Inspect		✓		✓		✓		✓		✓		✓		✓
Exhaust system (Leaks, damage, loose parts and foreign material)	Inspect	✓	✓	✓	✓	✓	✓	✓	✓	✓	✓	✓	✓	✓	✓
Steering linkage, ball joints, suspension, tie-rod ends, driveshaft and u-joints: lubricate if equipped with grease fittings	Inspect/ Lubricate	✓	✓	✓	✓	✓	✓	✓	✓	✓	✓	✓	✓	✓	✓
Drive belt	Inspect	✓	✓	✓	✓	✓	✓	✓	✓	✓	✓	✓	✓	✓	✓
Battery performance	Inspect	✓	✓	✓	✓	✓	✓	✓	✓	✓	✓	✓	✓	✓	✓
Horn, exterior lamps, turn signals and hazard warning light operation	Inspect	✓	✓	✓	✓	✓	✓	✓	✓	✓	✓	✓	✓	✓	✓
Engine air filter	Inspect	✓	✓	✓	✓	✓	✓	✓	✓	✓	✓	✓	✓	✓	✓
Windshield for cracks, chips and pitting	Inspect	✓	✓	✓	✓	✓	✓	✓	✓	✓	✓	✓	✓	✓	✓
Engine air filter	Replace				✓				✓				✓		
Auto trans fluid, filter	Replace								✓						
Oil and fluid leaks	Inspect	✓	✓	✓	✓	✓	✓	✓	✓	✓	✓	✓	✓	✓	✓
Rear differential fluid	Replace	At 150,000 miles													
Repack front wheel bearings and replace seals (2X4)	Inspect/ Repack								✓						
Spark plugs	Replace												✓		
Drive belt	Replace								✓						
Engine coolant	Replace														✓
Shocks and other suspension components for leaks and damage	Inspect	✓	✓	✓	✓	✓	✓	✓	✓	✓	✓	✓	✓	✓	✓
Windshield wiper spray and wiper operation	Inspect	✓	✓	✓	✓	✓	✓	✓	✓	✓	✓	✓	✓	✓	✓
Transfer case fluid (4X4)	Replace	At 150,000 miles													
Manual transmission fluid	Replace														✓
Front differential fluid (4X4)	Replace	At 150,000 miles													
Fuel filter	Replace				✓				✓				✓		

For extensive idling and or low speed driving, change engine oil and filter every 5,000 miles, 6 months or 200 hours of engine operation.

25759_RANG_C0014

SCHEDULED MAINTENANCE INTERVALS

Ford Ranger - Severe

SERVICE ITEM	SERVICE ACTION	VEHICLE MILEAGE INTERVAL (x1000)											
		5	10	15	20	25	30	35	40	45	50	55	60
Manual transmission fluid	Replace												✓
Auto transmission fluid and filter	Replace						✓						✓
Repack Front Wheel bearing and replace seals (4X2)							✓						✓
Battery performance	Inspect	✓	✓	✓	✓	✓	✓	✓	✓	✓	✓	✓	✓
Brake system	Inspect	✓	✓	✓	✓	✓	✓	✓	✓	✓	✓	✓	✓
Cooling system, hoses, clamps & coolant strength	Inspect	✓	✓	✓	✓	✓	✓	✓	✓	✓	✓	✓	✓
Drive belt	Inspect	✓	✓	✓	✓	✓	✓	✓	✓	✓	✓	✓	✓
Drive belt	Replace												✓
Engine air filter	Inspect	✓	✓	✓	✓	✓	✓	✓	✓	✓	✓	✓	✓
Engine air filter	Replace						✓						✓
Engine coolant	Replace	At 105,000 miles											
Engine oil & filter	Replace	✓	✓	✓	✓	✓	✓	✓	✓	✓	✓	✓	✓
Exhaust system (Leaks, damage, loose parts and foreign material)	Inspect	✓	✓	✓	✓	✓	✓	✓	✓	✓	✓	✓	✓
Fluid levels (all)	Top off	✓	✓	✓	✓	✓	✓	✓	✓	✓	✓	✓	✓
Inspect wheels and related components for abnormal noise, wear, looseness or drag	Inspect	✓	✓	✓	✓	✓	✓	✓	✓	✓	✓	✓	✓
Oil and fluid leaks	Inspect	✓	✓	✓	✓	✓	✓	✓	✓	✓	✓	✓	✓
Radiator, coolers, heater and air conditioning hoses	Inspect	✓	✓	✓	✓	✓	✓	✓	✓	✓	✓	✓	✓
Rear differential fluid	Replace	At 150,000 miles											
Rotate tires, inspect tread wear, measure tread depth and check pressure	Rotate/Inspect	✓	✓	✓	✓	✓	✓	✓	✓	✓	✓	✓	✓
Shocks and other suspension components for leaks and damage	Inspect	✓	✓	✓	✓	✓	✓	✓	✓	✓	✓	✓	✓
Spark plugs	Replace												✓
Steering linkage, ball joints, suspension and tie-rod ends, lubricate if equipped with	Inspect/Lubricate	✓	✓	✓	✓	✓	✓	✓	✓	✓	✓	✓	✓
Windshield wiper spray and wiper operation	Inspect	✓	✓	✓	✓	✓	✓	✓	✓	✓	✓	✓	✓
Windshield for cracks, chips and pitting	Inspect												
Fuel filter	Replace			✓			✓			✓			✓
Front differential fluid (4X4)	Replace	At 150,000 miles											
Transfer case fluid (4X4)	Replace												✓

For extensive idling and or low speed driving, change engine oil and filter every 5,000 miles, 6 months or 200 hours of engine operation.

25759_RANG_C0015

PRECAUTIONS

Before servicing any vehicle, please be sure to read all of the following precautions, which deal with personal safety, prevention of component damage, and important points to take into consideration when servicing a motor vehicle:

- Never open, service or drain the radiator or cooling system when the engine is hot; serious burns can occur from the steam and hot coolant.
- Observe all applicable safety precautions when working around fuel. Whenever servicing the fuel system, always work in a well-ventilated area. Do not allow fuel spray or vapors to come in contact with a spark, open flame, or excessive heat (a hot drop light, for example). Keep a dry chemical fire extinguisher near the work area. Always keep fuel in a container specifically designed for fuel storage; also, always properly seal fuel containers to avoid the possibility of fire or explosion. Refer to the additional fuel system precautions later in this section.
- Fuel injection systems often remain pressurized, even after the engine has been turned **OFF**. The fuel system pressure must be relieved before disconnecting any fuel lines. Failure to do so may result in fire and/or personal injury.
- Brake fluid often contains polyglycol ethers and polyglycols. Avoid contact with the eyes and wash your hands thoroughly after handling brake fluid. If you do get brake fluid in your eyes, flush your eyes with clean, running water for 15 minutes. If eye irritation persists, or if you have taken brake fluid internally, IMMEDIATELY seek medical assistance.
- The EPA warns that prolonged contact with used engine oil may cause a number of skin disorders, including cancer. You should make every effort to minimize your exposure to used engine oil. Protective gloves should be worn when changing oil. Wash your hands and any other exposed skin areas as soon as possible after exposure to used engine oil. Soap and water, or waterless hand cleaner should be used.
- All new vehicles are now equipped with an air bag system, often referred to as a Supplemental Restraint System (SRS) or Supplemental Inflatable Restraint (SIR) system. The system must be disabled before performing service on or around system components, steering column, instrument panel components, wiring and sensors. Failure to follow safety and disabling procedures could result in accidental air bag deployment, possible personal injury and unnecessary system repairs.
- Always wear safety goggles when working with, or around, the air bag system. When carrying a non-deployed air bag, be sure the bag and trim cover are pointed away from your body. When placing a non-deployed air bag on a work surface, always face the bag and trim cover upward, away from the surface. This will reduce the motion of the module if it is accidentally deployed. Refer to the additional air bag system precautions later in this section.
- Clean, high quality brake fluid from a sealed container is essential to the safe and proper operation of the brake system. You should always buy the correct type of brake fluid for your vehicle. If the brake fluid becomes contaminated, completely flush the system with new fluid. Never reuse any brake fluid. Any brake fluid that is removed from the system should be discarded. Also, do not allow any brake fluid to come in contact with a painted surface; it will damage the paint.
- Never operate the engine without the proper amount and type of engine oil; doing so WILL result in severe engine damage.
- Timing belt maintenance is extremely important. Many models utilize an interference-type, non-freewheeling engine. If the timing belt breaks, the valves in the cylinder head may strike the pistons, causing potentially serious (also time-consuming and expensive) engine damage. Refer to the maintenance interval charts for the recommended replacement interval for the timing belt, and to the timing belt section for belt replacement and inspection.
- Disconnecting the negative battery cable on some vehicles may interfere with the functions of the on-board computer system(s) and may require the computer to undergo a relearning process once the negative battery cable is reconnected.
- When servicing drum brakes, only disassemble and assemble one side at a time, leaving the remaining side intact for reference.
- Only an MVAC-trained, EPA-certified automotive technician should service the air conditioning system or its components.

BRAKES — ANTI-LOCK BRAKE SYSTEM (ABS)

GENERAL INFORMATION

PRECAUTIONS

- Certain components within the ABS system are not intended to be serviced or repaired individually.
- Do not use rubber hoses or other parts not specifically specified for and ABS system. When using repair kits, replace all parts included in the kit. Partial or incorrect repair may lead to functional problems and require the replacement of components.
- Lubricate rubber parts with clean, fresh brake fluid to ease assembly. Do not use shop air to clean parts; damage to rubber components may result.
- Use only DOT 3 brake fluid from an unopened container.
- If any hydraulic component or line is removed or replaced, it may be necessary to bleed the entire system.
- A clean repair area is essential. Always clean the reservoir and cap thoroughly before removing the cap. The slightest amount of dirt in the fluid may plug an orifice and impair the system function. Perform repairs after components have been thoroughly cleaned; use only denatured alcohol to clean components. Do not allow ABS components to come into contact with any substance containing mineral oil; this includes used shop rags.
- The Anti-Lock control unit is a microprocessor similar to other computer units in the vehicle. Ensure that the ignition switch is **OFF** before removing or installing controller harnesses. Avoid static electricity discharge at or near the controller.
- If any arc welding is to be done on the vehicle, the control unit should be unplugged before welding operations begin.

SPEED SENSORS

REMOVAL & INSTALLATION

Front

2WD Vehicles

See Figure 1.

1. With the vehicle in NEUTRAL, position it on a hoist.
2. Disconnect the wheel speed sensor electrical connector.
3. Remove the wheel speed sensor harness bolt and unclip the retainers.

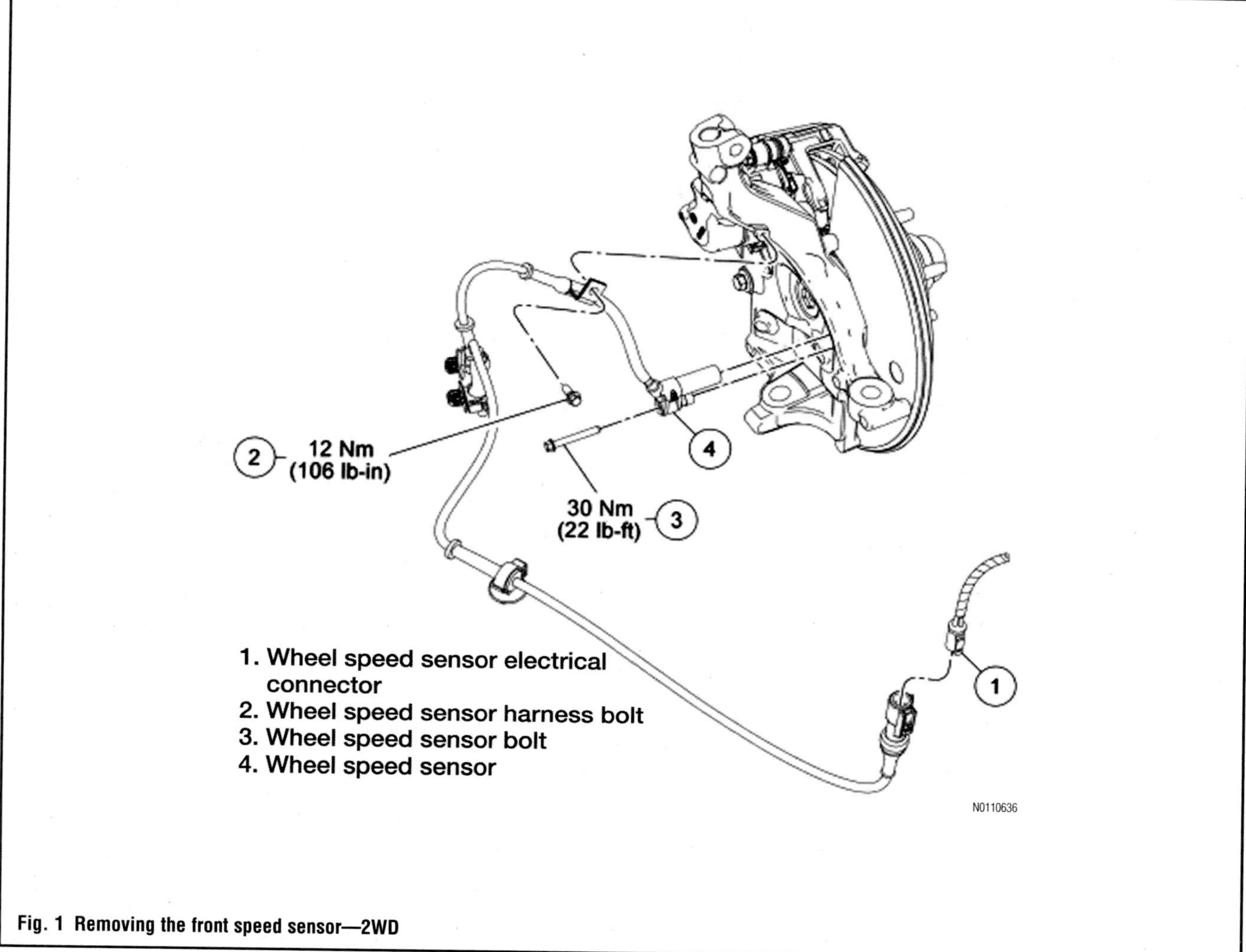

Fig. 1 Removing the front speed sensor—2WD

4. Remove the wheel speed sensor bolt and the wheel speed sensor.

➡Plug the sensor cavity and thoroughly clean the sensor mounting surface. Apply a light coating of the specified grease to the mounting surface.

5. To install, reverse the removal procedure. Refer to illustration for torque values.

4WD Vehicles

See Figure 2.

1. Remove the brake disc shield.
2. Disconnect the wheel speed sensor electrical connector.
3. Remove the wheel speed sensor harness bolt and unclip the retainers.
4. Remove the wheel speed sensor bolt and the wheel speed sensor.

➡Plug the sensor cavity and thoroughly clean the sensor mounting surface. Apply a light coating of the specified grease to the mounting surface.

5. To install, reverse the removal procedure. Refer to illustration for torque values.

Rear

See Figures 3 and 4.

1. With the vehicle in NEUTRAL, position it on a hoist.
2. Disconnect the wheel speed sensor electrical connector.
3. If the right rear wheel speed sensor is being removed, remove the wheel speed sensor pin-type retainer from the axle housing.
4. If the left rear wheel speed sensor is being removed, remove the wheel speed sensor retaining clip from the parking brake cable.
5. Disconnect the wheel speed sensor grommet retainers and pin-type retainers.
6. Remove the wheel speed sensor bolt.
7. Remove the wheel speed sensor.
8. To install, reverse the removal procedure. Refer to illustrations for torque values.

1
2
15 Nm
(133 lb-in)
4
3
18 Nm
(159 lb-in)
N0110637

1. Wheel speed sensor electrical connector
2. Wheel speed sensor harness bolt
3. Wheel speed sensor bolt
4. Wheel speed sensor

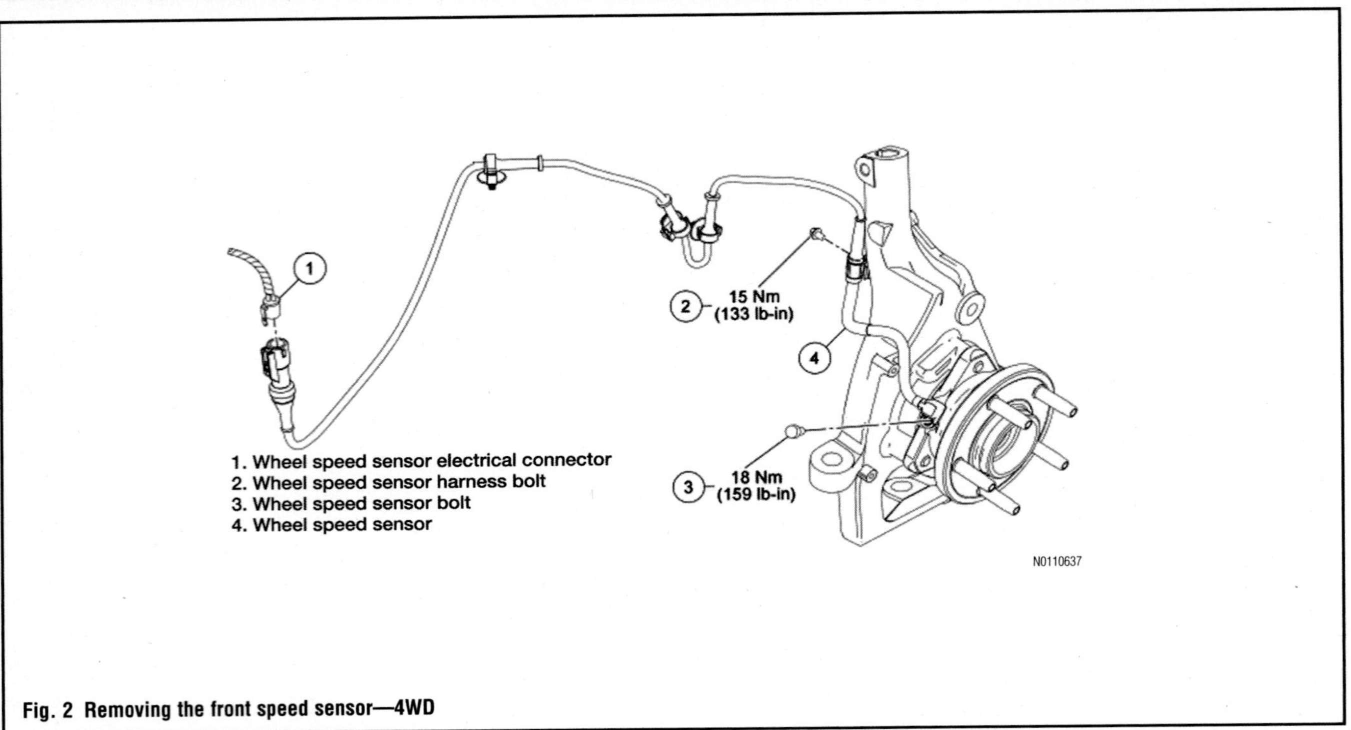

Fig. 2 Removing the front speed sensor—4WD

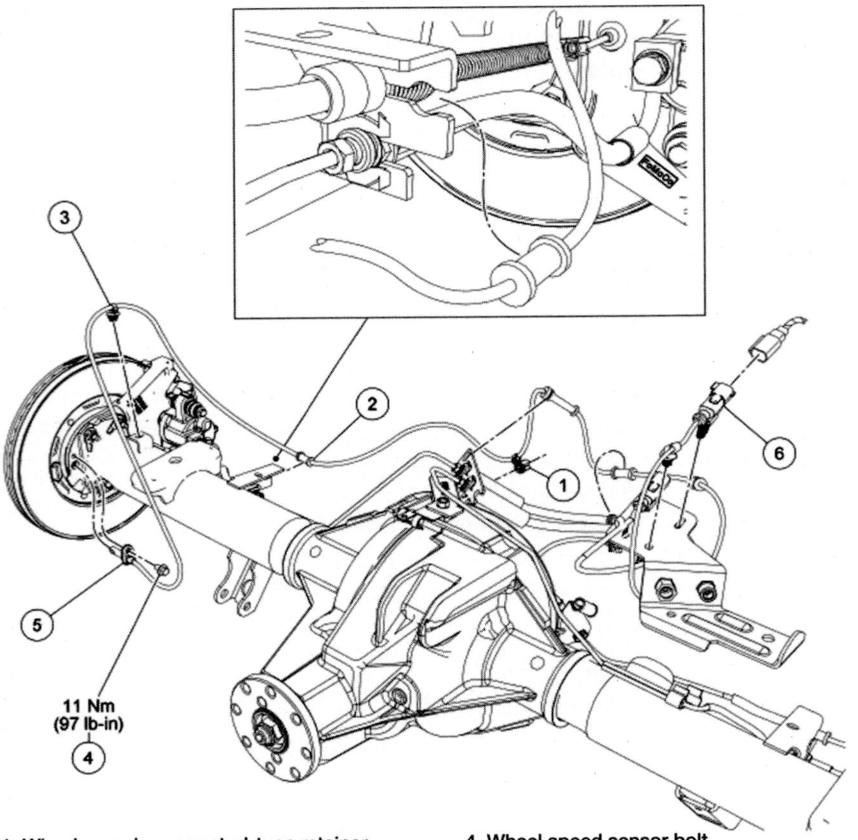

3
2
1
6
5
11 Nm
(97 lb-in)
4

1. Wheel speed sensor stud-type retainer
2. Wheel speed sensor grommet retainer
3. Wheel speed sensor harness pin-type retainer
4. Wheel speed sensor bolt
5. Wheel speed sensor
6. Wheel speed sensor electrical connector

N0110632

Fig. 3 Removing the right rear wheel speed sensor

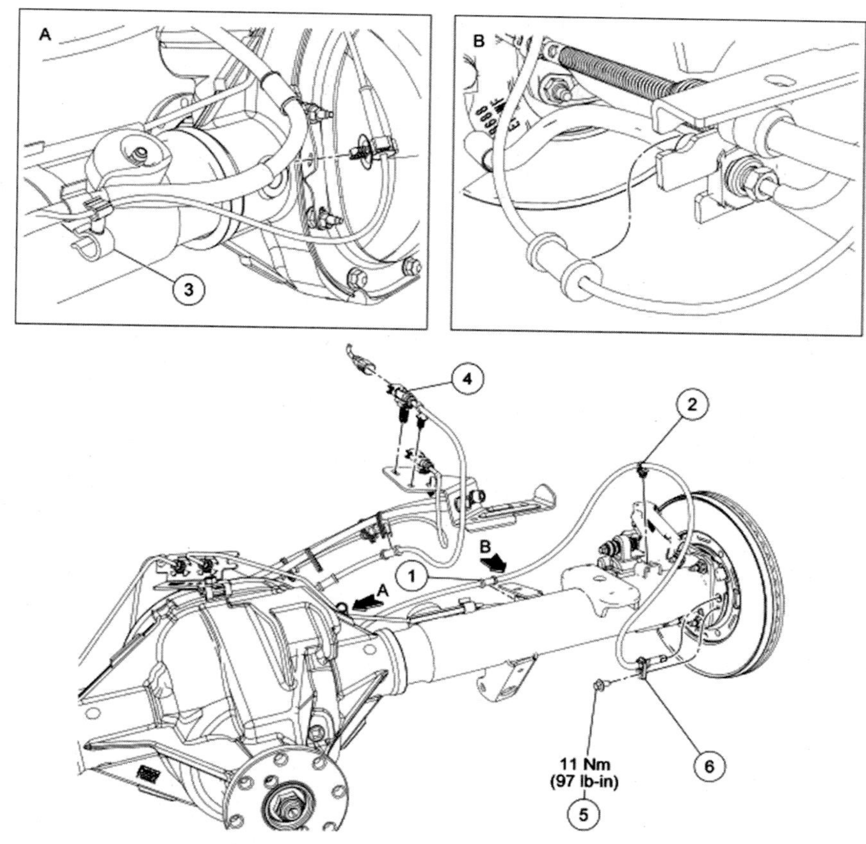

Fig. 4 Removing the left rear wheel speed sensor

BRAKES

BLEEDING THE BRAKE SYSTEM

BLEEDING PROCEDURE

BLEEDING PROCEDURE

Pressure Bleeding

⁂ WARNING

Do not use any fluid other than clean brake fluid meeting manufacturer's specification. Additionally, do not use brake fluid that has been previously drained. Following these instructions will help prevent system contamination, brake component damage and the risk of serious personal injury.

⁂ CAUTION

Brake fluid contains polyglycol ethers and polyglycols. Avoid contact with the eyes and wash your hands thoroughly after handling brake fluid. If you do get brake fluid in your eyes, flush your eyes with clean, running water for 15 minutes. If eye irritation persists, or if you have taken brake fluid internally, IMMEDIATELY seek medical assistance.

➡When any part of the hydraulic system has been disconnected for repair or installation of new components, air can get into the system and cause spongy brake pedal action. This requires bleeding of the hydraulic system after it has been correctly connected.

➡The Hydraulic Control Unit (HCU) bleeding procedure must be carried out if the HCU or any components upstream of the HCU are installed new.

➡Pressure bleed the brake system at 30-50 psi.

1. If equipped with a fire suppression system, depower the system, disconnect the negative battery cable and wait one minute.
2. Clean all dirt from and remove the brake master cylinder filler cap. Fill the brake master cylinder reservoir with clean, specified brake fluid.

➡Master cylinder pressure bleeder adapter tools are available from various manufacturers of pressure bleeding equipment. Follow the instructions of the manufacturer when installing the adapter.

3. Install the bleeder adapter to the brake master cylinder reservoir and attach the bleeder tank hose to the fitting on the adapter.
4. Place a box-end wrench on the master cylinder bleeder screw. Attach a rubber drain hose to the bleeder screw and sub-

merge the free end of the hose in a container partially filled with clean, specified brake fluid.

➡**Make sure the bleeder tank contains enough clean, specified brake fluid to complete the bleeding operation.**

5. Open the valve on the bleeder tank.
6. Apply 30-50 psi to the brake system.
7. Loosen the bleeder screw and leave open until clear, bubble-free brake fluid flows into the container.
8. Remove the brake caliper bleeder screw cap and place a box-end wrench on the bleeder screw. Attach a rubber drain hose to the RH rear brake caliper bleeder screw, and submerge the free end of the hose in a container partially filled with clean, specified brake fluid.
9. Loosen the bleeder screw and leave open until clear, bubble-free brake fluid flows into the container.
10. Remove the rubber hose and install the bleeder screw cap. Tighten the brake caliper bleeder screw to specification.
11. Repeat Steps 5 through 7 for the LH rear, RH front and LH front bleeder screws in this order.
12. Release the bleeder tank pressure and close the bleeder tank valve. Remove the tank hose from the adapter and remove the adapter.
13. Install the reservoir cap.

➡**If the brake pedal remains spongy, air may be trapped in the HCU.**

14. If the brake pedal remains spongy after pressure bleeding, carry out the ABS HCU bleeding procedure in this section with the scan tool.
15. If equipped with a fire suppression system, repower the system by connecting the negative battery cable.

Manual Bleeding

WARNING

Do not use any fluid other than clean brake fluid meeting manufacturer's specification. Additionally, do not use brake fluid that has been previously drained. Following these instructions will help prevent system contamination, brake component damage and the risk of serious personal injury.

CAUTION

Brake fluid contains polyglycol ethers and polyglycols. Avoid contact with the eyes and wash your hands thoroughly after handling brake fluid. If you do get brake fluid in your eyes, flush your eyes with clean, running water for 15 minutes. If eye irritation persists, or if you have taken brake fluid internally, IMMEDIATELY seek medical assistance.

1. If equipped with a fire suppression system, depower the system, disconnect the negative battery cable and wait one minute.
2. Clean all dirt from the brake master cylinder filler cap and remove the filler cap.
3. Fill the brake master cylinder reservoir with clean, specified brake fluid.
4. Place a box-end wrench on the master cylinder bleeder screw. Attach a rubber drain hose to the bleeder screw and submerge the free end of the hose in a container partially filled with clean, specified brake fluid.
5. Loosen the bleeder screw and leave open until clear, bubble-free brake fluid flows into the container.
6. Remove the rubber hose.
7. Remove the brake caliper bleeder screw cap and place a box end wrench on the RH rear bleeder screw. Attach a rubber drain hose to the bleeder screw and submerge the free end of the hose in a container partially filled with clean, specified brake fluid.
8. Have an assistant pump the brake pedal and then hold firm pressure on the brake pedal.
9. Loosen the bleeder screw until a stream of brake fluid comes out. While the assistant maintains pressure on the brake pedal, tighten the bleeder screw.
10. Repeat until clear, bubble-free fluid comes out.
11. Refill the brake master cylinder reservoir as necessary.
12. Tighten the brake caliper bleeder screw to specification.
13. Remove the rubber hose and install the bleeder screw cap.
14. Repeat Steps 7 through 13 for the LH rear, RH front and LH front bleeder screws in this order.
15. If equipped with a fire suppression system, repower the system. Connect the negative battery cable.

BLEEDING THE ABS SYSTEM

WARNING

Do not use any fluid other than clean brake fluid meeting manufacturer's specification. Additionally, do not use brake fluid that has been previously drained. Following these instructions will help prevent system contamination, brake component damage and the risk of serious personal injury.

CAUTION

Brake fluid contains polyglycol ethers and polyglycols. Avoid contact with the eyes and wash your hands thoroughly after handling brake fluid. If you do get brake fluid in your eyes, flush your eyes with clean, running water for 15 minutes. If eye irritation persists, or if you have taken brake fluid internally, IMMEDIATELY seek medical assistance.

➡**Follow the Pressure Bleeding or Manual Bleeding procedure steps to bleed the system.**

1. If equipped with a fire suppression system, depower the system, disconnect the negative battery cable and wait one minute.
2. Connect the scan tool and follow the ABS Service Bleed instructions.
3. Repeat the Pressure Bleeding or Manual Bleeding procedure steps to bleed the system.
4. If equipped with a fire suppression system, repower the system. Connect the negative battery cable.

FLUID FILL PROCEDURE

See Figure 5.

WARNING

Do not use any fluid other than clean brake fluid meeting manufacturer's specification. Additionally, do not use brake fluid that has been previously drained. Following these

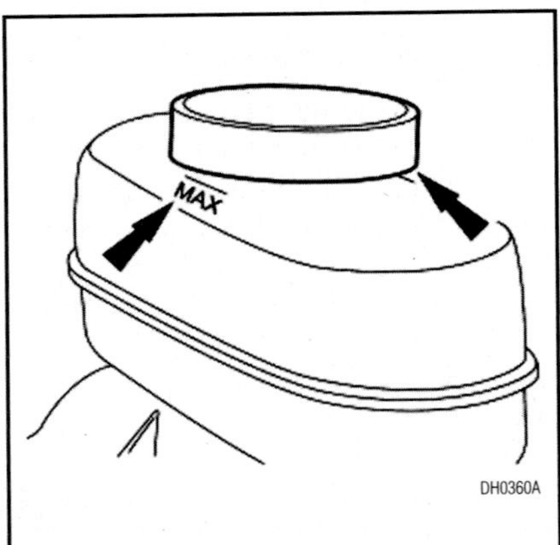

Fig. 5 Filling the brake master cylinder reservoir

instructions will help prevent system contamination, brake component damage and the risk of serious personal injury.

⁂ CAUTION

Brake fluid contains polyglycol ethers and polyglycols. Avoid contact with the eyes and wash your hands thoroughly after handling brake fluid. If you do get brake fluid in your eyes, flush your eyes with clean, running water for 15 minutes. If eye irritation persists, or if you have taken brake fluid internally, IMMEDIATELY seek medical assistance.

1. Clean all dirt from the brake master cylinder filler cap and remove the filler cap.
2. Fill the brake master cylinder reservoir with clean, specified brake fluid.

BRAKES

FRONT DISC BRAKES

⁂ CAUTION

Dust and dirt accumulating on brake parts during normal use may contain asbestos fibers from production or aftermarket brake linings. Breathing excessive concentrations of asbestos fibers can cause serious bodily harm. Exercise care when servicing brake parts. Do not sand or grind brake lining unless equipment used is designed to contain the dust residue. Do not clean brake parts with compressed air or by dry brushing. Cleaning should be done by dampening the brake components with a fine mist of water, then wiping the brake components clean with a dampened cloth. Dispose of cloth and all residue containing asbestos fibers in an impermeable container with the appropriate label. Follow practices prescribed by the Occupational Safety and Health Administration (OSHA) and the Environmental Protection Agency (EPA) for the handling, processing, and disposing of dust or debris that may contain asbestos fibers.

BRAKE CALIPER

REMOVAL & INSTALLATION

See Figure 6.

⁂ WARNING

Do not use any fluid other than clean brake fluid meeting manufacturer's specification. Additionally, do not use brake fluid that has been previously drained. Following these instructions will help prevent system contamination, brake component damage and the risk of serious personal injury.

⁂ CAUTION

Brake fluid contains polyglycol ethers and polyglycols. Avoid contact with the eyes and wash your hands thoroughly after handling brake fluid. If you do get brake fluid in your eyes, flush your eyes with clean, running water for 15 minutes. If eye irritation persists, or if you have taken brake fluid internally, IMMEDIATELY seek medical assistance.

1. If equipped with a fire suppression system, depower the system, disconnect the negative battery cable and wait one minute.
2. Remove the wheel and tire.
3. Remove the brake caliper flow bolt.
4. Discard the 2 copper washers.
5. Remove the 2 brake guide pin caliper bolts and the brake caliper.
6. Disconnect the brake pads from the caliper and remove the caliper.
7. Inspect the brake caliper for wear or damage. Inspect the guide pins and locating pins for wear or damage.
8. If leaks or damage are found, install a new brake caliper.

To install:

➡Make sure guide pin boots are correctly seated or damage to guide pins may occur.

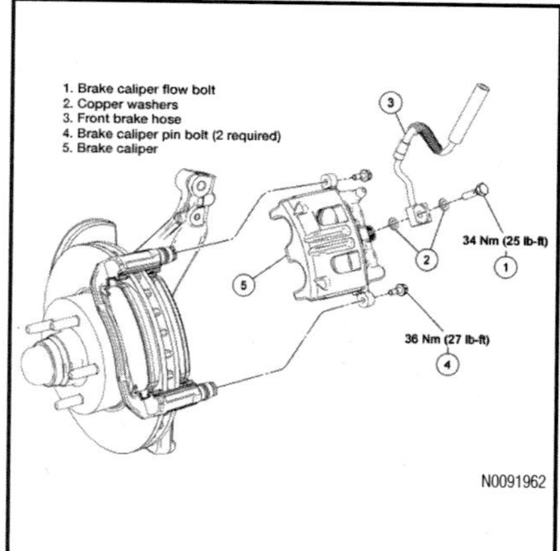

Fig. 6 Exploded view of the front caliper assembly

➡Tighten the lower brake caliper bolt first.

9. Install the brake caliper to the anchor plate and install the 2 brake caliper guide pin bolts. Tighten to 27 ft. lbs. (36 Nm).
10. Using 2 new copper washers, position the brake hose and install the brake caliper flow bolt. Tighten to 25 ft. lbs. (34 Nm).
11. Bleed the brake caliper.
12. Install the wheel and tire.
13. If equipped with a fire suppression system, repower the system. Connect the negative battery cable.

DISC BRAKE PADS

REMOVAL & INSTALLATION

See Figure 7.

⁂ WARNING

Do not use any fluid other than clean brake fluid meeting manufacturer's specification. Additionally, do not use brake fluid that has been previously drained. Following these instructions will help prevent system contamination, brake component damage and the risk of serious personal injury.

⁂ CAUTION

Brake fluid contains polyglycol ethers and polyglycols. Avoid contact with the eyes and wash your hands thoroughly after handling brake fluid. If you do get brake fluid in your eyes, flush your eyes with clean, running water for 15 minutes. If eye irritation persists, or if you have taken brake fluid internally, IMMEDIATELY seek medical assistance.

➡Do not spill brake fluid on painted or plastic surfaces or damage to the surface may occur. If brake fluid is spilled onto a painted or plastic surface, immediately wash the surface with water.

1. Check the brake fluid level in the brake master cylinder reservoir.
2. If required, remove the fluid until the brake master cylinder reservoir is half full.
3. Remove the wheel and tire.

➡Do not pry in the caliper sight hole to retract the pistons, as this may damage the pistons and boots.

➡Do not allow the brake caliper to hang from the brake hose or damage to the hose may occur.

4. Remove the 2 brake caliper guide pin bolts and position the caliper aside.
5. Support the caliper using mechanic's wire.

➡Do not remove the anchor pins unless installing new pins.

6. Inspect the anchor plate guide pins. They should slide in and out of the anchor plates with no binding.
7. Check the boots for cracks or tears. If the pins do not slide easily or the boots are cracked or torn, install new boots and pins. Lubricate the pins using the specified silicone brake caliper grease.
8. Inspect the brake pads for wear and contamination.

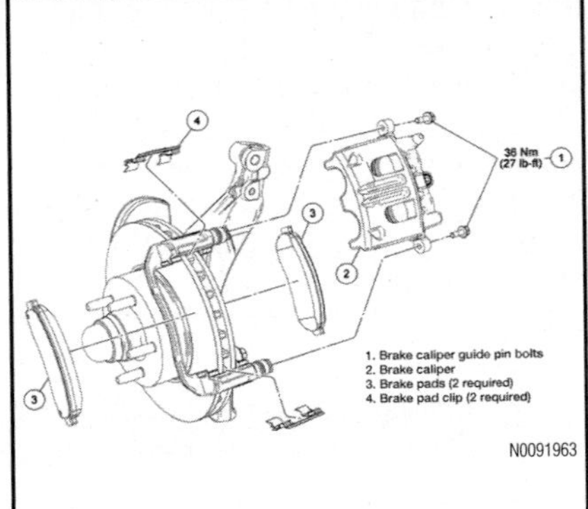

Fig. 7 Exploded view of the brake pad assembly

9. Inspect the brake disc. Machine or install a new front brake disc as necessary.

To install:

➡Do not allow grease, oil brake fluid or other contaminants to contact the pad lining material, or damage to components may occur. Do not install contaminated pads.

➡If installing new brake pads, install all new hardware as supplied with the brake pad kit.

10. Install the 2 new brake pad clips and the 2 brake pads.

➡Protect the piston and boots when pushing the caliper piston into the caliper piston bores or damage to components may occur.

11. If installing new brake pads, using a C-clamp and a worn brake pad, compress the disc brake caliper pistons into the caliper.

➡Tighten the bottom caliper bolt before tightening the top caliper bolt or damage to guide pins may occur.

➡Make sure the caliper pin boots are correctly seated to prevent damage to the guide pins.

12. Position the brake caliper and install the 2 caliper guide pin bolts.
13. Install the wheel and tire.
14. Fill the brake master cylinder reservoir with clean, specified brake fluid.
15. Apply the brakes several times to verify correct brake operation.

BRAKES — REAR DISC BRAKES

✲✲ CAUTION

Dust and dirt accumulating on brake parts during normal use may contain asbestos fibers from production or aftermarket brake linings. Breathing excessive concentrations of asbestos fibers can cause serious bodily harm. Exercise care when servicing brake parts. Do not sand or grind brake lining unless equipment used is designed to contain the dust residue. Do not clean brake parts with compressed air or by dry brushing. Cleaning should be done by dampening the brake components with a fine mist of water, then wiping the brake components clean with a dampened cloth. Dispose of cloth and all residue containing asbestos fibers in an impermeable container with the appropriate label. Follow practices prescribed by the Occupational Safety and Health Administration (OSHA) and the Environmental Protection Agency (EPA) for the handling, processing, and disposing of dust or debris that may contain asbestos fibers.

✲✲ WARNING

Do not use any fluid other than clean brake fluid meeting manufacturer's specification. Additionally, do not use brake fluid that has been previously drained. Following these instructions will help prevent system contamination, brake component damage and the risk of serious personal injury.

✲✲ CAUTION

Brake fluid contains polyglycol ethers and polyglycols. Avoid contact with the eyes and wash your hands thoroughly after handling brake fluid. If you do get brake fluid in your eyes, flush your eyes with clean, running water for 15 minutes. If eye irritation persists, or if you have taken brake fluid internally, IMMEDIATELY seek medical assistance.

➡Do not spill brake fluid on painted or plastic surfaces or damage to the surface may occur. If brake fluid is spilled onto a painted or plastic surface, immediately wash the surface with water.

BRAKE CALIPER

REMOVAL & INSTALLATION

See Figures 8 through 10.

1. Remove the wheel and tire.
2. Remove the brake caliper flow bolt and disconnect the brake hose from the brake caliper.
3. Remove and discard the copper washers.
4. Plug the brake hose.

➡Hand tools only must be used to remove the brake noise damper or damage to the damper may occur.

➡Do not remove the guide pin stud bolt by twisting on the noise damper or damage to the damper may occur.

5. Position aside the brake noise damper dust cover and remove the brake noise damper.

➡Do not remove the guide pin bolt, guide pin stud bolt or guide pin boots unless a problem is suspected. The guide pins are meant to be sealed for life and are not repairable.

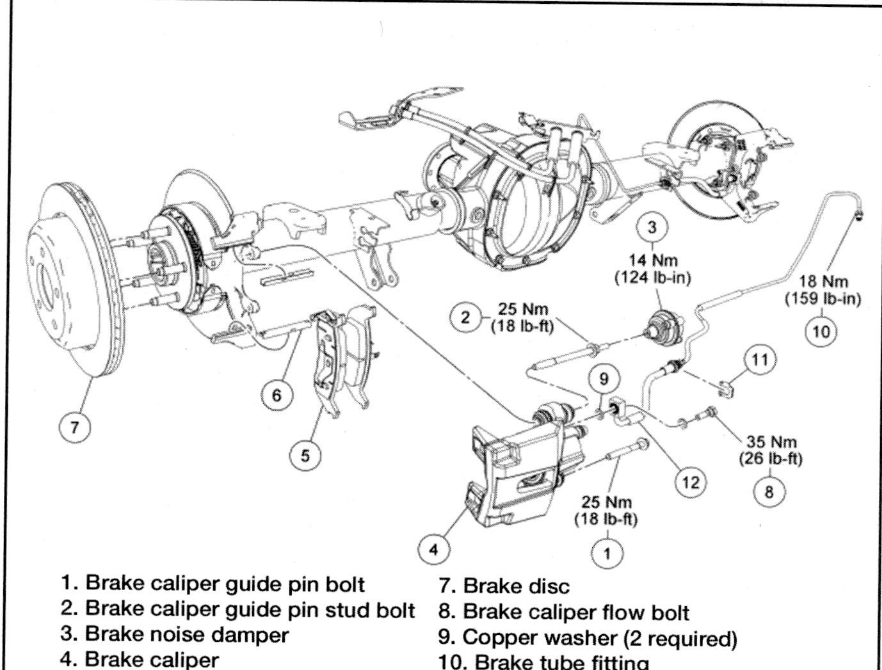

Fig. 8 Exploded view of the rear disc brake system—1 of 3

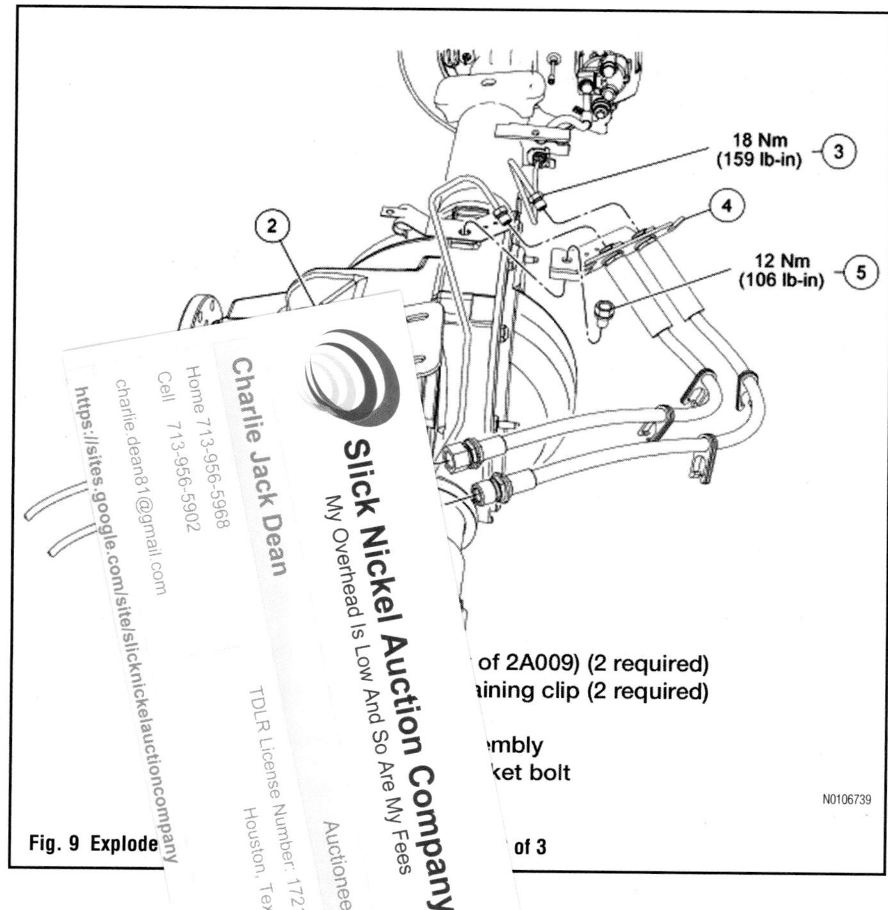

Fig. 9 Explode... of 3

6. Loosen the brake caliper guide pin bolt and guide pin stud bolt, position (slide) back and remove the brake caliper.

To install:

➡Make sure the anti-rattle clips are correctly positioned. Install new clips if worn or damaged.

Position the anti-rattle clip on the anchor plate rail.

➡When installed, the locator notch on the brake pads will be located at the upper end of the rear disc brake caliper.

7. Refer to illustrations for torque values.
8. Position the brake caliper and install the brake caliper guide pin bolt and the brake caliper guide pin stud bolt.

➡Hand tools only must be used to install the brake noise damper or damage to the damper may occur.

9. Install the brake noise damper.
10. Position back the brake noise damper dust cover
11. Position the brake hose and install the brake caliper flow bolt using 2 new copper washers.
12. Bleed the brake caliper.
13. Install the wheel and tire.

DISC BRAKE PADS

REMOVAL & INSTALLATION

See Figures 8 through 10.

1. Check the brake fluid level in the brake master cylinder reservoir.
2. If required, remove the fluid until the brake master cylinder reservoir is half full.
3. Remove the wheel and tire.

➡Hand tools only must be used to remove the brake noise damper or damage to the damper may occur.

➡Do not remove the guide pin stud bolt by twisting on the noise damper or damage to the damper may occur.

4. Position aside the brake noise damper dust cover and remove the brake noise damper.

➡Do not pry in the caliper sight hole to retract the pistons, as this can damage the pistons and boots.

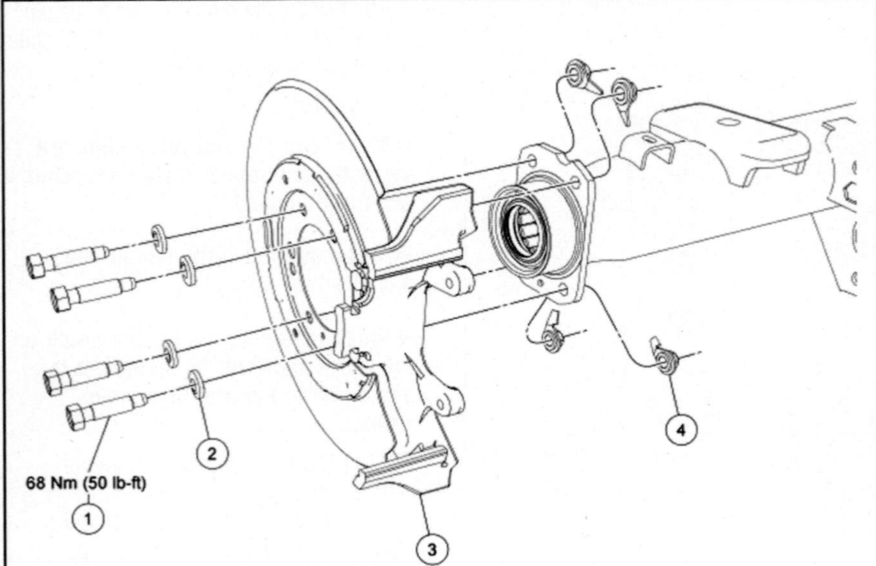

Fig. 10 Exploded view of the rear disc brake system—3 of 3

➡**Do not remove the guide pin bolt, guide pin stud bolt or guide pin boots unless a problem is suspected.**

5. The guide pins are meant to be sealed for life and are not repairable.

➡**Do not allow the brake caliper to hang from the brake hose or damage to the hose may occur.**

6. Remove the brake caliper guide pin bolt, brake caliper guide pin stud bolt and position the caliper aside.
7. Support the brake caliper using mechanic's wire.

➡**Do not allow grease, oil, brake fluid or other contaminants to contact the brake pads.**

8. Remove the brake pads.

➡**Protect the piston and boots when pushing the caliper piston into the caliper piston bores or damage to the piston or boot may occur.**

9. If installing new brake pads, using a suitable tool and a worn brake pad, compress the disc brake caliper pistons into the caliper.
10. To install, reverse the removal procedure.
11. Refer to illustrations for torque values.
12. Make sure the anti-rattle clips are clean and in good condition.
13. Fill the master cylinder with clean specified brake fluid.
14. Apply brakes several times to verify correct brake operation.

PARKING BRAKE SHOES

REMOVAL & INSTALLATION

See Figures 11 and 12.

⁂ CAUTION

Brake fluid contains polyglycol ethers and polyglycols. Avoid contact with the eyes and wash your hands thoroughly after handling brake fluid. If you do get brake fluid in your eyes, flush your eyes with clean, running water for 15 minutes. If eye irritation persists, or if you have taken brake fluid internally, IMMEDIATELY seek medical assistance.

➡**When servicing drum brakes, only dissemble and assemble one side at a time, leaving the remaining side intact for reference.**

⁂ WARNING

Clean, high quality brake fluid is essential to the safe and proper operation of the brake system. You

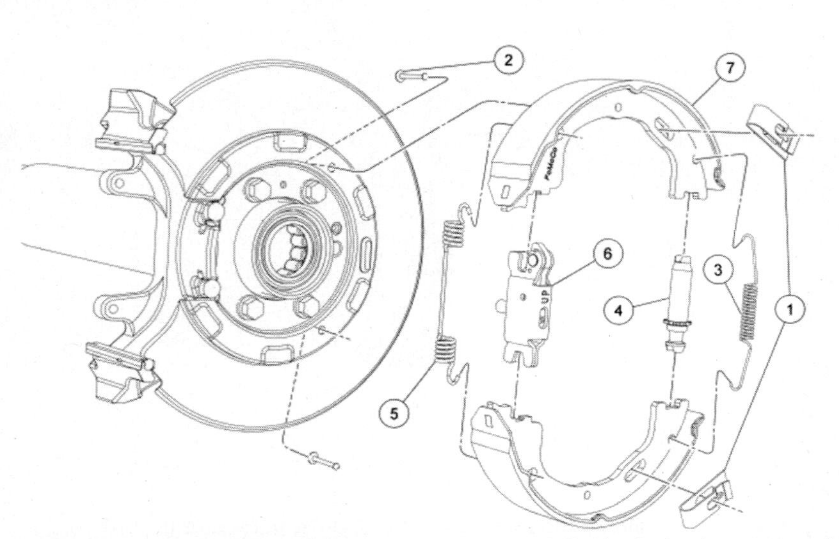

Fig. 11 Exploded view of the parking brake shoe assembly

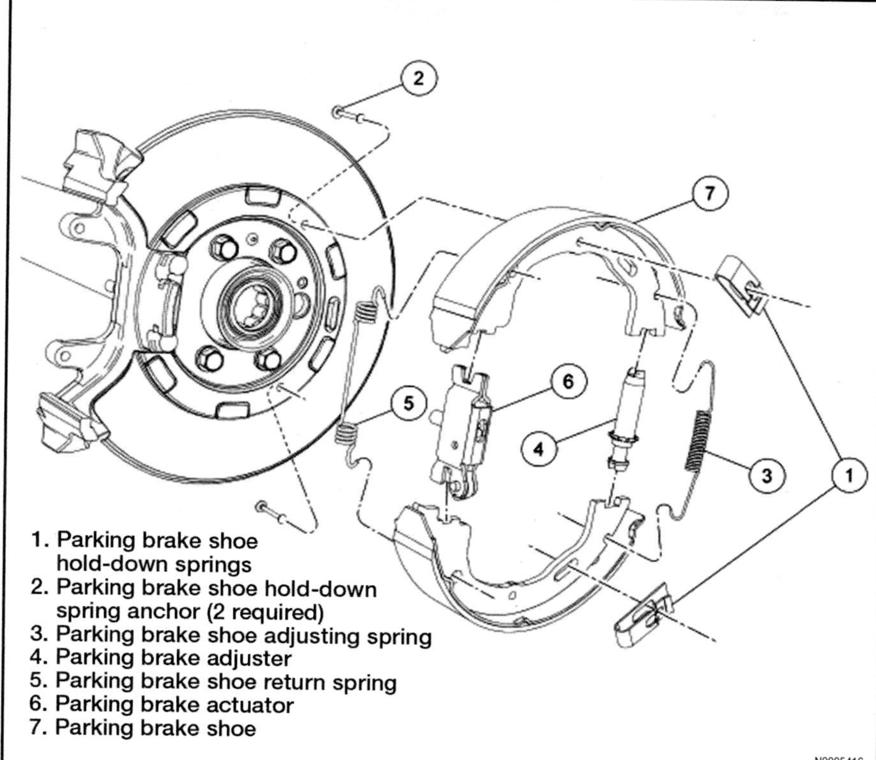

Fig. 12 Exploded view of the parking brake shoe assembly—With hub assembly removed

should always buy the highest quality brake fluid that is available. If the brake fluid becomes contaminated, drain and flush the system, then refill the master cylinder with new fluid. Never reuse any brake fluid. Any brake fluid that is removed from the system should be discarded. Also, do not allow any brake fluid to come in contact with a painted surface; it will damage the paint.

1. Remove the brake disc.
2. Remove the adjuster by removing the brake shoe return spring and the adjusting spring.

➡A sharp-pointed tool such as a scratch awl is useful in removing and installing the springs.

3. Remove the parking brake actuator.
4. Push the parking brake shoes toward each other then pull the parking brake actuator out. Unhook the parking brake cable end.
5. Remove the brake shoe hold-down springs.
6. Remove the parking brake shoes.
7. Inspect the components for excessive wear or damage and install new components as necessary.
8. To install, reverse the removal procedure.
9. Using the specified anti-seize lubricant, lubricate the brake shoe contact point before installation of the rear brake shoes.
10. Lubricate the adjusting screw threads with the specified anti-seize lubricant.
11. Adjust the parking brake shoes.
12. Adjust the parking brake cable tension.
13. If equipped with a fire suppression system, repower the system. Connect the negative battery cable.

ADJUSTMENT

See Figure 13.

➡Make sure the parking brake is fully released.

1. Using the release handle, release the parking brake control.
2. Remove the wheel and tire.

➡Do not allow the brake caliper and brake pads to hang from the brake hose or damage to the hose may occur.

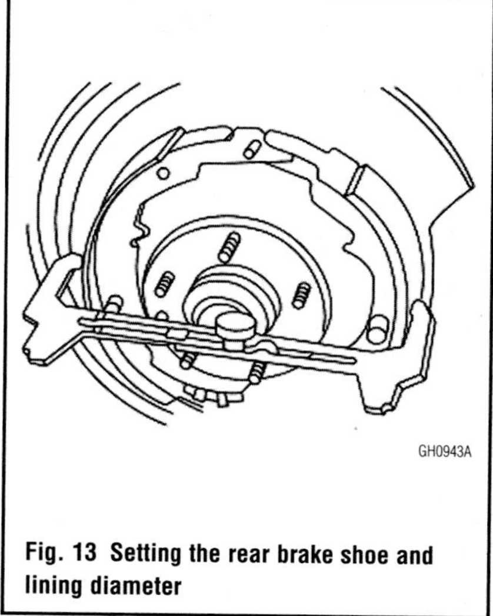

Fig. 13 Setting the rear brake shoe and lining diameter

3. Remove the 2 brake caliper guide pin bolts and position the caliper and brake pads aside.
4. Support the caliper using mechanic's wire.

➡If the brake disc binds on the rear parking brake shoes, remove the adjustment hole access plug and retract the parking brake shoes using an adjusting tool.

5. Insert the tool at the end of the access plug slot farthest from the brake caliper. Engage the adjuster and rotate by raising the end of the tool toward the backing plate. Remove the brake disc.
6. Inspect the parking brake shoes and drum for wear, damage or oil contamination. Install new components as necessary.
7. If the linings are oil contaminated, install a new rear axle oil seal.
8. Using a suitable brake adjusting gauge, measure the inside diameter of the drum portion of the rear brake disc. Record the measurement.
9. Using a suitable brake adjusting gauge, set the rear brake shoe and lining diameter to 0.020 inches less than the inside diameter of the drum portion of the rear brake disc.
10. Position the brake disc onto the hub.
11. Position the brake caliper and brake pads onto the anchor plate and install the 2 brake caliper guide pin bolts. Tighten to 18 ft. lbs. (25 Nm).
12. Test the parking brake for normal operation.
13. If equipped with a fire suppression system, repower the system. Connect the negative battery cable.

GENERAL INFORMATION

CAUTION

These vehicles are equipped with an air bag system. The system must be disarmed before performing service on, or around, system components, the steering column, instrument panel components, wiring and sensors. Failure to follow the safety precautions and the disarming procedure could result in accidental air bag deployment, possible injury and unnecessary system repairs.

SERVICE PRECAUTIONS

Disconnect and isolate the battery negative cable before beginning any airbag system component diagnosis, testing, removal, or installation procedures. Allow system capacitor to discharge for two minutes before beginning any component service. This will disable the airbag system. Failure to disable the airbag system may result in accidental airbag deployment, personal injury, or death.

Do not place an intact undeployed airbag face down on a solid surface. The airbag will propel into the air if accidentally deployed and may result in personal injury or death.

When carrying or handling an undeployed airbag, the trim side (face) of the airbag should be pointing away from the body to minimize possibility of injury if accidental deployment occurs. Failure to do this may result in personal injury or death.

Replace airbag system components with OEM replacement parts. Substitute parts may appear interchangeable, but internal differences may result in inferior occupant protection. Failure to do so may result in occupant personal injury or death.

Wear safety glasses, rubber gloves, and long sleeved clothing when cleaning powder residue from vehicle after an airbag deployment. Powder residue emitted from a deployed airbag can cause skin irritation. Flush affected area with cool water if irritation is experienced. If nasal or throat irritation is experienced, exit the vehicle for fresh air until the irritation ceases. If irritation continues, see a physician.

Do not use a replacement airbag that is not in the original packaging. This may result in improper deployment, personal injury, or death.

The factory installed fasteners, screws and bolts used to fasten airbag components have a special coating and are specifically designed for the airbag system. Do not use substitute fasteners. Use only original equipment fasteners listed in the parts catalog when fastener replacement is required.

During, and following, any child restraint anchor service, due to impact event or vehicle repair, carefully inspect all mounting hardware, tether straps, and anchors for proper installation, operation, or damage. If a child restraint anchor is found damaged in any way, the anchor must be replaced. Failure to do this may result in personal injury or death.

Deployed and non-deployed airbags may or may not have live pyrotechnic material within the airbag inflator.

Do not dispose of driver/passenger/curtain airbags or seat belt tensioners unless you are sure of complete deployment. Refer to the Hazardous Substance Control System for proper disposal.

Dispose of deployed airbags and tensioners consistent with state, provincial, local, and federal regulations.

After any airbag component testing or service, do not connect the battery negative cable. Personal injury or death may result if the system test is not performed first.

If the vehicle is equipped with the Occupant Classification System (OCS), do not connect the battery negative cable before performing the OCS Verification Test using the scan tool and the appropriate diagnostic information. Personal injury or death may result if the system test is not performed properly.

Never replace both the Occupant Restraint Controller (ORC) and the Occupant Classification Module (OCM) at the same time. If both require replacement, replace one, then perform the Airbag System test before replacing the other.

Both the ORC and the OCM store Occupant Classification System (OCS) calibration data, which they transfer to one another when one of them is replaced. If both are replaced at the same time, an irreversible fault will be set in both modules and the OCS may malfunction and cause personal injury or death.

If equipped with OCS, the Seat Weight Sensor is a sensitive, calibrated unit and must be handled carefully. Do not drop or handle roughly. If dropped or damaged, replace with another sensor. Failure to do so may result in occupant injury or death.

If equipped with OCS, the front passenger seat must be handled carefully as well. When removing the seat, be careful when setting on floor not to drop. If dropped, the sensor may be inoperative, could result in occupant injury, or possibly death.

If equipped with OCS, when the passenger front seat is on the floor, no one should sit in the front passenger seat. This uneven force may damage the sensing ability of the seat weight sensors. If sat on and damaged, the sensor may be inoperative, could result in occupant injury, or possibly death.

DISARMING THE SYSTEM

WARNING

Always wear eye protection when servicing a vehicle. Failure to follow this instruction may result in serious personal injury.

WARNING

Never probe the electrical connectors on air bag, Safety Canopy® or side air curtain modules. Failure to follow this instruction may result in the accidental deployment of these modules, which increases the risk of serious personal injury or death.

WARNING

Do not handle, move or change the original horizontal mounting position of the restraints control module (RCM) while the RCM is connected and the ignition switch is ON. Failure to follow this instruction may result in the accidental deployment of the Safety Canopy® and cause serious personal injury or death.

WARNING

To reduce the risk of accidental deployment, do not use any memory saver devices. Failure to follow this instruction may result in serious personal injury or death.

➡The air bag warning indicator illuminates when the correct Restraints Control Module (RCM) fuse is removed and the ignition is ON.

➡The Supplemental Restraint System (SRS) must be fully operational and free of faults before releasing the vehicle to the customer.

1. Turn all vehicle accessories OFF.
2. Turn the ignition to OFF.
3. At the Smart Junction Box (SJB), located below the RH side of the instrument panel, remove the RH lower cowl trim panel and remove RCM fuse 8 (10A) from the SJB. For additional information, refer to the Wiring Diagrams manual.
4. Turn the ignition ON and monitor the air bag warning indicator for at least 30 seconds. The air bag warning indicator will remain lit continuously (no flashing) if the correct RCM fuse has been removed. If the air bag warning indicator does not remain lit continuously, remove the correct RCM fuse before proceeding.
5. Turn the ignition OFF.

WARNING

Always deplete the backup power supply before repairing or installing any new front or side air bag supplemental restraint system (SRS) component and before servicing, removing, installing, adjusting or striking components near the front or side impact sensors or the restraints control module (RCM). Nearby components include doors, instrument panel, console, door latches, strikers, seats and hood latches. Refer to the Description and Operation portion of Supplemental Restraint System for location of the RCM and impact sensor(s).To deplete the backup power supply energy, disconnect the battery ground cable and wait at least 1 minute. Be sure to disconnect auxiliary batteries and power supplies (if equipped). Failure to follow these instructions may result in serious personal injury or death in the event of an accidental deployment.

6. Disconnect the battery ground cable and wait at least one minute.

ARMING THE SYSTEM

1. Turn the ignition from OFF to ON.
2. Install the RCM fuse 8 (10A) to the SJB and install the RH lower cowl trim panel.

WARNING

Make sure no one is in the vehicle and there is nothing blocking or placed in front of any air bag module when the battery is connected. Failure to follow these instructions may result in serious personal injury in the event of an accidental deployment.

3. Connect the battery ground cable.
4. Prove out the SRS as follows:
   a. Turn the ignition from ON to OFF.
   b. Wait 10 seconds, then turn the ignition to ON and monitor the air bag warning indicator with the air bag modules installed.
   c. The air bag warning indicator will light continuously for approximately 6 seconds and then turn off. If an SRS fault is present, the air bag warning indicator will: - fail to light. - remain lit continuously. - flash (RCM not configured).
   d. The air bag warning indicator may not illuminate until approximately 30 seconds after the ignition has been turned from the OFF to the ON position. This is the time required for the RCM to complete the testing of the SRS. If the air bag warning indicator is inoperative and a SRS fault exists, a chime will sound in a pattern of 5 sets of 5 beeps.
   e. If this occurs, the air bag warning indicator and any SRS fault discovered must be diagnosed and repaired. Clear all continuous RCM and Occupant Classification System Module (OCSM) DTCs using a scan tool.

CLOCKSPRING CENTERING

New Clockspring

➡A new clockspring is packaged in a centralized position and fixed in position with a key.

1. Remove the key from the clockspring, holding the rotor in its centralized position.
2. Do not allow the clockspring rotor to turn.

Recentering

WARNING

If the clockspring is not correctly centralized, it may fail prematurely. If in doubt, repeat the centralizing procedure. Failure to follow these instructions may increase the risk of serious personal injury or death in a crash.

➡Make sure the wheels are in the straight-ahead position.

➡If a clockspring has rotated out of center, follow through with this step.

1. Hold the clockspring outer housing stationary.

➡Overturning will destroy the clockspring. The internal ribbon wire acts as the stop and can be broken from its internal connection.

2. While holding the clockspring locking tab in the released position, turn the rotor counterclockwise, carefully feeling for the ribbon wire to run out of length and a slight resistance to be felt. Stop turning at this point.
3. While holding the clockspring locking tab in the released position, turn the clockspring clockwise approximately 2.25 turns. This is the center point of the clockspring.
4. Do not allow the rotor to turn from this position.

AUTOMATIC TRANSMISSION FLUID

DRAIN AND REFILL

1. With the vehicle in NEUTRAL, position it on a hoist.

➡If equipped, the transmission servo heat shield must be unclipped from the transmission fluid pan rail and positioned aside for transmission fluid pan removal.

2. If equipped, loosen the nut and position the heat shield aside.
3. Place a drain pan under the transmission fluid pan.
4. Drain transmission fluid.
5. Remove all the transmission fluid pan screws except for 2 in the front. Loosen the 2 front transmission fluid pan screws. Pry the rear of the transmission fluid pan down and allow fluid to drain.
6. After fluid is drained, remove the front 2 transmission fluid pan screws.

➡The transmission fluid pan gasket is reusable. Clean and inspect for damage, if not damaged, the gasket should be reused.

7. Remove the transmission fluid pan.
8. Remove the transmission fluid pan.
9. Remove the transmission fluid pan gasket.
10. Clean and inspect the transmission fluid pan and magnet. Clean all mating surfaces.

➡The transmission fluid pan gasket is reusable. Clean and inspect for damage, if not damaged, the gasket should be reused.

11. Install the transmission fluid pan.
12. Position the transmission fluid pan gasket on the transmission fluid pan.
13. Install and align the transmission fluid pan.
14. Loosely install the transmission fluid pan screws.
15. Tighten the transmission fluid pan screws in a crisscross sequence. Tighten to 7 ft. lbs. (10 Nm).
16. If equipped, position the servo heat shield over the servos and clip it to the pan rail and install the nut.
17. Fill the transmission.
18. Add 4 quarts of automatic transmission fluid to the transmission through the transmission fluid filler tube.
19. Start the engine. Move the selector lever through all the gear ranges, checking for engagements.
20. Fill the transmission to the correct level.
21. Using the scan tool, start and run the engine until the transmission is at normal operating temperature 150-170°F, check and adjust the transmission fluid level, and check for any leaks. If transmission fluid is needed, add fluid in increments of 0.5 pints until the correct level is achieved (fluid should be in the cross-hatched area of the fluid level indicator).

FILTER REPLACEMENT

Inline Filter

See Figures 14 through 17.

Transmission fluid in-line filter without auxiliary transmission fluid cooler.

➡Use the following guidelines for the in-line transmission fluid filter:

a. If the transmission was overhauled and the vehicle was equipped with an in-line transmission fluid filter, install a new in-line transmission fluid filter.
b. If the transmission was overhauled and the vehicle was not equipped with an in-line transmission fluid filter, install a new in-line transmission fluid filter kit.
c. If the transmission is being installed for a non-internal repair, do not install an in-line transmission fluid filter or filter kit.
d. If installing a new or a Ford-authorized remanufactured transmission, install the in-line transmission fluid filter that is supplied.

1. With the vehicle in NEUTRAL, position it on a hoist. Remove the retainer clips from the transmission fluid cooler tubes.
2. Disconnect the lower transmission fluid cooler tube fitting.
3. Remove the section of the return transmission fluid cooler tube, as illustrated.
   a. Clean and deburr the cut ends of the transmission fluid cooler tube.

➡Be sure the transmission fluid cooler tube is fully seated in the body of the fitting before final tightening of the ferrule nut.

4. Install the 2 ferrule connectors finger-tight onto each end of the transmission fluid cooler tube. Then tighten the nuts an additional one and a half turns to seat the ferrules in the connectors.

➡The filter has a bypass valve in it. The red arrow on the filter indicates the direction of the transmission fluid flow through the filter. The filter must be installed in the transmission fluid cooler tube with the red arrow pointing away from the transmission fluid cooler and toward the transmission (the return transmission fluid cooler tube has fluid coming out of the cooler going to the transmission). If the filter is not installed correctly, it will cause internal transmission damage.

➡Do not install any rubber hoses or tubing with a bend entering the filter greater than 60 degrees.

Using a suitable length of hose(s), install the filter. Tighten the clamps.

5. Connect the lower transmission fluid cooler tube nut. Tighten to 21 ft. lbs. (28 Nm).
6. Install the retainer clips on the transmission fluid cooler tubes.

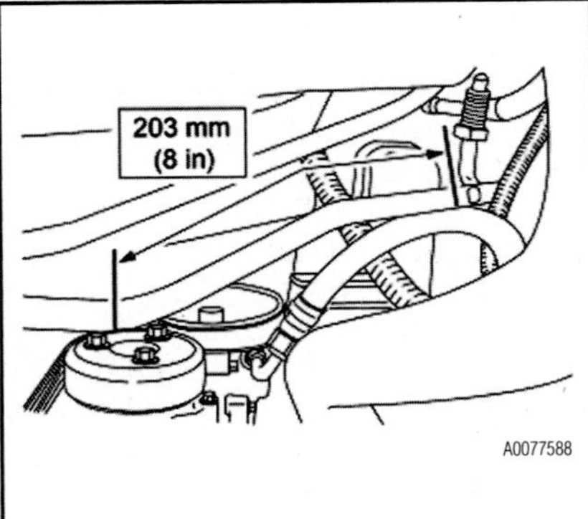

Fig. 14 Removing section of the return transmission fluid cooler tube

Fig. 15 Filter installation orientation

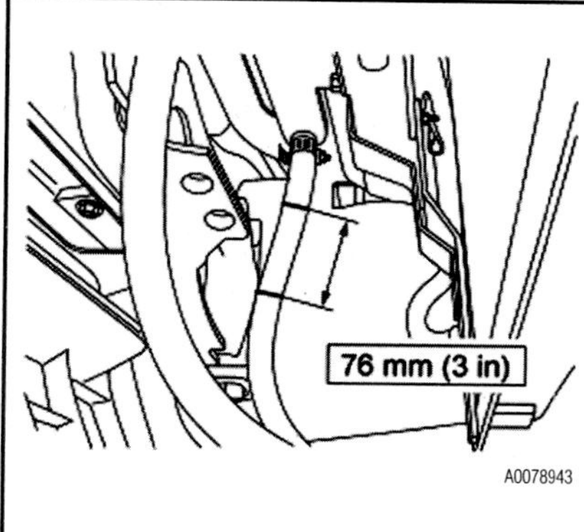

Fig. 16 Remove the section of the transmission fluid cooler tube

7. Clean a section of the transmission fluid pan and install the sticker.
8. Fill the transmission with transmission fluid.
9. Verify for correct operation.
10. Check the filter for leaks.

Transmission fluid in-line filter with an auxiliary transmission fluid cooler

11. With the vehicle in NEUTRAL, position it on a hoist.
12. Remove the section of the transmission fluid cooler tube, as illustrated.

➡The filter has a bypass valve in it. The red arrow on the filter indicates the direction of the transmission fluid flow through the filter. The filter must be installed in the transmission fluid cooler tube with the red arrow pointing away from the transmission fluid cooler and toward the transmission (the return transmission fluid cooler tube has fluid coming out of the cooler going to the transmission). If the filter is not installed correctly, it will cause internal transmission damage.

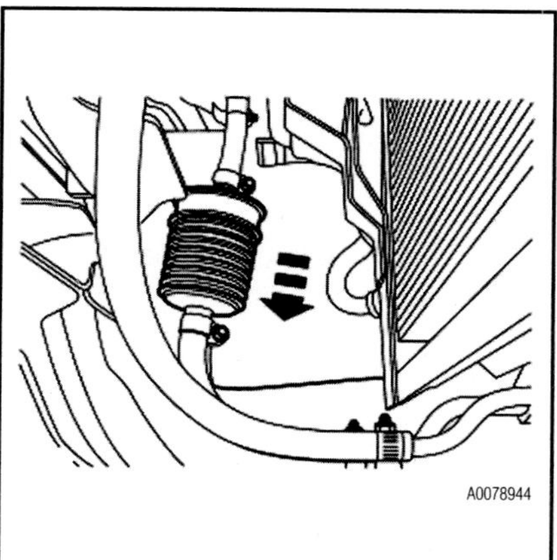

Fig. 17 Filter installation orientation

➡Do not install any rubber hoses or tubing with a bend entering the filter greater than 60 degrees.

Using 2 hose clamps, install the filter.

13. Clean a section of the transmission fluid pan and install the sticker.
14. Fill the transmission with transmission fluid.
15. Verify for correct operation.
16. Check the in-line filter connections for leaks.

MANUAL TRANSMISSION ASSEMBLY

REMOVAL & INSTALLATION

4WD Vehicles

See Figure 18.

1. Disconnect the battery ground cable.
2. Remove the upper gearshift lever, the outer gearshift lever boot and the console as an assembly.
3. With the vehicle in NEUTRAL, position it on a hoist.
4. Remove the catalytic converter. For additional information, refer to Catalytic Converter.
5. If transmission disassembly is required, remove the drain plug and drain the transmission fluid.
6. Install the drain plug after draining all the fluid. Tighten to 35 ft. lbs. (48 Nm).

➡To maintain initial driveshaft balance, index-mark the rear driveshaft yokes.

7. Remove the transfer case. For additional information, refer to Transfer Case.
8. Disconnect the wire harness from the crossmember.

➡Do not allow the transmission to hang freely or damage to the engine mounts will occur.

9. Position a suitable jack under the transmission. Secure the transmission to the jack with a safety strap.
10. Remove the 6 crossmember bolts.
11. Remove the 2 transmission mount nuts and the crossmember.
12. Remove the Heated Oxygen Sensor (HO2S) bracket nut and the bracket from the extension housing.
13. Remove the catalytic converter Y-pipe. For additional information, refer to Catalytic Converter.
14. Remove the fuel line/wiring harness nut bracket and remove the bracket from the transmission.
15. Disconnect the Vehicle Speed Sensor (VSS) electrical connector and the reverse lamp switch electrical connector. Then unclip the wiring harness from the transmission.
16. Detach the wiring harness from the transmission.

➡Do not allow the starter to hang freely or damage to the components may occur.

17. Remove the 3 bolts and the starter motor. Using mechanic's wire, position the starter aside.
18. Using the Hydraulic Line Disconnect Tool, disconnect the clutch hydraulic tube.
19. Using a suitable jack, support the engine.

➡Lower the transmission enough to gain access to the upper transmission-to-engine bolts.

20. Remove the 9 transmission-to-engine bolts.
21. Pull the transmission rearward until the input shaft is clear of the pressure plate, then lower the transmission from the vehicle.

To install:

⁂ WARNING

Do not breathe dust or use compressed air to blow dust from storage containers or friction components. Remove dust using government-approved techniques. Friction component dust may be a cancer and lung disease hazard. Exposure to potentially hazardous components may occur if dusts are created during repair of friction components, such as brake pads and clutch discs. Exposure may also cause irritation to skin, eyes and respiratory tract, and may cause allergic reactions and/or may lead to other chronic health

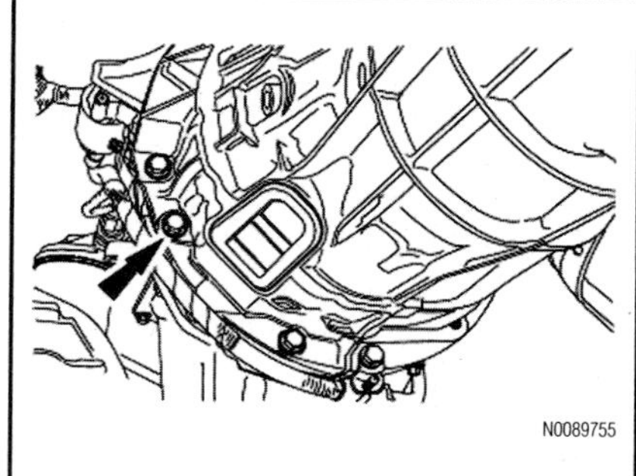

Fig. 18 Remove the 9 transmission-to-engine bolts

effects. If irritation persists, seek medical attention or advice. Failure to follow these instructions may result in serious personal injury.

22. Apply a thin coat of grease on the input shaft splines.

⁂ WARNING

Secure the assembly to the jack. Avoid any obstructions while lowering and raising the jack. Contact with obstructions may cause the assembly to fall off the jack, which may result in serious personal injury.

23. Raise and position the transmission to the engine.

➡Before securing the transmission to the engine, connect the hydraulic tube to the clutch slave cylinder.

24. Connect the clutch hydraulic tube.
25. Install the 9 transmission-to-engine bolts. Tighten to 41 ft. lbs. (55 Nm).
26. Install the starter motor and the 3 starter motor bolts.
27. Connect the Vehicle Speed Sensor (VSS) electrical connector and the reverse lamp switch electrical connector. Clip the wiring harness to the transmission.
28. Install the transmission mount and the 2 transmission mount bolts. Tighten to 72 ft. lbs. (98 Nm).
29. Install the Heated Oxygen Sensor (HO2S) bracket and nut to the extension housing. Tighten to 29 ft. lbs. (39 Nm).
30. Position the crossmember and the 2 transmission mount nuts. Do not tighten the nuts at this time.
31. Install the 6 crossmember bolts.
32. Tighten the transmission mount nuts to 72 ft. lbs. (98 Nm).
33. Tighten the crossmember bolts to 46 ft. lbs. (63 Nm).
34. Remove the transmission jack.
35. Connect the wire harness to the crossmember.
36. Install the transfer case.
37. Install the catalytic converter Y-pipe.
38. Fill the transmission with the specified type fluid and quantity of fluid.
39. Install the upper gearshift lever and gearshift lever boot as an assembly.
40. Connect the battery ground cable.

MANUAL TRANSMISSION FLUID

DRAIN AND REFILL

See Figure 19.

➡Position a suitable drain pan under the transmission.

1. Remove the drain plug and drain the transmission.
2. Clean and install the drain plug. Tighten to 35 ft. lbs. (48 Nm).

➡Before removing, clean the area around the fill plug.

3. Remove the fill plug.

➡Fill the transmission with the vehicle on a level surface.

➡Transmission capacity is 2.8 quarts.

4. Using a suitable oil suction gun, fill the transmission to the correct level with the specified fluid. The fluid must be just below the fill plug hole.
5. Install the fill plug. Tighten to 35 ft. lbs. (48 Nm).

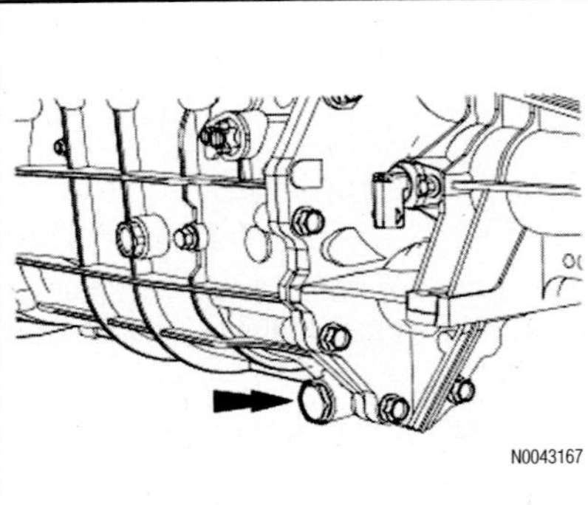

Fig. 19 Remove the drain plug and drain the transmission

CLUTCH

REMOVAL & INSTALLATION

See Figures 20 and 21.

⁂ WARNING

Do not breathe dust or use compressed air to blow dust from storage containers or friction components. Remove dust using government-approved techniques. Friction component dust may be a cancer and lung disease hazard. Exposure to potentially hazardous components may occur if dusts are created during repair of friction components, such as brake pads and clutch discs. Exposure may also cause irritation to skin, eyes and respiratory tract, and may cause allergic reactions and/or may lead to other chronic health effects. If irritation persists, seek medical attention or advice. Failure to follow these instructions may result in serious personal injury.

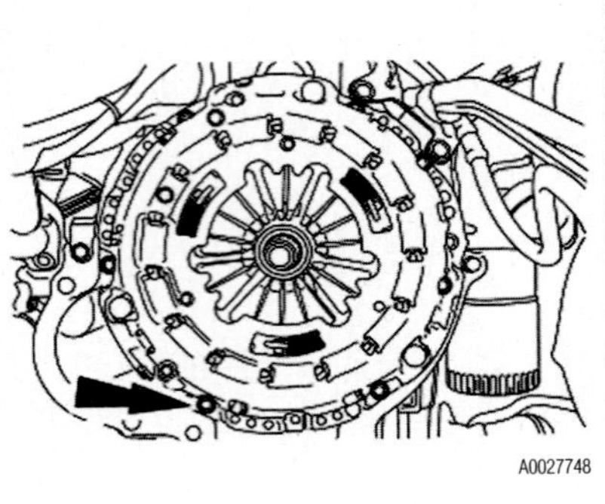

Fig. 20 Remove the 6 bolts, clutch pressure plate and the clutch disc

1. Remove the transmission.

➡If the clutch disc and pressure plate are to be reinstalled, bolts must be removed evenly or permanent damage to the diaphragm spring will occur, resulting in complete clutch release.

➡If the parts are to be reused, index-mark the clutch pressure plate to the flywheel.

2. Remove the 6 bolts, clutch pressure plate and the clutch disc.
3. Inspect the transmission pilot bearing:
   a. For misalignment and looseness in the crankshaft or flywheel.
   b. Needle rollers for scoring, discoloration, wear and broken rollers.
   c. Seal for damage and lubricant leakage.
4. Install a new transmission pilot bearing if any of these conditions are present.

➡Use emery cloth to remove minor imperfections in the clutch disc friction surface.

5. Inspect the clutch disc for:
   a. Oil and grease saturation.
   b. Worn and loose rivets at the hub.
   c. Broken springs.
   d. Wear and rust on the splines.
6. Install a new clutch disc if any of these conditions are present.

➡If necessary, use a suitable cleaning solution to remove any oil film from the clutch pressure plate friction surface.

7. Inspect the clutch pressure plate levers for heavy wear associated with binding. Also, inspect for substantial difference in lever wear. Inspect the clutch pressure plate friction surface for scoring, burning, heat checking, distortion, warping and dishing.

8. Install a new clutch pressure plate if any of these conditions are present.

➡If necessary, use a suitable cleaning solution to clean the flywheel clutch surface.

9. Inspect the flywheel for: Surface cracks, heat check, glazing, scoring and scratches or grooves.

10. For minor damage, finish the flywheel surface with coarse emery cloth or with a fine grade (400 grit) sandpaper. To polish the surface, stroke parallel to the machine lines.

11. Inspect the flywheel or ring gear for worn, chipped or broken teeth.

To install:

12. Lubricate the transmission pilot bearing with grease.

13. Adjust the clutch pressure plate.

a. Using a suitable press, press downward on the fingers until the adjusting ring moves freely.

b. Rotate the adjusting ring counterclockwise to compress the tension springs. Hold the adjusting ring in this position.

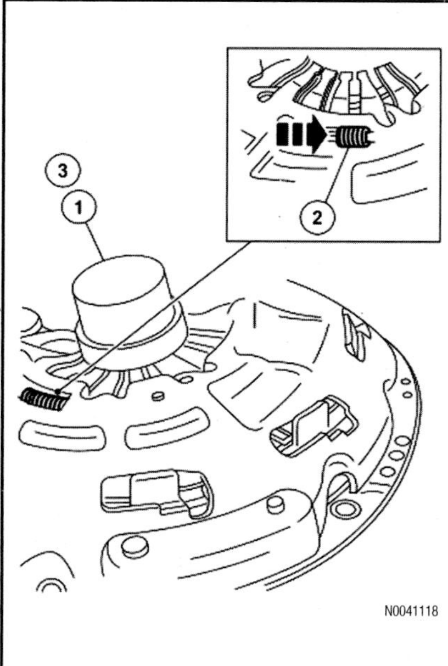

Fig. 21 Press (1), adjusting ring (2) and adjusting ring (3)

c. Release the pressure on the fingers. The adjusting ring will stay in the reset position.

14. Using a suitable clutch aligner, position the clutch disc on the flywheel.

➡If reusing the clutch pressure plate and flywheel, align the marks made during removal.

15. Using a suitable aligner, align the clutch disc and the clutch pressure plate. Install the 6 bolts and tighten in a cross pattern sequence. Tighten to 20 ft. lbs. (27 Nm).

➡Apply a thin film of Dow Corning® Molykote® G-n Metal Assembly Paste to the clutch slave cylinder bearing face.

➡Before securing the transmission to the engine, connect the hydraulic tube to the clutch slave cylinder.

16. Install the transmission.

PILOT BEARING

See Figures 22 and 23.

1. Using the Pilot Bearing Remover, remove the pilot bearing.

2. Inspect the pilot bearing for:

a. Misalignment and looseness in the flywheel.

b. Needle rollers for scoring, worn or broken needle rollers, inadequate grease or discoloration.

c. Seal leakage.

To install:

➡The pilot bearing can only be installed with the seal facing the transmission. The pilot bearing is pre-greased and does not require additional lubrication. A new pilot bearing must be installed whenever it is removed.

3. Using a soft-face hammer and the Pilot Bearing Installer, install the pilot bearing.

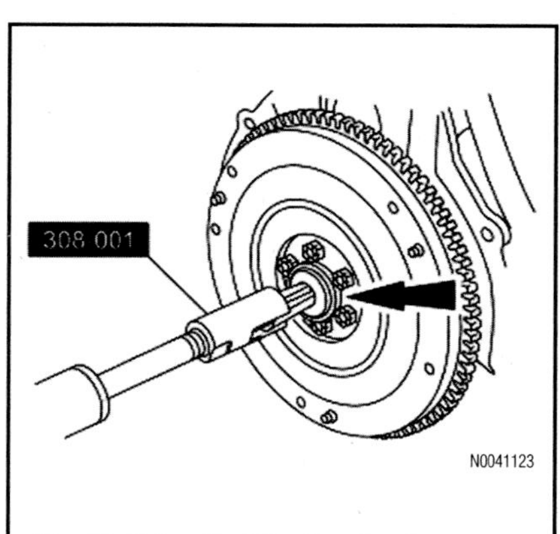

Fig. 22 Using the Pilot Bearing Remover

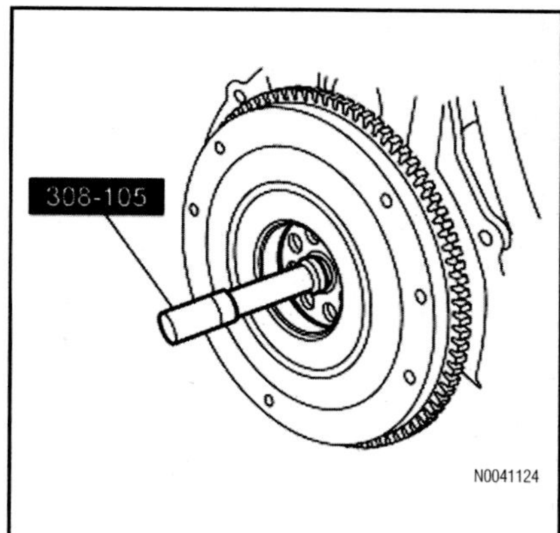

Fig. 23 Using a soft-face hammer and the Pilot Bearing Installer

TRANSFER CASE ASSEMBLY

DRAINING & FILLING

See Figure 24.

1. Remove the drain plug and drain the fluid.

2. Clean and install the drain plug after the fluid is drained. Tighten to 18 ft. lbs. (24 Nm).

➡Incorrect fluid fill may result in transfer case failure.

➡The fluid must be just below the fill plug hole. The fact that the fluid can be reached with a finger does not mean the fluid is at the correct level. Make sure the fluid is level with the filler opening for the correct fluid level.

3. Clean the area around the fill plug and remove. Fill the transfer case.

4. The total transfer case fill capacity is 2.5 pints.

5. Install the fill plug. Tighten to 18 ft. lbs. (24 Nm).

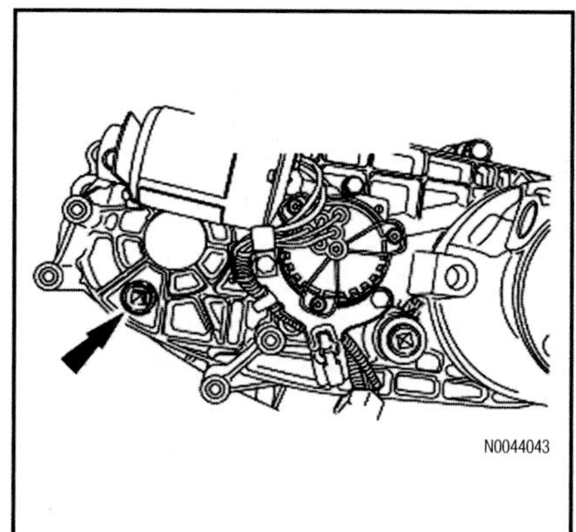

Fig. 24 Locating the drain plug

FRONT DRIVESHAFT

REMOVAL & INSTALLATION

4WD Vehicles

See Figures 25 and 26.

1. With the vehicle in NEUTRAL, position it on a hoist.
2. Index-mark the front driveshaft at both ends to maintain driveshaft balance.

➡If new bolts are not available, coat the threads of the original bolts with threadlock and sealer.

3. Remove and discard the 6 CV joint bolts and CV joint retainers. To install, tighten the new bolts evenly in a cross pattern to 22 ft. lbs. (30 Nm).

➡If new bolts are not available, coat the threads of the original bolts with threadlock and sealer.

4. Remove the 4 front driveshaft U-joint bolts and the U-joint straps.
5. Discard the bolts. To install, tighten the new bolts evenly and alternately to 14 ft. lbs. (19 Nm).
6. Remove the front driveshaft.

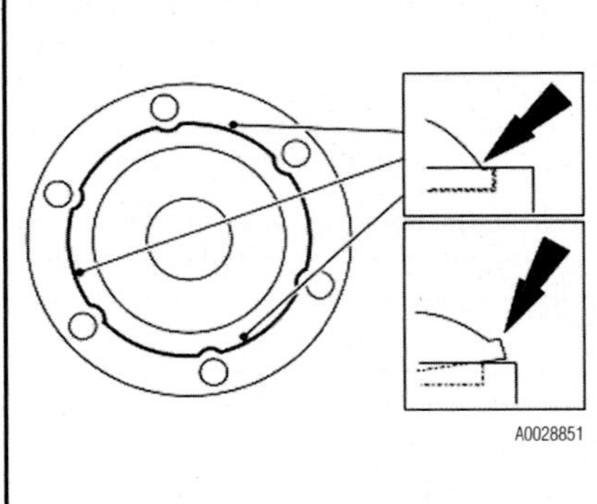

Fig. 26 CV joint cover orientation

➡The can (domed Constant Velocity [CV] joint housing cover) is pressed into the CV joint housing at the factory. When housed correctly, the can will appear as shown in the cut-away illustration (top box). Do not reseat the can in the CV joint housing if the can's flange is above the CV joint housing as shown in the cut-away illustration (bottom box) or vehicle damage may occur. Install a new driveshaft.

➡Tighten the Constant Velocity (CV) joint bolts evenly in a cross pattern or damage will occur to the CV joint.

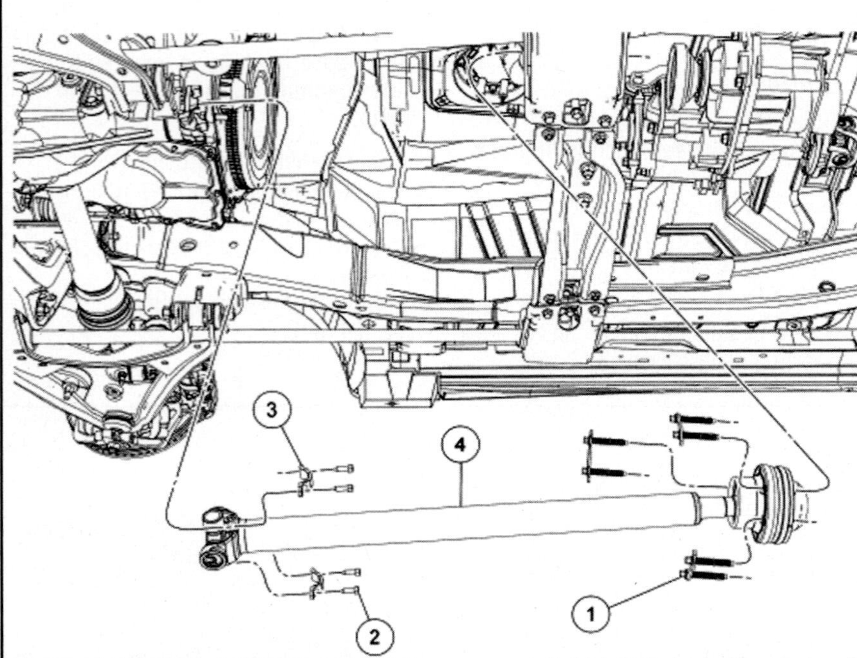

Fig. 25 Exploded view of the front driveshaft—4WD

➡Verify that the U-joint bearing caps are seated in the pinion yoke flange before tightening the U-joint strap bolts.

7. To install, reverse the removal procedure.

FRONT HALFSHAFT

REMOVAL & INSTALLATION

See Figures 27 and 28.

1. With the vehicle in NEUTRAL, position it on a hoist.
2. Remove the front wheel and tire.

➡Do not reuse the torque prevailing design hub nut and washer assembly or damage to the component may occur.

3. Remove and discard the hub nut and washer assembly. To install, tighten to 184 ft. lbs. (250 Nm).

➡Do not allow the disc brake caliper to hang suspended from the brake hose. Provide a suitable support.

4. Remove the 2 front disc brake anchor plate bolts from the knuckle. Lift the caliper assembly from the brake rotor and position the assembly aside.

➡Do not use a hammer to separate the outboard front wheel halfshaft joint from the wheel hub.

5. Damage to the outboard constant velocity (CV) joint stub shaft threads and internal CV joint components may result.
6. Using the Front Wheel Hub Remover, separate the outboard front wheel halfshaft joint from the wheel hub.
7. Support the front suspension lower arm.
8. Remove the nut and bolt retaining the upper ball joint to the front wheel knuckle. To install, tighten to 46 ft. lbs. (63 Nm).

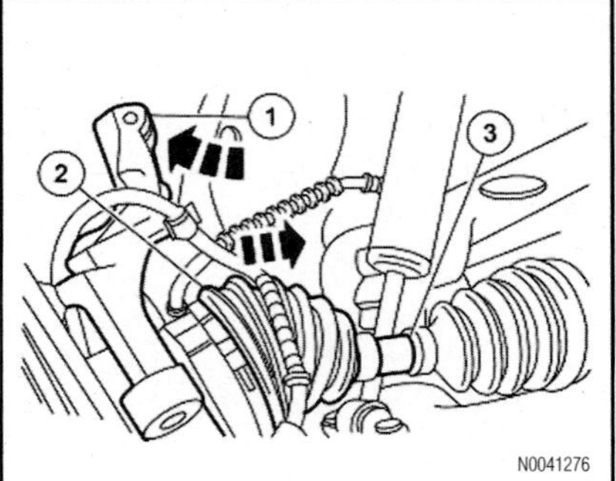

Fig. 27 Wheel hub (1), compress the front wheel halfshaft joint (2) and Remove the outboard front wheel halfshaft joint (3)

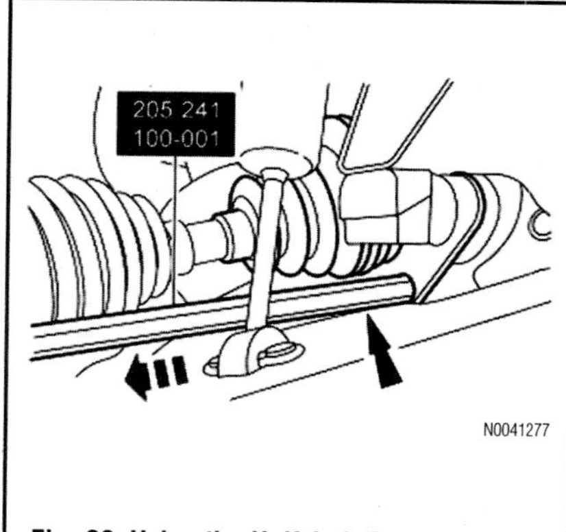

Fig. 28 Using the Halfshaft Remover and Slide Hammer

9. Using the Tie-Rod End Remover, separate the outer tie-rod end from the wheel spindle. To install, tighten to 59 ft. lbs. (80 Nm).

10. Remove the outboard front wheel halfshaft joint from the wheel hub.

a. Rotate the front wheel knuckle.

b. Compress the outboard front wheel halfshaft joint.

c. Remove the outboard front wheel halfshaft joint from the wheel hub.

11. Using the Halfshaft Remover and Slide Hammer, separate the inboard front wheel halfshaft joint from the front axle housing.

➡Do not damage the axle seal.

12. Remove the halfshaft assembly from the vehicle.

➡Do not reuse the torque prevailing design hub nut and washer assembly or damage to the components may occur.

➡Do not use power or impact tools to tighten the hub nut and washer assembly or damage to the components may occur.

➡Install a new retainer circlip in the groove in the LH inboard CV joint housing stub shaft before installing the halfshaft in the vehicle. To prevent the new retainer circlip from overexpanding when installing it, start one end in the groove and work the circlip over the shaft and into the groove.

13. To install, reverse the removal procedure.

FRONT PINION SEAL

REMOVAL & INSTALLATION

See Figures 29 through 33.

1. This operation disturbs the differential pinion bearing preload. Carefully reset the preload during assembly or damage to the component may occur.

2. With the vehicle in NEUTRAL, position it on a hoist.

3. Remove the front drivehaft assembly. For additional information, refer to Driveshaft.

4. Using a torque wrench, measure the torque required to maintain pinion rotation. Record the measurement.

5. Index-mark the pinion flange and the pinion stem.

6. Using the Drive Pinion Flange Holding Fixture, hold the pinion flange while removing the nut.

7. Using the 2 Jaw Puller, remove the pinion flange.

8. Inspect the pinion flange for burrs and damage. Inspect the end of the pinion flange that contacts the bearing cone, the nut counterbore and the seal surface for nicks. Discard the pinion flange as necessary.

Using the Torque Converter Fluid Seal Remover, and a suitable impact slide hammer, remove the pinion seal.

9. Remove the front axle drive pinion shaft oil slinger and the differential pinion bearing.

10. Remove and discard the collapsible spacer.

To install:

11. Verify that the splines on the pinion stem are free of burrs. If burrs are evident,

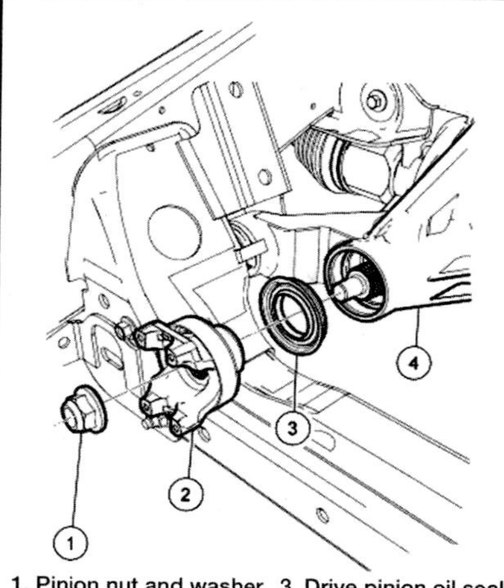

Fig. 29 Exploded view of the front pinion seal assembly

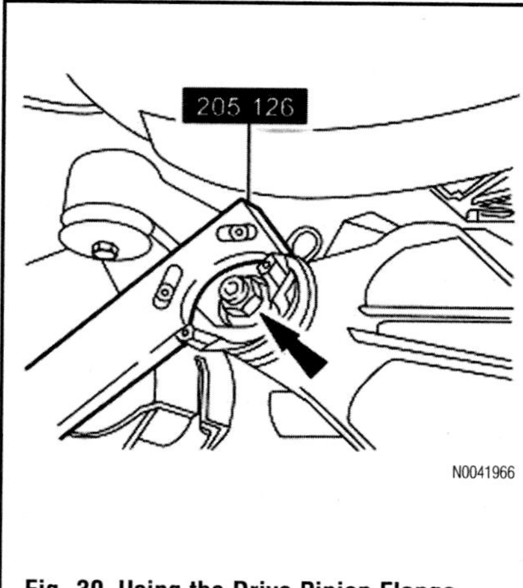

Fig. 30 Using the Drive Pinion Flange Holding Fixture

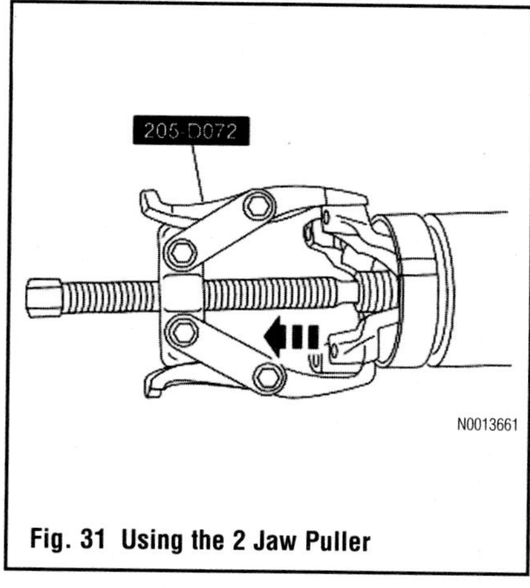

Fig. 31 Using the 2 Jaw Puller

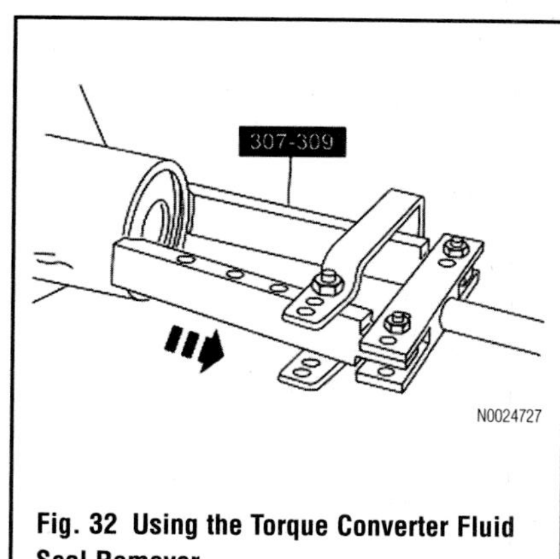

Fig. 32 Using the Torque Converter Fluid Seal Remover

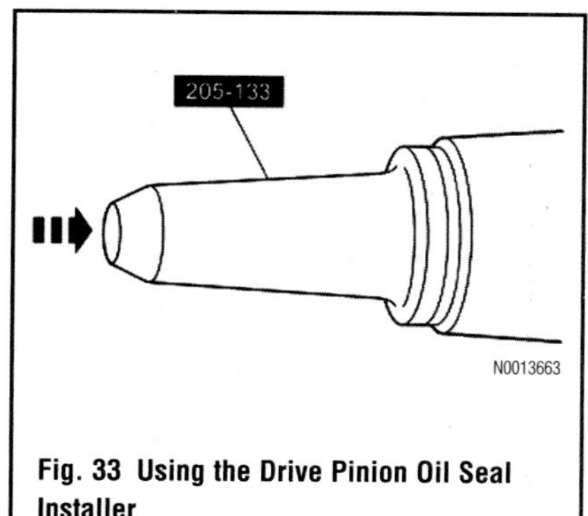

Fig. 33 Using the Drive Pinion Oil Seal Installer

remove them with a fine crocus cloth. Work in a rotating motion to wipe the pinion clean.

12. Clean the pinion seal bore.
13. Install a new collapsible spacer.
14. Install the original differential pinion bearing and the front axle drive pinion shaft oil slinger.
15. Lubricate the pinion seal with axle lubricant.
16. Using the Drive Pinion Oil Seal Installer, install the pinion seal.
17. Lubricate the pinion flange splines with axle lubricant.

NOTICE: Never use a metal hammer on the pinion flange or install the flange with power tools or component damage may occur. If necessary, use a plastic hammer to tap on a tight fitting flange.

18. Align the index marks and install the pinion flange.
19. Install the new pinion nut hand-tight.

➡Do not loosen the nut to reduce preload. Install a new collapsible spacer and nut if preload reduction is necessary or component damage may occur.

20. Using the Drive Pinion Flange Holding Fixture, hold the pinion flange while tightening the pinion nut to set the preload.
21. Tighten the nut, rotating the pinion occasionally to make sure the differential pinion bearings are seating correctly. Take frequent differential pinion bearing preload readings by rotating the pinion with a torque wrench. The final reading must be 5 inch lbs. more than the initial reading taken during removal.
22. Install the front driveshaft. For additional information, refer to Driveshaft.
23. Check the fluid level and, if necessary, fill the front axle with the correct type and quantity of lubricant. Refer to Specifications in this section.

REAR AXLE FLUID

DRAIN & REFILL

Refer to Rear Axle Housing Cover.

REAR AXLE HOUSING COVER

REMOVAL & INSTALLATION

See Figure 34.

1. With the vehicle in NEUTRAL, position it on a hoist.
2. Remove 2 nuts and position the parking brake cable and bracket aside.
3. Remove the differential housing cover.
4. Remove the 10 differential housing cover bolts and drain the lubricant from the rear axle housing.
5. Remove the differential housing cover.

To install:

➡Make sure the machined surfaces on the rear axle housing and the differential housing cover are clean and free of oil before installing the new silicone sealant. The inside of the rear axle must be covered when cleaning the machined surface to prevent contamination or damage to the component may occur.

6. Clean the gasket mating surface of the rear axle and the differential housing cover.
7. Apply a new continuous bead of sealant of the specified thickness to the differential housing cover.

➡The differential housing cover must be installed within 15 minutes of application of the silicone, or new sealant must be applied. If possible, allow one hour before filling with lubricant to make sure the silicone sealant has correctly cured.

8. Install the differential housing cover and the 10 bolts. Tighten to 33 ft. lbs. (45 Nm).
9. Position the parking brake cable and bracket. Install the 2 nuts. Tighten to 80 inch lbs. (9 Nm).

➡For Traction-Lok axles, before filling the rear axle with lubricant, first fill the rear axle with 4 oz of additive friction modifier.

➡Service refill capacities are determined by filling the rear axle with the specified lubricant to the level shown in the illustration.

10. Remove the filler plug and fill the rear axle with 2.4L (5 pt) with the specified lubricant and install the fill plug. Tighten to 38 ft. lbs. (52 Nm).

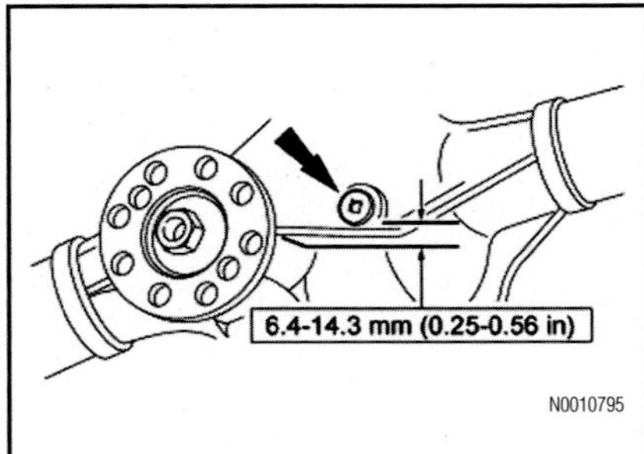

Fig. 34 Rear axle fill level

REAR AXLE SHAFT

REMOVE & INSTALLATION

See Figures 35 through 38.

1. Disconnect the negative battery cable.
2. Remove the brake disc.
3. Remove the differential housing cover.

➡Once the differential pinion shaft has been removed, turning the differential case or an axle shaft can cause the differential pinion gears to fall out of the assembly. This may result in damage to the component.

4. Remove the differential pinion shaft.
   a. Remove the differential pinion shaft lock bolt.
   b. Remove the differential pinion shaft.

➡Do not damage the rubber O-ring in the axle shaft U-washer groove.

5. Remove the axle shaft U-washer.
   a. Push the axle shaft inboard.
   b. Remove the U-washer.
6. Reinstall the differential pinion shaft.
   a. Push the axle shaft outboard.
   b. Install the differential pinion shaft.
   c. Install the differential pinion shaft lock bolt finger-tight.

➡Do not damage the wheel bearing oil seal.

7. Remove the axle shaft.

To install:

8. Lubricate the lip of the wheel bearing oil seal with grease.

➡Once the differential pinion shaft has been removed, turning the differential case or an axle shaft can cause the differential pinion gears to fall out of the assembly. This may result in chipped or damaged components.

9. Remove the differential pinion shaft.
   a. Remove the differential pinion shaft lock bolt and discard.
   b. Remove the differential pinion shaft.

➡Do not damage the wheel bearing oil seal.

10. Install the axle shaft.

➡Do not damage the rubber O-ring in the axle shaft U-washer groove.

11. Install the axle shaft U-washer.
    a. Position the U-washer on the button end of the axle shaft.

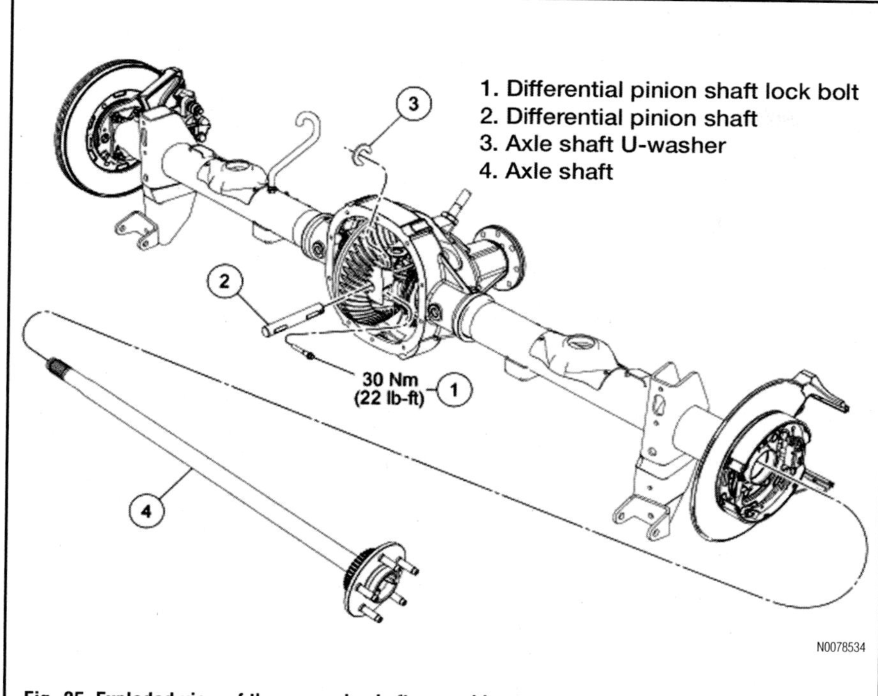

Fig. 35 Exploded view of the rear axle shaft assembly

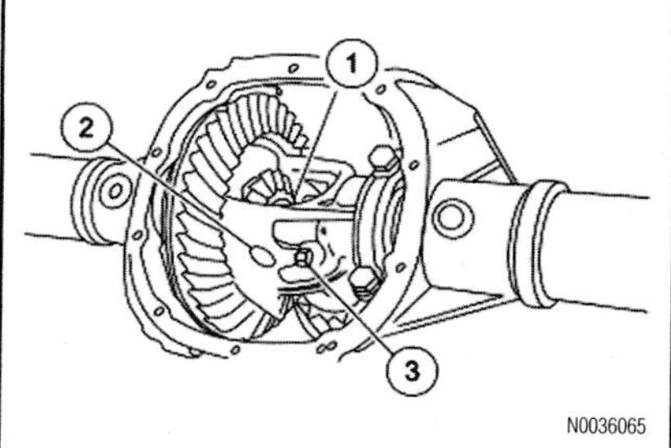

Fig. 38 Axle shaft outboard (1), differential pinion shaft (2) and differential pinion shaft lock bolt (3)

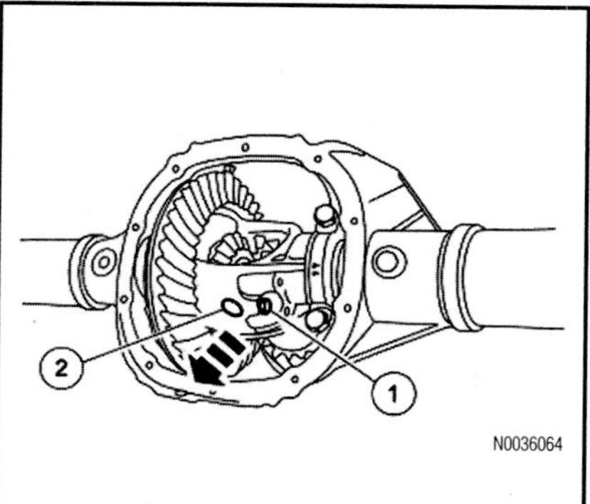

Fig. 36 Remove the differential pinion shaft lock bolt (1) and O-ring

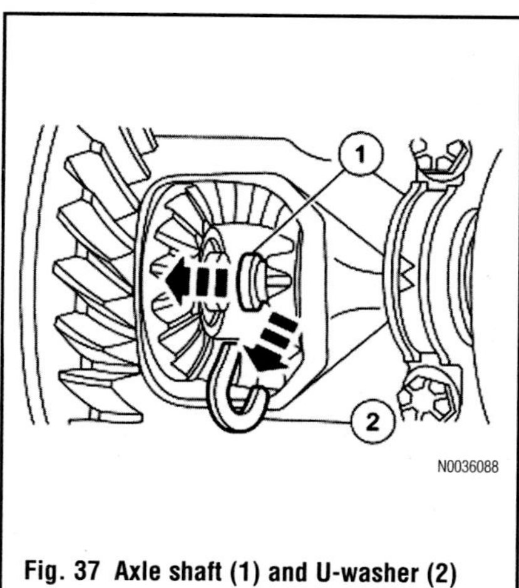

Fig. 37 Axle shaft (1) and U-washer (2)

b. Pull the axle shaft outward to seat the U-washer in the side gear.

12. Install the differential pinion shaft.

a. Align the hole in the differential pinion shaft with the lock bolt hole.

b. Install a new differential pinion shaft lock bolt. Tighten to 22 ft. lbs. (30 Nm).

13. Install the differential housing cover.

14. Install the brake disc.

REAR AXLE SHAFT BEARING & SEAL

REMOVAL & INSTALLATION

See Figures 39 through 42.

1. Disconnect the negative battery cable.
2. Remove the axle shaft.

➡If the wheel bearing oil seal is leaking, the axle housing vent may be plugged with foreign material.

➡If only the seal needs to be installed, use care to avoid damaging the seal bore.

3. Remove the oil seal from the axle tube. Discard the oil seal.
4. Inspect the rear wheel bearing and axle shaft bear surface for wear or damage.
5. If necessary, using the Slide Hammer and Axle Bearing Remover, remove the rear wheel bearing.

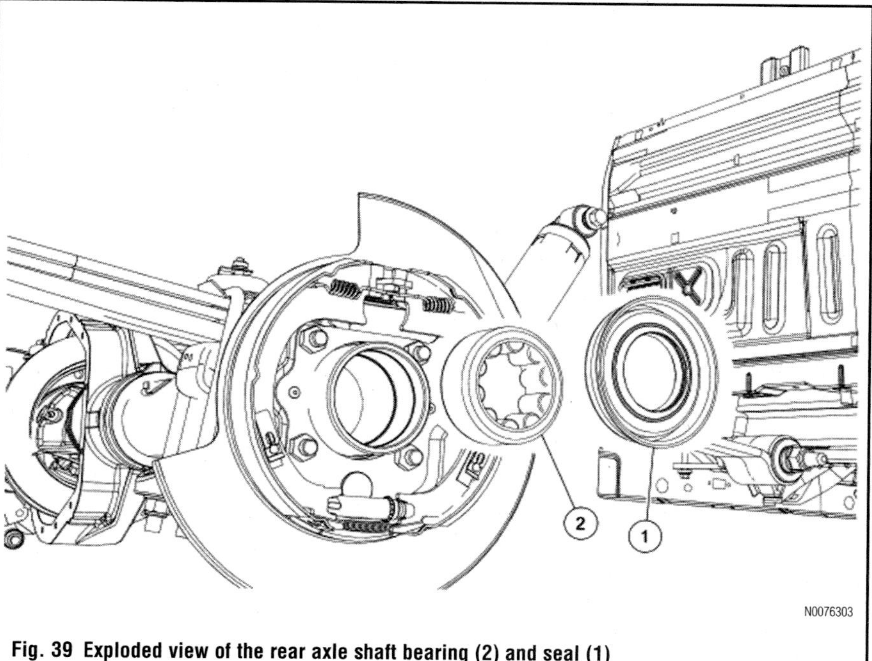

Fig. 39 Exploded view of the rear axle shaft bearing (2) and seal (1)

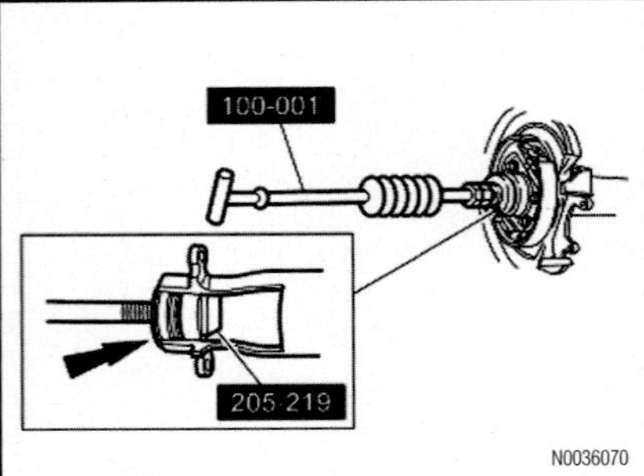

Fig. 40 Using the Slide Hammer and Axle Bearing Remover, remove the rear wheel bearing

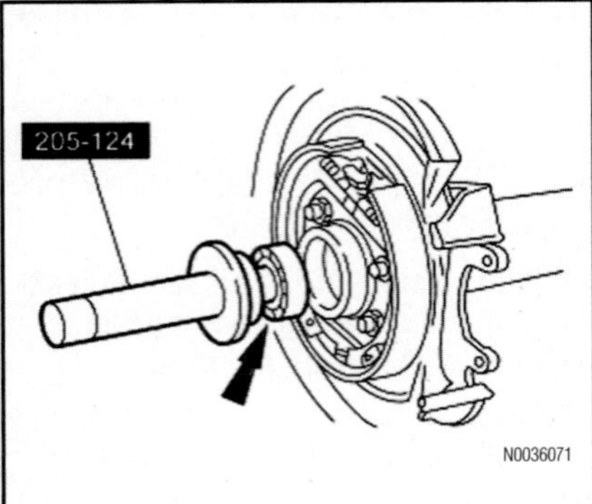

Fig. 41 Using the Axle Shaft Bearing Installer, install the rear wheel bearing

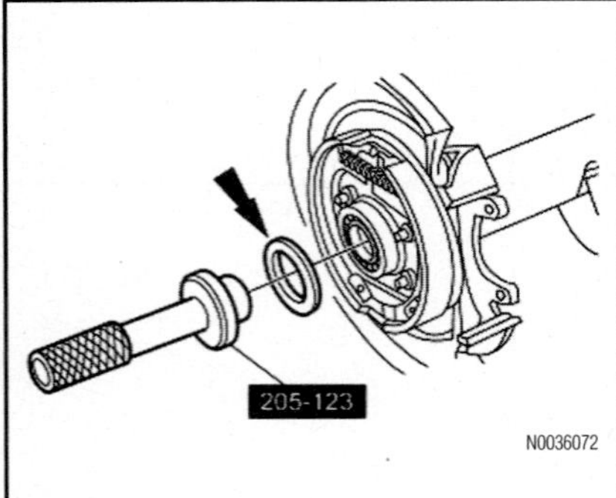

Fig. 42 Using the Axle Shaft Oil Seal Installer, install the wheel bearing oil seal

To install:

6. Using rear axle lubricant, lubricate the new rear wheel bearing.
7. Using the Axle Shaft Bearing Installer, install the rear wheel bearing.
8. Using long-life grease, lubricate the lip of the new wheel bearing oil seal.
9. Using the Axle Shaft Oil Seal Installer, install the wheel bearing oil seal.
10. Install the axle shaft.
11. Reconnect the negative battery cable.

REAR DRIVESHAFT

REMOVAL & INSTALLATION

4WD Vehicles

See Figures 43 and 44.

1. With the vehicle in NEUTRAL, position it on a hoist.
2. Index-mark the driveshaft flange to the rear axle pinion flange.
3. Index-mark the front flange and the transfer case flange.

➡If new bolts are not available, coat the threads of the original bolts with threadlock and sealer.

4. Remove and discard the 4 transfer case flange bolts. To install, tighten the new bolts evenly in a cross pattern to 83 ft. lbs. (112 Nm).

➡If new bolts are not available, coat the threads of the original bolts with threadlock and sealer.

5. Remove and discard the 4 rear axle flange bolts. To install, tighten the new bolts evenly in a cross pattern to 83 ft. lbs. (112 Nm).

➡The driveshaft flange fits tightly on the rear axle pinion flange pilot. Never hammer on the driveshaft or any of its components to disconnect the driveshaft flange from the pinion flange. Pry only in the area shown, with a suitable tool, to disconnect the driveshaft flange from the pinion flange.

6. Using a suitable tool, pry only in the area shown. Separate the driveshaft flange from the rear axle pinion flange.
7. Lower the driveshaft from the vehicle.

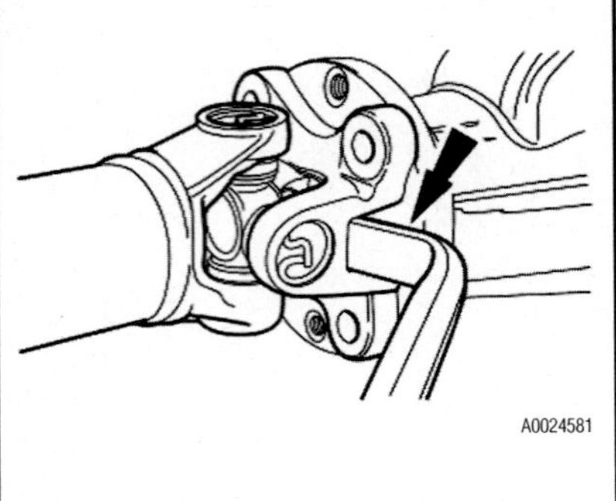

Fig. 44 Using a suitable tool, pry only in the area shown

➡The driveshaft flange fits tightly on the rear axle pinion flange pilot. To make sure that the driveshaft flange seats squarely on the pinion flange, tighten the bolts evenly in a cross pattern.

8. To install, reverse the removal procedure.

RWD Vehicles

See Figure 45.

1. With the vehicle in NEUTRAL, position it on a hoist.
2. Index-mark the driveshaft flange to the rear axle pinion flange and extension housing to maintain driveshaft balance.

➡Make sure the index marks on the extension housing and the driveshaft are aligned before separation.

➡After removing the driveshaft, place an index mark on the transmission output shaft that matches the transmission extension housing mark.

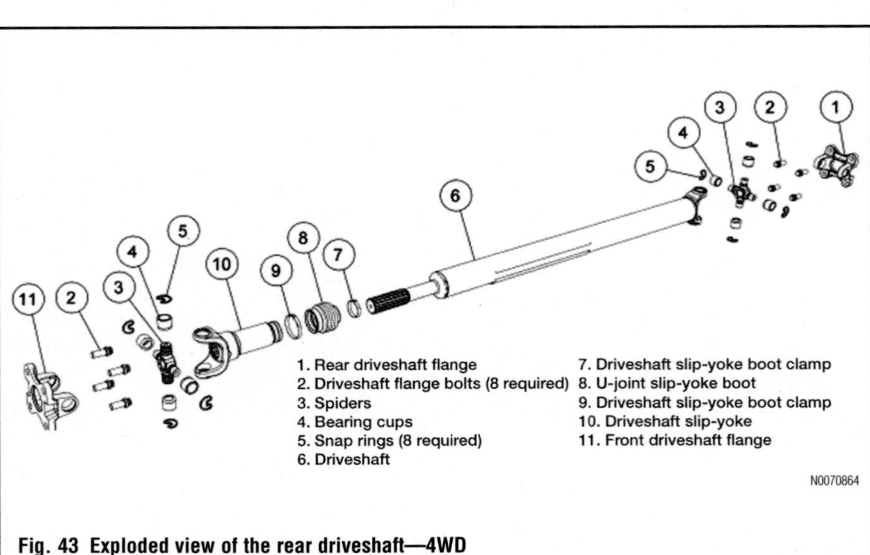

Fig. 43 Exploded view of the rear driveshaft—4WD

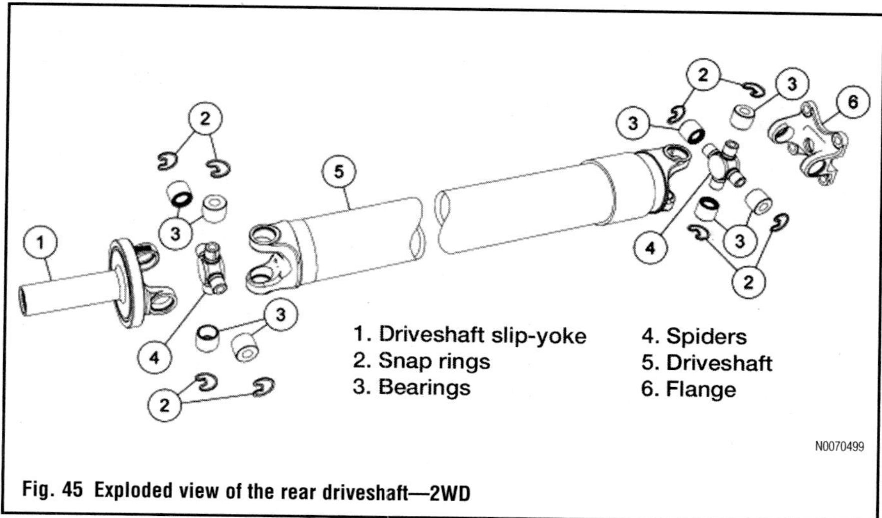

Fig. 45 Exploded view of the rear driveshaft—2WD

3. Index-mark the driveshaft and the extension housing.

➡If new bolts are not available, coat the threads of the original bolts with threadlock and sealer.

4. Remove and discard the 4 rear axle flange bolts. To install, tighten the new bolts evenly in a cross pattern to 83 ft. lbs. (112 Nm).

➡The driveshaft flange fits tightly on the rear axle pinion flange pilot. Never hammer on the driveshaft or any of its components to disconnect the driveshaft flange from the pinion flange. Pry only in the area shown, with a suitable tool, to disconnect the driveshaft flange from the pinion flange.

5. Using a suitable tool, pry only in the area shown. Separate the driveshaft flange from the rear axle pinion flange.
6. Lower the driveshaft and slide it off the output shaft.
7. Plug the extension housing to prevent fluid loss.

➡The driveshaft flange fits tightly on the rear axle pinion flange pilot. To make sure that the driveshaft flange seats squarely on the pinion flange, tighten the bolts evenly in a cross pattern.

8. To install, reverse the removal procedure.

REAR PINION SEAL

REMOVAL & INSTALLATION

See Figures 46 through 51.

➡Remove the rear brake discs to prevent brake drag during drive pinion bearing preload adjustment.

➡When removing the rear brake caliper in this procedure, it is not necessary to disconnect the hydraulic lines.

1. Remove the brake discs.
2. Remove the driveshaft and position the driveshaft aside.
3. Install a torque wrench on the nut and record the torque necessary to maintain rotation of the pinion through several revolutions.

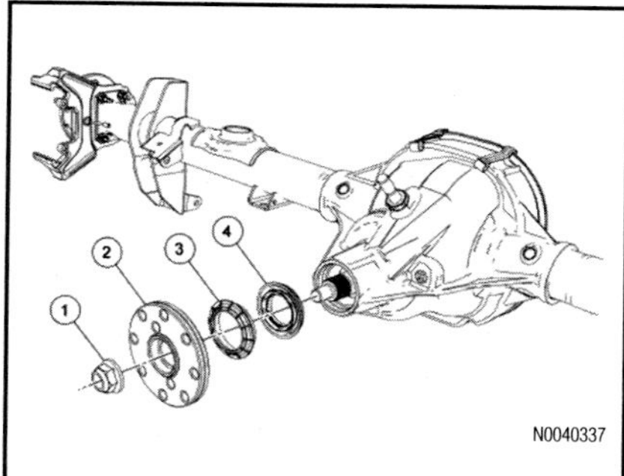

Fig. 46 Exploded view of the rear pinion seal and flange

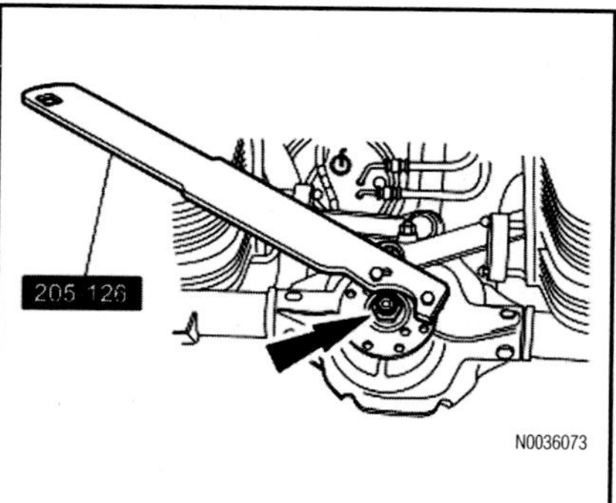

Fig. 47 Use the Drive Pinion Flange Holding Fixture

4. Use the Drive Pinion Flange Holding Fixture to hold the pinion flange while removing the nut.

Discard the nut.

5. Index-mark the pinion flange and the drive pinion stem for correct alignment during installation.
6. Using the 2 Jaw Puller, remove the pinion flange.
7. Force up on the metal flange of the drive pinion seal. Install gripping pliers and strike with a hammer until the drive pinion seal is removed.

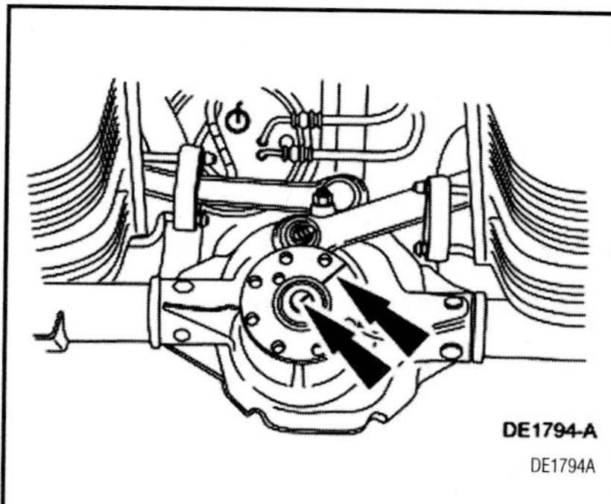

Fig. 48 Index-mark the pinion flange and the drive pinion stem

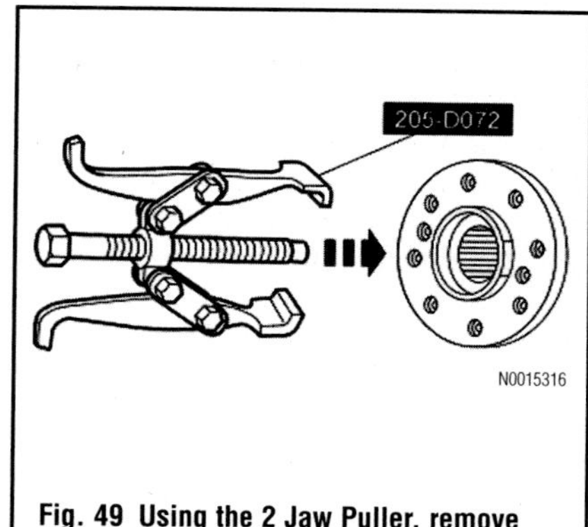

Fig. 49 Using the 2 Jaw Puller, remove the pinion flange

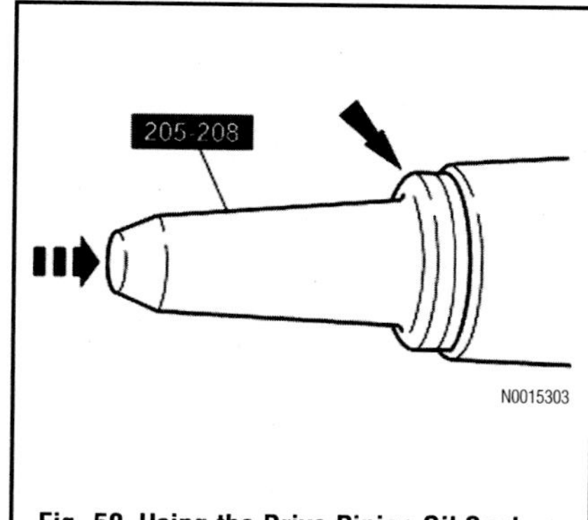

Fig. 50 Using the Drive Pinion Oil Seal Installer

8. Discard the seal.

To install:

9. Coat the new rear axle drive pinion seal lips with grease.

➡If the rear axle drive pinion seal becomes misaligned during installation, remove the seal and install a new seal.

10. Using the Drive Pinion Oil Seal Installer, install the rear axle drive pinion seal.
11. Lubricate the pinion flange splines with rear axle lubricant.

➡Disregard the index marks if installing a new pinion flange.

12. Position the pinion flange.
13. Using the Drive Pinion Flange Installer, install the pinion flange.
14. Position the new drive pinion nut.

➡Do not, under any circumstance, loosen the nut to reduce preload or component damage may occur. If it is necessary to reduce preload, install a new collapsible spacer and nut.

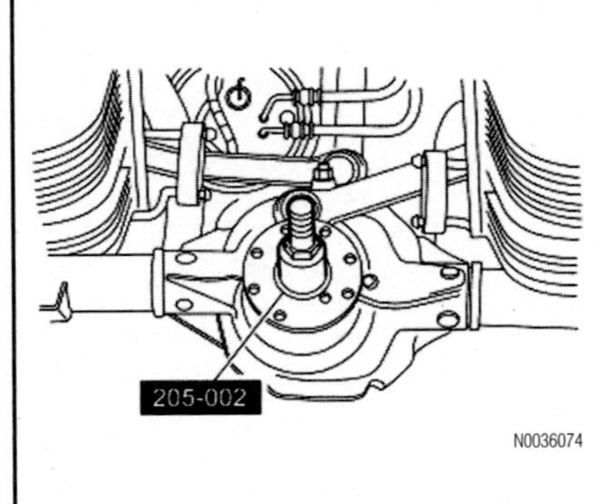

Fig. 51 Using the Drive Pinion Flange Installer

➡Remove the Drive Pinion Flange Holding Fixture while taking preload readings with the torque wrench.

15. Use the Drive Pinion Flange Holding Fixture to hold the pinion flange while tightening the nut.
16. Rotate the pinion occasionally to make sure the differential pinion bearings seat correctly. Take frequent differential pinion bearing preload readings by rotating the pinion with a Nm (lb-in) torque wrench.
17. If the preload recorded prior to disassembly is lower than the specification, tighten the nut to specification. If the preload recorded prior to disassembly is higher than the specification, tighten the nut to the original reading as recorded.
18. Install the drive shaft.
19. Install the brake discs.
20. Connect the negative battery cable.

ENGINE COOLING

ENGINE COOLANT

DRAIN, REFILL & BLEEDING PROCEDURE

WARNING

Always allow the engine to cool before opening the cooling system. Do not unscrew the coolant pressure relief cap when the engine is operating or the cooling system is hot. The cooling system is under pressure; steam and hot liquid can come out forcefully when the cap is loosened slightly. Failure to follow these instructions may result in serious personal injury.

➡The coolant must be recovered in a suitable, clean container for reuse. If the coolant is contaminated it must be recycled or disposed of correctly and replaced. Using contaminated coolant may damage cooling system components or the engine.

➡Always fill the cooling system with the manufacturer's specified coolant. If a non-specified coolant has been used the cooling system must be chemically flushed. Failure to follow these instructions may damage the engine or cooling system.

➡If cooling system stop leak pellets are used, Motorcraft Premium Gold Engine Coolant may darken from yellow to golden tan.

➡Less than 80% of the coolant capacity can be recovered with the engine in the vehicle. Dirty, rusty or contaminated coolant requires replacement.

1. With the vehicle in NEUTRAL, position it on a hoist.
2. Remove the degas bottle cap.
3. Place a suitable container below the radiator draincock. Drain the coolant.
4. Close the radiator draincock when finished draining.

Complete Drain

➡If cooling system stop leak pellets are used, Motorcraft Premium Gold Engine Coolant may darken from yellow to golden tan.

➡Less than 80% of the coolant capacity can be recovered with the engine in the vehicle. Dirty, rusty or contaminated coolant requires replacement.

5. With the vehicle in NEUTRAL, position it on a hoist.
6. Remove the degas bottle cap.
7. Place a suitable container below the radiator draincock. Drain the coolant.
8. Close the radiator draincock when finished.
9. Place a suitable container below the radiator lower hose and disconnect the hose from the thermostat housing.
10. Filling and Bleeding with a Vacuum Cooling System Filler

➡All air must be removed from the cooling system. Failure to remove all the air from the cooling system may result in engine damage.

➡Engine coolant provides boil protection, corrosion protection, freeze protection, and cooling efficiency to the engine and cooling components. In order to obtain these protections, maintain the engine coolant at the correct concentration and fluid level in the degas bottle. To maintain the integrity of the coolant and the cooling system:

11. Add Motorcraft® Premium Gold Engine Coolant or equivalent meeting Ford specification WSS-M97B51-A1 (yellow color). Use the same type of coolant that was originally used to fill the cooling system. Do not mix coolant types.
12. Do not add or mix with any other type of engine coolant. Mixing coolants may degrade the coolant's corrosion protection.
13. Do not add alcohol, methanol, or brine, or any engine coolants mixed with alcohol or methanol antifreeze. These can cause engine damage from overheating or freezing.
14. Ford Motor Company does NOT recommend the use of recycled engine coolant in vehicles originally equipped with Motorcraft® Premium Gold Engine Coolant since a Ford-approved recycling process is not yet available.

➡If cooling system stop leak pellets are used, Motorcraft Premium Gold Engine Coolant may darken from yellow to golden tan.

Install the vacuum cooling system filler and follow the manufacturer's instructions to fill and bleed the cooling system.

15. Recommended coolant concentration is 50/50 engine coolant to distilled water.
For extremely cold climates (less than -34°F):
16. It may be necessary to increase the coolant concentration above 50%.
17. NEVER increase the coolant concentration above 60%.
18. Maximum coolant concentration is 60/40 for cold weather areas.
19. A coolant concentration of 60% provides freeze point protection down to -58°F.
20. Engine coolant concentration above 60% decreases the overheat protection characteristics of the engine coolant and may damage the engine.
21. For extremely hot climates:
  a. It is still necessary to maintain the coolant concentration above 40%.
  b. NEVER decrease the coolant concentration below 40%.
  c. Minimum coolant concentration is 40/60 for warm weather areas.
  d. A coolant concentration of 40% provides freeze point protection down to -15°F.
  e. Engine coolant concentration below 40% decreases the corrosion and freeze protection characteristics of the engine coolant and may damage the engine.
22. Vehicles driven year-round in non-extreme climates should use a 50/50 mixture of engine coolant and distilled water for optimum cooling system and engine protection.

Filling and Bleeding without a Vacuum Cooling System Filler

➡Engine coolant provides freeze protection, boil protection, cooling efficiency and corrosion protection to the engine and cooling components. In order to obtain these protections, the engine coolant must be maintained at the correct concentration and fluid level. Incorrect coolant or coolant mixtures may damage cooling system components. To maintain the integrity of the coolant and the cooling system:

23. Add Motorcraft® Premium Gold Engine Coolant or equivalent meeting Ford specification WSS-M97B51-A1 (yellow color). Use the same type of coolant that was originally used to fill the cooling system. Do not mix coolant types.
24. Do not add or mix with any other type of engine coolant. Mixing coolants may degrade the coolant's corrosion protection.
25. Do not add alcohol, methanol, or brine, or any engine coolants mixed with alcohol or methanol antifreeze. These can cause engine damage from overheating or freezing.
26. Ford Motor Company does NOT recommend the use of recycled engine coolant in vehicles originally equipped with Motorcraft® Premium Gold Engine Coolant since a Ford-approved recycling process is not yet available.

➡If cooling system stop leak pellets are used, Motorcraft Premium Gold Engine Coolant may darken from yellow to golden tan.

27. Filling and bleeding procedure for use with partial drain
28. Make sure the radiator draincock is completely closed.
29. Add the correct engine coolant mixture to the degas bottle to 0.590 inches above the maximum fill level.
30. Recommended coolant concentration is 50/50 engine coolant to distilled water.
31. For extremely cold climates (less than -34°F):
  a. It may be necessary to increase the coolant concentration above 50%.
  b. NEVER increase the coolant concentration above 60%.
  c. Maximum coolant concentration is 60/40 for cold weather areas.
  d. A coolant concentration of 60% provides freeze point protection down to -58°F).
  e. Engine coolant concentration above 60% decreases the overheat protection characteristics of the engine coolant and may damage the engine.
32. For extremely hot climates:
  a. It is still necessary to maintain the coolant concentration above 40%.
  b. NEVER decrease the coolant concentration below 40%.
  c. Minimum coolant concentration is 40/60 for warm weather areas.
  d. A coolant concentration of 40% provides freeze point protection down to -15°F).
  e. Engine coolant concentration below 40% decreases the corrosion and freeze protection characteristics
  f. of the engine coolant and may damage the engine.
  g. Vehicles driven year-round in non-extreme climates should use a 50/50 mixture of engine coolant and distilled water for optimum cooling system and engine protection.
33. Install the degas bottle cap.

WARNING

Do not stand in line with or near the engine cooling fan blade when revving the engine. A damaged fan can separate during operation. Failure to follow this instruction may result in serious personal injury.

34. Start the engine and hold at 2,500 rpm engine speed for approximately 8 minutes until the thermostat opens.
35. Maintain 2,500 rpm engine speed for an additional 3 minutes.
36. Increase engine speed to 4,000 rpm and hold for 5 seconds.
37. Return engine speed to 2,500 rpm and hold for an additional 3 minutes.
38. Stop the engine and check for leaks.

Filling and bleeding procedure for use with complete drain

39. Install the radiator lower hose and close the radiator draincock.
40. Add the correct engine coolant mixture to the degas bottle to the maximum fill level.
41. Recommended coolant concentration is 50/50 engine coolant to distilled water.
42. For extremely cold climates (less than -34°F):
  a. It may be necessary to increase the coolant concentration above 50%.
  b. NEVER increase the coolant concentration above 60%.
  c. Maximum coolant concentration is 60/40 for cold weather areas.
  d. A coolant concentration of 60% provides freeze point protection down to -58°F.
  e. Engine coolant concentration above 60% decrease the overheat protection characteristics of the engine coolant and may damage the engine.
43. For extremely hot climates:
  a. It is still necessary to maintain the coolant concentration above 40%.
  b. NEVER decrease the coolant concentration below 40%.
  c. Minimum coolant concentration is 40/60 for warm weather areas.
  d. A coolant concentration of 40% provide freeze point protection down to -15°F.
  e. Engine coolant concentration below 40% decrease the corrosion and freeze protection characteristics of the engine coolant and may damage the engine.
  f. Vehicles driven year-round in non-extreme climates should use a 50/50 mixture of engine coolant and distilled water for optimum cooling system and engine protection.

WARNING

Do not stand in line with or near the engine cooling fan blade when revving the engine. A damaged fan can separate during operation. Failure to follow this instruction may result in serious personal injury.

44. Start the engine and run for approximately 10 seconds at 2,500 rpm to prime the heater circuit then turn the engine off.
45. Top off the coolant level to 0.6 inch above the max fill level.
46. Install the degas bottle cap.
47. Start the engine and hold at 2,500 rpm engine speed for approximately 8 minutes until the thermostat opens.
48. Maintain 2,500 rpm engine speed for an additional 3 minutes.
49. Increase engine speed to 4,000 rpm and hold for 5 seconds.
50. Return engine speed to 2,500 rpm and hold for an additional 3 minutes.
51. Repeat the previous 2 steps.
52. Stop the engine and check for leaks.
53. Verify correct fluid level after engine cools for 20 minutes. Top off the degas bottle to MAX line.

FLUSHING

1. Drain the cooling system.
2. Remove the thermostat. For additional information, refer to Thermostat in this section.
3. Install the thermostat housing without the thermostat.

➡Refer to the cooling system flusher manufacturer's operating instructions for specific vehicle hook-up.

4. Use an appropriate cooling system flusher to flush the engine and radiator.
5. Use premium cooling system flush.
6. Install the thermostat.

ENGINE FAN

REMOVAL & INSTALLATION

2.3L Engine

See Figure 52.

1. Remove the Air Cleaner (ACL) outlet pipe.
2. Remove the accessory drive belt. For additional information, refer to Accessory Drive Belt.
3. Using the Strap Wrench to hold the fan pulley, loosen the cooling fan clutch nut. To install, tighten to 41 ft. lbs. (55 Nm).
4. Remove the fan and clutch assembly.

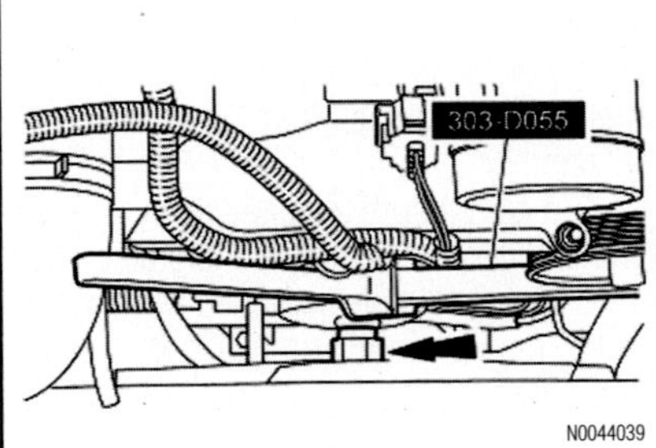

Fig. 52 Using the Strap Wrench

5. If necessary, remove the 4 fan-to-fan clutch bolts and separate the fan from the fan clutch.
6. To install, reverse the removal procedure.

4.0L Engine

See Figure 53.

1. Remove the Air Cleaner (ACL) outlet tube.
2. Remove the accessory drive belt. For additional information, refer to Accessory Drive Belt.
3. Using the Fan Pulley Holding Wrench and the Fan Clutch Nut Wrench, remove the fan and fan clutch assembly and position it inside the shroud. To install, tighten to 41 ft. lbs. (55 Nm).
4. Remove the 2 fan shroud bolts. Lift the fan and fan clutch assembly and the fan shroud together and remove from the vehicle.
5. Remove the 4 bolts and separate the fan from the fan clutch. To install, tighten to 62 inch lbs. (7 Nm).
6. To install, reverse the removal procedure.

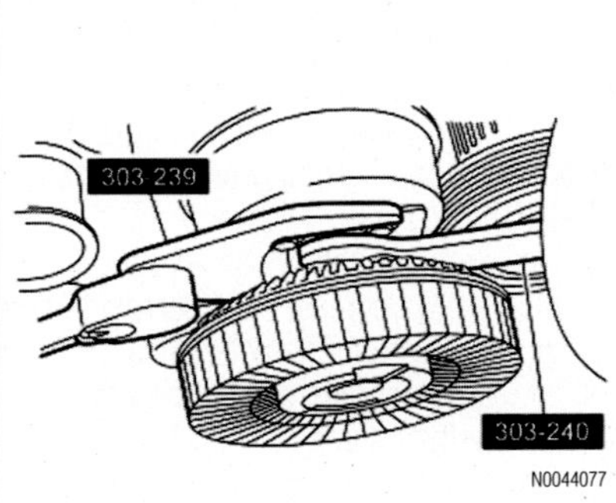

Fig. 53 Using the Fan Pulley Holding Wrench and the Fan Clutch Nut Wrench

RADIATOR

REMOVAL & INSTALLATION

2.3L Engine

See Figure 54.

1. Drain the cooling system.
2. Vehicles equipped with an automatic transmission: Disconnect the transmission cooling tubes from the radiator.

➡To avoid disturbing the transmission oil cooler fittings, use a back-up wrench.

3. Disconnect the degas bottle hose from the radiator and position the hose away from the radiator.
4. Disconnect the upper radiator hose from the radiator.
5. Remove the cooling fan and shroud.
6. Disconnect the lower radiator hose from the radiator.
7. Remove the bolts and the radiator.
8. Remove the 3 pushpins and the seal from the top of the radiator.

To install:

9. Install the seal and the 3 pushpins on the top of the radiator.
10. Position the radiator into the engine compartment and install the bolts.
11. Connect the lower radiator hose to the radiator.
12. Install the cooling fan and shroud.
13. Connect the upper radiator hose to the radiator.
14. Position the coolant overflow hose in the channel on top of the radiator, then connect the hose to the radiator.
15. Vehicles equipped with an automatic transmission: Connect the transmission cooling tubes to the radiator. Tighten to 20 ft. lbs. (27 Nm).

➡To avoid disturbing the transmission or cooler fittings, use a back-up wrench.

16. Fill and bleed the cooling system.

WARNING

Do not stand in line with or near the engine cooling fan blade when revving the engine. A damaged fan can separate during operation. Failure to follow this instruction may result in serious personal injury.

17. Operate the engine for several minutes and check the hoses and connections for leaks.
18. Check the transmission fluid level. Fill as needed.

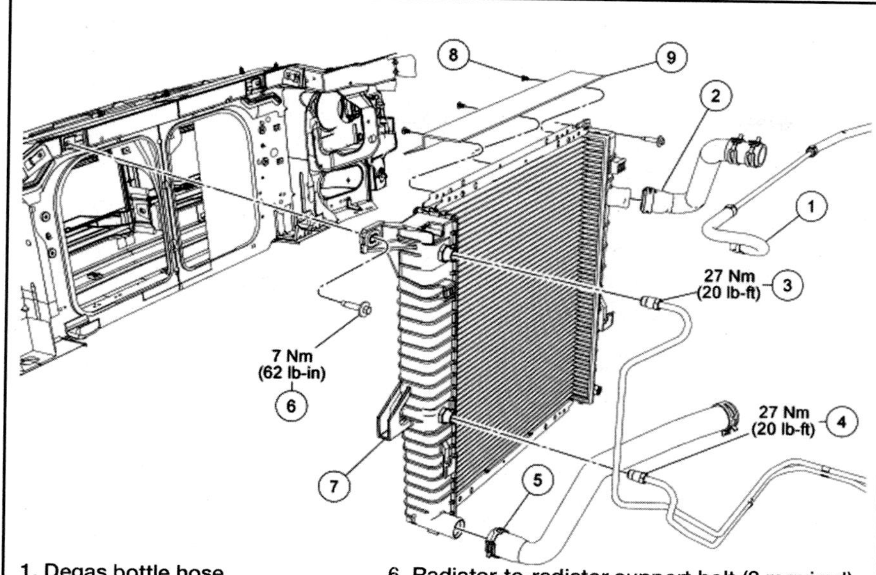

Fig. 54 Exploded view of the radiator and hoses—2.3L Engine

4.0L Engine

See Figure 55.

1. Drain the cooling system.
2. Disconnect the radiator overflow hose from the radiator.
3. Remove the cooling fan shroud.
4. Disconnect the upper radiator hose from the radiator.
5. Disconnect the lower radiator hose from the radiator.
6. Vehicles equipped with an automatic transmission; Disconnect the 2 transmission cooler tubes from the radiator.

➡To avoid disturbing the transmission oil cooler fittings, use a back-up wrench.

7. Remove the 2 bolts and the radiator.

To install:

8. Position the radiator and install the 2 bolts.
9. Vehicles equipped with an automatic transmission; Connect the 2 transmission cooler tubes to the radiator. Tighten to 18 ft. lbs. (25 Nm).

➡To avoid disturbing the transmission oil cooler fittings, use a back-up wrench.

10. Connect the lower radiator hose to the radiator.
11. Connect the upper radiator hose to the radiator.
12. Install the cooling fan shroud.
13. Connect the radiator overflow hose to the radiator.
14. Fill and bleed the cooling system.

✲✲ WARNING

Do not stand in line with or near the engine cooling fan blade when revving the engine. A damaged fan can separate during operation. Failure to follow this instruction may result in serious personal injury.

15. Operate the engine for several minutes and check the hoses and connections for leaks.
16. Vehicles equipped with an automatic transmission
17. Check the transmission fluid level. Fill as needed.

THERMOSTAT

REMOVAL & INSTALLATION

2.3L Engine

See Figure 56.

➡The thermostat and thermostat housing are serviced as an assembly.

1. Drain the cooling system.
2. Disconnect the lower radiator hose.
3. Disconnect the EGR valve heater hose.
4. Remove the bolts and the thermostat housing.
5. To install, reverse the removal procedure.
6. Clean and inspect the gasket, install a new gasket if necessary.

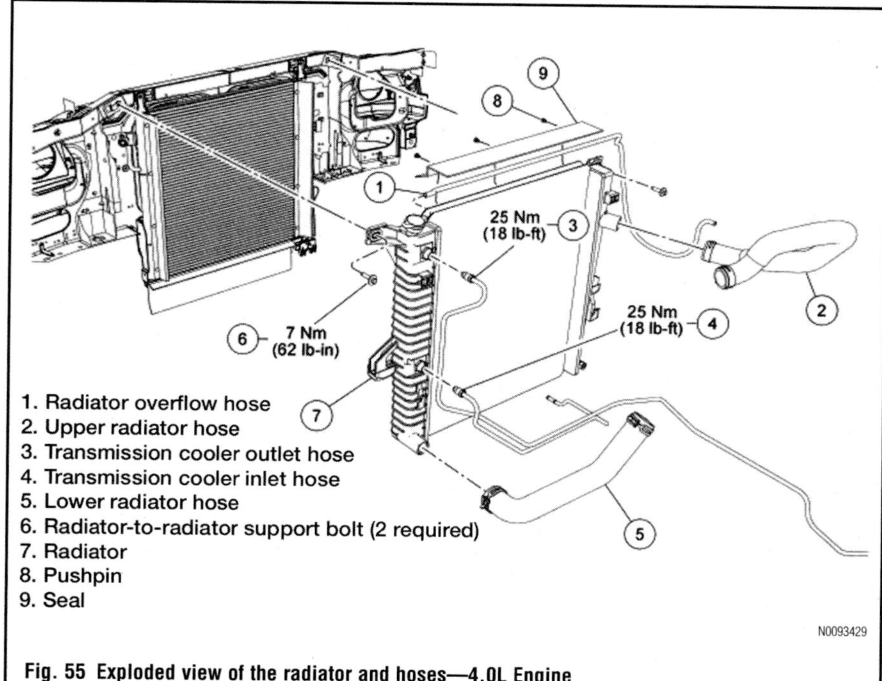

Fig. 55 Exploded view of the radiator and hoses—4.0L Engine

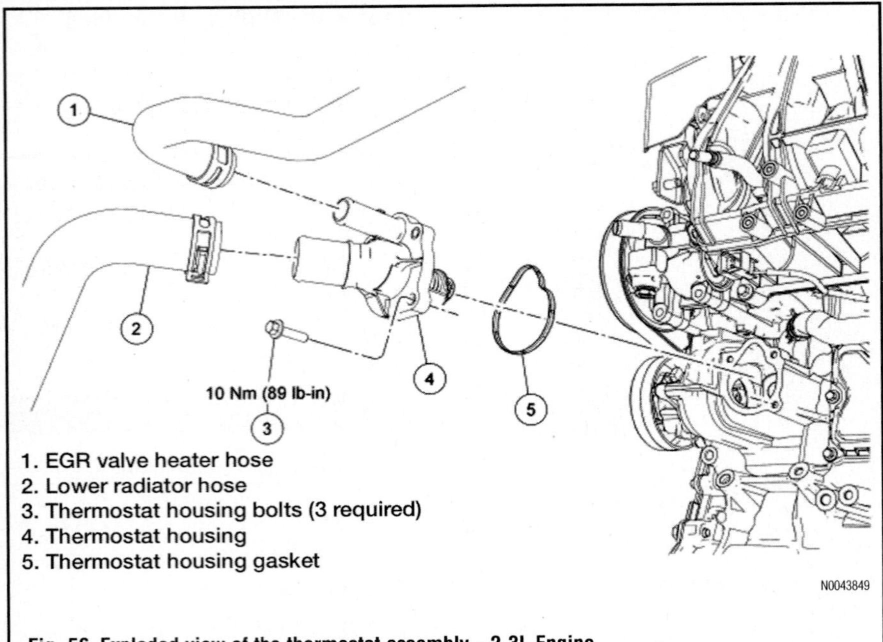

Fig. 56 Exploded view of the thermostat assembly—2.3L Engine

4.0L Engine

See Figure 57.

1. Drain the cooling system.
2. Remove the Air Cleaner (ACL) outlet tube.
3. Disconnect the upper radiator hose.
4. Remove the 3 bolts, the thermostat outlet housing and the thermostat.
5. Inspect the O-ring seal. Install a new O-ring seal if necessary.
6. To install, reverse the removal procedure.

WATER PUMP

REMOVAL & INSTALLATION

2.3L Engine

See Figure 58.

1. Remove the Air Cleaner (ACL) outlet pipe.
2. Drain the cooling system.
3. Remove the drive belt. For additional information, refer to Accessory Drive Belt.
4. Remove the 3 bolts and the coolant pump pulley.
5. Remove the 3 bolts and the coolant pump.

➡Lubricate the coolant pump O-ring seal with clean coolant.

6. To install, reverse the removal procedure. Refer to the illustration for torque values.

4.0L Engine

See Figure 59.

1. Drain the cooling system. For additional information, refer to Cooling System Draining, Filling and Bleeding in this section.
2. Loosen the 4 coolant pump pulley bolts.
3. Remove the accessory drive belt. For additional information, refer to Accessory Drive.
4. Remove the 4 bolts and the coolant pump pulley. To install, tighten to 18 ft. lbs. (25 Nm).
5. Remove the 4 bolts and the coolant pump.
6. Discard the O-ring seal. To install, tighten to 18 ft. lbs (25 Nm).

➡Do not rotate the coolant pump housing once installed in the engine. Damage to the O-ring seal can occur, causing the coolant pump to leak.

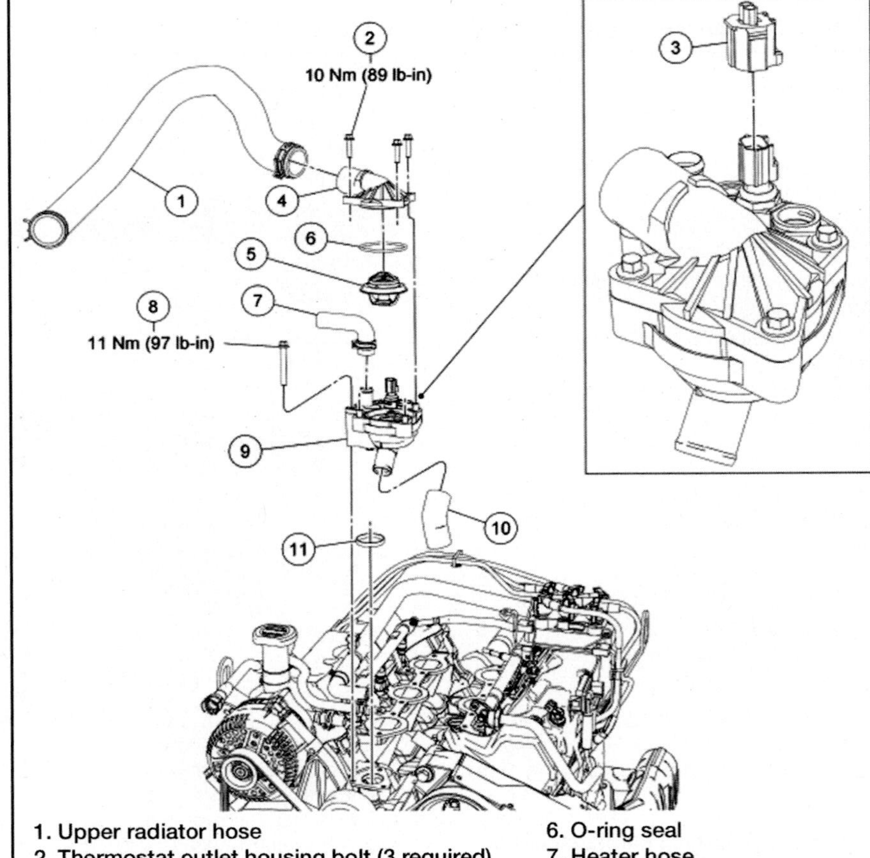

Fig. 57 Exploded view of the thermostat assembly—4.0L Engine

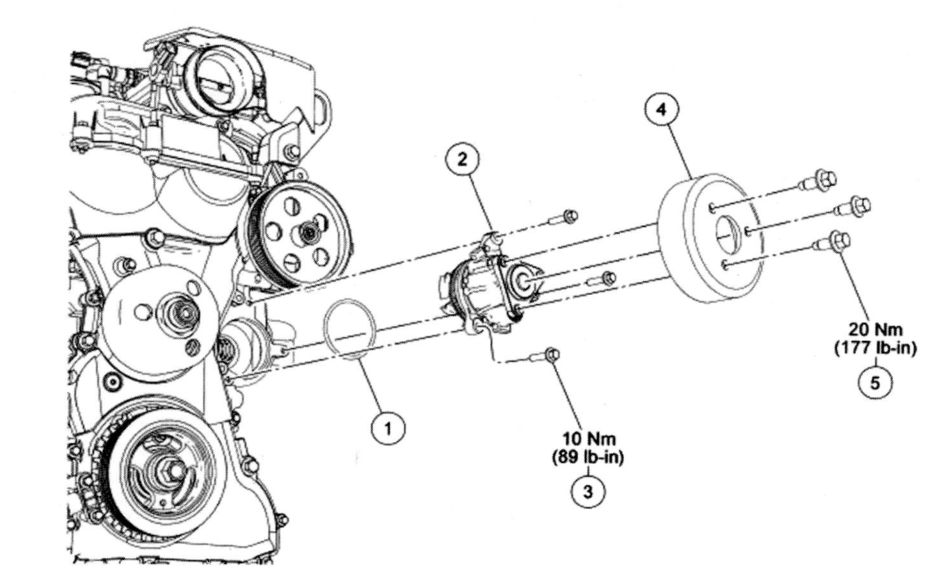

Fig. 58 Exploded view of the water pump—2.3L Engine

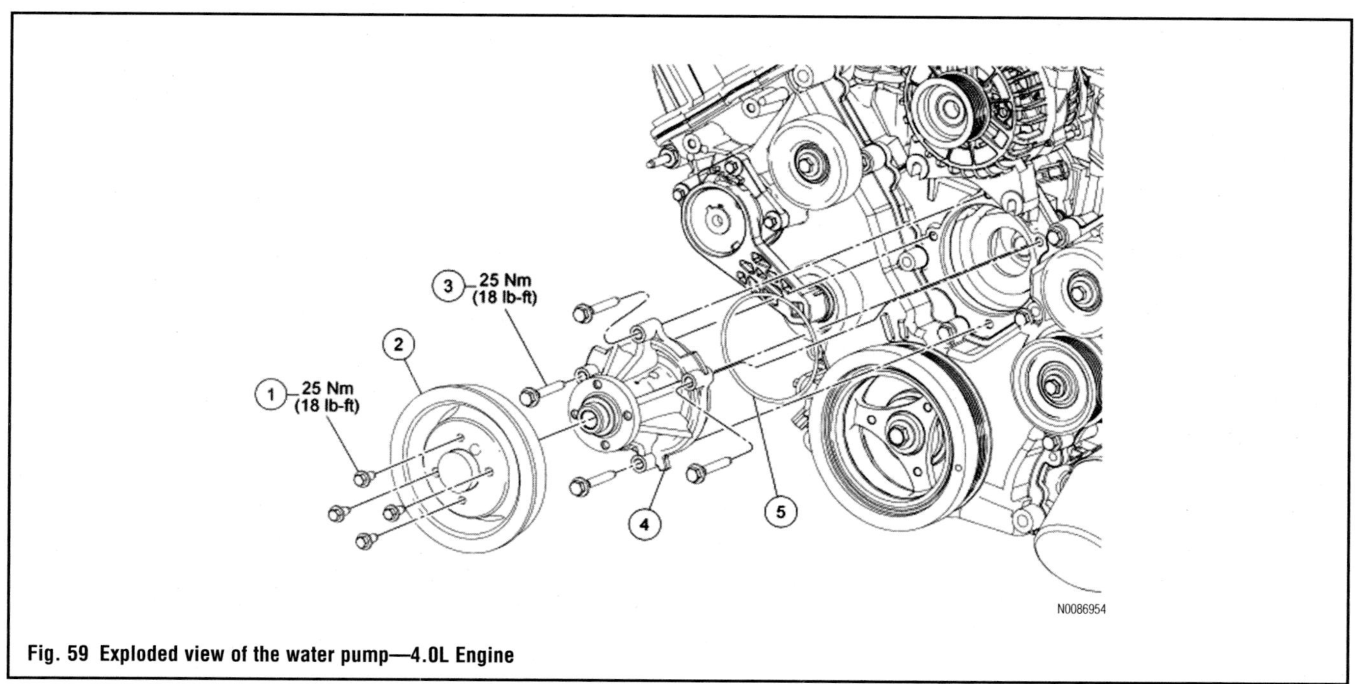

Fig. 59 Exploded view of the water pump—4.0L Engine

➡Align the mounting holes in the cylinder block with the mounting holes on the coolant pump prior to installing the coolant pump in the cylinder block.

➡Install a new O-ring seal and lubricate with clean engine coolant.

7. To install, reverse the removal procedure.

8. Clean all sealing surfaces with metal surface prep.

9. Fill and bleed the cooling system. For additional information, refer to Cooling System Draining, Filling and Bleeding in this section.

BATTERY

REMOVAL & INSTALLATION

See Figure 60.

✲✲ WARNING

Batteries contain sulfuric acid and produce explosive gases. Work in a well-ventilated area. Do not allow the battery to come in contact with flames, sparks or burning substances. Avoid contact with skin, eyes or clothing. Shield eyes when working near the battery to protect against possible splashing of acid solution. In case of acid contact with skin or eyes, flush immediately with water for a minimum of 15 minutes, then get prompt medical attention. If acid is swallowed, call a physician immediately. Failure to follow these instructions may result in serious personal injury.

✲✲ WARNING

Always deplete the backup power supply before repairing or installing any new front or side air bag supplemental restraint system (SRS) component and before servicing, removing, installing, adjusting or striking components near the front or side impact sensors or the restraints control module (RCM). Nearby components include doors, instrument panel, console, door latches, strikers, seats and hood latches.

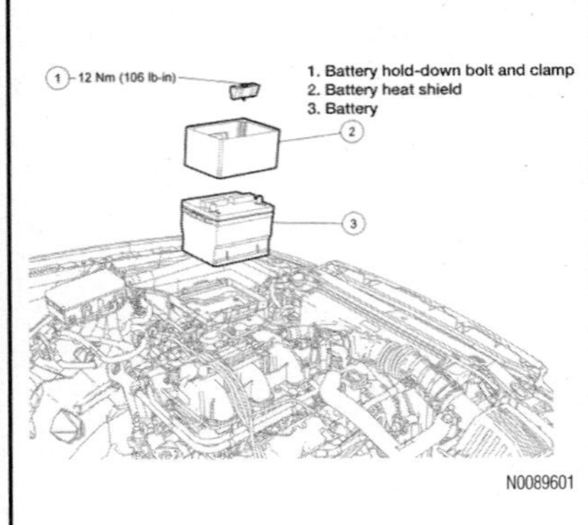

Fig. 60 Exploded view of the battery and tray

➡To deplete the backup power supply energy, disconnect the battery ground cable and wait at least 1 minute. Be sure to disconnect auxiliary batteries and power supplies (if equipped).

✲✲ WARNING

Failure to follow these instructions may result in serious personal injury or death in the event of an accidental deployment.

✲✲ WARNING

Always lift a plastic-cased battery with a battery carrier or with hands on opposite corners. Excessive pressure on the battery end walls may cause acid to flow through the vent caps, resulting in personal injury and/or damage to the vehicle or battery.

➡When the battery (or PCM) is disconnected and connected, some abnormal drive symptoms may occur while the vehicle relearns its adaptive strategy. The charging system setpoint may also vary. The vehicle may need to be driven to relearn its strategy.

1. Disconnect the battery.
2. Disconnect the battery ground cable.
3. Disconnect the positive battery cable.
4. Remove the bolt and the battery hold-down clamp.
5. Remove the battery.
6. To install, reverse the removal procedure.

BATTERY RECONNECT/RELEARN PROCEDURE

✲✲ WARNING

Batteries contain sulfuric acid and produce explosive gases. Work in a well-ventilated area. Do not allow the battery to come in contact with flames, sparks or burning substances. Avoid contact with skin, eyes or clothing. Shield eyes when working near the battery to protect against possible splashing of acid solution. In case of acid contact with skin or eyes, flush immediately with water for a minimum of 15 minutes, then get prompt medical attention. If acid is swallowed, call a physician immediately. Failure to follow these instructions may result in serious personal injury.

✲✲ WARNING

Always deplete the backup power supply before repairing or installing any new front or side air bag supplemental restraint system (SRS) component and before servicing, removing, installing, adjusting or striking components near the front or side impact sensors or the restraints control module (RCM). Nearby components include doors, instrument panel, console, door latches, strikers, seats and hood latches.

To deplete the backup power supply energy, disconnect the battery ground cable and wait at least 1 minute. Be sure to disconnect auxiliary batteries and power supplies (if equipped). Failure to follow these instructions may result in serious personal injury or death in the event of an accidental deployment.

✲✲ WARNING

Always lift a plastic-cased battery with a battery carrier or with hands on opposite corners. Excessive pressure on the battery end walls may cause acid to flow through the vent caps, resulting in personal injury and/or damage to the vehicle or battery.

➡When the battery (or PCM) is disconnected and connected, some abnormal drive symptoms may occur while the vehicle relearns its adaptive strategy. The charging system setpoint may also vary. The vehicle may need to be driven to relearn its strategy.

ALTERNATOR

REMOVAL & INSTALLATION

2.3L Engines

See Figure 61.

1. Disconnect the battery.
2. Remove the Air Cleaner (ACL) air cleaner outlet pipe.
3. Rotate the Front End Accessory Drive (FEAD) belt tensioner counterclockwise and position the accessory drive belt aside.
4. Remove the 2 bolts and position the alternator aside.
5. Disconnect the electrical connector from the alternator.
6. Position the protective cover aside, remove the nut and position the alternator B+ terminal aside.
7. Vehicles equipped with A/C; Remove the 2 bolts that secure the fan shroud and position the shroud aside.
8. Remove the alternator.
9. To install, reverse the removal procedure. Refer to the illustration for torque values.

4.0L Engines

See Figure 62.

1. Disconnect the battery.
2. Remove the Air Cleaner (ACL) outlet pipe.
3. Rotate the Front End Accessory Drive (FEAD) belt tensioner counterclockwise and position the accessory drive belt aside.
4. Disconnect the 2 electrical connectors from the alternator.
5. Position the protective cover aside, remove the nut and position the alternator B+ terminal aside.
6. Remove the 2 bolts from the alternator.
7. Remove the stud bolt, position the alternator harness bracket aside and remove the alternator.
8. To install, reverse the removal procedure. Refer to the illustration for torque values.

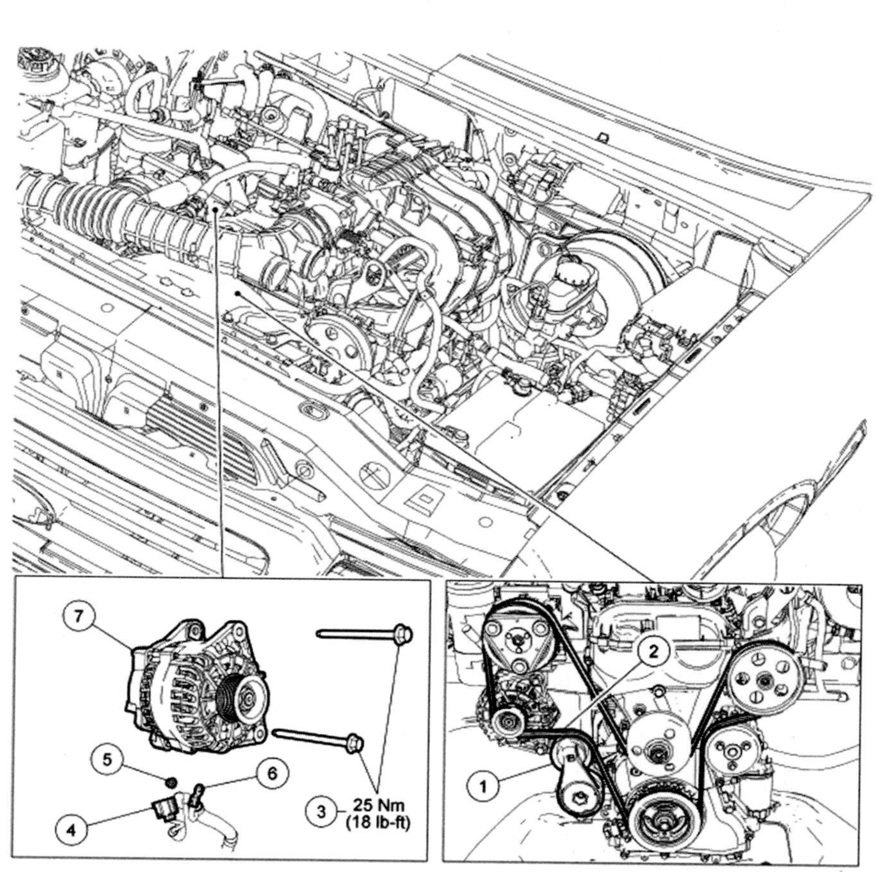

Fig. 61 Exploded view of the alternator and components—2.3L Engines

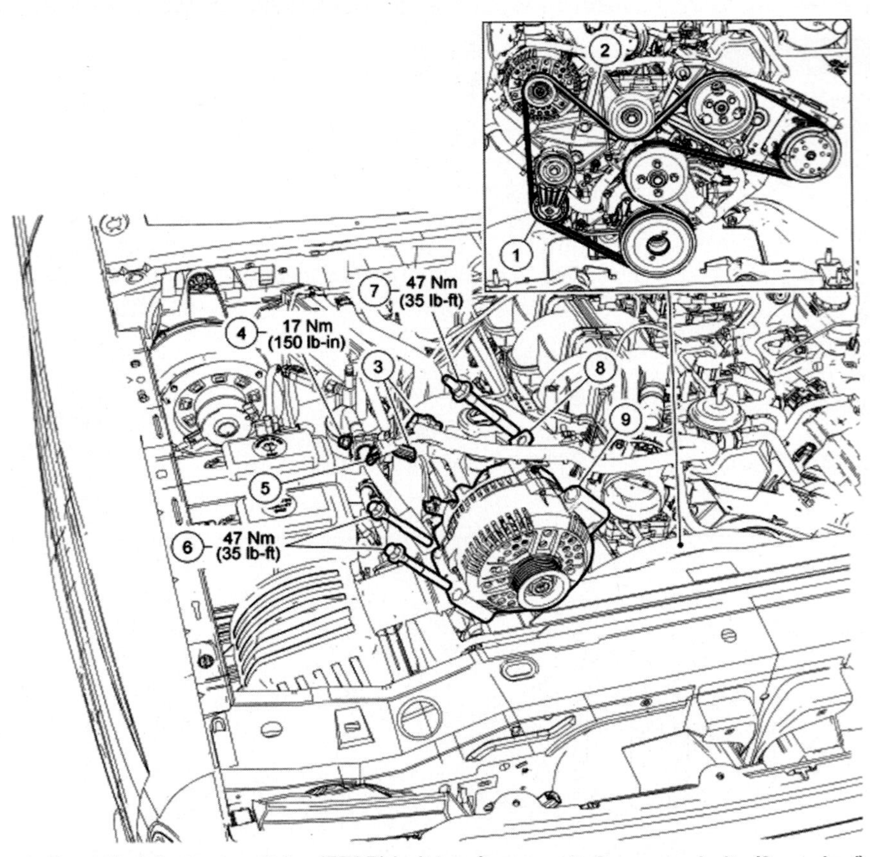

Fig. 62 Exploded view of the alternator and components—2.3L Engines

ENGINE ELECTRICAL

IGNITION SYSTEM

See Figures 63 and 64.

FIRING ORDER

4.0L engine: 1-4-2-5-3-6.

IGNITION COIL

REMOVAL & INSTALLATION

2.3L Engine

See Figure 65.

➡Do not pull on the spark plug wire as it may separate from the spark plug wire connector inside the spark plug wire boot.

➡Spark plug wires must be connected correctly. For additional information, refer to the Coil Terminal-to-Cylinder Relationship illustration. Failure to follow this instruction may result in poor engine performance.

1. Remove the spark plug wires by slightly twisting while pulling upwards.
2. Disconnect the ignition coil electrical connector.
3. Remove the 4 bolts and the ignition coil.

➡Wipe the coil towers with a clean cloth dampened with soap and water. Remove any soap film and dry with compressed air. Inspect for cracks, carbon tracking and dirt.

4. To install, reverse the removal procedure. Refer to the illustration for torque values.
5. Apply silicone dielectric compound to the inside of the spark plug wire boots prior to installation.

4.0L Engine

See Figure 66.

1. Disconnect the ignition coil electrical connector.

➡It is important to twist the spark plug wire boots while pulling upward, to avoid possible damage to the spark plug wire.

➡Spark plug wires must be connected to the correct ignition coil terminal. For additional information, refer to the Coil Terminal-to-Cylinder Relationship illustration. Failure to follow this instruction may result in poor engine performance.

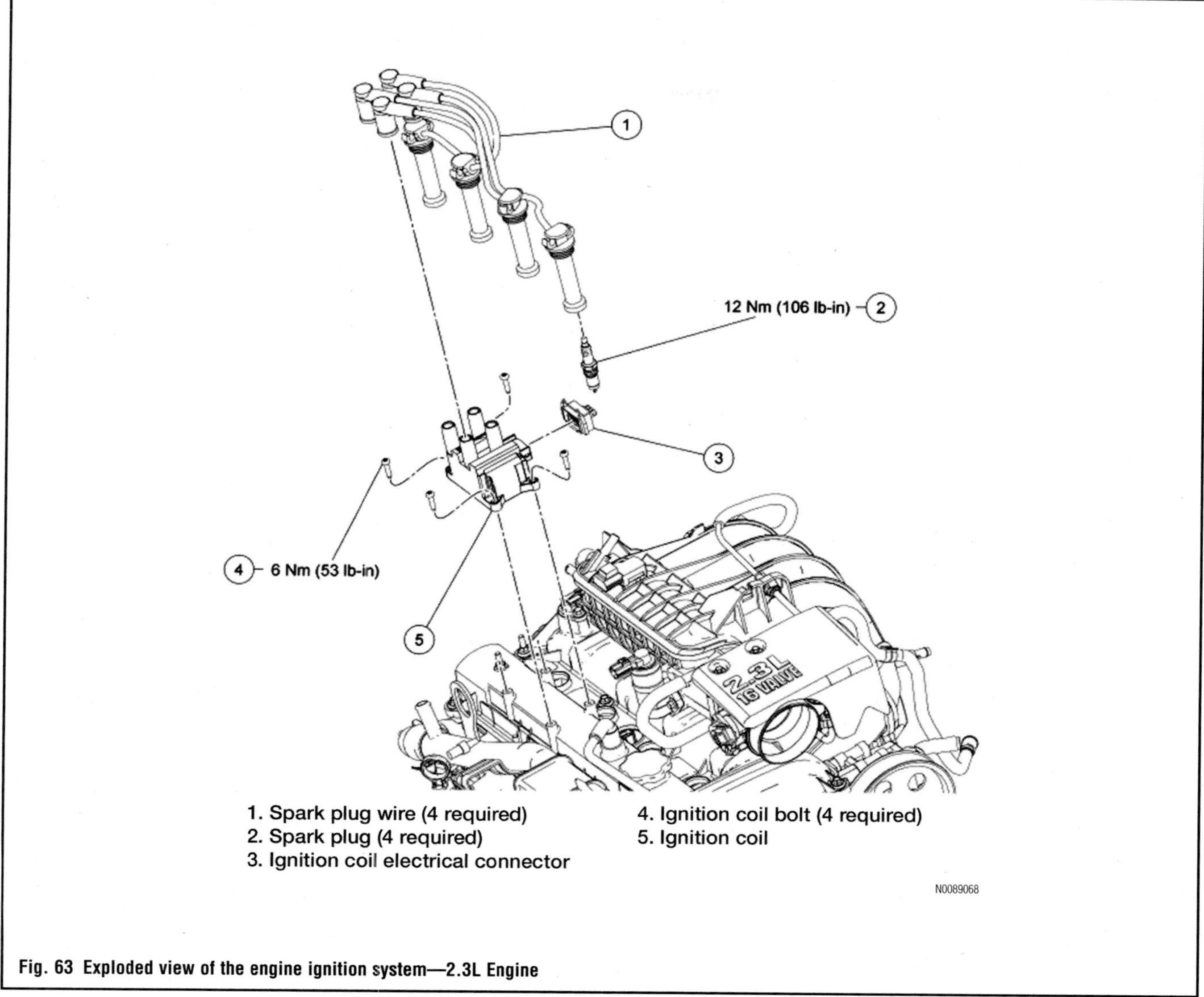

Fig. 63 Exploded view of the engine ignition system—2.3L Engine

2. Squeeze the locking tabs and twist while pulling upward, to disconnect the 6 spark plug wires from the ignition coil.
3. Remove the 4 bolts and the ignition coil.

➡Apply silicone dielectric compound to the inside of the spark plug wire coil boots.

➡Be sure to reinstall the radio ignition interference capacitor under the correct ignition coil mounting bolt.

4. To install, reverse the removal procedure. Refer to the illustration for torque values.

IGNITION TIMING

ADJUSTMENT

10 degrees Before Top Dead Center (BTDC) (not adjustable).

SPARK PLUGS

REMOVAL & INSTALLATION

1. Disconnect the negative battery cable.
2. Remove the ignition coil-on-plugs. For additional information, refer to Ignition Coil in this section.

➡Only use hand tools when removing or installing the spark plugs, or damage can occur to the cylinder head or spark plug.

➡Use compressed air to remove any foreign material from the spark plug well before removing the spark plugs.

3. Remove the spark plugs.
4. Inspect the spark plugs.
5. To install, reverse the removal procedure. Refer to the illustration for torque values.

INSPECTION

1. Inspect the spark plug for a bridged gap.
   a. Check for deposit build-up closing the gap between the electrodes. Deposits are caused by oil or carbon fouling.
   b. Install a new spark plug.
2. Check for oil fouling.
   a. Check for wet, black deposits on the insulator shell bore electrodes, caused by excessive oil entering the combustion chamber through worn rings and pistons, excessive valve-to-guide clearance or worn or loose bearings.
   b. Correct the oil leak concern.
   c. Install a new spark plug.
3. Inspect for carbon fouling. Look for black, dry, fluffy carbon deposits on the insulator tips, exposed shell surfaces and electrodes, caused by a spark plug

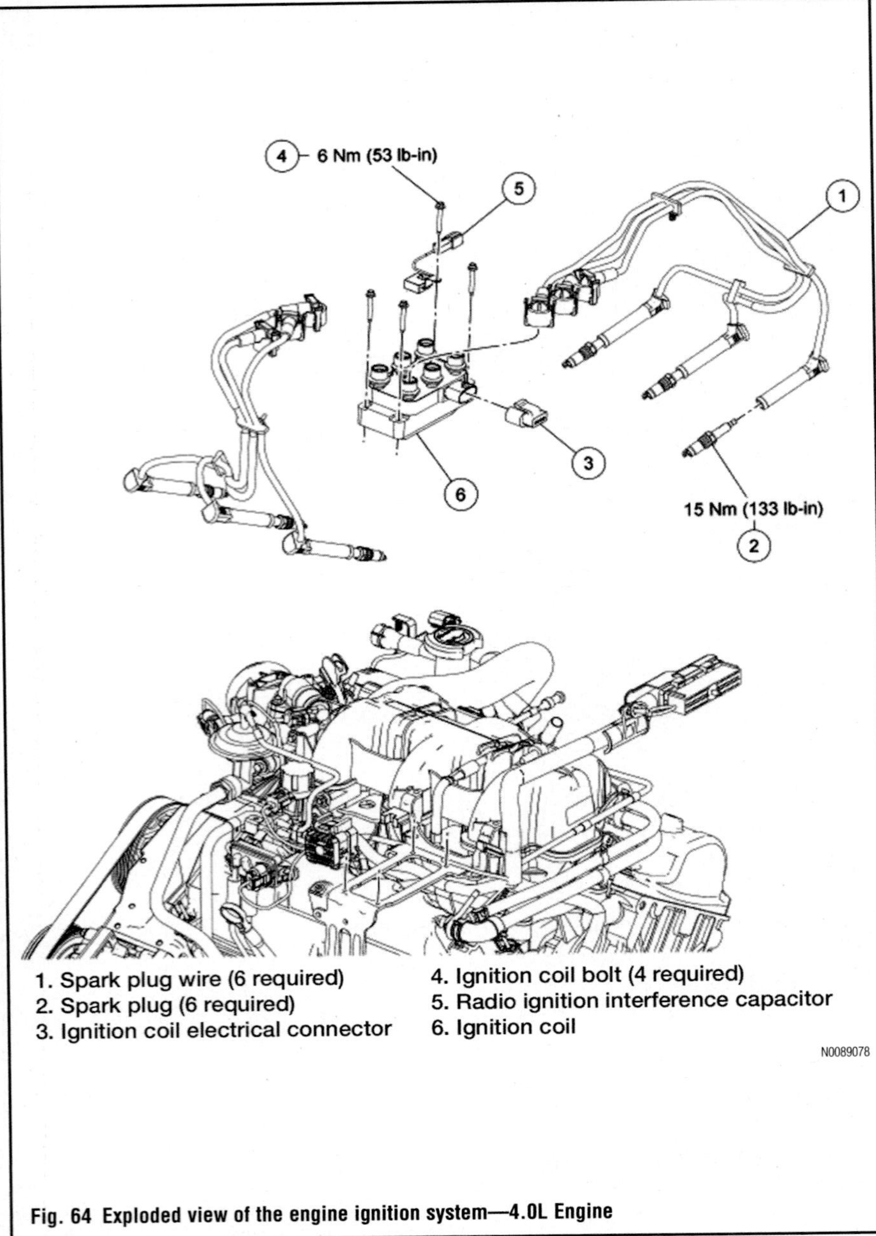

Fig. 64 Exploded view of the engine ignition system—4.0L Engine

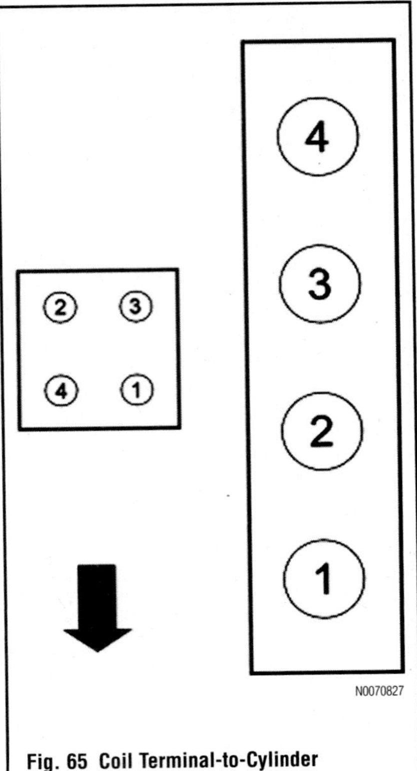

Fig. 65 Coil Terminal-to-Cylinder Relationship—2.3L Engine

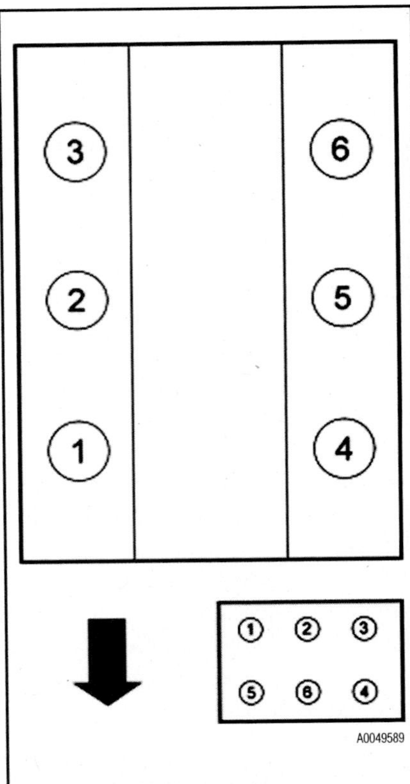

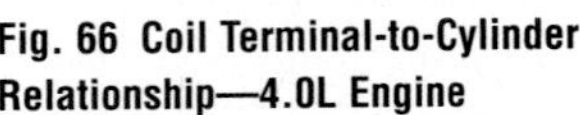

Fig. 66 Coil Terminal-to-Cylinder Relationship—4.0L Engine

with an incorrect heat range, dirty air cleaner, too rich a fuel mixture or excessive idling.

a. Install new spark plugs.

4. Inspect for normal burning.

a. Check for light tan or gray deposits on the firing tip.

5. Inspect for pre-ignition, identified by melted electrodes and a possibly damaged insulator. Metallic deposits on the insulator indicate engine damage. This may be caused by incorrect ignition timing, wrong type of fuel or the unauthorized installation of a heli-coil insert in place of the spark plug threads.

a. Install a new spark plug.

6. Inspect for overheating, identified by white or light gray spots and a bluish-burnt appearance of electrodes. This is caused by engine overheating, wrong type of fuel, loose spark plugs, spark plugs with an incorrect heat range, low fuel pump pressure or incorrect ignition timing.

a. Install a new spark plug.

7. Inspect for fused deposits, identified by melted or spotty deposits resembling bubbles or blisters. These are caused by sudden acceleration.

a. Install new spark plugs.

STARTER

REMOVAL & INSTALLATION

2.3L Engine

See Figure 67.

⁂ WARNING

Always disconnect the battery ground cable at the battery before disconnecting the starter motor battery terminal lead. If a tool is shorted at the starter motor battery terminal, the tool can quickly heat enough to cause a skin burn. Failure to follow this instruction may result in serious personal injury.

⁂ WARNING

With the vehicle in NEUTRAL, position it on a hoist.

1. Disconnect the battery ground cable.
2. Remove the LH front wheel and tire assembly.
3. Remove the 3 pushpins and the left front inner fender splash shield.
4. Remove the solenoid terminal cover from the terminals.
5. Remove the solenoid terminal nuts and disconnect the solenoid electrical connections.
6. Remove the ground cable retaining nut. Position the ground cable aside.
7. Remove the 2 starter motor stud bolts, the bolt and the starter motor.
8. To install, reverse the removal procedure. Refer to the illustration for torque values.

4.0L Engine

See Figure 68.

1. With the vehicle in NEUTRAL, position it on a hoist.

⁂ WARNING

Always disconnect the battery ground cable at the battery before disconnecting the starter motor battery terminal lead. If a tool is shorted at the starter motor battery terminal, the tool can quickly heat enough to cause a skin burn. Failure to follow this instruction may result in serious personal injury.

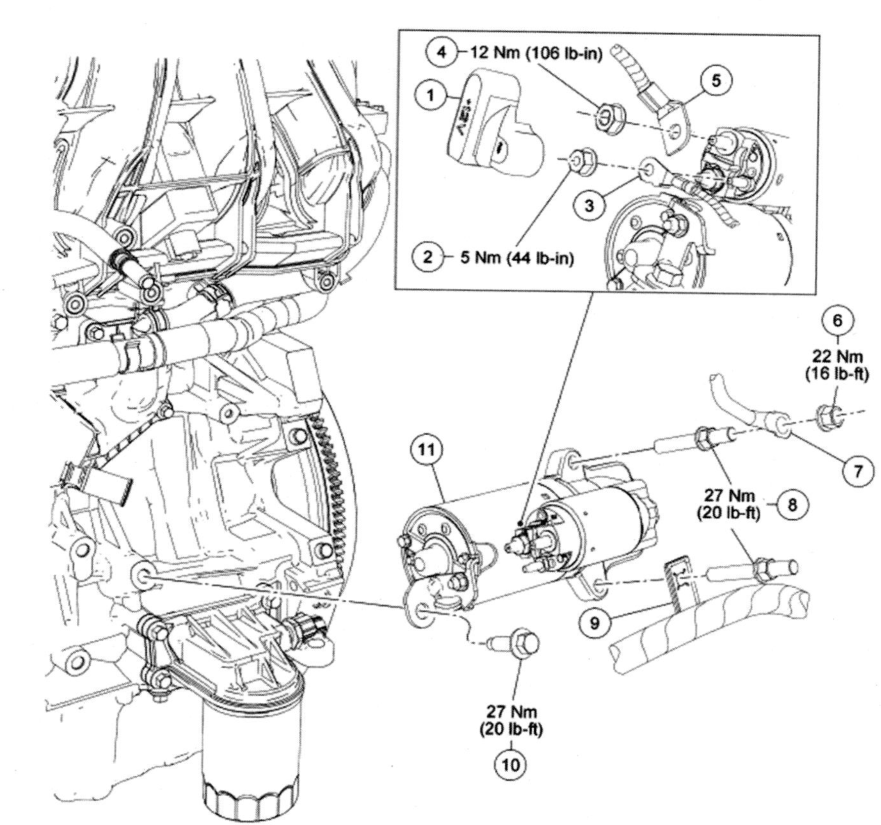

1. Starter solenoid terminal cover
2. Starter motor solenoid wire nut
3. Starter motor solenoid wire
4. Starter motor solenoid battery cable nut
5. Starter motor solenoid battery cable
6. Ground cable nut
7. Ground cable
8. Starter motor stud bolts (2 required)
9. Wiring harness retainer
10. Starter motor bolt
11. Starter motor

N0093046

Fig. 67 Exploded view of the starter assembly—2.3L Engines

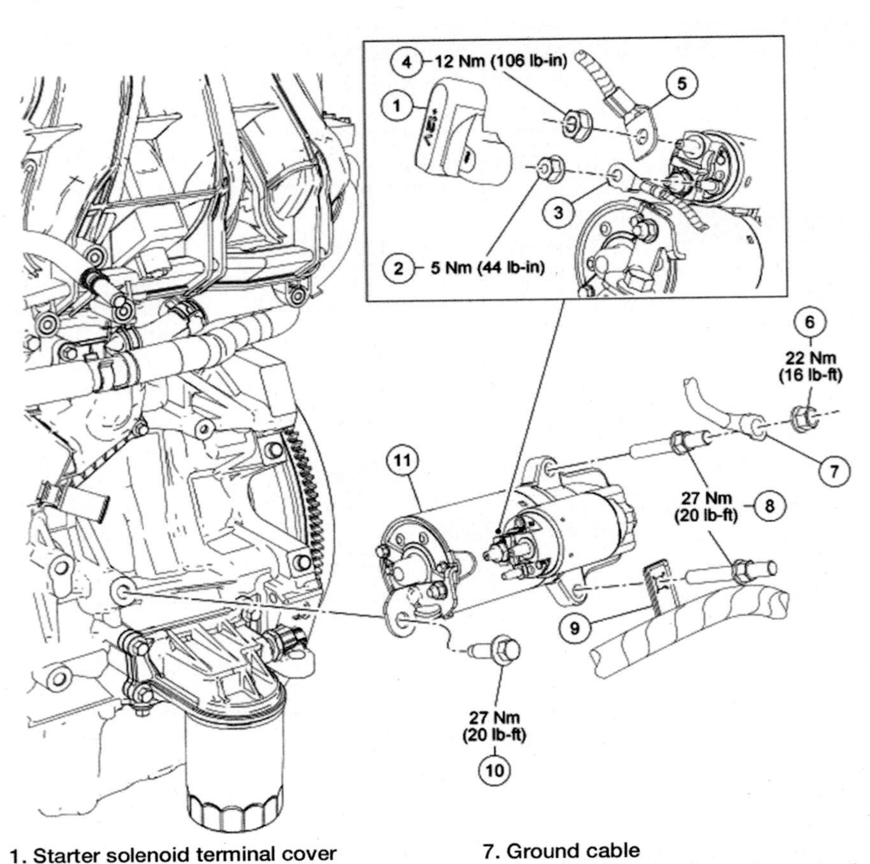

1. Starter solenoid terminal cover
2. Starter motor solenoid wire nut
3. Starter motor solenoid wire
4. Starter motor solenoid battery cable nut
5. Starter motor solenoid battery cable
6. Ground cable nut
7. Ground cable
8. Starter motor stud bolts (2 required)
9. Wiring harness retainer
10. Starter motor bolt
11. Starter motor

N0093046

Fig. 68 Exploded view of the starter assembly—4.0L Engines

2. Disconnect the battery ground cable.

➡A protective cap or boot is provided over the battery input terminal on all vehicle lines and must be reinstalled after repair. Failure to follow this instruction may result in damage to the vehicle.

3. Remove the starter motor solenoid terminal cover.
4. Remove the 2 nuts and disconnect the starter motor electrical connections.
5. Remove the nut and position the ground cable aside.
6. Remove the bolt, the stud bolt and the starter motor.
7. To install, tighten the bolts in the following sequence:
    a. Install the bolts finger-tight.
    b. Tighten the upper bolt.
    c. Tighten the lower stud bolt.
8. To install, reverse the removal procedure. Refer to the illustration for torque values.

ENGINE MECHANICAL

➡Disconnecting the negative battery cable may interfere with the functions of the on board computer systems and may require the computer to undergo a relearning process, once the negative battery cable is reconnected.

ACCESSORY DRIVE BELTS

ACCESSORY BELT ROUTING

See Figures 69 through 72.

Refer to the accompanying illustrations.

INSPECTION

Inspect for glazing, cracking, splitting, delaminating and shredding. Replace as necessary.

ADJUSTMENT

Adjustment is not possible or necessary.

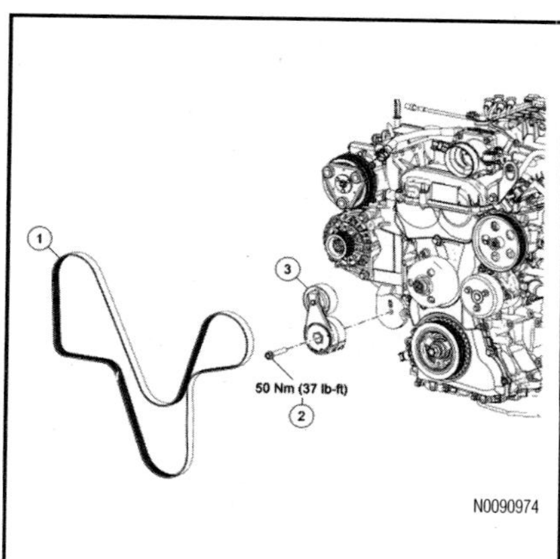

Fig. 69 Accessory belt routing—2.3L engines—With A/C

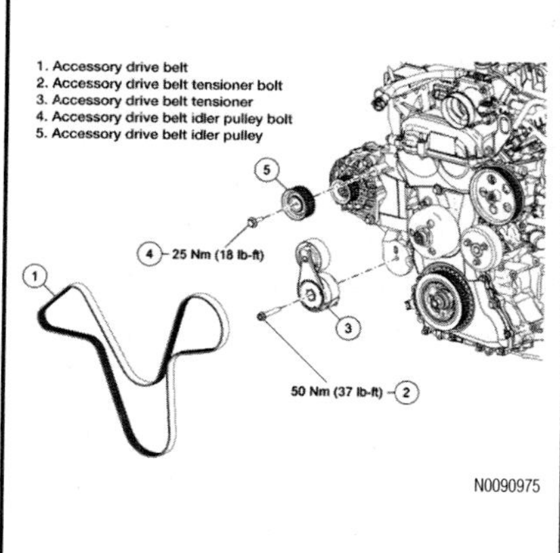

Fig. 70 Accessory belt routing—2.3L engines—Without A/C

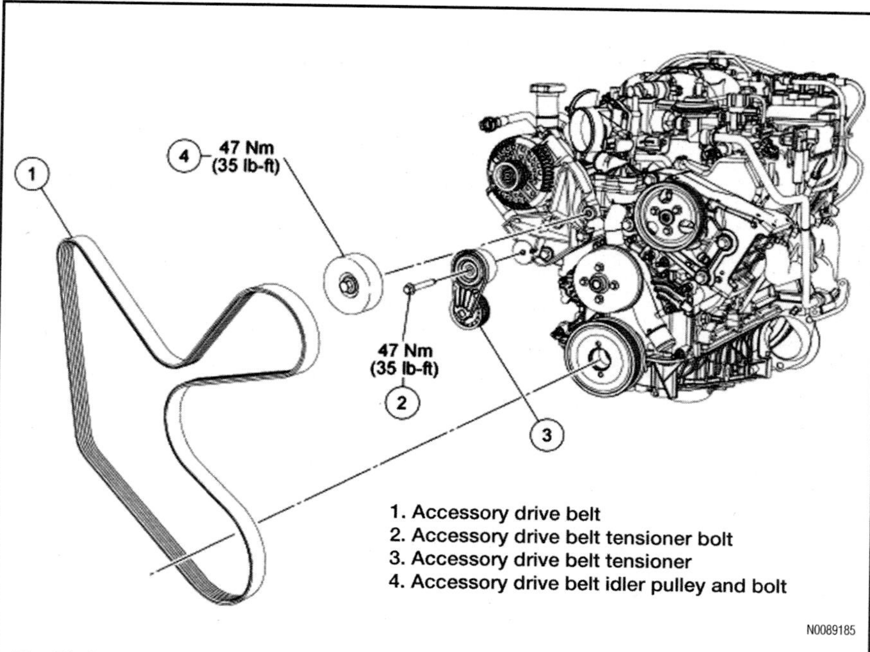

Fig. 71 Accessory belt routing—4.0L engines—Without A/C

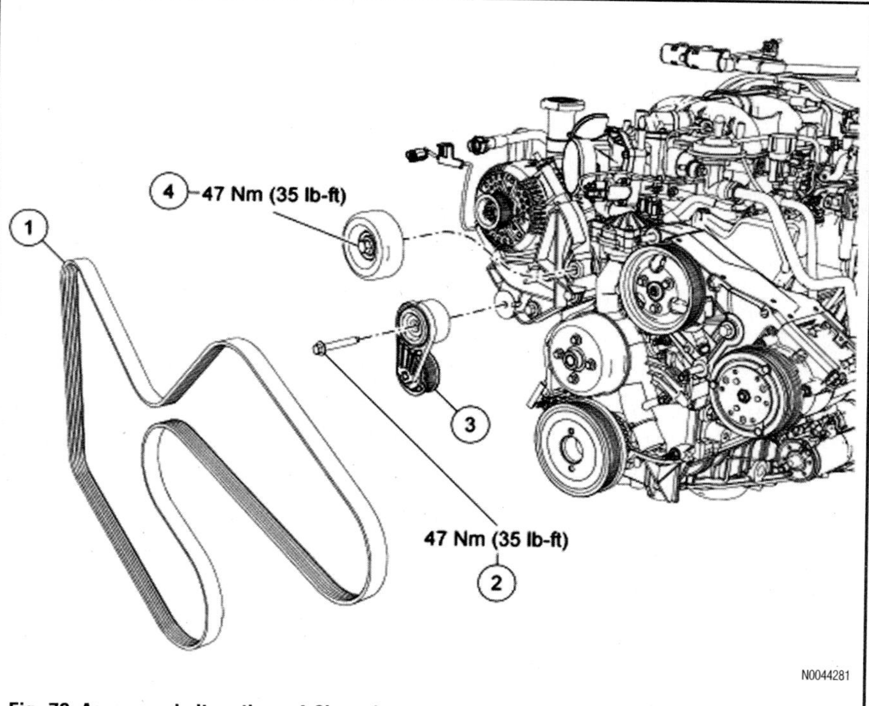

Fig. 72 Accessory belt routing—4.0L engines—With A/C

REMOVAL & INSTALLATION

1. Rotate the tensioner clockwise and remove the accessory drive belt.
2. To install, reverse the removal procedure.

AIR CLEANER

REMOVAL & INSTALLATION

See Figure 73.

1. Refer to the illustration to remove the air cleaner assembly.

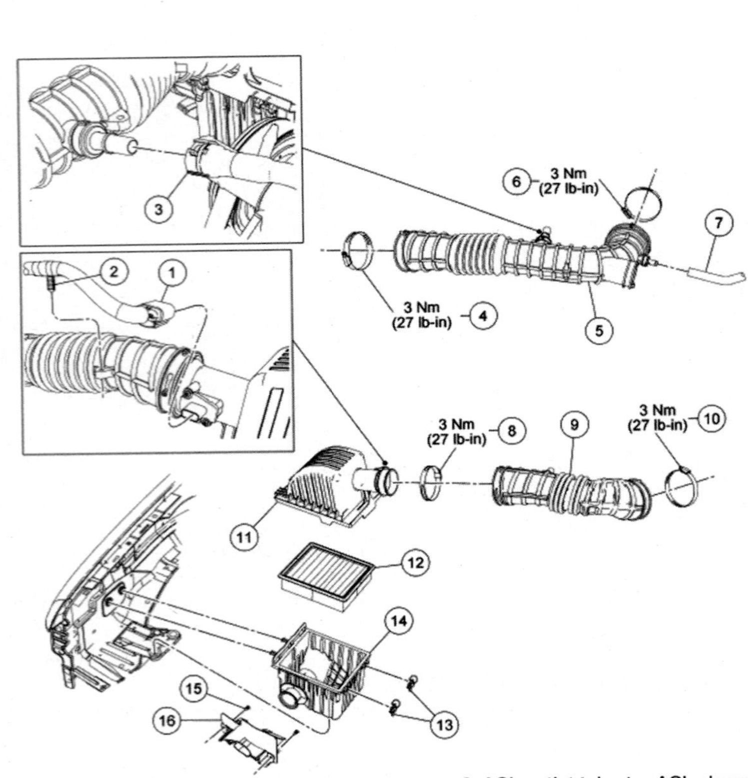

1. Mass Air Flow (MAF) sensor electrical connector
2. Wiring harness retainer. 2 required for 2.3L engines. 1 required for 4.0L engines
3. Crankcase ventilation tube quick connect coupling
4. Air Cleaner (ACL) outlet tube-to- ACL clamp (2.3L)
5. ACL outlet tube (2.3L)
6. ACL outlet tube-to-Throttle Body (TB) clamp (2.3L)
7. Brake booster vacuum hose
8. ACL outlet tube-to- ACL clamp (4.0L)
9. ACL outlet tube (4.0L)
10. ACL outlet tube-to- TB clamp (4.0L)
11. ACL cover
12. ACL element
13. ACL -to- ACL cover clips (2 required)
14. ACL
15. Air nozzle pushpin (2 required)
16. Air nozzle

N0091845

Fig. 73 Exploded view of the air cleaner assembly

2. If necessary, pry the engine Air Cleaner (ACL) from the base support bracket when removing the ACL.

FILTER/ELEMENT REPLACEMENT

1. Release the 2 Air Cleaner (ACL) cover retaining clips from the ACL cover.
2. Lift the ACL cover and remove the ACL element.
3. Installation:
   a. Lift the ACL cover and install the ACL element.

➡It is important that all hinge features are fully engaged from the cover to the tray after servicing the air filter element.

   b. Install the 2 ACL cover retaining clips to the ACL cover.

CAMSHAFT AND VALVE LIFTERS

INSPECTION

Camshaft Bearing Journal Diameter

See Figure 74.

➡Refer to the spec charts for specifications.

Camshaft End Play

See Figure 75.

➡Refer to the spec charts for specifications.

1. Using the Dial Indicator Gauge with Holding Fixture, measure the camshaft end play.

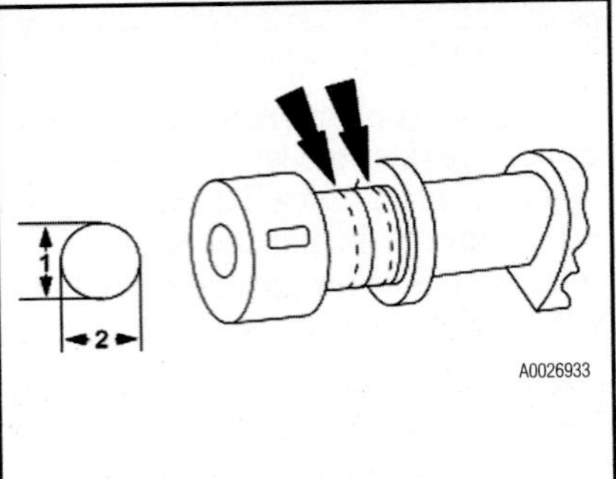

Fig. 74 Measure each camshaft journal diameter in 2 directions.

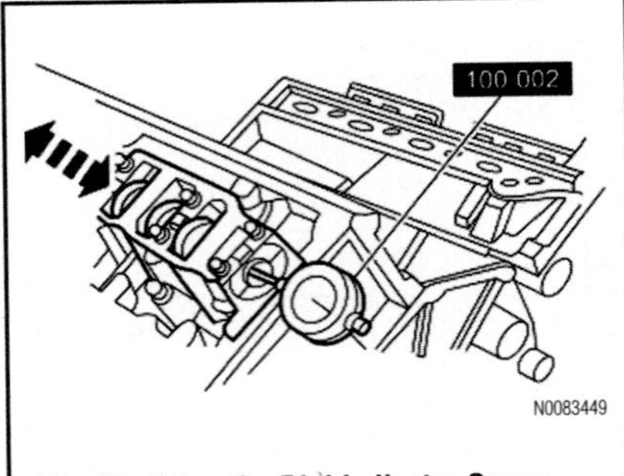

Fig. 75 Using the Dial Indicator Gauge with Holding Fixture, measure the camshaft end play

2. Position the camshaft to the rear of the cylinder head.
3. Zero the Dial Indicator Gauge.
4. Move the camshaft to the front of the cylinder head. Note and record the camshaft end play.
5. If camshaft end play exceeds specifications, install a new camshaft and recheck end play.
6. If camshaft end play exceeds specification after camshaft installation, install a new cylinder head.

Camshaft Journal To Bearing Clearance

See Figure 76.

➡Refer to the spec charts for specifications.

➡The camshaft journals must meet specifications before checking camshaft journal clearance.

1. Measure each camshaft bearing in 2 directions.
2. Subtract the camshaft journal diameter from the camshaft bearing diameter.

Camshaft Lobe Lift

See Figure 77.

➡Refer to the spec charts for specifications.

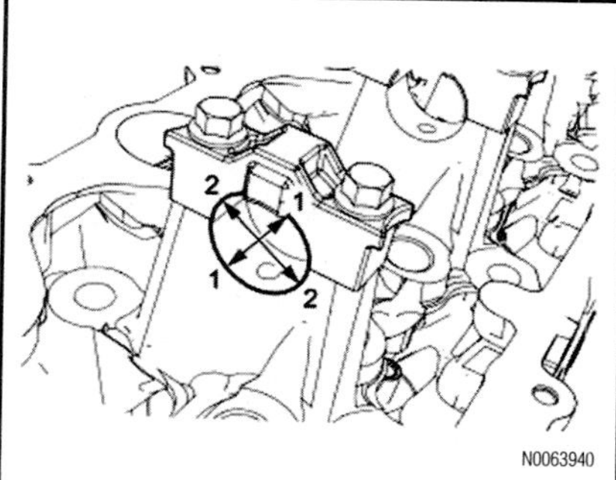

Fig. 76 Subtract the camshaft journal diameter from the camshaft bearing diameter.

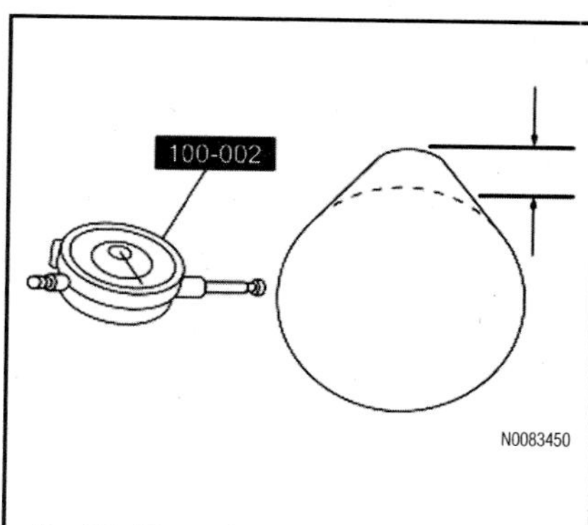

Fig. 77 Measuring camshaft intake/exhaust lobe lift

1. Use the Dial Indicator Gauge with Holding Fixture to measure camshaft intake/exhaust lobe lift.
2. Rotate the camshaft and subtract the lowest Dial Indicator Gauge reading from the highest Dial Indicator Gauge reading to figure the camshaft lobe lift.

Camshaft Runout

See Figures 78 and 79.

➡Refer to the spec charts for specifications.

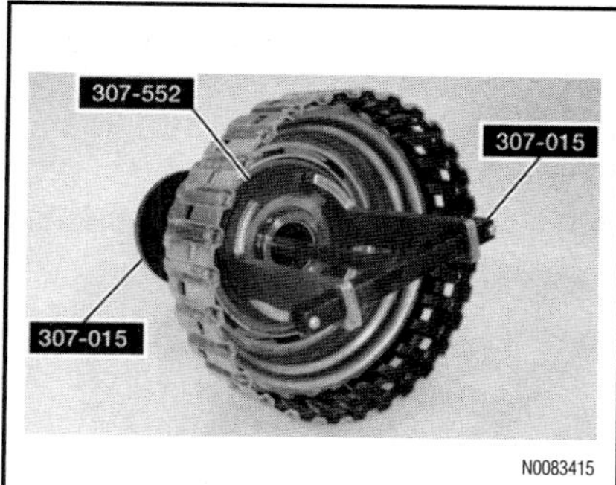

Fig. 78 Using the Dial Indicator Gauge with Holding Fixture, measure the camshaft runout

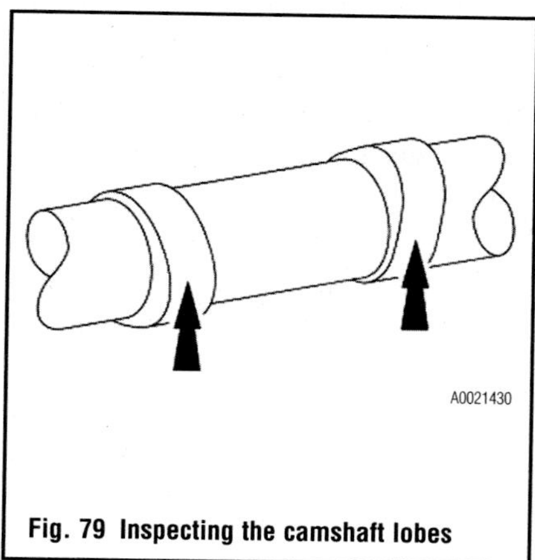

Fig. 79 Inspecting the camshaft lobes

➡Camshaft journals must be within specifications before checking runout.

1. Using the Dial Indicator Gauge with Holding Fixture, measure the camshaft runout.
2. Rotate the camshaft and subtract the lowest Dial Indicator Gauge reading from the highest Dial Indicator Gauge reading.

Camshaft Surface Inspection

Inspect the camshaft lobes for pitting or damage in the contact area. Minor pitting is acceptable outside the contact area.

REMOVAL & INSTALLATION

2.3L Engines

See Figures 80 and 81.

➡Do not loosen or remove the crankshaft pulley bolt without first installing the special tools as instructed in the crankshaft pulley procedure. The crankshaft pulley and the crankshaft timing sprocket are not keyed to the crankshaft. The crankshaft, the crankshaft sprocket and the pulley are fitted together by friction, using diamond washers between the flange faces on each part. For that reason, the crankshaft sprocket is also unfastened if the pulley bolt is loosened. Before any repair requiring loosening or removal of the crankshaft pulley bolt, the crankshaft and camshafts must be locked in place by the special tools, otherwise severe engine damage may occur.

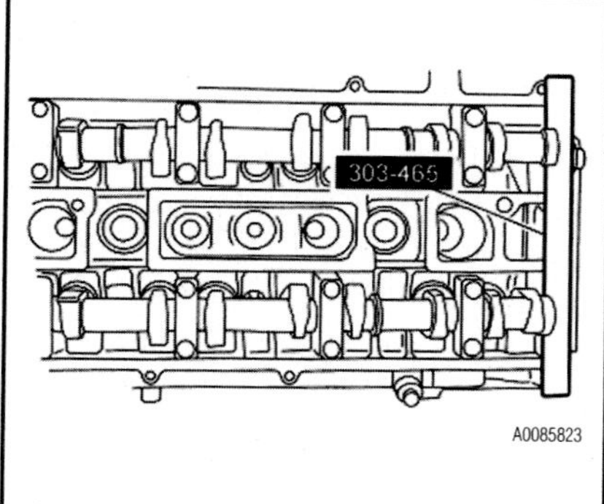

Fig. 80 Remove the Camshaft Alignment Plate

1. Remove the timing chain and sprockets. For additional information, refer to Timing Chain in this section.
2. Remove the Camshaft Alignment Plate.

➡Failure to follow the camshaft loosening procedure may result in damage to the camshafts.

➡Mark the location and orientation of each camshaft bearing cap.

➡Note the position of the lobes on the No. 1 cylinder before removing the camshafts for assembly reference.

3. Remove the camshafts from the engine.
4. Loosen the 20 camshaft bearing cap bolts, in sequence, one turn at a time.
5. Repeat the first step until all tension is released from the camshaft bearing caps.
6. Remove the 10 camshaft bearing caps.
7. Remove the 2 camshafts.

To install:

➡Install the camshafts with the alignment slots in the camshafts lined up so the Camshaft Alignment Plate can be installed without rotating the camshafts. Make sure the lobes on the No. 1 cylinder are in the same position as noted in the removal procedure. Rotating the camshafts when the timing chain is removed, or installing the camshafts 180 degrees out of position, may cause severe damage to the valves and pistons.

➡Lubricate the camshaft journals and bearing caps with clean engine oil prior to installation.

8. Position the camshafts and bearing caps in their original location and orientation. Loosely install the 20 bolts and tighten the bearing caps in the sequence shown in 3 stages:
   a. Stage 1: Tighten the camshaft bearing cap bolts one turn at a time until snug.
   b. Stage 2: Tighten the bolts to 72 inch lbs. (7 Nm).
   c. Stage 3: Tighten the bolts to 11 ft. lbs. (16 Nm).

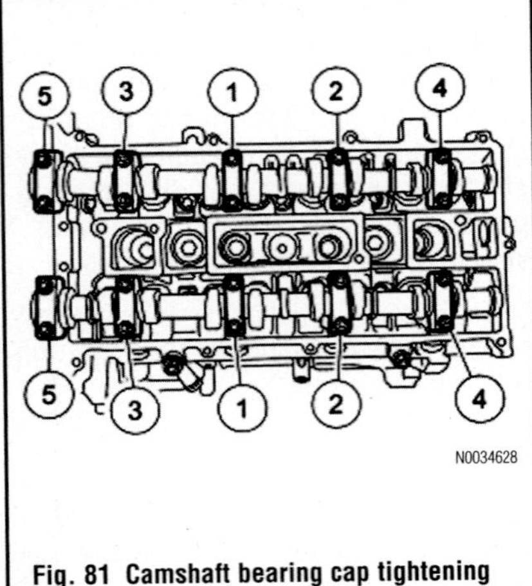

Fig. 81 Camshaft bearing cap tightening sequence

9. Install the timing chain and sprockets.

4.0L Engine

Roller Follower

See Figures 82 and 83.

1. With the vehicle in NEUTRAL, position it on a hoist.
2. Remove the valve covers. For additional information, refer to Valve Cover in this section.
3. Remove the engine fan.
4. Rotate the crankshaft until the camshaft for the cylinder being serviced is at base circle.

➡Mark each camshaft roller follower to make sure it is returned to its original position.

5. Using the Valve Spring Compressor, remove the camshaft roller followers.

➡The camshaft roller followers must be installed in their original positions.

➡Lubricate the camshaft roller followers with clean engine oil.

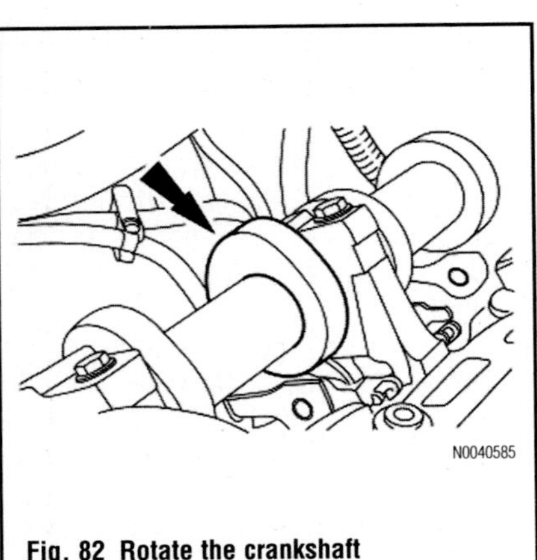

Fig. 82 Rotate the crankshaft

Fig. 83 Using the Valve Spring Compressor

6. To install, reverse the removal procedure.

Camshaft

See Figures 84 through 87.

1. Remove the camshaft roller followers.
2. Remove the RH hydraulic chain tensioner. For additional information, refer to Timing Chain.
3. RH side:
   a. Install the Camshaft Sprocket Holding Tool and Adapter on the rear of the RH cylinder head and tighten the top 2 clamp bolts to 89 inch lbs.

➡The RH camshaft sprocket is a LH-threaded bolt. Turning the bolt in the wrong direction can damage the bolt.

   b. Using the Torque Wrench Extension and the Camshaft Sprocket Nut Socket 303-565, loosen the camshaft sprocket bolt.
   c. Remove the camshaft sprocket bolt and position the RH camshaft sprocket aside.
4. LH side:
   a. Install the Camshaft Sprocket Holding Tool and Adapter on the front of the LH camshaft and tighten the 2 top clamp bolts to 89 inch lbs. (10 Nm).
   b. Loosen the camshaft sprocket bolt.
   c. Remove the bolt and position the LH camshaft sprocket aside.
5. Both sides:

➡Mark the position of the camshaft bearing caps so they can be installed in their original positions.

6. Remove the bolts in the sequence shown and remove the camshaft bearing caps.
7. Remove the camshaft.

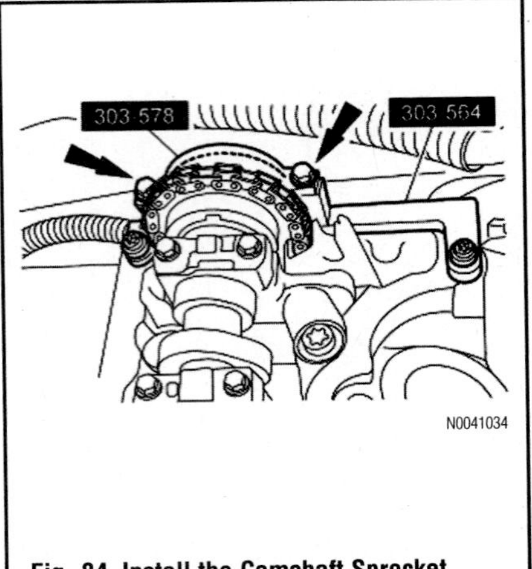

Fig. 84 Install the Camshaft Sprocket Holding Tool and Adapter

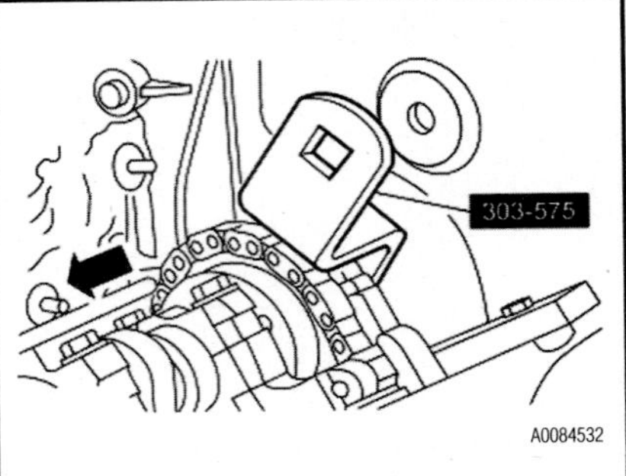

Fig. 85 Using the Torque Wrench Extension and the Camshaft Sprocket Nut Socket 303-565

To install:

8. Both sides:

➡Lubricate the camshafts with clean engine oil.

9. Install the camshaft.

➡Lubricate the camshaft bearing caps with clean engine oil.

➡The camshaft bearing caps must be installed in their original positions.

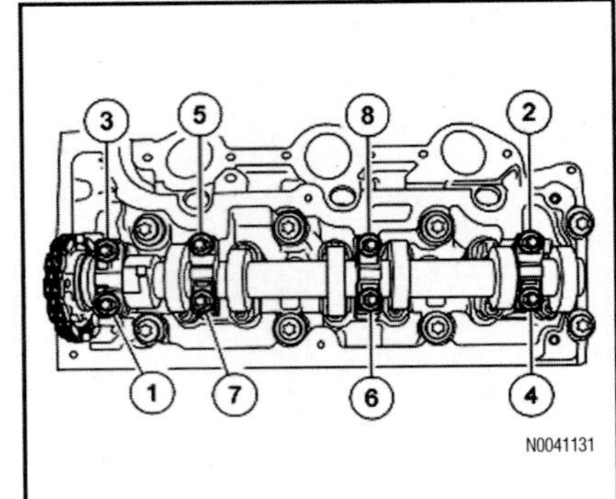

Fig. 86 Remove the bolts in the sequence shown

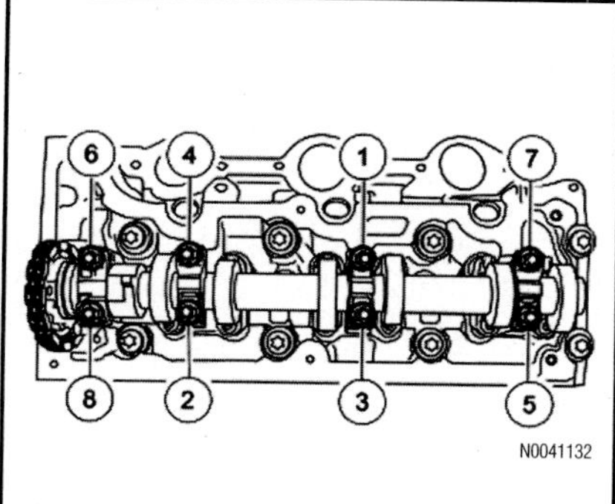

Fig. 87 Tighten the bolts in the sequence shown

➡After installing the bolts, check the camshaft for free rotation.

10. Install the camshaft bearing caps and the bolts.
11. Tighten the bolts in the sequence shown in 2 stages.
    a. Stage 1: Tighten to 53 inch lbs. (6 Nm).
    b. Stage 2: Tighten to 11 ft. lbs (16 Nm).
12. RH side:

➡The camshaft gear must turn freely on the camshaft. Do not tighten the bolt at this time.

    a. Install the RH camshaft sprocket and loosely install the bolt.
13. LH side:

➡The camshaft gear must turn freely on the camshaft. Do not tighten the bolt at this time.

    a. Install the LH camshaft sprocket and loosely install the bolt.
14. Both sides:
15. Retime the camshafts. For additional information, refer to Camshaft Timing in this section.
16. Install the camshaft roller followers.

Camshaft Timing

See Figures 88 through 90.

1. Remove the camshaft roller followers. For additional information, refer to Camshaft in this section.

➡The LH and RH camshafts must be retimed when either camshaft is disturbed.

2. Turn the crankshaft clockwise to position the No. 1 cylinder at Top Dead Center (TDC).

➡Do not rotate the engine counterclockwise. Rotating the engine counterclockwise will result in damage to the damper crank sensor speed wheel and incorrect timing of the engine.

3. If equipped, remove the nut and position the A/C hose aside.
4. Install the Crankshaft TDC Timing Tool on the crankshaft pulley timing ring.

➡While turning the crankshaft pulley, take care to not overturn the crankshaft pulley or damage to the crankshaft pulley timing ring may occur.

➡The Crankshaft TDC Timing Tool must be installed on the crankshaft pulley and should contact the engine block. This positions the engine at TDC.

5. Using the Strap Wrench, slowly turn the crankshaft counterclockwise until the TDC Timing Tool contacts the engine block in the slot
6. Install the Camshaft Sprocket Holding Tool and Adapter to the RH cylinder head and tighten the 2 top clamp bolts. Tighten to 7 ft. lbs. (10 Nm).

➡The RH camshaft sprocket bolt is a LH-threaded bolt.

7. Using the Torque Wrench Extension with the Camshaft Sprocket Nut Socket 303-565, loosen the RH camshaft sprocket bolt.
8. Loosen the top 2 Camshaft Sprocket Holding Tool clamp bolts.

➡The camshaft timing slots are off-center.

9. Position the camshaft timing slots below the centerline of the camshaft to correctly fit the Adapter and install the Camshaft Holding Tool and Adapter on the front of the RH cylinder head.
10. Remove the RH camshaft tensioner. Remove and discard the washer.
11. Install the Timing Chain Tensioner.

Fig. 88 Correctly fit the Adapter and install the Camshaft Holding Tool and Adapter

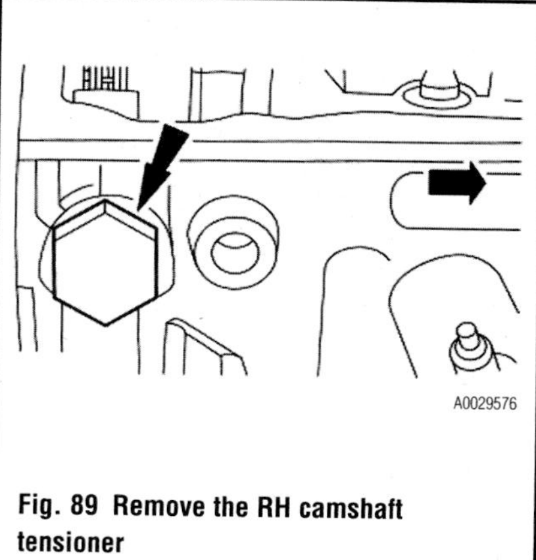

Fig. 89 Remove the RH camshaft tensioner

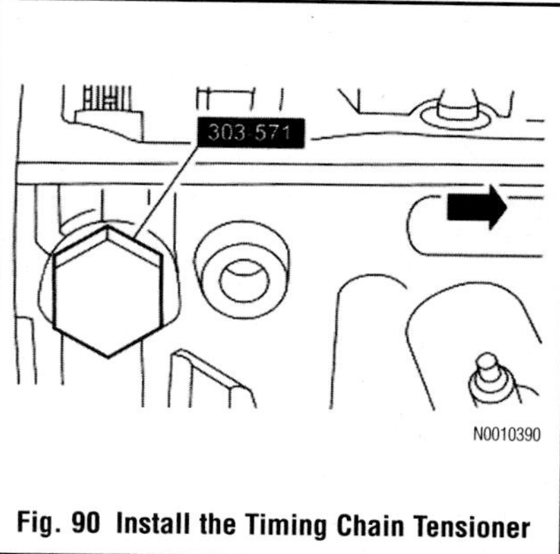

Fig. 90 Install the Timing Chain Tensioner

➡The RH camshaft sprocket bolt is a LH-threaded bolt.

12. Tighten the bolts.
13. Tighten the Camshaft Sprocket Holding Tool top 2 clamp bolts to 89 inch lbs. (10 Nm).
14. Using the Torque Wrench Extension with the Camshaft Sprocket Nut Socket 303-565, tighten the camshaft bolt.
15. Remove the Timing Chain Tensioner.

➡Install a new washer on the tensioner.

16. Install the RH camshaft tensioner. Tighten to 32 ft. lbs. (44 Nm).
17. Install the Camshaft Sprocket Holding Tool and Adapter on the front of the LH cylinder head and tighten the top 2 clamp bolts. Tighten to 7 ft. lbs. (10 Nm).
18. Loosen the LH camshaft sprocket bolt.
19. Loosen the top 2 clamp bolts on the Camshaft Sprocket Holding Tool to allow the camshaft sprocket to rotate freely.

➡The camshaft timing slots are off-center.

20. Position the camshaft timing slots below the centerline of the camshaft to

correctly fit the Adapter, and install the Camshaft Holding Tool and Adapter on the rear of the LH cylinder head.

21. Remove the LH camshaft tensioner.
22. Remove and discard the washer.
23. Install the Timing Chain Tensioner.
24. Tighten the bolts.
    a. Tighten the Camshaft Sprocket Holding Tool top 2 clamp bolts to 7 ft. lbs (10 Nm).
    b. Tighten the LH camshaft bolt to 63 ft. lbs. (85 Nm).
25. Remove the Timing Chain Tensioner.

➡Install a new washer on the tensioner.

26. Install the LH camshaft tensioner. Tighten to 32 ft. lbs. (44 Nm).
27. Install the camshaft roller followers. For additional information, refer to Camshaft in this section.

CATALYTIC CONVERTER

REMOVAL & INSTALLATION

See Figures 91 and 92.

➡Exhaust system will vary by wheelbase. Vehicle body removed from art for clarity.

Refer to the appropriate illustrations to remove the catalytic converter.

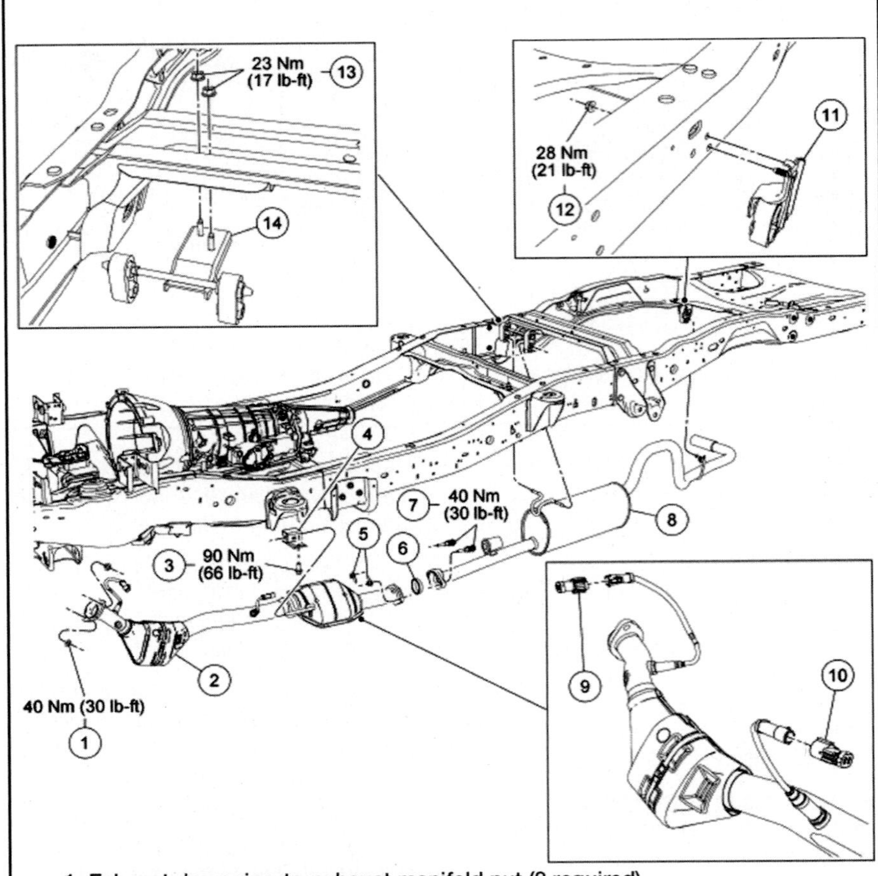

1. Exhaust downpipe-to-exhaust manifold nut (2 required)
2. Exhaust downpipe
3. Transmission mount and isolator-to-transmission bolt
4. Exhaust isolator
5. Exhaust downpipe-to-muffler and tail pipe assembly flag nuts (2 required)
6. Exhaust downpipe-to-muffler and tail pipe assembly gasket
7. Exhaust downpipe-to-muffler and tail pipe assembly bolts (2 required)
8. Muffler and tail pipe assembly
9. Heated Oxygen Sensor (HO2S) electrical connector
10. Catalyst Monitor Sensor (CMS) electrical connector
11. Tail pipe bracket and isolator assembly
12. Tail pipe bracket and isolator assembly nut
13. Muffler bracket and isolators assembly nuts (2 required)
14. Muffler bracket and isolators assembly

N0105561

Fig. 91 Exploded view of the exhaust system—2.3L engines

CRANKSHAFT FRONT SEAL

REMOVAL & INSTALLATION

2.3L Engine

See Figures 93 and 94.

➡Do not loosen or remove the crankshaft pulley bolt without first installing the special tools as instructed in the crankshaft pulley procedure. The crankshaft pulley and the crankshaft timing sprocket are not keyed to the crankshaft. The crankshaft, the crankshaft sprocket and the pulley are fitted together by friction, using diamond washers between the flange faces on each part. For that reason, the crankshaft sprocket is also unfastened if the pulley bolt is loosened. Before any repair requiring loosening or removal of the crankshaft pulley bolt, the crankshaft and camshafts must be locked in place by the special tools, otherwise severe engine damage can occur.

1. Remove the crankshaft pulley. For additional information, refer to Timing Chain in this section.

➡Use care not to damage the engine front cover or the crankshaft when removing the seal, or oil leakage may occur.

2. Using the Crankshaft Front Oil Seal Remover, remove the crankshaft front seal.

To install:

3. Lubricate the engine front cover and the crankshaft front seal inner lip with clean engine oil.
4. Using the Crankshaft Front Oil Seal Installer, install the crankshaft front seal into the engine front cover.
5. Install the crankshaft pulley.

4.0L Engine

See Figures 95 and 96.

1. Remove the crankshaft pulley. For additional information, refer to Timing Chain in this section.
2. Using the Crankshaft Front Oil Seal Remover, remove and discard the crankshaft front seal.

To install:

➡Lubricate the new front seal with clean engine oil.

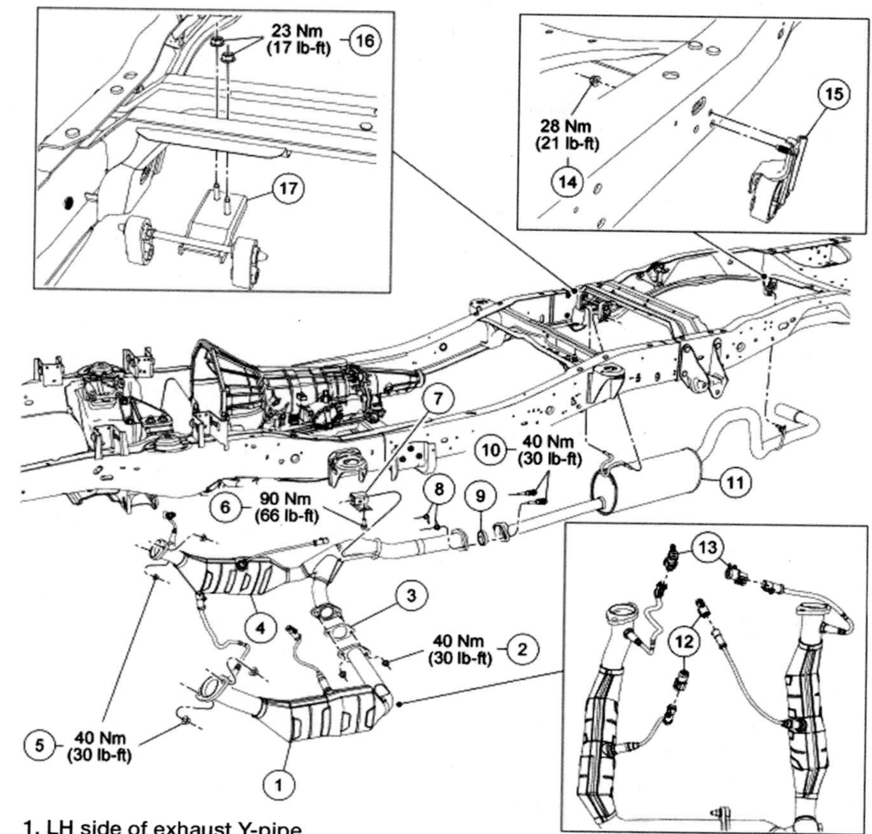

1. LH side of exhaust Y-pipe
2. LH side of exhaust Y-pipe-to-RH side of exhaust Y-pipe nut (2 required)
3. LH side of exhaust Y-pipe-to-RH side of exhaust Y-pipe gasket
4. RH side of exhaust Y-pipe
5. Exhaust Y-pipe assembly-to-exhaust manifold nuts (4 required)
6. Transmission mount and isolator-to-transmission bolt
7. Exhaust isolator
8. RH side of exhaust Y-pipe-to-muffler and tail pipe assembly flagnuts (2 required)
9. RH side of exhaust Y-pipe-to-muffler and tail pipe assembly gasket
10. RH side of exhaust Y-pipe-to-muffler and tail pipe assembly bolts (2 required)
11. Muffler and tail pipe assembly
12. Catalyst Monitor Sensor (CMS) electrical connectors
13. Heated Oxygen Sensor (HO2S) electrical connectors
14. Tail pipe bracket and isolator assembly nut
15. Tail pipe bracket and isolator assembly
16. Muffler bracket and isolators assembly nuts (2 required)
17. Muffler bracket and isolators assembly

N0093089

Fig. 92 Exploded view of the exhaust system—4.0L engines

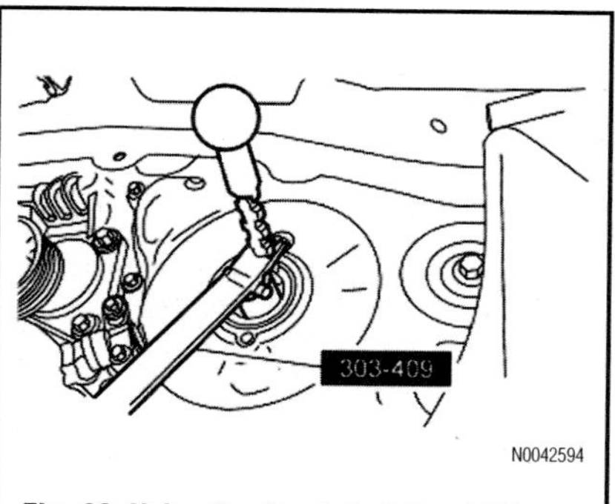

Fig. 93 Using the Crankshaft Front Oil Seal Remover

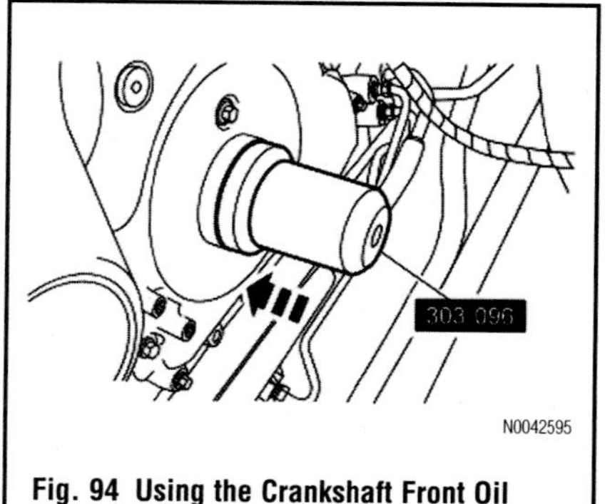

Fig. 94 Using the Crankshaft Front Oil Seal Installer

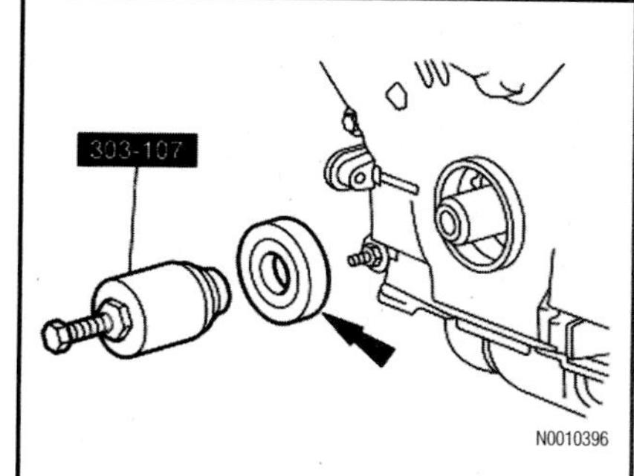

Fig. 95 Using the Crankshaft Front Oil Seal Remover

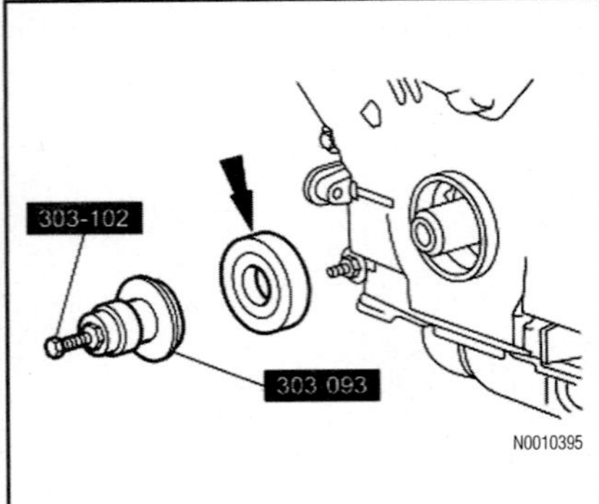

Fig. 96 Using the Front Cover Aligner and Crankshaft Vibration Damper Installer

3. Using the Front Cover Aligner and Crankshaft Vibration Damper Installer, install a new crankshaft front seal.
4. Install the crankshaft pulley.

CYLINDER HEAD

REMOVAL & INSTALLATION

2.3L Engines

See Figures 97 through 99.

1. Do not loosen or remove the crankshaft pulley bolt without first installing the special tools as instructed in the crankshaft pulley procedure. The crankshaft pulley and the crankshaft timing sprocket are not keyed to the crankshaft. The crankshaft, the crankshaft sprocket and the pulley are fitted together by friction, using diamond washers between the flange faces on each part. For that reason, the crankshaft sprocket is also unfastened if the pulley bolt is loosened. Before any repair requiring loosening or removal of the crankshaft pulley bolt, the crankshaft and camshafts must be locked in place by the special tools, otherwise severe engine damage can occur.
2. Disconnect the battery ground cable.
3. Remove the camshafts. For additional information, refer to Camshafts in this section.
4. Remove the exhaust manifold. For additional information, refer to Exhaust Manifold in this section.
5. Remove the fuel rail. For additional information, refer to Fuel System.
6. Remove the coolant hose retainer clip, the stud bolt and the ground cable.
7. Remove the EGR tube from the cylinder head.
8. Disconnect the EGR valve electrical connector.
9. Disconnect the EGR coolant hose and remove it from the hose bracket.

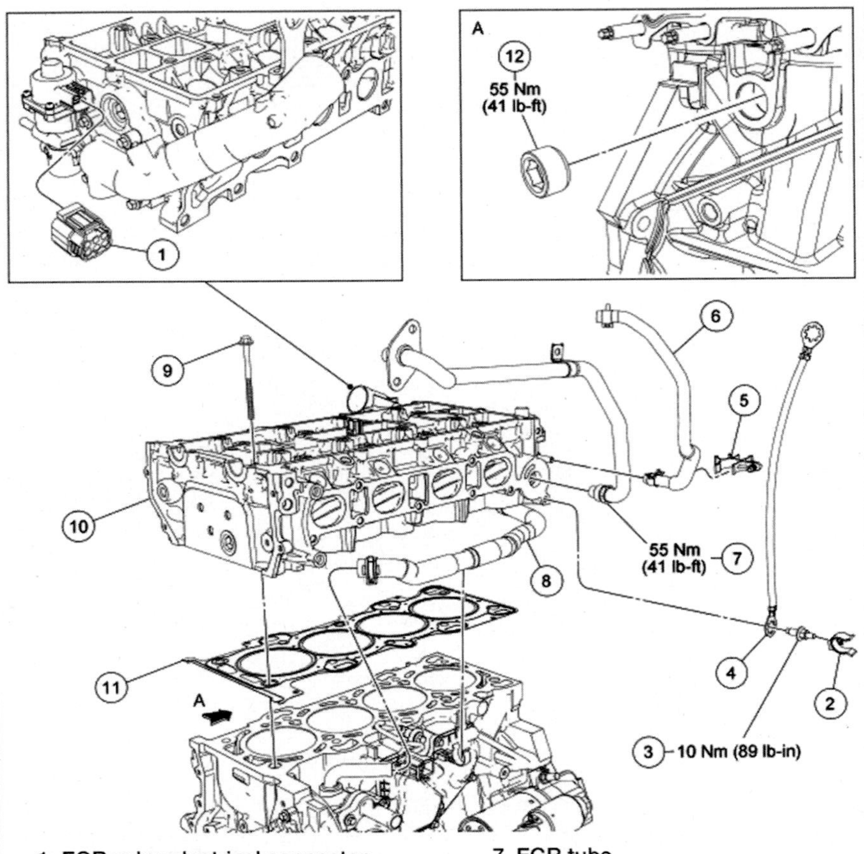

Fig. 97 Exploded view of the cylinder head assembly—2.3L Engines

10. Disconnect the coolant bypass hose.
11. Remove the cylinder block coolant drain plug.
12. Remove the 10 bolts and the cylinder head.
13. Discard the bolts.
14. Remove and discard the head gasket.

➡Do not use metal scrapers, wire brushes, power abrasive discs or other abrasive means to clean the sealing surfaces. These tools cause scratches and gouges that make leak paths. Use a plastic scraping tool to remove all traces of the head gasket.

➡Clean the sealing surface with silicone gasket remover and metal surface prep. Observe all warnings or cautions and follow all application directions contained on the packaging of the silicone gasket remover and the metal surface prep.

➡If there is no residual gasket material present, metal surface prep can be used to clean and prepare the surfaces.

15. Clean the cylinder head-to-cylinder block mating surfaces of both the cylinder head and the cylinder block in the following sequence.
    a. Remove any large deposits of silicone or gasket material with a plastic scraper.
    b. Apply silicone gasket remover, following package directions, and allow to set for several minutes.
    c. Remove the silicone gasket remover with a plastic scraper. A second application of silicone gasket remover may be required if residual traces of silicone or gasket material remain.

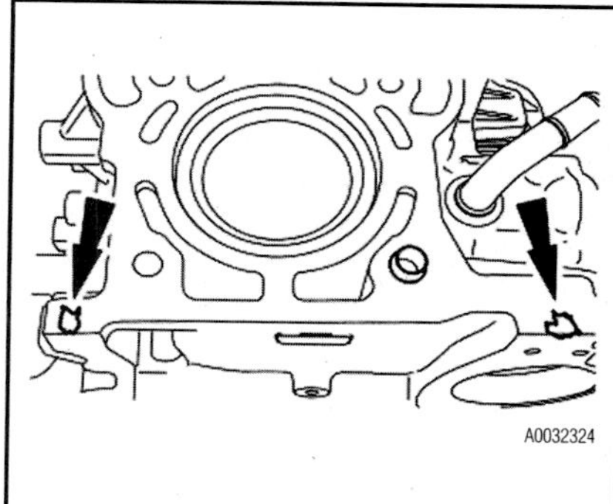

Fig. 98 Apply silicone gasket and sealant to the locations

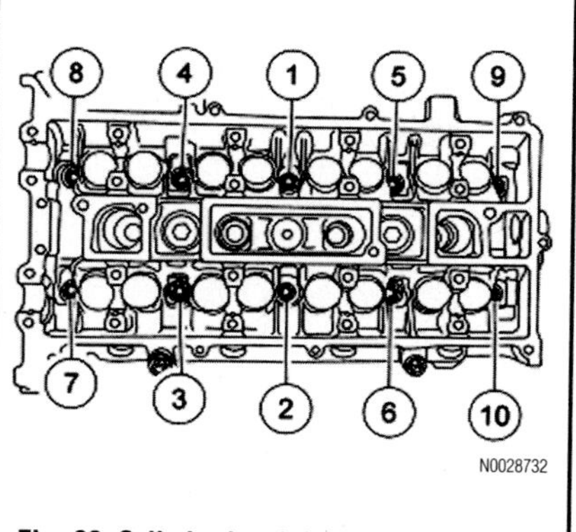

Fig. 99 Cylinder head tightening sequence

d. Apply metal surface prep, following package directions, to remove any remaining traces of oil or coolant, and to prepare the surfaces to bond with the new gasket. Do not attempt to make the metal shiny. Some staining of the metal surfaces is normal.

16. Support the cylinder head on a bench with the head gasket side up. Check the cylinder head distortion and the cylinder block distortion.

To install:

17. Clean the cylinder head bolt holes in the cylinder block. Make sure all coolant, oil or other foreign material is removed.

➡Do not use metal scrapers, wire brushes, power abrasive discs or other abrasive means to clean the sealing surfaces. These tools cause scratches and gouges, which make leak paths. Use a plastic scraping tool to remove all traces of old sealant.

➡Clean the sealing surface with silicone gasket remover and metal surface prep. Observe all warnings and cautions and follow all application directions contained on the packaging of the silicone gasket remover and metal surface prep.

➡If not secured within 4 minutes, the sealant must be removed and the sealing area cleaned. To clean the sealing area, use silicone gasket remover and metal surface prep. Observe all warnings and cautions and follow all application directions contained on the packaging of the silicone gasket remover and metal surface prep. Allow to dry until there is no sign of wetness, or 4 minutes, whichever is longer. Failure to follow this procedure can cause future oil leakage.

18. Apply silicone gasket and sealant to the locations shown.

19. Install a new cylinder head gasket.

➡If not secured within 4 minutes, the sealant must be removed and the sealing area cleaned. To clean the sealing area, use silicone gasket remover and metal surface prep. Observe all warnings and cautions and follow all application directions contained on the packaging of the silicone gasket remover and metal surface prep. Allow to dry until there is no sign of wetness, or 4 minutes, whichever is longer. Failure to follow this procedure can cause future oil leakage.

➡The cylinder head bolts are torque-to-yield and must not be reused. New cylinder head bolts must be installed.

➡Lubricate the cylinder head bolts with clean engine oil.

20. Install the cylinder head and the 10 new bolts. Tighten the bolts in the sequence shown, in 5 stages.

a. Stage 1: Tighten to 44 inch lbs. (5 Nm).

b. Stage 2: Tighten to 11 ft. lbs. (15 Nm).

c. Stage 3: Tighten to 33 ft. lbs. (45 Nm).

d. Stage 4: Tighten an additional 90 degrees.

e. Stage 5: Tighten an additional 90 degrees.

21. To complete installation, reverse the remaining removal procedure. Refer to exploded illustration for torque values.

4.0L Engines

See Figures 100 through 103.

1. With the vehicle in NEUTRAL, position it on a hoist.

2. Drain the engine cooling system.

3. Remove the intake manifold. For additional information, refer to Intake Manifold in this section.

4. Remove the cooling fan shroud. For additional information, refer to Engine Cooling.

5. Remove the roller followers. For additional information, refer to Camshaft in this section.

6. Rotate the accessory drive belt tensioner counterclockwise and remove the drive belt.

7. Disconnect the Engine Coolant Temperature (ECT) sensor electrical connector.

➡The coolant bypass hose will be removed with the thermostat housing.

8. Move the coolant bypass hose clamp off the coolant pump outlet.

9. Remove the 3 bolts and the thermostat housing and coolant bypass hose.

10. Remove the 4 bolts and the fuel rail and fuel injector assembly.

11. If equipped, remove the nut and position the A/C hose bracket aside.

➡Do not rotate the engine counterclockwise. Rotating the engine counterclockwise will result in damage to the damper crankshaft sensor speed wheel and incorrect timing of the engine.

➡The Crankshaft TDC Timing Tool must be installed on the damper and should contact the engine block. This positions the engine at Top Dead Center (TDC).

12. Install the Crankshaft TDC Timing Tool.

13. RH side:

a. Disconnect the alternator electrical connections and detach the wiring harness retainers.

b. Remove the bolt and the accessory drive belt tensioner.

c. Remove the 3 bolts and the alternator bracket assembly.

d. Disconnect the Crankshaft Position (CKP) sensor electrical connector.

e. Detach the 2 wiring harness retainers and position the wiring harness aside.

f. Remove and discard the 2 retainers.

g. Remove the 5 pushpins and the RH inner fender splash shield.

h. Remove the RH hydraulic timing chain tensioner.

i. Remove the RH exhaust manifold. For additional information, refer to Exhaust Manifold in this section.

j. Remove the bolt and position the wiring harness bracket aside.

k. Install the Camshaft Sprocket Holding Tool and the Adapter for 303-564. Tighten to 7 ft. lbs. (10 Nm).

➡The RH camshaft sprocket is a LH-threaded bolt. Turning the bolt in the wrong direction can damage the bolt.

14. Using the Torque Wrench Extension and the Camshaft Sprocket Nut Socket, remove the RH camshaft bolt.

Remove the RH timing drive cassette upper bolt.

➡Remove the camshaft sprocket from the timing chain to gain clearance to remove the cylinder head.

➡Hold the timing chain and cassette with a rubber band to aid in removal and to prevent the timing chain from falling into the cylinder block.

15. Remove the RH camshaft sprocket from the timing chain. Install a rubber band around the cassette and the timing chain.

16. LH side:

a. Remove the 4 bolts and position the power steering and A/C compressor bracket aside.

b. Remove the bolt and detach the wiring harness from the LH cylinder head.

c. Remove the bolt and the oil level indicator tube.

➡It is important to twist the spark plug wire boots while pulling upward to avoid possible damage to the spark plug wire.

➡Spark plug wires must be connected to the correct spark plug. Mark the spark plug locations before removing them.

d. Using the Spark Plug Wire Remover, disconnect the LH spark plug wires from the LH spark plugs and remove the ignition coil.

e. Remove the RH exhaust manifold. For additional information, refer to Exhaust Manifold in this section.

f. Remove the bolt and detach the ground strap.

g. Remove the LH side hydraulic timing chain tensioner.

h. Install the Camshaft Sprocket Holding Tool and the Adapter for 303-564. Tighten the top clamp bolts to 7 ft. lbs. (10 Nm).

i. Remove the LH camshaft sprocket bolt.

j. Remove the LH timing drive cassette upper bolt.

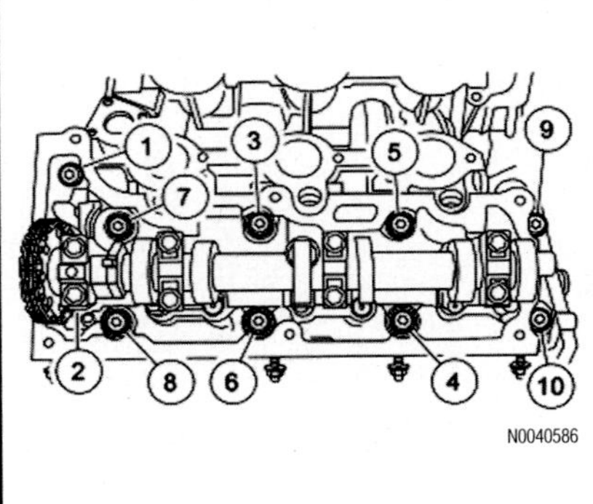

Fig. 100 Cylinder head removal sequence

➡Remove the camshaft sprocket from the timing chain to gain clearance to remove the cylinder head.

➡Hold the timing chain and cassette with a rubber band to aid in removal and to prevent the timing chain from falling into the cylinder block.

k. Remove the LH camshaft sprocket from the timing chain. Install a rubber band around the cassette and the timing chain.

17. Both sides:

➡To avoid damage to the timing chain cassette, an assistant will be required to help lift the cylinder head from the vehicle.

➡New cylinder head bolts must be installed. They are a torque-to-yield design and cannot be reused.

a. Remove the cylinder heads.

b. Remove the 10 cylinder head bolts in the sequence shown. Discard all bolts. Remove and discard the head gasket.

➡Do not use metal scrapers, wire brushes, power abrasive discs or other abrasive means to clean the sealing surfaces. These tools cause scratches and gouges which make leak paths.

c. Clean the cylinder head gasket surfaces with metal surface cleaner.

d. Support the cylinder head on a bench with the head gasket side up. Check the cylinder head distortion and the cylinder block distortion.

To install:

18. Both sides

a. Clean the cylinder head bolt holes in the cylinder block. Make sure all coolant, oil or other foreign material is removed.

b. Position the cylinder head gasket on the block.

19. RH side:

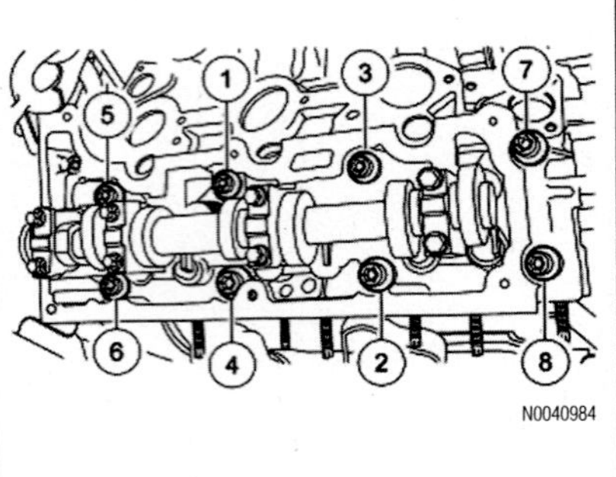

Fig. 101 RH cylinder head tightening sequence

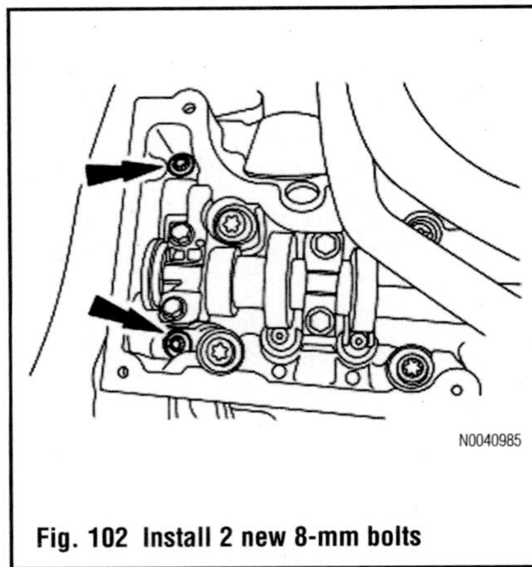

Fig. 102 Install 2 new 8-mm bolts

➡To avoid damage to the timing chain cassette, an assistant will be required to help position the cylinder head in the vehicle.

➡New cylinder head bolts must be installed. They are a torque-to-yield design and cannot be reused.

a. Install the cylinder head. Install 8 new 12-mm bolts and tighten in the sequence shown in 2 stages.

- Stage 1: Tighten to 9 ft. lbs. (12 Nm).
- Stage 2: Tighten to 18 ft. lbs. (25 Nm).

20. Install 2 new 8mm bolts. Tighten to 24 ft. lbs. (32 Nm).

21. Tighten the eight 12mm bolts in the sequence in 2 stages.

a. Stage 1: Tighten 90 degrees.

b. Stage 2: Tighten an additional 90 degrees.

➡The camshaft gear must turn freely on the camshaft. DO NOT tighten the bolt at this time.

c. Remove the rubber band. Install the camshaft sprocket and bolt.

d. Install the RH timing drive cassette upper bolt. Tighten to 7 ft. lbs. (10 Nm).

e. Position the wiring harness bracket and install the bolt. Tighten to 21 ft. lbs. (28 Nm).

22. Install the RH exhaust manifold. For additional information, refer to Exhaust Manifold in this section.

a. Install the RH inner fender splash shield and the 5 pushpins.

b. Install 2 new wiring harness retainers and attach the wiring harness.

c. Connect the CKP sensor electrical connector.

d. Position the alternator bracket and install the 3 bolts. Tighten to 31 ft. lbs. (42 Nm).

e. Position the accessory drive belt tensioner and install the bolt. Tighten to 35 ft. lbs. (47 Nm).

f. Connect the alternator electrical connectors and install the nut. Attach the wiring harness retainers.

23. LH side:

➡To avoid damage to the timing chain cassette, an assistant will be required to help position the cylinder head in the vehicle.

➡New cylinder head bolts must be installed. They are a torque-to-yield design and cannot be reused.

a. Install the cylinder head. Install 8 new 12-mm bolts and tighten in the sequence shown in 2 stages.

- Stage 1: Tighten to 9 ft. lbs. (12 Nm).
- Stage 2: Tighten to 18 ft. lbs. (25 Nm).

b. Install 2 new 8 mm bolts. Tighten to 24 ft. lbs. (32 Nm).

c. Tighten the eight 12 mm bolts in the sequence shown in 2 stages.

d. Stage 1: Tighten 90 degrees.

e. Stage 2: Tighten an additional 90 degrees.

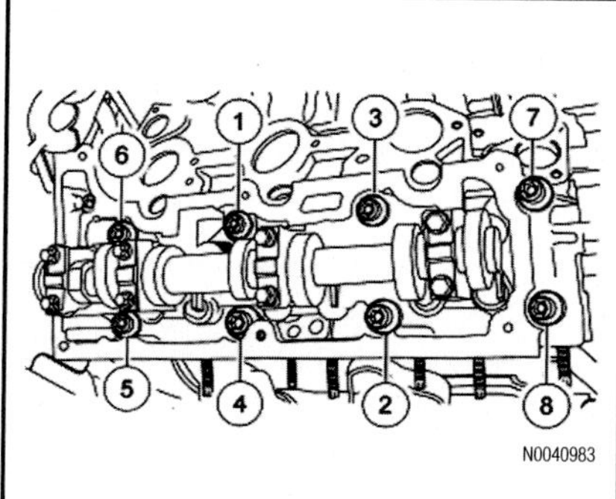

Fig. 103 LH cylinder head tightening sequence

➡The camshaft gear must turn freely on the camshaft. DO NOT tighten the bolt at this time.

24. Remove the rubber band. Install the camshaft sprocket and bolt.

25. Install the LH timing drive cassette upper bolt. Tighten to 9 ft. lbs. (12 Nm).

26. Position the ground strap and install the bolt. Tighten to 18 ft. lbs. (25 Nm).

27. To install, reverse the removal procedure.

28. Time the camshafts. For additional information, refer to Camshafts in this section.

29. Install the roller followers. For additional information, refer to Camshafts in this section.

30. Fill and bleed the engine cooling system. For additional information, refer to Engine Cooling.

ENGINE OIL & FILTER

REPLACEMENT

1. Remove the oil cap on top of the engine.
2. With the vehicle in NEUTRAL, position it on a hoist.
3. Position a oil receptacle under the vehicle.
4. Remove the oil pan drain plug until all the oil has fully drained. Install the oil pan plug.
5. Remove the oil filter and discard.
6. Lubricate the new oil filter seal with clean engine oil.
7. Install the oil filter.
8. Fill the engine with the recommended oil.
9. Check the dipstick for accurate fill levels.

EXHAUST MANIFOLD

REMOVAL & INSTALLATION

2.3L Engine

See Figure 104.

1. With the vehicle in NEUTRAL, position it on a hoist.
2. Disconnect the battery ground cable. For additional information, refer to Battery, Mounting and Cables.
3. Remove the accessory drive belt.
4. Drain the engine cooling system.
5. Remove the 2 exhaust downpipe flange nuts.
6. Disconnect the upper radiator hose and the degas bottle coolant hose from the front coolant outlet pipe.

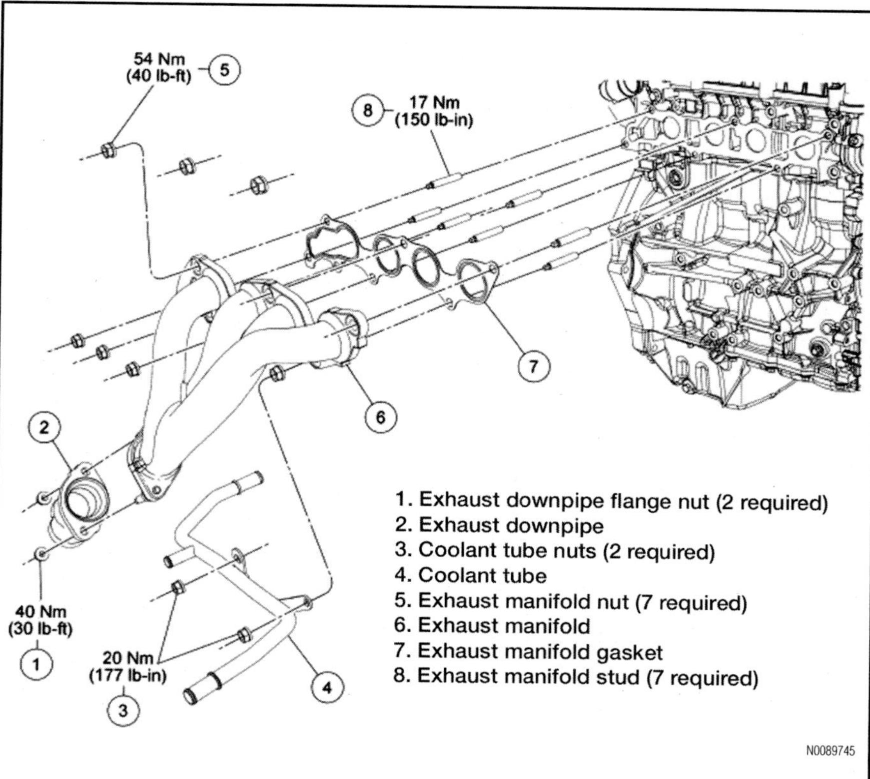

Fig. 104 Exploded view of the exhaust manifold—2.3L Engines

7. If equipped, remove the A/C compressor. For additional information, refer to Heating & Air Conditioning.

8. Disconnect the heater coolant hose from the front coolant outlet pipe.

9. Remove the oil level indicator, the 2 bolts and the oil level indicator tube.

10. Discard the O-ring seal.

11. Remove the 2 bolts and the front coolant outlet pipe.

12. Discard the O-ring seal.

13. Remove the 5 pushpins and position the right inner fender splash shield aside.

14. Remove the alternator and bracket. Refer to Alternator in Engine Electrical.

15. Remove the 2 nuts and position the coolant tube aside.

16. Remove the 7 nuts, the exhaust manifold and the gasket.

17. Discard the exhaust manifold nuts and the gasket.

18. Remove and discard the 7 exhaust manifold-to-cylinder head studs.

19. Clean and inspect the exhaust manifold.

➡Do not use metal scrapers, wire brushes, power abrasive discs or other abrasive means to clean the sealing surfaces. These tools cause scratches and gouges which make leak paths.

20. Clean and inspect the sealing surfaces with metal surface prep. Follow the directions on the packaging.

21. Observe all warnings and cautions and follow all application directions contained on the packaging of the metal surface prep.

To install:

22. To install, reverse the removal procedure. Refer to illustration for torque values.

23. Install 7 new exhaust manifold-to-cylinder head studs.

24. Install a new exhaust manifold gasket.

25. Position the exhaust manifold and install 7 new nuts.

26. Connect the battery ground cable. Fill and bleed the engine cooling system.

Left Hand Exhaust Manifold

See Figure 105.

1. With the vehicle in NEUTRAL, position it on a hoist.

2. Detach the differential feedback pressure EGR sensor from the exhaust manifold-to-EGR valve tube.

3. Remove the exhaust manifold-to-EGR valve tube.

4. Remove the 2 exhaust manifold-to-dual converter Y-pipe nuts.

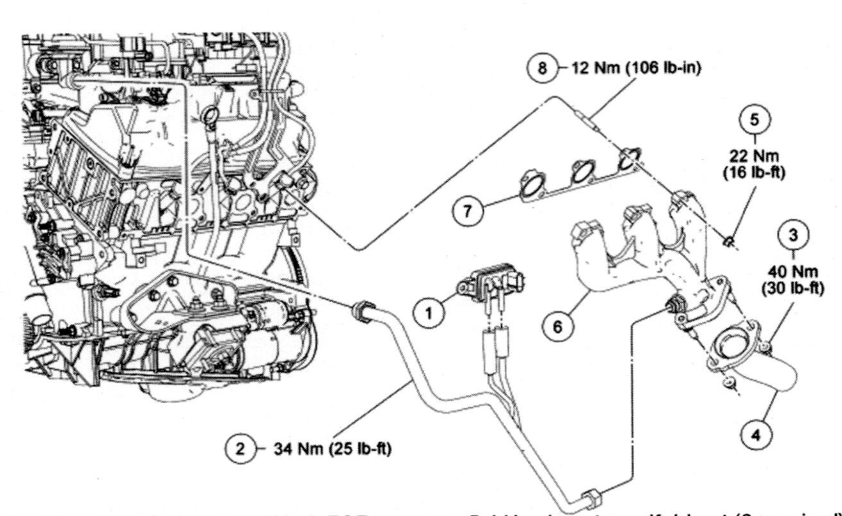

1. Differential pressure feedback EGR sensor
2. Exhaust manifold-to-EGR valve tube
3. LH exhaust manifold-to-dual converter Y-pipe nut (2 required)
4. Dual converter Y-pipe
5. LH exhaust manifold nut (6 required)
6. LH exhaust manifold
7. LH exhaust manifold gasket
8. LH exhaust manifold stud (6 required)

N0090742

Fig. 105 Exploded view of the LH exhaust manifold

5. Remove the 6 nuts, the LH exhaust manifold and the gasket.

6. Discard the nuts and gasket.

7. Clean and inspect the LH exhaust manifold.

8. Remove and discard the 6 LH exhaust manifold studs.

To install:

9. Reverse the removal procedure.

10. Refer to illustration for torque values.

11. Install the 6 new LH exhaust manifold studs.

12. Install the new LH exhaust manifold gasket, manifold and 6 new nuts.

13. Connect the EGR system module tube to the exhaust manifold.

Right Hand Exhaust Manifold

See Figure 106.

1. With the vehicle in NEUTRAL, position it on a hoist.

2. Remove the 2 exhaust manifold-to-dual converter Y-pipe nuts.

3. Remove the 6 nuts, the RH exhaust manifold and the gasket.

4. Discard the nuts and the gasket.

5. Remove and discard the 6 RH exhaust manifold studs.

To install:

6. Reverse the removal procedure.

7. Refer to illustration for torque values.

8. Clean and inspect the RH exhaust manifold.

9. Install 6 new RH exhaust manifold studs.

10. Position a new gasket and the RH exhaust manifold and install 6 new nuts.

11. Position the dual converter Y-pipe and install the 2 nuts.

INTAKE MANIFOLD

REMOVAL & INSTALLATION

2.3L Engine

See Figure 107.

⁂ WARNING

Before working on or disconnecting any of the fuel tubes or fuel system components, relieve the fuel system pressure to prevent accidental spraying of fuel. Fuel in the fuel system remains under high pressure, even when the engine is not running. Failure to follow this instruction may result in serious personal injury.

⁂ WARNING

Do not smoke, carry lighted tobacco or have an open flame of any type when working on or near any fuel-related component. Highly flammable mixtures are always present and may be ignited. Failure to follow

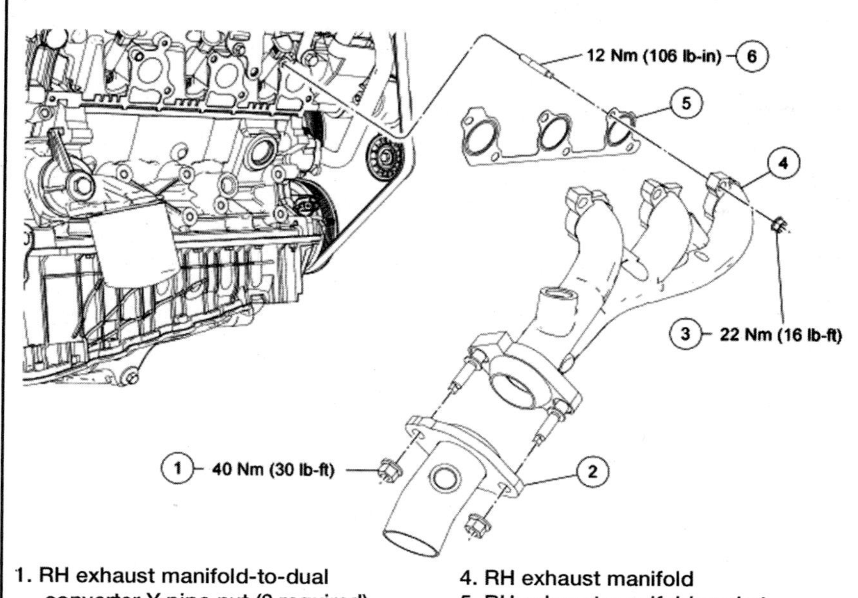

Fig. 106 Exploded view of the RH exhaust manifold and components

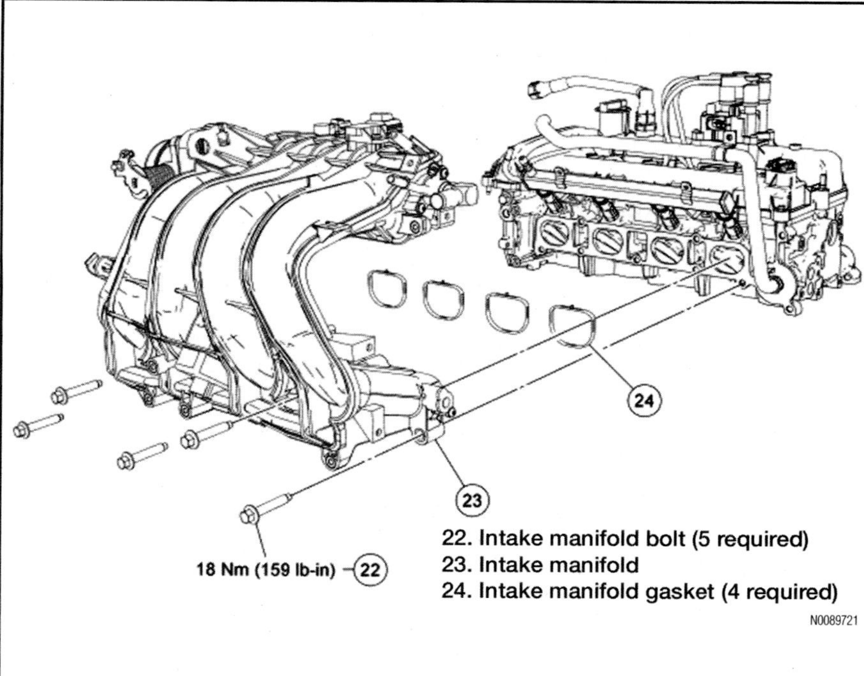

Fig. 107 Exploded view of the intake assembly—2.3L Engine

these instructions may result in serious personal injury.

WARNING

Do not carry personal electronic devices such as cell phones, pagers or audio equipment of any type when working on or near any fuel-related component. Highly flammable mixtures are always present and may be ignited. Failure to follow these instructions may result in serious personal injury.

WARNING

Always disconnect the battery ground cable at the battery when working on an evaporative emission (EVAP) system or fuel-related component. Highly flammable mixtures are always present and may be ignited. Failure to follow these instructions may result in serious personal injury.

1. Disconnect the negative battery cable.
2. Drain the engine cooling system.
3. Remove the Air Cleaner (ACL) outlet pipe.
4. Remove the 2 bolts and the Throttle Body (TB) shield.
5. Disconnect the acceleration control cable from the intake manifold and the TB.
6. If equipped, disconnect the speed control cable from the intake manifold and the TB.
7. Disconnect the Throttle Position (TP) sensor electrical connector.
8. Disconnect the Manifold Absolute Pressure (MAP) sensor electrical connector.
9. Disconnect the Idle Air Control (IAC) valve electrical connector.
10. Disconnect the vapor purge tube quick connect coupling.
11. Disconnect the engine vacuum harness, brake booster hose, the crankcase breather hose and the 2 coolant hoses.
12. Disconnect 2 engine wiring harness pin-type retainers from the intake manifold.
13. Disconnect the pin-type retainer from the rear of the intake manifold.
14. Remove the EGR tube support bracket bolt.
15. Remove the 2 bolts from the EGR tube flange.
16. Detach the fuel supply tube and the electrical connectors from the bracket and disconnect the Evaporative Emission (EVAP) tube quick connect coupling.
17. Disconnect the Knock Sensor (KS) electrical connector and disconnect the connector retainer from the intake manifold.
18. Remove the wiring harness pushpin from the bottom of the intake manifold.
19. Disconnect the fuel supply tube spring lock coupling.

➡Do not use metal scrapers, wire brushes, power abrasive discs or other abrasive means to clean the sealing surfaces. These tools cause scratches and gouges which make leak paths. Use a plastic scraping tool to remove all traces of old sealant.

20. Remove the 5 bolts and the intake manifold.

21. Clean the sealing surface of the cylinder head with silicone gasket remover and metal surface prep. Observe all warnings and cautions and follow all application directions contained on the packaging of the silicone gasket remover and metal surface prep.

22. Remove and discard the 4 intake manifold gaskets.

To install:

➡If the engine is repaired or replaced because of upper engine failure, typically including valve or piston damage, check the intake manifold for metal debris. If metal debris is found, install a new intake manifold. Failure to follow these instructions can result in engine damage.

23. Install 4 new intake manifold gaskets.

24. Position the intake manifold and install the 5 bolts. Tighten to 13 ft. lbs. (18 Nm).

25. Reverse the removal procedure.

26. Refer to illustration for torque values.

27. Fill and bleed the engine cooling system.

4.0L Engine

See Figure 108.

WARNING

Before working on or disconnecting any of the fuel tubes or fuel system components, relieve the fuel system pressure to prevent accidental spraying of fuel. Fuel in the fuel system remains under high pressure, even when the engine is not running. Failure to follow this instruction may result in serious personal injury.

WARNING

Do not smoke, carry lighted tobacco or have an open flame of any type when working on or near any fuel-related component. Highly flammable mixtures are always present and may be ignited. Failure to follow these instructions may result in serious personal injury.

WARNING

Do not carry personal electronic devices such as cell phones, pagers or audio equipment of any type when working on or near any fuel-related component. Highly flammable mixtures are always present and may be ignited. Failure to follow these instructions may result in serious personal injury.

WARNING

Always disconnect the battery ground cable at the battery when working on an evaporative emission (EVAP) system or fuel-related component. Highly flammable mixtures are always present and may be ignited. Failure to follow these instructions may result in serious personal injury.

1. Disconnect the battery ground cable.
2. Remove the Air Cleaner (ACL) outlet pipe.
3. Disconnect the accelerator cable from the Throttle Body (TB).
4. If equipped, disconnect the speed control actuator cable from the TB.
5. Disconnect the Throttle Position (TP) sensor electrical connector.
6. Detach the wiring harness retainer.
7. Disconnect the Idle Air Control (IAC) motor electrical connector.
8. Disconnect the EGR valve vacuum hose connector.
9. Disconnect the exhaust manifold-to-EGR valve tube from the EGR valve. Refer to Exhaust Manifold.
10. Disconnect the Evaporative Emission (EVAP) purge valve-to-intake manifold hose from the intake manifold.
11. Disconnect the EGR vacuum regulator solenoid electrical connector.
12. Disconnect the EGR vacuum regulator solenoid vacuum connector.
13. Disconnect the brake booster vacuum hose from the intake manifold.

➡It is important to twist the spark plug wire boots while pulling upward to avoid possible damage to the spark plug wire.

➡Spark plug wires must be connected to the correct ignition coil terminal. Mark the spark plug wire locations before removing them.

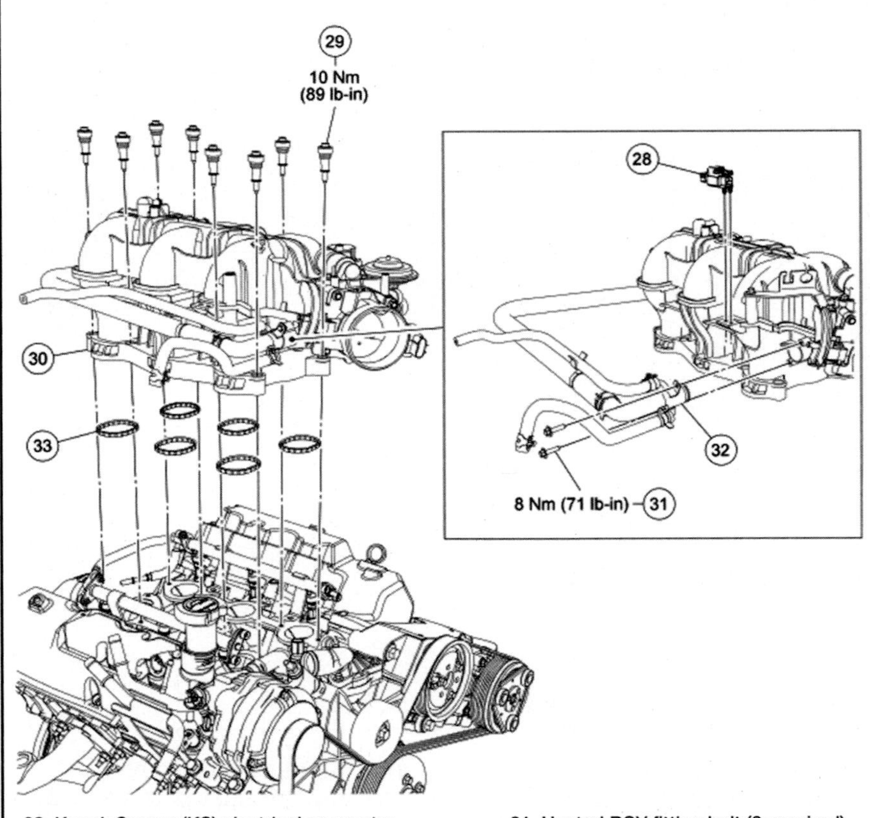

Fig. 108 Exploded view of the intake manifold—4.0L Engines

14. Disconnect the RH spark plug wires from the ignition coil.

15. Detach the RH spark plug wire retainer from the intake manifold and position the spark plug wires aside.

16. Disconnect the ignition coil electrical connector.

17. Detach the wiring harness retainer from the ignition coil bracket.

18. Detach the accelerator cable retainer from the ignition coil bracket.

19. Disconnect the radio interference capacitor electrical connector.

20. Remove the 4 bolts and position the ignition coil and bracket aside. Refer to Ignition Coil in Engine Electrical.

21. Disconnect the vacuum harness main vacuum connector from the intake manifold.

22. Remove the wiring harness-to-cowl bracket nut.

23. Disconnect the 3 PCM electrical connectors.

24. Remove the wiring harness ground wire stud bolt and position the wiring harness aside.

25. Detach the Knock Sensor (KS) electrical connector from the intake manifold.

26. Loosen the 8 bolts and lift up the intake manifold.

27. Remove the 2 heated PCV fitting bolts and detach the heated PCV fitting from the intake manifold.

28. Remove the intake manifold.

29. Inspect the intake manifold gaskets. Install new gaskets if necessary.

➡If the engine is repaired or replaced because of upper engine failure, typically including valve or piston damage, check the intake manifold for metal debris. If metal debris is found, install a new intake manifold. Failure to follow these instructions can result in engine damage.

30. To install, reverse the removal procedure.

OIL PAN

REMOVAL & INSTALLATION

2.3L Engine

See Figure 109.

1. With the vehicle in NEUTRAL, position it on a hoist.

2. Remove the engine cooling fan. For additional information, refer to Engine Cooling.

3. Remove the oil level indicator and tube.

➡Only the LH side of the engine will be raised.

4. Remove the LH engine support insulator-to-engine bracket nuts. Install the Lifting Eye.

5. Install the 3-Bar Engine Support Kit and raise the LH side of the engine approximately 1 inch.

6. Remove the drain plug and drain the engine oil. Install the drain plug when finished. Tighten to 21 ft. lbs. (28 Nm).

7. Detach the 2 wiring harness retainers from the engine front cover.

8. Remove the 4 engine front cover-to-oil pan bolts.

9. Remove the transmission bracket-to-transmission bolts.

10. Remove the 4 transmission-to-oil pan bolts.

➡To prevent damage to the transmission, do not loosen the transmission-to-engine bolts more than 0.19 inches.

11. Loosen the 7 transmission-to-cylinder block bolts 0.19 inches.

12. Slide the transmission rearward 5 mm (0.19 in).

➡If necessary, lift the rear of the transmission to remove the oil pan.

13. Remove the 13 oil pan bolts and the oil pan.

➡Do not use metal scrapers, wire brushes, power abrasive discs or other abrasive means to clean the sealing surfaces. These tools cause scratches and gouges, which make leak paths. Use a plastic scraping tool to remove all traces of old sealant.

14. Clean the sealing surface with silicone gasket remover and metal surface prep. Observe all warnings and cautions and follow all application directions contained on the packaging of the silicone gasket remover and metal surface prep.

To install:

➡Do not use metal scrapers, wire brushes, power abrasive discs or other abrasive means to clean the sealing surfaces. These tools cause scratches and gouges, which make leak paths. Use a plastic scraping tool to remove all traces of sealant.

➡If not secured within 4 minutes, the sealant must be removed and the sealing area cleaned. To clean the sealing area, use silicone gasket remover and metal surface prep. Observe all warnings and cautions and follow all application directions contained on the packaging of the silicone gasket remover and metal surface prep. Allow to dry until there is no sign of wetness, or 4 minutes, whichever is longer. Failure to follow this procedure can cause future oil leakage.

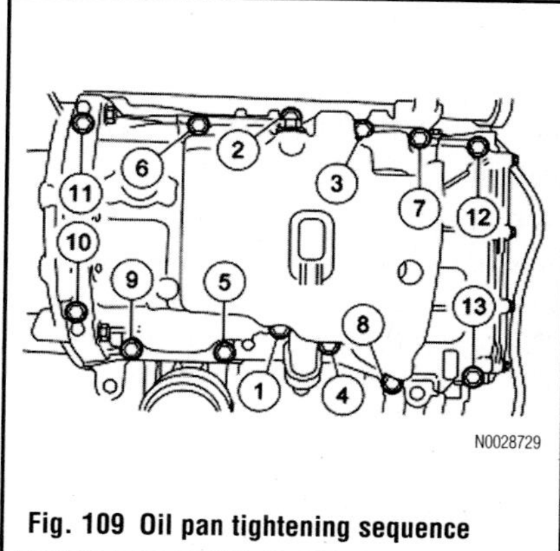

Fig. 109 Oil pan tightening sequence

➡If necessary, lift the rear of the transmission to install the oil pan.

15. Apply a 0.1 in bead of silicone gasket and sealant to the oil pan. Position the oil pan and install the 13 bolts finger-tight.

16. Install the 4 engine front cover-to-oil pan bolts. Tighten to 7 ft. lbs. (10 Nm).

17. Tighten the 13 oil pan bolts in the sequence shown. Tighten to 18 ft. lbs. (25 Nm).

18. Attach the 2 wiring harness retainers to the engine front cover.

19. Slide the transmission forward and tighten the 7 transmission-to-cylinder block bolts. Tighten to 35 ft. lbs. (48 Nm).

20. Install the 4 transmission-to-oil pan bolts. Tighten to 35 ft. lbs. (48 Nm).

21. Install the transmission bracket-to-transmission bolts. Tighten to 66 ft. lbs. (90 Nm).

22. Lower the engine and remove the 3-Bar Engine Support Kit and the Lifting Eye. Install the engine support insulator nuts. Tighten to 75 ft. lbs. (102 Nm).

23. Install the oil level indicator and tube.

24. Install the engine cooling fan. For additional information, refer to Engine Cooling.

25. Install a new oil filter.

26. Fill the engine with clean engine oil.

4.0L Engine

1. With the vehicle in NEUTRAL, position it on a hoist.

2. Remove the drain plug and drain the

engine oil. To install, tighten to 19 ft. lbs. (26 Nm).

3. Remove the bolts, the oil pan and the gasket. Discard the gasket. To install, tighten to 8 ft. lbs. (11 Nm).

➡Do not use metal scrapers, wire brushes, power abrasive discs or other abrasive means to clean sealing surfaces. These tools cause scratches and gouges which make leak paths. Use a plastic scraping tool to remove all traces of the old oil pan gasket.

4. Clean and inspect the sealing surfaces.
5. To install, reverse the removal procedure.
6. Fill the engine with clean engine oil.

OIL PUMP

REMOVAL & INSTALLATION

2.3L Engines

See Figures 110 through 112.

➡Do not loosen or remove the crankshaft pulley bolt without first installing the special tools as instructed in the crankshaft pulley procedure. The crankshaft pulley and the crankshaft timing sprocket are not keyed to the crankshaft. The crankshaft, the crankshaft sprocket and the pulley are fitted together by friction, using diamond washers between the flange faces on each part. For that reason, the crankshaft sprocket is also unfastened if the pulley bolt is loosened. Before any repair requiring loosening or removal of the crankshaft pulley bolt, the crankshaft and camshafts must be locked in place by the special tools, otherwise severe engine damage may occur.

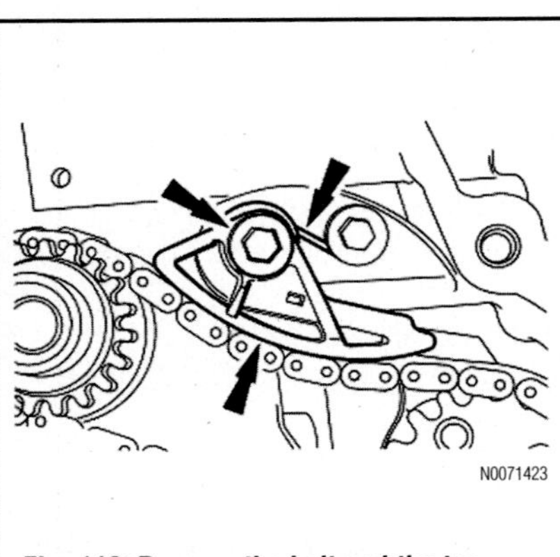

Fig. 110 Remove the bolt and the tensioner

1. Remove the engine front cover. For additional information, refer to Engine Front Cover in this section.
2. Remove the oil pump screen and pickup tube.
   a. Remove the oil pan.
   b. Remove the 4 bolts and the oil pump screen and pickup tube. Discard the gasket.
3. Remove the oil pump chain tensioner.
4. Release the tension on the tensioner spring.
5. Remove the bolt and the tensioner.
6. Remove the chain from the oil pump sprocket.
7. Remove the bolt and oil pump sprocket.
8. Remove the 4 bolts and the oil pump.

To install:

➡Clean the oil pump and cylinder block mating surfaces with metal surface prep. Observe all warnings and cautions and follow all application directions contained on the packaging of the metal surface prep. Allow to dry until there is no sign of wetness, or 4 minutes, whichever is longer. Failure to follow this procedure may cause future oil leakage.

9. Install the oil pump assembly. Tighten the 4 bolts in the sequence shown in 2 stages:
   a. Stage 1: Tighten to 89 inch lbs. (10 Nm).
   b. Stage 2: Tighten to 15 ft. lbs. (20 Nm).
10. Install the oil pump sprocket and bolt. Tighten to 18 ft. lbs. (25 Nm).
11. Install the chain onto the oil pump sprocket.
12. Install the oil pump chain tensioner and bolt.

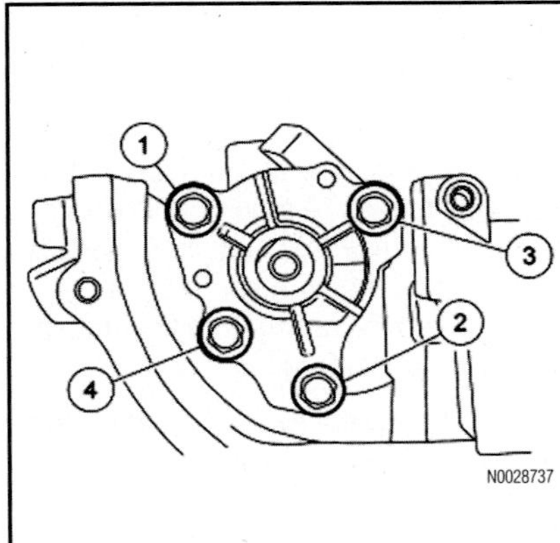

Fig. 111 Oil pump tightening sequence

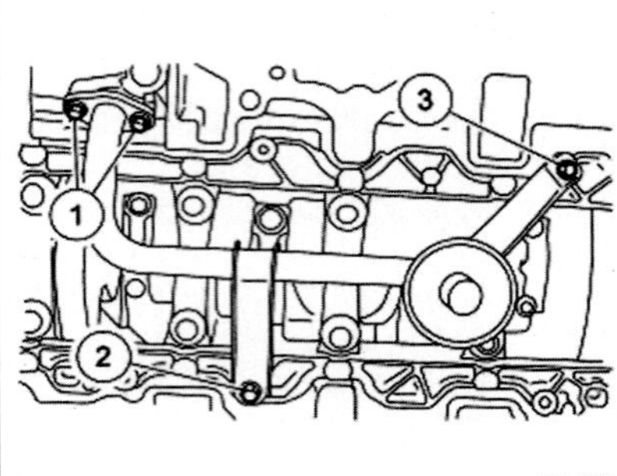

Fig. 112 Oil pump screen and pickup tube tightening sequence

13. Hook the tensioner spring around the shoulder bolt. Tighten to 89 inch lbs. (10 Nm).
14. Install the oil pump screen and pickup tube.

➡Clean the sealing surface with metal surface prep. Observe all warnings and cautions and follow all application directions contained on the packaging of the metal surface prep.

   a. Position a new oil pump pickup tube gasket and the pickup tube, and tighten the 4 bolts in the sequence shown to 7 ft. lbs. (10 Nm).
   b. Install the oil pan.
15. Install the engine front cover. For additional information, refer to Engine Front Cover in this section.

4.0L Engines

See Figures 113 through 116.

1. With the vehicle in NEUTRAL, position it on a hoist.
2. Disconnect the battery ground cable. For additional information, refer to Battery, Mounting and Cables.
3. Remove the Air Cleaner (ACL). For additional information, refer to Intake Air Distribution and Filtering.
4. Remove the starter. For additional information, refer to Starting System.
5. Remove the oil pan. For additional information, refer to Oil Pan in this section.
6. Remove the 2 bolts and position the fan shroud on the cooling fan.
7. Remove the oil level indicator.
8. Remove the 2 LH engine support insulator nuts.
9. Remove the A/C compressor and power steering bolt and use it to install the Engine Lifting Bracket.
10. Remove the 2 RH engine support insulator nuts.

11. Remove the heater tube assembly front bolt and use it to install the Engine Lifting Bracket.

12. Install the Engine Support Bar and the 2 Adapters for 303-290A and raise the engine 1 in.

13. Remove the bolt and position the transmission cooler tube bracket aside.

14. If equipped, remove the nut and position the A/C tube bracket aside.

15. Four-Wheel Drive (4WD) vehicles:

➡**Some vehicles are equipped with a 2-piece dual converter Y-pipe (LH and RH).**

a. Remove the dual converter Y-pipe. For additional information, refer to Exhaust System.

b. Secure the axle housing to a suitable jack.

➡**Any time bolts, washers, spacers or nuts are loosened in the front axle housing for any reason, install new components to prevent damage.**

c. Remove the 3 axle housing mounting bolts and lower the front axle housing approximately 1 inch.

d. Discard the front axle housing support bolts and nuts.

16. Remove the bolt and the oil pump screen and pickup tube.

17. Remove the 2 transmission-to-cylinder block cradle bolts.

➡**Note the location of the 2 Torx head bolts at the rear of the cylinder block cradle.**

18. Remove the 2 cylinder block cradle rear bolts.

19. Remove the 20 bolts and 2 nuts along the outside of the cylinder block cradle.

➡**Note the location of the 2 silver-colored bolts that have washer seals. They must be installed in the same position with new washer seals.**

20. Remove the 8 cylinder block cradle inner bolts and the 2 washer seals.

21. Discard the washer seals.

22. Remove the cylinder block cradle and the gasket.

23. Discard the gasket.

24. Remove the bolts and the oil pump.

To install:

25. Install the oil pump. Refer to exploded illustration for torque values.

➡**Failure to back off the 8 set screws can result in damage to the cylinder block cradle.**

26. Back the 8 set screws off until they are below the cylinder block cradle boss.

➡**Do not use metal scrapers, wire brushes, power abrasive discs or other abrasive means to clean the sealing surfaces. These tools cause scratches and gouges which make leak paths. Use a plastic scraping tool to remove all traces of the old cylinder block cradle gasket and sealant.**

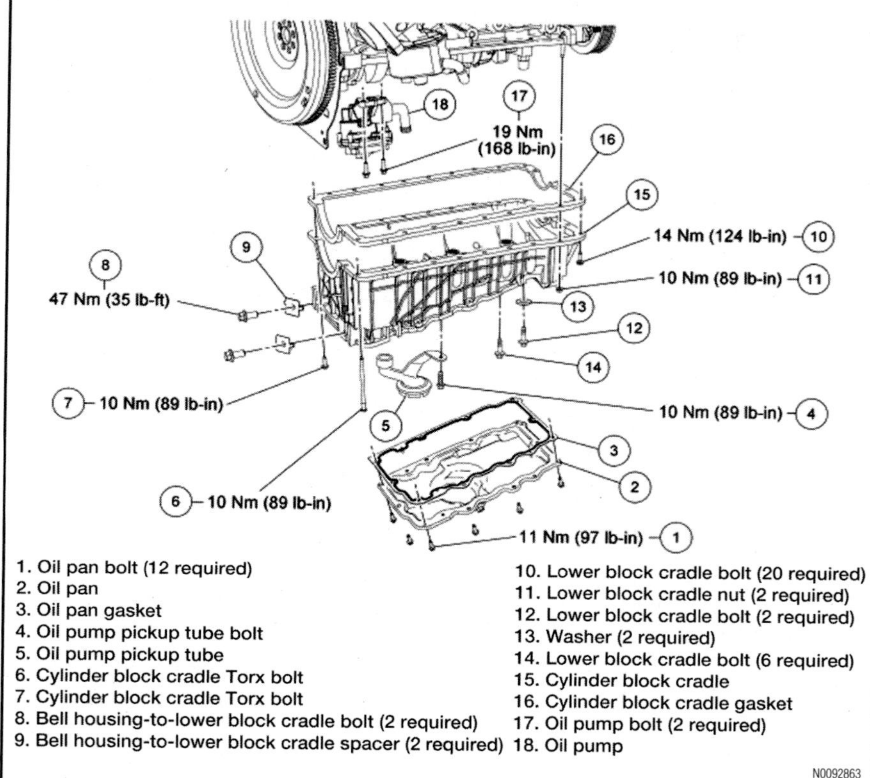

Fig. 113 Exploded view of the oil pump and related components—4.0L Engine

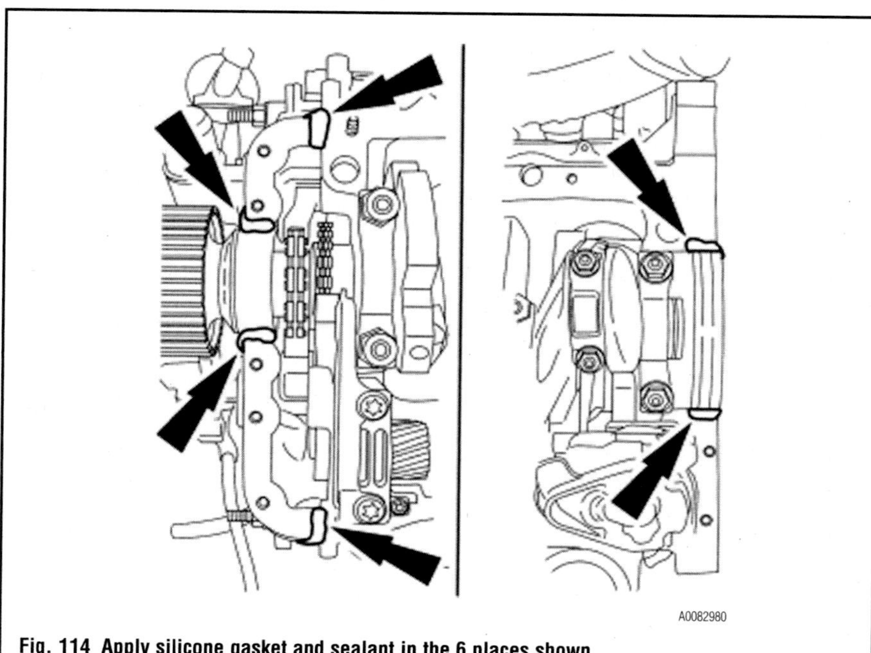

Fig. 114 Apply silicone gasket and sealant in the 6 places shown

➡Gasket material as well as silicone sealant may be present in the cavities in the main bearing cap. This material must be removed completely prior to assembly.

27. Clean the gasket mating surfaces, making sure all the sealant is removed from the cavities on the rear main bearing cap. To clean the sealing area, use a plastic scraping tool, silicone gasket remover and metal surface prep. Follow the directions on the packaging.

➡If not secured within 4 minutes, the sealant must be removed and the sealing area cleaned. To clean the sealing area, use silicone gasket remover and metal surface prep. Follow the directions on the packaging. Failure to follow this procedure can cause future oil leakage.

28. Apply silicone gasket and sealant in the 6 places shown.
29. Position a new gasket and the cylinder block cradle. Install the outer 20 bolts and 2 nuts finger-tight.
30. Install the 2 cylinder block cradle rear bolts finger-tight.
31. Install the 2 transmission-to-cylinder block cradle bolts. Tighten to 35 ft. lbs. (47 Nm).
32. Tighten the outer 20 bolts and 2 nuts. Tighten the nuts to 89 inch lbs. (10 Nm). Tighten the bolts to 10 ft. lbs. (14 Nm).
33. Tighten the 2 cylinder block cradle rear Torx bolts. Tighten to 89 inch lbs. (10 Nm).
34. Tighten the 8 set screws. Tighten to 27 inch lbs. (3 Nm).
35. Install the 2 silver-colored bolts and new washer seals finger-tight.
36. Install the 6 remaining inner bolts finger-tight.
37. Tighten the 8 inner bolts in the sequence shown in 2 stages.

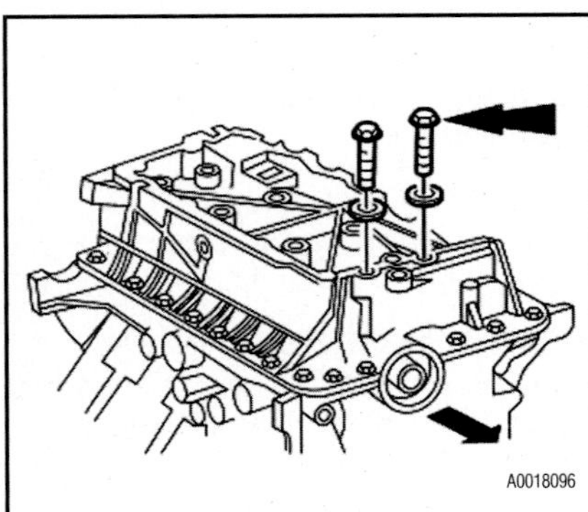

Fig. 115 Identifying the 2 silver-colored bolts

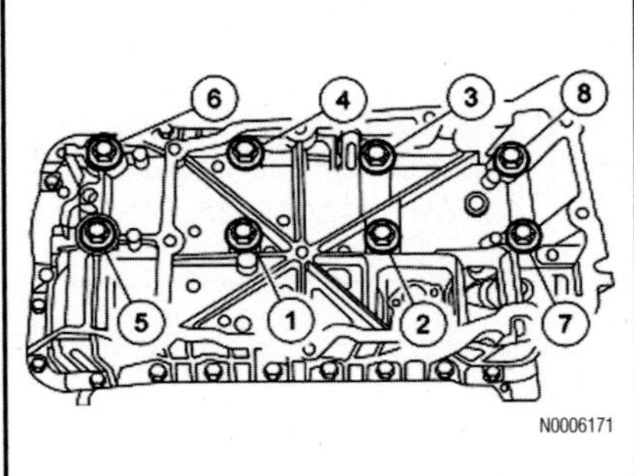

Fig. 116 8 inner bolts tightening sequence

a. Stage 1: Tighten to 11 ft. lbs. (15 Nm).
b. Stage 2: Tighten to 25 ft. lbs. (34 Nm).

38. Position the oil pump screen and pickup tube and install the bolt.

➡Any time bolts, washers, spacers or nuts are loosened in the front axle housing for any reason, install new components to prevent damage.

39. Raise the front axle housing into place and install new bolts and nuts. Tighten to 49 ft. lbs. (66 Nm).
40. Remove the jack.
41. Install the dual converter Y-pipe.
42. If equipped, position the A/C tube bracket and install the nut.
43. Position the transmission fluid cooler tube and install the bolt.
44. Lower the engine and remove the Engine Support Bar and the 2 Adapters for 303-209A.
45. Remove the Engine Lifting Bracket and install the coolant tube bolt.
46. Install the RH engine support insulator nuts. Tighten to 81 ft. lbs. (110 Nm).
47. Remove the Engine Lifting Bracket and install the power steering and A/C compressor bracket bolt. Tighten to 31 ft. lbs. (42 Nm).
48. Install the 2 LH engine support insulator nuts. Tighten to 81 ft. lbs. (110 Nm).
49. Install the oil level indicator.
50. Position the fan shroud and install the 2 bolts.
51. Install the oil pan. For additional information, refer to Oil Pan in this section.
52. Install the starter. For additional information, refer to Starting System.
53. Install the ACL outlet pipe.
54. Connect the battery ground cable.

REAR MAIN SEAL

REMOVAL & INSTALLATION

2.3L Engine

See Figures 117 and 118.

1. Remove the flywheel or flexplate.
2. Remove the oil pan. For additional information, refer to Oil Pan in this section.
3. Remove the 6 bolts and the crankshaft rear seal and retainer plate as an assembly.

To install:

4. Using the Crankshaft Rear Seal Installer, position the crankshaft rear seal with retainer plate onto the crankshaft.
5. Install the 6 crankshaft rear seal with retainer plate bolts.
6. Tighten in the sequence shown to 7 ft. lbs. (10 Nm).
7. Install the oil pan. For additional information, refer to Oil Pan in this section.
8. Install the flywheel or flexplate.

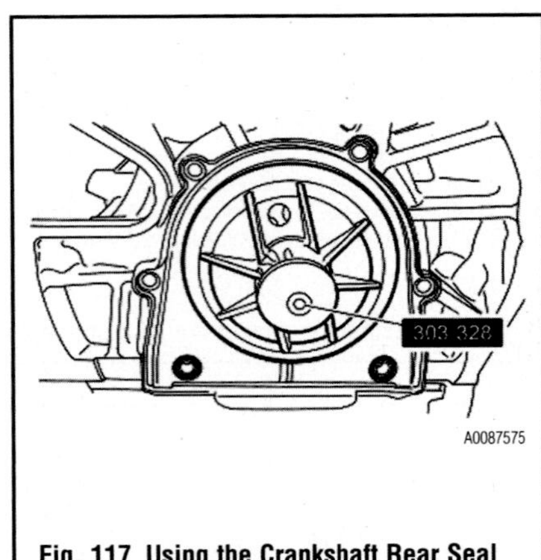

Fig. 117 Using the Crankshaft Rear Seal Installer

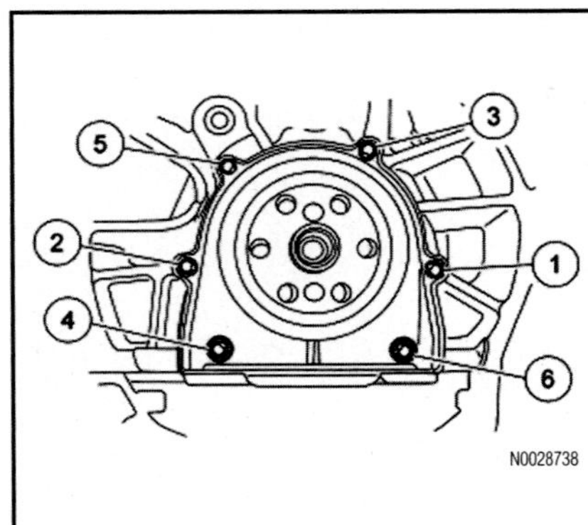

Fig. 118 Crankshaft rear seal tightening bolts

4.0L Engine

See Figures 119 through 122.

1. Remove the flexplate or flywheel.
2. Remove the spacer plate.

➡The original crankshaft rear seal does not have a speedy sleeve. Only a new replacement crankshaft rear seal comes with a speedy sleeve.

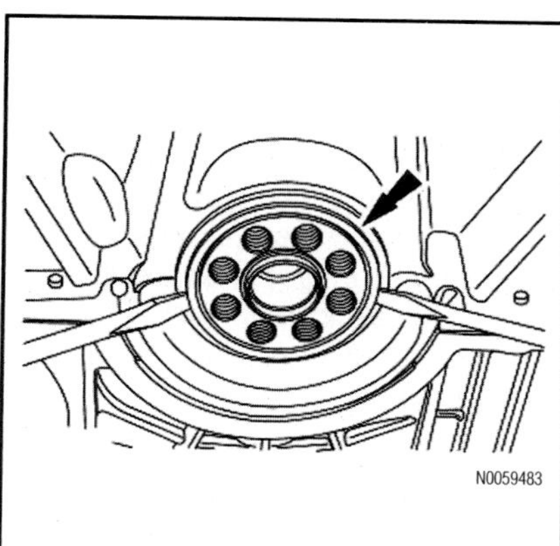

Fig. 119 Remove the speedy sleeve

Fig. 120 Using the Oil Seal Remover

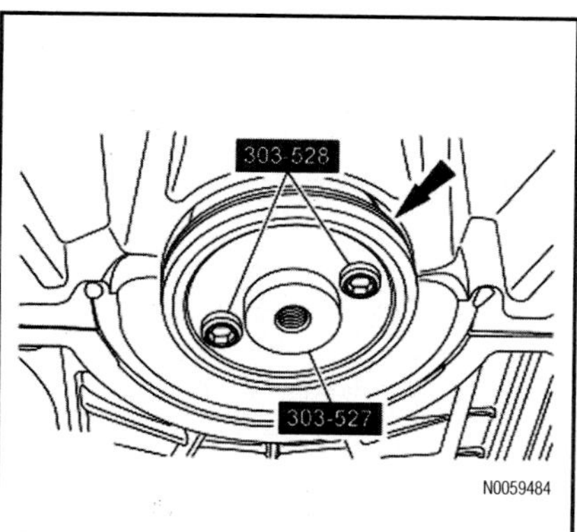

Fig. 121 Positioning the crankshaft rear seal with speedy sleeve

➡The crankshaft rear seal may have a metal speedy sleeve. This sleeve must be removed before attempting to remove the seal.

3. If necessary, remove the speedy sleeve using 2 screwdrivers or small pry bars.

➡Avoid scratching or damaging the crankshaft rear seal running surface during removal of the crankshaft rear seal.

4. Using the Oil Seal Remover, remove the crankshaft rear seal.

To install:

➡The new replacement crankshaft rear seal comes with a speedy sleeve. Do not remove the speedy sleeve, it must be installed with the crankshaft rear seal.

➡Be sure the crankshaft rear sealing surface is clean and free from any rust or corrosion. To clean the crankshaft rear seal surface area, use extra-fine emery cloth or extra-fine 0000 steel wool with metal surface prep.

5. Lubricate the crankshaft rear oil seal with clean engine oil.
6. Install the Crankshaft Rear Oil Seal Screws and Adapter.
7. Position the crankshaft rear seal with speedy sleeve around the Crankshaft Rear Oil Seal Screws and Adapter.
8. Using the Crankshaft Rear Oil Seal Installer, install the crankshaft rear seal with speedy sleeve.
9. Install the flexplate-to-crankshaft spacer.
10. Install the spacer plate.
11. Install the flexplate or flywheel.

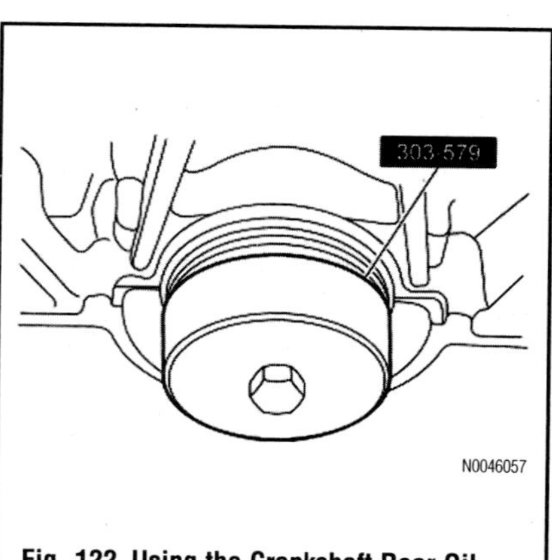

Fig. 122 Using the Crankshaft Rear Oil Seal Installer

TIMING CHAIN FRONT COVER

REMOVAL & INSTALLATION

2.3L Engines

See Figure 123.

➡Do not loosen or remove the crankshaft pulley bolt without first installing the special tools as instructed in the crankshaft pulley procedure. The crankshaft pulley and the crankshaft timing sprocket are not keyed to the crankshaft. The crankshaft, the crankshaft sprocket and the pulley are fitted together by friction, using diamond washers between the flange faces on each part. For that reason, the crankshaft sprocket is also unfastened if the pulley bolt is loosened. Before any repair requiring loosening or removal of the crankshaft pulley bolt, the crankshaft and camshafts must be locked in place by the special tools, otherwise severe engine damage can occur.

1. Remove the crankshaft pulley. For additional information, refer to Timing Chain in this section.
2. Remove the CPK sensor. Refer to Engine Performance.
3. Remove the bolt and the accessory drive belt tensioner.
4. Remove the 3 bolts and the coolant pump pulley.
5. Disconnect the Power Steering Pressure (PSP) switch electrical connector.
6. Remove the 3 bolts and position the power steering pump aside.

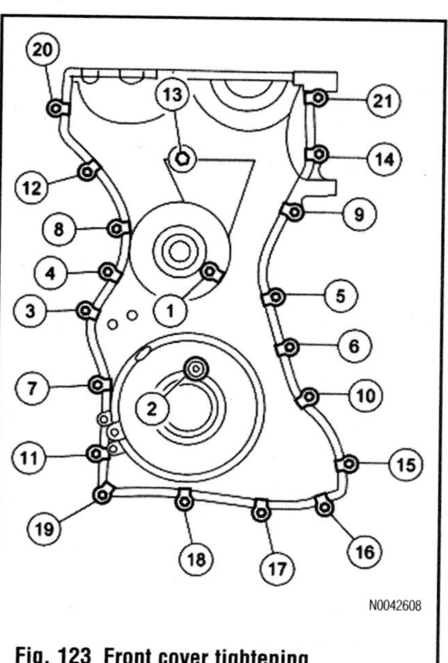

Fig. 123 Front cover tightening sequence—2.3L engine

➡This step is needed only if a new front cover is being installed.

7. Using a 3 jaw puller, remove the fan drive pulley. Refer to Engine Cooling.

➡There is one bolt behind the cooling fan drive pulley. This bolt can be accessed by lining up one of the holes in the pulley with the bolt.

8. Remove the 21 bolts and the engine front cover.

➡Do not use metal scrapers, wire brushes, power abrasive discs or other abrasive means to clean the sealing surfaces. These tools cause scratches and gouges, which make leak paths. Use a plastic scraping tool to remove all traces of old sealant.

9. Clean the sealing surface with silicone gasket remover and metal surface prep. Observe all warnings and cautions and follow all application directions contained on the packaging of the silicone gasket remover and metal surface prep.

To install:

➡This step is needed only if a new front cover is being installed.

10. Install the fan drive pulley, using a nut and bolt with flat washers.

➡Do not use metal scrapers, wire brushes, power abrasive discs or other abrasive means to clean the sealing surfaces. These tools cause scratches and gouges, which make leak paths. Use a plastic scraping tool to remove all traces of old sealant.

➡If not secured within 4 minutes, the sealant must be removed and the sealing area cleaned. To clean the sealing area, use silicone gasket remover and metal surface prep. Observe all warnings and cautions and follow all application directions contained on the packaging of the silicone gasket remover and metal surface prep. Allow to dry until there is no sign of wetness, or 4 minutes, whichever is longer. Failure to follow this procedure can cause future oil leakage.

11. Apply a 0.1 inch bead of silicone gasket and sealant to the cylinder head and oil pan joint areas. Apply a 0.1 inch bead of silicone gasket and sealant to the front cover.

12. Install the front cover. Tighten the 21 bolts in the sequence shown in 3 stages.

a. Stage 1: Tighten the seventeen 8 mm bolts and the stud bolt to 7 ft. lbs. (10 Nm).

b. Stage 2: Tighten the 10 mm bolt to 18 ft. lbs. (25 Nm).

c. Stage 3: Tighten the two 13 mm bolts to 35 ft. lbs. (48 Nm).

13. Position the power steering pump and install the bolts.

Tighten to 18 ft. lbs. (25 Nm).

14. Connect the PSP switch electrical connector.

15. Position the coolant pump pulley and install the 3 bolts.

16. Install the accessory drive belt tensioner and the bolt.

17. Install the crankshaft pulley.

18. Install a 6 mm x 18 mm bolt through the crankshaft pulley and thread it into the front cover.

19. Install the CKP.

4.0L Engines

See Figures 124 and 125.

➡During engine repair procedures, cleanliness is extremely important. Any foreign material, including any material created while cleaning gasket surfaces that enters the oil passages, coolant passages or the oil pan, can cause engine failure.

1. Drain the cooling system.
2. Remove the nut and detach the A/C hose bracket from the front cover.
3. Remove the 5 engine block cradle-to-engine front cover bolts.
4. If equipped, remove the 4 bolts and position the A/C compressor and power steering pump bracket aside.
5. Remove the alternator bracket. Refer to Alternator in Engine Electrical.
6. Disconnect the Crankshaft Position (CKP) sensor electrical connector.
7. Detach the wiring harness retainer.
8. Detach the 2 wiring harness anchors and position the wiring harness aside. Discard the 2 anchors.
9. Remove the bolt and detach the wiring harness from the LH cylinder head.
10. Position the bypass hose clamp off of the coolant pump outlet.
11. Disconnect the heater hose from the coolant pump.
12. Disconnect the lower radiator hose from the coolant pump.

➡Note the positions of the stud bolts for installation reference.

13. Remove the 5 bolts and the 5 stud bolts from the engine front cover. Discard the gasket.

To install:

➡Do not use metal scrapers, wire brushes, power abrasive discs or other abrasive means to clean sealing surfaces. These tools cause scratches and gouges which make leak paths.

14. Clean and inspect the gasket mating surfaces. Use silicone gasket remover and metal surface prep and a plastic or wooden scraping tool. Follow the directions on the packaging.

15. Position a new front cover gasket.

➡If not secured within 4 minutes, the sealant must be removed and the sealing area cleaned. To clean the sealing area, use silicone gasket remover and metal surface prep. Follow the directions on the packaging. Failure to follow this procedure can cause future oil leakage.

16. Apply silicone gasket and sealant to the oil pan and engine block mating surfaces.

17. Apply silicone gasket and sealant to the front cover in 2 places.

18. Install the 5 engine block cradle-to-engine front cover bolts. Tighten to 14 ft. lbs. (19 Nm).

19. To complete the installation, reverse the remaining removal procedure.

20. Fill the engine with clean engine oil.

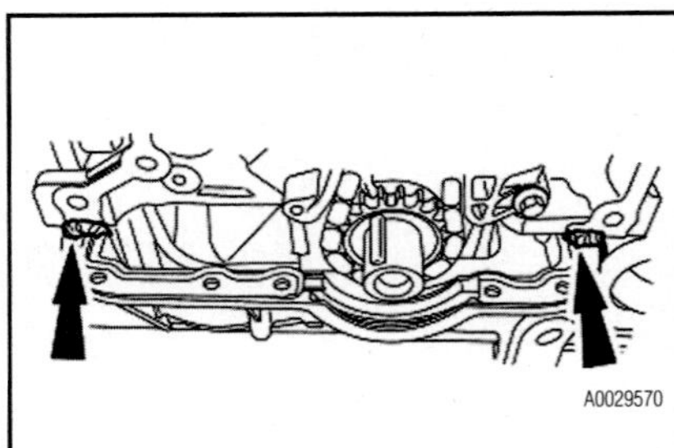

Fig. 124 Locating the oil pan and engine block mating surfaces

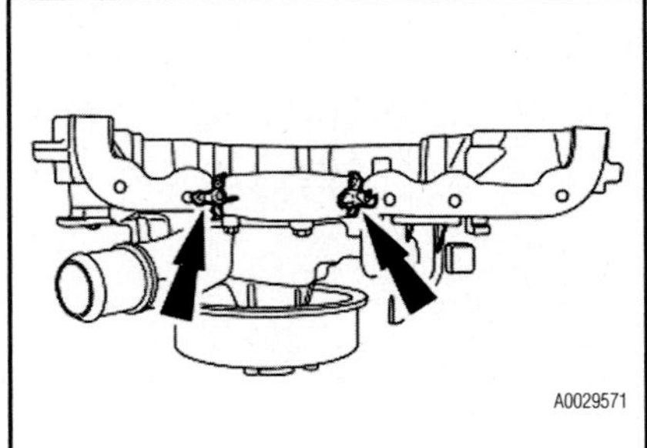

Fig. 125 Apply silicone gasket and sealant to the front cover in 2 places

21. Fill and bleed the engine cooling system.

TIMING CHAIN & SPROCKETS

REMOVAL & INSTALLATION

2.3L Engine

See Figure 126.

➡Do not loosen or remove the crankshaft pulley bolt without first installing the special tools as instructed in the crankshaft pulley procedure. The crankshaft pulley and the crankshaft timing sprocket are not keyed to the crankshaft. The crankshaft, the crankshaft sprocket and the pulley are fitted together by friction, using diamond washers between the flange faces on each part. For that reason, the crankshaft sprocket is also unfastened if the pulley bolt is loosened. Before any repair requiring loosening or removal of the crankshaft pulley bolt, the crankshaft and camshafts must be locked in place by the special tools, otherwise severe engine damage may occur.

1. Remove the engine front cover. For additional information, refer to Timing Chain Front Cover in this section.
2. Compress the timing chain tensioner in the following sequence.
3. Using a small pick, release and hold the ratchet mechanism.
4. While holding the ratchet mechanism in the released position, compress the tensioner by pushing the timing chain arm toward the tensioner.
5. Insert a paper clip into the hole to retain the tensioner.
6. Remove the 2 bolts and the timing chain tensioner.
7. Remove the RH timing chain guide.
8. Remove the timing chain.
9. Remove the 2 bolts and the LH timing chain guide.

➡Do not rely on the Camshaft Alignment Plate to prevent camshaft rotation. The tool or the camshaft may be damaged.

10. If necessary, remove the 2 bolts and the camshaft sprockets.
11. Use the flats on the camshaft to prevent camshaft rotation.

To install:

12. Remove the Camshaft Alignment Plate. Refer to Camshafts.

➡Do not rotate the camshafts. The valves and pistons may be damaged.

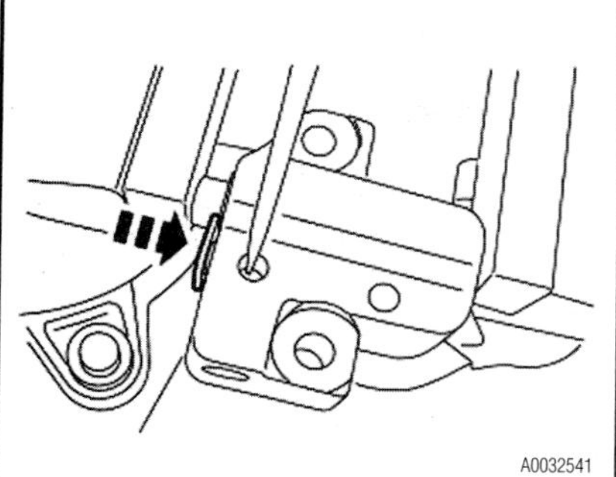

Fig. 126 Push the ratchet arm back into the tensioner housing

13. If the camshaft sprockets were not removed, use the flats on the camshafts to prevent camshaft rotation and loosen the 2 sprocket bolts.
14. If removed, install the camshaft sprockets and the 2 bolts. Do not tighten the bolts at this time.
15. Install the LH timing chain guide and the 2 bolts. Tighten to 7 ft. lbs. (10 Nm).
16. Install the timing chain.
17. Install the RH timing chain guide.

➡If the timing chain plunger and ratchet assembly are not pinned in the compressed position, follow the next 4 steps.

➡Do not compress the ratchet assembly. This will damage the ratchet assembly.

18. Using the edge of a vise, compress the timing chain tensioner plunger.
19. Using a small pick, push back and hold the ratchet mechanism.
20. While holding the ratchet mechanism, push the ratchet arm back into the tensioner housing.
21. Install a paper clip into the hole in the tensioner housing to hold the ratchet assembly and the plunger in during installation.
22. Position the timing chain tensioner and install the 2 bolts. Tighten to 7 ft. lbs. (10 Nm). Remove the paper clip to release the piston.
23. Install the Camshaft Alignment Plate.

➡Do not rely on the Camshaft Alignment Plate to prevent camshaft rotation. The tool or the camshafts may be damaged.

24. Using the flats on the camshafts to prevent camshaft rotation, tighten the 2 bolts. Tighten to 53 ft. lbs. (72 Nm).
25. Install the front cover. For additional information, refer to Timing Chain Front Cover in this section.

4.0L Engine

See Figures 127 through 129.

1. Remove the valve covers. For additional information, refer to Valve Cover in this section.
2. Remove the fuel rail. For additional information, refer to Fuel System.
3. Remove the engine front cover. For additional information, refer to Engine Front Cover in this section.
4. Remove the thermostat housing. For additional information, refer to Engine Cooling.
5. Remove all of the roller followers. For additional information, refer to Camshaft in this section.

➡The LH and RH camshafts must be retimed when either camshaft is disturbed.

6. Turn the crankshaft clockwise to position the No. 1 cylinder at Top Dead Center (TDC).
7. Remove the LH hydraulic chain tensioner.
8. Discard the washer.
9. Remove the LH camshaft sprocket bolt.
10. Install the Camshaft Sprocket Holding Tool and the Adapter for 303-564 and tighten the bolts to 7 ft. lbs. (10 Nm).
11. Remove the LH camshaft sprocket bolt.
12. Using the Crankshaft Holding Tool to prevent the crankshaft from turning, remove the jackshaft sprocket bolt.
13. Remove the 2 bolts and the primary chain tensioner.
14. Remove the primary chain and sprockets as an assembly.
15. Remove the LH cassette upper bolt.
16. Remove the LH cassette lower bolt and the LH cassette.

To install:

17. Refer to exploded illustration for torque values.

➡The camshaft chain sprockets must be oriented correctly. Position the LH cassette.

18. Install the LH cassette lower bolt.
19. Install the LH cassette upper bolt.
20. Install the jackshaft chain and sprockets as an assembly.
21. Install the jackshaft chain tensioner and the bolts.

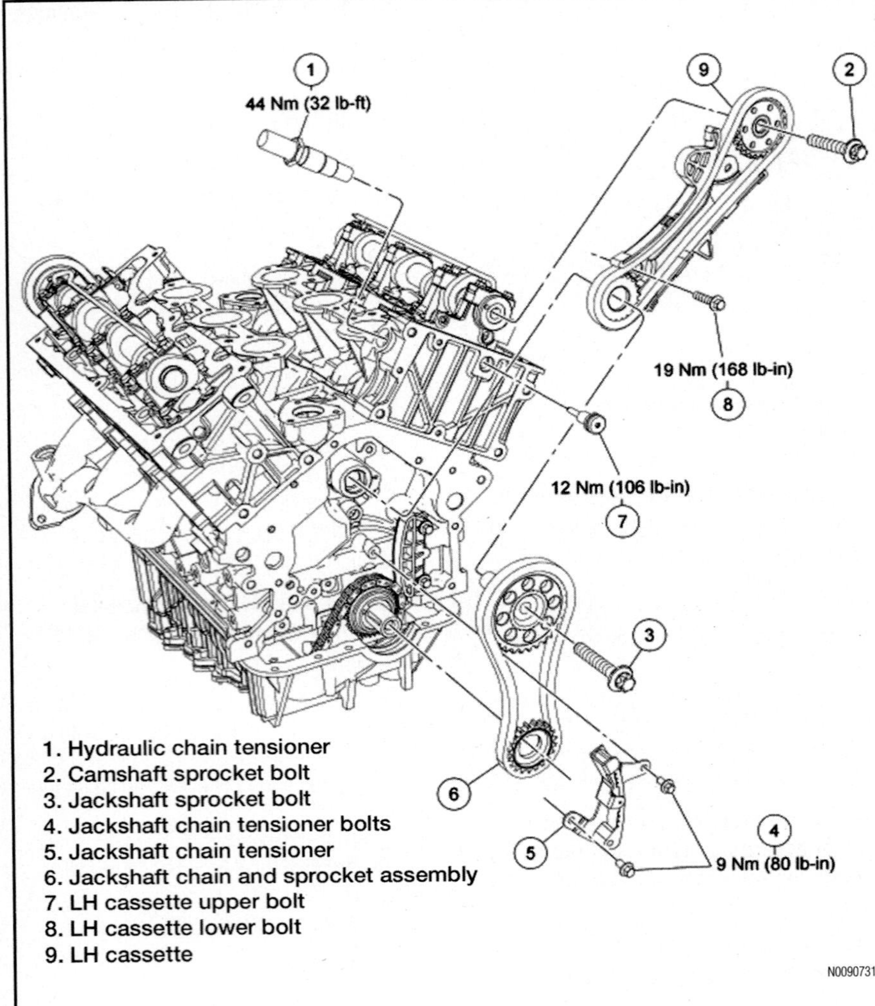

Fig. 127 Exploded view of the timing chain and sprocket assembly—4.0L Engine

22. Using the Crankshaft Holding Tool to prevent the crankshaft from turning, tighten the jackshaft sprocket bolt in 2 stages.
    a. Stage 1: Tighten to 33 ft. lbs. (45 Nm).

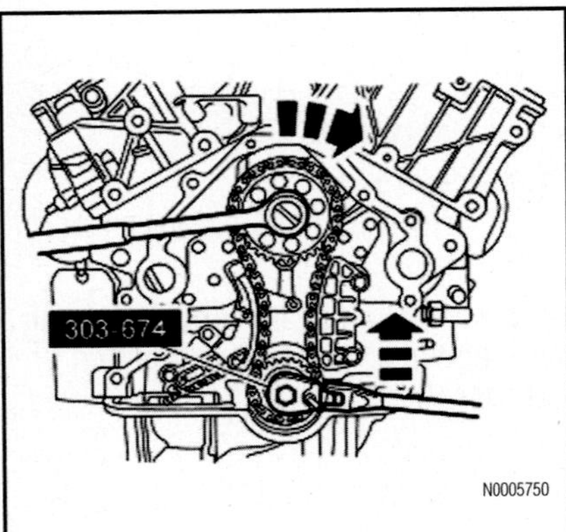

Fig. 128 Using the Crankshaft Holding Tool

    b. Stage 2: Tighten an additional 90 degrees.

23. Loosely install the camshaft sprocket bolt.
24. Install the engine front cover.

➡The LH and RH camshafts must be retimed when either camshaft is disturbed.

➡Install the LH hydraulic chain tensioner during camshaft timing.

25. Time the LH and RH camshafts. For additional information, refer to Camshafts in this section.
26. Install the camshaft roller followers. For additional information, refer to Camshafts in this section.
27. To complete installation, reverse the remaining removal procedure.
28. Fill and bleed the cooling system.

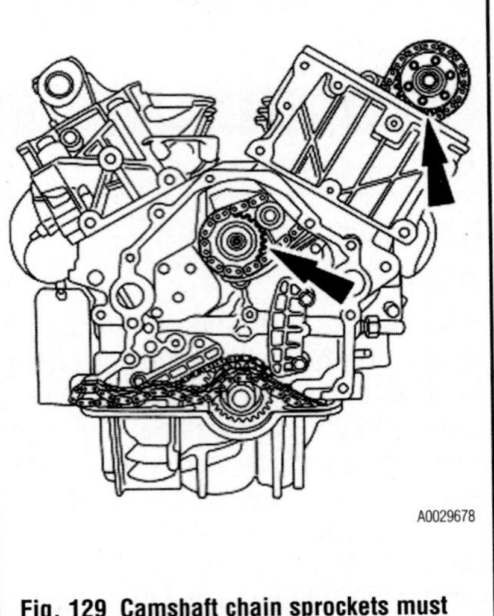

Fig. 129 Camshaft chain sprockets must be oriented correctly

VALVE COVERS

REMOVAL & INSTALLATION

2.3L Engine

See Figures 130 and 131.

1. Disconnect the battery ground cable.
2. Remove the intake manifold assembly. For additional information, refer to Intake Manifold in this section.
3. Position aside the Cylinder Head Temperature (CHT) sensor cover.
4. Disconnect the CHT sensor electrical connector.
5. Disconnect the engine wiring harness support bracket retainers from the valve cover studs.
6. Disconnect the spark plug wires from the spark plugs.
7. Disconnect the ignition coil electrical connector.
8. Remove the 4 bolts and the ignition coil and spark plug wires as an assembly.
9. Disconnect the Camshaft Position (CMP) sensor electrical connector.
10. Remove the bolt and the CMP sensor.
11. Disconnect the crankcase ventilation tube quick connect coupling.
12. Remove the 10 bolts, the 4 stud bolts and the valve cover.

➡Do not use metal scrapers, wire brushes, power abrasive discs or other abrasive means to clean the sealing surfaces. These tools cause scratches and gouges which make leak paths.

13. Clean and inspect the cylinder head sealing surfaces with metal surface prep and silicone gasket remover. Observe all warn-

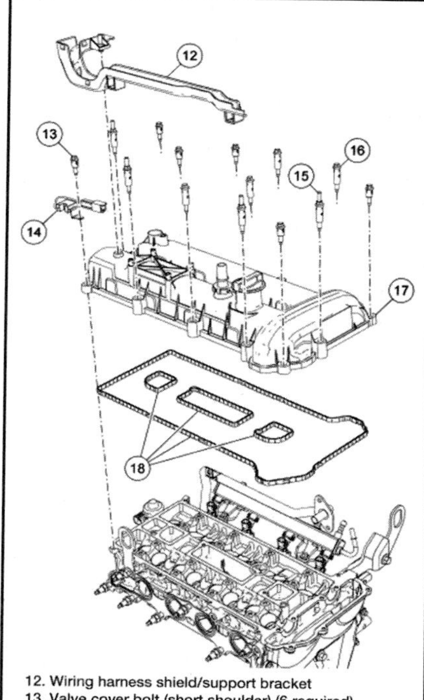

12. Wiring harness shield/support bracket
13. Valve cover bolt (short shoulder) (6 required)
14. Radio ignition interference capacitor
15. Valve cover stud bolt (4 required)
16. Valve cover bolt (medium shoulder) (4 required)
17. Valve cover
18. Valve cover seals (4 required)

N0042588

Fig. 130 Exploded view of the valve cover and components—2.3L Engine

ings and cautions and follow all application directions contained on the packaging of the silicone gasket remover and metal surface prep.

14. Remove and discard the 4 valve cover gaskets.

To install:

15. Install 4 new valve cover gaskets.
16. Position the valve cover and install the 10 bolts and 4 stud bolts in the sequence shown. Tighten to 7 ft. lbs. (10 Nm).

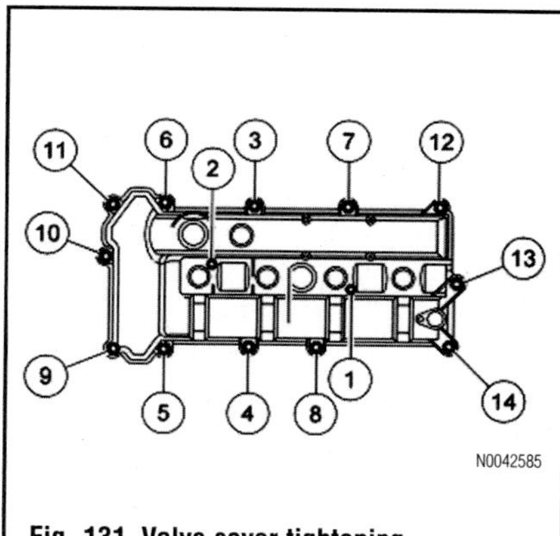

Fig. 131 Valve cover tightening sequence—2.3L Engine

17. To complete installation, reverse the remaining removal procedure.
18. Connect the battery ground cable.

4.0L Engine

LH Valve Cover

See Figure 132.

1. Detach the accelerator cable from the Throttle Body (TB) and the accelerator cable bracket.
2. Detach the exhaust manifold-to-EGR valve tube from the EGR valve. To install, tighten to 25 ft. lbs. (34 Nm).
3. Disconnect the Evaporative Emission (EVAP) purge valve-to-intake manifold tube from the intake manifold.
4. Detach the EVAP purge valve-to-intake manifold tube retainer.
5. Disconnect the differential pressure feedback EGR sensor electrical connector.
6. Detach the wiring harness retainer from the differential pressure feedback EGR sensor.
7. Remove the differential pressure feedback EGR sensor.
8. Disconnect the Camshaft Position (CMP) sensor electrical connector.
9. Disconnect the EGR vacuum regulator solenoid electrical connector.
10. Disconnect the EGR vacuum regulator solenoid vacuum connector.
11. Remove the 2 bolts and the EGR vacuum regulator solenoid. To install, tighten to 7 ft. lbs. (10 Nm).
12. Disconnect the wiring harness electrical connectors.
13. Remove the bolt and position the wiring harness connectors and bracket aside.

➡It is important to twist the spark plug wire boots while pulling upward to avoid possible damage to the spark plug wire.

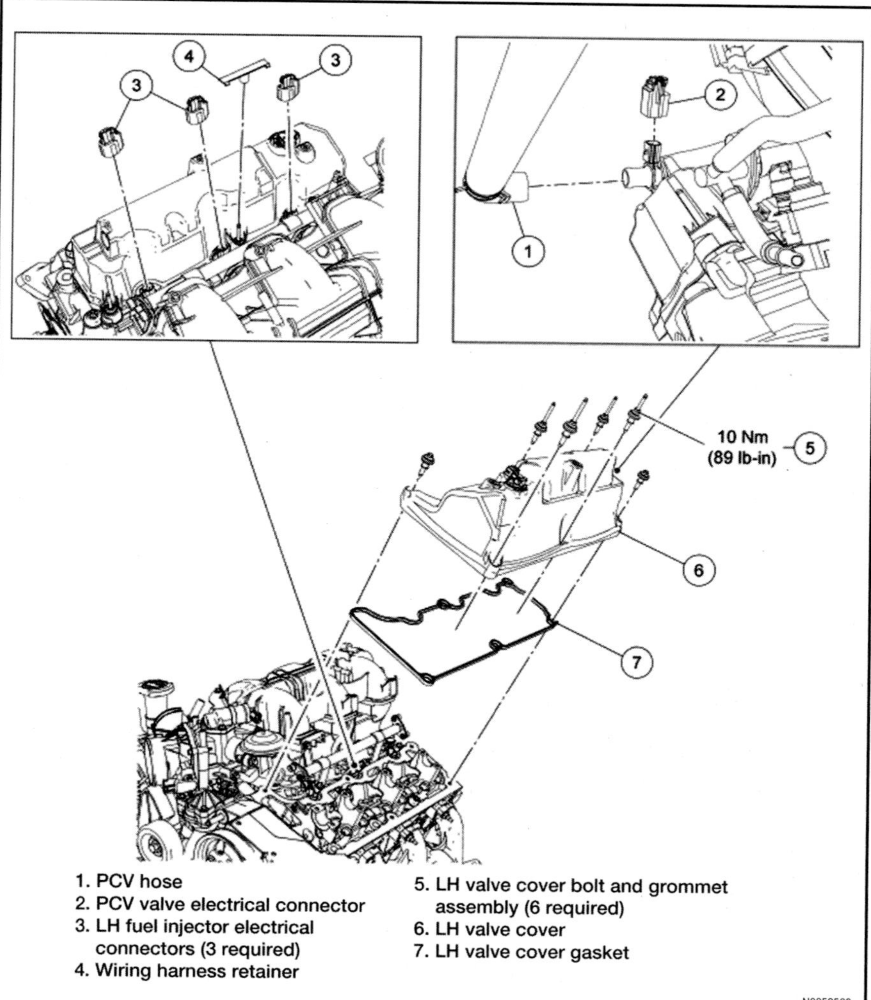

1. PCV hose
2. PCV valve electrical connector
3. LH fuel injector electrical connectors (3 required)
4. Wiring harness retainer
5. LH valve cover bolt and grommet assembly (6 required)
6. LH valve cover
7. LH valve cover gasket

N0052569

Fig. 132 Exploded view of the LH valve cover—4.0L Engine

➡Spark plug wires must be connected to the correct ignition coil terminal. Mark the spark plug wire locations before removing them.

14. Disconnect the LH spark plug wires from the ignition coil.
15. Detach the LH spark plug wire retainer from the ignition coil bracket.
16. Detach the LH spark plug wire retainer from the valve cover stud bolt.
17. Disconnect the ignition coil electrical connector.
18. Detach the wiring harness retainer from the ignition coil bracket.
19. Disconnect the radio interference capacitor electrical connector.
20. Detach the accelerator cable bracket from the ignition coil.
21. Remove the 4 bolts and position the ignition coil and bracket aside.
22. Disconnect the PCV hose from the PCV valve.
23. Disconnect the PCV valve electrical connector.
24. Disconnect the 3 LH fuel injector electrical connectors.
25. Detach the wiring harness retainer from the LH valve cover stud bolt.
26. Loosen the 6 bolt and grommet assemblies and remove the LH valve cover. To install, tighten to 7 ft. lbs. (10 Nm).

➡Do not use metal scrapers, wire brushes, power abrasive discs or other abrasive means to clean the sealing surfaces. These tools cause scratches and gouges which make leak paths.

27. Clean the sealing surfaces and inspect the LH valve cover gasket. Install a new gasket if necessary.
28. To install, reverse the removal procedure.

RH Valve Cover

See Figure 133.

1. Drain the cooling system.
2. Remove the Air Cleaner (ACL) outlet pipe.
3. Remove the upper radiator hose.
4. Disconnect the vacuum reservoir hose.
5. Disconnect the crankcase breather hose.
6. Vehicles equipped with an automatic transmission; Remove the transmission fluid level indicator tube nut and position the tube aside. To install, tighten to 17 ft. lbs. (23 Nm).
7. Disconnect the heated PCV coolant hose from the intake manifold heated PCV fitting.
8. Disconnect the heater hose from the thermostat housing.
9. Disconnect the heater hose from the front lower heater tube assembly.
10. Disconnect the heater hose from the rear upper heater tube assembly.
11. Disconnect the heater hose from the rear lower heater tube assembly.
12. Remove the 2 heater tube assembly bolts. To install, tighten the rear bolt to 17 ft. lbs. (23 Nm). To install, tighten the front bolt to 21 ft. lbs. (28 Nm).
13. Lift the heater tube assembly and detach the wiring harness retainer. Remove the heater tube assembly.
14. Disconnect the heater hose from the heater core and position the heater hose aside.
15. Disconnect the Mass Air Flow (MAF) sensor electrical connector.
16. Detach the MAF sensor wiring harness retainer from the alternator wiring harness and position the MAF sensor wiring harness aside.

➡It is important to twist the spark plug wire boots while pulling upward to avoid possible damage to the spark plug wire.

➡Spark plug wires must be connected to the correct spark plug. Mark spark plug wire locations before removing them.

➡Apply silicone brake caliper grease and dielectric compound to the inside of the spark plug wire boots before connecting them.

17. Using the Spark Plug Wire Remover, disconnect the RH spark plug wires from the spark plugs.
18. Detach the spark plug wire retainer from the valve cover stud bolt and position the spark plug wires aside.
19. Disconnect the RH fuel injector electrical connectors.
20. Detach the wiring harness retainer from the valve cover stud bolt and position the wiring harness aside.
21. Loosen the 6 bolt and grommet assemblies and remove the RH valve cover. To install, tighten to 7 ft. lbs. (10 Nm).

➡Do not use metal scrapers, wire brushes, power abrasive discs or other abrasive means to clean the sealing surfaces. These tools cause scratches and gouges which make leak paths.

22. Clean the sealing surfaces and inspect the RH valve cover gasket. Install a new gasket if necessary.
23. To install, reverse the removal procedure.

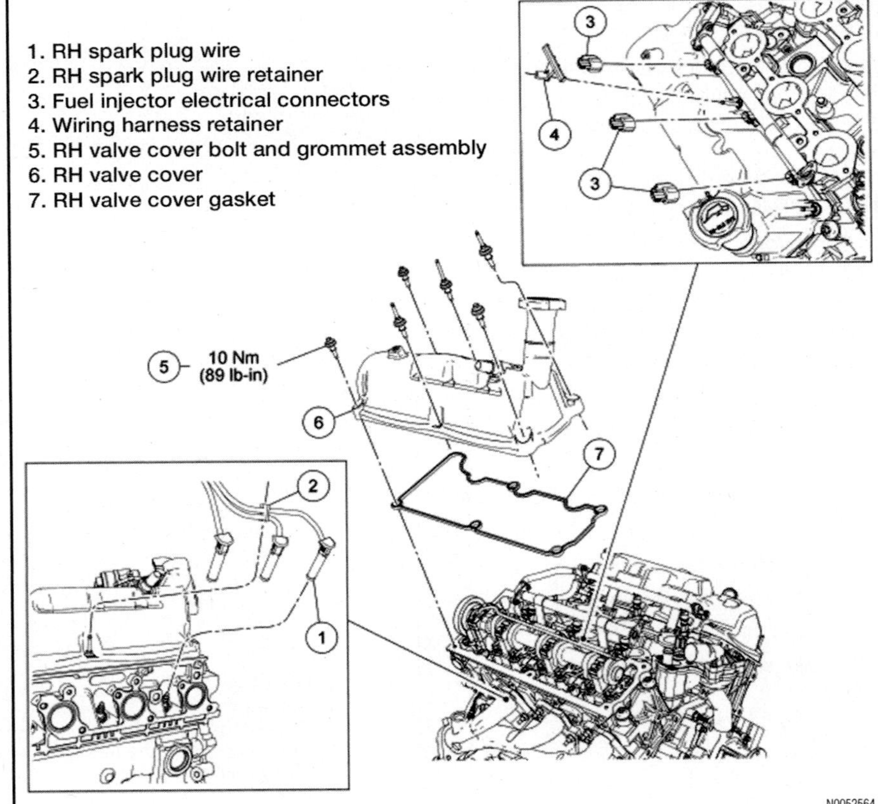

Fig. 133 Exploded view of the RH valve cover

ENGINE PERFORMANCE & EMISSION CONTROLS

CAMSHAFT POSITION (CMP) SENSOR

LOCATION

See Figures 134 and 135.

Refer to the accompanying illustrations.

REMOVAL & INSTALLATION

1. Disconnect the negative battery cable.
2. Disconnect the Camshaft Position (CMP) sensor electrical connector.
3. Remove the bolt and the CMP sensor and discard the O-ring seal.

➡Lubricate the new O-ring seal with clean engine oil prior to installation.

4. To install, reverse the removal procedure.

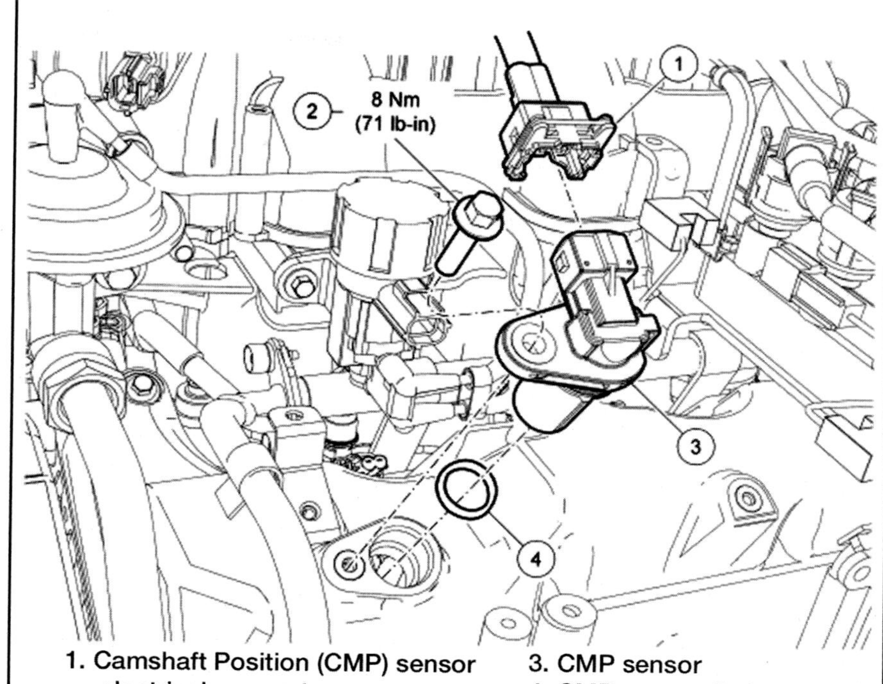

Fig. 135 Camshaft Position (CMP) sensor location—4.0L Engine

CRANKSHAFT POSITION (CKP) SENSOR

LOCATION

See Figures 136 and 137.

Refer to the accompanying illustrations.

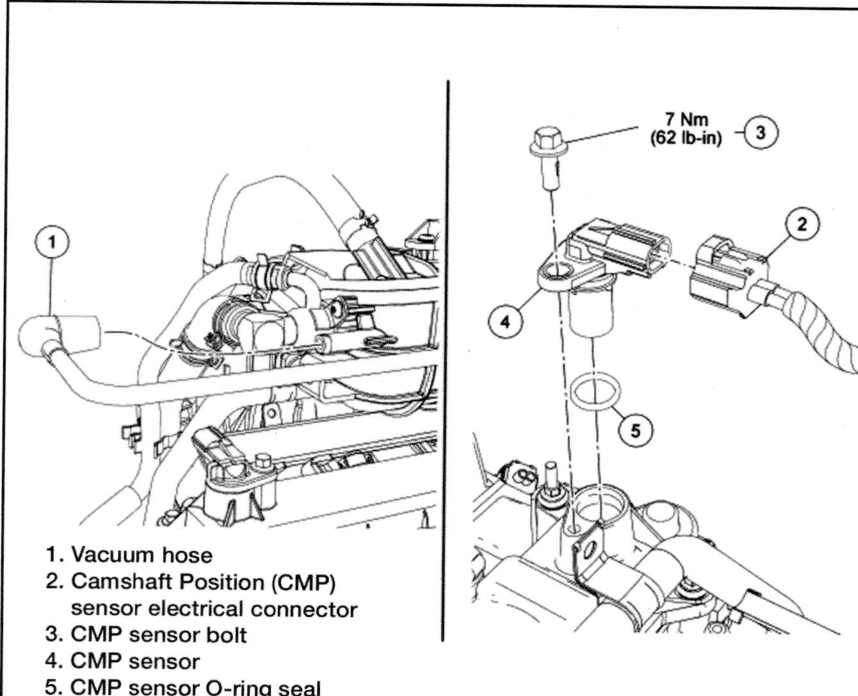

Fig. 134 Camshaft Position (CMP) sensor location—2.3L Engine

REMOVAL & INSTALLATION

2.3L Engine

See Figures 138 through 141.

1. With the vehicle in NEUTRAL, position it on a hoist.
2. Disconnect the Crankshaft Position (CKP) sensor electrical connector.
3. Remove the engine plug bolt.
4. Install the Crankshaft Timing Peg and turn the crankshaft pulley bolt to position the No. 1 cylinder at Top Dead Center (TDC).
5. Remove the 2 bolts and the CKP sensor.
6. Install the 6 mm x 18 mm bolt in the position shown.

To install:

➡Whenever the CKP sensor is removed, a new one must be installed using the Crankshaft Sensor Aligner.

7. Position the CKP sensor and loosely install the 2 bolts.
8. Adjust the CKP sensor with the Crankshaft Sensor Aligner and tighten the 2 bolts. Tighten to 62 inch lbs. (7 Nm).
9. Connect the CKP sensor electrical connector. Remove the 6 mm x 18 mm bolt.

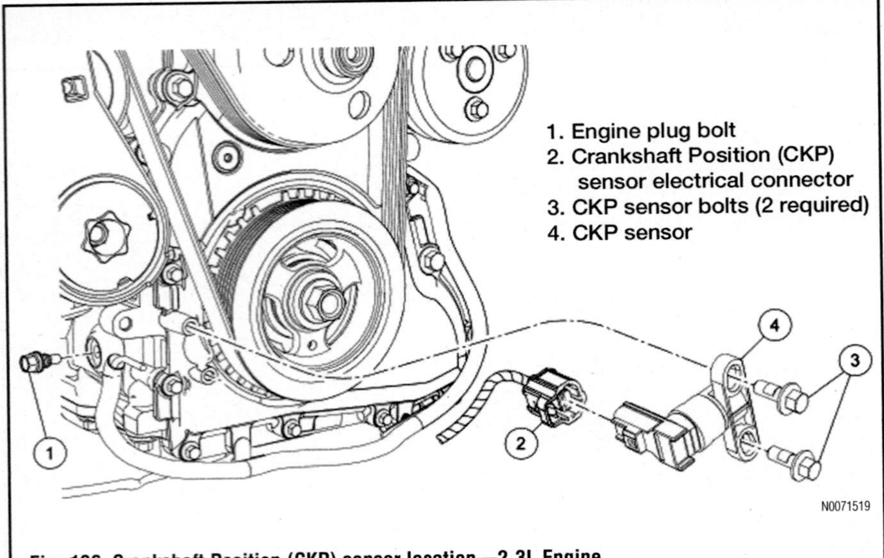

Fig. 136 Crankshaft Position (CKP) sensor location—2.3L Engine

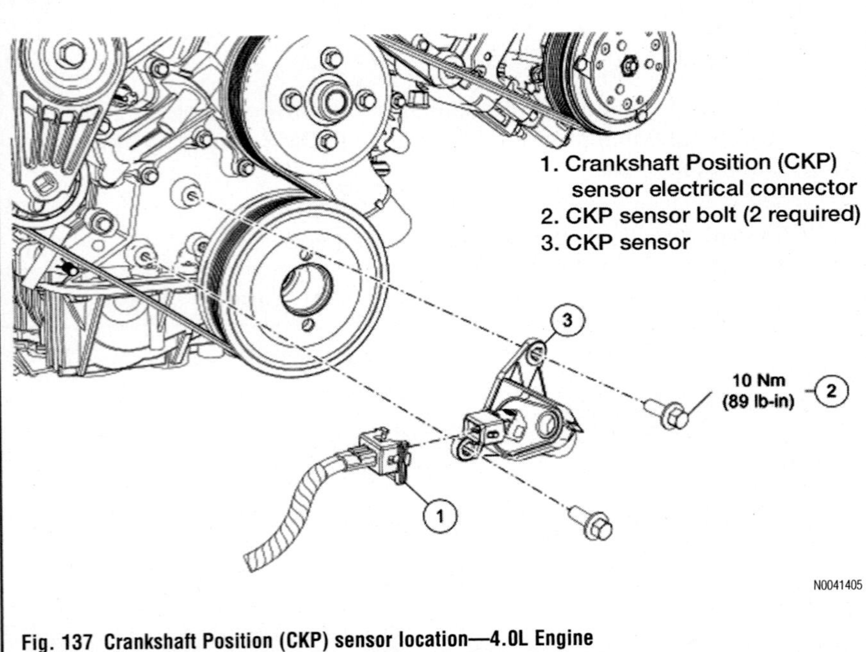

Fig. 137 Crankshaft Position (CKP) sensor location—4.0L Engine

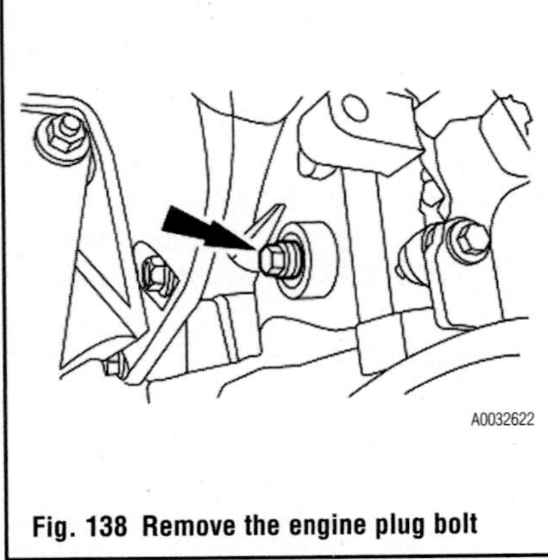

Fig. 138 Remove the engine plug bolt

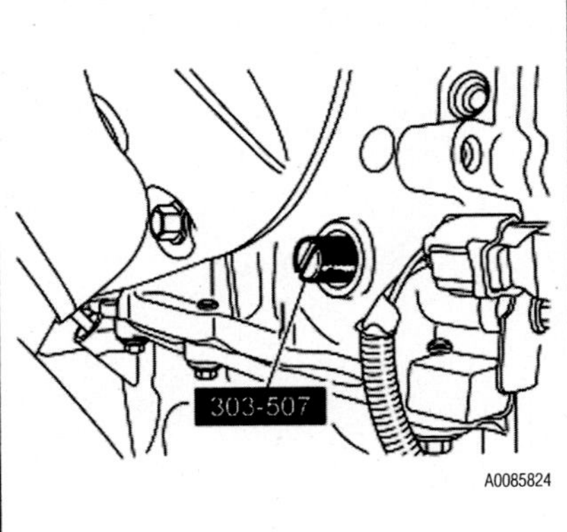

Fig. 139 Install the Crankshaft Timing Peg

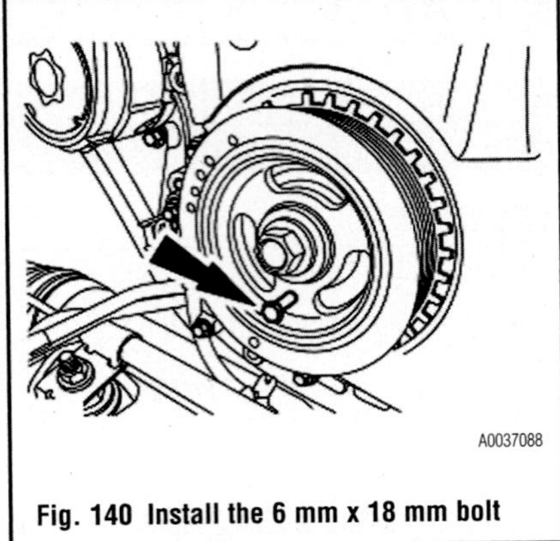

Fig. 140 Install the 6 mm x 18 mm bolt

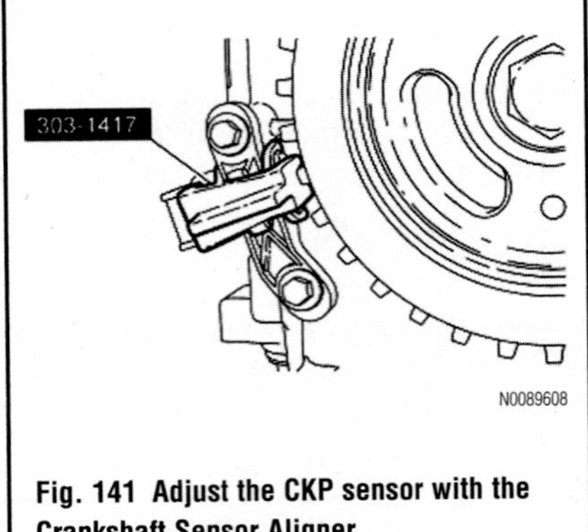

Fig. 141 Adjust the CKP sensor with the Crankshaft Sensor Aligner

10. Remove the Crankshaft Timing Peg.
11. Install the engine plug bolt. Tighten to 15 ft. lbs. (20 Nm).

4.0L Engine

1. Disconnect the negative battery cable.
2. Disconnect the Crankshaft Position (CKP) sensor electrical connector.
3. Remove the 2 bolts and the CKP sensor.
4. To install, reverse the removal procedure.

ELECTRONIC CONTROL MODULE (ECM)

REMOVAL & INSTALLATION

See Figure 142.

➡**Retrieve the module configuration. Carry out the module configuration retrieval steps of the Programmable Module Installation procedure.**

1. Remove the PCM wiring harness retainer nut.
2. Remove the ground wire stud bolt.
3. Disconnect the 3 PCM electrical connectors.
4. Remove the 2 nuts and the PCM.

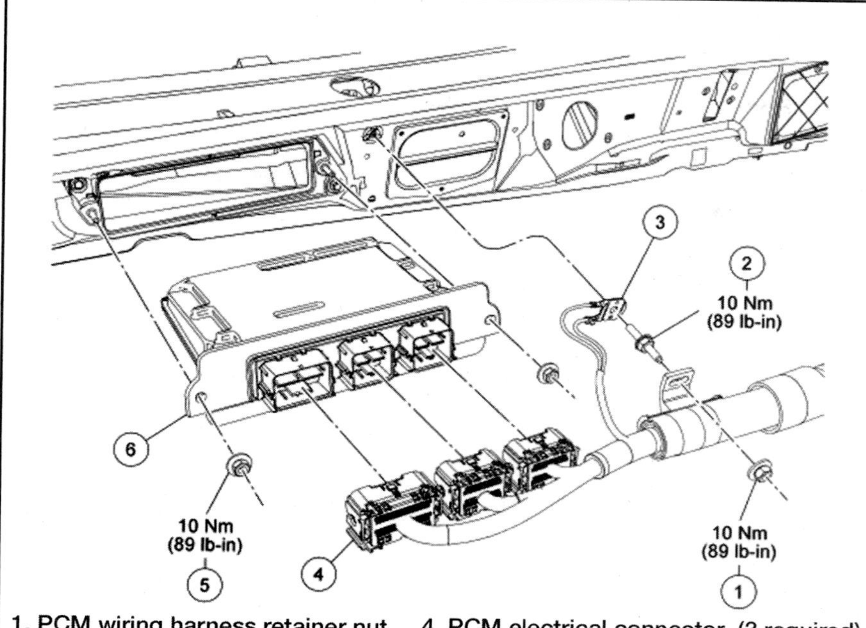

1. PCM wiring harness retainer nut
2. Ground wire stud bolt
3. Ground wire terminal (2 required)
4. PCM electrical connector (3 required)
5. PCM nuts
6. PCM

N0051798

Fig. 142 Removing the ECM

To install:

5. Install the PCM and the 2 nuts.
6. Connect the 3 PCM electrical connectors.
7. Position the ground wire terminals and install the stud bolt.
8. Install the PCM wiring harness retainer nut.

➡If a new PCM is installed, the parameters must be reset in both the PCM and the instrument cluster module or the vehicle will experience a Passive Anti-Theft System (PATS) no-start. This will occur even if the vehicle is not equipped with PATS.PATS vehicles and non- PATS vehicles have parameters in the instrument cluster module and the PCM and they both must be reset whenever a new PCM is installed.

9. Restore the module configurations for the instrument cluster module and the PCM. Carry out the module configuration restore steps of the Programmable Module Installation procedure.

MODULE CONFIGURATION

Programmable Module Installation (Pmi) Using The Integrated Diagnostic System (Ids) When The Original Module Is Available

➡Following module installation, some modules require a separate procedure be carried out. For instructions, refer to the specific module removal and installation procedures.

1. Connect the IDS and identify the vehicle as normal.
2. From the Toolbox icon, select Module Programming and press the check mark.
3. Select Programmable Module Installation.
4. Select the module that is being replaced.
5. Follow the on-screen instructions, turn the ignition key to the OFF position, and press the check mark.
6. Install the new module and press the check mark.
7. Follow the on-screen instructions, turn the ignition key to the ON position, and press the check mark.
8. The IDS downloads the data into the new module and displays Module Configuration Complete.
9. Test module for correct operation.

Programmable Module Installation (PMI) Using the Integrated Diagnostic System (IDS) When the Original Module is NOT Available

➡Following module installation, some modules require a separate procedure be carried out. For instructions, refer to the specific module removal and installation procedures.

10. Install the new module.
11. Connect the IDS and identify the vehicle as normal.
12. From the Toolbox icon, select Module Programming and press the check mark.
13. Select Programmable Module Installation.
14. Select the module that was replaced.
15. Follow the on-screen instructions, turn the ignition key to the OFF position, and press the check mark.
16. Follow the on-screen instructions, turn the ignition key to the ON position, and press the check mark.
17. If the data is not available, the IDS displays a screen stating to contact the As-Built Data Center.
18. Retrieve the data from the technician service publication website at this time and press the check mark.
19. Enter the module data and press the check mark.
20. The IDS downloads the data into the new module and displays Module Configuration Complete.
21. Test module for correct operation.

ENGINE COOLANT TEMPERATURE (ECT) SENSOR

LOCATION

See Figure 143.

Refer to the accompanying illustration.

REMOVAL & INSTALLATION

1. Drain the cooling system.
2. Disconnect the Engine Coolant Temperature (ECT) sensor electrical connector.
3. Remove the clip and the ECT sensor. Discard the O-ring seal.
4. To install, reverse the removal procedure.
5. Install a new O-ring seal.

HEATED OXYGEN SENSOR (HO2S)

LOCATION

Refer to Catalytic Converter in Engine Mechanical.

REMOVAL & INSTALLATION

See Figure 144.

1. With the vehicle in NEUTRAL, position it on a hoist.
2. Disconnect the Heated Oxygen Sensor (HO2S) electrical connector.

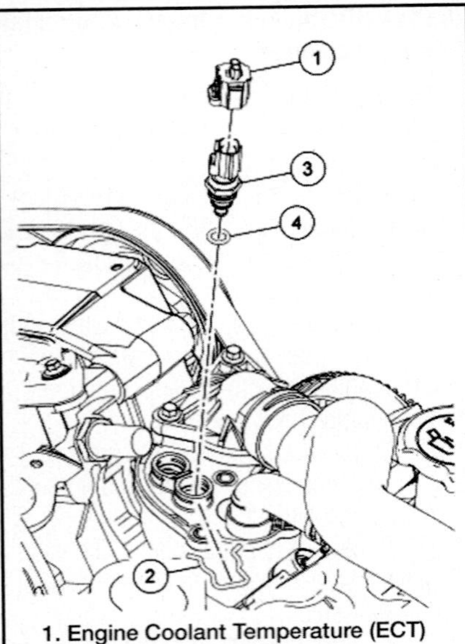

Fig. 143 ECT sensor location—4.0L Engines

➡If necessary, lubricate the HO2S with lock lubricant to assist in removal.

3. Using the Exhaust Gas Oxygen Sensor Socket, remove the HO2S.

To install:

4. Apply a light coat of nickel anti-seize lubricant to the threads of the HO2S.
5. Using the Exhaust Gas Oxygen Sensor Socket, install the HO2S.
6. Calculate the correct torque wrench setting for the following torque.
7. Using the Exhaust Gas Oxygen Sensor Socket, tighten to 35 ft. lbs. (48 Nm).
8. Connect the HO2S electrical connector.

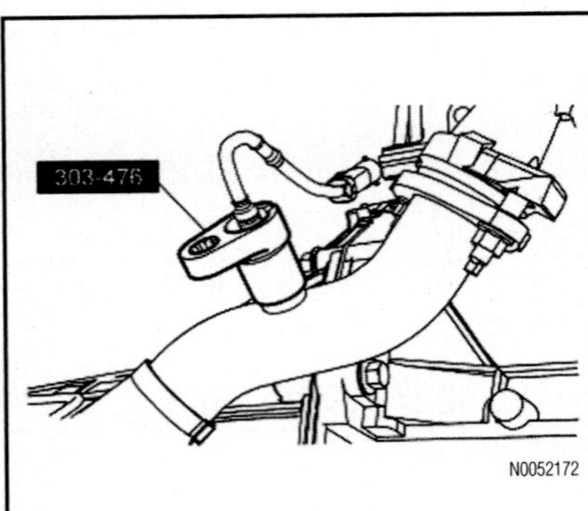

Fig. 144 Using the Exhaust Gas Oxygen Sensor Socket

KNOCK SENSOR (KS)

LOCATION

See Figures 145 and 146.

Refer to the accompanying illustrations.

REMOVAL & INSTALLATION

2.3L Engines

1. Disconnect the Knock Sensor (KS) electrical connector.

➡The KS is a one-time-use item and, if serviced, a new KS must be installed.

2. Remove the bolt and remove and discard the KS.
3. To install, reverse the removal procedure. Install a new KS.

4.0L Engines

1. Remove the intake manifold.
2. Disconnect the Knock Sensor (KS) electrical connector.
3. Remove the nut and the KS.
4. To install, reverse the removal procedure.

MANIFOLD ABSOLUTE PRESSURE (MAP) SENSOR

LOCATION

See Figure 147.

Refer to the accompanying illustration.

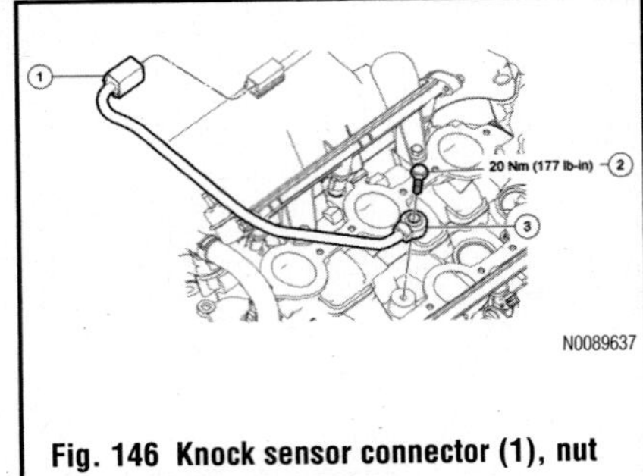

Fig. 146 Knock sensor connector (1), nut (2) and sensor (3)—2.3L Engine

REMOVAL & INSTALLATION

2.3L Engine

1. Disconnect the Manifold Absolute Pressure (MAP) sensor electrical connector.
2. Remove the bolt and lift the MAP sensor out of the intake manifold.
3. Discard the O-ring seal.
4. To install, reverse the removal procedure.
5. Install a new O-ring seal.

THROTTLE POSITION SENSOR (TPS)

LOCATION

See Figures 148 and 149.

Refer to the accompanying illustrations.

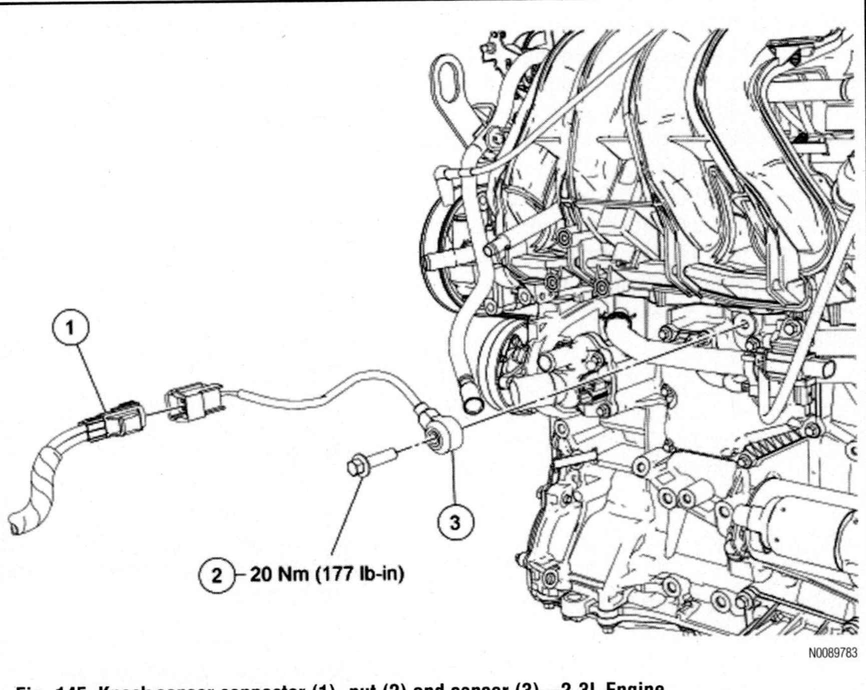

Fig. 145 Knock sensor connector (1), nut (2) and sensor (3)—2.3L Engine

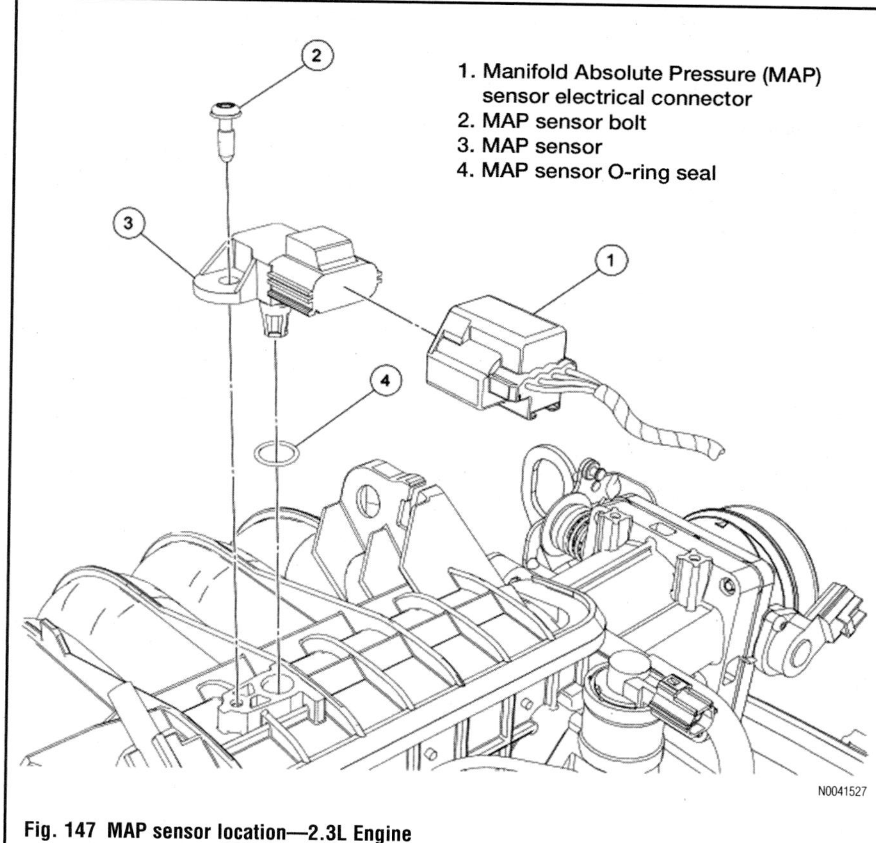

Fig. 147 MAP sensor location—2.3L Engine

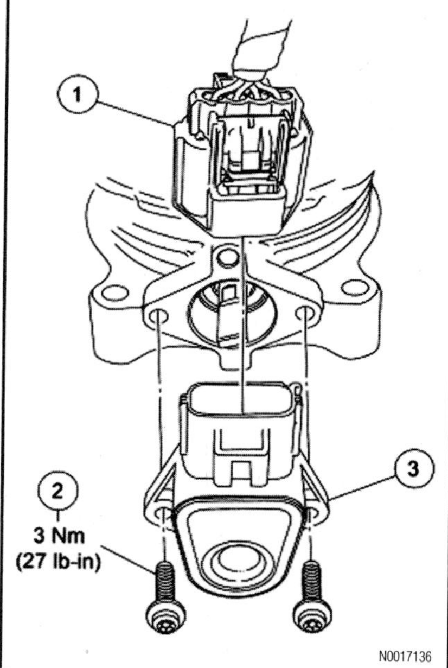

Fig. 148 Locating the TPS sensor connector (1), sensor (2) and screw (3)—2.3L Engine

Fig. 149 Locating the TPS sensor connector (1), sensor (2) and screw (3)—4.0L Engine

REMOVAL & INSTALLATION

2.3L Engine

1. Disconnect the Throttle Position (TP) sensor electrical connector.

➡Failure to remove the Throttle Position (TP) sensor screws in the following manner will result in damage to the screws. First, loosen the screws 1 to 2 full turns using a hand tool, and then use a suitable high-speed driver to complete the removal.

2. Remove and discard the 2 bolts and the TP sensor.

➡Do not use a high-speed driver to install the new screws or damage to the Throttle Position (TP) sensor may occur.

➡Do not reuse the TP sensor and screws. A new TP sensor and screws must be installed.

➡When installing the new TP sensor, make sure that the radial locator tab on the TP sensor is aligned with the radial locator hole on the Throttle Body (TB).

3. To install, reverse the removal procedure.
4. Install a new TP sensor and screws.

4.0L Engine

1. Remove the 3 bolts and the Throttle Body (TB) cover.
2. Disconnect the Throttle Position (TP) sensor electrical connector.

➡Failure to remove the Throttle Position (TP) sensor screws in the following manner will result in damage to the screws. First, loosen the screws 1 to 2 full turns using a hand tool, and then use a suitable high-speed driver to complete the removal.

3. Remove and discard the 2 bolts and the TP sensor.

➡Do not use a high-speed driver to install the new screws or the Throttle Position (TP) sensor may be damaged.

➡Do not reuse the TP sensor and screws. A new TP sensor and screws must be installed.

➡When installing the new TP sensor, make sure that the radial locator tab on the TP sensor is aligned with the radial locator hole on the TB.

4. To install, reverse the removal procedure.
5. Install a new TP sensor and screws.

FUEL SYSTEM SERVICE PRECAUTIONS

Safety is the most important factor when performing not only fuel system maintenance but any type of maintenance. Failure to conduct maintenance and repairs in a safe manner may result in serious personal injury or death. Maintenance and testing of the vehicle's fuel system components can be accomplished safely and effectively by adhering to the following rules and guidelines.

- To avoid the possibility of fire and personal injury, always disconnect the negative battery cable unless the repair or test procedure requires that battery voltage be applied.
- Always relieve the fuel system pressure prior to disconnecting any fuel system component (injector, fuel rail, pressure regulator, etc.), fitting or fuel line connection. Exercise extreme caution whenever relieving fuel system pressure to avoid exposing skin, face and eyes to fuel spray. Please be advised that fuel under pressure may penetrate the skin or any part of the body that it contacts.
- Always place a shop towel or cloth around the fitting or connection prior to loosening to absorb any excess fuel due to spillage. Ensure that all fuel spillage (should it occur) is quickly removed from engine surfaces. Ensure that all fuel soaked cloths or towels are deposited into a suitable waste container.
- Always keep a dry chemical (Class B) fire extinguisher near the work area.
- Do not allow fuel spray or fuel vapors to come into contact with a spark or open flame.
- Always use a back-up wrench when loosening and tightening fuel line connection fittings. This will prevent unnecessary stress and torsion to fuel line piping.
- Always replace worn fuel fitting O-rings with new Do not substitute fuel hose or equivalent where fuel pipe is installed.

**** CAUTION**

Do not smoke, carry lighted tobacco or have an open flame of any type when working on or near any fuel-related component. Highly flammable mixtures are always present and may be ignited. Failure to follow these instructions may result in serious personal injury.

**** CAUTION**

Do not carry personal electronic devices such as cell phones, pagers or audio equipment of any type when working on or near any fuel-related component. Highly flammable mixtures are always present and may be ignited. Failure to follow these instructions may result in serious personal injury.

**** CAUTION**

Before working on or disconnecting any of the fuel tubes or fuel system components, relieve the fuel system pressure to prevent accidental spraying of fuel. Fuel in the fuel system remains under high pressure, even when the engine is not running. Failure to follow this instruction may result in serious personal injury.

**** CAUTION**

When handling fuel, always observe fuel handling precautions and be prepared in the event of fuel spillage. Spilled fuel may be ignited by hot vehicle components or other ignition sources. Failure to follow these instructions may result in serious personal injury.

**** CAUTION**

Always disconnect the battery ground cable at the battery when working on an evaporative emission (EVAP) system or fuel-related component. Highly flammable mixtures are always present and may be ignited. Failure to follow these instructions may result in serious personal injury.

Before servicing the vehicle, make sure to also refer to the precautions in the beginning of this section as well.

RELIEVING FUEL SYSTEM PRESSURE

See Figures 150 and 151.

1. Before beginning this procedure, refer to the Fuel System Precautions.
2. Disconnect the battery ground cable.

➡2.3L shown, 4.0L similar.

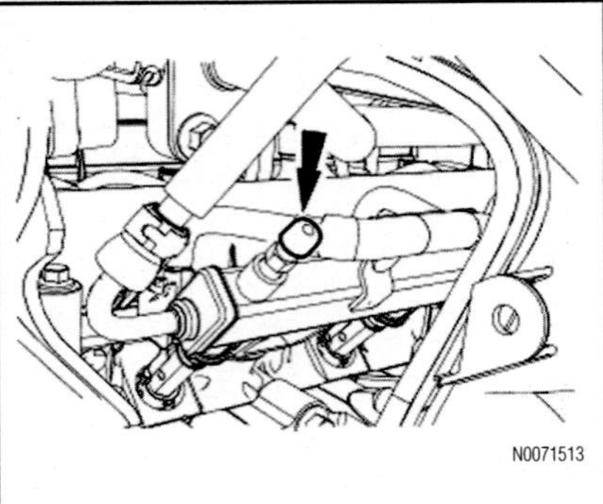

Fig. 150 Remove the cap from the fuel pressure relief valve

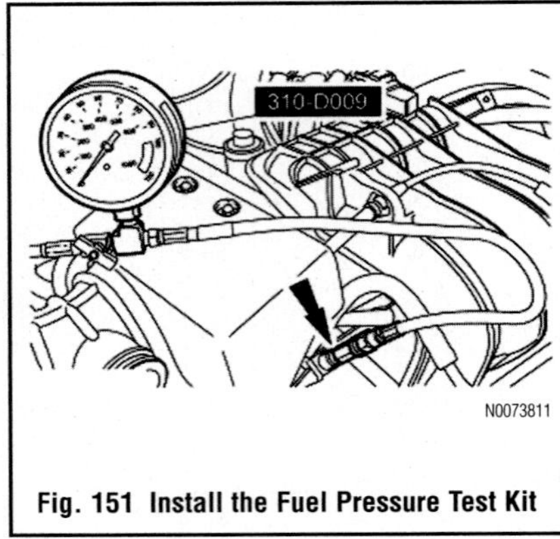

Fig. 151 Install the Fuel Pressure Test Kit

3. Remove the cap from the fuel pressure relief valve located on the fuel rail.

➡2.3L shown, 4.0L similar.

4. Install the Fuel Pressure Test Kit onto the fuel pressure relief valve.

➡Open the drain valve slowly to relieve the system pressure. This may drain fuel from the system.

5. Place fuel in a suitable container.
6. Open the drain valve on the Fuel Pressure Test Kit and relieve the fuel system pressure.

➡It may take more than one key cycle to pressurize the fuel system.

7. Upon completion of the fuel system repairs, cycle the ignition key and wait 3 seconds to pressurize the fuel system. Check for leaks before starting the engine.

FUEL FILTER

REMOVAL & INSTALLATION

See Figure 152.

1. Before beginning this procedure, refer to the Fuel System Precautions.

Fig. 152 Remove the fuel filter from the bracket

2. With the vehicle in NEUTRAL, position it on a hoist.
3. Release the fuel system pressure.
4. Disconnect the battery ground cable.

➡**Some residual fuel may remain in the fuel tubes and fuel filter after releasing the fuel system pressure. Upon disconnecting or removing any fuel-related component, carefully drain residual fuel into a suitable container.**

5. Disconnect the fuel supply and return tubes-to-fuel filter quick connect couplings.
6. Remove the fuel filter from the bracket.
7. To install, reverse the removal procedure.

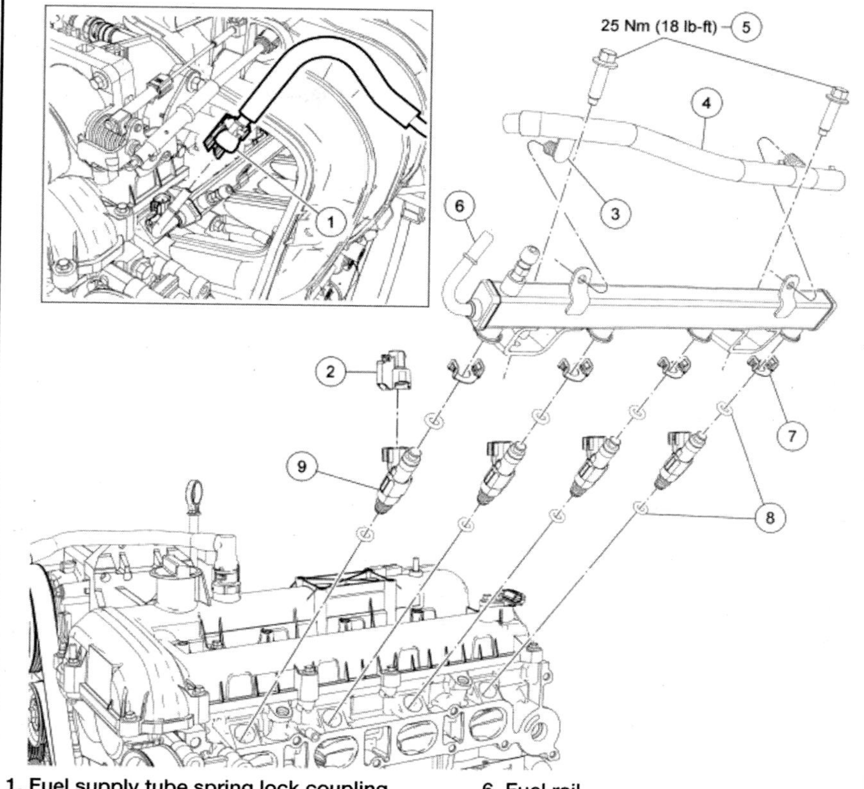

Fig. 153 Exploded view of the fuel rail and fuel injectors—2.3L Engine

FUEL INJECTORS

REMOVAL & INSTALLATION

⁂ WARNING

Shut off the electrical power to the air suspension system prior to hoisting or jacking an air suspension equipped vehicle. Failure to do so may result in unexpected inflation or deflation of the air springs, which may result in shifting of the vehicle during these operations. Failure to follow this instruction may result in serious personal injury.

2.3L Engine

See Figure 153.

1. Before beginning this procedure, refer to the Fuel System Precautions.
2. Disconnect the battery ground cable.
3. Release the fuel pressure.
4. Disconnect the 4 fuel injector electrical connectors.
5. Disconnect the fuel injector wiring harness pushpins from the fuel rail and position the wiring harness aside.
6. Disconnect the fuel supply tube spring lock coupling.

➡**Remove the fuel rail and the fuel injectors as an assembly.**

7. Remove the 2 bolts and the fuel rail and injector assembly.
8. Remove the retaining clips and separate the fuel injectors from the fuel rail.
9. Discard the fuel injector O-ring seals.

➡**Use O-ring seals that are made of special fuel-resistance material. The use of ordinary O-ring seals may cause the fuel system to leak.**

➡**Do not reuse the O-ring seals. The reuse of the O-ring seals may cause the fuel system to leak.**

➡**Lubricate the new O-ring seals with clean engine oil prior to installation.**

10. To install, reverse the removal procedure.
11. Install new O-ring seals onto the fuel injectors.

4.0L Engine

See Figure 154.

1. Before beginning this procedure, refer to the Fuel System Precautions.

➡**If used as a leverage device, the fuel rail may be damaged.**

2. Remove the intake manifold. For additional information, refer to Intake Manifold in Engine Mechanical.
3. Disconnect the fuel supply tube spring lock coupling.
4. Disconnect the 6 fuel injector electrical connectors.
5. Remove the 4 bolts and the fuel rail and fuel injectors as an assembly. Discard the bolts.
6. If necessary, remove the 4 fuel rail supply tube-to-fuel rail bolts and the fuel rail supply tube. Discard the O-ring seals.
7. If necessary, remove the fuel injectors from the fuel rail.

➡**Use O-ring seals that are made of special fuel-resistant material. The use**

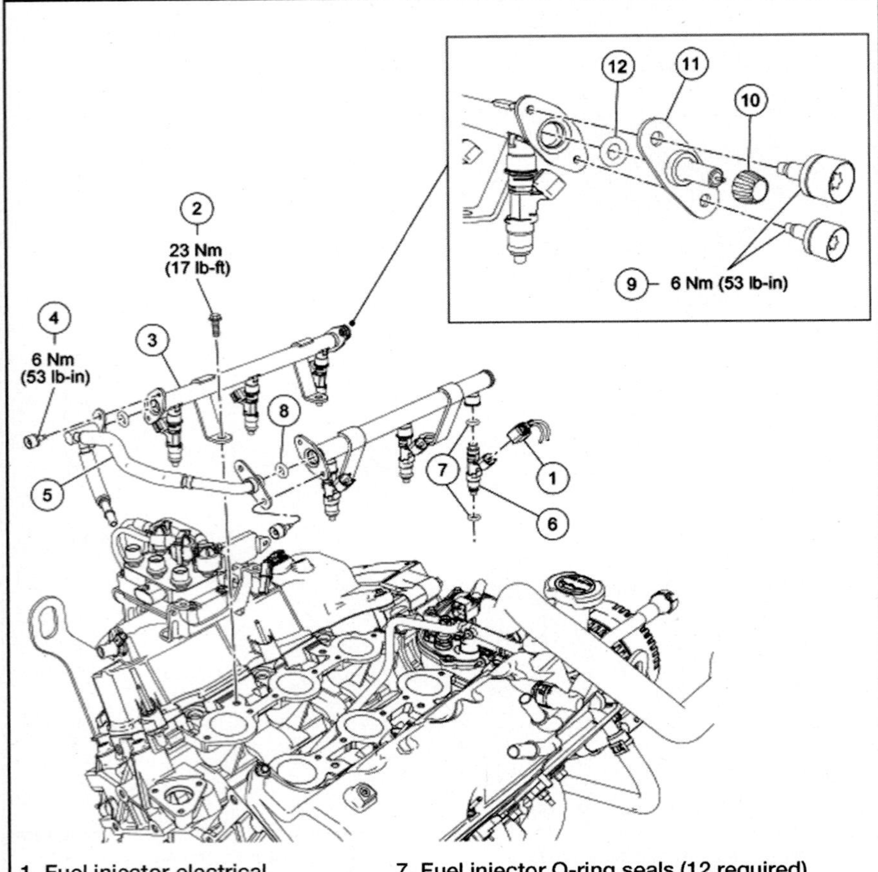

Fig. 154 Exploded view of the fuel rail and fuel injectors—4.0L Engine

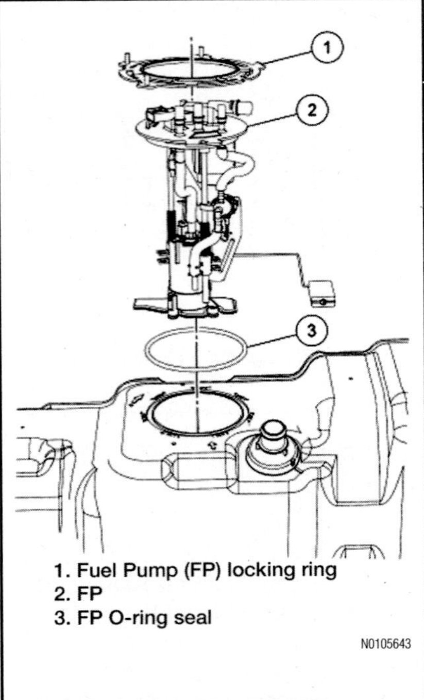

Fig. 155 Exploded view of the fuel pump assembly

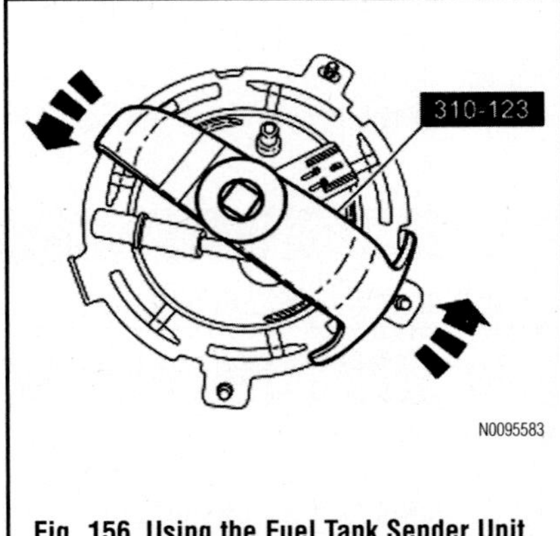

Fig. 156 Using the Fuel Tank Sender Unit Wrench

of ordinary O-ring seals may cause the fuel system to leak.

➡**Do not reuse O-ring seals. The reuse of O-ring seals may cause the fuel system to leak.**

➡**Lubricate the new O-ring seals with clean engine oil.**

➡**Use new fasteners to attach the fuel rail.**

8. To install, reverse the removal procedure.

FUEL PUMP

REMOVAL & INSTALLATION

See Figures 155 and 156.

1. Before beginning this procedure, refer to the Fuel System Precautions.
2. Remove the fuel tank. For additional information, refer to Fuel Tank in this section.
3. Clean the area around the Fuel Pump (FP) mounting flange.
4. Using the Fuel Tank Sender Unit Wrench, remove the FP locking ring.

➡**The Fuel Pump (FP) assembly must be removed and handled carefully to avoid damage to the float arm and filter.**

5. Remove the FP assembly.
6. Remove and discard the FP O-ring seal.

To install:

7. Clean the FP mounting flange and the fuel tank mounting surface.
8. Install a new FP O-ring seal.
9. Install the FP and sender assembly with the float toward the rear of the tank. Align the arrows molded into the tank and flange.
10. Install the FP locking ring while compressing the FP into the tank.
11. Using the Fuel Tank Sender Unit Wrench, tighten the FP locking ring until it locks in place.
12. Install the fuel tank. For additional information, refer to Fuel Tank in this section.

FUEL TANK

DRAINING

1. Before beginning this procedure, refer to the Fuel System Precautions.
2. Disconnect the battery ground cable.
3. Remove the fuel tank filler pipe cap.
4. Loosen the fuel tank filler pipe hose-to-fuel tank clamp.

5. Remove the fuel tank filler pipe from the fuel tank. Insert the Fuel Tank Drain Hose into the fuel tank.

➡**Follow the operating instructions supplied by the equipment manufacturer.**

6. Attach the Fuel Tank Drain Hose to the 30 Gallon Gasoline Hand Pump Storage Tanker and siphon the fuel from the fuel tank.

REMOVAL & INSTALLATION

See Figure 157.

1. Before beginning this procedure, refer to the Fuel System Precautions.
2. With vehicle in NEUTRAL, position it on a hoist.
3. Release the fuel system pressure.
4. Drain the fuel tank.
5. Remove the fuel tank support straps.
6. Partially lower the fuel tank for ease of access.
7. Remove the 3 nuts and the Fuel Pump (FP) module cover. To install, tighten to 80 inch lbs. (9 Nm).
8. Disconnect the FP electrical connector.
9. Disconnect the fuel tank filler pipe vent tube-to- FP quick connect coupling.
10. Disconnect the fuel supply tube-to- FP quick connect coupling and the fuel return tube-to- FP quick connect coupling.
11. Disconnect the rear fuel tank vapor tube and Fuel Tank Pressure (FTP) sensor assembly-to- FP quick connect coupling.
12. Disconnect the rear fuel tank vapor tube and FTP sensor assembly-to-fuel tank vent valve quick connect coupling at the rear of the fuel tank.
13. Lower the fuel tank.
14. To install, reverse the removal procedure.

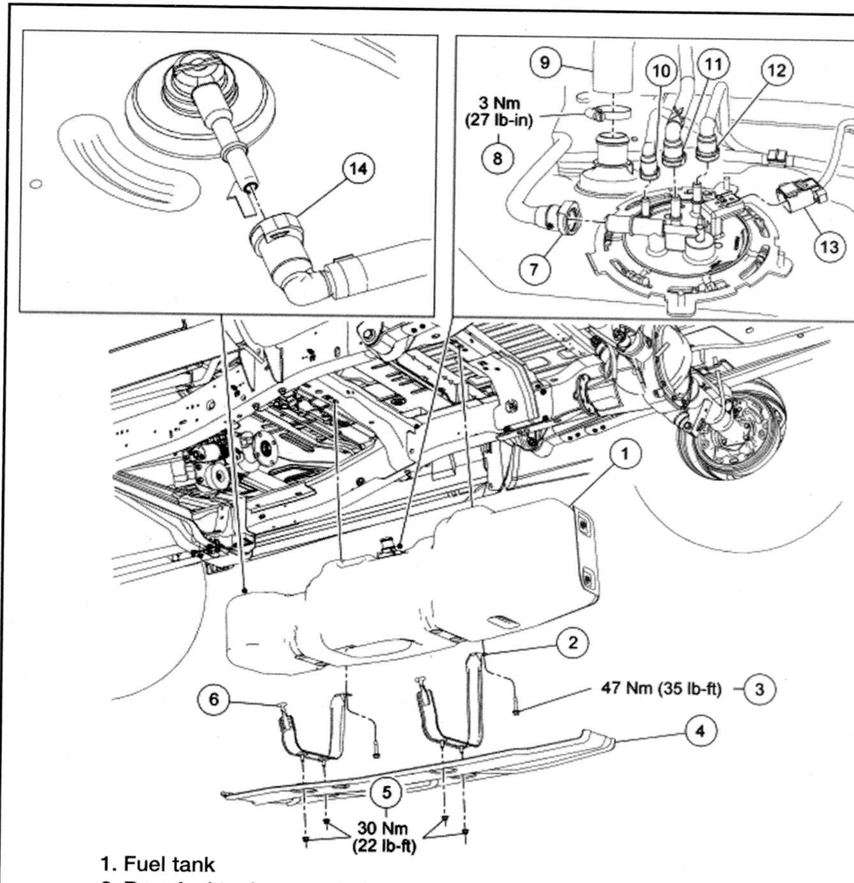

Fig. 157 Exploded view of the fuel tank

IDLE SPEED

ADJUSTMENT

Idle speed adjustment is not necessary or possible.

THROTTLE BODY

REMOVAL & INSTALLATION

2.3L Engine

See Figure 158.

1. Remove the Air Cleaner (ACL) outlet tube.
2. Remove the 2 bolts and the Throttle Body (TB) cover.
3. Disconnect the accelerator cable and, if equipped, the speed control cable.
4. Disconnect the Throttle Position (TP) sensor electrical connector.
5. Remove the 4 bolts and the TB.

To install:

6. Position the TB gasket, the TB and install the 4 bolts in a criss-cross pattern.
7. Inspect the TB gasket and install a new gasket as necessary.
8. Connect the TP sensor electrical connector.
9. Connect the accelerator cable and, if equipped, the speed control cable.
10. Position the TB cover and install the 2 bolts.
11. Install the ACL outlet tube.

4.0L Engine

See Figure 159.

1. Remove the Air Cleaner (ACL) outlet tube.
2. Disconnect the Throttle Position (TP) sensor electrical connector.
3. Disconnect the accelerator cable and, if equipped, the speed control cable.
4. Remove the 4 bolts and the Throttle Body (TB) and discard the TB gasket.
5. To install, reverse the removal procedure.
6. Install a new TB gasket.

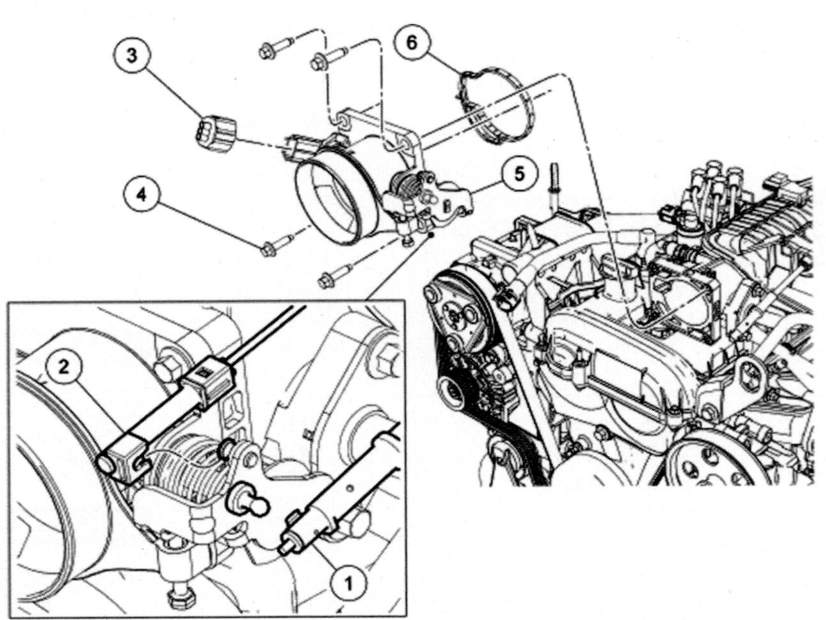

1. Accelerator cable
2. Speed control cable
3. Throttle Position (TP) sensor electrical connector
4. TP bolt (4 required)
5. Throttle Body (TB)
6. TB gasket

N0040488

Fig. 158 Exploded view of the throttle body—2.3L engine

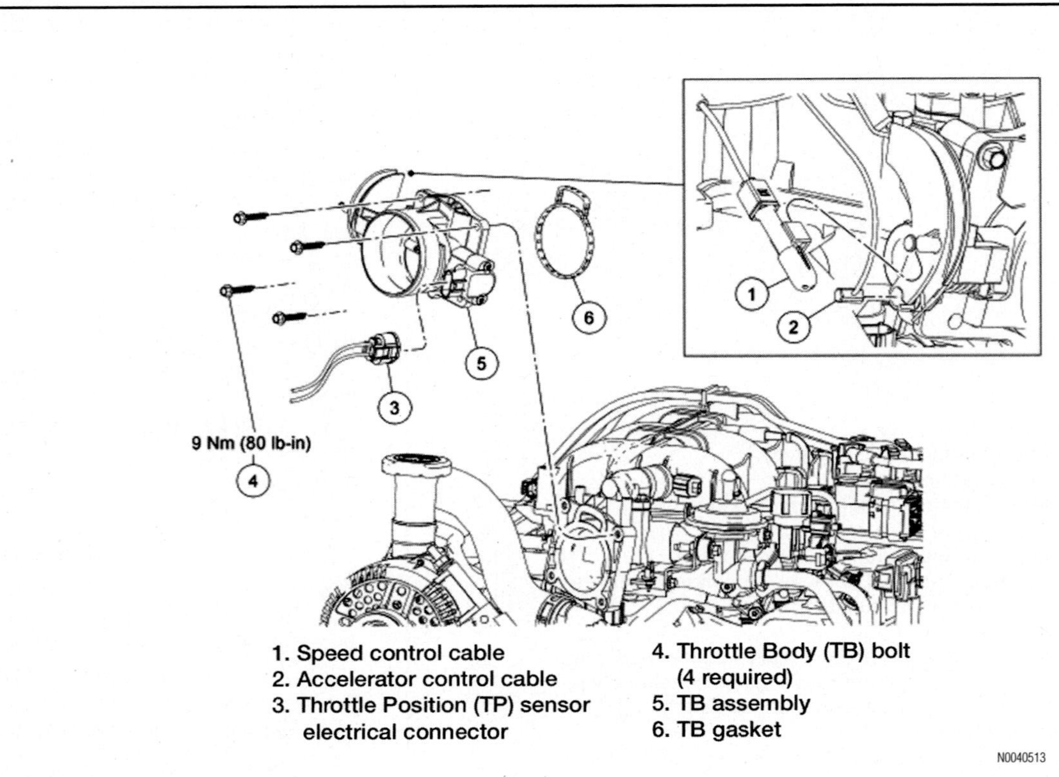

1. Speed control cable
2. Accelerator control cable
3. Throttle Position (TP) sensor electrical connector
4. Throttle Body (TB) bolt (4 required)
5. TB assembly
6. TB gasket

N0040513

Fig. 159 Exploded view of the throttle body—4.0L engine

HEATING & AIR CONDITIONING SYSTEM

BLOWER MOTOR

REMOVAL & INSTALLATION

See Figure 160.

1. Disconnect the negative battery cable.
2. Disconnect the speed control actuator electrical connector.
3. Remove the speed control actuator bolt and position the speed control actuator aside.
4. Disconnect the blower motor electrical connector.
5. Remove the blower motor vent tube.
6. Remove the 4 blower motor screws and the blower motor.
7. Remove the blower motor wheel clip.
8. Remove the blower motor wheel.
9. To install, reverse the removal procedure.

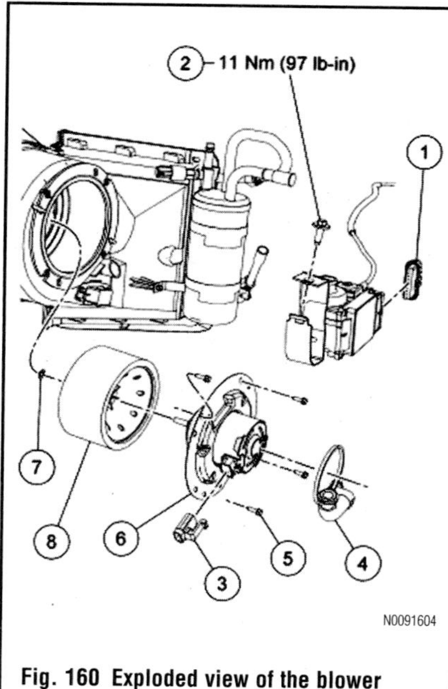

Fig. 160 Exploded view of the blower motor

HEATER CORE

REMOVAL & INSTALLATION

See Figures 161 through 164.

➡**If a heater core leak is suspected, the heater core must be leak tested before it is removed from the vehicle.**

Remove the evaporator core housing assembly :

➡**The evaporator core is not separately serviceable, it is serviced only with the evaporator core housing assembly.**

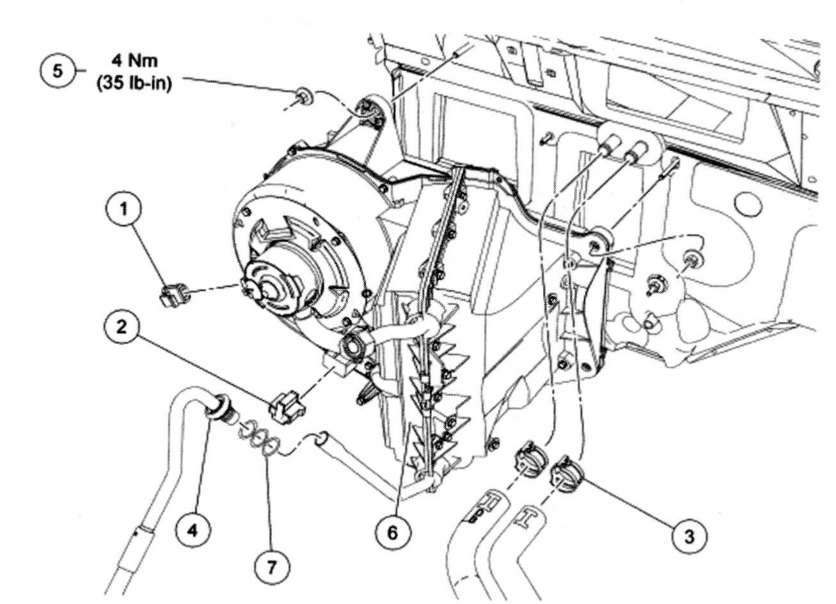

Fig. 161 Exploded view of the evaporator core housing assembly

➡**If an evaporator core leak is suspected, the evaporator core must be leak tested before it is removed from the vehicle.**

1. Drain the cooling system.
2. Recover the refrigerant.
3. Remove the Air Cleaner (ACL) outlet pipe.
4. Remove the suction accumulator.
5. Vehicles with 2.3L engine:
   a. Remove the A/C compressor.
   b. Remove the engine oil indicator and tube.
6. Vehicles with 4.0L engine:
   a. Position the coolant reservoir and windshield washer reservoir aside.
   b. Remove the 2 screws and 2 nuts.
   c. Position the reservoirs aside.
7. Vehicles with speed control:
   a. Disconnect the speed control actuator electrical connector.
   b. Remove the speed control actuator bolt and position the actuator aside.
   c. Detach the speed control cable from the evaporator core housing. To install, tighten to 8 ft. lbs. (11 Nm).
8. Disconnect the blower motor electrical connector.
9. Disconnect the blower motor resistor electrical connector.
10. Release the 2 heater hose clamps and disconnect the heater hoses from the heater core.
11. Detach the pin-type retainer and position the windshield washer hose aside.
12. Disconnect and detach the heater control valve vacuum hose.
13. Disconnect the vacuum supply hose near the evaporator core housing.
14. Disconnect the evaporator inlet fitting.
15. Discard the O-ring seals.

➡**The following step is carried out at the lower passenger side dash panel, inside the passenger compartment.**

16. Disconnect the vacuum hose connector and remove the nut.
17. Vehicles with 4.0L engine:
18. If equipped, remove the wheel splash guard.
19. Remove the RH fender splash shield.
20. Remove the 2 evaporator core housing nuts.
21. Remove the evaporator core housing.

Remove the Instrument Panel:

22. Remove the steering wheel.

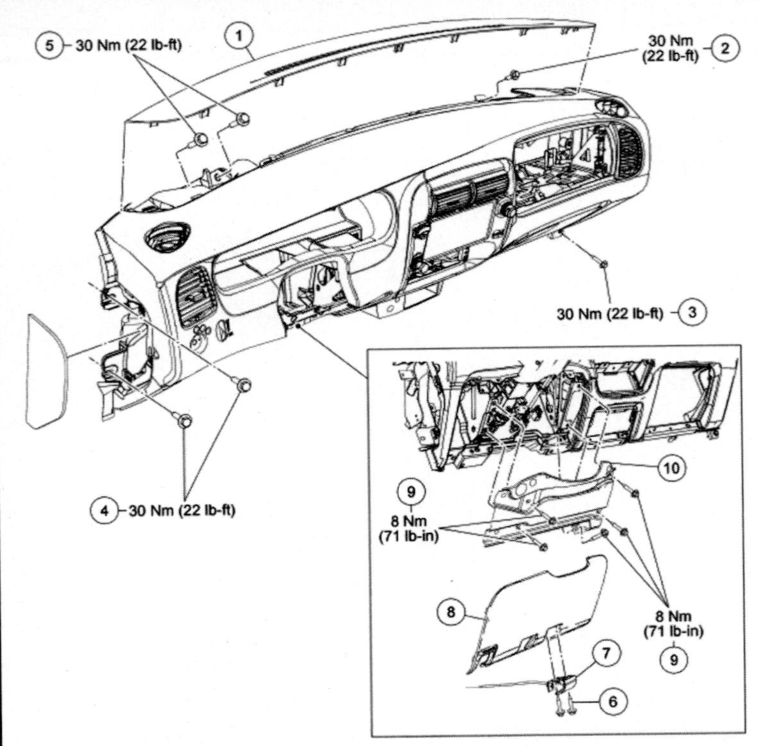

Fig. 162 Exploded view of the instrument panel

23. Remove the front seats.
24. Remove the 2 screws and position the parking brake release handle aside.
25. Remove the front door scuff plates.
26. Remove the LH and RH cowl side trim panels.
27. Remove the pin-type retainer.
28. Remove the cowl side trim panel.
29. Remove the 2 screws and position the hood release handle aside.
30. Remove the steering column opening trim panel.
31. Remove the 2 screws.
32. Remove the trim panel.
33. Remove the steering column opening cover reinforcement. Remove the 5 bolts.
34. Remove the reinforcement.
35. Disconnect the Brake Pedal Position (BPP) switch electrical connector.
36. If equipped, disconnect the Clutch Pedal Position (CPP) switch electrical connector.
37. If equipped, disconnect the selector lever cable from the steering column.
38. Disconnect the cable from the steering column shift tube lever.
39. Disconnect the cable from the steering column bracket.
40. Remove and discard the steering column shaft-to-steering column bolt and disconnect the steering column intermediate shaft.

➡A new steering column shaft-to-steering column bolt must be installed. To install, tighten to 21 ft. lbs. (28 Nm).

41. Remove the LH and RH A-pillar trim panels.
42. Remove the weatherstrip from the door.
43. Disconnect the electrical connectors and the ground wire from the RH cowl side trim panel.
44. Disconnect the LH side bulkhead electrical connector.
45. Press the release tab and pull the release lever.
46. Remove the audio unit.
47. Lower the glove compartment.
48. Press the release tabs inward while lowering the compartment.
49. Through the glove compartment opening, disconnect the blend door actuator electrical connector.
50. Through the glove compartment opening, disconnect the climate control vacuum harness connector.
51. Raise and secure the glove compartment.
52. Press the release tabs inward while raising the glove compartment.
53. Remove the instrument panel defroster opening grille.
54. Remove the instrument panel cowl top bolts. To install, tighten to 22 ft. lbs. (30 Nm).
55. If equipped, remove the floor console.
56. If not equipped with high-series floor console, remove the consolette mat.
57. Remove the screws and remove the Restraints Control Module (RCM) cover.
58. Remove the consolette base.
59. Remove the screws and remove the base.
60. Vehicles with manual transmission
    a. Remove the gearshift lever.
    b. Remove the screws and remove the manual transmission consolette.
61. All vehicles:

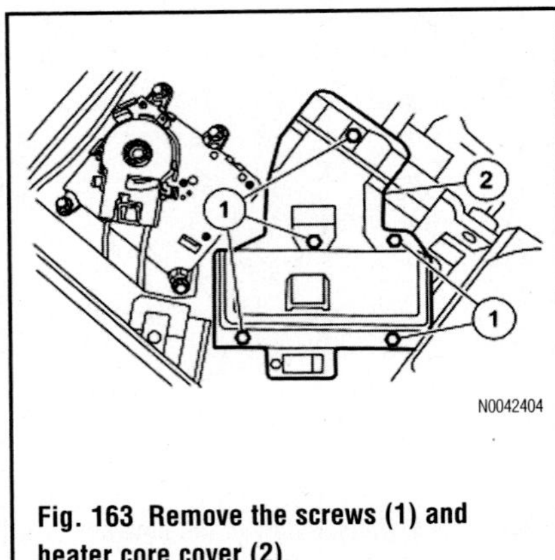

Fig. 163 Remove the screws (1) and heater core cover (2)

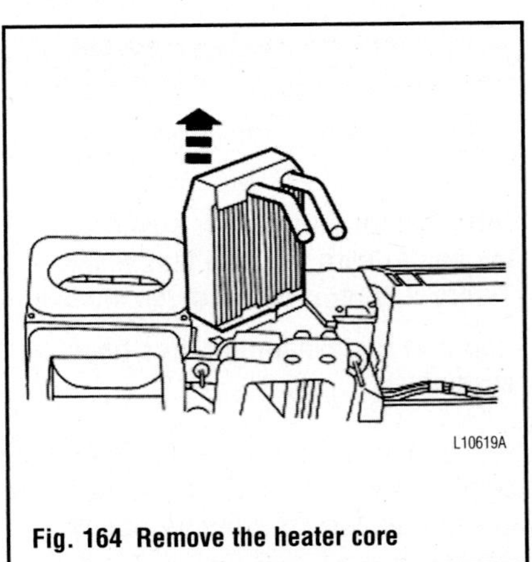

Fig. 164 Remove the heater core

a. Disconnect the RCM electrical connector.

b. Release the locking tab.

c. Disconnect the RCM electrical connector and ground strap bolt.

62. Pull the floor carpeting back.

63. Rear Wheel Drive (RWD) vehicles

a. Disconnect the instrument panel wiring harness.

b. Disconnect the electrical connector.

c. Release the retaining clips.

d. Remove the ground strap.

64. Four-Wheel Drive (4WD) vehicles:

a. Disconnect the instrument panel wiring harness.

b. From underneath the vehicle, release the instrument panel main harness at the transfer case.

c. Release the retaining clips.

d. Remove the ground strap.

65. Remove the instrument panel side finish panel.

66. Disconnect the door harness electrical connector.

67. Remove the RH side instrument panel bolt. To install, tighten to 22 ft. lbs. (30 Nm).

68. Remove the LH instrument panel cowl side bolts.

➡An assistant is required to carry out this step.

69. Position the instrument panel to gain access to the door harness electrical connector.

70. Disconnect the door harness electrical connector.

➡An assistant is required to carry out this step.

71. Remove the instrument panel.

72. Remove the PCM. For additional information, refer to Engine Performance.

73. Remove the PCM heat sink.

74. Remove the ground strap screw.

75. Remove the heat sink.

76. Remove the 4 nuts from the engine side of the dash panel. Position the plenum chamber on the vehicle floor.

77. Remove the heater core cover.

a. Remove the screws.

b. Remove the heater core cover.

78. Remove the heater core.

79. To install, reverse the removal procedure.

80. During installation, be sure to install a new oval foam seal around the heater core inlet and outlet tubes.

STEERING

POWER STEERING GEAR

REMOVAL & INSTALLATION

2WD Vehicles

See Figure 165.

➡When repairing the power steering system, care should be taken to prevent the entry of foreign material or failure of the power steering components may result.

1. Remove the front wheels and tires.
2. Place the steering wheel in the straight-ahead position and remove the ignition key.
3. Rotate the steering wheel until the steering column locks into position.
4. 4.0L engine; Remove the power steering fluid cooler.
5. Remove and discard the outer tie-rod end cotter pins and nuts. To install, tighten the new nut to 59 ft. lbs. (80 Nm).
6. Install new cotter pins.

➡Do not damage the tie-rod boot when installing the Tie-Rod End Remover.

➡Remove the adapter from the ball end of the Tie-Rod End Remover. Apply a small amount of grease to the tie-rod end stud and the ball of the Tie-Rod End Remover.

7. Using Tie-Rod End Remover, separate the outer tie-rod ends from the wheel spindles.

➡Do not allow the steering column to rotate while the steering column shaft

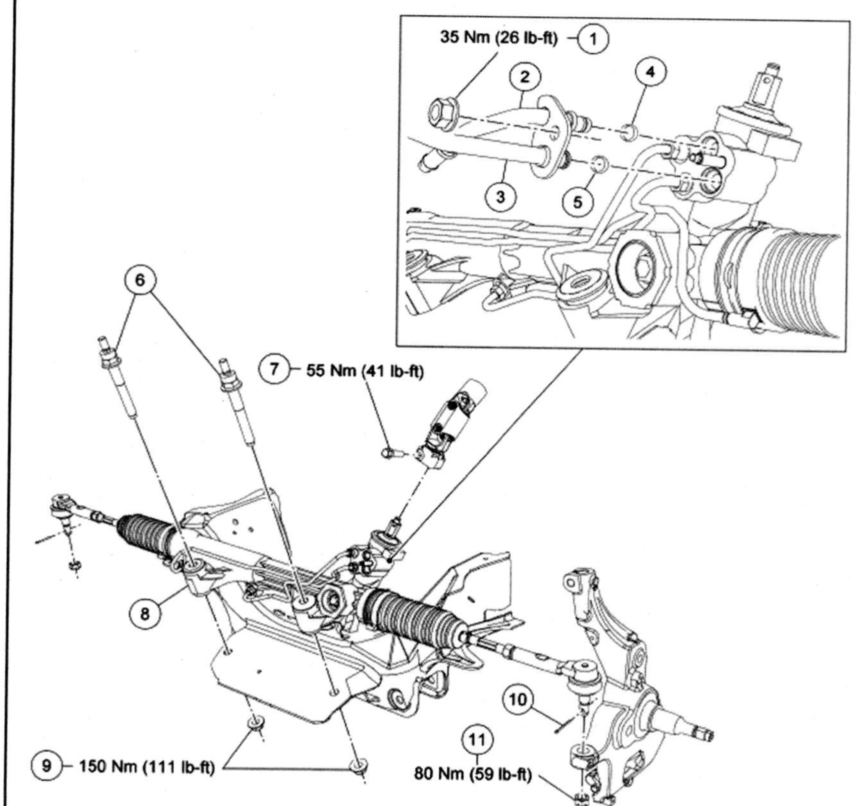

Fig. 165 Exploded view of the power steering gear assembly—2WD vehicles

is disconnected from the steering gear or damage to the clockspring may result. If there is evidence that the steering column has rotated, the clockspring must be removed and recentered. For additional information, refer to Supplemental Restraint System.

8. Remove the lower steering column shaft-to-steering gear bolt and disconnect the lower steering column shaft from the gear.
9. Discard the bolt. To install, tighten the new bolt to 41 ft. lbs. (55 Nm).
10. Remove the steering line clamp plate nut and disconnect the pressure and return lines.
11. Discard the O-ring seals. To install, tighten to 26 ft. lbs. (35 Nm).
12. Plug or cap the return line, pressure line and the steering gear ports to prevent the entry of dirt.

➡Hold the tops of the steering gear studs to avoid damaging the steering gear fluid transfer tubes.

13. Remove the 2 steering gear nuts and the 2 steering gear studs. To install, tighten to 111 ft. lbs. (150 Nm).
14. Remove the steering gear.
15. If necessary, remove the outer tie-rod ends.

➡New O-ring seals must be installed any time the power steering lines are disconnected from the steering gear or a fluid leak may occur.

16. To install, reverse the removal procedure.
17. Install new power steering line O-ring seals and cotter pins.
18. Fill the power steering system.
19. Check and, if necessary, adjust the front toe.

4WD Vehicles

See Figure 166.

➡When repairing the power steering system, care should be taken to prevent the entry of foreign material or failure of the power steering components may result.

1. Remove the front wheels and tires.
2. Place the steering wheel in the straight-ahead position and remove the ignition key.
3. Rotate the steering wheel until the steering column locks into position.
4. Remove the power steering fluid cooler. For additional information, refer to Power Steering Fluid Cooler in this section.
5. Loosen the tie-rod jam nuts.
6. Remove and discard the outer tie-rod end cotter pins and nuts.

➡Do not damage the tie-rod boot when installing the Tie-Rod End Remover.

➡Remove the adapter from the ball end of the Tie-Rod End Remover. Apply a small amount of grease to the tie-rod end stud and the ball of the Tie-Rod End Remover.

7. Using the Tie-Rod End Remover, separate the outer tie-rod ends from the wheel knuckles.
8. Remove the outer tie-rod ends.
9. Count and record the number of turns required to remove the outer tie-rod end.
10. Remove the stabilizer bar and link. For additional information, refer to Front Suspension.

➡Do not allow the steering column to rotate while the steering column shaft is disconnected from the steering gear or damage to the clockspring may result. If there is evidence that the steering column has rotated, the clockspring must be removed and recentered. For additional information, refer to Supplemental Restraint System.

11. Remove the lower steering column shaft-to-steering gear bolt and disconnect the shaft from the steering gear.
12. Discard the bolt.
13. Remove the steering line clamp plate nut and disconnect the pressure and return lines.
14. Discard the O-ring seals.

➡Hold the tops of the steering gear studs to avoid damaging the steering gear fluid transfer tubes.

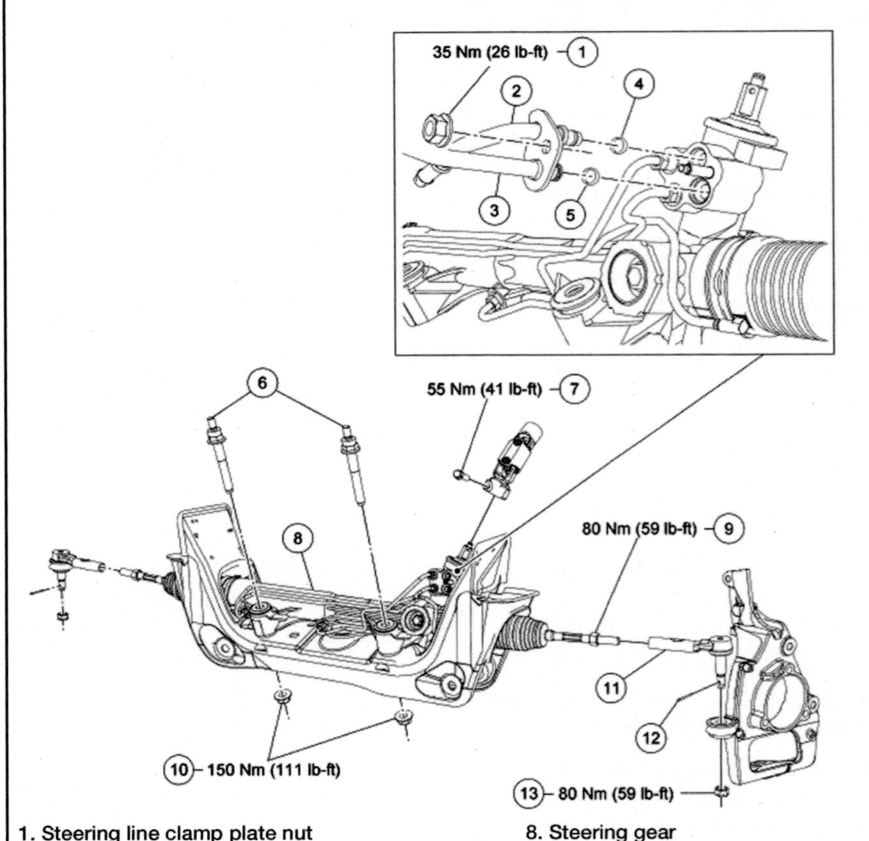

Fig. 166 Exploded view of the power steering gear assembly—4WD vehicles

15. Remove the 2 steering gear nuts and steering gear studs.

16. Rotate the steering gear control valve housing toward the front of the vehicle.

17. Turn the steering gear input shaft to the right until the stop is reached.

18. Move the steering gear as far to the RH side of the vehicle as possible.

19. Move the LH inner tie rod forward to clear the frame crossmember.

20. Remove the steering gear.

To install:

➡Handle the steering gear with caution to avoid damage to fluid transfer tubes and to avoid dimples in the steering gear bellows boot.

➡Make sure the steering gear input shaft is turned to the left until the stop is reached.

21. Turn the steering gear input shaft to the right until the stop is reached. Count and record the number of turns required.

➡Make sure the steering gear control valve housing is turned toward the front of the vehicle.

22. Install the steering gear into the RH opening of the crossmember.

➡Take care not to scuff or tear the steering gear bellows boots.

23. Move the steering gear as far to the RH side of the vehicle as possible.

24. Move the LH inner tie rod into the opening in the crossmember and move the steering gear into position.

25. To place the steering gear in the straight-ahead position, turn the steering gear input shaft to the left by one-half the number of turns previously recorded.

26. Rotate the steering gear control valve housing toward the rear of the vehicle.

27. Install the 2 steering gear studs.

➡Hold the tops of the steering gear studs to avoid damaging the steering gear fluid transfer tubes.

28. Install the 2 steering gear nuts. Tighten to 111 ft. lbs. (150 Nm).

➡New O-rings must be installed any time the lines are disconnected from the steering gear or a fluid leak may occur.

29. Position the pressure and return lines and install the steering line clamp plate nut. Tighten to 26 ft. lbs. (35 Nm).

➡Do not allow the steering column to rotate while the steering column shaft is disconnected from the steering gear or damage to the clockspring may result. If there is evidence that the steering column has rotated, the clockspring must be removed and re-centered. For additional information, refer to Supplemental Restraint System.

30. Connect the steering column shaft to the steering gear and install a new bolt. Tighten to 41 ft. lbs. (55 Nm).

31. Install the stabilizer bar and link.

32. Install the outer tie-rod ends.

33. Rotate the outer tie-rod ends the number of turns recorded during removal.

34. Position the outer tie-rod ends and install the new nuts and new cotter pins.

35. Check that the brake disc shields are not bent and are not in contact with the outer tie-rod end boots. Tighten to 59 ft. lbs. (80 Nm).

36. Install the power steering fluid cooler.

37. Tighten the tie-rod jam nuts. Tighten to 59 ft. lbs. (80 Nm).

38. Fill the power steering system.

39. Check and, if necessary, adjust the front toe.

POWER STEERING PUMP

REMOVAL & INSTALLATION

2.3L Engine

See Figures 167 and 168.

1. While repairing the power steering system, care should be taken to prevent the entry of foreign material or failure of the power steering components may result.

➡Do not allow power steering fluid to contact the accessory drive belt or the belt may be damaged.

2. Using a suitable suction device, remove the power steering fluid from the reservoir.

3. Remove the power steering pump pulley. Using the Power Steering Pump Pulley Remover, remove the power steering pump pulley.

4. Compress the clamp and disconnect the power steering pump supply hose.

5. Disconnect the pressure line-to-pump fitting.

6. Remove and discard the Teflon® seal. To install, tighten to 55 ft. lbs. (75 Nm).

7. Remove the 4 power steering pump bolts and the power steering pump. To install, tighten to 17 ft. lbs. (23 Nm).

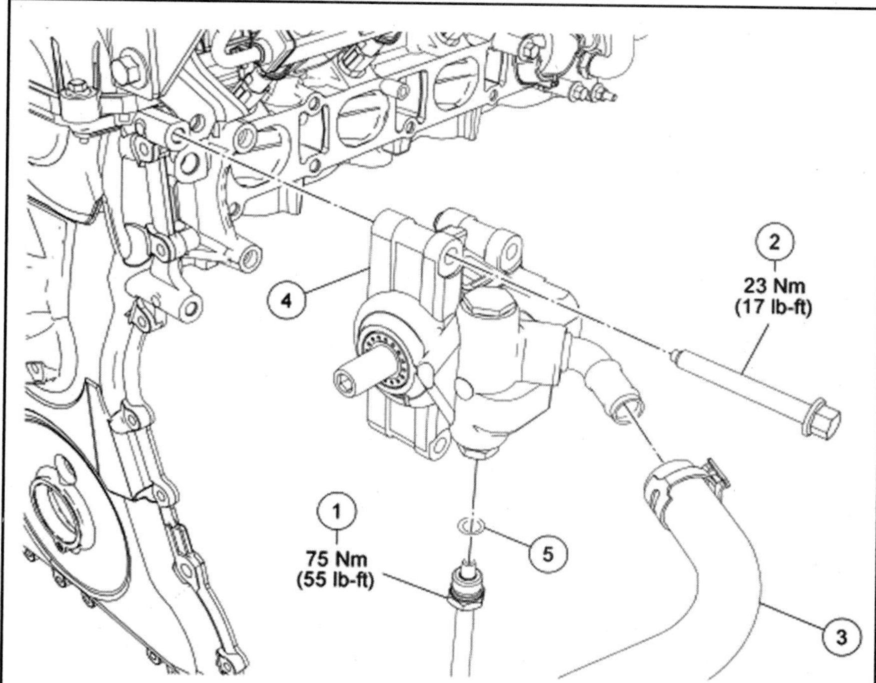

Fig. 167 Exploded view of the power steering pump assembly

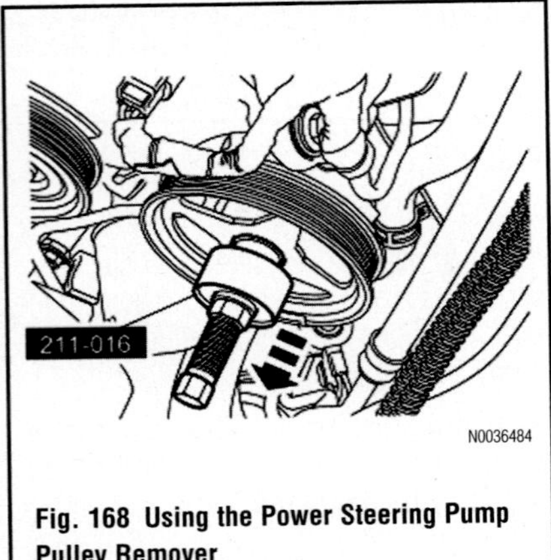

Fig. 168 Using the Power Steering Pump Pulley Remover

➡A new Teflon® seal must be installed any time the pressure line fitting is disconnected from the power steering pump or a fluid leak may occur.

8. To install, reverse the removal procedure.
9. Using the Teflon® Seal Installer Set, install a new Teflon® seal on the pressure line-to-pump fitting.
10. Fill the power steering system.

4.0L Engine

See Figure 169.

➡While repairing the power steering system, care should be taken to prevent the entry of foreign material or failure of the power steering components may result.

1. Disconnect the negative battery cable.
2. Using a suitable suction device, remove the power steering fluid from the reservoir.
3. Remove the engine cooling fan. For additional information, refer to Engine Cooling.
4. Remove the power steering pump pulley.
5. Compress the clamp and disconnect the power steering pump supply hose from the power steering fluid reservoir.
6. Disconnect the pressure line-to-pump fitting.
7. Discard the Teflon® seal.
8. Compress the clamp and disconnect the power steering pump supply hose from the power steering pump.
9. Remove the 3 bolts and the power steering pump.

➡When connecting a fitting with a Teflon® seal, a new Teflon® seal must be installed.

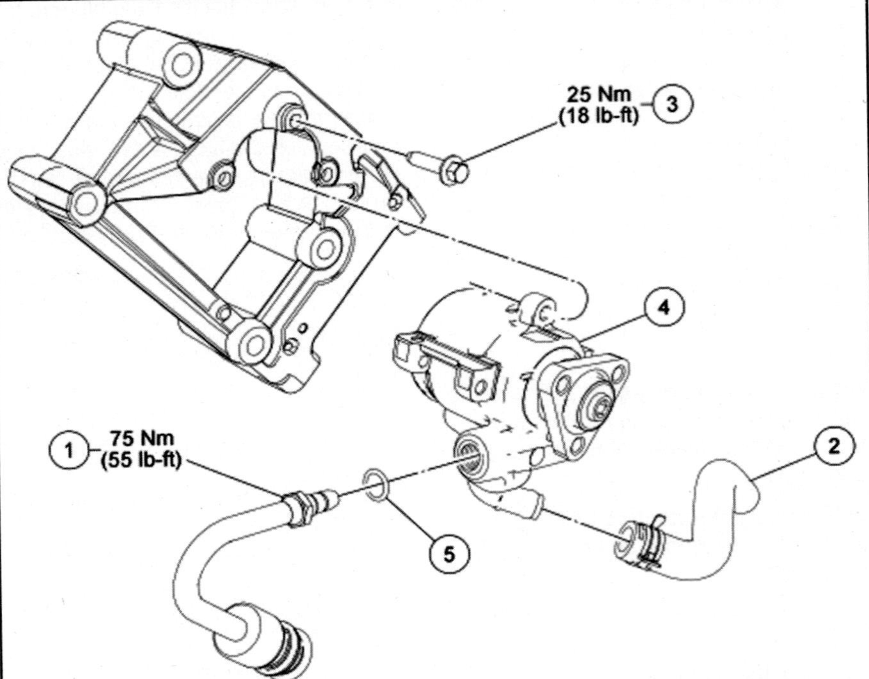

Fig. 169 Exploded view of the power steering pump—4.0L Engines

10. To install, reverse the removal procedure. Refer to the illustration for torque values.
11. Using the Teflon® Seal Installer Set, install a new Teflon® seal on the pressure line-to-pump fitting.
12. Fill the power steering system.

BLEEDING & FLUSHING

➡Do not mix fluid types. Any mixture or any unapproved fluid may lead to seal deterioration and leaks. A leak may ultimately cause loss of fluid, which may result in a loss of power steering assist.

1. Remove the power steering fluid reservoir cap.
2. Using a suitable suction device, remove the power steering fluid from the reservoir.
3. Release the clamp and disconnect the return hose from the reservoir.
    a. Remove the clamp from the hose and allow the remaining fluid to drain out of the reservoir.
4. Plug the power steering fluid reservoir inlet port.
5. Attach an extension hose to the return hose.

➡Do not reuse the power steering fluid that has been flushed from the power steering system.

6. Place the open end of the extension hose into a suitable container.
7. If equipped with Hydro-Boost®, apply the brake pedal 4 times.

➡Do not overfill the reservoir.

8. Fill the reservoir as needed with the specified fluid.

➡Do not allow the power steering pump to run completely dry of power steering fluid. Damage to the power steering pump may occur.

9. Start the engine while simultaneously turning the steering wheel to lock and then immediately turn the ignition switch to the OFF position.

➡Avoid turning the steering wheel without the engine running as this may cause air to be pulled into the steering gear.

➡Do not overfill the reservoir.

10. Fill the reservoir as needed with the specified fluid.
11. Repeat Steps 8 and 9, turning the steering wheel in the opposite direction

each time, until the fluid exiting the power steering fluid return hose is clean and clear of foreign material.

12. Remove the extension hose from the return hose.

13. Remove the plug from the fluid reservoir inlet port.

14. Install the clamp and connect the power steering return hose to the reservoir.

➡It is necessary to correctly fill the power steering system to remove any trapped air and completely fill the power steering system components.

15. If, after correctly filling the power steering system, there is power steering noise accompanied by evidence of aerated fluid and there are no fluid leaks, it may be necessary to purge the power steering system.

16. Fill the power steering system.

PURGING

See Figure 170.

➡If the air is not purged from the power steering system correctly, power steering pump failure may result. The condition may occur on pre-delivery vehicles with evidence of aerated fluid or on vehicles that have had steering component repairs.

1. If equipped with a fire suppression system, depower the system.

➡A whine heard from the power steering pump can be caused by air in the system. The power steering purge procedure must be carried out prior to any component repair for which power steering noise complaints are accompanied by evidence of aerated fluid.

2. Remove the power steering fluid reservoir cap.

3. Fill the reservoir as needed with the specified fluid.

4. Raise the front wheels off the floor.

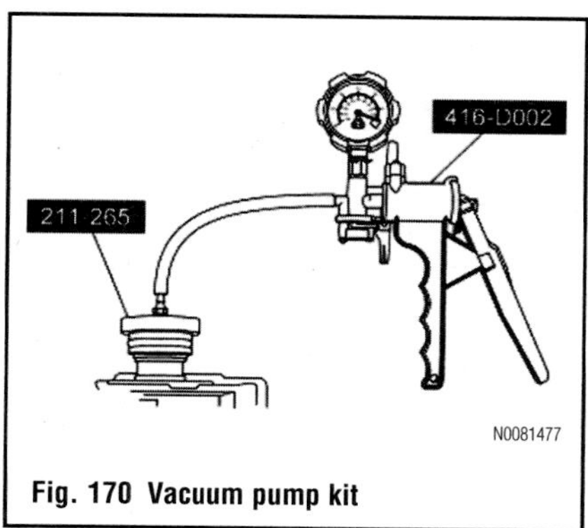

Fig. 170 Vacuum pump kit

5. Tightly insert the Power Steering Evacuation Cap into the reservoir and connect the Vacuum Pump Kit.

6. Start the engine.

7. Using the Vacuum Pump Kit, apply vacuum and maintain the maximum vacuum of 68-85 kPa (20-25 in-Hg).

8. If equipped with Hydro-Boost®, apply the brake pedal twice.

➡Do not hold the steering wheel against the stops for an extended amount of time. Damage to the power steering pump may occur.

9. Cycle the steering wheel fully from stop-to-stop 10 times.

10. Stop the engine.

11. Release the vacuum and remove the Vacuum Pump Kit.

➡Do not overfill the reservoir.

12. Fill the reservoir as needed.

13. Start the engine.

14. Install the Power Steering Evacuation Cap and the Vacuum Pump Kit. Apply and maintain the maximum vacuum of 68-85 kPa (20-25 in-Hg).

➡Do not hold the steering wheel against the stops for an extended amount of time. Damage to the power steering pump may occur.

15. Cycle the steering wheel fully from stop-to-stop 10 times.

16. Stop the engine, release the vacuum and remove the Vacuum Pump Kit and Power Steering Evacuation Cap.

➡Do not overfill the reservoir.

17. Fill the reservoir as needed and install the reservoir cap.

18. Visually inspect the power steering system for leaks.

FLUID FILL PROCEDURE

See Figure 171.

➡If the air is not purged from the power steering system correctly, premature power steering pump failure may result. The condition can occur on pre-delivery vehicles with evidence of aerated fluid or on vehicles that have had steering component repairs.

1. Remove the power steering fluid reservoir cap.

2. Install the Power Steering Evacuation Cap, Power Steering Fill Adapter Manifold and Vacuum Pump Kit as shown in the illustration.

➡The Power Steering Fill Adapter Manifold control valves are in the OPEN position when the points of the handles face the center of the Power Steering Fill Adapter Manifold.

3. Close the Power Steering Fill Adapter Manifold control valve (fluid side).

4. Open the Power Steering Fill Adapter Manifold control valve (vacuum side).

5. Using the Vacuum Pump Kit, apply 68–85 kPa (20–25 in-Hg) of vacuum to the power steering system.

6. Observe the Vacuum Pump Kit gauge for 30 seconds.

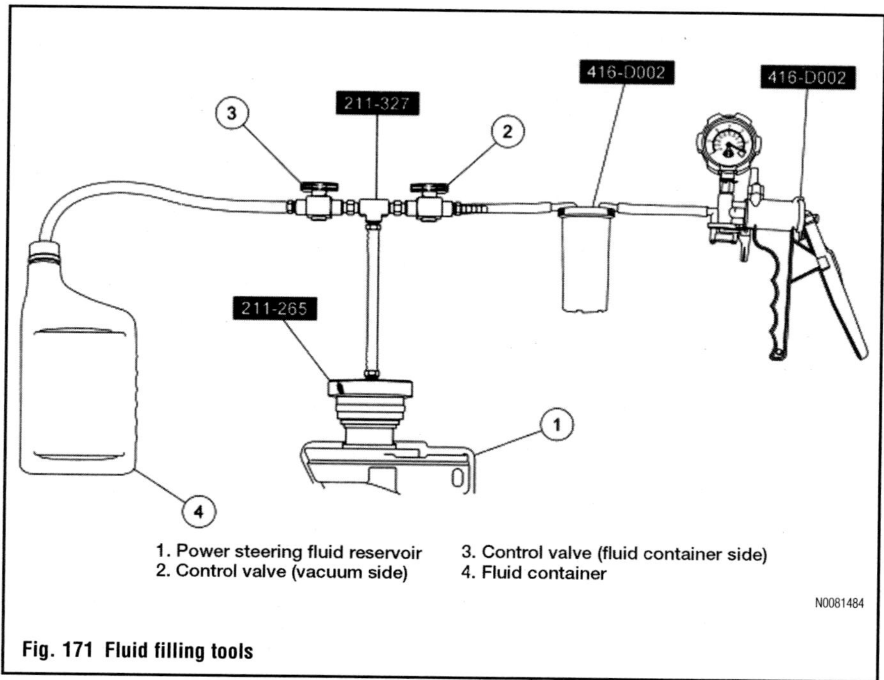

Fig. 171 Fluid filling tools

7. If the Vacuum Pump Kit gauge reading drops more than 3 kPa (0.88 in-Hg), correct any leaks in the power steering system or the Power Steering Evacuation Cap, Power Steering Fill Adapter Manifold and Vacuum Pump Kit before proceeding.

➡The Vacuum Pump Kit gauge reading will drop slightly during this step.

8. Slowly open the Power Steering Fill Adapter Manifold control valve (fluid side) until power steering fluid completely fills the hose and then close the control valve.

9. Using the Vacuum Pump Kit, apply 68–85 kPa (20–25 in-Hg) of vacuum to the power steering system.

10. Close the Power Steering Fill Adapter Manifold control valve (vacuum side).

11. Slowly open the Power Steering Fill Adapter Manifold control valve (fluid side).

12. Once power steering fluid enters the fluid reservoir and reaches the minimum fluid level indicator line on the reservoir, close the Power Steering Fill Adapter Manifold control valve (fluid side).

13. Remove the Power Steering Evacuation Cap, Power Steering Fill Adapter Manifold and Vacuum Pump Kit.

14. Install the reservoir cap.

➡Do not hold the steering wheel against the stops for an extended amount of time. Damage to the power steering pump may occur.

➡There will be a slight drop in the power steering fluid level in the reservoir when the engine is started.

Start the engine and turn the steering wheel from stop-to-stop.

Turn the ignition switch to the OFF position.

➡Do not overfill the reservoir.

15. Remove the reservoir cap and fill the reservoir with the specified fluid.

16. Install the reservoir cap.

SUSPENSION

FRONT SUSPENSION

COIL SPRING

REMOVAL & INSTALLATION

2WD Vehicles

See Figures 172 and 173.

WARNING

Do not apply heat or flame to the shock absorber or strut tube. The shock absorber and strut tube are gas pressurized and could explode if heated. Failure to follow this instruction may result in serious personal injury.

WARNING

Keep all body parts clear of shock absorbers or strut rods. Shock absorbers or struts can extend unassisted. Failure to follow this instruction may result in serious personal injury.

➡Suspension fasteners are critical parts because they affect performance of vital components and systems and their failure may result in major service expense. New parts must be installed with the same part number or an equivalent part if replacement is necessary. Do not use a replacement part of lesser quality or substitute design. Torque values must be used as specified during reassembly to make sure of correct retention of these parts.

1. Index-mark the lower arm to the frame with the vehicle in a static ground position (curb height).

2. Remove the wheel and tire.

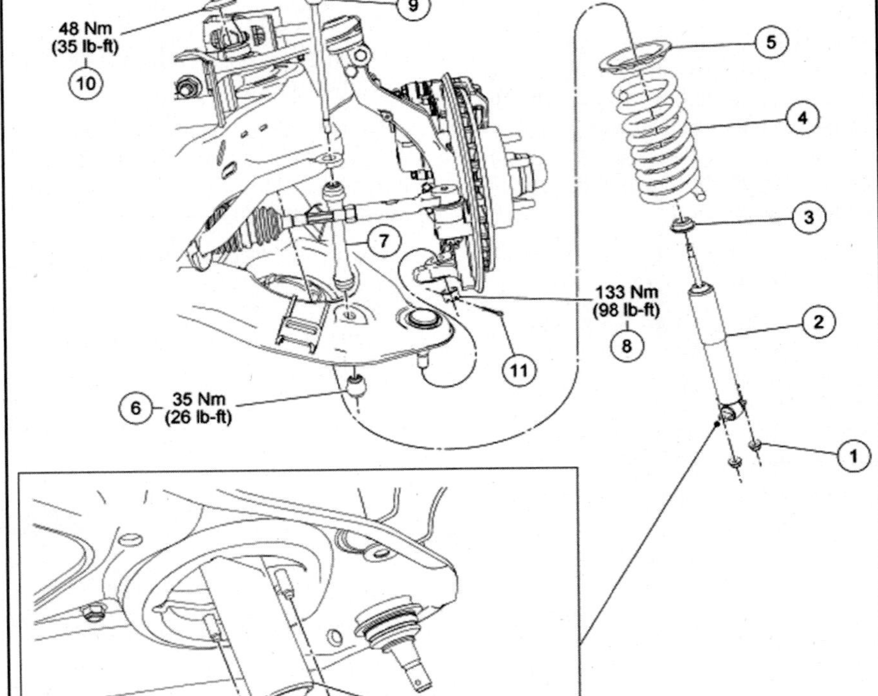

1. Lower shock nut (2 required)
2. Shock absorber
3. Shock absorber insulator
4. Coil spring
5. Coil spring insulator
6. Stabilizer bar link assembly
7. Stabilizer bar link and grommet
8. Lower ball joint nut
9. Stabilizer bar link stud and grommet
10. Shock absorber rod nut
11. Lower ball joint cotter pin

N0106458

Fig. 172 Exploded view of the spring and strut assembly

➡Do not allow the shaft to turn while removing the nut. Hold the flats on the shock rod using a suitable wrench or damage to the shock can result.

3. Remove and discard the shock absorber rod nut and washer assembly.
4. Remove and discard the 2 shock absorber lower nuts, and remove the shock absorber.
5. Remove the stabilizer bar link nut and grommet, then remove the link assembly.
6. Discard the nut.
7. Using the Coil Spring Compressor, compress the coil spring.
8. Remove and discard the lower ball joint cotter pin and nut.
9. Using a suitable jack, support the lower arm.

➡Do not damage the ball joint boot when installing the special tool.

10. Using the C-Frame and Screw Installer/Remover, separate the lower ball joint from the wheel spindle. Refer to Lower Ball Joint in this section.
11. Carefully remove the jack from under the lower arm.
12. Loosen the lower arm bolts and allow the lower arm to swing down.
13. Position the wheel spindle aside and remove the coil spring.

To install:

➡The end of the coil spring must cover the first hole and should not be visible in the second hole of the lower arm.

14. Refer to illustration for torque specifications.
15. Install the coil spring in the lower arm.
16. Using a suitable jack, support the lower arm.

➡Always install the cotter pin into the lower ball joint nut from outboard to inboard. Failure to do so will result in damage to the wheel and tire assembly.

17. Position the lower ball joint and install a new nut.
18. Install a new cotter pin.
19. Remove the jack from under the lower control arm.
20. Install the stabilizer bar link assembly in the following sequence.
21. Install the stabilizer bar link stud and grommet.
22. Install a new stabilizer bar link nut and grommet.
23. Remove the Coil Spring Compressor.
24. Position the shock absorber and install 2 new shock absorber lower nuts.
25. Install a new shock absorber rod nut and washer.
26. Position a suitable jack under the lower arm and raise the suspension until the index marks on the lower arm and the frame are aligned (curb height). Tighten to 148 ft. lbs. (200 Nm).
27. Remove the jack from under the lower control arm.

CONTROL LINKS

REMOVAL & INSTALLATION

Refer to Stabilizer Bar in this section.

LOWER BALL JOINT

REMOVAL & INSTALLATION

See Figures 174 through 178.

1. Remove the Steering Knuckle.
2. Remove and discard the lower ball joint snap ring.
3. Using the C-Frame and Screw Installer/Remover and Ball Joint Remover, remove the lower ball joint.

To install:

➡Do not damage the lower ball joint boot when installing the C-Frame and Screw Installer/Remover and Ball Joint Installer/Remover.

➡Clean and inspect the lower arm ball joint bore for damage before installing a new ball joint.

➡Make sure the new lower ball joint snap ring is fully seated.

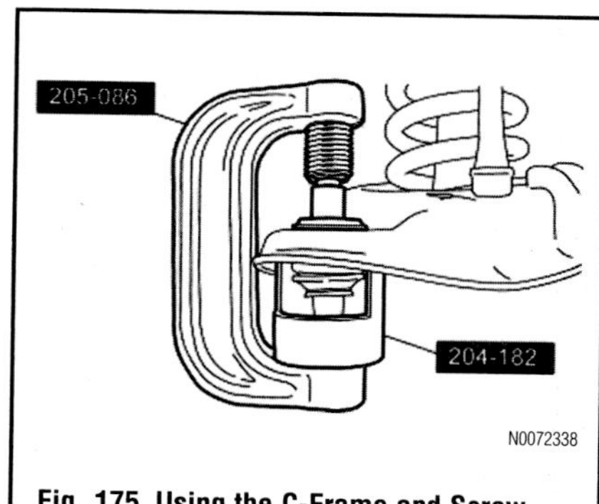

Fig. 175 Using the C-Frame and Screw Installer/Remover and Ball Joint Remover—2WD

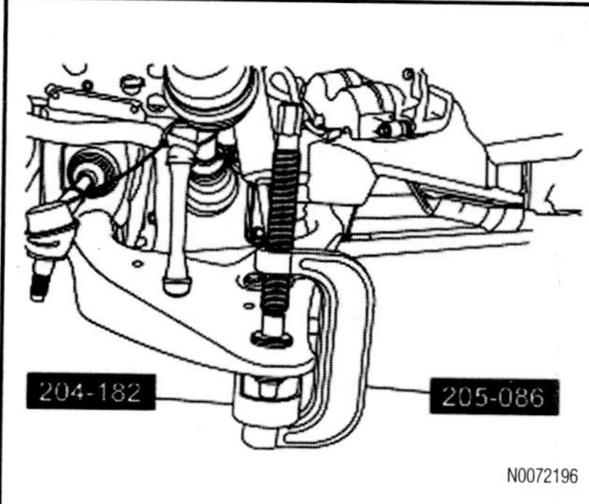

Fig. 176 Using the C-Frame and Screw Installer/Remover and Ball Joint Remover—4WD

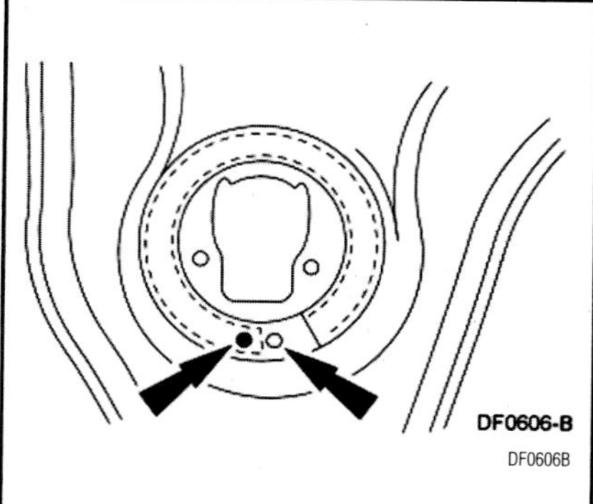

Fig. 173 The end of the coil spring must cover the first hole and should not be visible in the second hole

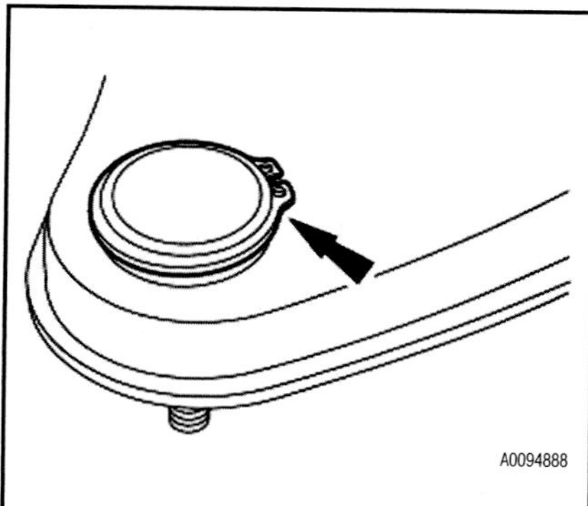

Fig. 174 Remove and discard the lower ball joint snap ring

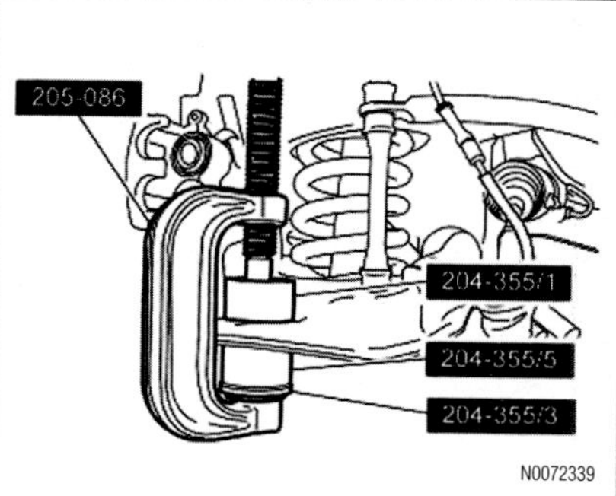

Fig. 177 Using the C-Frame and Screw Installer/Remover and Ball Joint Installer/Remover—2WD

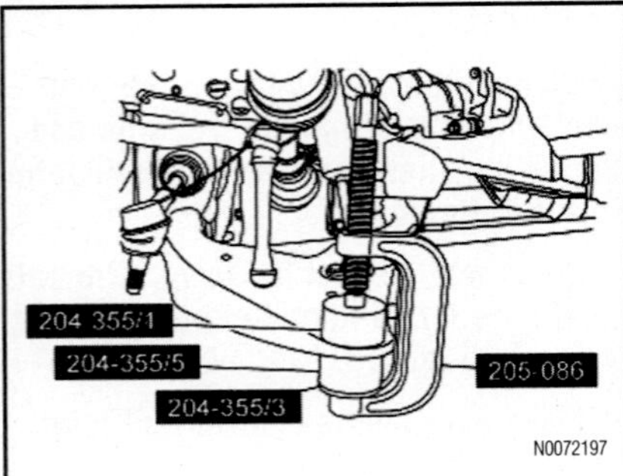

Fig. 178 Using the C-Frame and Screw Installer/Remover and Ball Joint Installer/Remover—4WD

4. Using the C-Frame and Screw Installer/Remover and Ball Joint Installer/Remover, install the lower ball joint.
5. Install the Steering Knuckle

LOWER CONTROL ARM

REMOVAL & INSTALLATION

Coil Spring System

See Figure 179.

➡**Suspension fasteners are critical parts because they affect performance of vital components and systems and their failure may result in major service expense. New parts must be installed with the same part number or an equivalent part if replacement is necessary. Do not use a replacement part of lesser quality or substitute design. Torque values must be used as specified during reassembly to make sure of correct retention of these parts.**

1. Remove the spring. For additional information, refer to Coil Spring in this section.
2. Remove and discard the 2 lower arm bolts, flagnuts and the lower control arm. If necessary, replace the jounce bumper and jounce bumper nut.
3. To install, reverse the removal procedure. Refer to illustration for torque specifications.
4. Check and, if necessary, align the front end.

Torsion Bar System

See Figure 180.

➡**Suspension fasteners are critical parts because they affect performance of vital components and systems and their failure may result in major service expense. New parts must be installed with the same part number or an equivalent part if replacement is necessary. Do not use a replacement part of lesser quality or substitute design. Torque values must be used as specified during reassembly to make sure of correct retention of these parts.**

1. Remove the torsion bar. For additional information, refer to Torsion Bar in this section.
2. Remove the wheel and tire.
3. Remove and discard the stabilizer bar link nut and grommet.
4. Remove the stabilizer link stud and grommet and the stabilizer link assembly.
5. Remove and discard the 2 lower shock nuts.
6. Remove and discard the lower ball joint cotter pin and nut.

➡**Do not use a hammer to separate the ball joint from the wheel spindle/knuckle or damage to the wheel spindle/knuckle will result.**

➡**Do not damage the ball joint boot while installing the special tool.**

7. Using the C-Frame and Screw Installer/Remover, separate the ball joint from the wheel spindle/knuckle.
8. Remove the lower arm bolts and nuts, and remove the front suspension lower arm.
9. Discard the 2 bolts and 2 nuts.

To install:

➡**Do not tighten the bolts at this time.**

10. Refer to illustration for torque specifications.
11. Position the lower arm and loosely install the 2 new lower arm bolts and the 2 lower arm nuts.
12. Position the ball joint and install the new ball joint nut.

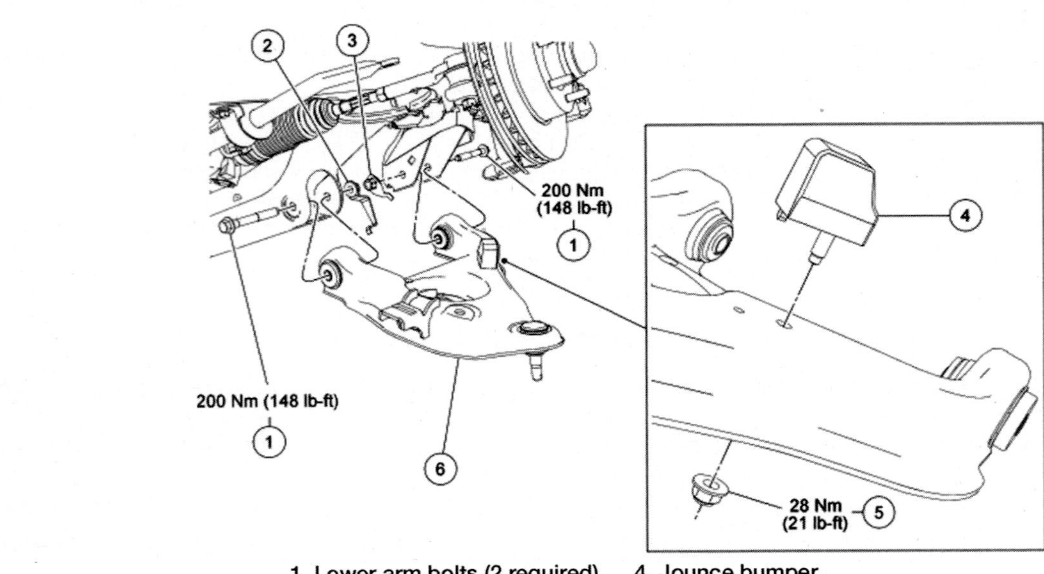

Fig. 179 Exploded view of the lower control arm—coil spring

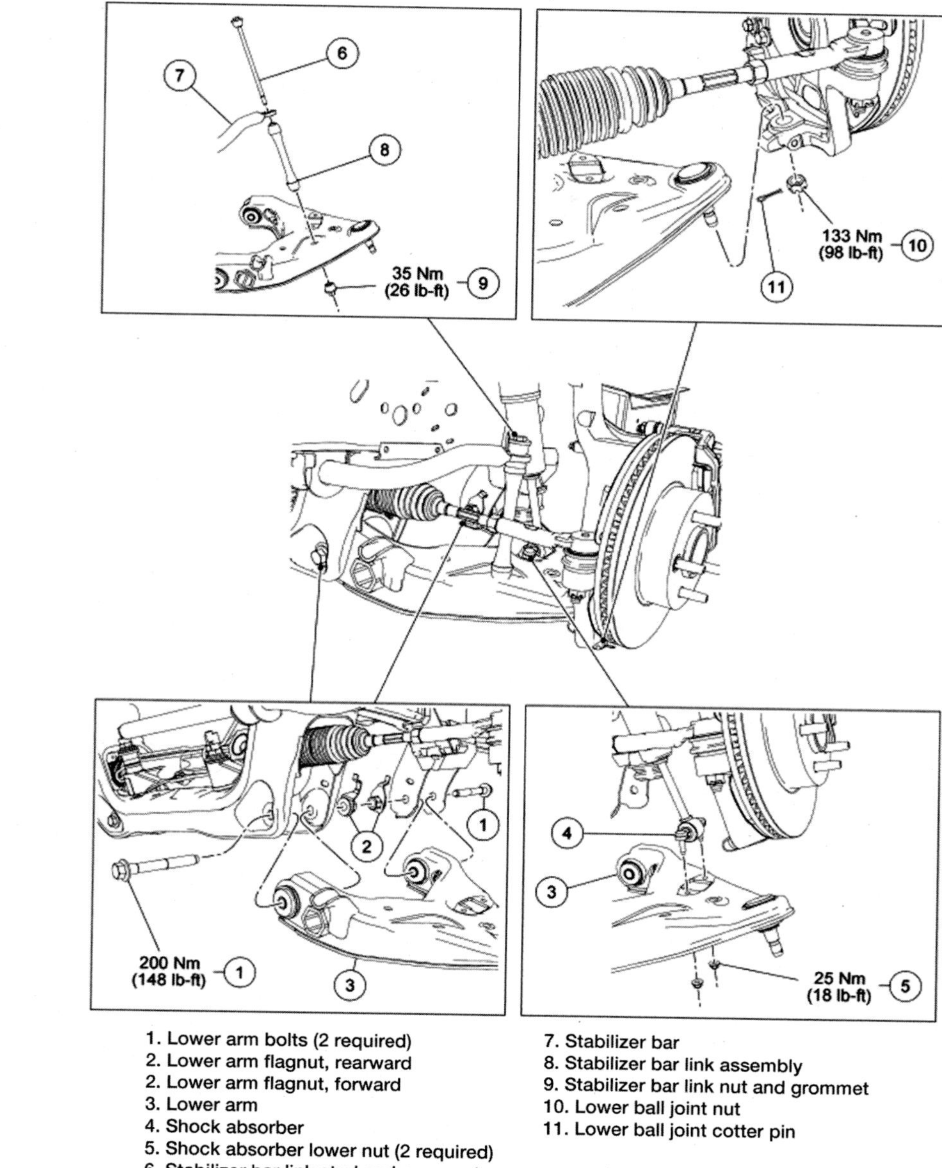

Fig. 180 Exploded view of the lower control arm—Torsion bar

➡Install the new cotter pin into the lower ball joint from outboard to inboard with the fingers bent together at a right angle. Failure to do so will result in damage to the wheel and tire assembly.

13. Install a new lower ball joint cotter pin.
14. Install the 2 new shock absorber lower nuts.
15. Install the stabilizer link stud and grommet and the stabilizer link assembly.
16. Install the wheel and tire.
17. With the weight of the vehicle on the wheel and tire, tighten the 2 lower arm bolts.

STABILIZER BAR

REMOVAL & INSTALLATION

See Figure 181.

➡Suspension fasteners are critical parts because they affect performance of vital components and systems and their failure may result in major service expense. New parts must be installed with the same part number or an equivalent part if replacement is necessary. Do not use a replacement part of lesser quality or substitute design. Torque values must be used as specified during reassembly to make sure of correct retention of these parts.

1. With the vehicle in NEUTRAL, position it on a hoist.
2. Remove and discard the front stabilizer bar link nuts and grommets.
3. Remove the front stabilizer bar link studs and the front stabilizer bar links.
4. Remove the 4 stabilizer bar bracket bolts, stabilizer bar, brackets and bushings.
5. Discard the stabilizer bar bracket bolts.

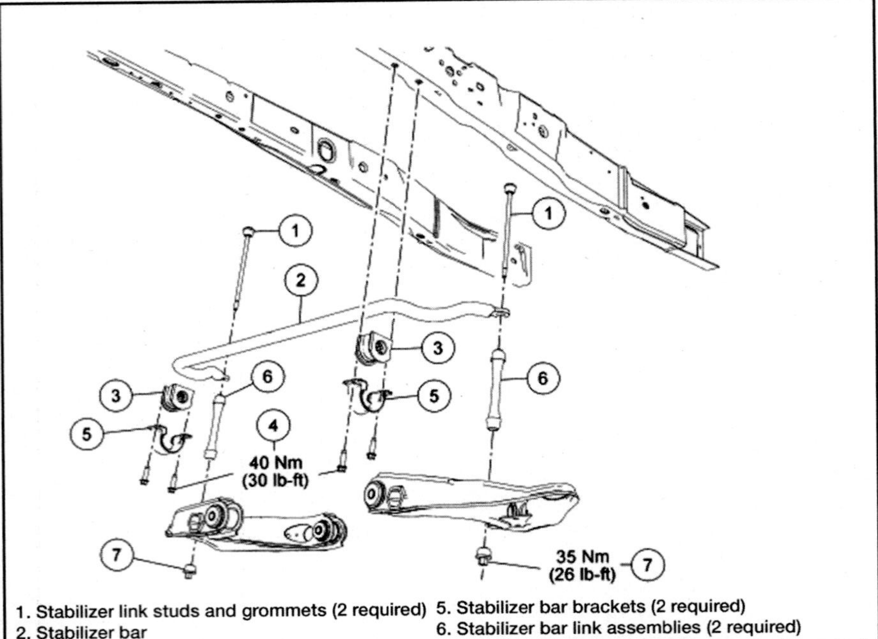

Fig. 181 Exploded view of the stabilizer bar and components

➡Inspect and clean the mating surfaces and the internal threads. Make sure all mating surfaces are free of foreign material and remove any thread locking compound from the internal threads.

➡In the event the stabilizer bar bracket bolts cannot be installed in the frame, remove the weld nut and replace with a flagnut (N807634-S441).

6. To install, reverse the removal procedure.
7. Refer to illustration for torque specifications.

STEERING KNUCKLE

REMOVAL & INSTALLATION

2WD Vehicles

See Figures 182 and 183.

➡Suspension fasteners are critical parts because they affect performance of vital components and systems and their failure may result in major service expense. New parts must be installed with the same part number or an equivalent part if replacement is necessary. Do not use a replacement part of lesser quality or substitute design. Torque values must be used as specified during reassembly to make sure of correct retention of these parts.

1. Remove the brake disc shield.
2. Remove the wheel speed sensor harness bolt.
3. Remove the wheel speed sensor bolt and disconnect the wheel speed sensor from the wheel spindle.
4. Remove and discard the outer tie-rod end cotter pin and nut.
5. Install a new cotter pin.

➡Do not use a hammer to separate the tie-rod end from the wheel spindle or damage to the wheel spindle will result.

➡Do not damage the tie-rod end boot when installing the special tool.

6. Using the C-Frame and Screw Installer/Remover, separate the outer tie-rod end from the wheel spindle.
7. Use a suitable jack to support the front suspension lower arm.
8. Remove and discard the upper ball joint nut and pinch bolt.
9. Disconnect the upper ball joint from the wheel spindle.

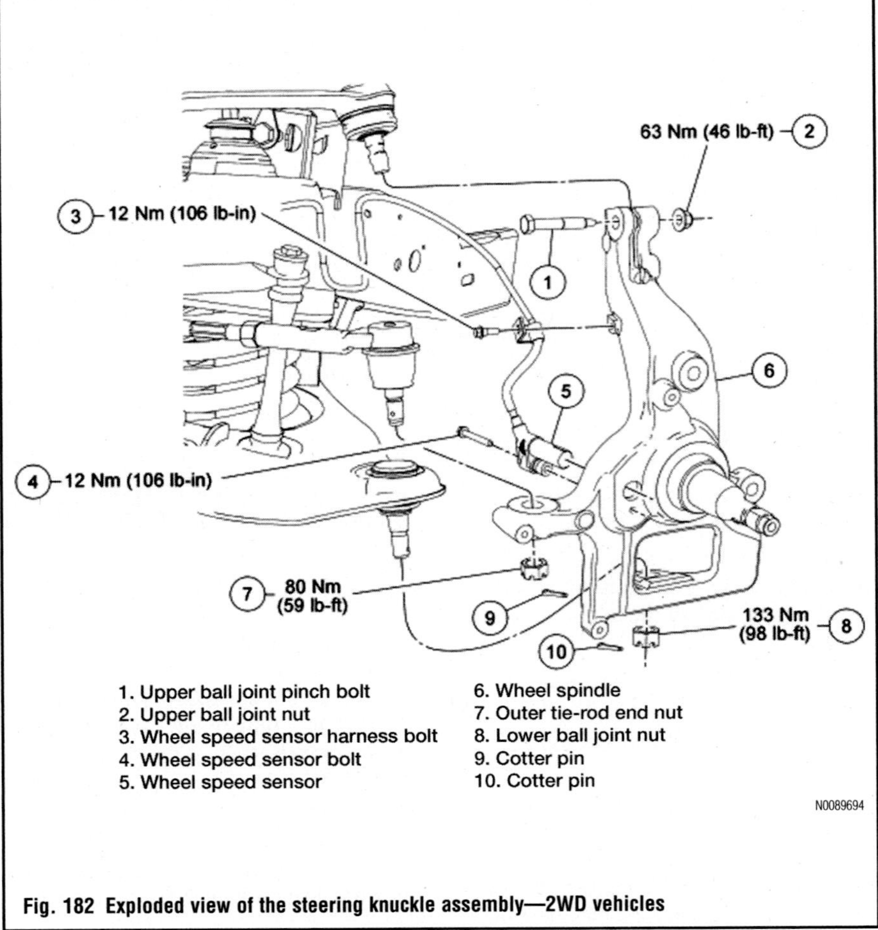

Fig. 182 Exploded view of the steering knuckle assembly—2WD vehicles

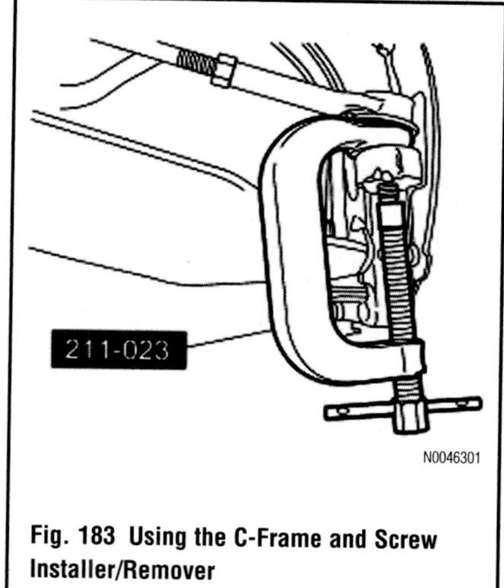

Fig. 183 Using the C-Frame and Screw Installer/Remover

10. Remove and discard the lower ball joint cotter pin and nut.
11. Install a new cotter pin.

➡Do not use a hammer to separate the ball joint from the wheel spindle or damage to the wheel spindle will result.

➡Do not damage the ball joint boot while installing the special tool.

12. Using the C-Frame and Screw Installer/Remover, separate the lower ball joint from the wheel spindle and remove the front wheel spindle.

➡Always install the cotter pins into the nuts from the outboard to inboard, with the fingers bent together at a right angle. Failure to do so will result in damage to the wheel and tire assembly.

13. To install, reverse the removal procedure.
14. Refer to exploded illustration for torque specifications.

4WD Vehicles

See Figure 184.

➡Suspension fasteners are critical parts because they affect performance of vital components and systems and their failure may result in major service expense. New parts must be installed with the same part number or an equivalent part if replacement is necessary. Do not use a replacement part of lesser quality or substitute design. Torque values must be used as specified during reassembly to make sure of correct retention of these parts.

1. Remove the wheel bearing and wheel hub. For additional information, refer to Wheel Bearing and Hub in this section.

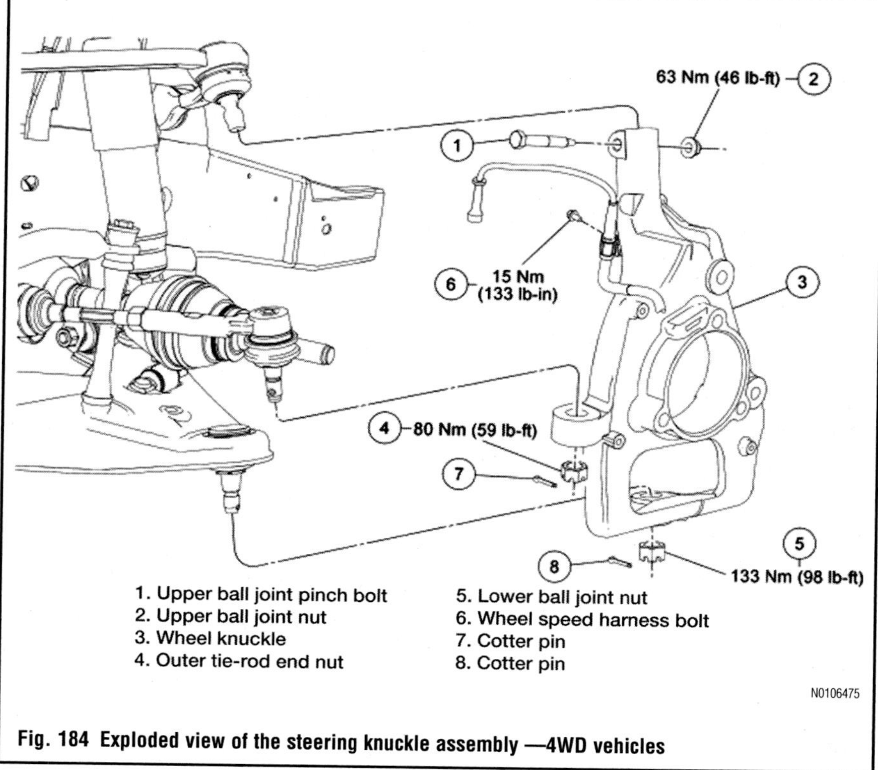

Fig. 184 Exploded view of the steering knuckle assembly —4WD vehicles

2. Remove the wheel speed sensor harness bolt.
3. Remove and discard the cotter pin and outer tie-rod end nut.
4. Install a new cotter pin.

➡Do not use a hammer to separate the outer tie-rod end from the wheel knuckle or damage to the wheel knuckle will result.

➡Do not damage the outer tie-rod end boot when installing the C-Frame and Screw Installer/Remover.

5. Using the C-Frame and Screw Installer/Remover, separate the outer tie-rod end from the front wheel knuckle.
6. Using a suitable jack, support the front suspension lower arm.
7. Remove and discard the lower ball joint cotter pin and nut.
8. Install a new cotter pin.

➡Do not use a hammer to separate the ball joint from the wheel knuckle or damage to wheel knuckle will result.

➡Do not damage the ball joint boot when installing the C-Frame and Screw Installer/Remover.

9. Using the C-Frame and Screw Installer/Remover, separate the ball joint from the wheel knuckle.
10. Remove and discard the upper ball joint pinch bolt and nut and remove the wheel knuckle.

➡Always install the cotter pin into the outer tie-rod end nut from the outboard to inboard, with the fingers bent together at a right angle. Failure to do so will result in damage to the wheel and tire assembly.

11. To install, reverse the removal procedure.
12. Refer to exploded illustration for torque specifications.
13. Check and, if necessary, align the front end.

TORSION BAR

REMOVAL & INSTALLATION

See Figures 185 and 186.

➡Suspension fasteners are critical parts because they affect performance of vital components and systems and their failure may result in major service expense. New parts must be installed with the same part number or an equivalent part if replacement is necessary. Do not use a replacement part of lesser quality or substitute design. Torque values must be used as specified during reassembly to make sure of correct retention of these parts.

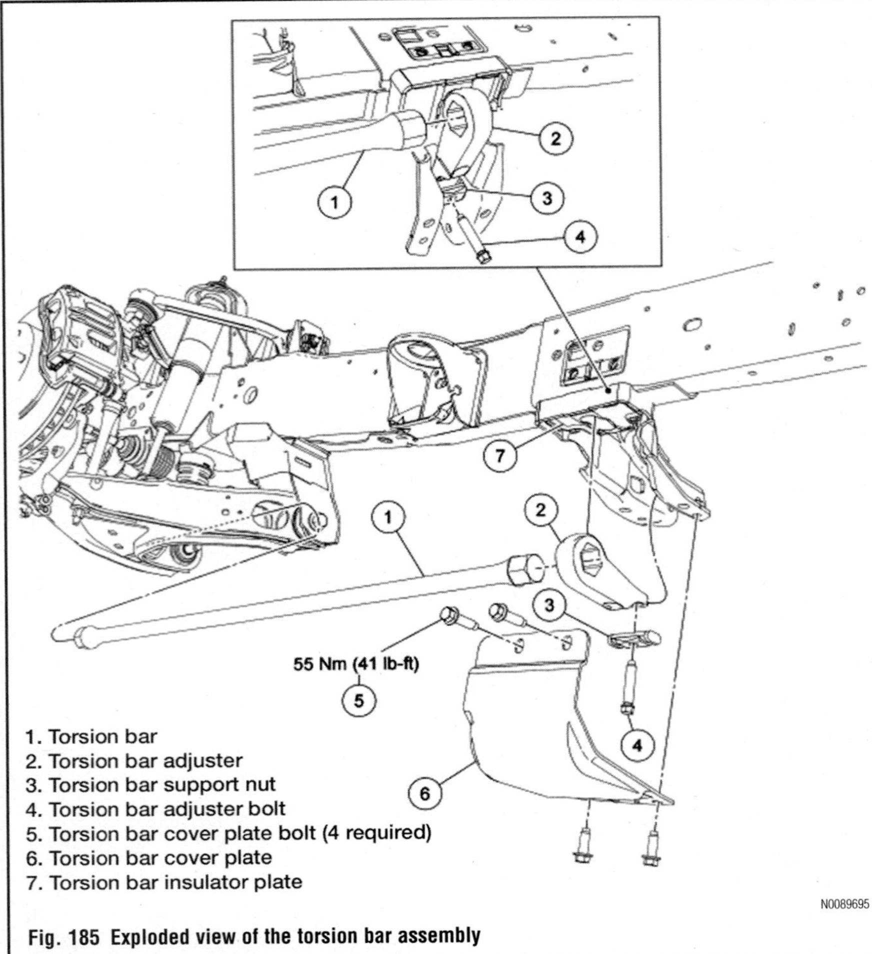

Fig. 185 Exploded view of the torsion bar assembly

1. With the vehicle in NEUTRAL, position it on a hoist.
2. Remove the torsion bar cover plate bolts and the torsion bar cover plate.

➡Before relieving the torsion bar tension, measure and record the measurement of the torsion bar adjustment bolt. This measurement will be used as the preset depth for the new torsion bar adjustment bolt during installation.

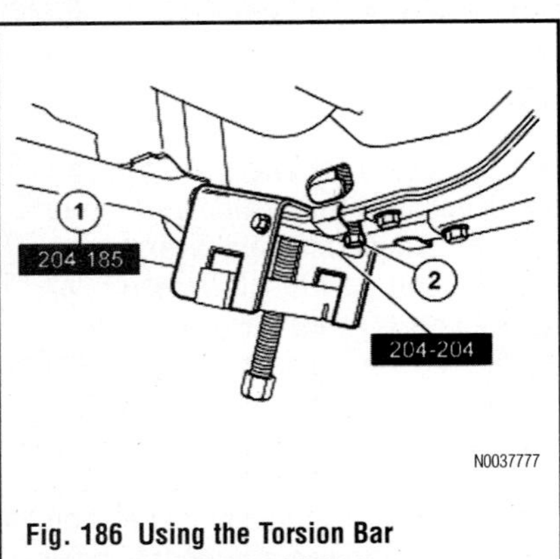

Fig. 186 Using the Torsion Bar Remover/Installer and Adapter

3. Make preliminary adjustment references.
4. Relieve the torsion bar tension.
    a. Position the Torsion Bar Remover/Installer and Adapter.
    b. Tighten the Torsion Bar Remover/Installer until the torsion bar adjuster lifts off the adjustment bolt.

➡The torsion bar adjustment bolt is coated with dry adhesive and must be replaced if it is backed off or removed. Failure to do so may cause the adjustment bolt to loosen during operation and cause a loss of vehicle alignment.

5. Remove and discard the torsion bar adjustment bolt and support nut.
6. Loosen the Torsion Bar Remover/Installer and Adapter until the tension is removed from the torsion bar.
7. Remove the torsion bar in the following sequence:
    a. Mark the torsion bar and the adjuster for correct installation.
    b. Remove the torsion bar insulator plate.
    c. Grasp the torsion bar and pull it free from the lower arm.

To install:

8. Refer to exploded illustration for torque specifications.
9. Position the torsion bar into lower arm.
10. Install the torsion bar adjuster in the following sequence.
    a. Align the marks on the torsion bar and the torsion bar adjuster, then install the torsion bar adjuster.
    b. Position the torsion bar insulator plate.

➡The torsion bar adjustment bolt is coated with dry adhesive and must be replaced if it is backed off or removed. Failure to do so may cause the adjustment bolt to loosen during operation and cause a loss of vehicle alignment.

11. Preload the torsion bar in the following sequence.
    a. Install the Torsion Bar Remover/Installer and Adapter.
    b. Tighten the Torsion Bar Remover/Installer until the new adjustment bolt and nut can be installed.
    c. Turn the adjustment bolt until the preliminary adjustment measurement (recorded length of the old adjustment bolt) is reached.
12. Remove the Torsion Bar Remover/Installer and Adapter.
13. Install the torsion bar cover plate and 4 cover plate bolts.
14. Adjust the ride height.
15. Check and if necessary, align the front end.

UPPER CONTROL ARM

REMOVAL & INSTALLATION

See Figure 187.

➡Suspension fasteners are critical parts because they affect performance of vital components and systems and their failure may result in major service expense. New parts must be installed with the same part number or an equivalent part if replacement is necessary. Do not use a replacement part of lesser quality or substitute design. Torque values must be used as specified during reassembly to make sure of correct retention of these parts.

1. Index-mark the lower arm to the frame with the vehicle in a static ground position (curb height).
2. Remove the wheel and tire.

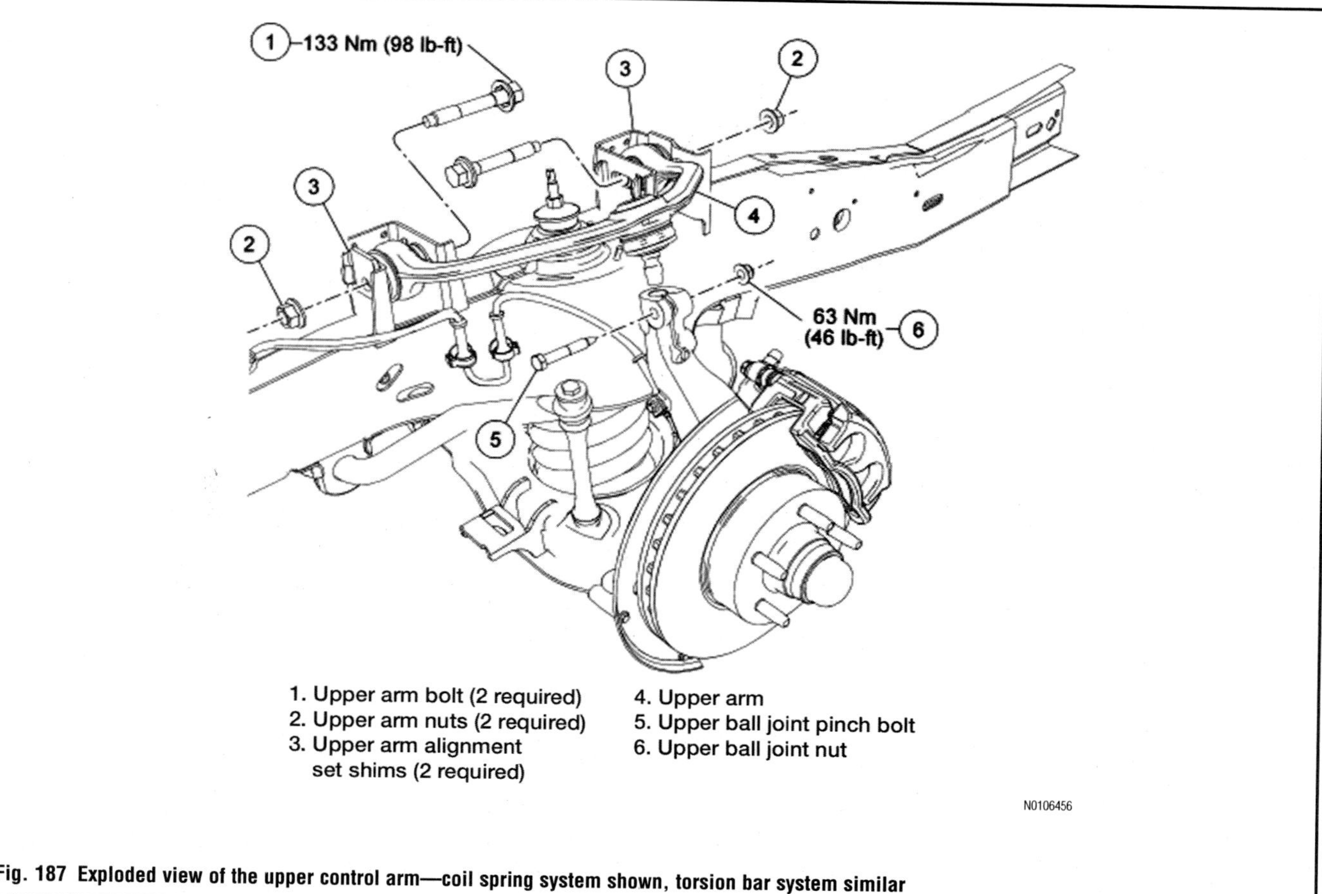

Fig. 187 Exploded view of the upper control arm—coil spring system shown, torsion bar system similar

3. Use a suitable jack to support the lower arm.

➡To avoid possible damage to the wheel spindle/knuckle, secure the wheel spindle/knuckle to keep it from tilting before removing the pinch bolt and nut.

4. Remove and discard the upper ball joint nut and pinch bolt, and separate the ball joint from the wheel spindle/knuckle.
5. Remove and discard the 2 upper arm nuts, bolts and set shims.
6. Remove the upper arm.

To install:

➡Do not tighten the bolts at this time.

➡Make sure that the set shims are installed in their original positions.

7. Refer to exploded illustration for torque specifications.
8. Position the upper arm and loosely install the 2 new upper arm bolts, set shims and 2 new nuts.
9. Install the upper ball joint and the new ball joint nut.
10. Position a suitable jack under the front suspension lower arm and raise the suspension until the index marks on the lower arm and the frame are aligned (curb height).

➡Make sure the upper arm bolts are held in place when tightening the nuts. Failure to do so may result in incorrect torque.

11. Tighten the upper arm bolts.
12. Install the wheel and tire.
13. Check and, if necessary, align the front end.

WHEEL BEARINGS

REMOVAL & INSTALLATION

4WD Vehicles

See Figures 188 and 189.

➡Suspension fasteners are critical parts because they affect performance of vital components and systems and their failure may result in major service expense. New parts must be installed with the same part number or an equivalent part if replacement is necessary. Do not use a replacement part of lesser quality or substitute design. Torque values must be used as specified during reassembly to make sure of correct retention of these parts.

1. Remove the wheel and tire.

➡Do not reuse the torque-prevailing designed halfshaft nut and washer assembly or damage to the component may occur.

2. Remove and discard the halfshaft nut and washer.

➡Do not use a hammer to separate the outboard Constant Velocity (CV) joint from the wheel bearing and hub. Damage to the outboard CV threads and to internal components may result.

3. Using the Front Wheel Hub Remover, separate the outboard CV joint from the wheel bearing and wheel hub.
4. Remove the bolt and detach the wheel speed sensor from the wheel bearing and wheel hub.

➡Do not allow the caliper and anchor plate assembly to hang from the brake hose or damage to the hose may occur.

5. Remove the brake caliper anchor

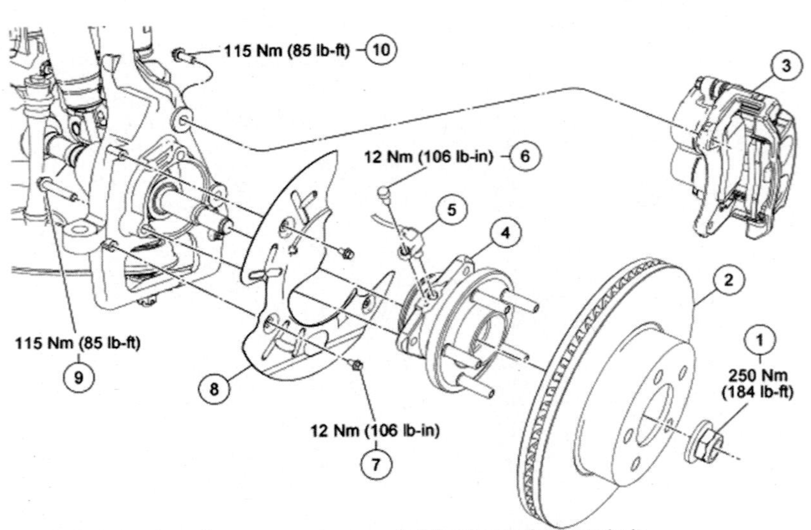

Fig. 188 Exploded view of the wheel bearing and hub assembly

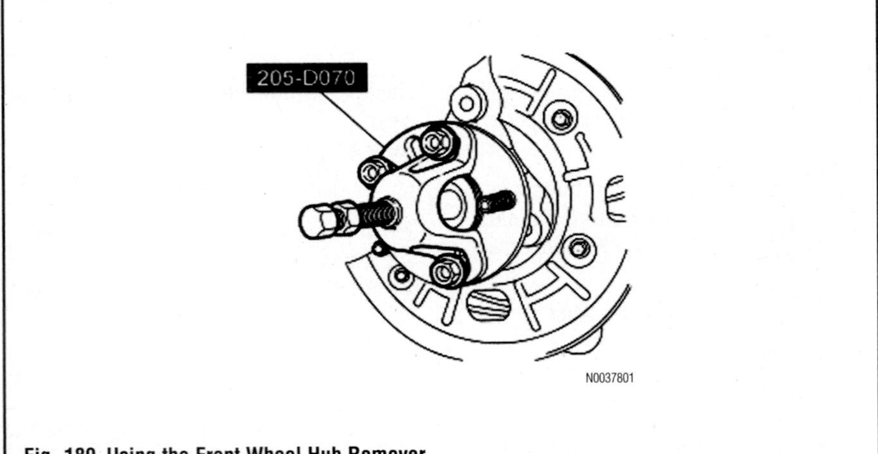

Fig. 189 Using the Front Wheel Hub Remover

plate bolts and position the caliper, pads and anchor plate assembly aside.

6. Support the caliper and anchor plate assembly using mechanic's wire.
7. Remove the brake disc.
8. Remove and discard the 3 brake disc shield bolts and remove the shield.

➡Do not overextend the Constant Velocity (CV) joint and boots when removing the wheel bearing and hub assembly or damage to the CV joint may occur.

9. Remove and discard the 3 bolts, and remove the wheel bearing and wheel hub.
10. To install, reverse the removal procedure.
11. Refer to exploded illustration for torque specifications.

LEAF SPRING

REMOVAL & INSTALLATION

See Figures 190 and 191.

➡Suspension fasteners are critical parts because they affect performance of vital components and systems and their failure may result in major service expense. New parts must be installed with the same part numbers or equivalent parts if replacement is necessary. Do not use replacement parts of lesser quality or substitute design. Torque values must be used as specified during reassembly to make sure of correct retention of these parts.

1. With the vehicle in NEUTRAL, position it on a hoist.
2. Using a suitable jack, support the rear axle.
3. Remove and discard the lower shock absorber bolt and nut.

➡When installing new U-bolts, the distance between the U-bolts should be 3.66 inches ± 0.12 inches. This is important for providing the correct U-bolt clamp load and retention of parts.

4. Remove and discard the 4 rear U-bolt nuts.

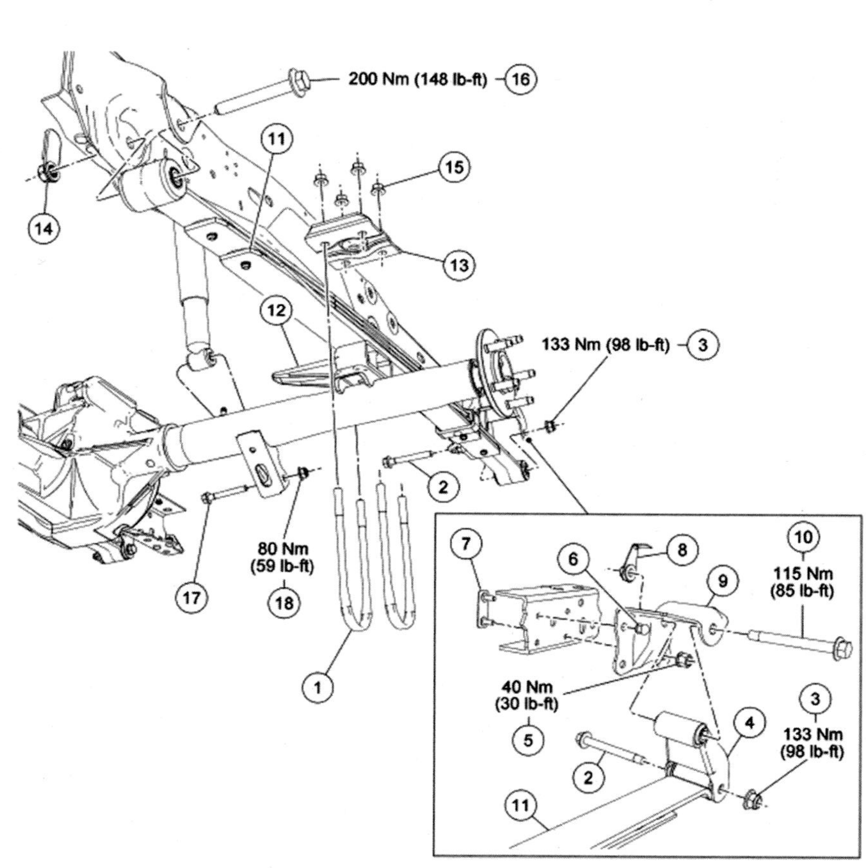

Fig. 190 Exploded view of the leaf spring assembly

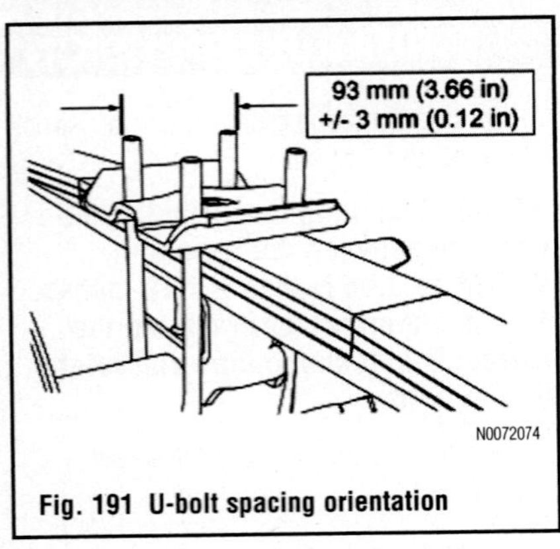

Fig. 191 U-bolt spacing orientation

5. Remove the U-bolts and the spring plate.
6. If equipped, carefully lower the rear axle and remove the rear spring spacer.
7. Remove and discard the spring-to-frame bracket bolt and flagnut.
8. Remove and discard the spring shackle-to-spring bolt and nut and remove the spring.
9. If necessary, remove the spring shackle.
10. Remove and discard the spring shackle-to-frame bracket bolt and flagnut.
11. Remove the shackle.

To install:

12. To install, reverse the removal procedure and note the following steps.
13. Refer to exploded illustration for torque specifications.
14. Tighten the U-bolt nuts in 4 stages:
    a. Stage 1: Tighten in a cross pattern to 22 ft. lbs. (30 Nm).
    b. Stage 2: Tighten in a cross pattern to 44 ft. lbs. (60 Nm).
    c. Stage 3: Tighten in a cross pattern to 66 ft. lbs. (90 Nm).
    d. Stage 4: Tighten in a cross pattern to 85 ft. lbs. (115 Nm).

FORD

Taurus

17

BRAKES 17-12

ANTI-LOCK BRAKE SYSTEM (ABS) 17-12
General Information.................17-12
Precautions.........................17-12
Speed Sensors........................17-12
Removal & Installation........17-12
BLEEDING THE BRAKE SYSTEM 17-14
Bleeding Procedure.................17-14
Bleeding Procedure 17-14
Bleeding the ABS System ...17-16
Brake Caliper Bleeding 17-16
Master Cylinder Bleeding 17-14
FRONT DISC BRAKES........17-16
Brake Caliper...........................17-16
Removal & Installation........17-16
Disc Brake...............................17-17
Removal & Installation........17-17
Disc Brake Pads......................17-17
Removal & Installation........17-17
Disc Brake Shield....................17-17
Removal & Installation........17-17
REAR DISC BRAKES 17-18
Brake Caliper...........................17-18
Removal & Installation........17-18
Disc Brake...............................17-18
Removal & Installation........17-18
Disc Brake Pads......................17-19
Removal & Installation........17-19
Disc Brake Shield....................17-20
Removal & Installation........17-20

CHASSIS ELECTRICAL 17-20

AIR BAG (SUPPLEMENTAL RESTRAINT SYSTEM) 17-20
General Information.................17-20
Arming the System 17-21
Disarming the System.........17-20
Service Precautions............17-20

DRIVE TRAIN 17-21

Automatic Transaxle Fluid.......17-21
Drain and Refill...................17-21
Front Driveshaft.......................17-23
Removal & Installation........17-23
Front Halfshaft.........................17-24
Removal & Installation........17-24
Rear Axle Assembly.................17-27
Removal & Installation........17-27
Rear Differential Housing Cover17-27
Removal & Installation........17-27
Rear Halfshaft..........................17-28
Removal & Installation........17-28
Rear Pinion Seal......................17-29
Removal & Installation........17-29
Rear Stub Shaft Seal 17-30
Removal & Installation........17-30
Transfer Case Assembly 17-21
Drain & Refill......................17-23
Removal & Installation........17-21

ENGINE COOLING 17-30

Coolant (Water) Pump.............17-30
Removal & Installation........17-30
Engine Coolant........................17-33
Draining Procedure.............17-33
Filling and Bleeding With Radiator Refiller........17-34
Filling and Bleeding Without Radiator Refiller...17-34
Engine Fan 17-35
Removal & Installation........17-35
Radiator...................................17-37
Removal & Installation........17-37
Thermostat 17-39
Removal & Installation........17-39

ENGINE ELECTRICAL 17-40

BATTERY SYSTEM............17-42
Battery....................................17-42
Removal & Installation........17-42
CHARGING SYSTEM 17-40
Alternator 17-40
Removal & Installation........17-40
IGNITION SYSTEM 17-41
Ignition Coil-On-Plug 17-41
Removal & Installation........17-41
Spark Plugs.............................17-41
Removal & Installation........17-41

STARTING SYSTEM 17-42
Starter 17-42
Removal & Installation........17-42

ENGINE MECHANICAL......17-43

Accessory Drive Belts 17-43
Accessory Belt Routing.............................17-43
Removal & Installation........17-43
Air Cleaner 17-45
Removal & Installation........17-45
Camshaft and Valve Lifters......17-46
Removal & Installation........17-46
Catalytic Converter..................17-65
Removal & Installation........17-65
Crankshaft Front Seal..............17-66
Removal & Installation........17-66
Cylinder Head 17-67
Removal & Installation........17-67
Engine Oil & Filter 17-76
Replacement 17-76
Exhaust Manifold 17-77
Removal & Installation........17-77
Intake Manifold 17-79
Removal & Installation........17-79
Oil Pump.................................17-81
Removal & Installation........17-81
Rear Main Seal........................17-83
Removal & Installation........17-83
Turbocharger 17-83
Removal & Installation........17-83
Valve Covers 17-86
Removal & Installation........17-86

ENGINE PERFORMANCE & EMISSION CONTROLS 17-92

Camshaft Position (CMP) Sensor 17-92
Location..............................17-92
Removal & Installation........17-92
Catalyst Monitor Sensor..........17-93
Removal & Installtion 17-93
Crankshaft Position (CKP) Sensor 17-93
Location..............................17-93
Removal & Installation........17-93

Cylinder Head Temperature (CHT) Sensor....17-93
Location....17-93
Removal & Installation....17-93
Fuel Rail Pressure (FRP) Sensor....17-94
Location....17-94
Removal & Installation....17-94
Heated Oxygen (HO2S) Sensor....17-95
Location....17-95
Removal & Installation....17-95
Intake Air Temperature (IAT) Sensor....17-96
Location....17-96
Removal & Installation....17-97
Knock Sensor (KS)....17-97
Location....17-97
Removal & Installation....17-97
Manifold Absolute Pressure (MAP) Sensor & Intake Air Temperature 2 (IAT2) Sensor....17-97
Removal & Installation....17-97
Powertrain Control Module (PCM)....17-97
Location....17-97
Removal & Installation....17-97
Throttle Position Sensor (TPS)....17-98
Removal & Installation....17-98
Turbocharger Boost Pressure (TCBP) / Charge Air cooler Temperature (CACT) Sensor .17-98
Location....17-98
Removal & Installation....17-98
Variable Camshaft Timing (VCT) Oil Control Solenoid...17-99
Location....17-99
Removal & Installation....17-99

FUEL....17-99

GASOLINE FUEL INJECTION SYSTEM....17-99
Fuel Filter....17-100
Removal & Installation....17-100
Fuel Injectors....17-100
Removal & Installation....17-100
Fuel Pump....17-100
Removal & Installation....17-100
Fuel Rail....17-102
Removal & Installtion....17-102
Fuel System Service Precautions....17-99
Fuel Tank....17-104
Draining....17-104
Removal & Installation....17-107
Relieving Fuel System Pressure....17-99
Throttle Body....17-108
Removal & Installation....17-108

HEATING & AIR CONDITIONING SYSTEM..17-110

Blower Motor....17-110
Removal & Installation....17-110
Heater Core....17-110
Removal & Installation....17-110

PRECAUTIONS....17-12

SPECIFICATIONS AND MAINTENANCE CHARTS....17-3

Brake Specifications....17-7
Camshaft Specifications....17-5
Capacities....17-4
Crankshaft and Connecting Rod Specifications....17-5
Engine and Vehicle Identification....17-3
Engine Tune-Up Specifications....17-3
Fluid Specifications....17-4
General Engine Specifications....17-3
Piston and Ring Specifications....17-5
Scheduled Maintenance Intervals....17-8–11
Tire, Wheel and Ball Joint Specifications....17-7
Torque Specifications....17-6
Valve Specifications....17-4
Wheel Alignment....17-6

STEERING....17-110

Power Steering Gear....17-110
Removal & Installation....17-110
Power Steering Pump....17-113
Fluid Fill Procedure....17-115
Purging....17-114
Removal & Installation....17-113

SUSPENSION....17-116

FRONT SUSPENSION....17-116
Lower Control Arm....17-116
Lower Control Arm Bushing Replacement....17-116
Removal & Installation....17-116
Stabilizer Bar....17-117
Removal & Installation....17-117
Stabilizer Bar Link....17-118
Removal & Installation....17-118
Strut & Spring Assembly....17-118
Removal & Installation....17-118
Wheel Bearing and Wheel Hub....17-119
Removal & Installation....17-119
Wheel Knuckle....17-120
Removal & Insatllation....17-120

REAR SUSPENSION....17-121
Lower Control Arm....17-121
Removal & Installation....17-121
Shock Absorber....17-122
Removal & Installation....17-122
Spring....17-123
Removal & Installtion....17-123
Stabilizer Bar....17-123
Removal & Installation....17-123
Stabilizer Bar Link....17-124
Removal & Installation....17-124
Toe Link....17-124
Removal & Installation....17-124
Trailing Arm....17-125
Removal & Installation....17-125
Upper Control Arm....17-126
Removal & Installation....17-126
Wheel Bearings and Wheel Hub....17-128
Removal & Installation....17-128
Wheel Knuckle....17-129
Removal & Installation....17-129

SPECIFICATIONS AND MAINTENANCE CHARTS

ENGINE AND VEHICLE IDENTIFICATION

Engine						
Code ①	Liters	Cu. In.	Cyl.	Fuel Sys.	Engine Type	Eng. Mfg.
W	3.5	214	6	MRFS ③	DOHC	Ford
T	3.5	214	6	GTDI ④	DOHC	Ford

Model Year	
Code ②	Year
A	2010
B	2011

① 8th position of VIN
② 10th position of VIN
③ 2-Speed Mechanical Returnless Fuel System (MRFS) with Sequential Multi-Port Fuel Injection (MFI)
④ Gasoline Turbocharged Direct Injection

25759_TAUR_C0001

GENERAL ENGINE SPECIFICATIONS

All measurements are given in inches.

Year	Model	Engine Displacement Liters (cc)	Engine ID/VIN	Fuel System Type	Net Horsepower @ rpm	Net Torque @ rpm (ft. lbs.)	Bore x Stroke (in.)	Com-pression Ratio	Oil Pressure @ rpm
2010	Taurus	3.5 (3496)	W	MRFS ①	263@6250	249@4500	3.64X3.41	10.3:1	30@1500
		3.5 (3496)	T	GTDI ②	365@5500	350@3500	3.64X3.49	10.0:1	30@1500
2011	Taurus	3.5 (3496)	W	MRFS ①	263@6250	249@4500	3.64X3.41	10.3:1	30@1500
		3.5 (3496)	T	GTDI ②	365@5500	350@3500	3.64X3.49	10.0:1	30@1500

① 2-Speed Mechanical Returnless Fuel System (MRFS) with Sequential Multi-Port Fuel Injection (MFI)
② Gasoline Turbocharged Direct Injection

25759_TAUR_C0002

ENGINE TUNE-UP SPECIFICATIONS

Year	Engine Displacement Liters (cc)	Engine ID/VIN	Spark Plug Gap (in.)	Ignition Timing (deg.)		Fuel Pump (psi)	Idle Speed (rpm)		Valve Clearance	
				MT	AT		MT	AT	Intake	Exhaust
2010	3.5 (3496)	W	0.051-0.057	N/A	①	65	N/A	①	0.0008-0.0027	0.0013-0.032
	3.5 (3496)	T	0.035	N/A	①	65	N/A	①	0.0008-0.0027	0.0013-0.032
2011	3.5 (3496)	W	0.051-0.057	N/A	①	65	N/A	①	0.0008-0.0027	0.0013-0.032
	3.5 (3496)	T	0.035	N/A	①	65	N/A	①	0.0008-0.0027	0.0013-0.032

① Controlled by the Powertrain Control Module (PCM) and cannot be manually adjusted

25759_TAUR_C0003

CAPACITIES

Year	Model	Engine Displacement Liters (cc)	Engine ID/VIN	Engine Oil with Filter (qts.)	Transmission/axle (pts.) Auto.	Transmission/axle (pts.) Manual	Drive Axle (pts.) Front	Drive Axle (pts.) Rear	Transfer Case (pts.)	Fuel Tank (gal.)	Cooling System (qts.)
2010	Taurus	3.5 (3496)	W	5.5	18.8	N/A	N/A	2.43	1.13	19	11.1
		3.5 (3496)	T	6	18.8	N/A	N/A	2.43	1.13	19	11.1
2011	Taurus	3.5 (3496)	W	5.5	18.8	N/A	N/A	2.43	1.13	19	11.1
		3.5 (3496)	T	6	18.8	N/A	N/A	2.43	1.13	19	11.1

NOTE: All capacities are approximate. Add fluid gradually and ensure a proper fluid level is obtained.

N/A - Not applicable

25759_TAUR_C0004

FLUID SPECIFICATIONS

Year	Model	Engine Disp. Liters	Engine Oil	Manual Trans.	Auto. Trans.	Drive Axle Front	Drive Axle Rear	Transfer Case	Power Steering Fluid	Brake Master Cylinder	Cooling System
2010	Taurus	3.5	①	N/A	MERCON® LV	N/A	80W-90	75W-140	MERCON® V	DOT 3	②
		3.5	①	N/A	MERCON® LV	N/A	80W-90	75W-140	MERCON® V	DOT 3	②
2011	Taurus	3.5	①	N/A	MERCON® LV	N/A	80W-90	75W-140	MERCON® V	DOT 3	②
		3.5	①	N/A	MERCON® LV	N/A	80W-90	75W-140	MERCON® V	DOT 3	②

DOT: Department Of Transpotation

N/A - Not Applicable

① 5W-20 Premium Synthetic Blend Motor Oil

② Motorcraft® Specialty Green Engine Coolant

25759_TAUR_C0005

VALVE SPECIFICATIONS

Year	Engine Displacement Liters (cc)	Engine ID/VIN	Seat Angle (deg.)	Face Angle (deg.)	Spring Test Pressure (lbs. @ in.)	Spring Free-Length (in.)	Spring Installed Height (in.)	Stem-to-Guide Clearance (in.) Intake	Stem-to-Guide Clearance (in.) Exhaust	Stem Diameter (in.) Intake	Stem Diameter (in.) Exhaust
2010	3.5 (3496)	W	44.5	44.5	53 @ 1.45	1.90	1.450	0.0008-0.0027	0.0013-0.0032	0.2157-0.2164	0.2151-0.2159
	3.5 (3496)	T	44.5	44.5	60 @ 1.45	2.170	1.450	0.0008-0.0027	0.0013-0.0032	0.2157-0.2164	0.2151-0.2159
2011	3.5 (3496)	W	44.5	44.5	53 @ 1.45	1.90	1.450	0.0008-0.0027	0.0013-0.0032	0.2157-0.2164	0.2151-0.2159
	3.5 (3496)	T	44.5	44.5	60 @ 1.45	2.170	1.450	0.0008-0.0027	0.0013-0.0032	0.2157-0.2164	0.2151-0.2159

25759_TAUR_C0006

CAMSHAFT SPECIFICATIONS

All measurements in inches unless noted

Year	Engine Displacement Liters (cc)	Engine Code/VIN	Journal Diameter	Brg. Oil Clearance	Shaft End-play	Runout	Journal Bore	Lobe Height	
								Intake	Exhaust
2010	3.5 (3496)	W	1.021-1.022	0.0029	0.0012-0.0066	0.0015	1.023-1.024	0.38	0.38
	3.5 (3496)	T	1.021-1.022	0.0029	0.0012-0.0066	0.0015	1.023-1.024	0.35	0.36
2011	3.5 (3496)	W	1.021-1.022	0.0029	0.0012-0.0066	0.0015	1.023-1.024	0.38	0.38
	3.5 (3496)	T	1.021-1.022	0.0029	0.0012-0.0066	0.0015	1.023-1.024	0.35	0.36

25759_TAUR_C0007

CRANKSHAFT AND CONNECTING ROD SPECIFICATIONS

All measurements are given in inches.

Year	Engine Displacement Liters (cc)	Engine ID/VIN	Crankshaft				Connecting Rod		
			Main Brg. Journal Dia.	Main Brg. Oi Clearance	Shaft End-play	Thrust on No.	Journal Diameter	Oil Clearance	Side Clearance
2010	3.5 (3496)	W	2.6570	0.0010-0.0016	0.0039-0.0114	3	2.204-2.2050	0.0007-0.0021	0.0068-0.0167
	3.5 (3496)	T	2.6570	0.0010-0.0016	0.0039-0.0114	3	2.204-2.2050	0.0007-0.0021	0.0068-0.0167
2011	3.5 (3496)	W	2.6570	0.0010-0.0016	0.0039-0.0114	3	2.204-2.2050	0.0007-0.0021	0.0068-0.0167
	3.5 (3496)	T	2.6570	0.0010-0.0016	0.0039-0.0114	3	2.204-2.2050	0.0007-0.0021	0.0068-0.0167

25759_TAUR_C0008

PISTON AND RING SPECIFICATIONS

All measurements are given in inches.

Year	Engine Displacement Liters	Engine ID/VIN	Piston Clearance	Ring Gap			Ring Side Clearance		
				Top Compression	Bottom Compression	Oil Control	Top Compression	Bottom Compression	Oil Control
2010	3.5 (3496)	W	0.0003-0.0017	0.0059-0.0098	0.0118-0.0216	0.0059-0.0177	0.0484-0.0492	0.0602-0.0610	N/A
	3.5 (3496)	T	0.0003-0.0017	0.0067-0.0106	0.0118-0.0216	0.0059-0.0177	0.0484-0.0492	0.0602-0.0610	N/A
2011	3.5 (3496)	W	0.0003-0.0017	0.0059-0.0098	0.0118-0.0216	0.0059-0.0177	0.0484-0.0492	0.0602-0.0610	N/A
	3.5 (3496)	T	0.0003-0.0017	0.0067-0.0106	0.0118-0.0216	0.0059-0.0177	0.0484-0.0492	0.0602-0.0610	N/A

N/A - Not Available

25759_TAUR_C0009

TORQUE SPECIFICATIONS

All readings in ft. lbs.

Year	Engine Disp. Liters (cc)	Engine ID/VIN	Cylinder Head Bolts	Main Bearing Bolts	Rod Bearing Bolts	Crankshaft Damper Bolts	Flexplate Bolts	Manifold Intake	Manifold Exhaust	Spark Plugs	Oil Pan Drain Plug
2010	3.5 (3496)	W	N/A	N/A	N/A	N/A	59	N/A	N/A	11	20
	3.5 (3496)	T	N/A	N/A	N/A	N/A	59	N/A	N/A	11	20
2011	3.5 (3496)	W	N/A	N/A	N/A	N/A	59	N/A	N/A	11	20
	3.5 (3496)	T	N/A	N/A	N/A	N/A	59	N/A	N/A	11	20

N/A - Not Avaiable

25759_TAUR_C0010

WHEEL ALIGNMENT

Year	Model		Caster Range (+/-Deg.)	Caster Preferred Setting (Deg.)	Camber Range (+/-Deg.)	Camber Preferred Setting (Deg.)	Toe-in (Deg.)
2010	Taurus	F	0.75	+3.2	0.75	-0.60	+0.20+/-0.20
		R	-	-	0.75	-1.00	+0.24+/-0.20
2011	Taurus	F	0.75	+3.2	0.75	-0.60	+0.20+/-0.20
		R	-	-	0.75	-1.00	+0.24+/-0.20

25759_TAUR_C0011

TIRE, WHEEL AND BALL JOINT SPECIFICATIONS

Year	Model	OEM Tires		Tire Pressures (psi)		Wheel	Ball Joint	Lug Nut
		Standard	Optional	Front	Rear	Size	Inspection	(ft. lbs.) ②
2010	Taurus	P235/60R17	①	40	40	17	NA	100
2011	Taurus	P235/60R17	①	40	40	17	NA	100

OEM: Original Equipment Manufacturer

PSI: Pounds Per Square Inch

NA: Information not available

① P235/55R18 99H Standard on the SEL model
P235/55R H Standard on the SEL AWD model
P255/45R V Standard on the Limited models
P255/45R V Standard on the SHO model

② The wheel nut torque specification is for clean, dry wheel stud and wheel nut threads

25759_TAUR_C0012

BRAKE SPECIFICATIONS

All measurements in inches unless noted

Year	Model		Brake Disc			Brake Drum Diameter			Minimum Pad/Lining Thickness		Brake Caliper	
			Original Thickness	Minimum Thickness	Max. Runout	Original Inside Diameter	Max. Wear Limit	Maximum Machine Diamter	Front	Rear	Bracket Bolts (ft. lbs.)	Mounting Bolts (ft. lbs.)
2010	Taurus	F	NA	①	0.002	-	-	-	0.118	-	111	44
		R	NA	0.393	0.002	-	-	-	-	0.118	81	21
2011	Taurus	F	NA	①	0.002	-	-	-	0.118	-	111	44
		R	NA	0.393	0.002	-	-	-	-	0.118	81	21

F: Front

R: Rear

NA: Information not available

① 1.122 - Vehicles Equipped With Inboard Vented Brake Disc
1.023 - Vehicles Equipped With Outboard Vented Brake Disc

25759_TAUR_C0013

SCHEDULED MAINTENANCE INTERVALS

2010 Taurus - Normal

		VEHICLE MILEAGE INTERVAL (x1000)													
Service Item	**Service Action**	**7.5**	**15**	**22.5**	**30**	**37.5**	**45**	**52.5**	**60**	**67.5**	**75**	**82.5**	**90**	**97.5**	**10.5**
Accesory drive belts	Inspect	✓	✓	✓	✓	✓	✓	✓	✓	✓	✓	✓	✓	✓	✓
Auto transmisison fluid	Replace	At 150,000 miles													
Battery performance	Inspect	✓	✓	✓	✓	✓	✓	✓	✓	✓	✓	✓	✓	✓	✓
Brake system (Pads/shoes/rotors/drums, brake lines and hoses, and parking brake system)	Inspect		✓		✓		✓		✓		✓		✓		✓
Cabin air filter	Inspect	✓	✓	✓	✓	✓	✓	✓	✓	✓	✓	✓	✓	✓	✓
Cabin air filter	Replace		✓		✓		✓		✓		✓		✓		✓
Rotate tires, inspect tread wear, measure tread depth and check pressure	Inspect/ Rotate	✓	✓	✓	✓	✓	✓	✓	✓	✓	✓	✓	✓	✓	✓
Engine oil & filter	Replace	✓	✓	✓	✓	✓	✓	✓	✓	✓	✓	✓	✓	✓	✓
Inspect wheels and related components for abnomal noise, wear, looseness or drag	Inspect	✓	✓	✓	✓	✓	✓	✓	✓	✓	✓	✓	✓	✓	✓
Steering linkage, ball joints, suspension, tie-rod ends, driveshaft and u-joints: lubricate if equipped with grease fittings	Inspect/ Lubricate	✓	✓	✓	✓	✓	✓	✓	✓	✓	✓	✓	✓	✓	✓
Halfshaft boots	Inspect	✓	✓	✓	✓	✓	✓	✓	✓	✓	✓	✓	✓	✓	✓
Cooling system, hoses, clamps & coolant strength	Inspect	✓	✓	✓	✓	✓	✓	✓	✓	✓	✓	✓	✓	✓	✓
Exhaust system (Leaks, damage, loose parts and foreign material)	Inspect	✓	✓	✓	✓	✓	✓	✓	✓	✓	✓	✓	✓	✓	✓
Climate-controlled seat filter (if equipped)	Replace				✓				✓				✓		
Engine air filter	Inspect	✓	✓	✓	✓	✓	✓	✓	✓	✓	✓	✓	✓	✓	✓
Engine air filter	Replace				✓				✓				✓		
Spark plugs	Replace												√		
Fluid levels (all)	Top off	✓	✓	✓	✓	✓	✓	✓	✓	✓	✓	✓	✓	✓	✓
Oil and fluid leaks	Inspect	✓	✓	✓	✓	✓	✓	✓	✓	✓	✓	✓	✓	✓	✓
Horn, exterior lamps, turn signals and hazard warning light operation	Inspect	✓	✓	✓	✓	✓	✓	✓	✓	✓	✓	✓	✓	✓	✓
Radiator, coolers, heater and air conditioning hoses	Inspect	✓	✓	✓	✓	✓	✓	✓	✓	✓	✓	✓	✓	✓	✓
Windshield wiper spray and wiper operation	Inspect	✓	✓	✓	✓	✓	✓	✓	✓	✓	✓	✓	✓	✓	✓
Windshield for cracks, chips and pitting	Inspect	✓	✓	✓	✓	✓	✓	✓	✓	✓	✓	✓	✓	✓	✓
Shocks struts and other suspension components for leaks and damage	Inspect	✓	✓	✓	✓	✓	✓	✓	✓	✓	✓	✓	✓	✓	✓
Engine coolant	Replace														✓

25759_TAUR_C0014

SCHEDULED MAINTENANCE INTERVALS

2010 Taurus - Severe

Service Item	Service Action	VEHICLE MILEAGE INTERVAL (x1000)																	
		5	10	15	20	25	30	35	40	45	50	55	60	65	70	75	80	85	90
Accessory drive belts	Inspect	✓	✓	✓	✓	✓	✓	✓	✓	✓	✓	✓	✓	✓	✓	✓	✓	✓	✓
Accessory drive belts	Replace	At 150,000 miles																	
Automatic transmission fluid	Replace						✓						✓						✓
Battery performance	Inspect	✓	✓	✓	✓	✓	✓	✓	✓	✓	✓	✓	✓	✓	✓	✓	✓	✓	✓
Brake system (Pads/shoes/rotors/drums, brake lines and hoses, and parking brake system)	Inspect	✓	✓	✓	✓	✓	✓	✓	✓	✓	✓	✓	✓	✓	✓	✓	✓	✓	✓
Spark plugs	Replace												✓						
Cabin air filter	Replace			✓			✓			✓			✓			✓			✓
Cabin air filter	Inspect	✓	✓	✓	✓	✓	✓	✓	✓	✓	✓	✓	✓	✓	✓	✓	✓	✓	✓
Climate-controlled seat filter (if equipped)	Replace						✓						✓						✓
Cooling system, hoses, clamps & coolant strength	Inspect	✓	✓	✓	✓	✓	✓	✓	✓	✓	✓	✓	✓	✓	✓	✓	✓	✓	✓
Engine air filter	Inspect	✓	✓	✓	✓	✓	✓	✓	✓	✓	✓	✓	✓	✓	✓	✓	✓	✓	✓
Engine air filter	Replace						✓						✓						✓
Exhaust system (Leaks, damage, loose parts and foreign material)	Inspect	✓	✓	✓	✓	✓	✓	✓	✓	✓	✓	✓	✓	✓	✓	✓	✓	✓	✓
Fluid levels (all)	Top off	✓	✓	✓	✓	✓	✓	✓	✓	✓	✓	✓	✓	✓	✓	✓	✓	✓	✓
Halfshaft boots	Inspect	✓	✓	✓	✓	✓	✓	✓	✓	✓	✓	✓	✓	✓	✓	✓	✓	✓	✓
Horn, exterior lamps, turn signals and hazard warning light operation	Inspect	✓	✓	✓	✓	✓	✓	✓	✓	✓	✓	✓	✓	✓	✓	✓	✓	✓	✓
Inspect wheels and related components for abnomal noise, wear, looseness or drag	Inspect	✓	✓	✓	✓	✓	✓	✓	✓	✓	✓	✓	✓	✓	✓	✓	✓	✓	✓
Oil and fluid leaks	Inspect	✓	✓	✓	✓	✓	✓	✓	✓	✓	✓	✓	✓	✓	✓	✓	✓	✓	✓
Radiator, coolers, heater and air conditioning hoses	Inspect	✓	✓	✓	✓	✓	✓	✓	✓	✓	✓	✓	✓	✓	✓	✓	✓	✓	✓
Rotate tires, inspect tread wear, measure tread depth and check pressure	Inspect	✓	✓	✓	✓	✓	✓	✓	✓	✓	✓	✓	✓	✓	✓	✓	✓	✓	✓
Shocks struts and other suspension components for leaks and damage	Inspect	✓	✓	✓	✓	✓	✓	✓	✓	✓	✓	✓	✓	✓	✓	✓	✓	✓	✓
Steering linkage, ball joints, suspension, tie-rod ends, driveshaft and u-joints: lubricate if equipped with grease fittings	Inspect/ Lubricate	✓	✓	✓	✓	✓	✓	✓	✓	✓	✓	✓	✓	✓	✓	✓	✓	✓	✓
Windshield wiper spray and wiper operation	Inspect	✓	✓	✓	✓	✓	✓	✓	✓	✓	✓	✓	✓	✓	✓	✓	✓	✓	✓
Windshield for cracks, chips and pitting	Inspect	✓	✓	✓	✓	✓	✓	✓	✓	✓	✓	✓	✓	✓	✓	✓	✓	✓	✓
Engine oil & filter	Replace	✓	✓	✓	✓	✓	✓	✓	✓	✓	✓	✓	✓	✓	✓	✓	✓	✓	✓
Engine coolant	Replace	At 105,000 miles																	

25759_TAUR_C0015

SCHEDULED MAINTENANCE INTERVALS

2011 Taurus - Normal

		MILEAGE INTERVAL AS INDICATED BY THE MESSAGE CENTER														
Service Item	**Service Action**	**1**	**2**	**3**	**4**	**5**	**6**	**7**	**8**	**9**	**10**	**11**	**12**	**13**	**14**	**15**
Engine oil & filter	Replace	✓	✓	✓	✓	✓	✓	✓	✓	✓	✓	✓	✓	✓	✓	✓
Rotate tires, inspect tread wear, measure tread depth and check pressure	Rotate/ Inspect	✓	✓	✓	✓	✓	✓	✓	✓	✓	✓	✓	✓	✓	✓	✓
Brake system (Pads/shoes/rotors/drums, brake lines and hoses, and parking brake system)	Inspect	✓	✓	✓	✓	✓	✓	✓	✓	✓	✓	✓	✓	✓	✓	✓
Steering linkage, ball joints, suspension, tie-rod ends, driveshaft and u-joints: lubricate if equipped with grease fittings	Inspect	✓	✓	✓	✓	✓	✓	✓	✓	✓	✓	✓	✓	✓	✓	✓
Cabin air filter	Replace		✓		✓		✓		✓		✓		✓		✓	
Climate-controlled seat filter (if equipped)	Replace			✓			✓			✓			✓			✓
Spark plugs	Replace										✓					
Engine coolant	Replace										✓					
Transmission fluid	Replace															✓
Accessory drive belts	Replace															✓
Accessory drive belts	Inspect	✓	✓	✓	✓	✓	✓	✓	✓	✓	✓	✓	✓	✓	✓	✓
Battery performance	Inspect	✓	✓	✓	✓	✓	✓	✓	✓	✓	✓	✓	✓	✓	✓	✓
Cooling system, hoses, clamps & coolant strength	Inspect	✓	✓	✓	✓	✓	✓	✓	✓	✓	✓	✓	✓	✓	✓	✓
Engine air filter	Inspect	✓	✓	✓	✓	✓	✓	✓	✓	✓	✓	✓	✓	✓	✓	✓
Engine air filter	Replace			✓			✓			✓			✓			✓
Exhaust system (Leaks, damage, loose parts and foreign material)	Inspect	✓	✓	✓	✓	✓	✓	✓	✓	✓	✓	✓	✓	✓	✓	✓
Fluid levels (all)	Top off	✓	✓	✓	✓	✓	✓	✓	✓	✓	✓	✓	✓	✓	✓	✓
Halfshaft boots	Inspect	✓	✓	✓	✓	✓	✓	✓	✓	✓	✓	✓	✓	✓	✓	✓
Horn, exterior lamps, turn signals and hazard warning light operation	Inspect	✓	✓	✓	✓	✓	✓	✓	✓	✓	✓	✓	✓	✓	✓	✓
Inspect wheels and related components for abnomal noise, wear, looseness or drag	Inspect	✓	✓	✓	✓	✓	✓	✓	✓	✓	✓	✓	✓	✓	✓	✓
Radiator, coolers, heater and air conditioning hoses	Inspect	✓	✓	✓	✓	✓	✓	✓	✓	✓	✓	✓	✓	✓	✓	✓
Shocks struts and other suspension components for leaks and damage	Inspect	✓	✓	✓	✓	✓	✓	✓	✓	✓	✓	✓	✓	✓	✓	✓
Windshield wiper spray and wiper operation	Inspect	✓	✓	✓	✓	✓	✓	✓	✓	✓	✓	✓	✓	✓	✓	✓
Windshield for cracks, chips and pitting	Inspect	✓	✓	✓	✓	✓	✓	✓	✓	✓	✓	✓	✓	✓	✓	✓

Oil change service intervals should be completed as indicated by the message center (Can be up to 1 year or 10,000 miles)

If the message center is prematurely reset or is inoperative, perform the oil change interval at 6 months or 5,000 miles from your last oil change.

25759_TAUR_C0016

SCHEDULED MAINTENANCE INTERVALS

2011 Taurus - Severe

Service Item	Service Action	MILEAGE INTERVAL AS INDICATED BY THE MESSAGE CENTER														
		1	2	3	4	5	6	7	8	9	10	11	12	13	14	15
Accessory drive belts	Inspect	✓	✓	✓	✓	✓	✓	✓	✓	✓	✓	✓	✓	✓	✓	✓
Accessory drive belts	Replace															✓
Battery performance	Inspect	✓	✓	✓	✓	✓	✓	✓	✓	✓	✓	✓	✓	✓	✓	✓
Automatic trans fluid	Replace			✓			✓			✓			✓			✓
Brake system (Pads/shoes/rotors/drums, brake lines and hoses, and parking brake system)	Inspect	✓	✓	✓	✓	✓	✓	✓	✓	✓	✓	✓	✓	✓	✓	✓
Cabin air filter	Inspect/ Service	✓	✓	✓	✓	✓	✓	✓	✓	✓	✓	✓	✓	✓	✓	✓
Climate-controlled seat filter (if equipped)	Replace			✓			✓			✓			✓			✓
Cooling system, hoses, clamps & coolant strength	Inspect	✓	✓	✓	✓	✓	✓	✓	✓	✓	✓	✓	✓	✓	✓	✓
Engine air filter	Inspect/ Service	✓	✓	✓	✓	✓	✓	✓	✓	✓	✓	✓	✓	✓	✓	✓
Engine coolant	Replace										✓					✓
Engine oil & filter	Replace	✓	✓	✓	✓	✓	✓	✓	✓	✓	✓	✓	✓	✓	✓	✓
Exhaust system (Leaks, damage, loose parts and foreign material)	Inspect	✓	✓	✓	✓	✓	✓	✓	✓	✓	✓	✓	✓	✓	✓	✓
Fluid levels (all)	Top off	✓	✓	✓	✓	✓	✓	✓	✓	✓	✓	✓	✓	✓	✓	✓
Halfshaft boots	Inspect	✓	✓	✓	✓	✓	✓	✓	✓	✓	✓	✓	✓	✓	✓	✓
Horn, exterior lamps, turn signals and hazard warning light operation	Inspect	✓	✓	✓	✓	✓	✓	✓	✓	✓	✓	✓	✓	✓	✓	✓
Inspect wheels and related components for abnomal noise, wear, looseness or drag	Inspect	✓	✓	✓	✓	✓	✓	✓	✓	✓	✓	✓	✓	✓	✓	✓
Oil and fluid leaks	Inspect	✓	✓	✓	✓	✓	✓	✓	✓	✓	✓	✓	✓	✓	✓	✓
Radiator, coolers, heater and air conditioning hoses	Inspect	✓	✓	✓	✓	✓	✓	✓	✓	✓	✓	✓	✓	✓	✓	✓
Rotate tires, inspect tread wear, measure tread depth and check pressure	Inspect/ Rotate	✓	✓	✓	✓	✓	✓	✓	✓	✓	✓	✓	✓	✓	✓	✓
Shocks struts and other suspension components for leaks and damage	Inspect	✓	✓	✓	✓	✓	✓	✓	✓	✓	✓	✓	✓	✓	✓	✓
Spark plugs	Replace						✓						✓			
Steering linkage, ball joints, suspension and tie-rod ends, lubricate if equipped with greases fittings	Inspect/L ubricate	✓	✓	✓	✓	✓	✓	✓	✓	✓	✓	✓	✓	✓	✓	✓
Windshield wiper spray and wiper operation	Inspect	✓	✓	✓	✓	✓	✓	✓	✓	✓	✓	✓	✓	✓	✓	✓
Windshield for cracks, chips and pitting	Inspect	✓	✓	✓	✓	✓	✓	✓	✓	✓	✓	✓	✓	✓	✓	✓

Oil change service intervals should be completed as indicated by the message center (Can be up to 1 year or 10,000 miles)

If the message center is prematurely reset or is inoperative, perform the oil change interval at 6 months or 5,000 miles from your last oil change.

25759_TAUR_C0017

PRECAUTIONS

Before servicing any vehicle, please be sure to read all of the following precautions, which deal with personal safety, prevention of component damage, and important points to take into consideration when servicing a motor vehicle:

- Never open, service or drain the radiator or cooling system when the engine is hot; serious burns can occur from the steam and hot coolant.
- Observe all applicable safety precautions when working around fuel. Whenever servicing the fuel system, always work in a well-ventilated area. Do not allow fuel spray or vapors to come in contact with a spark, open flame, or excessive heat (a hot drop light, for example). Keep a dry chemical fire extinguisher near the work area. Always keep fuel in a container specifically designed for fuel storage; also, always properly seal fuel containers to avoid the possibility of fire or explosion. Refer to the additional fuel system precautions later in this section.
- Fuel injection systems often remain pressurized, even after the engine has been turned **OFF**. The fuel system pressure must be relieved before disconnecting any fuel lines. Failure to do so may result in fire and/or personal injury.
- Brake fluid often contains polyglycol ethers and polyglycols. Avoid contact with the eyes and wash your hands thoroughly after handling brake fluid. If you do get brake fluid in your eyes, flush your eyes with clean, running water for 15 minutes. If eye irritation persists, or if you have taken brake fluid internally, IMMEDIATELY seek medical assistance.
- The EPA warns that prolonged contact with used engine oil may cause a number of skin disorders, including cancer. You should make every effort to minimize your exposure to used engine oil. Protective gloves should be worn when changing oil. Wash your hands and any other exposed skin areas as soon as possible after exposure to used engine oil. Soap and water, or waterless hand cleaner should be used.
- All new vehicles are now equipped with an air bag system, often referred to as a Supplemental Restraint System (SRS) or Supplemental Inflatable Restraint (SIR) system. The system must be disabled before performing service on or around system components, steering column, instrument panel components, wiring and sensors. Failure to follow safety and disabling procedures could result in accidental air bag deployment, possible personal injury and unnecessary system repairs.
- Always wear safety goggles when working with, or around, the air bag system. When carrying a non-deployed air bag, be sure the bag and trim cover are pointed away from your body. When placing a non-deployed air bag on a work surface, always face the bag and trim cover upward, away from the surface. This will reduce the motion of the module if it is accidentally deployed. Refer to the additional air bag system precautions later in this section.
- Clean, high quality brake fluid from a sealed container is essential to the safe and proper operation of the brake system. You should always buy the correct type of brake fluid for your vehicle. If the brake fluid becomes contaminated, completely flush the system with new fluid. Never reuse any brake fluid. Any brake fluid that is removed from the system should be discarded. Also, do not allow any brake fluid to come in contact with a painted surface; it will damage the paint.
- Never operate the engine without the proper amount and type of engine oil; doing so WILL result in severe engine damage.
- Timing belt maintenance is extremely important. Many models utilize an interference-type, non-freewheeling engine. If the timing belt breaks, the valves in the cylinder head may strike the pistons, causing potentially serious (also time-consuming and expensive) engine damage. Refer to the maintenance interval charts for the recommended replacement interval for the timing belt, and to the timing belt section for belt replacement and inspection.
- Disconnecting the negative battery cable on some vehicles may interfere with the functions of the on-board computer system(s) and may require the computer to undergo a relearning process once the negative battery cable is reconnected.
- When servicing drum brakes, only disassemble and assemble one side at a time, leaving the remaining side intact for reference.
- Only an MVAC-trained, EPA-certified automotive technician should service the air conditioning system or its components.

BRAKES

ANTI-LOCK BRAKE SYSTEM (ABS)

GENERAL INFORMATION

PRECAUTIONS

- Certain components within the ABS system are not intended to be serviced or repaired individually.
- Do not use rubber hoses or other parts not specifically specified for and ABS system. When using repair kits, replace all parts included in the kit. Partial or incorrect repair may lead to functional problems and require the replacement of components.
- Lubricate rubber parts with clean, fresh brake fluid to ease assembly. Do not use shop air to clean parts; damage to rubber components may result.
- Use only DOT 3 brake fluid from an unopened container.
- If any hydraulic component or line is removed or replaced, it may be necessary to bleed the entire system.
- A clean repair area is essential. Always clean the reservoir and cap thoroughly before removing the cap. The slightest amount of dirt in the fluid may plug an orifice and impair the system function. Perform repairs after components have been thoroughly cleaned; use only denatured alcohol to clean components. Do not allow ABS components to come into contact with any substance containing mineral oil; this includes used shop rags.
- The Anti-Lock control unit is a microprocessor similar to other computer units in the vehicle. Ensure that the ignition switch is **OFF** before removing or installing controller harnesses. Avoid static electricity discharge at or near the controller.
- If any arc welding is to be done on the vehicle, the control unit should be unplugged before welding operations begin.

SPEED SENSORS

REMOVAL & INSTALLATION

Front

See Figure 1.

1. Remove the wheel and tire.
2. Disconnect the wheel speed sensor electrical connector.
3. Remove the 2 scrivets and position aside the fender splash shield.
4. Remove the wheel speed sensor harness pin-type retainer.
5. Remove the 2 wheel speed sensor harness retainers.

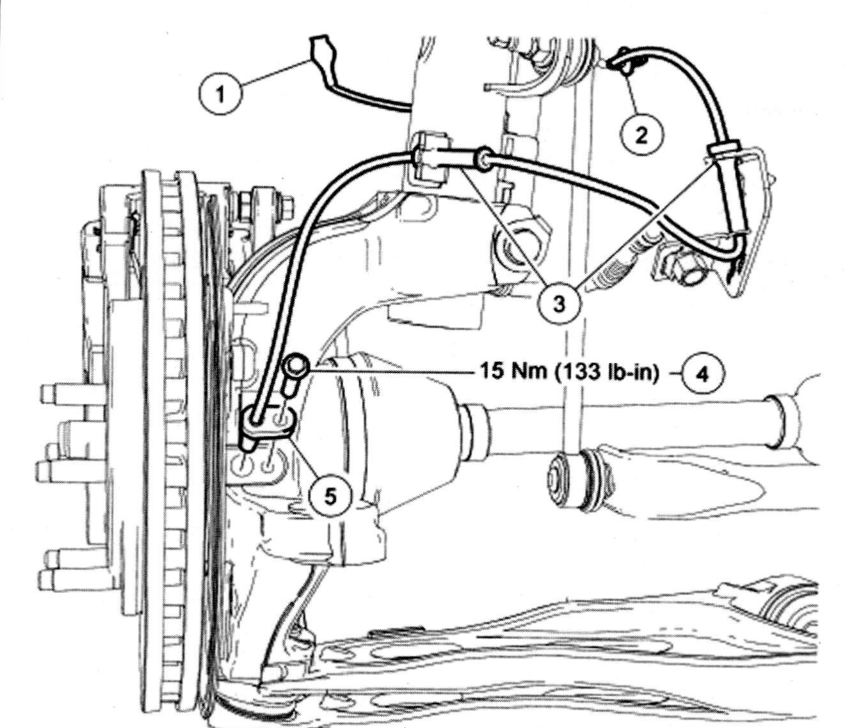

Fig. 1 Exploded view of the front wheel speed sensor

6. Remove the bolt and the wheel speed sensor.

To install:

7. Install the wheel speed sensor, and install the bolt. Tighten the bolt to 133 inch lbs. (15 Nm)
8. Install the 2 wheel speed sensor harness retainers.
9. Install the wheel speed sensor harness pin-type retainer.
10. Install the 2 scrivets and reposition the fender splash shield.
11. Connect the wheel speed sensor electrical connector.
12. Install the wheel and tire.

Rear

See Figure 2.

➡Make sure to correctly route and secure the wheel speed sensor harness in the rear subframe assembly or damage to the harness may occur.

1. With the vehicle in NEUTRAL, position it on a hoist.
2. Disconnect the wheel speed sensor electrical connector.
3. Detach the 2 wheel speed sensor pin-type retainers.
4. Detach the 2 wheel speed sensor harness retainers.

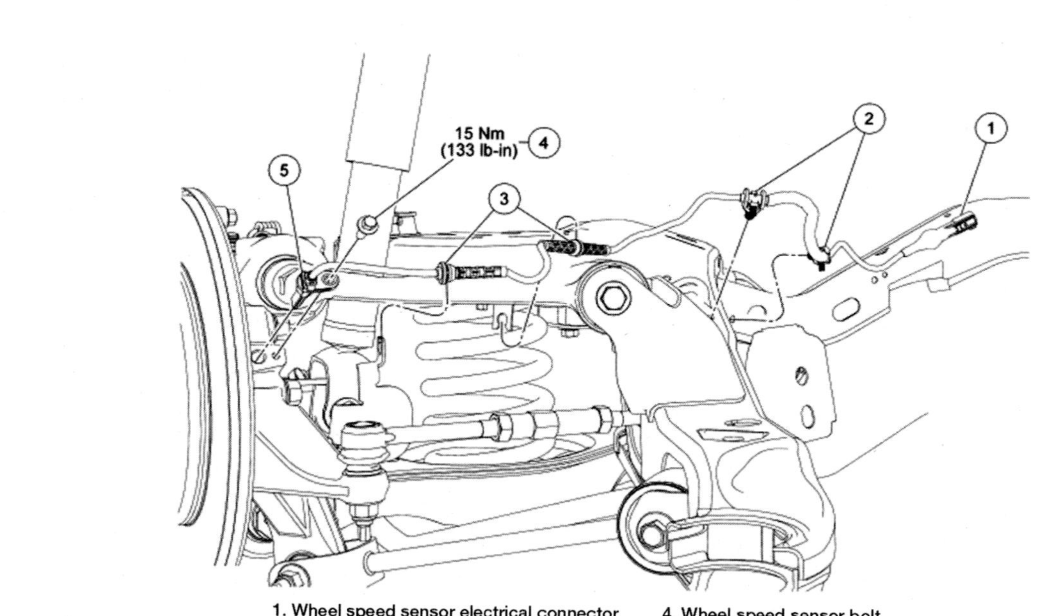

Fig. 2 Exploded view if the rear wheel speed sensor

5. Remove the wheel speed sensor bolt.

6. Remove the wheel speed sensor.

To install:

➡Make sure to correctly route and secure the wheel speed sensor harness in the rear subframe assembly or damage to the harness may occur.

7. Install the wheel speed sensor.

8. Install the wheel speed sensor bolt. Tighten the bolt to 133 inch lbs. (15 Nm).

9. Attach the 2 wheel speed sensor harness retainers.

10. Attach the 2 wheel speed sensor pin-type retainers.

11. Connect the wheel speed sensor electrical connector.

12. With the vehicle in NEUTRAL, lower the vehicle from hoist.

BRAKES — BLEEDING THE BRAKE SYSTEM

BLEEDING PROCEDURE

BLEEDING PROCEDURE

Pressure Bleeding Procedure

See Figure 3.

➡Use Special Tool (ST2834-A) Vehicle Communication Module (VCM) and Integrated Diagnostic System (IDS) software with appropriate hardware, or equivalent scan tool Material.

⁂ CAUTION

Do not use any fluid other than clean brake fluid meeting manufacturer's specification. Additionally, do not use brake fluid that has been previously drained. Following these instructions will help prevent system contamination, brake component damage and the risk of serious personal injury.

⁂ CAUTION

Carefully read cautionary information on product label. For additional information, consult the product Material Safety Data Sheet (MSDS) if available. Failure to follow these instructions may result in serious personal injury.

⁂ CAUTION

Do not allow the brake master cylinder to run dry during the bleeding operation. Master cylinder may be damaged if operated without fluid, resulting in degraded braking performance. Failure to follow this instruction may result in serious personal injury.

➡Do not spill brake fluid on painted or plastic surfaces or damage to the surface may occur. If brake fluid is spilled onto a painted or plastic surface, immediately wash the surface with water.

➡Pressure bleeding the brake system is preferred to manual bleeding.

➡The Hydraulic Control Unit (HCU) bleeding procedure must be carried out if the HCU or any components upstream of the HCU are installed new.

1. Clean all the dirt from around the brake fluid reservoir cap and remove the cap. Fill the brake master cylinder reservoir with clean, specified brake fluid.

➡Master cylinder pressure bleeder adapter tools are available from various manufacturers of pressure bleeding equipment. Follow the instructions of the manufacturer when installing the adapter.

2. Install the bleeder adapter to the brake master cylinder reservoir and attach the bleeder tank hose to the fitting on the adapter.

➡Make sure the bleeder tank contains enough specified brake fluid to complete the bleeding operation.

3. Open the valve on the bleeder tank. Apply 30-50 psi to the brake system.

4. Remove the RH rear bleeder cap and place a box-end wrench on the bleeder screw. Attach a rubber drain tube to the RH rear bleeder screw and submerge the free end of the tube in a container partially filled with clean, specified brake fluid.

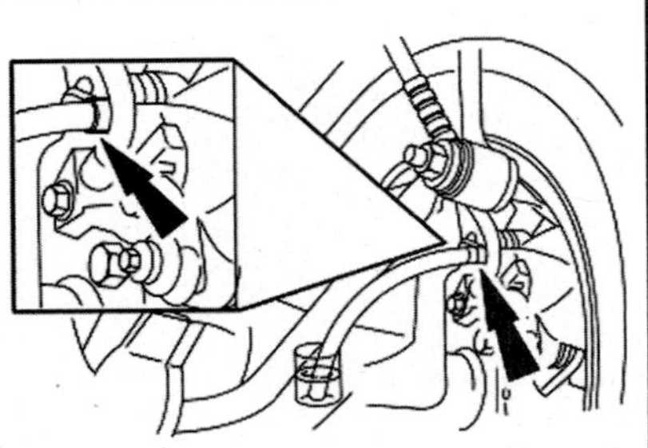

Fig. 3 Right-hand rear bleeder cap and screw location

➡Due to the complexity of the fluid path within the rear integral parking brake calipers, it is necessary to press and release the parking brake during the bleed procedure.

5. Loosen the RH rear bleeder screw. Leave open until clear, bubble-free brake fluid flows, then tighten the RH rear bleeder screw.
   - Press and release the parking brake 5 times.
   - Repeat until clear, bubble-free fluid comes out.

6. Tighten the RH rear bleeder screw. Tighten the rear bleeder screw to 89 inch lbs. (10 Nm).
   - Remove the rubber hose and install the bleeder screw cap.

7. Repeat Steps 5 and 6 for the LH rear brake caliper.

8. Continue bleeding the front of the system, going in order from the RH front brake caliper and then to the LH front brake caliper.
   - Tighten the front brake caliper bleeder screws. Tighten the front bleeder screw to 97 inch lbs. (11 Nm).

9. Close the bleeder tank valve and release the pressure. Remove the tank hose from the adapter and remove the adapter. Fill the reservoir with clean, specified brake fluid and install the reservoir cap.

Manual Bleeding Procedure

See Figure 3.

⁂ CAUTION

Do not use any fluid other than clean brake fluid meeting manufacturer's specification. Additionally, do not use brake fluid that has been previously drained. Following these instructions will help prevent system contamination, brake component damage and the risk of serious personal injury.

✻✻ CAUTION

Carefully read cautionary information on product label. For additional information, consult the product Material Safety Data Sheet (MSDS) if available. Failure to follow these instructions may result in serious personal injury.

✻✻ CAUTION

Do not allow the brake master cylinder to run dry during the bleeding operation. Master cylinder may be damaged if operated without fluid, resulting in degraded braking performance. Failure to follow this instruction may result in serious personal injury.

➡Do not spill brake fluid on painted or plastic surfaces or damage to the surface may occur. If brake fluid is spilled onto a painted or plastic surface, immediately wash the surface with water.

➡Pressure bleeding the brake system is preferred to manual bleeding.

➡The HCU bleeding procedure must be carried out if the HCU or any components upstream of the HCU are installed new.

1. Clean all the dirt from around the brake fluid reservoir cap and remove the cap. Fill the brake master cylinder reservoir with clean, specified brake fluid.
2. Remove the RH rear bleeder cap and place a box-end wrench on the bleeder screw. Attach a rubber drain tube to the RH rear bleeder screw and submerge the free end of the tube in a container partially filled with clean, specified brake fluid.
3. Have an assistant hold firm pressure on the brake pedal.

➡Due to the complexity of the fluid path within the rear integral parking brake calipers, it is necessary to press and release the parking brake during the bleed procedure.

4. Loosen the RH rear bleeder screw until a stream of brake fluid comes out. While the assistant maintains pressure on the brake pedal, tighten the RH rear bleeder screw.
   - Press and release the parking brake 5 times.
   - Repeat until clear, bubble-free fluid comes out.
   - Refill the brake master cylinder reservoir as necessary.
5. Tighten the RH rear bleeder screw to specification. Tighten the rear bleeder screw to 89 inch lbs. (10 Nm).
   - Remove the rubber hose and install the bleeder screw cap.
6. Repeat Steps 2 through 5 for the LH rear brake caliper.
7. Remove the RH front bleeder cap and place a box-end wrench on the bleeder screw. Attach a rubber drain tube to the RH front bleeder screw and submerge the free end of the tube in a container partially filled with clean, specified brake fluid.
8. Have an assistant hold firm pressure on the brake pedal.
9. Loosen the RH front bleeder screw until a stream of brake fluid comes out. While the assistant maintains pressure on the brake pedal, tighten the RH front bleeder screw. Tighten the front bleeder screw to 97 inch lbs. (11 Nm).
   - Repeat until clear, bubble-free fluid comes out.
   - Refill the brake master cylinder reservoir as necessary.
10. Tighten the RH front bleeder screw. Tighten the front bleeder screw to 97 inch lbs. (11 Nm).
    - Remove the rubber hose and install the bleeder screw cap.
11. Repeat Steps 7 through 10 for the LH front brake caliper bleeder screw.

Hydraulic Control Unit (HCU) Bleeding

➡Pressure bleeding the brake system is preferred to manual bleeding.

1. Follow the pressure bleeding or manual bleeding procedure steps to bleed the system.
2. Connect the scan tool and follow the ABS Service Bleed instructions.
3. Repeat the pressure bleeding or manual bleeding procedure steps to bleed the system.

MASTER CYLINDER BLEEDING

See Figure 4.

✻✻ CAUTION

Do not use any fluid other than clean brake fluid meeting manufacturer's specification. Additionally, do not use brake fluid that has been previously drained. Following these instructions will help prevent system contamination, brake component damage and the risk of serious personal injury.

✻✻ CAUTION

Carefully read cautionary information on product label. For EMERGENCY MEDICAL INFORMATION seek medical advice. Failure to follow these instructions may result in serious personal injury.

✻✻ CAUTION

Do not allow the brake master cylinder to run dry during the bleeding operation. Master cylinder may be damaged if operated without fluid, resulting in degraded braking performance. Failure to follow this instruction may result in serious personal injury.

➡Do not spill brake fluid on painted or plastic surfaces or damage to the surface may occur. If brake fluid is spilled onto a painted or plastic surface, immediately wash the surface with water.

➡When a new brake master cylinder has been installed or the system has been emptied, or partially emptied, it should be primed to prevent air from entering the system.

1. Disconnect the brake tubes from the master cylinder.
2. Install short brake tubes onto the primary and secondary ports with the ends submerged in the brake master cylinder reservoir.
3. Fill the brake master cylinder reservoir with clean, specified brake fluid.
4. Have an assistant pump the brake pedal until clear fluid flows from the brake tubes without air bubbles.
5. Remove the short brake tubes, and install the master cylinder brake tubes.
6. Bleed the brake system.

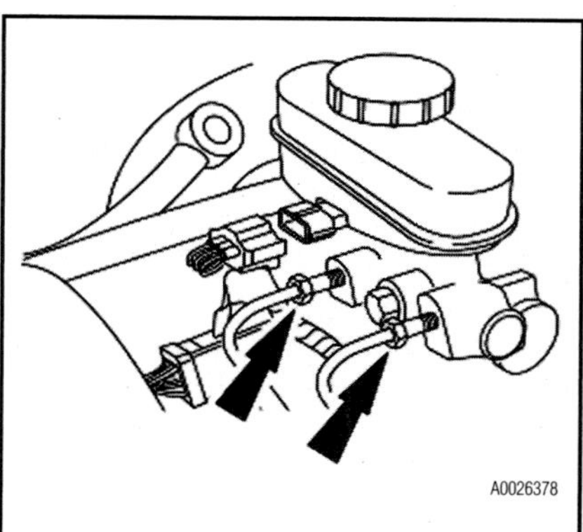

Fig. 4 Master cylinder and brake tubes

BRAKE CALIPER BLEEDING

See Figure 5.

**** CAUTION**

Do not use any fluid other than clean brake fluid meeting manufacturer's specification. Additionally, do not use brake fluid that has been previously drained. Following these instructions will help prevent system contamination, brake component damage and the risk of serious personal injury.

**** CAUTION**

Carefully read cautionary information on product label. For EMERGENCY MEDICAL INFORMATION seek medical advice. Failure to follow these instructions may result in serious personal injury.

**** CAUTION**

Do not allow the brake master cylinder to run dry during the bleeding operation. Master cylinder may be damaged if operated without fluid, resulting in degraded braking performance. Failure to follow this instruction may result in serious personal injury.

➡Do not spill brake fluid on painted or plastic surfaces or damage to the surface may occur. If brake fluid is spilled onto a painted or plastic surface, immediately wash the surface with water.

➡It is not necessary to do a complete brake system bleed if only the disc brake caliper was disconnected.

1. Remove the brake caliper bleeder screw cap and place a box-end wrench on the bleeder screw. Attach a rubber drain hose to the bleeder screw and submerge the free end of the hose in a container partially filled with clean, specified brake fluid.
2. Have an assistant pump the brake pedal and then hold firm pressure on the brake pedal.

➡Due to the complexity of the fluid path within the rear integral parking brake calipers, it is necessary to press and release the parking brake during the bleed procedure.

3. Loosen the bleeder screw until a stream of brake fluid comes out. While the assistant maintains pressure on the brake pedal, tighten the bleeder screw.
   - If bleeding a rear brake caliper, press and release the parking brake 5 times.
   - Repeat until clear, bubble-free fluid comes out.
   - Refill the brake master cylinder reservoir as necessary.

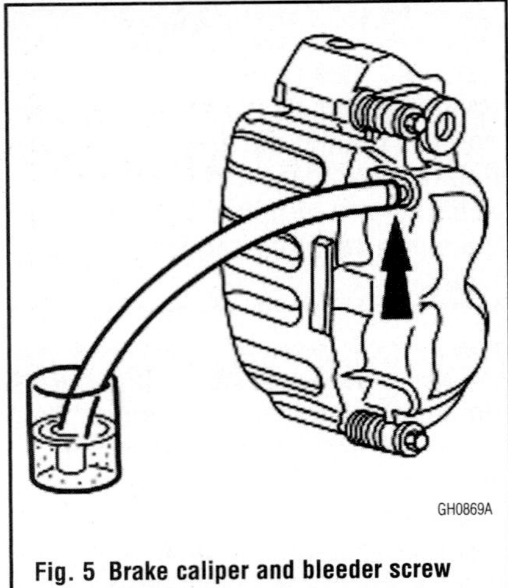

Fig. 5 Brake caliper and bleeder screw

4. Tighten the brake caliper bleeder screw, remove the rubber hose and install the bleeder screw cap.
   - Tighten the front brake caliper bleeder screws to specification. Tighten the front bleeder screw to 97 inch lbs. (11 Nm).
   - Tighten the rear brake caliper bleeder screws to specification. Tighten the rear bleeder screw to 89 inch lbs. (10 Nm).

BLEEDING THE ABS SYSTEM

For the Hydraulic Control Unit (HCU) Bleeding, it is preferred to use Pressure bleeding over the manual bleeding as outlined in this section.

BRAKES — FRONT DISC BRAKES

**** WARNING**

Dust and dirt accumulating on brake parts during normal use may contain asbestos fibers from production or aftermarket brake linings. Breathing excessive concentrations of asbestos fibers can cause serious bodily harm. Exercise care when servicing brake parts. Do not sand or grind brake lining unless equipment used is designed to contain the dust residue. Do not clean brake parts with compressed air or by dry brushing. Cleaning should be done by dampening the brake components with a fine mist of water, then wiping the brake components clean with a dampened cloth. Dispose of cloth and all residue containing asbestos fibers in an impermeable container with the appropriate label. Follow practices prescribed by the Occupational Safety and Health Administration (OSHA) and the Environmental Protection Agency (EPA) for the handling, processing, and disposing of dust or debris that may contain asbestos fibers.

BRAKE CALIPER

REMOVAL & INSTALLATION

**** CAUTION**

Do not use any fluid other than clean brake fluid meeting manufacturer's specification. Additionally, do not use brake fluid that has been previously drained. Following these instructions will help prevent system contamination, brake component damage and the risk of serious personal injury.

**** CAUTION**

Carefully read cautionary information on product label. For EMERGENCY MEDICAL INFORMATION seek medical advice. For additional information, consult the product Material Safety Data Sheet (MSDS) if available. Failure to follow these instructions may result in serious personal injury.

➡Do not spill brake fluid on painted or plastic surfaces or damage to the surface may occur. If brake fluid is spilled onto a painted or plastic surface, immediately wash the surface with water.

1. Remove the brake pads as outlined in this section.
2. Remove the brake caliper flow bolt and position the brake hose aside.
   - Discard the copper washers.
3. Remove the brake caliper.

To install:

4. Position the brake hose and install the brake caliper flow bolt.
   - Install new copper washers.
   - Tighten the bolt to 35 ft. lbs. (47 Nm).
5. Install the brake pads as outlined in this section.
6. Bleed the brake caliper as outlined in this section.

DISC BRAKE

REMOVAL & INSTALLATION

1. Remove the wheel and tire.

➡Do not allow the brake caliper to hang from the brake flexible hose or damage to the hose may occur.

2. Remove and discard the 2 anchor plate bolts and position the brake caliper and anchor plate assembly aside.
   - Support the brake caliper and anchor plate assembly using mechanic's wire.
3. Remove and discard the brake disc screw.
4. Thread a M10 bolt into the brake disc removal hole and tighten to press the disc off the hub.

To install:

5. Using specified brake parts cleaner, clean any residual sealant from the wheel knuckle and the brake caliper anchor plate.
6. Use specified brake parts cleaner to clean the brake disc and hub mating surfaces.
7. Apply a thin coat of anti-seize lubricant to the hub flange.
8. Install the brake disc.
9. Install a new brake disc screw. Tighten the screws to 177 inch lbs. (20 Nm).
10. Position the brake caliper and brake caliper anchor plate assembly and install 2 new bolts. Tighten the bolts to 111 ft. lbs. (150 Nm).
11. Install the wheel and tire.

DISC BRAKE PADS

REMOVAL & INSTALLATION

✲✲ CAUTION

Do not use any fluid other than clean brake fluid meeting manufacturer's specification. Additionally, do not use brake fluid that has been previously drained. Following these instructions will help prevent system contamination, brake component damage and the risk of serious personal injury.

✲✲ CAUTION

Carefully read cautionary information on product label. For EMERGENCY MEDICAL INFORMATION seek medical advice. For additional information, consult the product Material Safety Data Sheet (MSDS) if available. Failure to follow these instructions may result in serious personal injury.

✲✲ CAUTION

Always install new brake shoes or pads at both ends of an axle to reduce the possibility of brakes pulling vehicle to one side. Failure to follow this instruction may result in uneven braking and serious personal injury.

➡Do not spill brake fluid on painted or plastic surfaces or damage to the surface may occur. If brake fluid is spilled onto a painted or plastic surface, immediately wash the surface with water.

1. Check the brake fluid level in the brake master cylinder reservoir.
   - If required, remove the fluid until the brake master cylinder reservoir is half full.
2. Remove the wheel and tire.
3. Using a C-clamp, compress the pistons into the caliper housing.

➡Do not allow the brake caliper to hang from the brake hose or damage to the hose may occur.

4. Remove the 2 brake caliper guide pin bolts and position the caliper aside.
   - Support the caliper using mechanic's wire.
5. Remove the 2 brake pads and spring clips from the brake caliper anchor plate.
   - Discard the spring clips.

To install:

➡Do not allow grease, oil, brake fluid or other contaminants to contact the pad lining material, or damage to components may occur. Do not install contaminated pads.

➡If installing new brake pads, make sure to install all new hardware and lubricant supplied with the brake pad kit. Refer to the brake pad instruction sheet when applying lubricant.

6. Install the new spring clips and brake pads to the brake caliper anchor plate.
   - Apply equal amounts of specified lubricant to the brake caliper-to-brake pad contact points.

➡Make sure the caliper pin boots are correctly seated to prevent corrosion to the guide pins.

➡Make sure that the brake hose is not twisted when the caliper is positioned on the anchor plate to prevent abrasive damage.

7. Position the brake caliper onto the brake caliper anchor plate and install the 2 brake caliper guide pin bolts. Tighten the bolts to 53 ft. lbs. (72 Nm).
8. Install the wheel and tire.
9. If necessary, fill the brake master cylinder reservoir with clean, specified brake fluid.
10. Apply brakes several times to verify correct brake operation.

DISC BRAKE SHIELD

REMOVAL & INSTALLATION

1. Remove the brake disc as outlined in this section.
2. Remove the 3 bolts and the brake disc shield.

To install:

3. Install the 3 bolts and the brake disc shield. Tighten the bolts to 133 inch lbs. (15 Nm).
4. Install the brake disc as outlined in this section.

WARNING

Dust and dirt accumulating on brake parts during normal use may contain asbestos fibers from production or aftermarket brake linings. Breathing excessive concentrations of asbestos fibers can cause serious bodily harm. Exercise care when servicing brake parts. Do not sand or grind brake lining unless equipment used is designed to contain the dust residue. Do not clean brake parts with compressed air or by dry brushing. Cleaning should be done by dampening the brake components with a fine mist of water, then wiping the brake components clean with a dampened cloth. Dispose of cloth and all residue containing asbestos fibers in an impermeable container with the appropriate label. Follow practices prescribed by the Occupational Safety and Health Administration (OSHA) and the Environmental Protection Agency (EPA) for the handling, processing, and disposing of dust or debris that may contain asbestos fibers.

BRAKE CALIPER

REMOVAL & INSTALLATION

See Figure 6.

CAUTION

Do not use any fluid other than clean brake fluid meeting manufacturer's specification. Additionally, do not use brake fluid that has been previously drained. Following these instructions will help prevent system contamination, brake component damage and the risk of serious personal injury.

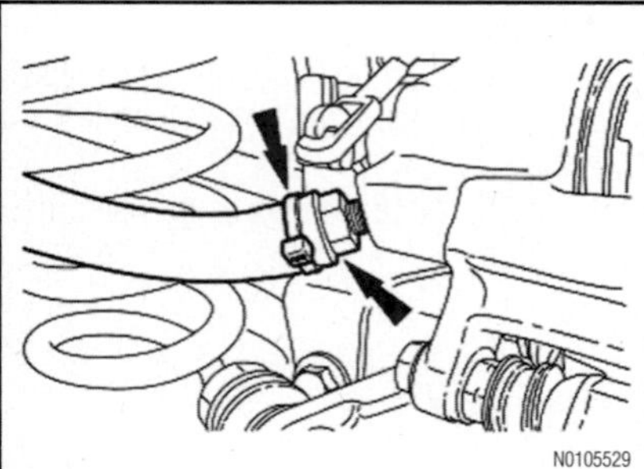

Fig. 6 Flexible hose protective sleeve and tie strap location

CAUTION

Carefully read cautionary information on product label. For EMERGENCY MEDICAL INFORMATION seek medical advice. For additional information, consult the product Material Safety Data Sheet (MSDS) if available. Failure to follow these instructions may result in serious personal injury.

➡Do not spill brake fluid on painted or plastic surfaces or damage to the surface may occur. If brake fluid is spilled onto a painted or plastic surface, immediately wash the surface with water.

All Calipers

1. Release the parking brake cable tension as outlined in this section.
   - Disconnect the parking brake cable from the subframe bracket and the caliper.
   - Position the parking brake cable aside.

Left-Hand Calipers With Flow Bolt Brake Hose Attachment

2. Remove the brake caliper flow bolt and the brake caliper.
   - Discard the 2 copper washers.

Calipers with Threaded Fitting Brake Hose Attachment

3. Remove the brake flexible hose as outlined in this section.

All Calipers

CAUTION

Always install new brake shoes or pads at both ends of an axle to reduce the possibility of brakes pulling vehicle to one side. Failure to follow this instruction may result in uneven braking and serious personal injury.

➡When the brake pads are separated from the brake caliper, new brake pads must be installed to prevent brake noise and shudder. The brake pads are one-time-use only.

4. Remove and discard the brake pads as outlined in this section.

To install:

➡During installation, make sure that the brake flexible hose does not become twisted or damage to hose may occur.

➡If equipped, verify correct installation of the brake flexible hose protective sleeve and tie strap.

All Calipers

CAUTION

Always install new brake shoes or pads at both ends of an axle to reduce the possibility of brakes pulling vehicle to one side. Failure to follow this instruction may result in uneven braking and serious personal injury.

➡When the brake pads are separated from the brake caliper, new brake pads must be installed to prevent brake noise and shudder. The brake pads are one-time-use only.

5. Install the brake pads as outlined in this section.

Calipers With Threaded Fitting Brake Hose Attachment

6. Install the brake flexible hose as outlined in this section.

Left-Hand Calipers With Flow Bolt Brake Hose Attachment

7. Install the brake caliper flow bolt and the brake caliper.
   - Install 2 New copper washers. Tighten the bolts to 22 ft. lbs. (30 Nm).

All Calipers

8. Engage the parking brake cable tension as outlined in this section.
   - Connect the parking brake cable from the subframe bracket and the caliper.
   - Reposition the parking brake cable.
9. Bleed the caliper as outlined in this section.

DISC BRAKE

REMOVAL & INSTALLATION

1. Remove the wheel and tire.

➡Do not allow the caliper to hang from the brake hose or damage to the hose can occur.

2. Remove and discard the 2 brake caliper anchor plate bolts and position the brake caliper and anchor plate assembly aside.
   - Support the brake caliper and anchor plate assembly using mechanic's wire.
3. Remove and discard the brake disc screw.

4. Thread a M10 bolt into the brake disc removal hole and tighten to press the disc off the hub.

To install:

5. Clean any rust or foreign material from brake disc and wheel hub.
   - Use specified brake parts cleaner to clean the brake disc and hub mating surfaces.
6. Apply a thin coat of specified anti-seize lubricant to the hub flange.
7. Install the brake disc.
8. Install a new brake disc screw. Tighten the screw to 177 inch lbs. (20 Nm).
9. Position the brake caliper and brake caliper anchor plate assembly and install 2 new bolts. Tighten the bolts to 76 ft. lbs. (103 Nm).
   a. Apply brakes several times to verify correct brake operation.
10. Install the wheel and tire.

DISC BRAKE PADS

REMOVAL & INSTALLATION

See Figures 7 and 8.

***** CAUTION**

Do not use any fluid other than clean brake fluid meeting manufacturer's specification. Additionally, do not use brake fluid that has been previously drained. Following these instructions will help prevent system contamination, brake component damage and the risk of serious personal injury.

***** CAUTION**

Carefully read cautionary information on product label. For EMERGENCY MEDICAL INFORMATION seek medical advice. For additional information, consult the product Material Safety Data Sheet (MSDS) if available. Failure to follow these instructions may result in serious personal injury.

***** CAUTION**

Always install new brake shoes or pads at both ends of an axle to reduce the possibility of brakes pulling vehicle to one side. Failure to follow this instruction may result in uneven braking and serious personal injury.

➡Do not spill brake fluid on painted or plastic surfaces or damage to the surface may occur. If brake fluid is spilled onto a painted or plastic surface, immediately wash the surface with water.

1. Check the brake fluid level in the brake fluid reservoir.
   - If required, remove fluid until the brake master cylinder reservoir is half full.
2. Remove the wheel and tire.
3. Remove the brake caliper bolts.

➡Do not allow the caliper to hang from the brake hose or damage to the hose may occur.

➡Care must be taken when servicing rear brake components without disconnecting the parking brake cable from the brake caliper lever. Carefully position the caliper aside using a suitable support or damage to the parking brake cable end fittings may occur.

4. Using hand force and a rocking motion, separate the brake caliper from the anchor plate. Position the brake caliper aside.
   - Support the caliper with mechanic's wire.

➡When the brake pads are separated from the brake caliper, new brake pads must be installed to prevent brake noise and shudder. The brake pads are one-time use only.

5. Remove and discard the 2 brake pads and spring clips from the brake caliper anchor plate.

➡Do not remove the anchor plate guide pins. The guide pins are press fit to the brake caliper anchor plate. If the guide pins are damaged, a new anchor plate must be installed.

6. Inspect the brake caliper anchor plate assembly.
   - Check the guide pins and boots for binding or damage.
   - Install a new brake caliper anchor plate if it is worn or damaged.

To install:

➡A moderate to heavy force toward the caliper piston must be applied. If sufficient force is not applied, the internal park brake mechanism clutch cone will not engage and the piston will not compress.

7. Using the Rear Caliper Piston Adjuster (or equivalent such as OTC tool 7317A), rotate the caliper piston clockwise to compress the piston into its cylinder.

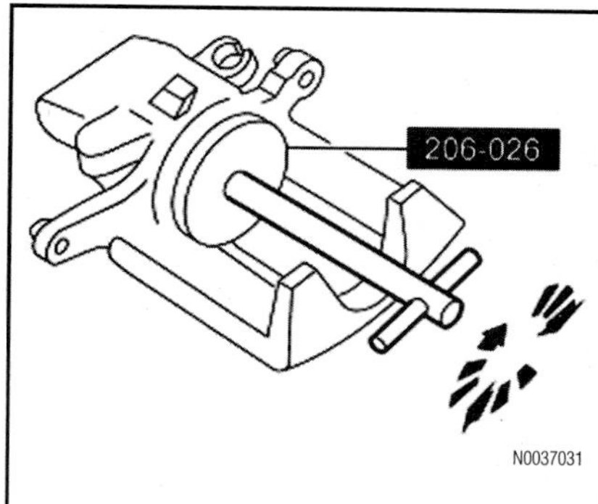

Fig. 7 Using a rear caliper piston adjuster, rotate the caliper piston clockwise to compress the piston into its cylinder.

8. Clean the residual adhesive from the brake caliper fingers and piston using specified brake parts cleaner.
9. Position the notch in the caliper piston so that it will correctly align with the pin on the backside of the inboard brake pad.

➡Do not allow grease, oil, brake fluid or other contaminants to contact the pad lining material, or damage to components may occur. Do not install contaminated pads.

10. Install the new spring clips and brake pads to the brake caliper anchor plate.

➡During installation, make sure brake flexible hose does not become twisted. A twisted brake hose may make contact with other components causing damage to the hose.

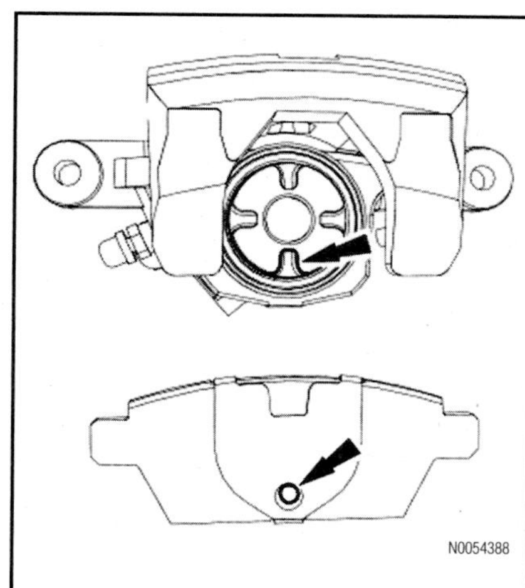

Fig. 8 Position the notch in the caliper piston so that it will correctly align with the pin on the backside of the inboard brake pad.

11. Position the brake caliper and install the 2 bolts. Tighten the bolts to 24 ft. lbs. (33 Nm).

12. If necessary, fill the brake fluid reservoir with clean, specified brake fluid.

- Apply brakes several times to verify correct brake operation.

13. Install the wheel and tire.

DISC BRAKE SHIELD

REMOVAL & INSTALLATION

1. Remove the wheel hub and bearing.

2. Remove the 3 bolts and the brake disc shield.

To install:

3. Install the brake disc shield and the 3 bolts. Tighten the bolts to 133 inch lbs. (15 Nm).

4. Install the wheel hub and bearing.

CHASSIS ELECTRICAL

AIR BAG (SUPPLEMENTAL RESTRAINT SYSTEM)

GENERAL INFORMATION

** WARNING

These vehicles are equipped with an air bag system. The system must be disarmed before performing service on, or around, system components, the steering column, instrument panel components, wiring and sensors. Failure to follow the safety precautions and the disarming procedure could result in accidental air bag deployment, possible injury and unnecessary system repairs.

SERVICE PRECAUTIONS

Disconnect and isolate the battery negative cable before beginning any airbag system component diagnosis, testing, removal, or installation procedures. Allow system capacitor to discharge for two minutes before beginning any component service. This will disable the airbag system. Failure to disable the airbag system may result in accidental airbag deployment, personal injury, or death.

Do not place an intact undeployed airbag face down on a solid surface. The airbag will propel into the air if accidentally deployed and may result in personal injury or death.

When carrying or handling an undeployed airbag, the trim side (face) of the airbag should be pointing towards the body to minimize possibility of injury if accidental deployment occurs. Failure to do this may result in personal injury or death.

Replace airbag system components with OEM replacement parts. Substitute parts may appear interchangeable, but internal differences may result in inferior occupant protection. Failure to do so may result in occupant personal injury or death.

Wear safety glasses, rubber gloves, and long sleeved clothing when cleaning powder residue from vehicle after an airbag deployment. Powder residue emitted from a deployed airbag can cause skin irritation. Flush affected area with cool water if irritation is experienced. If nasal or throat irritation is experienced, exit the vehicle for fresh air until the irritation ceases. If irritation continues, see a physician.

Do not use a replacement airbag that is not in the original packaging. This may result in improper deployment, personal injury, or death.

The factory installed fasteners, screws and bolts used to fasten airbag components have a special coating and are specifically designed for the airbag system. Do not use substitute fasteners. Use only original equipment fasteners listed in the parts catalog when fastener replacement is required.

During, and following, any child restraint anchor service, due to impact event or vehicle repair, carefully inspect all mounting hardware, tether straps, and anchors for proper installation, operation, or damage. If a child restraint anchor is found damaged in any way, the anchor must be replaced. Failure to do this may result in personal injury or death.

Deployed and non-deployed airbags may or may not have live pyrotechnic material within the airbag inflator.

Do not dispose of driver/passenger/curtain airbags or seat belt tensioners unless you are sure of complete deployment. Refer to the Hazardous Substance Control System for proper disposal.

Dispose of deployed airbags and tensioners consistent with state, provincial, local, and federal regulations.

After any airbag component testing or service, do not connect the battery negative cable. Personal injury or death may result if the system test is not performed first.

If the vehicle is equipped with the Occupant Classification System (OCS), do not connect the battery negative cable before performing the OCS Verification Test using the scan tool and the appropriate diagnostic information. Personal injury or death may result if the system test is not performed properly.

Never replace both the Occupant Restraint Controller (ORC) and the Occupant Classification Module (OCM) at the same time. If both require replacement, replace one, then perform the Airbag System test before replacing the other.

Both the ORC and the OCM store Occupant Classification System (OCS) calibration data, which they transfer to one another when one of them is replaced. If both are replaced at the same time, an irreversible fault will be set in both modules and the OCS may malfunction and cause personal injury or death.

If equipped with OCS, the Seat Weight Sensor is a sensitive, calibrated unit and must be handled carefully. Do not drop or handle roughly. If dropped or damaged, replace with another sensor. Failure to do so may result in occupant injury or death.

If equipped with OCS, the front passenger seat must be handled carefully as well. When removing the seat, be careful when setting on floor not to drop. If dropped, the sensor may be inoperative, could result in occupant injury, or possibly death.

If equipped with OCS, when the passenger front seat is on the floor, no one should sit in the front passenger seat. This uneven force may damage the sensing ability of the seat weight sensors. If sat on and damaged, the sensor may be inoperative, could result in occupant injury, or possibly death.

DISARMING THE SYSTEM

1. Ensure the ignition is off.

2. Remove the Smart Junction Box (SJB) cover located below the left side of the instrument panel. Remove the Restraints Control Module (RCM) fuse 32 (10-amp).

3. Turn the ignition on and watch the air bag indicator for 30 seconds. The indicator light will remain lit constantly if the correct fuse has been removed. If the light is not on steadily, remove the correct fuse and check the light again.

4. Turn the ignition switch off.

5. Disconnect the negative battery cable and wait one minute.

ARMING THE SYSTEM

1. Turn the ignition switch on.
2. Install Restraints Control Module (RCM) fuse 32 (10-amp) and the fuse cover.
3. Turn the ignition off.
4. Connect the negative battery cable.
5. Turn the ignition on and then off. Wait 10 seconds and turn the key back on. Watch the air bag indicator. The indicator light will remain lit constantly for 6 seconds and then go off. If the indicator does not turn on and then off, diagnose the air bag system
6. Clear all Diagnostic Trouble Codes (DTC) using a diagnostic tool.

DRIVE TRAIN

AUTOMATIC TRANSAXLE FLUID

DRAIN AND REFILL

See Figure 9.

All Vehicles

1. With the vehicle in NEUTRAL, position it on a hoist.

➡If an internal problem is suspected, drain the transmission fluid through a paper filter. A small amount of metal or friction particles may be found from normal wear. If an excessive amount of metal or friction material is present, the transaxle will need to be overhauled.

2. Remove the transmission fluid drain plug and allow the transmission fluid to drain. Install the transmission fluid drain plug. Tighten the drain plug to 80 inch lbs. (9 Nm).

Vehicles Without 3.5L Turbo

3. Remove the transmission fluid level indicator. If the transaxle was removed and disassembled, fill the transaxle with 6.5 qt. of clean transmission fluid. If the main control cover was removed for in-vehicle repair, fill the transaxle with 4.5 qt. of clean transmission fluid.

Vehicles With 3.5L Turbo

4. Clean the area around the clamp that connects the Air Cleaner (ACL) to the ACL outlet pipe.
5. If equipped, remove the bolt cover.

➡Do not disconnect the Intake Air Temperature (IAT) sensor electrical connector.

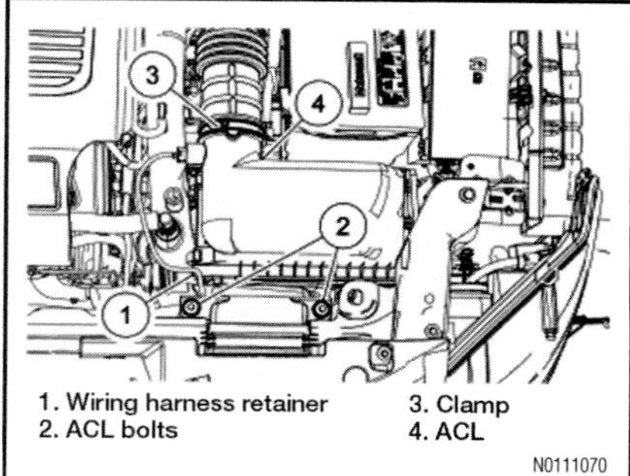

Fig. 9 Removal of the ACL bracket and the ACL outlet hose

6. Remove the ACL from the ACL bracket and the ACL outlet hose.
   a. Remove the wiring harness retainer from the ACL by pulling It up.
   b. Remove the 2 ACL bolts.
   c. Loosen the clamp.
   d. Pull up on the ACL to remove it from the 2 rubber grommets and position it aside with the IAT sensor electrical connector still connected.
7. With the IAT sensor connected, rotate the ACL 90 degrees to access the transmission fluid level indicator. Install the ACL in the outlet pipe and tighten the clamp. Tighten the clamp to 44 inch lbs. (5 Nm).
8. Remove the transmission fluid level indicator. If the transaxle was removed and disassembled, fill the transaxle with 6.2L (6.5 qt) of clean transmission fluid. If the main control cover was removed for in-vehicle repair, fill the transaxle with 4.3L (4.5 qt) of clean transmission fluid.

All Vehicles

9. Start the engine and let it run for 3 minutes. Move the range selector lever into each gear position and allow engagement for a minimum of ten seconds. Check the transmission fluid level by installing and removing the transmission fluid level indicator. When installing the transmission fluid level indicator, be sure it is seated and rotate it clockwise to the locked position. Adjust the transmission fluid level.
   a. Correct transmission fluid level at normal operating temperature 180°F-200°F (82°C-93°C).
   b. Low transmission fluid level.
   c. High transmission fluid level.

Vehicles With 3.5L Turbo

10. Turn the engine off, loosen the clamp and remove the ACL assembly from the ACL outlet pipe and position it aside with the IAT sensor electrical connector connected.
11. Install the ACL.
   a. Position the ACL assembly in the ACL outlet pipe and push down to install it in the 2 rubber grommets. Tighten the clamp to 44 inch lbs. (5 Nm).
   b. Install the 2 ACL bolts. Tighten the bolts to 44 inch lbs. (5 Nm).
   c. Install the wiring harness retainer on the ACL.
12. If equipped, install the bolt cover.

TRANSFER CASE ASSEMBLY

REMOVAL & INSTALLATION

3.5L Engine, Except Turbo

See Figures 10 and 11.

1. With the vehicle in NEUTRAL, position it on a hoist.
2. Remove the RH halfshaft as outlined in this section.
3. Remove the RH catalytic converter as outlined in the Engine Mechanical Section.

➡To maintain the initial driveshaft balance, index-mark the driveshaft flange and the output flange.

4. Remove the 4 driveshaft-to-output flange bolts, then disconnect the driveshaft from the output flange. Position the driveshaft aside.
5. Remove the 5 Power Transfer Unit (PTU) support bracket bolts and the support bracket.
6. Position the engine roll restrictor aside.
   a. Remove the 2 engine roll restrictor-to-transaxle bolts.
   b. Loosen the rear engine roll restrictor bolt and pivot the roll restrictor downward.

➡Position a drain pan under the vehicle.

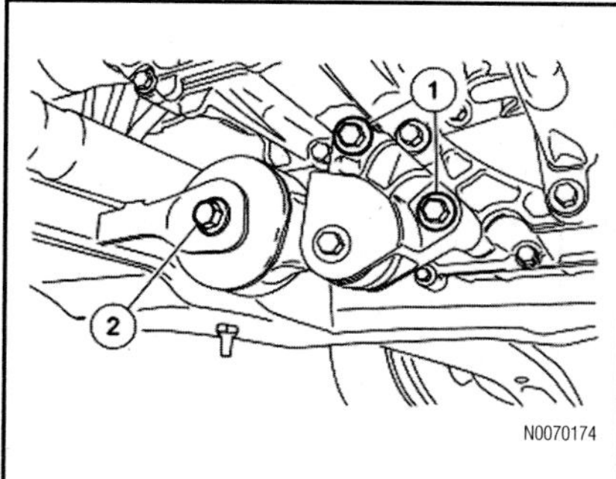

Fig. 10 Engine roll restrictor-to-transaxle bolts

7. Remove the 5 PTU bolts. Pull the PTU outward and separate it from the transaxle. Rotate the output flange upward, then turn it and remove the PTU from the vehicle.

8. Using a small screwdriver remove and discard the compression seal.

To install:

➡A new compression seal must be installed whenever the Power Transfer Unit (PTU) is removed from the vehicle.

9. Using a suitable tool, install the new compression seal.

10. Position the PTU and install the 5 PTU bolts. Tighten the bolts to 66 ft. lbs. (90 Nm).

11. Position the PTU support bracket and install the 3 PTU support bracket-to-engine bolts. Tighten the bolts to 35 ft. lbs. (48 Nm).

12. Install the 2 PTU support bracket-to-transaxle bolts. Tighten the bolts to 35 ft. lbs. (48 Nm).

13. Position the engine roll restrictor to the transaxle and install the 2 bolts. Tighten the engine roll restrictor-to-transaxle bolts to 76 ft. lbs. (103 Nm), and tighten the rear engine roll restrictor bolt to 66 ft. lbs. (90 Nm).

➡Line up the index marks made during removal.

14. Install the 4 driveshaft-to-output flange bolts. Tighten the bolts to 52 ft. lbs. (70 Nm).

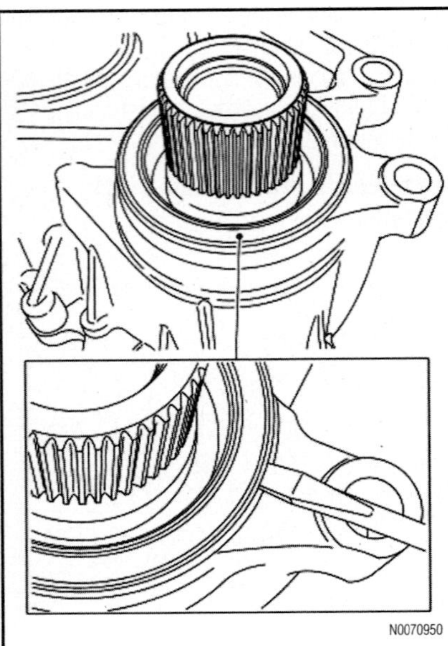

Fig. 11 Remove and discard the compression seal

15. Install the RH catalytic converter as outlined in the Engine Mechanical Section.

16. Install the RH front halfshaft as outlined in this section.

17. Inspect the transmission fluid level and add clean, specified fluid as necessary.

3.5L Turbo Engine

See Figures 12 through 15.

1. With the vehicle in NEUTRAL, position it on a hoist.

➡Use a steering wheel holding device (such as Hunter® 28-75-1 or equivalent).

2. Using a suitable holding device, hold the steering wheel in the straight-ahead position.

3. Remove the 4 retainers and the underbody shield.

4. Remove the RH halfshaft as outlined in this section.

5. Remove the RH catalytic converter as outlined in the Engine Mechanical Section.

➡To maintain the initial driveshaft balance, index-mark the driveshaft flange and the output flange.

6. Remove the 4 driveshaft-to-output flange bolts, then disconnect the driveshaft from the output flange. Position the driveshaft aside.

➡Do not allow the intermediate shaft to rotate while it is disconnected from the gear or damage to the clockspring may occur. If there is evidence that the intermediate shaft has rotated, the clockspring must be removed and recentered. Refer to the Chassis Electrical Section.

7. Remove the steering shaft bolt and disconnect the steering column shaft from the steering gear. Discard the bolt.

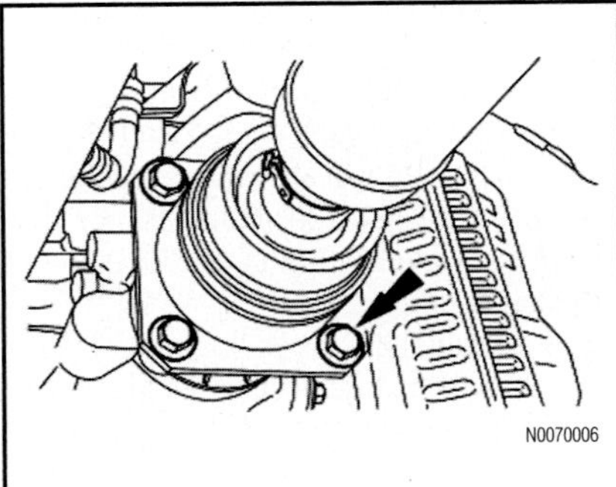

Fig. 12 Driveshaft-to-output flange bolts removal

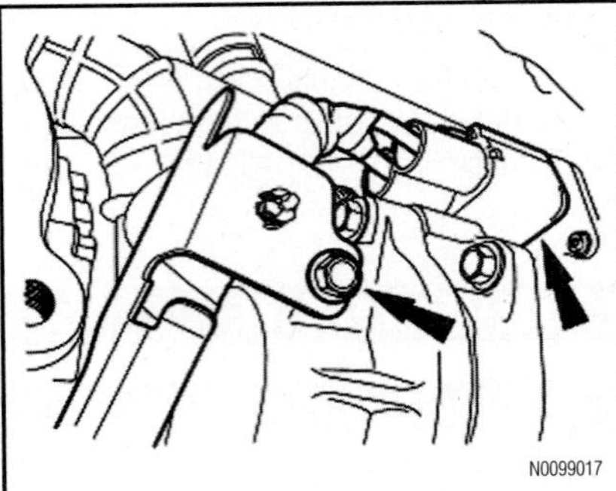

Fig. 13 Remove the bolt and disconnect the 2 Electronic Power Assist Steering (EPAS) electrical connectors and the wiring retainer

8. Remove the bolt and disconnect the 2 Electronic Power Assist Steering (EPAS) electrical connectors and the wiring retainer.

9. Remove the 3 bolts and the RH turbocharger lower bracket.

10. Remove the 3 bolts and the Power Transfer Unit (PTU) support bracket.

11. Position the rear engine roll restrictor aside in the following sequence.

a. Remove the 2 engine roll restrictor-to-transaxle bolts.

b. Loosen the engine roll restrictor-to-frame bolt and pivot the roll restrictor downward.

12. Remove the front engine roll restrictor bolt and position the engine roll restrictor aside.

13. Position a jackstand under the rear of the subframe.

➡RH shown, LH similar.

14. Remove the subframe bracket-to-body bolts.

15. Remove the subframe rear bolts and the subframe brackets. Discard the bolts.

16. Position a jackstand under the front roll restrictor bracket and raise the engine far enough to allow the PTU to be removed.

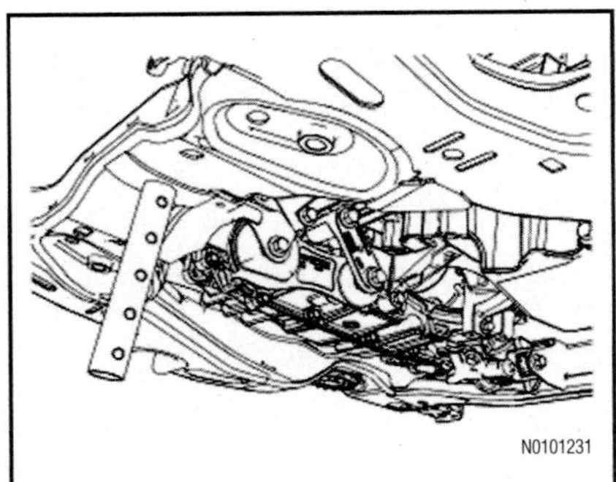

Fig. 14 Position a jackstand under the rear of the subframe

➡**Position a drain pan under the vehicle.**

17. Remove the 5 PTU bolts. Pull the PTU outward to separate it from the transaxle. Rotate the output flange upward, then turn it and remove the PTU from the vehicle.

18. Using a small screwdriver, remove and discard the compression seal.

To install:

➡**A new compression seal must be installed whenever the Power Transfer Unit (PTU) is removed from the vehicle.**

19. Using a suitable tool, install the new compression seal.

20. Position the PTU and install the 5 bolts. Tighten the bolts to 66 ft. lbs. (90 Nm).

21. Lower the engine and remove the jackstand from the front of the roll restrictor.

22. Using the jackstand, raise the subframe into the installed position.

23. Position the subframe brackets and loosely install the 4 bolts.

24. Install the 2 subframe rear bolts. Tighten the bolts to 111 ft. lbs. (150 Nm).

25. Tighten the 4 subframe bracket-to-body bolts to 41 ft. lbs. (55 Nm).

26. Remove the jackstand from the subframe.

27. Position the front engine roll restrictor to the bracket and install the bolt. Tighten the bolt to 66 ft. lbs. (90 Nm).

28. Position the rear engine roll restrictor to the transaxle and install the 3 bolts. Tighten the engine roll restrictor-to-transaxle bolts to 76 ft. lbs. (103 Nm), and the rear engine roll restrictor bolt to 66 ft. lbs. (90 Nm).

29. Position the PTU support bracket in place and install the 3 bolts. Tighten the bolts to 35 ft. lbs. (48 Nm).

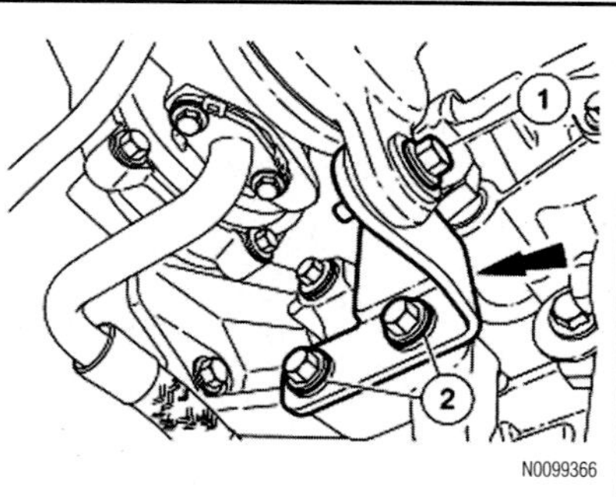

Fig. 15 Turbocharger lower bracket installation. Tighten the bolt (1) to 168 inch lbs. (19 Nm), and tighten the bolts (2) to 35 ft. lbs. (48 Nm)

30. Install the RH turbocharger lower bracket and the 3 bolts.

31. Connect the 2 Electronic Power Assist Steering (EPAS) electrical connectors (1 shown) and attach the wiring retainer (not shown) and install the bolt Tighten the bolt to 80 inch lbs. (9 Nm).

➡**Do not allow the intermediate shaft to rotate while it is disconnected from the gear or damage to the clockspring may occur. If there is evidence that the intermediate shaft has rotated, the clockspring must be removed and recentered. Refer to the Chassis Electrical Section.**

32. Install the steering intermediate shaft onto the steering gear and install a new bolt. Tighten the bolt to 177 inch lbs. (20 Nm).

➡**Align the index marks made during removal.**

33. Install the 4 driveshaft-to-output flange bolts. Tighten the bolts to 52 ft. lbs. (70 Nm).

34. Install the RH catalytic converter as outlined in the Engine Mechanical Section.

35. Install the RH front halfshaft as outlined in this section.

36. Install the underbody shield and the 4 retainers.

37. Remove the locking device from the steering wheel.

38. Inspect the transmission fluid level and add clean, specified fluid as necessary.

DRAIN & REFILL

See Figure 16.

➡**A new Power Transfer Unit (PTU) must be installed any time the PTU has been submerged in water.**

➡**The Power Transfer Unit (PTU) is not to be drained unless contamination is suspected. To drain the PTU fluid, the PTU must be removed from the vehicle. The fluid that is drained may appear black and have a pungent odor. Do not mistake this for contaminated fluid.**

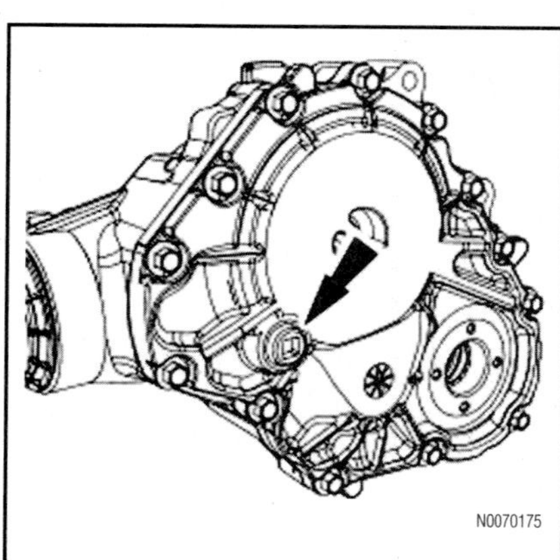

Fig. 16 Power transfer unit (PTU) fluid filler plug

➡**Fill level checks are done in-vehicle only. Let the vehicle sit 10 minutes after the road test before checking the fluid level.**

1. With the vehicle in NEUTRAL, position it on a hoist.

2. Clean the area around the filler plug before removing.

3. Remove and discard the filler plug.

4. With the vehicle on a flat, level surface, fill the PTU with lubricant. The fluid must be even with the bottom of the fill opening. Fluid capacity is 18 oz.

5. Install a new filler plug. Tighten the plug to 177 inch lbs. (20 Nm).

FRONT DRIVESHAFT

REMOVAL & INSTALLATION

See Figure 17.

➡**All driveshaft assemblies are balanced. If undercoating the vehicle, protect the driveshaft to prevent overspray of any undercoating material.**

1. The driveshaft assembly consists of the following:

   a. Rubber-isolated center support bearing

   b. CV joints at each end of the shaft

   c. U-joint at the center support

   d. Assembly balanced with traditional balance weights

   e. Lubed-for-life joints requiring no periodic lubrication

   f. Unique bolt and washer assembly for the rear CV joint

2. The driveshaft transfers torque from the Power Transfer Unit (PTU) to the rear axle. It is attached to the PTU flange with a CV joint. The 2-piece shaft is connected by a staked U-joint located rearward of the driveshaft center bearing and attached to the Rear Drive Unit (RDU) at the active torque coupling. The driveshaft joints allow the smooth continuous rotation of the driveshaft through the allowable angle planes and length variations required in normal vehicle operation. The driveshaft is always turning at front wheel speed. The driveshaft is not serviceable. A new driveshaft must be installed if worn or damaged.

➡**Index-mark both driveshaft flanges.**

3. With the vehicle in NEUTRAL, position it on a hoist.

4. Remove the muffler and tailpipe.
5. Remove the 4 exhaust support brace bolts and the exhaust brace.

➡Do not reuse the bolt and washer assemblies for the rear Constant Velocity (CV) joint flange. Install new assemblies or damage to the vehicle may occur.

6. Remove and discard the 3 Rear Drive Unit (RDU) pinion flange bolt and washer assemblies.
7. Separate the driveshaft CV flange from the RDU flange using a flat-blade screwdriver.

➡Do not reuse the Constant Velocity (CV) joint bolts. Install new bolts or damage to the vehicle may occur.

8. Remove and discard the 4 Power Transfer Unit (PTU) flange bolts.
9. Using a suitable prybar, separate the driveshaft flange from the PTU flange.
10. With the help of an assistant, remove the 2 outer center bearing bracket bolts and the driveshaft.
11. If necessary, remove the 2 inner center bearing bolts and remove the bracket.

➡If a driveshaft is installed and driveshaft vibration is encountered after installation, index the driveshaft. Refer to the General Information in this section.

To install:

➡If a driveshaft is installed and driveshaft vibration is encountered after installation, index the driveshaft. Refer to the General Information in this section.

12. If necessary, install the 2 inner center bearing bolts and install the bracket. Tighten the bolts to 177 inch lbs. (20 Nm).
13. With the help of an assistant, install the 2 outer center bearing bracket bolts and the driveshaft. Tighten the bolts to 22 ft. lbs. (30 Nm).
14. Install the driveshaft flange to the PTU flange.
15. Install 4 New Power Transfer Unit (PTU) flange bolts. Tighten the bolts to 52 ft. lbs. (70 Nm).

➡Do not reuse the Constant Velocity (CV) joint bolts. Install new bolts or damage to the vehicle may occur.

16. Install the driveshaft CV flange to the RDU flange using a flat-blade screwdriver.
17. Install 3 New Rear Drive Unit (RDU) pinion flange bolt and washer assemblies. Tighten the bolt to 18 ft. lbs. (25 Nm).

➡Do not reuse the bolt and washer assemblies for the rear Constant Velocity (CV) joint flange. Install new assemblies or damage to the vehicle may occur.

18. Install 4 new exhaust support brace bolts and the exhaust brace. Tighten the bolts to 22 ft. lbs. (30 Nm).
19. Install the muffler and tailpipe.
20. With the vehicle in NEUTRAL, lower it from the hoist.
21. The driveshaft transfers torque from the Power Transfer Unit (PTU) to the rear axle. It is attached to the PTU flange with a CV joint. The 2-piece shaft is connected by a staked U-joint located rearward of the driveshaft center bearing and attached to the Rear Drive Unit (RDU) at the active torque coupling. The driveshaft joints allow the smooth continuous rotation of the driveshaft through the allowable angle planes and length variations required in normal vehicle operation. The driveshaft is always turning at front wheel speed. The driveshaft is not serviceable. A new driveshaft must be installed if worn or damaged.

➡Index-mark both driveshaft flanges.

22. The driveshaft assembly consists of the following:
    a. Rubber-isolated center support bearing
    b. CV joints at each end of the shaft
    c. U-joint at the center support
    d. Assembly balanced with traditional balance weights
    e. Lubed-for-life joints requiring no periodic lubrication
    f. Unique bolt and washer assembly for the rear CV joint

➡All driveshaft assemblies are balanced. If undercoating the vehicle, protect the driveshaft to prevent overspray of any undercoating material.

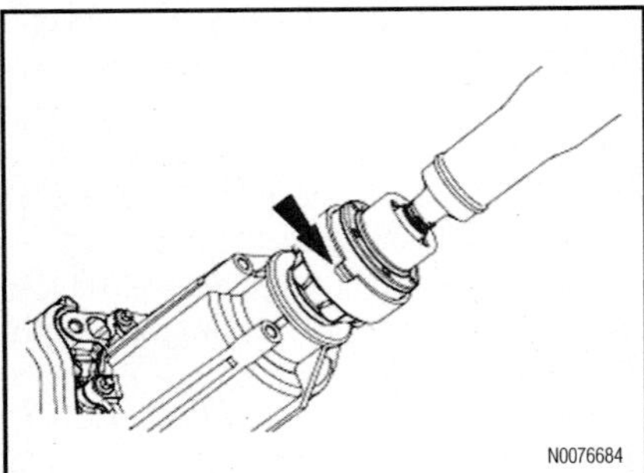

Fig. 17 Separate the driveshaft CV flange from the RDU flange using a flat-blade screwdriver in the area

FRONT HALFSHAFT

REMOVAL & INSTALLATION

Left-Hand

See Figures 18 and 19.

1. With the vehicle in NEUTRAL, position it on a hoist.
2. Remove the wheel and tire.

➡Apply the brake to keep the halfshaft from rotating.

3. Remove the wheel hub nut.
    a. Do not discard at this time.

➡Use care when releasing the lower arm and knuckle into the resting position or damage to the ball joint seal or Constant Velocity (CV) boot may occur.

➡Use the hex-holding feature to prevent the stud from turning while removing the nut.

4. Remove and discard the lower ball joint nut.
    a. Separate the ball joint from the wheel knuckle.
5. Using the Front Wheel Hub Remover, separate the halfshaft from the wheel hub.
6. Pull the wheel knuckle outboard and rotate it toward the rear of the vehicle.

➡The sharp edges on the stub shaft splines can slice or puncture the oil seal. Use care when inserting the stub shaft into the transmission or damage to the component may occur.

7. Using the Slide Hammer and Halfshaft Remover, remove the halfshaft from the transmission.
8. Remove and discard the circlip from the stub shaft.
9. Inspect the halfshaft hub for wear or damage and install a new halfshaft, if necessary.
    a. Inspect the differential seal surface.

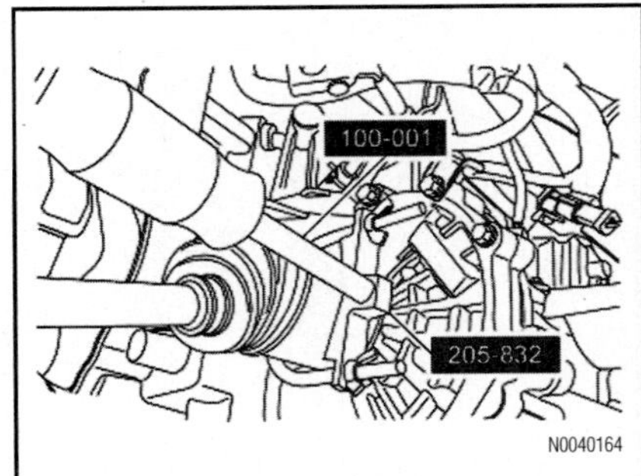

Fig. 18 Halfshaft from transmission removal

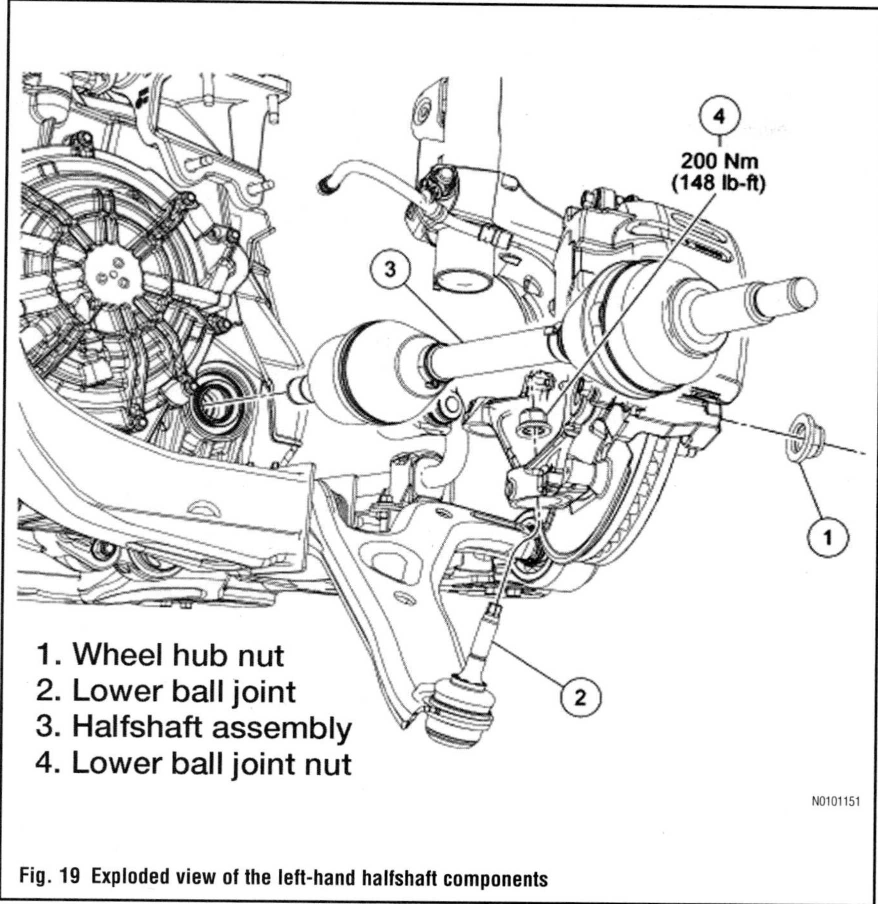

Fig. 19 Exploded view of the left-hand halfshaft components

b. Inspect the halfshaft bushing surface. If this surface is damaged, inspect the halfshaft bushing for damage.

c. Inspect the differential side gear splines.

To install:

➡The circlips are unique in size and shape for each shaft. Make sure to use the specified circlip for the application or vehicle damage may occur.

10. Install the correct new circlip on the inboard stub shaft.

➡After insertion, pull the halfshaft inner end to make sure the circlip is locked.

11. Push the stub shaft into the transmission so the circlip locks into the differential side gear.
12. Rotate the wheel knuckle into position and insert the halfshaft into the wheel hub.
13. Position the lower ball joint into the wheel knuckle and install the new nut. Tighten the nut to 148 ft. lbs. (200 Nm).

➡Do not tighten the wheel hub nut with the vehicle on the ground. The nut must be tightened to specification before the vehicle is lowered onto the wheels. Wheel bearing damage will occur if the wheel bearing is loaded with the weight of the vehicle applied.

➡Apply the brake to keep the halfshaft from rotating.

14. Using the previously removed wheel hub nut, seat the halfshaft. Tighten the nut to 258 ft. lbs. (350 Nm).
    a. Remove and discard the wheel hub nut.

➡The wheel hub nut contains a one-time locking chemical that is activated by the heat created when it is tightened. Install and tighten the new wheel hub nut to specification within 5 minutes of starting it on the threads. Always install a new wheel hub nut after loosening or when not tightened within the specified time or damage to the components can occur.

➡Apply the brake to keep the halfshaft from rotating.

15. Install a new wheel hub nut. Tighten the nut to 258 ft. lbs. (350 Nm).
16. Install the front wheel and tire.

Right-Hand

See Figures 20 through 24.

All Vehicles

1. With the vehicle in NEUTRAL, position it on a hoist.
2. Remove the wheel and tire.

➡Apply the brake to keep the halfshaft from rotating.

3. Remove the wheel hub nut.
    a. Do not discard at this time.

All-Wheel Drive (AWD) Vehicles

4. Remove the front RH brake disc as outlined in the Brakes Section.

All Vehicles

5. Remove the bolt from the brake hose bracket.

➡Suspension fasteners are critical parts because they affect performance of vital components and systems and their failure may result in major service expense. New parts must be installed with the same part number or equivalent part, if replacement is necessary. Do not use a replacement part of lesser quality or substitute design. Torque values must be used as specified during reassembly to make sure of correct retention of these parts.

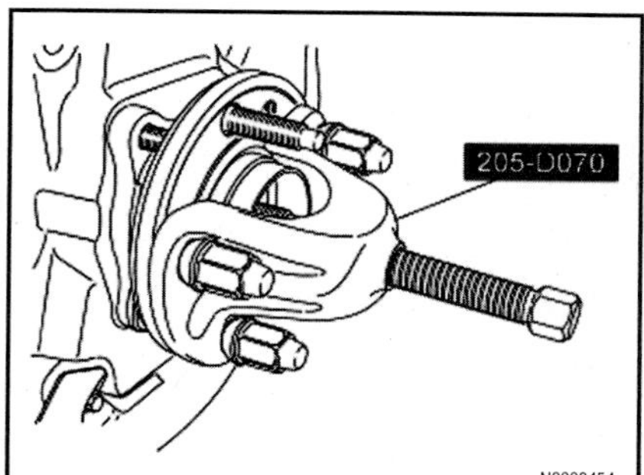

Fig. 20 Use the front wheel hub remover to separate the halfshaft from the wheel hub

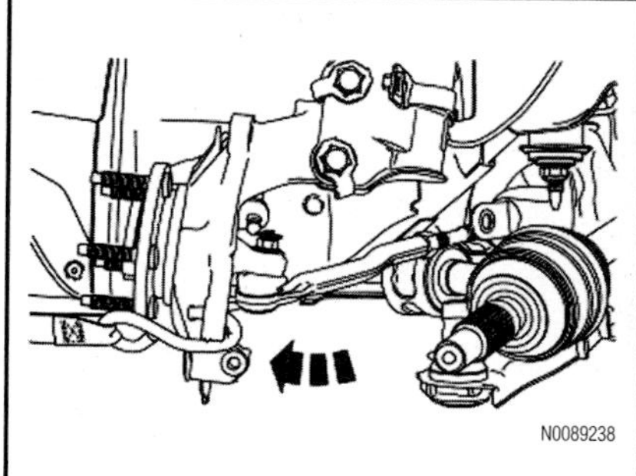

Fig. 21 Pull the wheel knuckle outboard and rotate it toward the rear of the vehicle

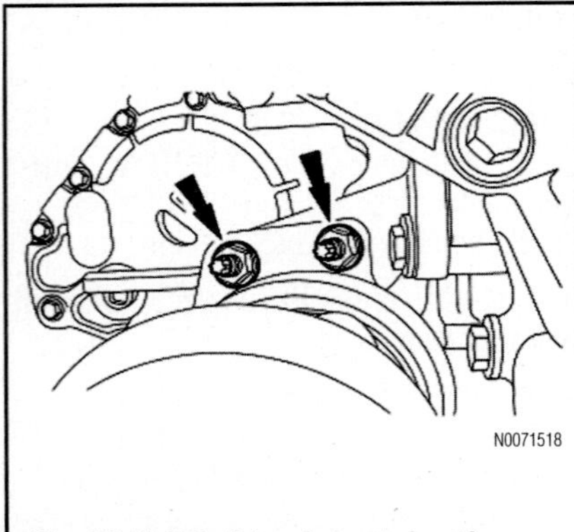

Fig. 22 Halfshaft bracket nuts location

➡Use care when releasing the lower arm and knuckle into the resting position or damage to the ball joint seal or Constant Velocity (CV) boot may occur.

➡Use the hex-holding feature to prevent the stud from turning while removing the nut.

6. Remove and discard the lower ball joint nut.
   a. Separate the lower ball joint from the wheel knuckle.
7. Using the Front Wheel Hub Remover, separate the halfshaft from the wheel hub.
8. Pull the wheel knuckle outboard and rotate it toward the rear of the vehicle.
   a. Secure the wheel knuckle assembly.
9. Remove the 2 lower scrivets from the rubber shield and position the shield aside.

Without 3.5L Turbo

10. Remove the 2 halfshaft bracket nuts.
11. Remove the intermediate and halfshaft assembly.
    a. Inspect the intermediate shaft for pitting or damage in the seal contact area. Replace if necessary.
12. Inspect the halfshaft hub for wear or damage and install a new halfshaft, if necessary.
    a. Inspect the differential seal surface.
    b. Inspect the halfshaft bushing surface. If this surface is damaged, inspect the halfshaft bushing for damage.
    c. Inspect the differential side gear splines.

With 3.5L Turbo

13. Separate the halfshaft from the intermediate shaft and remove the halfshaft.

To install:

AWD vehicles

➡A new Power Transfer Unit (PTU) shaft seal must be installed whenever the intermediate shaft is removed or damage to the components can occur.

14. Install a new intermediate shaft seal and deflector as outlined in Transfer Case in this section.

With 3.5L Turbo

15. Install the halfshaft to the intermediate shaft.

Without 3.5L Turbo

16. Install the intermediate and halfshaft assembly and the 2 halfshaft bracket nuts. Tighten the nuts to 18 ft. lbs. (25 Nm).

All Vehicles

17. Rotate the wheel knuckle into position and insert the halfshaft into the wheel hub.
18. Position the lower ball joint into the wheel knuckle and install the new nut. Tighten the nut to 148 ft. lbs. (200 Nm).
19. Position the brake hose bracket and install the bolt. Tighten the bolt to 22 ft. lbs. (30 Nm).
20. Install the 2 scrivets in the rubber shield.

AWD Vehicles

21. Install the RH brake disc. For additional information, refer to Front Disc Brake.

All Vehicles

➡Do not tighten the front wheel hub nut with the vehicle on the ground. The nut must be tightened to specification before the vehicle is lowered onto the wheels. Wheel bearing damage will occur if the wheel bearing is loaded with the weight of the vehicle applied.

➡Apply the brake to keep the halfshaft from rotating.

22. Using the previously removed wheel hub nut, seat the halfshaft. Tighten the nut to 258 ft. lbs. (350 Nm).
    a. Remove and discard the wheel hub nut.

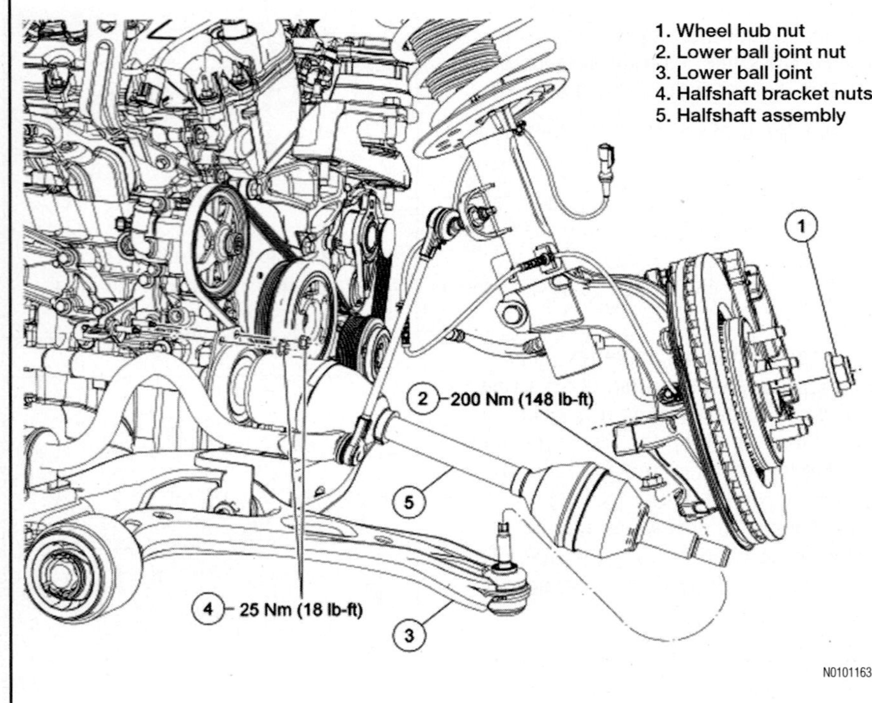

Fig. 23 Exploded view of the right-hand halfshaft components

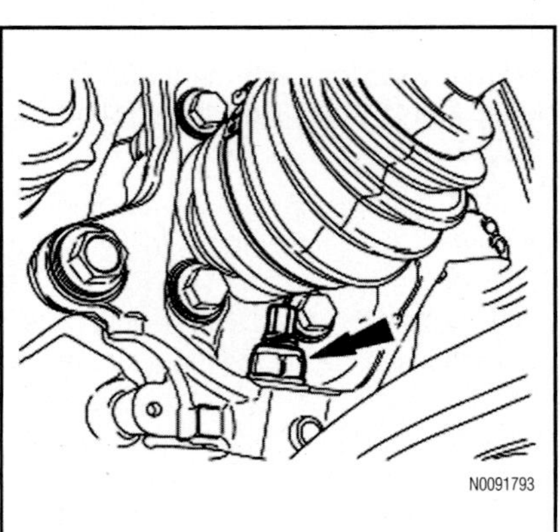

Fig. 24 Lower ball joint to wheel knuckle nut location

➡**The wheel hub nut contains a one-time locking chemical that is activated by the heat created when it is tightened. Install and tighten the new wheel hub nut to specification within 5 minutes of starting it on the threads. Always install a new wheel hub nut after loosening or when not tightened within the specified time or damage to the components can occur.**

➡**Apply the brake to keep the halfshaft from rotating.**

23. Install a new wheel hub nut. Tighten the nut to 258 ft. lbs. (350 Nm).
24. Install the wheel and tire.

Intermediate Shaft—3.5L Turbo

See Figure 25.

➡**The intermediate shaft seal in the Power Transfer Unit (PTU) must be replaced whenever the intermediate shaft is removed or a leak may occur.**

1. Remove the right halfshaft assembly.
2. Remove the 2 intermediate shaft support bracket bolts and the intermediate shaft.
3. Remove and discard the circlip from the outboard end of the intermediate shaft.

To install:

4. Install a new 1.181 in. (30 mm) circlip on the outboard end of the intermediate shaft.
5. Install a new intermediate shaft seal in the Power Transfer Unit (PTU) as outlined in this section.
6. Position the intermediate shaft in the PTU and engage the intermediate shaft splines with the PTU gears.
7. Install the 2 intermediate shaft support bracket bolts. Tighten the bolts to 30 ft. lbs. (40 Nm).
8. Install the right halfshaft as outlined in this section.

REAR AXLE ASSEMBLY

REMOVAL & INSTALLATION

See Figures 26 and 27.

1. Remove the driveshaft assembly. For additional information, refer to Driveshaft.
2. Remove the rear halfshafts as outlined in this section.
3. Remove the stabilizer bar as outlined in the Suspension Section.
4. Position a suitable transmission hydraulic jack to the axle housing.
   a. Securely strap the jack to the housing.

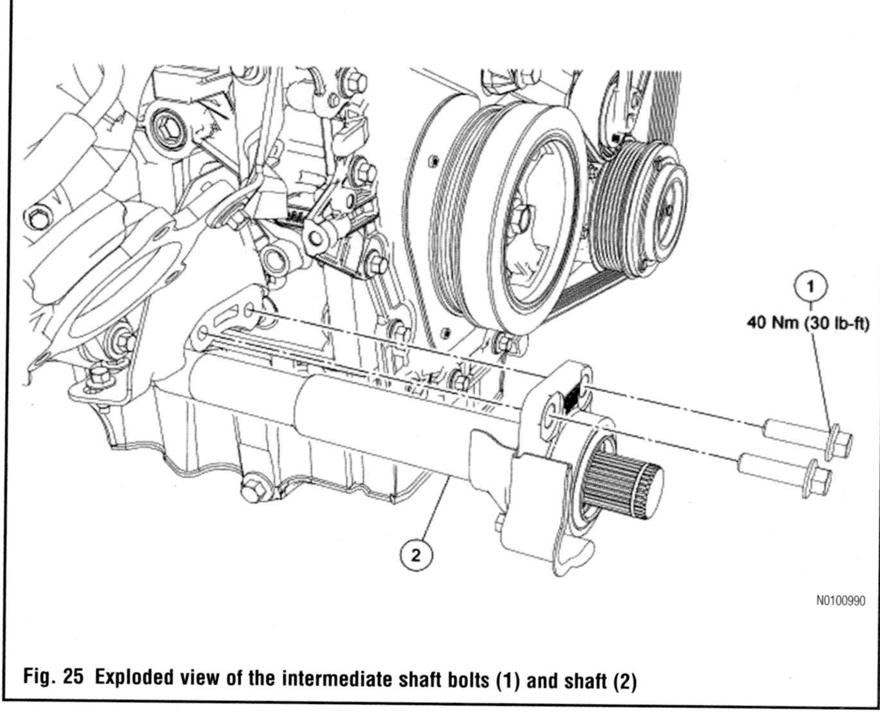

Fig. 25 Exploded view of the intermediate shaft bolts (1) and shaft (2)

5. Remove the 4 differential housing-to-front insulator bracket bolts.
6. Remove the 6 side insulator bracket-to-rear axle differential bolts.
7. Lower the axle to gain clearance to the Active Torque Coupling (ATC) electrical connector and disconnect the connector.
8. Remove the axle assembly.

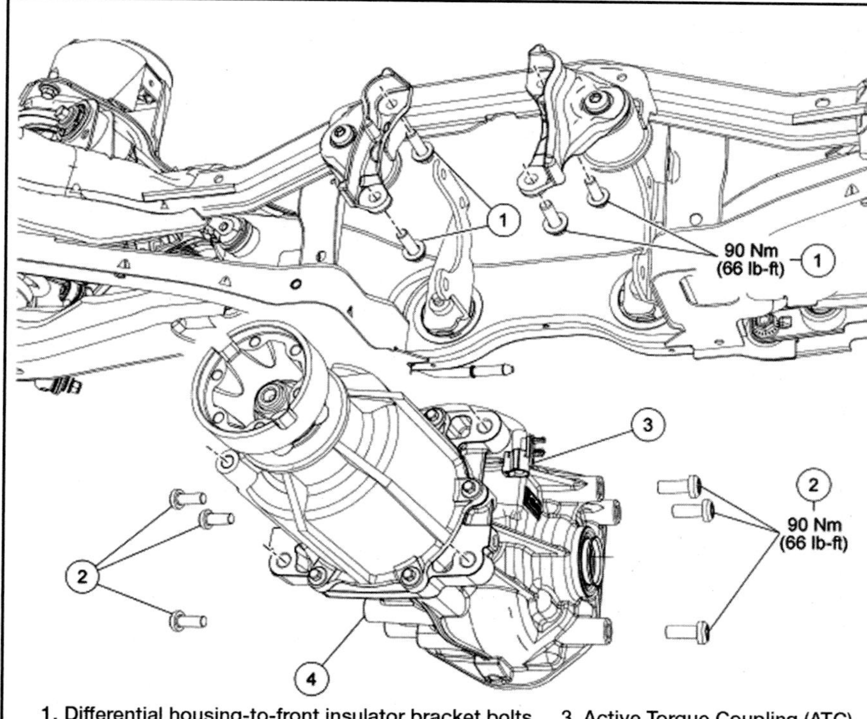

Fig. 26 Exploded view of the rear axle mounting

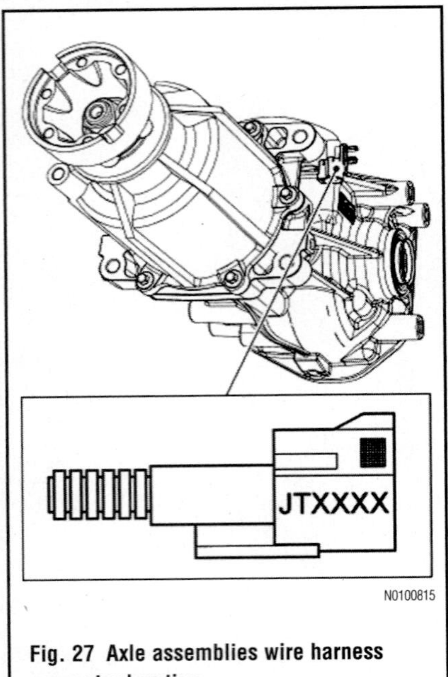

Fig. 27 Axle assemblies wire harness connector location

To install:

➡If replacing the axle assembly, the 4X4 control module will need to be reconfigured with the new Active Torque Coupling (ATC) bar code information. If the new bar code information does not match the existing 4X4 control module information, driveline damage or driveability concerns can occur.

➡The ATC bar code can be found etched on the ATC wire harness connector of the new axle assembly.

➡Record the bar code identification number from the new axle assemblies wire harness connector.

9. Position the axle housing on a suitable transmission hydraulic jack.
   a. Securely strap the jack to the housing.
10. Raise the axle and connect the ATC electrical connector.
11. Install the 6 side insulator bracket-to-rear axle differential bolts. Tighten the bolts to 66 ft. lbs. (90 Nm).
12. Install the 4 differential housing-to-front insulator bracket bolts. Tighten the bolts to 66 ft. lbs. (90 Nm).
13. Install the stabilizer bar as outlined in the Suspension Section.
14. Install the rear halfshafts as outlined in this section.
15. Install the driveshaft assembly as outlined in this section.
16. Using the scan tool, program the 4-digit bar code information retrieved from the new axle assembly harness connector into the 4X4 control module using the ATC Bar Code Entry service function.
17. The scan tool will verify that the numbers entered are valid and display a message if the information is not correct.

REAR DIFFERENTIAL HOUSING COVER

REMOVAL & INSTALLATION

1. With the vehicle in NEUTRAL, position it on a hoist. For additional information, refer to Jacking and Lifting.
2. If equipped, remove the exhaust insulator located near the differential housing cover using soapy water.

➡Drain the differential fluid into a suitable drain pan.

3. Remove the 10 bolts and the rear differential housing cover.
   a. Drain the differential fluid from the housing.

To install:

➡Make sure the machined surfaces on the rear axle housing and the differential housing cover are clean and free of oil before installing the new silicone sealant. The inside of the rear axle must be covered when cleaning the machined surface to prevent contamination.

4. Clean the gasket mating surfaces of the differential housing and the differential housing cover.

➡The differential housing cover must be installed within 15 minutes of application of the silicone, or new silicone must be applied. If possible, allow one hour before filling with lubricant to make sure the silicone has correctly cured.

5. Apply a new continuous bead of clear silicone rubber as shown in the illustration.
6. Install the differential housing cover and the 10 bolts. Tighten the bolts to 17 ft. lbs. (23 Nm).
7. Remove the filler plug and fill the rear axle with 2.43 pt. of rear axle lubricant, 0.118-0.196 inches below the bottom of the filler hole.
   a. Install the filler plug and tighten to 21 ft. lbs. (29 Nm).
8. If equipped, install the exhaust insulator located near the differential housing cover.

REAR HALFSHAFT

REMOVAL & INSTALLATION

See Figures 28 and 29.

➡Suspension fasteners are critical parts because they affect performance of vital components and systems and their failure may result in major service expense. New parts must be installed with the same part numbers or equivalent part, if replacement is necessary. Do not use a replacement part of lesser quality or substitute design. Torque values must be used as specified during reassembly to make sure of correct retention of these parts.

1. Measure the distance from the center of the wheel hub to the lip of the fender with the vehicle in a level, static ground position (curb height).
2. Remove the wheel and tire.
3. Remove the wheel hub nut.
   a. Do not discard at this time.

➡Do not allow the caliper to hang from the brake hose or damage to the hose can occur.

4. Remove and discard the 2 brake caliper anchor plate bolts and position the brake caliper and anchor plate assembly aside.
   a. Support the brake caliper and anchor plate assembly using mechanic's wire.

➡Use the hex-holding feature to prevent the stabilizer bar link stud from turning while removing or installing the nut.

5. Remove and discard the stabilizer bar link upper nut and disconnect the link.
6. Remove and discard the toe link-to-wheel knuckle nut and disconnect the link.
7. Remove the wheel speed sensor bolt.
   a. Disconnect the wheel speed sensor harness retainers and position the sensor and harness aside.
8. Position a screw-type jackstand under the lower arm.
9. Remove and discard the upper arm-to-wheel knuckle nut and bolt and disconnect the knuckle from the upper arm.
10. Remove and discard the shock absorber lower bolt and disconnect the shock absorber from the knuckle bracket.
11. Loosen, but do not remove the lower arm-to-wheel knuckle bolt.
12. Using the Front Hub Remover, separate the halfshaft outer CV joint from the hub bearing.

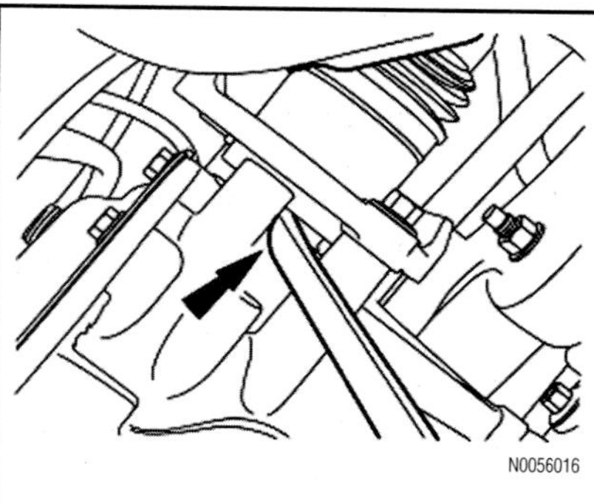

Fig. 28 Halfshaft inner CV joint from the differential removal

13. Swing the wheel knuckle outward and remove the halfshaft outer CV joint from the hub bearing.

➡**Do not damage the oil seal when removing the axle halfshaft from the differential.**

14. Using a suitable pry bar, remove the halfshaft inner CV joint from the differential.
  a. Remove the halfshaft from the vehicle.
15. Remove and discard the circlip from the halfshaft.

To install:

➡**Before tightening suspension bushing fasteners, use a jackstand to raise the rear suspension until the distance between the center of the hub and the lip of the fender is equal to the measurement taken in the removal procedure (curb height).**

➡**The circlips are unique in size and shape for each shaft. Make sure to use the specified circlip for the application or vehicle damage may occur.**

16. Install a new circlip on the halfshaft.
17. Using the Axle Seal Protector, install the halfshaft inner CV joint into the differential.

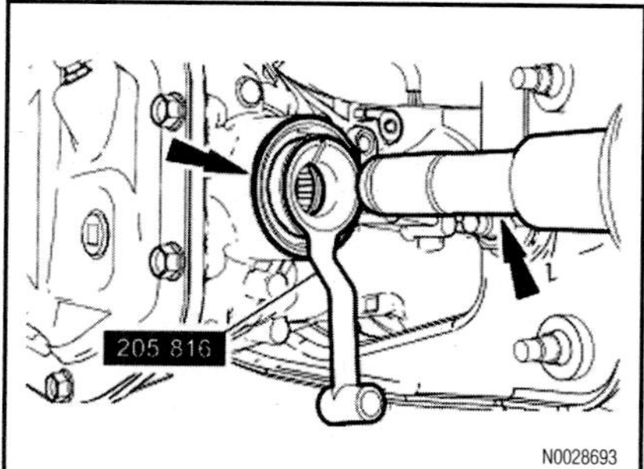

Fig. 29 Using the axle seal protector, install the halfshaft inner CV joint into the differential

  a. Make sure the circlip locks in the side gear.
18. Swing the wheel knuckle inward and install the halfshaft outer CV joint through the hub bearing.
19. Position the wheel knuckle to the upper arm and loosely install a new nut and bolt.
20. Position the shock absorber and loosely install a new bolt.
21. Position the wheel speed sensor harness in the retainers and install the sensor and bolt. Tighten the bolt to 133 inch lbs. (15 Nm).
22. Position the toe link and loosely install a new toe link-to-wheel knuckle nut.
23. Position a suitable jackstand under the lower control arm at the shock and spring assembly attachment point and raise the rear suspension until the distance between the center of the hub and the lip of the fender is equal to the measurement taken in Step 1 of the procedure (curb height).

➡**A slotted upper arm allows for the rear suspension camber to be adjusted by pushing inward or pulling outward on the wheel knuckle while tightening the upper arm-to-wheel knuckle nut.**

24. With the wheel knuckle pushed inward for maximum negative camber, tighten the upper arm-to-wheel knuckle nut to 148 ft. lbs. (200 Nm).
25. Tighten the lower arm-to-wheel knuckle bolt to 196 ft. lbs. (265 Nm).
26. Tighten the shock absorber lower bolt to 129 ft. lbs. (175 Nm).
27. Tighten the toe link-to-wheel knuckle nut to 59 ft. lbs. (80 Nm).

➡**Use the hex-holding feature to prevent the stabilizer bar link stud from turning while removing or installing the nut.**

28. Connect the stabilizer bar link and install a new stabilizer bar link upper nut. Tighten the nut to 41 ft. lbs. (55 Nm).
29. Position the brake caliper and anchor plate assembly and install the 2 bolts. Tighten the bolts to 76 ft. lbs. (103 Nm).

➡**Do not tighten the wheel hub nut with the vehicle on the ground. The nut must be tightened to specification before the vehicle is lowered onto the wheels. Wheel bearing damage will occur if the wheel bearing is loaded with the weight of the vehicle applied.**

➡**Apply the brake to keep the halfshaft from rotating.**

30. Use the previously removed hub nut to seat the halfshaft. Tighten the nut to 258 ft. lbs. (350 Nm).
  a. Remove and discard the hub nut.

➡**The wheel hub nut contains a one-time locking chemical that is activated by the heat created when it is tightened. Install and tighten the new wheel hub nut to specification within 5 minutes of starting it on the threads. Always install a new wheel hub nut after loosening or when not tightened within the specified time or damage to the components can occur.**

➡**Apply the brake to keep the halfshaft from rotating.**

31. Install a new hub nut. Tighten the nut to 258 ft. lbs. (350 Nm).
32. Install the wheel and tire.
33. Check and if necessary, adjust the rear toe as outlined in the Suspension Section.

REAR PINION SEAL

REMOVAL & INSTALLATION

See Figure 30.

1. Remove the driveshaft as outlined in this section.
2. Using the Drive Pinion Flange Holding Fixture, hold the pinion flange and remove the nut.
  a. Discard the nut.
3. Index-mark the location of the pinion to the yoke.
4. Using the 2 Jaw Puller, remove the pinion flange.
5. Using the Torque Converter Fluid Seal Remover and Slide Hammer, remove the seal.

To install:

➡**Make sure that the mating surface is clean before installing the new seal.**

6. Using the Pinion Seal Replacer, install the seal.

➡**Lubricate the pinion flange with grease.**

7. Line up the index marks and position the pinion flange.
8. Using the Drive Pinion Flange Holding Fixture, install the new pinion nut. Tighten the nut to 180 ft. lbs. (244 Nm).
9. Install the driveshaft as outlined in this section.

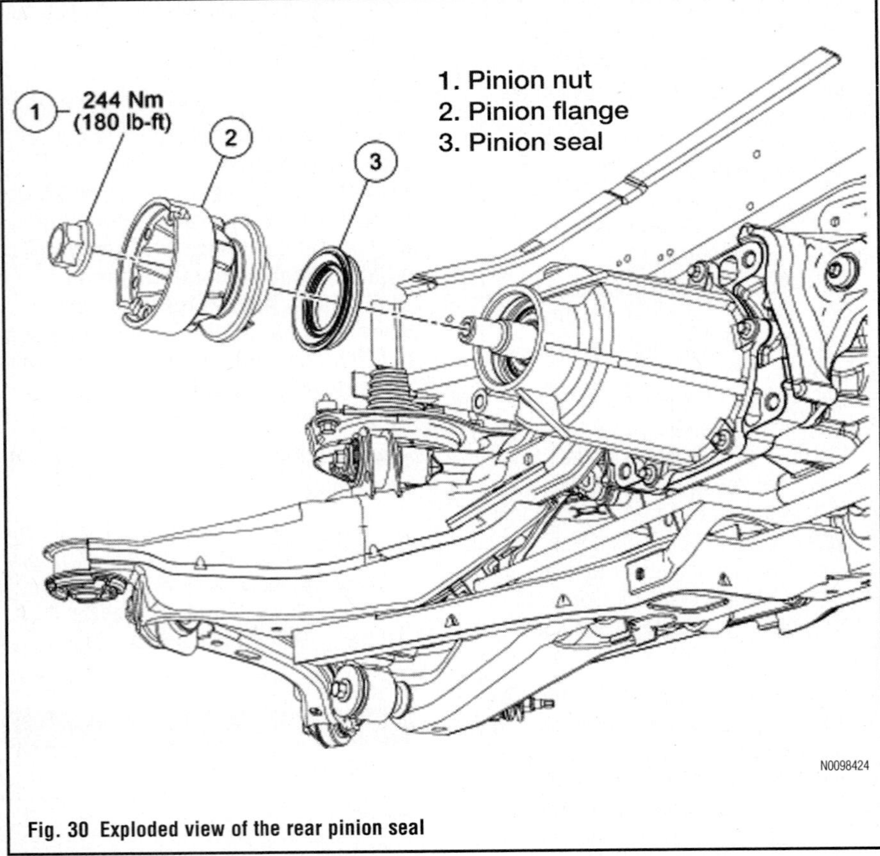

Fig. 30 Exploded view of the rear pinion seal

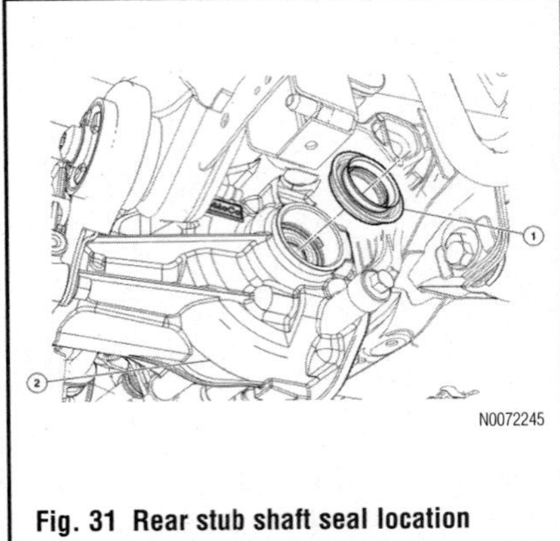

Fig. 31 Rear stub shaft seal location

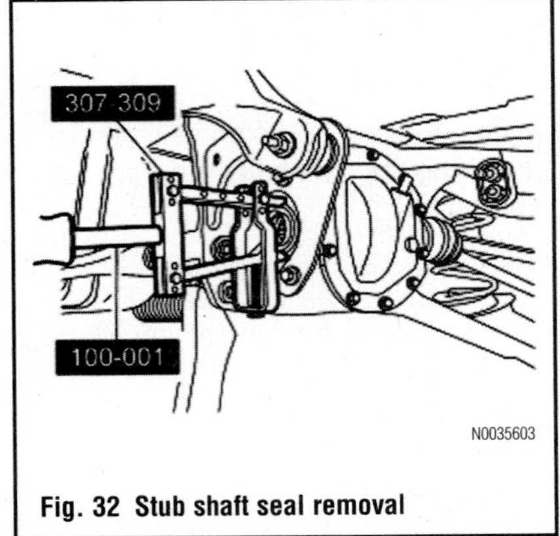

Fig. 32 Stub shaft seal removal

REAR STUB SHAFT SEAL

REMOVAL & INSTALLATION

See Figures 31 and 32.

➡The Rear Drive Unit (RDU) does not have stub shaft pilot bearings. It has stub shaft seals only.

1. Remove the halfshaft assembly as outlined in this section.
2. Using the Torque Converter Fluid Seal Remover and Slide Hammer, remove the stub shaft seal.

To install:

➡Lubricate the new stub shaft seal with grease.

3. Using the Front Axle Oil Seal Installer and Handle, install the stub shaft pilot bearing housing seal.
4. Install the halfshaft assembly as outlined in this section.

ENGINE COOLING

COOLANT (WATER) PUMP

REMOVAL & INSTALLATION

See Figures 33 through 48.

➡During engine repair procedures, cleanliness is extremely important. Any foreign material, including any material created while cleaning gasket surfaces, that enters the oil passages, coolant passages or the oil pan may cause engine failure.

➡On early build engines, the timing chain rides on the inner side of the RH timing chain guide. Late build engines are equipped with a different design RH timing chain guide that requires the timing chain to ride on the outer side of the RH timing chain guide. For service, all replacement RH timing chain guides will be the late build design.

All Vehicles

1. With the vehicle in NEUTRAL, position it on a hoist.
2. Drain the cooling system as outlined in this section.
3. Remove the engine front cover as outlined in the Engine Mechanical Section.
4. Remove and discard the engine oil filter.

Engines Equipped With Early Build RH Timing Chain Guides

5. Rotate the crankshaft clockwise and align the timing marks on the Variable Camshaft Timing (VCT) assemblies.

Engines Equipped With Late Build/Replacement RH Timing Chain Guides

6. Rotate the crankshaft clockwise and align the timing marks on the VCT assemblies.

All Vehicles

➡The Camshaft Holding Tool will hold the camshafts in the Top Dead Center (TDC) position.

7. Install the Camshaft Holding Tool onto the flats of the LH camshafts.

➡The Camshaft Holding Tool will hold the camshafts in the TDC position.

8. Install the Camshaft Holding Tool onto the flats of the RH camshafts.

Fig. 33 Rotate the crankshaft clockwise and align the timing marks on the Variable Camshaft Timing (VCT) assemblies

Fig. 34 Rotate the crankshaft clockwise and align the timing marks on the Variable Camshaft Timing (VCT) assemblies

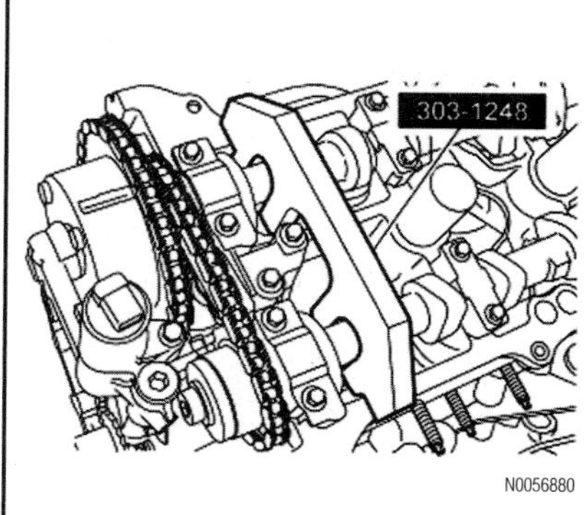

Fig. 35 Install the camshaft holding tool onto the flats of the LH camshafts, RH similar

Fig. 36 RH VCT housing bolts, LH similar

9. Remove the 3 bolts and the RH VCT housing.
10. Remove the 3 bolts and the LH VCT housing.
11. Remove the 2 bolts and the primary timing chain tensioner.
12. Remove the primary timing chain tensioner arm.
13. Remove the 2 bolts and the lower LH primary timing chain guide.
14. Remove the primary timing chain.
15. Remove the 2 bolts and the upper LH primary timing chain guide.

Engines Equipped With Early Build RH Timing Chain Guides

16. Remove the RH primary timing chain guide lower bolt.

Fig. 37 Primary timing chain tensioner bolt location

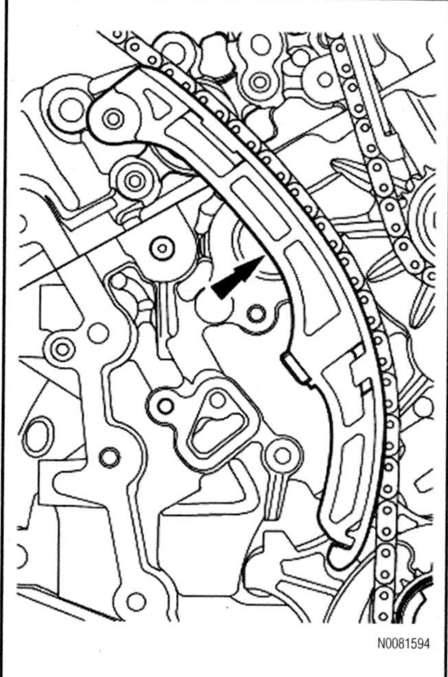

Fig. 38 Primary timing chain tensioner arm

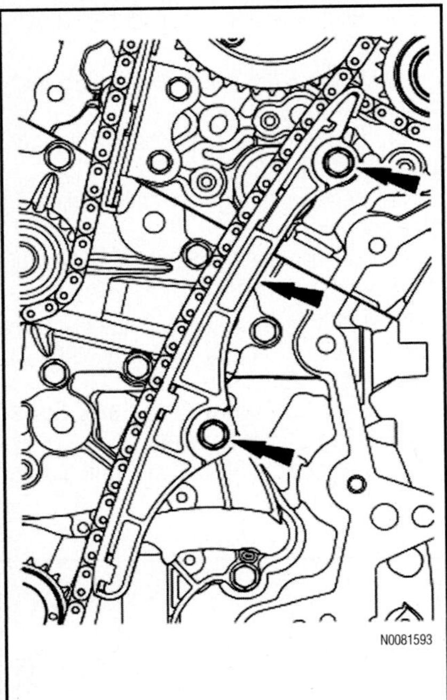

Fig. 39 LH primary timing chain guide

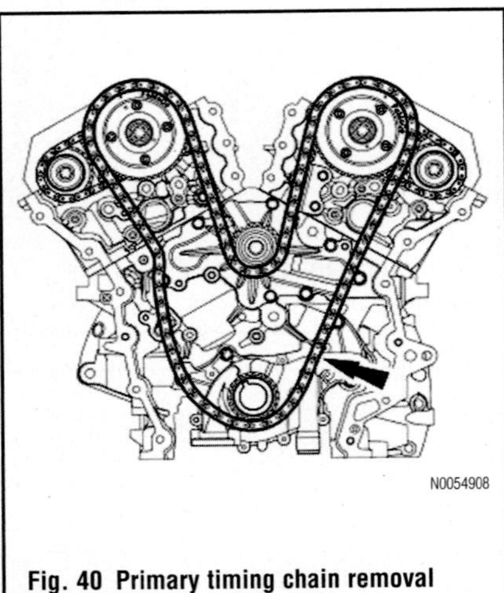

Fig. 40 Primary timing chain removal

➡**The RH primary timing chain guide must be repositioned to allow the coolant pump to be removed.**

17. Loosen the RH primary timing chain guide upper bolt.
   a. Rotate the guide and tighten the bolt.

Engines Equipped With Late Build/Replacement RH Timing Chain Guides

18. Remove the RH primary timing chain guide lower bolt.

➡**The RH primary timing chain guide must be repositioned to allow the coolant pump to be removed.**

19. Loosen the RH primary timing chain guide upper bolt.

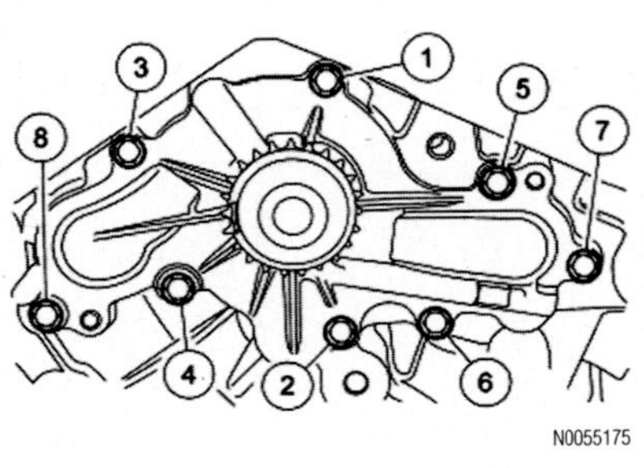

Fig. 41 Coolant pump removal & installation. Tighten the bolts in the proper sequence

   a. Rotate the guide and tighten the bolt.

All Vehicles

20. Place clean lint-free shop towels in the oil pan opening to prevent coolant from entering the oil pan during coolant pump removal.
21. Remove the 8 bolts and the coolant pump.

To install:

All Vehicles

➡**Clean and inspect all sealing surfaces.**

22. Install the coolant pump and the 8 bolts. Tighten the bolts to 89 inch lbs. (10 Nm).
23. Remove all of the shop towels from the oil pan opening.

➡**Any coolant that has accumulated in the oil pan must be drained from the pan and any residual coolant cleaned from the front of the engine and oil pan. Failure to remove all traces of the coolant can result in oil contamination and severe engine damage.**

24. Remove the oil pan drain plug and allow any accumulated coolant to drain.
   a. Remove any residual coolant from the front of the engine and the oil pan using regulated, compressed air and clean, lint-free shop towels.
   b. Install the oil pan drain plug. Tighten the drain plug to 20 ft. lbs. (27 Nm).

Engines Equipped With Late Build/Replacement RH Timing Chain Guides

25. Loosen the RH primary timing chain guide upper bolt.
   a. Position the RH primary timing chain guide and install the lower bolt. Tighten the bolts to 89 inch lbs. (10 Nm).

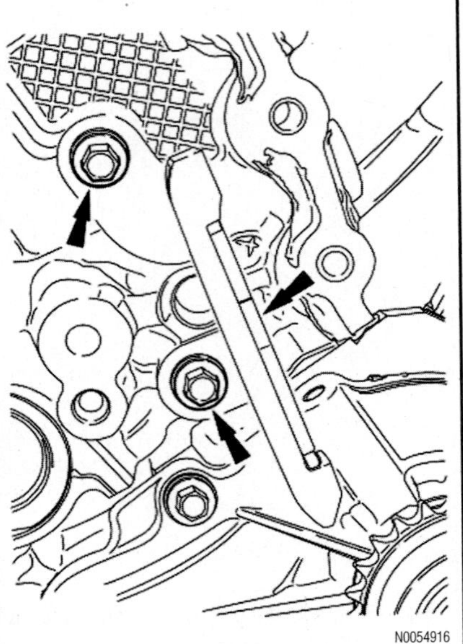

Fig. 42 RH primary timing chain guide upper and lower bolt locations. LH primary timing chain guide upper similar.

Engines Equipped With Early Build RH Timing Chain Guides

26. Loosen the RH primary timing chain guide upper bolt.
   a. Position the RH primary timing chain guide and install the lower bolt. Tighten the bolts to 89 inch lbs. (10 Nm).

All Vehicles

27. Install the primary timing chain with the colored links aligned with the timing marks on the VCT assemblies and the crankshaft sprocket.
28. Install the upper LH primary timing chain guide and the 2 bolts. Tighten the bolts to 89 inch lbs. (10 Nm).

Fig. 43 Install the primary timing chain with the colored links aligned with the timing marks on the VCT assemblies and the crankshaft sprocket

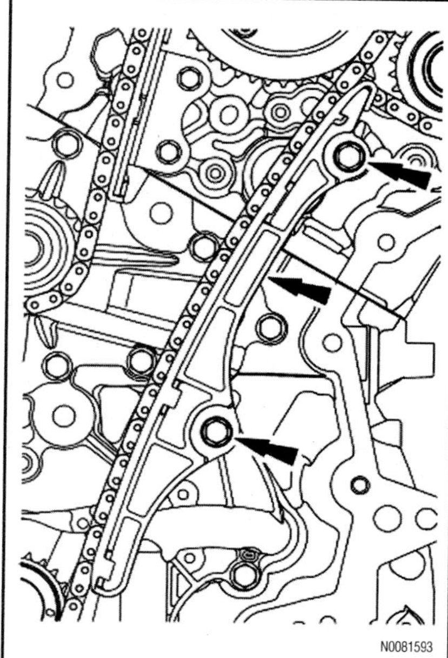

Fig. 44 Install the lower LH primary timing chain guide

29. Install the lower LH primary timing chain guide and the 2 bolts. Tighten the bolts to 89 inch lbs. (10 Nm).

30. Install the primary timing chain tensioner arm.

31. Reset the primary timing chain tensioner.

a. Rotate the lever counterclockwise.

b. Using a soft-jawed vise, compress the plunger.

c. Align the hole in the lever with the hole in the tensioner housing.

d. Install a suitable lockpin.

Fig. 45 Reset the primary timing chain tensioner arm

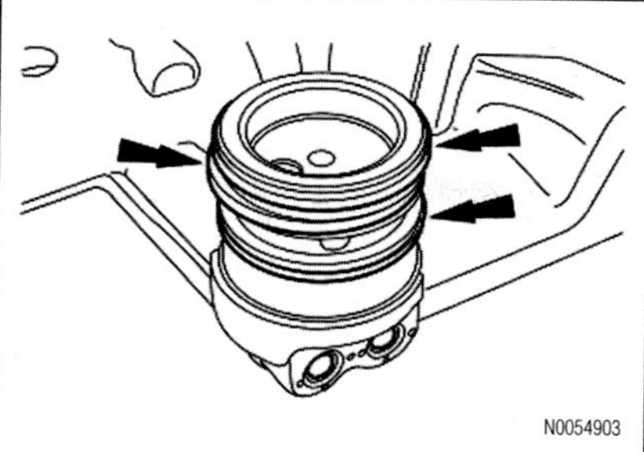

Fig. 46 Inspect the VCT housing seals for damage

➡It may be necessary to rotate the crankshaft slightly to remove slack from the timing chain and install the tensioner.

32. Install the primary tensioner and the 2 bolts. Tighten the bolts to 89 inch lbs. (10 Nm).

a. Remove the lockpin.

33. As a post check, verify correct alignment of all timing marks.

34. Inspect the VCT housing seals for damage and replace if necessary.

➡Make sure the dowels on the VCT housing are fully engaged in the cylinder head prior to tightening the bolts.

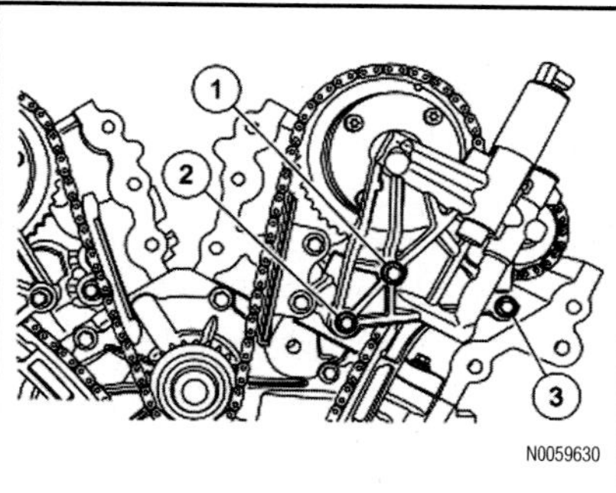

Fig. 47 Install the LH VCT housing and tighten the bolts in sequence shown

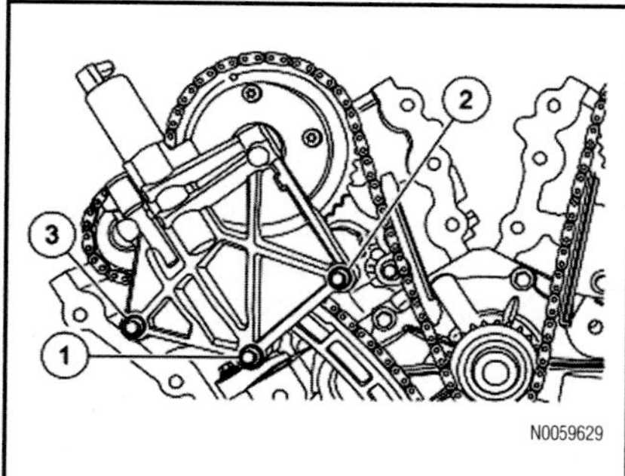

Fig. 48 Install the RH VCT housing and tighten the bolts in sequence shown

35. Install the LH VCT housing and the 3 bolts. Tighten the bolts to 89 inch lbs. (10 Nm).

➡Make sure the dowels on the VCT housing are fully engaged in the cylinder head prior to tightening the bolts.

36. Install the RH VCT housing and the 3 bolts. Tighten the bolts to 89 inch lbs. (10 Nm).

➡Lubricate the engine oil filter gasket with clean engine oil prior to installing the oil filter.

37. Install a new engine oil filter. Tighten the engine oil filter to 44 inch lbs. (5 Nm), and then rotate an additional 180°.

38. Install the engine front cover as outlined in the Engine Mechanical Section.

39. Fill and bleed the cooling system as outlined in this section.

ENGINE COOLANT

DRAINING PROCEDURE

See Figure 49.

1. With the vehicle in NEUTRAL, position it on a hoist. For additional information, refer to Jacking and Lifting.

✲✲ CAUTION

Always allow the engine to cool before opening the cooling system. Do not unscrew the coolant pressure relief cap when the engine is operating or the cooling system is hot. The cooling system is under pressure; steam and hot liquid can come out forcefully when the cap is loosened slightly. Failure to follow these instructions may result in serious personal injury.

➡The coolant must be recovered in a suitable, clean container for reuse. If the coolant is contaminated, it must be recycled or disposed of correctly. Using contaminated coolant may result in damage to the engine or cooling system components.

➡The engine cooling system is filled with Motorcraft® Specialty Green Engine Coolant. Mixing coolant types degrades the corrosion protection of Motorcraft® Specialty Green Engine Coolant.

➡Genuine Mazda® Extended Life Coolant and Motorcraft® Specialty Green Engine Coolant are very sensitive to light. Do NOT allow these

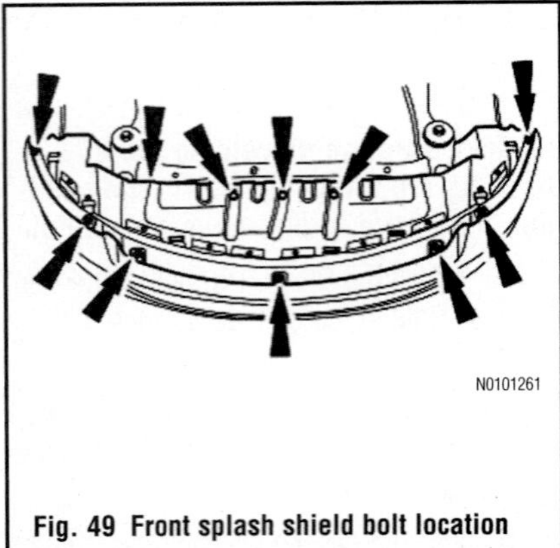
Fig. 49 Front splash shield bolt location

products to be exposed to ANY LIGHT for more than a day or two. Extended light exposure causes these products to degrade.

➡Stop-leak style pellets/products must not be used as an additive in this engine cooling system. The addition of stop-leak style pellets/products may clog or damage the cooling system, resulting in degraded cooling system performance and/or failure.

➡Less than 80% of coolant capacity can be recovered with the engine in the vehicle. Dirty, rusty or contaminated coolant requires replacement. Release the pressure in the cooling system by slowly turning the pressure relief cap one half to one turn counterclockwise to the first stop on the filler neck. When the pressure has been released, remove the pressure relief cap.

2. Remove the 7 bolts, 3 pin-type retainers and the front splash shield.
3. Place a suitable container below the radiator draincock. Open the radiator draincock and drain the coolant.
4. Close the radiator draincock.
5. Install the front splash shield, 3 pin-type retainers and the 7 bolts, when the cooling system or engine service is finished.

FILLING AND BLEEDING WITH RADIATOR REFILLER

See Figure 50.

1. Install the RADIATOR REFILLER and follow the manufacturer's instructions to fill and bleed the cooling system.
   a. Recommended coolant concentration is 50/50 ethylene glycol to distilled water.
   b. Maximum coolant concentration is 60/40 for cold weather areas.
   c. Minimum coolant concentration is 40/60 for warm weather areas.

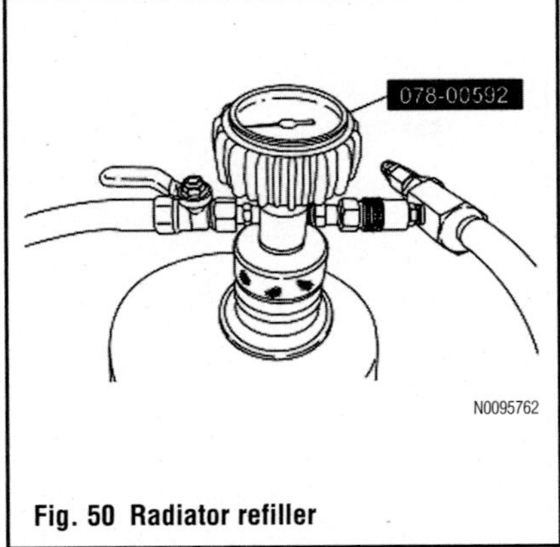

Fig. 50 Radiator refiller

FILLING AND BLEEDING WITHOUT RADIATOR REFILLER

➡Engine coolant provides freeze protection, boil protection, cooling efficiency and corrosion protection to the engine and cooling components. In order to obtain these protections, the engine coolant must be maintained at the correct concentration and fluid level. To maintain the integrity of the coolant and the cooling system:

➡Genuine Mazda® Extended Life Coolant and Motorcraft® Specialty Green Engine Coolant are very sensitive to light. Do NOT allow these products to be exposed to ANY LIGHT for more than a day or two. Extended light exposure causes these products to degrade.

➡Add Motorcraft® Specialty Green Engine Coolant to the cooling system.

➡Do not add alcohol, methanol or brine, or any engine coolants mixed with alcohol or methanol antifreeze. These can cause engine damage from overheating or freezing.

➡Ford Motor Company does NOT recommend the use of recycled engine coolant in vehicles.

➡Stop-leak style pellets/products must not be used as an additive in this engine cooling system. The addition of stop-leak style pellets/products may clog or damage the cooling system, resulting in degraded cooling system performance and/or failure.

1. Open the degas bottle cap and fill the degas bottle to 0.984 inch (25 mm) above the top of the COLD FILL RANGE.
   a. Recommended coolant concentration is 50/50 ethylene glycol to distilled water.
   b. Maximum coolant concentration is 60/40 for cold weather areas.
   c. Minimum coolant concentration is 40/60 for warm weather areas.
2. Close the degas bottle cap.
3. Turn the HVAC system to OFF.
4. Run the engine at 3,500 rpm for 30 seconds.

➡If the engine overheats or the fluid level drops below the top of the COLD FILL RANGE, shut off the engine and add fluid to 0.984 inch (25 mm) above the top of the COLD FILL RANGE once the engine cools.

5. Turn the engine off for 1 minute to purge any large air pockets.
6. Start the engine and let idle until the engine reaches normal operating temperature and the thermostat is fully open. A fully open thermostat can be verified by the radiator fan cycling on at least once.
7. Run the engine at 3,500 rpm for 30 seconds.
8. Run the engine at idle for 30 seconds.

➡If the engine overheats or the fluid level drops below the top of the COLD FILL RANGE, shut off the engine and add fluid to 0.984 inch (25 mm) above the top of the COLD FILL RANGE once the engine cools.

9. Turn the engine off for 1 minute.
10. Repeat Steps 7 through 9 a total of 10 times to remove any remaining air trapped in the system.

CAUTION

Always allow the engine to cool before opening the cooling system. Do not unscrew the coolant pressure relief cap when the engine is operating or the cooling system is hot. The cooling system is under pressure; steam and hot liquid can come out forcefully when the cap is loosened slightly. Failure to follow these instructions may result in serious personal injury.

11. Check the engine coolant level in the degas bottle and fill to 0.984 inch (25 mm) above the top of the COLD FILL RANGE when warm or to the top of the COLD FILL RANGE line when cold.
12. Install the degas bottle cap to at least one audible "click."

ENGINE FAN

REMOVAL & INSTALLATION

3.5L Engine, Except Turbo

See Figure 51.

1. With the vehicle in NEUTRAL, position it on a hoist.
2. Remove the Air Cleaner (ACL) assembly as outlined in the Engine Mechanical Section.
3. If equipped, detach the block heater wiring harness retainers from the engine wiring harness.
4. Disconnect the cooling fan motor electrical connector and detach the all the wiring harness retainers from the shroud.
5. Detach the 2 wiring harness retainers from the radiator support.
6. Detach the hood release cable retainer from the cooling fan motor and shroud.
7. Detach the upper radiator hose from the cooling fan motor and shroud.
8. Release the tab through the access hole and remove the upper radiator hose support.
9. Remove the 2 bolts and the cooling fan motor and shroud.

To install:

10. Install the 2 bolts and the cooling fan motor and shroud. Tighten the bolts to 53 inch lbs. (6 Nm).
11. Engage the tab through the access hole and install the upper radiator hose support.
12. Attach the upper radiator hose from the cooling fan motor and shroud.
13. Attach the hood release cable retainer from the cooling fan motor and shroud.
14. Attach the 2 wiring harness retainers from the radiator support.
15. Connect the cooling fan motor electrical connector and detach the all the wiring harness retainers to the shroud.
16. If equipped, attach the block heater wiring harness retainers to the engine wiring harness.
17. Install the Air Cleaner (ACL) assembly as outlined in the Engine Mechanical Section.
18. With the vehicle in NEUTRAL, lower from hoist.

3.5L Turbo Engine

See Figures 52 through 54.

➡Whenever turbocharger air intake system components are removed, always cover open ports to protect from

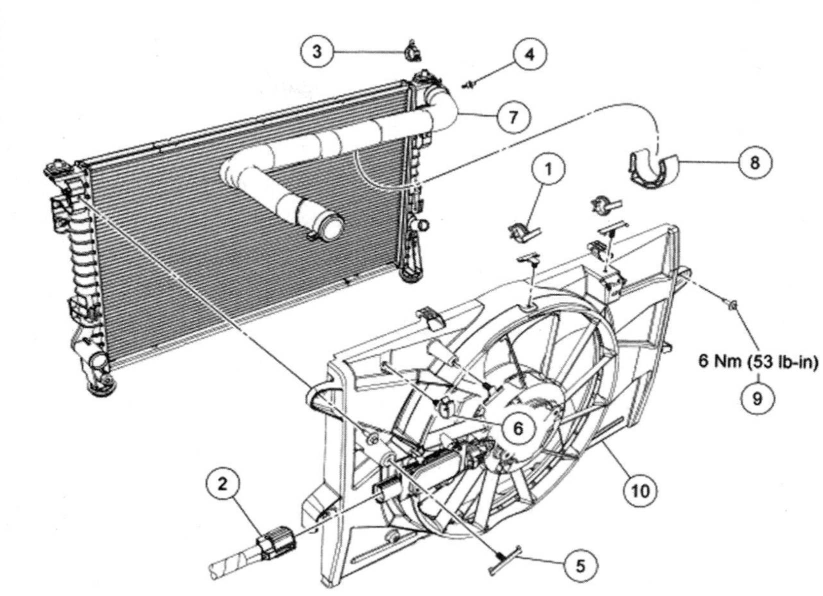

Fig. 51 Cooling fan motor and shroud—3.5L engine, except Turbo

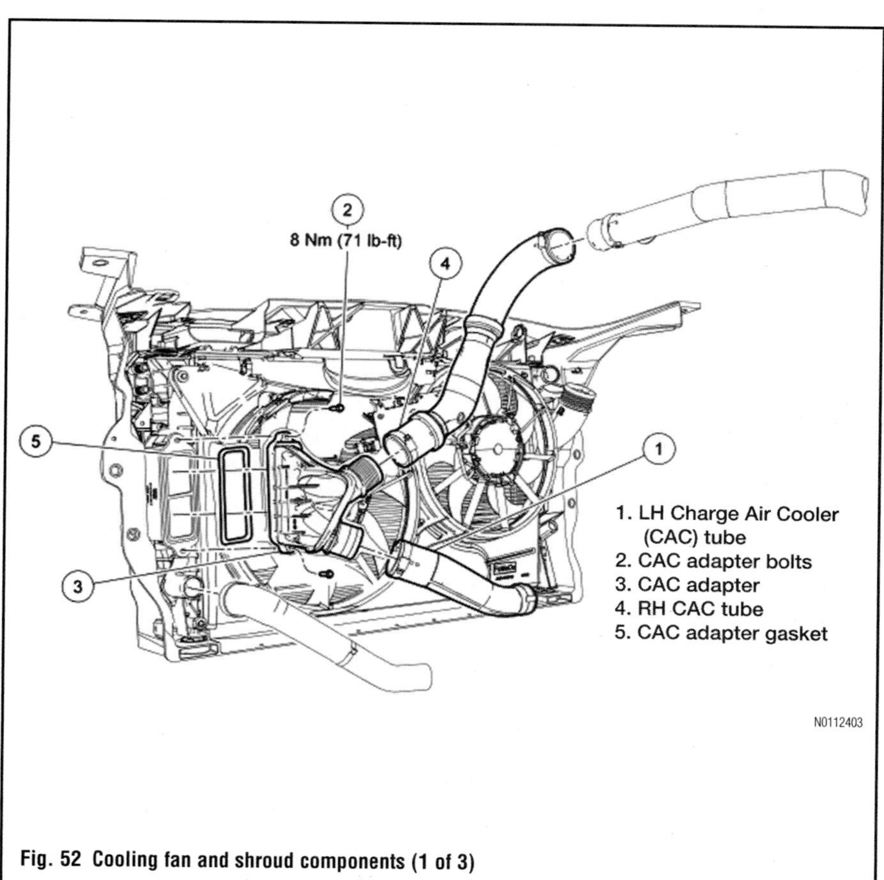

Fig. 52 Cooling fan and shroud components (1 of 3)

debris. It is important that no foreign material enter the system. The turbocharger compressor vanes are susceptible to damage from even small particles. All components should be inspected and cleaned, if necessary, prior to installation or reassembly.

1. With the vehicle in NEUTRAL, position it on a hoist. For additional information, refer to Jacking and Lifting.
2. Disconnect the cooling fan motor electrical connector.
3. Remove the 4 retainers and the underbody shield.

➡Index-mark the LH Charge Air Cooler (CAC) tube position for reference during installation.

4. Working from below disconnect the LH CAC tube from the CAC adapter.
5. Remove the lower bolt from the CAC adapter.
6. Detach the lower radiator hose retainer from the cooling fan and shroud.
7. Remove the Air Cleaner (ACL) assembly and ACL outlet pipe as outlined in the Engine Mechanical Section.

➡Index-mark the RH CAC tube position for reference during installation.

8. Remove the RH CAC.
9. Remove the upper bolt and the CAC adapter.
    a. Inspect and install a new CAC adapter gasket, if necessary.
10. Disconnect the crankcase vent tube quick connect coupling and remove the crankcase vent tube.
11. If equipped, detach the block heater wiring harness retainers from the engine wiring harness.
12. Detach all the wiring harness retainers from the cooling fan and shroud and radiator grille support.
13. Disconnect the LH Heated Oxygen Sensor (HO2S) electrical connector.
    a. Detach the HO2S connector retainer from the bracket.
14. Remove the 2 bolts and the cooling fan motor and shroud.

To install:

15. Install the cooling fan motor and shroud and the 2 bolts. Tighten the bolts to 53 inch lbs. (6 Nm).
16. Connect the LH HO2S electrical connector.
    a. Attach the HO2S connector retainer to the bracket.
17. Attach all the wiring harness retainers to the cooling fan and shroud and radiator grille support.

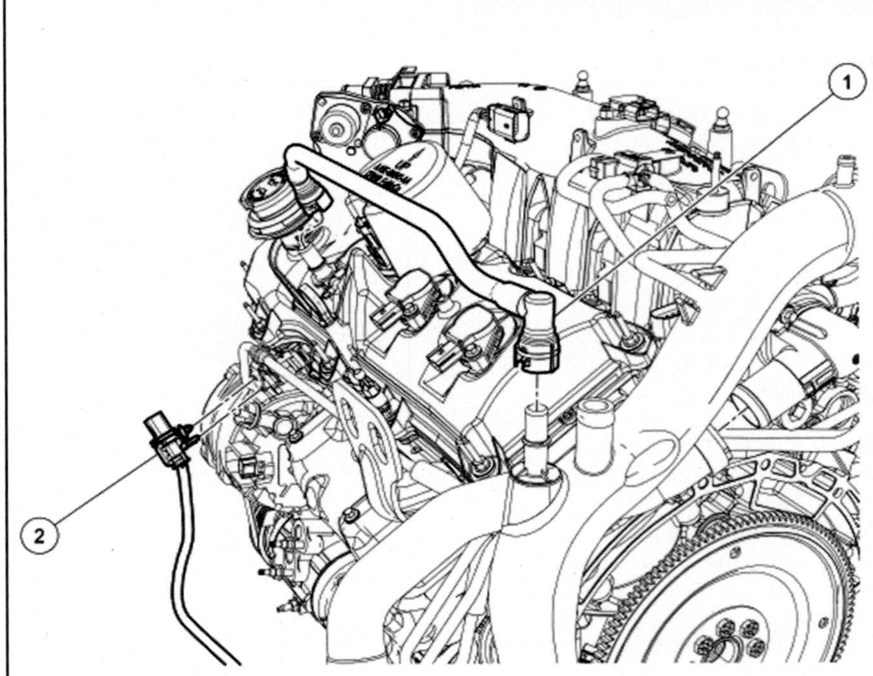

Fig. 53 Cooling fan and shroud components (2 of 3)

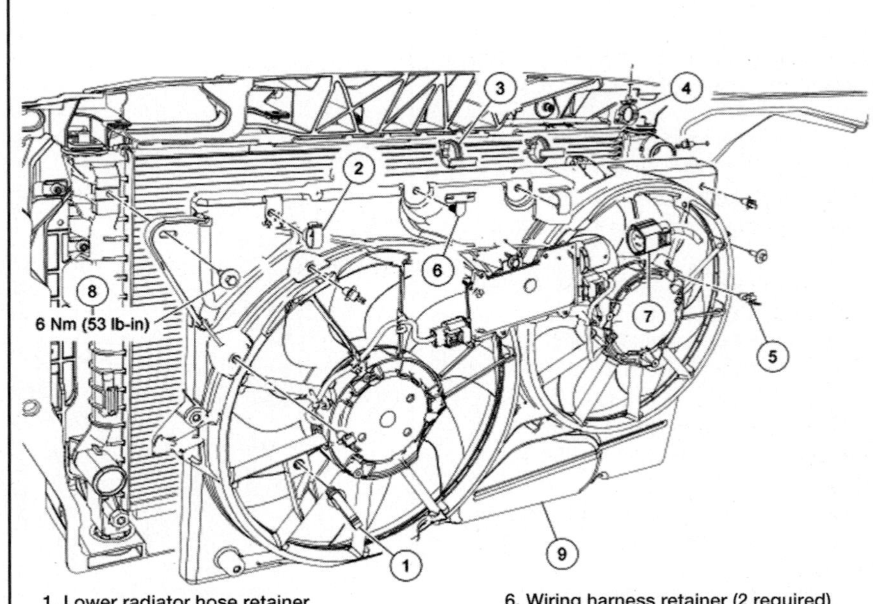

Fig. 54 Cooling fan and shroud components (3 of 3)

18. If equipped, attach the block heater wiring harness retainers to the engine wiring harness.

19. Install the crankcase vent tube quick connect coupling.

20. Install the CAC adapter gasket, adapter and the upper bolt.

a. Do not tighten the bolt at this time.

21. Install the lower bolt for the CAC adapter. Tighten the bolt to 71 inch lbs. (8 Nm).

22. Tighten the upper CAC adapter bolt. Tighten the bolt to 71 inch lbs. (8 Nm).

➡Align the marks for the RH CAC tube.

23. Install the RH CAC tube. Tighten the tube to 44 inch lbs. (5 Nm).

24. Install the ACL outlet pipe and ACL assembly as outlined in the Engine Mechanical Section.

25. Attach the lower radiator hose retainer to the cooling fan and shroud.

➡Align the marks for the LH CAC tube.

26. Connect the LH CAC tube to the CAC adapter. Tighten the tube to 44 inch lbs. (5 Nm).

27. Install the underbody shield and the 4 retainers.

28. Connect the cooling fan motor electrical connector.

RADIATOR

REMOVAL & INSTALLATION

3.5L Engine, Except Turbo

See Figures 55 and 56.

1. Drain the cooling system as outlined in this section.

2. Remove the cooling fan motor and shroud as outlined in this section.

3. Remove the front bumper cover.

4. Disconnect the upper radiator hose and lower degas bottle hose from the radiator.

5. Disconnect the lower radiator hose from the radiator.

6. Remove the 2 radiator support brackets bolts and position the radiator toward the engine.

7. Remove the 2 A/C condenser bolts from the radiator and separate the condenser from the radiator.

➡Make sure the bottom radiator insulators are in place when installing the radiator.

8. Remove the radiator.

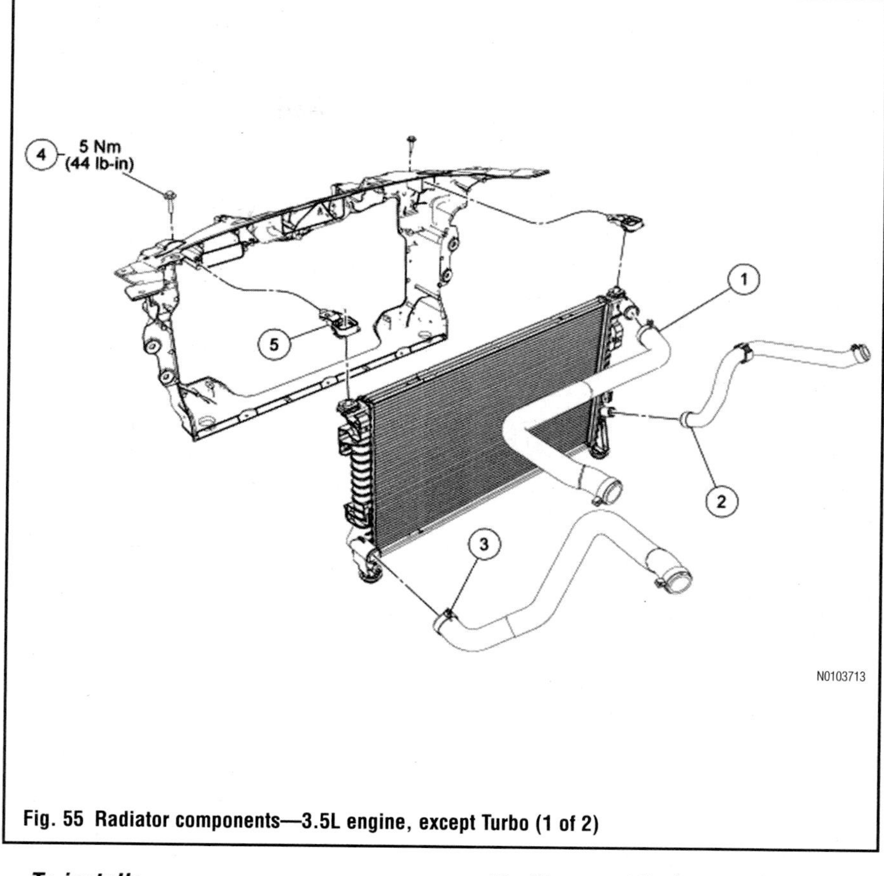

Fig. 55 Radiator components—3.5L engine, except Turbo (1 of 2)

To install:

➡Make sure the bottom radiator insulators are in place when installing the radiator.

9. Install the radiator.

10. Install the 2 A/C condenser bolts to the radiator and separate the condenser to the radiator. Tighten the bolts to 53 inch lbs. (6 Nm).

11. Install the 2 radiator support brackets bolts and position the radiator toward the engine. Tighten the bolts to 44 inch lbs. (5 Nm).

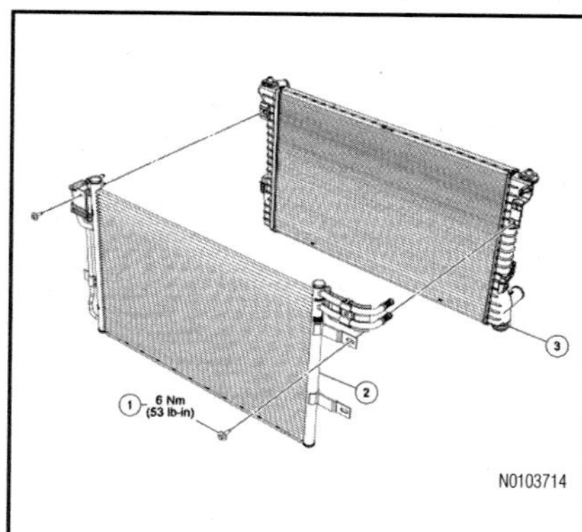

Fig. 56 Radiator components—3.5L engine, except Turbo (2 of 2)

12. Disconnect the lower radiator hose from the radiator.

13. Disconnect the upper radiator hose and lower degas bottle hose from the radiator.

14. Remove the front bumper cover.

15. Remove the cooling fan motor and shroud as outlined in this section.

16. Drain the cooling system as outlined in this section.

17. Fill and bleed the cooling system as outlined in this section.

3.5L Turbo Engine

See Figures 57 through 60.

➡Whenever turbocharger air intake system components are removed, always cover open ports to protect from debris. It is important that no foreign material enter the system. The turbocharger compressor vanes are susceptible to damage from even small particles. All components should be inspected and cleaned, if necessary, prior to installation or reassembly.

1. Drain the cooling system as outlined in this section.

2. Remove the cooling fan motor and shroud as outlined in this section.

3. Remove the front bumper cover.
4. Remove the noise generator as outlined in the Engine Mechanical Section.
5. Disconnect the Turbocharger Boost Pressure (TCBP)/Charge Air Cooler Temperature (CACT) sensor electrical connector.

➡**Index-mark the Charge Air Cooler (CAC) outlet pipe position for reference during installation.**

6. Remove the CAC outlet pipe.
7. Disconnect the lower radiator hose from the radiator.
8. Disconnect the upper radiator hose and lower degas bottle hose from the radiator.
9. Detach the 4 radiator grille air deflector pin-type retainers and remove the RH and LH radiator grille air deflectors.
10. Remove the 2 A/C condenser bolts from the CAC and separate the A/C condenser from the CAC.
11. Remove the 2 radiator support bracket bolts and position the radiator toward the engine.
12. Remove the 2 bolts and separate the CAC from the radiator.

➡**Make sure the bottom radiator insulators are in place when installing the radiator.**

13. Remove the radiator.

To install:

➡**Make sure the bottom radiator insulators are in place when installing the radiator.**

14. Install the radiator.
15. Install the 2 bolts and separate the CAC to the radiator. Tighten the bolts to 53 inch lbs. (6 Nm).
16. Install the 2 radiator support bracket bolts and position the radiator away from the engine. Tighten the bolts to 44 inch lbs. (5 Nm).
17. Install the 2 A/C condenser bolts to the CAC and separate the A/C condenser to

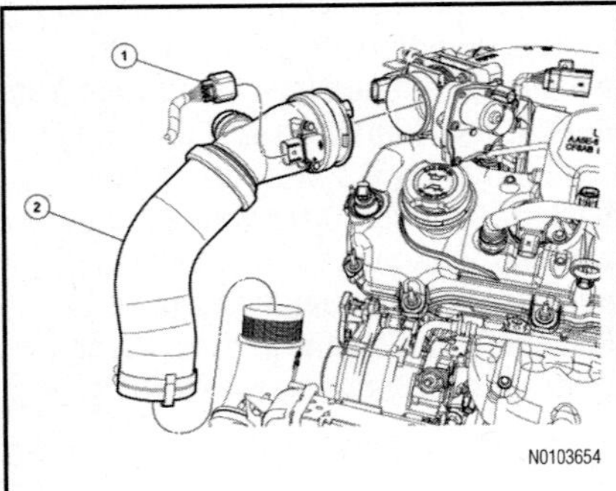

Fig. 57 Radiator components—3.5L Turbo (1 of 4)

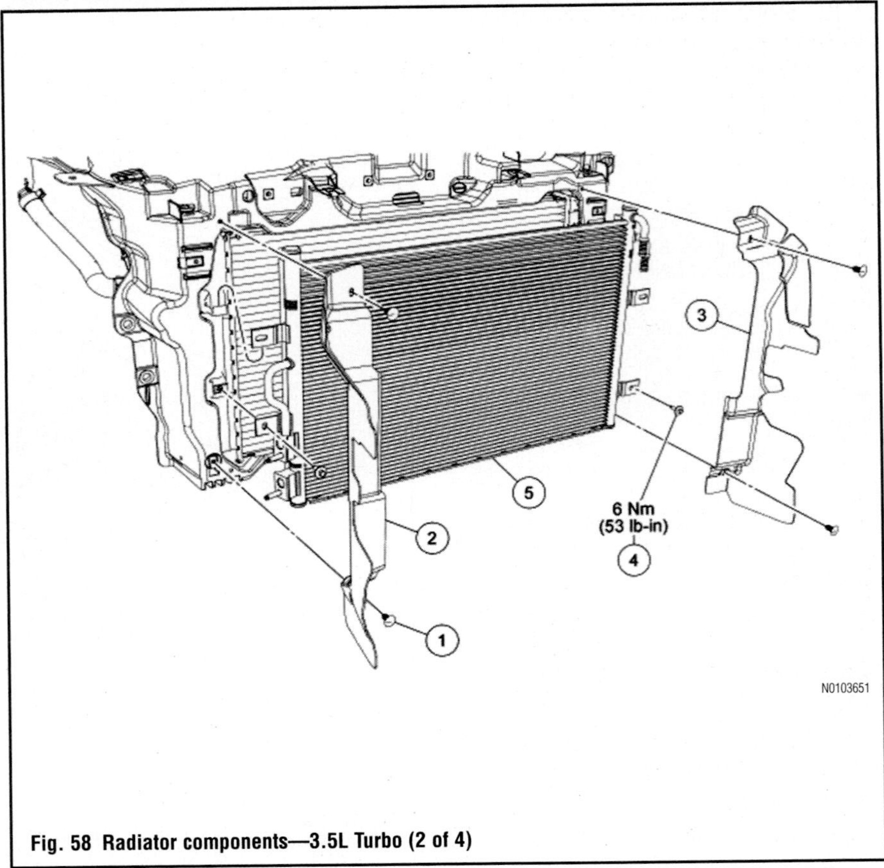

Fig. 58 Radiator components—3.5L Turbo (2 of 4)

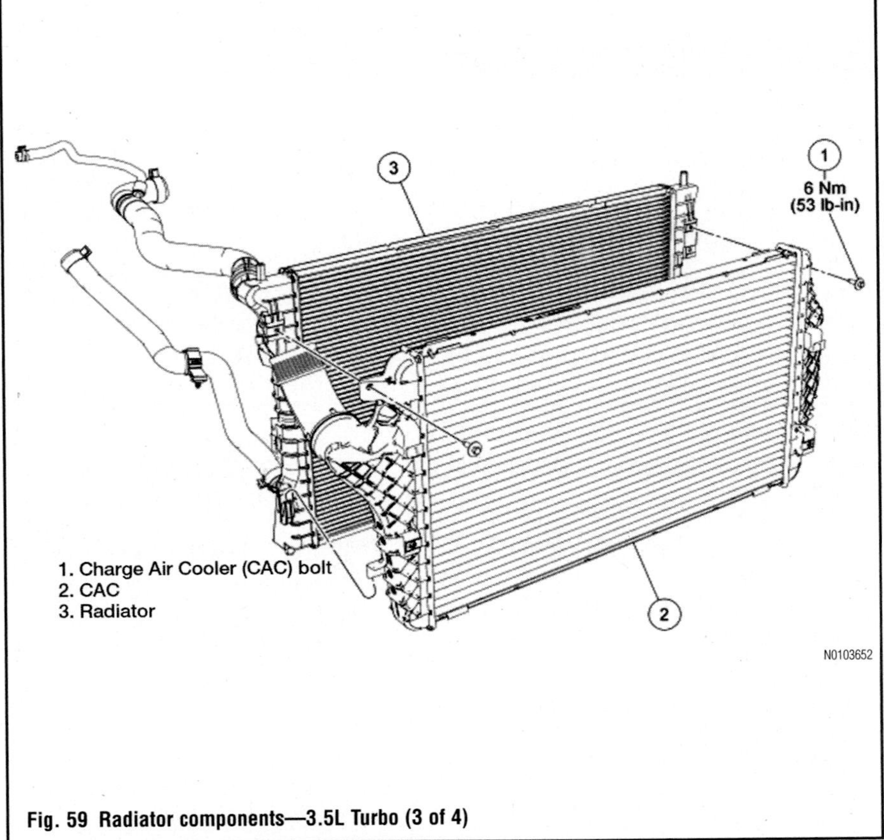

Fig. 59 Radiator components—3.5L Turbo (3 of 4)

the CAC. Tighten the bolts to 53 inch lbs. (6 Nm).

18. Attach the 4 radiator grille air deflector pin-type retainers and install the RH and LH radiator grille air deflectors.

19. Connect the upper radiator hose and lower degas bottle hose to the radiator.

20. Connect the lower radiator hose to the radiator.

➡Index-mark the Charge Air Cooler (CAC) outlet pipe position for reference during installation.

21. Install the CAC outlet pipe. Tighten the outlet pipe to 44 inch lbs. (5 Nm).

22. Connect the Turbocharger Boost Pressure (TCBP)/Charge Air Cooler Temperature (CACT) sensor electrical connector.

23. Install the noise generator as outlined in the Engine Mechanical Section.

24. Install the front bumper cover.

25. Install the cooling fan motor and shroud as outlined in this section.

26. Fill the cooling system as outlined in this section.

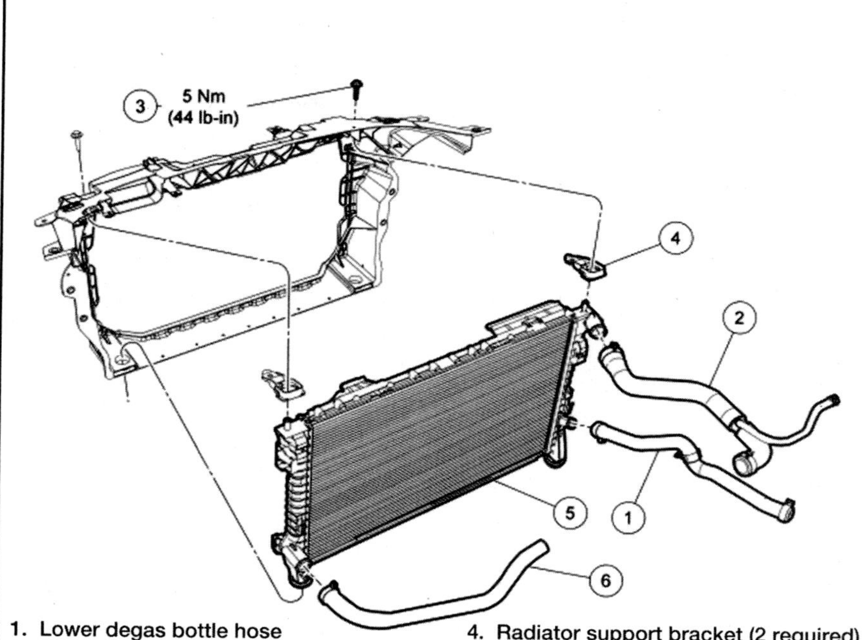

Fig. 60 Radiator components—3.5L Turbo (4 of 4)

THERMOSTAT

REMOVAL & INSTALLATION

See Figure 61.

1. Drain the cooling system as outlined in this section.

2. Remove the engine Air Cleaner (ACL) outlet pipe as outlined in the Engine Mechanical Section.

3. Remove the 2 bolts and position aside the thermostat housing.

   a. On Gasoline Turbocharged Direct Injection (3.5L Turbo) vehicles, clean the bolts and apply Thread Sealant with PTFE before installing the bolts.

4. Remove the O-ring seal and thermostat.

   a. Clean and inspect the O-ring seal. Install a new seal if necessary.

➡Genuine Mazda® Extended Life Coolant and Motorcraft® Specialty Green Engine Coolant are very sensitive to light. Do NOT allow these products to be exposed to ANY LIGHT for more than a day or two. Extended light exposure causes these products to degrade.

➡Lubricate the thermostat O-ring seal with clean engine coolant.

To install:

➡Genuine Mazda® Extended Life Coolant and Motorcraft® Specialty Green Engine Coolant are very sensi-

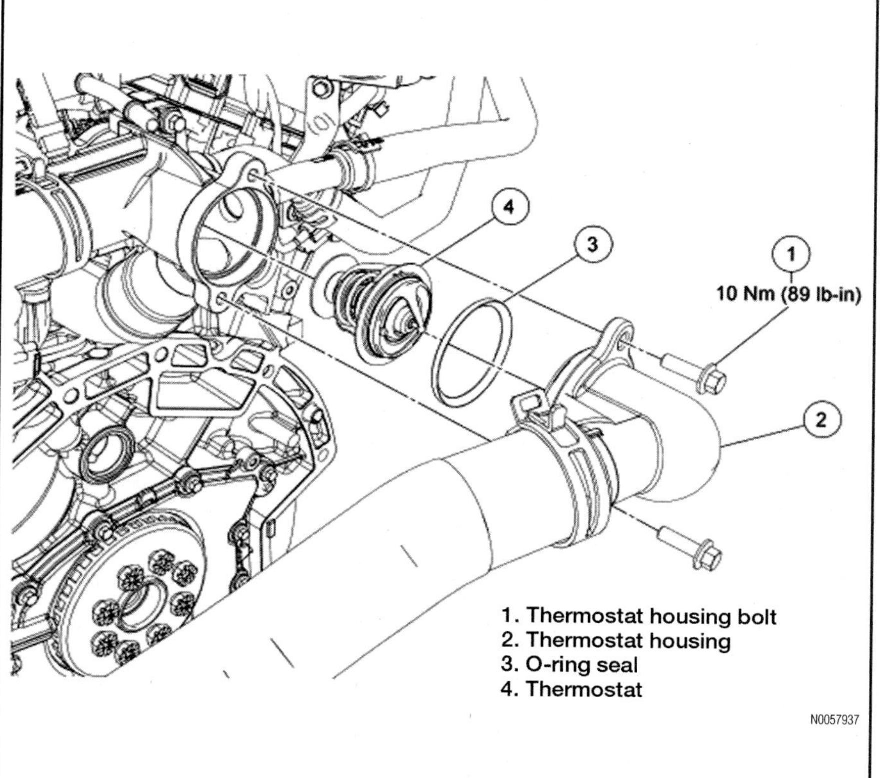

Fig. 61 Thermostat components (3.5L shown, 3.5L Turbo similar)

tive to light. Do NOT allow these products to be exposed to ANY LIGHT for more than a day or two. Extended light exposure causes these products to degrade.

➡Lubricate the thermostat O-ring seal with clean engine coolant.

5. Remove the O-ring seal and thermostat.
   a. Clean and inspect the O-ring seal. Install a new seal if necessary.
6. Remove the 2 bolts and position aside the thermostat housing.
   a. On Gasoline Turbocharged Direct Injection (3.5L Turbo) vehicles, clean the bolts and apply Thread Sealant with PTFE before installing the bolts. Tighten the bolts to 89 inch lbs. (10 Nm).
7. Remove the engine Air Cleaner (ACL) outlet pipe as outlined in the Engine Mechanical Section.
8. Drain the cooling system as outlined in this section.
9. Fill and bleed the cooling system as outlined in this section.

ENGINE ELECTRICAL

CHARGING SYSTEM

ALTERNATOR

REMOVAL & INSTALLATION

See Figure 62.

All Vehicles

1. Disconnect the battery. For additional information, refer to Battery, Mounting and Cables.
2. Remove the engine cover.

3.5L non-Turbo

3. Position the upper radiator hose aside and remove the radiator hose support cradle.
4. Rotate the accessory drive belt tensioner and remove the accessory drive belt from the generator.

3.5L Turbo

5. Remove A/C compressor. For additional information, refer to Climate Control.

All Vehicles

6. Position the generator protective cover aside, remove the B+ nut and position the B+ terminal aside.
7. Disconnect the generator electrical connector and position the harness aside.
8. Remove the upper generator nut and loosen the lower generator bolt completely. Leave the bolt in the generator.
9. Remove the upper generator stud.
10. Remove the generator.

To install:

All Vehicles

11. Position the generator and install the lower generator bolt.
    a. Hand-tighten the bolt at this time.
12. Install the upper generator stud and nut. Tighten the stud to 71 inch lbs. (8 Nm), and the nut to 35 ft. lbs. (47 Nm).
13. Tighten the lower generator bolt to 35 ft. lbs. (47 Nm).
14. Connect the generator electrical connector and install the B+ nut. Tighten the nut to 150 inch lbs. (17 Nm).

3.5L Turbo

15. Install the A/C compressor.

3.5L non-Turbo

16. Rotate the accessory drive belt tensioner and install the accessory drive belt on the generator.
17. Install the upper radiator hose support cradle and reposition the upper radiator hose into the cradle.

All Vehicles

18. Install the engine cover.
19. Connect the battery cable.

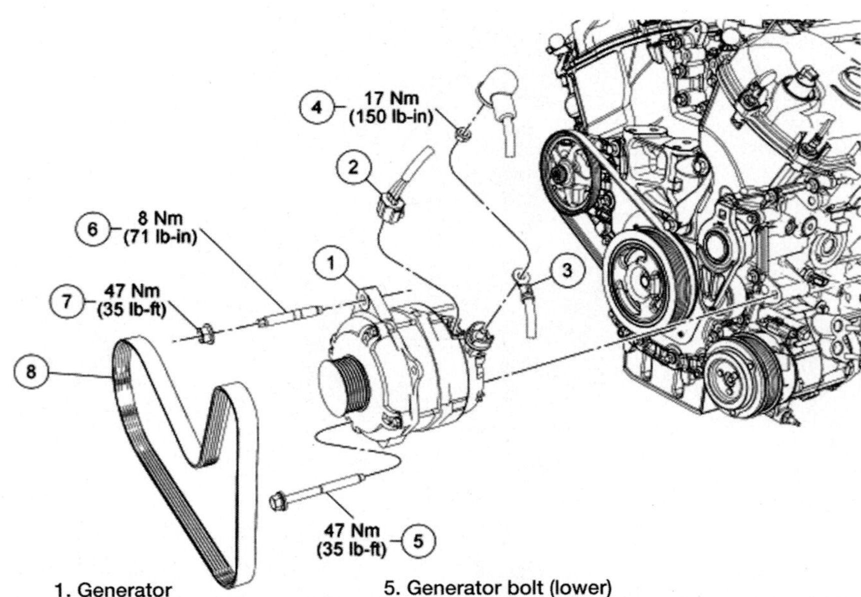

Fig. 62 Alternator components

IGNITION COIL-ON-PLUG

REMOVAL & INSTALLATION

3.5L Engine, Except Turbo

LH Side

1. Disconnect the crankcase ventilation tube-to-valve cover fitting quick connect coupling and position aside.

RH Side

➡The upper intake manifold must be removed to access the RH ignition coil-on-plugs.

2. Remove the upper intake manifold as outlined in the Engine Mechanical Section.

Both Sides

3. Disconnect the 6 ignition coil-on-plug electrical connectors.

➡When removing the ignition coil-on-plugs, a slight twisting motion will break the seal and ease removal.

4. Remove the 6 bolts and the 6 ignition coil-on-plugs.

To install, tighten to 62 inch lbs. (7 Nm).

5. Inspect the coil seals for rips, nicks or tears. Remove and discard any damaged coil seals.
   a. To install, slide the new coil seal onto the coil until it is fully seated at the top of the coil.

To install:

Both Sides

6. Inspect the coil seals for rips, nicks or tears. Install any new coil seals.
   a. To install, slide the new coil seal onto the coil until it is fully seated at the top of the coil.

➡When installing the ignition coil-on-plugs, a slight twisting motion will help ease installation.

7. Install the 6 bolts and the 6 ignition coil-on-plugs. Tighten the bolts to 62 inch lbs. (7 Nm).
8. Connect the 6 ignition coil-on-plug electrical connectors.

RH Side

➡The upper intake manifold must be removed to access the RH ignition coil-on-plugs.

9. Install the upper intake manifold as outlined in the Engine Mechanical Section.

LH Side

10. Connect the crankcase ventilation tube-to-valve cover fitting quick connect coupling and position aside.
11. Apply a small amount of dielectric grease to the inside of the ignition coil-on-plug boots before attaching to the spark plugs.

3.5L Turbo Engine

See Figure 63.

LH Side

1. Remove the fuel injection pump noise insulator shield.
2. Disconnect the crankcase ventilation tube-to-valve cover fitting quick connect coupling.

Both Sides

3. Disconnect the 6 ignition coil-on-plug electrical connectors.

➡When removing the ignition coil-on-plugs, a slight twisting motion will break the seal and ease removal.

4. Remove the 6 bolts and the 6 ignition coil-on-plugs.

To install, tighten to 62 inch lbs. (7 Nm).

5. Inspect the coil seals for rips, nicks or tears. Remove and discard any damaged coil seals.

To install, slide the new coil seal onto the coil until it is fully seated at the top of the coil.

To install:

Both Sides

6. Inspect the coil seals for rips, nicks or tears. Install any new coil seals.
   a. To install, slide the new coil seal onto the coil until it is fully seated at the top of the coil.

➡When installing the ignition coil-on-plugs, a slight twisting motion will ease installation.

7. Install the 6 bolts and the 6 ignition coil-on-plugs. Tighten the bolts to 62 inch lbs. (7 Nm).

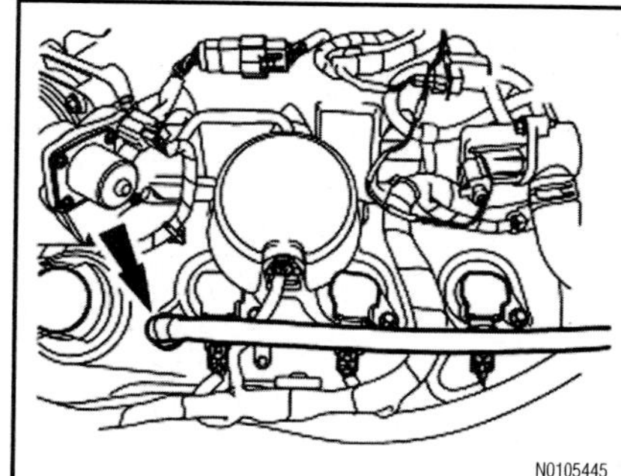

Fig. 63 Crankcase ventilation tube-to-valve cover fitting quick connect coupling

8. Connect the 6 ignition coil-on-plug electrical connectors.

LH Side

9. Connect the crankcase ventilation tube-to-valve cover fitting quick connect coupling.
10. Install the fuel injection pump noise insulator shield.
11. Apply a small amount of dielectric grease to the inside of the ignition coil-on-plug boots before attaching to the spark plugs.

SPARK PLUGS

REMOVAL & INSTALLATION

3.5L Engine, Except Turbo

1. Remove the 6 ignition coil-on-plugs as outlined in this section.

➡Only use hand tools when removing or installing the spark plugs, or damage may occur to the cylinder head or spark plug.

➡Use compressed air to remove any foreign material in the spark plug well before removing the spark plugs.

2. Remove the 6 spark plugs.
3. Inspect the 6 spark plugs.

To install:

4. Inspect the 6 spark plugs.

➡Only use hand tools when removing or installing the spark plugs, or damage may occur to the cylinder head or spark plug.

➡Use compressed air to remove any foreign material in the spark plug well before installing the spark plugs.

5. Install the 6 spark plugs. Tighten the spark plugs to 133 inch lbs. (15 Nm).
6. Install the 6 ignition coil-on-plugs as outlined in this section.
7. Adjust the spark plug gap as necessary to 0.051–0.057 inches.

3.5L Turbo Engine

1. Remove the 6 ignition coil-on-plugs as outlined in this section.

➡Only use hand tools when removing or installing the spark plugs, or damage may occur to the cylinder head or spark plug.

➡Use compressed air to remove any foreign material in the spark plug well before removing the spark plugs.

2. Remove the 6 spark plugs.
3. Inspect the 6 spark plugs.

To install:

4. Inspect the 6 spark plugs.

➡Only use hand tools when removing or installing the spark plugs, or damage may occur to the cylinder head or spark plug.

➡Use compressed air to remove any foreign material in the spark plug well before installing the spark plugs.

5. Install the 6 spark plugs. Tighten the spark plugs to 133 inch lbs. (15 Nm).
6. Install the 6 ignition coil-on-plugs as outlined in this section.
7. Adjust the spark plug gap as necessary to 0.032–0.038 inches.

ENGINE ELECTRICAL — BATTERY SYSTEM

BATTERY

REMOVAL & INSTALLATION

⁂ CAUTION

Batteries contain sulfuric acid and produce explosive gases. Work in a well-ventilated area. Do not allow the battery to come in contact with flames, sparks or burning substances. Avoid contact with skin, eyes or clothing. Shield eyes when working near the battery to protect against possible splashing of acid solution. In case of acid contact with skin or eyes, flush immediately with water for a minimum of 15 minutes, then get prompt medical attention. If acid is swallowed, call a physician immediately. Failure to follow these instructions may result in serious personal injury.

⁂ CAUTION

Always lift a plastic-cased battery with a battery carrier or with hands on opposite corners. Excessive pressure on the battery end walls may cause acid to flow through the vent caps, resulting in personal injury and/or damage to the vehicle or battery.

⁂ CAUTION

When directed to drive the vehicle as part of this test, drive the vehicle on a hard surface in an area without traffic to prevent a crash. Failure to follow these instructions may result in personal injury.

1. Disconnect the battery.
2. Remove the 2 nuts and the battery hold-down clamp.
3. Remove the battery.

To install:

4. Install the battery.
5. Install the 2 nuts and the battery hold-down clamp. Tighten the nuts to 27 inch lbs. (3 Nm).
6. Connect the battery.

ENGINE ELECTRICAL — STARTING SYSTEM

STARTER

REMOVAL & INSTALLATION

See Figures 64 and 65.

⁂ CAUTION

Always disconnect the battery ground cable at the battery before disconnecting the starter motor battery terminal lead. If a tool is shorted at the starter motor battery terminal, the tool can quickly heat enough to cause a skin burn. Failure to follow this instruction may result in serious personal injury.

1. Disconnect the battery ground cable.
2. Remove the Air Cleaner (ACL) outlet pipe and ACL assembly as outlined in the Engine Mechanical Section.
3. Disconnect the transmission shift cable and adjustment lock from the transmission manual control lever.
4. Disconnect the transmission shift cable rotating slide snap and position aside the transmission cable.
5. Remove the nut and the transmission manual control lever.

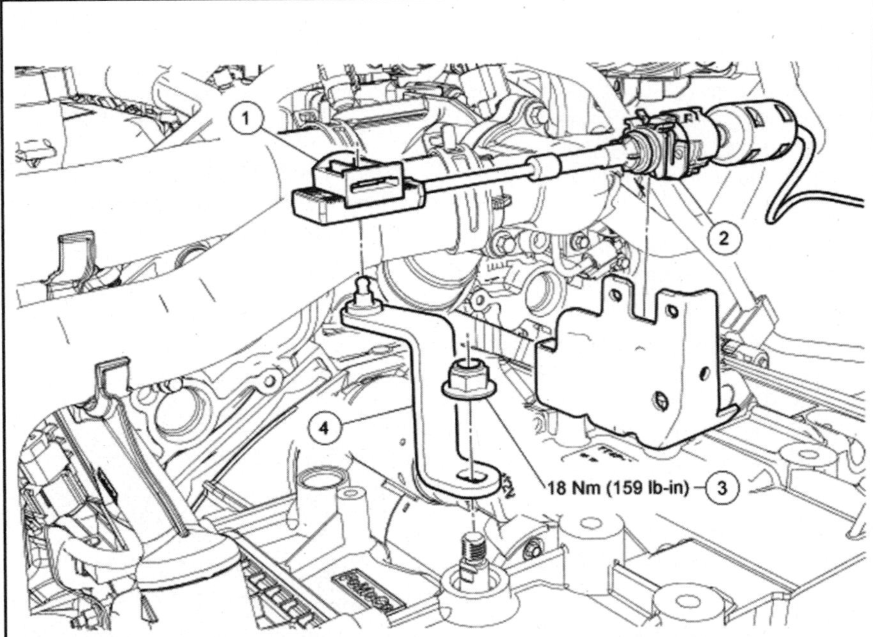

1. Transmission shift cable adjustment lock
2. Transmission shift cable rotating slide snap
3. Transmission manual control lever nut
4. Transmission manual control lever

N0081282

Fig. 64 Starter motor (1 of 2)

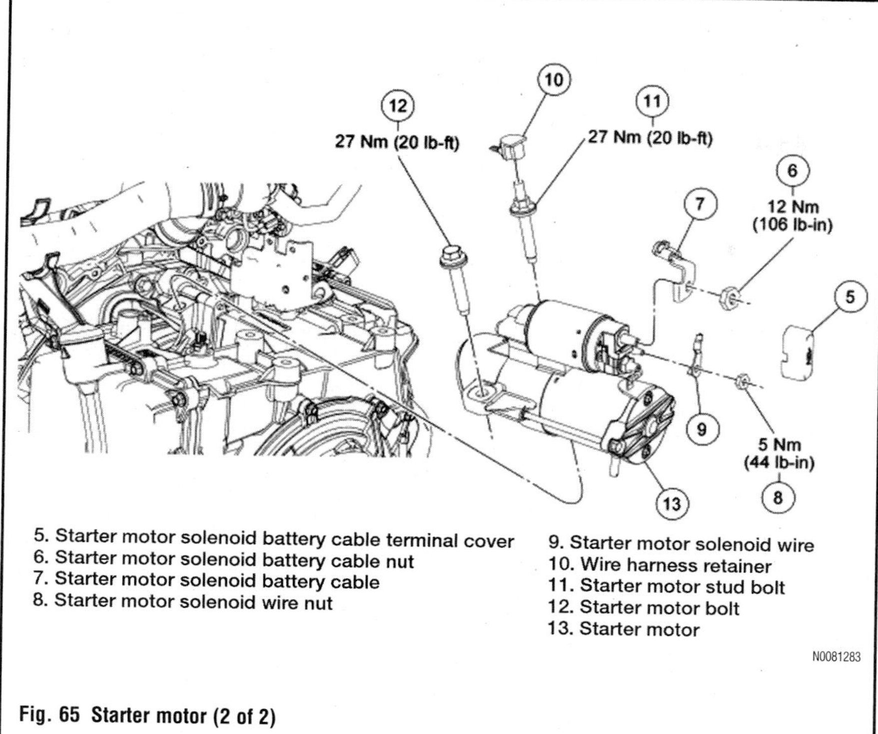

Fig. 65 Starter motor (2 of 2)

6. Remove the starter motor terminal cover.
7. Remove the starter motor solenoid battery cable nut.
8. Remove the starter motor solenoid wire nut.
9. Disconnect the wiring harness retainer from the starter motor stud bolt.
10. Remove the starter motor stud bolt, bolt and the starter motor.

To install:

CAUTION

Always disconnect the battery ground cable at the battery before disconnecting the starter motor battery terminal lead. If a tool is shorted at the starter motor battery terminal, the tool can quickly heat enough to cause a skin burn. Failure to follow this instruction may result in serious personal injury.

11. Install the starter motor stud bolt, bolt and the starter motor. Tighten the bolt to 20 ft. lbs. (27 Nm).
12. Connect the wiring harness retainer to the starter motor stud bolt.
13. Install the starter motor solenoid wire nut. Tighten the nut to 44 inch lbs. (5 Nm).
14. Install the starter motor solenoid battery cable nut. Tighten the nut to 106 inch lbs. (12 Nm).
15. Install the starter motor terminal cover.
16. Install the nut and the transmission manual control lever. Tighten the nut to 159 inch lbs. (18 Nm).
17. Connect the transmission shift cable rotating slide snap and position aside the transmission cable.
18. Connect the transmission shift cable and adjustment lock to the transmission manual control lever.
19. Install the Air Cleaner (ACL) outlet pipe and ACL assembly as outlined in the Engine Mechanical Section.
20. Connect the battery ground cable.

ENGINE MECHANICAL

➡Disconnecting the negative battery cable may interfere with the functions of the on board computer systems and may require the computer to undergo a relearning process, once the negative battery cable is reconnected.

ACCESSORY DRIVE BELTS

ACCESSORY BELT ROUTING

See Figures 66 through 68.

Refer to the accompanying illustrations.

REMOVAL & INSTALLATION

3.5L Engine, Except Turbo

➡Under no circumstances should the accessory drive belt, tensioner or pulleys be lubricated as potential damage to the belt material and tensioner damping mechanism will occur. Do not apply any fluids or belt dressing to the accessory drive belt or pulleys.

1. With the vehicle in NEUTRAL, position it on a hoist.
2. Working from the top of the vehicle, rotate the accessory drive belt tensioner clockwise and remove the accessory drive belt from the generator pulley.

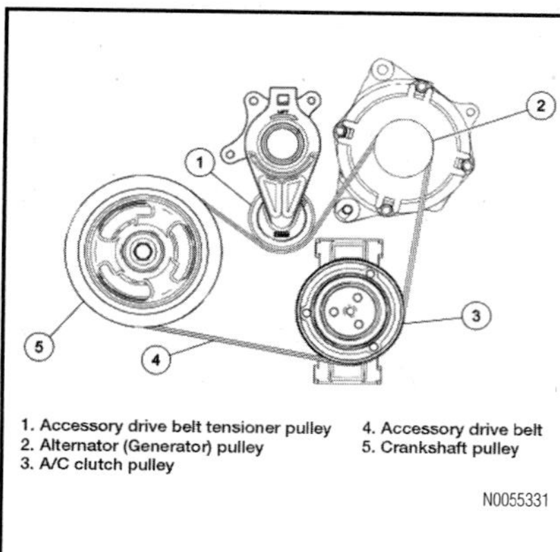

Fig. 66 Accessory drive belt routing

3. Remove the 7 pin-type retainers and the RH splash shield.
4. Working from under the vehicle, remove the accessory drive belt.

To install:

CAUTION

Working from under the vehicle, position the accessory drive belt on all pulleys, with the exception of the generator pulley.

➡After installation, make sure the accessory drive belt is correctly seated on all pulleys.

5. Working from the top of the vehicle, rotate the accessory drive belt tensioner clockwise and install the accessory drive belt on the generator pulley.

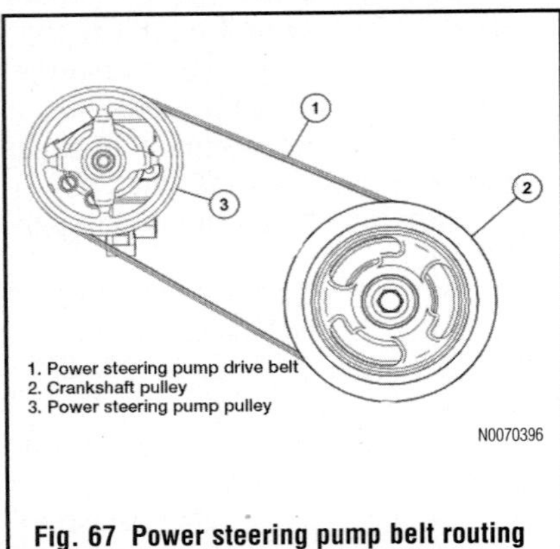

Fig. 67 Power steering pump belt routing

6. Install the RH splash shield and the 7 pin-type retainers.

3.5L Turbo Engine

➡Under no circumstances should the accessory drive belt, tensioner or pulleys be lubricated as potential damage to the belt material and tensioner damping mechanism will occur. Do not apply any fluids or belt dressing to the accessory drive belt or pulleys.

1. With the vehicle in NEUTRAL, position it on a hoist. For additional information, refer to Jacking and Lifting.
2. Remove the RH front wheel and tire.
3. Remove the 7 pin-type retainers and the RH splash shield.
4. Working from under the vehicle, rotate the accessory drive belt tensioner clockwise and remove the accessory drive belt.

To install:

5. Working from under the vehicle, position the accessory drive belt on all pulleys with the exception of the crankshaft pulley.

➡After installation, make sure the accessory drive belt is correctly seated on all pulleys.

6. Rotate the accessory drive belt tensioner clockwise and install the accessory drive belt on the crankshaft pulley.
7. Install the RH splash shield and the 7 pin-type retainers.
8. Install the RH front wheel and tire.

Power Steering Pump Belt

See Figures 69 through 72.

⁂ WARNING

Under no circumstances should the accessory drive belt, tensioner or pulleys be lubricated as potential damage to the belt material and tensioner damping mechanism will occur. Do not apply any fluids or belt dressing to the accessory drive belt or pulleys.

1. Working from the top of the vehicle, rotate the accessory drive belt tensioner clockwise and remove the accessory drive belt from the generator pulley.
2. Remove the RF wheel and tire.
3. Remove the 7 pin-type retainers and the RH splash shield.
4. Position the accessory drive belt off the crankshaft pulley.
5. Position the Stretchy Belt Remover on the power steering pump pulley belt.

➡Feed the Stretchy Belt Remover on to the power steering pump pulley approximately 90 degrees.

6. Turn the crankshaft clockwise and feed the Stretchy Belt Remover evenly on the power steering pump pulley.
7. Remove the power steering pump belt.
   a. Fold the Stretchy Belt Remover under the inside of the power steering pump belt as shown.
   b. In one quick motion, firmly pull the Stretchy Belt Remover out of the RH fender well, removing the coolant pump belt.

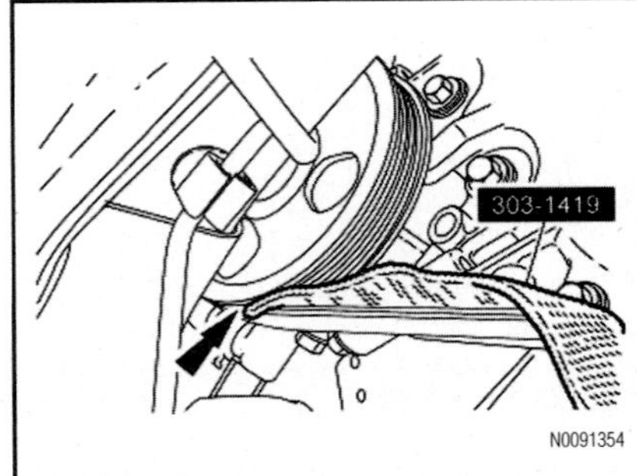

Fig. 69 Position the Stretchy Belt Remover on the power steering pump pulley belt

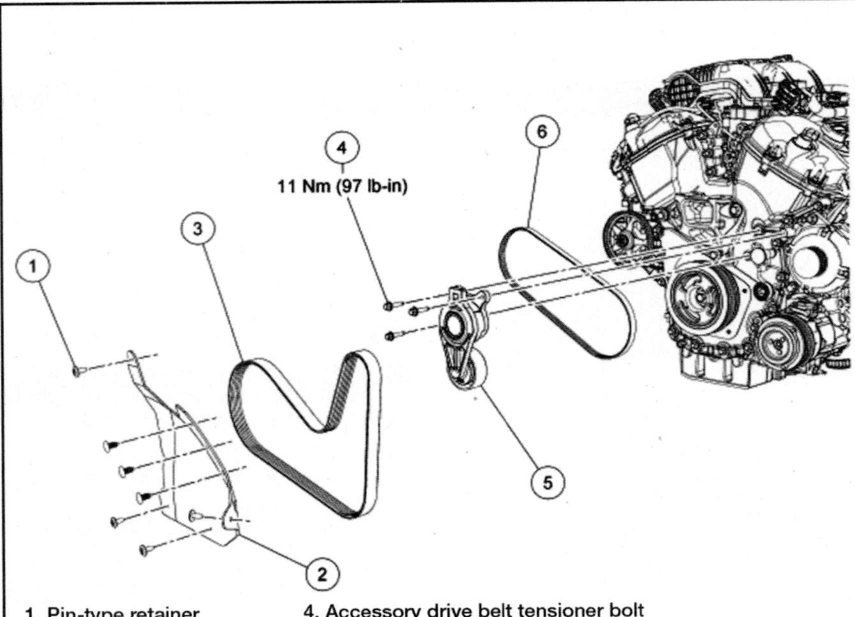

Fig. 68 Front end accessory drive components

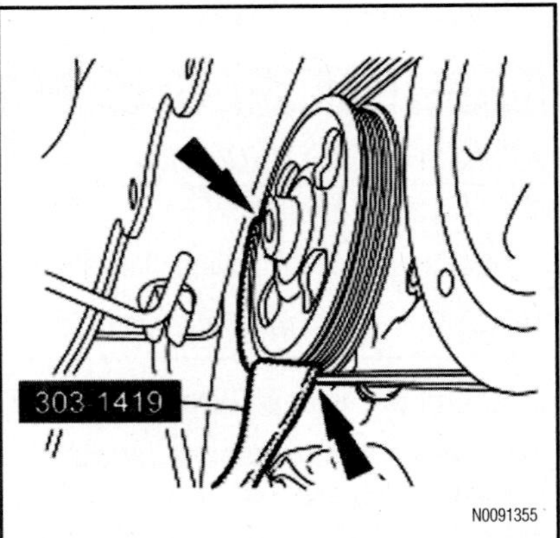

Fig. 70 Turn the crankshaft clockwise and feed the Stretchy Belt Remover evenly on the power steering pump pulley

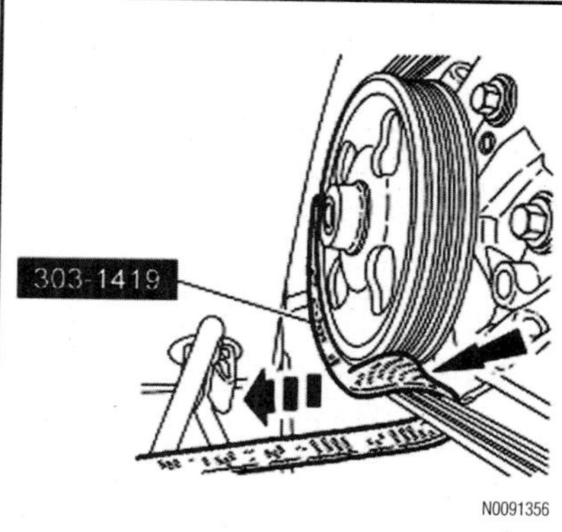

Fig. 71 In one quick motion, firmly pull the Stretchy Belt Remover out of the RH fender well, removing the coolant pump belt

To install:

8. Install the power steering drive belt on the crankshaft pulley.

➡After installation, make sure the power steering drive belt is correctly seated on the crankshaft and power steering pump pulleys.

9. Position the power steering drive belt around the Stretchy Belt Installer Tool and the power steering pump pulley. Make sure the belt is engaged with the power steering pump pulley and rotate the crankshaft clockwise to install the power steering drive belt.
10. Position the accessory drive belt on the crankshaft pulley.

➡After installation, make sure the accessory drive belt is correctly seated on all pulleys.

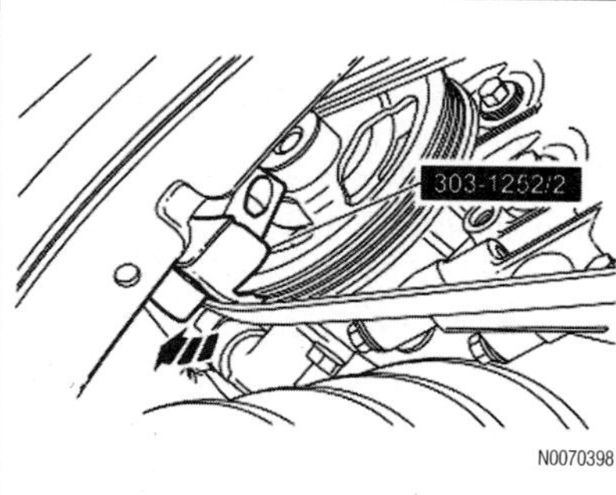

Fig. 72 Position the power steering drive belt around the Stretchy Belt Installer Tool and the power steering pump pulley. Make sure the belt is engaged with the power steering pump pulley and rotate the crankshaft clockwise to install the power steering drive belt

11. Working from the top of the vehicle, rotate the accessory drive belt tensioner clockwise and install the accessory drive belt.
12. Install the RH splash shield and the 7 pin-type retainers.
13. Install the RF tire and wheel.

AIR CLEANER

REMOVAL & INSTALLATION

3.5L Engine, Except Turbo

1. Disconnect the Mass Air Flow (MAF) sensor electrical connector.
2. Loosen the clamp and disconnect the Air Cleaner (ACL) outlet pipe from the ACL.
3. Remove the 2 bolts from the ACL assembly.

➡No tools are required to remove the ACL assembly. Removal should be carried out using hands only.

4. Separate the 2 ACL feet from the rubber grommets and remove the ACL assembly.

➡Make sure that the 2 ACL feet are seated into the rubber grommets under the ACL assembly.

➡The ACL outlet pipe should be securely sealed to prevent unmetered air from entering the engine.

To install:

➡The ACL outlet pipe should be securely sealed to prevent unmetered air from entering the engine.

➡Make sure that the 2 ACL feet are seated into the rubber grommets under the ACL assembly.

➡No tools are required to install the ACL assembly. Installation should be carried out using hands only.

5. Install the 2 ACL feet to the rubber grommets and install the ACL assembly.
6. Install the 2 bolts to the ACL assembly. Tighten the bolts to 44 inch lbs. (5 Nm).
7. Connect the ACL outlet pipe to the ACL and Tighten the clamp. Tighten the clamp to 44 inch lbs. (5 Nm).
8. Connect the Mass Air Flow (MAF) sensor electrical connector.

3.5L Turbo Engine

➡Whenever turbocharger air intake system components are removed, always cover open ports to protect from debris. It is important that no foreign material enter the system. The turbocharger compressor vanes are susceptible to damage from even small particles. All components should be inspected and cleaned, if necessary, prior to installation or reassembly.

1. Disconnect the Intake Air Temperature 2 (IAT2) sensor electrical connector.
2. Release the IAT2 sensor wiring harness pin-type retainer from the Air Cleaner (ACL) cover.
3. Loosen the clamp and disconnect the ACL outlet pipe from the ACL.
4. If equipped, remove the bolt cover.
5. Remove the 2 bolts from the ACL assembly.

➡No tools are required to remove the ACL assembly. Removal should be carried out using hands only.

6. Separate the 2 ACL feet from the rubber grommets and remove the ACL assembly.

➡Make sure that the 2 ACL feet are seated into the rubber grommets under the ACL assembly.

➡The ACL outlet pipe should be securely sealed to prevent unmetered air from entering the engine.

➡Utilize the alignment features to make sure the ACL outlet tube is seated within 2 mm of the stops.

To install:

➡Whenever turbocharger air intake system components are installed, always cover open ports to protect from debris. It is important that no foreign material enter the system. The turbocharger compressor vanes are susceptible to damage from even small particles. All components should be inspected and cleaned, if necessary, prior to installation or reassembly.

➡Utilize the alignment features to make sure the ACL outlet tube is seated within 2 mm of the stops.

➡The ACL outlet pipe should be securely sealed to prevent unmetered air from entering the engine.

➡Make sure that the 2 ACL feet are seated into the rubber grommets under the ACL assembly.

➡No tools are required to install the ACL assembly. Installation should be carried out using hands only.

7. Install the 2 ACL feet from the rubber grommets and install the ACL assembly.

8. Install the 2 bolts from the ACL assembly. Tighten the bolts to 44 inch lbs. (5 Nm).
9. If equipped, install the bolt cover.
10. Connect the ACL outlet pipe to the ACL and Tighten the clamp. Tighten the clamp to 44 inch lbs. (5 Nm).
11. Engage the IAT2 sensor wiring harness pin-type retainer to the Air Cleaner (ACL) cover.
12. Connect the Intake Air Temperature 2 (IAT2) sensor electrical connector.

CAMSHAFT AND VALVE LIFTERS

REMOVAL & INSTALLATION

3.5L Engine, Except Turbo

See Figures 75 through 81.

WARNING

During engine repair procedures, cleanliness is extremely important. Any foreign material, including any material created while cleaning gasket surfaces, that enters the oil passages, coolant passages or the oil pan may cause engine failure.

WARNING

Early build engines have 11 fastener valve covers, late build engines have 9 fastener valve covers. Do not attempt to install bolts in the 2 empty late build valve cover holes or damage to the valve cover will occur.

➡On early build engines, the timing chain rides on the inner side of the RH timing chain guide. Late build engines are equipped with a different design RH timing chain guide that requires the timing chain to ride on the outer side of the RH timing chain guide. For service, all replacement RH timing chain guides will be the late build design.

All Camshafts

1. With the vehicle in NEUTRAL, position it on a hoist.
2. Recover the A/C system.
3. Remove the cowl panel grille.
4. Detach the brake booster vacuum hose retainer from the strut tower brace.
5. Remove the 4 nuts and the strut tower brace.
6. Release the fuel system pressure as outlined in the Fuel System Section.
7. Remove the engine Air Cleaner (ACL) and ACL outlet pipe as outlined in this section.
8. Remove the battery tray.
9. Disconnect the engine wiring harness electrical connector.
10. Remove the nut and disconnect the 2 power feed wires from the positive battery terminal.
11. Remove the nut and disconnect the ground cable from the negative battery terminal.
12. Drain the cooling system as outlined in the Engine Cooling Section.
13. Remove the LF wheel and tire.
14. Remove the accessory drive belt and the power steering belt as outlined in this section.
15. Remove the 3 pushpins, 7 screws and the front valance.
16. Disconnect the power steering cooler tube located at the left front subframe and drain the power steering fluid into a suitable container.
17. Remove the nut and disconnect the A/C tube.
    a. Discard the O-ring seal and gasket seal.
18. Remove the nut and the A/C tube.
    a. Discard the O-ring seal and gasket seal.
19. Remove the degas bottle.
20. Disconnect the vacuum hose and the Evaporative Emission (EVAP) tube from the upper intake manifold.
21. Detach the EVAP tube pin-type retainer from the upper intake manifold.
22. Remove the EVAP canister purge valve as outlined in the Engine Performance & Emission Controls Section.
23. Disconnect the PCM and engine harness electrical connectors.
    a. Detach the wiring harness retainer.
24. Disconnect the 2 PCM electrical connectors.
25. Remove the engine wiring harness retainer from the bulkhead.
    a. Push the wiring harness retainer tab in.
    b. Slide the wiring harness up and out of the bulkhead.
26. Disconnect the upper radiator hose, lower radiator hose and 2 heater hoses from the thermostat housing.
27. Disconnect the transaxle control cable from the control lever.
28. Disconnect the transaxle control cable from the shift cable bracket and detach the wiring harness pin-type retainer.
29. If equipped, detach the engine block heater harness from the radiator support.
30. Disconnect the A/C pressure switch and remove the nut and disconnect the upper A/C tube from the condenser.
    a. Discard the O-ring seal.
31. Disconnect the fuel supply tube from the fuel rail as outlined in the Fuel System Section.
32. Detach the engine wiring harness retainer.
33. Detach the wire harness retainer from the RH valve cover stud bolt.
34. Remove the bolt and the ground cable from the engine.
35. Disconnect the hose from the power steering reservoir.

➡Use a steering wheel holding device (such as Hunter® 28-75-1 or equivalent).

36. Using a suitable holding device, hold the steering wheel in the straight-ahead position.

➡Apply the brake to keep the half-shafts from rotating.

37. Remove the RH and LH halfshaft nuts.
    a. Do not discard at this time.
38. Using the Front Wheel Hub Remover, separate the RH and LH halfshaft from the wheel hubs.
39. Remove the 2 lower scrivets from the rubber shield and position the shield aside.
40. Remove the bolt from the RH brake hose bracket.

WARNING

Do not allow the intermediate shaft to rotate while it is disconnected from the gear or damage to the clock-spring may occur. If there is evidence that the intermediate shaft has rotated, the clockspring must be removed and recentered as outlined in the Chassis Electrical Section.

➡Index-mark the steering column shaft position to the steering gear for reference during installation.

41. Remove the bolt and disconnect the steering column shaft from the steering gear.
    a. Discard the bolt.
42. Remove the 4 Y-pipe-to-catalytic converter nuts.
    a. Discard the nuts.
43. Remove the 2 Y-pipe flange nuts.
    a. Detach the exhaust hanger and remove the Y-pipe.
    b. Discard the gaskets and nuts.

All-Wheel Drive (AWD) Vehicles

➡Index-mark the driveshaft for installation.

44. Remove and discard the 4 bolts and support the driveshaft with a length of mechanic's wire.

All Camshafts

45. Remove the drain plug and drain the engine oil.
   a. Install the drain plug and tighten to 20 ft. lbs. (27 Nm).
46. Remove and discard the engine oil filter.
47. Remove the Power Steering Pressure (PSP) tube bracket-to-steering gear bolt.
48. Remove the bolt, rotate the clamp plate clockwise and disconnect the PSP tube from the steering gear.
   a. Discard the O-ring seal.
49. Remove the 2 rear engine roll restrictor-to-transaxle bolts.
50. Remove the 2 front engine roll restrictor-to-transaxle bolts.
51. Remove and discard the upper stabilizer link nuts.

➡The hex-holding feature can be used to prevent turning of the stud while removing the nuts.

52. Remove and discard the tie-rod end nuts.
   a. Separate the tie-rod ends from the wheel knuckles.

⁂ WARNING

Suspension fasteners are critical parts because they affect performance of vital components and systems and their failure may result in major service expense. New parts must be installed with the same part number or equivalent part, if replacement is necessary. Do not use a replacement part of lesser quality or substitute design. Torque values must be used as specified during reassembly to make sure of correct retention of these parts.

⁂ WARNING

Use care when releasing the lower arm and knuckle into the resting position or damage to the ball joint seal or Constant Velocity (CV) boot may occur.

➡Use the hex-holding feature to prevent the stud from turning while removing the nut.

53. Remove and discard the lower ball joint-to-wheel knuckle nuts.
   a. Separate the lower ball joints from the wheel knuckles.
54. Position the Powertrain Lift under the subframe assembly.
55. Remove the subframe bracket-to-body bolts.
56. Remove the rear subframe bolts and the subframe brackets.
57. Remove the front subframe bolts.
58. Lower the subframe assembly from the vehicle.
59. Pull the RH wheel knuckle outward and rotate it toward the rear of the vehicle.
   a. Secure the RH wheel knuckle assembly.
60. Remove the 2 intermediate shaft bracket nuts.
61. Remove the intermediate and halfshaft assembly.

⁂ WARNING

The sharp edges on the stub shaft splines can slice or puncture the oil seal. Use care when inserting the stub shaft into the transmission or damage to the component may occur.

62. Using the Slide Hammer and Halfshaft Remover, remove the halfshaft from the transmission.
63. Remove and discard the circlip from the stub shaft.
64. Remove the 2 RH halfshaft support bracket studs.
65. Remove the 4 bolts and the RH halfshaft support bracket.
66. Remove the 2 secondary latches from the transmission fluid cooler tubes at the transmission fluid cooler thermal bypass valve.
67. Using the Transmission Cooler Tube Disconnect Tool, disconnect the transmission fluid cooler tubes from the transmission fluid cooler thermal bypass valve.

➡Position a block of wood under the transaxle.

68. Install the Powertrain Lift and Universal Adapter Brackets.
69. Remove the transaxle mount through bolt and nut.
70. Remove the bolt, 3 nuts and the transaxle mount bracket.
71. Remove the nut, bolt and engine mount brace.
72. Remove the 4 engine mount nuts.
73. Remove the 3 bolts and the engine mount.
74. Lower the engine and transaxle assembly from the vehicle.
75. Disconnect the PCV hose from the PCV valve.
76. Disconnect the Throttle Body (TB) electrical connector.
77. Detach the wiring harness retainers from the upper intake manifold.
78. Remove the upper intake manifold support bracket bolt.
79. Remove the wire harness pin-type retainer and the fuel tube bracket bolt from the upper intake manifold.

⁂ WARNING

If the engine is repaired or replaced because of upper engine failure, typically including valve or piston damage, check the intake manifold for metal debris. If metal debris is found, install a new intake manifold. Failure to follow these instructions can result in engine damage.

80. Remove the 6 bolts and the upper intake manifold.
   a. Discard the gaskets.
81. Disconnect the RH catalyst monitor electrical connector.
82. Disconnect the RH Variable Camshaft Timing (VCT) solenoid electrical connector.
83. Disconnect the 3RH coil-on-plug electrical connectors.
84. Detach all of the wiring harness retainers from the RH valve cover and stud bolts.
85. Disconnect the LH VCT solenoid electrical connector.
86. Disconnect the 3 LH coil-on-plug electrical connectors.
87. Detach all of the wiring harness retainers from the LH valve cover and stud bolts.
88. Remove the 6 bolts and the 6 coil-on-plug assemblies.
89. Disconnect the PSP switch electrical connector.
90. Remove the PSP tube bracket-to-power steering pump bolt.
91. Remove the nut and the PSP tube bracket from the RH valve cover stud bolt.
92. Remove the 3 bolts and position aside the power steering pump.
93. Remove the 3 bolts and the accessory drive belt tensioner.

Early Build Vehicles

94. Loosen the 11 stud bolts and remove the LH valve cover. Discard the gasket.
95. Loosen the bolt, the 10 stud bolts and remove the RH valve cover. Discard the gasket.

Late Build Vehicles

96. Loosen the 9 stud bolts and remove the LH valve cover. Discard the gasket.
97. Loosen the 9 stud bolts and remove the RH valve cover. Discard the gasket.

All Vehicles

➡VCT solenoid seal removal shown, spark plug tube seal removal similar.

98. Inspect the VCT solenoid seals and the spark plug tube seals. Install new seals if damaged.
   a. Using the VCT Spark Plug Tube Seal Remover and Handle, remove the seal(s).
99. Using the Strap Wrench, remove the crankshaft pulley bolt and washer.
   a. Discard the bolt.
100. Using the 3 Jaw Puller, remove the crankshaft pulley.
101. Using the Oil Seal Remover, remove and discard the crankshaft front seal.
102. Remove the 2 bolts and the engine mount bracket.

➡Only use hand tools to remove the studs.

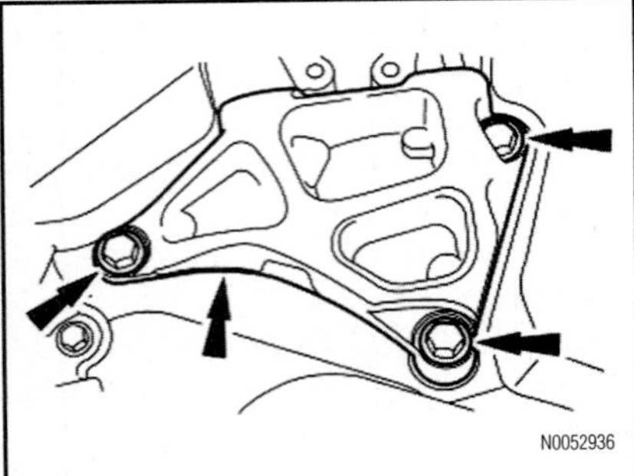

Fig. 73 Removal of the engine mount bracket bolts

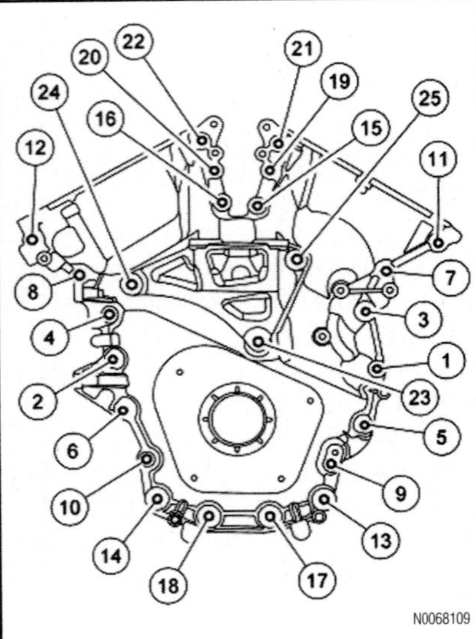

Fig. 74 Removal & installation of the 22 engine front cover bolts and the 3 engine mount bolts

103. Remove the 2 engine mount studs.
104. Remove the 3 bolts and the engine mount bracket.
105. Remove the 22 engine front cover bolts.
106. Install 6 of the engine front cover bolts (finger tight) into the 6 threaded holes in the engine front cover.
   a. Tighten the bolts one turn at a time in a crisscross pattern until the engine front cover-to-cylinder block seal is released.
   b. Remove the engine front cover.

WARNING

Only use a 3M(tm) Roloc® Bristle Disk (2-in white, part number 07528) to clean the engine front cover. Do not use metal scrapers, wire brushes or any other power abrasive disk to clean the engine front cover. These tools cause scratches and gouges that make leak paths.

107. Clean the engine front cover using a 3M® Roloc® Bristle Disk (2-in white, part number 07528) in a suitable tool turning at the recommended speed of 15,000 rpm.
   a. Thoroughly wash the engine front cover to remove any foreign material, including any abrasive particles created during the cleaning process.

WARNING

Place clean, lint-free shop towels over exposed engine cavities. Carefully remove the towels so foreign material is not dropped into the engine. Any foreign material (including any material created while cleaning gasket surfaces) that enters the oil passages or the oil pan, may cause engine failure.

WARNING

Do not use wire brushes, power abrasive discs or 3M® Roloc® Bristle Disk (2-in white, part number 07528) to clean the sealing surfaces. These tools cause scratches and gouges that make leak paths. They also cause contamination that will cause premature engine failure. Remove all traces of sealant, including any sealant from the inner surface of the cylinder block and cylinder head.

108. Clean the sealing surfaces of the cylinder heads, the cylinder block and the oil pan in the following sequence.
   a. Remove any large deposits of silicone or gasket material.
   b. Apply silicone gasket remover and allow to set for several minutes.
   c. Remove the silicone gasket remover. A second application of silicone gasket remover may be required if residual traces of silicone or gasket material remain.
   d. Apply metal surface prep, to remove any remaining traces of oil or coolant and to prepare the surfaces to bond. Do not attempt to make the metal shiny. Some staining of the metal surfaces is normal.
   e. Make sure the 2 locating dowel pins are seated correctly in the cylinder block.

Engines Equipped With Early Build RH Timing Chain Guides

109. Rotate the crankshaft clockwise and align the timing marks on the VCT assemblies.

Engines Equipped With Late Build/Replacement RH Timing Chain Guides

110. Rotate the crankshaft clockwise and align the timing marks on the VCT assemblies as shown.

All Camshafts

➡The Camshaft Holding Tool will hold the camshafts in the Top Dead Center (TDC) position.

111. Install the Camshaft Holding Tool onto the flats of the LH camshafts.

➡The Camshaft Holding Tool will hold the camshafts in the TDC position.

112. Install the Camshaft Holding Tool onto the flats of the RH camshafts.
113. Remove the 3 bolts and the RH VCT housing.
114. Remove the 3 bolts and the LH VCT housing.

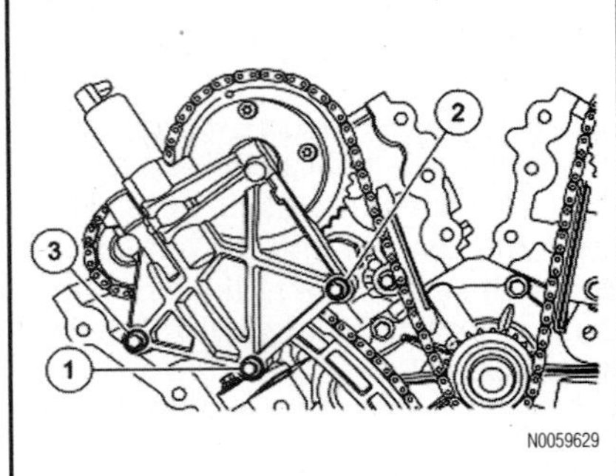

Fig. 75 Removal & installation of the RH VCT housing, and 3 bolts. Tighten in the sequence shown

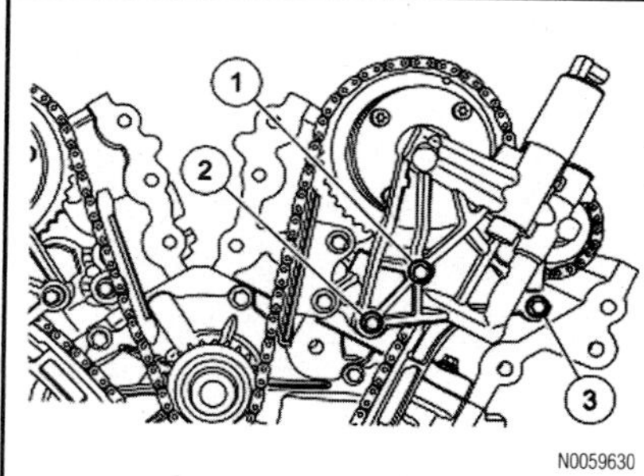

Fig. 76 Removal & installation of the LH VCT housing, and 3 bolts. Tighten in the sequence shown

115. Remove the 2 bolts and the primary timing chain tensioner.

116. Remove the primary timing chain tensioner arm.

117. Remove the 2 bolts and the lower LH primary timing chain guide.

118. Remove the primary timing chain.

LH Camshafts

119. Compress the LH secondary timing chain tensioner and install a suitable lock-pin to retain the tensioner in the collapsed position.

➡The VCT bolt and the exhaust camshaft bolt must be discarded and new ones installed. However, the exhaust camshaft washer is reusable.

120. Remove and discard the LH VCT assembly bolt and the LH exhaust camshaft sprocket bolt.

a. Remove the LH VCT assembly, secondary timing chain and the LH exhaust camshaft sprocket as an assembly.

➡When the Camshaft Holding Tool is removed, valve spring pressure will rotate the LH camshafts approximately 3 degrees to a neutral position.

121. Remove the Camshaft Holding Tool from the LH camshafts.

⁂ WARNING

The camshafts must remain in the neutral position during removal or engine damage may occur.

122. Verify the LH camshafts are in the neutral position.

➡Cylinder head camshaft bearing caps are numbered to verify that they are assembled in their original positions.

123. Remove the bolts and the LH camshaft bearing caps.

a. Remove the LH camshafts.

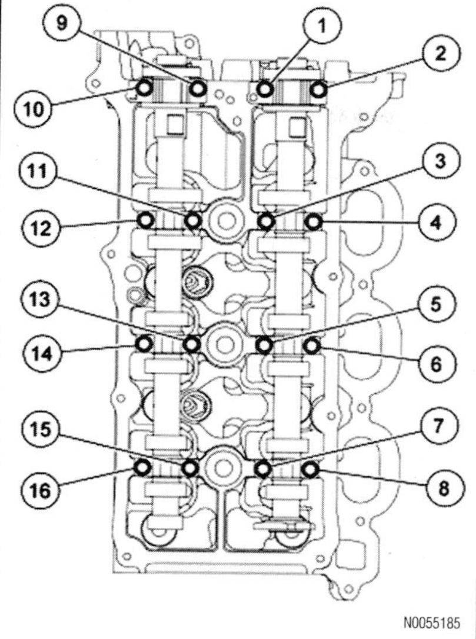

Fig. 77 Removal & installation of the LH camshaft bearing caps (8), and the bolts (16)

RH Camshafts

124. Compress the RH secondary timing chain tensioner and install a suitable lock-pin to retain the tensioner in the collapsed position.

➡The VCT bolt and the exhaust camshaft bolt must be discarded and new ones installed. However, the exhaust camshaft washer is reusable.

125. Remove and discard the RH VCT assembly bolt and the RH exhaust camshaft sprocket bolt.

a. Remove the RH VCT assembly, secondary timing chain and the RH exhaust camshaft sprocket as an assembly.

126. Remove the Camshaft Holding Tool from the RH camshafts.

⁂ WARNING

The camshafts must remain in the neutral position during removal or engine damage may occur.

127. Rotate the RH camshafts counterclockwise to the neutral position.

➡Cylinder head camshaft bearing caps are numbered to verify that they are assembled in their original positions.

128. Remove the bolts and the RH camshaft bearing caps.

a. Remove the RH camshafts.

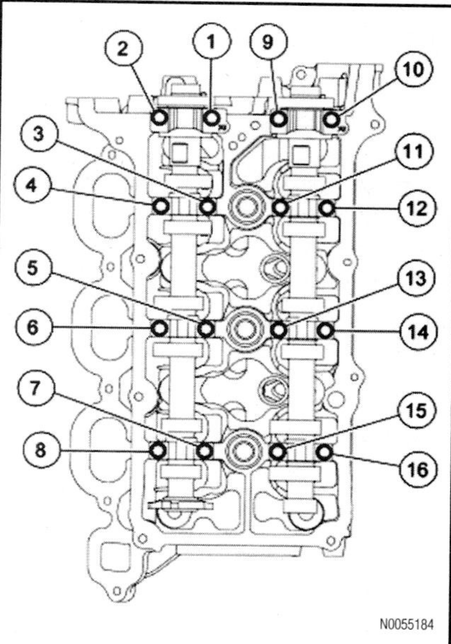

Fig. 78 Removal & installation of the RH camshaft bearing caps (8), and the bolts (16)

To install:

⁂ CAUTION

Do not smoke, carry lighted tobacco or have an open flame of any type when working on or near any fuel-related component. Highly flammable mixtures are always present and may be ignited. Failure to follow these instructions may result in serious personal injury.

⁂ WARNING

During engine repair procedures, cleanliness is extremely important. Any foreign material, including any material created while cleaning gasket surfaces that enters the oil passages, coolant passages or the oil pan, may cause engine failure.

⁂ WARNING

Early build engines have 11 fastener valve covers, late build engines have 9 fastener valve covers. Do not attempt to install bolts in the 2 empty late build valve cover holes or damage to the valve cover will occur.

➡On early build engines, the timing chain rides on the inner side of the RH timing chain guide. Late built engines are equipped with a different design RH timing chain guide that requires the timing chain to ride on the outer side of

the RH timing chain guide. For service, all replacement RH timing chain guides will be the late build design.

All Camshafts

WARNING

The crankshaft must remain in the freewheeling position (crankshaft dowel pin at 9 o'clock) until after the camshafts are installed and the valve clearance is checked/adjusted. Do not turn the crankshaft until instructed to do so. Failure to follow this process will result in severe engine damage.

129. Rotate the crankshaft counterclockwise until the crankshaft dowel pin is in the 9 o'clock position.

LH Camshafts

WARNING

The camshafts must remain in the neutral position during removal or engine damage may occur.

➡Coat the camshafts with clean engine oil prior to installation.

130. Position the camshafts onto the LH cylinder head in the neutral position.

➡Cylinder head camshaft bearing caps are numbered to verify that they are assembled in their original positions.

131. Install the 8 camshaft caps and the 16 bolts. Tighten the bolts to 89 inch lbs. (10 Nm).

RH Camshafts

WARNING

The camshafts must remain in the neutral position during removal or engine damage may occur.

➡Coat the camshafts with clean engine oil prior to installation.

132. Position the camshafts onto the RH cylinder head in the neutral position as shown.

➡Cylinder head camshaft bearing caps are numbered to verify that they are assembled in their original positions.

133. Install the 8 camshaft caps and the 16 bolts. Tighten the bolts to 89 inch lbs. (10 Nm).

All Camshafts

WARNING

If any components are installed new, the engine valve clearance must be checked/adjusted or engine damage may occur.

➡Use a camshaft sprocket bolt to turn the camshafts.

134. Using a feeler gauge, confirm that the valve tappet clearances are within specification. If valve tappet clearances are not within specification, the clearance must be adjusted by installing new valve tappet(s) of the correct size. Refer to Valve Clearance Check in this section.

LH Camshafts

➡Use a camshaft sprocket bolt to turn the camshafts.

135. Rotate the LH camshafts to the Top Dead Center (TDC) position and install the Camshaft Holding Tool on the flats of the camshafts.

136. Assemble the LH Variable Camshaft Timing (VCT) assembly, the LH exhaust camshaft sprocket and the LH secondary timing chain.

a. Align the colored links with the timing marks.

137. Position the LH secondary timing assembly onto the camshafts.

138. Install the new VCT bolt and new exhaust camshaft bolt and the original washer. Tighten in 4 stages.

a. Stage 1: Tighten to 30 ft. lbs. (40 Nm).

b. Stage 2: Loosen one full turn.

c. Stage 3: Tighten to 89 inch lbs. (10 Nm).

d. Stage 4: Tighten 90 degrees.

139. Remove the lockpin from the LH secondary timing chain tensioner.

RH Camshafts

➡Use a camshaft sprocket bolt to turn the camshafts.

140. Rotate the RH camshafts to the TDC position and install the Camshaft Holding Tool on the flats of the camshafts.

141. Assemble the RH VCT assembly, the RH exhaust camshaft sprocket and the RH secondary timing chain.

a. Align the colored links with the timing marks.

142. Position the RH secondary timing assembly onto the camshafts.

143. Install the new VCT bolt and new exhaust camshaft bolt and the original washer. Tighten in 4 stages.

a. Stage 1: Tighten to 30 ft. lbs. (40 Nm).

b. Stage 2: Loosen one full turn.

c. Stage 3: Tighten to 89 inch lbs. (10 Nm).

Fig. 79 Installation of the primary timing chain with the colored links aligned with the timing marks on the VCT assemblies

d. Stage 4: Tighten 90 degrees.

144. Remove the lockpin from the RH secondary timing chain tensioner.

All Camshafts

145. Rotate the crankshaft clockwise 60 degrees to the TDC position (crankshaft dowel pin at 11 o'clock).

146. Install the primary timing chain with the colored links aligned with the timing marks on the VCT assemblies and the crankshaft sprocket.

147. Install the lower LH primary timing chain guide and the 2 bolts. Tighten the bolts to 89 inch lbs. (10 Nm).

148. Install the primary timing chain tensioner arm.

149. Reset the primary timing chain tensioner.

a. Rotate the lever counterclockwise.

b. Using a soft-jawed vise, compress the plunger.

c. Align the hole in the lever with the hole in the tensioner housing.

d. Install a suitable lockpin.

➡It may be necessary to rotate the crankshaft slightly to remove slack from the timing chain and install the tensioner.

150. Install the primary tensioner and the 2 bolts. Tighten the bolts to 89 inch lbs. (10 Nm).

a. Remove the lockpin.

151. As a post-check, verify correct alignment of all timing marks.

152. Inspect the VCT housing seals for damage and replace as necessary.

WARNING

Make sure the dowels on the Variable Camshaft Timing (VCT) housing are fully engaged in the cylinder head

prior to tightening the bolts. Failure to follow this process will result in severe engine damage.

153. Install the LH VCT housing and the 3 bolts. Tighten the bolts to 89 inch lbs. (10 Nm).

WARNING

Make sure the dowels on the Variable Camshaft Timing (VCT) housing are fully engaged in the cylinder head prior to tightening the bolts. Failure to follow this process will result in severe engine damage.

154. Install the RH VCT housing and the 3 bolts. Tighten the bolts to 89 inch lbs. (10 Nm).

155. Install the Alignment Pins.

WARNING

Failure to use Motorcraft® High Performance Engine RTV Silicone may cause the engine oil to foam excessively and result in serious engine damage.

➡The engine front cover and bolts 17, 18, 19 and 20 must be installed within 4 minutes of the initial sealant application. The remainder of the engine front cover bolts and the engine mount bracket bolts must be installed and tighten within 35 minutes of the initial sealant application. If the time limits are exceeded, the sealant must be removed, the sealing area cleaned and sealant reapplied. To clean the sealing area, use silicone gasket remover and metal surface prep. Failure to follow this procedure can cause future oil leakage.

156. Apply a 0.11 inch (3.0 mm) bead of Motorcraft® High Performance Engine RTV Silicone to the engine front cover sealing surfaces including the 3 engine mount bracket bosses.

a. Apply a 5.5 mm (0.21 in) bead of Motorcraft® High Performance Engine RTV Silicone to the oil pan-to-cylinder block joint and the cylinder head-to-cylinder block joint areas of the engine front cover in 5 places as indicated.

➡Make sure the 2 locating dowel pins are seated correctly in the cylinder block.

157. Install the engine front cover and bolts 17, 18, 19 and 20. Tighten the bolts to 27 inch lbs. (3 Nm).

158. Remove the Alignment Pins.

➡Do not tighten the bolts at this time.

159. Install the engine mount bracket and the 3 bolts.

WARNING

Do not expose the Motorcraft® High Performance Engine RTV Silicone to engine oil for at least 90 minutes after installing the engine front cover. Failure to follow this instruction may cause oil leakage.

160. Install the remaining engine front cover bolts. Tighten all of the engine front cover bolts and engine mount bracket bolts in the sequence shown in 2 stages:

a. Stage 1: Tighten bolts 1 thru 22 to 89 inch lbs. (10 Nm) and bolts 23, 24 and 25 to 133 inch lbs. (15 Nm).

b. Stage 2: Tighten bolts 1 thru 22 to 18 ft. lbs. (24 Nm) and bolts 23, 24 and 25 to 55 ft. lbs. (75 Nm).

WARNING

The thread sealer on the engine mount studs (including new engine mount studs if applicable) must be cleaned off with a wire brush and new Threadlock and Sealer applied prior to installing the engine mount studs. Failure to follow this procedure may result in damage to the engine mount studs or engine.

161. Install the engine mount studs in the following sequence.

a. Clean the front cover engine mount stud holes with pressurized air to remove any foreign material.

b. Clean all the thread sealer from the engine mount studs (old and new studs).

c. Apply new Threadlock and Sealer to the engine mount stud threads.

d. Install the 2 engine mount studs. Tighten the stud mounts to 177 inch lbs. (20 Nm).

162. Install the engine mount bracket and the 2 bolts. Tighten the bolts to 18 ft. lbs. (24 Nm).

➡Apply clean engine oil to the crankshaft front seal bore in the engine front cover.

163. Using the Crankshaft Vibration Damper Installer and Front Crankshaft Seal Installer, install a new crankshaft front seal.

➡Lubricate the outside diameter sealing surfaces with clean engine oil.

164. Using the Crankshaft Vibration Damper Installer and Front Cover Oil Seal Installer, install the crankshaft pulley.

165. Using the Strap Wrench, install the crankshaft pulley washer and new bolt and tighten in 4 stages.

a. Stage 1: Tighten to 89 ft. lbs. (120 Nm).

b. Stage 2: Loosen one full turn.

c. Stage 3: Tighten to37 ft. lbs. (50 Nm).

d. Stage 4: Tighten an additional 90 degrees.

166. Install the accessory drive belt tensioner and the 3 bolts. Tighten the bolts to 97 inch lbs. (11 Nm).

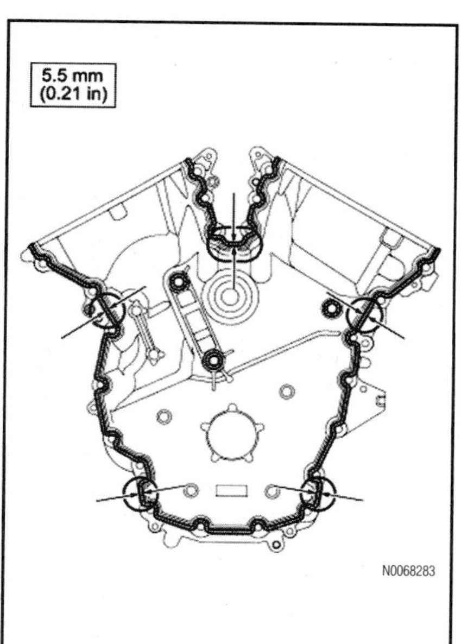

Fig. 80 Engine front cover silicone bead placement

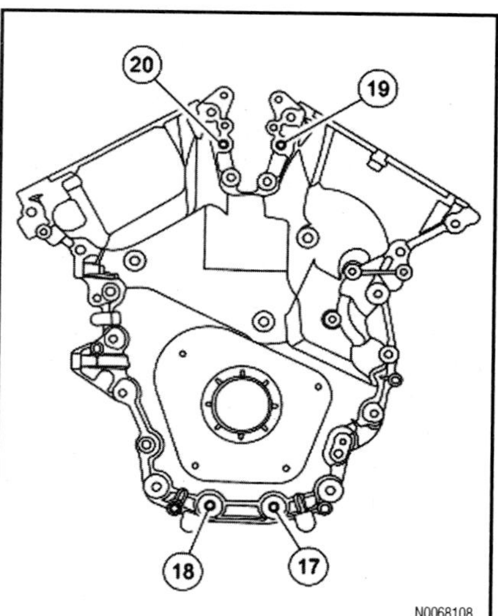

Fig. 81 Install the engine front cover and bolts 17, 18, 19 and 20. Tighten in sequence shown

167. Install the power steering pump and the 3 bolts. Tighten the bolts to 18 ft. lbs. (25 Nm).

➡Installation of new seals is only required if damaged seals were removed during disassembly of the engine.

➡Spark plug tube seal installation shown, VCT seal solenoid installation similar.

168. Using the VCT Spark Plug Tube Seal Installer and Handle, install new VCT solenoid and/or spark plug tube seals.

WARNING

Failure to use Motorcraft® High Performance Engine RTV Silicone may cause the engine oil to foam excessively and result in serious engine damage.

➡If the valve cover is not installed and the fasteners tightened within 4 minutes, the sealant must be removed and the sealing area cleaned. To clean the sealing area, use silicone gasket remover and metal surface prep. Failure to follow this procedure can cause future oil leakage.

169. Apply an 0.31 inch (8 mm) bead of Motorcraft® High Performance Engine RTV Silicone to the engine front cover-to-RH cylinder head joints.

Early Build Vehicles

170. Using a new gasket, install the RH valve cover, bolt and the 10 stud bolts. Tighten the bolts to 89 inch lbs. (10 Nm). Refer to the sequence in the Valve Cover procedure.

Late Build Vehicles

171. Using a new gasket, install the RH valve cover and tighten the 9 stud bolts. Tighten the bolts to 89 inch lbs. (10 Nm). Refer to the sequence in the Valve Cover procedure.

All Vehicles

WARNING

Failure to use Motorcraft® High Performance Engine RTV Silicone may cause the engine oil to foam excessively and result in serious engine damage.

➡If the valve cover is not installed and the fasteners tightened within 4 minutes, the sealant must be removed and the sealing area cleaned. To clean the sealing area, use silicone gasket remover and metal surface prep. Failure to follow this procedure can cause future oil leakage.

172. Apply an 0.31 inch (8 mm) bead of Motorcraft® High Performance Engine RTV Silicone to the engine front cover-to-LH cylinder head joints.

Early Build Vehicles

173. Using a new gasket, install the LH valve cover and 11 stud bolts. Tighten the bolts to 89 inch lbs. (10 Nm).

Late Build Vehicles

174. Using a new gasket, install the LH valve cover tighten the 9 stud bolts. Tighten the bolts to 89 inch lbs. (10 Nm).

All Vehicles

175. Install the PSP tube bracket and nut to the RH valve cover stud bolt. Tighten the bolt to 62 inch lbs. (7 Nm).

176. Install the PSP tube bracket bolt. Tighten the bolt to 89 inch lbs. (10 Nm).

177. Connect the PSP switch electrical connector.

178. Install the 6 coil-on-plug assemblies and the 6 bolts. Tighten the bolts to 62 inch lbs. (7 Nm).

179. Attach all of the wiring harness retainers to the LH valve cover and stud bolts.

180. Connect the 3 LH coil-on-plug electrical connectors.

181. Connect the LH VCT solenoid electrical connector.

182. Attach all of the wiring harness retainers to the RH valve cover and stud bolts.

183. Connect the 3 RH coil-on-plug electrical connectors.

184. Connect the RH VCT solenoid electrical connector.

185. Connect the RH CMS electrical connector.

WARNING

If the engine is repaired or replaced because of upper engine failure, typically including valve or piston damage, check the intake manifold for metal debris. If metal debris is found, install a new intake manifold. Failure to follow these instructions can result in engine damage.

186. Using a new gasket, install the upper intake manifold and the 6 bolts. Tighten the bolts to 89 inch lbs. (10 Nm). Refer to the Intake Manifold procedure for the tightening sequence.

187. Install the fuel tube bracket bolt to the upper intake manifold and install the wiring harness pin-type retainer. Tighten the bolt to 53 inch lbs. (6 Nm).

188. Install the upper intake manifold support bracket bolt. Tighten the bolt to 89 inch lbs. (10 Nm).

189. Attach the wiring harness retainers to the upper intake manifold.

190. Connect the Throttle Body (TB) electrical connector.

191. Connect the PCV hose to the PCV valve.

192. Raise the engine and transaxle assembly into the vehicle.

193. Install the engine mount and the 3 bolts. Tighten the bolts to 66 ft. lbs. (90 Nm).

194. Install the 4 engine mount nuts. Tighten the nuts to 46 ft. lbs. (63 Nm).

195. Install the engine mount brace, the nut and the bolt. Tighten the nut and bolt to 177 inch lbs. (20 Nm).

196. Install the transaxle support insulator bracket, 3 nuts and the bolt. Tighten the nuts to 46 ft. lbs. (63 Nm), and the bolt to 41 ft. lbs. (55 Nm).

197. Install the transaxle support insulator through bolt and nut. Tighten the bolt to 129 ft. lbs. (175 Nm).

All-Wheel Drive (AWD)

➡A new Power Transfer Unit (PTU) seal must be installed whenever the intermediate shaft is removed.

198. Install a new PTU seal as outlined in the Drive Train Section.

All Camshafts

199. Connect the transaxle cooler tubes and install the 2 secondary latches.

200. Install the RH halfshaft support bracket and the 4 bolts.

a. Tighten the halfshaft support-to-cylinder block bolts to 30 ft. lbs. (40 Nm).

b. Tighten the catalytic converter-to-halfshaft support bolts to 177 inch lbs. (20 Nm).

201. Install the 2 halfshaft support bracket studs. Tighten the studs to 89 inch lbs. (10 Nm).

WARNING

The circlips are unique in size and shape for each shaft. Make sure to use the specified circlip for the application or vehicle damage may occur.

202. Install the correct new circlip on the inboard stub shaft.

➡After insertion, pull the halfshaft inner end to make sure the circlip is locked.

203. Push the stub shaft into the transmission so the circlip locks into the differential side gear.

204. Rotate the LH wheel knuckle into position and insert the LH halfshaft into the wheel hub.

205. Install the intermediate and halfshaft assembly and the 2 bolts. Tighten the bolts to 18 ft. lbs. (25 Nm).

206. Rotate the RH wheel knuckle into position and insert the RH halfshaft into the wheel hub.

207. Using the Powertrain Lift, raise the subframe into the installed position.

208. Install the 2 front subframe bolts. Tighten the bolts to 148 ft. lbs. (200 Nm).

209. Position the subframe brackets and install the 4 bolts finger-tight.

210. Install the 2 rear subframe bolts. Tighten the bolts to 111 ft. lbs. (150 Nm).

211. Install the 4 subframe bracket-to-body bolts. Tighten the bolts to 41 ft. lbs. (55 Nm).

212. Position the ball joints into the wheel knuckles. Install the new ball joint nuts. Tighten the nuts to 148 ft. lbs. (200 Nm).

➡The hex-holding feature can be used to prevent turning of the stud while removing the nuts.

213. Install new tie-rod end nuts. Tighten the nuts to 111 ft. lbs. (150 Nm).

214. Install new upper stabilizer bar link nuts. Tighten the nuts to 111 ft. lbs. (150 Nm).

215. Install the 2 front engine roll restrictor-to-transaxle bolts. Tighten the bolts to 66 ft. lbs. (90 Nm).

216. Install the 2 rear engine roll restrictor-to-transaxle bolts. Tighten the bolts to 66 ft. lbs. (90 Nm).

217. Using a new O-ring seal, install the PSP tube onto the steering gear, rotate the clamp plate and install the bolt. Tighten the bolt to 18 ft. lbs. (25 Nm).

218. Install the PSP tube bracket-to-steering gear bolt. Tighten the bolt to 89 inch lbs. (10 Nm).

➡Lubricate the engine oil filter gasket with clean engine oil prior to installing the oil filter.

219. Install a new engine oil filter. Tighten the oil filter to 44 inch lbs. (5 Nm), and then rotate an additional 180 degrees.

AWD Vehicles

220. Line up the index marks on the rear driveshaft to the index marks on the PTU flange made during removal and install the 4 bolts. Tighten the bolts to 52 ft. lbs. (70 Nm).

All Camshafts

221. Using a new gasket, install the Y-pipe and install the 2 new nuts. Tighten the nuts to 30 ft. lbs. (40 Nm).

a. Attach the exhaust hanger.

222. Install the Y-pipe assembly and 4 new nuts. Tighten the nuts to 30 ft. lbs. (40 Nm).

**** WARNING**

Do not allow the intermediate shaft to rotate while it is disconnected from the gear or damage to the clockspring may occur. If there is evidence that the intermediate shaft has rotated, the clockspring must be removed and recentered. Refer to the Chassis Electrical Section.

➡Align the index marks made during removal.

223. Install the steering intermediate shaft onto the steering gear and install a new bolt. Tighten the bolt to 17 ft. lbs. (23 Nm).

224. Position the RH brake hose bracket and install the bolt. Tighten the bolt to 22 ft. lbs. (30 Nm).

225. Position the rubber shield and install the 2 lower scrivets.

**** WARNING**

Do not tighten the wheel hub nut with the vehicle on the ground. The nut must be tightened to specification before the vehicle is lowered onto the wheels. Wheel bearing damage will occur if the wheel bearing is loaded with the weight of the vehicle applied.

➡Apply the brake to keep the halfshaft from rotating.

226. Using the previously removed RH and LH wheel hub nuts, seat the halfshaft. Tighten the nuts to 258 ft. lbs. (350 Nm).

a. Remove and discard the wheel hub nuts.

**** WARNING**

The wheel hub nut contains a one-time locking chemical that is activated by the heat created when it is tightened. Install and tighten the new wheel hub nut to specification within 5 minutes of starting it on the threads. Always install a new wheel hub nut after loosening or when not tightened within the specified time or damage to the components can occur.

➡Apply the brake to keep the halfshaft from rotating.

227. Install a new RH and LH wheel hub nut. Tighten the nut to 258 ft. lbs. (350 Nm).

228. Connect the hose to the power steering reservoir.

229. Install the oil level indicator.

230. Install the ground cable and bolt. Tighten the bolt to 106 inch lbs. (12 Nm).

231. Attach the wire harness retainer to the RH valve cover stud bolt.

232. Attach the engine wiring harness retainer.

233. Connect the fuel supply tube to the fuel rail.

234. Using a new O-ring seal, connect the upper A/C tube to the condenser and install the nut and connect the A/C pressure switch electrical connector. Tighten the nut to 133 inch lbs. (15 Nm).

235. If equipped, attach the block heater wiring harness retainer to the radiator and power steering tube.

236. Connect the transaxle control cable to the shift cable bracket.

237. Connect the transaxle control cable to the control lever.

238. Connect the upper radiator hose, lower radiator hose and heater hose to the thermostat housing.

239. Install the engine wiring harness retainer to the bulkhead.

a. Slide the wiring harness in the bulkhead.

b. Make sure the wiring harness retainer tab is below the bulkhead lip.

240. Connect the 2 PCM electrical connectors.

241. Connect the PCM and engine harness electrical connectors.

a. Attach the wiring harness retainer.

242. Install the Evaporative Emission (EVAP) canister purge valve as outlined in the Engine Performance & Emission Controls Section.

243. Attach the EVAP tube pin-type retainer to the upper intake manifold.

244. Connect the vacuum hose and the EVAP tube to the upper intake manifold.

245. Install the degas bottle.

246. Using a new O-ring seal and gasket seal, install the A/C tube and the nut. Tighten the nut to 133 inch lbs. (15 Nm).

247. Using a new O-ring seal and gasket seal, connect the A/C tube and install the nut. Tighten the nut to 133 inch lbs. (15 Nm).

248. Connect the power steering cooler tube.

249. Install the front valance, 3 pushpins and 7 screws.

250. Install the accessory drive belt and the power steering belt as outlined in this section.

251. Install the LF wheel and tire.

252. Connect the ground cable to the negative battery terminal and install the nut. Tighten the nut to 53 inch lbs. (6 Nm).

253. Connect the power feed wire to the positive battery terminal and install the nut. Tighten the nut to 53 inch lbs. (6 Nm).

254. Connect the engine wiring harness electrical connector.

255. Install the battery tray.

256. Install the engine Air Cleaner (ACL) and ACL outlet pipe as outlined in this section.

257. Install the strut tower brace and the 4 nuts. Tighten the nuts to 26 ft. lbs. (35 Nm).

258. Attach the brake booster vacuum hose retainers to the strut tower brace.

259. Install the cowl panel grille as outlined in the Body and Paint Section.

WARNING

Do not expose the Motorcraft® High Performance Engine RTV Silicone to engine oil for at least 90 minutes after installing the engine front cover. Failure to follow this instruction may cause oil leakage.

260. Fill the engine with clean engine oil.

261. Fill and bleed the cooling system as outlined in the Engine Cooling Section.

262. Fill the power steering system as outlined in the Steering Section.

263. Recharge the A/C system as outlined in the Heating, Ventilation & Air Conditioning Section.

3.5L Turbo Engine

See Figures 82 through 101.

CAUTION

Do not smoke, carry lighted tobacco or have an open flame of any type when working on or near any fuel-related component. Highly flammable mixtures are always present and may be ignited. Failure to follow these instructions may result in serious personal injury.

WARNING

During engine repair procedures, cleanliness is extremely important. Any foreign material, including any material created while cleaning gasket surfaces, that enters the oil passages, coolant passages or the oil pan may cause engine failure.

WARNING

Whenever turbocharger air intake system components are removed, always cover open ports to protect from debris. It is important that no foreign material enter the system. The turbocharger compressor vanes are susceptible to damage from even small particles. All components should be inspected and cleaned, if necessary, prior to installation or reassembly.

➡On early build engines, the timing chain rides on the inner side of the RH timing chain guide. Late build engines are equipped with a different design RH timing chain guide that requires the timing chain to ride on the outer side of the RH timing chain guide. For service, all replacement RH timing chain guides will be the late build design.

All Camshafts

1. With the vehicle in NEUTRAL, position it on a hoist.

➡Use a steering wheel holding device (such as Hunter® 28-75-1 or equivalent).

2. Using a steering wheel holding device, hold the steering wheel in the straight-ahead position.

3. Release the fuel system pressure as outlined in the Fuel System Section.

4. Recover the A/C system as outlined in the Heating, Ventilation & Air conditioning.

5. Disconnect the LH Heated Oxygen Sensor (HO2S) electrical connector.
    a. Detach the HO2S connector retainer from the bracket.

6. Remove the 4 retainers and the underbody shield.

7. Remove the 7 bolts, 3 pin-type retainers and the front splash shield.

8. Drain the cooling system as outlined in the Engine Cooling Section.

9. Remove the front wheels and tires.

10. Remove the 2 lower scrivets from the rubber shield and position the shield aside.

➡Apply the brake to keep the halfshafts from rotating.

11. Remove the RH and LH halfshaft nuts.
    a. Do not discard at this time.

12. Using the Front Wheel Hub Remover, separate the RH and LH halfshaft from the wheel hubs.

13. Remove the bolt from the RH brake hose bracket.

14. Remove the LH and RH catalytic converters as outlined in this section.

15. Remove the 2 rear engine roll restrictor-to-transaxle bolts.

16. Remove the 2 front engine roll restrictor-to-transaxle bolts.

17. Remove and discard the upper stabilizer link nuts.

➡The hex-holding feature can be used to prevent turning of the stud while removing the nut.

18. Remove and discard the tie-rod end nuts.
    a. Separate the tie-rod ends from the wheel knuckles.

WARNING

Suspension fasteners are critical parts because they affect performance of vital components and systems and their failure may result in major service expense. New parts must be installed with the same part number or equivalent part, if replacement is necessary. Do not use a replacement part of lesser quality or substitute design. Torque values must be used as specified during reassembly to make sure of correct retention of these parts.

WARNING

Use care when releasing the lower arm and knuckle into the resting position or damage to the ball joint seal or Constant Velocity (CV) boot may occur.

➡Use the hex-holding feature to prevent the stud from turning while removing the nut.

19. Remove and discard the lower ball joint-to-wheel knuckle nuts.
    a. Separate the lower ball joints from the wheel knuckles.

WARNING

Do not allow the intermediate shaft to rotate while it is disconnected from the gear or damage to the clockspring may occur. If there is evidence that the intermediate shaft has rotated, the clockspring must be removed and recentered. Refer to the Supplemental Restraint System in the Chassis Electrical Section.

20. Remove the bolt and disconnect the steering column shaft from the steering gear.
    a. Discard the bolt.

21. Remove the bolt and disconnect the 2 Electronic Power Assist Steering (EPAS)

electrical connectors, and the wiring retainer.

22. Position the Powertrain Lift under the subframe assembly.
23. Remove the subframe bracket-to-body bolts.
24. Remove the rear subframe bolts and the subframe brackets.
25. Remove the front subframe bolts.
26. Lower the subframe assembly from the vehicle.
27. Pull the RH wheel knuckle outward and rotate it toward the rear of the vehicle.
    a. Secure the RH wheel knuckle assembly.
28. Remove the 2 halfshaft bracket bolts.
29. Remove the intermediate and halfshaft assembly.
    a. Inspect the intermediate shaft for pitting or damage in the seal contact area. Replace if necessary.

WARNING

The sharp edges on the stub shaft splines can slice or puncture the oil seal. Use care when inserting the stub shaft into the transmission or damage to the component may occur.

30. Using the Slide Hammer and Halfshaft Remover, remove the halfshaft from the transmission.
31. Remove and discard the circlip from the stub shaft.
32. Remove the cowl panel grille as outlined in the Body and Paint Section.
33. Detach the 2 brake booster vacuum hose retainers from the strut tower brace.
34. Remove the 4 nuts and the strut tower brace.
35. Disconnect the PCM and engine harness electrical connectors.
    a. Detach the wiring harness retainer.
36. Disconnect the 2 PCM electrical connectors.
37. Remove the engine wiring harness retainer from the bulkhead.
    a. Push the wiring harness retainer tab in.
    b. Slide the wiring harness up and out of the bulkhead.
38. Remove the nut and disconnect the A/C tube.
    a. Discard the O-ring seal and gasket seal.
39. Remove the nut and the A/C tube.
    a. Discard the O-ring seal and gasket seal.
40. Remove the degas bottle.
41. Remove the engine Air Cleaner (ACL) and ACL outlet pipe as outlined in this section.
42. Remove the noise generator. Refer to the Intake Air System Components as outlined in this section.
43. Disconnect the Turbocharger Boost Pressure (TCBP)/Charge Air Cooler Temperature (CACT) sensor electrical connector.
44. Loosen the 2 clamps and remove the CAC outlet pipe.
45. Remove the battery tray.
46. Disconnect the engine wiring harness electrical connector.
47. Remove the nut and disconnect the ground cable from the negative battery terminal.
48. Remove the nut and disconnect the power feed wires from the positive battery terminal.
49. Disconnect the brake booster vacuum quick connect coupling as outlined in the Fuel System Section.
50. Disconnect the transaxle control cable from the control lever.
51. Disconnect the transaxle control cable from the shift cable bracket.
    a. Detach the wiring harness pin-type retainer.
52. Loosen the 2 clamps and remove the RH CAC tube.
53. Disconnect the 2 heater hoses from the intake manifold.
54. Remove the bolt and ground wire from the engine front cover.
55. Disconnect the upper radiator hose from the intake manifold coolant tube.
56. If equipped, detach the engine block heater harness from the radiator support wiring harness.
57. Disconnect the Evaporative Emission (EVAP) tube quick connect coupling as outlined in the Fuel System Section.
58. Disconnect the EVAP valve electrical connector and detach from the intake manifold.
59. Disconnect the quick connect coupling from the intake manifold and remove the EVAP tube assembly as outlined in the Fuel System Section.
60. Disconnect the fuel supply tube as outlined in the Fuel System.

➡Index-mark the driveshaft for installation.

61. Remove and discard the 4 bolts and position aside the driveshaft.
62. Remove the drain plug and drain the engine oil. Install the drain plug and tighten the plug to 20 ft. lbs. (27 Nm).
63. Remove and discard the engine oil filter.
64. Remove the A/C tube bracket bolt from the rear of the compressor.
65. Remove the nut and disconnect the upper A/C tube from the compressor.
    a. Discard the O-ring seal and gasket seal.
66. Loosen the clamp and disconnect the lower LH CAC tube from the LH turbocharger.
67. Detach the lower radiator hose retainer from the cooling fan and shroud.
68. Disconnect the lower radiator hose from the radiator.
69. Remove the 2 secondary latches from the transmission fluid cooler tubes at the transmission fluid cooler thermal bypass valve.
70. Using the Transmission Cooler Line Disconnect Tool, disconnect the transmission fluid cooler tubes from the transmission fluid cooler thermal bypass valve.
71. Remove the 3 bolts and the RH turbocharger lower bracket.
72. Remove the 2 bolts and the RH halfshaft support bracket.
73. Remove the 3 bolts and the Power Transfer Unit (PTU) support bracket.
74. Remove the 5 bolts and the PTU.

➡Position a block of wood under the transaxle.

75. Install the Powertrain Lift and Universal Adapter Brackets.
76. Remove the 3 nuts and the bolt from the transaxle support insulator bracket-to-transaxle.
77. Remove the 4 engine mount nuts.
78. Remove the 3 bolts and the engine mount.
79. Lower the engine and transaxle assembly from the vehicle.
80. Disconnect the 2 quick connect couplings and remove the crankcase vent tube as outlined in the Fuel System Section.
81. Remove the nut and the A/C tube from the compressor.
    a. Discard the O-ring seal and gasket seal.
82. Disconnect the brake vacuum tube from the intake manifold.
83. Disconnect the 2 quick connect couplings and remove the PCV tube as outlined in the Fuel System Section.
84. If equipped, disconnect the 2 heated PCV electrical connectors.
85. Disconnect the LH turbocharger bypass valve electrical connector.

➡Index-mark the hoses for installation.

86. Disconnect the turbocharger wastegate regulating valve hoses from the RH CAC tube and turbocharger wastegate regulating valve.

87. Loosen the clamp and remove the LH turbocharger intake tube from the LH turbocharger.

88. Disconnect the RH turbocharger bypass valve electrical connector.

89. Loosen the clamp and remove the RH CAC tube from the RH turbocharger.

90. Loosen the clamp and remove the RH turbocharger intake pipe from the RH turbocharger.

⁂ WARNING

The compression limiter bushing may fall out of the mounting bracket grommet on the turbocharger intake tube during service. Make sure the bushing is in place when reinstalling the tube or damage to the tube may occur.

91. Remove the nut from the RH valve cover stud bolt for the RH turbocharger intake tube.

⁂ WARNING

The compression limiter bushing may fall out of the mounting bracket grommet on the Charge Air Cooler (CAC) tube during service. Make sure the bushing is in place when reinstalling the tube or damage to the tube may occur.

92. Remove the RH CAC tube nut from the intake manifold and remove the RH CAC tube and turbocharger intake tube as an assembly.

93. Remove the noise insulator shield for the fuel injection pump and disconnect the electrical connector.

94. Disconnect the Throttle Position (TP) sensor and electronic TB electrical connectors.

95. Disconnect the LH Variable Camshaft Timing (VCT) solenoid electrical connector.

96. Disconnect the Engine Oil Pressure (EOP) electrical connector.

a. Detach the wiring harness retainer from the block.

97. Disconnect the 3 LH ignition coil-on-plug electrical connectors.

98. Remove the lower radiator hose from the thermostat housing.

99. Remove the engine cover mounting stud from the LH valve cover stud bolt.

100. Detach all the wiring harness retainers from the LH valve cover and stud bolts.

101. Remove the nut and the oil supply tube bracket from the LH valve cover stud bolt.

102. Remove the oil level indicator.

103. Detach and disconnect the 2 fuel injector wiring harness electrical connectors.

104. Disconnect the Manifold Absolute Pressure (MAP)/Intake Air Temperature 2 (IAT2) sensor electrical connector.

105. Disconnect the turbocharger wastegate regulating valve electrical connector.

106. Detach the 2 wire harness-to-intake manifold retainers.

107. Remove the fuel tube-to-engine front cover bracket bolt and position the fuel tube aside.

108. Disconnect the 2 turbocharger coolant hoses from the intake manifold.

⁂ WARNING

If the engine is repaired or replaced because of upper engine failure, typically including valve or piston damage, check the intake manifold for metal debris. If metal debris is found, install a new intake manifold. Failure to follow these instructions can result in engine damage.

➡Note the routing of the 2 fuel rail wiring harnesses for installation.

109. Remove the 12 bolts and the intake manifold (refer to the Intake Manifold procedure for more information):

a. Remove and discard the intake manifold, coolant crossover and thermostat housing gaskets.

b. Clean and inspect all sealing surfaces.

110. Disconnect the RH VCT solenoid electrical connector and detach the 2 wiring harness retainers.

111. Disconnect the 3 RH ignition coil-on-plug electrical connectors.

112. Detach all the wiring harness retainers from the RH valve cover and stud bolts.

Early Build Vehicles

113. Remove the nut for the high pressure fuel tube from the LH valve cover stud bolt.

Late Build Vehicles

114. Remove the high pressure fuel tube bolt from the LH cylinder head.

All Vehicles

➡To release the fuel pressure in the high pressure fuel tube, wrap the flare nuts with a shop towel to absorb any residual fuel pressure during the loosening of the flare nuts.

115. Remove the high pressure fuel tube flare nut from the fuel injection pump. Remove the 2 high pressure fuel tube flare nuts from the fuel rails and remove the high pressure fuel tube assembly.

116. Remove the 2 bolts and the fuel injection pump.

117. Remove the fuel injection pump mounting plate.

118. Remove the fuel injection pump roller tappet.

a. Inspect the fuel injection pump roller tappet as outlined in the Fuel System Section.

➡When removing the ignition coil-on-plugs, a slight twisting motion will break the seal and ease removal.

119. Remove the 3 bolts and the 3 LH ignition coil-on-plugs.

➡When removing the ignition coil-on-plugs, a slight twisting motion will break the seal and ease removal.

120. Remove the 3 bolts and the 3 RH ignition coil-on-plugs.

121. Loosen the 10 stud bolts and remove the LH valve cover. Discard the gasket.

122. Loosen the 11 stud bolts and remove the RH valve cover. Discard the gasket.

➡VCT solenoid seal removal shown, spark plug tube seal removal similar.

123. Inspect the VCT solenoid seals and the spark plug tube seals. Install new seals if damaged.

a. Using the VCT Spark Plug Tube Seal Remover and Handle, remove the seal(s).

124. Rotate the accessory drive belt tensioner clockwise and remove the accessory drive belt.

125. Remove the 3 bolts and the accessory drive belt tensioner.

126. Using the Strap Wrench, remove the crankshaft pulley bolt and washer.

a. Discard the bolt.

127. Using the 3 Jaw Puller, remove the crankshaft pulley.

128. Using the Oil Seal Remover, remove and discard the crankshaft front seal.

129. Remove the HO2S connector bracket stud bolt from the engine front cover.

➡Only use hand tools to remove the studs.

130. Remove the 2 engine mount studs.

131. Remove the 3 bolts and the engine mount bracket.

132. Remove the 22 engine front cover bolts.

133. Install 6 of the engine front cover bolts (finger-tight) into the 6 threaded holes in the engine front cover.

a. Tighten the bolts one turn at a time in a crisscross pattern until the engine front cover-to-cylinder block seal is released.

b. Remove the engine front cover.

⁂ WARNING

Only use a 3M® Roloc® Bristle Disk (2-in white, part number 07528) to clean the engine front cover. Do not use metal scrapers, wire brushes or any other power abrasive disk to clean the engine front cover. These tools cause scratches and gouges that make leak paths.

134. Clean the engine front cover using a 3M® Roloc® Bristle Disk (2-in white, part number 07528) in a suitable tool turning at the recommended speed of 15,000 rpm.

a. Thoroughly wash the engine front cover to remove any foreign material, including any abrasive particles created during the cleaning process.

⁂ WARNING

Place clean, lint-free shop towels over exposed engine cavities. Carefully remove the towels so foreign material is not dropped into the engine. Any foreign material (including any material created while cleaning gasket surfaces) that enters the oil passages or the oil pan, may cause engine failure.

⁂ WARNING

Do not use wire brushes, power abrasive discs or 3M® Roloc® Bristle Disk (2-in white, part number 07528) to clean the sealing surfaces. These tools cause scratches and gouges that make leak paths. They also cause contamination that will cause premature engine failure. Remove all traces of sealant, including any sealant from the inner surface of the cylinder block and cylinder head.

135. Clean the sealing surfaces of the cylinder heads, the cylinder block and the oil pan in the following sequence.

a. Remove any large deposits of silicone or gasket material.

b. Apply silicone gasket remover and allow to set for several minutes.

c. Remove the silicone gasket remover. A second application of silicone gasket remover may be required if residual traces of silicone or gasket material remain.

d. Apply metal surface prep, to remove any remaining traces of oil or coolant and to prepare the surfaces to bond. Do not attempt to make the metal shiny. Some staining of the metal surfaces is normal.

e. Make sure the 2 locating dowel pins are seated correctly in the cylinder block.

Engines Equipped With Early Build RH Timing Chain Guides

136. Rotate the crankshaft clockwise and align the timing marks on the VCT assemblies as shown.

Engines Equipped With Late Build/Replacement RH Timing Chain Guides

137. Rotate the crankshaft clockwise and align the timing marks on the VCT assemblies as shown.

All Camshafts

➡The Camshaft Holding Tool will hold the camshafts in the Top Dead Center (TDC) position.

138. Install the Camshaft Holding Tool onto the flats of the LH camshafts.

➡The Camshaft Holding Tool will hold the camshafts in the TDC position.

139. Install the Camshaft Holding Tool onto the flats of the RH camshafts.

140. Remove the 3 bolts and the RH VCT housing.

141. Remove the 3 bolts and the LH VCT housing.

142. Remove the 2 bolts and the primary timing chain tensioner.

143. Remove the primary timing chain tensioner arm.

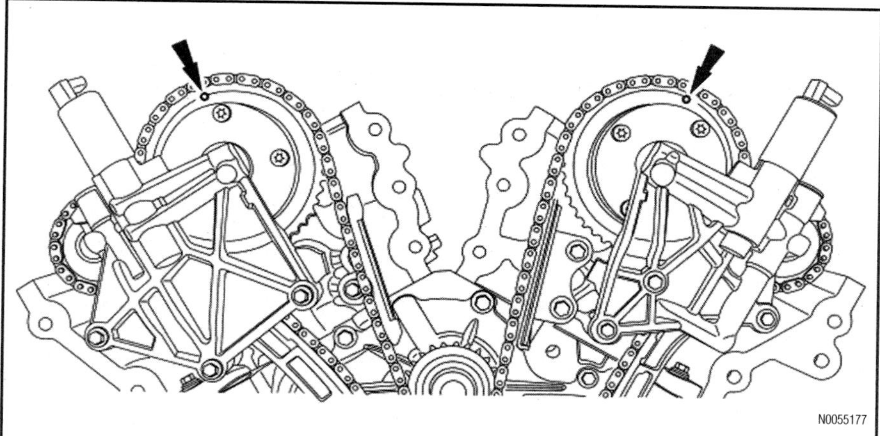

Fig. 82 Rotate the crankshaft clockwise and align the timing marks on the VCT assemblies—Early Build

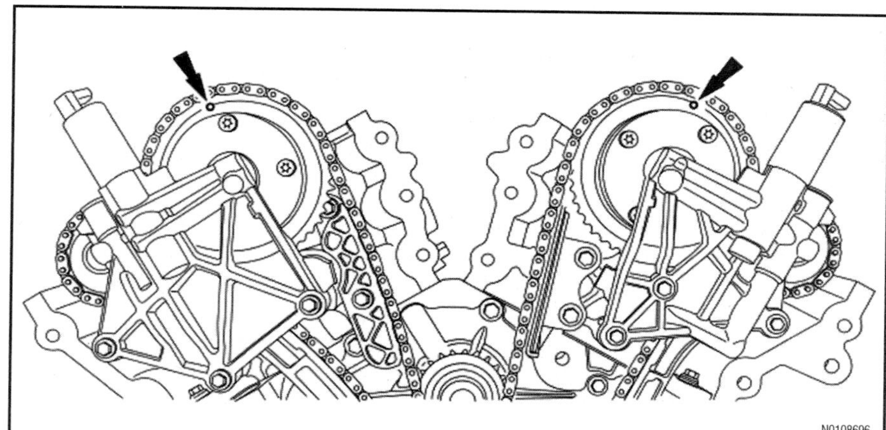

Fig. 83 Rotate the crankshaft clockwise and align the timing marks on the VCT assemblies—Late Build/Replacement

144. Remove the 2 bolts and the lower LH primary timing chain guide.

145. Remove the primary timing chain.

LH Camshafts

146. Compress the LH secondary timing chain tensioner and install a suitable lock-pin to retain the tensioner in the collapsed position.

➡The VCT bolt and the exhaust camshaft bolt must be discarded and new ones installed. However, the exhaust camshaft washer is reusable.

147. Remove and discard the LH VCT assembly bolt and the LH exhaust camshaft sprocket bolt.

a. Remove the LH VCT assembly, secondary timing chain and the LH exhaust camshaft sprocket as an assembly.

➡When the Camshaft Holding Tool is removed, valve spring pressure will rotate the LH camshafts approximately 3 degrees to a neutral position.

148. Remove the Camshaft Holding Tool from the LH camshafts.

⁂ WARNING

The camshafts must remain in the neutral position during removal or engine damage may occur.

149. Verify the LH camshafts are in the neutral position.

➡Cylinder head camshaft bearing caps are numbered to verify that they are assembled in their original positions.

150. Remove the bolts and the LH camshaft bearing caps.

a. Remove the LH camshafts.

RH Camshafts

151. Compress the RH secondary timing chain tensioner and install a suitable lock-pin to retain the tensioner in the collapsed position.

➡The VCT bolt and the exhaust camshaft bolt must be discarded and new ones installed. However, the exhaust camshaft washer is reusable.

152. Remove and discard the RH VCT assembly bolt and the RH exhaust camshaft sprocket bolt.

a. Remove the RH VCT assembly, secondary timing chain and the RH exhaust camshaft sprocket as an assembly.

153. Remove the Camshaft Holding Tool from the RH camshafts.

⁂ WARNING

The camshafts must remain in the neutral position during removal or engine damage may occur.

154. Rotate the RH camshafts counterclockwise to the neutral position.

➡Cylinder head camshaft bearing caps are numbered to verify that they are assembled in their original positions.

155. Remove the bolts and the RH camshaft bearing caps.

a. Remove the RH camshafts.

To install:

⁂ CAUTION

Do not smoke, carry lighted tobacco or have an open flame of any type when working on or near any fuel-related component. Highly flammable mixtures are always present and may be ignited. Failure to follow these instructions may result in serious personal injury.

⁂ WARNING

Whenever turbocharger air intake system components are removed, always cover open ports to protect from debris. It is important that no foreign material enter the system. The turbocharger compressor vanes are susceptible to damage from even small particles. All components should be inspected and cleaned, if necessary, prior to installation or reassembly.

⁂ WARNING

During engine repair procedures, cleanliness is extremely important. Any foreign material, including any material created while cleaning gasket surfaces that enters the oil passages, coolant passages or the oil pan, may cause engine failure.

➡On early build engines, the timing chain rides on the inner side of the RH timing chain guide. Late build engines are equipped with a different design RH timing chain guide that requires the timing chain to ride on the outer side of the RH timing chain guide. For service, all replacement RH timing chain guides will be the late build design.

All Camshafts

⁂ WARNING

The crankshaft must remain in the freewheeling position (crankshaft dowel pin at 9 o'clock) until after the camshafts are installed and the valve clearance is checked/adjusted. Do not turn the crankshaft until instructed to do so. Failure to follow this process will result in severe engine damage.

156. Rotate the crankshaft counterclockwise until the crankshaft dowel pin is in the 9 o'clock position.

LH Camshafts

⁂ WARNING

The camshafts must remain in the neutral position during installation or engine damage may occur.

➡Coat the camshafts with clean engine oil prior to installation.

157. Position the camshafts onto the LH cylinder head in the neutral position.

➡Cylinder head camshaft bearing caps are numbered to verify that they are assembled in their original positions.

158. Install the 8 camshaft caps and the 16 bolts. Tighten the 16 camshaft bolts to 89 inch lbs. (10 Nm) in the proper sequence.

RH Camshafts

⁂ WARNING

The camshafts must remain in the neutral position during installation or engine damage may occur.

➡Coat the camshafts with clean engine oil prior to installation.

159. Position the camshafts onto the RH cylinder head in the neutral position.

Fig. 84 Position the camshafts onto the LH cylinder head in the neutral position

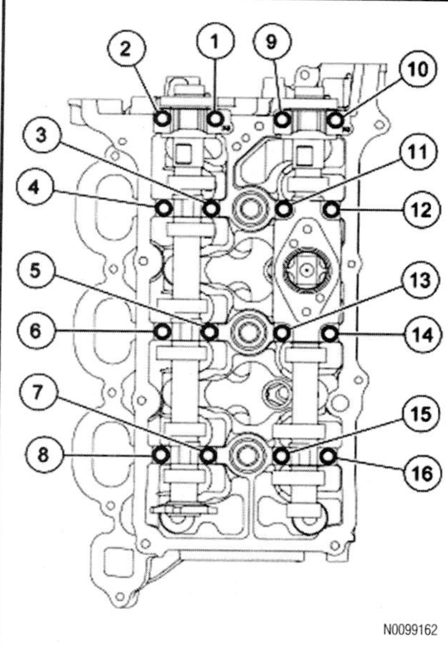

Fig. 85 Installation of the 8 camshaft caps and 16 bolts—LH camshaft

Fig. 86 Position the camshafts onto the RH cylinder head in the neutral position

➡Cylinder head camshaft bearing caps are numbered to verify that they are assembled in their original positions.

160. Install the 8 camshaft caps and the 16 bolts. Tighten the 16 camshaft bolts to 89 inch lbs. (Nm) in the proper sequence.

All Camshafts

⁂ WARNING

If any components are installed new, the engine valve clearance must be checked/adjusted or engine damage may occur.

➡Use a camshaft sprocket bolt to turn the camshafts.

161. Using a feeler gauge, confirm that the valve tappet clearances are within specification. If valve tappet clearances are not within specification, the clearance must be adjusted by installing new valve tappet(s) of the correct size.

LH Camshafts

➡Use a camshaft sprocket bolt to turn the camshafts.

162. Rotate the LH camshafts to the Top Dead Center (TDC) position and install the Camshaft Holding Tool on the flats of the camshafts.

163. Assemble the LH Variable Camshaft Timing (VCT) assembly, the LH exhaust camshaft sprocket and the LH secondary timing chain.

a. Align the colored links with the timing marks.

164. Position the LH secondary timing assembly onto the camshafts.

165. Install 2 new bolts and the original washer. Tighten in 4 stages.

a. Stage 1: Tighten to 30 ft. lbs. (40 Nm).

b. Stage 2: Loosen one full turn.

c. Stage 3: Tighten to 89 inch lbs. (10 Nm).

d. Stage 4: Tighten 90 degrees.

166. Remove the lockpin from the LH secondary timing chain tensioner.

RH Camshafts

➡Use a camshaft sprocket bolt to turn the camshafts.

167. Rotate the RH camshafts to the TDC position and install the Camshaft Holding Tool on the flats of the camshafts.

168. Assemble the RH VCT assembly, the RH exhaust camshaft sprocket and the RH secondary timing chain.

a. Align the colored links with the timing marks.

169. Position the RH secondary timing assembly onto the camshafts.

170. Install 2 new bolts and the original washer. Tighten in 4 stages.

a. Stage 1: Tighten to 30 ft. lbs. (40 Nm).

b. Stage 2: Loosen one full turn.

c. Stage 3: Tighten to 89 inch lbs. (10 Nm).

d. Stage 4: Tighten 90 degrees.

171. Remove the lockpin from the RH secondary timing chain tensioner.

All Camshafts

172. Rotate the crankshaft clockwise 60 degrees to the TDC position (crankshaft dowel pin at 11 o'clock).

173. Install the primary timing chain with the colored links aligned with the timing marks on the VCT assemblies and the crankshaft sprocket.

174. Install the lower LH primary timing chain guide and the 2 bolts. Tighten the bolts to 89 inch lbs. (10 Nm).

175. Install the primary timing chain tensioner arm.

176. Reset the primary timing chain tensioner.

a. Rotate the lever counterclockwise.

b. Using a soft-jawed vise, compress the plunger.

c. Align the hole in the lever with the hole in the tensioner housing.

d. Install a suitable lockpin.

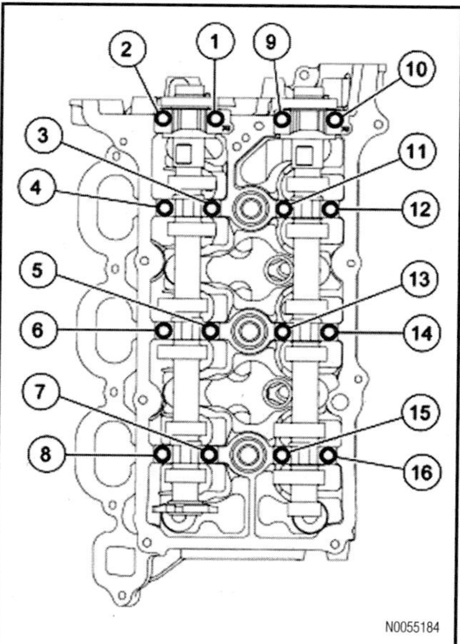

Fig. 87 Installation of the 8 camshaft caps and 16 bolts—RH camshaft

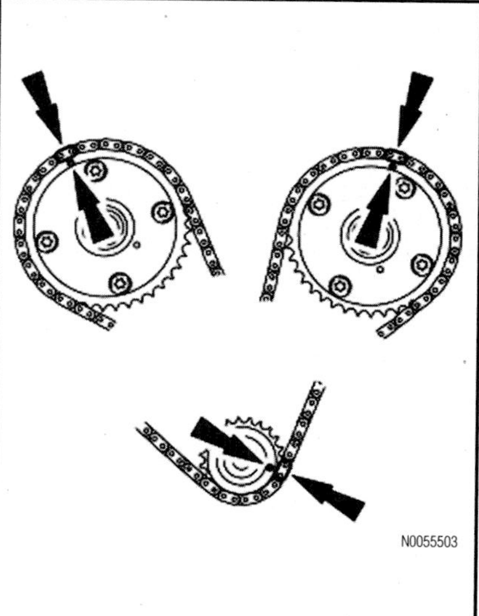

Fig. 88 Install the primary timing chain with the colored links aligned with the timing marks on the VCT assemblies and the crankshaft sprocket

➡It may be necessary to rotate the crankshaft slightly to remove slack from the timing chain and install the tensioner.

177. Install the primary tensioner and the 2 bolts. Tighten the bolts to 89 inch lbs. (10 Nm).
    a. Remove the lockpin.
178. As a post-check, verify correct alignment of all timing marks.
179. Inspect the VCT housing seals for damage and replace as necessary.

⁂ WARNING

Make sure the dowels on the Variable Camshaft Timing (VCT) housing are fully engaged in the cylinder head prior to tightening the bolts. Failure to follow this process will result in severe engine damage.

180. Install the LH VCT housing and the 3 bolts. Tighten the bolts to 89 inch lbs. (10 Nm).

⁂ WARNING

Make sure the dowels on the Variable Camshaft Timing (VCT) housing are fully engaged in the cylinder head prior to tightening the bolts. Failure to follow this process will result in severe engine damage.

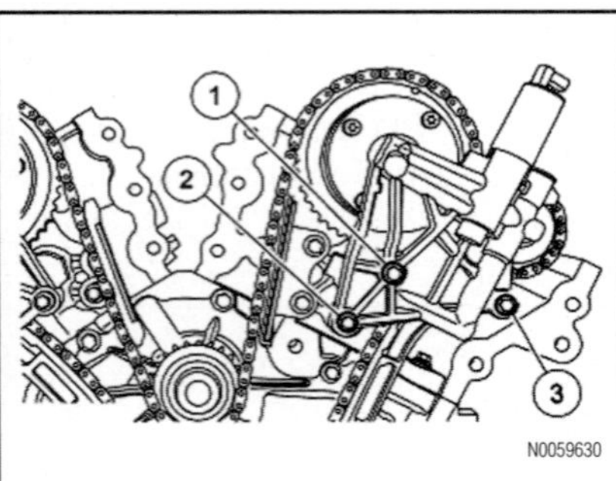

Fig. 89 Installation of the LH VCT housing and the 3 bolts

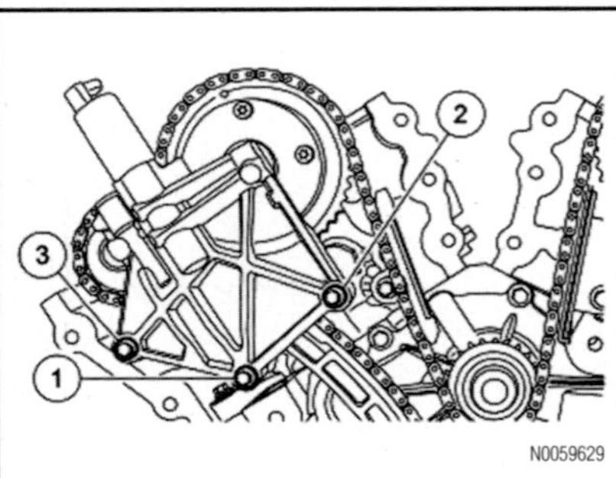

Fig. 90 Installation of the RH VCT housing and the 3 bolts

181. Install the RH VCT housing and the 3 bolts. Tighten the bolts to 89 inch lbs. (10 Nm).
182. Install the Alignment Pins.

⁂ WARNING

Failure to use Motorcraft® High Performance Engine RTV Silicone may cause the engine oil to foam excessively and result in serious engine damage.

➡The engine front cover and bolts 17, 18, 19 and 20 must be installed within 4 minutes of the initial sealant application. The remainder of the engine front cover bolts and the engine mount bracket bolts must be installed and tightened within 35 minutes of the initial sealant application. If the time limits are exceeded, the sealant must be removed, the sealing area cleaned and sealant reapplied. To clean the sealing area, use silicone gasket remover and metal surface prep. Failure to follow this procedure can cause future oil leakage.

➡Apply a 0.11 inch (3.0 mm) bead of Motorcraft® High Performance Engine RTV Silicone to the engine front cover sealing surfaces including the 3 engine mount bracket bosses.

➡Apply a 0.21 inch (5.5 mm) bead of Motorcraft® High Performance Engine RTV Silicone to the oil pan-to-cylinder block joint and the cylinder head-to-cylinder block joint areas of the engine front cover in 5 places as indicated.

➡Make sure the 2 locating dowel pins are seated correctly in the cylinder block.

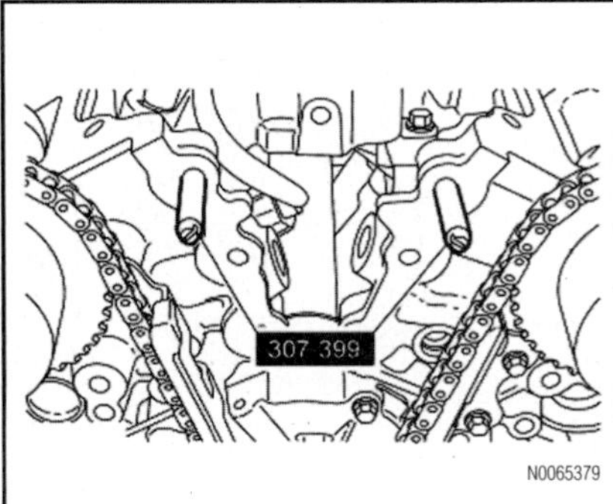

Fig. 91 Alignment pin location

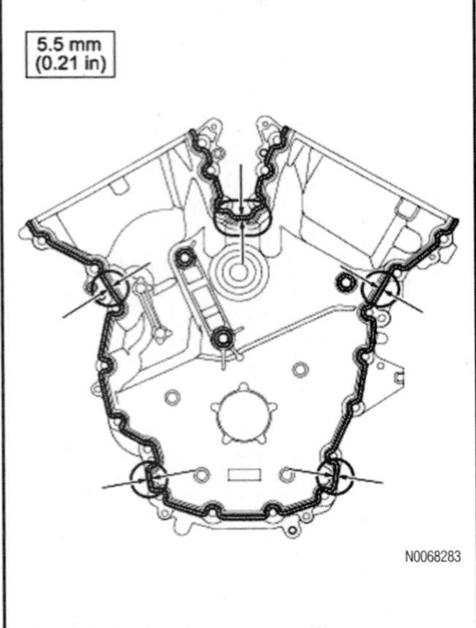

Fig. 92 Engine front cover silicone application locations

183. Install the engine front cover and bolts. Tighten the bolts to 27 inch lbs. (3 Nm).
184. Remove the Alignment Pins.

➡Do not tighten the bolts at this time.

185. Install the engine mount bracket and the 3 bolts.

⁂ WARNING

Do not expose the Motorcraft® High Performance Engine RTV Silicone to engine oil for at least 90 minutes after installing the engine front cover. Failure to follow this instruction may cause oil leakage.

186. Install the remaining engine front cover bolts. Tighten all of the engine front cover bolts and engine mount bracket bolts in the proper sequence.
    a. Stage 1: Tighten bolts 1 thru 22 to 89 inch lbs. (10 Nm) and bolts 23, 24 and 25 to 133 inch lbs. (15 Nm).
    b. Stage 2: Tighten bolts 1 thru 22 to 18 ft. lbs. (24 Nm) and bolts 23, 24 and 25 to 55 ft. lbs. (75 Nm).

⁂ WARNING

The thread sealer on the engine mount studs (including new engine mount studs if applicable) must be cleaned off with a wire brush and new Threadlock and Sealer applied prior to installing the engine mount studs. Failure to follow this procedure may result in damage to the engine mount studs or engine.

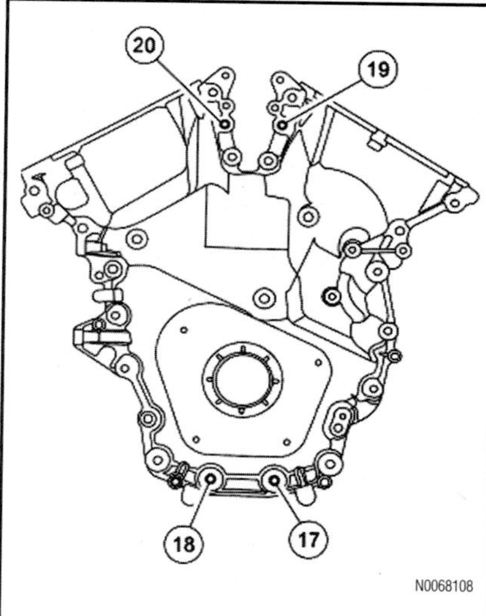

Fig. 93 Installation of the engine front cover bolts 17, 18, 19 and 20

187. Install the engine mount studs in the following sequence.

a. Clean the front cover engine mount stud holes with pressurized air to remove any foreign material.

b. Clean all the thread sealer from the engine mount studs (old and new studs).

c. Apply new Threadlock and Sealer to the engine mount stud threads.

d. Install the 2 engine mount studs. Tighten the studs to 177 inch lbs. (20 Nm).

188. Install the Heated Oxygen Sensor (HO2S) connector bracket and stud bolt to the engine front cover. Tighten the bolt to 89 inch lbs. (10 Nm).

➡Apply clean engine oil to the crankshaft front seal bore in the engine front cover.

189. Using the Crankshaft Vibration Damper Installer and Front Crankshaft Seal Installer, install a new crankshaft front seal.

➡Lubricate the outside diameter sealing surfaces with clean engine oil.

190. Using the Crankshaft Vibration Damper Installer and Front Cover Oil Seal Installer, install the crankshaft pulley.

191. Using the Strap Wrench, install the crankshaft pulley washer and new bolt and tighten in 4 stages.

a. Stage 1: Tighten to 89 ft. lbs. (120 Nm).

b. Stage 2: Loosen one full turn.

c. Stage 3: Tighten to 37 ft. lbs. (50 Nm).

d. Stage 4: Tighten an additional 90 degrees.

192. Install the accessory drive belt tensioner and the 3 bolts. Tighten the bolts to 97 inch lbs. (11 Nm).

193. Rotate the accessory drive belt tensioner clockwise and install the accessory drive belt.

➡Installation of new seals is only required if damaged seals were removed during disassembly of the engine.

➡Spark plug tube seal installation shown, VCT solenoid seal installation similar.

194. Using the VCT Spark Plug Tube Seal Installer and Handle, install new VCT solenoid and/or spark plug tube seals.

WARNING

Failure to use Motorcraft® High Performance Engine RTV Silicone may cause the engine oil to foam excessively and result in serious engine damage.

➡If the valve cover is not installed and the fasteners tightened within 4 minutes, the sealant must be removed and the sealing area cleaned. To clean the sealing area, use silicone gasket remover and metal surface prep. Failure to follow this procedure can cause future oil leakage.

195. Apply an 0.31 inch (8 mm) bead of Motorcraft® High Performance Engine RTV Silicone to the engine front cover-to-RH cylinder head joints.

196. Using a new gasket, install the RH valve cover and tighten the 11 stud bolts. Tighten the stud bolts to 89 inch lbs. (10 Nm). Refer to the Valve Cover procedure for tightening sequence.

WARNING

Failure to use Motorcraft® High Performance Engine RTV Silicone may cause the engine oil to foam excessively and result in serious engine damage.

➡If the valve cover is not installed and the fasteners tightened within 4 minutes, the sealant must be removed and the sealing area cleaned. To clean the sealing area, use silicone gasket remover and metal surface prep. Failure to follow this procedure can cause future oil leakage.

197. Apply an 0.31 inch (8 mm) bead of Motorcraft® High Performance Engine RTV Silicone to the engine front cover-to-LH cylinder head joints.

198. Using a new gasket, install the LH valve cover and tighten the 10 stud bolts. Tighten the stud bolts to 89 inch lbs. (10 Nm). Refer to the Valve Cover procedure for the tightening sequence.

199. Install 3 RH ignition coil-on-plugs and the 3 bolts. Tighten the bolts to 62 inch lbs. (7 Nm).

200. Install 3 LH ignition coil-on-plugs and the 3 bolts. Tighten the bolts to 62 inch lbs. (7 Nm).

➡The cam lobe for the fuel injection pump must be at Bottom Dead Center (BDC) for the fuel injection pump installation.

201. Using the crankshaft pulley bolt, turn the crankshaft until the fuel injection pump cam lobe is at BDC.

➡Valve cover is removed for clarity.

➡Apply clean engine oil to the fuel injection pump mounting pedestal bore.

202. Install the fuel injection pump roller tappet.

➡Apply clean engine oil to the fuel injection pump mounting plate seal.

203. Inspect the fuel injection pump mounting plate-to-valve cover gasket and replace if necessary.

➡Apply clean engine oil to the fuel injection pump mounting plate O-ring seals.

204. Inspect the 2 fuel injection pump mounting plate O-ring seals and replace if necessary.

➡Apply clean engine oil to the fuel injection pump O-ring seal.

205. Install the fuel injection pump on the fuel injection pump mounting plate.

➡Clean the fuel injection pump bolts and apply Thread Sealant with PTFE to the bolts.

➡Start the fuel injection pump bolts by hand then simultaneously tighten.

206. Install the fuel injection pump and the 2 bolts. Tighten the bolts to 89 inch lbs. (10 Nm), then tighten an additional 45°

207. Connect the high pressure fuel tube flare nut to the fuel injection pump. Connect the 2 high pressure fuel tube flare nuts to the fuel rails. Tighten the nuts to 22 ft. lbs. (30 Nm).

Late Build Vehicles

208. Install the bolt for the high pressure fuel tube to the LH cylinder head. Tighten the bolt to 53 inch lbs. (6 Nm).

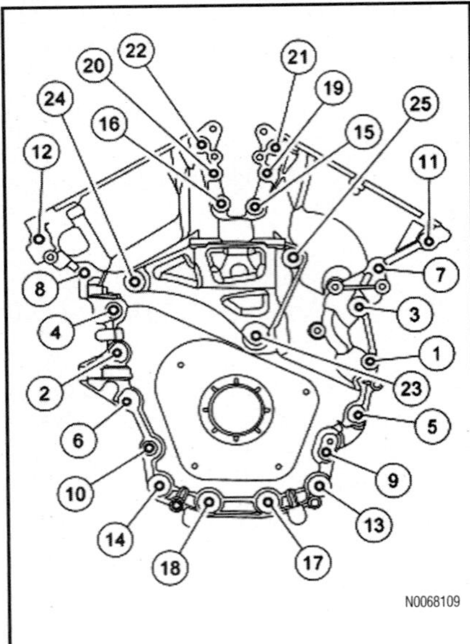

Fig. 94 Installation of the remaining engine front cover bolts

Early build vehicles

209. Install the nut for the high pressure fuel tube to the LH valve cover stud bolt. Tighten the nut to 53 inch lbs. (6 Nm).

All Vehicles

210. Attach the wiring harness retainers to the RH valve cover and stud bolt.

211. Connect the 3 RH ignition coil-on-plug electrical connectors.

212. Connect the RH VCT solenoid electrical connector and attach the 2 wiring harness retainers.

WARNING

If the engine is repaired or replaced because of upper engine failure, typically including valve or piston damage, check the intake manifold for metal debris. If metal debris is found, install a new intake manifold. Failure to follow these instructions can result in engine damage.

➡Make sure the fuel rail wiring harnesses are routed correct.

➡Installing the 2 long bolts first will aid in installing the intake manifold.

213. Using new intake manifold, coolant crossover and thermostat housing gaskets, install the intake manifold and the 12 bolts. Tighten the bolts to 89 inch lbs. (10 Nm). Refer to the Intake Manifold procedure for the tightening sequence.

214. Connect the 2 turbocharger coolant hoses to the intake manifold.

215. Position the fuel tube and install the fuel tube-to-engine front cover bracket bolt. Tighten the bolt to 89 inch lbs. (10 Nm).

216. Attach the 2 wire harness-to-intake manifold retainers.

217. Connect the turbocharger wastegate regulating valve electrical connector.

218. Connect the Manifold Absolute Pressure (MAP)/Intake Air Temperature 2 (IAT2) sensor electrical connector.

219. Connect and attach the 2 fuel injector wiring harness electrical connectors.

220. Install the oil level indicator.

221. Install the oil supply tube bracket on the LH valve cover stud bolt and install the nut. Tighten the nut to 71 inch lbs. (8 Nm).

222. Attach all the wiring harness retainers to the LH valve cover and stud bolts.

223. Install the engine cover mounting stud to the LH valve cover stud bolt. Tighten the bolt to 53 inch lbs. (6 Nm).

224. Install the lower radiator hose to the thermostat housing.

225. Connect the 3 LH ignition coil-on-plug electrical connectors.

226. Connect the Engine Oil Pressure (EOP) electrical connector.

a. Attach the wiring harness retainer to the block.

227. Connect the LH VCT solenoid electrical connector.

228. Connect the Throttle Position (TP) and electronic Throttle Body (TB) electrical connectors.

229. Connect the fuel injection pump electrical connector and install the insulated cover.

WARNING

The compression limiter bushing may fall out of the mounting bracket grommet on the Charge Air Cooler (CAC) tube during service. Make sure the bushing is in place when reinstalling the tube or damage to the tube may occur.

230. Install the RH Charge Air Cooler (CAC) tube and turbocharger intake tube as an assembly and install the RH CAC tube nut to the intake manifold. Tighten the nut to 53 inch lbs. (6 Nm).

WARNING

The compression limiter bushing may fall out of the mounting bracket grommet on the turbocharger intake tube during service. Make sure the bushing is in place when reinstalling the tube or damage to the tube may occur.

231. Install the RH turbocharger intake tube to the valve cover stud bolt and install the nut. Tighten the nut to 53 inch lbs. (6 Nm).

➡Align the index marks for the RH turbocharger intake pipe.

232. Install the RH turbocharger intake pipe to the RH turbocharger and tighten the clamp. Tighten the clamp to 44 inch lbs. (5 Nm).

➡Align the index marks for the RH CAC tube.

233. Install the RH CAC tube to the RH turbocharger and tighten the clamp. Tighten the clamp to 44 inch lbs. (5 Nm).

234. Connect the RH turbocharger bypass valve electrical connector.

➡Align the index marks for the LH turbocharger intake tube.

235. Install the LH turbocharger intake tube to the LH turbocharger and tighten the clamp. Tighten the clamp to 44 inch lbs. (5 Nm).

236. Install the turbocharger wastegate regulating valve hoses to the turbocharger wastegate regulating valve and to the RH CAC tube.

237. Connect the LH turbocharger bypass valve electrical connector.

238. If equipped, connect the 2 heated PCV electrical connectors.

239. Install the PCV tube and connect the 2 quick connect couplings as outlined in the Fuel System Section.

240. Connect the brake vacuum tube to the intake manifold.

241. Using a new O-ring seal and gasket seal, connect the A/C tube to the compressor and install the nut. Tighten the nut to 133 inch lbs. (15 Nm).

242. Install the crankcase vent tube and connect the 2 quick connect couplings as outlined in the Fuel System Section.

243. Raise the engine and transaxle assembly into the vehicle.

244. Install the engine mount and the 3 bolts. Tighten the bolts to 66 ft. lbs. (90 Nm).

245. Install the 4 engine mount nuts. Tighten the nuts to 46 ft. lbs. (63 Nm).

246. Install the bolt and the 3 nuts to the transaxle support insulator bracket-to-transaxle. Tighten the bolt to 59 ft. lbs. (80 Nm), and the nuts to 46 ft. lbs. (63 Nm).

➡A new compression seal must be installed whenever the Power Transfer Unit (PTU) is removed from the vehicle.

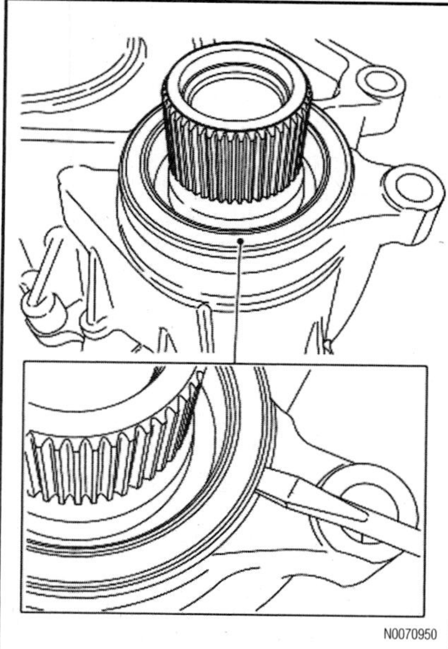

Fig. 95 Power Transfer Unit compression seal location

247. Using a small screwdriver, remove the compression seal and discard.
248. Using a soft face hammer, install the new compression seal.
249. Position the PTU in place and install the 5 bolts. Tighten the bolts to 66 ft. lbs. (90 Nm).
250. Position the PTU support bracket in place and install the 3 bolts.
251. Install the RH halfshaft support bracket and the 2 bolts. Tighten the bolts to 30 ft. lbs. (40 Nm).
252. Install the RH turbocharger lower bracket and the 3 bolts.
253. Connect the transaxle cooler tubes and install the 2 secondary latches.
254. Connect the lower radiator hose to the radiator.

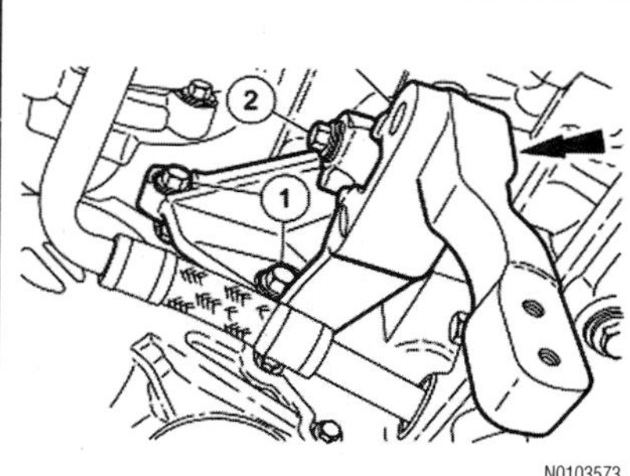

Fig. 96 PTU support bracket bolt installation. Tighten the "1" bolt to 35 ft. lbs. (48 Nm), and the "2" bolt to 52 ft. lbs. (70 Nm).

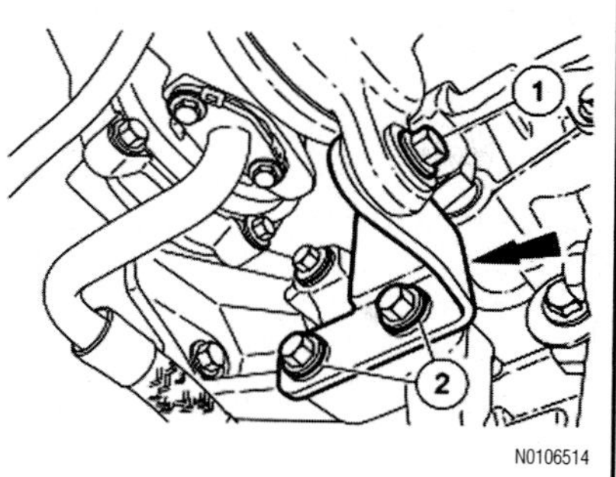

Fig. 97 RH turbocharger lower bracket installation. Tighten the "1" bolt to 168 inch lbs. (19 Nm), and the "2" to 35 ft. lbs. (48 Nm).

255. Attach the lower radiator hose retainer to the cooling fan and shroud.

➡Align the index marks for the LH CAC tube.

256. Connect the lower LH CAC tube to the LH turbocharger and tighten the clamp. Tighten the clamp to 44 inch lbs. (5 Nm).
257. Using a new O-ring seal and gasket seal, install the upper A/C tube to the A/C compressor and install the nut. Tighten the nut to 133 inch lbs. (15 Nm).
258. Install the A/C tube bracket and bolt to the rear of the A/C compressor. Tighten the bolt to 18 ft. lbs. (25 Nm).

➡Lubricate the engine oil filter gasket with clean engine oil prior to installing the oil filter.

259. Install a new engine oil filter. Tighten the filter to 44 inch lbs. (5 Nm), and then rotate an additional 180°.
260. Line up the index marks on the rear driveshaft to the index marks on the PTU flange made during removal and install the 4 new bolts. Tighten the 52 ft. lbs. (70 Nm).
261. Connect the fuel supply tube as outlined in the Fuel System Section.
262. Install the Evaporative Emission (EVAP) tube assembly and connect the quick connect coupling to the intake manifold.
263. Connect the EVAP valve electrical connector and attach to the intake manifold.
264. Connect the EVAP tube quick connect coupling as outlined in the Fuel System Section.
265. If equipped, attach the engine block heater harness to the radiator support wiring harness.
266. Connect the upper radiator hose to the intake manifold coolant tube.
267. Install the ground wire and bolt to the engine front cover. Tighten the bolt to 89 inch lbs. (10 Nm).
268. Connect the 2 heater hoses to the intake manifold.

➡Align the index marks for the RH CAC tube.

269. Install the RH CAC tube and tighten the clamps. Tighten the clamps to 44 inch lbs. (5 Nm).
270. Attach the wiring harness pin-type retainer and connect the transaxle control cable to the shift cable bracket.
271. Connect the transaxle control cable to the control lever.
272. Connect the quick connect coupling to the brake booster as outlined in the Fuel System Section.
273. Connect the power feed wires to the positive battery terminal and install the nut. Tighten the nut to 53 inch lbs. (6 Nm).
274. Connect the ground cable to the negative battery terminal and install the nut. Tighten the nut to 53 inch lbs. (6 Nm).
275. Connect the engine wiring harness electrical connector.
276. Install the battery tray.

➡Align the index marks for the CAC outlet pipe.

277. Install the CAC outlet pipe and tighten the clamps. Tighten the clamps to 44 inch lbs. (5 Nm).
278. Connect the Turbocharger Boost Pressure (TCBP)/Charge Air Cooler Temperature (CACT) sensor electrical connector.
279. Install the noise generator as outlined in Intake Air distribution and Filtering in this section.
280. Install the engine Air Cleaner (ACL) and ACL outlet pipe as outlined in Intake Air distribution and Filtering in this section.
281. Install the degas bottle.
282. Using a new O-ring seal and gasket seal, install the A/C tube and the nut. Tighten the nut to 133 inch lbs. (15 Nm).
283. Using a new O-ring seal and gasket seal, connect the A/C tube and install the nut. Tighten the nut to 133 inch lbs. (15 Nm).
284. Install the engine wiring harness retainer to the bulkhead.
  a. Slide the wiring harness in the bulkhead.
  b. Make sure the wiring harness retainer tab is below the bulkhead lip.
285. Attach the wiring harness retainer and connect the electrical connector.
286. Connect the 2 PCM electrical connectors.
287. Install the strut tower brace and the 4 nuts. Tighten the nuts to 22 ft. lbs. (30 Nm).

288. Attach the 2 brake booster vacuum hose retainers to the strut tower brace.

289. Install the cowl panel grille as outlined in the Body and Paint Section.

WARNING

The circlips are unique in size and shape for each shaft. Make sure to use the specified circlip for the application or vehicle damage may occur.

290. Install the correct new circlip on the inboard stub shaft.

➡**After insertion, pull the halfshaft inner end to make sure the circlip is locked.**

291. Push the stub shaft into the transmission so the circlip locks into the differential side gear.

292. Rotate the LH wheel knuckle into position and insert the LH halfshaft into the wheel hub.

WARNING

A new Power Transfer Unit (PTU) shaft seal must be installed whenever the intermediate shaft is removed or damage to the components can occur.

293. Install a new intermediate shaft seal and deflector as outlined in this section.

294. Install the intermediate and halfshaft assembly and the 2 bolts. Tighten the bolts to 18 ft. lbs. (25 Nm).

295. Rotate the RH wheel knuckle into position and insert the RH halfshaft into the wheel hub.

296. Using the Powertrain Lift, raise the subframe into the installed position.

297. Install the 2 front subframe bolts. Tighten the bolts to 148 ft. lbs. (200 Nm).

298. Position the subframe brackets and install the 4 bolts finger-tight.

299. Install the 2 rear subframe bolts. Tighten the bolts to 111 ft. lbs. (150 Nm).

300. Tighten the 4 subframe bracket-to-body bolts to 41 ft. lbs. (55 Nm).

301. Connect the 2 Electronic Power Assist Steering (EPAS) electrical connectors and attach the wiring retainer and install the bolt. Tighten the bolt to 80 inch lbs. (9 Nm).

WARNING

Do not allow the intermediate shaft to rotate while it is disconnected from the gear or damage to the clockspring may occur. If there is evidence that the intermediate shaft has rotated, the clockspring must be removed and recentered as outlined in the Chassis Electrical Section.

302. Install the steering intermediate shaft onto the steering gear and install a new bolt. Tighten the bolt to 177 inch lbs. (20 Nm).

303. Position the ball joints into the wheel knuckles. Install the new ball joint nuts. Tighten the nuts to 148 ft. lbs. (200 Nm).

➡**The hex-holding feature can be used to prevent turning of the stud while installing the nuts.**

304. Install new tie-rod end nuts. Tighten the nuts to 111 ft. lbs. (150 Nm).

305. Install new upper stabilizer bar link nuts. Tighten the nuts to 111 ft. lbs. (150 Nm).

306. Install the 2 front engine roll restrictor-to-transaxle bolts. Tighten the bolts to 66 ft. lbs. (90 Nm).

307. Install the 2 rear engine roll restrictor-to-transaxle bolts. Tighten the bolts to 66 ft. lbs. (90 Nm).

308. Install the RH and LH catalytic converters as outlined in this section.

309. Position the RH brake hose bracket and install the bolt. Tighten the bolt to 22 ft. lbs. (30 Nm).

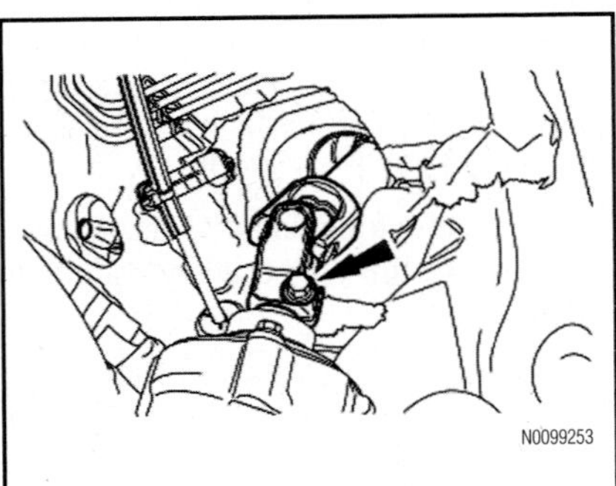

Fig. 98 Steering intermediate shaft to steering gear installation

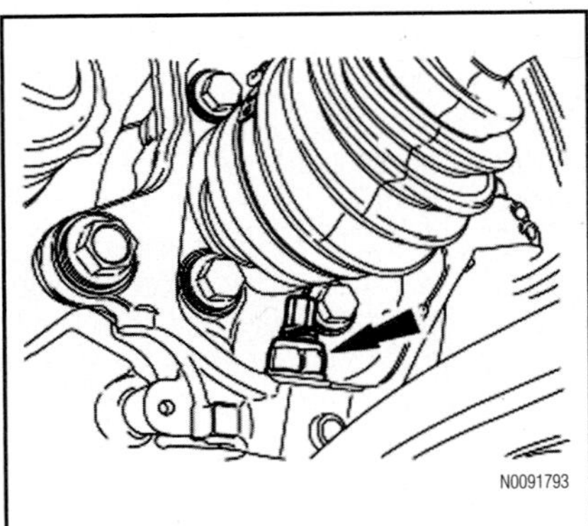

Fig. 99 Ball joints to wheel knuckles installation

WARNING

Do not tighten the wheel hub nut with the vehicle on the ground. The nut must be tightened to specification before the vehicle is lowered onto the wheels. Wheel bearing damage will occur if the wheel bearing is loaded with the weight of the vehicle applied.

➡**Apply the brake to keep the halfshaft from rotating.**

310. Using the previously removed RH and LH wheel hub nuts, seat the halfshaft. Tighten the nuts to 258 ft. lbs. (350 Nm).

a. Remove and discard the wheel hub nuts.

WARNING

The wheel hub nut contains a one-time locking chemical that is activated by the heat created when it is tightened. Install and tighten the new wheel hub nut to specification within 5 minutes of starting it on the threads. Always install a new wheel hub nut after loosening or when not

Fig. 100 Front engine roll restrictor-to-transaxle installation

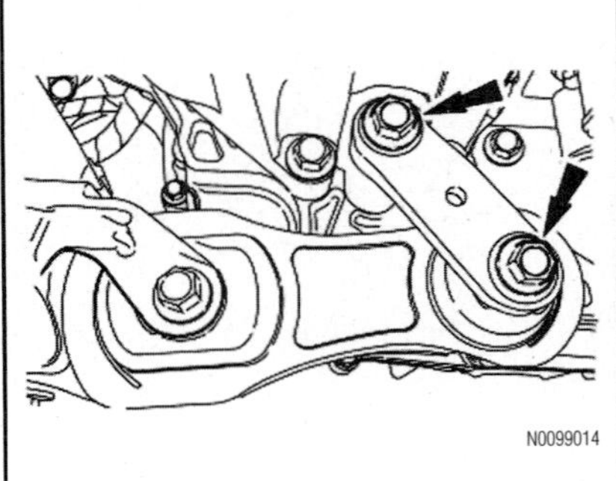

Fig. 101 Rear engine roll restrictor-to-transaxle installation

tightened within the specified time or damage to the components can occur.

➡Apply the brake to keep the halfshaft from rotating.

311. Install a new RH and LH wheel hub nut. Tighten the nut to 258 ft. lbs. (350 Nm).
312. Install the 2 scrivets in the rubber shield.
313. Install the front wheels and tires.
314. Fill the engine with clean engine oil.
315. Fill and bleed the cooling system as outlined in the Engine Cooling Section.
316. Install the front splash shield, 3 pin-type retainers and the 7 bolts, when the coolant system or engine service is finished.
317. Install the underbody shield and the 4 retainers.
318. Connect the LH Heated Oxygen Sensor (HO2S) electrical connector.
   a. Attach the HO2S connector retainer to the bracket.
319. Fill the engine with clean engine oil.
320. Refill the transaxle fluid as outlined in the Drive Train Section.
321. Recharge the A/C system as outlined in the Heating , Ventilation & Air Conditioning Section.

CATALYTIC CONVERTER

REMOVAL & INSTALLATION

3.5L Engine, Except Turbo

Left-Hand

➡Always install new fasteners and gaskets. Clean flange faces prior to new gasket installation to make sure of correct sealing.

1. With the vehicle in NEUTRAL, position it on a hoist.
2. Disconnect the LH Catalyst Monitor Sensor (CMS) electrical connector.
3. Remove the exhaust Y-pipe.
4. Remove the 2 catalytic converter support bracket-to-transmission bolts.
5. Remove the 4 nuts and the LH catalytic converter.
   a. Discard the nuts and gasket.
6. Inspect the exhaust manifold studs for damage.
   a. If damaged, or if stud comes out when removing the nut, replace the stud.

To install:

➡Always install new fasteners and gaskets. Clean flange faces prior to new gasket installation to make sure of correct sealing.

7. Inspect the exhaust manifold studs for damage.
   a. If damaged, or if stud comes out when removing the nut, replace the stud. Tighten the nut to 18 ft. lbs. (25 Nm).
8. Install the 4 nuts and the LH catalytic converter.
   a. Discard the nuts and gasket. Using a new gasket and nuts, tighten the nuts to 30 ft. lbs. (40 Nm).
9. Install the 2 catalytic converter support bracket-to-transmission bolts. Tighten the bolts to 35 ft. lbs. (48 Nm).
10. Install the exhaust Y-pipe.
11. Connect the LH Catalyst Monitor Sensor (CMS) electrical connector.
12. With the vehicle in NEUTRAL, lower it from the hoist.

Right-Hand

➡Always install new fasteners and gaskets. Clean flange faces prior to new gasket installation to make sure of correct sealing.

1. With the vehicle in NEUTRAL, position it on a hoist.
2. Remove the exhaust Y-pipe.
3. Remove the RH Catalyst Monitor Sensor (CMS) as outlined in the Engine Performance & Emission Controls Section.
4. Remove the 2 bracket-to-RH catalytic converter bolts.
5. Remove the 4 nuts and the RH catalytic converter.
   a. Discard the nuts and gasket.
6. Inspect the exhaust manifold studs for damage.
   a. If damaged or if stud comes out when removing the nut, replace the stud.

To install:

➡Always install new fasteners and gaskets. Clean flange faces prior to new gasket installation to make sure of correct sealing.

7. Inspect the exhaust manifold studs for damage.
   a. If damaged or if stud comes out when removing the nut, replace the stud. Tighten the nut to 18 ft. lbs. (25 Nm).
8. Install the 4 nuts and the RH catalytic converter.
   a. Discard the nuts and gasket. Using a new gasket and nuts, tighten the nuts to 30 ft. lbs. (40 Nm).
9. Install the 2 bracket-to-RH catalytic converter bolts. Tighten the bolts to 177 inch lbs. (20 Nm).
10. Install the RH Catalyst Monitor Sensor (CMS) as outlined in the Engine Performance & Emission Controls Section.
11. Install the exhaust Y-pipe.
12. With the vehicle in NEUTRAL, lower it from the hoist.

3.5L Turbo Engine

Left-Hand

➡Always install new fasteners and gaskets. Clean flange faces prior to new gasket installation to make sure of correct sealing.

1. With the vehicle in NEUTRAL, position it on a hoist.
2. Remove the LH Heated Oxygen Sensor (HO2S) as outlined in the Engine Performance & Emission Controls Section.
3. Remove the LH exhaust flexible pipe.
4. Disconnect the LH Catalyst Monitor Sensor (CMS) electrical connector.
5. Remove the 3 LH catalytic converter-to-turbocharger nuts and the catalytic converter.
   a. Discard the nuts and gasket.
6. Inspect the LH turbocharger-to-catalytic converter studs for damage.
   a. If damaged or if a stud comes out when removing the nut, replace the stud.

To install:

➡Always install new fasteners and gaskets. Clean flange faces prior to new gasket installation to make sure of correct sealing.

7. Inspect the LH turbocharger-to-catalytic converter studs for damage.
   a. If damaged or if a stud comes out when removing the nut, replace the stud. Tighten the nut to 18 ft. lbs. (25 Nm).
8. Install the 3 LH catalytic converter-to-turbocharger nuts and the catalytic converter.
   a. Discard the nuts and gasket. Using a new gasket and nuts, tighten the nuts to 30 ft. lbs. (40 Nm).
9. Connect the LH Catalyst Monitor Sensor (CMS) electrical connector.
10. Install the LH exhaust flexible pipe.
11. Install the LH Heated Oxygen Sensor (HO2S) as outlined in the Engine Performance & Emission Controls Section.
12. With the vehicle in NEUTRAL, lower it from the hoist.

Right-Hand

➡Always install new fasteners and gaskets. Clean flange faces prior to new gasket installation to make sure of correct sealing.

1. With the vehicle in NEUTRAL, position it on a hoist.
2. Remove the RH front wheel and tire.
3. Disconnect the RH Heated Oxygen Sensor (HO2S) electrical connector.
   a. Detach the HO2S electrical connector retainer from the bracket.
4. Remove the LH and RH exhaust flexible pipes.
5. Disconnect the RH Catalyst Monitor Sensor (CMS) electrical connector.
6. Remove the 3 RH catalytic converter-to-turbocharger nuts and the converter.
   a. Discard the nuts and gasket.
7. Inspect the RH turbocharger-to-catalytic converter studs for damage.
   a. If damaged or if a stud comes out when removing the nut, replace the stud.

To install:

➡Always install new fasteners and gaskets. Clean flange faces prior to new gasket installation to make sure of correct sealing.

8. Inspect the RH turbocharger-to-catalytic converter studs for damage.
   a. If damaged or if a stud comes out when removing the nut, replace the stud. Tighten the nut to 18 ft. lbs. (25 Nm).
9. Install the 3 RH catalytic converter-to-turbocharger nuts and the converter.
   a. Discard the nuts and gasket. Using a new gasket and nuts, tighten nuts to 30 ft. lbs. (40 Nm).
10. Connect the RH Catalyst Monitor Sensor (CMS) electrical connector.
11. Install the LH and RH exhaust flexible pipes.
12. Connect the RH Heated Oxygen Sensor (HO2S) electrical connector.
   a. Attach the HO2S electrical connector retainer to the bracket.
13. Install the RH front wheel and tire.
14. With the vehicle in NEUTRAL, lower it from the hoist.

CRANKSHAFT FRONT SEAL

REMOVAL & INSTALLATION

1. With the vehicle in NEUTRAL, position it on a hoist.
2. Remove the crankshaft pulley.
3. Using the Oil Seal Remover, remove and discard the crankshaft front seal.
   a. Clean all sealing surfaces with metal surface prep.

To install:

➡Apply clean engine oil to the crankshaft front seal bore in the engine front cover.

4. Using the Front Crankshaft Seal Installer and Crankshaft Vibration Damper Installer, install a new crankshaft front seal.
5. Install the crankshaft pulley.
6. With the vehicle in NEUTRAL, lower it from the hoist.

CYLINDER HEAD

REMOVAL & INSTALLATION

3.5L Engine, Except Turbo

Left-Hand

See Figures 102 through 105.

⁂ WARNING

During engine repair procedures, cleanliness is extremely important. Any foreign material, including any material created while cleaning gasket surfaces, that enters the oil passages, coolant passages or the oil pan, may cause engine failure.

1. Remove the LH camshafts.
2. Disconnect the 6 fuel injector electrical connectors.
3. Disconnect the Cylinder Head Temperature (CHT) sensor electrical connector.
4. Disconnect the LH Camshaft Position (CMP) sensor electrical connector.
5. Remove the bolt and the LH CMP sensor.
6. Disconnect the LH Heated Oxygen Sensor (HO2S) electrical connector.
7. Disconnect the LH Catalyst Monitor Sensor (CMS) electrical connector.
8. Detach the wiring harness retainer from the rear of the LH cylinder head.
9. Remove the nut and disconnect the generator B+ cable.
10. Disconnect the generator electrical connector.
11. Remove the nut, bolt and the generator.
   a. Remove the generator stud.
12. Disconnect the Engine Oil Pressure (EOP) switch electrical connector and the wiring harness pin-type retainer.
   a. Remove the wiring harness from the engine.
13. Remove the 2 LH catalytic converter bracket bolts.
14. Remove the 4 nuts and the LH catalytic converter.
   a. Discard the nuts and the gasket.
15. Remove the 3 bolts and the LH exhaust manifold heat shield.
16. Remove the 6 nuts and the LH exhaust manifold.
   a. Discard the nuts and the exhaust manifold gasket.
17. Clean and inspect the LH exhaust manifold.
18. Remove and discard the 6 LH exhaust manifold studs.
19. Remove the LH cylinder block drain plug.
   a. Allow coolant to drain from the cylinder block.
20. Remove the 4 nuts and the RH catalytic converter.
   a. Discard the nuts and gasket.
21. If equipped, remove the heat shield and disconnect the block heater electrical connector.
   a. Remove the block heater wiring harness from the engine.
22. Remove the RH cylinder block drain plug or, if equipped, the block heater.
   a. Allow coolant to drain from the cylinder block.
23. Remove the coolant bypass hose from the thermostat housing.
24. Remove the 4 bolts and the fuel rail and injectors as an assembly.
25. Remove the 3 thermostat housing-to-lower intake manifold bolts.
   a. Remove the thermostat housing and discard the gasket and O-ring seal.

⁂ WARNING

If the engine is repaired or replaced because of upper engine failure, typically including valve or piston damage, check the intake manifold for metal debris. If metal debris is

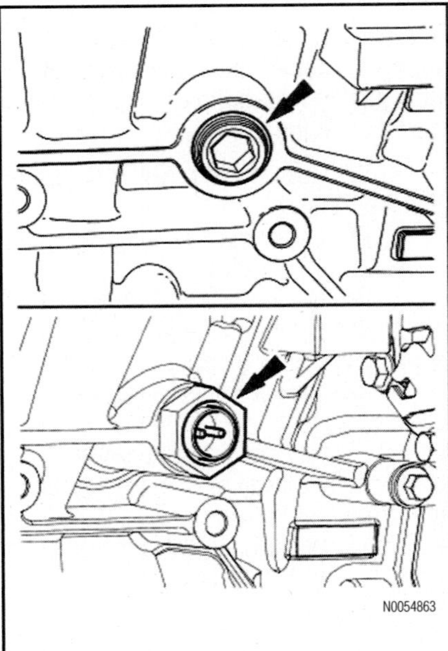

Fig. 102 Engine coolant drain plug location

found, install a new intake manifold. Failure to follow these instructions can result in engine damage.

26. Remove the 10 bolts and the lower intake manifold.
    a. Discard the gaskets.
27. Remove the 2 bolts and the upper LH primary timing chain guide.
28. Remove the 2 bolts and the LH secondary timing chain tensioner.

➡If the components are to be reinstalled, they must be installed in the same positions. Mark the components for installation into their original locations.

29. Remove the valve tappets from the cylinder head.
30. Inspect the valve tappets.
31. Remove and discard the M6 bolt.

WARNING

Place clean, lint-free shop towels over exposed engine cavities. Carefully remove the towels so foreign material is not dropped into the engine. Any foreign material (including any material created while cleaning gasket surfaces) that enters the oil passages or the oil pan, may cause engine failure.

WARNING

Aluminum surfaces are soft and may be scratched easily. Never place the cylinder head gasket surface, unprotected, on a bench surface.

➡The cylinder head bolts must be discarded and new bolts must be installed. They are a tighten-to-yield design and cannot be reused.

32. Remove and discard the 8 bolts from the cylinder head.
    a. Remove the cylinder head.
    b. Discard the cylinder head gasket.

WARNING

Do not use metal scrapers, wire brushes, power abrasive discs or other abrasive means to clean the sealing surfaces. These tools cause scratches and gouges that make leak paths. Use a plastic scraping tool to remove all traces of the head gasket.

➡Observe all warnings or cautions and follow all application directions contained on the packaging of the silicone gasket remover and the metal surface prep.

➡If there is no residual gasket material present, metal surface prep can be used to clean and prepare the surfaces.

33. Clean the cylinder head-to-cylinder block mating surfaces of both the cylinder heads and the cylinder block in the following sequence.
    a. Remove any large deposits of silicone or gasket material with a plastic scraper.
    b. Apply silicone gasket remover, following package directions, and allow to set for several minutes.
    c. Remove the silicone gasket remover with a plastic scraper. A second application of silicone gasket remover may be required if residual traces of silicone or gasket material remain.
    d. Apply metal surface prep, following package directions, to remove any remaining traces of oil or coolant and to prepare the surfaces to bond with the new gasket. Do not attempt to make the metal shiny. Some staining of the metal surfaces is normal.
34. Support the cylinder head on a bench with the head gasket side up. Check the cylinder head distortion and the cylinder block distortion.

To install:

WARNING

During engine repair procedures, cleanliness is extremely important. Any foreign material, including any material created while cleaning gasket surfaces that enters the oil passages, coolant passages or the oil pan, may cause engine failure.

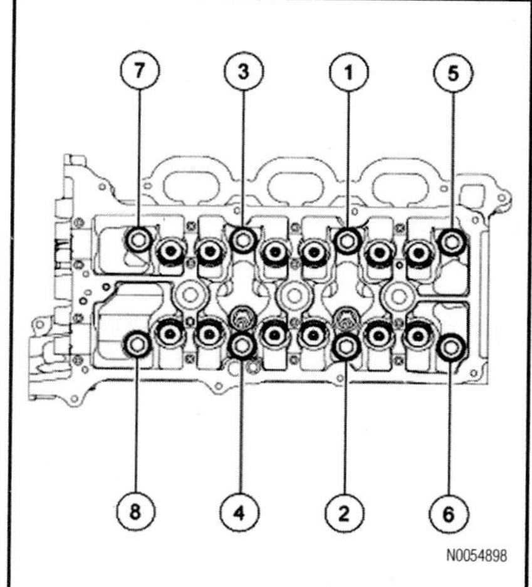

Fig. 103 LH cylinder head and tightening sequence

35. Install a new gasket, the LH cylinder head and 8 new bolts. Tighten in the proper sequence in 5 stages:
    a. Stage 1: Tighten to 177 inch lbs. (20 Nm).
    b. Stage 2: Tighten to 26 ft. lbs. (35 Nm).
    c. Stage 3: Tighten 90 degrees.
    d. Stage 4: Tighten 90 degrees.
    e. Stage 5: Tighten 90 degrees.
36. Install the M6 bolt. Tighten the bolt to 89 inch lbs. (10 Nm).

➡The valve tappets must be installed in their original positions.

➡Coat the valve tappets with clean engine oil prior to installation.

37. Install the valve tappets.
38. Install the LH secondary timing chain tensioner and the 2 bolts. Tighten the bolts to 89 inch lbs. (10 Nm).
39. Install the upper LH primary timing chain guide and the 2 bolts. Tighten the bolts to 89 inch lbs. (10 Nm).

WARNING

If the engine is repaired or replaced because of upper engine failure, typically including valve or piston damage, check the intake manifold for metal debris. If metal debris is found, install a new intake manifold. Failure to follow these instructions can result in engine damage.

40. Using new gaskets, install the lower intake manifold and the 10 bolts.
    a. Tighten in the proper sequence to 89 inch lbs. (10 Nm). Refer to the Intake Manifold procedure for the sequence.
41. Using a new gasket and O-ring seal, install the thermostat housing and the 3 bolts. Tighten the bolts to 89 inch lbs. (10 Nm).

WARNING

Use O-ring seals that are made of special fuel-resistant material. The use of ordinary O-rings may cause the fuel system to leak. Do not reuse the O-ring seals.

➡The upper and lower O-ring seals are not interchangeable.

42. Install new fuel injector O-ring seals.
    a. Remove the retaining clips and separate the fuel injectors from the fuel rail.

b. Remove and discard the O-ring seals.

c. Install new O-ring seals and lubricate with clean engine oil.

d. Install the fuel injectors and the retaining clips onto the fuel rail.

43. Install the fuel rail and injectors as an assembly and install the 4 bolts. Tighten the bolts to 89 inch lbs. (10 Nm).

44. Install the coolant bypass hose to the thermostat housing.

45. Install the RH cylinder block drain plug or, if equipped, the block heater. Tighten the drain plug to 30 ft. lbs. (40 Nm).

46. If equipped, install the block heater wiring harness onto the engine.

a. Connect the block heater electrical connector and install the heat shield.

47. Using a new gasket, install the RH catalytic converter and 4 new nuts. Tighten the nuts to 30 ft. lbs. (40 Nm).

48. Install the LH cylinder block drain plug. Tighten the drain plug to 177 inch lbs. (20 Nm), plus an additional 180°.

49. Install 6 new LH exhaust manifold studs. Tighten the studs to 106 inch lbs. (12 Nm).

⁂ WARNING

Failure to tighten the exhaust manifold nuts to specification a second time will cause the exhaust manifold to develop an exhaust leak.

50. Using a new gasket, install the LH exhaust manifold and 6 new nuts. Tighten in 2 stages in the proper sequence (refer to the Exhaust Manifold procedure):

a. Stage 1: Tighten to 177 inch lbs. (20 Nm).

b. Stage 2: Tighten to 18 ft. lbs. (25 Nm).

51. Install the LH exhaust manifold heat shield and the 3 bolts. Tighten the bolts to 89 inch lbs. (10 Nm).

52. Using a new gasket, install the LH catalytic converter and 4 new nuts. Tighten the nuts to 30 ft. lbs. (40 Nm).

53. Install the LH catalytic converter bracket bolts. Tighten the bolts to 177 inch lbs. (20 Nm).

54. Attach the Engine Oil Pressure (EOP) switch wiring harness pin-type retainer.

55. Install the stud, generator and the nut and bolt. Tighten the stud to 106 inch lbs. (12 Nm), and tighten the nut and bolt to 35 ft. lbs. (48 Nm).

56. Connect the generator electrical connector.

57. Connect the generator B+ cable and install the nut. Tighten the nut to 150 inch lbs. (17 Nm).

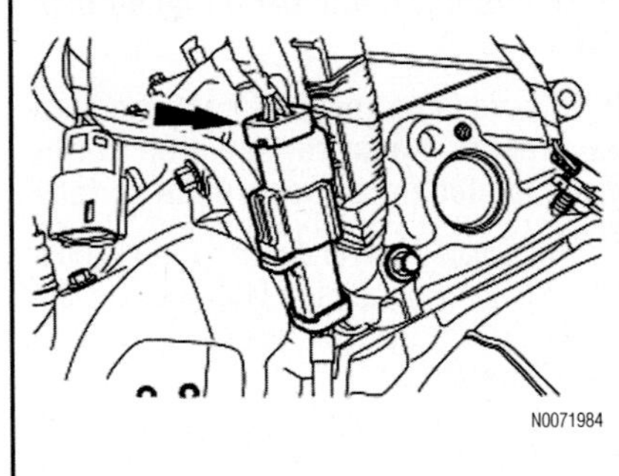

Fig. 104 LH catalyst monitor sensor (CMS) electrical connector

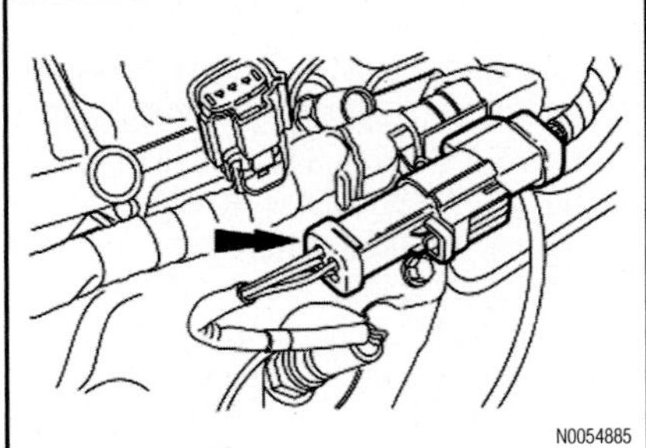

Fig. 105 LH heated oxygen sensor (HO2S) electrical connector

58. Attach the pin-type wire harness retainer to the rear of LH cylinder head.

59. Connect the LH Catalyst Monitor Sensor (CMS) electrical connector.

60. Connect the LH Heated Oxygen Sensor (HO2S) electrical connector.

61. Install the LH Camshaft Position (CMP) sensor and the bolt. Tighten the bolt to 89 inch lbs. (10 Nm).

62. Connect the LH CMP sensor electrical connector.

63. Connect the Cylinder Head Temperature (CHT) sensor electrical connector.

64. Connect the 6 fuel injector electrical connectors (3 shown).

65. Install the LH camshafts.

Right-Hand

See Figures 106 through 110.

⁂ WARNING

During engine repair procedures, cleanliness is extremely important. Any foreign material, including any material created while cleaning gasket surfaces, that enters the oil passages, coolant passages or the oil pan, may cause engine failure.

➡On early build engines, the timing chain rides on the inner side of the RH timing chain guide. Late build engines are equipped with a different design RH timing chain guide that requires the timing chain to ride on the outer side of the RH timing chain guide. For service, all replacement RH timing chain guides will be the late build design.

All Vehicles

1. Remove the RH camshafts. For additional information, refer to Camshaft in this section.

2. Disconnect the RH Heated Oxygen Sensor (HO2S) electrical connector.

3. Disconnect the RH Camshaft Position (CMP) sensor electrical connector.

4. Remove the bolt and the RH CMP sensor.

5. Remove the bolt and the Power Steering Pressure (PSP) tube bracket from the RH cylinder head.

6. Remove the bolt and the ground wire.

7. Disconnect the 6 fuel injector electrical connectors (3 shown).

8. Disconnect the Cylinder Head Temperature (CHT) sensor electrical connector.

9. Disconnect the LH Catalyst Monitor Sensor (CMS) electrical connector.

10. Remove the 2 LH catalytic converter bracket bolts.

11. Remove the 4 nuts and the LH catalytic converter.

a. Discard the nuts and the gasket.

12. Remove the LH cylinder block drain plug.

a. Allow coolant to drain from the cylinder block.

13. Remove the 4 nuts and the RH catalytic converter.

a. Discard the nuts and gasket.

14. If equipped, remove the heat shield and disconnect the block heater electrical connector.

a. Remove the block heater wiring harness from the engine.

15. Remove the RH cylinder block drain plug or, if equipped, the block heater.

a. Allow coolant to drain from the cylinder block.

16. Remove the 3 bolts and the RH exhaust manifold heat shield.

17. Remove the 6 nuts and the RH exhaust manifold.

a. Discard the nuts and exhaust manifold gaskets.

18. Clean and inspect the RH exhaust manifold as outlined in this section.

19. Remove and discard the 6 RH exhaust manifold studs.

Engines Equipped With Early Build RH Timing Chain Guides

20. Remove the 2 bolts and the RH primary timing chain guide.

Engines Equipped With Late Build/Replacement RH Timing Chain Guides

21. Remove the 2 bolts and the RH primary timing chain guide.

All Vehicles

22. Remove the bolts and the RH secondary timing chain tensioner.
23. Remove the 2 bolts and the engine lifting eye.

➡Index-mark the location of the bracket on the cylinder head for installation.

24. Remove the bolt and the upper intake manifold support bracket.
25. Remove the coolant bypass hose from the thermostat housing.
26. Remove the 4 bolts and the fuel rail and injectors as an assembly.
27. Remove the 3 thermostat housing-to-lower intake manifold bolts.
    a. Remove the thermostat housing and discard the gasket and O-ring seal.

⁂ WARNING

If the engine is repaired or replaced because of upper engine failure, typically including valve or piston damage, check the intake manifold for metal debris. If metal debris is found, install a new intake manifold. Failure to follow these instructions can result in engine damage.

28. Remove the 10 bolts and the lower intake manifold.
    a. Discard the gaskets.
29. Disconnect and remove the CHT sensor jumper harness.

➡If the components are to be reinstalled, they must be installed in the same positions. Mark the components for installation into their original locations.

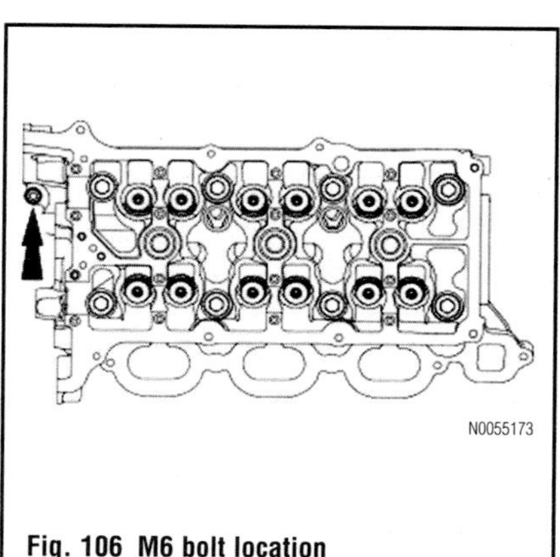

Fig. 106 M6 bolt location

30. Remove the valve tappets from the cylinder head.
31. Inspect the valve tappets.
32. Remove and discard the M6 bolt.

⁂ WARNING

Place clean, lint-free shop towels over exposed engine cavities. Carefully remove the towels so foreign material is not dropped into the engine. Any foreign material (including any material created while cleaning gasket surfaces) that enters the oil passages or the oil pan, may cause engine failure.

⁂ WARNING

Aluminum surfaces are soft and may be scratched easily. Never place the cylinder head gasket surface, unprotected, on a bench surface.

➡The cylinder head bolts must be discarded and new bolts must be installed. They are a tighten-to-yield design and cannot be reused.

33. Remove and discard the 8 bolts from the cylinder head.
    a. Remove the cylinder head.
    b. Discard the cylinder head gasket.

➡Do not use metal scrapers, wire brushes, power abrasive discs or other abrasive means to clean the sealing surfaces. These tools cause scratches and gouges that make leak paths. Use a plastic scraping tool to remove all traces of the head gasket.

➡Observe all warnings or cautions and follow all application directions contained on the packaging of the silicone gasket remover and the metal surface prep.

➡If there is no residual gasket material present, metal surface prep can be used to clean and prepare the surfaces.

34. Clean the cylinder head-to-cylinder block mating surfaces of both the cylinder heads and the cylinder block in the following sequence.
    a. Remove any large deposits of silicone or gasket material with a plastic scraper.
    b. Apply silicone gasket remover, following package directions, and allow to set for several minutes.
    c. Remove the silicone gasket remover with a plastic scraper. A second application of silicone gasket remover may be required if residual traces of silicone or gasket material remain.
    d. Apply metal surface prep, following package directions, to remove any remaining traces of oil or coolant and to prepare the surfaces to bond with the new gasket. Do not attempt to make the metal shiny. Some staining of the metal surfaces is normal.
35. Support the cylinder head on a bench with the head gasket side up. Check the cylinder head distortion and the cylinder block distortion.

To install:

⁂ WARNING

During engine repair procedures, cleanliness is extremely important. Any foreign material, including any material created while cleaning gasket surfaces that enters the oil passages, coolant passages or the oil pan, may cause engine failure.

➡On early build engines, the timing chain rides on the inner side of the RH timing chain guide. Late built engines are equipped with a different design RH timing chain guide that requires the timing chain to ride on the outer side of the RH timing chain guide. For service, all replacement RH timing chain guides will be the late build design.

All Vehicles

36. Install a new gasket, the RH cylinder head and 8 new bolts. Tighten in the sequence shown in 5 stages:
    a. Stage 1: Tighten to 177 inch lbs. (20 Nm).

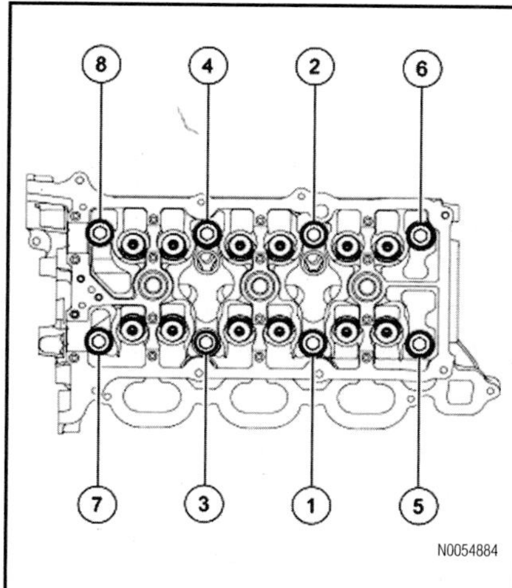

Fig. 107 RH cylinder head installation and tightening sequence

b. Stage 2: Tighten to 26 ft. lbs. (35 Nm).
c. Stage 3: Tighten 90 degrees.
d. Stage 4: Tighten 90 degrees.
e. Stage 5: Tighten 90 degrees.

37. Install the M6 bolt. Tighten the bolt to 89 inch lbs. (10 Nm).

➡**The valve tappets must be installed in their original positions.**

➡**Coat the valve tappets with clean engine oil prior to installation.**

38. Install the valve tappets.
39. Install and connect the Cylinder Head Temperature (CHT) sensor jumper harness.

WARNING

If the engine is repaired or replaced because of upper engine failure, typically including valve or piston damage, check the intake manifold for metal debris. If metal debris is found, install a new intake manifold. Failure to follow these instructions can result in engine damage.

40. Using new gaskets, install the lower intake manifold and the 10 bolts. Tighten the bolts to 89 inch lbs. (10 Nm). Refer to the Intake Manifold procedure.
41. Using a new gasket and O-ring seal, install the thermostat housing and the 3 bolts. Tighten the bolts to 89 inch lbs. (10 Nm).

WARNING

Use O-ring seals that are made of special fuel-resistant material. The use of ordinary O-rings may cause the fuel system to leak. Do not reuse the O-ring seals.

➡**The upper and lower O-ring seals are not interchangeable.**

42. Install new fuel injector O-ring seals.
a. Remove the retaining clips and separate the fuel injectors from the fuel rail.
b. Remove and discard the O-ring seals.
c. Install new O-ring seals and lubricate with clean engine oil.
d. Install the fuel injectors and the retaining clips onto the fuel rail.

43. Install the fuel rail and injectors as an assembly and install the 4 bolts. Tighten the bolts to 89 inch lbs. (10 Nm).
44. Install the coolant bypass hose to the thermostat housing.

➡**Align the bracket with the index mark made during removal.**

45. Install the upper intake manifold support bracket and the bolt. Tighten the bolt to 89 inch lbs. (10 Nm).
46. Install the engine lifting eye and the 2 bolts. Tighten the bolts to 18 ft. lbs. (24 Nm).
47. Install the RH secondary timing chain tensioner and the 2 bolts. Tighten the bolts to 89 inch lbs. (10 Nm).

Engines Equipped With Late Build/Replacement RH Timing Chain Guides

48. Install the RH primary timing chain guide and the 2 bolts. Tighten the bolts to 89 inch lbs. (10 Nm).

Engines Equipped With Early Build RH Timing Chain Guides

49. Install the RH primary timing chain guide and the 2 bolts. Tighten the bolts to 89 inch lbs. (10 Nm).

All Vehicles

50. Install 6 new RH exhaust manifold studs. Tighten the studs to 106 inch lbs. (12 Nm).

WARNING

Failure to tighten the exhaust manifold nuts to specification a second time will cause the exhaust manifold to develop an exhaust leak.

51. Using a new gasket, install the RH exhaust manifold and 6 new nuts. Tighten in 2 stages in the sequence given in the Exhaust Manifold procedure:
a. Stage 1: Tighten to 177 inch lbs. (20 Nm).
b. Stage 2: Tighten to 18 ft. lbs. (25 Nm).

52. Install the RH exhaust manifold heat shield and the 3 bolts. Tighten the bolts to 89 inch lbs. (10 Nm).
53. Install the RH cylinder block drain plug or, if equipped, the block heater. Tighten the bolts to 30 ft. lbs. (40 Nm).
54. If equipped, install the block heater wiring harness onto the engine.

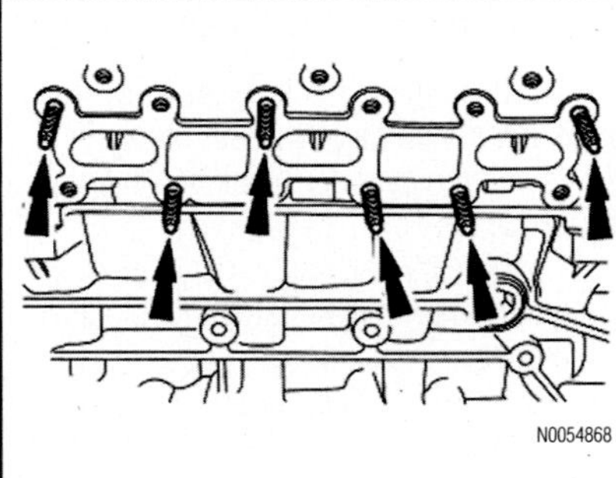

Fig. 108 RH exhaust manifold studs location

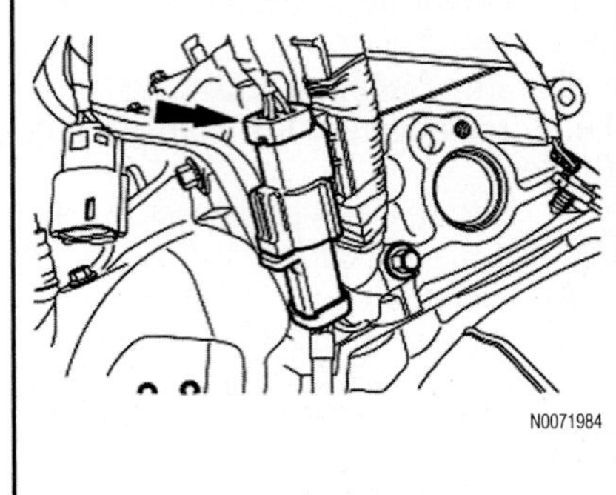

Fig. 109 LH catalyst monitor sensor (CMS) electrical connector

a. Connect the block heater electrical connector and install the heat shield.

55. Using a new gasket, install the RH catalytic converter and 4 new nuts. Tighten the nuts to 30 ft lb. (40 Nm).
56. Install the LH cylinder block drain plug. Tighten the drain plug to 177 inch lbs. (20 Nm) plus an additional 180 degrees.
57. Using a new gasket, install the LH catalytic converter and 4 new nuts. Tighten the nuts to 30 ft. lbs. (40 Nm).
58. Install the 2 LH catalytic converter bracket bolts. Tighten the bolts to 177 inch lbs. (20 Nm).
59. Connect the LH Catalyst Monitor Sensor (CMS) electrical connector.
60. Connect the CHT sensor electrical connector.
61. Connect the 6 fuel injector electrical connectors.
62. Install the ground wire and the bolt. Tighten the bolt to 89 inch lbs. (10 Nm).
63. Install the Power Steering Pressure (PSP) tube bracket and the bolt to the RH cylinder head. Tighten the bolt to 89 inch lbs. (10 Nm).
64. Install the RH Camshaft Position (CMP) sensor and the bolt. Tighten the bolt to 89 inch lbs. (10 Nm).

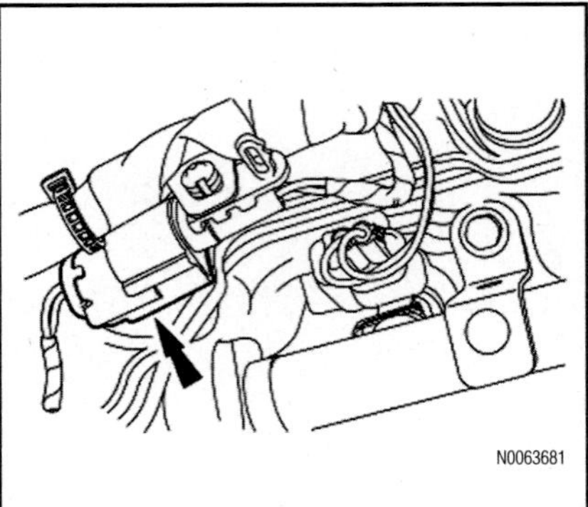

Fig. 110 CHT sensor electrical connector

65. Connect the RH CMP sensor electrical connector.

66. Connect the RH Heated Oxygen Sensor (HO2S) electrical connector.

67. Install the RH camshafts as outlined in this section.

3.5L Turbo Engine

Left-Hand

See Figures 111 through 119.

**** WARNING**

During engine repair procedures, cleanliness is extremely important. Any foreign material, including any material created while cleaning gasket surfaces, that enters the oil passages, coolant passages or the oil pan, may cause engine failure.

**** WARNING**

Whenever turbocharger air intake system components are removed, always cover open ports to protect from debris. It is important that no foreign material enter the system. The turbocharger compressor vanes are susceptible to damage from even small particles. All components should be inspected and cleaned, if necessary, prior to installation or reassembly.

1. Remove the fuel rails as outlined in the Fuel System Section.
2. Remove the LH camshafts as outlined in this section.
3. Disconnect the LH Camshaft Position (CMP) sensor electrical connector.
4. Remove the bolt and the LH CMP sensor.
5. Detach the wiring harness retainer from the rear of the LH cylinder head.
6. Remove the coolant tube bracket-to-cylinder head nut.
7. Remove the nut and disconnect the generator B+ cable.
8. Disconnect the generator electrical connector.
9. Remove the nut, bolt and the generator.
   a. Remove the generator stud.
10. Remove the 3 bolts and the LH exhaust manifold heat shield.
11. Disconnect the turbocharger wastegate regulating valve hose from the LH turbocharger assembly.
12. Remove the 2 bolts and the LH turbocharger oil return tube from the turbocharger.
    a. Remove and discard the gasket.
13. Remove the LH oil supply tube secondary latch.
14. Using the Spring Lock Coupling Disconnect Tool, remove the LH oil supply tube from the quick connect fitting.
    a. Inspect and if necessary, replace the quick connect fitting.
15. Remove the 2 coolant tube banjo bolts and the LH turbocharger coolant tubes and sealing washers.
    a. Discard the sealing washers.
16. Remove the LH turbocharger oil supply tube banjo bolt.
    a. Discard the sealing washer.
    b. Discard the oil supply tube filter.
17. Remove the 2 bolts and the lower LH turbocharger-to-cylinder block bracket.
18. Remove the 2 bolts and the upper LH turbocharger bracket-to-cylinder block bracket.
19. Remove the 8 LH exhaust manifold nuts and the exhaust manifold and turbocharger assembly.
    a. Discard the exhaust manifold gasket and nuts.
20. Clean and inspect the LH exhaust manifold as outlined in this section.
21. Remove and discard the 8 LH exhaust manifold studs.

**** WARNING**

Do not use metal scrapers, wire brushes, power abrasive discs or other abrasive means to clean the sealing surfaces. These may cause scratches and gouges resulting in leak paths. Use a plastic scraper to clean the sealing surfaces.

22. Clean the exhaust manifold mating surface of the cylinder head with metal surface prep. Follow the directions on the packaging.
23. Remove the LH cylinder block drain plug.
    a. Allow coolant to drain from the cylinder block.
24. If equipped, remove the heat shield and disconnect the block heater electrical connector.
    a. Remove the block heater wiring harness from the engine.
25. Remove the RH cylinder block drain plug or, if equipped, the block heater.
    a. Allow coolant to drain from the cylinder block.
26. Remove the 2 bolts and the upper LH primary timing chain guide.
27. Remove the 2 bolts and the LH secondary timing chain tensioner.

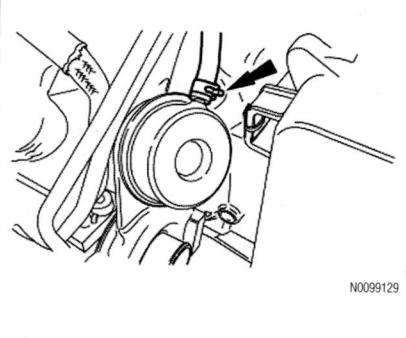

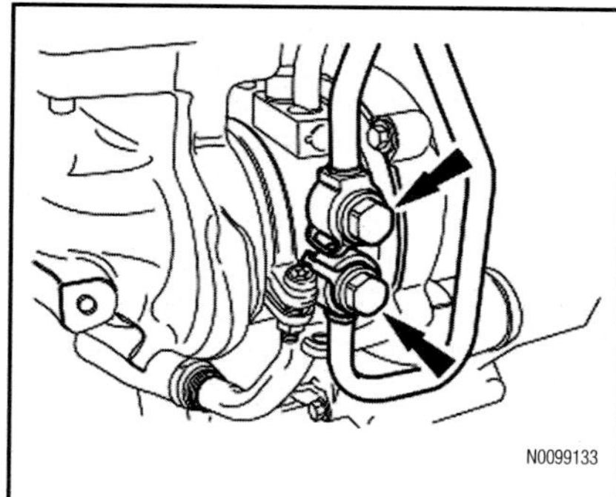

Fig. 112 Turbocharger coolant tubes and banjo bolts—left-hand

N0099129

Fig. 111 Turbocharger wastegate regulating valve hose—left-hand location

N0100452

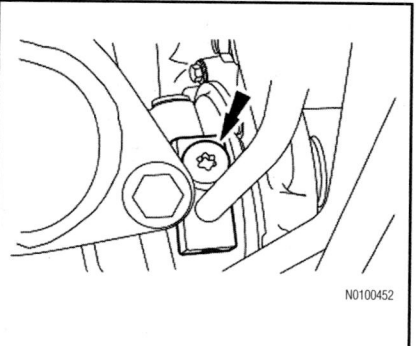

Fig. 113 Turbocharger oil supply tube banjo bolt—left-hand

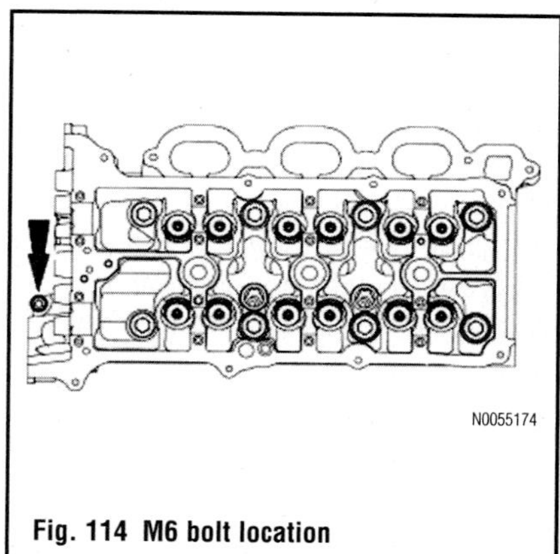

Fig. 114 M6 bolt location

➡**If the components are to be reinstalled, they must be installed in the same positions. Mark the components for installation into their original locations.**

28. Remove the valve tappets from the cylinder head.
29. Inspect the valve tappets as outlined in this section.
30. Remove and discard the M6 bolt.

⁂ WARNING

Place clean, lint-free shop towels over exposed engine cavities. Carefully remove the towels so foreign material is not dropped into the engine. Any foreign material (including any material created while cleaning gasket surfaces) that enters the oil passages or the oil pan, may cause engine failure.

⁂ WARNING

Aluminum surfaces are soft and may be scratched easily. Never place the cylinder head gasket surface, unprotected, on a bench surface.

➡**The cylinder head bolts must be discarded and new bolts must be installed. They are a torque-to-yield design and cannot be reused.**

31. Remove and discard the 8 bolts from the cylinder head.
    a. Remove the cylinder head.
    b. Discard the cylinder head gasket.

⁂ WARNING

Do not use metal scrapers, wire brushes, power abrasive discs or other abrasive means to clean the sealing surfaces. These tools cause scratches and gouges that make leak paths. Use a plastic scraping tool to remove all traces of the head gasket.

➡**Observe all warnings or cautions and follow all application directions contained on the packaging of the silicone gasket remover and the metal surface prep.**

➡**If there is no residual gasket material present, metal surface prep can be used to clean and prepare the surfaces.**

32. Clean the cylinder head-to-cylinder block mating surfaces of both the cylinder heads and the cylinder block in the following sequence.
    a. Remove any large deposits of silicone or gasket material with a plastic scraper.
    b. Apply silicone gasket remover, following package directions, and allow to set for several minutes.
    c. Remove the silicone gasket remover with a plastic scraper. A second application of silicone gasket remover may be required if residual traces of silicone or gasket material remain.
    d. Apply metal surface prep, following package directions, to remove any remaining traces of oil or coolant and to prepare the surfaces to bond with the new gasket. Do not attempt to make the metal shiny. Some staining of the metal surfaces is normal.
33. Support the cylinder head on a bench with the head gasket side up. Check the cylinder head distortion and the cylinder block distortion as outlined in this section

To install:

⁂ WARNING

During engine repair procedures, cleanliness is extremely important. Any foreign material, including any material created while cleaning gasket surfaces that enters the oil passages, coolant passages or the oil pan, may cause engine failure.

⁂ WARNING

Whenever turbocharger air intake system components are removed, always cover open ports to protect from debris. It is important that no foreign material enter the system. The turbocharger compressor vanes are susceptible to damage from even small particles. All components should be inspected and cleaned, if necessary, prior to installation or reassembly.

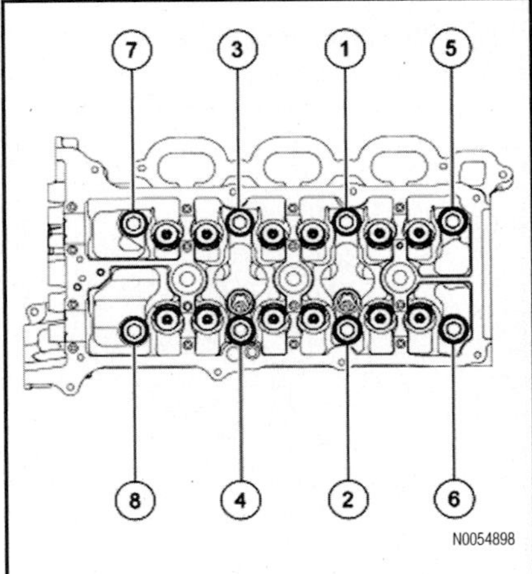

Fig. 115 LH cylinder head installation and tightening sequence

34. Install a new gasket, the LH cylinder head and 8 new bolts. Tighten in the proper sequence in 5 Stages:
    a. Stage 1: Tighten to 177 inch lbs. (20 Nm).
    b. Stage 2: Tighten to 26 ft. lbs. (35 Nm).
    c. Stage 3: Tighten 90 degrees.
    d. Stage 4: Tighten 90 degrees.
    e. Stage 5: Tighten 90 degrees.
35. Install the cylinder head M6 bolt. Tighten the bolt to 89 inch lbs. (10 Nm).

➡**The valve tappets must be installed in their original positions.**

➡**Coat the valve tappets with clean engine oil prior to installation.**

36. Install the valve tappets.
37. Install the LH secondary timing chain tensioner and the 2 bolts. Tighten the bolts to 89 inch lbs. (10 Nm).
38. Install the upper LH primary timing chain guide and the 2 bolts. Tighten the bolts to 89 inch lbs. (10 Nm).
39. Install the RH cylinder block drain plug or, if equipped, the block heater. Tighten the drain plug to 30 ft. lbs. (40 Nm).
40. If equipped, install the block heater wiring harness onto the engine.
    a. Connect the block heater electrical connector and install the heat shield.
41. Install the LH cylinder block drain plug. Tighten the drain plug to 177 inch lbs. (20 Nm) plus an additional 180°.
42. Install 8 new LH exhaust manifold studs. Tighten the studs to 106 inch lbs. (12 Nm).

⁂ WARNING

Failure to tighten the exhaust manifold nuts to specification a second

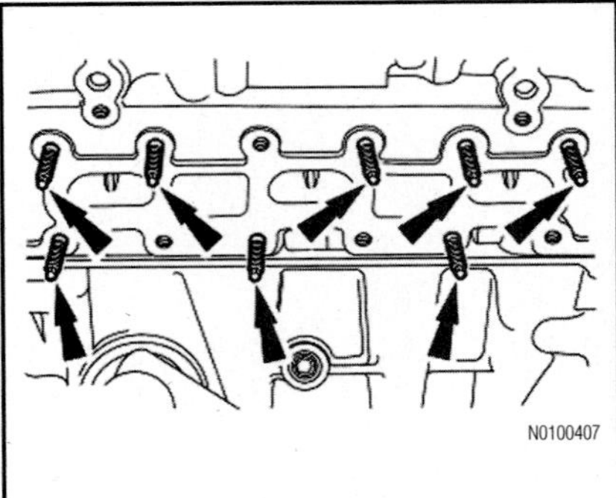

Fig. 116 LH exhaust manifold studs location

time will cause the exhaust manifold to develop an exhaust leak.

43. Install a new gasket, LH exhaust manifold and turbocharger assembly and 8 new nuts. Tighten the nuts in 2 stages in the sequence given in the Exhaust Manifold procedure:
    a. Stage 1: Tighten to 133 inch lbs. (15 Nm).
    b. Stage 2: Tighten to 177 inch lbs. (20 Nm).
44. Install the upper turbocharger bracket-to-cylinder block and the 2 bolts.
    a. Do not tighten the bolts at this time.
45. Install the lower turbocharger-to-cylinder block bracket and the 2 bolts.
    a. Do not tighten the bolts at this time.

WARNING

The next 4 steps must be performed in order or damage to the turbocharger may occur.

46. Tighten the upper turbocharger bracket-to-turbocharger bolt. Tighten the bolt to 168 inch lbs. (19 Nm).
47. Tighten the upper turbocharger bracket-to-cylinder block bolt. Tighten the bolt to 18 ft. lbs. (25 Nm).
48. Tighten the lower turbocharger bracket-to-turbocharger bolt. Tighten the bolt to 168 inch lbs. (19 Nm).

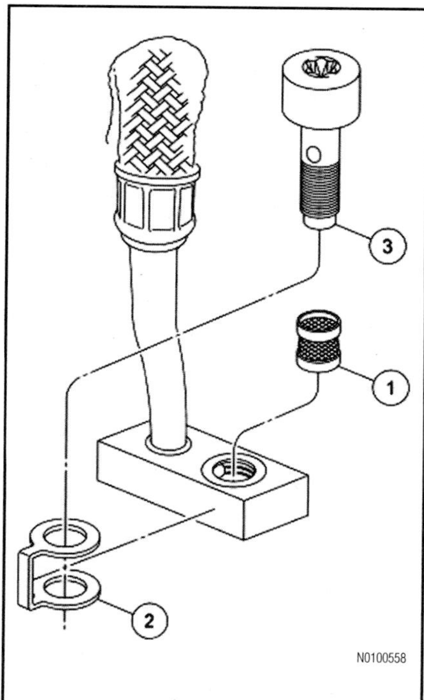

Fig. 117 Oil supply tube filter, washer and bolt

49. Tighten the lower turbocharger bracket-to-cylinder block bolt. Tighten the bolt to 97 inch lbs. (11 Nm).
50. Install the oil supply tube filter, washer and bolt.
    a. Install a new oil supply tube filter in the oil supply tube block.
    b. Slide the new washer onto the oil supply tube block.
    c. Install the banjo bolt into the oil supply tube block.
51. Install the LH turbocharger oil supply tube. Tighten the bolt to 26 ft. lbs. (35 Nm).
52. Using 2 new sealing washers, install the 2 LH turbocharger coolant tubes and the banjo bolts. Tighten the bolts to 27 ft. lbs. (37 Nm).
53. If necessary, install the LH cylinder head turbocharger oil supply quick connect fitting. Tighten the fitting to 142 inch lbs. (16 Nm).

➡Listen for audible click when installing the oil supply tube into the quick connect fitting.

54. Install the LH oil supply tube into the quick connect fitting.
55. Install the LH oil supply tube secondary latch.

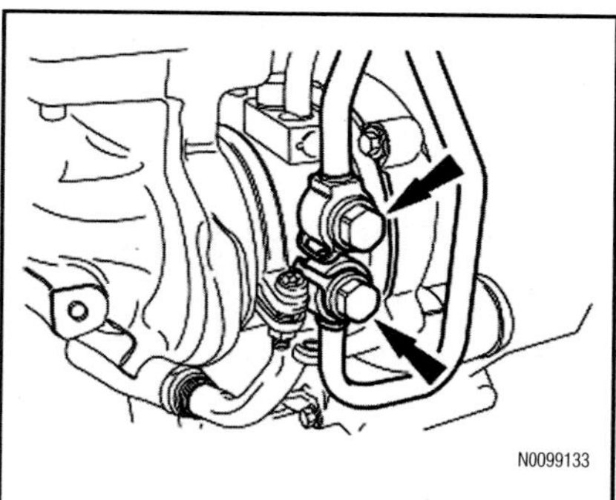

Fig. 118 LH turbocharger coolant tubes and banjo bolts

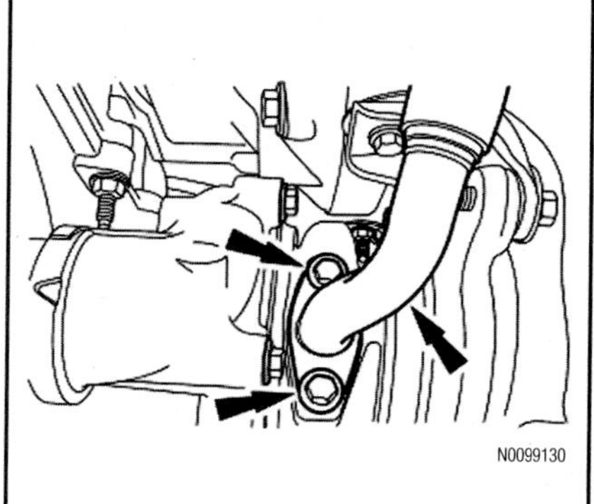

Fig. 119 Turbocharger oil return tube

56. Install a new gasket, turbocharger oil return tube and the 2 bolts. Tighten the bolts to 89 inch lbs. (10 Nm).

➡Make sure the turbocharger wastegate regulating valve hose does not contact the exhaust manifold heat shield.

57. Connect the turbocharger wastegate regulating valve hose to the LH turbocharger assembly.
58. Install the LH exhaust manifold heat shield and the 3 bolts. Tighten the bolts to 124 inch lbs. (14 Nm).
59. Install the stud, generator and the nut and bolt. Tighten the stud to 71 inch lbs. (8 Nm), and the nut & bolt to 35 ft. lbs. (47 Nm).
60. Connect the generator electrical connector.
61. Connect the generator B+ cable and install the nut. Tighten the nut to 150 inch lbs. (17 Nm).
62. Install the LH coolant tube bracket-to-cylinder head nut. Tighten the nut to 89 inch lbs. (10 Nm).
63. Attach the pin-type wire harness retainer to the rear of LH cylinder head.
64. Install the LH Camshaft Position (CMP) sensor and the bolt. Tighten the bolt to 89 inch lbs. (10 Nm).
65. Connect the LH CMP sensor electrical connector.
66. Install the LH camshafts as outlined in this section.
67. Install the fuel rails as outlined in the Fuel System Section.

Right-Hand

See Figures 120 through 128.

WARNING

During engine repair procedures, cleanliness is extremely important. Any foreign material, including any material created while cleaning gasket surfaces, that enters the oil passages, coolant passages or the oil pan, may cause engine failure.

WARNING

Whenever turbocharger air intake system components are removed, always cover open ports to protect from debris. It is important that no foreign material enter the system. The turbocharger compressor vanes are susceptible to damage from even small particles. All components should be inspected and cleaned, if necessary, prior to installation or reassembly.

➡On early build engines, the timing chain rides on the inner side of the RH timing chain guide. Late build engines are equipped with a different design RH timing chain guide that requires the timing chain to ride on the outer side of the RH timing chain guide. For service, all replacement RH timing chain guides will be the late build design.

All Vehicles

1. Remove the fuel rails as outlined in the Fuel System Section.
2. Remove the RH camshafts as outlined in this section.
3. Disconnect the RH Camshaft Position (CMP) sensor electrical connector.
4. Remove the bolt and the RH CMP sensor.
5. Remove the bolt and the ground wire.
6. Remove the bolt and the radio capacitor from the RH cylinder head.
7. Disconnect the Cylinder Head Temperature (CHT) sensor electrical connector from the rear of the RH cylinder head.
8. Remove the 5 bolts and the 2 upper RH exhaust manifold heat shields.
9. Disconnect the turbocharger wastegate regulating valve hose from the RH turbocharger assembly.

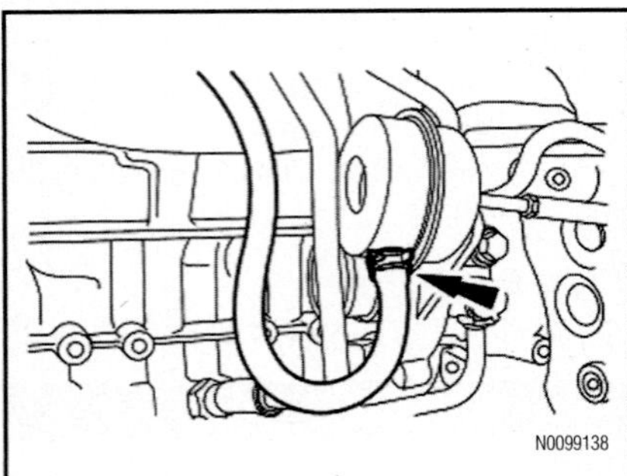

Fig. 120 Turbocharger wastegate regulating valve

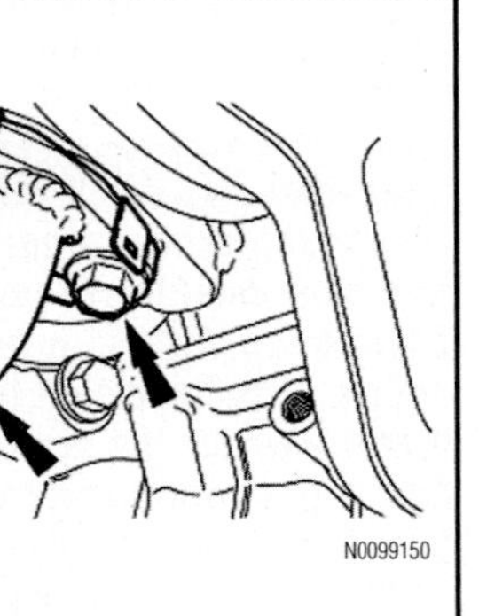

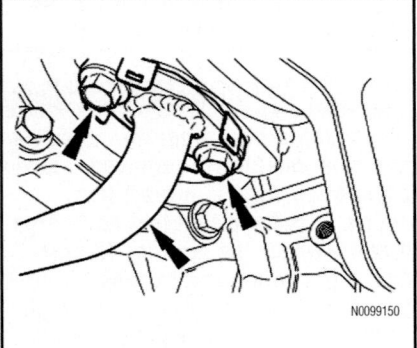

Fig. 121 Turbocharger oil return tube

10. Remove the 2 bolts and the turbocharger oil return tube from the RH turbocharger.
    a. Remove and discard the gasket.
11. Remove the oil supply tube secondary latch.
12. Using the Spring Lock Coupling Disconnect Tool, remove the RH turbocharger oil supply tube from the quick connect fitting.
    a. Inspect and if necessary, replace the quick connect fitting.
13. Remove the 2 coolant tube banjo bolts and the RH turbocharger coolant tubes and sealing washers.
    a. Discard the sealing washers.
14. Remove the coolant tube bracket-to-cylinder head bolt.
15. Remove the 3 bolts and the upper turbocharger-to-cylinder block bracket.
16. Remove the 3 exhaust manifold-to-turbocharger bolts and the turbocharger assembly.
    a. Discard the gasket and bolts.
17. Remove the RH turbocharger oil supply tube banjo bolt.
    a. Discard the sealing washer.
    b. Discard the oil supply tube filter.
18. Remove the 8 nuts and the RH exhaust manifold.
    a. Discard the nuts and exhaust manifold gaskets.
19. Clean and inspect the RH exhaust manifold as outlined in this section.
20. Remove and discard the 8 RH exhaust manifold studs.

⁂ WARNING

Do not use metal scrapers, wire brushes, power abrasive discs or other abrasive means to clean the sealing surfaces. These may cause scratches and gouges resulting in leak paths. Use a plastic scraper to clean the sealing surfaces.

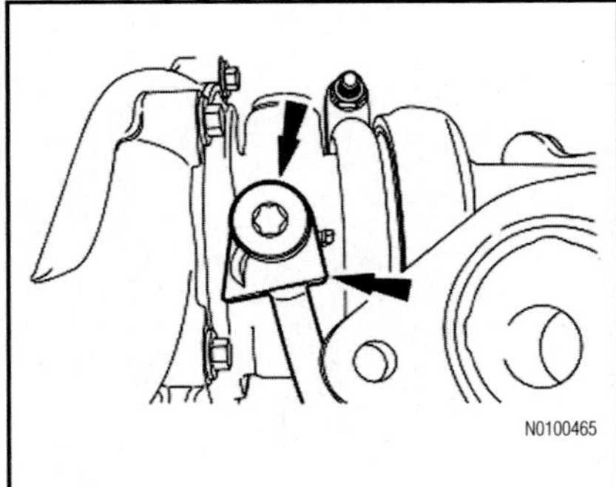

Fig. 122 RH turbocharger oil supply tube banjo bolt location

21. Clean the exhaust manifold mating surface of the cylinder head with metal surface prep. Follow the directions on the packaging.
22. Remove the LH cylinder block drain plug.
    a. Allow coolant to drain from the cylinder block.
23. If equipped, remove the heat shield and disconnect the block heater electrical connector.
    a. Remove the block heater wiring harness from the engine.
24. Remove the RH cylinder block drain plug or, if equipped, the block heater.
    a. Allow coolant to drain from the cylinder block.

Engines Equipped With Early Build RH Timing Chain Guides

25. Remove the 2 bolts and the RH primary timing chain guide.

Engines Equipped With Late Build/Replacement RH Timing Chain Guides

26. Remove the 2 bolts and the RH primary timing chain guide.

All Vehicles

27. Remove the bolts and the RH secondary timing chain tensioner.
28. Remove the 2 bolts and the RH engine lifting eye.

➡If the components are to be reinstalled, they must be installed in the same positions. Mark the components for installation into their original locations.

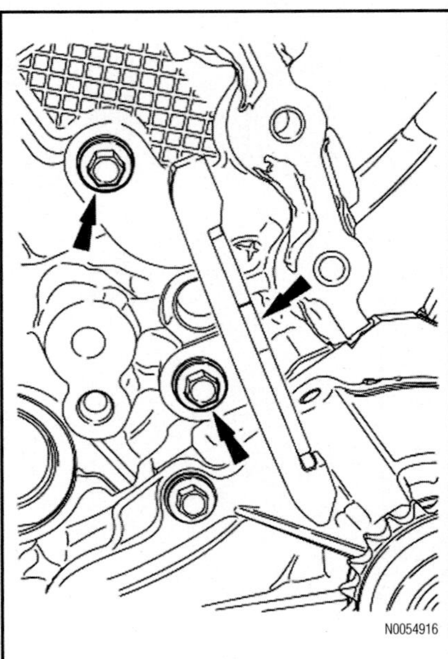

Fig. 123 Early build RH primary timing chain guide location

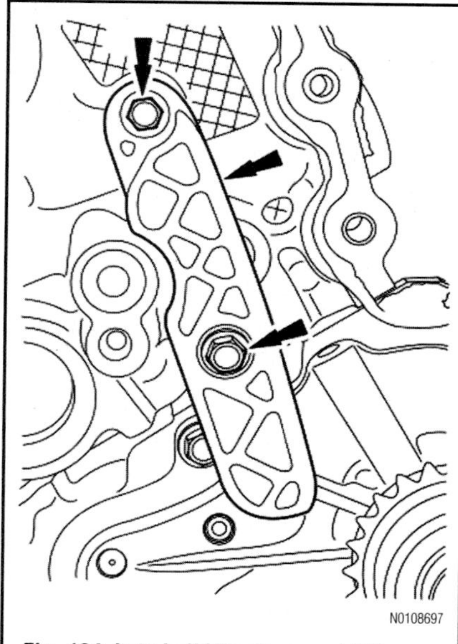

Fig. 124 Late build/Replacement RH timing chain guides

29. Remove the valve tappets from the cylinder head.
30. Inspect the valve tappets as outlined in this section.
31. Remove and discard the M6 bolt.

WARNING

Place clean, lint-free shop towels over exposed engine cavities. Carefully remove the towels so foreign material is not dropped into the engine. Any foreign material (including any material created while cleaning gasket surfaces) that enters the oil passages or the oil pan, may cause engine failure.

➡Aluminum surfaces are soft and may be scratched easily. Never place the cylinder head gasket surface, unprotected, on a bench surface.

➡The cylinder head bolts must be discarded and new bolts must be installed. They are a torque-to-yield design and cannot be reused.

32. Remove and discard the 8 bolts from the cylinder head.
    a. Remove the cylinder head.
    b. Discard the cylinder head gasket.

WARNING

Do not use metal scrapers, wire brushes, power abrasive discs or other abrasive means to clean the sealing surfaces. These tools cause scratches and gouges that make leak paths. Use a plastic scraping tool to remove all traces of the head gasket.

➡Observe all warnings or cautions and follow all application directions contained on the packaging of the silicone gasket remover and the metal surface prep.

➡If there is no residual gasket material present, metal surface prep can be used to clean and prepare the surfaces.

33. Clean the cylinder head-to-cylinder block mating surfaces of both the cylinder heads and the cylinder block in the following sequence.
    a. Remove any large deposits of silicone or gasket material with a plastic scraper.
    b. Apply silicone gasket remover, following package directions, and allow to set for several minutes.
    c. Remove the silicone gasket remover with a plastic scraper. A second application of silicone gasket remover may be required if residual traces of silicone or gasket material remain.
    d. Apply metal surface prep, following package directions, to remove any remaining traces of oil or coolant and to prepare the surfaces to bond with the new gasket. Do not attempt to make the metal shiny. Some staining of the metal surfaces is normal.
34. Support the cylinder head on a bench with the head gasket side up. Check the cylinder head distortion and the cylinder block distortion as outlined in this section.

To install:

WARNING

During engine repair procedures, cleanliness is extremely important. Any foreign material, including any material created while cleaning gasket surfaces that enters the oil passages, coolant passages or the oil pan, may cause engine failure.

WARNING

Whenever turbocharger air intake system components are removed, always cover open ports to protect from debris. It is important that no foreign material enter the system. The turbocharger compressor vanes are susceptible to damage from even small particles. All components should be inspected and cleaned, if necessary, prior to installation or reassembly.

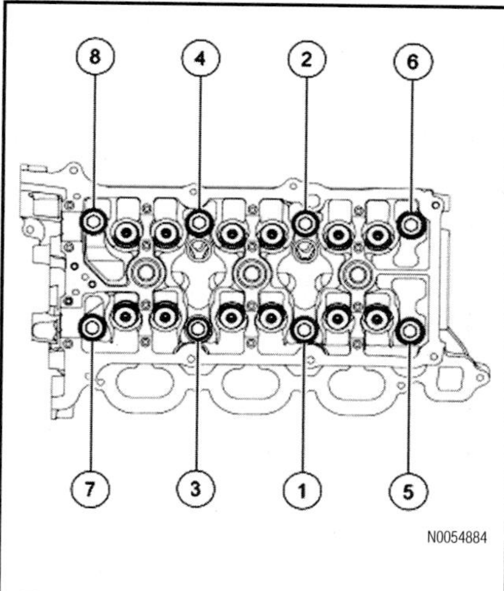

Fig. 125 RH cylinder head installation and tightening sequence

➡On early build engines, the timing chain rides on the inner side of the RH timing chain guide. Late build engines are equipped with a different design RH timing chain guide that requires the timing chain to ride on the outer side of the RH timing chain guide. For service, all replacement RH timing chain guides will be the late build design.

All Vehicles

35. Install a new gasket, the RH cylinder head and 8 new bolts. Tighten in the proper sequence:
    a. Stage 1: Tighten to 177 inch lbs. (20 Nm).
    b. Stage 2: Tighten to 26 ft. lbs. (35 Nm).
    c. Stage 3: Tighten 90 degrees.
    d. Stage 4: Tighten 90 degrees.
    e. Stage 5: Tighten 90 degrees.
36. Install the cylinder head M6 bolt. Tighten the bolt to 89 inch lbs. (10 Nm).

➡The valve tappets must be installed in their original positions.

➡Coat the valve tappets with clean engine oil prior to installation.

37. Install the valve tappets.
38. Install the RH engine lifting eye and the 2 bolts. Tighten the bolts 18 ft. lbs. (24 Nm).
39. Install the RH secondary timing chain tensioner and the 2 bolts. Tighten the bolts to 89 inch lbs. (10 Nm).

Engines Equipped With Early Build RH Timing Chain Guides

40. Install the RH primary timing chain guide and the 2 bolts. Tighten the bolts to 89 inch lbs. (10 Nm).

Engines Equipped With Late Build/Replacement RH Timing Chain Guides

41. Install the RH primary timing chain guide and the 2 bolts. Tighten the bolts to 89 inch lbs. (10 Nm).

All Vehicles

42. Install the RH cylinder block drain plug or, if equipped, the block heater. Tighten the drain plug to 30 ft. lbs. (40 Nm).

43. If equipped, install the block heater wiring harness onto the engine.

a. Connect the block heater electrical connector and install the heat shield.

44. Install the LH cylinder block drain plug. Tighten the drain plug to 177 inch lbs. (20 Nm). Plus an additional 180 degrees.

45. Install 8 new RH exhaust manifold studs. Tighten the studs to 106 inch lbs. (12 Nm).

WARNING

Failure to tighten the exhaust manifold nuts to specification a second time will cause the exhaust manifold to develop an exhaust leak.

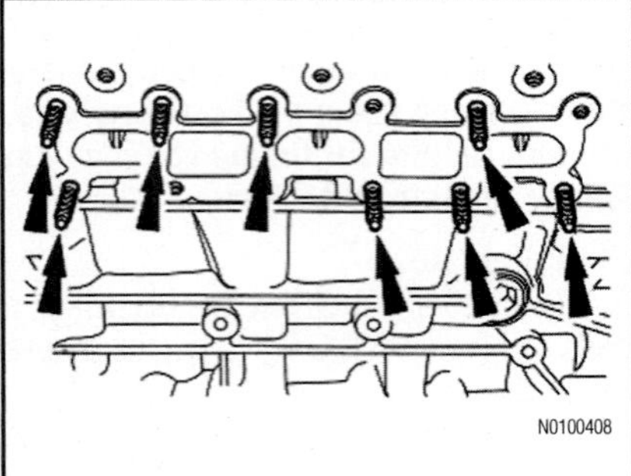

Fig. 126 RH exhaust manifold studs location

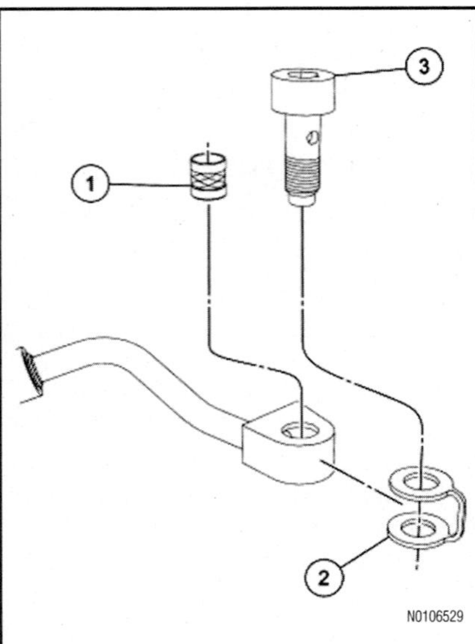

Fig. 127 Oil supply tube filter, washer and bolt location

46. Install a new gasket, RH exhaust manifold and 8 new nuts. Tighten in 2 stages in the proper sequence given in the Exhaust Manifold procedure:

a. Stage 1: Tighten to 133 inch lbs. (15 Nm).

b. Stage 2: Tighten to 177 inch lbs. (20 Nm).

47. Install the oil supply tube filter, washer and bolt.

a. Install a new oil supply tube filter in the oil supply tube block.

b. Slide the new washer onto the oil supply tube block.

c. Install the banjo bolt into the oil supply tube block.

48. Install the RH turbocharger oil supply tube. Tighten the bolt to 26 ft. lbs. (35 Nm).

49. Install a new gasket, the turbocharger and the 3 new exhaust manifold-to-turbocharger bolts. Tighten the bolts to 33 ft. lbs. (45 Nm).

50. Install the upper turbocharger-to-cylinder block bracket and the 3 bolts and position the bracket as far clockwise as possible and tighten the bolts in the following sequence:

a. Tighten the lower bolt to 19 ft. lbs. (26 Nm).

b. Tighten the upper bolt to 19 ft. lbs. (26 Nm).

c. Tighten the turbocharger bolt to 168 inch lbs. (19 Nm).

51. Using 2 new sealing washers, install the 2 RH turbocharger coolant tubes and banjo bolts. Tighten the bolts to 27 ft. lbs. (37 Nm).

52. Install the coolant tube bracket-to-cylinder head bolt. Tighten the bolt to 89 inch lbs. (10 Nm).

53. If necessary, install the RH cylinder head turbocharger oil supply quick connect fitting. Tighten the quick connect fitting to 142 inch lbs. (16 Nm).

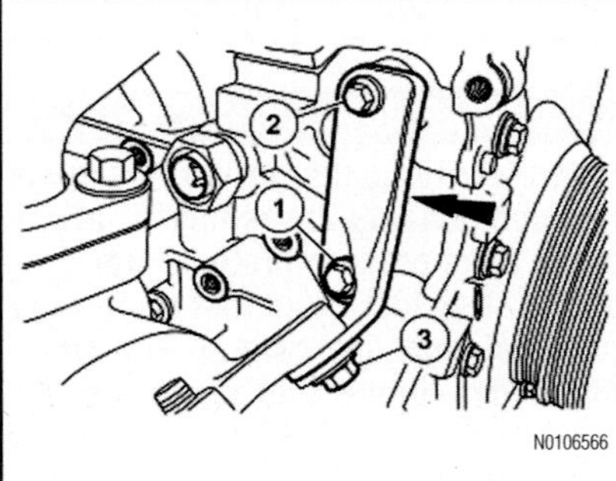

Fig. 128 Upper turbocharger-to-cylinder block bracket installation

➡Listen for audible click when installing the oil supply tube into the quick connect fitting.

54. Install the RH oil supply tube into the quick connect fitting.

55. Install the oil supply tube secondary latch.

56. Install a new gasket and the RH turbocharger oil return tube and the 2 bolts. Tighten the bolts to 89 inch lbs. (10 Nm).

➡Make sure the turbocharger wastegate regulating valve hose does not contact the exhaust manifold heat shield.

57. Connect the turbocharger wastegate regulating valve hose to the RH turbocharger assembly.

➡Make sure the heat shield does not contact the wastegate arm.

58. Install the 2 upper RH exhaust manifold heat shield and the 5 bolts. Tighten the bolts to 124 inch lbs. (14 Nm).

59. Connect the Cylinder Head Temperature (CHT) sensor electrical connector to the rear of the RH cylinder head.

60. Install the radio capacitor and bolt to the RH cylinder head. Tighten the bolt to 89 inch lbs. (10 Nm).

61. Install the ground wire and the bolt. Tighten the bolt to 89 inch lbs. (10 Nm).

62. Install the RH Camshaft Position (CMP) sensor and the bolt. Tighten the bolt to 89 inch lbs. (10 Nm).

63. Connect the RH CMP sensor electrical connector.

64. Install the RH camshafts as outlined in this section.

65. Install the fuel rails as outlined in the Fuel System Section.

ENGINE OIL & FILTER

REPLACEMENT

3.5L Engine, Except Turbo

1. With the vehicle in NEUTRAL, position it on a hoist.

2. Remove and discard the engine oil filter.

3. Remove the 3 bolts and the oil filter adapter.

a. Discard the gasket.

4. Clean and inspect all sealing surfaces.

To install:

5. Clean and inspect all sealing surfaces.

6. Install the 3 bolts and the oil filter adapter. Tighten to 89 inch lbs. (10 Nm).

➡Lubricate the engine oil filter gasket with clean engine oil prior to installing the oil filter.

7. Install a new engine oil filter. Tighten the filter to 44 inch lbs. (5 Nm) and then rotate an additional 180 degrees.
8. With the vehicle in NEUTRAL, lower it from the hoist.

3.5L Turbo Engine

1. With the vehicle in NEUTRAL, position it on a hoist.
2. Remove and discard the engine oil filter.
3. Remove the 3 bolts and the oil filter adapter.
   a. Discard the gasket.
   b. Clean and inspect all sealing surfaces.

To install:

4. Using a new gasket, install the oil filter adapter and the 3 bolts. Tighten bolts 89 inch lbs. (10 Nm).

➡Lubricate the engine oil filter gasket with clean engine oil prior to installing the oil filter.

5. Install a new engine oil filter. Tighten the filter to 44 inch lbs. (5 Nm) and then rotate an additional 180 degrees.

EXHAUST MANIFOLD

REMOVAL & INSTALLATION

3.5L Engine, Except Turbo

Left-Hand

See Figure 129.

1. Remove the LH catalytic converter as outlined in this section.
2. Remove the LH Heated Oxygen Sensor (HO2S) as outlined in the Engine Performance & Emission Controls Section.
3. Remove the 3 bolts and the LH exhaust manifold heat shield.
4. Remove the 6 nuts and the LH exhaust manifold.
   a. Discard the nuts and gasket.
5. Clean and inspect the LH exhaust manifold as outlined in this section.
6. Remove and discard the 6 LH exhaust manifold studs.

✻✻ WARNING

Do not use metal scrapers, wire brushes, power abrasive discs or other abrasive means to clean the sealing surfaces. These may cause scratches and gouges resulting in leak paths. Use a plastic scraper to clean the sealing surfaces.

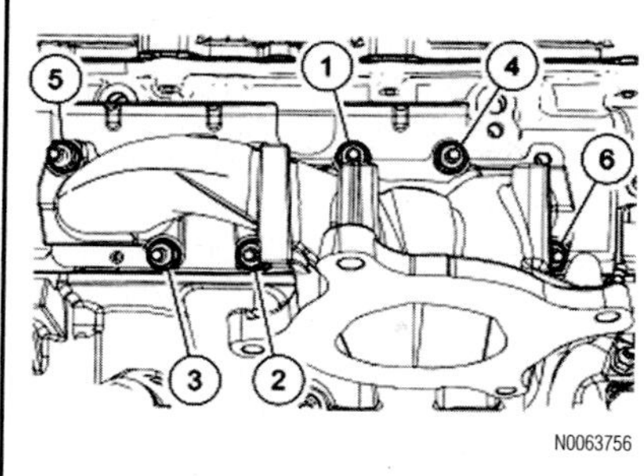

Fig. 129 LH exhaust manifold—3.5L engine, except Turbo

7. Clean the exhaust manifold mating surface of the cylinder head with metal surface prep. Follow the directions on the packaging.

To install:

8. Install 6 new LH exhaust manifold studs. Tighten the studs to 106 inch lbs. (12 Nm).

✻✻ WARNING

Failure to tighten the exhaust manifold nuts to specification a second time will cause the exhaust manifold to develop an exhaust leak.

9. Using a new gasket, install the LH exhaust manifold and 6 new nuts. Tighten the nuts in 2 stages in the proper sequence.
   a. Stage 1: Tighten to 177 inch lbs. (20 Nm).
   b. Stage 2: Tighten to 18 ft. lbs. (25 Nm).
10. Install the LH exhaust manifold heat shield and the 3 bolts. Tighten the bolts to 89 inch lbs. (10 Nm).
11. Install the LH HO2S as outlined in the Engine Performance & Emission Controls Section.
12. Install the LH catalytic converter as outlined in this section.

Right-Hand

See Figure 130.

1. Remove the RH catalytic converter as outlined in this section.
2. Disconnect the RH Heated Oxygen Sensor (HO2S) electrical connector.
3. Remove the 6 nuts and the RH exhaust manifold.
   a. Discard the nuts and gasket.
4. Clean and inspect the RH exhaust manifold as outlined in this section.
5. Remove and discard the 6 RH exhaust manifold studs.

✻✻ WARNING

Do not use metal scrapers, wire brushes, power abrasive discs or other abrasive means to clean the sealing surfaces. These may cause scratches and gouges resulting in leak paths. Use a plastic scraper to clean the sealing surfaces.

6. Clean the exhaust manifold mating surface of the cylinder head with metal surface prep. Follow the directions on the packaging.

To install:

7. Install 6 new RH exhaust manifold studs. Tighten to 106 inch lbs. (12 Nm).

✻✻ WARNING

Failure to tighten the exhaust manifold nuts to specification a second time will cause the exhaust manifold to develop an exhaust leak.

8. Using a new gasket, install the RH exhaust manifold and 6 new nuts. Tighten in 2 stages in the proper sequence.
   a. Stage 1: Tighten to 177 inch lbs. (20 Nm).
   b. Stage 2: Tighten to 18 ft. lbs. (25 Nm).
9. Connect the RH HO2S electrical connector.
10. Install the RH catalytic converter as outlined in this section.

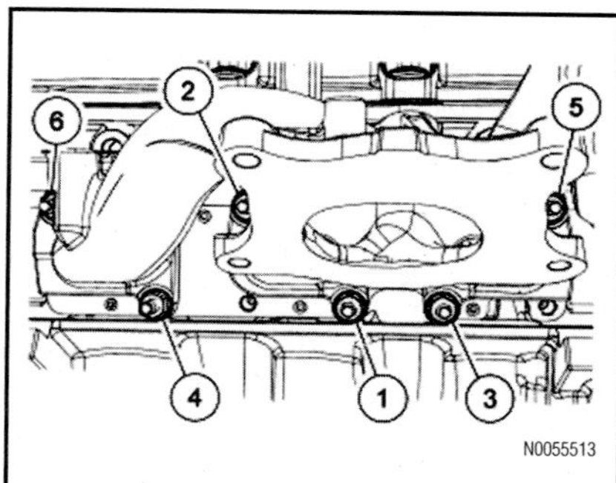

Fig. 130 RH exhaust manifold—3.5L engine, except Turbo

3.5L Turbo Engine

Left-Hand

See Figures 131 through 133.

✱✱ WARNING

Whenever turbocharger air intake system components are removed, always cover open ports to protect from debris. It is important that no foreign material enter the system. The turbocharger compressor vanes are susceptible to damage from even small particles. All components should be inspected and cleaned, if necessary, prior to installation or reassembly.

1. Remove the 2 top LH exhaust manifold heat shield bolts.
2. Remove the LH catalytic converter as outlined in this section.
3. Remove the bottom bolt and the LH exhaust manifold heat shield.
4. Remove the 2 bolts and the LH upper turbocharger bracket.
5. Loosen the 2 bolts for the LH lower turbocharger bracket.
6. Remove the 3 LH turbocharger-to-exhaust manifold bolts.
   a. Discard the gasket.
7. Remove the 5 top LH exhaust manifold nuts.
   a. Discard the nuts.
8. Remove the 3 bottom nuts and the LH exhaust manifold.
   a. Discard the nuts and gasket.
9. Clean and inspect the LH exhaust manifold as outlined in this section.
10. Remove and discard the 8 LH exhaust manifold studs.

✱✱ WARNING

Do not use metal scrapers, wire brushes, power abrasive discs or other abrasive means to clean the sealing surfaces. These may cause scratches and gouges resulting in leak paths. Use a plastic scraper to clean the sealing surfaces.

11. Clean the exhaust manifold mating surface of the cylinder head with metal surface prep. Follow the directions on the packaging.

To install:

12. Install 8 new LH exhaust manifold studs. Tighten the studs to 106 inch lbs. (12 Nm).

✱✱ WARNING

Failure to tighten the exhaust manifold nuts to specification a second time will cause the exhaust manifold to develop an exhaust leak.

13. Install a new gasket, LH exhaust manifold and 8 new nuts. Tighten in 2 stages in the proper sequence.
   a. Stage 1: Tighten to 133 inch lbs. (15 Nm).
   b. Stage 2: Tighten to 177 inch lbs. (20 Nm).
14. Install a new gasket and the 3 turbocharger-to-exhaust manifold bolts. Tighten the bolts to 33 ft. lbs. (45 Nm).
15. Install the upper turbocharger bracket and the 2 bolts.
   a. Do not tighten the bolts at this time.

✱✱ WARNING

The next 4 steps must be performed in order or damage to the turbocharger may occur.

16. Tighten the upper turbocharger bracket-to-turbocharger bolt. Tighten the bolt to 168 inch lbs. (19 Nm).
17. Tighten the upper turbocharger bracket-to-cylinder block bolt. Tighten the bolt to 18 ft. lbs. (25 Nm).
18. Tighten the lower turbocharger bracket-to-turbocharger bolt. Tighten the bolt to 168 inch lbs. (19 Nm).

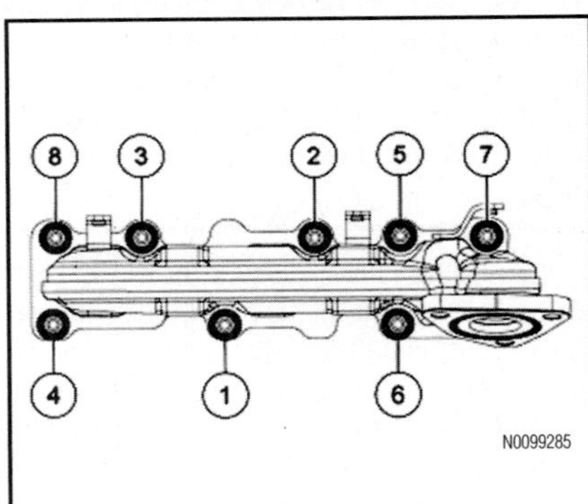

Fig. 131 LH exhaust manifold–3.5L Turbo

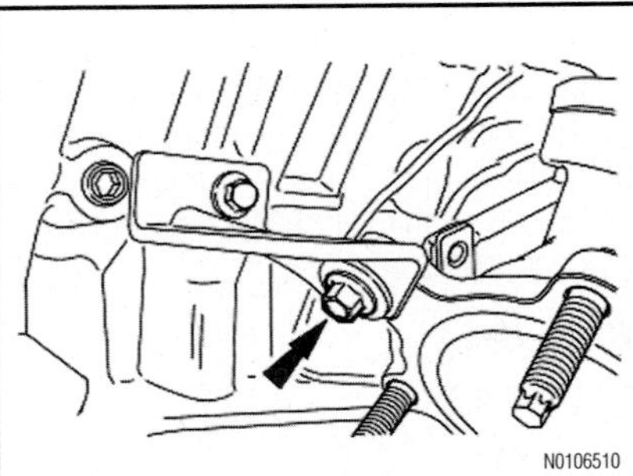

Fig. 132 Upper turbocharger bracket-to-turbocharger

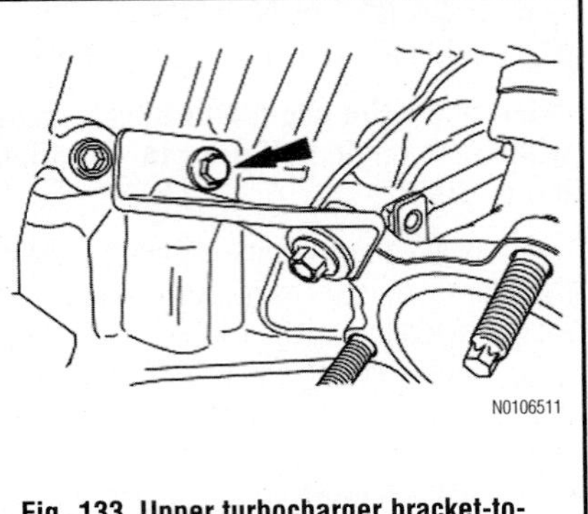

Fig. 133 Upper turbocharger bracket-to-cylinder block bolt

19. Tighten the lower turbocharger bracket-to-cylinder block bolt. Tighten the bolt to 97 inch lbs. (11 Nm).
20. Install the LH exhaust manifold heat shield and the bottom bolt.
   a. Do not tighten the bolt at this time.
21. Install the LH catalytic converter as outlined in this section.
22. Install the 2 top LH exhaust manifold heat shield bolts. Tighten the bolts to 124 inch lbs. (14 Nm).
23. Tighten the LH exhaust manifold heat shield bottom bolt. Tighten the bolt to 124 inch lbs. (14 Nm).

Right-Hand

See Figure 134.

✱✱ WARNING

Whenever turbocharger air intake system components are removed, always cover open ports to protect from debris. It is important that no foreign material enter the system. The turbocharger compressor vanes are susceptible to damage from even small particles. All components should be inspected and cleaned, if necessary, prior to installation or reassembly.

1. Remove the RH turbocharger as outlined in the Fuel System Section.
2. Remove the 8 nuts and the RH exhaust manifold.
   a. Discard the nuts and exhaust manifold gasket.
3. Clean and inspect the RH exhaust manifold as outlined in this section.
4. Remove and discard the 8 RH exhaust manifold studs.

✱✱ WARNING

Do not use metal scrapers, wire brushes, power abrasive discs or other abrasive means to clean the

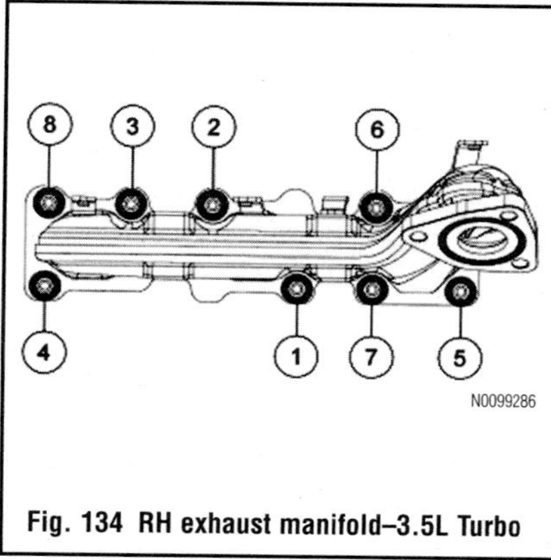

Fig. 134 RH exhaust manifold–3.5L Turbo

sealing surfaces. These may cause scratches and gouges resulting in leak paths. Use a plastic scraper to clean the sealing surfaces.

5. Clean the exhaust manifold mating surface of the cylinder head with metal surface prep. Follow the directions on the packaging.

To install:

6. Install 8 new RH exhaust manifold studs. Tighten the studs to 106 inch lbs. (12 Nm).

**** WARNING**

Failure to tighten the exhaust manifold nuts to specification a second time will cause the exhaust manifold to develop an exhaust leak.

7. Install a new gasket, RH exhaust manifold and 8 new nuts. Tighten in 2 stages in the proper sequence.
   a. Stage 1: Tighten to 133 inch lbs. (15 Nm).
   b. Stage 2: Tighten to 177 inch lbs. (20 Nm).
8. Install the RH turbocharger as outlined in the Fuel System Section.

INTAKE MANIFOLD

REMOVAL & INSTALLATION

3.5L Engine, Except Turbo

Lower

See Figure 135.

**** WARNING**

During engine repair procedures, cleanliness is extremely important. Any foreign material, including any material created while cleaning gasket surfaces that enters the oil passages, coolant passages or the oil pan, may cause engine failure.

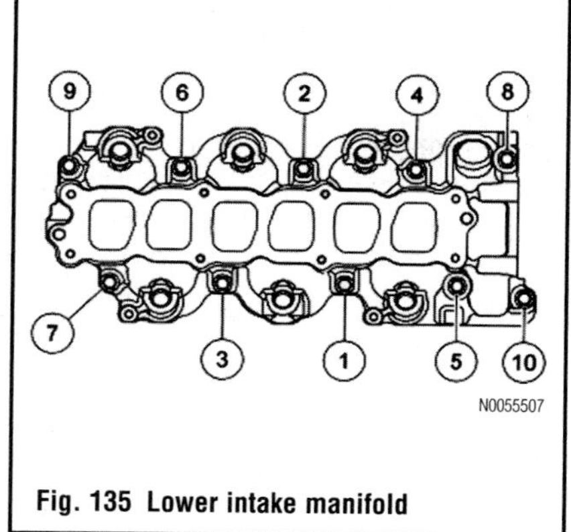

Fig. 135 Lower intake manifold

1. Remove the fuel rail as outlined in the Fuel System Section.
2. Drain the cooling system as outlined in the Engine Cooling Section.
3. Remove the 3 thermostat housing-to-lower intake manifold bolts.
4. Remove the 10 bolts and the lower intake manifold.
   a. Remove and discard the intake manifold and thermostat housing gaskets.
   b. Clean and inspect all sealing surfaces.

To install:

**** WARNING**

If the engine is repaired or replaced because of upper engine failure, typically including valve or piston damage, check the intake manifold for metal debris. If metal debris is found, install a new intake manifold. Failure to follow these instructions can result in engine damage.

5. Using new intake manifold and thermostat housing gaskets, install the lower intake manifold and the 10 bolts. Tighten the bolts in the proper sequence to 89 inch lbs. (10 Nm).
6. Install the 3 thermostat housing-to-lower intake manifold bolts. Tighten to 89 inch lbs. (10 Nm).
7. Install the fuel rail as outlined in the Fuel System Section.
8. Fill and bleed the cooling system as outlined in the Engine Cooling Section.

Upper

See Figure 136.

1. Remove the Air Cleaner (ACL) outlet pipe as outlined in this section.
2. Disconnect the Throttle Body (TB) electrical connector.
3. Disconnect the Evaporative Emission (EVAP) tube from the intake manifold.
4. Detach the EVAP tube pin-type retainer from the upper intake manifold.
5. Disconnect the brake booster vacuum hose from the intake manifold.
6. Disconnect the PCV tube from the PCV valve.
7. Detach the wiring harness retainers from the upper intake manifold.
8. Remove the upper intake manifold support bracket bolt.
9. Remove the fuel tube bracket bolt.
10. Remove the 6 bolts and the upper intake manifold.
    a. Remove and discard the gaskets.
    b. Clean and inspect all of the sealing surfaces of the upper and lower intake manifold.

To install:

**** WARNING**

If the engine is repaired or replaced because of upper engine failure, typically including valve or piston damage, check the intake manifold for metal debris. If metal debris is found, install a new intake manifold. Failure to follow these instructions can result in engine damage.

11. Using new gaskets, install the upper intake manifold and the 6 bolts. Tighten the bolts in the proper sequence to 89 inch lbs. (10 Nm).
12. Install the fuel tube bracket bolt. Tighten the bolt to 53 inch lbs. (6 Nm).
13. Install the upper intake manifold support bracket bolt. Tighten the bolt to 89 inch lbs. (10 Nm).

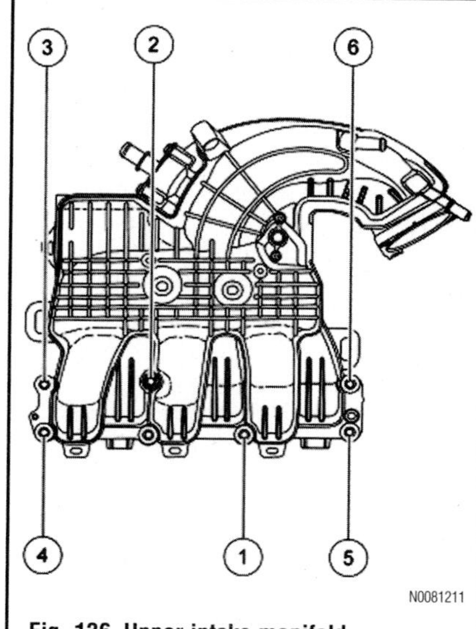

Fig. 136 Upper intake manifold

14. Attach the wiring harness retainers to the upper intake manifold.

15. Connect the PCV tube to the PCV valve.

16. Connect the brake booster vacuum hose to the intake manifold.

17. Connect the EVAP tube to the intake manifold.

18. Attach the EVAP tube pin-type retainer to the upper intake manifold.

19. Connect the TB electrical connector.

20. Install the ACL outlet pipe as outlined in this section.

3.5L Turbo Engine

See Figure 137.

WARNING

During engine repair procedures, cleanliness is extremely important. Any foreign material, including any material created while cleaning gasket surfaces that enters the oil passages, coolant passages or the oil pan, may cause engine failure.

WARNING

Whenever turbocharger air intake system components are removed, always cover open ports to protect from debris. It is important that no foreign material enter the system. The turbocharger compressor vanes are susceptible to damage from even small particles. All components should be inspected and cleaned, if necessary, prior to installation or reassembly.

1. Drain the cooling system as outlined in the Engine Cooling Section.
2. Remove the Air Cleaner (ACL) outlet pipe as outlined in this section.
3. Disconnect the LH turbocharger bypass valve electrical connector.
4. Disconnect the LH turbocharger bypass valve hose from the RH Charge Air Cooler (CAC) tube.
5. Disconnect the turbocharger wastegate regulating valve hose from the RH CAC tube.
6. Disconnect the RH turbocharger bypass valve electrical connector.
7. Disconnect the RH turbocharger bypass valve hose from the RH turbocharger intake tube.

WARNING

The compression limiter bushing may fall out of the mounting bracket grommet on the Charge Air Cooler (CAC) tube during service. Make sure the bushing is in place when reinstalling the tube or damage to the tube may occur.

8. Remove the RH CAC tube nut from the intake manifold.
9. Loosen the clamp and remove the RH CAC tube.
10. Loosen the clamp and remove the RH CAC tube from the RH turbocharger.
11. Remove the noise generator.
12. Loosen the clamp and position CAC outlet pipe-to-Throttle Body (TB) aside.
13. Disconnect the Throttle Position (TP) sensor and electronic TB electrical connectors.
14. Disconnect the quick connect coupling Evaporative Emission (EVAP) tube from the intake manifold.
15. Detach the EVAP purge valve from the intake manifold.
16. Disconnect the brake booster vacuum hose from the intake manifold.
17. Remove the fuel tube-to-engine front cover bracket bolt and position the fuel tube aside.
18. Disconnect the PCV tube quick connect coupling from the intake manifold.
19. If equipped, disconnect the heated PCV valve electrical connector from the intake manifold.
20. Detach and disconnect the 2 fuel injector wiring harness electrical connectors.
21. Disconnect the Manifold Absolute Pressure (MAP)/Intake Air Temperature 2 (IAT2) sensor electrical connector.

➡Mark the location of each hose for installation.

22. Disconnect the 2 hoses from the turbocharger wastegate regulating valve.
23. Disconnect the turbocharger wastegate regulating valve electrical connector.
24. Detach the 2 wire harness-to-intake manifold retainers.
25. Detach the 2 wire harness retainer from the LH valve cover stud bolt.
26. Detach the 2 wire harness retainer from the LH valve cover.
27. Disconnect the 2 coolant heater hoses from the intake manifold.
28. Disconnect the 2 turbocharger coolant hoses from the intake manifold.
29. Disconnect the lower radiator hose from the thermostat housing.
30. Remove the bolt and ground wire from the engine front cover.
31. Disconnect the upper radiator hose at the intake manifold and position the hose aside.

➡Note the routing of the 2 fuel rail wiring harnesses for installation.

32. Remove the 12 bolts and the intake manifold.
    a. Remove and discard the intake manifold, coolant crossover and thermostat housing gaskets.
    b. Clean and inspect all sealing surfaces.

To install:

WARNING

If the engine is repaired or replaced because of upper engine failure, typically including valve or piston damage, check the intake manifold for metal debris. If metal debris is found, install a new intake manifold. Failure to follow these instructions can result in engine damage.

➡Make sure the fuel rail wiring harnesses are routed correctly.

➡Installing the 2 long bolts first will aid in installing the intake manifold.

33. Using new intake manifold, coolant crossover and thermostat housing gaskets, install the intake manifold and the 12 bolts. Tighten the bolts in the proper sequence to 89 inch lbs. (10 Nm).
34. Connect the upper radiator hose to the intake manifold.
35. Install the ground wire and bolt to the engine front cover. Tighten the bolt to 89 inch lbs. (10 Nm).

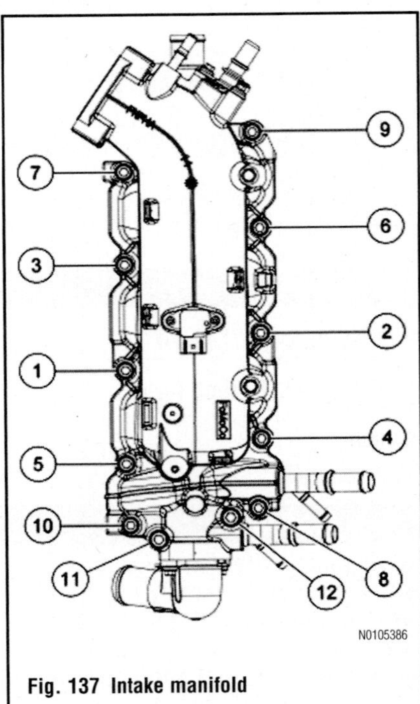

Fig. 137 Intake manifold

36. Connect the lower radiator hose to the thermostat housing.

37. Connect the 2 turbocharger coolant hoses from the intake manifold.

38. Connect the 2 coolant heater hoses from the intake manifold.

39. Attach the 2 wire harness retainers to the LH valve cover.

40. Attach the 2 wire harness retainers to the LH valve cover stud bolt.

41. Attach the 2 wire harness-to-intake manifold retainers.

42. Connect the turbocharger wastegate regulating valve electrical connector.

43. Connect the 2 hoses to the wastegate control valve.

44. Connect the MAP / IAT2 sensor electrical connector.

45. Connect and attach the 2 fuel injector wiring harness electrical connectors.

46. If equipped, connect the heated PCV valve electrical connector.

47. Connect the PCV tube quick connect coupling to the intake manifold.

48. Position the fuel tube and install the fuel tube-to-engine front cover bracket bolt. Tighten the bolt to 89 inch lbs. (10 Nm).

49. Connect the brake vacuum tube to the intake manifold.

50. Attach the EVAP purge valve to the intake manifold.

51. Connect the quick connect coupling EVAP tube to the intake manifold.

➡Align the index marks for the outlet pipe.

52. Connect the TP sensor and electronic TB electrical connectors.

➡Align the index marks for the CAC outlet pipe.

53. Position CAC outlet pipe on the TB and tighten the clamp. Tighten the clamp to 44 inch lbs. (5 Nm).

54. Install the noise generator as outlined in this section.

➡Align the index marks for the RH CAC tube.

55. Install the RH CAC tube to the RH turbocharger and tighten the clamp. Tighten the clamp to 44 inch lbs. (5 Nm).

➡Align the index marks for the RH CAC tube.

56. Install the RH CAC tube and tighten the clamp. Tighten the clamp to 44 inch lbs. (5 Nm).

⁂ WARNING

The compression limiter bushing may fall out of the mounting bracket grommet on the Charge Air Cooler (CAC) tube during service. Make sure the bushing is in place when reinstalling the tube or damage to the tube may occur.

57. Install the RH CAC tube and the RH CAC tube nut to the intake manifold. Tighten the nut to 53 inch lbs. (6 Nm).

58. Connect the RH turbocharger bypass valve hose to the RH turbocharger intake tube.

59. Connect the RH turbocharger bypass valve electrical connector.

60. Connect the turbocharger wastegate regulating valve hose to the RH CAC tube.

61. Connect the LH turbocharger bypass valve electrical connector and the turbocharger bypass valve hose.

62. Install the ACL outlet pipe as outlined in this section.

63. Fill and bleed the cooling system as outlined in the Engine Cooling Section.

OIL PUMP

REMOVAL & INSTALLATION

See Figures 138 through 144.

⁂ WARNING

During engine repair procedures, cleanliness is extremely important. Any foreign material, including any material created while cleaning gasket surfaces, that enters the oil passages, coolant passages or the oil pan may cause engine failure.

➡On early build engines, the timing chain rides on the inner side of the RH timing chain guide. Late build engines are equipped with a different design RH timing chain guide that requires the timing chain to ride on the outer side of the RH timing chain guide. For service, all replacement RH timing chain guides will be the late build design.

All Vehicles

1. Remove the engine front cover as outlined in this section.

Engines Equipped With Early Build RH Timing Chain Guides

2. Rotate the crankshaft clockwise and align the timing marks on the Variable Camshaft Timing (VCT) assemblies.

Engines Equipped With Late Build/Replacement RH Timing Chain Guides

3. Rotate the crankshaft clockwise and align the timing marks on the VCT assemblies.

All Vehicles

➡The Camshaft Holding Tool will hold the camshafts in the Top Dead Center (TDC) position.

4. Install the Camshaft Holding Tool onto the flats of the LH camshafts.

➡The Camshaft Holding Tool will hold the camshafts in the TDC position.

5. Install the Camshaft Holding Tool onto the flats of the RH camshafts.

6. Remove the 3 bolts and the RH VCT housing.

7. Remove the 3 bolts and the LH VCT housing.

8. Remove the 2 bolts and the primary timing chain tensioner.

9. Remove the primary timing chain tensioner arm.

10. Remove the 2 bolts and the lower LH primary timing chain guide.

11. Remove the primary timing chain.

Fig. 138 Early Build RH Timing Chain Guides

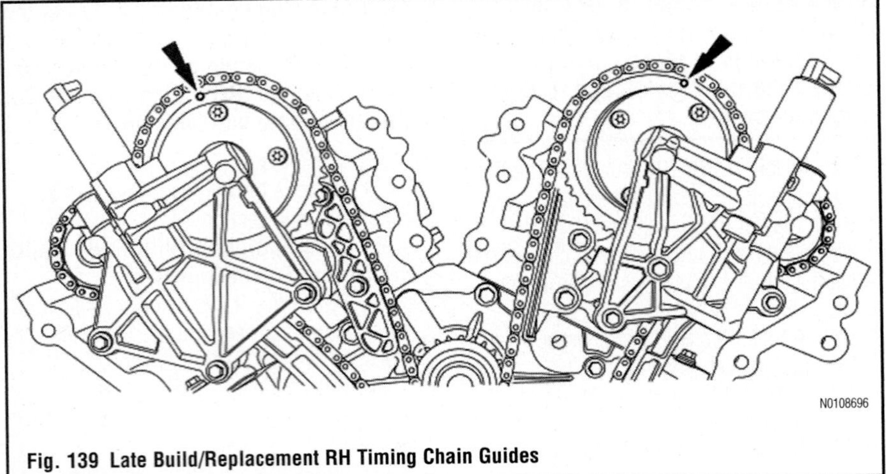
Fig. 139 Late Build/Replacement RH Timing Chain Guides

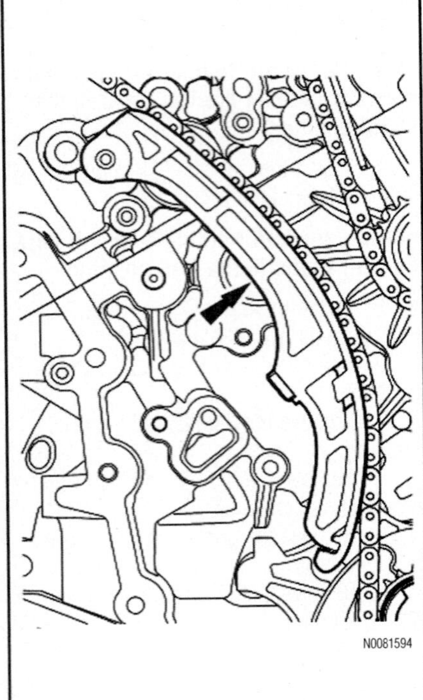
Fig. 140 Primary timing chain tensioner arm

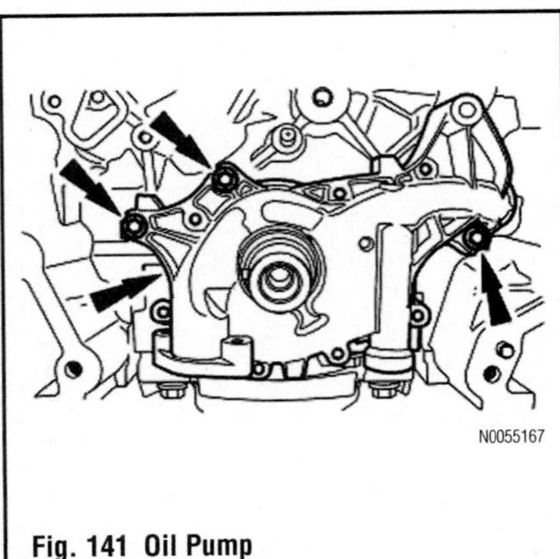
Fig. 141 Oil Pump

12. Remove the crankshaft timing chain sprocket.
13. Remove the 2 bolts and the oil pump screen and pickup tube.
    a. Discard the O-ring seal.
14. Remove the 3 bolts and the oil pump.

To install:

15. Install the oil pump and the 3 bolts. Tighten the bolts to 89 inch lbs. (10 Nm).
16. Using a new O-ring seal, install the oil pump screen and pickup tube and the 2 bolts. Tighten the bolts to 89 inch lbs. (10 Nm).
17. Install the crankshaft timing chain sprocket.
18. Install the primary timing chain with the colored links aligned with the timing marks on the VCT assemblies and the crankshaft sprocket.
19. Install the LH primary timing chain guide and the 2 bolts. Tighten the bolts to 89 inch lbs. (10 Nm).

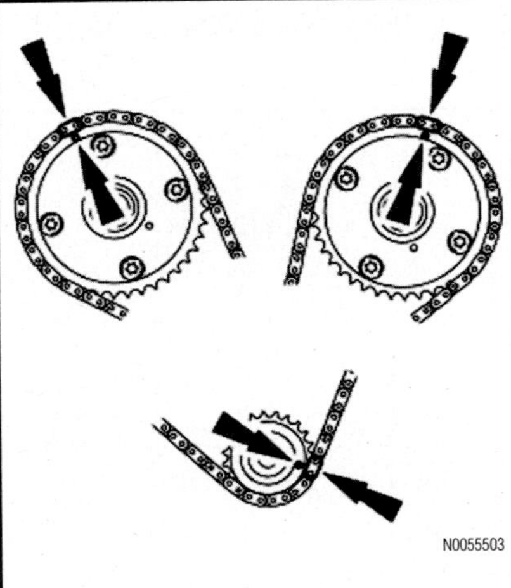
Fig. 142 Install the primary timing chain with the colored links aligned with the timing marks on the VCT assemblies and the crankshaft sprocket

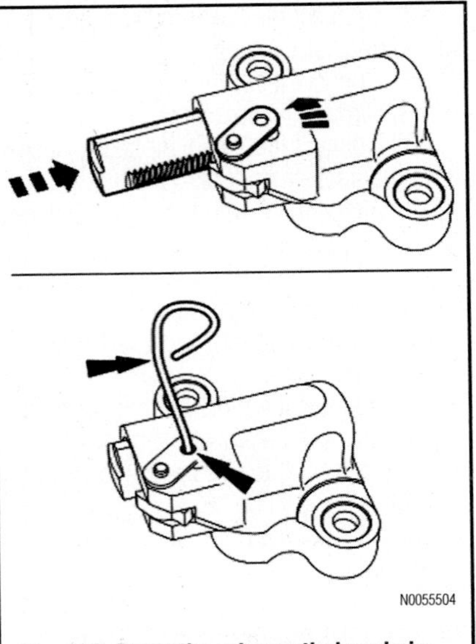
Fig. 143 Reset the primary timing chain tensioner

20. Install the primary timing chain tensioner arm.
21. Reset the primary timing chain tensioner.
    a. Rotate the lever counterclockwise.
    b. Using a soft-jawed vise, compress the plunger.
    c. Align the hole in the lever with the hole in the tensioner housing.
    d. Install a suitable lockpin.

➡It may be necessary to rotate the crankshaft slightly to remove slack from the timing chain and install the tensioner.

22. Install the primary tensioner and the 2 bolts. Tighten the bolts to 89 inch lbs. (10 Nm).
    a. Remove the lockpin.
23. As a post-check, verify correct alignment of all timing marks.
24. Inspect the VCT housing seals for damage and replace as necessary.

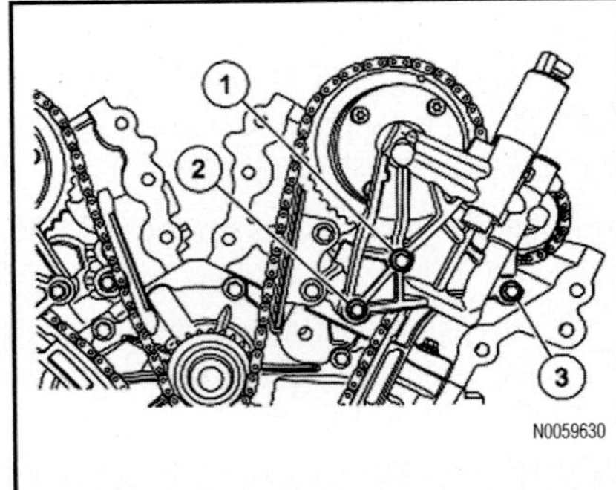

Fig. 144 Install the LH VCT housing and the 3 bolts

WARNING

Make sure the dowels on the Variable Camshaft Timing (VCT) housing are fully engaged in the cylinder head prior to tightening the bolts. Failure to follow this process will result in severe engine damage.

25. Install the LH VCT housing and the 3 bolts. Tighten the bolts to 89 inch lbs. (10 Nm) in the proper sequence.

WARNING

Make sure the dowels on the Variable Camshaft Timing (VCT) housing are fully engaged in the cylinder head prior to tightening the bolts. Failure to follow this process will result in severe engine damage.

26. Install the RH VCT housing and the 3 bolts. Tighten the bolts to 89 inch lbs. (10 Nm) in the proper sequence.
27. Install the engine front cover as outlined in this section.

REAR MAIN SEAL

REMOVAL & INSTALLATION

3.5L Engine, Except Turbo

See Figure 145.

1. With the vehicle in NEUTRAL, position it on a hoist.
2. Remove the flexplate.
3. Remove the crankshaft sensor ring.
4. Using the Crankshaft Rear Oil Seal Remover and Slide Hammer, remove and discard the crankshaft rear seal.
5. Clean all sealing surfaces with metal surface prep.

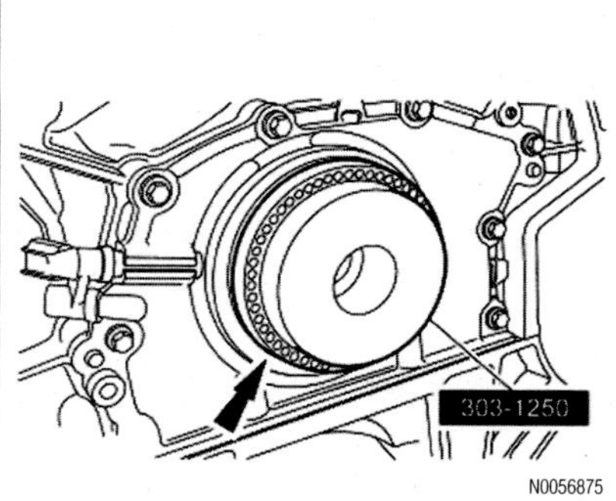

Fig. 145 Position the Rear Main Seal Installer onto the end of the crankshaft and slide a new crankshaft rear seal onto the tool

To install:

➡**Lubricate the seal lips and bore with clean engine oil prior to installation.**

6. Position the Rear Main Seal Installer onto the end of the crankshaft and slide a new crankshaft rear seal onto the tool.
7. Using the Rear Main Seal Installer and Handle, install the new crankshaft rear seal.
8. Install the crankshaft sensor ring.
9. Install the flexplate.

3.5L Turbo Engine

See Figure 145.

1. Remove the flexplate.
2. Remove the crankshaft sensor ring.
3. Using the Crankshaft Rear Oil Seal Remover and Slide Hammer, remove and discard the crankshaft rear seal.
4. Clean all sealing surfaces with metal surface prep

To install:

➡**Lubricate the seal lips and bore with clean engine oil prior to installation.**

5. Position the Rear Main Seal Installer onto the end of the crankshaft and slide a new crankshaft rear seal onto the tool.
6. Using the Rear Main Seal Installer and Handle, install the new crankshaft rear seal.
7. Install the crankshaft sensor ring.
8. Install the flexplate.
9. Using the scan tool, perform the Misfire Monitor Neutral Profile Correction procedure, following the on-screen instructions.

TURBOCHARGER

REMOVAL & INSTALLATION

Left-Hand

See Figures 146 through 148.

WARNING

Whenever turbocharger air intake system components are removed, always cover open ports to protect from debris. It is important that no foreign material enter the system. The turbocharger compressor vanes are susceptible to damage from even small particles. All components should be inspected and cleaned, if necessary, prior to installation or reassembly.

1. With the vehicle in NEUTRAL, position it on a hoist.
2. Remove the Air Cleaner (ACL) assembly as outlined in the Engine Section.
3. Disconnect the wastegate control valve hose from the LH turbocharger assembly.
4. Remove the 2 bolts from the top of the LH exhaust manifold heat shield.
5. Loosen the clamp and remove the LH turbocharger intake tube from the turbocharger.
6. Remove the LH turbocharger oil supply tube bolt and sealing washer.
   a. Discard the sealing washer and oil supply tube filter.
7. Drain the cooling system as outlined in the Engine Cooling Section.
8. Remove the LH catalytic converter as outlined in this section.
9. Remove the bottom bolt and the LH exhaust manifold heat shield.
10. Remove the 2 LH oil return tube-to-turbocharger bolts.
    a. Remove and discard the gasket.
11. Remove the LH turbocharger oil return tube from the oil pan.
    a. Discard the 2 O-ring seals.
12. Remove the 2 coolant tube banjo bolts and the LH turbocharger coolant tubes.

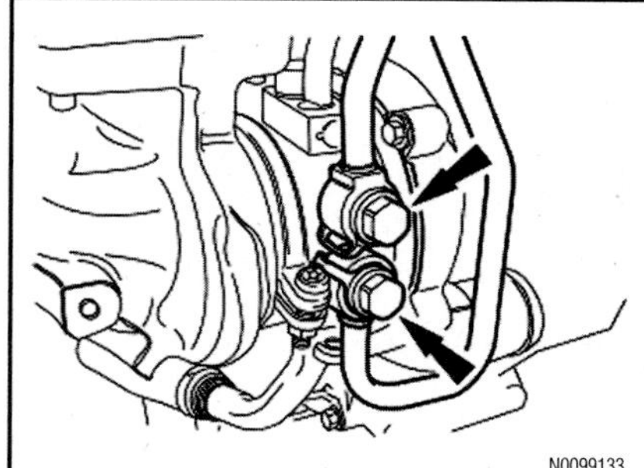

Fig. 146 Remove the 2 coolant tube banjo bolts and the LH turbocharger coolant tubes

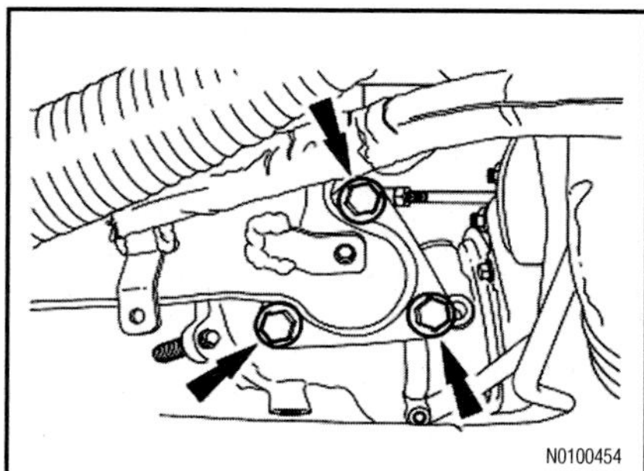

Fig. 147 Remove the 3 exhaust manifold-to-LH turbocharger bolts

a. Discard the sealing washers.

13. Loosen the clamp and remove the LH CAC tube from the LH turbocharger.

14. Remove the 3 exhaust manifold-to-LH turbocharger bolts.

a. Discard the gasket and bolts.

15. Remove the 2 bolts and the lower LH turbocharger-to-cylinder block bracket.

16. Remove the upper LH turbocharger bracket-to-turbocharger bolt and the turbocharger assembly.

To install:

⁂ WARNING

The upper LH turbocharger bracket bolt must be loosened in order to perform the tightening sequence or damage to the turbocharger may occur.

17. Loosen the upper LH turbocharger bracket bolt.

18. Install a new LH exhaust manifold-to-turbocharger gasket.

19. Install the turbocharger assembly and install upper LH turbocharger bracket-to-turbocharger bolt.

a. Do not tighten the bolts at this time.

20. Install the lower LH turbocharger-to-cylinder block bracket and the 2 bolts.

a. Do not tighten the bolts at this time.

21. Install the 3 new LH exhaust manifold-to-turbocharger bolts. Tighten the bolts to 33 ft. lbs. (45 Nm).

⁂ CAUTION

The next 4 steps must be performed in the order written or damage to the turbocharger may occur.

22. Tighten the upper LH turbocharger bracket-to-turbocharger bolt. Tighten the bolt to 168 inch lbs. (19 Nm).

23. Tighten the upper LH turbocharger bracket-to-cylinder block bolt. Tighten the bolts to 18 ft. lbs. (25 Nm).

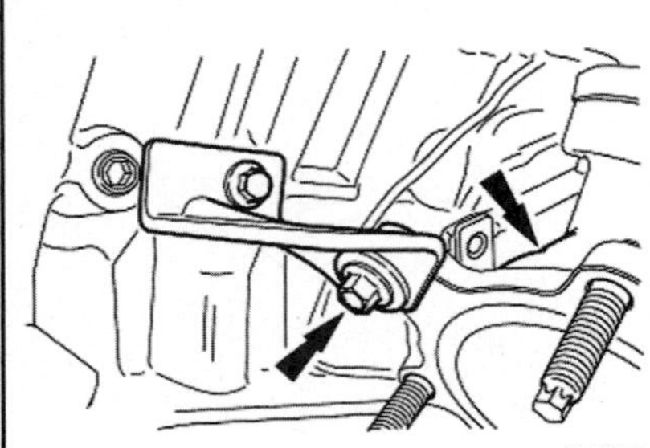

Fig. 148 Install the turbocharger assembly and install upper LH turbocharger bracket-to-turbocharger bolt

24. Tighten the lower LH turbocharger bracket-to-turbocharger bolt. Tighten the bolt to 168 inch lbs. (19 Nm).

25. Tighten the lower LH turbocharger bracket-to-cylinder block bolt. Tighten the bolt to 97 inch lbs. (11 Nm).

➡Align the index marks for the LH CAC tube.

26. Install the LH CAC tube on the LH turbocharger and tighten the clamp. Tighten the clamp to 44 inch lbs. (5 Nm).

27. Using 2 new sealing washers, install the 2 coolant tube banjo bolts. Tighten the bolts to 27 ft. lbs. (37 Nm).

➡Lubricate the oil pan bore with clean engine oil.

28. Using 2 new O-ring seals, install the LH turbocharger oil return tube to the oil pan.

29. Using a new gasket, install the LH turbocharger oil return tube and the 2 bolts. Tighten the bolts to 89 inch lbs. (10 Nm).

➡Align the marks for the LH turbocharger intake tube.

30. Install LH turbocharger intake tube and tighten the clamp. Tighten the clamp to 44 inch lbs. (5 Nm).

31. Install the oil supply tube filter, washer and bolt.

a. Install the new oil supply tube filter in the oil supply tube block.

b. Slide the new washer onto the oil supply tube block.

c. Install the bolt into the oil supply tube block.

32. Install the LH turbocharger oil supply tube. Tighten the bolt to 26 ft. lbs. (35 Nm).

➡Make sure the turbocharger wastegate regulating valve hose does not contact the exhaust manifold heat shield.

33. Connect the wastegate control valve hose to the LH turbocharger assembly.

34. Install the LH exhaust manifold heat shield and the bottom bolt.

a. Do not tighten the bolts at this time.

35. Install the 2 top LH exhaust manifold heat shield bolts. Tighten the bolt to 124 inch lbs. (14 Nm).

36. Tighten the LH exhaust manifold heat shield bottom bolt. Tighten the bolt to 124 inch lbs. (14 Nm).

37. Install the LH catalytic converter as outlined in this section.

38. Fill and bleed the cooling system as outlined in the Engine Cooling Section.

39. Install the ACL assembly as outlined in this section.

Right-Hand

See Figures 149 through 158.

⁂ WARNING

Whenever turbocharger air intake system components are removed, always cover open ports to protect from debris. It is important that no foreign material enter the system. The turbocharger compressor vanes are susceptible to damage from even small particles. All components should be inspected and cleaned, if necessary, prior to installation or reassembly.

1. With the vehicle in NEUTRAL, position it on a hoist.

➡Use a steering wheel holding device (such as Hunter® 28-75-1 or equivalent).

2. Using a suitable holding device, hold the steering wheel in the straight-ahead position.

3. Remove the 4 retainers and the underbody shield.

4. Drain the cooling system as outlined in the Engine Cooling Section.

5. Remove the RH catalytic converter as outlined in this section.

6. Remove the front subframe as outlined in the Body and Paint Section.

7. Remove the RH turbocharger oil supply tube secondary latch.

8. Using a Spring Lock Coupling Disconnect Tool, remove the RH turbocharger oil supply tube from the quick connect fitting.

a. Inspect and if necessary, replace the quick connect fitting.

9. Remove the lower RH exhaust manifold heat shield bolt.

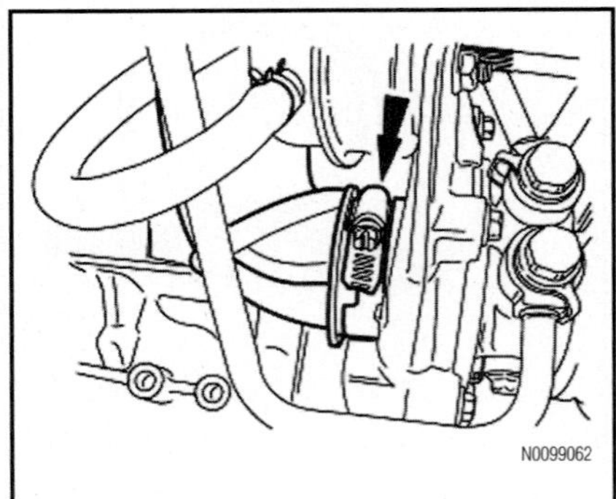

Fig. 149 Remove the RH turbocharger intake pipe from the RH turbocharger

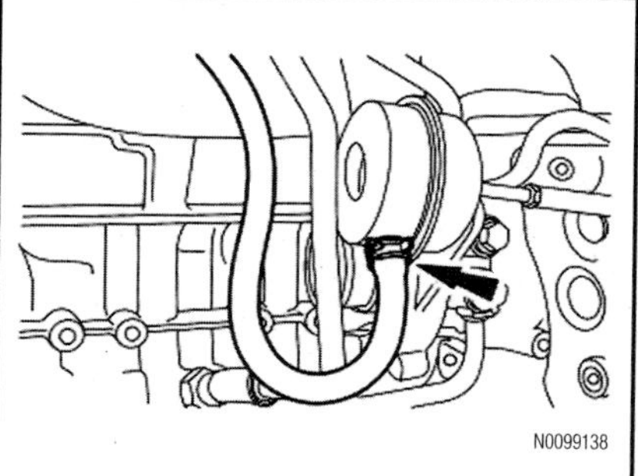
Fig. 150 Turbocharger wastegate regulating valve hose from the RH turbocharger assembly

10. Loosen the clamp and remove the RH turbocharger intake pipe from the RH turbocharger.
11. Disconnect the turbocharger wastegate regulating valve hose from the RH turbocharger assembly.
12. Remove the 3 bolts and the RH turbocharger lower bracket.
13. Remove the 2 bolts and the RH turbocharger oil return tube from the turbocharger.
   a. Remove and discard the gasket.
14. Remove the RH turbocharger oil return tube from the cylinder block.
   a. Discard the 2 O-ring seals.

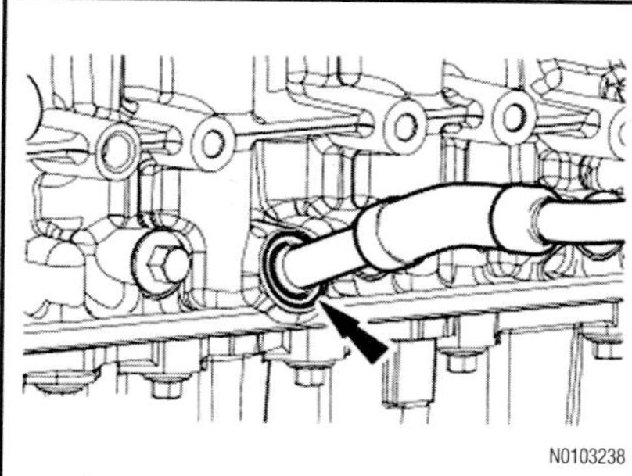
Fig. 151 Remove the RH turbocharger oil return tube from the cylinder block

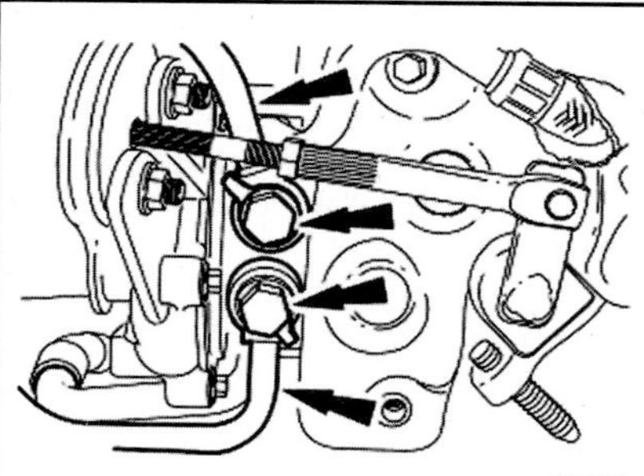
Fig. 152 Remove the 2 coolant tube banjo bolts and the RH turbocharger coolant tubes

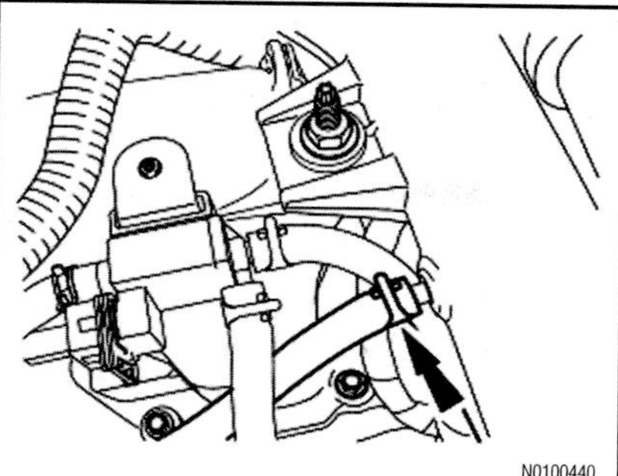
Fig. 153 Turbocharger wastegate regulating valve hose from the RH Charge Air Cooler (CAC) tube

15. Remove the 2 coolant tube banjo bolts and the RH turbocharger coolant tubes.
   Discard the sealing washers.
16. Detach the 2 vacuum hose retainers from the strut tower brace.
17. Remove the 4 nuts and the strut tower brace.
18. Disconnect the LH turbocharger bypass valve electrical connector and the turbocharger bypass valve hose.
19. Remove the turbocharger wastegate regulating valve hose from the RH Charge Air Cooler (CAC) tube.
20. Disconnect the RH turbocharger bypass valve electrical connector.
21. Disconnect the RH turbocharger bypass valve hose.
22. Remove the RH CAC tube nut from the intake manifold.
23. Loosen the clamp and remove the RH CAC tube.
24. Loosen the clamp and remove the RH CAC tube from the RH turbocharger.
25. Remove the 4 bolts and the 2 upper RH exhaust manifold heat shields.
26. Remove the 2 bolts and the RH engine lifting eye.
27. Remove the 3 RH exhaust manifold-to-turbocharger bolts.

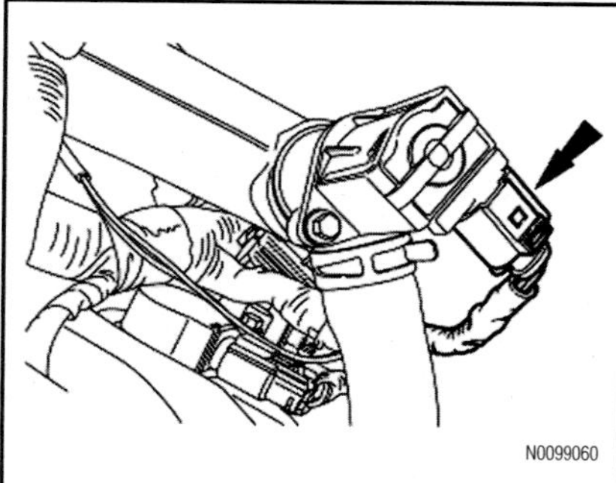
Fig. 154 RH turbocharger bypass valve electrical connector

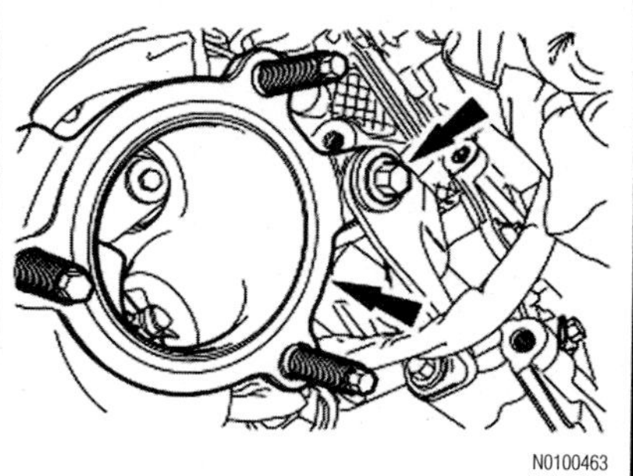
Fig. 155 Upper RH turbocharger-to-cylinder block bracket bolt and the RH turbocharger assembly

   a. Discard the gasket.
28. Remove the upper RH turbocharger-to-cylinder block bracket bolt and the RH turbocharger assembly.
29. Remove the RH turbocharger oil supply tube banjo bolt.
   a. Discard the sealing washer and oil supply tube filter.

To install:

30. Install the oil supply tube filter, washer and bolt.
   a. Install the new oil supply tube filter in the oil supply tube block.
   b. Slide the new washer onto the oil supply tube block.
   c. Install the bolt into the oil supply tube block.
31. Install the RH turbocharger oil supply tube. Tighten the bolt to 26 ft. lbs. (35 Nm).

WARNING

The upper RH turbocharger bracket bolts must be loosened in order to perform the tightening sequence or damage to the turbocharger may occur.

32. Loosen the 2 bolts for the upper RH turbocharger-to-cylinder block bracket.
33. Install a new RH exhaust manifold-to-turbocharger gasket.
34. Install the RH turbocharger assembly and the upper RH turbocharger-to-cylinder block bracket bolt.
   a. Do not tighten the bolts at this time.
35. Install the 3 new RH exhaust manifold-to-turbocharger bolts. Tighten the bolts to 33 ft. lbs. (45 Nm).
36. Install the RH engine lifting eye and the 2 bolts. Tighten the bolts to 18 ft. lbs. (24 Nm).
37. Install the 2 upper RH exhaust manifold heat shields and the 4 bolts. Tighten the bolts to 124 inch lbs. (14 Nm).

➡Align the index marks for the RH CAC tube.

38. Install the RH CAC tube to the RH turbocharger and tighten the clamp. Tighten the clamp to 44 inch lbs. (5 Nm).

➡Align the index marks for the RH CAC tube.

39. Install the RH CAC and tighten the clamp. Tighten the clamp to 44 inch lbs. (5 Nm).
40. Install the RH CAC tube and the RH CAC tube nut to the intake manifold. Tighten the nut to 53 inch lbs. (6 Nm).
41. Connect the RH turbocharger bypass valve hose.
42. Connect the RH turbocharger bypass valve electrical connector.
43. Install the turbocharger wastegate regulating valve hose to the RH CAC tube.
44. Connect the LH turbocharger bypass valve electrical connector and the turbocharger bypass valve hose.
45. Install the strut tower brace and the 4 nuts. Tighten the nuts to 22 ft. lbs. (30 Nm).
46. Attach the 2 brake booster vacuum hose retainers to the strut tower brace.
47. Position the upper RH turbocharger-to-cylinder block bracket as far clockwise as possible and tighten the bolts in the proper sequence as follows:
    a. Tighten the lower cylinder block bracket bolt to 19 ft. lbs. (26 Nm).
    b. Tighten the upper cylinder block bracket bolt to 19 ft. lbs. (26 Nm).
    c. Tighten the cylinder block bracket-to-turbocharger bolt to 168 inch lbs. (19 Nm).
48. Using 2 new sealing washers, install the 2 RH turbocharger coolant tube banjo bolts. Tighten the bolts to 27 ft. lbs. (37 Nm).

➡Lubricate the cylinder block bore with clean engine oil.

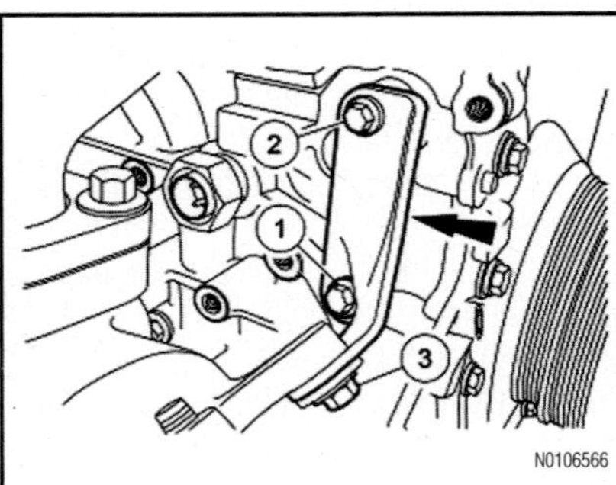

Fig. 156 Upper RH turbocharger-to-cylinder block bracket

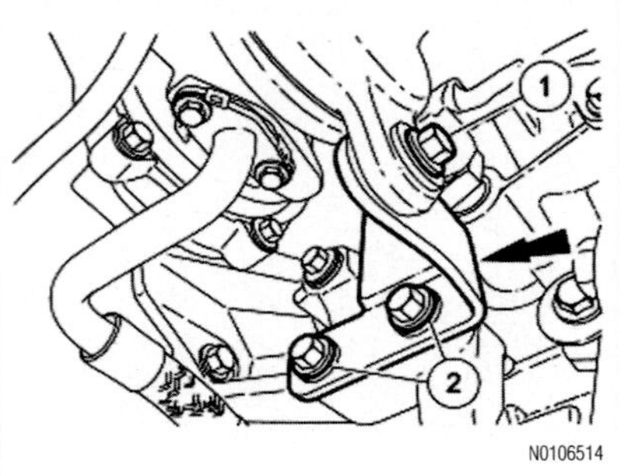

Fig. 157 Lower RH turbocharger bracket-to-cylinder block bolts

49. Using 2 new O-ring seals, install the RH turbocharger oil return tube in the cylinder block.
50. Install a new gasket and install the RH turbocharger oil return tube and the 2 bolts. Tighten the bolts to 89 inch lbs. (10 Nm).
51. Install the lower RH turbocharger bracket and the 3 bolts and tighten in proper sequence as follows:
    a. Tighten the lower RH turbocharger bracket-to-turbocharger bolt to 168 inch lbs. (19 Nm).
    b. Tighten the 2 lower RH turbocharger bracket-to-cylinder block bolts to 35 ft. lbs. (48 Nm).

➡Make sure the turbocharger wastegate regulating valve hose does not contact the exhaust manifold heat shield.

52. Connect the turbocharger wastegate regulating valve hose to the RH turbocharger.

➡Align the index marks for the RH turbocharger intake pipe.

53. Install the RH turbocharger intake pipe to the RH turbocharger and tighten the clamp. Tighten the clamp to 44 inch lbs. (5 Nm).

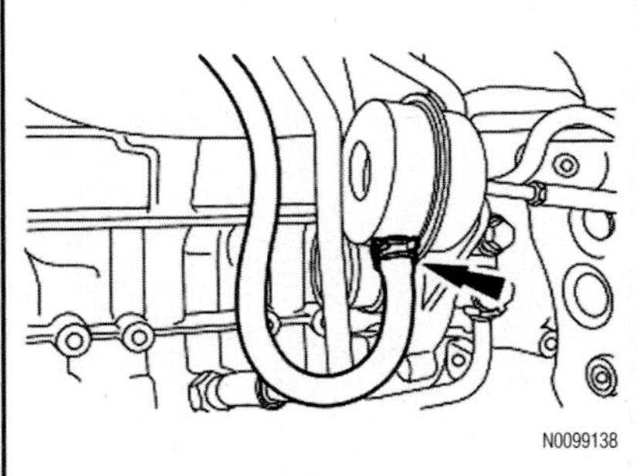

Fig. 158 Turbocharger wastegate regulating valve hose to the RH turbocharger

54. Install the lower RH exhaust manifold heat shield bolt. Tighten the bolt to 124 inch lbs. (14 Nm).

➡Listen for audible click when installing the oil supply tube into the quick connect fitting.

55. Install the RH turbocharger oil supply tube into the quick connect fitting.
56. Install the RH turbocharger oil supply tube secondary latch.
57. Install the front subframe as outlined in the Body and Paint Section.
58. Install the RH catalytic converter as outlined in this section.
59. Fill and bleed the cooling system as outlined in the Engine Cooling Section.
60. Install the underbody shield and the 4 retainers.

VALVE COVERS

REMOVAL & INSTALLATION

3.5L Engine, Except Turbo

Left-Hand

See Figures 159 and 160.

WARNING

During engine repair procedures, cleanliness is extremely important. Any foreign material, including any material created while cleaning gasket surfaces that enters the oil passages, coolant passages or the oil pan, may cause engine failure.

WARNING

Early build engines have 11 fastener valve covers, late build engines have 9 fastener valve covers. Do not attempt to install bolts in the 2 empty late build valve cover holes or damage to the valve cover will occur.

All Vehicles

1. Remove the LH ignition coils as outlined in the Engine Electrical Section.
2. Remove the oil level indicator.
3. Disconnect the LH Variable Camshaft Timing (VCT) solenoid electrical connector.
4. Detach all of the wiring harness retainers from the LH valve cover stud bolts.
5. Disconnect the 3 LH fuel injector electrical connectors.

Early Build Vehicles

6. Loosen the 11 stud bolts and remove the LH valve cover.
    a. Discard the gasket.

Late Build Vehicles

7. Loosen the 9 stud bolts and remove the LH valve cover.

a. Discard the gasket.

All Vehicles

➡VCT solenoid seal removal shown, spark plug tube seal removal similar.

8. Inspect the VCT solenoid seals and the spark plug tube seals. Remove any damaged seals.

a. Using the VCT Spark Plug Tube Seal Remover and Handle, remove the seal(s).

9. Clean the valve cover, cylinder head and engine front cover sealing surfaces with metal surface prep.

To install:

All Vehicles

➡Installation of new seals is only required if damaged seals were removed during disassembly of the engine.

➡Spark plug tube seal installation shown, VCT solenoid seal installation similar.

10. Using the VCT Spark Plug Tube Seal Installer and Handle, install new VCT solenoid and/or spark plug tube seals.

⁂ WARNING

Failure to use the correct Motorcraft® High Performance Engine RTV Silicone may cause the engine oil to foam excessively and result in serious engine damage.

➡If the valve cover is not installed and the fasteners tightened within 4 minutes, the sealant must be removed and the sealing area cleaned.

➡To clean the sealing area, use silicone gasket remover and metal surface prep. Failure to follow this procedure can cause future oil leakage.

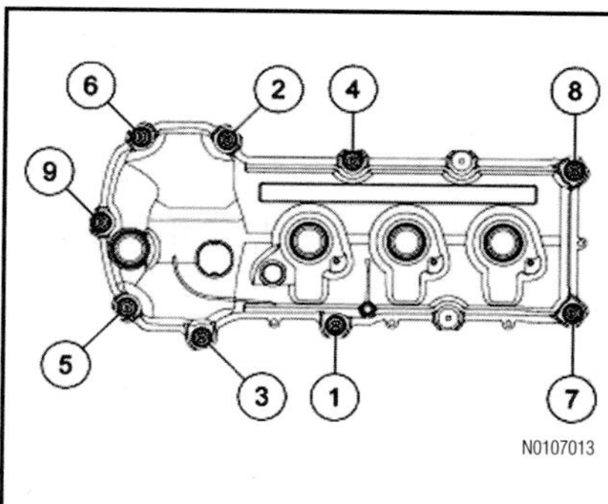

Fig. 159 LH valve cover tightening sequence—Late Build Vehicles

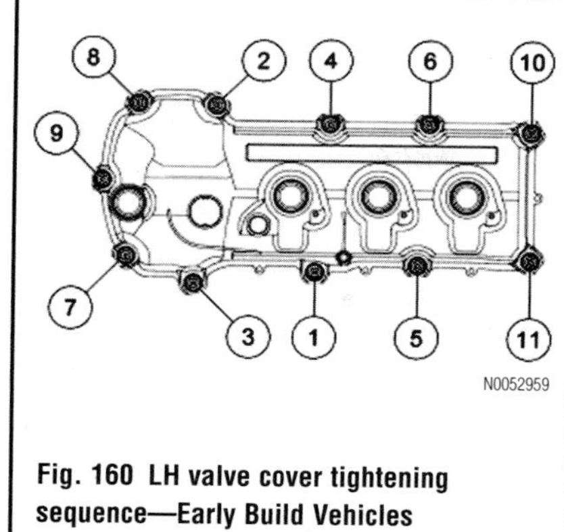

Fig. 160 LH valve cover tightening sequence—Early Build Vehicles

11. Apply an 0.31 inch (8 mm) bead of Motorcraft® High Performance Engine RTV Silicone to the engine front cover-to-LH cylinder head joints.

Late Build Vehicles

12. Using a new gasket, install the LH valve cover and tighten the 9 stud bolts. Tighten the stud bolts to 89 inch lbs. (10 Nm) in the proper sequence.

Early Build Vehicles

13. Using a new gasket, install the LH valve cover and tighten the 11 stud bolts. Tighten the stud bolts to 89 inch lbs. (10 Nm) in the proper sequence.

All Vehicles

14. Connect the 3 LH fuel injector electrical connectors.

15. Attach all of the wiring harness retainers to the LH valve cover stud bolts.

16. Connect the LH VCT solenoid electrical connector.

17. Install the oil level indicator.

18. Install the LH ignition coils as outlined in the Engine Electrical Section.

Right-Hand

See Figures 161 through 163.

⁂ WARNING

During engine repair procedures, cleanliness is extremely important. Any foreign material, including any material created while cleaning gasket surfaces that enters the oil passages, coolant passages or the oil pan, may cause engine failure.

⁂ WARNING

Early build engines have 11 fastener valve covers, late build engines have 9 fastener valve covers. Do not attempt to install bolts in the 2 empty late build valve cover holes or damage to the valve cover will occur.

All Vehicles

1. Remove the RH ignition coils as outlined in the Engine Electrical Section.

2. Detach and disconnect the RH Heated Oxygen Sensor (HO2S) electrical connector.

3. Detach and disconnect the RH Catalyst Monitor Sensor (CMS) electrical connector.

4. Disconnect the RH Variable Camshaft Timing (VCT) solenoid electrical connector.

5. Disconnect the 3 RH fuel injector electrical connectors.

6. Detach all of the wiring harness retainers from the RH valve cover stud bolts.

7. Remove the nut and the Power Steering Pressure (PSP) tube bracket from the valve cover stud bolt.

Early Build Vehicles

➡It is necessary to reposition the A/C tubes to remove the valve cover.

8. Loosen the bolt, the 10 stud bolts and remove the RH valve cover.

a. Discard the gasket.

Late Build Vehicles

➡It is necessary to reposition the A/C tubes to remove the valve cover.

9. Loosen the 9 stud bolts and remove the RH valve cover.

a. Discard the gasket.

All Vehicles

➡VCT solenoid seal removal shown, spark plug tube seal removal similar.

10. Inspect the VCT solenoid seals and the spark plug tube seals. Remove any damaged seals.

a. Using the VCT Spark Plug Tube Seal Remover and Handle, remove the seal(s).

11. Clean the valve cover, cylinder head and engine front cover sealing surfaces with metal surface prep.

To install:

All Vehicles

➡Installation of new seals is only required if damaged seals were removed during disassembly of the engine.

➡Spark plug tube seal installation shown, VCT solenoid seal installation similar.

12. Using the VCT Spark Plug Tube Seal Installer and Handle, install a new VCT solenoid and/or spark plug tube seals.

⁂ WARNING

Failure to use Motorcraft® High Performance Engine RTV Silicone may cause the engine oil to foam excessively and result in serious engine damage.

➡If the valve cover is not installed and the fasteners tightened within 4 minutes, the sealant must be removed and the sealing area cleaned. To clean the sealing area, use silicone gasket remover and metal surface prep. Failure to follow this procedure can cause future oil leakage.

Apply an 0.31 inch (8 mm) bead of Motorcraft® High Performance Engine RTV Silicone to the engine front cover-to-RH cylinder head joints.

Late Build Vehicles

13. Using a new gasket, install the RH valve cover and tighten the 9 stud bolts. Tighten the stud bolts to 89 inch lbs. (89 Nm) in the proper sequence.

Early Build Vehicles

14. Using a new gasket, install the RH valve cover and tighten the bolt and the 10 stud bolts. Tighten the stud bolts to 89 inch lbs. (10 Nm) in the proper sequence.

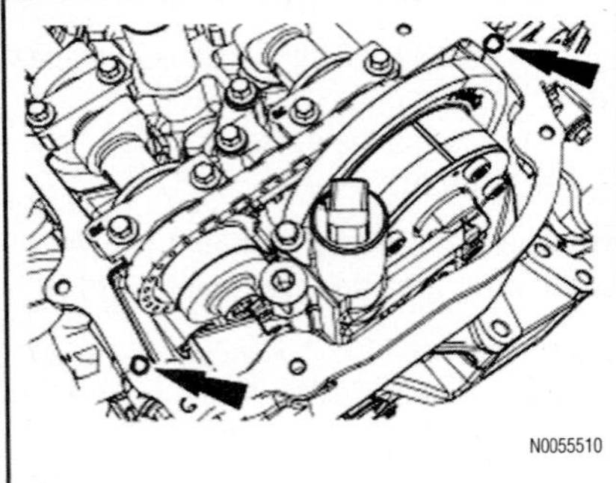

Fig. 161 Engine front cover-to-RH cylinder head joints

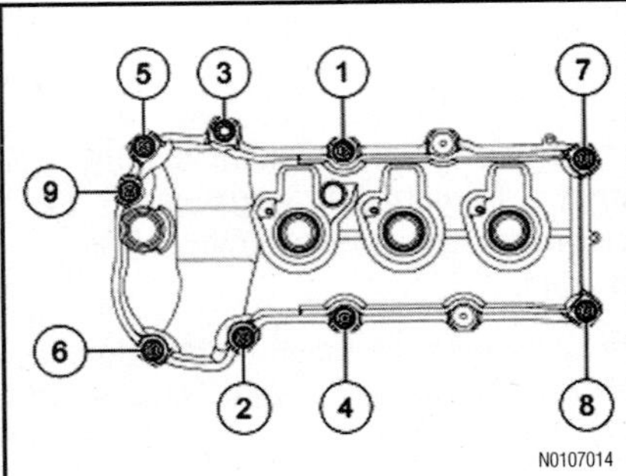

Fig. 162 RH valve cover—Late Build Vehicles

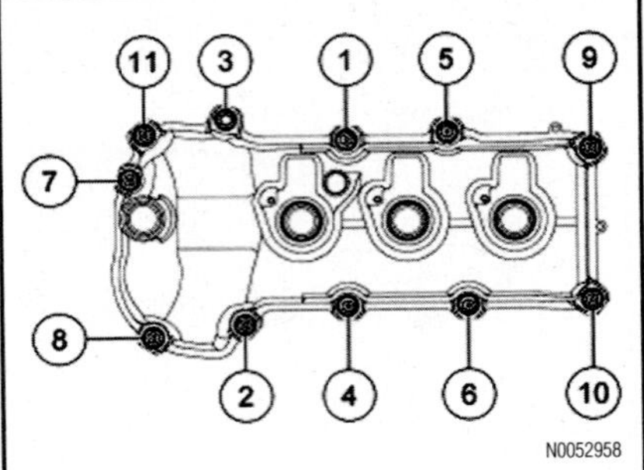

Fig. 163 RH valve cover—Early Build Vehicles

All Vehicles

15. Install the PSP tube bracket on the valve cover stud bolt and install the nut. Tighten the nut to 62 inch lbs. (7 Nm).

16. Attach all of the wiring harness retainers to the RH valve cover stud bolts.

17. Connect the 3 RH fuel injector electrical connectors.

18. Connect the RH VCT solenoid electrical connector.

19. Connect the RH CMS electrical connector.

20. Connect the RH HO2S electrical connector.

21. Install the RH ignition coils as outlined in the Engine Electrical Section.

3.5L Turbo Engine

Left-Hand

See Figures 164 through 168.

⁂ WARNING

During engine repair procedures, cleanliness is extremely important. Any foreign material, including any material created while cleaning gasket surfaces that enters the oil passages, coolant passages or the oil pan, may cause engine failure.

⁂ WARNING

Whenever turbocharger air intake system components are removed, always cover open ports to protect from debris. It is important that no foreign material enter the system. The turbocharger compressor vanes are susceptible to damage from even small particles. All components should be inspected and cleaned, if necessary, prior to installation or reassembly.

All Vehicles

1. Release the fuel system pressure as outlined in the Fuel System Section

2. Disconnect the Turbocharger Boost Pressure (TCBP)/Charge Air Cooler Temperature (CACT) sensor electrical connector.

3. Remove the noise generator as outlined in this section.

4. Loosen the 2 clamps and remove the Charge Air Cooler (CAC) outlet pipe.

5. Disconnect the 2 quick connect couplings and remove the crankcase vent tube as outlined in the Fuel System Section.

6. Remove the fuel injection pump noise insulator shield.

7. Remove the oil level indicator.

Early Build Vehicles

8. Remove the intake manifold as outlined in this section.

9. Remove the nut for the high pressure fuel tube from the LH valve cover stud bolt.

➡To release the fuel pressure in the high-pressure fuel tubes, wrap the flare nut with a shop towel to absorb any residual fuel pressure during the loosening of the flare nuts.

10. Remove the high pressure fuel tube flare nut from the fuel injection pump.

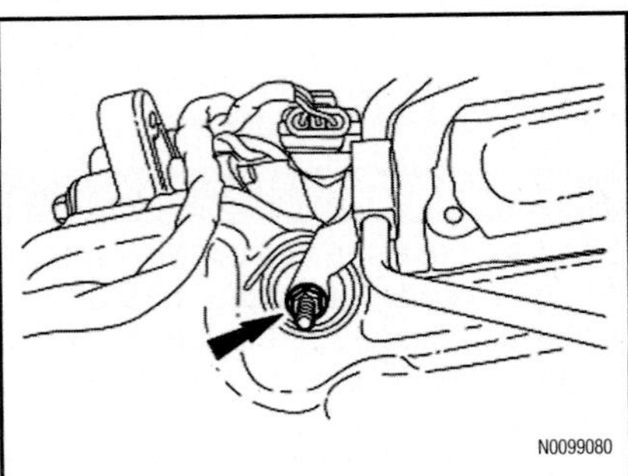

Fig. 164 High pressure fuel tube from the LH valve cover stud bolt

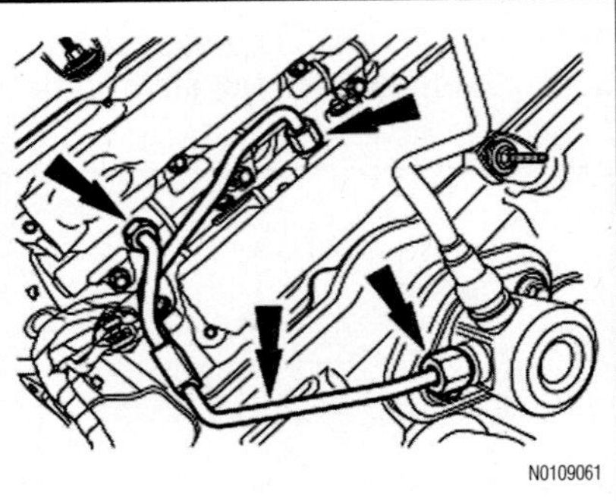

Fig. 165 Remove the high pressure fuel tube flare nut from the fuel injection pump. Remove the 2 high pressure fuel tube flare nuts from the fuel rails and remove the high pressure fuel tube assembly

Remove the 2 high pressure fuel tube flare nuts from the fuel rails and remove the high pressure fuel tube assembly.

Late Build Vehicles

11. Remove the Throttle Body (TB) as outlined in the Fuel System Section.
12. Disconnect the LH turbocharger bypass valve electrical connector.
13. Disconnect the LH turbocharger bypass valve hose from the RH CAC tube.
14. Disconnect the turbocharger wastegate regulating valve hose from the RH CAC tube.
15. Disconnect the RH turbocharger bypass valve electrical connector.
16. Disconnect the RH turbocharger bypass valve hose from the RH turbocharger intake tube.

⁂ WARNING

The compression limiter bushing may fall out of the mounting bracket grommet on the Charge Air Cooler (CAC) tube during service. Make sure the bushing is in place when reinstalling the tube or damage to the tube may occur.

17. Remove the RH CAC tube nut from the intake manifold.
18. Loosen the clamp and remove the RH CAC tube.
19. Loosen the clamp and remove the RH CAC tube from the RH turbocharger.

All Vehicles

20. Remove the fuel injection pump as outlined in the Fuel System Section.
21. Disconnect the LH Variable Camshaft Timing (VCT) solenoid electrical connector.
22. Remove the engine cover mounting stud from the LH valve cover stud bolt.
23. Detach all of the wiring harness retainers from the LH valve cover stud bolts.
24. Remove the nut and the oil supply tube bracket from the LH valve cover stud bolt.
25. Disconnect the 3 LH ignition coil-on-plug electrical connectors.

➡When removing the ignition coil-on-plugs, a slight twisting motion will break the seal and ease removal.

26. Remove the 3 bolts and the 3 LH ignition coil-on-plugs.
27. Loosen the 10 stud bolts and remove the LH valve cover.
    a. Discard the gasket.

➡VCT solenoid seal removal shown, spark plug tube seal removal similar.

28. Inspect the VCT solenoid seals and the spark plug tube seals. Remove any damaged seals.
    a. Using the VCT Spark Plug Tube Seal Remover and Handle, remove the seal(s).
29. Clean the valve cover, cylinder head and engine front cover sealing surfaces with metal surface prep.

To install:

All Vehicles

➡Installation of new seals is only required if damaged seals were removed during disassembly of the engine.

➡Spark plug tube seal installation shown, VCT solenoid seal installation similar.

30. Using the VCT Spark Plug Tube Seal Installer and Handle, install new VCT solenoid and/or spark plug tube seals.

⁂ WARNING

Failure to use the correct Motorcraft® High Performance Engine RTV Silicone may cause the engine oil to foam excessively and result in serious engine damage.

➡If the valve cover is not installed and the fasteners tightened within 4 minutes, the sealant must be removed and the sealing area cleaned. To clean the sealing area, use silicone gasket remover and metal surface prep. Failure to follow these instructions can cause future oil leakage.

31. Apply an 0.31 inch (8 mm) bead of Motorcraft® High Performance Engine RTV Silicone to the engine front cover-to-LH cylinder head joints.
32. Using a new gasket, install the LH valve cover and tighten the 10 stud bolts.

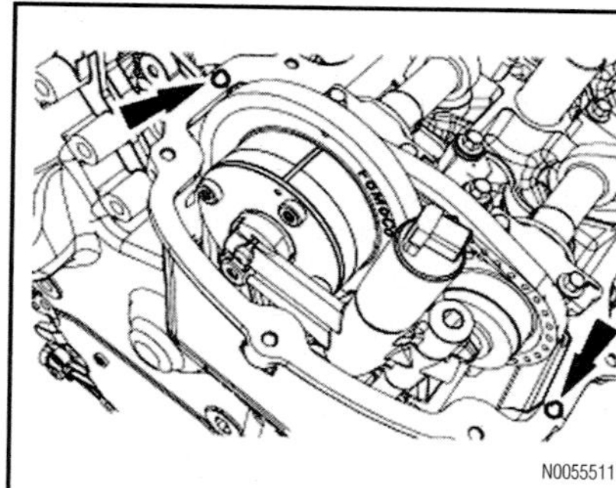

Fig. 166 Apply an 0.31 inch (8 mm) bead of Motorcraft® High Performance Engine RTV Silicone to the engine front cover-to-LH cylinder head joints

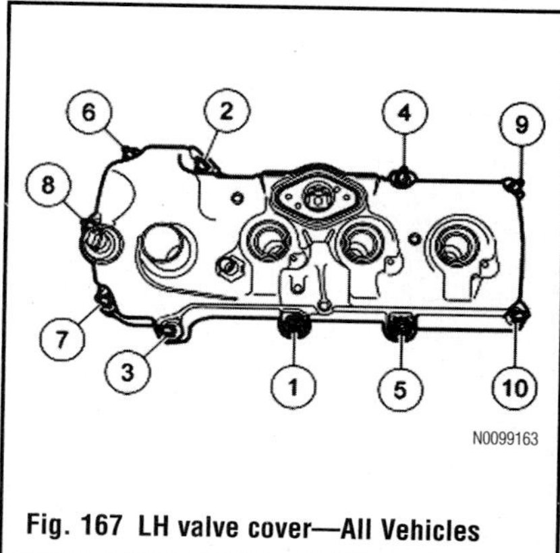

Fig. 167 LH valve cover—All Vehicles

Tighten the stud bolts to 89 inch lbs. (10 Nm) in the proper sequence.

33. Install 3 LH ignition coil-on-plugs and the 3 bolts. Tighten the bolts to 62 inch lbs. (7 Nm).
34. Connect the 3 LH ignition coil-on-plug electrical connectors.
35. Install the oil supply tube bracket on the LH valve cover stud bolt and install the nut. Tighten the bolt to 71 inch lbs. (8 Nm).
36. Attach all of the wiring harness retainers to the LH valve cover and stud bolts.
37. Install the engine cover mounting stud to the LH valve cover stud bolt. Tighten the bolt to 53 inch lbs. (6 Nm).
38. Connect the LH VCT solenoid electrical connector.
39. Install the fuel injection pump as outlined in the Fuel System Section.

Late Build Vehicles

➡Align the index marks for the RH CAC tube.

40. Install the RH CAC tube to the RH turbocharger and tighten the clamp. Tighten the clamp to 44 inch lbs. (5 Nm).

➡Align the index marks for the RH CAC tube.

41. Install the RH CAC tube and tighten the clamp. Tighten the clamp to 44 inch lbs. (5 Nm).

⁂ WARNING

The compression limiter bushing may fall out of the mounting bracket grommet on the Charge Air Cooler (CAC) tube during service. Make sure the bushing is in place when reinstalling the tube or damage to the tube may occur.

42. Install the RH CAC tube and the RH CAC tube nut to the intake manifold. Tighten the nut to 53 inch lbs. (6 Nm).

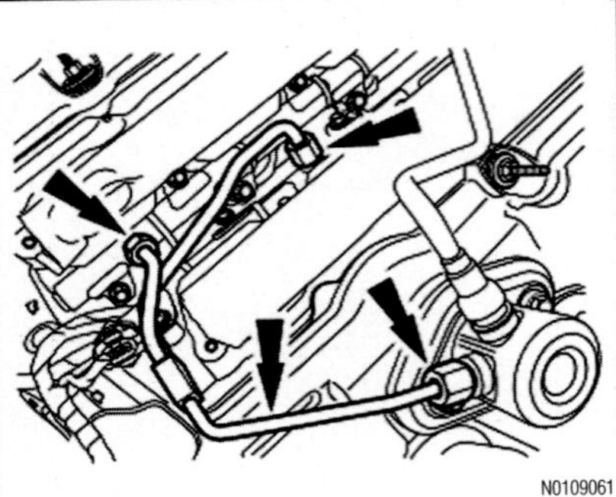

Fig. 168 High pressure fuel tube flare nut to the fuel injection pump and the 2 high pressure fuel tube flare nuts to the fuel rails

43. Connect the RH turbocharger bypass valve hose to the RH turbocharger intake tube.
44. Connect the RH turbocharger bypass valve electrical connector.
45. Connect the turbocharger wastegate regulating valve hose to the RH CAC tube.
46. Connect the LH turbocharger bypass valve electrical connector and the turbocharger bypass valve hose.
47. Install the Throttle Body as outlined in the Fuel System Section.

Early Build Vehicles

48. Connect the high pressure fuel tube flare nut to the fuel injection pump and the 2 high pressure fuel tube flare nuts to the fuel rails. Tighten the nuts to 22 ft. lbs. (30 Nm).
49. Install the nut for the high pressure fuel tube on the LH valve cover stud bolt. Tighten the bolt to 53 inch lbs. (6 Nm).
50. Install the intake manifold as outlined in this section.

All Vehicles

51. Install the oil level indicator.
52. Install the fuel injection pump noise insulator shield.
53. Install the crankcase vent tube and connect the 2 quick connect couplings as outlined in the Fuel System Section.

➡Align the index marks for the CAC outlet pipe.

54. Install the CAC outlet pipe and tighten the 2 clamps. Tighten the clamps to 44 inch lbs. (5 Nm).
55. Install the noise generator as outlined in this section.
56. Connect the TCBP / CACT sensor electrical connector.

Right-Hand

See Figure 169.

✱✱ WARNING

During engine repair procedures, cleanliness is extremely important. Any foreign material, including any material created while cleaning gasket surfaces that enters the oil passages, coolant passages or the oil pan, may cause engine failure.

✱✱ WARNING

Whenever turbocharger air intake system components are removed, always cover open ports to protect from debris. It is important that no foreign material enter the system. The turbocharger compressor vanes are susceptible to damage from even small particles. All components should be inspected and cleaned, if necessary, prior to installation or reassembly.

1. Release the fuel system pressure as outlined in the Fuel System Section.
2. Disconnect the LH turbocharger bypass valve electrical connector.
3. Disconnect the turbocharger bypass valve hose from the RH Charge Air Cooler (CAC) tube.
4. Remove the turbocharger wastegate regulating valve hose from the RH CAC tube.
5. Disconnect the RH turbocharger bypass valve electrical connector.
6. Disconnect the RH turbocharger bypass valve hose from the RH turbocharger intake tube.

✱✱ WARNING

The compression limiter bushing may fall out of the mounting bracket grommet on the Charge Air Cooler (CAC) tube during service. Make sure the bushing is in place when reinstalling the tube or damage to the tube may occur.

7. Remove the RH CAC tube nut from the intake manifold.
8. Loosen the clamp and remove the RH CAC tube.
9. Loosen the clamp and remove the RH CAC tube.
10. Detach the 2 brake booster vacuum hose retainers from the strut tower brace and position aside.
11. Disconnect the fuel supply tube as outlined in the Fuel System Section.
12. Remove the fuel tube-to-engine front cover bracket bolt and position the fuel tube aside.
13. Disconnect the RH fuel injector wiring harness electrical connector.
14. Disconnect the Evaporative Emission (EVAP) tube quick connect coupling as outlined in the Fuel System Section.
15. Disconnect the EVAP valve electrical connector and detach from the intake manifold.
16. Disconnect the quick connect coupling from the intake manifold and remove the EVAP tube assembly as outlined in the Fuel System Section.
17. Disconnect the 2 quick connect couplings and remove the PCV tube as outlined in the Fuel System Section.
18. If equipped, disconnect the 2 heated PCV electrical connectors.
19. Disconnect the RH Variable Camshaft Timing (VCT) solenoid electrical connector and detach the 2 wiring harness retainers.
20. Disconnect the 3 RH ignition coil-on-plugs electrical connectors.
21. Detach all of the wiring harness retainers from the RH valve cover and stud bolts position aside.

➡When removing the ignition coil-on-plugs, a slight twisting motion will break the seal and ease removal.

22. Remove the 3 bolts and the 3 RH ignition coil-on-plugs.
23. Loosen the clamp and remove the RH turbocharger intake tube from the RH turbocharger intake pipe.

✱✱ WARNING

The compression limiter bushing may fall out of the mounting bracket grommet on the turbocharger intake tube during service. Make sure the bushing is in place when reinstalling the tube or damage to the tube may occur.

24. Remove the nut from the RH valve cover stud bolt and position the RH turbocharger intake tube off the RH valve cover stud bolt.
25. Loosen the 11 stud bolts and remove the RH valve cover.
    a. Discard the gasket.

➡VCT solenoid seal removal shown, spark plug tube seal removal similar.

26. Inspect the VCT solenoid seals and the spark plug tube seals. Remove any damaged seals.
    a. Using the VCT Spark Plug Tube

Seal Remover and Handle, remove the seal(s).

27. Clean the valve cover, cylinder head and engine front cover sealing surfaces with metal surface prep.

To install:

➡Installation of new seals is only required if damaged seals were removed during disassembly of the engine.

➡Spark plug tube seal installation shown, VCT solenoid seal installation similar.

28. Using the VCT Spark Plug Tube Seal Installer and Handle, install new VCT solenoid and/or spark plug tube seals.

⁂ WARNING

Failure to use Motorcraft® High Performance Engine RTV Silicone may cause the engine oil to foam excessively and result in serious engine damage.

➡If the valve cover is not installed and the fasteners tightened within 4 minutes, the sealant must be removed and the sealing area cleaned.

➡To clean the sealing area, use silicone gasket remover and metal surface prep. Failure to follow this procedure can cause future oil leakage.

29. Apply an 0.31 inch (8 mm) bead of Motorcraft® High Performance Engine RTV Silicone to the engine front cover-to-RH cylinder head joints.

30. Using a new gasket, install the RH valve cover and tighten the 11 stud bolts. Tighten the bolts to 89 inch lbs. (10 Nm) in the proper sequence.

⁂ WARNING

The compression limiter bushing may fall out of the mounting bracket grommet on the turbocharger intake tube during service. Make sure the bushing is in place when reinstalling the tube or damage to the tube may occur.

31. Position the RH turbocharger intake tube and install the nut to the RH valve cover stud bolt. Tighten the bolt to 53 inch lbs. (6 Nm).

➡Align the index marks for the RH turbocharger intake tube.

32. Install the RH turbocharger intake tube to the RH turbocharger intake pipe and tighten the clamp. Tighten the clamp to 44 inch lbs. (5 Nm).

33. Install 3 RH ignition coil-on-plugs and the 3 bolts. Tighten the bolts to 62 inch lbs. (7 Nm).

34. Attach all of the wiring harness retainers to the RH valve cover and stud bolts.

35. Connect the 3 RH ignition coil-on-plug electrical connectors.

36. Connect the RH VCT solenoid electrical connector and attach the 2 wiring harness retainers.

37. If equipped, connect the 2 heated PCV electrical connectors.

38. Install the PCV tube and connect the 2 quick connect couplings as outlined in the Fuel System Section.

39. Install the EVAP tube assembly and connect the quick connect coupling to the intake manifold.

40. Connect the EVAP valve electrical connector and attach to the intake manifold.

41. Connect the EVAP tube quick connect coupling as outlined in the Fuel System Section.

42. Connect the RH fuel injector wiring harness electrical connector.

43. Position the fuel tube and install the fuel tube-to-engine front cover bracket bolt. Tighten the bolt to 89 inch lbs. (10 Nm).

44. Connect the fuel supply tube as outlined in the Fuel System Section.

45. Attach the 2 brake booster vacuum hose retainers to the strut tower brace.

➡Align the index marks for the RH CAC tube.

46. Install the RH CAC tube to the RH turbocharger and tighten the clamp. Tighten the clamp to 44 inch lbs. (5 Nm).

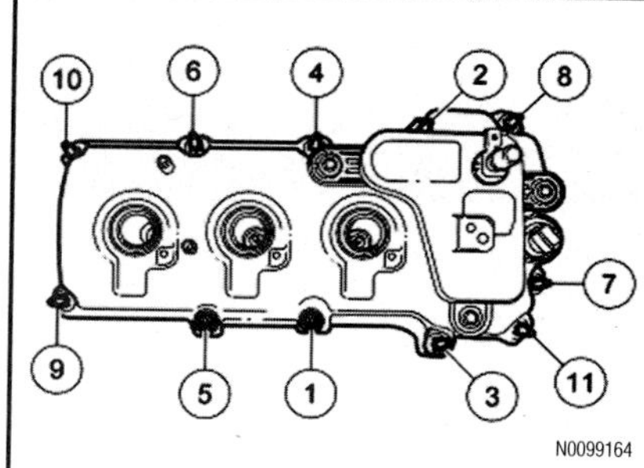

Fig. 169 Using a new gasket, install the RH valve cover and tighten the 11 stud bolts

➡Align the index marks for the RH CAC tube.

47. Install the RH CAC tube and tighten the clamp. Tighten the clamp to 44 inch lbs. (5 Nm).

⁂ WARNING

The compression limiter bushing may fall out of the mounting bracket grommet on the Charge Air Cooler (CAC) tube during service. Make sure the bushing is in place when reinstalling the tube or damage to the tube may occur.

48. Install the RH CAC tube and turbocharger intake tube as an assembly and install the RH CAC tube nut to the intake manifold. Tighten the nut to 53 inch lbs. (6 Nm).

49. Connect the RH turbocharger bypass valve hose to the RH turbocharger intake tube.

50. Connect the RH turbocharger bypass valve electrical connector.

51. Install the turbocharger wastegate regulating valve hose to the RH CAC tube.

52. Connect the turbocharger bypass valve hose to the RH CAC tube.

53. Connect the LH turbocharger bypass valve electrical connector.

CAMSHAFT POSITION (CMP) SENSOR

LOCATION

See Figures 170 and 171.

Refer to the accompanying illustrations.

REMOVAL & INSTALLATION

3.5L Engine, Except Turbo

1. Remove the Air Cleaner (ACL) outlet pipe and the ACL as outlined in the Engine Mechanical Section.
2. Disconnect the Camshaft Position (CMP) sensor electrical connector.

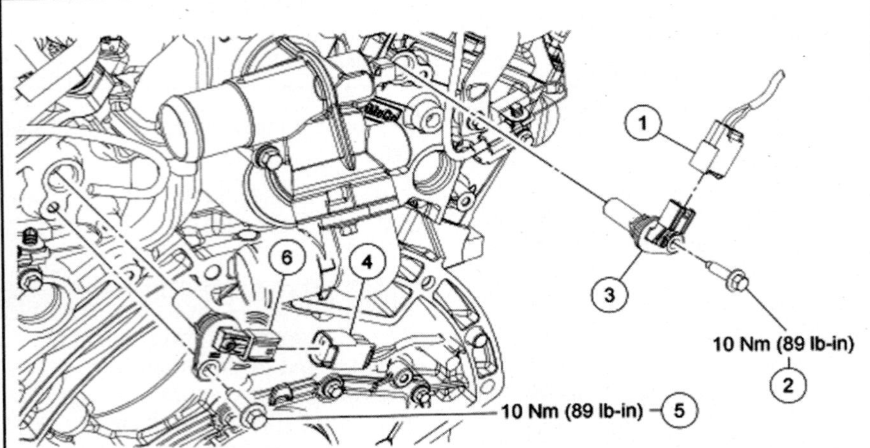

Fig. 170 Camshaft Position (CMP) sensor locations—3.5L engine, except Turbo

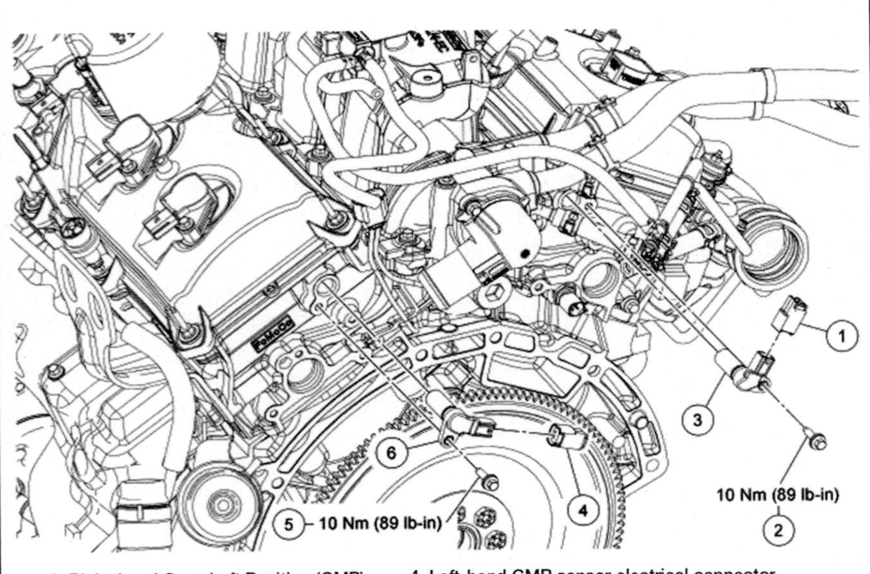

Fig. 171 Camshaft Position (CMP) sensors locations—3.5L Turbo engine

3. Remove the bolt and the CMP sensor.

➡Lubricate the CMP sensor O-ring seal with clean engine oil.

To install:

➡Lubricate the CMP sensor O-ring seal with clean engine oil.

4. Install the bolt and the CMP sensor. Tighten the bolt to 89 inch lbs. (10 Nm).
5. Connect the Camshaft Position (CMP) sensor electrical connector.
6. Install the Air Cleaner (ACL) outlet pipe and the ACL as outlined in the Engine Mechanical Section.

3.5L Turbo Engine

Both Sensors

1. Remove the Air Cleaner (ACL) outlet pipe and the ACL as outlined in the Engine Mechanical Section.

RH Sensor

2. Position the RH turbocharger intake tube aside as outlined in the Engine Mechanical Section.

LH Sensor

3. Position the LH turbocharger intake tube aside as outlined in the Engine Mechanical Section.

Both Sensors

4. Disconnect the Camshaft Position (CMP) sensor electrical connector.
5. Remove the bolt and the CMP sensor.

➡Lubricate the CMP sensor O-ring seal with clean engine oil.

To install:

➡Lubricate the CMP sensor O-ring seal with clean engine oil.

Both Sensors

6. Install the bolt and the CMP sensor. Tighten the bolt to 89 inch lbs. (10 Nm).
7. Connect the Camshaft Position (CMP) sensor electrical connector.

LH Sensor

8. Position the LH turbocharger intake tube as outlined in the Engine Mechanical Section.

RH Sensor

9. Position the RH turbocharger intake tube as outlined in the Engine Mechanical Section.

Both Sensors

10. Install the Air Cleaner (ACL) outlet pipe and the ACL as outlined in the Engine Mechanical Section.

CATALYST MONITOR SENSOR

REMOVAL & INSTALLTION

All Sensors

1. With the vehicle in NEUTRAL, position it on a hoist.

All Sensors Except The RH 3.5L Turbo Sensor

2. Disconnect the Catalyst Monitor Sensor (CMS) electrical connector.

RH 3.5L Turbo Sensor

3. Disconnect the CMS electrical connector.
   a. Detach the wiring retainer from the rear engine roll restrictor bracket.

All Sensors

➡If necessary, lubricate the sensor threads with penetrating and lock lubricant to assist in removal.

4. Using the Exhaust Gas Oxygen Sensor Socket, remove the CMS.
   a. Calculate the correct torque wrench setting for the following torque.

➡Apply a light coat of anti-seize lubricant to the threads of the CMS.

To install:

➡Apply a light coat of anti-seize lubricant to the threads of the CMS.

All Sensors

➡If necessary, lubricate the sensor threads with penetrating and lock lubricant to assist in installation.

5. Using the Exhaust Gas Oxygen Sensor Socket, install the CMS.
   a. Calculate the correct torque wrench setting. Tighten to 48 Nm (35 lb-ft).

RH 3.5L Turbo Sensor

6. Connect the CMS electrical connector.
   a. Attach the wiring retainer to the rear engine roll restrictor bracket.

All Sensors Except The RH 3.5L Turbo Sensor

7. Connect the Catalyst Monitor Sensor (CMS) electrical connector.

All Sensors

8. With the vehicle in NEUTRAL, lower from the hoist.

CRANKSHAFT POSITION (CKP) SENSOR

LOCATION

See Figure 172.

Refer to the accompanying illustration.

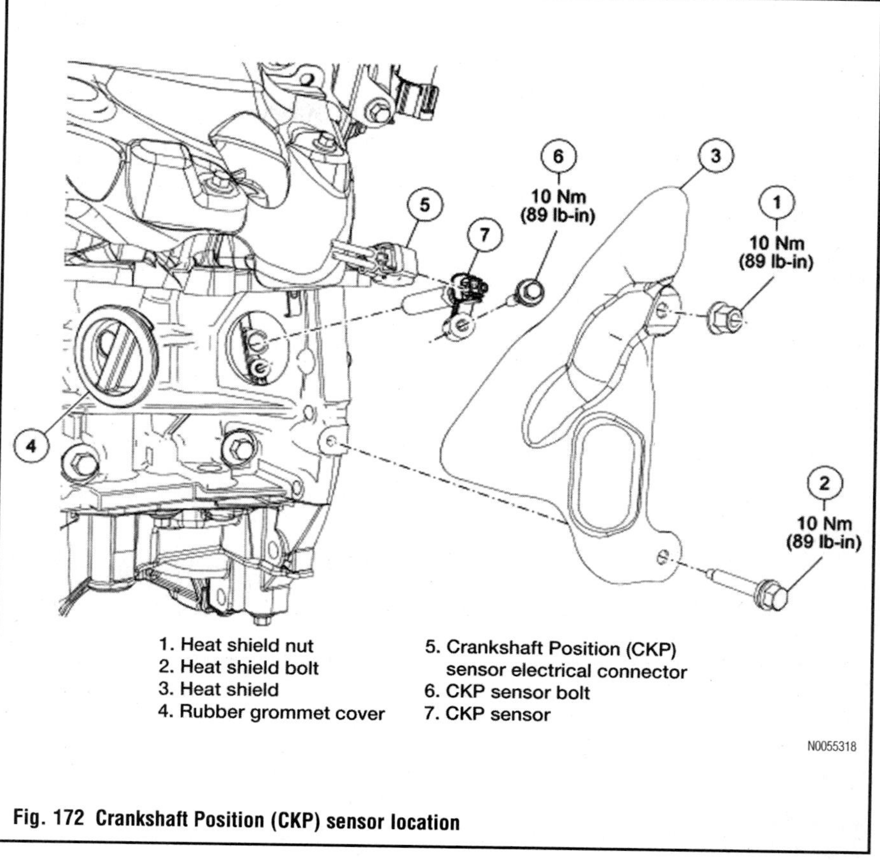

Fig. 172 Crankshaft Position (CKP) sensor location

REMOVAL & INSTALLATION

All Vehicles

1. With the vehicle in NEUTRAL, position it on a hoist.

All Vehicles Except 3.5L Turbo

2. Remove the LH catalytic converter as outlined in the Engine Mechanical Section.
3. Remove the bolt, nut and the heat shield.

3.5L Turbo

4. Remove the LH turbocharger as outlined in the Fuel System Section.
5. Remove the nut and the heat shield.

All Vehicles

6. Remove the rubber grommet cover.
7. Disconnect the Crankshaft Position (CKP) sensor electrical connector.
8. Remove the bolt and the CKP sensor.

To install:

All Vehicles

9. Install the bolt and the CKP sensor. Tighten the bolt to 89 inch lbs. (10 Nm).
10. Connect the Crankshaft Position (CKP) sensor electrical connector.
11. Install the rubber grommet cover.

3.5L Turbo

12. Install the nut and the heat shield. Tighten the nut to 89 inch lbs. (10 Nm).
13. Install the LH turbocharger as outlined in the Fuel System Section.

All Vehicles Except 3.5L Turbo

14. Install the bolt, nut and the heat shield. Tighten the bolt to 89 inch lbs. (10 Nm).
15. Install the LH catalytic converter as outlined in the Engine Mechanical Section.

All Vehicles

16. With the vehicle in NEUTRAL, position it on a hoist.

3.5L Turbo

17. Using the scan tool, perform the Misfire Monitor Neutral Profile Correction procedure, following the on-screen instructions.

CYLINDER HEAD TEMPERATURE (CHT) SENSOR

LOCATION

See Figures 173 and 174.

REMOVAL & INSTALLATION

3.5L Engine, Except Turbo

1. Remove the lower intake manifold as outlined in the Engine Mechanical Section.
2. Disconnect the Cylinder Head Temperature (CHT) sensor electrical connector.
3. Remove and discard the CHT sensor.

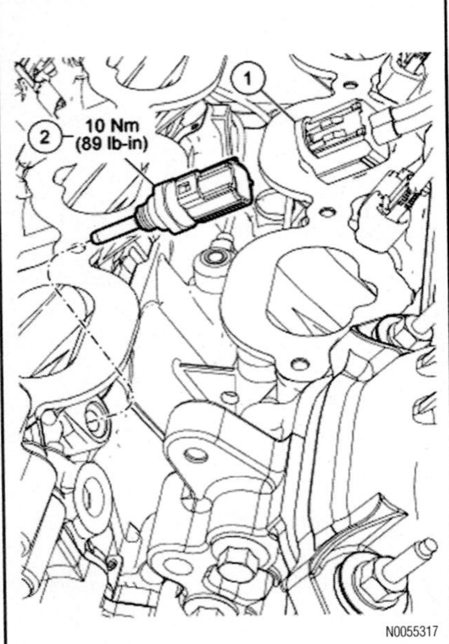

Fig. 173 Cylinder Head Temperature (CHT) Sensor [CHT sensor electrical connector (1), CHT sensor (2)]—3.5L engine, except Turbo

To install:

⁂ WARNING

Do not reuse the CHT sensor. Install a new sensor.

4. Install the CHT sensor. Tighten the sensor to 89 inch lbs. (10 Nm).
5. Connect the Cylinder Head Temperature (CHT) sensor electrical connector.
6. Install the lower intake manifold as outlined in the Engine Mechanical Section.

3.5L Turbo Engine

1. Remove the Air Cleaner (ACL) outlet pipe and the ACL as outlined in the Engine Mechanical Section.
2. Remove the ACL-to-LH and ACL-to-RH turbocharger intake tubes as outlined in the Engine Mechanical Section.
3. Disconnect the Cylinder Head Temperature (CHT) sensor electrical connector.
4. Remove and discard the CHT sensor.

To install:

⁂ WARNING

Do not reuse the CHT sensor. Install a new sensor.

5. Install the CHT sensor. Tighten the sensor to 89 inch lbs. (10 Nm).
6. Connect the Cylinder Head Temperature (CHT) sensor electrical connector.
7. Install the ACL -to-LH and ACL -to-RH turbocharger intake tubes as outlined in the Engine Mechanical Section.
8. Install the Air Cleaner (ACL) outlet pipe and the ACL as outlined in the Engine Mechanical Section.

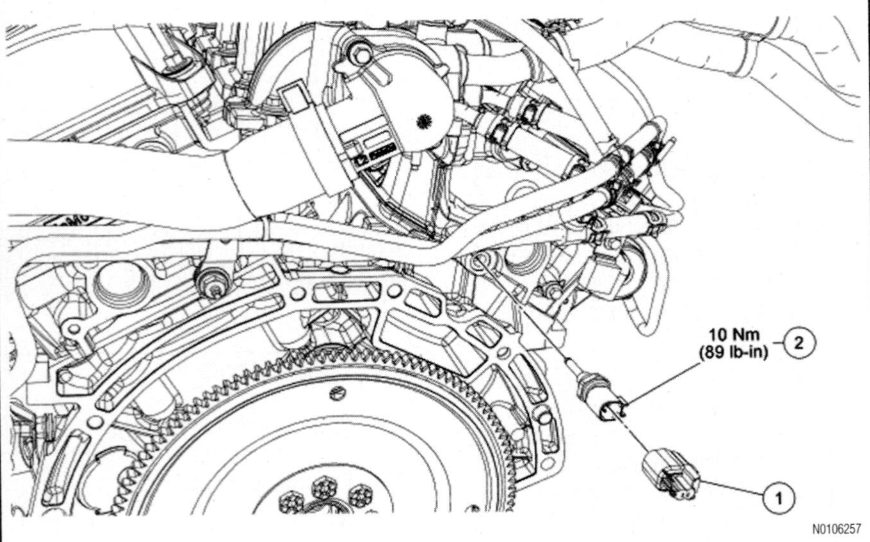

Fig. 174 Cylinder Head Temperature (CHT) Sensor [CHT sensor electrical connector (1), CHT sensor (2)]–3.5L Turbo engine

FUEL RAIL PRESSURE (FRP) SENSOR

LOCATION

See Figures 175 and 176.

Refer to the accompanying illustrations.

REMOVAL & INSTALLATION

⁂ CAUTION

Do not smoke, carry lighted tobacco or have an open flame of any type when working on or near any fuel-related component. Highly flammable mixtures are always present and may be ignited. Failure to follow these instructions may result in serious personal injury.

⁂ CAUTION

Before working on or disconnecting any of the fuel tubes or fuel system components, relieve the fuel system pressure to prevent accidental spraying of fuel. Fuel in the fuel system remains under high pressure, even when the engine is not running. Failure to follow this instruction may result in serious personal injury.

1. Release the fuel system pressure as outlined in the Fuel System Section.
2. Disconnect the battery ground cable.
3. Remove the intake manifold as outlined in the Engine Mechanical Section.
4. Disconnect the Fuel Rail Pressure (FRP) sensor electrical connector.
5. Remove the FRP sensor.

To install:

⁂ CAUTION

Do not smoke, carry lighted tobacco or have an open flame of any type when working on or near any fuel-related component. Highly flammable mixtures are always present and may be ignited. Failure to follow these instructions may result in serious personal injury.

⁂ CAUTION

Before working on or disconnecting any of the fuel tubes or fuel system components, relieve the fuel system pressure to prevent accidental spraying of fuel. Fuel in the fuel system remains under high pressure, even when the engine is not running. Failure to follow this instruction may result in serious personal injury.

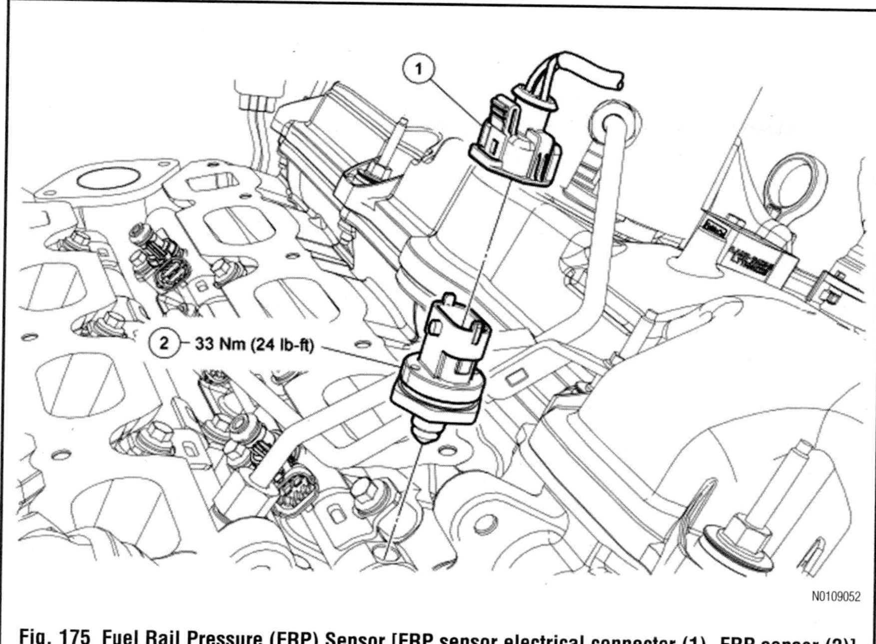

Fig. 175 Fuel Rail Pressure (FRP) Sensor [FRP sensor electrical connector (1), FRP sensor (2)]

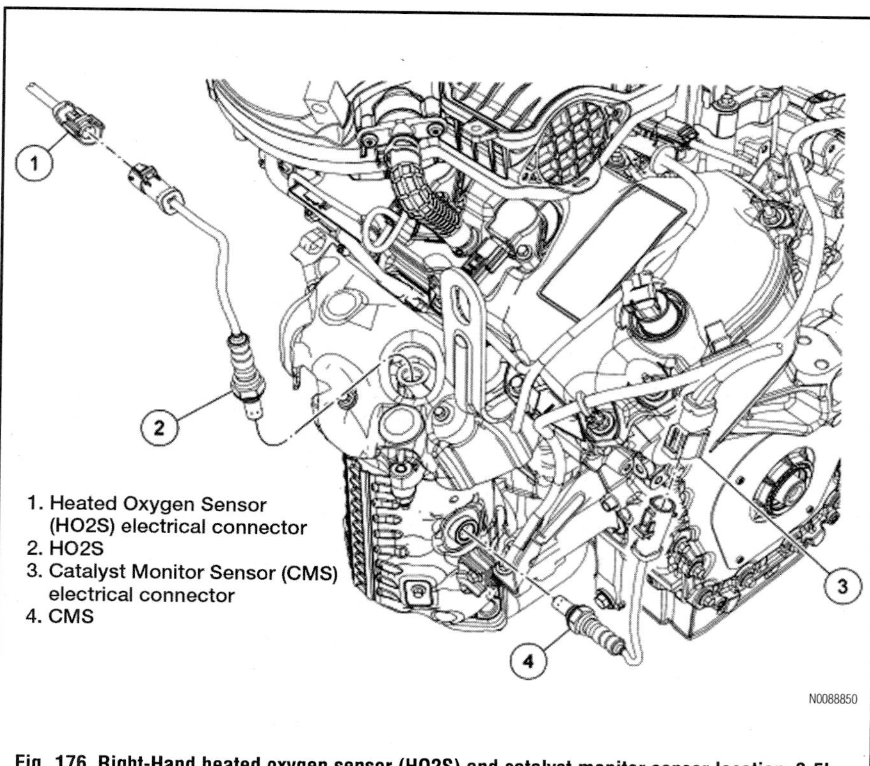

Fig. 176 Right-Hand heated oxygen sensor (HO2S) and catalyst monitor sensor location–3.5L

6. Install the FRP sensor. Tighten the sensor to 24 ft. lbs. (33 Nm).
7. Connect the Fuel Rail Pressure (FRP) sensor electrical connector.
8. Install the intake manifold as outlined in the Engine Mechanical Section.
9. Connect the battery ground cable.
10. Pressurize the fuel system pressure as outlined in the Fuel System Section.

HEATED OXYGEN (HO2S) SENSOR

LOCATION

See Figures 177 and 178.

Refer to the accompanying illustrations.

REMOVAL & INSTALLATION

See Figures 179 and 180.

All RH Sensors

1. With the vehicle in NEUTRAL, position it on a hoist.

RH 3.5L Turbo Sensor

2. Disconnect the Heated Oxygen Sensor (HO2S) electrical connector.
   a. Detach the HO2S electrical connector retainer from the bracket.

LH 3.5L Turbo Sensor

3. Remove the 4 retainers and the underbody shield.
4. Disconnect the LH HO2S electrical connector.
   a. Detach the HO2S connector retainer from the bracket.

All Sensors Except Turbo

5. Disconnect the HO2S electrical connector.

All Sensors

➡If necessary, lubricate the sensor threads with penetrating and lock lubricant to assist in removal.

6. Using the Exhaust Gas Oxygen Sensor Socket, remove the HO2S.
   a. Calculate the correct torque wrench setting.

➡Apply a light coat of anti-seize lubricant to the threads of the HO2S.

To install:

All Sensors

➡Apply a light coat of anti-seize lubricant to the threads of the HO2S.

➡If necessary, lubricate the sensor threads with penetrating and lock lubricant to assist in removal.

7. Using the Exhaust Gas Oxygen Sensor Socket, install the HO2S.
   a. Calculate the correct torque wrench setting. Tighten the sensor to 35 ft. lbs. (48 Nm).

All Sensors Except Turbo

8. Connect the HO2S electrical connector.

LH 3.5L Turbo Sensor

9. Install the 4 retainers and the underbody shield.
10. Connect the LH HO2S electrical connector.
   a. Attach the HO2S connector retainer to the bracket.

RH 3.5L Turbo Sensor

11. Connect the Heated Oxygen Sensor (HO2S) electrical connector.
   a. Attach the HO2S electrical connector retainer to the bracket.

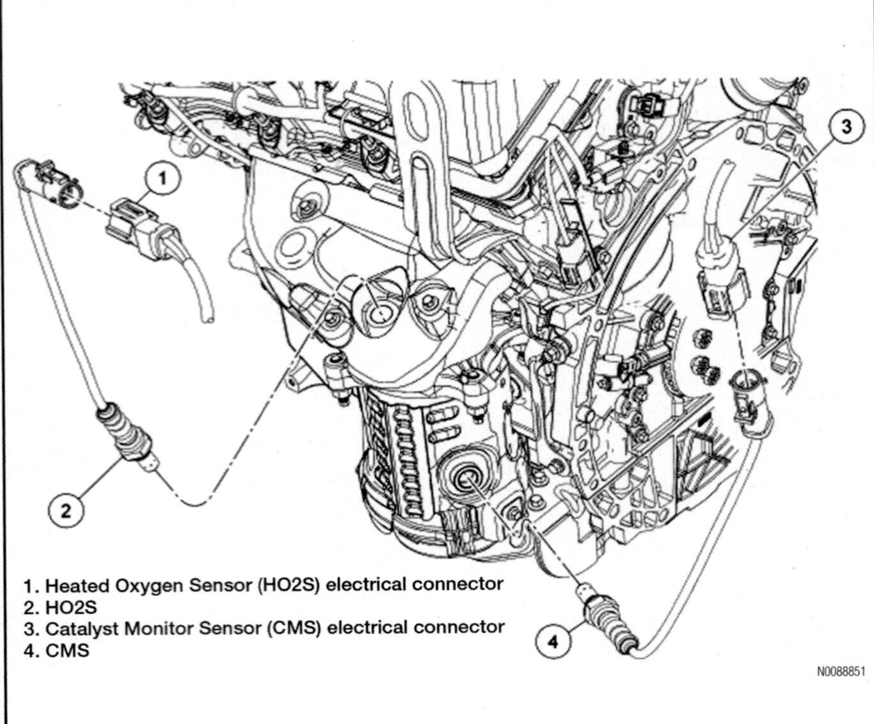

Fig. 177 Left-Hand heated oxygen sensor (HO2S) and catalyst monitor sensor location–3.5L

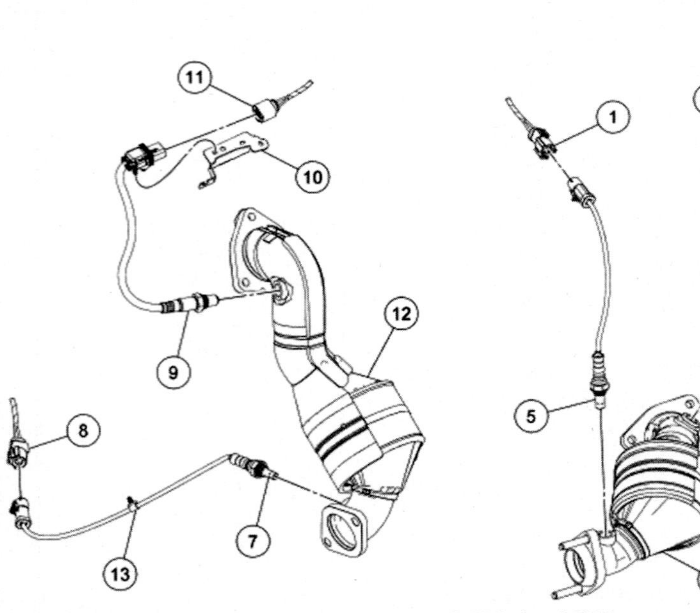
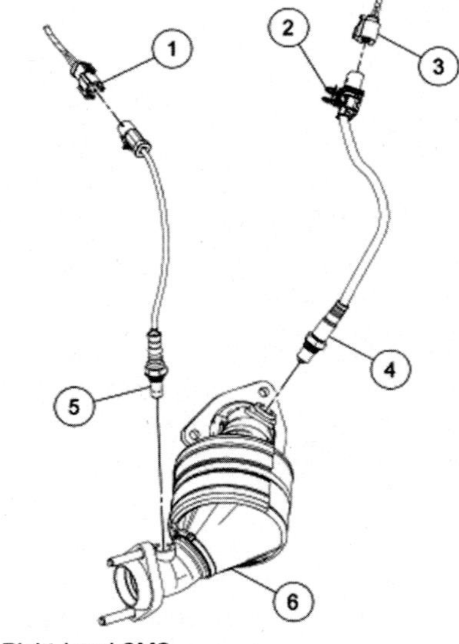

1. Left-hand Catalyst Monitor Sensor (CMS) electrical connector
2. Left-hand Heated Oxygen Sensor (HO2S) electrical connector retainer
3. Left-hand HO2S electrical connector
4. Left-hand HO2S
5. Left-hand CMS
6. Left-hand catalytic converter
7. Right-hand CMS
8. Right-hand CMS electrical connector
9. Right-hand HO2S
10. Right-hand HO2S connector bracket
11. Right-hand HO2S electrical connector
12. Right-hand catalytic converter
13. Right-hand CMS wiring retainer

Fig. 178 Heated oxygen sensor (HO2S) and catalyst monitor sensor location–3.5L Turbo

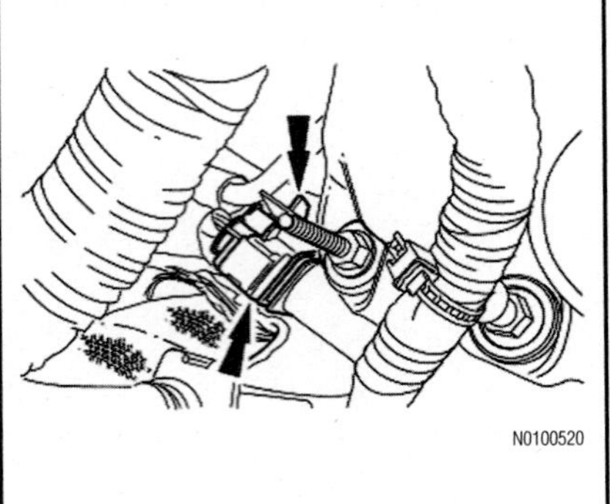

Fig. 179 Heated Oxygen Sensor (HO2S) electrical connector

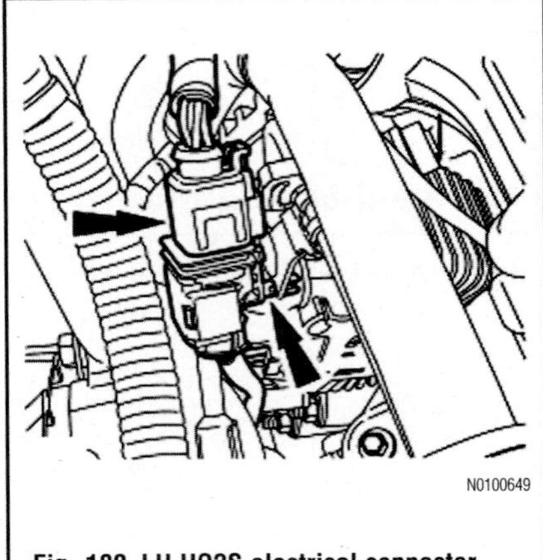

Fig. 180 LH HO2S electrical connector

All RH Sensors

12. With the vehicle in NEUTRAL, lower it from the hoist.

INTAKE AIR TEMPERATURE (IAT) SENSOR

LOCATION

See Figure 181.

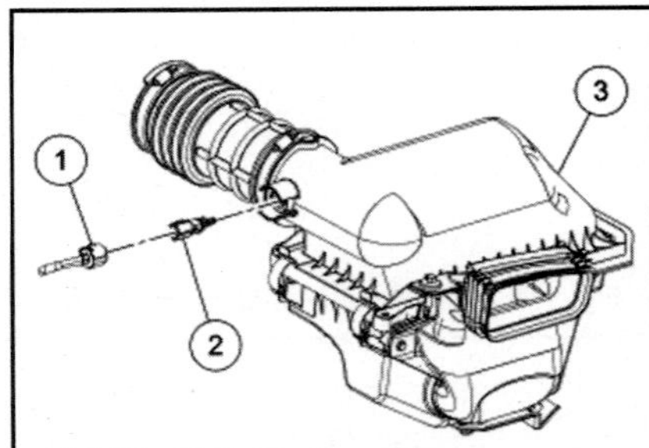

1. Intake Air Temperature (IAT) sensor electrical connector
2. IAT sensor
3. Air Cleaner (ACL) assembly

N0103522

Fig. 181 Intake Air Temperature (IAT) sensor location

REMOVAL & INSTALLATION

1. Disconnect the Intake Air Temperature (IAT) sensor electrical connector.
2. Remove the IAT sensor.
   a. Lift the tab and turn the IAT sensor counterclockwise to remove.

To install:

3. Install the IAT sensor.
   a. Push the tab and turn the IAT sensor clockwise to install.
4. Connect the Intake Air Temperature (IAT) sensor electrical connector.
5. Make sure the IAT sensor tab is fully seated during installation.

KNOCK SENSOR (KS)

LOCATION

See Figures 182 and 183.

Refer to the accompanying illustrations.

REMOVAL & INSTALLATION

3.5L Engine, Except Turbo

1. Remove the thermostat housing as outlined in the Engine Cooling Section.
2. Remove the lower intake manifold as outlined in the Engine Mechanical Section.
3. Remove the coolant tube.

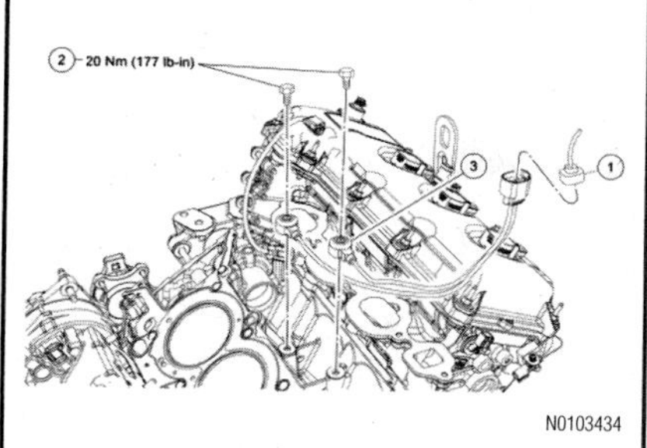

Fig. 183 Knock Sensor (KS) location–3.5L Turbo engine

   a. Discard the O-ring seal.
4. Disconnect the Knock Sensor (KS) electrical connector.
5. Remove the 2 bolts and the KS.

To install:

6. Install the 2 bolts and the KS. Tighten to 177 inch lbs. (20 Nm).
7. Connect the Knock Sensor (KS) electrical connector.
8. Install the coolant tube.
   a. Discard the O-ring seal.
9. Install the lower intake manifold as outlined in the Engine Mechanical Section.

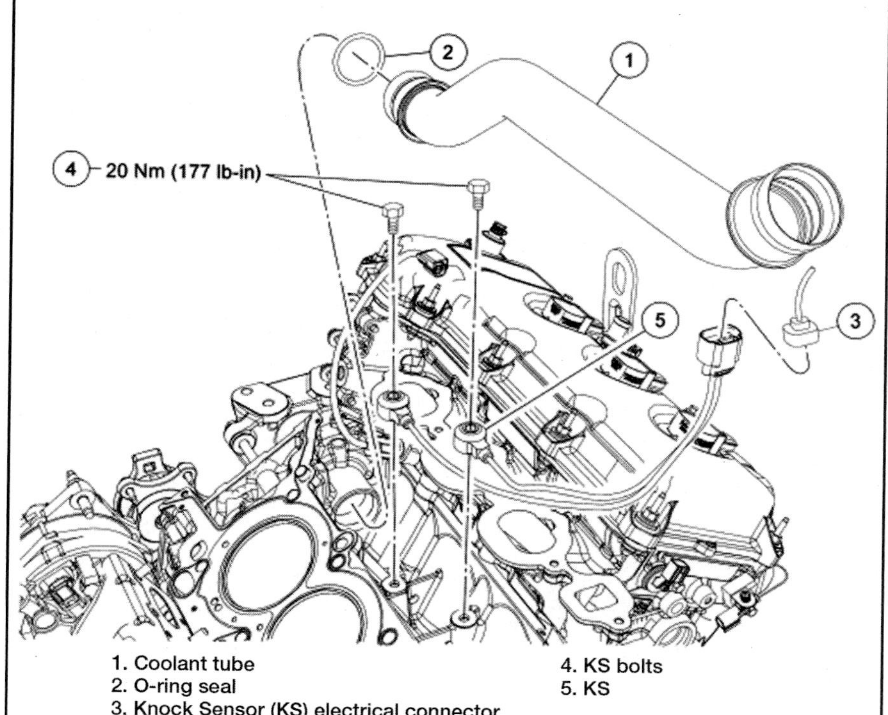

Fig. 182 Knock Sensor (KS) location–3.5L engine, except Turbo

10. Install the thermostat housing as outlined in the Engine Cooling Section.
11. Lubricate the new O-ring seal with clean engine coolant.

3.5L Turbo Engine

1. Remove the coolant inlet pipe.
2. Remove the fuel rail as outlined in the Fuel System Section.
3. Disconnect the Knock Sensor (KS) electrical connector.
4. Remove the 2 bolts and the KS.

To install:

5. Install the 2 bolts and the KS. Tighten the bolts to 177 inch lbs. (20 Nm).
6. Connect the Knock Sensor (KS) electrical connector.
7. Install the fuel rail as outlined in the Fuel System Section.
8. Install the coolant inlet pipe.

MANIFOLD ABSOLUTE PRESSURE (MAP) SENSOR & INTAKE AIR TEMPERATURE 2 (IAT2) SENSOR

REMOVAL & INSTALLATION

➡The Turbocharger Boost Pressure (TCBP)/Charge Air Cooler Temperature (CACT) sensor and the Manifold Absolute Pressure (MAP)/ Intake Air Temperature 2 (IAT2) sensor are not interchangeable.

1. Disconnect the MAP / IAT2 sensor electrical connector.
2. Remove the 2 screws and the MAP / IAT2 sensor.

To install:

3. Lubricate the MAP / IAT2 sensor O-ring seal with clean engine oil.
4. Install the MAP / IAT2 sensor and the 2 screws. Tighten the screws to 53 inch lbs. (6 Nm).
5. Connect the MAP / IAT2 sensor electrical connector.

POWERTRAIN CONTROL MODULE (PCM)

LOCATION

See Figure 184.

Refer to the accompanying illustration.

REMOVAL & INSTALLATION

➡PCM installation DOES NOT require new keys or programming of keys.

1. Retrieve the module configuration. Carry out the module configuration retrieval

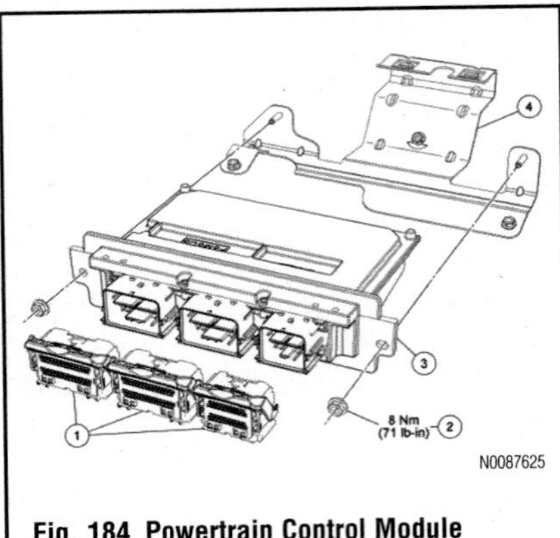

Fig. 184 Powertrain Control Module (PCM) location

steps of the Programmable Module Installation (PMI) procedure.

2. Remove the cowl panel grille as outlined in the Body and Paint Section.
3. Disconnect the 3 PCM electrical connectors.
4. Remove the 2 nuts and the PCM.

To install:

5. Install the PCM and the 2 nuts. Tighten the nuts to 71 inch lbs. (8 Nm).
6. Connect the 3 PCM electrical connectors.
7. Install the cowl panel grille as outlined in the Body and Paint Section.
8. Restore the module configuration. Carry out the module configuration restore steps of the Programmable Module Installation (PMI) procedure.
9. Reprogram the Passive Anti-Theft System (PATS). Carry out the Parameter Reset procedure as outlined in the Chassis Electrical Section.
10. Using the scan tool, perform the Misfire Monitor Neutral Profile Correction procedure, following the on-screen instructions.

THROTTLE POSITION SENSOR (TPS)

REMOVAL & INSTALLATION

See Figures 185 and 186.

1. Remove the Charge Air Cooler (CAC) outlet pipe as outlined in the Engine Mechanical Section.
2. Disconnect the Throttle Position (TP) sensor electrical connector.

⁂ WARNING

Do not put direct heat on the Throttle Position (TP) sensor or any other plastic parts because heat damage may occur. Damage may also occur if Electronic Throttle Body (ETB) temperature exceeds 248°F (120°C).

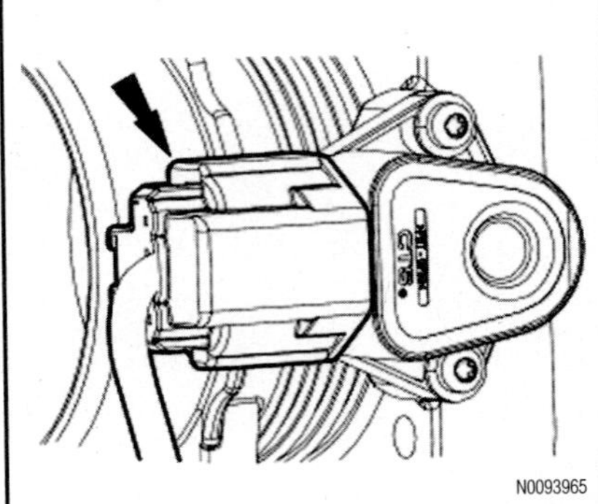

Fig. 185 Throttle Position (TP) sensor electrical connector

➡Do not use power tools.

3. Remove the TP sensor.
   a. Using a suitable heat gun, apply heat to the top of the Electronic Throttle Body (ETB) until the top TP sensor bolt ear reaches approximately 130°F (55°C), this should take no more than 3 minutes using an 1,100-watt heat gun. The heat gun should be about 1 inch (25.4 mm) away from the ETB.
   b. Monitor the temperature of the top TP sensor bolt ear on the ETB with a suitable temperature measuring device, such as a digital temperature laser or infrared thermometer, while heating the ETB.
   c. Using hand tools, quickly remove the bolt farthest from the heat source first and discard.
   d. Using hand tools, remove the remaining bolt and discard.
   e. Remove and discard the TP sensor.

To install:

➡When installing the new TP sensor, make sure that the radial locator tab on the TP sensor is aligned with the radial locator hole on the ETB.

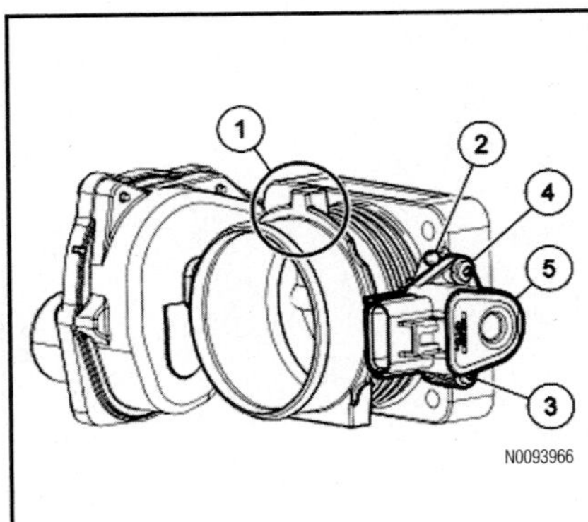

Fig. 186 Throttle Body Sensor

➡Do not use power tools.

4. Install the new TP sensor.
   a. Using hand tools, install the 2 new bolts. Tighten the bolts to 27 inch lbs. (3 Nm).
5. Connect the TP sensor electrical connector.
6. Install the CAC outlet pipe as outlined in the Engine Mechanical Section.

TURBOCHARGER BOOST PRESSURE (TCBP) / CHARGE AIR COOLER TEMPERATURE (CACT) SENSOR

LOCATION

See Figure 187.

Refer to the accompanying illustration.

REMOVAL & INSTALLATION

➡Turbocharger Boost Pressure (TCBP)/ Charge Air Cooler Temperature (CACT)sensor and the Manifold Absolute Pressure (MAP)/Intake Air Temperature 2 (IAT2) sensor are not interchangeable.

1. Disconnect the TCBP / CACT sensor electrical connector.
2. Remove the 2 screws and the TCBP / CACT sensor.

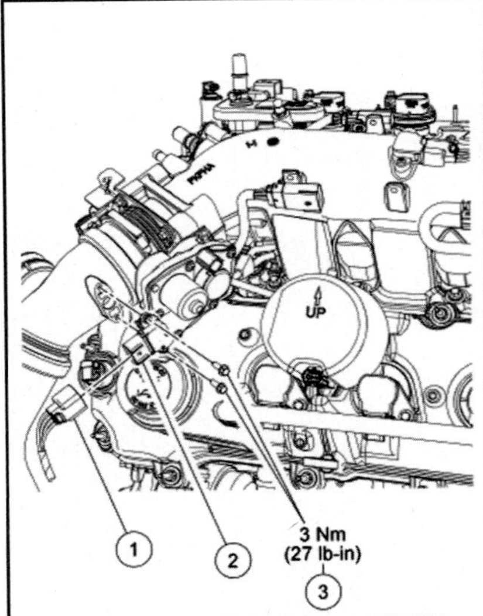

Fig. 187 Turbocharger boost pressure (TCBP) / Charge air cooler temperature (CACT) Sensor location

To install:

3. Lubricate the TCBP / CACT sensor O-ring seal with clean engine oil.
4. Install the TCBP / CACT sensor and the 2 screws. Tighten the screws to 27 inch lbs. (3 Nm).
5. Connect the TCBP / CACT sensor electrical connector.

VARIABLE CAMSHAFT TIMING (VCT) OIL CONTROL SOLENOID

LOCATION

See Figure 188.

Refer to the accompanying illustration.

REMOVAL & INSTALLATION

1. Remove the LH or RH valve cover as outlined in the Engine Mechanical Section.
2. Remove the bolt and the Variable Camshaft Timing (VCT) oil control solenoid.

To install:

3. Remove the bolt and the Variable Camshaft Timing (VCT) oil control solenoid. Tighten the bolt to 89 inch lbs. (10 Nm).
4. Remove the LH or RH valve cover as outlined in the Engine Mechanical Section.

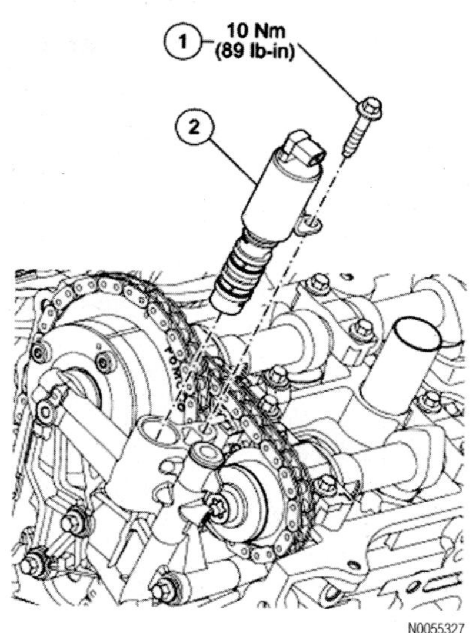

Fig. 188 Variable camshaft timing (VCT) oil control solenoid location. Variable camshaft timing (VCT) oil control solenoid bolt (1), VCT oil control solenoid (2)

FUEL

GASOLINE FUEL INJECTION SYSTEM

FUEL SYSTEM SERVICE PRECAUTIONS

Safety is the most important factor when performing not only fuel system maintenance but any type of maintenance. Failure to conduct maintenance and repairs in a safe manner may result in serious personal injury or death. Maintenance and testing of the vehicle's fuel system components can be accomplished safely and effectively by adhering to the following rules and guidelines.

- To avoid the possibility of fire and personal injury, always disconnect the negative battery cable unless the repair or test procedure requires that battery voltage be applied.
- Always relieve the fuel system pressure prior to disconnecting any fuel system component (injector, fuel rail, pressure regulator, etc.), fitting or fuel line connection. Exercise extreme caution whenever relieving fuel system pressure to avoid exposing skin, face and eyes to fuel spray. Please be advised that fuel under pressure may penetrate the skin or any part of the body that it contacts.
- Always place a shop towel or cloth around the fitting or connection prior to loosening to absorb any excess fuel due to spillage. Ensure that all fuel spillage (should it occur) is quickly removed from engine surfaces. Ensure that all fuel soaked cloths or towels are deposited into a suitable waste container.
- Always keep a dry chemical (Class B) fire extinguisher near the work area.
- Do not allow fuel spray or fuel vapors to come into contact with a spark or open flame.
- Always use a back-up wrench when loosening and tightening fuel line connection fittings. This will prevent unnecessary stress and torsion to fuel line piping.
- Always replace worn fuel fitting O-rings with new Do not substitute fuel hose or equivalent where fuel pipe is installed.

Before servicing the vehicle, make sure to also refer to the precautions in the beginning of this section as well.

RELIEVING FUEL SYSTEM PRESSURE

See Figure 189.

CAUTION

Do not smoke, carry lighted tobacco or have an open flame of any type when working on or near any fuel-related component. Highly flammable mixtures are always present and may be ignited. Failure to follow these instructions may result in serious personal injury.

CAUTION

Do not carry personal electronic devices such as cell phones, pagers or audio equipment of any type when working on or near any fuel-related component. Highly flammable mixtures are always present and may be ignited. Failure to follow these instructions may result in serious personal injury.

CAUTION

Before working on or disconnecting any of the fuel tubes or fuel system components, relieve the fuel system pressure to prevent accidental spraying of fuel. Fuel in the fuel system remains under high pressure, even when the engine is not running. Failure to follow this instruction may result in serious personal injury.

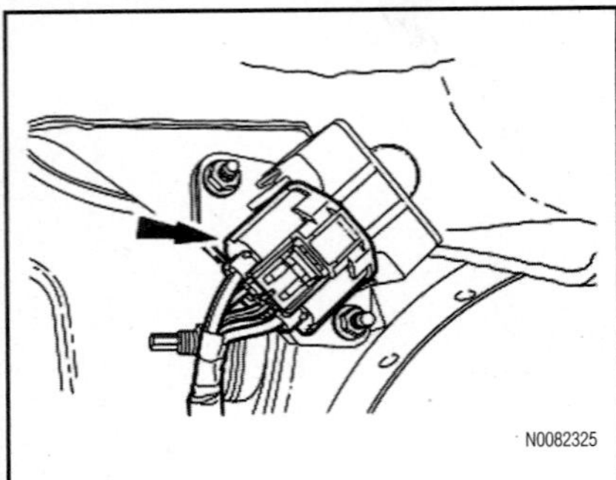

Fig. 189 FP control module electrical connector

⁂ CAUTION

When handling fuel, always observe fuel handling precautions and be prepared in the event of fuel spillage. Spilled fuel may be ignited by hot vehicle components or other ignition sources. Failure to follow these instructions may result in serious personal injury.

⁂ CAUTION

Always disconnect the battery ground cable at the battery when working on an evaporative emission (EVAP) system or fuel-related component. Highly flammable mixtures are always present and may be ignited. Failure to follow these instructions may result in serious personal injury.

➡Refer to Description and Operation, Intelligent Access with Push Button Start in the Chassis Electrical Section Passive Anti-Theft System (PATS) to review the procedures for achieving the various ignition states (ignition OFF, ignition in ACCESSORY, ignition ON and ignition START) on vehicles with this feature.

All Vehicles

➡The Fuel Pump (FP) control module is mounted to the panel behind the rear seat backrest cushion. The FP control module electrical connector can be accessed through the luggage compartment.

1. Disconnect the FP module electrical connector.
2. Start the engine and allow it to idle until it stalls.
3. Turn the ignition to the OFF position.

3.5L Turbo

➡On vehicles equipped with Gasoline Turbocharged Direct Injection (GTDI), it is necessary to release the high system fuel pressure prior to disconnecting a low pressure fuel tube quick connect coupling.

➡To release the fuel pressure in the high pressure fuel tube, wrap the flare nut with a shop towel to absorb any residual fuel pressure during the loosening of the flare nut.

4. Disconnect the high pressure fuel tube-to-fuel injection pump flare nut.

All Vehicles

5. When the fuel system service is complete, reconnect the FP control module electrical connector.

➡It may take more than one ignition cycle to pressurize the fuel system.

6. Cycle the ignition and wait 3 seconds to pressurize the fuel system.

➡Carry out an ignition ON engine OFF visual inspection for fuel leaks prior to starting the engine.

7. Start the engine and check for leaks.

FUEL FILTER

REMOVAL & INSTALLATION

A Lifetime Fuel Filter is used and serviced as part of the Fuel Pump (FP) module.

FUEL INJECTORS

REMOVAL & INSTALLATION

The fuel injectors are serviced with the fuel rail.

FUEL PUMP

REMOVAL & INSTALLATION

See Figures 190 and 191.

⁂ CAUTION

Do not smoke, carry lighted tobacco or have an open flame of any type when working on or near any fuel-related component. Highly flammable mixtures are always present and may be ignited. Failure to follow these instructions may result in serious personal injury.

⁂ CAUTION

Do not carry personal electronic devices such as cell phones, pagers or audio equipment of any type when working on or near any fuel-related component. Highly flammable mixtures are always present and may be ignited. Failure to follow these instructions may result in serious personal injury.

⁂ CAUTION

Before working on or disconnecting any of the fuel tubes or fuel system components, relieve the fuel system pressure to prevent accidental spraying of fuel. Fuel in the fuel system remains under high pressure, even when the engine is not running. Failure to follow this instruction may result in serious personal injury.

⁂ CAUTION

When handling fuel, always observe fuel handling precautions and be prepared in the event of fuel spillage. Spilled fuel may be ignited by hot vehicle components or other ignition sources. Failure to follow these instructions may result in serious personal injury.

⁂ CAUTION

Always disconnect the battery ground cable at the battery when working on an evaporative emission (EVAP) system or fuel-related component. Highly flammable mixtures are always present and may be ignited. Failure to follow these instructions may result in serious personal injury.

All Vehicles

1. Release the fuel system pressure.
2. Disconnect the battery ground cable.
3. Remove the rear seat lower cushion.
4. Remove the Fuel Pump (FP) module access cover.

➡Clean the FP module connections, couplings, flange surfaces and the immediate surrounding area of any dirt or foreign material.

5. Disconnect the FP module electrical connector.
6. Disconnect the fuel tank wiring harness electrical connector.
7. Disconnect the Fuel Tank Pressure (FTP) sensor electrical connector.

➡Place absorbent toweling in the immediate surrounding area in case of fuel spillage.

8. Disconnect the fuel tank jumper tube-to- FP module quick connect coupling.

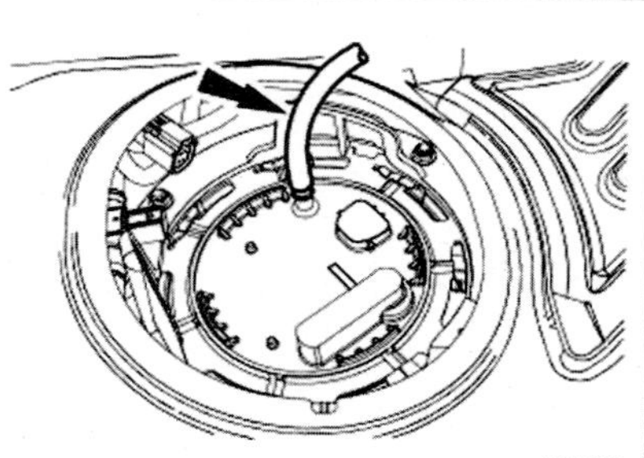

Fig. 190 Attach the Fuel Storage Tanker tube to the FP module outlet fitting and remove one fourth (approximately 5 gallons) of the fuel from a completely full tank, lowering the fuel level below the FP module mounting flange

9. Attach the Fuel Storage Tanker tube to the FP module outlet fitting and remove one fourth (approximately 5 gallons) of the fuel from a completely full tank, lowering the fuel level below the FP module mounting flange.

All-Wheel Drive (AWD) Vehicles

10. Remove the Evaporative Emission (EVAP) canister.

11. Remove the driveshaft as outlined in the Drive Train Section.

12. Position the Powertrain Lift under the fuel tank.

13. Loosen the 2 rear fuel tank strap bolts.

14. Remove the 2 front fuel tank strap bolts.

➡Install a suitable cap on the FP module port to avoid fuel spillage when lowering the front of the fuel tank.

15. Partially lower the front of the fuel tank to access the FP module shield nuts.

16. Remove the 3 nuts and the FP module shield.

➡The fuel tank must be placed back into the installed position prior to FP module removal to avoid fuel spillage.

17. Raise the fuel tank into the installed position and reinstall the 2 front fuel tank strap bolts.

All Vehicles

➡Carefully install the Fuel Tank Sender Unit Wrench to avoid damaging the FP module when removing the lock ring.

18. Install the Fuel Tank Sender Unit Wrench, remove the FP module lock ring.

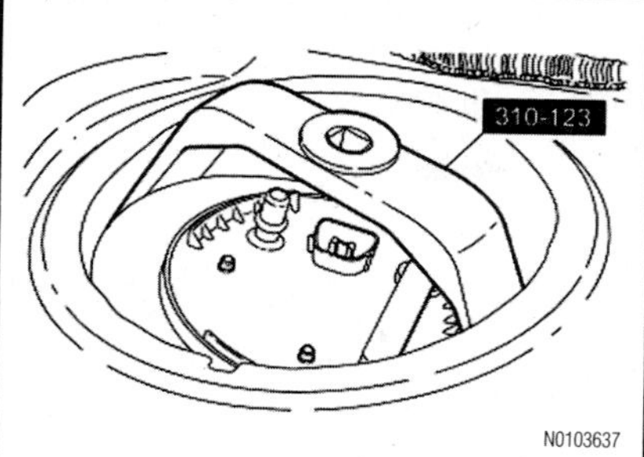

Fig. 191 Install the Fuel Tank Sender Unit Wrench, remove the FP module lock ring

AWD Vehicles

WARNING

The Fuel Pump (FP) module must be handled carefully to avoid damage to the float arm.

19. Carefully lift the FP module out of the fuel tank allowing access and disconnect the FP module internal quick connect coupling.

All Vehicles

WARNING

The Fuel Pump (FP) module must be handled carefully to avoid damage to the float arm.

➡The FP module will have residual fuel remaining internally, drain into a suitable container.

20. Completely remove the FP module from the fuel tank.

➡Inspect the surfaces of the FP module flange and fuel tank O-ring seal contact surfaces. Do not polish or adjust the O-ring seal contact area of the fuel tank flange or the fuel tank. Install a new FP module or fuel tank if the O-ring seal contact area is bent, scratched or corroded.

21. Remove and discard the FP module O-ring seal.

➡Make sure to install a new FP module O-ring seal.

➡To install, apply clean engine oil to the O-ring seal.

To install:

➡Make sure the alignment arrows on the fuel pump module and the fuel tank meet before tightening the FP module lock ring.

➡Tighten the FP lock ring until it meets the stop tabs on the fuel tank.

All Vehicles

➡Make sure to install a new FP module O-ring seal.

➡To install, apply clean engine oil to the O-ring seal.

➡Inspect the surfaces of the FP module flange and fuel tank O-ring seal contact surfaces. Do not polish or adjust the O-ring seal contact area of the fuel tank flange or the fuel tank. Install a new FP module or fuel tank if the O-ring seal contact area is bent, scratched or corroded.

Remove and discard the FP module O-ring seal.

WARNING

The Fuel Pump (FP) module must be handled carefully to avoid damage to the float arm.

➡The FP module will have residual fuel remaining internally, drain into a suitable container.

22. Completely install the FP module from the fuel tank.

AWD Vehicles

WARNING

The Fuel Pump (FP) module must be handled carefully to avoid damage to the float arm.

23. Connect the FP module internal quick connect coupling, and carefully lower the FP module into the fuel tank.

All Vehicles

➡Carefully install the Fuel Tank Sender Unit Wrench to avoid damaging the FP module when removing the lock ring.

24. Install the Fuel Tank Sender Unit Wrench, install the FP module lock ring.

All-Wheel Drive (AWD) Vehicles

➡The fuel tank must be placed back into the installed position prior to FP module installation to avoid fuel spillage.

25. Raise the fuel tank into the installed position and reinstall the 2 front fuel tank strap bolts.

26. Install the 3 nuts and the FP module shield. Tighten the nuts to 80 inch lbs. (9 Nm).

➡Install a suitable cap on the FP module port to avoid fuel spillage when lowering the front of the fuel tank.

27. Partially lower the front of the fuel tank to access the FP module shield nuts.
28. Install the 2 front fuel tank strap bolts. Tighten the bolts to 26 ft. lbs. (35 Nm).
29. Tighten the 2 rear fuel tank strap bolts.
    a. Calculate the correct torque wrench setting. To install, use a torque adapter and tighten the bolts to 26 ft. lbs. (35 Nm).
30. Position the Powertrain Lift under the fuel tank.
31. Remove the driveshaft as outlined in the Drive Train Section.
32. Remove the Evaporative Emission (EVAP) canister.

All Vehicles

33. Attach the Fuel Storage Tanker tube to the FP module outlet fitting and remove one fourth (approximately 5 gallons) of the fuel from a completely full tank, lowering the fuel level below the FP module mounting flange.

➡Place absorbent toweling in the immediate surrounding area in case of fuel spillage.

34. Disconnect the fuel tank jumper tube-to- FP module quick connect coupling.
35. Disconnect the Fuel Tank Pressure (FTP) sensor electrical connector.
36. Disconnect the fuel tank wiring harness electrical connector.

➡Clean the FP module connections, couplings, flange surfaces and the immediate surrounding area of any dirt or foreign material.

37. Disconnect the FP module electrical connector.
38. Remove the Fuel Pump (FP) module access cover.
39. Remove the rear seat lower cushion.
40. Disconnect the battery ground cable.
41. Release the fuel system pressure.

FUEL RAIL

REMOVAL & INSTALLTION

3.5L Engine, Except Turbo

See Figures 192 and 193.

⁂ CAUTION

Do not smoke, carry lighted tobacco or have an open flame of any type when working on or near any fuel-related component. Highly flammable mixtures are always present and may be ignited. Failure to follow these instructions may result in serious personal injury.

⁂ CAUTION

Before working on or disconnecting any of the fuel tubes or fuel system components, relieve the fuel system pressure to prevent accidental spraying of fuel. Fuel in the fuel system remains under high pressure, even when the engine is not running. Failure to follow this instruction may result in serious personal injury.

⁂ CAUTION

Do not carry personal electronic devices such as cell phones, pagers or audio equipment of any type when working on or near any fuel-related component. Highly flammable mixtures are always present and may be ignited. Failure to follow these instructions may result in serious personal injury.

⁂ CAUTION

Always disconnect the battery ground cable at the battery when working on an evaporative emission (EVAP) system or fuel-related component. Highly flammable mixtures are always present and may be ignited. Failure to follow these instructions may result in serious personal injury.

⁂ CAUTION

Clean all fuel residue from the engine compartment. If not removed, fuel residue may ignite when the engine is returned to operation. Failure to follow this instruction may result in serious personal injury.

1. Release the fuel system pressure.
2. Disconnect the battery ground cable.
3. Remove the upper intake manifold as outlined in the Engine Section.
4. Detach the fuel tube routing clips from the fuel rail.
5. Disconnect the fuel jumper tube-to-fuel rail spring lock coupling.
6. Disconnect the 6 fuel injector electrical connectors.
7. Remove the 4 fuel rail bolts.

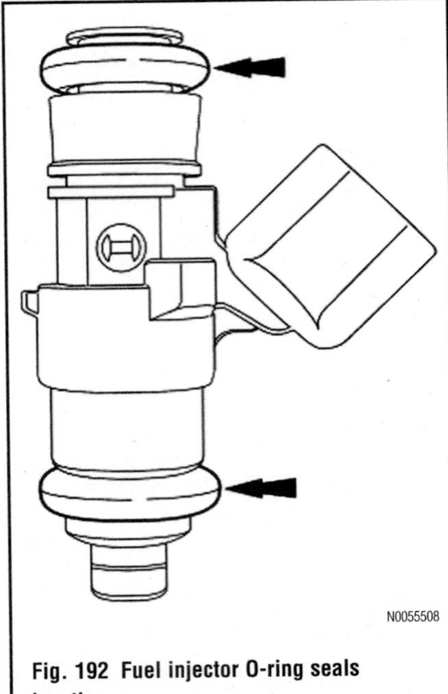

Fig. 192 Fuel injector O-ring seals location

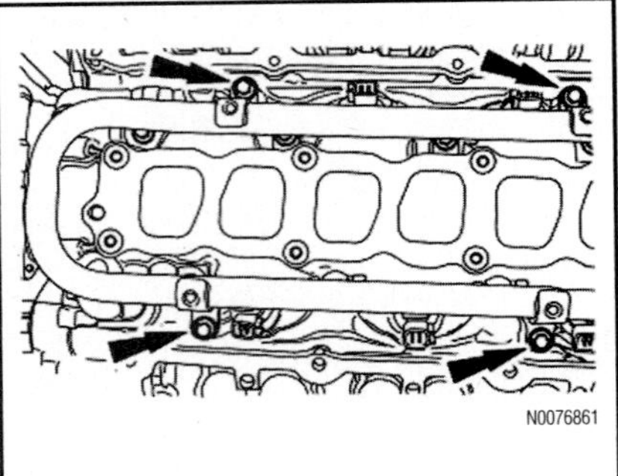

Fig. 193 Fuel rail and injectors assembly installation

8. Remove the fuel rail and injectors as an assembly.
9. Remove the 6 fuel injector clips and the 6 fuel injectors.
10. Remove and discard the 12 fuel injector O-ring seals.

To install:

⁂ WARNING

Use O-ring seals that are made of special fuel-resistant material. The use of ordinary O-rings may cause the fuel system to leak. Do not reuse the O-ring seals.

➡The upper and lower fuel injector O-ring seals are similar in appearance, but are not interchangeable.

11. Install the new O-ring seals onto the fuel injectors and lubricate them with clean engine oil.

12. Install the 6 fuel injectors and the 6 fuel injector clips into the fuel rail.
13. Install the fuel rail and fuel injectors as an assembly.
14. Install the 4 fuel rail bolts. Tighten the bolts to 89 inch lbs. (10 Nm).
15. Connect the 6 fuel injector electrical connectors.
16. Connect the fuel jumper tube-to-fuel rail spring lock coupling. For additional information, refer to Fuel System — General Information.
17. Attach the fuel tube routing clips to the fuel rail.
18. Install the upper intake manifold as outlined in the Engine Section.
19. Connect the battery ground cable.

3.5L Turbo Engine

See Figures 194 and 195.

All Vehicles

CAUTION

Do not smoke, carry lighted tobacco or have an open flame of any type when working on or near any fuel-related component. Highly flammable mixtures are always present and may be ignited. Failure to follow these instructions may result in serious personal injury.

CAUTION

Do not carry personal electronic devices such as cell phones, pagers or audio equipment of any type when working on or near any fuel-related component. Highly flammable mixtures are always present and may be ignited. Failure to follow these instructions may result in serious personal injury.

CAUTION

When handling fuel, always observe fuel handling precautions and be prepared in the event of fuel spillage. Spilled fuel may be ignited by hot vehicle components or other ignition sources. Failure to follow these instructions may result in serious personal injury.

CAUTION

Before working on or disconnecting any of the fuel tubes or fuel system components, relieve the fuel system pressure to prevent accidental spraying of fuel. Fuel in the fuel system remains under high pressure, even when the engine is not running. Failure to follow this instruction may result in serious personal injury.

CAUTION

Clean all fuel residue from the engine compartment. If not removed, fuel residue may ignite when the engine is returned to operation. Failure to follow this instruction may result in serious personal injury.

CAUTION

Always disconnect the battery ground cable at the battery when working on an evaporative emission (EVAP) system or fuel-related component. Highly flammable mixtures are always present and may be ignited. Failure to follow these instructions may result in serious personal injury.

➡A clean working environment is essential to prevent dirt or foreign material contamination.

1. Release the fuel system pressure as outlined in this section.
2. Disconnect the battery ground cable. For additional information, refer to Battery, Mounting and Cables.
3. Remove the intake manifold as outlined in the Engine Section.
4. Remove the fuel injection pump noise insulator shield.

Early Build Vehicles

5. Remove the high pressure fuel tube nut.

Late Build Vehicles

6. Remove the high pressure fuel tube bolt.

All Vehicles

➡To release the fuel pressure in the high pressure fuel tube, wrap the flare nuts with a shop towel to absorb any residual fuel pressure during the loosening of the flare nuts.

7. Loosen the 3 flare nuts and remove the high pressure fuel tube.
8. Disconnect the Fuel Rail Pressure (FRP) sensor electrical connector.

WARNING

It is very important to note the routing of the fuel charge wire harnesses on the fuel rails and index-mark the location of the tie straps prior to removal or damage may occur to the wire harnesses during installation.

➡Use compressed air and remove any dirt or foreign material from the cylinder head, block and general surrounding area of the fuel rail and injectors.

9. Cut, remove and discard the fuel charge wiring harness tie straps.

WARNING

Pull out the fuel rails in the direction of the fuel injector axis or damage may occur to the fuel injectors.

➡When removing the fuel rails, the fuel injectors may remain in the fuel rails but normally remain in the cylinder heads and require the use of a Fuel Injector Remover tool to extract.

10. Remove and discard the 6 bolts and remove the LH fuel rail.
11. Remove and discard the 6 bolts and remove the RH fuel rail.
12. Disconnect the 6 fuel injector electrical connectors and remove the 2 fuel charge wire harnesses.
13. Remove and discard the 6 upper fuel injector O-ring seals.
14. Remove and discard the 6 fuel injector clips.
15. Using the Slide Hammer and the Fuel Injector Remover, remove the 6 fuel injectors.

To install:

All Vehicles

➡A clean working environment is essential to prevent dirt or foreign material contamination.

➡Make sure to thoroughly clean any residual fuel or foreign material from the cylinder head, block and the general surrounding area of the fuel rails and injectors.

16. Using the Fuel Injector Brush, clean the fuel injector orifices.

WARNING

Do not attempt to cut the lower Teflon® seal without first pulling it away from the fuel injector or damage to the injector may occur.

➡Be very careful when removing the lower Teflon® seals, not to scratch, nick or gouge the fuel injectors.

17. Pull the lower Teflon® seal away from the injector with narrow tip pliers.

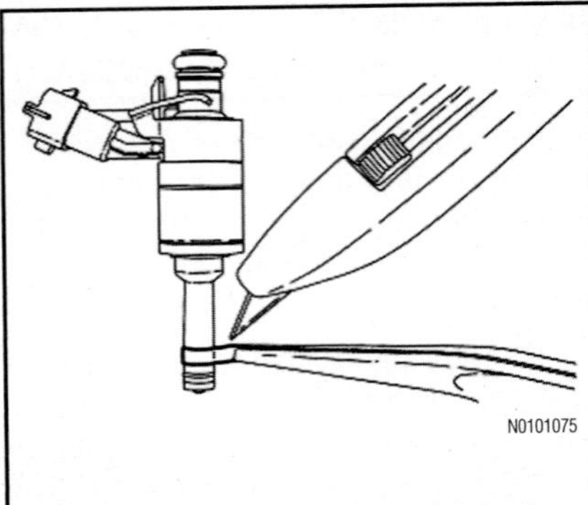

Fig. 194 Carefully cut and discard the 6 lower fuel injector Teflon® seals

18. Carefully cut and discard the 6 lower fuel injector Teflon® seals.

➡Do not lubricate the 6 new lower Teflon® fuel injector seals.

19. Install the new lower Teflon® seals on the narrow end of the Arbor (part of the Fuel Injector Seal Installer), then install the Arbor on the fuel injector tips.

⁂ WARNING

Once the Teflon® seal is installed on the Arbor, it should immediately be installed onto the fuel injector to avoid excessive expansion of the seal.

20. Using the Pusher Tool (part of the Fuel Injector Seal Installer), slide the Teflon® seals off of the Arbor and into the groove on the fuel injectors.
21. Place the Adjustment Ring (part of the Fuel Injector Seal Installer) beveled side first, over the fuel injector tip until it bottoms out against the fuel injector and turn 180 degrees.
    a. After one minute, turn the Adjustment Ring back 180 degrees and remove.

⁂ WARNING

It is very important to note the routing of the fuel charge wiring harnesses on the fuel rails and index-mark the location of the tie straps prior to removal or damage may occur to the wire harnesses during installation.

22. Install the fuel charge wire harnesses and tie straps to the index-marked locations on the fuel rails. Start by attaching the first tie strap farthest down the wire harness and continue to the connector end of the harness, leaving ample slack between the fuel injectors.
23. Connect the FRP sensor electrical connector.

⁂ WARNING

Use fuel injector O-ring seals that are made of special fuel-resistant material. The use of ordinary O-ring seals may cause the fuel system to leak. Do not reuse the O-ring seals.

➡To install, apply clean engine oil to the 6 new upper fuel injector O-ring seals only. Do not lubricate the lower fuel injector Teflon® seals.

➡Inspect the fuel injector support disks and replace if necessary.

24. Install the 6 new upper fuel injector O-ring seals.
25. Install the 6 new fuel injector clips.

➡The anti-rotation device on the fuel injector has to slip into the groove of the fuel rail cup.

26. Install the 6 fuel injectors into the fuel rails and connect the 6 electrical connectors.

⁂ WARNING

It is very important to visually inspect the routing of the fuel charge wire harness to make sure that they will not be pinched or damaged between the fuel rail and the cylinder head during installation.

➡Tighten the bolts in a method that draws the fuel rail evenly to the head, preventing a rocking motion.

27. Install the 6 new bolts and the RH fuel rail assembly.
    a. Push down on the fuel rail face above the injectors and begin tightening the outer bolts first and then proceed inward.

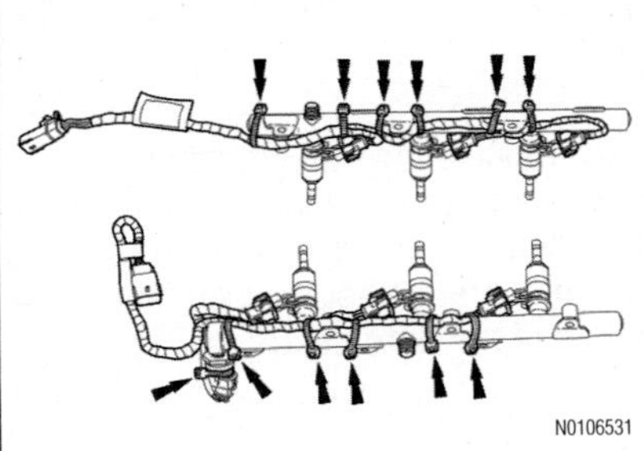

Fig. 195 Install the fuel charge wire harnesses and tie straps to the index-marked locations on the fuel rails. Start by attaching the first tie strap farthest down the wire harness and continue to the connector end of the harness, leaving ample slack between the fuel injectors

    b. To install, tighten the bolts to 89 inch lbs. (10 Nm), and then tighten an additional 45 degrees.

⁂ WARNING

It is very important to visually inspect the routing of the fuel charge wire harness to make sure that they will not be pinched or damaged between the fuel rail and the cylinder head during installation.

➡Tighten the bolts in a method that draws the fuel rail evenly to the head, preventing a rocking motion.

28. Install the 6 new bolts and the LH fuel rail assembly.
    a. Push down on the fuel rail face above the injectors and begin tightening the outer bolts first and proceed inward.
    b. To install, tighten the bolts to 89 inch lbs. (10 Nm), and then tighten an additional 45 degrees.

➡To install, apply clean engine oil to the threads of the 3 high-pressure fuel tube flare nuts.

29. Install the high-pressure fuel tube and tighten the 3 flare nuts. Tighten the nuts to 22 ft. lbs. (30 Nm).

Early Build Vehicles

30. Install the high-pressure fuel tube nut. Tighten the nut to 53 inch lbs. (6 Nm).

Late Build Vehicles

31. Install the high-pressure fuel tube bolt. Tighten the bolt to 53 inch lbs. (6 Nm).

All Vehicles

32. Install the fuel injection pump noise insulator shield.
33. Install the intake manifold as outlined in the Engine Mechanical Section.
34. Connect the battery ground cable.

FUEL TANK

DRAINING

⁂ CAUTION

Do not smoke, carry lighted tobacco or have an open flame of any type when working on or near any fuel-related component. Highly flammable mixtures are always present and may be ignited. Failure to follow these instructions may result in serious personal injury.

⁂ CAUTION

Do not carry personal electronic devices such as cell phones, pagers

or audio equipment of any type when working on or near any fuel-related component. Highly flammable mixtures are always present and may be ignited. Failure to follow these instructions may result in serious personal injury.

**** CAUTION**

Before working on or disconnecting any of the fuel tubes or fuel system components, relieve the fuel system pressure to prevent accidental spraying of fuel. Fuel in the fuel system remains under high pressure, even when the engine is not running. Failure to follow this instruction may result in serious personal injury.

**** CAUTION**

When handling fuel, always observe fuel handling precautions and be prepared in the event of fuel spillage. Spilled fuel may be ignited by hot vehicle components or other ignition sources. Failure to follow these instructions may result in serious personal injury.

**** CAUTION**

Always disconnect the battery ground cable at the battery when working on an evaporative emission (EVAP) system or fuel-related component. Highly flammable mixtures are always present and may be ignited. Failure to follow these instructions may result in serious personal injury.

L-Shaped

See Figures 196 through 203.

1. Release the fuel system pressure as outlined in this section.
2. Disconnect the battery ground cable.
3. Remove the rear seat lower cushion.
4. Remove the Fuel Pump (FP) module access cover.

➡Clean the FP module connections, couplings, flange surfaces and the immediate surrounding area of any dirt or foreign material.

5. Disconnect the FP module electrical connector.
6. Disconnect the fuel tank wiring harness electrical connector.
7. Disconnect the Fuel Tank Pressure (FTP) sensor electrical connector.

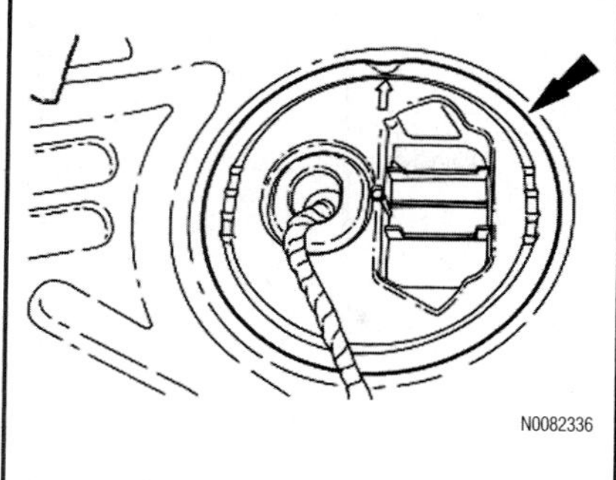

Fig. 196 Remove the Fuel Pump (FP) module access cover

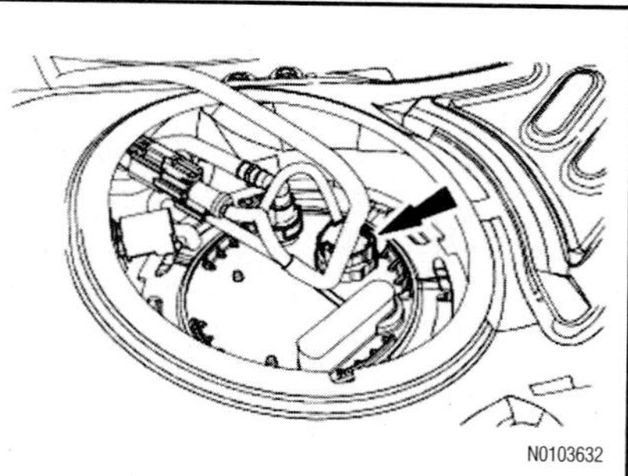

Fig. 197 Disconnect the FP module electrical connector

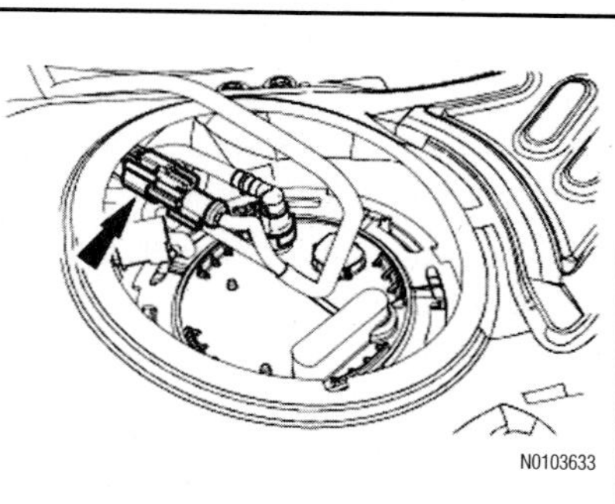

Fig. 198 Disconnect the fuel tank wiring harness electrical connector

➡Place absorbent toweling in the immediate surrounding area in case of fuel spillage.

8. Disconnect the fuel tank jumper tube-to-FP module quick connect coupling.
9. Attach the Fuel Storage Tanker tube to the FP module outlet fitting and remove one fourth (approximately 5 gallons) of the fuel from a completely full tank, lowering the fuel level below the FP module flange.

**** WARNING**

Carefully install the Fuel Tank Sender Unit Wrench to avoid damaging the Fuel Pump (FP) module when removing the lock ring.

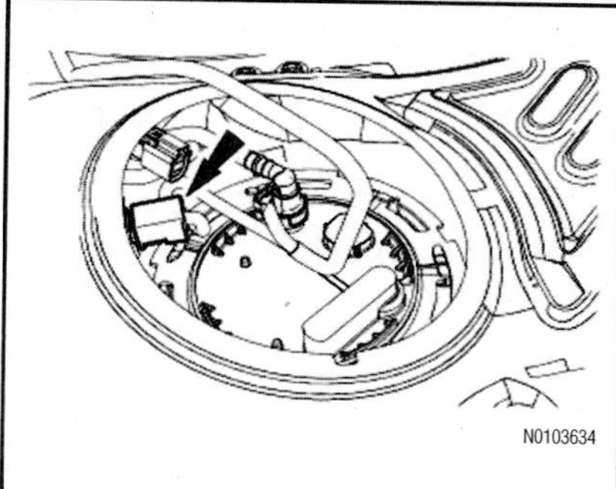

Fig. 199 Disconnect the Fuel Tank Pressure (FTP) sensor electrical connector

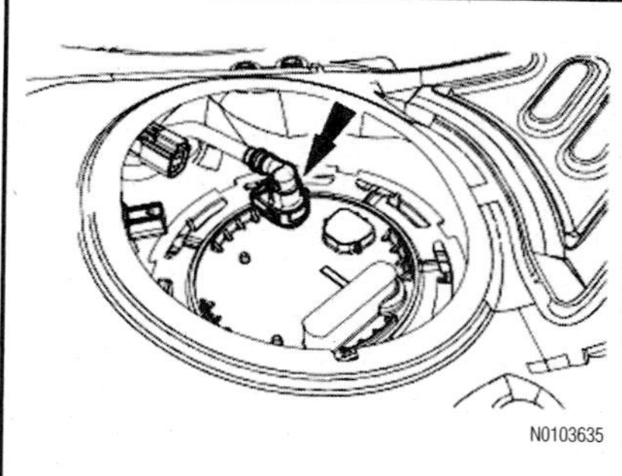

Fig. 200 Disconnect the fuel tank jumper tube-to- FP module quick connect coupling

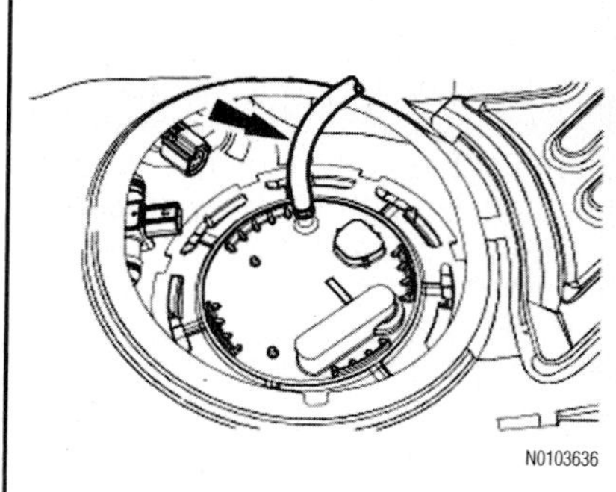

Fig. 201 Attach the Fuel Storage Tanker tube to the FP module outlet fitting and remove one fourth (approximately 5 gallons) of the fuel from a completely full tank, lowering the fuel level below the FP module flange

➡Make sure to install a new FP module O-ring seal.

10. Install the Fuel Tank Sender Unit Wrench and remove the FP module lock ring.

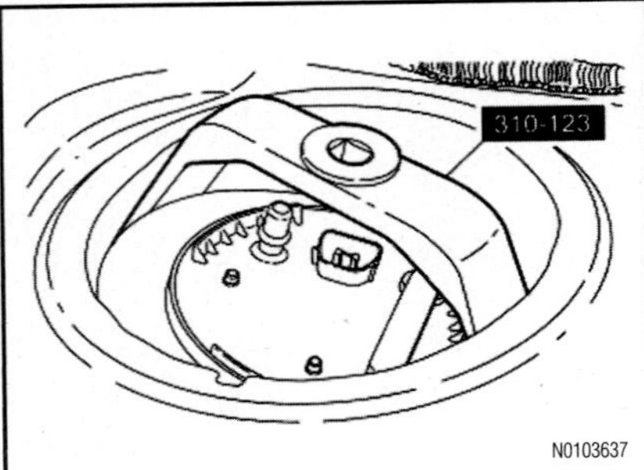

Fig. 202 Install the Fuel Tank Sender Unit Wrench and remove the FP module lock ring

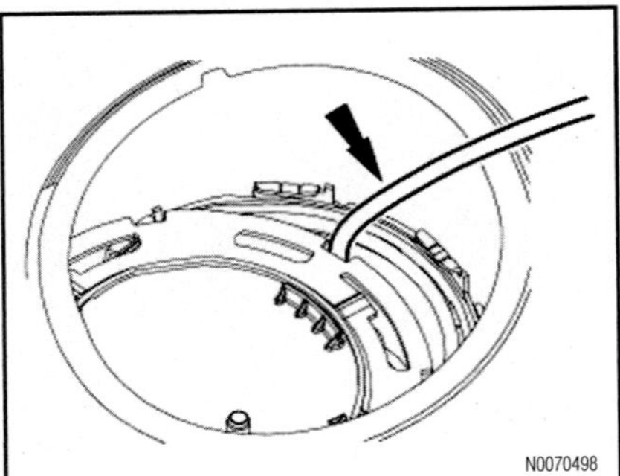

Fig. 203 Position the FP module aside, insert the tube from the fuel storage tanker into the FP module aperture and remove as much fuel as possible from the fuel tank

WARNING

The Fuel Pump (FP) module must be handled carefully to avoid damage to the float arm and filter.

11. Position the FP module aside, insert the tube from the fuel storage tanker into the FP module aperture and remove as much fuel as possible from the fuel tank.

Saddle Type

See Figures 204 through 211.

1. Release the fuel system pressure as outlined in this section.
2. Disconnect the battery ground cable.
3. Remove the rear seat lower cushion.
4. Remove the Fuel Pump (FP) module access cover.

➡Clean the FP module connections, couplings, flange surfaces and the immediate surrounding area of any dirt or foreign material.

5. Disconnect the FP module electrical connector.
6. Disconnect the fuel tank wiring harness electrical connector.

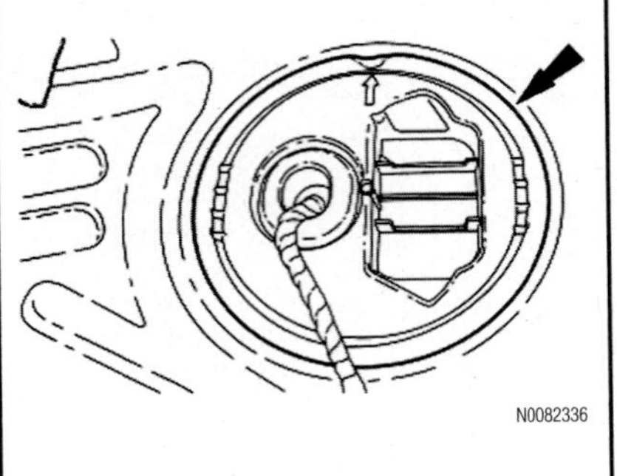

Fig. 204 Remove the Fuel Pump (FP) module access cover

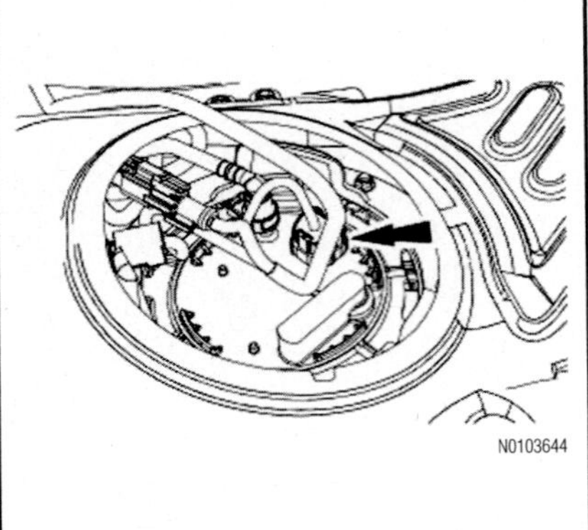

Fig. 205 Disconnect the FP module electrical connector

7. Disconnect the Fuel Tank Pressure (FTP) sensor electrical connector.

➡Place absorbent toweling in the immediate surrounding area in case of fuel spillage.

8. Disconnect the fuel tank jumper tube-to-FP module quick connect coupling.
9. Attach the Fuel Storage Tanker tube to the FP module outlet fitting and remove one fourth (approximately 5 gallons) of the fuel from a completely full tank, lowering the fuel level below the fuel level sensor flange.
10. Remove the fuel level sensor access cover.

➡Clean the fuel level sensor connections, couplings, flange surfaces and the immediate surrounding area of any dirt or foreign material.

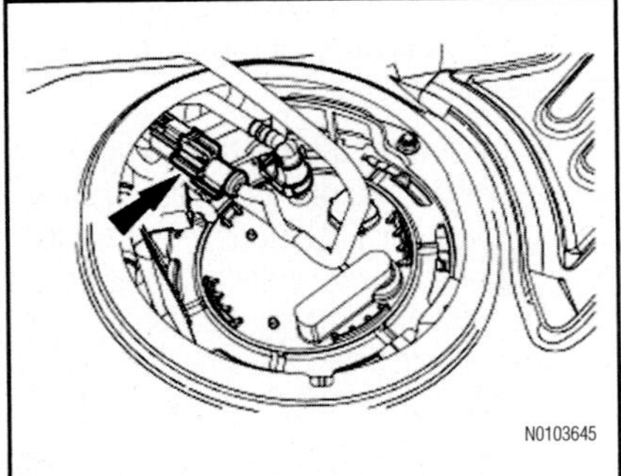

Fig. 206 Disconnect the fuel tank wiring harness electrical connector

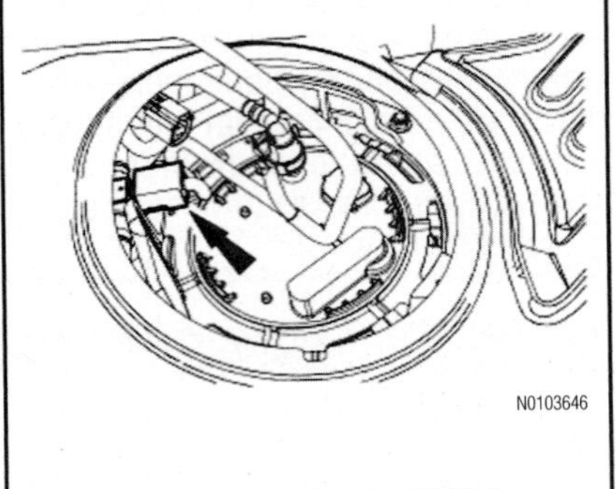

Fig. 207 Disconnect the Fuel Tank Pressure (FTP) sensor electrical connector

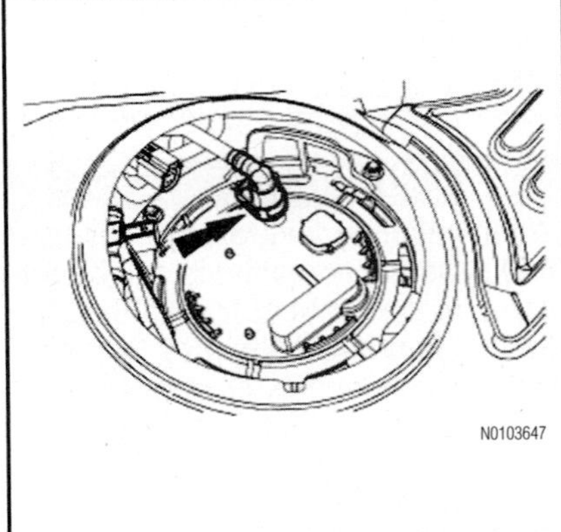

Fig. 208 Disconnect the fuel tank jumper tube-to- FP module quick connect coupling

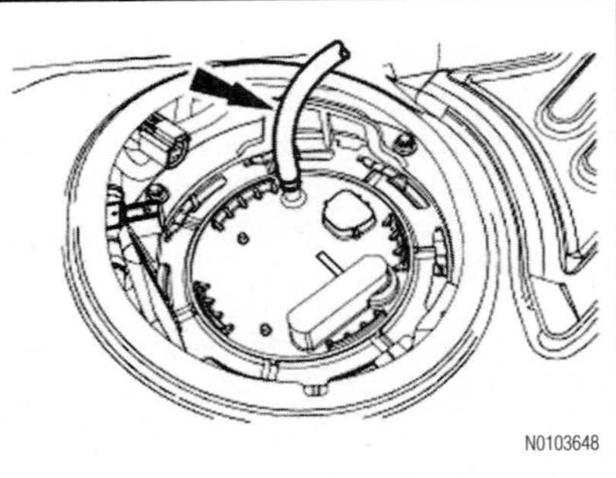

Fig. 209 Attach the Fuel Storage Tanker tube to the FP module outlet fitting and remove one fourth (approximately 5 gallons) of the fuel from a completely full tank, lowering the fuel level below the fuel level sensor flange

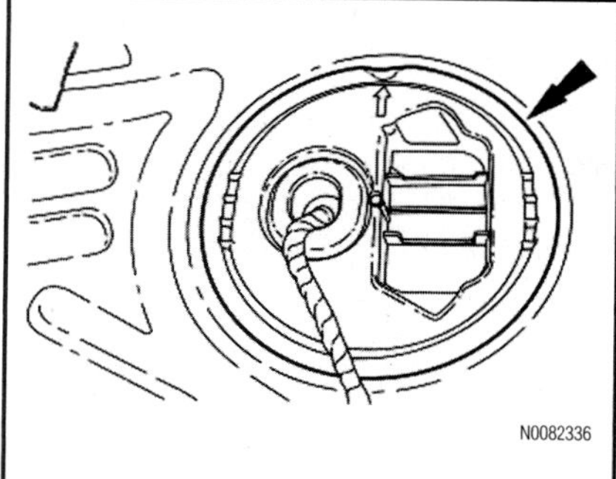

Fig. 210 Remove the fuel level sensor access cover

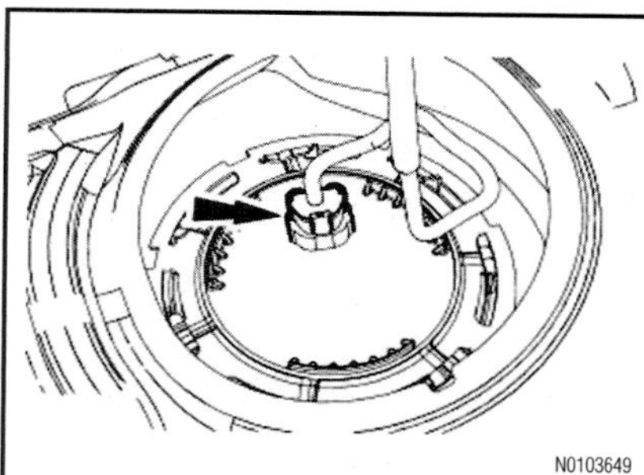

Fig. 211 Disconnect the fuel level sensor electrical connector

11. Disconnect the fuel level sensor electrical connector.

➡Carefully install the Fuel Tank Sender Unit Wrench to avoid damaging the fuel level sensor when removing the lock ring.

➡Place absorbent toweling in the immediate surrounding area in case of fuel spillage.

➡Make sure to install a new fuel level sensor O-ring seal.

12. Install the Fuel Tank Sender Unit Wrench and remove the fuel level sensor lock ring.

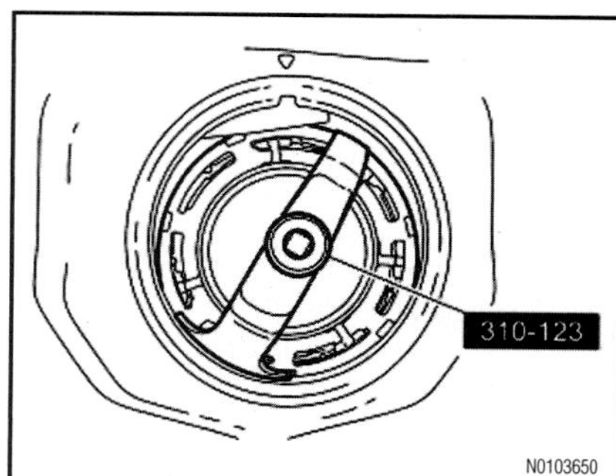

Fig. 212 Install the Fuel Tank Sender Unit Wrench and remove the fuel level sensor lock ring

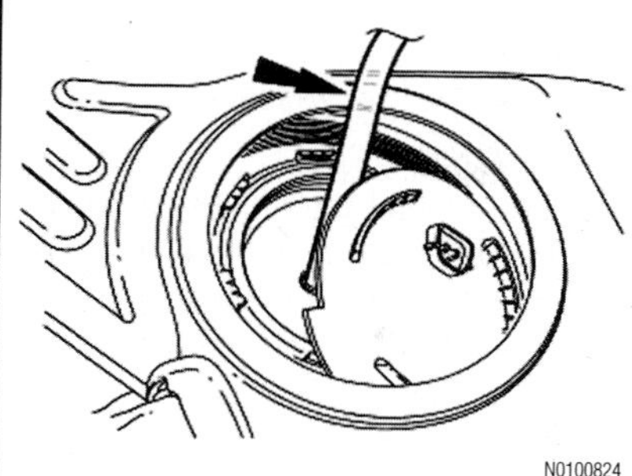

Fig. 213 Position the fuel level sensor aside, insert the tube from the Fuel Storage Tanker into the fuel level sensor aperture and remove as much of the remaining fuel as possible from the fuel tank

13. Position the fuel level sensor aside, insert the tube from the Fuel Storage Tanker into the fuel level sensor aperture and remove as much of the remaining fuel as possible from the fuel tank.

REMOVAL & INSTALLATION

**** CAUTION**

Do not smoke, carry lighted tobacco or have an open flame of any type when working on or near any fuel-related component. Highly flammable mixtures are always present and may be ignited. Failure to follow these instructions may result in serious personal injury.

**** CAUTION**

Do not carry personal electronic devices such as cell phones, pagers or audio equipment of any type when working on or near any fuel-related component. Highly flammable mixtures are always present and may be ignited. Failure to follow these instructions may result in serious personal injury.

**** CAUTION**

Before working on or disconnecting any of the fuel tubes or fuel system components, relieve the fuel system pressure to prevent accidental spraying of fuel. Fuel in the fuel system remains under high pressure, even when the engine is not running. Failure to follow this instruction may result in serious personal injury.

**** CAUTION**

When handling fuel, always observe fuel handling precautions and be prepared in the event of fuel spillage. Spilled fuel may be ignited by hot vehicle components or other ignition sources. Failure to follow these instructions may result in serious personal injury.

**** CAUTION**

Always disconnect the battery ground cable at the battery when working on an evaporative emission (EVAP) system or fuel-related component. Highly flammable mixtures are always present and may be ignited. Failure to follow these instructions may result in serious personal injury.

L-Shaped

1. With the vehicle in NEUTRAL, position it on a hoist.
2. Drain the fuel tank as outlined in this section.
3. Remove the muffler and tail pipe assembly.

➡Some residual fuel may remain in the fuel tank filler pipe after draining the fuel tank. Carefully drain any residual fuel into a suitable container.

4. Release the clamp and remove the fuel tank filler pipe hose from the fuel tank.
5. Disconnect the fuel vapor tube assembly-to-fuel tank filler pipe recirculation tube quick connect coupling as outlined in this section.
6. Disconnect the fuel tank jumper tube-to-fuel tube quick connect coupling as outlined in this section.
7. Release the fresh air hose vent cap and pin-type retainer from the body.

➡Clean the Evaporative Emission (EVAP) canister vent solenoid electrical connector and the immediate surrounding area of any dirt or foreign material.

8. Disconnect the EVAP canister vent solenoid electrical connector.
9. Disconnect the fresh air hose-to-dust separator fitting.
10. Disconnect the fuel vapor tube assembly-to- EVAP canister quick connect coupling as outlined in this section.
11. Position the Powertrain Lift under the fuel tank.

➡**Do not bend or distort the fuel tank straps.**

12. Remove the 4 bolts and the 2 fuel tank straps.
13. Carefully lower and remove the fuel tank from the vehicle.

To install:

14. Carefully lower and remove the fuel tank from the vehicle.

➡**Do not bend or distort the fuel tank straps.**

15. Install the 4 bolts and the 2 fuel tank straps. Tighten the bolts to 26 ft. lbs. (35 Nm).
16. Position the Powertrain Lift under the fuel tank.
17. Connect the fuel vapor tube assembly-to- EVAP canister quick connect coupling as outlined in this section.
18. Connect the fresh air hose-to-dust separator fitting.
19. Connect the EVAP canister vent solenoid electrical connector.

➡**Clean the Evaporative Emission (EVAP) canister vent solenoid electrical connector and the immediate surrounding area of any dirt or foreign material.**

20. Engage the fresh air hose vent cap and pin-type retainer to the body.
21. Connect the fuel tank jumper tube-to-fuel tube quick connect coupling as outlined in this section.
22. Connect the fuel vapor tube assembly-to-fuel tank filler pipe recirculation tube quick connect coupling as outlined in this section.

➡**Some residual fuel may remain in the fuel tank filler pipe after draining the fuel tank. Carefully drain any residual fuel into a suitable container.**

23. Release the clamp and install the fuel tank filler pipe hose to the fuel tank. Tighten the clamp to 27 inch lbs. (3 Nm).
24. Install the muffler and tail pipe assembly as outlined in the Engine Mechanical Section.
25. Fill the fuel tank as outlined in this section.
26. With the vehicle in NEUTRAL, lower it from the hoist.

Saddle Type

1. With the vehicle in NEUTRAL, position it on a hoist.
2. Remove the muffler and tail pipe as outlined in the Engine Mechanical Section.
3. Drain the fuel tank as outlined in the section.
4. Remove the driveshaft as outlined in the Drive Train Section.
5. Remove the Evaporative Emission (EVAP) canister.

➡**Some residual fuel may remain in the fuel tank filler pipe after draining the fuel tank. Carefully drain any residual fuel into a suitable container.**

6. Release the clamp and remove the fuel tank filler pipe hose from the fuel tank.
7. Disconnect the fuel vapor tube assembly-to-fuel tank filler pipe recirculation tube quick connect coupling as outlined in this section.
8. Disconnect the fuel tank jumper tube-to-fuel tube quick connect coupling as outlined in this section.
9. Release the fresh air hose vent cap and pin-type retainer from the body.
10. Position the Powertrain Lift under the fuel tank.
11. Loosen the 2 rear fuel tank strap bolts.
    a. Calculate the correct torque wrench setting for the following torque.
12. Remove the 2 front fuel tank strap bolts.

➡**Do not bend or distort the fuel tank straps.**

13. Release the 2 straps from the fuel tank and carefully position aside.
14. Carefully lower and remove the fuel tank from the vehicle.

To install:

15. Carefully lower and remove the fuel tank from the vehicle.

➡**Do not bend or distort the fuel tank straps.**

16. Engage the 2 straps to the fuel tank and carefully reposition.
17. Install the 2 front fuel tank strap bolts. Tighten the bolts to 26 ft. lbs. (35 Nm).
18. Tighten the 2 rear fuel tank strap bolts.
    a. Calculate the correct torque wrench setting for the following torque. To install, use a torque adapter and tighten the bolts to 26 ft. lbs. (35 Nm).
19. Position the Powertrain Lift under the fuel tank.
20. Engage the fresh air hose vent cap and pin-type retainer to the body.
21. Connect the fuel tank jumper tube-to-fuel tube quick connect coupling as outlined in this section.
22. Connect the fuel vapor tube assembly-to-fuel tank filler pipe recirculation tube quick connect coupling as outlined in this section.

➡**Some residual fuel may remain in the fuel tank filler pipe after draining the fuel tank. Carefully drain any residual fuel into a suitable container.**

23. Engage the clamp and install the fuel tank filler pipe hose to the fuel tank. Tighten the clamp to 27 inch lbs. (3 Nm).
24. Install the Evaporative Emission (EVAP) canister.
25. Install the driveshaft as outlined in the Drive Train Section.
26. Fill the fuel tank as outlined in the section.
27. Install the muffler and tail pipe.
28. With the vehicle in NEUTRAL, lower the vehicle from the hoist.

THROTTLE BODY

REMOVAL & INSTALLATION

3.5L Engine, Except Turbo

See Figure 214.

1. Remove the Air Cleaner (ACL) outlet pipe.
2. Disconnect the electronic throttle control electrical connector.
3. Remove the 4 bolts and the Throttle Body (TB).
    a. Discard the TB gasket.

➡**Install a new TB gasket.**

To install:

➡**Install a new TB gasket**

4. Install the 4 bolts and the Throttle Body (TB). Tighten the bolts to 89 inch lbs. (10 Nm).
5. Connect the electronic throttle control electrical connector.
6. Install the Air Cleaner (ACL) outlet pipe as outlined in the Engine Mechanical Section.

3.5L Turbo Engine

See Figure 215.

1. Disconnect the Throttle Position (TP) sensor electrical connector.
2. Disconnect the Throttle Actuator Control (TAC) electrical connector.
3. Loosen the clamp and disconnect the Charge Air Cooler (CAC) outlet pipe-to-Throttle Body (TB).
4. Remove the 4 bolts, the TB and the TP sensor shield bracket.

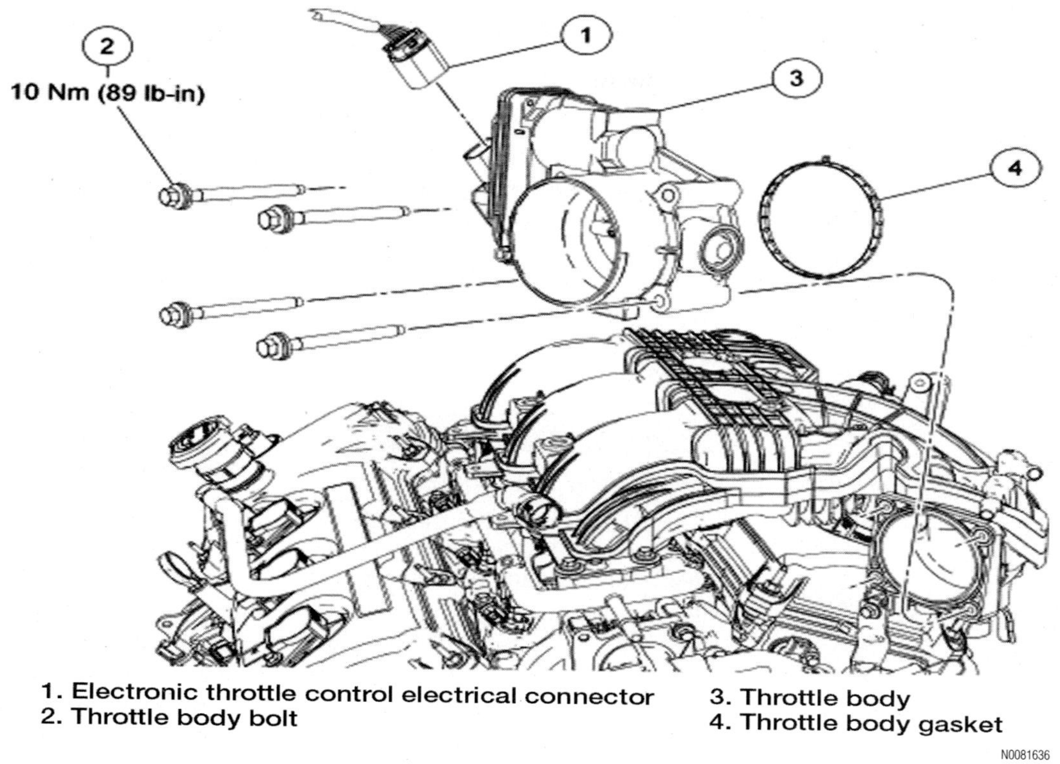

Fig. 214 Throttle Body—3.5L engine, except Turbo

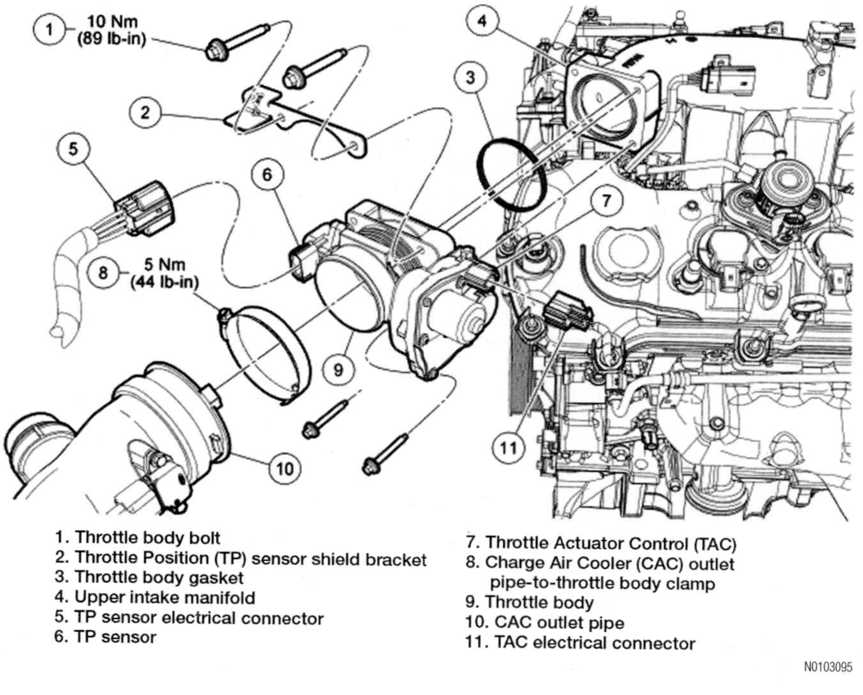

Fig. 215 Throttle Body—3.5L Turbo

a. Discard the TB gasket.

To install:

➡Install a new TB gasket.

5. Install the 4 bolts, the TB and the TP sensor shield bracket. Tighten the bolts to 89 inch lbs. (10 Nm).

6. Tighten the clamp and connect the Charge Air Cooler (CAC) outlet pipe-to-Throttle Body (TB). Tighten the clamp to 44 inch lbs. (5 Nm).

7. Connect the Throttle Actuator Control (TAC) electrical connector.

8. Connect the Throttle Position (TP) sensor electrical connector.

HEATING & AIR CONDITIONING SYSTEM

BLOWER MOTOR

REMOVAL & INSTALLATION

See Figure 216.

1. Remove the 3 RH lower instrument panel insulator screws and the RH lower instrument panel insulator.

2. Disconnect the blower motor electrical connector.

3. Detach the 2 blower motor vent tube clips and position the tube downward to detach it from the heater core and evaporator core housing.

4. Rotate the blower motor counterclockwise to detach it from the heater core and evaporator core housing and remove the blower motor.

To install:

5. Install the blower motor, and rotate the blower motor clockwise to attach it to the heater core and evaporator core housing.

6. Position the tube upward to attach it to the heater core and evaporator core housing, and attach the 2 blower motor vent tube clips.

7. Connect the blower motor electrical connector.

8. Install the RH lower instrument panel insulator, and install the 3 RH lower instrument panel insulator screws.

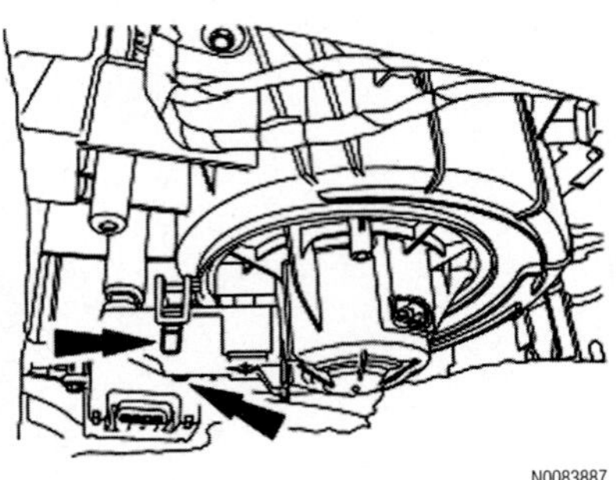

Fig. 216 Detach the 2 blower motor vent tube clips and position the tube downward to detach it from the heater core and evaporator core housing

HEATER CORE

REMOVAL & INSTALLATION

➡If a heater core leak is suspected, the heater core must be pressure leak tested before it is removed from the vehicle.

1. Remove the heater core and evaporator core housing.

2. Remove the dash panel seal.

3. Remove the 3 heater core tube support bracket screws and heater core tube support bracket.

4. Remove the 10 plenum chamber screws and separate the heater core and evaporator housing.

5. Remove the heater core and seal assembly.

To install:

6. Install the heater core and seal assembly.

7. Install the 10 plenum chamber screws and separate the heater core and evaporator housing.

8. Install the 3 heater core tube support bracket screws and heater core tube support bracket.

9. Install the dash panel seal.

10. Install the heater core and evaporator core housing.

STEERING

POWER STEERING GEAR

REMOVAL & INSTALLATION

Electronic Power Assist Steering (EPAS)

See Figures 217 and 218.

➡Use a steering wheel holding device (such as Hunter® 28-75-1 or equivalent).

1. Using a suitable holding device, hold the steering wheel in the straight-ahead position.

2. Remove the wheels and tires.

⁂ WARNING

Do not allow the steering column to rotate while the steering column shaft is disconnected from the steering gear or damage to the clockspring may occur. If there is evidence that the steering column has rotated, the clockspring must be removed and recentered as outlined in the Chassis Electrical Section.

3. Remove the bolt and disconnect the steering column shaft from the steering gear.

a. Discard the bolt.

4. Remove the 2 stabilizer bar link upper nuts.

a. Discard the nuts.

5. Remove the 2 outer tie-rod end nuts and separate the tie-rod ends from the wheel knuckle.

6. Remove the 4 retainers and the underbody shield.

7. Remove the RH and LH exhaust flexible pipes. For additional information, refer to Exhaust System.

8. Remove the 2 front and rear engine roll restrictor bolts.

9. Position the Powertrain Lift Table under the subframe.

10. Remove the 2 front subframe rearward bolts, the 4 support bracket bolts and the 2 subframe support brackets.

a. Loosen the 2 front subframe forward bolts.

11. Lower the subframe to gain access to the steering gear.

12. Remove the wiring harness bracket bolt.

13. Disconnect the 2 Electronic Power Assist Steering (EPAS) electrical connectors and the wiring retainer.

➡Position the stabilizer bar to the full up position.

14. Remove the 2 steering gear bolts.

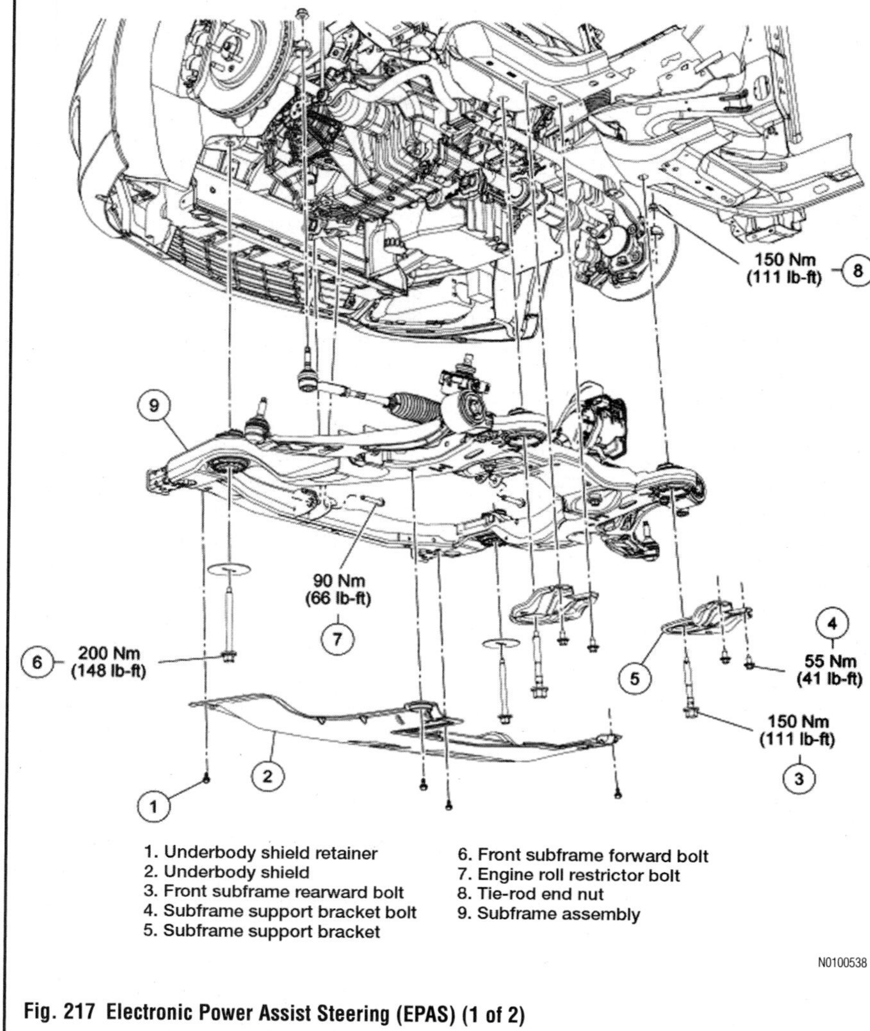

Fig. 217 Electronic Power Assist Steering (EPAS) (1 of 2)

a. Remove the steering gear from the RH side of the vehicle.

To install:

15. Position the steering gear and install the 2 bolts. Tighten the bolts to 122 ft. lbs. (165 Nm).
16. Connect the 2 EPAS electrical connectors and the wiring retainer.
17. Position the wiring harness bracket and install the bolt. Tighten the bolt to 80 inch lbs. (9 Nm).
18. Raise the subframe.
19. Position the 2 subframe support brackets and install the 4 bolts finger-tight.
20. Install the 2 front subframe rearward bolts. Tighten the rearward bolts to 111 ft. lbs. (150 Nm), and tighten the forward bolts to 148 ft. lbs. (200 Nm).
21. Tighten the 4 subframe support bracket bolts to 41 ft. lbs. (55 Nm).
22. Install the 2 front and rear engine roll restrictor bolts. Tighten the bolts to 66 ft. lbs. (90 Nm).
23. Install the RH and LH exhaust flexible pipes as outlined in the Engine Mechanical Section.
24. Position the underbody shield and install the 4 retainers.
25. Position the 2 outer tie-rod ends and install the nuts. Tighten the nuts to 111 ft. lbs. (150 Nm).
26. Connect the stabilizer bar links and install the 2 nuts. Tighten the new nuts to 111 ft. lbs. (150 Nm).

WARNING

Do not allow the steering column to rotate while the steering column shaft is disconnected from the steering gear or damage to the clockspring may occur. If there is evidence that the steering column has rotated, the clockspring must be removed and recentered as outlined in the Chassis Electrical Section.

27. With the locator on the input shaft correctly aligned, connect the steering column shaft to the steering gear and install the new bolt. Tighten the bolt to 177 inch lbs. (20 Nm).
28. Install the wheels and tires.

Hydraulic Power Assist Steering (HPAS)

See Figures 219 and 220.

All Vehicles

WARNING

When repairing the power steering system, care should be taken to prevent the entry of foreign material or failure of the power steering components may occur.

➡Use a steering wheel holding device (such as Hunter® 28-75-1 or equivalent).

1. Using a suitable holding device, hold the steering wheel in the straight-ahead position.
2. Remove the wheels and tires.

➡The hex-holding feature can be used to prevent turning of the stud while removing the nut.

3. Remove the 2 tie-rod end nuts and disconnect the tie-rod ends from the wheel knuckles.
4. Remove the pressure line bracket-to-steering gear bolt.

WARNING

Whenever the power steering lines are disconnected, new O-ring seals must be installed. Make sure that the O-ring seals are installed in the correct order or a fluid leak may occur.

5. Remove the power steering line clamp plate bolt.
   a. Rotate the clamp plate and disconnect the pressure and return lines from the steering gear.
   b. Discard the 2 O-ring seals.

WARNING

Do not allow the steering column shaft to rotate while the lower shaft is disconnected or damage to the clockspring may result. If there is evidence that the shaft has rotated, the clockspring must be removed and recentered. For additional information, refer to Supplemental Restraint System.

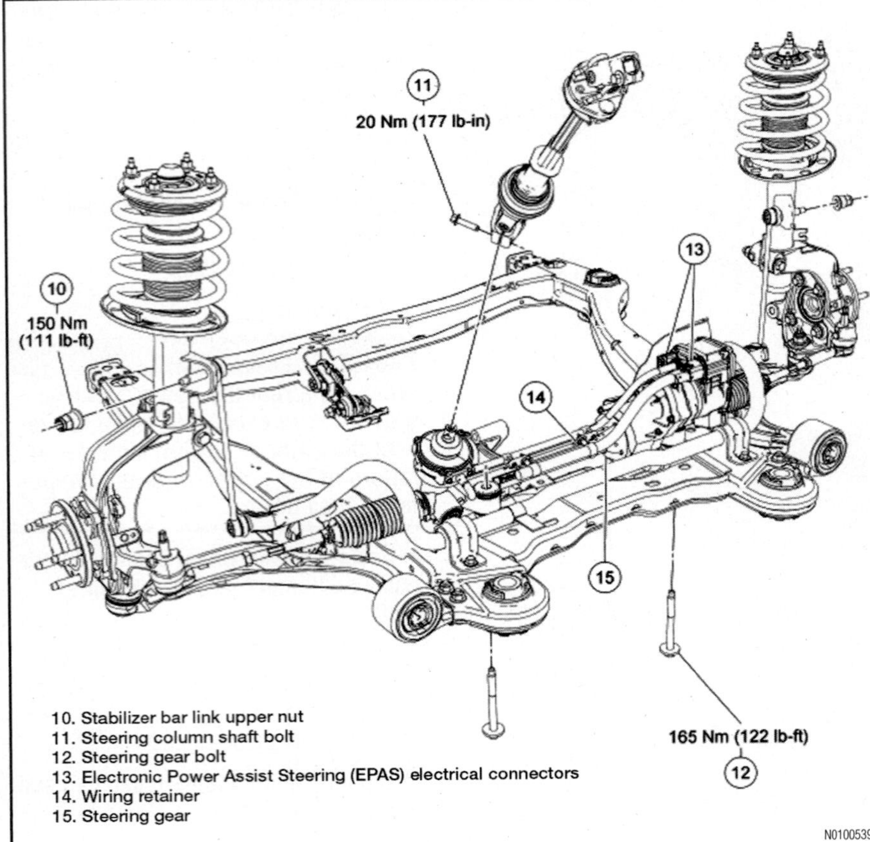

Fig. 218 Electronic Power Assist Steering (EPAS) (2 of 2)

6. Remove the steering column shaft-to-steering gear bolt and disconnect the shaft from the steering gear.
   a. Discard the bolt.

➡The hex-holding feature can be used to prevent turning of the stud while removing the nut.

7. Remove and discard the 2 stabilizer bar link upper nuts.
   a. Position the stabilizer bar and links upward.

All-Wheel Drive (AWD) Vehicles

8. Remove and discard the 4 stabilizer bar bracket bolts.
   a. Position the stabilizer bar and links upward.

All Vehicles

9. If equipped, remove the steering gear heat shield-to-subframe pushpin.
10. Remove and discard the 2 steering gear nuts and bolts.
    a. Stage 1: Tighten to 40 Nm (30 lb-ft).
    b. Stage 2: Tighten an additional 180 degrees.
11. Remove the steering gear from the left side of the vehicle.

➡NOTE: Whenever the power steering lines are disconnected, new O-ring seals must be installed.

To install:

All Vehicles

➡NOTE: Whenever the power steering lines are disconnected, new O-ring seals must be installed.

12. Install the steering gear to the left side of the vehicle.
13. Install and discard the 2 steering gear nuts and bolts.
    a. To install, tighten the 2 new nuts and bolts in 2 stages:
    b. Stage 1: Tighten to 30 ft. lbs. (40 Nm).
    c. Stage 2: Tighten an additional 180 degrees.
14. If equipped, install the steering gear heat shield-to-subframe pushpin.

All-Wheel Drive (AWD) Vehicles

15. Install and discard the 4 stabilizer bar bracket bolts. Tighten the 4 new bolts to 41 ft. lbs. (55 Nm).
    a. Position the stabilizer bar and links upward.

All Vehicles

➡The hex-holding feature can be used to prevent turning of the stud while removing the nut.

16. Install the 2 new stabilizer bar link upper nuts. Tighten the 2 new nuts to 111 ft. lbs. (150 Nm).
    a. Position the stabilizer bar and links upward.

WARNING

Do not allow the steering column shaft to rotate while the lower shaft is disconnected or damage to the clockspring may result. If there is evidence that the shaft has rotated, the clockspring must be removed and recentered. For additional information, refer to Supplemental Restraint System.

17. Install the steering column shaft-to-steering gear bolt and connect the shaft from the steering gear. Tighten the new bolt to 18 ft. lbs. (25 Nm).

WARNING

Whenever the power steering lines are disconnected, new O-ring seals must be installed. Make sure that the O-ring seals are installed in the correct order or a fluid leak may occur.

18. Install the power steering line clamp plate bolt.
    a. Rotate the clamp plate and connect the pressure and return lines to the steering gear. Tighten the clamp to 17 ft lb. (23 Nm).
19. Install the pressure line bracket-to-steering gear bolt. Tighten the bolt to 17 ft. lbs. (23 Nm).

➡The hex-holding feature can be used to prevent turning of the stud while removing the nut.

20. Install the 2 tie-rod end nuts and connect the tie-rod ends to the wheel knuckles. Tighten the nuts to 111 ft. lbs. (150 Nm).
21. Install the wheels and tires.

WARNING

When repairing the power steering system, care should be taken to prevent the entry of foreign material or failure of the power steering components may occur.

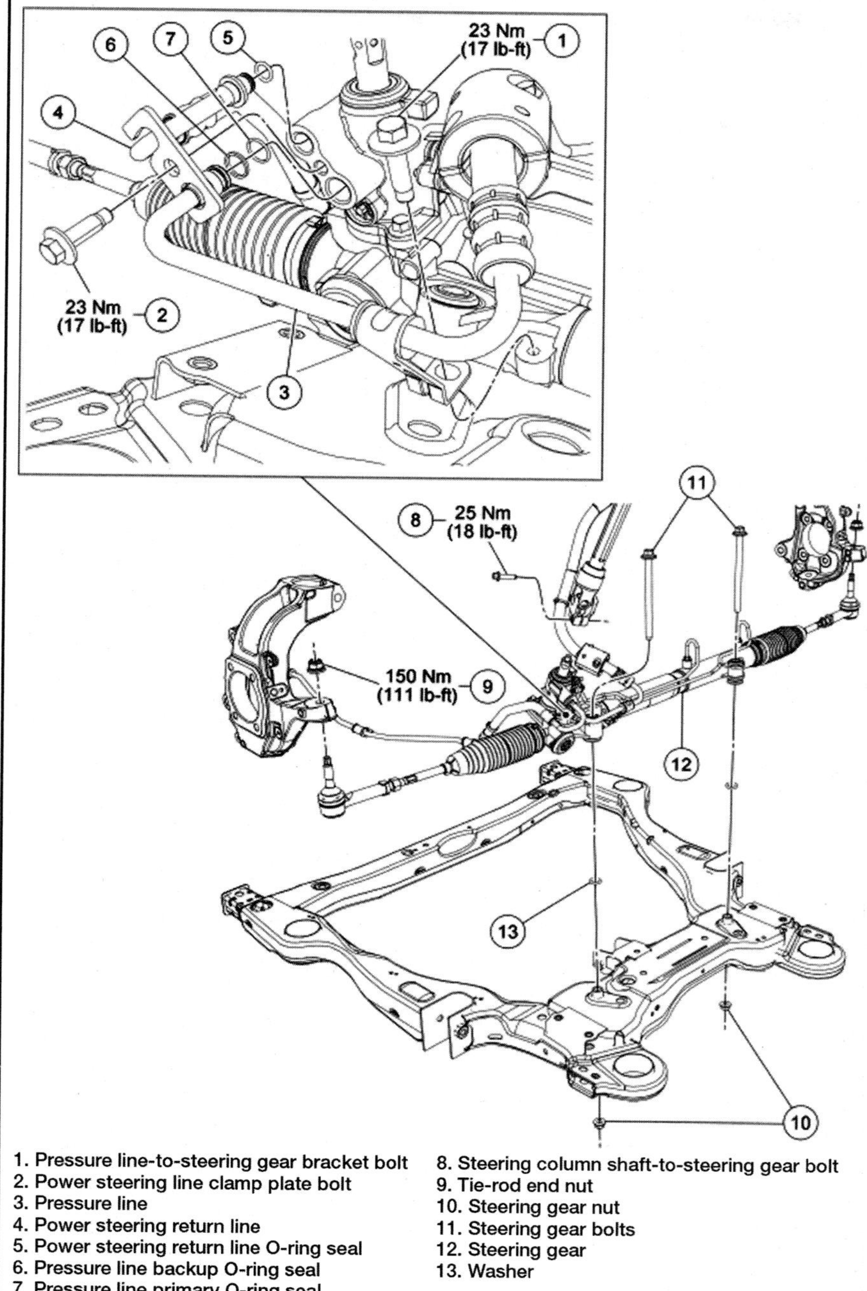

Fig. 219 Hydraulic Power Assist Steering (HPAS) (1 of 2)

➡Use a steering wheel holding device (such as Hunter® 28-75-1 or equivalent).

22. Using a suitable holding device, hold the steering wheel in the straight-ahead position.
23. Fill the power steering system.
24. Check and, if necessary, adjust the front toe.

POWER STEERING PUMP

REMOVAL & INSTALLATION

See Figures 221 through 224.

WARNING

While repairing the power steering system, care should be taken to prevent the entry of foreign material or failure of the power steering components may result.

1. With the vehicle in NEUTRAL, position it on a hoist.
2. Using a suitable suction device, siphon the power steering fluid from the power steering fluid reservoir.
3. Remove the 7 pin-type retainers and the RH splash shield.
4. Position the Stretchy Belt Remover on the power steering pump pulley belt.

➡Feed the Stretchy Belt Remover onto the power steering pump pulley approximately 90 degrees.

5. Turn the crankshaft clockwise and feed the Stretchy Belt Remover evenly on the power steering pump pulley.
6. Remove the power steering pump belt.
   a. Fold the Stretchy Belt Remover under the inside of the power steering pump belt.
   b. In one quick motion, firmly pull the Stretchy Belt Remover out of the RH fender well, removing the power steering pump belt.
7. Release the clamp and disconnect the power steering fluid reservoir-to-pump supply hose from the power steering pump.
   a. Detach the supply hose retainer from the pressure line bracket.
8. Remove the pressure line bracket-to-engine bolt.
9. Remove the 3 power steering pump bolts.
10. Holding the power steering pump with a punch inserted into a mounting bolt cavity, disconnect the pressure line fitting-to-power steering pump.

To install:

WARNING

A new Teflon® seal must be installed any time the pressure line is disconnected from the power steering pump or a fluid leak may occur.

11. Using the Teflon® Seal Installer Set, install a new Teflon® seal on the power steering pressure line fitting.
12. Holding the power steering pump with a punch inserted into a mounting cavity, connect the pressure line fitting-to-power steering pump.

    Tighten the pressure line fitting to 55 ft. lbs. (75 Nm).
13. Position the power steering pump and install the 3 bolts. Tighten the bolts to 18 ft. lbs. (25 Nm).
14. Position the bracket and install the pressure line bracket-to-engine bolt. Tighten the bolt to 80 inch lbs. (9 Nm).

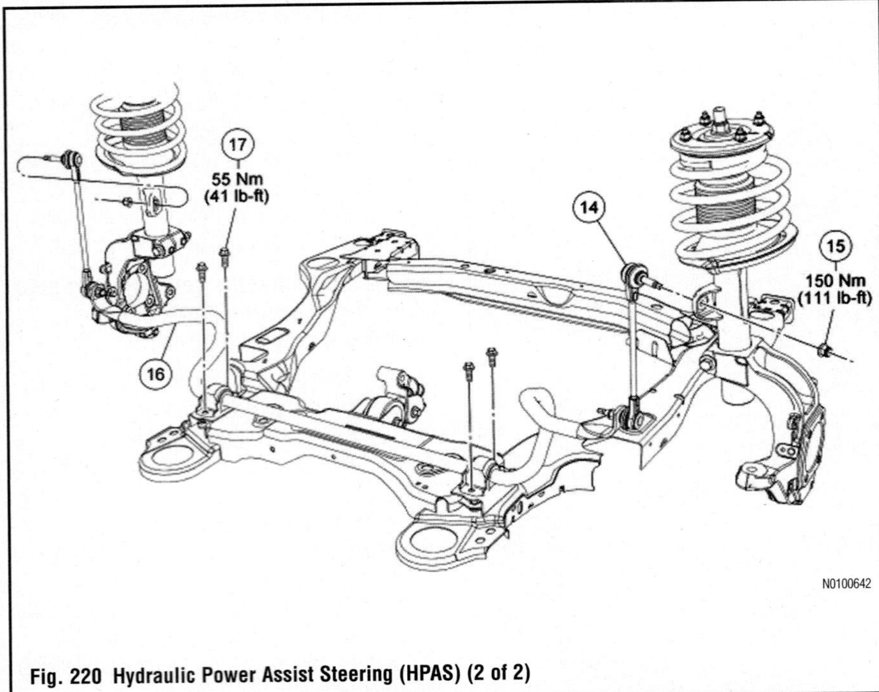

Fig. 220 Hydraulic Power Assist Steering (HPAS) (2 of 2)

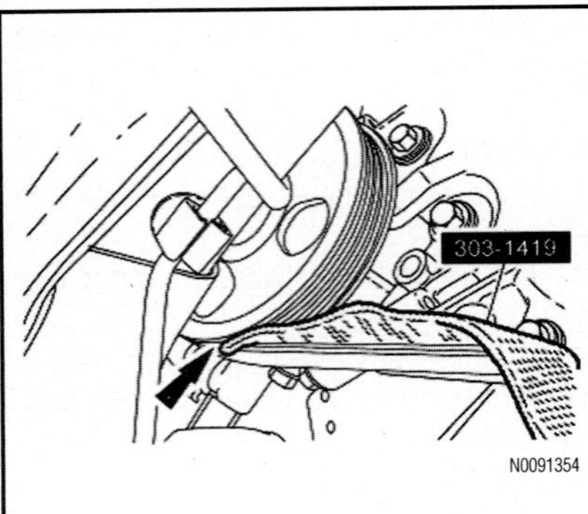

Fig. 221 Position the Stretchy Belt Remover on the power steering pump pulley belt

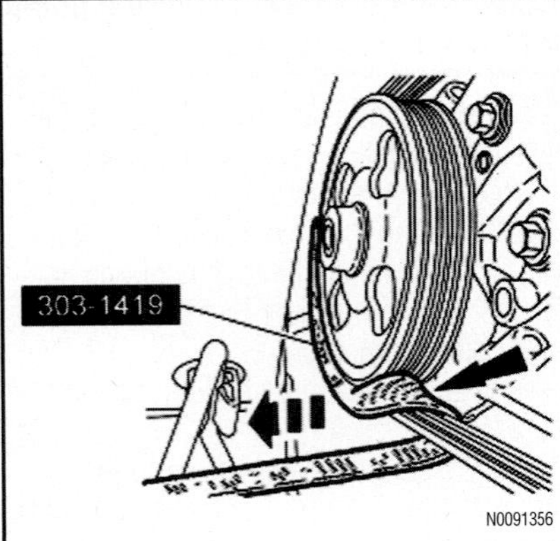

Fig. 222 Fold the Stretchy Belt Remover under the inside of the power steering pump belt

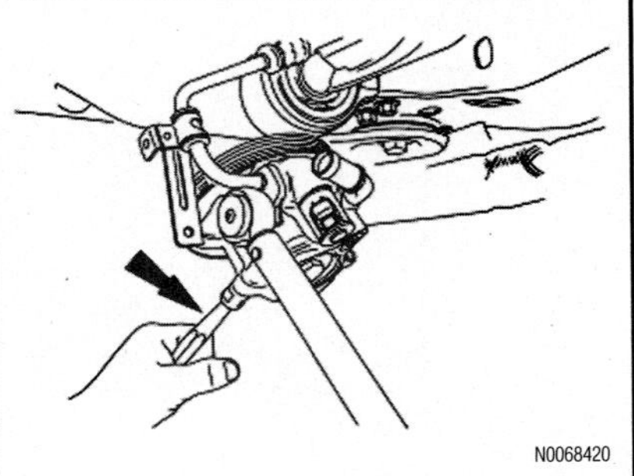

Fig. 223 Holding the power steering pump with a punch inserted into a mounting bolt cavity, disconnect the pressure line fitting-to-power steering pump

15. Release the clamp and connect the power steering fluid cooler-to-pump supply hose.
    a. Attach the supply hose retainer to the pressure line bracket.
16. Using the Stretchy Belt Installer Tool, install the power steering pump belt onto the power steering pump pulley.
    a. Install the Stretchy Belt Installer Tool, between the power steering pump belt and pulley and turn the crankshaft bolt clockwise.
17. Install the RH inner fender splash shield.
18. Fill the power steering system.

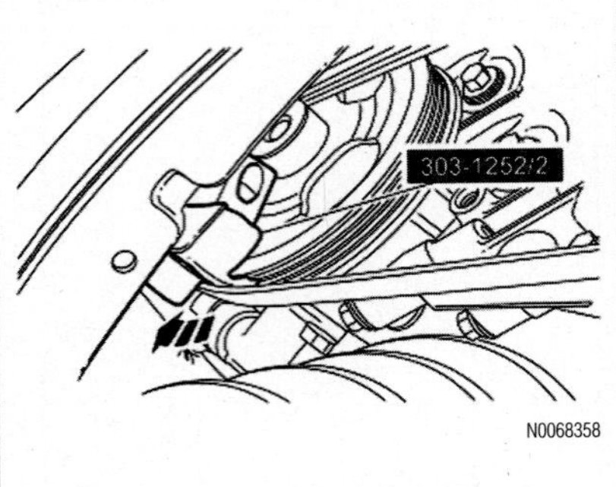

Fig. 224 Install the Stretchy Belt Installer Tool, between the power steering pump belt and pulley and turn the crankshaft bolt clockwise

PURGING

WARNING

If the air is not purged from the power steering system correctly, premature power steering pump failure may result. The condition may occur on pre-delivery vehicles with evidence of aerated fluid or on vehicles that have had steering component repairs.

➡A whine heard from the power steering pump can be caused by air in the system. The power steering purge procedure must be carried out prior to any component repair for which power steering noise complaints are accompanied by evidence of aerated fluid.

1. Remove the power steering reservoir cap. Check the fluid.
2. Raise the front wheels off the floor.
3. Tightly insert the Power Steering Evacuation Cap into the reservoir and connect the Vacuum Pump Kit.
4. Start the engine.
5. Using the Vacuum Pump Kit, apply vacuum and maintain the maximum vacuum of 68-85 kPa (20-25 in-Hg).
    a. If the Vacuum Pump Kit does not maintain vacuum, check the power steering system for leaks before proceeding.
6. If equipped with Hydro-Boost®, apply the brake pedal 4 times.

WARNING

Do not hold the steering wheel against the stops for an extended amount of time. Damage to the power steering pump may occur.

7. Cycle the steering wheel fully from stop-to-stop 10 times.

8. Stop the engine.
9. Release the vacuum and remove the Vacuum Pump Kit and the Power Steering Evacuation Cap.

➡**Do not overfill the reservoir.**

10. Fill the reservoir as needed with the specified fluid.
11. Start the engine.
12. Install the Power Steering Evacuation Cap and the Vacuum Pump Kit. Apply and maintain the maximum vacuum of 20-25 in-Hg (68-85 kPa).

WARNING

Do not hold the steering wheel against the stops for an extended amount of time. Damage to the power steering pump may occur.

13. Cycle the steering wheel fully from stop-to-stop 10 times.
14. Stop the engine, release the vacuum and remove the Vacuum Pump Kit and the Power Steering Evacuation Cap.

➡**Do not overfill the reservoir.**

15. Fill the reservoir as needed with the specified fluid and install the reservoir cap.
16. Visually inspect the power steering system for leaks.

FLUID FILL PROCEDURE

See Figure 225.

WARNING

If the air is not purged from the power steering system correctly, premature power steering pump failure may result. The condition can occur on pre-delivery vehicles with evidence of aerated fluid or on vehicles that have had steering component repairs.

1. Remove the power steering fluid reservoir cap.
2. Install the Power Steering Evacuation Cap, Power Steering Fill Adapter Manifold and Vacuum Pump Kit as shown in the illustration.

➡**The Power Steering Fill Adapter Manifold control valves are in the OPEN position when the points of the handles face the center of the Power Steering Fill Adapter Manifold.**

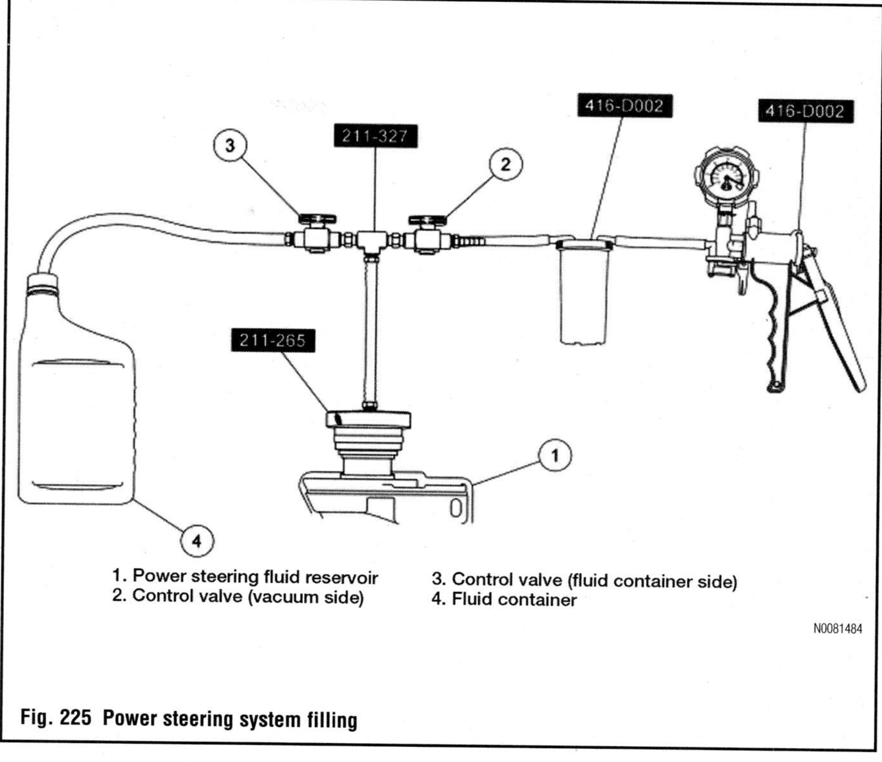

Fig. 225 Power steering system filling

3. Close the Power Steering Fill Adapter Manifold control valve (fluid side).
4. Open the Power Steering Fill Adapter Manifold control valve (vacuum side).
5. Using the Vacuum Pump Kit, apply 20-25 in-Hg (68-85 kPa) of vacuum to the power steering system.
6. Observe the Vacuum Pump Kit gauge for 30 seconds.
7. If the Vacuum Pump Kit gauge reading drops more than 0.88 in-Hg (3 kPa), correct any leaks in the power steering system or the Power Steering Evacuation Cap, Power Steering Fill Adapter Manifold and Vacuum Pump Kit before proceeding.

➡**The Vacuum Pump Kit gauge reading will drop slightly during this step.**

8. Slowly open the Power Steering Fill Adapter Manifold control valve (fluid side) until power steering fluid completely fills the hose and then close the control valve.
9. Using the Vacuum Pump Kit, apply 20-25 in-Hg (68-85 kPa) of vacuum to the power steering system.
10. Close the Power Steering Fill Adapter Manifold control valve (vacuum side).
11. Slowly open the Power Steering Fill Adapter Manifold control valve (fluid side).
12. Once power steering fluid enters the fluid reservoir and reaches the minimum fluid level indicator line on the reservoir, close the Power Steering Fill Adapter Manifold control valve (fluid side).
13. Remove the Power Steering Evacuation Cap, Power Steering Fill Adapter Manifold and Vacuum Pump Kit.
14. Install the reservoir cap.

WARNING

Do not hold the steering wheel against the stops for an extended amount of time. Damage to the power steering pump may occur.

➡**There will be a slight drop in the power steering fluid level in the reservoir when the engine is started.**

15. Start the engine and turn the steering wheel from stop-to-stop.
16. Turn the ignition switch to the OFF position.

➡**Do not overfill the reservoir.**

17. Remove the reservoir cap and fill the reservoir with the specified fluid.
18. Install the reservoir cap.

LOWER CONTROL ARM

REMOVAL & INSTALLATION

WARNING

Suspension fasteners are critical parts because they affect performance of vital components and systems and their failure may result in major service expense. New parts must be installed with the same part numbers or equivalent part, if replacement is necessary. Do not use a replacement part of lesser quality or substitute design. Torque values must be used as specified during reassembly to make sure of correct retention of these parts.

1. Remove the wheel and tire.

➡Use the hex-holding feature to prevent the stud from turning while removing the nut.

2. Using a crowfoot wrench, remove and discard the lower ball joint nut.

WARNING

Use care when releasing the lower arm and knuckle into the resting position or damage to the ball joint seal may occur.

3. Push the lower arm downward until the ball joint is clear of the wheel knuckle.
4. Remove and discard the lower arm forward bolt.
5. Remove and discard the lower arm rearward nuts and bolts.
   a. Install the new lower arm rearward bolts from the bottom of the lower arm bushing with the nuts on top.
6. If necessary, remove the lower arm rearward bushing. For additional information, refer to Lower Arm Bushing in this section.

WARNING

The lower arm forward bolt must be tightened with the weight of the vehicle on the wheels and tires or damage to the bushings may occur.

To install:

WARNING

Suspension fasteners are critical parts because they affect performance of vital components and systems and their failure may result in major service expense. New parts must be installed with the same part numbers or equivalent part, if replacement is necessary. Do not use a replacement part of lesser quality or substitute design. Torque values must be used as specified during reassembly to make sure of correct retention of these parts.

WARNING

The lower arm forward bolt must be tightened with the weight of the vehicle on the wheels and tires or damage to the bushings may occur.

7. If necessary, install the lower arm rearward bushing.
8. Install and use a new lower arm rearward nuts and bolts. Tighten the new nuts to 73 ft. lbs. (99 Nm).
   a. Install the new lower arm rearward bolts from the bottom of the lower arm bushing with the nuts on top.
9. Install and use a new lower arm forward bolt. Tighten the new bolt to 136 ft. lbs. (185 Nm).

WARNING

Use care when releasing the lower arm and knuckle into the resting position or damage to the ball joint seal may occur.

10. Push the lower arm upward until the ball joint is in the wheel knuckle.

➡Use the hex-holding feature to prevent the stud from turning while removing the nut.

11. Using a crowfoot wrench, install and use a new lower ball joint nut. Tighten the nut to 148 ft. lbs. (200 Nm).
12. Install the wheel and tire.

LOWER CONTROL ARM BUSHING REPLACEMENT

See Figures 226 and 227.

1. Remove the lower arm as outlined above.
2. Index-mark the bushing-to-lower arm position for reference during the installation procedure.

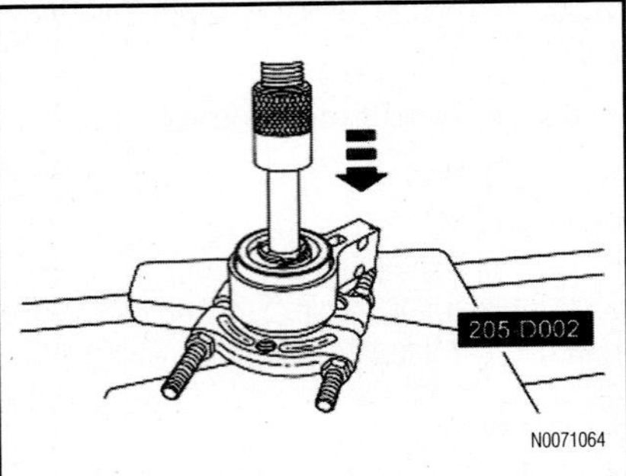

Fig. 226 Using the Drive Pinion Bearing Cone Remover, a suitable press and adapters, remove the lower arm bushing

➡The Drive Pinion Bearing Cone Remover is used to secure the lower arm bushing while separating the bushing from the lower arm.

3. Using the Drive Pinion Bearing Cone Remover, a suitable press and adapters, remove the lower arm bushing.

To install:

➡The Drive Pinion Bearing Cone Remover is used to clamp and hold the lower arm while installing the bushing.

4. Install the Drive Pinion Bearing Cone Remover onto the lower arm.
5. Transfer the index mark to the new lower arm bushing.

➡The Drive Pinion Bearing Cone Remover is used to clamp and hold the lower arm while installing the bushing.

6. Align the index marks and using the Drive Pinion Bearing Cone Remover, a suitable press and adapters, install a new lower arm bushing.
7. Install the lower arm.

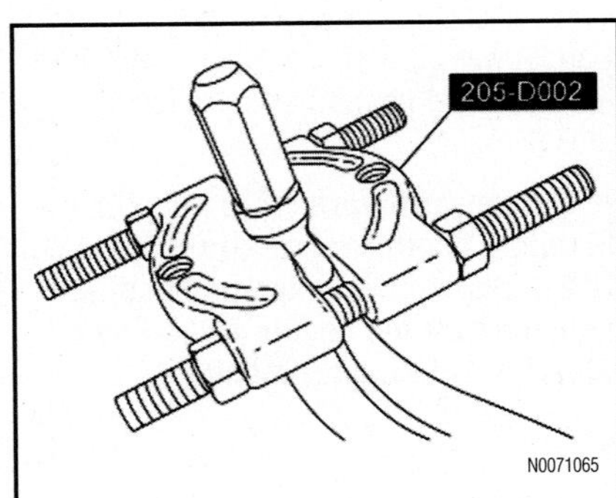

Fig. 227 Install the Drive Pinion Bearing Cone Remover onto the lower arm

STABILIZER BAR

REMOVAL & INSTALLATION

See Figures 228 through 230.

✲✲ WARNING

Suspension fasteners are critical parts because they affect performance of vital components and systems and their failure may result in major service expense. New parts must be installed with the same part numbers or equivalent part, if replacement is necessary. Do not use a replacement part of lesser quality or substitute design. Torque values must be used as specified during reassembly to make sure of correct retention of these parts.

➡Make sure the steering wheel is in the unlocked position.

➡The stabilizer bushing and bracket are part of the stabilizer bar assembly. The stabilizer bar will not turn easily in the bushing.

All Vehicles

1. With the vehicle in NEUTRAL, position it on a hoist.
2. Disconnect the Heated Oxygen Sensor (HO2S) electrical connector and unclip the connector from the subframe.

All-Wheel Drive (AWD) Vehicles

3. Remove the exhaust Y-pipe as outlined in the Engine Mechanical Section.

All Vehicles

✲✲ WARNING

Do not use power tools to remove the stabilizer bar link nut. Damage to the stabilizer link ball joint or boot may occur.

➡To remove the stabilizer bar link nut, first loosen the nut, then use the hex-holding feature to prevent the ball joint from turning while removing the stabilizer bar link nut.

Fig. 228 Disconnect the Heated Oxygen Sensor (HO2S) electrical connector and unclip the connector from the subframe

4. Remove and discard the stabilizer bar link lower nuts.

➡No special tools are necessary to separate the tie rod from the front knuckle; use a mallet to loosen the joint.

5. Remove and discard both tie-rod end nuts and separate the tie-rod ends from the knuckles.

➡Install the new lower arm rearward bolts from the bottom of the lower arm bushing with the nuts on top.

6. Remove and discard the 4 lower arm rearward nuts and bolts.
7. Remove and discard the 2 lower arm forward bolts. Position both lower arms aside.
8. Using a suitable screw-type jackstand, support the rear of the subframe.
9. Remove the 2 steering gear nuts and bolts.
   a. Vehicles with Electronic Power Assist Steering (EPAS)
   b. Vehicles with Hydraulic Power Assist Steering (HPAS)
10. Remove and discard the 4 subframe bracket bolts.
11. Remove and discard the subframe forward bolts.
12. Remove and discard the subframe rearward bolts.
   a. Vehicles with EPAS
   b. Vehicle with HPAS

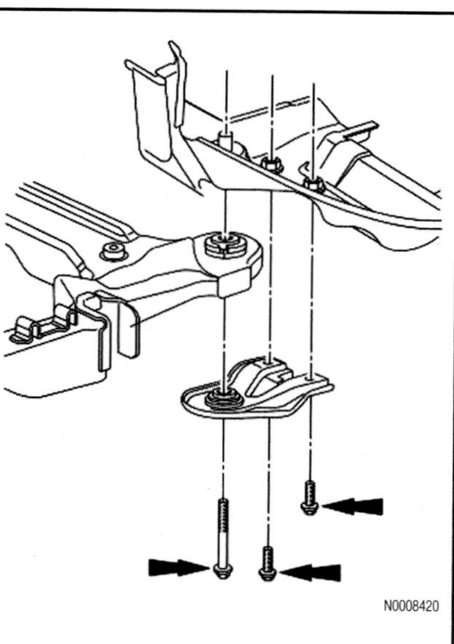

Fig. 229 Remove and discard the subframe rearward bolts

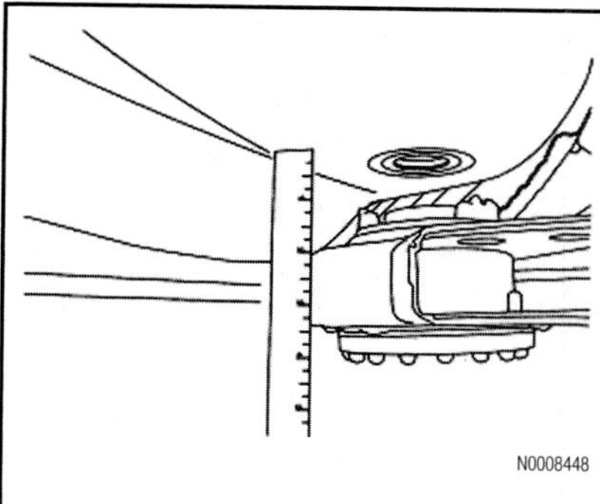

Fig. 230 Lower the rear of the subframe approximately 21 inch (51 mm)

13. Lower the rear of the subframe approximately 21 inch (51 mm).
14. Remove and discard the LH and RH stabilizer bar bracket bolts.
15. Remove the stabilizer bar by guiding it between the subframe and the steering gear toward the RH side of the vehicle.

To install:

✲✲ WARNING

Suspension fasteners are critical parts because they affect performance of vital components and systems and their failure may result in major service expense. New parts must be installed with the same part numbers or equivalent part, if replacement is necessary. Do not use a replacement part of lesser quality or substitute design. Torque values must be used as specified during reassembly to make sure of correct retention of these parts.

➡Make sure the steering wheel is in the unlocked position.

➡The stabilizer bushing and bracket are part of the stabilizer bar assembly. The stabilizer bar will not turn easily in the bushing.

16. Install the stabilizer bar by guiding it between the subframe and the steering gear away from the RH side of the vehicle.

All Vehicles

17. Install and use new LH and RH stabilizer bar bracket bolts. Tighten the new bolts to 41 ft. lbs. (55 Nm).
18. Raise the rear of the subframe approximately 21 inch (51 mm).
19. Install and use new subframe rearward bolts.
   a. Vehicles with EPAS tighten the new bolts to 111 ft. lbs. (150 Nm).
   b. Vehicle with HPAS, tighten the new bolts to 130 ft. lbs. (175 Nm).

20. Install and use new subframe forward bolts. Tighten the new bolts to 148 ft. lbs. (200 Nm).
21. Install and use 4 new subframe bracket bolts. Tighten the new bolts to 41 ft. lbs. (55 Nm).
22. Install the 2 steering gear nuts and bolts.
   a. Vehicles with Electronic Power Assist Steering (EPAS), tighten the nuts to 122 ft. lbs. (65 Nm).
   b. Vehicles with Hydraulic Power Assist Steering (HPAS), tighten the new nuts to 86 ft. lbs. (117 Nm).
23. Using a suitable screw-type jackstand, support the rear of the subframe.
24. Install and use 2 new 2 lower arm forward bolts. Reposition both lower arms. Tighten the new bolts to 136 ft. lbs. (185 Nm).

➡Install the new lower arm rearward bolts from the bottom of the lower arm bushing with the nuts on top.

25. Install and use 4 new 4 lower arm rearward nuts and bolts. Tighten the new bolts to 73 ft. lbs. (99 Nm).

➡No special tools are necessary to separate the tie rod from the front knuckle; use a mallet to loosen the joint.

26. Install and new tie-rod end nuts and separate the tie-rod ends to the knuckles. Tighten the new nuts to 111 ft. lbs. (150 Nm).

✲✲ WARNING

Do not use power tools to install the stabilizer bar link nut. Damage to the stabilizer link ball joint or boot may occur.

➡To install the stabilizer bar link nut, use the hex-holding feature to prevent the ball joint from turning while installing the stabilizer bar link nut, then tighten the nut.

27. Install and use new stabilizer bar link lower nuts. Tighten the new nuts to 111 ft. lbs. (150 Nm).

All-Wheel Drive (AWD) Vehicles

28. Install the exhaust Y-pipe as outlined in the Engine Mechanical Section.

All Vehicles

29. Connect the Heated Oxygen Sensor (HO2S) electrical connector and clip the connector to the subframe.
30. With the vehicle in NEUTRAL, lower from the hoist.

STABILIZER BAR LINK

REMOVAL & INSTALLATION

✲✲ WARNING

Suspension fasteners are critical parts because they affect performance of vital components and systems and their failure may result in major service expense. New parts must be installed with the same part numbers or equivalent part, if replacement is necessary. Do not use a replacement part of lesser quality or substitute design. Torque values must be used as specified during reassembly to make sure of correct retention of these parts.

1. With the vehicle in NEUTRAL, position it on a hoist. For additional information, refer to Jacking and Lifting.

✲✲ WARNING

Do not use power tools to remove the stabilizer bar link nuts. Damage to the stabilizer bar link ball joints or boots may occur.

➡To remove the stabilizer bar link nuts, first loosen the nuts, then use the hex-holding feature to prevent the stabilizer bar link ball joints from turning while removing the stabilizer bar link nuts.

2. Remove and discard the stabilizer bar link lower nut.
3. Remove and discard the stabilizer bar link upper nut.
4. Remove the stabilizer bar link.

➡To install the nuts, use the hex-holding feature to prevent the stabilizer link ball joints from turning while installing the nuts until snug. Finally, tighten the nuts using a socket and a torque wrench.

To install:

➡To install the nuts, use the hex-holding feature to prevent the stabilizer link ball joints from turning while installing the nuts until snug. Finally, tighten the nuts using a socket and a torque wrench.

5. Install the stabilizer bar link.
6. Install and use a new stabilizer bar link upper nut. Tighten the new nut to 111 ft. lbs. (150 Nm).
7. Install and a new stabilizer bar link lower nut. Tighten the new nut to 111 ft. lbs. (150 Nm).

✲✲ WARNING

Do not use power tools to remove the stabilizer bar link nuts. Damage to the stabilizer bar link ball joints or boots may occur.

➡To install the stabilizer bar link nuts, use the hex-holding feature to prevent the stabilizer bar link ball joints from turning while removing the stabilizer bar link nuts, and then tighten the nuts.

✲✲ WARNING

Suspension fasteners are critical parts because they affect performance of vital components and systems and their failure may result in major service expense. New parts must be installed with the same part numbers or equivalent part, if replacement is necessary. Do not use a replacement part of lesser quality or substitute design. Torque values must be used as specified during reassembly to make sure of correct retention of these parts.

8. With the vehicle in NEUTRAL, lower from the hoist.

STRUT & SPRING ASSEMBLY

REMOVAL & INSTALLATION

See Figure 231.

✲✲ CAUTION

Do not apply heat or flame to the shock absorber or strut tube. The shock absorber and strut tube are gas pressurized and could explode if heated. Failure to follow this instruction may result in serious personal injury.

✲✲ CAUTION

Keep all body parts clear of shock absorbers or strut rods. Shock absorbers or struts can extend unassisted. Failure to follow this instruction may result in serious personal injury.

✲✲ WARNING

Suspension fasteners are critical parts because they affect performance of vital components and systems and their failure may result in major service expense. New parts

must be installed with the same part numbers or equivalent part, if replacement is necessary. Do not use a replacement part of lesser quality or substitute design. Torque values must be used as specified during reassembly to make sure of correct retention of these parts.

➡Make sure the steering wheel is in the unlocked position.

1. Loosen the upper strut mount nuts.
2. Remove the wheel and tire.

➡Do not discard the wheel hub nut at this time.

3. Remove the wheel hub nut.
4. Remove the brake disc.

➡No special tools are necessary to separate the tie rod from the front knuckle; use a mallet to loosen the joint.

5. Remove and discard the tie-rod end nut, then separate the tie rod from the wheel knuckle.
6. Remove and discard the stabilizer bar link upper nut.
7. Detach the wheel speed sensor harness from the strut.
8. Remove the bolt and the wheel speed sensor from the wheel knuckle. Position the wheel speed sensor aside.

➡Use the hex-holding feature to prevent the stud from turning while removing the nut.

9. Using a crowfoot wrench, remove and discard the lower ball joint nut.

✻✻ WARNING

Use care when releasing the lower arm and knuckle into the resting position or damage to the ball joint seal may occur.

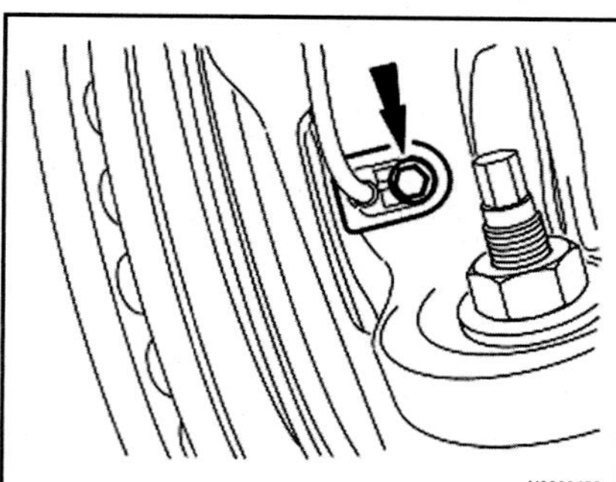

Fig. 231 Remove the bolt and the wheel speed sensor from the wheel knuckle. Position the wheel speed sensor aside

10. Push the lower arm downward until the ball joint is clear of the wheel knuckle.

✻✻ WARNING

Do not allow the halfshaft to move outboard. Overextension of the tripod Constant Velocity (CV) joint may result in separation of internal parts, causing failure of the halfshaft.

11. Using the Front Wheel Hub Remover, press the halfshaft from the wheel bearing and hub. Support the halfshaft in a level position.
12. Remove and discard the 4 upper strut mount nuts.
13. Remove the wheel knuckle and the strut and spring as an assembly.
14. Remove and discard the strut-to-wheel knuckle nut and flagbolt.
15. Separate the strut and spring assembly from the wheel knuckle.

To install:

16. Position the wheel knuckle onto the strut and spring and install a new strut-to-wheel knuckle nut and flagbolt. Tighten the nut to 129 ft. lbs. (175 Nm).
17. Install the wheel knuckle and the strut and spring as an assembly.
18. Loosely install the 4 new upper strut mount nuts.
19. While supporting the halfshaft in a level position, install the halfshaft into the wheel bearing and hub.

✻✻ WARNING

Use care not to damage the ball joint seal while installing the ball joint stud into the wheel knuckle.

20. Push the lower arm downward and install the ball joint stud into the wheel knuckle.

➡Use the hex-holding feature to prevent the stud from turning while installing the nut.

21. Using a crowfoot wrench, install the new lower ball joint nut. Tighten the nut to 148 ft. lbs. (200 Nm).
22. Position the wheel speed sensor and install the bolt. Tighten the bolt to 133 inch lbs. (15 Nm).
23. Attach the wheel speed sensor harness to the strut.
24. Install the new stabilizer bar link upper nut. Tighten the nut to 111 ft. lbs. (150 Nm).
25. Position the tie-rod end stud into the wheel knuckle and install a new tie-rod end nut. Tighten the nut to 111 ft. lbs. (150 Nm).
26. Install the brake disc.

✻✻ WARNING

Do not tighten the front wheel hub nut with the vehicle on the ground. The nut must be tightened to specification before the vehicle is lowered onto the wheels. Wheel bearing damage will occur if the wheel bearing is loaded with the weight of the vehicle applied.

➡Apply the brake to keep the halfshaft from rotating.

27. Using the previously removed hub nut, seat the halfshaft. Tighten the nut to 258 ft. lbs. (350 Nm).
28. Remove and discard the hub nut.

✻✻ WARNING

The wheel hub nut contains a one-time locking chemical that is activated by the heat created when it is tightened. Install and tighten the new wheel hub nut to specification within 5 minutes of starting it on the threads. Always install a new wheel hub nut after loosening or when not tightened within the specified time or damage to the components can occur.

➡Apply the brake to keep the halfshaft from rotating.

29. Install a new hub nut. Tighten the nut to 258 ft. lbs. (350 Nm).
30. Install the wheel and tire.
31. Tighten the 4 upper strut mount nuts to 22 ft. lbs. (30 Nm).

WHEEL BEARING AND WHEEL HUB

REMOVAL & INSTALLATION

See Figure 232.

✻✻ WARNING

Suspension fasteners are critical parts because they affect performance of vital components and systems and their failure may result in major service expense. New parts must be installed with the same part numbers or equivalent part, if replacement is necessary. Do not use a replacement part of lesser quality or substitute design. Torque values must be used as specified during reassembly to make sure of correct retention of these parts.

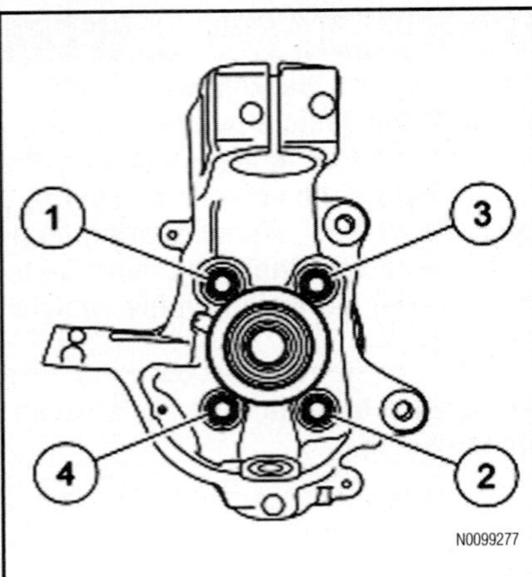

Fig. 232 Wheel bearing and wheel hub bolts location

1. Remove the wheel knuckle.
2. Remove and discard the 4 wheel bearing and wheel hub bolts, then separate the wheel bearing and wheel hub from the wheel knuckle.

✻✻ WARNING

The wheel knuckle bore must be clean enough to allow the wheel bearing and wheel hub to seat completely by hand. Do not press or draw the wheel hub and bearing into place or damage to the bearing may occur.

3. Clean and inspect the knuckle bearing bore. If the wheel knuckle is cracked, install a new wheel knuckle.

➡Make sure the wheel hub-to-wheel knuckle mating surfaces are clean and free of any adhesive. Failure to clean the adhesive from both surfaces may cause bearing damage.

4. Using a clean shop towel, clean the wheel hub-to-knuckle mating surfaces.

To install:

✻✻ WARNING

The wheel knuckle bore must be clean enough to allow the wheel bearing and wheel hub to seat completely by hand. Do not press or draw the wheel hub and bearing into place or damage to the bearing may occur.

5. Clean and inspect the knuckle bearing bore. If the wheel knuckle is cracked, install a new wheel knuckle.

➡Make sure the wheel hub-to-wheel knuckle mating surfaces are clean and free of any adhesive. Failure to clean the adhesive from both surfaces may cause bearing damage.

6. Using a clean shop towel, clean the wheel hub-to-knuckle mating surfaces.
7. Install separate the wheel bearing and wheel hub from the wheel knuckle, and then use 4 new wheel bearing and wheel hub bolts.
   a. To install, tighten the new bolts to 98 ft. lbs. (133 Nm).

✻✻ WARNING

Suspension fasteners are critical parts because they affect performance of vital components and systems and their failure may result in major service expense. New parts must be installed with the same part numbers or equivalent part, if replacement is necessary. Do not use a replacement part of lesser quality or substitute design. Torque values must be used as specified during reassembly to make sure of correct retention of these parts.

8. Install the wheel knuckle.
9. Lubricate the hub-to-brake disc surface with anti-seize lubricant before installing the brake disc.

WHEEL KNUCKLE

REMOVAL & INSATLLATION

See Figure 233.

✻✻ WARNING

Suspension fasteners are critical parts because they affect performance of vital components and systems and their failure may result in major service expense. New parts must be installed with the same part numbers or equivalent part, if replacement is necessary. Do not use a replacement part of lesser quality or substitute design. Torque values must be used as specified during reassembly to make sure of correct retention of these parts.

1. Remove the wheel and tire.

➡Do not discard the wheel hub nut at this time.

2. Remove the wheel hub nut.
3. Remove the brake disc.

➡No special tools are necessary to separate the tie rod from the front knuckle; use a mallet to loosen the joint.

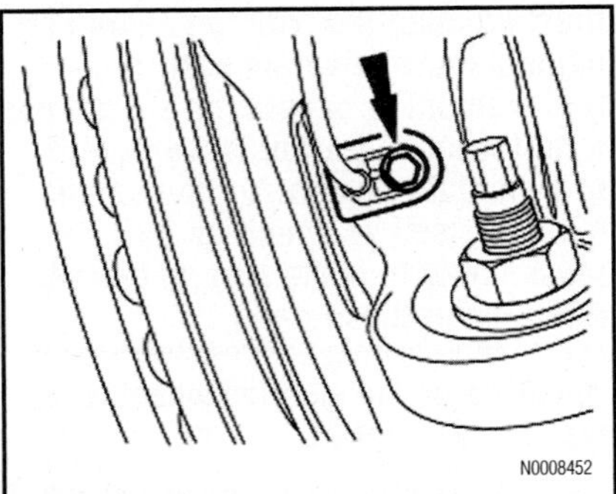

Fig. 233 Remove the bolt and the wheel speed sensor from the wheel knuckle. Position the wheel speed sensor aside

4. Remove and discard the tie-rod end nut, then separate the tie rod from the wheel knuckle.
5. Remove the bolt and the wheel speed sensor from the wheel knuckle. Position the wheel speed sensor aside.

➡Use the hex-holding feature to prevent the stud from turning while removing the nut.

6. Using a crowfoot wrench, remove and discard the lower ball joint nut.
7. Push the lower arm downward until the ball joint is clear of the wheel knuckle.

✻✻ WARNING

Do not allow the halfshaft to move outboard. Overextension of the tripod Constant Velocity (CV) joint may result in separation of internal parts, causing failure of the halfshaft.

8. Using the Front Wheel Hub Remover, press the halfshaft from the wheel bearing and hub. Support the halfshaft in a level position.
9. Remove and discard the strut-to-wheel knuckle nut and flagbolt.
10. Remove the wheel knuckle.
    a. If necessary, remove the wheel hub and bearing.

To install:

11. Position the wheel knuckle and install a new strut-to-wheel knuckle nut and flagbolt. Tighten the nut and flagbolt to 129 ft. lbs. (175 Nm).
12. While supporting the halfshaft in a level position, install the halfshaft into the wheel bearing and hub.

✻✻ WARNING

Use care not to damage the ball joint seal while installing the ball joint stud into the wheel knuckle.

13. Push the lower arm downward and install the ball joint stud into the wheel knuckle.

➡Use the hex-holding feature to prevent the stud from turning while installing the nut.

14. Using a crowfoot wrench, install the new lower ball joint nut. Tighten the nut to 148 ft. lbs. (200 Nm).
15. Position the wheel speed sensor and install the bolt. Tighten the bolt to 133 inch lbs. (15 Nm).
16. Position the tie-rod end stud into the wheel knuckle and install a new tie-rod end nut. Tighten the nut to 111 ft. lbs. (150 Nm).
17. Install the brake disc.

⁂ WARNING

Do not tighten the front wheel hub nut with the vehicle on the ground. The nut must be tightened to specification before the vehicle is lowered onto the wheels. Wheel bearing damage will occur if the wheel bearing is loaded with the weight of the vehicle applied.

➡Apply the brake to keep the halfshaft from rotating.

18. Using the previously removed hub nut, seat the halfshaft. Tighten the nut to 258 ft. lbs. (350 Nm).
    a. Remove and discard the hub nut.

⁂ WARNING

The wheel hub nut contains a one-time locking chemical that is activated by the heat created when it is tightened. Install and tighten the new wheel hub nut to specification within 5 minutes of starting it on the threads. Always install a new wheel hub nut after loosening or when not tightened within the specified time or damage to the components can occur.

➡Apply the brake to keep the halfshaft from rotating.

19. Install a new hub nut. Tighten the nut to 258 ft. lbs. (350 Nm).
20. Install the wheel and tire.

SUSPENSION

REAR SUSPENSION

LOWER CONTROL ARM

REMOVAL & INSTALLATION

See Figure 234.

⁂ WARNING

Suspension fasteners are critical parts because they affect performance of vital components and systems and their failure may result in major service expense. New parts must be installed with the same part numbers or equivalent part, if replacement is necessary. Do not use a replacement part of lesser quality or substitute design. Torque values must be used as specified during reassembly to make sure of correct retention of these parts.

1. Measure the distance from the center of the wheel hub to the lip of the fender with the vehicle in a level, static ground position (curb height).
2. Remove the wheel and tire.

➡Use the hex-holding feature to prevent the stabilizer bar link stud from turning while removing the nut.

3. Remove both stabilizer bar link upper nuts and disconnect the links from the wheel knuckle.
    a. Discard the nuts.
4. Position a screw-type jackstand under the lower arm.
5. Remove and discard the lower arm-to-knuckle bolt and nut.

➡Do not remove the lower arm inner bolt at this time.

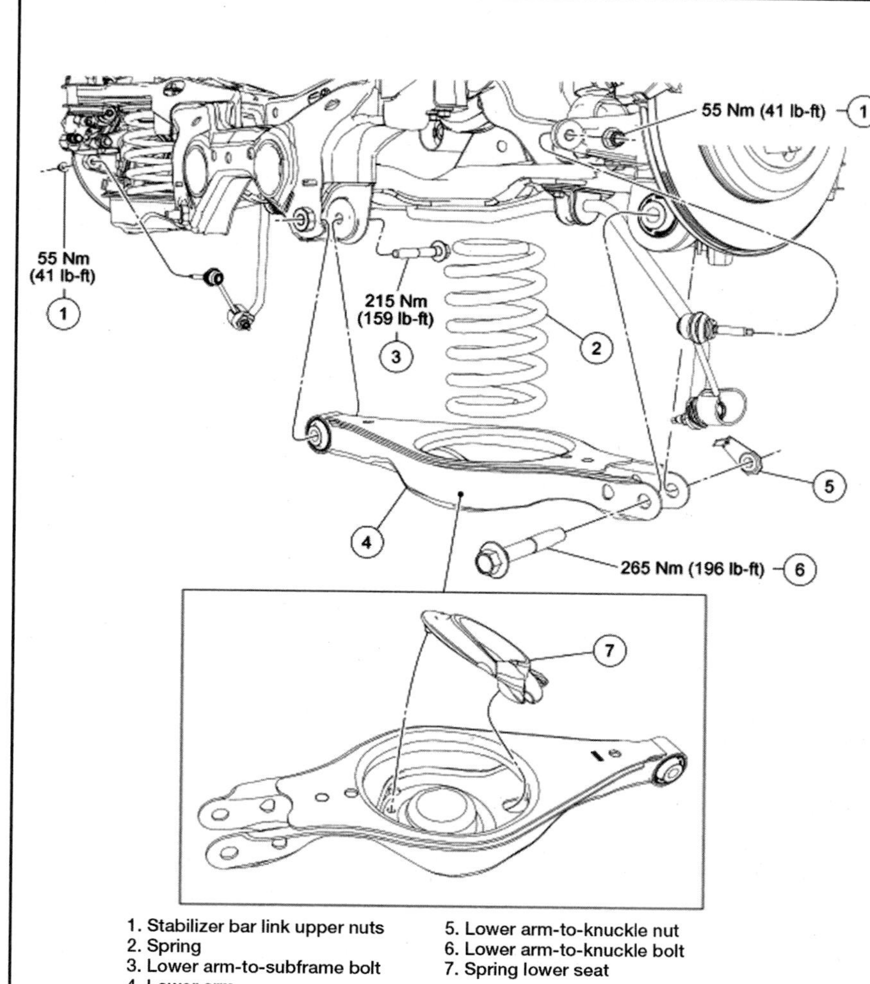

Fig. 234 Lower arm (FWD vehicle shown, AWD vehicle similar)

6. Loosen the lower arm inner bolt.
7. Lower the jackstand and remove the spring.
8. Remove the lower arm inner bolt and lower arm.
   a. Discard the bolt.

To install:

➡Before tightening the lower arm bolts, use a jackstand to raise the rear suspension until the distance between the center of the hub and the lip of the fender is equal to the measurement taken in the Removal procedure (curb height).

9. Position the lower arm and loosely install the new lower arm inner bolt.

➡Make sure the lower spring seat is properly positioned in the lower arm.

10. Install the spring and position the screw-type jackstand under the lower arm.

➡Do not tighten the lower arm nut at this time.

11. Raise the jackstand and loosely install the new lower arm-to-knuckle bolt and nut.
12. Using the jackstand, raise the rear suspension until the distance between the center of the hub and the lip of the fender is equal to the measurement taken in the Removal procedure (curb height).
13. Tighten the lower arm-to-subframe bolt to 159 ft. lbs. (215 Nm).
14. Tighten the lower arm-to-knuckle bolt to 196 ft. lbs. (265 Nm).

➡Use the hex-holding feature to prevent the stabilizer bar link stud from turning while removing the nut.

15. Position the stabilizer bar links and install 2 new stabilizer bar link upper nuts. Tighten the nuts to 41 ft. lbs. (55 Nm).

SHOCK ABSORBER

REMOVAL & INSTALLATION

See Figure 235.

⁂ WARNING

Suspension fasteners are critical parts because they affect performance of vital components and systems and their failure may result in major service expense. New parts must be installed with the same part numbers or equivalent part, if replacement is necessary. Do not use a replacement part of lesser quality or substitute design. Torque values must be used as specified during reassembly to make sure of correct retention of these parts.

➡Use the hex-holding feature on the stock rod nut to prevent the shock rod from rotating when removing or installing the shock rod nut.

1. Pull back the luggage compartment side trim panel to gain access to the shock absorber upper nut.
2. Remove and discard the shock absorber upper mount nut.
3. Remove the wheel and tire.

➡Use the hex-holding feature to prevent the stabilizer bar link stud from turning while removing or installing the nut.

4. Remove and discard the stabilizer bar link upper nut and disconnect the link from the wheel knuckle.
5. Remove and discard the shock absorber lower bolt and remove the shock absorber.

To install:

6. Install and discard the shock absorber lower bolt and remove the shock absorber. Tighten the new bolt to 129 ft. lbs. (175 Nm).

➡Use the hex-holding feature to prevent the stabilizer bar link stud from turning while removing or installing the nut.

7. Install and discard the stabilizer bar link upper nut and connect the link to the wheel knuckle. Tighten the new nut to 41 ft. lbs. (55 Nm).
8. Install the wheel and tire.
9. Install and discard the shock absorber upper mount nut. Tighten the new nut to 41 ft. lbs. (55 Nm).

⁂ WARNING

Suspension fasteners are critical parts because they affect performance of vital components and systems and their failure may result in major service expense. New parts must be installed with the same part numbers or equivalent part, if replacement is necessary. Do not use a replacement part of lesser quality or substitute design. Torque values must be used as specified during reassembly to make sure of correct retention of these parts.

➡Use the hex-holding feature on the stock rod nut to prevent the shock rod from rotating when removing or installing the shock rod nut.

10. Pull back the luggage compartment side trim panel to gain access to the shock absorber upper nut.

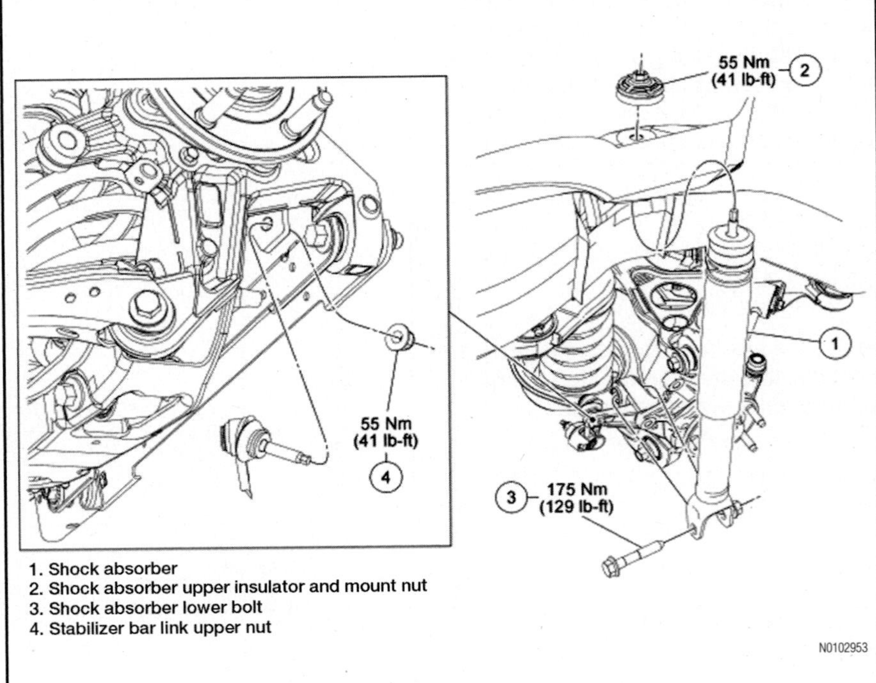

Fig. 235 Shock absorber

SPRING

REMOVAL & INSTALLTION

See Figure 236.

⁂ WARNING

Suspension fasteners are critical parts because they affect performance of vital components and systems and their failure may result in major service expense. New parts must be installed with the same part numbers or equivalent part, if replacement is necessary. Do not use a replacement part of lesser quality or substitute design. Torque values must be used as specified during reassembly to make sure of correct retention of these parts.

1. Measure the distance from the center of the wheel hub to the lip of the fender with the vehicle in a level, static ground position (curb height).
2. Remove the wheel and tire.

➡Use the hex-holding feature to prevent the stabilizer bar link studs from turning while removing the nuts.

3. Remove and discard the 2 stabilizer bar link upper nuts.
   a. Position the stabilizer bar away from the lower arm.
4. Using a suitable jackstand, support the lower arm.
5. Loosen the lower arm-to-subframe bolt.
6. Remove and discard the lower arm-to wheel knuckle bolt.
7. Lower the jackstand and remove the spring.

➡Make sure the lower spring seat is properly positioned in the lower arm.

8. Inspect the upper and lower spring seats for damage and, if necessary, install new spring seats.

To install:

➡Before tightening the lower arm bolts, use a jackstand to raise the rear suspension until the distance between the center of the hub and the lip of the fender is equal to the measurement taken in the Removal procedure (curb height).

9. Install the spring and position the jackstand under the lower arm.
10. Raise the jackstand and loosely install a new lower arm-to-wheel knuckle bolt.

➡Use the hex-holding feature to prevent the stabilizer bar link studs from turning while installing the nuts.

11. Position the stabilizer bar and links and install 2 new stabilizer bar link upper nuts. Tighten the nuts to 41 ft. lbs. (55 Nm).
12. Using the jackstand, raise the rear suspension until the distance between the center of the hub and the lip of the fender is equal to the measurement taken in the Removal procedure (curb height).
13. Tighten the lower arm-to-wheel knuckle bolt to 196 ft. lbs. (265 Nm).
14. Tighten the lower arm-to-subframe bolt to 159 ft. lbs. (215 Nm).
15. Install the wheel and tire.

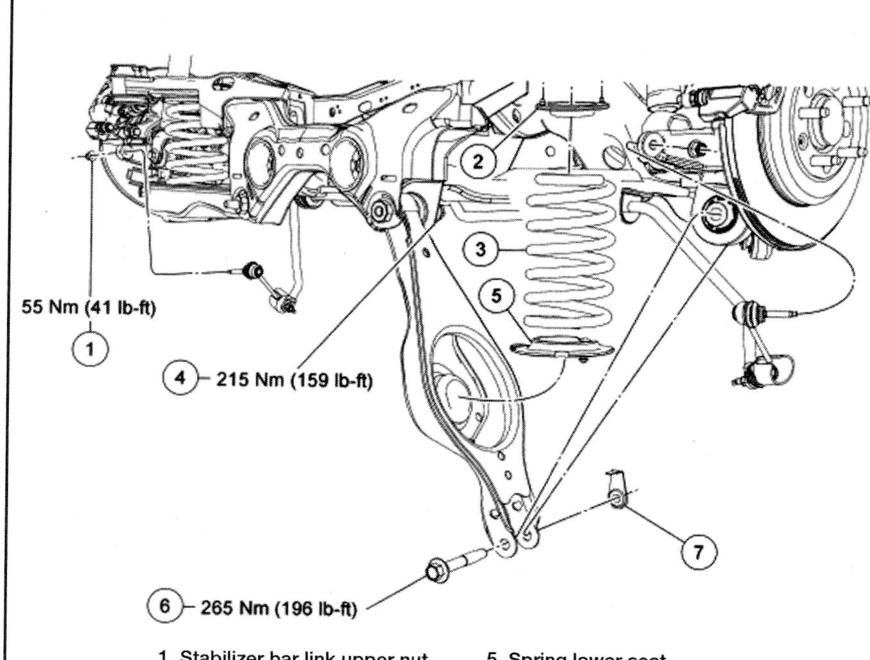

Fig. 236 Spring components

STABILIZER BAR

REMOVAL & INSTALLATION

See Figures 237 and 238.

⁂ WARNING

Suspension fasteners are critical parts because they affect performance of vital components and systems and their failure may result in major service expense. New parts must be installed with the same part numbers or equivalent part, if replacement is necessary. Do not use a replacement part of lesser quality or substitute design. Torque values must be used as specified during reassembly to make sure of correct retention of these parts.

➡Use the hex-holding feature to prevent the stabilizer bar link stud from turning while removing or installing the nut.

1. With the vehicle in NEUTRAL, position it on a hoist.
2. Support the exhaust system with a suitable jackstand, disconnect the 2 muffler and tail pipe isolators and lower the exhaust approximately 2 inch (50.8 mm).
3. Remove and discard the 2 stabilizer bar link lower nuts.
4. Remove and discard the 4 stabilizer bar bracket bolts.
5. Remove the stabilizer bar.

To install:

6. Remove the stabilizer bar.
7. Remove and discard the 4 stabilizer bar bracket bolts. Tighten the new bolts to 41 ft. lbs. (55 Nm).
8. Remove and discard the 2 stabilizer bar link lower nuts. Tighten the new nuts to 46 ft. lbs. (63 Nm).

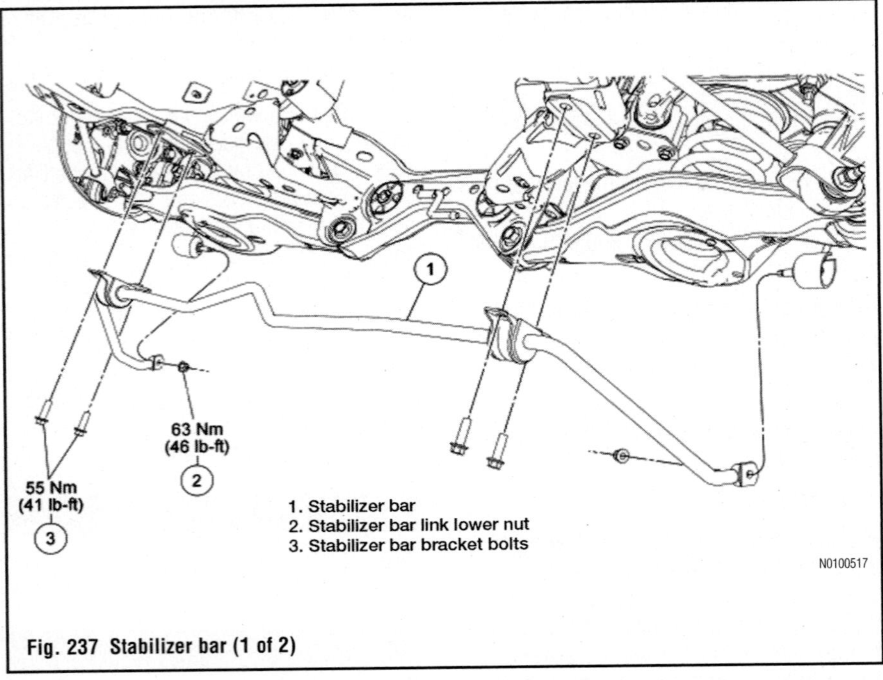

Fig. 237 Stabilizer bar (1 of 2)

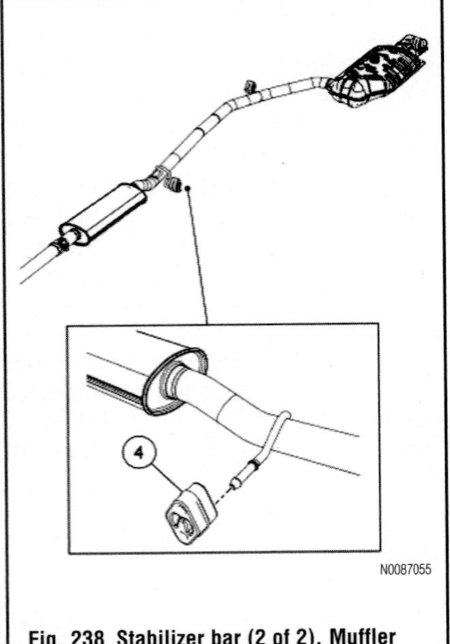

Fig. 238 Stabilizer bar (2 of 2). Muffler and tail pipe isolator (4)

9. Support the exhaust system with a suitable jackstand, disconnect the 2 muffler and tail pipe isolators and lower the exhaust approximately 2 inch (50.8 mm).

WARNING

Suspension fasteners are critical parts because they affect performance of vital components and systems and their failure may result in major service expense. New parts must be installed with the same part numbers or equivalent part, if replacement is necessary. Do not use a replacement part of lesser quality or substitute design. Torque values must be used as specified during reassembly to make sure of correct retention of these parts.

➡Use the hex-holding feature to prevent the stabilizer bar link stud from turning while removing or installing the nut.

10. With the vehicle in NEUTRAL, position it on a hoist.

STABILIZER BAR LINK

REMOVAL & INSTALLATION

WARNING

Suspension fasteners are critical parts because they affect performance of vital components and systems and their failure may result in major service expense. New parts must be installed with the same part numbers or equivalent part, if replacement is necessary. Do not use a replacement part of lesser quality or substitute design. Torque values must be used as specified during reassembly to make sure of correct retention of these parts.

➡Use the hex-holding feature to prevent the stabilizer bar link stud from turning while removing or installing the nut.

1. Remove and discard the stabilizer bar link lower nut.
2. Remove the stabilizer bar link upper nut and stabilizer bar link.
   a. Discard the nut.

To install:

3. Remove the stabilizer bar link upper nut and stabilizer bar link.
   a. Discard the nut. Tighten the new nut to 41 ft. lbs. (55 Nm).

WARNING

Suspension fasteners are critical parts because they affect performance of vital components and systems and their failure may result in major service expense. New parts must be installed with the same part numbers or equivalent part, if replacement is necessary. Do not use a replacement part of lesser quality or substitute design. Torque values must be used as specified during reassembly to make sure of correct retention of these parts.

➡Use the hex-holding feature to prevent the stabilizer bar link stud from turning while removing or installing the nut.

4. Remove and discard the stabilizer bar link lower nut. Tighten the new nut to 46 ft. lbs. (63 Nm).

TOE LINK

REMOVAL & INSTALLATION

See Figure 239.

WARNING

Suspension fasteners are critical parts because they affect performance of vital components and systems and their failure may result in major service expense. New parts must be installed with the same part numbers or equivalent part, if replacement is necessary. Do not use a replacement part of lesser quality or substitute design. Torque values must be used as specified during reassembly to make sure of correct retention of these parts.

1. Measure the distance from the center of the wheel hub to the lip of the fender with the vehicle in a level, static ground position (curb height).
2. Remove the wheel and tire.
3. Use a jackstand to raise the rear suspension until the distance between the

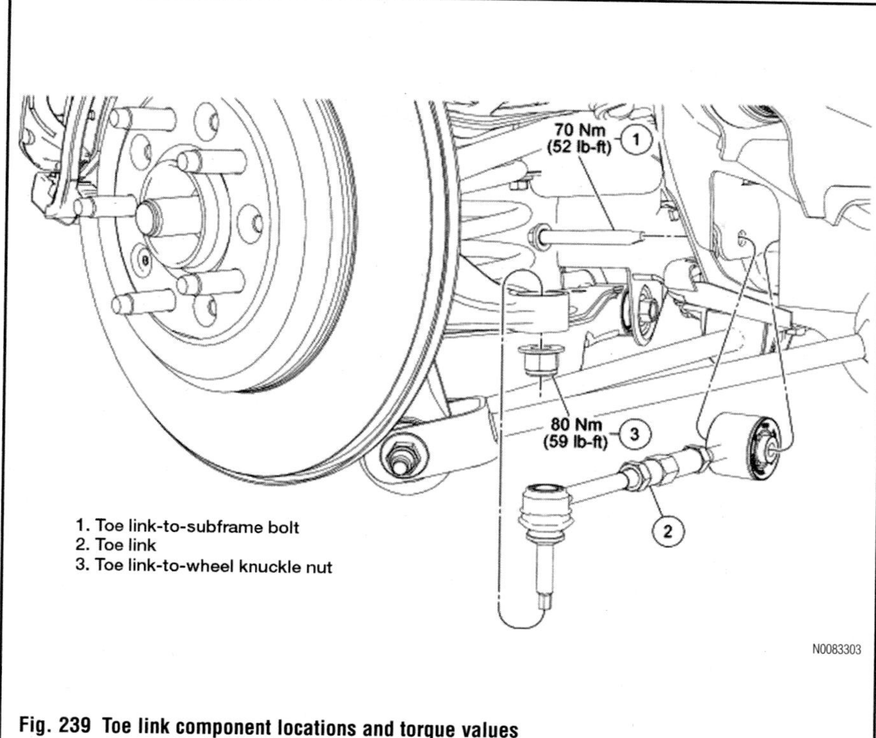

Fig. 239 Toe link component locations and torque values

center of the hub and the lip of the fender is equal to the measurement taken in Step 1 of the procedure (curb height).

4. Remove and discard the toe link-to-wheel knuckle nut.
5. Remove and discard the toe link-to-subframe bolt.

To install:

6. Install and discard the toe link-to-subframe bolt. Tighten the new bolt to 52 ft. lbs. (70 Nm).
7. Install and discard the toe link-to-wheel knuckle nut. Tighten the new nut to 59 ft. lbs. (80 Nm).
8. Use a jackstand to raise the rear suspension until the distance between the center of the hub and the lip of the fender is equal to the measurement taken in Step 1 of the procedure (curb height).
9. Install the wheel and tire.

WARNING

Suspension fasteners are critical parts because they affect performance of vital components and systems and their failure may result in major service expense. New parts must be installed with the same part numbers or equivalent part, if replacement is necessary. Do not use a replacement part of lesser quality or substitute design. Torque values must be used as specified during reassembly to make sure of correct retention of these parts.

10. Measure the distance from the center of the wheel hub to the lip of the fender with the vehicle in a level, static ground position (curb height).

Check and, if necessary, adjust the rear toe.

TRAILING ARM

REMOVAL & INSTALLATION

See Figure 240.

WARNING

Suspension fasteners are critical parts because they affect performance of vital components and systems and their failure may result in major service expense. New parts must be installed with the same part numbers or equivalent part, if replacement is necessary. Do not use a replacement part of lesser quality or substitute design. Torque values must be used as specified during reassembly to make sure of correct retention of these parts.

1. Measure the distance from the center of the wheel hub to the lip of the fender with the vehicle in a level, static ground position (curb height).
2. Remove the wheel and tire.
3. Use a jackstand to raise the rear suspension until the distance between the center of the hub and the lip of the fender is equal to the measurement taken in Step 1 of the procedure (curb height).
4. Remove and discard the trailing arm-to-knuckle nut and bolt.
5. Remove and discard the trailing arm-to-subframe bolt.

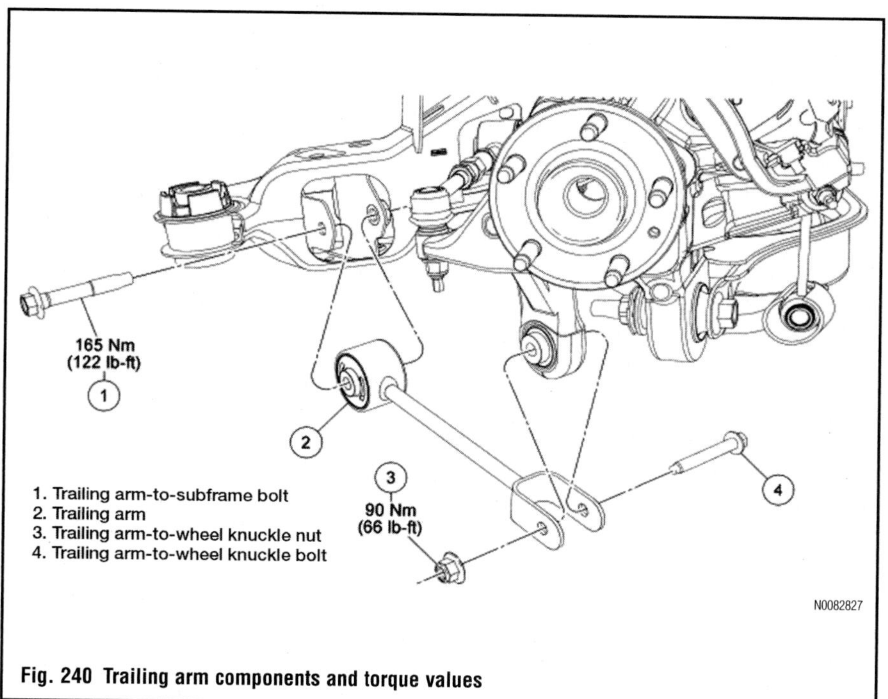

Fig. 240 Trailing arm components and torque values

To install:

6. Install and discard the trailing arm-to-subframe bolt. Tighten the new bolt to 122 ft. lbs. (165 Nm).
7. Install and discard the trailing arm-to-knuckle nut and bolt. Tighten the new nut to 66 ft. lbs. (90 Nm).
8. Use a jackstand to raise the rear suspension until the distance between the center of the hub and the lip of the fender is equal to the measurement taken in Step 1 of the procedure (curb height).
9. Install the wheel and tire.

WARNING

Suspension fasteners are critical parts because they affect performance of vital components and systems and their failure may result in major service expense. New parts must be installed with the same part numbers or equivalent part, if replacement is necessary. Do not use a replacement part of lesser quality or substitute design. Torque values must be used as specified during reassembly to make sure of correct retention of these parts.

10. Measure the distance from the center of the wheel hub to the lip of the fender with the vehicle in a level, static ground position (curb height).

UPPER CONTROL ARM

REMOVAL & INSTALLATION

See Figures 241 through 244.

WARNING

Suspension fasteners are critical parts because they affect performance of vital components and systems and their failure may result in major service expense. New parts must be installed with the same part numbers or equivalent part, if replacement is necessary. Do not use a replacement part of lesser quality or substitute design. Torque values must be used as specified during reassembly to make sure of correct retention of these parts.

1. Measure the distance from the center of the wheel hub to the lip of the fender with the vehicle in a level, static ground position (curb height).
2. Remove the rear wheels and tires.
3. Remove LH and RH parking brake cable bracket bolts.

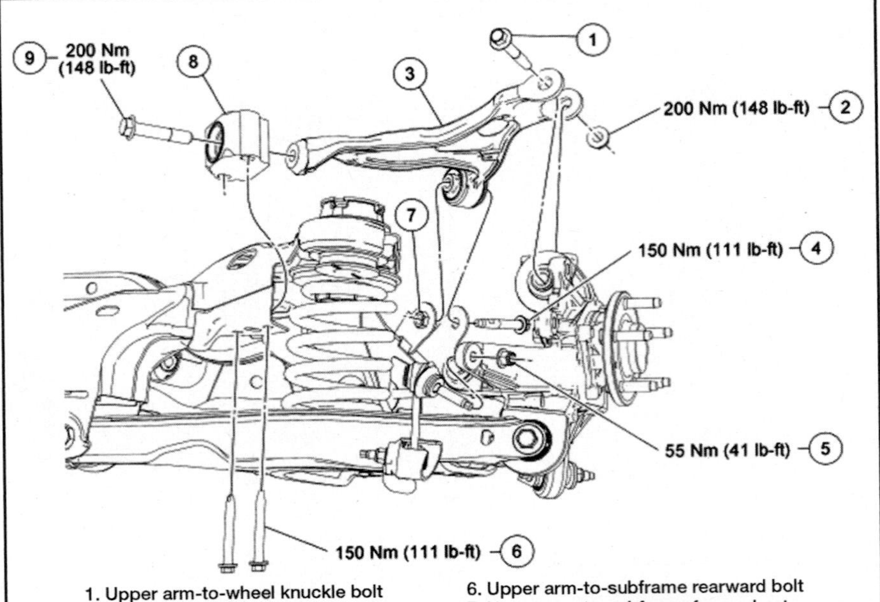

Fig. 241 Upper arm components (1 of 3)

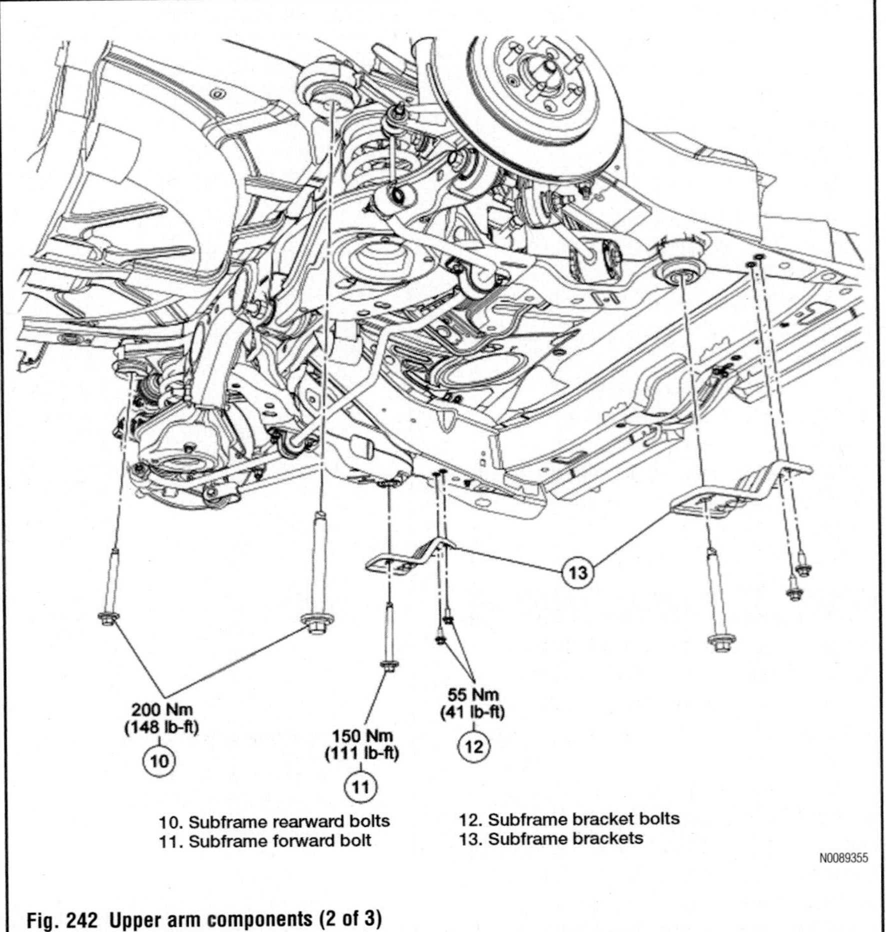

Fig. 242 Upper arm components (2 of 3)

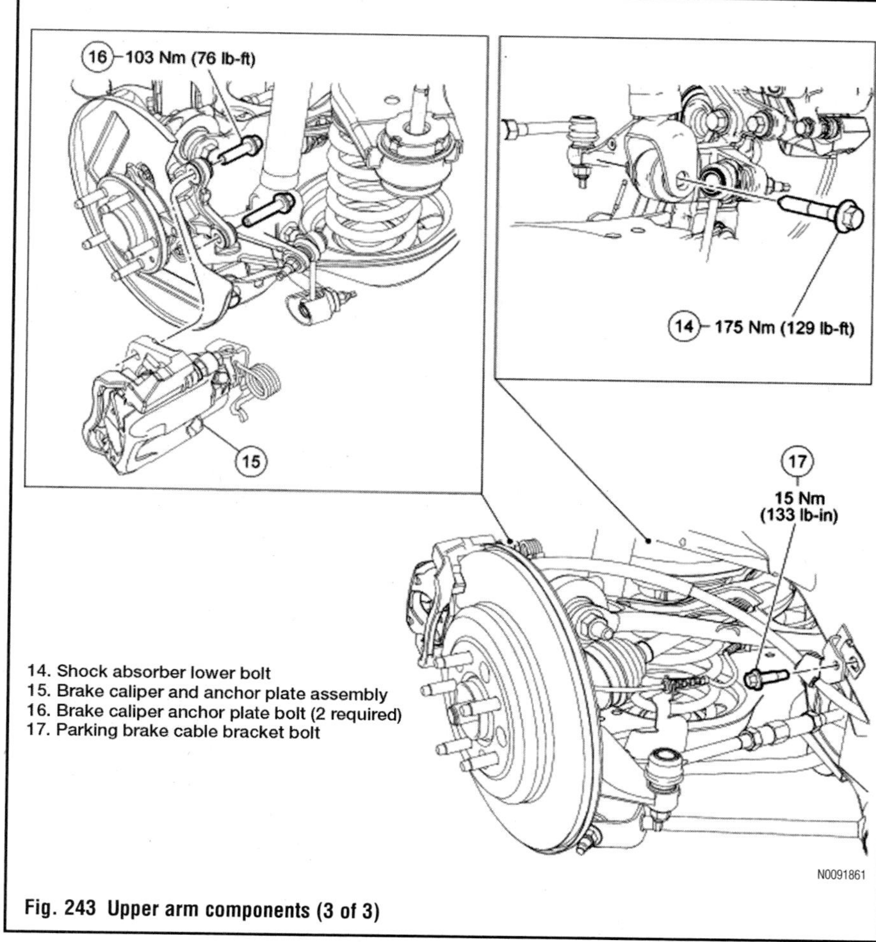

Fig. 243 Upper arm components (3 of 3)

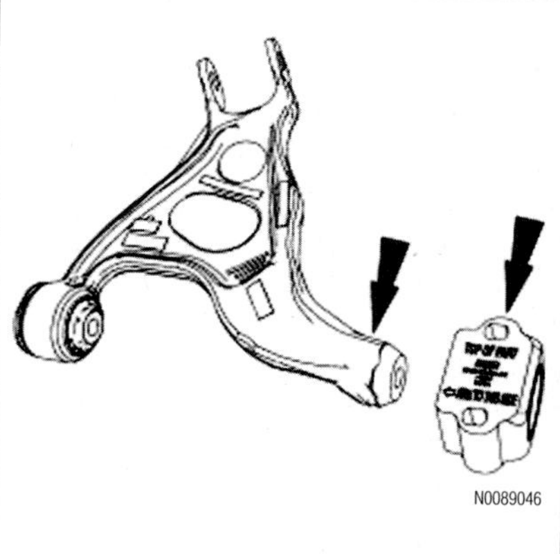

Fig. 244 With the upper arm positioned so the top side is facing up and the upper arm bushing is positioned with the TOP OF PART facing up and the ARM TO THIS SIDE arrow is pointing toward the upper arm. Install the upper arm bushing

WARNING

Do not allow the brake caliper to hang from the brake flexible hose or damage to the hose may occur.

4. Remove the 4 brake caliper anchor plate bolts and position the LH and RH brake caliper and anchor plate assemblies aside.
   a. Support the brake caliper and anchor plate assemblies using mechanic's wire.
5. Position screw-type jackstands under the LH and RH wheel knuckles.
6. Remove and discard the upper arm-to-knuckle bolt and nut.
7. Remove and discard the 2 upper arm-to-subframe rearward bolts.

➡Use the hex-holding feature to prevent the stabilizer bar link stud from turning while removing or installing the nut.

8. Remove and discard the LH and RH stabilizer bar link upper nuts and disconnect the links from the stabilizer bar.
9. Remove and discard the LH and RH lower shock bolts.
10. Remove and discard the 4 subframe bracket bolts.
11. Remove and discard the 2 subframe forward bolts and remove the 2 subframe brackets.
12. Remove and discard the 2 subframe rearward bolts and lower the subframe enough to allow removal of the upper arm forward bolt.
13. Remove and discard the upper arm-to-subframe forward bolt and nut.
   a. Remove the upper arm.
14. If service to the upper arm rearward bushing is required, remove the upper arm bushing bolt and remove the upper arm bushing.
   a. Discard the bolt.

To install:

➡Before tightening the shock absorber lower bolts and upper arm nut and bolts, use a jackstand to raise the rear suspension until the distance between the center of the hub and the lip of the fender is equal to the measurement taken in the Removal procedure (curb height).

15. If removed, install the upper arm bushing onto the upper arm in the following sequence.
   a. With the upper arm positioned so the top side is facing up and the upper arm bushing is positioned with the TOP OF PART facing up and the ARM TO THIS SIDE arrow is pointing toward the upper arm. Install the upper arm bushing.
   b. Install a new upper arm rearward bushing bolt and tighten to 148 ft. lbs. (200 Nm).
16. Position the upper arm and loosely install the new upper arm-to-subframe forward bolt and nut.
17. Raise the subframe and install 2 new subframe rearward bolts. Tighten the bolts to 148 ft. lbs. (200 Nm).
18. Position the 2 subframe brackets and install 4 new subframe bracket bolts. Tighten the bolts to 41 ft. lbs. (55 Nm).
19. Install 2 new subframe forward bolts. Tighten the bolts to 111 ft. lbs. (150 Nm).
20. Loosely install new LH and RH shock absorber lower bolts.

➡Use the hex-holding feature to prevent the stabilizer bar link stud from turning while removing or installing the nut.

21. Connect the LH and RH stabilizer bar links to the stabilizer bar and install the new nuts. Tighten the nuts to 41 ft. lbs. (55 Nm).
22. Loosely install 2 new upper arm-to-subframe rearward bolts.
23. Loosely install a new upper arm-to-knuckle bolt and nut.
24. Position the LH and RH brake caliper

and anchor plate assemblies and install the 4 anchor plate bolts. Tighten the bolts to 76 ft. lbs. (103).

25. Install LH and RH parking brake cable bracket bolts. Tighten the bolts to 133 inch lbs. (15 Nm).

26. Using the screw-type jackstand, raise the rear suspension until the distance between the center of the hub and the lip of the fender is equal to the measurement taken in the removal procedure (curb height).

27. Tighten the upper arm-to-subframe forward bolt to 111 ft. lbs. (150 Nm).

28. Tighten the LH and RH shock absorber lower bolts to 129 ft. lbs. (175 Nm).

29. Tighten the 2 upper arm-to-subframe rearward bolts to 111 ft. lbs. (150 Nm).

➡A slotted upper arm allows for the rear suspension camber to be adjusted by pushing inward or pulling outward on the wheel knuckle while tightening the upper arm-to-wheel knuckle nut.

30. With the wheel knuckle pushed inward for maximum negative camber, tighten the upper arm-to-wheel knuckle nut to 148 ft. lbs. (200 Nm).

31. Remove the 2 jackstands.

32. Install the rear wheels and tires.

33. Check and, if necessary, adjust the rear camber.

WHEEL BEARINGS AND WHEEL HUB

REMOVAL & INSTALLATION

See Figure 245.

All Vehicles

⁂ WARNING

Suspension fasteners are critical parts because they affect performance of vital components and systems and their failure may result in major service expense. New parts must be installed with the same part numbers or equivalent part, if replacement is necessary. Do not use a replacement part of lesser quality or substitute design. Torque values must be used as specified during reassembly to make sure of correct retention of these parts.

1. Remove the brake disc.
2. Remove the wheel speed sensor bolt and position the sensor aside.

All-Wheel Drive (AWD) Vehicles

➡Do not discard the nut at this time.

3. Remove the wheel hub nut.
4. Using the Front Wheel Hub Remover, separate the halfshaft from the wheel hub.

All Vehicles

5. Remove the 4 bolts and the wheel bearing and wheel hub.
   a. Discard the bolts.

⁂ WARNING

The wheel knuckle bore must be clean enough to allow the wheel bearing and wheel hub to seat completely by hand. Do not press or draw the wheel hub and bearing into place or damage to the bearing may occur.

⁂ WARNING

Make sure the wheel hub-to-knuckle mating surfaces are clean and free of any adhesive. Failure to clean adhesive from both surfaces may cause bearing damage.

6. Using a clean shop towel, clean the wheel knuckle-to-mating surfaces and inspect the knuckle bearing bore.
   a. If the wheel knuckle is cracked, install a new wheel knuckle.

To install:

All Vehicles

7. Install the wheel bearing and wheel hub assembly.
8. Install the 4 new wheel bearing and wheel hub bolts. Tighten the bolts to 98 ft. lbs. (133 Nm) in a cross-pattern.
9. Install the brake disc.
10. Position the wheel speed sensor and install the bolt. Tighten the bolt to 133 inch lbs. (15 Nm).

AWD Vehicles

⁂ WARNING

Do not tighten the rear wheel hub nut with the vehicle on the ground. The nut must be tightened to specification before the vehicle is lowered to the ground. Wheel bearing damage will occur if the wheel bearing is loaded

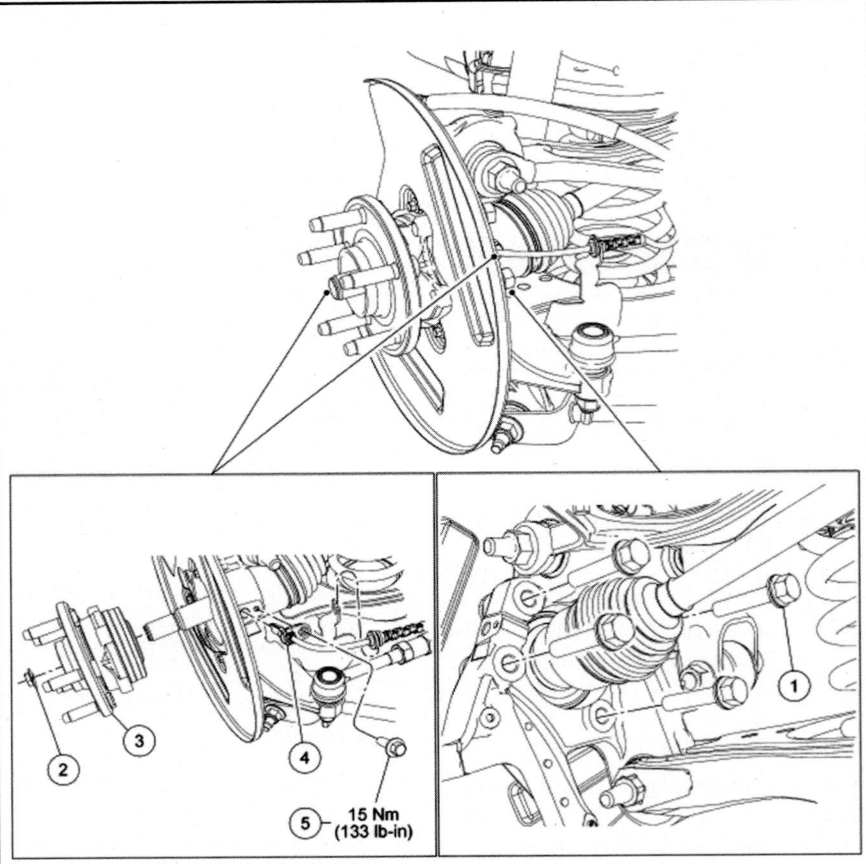

Fig. 245 Wheel bearing and wheel hub components. AWD shown, FWD similar

with the weight of the vehicle applied.

➡Apply the brake to keep the halfshaft from rotating.

11. Position the halfshaft in the hub and use the previously removed wheel hub nut to seat the halfshaft. Tighten the nut to 258 ft. lbs. (350 Nm).
    a. Remove and discard the nut.

**** WARNING**

Install and tighten the new wheel hub nut to specification within 5 minutes of starting it on the threads. Always install a new wheel hub nut after loosening or when not tightening within the specified time or damage to the components may occur.

12. Install a new wheel hub nut. Tighten the nut to 258 ft. lbs. (350 Nm).

WHEEL KNUCKLE

REMOVAL & INSTALLATION

AWD Vehicles

See Figures 246 through 248.

**** WARNING**

Suspension fasteners are critical parts because they affect performance of vital components and systems and their failure may result in major service expense. New parts must be installed with the same part numbers or equivalent part, if replacement is necessary. Do not use a replacement part of lesser quality or substitute design. Torque values must be used as specified during reassembly to make sure of correct retention of these parts.

1. Measure the distance from the center of the wheel hub to the lip of the fender with the vehicle in a level, static ground position (curb height).
2. Remove the wheel bearing and wheel hub. For additional information, refer to Wheel Bearing and Wheel Hub in this section.
3. Using a suitable jackstand, support the lower arm.
4. Remove and discard the trailing arm-to-wheel knuckle nut and bolt.

➡Use the hex-holding feature to prevent the stabilizer bar link stud from turning while removing or installing the nut.

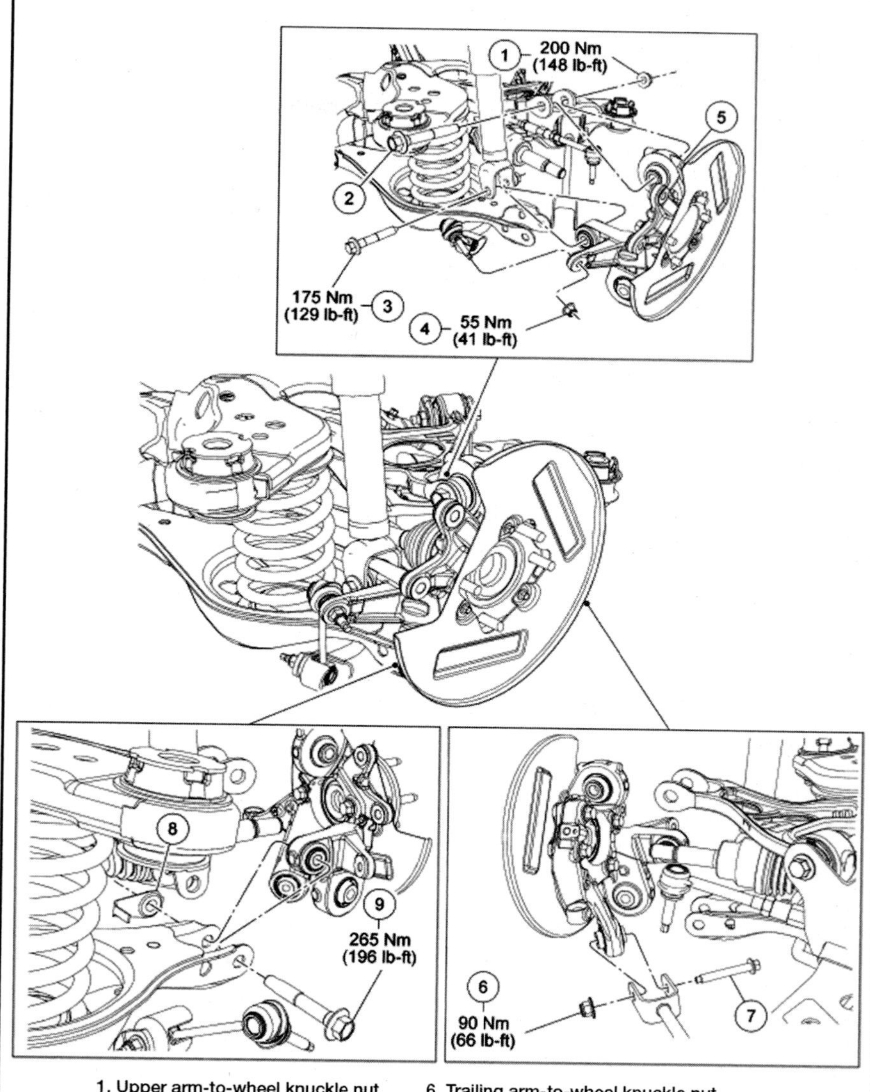

Fig. 246 Wheel knuckle—AWD (1 of 3)

5. Remove and discard the stabilizer bar link upper nut and disconnect the link.
6. Remove and discard the shock absorber lower bolt and disconnect the shock absorber from the knuckle bracket.
7. Remove and discard the toe link-to-knuckle nut.
8. Remove and discard the upper arm-to-wheel knuckle nut and bolt and disconnect the upper arm from the knuckle.
9. Remove and discard the lower arm-to-wheel knuckle nut and bolt.
10. Lower the jackstand, slide the knuckle off the toe link and remove the knuckle.
11. If necessary, remove the 3 brake disc shield bolts and remove the shield.

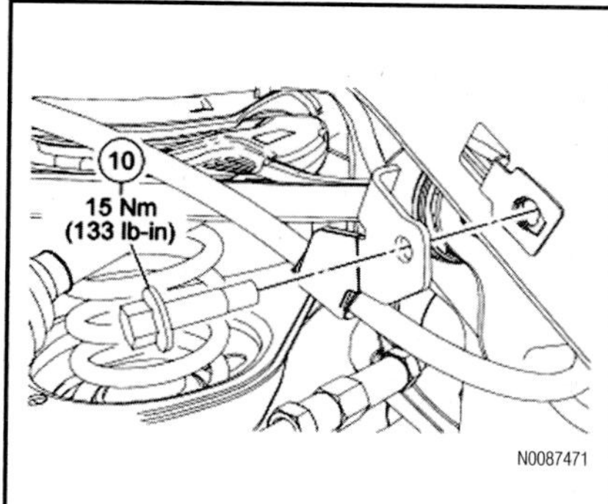

Fig. 247 Wheel knuckle—AWD (2 of 3). Parking brake cable bracket bolt (10)

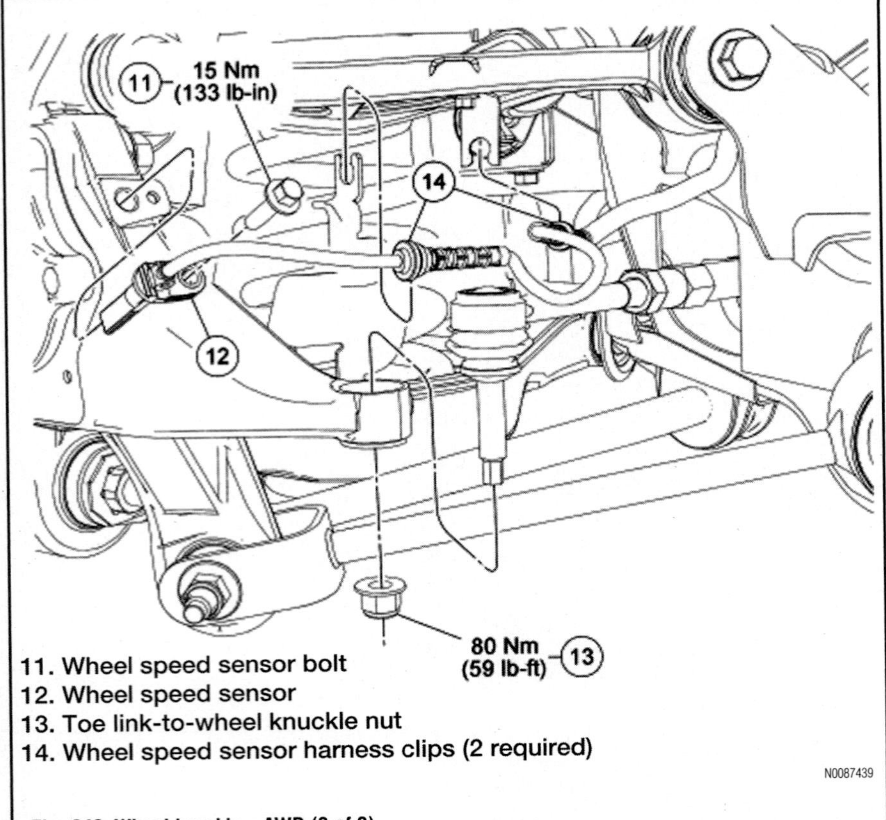

Fig. 248 Wheel knuckle—AWD (3 of 3)

To install:

➡Before tightening suspension bushing fasteners, use a jackstand to raise the rear suspension until the distance between the center of the hub and the lip of the fender is equal to the measurement taken in the removal procedure (curb height).

12. If removed, install the brake disc shield. Tighten the 3 bolts to 133 inch lbs. (15 Nm).
13. Position the wheel knuckle onto the toe link and loosely install a new lower arm-to-wheel knuckle nut and bolt.
14. Loosely install a new toe link-to-knuckle nut.
15. Connect the shock absorber to the knuckle and loosely install a new shock absorber lower bolt.

➡Use the hex-holding feature to prevent the stabilizer bar link stud from turning while removing or installing the nut.

16. Connect the stabilizer bar link and install a new stabilizer bar link upper nut. Tighten the nut to 41 ft. lbs. (55 Nm).
17. Loosely install a new trailing arm-to-wheel knuckle nut and bolt.
18. Raise the jackstand and loosely install a new upper arm-to-wheel knuckle nut and bolt.
19. Position a suitable jackstand under the lower control arm at the shock and spring assembly attachment point and raise the rear suspension until the distance between the center of the hub and the lip of the fender is equal to the measurement taken in Step 1 of the procedure (curb height).

➡A slotted upper arm allows for the rear suspension camber to be adjusted by pushing inward or pulling outward on the wheel knuckle while tightening the upper arm-to-wheel knuckle nut.

20. With the wheel knuckle pushed inward for maximum negative camber, tighten the upper arm-to-wheel knuckle nut to 200 Nm (148 lb-ft).
21. Tighten the lower arm-to-wheel knuckle bolt to 196 ft. lbs. (265 Nm).
22. Tighten the shock absorber bolt to 129 ft. lbs. (175 Nm).
23. Tighten the trailing arm-to-wheel knuckle nut to 66 ft. lbs. (90 Nm).
24. Tighten the toe link-to-wheel knuckle nut to 59 ft. lbs. (80 Nm).
25. Install the wheel bearing and wheel hub as outlined in this section.
26. Check and if necessary, adjust the rear toe.

FWD Vehicles

See Figures 249 and 250.

⁂ WARNING

Suspension fasteners are critical parts because they affect performance of vital components and systems and their failure may result in major service expense. New parts must be installed with the same part numbers or equivalent part, if replacement is necessary. Do not use a replacement part of lesser quality or substitute design. Torque values must be used as specified during reassembly to make sure of correct retention of these parts.

1. Measure the distance from the center of the wheel hub to the lip of the fender with the vehicle in a level, static ground position (curb height).
2. Remove the wheel and tire.
3. Remove the brake disc.
4. Using a suitable jackstand, support the lower arm.
5. Remove and discard the trailing arm-to-wheel knuckle nut and bolt.

➡Use the hex-holding feature to prevent the stabilizer bar link stud from turning while removing the nut.

6. Remove and discard the stabilizer bar link upper nut and disconnect the link.
7. Remove and discard the shock absorber lower bolt and disconnect the shock absorber.
8. Remove the wheel speed sensor bolt, disconnect the harness and position the sensor and harness assembly aside.
9. Remove and discard the toe link-to-knuckle nut.
10. Remove and discard the upper arm-to-wheel knuckle nut and bolt and disconnect the upper arm from the knuckle.
11. Remove and discard the lower arm-to-wheel knuckle nut and bolt.
12. Lower the jackstand, slide the knuckle off the toe link and remove the knuckle.

To install:

➡Before tightening any suspension bushing fasteners, use a jackstand to raise the rear suspension until the distance between the center of the hub

and the lip of the fender is equal to the measurement taken in the removal procedure (curb height).

13. Position the wheel knuckle onto the toe link and loosely install a new lower arm-to-wheel knuckle nut and bolt.

14. Loosely install a new toe link-to-knuckle nut.

15. Position the wheel speed sensor harness and install the wheel speed sensor and bolt. Tighten the bolt to 133 inch lbs. (15 Nm).

16. Connect the shock absorber to the knuckle and loosely install a new shock absorber lower bolt.

17. Connect the stabilizer bar link and install a new stabilizer bar link upper nut. Tighten the nut to 41 ft. lbs. (55 Nm).

➡Use the hex-holding feature to prevent the stabilizer bar link stud from turning while removing or installing the nut.

18. Loosely install a new trailing arm-to-wheel knuckle nut and bolt.

19. Loosely install a new upper arm-to-wheel knuckle nut and bolt.

20. Position a suitable jackstand under the lower control arm at the shock and

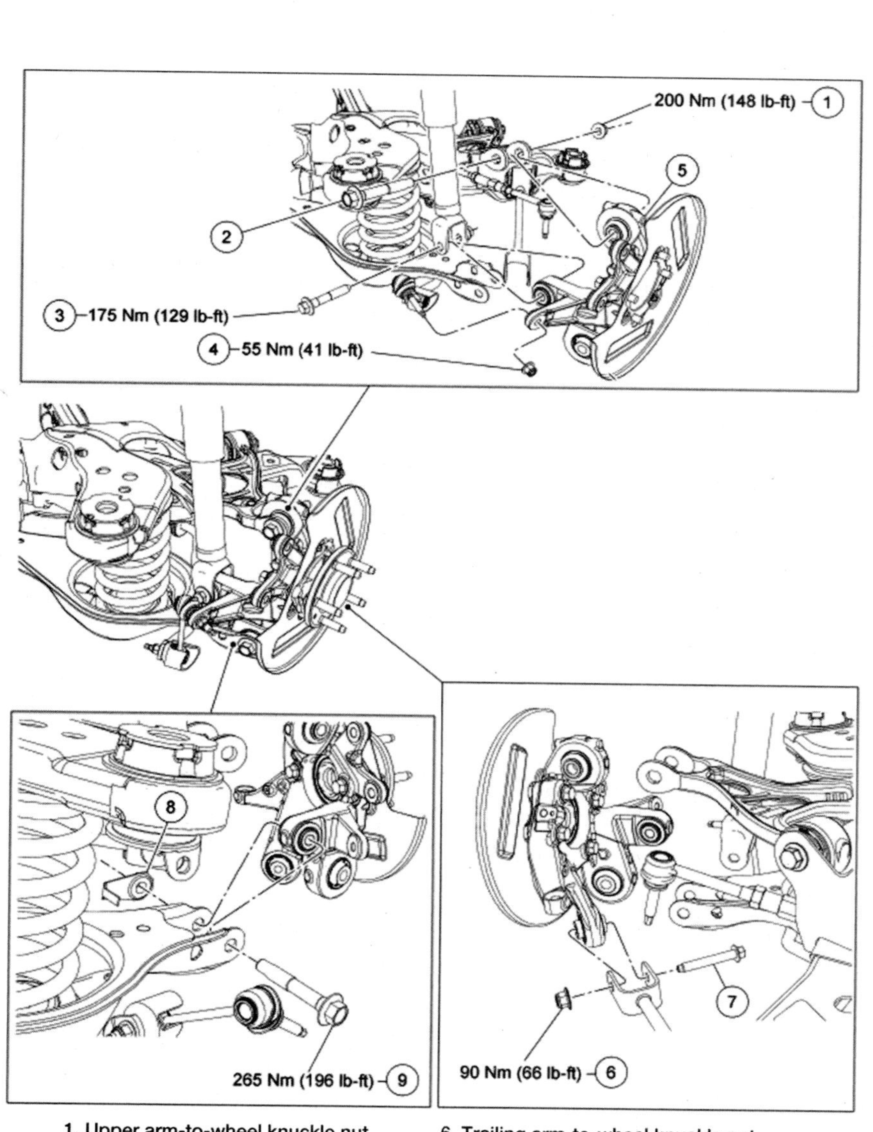

Fig. 249 Wheel knuckle—FWD (1 of 2)

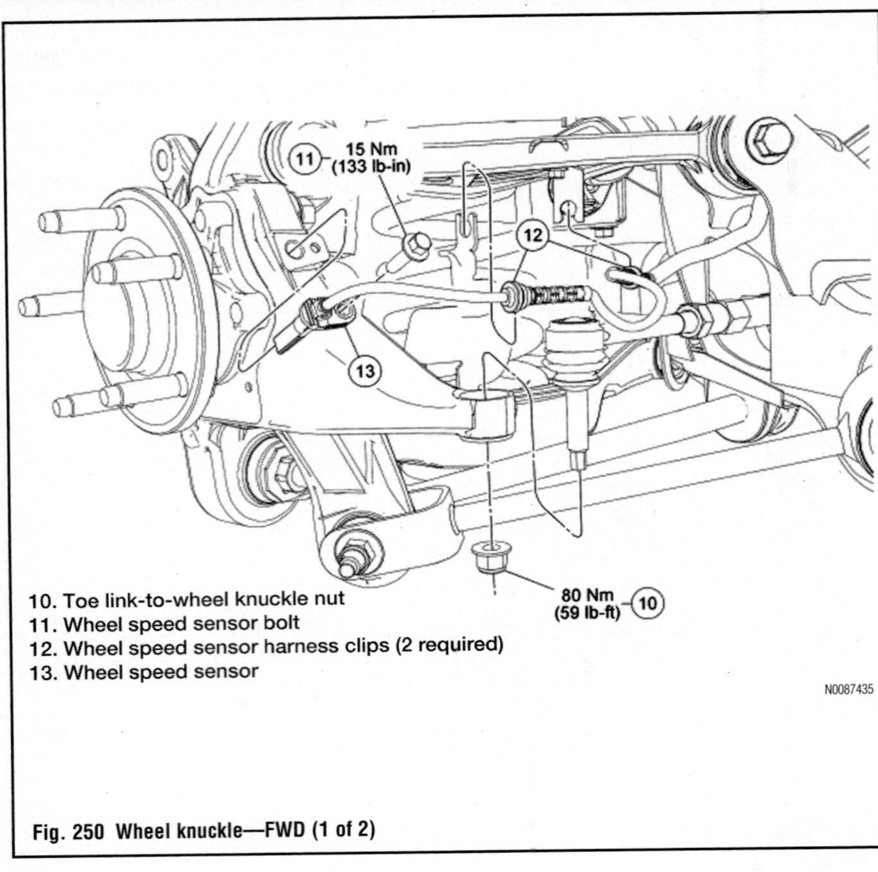

Fig. 250 Wheel knuckle—FWD (1 of 2)

spring assembly attachment point and raise the rear suspension until the distance between the center of the hub and the lip of the fender is equal to the measurement taken in Step 1 of the procedure (curb height).

➡A slotted upper arm allows for the rear suspension camber to be adjusted by pushing inward or pulling outward on the wheel knuckle while tightening the upper arm-to-wheel knuckle nut.

21. With the wheel knuckle pushed inward for maximum negative camber, tighten the upper arm-to-wheel knuckle nut to 148 ft. lbs. (200 Nm).
22. Tighten the lower arm-to-wheel knuckle bolt to 196 ft. lbs. (265 Nm).
23. Tighten the shock absorber bolt to 129 ft. lbs. (175 Nm).
24. Tighten the trailing arm-to-wheel knuckle nut to 66 ft. lbs. (90 Nm).
25. Tighten the toe link-to-knuckle nut to 59 ft. lbs. (80 Nm).
26. Install the brake disc.
27. Install the wheel and tire.
28. Check and if necessary, adjust the rear toe.

FORD

Transit Connect

18

BRAKES 18-10

ANTI-LOCK BRAKE SYSTEM (ABS) 18-10
General Information................18-10
Precautions........................18-10
Speed Sensors.......................18-10
Removal & Installation........18-10

BLEEDING THE BRAKE SYSTEM 18-12
Bleeding Procedure................18-12
Bleeding Procedure 18-12
Bleeding the ABS System ...18-13
Brake Line Bleeding............18-13
Fluid Fil Procedure.............18-13
Master Cylinder Bleeding ...18-13

FRONT DISC BRAKES........18-14
Brake Caliper..........................18-14
Removal & Installation........18-14
Disc Brake Pads.....................18-15
Removal & Installation........18-15

PARKING BRAKE..............18-17
Parking Brake Cables.............18-17
Adjustment 18-17
Parking Brake Shoes..............18-17
Removal & Installation........18-17

REAR DRUM BRAKES........18-15
Brake Drum 18-15
Removal & Installation........18-15
Brake Shoes 18-16
Adjustment 18-17
Removal & Installation........18-16

CHASSIS ELECTRICAL 18-17

AIR BAG (SUPPLEMENTAL RESTRAINT SYSTEM) 18-17
General Information................18-17
Arming the System 18-18
Clockspring Centering........18-19
Disarming the System.........18-18
Service Precautions...........18-17

DRIVE TRAIN 18-20

Automatic Transaxle Fluid.......18-20
Drain and Refill...................18-20
Front Halfshaft.........................18-20
Removal & Installation........18-20

ENGINE COOLING...........18-21

Engine Coolant........................18-21
Bleeding 18-22
Drain & Refill Procedure.....18-21
Flushing.............................18-22
Engine Fan 18-24
Removal & Installation........18-24
Radiator..................................18-24
Removal & Installation........18-24
Thermostat 18-24
Removal & Installation........18-24
Water Pump 18-25
Removal & Installation........18-25

ENGINE ELECTRICAL 18-26

BATTERY SYSTEM............18-26
Battery....................................18-26
Battery Reconnect/Relearn Procedure........................18-27
Removal & Installation........18-26

CHARGING SYSTEM 18-28
Alternator 18-28
Removal & Installation........18-28

IGNITION SYSTEM 18-29
Firing Order............................18-29
Ignition Coil 18-29
Removal & Installation........18-29
Ignition Timing.......................18-29
Adjustment 18-29
Spark Plugs............................18-29
Removal & Installation........18-29

STARTING SYSTEM 18-31
Starter 18-31
Removal & Installation........18-31

ENGINE MECHANICAL......18-31

Accessory Drive Belts 18-31
Accessory Belt Routing.......18-31
Adjustment 18-31
Inspection 18-31
Removal & Installation........18-31
Air Cleaner 18-31
Filter/Element Replacement....................18-32
Removal & Installation........18-31
Camshaft and Valve Lifters......18-32
Inspection 18-32
Removal & Installation........18-35
Catalytic Converter 18-37
Removal & Installation........18-37
Crankshaft Front Seal 18-39
Removal & Installation........18-39
Cylinder Head 18-39
Removal & Installation........18-39
Engine Oil & Filter 18-42
Replacement 18-42
Exhaust Manifold 18-42
Removal & Installation........18-42
Intake Manifold 18-43
Removal & Installation........18-43
Oil Pan 18-44
Removal & Installation........18-44
Oil Pump.................................18-45
Removal & Installation........18-45
Piston and Ring.......................18-46
Positioning 18-46
Rear Main Seal.......................18-47
Removal & Installation........18-47
Timing Chain & Sprockets.............................18-50
Removal & Installation........18-50
Timing Chain Front Cover.......18-48
Removal & Installation........18-48
Valve Covers 18-51
Removal & Installation........18-51
Valve Lash..............................18-52
Adjustment 18-52

ENGINE PERFORMANCE & EMISSION CONTROLS 18-53

Camshaft Position (CMP) Sensor 18-53
Location.............................18-53
Removal & Installation........18-53
Crankshaft Position (CKP) Sensor 18-53
Location.............................18-53
Removal & Installation........18-53
Cylinder Head Temperature (CHT) Sensor.......................18-54
Location.............................18-54
Removal & Installation........18-54

Heated Oxygen Sensor (HO2S) ... 18-54
Location ... 18-54
Removal & Installation ... 18-54
Knock Sensor (KS) ... 18-55
Location ... 18-55
Removal & Installation ... 18-55
Mass Air Flow (MAF) Sensor ... 18-55
Location ... 18-55
Removal & Installation ... 18-55
Output Shaft Speed (OSS) Sensor ... 18-55
Location ... 18-55
Removal & Installation ... 18-55
Powertrain Control Module (PCM) ... 18-56
Location ... 18-56
Parameter Reset Procedure ... 18-57
Programmable Module Installation (PMI) Procedure ... 18-58
Removal & Installation ... 18-56
Throttle Position Sensor (TPS) ... 18-58
Location ... 18-58
Removal & Installation ... 18-58

FUEL ... 18-58

GASOLINE FUEL INJECTION SYSTEM ... 18-58
Fuel Filter ... 18-59
Removal & Installation ... 18-59
Fuel Injectors ... 18-59
Removal & Installation ... 18-59
Fuel Pump Module ... 18-60
Removal & Installation ... 18-60
Fuel System Service Precautions ... 18-58
Fuel Tank ... 18-61
Draining ... 18-61
Removal & Installation ... 18-62
Idle Speed ... 18-63
Adjustment ... 18-63
Relieving Fuel System Pressure ... 18-58
Throttle Body ... 18-63
Removal & Installation ... 18-63

HEATING & AIR CONDITIONING SYSTEM ... 18-64
Blower Motor ... 18-64
Removal & Installation ... 18-64
Heater Core ... 18-64
Removal & Installation ... 18-64

PRECAUTIONS ... 18-10

SPECIFICATIONS AND MAINTENANCE CHARTS ... 18-3
Brake Specifications ... 18-7
Camshaft Specifications ... 18-5
Capacities ... 18-4
Crankshaft and Connecting Rod Specifications ... 18-5
Engine and Vehicle Identification ... 18-3
Engine Tune-Up Specifications ... 18-3
Fluid Specifications ... 18-4
General Engine Specifications ... 18-3
Piston and Ring Specifications ... 18-5
Scheduled Maintenance Intervals ... 18-8
Tire, Wheel and Ball Joint Specifications ... 18-7
Torque Specifications ... 18-6
Valve Specifications ... 18-4
Wheel Alignment ... 18-6

STEERING ... 18-66
Power Steering Gear ... 18-66
Removal & Installation ... 18-66
Power Steering Pump ... 18-67
Bleeding ... 18-69
Fluid Fill Procedure ... 18-69
Removal & Installation ... 18-67

SUSPENSION ... 18-70

FRONT SUSPENSION ... 18-70
Control Links ... 18-70
Removal & Installation ... 18-70
Lower Ball Joint ... 18-70
Removal & Installation ... 18-70
Lower Control Arm ... 18-70
Removal & Installation ... 18-70
Stabilizer Bar ... 18-71
Removal & Installation ... 18-71
Steering Knuckle ... 18-73
Removal & Installation ... 18-73
Strut & Spring Assembly ... 18-75
Overhaul ... 18-76
Removal & Installation ... 18-75
Wheel Bearings ... 18-76
Adjustment ... 18-78
Removal & Installation ... 18-76

REAR SUSPENSION ... 18-78
Leaf Spring ... 18-78
Removal & Installation ... 18-78
Shock Absorbers ... 18-79
Removal & Installation ... 18-79
Testing ... 18-80
Stabilizer Bar & Link ... 18-80
Removal & Installation ... 18-80
Wheel Bearings ... 18-81
Adjustment ... 18-81
Removal & Installation ... 18-81
Wheel Spindle ... 18-81
Removal & Installation ... 18-81

SPECIFICATIONS AND MAINTENANCE CHARTS

ENGINE AND VEHICLE IDENTIFICATION

Engine						
Code ①	Liters (cc)	Cu. In.	Cyl.	Fuel Sys.	Engine Type	Eng. Mfg.
N	2.0	122	4	SFI	DOHC	Ford

Model Year	
Code ②	Year
A	2010
B	2011

SFI: Sequential Fuel Injection

DOHC: Double Overhead Camshafts

① 8th position of VIN

② 10th position of VIN

25759_TRAN_C0001

GENERAL ENGINE SPECIFICATIONS

All measurements are given in inches.

Year	Model	Engine Displacement Liters (VIN)	Fuel System Type	Net Horsepower @ rpm	Net Torque @ rpm (ft. lbs.)	Bore x Stroke (in.)	Com-pression Ratio	Oil Pressure @ rpm
2010	Transit Connect	2.0 (N)	SFI	136@6,300	128@4,750	3.44 x 3.27	10.0:1	29-39@2,000
2011	Transit Connect	2.0 (N)	SFI	136@6,300	128@4,750	3.44 x 3.27	10.0:1	29-39@2,000

25759_TRAN_C0002

ENGINE TUNE-UP SPECIFICATIONS

Year	Engine Displacement Liters	Engine ID/VIN	Spark Plug Gap (in.)	Ignition Timing (deg.)		Fuel Pump (psi)	Idle Speed (rpm)		Valve Clearance	
				MT	AT		MT	AT	Intake	Exhaust
2010	2.0	N	0.049-0.053	10B	10B	55	①	①	0.008-0.011	0.010-0.013
2011	2.0	N	0.049-0.053	10B	10B	55	①	①	0.008-0.011	0.010-0.013

NOTE: The Vehicle Emission Control Information label often reflects specification changes made during production.
The label figures must be used if they differ from those in this chart.

B: Before Top Dead Center

① Ignition timing is preset and cannot be adjusted

25759_TRAN_C0003

CAPACITIES

Year	Model	Engine Displacement Liters (VIN)	Engine Oil with Filter (qts.)	Transmission/axle (pts.) Auto.	Transmission/axle (pts.) Manual	Drive Axle (pts.) Front	Drive Axle (pts.) Rear	Transfer Case (pts.)	Fuel Tank (gal.)	Cooling System (qts.)
2010	Transit Connect	2.0 (N)	4.5	14.0	N/A	N/A	N/A	N/A	15.4	6.1
2011	Transit Connect	2.0 (N)	4.5	14.0	N/A	N/A	N/A	N/A	15.4	6.1

NOTE: All capacities are approximate. Add fluid gradually and ensure a proper fluid level is obtained.

N/A: Not Applicable

25759_TRAN_C0004

FLUID SPECIFICATIONS

Year	Model	Engine Disp. Liters	Engine Oil	Manual Trans.	Auto. Trans.	Drive Axle Front	Drive Axle Rear	Power Steering Fluid	Brake Master Cylinder	Cooling System
2010	Transit Connect	2.0	5W-20	N/A	Mercon® LV ATF	N/A	N/A	Mercon® V ATF	DOT 4	①
2011	Transit Connect	2.0	5W-20	N/A	Mercon® LV ATF	N/A	N/A	Mercon® V ATF	DOT 4	①

DOT: Department Of Transportation

N/A: Not Applicable

① Motorcraft® Specialty Orange Engine Coolant with Bittering Agent or equivalent

25759_TRAN_C0005

VALVE SPECIFICATIONS

Year	Engine Displacement Liters	Engine ID/VIN	Seat Angle (deg.)	Face Angle (deg.)	Spring Test Pressure (lbs. @ in.)	Spring Free-Length (in.)	Spring Installed Height (in.)	Stem-to-Guide Clearance (in.) Intake	Stem-to-Guide Clearance (in.) Exhaust	Stem Diameter (in.) Intake	Stem Diameter (in.) Exhaust
2010	2.0	N	45	45	①	1.768	1.492	0.0001	0.0001	0.2153-0.2159	0.2151-0.2157
2011	2.0	N	45	45	①	1.768	1.492	0.0001	0.0001	0.2153-0.2159	0.2151-0.2157

① Intake: 0.35 inch@97.03 lbs.; Exhaust: 0.29 inch@93.34 lbs.

25759_TRAN_C0006

CAMSHAFT SPECIFICATIONS

All measurements in inches unless noted

Year	Engine Displacement Liters	Engine Code/VIN	Journal Diameter	Brg. Oil Clearance	Shaft End-play	Runout	Journal Bore	Lobe Height Intake	Lobe Height Exhaust
2010	2.0	N	0.9820-0.9830	0.0010-0.0030	0.0030-0.0090	0.0010	0.9840-0.9850	0.3240	0.3070
2011	2.0	N	0.9820-0.9830	0.0010-0.0030	0.0030-0.0090	0.0010	0.9840-0.9850	0.3240	0.3070

25759_TRAN_C0007

CRANKSHAFT AND CONNECTING ROD SPECIFICATIONS

All measurements are given in inches.

Year	Engine Displacement Liters	Engine ID/VIN	Crankshaft Main Brg. Journal Dia.	Crankshaft Main Brg. Oil Clearance	Crankshaft Shaft End-play	Crankshaft Thrust on No.	Connecting Rod Journal Diameter	Connecting Rod Oil Clearance	Connecting Rod Side Clearance
2010	2.0	N	2.0460-2.0470	0.0007-0.0018	0.0080-0.0160	3	1.9670-1.9680	0.0010-0.0020	0.0760-0.1200
2011	2.0	N	2.0460-2.0470	0.0007-0.0018	0.0080-0.0160	3	1.9670-1.9680	0.0010-0.0020	0.0760-0.1200

25759_TRAN_C0008

PISTON AND RING SPECIFICATIONS

All measurements are given in inches.

Year	Engine Displacement Liters	Engine ID/VIN	Piston Clearance	Ring Gap Top Compression	Ring Gap Bottom Compression	Ring Gap Oil Control	Ring Side Clearance Top Compression	Ring Side Clearance Bottom Compression	Ring Side Clearance Oil Control
2010	2.0	N	0.0009-0.0017	0.0060-0.0120	0.0120-0.0180	0.0070-0.0270	0.0008-0.0013	0.0004-0.0011	0.0025-0.0054
2011	2.0	N	0.0009-0.0017	0.0060-0.0120	0.0120-0.0180	0.0070-0.0270	0.0008-0.0013	0.0004-0.0011	0.0025-0.0054

25759_TRAN_C0009

TORQUE SPECIFICATIONS

All readings in ft. lbs.

Year	Engine Disp. Liters	Engine ID/VIN	Cylinder Head Bolts	Main Bearing Bolts	Rod Bearing Bolts	Crankshaft Damper Bolts	Flywheel Bolts	Manifold Intake	Manifold Exhaust	Spark Plugs	Oil Pan Drain Plug
2010	2.0	N	①	②	③	④	⑤	13	⑥	9	21
2011	2.0	N	①	②	③	④	⑤	13	⑥	9	21

① Step 1: 44 inch lbs.
Step 2: 133 inch lbs.
Step 3: 33 ft. lbs.
Step 4: Plus 90 degrees
Step 5: Plus 90 degrees

② Apply engine oil to bolts
Step 1: 44 inch lbs.
Step 2: 18 ft. lbs.
Step 3: Plus 90 degrees

③ Step 1: 21 ft. lbs.
Step 2: Plus 90 degrees

④ Step 1: 74 ft. lbs.
Step 2: Plus 90 degrees

⑤ Step 1: 37 ft. lbs.
Step 2: 50 ft. lbs.
Step 3: 83 ft. lbs.

⑥ Step 1: 35 ft. lbs.
Step 2: 35 ft. lbs.

25759_TRAN_C0010

WHEEL ALIGNMENT

Year	Model		Caster Range (+/-Deg.)	Caster Preferred Setting (Deg.)	Camber Range (+/-Deg.)	Camber Preferred Setting (Deg.)	Toe-in (in.)
2010	Transit Connect	F	1.00	1.80	1.00	-0.61	0.43 +/- 0.15
		R	N/A	N/A	1.00	-1.00	0.30 +/- 0.30
2011	Transit Connect	F	1.00	1.80	1.00	-0.61	0.43 +/- 0.15
		R	N/A	N/A	1.00	-1.00	0.30 +/- 0.30

N/A: Not Applicable

25759_TRAN_C0011

TIRE, WHEEL AND BALL JOINT SPECIFICATIONS

Year	Model	OEM Tires Standard	OEM Tires Optional	Tire Pressures (psi) Front	Tire Pressures (psi) Rear	Wheel Size	Ball Joint Inspection	Lug Nut (ft. lbs.)
2010	Transit Connect	P205/65/R15	NA	①	①	NA	②	66
2011	Transit Connect	P205/65/R15	NA	①	①	NA	②	66

OEM: Original Equipment Manufacturer

PSI: Pounds Per Square Inch

NA: Information not available

① Always refer to the owner's manual and/or vehicle label

② Replace if ball joint deflection is more than 0.008 inch

25759_TRAN_C0012

BRAKE SPECIFICATIONS

All measurements in inches unless noted

Year	Model		Brake Disc Original Thickness	Brake Disc Minimum Thickness	Brake Disc Max. Runout	Brake Drum Diameter Original Inside Diameter	Brake Drum Diameter Max. Wear Limit	Brake Drum Diameter Maximum Machine Diameter	Minimum Pad/Lining Thickness Front	Minimum Pad/Lining Thickness Rear	Brake Caliper Bracket Bolts (ft. lbs.)	Brake Caliper Guide Pin Bolts (ft. lbs.)
2010	Transit Connect	F	N/S	0.866	0.002	N/A	N/A	N/A	0.078	N/A	98	22
		R	N/A	N/A	N/A	N/S	9.062	N/S	N/A	0.039	N/A	N/A
2011	Transit Connect	F	N/S	0.866	0.002	N/A	N/A	N/A	0.078	N/A	98	22
		R	N/A	N/A	N/A	N/S	9.062	N/S	N/A	0.039	N/A	N/A

F: Front

R: Rear

N/A: Not Applicable

N/S: Not Specified

25759_TRAN_C0013

SCHEDULED MAINTENANCE INTERVALS

TRANSIT CONNECT - NORMAL SERVICE

		VEHICLE MILEAGE INTERVAL (x1000)													
TO BE SERVICED	SERVICE ACTION	7.5	15	22.5	30	37.5	45	52.5	60	67.5	75.0	82.5	90.0	97.5	10.5
Accessory drive belt	Replace	At 150,000 miles													
Accessory drive belt	Inspect	✓	✓	✓	✓	✓	✓	✓	✓	✓	✓	✓	✓	✓	✓
Auto trans. fluid & filter	Replace	At 150,000 miles													
Battery performance	Inspect	✓	✓	✓	✓	✓	✓	✓	✓	✓	✓	✓	✓	✓	✓
Brake system (Pads/shoes/rotors/drums, brake lines and hoses, and parking brake system)	Inspect		✓		✓		✓		✓		✓		✓		✓
Cooling system, hoses, clamps	Inspect		✓		✓		✓		✓		✓		✓		✓
Engine air filter	Replace				✓				✓				✓		
Engine air filter	Inspect	✓	✓	✓	✓	✓	✓	✓	✓	✓	✓	✓	✓	✓	✓
Engine coolant	Replace														√
Engine oil & filter	Replace	✓	✓	✓	✓	✓	✓	✓	✓	✓	✓	✓	✓	✓	✓
Exhaust system (Leaks, damage, loose parts and foreign material)	Inspect		✓		✓		✓		✓		✓		✓		✓
Fluid levels (all)	Top off	✓	✓	✓	✓	✓	✓	✓	✓	✓	✓	✓	✓	✓	✓
Halfshaft boots	Inspect		✓		✓		✓		✓		✓		✓		✓
Inspect wheels and related	Inspect	✓	✓	✓	✓	✓	✓	✓	✓	✓	✓	✓	✓	✓	✓
Oil and fluid leaks	Inspect	✓	✓	✓	✓	✓	✓	✓	✓	✓	✓	✓	✓	✓	✓
Radiator, coolers, heater and	Inspect	✓	✓	✓	✓	✓	✓	✓	✓	✓	✓	✓	✓	✓	✓
Rotate tires, inspect tread wear, measure tread depth and check pressure	Rotate/ Inspect	✓	✓	✓	✓	✓	✓	✓	✓	✓	✓	✓	✓	✓	✓
Spark plugs	Replace														√
Steering linkage, ball joints, suspension, tie-rod ends, driveshaft and u-joints: lubricate	Inspect/ Lubricate		✓		✓		✓		✓		✓		✓		✓
Suspension components for leaks and damage	Inspect	✓	✓	✓	✓	✓	✓	✓	✓	✓	✓	✓	✓	✓	✓
Torque rear U-bolts	Tighten		✓		✓		✓		✓		✓		✓		✓
Windshield for cracks, chips	Inspect	✓	✓	✓	✓	✓	✓	✓	✓	✓	✓	✓	✓	✓	✓
Windshield wiper spray and	Inspect	✓	✓	✓	✓	✓	✓	✓	✓	✓	✓	✓	✓	✓	✓
Cabin air filter (If equipped)	Replace		✓		✓		✓		✓		✓		✓		✓

25759_TRAN_C0014

SCHEDULED MAINTENANCE INTERVALS

FORD TRANSIT CONNECT - SEVERE SERVICE

TO BE SERVICED	SERVICE ACTION	VEHICLE MILEAGE INTERVAL (x1000)											
		5	10	15	20	25	30	35	40	45	50	55	60
Accessory drive belt	Inspect	✓	✓	✓	✓	✓	✓	✓	✓	✓	✓	✓	✓
Accessory drive belt	Replace	At 150,000 miles											
Automatic transaxle fluid & filter	Replace						✓						✓
Battery performance	Inspect	✓	✓	✓	✓	✓	✓	✓	✓	✓	✓	✓	✓
Brake system (Pads/shoes/rotors/drums, brake lines and hoses, and parking brake system)	Inspect	✓	✓	✓	✓	✓	✓	✓	✓	✓	✓	✓	✓
Cooling system, hoses, clamps & coolant strength	Inspect	✓	✓	✓	✓	✓	✓	✓	✓	✓	✓	✓	✓
Engine air filter	Inspect	✓	✓	✓	✓	✓	✓	✓	✓	✓	✓	✓	✓
Cabin air filter (If equipped)	Inspect	✓	✓	✓	✓	✓	✓	✓	✓	✓	✓	✓	✓
Engine coolant	Replace	At 105,000 miles											
Engine oil & filter	Replace	✓	✓	✓	✓	✓	✓	✓	✓	✓	✓	✓	✓
Exhaust system (Leaks, damage, loose parts and foreign material)	Inspect	✓	✓	✓	✓	✓	✓	✓	✓	✓	✓	✓	✓
Fluid levels (all)	Top off	✓	✓	✓	✓	✓	✓	✓	✓	✓	✓	✓	✓
Halfshaft boots	Inspect	✓	✓	✓	✓	✓	✓	✓	✓	✓	✓	✓	✓
Inspect wheels and related components for abnomal noise, wear, looseness or drag	Inspect	✓	✓	✓	✓	✓	✓	✓	✓	✓	✓	✓	✓
Oil and fluid leaks	Inspect	✓	✓	✓	✓	✓	✓	✓	✓	✓	✓	✓	✓
Radiator, coolers, heater and air conditioning hoses	Inspect	✓	✓	✓	✓	✓	✓	✓	✓	✓	✓	✓	✓
Rotate tires, inspect tread wear, measure tread depth and check pressure	Inspect/ Rotate	✓	✓	✓	✓	✓	✓	✓	✓	✓	✓	✓	✓
Spark plugs	Replace												✓
Steering linkage, ball joints, suspension and tie-rod ends, lubricate if equipped with greases fittings	Inspect/ Lubricate	✓	✓	✓	✓	✓	✓	✓	✓	✓	✓	✓	✓
Suspension components for leaks and damage	Inspect	✓	✓	✓	✓	✓	✓	✓	✓	✓	✓	✓	✓
Torque rear U-bolts	Tighten			✓			✓			✓			✓
Windshield for cracks, chips and pitting	Inspect	✓	✓	✓	✓	✓	✓	✓	✓	✓	✓	✓	✓
Windshield wiper spray and wiper operation	Inspect	✓	✓	✓	✓	✓	✓	✓	✓	✓	✓	✓	✓

For extensive idling and or low speed driving, change engine oil and filter every 5,000 miles, 6 months or 200 hours of engine operation.

25759_TRAN_C0015

PRECAUTIONS

Before servicing any vehicle, please be sure to read all of the following precautions, which deal with personal safety, prevention of component damage, and important points to take into consideration when servicing a motor vehicle:

- Never open, service or drain the radiator or cooling system when the engine is hot; serious burns can occur from the steam and hot coolant.
- Observe all applicable safety precautions when working around fuel. Whenever servicing the fuel system, always work in a well-ventilated area. Do not allow fuel spray or vapors to come in contact with a spark, open flame, or excessive heat (a hot drop light, for example). Keep a dry chemical fire extinguisher near the work area. Always keep fuel in a container specifically designed for fuel storage; also, always properly seal fuel containers to avoid the possibility of fire or explosion. Refer to the additional fuel system precautions later in this section.
- Fuel injection systems often remain pressurized, even after the engine has been turned **OFF**. The fuel system pressure must be relieved before disconnecting any fuel lines. Failure to do so may result in fire and/or personal injury.
- Brake fluid often contains polyglycol ethers and polyglycols. Avoid contact with the eyes and wash your hands thoroughly after handling brake fluid. If you do get brake fluid in your eyes, flush your eyes with clean, running water for 15 minutes. If eye irritation persists, or if you have taken brake fluid internally, IMMEDIATELY seek medical assistance.
- The EPA warns that prolonged contact with used engine oil may cause a number of skin disorders, including cancer. You should make every effort to minimize your exposure to used engine oil. Protective gloves should be worn when changing oil. Wash your hands and any other exposed skin areas as soon as possible after exposure to used engine oil. Soap and water, or waterless hand cleaner should be used.
- All new vehicles are now equipped with an air bag system, often referred to as a Supplemental Restraint System (SRS) or Supplemental Inflatable Restraint (SIR) system. The system must be disabled before performing service on or around system components, steering column, instrument panel components, wiring and sensors. Failure to follow safety and disabling procedures could result in accidental air bag deployment, possible personal injury and unnecessary system repairs.
- Always wear safety goggles when working with, or around, the air bag system. When carrying a non-deployed air bag, be sure the bag and trim cover are pointed away from your body. When placing a non-deployed air bag on a work surface, always face the bag and trim cover upward, away from the surface. This will reduce the motion of the module if it is accidentally deployed. Refer to the additional air bag system precautions later in this section.
- Clean, high quality brake fluid from a sealed container is essential to the safe and proper operation of the brake system. You should always buy the correct type of brake fluid for your vehicle. If the brake fluid becomes contaminated, completely flush the system with new fluid. Never reuse any brake fluid. Any brake fluid that is removed from the system should be discarded. Also, do not allow any brake fluid to come in contact with a painted surface; it will damage the paint.
- Never operate the engine without the proper amount and type of engine oil; doing so WILL result in severe engine damage.
- Timing belt maintenance is extremely important. Many models utilize an interference-type, non-freewheeling engine. If the timing belt breaks, the valves in the cylinder head may strike the pistons, causing potentially serious (also time-consuming and expensive) engine damage. Refer to the maintenance interval charts for the recommended replacement interval for the timing belt, and to the timing belt section for belt replacement and inspection.
- Disconnecting the negative battery cable on some vehicles may interfere with the functions of the on-board computer system(s) and may require the computer to undergo a relearning process once the negative battery cable is reconnected.
- When servicing drum brakes, only disassemble and assemble one side at a time, leaving the remaining side intact for reference.
- Only an MVAC-trained, EPA-certified automotive technician should service the air conditioning system or its components.

BRAKES

ANTI-LOCK BRAKE SYSTEM (ABS)

GENERAL INFORMATION

PRECAUTIONS

- Certain components within the ABS system are not intended to be serviced or repaired individually.
- Do not use rubber hoses or other parts not specifically specified for and ABS system. When using repair kits, replace all parts included in the kit. Partial or incorrect repair may lead to functional problems and require the replacement of components.
- Lubricate rubber parts with clean, fresh brake fluid to ease assembly. Do not use shop air to clean parts; damage to rubber components may result.
- Use only DOT 3 brake fluid from an unopened container.
- If any hydraulic component or line is removed or replaced, it may be necessary to bleed the entire system.
- A clean repair area is essential. Always clean the reservoir and cap thoroughly before removing the cap. The slightest amount of dirt in the fluid may plug an orifice and impair the system function. Perform repairs after components have been thoroughly cleaned; use only denatured alcohol to clean components. Do not allow ABS components to come into contact with any substance containing mineral oil; this includes used shop rags.
- The Anti-Lock control unit is a microprocessor similar to other computer units in the vehicle. Ensure that the ignition switch is **OFF** before removing or installing controller harnesses. Avoid static electricity discharge at or near the controller.
- If any arc welding is to be done on the vehicle, the control unit should be unplugged before welding operations begin.

SPEED SENSORS

REMOVAL & INSTALLATION

Front Speed Sensor

See Figure 1.

1. Before servicing the vehicle, refer to the Precautions Section.
2. Raise and safely support the vehicle.
3. Remove the wheel and tire.
4. Remove the wheel speed sensor bolt.

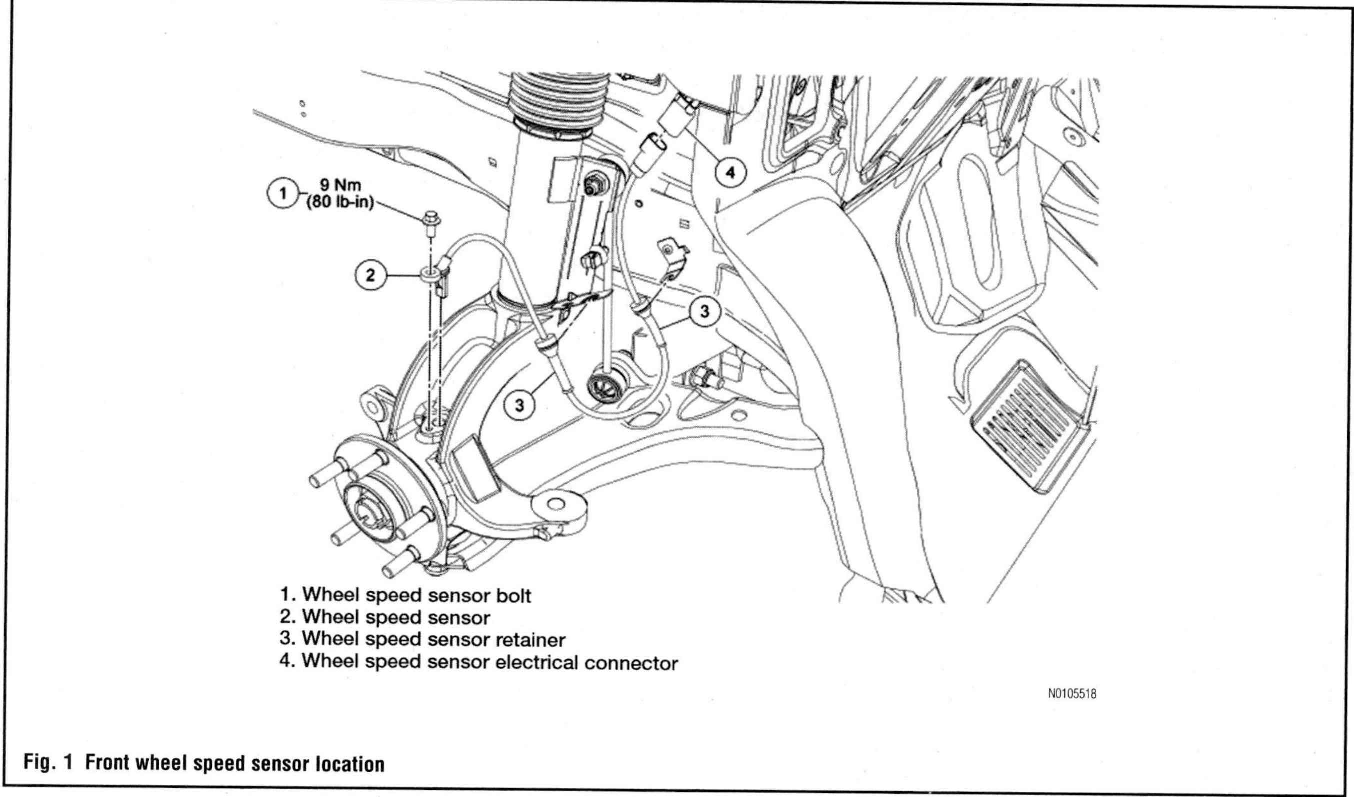

Fig. 1 Front wheel speed sensor location

5. Disconnect the wheel speed sensor electrical connector.
   - Remove the sensor by pulling the sensor grommets out of the clips.

To install:

6. Installation is the reverse of the removal procedure.
7. Tighten the wheel speed sensor bolt to 80 inch lbs. (9 Nm).

Rear Speed Sensor

See Figure 2.

1. Before servicing the vehicle, refer to the Precautions Section.
2. Raise and safely support the vehicle.
3. Place the vehicle in NEUTRAL.
4. Remove the wheel speed sensor bolt.

➡Not all the clips are part of the sensor assembly and may not be reusable.

5. Disconnect the wheel speed sensor electrical connector.
   - Remove the sensor by detaching the pin-type retainer and pulling the sensor grommets out of the clips.

To install:

6. Installation is the reverse of the removal procedure.
7. Tighten the wheel speed sensor bolt to 80 inch lbs. (9 Nm).

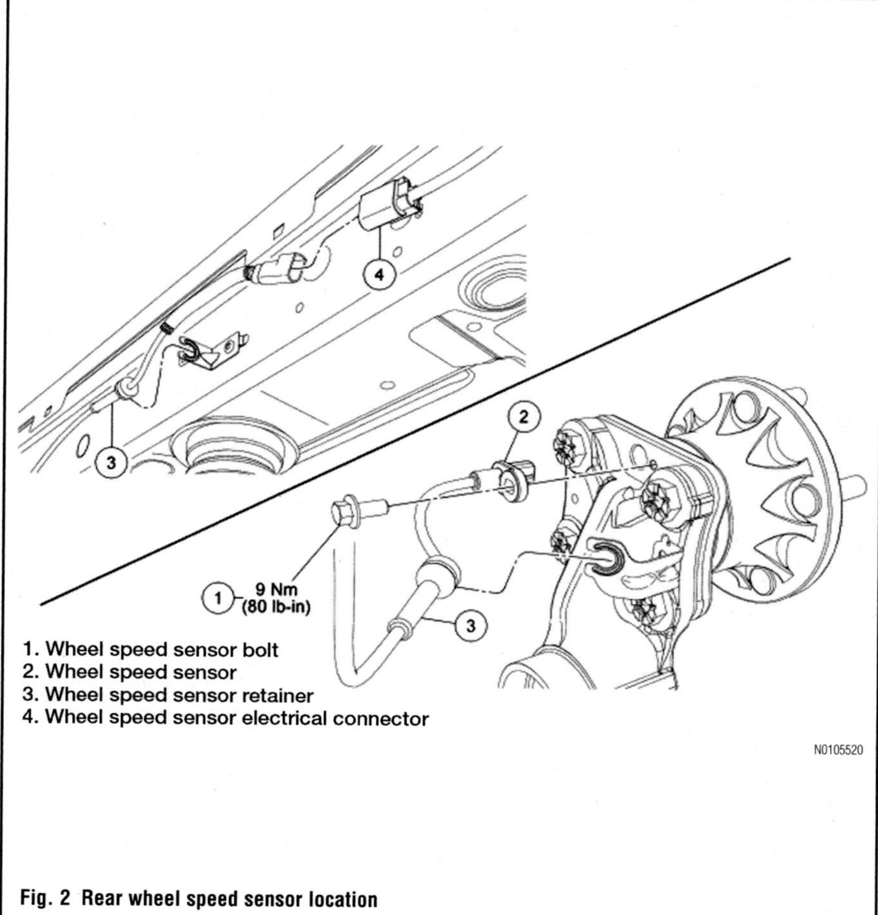

Fig. 2 Rear wheel speed sensor location

BLEEDING PROCEDURE

BLEEDING PROCEDURE

Manual Bleeding

WARNING

Do not use any fluid other than clean brake fluid meeting manufacturer's specification. Additionally, do not use brake fluid that has been previously drained. Following these instructions will help prevent system contamination, brake component damage, and the risk of serious personal injury.

CAUTION

Brake fluid contains polyglycol ethers and polyglycols. Avoid contact with the eyes. Wash hands thoroughly after handling. If brake fluid contacts the eyes, flush the eyes for 15 minutes with cold running water. Get medical attention if irritation persists. If taken internally, drink water and induce vomiting. Get medical attention immediately. Failure to follow these instructions may result in personal injury.

WARNING

Do not allow the brake master cylinder to run dry during the bleeding operation. The master cylinder may be damaged if operated without fluid, resulting in degraded braking performance.

WARNING

Do not spill brake fluid on painted or plastic surfaces or damage to the surface may occur. If brake fluid is spilled onto a painted or plastic surface, immediately wash the surface with water.

➡Pressure bleeding the brake system is preferred to manual bleeding.

1. Before servicing the vehicle, refer to the Precautions Section.
2. Clean all dirt from around the brake fluid reservoir cap and remove the filler cap.
3. Fill the brake master cylinder reservoir with clean, specified brake fluid.
4. Remove the RR bleeder screw cap and place a box-end wrench on the bleeder screw. Attach a rubber drain hose to the RR bleeder screw and submerge the free end of the hose in a container partially filled with clean, specified brake fluid.
5. Have an assistant pump and then hold firm pressure on the brake pedal.
6. Loosen the RR bleeder screw until a stream of brake fluid comes out. While an assistant maintains pressure on the brake pedal, tighten the RR bleeder screw.
7. Repeat until clear, bubble-free fluid comes out.
8. Refill the brake master cylinder reservoir as necessary.
9. Tighten the RR bleeder screw to 71 inch lbs. (8 Nm).
10. Remove the rubber hose and install the bleeder screw cap.
11. Repeat the procedure for the LR, RF, and then LF bleeder screws.

Pressure Bleeding

WARNING

Do not use any fluid other than clean brake fluid meeting manufacturer's specification. Additionally, do not use brake fluid that has been previously drained. Following these instructions will help prevent system contamination, brake component damage, and the risk of serious personal injury.

CAUTION

Brake fluid contains polyglycol ethers and polyglycols. Avoid contact with the eyes. Wash hands thoroughly after handling. If brake fluid contacts the eyes, flush the eyes for 15 minutes with cold running water. Get medical attention if irritation persists. If taken internally, drink water and induce vomiting. Get medical attention immediately. Failure to follow these instructions may result in personal injury.

WARNING

Do not allow the brake master cylinder to run dry during the bleeding operation. The master cylinder may be damaged if operated without fluid, resulting in degraded braking performance.

WARNING

Do not spill brake fluid on painted or plastic surfaces or damage to the surface may occur. If brake fluid is spilled onto a painted or plastic surface, immediately wash the surface with water.

➡Pressure bleeding the brake system is preferred to manual bleeding.

1. Before servicing the vehicle, refer to the Precautions Section.
2. Clean all dirt from the brake master cylinder filler cap and remove the filler cap.
3. Fill the brake master cylinder reservoir with clean, specified brake fluid.

➡Master cylinder pressure bleeder adapter tools are available from various manufacturers of pressure bleeding equipment. Follow the instructions of the manufacturer when installing the adapter.

4. Install the bleeder adapter to the brake master cylinder reservoir, and attach the bleeder tank hose to the fitting on the adapter.
5. Make sure the bleeder tank contains enough clean, specified brake fluid to complete the bleeding operation.
6. Open the valve on the bleeder tank.
7. Apply 15–58 psi (100–400 kPa) to the brake system.
8. Remove the RR bleeder screw cap and place a box-end wrench on the bleeder screw. Attach a rubber drain hose to the RR bleeder screw and submerge the free end of the hose in a container partially filled with clean, specified brake fluid.
9. Loosen the RR bleeder screw. Leave open until clear, bubble-free brake fluid flows, then tighten the RR bleeder screw to 71 inch lbs. (8 Nm).
10. Continue bleeding the rest of the system, going in order from the LR bleeder screw to the RF bleeder screw, ending with the LF bleeder screw.
11. Tighten the bleeder screws to 71 inch lbs. (8 Nm).
12. Close the bleeder tank valve. Remove the tank hose from the adapter and remove the adapter. Fill the reservoir with clean, specified brake fluid and install the reservoir cap.

MASTER CYLINDER BLEEDING

See Figure 3.

**** WARNING**

Do not use any fluid other than clean brake fluid meeting manufacturer's specification. Additionally, do not use brake fluid that has been previously drained. Following these instructions will help prevent system contamination, brake component damage, and the risk of serious personal injury.

**** CAUTION**

Brake fluid contains polyglycol ethers and polyglycols. Avoid contact with the eyes. Wash hands thoroughly after handling. If brake fluid contacts the eyes, flush the eyes for 15 minutes with cold running water. Get medical attention if irritation persists. If taken internally, drink water and induce vomiting. Get medical attention immediately. Failure to follow these instructions may result in personal injury.

**** WARNING**

Do not allow the brake master cylinder to run dry during the bleeding operation. The master cylinder may be damaged if operated without fluid, resulting in degraded braking performance.

**** WARNING**

Do not spill brake fluid on painted or plastic surfaces or damage to the surface may occur. If brake fluid is spilled onto a painted or plastic surface, immediately wash the surface with water.

➡When the brake master cylinder has been installed new or the system has been emptied or partially emptied, it must be primed to prevent air from entering the system.

1. Before servicing the vehicle, refer to the Precautions Section.
2. Remove the battery tray.
3. Remove the battery ground cable bolt and position the cable aside.
4. Loosen the Battery Junction Box (BJB) mounting screw.
5. Press the locking tab, disconnect the BJB from the bracket and position the BJB aside.

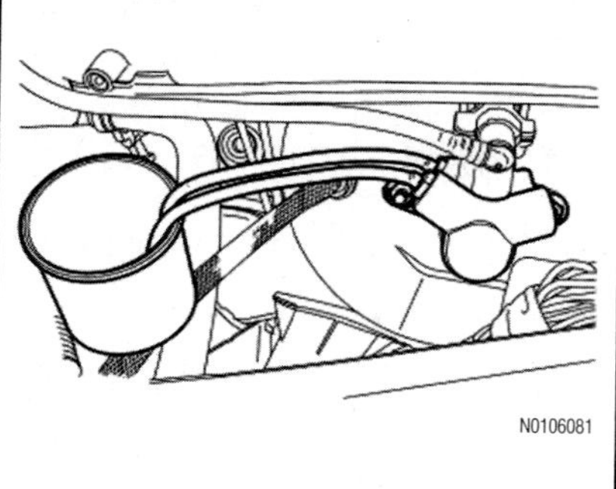

Fig. 3 Short brake tubes installed for master cylinder bleeding

➡The brake tubes must be installed in the same position and orientation as removed.

6. Disconnect the brake tube fittings at the master cylinder. Loosen the master cylinder brake tube fittings at the Hydraulic Control Unit (HCU) to allow the brake tubes to move without being damaged.
7. Install short brake tubes onto the primary and secondary ports with the ends submerged in a container partially filled with clean, specified brake fluid.
8. Have an assistant pump the brake pedal until clear fluid flows from the brake tubes without air bubbles.
9. Remove the short brake tubes, and install the master cylinder brake tubes. Tighten the brake tube fittings to 17 ft. lbs. (23 Nm).
10. Position the BJB and engage the locking tab.
11. Tighten the BJB mounting screw.
12. Position the battery ground cable and install the bolt. Tighten the bolt to 89 inch lbs. (10 Nm).
13. Install the battery tray.
14. Bleed the brake system. Refer to Bleeding The Brake System, Bleeding Procedure.

BRAKE LINE BLEEDING

Refer to Bleeding Procedure, Manual Bleeding or Pressure Bleeding.

BLEEDING THE ABS SYSTEM

**** WARNING**

Do not use any fluid other than clean brake fluid meeting manufacturer's specification. Additionally, do not use brake fluid that has been previously drained. Following these instructions will help prevent system contamination, brake component damage, and the risk of serious personal injury.

**** CAUTION**

Brake fluid contains polyglycol ethers and polyglycols. Avoid contact with the eyes. Wash hands thoroughly after handling. If brake fluid contacts the eyes, flush the eyes for 15 minutes with cold running water. Get medical attention if irritation persists. If taken internally, drink water and induce vomiting. Get medical attention immediately. Failure to follow these instructions may result in personal injury.

**** WARNING**

Do not allow the brake master cylinder to run dry during the bleeding operation. Master cylinder may be damaged if operated without fluid, resulting in degraded braking performance.

**** WARNING**

Do not spill brake fluid on painted or plastic surfaces or damage to the surface may occur. If brake fluid is spilled onto a painted or plastic surface, immediately wash the surface with water.

➡Pressure bleeding the brake system is preferred to manual bleeding.

1. Before servicing the vehicle, refer to the Precautions Section.
2. Follow the Pressure Bleeding or Manual Bleeding procedure steps to bleed the system.
3. Connect the scan tool and follow the ABS Service Bleed instructions.
4. Repeat the Pressure Bleeding or Manual Bleeding procedure steps to bleed the system.

FLUID FILL PROCEDURE

**** WARNING**

Do not use any fluid other than clean brake fluid meeting manufacturer's specification. Additionally, do not use brake fluid that has been previously drained. Following these instructions will help prevent system contamination, brake component damage, and the risk of serious personal injury.

✲✲ CAUTION

Brake fluid contains polyglycol ethers and polyglycols. Avoid contact with the eyes. Wash hands thoroughly after handling. If brake fluid contacts the eyes, flush the eyes for 15 minutes with cold running water. Get medical attention if irritation persists. If taken internally, drink water and induce vomiting. Get medical attention immediately. Failure to follow these instructions may result in personal injury.

✲✲ WARNING

Do not allow the brake master cylinder to run dry during the bleeding operation. Master cylinder may be damaged if operated without fluid, resulting in degraded braking performance.

✲✲ WARNING

Do not spill brake fluid on painted or plastic surfaces or damage to the surface may occur. If brake fluid is spilled onto a painted or plastic surface, immediately wash the surface with water.

1. Before servicing the vehicle, refer to the Precautions Section.
2. Clean all dirt from around the brake fluid reservoir cap and remove the filler cap.
3. Fill the brake master cylinder reservoir with clean, specified brake fluid.

BRAKES

FRONT DISC BRAKES

✲✲ CAUTION

Dust and dirt accumulating on brake parts during normal use may contain asbestos fibers from production or aftermarket brake linings. Breathing excessive concentrations of asbestos fibers can cause serious bodily harm. Exercise care when servicing brake parts. Do not sand or grind brake lining unless equipment used is designed to contain the dust residue. Do not clean brake parts with compressed air or by dry brushing. Cleaning should be done by dampening the brake components with a fine mist of water, then wiping the brake components clean with a dampened cloth. Dispose of cloth and all residue containing asbestos fibers in an impermeable container with the appropriate label. Follow practices prescribed by the Occupational Safety and Health Administration (OSHA) and the Environmental Protection Agency (EPA) for the handling, processing, and disposing of dust or debris that may contain asbestos fibers.

✲✲ WARNING

Do not use any fluid other than clean brake fluid meeting manufacturer's specification. Additionally, do not use brake fluid that has been previously drained. Following these instructions will help prevent system contamination, brake component damage, and the risk of serious personal injury.

✲✲ CAUTION

Brake fluid contains polyglycol ethers and polyglycols. Avoid contact with the eyes. Wash hands thoroughly after handling. If brake fluid contacts the eyes, flush the eyes for 15 minutes with cold running water. Get medical attention if irritation persists. If taken internally, drink water and induce vomiting. Get medical attention immediately. Failure to follow these instructions may result in personal injury.

✲✲ WARNING

Do not spill brake fluid on painted or plastic surfaces or damage to the surface may occur. If brake fluid is spilled onto a painted or plastic surface, immediately wash the surface with water.

BRAKE CALIPER

REMOVAL & INSTALLATION

See Figure 4.

1. Before servicing the vehicle, refer to the Precautions Section.
2. Raise and safely support the vehicle.
3. Remove the wheel and tire.

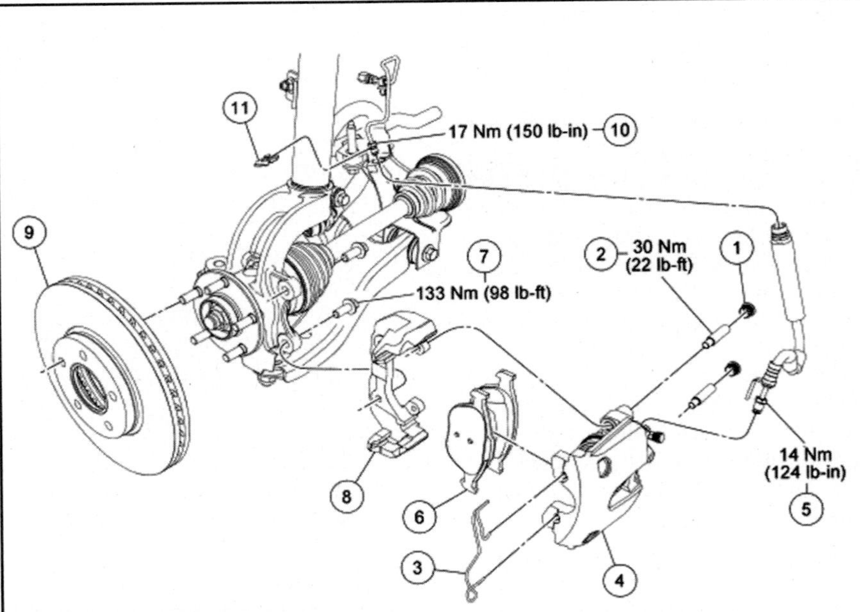

Fig. 4 Front disc brake system—exploded view

4. Remove the brake pad anti-rattle spring.
5. Disconnect the brake flexible hose fitting from the brake caliper.
6. Remove the 2 guide pin bolt covers and the 2 brake caliper guide pin bolts.
7. Remove the brake caliper.

To install:

8. To install, reverse the removal procedure and note the following:
   - Apply silicone grease to the brake pad-to-brake caliper contact points
   - Make sure the holding feature on the brake flexible hose is aligned with the notch on the brake caliper
   - Tighten the brake caliper to 22 ft. lbs. (30 Nm)
   - Tighten the brake flexible hose fitting to 10 ft. lbs. (14 Nm)
9. Bleed the brake caliper.

DISC BRAKE PADS

REMOVAL & INSTALLATION

See Figure 4.

**** CAUTION**

Always install new brake shoes or pads at both ends of an axle to reduce the possibility of brakes pulling vehicle to one side. Failure to follow this instruction may result in uneven braking and serious personal injury.

1. Before servicing the vehicle, refer to the Precautions Section.
2. Check the brake fluid level in the brake master cylinder reservoir.

➡If required, remove the fluid until the brake master cylinder reservoir is half full.

3. Raise and safely support the vehicle.
4. Remove the wheel and tire assembly.
5. Remove the brake pad anti-rattle spring.

**** WARNING**

Do not pry in the caliper sight hole to retract the pistons, as this can damage the pistons and boots.

**** WARNING**

Do not allow the brake caliper to hang from the brake caliper flexible hose or damage to the hose may occur.

6. Remove the 2 guide pin bolt covers and the 2 brake caliper guide pin bolts.
7. Position the caliper aside. Support the caliper using mechanic's wire.
8. Remove the 2 brake pads.

To install:

**** WARNING**

Protect the caliper pistons and boots when pushing the caliper pistons into the caliper piston bores or damage to components may occur.

9. If installing new brake pads, using a C-clamp and a worn brake pad, compress the disc brake caliper pistons into the caliper.
10. To install, reverse the removal procedure and note the following:
    - Apply silicone grease to the brake pad-to-brake caliper contact points
    - Tighten the caliper bolts to 22 ft. lbs. (30 Nm).
    - Fill master cylinder reservoir with specified brake fluid
11. Apply brakes several times to verify correct brake operation

BRAKES — REAR DRUM BRAKES

**** CAUTION**

Dust and dirt accumulating on brake parts during normal use may contain asbestos fibers from production or aftermarket brake linings. Breathing excessive concentrations of asbestos fibers can cause serious bodily harm. Exercise care when servicing brake parts. Do not sand or grind brake lining unless equipment used is designed to contain the dust residue. Do not clean brake parts with compressed air or by dry brushing. Cleaning should be done by dampening the brake components with a fine mist of water, then wiping the brake components clean with a dampened cloth. Dispose of cloth and all residue containing asbestos fibers in an impermeable container with the appropriate label. Follow practices prescribed by the Occupational Safety and Health Administration (OSHA) and the Environmental Protection Agency (EPA) for the handling, processing, and disposing of dust or debris that may contain asbestos fibers.

BRAKE DRUM

REMOVAL & INSTALLATION

See Figure 5.

**** CAUTION**

Do not breathe dust or use compressed air to blow dust from storage containers or friction components. Remove dust using government-approved techniques. Friction component dust may be a cancer and lung disease hazard. Exposure to potentially hazardous components may occur if dusts are created during repair of friction components, such as brake pads and clutch discs. Exposure may also cause irritation to skin, eyes and respiratory tract, and may cause allergic reactions and/or may lead to other chronic health effects. If irritation persists, seek medical attention or advice. Failure to follow these instructions may result in serious personal injury.

➡Make sure that the parking brake control is fully released.

1. Before servicing the vehicle, refer to the Precautions Section.
2. Remove the wheel and tire.

**** WARNING**

Use of a brake drum puller or a torch is not recommended. Brake drum distortion may result.

➡If the brake drum is rusted to the axle shaft pilot diameter, tap the center of the brake drum between the wheel studs.

3. Remove the brake drum.
4. To install, reverse the removal procedure.
5. Adjust the rear brakes. Refer to Brake Shoes, Adjustment.

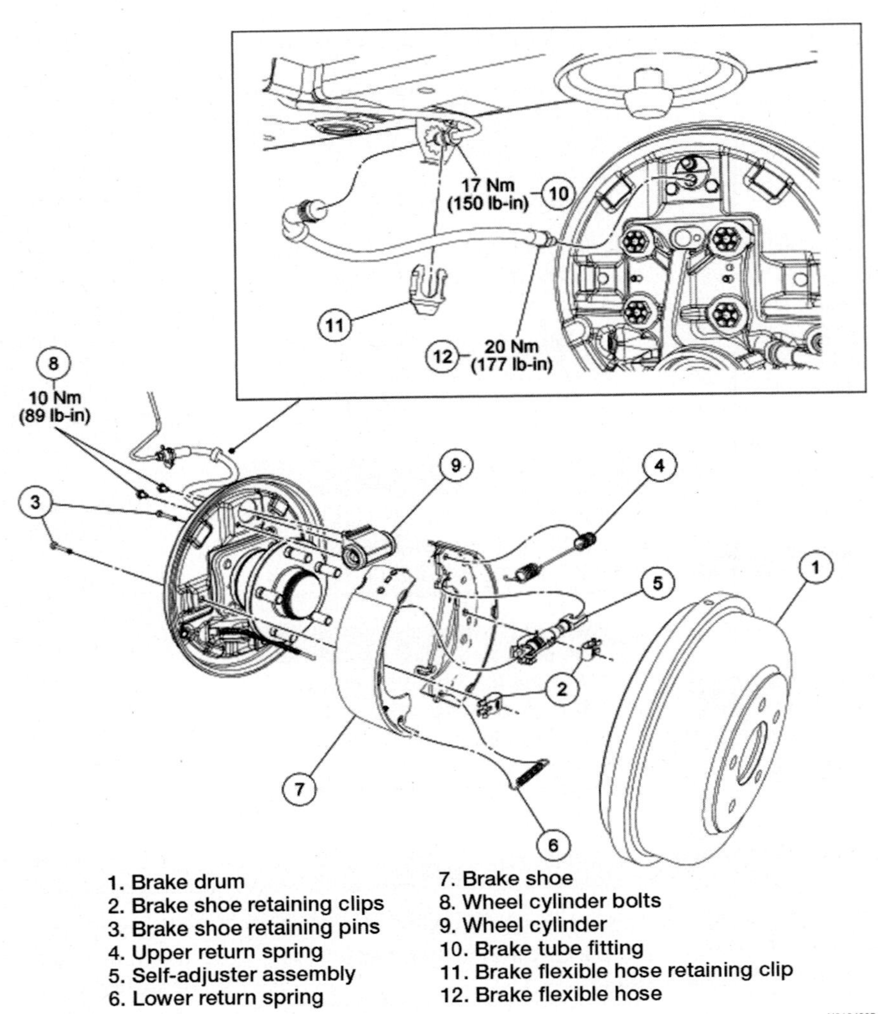

Fig. 6 Rear drum brake system—exploded view

BRAKE SHOES

REMOVAL & INSTALLATION

See Figure 5.

CAUTION

Always install new brake shoes or pads at both ends of an axle to reduce the possibility of brakes pulling vehicle to one side. Failure to follow this instruction may result in uneven braking and serious personal injury.

1. Before servicing the vehicle, refer to the Precautions Section.
2. Remove the parking brake control boot.
   a. Release the boot clip.
   b. Lift the boot upward and over the parking brake control handle.

➡Make sure the rear brakes are cool to the touch.

3. Move the parking brake control to the fully released position.
4. Relieve the tension on the parking brake cable in the following sequence.
   a. Remove and discard the retaining clip.
   b. Loosen the adjustment nut.
5. Remove the brake drum. Refer to Brake Drum, removal & installation.
6. Remove the brake shoe retaining clips and pins.
7. Remove the upper return spring.
8. Remove the self-adjuster and spring assembly.
9. Remove the lower return spring.
10. Remove the leading brake shoe, the trailing brake shoe and parking brake actuator lever assembly.

To install:

11. Using specified brake parts cleaner, clean and dry the brake shoe contact points on the backing plate.
12. Apply a thin coat of the specified silicone grease to the brake shoe contact points on the backing plate.
13. To install, reverse the removal procedure.
14. Adjust the parking brake cable. Refer to Adjustment procedure.

ADJUSTMENT

See Figures 6 and 7.

1. Before servicing the vehicle, refer to the Precautions Section.
2. Remove the brake drum. Refer to Brake Drum, removal & installation.
3. Using the Brake Adjustment Gauge, measure the inside diameter of the brake drum.
4. Position the Brake Adjustment Gauge on the brake shoes and linings and adjust accordingly.
5. Install the brake drum. Refer to Brake Drum, removal & installation.

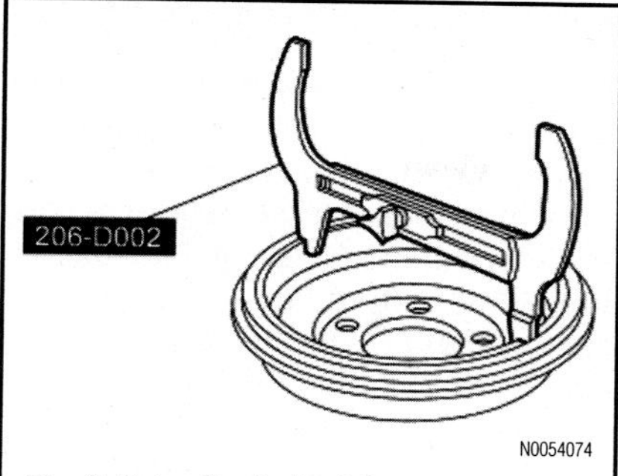

Fig. 6 Using the Brake Adjustment Gauge to measure the inside diameter of the brake drum

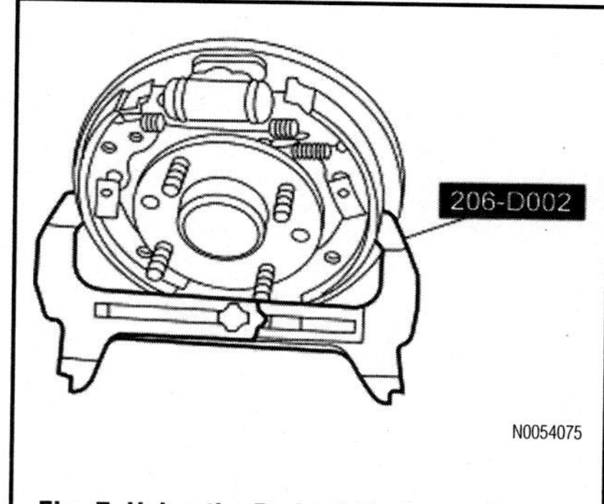

Fig. 7 Using the Brake Adjustment Gauge to measure the brake shoe and linings

BRAKES

PARKING BRAKE

PARKING BRAKE CABLES

ADJUSTMENT

1. Before servicing the vehicle, refer to the Precautions Section.
2. Remove the parking brake control boot.
3. Release the parking brake.
4. Loosen parking brake cable adjustment nut until there is no tension in the cable.
5. Apply the service brakes several times to verify the rear brake shoes are correctly adjusted.
6. Raise the parking brake control 7 clicks.

➡If rear cables are installed new, tighten parking brake adjustment nut to 44 inch lbs. (5 Nm) and loosen then tighten to 27 inch lbs. (3 Nm).

7. Tighten the parking brake cable adjustment nut to 27 inch lbs. (3 Nm).
8. Apply and release the parking brake control several times with sufficient force to settle the parking brake system.
9. Release the parking brake control to its lowest position.
10. Rotate the rear wheels to make sure the brake shoes do not drag.
11. Install the parking brake control boot.

PARKING BRAKE SHOES

REMOVAL & INSTALLATION

On drum brakes, the parking brakes utilize the regular service brakes. Refer to Rear Drum Brakes, Brake Shoes, removal & installation.

CHASSIS ELECTRICAL

AIR BAG (SUPPLEMENTAL RESTRAINT SYSTEM)

GENERAL INFORMATION

CAUTION

These vehicles are equipped with an air bag system. The system must be disarmed before performing service on, or around, system components, the steering column, instrument panel components, wiring and sensors. Failure to follow the safety precautions and the disarming procedure could result in accidental air bag deployment, possible injury and unnecessary system repairs.

SERVICE PRECAUTIONS

Disconnect and isolate the battery negative cable before beginning any airbag system component diagnosis, testing, removal, or installation procedures. Allow system capacitor to discharge for two minutes before beginning any component service. This will disable the airbag system. Failure to disable the airbag system may result in accidental airbag deployment, personal injury, or death.

Do not place an intact undeployed airbag face down on a solid surface. The airbag will propel into the air if accidentally deployed and may result in personal injury or death.

When carrying or handling an undeployed airbag, the trim side (face) of the airbag should be pointing away from the body to minimize possibility of injury if accidental deployment occurs. Failure to do this may result in personal injury or death.

Replace airbag system components with OEM replacement parts. Substitute parts may appear interchangeable, but internal differences may result in inferior occupant protection. Failure to do so may result in occupant personal injury or death.

Wear safety glasses, rubber gloves, and long sleeved clothing when cleaning powder residue from vehicle after an airbag deployment. Powder residue emitted from a deployed airbag can cause skin irritation. Flush affected area with cool water if irritation is experienced. If nasal or throat irritation is experienced, exit the vehicle for fresh air until the irritation ceases. If irritation continues, see a physician.

Do not use a replacement airbag that is not in the original packaging. This may result in improper deployment, personal injury, or death.

The factory installed fasteners, screws and bolts used to fasten airbag components have a special coating and are specifically designed for the airbag system. Do not use substitute fasteners. Use only original equipment fasteners listed in the parts catalog when fastener replacement is required.

During, and following, any child restraint anchor service, due to impact event or vehicle repair, carefully inspect all mounting hardware, tether straps, and anchors for proper installation, operation, or damage. If a child restraint anchor is found damaged in any way, the anchor must be replaced. Failure to do this may result in personal injury or death.

Deployed and non-deployed airbags may or may not have live pyrotechnic material within the airbag inflator.

Do not dispose of driver/passenger/ curtain airbags or seat belt tensioners unless you are sure of complete deployment. Refer to the Hazardous Substance Control System for proper disposal.

Dispose of deployed airbags and tensioners consistent with state, provincial, local, and federal regulations.

After any airbag component testing or service, do not connect the battery negative cable. Personal injury or death may result if the system test is not performed first.

If the vehicle is equipped with the Occupant Classification System (OCS), do not connect the battery negative cable before performing the OCS Verification Test using the scan tool and the appropriate diagnostic information. Personal injury or death may result if the system test is not performed properly.

Never replace both the Occupant Restraint Controller (ORC) and the Occupant Classification Module (OCM) at the same time. If both require replacement, replace one, then perform the Airbag System test before replacing the other.

Both the ORC and the OCM store Occupant Classification System (OCS) calibration data, which they transfer to one another when one of them is replaced. If both are replaced at the same time, an irreversible fault will be set in both modules and the OCS may malfunction and cause personal injury or death.

If equipped with OCS, the Seat Weight Sensor is a sensitive, calibrated unit and must be handled carefully. Do not drop or handle roughly. If dropped or damaged, replace with another sensor. Failure to do so may result in occupant injury or death.

If equipped with OCS, the front passenger seat must be handled carefully as well. When removing the seat, be careful when setting on floor not to drop. If dropped, the sensor may be inoperative, could result in occupant injury, or possibly death.

If equipped with OCS, when the passenger front seat is on the floor, no one should sit in the front passenger seat. This uneven force may damage the sensing ability of the seat weight sensors. If sat on and damaged, the sensor may be inoperative, could result in occupant injury, or possibly death.

DISARMING THE SYSTEM

CAUTION

Always wear eye protection when servicing a vehicle. Failure to follow this instruction may result in serious personal injury.

CAUTION

Never disassemble or tamper with safety belt buckle/retractor pretensioners or adaptive load limiting retractors or probe the electrical connectors. Failure to follow this instruction may result in the accidental deployment of the safety belt pretensioners or adaptive load limiting retractors which increases the risk of serious personal injury or death.

CAUTION

To reduce the risk of accidental deployment, do not use any memory saver devices. Failure to follow this instruction may result in serious personal injury or death.

➡The air bag warning indicator illuminates when the correct Restraints Control Module (RCM) fuse is removed and the ignition is ON.

1. Before servicing the vehicle, refer to the Precautions Section.
2. Turn all vehicle accessories OFF.
3. Turn the ignition to OFF.
4. At the Central Junction Box (CJB), located below the LH side of the instrument panel, remove RCM fuse 162 (7.5A) from the CJB.
5. Turn the ignition ON and monitor the air bag indicator for at least 30 seconds. The air bag indicator will remain lit continuously (no flashing) if the correct fuse has been removed. If the air bag warning indicator does not remain lit continuously, remove the correct RCM fuse before proceeding.
6. Turn the ignition OFF.

CAUTION

Turn the ignition OFF and wait one minute to deplete the backup power supply. Failure to follow this instruction may result in serious personal injury or death in the event of an accidental deployment.

7. Disconnect the battery ground cable and wait at least one minute.

ARMING THE SYSTEM

CAUTION

Always wear eye protection when servicing a vehicle. Failure to follow this instruction may result in serious personal injury.

CAUTION

Never disassemble or tamper with safety belt buckle/retractor pretensioners or adaptive load limiting retractors or probe the electrical connectors. Failure to follow this instruction may result in the accidental deployment of the safety belt pretensioners or adaptive load limiting retractors which increases the risk of serious personal injury or death.

CAUTION

To reduce the risk of accidental deployment, do not use any memory saver devices. Failure to follow this instruction may result in serious personal injury or death.

➡The air bag warning indicator illuminates when the correct Restraints Control Module (RCM) fuse is removed and the ignition is ON.

1. Before servicing the vehicle, refer to the Precautions Section.
2. Turn the ignition from OFF to ON with the battery ground cable disconnected.
3. Install the RCM fuse 162 (7.5A) to the CJB.

CAUTION

Make sure no one is in the vehicle and there is nothing blocking or placed in front of any air bag module when the battery is connected. Failure to follow these instructions may result in serious personal injury in the event of an accidental deployment.

4. Connect the battery ground cable.
5. Prove out the SRS as follows:
   a. Turn the ignition from ON to OFF.
   b. Wait 10 seconds, then turn the ignition back to ON and monitor the air bag warning indicator with the air bag modules installed. The air bag warning indicator will light continuously for approximately 6 seconds and then turn off.
   - If an air bag SRS fault is present, the air bag warning indicator will fail to light, remain lit continuously, or flash
   - The air bag warning indicator may not illuminate until approximately 30 seconds after the ignition has been turned from the OFF to the ON position. This is the time required for the RCM to complete the testing of the SRS

- If the air bag warning indicator is inoperative and a SRS fault exists, a chime will sound in a pattern of 5 sets of 5 beeps. If this occurs, the air bag warning indicator and any SRS fault discovered must be diagnosed and repaired. Clear all CMDTCs from the RCM and OCSM using a scan tool.

CLOCKSPRING CENTERING

See Figure 8

⁂ CAUTION

Whenever working near any of the SRS components, such as the impact sensors, the air bag module, steering column, and instrument panel, disable the SRS. Refer to Disarming The System.

⁂ CAUTION

Incorrect centralization may result in premature component failure. If in doubt when centralizing the clockspring, repeat the centralizing procedure. Failure to follow this instruction may result in personal injury.

⁂ CAUTION

If installing a new clockspring, DO NOT remove the clockspring anti-rotation key until the steering wheel is installed. If the anti-rotation key has been removed before installing the steering wheel, the clockspring must be centered. Failure to follow this instruction may result in component damage and/or system failure.

1. Before servicing the vehicle, refer to the Precautions Section.
2. Install the clockspring and 4 screws.
3. Connect the electrical connector.

➡If a new clockspring was installed and the anti-rotation key has not been removed, the clockspring is already centered.

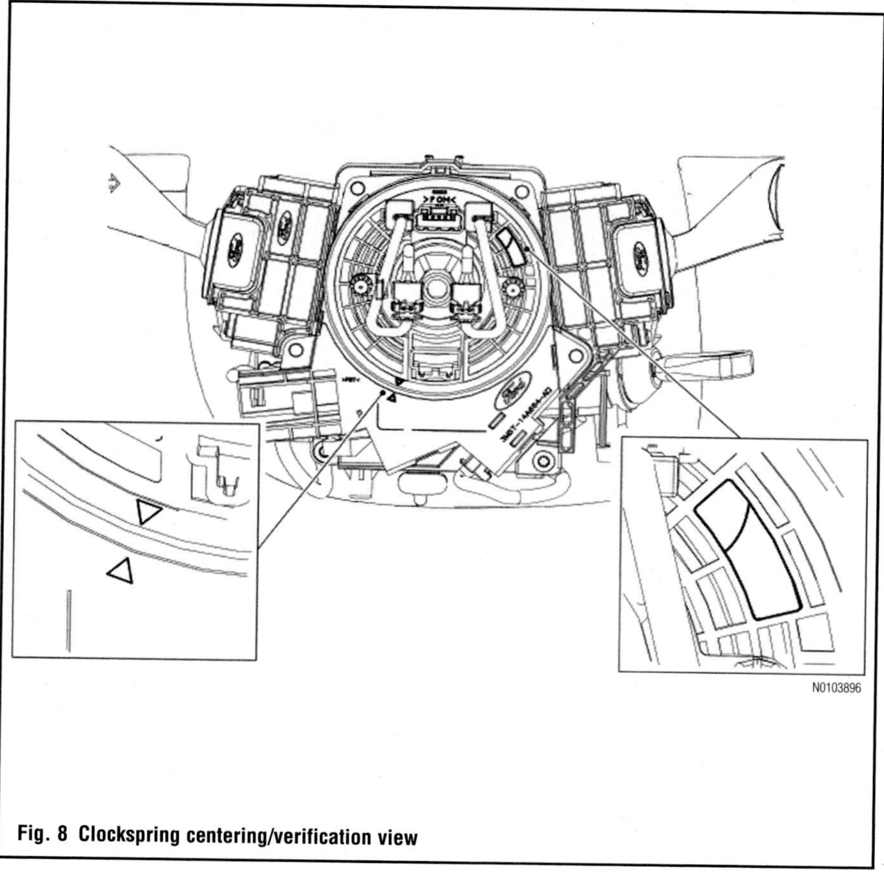

Fig. 8 Clockspring centering/verification view

4. If a new clockspring was installed and the anti-rotation key has been removed or the same clockspring is being installed, rotate the clockspring inner rotor counter-clockwise and carefully feel for the ribbon wire to run out of length with slight resistance. Stop rotating the clockspring inner rotor at this point.
5. Starting with the clockspring inner rotor, wiring and connector in the 12 o'clock position, rotate the inner rotor clockwise through 3 revolutions to center the clockspring.
6. Verify that the clockspring is correctly centered by observing that after 3 revolutions:
    a. The clockspring rotor window is in the 2 o'clock position and the electrical ribbon is visible in the window.
    b. The 2 arrows located on the inner and outer rotor of the clockspring line up in the 7 o'clock position.
    c. The clockspring inner rotor, wiring and connector are in the 12 o'clock position.

⁂ WARNING

To prevent damage to the clockspring, make sure the road wheels are in the straight-ahead position.

➡The clockspring inner rotor, wiring and connector must be in the 12 o'clock position to install the steering wheel.

7. If a new clockspring was installed, remove the anti-rotation key. Install the steering wheel.

DRIVE TRAIN

AUTOMATIC TRANSAXLE FLUID

DRAIN AND REFILL

See Figures 9 through 11.

**** WARNING**

During this procedure, to prevent damage to the transaxle, do not run the engine above idle.

1. Before servicing the vehicle, refer to the Precautions Section.
2. With the vehicle in NEUTRAL, position it on a hoist.
3. Disconnect the transmission fluid cooler outlet tube from the transmission fluid cooler and position it aside.
4. Attach a length of suitable drain hose to the transmission fluid cooler.
5. Insert the drain hose into a calibrated 10.5 quart (10L) container.

➡If the transmission fluid return rate is less than 1.0 qt. (0.95L) in 30 seconds, or if the return hose pulsates, check for restrictions at the pump, transmission fluid cooler or transmission fluid cooler tubes.

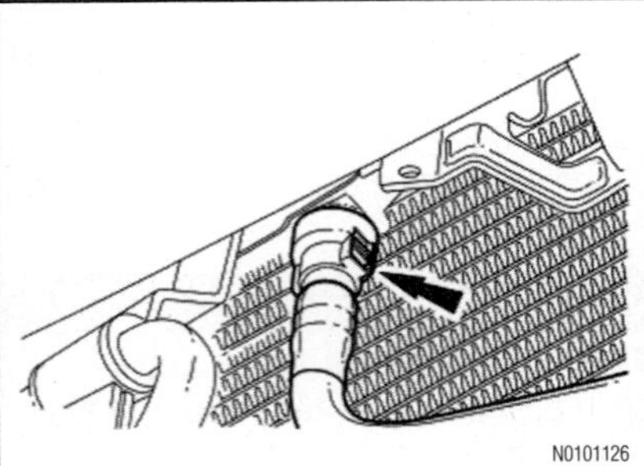

Fig. 9 Disconnect the transmission fluid cooler outlet tube from the transmission fluid cooler

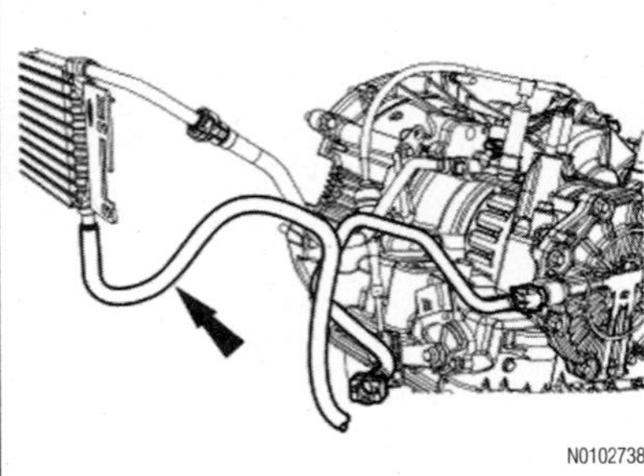

Fig. 10 Attach suitable drain hose to the transmission fluid cooler

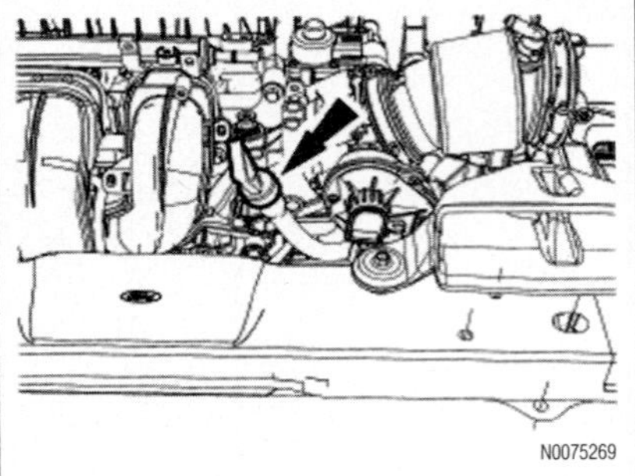

Fig. 11 Transmission fluid level indicator and transaxle filler tube location

6. Run the engine at idle and pump out 3.17 qts. (3L) of transmission fluid.
7. Switch the engine OFF.
8. Remove the transmission fluid level indicator from the transaxle filler tube.
9. Add 3.17 qts. (3L) of transmission fluid to the transaxle.
10. Run the engine at idle and pump out 3.17 qts. (3L) of transmission fluid.
11. Switch the engine OFF.
12. Add 3.17 qts. (3L) of transmission fluid to the transaxle.
13. Run the engine at idle and pump out 3.17 qts. (3L) of transmission fluid.
14. Switch the engine OFF.
15. Remove the length of drain hose from the transmission fluid cooler.
16. Connect the transmission fluid cooler outlet tube to the transmission fluid cooler.
17. Lower the vehicle.
18. Add 3.17 qts. (3L) of transmission fluid to the transaxle.
19. Install the transmission fluid level indicator into the transaxle filler tube.
20. Run the engine.
21. Check the transmission fluid level and fill to the proper level, as needed.

FRONT HALFSHAFT

REMOVAL & INSTALLATION

Left Side Halfshaft

See Figures 12 through 16.

1. Before servicing the vehicle, refer to the Precautions Section.
2. With the vehicle in NEUTRAL, position it on a hoist.
3. Remove the LH wheel and tire.
4. Remove and discard the wheel hub nut.
5. Remove and discard the lower ball joint nut.

**** WARNING**

Use care when releasing the lower arm and wheel knuckle into the resting position or damage to the ball joint seal may occur.

6. Using the Ball Joint Separator and Adapter, separate the lower arm from the ball joint stud.

**** WARNING**

The inner joint must not be bent more than 18 degrees. The outer joint must not be bent more than 45 degrees. Damage to the halfshaft may occur.

7. Using the Front Wheel Hub Remover, press out the halfshaft from the wheel hub and detach the LH halfshaft from the wheel hub. Support the halfshaft.

**** WARNING**

Do not damage the transaxle seal when removing the LH halfshaft.

8. Using the Slide Hammer, the extension from the Halfshaft Remover and the Halfshaft (Plate) Remover, remove the LH halfshaft from the transaxle.

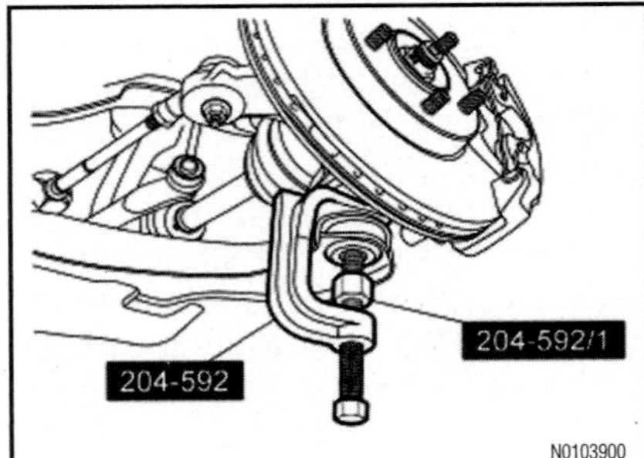

Fig. 12 Using the Ball Joint Separator and Adapter to separate the lower arm from the ball joint stud

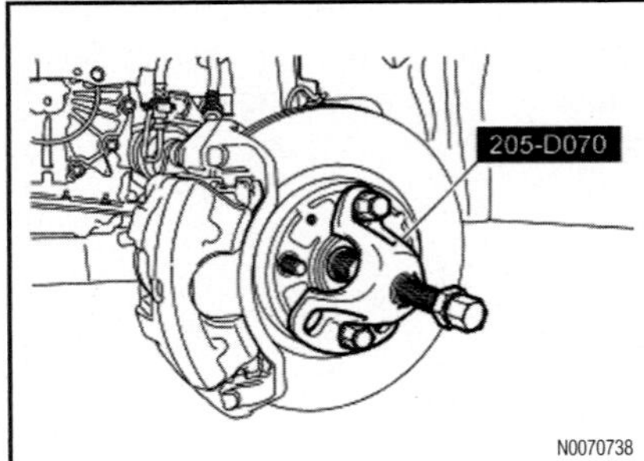

Fig. 13 Using the Front Wheel Hub Remover, press out the halfshaft from the wheel hub

9. Remove and discard the halfshaft circlip.

To install:

10. Install a new halfshaft circlip.

➡Make sure the circlip is fully engaged by pulling on the joint housing.

11. Install the LH halfshaft into the transaxle.
12. Using the Halfshaft Installer, install the LH halfshaft into the wheel hub.
13. Insert the lower arm ball joint stud into the lower arm and install a new nut. Tighten to 111 ft. lbs. (150 Nm).

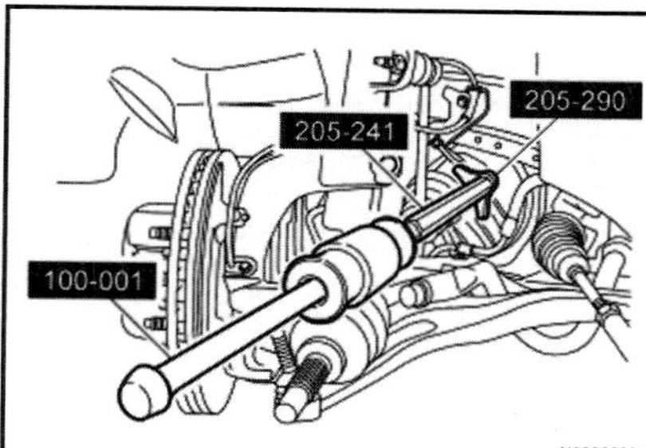

Fig. 14 Using the Slide Hammer, the extension from the Halfshaft Remover and the Halfshaft (Plate) Remover, remove the LH halfshaft from the transaxle

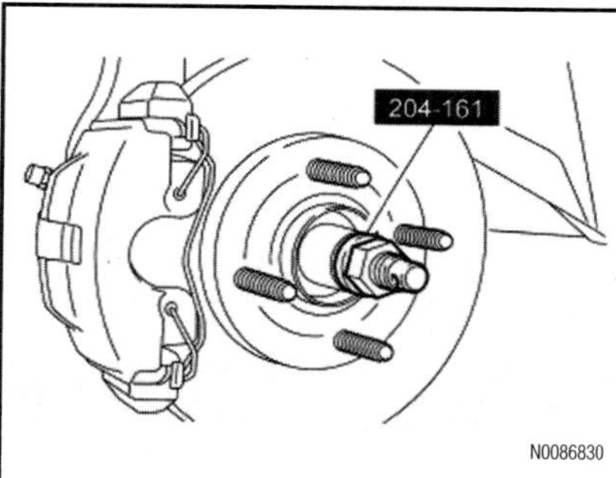

Fig. 15 Using the Halfshaft Installer, install the LH halfshaft into the wheel hub

⁂ WARNING

Install and tighten the new wheel hub nut to specification. Always install a new wheel hub nut after loosening or when not tightened to specification or damage to the components may occur.

➡Apply the brake to keep the halfshaft from rotating.

14. Install a new wheel hub nut. Tighten to 207 ft. lbs. (280 Nm).
15. Install the wheels and tire. Tighten the wheel nuts in a star pattern to 66 ft. lbs. (90 Nm).
16. Top off the transmission fluid level, as needed.

Right Side Halfshaft

See Figures 13, 17 through 19.

1. Before servicing the vehicle, refer to the Precautions Section.
2. With the vehicle in NEUTRAL, position it on a hoist.
3. Remove the wheel and tire.
4. Remove and discard the wheel hub nut.
5. Remove and discard the lower ball joint nut.

⁂ WARNING

Use care when releasing the lower arm and wheel knuckle into the resting position or damage to the ball joint seal may occur.

6. Using the Ball Joint Separator and Adapter, separate the lower arm from the ball joint stud.

⁂ WARNING

The inner joint must not be bent more than 18 degrees. The outer joint must not be bent more than 45 degrees. Damage to the halfshaft may occur.

7. Using the Front Wheel Hub Remover, press out the halfshaft from the wheel hub and detach the RH halfshaft from the wheel hub. Support the halfshaft assembly.
8. Remove and discard the intermediate shaft bearing strap and the 2 nuts.

⁂ WARNING

Do not damage the transaxle seal when removing the RH halfshaft assembly.

9. Remove the RH halfshaft assembly.

To install:

10. Install the RH halfshaft assembly into the transaxle.
11. Install a new intermediate shaft bearing strap and 2 new nuts. Tighten to 18 ft. lbs. (25 Nm).
12. Using the Halfshaft Installer, install the RH halfshaft into the wheel hub.
13. Insert the ball joint stud into the lower arm and install a new nut. Tighten to 111 ft. lbs. (150 Nm).

⁂ WARNING

Install and tighten the new wheel hub nut to specification. Always install a new wheel hub nut after loosening or when not tightened to specification or damage to the components may occur.

➡Apply the brake to keep the halfshaft from rotating.

14. Install a new wheel hub nut. Tighten to 207 ft. lbs. (280 Nm).
15. Install the wheel and tire. Tighten the wheel nuts in a star pattern to 66 ft. lbs. (90 Nm).
16. Top off the transmission fluid level as needed.

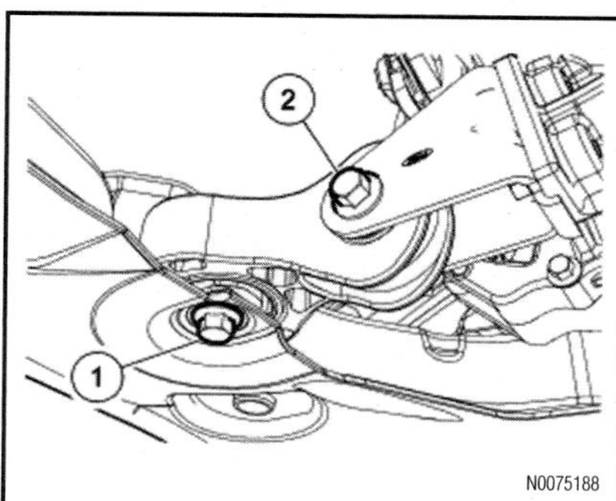

Fig. 16 Left side halfshaft—exploded view

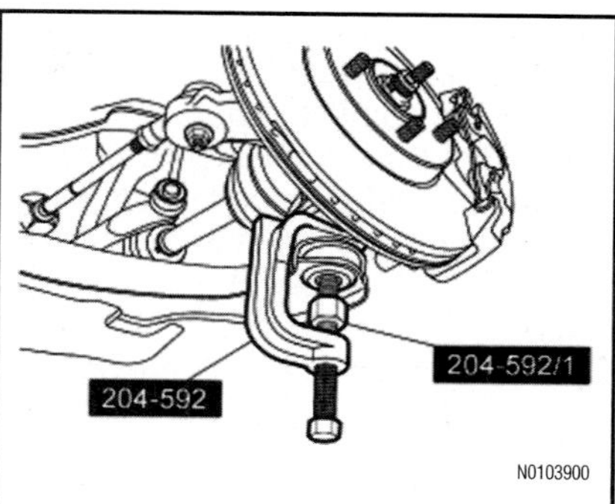

Fig. 17 Using the Ball Joint Separator and Adapter

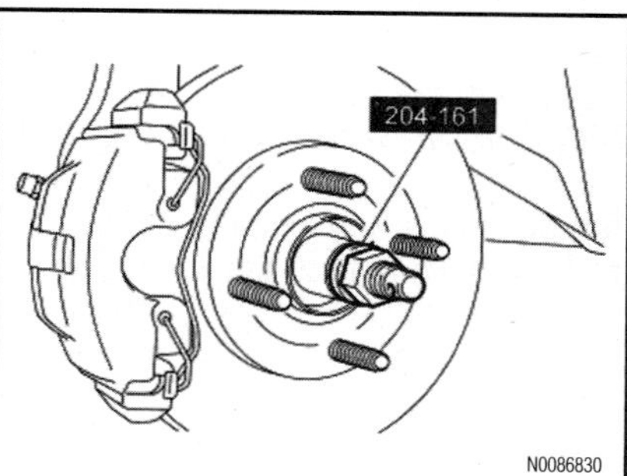

Fig. 18 Using the Halfshaft Installer, install the halfshaft into the wheel hub (left side shown)

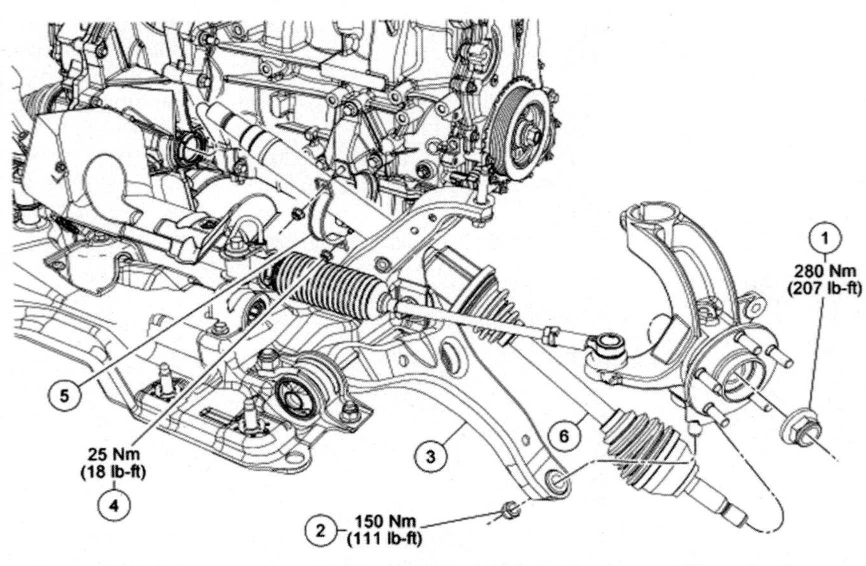

Fig. 19 Right side halfshaft assembly—exploded view

ENGINE COOLING

ENGINE COOLANT

DRAIN & REFILL PROCEDURE

CAUTION

Always allow the engine to cool before opening the cooling system. Do not unscrew the coolant pressure relief cap when the engine is operating or the cooling system is hot. The cooling system is under pressure; steam and hot liquid can come out forcefully when the cap is loosened slightly. Failure to follow these instructions may result in serious personal injury.

➡The coolant must be recovered in a suitable, clean container for reuse. If the coolant is contaminated, it must be recycled or disposed of correctly. Using contaminated coolant may result in damage to the engine or cooling system components.

WARNING

The engine cooling system is filled with Motorcraft® Specialty Orange Engine Coolant. Mixing coolant types degrades the corrosion protection of Motorcraft® Specialty Orange Engine Coolant. Do not mix coolant types. Failure to follow these instructions may result in engine or cooling system damage.

➡The addition of stop leak pellets may darken engine coolant.

➡Ford Motor Company does NOT recommend the use of recycled engine coolant in vehicles.

➡Less than 80 percent of coolant capacity can be recovered with the engine in the vehicle. Dirty, rusty, or contaminated coolant requires replacement.

Engine coolant provides boil protection, corrosion protection, freeze protection, and cooling efficiency to the engine and cooling components. In order to obtain these protections, maintain the engine coolant at the correct concentration and fluid level in the degas bottle. To maintain the integrity of the coolant and the cooling system:

- Add Motorcraft® Specialty Orange Engine Coolant, or equivalent, meeting Ford specification. Do not mix coolant types

- Do not add or mix with any other type of engine coolant. Mixing coolants may degrade the coolant's corrosion protection
- Do not add alcohol, methanol, or brine, or any engine coolants mixed with alcohol or methanol antifreeze. These can cause engine damage from overheating or freezing

Recommended coolant concentration is 50/50 ethylene glycol to distilled water.

For extremely cold climates (less than -33°F (-36°C):

- It may be necessary to increase the coolant concentration above 50 percent
- NEVER increase the coolant concentration above 60 percent
- Maximum coolant concentration is 60/40 for cold weather areas
- A coolant concentration of 60 percent will provide freeze point protection down to -62°F (-52°C)
- Engine coolant concentration above 60 percent will decrease the overheat protection characteristics of the engine coolant and may damage the engine

For extremely hot climates:

- It is still necessary to maintain the coolant concentration above 40 percent
- NEVER decrease the coolant concentration below 40 percent
- Minimum coolant concentration is 40/60 for warm weather areas
- A coolant concentration of 40 percent will provide freeze point protection down to -11°F (-24°C)
- Engine coolant concentration below 40 percent will decrease the corrosion and freeze protection characteristics of the engine coolant and may damage the engine

Vehicles driven year-round in non-extreme climates should use a 50/50 mixture of engine coolant and distilled water for optimum cooling system and engine protection.

Draining Engine Coolant

1. Before servicing the vehicle, refer to the Precautions Section.
2. With the vehicle in NEUTRAL, position it on a hoist.
3. Release the pressure in the cooling system by slowly turning the pressure relief cap ½ turn counterclockwise. When the pressure is released, remove the pressure relief cap.
4. Place a suitable container below the radiator drain valve.
5. Open the radiator drain valve and allow the coolant to drain.
6. Close the radiator drain valve.

Filling & Bleeding—With A Radiator Refiller

See Figure 20.

1. Before servicing the vehicle, refer to the Precautions Section.
2. Install the RADIATOR REFILLER and follow the manufacturer's instructions to fill and bleed the cooling system.

Filling & Bleeding—Without A Radiator Refiller

1. Before servicing the vehicle, refer to the Precautions Section.
2. Fill the degas bottle to the max level mark with the recommended type and concentration of engine coolant.
3. Install the degas bottle pressure relief cap.

WARNING

If the engine overheats or the fluid level in the degas bottle drops below the MAX fill line, allow the engine to cool. Once engine is cool, add coolant to the degas bottle to the MAX fill line. Failure to follow these instructions may result in engine damage.

4. Start the engine, run and hold at 2,500 RPM for approximately 8 minutes until the thermostat opens, then for another 3 minutes after the thermostat opens.
5. Increase the engine speed briefly to 4,000 RPM and hold for approximately 5 seconds.
6. Return the engine speed to 2,500 RPM and hold for another 3 minutes.
7. Shut the engine OFF and allow to cool.
8. Check the engine for any leaks.
9. Check the coolant level in the degas bottle and fill to the MAX fill line as necessary.

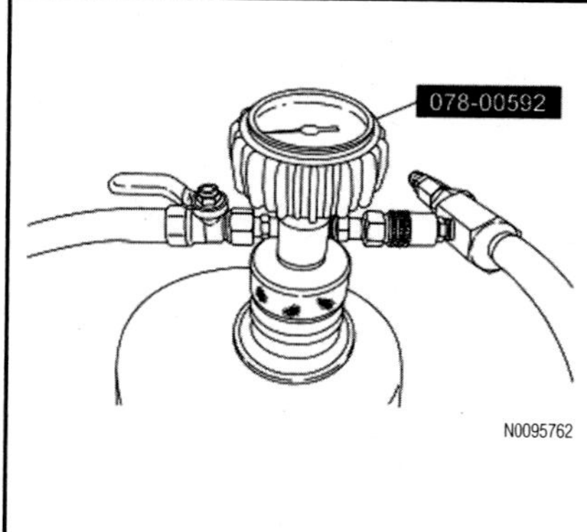

Fig. 20 View of radiator refiller installed

BLEEDING

Refer to Filling & Bleeding—With or Without A Radiator Refiller in the Drain & Refill Procedure.

FLUSHING

CAUTION

Always allow the engine to cool before opening the cooling system. Do not unscrew the coolant pressure relief cap when the engine is operating or the cooling system is hot. The cooling system is under pressure; steam and hot liquid can come out forcefully when the cap is loosened slightly. Failure to follow these instructions may result in serious personal injury.

➡To remove rust, sludge and other foreign material from the cooling system, use cooling system flush that is safe for use with aluminum radiators. This cleaning restores cooling system efficiency and helps prevent overheating. A pulsating or reversed direction of flushing water will loosen sediment more quickly than a steady flow in the normal coolant flow direction.

➡In severe cases where cleaning solvents will not clean the cooling system efficiently, it will be necessary to use the pressure flushing method using cooling system flusher. Dispose of old coolant and flushing water contaminated with antifreeze and cleaning chemicals in accordance with local, state or federal laws.

1. Before servicing the vehicle, refer to the Precautions Section.
2. Add premium cooling system flush to the cooling system and follow the directions on the package.
3. Drain the cooling system.
4. Remove the radiator. For additional information, refer to Radiator, removal & installation.

WARNING

Radiator internal pressure must not exceed 20 psi (138 kPa). Damage to the radiator can result.

5. Backflush the radiator with the radiator in an upside-down position and a high-pressure hose in the lower hose location.

➡The thermostat and housing are serviced as an assembly.

6. Remove the thermostat housing. Refer to Thermostat, removal & installation.
7. Position a high-pressure water hose into the engine through the engine return and backflush the engine.
8. Install the thermostat housing.
9. Install the radiator.
10. Fill and bleed the cooling system. Refer to Filling & Bleeding—With or Without A Radiator Refiller in the Drain & Refill Procedure.

ENGINE FAN

REMOVAL & INSTALLATION

See Figure 21.

1. Before servicing the vehicle, refer to the Precautions Section.
2. With the vehicle in NEUTRAL, position it on a hoist.
3. Disconnect the cooling fan motor and shroud resistor electrical connector.
4. Disconnect the RH and LH cooling fan motor electrical connector. Detach the LH cooling fan motor wiring harness pin-type retainer.
5. Remove the 2 nuts and the cooling fan motor and shroud.
6. To install, reverse the removal procedure.
   - Tighten the attaching nuts to 44 inch lbs. (5 Nm)

RADIATOR

REMOVAL & INSTALLATION

See Figures 22 and 23.

1. Before servicing the vehicle, refer to the Precautions Section.
2. Drain the cooling system. Refer to Engine Coolant, Drain & Refill Procedure.
3. Remove the 2 bolts, pin-type retainer, and the LH front splash shield.
4. Disconnect the upper radiator and degas bottle hoses from the radiator.
5. Remove the cooling fan motor and shroud. Refer to Engine Fan, removal & installation.
6. Remove the 2 cooling fan and shroud bolts from the radiator.

➡The 2 side lower air deflectors may become detached when positioning the lower air deflector aside.

7. Remove the 4 pin-type retainers and position the lower air deflector aside.

5 Nm (44 lb-in) 5

1. Cooling fan motor and shroud resistor electrical connector
2. RH cooling fan motor electrical connector
3. LH cooling fan motor electrical connector
4. LH cooling fan motor wiring harness pin-type retainer
5. Cooling fan motor and shroud nut (2 required)
6. Cooling fan motor and shroud

N0105945

Fig. 21 View of engine cooling fan and related components

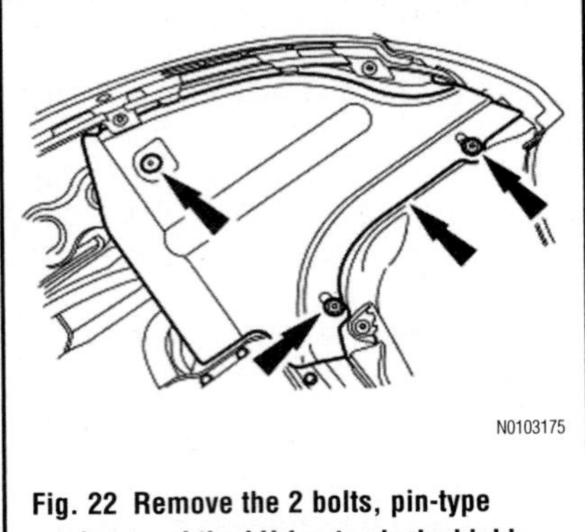

Fig. 22 Remove the 2 bolts, pin-type retainer, and the LH front splash shield

8. Disconnect the lower radiator hose from the radiator.
9. Remove the A/C tube bracket nut from the RH side of the lower radiator support.
10. Position a jackstand below the lower radiator support to support the cooling module.

➡The cooling module will have to be lifted upward to remove the lower radiator support and then positioned back onto the jackstand.

11. Remove the 4 bolts and the lower radiator support.
12. Slide the radiator towards the LH side of vehicle to separate the radiator from the A/C condenser core and remove the radiator.

To install:

13. To install, reverse the removal procedure.
14. Tighten the 4 bolts of the lower radiator support to 18 ft. lbs. (25 Nm).
15. Tighten the A/C tube bracket nut on the RH side of the lower radiator support to 80 inch lbs. (9 Nm).
16. Fill and bleed the cooling system. Refer to Engine Coolant, Drain & Refill Procedure.

THERMOSTAT

REMOVAL & INSTALLATION

See Figure 24.

➡The thermostat and thermostat housing are serviced as an assembly.

1. Before servicing the vehicle, refer to the Precautions Section.
2. Drain the cooling system. Refer to Engine Coolant, Drain & Refill Procedure.
3. Remove the power steering pump. Refer to Power Steering Pump, removal & installation.

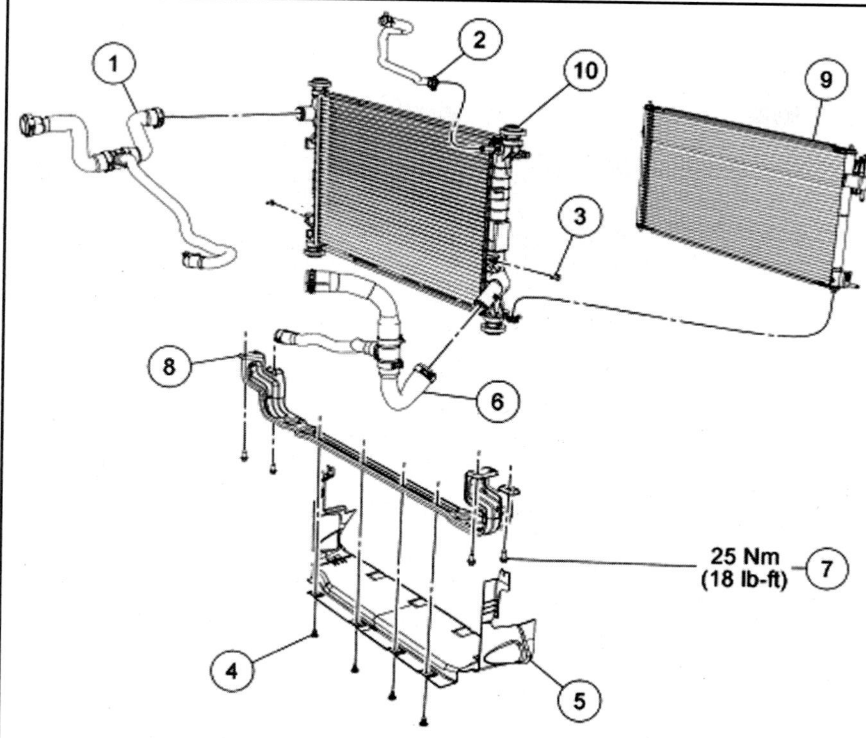

Fig. 23 View of radiator installation

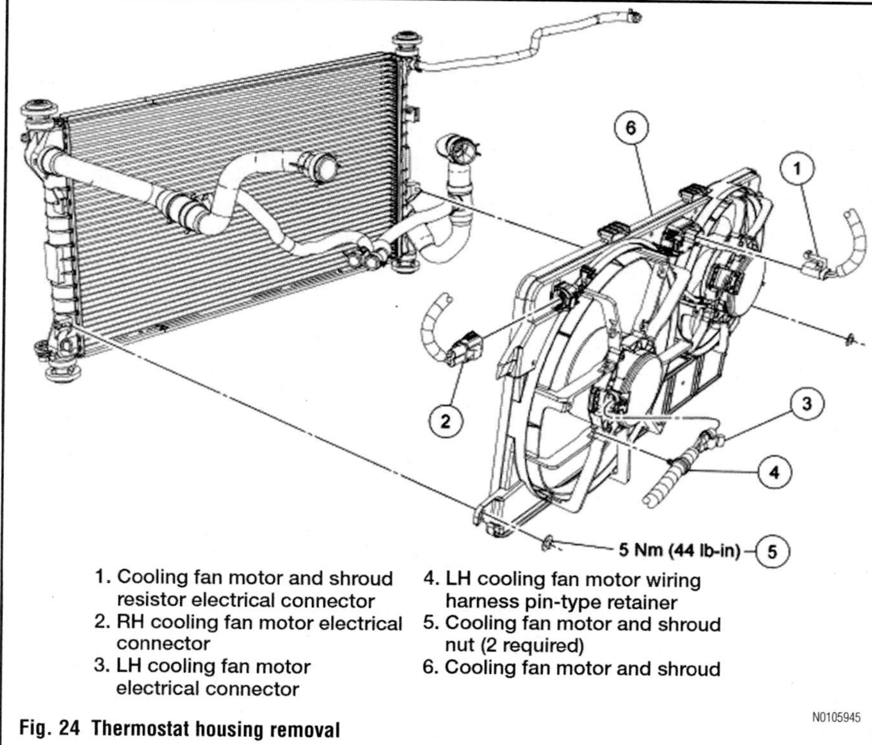

Fig. 24 Thermostat housing removal

4. Disconnect the Knock Sensor (KS) electrical connector.

5. Disconnect the heater hose at the thermostat housing.

6. Disconnect the lower radiator hose at the thermostat housing.

7. Remove the 3 bolts and the thermostat housing.

8. Remove and discard the thermostat housing seal.

To install:

9. Lubricate the thermostat housing seal with clean engine coolant.

10. To install, reverse the removal procedure.

11. Tighten the thermostat housing bolts to 89 inch lbs. (10 Nm).

12. Fill and bleed the cooling system. Refer to Engine Coolant, Drain & Refill Procedure.

WATER PUMP

REMOVAL & INSTALLATION

See Figure 25.

1. Before servicing the vehicle, refer to the Precautions Section.

2. Drain the cooling system. Refer to Engine Coolant, Drain & Refill Procedure.

3. Loosen the 3 coolant pump pulley bolts.

4. Remove the accessory drive belt. Refer to Accessory Drive Belts, removal & installation.

5. Remove the 3 coolant pump pulley bolts and the pulley.

6. Remove the 3 coolant pump bolts and the coolant pump.

To install:

⁂ WARNING

Make sure the coolant pump is correctly seated to the engine block before installing and tightening the fasteners, or damage to the coolant pump may occur.

7. Install a new coolant pump O-ring seal and lubricate with clean engine coolant.

8. To install, reverse the removal procedure.

9. Tighten the coolant pump bolts to 89 inch lbs. (10 Nm).

10. Tighten the 3 coolant pump pulley bolts to 15 ft. lbs. (20 Nm).

11. Fill and bleed the cooling system. Refer to Engine Coolant, Drain & Refill Procedure.

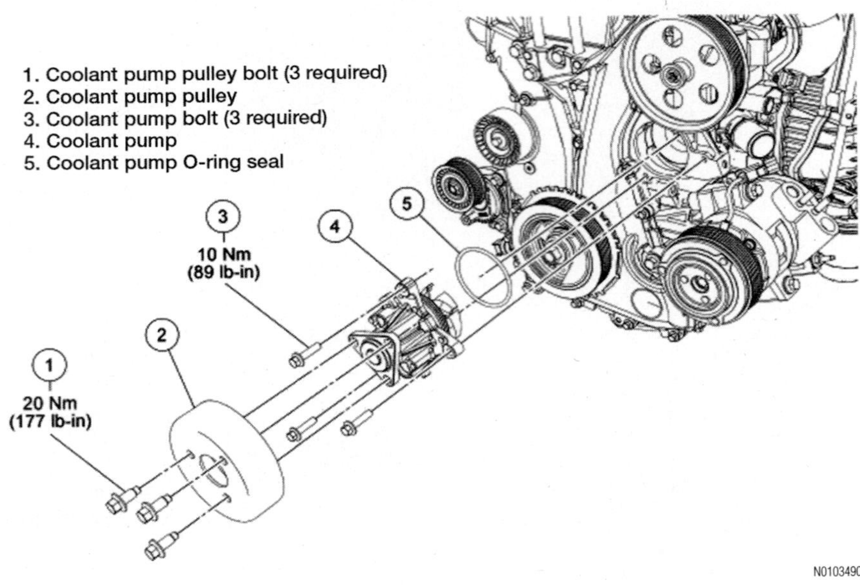

Fig. 25 Exploded view of coolant pump

ENGINE ELECTRICAL

BATTERY SYSTEM

BATTERY

REMOVAL & INSTALLATION

See Figure 26.

CAUTION

Batteries contain sulfuric acid and produce explosive gases. Work in a well-ventilated area. Do not allow the battery to come in contact with flames, sparks or burning substances. Avoid contact with skin, eyes or clothing. Shield eyes when working near the battery to protect against possible splashing of acid solution. In case of acid contact with skin or eyes, flush immediately with water for a minimum of 15 minutes, then get prompt medical attention. If acid is swallowed, call a physician immediately. Failure to follow these instructions may result in serious personal injury.

WARNING

Always lift a plastic-cased battery with a battery carrier or with hands on opposite corners. Excessive pressure on the battery end walls may cause acid to flow through the vent caps, resulting in personal injury and/or damage to the vehicle or battery.

CAUTION

Always deplete the backup power supply before repairing or installing any new front or side air bag Supplemental Restraint System (SRS) component and before servicing, removing, installing, adjusting or striking components near the front or side impact sensors or the Restraints Control Module (RCM). Nearby components include doors, instrument panel, console, door latches, strikers, seats and hood latches.

CAUTION

To deplete the backup power supply energy, disconnect the battery ground cable and wait at least 1 minute. Be sure to disconnect auxiliary batteries and power supplies (if equipped). Failure to follow these instructions may result in serious personal injury or death in the event of an accidental deployment.

CAUTION

Battery posts, terminals and related accessories contain lead and lead components. Wash hands after handling. Failure to follow these instructions may result in serious personal injury.

1. Before servicing the vehicle, refer to the Precautions Section.
2. Disconnect the battery ground terminal.
3. Open the positive battery terminal access panel.

➡When disconnecting the battery ground cable to interrupt power to the vehicle electrical system, disconnect the battery ground cable only. It is not necessary to disconnect the positive battery cable.

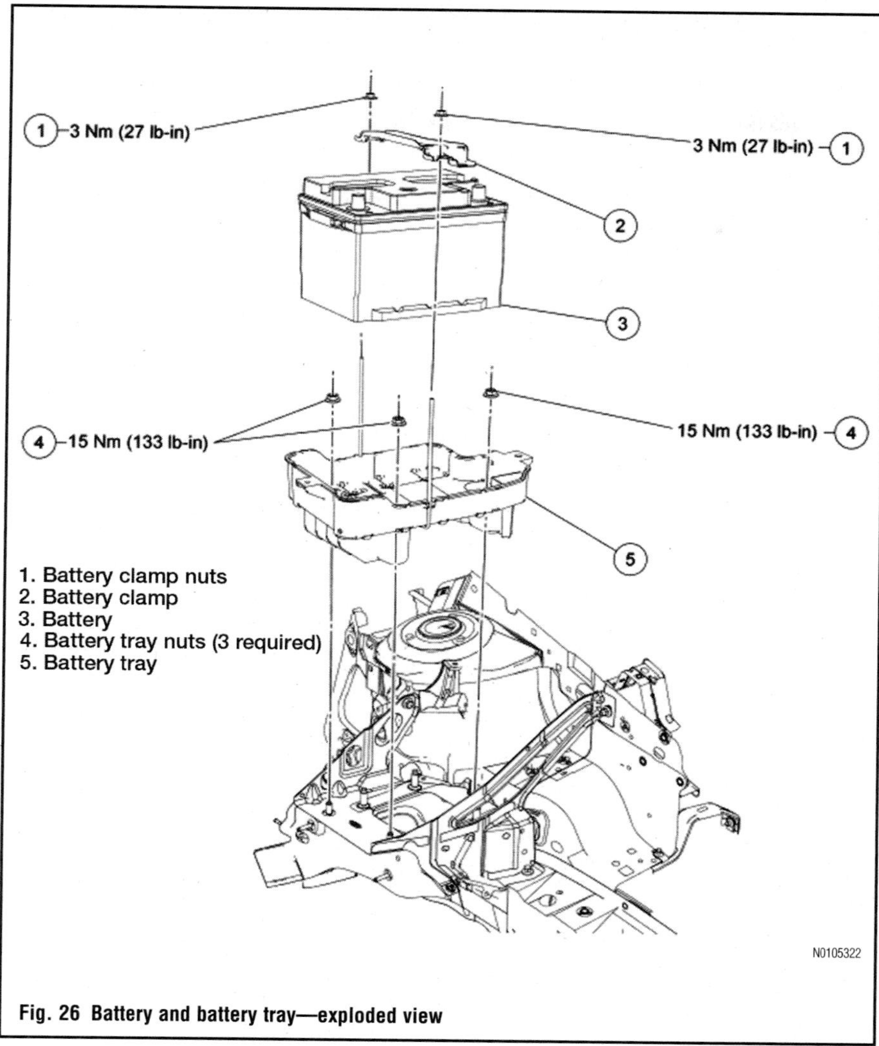

Fig. 26 Battery and battery tray—exploded view

4. Disconnect the positive battery terminal.
5. Open the wire harness clamp and remove the harness from the clamp.
6. Thread the wire harness retainer off of the battery hold-down stud.
7. Remove the 2 nuts from the battery clamp and remove the clamp.
8. Remove the battery.

To install:

9. To install, reverse the removal procedure.
10. Install and close the positive battery terminal cover.
11. Tighten the 2 nuts on the battery clamp to 27 inch lbs. (3 Nm).
12. Connect the positive battery terminal and then the negative battery terminal. Tighten to 44 inch lbs. (5 Nm).
13. Reset electronic systems as necessary. Refer to Battery Reconnect/Relearn Procedure.

BATTERY RECONNECT/RELEARN PROCEDURE

⁂ CAUTION

Always deplete the backup power supply before repairing or installing any new front or side air bag Supplemental Restraint System (SRS) component and before servicing, removing, installing, adjusting, or striking components near the front or side impact sensors or the Restraints Control Module (RCM). Nearby components include doors, instrument panel, console, door latches, strikers, seats, and hood latches.

1. Before servicing the vehicle, refer to the Precautions Section.
2. To deplete the backup power supply energy, disconnect the battery ground cable and wait at least 1 minute. Be sure to disconnect auxiliary batteries and power supplies (if equipped).

⁂ CAUTION

Battery posts, terminals and related accessories contain lead and lead components. Wash hands after handling. Failure to follow these instructions may result in serious personal injury.

3. When the battery (or PCM) is disconnected and connected, some abnormal drive symptoms may occur while the vehicle relearns its adaptive strategy. The charging system set point may also vary. The vehicle may need to be driven to relearn its strategy.

ALTERNATOR

REMOVAL & INSTALLATION

See Figures 27 and 28.

1. Before servicing the vehicle, refer to the Precautions Section.
2. With the vehicle in NEUTRAL, position it on a hoist.

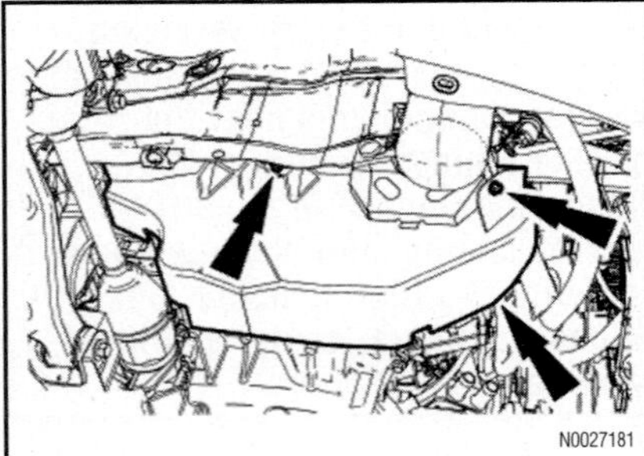

Fig. 27 Remove the accessory drive splash shield

3. Disconnect the battery. For additional information, refer to Battery, removal & installation.
4. Disconnect the alternator electrical connector.
5. Remove the RH halfshaft. Refer to Front Halfshaft, removal & installation.
6. Remove the 3 bolts and the center support bracket.
7. Remove the 2 screws and the accessory drive splash shield.
8. Rotate the Front End Accessory Drive (FEAD) belt tensioner clockwise and remove the belt from the alternator drive pulley. Position the FEAD belt aside.
9. Release the 2 retainers and remove the lower alternator air duct.
10. Position the protective cover aside, remove the nut and position the alternator B+ terminal aside.
11. Remove the 2 alternator mounting nuts.
12. Remove the 2 alternator studs.
13. Remove the alternator mounting bolt and the alternator.
14. If necessary, remove the bolt and the alternator upper air duct.

To install:

15. If removed, install the alternator upper air duct and the bolt.
16. Install the alternator and alternator mounting bolt. Hand-tighten the bolt. Do not tighten the bolt at this time.
17. Install the 2 alternator studs. Tighten to 18 ft. lbs. (24 Nm).
18. Install the 2 alternator mounting nuts. Tighten to 35 ft. lbs. (47 Nm).
19. Tighten the alternator bolt. Tighten to 35 ft. lbs. (47 Nm).
20. Position the alternator B+ terminal on the alternator and install the nut. Tighten the nut to 106 inch lbs.

1. Center support bracket
2. Front End Accessory Drive (FEAD) belt
3. Alternator lower air duct
4. Center support bracket bolt (3 required)
5. Alternator B+ terminal nut
6. Alternator B+ terminal
7. Alternator bolt
8. Alternator mounting nuts (2 required)
9. Alternator
10. Alternator mounting studs (2 required)
11. Alternator upper air duct

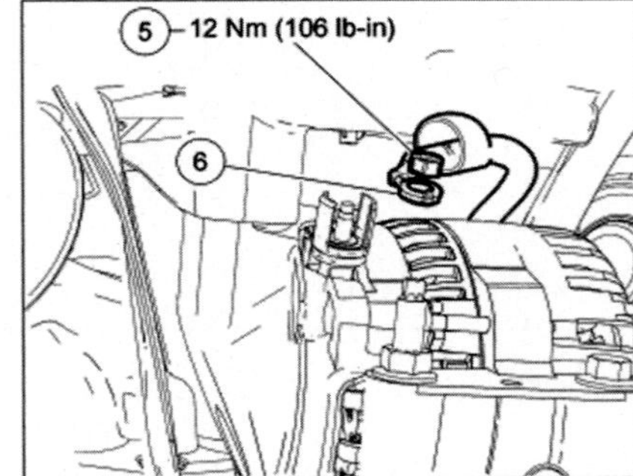

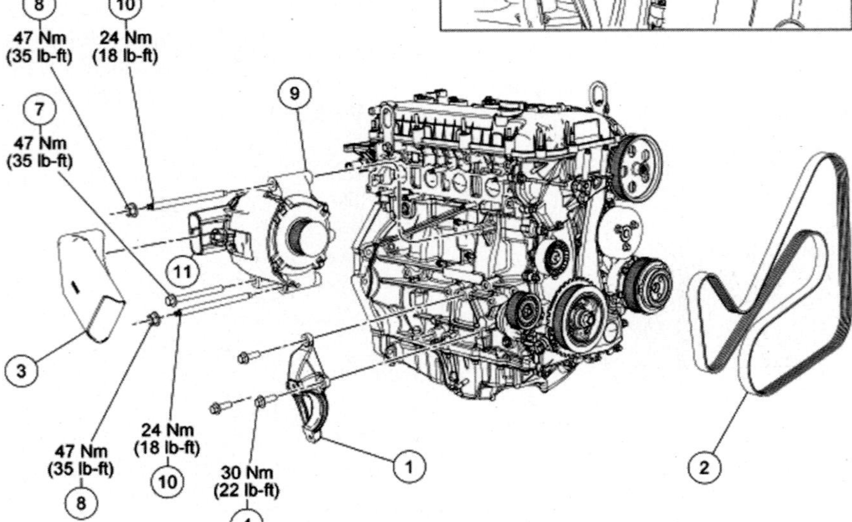

Fig. 28 Alternator and related components—exploded view

(12 Nm) and position the protective cover on the nut.

21. Install the lower alternator air duct.

22. Rotate the FEAD belt tensioner clockwise and install the FEAD belt.

23. Position the accessory drive splash shield and install the 2 screws. Tighten the screws to 44 inch lbs. (5 Nm).

24. Install the center support bracket and the 3 bolts. Tighten the bolts to 22 ft. lbs. (30 Nm).

25. Install the RH halfshaft. Refer to Front Halfshaft, removal & installation.

26. Connect the alternator electrical connector.

27. Connect the battery. Refer to Battery, removal & installation.

ENGINE ELECTRICAL

IGNITION SYSTEM

FIRING ORDER

2.0L Engine firing order: 1–3–4–2

IGNITION COIL

REMOVAL & INSTALLATION

See Figure 29.

1. Before servicing the vehicle, refer to the Precautions Section.

2. Disconnect the ignition coil-on-plug electrical connector.

➡**When removing the ignition coil-on-plugs, a slight twisting motion will break the seal and ease removal.**

3. Remove the bolt and the ignition coil.

To install:

4. Inspect the coil boots for rips, nicks or tears. Remove and discard any damaged coil boots.

5. To install a new coil boot, slide the new coil boot onto the coil until it is fully seated at the top of the coil.

6. Apply silicone dielectric compound to the inside of the ignition coil boot.

7. Install the ignition coil and tighten the bolt to 89 inch lbs. (10 Nm).

8. Connect the ignition coil-on-plug electrical connector.

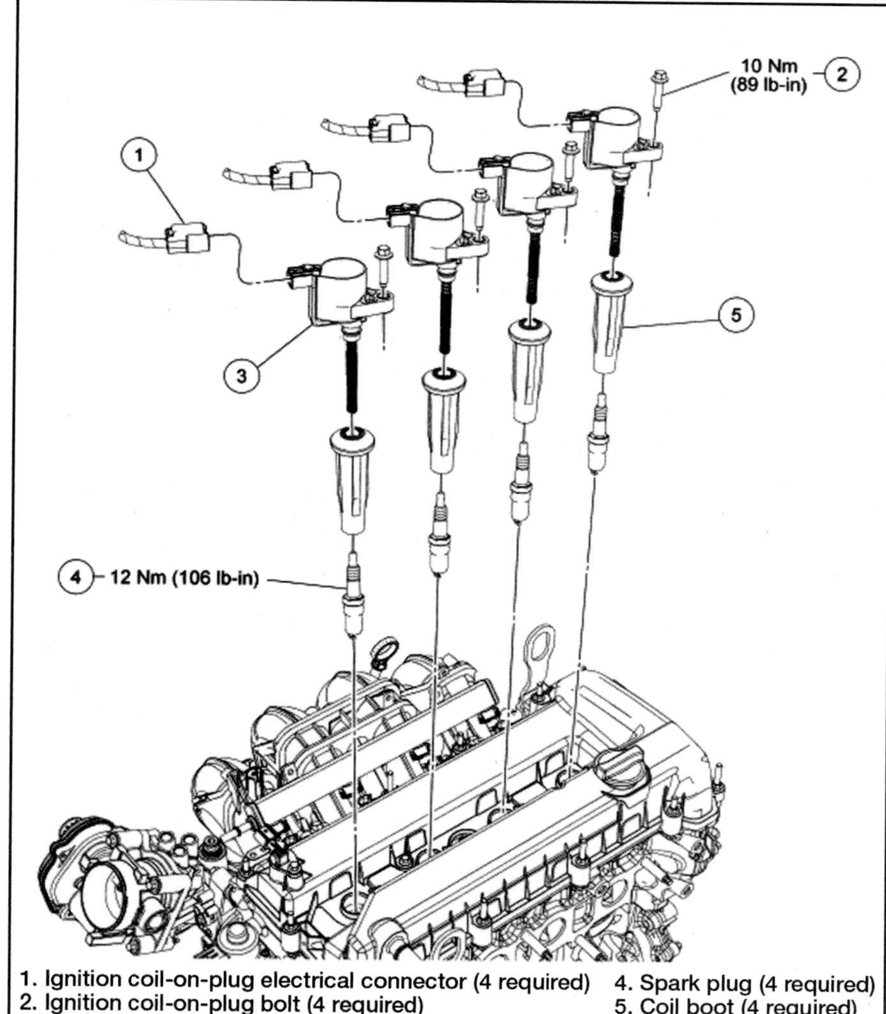

Fig. 29 Engine ignition components—exploded view

IGNITION TIMING

ADJUSTMENT

The ignition timing is controlled by the Powertrain Control Module (PCM). No adjustment is necessary.

SPARK PLUGS

REMOVAL & INSTALLATION

See Figures 30 and 31.

1. Before servicing the vehicle, refer to the Precautions Section.

2. Remove the ignition coil. Refer to Ignition Coil, removal & installation.

⁂ WARNING

Only use hand tools when removing or installing the spark plugs, or damage can occur to the cylinder head or spark plug.

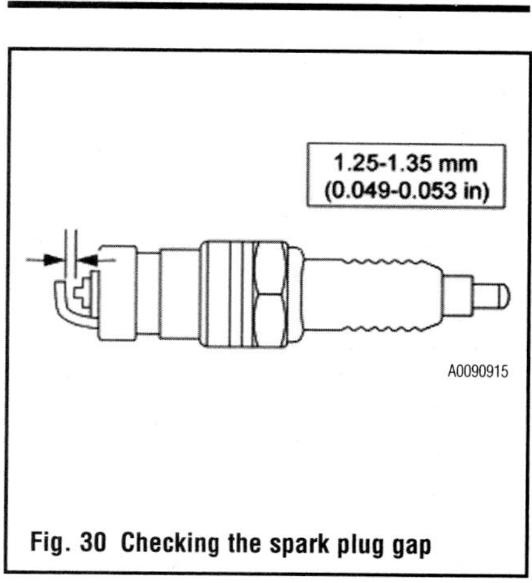

Fig. 30 Checking the spark plug gap

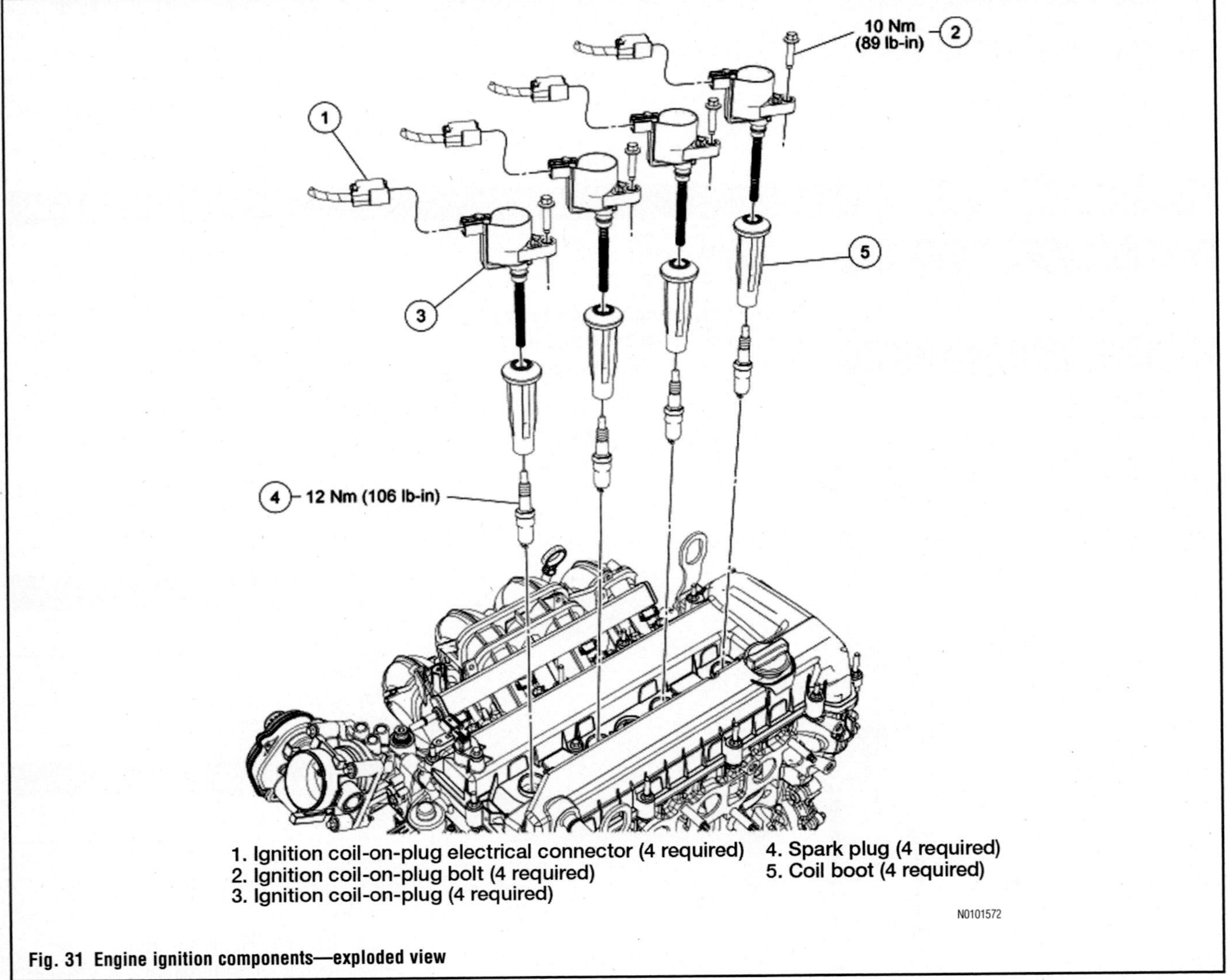

Fig. 31 Engine ignition components—exploded view

3. Use compressed air to remove any foreign material in the spark plug wells prior to removing the spark plugs.
4. Remove the spark plug.

To install:

5. Inspect the removed spark plugs.
6. Check and adjust the spark plug gap, as necessary.
7. Install the spark plugs and tighten to 106 inch lbs. (12 Nm).
8. Install the ignition coils. Refer to Ignition Coil, removal & installation.

ENGINE ELECTRICAL

STARTER

REMOVAL & INSTALLATION

See Figure 32.

1. Before servicing the vehicle, refer to the Precautions Section.
2. With the vehicle in NEUTRAL, position it on a hoist.
3. Disconnect the battery ground cable. For additional information, refer to Battery, removal & installation.
4. Remove the starter solenoid wire nut.
5. Remove the starter solenoid battery cable nut and the starter motor solenoid wire harness terminal cover.
6. Detach the Engine Oil Pressure (EOP) switch wire harness retainer from the starter stud bolt.
7. Remove the power steering tube bracket nut and position the power steering tube and bracket aside.
8. Remove the upper bolt, the lower stud bolt from the starter motor.
9. Remove the starter motor.

To install:

10. Install the starter motor into position.
    a. Install the upper bolt and lower stud bolt finger-tight.
    b. Tighten the upper bolt to 26 ft. lbs. (35 Nm).
    c. Tighten the lower stud bolt to 26 ft. lbs. (35 Nm).
11. Position the power steering tube and bracket. Tighten the bracket nut to 15 ft. lbs. (20 Nm).

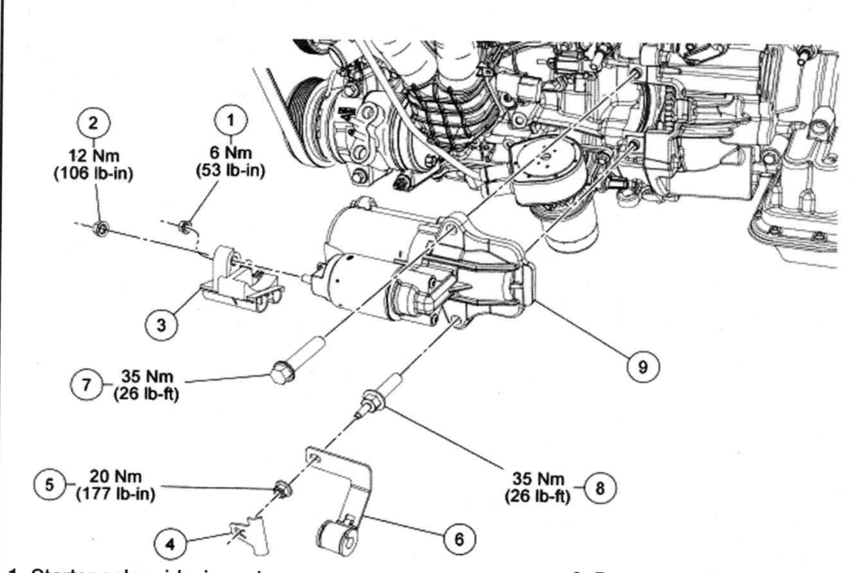

Fig. 32 View of starter motor mounting

12. Install the starter solenoid battery cable nut and tighten to 106 inch lbs. (12 Nm).
13. Install the starter solenoid wire nut and tighten to 53 inch lbs. (6 Nm).
14. Install the starter motor solenoid wire harness terminal cover.
15. Connect the battery ground cable. For additional information, refer to Battery, removal & installation.

ENGINE MECHANICAL

➡Disconnecting the negative battery cable may interfere with the functions of the on board computer systems and may require the computer to undergo a relearning process, once the negative battery cable is reconnected.

ACCESSORY DRIVE BELTS

ACCESSORY BELT ROUTING

See Figure 33.

Refer to the accompanying illustration.

INSPECTION

Inspect the drive belt for signs of glazing or cracking. A glazed belt will be perfectly smooth from slippage, while a good belt will have a slight texture of fabric visible. Cracks will usually start at the inner edge of the belt and run outward. All worn or damaged drive belts should be replaced immediately.

ADJUSTMENT

Accessory belt tension is automatically maintained by a spring-loaded tensioner. No adjustment is necessary.

REMOVAL & INSTALLATION

See Figures 33 and 34.

1. Before servicing the vehicle, refer to the Precautions Section.
2. With the vehicle in NEUTRAL, position it on a hoist.
3. Remove the 2 bolts and the accessory drive belt splash shield.
4. Using the hex feature, rotate the accessory drive belt tensioner clockwise and remove the accessory drive belt.

To install:

5. Rotate the accessory drive belt tensioner clockwise.
6. Route the drive belt.
7. Slowly release the tensioner.
8. Install the splash shield and tighten the 2 mounting bolts to 80 inch lbs. (9 Nm).

AIR CLEANER

REMOVAL & INSTALLATION

See Figure 35.

1. Before servicing the vehicle, refer to the Precautions Section.
2. Disconnect the Mass Air Flow (MAF) sensor electrical connector.
3. Loosen the clamp and disconnect the Air Cleaner (ACL) outlet pipe from the ACL cover.

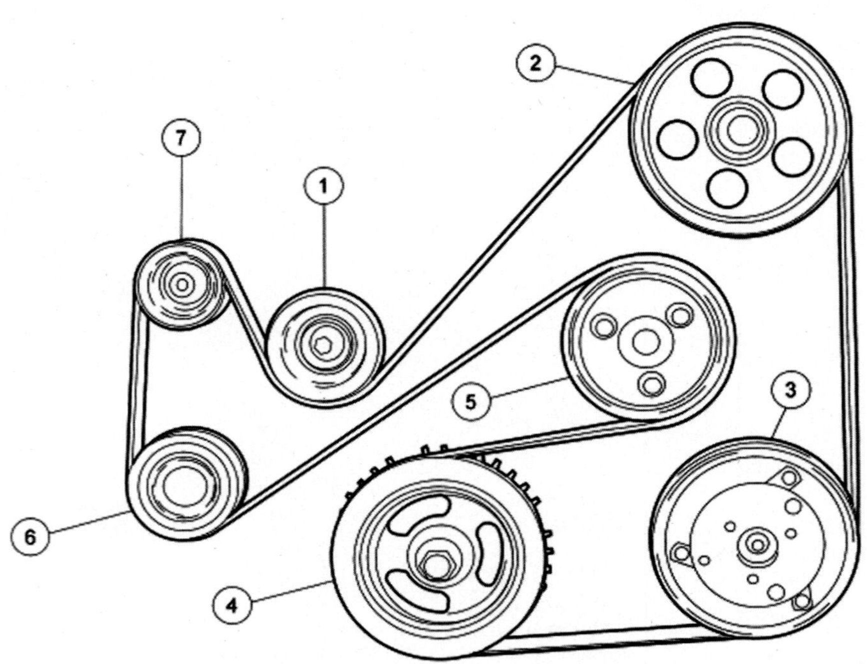

Fig. 33 Accessory drive belt routing

4. Remove the 2 ACL assembly bolts.

➡**No tools are required to remove the ACL assembly. Removal should be carried out using hands only.**

Fig. 34 Drive belt tensioner hex feature shown

5. Release the ACL assembly from the body isolator.
6. Remove the ACL assembly.

To install:

➡**Make sure the ACL assembly is seated into the body isolator.**

➡**The ACL outlet pipe should be securely sealed to prevent unmetered air from entering the engine.**

7. Install the ACL assembly and tighten the 2 assembly bolts to 71 inch lbs. (8 Nm).
8. Install the ACL outlet pipe and clamp to the ACL cover. Tighten the clamp to 27 inch lbs. (3 Nm).
9. Connect the MAF sensor electrical connector.

FILTER/ELEMENT REPLACEMENT

See Figure 36

1. Before servicing the vehicle, refer to the Precautions Section.
2. Disconnect the Mass Air Flow (MAF) sensor electrical connector.
3. Loosen the clamp and separate the Air Cleaner (ACL) outlet pipe from the ACL cover.
4. Remove the ACL cover.
5. Remove the ACL element.
6. Installation is the reverse of the removal procedure.

CAMSHAFT AND VALVE LIFTERS

INSPECTION

Camshaft Bearing Journal Diameter

See Figure 37.

1. Before servicing the vehicle, refer to the Precautions Section.
2. Measure each camshaft journal diameter in 2 directions.
   - Camshaft journal diameter specification: 0.982–0.983 inch

Camshaft End Play

1. Before servicing the vehicle, refer to the Precautions Section.

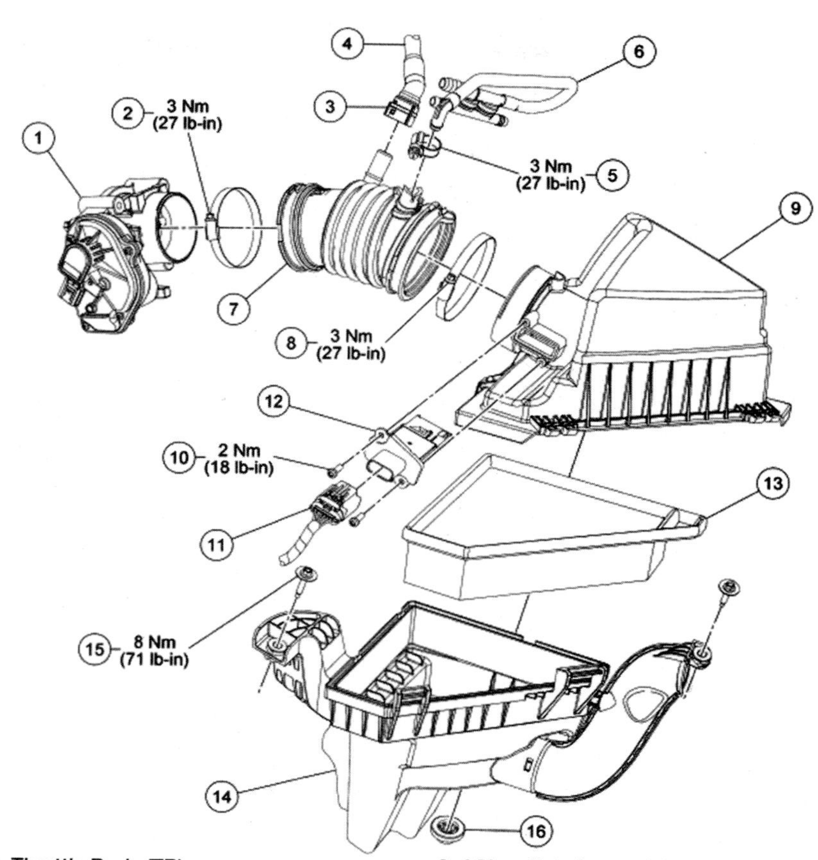

1. Throttle Body (TB)
2. Air Cleaner (ACL) outlet pipe-to-TB clamp
3. Crankcase ventilation tube-to-ACL outlet pipe quick connect coupling
4. Crankcase ventilation tube
5. Power brake booster aspirator tube-to-ACL outlet pipe clamp
6. Power brake booster aspirator tube
7. ACL outlet pipe
8. ACL outlet pipe-to-ACL cover clamp
9. ACL cover (part of 9600)
10. Mass Air Flow (MAF) screw (2 required)
11. MAF sensor electrical connector
12. MAF sensor
13. ACL element
14. ACL assembly
15. ACL assembly bolt (2 required)
16. ACL-to-body isolator

N0101419

Fig. 35 Intake air system components—exploded view

2. Using the Dial Indicator Gauge with Holding Fixture, measure the camshaft end play.
3. Position the camshaft to the rear of the cylinder head.
4. Zero the Dial Indicator Gauge.
5. Move the camshaft to the front of the cylinder head. Note and record the camshaft end play.
    a. If camshaft end play exceeds specifications, install a new camshaft and recheck end play.
    b. If camshaft end play exceeds specification after camshaft installation, install a new cylinder head.
    - Camshaft end play specification: 0.003–0.009 inch

Camshaft Journal To Bearing Clearance

1. Before servicing the vehicle, refer to the Precautions Section.

➡The camshaft journals must meet specifications before checking camshaft journal clearance.

2. Measure each camshaft bearing in 2 directions.
3. Subtract the camshaft journal diameter from the camshaft bearing diameter to determine bearing oil clearance.
    - Camshaft bearing oil clearance specification: 0.001–0.003 inch

Camshaft Lobe Lift

See Figure 38.

1. Before servicing the vehicle, refer to the Precautions Section.
2. Use the Dial Indicator Gauge with Holding Fixture to measure camshaft intake/exhaust lobe lift.
3. Rotate the camshaft and subtract the lowest Dial Indicator Gauge reading from the highest Dial Indicator Gauge reading to figure the camshaft lobe lift.
    - Camshaft lobe lift specification: Intake 0.324 inch; Exhaust 0.307 inch

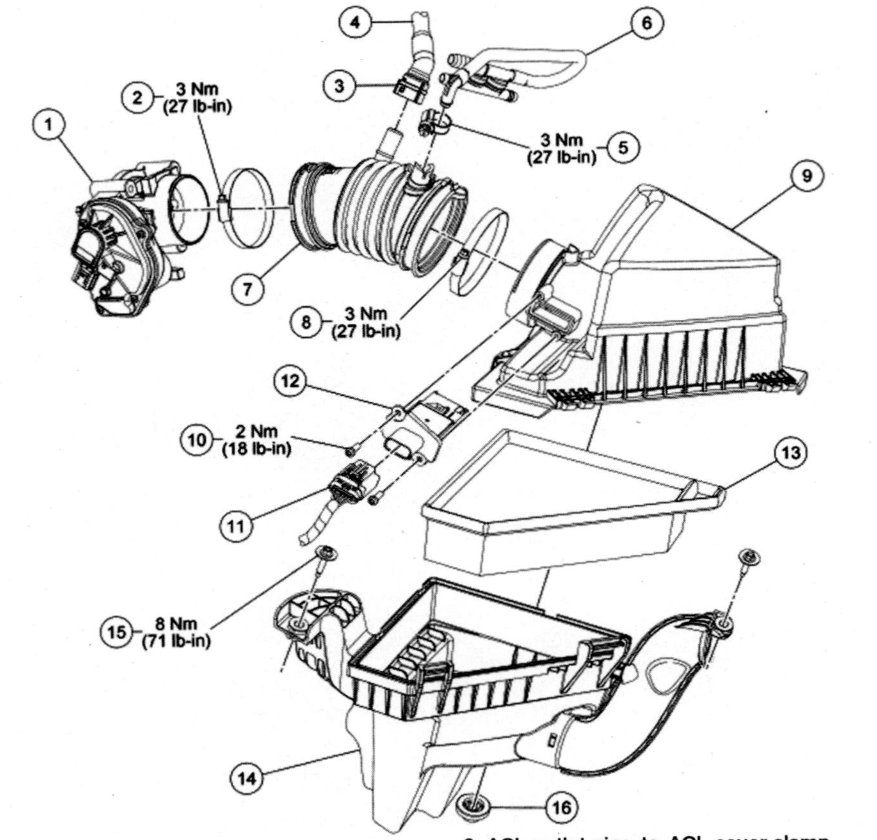

1. Throttle Body (TB)
2. Air Cleaner (ACL) outlet pipe-to-TB clamp
3. Crankcase ventilation tube-to-ACL outlet pipe quick connect coupling
4. Crankcase ventilation tube
5. Power brake booster aspirator tube-to-ACL outlet pipe clamp
6. Power brake booster aspirator tube
7. ACL outlet pipe
8. ACL outlet pipe-to-ACL cover clamp
9. ACL cover (part of 9600)
10. Mass Air Flow (MAF) screw (2 required)
11. MAF sensor electrical connector
12. MAF sensor
13. ACL element
14. ACL assembly
15. ACL assembly bolt (2 required)
16. ACL-to-body isolator

N0101419

Fig. 36 Intake air system components—exploded view

Camshaft Runout

See Figure 39.

1. Before servicing the vehicle, refer to the Precautions Section.

➡**Camshaft journals must be within specifications before checking runout.**

2. Using the Dial Indicator Gauge with Holding Fixture, measure the camshaft runout.

3. Rotate the camshaft and subtract the lowest Dial Indicator Gauge reading from the highest Dial Indicator Gauge reading.

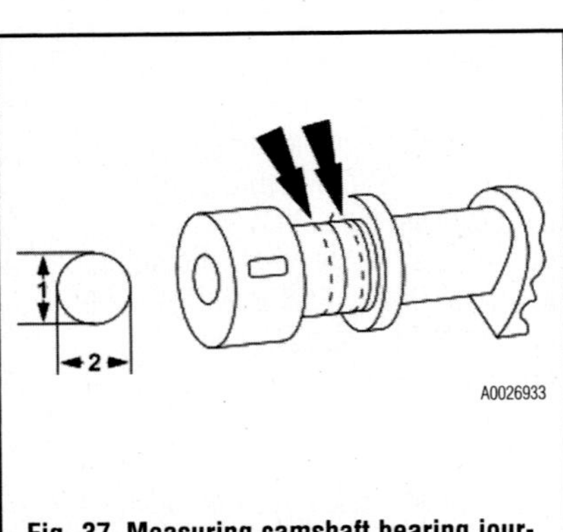

Fig. 37 Measuring camshaft bearing journal diameter

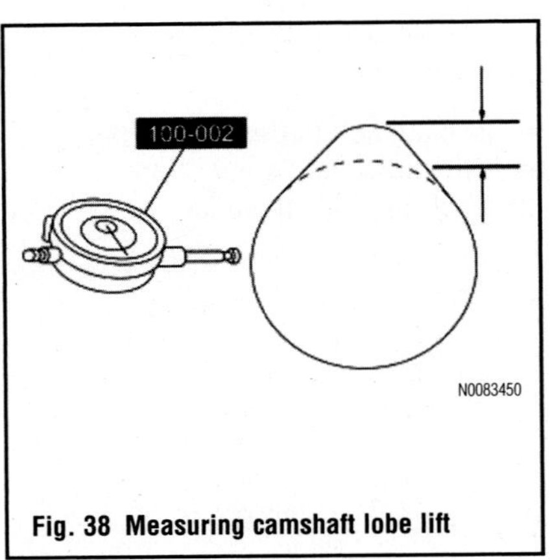

Fig. 38 Measuring camshaft lobe lift

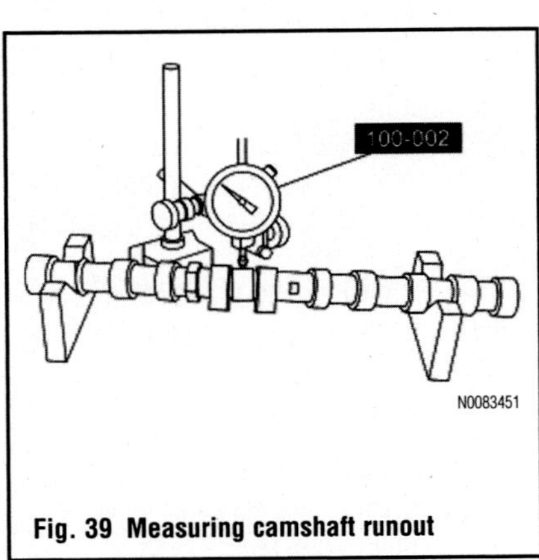

Fig. 39 Measuring camshaft runout

- Camshaft runout specification: 0.0010 inch

Camshaft Surface

See Figure 40.

1. Before servicing the vehicle, refer to the Precautions Section.
2. Inspect camshaft lobes for pitting or damage in the contact area. Minor pitting is acceptable outside the contact area.

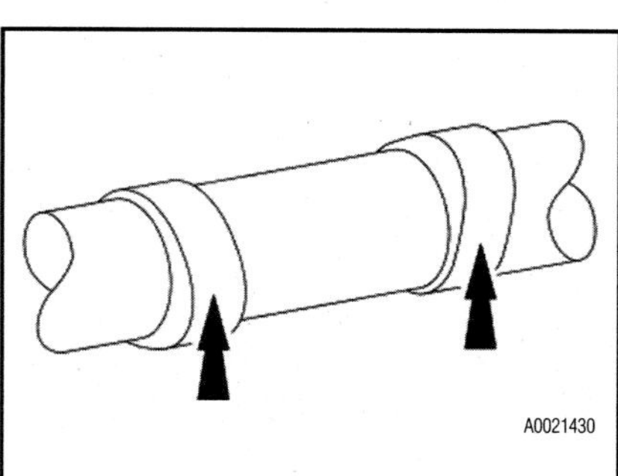

Fig. 40 Camshaft lobe contact area inspection

Valve Clearance Check

Refer to Valve Lash, Adjustment.

REMOVAL & INSTALLATION

See Figures 41 through 47.

WARNING

During engine repair procedures, cleanliness is extremely important. Any foreign material (including any material created while cleaning gasket surfaces) that enters the oil passages, coolant passages or the oil pan can cause engine failure.

WARNING

Do not rotate the camshafts unless instructed to in this procedure. Rotating the camshafts or crankshaft with timing components loosened or removed can cause serious damage to the valves and pistons.

1. Before servicing the vehicle, refer to the Precautions Section.
2. With the vehicle in NEUTRAL, position it on a hoist.
3. Remove the coolant expansion tank.
4. Remove the RF wheel and tire.
5. Check the valve clearance. Refer to Valve Lash, Adjustment.
6. Remove the accessory drive belt. Refer to Accessory Drive Belts, removal & installation.

WARNING

Failure to position the No. 1 piston at Top Dead Center (TDC) can result in damage to the engine. Turn the engine in the normal direction of rotation only.

7. Using the crankshaft pulley bolt, turn the crankshaft clockwise to position the No. 1 piston at TDC. The hole in the crankshaft pulley should be in the 6 o'clock position.

WARNING

The Camshaft Alignment Plate is for camshaft alignment only. Using this tool to prevent engine rotation can result in engine damage.

➡The camshaft timing slots are offset. If the Camshaft Alignment Plate cannot be installed, rotate the crankshaft one complete revolution clockwise to correctly position the camshafts.

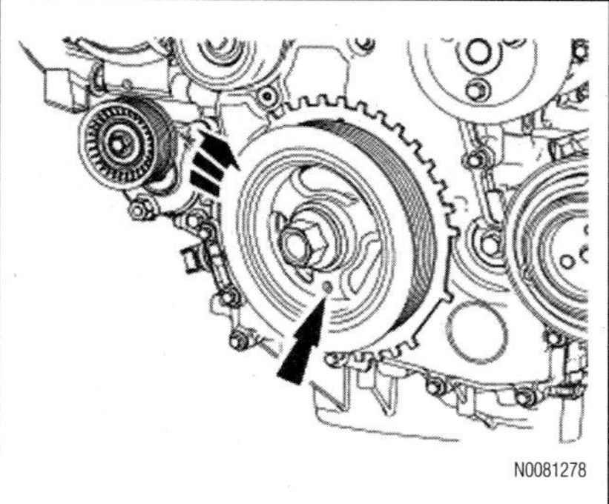

Fig. 41 Turn the crankshaft clockwise to position the No. 1 piston at TDC. The hole in the crankshaft pulley should be in the 6 o'clock position

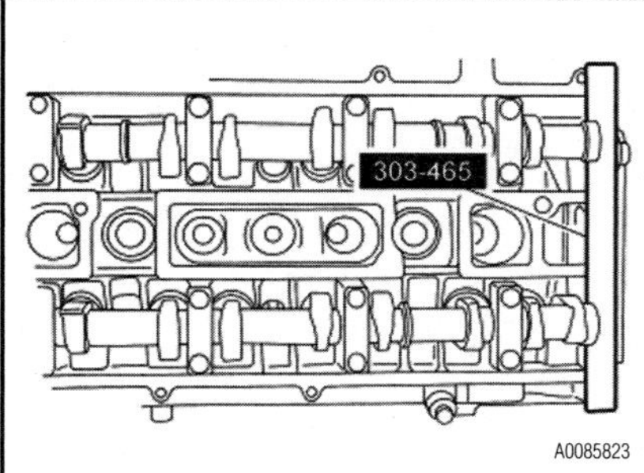

Fig. 42 Install the Camshaft Alignment Plate in the slots on the rear of both camshafts

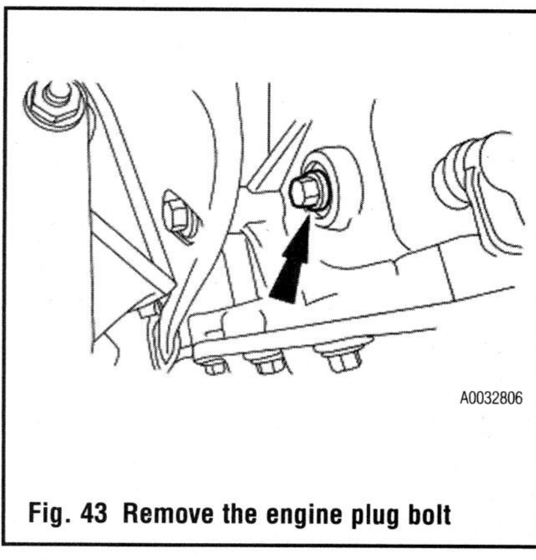

Fig. 43 Remove the engine plug bolt

8. Install the Camshaft Alignment Plate in the slots on the rear of both camshafts.
9. Remove the engine plug bolt.

➡The Crankshaft TDC Timing Peg will contact the crankshaft and prevent it from turning past TDC. However, the crankshaft can still be rotated in the counterclockwise direction. The crankshaft must remain at the TDC position during the camshaft removal and installation.

10. Install the Crankshaft TDC Timing Peg.
11. Install a standard 0.24 inch (6mm) x 0.71 inch (18mm) bolt through the crankshaft pulley and thread it into the front cover.

➡Only hand-tighten the bolt or damage to the front cover can occur.

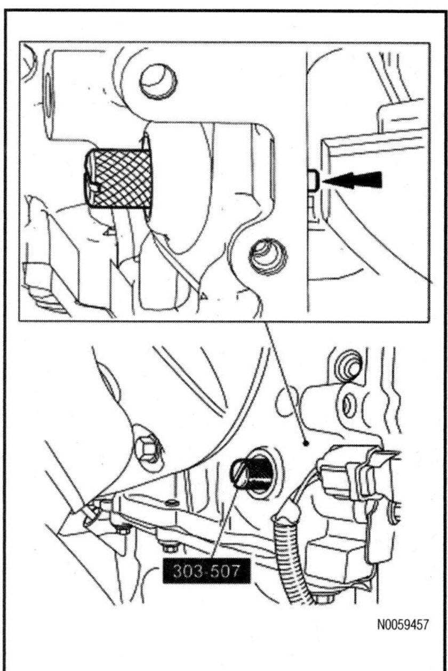

Fig. 44 Install the Crankshaft TDC Timing Peg

12. Remove the front cover lower timing hole plug from the engine front cover.

13. Remove the front cover upper timing hole plug from the engine front cover.

14. Reposition the Camshaft Alignment Plate to the slot on the rear of the intake camshaft only.

➡Releasing the ratcheting mechanism in the timing chain tensioner allows the plunger to collapse and create slack in the timing chain. Installing an M6 x 1.18 inch (30mm) bolt into the upper front cover timing hole will hold the tensioner arm in a retracted position and allow enough slack in the timing chain for removal of the exhaust camshaft gear.

15. Using a small pick tool, unlock the chain tensioner ratchet through the lower front cover timing hole.

   a. Using the flats of the camshaft, have an assistant rotate the exhaust camshaft clockwise to collapse the timing chain tensioner plunger.

   b. Insert an M6 x 1.18 inch (30mm) bolt into the upper front cover timing hole to hold the tensioner arm in place.

16. Remove the Camshaft Alignment Plate.

17. Using the flats on the camshaft to prevent camshaft rotation, remove the bolt and exhaust camshaft drive gear.

18. Remove the timing chain from the intake camshaft drive gear.

19. Using the flats on the camshaft to prevent camshaft rotation, remove the bolt and intake camshaft drive gear.

20. Mark the position of the camshaft lobes on the No. 1 cylinder for installation reference.

⁂ WARNING

Failure to follow the camshaft loosening procedure can result in damage to the camshafts.

➡Mark the location and orientation of each camshaft bearing cap.

21. Remove the camshafts from the engine.

   a. Loosen the camshaft bearing cap bolts, in sequence, one turn at a time.

   b. Repeat the first step until all tension is released from the camshaft bearing caps.

   c. Remove the camshaft bearing caps.

   d. Remove the camshafts.

To install:

⁂ WARNING

Install the camshafts with the alignment slots in the camshafts lined up so the Camshaft Alignment Plate can be installed without rotating the camshafts. Make sure the lobes on the No. 1 cylinder are in the same position as noted in the removal procedure. Rotating the camshafts when the timing chain is removed, or installing the camshafts 180° out of position can cause severe damage to the valves and pistons.

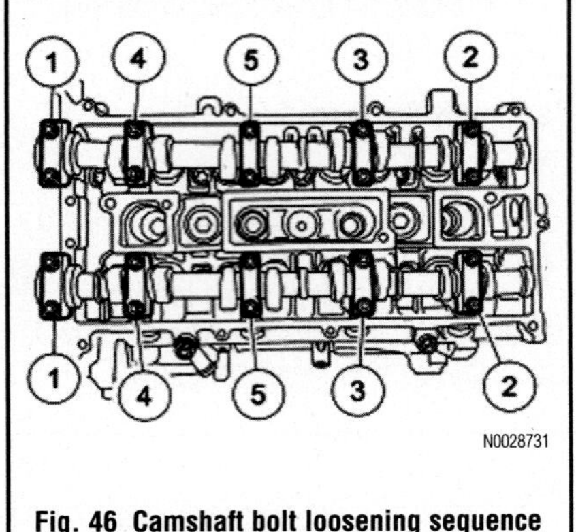

Fig. 46 Camshaft bolt loosening sequence

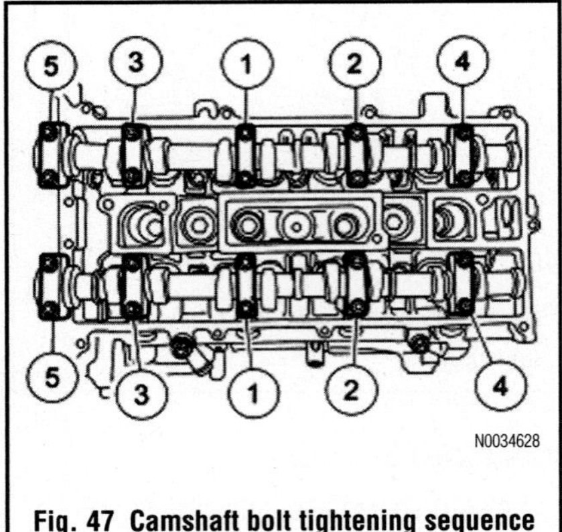

Fig. 47 Camshaft bolt tightening sequence

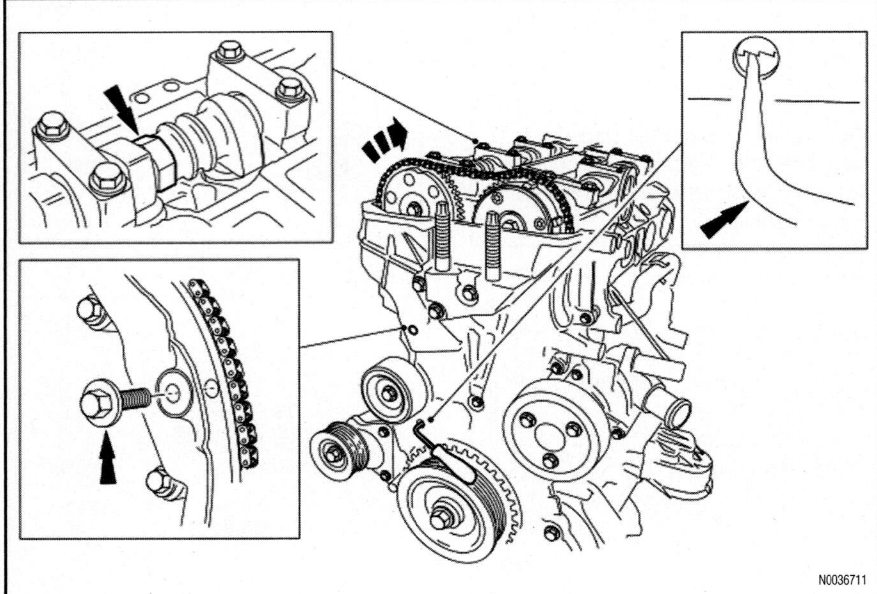

Fig. 45 Using a small pick tool, unlock the chain tensioner ratchet through the lower front cover timing hole

➡Lubricate the camshaft journals and bearing caps with clean engine oil.

22. Install the camshafts and bearing caps in their original location and orientation. Tighten the bearing caps in the sequence shown in 3 stages:

- Stage 1: Tighten the camshaft bearing cap bolts one turn at a time until finger-tight
- Stage 2: Tighten to 62 inch lbs. (7 Nm)
- Stage 3: Tighten to 12 ft. lbs. (16 Nm)

23. Install the Camshaft Alignment Plate.

24. Install the intake camshaft drive gear and hand-tighten the bolt.

25. Install the timing chain on the intake camshaft drive gear.

➡The timing chain must be correctly engaged on the teeth of the crankshaft timing sprocket and the intake camshaft drive gear in order to install the exhaust camshaft drive gear onto the exhaust camshaft.

26. Position the exhaust camshaft drive gear in the timing chain and install the gear and bolt on the exhaust camshaft. Hand-tighten the bolt.

➡**Releasing the tensioner arm will remove the slack from the timing chain release.**

27. Remove the M6 x 1.18 inch (30mm) bolt from the upper front cover timing hole to unlock the tensioner arm.

⁂ WARNING

The Camshaft Alignment Plate is for camshaft alignment only. Using this tool to prevent engine rotation can result in engine damage.

28. Using the flats on the camshafts to prevent camshaft rotation, tighten the camshaft drive gear bolts to 53 ft. lbs. (72 Nm).
29. Remove the Camshaft Alignment Plate.
30. Remove the 0.24 inch (6mm) x 0.71 inch (18mm) bolt from the crankshaft damper.
31. Remove the Crankshaft TDC Timing Peg.
32. Install the front cover upper timing hole plug. Tighten to 89 inch lbs. (10 Nm).
33. Apply silicone gasket and sealant to the threads of the front cover lower timing hole plug. Install the plug and tighten to 106 inch lbs. (12 Nm).
34. Install the engine plug bolt. Tighten to 15 ft. lbs. (20 Nm).
35. Install the accessory drive belt. Refer to Accessory Drive Belts, removal & installation.
36. Install the RF wheel and tire assembly. Tighten the wheel nuts in a star pattern to 100 ft. lbs. (135 Nm).
37. Install the valve cover. Refer to Valve Covers, removal & installation.
38. Install the coolant expansion tank.

CATALYTIC CONVERTER

REMOVAL & INSTALLATION

Catalytic Converter—Mounted To Exhaust Manifold

See Figures 48 through 49.

⁂ WARNING

The exhaust hanger isolators are constructed from a special material. Use only the correct specification exhaust hanger isolators or damage to the exhaust system may occur.

⁂ WARNING

Do not use oil or grease-based lubricants on the insulators. They may cause deterioration of the rubber. Oil or grease-based lubricants on the insulators may cause the exhaust hanger insulator to separate from the exhaust hanger bracket during vehicle operation.

➡**Check the exhaust hanger isolators for damage and fatigue. Install new exhaust hanger isolators as required.**

➡**The exhaust system has 2 catalytic converters: a catalytic converter mounted to the exhaust manifold and an underbody catalytic converter that is serviced with the muffler and tailpipe.**

1. Before servicing the vehicle, refer to the Precautions Section.
2. With the vehicle in NEUTRAL, position it on a hoist.
3. Disconnect the Catalyst Monitor Sensor (CMS) electrical connector. Detach the wiring retainer.
4. Remove the 2 upper catalytic converter heat shield bolts.
5. Remove the muffler and tailpipe.
6. Detach the 3 CMS wiring retainers.

⁂ WARNING

Do not excessively bend or twist the exhaust flexible pipe. Failure to follow these instructions may cause damage to the exhaust flexible pipe.

7. Support the exhaust flexible pipe with a support wrap or suitable splint.
8. Remove the 2 lower bolts and position aside the catalytic converter heat shield.
9. Remove the 2 bolts and the steering gear heat shield.
10. Remove the engine support bracket-to-catalytic converter bolt.

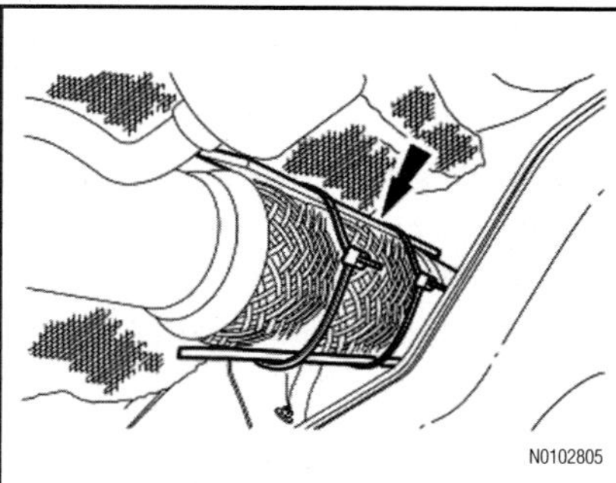

Fig. 48 Support the exhaust flexible pipe with a support wrap or suitable splint

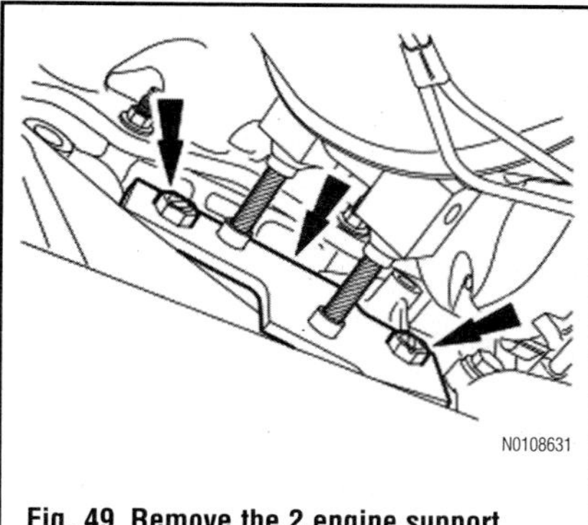

Fig. 49 Remove the 2 engine support bracket-to-engine block bolts

11. Remove the 2 engine support bracket-to-engine block bolts. Remove the engine support bracket.
12. Detach the 2 catalytic converter exhaust hanger isolators.
13. Remove and discard the 2 exhaust manifold-to-catalytic converter nuts.
14. Remove the catalytic converter.
15. Discard the gasket.

To install:

16. To install, reverse the removal procedure.
17. Install new gaskets and nuts.
18. Tighten the exhaust manifold-to-catalytic converter nuts to 18 ft. lbs. (25 Nm).
19. Tighten the 2 engine support bracket-to-engine block bolts to 35 ft. lbs. (47 Nm).
20. Tighten the engine support bracket-to-catalytic converter bolt to 18 ft. lbs. (25 Nm).
21. Tighten the 2 bolts for the steering gear heat shield to 62 inch lbs. (7 Nm).
22. Tighten the 2 lower bolts for the catalytic converter heat shield to 89 inch lbs. (10 Nm).
23. Tighten the 2 upper catalytic converter heat shield bolts to 89 inch lbs. (10 Nm).

Catalytic Converter—Underbody

See Figure 50.

➡**The exhaust system has 2 catalytic converters: a catalytic converter mounted to the exhaust manifold and an underbody catalytic converter that is serviced with the muffler and tailpipe.**

⁂ WARNING

The exhaust hanger isolators are constructed from a special material. Use only the correct specification exhaust hanger isolators or damage to the exhaust system may occur.

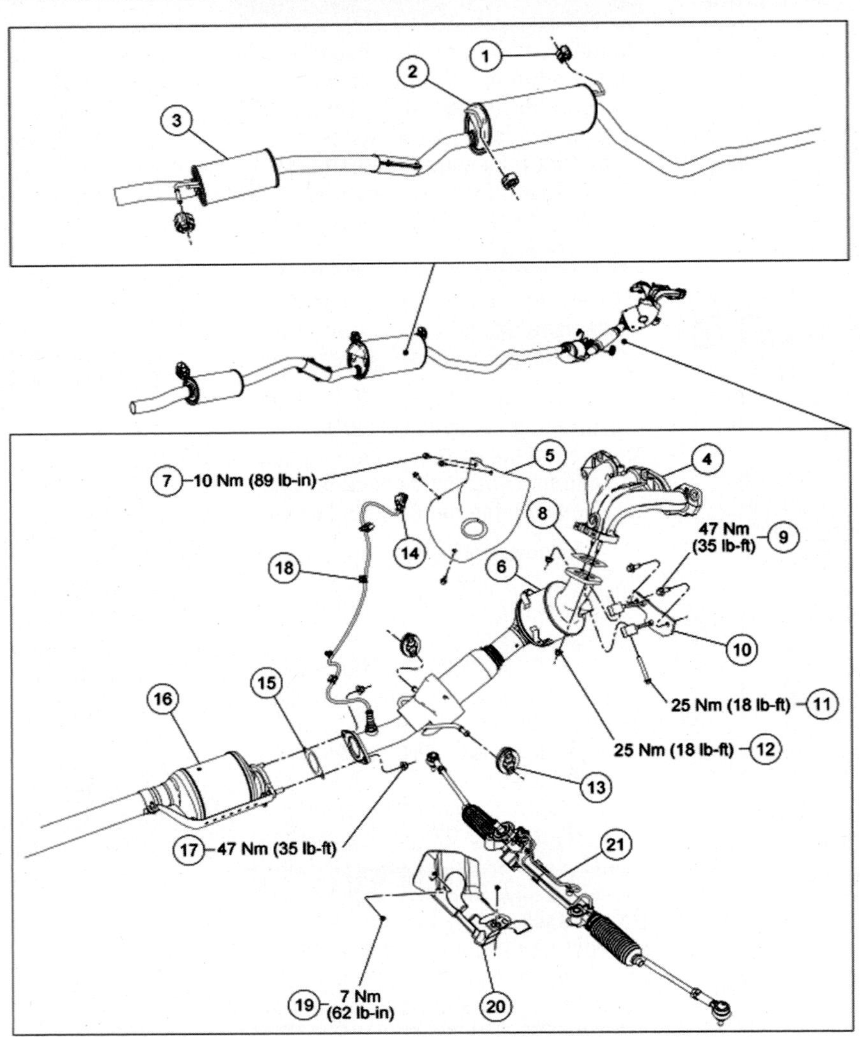

1. Muffler and tailpipe exhaust hanger isolator (3 required)
2. Muffler
3. Resonator
4. Exhaust manifold
5. Catalytic converter heat shield
6. Catalytic converter
7. Catalytic converter heat shield bolt
8. Gasket
9. Engine support bracket-to-engine block bolt (2 required)
10. Engine support bracket
11. Engine support bracket-to-catalytic converter bolt
12. Exhaust manifold-to-catalytic converter nut (2 required)
13. Catalytic converter exhaust hanger isolator (2 required)
14. Catalyst Monitor Sensor (CMS) electrical connector
15. Gasket
16. Underbody catalytic converter
17. Catalytic converter-to-muffler and tailpipe nut
18. CMS wiring retainer (4 required)
19. Steering gear heat shield bolt (2 required)
20. Steering gear heat shield
21. Steering gear

N0108625

Fig. 50 Exhaust system—exploded view

WARNING

Do not use oil or grease-based lubricants on the insulators. They may cause deterioration of the rubber. Oil or grease-based lubricants on the insulators may cause the exhaust hanger insulator to separate from the exhaust hanger bracket during vehicle operation.

➡Check the exhaust hanger isolators for damage and fatigue. Install new exhaust hanger isolators as required.

➡If replacement is not required, the production underbody catalytic converter and muffler and tailpipe assembly can be removed and installed as one piece. It is only necessary to cut the production exhaust to enable the service section(s) to be fitted. Before cutting any part of the exhaust system, check that the position of the cut is correct in comparison to the service section(s) being installed.

1. Before servicing the vehicle, refer to the Precautions Section.
2. With the vehicle in NEUTRAL, position it on a hoist.

➡It may be necessary to lubricate the catalytic converter-to-muffler and

tailpipe nuts and studs with penetrating and lock lubricant to assist in removal.

3. Remove the 2 catalytic converter-to-muffler and tailpipe nuts. Discard the nuts and gasket.
4. Detach the 3 exhaust hanger isolators and remove the muffler and tailpipe assembly.
5. Make the appropriate cut(s) to the muffler and tailpipe assembly to service the underbody catalytic converter, muffler or tailpipe.

To install:

6. Thoroughly clean the sealing surfaces of the flanges using a finishing pad.
7. Install the service clamp(s). Do not tighten the service clamp(s) at this time.
8. Position the muffler and tailpipe assembly and attach the 3 exhaust hanger isolators.
9. Install a new gasket and 2 new catalytic converter-to-muffler and tailpipe nuts. Tighten to 35 ft. lbs. (47 Nm).
10. Align the muffler and tailpipe assembly and tighten the service clamp(s). Tighten to 35 ft. lbs. (47 Nm).

CRANKSHAFT FRONT SEAL

REMOVAL & INSTALLATION

See Figures 51 and 52.

WARNING

Do not loosen or remove the crankshaft pulley bolt without first installing the special tools as instructed in this procedure. The crankshaft pulley and the crankshaft timing sprocket are not keyed to the crankshaft. The crankshaft, the crankshaft sprocket and the pulley are fitted together by friction, using diamond washers between the flange faces on each part. For that reason, the crankshaft sprocket is also unfastened if the pulley bolt is loosened. Before any repair requiring loosening or removal of the crankshaft pulley bolt, the crankshaft and camshafts must be locked in place by the special service tools, otherwise severe engine damage can occur.

WARNING

During engine repair procedures, cleanliness is extremely important. Any foreign material, including any material created while cleaning gasket surfaces, that enters the oil passages, coolant passages or the oil pan can cause engine failure.

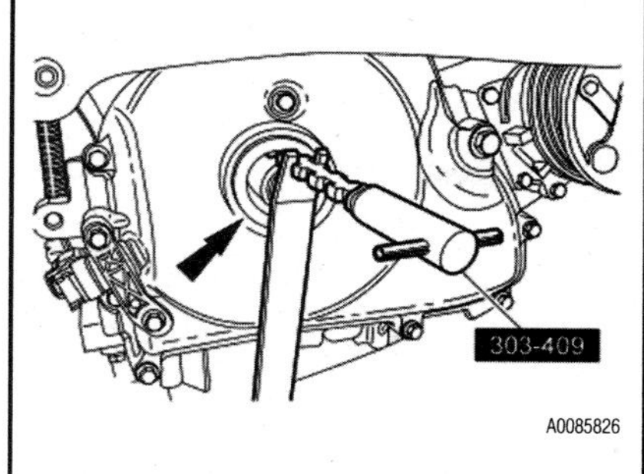

Fig. 51 Using the Oil Seal Remover to remove the crankshaft front oil seal

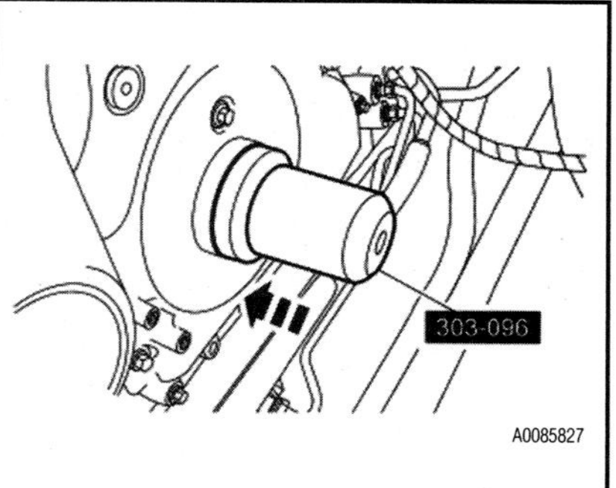

Fig. 52 Using the Oil Seal Remover to remove the crankshaft front oil seal

1. Before servicing the vehicle, refer to the Precautions Section.
2. Remove the crankshaft pulley.

➡Use care not to damage the engine front cover or the crankshaft when removing the seal.

3. Using the Oil Seal Remover, remove the crankshaft front oil seal.

To install:

➡Remove the through-bolt from the Camshaft Front Oil Seal Installer.

4. Lubricate the oil seal with clean engine oil.
5. Using the Camshaft Front Oil Seal Installer, install the crankshaft front oil seal.
6. Install the crankshaft pulley.

CYLINDER HEAD

REMOVAL & INSTALLATION

See Figures 53 through 59.

WARNING

Do not loosen or remove the crankshaft pulley bolt without first installing the special tools as instructed in this procedure. The crankshaft pulley and the crankshaft timing sprocket are not keyed to the crankshaft. The crankshaft, the crankshaft sprocket and the pulley are fitted together by friction, using diamond washers between the flange faces on each part. For that reason, the crankshaft sprocket is also unfastened if the pulley bolt is loosened. Before any repair requiring loosening or removal of the crankshaft pulley bolt, the crankshaft and camshafts must be locked in place by the special service tools, otherwise severe engine damage can occur.

WARNING

During engine repair procedures, cleanliness is extremely important. Any foreign material, including any material created while cleaning gasket surfaces, that enters the oil passages, coolant passages or the oil pan can cause engine failure.

1. Before servicing the vehicle, refer to the Precautions Section.
2. With the vehicle in NEUTRAL, position it on a hoist.
3. Release the fuel system pressure. Refer to Relieving Fuel System Pressure.
4. Depower the Supplemental Restraint System (SRS). Refer to Air Bag (Supplemental Restraint System), Disarming The System.
5. Remove the battery tray. Refer to Battery, removal & installation.
6. Remove the alternator. Refer to Alternator, removal & installation.
7. Remove the exhaust manifold. Refer to Exhaust Manifold, removal & installation.
8. Clean and inspect the exhaust manifold flange.

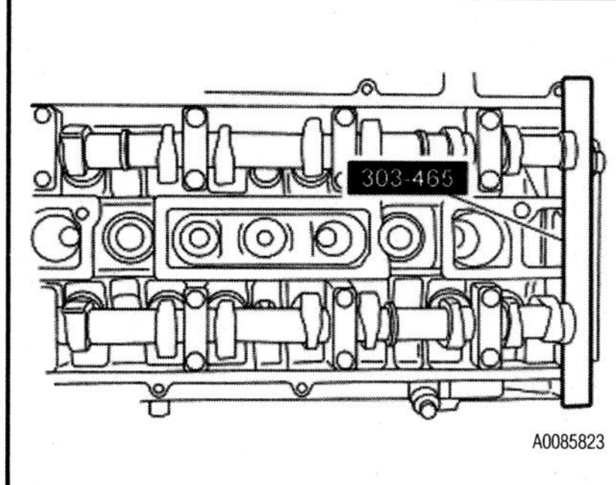

Fig. 53 Remove the Camshaft Alignment Plate

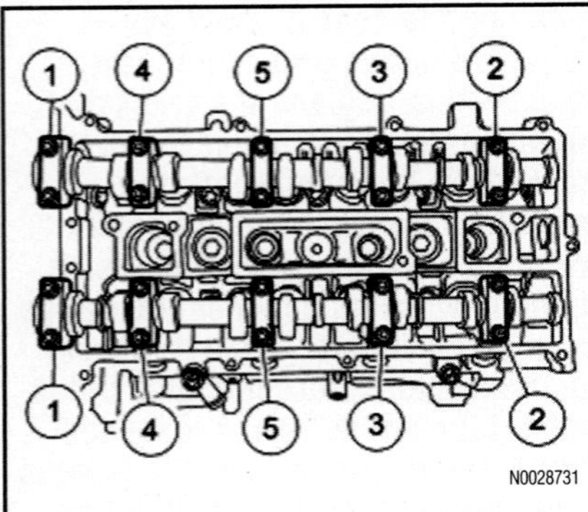

Fig. 54 Loosen the camshaft bearing cap bolts, in sequence, one turn at a time

9. Drain the cooling system. Refer to Engine Coolant, Drain & Refill Procedure.

10. Check the valve clearance. Refer to Valve Lash, Adjustment.

11. Remove the engine oil filter and discard.

12. Remove the intake manifold. Refer to Intake Manifold, removal & installation.

13. Remove the timing drive components. Refer to Timing Chain & Sprockets, removal & installation.

14. Remove the Camshaft Alignment Plate.

15. Mark the position of the camshaft lobes on the No. 1 cylinder for installation reference.

WARNING

Failure to follow the camshaft loosening procedure may result in damage to the camshafts.

➡Mark the location and orientation of each camshaft bearing cap.

16. Remove the camshafts from the engine.

a. Loosen the camshaft bearing cap bolts, in sequence, one turn at a time.

b. Repeat the first step until all tension is released from the camshaft bearing caps.

c. Remove the camshaft bearing caps.

d. Remove the camshafts.

➡If the camshafts and valve tappets are to be reused, mark the location of the valve tappets to make sure they are assembled in their original positions.

17. Remove the valve tappets.

➡The number on the valve tappets only reflects the digits that follow the decimal. For example, a tappet with the number 0.650 has the thickness of 3.650 mm.

18. Inspect the valve tappets.

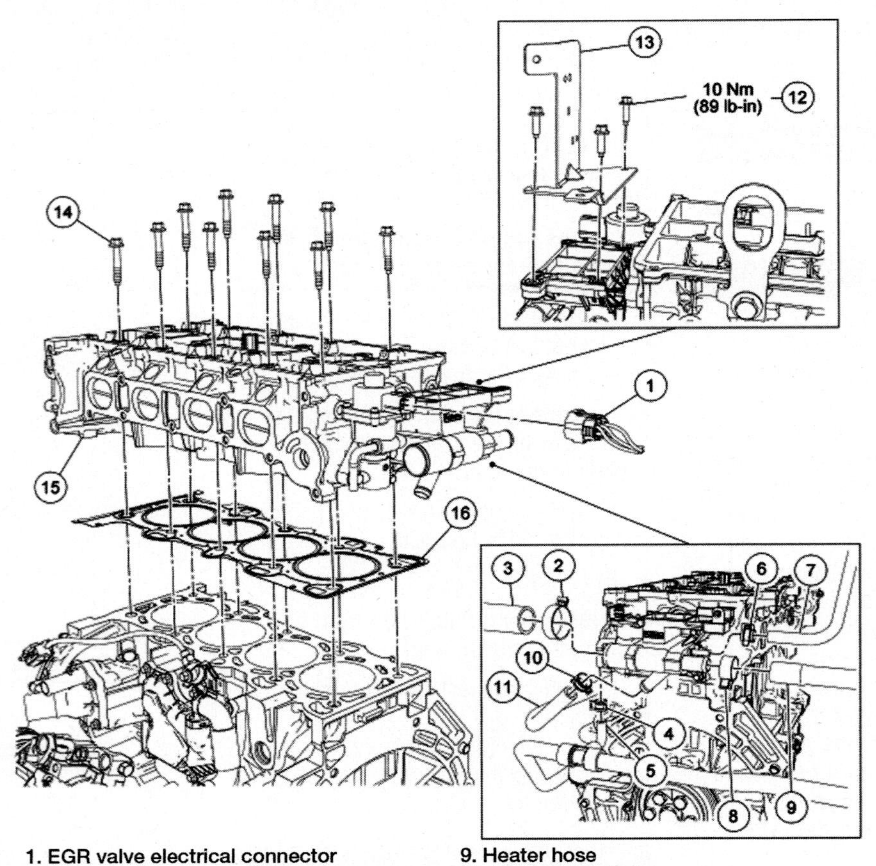

Fig. 55 Cylinder head—exploded view

19. Remove the 3 bolts and position the wiring harness and bracket aside.

20. Disconnect the EGR valve electrical connector.

21. Disconnect the coolant hoses from the coolant bypass.

22. Disconnect the EGR coolant hose.

23. Lower the engine and remove the Engine Support Bar.

24. Remove the 10 bolts and the cylinder head. Discard the bolts.

25. Remove and discard the head gasket.

To install:

26. Inspect the cylinder head mating surfaces.

WARNING

Do not use metal scrapers, wire brushes, power abrasive discs or other abrasive means to clean the sealing surfaces. These tools cause scratches and gouges that make leak paths. Use a plastic scraping tool to remove all traces of the head gasket.

➡Observe all warnings or cautions and follow all application directions contained on the packaging of the silicone gasket remover and the metal surface prep.

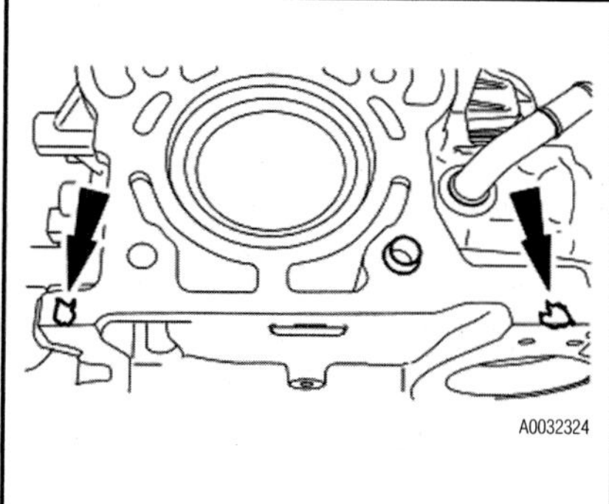

Fig. 56 Apply silicone gasket and sealant to the locations shown

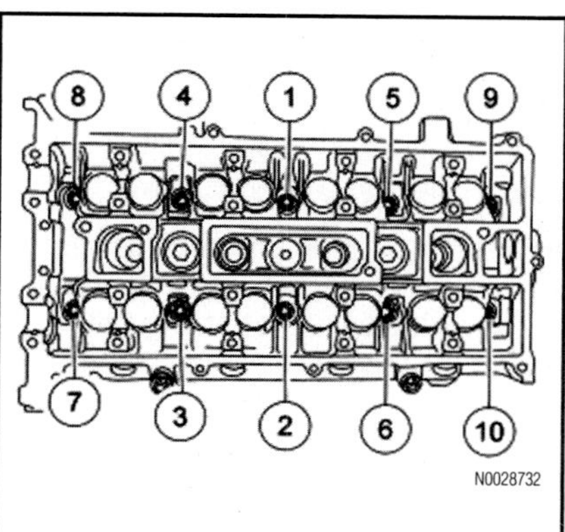

Fig. 57 Cylinder head tightening sequence

➡If there is no residual gasket material present, metal surface prep can be used to clean and prepare the surfaces.

27. Clean the cylinder head-to-cylinder block mating surface of both the cylinder head and the cylinder block in the following sequence.

a. Remove any large deposits of silicone or gasket material with a plastic scraper.

b. Apply silicone gasket remover, following package directions, and allow to set for several minutes.

c. Remove the silicone gasket remover with a plastic scraper. A second application of silicone gasket remover may be required if residual traces of silicone or gasket material remain.

d. Apply metal surface prep, following package directions, to remove any traces of oil or coolant, and to prepare the surfaces to bond with the new gasket. Do not attempt to make the metal shiny. Some staining of the metal surfaces is normal.

28. Clean the cylinder head bolt holes in the cylinder block. Make sure all coolant, oil or other foreign material is removed.

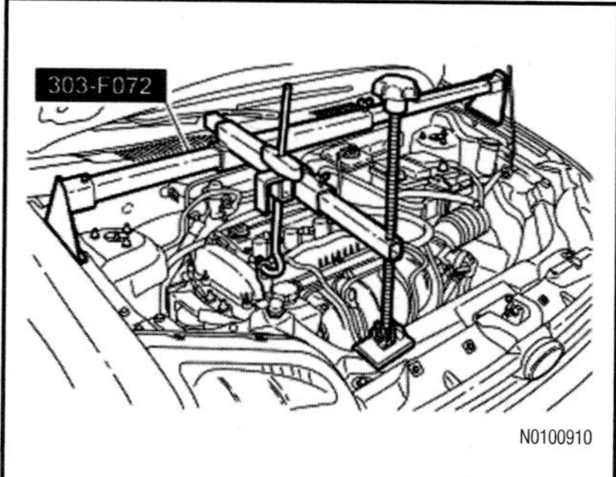

Fig. 58 Install the Engine Support Bar and raise the engine

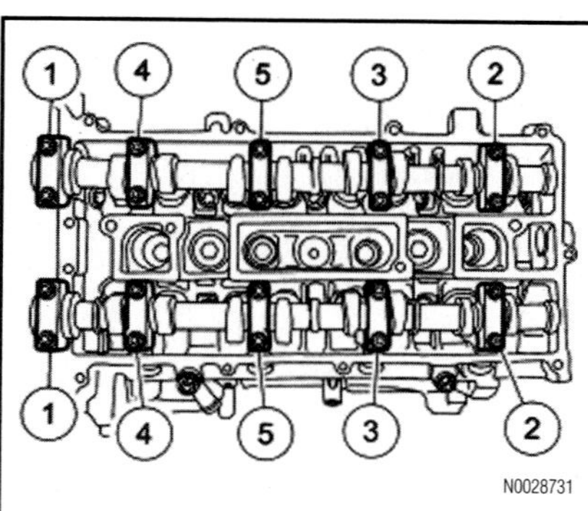

Fig. 59 Camshaft bearing cap bolt tightening sequence

29. Support the cylinder head on a bench with the head gasket side up. Check the cylinder head distortion and the cylinder block distortion.

30. Apply silicone gasket and sealant to the locations shown.

31. Install a new cylinder head gasket.

➡The cylinder head bolts are torque-to-yield and must not be reused. New cylinder head bolts must be installed.

32. Install the cylinder head and the 10 new bolts. Tighten the bolts in the sequence shown in 5 stages.

- Stage 1: Tighten to 44 inch lbs. (5 Nm)
- Stage 2: Tighten to 11 ft. lbs. (15 Nm)
- Stage 3: Tighten to 33 ft. lbs. (45 Nm)
- Stage 4: Turn 90 degrees
- Stage 5: Turn an additional 90 degrees

33. Install the Engine Support Bar and raise the engine.

34. Install the EGR coolant hose.

35. Connect the coolant hoses onto the coolant bypass.

36. Connect the EGR valve electrical connector.

37. Position the wire harness bracket and install the 3 bolts. Tighten to 89 inch lbs. (10 Nm).

➡Lubricate the valve tappets with clean engine oil.

38. Install the valve tappets in their original positions.

WARNING

Install the camshafts with the alignment notches in the camshafts lined up so the camshaft alignment plate can be installed. Make sure the lobes on the No. 1 cylinder are in the same position at noted in the removal procedure. Failure to follow this procedure can cause severe damage to the valves and pistons.

39. Lubricate the camshaft journals and bearing caps with clean engine oil.

40. Install the camshafts and bearing caps in their original location and orientation. Tighten the bearing caps in the sequence shown in 3 stages:

- Stage 1: Tighten the camshaft bearing cap bolts, one turn at a time, until the cam is fully seated

- Stage 2: Tighten to 62 inch lbs. (7 Nm)
- Stage 3: Tighten to 12 ft. lbs. (16 Nm)

41. Install the timing drive components. Refer to Timing Chain & Sprockets, removal & installation.
42. Install the valve cover. Refer to Valve Covers, removal & installation.
43. Install the intake manifold. Refer to Intake Manifold, removal & installation.
44. Install the exhaust manifold. Refer to Exhaust Manifold, removal & installation.
45. Install the alternator. Refer to Alternator, removal & installation.
46. Install the battery tray. Refer to Battery, removal & installation.
47. Drain the engine oil. Install the drain plug and tighten to 21 ft. lbs. (28 Nm).
48. Lubricate the engine oil filter gasket with clean engine oil prior to installing the oil filter. Install a new engine oil filter. Tighten the oil filter ¾ turn after the oil filter gasket makes contact with the oil filter adapter.
49. Fill the engine with the proper type and amount of clean engine oil.
50. Fill and bleed the cooling system. Refer to Engine Coolant, Drain & Refill Procedure.
51. Repower the SRS. Refer to Air Bag (Supplemental Restraint System), Arming The System.

ENGINE OIL & FILTER

REPLACEMENT

See Figures 60 and 61.

CAUTION

Prolonged and repeated contact with used engine oil may cause skin cancer. Try to avoid direct skin contact with used oil. If skin contact is made, wash thoroughly with soap or hand cleaner as soon as possible. Wear protective clothing, including impervious gloves where practicable. Where there is a risk of eye contact, eye protection should be worn, for example, chemical goggles or face shields; in addition an eye wash facility should be provided.

CAUTION

Hot oil can scald.

➡Use only engine oil with the American Petroleum Institute (API) Certified For Gasoline Engines "Starburst" symbol. It is highly recommended to use SAE 5W-20 oil.

1. Before servicing the vehicle, refer to the Precautions Section.
2. Before draining the engine oil, check the engine for oil leakage. If any sign of leakage is found, make sure to correct the defective part before proceeding to the following procedure.
3. Drain the engine oil by removing the drain plug.
4. Wipe the drain plug and its mounting surface clean. Reinstall the drain plug with a new gasket, if applicable, and tighten the drain plug to 21 ft. lbs. (28 Nm).
5. Remove the oil filter with an oil filter wrench.

To install:

6. Wipe the oil filter mounting surface clean.

➡Lubricate the engine oil filter gasket with clean engine oil prior to installing the oil filter.

7. Install the new oil filter by hand until the filter O-ring touches the filter mounting surface.

➡To tighten the oil filter properly, it is important to accurately identify the position at which the filter O-ring first contacts the mounting surface.

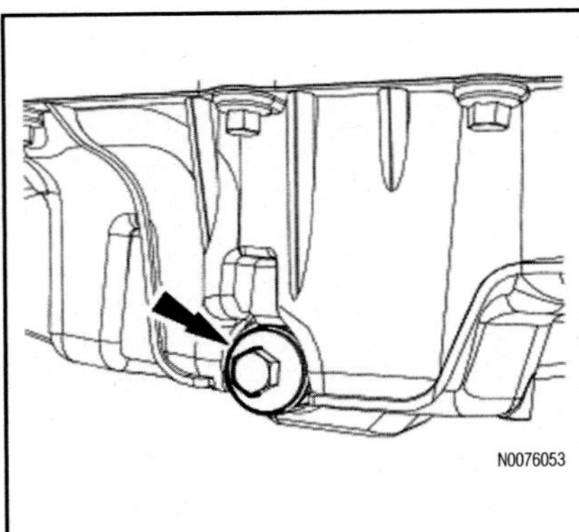

Fig. 60 Engine oil drain plug location

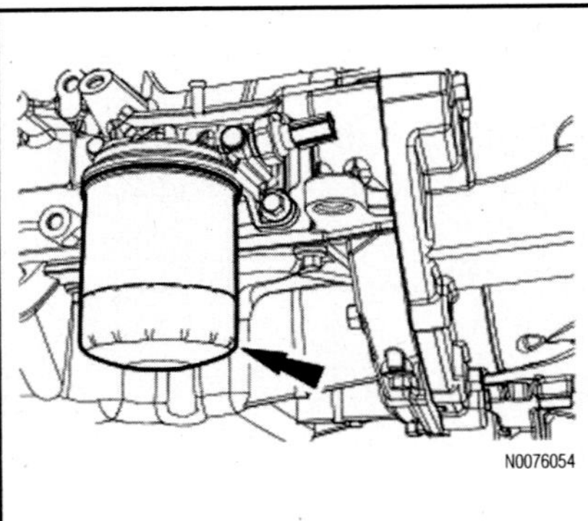

Fig. 61 Oil filter location

8. Tighten the oil filter ¾ turn from the point of contact with the filter mounting surface.
9. Refill the engine oil to the specified amount.

➡Engine oil capacity is specified below. However, note that the amount of oil required when actually changing the oil may somewhat differ from the data depending on various conditions (temperature, viscosity, etc.)

- Oil pan plus oil filter capacity: About 4.5 quarts (4.3 liters)

10. Check the oil filter and drain plug for oil leakage.
11. Start and run the engine for 3 minutes. After stopping the engine, wait for 5 minutes. Then, confirm that the specified amount of engine oil has been refilled.

EXHAUST MANIFOLD

REMOVAL & INSTALLATION

See Figures 62 and 63.

1. Before servicing the vehicle, refer to the Precautions Section.
2. With the vehicle in NEUTRAL, position it on a hoist.
3. Remove the catalytic converter. Refer to Catalytic Converter, removal & installation.
4. Disconnect the Heated Oxygen Sensor (HO2S) electrical connector. Detach the wiring retainer.
5. Remove the 4 exhaust manifold heat shield bolts and the heat shield.
6. Remove and discard the 7 exhaust manifold nuts.
7. Remove the exhaust manifold and discard the exhaust manifold gasket.
8. Remove and discard the 7 exhaust manifold studs.
9. Clean and inspect the exhaust manifold.

To install:

10. Install the 7 new exhaust manifold studs. Tighten to 13 ft. lbs. (17 Nm).

➡Failure to tighten the catalytic converter nuts to specification before installing the converter bracket bolts may cause the converter to develop an exhaust leak.

11. Install a new exhaust manifold gasket, the exhaust manifold and 7 new nuts in the sequence shown:

Fig. 62 Exhaust manifold tightening sequence shown

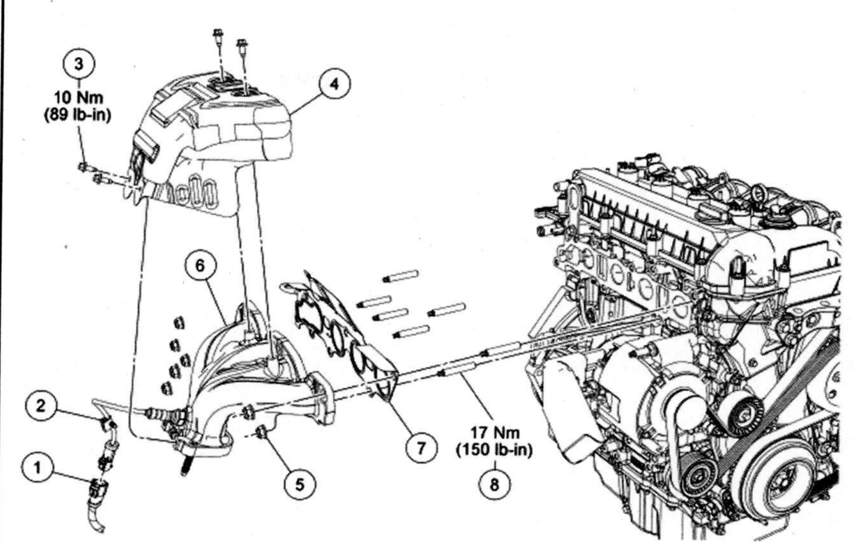

Fig. 63 Exhaust manifold and related components—exploded view

- Stage 1: Tighten to 35 ft. lbs. (48 Nm).
- Stage 2: Tighten to 35 ft. lbs. (48 Nm).

12. Install the exhaust manifold heat shield and the 4 bolts. Tighten to 89 inch lbs. (10 Nm).
13. Connect the HO2S electrical connector. Attach the wiring retainer.
14. Install the catalytic converter. Refer to Catalytic Converter, removal & installation.

INTAKE MANIFOLD

REMOVAL & INSTALLATION

See Figures 64 through 67.

1. Before servicing the vehicle, refer to the Precautions Section.
2. With vehicle in NEUTRAL, position it on a hoist.
3. Remove the Air Cleaner (ACL) and outlet pipe. Refer to Air Cleaner, removal & installation.
4. Remove the oil level indicator and tube.
5. Remove the fuel rail. Refer to Fuel Injectors, removal & installation.
6. Remove the transaxle fluid indicator.
7. Remove the intake manifold lower bolt.
8. Detach the engine wiring harness pin-type retainer from the intake manifold.
9. Disconnect the Engine Oil Pressure (EOP) switch electrical connector and detach the wire harness retainer from the starter stud bolt.
10. Disconnect the electronic throttle control electrical connector.
11. Disconnect the fuel vapor return hose.
12. Disconnect the power brake booster vacuum tube.
    a. Depress the quick release locking ring.
    b. Pull the vacuum tube out of the quick release fitting.
13. Disconnect the Manifold Absolute Pressure (MAP) sensor electrical connector.
14. Detach the wiring harness retainer from the intake manifold and disconnect the Knock Sensor (KS) electrical connector.
15. Detach the 4 wiring harness pin-type retainers from the intake manifold.

➡The 2 intake manifold bolts differ in length from rest of the bolts and also retain a crash bracket to the intake manifold. The 2 bolts are equipped with an attachment feature that allows them to be loosened but remain attached to the intake manifold. Do not attempt to remove the 2 bolts or the crash bracket from the intake manifold.

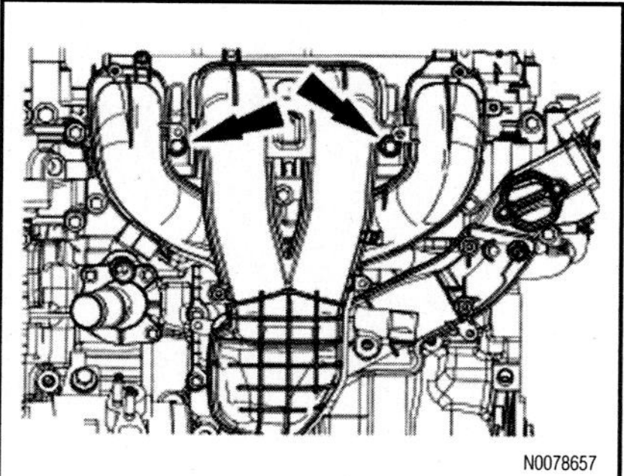

Fig. 64 Loosen the 2 intake manifold bolts shown

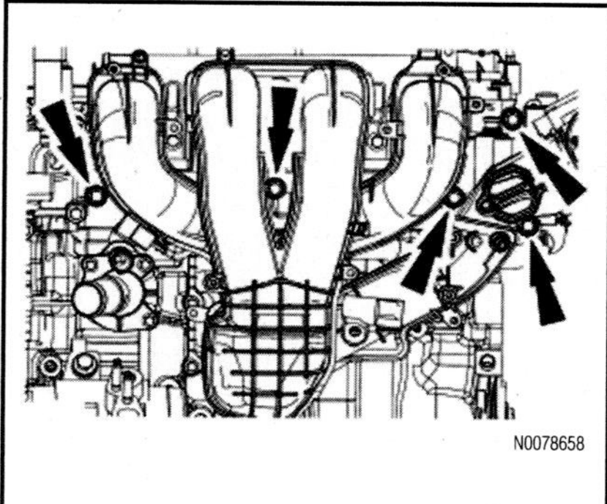

Fig. 65 Remove the 5 intake manifold bolts shown

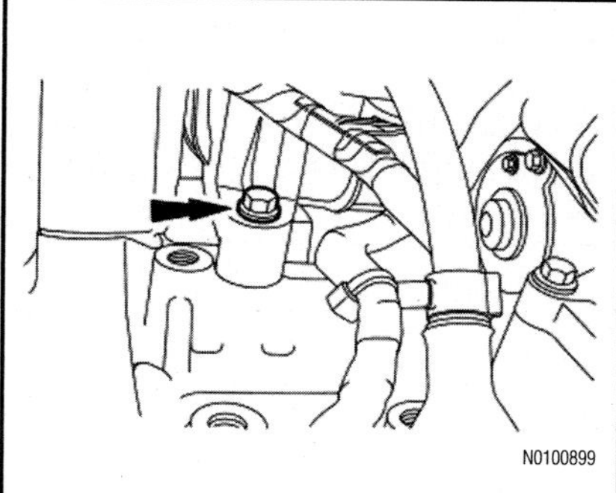

Fig. 66 Install the lower intake manifold bolt

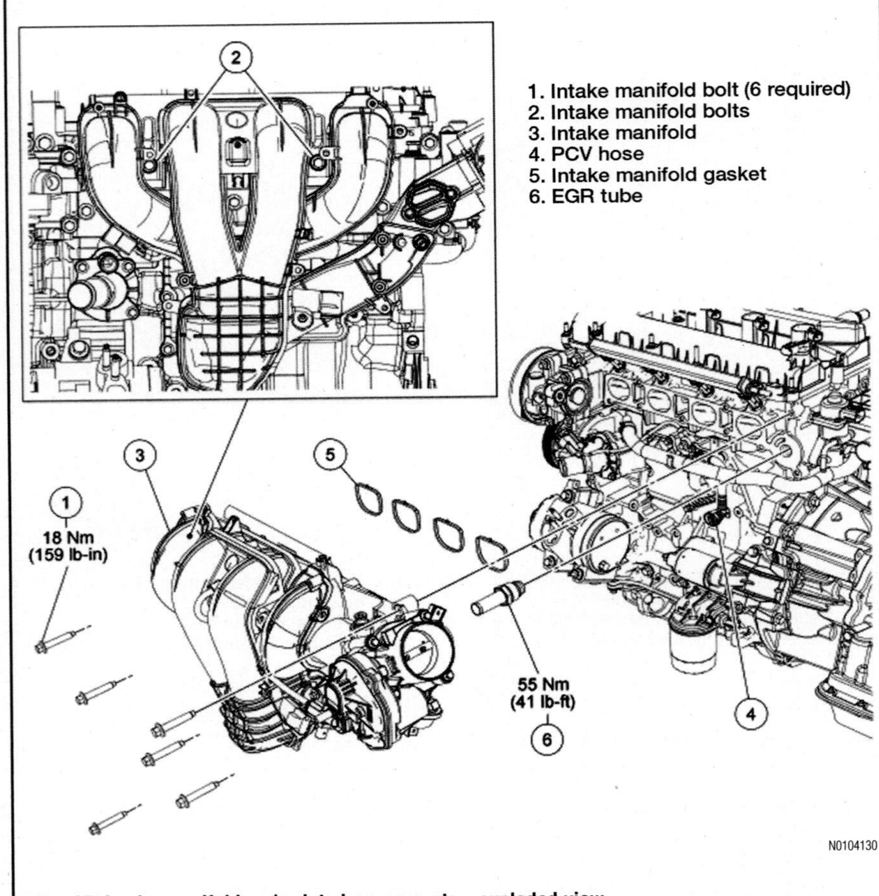

Fig. 67 Intake manifold and related components—exploded view

16. Loosen the 2 intake manifold bolts.
17. Remove the 5 intake manifold bolts.
18. Remove the EGR tube from the cylinder head.
19. Disconnect the PCV hose and remove the intake manifold.

To install:

WARNING

If the engine is repaired or replaced because of upper engine failure, typically including valve or piston damage, check the intake manifold for metal debris. If metal debris is found, install a new intake manifold. Failure to follow these instructions can result in engine damage.

20. Inspect and install new intake manifold gaskets if necessary.
21. Position the intake manifold and connect the PCV hose.
22. Install the EGR tube. Tighten to 41 ft. lbs. (55 Nm).
23. Attach the wiring harness retainer to the intake manifold and connect the KS electrical connector.
24. Install the intake manifold and hand-tighten the 2 intake manifold bolts that are equipped with an attachment feature that allows them to be loosened but remain attached to the intake manifold.
25. Install the 5 intake manifold mounting bolts.
26. Tighten all 7 intake manifold bolts to 13 ft. lbs. (18 Nm).
27. Attach the 4 wiring harness pin-type retainers to the intake manifold.
28. Connect the MAP sensor electrical connector.
29. Connect the power brake booster vacuum tube. Push the vacuum tube into the quick release fitting.
30. Connect the fuel vapor return hose.
31. Connect the electronic throttle control electrical connector.
32. Connect the EOP switch electrical connector and attach the wire harness retainer to the starter stud bolt.
33. Attach the engine wiring harness pin-type retainer to the intake manifold.
34. Install the lower intake manifold bolt. Tighten to 13 ft. lbs. (18 Nm).
35. Install the transaxle fluid indicator.
36. Install the fuel rail. Refer to Fuel Injectors, removal & installation.
37. Install the oil level indicator and tube.
38. Install the Air Cleaner (ACL) and outlet pipe. Refer to Air Cleaner, removal & installation.

OIL PAN

REMOVAL & INSTALLATION

See Figures 68 through 70.

1. Before servicing the vehicle, refer to the Precautions Section.
2. With the vehicle in NEUTRAL, position it on a hoist.
3. Remove the battery tray. For additional information, refer to Battery, removal & installation.

WARNING

To prevent damage to the transmission, do not loosen the transmission-to-engine bolts more than 0.19 inch (5mm).

4. Loosen the upper bellhousing-to-engine bolt and stud bolt 0.19 inch (5mm).
5. Remove the oil level indicator and tube.
6. Loosen the 2 LH bellhousing-to-engine bolts 0.19 inch (5mm).
7. Loosen the RH engine-to-bellhousing bolt and stud bolt 0.19 inch (5mm).
8. Remove the 2 bellhousing-to-oil pan bolts.
9. Remove the 2 oil pan-to-bellhousing bolts.
10. Slide the transaxle rearward 0.19 inch (5mm).
11. Remove the 2 bolts and the accessory drive belt splash shield.
12. Drain the engine oil. Install the drain plug and tighten to 21 ft. lbs. (28 Nm).

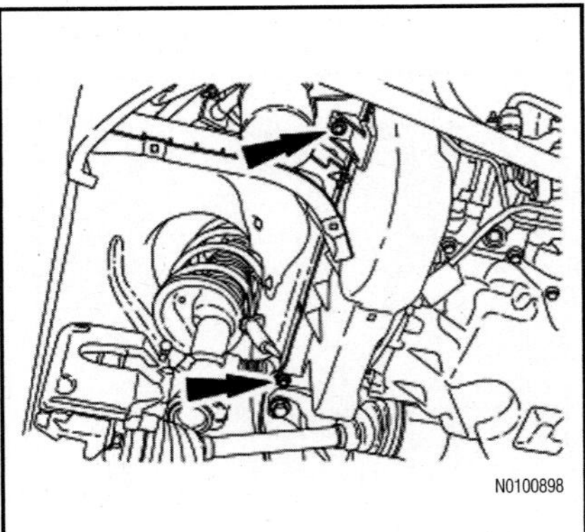

Fig. 68 Remove the 2 bolts and the accessory drive belt splash shield

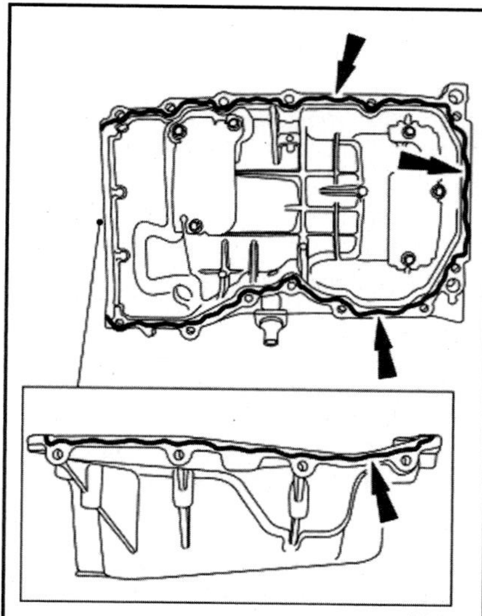

Fig. 69 Apply a bead of sealant to the areas indicated

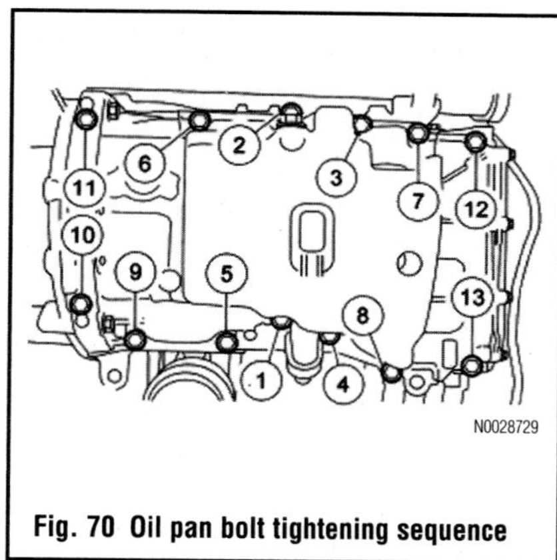

Fig. 70 Oil pan bolt tightening sequence

13. Remove the 4 engine front cover-to-oil pan bolts.
14. Remove the 13 bolts and the oil pan.

To install:

WARNING

Do not use metal scrapers, wire brushes, power abrasive discs or other abrasive means to clean the sealing surfaces. These tools cause scratches and gouges, which make leak paths. Use a plastic scraping tool to remove traces of sealant.

15. Clean and inspect all mating surfaces.

➡If the oil pan is not secured within 10 minutes of sealant application, the sealant must be removed and the sealing area cleaned with metal surface prep. Allow to dry until there is no sign of wetness, or 10 minutes, whichever is longer. Failure to follow this procedure can cause future oil leakage.

16. Apply a 0.09 inch (2.5mm) bead of silicone gasket and sealant to the oil pan-to-engine block and to the oil pan-to-engine front cover mating surface.
17. Position the oil pan onto the engine and install the 13 oil pan bolts finger-tight.

➡The engine front cover-to-oil pan bolts must be tightened first to align the front surface of the oil pan flush with the front surface of the engine block.

18. Install the 4 engine front cover-to-oil pan bolts. Tighten to 89 inch lbs. (10 Nm).
19. Tighten the oil pan bolts to 18 ft. lbs. (25 Nm) in the sequence shown.
20. Install the accessory drive belt splash shield and the 2 bolts. Tighten to 80 inch lbs. (9 Nm).
21. Alternate tightening the 1 LH bellhousing-to-engine and 1 RH engine-to-bellhousing lower bolts to slide the transaxle and engine together. Tighten to 35 ft. lbs. (48 Nm).
22. Tighten the remaining LH bellhousing-to-engine bolt and the remaining rear engine-to-bellhousing stud bolt. Tighten to 35 ft. lbs. (48 Nm).
23. Install the 2 bellhousing-to-oil pan bolts. Tighten to 35 ft. lbs. (48 Nm).
24. Install the 2 oil pan-to-bellhousing bolts. Tighten to 35 ft. lbs. (48 Nm).
25. Install the oil level indicator and tube.
26. Tighten the top bellhousing-to-engine bolt and stud bolt. Tighten to 35 ft. lbs. (48 Nm).
27. Install the battery tray. For additional information, refer to Battery, removal & installation.
28. Fill the engine with the proper type and amount of clean engine oil.

OIL PUMP

REMOVAL & INSTALLATION

See Figures 71 through 76.

1. Before servicing the vehicle, refer to the Precautions Section.
2. With the engine in NEUTRAL, position it on a hoist.
3. Remove the engine front cover. Refer to Timing Chain Front Cover, removal & installation.
4. Remove the oil level indicator and tube.
5. Drain the engine oil, then install the drain plug and tighten to 21 ft. lbs. (28 Nm).
6. Remove the 2 oil pan-to-bellhousing bolts.
7. Remove the 2 bellhousing-to-oil pan bolts.
8. Remove the 13 bolts and the oil pan.

➡Discard the gasket and clean and inspect the gasket mating surfaces.

9. Remove the 2 bolts and the oil pump screen and pickup tube.
10. Remove the oil pump drive chain tensioner.
    a. Release the tension on the tensioner spring.
    b. Remove the tensioner and the 2 shoulder bolts.
11. Remove the chain from the oil pump sprocket.
12. Remove the bolt and oil pump sprocket.
13. Remove the 4 bolts and the oil pump.

To install:

14. Clean the oil pump and cylinder block mating surfaces with metal surface prep.
15. Install the oil pump assembly. Tighten the 4 bolts in the sequence shown in 2 stages:

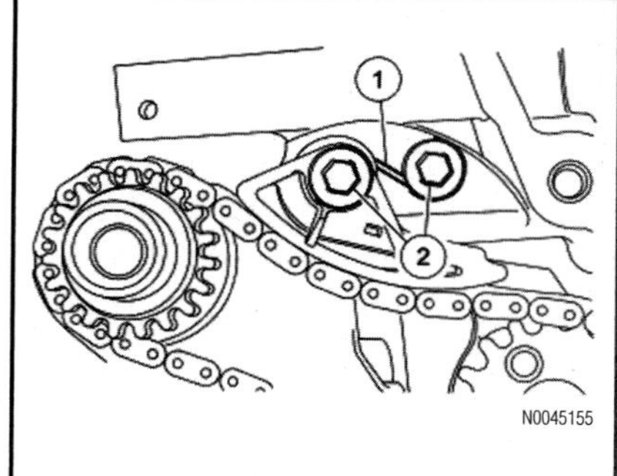

Fig. 71 Remove the oil pump drive chain tensioner

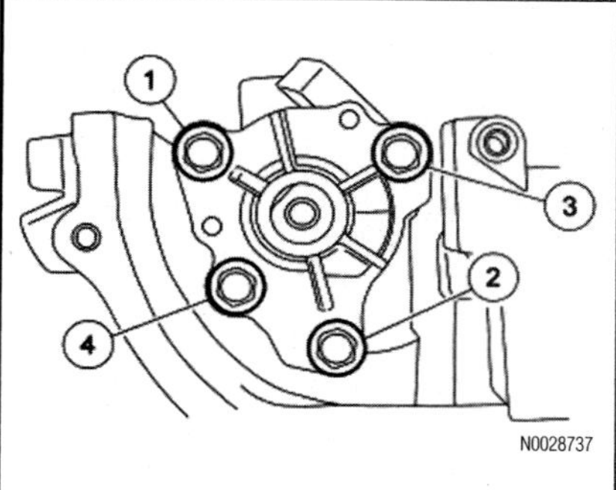

Fig. 72 Oil pump assembly bolt tightening sequence

- Stage 1: Tighten to 89 inch lbs. (10 Nm)
- Stage 2: Tighten to 15 ft. lbs. (20 Nm)

16. Install the oil pump sprocket and bolt. Tighten to 18 ft. lbs. (25 Nm).
17. Install the chain onto the oil pump sprocket.
18. Install the oil pump drive chain tensioner shoulder bolt. Tighten to 89 inch lbs. (10 Nm).
19. Install the oil pump chain tensioner and bolt. Hook the tensioner spring around the shoulder bolt. Tighten to 89 inch lbs. (10 Nm).
20. Install the oil pump screen and pickup tube and the 2 bolts. Tighten to 89 inch lbs. (10 Nm).

⁂ WARNING

Do not use metal scrapers, wire brushes, power abrasive discs or other abrasive means to clean the sealing surfaces. These tools cause scratches and gouges, which make leak paths. Use a plastic scraping tool to remove traces to sealant.

21. Clean all mating surfaces with metal surface prep.

➡If the oil pan is not secured within 10 minutes of sealant application, the sealant must be removed and the sealing area cleaned with metal surface prep. Allow to dry until there is no sign of wetness, or 10 minutes, whichever is longer. Failure to follow this procedure can cause future oil leakage.

22. Apply a 0.09 inch (2.5mm) bead of sealant gasket and sealant to the oil pan. Position the oil pan onto the engine and install the 2 rear oil pan bolts finger-tight.
23. Using a suitable straight edge, align the front surface of the oil pan flush with the front surface of the engine block.

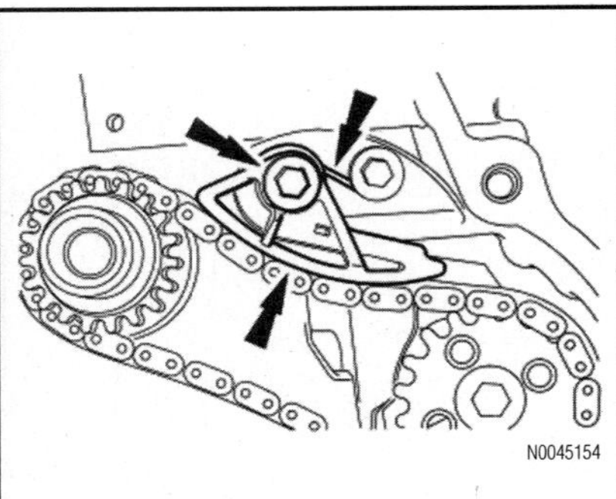

Fig. 73 Install the oil pump chain tensioner and bolt

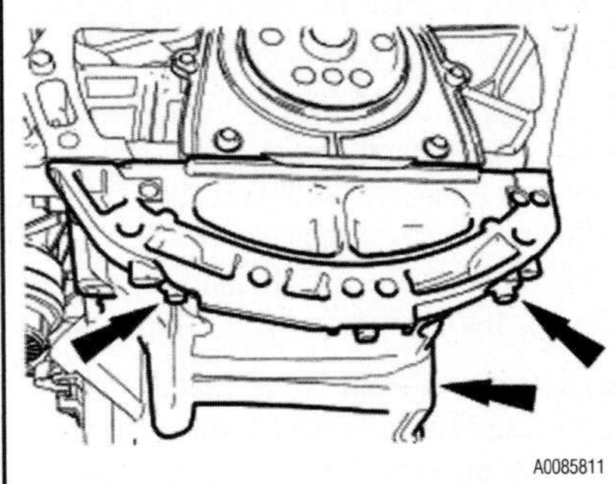

Fig. 74 Position the oil pan onto the engine and install the 2 rear oil pan bolts finger-tight

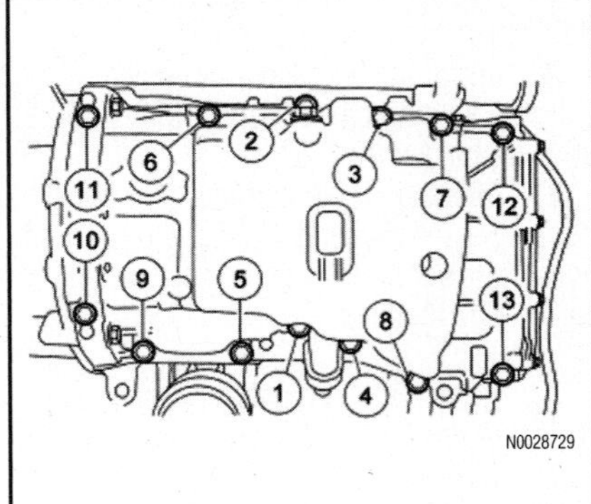

Fig. 75 Oil pan bolt tightening sequence

24. Install the remaining oil pan bolts. Tighten in sequence to 18 ft. lbs. (25 Nm).
25. Install the 2 bellhousing-to-oil pan bolts. Tighten to 35 ft. lbs. (48 Nm).
26. Install the 4 oil pan-to-bellhousing bolts. Tighten to 35 ft. lbs. (48 Nm).
27. Install the oil level indicator and tube.
28. Install the engine front cover. Refer to Timing Chain Front Cover, removal & installation.
29. Fill the engine with the proper type and amount of clean engine oil.

PISTON AND RING

POSITIONING

See Figures 77 and 79.

The arrow on the top of the piston points towards the front of the engine.

The piston compression upper and lower ring should be installed with the paint mark on the outside diameter circumference of the ring to be positioned on the right side of the ring gap. The lower compression ring can also be installed with the undercut side downward.

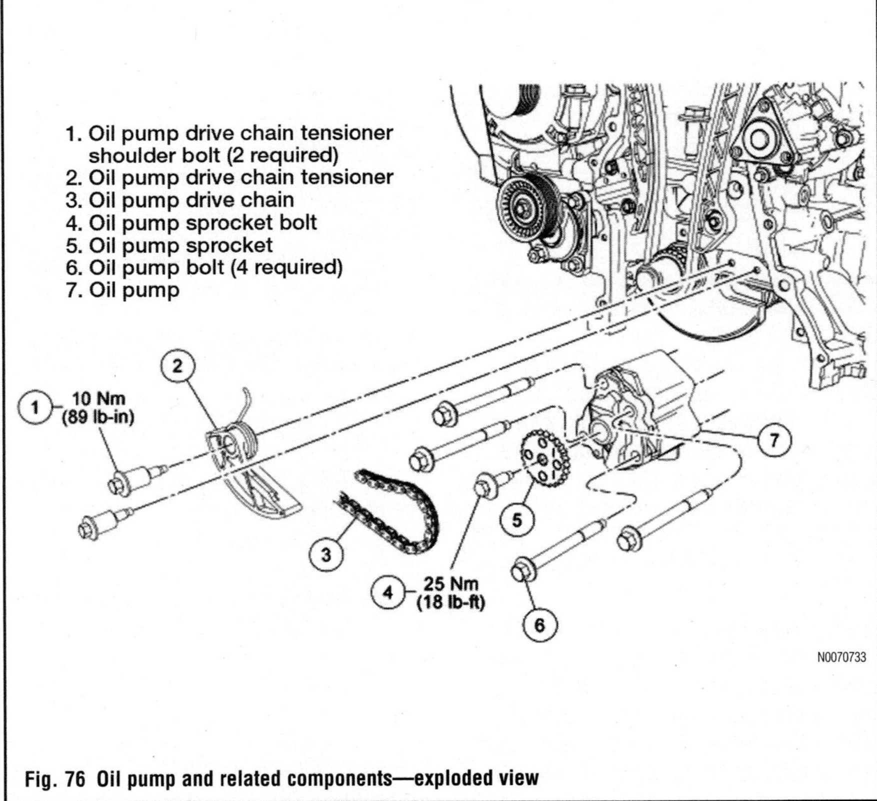

Fig. 76 Oil pump and related components—exploded view

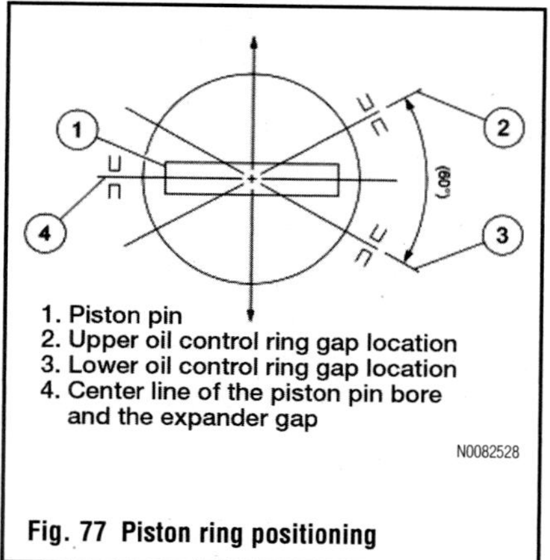

Fig. 77 Piston ring positioning

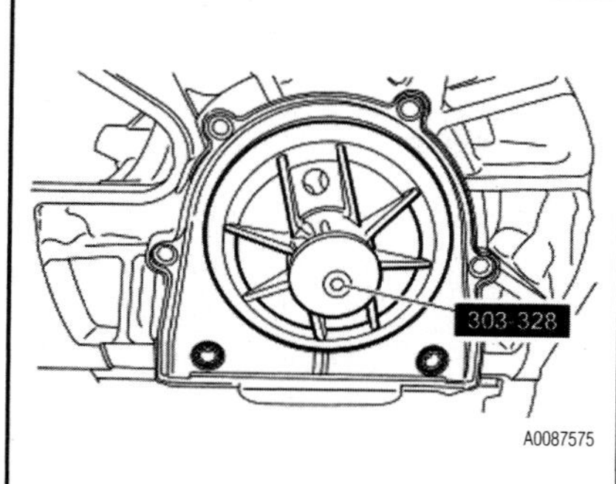

Fig. 79 Using the Crankshaft Rear Main Oil Seal Installer

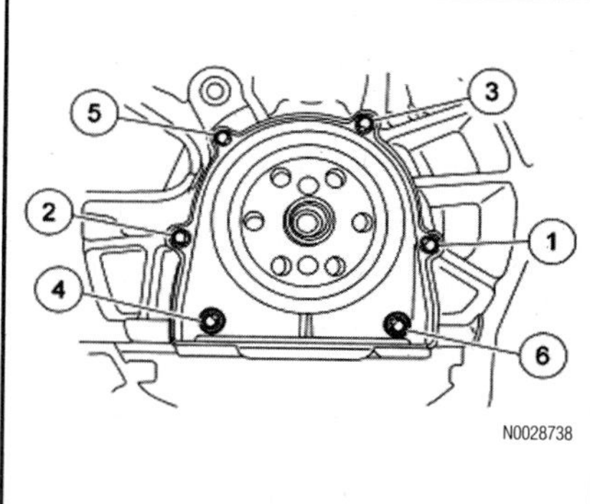

Fig. 80 Crankshaft rear seal with retainer plate bolt tightening sequence

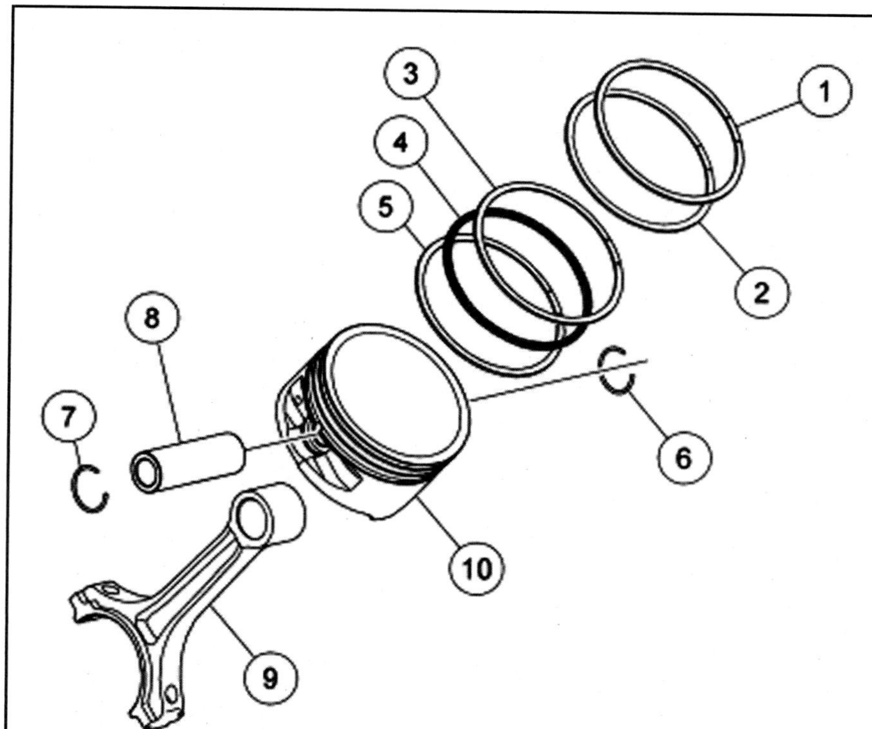

Fig. 78 Piston and ring assembly—exploded view

REAR MAIN SEAL

REMOVAL & INSTALLATION

See Figures 74, 80 through 83.

1. Before servicing the vehicle, refer to the Precautions Section.
2. With the vehicle in NEUTRAL, position it on a hoist.
3. Remove the flexplate.
4. Drain the engine oil. Install the drain plug and tighten to 21 ft. lbs. (28 Nm).
5. Remove the oil level indicator and tube.

WARNING

If the oil pan is not removed, damage to the rear oil seal retainer joint can occur.

6. Remove the 17 bolts and the oil pan.
7. Remove the 6 bolts and the crankshaft rear seal with retainer plate.

To install:

8. Using the Crankshaft Rear Main Oil Seal Installer, position the crankshaft rear oil seal with retainer plate onto the crankshaft.
9. Install the crankshaft rear seal with retainer plate and 6 bolts. Tighten in sequence to 89 inch lbs. (10 Nm).

WARNING

Do not use metal scrapers, wire brushes, power abrasive discs or other abrasive means to clean the sealing surfaces. These tools cause scratches and gouges, which make leak paths. Use a plastic scraping tool to remove traces of sealant.

10. Clean and inspect all the oil pan, cylinder block, and front cover flange mating surfaces.

➡If not secured within 4 minutes, the sealant must be removed and the sealing area cleaned. To clean the sealing area, use silicone gasket remover and metal surface prep. Follow the directions on the packaging. Failure to follow this procedure can cause future oil leakage.

➡The oil pan must be installed and the bolts tightened within 4 minutes of applying the silicone gasket and sealant.

11. Apply a 0.09 inch (2.5mm) bead of silicone gasket and sealant to the oil pan.
12. Install the oil pan and the 2 bolts finger-tight.
13. Install the 4 front cover-to-oil pan bolts. Tighten to 89 inch lbs. (10 Nm).

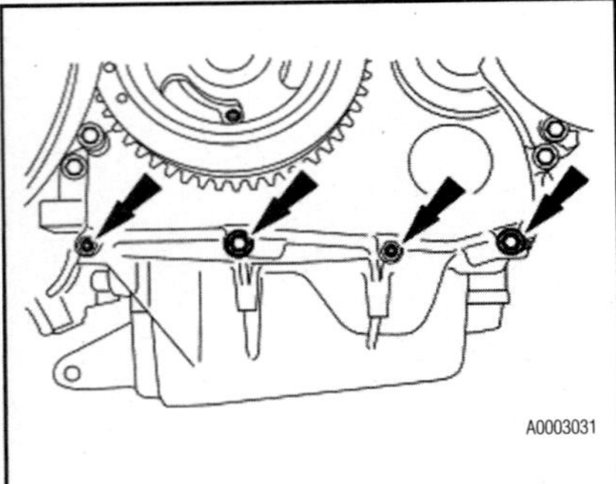

Fig. 81 Install the 4 engine front cover-to-oil pan bolts

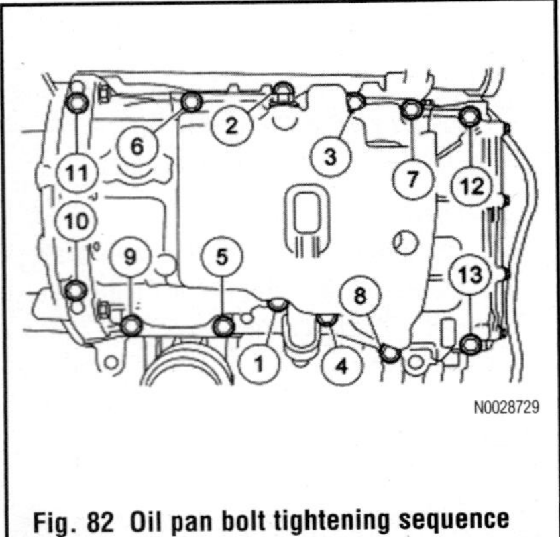

Fig. 82 Oil pan bolt tightening sequence

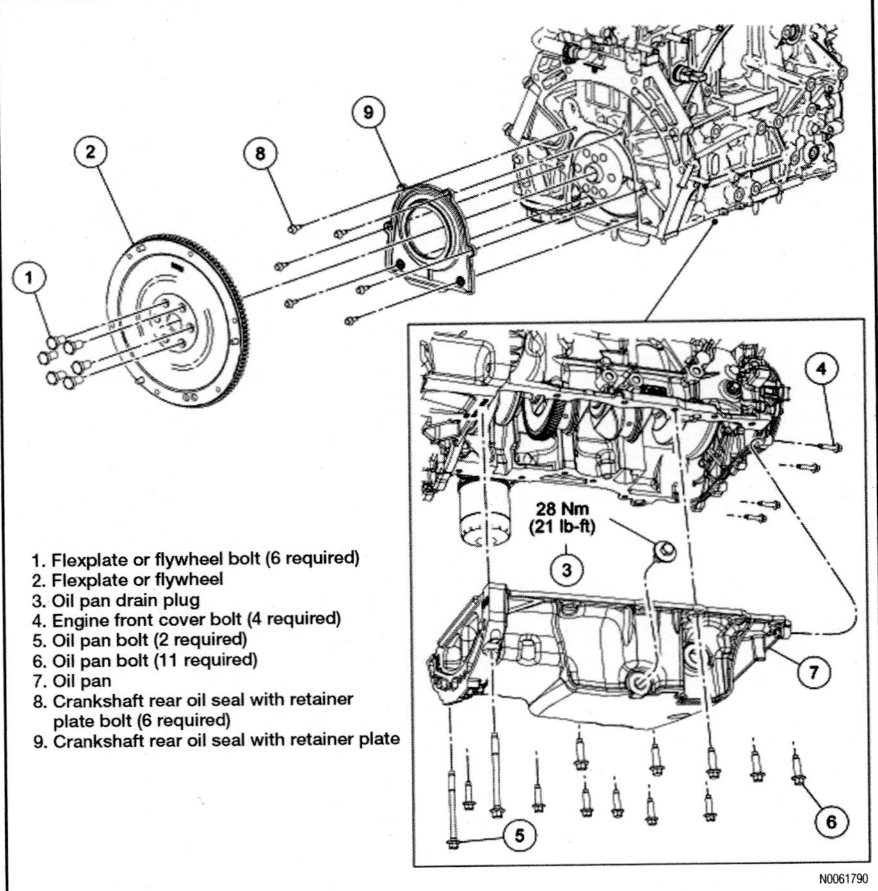

Fig. 83 Exploded view of crankshaft rear seal and related components

14. Install the remaining oil pan bolts. Tighten in sequence to 18 ft. lbs. (25 Nm).
15. Install the oil level indicator and tube.
16. Install the flywheel or flexplate.
17. Fill the engine with the proper type and amount of clean engine oil.

TIMING CHAIN FRONT COVER

REMOVAL & INSTALLATION

See Figures 84 through 90.

⁂ WARNING

Do not loosen or remove the crankshaft pulley bolt without first installing the special tools as instructed in this procedure. The crankshaft pulley and the crankshaft timing sprocket are not keyed to the crankshaft. The crankshaft, the crankshaft sprocket and the pulley are fitted together by friction, using diamond washers between the flange faces on each part. For that reason, the crankshaft sprocket is also unfastened if the pulley bolt is loosened. Before any repair requiring loosening or removal of the crankshaft pulley bolt, the crankshaft and camshafts must be locked in place by the special service tools, otherwise severe engine damage can occur.

⁂ WARNING

During engine repair procedures, cleanliness is extremely important. Any foreign material, including any material created while cleaning gasket surfaces, that enters the oil passages, coolant passages or the oil pan can cause engine failure.

1. Before servicing the vehicle, refer to the Precautions Section.
2. With the vehicle in NEUTRAL, position it on a hoist.
3. Depower the Supplemental Restraint System (SRS). Refer to Air Bag (Supplemental Restraint System), Disarming The System.
4. Loosen the 3 coolant pump pulley bolts.
5. Remove the crankshaft pulley.
6. Disconnect the Crankshaft Position (CKP) sensor electrical connector. Detach the 2 wiring harness retainers from the engine front cover.
7. Remove the 2 bolts and the CKP sensor.

⁂ WARNING

Use care not to damage the engine front cover or the crankshaft when removing the seal.

8. Using the Oil Seal Remover, remove the crankshaft front oil seal.
9. Remove the 3 bolts and the coolant pump pulley.
10. Remove the coolant expansion tank.
11. Remove the power steering pump. Refer to Power Steering Pump, removal & installation.
12. Remove the engine mount.
13. Slightly raise the engine for access to the accessory drive idler pulley.
14. Remove the accessory drive idler pulley.

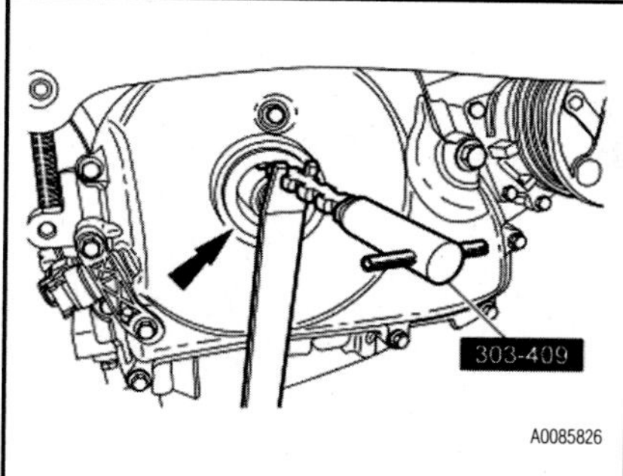

Fig. 84 Using the Oil Seal Remover to remove the crankshaft front oil seal

15. Remove the bolts and the engine front cover.

To install:

WARNING

Do not use metal scrapers, wire brushes, power abrasive disks or other abrasive means to clean sealing surfaces. These tools cause scratches and gouges which make leak paths.

16. Clean and inspect the mounting surfaces of the engine and the front cover.

➡The engine front cover must be installed and the bolts tightened within 4 minutes of applying the silicone gasket and sealant.

17. Apply a 0.09 (2.5mm) bead of silicone gasket and sealant to the cylinder head and oil pan joint areas. Apply a 0.09 (2.5mm) bead of silicone gasket and sealant to the front cover.

18. Install the engine front cover. Tighten the bolts in sequence, to the following specifications:

a. Tighten the 8mm bolts to 89 inch lbs. (10 Nm).

b. Tighten the 13mm bolts to 35 ft. lbs. (48 Nm).

19. Install the accessory drive idler pulley.

20. Lower the engine to the installed position.

21. Install the engine mount.

22. Install the power steering pump.

23. Install the coolant expansion tank.

24. Install the coolant pump pulley and the 3 bolts. Do not tighten at this time.

➡Remove the through-bolt from the Camshaft Front Oil Seal Installer.

25. Lubricate the oil seal with clean engine oil.

26. Using the Camshaft Front Oil Seal Installer, install the crankshaft front oil seal.

27. Install the crankshaft pulley.

WARNING

Only hand-tighten the crankshaft pulley holding bolt or damage to the front cover can occur.

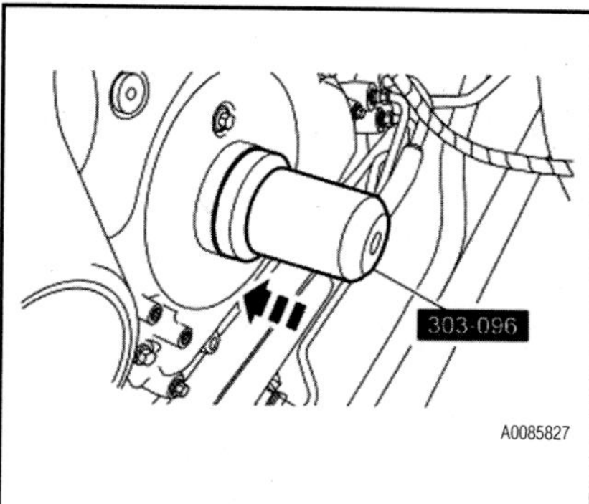

Fig. 87 Using the Camshaft Front Oil Seal Installer

28. Install a standard 6mm x 18mm bolt through the crankshaft pulley and thread it into the front cover.

29. Install the CKP sensor and the 2 bolts. Do not tighten the bolts at this time.

30. Using the Crankshaft Sensor Aligner, adjust the CKP sensor. Tighten the 2 bolts to 62 inch lbs. (7 Nm).

31. Connect the CKP sensor electrical connector. Attach the 2 wiring harness retainers to the engine front cover.

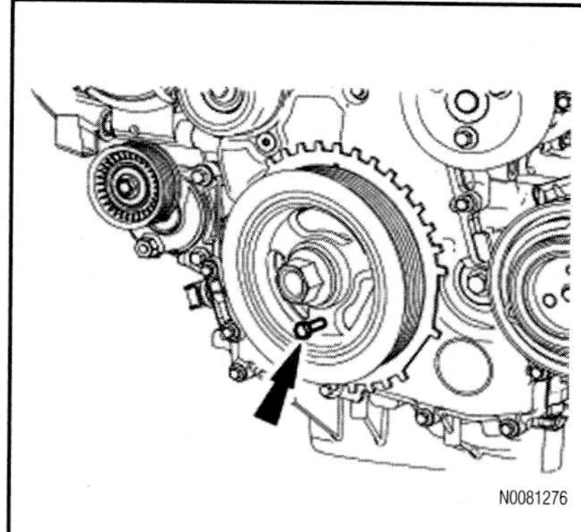

Fig. 88 Install a standard 6mm x 18mm bolt through the crankshaft pulley and thread it into the front cover

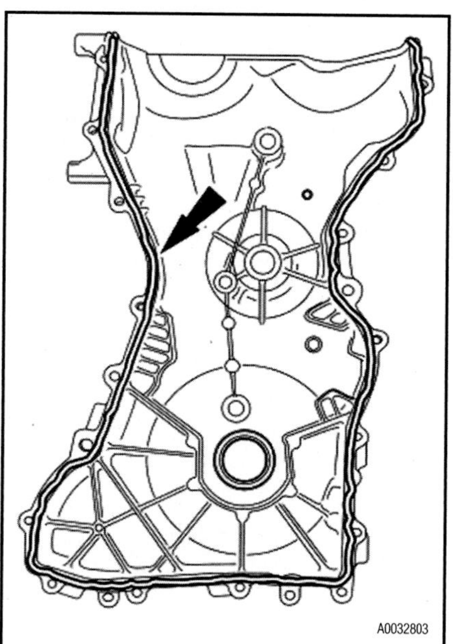

Fig. 85 Apply a bead of silicone gasket sealant in the area shown

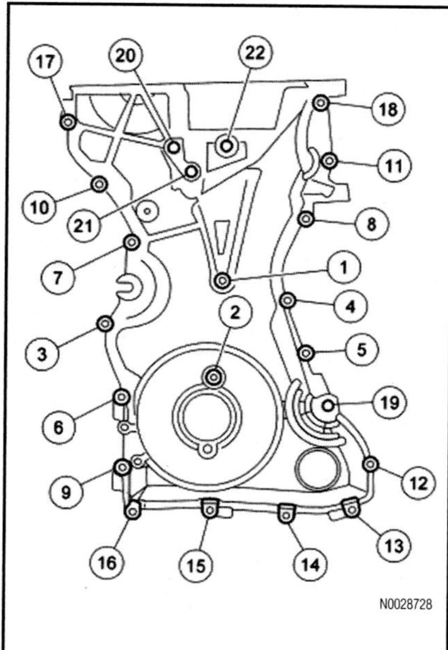

Fig. 86 Engine front cover bolt tightening sequence

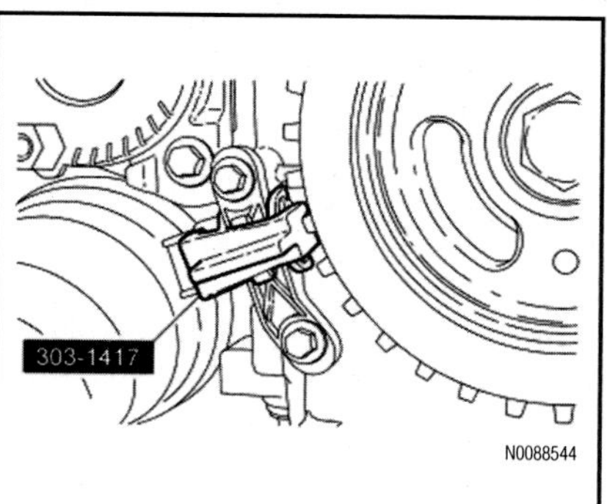

Fig. 89 Crankshaft Sensor Aligner installed

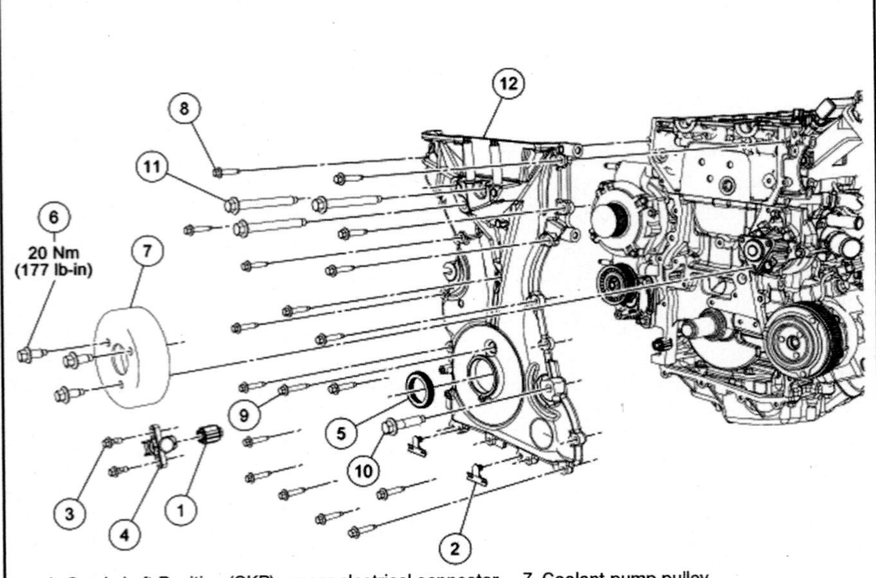

Fig. 90 Exploded view of engine front cover and related components

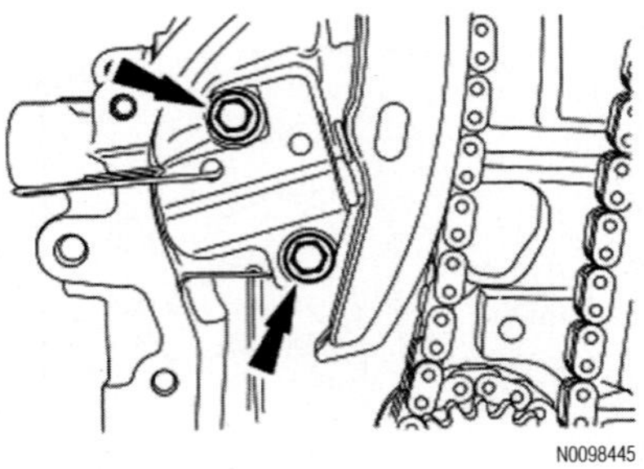

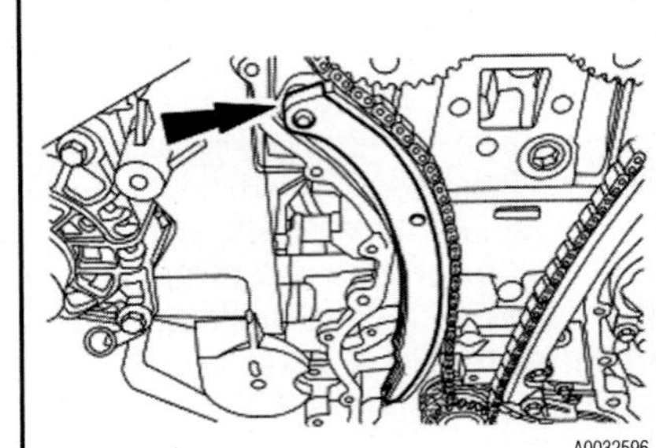

Fig. 91 With paper clip in hole to retain tensioner, remove bolts and timing chain tensioner

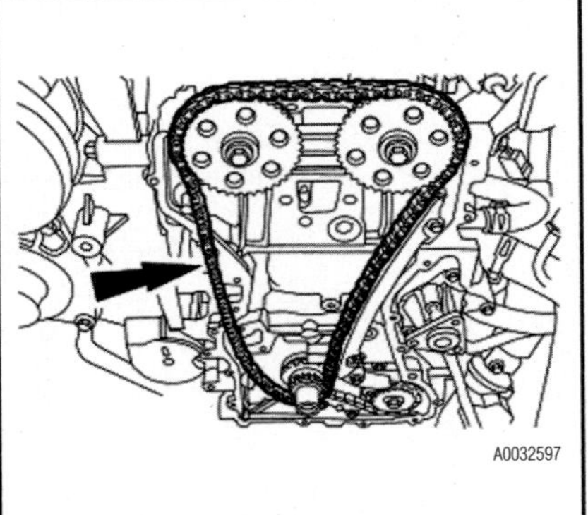

Fig. 92 Remove the RH timing chain guide

32. Remove the 6mm x 18mm bolt from the crankshaft pulley.
33. Tighten the coolant pump pulley bolts. Tighten to 15 ft. lbs. (20 Nm).
34. Repower the SRS. Refer to Air Bag (Supplemental Restraint System), Arming The System.
35. Fill the power steering system with the proper type and amount of fluid.

TIMING CHAIN & SPROCKETS

REMOVAL & INSTALLATION

See Figures 91 through 95.

WARNING

Do not loosen or remove the crankshaft pulley bolt without first installing the special tools as instructed in this procedure. The crankshaft pulley and the crankshaft timing sprocket are not keyed to the crankshaft. The crankshaft, the crankshaft sprocket and the pulley are fitted together by friction, using diamond washers between the flange faces on each part. For that reason, the crankshaft sprocket is also unfastened if the pulley bolt is loosened. Before any repair requiring loosening or removal of the crankshaft pulley bolt, the crankshaft and camshafts must be locked in place by the special service tools, otherwise severe engine damage can occur.

WARNING

During engine repair procedures, cleanliness is extremely important. Any foreign material, including any material created while cleaning gasket surfaces, that enters the oil passages, coolant passages or the oil pan can cause engine failure.

1. Before servicing the vehicle, refer to the Precautions Section.
2. With the vehicle in NEUTRAL, position it on a hoist.
3. Remove the engine front cover. Refer to Timing Chain Front Cover, removal & installation.
4. Compress the timing chain tensioner in the following sequence.
   a. Using a small pick, release and hold the ratchet mechanism.
   b. While holding the ratchet mechanism in the released position, compress the tensioner by pushing the timing chain arm toward the tensioner.

Fig. 93 Remove the timing chain

Fig. 94 Install the LH timing chain guide and bolts

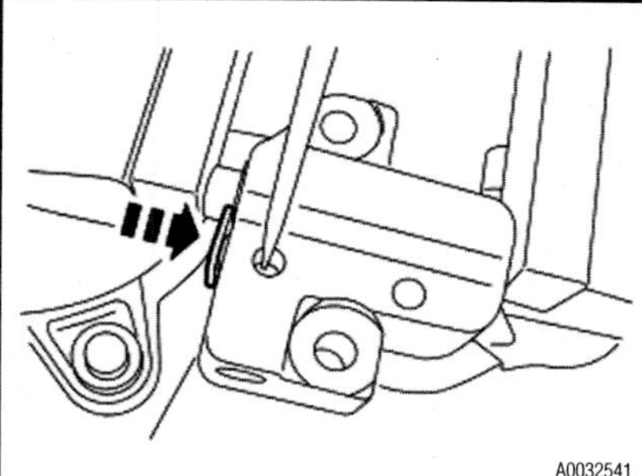

Fig. 95 While holding the ratchet mechanism, push the ratchet arm back into the tensioner housing

c. Insert a paper clip, or equivalent, into the hole to retain the tensioner.

5. Remove the 2 bolts and the timing chain tensioner.
6. Remove the RH timing chain guide.
7. Remove the timing chain.
8. Remove the bolts and the LH timing chain guide.

⁂ WARNING

Do not rely on the Camshaft Alignment Plate to prevent camshaft rotation. Damage to the tool or the camshaft can occur.

9. Remove the bolts and the camshaft drive gears. Use the flats on the camshaft to prevent camshaft rotation.

To install:

10. Install the camshaft drive gears and the bolts. Do not tighten the bolts at this time.
11. Install the LH timing chain guide and bolts. Tighten to 89 inch lbs. (10 Nm).
12. Install the timing chain.
13. Install the RH timing chain guide.

➡If the timing chain tensioner plunger and ratchet assembly are not pinned in the compressed position, follow the next 4 steps.

⁂ WARNING

Do not compress the ratchet assembly. This will damage the ratchet assembly.

14. Using the edge of a vise, compress the timing chain tensioner plunger.
15. Using a small pick, push back and hold the ratchet mechanism.
16. While holding the ratchet mechanism, push the ratchet arm back into the tensioner housing.
17. Install a paper clip into the hole in the tensioner housing to hold the ratchet assembly and the plunger in during installation.
18. Install the timing chain tensioner and the 2 bolts. Tighten to 89 inch lbs. (10 Nm).
19. Remove the paper clip to release the piston.

⁂ WARNING

The Camshaft Alignment Plate is for camshaft alignment only. Using this tool to prevent engine rotation can result in engine damage.

20. Using the flats on the camshafts to prevent camshaft rotation, tighten the camshaft drive gear bolts. Tighten to 53 ft. lbs. (72 Nm).
21. Install the front cover. Refer to Timing Chain Front Cover, removal & installation.

VALVE COVERS

REMOVAL & INSTALLATION

See Figures 96 through 98.

⁂ WARNING

During engine repair procedures, cleanliness is extremely important. Any foreign material, including any material created while cleaning gasket surfaces, that enters the oil passages, coolant passages or the oil pan can cause engine failure.

1. Before servicing the vehicle, refer to the Precautions Section.
2. Disconnect the Camshaft Position (CMP) sensor electrical connector.
3. Disconnect the 4 ignition coil-on-plug electrical connectors.
4. Remove the 4 ignition coil-to-valve cover bolts and the ignition coils.
5. Lift up the connector boot and disconnect the Cylinder Head Temperature (CHT) sensor electrical connector.
6. Disconnect the crankcase breather tube from the valve cover.
7. Detach all of the wiring harness retainers from the valve cover stud bolts.
8. Disconnect the alternator electrical connector.
9. Remove the radio interference capacitor bracket bolt.
10. Remove the radio interference capacitor ground bolt and position the bracket aside.
11. Remove the 14 valve cover retainers, the valve cover and gasket.
12. Discard the valve cover gasket.

To install:

⁂ WARNING

Do not use metal scrapers, wire brushes, power abrasive discs or other abrasive means to clean the sealing surfaces. These tools cause scratches and gouges which make leak paths.

13. Clean and inspect the sealing surfaces.
14. Apply silicone gasket and sealant to the locations shown.

➡The valve cover must be secured within 4 minutes of silicone gasket application. If the valve cover is not secured within 4 minutes, the sealant must be removed and the sealing area cleaned with metal surface prep.

15. Install the valve cover, a new gasket, and the 14 retainers. Tighten in sequence to 89 inch lbs. (10 Nm).
16. Position the radio interference capacitor bracket and install the bolt. Tighten to 89 inch lbs. (10 Nm).
17. Install the radio interference capacitor ground bolt. Tighten to 89 inch lbs. (10 Nm).

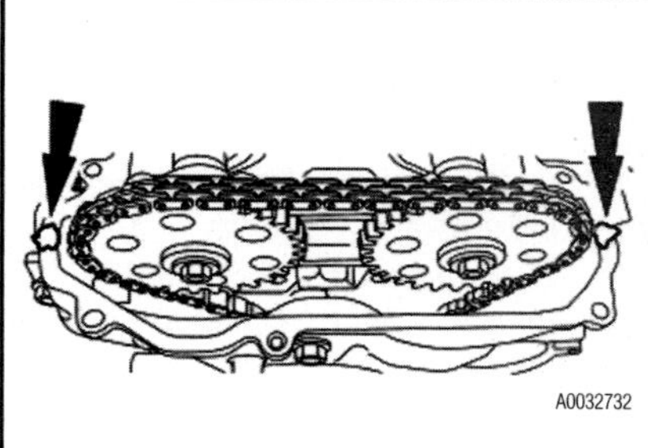

Fig. 96 Apply silicone gasket and sealant to the locations shown

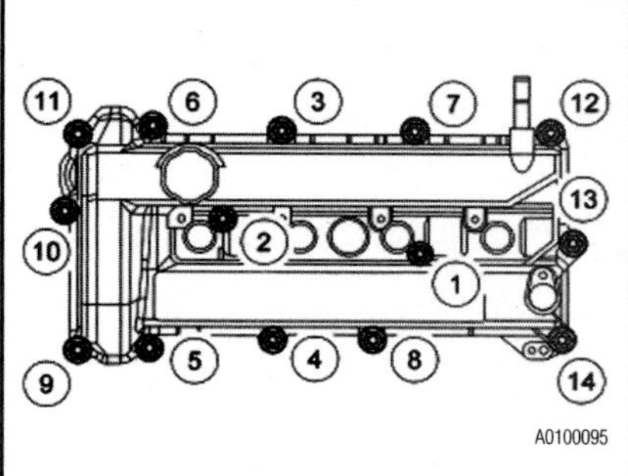

Fig. 97 Valve cover retainer tightening sequence

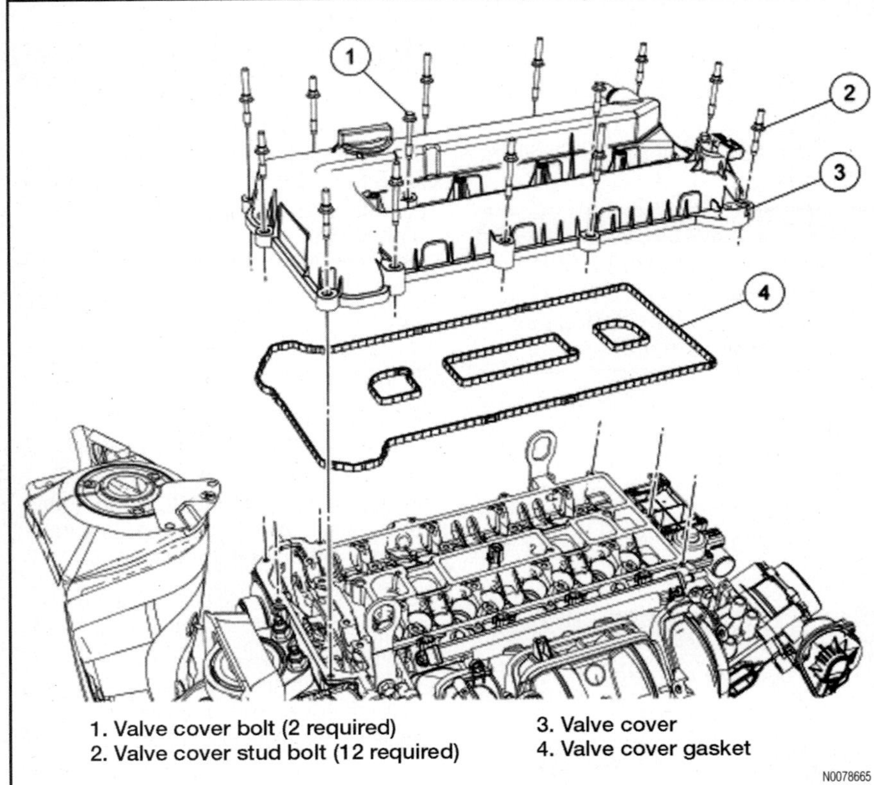

Fig. 98 Valve cover components—exploded view

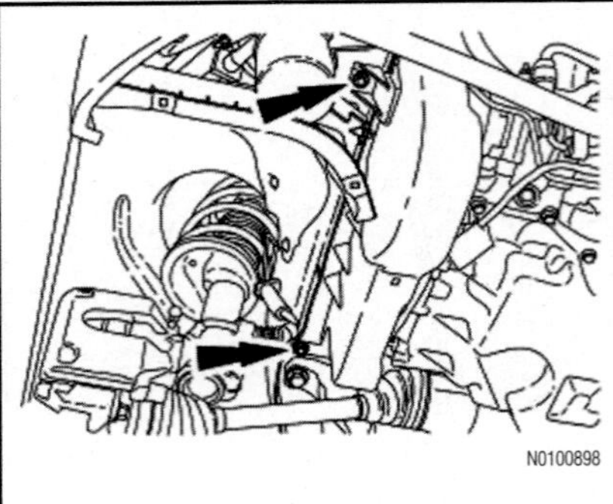

Fig. 99 Remove the accessory drive belt splash shield

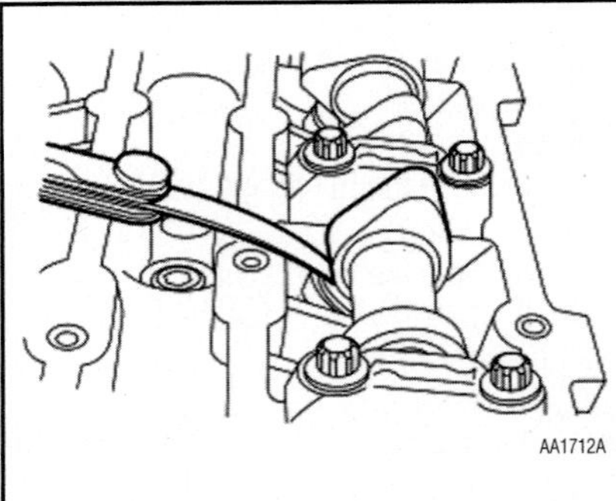

Fig. 100 Use a feeler gauge to measure valve clearance

18. Connect the alternator electrical connector.
19. Attach all of the wiring harness retainers to the valve cover stud bolts.
20. Connect the crankcase breather tube on the valve cover.
21. Connect the CHT sensor electrical connector and install the connector boot.
22. Install the ignition coils and the 4 ignition coil-to-valve cover bolts. Tighten to 89 inch lbs. (10 Nm).
23. Connect the 4 ignition coil-on-plug electrical connectors.
24. Connect the CMP sensor electrical connector.

VALVE LASH

ADJUSTMENT

See Figures 99 and 100.

1. Before servicing the vehicle, refer to the Precautions Section.
2. Remove the valve cover. Refer to Valve Cover, removal & installation.
3. Remove the 2 bolts and accessory drive belt splash shield.

**** WARNING**

Turn the engine clockwise only, and use the crankshaft bolt only.

➡Measure each valve's clearance at base circle, with the lobe pointed away from the tappet, before removing the camshafts. Failure to measure all clearances prior to removing the camshafts will necessitate repeated removal and installation and wasted labor time.

4. Use a feeler gauge to measure each valve's clearance and record its location.
   a. Intake valve specifications:
      - Nominal clearance: 0.0095 inch (0.25mm)
      - Acceptable installed clearance: 0.008–0.011 inch (0.22–0.28mm)
   b. Exhaust valve specifications:
      - Nominal clearance: 0.0115 inch (0.030mm)
      - Acceptable installed clearance: 0.010–0.013 inch (0.27–0.33mm)

➡The number on the valve tappet only reflects the digits that follow the decimal. For example, a tappet with the number 0.650 has the thickness of 3.650mm.

5. Select tappets using this formula: tappet thickness = measured clearance + the existing tappet thickness - nominal clearance. Select the closest tappet size to the ideal tappet thickness available and mark the installation location.
6. If any tappets do not measure within specifications, install new tappets in these locations.
7. Install the 2 bolts and accessory drive belt splash shield. Tighten to 80 inch lbs. (9 Nm).

ENGINE PERFORMANCE & EMISSION CONTROLS

CAMSHAFT POSITION (CMP) SENSOR

LOCATION

See Figure 101.

Refer to the accompanying illustration.

REMOVAL & INSTALLATION

See Figure 101.

1. Before servicing the vehicle, refer to the Precautions Section.
2. Disconnect the Camshaft Position (CMP) sensor electrical connector.
3. Remove the bolt and the CMP sensor.

To install:

4. Lubricate the O-ring with clean engine oil.
5. Install the CMP sensor into position. Tighten the bolt to 62 inch lbs. (7 Nm).
6. Connect the CMP sensor electrical connector.

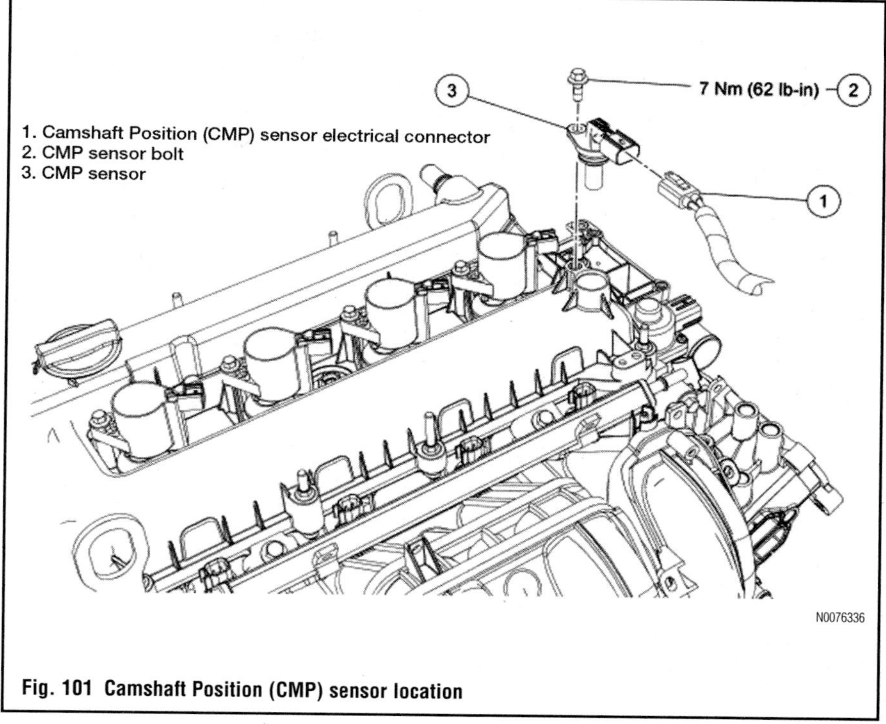

Fig. 101 Camshaft Position (CMP) sensor location

CRANKSHAFT POSITION (CKP) SENSOR

LOCATION

See Figure 102.

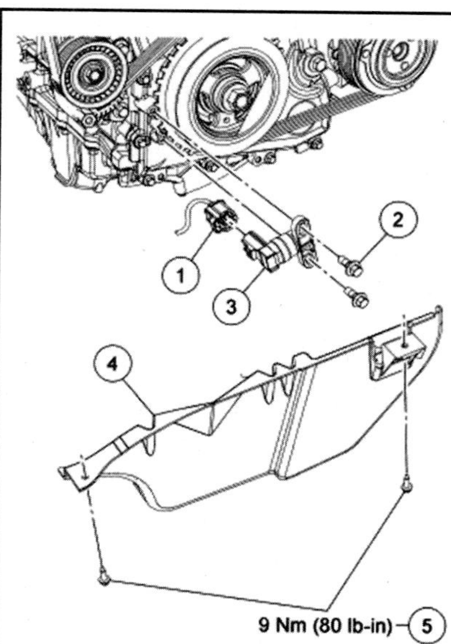

Fig. 102 Crankshaft Position (CKP) sensor location

Refer to the accompanying illustration.

REMOVAL & INSTALLATION

See Figures 103 through 108.

1. Before servicing the vehicle, refer to the Precautions Section.
2. With the vehicle in NEUTRAL, position it on a hoist.
3. Remove the 2 bolts and the accessory drive belt splash shield.
4. Disconnect the Crankshaft Position (CKP) sensor electrical connector.
5. Turn the crankshaft clockwise until the hole in the crankshaft pulley is in the 3 o'clock position.

➡The cylinder block plug is located on the exhaust side of the engine block near the CKP sensor.

6. Remove the cylinder block plug.

➡When the crankshaft contacts the Crankshaft TDC Timing Peg, the No. 1 cylinder will be at Top Dead Center (TDC).

7. Install the crankshaft TDC Timing Peg.
8. Turn the crankshaft clockwise until the crankshaft contacts the Crankshaft TDC Timing Peg.
9. Remove the CKP sensor retaining bolts and the sensor.

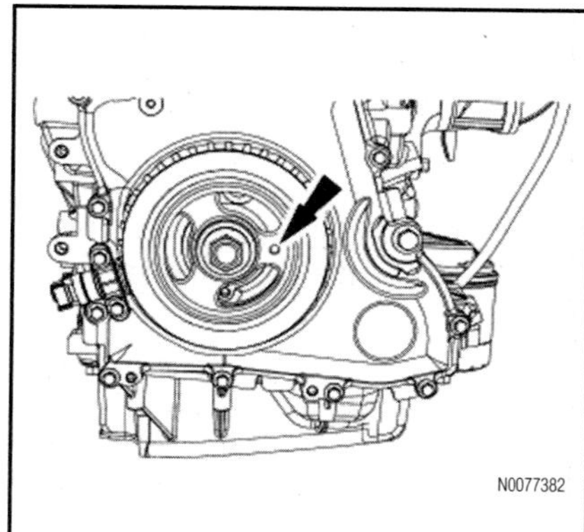

Fig. 103 Turn the crankshaft clockwise until the hole in the crankshaft pulley is in the 3 o'clock position

Fig. 104 Remove the cylinder block plug

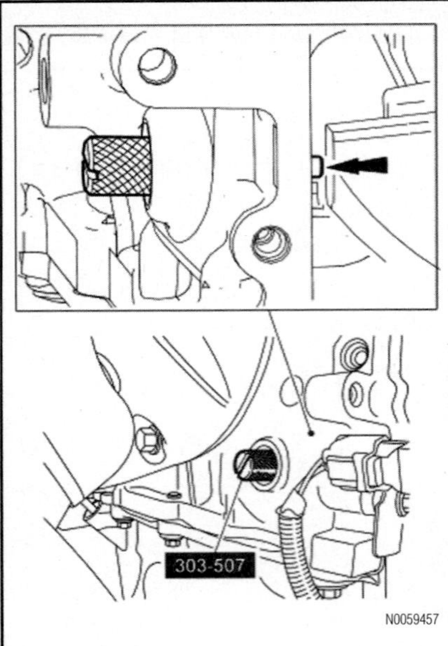

Fig. 105 View of crankshaft TDC Timing Peg installed

WARNING

Only hand-tighten the bolt through the crankshaft pulley or damage to the front cover can occur.

10. Install a 6mm x 18mm standard bolt into the crankshaft pulley.

To install:

11. Install the CKP sensor, but do not tighten the 2 bolts at this time.
12. Using the Crankshaft Sensor Aligner, adjust the CKP sensor. Tighten the 2 CKP sensor bolts to 62 inch lbs. (7 Nm).
13. Connect the CKP sensor electrical connector.

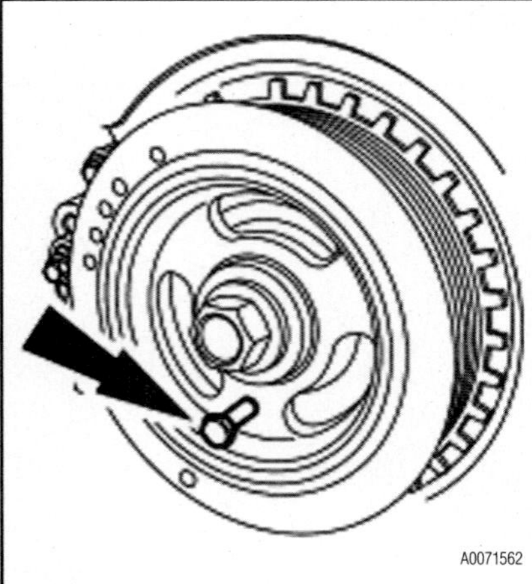

Fig. 106 Install a standard bolt into the crankshaft pulley

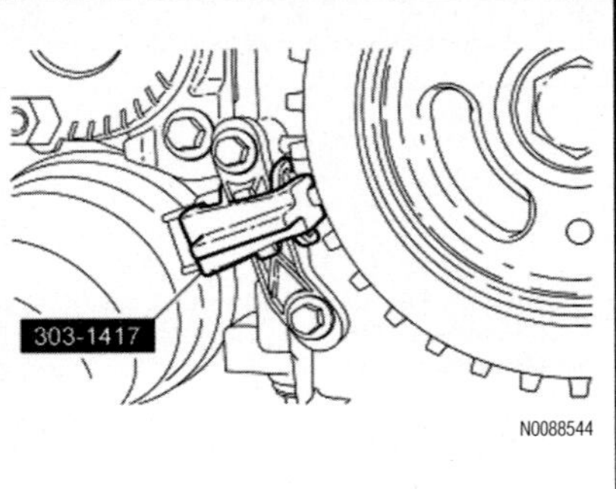

Fig. 107 Crankshaft Sensor Aligner installed

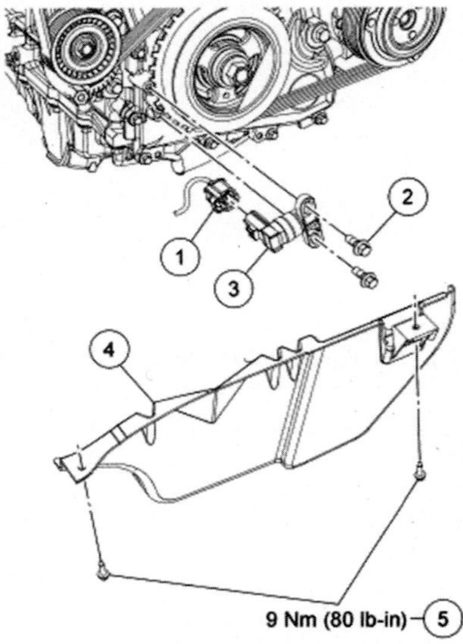

Fig. 108 Crankshaft Position (CKP) sensor location

14. Remove the 6mm x 18mm bolt from the crankshaft pulley.
15. Remove the Crankshaft TDC Timing Peg.
16. Install the cylinder block plug. Tighten to 15 ft. lbs. (20 Nm).
17. Install the accessory drive belt splash shield and the 2 bolts. Tighten to 80 inch lbs. (9 Nm).

CYLINDER HEAD TEMPERATURE (CHT) SENSOR

LOCATION

See Figure 109.

Refer to the accompanying illustration.

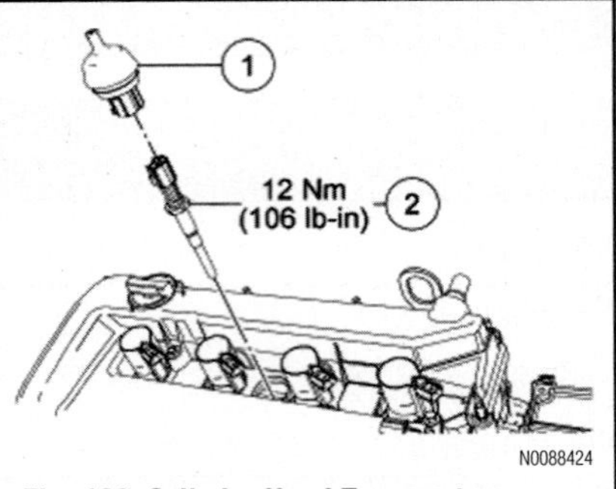

Fig. 109 Cylinder Head Temperature (CHT) sensor (2) and electrical connector (1) location

REMOVAL & INSTALLATION

See Figure 109.

1. Before servicing the vehicle, refer to the Precautions Section.
2. Pull back the Cylinder Head Temperature (CHT) sensor cover and disconnect the electrical connector.
3. Remove the CHT sensor.
4. Installation is the reverse of the removal procedure.
    - Tighten the CHT sensor to 106 inch lbs. (12 Nm).

HEATED OXYGEN SENSOR (HO2S)

LOCATION

See Figure 110.

Refer to the accompanying illustration.

REMOVAL & INSTALLATION

See Figure 110.

➡For installation and removal of the Catalyst Monitor Sensor (CMS), follow the same procedure used for the Heated Oxygen Sensor (HO2S).

1. Before servicing the vehicle, refer to the Precautions Section.
2. Disconnect the electrical connector and detach the wiring retainer.

➡If necessary, lubricate the sensor threads with penetrating and lock lubricant to assist in removal.

3. Using the Exhaust Gas Oxygen Sensor Socket, remove the HO2S.

To install:

WARNING

Make sure that the sensor wiring is routed away from hot surfaces and sharp edges or damage to the wiring may occur.

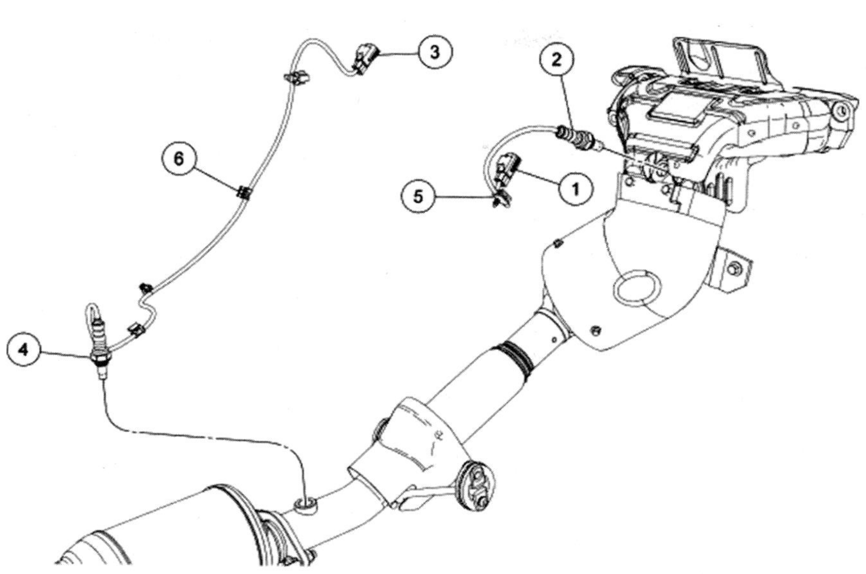

Fig. 110 Heated Oxygen Sensor (HO2S) and Catalyst Monitor Sensor (CMS) location

4. Apply a light coat of anti-seize lubricant to the threads of the HO2S.
5. Install the HO2S and tighten to 35 ft. lbs. (48 Nm).
6. Connect the electrical connector. Make sure that the electrical connector locking tab is engaged.

KNOCK SENSOR (KS)

LOCATION

See Figure 111.

Refer to the accompanying illustration.

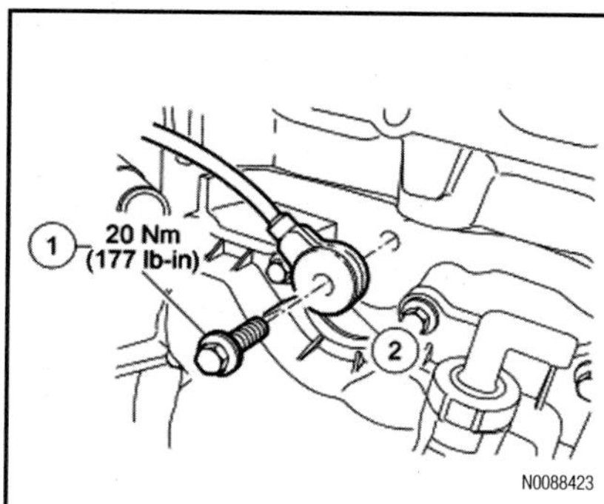

Fig. 111 Knock Sensor (KS) (2) and bolt (1) location

REMOVAL & INSTALLATION

See Figure 111.

1. Before servicing the vehicle, refer to the Precautions Section.
2. Remove the intake manifold. Refer to Intake Manifold, removal & installation.

➡The Knock Sensor (KS) must not touch the crankcase vent oil separator.

3. Remove the bolt and the KS.
4. To install, reverse the removal procedure. Tighten the KS to 15 ft. lbs. (20 Nm).

MASS AIR FLOW (MAF) SENSOR

LOCATION

See Figure 112.

Refer to the accompanying illustration.

REMOVAL & INSTALLATION

See Figure 112.

1. Before servicing the vehicle, refer to the Precautions Section.
2. Disconnect the Mass Air Flow (MAF) sensor electrical connector.
3. Remove the MAF sensor retaining screws.
4. Remove the MAF sensor.
5. Installation is the reverse of the removal procedure.

OUTPUT SHAFT SPEED (OSS) SENSOR

LOCATION

See Figure 113.

The Output Shaft Speed (OSS) sensor is an inductive sensor which detects the vehicle speed by means of a rotor on the differential. The OSS sensor is located in the transaxle housing above the rotor in the differential.

REMOVAL & INSTALLATION

See Figure 113.

1. Before servicing the vehicle, refer to the Precautions Section.
2. With the vehicle in NEUTRAL, position it on a hoist.
3. Place a drain pan beneath the Output Shaft Speed (OSS) sensor.
4. Remove the OSS sensor.
   a. Disconnect the electrical connector.
   b. Remove the bolt.
   c. Inspect the OSS bore.

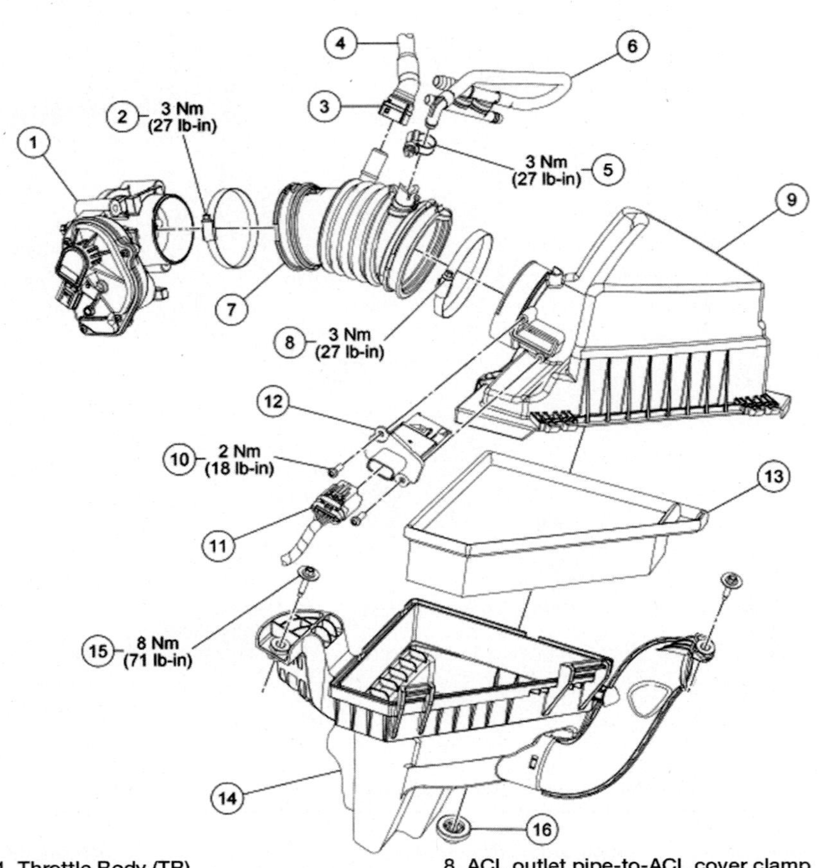

Fig. 112 Air Cleaner (ACL) assembly with Mass Air Flow (MAF) sensor and related components location

To install:

5. Inspect the O-ring seal for nicks or cuts; install a new O-ring if necessary.

➡**Apply a light coat of clean transmission fluid to the O-ring before installation.**

6. Install the OSS sensor. Tighten to 89 inch lbs. (10 Nm). Connect the electrical connector.
7. Lower the vehicle.
8. Check the transmission fluid level and add transmission fluid as necessary.
9. Start the engine and move the transaxle range selector lever through all gear positions.

POWERTRAIN CONTROL MODULE (PCM)

LOCATION

See Figure 114.

The Powertrain Control Module (PCM) is located in the engine compartment above the transaxle.

REMOVAL & INSTALLATION

See Figure 115.

➡**PCM installation DOES NOT require new keys or programming of keys, only a Parameter Reset of the Passive Anti-Theft System (PATS).**

1. Before servicing the vehicle, refer to the Precautions Section.
2. Retrieve the module configuration. Carry out the module configuration retrieval steps of the Programmable Module Installation (PMI) procedure.
3. Remove the Air Cleaner (ACL) outlet pipe and the ACL assembly. Refer to Air Cleaner, removal & installation.
4. Disconnect the 3 PCM electrical connectors.
5. Remove the 2 bolts and the PCM.

To install:

6. Install the PCM and the 2 bolts. Tighten to 71 inch lbs. (8 Nm).
7. Connect the 3 PCM electrical connectors.

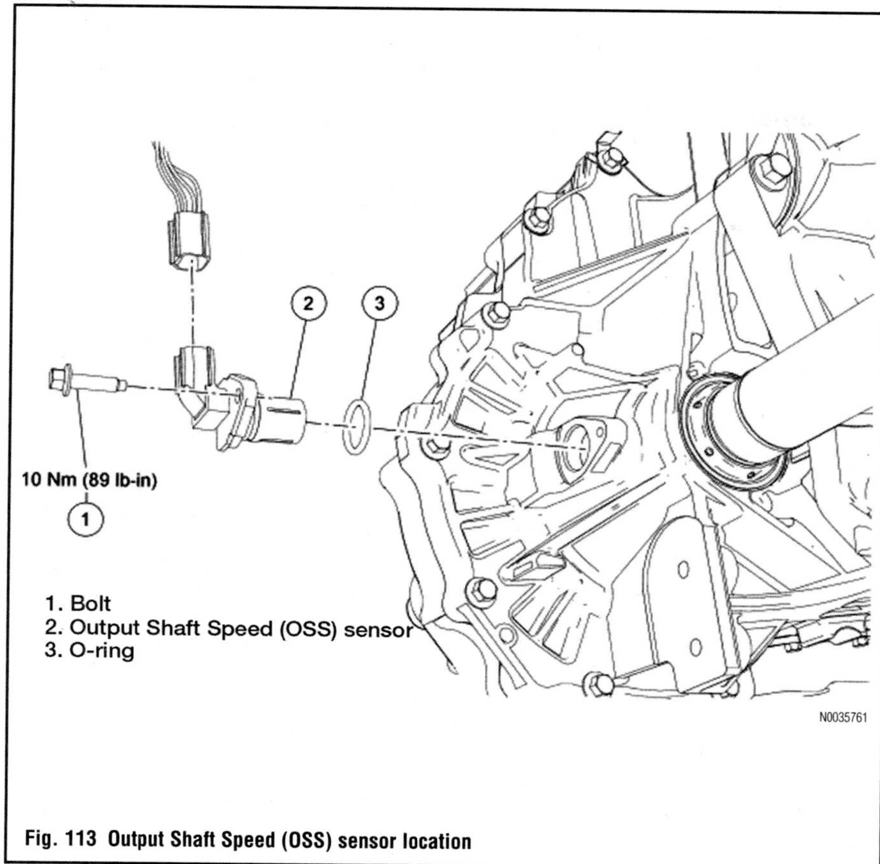

Fig. 113 Output Shaft Speed (OSS) sensor location

8. Install the ACL outlet pipe and the air cleaner assembly.

9. Restore the module configuration. Carry out the module configuration restore steps of the Programmable Module Installation (PMI) procedure.

10. Reprogram the PATS. Carry out the Parameter Reset procedure.

PARAMETER RESET PROCEDURE

➡A minimum of 2 Passive Anti-Theft System (PATS) keys must be programmed into the Instrument Cluster (IC) to complete this procedure and allow the vehicle to start.

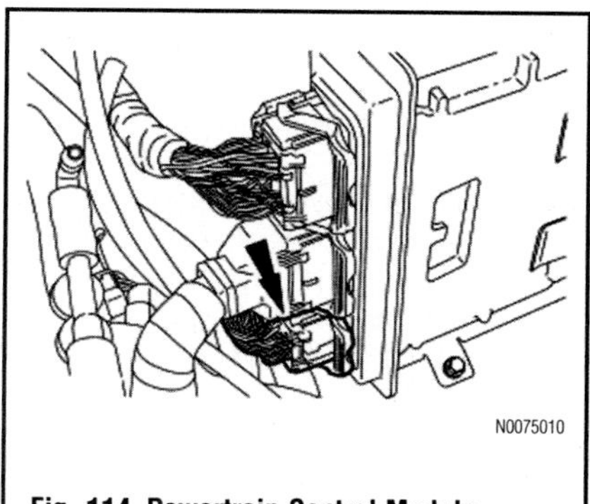

Fig. 114 Powertrain Control Module (PCM) location

1. Before servicing the vehicle, refer to the Precautions Section.

2. Turn the key from the OFF position to the ON position.

3. From the scan tool, follow the on-screen instructions to ENTER SECURITY ACCESS.

4. From the scan tool, select: Parameter Reset and follow the on-screen instructions.

➡If the IC or the IC and the PCM were replaced, updated or reconfigured, follow Steps 5–10. All vehicle keys are erased during the parameter reset procedure. Verify at least 2 vehicle keys are available prior to carrying out the PATS parameter reset. If only the PCM was replaced, go to Step 10.

5. From the scan tool, select: Ignition Key Code Erase and follow the on-screen instructions.

6. Turn the key to the OFF position and disconnect the scan tool.

7. Turn the key to the ON position for 6 seconds.

8. Turn the key to the OFF position and remove the key.

9. Insert the second PATS key into the ignition lock cylinder and turn the key to the ON position for 6 seconds.

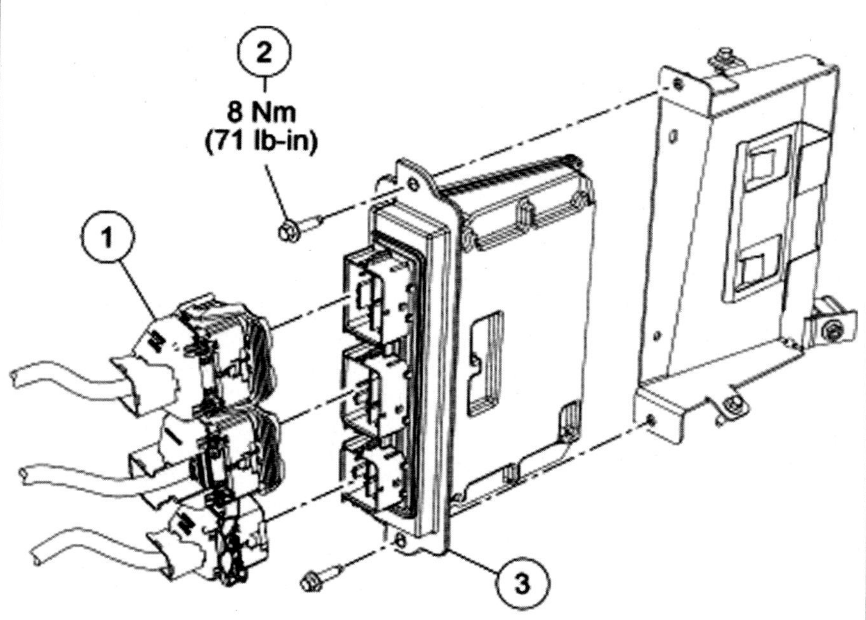

Fig. 115 Expanded view of the Powertrain Control Module (PCM)

10. Both keys should now start the vehicle.

11. Program the Remote Keyless Entry (RKE) transmitter portion of the Integrated Keyhead Transmitter (IKT) PATS keys, as needed.

PROGRAMMABLE MODULE INSTALLATION (PMI) PROCEDURE

When Original Module Is Available

➡Following module installation, some modules require a separate procedure be carried out. For instructions, refer to the specific module removal and installation procedures.

1. Before servicing the vehicle, refer to the Precautions Section.
2. Connect the Integrated Diagnostic System (IDS) and identify the vehicle as normal.
3. From the Toolbox icon, select Module Programming and press the check mark.
4. Select Programmable Module Installation.
5. Select the module that is being replaced.
6. Follow the on-screen instructions, turn the ignition key to the OFF position, and press the check mark.
7. Install the new module and press the check mark.
8. Follow the on-screen instructions, turn the ignition key to the ON position, and press the check mark.
9. The IDS downloads the data into the new module and displays Module Configuration Complete.
10. Test module for correct operation.

When Original Module Is NOT Available

➡Following module installation, some modules require a separate procedure be carried out. For instructions, refer to the specific module removal and installation procedures.

1. Before servicing the vehicle, refer to the Precautions Section.
2. Install the new module.
3. Connect the Integrated Diagnostic System (IDS) and identify the vehicle as normal.
4. From the Toolbox icon, select Module Programming and press the check mark.
5. Select Programmable Module Installation.
6. Select the module that was replaced.
7. Follow the on-screen instructions, turn the ignition key to the OFF position, and press the check mark.
8. Follow the on-screen instructions, turn the ignition key to the ON position, and press the check mark.
9. If the data is not available, the IDS displays a screen stating to contact the As-Built Data Center. Retrieve the data from the technician service publication website at this time and press the check mark.
10. Enter the module data and press the check mark.
11. The IDS downloads the data into the new module and displays Module Configuration Complete.
12. Test module for correct operation.

THROTTLE POSITION SENSOR (TPS)

LOCATION

The Throttle Position (TP) sensor is located on the Throttle Body (TB).

REMOVAL & INSTALLATION

The Throttle Position Sensor (TPS) is integral to the electronic throttle body. Refer to Throttle Body, removal & installation.

FUEL — GASOLINE FUEL INJECTION SYSTEM

FUEL SYSTEM SERVICE PRECAUTIONS

Safety is the most important factor when performing not only fuel system maintenance but any type of maintenance. Failure to conduct maintenance and repairs in a safe manner may result in serious personal injury or death. Maintenance and testing of the vehicle's fuel system components can be accomplished safely and effectively by adhering to the following rules and guidelines.

- To avoid the possibility of fire and personal injury, always disconnect the negative battery cable unless the repair or test procedure requires that battery voltage be applied.
- Always relieve the fuel system pressure prior to disconnecting any fuel system component (injector, fuel rail, pressure regulator, etc.), fitting or fuel line connection. Exercise extreme caution whenever relieving fuel system pressure to avoid exposing skin, face and eyes to fuel spray. Please be advised that fuel under pressure may penetrate the skin or any part of the body that it contacts.
- Always place a shop towel or cloth around the fitting or connection prior to loosening to absorb any excess fuel due to spillage. Ensure that all fuel spillage (should it occur) is quickly removed from engine surfaces. Ensure that all fuel soaked cloths or towels are deposited into a suitable waste container.
- Always keep a dry chemical (Class B) fire extinguisher near the work area.
- Do not allow fuel spray or fuel vapors to come into contact with a spark or open flame.
- Always use a back-up wrench when loosening and tightening fuel line connection fittings. This will prevent unnecessary stress and torsion to fuel line piping.
- Always replace worn fuel fitting O-rings with new Do not substitute fuel hose or equivalent where fuel pipe is installed.

Before servicing the vehicle, make sure to also refer to the precautions in the beginning of this section as well.

RELIEVING FUEL SYSTEM PRESSURE

See Figure 116.

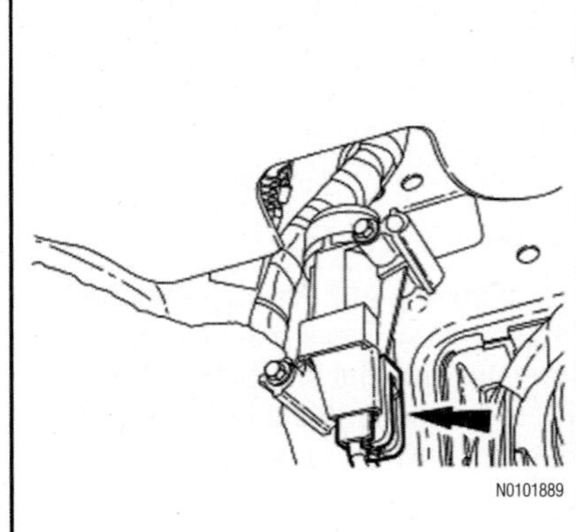

Fig. 116 Disconnect the Inertia Fuel Shutoff (IFS) switch electrical connector

CAUTION

Do not smoke, carry lighted tobacco or have an open flame of any type when working on or near any fuel-related component. Highly flammable mixtures are always present and may be ignited. Failure to follow these instructions may result in serious personal injury.

❊❊ CAUTION

Do not carry personal electronic devices such as cell phones, pagers or audio equipment of any type when working on or near any fuel-related component. Highly flammable mixtures are always present and may be ignited. Failure to follow these instructions may result in serious personal injury.

❊❊ CAUTION

Before working on or disconnecting any of the fuel tubes or fuel system components, relieve the fuel system pressure to prevent accidental spraying of fuel. Fuel in the fuel system remains under high pressure, even when the engine is not running. Failure to follow this instruction may result in serious personal injury.

❊❊ CAUTION

When handling fuel, always observe fuel handling precautions and be prepared in the event of fuel spillage. Spilled fuel may be ignited by hot vehicle components or other ignition sources. Failure to follow these instructions may result in serious personal injury.

1. Before servicing the vehicle, refer to the Precautions Section.
2. Remove the RF lower cowl trim panel.
3. Disconnect the Inertia Fuel Shutoff (IFS) switch electrical connector.
4. Start the engine and allow it to idle until it stalls.
5. After the engine stalls, crank the engine for approximately 5 seconds to make sure the fuel system pressure has been released.
6. Turn the ignition switch to the OFF position.
7. When fuel system service is complete, reconnect the IFS switch electrical connector.

➡It may take more than one key cycle to pressurize the fuel system.

8. Cycle the ignition key and wait 3 seconds to pressurize the fuel system. Check for leaks before starting the engine.
9. Start the vehicle and check the fuel system for leaks.
10. Install the RF lower cowl trim panel.

FUEL FILTER

REMOVAL & INSTALLATION

A lifetime fuel filter is serviced as part of the fuel pump module. Refer to Fuel Pump Module, removal & installation.

FUEL INJECTORS

REMOVAL & INSTALLATION

See Figures 117 and 118.

❊❊ CAUTION

Do not smoke, carry lighted tobacco or have an open flame of any type when working on or near any fuel-related component. Highly flammable mixtures are always present and may be ignited. Failure to follow these instructions may result in serious personal injury.

❊❊ CAUTION

Before working on or disconnecting any of the fuel tubes or fuel system components, relieve the fuel system pressure to prevent accidental spraying of fuel. Fuel in the fuel system remains under high pressure, even when the engine is not running. Failure to follow this instruction may result in serious personal injury.

❊❊ CAUTION

Clean all fuel residue from the engine compartment. If not removed, fuel residue may ignite when the engine is returned to operation. Failure to follow this instruction may result in serious personal injury.

❊❊ CAUTION

Do not carry personal electronic devices such as cell phones, pagers or audio equipment of any type when working on or near any fuel-related component. Highly flammable mixtures are always present and may be ignited. Failure to follow these instructions may result in serious personal injury.

❊❊ CAUTION

Always disconnect the battery ground cable at the battery when working on a fuel-related component. Highly flammable mixtures are always present and may be ignited. Failure to follow these instructions may result in serious personal injury.

➡The fuel injectors are serviced with the fuel rail.

1. Before servicing the vehicle, refer to the Precautions Section.
2. Release the fuel system pressure. Refer to Relieving Fuel System Pressure.
3. Disconnect the battery ground cable. For additional information, refer to Battery, removal & installation.
4. Disconnect the 4 fuel injector electrical connectors.
5. Insert the Spring Lock Coupling Disconnect Tool into the spring lock coupling and release the fuel jumper tube from the fuel rail.
6. Remove the 2 bolts and the fuel rail and injectors.
7. Remove the fuel injector retaining clips and the fuel injectors. Remove and discard the O-ring seals.

To install:

➡Use O-ring seals that are made of special fuel resistant material. Use of ordinary O-rings can cause the fuel system to leak. Do not reuse the O-ring seals.

8. Install new O-ring seals and lubricate them with clean engine oil.
9. To install, reverse the removal procedure.
   - Tighten the fuel rail bolts to 18 ft. lbs. (25 Nm).

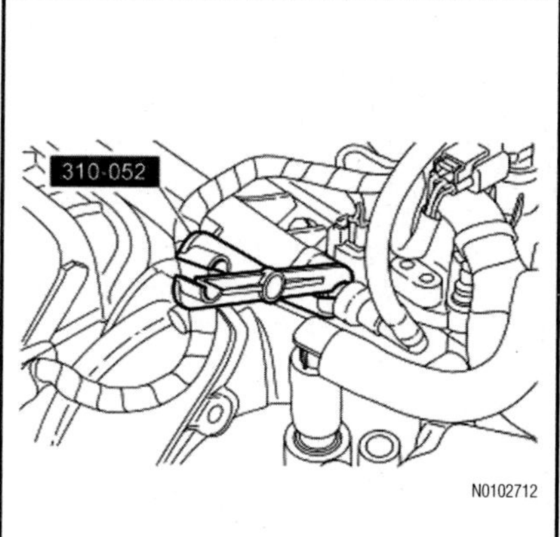

Fig. 117 Using the Spring Lock Coupling Disconnect Tool to release the fuel jumper tube from the fuel rail

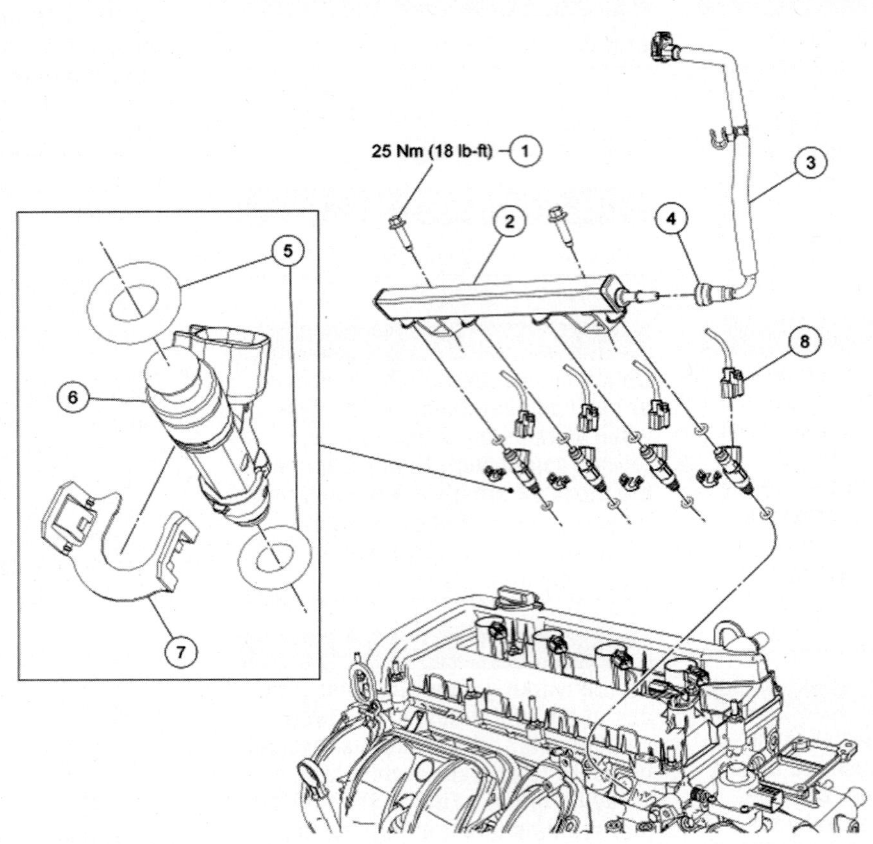

Fig. 118 Fuel rail and fuel injectors—exploded view

FUEL PUMP MODULE

REMOVAL & INSTALLATION

See Figures 119 and 120.

⁂ CAUTION

Do not smoke, carry lighted tobacco or have an open flame of any type when working on or near any fuel-related component. Highly flammable mixtures are always present and may be ignited. Failure to follow these instructions may result in serious personal injury.

⁂ CAUTION

Before working on or disconnecting any of the fuel tubes or fuel system components, relieve the fuel system pressure to prevent accidental spraying of fuel. Fuel in the fuel system remains under high pressure, even when the engine is not running. Failure to follow this instruction may result in serious personal injury.

⁂ CAUTION

Clean all fuel residue from the engine compartment. If not removed, fuel residue may ignite when the engine is returned to operation. Failure to follow this instruction may result in serious personal injury.

⁂ CAUTION

Do not carry personal electronic devices such as cell phones, pagers or audio equipment of any type when working on or near any fuel-related component. Highly flammable mixtures are always present and may be ignited. Failure to follow these instructions may result in serious personal injury.

⁂ CAUTION

Always disconnect the battery ground cable at the battery when working on a fuel-related component. Highly flammable mixtures are always present and may be ignited. Failure to follow these instructions may result in serious personal injury.

1. Before servicing the vehicle, refer to the Precautions Section.
2. Remove the fuel tank. Refer to Fuel Tank, removal & installation.

➡Clean the Fuel Pump (FP) module connections, couplings, flange surfaces and the immediate surrounding area of any dirt or foreign material.

Fig. 119 Fuel Tank Sender Unit Wrench installed to remove FP module lock ring

3. Disconnect the fuel supply tube-to-FP module quick connect coupling.

⁂ WARNING

Carefully install the lock ring wrench to avoid damaging the FP module when removing the lock ring.

4. Install the Fuel Tank Sender Unit Wrench and remove the FP module lock ring.

⁂ WARNING

The Fuel Pump (FP) module must be handled carefully to avoid damage to the float arm.

➡The FP module will have residual fuel remaining internally, drain into a suitable container.

5. Completely remove the FP module from the fuel tank.
6. Remove and discard the FP module O-ring seal.

To install:

7. Inspect the mating surfaces of the FP module flange and the fuel tank O-ring seal contact surfaces. Do not polish or adjust the O-ring seal contact area of the fuel tank flange or the fuel tank. Install a new FP module or fuel tank if the O-ring seal contact area is bent, scratched or corroded.
8. Apply clean engine oil to the new FP module O-ring seal.
9. To install, reverse the removal procedure.
10. Start the engine and check for leaks.

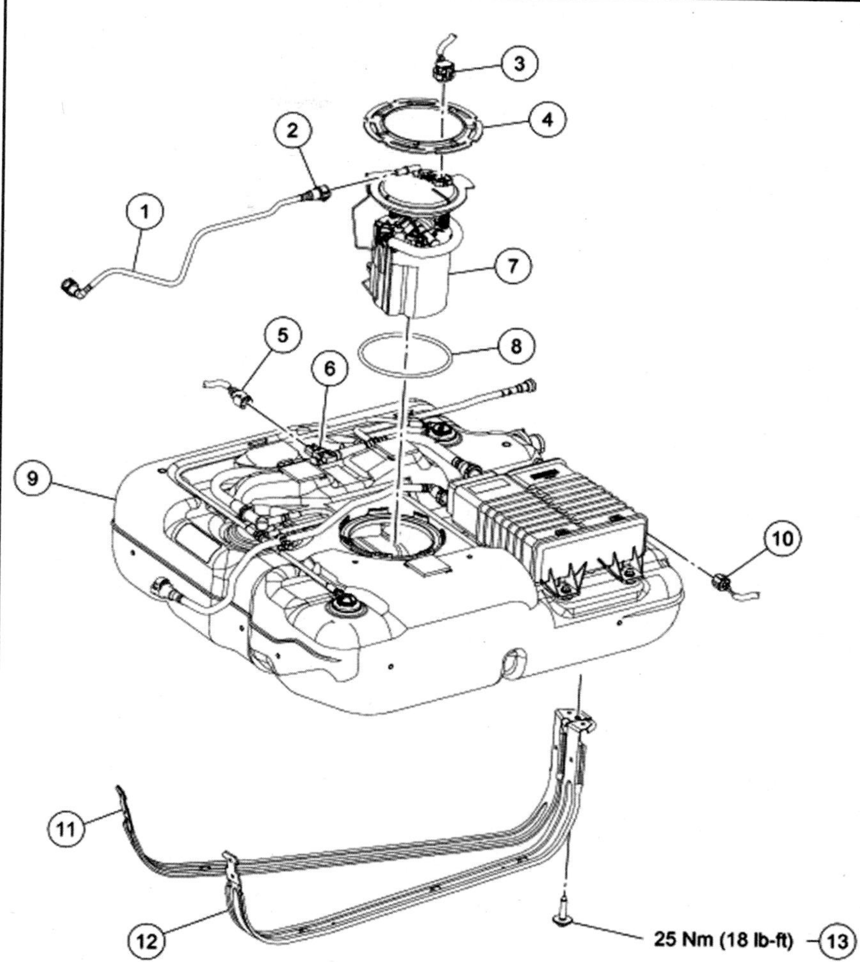

1. Fuel jumper tube
2. Fuel jumper tube-to-Fuel Pump (FP) module quick connect coupling
3. FP module electrical connector
4. FP module lock ring
5. Fuel Tank Pressure (FTP) sensor electrical connector
6. FTP sensor
7. FP module
8. FP module O-ring seal
9. Fuel tank
10. Evaporative Emission (EVAP) canister vent solenoid electrical connector
11. RH fuel tank strap
12. LH fuel tank strap
13. Fuel tank strap bolt

N0101916

Fig. 120 Fuel pump module, fuel tank, and related components—exploded view

FUEL TANK

DRAINING

⁂ CAUTION

Do not smoke, carry lighted tobacco or have an open flame of any type when working on or near any fuel-related component. Highly flammable mixtures are always present and may be ignited. Failure to follow these instructions may result in serious personal injury.

⁂ CAUTION

Before working on or disconnecting any of the fuel tubes or fuel system components, relieve the fuel system pressure to prevent accidental spraying of fuel. Fuel in the fuel system remains under high pressure, even when the engine is not running. Failure to follow this instruction may result in serious personal injury.

⁂ CAUTION

Clean all fuel residue from the engine compartment. If not removed, fuel residue may ignite when the engine is returned to operation. Failure to follow this instruction may result in serious personal injury.

✱✱ CAUTION

Do not carry personal electronic devices such as cell phones, pagers or audio equipment of any type when working on or near any fuel-related component. Highly flammable mixtures are always present and may be ignited. Failure to follow these instructions may result in serious personal injury.

✱✱ CAUTION

Always disconnect the battery ground cable at the battery when working on a fuel-related component. Highly flammable mixtures are always present and may be ignited. Failure to follow these instructions may result in serious personal injury.

✱✱ CAUTION

Remove the fuel filler cap slowly. The fuel system may be under pressure. If the fuel filler cap is venting vapor or if you hear a hissing sound, wait until it stops before completely removing the fuel filler cap. Otherwise, fuel may spray out. Failure to follow these instructions may result in serious personal injury.

1. Before servicing the vehicle, refer to the Precautions Section.
2. Disconnect the battery ground cable. For additional information, refer to Battery, removal & installation.
3. Carefully turn the fuel tank filler cap counterclockwise approximately 1/4 turn until the threads disengage and position aside.

➡The safety valve is located at the inlet of the fuel tank.

4. Insert a suitable drain tube into the fuel tank filler pipe until it enters the fuel tank inlet, opening the safety valve.
5. Attach the special tool, Fuel Storage Tanker, to the drain tube and remove as much fuel as possible from the fuel tank.

REMOVAL & INSTALLATION

See Figures 121 and 122.

✱✱ CAUTION

Do not smoke, carry lighted tobacco or have an open flame of any type when working on or near any fuel-related component. Highly flammable mixtures are always present and may be ignited. Failure to follow these instructions may result in serious personal injury.

✱✱ CAUTION

Do not carry personal electronic devices such as cell phones, pagers or audio equipment of any type when working on or near any fuel-related component. Highly flammable mixtures are always present and may be ignited. Failure to follow these instructions may result in serious personal injury.

✱✱ CAUTION

When handling fuel, always observe fuel handling precautions and be prepared in the event of fuel spillage. Spilled fuel may be ignited by hot vehicle components or other ignition sources. Failure to follow these instructions may result in serious personal injury.

✱✱ CAUTION

Before working on or disconnecting any of the fuel tubes or fuel system components, relieve the fuel system pressure to prevent accidental spraying of fuel. Fuel in the fuel system remains under high pressure, even when the engine is not running. Failure to follow this instruction may result in serious personal injury.

✱✱ CAUTION

Always disconnect the battery ground cable at the battery when working on an evaporative emission (EVAP) system or fuel-related component. Highly flammable mixtures are always present and may be ignited. Failure to follow these instructions may result in serious personal injury.

1. Before servicing the vehicle, refer to the Precautions Section.
2. With the vehicle in NEUTRAL, position it on a hoist.
3. Release the fuel system pressure. Refer to Relieving Fuel System Pressure.
4. Disconnect the battery ground cable. For additional information, refer to Battery, removal & installation.
5. Drain the fuel tank. Refer to Fuel Tank, removal & installation.

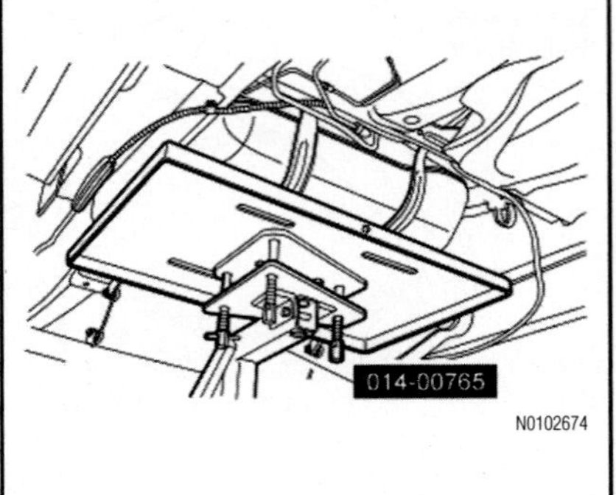

Fig. 121 Install a Powertrain Lift under the fuel tank

6. Remove the muffler and tailpipe.
7. Remove the 11 nuts, 2 screws, and the front and rear fuel tank heat shields.
8. Disconnect the fuel jumper tube-to-fuel supply tube quick connect coupling.
9. Disconnect the fuel vapor jumper tube-to-fuel vapor tube quick connect coupling.

➡Some residual fuel may remain in the fuel tank filler pipe after draining the fuel tank. Carefully drain any remaining fuel into a suitable container.

10. Release the clamp and remove the fuel tank filler pipe hose from the fuel tank.
11. Disconnect the fuel vapor tube assembly-to-fuel tank filler pipe recirculation tube quick connect coupling.
12. Disconnect the fuel tank filler pipe fresh air hose from the Evaporative Emission (EVAP) canister.
13. Install a Powertrain Lift under the fuel tank.
14. Remove the bolt and the fuel tank straps.

✱✱ WARNING

Be very careful when lowering the fuel tank so the fuel tank wiring harness is not damaged.

15. Partially lower the fuel tank for access.
16. Disconnect the Fuel Pump (FP) module, EVAP canister vent solenoid and Fuel Tank Pressure (FTP) sensor electrical connectors.
17. Completely lower and remove the fuel tank.

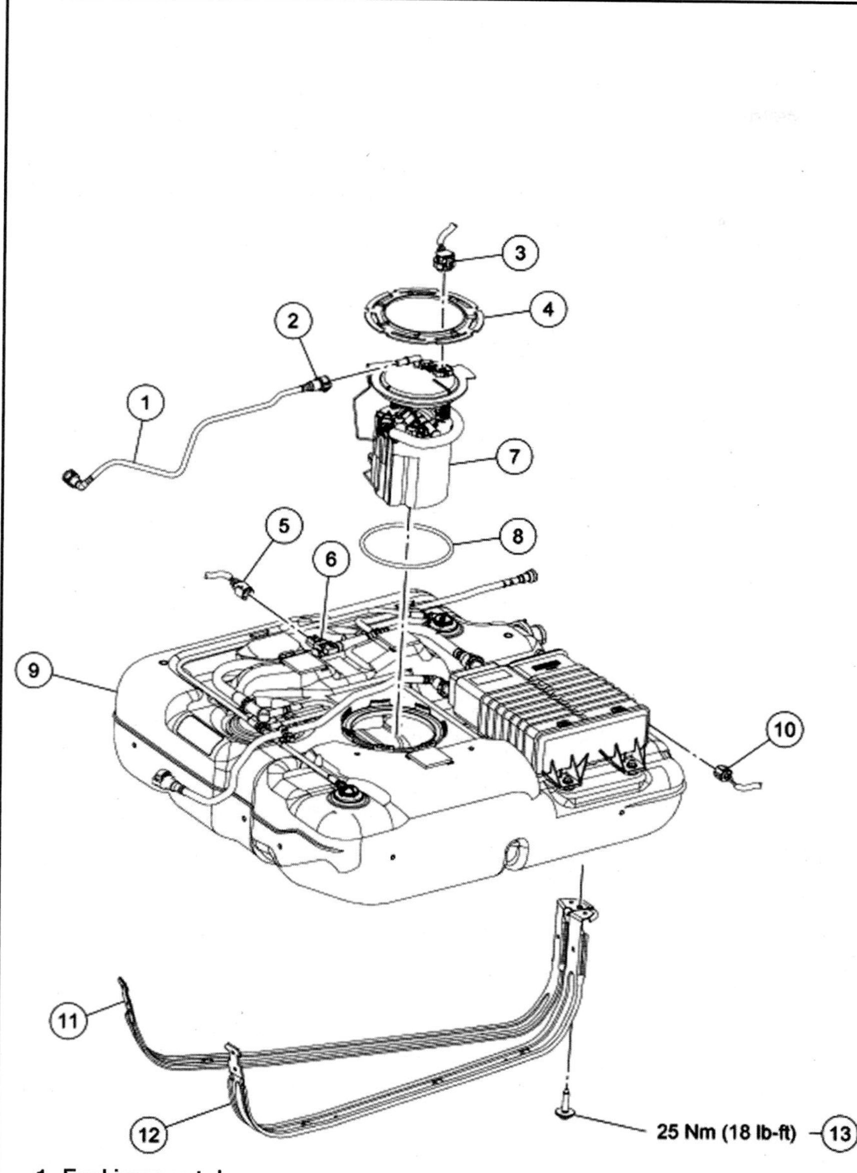

Fig. 122 Fuel pump module, fuel tank, and related components—exploded view

To install:

18. To install, reverse the removal procedure and note the following:
    - Tighten the fuel tank filler pipe hose clamp to 35 inch lbs. (4 Nm).
    - Tighten the fuel tank strap bolts to 18 ft. lbs. (25 Nm).
19. Pressurize the fuel system and check for leakage.

IDLE SPEED

ADJUSTMENT

The idle speed is controlled by the Powertrain Control Module (PCM).

THROTTLE BODY

REMOVAL & INSTALLATION

See Figures 123 and 124.

1. Before servicing the vehicle, refer to the Precautions Section.
2. Remove the Air Cleaner (ACL) outlet pipe. Refer to Air Cleaner, removal & installation.
3. Disconnect the electronic throttle control electrical connector.
4. Remove the 4 bolts and the Throttle Body (TB).
5. To install, reverse the removal procedure and note the following:
    - Inspect the TB gasket and install new as necessary.
    - Tighten the throttle body retaining bolts in sequence to 89 inch lbs. (10 Nm).

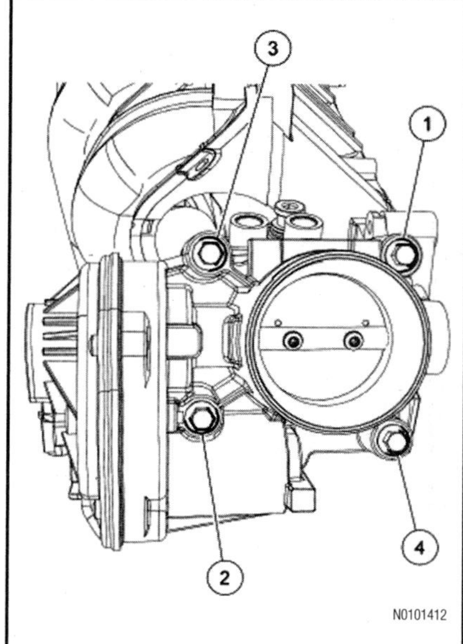

Fig. 123 Throttle body bolt tightening sequence

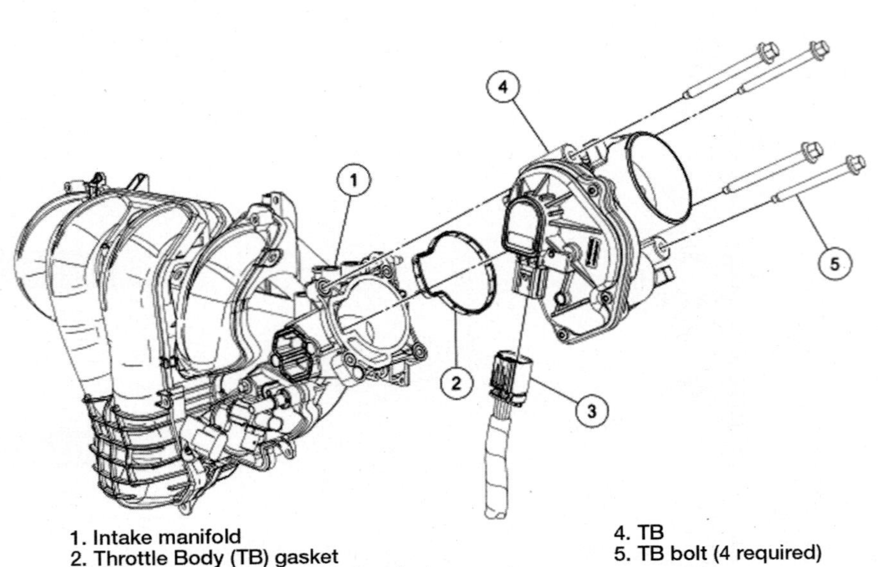

Fig. 124 Throttle body and related components—exploded view

HEATING & AIR CONDITIONING SYSTEM

BLOWER MOTOR

REMOVAL & INSTALLATION

See Figures 125 and 126.

1. Before servicing the vehicle, refer to the Precautions Section.
2. Remove the RH lower instrument panel insulator.
3. Remove the floor duct screw and the floor duct.
4. Disconnect the blower motor electrical connector.
5. Remove the 3 blower motor screws.
6. Remove the blower motor.
7. To install, reverse the removal procedure.

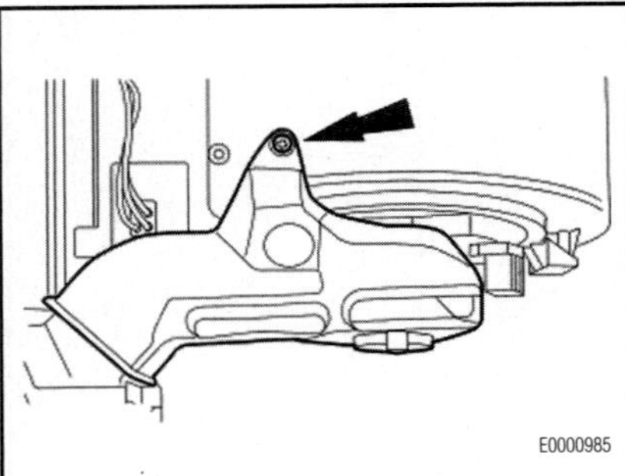

Fig. 125 Remove the floor duct screw and the floor duct

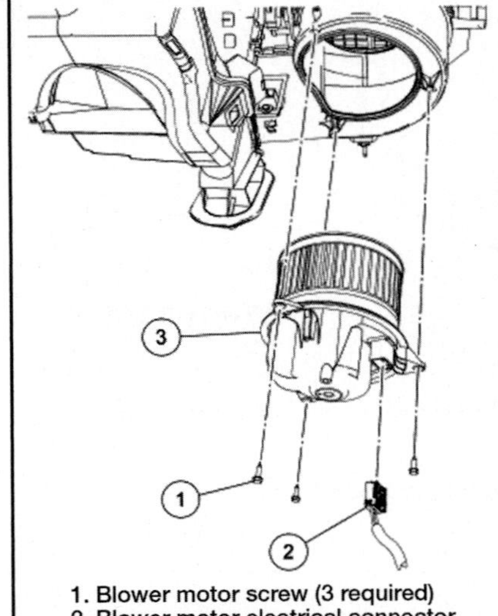

Fig. 126 Blower motor removal

HEATER CORE

REMOVAL & INSTALLATION

See Figures 125, 127 through 132.

➡If a heater core leak is suspected, the heater core must be leak tested before it is removed from the vehicle.

1. Before servicing the vehicle, refer to the Precautions Section.
2. With the vehicle in NEUTRAL, position it on a hoist.
3. Drain the engine coolant. For additional information, refer to Engine Coolant, Drain & Refill Procedure.
4. Remove the floor console.
5. Remove the RH lower instrument panel insulator.
6. Remove the screw and the floor duct.
7. Release the 2 heater hose clamps and disconnect the heater hoses from the heater core.
8. Remove the 6 in-vehicle crossbeam bracket bolts and remove the brackets.
9. Remove the LH floor duct clip between the heater core and evaporator core housing and the dash panel.
10. Remove the LH floor duct.
    a. Remove the LH floor duct screw.
    b. Remove the LH floor duct.
11. Remove the RH floor duct.
    a. Remove the RH floor duct clip.
    b. Remove the RH floor duct screw.
    c. Remove the RH floor duct.
12. Remove the heater core cover.
    a. Remove the 2 heater core cover screws.

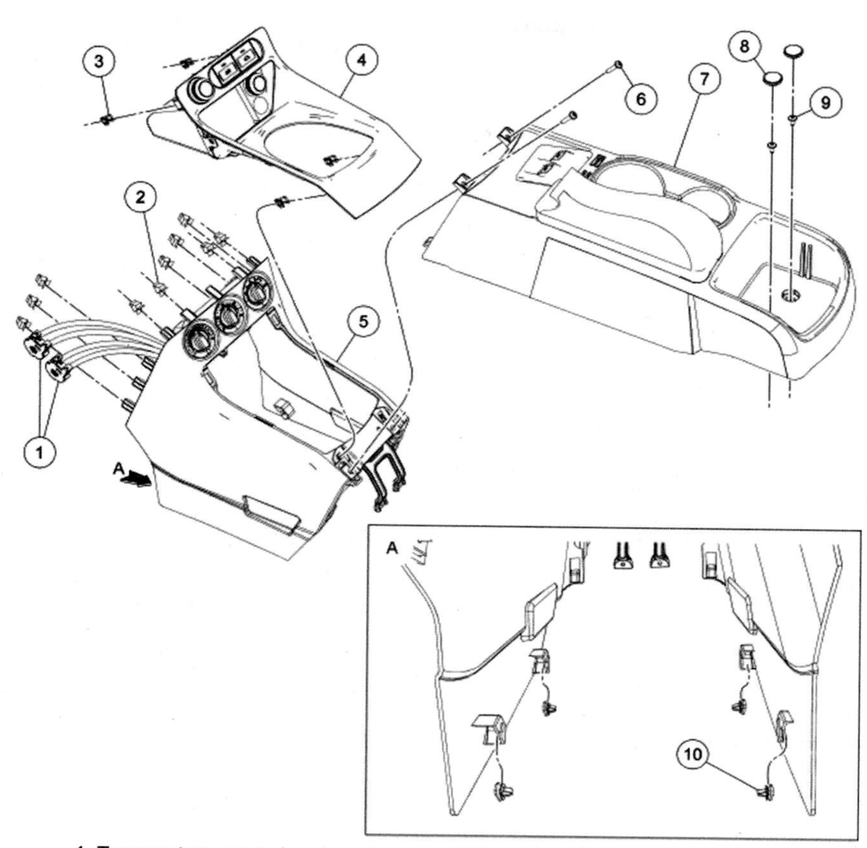

Fig. 127 Floor console—expanded view

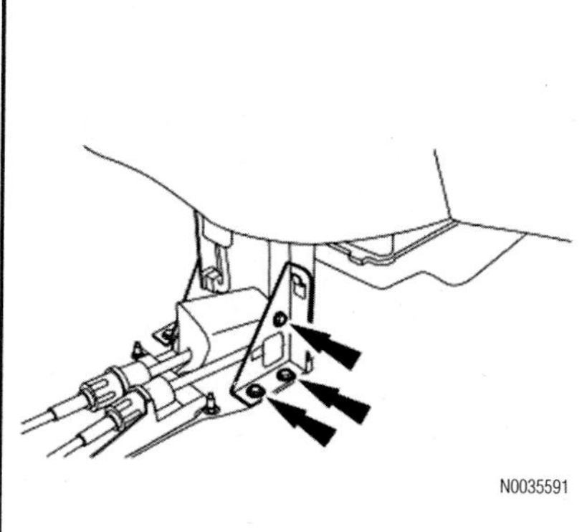

Fig. 128 Remove the 6 in-vehicle cross-beam bracket bolts and remove the brackets (RH shown)

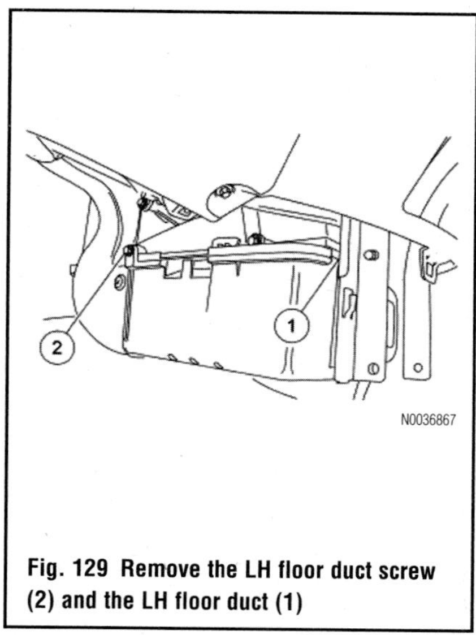

Fig. 129 Remove the LH floor duct screw (2) and the LH floor duct (1)

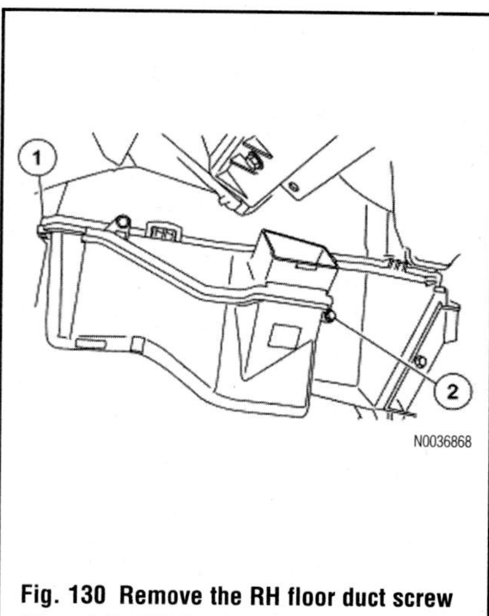

Fig. 130 Remove the RH floor duct screw (2) and the RH floor duct (1)

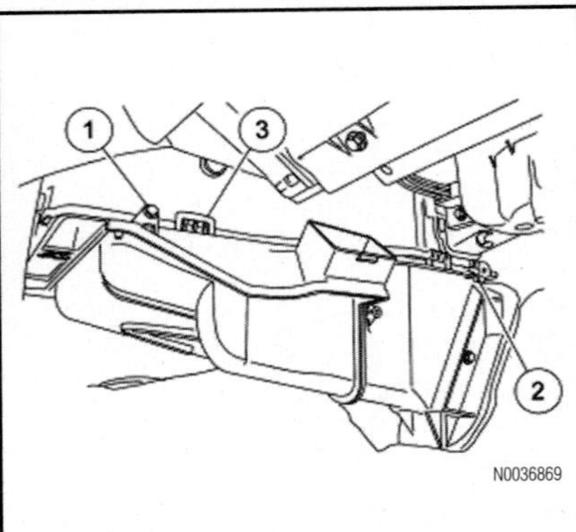

Fig. 131 Remove the heater core cover screws (1) and clips (3) and remove the heater core cover (2)

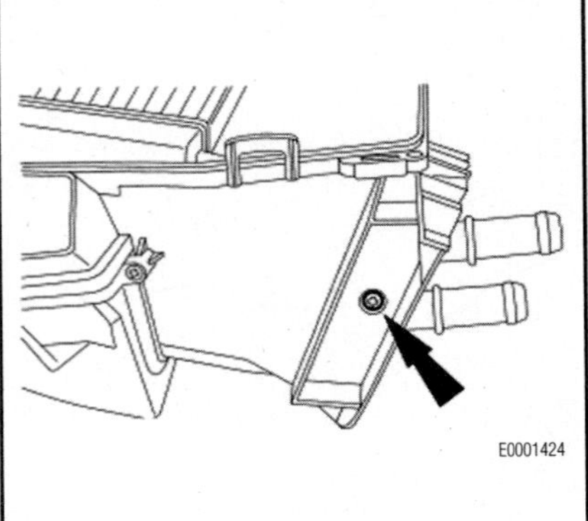

Fig. 132 Remove the heater core tube bracket screw

b. Remove the 2 heater core cover clips.

c. Release the heater core cover tab and remove the heater core cover and heater core as an assembly.

13. Remove the heater core tube bracket screw.

14. Remove the heater core.

To install:

15. To install, reverse the removal procedure.

16. Tighten the 6 in-vehicle crossbeam bracket bolts to 18 ft. lbs. (25 Nm).

17. Fill and bleed the engine cooling system. Refer to Engine Coolant, Drain & Refill Procedure.

18. Run the engine and check for coolant leakage.

STEERING

POWER STEERING GEAR

REMOVAL & INSTALLATION

See Figures 133 through 135.

WARNING

Steering fasteners are critical parts because they affect performance of vital components and systems and their failure may result in major service expense. New parts must be installed with the same part numbers or equivalent part, if replacement is necessary. Do not use a replacement part of lesser quality or substitute design. Torque values must be used as specified during reassembly to make sure of correct retention of these parts.

WARNING

While repairing the power steering system, care should be taken to prevent the entry of foreign material or failure of the power steering components may result.

1. Before servicing the vehicle, refer to the Precautions Section.

2. Using a suitable holding device, hold the steering wheel in the straight-ahead position.

3. Remove the stabilizer bar. Refer to Stabilizer Bar, removal & installation.

➡Use the hex-holding feature to prevent turning of the stud while removing the outer tie-rod end nuts.

4. Remove and discard the 2 outer tie-rod end nuts.

5. Using the Ball Joint Separator and Adapter, disconnect the outer tie-rod ends from the wheel knuckles.

6. Remove the steering line-to-steering gear retainer bolt and the retainer.

7. Disconnect the pressure line from the steering gear.

a. Remove the steering line clamp plate bolt and rotate the clamp plate.

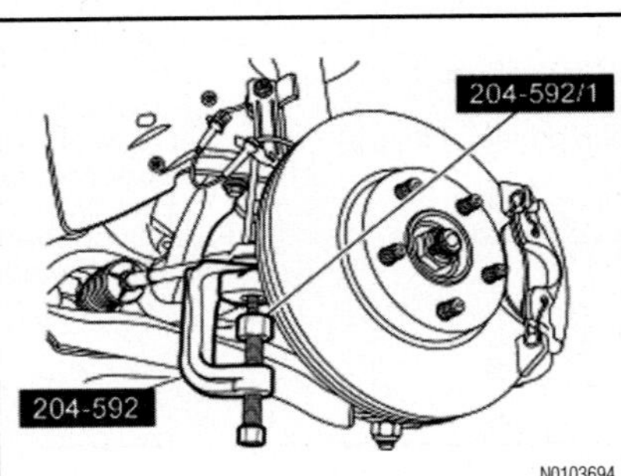

Fig. 133 Using the Ball Joint Separator and Adapter, disconnect the outer tie-rod ends from the wheel knuckles

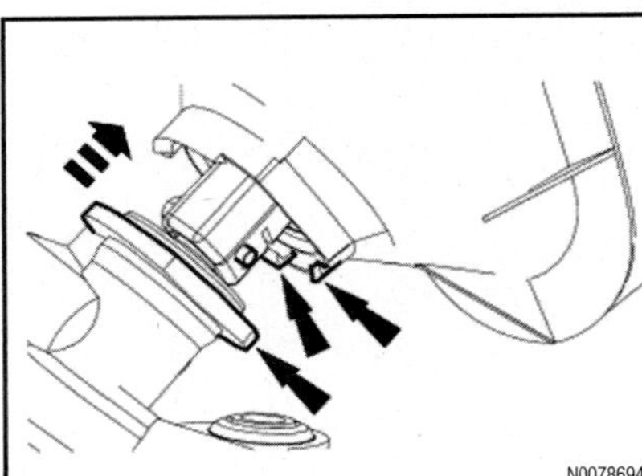

Fig. 134 Pull out on the dash seal tabs and push the dash seal upward to detach it from the steering gear

b. Discard the O-ring seal.

8. Disconnect the return hose from the steering gear. Discard the O-ring seal.

9. Remove the 2 bolts and the steering gear heat shield.

10. Pull out on the dash seal tabs and push the dash seal upward to detach it from the steering gear. Position the dash seal aside.

11. Remove the bolt and disconnect the lower steering column shaft from the steering gear. Discard the bolt.

12. Remove the 2 steering gear bolts and the steering gear.

To install:

➡New O-ring seals must be installed any time the pressure and return lines are disconnected from the steering gear or a fluid leak may occur.

13. Install 2 new O-ring seals on the pressure and return lines.

14. Position the steering gear and install the 2 bolts. Tighten to 59 ft. lbs. (80 Nm).

WARNING

Install a new steering column shaft bolt. Reuse could result in bolt failure and loss of vehicle control. Failure to follow this instruction may result in serious injury to vehicle occupant(s).

15. Connect the lower steering column shaft to the steering gear and install the new bolt. Tighten to 21 ft. lbs. (28 Nm).

16. Install the dash seal to the steering gear.

- Center the dash seal on the steering gear and pull down to attach it to the steering gear

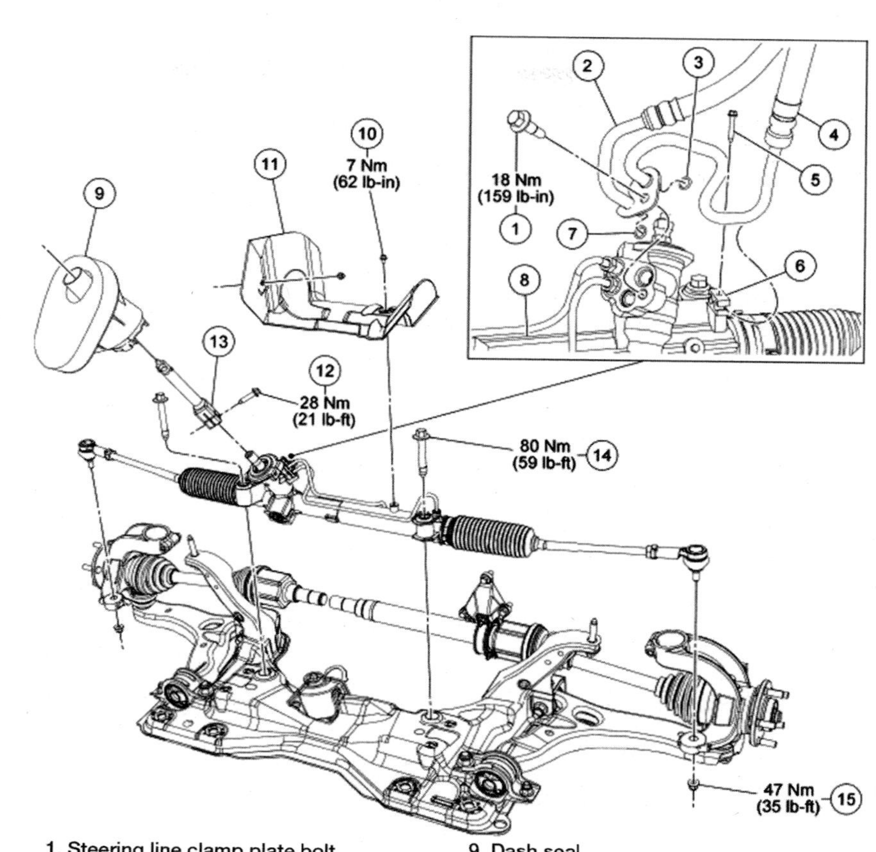

Fig. 135 Power steering gear and related components—exploded view

17. Position the steering gear heat shield and install the 2 bolts. Tighten to 62 inch lbs. (7 Nm).

18. Install the pressure and return lines to the steering gear, rotate the steering line clamp plate and install the bolt. Tighten to 13 ft. lbs. (18 Nm).

19. Position the steering line retainer and install the bolt.

20. Install the stabilizer bar. Refer to Stabilizer Bar, removal & installation.

WARNING

Do not reuse a tie rod-to-wheel knuckle nut. This can result in nut failure and loss of steering control. Failure to follow this instruction may result in serious injury to vehicle occupant(s).

21. Position the outer tie-rod ends in the wheel knuckles and install the 2 new nuts. Tighten to 35 ft. lbs. (47 Nm).

22. Fill the power steering system with the proper type and amount of fluid. For additional information, refer to Power Steering Pump, Fluid Fill Procedure.

23. Check and, if necessary, adjust the front toe.

POWER STEERING PUMP

REMOVAL & INSTALLATION

See Figures 136 through 139.

WARNING

While repairing the power steering system, care should be taken to prevent the entry of foreign material or failure of the power steering components may occur.

WARNING

Do not allow power steering fluid to contact the accessory drive belt or damage to the belt may occur.

1. Before servicing the vehicle, refer to the Precautions Section.

2. With a suitable suction device, remove the power steering fluid from the fluid reservoir.

3. With the vehicle in NEUTRAL, position it on a hoist.

4. Remove the 2 bolts and the accessory drive belt splash shield.

5. Rotate the accessory drive belt tensioner clockwise and position the accessory

Fig. 136 Using the Power Steering Pump Pulley Remover, remove the power steering pump pulley

drive belt away from the power steering pump pulley.

6. Using the Power Steering Pump Pulley Remover, remove the power steering pump pulley.

7. Disconnect the pressure line fitting from the power steering pump.

8. Release the clamp and disconnect the return hose from the power steering pump.

9. Remove the 4 bolts and the power steering pump and fluid reservoir.

10. Remove and discard the Teflon® seal from the pressure line fitting.

WARNING

Use a slight twisting motion when removing the reservoir and carefully pull it away from the pump on the same axis as the reservoir outlet tube to avoid damaging the reservoir.

➡Whenever the fluid reservoir is separated from the pump, new O-ring seals must be installed or a fluid leak may occur.

11. If necessary, remove the power steering fluid reservoir from the power steering pump and discard the O-ring seals.

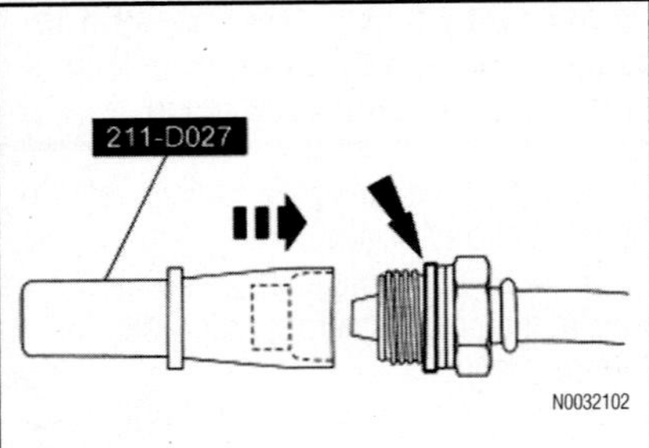

Fig. 137 Using the Teflon® Seal Installer Set, install a new Teflon® seal on the pressure line fitting

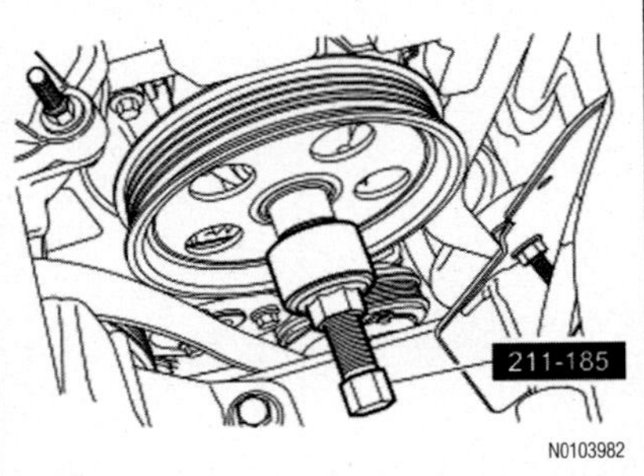

Fig. 138 Using the Power Steering Pump Pulley Installer, install the power steering pump pulley

To install:

12. If removed, install the power steering fluid reservoir to the power steering pump using new O-ring seals.

13. Using the Teflon® Seal Installer Set, install a new Teflon® seal on the pressure line fitting.

14. Install the 4 bolts and the power steering pump and fluid reservoir. Tighten to 18 ft. lbs. (25 Nm).

15. Connect the return hose to the power steering pump and install the clamp.

16. Connect the pressure line fitting to the power steering pump. Tighten to 48 ft. lbs. (65 Nm).

➡Make sure the pulley is flush with the end of the power steering pump shaft during installation.

17. Using the Power Steering Pump Pulley Installer, install the power steering pump pulley.

18. Rotate the tensioner clockwise and position the accessory drive belt on the power steering pump pulley.

19. Position the accessory drive belt splash shield and install the 2 bolts. Tighten to 80 inch lbs. (9 Nm).

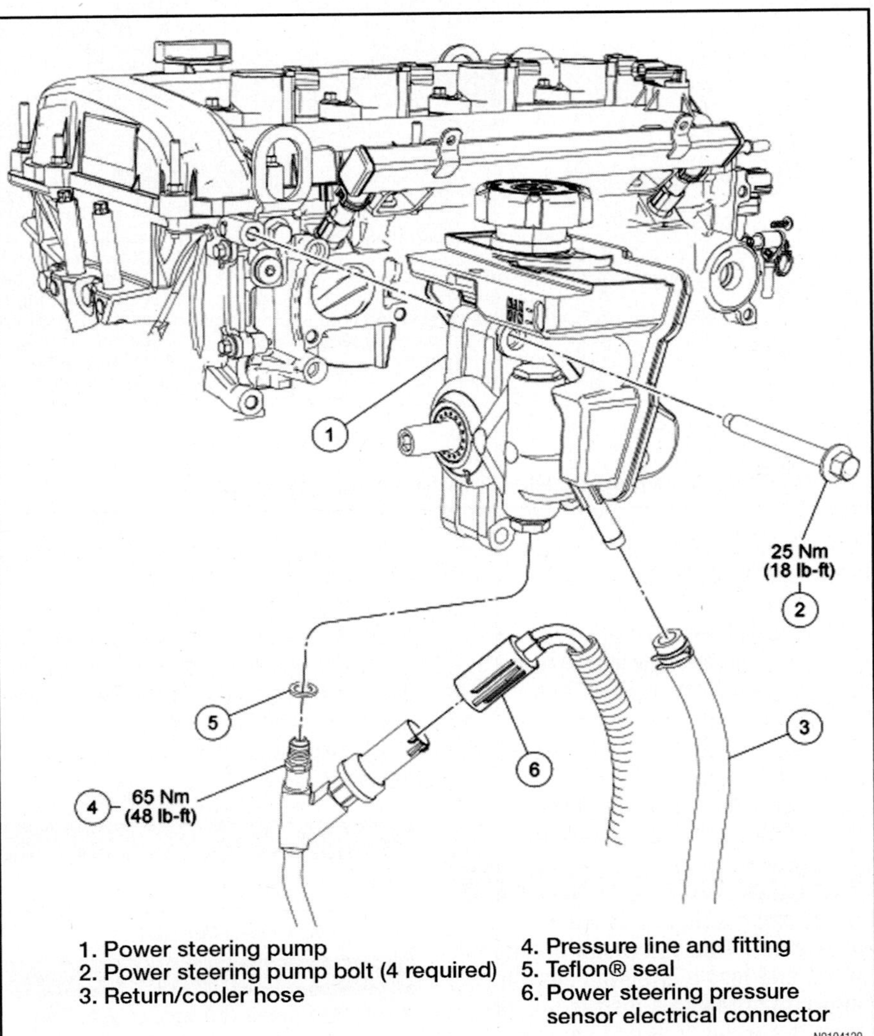

Fig. 139 View of power steering pump installation

20. Fill the power steering system. Refer to Fluid Fill Procedure.

BLEEDING

See Figure 140.

WARNING

If the air is not purged from the power steering system correctly, premature power steering pump failure may result. The condition may occur on pre-delivery vehicles with evidence of aerated fluid or on vehicles that have had steering component repairs.

➡A whine heard from the power steering pump can be caused by air in the system. The power steering purge procedure must be carried out prior to any component repair for which power steering noise complaints are accompanied by evidence of aerated fluid.

1. Before servicing the vehicle, refer to the Precautions Section.
2. Remove the power steering reservoir cap. Check the fluid.
3. Raise the front wheels off the floor.
4. Tightly insert the Power Steering Evacuation Cap into the reservoir and connect the Vacuum Pump Kit.
5. Start the engine.
6. Using the Vacuum Pump Kit, apply vacuum and maintain the maximum vacuum of 20–25 inches Hg (68–85 kPa).
7. If the Vacuum Pump Kit does not maintain vacuum, check the power steering system for leaks before proceeding.
8. If equipped with Hydro-Boost®, apply the brake pedal 4 times.

WARNING

Do not hold the steering wheel against the stops for an extended amount of time. Damage to the power steering pump may occur.

9. Cycle the steering wheel fully from stop-to-stop 10 times.
10. Stop the engine.
11. Release the vacuum and remove the Vacuum Pump Kit and the Power Steering Evacuation Cap.

➡Do not overfill the reservoir.

12. Fill the reservoir as needed with the specified fluid.
13. Repeat steps 4–12
14. Install the reservoir cap.
15. Visually inspect the power steering system for leaks.

FLUID FILL PROCEDURE

See Figure 141.

WARNING

If the air is not purged from the power steering system correctly, premature power steering pump failure may result. The condition can occur on pre-delivery vehicles with evidence of aerated fluid or on vehicles that have had steering component repairs.

1. Before servicing the vehicle, refer to the Precautions Section.
2. Remove the power steering fluid reservoir cap.
3. Install the Power Steering Evacuation Cap, Power Steering Fill Adapter Manifold, and Vacuum Pump Kit.

➡The Power Steering Fill Adapter Manifold control valves are in the OPEN position when the points of the handles face the center of the Power Steering Fill Adapter Manifold.

4. Close the Power Steering Fill Adapter Manifold control valve (fluid side).
5. Open the Power Steering Fill Adapter Manifold control valve (vacuum side).
6. Using the Vacuum Pump Kit, apply 20–25 inches Hg (68–85 kPa) of vacuum to the power steering system.
7. Observe the Vacuum Pump Kit gauge for 30 seconds.
8. If the Vacuum Pump Kit gauge reading drops more than 0.88 inch Hg (3 kPa), correct any leaks in the power steering system or the Power Steering Evacuation Cap, Power Steering Fill Adapter Manifold, and Vacuum Pump Kit before proceeding.

➡The Vacuum Pump Kit gauge reading will drop slightly during this next step.

9. Slowly open the Power Steering Fill Adapter Manifold control valve (fluid side) until power steering fluid completely fills the hose and then close the control valve.

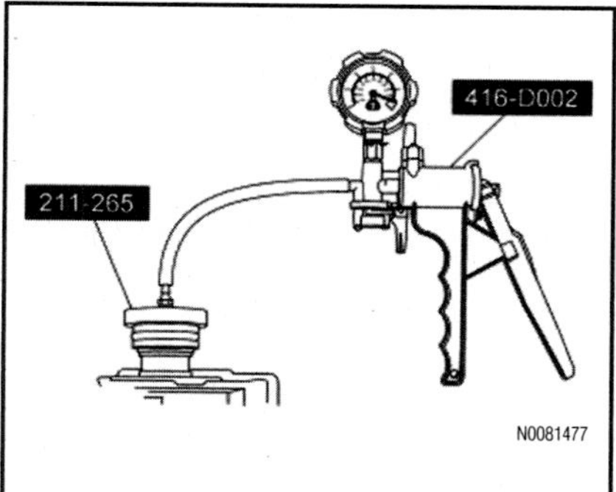

Fig. 140 Power Steering Evacuation Cap and Vacuum Pump Kit installed to vehicle

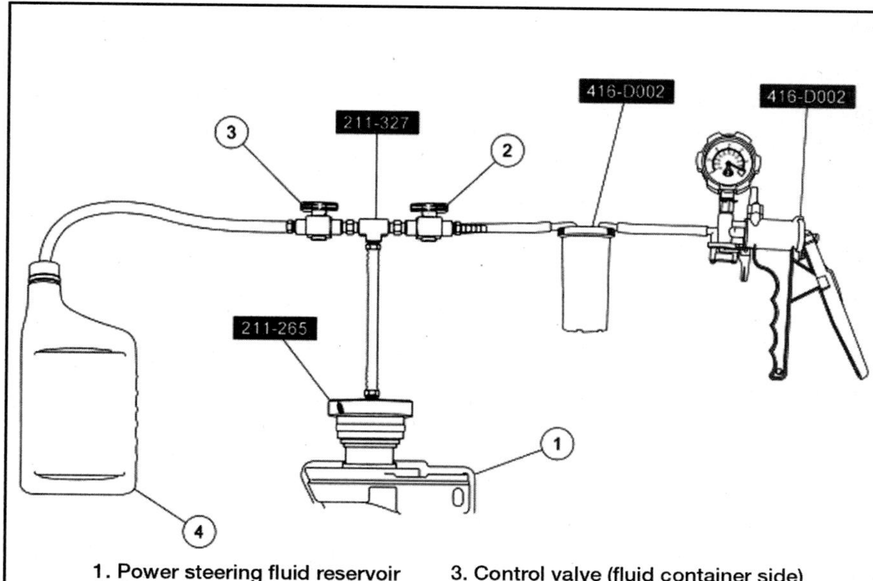

Fig. 141 Install the Power Steering Evacuation Cap, Power Steering Fill Adapter Manifold, and Vacuum Pump Kit

10. Using the Vacuum Pump Kit, apply 20–25 inches Hg (68–85 kPa) of vacuum to the power steering system.

11. Close the Power Steering Fill Adapter Manifold control valve (vacuum side).

12. Slowly open the Power Steering Fill Adapter Manifold control valve (fluid side).

13. Once power steering fluid enters the fluid reservoir and reaches the minimum fluid level indicator line on the reservoir, close the Power Steering Fill Adapter Manifold control valve (fluid side).

14. Remove the Power Steering Evacuation Cap, Power Steering Fill Adapter Manifold, and Vacuum Pump Kit.

15. Install the reservoir cap.

WARNING

Do not hold the steering wheel against the stops for an extended amount of time. Damage to the power steering pump may occur.

➡There will be a slight drop in the power steering fluid level in the reservoir when the engine is started.

16. Start the engine and turn the steering wheel from stop-to-stop.

17. Turn the ignition switch to the OFF position.

➡Do not overfill the reservoir.

18. Remove the reservoir cap and fill the reservoir with the specified fluid.

19. Install the reservoir cap.

SUSPENSION

FRONT SUSPENSION

CONTROL LINKS

REMOVAL & INSTALLATION

See Figure 142.

WARNING

Suspension fasteners are critical parts because they affect performance of vital components and systems and their failure may result in major service expense. New parts must be installed with the same part numbers or equivalent part, if replacement is necessary. Do not use a replacement part of lesser quality or substitute design. Torque values must be used as specified during reassembly to make sure of correct retention of these parts.

WARNING

Do not use power tools to remove or install the stabilizer bar link nuts.

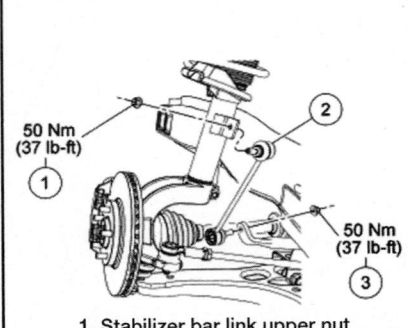

Fig. 142 View of stabilizer bar link installation

Damage to the stabilizer bar link ball joints and boots may occur.

WARNING

Do not hold the stabilizer bar link boot with any tool or damage to the boot may occur.

1. Before servicing the vehicle, refer to the Precautions Section.

2. With the vehicle in NEUTRAL, position it on a hoist.

➡Use the hex-holding feature to prevent the ball stud from turning while removing or installing the stabilizer bar link nuts.

3. Remove and discard the stabilizer bar link upper and lower nuts.

4. Remove the stabilizer bar link.

To install:

5. To install, reverse the removal procedure.

6. Tighten the stabilizer bar link upper and lower nuts to 37 ft. lbs. (50 Nm).

LOWER BALL JOINT

REMOVAL & INSTALLATION

See Figure 143.

The manufacturer does not provide a specific removal and installation procedure for this component. Use the illustration as a guide when servicing this component.

LOWER CONTROL ARM

REMOVAL & INSTALLATION

See Figures 144 and 145

WARNING

Suspension fasteners are critical parts because they affect performance of vital components and systems and their failure may result in major service expense. New parts must be installed with the same part numbers or equivalent part, if replacement is necessary. Do not use a replacement part of lesser quality or substitute design. Torque values must be used as specified during reassembly to make sure of correct retention of these parts.

1. Before servicing the vehicle, refer to the Precautions Section.

2. Remove the wheel and tire.

3. Remove and discard the ball joint nut.

WARNING

Use care when releasing the lower arm and wheel knuckle into the resting position or damage to the ball joint seal may occur.

4. Using the Ball Joint Separator and Adapter, separate the lower arm from the ball joint stud.

5. Remove and discard the lower arm bracket inboard and outboard nuts and bolts.

6. Remove and discard the lower arm forward nut and bolt.

7. Remove the lower arm.

To install:

WARNING

To prevent incorrect clamp load or component damage, install the fasteners in their original orientation. Install the lower arm bushing clamp bolts with their heads facing down.

➡Do not tighten the nuts and bolts at this time.

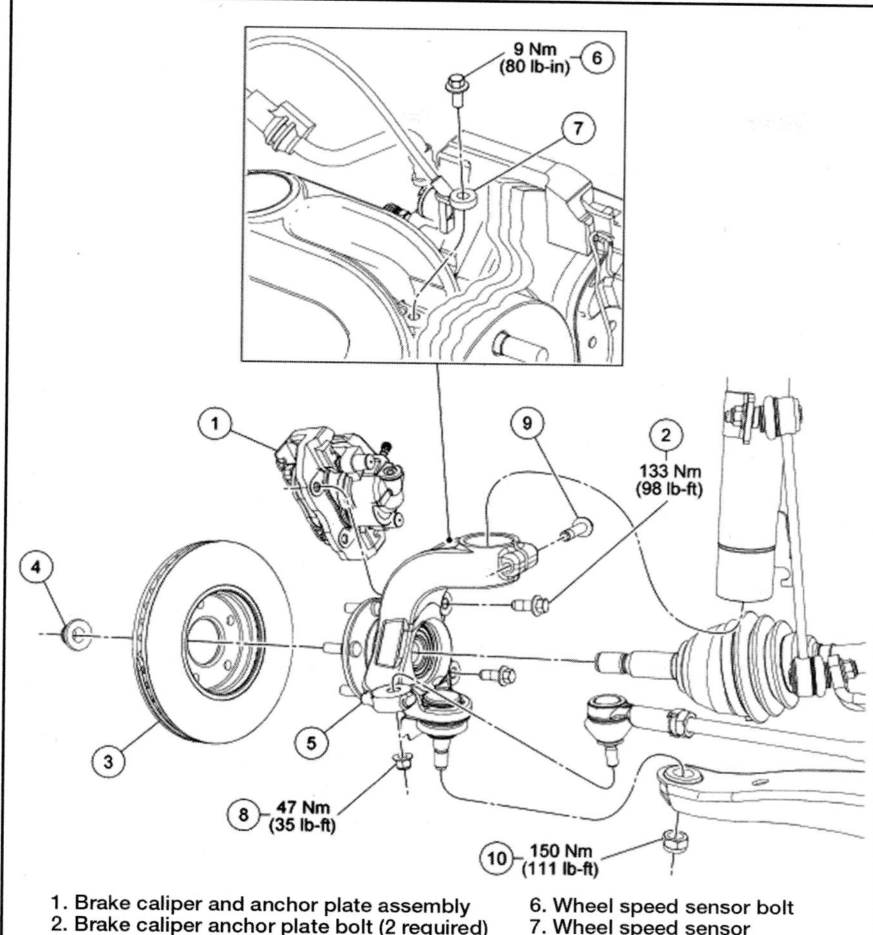

Fig. 143 Wheel knuckle and related components—exploded view

8. Position the lower arm and loosely install the forward bolt and nut.
9. Loosely install the lower arm bracket inboard and outboard bolts and nuts.
10. Position the ball joint into the lower arm and install the ball joint nut. Tighten to 111 ft. lbs. (150 Nm).

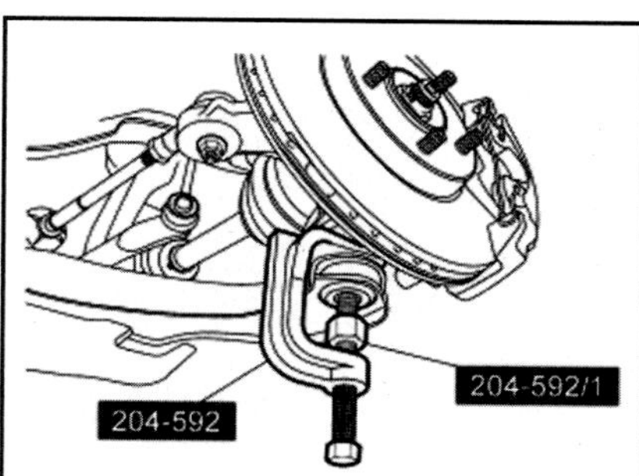

Fig. 144 Using the Ball Joint Separator and Adapter, separate the lower arm from the ball joint stud

11. Install the wheels and tires. Tighten the wheel nuts in a star pattern to 66 ft. lbs. (90 Nm).
12. Lower the hoist so the weight of the vehicle is resting on the wheels and tires.
13. Tighten the lower arm forward nut to 140 ft. lbs. (190 Nm).
14. Tighten the lower arm bracket inboard nut to 178 ft. lbs. (240 Nm).
15. Tighten the lower arm bracket outboard nut to 74 ft. lbs. (100 Nm).
16. Check and, if necessary, align the front end.

STABILIZER BAR

REMOVAL & INSTALLATION

See Figures 146 through 149.

⁂ WARNING

Suspension fasteners are critical parts because they affect performance of vital components and systems and their failure may result in major service expense. New parts must be installed with the same part numbers or equivalent part, if replacement is necessary. Do not use a replacement part of lesser quality or substitute design. Torque values must be used as specified during reassembly to make sure of correct retention of these parts.

1. Before servicing the vehicle, refer to the Precautions Section.
2. Turn the steering wheel to the straight-ahead position and turn the ignition switch to the OFF position.
3. Remove and discard the steering column shaft-to-steering column bolt.

⁂ WARNING

Do not allow the steering column to rotate while the steering column shaft is disconnected or damage to the clockspring may result. If there is evidence that the steering column has rotated, the clockspring must be removed and recentered. For additional information, refer to Clockspring Centering.

4. Disconnect the steering column shaft from the steering column.
5. Remove the wheel and tire.
6. Remove and discard the stabilizer bar link lower nuts. Pull downward on the stabilizer bar and detach the stabilizer bar links.
7. Using a suitable transmission jack, support the subframe.
8. Index-mark the subframe position.
9. Remove and discard the 4 rearward and 2 forward subframe bolts.
10. Unclip the Heated Oxygen Sensor (HO2S) harness from the steering gear heat shield.
11. Disconnect the 2 catalytic converter exhaust hanger isolators.
12. Lower the subframe approximately 4 inches (100mm) to gain access to the stabilizer bar.
13. Remove and discard the 4 subframe washers.
14. Remove the 4 stabilizer bar bracket bolts, the RH heat shield and 2 brackets. Discard the bolts.
15. Remove the stabilizer bar bushings.
16. While pushing upward (slightly) on the catalytic converter, remove the stabilizer bar towards the rear of the vehicle.

To install:

17. While pushing upward (slightly) on the catalytic converter, install the stabilizer bar.

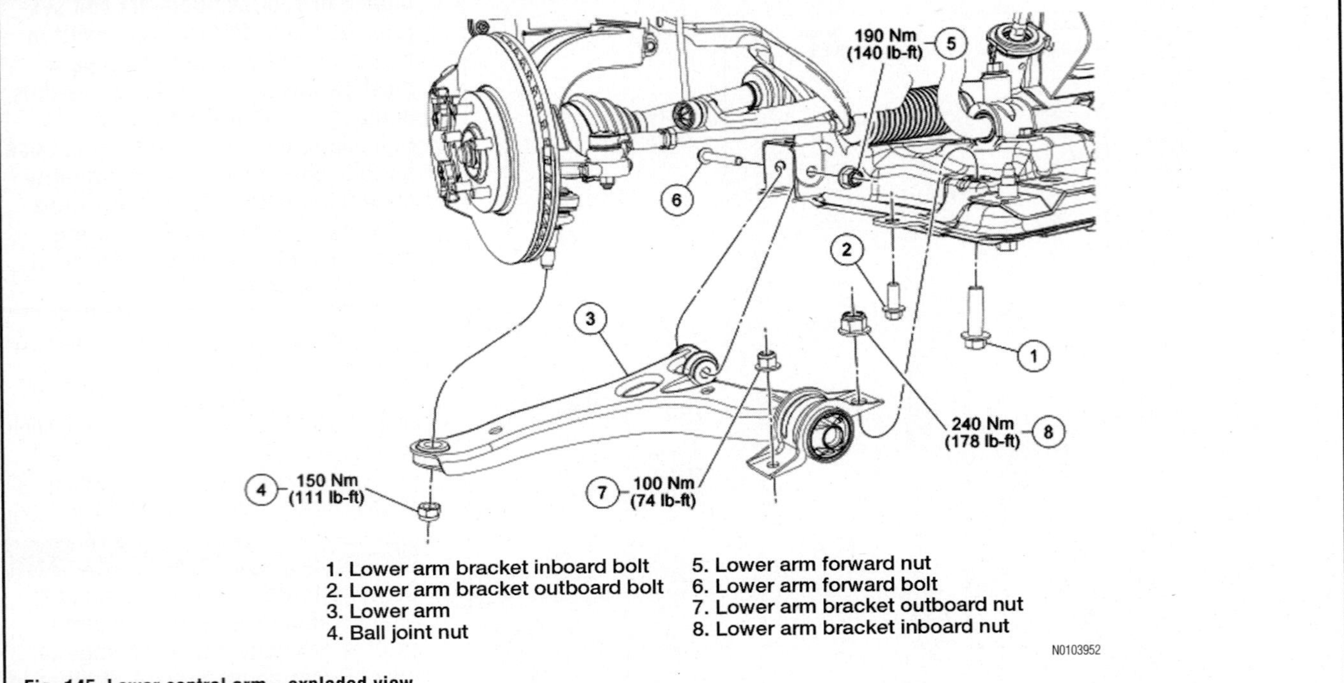

Fig. 145 Lower control arm—exploded view

⁂ WARNING

The stabilizer bar bushings must be positioned correctly on the flats of the stabilizer bar or damage to the bushings may occur.

⁂ WARNING

Do not apply any type of lubricant to the stabilizer bar or bushings or damage to the bushings may occur.

18. Install the stabilizer bar bushings.

⁂ WARNING

Make sure that the stabilizer bar brackets are installed with the rounded bolt tab edge of the bracket facing towards the front of the vehicle or damage to the bushings may occur.

⁂ WARNING

Make sure that the stabilizer bar bushings remain in the correct position while positioning the brackets and installing the bolts or damage to the bushings may occur.

➡Do not fully tighten the stabilizer bar bracket bolts at this time.

19. Position the 2 stabilizer bar brackets and install the 4 new bolts. Tighten until snug.
20. With the stabilizer bar in a vertical plane, use cable straps or mechanic's wire and set it to specification.
21. Tighten the stabilizer bar bracket bolts. Tighten alternately and evenly to 52 ft. lbs. (70 Nm).
22. Remove the cable straps or mechanic's wire.
23. Install the 4 new subframe washers.

➡Do not fully tighten the subframe bolts at this time.

24. Raise the subframe into position using the index marks made during removal and install the 2 forward and 4 rearward subframe bolts. Tighten the bolts until snug.

➡While tightening the subframe bolts, make sure the subframe does not move.

25. Tighten the 4 rearward subframe bolts. Tighten to 148 ft. lbs. (200 Nm).
26. Tighten the 2 forward subframe bolts. Tighten to 92 ft. lbs. (125 Nm).

Fig. 146 Remove and discard the 4 subframe washers

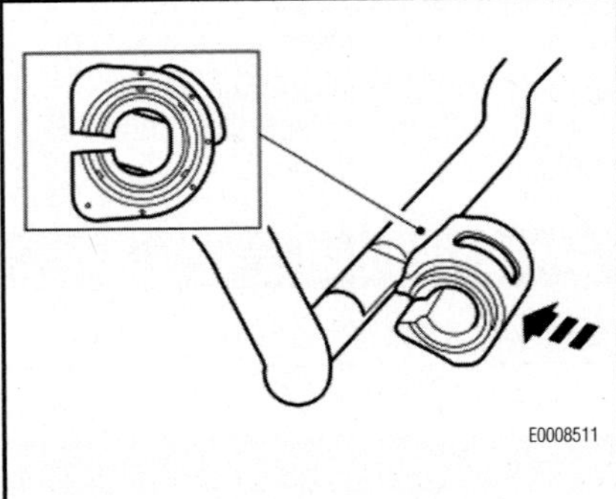

Fig. 147 Install the stabilizer bar bushings as shown

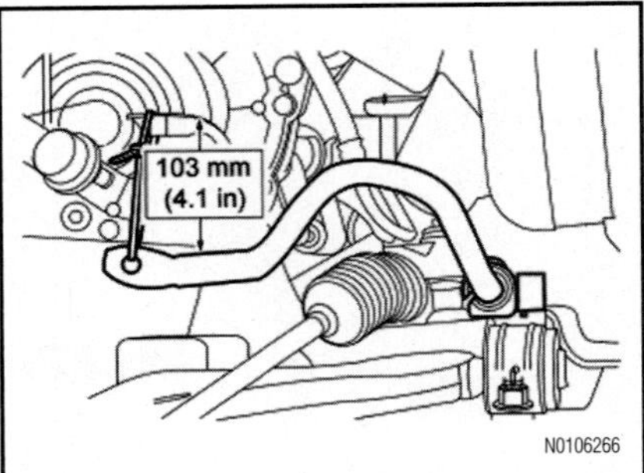

Fig. 148 Use cable straps or mechanic's wire to set the stabilizer bar to specification shown

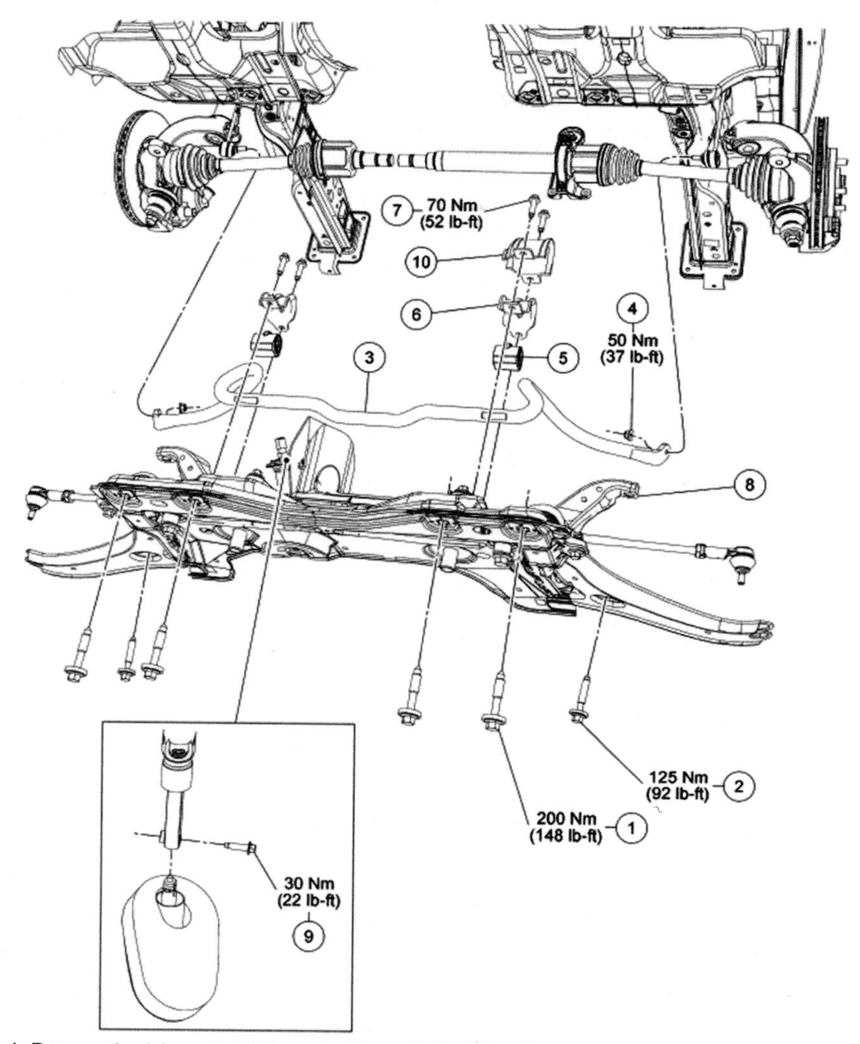

Fig. 149 Stabilizer bar and related components—exploded view

27. Clip the HO2S harness to the steering gear heat shield.
28. Connect the 2 catalytic converter exhaust hanger isolators.
29. Attach the stabilizer bar links to the stabilizer bar and install the new nuts. Tighten to 37 ft. lbs. (50 Nm).
30. Install the wheels and tires. Tighten the wheel nuts in a star pattern to 66 ft. lbs. (90 Nm).
31. Connect the steering column shaft to the steering column.

WARNING

Do not reuse steering column shaft bolts. This may result in fastener failure and steering column shaft detachment or loss of steering control. Failure to follow this instruction may result in serious injury to vehicle occupant(s).

32. Install the new bolt steering column shaft-to-steering column bolt. Tighten to 22 ft. lbs. (30 Nm).
33. Check and, if necessary, align the front suspension.

STEERING KNUCKLE

REMOVAL & INSTALLATION

See Figures 150 through 155

WARNING

Suspension fasteners are critical parts because they affect performance of vital components and systems and their failure may result in major service expense. New parts must be installed with the same part numbers or equivalent part, if replacement is necessary. Do not use a replacement part of lesser quality or substitute design. Torque values must be used as specified during reassembly to make sure of correct retention of these parts.

1. Before servicing the vehicle, refer to the Precautions Section.
2. Loosen the 3 upper strut mount nuts 5 turns.
3. Remove the wheel and tire.
4. Remove and discard the wheel hub nut.
5. Remove the brake hose retainer clip.

WARNING

Do not allow the brake caliper to hang from the brake hose or damage to the hose can occur.

6. Remove the 2 brake caliper anchor plate bolts and position the caliper and anchor plate assembly aside. Support the caliper assembly using mechanic's wire.
7. Remove the brake disc.
8. Remove the wheel speed sensor bolt and position the sensor aside.

➡Leave the tie-rod end nut in place or damage to the tie-rod end may occur.

9. Loosen the tie-rod end nut.
10. Using the Ball Joint Separator and Adapter, disconnect the tie-rod end from the wheel knuckle. Remove and discard the tie-rod end nut.

➡Use the hex-holding feature when removing or installing the lower ball joint nut.

11. Remove and discard the ball joint nut.

WARNING

Do not use a prying device or separator fork between the ball joint and the wheel knuckle. Damage to the ball joint or ball joint seal may result.

12. Using the Ball Joint Separator and Adapter, separate the ball joint from the wheel knuckle.

WARNING

The inner Constant Velocity (CV) joint must not be bent more than 18 degrees and the outer CV joint must not be bent more than 45 degrees or damage to the halfshaft may occur.

13. Using the Front Wheel Hub Remover, press out the halfshaft from the wheel hub and detach the halfshaft from the wheel hub. Support the halfshaft.
14. Remove and discard the wheel knuckle-to-strut bolt.
15. Remove the wheel knuckle.

To install:

WARNING

The wheel knuckle-to-strut bolt is tightened in 2 stages. Failure to follow these instructions may result in incorrect clamp load and component damage.

16. Position the wheel knuckle and install a new wheel knuckle-to-strut bolt.
    - Stage 1: Tighten to 74 ft. lbs. (100 Nm)
    - Stage 2: Tighten an additional 90°
17. Insert the halfshaft into the wheel hub.

➡Use the hex-holding feature when removing or installing the lower ball joint nut.

18. Insert the ball joint into the lower arm and install a new nut. Tighten to 111 ft. lbs. (150 Nm).
19. Attach the tie-rod end to the wheel knuckle and install a new nut. Tighten to 35 ft. lbs. (47 Nm).
20. Position the wheel speed sensor and install the bolt. Tighten to 80 inch lbs. (9 Nm).
21. Install the brake disc.
22. Position the caliper and anchor plate assembly and install the 2 bolts. Tighten to 98 ft. lbs. (133 Nm).
23. Install the brake hose retainer clip.
24. Tighten the 3 upper strut mount nuts to 18 ft. lbs. (25 Nm).
25. Using the Halfshaft Installer, install the halfshaft into the wheel hub.

E0002158

Fig. 150 Loosen the 3 upper strut mount nuts 5 turns

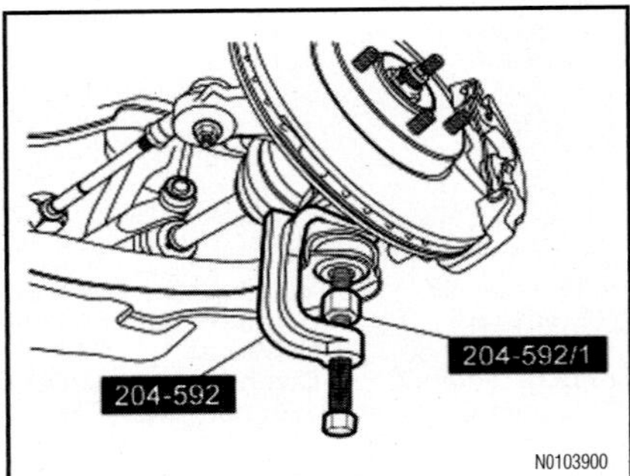

Fig. 152 Using the Ball Joint Separator and Adapter, separate the ball joint from the wheel knuckle

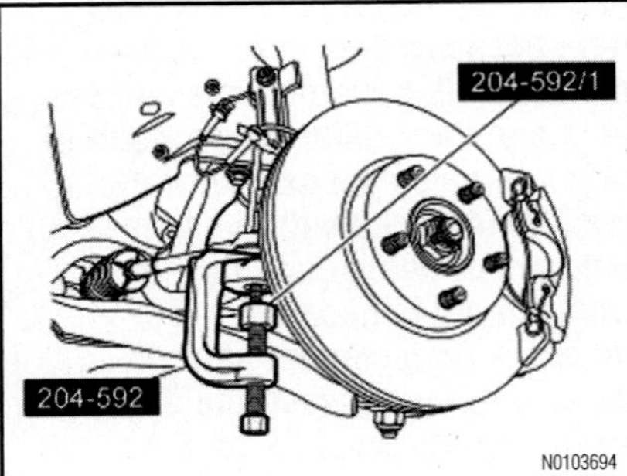

Fig. 151 Using the Ball Joint Separator and Adapter, disconnect the tie-rod end from the wheel knuckle

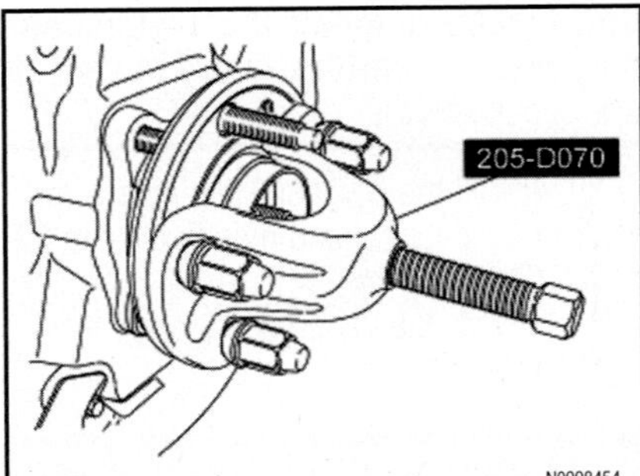

Fig. 153 Using the Front Wheel Hub Remover, press out the halfshaft from the wheel hub

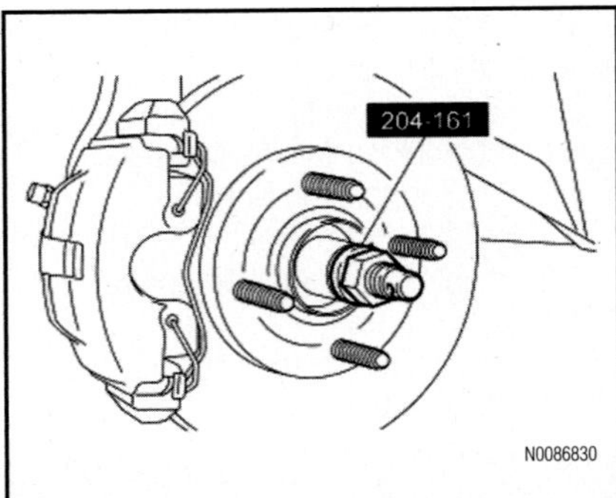

Fig. 154 Using the Halfshaft Installer, install the halfshaft into the wheel hub

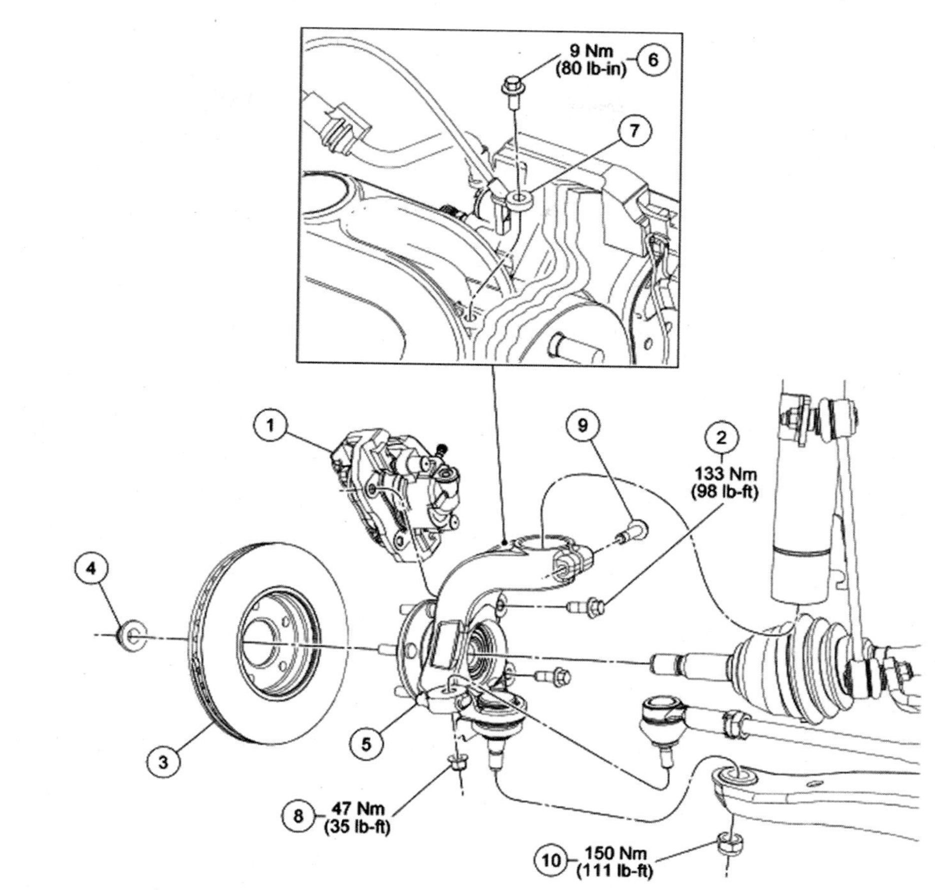

Fig. 155 Wheel knuckle and related components—exploded view

WARNING

Do not tighten the wheel hub nut with the vehicle on the ground. The nut must be tightened to specification before the vehicle is lowered onto the wheels. Wheel bearing damage will occur if the wheel bearing is loaded with the weight of the vehicle applied.

WARNING

Install and tighten the new wheel hub nut to specification in a continuous rotation. Always install a new wheel hub nut after loosening or when not tightened to specification in a continuous rotation or damage to the component may occur.

➡Apply the brake to keep the halfshaft from rotating.

26. Install the new wheel hub nut. Tighten to 207 ft. lbs. (280 Nm) in a continuous rotation.
27. Install the wheel and tire. Tighten the wheel nuts in a star pattern to 66 ft. lbs. (90 Nm).

STRUT & SPRING ASSEMBLY

REMOVAL & INSTALLATION

See Figure 156.

WARNING

Suspension fasteners are critical parts because they affect performance of vital components and systems and their failure may result in major service expense. New parts must be installed with the same part numbers or equivalent part, if replacement is necessary. Do not use a replacement part of lesser quality or substitute design. Torque values must be used as specified during reassembly to make sure of correct retention of these parts.

1. Before servicing the vehicle, refer to the Precautions Section.
2. Remove the wheel and tire.
3. Detach the brake hose from the support bracket.
4. Remove the stabilizer bar link upper nut and detach the link from the strut.
5. Remove the wheel knuckle-to-strut bolt.

WARNING

The inner Constant Velocity (CV) joint must not be bent more than 18 degrees and the outer CV joint must not be bent more than 45 degrees or damage to the halfshaft may occur.

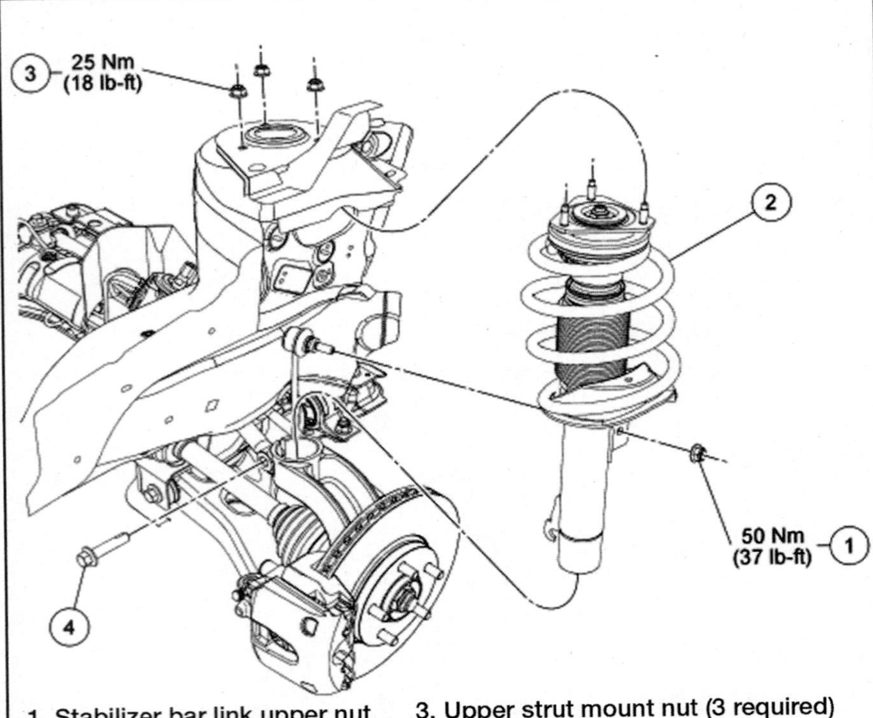

Fig. 156 Strut and spring assembly installation

6. Detach the wheel knuckle from the strut and spring assembly. Support the wheel knuckle and halfshaft using mechanic's wire.

WARNING

Support the strut and spring assembly to prevent damage.

7. Remove the upper strut mount nuts and the strut and spring assembly.

To install:

8. To install, reverse the removal procedure.
9. Tighten the upper strut mount nuts to 18 ft. lbs. (25 Nm).

WARNING

The wheel knuckle-to-strut bolt is tightened in 2 stages. Failure to follow these instructions may result in incorrect clamp load and component damage.

10. Tighten the wheel knuckle-to-strut bolt.
    - Stage 1: To install, tighten to 74 ft. lbs. (100 Nm)
    - Stage 2: Tighten an additional 90°
11. Tighten the stabilizer bar link upper nut to 37 ft. lbs. (50 Nm).
12. Check and, if necessary, align the front end.

OVERHAUL

See Figure 157.

WARNING

Suspension fasteners are critical parts because they affect performance of vital components and systems and their failure can result in major service expense. A new part with the same part number must be installed if installation is necessary. Do not use a new part of lesser quality or substitute design. Torque values must be used as specified during reassembly to make sure of correct retention of these parts.

1. Before servicing the vehicle, refer to the Precautions Section.
2. Remove the strut and spring assembly. Refer to Strut & Spring Assembly, removal & installation.

CAUTION

Keep all body parts clear of shock absorbers or strut rods. Shock absorbers or struts can extend unassisted. Failure to follow this instruction may result in serious personal injury.

3. Using a suitable coil spring compressor, compress the spring.

➡Use the hex-holding feature to prevent the strut rod from rotating while removing the nut.

4. Remove and discard the strut rod nut.
5. Remove the upper strut mount, spring upper seat and dust boot.
6. Remove the strut and jounce bumper.
7. Carefully remove the spring from the spring compressor.

WARNING

Make sure the upper strut mount is correctly seated before assembly or damage to the upper mount may occur.

8. To assemble, reverse the disassembly procedure.
9. Tighten the strut rod nut to 43 ft. lbs. (58 Nm).

WHEEL BEARINGS

REMOVAL & INSTALLATION

See Figures 158 through 163.

1. Before servicing the vehicle, refer to the Precautions Section.
2. Remove the wheel knuckle. Refer to Steering Knuckle, removal & installation.
3. Remove and discard the snap ring.

➡If removing the wheel hub, a new wheel bearing must be installed. The bearing inner race may remain on the wheel hub.

4. Using the Bushing Remover/Installer and Bearing Puller, remove the wheel hub.

WARNING

The special tools must be used to prevent damage to the hub. If the hub is damaged, a new hub must be installed.

WARNING

Do not use heat to remove the bearing inner ring or damage to the bearing may occur.

➡The following step is necessary if the inner wheel bearing race remains on the wheel hub after removing the wheel hub.

5. Using the Bushing Remover/Installer and Bearing Puller, remove the bearing inner race from the wheel hub.

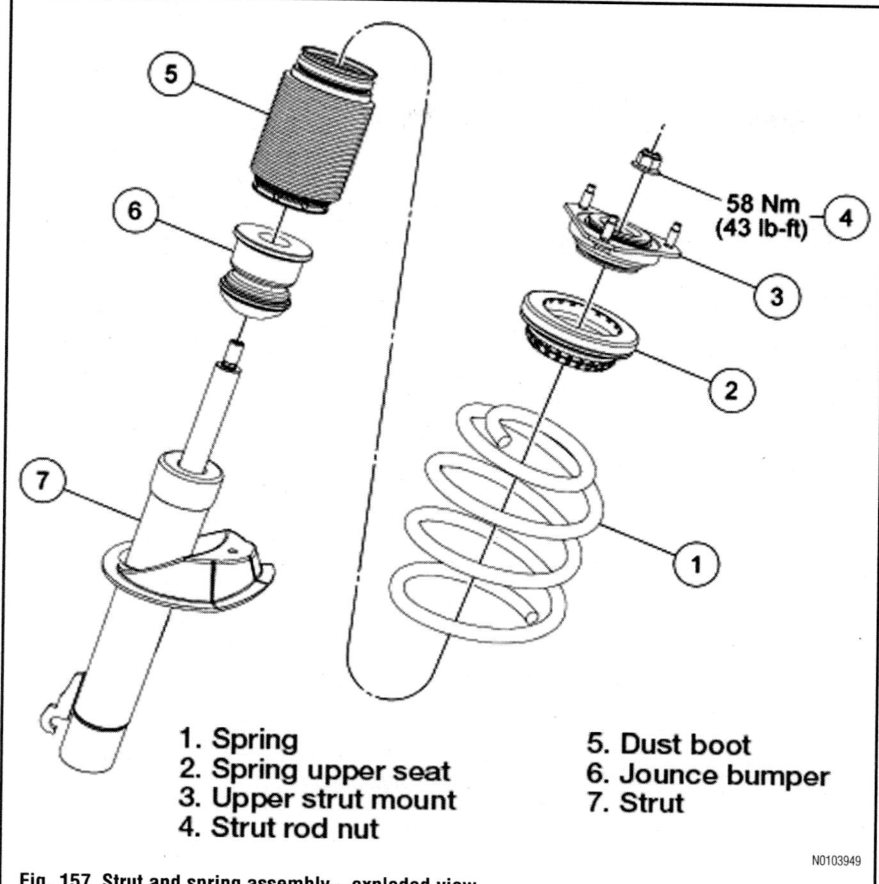

Fig. 157 Strut and spring assembly—exploded view

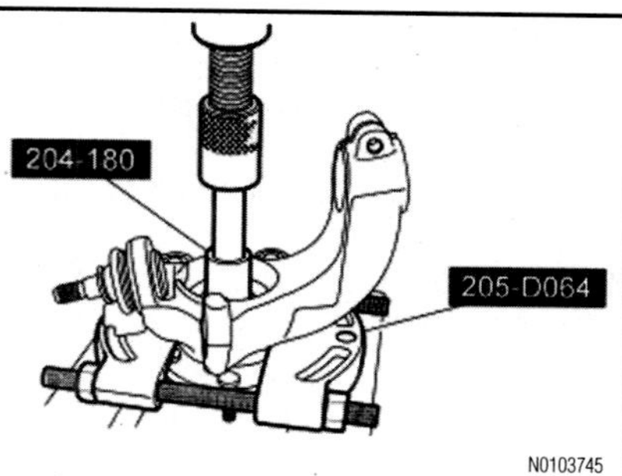

Fig. 158 Using the Bushing Remover/Installer and Bearing Puller, remove the wheel hub

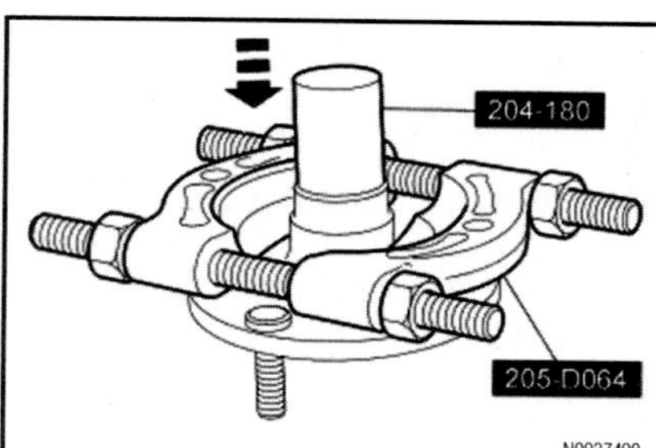

Fig. 159 Using the Bushing Remover/Installer and Bearing Puller, remove the bearing inner race from the wheel hub

6. Using the Axle Shaft Bearing Cup Installer and Wheel Speed Sensor Ring Installer, remove the bearing from the wheel knuckle.

To install:

WARNING

Once the wheel bearing is installed, make sure the wheel speed sensor ring on the bearing and the sensor hole on the wheel knuckle are clean or damage to the wheel speed sensor or sensor ring may occur.

➡Make sure the wheel bearing is installed into the wheel knuckle with the wheel speed sensor ring (black in color) toward the inner face of the wheel knuckle.

7. Using the Tri-Beam Suspension Service Set Adapter, install the new wheel bearing.

8. Using the Bearing Cup Remover/Installer and the Drive Pinion Bearing Cup Installer, install the wheel hub.

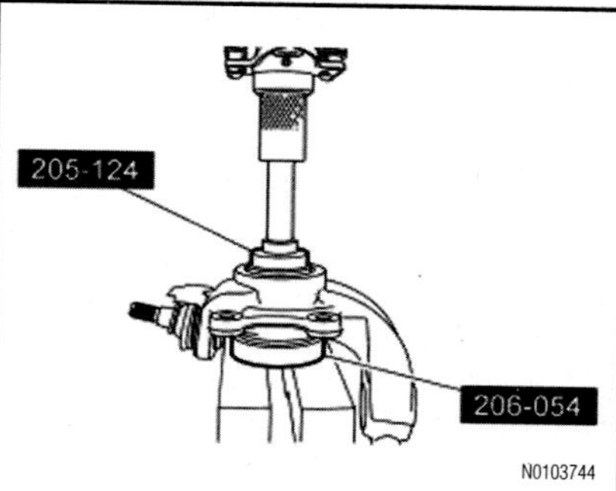

Fig. 160 Using the Axle Shaft Bearing Cup Installer and Wheel Speed Sensor Ring Installer, remove the bearing from the wheel knuckle

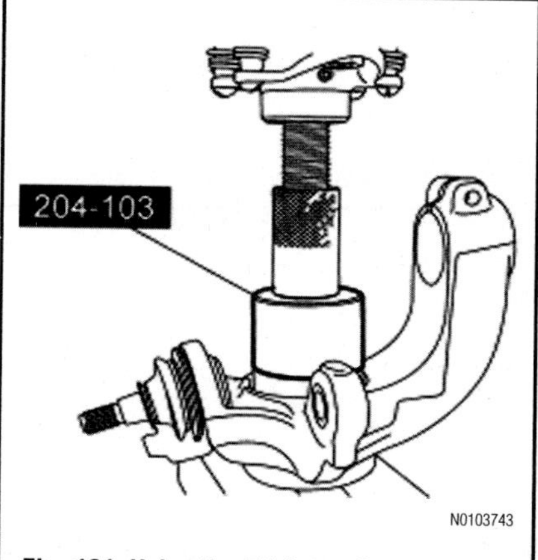

Fig. 161 Using the Tri-Beam Suspension Service Set Adapter to install the new wheel bearing

➡Make sure the wheel speed sensor hole in the wheel knuckle is not blocked by the snap ring. The sensor hole must be positioned between the ends of the snap ring.

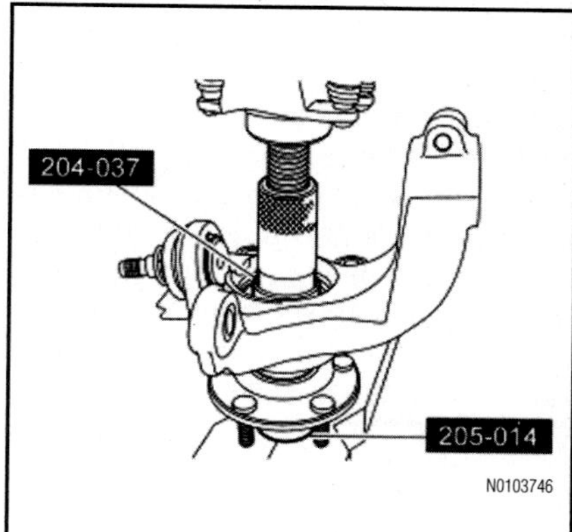

Fig. 162 Using the Bearing Cup Remover/Installer and the Drive Pinion Bearing Cup Installer, install the wheel hub

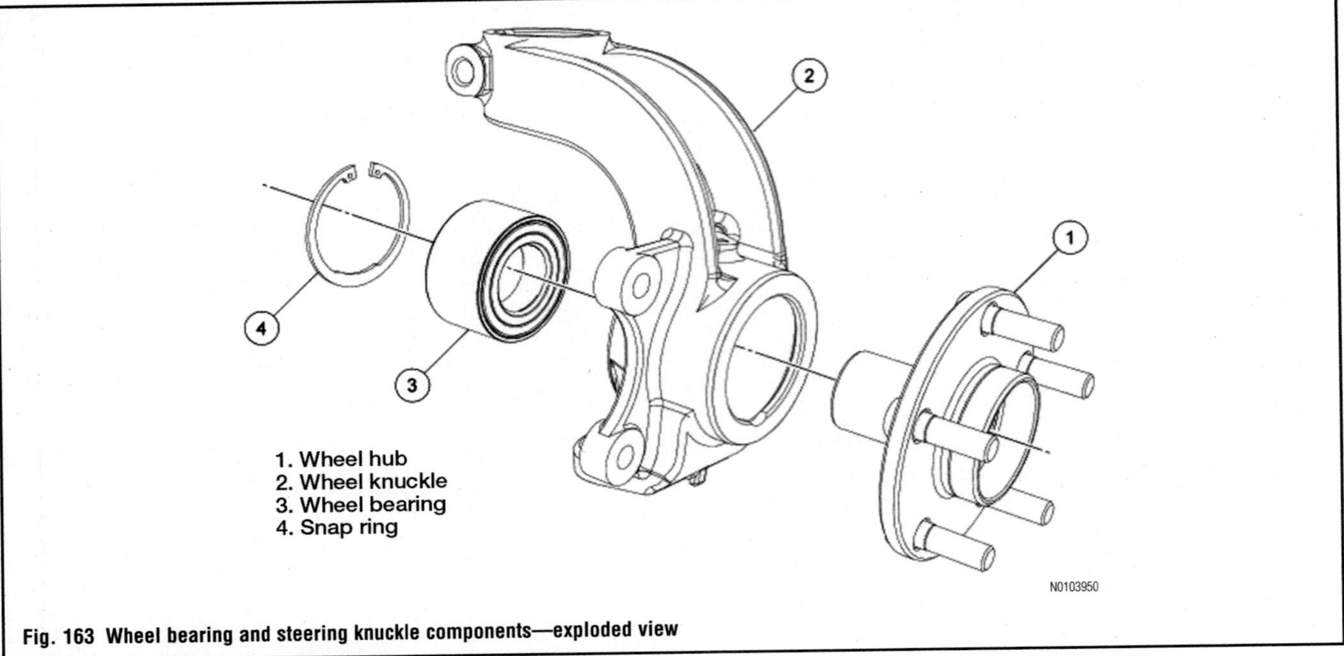

Fig. 163 Wheel bearing and steering knuckle components—exploded view

9. Install the new snap ring.
10. Install the wheel knuckle. For additional information, refer to Wheel Knuckle in this section.

ADJUSTMENT

The bearings on the front and rear wheels are a one piece cartridge design and cannot be adjusted. If wheel bearing play is excessive, check the wheel hub retainer nut for proper torque. If the torque is correct, replacement of the wheel bearing is required.

SUSPENSION

LEAF SPRING

REMOVAL & INSTALLATION

See Figure 164.

WARNING

Suspension fasteners are critical parts because they affect performance of vital components and systems and their failure may result in major service expense. New parts must be installed with the same part numbers or equivalent part, if replacement is necessary. Do not use a replacement part of lesser quality or substitute design. Torque values must be used as specified during reassembly to make sure of correct retention of these parts.

1. Before servicing the vehicle, refer to the Precautions Section.
2. Remove the wheel and tire.
3. Using a suitable jack, support the rear axle.
4. Remove and discard the shock absorber lower nut and bolt.
5. Remove the 4 U-bolt nuts, the 2 U-bolts and the U-bolt guide plate. Discard the U-bolts and nuts.
6. Remove and discard the body bracket-to-spring bolt and nut.
7. Remove and discard the shackle-to-body nut and bolt.

WARNING

To avoid damage to the brake hose, make sure the axle is only lowered enough to allow for removal of the spring.

8. Lower the jack and remove the spring.
9. Remove the shackle-to-spring nut, bolt and shackle. Discard the bolt and nut.

To install:

WARNING

Do not tighten the suspension fasteners until the installation procedure is complete and the weight of the vehicle is resting on the wheel and tire assemblies or incorrect clamp load and bushing damage may occur.

10. Inspect the inner and outer body bushings and install new bushings as necessary.
11. Position the shackle and install the new shackle-to-spring nut and bolt. Tighten the nut until snug.
12. Using a suitable jack, support the rear axle.
13. Position the spring and install the body bracket-to spring bolt and nut. Tighten the nut until snug.
14. Install the new shackle-to-body bolt and nut. Tighten the nut until snug.
15. Position the U-bolt guide plate and install the 2 new U-bolts and 4 new nuts. Tighten until snug.
16. Install the new shock absorber lower nut and bolt. Tighten until snug.
17. Lower and remove the jack.
18. Install the wheel and tire. Tighten the wheel nuts in a star pattern to 66 ft. lbs. (90 Nm).
19. Lower the vehicle until the weight of the vehicle is resting on the wheels and tires (curb height).
20. Tighten the shackle-to-body nut to 85 ft. lbs. (115 Nm).

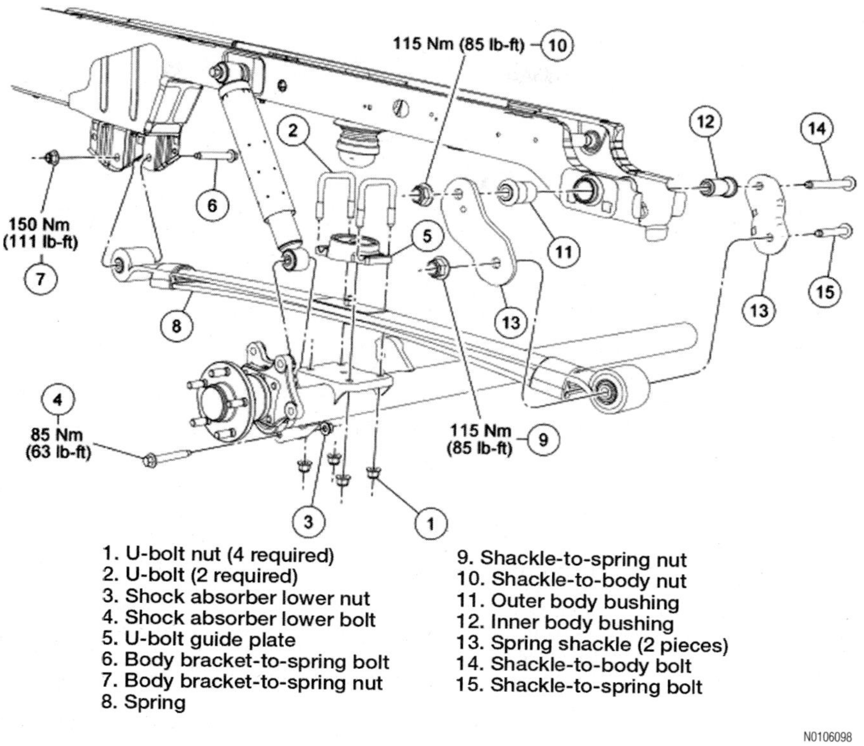

1. U-bolt nut (4 required)
2. U-bolt (2 required)
3. Shock absorber lower nut
4. Shock absorber lower bolt
5. U-bolt guide plate
6. Body bracket-to-spring bolt
7. Body bracket-to-spring nut
8. Spring
9. Shackle-to-spring nut
10. Shackle-to-body nut
11. Outer body bushing
12. Inner body bushing
13. Spring shackle (2 pieces)
14. Shackle-to-body bolt
15. Shackle-to-spring bolt

N0106098

Fig. 164 Leaf spring and related components—exploded view

21. Tighten the body bracket-to-spring nut to 111 ft. lbs. (150 Nm).

22. Tighten the shackle-to-spring nut to 85 ft. lbs. (115 Nm).

➡Tighten the U-bolt nuts evenly in a cross-type pattern.

23. Tighten the U-bolts nuts to 92 ft. lbs. (125 Nm).

24. Tighten the shock absorber lower nut to 63 ft. lbs. (85 Nm).

SHOCK ABSORBERS

REMOVAL & INSTALLATION

See Figure 165.

⁂ WARNING

Suspension fasteners are critical parts because they affect performance of vital components and systems and their failure may result in major service expense. New parts must be installed with the same part numbers or equivalent part, if replacement is necessary. Do not use a replacement part of lesser quality or substitute design. Torque values must be used as specified during reassembly

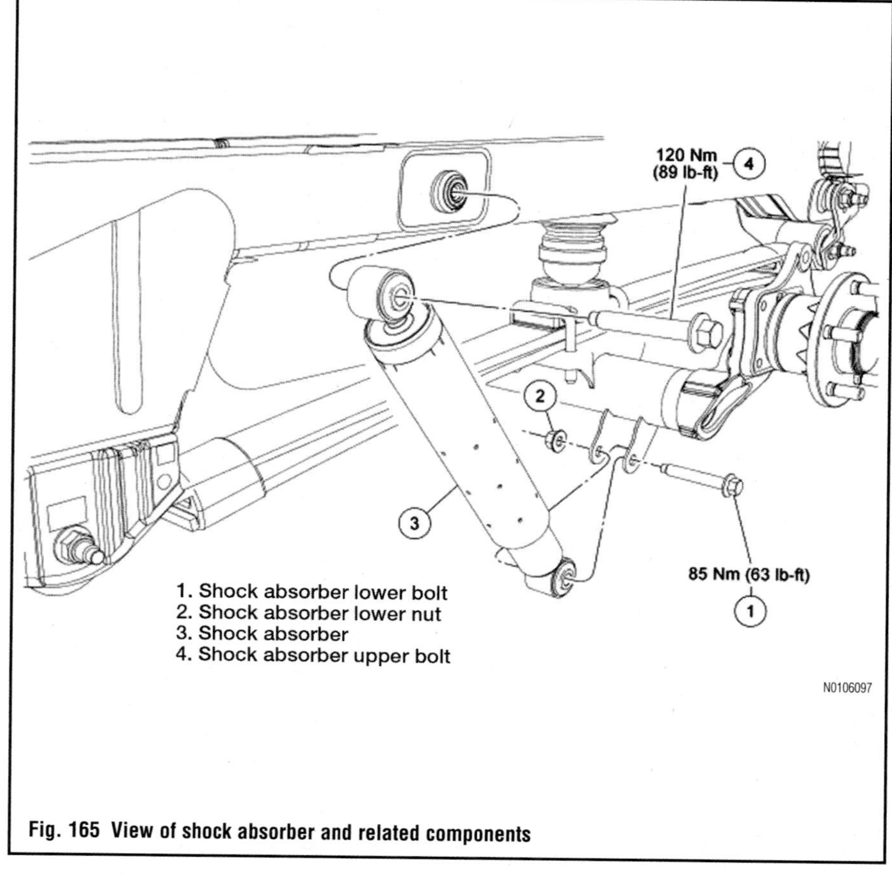

Fig. 165 View of shock absorber and related components

to make sure of correct retention of these parts.

1. Before servicing the vehicle, refer to the Precautions Section.
2. With the vehicle in NEUTRAL, position it on a hoist.
3. Remove and discard the shock absorber lower nut and bolt.
4. Remove and discard the shock absorber upper bolt.
5. Remove the shock absorber.

To install:

WARNING

Do not tighten the shock absorber fasteners until the installation procedure is complete and the weight of the vehicle is resting on the wheel and tire assemblies or incorrect clamp load and bushing damage may occur.

6. Position the shock absorber and loosely install the shock absorber upper bolt.
7. Loosely install shock absorber lower bolt and nut.
8. Lower the vehicle until the weight of the vehicle is resting on the wheels and tires.
9. Tighten the shock absorber upper bolt to 89 ft. lbs. (120 Nm).
10. Tighten the shock absorber lower bolt to 63 ft. lbs. (85 Nm).

TESTING

The easiest test of the shock absorber is to simply push down on one corner of the unladen vehicle and release it. Observe the motion of the body as it is released. In most cases, it will come up beyond its original rest position, dip back below it, and settle quickly to rest. This shows that the damper is controlling the spring action. Any tendency to excessive pitch (up-and-down) motion or failure to return to rest within 2–3 cycles, is a sign of poor function within the shock absorber.

Oil-filled shocks may have a light film of oil around the seal, resulting from normal breathing and air exchange. This should NOT be taken as a sign of failure, but any sign of thick or running oil indicates failure. Gas-filled shocks may also show some film at the shaft; if the gas has leaked out, the shock will have almost no resistance to motion.

While each shock absorber can be replaced individually, it is recommended that they be changed as a pair (both front or both rear) to maintain equal response on both sides of the vehicle. If one side has failed, its mate may also be weak.

1. Before servicing the vehicle, refer to the Precautions Section.
2. Check the rubber parts for damage or deterioration.
3. Check the spring for correct height, deformation, deterioration, or damage.
4. Check the shock absorber for abnormal resistance or unusual sounds.
5. Check for oil seepage around seals.
6. Replace as needed.

STABILIZER BAR & LINK

REMOVAL & INSTALLATION

See Figure 166.

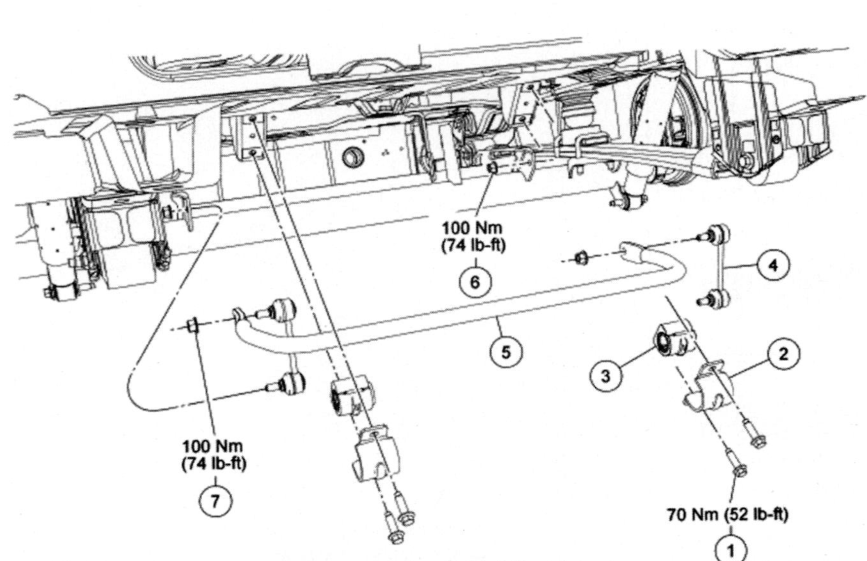

Fig. 166 Stabilizer bar and link components—exploded view

⁂ WARNING

Suspension fasteners are critical parts because they affect performance of vital components and systems and their failure may result in major service expense. New parts must be installed with the same part numbers or equivalent part, if replacement is necessary. Do not use a replacement part of lesser quality or substitute design. Torque values must be used as specified during reassembly to make sure of correct retention of these parts.

⁂ WARNING

Do not use power tools to remove or install the stabilizer bar link nuts. Damage to the stabilizer bar link ball joints and boots may occur.

⁂ WARNING

Do not hold the stabilizer bar link boot with any tool or damage to the boot may occur.

1. Before servicing the vehicle, refer to the Precautions Section.
2. With the vehicle in NEUTRAL, position it on a hoist.

➡Use the hex-holding feature to prevent the ball stud from turning while removing or installing the stabilizer bar link nut.

3. Remove and discard the 2 stabilizer bar link lower nuts.
4. Remove and discard the 4 stabilizer bar bracket bolts. Remove the stabilizer bar brackets and stabilizer bar.
5. Remove and discard the 2 stabilizer bar link upper nuts.

To install:

6. To install, reverse the removal procedure.
7. Tighten the 2 stabilizer bar link upper nuts to 74 ft. lbs. (100 Nm).
8. Tighten the 4 stabilizer bar bracket bolts to 52 ft. lbs. (70 Nm).
9. Tighten the 2 stabilizer bar link lower nuts to 74 ft. lbs. (100 Nm).

WHEEL BEARINGS

REMOVAL & INSTALLATION

See Figure 167.

1. Before servicing the vehicle, refer to the Precautions Section.
2. Remove the brake drum. For additional information, refer to Brake Drum, removal & installation.
3. Remove the dust cap.
4. Remove and discard the wheel hub nut.
5. Remove the wheel bearing and wheel hub.

To install:

6. To install, reverse the removal procedure.
7. Tighten the wheel hub nut to 251 ft. lbs. (340 Nm).

ADJUSTMENT

The bearings on the front and rear wheels are a one piece cartridge design and cannot be adjusted. If wheel bearing play is excessive, check the wheel hub retainer nut for proper torque. If the torque is correct, replacement of the wheel bearing is required.

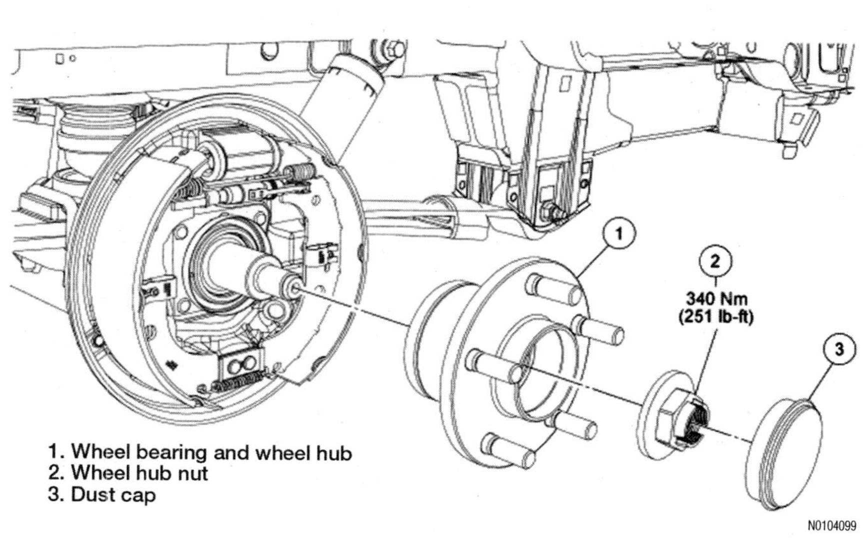

Fig. 167 Wheel bearing and wheel hub (rear)—exploded view

WHEEL SPINDLE

REMOVAL & INSTALLATION

See Figure 168.

⁂ WARNING

Suspension fasteners are critical parts because they affect performance of vital components and systems and their failure may result in major service expense. New parts must be installed with the same part numbers or equivalent part, if replacement is necessary. Do not use a replacement part of lesser quality or substitute design. Torque values must be used as specified during reassembly to make sure of correct retention of these parts.

1. Before servicing the vehicle, refer to the Precautions Section.
2. Remove the wheel bearing and wheel hub. Refer to Wheel Bearings, removal & installation.
3. Remove the wheel speed sensor bolt and position the wheel speed sensor aside.
4. Remove the 4 wheel spindle bolts and the wheel spindle. Discard the bolts.

To install:

5. To install, reverse the removal procedure.
6. Tighten the 4 new wheel spindle bolts to 89 ft. lbs. (120 Nm).
7. Tighten the wheel speed sensor bolt to 80 inch lbs. (9 Nm).

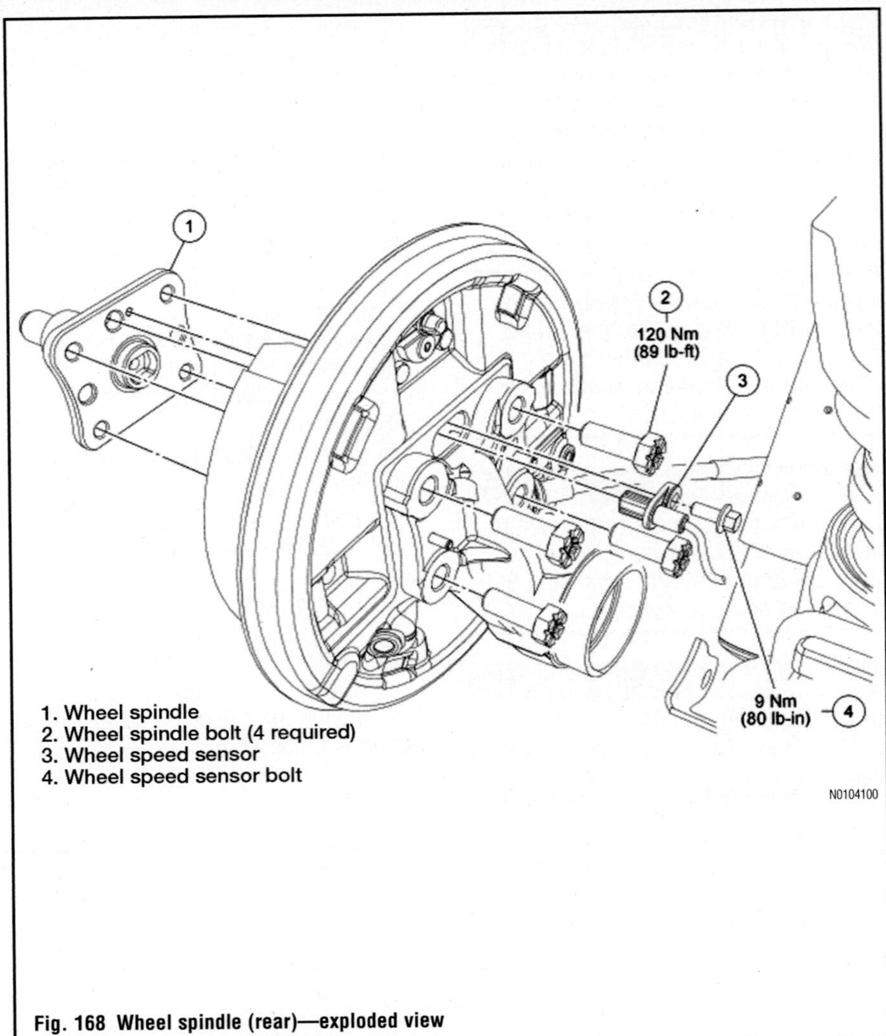

Fig. 168 Wheel spindle (rear)—exploded view

FORD, LINCOLN AND MERCURY

Diagnostic Trouble Codes

DIAGNOSTIC TROUBLE CODES DTC-1

OBD II Trouble Code List (P0xxx Codes) DTC-2
OBD II Trouble Code List (P1xxx Codes) DTC-29
OBD II Trouble Code List (P2xxx Codes) DTC-36
OBD II Trouble Code List (Uxxxx Codes) DTC-42
OBD II Vehicle Applications DTC-1
Ford DTC-1
Lincoln DTC-1
Mercury DTC-1
Introduction DTC-1

DIAGNOSTIC TROUBLE CODES

OBD II VEHICLE APPLICATIONS

FORD

Fiesta
2011
- 1.6L .... VIN J

Flex
2010–2011
- 3.5L .... VIN W
- 3.5L .... VIN T

Focus
2010–2011
- 2.0L .... VIN N

Fusion, Fusion Hybrid
2010–2011
- 2.5L .... VIN 3
- 2.5L .... VIN A
- 3.0L .... VIN G
- 3.5L .... VIN C

Mustang
2008–2010
- 3.7L .... VIN M
- 4.0L .... VIN N
- 4.6L .... VIN H
- 5.0L .... VIN F
- 5.4L .... VIN S

Ranger
2010–2011
- 2.3L .... VIN D
- 4.0L .... VIN E

Taurus
2010–2011
- 3.5L .... VIN W
- 3.5L .... VIN T

Transit Connect
2010–2011
- 2.0L .... VIN N

LINCOLN

MKS
2010–2011
- 3.5L .... VIN T
- 3.7L .... VIN R

MKT
2010–2011
- 3.5L .... VIN T
- 3.7L .... VIN R

MKZ
2010–2011
- 3.5L .... VIN C

MERCURY

Milan, Milan Hybrid
2010–2011
- 2.5L .... VIN 3
- 2.5L .... VIN A
- 3.0L .... VIN G
- 3.5L .... VIN C

INTRODUCTION

To use this information, first read and record all codes in memory along with any Freeze Frame data. *If the PCM reset function is done prior to recording any data, all codes and freeze frame data will be lost!* Look up the desired code by DTC number, Code Title and Conditions (enable criteria) that indicate why a code set, and how to drive the vehicle.

OBD II Trouble Code List (P0xxx Codes)

DTC	Trouble Code Title, Conditions, Possible Causes
DTC: P0001	**Fuel Volume Regulator Control Circuit/Open:** The powertrain control module (PCM) monitors the fuel volume regulator (FVR) and fuel volume regulator return (FVRRTN) circuits to the PCM for high and low voltage.
DTC: P0003	**Fuel Volume Regulator Control Circuit Low:** The powertrain control module (PCM) monitors the fuel volume regulator (FVR) and fuel volume regulator return (FVRRTN) circuits to the PCM for high and low voltage.
DTC: P0004	**Fuel Volume Regulator Control Circuit High:** The powertrain control module (PCM) monitors the fuel volume regulator (FVR) and fuel volume regulator return (FVRRTN) circuits to the PCM for high and low voltage.
DTC: P000A	**Intake A Camshaft Position Slow Response Bank 1:** The powertrain control module (PCM) monitors and evaluates the response of the actual position on a target position change. The setpoint and camshaft position are saved at the beginning of a setpoint change. If this change over time is large enough (gradient), the camshaft phasing change is evaluated. If the change after the diagnostic time is smaller than a threshold, a slow response is detected, and if the value is greater, then there is no concern. By detecting a concern, an antibounce counter is incremented otherwise the counter is decremented. If the counter exceeds an adjustable limit, this DTC sets.
DTC: P000B	**Exhaust B Camshaft Position Slow Response Bank 1:** The powertrain control module (PCM) monitors and evaluates the response of the actual position on a target position change. The setpoint and camshaft position are saved at the beginning of a setpoint change. If this change over time is large enough (gradient), the camshaft phasing change is evaluated. If the change after the diagnostic time is smaller than a threshold, a slow response is detected, and if the value is greater, then there is no concern. By detecting a concern, an antibounce counter is incremented, otherwise the counter is decremented. If the counter exceeds an adjustable limit, this DTC sets.
DTC: P0010	**Intake Camshaft Position Actuator Circuit/Open (Bank 1):** The powertrain control module (PCM) monitors the variable camshaft timing (VCT) circuit to the PCM for high and low voltage. The test fails if the voltage exceeds or falls below a calibrated limit for a calibrated amount of time.
DTC: P0011	**Intake Camshaft Position Timing - Over-Advanced (Bank 1):** The powertrain control module (PCM) monitors the variable camshaft timing (VCT) position for an over-advanced camshaft timing. The test fails when the camshaft timing exceeds a maximum calibrated value or remains in an advanced position.
DTC: P0012	**Intake Camshaft Position Timing - Over-Retarded (Bank 1):** The powertrain control module (PCM) monitors the variable camshaft timing (VCT) position for over-retarded camshaft timing. The test fails when the camshaft timing exceeds a maximum calibrated value or remains in a retarded position.
DTC: P0013	**Exhaust Camshaft Position Actuator Circuit/Open (Bank 1):** The powertrain control module (PCM) monitors the variable camshaft timing (VCT) circuit for high and low voltage. The test fails if the voltage exceeds a calibrated limit for a calibrated amount of time.
DTC: P0014	**Exhaust Camshaft Position Timing - Over-Advanced (Bank 1):** The powertrain control module (PCM) monitors the variable camshaft timing (VCT) position for an over-advanced camshaft timing. The test fails when the camshaft timing exceeds a maximum calibrated value or remains in an advanced position.
DTC: P0015	**Exhaust Camshaft Position Timing - Over-Retarded (Bank 1):** The powertrain control module (PCM) monitors the variable camshaft timing (VCT) position for over-retarded camshaft timing. The test fails when the camshaft timing exceeds a maximum calibrated value or remains in a retarded position.
DTC: P0016	**Crankshaft Position - Camshaft Position Correlation - Bank 1 Sensor A:** The powertrain control module (PCM) monitors the variable camshaft timing (VCT) position for a misalignment between the camshaft and crankshaft. The test fails when the misalignment is 1 tooth or greater. This DTC can also set due to VCT system concerns (oil contamination or VCT solenoid stuck).
DTC: P0017	**Crankshaft Position - Camshaft Position Correlation - Bank 1 Sensor B:** The powertrain control module (PCM) monitors the variable camshaft timing (VCT) position for a misalignment between the camshaft and crankshaft. The test fails when the misalignment is 1 tooth or greater. This DTC can also set due to VCT system concerns (oil contamination or VCT solenoid stuck).
DTC: P0018	**Crankshaft Position - Camshaft Position Correlation - Bank 2 Sensor A:** The powertrain control module (PCM) monitors the variable camshaft timing (VCT) position for a misalignment between the camshaft and crankshaft. The test fails when the misalignment is 1 tooth or greater. This DTC can also set due to VCT system concerns (oil contamination or VCT solenoid stuck).

DTC	Trouble Code Title, Conditions, Possible Causes
DTC: P0019	**Crankshaft Position - Camshaft Position Correlation - Bank 2 Sensor B:** The powertrain control module (PCM) monitors the variable camshaft timing (VCT) position for a misalignment between the camshaft and crankshaft. The test fails when the misalignment is 1 tooth or greater. This DTC can also set due to VCT system concerns (oil contamination or VCT solenoid stuck).
DTC: P0020	**Intake Camshaft Position Actuator Circuit/Open (Bank 2):** The powertrain control module (PCM) monitors the variable camshaft timing (VCT) circuit for high and low voltage. The test fails if the voltage exceeds a calibrated limit for a calibrated amount of time.
DTC: P0021	**Intake Camshaft Position Timing - Over-Advanced (Bank 2):** The powertrain control module (PCM) monitors the variable camshaft timing (VCT) position for an over-advanced camshaft timing. The test fails when the camshaft timing exceeds a maximum calibrated value or remains in an advanced position.
DTC: P0022	**Intake Camshaft Position Timing - Over-Retarded (Bank 2):** The powertrain control module (PCM) monitors the variable camshaft timing (VCT) position for over-retarded camshaft timing. The test fails when the camshaft timing exceeds a maximum calibrated value or remains in a retarded position.
DTC: P0023	**Exhaust Camshaft Position Actuator Circuit/Open (Bank 2):** The powertrain control module (PCM) monitors the variable camshaft timing (VCT) circuit for high and low voltage. The test fails if the voltage exceeds a calibrated limit for a calibrated amount of time.
DTC: P0024	**Exhaust Camshaft Position Timing - Over-Advanced (Bank 2):** The powertrain control module (PCM) monitors the variable camshaft timing (VCT) position for an over-advanced camshaft timing. The test fails when the camshaft timing exceeds a maximum calibrated value or remains in an advanced position.
DTC: P0025	**Exhaust Camshaft Position Timing - Over-Retarded (Bank 2):** The powertrain control module (PCM) monitors the variable camshaft timing (VCT) position for over-retarded camshaft timing. The test fails when the camshaft timing exceeds a maximum calibrated value or remains in a retarded position.
DTC: P0030	**HO2S Heater Control Circuit (Bank 1, Sensor 1) (For Vehicles With HO2S (4-pin)):** The powertrain control module (PCM) monitors the heater in the heated oxygen sensor (HO2S) for correct operation. The PCM controls the heater on and off duty cycle to maintain a calibrated temperature. The test fails when the sensor does not warm up to the required temperature in a calibrated amount of time. The test also fails when the PCM is not able to maintain the required temperature after the sensor is warm.
DTC: P0031	**HO2S Heater Control Circuit Low (Bank 1, Sensor 1):** The powertrain control module (PCM) monitors the heater in the heated oxygen sensor (HO2S) for correct operation. The PCM controls the heater on and off duty cycle to maintain a calibrated temperature. The test fails when the sensor does not warm up to the required temperature in a calibrated amount of time. The test also fails when the PCM is not able to maintain the required temperature after the sensor is warm.
DTC: P0032	**HO2S Heater Control Circuit High (Bank 1, Sensor 1):** The powertrain control module (PCM) monitors the heater in the heated oxygen sensor (HO2S) for correct operation. The PCM controls the heater on and off duty cycle to maintain a calibrated temperature. The test fails when the sensor does not warm up to the required temperature in a calibrated amount of time. The test also fails when the PCM is not able to maintain the required temperature after the sensor is warm.
DTC: P0034	**Turbocharger/Supercharger Bypass Valve A Control Circuit Low:** The powertrain control module (PCM) continuously monitors the TCBY circuit for concerns. This DTC sets when the PCM detects a short to ground in the circuit.
DTC: P0035	**Turbocharger/Supercharger Bypass Valve A Control Circuit High:** The powertrain control module (PCM) continuously monitors the TCBY circuit for concerns. This DTC sets when the PCM detects an open circuit or high voltage in the circuit.
DTC: P0036	**HO2S Heater Control Circuit (Bank 1, Sensor 2):** The powertrain control module (PCM) monitors the heater in the heated oxygen sensor (HO2S) for correct operation. The PCM controls the heater on and off duty cycle to maintain a calibrated temperature. The test fails when the sensor does not warm up to the required temperature in a calibrated amount of time. The test also fails when the PCM is not able to maintain the required temperature after the sensor is warm.
DTC: P0037	**HO2S Heater Control Circuit Low (Bank 1, Sensor 2):** The powertrain control module (PCM) monitors the heater in the heated oxygen sensor (HO2S) for correct operation. The PCM controls the heater on and off duty cycle to maintain a calibrated temperature. The test fails when the sensor does not warm up to the required temperature in a calibrated amount of time. The test also fails when the PCM is not able to maintain the required temperature after the sensor is warm.

DTC	Trouble Code Title, Conditions, Possible Causes
DTC: P0038	**HO2S Heater Control Circuit High (Bank 1, Sensor 2):** The powertrain control module (PCM) monitors the heater in the heated oxygen sensor (HO2S) for correct operation. The PCM controls the heater on and off duty cycle to maintain a calibrated temperature. The test fails when the sensor does not warm up to the required temperature in a calibrated amount of time. The test also fails when the PCM is not able to maintain the required temperature after the sensor is warm.
DTC: P0040	**Oxygen Sensor Signals Swapped Bank 1 Sensor 1/Bank 2 Sensor 1:** The heated oxygen sensor (HO2S) monitor determines if the HO2S signal response for a fuel shift corresponds to the correct engine bank. The test fails when there is no response from the HO2S being tested.
DTC: P0041	**Oxygen Sensor Signals Swapped Bank 1 Sensor 2/Bank 2 Sensor 2:** The heated oxygen sensor (HO2S) monitor determines if the HO2S signal response for a fuel shift corresponds to the correct engine bank. The test fails when there is no response from the HO2S being tested.
DTC: P0050	**HO2S Heater Control Circuit (Bank 2, Sensor 1) (For Vehicles With HO2S (4-pin)):** The powertrain control module (PCM) monitors the heater in the heated oxygen sensor (HO2S) for correct operation. The PCM controls the heater on and off duty cycle to maintain a calibrated temperature. The test fails when the sensor does not warm up to the required temperature in a calibrated amount of time. The test also fails when the PCM is not able to maintain the required temperature after the sensor is warm.
DTC: P0053	**HO2S Heater Resistance (Bank 1, Sensor 1):** Heater current requirements too low or high in the heated oxygen sensor (HO2S) heater control circuit.
DTC: P0054	**HO2S Heater Resistance (Bank 1, Sensor 2):** Heater current requirements too low or high in the heated oxygen sensor (HO2S) heater control circuit.
DTC: P0059	**HO2S Heater Resistance (Bank 2, Sensor 1):** Heater current requirements too low or high in the heated oxygen sensor (HO2S) heater control circuit.
DTC: P0060	**HO2S Heater Resistance (Bank 2, Sensor 2):** Heater current requirements too low or high in the heated oxygen sensor (HO2S) heater control circuit.
DTC: P0068	**Manifold Absolute Pressure (MAP)/Mass Air Flow (MAF) - Throttle Position Correlation (For Vehicles With An Idle Air Control (IAC) Valve):** The powertrain control module (PCM) monitors a vehicle operation rationality check, by comparing sensed throttle position to mass air flow readings. If during a key on engine running (KOER) self-test, the comparison of the throttle position (TP) sensor and MAF sensor readings are not consistent with the calibrated load values, the test fails and a DTC is stored in continuous memory.
DTC: P0071	**Ambient Air Temperature Sensor Circuit Range/Performance:** The powertrain control module (PCM) continuously monitors this sensor for concerns. This DTC sets when the ambient air temperature (AAT) sensor reading does not correlate with the other temperature sensor readings at ignition ON. The PCM runs this logic after an engine off and a calibrated soak period, typically 6 - 8 hours. This soak period allows the AAT sensor and the other temperature sensors to stabilize and not differ by greater than a calibrated value, typically 18°C (32.4°F).
DTC: P0072	**Ambient Air Temperature Sensor Circuit Low:** The DTC indicates the sensor signal is less than the self-test minimum.
DTC: P0073	**Ambient Air Temperature Sensor Circuit High:** The DTC indicates the sensor signal is greater than the self-test maximum.
DTC: P0074	**Ambient Air Temperature Sensor Circuit Intermittent/Erratic:** The powertrain control module (PCM) continuously monitors the AAT circuit for concerns. This DTC sets if the PCM detects a sudden change in the ambient air temperature (AAT) sensor signal that changes beyond the minimum or maximum calibrated limit.
DTC: P007B	**Charge Air Cooler Temperature Sensor Circuit Range/Performance (Bank 1):** The powertrain control module (PCM) continuously monitors this sensor for concerns. This DTC sets when the CAC_T PID does not correlate with the IAT or the IAT2 PIDs at ignition ON. It will also set if the IAT PID reading is greater than a maximum calibrated value while driving.
DTC: P007C	**Charge Air Cooler Temperature Sensor Circuit Low (Bank 1):** The powertrain control module (PCM) continuously monitors the CACT circuit for concerns. The test fails when the temperature is greater than the calibrated value for the sensor or a short to ground is detected in the circuit.
DTC: P007D	**Charge Air Cooler Temperature Sensor Circuit High (Bank 1):** The powertrain control module (PCM) continuously monitors the CACT circuit for concerns. The test fails when the temperature is lower than the calibrated value for the sensor or an open or short to voltage is detected in the circuit.
DTC: P0087	**Fuel Rail/System Pressure - Too Low:** The powertrain control module (PCM) regulates the fuel rail pressure by controlling the fuel volume regulator. When the PCM is no longer capable of maintaining the fuel pressure within the calibrated parameters, the DTC is set.

DTC	Trouble Code Title, Conditions, Possible Causes
DTC: P0088	**Fuel Rail/System Pressure - Too High:** The powertrain control module (PCM) regulates the fuel rail pressure by controlling the fuel volume regulator. When the PCM is no longer capable of maintaining the fuel pressure within the calibrated parameters, the DTC is set.
DTC: P008A	**Low Pressure Fuel System Pressure - Too Low:** The powertrain control module (PCM) monitors the fuel pressure sensor. This DTC sets when the low pressure fuel system falls below an expected threshold.
DTC: P008B	**Low Pressure Fuel System Pressure - Too High:** The powertrain control module (PCM) monitors the fuel pressure sensor. This DTC sets when the low pressure fuel system rises above an expected threshold.
DTC: P0096	**Intake Air Temperature Sensor 2 Circuit Range/Performance (Bank 1):** The powertrain control module (PCM) continuously monitors this sensor for concerns. This DTC sets when the intake air temperature 2 (IAT2) PID does not correlate with the charge air cooler temperature (CAC_T) or the intake air temperature (IAT) PIDs at ignition ON. It will also set if the IAT2 PID exceeds the maximum calibrated temperature threshold while driving.
DTC: P0097	**Intake Air Temperature Sensor 2 Circuit Low:** Indicates the sensor signal is less than the self-test minimum. The intake air temperature 2 (IAT2) sensor minimum is 0.2 volt.
DTC: P0098	**Intake Air Temperature Sensor 2 Circuit High:** Indicates the sensor signal is greater than the self-test maximum. The intake air temperature 2 (IAT2) sensor maximum is 4.6 volts.
DTC: P009A	**Intake Air Temperature /Ambient Air Temperature Correlation:** The DTC indicates that the intake air temperature (IAT) and ambient air temperature (AAT) sensor readings differ by greater than a calibrated value.
DTC: P00BA	**Low Fuel Pressure Forced Limited Power:** This DTC sets when the fuel delivery volume is less than the requested fuel delivery volume and the PCM has reduced engine power as a result.
DTC: P00BB	**Fuel Injector Insufficient Flow - Forced Limited Power:** This DTC sets when the requested fuel delivery volume is greater than the fuel injector's maximum delivery volume.
DTC: P00C1	**Turbocharger/Supercharger Bypass Valve B Control Circuit Low:** The powertrain control module (PCM) continuously monitors the TCBY2 circuit for concerns. This DTC sets when the PCM detects a short to ground in the circuit.
DTC: P00C2	**Turbocharger/Supercharger Bypass Valve B Control Circuit High:** The powertrain control module (PCM) continuously monitors the TCBY2 circuit for concerns. This DTC sets when the PCM detects an open circuit or high voltage in the circuit.
DTC: P00C6	**Fuel Rail Pressure Too Low - Engine Cranking:** The high pressure fuel system must reach a minimum pressure threshold before the engine can be started. If the high pressure fuel system cannot achieve this threshold within a certain time and crankshaft rotation limits, the powertrain control module (PCM) attempts to start the engine at fuel pump pressure and sets DTC P00C6.
DTC: P00CE	**Intake Air Temperature Measurement System - Multiple Sensor Correlation:** The powertrain control module (PCM) monitors the intake air system for concerns at ignition start. The test fails when the intake air temperature (IAT), charge air cooler temperature (CAC_T) and the intake air temperature 2 (IAT2) parameter identifications (PIDs) are each more than 16.67° C (30° F) different from each other at start up. The DTC sets when the PCM detects that each sensor is out of the calibrated range at engine start up after a soak period of at least 6 hours when a block heater is not used.
DTC: P0100	**Mass or Volume Air Flow A Circuit:** The powertrain control module (PCM) continuously monitors this sensor for concerns. The mass airflow (MAF) sensor is monitored for a low sensor frequency. This DTC sets if the sensor frequency changes below a minimum calibrated limit for greater than 0.5 seconds.
DTC: P0101	**Mass or Volume Air Flow A Circuit Range/Performance:** The powertrain control module (PCM) continuously monitors the mass airflow (MAF) sensor for concerns. This DTC sets if the PCM detects that the actual airflow is less or greater than the modeled airflow by greater than a calibrated value for 2.4 seconds.
DTC: P0102	**Mass or Volume Air Flow A Circuit Low:** The mass air flow (MAF) sensor circuit is monitored by the powertrain control module (PCM) for low air flow (or voltage) input through the comprehensive component monitor (CCM). If during key on, engine running (KOER) the air flow (or voltage) changes below a minimum calibrated limit, the test fails.

DTC	Trouble Code Title, Conditions, Possible Causes
DTC: P0102	**Mass or Volume Air Flow A Circuit Low Input:** The mass air flow (MAF) sensor circuit is monitored by the powertrain control module (PCM) for low air flow (or voltage) input through the comprehensive component monitor (CCM). If during ignition on engine running the air flow (or voltage) changes below a minimum calibrated limit, the test fails.
DTC: P0103	**Mass or Volume Air Flow A Circuit High Input:** The mass air flow (MAF) sensor circuit is monitored by the PCM for high air flow (or voltage) input through the comprehensive component monitor (CCM). If during KOEO, or KOER, the air flow (or voltage) changes above a maximum calibrated limit, the test fails.
DTC: P0104	**Mass or Volume Air Flow A Circuit Intermittent/Erratic:** A concern exists in the mass air flow (MAF) sensor A circuit, or the air tube containing the sensor, causing an incorrect air flow reading.
DTC: P0106	**Manifold Absolute Pressure (MAP/BARO) Sensor Range/Performance (For All Others):** MAP sensor input to the powertrain control module (PCM) is monitored and is not within the calibrated value.
DTC: P0106	**Manifold Absolute Pressure (MAP/BARO) Sensor Range/Performance (For Vehicles With 3.5L GTDI Engine):** The powertrain control module (PCM) continuously monitors this sensor for concerns. This DTC sets when the manifold absolute pressure (MAP) PID does not correlate with the barometric pressure (BARO) or the throttle intake pressure (TIP_PRS_BOOST) PIDs at ignition ON. It will also set if the MAP and TIP_PRS_BOOST PIDs fail to correlate when running and the TIP_PRS_BOOST PID does not correlate with the BARO PID at idle.
DTC: P0107	**Manifold Absolute Pressure (MAP)/Barometric Pressure (BARO) Sensor Low:** MAP sensor operating voltage is below the minimum calibrated parameter of 0.024 volt.
DTC: P0108	**Manifold Absolute Pressure (MAP)/Barometric Pressure (BARO) Sensor High:** Sensor operating voltage is greater than 4.96 volts. As a result, it failed above the maximum allowable calibrated parameter.
DTC: P0109	**Manifold Absolute Pressure (MAP)/Barometric Pressure (BARO) Sensor Intermittent:** The sensor signal to the powertrain control module (PCM) is failing intermittently.
DTC: P0111	**Intake Air Temperature (IAT) Sensor 1 Circuit Range/Performance (For All Others):** Indicates the IAT rationality test has failed. This DTC indicates the IAT value is higher than a calibrated value. This could prevent one or more on board diagnostic (OBD) monitors from completing. The powertrain control module (PCM) runs this logic after an engine off and a calibrated soak period (typically 6 hours). This soak period allows IAT and engine coolant temperature (ECT) or cylinder head temperature (CHT) to stabilize and not differ by more than a calibrated value. DTC P0111 sets when the IAT at engine start exceeds the ECT or CHT by more than a calibrated value, typically 17°C (30°F).
DTC: P0111	**Intake Air Temperature (IAT) Sensor 1 Circuit Range/Performance (For Vehicles With 3.5L GTDI Engine):** The powertrain control module (PCM) continuously monitors this sensor for concerns. This DTC sets when either of the following condition is present. When the intake air temperature (IAT) parameter identification (PID) does not correlate with the charge air cooler temperature (CAC_T) or the intake air temperature 2 (IAT2) PIDs at ignition on. When the IAT PID exceeds the maximum calibrated temperature threshold while driving.
DTC: P0112	**Intake Air Temperature (IAT) Sensor 1 Circuit Low:** Indicates the sensor signal is less than the self-test minimum. The IAT sensor minimum is 0.2 volt or 121°C (250°F).
DTC: P0113	**Intake Air Temperature (IAT) Sensor 1 Circuit High:** The DTC indicates the sensor signal is greater than the self-test maximum.
DTC: P0114	**Intake Air Temperature (IAT) Sensor 1 Intermittent/Erratic:** Indicates the IAT sensor signal was intermittent during the comprehensive component monitor.
DTC: P0116	**Engine Coolant Temperature (ECT) Sensor 1 Circuit Range/Performance:** Indicates the engine coolant temperature rationality test has failed. This DTC indicates the ECT or cylinder head temperature (CHT) value is higher than the calibrated value. This could prevent one or more on board diagnostic (OBD) monitors from completing. The powertrain control module (PCM) runs this logic after an engine off and a calibrated soak period (typically 6 hours). This soak period allows the intake air temperature (IAT) and the CHT or ECT to stabilize and not differ by more than a calibrated value. DTC P0116 sets when all of the following conditions are met: The ECT at engine start exceeds the IAT at engine start by more than a calibrated value, typically 17°C (30°F).The ECT exceeds a calibrated value, typically 107°C (225°F).The fuel system, heated oxygen and misfire monitors have not completed. The calibrated time to set DTC P0116 has expired.
DTC: P0117	**Engine Coolant Temperature (ECT) Sensor 1 Circuit Low:** Indicates the sensor signal is less than the self-test minimum. The ECT sensor minimum is 0.2 volt or 121°C (250°F).
DTC: P0118	**Engine Coolant Temperature (ECT) Sensor 1 Circuit High:** Indicates the sensor signal is greater than the self-test maximum. The ECT sensor maximum is 4.6 volts or -50°C (-58°F).

DTC	Trouble Code Title, Conditions, Possible Causes
DTC: P0119	**Engine Coolant Temperature (ECT) Sensor 1 Circuit Intermittent/Erratic:** Indicates the ECT circuit became intermittently open or short while the engine was running. On vehicles that are not equipped with an ECT sensor, the cylinder head temperature (CHT) sensor sets this DTC.
DTC: P011E	**Engine Coolant Temperature 1/Ambient Air Temperature Correlation:** The DTC indicates that the engine coolant temperature (ECT) and ambient air temperature (AAT) sensor readings differ by greater than a calibrated value.
DTC: P0121	**Throttle/Pedal Position Sensor A Circuit Range/Performance (For All Others):** The electronic throttle control (ETC) throttle position (TP) sensor 1 circuit was flagged as a concern by the powertrain control module (PCM) indicating an out of range in either the closed or wide open throttle (WOT) modes.
DTC: P0121	**Throttle/Pedal Position Sensor A Circuit Range/Performance (For Vehicles With An Idle Air Control (IAC) Valve):** The throttle position (TP) sensor circuit is monitored by the powertrain control module (PCM) for a non-closed throttle position at idle. The test fails if the key on engine running (KOER) self-test terminates upon placing the transmission gear selector in DRIVE or REVERSE or the TP closed throttle position is not achieved when closing the throttle (idle) after opening it (in PARK or NEUTRAL).
DTC: P0122	**Throttle/Pedal Position Sensor A Circuit Low (For Vehicles With An Idle Air Control (IAC) Valve):** The throttle position (TP) sensor circuit is monitored by the powertrain control module (PCM) for a high TP rotation angle (or voltage) input through the comprehensive component monitor (CCM). The test fails if the TP rotation angle (or voltage) changes above the maximum calibrated limit.
DTC: P0122	**Throttle/Pedal Position Sensor A Circuit Low:** The electronic throttle control (ETC) throttle position (TP) sensor 1 circuit was flagged as a concern by the powertrain control module (PCM) indicating a low voltage or open circuit.
DTC: P0123	**Throttle/Pedal Position Sensor A Circuit High (For All Others):** The electronic throttle control (ETC) throttle position (TP) sensor 1 circuit was flagged as a concern by the powertrain control module (PCM) indicating a high voltage.
DTC: P0123	**Throttle/Pedal Position Sensor A Circuit High (For Vehicles With An Idle Air Control (IAC) Valve):** The throttle position (TP) sensor circuit is monitored by the powertrain control module (PCM) for a high TP rotation angle (or voltage) input through the comprehensive component monitor (CCM). The test fails if the TP rotation angle (or voltage) changes above the maximum calibrated limit.
DTC: P0125	**Insufficient Coolant Temperature For Closed Loop Fuel Control:** Indicates the engine coolant temperature (ECT) or the cylinder head temperature (CHT) sensor has not achieved the required temperature level to enter closed loop operating conditions within a specified amount of time after starting the engine.
DTC: P0127	**Intake Air Temperature (IAT) Too High:** Indicates the intake air temperature 2 (IAT2) sensor has detected a concern in the charge air cooler (CAC) system.
DTC: P0128	**Coolant Thermostat (Coolant Temperature Below Thermostat Regulating Temperature):** Indicates the thermostat monitor has not achieved the required engine operating temperature within a specified amount of time after starting the engine.
DTC: P012B	**Turbocharger/Supercharger Inlet Pressure Sensor Circuit Range/Performance:** Manifold absolute pressure (MAP) sensor input to the powertrain control module (PCM) is monitored and is not within the calibrated value.
DTC: P012C	**Turbocharger/Supercharger Inlet Pressure Sensor Circuit Low:** Manifold absolute pressure MAP sensor operating voltage is below the minimum calibrated parameter of 0.25 volt.
DTC: P012D	**Turbocharger/Supercharger Inlet Pressure Sensor Circuit High:** Manifold absolute pressure (MAP) sensor operating voltage is above the maximum calibrated parameter of 5 volts.
DTC: P012E	**Turbocharger/Supercharger Inlet Pressure Sensor Circuit Intermittent/Erratic:** The sensor signal to the powertrain control module (PCM) is intermittent.
DTC: P0130	**O2 Circuit (Bank 1, Sensor 1):** The powertrain control module (PCM) monitors the heated oxygen sensor (HO2S) for a circuit concern. The test fails when the PCM detects a concern with one of the circuits used to determine the oxygen content in the exhaust gas.
DTC: P0131	**O2 Circuit Low Voltage (Bank 1, Sensor 1):** The powertrain control module (PCM) monitors the heated oxygen sensor (HO2S) for a circuit concern. This DTC sets when the PCM detects a concern with one of the circuits used to determine the oxygen content in the exhaust gas.

DTC	Trouble Code Title, Conditions, Possible Causes
DTC: P0132	**02 Circuit High Voltage (Bank 1, Sensor 1) (For Vehicles With HO2S (4-pin)):** The heated oxygen sensor (HO2S) signals are monitored for an over voltage condition. For Fiesta, this DTC sets if the HO2S signal voltage is 1.1 volts or greater. For all others, this DTC sets if the HO2S signal voltage is 1.5 volts or greater.
DTC: P0132	**02 Circuit High Voltage (Bank 1, Sensor 1) (For Vehicles With Universal HO2S):** The powertrain control module (PCM) monitors the heated oxygen sensor (HO2S) for a circuit concern. This DTC sets when the PCM detects a concern with one of the circuits used to determine the oxygen content in the exhaust gas.
DTC: P0133	**02 Circuit Slow Response (Bank 1, Sensor 1):** The powertrain control module (PCM) monitors oxygen sensor response time by commanding a calibrated fuel control routine. This routine sets the air fuel ratio to a calibrated limit to produce a predictable oxygen sensor signal amplitude. For vehicles with universal heated oxygen sensors (HO2S), the test fails if the oxygen sensor signal does not reach the predicted amplitude within a predetermined response time. For vehicles with heated oxygen sensors (HO2S), the test fails when the oxygen sensor amplitude is less than the predicted minimum amplitude limit.
DTC: P0134	**02 Circuit No Activity Detected (Bank 1, Sensor 1):** The powertrain control module (PCM) monitors the heated oxygen sensor (HO2S) for a lack of movement concern. If the sensor signal value is not changing from the default value, the PCM commands an oscillating air/fuel ratio attempting to detect some movement in the signal value. The test fails when the PCM is unable to detect movement in the sensor signal while the air/fuel ratio is oscillating.
DTC: P0135	**02 Heater Circuit (Bank 1, Sensor 1):** During testing the heated oxygen sensor, (HO2S) heaters are checked for open and short circuits and excessive current draw. The test fails when the current draw exceeds a calibrated limit or an open or short circuit is detected.
DTC: P0136	**02 Circuit (Bank 1, Sensor 2):** This DTC sets when the powertrain control module (PCM) detects a concern with one of the circuits used to determine the oxygen content in the exhaust gas.
DTC: P0137	**02 Sensor Circuit Low Voltage (Bank 1 Sensor 2):** The powertrain control module (PCM) monitors the heated oxygen sensor (HO2S) for a circuit concern. This DTC sets when the PCM detects a concern with the circuit used to determine the oxygen content in the exhaust gas.
DTC: P0138	**02 Circuit High Voltage (Bank 1, Sensor 2):** The heated oxygen sensor (HO2S) signals are monitored for an over voltage condition. The DTC sets when the HO2S signal voltage is 1.5 volts or greater.
DTC: P0139	**02 Circuit Slow Response (Bank 1, Sensor 2):** The heated oxygen sensor (HO2S) monitor tracks the rate of voltage change during the rise and fall of the HO2S signal. When the rate of voltage change is less than a calibrated value, the powertrain control module (PCM) begins to modify the fuel trim attempting to increase the HO2S voltage switch rate. This DTC sets when the PCM is at the allowable limit or has exceeded an allowable length of time for fuel trim modification, without detecting an acceptable rate of voltage change.
DTC: P013A	**02 Sensor Slow Response - Rich to Lean (Bank 1, Sensor 2):** During a deceleration fuel shut-off (DFSO) event, the powertrain control module (PCM) monitors how quickly the rear heated oxygen sensor (HO2S) switches from rich to lean. The measured rate of the rich to lean switch is compared to a calibrated fault threshold value. The threshold value takes into account the level of oxygen in the catalyst, which has an impact on how quickly the rich to lean switch occurs. The test fails when the measured value is slower than the threshold value.
DTC: P013B	**02 Sensor Slow Response - Lean to Rich Bank 1, Sensor 2:** During a deceleration fuel shut-off (DFSO) event, the powertrain control module (PCM) monitors how quickly the rear heated oxygen sensor (HO2S) switches from lean to rich. The measured rate of the lean to rich switch is compared to a calibrated fault threshold value. The measured rate of the lean to rich switch is compared to a calibrated fault threshold value. This DTC sets if the measured value is slower than the threshold value.
DTC: P013C	**02 Sensor Slow Response - Rich to Lean (Bank 2, Sensor 2):** During a deceleration fuel shut-off (DFSO) event, the powertrain control module (PCM) monitors how quickly the rear heated oxygen sensor (HO2S) switches from rich to lean. The measured rate of the rich to lean switch is compared to a calibrated fault threshold value. The threshold value takes into account the level of oxygen in the catalyst, which has an impact on how quickly the rich to lean switch occurs. The test fails when the measured value is slower than the threshold value.

DTC	Trouble Code Title, Conditions, Possible Causes
DTC: P013E	**Sensor Delayed Response - Rich to Lean (Bank 1, Sensor 2):** During a deceleration fuel shut-off (DFSO) event, the powertrain control module (PCM) monitors the rear heated oxygen sensor (HO2S) signal to determine if the signal is stuck in range. The PCM expects the signal to exceed a calibrated rich or lean value within a calibrated amount of time. If the signal voltage remains less than the rich value after a number of occurrences, the PCM intrusively controls the fuel system rich over increasing time periods in an attempt to force the signal to greater than the calibrated rich value. The test fails when after three consecutive intrusive attempts the signal cannot be forced greater than the calibrated rich value. In addition, if the signal voltage remains greater than the lean value after a calibrated amount of time with the fuel injectors off, a counter is incremented. The test fails when after three consecutive occurrences the signal is not less than the calibrated lean value.
DTC: P0140	**O2 Circuit No Activity Detected (Bank 1, Sensor 2):** The powertrain control module (PCM) monitors the heated oxygen sensor (HO2S) for a lack of movement concern. If the sensor signal value is not changing from the default value, the PCM commands an oscillating air/fuel ratio attempting to detect some movement in the signal value. The test fails when the PCM is unable to detect movement in the sensor signal while the air/fuel ratio is oscillating.
DTC: P0141	**O2 Heater Circuit (Bank 1, Sensor 2):** During testing the heated oxygen sensor, (HO2S) heaters are checked for open and short circuits and excessive current draw. The test fails when the current draw exceeds a calibrated limit or an open or short circuit is detected.
DTC: P0148	**Fuel Delivery Error:** At least one bank is lean at wide open throttle (WOT).
DTC: P014A	**Sensor Delayed Response - Rich to Lean (Bank 2, Sensor 2):** During a deceleration fuel shut-off (DFSO) event, the powertrain control module (PCM) monitors the rear heated oxygen sensor (HO2S) signal to determine if the signal is stuck in range. The PCM expects the signal to exceed a calibrated rich or lean value within a calibrated amount of time. If the signal voltage remains less than the rich value after a number of occurrences, the PCM intrusively controls the fuel system rich over increasing time periods in an attempt to force the signal to greater than the calibrated rich value. The test fails when, after three consecutive intrusive attempts, the signal cannot be forced greater than the calibrated rich value. In addition, if the signal voltage remains greater than the lean value after a calibrated amount of time with the fuel injectors off, a counter is incremented. The test fails when after three consecutive occurrences the signal is not less than the calibrated lean value.
DTC: P0150	**O2 Circuit (Bank 2, Sensor 1):** The powertrain control module (PCM) monitors the heated oxygen sensor (HO2S) for a circuit concern. This DTC sets when the PCM detects a concern with one of the circuits used to determine the oxygen content in the exhaust gas.
DTC: P0151	**O2 Circuit Low Voltage (Bank 2, Sensor 1):** The powertrain control module (PCM) monitors the heated oxygen sensor (HO2S) for a circuit concern. This DTC sets when the PCM detects a concern with one of the circuits used to determine the oxygen content in the exhaust gas.
DTC: P0152	**O2 Circuit High Voltage (Bank 2, Sensor 1):** The powertrain control module (PCM) monitors the heated oxygen sensor (HO2S) for a circuit concern. This DTC sets when the PCM detects a concern with one of the circuits used to determine the oxygen content in the exhaust gas.
DTC: P0153	**O2 Circuit Slow Response (Bank 2, Sensor 1):** The powertrain control module (PCM) monitors oxygen sensor response time by commanding a calibrated fuel control routine. This routine sets the air fuel ratio to a calibrated limit to produce a predictable oxygen sensor signal amplitude. For vehicles with universal heated oxygen sensors (HO2S), the test fails if the oxygen sensor signal does not reach the predicted amplitude within a predetermined response time. For vehicles with heated oxygen sensors (HO2S), the test fails when the oxygen sensor amplitude is less than the predicted minimum amplitude limit.
DTC: P0154	**O2 Circuit No Activity Detected (Bank 2, Sensor 1):** The powertrain control module (PCM) monitors the heated oxygen sensor (HO2S) for a lack of movement concern. If the sensor signal value is not changing from the default value, the PCM commands an oscillating air/fuel ratio attempting to detect some movement in the signal value. The test fails when the PCM is unable to detect movement in the sensor signal while the air/fuel ratio is oscillating.
DTC: P0155	**O2 Heater Circuit (Bank 2, Sensor 1):** During testing the heated oxygen sensor, (HO2S) heaters are checked for open and short circuits and excessive current draw. The test fails when the current draw exceeds a calibrated limit or an open or short circuit is detected.
DTC: P0157	**O2 Sensor Circuit Low Voltage (Bank 2 Sensor 2):** The powertrain control module (PCM) monitors the heated oxygen sensor (HO2S) for a circuit concern. This DTC sets when the PCM detects a concern with the circuit used to determine the oxygen content in the exhaust gas.
DTC: P0158	**O2 Circuit High Voltage (Bank 2, Sensor 2) (For Vehicles With HO2S (4-pin)):** The heated oxygen sensor (HO2S) signals are monitored for an over voltage condition. For Fiesta, this DTC sets if the HO2S signal voltage is 1.1 volts or greater. For all others, this DTC sets if the HO2S signal voltage is 1.5 volts or greater.

DTC	Trouble Code Title, Conditions, Possible Causes
DTC: P0158	**O2 Circuit High Voltage (Bank 2, Sensor 2):** The powertrain control module (PCM) monitors the heated oxygen sensor (HO2S) for a circuit concern. This DTC sets when the PCM detects a concern with one of the circuits used to determine the oxygen content in the exhaust gas.
DTC: P0159	**O2 Circuit Slow Response (Bank 2, Sensor 2):** The heated oxygen sensor (HO2S) monitor tracks the rate of voltage change during the rise and fall of the HO2S signal. When the rate of voltage change is less than a calibrated value, the powertrain control module (PCM) begins to modify the fuel trim attempting to increase the HO2S voltage switch rate. The DTC sets when the PCM is at the allowable limit or has exceeded an allowable length of time for fuel trim modification, without detecting an acceptable rate of voltage change.
DTC: P0161	**O2 Heater Circuit (Bank 2, Sensor 2):** During testing the heated oxygen sensor, (HO2S) heaters are checked for open and short circuits and excessive current draw. The test fails when the current draw exceeds a calibrated limit or an open or short circuit is detected.
DTC: P016A	**O2 Sensor Not Ready (Bank 1, Sensor 1):** The heated oxygen sensor (HO2S) monitor tracks the rate of voltage change during the rise and fall of the HO2S signal. When the rate of voltage change is less than a calibrated value, the powertrain control module (PCM) begins to modify the fuel trim attempting to increase the HO2S voltage switch rate. This DTC sets when the PCM is at the allowable limit or has exceeded an allowable length of time for fuel trim modification, without detecting an acceptable rate of voltage change.
DTC: P0171	**System Too Lean (Bank 1):** The adaptive fuel strategy continuously monitors the fuel delivery hardware. The test fails when the adaptive fuel tables reach a rich calibrated limit. Refer to Section 1, Powertrain Control Software, and Fuel Trim for additional information.
DTC: P0172	**System Too Rich (Bank 1):** The adaptive fuel strategy continuously monitors the fuel delivery hardware. The test fails when the adaptive fuel tables reach a lean calibrated limit. Refer to Section 1, Powertrain Control Software Fuel Trim for more information.
DTC: P0174	**System Too Lean (Bank 2):** The adaptive fuel strategy continuously monitors the fuel delivery hardware. The test fails when the adaptive fuel tables reach a rich calibrated limit. Refer to Section 1, Powertrain Control Software, and Fuel Trim for additional information.
DTC: P0175	**System Too Rich (Bank 2):** The adaptive fuel strategy continuously monitors the fuel delivery hardware. The test fails when the adaptive fuel tables reach a lean calibrated limit. Refer to Section 1, Powertrain Control Software, and Fuel Trim for additional information.
DTC: P0180	**Fuel Temperature Sensor A Circuit:** The comprehensive component monitor (CCM) monitors the fuel temperature sensor circuit to the powertrain control module (PCM) for low and high voltage. The test fails if the voltage falls below or exceeds a calibrated limit and amount of time during testing.
DTC: P0181	**Fuel Temperature Sensor A Circuit Range/Performance:** The comprehensive component monitor (CCM) monitors the fuel temperature sensor for acceptable operating temperature. The test fails if the voltage falls below or exceeds a calibrated limit, for a calibrated amount of time during testing.
DTC: P0182	**Fuel Temperature Sensor A Circuit Low:** The comprehensive component monitor (CCM) monitors the fuel temperature sensor circuit to the powertrain control module (PCM) for low voltage. The test fails if the voltage falls below a calibrated limit for a calibrated amount of time during testing.
DTC: P0183	**Fuel Temperature Sensor A Circuit High:** The comprehensive component monitor (CCM) monitors the fuel temperature sensor circuit to the powertrain control module (PCM) for high voltage. The test fails if the voltage exceeds a calibrated limit for a calibrated amount of time during testing.
DTC: P018C	**Fuel Pressure Sensor B Circuit Low:** The comprehensive component monitor (CCM) monitors the fuel pressure sensor circuit to the powertrain control module (PCM) for low voltage. The test fails if the voltage falls below a calibrated limit for a calibrated amount of time during testing.
DTC: P018D	**Fuel Pressure Sensor B Circuit High:** The comprehensive component monitor (CCM) monitors the fuel pressure sensor circuit to the powertrain control module (PCM) for high voltage. The test fails if the voltage exceeds a calibrated limit for a calibrated amount of time during testing.
DTC: P0190	**Fuel Rail Pressure Sensor A Circuit:** The comprehensive component monitor (CCM) monitors the fuel rail pressure (FRP) sensor to the powertrain control module (PCM) for VREF voltage. The test fails when the VREF voltage from the PCM drops to a voltage less than a minimum calibrated value.
DTC: P0191	**Fuel Rail Pressure Sensor A Circuit Range/Performance:** The comprehensive component monitor (CCM) checks the fuel rail pressure (FRP) sensor for an acceptable fuel pressure. The test fails when the difference between the fuel rail pressure requested by the PCM and the fuel rail pressure delivered exceeds 138 kPa (20 psi) for greater than 8 seconds.

DTC	Trouble Code Title, Conditions, Possible Causes
DTC: P0192	**Fuel Rail Pressure Sensor A Circuit Low:** The comprehensive component monitor (CCM) monitors the fuel rail pressure (FRP) sensor circuit to the powertrain control module (PCM) for low voltage. The test fails if the voltage falls below a calibrated limit for a calibrated amount of time during testing.
DTC: P0193	**Fuel Rail Pressure Sensor A Circuit High:** The comprehensive component monitor (CCM) monitors the fuel rail pressure (FRP) sensor circuit to the powertrain control module (PCM) for high voltage. The test fails if the voltage exceeds a calibrated limit for a calibrated amount of time during testing.
DTC: P0196	**Engine Oil Temperature (EOT) Sensor Circuit Range/Performance:** Indicates the value from the EOT sensor is not within the powertrain control module (PCM) predicted engine oil temperature range, based on other PCM inputs.
DTC: P0197	**Engine Oil Temperature (EOT) Sensor Circuit Low:** Indicates EOT signal voltage is low (high temperature).
DTC: P0198	**Engine Oil Temperature (EOT) Sensor Circuit High:** Indicates EOT signal voltage is high (low temperature).
DTC: P0201	**Injector Circuit/Open - Cylinder 1:** The comprehensive component monitor (CCM) monitors the operation of the fuel injector drivers in the powertrain control module (PCM). The test fails when the fuel injector circuitry is inoperative.
DTC: P0202	**Injector Circuit/Open - Cylinder 2:** The comprehensive component monitor (CCM) monitors the operation of the fuel injector drivers in the powertrain control module (PCM). The test fails when the fuel injector circuitry is inoperative.
DTC: P0203	**Injector Circuit/Open - Cylinder 3:** The comprehensive component monitor (CCM) monitors the operation of the fuel injector drivers in the powertrain control module (PCM). The test fails when the fuel injector circuitry is inoperative.
DTC: P0204	**Injector Circuit/Open - Cylinder 4:** The comprehensive component monitor (CCM) monitors the operation of the fuel injector drivers in the powertrain control module (PCM). The test fails when the fuel injector circuitry is inoperative.
DTC: P020x	**Injector Circuit/Open - Cylinder X (For Vehicles With Direct Fuel Injection):** **NOTE: x represents injector numbers 1 through 9.** The comprehensive component monitor (CCM) monitors the operation of the fuel injector drivers in the powertrain control module (PCM). The test fails when the fuel injector circuitry is inoperative.
DTC: P020x	**Injector Circuit/Open - Cylinder X (For All Others):** **NOTE: x represents injector numbers 1 through 9.** The comprehensive component monitor (CCM) monitors the operation of the fuel injector drivers in the powertrain control module (PCM). The test fails when the fuel injector circuitry is inoperative.
DTC: P0217	**Engine Coolant Over-Temperature Condition (For Vehicles With 3.5L GTDI Engine):** Indicates an engine overheat condition was detected by the engine temperature sensor (CHT or ECT depending how the vehicle is equipped).
DTC: P0217	**Engine Coolant Over-Temperature Condition (For All Others):** Indicates an engine overheat condition was detected by the engine temperature sensor (CHT or ECT depending how the vehicle is equipped).
DTC: P0218	**Transmission Fluid Temperature Over-Temperature Condition:** Indicates a transmission overheat condition was sensed by the transmission fluid temperature (TFT) sensor.
DTC: P0219	**Engine Over Speed Condition:** Indicates the vehicle has been operated in a manner, which caused the engine speed to exceed a calibrated limit. The engine RPM is continuously monitored and evaluated by the powertrain control module (PCM). This DTC sets when the RPM exceeds the calibrated limit set within the PCM.
DTC: P0221	**Throttle/Pedal Position Sensor/Switch B Circuit Range/Performance:** The electronic throttle control (ETC) throttle position (TP) sensor 2 circuit was flagged as a concern by the powertrain control module (PCM) indicating an out of range in either the closed or wide open throttle (WOT) modes.
DTC: P0222	**Throttle/Pedal Position Sensor/Switch B Circuit Low:** The electronic throttle control (ETC) throttle position (TP) sensor 2 circuit was flagged as a concern by the powertrain control module (PCM) indicating a low voltage, or open circuit.

DTC	Trouble Code Title, Conditions, Possible Causes
DTC: P0223	**Throttle/Pedal Position Sensor/Switch B Circuit High:** The electronic throttle control (ETC) throttle position (TP) sensor 2 circuit was flagged as a concern by the powertrain control module (PCM) indicating a high voltage.
DTC: P0230	**Fuel Pump Primary Circuit:** The powertrain control module (PCM) monitors the fuel pump (FP) circuit output from the PCM. The test fails when the FP output is commanded ON (grounded) and excessive current draw is detected on the FP circuit. The test also fails when the FP output is commanded OFF and voltage is not detected on the FP circuit. The PCM expects to detect VPWR voltage coming through the fuel pump relay coil to the FP circuit.
DTC: P0231	**Fuel Pump Secondary Circuit Low:** The powertrain control module (PCM) monitors the fuel pump monitor (FPM) circuit. The test fails if the PCM commands the fuel pump ON and B+ voltage is not detected on the FPM circuit.
DTC: P0232	**Fuel Pump Secondary Circuit High:** The powertrain control module (PCM) monitors the fuel pump monitor (FPM) circuit. This test fails when the PCM detects voltage on the FPM circuit while the fuel pump is commanded OFF. The FPM circuit is wired to a pull-up voltage inside the PCM. The FPM circuit goes high if, with the ignition ON, engine OFF and the fuel pump commanded OFF, the FPM/FP PWR circuit loses its path to ground through the fuel pump. The FPM circuit also goes high if the FPM/FP PWR circuit is short to voltage.
DTC: P0234	**Turbocharger/Supercharger A Overboost Condition:** The powertrain control module (PCM) continuously monitors the turbocharger system for an overboost condition. The PCM checks for a maximum throttle intake pressure (TIP) PID reading during engine operation, which indicates an overboost condition. This DTC sets when the PCM detects that the actual throttle intake pressure is greater than the desired throttle intake pressure by 27.6 kPa (4 psi) or more for 5 seconds.
DTC: P0236	**Turbocharger/Supercharger Boost Sensor A Circuit Range/Performance:** The powertrain control module (PCM) continuously monitors this sensor for concerns. This DTC sets when either of the following conditions is present. When the throttle intake pressure (TIP_PRS_BOOST) parameter identification (PID) does not correlate with the barometric pressure (BARO) or the manifold absolute pressure (MAP) PIDs at ignition on. When the turbocharger boost pressure (TCBP) sensor does not correlate with the BARO sensor at idle and the TCBP sensor and MAP sensor fail to correlate while driving.
DTC: P0237	**Turbocharger/Supercharger Boost Sensor A Circuit Low:** The powertrain control module (PCM) continuously monitors the TCBP circuit for concerns. This DTC sets when the PCM detects a short to ground in the circuit.
DTC: P0238	**Turbocharger/Supercharger Boost Sensor A Circuit High:** The powertrain control module (PCM) continuously monitors the TCBP circuit for concerns. This DTC sets when the PCM detects an open circuit or high voltage in the circuit.
DTC: P0245	**Turbocharger/Supercharger Wastegate Solenoid A Low:** The powertrain control module (PCM) continuously monitors the TCWRVS circuit for concerns. This DTC sets when the PCM detects a short to ground in the circuit.
DTC: P0246	**Turbocharger/Supercharger Wastegate Solenoid A High:** The powertrain control module (PCM) continuously monitors the TCWRVS circuit for concerns. This DTC sets when the PCM detects an open circuit or high voltage in the circuit.
DTC: P025A	**Fuel Pump Module Control Circuit/Open:** The powertrain control module (PCM) monitors the fuel pump command (FPC) circuit for a concern. When the PCM commands the fuel pump (FP) on, the PCM is able to detect a short to voltage on the FPC circuit. When the PCM commands the FP off, the PCM is able to detect an open circuit or a short to ground on the FPC circuit. The test fails if the voltage is less than or greater than a calibrated limit, for a calibrated amount of time.
DTC: P025B	**Fuel Pump Module A Control Circuit Range/Performance:** The fuel pump control module monitors the duty cycle and frequency of the signal it receives from the powertrain control module (PCM). The fuel pump control module determines if the signal from the PCM on the fuel pump command (FPC) circuit is a valid duty cycle and frequency. If the duty cycle or frequency is invalid, the fuel pump control module sends a 20% duty cycle signal on the fuel pump monitor (FPM) circuit to report the concern to the PCM. The test fails when the fuel pump control module is still reporting that it is receiving an invalid duty cycle or frequency from the PCM after a calibrated amount of time.
DTC: P025C	**Fuel Pump Module A Control Circuit Low:** The powertrain control module (PCM) monitors the fuel pump command (FPC) circuit for a concern. When the PCM commands the fuel pump (FP) ON, the PCM is able to detect a short to voltage on the FPC circuit. When the PCM commands the FP OFF, the PCM is able to detect an open circuit or a short to ground on the FPC circuit. The test fails if the voltage is less than or greater than a calibrated limit, for a calibrated amount of time.

DTC	Trouble Code Title, Conditions, Possible Causes
DTC: P025D	**Fuel Pump Module A Control Circuit High:** The powertrain control module (PCM) monitors the fuel pump command (FPC) circuit for a concern. When the PCM commands the fuel pump (FP) ON, the PCM is able to detect a short to voltage on the FPC circuit. When the PCM commands the FP OFF, the PCM is able to detect an open circuit or a short to ground on the FPC circuit. The test fails if the voltage is less than or greater than a calibrated limit, for a calibrated amount of time.
DTC: P025E	**Turbocharger/Supercharger Boost Sensor A Intermittent/Erratic:** The powertrain control module (PCM) continuously monitors the TCBP circuit for concerns. The test fails when the PCM detects ten intermittent events during a single drive cycle.
DTC: P0261	**Cylinder 1 Injector Circuit Low:** The powertrain control module (PCM) monitors the output of the fuel injector circuits and sets a DTC when it detects the output is not within a calibrated limit.
DTC: P0262	**Cylinder 1 Injector Circuit High:** The powertrain control module (PCM) monitors the output of the fuel injector circuits and sets a DTC when it detects the output is not within a calibrated limit.
DTC: P0264	**Cylinder 2 Injector Circuit Low:** The powertrain control module (PCM) monitors the output of the fuel injector circuits and sets a DTC when it detects the output is not within a calibrated limit.
DTC: P0265	**Cylinder 2 Injector Circuit High:** The powertrain control module (PCM) monitors the output of the fuel injector circuits and sets a DTC when it detects the output is not within a calibrated limit.
DTC: P0267	**Cylinder 3 Injector Circuit Low:** The powertrain control module (PCM) monitors the output of the fuel injector circuits and sets a DTC when it detects the output is not within a calibrated limit.
DTC: P0268	**Cylinder 3 Injector Circuit High:** The powertrain control module (PCM) monitors the output of the fuel injector circuits and sets a DTC when it detects the output is not within a calibrated limit.
DTC: P0270	**Cylinder 4 Injector Circuit Low:** The powertrain control module (PCM) monitors the output of the fuel injector circuits and sets a DTC when it detects the output is not within a calibrated limit.
DTC: P0271	**Cylinder 4 Injector Circuit High:** The powertrain control module (PCM) monitors the output of the fuel injector circuits and sets a DTC when it detects the output is not within a calibrated limit.
DTC: P027A	**Fuel Pump Module B Control Circuit/Open:** The powertrain control module (PCM) monitors the fuel pump command (FPC) circuit for a concern. When the PCM commands the fuel pump (FP) ON, the PCM is able to detect a short to voltage on the FPC circuit. When the PCM commands the FP OFF, the PCM is able to detect an open circuit or a short to ground on the FPC circuit. The test fails if the voltage is less than or greater than a calibrated limit, for a calibrated amount of time.
DTC: P027B	**Fuel Pump Module Control Circuit Range/Performance:** The fuel pump control module 2 monitors the duty cycle and frequency of the signal it receives from the powertrain control module (PCM). The fuel pump control module 2 determines if the signal from the PCM on the fuel pump command (FPC) circuit is a valid duty cycle and frequency. If the duty cycle or frequency is invalid, the fuel pump control module 2 sends a 20% duty cycle signal on the fuel pump monitor 2 (FPM2) circuit to report the concern to the PCM. The test fails when the fuel pump control module 2 is still reporting that it is receiving an invalid duty cycle or frequency from the PCM after a calibrated amount of time.
DTC: P0297	**Vehicle Over Speed Condition:** Indicates the vehicle has been operated in a manner, which caused the vehicle speed to exceed a calibration limit. The vehicle speed is continuously monitored and evaluated by the powertrain control module (PCM). This DTC is set when the vehicle speed exceeds the calibrated limit set within the PCM. For additional information on the vehicle speed limiter, refer to Section 1, Powertrain Control Software.
DTC: P0297	**Vehicle Over Speed Condition:** Indicates the vehicle has been operated in a manner, which caused the vehicle speed to exceed a calibration limit. The vehicle speed is continuously monitored and evaluated by the powertrain control module (PCM). The DTC is set when the vehicle speed exceeds the calibrated limit set within the PCM. For additional information on the vehicle speed limiter, refer to Section 1, Powertrain Control Software.

DTC	Trouble Code Title, Conditions, Possible Causes
DTC: P0298	**Engine Oil Over Temperature Condition:** Indicates the engine oil temperature protection strategy in the powertrain control module (PCM) has been activated. This temporarily prohibits high engine speed operation by disabling injectors, to reduce the risk of engine damage from high engine oil temperature. On engines equipped with an oil temperature sensor, the PCM reads oil temperature to determine if it is excessive. When an oil temperature sensor is not present, the PCM uses an oil algorithm to determine actual temperature. Engine shutdown strategy function is the same on vehicles with and without oil temperature sensors.
DTC: P0299	**Turbocharger/Supercharger A Underboost Condition:** The powertrain control module (PCM) continuously monitors the turbocharger system for an underboost condition. The PCM checks for a minimum throttle intake pressure (TIP) PID reading during engine operation, which indicates an underboost condition. This DTC sets when the PCM detects that the actual throttle intake pressure is less than the desired throttle intake pressure by 27.6 kPa (4 psi) or more for 5 seconds.
DTC: P0300	**Random Misfire Detected:** The random misfire DTC indicates multiple cylinders are misfiring or the powertrain control module (PCM) cannot identify which cylinder is misfiring.
DTC: P0301	**Cylinder 1 Misfire Detected:** The misfire detection monitor is designed to monitor engine misfire and identify the specific cylinder in which the misfire has occurred. Misfire is defined as lack of combustion in a cylinder due to absence of spark, incorrect fuel metering, incorrect compression, or any other cause.
DTC: P0301	**Cylinder 1 Misfire Detected:** The misfire detection monitor is designed to monitor engine misfire and identify the specific cylinder in which the misfire has occurred. Misfire is defined as lack of combustion in a cylinder due to absence of spark, poor fuel metering, poor compression, or any other cause.
DTC: P0302	**Cylinder Number 2 Misfire Detected:** The misfire detection monitor is designed to monitor engine misfire and identify the specific cylinder in which the misfire has occurred. Misfire is defined as lack of combustion in a cylinder due to absence of spark, poor fuel metering, poor compression, or any other cause. **NOTE: The Malfunction Indicator Lamp (MIL) blinks once per second when a misfire severe enough to cause catalyst damage is detected. If the MIL is on steady state due to a misfire, this indicates the threshold for emissions was exceeded and caused the vehicle to fail an inspection and maintenance tailpipe test.**
DTC: P0303	**Cylinder 3 Misfire Detected:** The misfire detection monitor is designed to monitor engine misfire and identify the specific cylinder in which the misfire has occurred. Misfire is defined as lack of combustion in a cylinder due to absence of spark, poor fuel metering, poor compression, or any other cause. **NOTE: The Malfunction Indicator Lamp (MIL) blinks once per second when a misfire severe enough to cause catalyst damage is detected. If the MIL is on steady state due to a misfire, this indicates the threshold for emissions was exceeded and caused the vehicle to fail an inspection and maintenance tailpipe test.**
DTC: P0304	**Cylinder Number 4 Misfire Detected:** The misfire detection monitor is designed to monitor engine misfire and identify the specific cylinder in which the misfire has occurred. Misfire is defined as lack of combustion in a cylinder due to absence of spark, poor fuel metering, poor compression, or any other cause. **NOTE: The Malfunction Indicator Lamp (MIL) blinks once per second when a misfire severe enough to cause catalyst damage is detected. If the MIL is on steady state due to a misfire, this indicates the threshold for emissions was exceeded and caused the vehicle to fail an inspection and maintenance tailpipe test.**
DTC: P0305	**Cylinder Number 5 Misfire Detected:** The misfire detection monitor is designed to monitor engine misfire and identify the specific cylinder in which the misfire has occurred. Misfire is defined as lack of combustion in a cylinder due to absence of spark, poor fuel metering, poor compression, or any other cause. **NOTE: The Malfunction Indicator Lamp (MIL) blinks once per second when a misfire severe enough to cause catalyst damage is detected. If the MIL is on steady state due to a misfire, this indicates the threshold for emissions was exceeded and caused the vehicle to fail an inspection and maintenance tailpipe test.**
DTC: P0306	**Cylinder Number 6 Misfire Detected:** The misfire detection monitor is designed to monitor engine misfire and identify the specific cylinder in which the misfire has occurred. Misfire is defined as lack of combustion in a cylinder due to absence of spark, poor fuel metering, poor compression, or any other cause. **NOTE: The Malfunction Indicator Lamp (MIL) blinks once per second when a misfire severe enough to cause catalyst damage is detected. If the MIL is on steady state due to a misfire, this indicates the threshold for emissions was exceeded and caused the vehicle to fail an inspection and maintenance tailpipe test.**

DTC	Trouble Code Title, Conditions, Possible Causes
DTC: P0307	**Cylinder Number 7 Misfire Detected:** The misfire detection monitor is designed to monitor engine misfire and identify the specific cylinder in which the misfire has occurred. Misfire is defined as lack of combustion in a cylinder due to absence of spark, poor fuel metering, poor compression, or any other cause. **NOTE: The Malfunction Indicator Lamp (MIL) blinks once per second when a misfire severe enough to cause catalyst damage is detected. If the MIL is on steady state due to a misfire, this indicates the threshold for emissions was exceeded and caused the vehicle to fail an inspection and maintenance tailpipe test.**
DTC: P0308	**Cylinder Number 8 Misfire Detected:** The misfire detection monitor is designed to monitor engine misfire and identify the specific cylinder in which the misfire has occurred. Misfire is defined as lack of combustion in a cylinder due to absence of spark, poor fuel metering, poor compression, or any other cause. **NOTE: The Malfunction Indicator Lamp (MIL) blinks once per second when a misfire severe enough to cause catalyst damage is detected. If the MIL is on steady state due to a misfire, this indicates the threshold for emissions was exceeded and caused the vehicle to fail an inspection and maintenance tailpipe test.**
DTC: P0313	**Misfire Detected with Low Fuel:** The powertrain control module (PCM) continuously monitors the ignition system for concerns. This DTC sets if the PCM detects that the actual fuel volume is less than the requested fuel volume that results in a misfire condition.
DTC: P0315	**Crankshaft Position System Variation Not Learned:** The powertrain control module (PCM) is unable to learn and correct for mechanical inaccuracies in crankshaft pulse wheel tooth spacing. This DTC disables the misfire monitor.
DTC: P0316	**Misfire Detected On Startup (First 1000 Revolutions):** DTC P0316 sets in addition to any type B misfire DTC, which occurs in the first 1,000 revolution test interval following engine start.
DTC: P0320	**Ignition/Distributor Engine Speed Input Circuit:** The ignition engine speed sensor input signal to powertrain control module (PCM) is continuously monitored. The test fails when the signal indicates two successive erratic profile ignition pickup (PIP) pulses occurred.
DTC: P0322	**Ignition/Distributor Engine Speed Input Circuit No Signal:** The ignition engine speed sensor input signal to powertrain control module (PCM) is continuously monitored after one normal camshaft signal is detected and the starter motor is engaged, or the camshaft speed exceeds the equivalent speed of engine idle. The test fails when one or more full camshaft revolutions have elapsed without profile ignition pickup (PIP) pulses.
DTC: P0325	**Knock Sensor 1 Circuit (Bank 1:** The knock sensor detects vibrations upon increase and decrease in engine RPM. The knock sensor generates a voltage based on this vibration. If the voltage goes outside a calibrated level, a DTC is set.
DTC: P0326	**Knock Sensor 1 Circuit Range/Performance (Bank 1):** The knock sensor (KS) detects vibrations upon increase and decrease in engine RPM. The knock sensor generates a voltage based on this vibration. A DTC is set if the voltage goes outside a calibrated level.
DTC: P0327	**Knock Sensor 1 Circuit Low (Bank 1):** The knock sensor (KS) detects vibrations upon increase and decrease in engine RPM. The KS generates a voltage based on this vibration. This DTC sets if the voltage goes outside a calibrated level.
DTC: P0328	**Knock Sensor 1 Circuit High (Bank 1):** The knock sensor (KS) detects vibrations upon increase and decrease in engine RPM. The KS generates a voltage based on this vibration. This DTC sets if the voltage goes outside a calibrated level.
DTC: P0330	**Knock Sensor 2 Circuit (Bank 2):** The knock sensor (KS) detects vibrations upon increase and decrease in engine RPM. The KS generates a voltage based on this vibration. This DTC sets if the voltage goes outside a calibrated level.
DTC: P0331	**Knock Sensor 2 Circuit Range/Performance (Bank 2):** The knock sensor (KS) detects vibrations upon increase and decrease in engine RPM. The knock sensor generates a voltage based on this vibration. A DTC is set if the voltage goes outside a calibrated level.
DTC: P0332	**Knock Sensor 2 Circuit Low (Bank 2):** The knock sensor (KS) detects vibrations upon increase and decrease in engine RPM. The KS generates a voltage based on this vibration. This DTC sets if the voltage goes outside a calibrated level.
DTC: P0333	**Knock Sensor 2 Circuit High (Bank 2):** The knock sensor (KS) detects vibrations upon increase and decrease in engine RPM. The KS generates a voltage based on this vibration. This DTC sets if the voltage goes outside a calibrated level.
DTC: P0335	**Crankshaft Position Sensor A Circuit:** The powertrain control module (PCM) continuously monitors this sensor for concerns. This DTC sets when the PCM detects that the crankshaft position (CKP) sensor signal is missing for greater than a calibrated number of camshaft revolutions.

DTC	Trouble Code Title, Conditions, Possible Causes
DTC: P0336	**Crankshaft Position Sensor A Circuit Range/Performance:** This DTC sets when the input signal to the powertrain control module (PCM) from the crankshaft position (CKP) sensor is erratic.
DTC: P0340	**Camshaft Position Sensor A Circuit (Bank 1 or single sensor):** This DTC sets when the powertrain control module (PCM) can no longer detect the signal from the camshaft position (CMP) sensor on bank 1 (vehicles with a single CMP sensor per bank) or bank 1, sensor 1 (vehicles with dual CMP sensors per bank).
DTC: P0341	**Camshaft Position Sensor A Circuit Range/Performance (Bank 1 or single sensor):** The powertrain control module (PCM) monitors the camshaft position (CMP) sensor for a noisy signal.
DTC: P0344	**Camshaft Position Sensor A Circuit Intermittent (Bank 1 or single sensor):** The test fails when the powertrain control module (PCM) detects an intermittent signal from the camshaft position (CMP) sensor.
DTC: P0345	**Camshaft Position Sensor A Circuit (Bank 2):** This DTC sets when the powertrain control module (PCM) can no longer detect the signal from the camshaft position (CMP) sensor on bank 2 (vehicles with a single CMP sensor per bank) or bank 2, sensor 1 (vehicles with dual CMP sensors per bank).
DTC: P0345	**Camshaft Position Sensor A Circuit (Bank 2):** The test fails when the powertrain control module (PCM) can no longer detect the signal from the camshaft position (CMP) sensor on bank 2.
DTC: P0346	**Camshaft Position Sensor A Circuit Range/Performance (Bank 2):** The powertrain control module (PCM) monitors the camshaft position (CMP) sensor for a noisy signal.
DTC: P0349	**Camshaft Position Sensor A Circuit Intermittent (Bank 2):** The test fails when the powertrain control module (PCM) detects an intermittent signal from the camshaft position (CMP) sensor.
DTC: P0351	**Ignition Coil A Primary/Secondary Circuit:** Each ignition primary circuit is continuously monitored. The test fails when the powertrain control module (PCM) does not receive a valid ignition diagnostic monitor (IDM) pulse signal from the ignition module (integrated in the PCM).
DTC: P0352	**Ignition Coil B Primary/Secondary Circuit:** Each ignition primary circuit is continuously monitored. The test fails when the powertrain control module (PCM) does not receive a valid ignition diagnostic monitor (IDM) pulse signal from the ignition module (integrated in the PCM).
DTC: P0353	**Ignition Coil C Primary/Secondary Circuit:** Each ignition primary circuit is continuously monitored. The test fails when the powertrain control module (PCM) does not receive a valid ignition diagnostic monitor (IDM) pulse signal from the ignition module (integrated in the PCM).
DTC: P0354	**Ignition Coil D Primary/Secondary Circuit:** Each ignition primary circuit is continuously monitored. The test fails when the powertrain control module (PCM) does not receive a valid ignition diagnostic monitor (IDM) pulse signal from the ignition module (integrated in the PCM).
DTC: P0355	**Ignition Coil E Primary/Secondary Circuit:** Each ignition primary circuit is continuously monitored. The test fails when the powertrain control module (PCM) does not receive a valid ignition diagnostic monitor (IDM) pulse signal from the ignition module (integrated in the PCM).
DTC: P0356	**Ignition Coil F Primary/Secondary Circuit:** Each ignition primary circuit is continuously monitored. The test fails when the powertrain control module (PCM) does not receive a valid ignition diagnostic monitor (IDM) pulse signal from the ignition module (integrated in the PCM).
DTC: P0357	**Ignition Coil G Primary/Secondary Circuit:** Each ignition primary circuit is continuously monitored. The test fails when the powertrain control module (PCM) does not receive a valid ignition diagnostic monitor (IDM) pulse signal from the ignition module (integrated in the PCM).
DTC: P0358	**Ignition Coil H Primary/Secondary Circuit:** Each ignition primary circuit is continuously monitored. The test fails when the powertrain control module (PCM) does not receive a valid ignition diagnostic monitor (IDM) pulse signal from the ignition module (integrated in the PCM).
DTC: P0359	**Ignition Coil I Primary/Secondary Circuit:** Each ignition primary circuit is continuously monitored. The test fails when the powertrain control module (PCM) does not receive a valid ignition diagnostic monitor (IDM) pulse signal from the ignition module (integrated in the PCM).
DTC: P0360	**Ignition Coil J Primary/Secondary Circuit:** Each ignition primary circuit is continuously monitored. The test fails when the powertrain control module (PCM) does not receive a valid ignition diagnostic monitor (IDM) pulse signal from the ignition module (integrated in the PCM).
DTC: P0365	**Camshaft Position Sensor B Circuit (Bank 1 or Single Sensor):** The test fails when the powertrain control module (PCM) can no longer detect the signal from the camshaft position (CMP) sensor on bank 1.

DTC	Trouble Code Title, Conditions, Possible Causes
DTC: P0366	**Camshaft Position Sensor B Circuit Range/Performance (Bank 1 or Single Sensor):** The powertrain control module (PCM) monitors the camshaft position (CMP) sensor for a noisy signal.
DTC: P0369	**Camshaft Position Sensor B Circuit Intermittent (Bank 1):** The test fails when the powertrain control module (PCM) detects an intermittent signal from the camshaft position (CMP) sensor.
DTC: P0390	**Camshaft Position Sensor B Circuit (Bank 2):** This DTC sets when the powertrain control module (PCM) can no longer detect the signal from the camshaft position (CMP) sensor (bank 2, sensor 2).
DTC: P0391	**Camshaft Position Sensor B Circuit Range/Performance (Bank 2):** The powertrain control module (PCM) monitors the camshaft position (CMP) sensor for a noisy signal.
DTC: P0394	**Camshaft Position Sensor B Circuit Intermittent (Bank 2):** The test fails when the powertrain control module (PCM) detects an intermittent signal from the camshaft position (CMP) sensor.
DTC: P0400	**Exhaust Gas Recirculation (EGR) Flow:** The electric EGR (EEGR) system is monitored once per drive cycle at high and low load conditions. The test fails when a concern is detected by powertrain control module (PCM) calculations indicating the EGR flow is less or greater than expected.
DTC: P0401	**Exhaust Gas Recirculation (EGR) Flow Insufficient Detected:** The EGR system is monitored during steady state driving conditions while the EGR is commanded on. The test fails when the signal from the differential pressure feedback EGR sensor indicates that EGR flow is less than the desired minimum.
DTC: P0402	**Exhaust Gas Recirculation (EGR) Flow Excessive Detected:** The EGR system is monitored for undesired EGR flow during idle. The EGR monitor looks at the differential pressure feedback EGR (DPFE) signal at idle and compares it to the stored signal measured during ignition on engine off. The test does not pass when the signal at idle is greater than at ignition on engine off by a calibrated amount.
DTC: P0403	**Exhaust Gas Recirculation (EGR) Control Circuit:** The electric EGR (EEGR) system is continuously monitored to check the four EEGR motor coils, circuits, and the powertrain control module (PCM) for opens, shorts to voltage and ground. If a concern is detected, the EEGR system is disabled and additional monitoring is suspended for the remainder of the drive until the next drive cycle.
DTC: P0403	**Exhaust Gas Recirculation (EGR) Control Circuit (For All Others):** This test checks the electrical function of the EGR vacuum regulator solenoid. The test fails when the EVR circuit voltage is either too high or too low when compared to the expected voltage range. The EGR system must be enabled for the test to be completed.
DTC: P0405	**Exhaust Gas Recirculation (EGR) Sensor A Circuit Low:** The EGR monitor checks the differential pressure feedback EGR sensor signal to the powertrain control module (PCM) for low voltage. The test fails when the average voltage to the PCM drops to a voltage less than the minimum calibrated value.
DTC: P0406	**Exhaust Gas Recirculation (EGR) Sensor A Circuit High:** The EGR monitor checks the EGR sensor signal to the powertrain control module (PCM) for high voltage. The test fails when the average voltage to the PCM exceeds the maximum calibrated value.
DTC: P0420	**Catalyst System Efficiency Below Threshold (Bank 1):** Indicates the catalyst system efficiency is below the acceptable threshold.
DTC: P0430	**Catalyst System Efficiency Below Threshold (Bank 2):** Indicates the bank 2 catalyst system efficiency is below the acceptable threshold.
DTC: P0442	**Evaporative Emission System Leak Detected (Small Leak):** The powertrain control module (PCM) monitors the complete evaporative emission (EVAP) control system for the presence of a small fuel vapor leak. System failure occurs when a fuel vapor leak from an opening as small as 1.016 mm (0.040 in) is detected by the EVAP running loss monitor test.
DTC: P0443	**Evaporative Emission System Purge Control Valve Circuit:** The powertrain control module (PCM) monitors the state of the evaporative emission (EVAP) canister purge valve circuit output driver. The test fails when the signal moves outside the minimum or maximum limit for the commanded state.
DTC: P0444	**Evaporative Emission System Purge Control Valve A Circuit Open:** The powertrain control module (PCM) monitors the state of the evaporative emission (EVAP) canister purge valve circuit output driver. The test fails when the signal moves outside the minimum or maximum limit for the commanded state.
DTC: P0446	**Evaporative Emission System Vent Control Circuit:** Monitors the EVAP canister vent solenoid circuit for an electrical failure. The test fails when the signal moves outside the minimum or maximum allowable calibrated parameters for a specified EVAP canister vent duty cycle by powertrain control module (PCM) command.

DTC	Trouble Code Title, Conditions, Possible Causes
DTC: P0450	**Evaporative Emission System Pressure Sensor/Switch:** The powertrain control module (PCM) monitors the evaporative emission (EVAP) system natural vacuum leak detection (NVLD) module vacuum switch input signal to the PCM. The test fails when the signal input is not responding as expected.
DTC: P0451	**Evaporative Emission System Pressure Sensor/Switch Range/Performance:** This DTC sets for a fuel tank pressure (FTP) sensor range (offset) concern. The FTP sensor output is offset by greater than 1.7 inches of water or less than -1.7 inches of water.
DTC: P0451	**Evaporative Emission System Pressure Sensor/Switch Range/Performance (For Vehicles With NVLD Module):** This DTC sets if the natural vacuum leak detection (NVLD) module pressure switch does not respond to pressure changes in the EVAP system.
DTC: P0452	**Evaporative Emission System Pressure Sensor/Switch Low (For All Others):** The powertrain control module (PCM) monitors the evaporative emission (EVAP) control system fuel tank pressure (FTP) sensor input signal to the PCM. The test fails when the signal average drops below a minimum allowable calibrated parameter.
DTC: P0452	**Evaporative Emission System Pressure Sensor/Switch Low (For Vehicles With NVLD Module):** The natural vacuum leak detection (NVLD) module monitors the position of the NVLD module pressure switch. This DTC sets if the NVLD module pressure switch voltage is out of range low.
DTC: P0453	**Evaporative Emission System Pressure Sensor/Switch High (For All Others):** The powertrain control module (PCM) monitors the evaporative emission (EVAP) control system fuel tank pressure (FTP) sensor input signal to the PCM. The test fails when the signal average jumps above a minimum allowable calibrated parameter.
DTC: P0453	**Evaporative Emission System Pressure Sensor/Switch High (For Vehicles With NVLD Module):** The natural vacuum leak detection (NVLD) module monitors the position of the NVLD module pressure switch. This DTC sets if the NVLD module pressure switch voltage is out of range high.
DTC: P0454	**Evaporative Emission System Pressure Sensor/Switch Intermittent:** The fuel tank pressure changes greater than 14 inches of water in 0.10 seconds.
DTC: P0455	**Evaporative Emission System Leak Detected (Gross Leak/No Flow):** The powertrain control module (PCM) monitors the complete evaporative emission (EVAP) control system for no purge flow, the presence of a large fuel vapor leak, or multiple small fuel vapor leaks. System failure occurs when no purge flow, which is attributed to fuel vapor blockages or restrictions, a large fuel vapor leak, or multiple fuel vapor leaks are detected by the EVAP running loss monitor test with the engine running, but not at idle.
DTC: P0456	**Evaporative Emission System Leak Detected (Very Small Leak):** The powertrain control module (PCM) monitors the complete evaporative emission (EVAP) control system for the presence of a very small fuel vapor leak. The system failure occurs when a fuel vapor leak from an opening as small as 0.508 mm (0.020 inch) is detected by the EVAP running loss monitor test.
DTC: P0457	**Evaporative Emission System Leak Detected (Fuel Cap Loose/Off):** The powertrain control module (PCM) continuously monitors the fuel level and retains the last updated value prior to the ignition switch being placed in the OFF position. After the ignition switch is placed in the ON position, a new fuel level is taken and compared to the level recorded at ignition OFF. If the fuel level has increased, a flag is set in the PCM indicating the vehicle was refueled. This DTC sets if the evaporative emission (EVAP) monitor detects a gross leak while the refueling flag is set and a loose fuel filler cap or an incorrectly sealed fuel tank filler pipe (if equipped) is suspected. On most vehicles when the DTC sets, either the check fuel cap indicator illuminates or a message on the instrument panel cluster (IPC) displays to instruct the driver to check the fuel cap or capless fuel tank filler pipe (if equipped).
DTC: P0458	**Evaporative Emission System Purge Control Valve Circuit Low:** The powertrain control module (PCM) monitors the state of the evaporative emission (EVAP) canister purge valve circuit output driver. The test fails when the signal moves outside the minimum or maximum limit for the commanded state.
DTC: P0459	**Evaporative Emission System Purge Control Valve Circuit High:** The powertrain control module (PCM) monitors the state of the evaporative emission (EVAP) canister purge valve circuit output driver. The test fails when the signal moves outside the minimum or maximum limit for the commanded state.
DTC: P0460	**Fuel Level Sensor A Circuit:** The powertrain control module (PCM) monitors the fuel level input (FLI) communications network message for a concern. The PCM calculates the amount of fuel used during operation. The test fails when the PCM determines the value of the FLI signal is stuck. This DTC sets if the FLI signal does not change or does not correspond with the calculated fuel usage.
DTC: P0461	**Fuel Level Sensor A Circuit Range/Performance:** The powertrain control module (PCM) monitors the fuel level input (FLI) communications network message for a concern. The test fails when the FLI signal repeatedly moves in and out of range, exceeding the minimum or maximum allowable calibrated parameters for a specified fuel fill percentage in the fuel tank.

DTC	Trouble Code Title, Conditions, Possible Causes
DTC: P0462	**Fuel Level Sensor A Circuit Low:** The powertrain control module (PCM) monitors the fuel level input (FLI) communications network message for a concern. The test fails when the FLI signal is less than the minimum allowable calibrated parameter for a specified fuel fill percentage in the fuel tank.
DTC: P0463	**Fuel Level Sensor A Circuit High:** The powertrain control module (PCM) monitors the fuel level input (FLI) communications network message for a concern. The test fails when the FLI signal is greater than the maximum allowable calibrated parameter for a specified fuel fill percentage in the fuel tank.
DTC: P0480	**Fan 1 Control Circuit (For Variable Speed Electric Cooling Fan):** This test checks the fan control variable (FCV) output circuit. This DTC sets if the powertrain control module (PCM) detects the voltage on the FCV circuit is not within the expected range.
DTC: P0480	**Fan 1 Control Circuit (For Cooling Fan Clutch):** This test checks the fan control variable (FCV) output circuit for the cooling fan clutch. This DTC sets if the powertrain control module (PCM) detects the voltage on the FCV circuit is not within the expected range.
DTC: P0480	**Fan 1 Control Circuit (For Relay Controlled Electric Cooling Fan):** Monitors the low fan control (LFC) primary circuit output from the powertrain control module (PCM). The test fails when the PCM grounds the LFC circuit and excessive current draw is detected on the LFC circuit; or with the LFC circuit not grounded by the PCM the voltage is not detected on the LFC circuit, (the PCM expects to detect VPWR voltage coming through the low speed fan control relay coil to the LFC circuit).
DTC: P0481	**Fan 2 Control Circuit:** Monitors the high fan control (HFC) primary circuit output from the powertrain control module (PCM). The test fails when the HFC output is commanded on (grounded) and excessive current draw is detected on the HFC circuit; or when the HFC circuit is commanded off and voltage is not detected on the HFC circuit (the PCM expects to detect VPWR voltage through the high speed FC relay coil to the HFC circuit).
DTC: P0496	**Evaporative Emission System High Purge Flow:** The powertrain control module (PCM) monitors the complete evaporative emission (EVAP) control system for high purge flow.
DTC: P0497	**Evaporative Emission System Low Purge Flow:** The powertrain control module (PCM) monitors the complete evaporative emission (EVAP) control system for low purge flow.
DTC: P0500	**Vehicle Speed Sensor (VSS) A:** Indicates the powertrain control module (PCM) detected an error in the vehicle speed information. Vehicle speed data is received from either the VSS, the transfer case speed sensor (TCSS) or the anti-lock brake system (ABS) control module. If the engine RPM is above the torque converter stall speed (automatic transmission) and the engine load is high, it can be inferred that the vehicle must be moving. If there is insufficient vehicle speed data input, a concern is indicated and this DTC sets. On most vehicle applications, the malfunction indicator lamp (MIL) illuminates when this DTC sets.
DTC: P0501	**Vehicle Speed Sensor A Range/Performance:** Engine started; then with the engine speed more than the TCC stall speed, the PCM detected a problem with the vehicle speed data.
DTC: P0503	**Vehicle Speed Sensor (VSS) A Intermittent/Erratic/High:** Indicates incorrect or noisy VSS performance. Vehicle speed data is received from either the VSS, the transfer case speed sensor (TCSS), or the anti-lock brake system (ABS) control module.
DTC: P0504	**Brake Switch Correlation:** The PCM does a comparison test between the brake pedal switch (BPS) and the brake pedal position (BPP) switch.
DTC: P0505	**Idle Air Control (IAC) System:** The powertrain control module (PCM) attempts to control engine speed during the key on, engine running (KOER) self-test. The test fails when the desired RPM could not be reached or controlled during the self-test.
DTC: P0506	**Idle Air Control System RPM Lower Than Expected:** This DTC sets when the powertrain control module (PCM) detects actual engine speed that is lower than the desired RPM.
DTC: P0507	**Idle Air Control System RPM Higher Than Expected:** This DTC sets when the powertrain control module (PCM) detects actual engine speed that is greater than the desired RPM.
DTC: P050A	**Cold Start Idle Air Control Performance (For Vehicles With An Idle Air Control (IAC) Valve):** The cold start emission reduction monitor has detected an airflow performance deficiency. The cold start emission reduction monitor validates the operation of the components of the system required to achieve the cold start emission reduction strategy, retarded spark timing (P050B) and elevated idle airflow (P050A). When the idle airflow test portion of the cold start emission reduction strategy is enabled, the idle air control system requests a higher idle RPM to increase the engine airflow. The cold start emission reduction monitor compares the actual airflow measured by the mass airflow (MAF) sensor to the requested powertrain control module (PCM) airflow. This DTC sets when the airflow is less than the calibrated limit.

DTC	Trouble Code Title, Conditions, Possible Causes
DTC: P050A	**Cold Start Idle Air Control Performance:** The monitor compares the actual measured engine speed to the engine speed requested by the powertrain control module (PCM). This DTC sets when the difference between desired and actual engine speed exceeds the calibrated threshold.
DTC: P050B	**Cold Start Ignition Timing Performance:** The monitor compares commanded spark timing to the spark timing desired by the powertrain control module (PCM). This DTC sets when the difference between desired and commanded spark timing exceeds the calibrated threshold.
DTC: P050E	**Cold Start Engine Exhaust Temperature Out of Range:** The powertrain control module (PCM) calculates the actual catalyst warm up temperature during a cold start. The PCM then compares the actual catalyst temperature to the expected catalyst temperature model. The difference between the actual and expected temperatures is a ratio. This DTC sets when this ratio exceeds the calibrated value and the malfunction indicator lamp (MIL) illuminates.
DTC: P050E	**Cold Start Engine Exhaust Temperature Out of Range (For Vehicles With An Idle Air Control (IAC) Valve):** The powertrain control module (PCM) attempts to control engine speed during the key on, engine running (KOER) self-test. The test fails when the desired RPM could not be reached or controlled during the self-test.
DTC: P0511	**Idle Air Control (IAC) Circuit:** This DTC sets when the powertrain control module (PCM) detects an electrical load failure on the IAC output circuit.
DTC: P0512	**Starter Request Circuit:** Indicates the one touch integrated starting system voltage circuit to the starter relay has a short to voltage.
DTC: P0528	**Fan Speed Sensor Circuit No Signal:** The powertrain control module (PCM) uses the fan speed sensor (FSS) input to monitor the cooling fan clutch speed. If the indicated fan speed is lower than the calibrated value during the key on engine running (KOER) self-test, the DTC is set.
DTC: P052A	**Cold Start Camshaft Position Timing Over-Advanced (Bank 1):** The powertrain control module (PCM) monitors the variable camshaft timing (VCT) position for an over-advanced camshaft timing during cold start up. The test fails when the camshaft timing exceeds a maximum calibrated value or remains in an advanced position.
DTC: P052B	**Cold Start Camshaft Position Timing Over-Retarded (Bank 1):** The powertrain control module (PCM) monitors the variable camshaft timing (VCT) position for over-retarded camshaft timing during cold start up. The test fails when the camshaft timing exceeds a maximum calibrated value or remains in a retarded position.
DTC: P052C	**Cold Start Camshaft Position Timing Over-Advanced (Bank 2):** The powertrain control module (PCM) monitors the variable camshaft timing (VCT) position for an over-advanced camshaft timing during cold start up. The test fails when the camshaft timing exceeds a maximum calibrated value or remains in an advanced position.
DTC: P052D	**Cold Start Camshaft Position Timing Over-Retarded (Bank 2):** The powertrain control module (PCM) monitors the variable camshaft timing (VCT) position for over-retarded camshaft timing during cold start up. The test fails when the camshaft timing exceeds a maximum calibrated value or remains in a retarded position.
DTC: P053A	**Positive Crankcase Ventilation (PCV) Heater Control Circuit / Open:** This DTC sets when the powertrain control module (PCM) detects that the actual PCVHC circuit voltage is less than the desired voltage.
DTC: P053F	**Cold Start Fuel Pressure Performance:** The PCM monitors fuel rail pressure to control split injection. This DTC sets if the fuel rail pressure falls outside a calibrated threshold limit for controlling split injection during a cold start.
DTC: P054A	**Cold Start Exhaust (B) Camshaft Position Timing Over-Advanced (Bank 1):** The powertrain control module (PCM) monitors the variable camshaft timing (VCT) position for an over-advanced camshaft timing during cold start up. The test fails when the camshaft timing exceeds a maximum calibrated value or remains in an advanced position.
DTC: P054B	**Cold Start Exhaust (B) Camshaft Position Timing Over-Retarded (Bank 1):** The powertrain control module (PCM) monitors the variable camshaft timing (VCT) position for over-retarded camshaft timing during cold start up. The test fails when the camshaft timing exceeds a maximum calibrated value or remains in a retarded position.
DTC: P054C	**Cold Start Exhaust (B) Camshaft Position Timing Over-Advanced (Bank 2):** The powertrain control module (PCM) monitors the variable camshaft timing (VCT) position for an over-advanced camshaft timing during cold start up. The test fails when the camshaft timing exceeds a maximum calibrated value or remains in an advanced position.
DTC: P054D	**Cold Start Exhaust (B) Camshaft Position Timing Over-Retarded (Bank 2):** The powertrain control module (PCM) monitors the variable camshaft timing (VCT) position for over-retarded camshaft timing during cold start up. The test fails when the camshaft timing exceeds a maximum calibrated value or remains in a retarded position.
DTC: P0552	**Power Steering Pressure (PSP) Sensor/Switch Circuit Low:** Indicates the PSP sensor input signal was less than the self-test minimum.

DTC	Trouble Code Title, Conditions, Possible Causes
DTC: P0553	**Power Steering Pressure (PSP) Sensor Circuit High Input:** Indicates the PSP sensor input signal was greater than the self-test maximum.
DTC: P0562	**System Voltage Low:** This DTC is set when the Powertrain Control Module (PCM) detects low system voltage. **NOTE: System voltage is monitored by the PCM. When the voltage is above or below a calibrated value, internal counter increments until a DTC is set.**
DTC: P0562	**System Voltage Low:** This DTC sets when the transaxle control module (TCM) detects low system voltage or when the ignition is turned to the OFF position and the vehicle travels for an additional 10 seconds. A vehicle shutdown can set this DTC and illuminate the hazard warning indicator.
DTC: P0563	**System Voltage High:** This DTC is set when the Powertrain Control Module (PCM) detects high system voltage. **NOTE: System voltage is monitored by the PCM. When the voltage is above or below a calibrated value, internal counter increments until a DTC is set.**
DTC: P0571	**Brake Switch A Circuit:** The purpose of this DTC is to check whether the brake switch has toggled or not during the key on engine running (KOER) test.
DTC: P0572	**Brake Switch A Circuit Low:** This DTC indicates the brake switch is stuck in the ON position.
DTC: P0573	**Brake Switch A Circuit High:** This DTC indicates the brake switch is stuck in the OFF position.
DTC: P0579	**Cruise Control Multifunction Input A Circuit Range / Performance:** This DTC indicates the speed control is inoperative.
DTC: P0581	**Cruise Control Multifunction Input A Circuit High:** This DTC indicates the speed control is inoperative.
DTC: P0600	**Serial Communication Link:** Indicates an error occurred in the powertrain control module (PCM). This DTC may set alone or in combination with P2105.
DTC: P0602	**Powertrain Control Module (PCM) Programming Error:** This DTC indicates a programming error within the vehicle ID (VID) block.
DTC: P0603	**Internal Control Module Keep Alive Memory (KAM) Error:** Indicates the powertrain control module (PCM) has experienced an internal memory concern. However, there are external items that can cause this DTC.
DTC: P0604	**Internal Control Module Random Access Memory (RAM) Error:** Indicates the powertrain control module (PCM) RAM has been corrupted.
DTC: P0605	**Internal Control Module Read Only Memory (ROM) Error:** The powertrain control module (PCM) ROM has been corrupted.
DTC: P0606	**Control Module Processor:** This DTC indicates an internal powertrain control module (PCM) communication error.
DTC: P0607	**Control Module Performance:** Indicates that the powertrain control module (PCM) internal central processing unit (CPU) has encountered an error. The PCM monitors itself and carries out internal checks of its own CPU. This DTC sets if any of these checks returns an incorrect value.
DTC: P060A	**Internal Control Module Monitoring Processor Performance:** Indicates an error occurred in the powertrain control module (PCM). This DTC may set in combination with P2105.
DTC: P060B	**Internal Control Module A/D Processing Performance:** Indicates an error occurred in the powertrain control module (PCM). This DTC may set in combination with P2104 or P2110.
DTC: P060C	**Internal Control Module Main Processor Performance:** Indicates an internal error occurred in the powertrain control module (PCM) or a transmission range (TR) sensor concern.
DTC: P060D	**Internal Control Module Accelerator Pedal Position Performance:** Indicates an error occurred in the powertrain control module (PCM). If the PCM detects a concern identifying an issue with an accelerator pedal position (APP) sensor signal or with processing the brake pedal sensor input, the DTC is set.
DTC: P0610	**Control Module Vehicle Options Error:** Indicates a powertrain control module (PCM) vehicle options error.
DTC: P0613	**Transaxle Control Module (TCM) Processor:** This DTC indicates a TCM internal error.

DTC	Trouble Code Title, Conditions, Possible Causes
DTC: P0616	**Starter Relay Circuit Low:** The PCM detects a malfunction in the starting system.
DTC: P0617	**Starter Relay Circuit High:** The PCM detects a malfunction in the starting system.
DTC: P061A	**Internal Control Module Torque Performance:** Indicates a torque calculation error occurred in the powertrain control module (PCM).
DTC: P061B	**Internal Control Module Torque Calculation Performance:** Indicates a calculation error occurred in the Powertrain Control Module (PCM).
DTC: P061C	**Internal Control Module Engine RPM Performance:** Indicates a calculation error occurred in the powertrain control module (PCM).
DTC: P061D	**Internal Control Module Engine Air Mass Performance:** Indicates an error occurred in the powertrain control module (PCM).
DTC: P061F	**Internal Control Module Throttle Actuator Controller Performance:** Indicates an error occurred in the Powertrain Control Module (PCM).
DTC: P0620	**Generator Control Circuit:** The powertrain control module (PCM) monitors the generator circuits and sets this DTC when the PCM detects a concern.
DTC: P0622	**Generator Field Terminal Circuit:** The Powertrain Control Module (PCM) monitors the generator load from the generator/regulator in the form of frequency. The frequency range is determined by the temperature of the voltage regulator, where 97% indicates a full load, and less than 6% indicates no load.
DTC: P0625	**Generator Field Terminal Circuit Low:** The Powertrain Control Module (PCM) monitors generator load from the generator/regulator in the form of frequency The concern indicates the input is lower than the load should be in normal operation The load input could be low when no generator output exists.
DTC: P0626	**Generator Field Terminal Circuit High:** The Powertrain Control Module (PCM) monitors generator load from the generator/regulator in the form of frequency The concern indicates the input is higher than the load should be in normal operation The load input could be high when a battery short to ground exists.
DTC: P0627	**Fuel Pump A Control Circuit/Open:** The fuel pump control module monitors the fuel pump assembly and secondary circuits for a concern. If the fuel pump control module detects a concern with the fuel pump assembly or secondary circuits, the fuel pump control module sends an 80% duty cycle signal on the fuel pump monitor (FPM) circuit to report the concern to the powertrain control module (PCM). The test fails when the fuel pump control module is still reporting a concern with the fuel pump assembly or secondary circuits after a calibrated amount of time.
DTC: P062C	**Internal Control Module Vehicle Speed Performance:** Indicates an error occurred in the powertrain control module (PCM).
DTC: P062F	**Internal Control Module EEPROM Error:** Indicates the powertrain control module (PCM) electrically erasable programmable read only memory (EEPROM) has been corrupted.
DTC: P062F	**Internal Control Module EEPROM Error:** The Transmission control module (TCM) read only memory (ROM) has been corrupted.
DTC: P0630	**VIN Not Programmed or Incompatible - ECM/PCM:** The PCM has a programming error.
DTC: P0642	**Sensor Reference Voltage A Circuit Low:** Indicates the reference voltage (VREF) circuit is less than VREF minimum.
DTC: P0643	**Sensor Reference Voltage A Circuit High:** Indicates the reference voltage (VREF) circuit is greater than VREF maximum.
DTC: P064D	**Internal Control Module O2 Sensor Processor Performance - Bank 1:** The powertrain control module (PCM) monitors the application-specific integrated circuit that controls and monitors the universal heated oxygen sensor (HO2S). The test fails when the PCM detects an internal circuit or communication concern.
DTC: P064E	**Internal Control Module O2 Sensor Processor Performance - Bank 2:** The powertrain control module (PCM) monitors the application-specific integrated circuit that controls and monitors the heated oxygen sensor (HO2S). The test fails when the PCM detects an internal circuit or communication concern.

DTC	Trouble Code Title, Conditions, Possible Causes
DTC: P0652	**Sensor Reference Voltage B Circuit Low:** Indicates the electronic throttle control reference voltage (ETCREF) circuit is less than VREF minimum.
DTC: P0653	**Sensor Reference Voltage B Circuit High:** Indicates the electronic throttle control reference voltage (ETCREF) circuit is greater than VREF maximum.
DTC: P0657	**Actuator Supply Voltage A Circuit Open:** Transaxle solenoid power control provides power to all the solenoids. This DTC sets if the transaxle solenoid power control circuit is open.
DTC: P065B	**Generator Control Circuit Range/Performance:** The Powertrain Control Module (PCM) reads the GENLI and sends a DTC through the network when the signal frequency of GENLI indicates a concern. **NOTE: An IMTVM PID reading may indicate a fault.**
DTC: P065C	**Generator Mechanical Performance:** The Powertrain Control Module (PCM) reads the GENLI and sends a DTC through the network when the signal frequency of GENLI indicates a concern. **NOTE: An IMTVM PID reading may indicate a fault.**
DTC: P0660	**Intake Manifold Tuning Valve (IMTV) Control Circuit Open - Bank 1:** The IMTV system is monitored for failure during continuous, key ON engine OFF (KOEO) or key ON engine running (KOER) self-tests. The test fails when the signal is greater or less, than an expected calibrated range.
DTC: P0663	**Intake Manifold Tuning Valve (IMTV) Control Circuit Open - Bank 2:** The IMTV system is monitored for failure during continuous, key ON engine OFF (KOEO) or key ON engine running (KOER) self-tests. The test fails when the signal is greater or less, than an expected calibrated range.
DTC: P0685	**Electronic Control Module (ECM)/Powertrain Control Module (PCM) Power Relay Control Circuit/Open:** This DTC sets when the ignition switch position run (ISP-R) circuit indicates the ignition is in the OFF, ACC, or LOCK position, and the amount of time the PCM remains powered through the PCM power relay exceeds a predetermined amount of time.
DTC: P0686	**Electronic Control Module (ECM)/Powertrain Control Module (PCM) Power Relay Control Circuit Low:** This DTC sets when the ignition switch position run (ISP-R) circuit indicates the ignition is in the OFF, ACC, or LOCK position, and the amount of time the PCM remains powered through the PCM power relay exceeds a predetermined amount of time.
DTC: P0687	**Electronic Control Module (ECM)/Powertrain Control Module (PCM) Power Relay Control Circuit High:** This DTC sets when the ignition switch position run (ISP-R) circuit indicates the ignition is in the OFF, ACC, or LOCK position, and the amount of time the PCM remains powered through the PCM power relay exceeds a predetermined amount of time.
DTC: P0689	**Electronic Control Module (ECM)/Powertrain Control Module (PCM) Power Relay Sense Circuit Low:** The powertrain control module (PCM) monitors the voltage on the ignition switch position run (ISP-R) and the fuel injector power monitor (INJPWRM) circuits. This DTC sets when the voltage on the ISP-R and the INJPWRM circuit voltages do not correspond for a calibrated period of time.
DTC: P068A	**ECM/PCM Power Relay De-Energized - Too Early:** This DTC sets when the powertrain control module (PCM) power relay is de-energized too early.
DTC: P0690	**Electronic Control Module (ECM)/Powertrain Control Module (PCM) Power Relay Sense Circuit High:** The powertrain control module (PCM) monitors the voltage on the ignition switch position run (ISP-R) and the fuel injector power monitor (INJPWRM) circuits. This DTC sets when the voltage on the ISP-R and the INJPWRM circuit voltages do not correspond for a calibrated period of time.
DTC: P0691	**Fan 1 Control Circuit Low:** This DTC sets when the powertrain control module (PCM) detects that the fan control (FC) circuit voltage is less than the desired voltage.
DTC: P0692	**Fan 1 Control Circuit High:** This DTC sets when the powertrain control module (PCM) detects that the fan control (FC) circuit voltage is greater than the desired voltage.
DTC: P06B6	**Internal Control Module Knock Sensor Processor 1 Performance:** The powertrain control module (PCM) has detected an error condition with the knock sensor (KS) processor integrated circuit.
DTC: P06B8	**Internal Control Module Non-Volatile Random Access Memory (NVRAM) Error:** This DTC indicates a concern with the ability of the powertrain control module (PCM) to correctly store permanent DTCs.
DTC: P06D1	**Internal Control Module Ignition Coil Control Module Performance:** The powertrain control module (PCM) has detected an error with the ignition coil driver and diagnostic circuit.
DTC: P0700	**Transmission Control System (Malfunction Indicator Lamp [MIL] Request):** This DTC indicates the powertrain control module (PCM) received a MIL request controller area network CAN message from the transaxle control module (TCM).

DTC	Trouble Code Title, Conditions, Possible Causes
DTC: P0701	**Transmission control system range/performance:** The PCM has detected an intermittent clutch ON fault. Vehicle decelerates during upshift or hangs in gear DTCs P2700 (A) clutch, P2701 (B) clutch, P2702 (C) clutch, P2703 (D) clutch and/or P2704 (E) clutch may set
DTC: P0702	**Battery voltage out of range:** The PCM has detected a voltage level above or below the accepted voltage range. Maximum line pressure DTCs P0882 and/or P0883 may set
DTC: P0703	**Brake Switch B Input Circuit:** Indicates the powertrain control module (PCM) did not receive a brake pedal position (BPP) input.
DTC: P0704	**Clutch Switch Input Circuit:** When the clutch pedal is applied, the voltage goes to low. This DTC sets if the powertrain control module (PCM) does not see this change from high to low.
DTC: P0705	**Transmission Range Sensor A Circuit (PRNDL) Input:** TR circuits indicating an invalid pattern with multiple inputs (besides REVERSE input). Condition caused by a short to ground or an open in P/N, R, D or L circuits. This DTC can be set by an incorrectly adjusted TR sensor. Increase in control pressure (harsh shifts). Defaults to D for an invalid position.
DTC: P0706	**Transmission Range Sensor A Circuit Range/Performance:** TR sensor stuck in transition zone and possible no crank condition. Only PARK, REVERSE, NEUTRAL and 5th gear available.
DTC: P0707	**Transmission Range Sensor A Circuit Low:** Key on or engine running; and the PCM detected the Digital Transmission Range (DTR) or Transmission Range sensor (TR) input was more than the self-test maximum range in the test.
DTC: P0708	**Transmission Range Sensor High Input:** * Key on or engine running* TR sensor signal is above threshold of 4.87 volts* TR sensor indicates a stuck position* No adaptive or self-learning strategy
DTC: P0709	**TR sensor A circuit intermittent :** The PCM has detected a TR signal duty cycle is not out of range but is invalid. Engine may not crank. Default to 5th gear if DTC sets after engine running Maximum line pressure DTC P1702 may set
DTC: P0710	**Transmission Fluid Temperature Sensor A Circuit:** The transaxle control module (TCM) uses the transmission fluid temperature (TFT) sensor to continuously monitor the fluid temperature. This DTC indicates the concern in TFT sensor or circuit.
DTC: P0711	**TFT sensor A circuit range/performance:** PCM has detected no TFT sensor change during operation. The TFT sensor is stuck below 21°C (70°F) or above 107°C (225°F) or the temperature did not change by 8°F during a drive cycle. Transmission Control Indicator Lamp (TCIL) flashing Wrench light illuminated Default to 1st or 3rd gear
DTC: P0712	**TFT sensor A circuit low:** PCM detected a temperature greater than 171°C (340°F) for at least 2.5 seconds (grounded circuit).TCIL flashing Wrench light illuminated Default to 1st gear DTC P0710 may set
DTC: P0713	**TFT sensor A circuit high:** PCM detected a temperature less than -45°C (-50°F) for at least 2.5 seconds (open circuit).TCIL flashing Wrench light illuminated Default to 1st gear DTC P0710 may set
DTC: P0715	**Turbine Shaft Speed (TSS) sensor A circuit:** PCM indicated 0 rpm from the TSS sensor when the Output Shaft Speed (OSS) sensor indicated rpm greater than 0.Wrench light illuminated. Default to 5th gear Maximum line pressure DTC P0717 may set
DTC: P0716	**Turbine Shaft Speed (TSS) Performance:** * PCM has detected a loss or noisy TSS signal during operation.
DTC: P0717 PCM	**TSS sensor A circuit no signal:** PCM has not detected a TSS sensor signal during operation. TCIL flashing Wrench light illuminated Default to 5th gear Maximum line pressure DTC P0715 may set
DTC: P0718	**TSS sensor A circuit intermittent:** PCM has detected an intermittent (noise) in the TSS sensor signal during operation. TCIL ON or TCIL flashing. Poor shift quality.
DTC: P0720	**Output Shaft Speed (OSS) Sensor Circuit:** The OSS sensor inputs a signal to the powertrain control module (PCM) based on the speed of the output shaft of the transmission.

DTC	Trouble Code Title, Conditions, Possible Causes
DTC: P0720	**Output Shaft Speed (OSS) Sensor Circuit:** The OSS sensor inputs a signal to the Powertrain Control Module (PCM) based on the speed of the output shaft of the transmission. **NOTE: Verify the sensor signal output varies with the vehicle speed.**
DTC: P0721	**Output Shaft Speed (OSS) Sensor Circuit Range/Performance:** The OSS sensor signal is very sensitive to noise. This noise distorts the input to the Powertrain Control Module (PCM). **NOTE: Check the routing of the harness, and the wiring and the connector for damage.**
DTC: P0722	**Output Shaft Speed (OSS) Sensor Circuit No Signal:** The OSS sensor failed to provide a signal to the Powertrain Control Module (PCM) upon initial movement of vehicle. **NOTE: Check the wiring, connector, and sensor for damage.**
DTC: P0723	**Output Shaft Speed (OSS) Sensor Circuit Intermittent:** The OSS sensor signal to the powertrain control module (PCM) is irregular or interrupted.
DTC: P0726	**Engine Speed Input Circuit Range/Performance:** The transaxle control module (TCM) calculates an engine speed and compares it to the engine speed received from the powertrain control module (PCM). This DTC is set when the RPM difference between the calculated and received speeds is greater than 1,000 RPM.
DTC: P0727	**Engine Speed Input Circuit No Signal:** The transaxle control module (TCM) continuously monitors the clean tachometer output (CTO) circuit from the powertrain control module (PCM) for an engine speed signal. This DTC is set when if there is a CTO circuit concern.
DTC: P0729	**Incorrect Sixth Gear Ratio:** Engine started, vehicle operating with 6th Gear commanded "on", and the PCM detected an incorrect 6th gear ratio during the test. **NOTE: Verify harness and connector integrity and correct installation of the OSS sensor.**
DTC: P0730	**Gear Ratio Error:** Engine running, and the vehicle is in motion, the PCM has detected an incorrect gear ratio during the test
DTC: P0731	**Incorrect First Gear Ratio:** Engine started, vehicle operating with 1st Gear commanded "on", and the PCM detected an incorrect 1st gear ratio during the test. **NOTE: Verify harness and connector integrity and correct installation of the OSS sensor. Will turn on TCIL.**
DTC: P0732	**Incorrect Second Gear Ratio:** Engine started, vehicle operating with 2nd Gear commanded "on", and the PCM detected an incorrect 2nd gear ratio during the test. **NOTE: Verify harness and connector integrity and correct installation of the OSS sensor. Will turn on TCIL.**
DTC: P0733	**Incorrect Third Gear Ratio:** Engine started, vehicle operating with 3rd Gear commanded "on", and the PCM detected an incorrect 3rd gear ratio during the test. **NOTE: Verify harness and connector integrity and correct installation of the OSS sensor. Will turn on TCIL.**
DTC: P0734	**Incorrect Fourth Gear Ratio:** Engine started, vehicle operating with 4th Gear commanded "on", and the PCM detected an incorrect 4th gear ratio during the test. **NOTE: Verify harness and connector integrity and correct installation of the OSS sensor. Will turn on TCIL.**
DTC: P0735	**Incorrect Fifth Gear Ratio:** Engine started, vehicle operating with 5th Gear commanded "on", and the PCM detected an incorrect 5th gear ratio during the test.
DTC: P0736	**Incorrect Reverse Gear Ratio:** Engine started Vehicle operating in Reverse. The TCM detected no reverse gear ratio. • Reverse gear solenoid is damaged or not installed properly
DTC: P0740	**TCC Solenoid Circuit Malfunction:** Key on, KOEO Self-Test enabled and the PCM did not detect any voltage drop across the TCC solenoid circuit during the test period.
DTC: P0741	**Torque Converter Clutch (TCC) Failed Off:** Non-electrical TCC solenoid stuck off.* TCC mechanical failure.* TCC regulator apply valve stuck in TCC release position.* TCC control valve stuck in TCC release position.* TCC failed to apply 3 consecutive times.
DTC: P0742	**TCC solenoid circuit stuck on:** The PCM has detected a TCC solenoid control circuit shorted to ground. TCC is disabled. Poor launch performance. Default to 5th gear DTC P0743 may set
DTC: P0743	**Torque Converter Clutch (TCC) Electrical Fault:** Failure Mode Effects Management action opens the transaxle solenoid power control, removing power from all solenoids* Harsh engagements.* Poor launch performance (due to 5th gear drive away)* No shifts
DTC: P0744	**TCC solenoid circuit intermittent:** The PCM has detected a TCC solenoid control circuit shorted to power. TCC is disabled DTC P0743 may set

DTC	Trouble Code Title, Conditions, Possible Causes
DTC: P0745	**Pressure Control Solenoid A or Circuit Fault:** PCA functional fault-low pressure.
DTC: P0748	**Line Pressure Control (LPC) Solenoid Electrical Fault:** Failed to minimum line pressure.* Failure Mode Effects Management action opens the transaxle solenoid power control, removing power from all solenoids* Harsh engagements.* Poor launch performance (due to 5th gear drive away).
DTC: P0750	**A/T Shift Solenoid 1/A Circuit Malfunction:** Engine started, vehicle driven with the solenoid applied, and the PCM detected an unexpected voltage condition on the SS1/A solenoid circuit was incorrect during the test.
DTC: P0751	**Shift Solenoid A Performance/Stuck Off:** Neutral conditions or flares on downshifts from 5th or 6th gear.* Gears 1 through 4 are disabled — leaving 5th and 6th gears as the only forward gears.* Erratic shifting* Harsh engagements* Neutral conditions* Poor launch performance* Harsh reverse engagements
DTC: P0752	**Shift Solenoid A Performance/Stuck On:** * Neutral conditions or flares on downshifts from 5th or 6th gear.* Gears 1 through 4 are disabled — leaving 5th and 6th gears as the only forward gears.* Erratic shifting* Harsh engagements* Neutral conditions* Poor launch performance* Harsh reverse engagements
DTC: P0753	**Shift Solenoid A Circuit Malfunction:** The PCM sets this DTC along with one or more specific electrical DTCs. TCIL flashing Wrench light illuminated 5th and 6th gear only DTCs P0750, P0973 and/or P0974 may set
DTC: P0754	**Shift Solenoid A Intermittent:** * Unexpected upshifts* Unexpected downshifts* Unexpected flairs* Neutral conditions.
DTC: P0755	**A/T Shift Solenoid 2/B Circuit Malfunction:** Key on, KOEO Self-Test enabled, Shift Solenoid 2/B applied, and the PCM detected an unexpected voltage condition on the Shift Solenoid 2/B circuit during the CCM test period.
DTC: P0756	**Shift Solenoid B Performance/Stuck Off:** * Flares or neutral conditions on shifts into 3rd or 5th gear.* PCM will command 3 shifts into 3rd or 5th gear* If direct clutch is failed off the driver will notice flares or neutral conditions that last one second or so.* 3rd and 5th gears are disabled,* Transmission hangs in 2nd on acceleration until driver tips out to closed pedal (done to protect overdrive clutch)
DTC: P0757	**Shift Solenoid B Stuck On:** Vehicle deceleration on shift into 2nd, 4th or 6th gear.* Harsh 1-3 shift* Poor launch performance - lack of shifts
DTC: P0758	**Shift Solenoid B Circuit Malfunction:** Engine started, vehicle driven with the solenoid applied, and the PCM detected an unexpected voltage condition on the SSB solenoid circuit was incorrect during the test.
DTC: P0759	**Shift Solenoid B Intermittent:** * Unexpected upshifts* Unexpected downshifts* Unexpected flairs* Neutral conditions.
DTC: P0760	**A/T Shift Solenoid 4/D Circuit Malfunction:** Engine started, vehicle driven with Shift Solenoid 4/D applied, and the PCM detected an unexpected voltage condition on Shift Solenoid 4/D circuit during the CCM continuous test.
DTC: P0760	**Shift Solenoid C Circuit Malfunction:** Engine started, vehicle driven with the solenoid applied, and the PCM detected an unexpected voltage condition on the SSC solenoid circuit was incorrect during the test.
DTC: P0761	**Shift Solenoid C Functional Failure:** * PCM detected a mechanical or hydraulic failure while operating the Shift Solenoid C.* Not all gears present
DTC: P0762	**Shift Solenoid C Functional Failure:** * PCM detected a mechanical or hydraulic failure while operating the Shift Solenoid C.* Not all gears present
DTC: P0763	**Shift Solenoid C Circuit Malfunction:** Engine started, vehicle driven with the solenoid applied, and the PCM detected an unexpected voltage condition on the SSC solenoid circuit was incorrect during the test.
DTC: P0764	**Shift Solenoid C Intermittent:** * Unexpected upshifts* Unexpected downshifts* Unexpected flairs* Neutral conditions.
DTC: P0765	**Shift Solenoid D Circuit Failure:** Engine started, vehicle driven with the solenoid applied, and the PCM detected an unexpected voltage condition on the SSD solenoid circuit was incorrect during the test.

DTC	Trouble Code Title, Conditions, Possible Causes
DTC: P0766	**SSD performance/stuck off:** PCM commanded SSD on but detected a ratio error (mechanical failure).3rd gear only. Delayed or no reverse engagement Neutral or flair condition DTCs P2703 and/or P2704 may set
DTC: P0767	**SSD stuck on:** PCM commanded SSD off but detected a ratio error (mechanical failure).4th, 5th and 6th gear only Early upshift Stuck in 4th DTC P2704 may set
DTC: P0768	**Shift Solenoid D Circuit Failure:** Engine started, vehicle driven with the solenoid applied, and the PCM detected an unexpected voltage condition on the SSD solenoid circuit was incorrect during the test.
DTC: P0769	**Shift Solenoid D Circuit Intermittent:** The PCM sets this DTC when an intermittent condition (open, short to power or ground) occurs three times for less than 5 seconds with each occurrence. Unexpected upshifts, downshifts, flairs or neutral conditions.
DTC: P0770	**A/T Shift Solenoid 5/E Functional Failure:** Functional Failure (Stuck ON) or Main Control System Failure. (shift valves, orifices and sealing)
DTC: P0771	**Shift Solenoid E Functional Failure:** * PCM detected a mechanical or hydraulic failure while operating the Shift Solenoid E.* Not all gears present
DTC: P0772	**Shift Solenoid E Performance/Stuck On:** Functional Failure (Stuck ON) or Main Control System Failure. (shift valves, orifices and sealing)
DTC: P0773	**Shift Solenoid E Electrical:** * Failure Mode Effect Management for P0770
DTC: P0774	**SSE intermittent:** The PCM sets this DTC when an intermittent condition (open, short to power or ground) occurs but does not set DTC P0770. Transmission hangs in 1st gear or may be stuck in 3rd gear
DTC: P0775	**Pressure Control Solenoid B (PCB):** Functional fault, Low pressure or circuit fault. Incorrect shift pattern indicating mechanical or hydraulic failure of the transmission
DTC: P0778	**Pressure Control Solenoid B (PCB) Circuit Failure:** Electrical failure of the solenoid detected, 2nd and 5th gear.
DTC: P0780	**Transaxle Valve Stuck:** * Increased RPM during shifts* Slipping or erratic shifting
DTC: P0791	**Intermediate Shaft Speed Sensor No Signal:** Insufficient input from the intermediate shaft speed sensor. PCM has detected a loss of the intermediate shaft speed sensor signal during operation. Harsh shifts.
DTC: P0794	**Intermediate Shaft Speed Sensor Signal Noise:** Intermediate shaft speed sensor signal noisy. PCM has detected a loss of the intermediate shaft speed sensor signal during operation. Harsh shifts.
DTC: P0795	**Pressure Control Solenoid C (PCC) Circuit Fault:** Incorrect shift pattern indicating mechanical or hydraulic failure of the transmission.
DTC: P0798	**Pressure Control Solenoid C (PCC) Circuit Fault:** Electrical failure of the solenoid detected. Incorrect gear ratio in 4th and 5th gear.
DTC: P0813	**Reverse Lamp Circuit Short/Open:** * Reverse lamps always illuminated* Reverse lamps inoperative
DTC: P0815	**Upshift Switch Circuit:** Key on or engine running; and the PCM detected an incorrect up shift.
DTC: P0817	**Starter Lock Circuit Failed:** Ignition switch is ON, TCM and PCM communication is normal. No voltage is detected on the start lock circuit for more than 0.1 second or a continuous 12-volt output is detected for more than 0.1 second.
DTC: P0819	**Select Shift Switch Output Circuit Failure:** * No manual up/down shift available
DTC: P0830	**Clutch Pedal Switch A Circuit:** The powertrain control module (PCM) monitors the clutch pedal position (CPP) bottom of travel (CPP-BT) switch only during the calibrated engine speed range (cranking speed range). This DTC sets when the CPP-BT switch does not indicate that the clutch is disengaged (clutch pedal pressed) when the engine is cranked.

DTC	Trouble Code Title, Conditions, Possible Causes
DTC: P0833	**Clutch Pedal Switch B Circuit:** The powertrain control module (PCM) monitors the clutch pedal position (CPP) top of travel (CPP-TT) switch only during the calibrated engine speed range (cranking speed range). This DTC sets when the CPP-TT does not indicate that the clutch is disengaged (clutch pedal pressed) when the engine is cranked.
DTC: P0840	**Transmission Fluid Pressure Sensor/Switch A Circuit:** The Transmission Control Module (TCM) monitors the transmission fluid pressure. This DTC sets when the TCC does not see the proper transmission fluid pressure. **NOTE: Check for the correct fluid level and condition.**
DTC: P0867	**Transmission Fluid Pressure:** The control valve test raises line pressure to insure that the clutch control bypass valve (multiplex valve) is latched, and turns on SSE to test for a stuck TCC control valve under steady state operation in 4th, 5th and 6th gear. If the ratio breaks away, the test is aborted. If enough ratio break away occurs, the DTC is set.
DTC: P0882	**Transmission Control Module (TCM) power input signal low:** The TCM has detected a voltage level below 9 volts. Default to 3rd or 5th gear. Battery voltage below 9 volts Maximum line pressure
DTC: P0883	**TCM power input signal high:** The TCM has detected a voltage level above 21 volts. Default to 3rd or 5th gear. Battery voltage above 21 volts maximum line pressure may set DTC P0702
DTC: P0960	**Line Pressure Control (LPC) Solenoid Circuit Open:** * Maximum LPC pressure* Harsh engagements and shifts
DTC: P0961	**PCA control circuit range/performance:** The PCM has detected the PCA control circuit shorted to ground but not long enough to set DTC P0962.Wrench light illuminated, Intermittent condition. Minimum line pressure
DTC: P0962	**Line Pressure Control (LPC) Solenoid Short to Ground:** * Maximum LPC pressure* Harsh engagements and shifts
DTC: P0963	**Line Pressure Control (LPC) Solenoid Short to Voltage:** * Maximum LPC pressure* Harsh engagements and shifts
DTC: P0964	**PCB solenoid circuit open:** Voltage through PCB solenoid is checked. Error is noted if tolerance is exceeded.
DTC: P0966	**PCB solenoid circuit failure, short to ground:** Voltage through PCB solenoid is checked. An error will be noted if tolerance is exceeded No 2nd and 5th gear.
DTC: P0967	**PCB solenoid short to battery voltage, short to ground:** Voltage through PCB solenoid is checked. An error will be noted if tolerance is exceeded. Short to battery power: harsh shift and engagements. Short to ground — No 2nd and 4th gear.
DTC: P0968	**PCC solenoid circuit open:** Voltage through PCC solenoid is checked. Error is noted if tolerance is exceeded.
DTC: P0970	**PCC solenoid circuit failure, short to ground:** Voltage through PCC solenoid is checked. An error will be noted if tolerance is exceeded. No 4th and 5th gear.
DTC: P0971	**PCC solenoid short to power, short to ground:** Voltage through PCC solenoid is checked. An error will be noted if tolerance is exceeded. Short to battery power: harsh shift and engagements. Short to ground — No 4th and 5th gear.
DTC: P0973	**Shift Solenoid (SSA) Short To Ground (VFS-1):** SSA (VFS-1) circuit or solenoid failure. Mechanical limp-home mode, default to 3rd or 5th gear. May turn on MIL.
DTC: P0974	**Shift Solenoid A (SSA) Short to Voltage:** * Forward clutch is failed off* Neutral condition or flare when fault occurs.* Poor launch due to 5th gear drive away
DTC: P0975	**Shift Solenoid B (SSA) Solenoid Failure (VFS-2):** SSA (VFS-2) circuit or solenoid failure. Mechanical limp-home mode, default to 3rd or 5th gear. May turn on MIL.
DTC: P0976	**Shift Solenoid B Short to Ground:** * Failure Mode Effects Management action opens the transaxle solenoid power control, removing power from all solenoids.* Harsh engagements.* Poor launch performance (due to 5th gear drive away).* No TCC apply.* No shifts.
DTC: P0977	**Shift Solenoid B (SSB) Short to Voltage:** * Direct clutch failed on* Harsh engagements.* Poor launch performance (due to 3rd gear drive away).

DTC	Trouble Code Title, Conditions, Possible Causes
DTC: P0978	**Shift Solenoid C Circuit Failure:** No shift engagements* No adaptive or self-learning strategy* Incorrect current detected by TCM
DTC: P0979	**Shift Solenoid C (SSC) Circuit Low :** The PCM detected 0 volts on the SSC circuit. Short to ground detected. Wrench light illuminated. Default to 5th gear. Maximum line pressure DTC P0763 may set
DTC: P0980	**Shift Solenoid C (SSC) Short to Voltage:** * Neutral condition before diagnostics disables 2nd and 6th gears* Erratic, delayed or harsh shifts
DTC: P0981	**Shift Solenoid D Circuit Failure:** * No shift engagements* No adaptive or self-learning strategy* Incorrect current detected by TCM. May turn on MIL. **NOTE: Will turn on the TCIL.**
DTC: P0982	**Shift Solenoid D (SSD) Short to Ground:** * Failure Mode Effects Management action opens the transaxle solenoid power control, removing power from all solenoids.* Harsh engagements.* Poor launch performance (due to 5th gear drive away).* No TCC apply.* No shifts.
DTC: P0983	**Shift Solenoid D (SSD) Short to Voltage:** * O/D clutch failed on, only 4th, 5th and 6th gears available* Harsh engagements* Poor launch due to 4th gear drive away
DTC: P0984	**Shift Solenoid E Functional Failure:** * PCM detected a mechanical or hydraulic failure while operating the Shift Solenoid E or main control valves.* Not all gears present
DTC: P0985	**Shift Solenoid E Short to Ground:** * No engagements* No adaptive or self-learning
DTC: P0986	**Shift Solenoid E Short to Voltage:** * During self test, voltage in SSE circuit tolerance is exceeded* No engagements* No adaptive or self-learning strategy
DTC: P0997	**Shift Solenoid F Circuit Failure:** * No engagements* No adaptive or self-learning strategy* Incorrect current detected by the TCM
DTC: P0998	**Shift Solenoid F Short to Ground:** * No engagements* No adaptive or self-learning strategy* SSF circuit voltage exceeded tolerance during self test
DTC: P0999	**Shift Solenoid F Short to Voltage:** * During self test, voltage in SSF circuit tolerance is exceeded* No engagements* No adaptive or self-learning strategy
DTC: P0A5A	**Generator Current Sensor Circuit Range/Performance:** Engine running, the Powertrain Control Module (PCM) detects that the generator field control circuit has a malfunction.
DTC: P0A5B	**Generator Current Sensor Circuit Low:** Engine running, the Powertrain Control Module (PCM) detects that the generator field control circuit has a malfunction.
DTC: P0A5C	**Generator Current Sensor Circuit High:** Engine running, the Powertrain Control Module (PCM) detects that the generator field control circuit has a malfunction.

OBD II Trouble Code List (P1xxx Codes)

DTC	Trouble Code Title, Conditions, Possible Causes
DTC: P1000	**On-Board Diagnostic (OBD) Systems Readiness Test Not Complete:** The OBD monitors are carried out during the OBD drive cycle. This DTC is stored in continuous memory if any of the OBD monitors do not carry out their full diagnostic check. This DTC is not supported on all vehicles. Refer to Section 2, On Board Diagnostic (OBD) Drive Cycle for additional information.
DTC: P1001	**Key On Engine Running (KOER) Not Able To Complete, KOER Aborted:** This non-malfunction indicator lamp (MIL) DTC sets when the KOER self-test does not complete in the time allowed.
DTC: P1100	**Mass Air Flow (MAF) Sensor Circuit Intermittent:** The MAF sensor circuit is monitored by the powertrain control module (PCM) for sudden voltage (or air flow) input change through the comprehensive component monitor (CCM). If during the last 40 warm-up cycles in ignition on, engine running the PCM detects a voltage (or air flow) change beyond the minimum or maximum calibrated limit, a continuous memory DTC is stored.
DTC: P1101	**Mass Air Flow (MAF) Sensor Out of Self-Test Range:** The MAF sensor circuit is monitored by the powertrain control module (PCM) for an out of range air flow (or voltage) input. If, during key on engine off (KOEO), the air flow voltage signal is greater than 0.27 volt the test fails. Likewise, if, during key on, engine running (KOER), the air flow voltage signal is not within 0.46 volt to 2.44 volts, the test fails.

DTC	Trouble Code Title, Conditions, Possible Causes
DTC: P1112	**Intake Air Temperature (IAT) Circuit Intermittent:** Indicates the IAT sensor signal was intermittent.
DTC: P1114	**Intake Air Temperature 2 (IAT2) Circuit Low (Supercharged/Turbocharged engines):** Indicates the sensor signal is less than the self-test minimum. The IAT2 sensor minimum is 0.2 volt.
DTC: P1115	**Intake Air Temperature 2 (IAT2) Circuit High (Supercharged/Turbocharged engines):** Indicates the sensor signal is greater than the self-test maximum. The IAT2 sensor maximum is 4.6 volts.
DTC: P1116	**Engine Coolant Temperature (ECT) Sensor Out of Self-Test Range:** Indicates the ECT sensor is out of self-test range. The correct range is 0.3 to 3.7 volts.
DTC: P1117	**Engine Coolant Temperature (ECT) Sensor Circuit Intermittent:** Indicates the ECT circuit became intermittently open or short while the engine was running.
DTC: P1120	**Throttle Position Sensor A Out Of Range Low (Ratch Too Low):** The throttle position (TP) sensor circuit is monitored by the powertrain control module (PCM) for a low TP rotation angle or voltage input below the closed throttle position through the comprehensive component monitor (CCM). The test fails if the TP rotation angle or voltage remains within the calibrated self-test range, but falls between 3.42-9.85% (0.17-0.49 volt).
DTC: P1124	**Throttle Position Sensor A Out Of Self-Test Range:** During key on engine off (KOEO) and key on engine running (KOER) self-tests, the powertrain control module (PCM) monitors the electronic throttle control (ETC) throttle position (TP) sensor inputs to determine if the TP1 and TP2 signals are less than an expected value. If either TP1 or TP2 is greater than the expected value, the DTC is set.
DTC: P1127	**Exhaust Temperature Out of Range, O2 Sensor Tests Not Completed:** The heated oxygen sensor (HO2S) monitor uses an exhaust temperature model to determine when the HO2S heaters are cycled ON. The test fails when the inferred exhaust temperature is below a minimum calibrated value.
DTC: P1145	**Calculated Torque Error:** This DTC indicates the engine was overproducing torque and overcharging the traction battery, when its operating temperature was below the calibrated threshold. To protect the traction battery the powertrain control module (PCM) disabled the fuel injectors.
DTC: P115E	**Throttle Actuator Control (TAC) Throttle Body Air Flow Trim at Max Limit:** During idle, the powertrain control module (PCM) monitors the throttle angle and air flow. If the air flow is determined to be less than expected, the PCM adjusts the throttle angle to compensate. The air flow reduction is typically the result of engine deposit buildup around the throttle plate. This DTC indicates the PCM has reached the maximum allowed compensation and is no longer able to compensate for the buildup.
DTC: P117A	**Engine Oil Over Temperature — Forced Limited Power:** Indicates the engine oil protection strategy is enabled when the engine oil temperature reaches a predetermined level in the powertrain control module (PCM). The PCM then limits the engine RPMs until the engine oil temperature returns to normal.
DTC: P1184	**Engine Oil Temperature (EOT) Sensor Out of Self-Test Range:** Indicates the EOT sensor signal was out of self-test range.
DTC: P1227	**Wastegate Failed Closed (Over pressure):** Indicates that boost pressure is continuously higher than desired.
DTC: P1228	**Wastegate Failed Open (Under pressure):** Indicates that boost pressure is continuously lower than desired.
DTC: P1229	**Charge Air Cooler (CAC) Pump Driver:** This DTC sets when the powertrain control module (PCM) commands the supercharger CAC pump to operate but no current is detected.
DTC: P1233	**Fuel Pump Driver Module Disabled or Off Line:** The powertrain control module (PCM) monitors the fuel pump monitor (FPM) circuit from the fuel pump driver module (FPDM). With the ignition ON, engine OFF or ignition ON, engine running the FPDM continuously sends a duty cycle signal to the PCM through the FPM circuit. The test fails if the PCM stops receiving the duty cycle signal.
DTC: P1234	**Fuel Pump Driver Module Disabled or Off Line:** The powertrain control module (PCM) monitors the fuel pump monitor 2 (FPM2) circuit from the fuel pump driver module 2 (FPDM2). With the ignition ON, engine OFF or ignition ON, engine running the FPDM2 continuously sends a duty cycle signal to the PCM through the FPM2 circuit. The test fails if the PCM stops receiving the duty cycle signal.
DTC: P1235	**Fuel Pump Control Out Of Range:** This DTC indicates the fuel pump driver module (FPDM) detected an invalid or missing fuel pump (FP) duty cycle signal on the fuel pump control (FPC) circuit from the powertrain control module (PCM). The FPDM sends a message to the PCM through the fuel pump monitor (FPM) circuit, indicating this concern was detected. The PCM sets the DTC when the message is received.

DTC	Trouble Code Title, Conditions, Possible Causes
DTC: P1236	**Fuel Pump Control Out Of Range:** This DTC indicates the fuel pump driver module 2 (FPDM2) detected an invalid or missing fuel pump (FP) duty cycle signal on the fuel pump control (FPC) circuit from the powertrain control module (PCM). The FPDM2 sends a message to the PCM through the fuel pump monitor 2 (FPM2) circuit, indicating this concern was detected. The PCM sets the DTC when the message is received.
DTC: P1237	**Fuel Pump Secondary Circuit:** This DTC indicates the fuel pump driver module (FPDM) detected a fuel pump secondary circuit concern. The FPDM sends a message to the powertrain control module (PCM) through the fuel pump monitor (FPM) circuit indicating this concern was detected. The PCM sets the DTC when the message is received.
DTC: P1238	**Fuel Pump Secondary Circuit:** This DTC indicates the fuel pump driver module (FPDM2) detected a fuel pump secondary circuit concern. The FPDM2 sends a message to the powertrain control module (PCM) through the fuel pump monitor (FPM2) circuit, indicating this concern was detected. The PCM sets the DTC when the message is received.
DTC: P1244	**Alternator Load High Input:** The Powertrain Control Module (PCM) monitors generator load from the generator/regulator in the form of frequency. The concern indicates the input is higher than the load should be in normal operation. The load input could be high when a battery short to ground exists.
DTC: P1245	**Alternator Load High Low:** The Powertrain Control Module (PCM) monitors generator load from the generator/regulator in the form of frequency. The concern indicates the input is lower than the load should be in normal operation. The load input could be low when no generator output exists.
DTC: P1246	**Alternator Load Circuit Impute:** The Powertrain Control Module (PCM) monitors the generator load from the generator/regulator in the form of frequency. The frequency range is determined by the temperature of the voltage regulator, where 97% indicates a full load, and less than 6% indicates no load.
DTC: P1260	**Theft Detected, Vehicle Immobilized:** This DTC can be set if the passive anti-theft system (PATS) has determined a theft, condition existed and the engine is disabled or an engine start was attempted using a non-PATS key. This DTC is a good indicator to check the PATS for DTCs. The DTC can also be set when a new instrument cluster (IC), instrument panel cluster (IPC) or powertrain control module (PCM) is installed without correctly programming either module even if the vehicle is not equipped with PATS.
DTC: P1270	**Engine RPM or Vehicle Speed Limiter Reached:** Indicates the vehicle has been operated in a manner, which caused the engine or vehicle to exceed a calibration limit. The engine RPM and vehicle speed are continuously monitored and evaluated by the powertrain control module (PCM). The DTC is set when the RPM or vehicle speed falls out of a calibrated range. For additional information on the engine RPM/vehicle speed limiter, refer to Section 1, Powertrain Control Software.
DTC: P1285	**Cylinder Head Over Temperature Condition:** Indicates an engine overheat condition was sensed by the cylinder head temperature (CHT) sensor.
DTC: P1288	**Cylinder Head Temperature (CHT) Sensor Out of Self-Test Range:** Indicates the CHT sensor is out of self-test range. The engine is not at a normal operating temperature.
DTC: P1289	**Cylinder Head Temperature (CHT) Sensor Circuit High:** Indicates a CHT sensor circuit open.
DTC: P128A	**Cylinder Head Temperature (CHT) Sensor Circuit Intermittent/Erratic:** Indicates the CHT circuit became intermittently open or short while the engine was running.
DTC: P1290	**Cylinder Head Temperature (CHT) Sensor Circuit Low:** Indicates a CHT sensor circuit short to ground.
DTC: P1299	**Cylinder Head Over Temperature Protection Active:** Indicates an engine overheat condition was detected by the cylinder head temperature (CHT) sensor. A failure mode effects management (FMEM) strategy called fail-safe cooling was activated to cool the engine.
DTC: P130D	**Engine Knock/Combustion Performance - Forced Limited Power:** The powertrain control module (PCM) continuously monitors the knock system for concerns. This DTC sets when the PCM detects that the knock sensor (KS) voltage has exceeded a maximum value greater than a calibrated number of times within a set time period.
DTC: P1336	**Crankshaft/Camshaft Sensor Range/Performance:** The input signal to the powertrain control module (PCM) from the crankshaft position (CKP) sensor or the camshaft position (CMP) sensor is erratic.

DTC	Trouble Code Title, Conditions, Possible Causes
DTC: P1397	**System Voltage Out Of Self -Test Range:** This DTC indicates that the 12-volt system voltage is too high or too low during the key on engine off (KOEO) or key on engine running (KOER) self-test. It sets if the system voltage falls below or exceeds the calibrated threshold at any time during the KOEO or KOER self-test.
DTC: P1405	**Differential Pressure Feedback Sensor Upstream Hose Off or Plugged:** While driving, the exhaust gas recirculation (EGR) monitor commands the EGR valve closed and checks the differential pressure across the EGR orifice. The test fails when the signal from the differential pressure feedback EGR sensor indicates EGR flow is in the negative direction.
DTC: P1406	**Differential Pressure Feedback Sensor Downstream Hose Off or Plugged:** While driving, the exhaust gas recirculation (EGR) monitor commands the EGR valve closed and checks the differential pressure across the EGR orifice. The test fails when the signal from the differential pressure feedback EGR sensor continues to indicate EGR flow even after the EGR valve is commanded closed.
DTC: P1408	**Exhaust Gas Recirculation (EGR) Flow Out Of Self-Test Range:** This test is carried out during the key on engine running (KOER) on demand self-test only. The EGR system is commanded on at a fixed engine speed. The test does not pass and the DTC is set when the measured EGR flow falls above or below the required calibration.
DTC: P1409	**Exhaust Gas Recirculation (EGR) Vacuum Regulator Solenoid Circuit:** This test checks the electrical function of the EGR vacuum regulator solenoid. The test fails when the EVR circuit voltage is either too high or too low when compared to the expected voltage range. The EGR system must be enabled for the test to be completed.
DTC: P144A	**Evaporative Emission System Purge Vapor Line Restricted/Blocked:** The powertrain control module (PCM) monitors the evaporative emission (EVAP) system for a blocked fuel vapor tube between the fuel tank pressure (FTP) sensor and the fuel tank. During the initial phase of the EVAP monitor, the PCM closes the canister vent and a vacuum develops in the fuel vapor tubes and lines and in the fuel tank. The PCM monitors the FTP sensor to determine the amount of vacuum and how quickly the vacuum increases. The rate at which the vacuum increases is compared to an expected value. If the vacuum increases quicker than expected, a blocked fuel vapor tube is suspected and an intrusive test is carried out in the final phase of the EVAP monitor. If the intrusive test confirms a blockage a counter is incremented and once the counter reaches a calibrated number of completions, the DTC is set.
DTC: P144C	**Evaporative Emission System Purge Check Valve Performance:** The powertrain control module (PCM) tests the EVAP canister purge check valve for a stuck open condition. The EVAP canister purge check valve test is performed during minimal boost conditions, once per drive cycle, when entry conditions are met. This DTC sets if the fuel tank pressure exceeds a calibrated amount within a specified amount of time during the test.
DTC: P1450	**Unable to Bleed Up Fuel Tank Vacuum:** Monitors the fuel vapor vacuum and pressure in the fuel tank. System failure occurs when the evaporative emission (EVAP) running loss monitor detects excessive fuel tank vacuum with the engine running, but not at idle.
DTC: P1451	**Evaporative Emission System Vent Control Circuit:** Monitors the EVAP canister vent solenoid circuit for an electrical failure. The test fails when the signal moves outside the minimum or maximum allowable calibrated parameters for a specified EVAP canister vent duty cycle by powertrain control module (PCM) command.
DTC: P145E	**PCV Heater Control B Circuit:** This DTC sets when the powertrain control module (PCM) detects the actual PCVHF circuit voltage is less than or greater than the desired voltage.
DTC: P1474	**Fan Control Primary Circuit:** Monitors the low fan control (LFC) primary circuit output from the powertrain control module (PCM). The test fails if the PCM grounds the LFC circuit, excessive current draw is detected on the LFC circuit or with the LFC circuit not grounded by the PCM, and voltage is not detected on the LFC circuit (the PCM expects to detect VPWR voltage coming through the low speed FC relay coil to the LFC circuit).
DTC: P1479	**High Fan Control Primary Circuit:** Monitors the high fan control (HFC) primary circuit output from the powertrain control module (PCM). The test fails if the HFC output commanded on (grounded), excessive current draw is detected on the HFC circuit or, with the HFC circuit commanded off, voltage is not detected on the HFC circuit (the PCM expects to detect VPWR voltage through the high speed FC relay coil to the HFC circuit).
DTC: P1489	**PCV Heater Control Circuit:** This DTC sets when the powertrain control module (PCM) detects that the actual PCVHC circuit voltage is less than or greater than the desired voltage.
DTC: P1500	**Vehicle Speed Sensor (VSS):** Indicates the VSS input signal was intermittent. This DTC sets when a VSS concern interferes with other on-board diagnostics (OBD) tests, such as the catalyst efficiency monitor, the EVAP monitor or the HO2S monitor.

DTC	Trouble Code Title, Conditions, Possible Causes
DTC: P1501	**Vehicle Speed Sensor (VSS) Out of Self-Test Range:** Indicates the VSS input signal is out of self-test range. If the PCM detects a VSS input signal, any time during the self-test, the DTC P1501 sets and the test aborts.
DTC: P1502	**Vehicle Speed Sensor (VSS) Intermittent:** Indicates the powertrain control module (PCM) detected an error in the vehicle speed information. Vehicle speed data is received from either the VSS, transfer case speed sensor (TCSS) or anti-lock brake system (ABS) control module. This DTC sets the same way as P0500. However, it is intended to flash the transmission control indicator lamp (TCIL) for first time VSS circuit error.
DTC: P1504	**Idle Air Control (IAC) Circuit:** This DTC sets when the powertrain control module (PCM) detects an electrical load failure on the IAC output circuit.
DTC: P1506	**Idle Air Control (IAC) Overspeed Error:** This DTC sets when the powertrain control module (PCM) detects an engine idle speed that is greater than the desired RPM.
DTC: P1507	**Idle Air Control (IAC) Underspeed Error:** This DTC sets when the powertrain control module (PCM) detects an engine idle speed that is less than the desired RPM.
DTC: P1548	**Engine Air Filter Restriction:** The powertrain control module (PCM) monitors the manifold absolute pressure at various engine speeds during wide open throttle (WOT) operation, and compares the information to a calibrated value. This DTC sets if the airflow is out of range.
DTC: P1550	**Power Steering Pressure (PSP) Sensor Out of Self-Test Range:** The PSP sensor input signal to the powertrain control module (PCM) is continuously monitored. The test fails when the signal falls out of a maximum or minimum calibrated range.
DTC: P1561	**Brake Line Pressure Sensor Circuit:** If a short to voltage or an open condition exists on any of the 3 circuits or if the transducer is indicating high pressure for more than 5 seconds while the Brake Pedal Position (BPP) switch (also known as the stop lamp switch) is indicating no brake application, DTC P1561 will be set.
DTC: P1572	**Brake Pedal Switch Circuit:** Indicates the brake input rationality test for brake pedal position (BPP) and brake pressure switch (BPS) has detected a concern. One or both inputs to the powertrain control module (PCM) did not change state when expected. On some vehicles with stability assist, the BPP switch is connected to the anti-lock brake system (ABS) control module and the ABS generates a driver brake application signal, which is then sent to the PCM.
DTC: P1575	**Pedal Position Out Of Self Test Range:** During key on engine off (KOEO) self-test, the powertrain control module (PCM) monitors the accelerator pedal position (APP) sensor inputs to determine if the APP1 and APP2 signals are less than an expected value. If either APP1 or APP2 is greater than the expected value, the DTC is set.
DTC: P1588	**Throttle Control Detected Loss Of Return Spring:** The powertrain control module (PCM) tests the electronic throttle for the ability of the throttle plate to return to the default (limp home) position from both the open and closed positions. This DTC sets if the throttle does not return to the default (limp home) position.
DTC: P160A	**Control Module Vehicle Options Reconfiguration Error:** Indicates a powertrain control module (PCM) vehicle reconfiguration error.
DTC: P161A	**Incorrect Response from Immobilizer Control Module:** The BCM ID received by the PCM does not match the ID stored in the PCM memory. CARRY OUT a parameter reset. REFER to Passive Anti-Theft System (PATS) Parameter Reset. CLEAR the DTCs. REPEAT the self-test.
DTC: P1633	**Keep Alive Power (KAPWR) Voltage Too Low:** Indicates the KAPWR circuit has experienced a voltage interrupt.
DTC: P1635	**Tire/Axle Ratio Out of Acceptable Range:** This DTC indicates the tire and axle information contained in the vehicle identification (VID) block does not match the vehicle hardware.
DTC: P1636	**Inductive Signature Chip Communication Error:** Indicates the powertrain control module (PCM) has lost communication with the inductive signature chip.
DTC: P1639	**Vehicle ID (VID) Block Corrupted, Not Programmed:** This DTC indicates the VID block is not programmed or the information within is corrupt.
DTC: P163E	**TCM programming error:** The TCM has detected an invalid checksum. Default to 1st or 3rd gear Maximum line pressure

DTC	Trouble Code Title, Conditions, Possible Causes
DTC: P1640	**Powertrain DTCs Available in Another Module:** Vehicles using a secondary engine control module can request that the powertrain control module (PCM) illuminate the malfunction indicator lamp (MIL) when a failure occurs which affects emissions.
DTC: P1646	**Linear O2 Sensor Control Chip (Bank 1):** The powertrain control module (PCM) monitors the application-specific integrated circuit that controls and monitors the heated oxygen sensor (HO2S). The test fails when the PCM detects an internal circuit or communication concern.
DTC: P1647	**Linear O2 Sensor Control Chip (Bank 2):** The powertrain control module (PCM) monitors the application-specific integrated circuit that controls and monitors the heated oxygen sensor (HO2S). The test fails when the PCM detects an internal circuit or communication concern.
DTC: P164A	**O2 Sensor Positive Current Trim Circuit Performance (Bank 1 Sensor 1):** A resistor is installed in the universal heated oxygen sensor (HO2S) connector for part to part variance. The powertrain control module (PCM) determines the value of this resistor by taking multiple measurements of the resistor during each key on event. The PCM uses this value in order to compensate for the variance in the pumping current signal. The test fails if the PCM receives an inconsistent or erratic measurement of the resistor.
DTC: P164B	**O2 Sensor Positive Current Trim Circuit Performance (Bank 2 Sensor 1):** A resistor is installed in the universal heated oxygen sensor (HO2S) connector for part to part variance. The powertrain control module (PCM) determines the value of this resistor by taking multiple measurements of the resistor during each ignition ON event. The PCM uses this value to compensate for the variance in the pumping current signal. The test fails if the PCM receives an inconsistent or erratic measurement of the resistor.
DTC: P1650	**Power Steering Pressure (PSP) Switch Out of Self-Test Range:** In the key on engine off (KOEO) self-test, this DTC indicates the PSP input to the powertrain control module (PCM) is high. In the key on engine running (KOER) self-test, this DTC indicates the PSP input did not change state.
DTC: P1674	**Control Module Software Corrupted:** Indicates an error occurred in the powertrain control module (PCM). This DTC sets in combination with P2105.
DTC: P1700	**Transmission indeterminate failure:** Internal component failure. Direct One-Way Clutch (OWC) failure. Failure Mode Effects Management becomes active — engine rpm limited to 4,000 rpm. Failed a neutral condition in 1st, 3rd or 4th gear in automatic Mode. Only 2nd and 5th gear available.
DTC: P1702	**Transmission Range Sensor Circuit Failure:** * Increased control pressure causes harsh shifts* Transmission defaults to Drive
DTC: P1703	**Brake Switch Out of Self-Test Range:** Indicates that during the key on engine off (KOEO) self-test, the brake pedal position (BPP) signal was high, or during the key on engine running (KOER) self-test, the BPP signal did not cycle high and low.
DTC: P1704	**TR Sensor not in P or N positions during KOEO / KOER :** TR sensor or transmission selector lever cable incorrectly adjusted or TR circuit failure.
DTC: P1705	**Transmission Range Sensor Out of Self-Test Range:** Key on, KOEO Self Test enabled, and the PCM detected it did not receive a Transmission Range (TR) sensor signal in Park or Neutral position. **NOTE: Verify the gear selector is in PARK/NEUTRAL.**
DTC: P1709	**Park/Neutral Position (PNP) Switch Out of Self-Test Range:** This DTC indicates that the voltage is high when it should be low. Refer to Automatic Transmission/Transaxle Section.
DTC: P1710	**Transmission Stuck in Midrange:** * Occasional hard shifts* PCM does not detect a change in fluid temperature
DTC: P1711	**TFT Sensor Out of Self-Test Range:** Key on, KOER Self Test enabled; or engine running with the KOER Self Test enabled, and the PCM detected the Transmission Fluid Temperature (TFT) sensor was more than or less than the calibrated range (25°F to 240°F) during the self-test.
DTC: P1713	**TFT Sensor No Activity or TFT Sensor Circuit Low Input:** Engine started, VSS over 1 mph, and the PCM did not detect any change in the TFT low range circuit during the self-test.
DTC: P1714	**Transmission Control System Malfunction:** Engine started, VSS over 1 mph, and the PCM did not detect any change in the TFT low range circuit during the self-test.
DTC: P1715	**Transmission Control System Malfunction:** Engine started, VSS over 1 mph, and the PCM detected a mechanical problem in the Shift Solenoid 'B' (SSB) during the test.
DTC: P1716	**Transmission Control System Malfunction:** Engine started, VSS over 1 mph, and the PCM detected a problem in the Transmission Control system during the self-test.

DTC	Trouble Code Title, Conditions, Possible Causes
DTC: P1717	**Transmission Control System Malfunction:** Engine started, VSS over 1 mph, and the PCM detected a problem in the Transmission Control system during the self-test.
DTC: P1718	**TFT Sensor No Activity Or TFT Sensor Circuit High Input:** Engine started, VSS over 1 mph, and the PCM did not detect any change in the TFT high range circuit during the self-test.
DTC: P1729	**4x4L Switch:** The 4x4L switch is an on/off switch. If the powertrain control module (PCM) does not sense appropriate voltage when the switch is cycled on and off, a DTC sets for mechanical shift on the fly (MSOF) systems.
DTC: P1740	**Torque Converter Clutch (TCC) Solenoid Mechanical Malfunction:** Engine started, vehicle speed more than 20 mph, and the PCM detected that TCC lockup did not occur (the lockup event is inferred from other inputs).
DTC: P1744	**Torque Converter Clutch (TCC) System Mechanically Stuck In Off Position:** Engine started, vehicle in gear at Cruise speed, and the PCM detected the Torque Converter Clutch system had failed with the TCC in the mechanically "off" position.
DTC: P1780	**Transmission Control Switch (TCS) Out of Self-Test Range:** During key on engine running (KOER) self-test, the TCS must be cycled, or a DTC is set.
DTC: P1781	**4x4L Switch Out of Self-Test Range:** The 4x4L switch is an on/off switch. If the powertrain control module (PCM) does not sense low voltage when the switch is on, the DTC sets.
DTC: P1783	**Transmission Over-Temperature Malfunction:** Engine started, engine runtime more than 5 minutes, vehicle in gear at Cruise speed, and the PCM detected the TFT sensor signal was more than 300°F during the CCM test period.
DTC: P1793	**Ignition Supply Malfunction:** The powertrain control module (PCM) monitors the ignition switch position run (ISP-R) circuit. This DTC sets if the voltage drops below 7 volts or rises above 16 volts.
DTC: P181F	**Clutch Control System Performance:** AWD operation may be limited
DTC: P1824	**4 Wheel Drive (4WD) Clutch Relay Circuit Failure:** The 4X4 control module detects a short to ground on the Active Torque Coupling (ATC) solenoid feedback circuit
DTC: P1825	**4 Wheel Drive (4WD) Clutch Relay Open Circuit:** The 4X4 control module detects an open or short to ground on the ATC solenoid command or feedback circuit for more than 2 seconds
DTC: P187B	**Tire/Axle Out of Acceptable Range:** -The PCM detects an inappropriate size mini spare or road wheels/tires (greater than 7% difference in size across the front and rear axle or greater than 14% difference in size at one wheel on either the front or rear axle) installed.-AWD Disabled or-AWD Limited Functionality
DTC: P188B	**All Wheel Drive (AWD) Clutch Control Circuit:** When the AWD relay module detects an open, a short to power or ground on the ATC solenoid voltage supply and or return circuit, this DTC is set and the AWD relay module shuts off current to the ATC solenoid.
DTC: P188C	**All Wheel Drive (AWD) Relay Module Communication Circuit:** The PCM detects an open, a short to ground or voltage on the command circuit. The AWD operation may be disabled.
DTC: P188D	**All Wheel Drive (AWD) Relay Module Feedback Circuit:** - The PCM detects an open, a short to ground or voltage on the feedback circuit- The AWD relay module may not allow All-Wheel Drive (AWD) operation.
DTC: P1900	**Output Shaft Speed (OSS) Sensor Circuit Intermittent:** The OSS sensor signal to the powertrain control module (PCM) is irregular or interrupted.
DTC: P1901	**Turbine Shaft Speed (TSS) Sensor Circuit Intermittent:** The TSS sensor signal to the powertrain control module (PCM) is irregular or interrupted.
DTC: P1910	**Reverse Lamp Control Circuit/Open:** Engine started, vehicle in reverse, and the PCM detected no backup lamps. Backup lamp driver control circuit failed.
DTC: P1921	**Transmission Range Signal:** The transaxle control module (TCM) continuously monitors the controller area network (CAN) for a transmission range message from the powertrain control module (PCM). This DTC sets when the received message does not match the actual transmission range.

OBD II Trouble Code List (P2xxx Codes)

DTC	Trouble Code Title, Conditions, Possible Causes
DTC: P2004	**Intake Manifold Runner Control (IMRC) Stuck Open (Bank 1):** This DTC sets when the IMRC is commanded closed, but the IMRC monitor indicates open.
DTC: P2005	**Intake Manifold Runner Control (IMRC) Stuck Open (Bank 2):** This DTC sets when the IMRC is commanded closed, but the IMRC monitor indicates open.
DTC: P2006	**Intake Manifold Runner Control (IMRC) Stuck Closed (Bank 1):** This DTC sets when the IMRC is commanded open, but the IMRC monitor indicates closed.
DTC: P2007	**Intake Manifold Runner Control (IMRC) Stuck Closed (Bank 2):** This DTC sets when the IMRC is commanded open, but the IMRC monitor indicates closed.
DTC: P2008	**Intake Manifold Runner Control (IMRC) Circuit Open (Bank 1):** This DTC indicates a failure in the IMRC primary control circuit.
DTC: P2014	**Intake Manifold Runner Position Sensor/Switch Circuit (Bank 1):** The intake manifold runner control (IMRC) system is monitored for failure during continuous or key on engine off (KOEO) self-test. Each DTC distinguishes the corresponding bank for IMRC actuator assemblies with dual monitor switches. The test fails when the signal on the monitor pin is outside an expected calibrated range.
DTC: P2015	**Intake Manifold Runner Position Sensor/Switch Circuit Range/Performance (Bank 1):** The intake manifold runner control (IMRC) system is monitored for failures. Each DTC distinguishes the corresponding bank. The test fails when the system detects the presence of a broken or persistently out of range linkage.
DTC: P2020	**Intake Manifold Runner Position Sensor/Switch Circuit Range/Performance (Bank 2):** The intake manifold runner control (IMRC) system is monitored for failures. Each DTC distinguishes the corresponding bank. The test fails when the system detects the presence of a broken or persistently out of range linkage.
DTC: P2025	**Evaporative Emissions Fuel Vapor Temperature Sensor Circuit Performance:** The powertrain control module (PCM) monitors the natural vacuum leak detection (NVLD) module input for expected NVLD ambient temperature sensor values. This DTC sets when the input is outside a calibrated set of limits.
DTC: P2026	**Evaporative Emissions Fuel Vapor Temperature Sensor Circuit Low Voltage:** The powertrain control module (PCM) monitors the natural vacuum leak detection (NVLD) module input for expected NVLD ambient temperature sensor values. This DTC sets when the input is outside a calibrated set of limits.
DTC: P2027	**Evaporative Emissions Fuel Vapor Temperature Sensor Circuit High Voltage:** The powertrain control module (PCM) monitors the natural vacuum leak detection (NVLD) module input for expected NVLD ambient temperature sensor values. This DTC sets when the input is outside a calibrated set of limits.
DTC: P2065	**Fuel Level Sensor B Circuit:** Fuel level information is sent to the powertrain control module (PCM) on the communication link.
DTC: P2066	**Fuel Level Sensor B Circuit Range/Performance:** Fuel level information is sent to the powertrain control module (PCM) on the communication link.
DTC: P2067	**Fuel Level Sensor B Circuit Low:** Fuel level information is sent to the powertrain control module (PCM) on the communication link.
DTC: P2068	**Fuel Level Sensor B Circuit High:** Fuel level information is sent to the powertrain control module (PCM) on the communication link.
DTC: P2070	**Intake Manifold Tuning Valve (IMTV) Stuck Open Bank 1:** The IMTV system is monitored for failure during continuous, key on engine off (KOEO), or key on engine running (KOER) self-tests. The test fails when the signal is more or less than an expected calibrated range.
DTC: P2071	**Intake Manifold Tuning Valve (IMTV) Stuck Closed Bank 1:** The IMTV system is monitored for failure during continuous, key on engine off (KOEO), or key on engine running (KOER) self-tests. The test fails when the signal is more or less than an expected calibrated range.
DTC: P2072	**Throttle Actuator Control (TAC) System - Ice Breakage:** This DTC only identifies that the strategy has carried out several open and close cycles to remove potential ice build up. This DTC does not imply any system concerns, only that the mode has occurred, and that mode may be causing a long start time.
DTC: P2088	**A Camshaft Position Actuator Control Circuit Low Bank 1:** The powertrain control module (PCM) monitors the variable camshaft timing (VCT) circuit for high and low voltage. The test fails if the voltage exceeds a calibrated limit for a calibrated amount of time.

DTC	Trouble Code Title, Conditions, Possible Causes
DTC: P2089	**A Camshaft Position Actuator Control Circuit High Bank 1:** The powertrain control module (PCM) monitors the variable camshaft timing (VCT) circuit for high and low voltage. The test fails if the voltage exceeds a calibrated limit for a calibrated amount of time.
DTC: P2090	**B Camshaft Position Actuator Control Circuit Low Bank 1:** The powertrain control module (PCM) monitors the variable camshaft timing (VCT) circuit for high and low voltage. The test fails if the voltage exceeds a calibrated limit for a calibrated amount of time.
DTC: P2091	**B Camshaft Position Actuator Control Circuit High Bank 1:** The powertrain control module (PCM) monitors the variable camshaft timing (VCT) circuit for high and low voltage. The test fails if the voltage exceeds a calibrated limit for a calibrated amount of time.
DTC: P2096	**Post Catalyst Fuel Trim System Too Lean Bank 1:** The powertrain control module (PCM) monitors the correction value from downstream heated oxygen sensor (HO2S) as part of the fore-aft oxygen sensor control routine. The test fails when the correction value is greater than a calibrated limit.
DTC: P2097	**Post Catalyst Fuel Trim System Too Rich Bank 1:** The powertrain control module (PCM) monitors the correction value from downstream heated oxygen sensor (HO2S) as part of the fore-aft oxygen sensor control routine. The test fails when the correction value is greater than a calibrated limit.
DTC: P2098	**Post Catalyst Fuel Trim System Too Lean Bank 2:** The powertrain control module (PCM) monitors the correction value from downstream heated oxygen sensor (HO2S) as part of the fore-aft oxygen sensor control routine. The test fails when the correction value is greater than a calibrated limit.
DTC: P2099	**Post Catalyst Fuel Trim System Too Rich Bank 2:** The powertrain control module (PCM) monitors the correction value from downstream heated oxygen sensor (HO2S) as part of the fore-aft oxygen sensor control routine. The test fails when the correction value is greater than a calibrated limit.
DTC: P2100	**Throttle Actuator Control (TAC) Motor Circuit/Open:** A powertrain control module (PCM) fault flag is set indicating the motor circuit is open. May require cycling the ignition.
DTC: P2101	**Throttle Actuator Control (TAC) Motor Range/Performance:** A powertrain control module (PCM) fault flag is set indicating the motor circuit is open, and may require cycling the ignition.
DTC: P2104	**Throttle Actuator Control (TAC) System - Forced Idle:** The TAC system is in the failure mode effects management (FMEM) mode of forced idle.
DTC: P2105	**Throttle Actuator Control (TAC) System - Forced Engine Shutdown:** The TAC system is in the failure mode effects management (FMEM) mode of forced engine shutdown.
DTC: P2107	**Throttle Actuator Control (TAC) Module Processor:** The electronic throttle control (ETC) area of the powertrain control module (PCM) failed the self-test. The concern could be the result of an incorrect throttle position (TP) command, or TAC motor wires shorted together.
DTC: P2109	**Throttle/Pedal Position Sensor A Minimum Stop Performance:** The powertrain control module (PCM) monitors the electronic throttle for the ability of the throttle plate to reach the lower mechanical stop position within a calibrated amount of time at ignition ON. This DTC sets if the throttle plate does not reach the lower mechanical stop position within a calibrated amount of time.
DTC: P2110	**Throttle Actuator Control (TAC) System - Forced Limited RPM:** The TAC system is in the failure mode effects management (FMEM) mode of forced limited RPM.
DTC: P2111	**Throttle Actuator Control (TAC) System - Stuck Open:** This powertrain control module (PCM) fault status indicates the throttle plate is at a greater angle than commanded.
DTC: P2112	**Throttle Actuator Control (TAC) System - Stuck Closed:** This powertrain control module (PCM) fault status indicates the throttle plate is at a lower angle than commanded.
DTC: P2118	**Throttle Actuator A Control Motor Current Range/Performance:** The powertrain control module (PCM) monitors the electronic throttle control (ETC) operation for a high current condition. This DTC sets if the current necessary to operate the throttle actuator control (TAC) motor is higher than a calibrated limit.
DTC: P2119	**Throttle Actuator A Control Throttle Body Range/Performance:** This powertrain control module (PCM) fault status indicates the throttle plate is at an angle other than commanded.
DTC: P2121	**Throttle/Pedal Position Sensor/Switch D Circuit Range/Performance:** The accelerator pedal position (APP) sensor fault flag is set for sensor 1 by the powertrain control module (PCM), indicating the signal is out of the normal self-test operating range.
DTC: P2122	**Throttle/Pedal Position Sensor/Switch D Circuit Low:** The accelerator pedal position (APP) sensor 1 is out of self-test range low.

DTC	Trouble Code Title, Conditions, Possible Causes
DTC: P2123	**Throttle/Pedal Position Sensor/Switch D Circuit High:** The accelerator pedal position (APP) sensor 1 is out of self-test range high.
DTC: P2126	**Throttle/Pedal Position Sensor/Switch E Circuit Range/Performance:** The accelerator pedal position (APP) sensor fault flag is set for sensor 2 by the powertrain control module (PCM), indicating the signal is out of the normal self-test operating range.
DTC: P2127	**Throttle/Pedal Position Sensor/Switch E Circuit Low:** The accelerator pedal position (APP) sensor 2 is out of self-test range low.
DTC: P2128	**Throttle/Pedal Position Sensor/Switch E Circuit High:** The accelerator pedal position (APP) sensor 2 is out of self-test range high.
DTC: P2131	**Throttle/Pedal Position Sensor/Switch F Circuit Range/Performance:** The accelerator pedal position (APP) sensor fault flag is set for sensor 3 by the powertrain control module (PCM), indicating the signal is out of the normal self-test operating range.
DTC: P2132	**Throttle/Pedal Position Sensor/Switch F Circuit Low:** The accelerator pedal position (APP) sensor 3 is out of self-test range low.
DTC: P2133	**Throttle/Pedal Position Sensor/Switch F Circuit High:** The accelerator pedal position (APP) sensor 3 is out of self-test range high.
DTC: P2135	**Throttle/Pedal Position Sensor/Switch A/B Voltage Correlation:** The powertrain control module (PCM) flagged a concern indicating that throttle position (TP) voltage PIDs TP1 and TP2 disagree by greater than a calibrated limit.
DTC: P2138	**Throttle/Pedal Position Sensor/Switch D/E Voltage Correlation:** The powertrain control module (PCM) monitors the accelerator pedal position (APP) sensor for a concern. The PCM compares the accelerator pedal position information from the APP sensor inputs, APP1 and APP2. The DTC sets if the APP sensor inputs APP1 and APP2 disagree on the position of the accelerator pedal by greater than an expected value.
DTC: P2163	**Throttle/Pedal Position Sensor A Maximum Stop Performance:** The powertrain control module (PCM) monitors the electronic throttle for the ability of the throttle plate to reach the upper mechanical stop position within a calibrated amount of time at ignition ON. This DTC sets if the throttle plate does not reach the upper mechanical stop position within a calibrated amount of time.
DTC: P2176	**Throttle Actuator A Control System - Idle Position Not Learned:** The electronic throttle control (ETC) system of the powertrain control module (PCM) detected a concern. This DTC sets if the PCM is unable to learn the calibrated throttle positions.
DTC: P2195	**O2 Sensor Signal Biased/Stuck Lean - Bank 1, Sensor 1:** A heated oxygen sensor (HO2S) indicating lean at the end of a test is trying to correct for an over-rich condition. The test fails when the fuel control system no longer detects switching for a calibrated amount of time.
DTC: P2196	**O2 Sensor Signal Biased/Stuck Rich - Bank 1, Sensor 1:** A heated oxygen sensor (HO2S) indicating rich at the end of a test is trying to correct for an over-lean condition. The test fails when the fuel control system no longer detects switching for a calibrated amount of time.
DTC: P2197	**O2 Sensor Signal Biased/Stuck Lean - Bank 2, Sensor 1:** A heated oxygen sensor (HO2S) indicating lean at the end of a test is trying to correct for an over-rich condition. The test fails when the fuel control system no longer detects switching for a calibrated amount of time.
DTC: P2198	**O2 Sensor Signal Biased/Stuck Rich - Bank 2, Sensor 1:** A heated oxygen sensor (HO2S) indicating rich at the end of a test is trying to correct for an over-lean condition. The test fails when the fuel control system no longer detects switching for a calibrated amount of time.
DTC: P219A	**Bank 1 Air/Fuel Ratio Imbalance:** The air fuel imbalance monitor is designed to detect differences in the air fuel ratio between cylinders per engine bank. The test fails if the air fuel ratio difference per cylinder is greater than a calculated amount.
DTC: P219B	**Bank 2 Air/Fuel Ratio Imbalance:** The air fuel imbalance monitor is designed to detect differences in the air fuel ratio between cylinders per engine bank. The test fails if the air fuel ratio difference per cylinder is greater than a calculated amount.
DTC: P2227	**Barometric Pressure Sensor A Circuit Range/Performance** The powertrain control module (PCM) continuously monitors this sensor for concerns. The test fails when the barometric pressure (BARO) PID does not correlate with the throttle intake pressure (TIP) or the manifold absolute pressure (MAP) PIDs at ignition ON. This DTC sets when the PCM detects an out of range condition in the control circuit.

DTC	Trouble Code Title, Conditions, Possible Causes
DTC: P2228	**Barometric Pressure Sensor A Circuit Low:** Checks whether the BARO reading is abnormally low, indicating an extreme high altitude.
DTC: P2229	**Barometric Pressure Sensor A Circuit High:** Checks whether the BARO reading is abnormally high, indicating an extreme low altitude.
DTC: P2237	**O2 Sensor Positive Current Control Circuit Open - Bank 1, Sensor 1:** The powertrain control module (PCM) monitors the universal heated oxygen sensor (HO2S) for a circuit concern. This DTC sets when the PCM detects a concern with the circuit used to determine the oxygen content in the exhaust gas.
DTC: P2240	**O2 Sensor Positive Current Control Circuit Open - Bank 2, Sensor 1:** The powertrain control module (PCM) monitors the universal heated oxygen sensor (HO2S) for a circuit concern. This DTC sets when the PCM detects a concern with the circuit used to determine the oxygen content in the exhaust gas.
DTC: P2243	**O2 Sensor Reference Voltage Circuit Open - Bank 1, Sensor 1:** The powertrain control module (PCM) monitors the universal heated oxygen sensor (HO2S) for a circuit concern. This DTC sets when the PCM detects a concern with the circuit used to determine the oxygen content in the exhaust gas.
DTC: P2247	**O2 Sensor Reference Voltage Circuit Open - Bank 2, Sensor 1:** The powertrain control module (PCM) monitors the universal heated oxygen sensor (HO2S) for a circuit concern. This DTC sets when the PCM detects a concern with the circuit used to determine the oxygen content in the exhaust gas.
DTC: P2251	**O2 Sensor Negative Current Control Circuit Open - Bank 1, Sensor 1:** The powertrain control module (PCM) monitors the universal heated oxygen sensor (HO2S) for a circuit concern. This DTC sets when the PCM detects a concern with the circuit used to determine the oxygen content in the exhaust gas.
DTC: P2254	**O2 Sensor Negative Current Control Circuit Open - Bank 2, Sensor 1:** The powertrain control module (PCM) monitors the universal heated oxygen sensor (HO2S) for a circuit concern. This DTC sets when the PCM detects a concern with the circuit used to determine the oxygen content in the exhaust gas.
DTC: P2270	**O2 Sensor Signal Stuck Lean - Bank 1, Sensor 2:** The downstream heated oxygen sensor (HO2S) is forced rich and lean and monitored by the powertrain control module (PCM). The test fails if the PCM does not detect the output of the HO2S in a calibrated amount of time.
DTC: P2271	**O2 Sensor Signal Stuck Rich - Bank 1, Sensor 2:** The downstream heated oxygen sensor (HO2S) is forced rich and lean and monitored by the powertrain control module (PCM). The test fails if the PCM does not detect the output of the HO2S in a calibrated amount of time.
DTC: P2272	**O2 Sensor Signal Stuck Lean - Bank 2, Sensor 2:** The downstream heated oxygen sensor (HO2S) is forced rich and lean and monitored by the powertrain control module (PCM). The test fails if the PCM does not detect the output of the HO2S in a calibrated amount of time.
DTC: P2273	**O2 Sensor Signal Stuck Rich - Bank 2, Sensor 2:** The downstream heated oxygen sensor (HO2S) is forced rich and lean and monitored by the powertrain control module (PCM). The test fails if the PCM does not detect the output of the HO2S in a calibrated amount of time.
DTC: P2279	**Intake Air System Leak:** This DTC indicates the engine was overproducing torque and overcharging the traction battery when its operating temperature was within normal range. To protect the traction battery the powertrain control module (PCM) disabled the fuel injectors.
DTC: P2282	**Air Leak Between Throttle Body and Intake Valve:** This DTC sets when the powertrain control module (PCM) detects an air leak that exceeds a predetermined limit for greater than 5 seconds. If the air flow entering the engine exceeds the air flow through the throttle, a leak is detected and this diagnostic fails.
DTC: P2297	**O2 Sensor Out of Range During Deceleration (Bank 1, Sensor 1):** During a deceleration fuel shut-off (DFSO) event, the powertrain control module (PCM) monitors how quickly the rear heated oxygen sensor (HO2S) switches from rich to lean. The measured rate of the rich to lean switch is compared to a calibrated threshold value. The threshold value takes into account the level of oxygen in the catalyst, which has an impact on how quickly the rich to lean switch occurs. The test fails when the measured value is slower than the threshold value.
DTC: P2300	**Ignition Coil A Primary Control Circuit Low:** The powertrain control module (PCM) continuously monitors the ignition system for concerns. This DTC sets when the PCM detects a short to ground in the circuit.
DTC: P2301	**Ignition Coil A Primary Control Circuit High:** The powertrain control module (PCM) continuously monitors the ignition system for concerns. This DTC sets when the PCM detects a short to voltage in the circuit.
DTC: P2303	**Ignition Coil B Primary Control Circuit Low:** The powertrain control module (PCM) continuously monitors the ignition system for concerns. This DTC sets when the PCM detects a short to ground in the circuit.

DTC	Trouble Code Title, Conditions, Possible Causes
DTC: P2304	**Ignition Coil B Primary Control Circuit High:** The powertrain control module (PCM) continuously monitors the ignition system for concerns. This DTC sets when the PCM detects a short to voltage in the circuit.
DTC: P2306	**Ignition Coil C Primary Control Circuit Low:** The powertrain control module (PCM) continuously monitors the ignition system for concerns. This DTC sets when the PCM detects a short to ground in the circuit.
DTC: P2307	**Ignition Coil C Primary Control Circuit High:** The powertrain control module (PCM) continuously monitors the ignition system for concerns. This DTC sets when the PCM detects a short to voltage in the circuit.
DTC: P2309	**Ignition Coil D Primary Control Circuit Low:** The powertrain control module (PCM) continuously monitors the ignition system for concerns. This DTC sets when the PCM detects a short to ground in the circuit.
DTC: P2310	**Ignition Coil D Primary Control Circuit High:** The powertrain control module (PCM) continuously monitors the ignition system for concerns. This DTC sets when the PCM detects a short to voltage in the circuit.
DTC: P2312	**Ignition Coil E Primary Control Circuit Low:** The powertrain control module (PCM) continuously monitors the ignition system for concerns. This DTC sets when the PCM detects a short to ground in the circuit.
DTC: P2313	**Ignition Coil E Primary Control Circuit High:** The powertrain control module (PCM) continuously monitors the ignition system for concerns. This DTC sets when the PCM detects a short to voltage in the circuit.
DTC: P2315	**Ignition Coil F Primary Control Circuit Low:** The powertrain control module (PCM) continuously monitors the ignition system for concerns. This DTC sets when the PCM detects a short to ground in the circuit.
DTC: P2316	**Ignition Coil F Primary Control Circuit High:** The powertrain control module (PCM) continuously monitors the ignition system for concerns. This DTC sets when the PCM detects a short to voltage in the circuit.
DTC: P2418	**Evaporative Emission Control System Switching Valve Control Circuit/Open:** The powertrain control module (PCM) monitors the state of the fuel vapor vent valve circuit output driver. The test fails when the signal moves outside the minimum or maximum limit for the commanded state.
DTC: P2450	**Evaporative Emission Control System Switching Valve Performance or Stuck Open:** The powertrain control module (PCM) monitors the fuel vapor vent valve for correct operation. During the evaporative emission (EVAP) monitor cruise test after verifying a 1.02 mm (0.040 inch) leak is not present, the PCM commands the fuel vapor vent valve closed while a vacuum is present in the fuel tank and opens the canister vent. If the fuel vapor vent does not close, the vacuum in the tank is quickly lost. If the rate of loss exceeds a calibrated threshold, the DTC is set.
DTC: P2510	**ECM / PCM Power Relay Sense Circuit Range/Performance:** The powertrain control module (PCM) monitors the voltage on the ignition switch position run (ISP-R) and the fuel injector power monitor (INJPWRM) circuits. This DTC sets when the voltage on the ISP-R and the INJPWRM circuit voltages do not correspond for a calibrated period of time.
DTC: P2531	**Ignition Switch Run Position Circuit Low:** The PCM carries out a logic check on the ISP-R and ISP-R/S circuits. When the powertrain control module (PCM) detects the ISP-R circuit low when it is expected to be high, this DTC sets.
DTC: P2533	**Ignition Switch Run/Start Position Circuit:** The powertrain control module (PCM) carries out a logic check on the ISP-R and ISP-R/S circuits. The PCM sets this DTC when a concern is detected.
DTC: P2535	**Ignition Switch Run/Start Position Circuit High:** The powertrain control module (PCM) carries out a logic check on the ISP-R and ISP-R/S circuits. If the ISP-R/S circuit stays high longer than a calibrated amount of time, or is high when the PCM when it is expected to be low, this DTC sets.
DTC: P260F	**Evaporative System Monitoring Processor Performance:** This DTC sets when a concern is detected internal to the powertrain control module (PCM). The microprocessor that controls the engine off natural vacuum (EONV) leak check monitor is separate from the main processor within the PCM.
DTC: P2610	**Electronic Control Module (ECM)/Powertrain Control Module (PCM) Internal Engine Off Timer Performance:** Indicates an error in the internal PCM engine off timer processor. The test fails when the difference between the engine off time and the central processing unit (CPU) time exceeds a calibrated limit for a calibrated amount of time.

DTC	Trouble Code Title, Conditions, Possible Causes
DTC: P2626	**O2 Sensor Positive Current Trim Circuit/Open (Bank 1 Sensor 1):** During deceleration fuel shut-off (DFSO) the powertrain control module (PCM) monitors the integrity of the universal heated oxygen sensor (HO2S) UO2SPCT circuit by comparing the actual oxygen sensor voltage signal to an expected oxygen sensor voltage signal. The test fails when the actual oxygen sensor voltage exceeds the maximum expected voltage threshold for a specified amount of time.
DTC: P2627	**O2 Sensor Pumping Current Trim Circuit Low Bank 1, Sensor 1:** A resistor is installed in the universal heated oxygen sensor (HO2S) connector for part to part variance. The powertrain control module (PCM) determines the value of this resistor by taking multiple measurements of the resistor during each key on event. The PCM uses this value in order to compensate for the variance in the pumping current signal. The test fails if the PCM determines the resistance value is too high.
DTC: P2628	**O2 Sensor Positive Current Trim Circuit High (Bank 1 Sensor 1):** The powertrain control module (PCM) monitors the universal heated oxygen sensor (HO2S) for a circuit concern. This DTC sets when the PCM detects a concern with the circuit used to determine the oxygen content in the exhaust gas.
DTC: P2629	**O2 Sensor Positive Current Trim Circuit/Open (Bank 2 Sensor 1):** During deceleration fuel shut-off (DFSO) the powertrain control module (PCM) monitors the integrity of the universal heated oxygen sensor (HO2S) UO2SPCT circuit by comparing the actual oxygen sensor voltage signal to an expected oxygen sensor voltage signal. The test fails when the actual oxygen sensor voltage exceeds the maximum expected voltage threshold for a specified amount of time.
DTC: P2630	**O2 Sensor Pumping Current Trim Circuit Low Bank 2, Sensor 1:** A resistor is installed in the universal heated oxygen sensor (HO2S) connector for part to part variance. The powertrain control module (PCM) determines the value of this resistor by taking multiple measurements of the resistor during each key on event. The PCM uses this value in order to compensate for the variance in the pumping current signal. The test fails if the PCM determines the resistance value is too high.
DTC: P2631	**O2 Sensor Positive Current Trim Circuit High (Bank 2 Sensor 1):** The powertrain control module (PCM) monitors the universal heated oxygen sensor (HO2S) for a circuit concern. This DTC sets when the PCM detects a concern with the circuit used to determine the oxygen content in the exhaust gas.
DTC: P2632	**Fuel Pump B Control Circuit/Open:** The fuel pump control module 2 monitors the fuel pump assembly and secondary circuits for a concern. If the fuel pump control module 2 detects a concern with the fuel pump assembly or secondary circuits, the fuel pump control module 2 sends an 80% duty cycle signal on the fuel pump monitor 2 (FPM2) circuit to report the concern to the powertrain control module (PCM). The test fails when the fuel pump control module 2 is still reporting a concern with the fuel pump assembly or secondary circuits after a calibrated amount of time.
DTC: P2700	**Transmission Forward Clutch Performance:** * Wrench (TCIL) light is illuminated
DTC: P2701	**Transmission Direct Clutch Performance:** * Wrench (TCIL) light is illuminated
DTC: P2702	**Transmission Intermediate Clutch Performance:** * Wrench (TCIL) light is illuminated
DTC: P2703	**Transmission Low/Reverse Clutch Performance:** * No engine braking in 1st gear* Erratic shifting as the diagnostics isolates the fault to low/reverse clutch failed off.* Delayed or no reverse engagement.
DTC: P2704	**Transmission Overdrive Clutch Performance:** * Overdrive clutch failed off
DTC: P2705	**Transmission One Way Clutch (OWC) Failed:** * Neutral conditions when 1st gear is commanded.* Erratic shifting as the diagnostic isolates the cause of the neutral condition to the OWC being failed.* Poor launch performance (due to 2nd gear drive away).* Harsh engagements.
DTC: P2758	**TCC pressure control solenoid stuck on:** The PCM commanded TCC off but TCC did not release. (mechanical error)Wrench light illuminated. Engine stalls or is lugging. DTC P1744 may set
DTC: P2760	**TCC Pressure Control Solenoid Intermittent:** * Poor launch performance (due to 5th gear drive away).* No TCC apply.* No shifts.
DTC: P2783	**Torque Converter Temperature Too High:** * Torque converter temperature too high.* Erratic shifts, vehicle disengages at a stop while in drive or low, early TCC apply.* Test will run in 3rd gear or higher when valve 2 is in the latched position, pointing SSD at overdrive clutch when the TCC is commanded open. SSE is turned on, if the control valve is stuck, this will cause the TCC to apply even though the TCC solenoid is off.

DTC	Trouble Code Title, Conditions, Possible Causes
DTC: P2800	**Transmission Range Sensor B Circuit (PRNDL Input):** The powertrain control module (PCM) checks the gear selector position by monitoring two independent voltage signals from the transmission range (TR) sensor. The TR voltages are then compared to an allowed voltage range for each gear. The test fails when the compared voltages are out of range. This DTC indicates that one TR signal is more than one band away from the majority.
DTC: P2801	**Transmission Range Sensor B Circuit Range/Performance:** The powertrain control module (PCM) checks the gear selector position by monitoring two independent voltage signals from the transmission range (TR) sensor. The TR voltages are then compared to an allowed voltage range for each gear. The test fails when the compared voltages are out of range. This DTC indicates that two or more TR signals are low or high.
DTC: P2802	**Transmission Range Sensor B Circuit Low:** The powertrain control module (PCM) checks the gear selector position by monitoring three independent voltage signals from the transmission range (TR) sensor. The TR voltages are then compared to an allowed voltage range for each gear. The test fails when the compared voltages are out of range. This DTC indicates that one TR signal is low.
DTC: P2803	**Transmission Range Sensor B Circuit High:** The powertrain control module (PCM) checks the gear selector position by monitoring two independent voltage signals from the transmission range (TR) sensor. The TR voltages are then compared to an allowed voltage range for each gear. The test fails when the compared voltages are out of range. This DTC indicates that one TR signal is high.
DTC: P2805	**Transmission Range Sensor A/B Correlation:** The powertrain control module (PCM) checks the gear selector position by monitoring two independent voltage signals from the transmission range (TR) sensor. The TR voltages are then compared to an allowed voltage range for each gear. The test fails when the compared voltages are out of range. This DTC indicates that all two TR sensors disagree but are still within range.
DTC: P2806	**Transmission Range Sensor Alignment:** The transaxle control module (TCM) monitors vehicle speed and gear position. This DTC indicates that vehicle speed exceeded the maximum calibrated speed in PARK.
DTC: P2A01	**O2 Circuit Range / Performance Bank 1, Sensor 2:** The powertrain control module (PCM) monitors the heated oxygen sensor (HO2S) for an out of range low voltage concern. This DTC sets if the HO2S voltage is out of range low for a calibrated period of time.
DTC: P2A04	**O2 Circuit Range / Performance Bank 2, Sensor 2:** The powertrain control module (PCM) monitors the heated oxygen sensor (HO2S) for an out of range low voltage concern. This DTC sets if the HO2S voltage is out of range low for a calibrated period of time.

OBD II Trouble Code List (Uxxxx Codes)

DTC	Trouble Code Title, Conditions, Possible Causes
DTC: U0001	**High Speed CAN Communication Bus:** The module could not communicate on the network at a point in time. Diagnose the High Speed Controller Area Network (HS-CAN) bus. The ABS module communicates with the scan tool through the High Speed Controller Area Network (HS-CAN). Circuits (W/L) (HS-CAN +) and (W) (HS-CAN -) provide the network connection to the ABS module. The ABS module shares the HS-CAN network with the PCM, the 4X4 module, the Instrument Cluster (IC), the Restraints Module (RCM), the Power Steering Module (PSCM) and the Occupant Classification Sensor Module (OCSM). Voltage for the ABS module is provided by circuits (GY), (R) and (Y/R). Ground is provided by circuit (B/G).
DTC: U0073	**Control Module Communication Bus A Off:** This DTC is set when the controller area network (CAN) between the powertrain control module (PCM) and data link connector (DLC) is open.
DTC: U0100	**Lost Communication With Electronic Control Module (ECM)/Powertrain Control Module (PCM) A:** The transaxle control module (TCM) continuously monitors controller area network (CAN) for messages from the powertrain control module (PCM). This DTC sets when TCM stops receiving PCM messages for a set amount of time.
DTC: U0101	**Lost Communication With Transaxle Control Module (TCM):** The powertrain control module (PCM) continuously monitors controller area network (CAN) for messages from the TCM. This DTC sets when the PCM does not receive the TCM message within the defined amount of time.
DTC: U0109	**Lost Communication With Fuel Pump Control Module:** The powertrain control module (PCM) monitors the fuel pump monitor (FPM) circuit for the presence of a duty cycled signal. If the FPM circuit is fixed at a low or high voltage, the PCM begins to increment a counter. The test fails when the PCM is still not detecting a duty cycled signal on the FPM circuit after a calibrated amount of time.
DTC: U0111	**Lost Communication With Battery Energy Control Module A:** The transaxle control module (TCM) continuously monitors controller area network (CAN) for messages from the traction battery control module (TBCM). This DTC sets when TCM stops receiving TBCM messages for a set amount of time.

DTC	Trouble Code Title, Conditions, Possible Causes
DTC: U0120	**Lost Communication With Starter/Generator Control Module:** The powertrain control module (PCM) continuously monitors controller area network (CAN) for messages from the Starter/Generator Control Module. This DTC sets when the PCM does not receive the message within the defined amount of time.
DTC: U0121	**Lost Communication With Anti-lock Brake System (ABS) Control Module:** The powertrain control module (PCM) continuously monitors the controller area network (CAN) for messages from the ABS. This DTC sets when the PCM fails to receive the ABS message within the defined amount of time.
DTC: U0129	**Lost Communications with Brake System Control Module:** The powertrain control module (PCM) continuously monitors the controller area network (CAN) for messages from the anti-lock brake system (ABS). This DTC sets when the PCM does not receive the ABS message within the defined amount of time. When this DTC is set, the regenerative braking is disabled until the next driving cycle.
DTC: U0140	**Lost Communication With Body Control Module:** The powertrain control module (PCM) continuously monitors controller area network (CAN) for messages from body control module (BCM). This DTC sets when the PCM does not receive the BCM message within the defined amount of time.
DTC: U0155	**Lost Communication With Instrument Panel Cluster Control Module:** The powertrain control module (PCM) continuously monitors the controller area network (CAN) for messages from the instrument panel cluster. This DTC sets when the PCM does not receive the instrument panel cluster message within the defined amount of time.
DTC: U016C	**Lost Communication With Fuel Pump Control Module B:** The powertrain control module (PCM) monitors the fuel pump monitor 2 (FPM2) circuit for the presence of a duty cycled signal. If the FPM2 circuit is fixed at a low or high voltage, the PCM begins to increment a counter. The test fails when the PCM is still not detecting a duty cycled signal on the FPM2 circuit after a calibrated amount of time.
DTC: U0294	**Lost Communication With Powertrain Control Monitor Module:** The transaxle control module (TCM) continuously monitors the controller area network (CAN) for messages from the powertrain control module (PCM) quizzer. This DTC is set when the TCM stops receiving the PCM messages for a set amount of time.
DTC: U029F	**Lost Communication with Evaporative Emission System Leak Detection Control Module:** Network DTC concerns occur during module-to-module communication.
DTC: U0300	**Internal Control Module Software Incompatibility:** This DTC indicates there are incompatible software levels within the powertrain control module (PCM) that control the electronic throttle control (ETC) monitor system. The ETC monitor system uses multiple microprocessors within the PCM, each having its own software level and function. The microprocessors must have the correct level of software in order to communicate and function together.
DTC: U0402	**Invalid Data Received From TCM:** Network DTC concerns occur during module-to-module communication.
DTC: U0412	**Invalid Data Received From BECM A:** The transmission control module (TCM) continuously monitors the controller area network (CAN) for messages from the battery energy control module (BECM). This DTC is set when the message received from the BECM is out of expected range or contains invalid data.
DTC: U0415	**Invalid Data Received From ABS Control Module:** Network DTC concerns occur during module-to-module communication.
DTC: U0418	**Invalid Data Received From Brake System Control Module:** The powertrain control module (PCM) continuously monitors controller area network (CAN) for messages from the anti-lock brake system (ABS) module. This DTC sets when the PCM does not receive the ABS message within a defined time period, or when the message received is out of expected range, or if the message received contains invalid data. When this DTC is set, the regenerative braking is disabled until the next driving cycle.
DTC: U0422	**Invalid Data Received From Body Control Module:** Network DTC concerns occur during module-to-module communication.
DTC: U0423	**Invalid Data Received From IPC:** Network DTC concerns occur during module-to-module communication.
DTC: U0469	**Invalid Data Received From Starter / Generator Control Module:** Network DTC concerns occur during module-to-module communication.
DTC: U05A0	**Invalid Data Received from Evaporative Emission System Leak Detection Control Module:** Network DTC concerns occur during module-to-module communication.

DTC	Trouble Code Title, Conditions, Possible Causes
DTC: U1039	**SCP (J1850) Invalid or Missing Data for Vehicle Speed:** Network DTC(s) occur during module-to-module communication concerns. Two types of network concerns can be categorized: Invalid data network a concern - data is transferred within the normal inter-module message, but contains known invalid data. The transmitting module logs a DTC related to the invalid data concern. Missing message network concerns - missing message concerns are logged by the module upon failure to receive a message from another module within a defined retry period.
DTC: U210B	**Lost Communication Between Fuel Pump Control Module and Restraints Control Module:** The fuel pump control module monitors the duty cycle and frequency of the signal it receives from the restraints control module (RCM). The fuel pump control module determines if the signal on the event notification signal (ENS) circuit from the RCM is a valid duty cycle and frequency. If the duty cycle or frequency is invalid, the fuel pump control module sends a 40% duty cycle signal on the fuel pump monitor (FPM) circuit to report the concern to the powertrain control module (PCM). The test fails when the fuel pump control module is still reporting that it is receiving an invalid duty cycle or frequency from the RCM after a calibrated amount of time.
DTC: U210C	**Lost Communication Between Fuel Pump Control Module B and Restraints Control Module:** The fuel pump control module 2 monitors the duty cycle and frequency of the signal it receives from the restraints control module (RCM). The fuel pump control module 2 determines if the signal on the event notification signal (ENS) circuit from the RCM is a valid duty cycle and frequency. If the duty cycle or frequency is invalid, the fuel pump control module 2 sends a 40% duty cycle signal on the fuel pump monitor 2 (FPM2) circuit to report the concern to the PCM. The test fails when the fuel pump control module 2 is still reporting that it is receiving an invalid duty cycle or frequency from the RCM after a calibrated amount of time.
DTC: U300C	**Ignition Input Off/On/Start:** The powertrain control module (PCM) monitors the ignition key state. This DTC sets when the key state is not available.

GLOSSARY

ABS: Anti-lock braking system. An electro-mechanical braking system which is designed to minimize or prevent wheel lock-up during braking.

ABSOLUTE PRESSURE: Atmospheric (barometric) pressure plus the pressure gauge reading.

ACCELERATOR PUMP: A small pump located in the carburetor that feeds fuel into the air/fuel mixture during acceleration.

ACCUMULATOR: A device that controls shift quality by cushioning the shock of hydraulic oil pressure being applied to a clutch or band.

ACTUATING MECHANISM: The mechanical output devices of a hydraulic system, for example, clutch pistons and band servos.

ACTUATOR: The output component of a hydraulic or electronic system.

ADVANCE: Setting the ignition timing so that spark occurs earlier before the piston reaches top dead center (TDC).

ADAPTIVE MEMORY (ADAPTIVE STRATEGY): The learning ability of the TCM or PCM to redefine its decision-making process to provide optimum shift quality.

AFTER TOP DEAD CENTER (ATDC): The point after the piston reaches the top of its travel on the compression stroke.

AIR BAG: Device on the inside of the car designed to inflate on impact of crash, protecting the occupants of the car.

AIR CHARGE TEMPERATURE (ACT) SENSOR: The temperature of the airflow into the engine is measured by an ACT sensor, usually located in the lower intake manifold or air cleaner.

AIR CLEANER: An assembly consisting of a housing, filter and any connecting ductwork. The filter element is made up of a porous paper, sometimes with a wire mesh screening, and is designed to prevent airborne particles from entering the engine through the carburetor or throttle body.

AIR INJECTION: One method of reducing harmful exhaust emissions by injecting air into each of the exhaust ports of an engine. The fresh air entering the hot exhaust manifold causes any remaining fuel to be burned before it can exit the tailpipe.

AIR PUMP: An emission control device that supplies fresh air to the exhaust manifold to aid in more completely burning exhaust gases.

AIR/FUEL RATIO: The ratio of air-to-gasoline by weight in the fuel mixture drawn into the engine.

ALDL (assembly line diagnostic link): Electrical connector for scanning ECM/PCM/TCM input and output devices.

ALIGNMENT RACK: A special drive-on vehicle lift apparatus/measuring device used to adjust a vehicle's toe, caster and camber angles.

ALL WHEEL DRIVE: Term used to describe a full time four wheel drive system or any other vehicle drive system that continuously delivers power to all four wheels. This system is found primarily on station wagon vehicles and SUVs not utilized for significant off road use.

ALTERNATING CURRENT (AC): Electric current that flows first in one direction, then in the opposite direction, continually reversing flow.

ALTERNATOR: A device which produces AC (alternating current) which is converted to DC (direct current) to charge the car battery.

AMMETER: An instrument, calibrated in amperes, used to measure the flow of an electrical current in a circuit. Ammeters are always connected in series with the circuit being tested.

AMPERAGE: The total amount of current (amperes) flowing in a circuit.

AMPLIFIER: A device used in an electrical circuit to increase the voltage of an output signal.

AMP/HR. RATING (BATTERY): Measurement of the ability of a battery to deliver a stated amount of current for a stated period of time. The higher the amp/hr. rating, the better the battery.

AMPERE: The rate of flow of electrical current present when one volt of electrical pressure is applied against one ohm of electrical resistance.

ANALOG COMPUTER: Any microprocessor that uses similar (analogous) electrical signals to make its calculations.

ANODIZED: A special coating applied to the surface of aluminum valves for extended service life.

ANTIFREEZE: A substance (ethylene or propylene glycol) added to the coolant to prevent freezing in cold weather.

ANTI-FOAM AGENTS: Minimize fluid foaming from the whipping action encountered in the converter and planetary action.

ANTI-WEAR AGENTS: Zinc agents that control wear on the gears, bushings, and thrust washers.

ANTI-LOCK BRAKING SYSTEM: A supplementary system to the base hydraulic system that prevents sustained lock-up of the wheels during braking as well as automatically controlling wheel slip.

ANTI-ROLL BAR: See stabilizer bar.

ARC: A flow of electricity through the air between two electrodes or contact points that produces a spark.

ARMATURE: A laminated, soft iron core wrapped by a wire that converts electrical energy to mechanical energy as in a motor or relay. When rotated in a magnetic field, it changes mechanical energy into electrical energy as in a generator.

ATDC: After Top Dead Center.

ATF: Automatic transmission fluid.

ATMOSPHERIC PRESSURE: The pressure on the Earth's surface caused by the weight of the air in the atmosphere. At sea level, this pressure is 14.7 psi at 32°F (101 kPa at 0°C).

ATOMIZATION: The breaking down of a liquid into a fine mist that can be suspended in air.

AUXILIARY ADD-ON COOLER: A supplemental transmission fluid cooling device that is installed in series with the heat exchanger (cooler), located inside the radiator, to provide additional support to cool the hot fluid leaving the torque converter.

AUXILIARY PRESSURE: An added fluid pressure that is introduced into a regulator or balanced valve system to control valve movement. The auxiliary pressure itself can be either a fixed or a variable value. (See balanced valve; regulator valve.)

AWD: All wheel drive.

AXIAL FORCE: A side or end thrust force acting in or along the same plane as the power flow.

AXIAL PLAY: Movement parallel to a shaft or bearing bore.

AXLE CAPACITY: The maximum load-carrying capacity of the axle itself, as specified by the manufacturer. This is usually a higher number than the GAWR.

AXLE RATIO: This is a number (3.07:1, 4.56:1, for example) expressing the ratio between driveshaft revolutions and wheel revolutions. A low numerical ratio allows the engine to work easier because it doesn't have to turn as fast. A high numerical ratio means that the engine has to turn more rpm's to move the wheels through the same number of turns.

BACKFIRE: The sudden combustion of gases in the intake or exhaust system that results in a loud explosion.

BACKLASH: The clearance or play between two parts, such as meshed gears.

BACKPRESSURE: Restrictions in the exhaust system that slow the exit of exhaust gases from the combustion chamber.

BAKELITE®: A heat resistant, plastic insulator material commonly used in printed circuit boards and transistorized components.

BALANCED VALVE: A valve that is positioned by opposing auxiliary hydraulic pressures and/or spring force. Examples include mainline regulator, throttle, and governor valves. (See regulator valve.)

BAND: A flexible ring of steel with an inner lining of friction material. When tightened around the outside of a drum, a planetary member is held stationary to the transmission/transaxle case.

BALL BEARING: A bearing made up of hardened inner and outer races between which hardened steel balls roll.

BALL JOINT: A ball and matching socket connecting suspension components (steering knuckle to lower control arms). It permits rotating movement in any direction between the components that are joined.

BARO (BAROMETRIC PRESSURE SENSOR): Measures the change in the intake manifold pressure caused by changes in altitude.

BAROMETRIC MANIFOLD ABSOLUTE PRESSURE (BMAP) SENSOR: Operates similarly to a conventional MAP sensor; reads intake manifold pressure and is also responsible for determining altitude and barometric pressure prior to engine operation.

BAROMETRIC PRESSURE: (See atmospheric pressure.)

BALLAST RESISTOR: A resistor in the primary ignition circuit that lowers voltage after the engine is started to reduce wear on ignition components.

BATTERY: A direct current electrical storage unit, consisting of the basic active materials of lead and sulfuric acid, which converts chemical energy into electrical energy. Used to provide current for the operation of the starter as well as other equipment, such as the radio, lighting, etc.

BEAD: The portion of a tire that holds it on the rim.

BEARING: A friction reducing, supportive device usually located between a stationary part and a moving part.

BEFORE TOP DEAD CENTER (BTDC): The point just before the piston reaches the top of its travel on the compression stroke.

BELTED TIRE: Tire construction similar to bias-ply tires, but using two or more layers of reinforced belts between body plies and the tread.

BEZEL: Piece of metal surrounding radio, headlights, gauges or similar components; sometimes used to hold the glass face of a gauge in the dash.

BIAS-PLY TIRE: Tire construction, using body ply reinforcing cords which run at alternating angles to the center line of the tread.

BI-METAL TEMPERATURE SENSOR: Any sensor or switch made of two dissimilar types of metal that bend when heated or cooled due to the different expansion rates of the alloys. These types of sensors usually function as an on/off switch.

BLOCK: See Engine Block.

BLOW-BY: Combustion gases, composed of water vapor and unburned fuel, that leak past the piston rings into the crankcase during normal engine operation. These gases are removed by the PCV system to prevent the buildup of harmful acids in the crankcase.

BOOK TIME: See Labor Time.

BOOK VALUE: The average value of a car, widely used to determine trade-in and resale value.

BOOST VALVE: Used at the base of the regulator valve to increase mainline pressure.

BORE: Diameter of a cylinder.

BRAKE CALIPER: The housing that fits over the brake disc. The caliper holds the brake pads, which are pressed against the discs by the caliper pistons when the brake pedal is depressed.

BRAKE HORSEPOWER (BHP): The actual horsepower available at the engine flywheel as measured by a dynamometer.

BRAKE FADE: Loss of braking power, usually caused by excessive heat after repeated brake applications.

BRAKE HORSEPOWER: Usable horsepower of an engine measured at the crankshaft.

BRAKE PAD: A brake shoe and lining assembly used with disc brakes.

BRAKE PROPORTIONING VALVE: A valve on the master cylinder which restricts hydraulic brake pressure to the wheels to a specified amount, preventing wheel lock-up.

BREAKAWAY: Often used by Chrysler to identify first-gear operation in D and 2 ranges. In these ranges, first-gear operation depends on a one-way roller clutch that holds on acceleration and releases (breaks away) on deceleration, resulting in a freewheeling coast-down condition.

BRAKE SHOE: The backing for the brake lining. The term is, however, usually applied to the assembly of the brake backing and lining.

BREAKER POINTS: A set of points inside the distributor, operated by a cam, which make and break the ignition circuit.

BRINNELLING: A wear pattern identified by a series of indentations at regular intervals. This condition is caused by a lack of lube, overload situations, and/or vibrations.

BTDC: Before Top Dead Center.

BUMP: Sudden and forceful apply of a clutch or band.

BUSHING: A liner, usually removable, for a bearing; an anti-friction liner used in place of a bearing.

CALIFORNIA ENGINE: An engine certified by the EPA for use in California only; conforms to more stringent emission regulations than Federal engine.

CALIPER: A hydraulically activated device in a disc brake system, which is mounted straddling the brake rotor (disc). The caliper contains at least one piston and two brake pads. Hydraulic pressure on the piston(s) forces the pads against the rotor.

CAPACITY: The quantity of electricity that can be delivered from a unit, as from a battery in ampere-hours, or output, as from a generator.

CAMBER: One of the factors of wheel alignment. Viewed from the front of the car, it is the inward or outward tilt of the wheel. The top of the tire will lean outward (positive camber) or inward (negative camber).

CAMSHAFT: A shaft in the engine on which are the lobes (cams) which operate the valves. The camshaft is driven by the crankshaft, via a belt, chain or gears, at one half the crankshaft speed.

CAPACITOR: A device which stores an electrical charge.

CARBON MONOXIDE (CO): A colorless, odorless gas given off as a normal byproduct of combustion. It is poisonous and extremely dangerous in confined areas, building up slowly to toxic levels without warning if adequate ventilation is not available.

CARBURETOR: A device, usually mounted on the intake manifold of an engine, which mixes the air and fuel in the proper proportion to allow even combustion.

CASTER: The forward or rearward tilt of an imaginary line drawn through the upper ball joint and the center of the wheel. Viewed from the sides, positive caster (forward tilt) lends directional stability, while negative caster (rearward tilt) produces instability.

CATALYTIC CONVERTER: A device installed in the exhaust system, like a muffler, that converts harmful byproducts of combustion into carbon dioxide and water vapor by means of a heat-producing chemical reaction.

CENTRIFUGAL ADVANCE: A mechanical method of advancing the spark timing by using flyweights in the distributor that react to centrifugal force generated by the distributor shaft rotation.

CENTRIFUGAL FORCE: The outward pull of a revolving object, away from the center of revolution. Centrifugal force increases with the speed of rotation.

CETANE RATING: A measure of the ignition value of diesel fuel. The higher the cetane rating, the better the fuel. Diesel fuel cetane rating is roughly comparable to gasoline octane rating.

CHECK VALVE: Any one-way valve installed to permit the flow of air, fuel or vacuum in one direction only.

CHOKE: The valve/plate that restricts the amount of air entering an engine on the induction stroke, thereby enriching the air/fuel ratio.

CHUGGLE: Bucking or jerking condition that may be engine related and may be most noticeable when converter clutch is engaged; similar to the feel of towing a trailer.

CIRCLIP: A split steel snapring that fits into a groove to hold various parts in place.

CIRCUIT BREAKER: A switch which protects an electrical circuit from overload by opening the circuit when the current flow exceeds a pre-determined level. Some circuit breakers must be reset manually, while most reset automatically.

CIRCUIT: Any unbroken path through which an electrical current can flow. Also used to describe fuel flow in some instances.

CIRCUIT, BYPASS: Another circuit in parallel with the major circuit through which power is diverted.

CIRCUIT, CLOSED: An electrical circuit in which there is no interruption of current flow.

CIRCUIT, GROUND: The non-insulated portion of a complete circuit used as a common potential point. In automotive circuits, the ground is composed of metal parts, such as the engine, body sheet metal, and frame and is usually a negative potential.

CIRCUIT, HOT: That portion of a circuit not at ground potential. The hot circuit is usually insulated and is connected to the positive side of the battery.

CIRCUIT, OPEN: A break or lack of contact in an electrical circuit, either intentional (switch) or unintentional (bad connection or broken wire).

CIRCUIT, PARALLEL: A circuit having two or more paths for current flow with common positive and negative tie points. The same voltage is applied to each load device or parallel branch.

CIRCUIT, SERIES: An electrical system in which separate parts are connected end to end, using one wire, to form a single path for current to flow.

CIRCUIT, SHORT: A circuit that is accidentally completed in an electrical path for which it was not intended.

CLAMPING (ISOLATION) DIODES: Diodes positioned in a circuit to prevent self-induction from damaging electronic components.

CLEARCOAT: A transparent layer which, when sprayed over a vehicle's paint job, adds gloss and depth as well as an additional protective coating to the finish.

CLUTCH: Part of the power train used to connect/disconnect power to the rear wheels.

CLUTCH, FLUID: The same as a fluid coupling. A fluid clutch or coupling performs the same function as a friction clutch by utilizing fluid friction and inertia as opposed to solid friction used by a friction clutch. (See fluid coupling.)

CLUTCH, FRICTION: A coupling device that provides a means of smooth and positive engagement and disengagement of engine torque to the vehicle powertrain. Transmission of power through the clutch is accomplished by bringing one or more rotating drive members into contact with complementing driven members.

COAST: Vehicle deceleration caused by engine braking conditions.

COEFFICIENT OF FRICTION: The amount of surface tension between two contacting surfaces; identified by a scientifically calculated number.

COIL: Part of the ignition system that boosts the relatively low voltage supplied by the car's electrical system to the high voltage required to fire the spark plugs.

COMBINATION MANIFOLD: An assembly which includes both the intake and exhaust manifolds in one casting.

COMBINATION VALVE: A device used in some fuel systems that routes fuel vapors to a charcoal storage canister instead of venting them into the atmosphere. The valve relieves fuel tank pressure and allows fresh air into the tank as the fuel level drops to prevent a vapor lock situation.

COMBUSTION CHAMBER: The part of the engine in the cylinder head where combustion takes place.

COMPOUND GEAR: A gear consisting of two or more simple gears with a common shaft.

COMPOUND PLANETARY: A gearset that has more than the three elements found in a simple gearset and is constructed by combining members of two planetary gearsets to create additional gear ratio possibilities.

COMPRESSION CHECK: A test involving removing each spark plug and inserting a gauge. When the engine is cranked, the gauge will record a pressure reading in the individual cylinder. General operating condition can be determined from a compression check.

COMPRESSION RATIO: The ratio of the volume between the piston and cylinder head when the piston is at the bottom of its stroke (bottom dead center) and when the piston is at the top of its stroke (top dead center).

COMPUTER: An electronic control module that correlates input data according to prearranged engineered instructions; used for the management of an actuator system or systems.

CONDENSER: An electrical device which acts to store an electrical charge, preventing voltage surges.

2. A radiator-like device in the air conditioning system in which refrigerant gas condenses into a liquid, giving off heat.

CONDUCTOR: Any material through which an electrical current can be transmitted easily.

CONNECTING ROD: The connecting link between the crankshaft and piston.

CONSTANT VELOCITY JOINT: Type of universal joint in a halfshaft assembly in which the output shaft turns at a constant angular velocity without variation, provided that the speed of the input shaft is constant.

CONTINUITY: Continuous or complete circuit. Can be checked with an ohmmeter.

CONTROL ARM: The upper or lower suspension components which are mounted on the frame and support the ball joints and steering knuckles.

CONVENTIONAL IGNITION: Ignition system which uses breaker points.

CONVERTER: (See torque converter.)

CONVERTER LOCKUP: The switching from hydrodynamic to direct mechanical drive, usually through the application of a friction element called the converter clutch.

COOLANT: Mixture of water and anti-freeze circulated through the engine to carry off heat produced by the engine.

CORROSION INHIBITOR: An inhibitor in ATF that prevents corrosion of bushings, thrust washers, and oil cooler brazed joints.

COUNTERSHAFT: An intermediate shaft which is rotated by a mainshaft and transmits, in turn, that rotation to a working part.

COUPLING PHASE: Occurs when the torque converter is operating at its greatest hydraulic efficiency. The speed differential between the impeller and the turbine is at its minimum. At this point, the stator freewheels, and there is no torque multiplication.

CRANKCASE: The lower part of an engine in which the crankshaft and related parts operate.

CRANKSHAFT: Engine component (connected to pistons by connecting rods) which converts the reciprocating (up and down) motion of pistons to rotary motion used to turn the driveshaft.

CURB WEIGHT: The weight of a vehicle without passengers or payload, but including all fluids (oil, gas, coolant, etc.) and other equipment specified as standard.

CURRENT: The flow (or rate) of electrons moving through a circuit. Current is measured in amperes (amp).

CURRENT FLOW CONVENTIONAL: Current flows through a circuit from the positive terminal of the source to the negative terminal (plus to minus).

CURRENT FLOW, ELECTRON: Current or electrons flow from the negative terminal of the source, through the circuit, to the positive terminal (minus to plus).

CV-JOINT: Constant velocity joint.

CYCLIC VIBRATIONS: The off-center movement of a rotating object that is affected by its initial balance, speed of rotation, and working angles.

CYLINDER BLOCK: See engine block.

CYLINDER HEAD: The detachable portion of the engine, usually fastened to the top of the cylinder block and containing all or most of the combustion chambers. On overhead valve engines, it contains the valves and their operating parts. On overhead cam engines, it contains the camshaft as well.

CYLINDER: In an engine, the round hole in the engine block in which the piston(s) ride.

DATA LINK CONNECTOR (DLC): Current acronym/term applied to the federally mandated, diagnostic junction connector that is used to monitor ECM/PC/TCM inputs, processing strategies, and outputs including diagnostic trouble codes (DTCs).

DEAD CENTER: The extreme top or bottom of the piston stroke.

DECELERATION BUMP: When referring to a torque converter clutch in the applied position, a sudden release of the accelerator pedal causes a forceful reversal of power through the drivetrain (engine braking), just prior to the apply plate actually being released.

DELAYED (LATE OR EXTENDED): Condition where shift is expected but does not occur for a period of time, for example, where clutch or band engagement does not occur as quickly as expected during part throttle or wide open throttle apply of accelerator or when manually downshifting to a lower range.

DETENT: A spring-loaded plunger, pin, ball, or pawl used as a holding device on a ratchet wheel or shaft. In automatic transmissions, a detent mechanism is used for locking the manual valve in place.

DETENT DOWNSHIFT: (See kickdown.)

DETERGENT: An additive in engine oil to improve its operating characteristics.

DETONATION: An unwanted explosion of the air/fuel mixture in the combustion chamber caused by excess heat and compression, advanced timing, or an overly lean mixture. Also referred to as "ping".

DEXRON®: A brand of automatic transmission fluid.

DIAGNOSTIC TROUBLE CODES (DTCs): A digital display from the control module memory that identifies the input, processor, or output device circuit that is related to the powertrain emission/driveability malfunction detected. Diagnostic trouble codes can be read by the MIL to flash any codes or by using a handheld scanner.

DIAPHRAGM: A thin, flexible wall separating two cavities, such as in a vacuum advance unit.

DIESELING: The engine continues to run after the car is shut off; caused by fuel continuing to be burned in the combustion chamber.

DIFFERENTIAL: A geared assembly which allows the transmission of motion between drive axles, giving one axle the ability to rotate faster than the other, as in cornering.

DIFFERENTIAL AREAS: When opposing faces of a spool valve are acted upon by the same pressure but their areas differ in size, the face with the larger area produces the differential force and valve movement. (See spool valve.)

DIFFERENTIAL FORCE: (See differential areas)

DIGITAL READOUT: A display of numbers or a combination of numbers and letters.

DIGITAL VOLT OHMMETER: An electronic diagnostic tool used to measure voltage, ohms and amps as well as several other functions, with the readings displayed on a digital screen in tenths, hundredths and thousandths.

DIODE: An electrical device that will allow current to flow in one direction only.

DIRECT CURRENT (DC): Electrical current that flows in one direction only.

DIRECT DRIVE: The gear ratio is 1:1, with no change occurring in the torque and speed input/output relationship.

DISC BRAKE: A hydraulic braking assembly consisting of a brake disc, or rotor, mounted on an axle shaft, and a caliper assembly containing, usually two brake pads which are activated by hydraulic pressure. The pads are forced against the sides of the disc, creating friction which slows the vehicle.

DISPERSANTS: Suspend dirt and prevent sludge buildup in a liquid, such as engine oil.

DOUBLE BUMP (DOUBLE FEEL): Two sudden and forceful applies of a clutch or band.

DISPLACEMENT: The total volume of air that is displaced by all pistons as the engine turns through one complete revolution.

DISTRIBUTOR: A mechanically driven device on an engine which is responsible for electrically firing the spark plug at a pre-determined point of the piston stroke.

DOHC: Double overhead camshaft.

DOUBLE OVERHEAD CAMSHAFT: The engine utilizes two camshafts mounted in one cylinder head. One camshaft operates the exhaust valves, while the other operates the intake valves.

DOWEL PIN: A pin, inserted in mating holes in two different parts allowing those parts to maintain a fixed relationship.

DRIVELINE: The drive connection between the transmission and the drive wheels.

DRIVE TRAIN: The components that transmit the flow of power from the engine to the wheels. The components include the clutch, transmission, driveshafts (or axle shafts in front wheel drive), U-joints and differential.

DRUM BRAKE: A braking system which consists of two brake shoes and one or two wheel cylinders, mounted on a fixed backing plate, and a brake drum, mounted on an axle, which revolves around the assembly.

DRY CHARGED BATTERY: Battery to which electrolyte is added when the battery is placed in service.

DVOM: Digital volt ohmmeter

DWELL: The rate, measured in degrees of shaft rotation, at which an electrical circuit cycles on and off.

DYNAMIC: An application in which there is rotating or reciprocating motion between the parts.

EARLY: Condition where shift occurs before vehicle has reached proper speed, which tends to labor engine after upshift.

EBCM: See Electronic Control Unit (ECU).

ECM: See Electronic Control Unit (ECU).

ECU: Electronic control unit.

ELECTRODE: Conductor (positive or negative) of electric current.

ELECTROLYSIS: A surface etching or bonding of current conducting transmission/transaxle components that may occur when grounding straps are missing or in poor condition.

ELECTROLYTE: A solution of water and sulfuric acid used to activate the battery. Electrolyte is extremely corrosive.

ELECTROMAGNET: A coil that produces a magnetic field when current flows through its windings.

ELECTROMAGNETIC INDUCTION: A method to create (generate) current flow through the use of magnetism.

ELECTROMAGNETISM: The effects surrounding the relationship between electricity and magnetism.

ELECTROMOTIVE FORCE (EMF): The force or pressure (voltage) that causes current movement in an electrical circuit.

ELECTRONIC CONTROL UNIT: A digital computer that controls engine (and sometimes transmission, brake or other vehicle system) functions based on data received from various sensors. Examples used by some manufacturers include Electronic Brake Control Module (EBCM), Engine Control Module (ECM), Powertrain Control Module (PCM) or Vehicle Control Module (VCM).

ELECTRONIC IGNITION: A system in which the timing and firing of the spark plugs is controlled by an electronic control unit, usually called a module. These systems have no points or condenser.

ELECTRONIC PRESSURE CONTROL (EPC) SOLENOID: A specially designed solenoid containing a spool valve and spring assembly to control fluid mainline pressure. A variable current flow, controlled by the ECM/PCM, varies the internal force of the solenoid on the spool valve and resulting mainline pressure. (See variable force solenoid.)

ELECTRONICS: Miniaturized electrical circuits utilizing semiconductors, solid-state devices, and printed circuits. Electronic circuits utilize small amounts of power.

ELECTRONIFICATION: The application of electronic circuitry to a mechanical device. Regarding automatic transmissions, electrification is incorporated into converter clutch lockup, shift scheduling, and line pressure control systems.

ELECTROSTATIC DISCHARGE (ESD): An unwanted, high-voltage electrical current released by an individual who has taken on a static charge of electricity. Electronic components can be easily damaged by ESD.

ELEMENT: A device within a hydrodynamic drive unit designed with a set of blades to direct fluid flow.

ENAMEL: Type of paint that dries to a smooth, glossy finish.

END BUMP (END FEEL OR SLIP BUMP): Firmer feel at end of shift when compared with feel at start of shift.

END-PLAY: The clearance/gap between two components that allows for expansion of the parts as they warm up, to prevent binding and to allow space for lubrication.

ENERGY: The ability or capacity to do work.

ENGINE: The primary motor or power apparatus of a vehicle, which converts liquid or gas fuel into mechanical energy.

ENGINE BLOCK: The basic engine casting containing the cylinders, the crankshaft main bearings, as well as machined surfaces for the mounting of other components such as the cylinder head, oil pan, transmission, etc.

ENGINE BRAKING: Use of engine to slow vehicle by manually downshifting during zero-throttle coast down.

ENGINE CONTROL MODULE (ECM): Manages the engine and incorporates output control over the torque converter clutch solenoid. (Note: Current designation for the ECM in late model vehicles is PCM.)

ENGINE COOLANT TEMPERATURE (ECT) SENSOR: Prevents converter clutch engagement with a cold engine; also used for shift timing and shift quality.

EP LUBRICANT: EP (extreme pressure) lubricants are specially formulated for use with gears involving heavy loads (transmissions, differentials, etc.).

ETHYL: A substance added to gasoline to improve its resistance to knock, by slowing down the rate of combustion.

ETHYLENE GLYCOL: The base substance of antifreeze.

EXHAUST MANIFOLD: A set of cast passages or pipes which conduct exhaust gases from the engine.

FAIL-SAFE (BACKUP) CONTROL: A substitute value used by the PCM/TCM to replace a faulty signal from an input sensor. The temporary value allows the vehicle to continue to be operated.

FAST IDLE: The speed of the engine when the choke is on. Fast idle speeds engine warm-up.

FEDERAL ENGINE: An engine certified by the EPA for use in any of the 49 states (except California).

FEEDBACK: A circuit malfunction whereby current can find another path to feed load devices.

FEELER GAUGE: A blade, usually metal, of precisely predetermined thickness, used to measure the clearance between two parts.

FILAMENT: The part of a bulb that glows; the filament creates high resistance to current flow and actually glows from the resulting heat.

FINAL DRIVE: An essential part of the axle drive assembly where final gear reduction takes place in the powertrain. In RWD applications and north-south FWD applications, it must also change the power flow direction to the axle shaft by ninety degrees. (Also see axle ratio).

FIRING ORDER: The order in which combustion occurs in the cylinders of an engine. Also the order in which spark is distributed to the plugs by the distributor.

FIRM: A noticeable quick apply of a clutch or band that is considered normal with medium to heavy throttle shift; should not be confused with harsh or rough.

FLAME FRONT: The term used to describe certain aspects of the fuel explosion in the cylinders. The flame front should move in a controlled pattern across the cylinder, rather than simply exploding immediately.

FLARE (SLIPPING): A quick increase in engine rpm accompanied by momentary loss of torque; generally occurs during shift.

FLAT ENGINE: Engine design in which the pistons are horizontally opposed. Porsche, Subaru and some old VW are common examples of flat engines.

FLAT RATE: A dealership term referring to the amount of money paid to a technician for a repair or diagnostic service based on that particular service versus dealership's labor time (NOT based on the actual time the technician spent on the job).

FLAT SPOT: A point during acceleration when the engine seems to lose power for an instant.

FLOODING: The presence of too much fuel in the intake manifold and combustion chamber which prevents the air/fuel mixture from firing, thereby causing a no-start situation.

FLUID: A fluid can be either liquid or gas. In hydraulics, a liquid is used for transmitting force or motion.

FLUID COUPLING: The simplest form of hydrodynamic drive, the fluid coupling consists of two look-alike members with straight radial varies referred to as the impeller (pump) and the turbine. Input torque is always equal to the output torque.

FLUID DRIVE: Either a fluid coupling or a fluid torque converter. (See hydrodynamic drive units.)

FLUID TORQUE CONVERTER: A hydrodynamic drive that has the ability to act both as a torque multiplier and fluid coupling. (See hydrodynamic drive units; torque converter.)

FLUID VISCOSITY: The resistance of a liquid to flow. A cold fluid (oil) has greater viscosity and flows more slowly than a hot fluid (oil).

FLYWHEEL: A heavy disc of metal attached to the rear of the crankshaft. It smoothes the firing impulses of the engine and keeps the crankshaft turning during periods when no firing takes place. The starter also engages the flywheel to start the engine.

FOOT POUND (ft. lbs., lbs. ft. or sometimes, ft. lb.): The amount of energy or work needed to raise an item weighing one pound, a distance of one foot.

FREEZE PLUG: A plug in the engine block which will be pushed out if the coolant freezes. Sometimes called expansion plugs, they protect the block from cracking should the coolant freeze.

FRICTION: The resistance that occurs between contacting surfaces. This relationship is expressed by a ratio called the coefficient of friction (CL).

FRICTION, COEFFICIENT OF: The amount of surface tension between two contacting surfaces; expressed by a scientifically calculated number.

FRONT END ALIGNMENT: A service to set caster, camber and toe-in to the correct specifications. This will ensure that the car steers and handles properly and that the tires wear properly.

FRICTION MODIFIER: Changes the coefficient of friction of the fluid between the mating steel and composition clutch/band surfaces during the engagement process and allows for a certain amount of intentional slipping for a good "shift-feel".

FRONTAL AREA: The total frontal area of a vehicle exposed to air flow.

FUEL FILTER: A component of the fuel system containing a porous paper element used to prevent any impurities from entering the engine through the fuel system. It usually takes the form of a canister-like housing, mounted in-line with the fuel hose, located anywhere on a vehicle between the fuel tank and engine.

FUEL INJECTION: A system replacing the carburetor that sprays fuel into the cylinder through nozzles. The amount of fuel can be more precisely controlled with fuel injection.

FULL FLOATING AXLE: An axle in which the axle housing extends through the wheel giving bearing support on the outside of the housing. The front axle of a four-wheel drive vehicle is usually a full floating axle, as are the rear axles of many larger (1 ton and over) pick-ups and vans.

FULL-TIME FOUR-WHEEL DRIVE: A four-wheel drive system that continuously delivers power to all four wheels. A differential between the front and rear driveshafts permits variations in axle speeds to control gear wind-up without damage.

FULL THROTTLE DETENT DOWNSHIFT: A quick apply of accelerator pedal to its full travel, forcing a downshift.

FUSE: A protective device in a circuit which prevents circuit overload by breaking the circuit when a specific amperage is present. The device is constructed around a strip or wire of a lower amperage rating than the circuit it is designed to protect. When an amperage higher than that stamped on the fuse is present in the circuit, the strip or wire melts, opening the circuit.

FUSIBLE LINK: A piece of wire in a wiring harness that performs the same job as a fuse. If overloaded, the fusible link will melt and interrupt the circuit.

FWD: Front wheel drive.

GAWR: (Gross axle weight rating) the total maximum weight an axle is designed to carry.

GCW: (Gross combined weight) total combined weight of a tow vehicle and trailer.

GARAGE SHIFT: initial engagement feel of transmission, neutral to reverse or neutral to a forward drive.

GARAGE SHIFT FEEL: A quick check of the engagement quality and responsiveness of reverse and forward gears. This test is done with the vehicle stationary.

GEAR: A toothed mechanical device that acts as a rotating lever to transmit power or turning effort from one shaft to another. (See gear ratio.)

GEAR RATIO: A ratio expressing the number of turns a smaller gear will make to turn a larger gear through one revolution. The ratio is found by dividing the number of teeth on the smaller gear into the number of teeth on the larger gear.

GEARBOX: Transmission

GEAR REDUCTION: Torque is multiplied and speed decreased by the factor of the gear ratio. For example, a 3:1 gear ratio changes an input torque of 180 ft. lbs. and an input speed of 2700 rpm to 540 Ft. lbs. and 900 rpm, respectively. (No account is taken of frictional losses, which are always present.)

GEARTRAIN: A succession of intermeshing gears that form an assembly and provide for one or more torque changes as the power input is transmitted to the power output.

GEL COAT: A thin coat of plastic resin covering fiberglass body panels.

GENERATOR: A device which produces direct current (DC) necessary to charge the battery.

GOVERNOR: A device that senses vehicle speed and generates a hydraulic oil pressure. As vehicle speed increases, governor oil pressure rises.

GROUND CIRCUIT: (See circuit, ground.)

GROUND SIDE SWITCHING: The electrical/electronic circuit control switch is located after the circuit load.

GVWR: (Gross vehicle weight rating) total maximum weight a vehicle is designed to carry including the weight of the vehicle, passengers, equipment, gas, oil, etc.

HALOGEN: A special type of lamp known for its quality of brilliant white light. Originally used for fog lights and driving lights.

HARD CODES: DTCs that are present at the time of testing; also called continuous or current codes.

HARSH(ROUGH): An apply of a clutch or band that is more noticeable than a firm one; considered undesirable at any throttle position.

HEADER TANK: An expansion tank for the radiator coolant. It can be located remotely or built into the radiator.

HEAT RANGE: A term used to describe the ability of a spark plug to carry away heat. Plugs with longer nosed insulators take longer to carry heat off effectively.

HEAT RISER: A flapper in the exhaust manifold that is closed when the engine is cold, causing hot exhaust gases to heat the intake manifold providing better cold engine operation. A thermostatic spring opens the flapper when the engine warms up.

HEAVY THROTTLE: Approximately three-fourths of accelerator pedal travel.

HEMI: A name given an engine using hemispherical combustion chambers.

HERTZ (HZ): The international unit of frequency equal to one cycle per second (10,000 Hertz equals 10,000 cycles per second).

HIGH-IMPEDANCE DVOM (DIGITAL VOLT-OHMMETER): This styled device provides a built-in resistance value and is capable of limiting circuit current flow to safe milliamp levels.

HIGH RESISTANCE: Often refers to a circuit where there is an excessive amount of opposition to normal current flow.

HORSEPOWER: A measurement of the amount of work; one horsepower is the amount of work necessary to lift 33,000 lbs. one foot in one minute. Brake horsepower (bhp) is the horsepower delivered by an engine on a dynamometer. Net horsepower is the power remaining (measured at the flywheel of the engine) that can be used to turn the wheels after power is consumed through friction and running the engine accessories (water pump, alternator, air pump, fan etc.)

HOT CIRCUIT: (See circuit, hot; hot lead.)

HOT LEAD: A wire or conductor in the power side of the circuit. (See circuit, hot.)

HOT SIDE SWITCHING: The electrical/electronic circuit control switch is located before the circuit load.

HUB: The center part of a wheel or gear.

HUNTING (BUSYNESS): Repeating quick series of up-shifts and downshifts that causes noticeable change in engine rpm, for example, as in a 4-3-4 shift pattern.

HYDRAULICS: The use of liquid under pressure to transfer force of motion.

HYDROCARBON (HC): Any chemical compound made up of hydrogen and carbon. A major pollutant formed by the engine as a by-product of combustion.

HYDRODYNAMIC DRIVE UNITS: Devices that transmit power solely by the action of a kinetic fluid flow in a closed recirculating path. An impeller energizes the fluid and discharges the high-speed jet stream into the turbine for power output.

HYDROMETER: An instrument used to measure the specific gravity of a solution.

HYDROPLANING: A phenomenon of driving when water builds up under the tire tread, causing it to lose contact with the road. Slowing down will usually restore normal tire contact with the road.

HYPOID GEARSET: The drive pinion gear may be placed below or above the centerline of the driven gear; often used as a final drive gearset.

IDLE MIXTURE: The mixture of air and fuel (usually about 14:1) being fed to the cylinders. The idle mixture screw(s) are sometimes adjusted as part of a tune-up.

IDLER ARM: Component of the steering linkage which is a geometric duplicate of the steering gear arm. It supports the right side of the center steering link.

IMPELLER: Often called a pump, the impeller is the power input (drive) member of a hydrodynamic drive. As part of the torque converter cover, it acts as a centrifugal pump and puts the fluid in motion.

INCH POUND (inch lbs.; sometimes in. lb. or in. lbs.): One twelfth of a foot pound.

INDUCTANCE: The force that produces voltage when a conductor is passed through a magnetic field.

INDUCTION: A means of transferring electrical energy in the form of a magnetic field. Principle used in the ignition coil to increase voltage.

INITIAL FEEL: A distinct firmer feel at start of shift when compared with feel at finish of shift.

INJECTOR: A device which receives metered fuel under relatively low pressure and is activated to inject the fuel into the engine under relatively high pressure at a predetermined time.

INPUT: In an automatic transmission, the source of power from the engine is absorbed by the torque converter, which provides the power input into the transmission. The turbine drives the input(turbine)shaft.

INPUT SHAFT: The shaft to which torque is applied, usually carrying the driving gear or gears.

INTAKE MANIFOLD: A casting of passages or pipes used to conduct air or a fuel/air mixture to the cylinders.

INTERNAL GEAR: The ring-like outer gear of a planetary gearset with the gear teeth cut on the inside of the ring to provide a mesh with the planet pinions.

ISOLATION (CLAMPING) DIODES: Diodes positioned in a circuit to prevent self-induction from damaging electronic components.

IX ROTARY GEAR PUMP: Contains two rotating members, one shaped with internal gear teeth and the other with external gear teeth. As the gears separate, the fluid fills the gaps between gear teeth, is pulled across a crescent-shaped divider, and then is forced to flow through the outlet as the gears mesh.

IX ROTARY LOBE PUMP: Sometimes referred to as a gerotor type pump. Two rotating members, one shaped with internal lobes and the other with external lobes, separate and then mesh to cause fluid to flow.

JOURNAL: The bearing surface within which a shaft operates.

JUMPER CABLES: Two heavy duty wires with large alligator clips used to provide power from a charged battery to a discharged battery mounted in a vehicle.

JUMPSTART: Utilizing the sufficiently charged battery of one vehicle to start the engine of another vehicle with a discharged battery by the use of jumper cables.

KEY: A small block usually fitted in a notch between a shaft and a hub to prevent slippage of the two parts.

KICKDOWN: Detent downshift system; either linkage, cable, or electrically controlled.

KILO: A prefix used in the metric system to indicate one thousand.

KNOCK: Noise which results from the spontaneous ignition of a portion of the air-fuel mixture in the engine cylinder caused by overly advanced ignition timing or use of incorrectly low octane fuel for that engine.

KNOCK SENSOR: An input device that responds to spark knock, caused by over advanced ignition timing.

LABOR TIME: A specific amount of time required to perform a certain repair or diagnostic service as defined by a vehicle or after-market manufacturer .

LACQUER: A quick-drying automotive paint.

LATE: Shift that occurs when engine is at higher than normal rpm for given amount of throttle.

LIGHT-EMITTING DIODE (LED): A semiconductor diode that emits light as electrical current flows through it; used in some electronic display devices to emit a red or other color light.

LIGHT THROTTLE: Approximately one-fourth of accelerator pedal travel.

LIMITED SLIP: A type of differential which transfers driving force to the wheel with the best traction.

LIMP-IN MODE: Electrical shutdown of the transmission/ transaxle output solenoids, allowing only forward and reverse gears that are hydraulically energized by the manual valve. This permits the vehicle to be driven to a service facility for repair.

LIP SEAL: Molded synthetic rubber seal designed with an outer sealing edge (lip) that points into the fluid containing area to be sealed. This type of seal is used where rotational and axial forces are present.

LITHIUM-BASE GREASE: Chassis and wheel bearing grease using lithium as a base. Not compatible with sodium-base grease.

LOAD DEVICE: A circuit's resistance that converts the electrical energy into light, sound, heat, or mechanical movement.

LOAD RANGE: Indicates the number of plies at which a tire is rated. Load range B equals four-ply rating; C equals six-ply rating; and, D equals an eight-ply rating.

LOAD TORQUE: The amount of output torque needed from the transmission/transaxle to overcome the vehicle load.

LOCKING HUBS: Accessories used on part-time four-wheel drive systems that allow the front wheels to be disengaged from the drive train when four-wheel drive is not being used. When four-wheel drive is desired, the hubs are engaged, locking the wheels to the drive train.

LOCKUP CONVERTER: A torque converter that operates hydraulically and mechanically. When an internal apply plate (lockup plate) clamps to the torque converter cover, hydraulic slippage is eliminated.

LOCK RING: See Circlip or Snapring

MAGNET: Any body with the property of attracting iron or steel.

MAGNETIC FIELD: The area surrounding the poles of a magnet that is affected by its attraction or repulsion forces.

MAIN LINE PRESSURE: Often called control pressure or line pressure, it refers to the pressure of the oil leaving the pump and is controlled by the pressure regulator valve.

MALFUNCTION INDICATOR LAMP (MIL): Previously known as a check engine light, the dash-mounted MIL illuminates and signals the driver that an emission or driveability problem with the powertrain has been detected by the ECM/PCM. When this occurs, at least one diagnostic trouble code (DTC) has been stored into the control module memory.

MANIFOLD ABSOLUTE PRESSURE (MAP) SENSOR: Reads the amount of air pressure (vacuum) in the engine's intake manifold system; its signal is used to analyze engine load conditions.

MANIFOLD VACUUM: Low pressure in an engine intake manifold formed just below the throttle plates. Manifold vacuum is highest at idle and drops under acceleration.

MANIFOLD: A casting of passages or set of pipes which connect the cylinders to an inlet or outlet source.

MANUAL LEVER POSITION SWITCH (MLPS): A mechanical switching unit that is typically mounted externally to the transmission/transaxle to inform the PCM/ECM which gear range the driver has selected.

MANUAL VALVE: Located inside the transmission/transaxle, it is directly connected to the driver's shift lever. The position of the manual valve determines which hydraulic circuits will be charged with oil pressure and the operating mode of the transmission.

MANUAL VALVE LEVER POSITION SENSOR (MVLPS): The input from this device tells the TCM what gear range was selected.

MASS AIR FLOW (MAF) SENSOR: Measures the airflow into the engine.

MASTER CYLINDER: The primary fluid pressurizing device in a hydraulic system. In automotive use, it is found in brake and hydraulic clutch systems and is pedal activated, either directly or, in a power brake system, through the power booster.

MacPherson STRUT: A suspension component combining a shock absorber and spring in one unit.

MEDIUM THROTTLE: Approximately one-half of accelerator pedal travel.

MEGA: A metric prefix indicating one million.

MEMBER: An independent component of a hydrodynamic unit such as an impeller, a stator, or a turbine. It may have one or more elements.

MERCON: A fluid developed by Ford Motor Company in 1988. It contains a friction modifier and closely resembles operating characteristics of Dexron.

METAL SEALING RINGS: Made from cast iron or aluminum, their primary application is with dynamic components involving pressure sealing circuits of rotating members. These rings are designed with either butt or hook lock end joints.

METER (ANALOG): A linear-style meter representing data as lengths; a needle-style instrument interfacing with logical numerical increments. This style of electrical meter uses relatively low impedance internal resistance and cannot be used for testing electronic circuitry.

METER (DIGITAL): Uses numbers as a direct readout to show values. Most meters of this style use high impedance internal resistance and must be used for testing low current electronic circuitry.

MICRO: A metric prefix indicating one-millionth (0.000001).

MILLI: A metric prefix indicating one-thousandth (0.001).

MINIMUM THROTTLE: The least amount of throttle opening required for upshift; normally close to zero throttle.

MISFIRE: Condition occurring when the fuel mixture in a cylinder fails to ignite, causing the engine to run roughly.

MODULE: Electronic control unit, amplifier or igniter of solid state or integrated design which controls the current flow in the ignition primary circuit based on input from the pick-up coil. When the module opens the primary circuit, high secondary voltage is induced in the coil.

MODULATED: In an electronic-hydraulic converter clutch system (or shift valve system), the term modulated refers to the pulsing of a solenoid, at a variable rate. This action controls the buildup of oil pressure in the hydraulic circuit to allow a controlled amount of clutch slippage.

MODULATED CONVERTER CLUTCH CONTROL (MCCC): A pulse width duty cycle valve that controls the converter lockup apply pressure and maximizes smoother transitions between lock and unlock conditions.

MODULATOR PRESSURE (THROTTLE PRESSURE): A hydraulic signal oil pressure relating to the amount of engine load, based on either the amount of throttle plate opening or engine vacuum.

MODULATOR VALVE: A regulator valve that is controlled by engine vacuum, providing a hydraulic pressure that varies in relation to engine torque. The hydraulic torque signal functions to delay the shift pattern and provide a line pressure boost. (See throttle valve.)

MOTOR: An electromagnetic device used to convert electrical energy into mechanical energy.

MULTIPLE-DISC CLUTCH: A grouping of steel and friction lined plates that, when compressed together by hydraulic pressure acting upon a piston, lock or unlock a planetary member.

MULTI-WEIGHT: Type of oil that provides adequate lubrication at both high and low temperatures.

needed to move one amp through a resistance of one ohm.

MUSHY: Same as soft; slow and drawn out clutch apply with very little shift feel.

MUTUAL INDUCTION: The generation of current from one wire circuit to another by movement of the magnetic field surrounding a current-carrying circuit as its ampere flow increases or decreases.

NEEDLE BEARING: A bearing which consists of a number (usually a large number) of long, thin rollers.

NITROGEN OXIDE (NOx): One of the three basic pollutants found in the exhaust emission of an internal combustion engine. The amount of NOx usually varies in an inverse proportion to the amount of HC and CO.

NONPOSITIVE SEALING: A sealing method that allows some minor leakage, which normally assists in lubrication.

02 SENSOR: Located in the engine's exhaust system, it is an input device to the ECM/PCM for managing the fuel delivery and ignition system. A scanner can be used to observe the fluctuating voltage readings produced by an 02 sensor as the oxygen content of the exhaust is analyzed.

O-RING SEAL: Molded synthetic rubber seal designed with a circular cross-section. This type of seal is used primarily in static applications.

OBD II (ON-BOARD DIAGNOSTICS, SECOND GENERATION): Refers to the federal law mandating tighter control of 1996 and newer vehicle emissions, active monitoring of related devices, and standardization of terminology, data link connectors, and other technician concerns.

OCTANE RATING: A number, indicating the quality of gasoline based on its ability to resist knock. The higher the number, the better the quality. Higher compression engines require higher octane gas.

OEM: Original Equipment Manufactured. OEM equipment is that furnished standard by the manufacturer.

OFFSET: The distance between the vertical center of the wheel and the mounting surface at the lugs. Offset is positive if the center is outside the lug circle; negative offset puts the center line inside the lug circle.

OHM'S LAW: A law of electricity that states the relationship between voltage, current, and resistance. Volts = amperes x ohms

OHM: The unit used to measure the resistance of conductor-to-electrical flow. One ohm is the amount of resistance that limits current flow to one ampere in a circuit with one volt of pressure.

OHMMETER: An instrument used for measuring the resistance, in ohms, in an electrical circuit.

ONE-WAY CLUTCH: A mechanical clutch of roller or sprag design that resists torque or transmits power in one direction only. It is used to either hold or drive a planetary member.

ONE-WAY ROLLER CLUTCH: A mechanical device that transmits or holds torque in one direction only.

OPEN CIRCUIT: A break or lack of contact in an electrical circuit, either intentional (switch) or unintentional (bad connection or broken wire).

ORIFICE: Located in hydraulic oil circuits, it acts as a restriction. It slows down fluid flow to either create back pressure or delay pressure buildup downstream.

OSCILLOSCOPE: A piece of test equipment that shows electric impulses as a pattern on a screen. Engine performance can be analyzed by interpreting these patterns.

OUTPUT SHAFT: The shaft which transmits torque from a device, such as a transmission.

OUTPUT SPEED SENSOR (OSS): Identifies transmission/transaxle output shaft speed for shift timing and may be used to calculate TCC slip; often functions as the VSS (vehicle speed sensor).

OVERDRIVE: (1.) A device attached to or incorporated in a transmission/transaxle that allows the engine to turn less than one full revolution for every complete revolution of the wheels. The net effect is to reduce engine rpm, thereby using less fuel. A typical overdrive gear ratio would be .87:1, instead of the normal 1:1 in high gear. (2.) A gear assembly which produces more shaft revolutions than that transmitted to it.

OVERDRIVE PLANETARY GEARSET: A single planetary gearset designed to provide a direct drive and overdrive ratio. When coupled to a three-speed transmission/transaxle configuration, a four-speed/overdrive unit is present.

OVERHEAD CAMSHAFT (OHC): An engine configuration in which the camshaft is mounted on top of the cylinder head and operates the valve either directly or by means of rocker arms.

OVERHEAD VALVE (OHV): An engine configuration in which all of the valves are located in the cylinder head and the camshaft is located in the cylinder block. The camshaft operates the valves via lifters and pushrods.

OVERRUNCLUTCH: Another name for a one-way mechanical clutch. Applies to both roller and sprag designs.

OVERSTEER: The tendency of some vehicles, when steering into a turn, to over-respond or steer more than required, which could result in excessive slip of the rear wheels. Opposite of under-steer.

OXIDATION STABILIZERS: Absorb and dissipate heat. Automatic transmission fluid has high resistance to varnish and sludge buildup that occurs from excessive heat that is generated primarily in the torque converter. Local temperatures as high as 6000F (3150C) can occur at the clutch plates during engagement, and this heat must be absorbed and dissipated. If the fluid cannot withstand the heat, it burns or oxidizes, resulting in an almost immediate destruction of friction materials, clogged filter screen and hydraulic passages, and sticky valves.

OXIDES OF NITROGEN: See nitrogen oxide (NOx).

OXYGEN SENSOR: Used with a feedback system to sense the presence of oxygen in the exhaust gas and signal the computer which can use the voltage signal to determine engine operating efficiency and adjust the air/fuel ratio.

PARALLEL CIRCUIT: (See circuit, parallel.)

PARTS WASHER: A basin or tub, usually with a built-in pump mechanism and hose used for circulating chemical solvent for the purpose of cleaning greasy, oily and dirty components.

PART-TIME FOUR WHEEL DRIVE: A system that is normally in the two wheel drive mode and only runs in four-wheel drive when the system is manually engaged because more traction is desired. Two or four wheel drive is normally selected by a lever to engage the front axle, but if locking hubs are used, these must also be manually engaged in the Lock position. Otherwise, the front axle will not drive the front wheels.

PASSIVE RESTRAINT: Safety systems such as air bags or automatic seat belts which operate with no action required on the part of the driver or passenger. Mandated by Federal regulations on all vehicles sold in the U.S. after 1990.

PAYLOAD: The weight the vehicle is capable of carrying in addition to its own weight. Payload includes weight of the driver, passengers and cargo, but not coolant, fuel, lubricant, spare tire, etc.

PCM: Powertrain control module.

PCV VALVE: A valve usually located in the rocker cover that vents crankcase vapors back into the engine to be reburned.

PERCOLATION: A condition in which the fuel actually "boils," due to excessive heat. Percolation prevents proper atomization of the fuel causing rough running.

PICK-UP COIL: The coil in which voltage is induced in an electronic ignition.

PING: A metallic rattling sound produced by the engine during acceleration. It is usually due to incorrect ignition timing or a poor grade of gasoline.

PINION: The smaller of two gears. The rear axle pinion drives the ring gear which transmits motion to the axle shafts.

PINION GEAR: The smallest gear in a drive gear assembly.

PISTON: A disc or cup that fits in a cylinder bore and is free to move. In hydraulics, it provides the means of converting hydraulic pressure into a usable force. Examples of piston applications are found in servo, clutch, and accumulator units.

PISTON RING: An open-ended ring which fits into a groove on the outer diameter of the piston. Its chief function is to form a seal between the piston and cylinder wall. Most automotive pistons have three rings: two for compression sealing; one for oil sealing.

PITMAN ARM: A lever which transmits steering force from the steering gear to the steering linkage.

PLANET CARRIER: A basic member of a planetary gear assembly that carries the pinion gears.

PLANET PINIONS: Gears housed in a planet carrier that are in constant mesh with the sun gear and internal gear. Because they have their own independent rotating centers, the pinions are capable of rotating around the sun gear or the inside of the internal gear.

PLANETARY GEAR RATIO: The reduction or overdrive ratio developed by a planetary gearset.

PLANETARY GEARSET: In its simplest form, it is made up of a basic assembly group containing a sun gear, internal gear, and planet carrier. The gears are always in constant mesh and offer a wide range of gear ratio possibilities.

PLANETARY GEARSET (COMPOUND): Two planetary gearsets combined together.

PLANETARY GEARSET (SIMPLE): An assembly of gears in constant mesh consisting of a sun gear, several pinion gears mounted in a carrier, and a ring gear. It provides gear ratio and direction changes, in addition to a direct drive and a neutral.

PLY RATING: A. rating given a tire which indicates strength (but not necessarily actual plies). A two-ply/four-ply rating has only two plies, but the strength of a four-ply tire.

POLARITY: Indication (positive or negative) of the two poles of a battery.

PORT: An opening for fluid intake or exhaust.

POSITIVE SEALING: A sealing method that completely prevents leakage.

POTENTIAL: Electrical force measured in volts; sometimes used interchangeably with voltage.

POWER: The ability to do work per unit of time, as expressed in horsepower; one horsepower equals 33,000 ft. lbs. of work per minute, or 550 ft. lbs. of work per second.

POWER FLOW: The systematic flow or transmission of power through the gears, from the input shaft to the output shaft.

POWER-TO-WEIGHT RATIO: Ratio of horsepower to weight of car.

POWERTRAIN: See Drivetrain.

POWERTRAIN CONTROL MODULE (PCM): Current designation for the engine control module (ECM). In many cases, late model vehicle control units manage the engine as well as the transmission. In other settings, the PCM controls the engine and is interfaced with a TCM to control transmission functions.

Ppm: Parts per million; unit used to measure exhaust emissions.

PREIGNITION: Early ignition of fuel in the cylinder, sometimes due to glowing carbon deposits in the combustion chamber. Preignition can be damaging since combustion takes place prematurely.

PRELOAD: A predetermined load placed on a bearing during assembly or by adjustment.

PRESS FIT: The mating of two parts under pressure, due to the inner diameter of one being smaller than the outer diameter of the other, or vice versa; an interference fit.

PRESSURE: The amount of force exerted upon a surface area.

PRESSURE CONTROL SOLENOID (PCS): An output device that provides a boost oil pressure to the mainline regulator valve to control line pressure. Its operation is determined by the amount of current sent from the PCM.

PRESSURE GAUGE: An instrument used for measuring the fluid pressure in a hydraulic circuit.

PRESSURE REGULATOR VALVE: In automatic transmissions, its purpose is to regulate the pressure of the pump output and supply the basic fluid pressure necessary to operate the transmission. The regulated fluid pressure may be referred to as mainline pressure, line pressure, or control pressure.

PRESSURE SWITCH ASSEMBLY (PSA): Mounted inside the transmission, it is a grouping of oil pressure switches that inputs to the PCM when certain hydraulic passages are charged with oil pressure.

PRESSURE PLATE: A spring-loaded plate (part of the clutch) that transmits power to the driven (friction) plate when the clutch is engaged.

PRIMARY CIRCUIT: The low voltage side of the ignition system which consists of the ignition switch, ballast resistor or resistance wire, bypass, coil, electronic control unit and pick-up coil as well as the connecting wires and harnesses.

PROFILE: Term used for tire measurement (tire series), which is the ratio of tire height to tread width.

PROM (PROGRAMMABLE READ-ONLY MEMORY): The heart of the computer that compares input data and makes the engineered program or strategy decisions about when to trigger the appropriate output based on stored computer instructions.

PULSE GENERATOR: A two-wire pickup sensor used to produce a fluctuating electrical signal. This changing signal is read by the controller to determine the speed of the object and can be used to measure transmission/transaxle input speed, output speed, and vehicle speed.

PSI: Pounds per square inch; a measurement of pressure.

PULSE WIDTH DUTY CYCLE SOLENOID (PULSE WIDTH MODULATED SOLENOID): A computer-controlled solenoid that turns on and off at a variable rate producing a modulated oil pressure; often referred to as a pulse width modulated (PWM) solenoid. Employed in many electronic automatic transmissions and transaxles, these solenoids are used to manage shift control and converter clutch hydraulic circuits.

PUSHROD: A steel rod between the hydraulic valve lifter and the valve rocker arm in overhead valve (OHV) engines.

PUMP: A mechanical device designed to create fluid flow and pressure buildup in a hydraulic system.

QUARTER PANEL: General term used to refer to a rear fender. Quarter panel is the area from the rear door opening to the tail light area and from rear wheel well to the base of the trunk and roof-line.

RACE: The surface on the inner or outer ring of a bearing on which the balls, needles or rollers move.

RACK AND PINION: A type of automotive steering system using a pinion gear attached to the end of the steering shaft. The pinion meshes with a long rack attached to the steering linkage.

RADIAL TIRE: Tire design which uses body cords running at right angles to the center line of the tire. Two or more belts are used to give tread strength. Radials can be identified by their characteristic sidewall bulge.

RADIATOR: Part of the cooling system for a water-cooled engine, mounted in the front of the vehicle and connected to the engine with rubber hoses. Through the radiator, excess combustion heat is dissipated into the atmosphere through forced convection using a water and glycol based mixture that circulates through, and cools, the engine.

RANGE REFERENCE AND CLUTCH/BAND APPLY CHART: A guide that shows the application of clutches and bands for each gear, within the selector range positions. These charts are extremely useful for understanding how the unit operates and for diagnosing malfunctions.

RAVIGNEAUX GEARSET: A compound planetary gearset that features matched dual planetary pinions (sets of two) mounted in a single planet carrier. Two sun gears and one ring mesh with the carrier pinions.

REACTION MEMBER: The stationary planetary member, in a planetary gearset, that is grounded to the transmission/transaxle case through the use of friction and wedging devices known as bands, disc clutches, and one-way clutches.

REACTION PRESSURE: The fluid pressure that moves a spool valve against an opposing force or forces; the area on which the opposing force acts. The opposing force can be a spring or a combination of spring force and auxiliary hydraulic force.

REACTOR, TORQUE CONVERTER: The reaction member of a fluid torque converter, more commonly called a stator. (See stator.)

REAR MAIN OIL SEAL: A synthetic or rope-type seal that prevents oil from leaking out of the engine past the rear main crankshaft bearing.

RECIRCULATING BALL: Type of steering system in which recirculating steel balls occupy the area between the nut and worm wheel, causing a reduction in friction.

RECTIFIER: A device (used primarily in alternators) that permits electrical current to flow in one direction only.

REDUCTION: (See gear reduction.)

REGULATOR VALVE: A valve that changes the pressure of the oil in a hydraulic circuit as the oil passes through the valve by bleeding off (or exhausting) some of the volume of oil supplied to the valve.

REFRIGERANT 12 (R-12) or 134 (R-134): The generic name of the refrigerant used in automotive air conditioning systems.

REGULATOR: A device which maintains the amperage and/or voltage levels of a circuit at predetermined values.

RELAY: A switch which automatically opens and/or closes a circuit.

RELAY VALVE: A valve that directs flow and pressure. Relay valves simply connect or disconnect interrelated passages without restricting the fluid flow or changing the pressure.

RELIEF VALVE: A spring-loaded, pressure-operated valve that limits oil pressure buildup in a hydraulic circuit to a predetermined maximum value.

RELUCTOR: A wheel that rotates inside the distributor and triggers the release of voltage in an electronic ignition.

RESERVOIR: The storage area for fluid in a hydraulic system; often called a sump.

RESIN: A liquid plastic used in body work.

RESIDUAL MAGNETISM: The magnetic strength stored in a material after a magnetizing field has been removed.

RESISTANCE: The opposition to the flow of current through a circuit or electrical device, and is measured in ohms. Resistance is equal to the voltage divided by the amperage.

RESISTOR SPARK PLUG: A spark plug using a resistor to shorten the spark duration. This suppresses radio interference and lengthens plug life.

RESISTOR: A device, usually made of wire, which offers a preset amount of resistance in an electrical circuit.

RESULTANT FORCE: The single effective directional thrust of the fluid force on the turbine produced by the vortex and rotary forces acting in different planes.

RETARD: Set the ignition timing so that spark occurs later (fewer degrees before TDC).

RHEOSTAT: A device for regulating a current by means of a variable resistance.

RING GEAR: The name given to a ring-shaped gear attached to a differential case, or affixed to a flywheel or as part of a planetary gear set.

ROADLOAD: grade.

ROCKER ARM: A lever which rotates around a shaft pushing down (opening) the valve with an end when the other end is pushed up by the pushrod. Spring pressure will later close the valve.

ROCKER PANEL: The body panel below the doors between the wheel opening.

ROLLER BEARING: A bearing made up of hardened inner and outer races between which hardened steel rollers move.

ROLLER CLUTCH: A type of one-way clutch design using rollers and springs mounted within an inner and outer cam race assembly.

ROTARY FLOW: The path of the fluid trapped between the blades of the members as they revolve with the rotation of the torque converter cover (rotational inertia).

ROTOR: (1.) The disc-shaped part of a disc brake assembly, upon which the brake pads bear; also called, brake disc. (2.) The device mounted atop the distributor shaft, which passes current to the distributor cap tower contacts.

ROTARY ENGINE: See Wankel engine.

RPM: Revolutions per minute (usually indicates engine speed).

RTV: A gasket making compound that cures as it is exposed to the atmosphere. It is used between surfaces that are not perfectly machined to one another, leaving a slight gap that the RTV fills and in which it hardens. The letters RTV represent room temperature vulcanizing.

RUN-ON: Condition when the engine continues to run, even when the key is turned off. See dieseling.

SEALED BEAM: A automotive headlight. The lens, reflector and filament from a single unit.

SEATBELT INTERLOCK: A system whereby the car cannot be started unless the seatbelt is buckled.

SECONDARY CIRCUIT: The high voltage side of the ignition system, usually above 20,000 volts. The secondary includes the ignition coil, coil wire, distributor cap and rotor, spark plug wires and spark plugs.

SELF-INDUCTION: The generation of voltage in a current-carrying wire by changing the amount of current flowing within that wire.

SEMI-CONDUCTOR: A material (silicon or germanium) that is neither a good conductor nor an insulator; used in diodes and transistors.

SEMI-FLOATING AXLE: In this design, a wheel is attached to the axle shaft, which takes both drive and cornering loads. Almost all solid axle passenger cars and light trucks use this design.

SENDING UNIT: A mechanical, electrical, hydraulic or electromagnetic device which transmits information to a gauge.

SENSOR: Any device designed to measure engine operating conditions or ambient pressures and temperatures. Usually electronic in nature and designed to send a voltage signal to an on-board computer, some sensors may operate as a simple on/off switch or they may provide a variable voltage signal (like a potentiometer) as conditions or measured parameters change.

SERIES CIRCUIT: (See circuit, series.)

SERPENTINE BELT: An accessory drive belt, with small multiple v-ribs, routed around most or all of the engine-powered accessories such as the alternator and power steering pump. Usually both the front and the back side of the belt comes into contact with various pulleys.

SERVO: In an automatic transmission, it is a piston in a cylinder assembly that converts hydraulic pressure into mechanical force and movement; used for the application of the bands and clutches.

SHIFT BUSYNESS: When referring to a torque converter clutch, it is the frequent apply and release of the clutch plate due to uncommon driving conditions.

SHIFT VALVE: Classified as a relay valve, it triggers the automatic shift in response to a governor and a throttle signal by directing fluid to the appropriate band and clutch apply combination to cause the shift to occur.

SHIM: Spacers of precise, predetermined thickness used between parts to establish a proper working relationship.

SHIMMY: Vibration (sometimes violent) in the front end caused by misaligned front end, out of balance tires or worn suspension components.

SHORT CIRCUIT: An electrical malfunction where current takes the path of least resistance to ground (usually through damaged insulation). Current flow is excessive from low resistance resulting in a blown fuse.

SHUDDER: Repeated jerking or stick-slip sensation, similar to chuggle but more severe and rapid in nature, that may be most noticeable during certain ranges of vehicle speed; also used to define condition after converter clutch engagement.

SIMPSON GEARSET: A compound planetary gear train that integrates two simple planetary gearsets referred to as the front planetary and the rear planetary.

SINGLE OVERHEAD CAMSHAFT: See overhead camshaft.

SKIDPLATE: A metal plate attached to the underside of the body to protect the fuel tank, transfer case or other vulnerable parts from damage.

SLAVE CYLINDER: In automotive use, a device in the hydraulic clutch system which is activated by hydraulic force, disengaging the clutch.

SLIPPING: Noticeable increase in engine rpm without vehicle speed increase; usually occurs during or after initial clutch or band engagement.

SLUDGE: Thick, black deposits in engine formed from dirt, oil, water, etc. It is usually formed in engines when oil changes are neglected.

SNAP RING: A circular retaining clip used inside or outside a shaft or part to secure a shaft, such as a floating wrist pin.

SOFT: Slow, almost unnoticeable clutch apply with very little shift feel.

SOFTCODES: DTCs that have been set into the PCM memory but are not present at the time of testing; often referred to as history or intermittent codes.

SOHC: Single overhead camshaft.

SOLENOID: An electrically operated, magnetic switching device.

SPALLING: A wear pattern identified by metal chips flaking off the hardened surface. This condition is caused by foreign particles, overloading situations, and/or normal wear.

SPARK PLUG: A device screwed into the combustion chamber of a spark ignition engine. The basic construction is a conductive core inside of a ceramic insulator, mounted in an outer conductive base. An electrical charge from the spark plug wire travels along the conductive core and jumps a preset air gap to a grounding point or points at the end of the conductive base. The resultant spark ignites the fuel/air mixture in the combustion chamber.

SPECIFIC GRAVITY (BATTERY): The relative weight of liquid (battery electrolyte) as compared to the weight of an equal volume of water.

SPLINES: Ridges machined or cast onto the outer diameter of a shaft or inner diameter of a bore to enable parts to mate without rotation.

SPLIT TORQUE DRIVE: In a torque converter, it refers to parallel paths of torque transmission, one of which is mechanical and the other hydraulic.

SPONGY PEDAL: A soft or spongy feeling when the brake pedal is depressed. It is usually due to air in the brake lines.

SPOOLVALVE: A precision-machined, cylindrically shaped valve made up of lands and grooves. Depending on its position in the valve bore, various interconnecting hydraulic circuit passages are either opened or closed.

SPRAG CLUTCH: A type of one-way clutch design using cams or contoured-shaped sprags between inner and outer races. (See one-way clutch.)

SPRUNG WEIGHT: The weight of a car supported by the springs.

SQUARE-CUT SEAL: Molded synthetic rubber seal designed with a square- or rectangular-shaped cross-section. This type of seal is used for both dynamic and static applications.

SRS: Supplemental restraint system

STABILIZER (SWAY) BAR: A bar linking both sides of the suspension. It resists sway on turns by taking some of added load from one wheel and putting it on the other.

STAGE: The number of turbine sets separated by a stator. A turbine set may be made up of one or more turbine members. A three-element converter is classified as a single stage.

STALL: In fluid drive transmission/transaxle applications, stall refers to engine rpm with the transmission/transaxle engaged and the vehicle stationary; throttle valve can be in any position between closed and wide open.

STALL SPEED: In fluid drive transmission/transaxle applications, stall speed refers to the maximum engine rpm with the transmission/transaxle engaged and vehicle stationary, when the throttle valve is wide open. (See stall; stall test.)

STALL TEST: A procedure recommended by many manufacturers to help determine the integrity of an engine, the torque converter stator, and certain clutch and band combinations. With the shift lever in each of the forward and reverse positions and with the brakes firmly applied, the accelerator pedal is momentarily pressed to the wide open throttle (WOT) position. The engine rpm reading at full throttle can provide clues for diagnosing the condition of the items listed above.

STALL TORQUE: The maximum design or engineered torque ratio of a fluid torque converter, produced under stall speed conditions. (See stall speed.)

STARTER: A high-torque electric motor used for the purpose of starting the engine, typically through a high ratio geared drive connected to the flywheel ring gear.

STATIC: A sealing application in which the parts being sealed do not move in relation to each other.

STATOR (REACTOR): The reaction member of a fluid torque converter that changes the direction of the fluid as it leaves the turbine to enter the impeller vanes. During the torque multiplication phase, this action assists the impeller's rotary force and results in an increase in torque.

STEERING GEOMETRY: Combination of various angles of suspension components (caster, camber, toe-in); roughly equivalent to front end alignment.

STRAIGHT WEIGHT: Term designating motor oil as suitable for use within a narrow range of temperatures. Outside the narrow temperature range its flow characteristics will not adequately lubricate.

STROKE: The distance the piston travels from bottom dead center to top dead center.

SUBSTITUTION: Replacing one part suspected of a defect with a like part of known quality.

SUMP: The storage vessel or reservoir that provides a ready source of fluid to the pump. In an automatic transmission, the sump is the oil pan. All fluid eventually returns to the sump for recycling into the hydraulic system.

SUN GEAR: In a planetary gearset, it is the center gear that meshes with a cluster of planet pinions.

SUPERCHARGER: An air pump driven mechanically by the engine through belts, chains, shafts or gears from the crankshaft. Two general types of supercharger are the positive displacement and centrifugal type, which pump air in direct relationship to the speed of the engine.

SUPPLEMENTAL RESTRAINT SYSTEM: See air bag.

SURGE: Repeating engine-related feeling of acceleration and deceleration that is less intense than chuggle.

SWITCH: A device used to open, close, or redirect the current in an electrical circuit.

SYNCHROMESH: A manual transmission/transaxle that is equipped with devices (synchronizers) that match the gear speeds so that the transmission/transaxle can be downshifted without clashing gears.

SYNTHETIC OIL: Non-petroleum based oil.

TACHOMETER: A device used to measure the rotary speed of an engine, shaft, gear, etc., usually in rotations per minute.

TDC: Top dead center. The exact top of the piston's stroke.

TEFLON SEALING RINGS: Teflon is a soft, durable, plastic-like material that is resistant to heat and provides excellent sealing. These rings are designed with either scarf-cut joints or as one-piece rings. Teflon sealing rings have replaced many metal ring applications.

TERMINAL: A device attached to the end of a wire or cable to make an electrical connection.

TEST LIGHT, CIRCUIT-POWERED: Uses available circuit voltage to test circuit continuity.

TEST LIGHT, SELF-POWERED: Uses its own battery source to test circuit continuity.

THERMISTOR: A special resistor used to measure fluid temperature; it decreases its resistance with increases in temperature.

THERMOSTAT: A valve, located in the cooling system of an engine, which is closed when cold and opens gradually in response to engine heating, controlling the temperature of the coolant and rate of coolant flow.

THERMOSTATIC ELEMENT: A heat-sensitive, spring-type device that controls a drain port from the upper sump area to the lower sump. When the transaxle fluid reaches operating temperature, the port is closed and the upper sump fills, thus reducing the fluid level in the lower sump.

THROTTLE POSITION (TP) SENSOR: Reads the degree of throttle opening; its signal is used to analyze engine load conditions. The ECM/PCM decides to apply the TCC, or to disengage it for coast or load conditions that need a converter torque boost.

THROTTLE PRESSURE/MODULATOR PRESSURE: A hydraulic signal oil pressure relating to the amount of engine load, based on either the amount of throttle plate opening or engine vacuum.

THROTTLE VALVE: A regulating or balanced valve that is controlled mechanically by throttle linkage or engine vacuum. It sends a hydraulic signal to the shift valve body to control shift timing and shift quality. (See balanced valve; modulator valve.)

THROW-OUT BEARING: As the clutch pedal is depressed, the throwout bearing moves against the spring fingers of the pressure plate, forcing the pressure plate to disengage from the driven disc.

TIE ROD: A rod connecting the steering arms. Tie rods have threaded ends that are used to adjust toe-in.

TIE-UP: Condition where two opposing clutches are attempting to apply at same time, causing engine to labor with noticeable loss of engine rpm.

TIMING BELT: A square-toothed, reinforced rubber belt that is driven by the crankshaft and operates the camshaft.

TIMING CHAIN: A roller chain that is driven by the crankshaft and operates the camshaft.

TIRE ROTATION: Moving the tires from one position to another to make the tires wear evenly.

TOE-IN (OUT): A term comparing the extreme front and rear of the front tires. Closer together at the front is toe-in; farther apart at the front is toe-out.

TOP DEAD CENTER (TDC): The point at which the piston reaches the top of its travel on the compression stroke.

TORQUE: Measurement of turning or twisting force, expressed as foot-pounds or inch-pounds.

TORQUE CONVERTER: A turbine used to transmit power from a driving member to a driven member via hydraulic action, providing changes in drive ratio and torque. In automotive use, it links the driveplate at the rear of the engine to the automatic transmission.

TORQUE CONVERTER CLUTCH: The apply plate (lockup plate) assembly used for mechanical power flow through the converter.

TORQUE PHASE: Sometimes referred to as slip phase or stall phase, torque multiplication occurs when the turbine is turning at a slower speed than the impeller, and the stator is reactionary (stationary). This sequence generates a boost in output torque.

TORQUE RATING (STALL TORQUE): The maximum torque multiplication that occurs during stall conditions, with the engine at wide open throttle (WOT) and zero turbine speed.

TORQUE RATIO: An expression of the gear ratio factor on torque effect. A 3:1 gear ratio or 3:1 torque ratio increases the torque input by the ratio factor of 3. Input torque (100 ft. lbs.) x 3 = output torque (300 ft. lbs.)

TRACTION: The amount of usable tractive effort before the drive wheels slip on the road contact surface.

TORSION BAR SUSPENSION: Long rods of spring steel which take the place of springs. One end of the bar is anchored and the other arm (attached to the suspension) is free to twist. The bars' resistance to twisting causes springing action.

TRACK: Distance between the centers of the tires where they contact the ground.

TRACTION CONTROL: A control system that prevents the spinning of a vehicle's drive wheels when excess power is applied.

TRACTIVE EFFORT: The amount of force available to the drive wheels, to move the vehicle.

TRANSAXLE: A single housing containing the transmission and differential. Transaxles are usually found on front engine/front wheel drive or rear engine/rear wheel drive cars.

TRANSDUCER: A device that changes energy from one form to another. For example, a transducer in a microphone changes sound energy to electrical energy. In automotive air-conditioning controls used in automatic temperature systems, a transducer changes an electrical signal to a vacuum signal, which operates mechanical doors.

TRANSMISSION: A powertrain component designed to modify torque and speed developed by the engine; also provides direct drive, reverse, and neutral.

TRANSMISSION CONTROL MODULE (TCM): Manages transmission functions. These vary according to the manufacturer's product design but may include converter clutch operation, electronic shift scheduling, and mainline pressure.

TRANSMISSION FLUID TEMPERATURE (TFT) SENSOR: Originally called a transmission oil temperature (TOT) sensor, this input device to the ECM/PCM senses the fluid temperature and provides a resistance value. It operates on the thermistor principle.

TRANSMISSION INPUT SPEED (TIS) SENSOR: Measures turbine shaft (input shaft) rpm's and compares to engine rpm's to determine torque converter slip. When compared to the transmission output speed sensor or VSS, gear ratio and clutch engagement timing can be determined.

TRANSMISSION OIL TEMPERATURE (TOT) SENSOR: (See transmission fluid temperature (TFT) sensor.)

TRANSMISSION RANGE SELECTOR (TRS) SWITCH: Tells the module which gear shift position the driver has chosen.

TRANSFER CASE: A gearbox driven from the transmission that delivers power to both front and rear driveshafts in a four-wheel drive system. Transfer cases usually have a high and low range set of gears, used depending on how much pulling power is needed.

TRANSISTOR: A semi-conductor component which can be actuated by a small voltage to perform an electrical switching function.

TREAD WEAR INDICATOR: Bars molded into the tire at right angles to the tread that appear as horizontal bars when 1/16 in. of tread remains.

TREAD WEAR PATTERN: The pattern of wear on tires which can be "read" to diagnose problems in the front suspension.

TUNE-UP: A regular maintenance function, usually associated with the replacement and adjustment of parts and components in the electrical and fuel systems of a vehicle for the purpose of attaining optimum performance.

TURBINE: The output (driven) member of a fluid coupling or fluid torque converter. It is splined to the input (turbine) shaft of the transmission.

TURBOCHARGER: An exhaust driven pump which compresses intake air and forces it into the combustion chambers at higher than atmospheric pressures. The increased air pressure allows more fuel to be burned and results in increased horsepower being produced.

TURBULENCE: The interference of molecules of a fluid (or vapor) with each other in a fluid flow.

TYPE F: Transmission fluid developed and used by Ford Motor Company up to 1982. This fluid type provides a high coefficient of friction.

TYPE 7176: The preferred choice of transmission fluid for Chrysler automatic transmissions and transaxles. Developed in 1986, it closely resembles Dexron and Mercon. Type 7176 is the recommended service fill fluid for all Chrysler products utilizing a lockup torque converter dating back to 1978.

U-JOINT (UNIVERSAL JOINT): A flexible coupling in the drive train that allows the driveshafts or axle shafts to operate at different angles and still transmit rotary power.

UNDERSTEER: The tendency of a car to continue straight ahead while negotiating a turn.

UNIT BODY: Design in which the car body acts as the frame.

UNLEADED FUEL: Fuel which contains no lead (a common gasoline additive). The presence of lead in fuel will destroy the functioning elements of a catalytic converter, making it useless.

UNSPRUNG WEIGHT: The weight of car components not supported by the springs (wheels, tires, brakes, rear axle, control arms, etc.).

UPSHIFT: A shift that results in a decrease in torque ratio and an increase in speed.

VACUUM: A negative pressure; any pressure less than atmospheric pressure.

VACUUM ADVANCE: A device which advances the ignition timing in response to increased engine vacuum.

VACUUM GAUGE: An instrument used for measuring the existing vacuum in a vacuum circuit or chamber. The unit of measure is inches (of mercury in a barometer).

VACUUM MODULATOR: Generates a hydraulic oil pressure in response to the amount of engine vacuum.

VALVES: Devices that can open or close fluid passages in a hydraulic system and are used for directing fluid flow and controlling pressure.

VALVE BODY ASSEMBLY: The main hydraulic control assembly of the transmission/transaxle that contains numerous valves, check balls, and other components to control the distribution of pressurized oil throughout the transmission.

VALVE CLEARANCE: The measured gap between the end of the valve stem and the rocker arm, cam lobe or follower that activates the valve.

VALVE GUIDES: The guide through which the stem of the valve passes. The guide is designed to keep the valve in proper alignment.

VALVE LASH (clearance): The operating clearance in the valve train.

VALVE TRAIN: The system that operates intake and exhaust valves, consisting of camshaft, valves and springs, lifters, pushrods and rocker arms.

VAPOR LOCK: Boiling of the fuel in the fuel lines due to excess heat. This will interfere with the flow of fuel in the lines and can completely stop the flow. Vapor lock normally only occurs in hot weather.

VARIABLE DISPLACEMENT (VARIABLE CAPACITY) VANE PUMP: Slipper-type vanes, mounted in a revolving rotor and contained within the bore of a movable slide, capture and then force fluid to flow. Movement of the slide to various positions changes the size of the vane chambers and the amount of fluid flow. **Note:** GM refers to this pump design as variable displacement, and Ford terms it variable capacity.

VARIABLE FORCE SOLENOID (VFS): Commonly referred to as the electronic pressure control (EPC) solenoid, it replaces the cable/linkage style of TV system control and is integrated with a spool valve and spring assembly to control pressure. A variable computer-controlled current flow varies the internal force of the solenoid on the spool valve and resulting control pressure.

VARIABLE ORIFICE THERMAL VALVE: Temperature-sensitive hydraulic oil control device that adjusts the size of a circuit path opening. By altering the size of the opening, the oil flow rate is adapted for cold to hot oil viscosity changes.

VARNISH: Term applied to the residue formed when gasoline gets old and stale.

VCM: See Electronic Control Unit (ECU).

VEHICLE SPEED SENSOR (VSS): Provides an electrical signal to the computer module, measuring vehicle speed, and affects the torque converter clutch engagement and release.

VESPEL SEALING RINGS: Hard plastic material that produces excellent sealing in dynamic settings. These rings are found in late versions of the 4T60 and in all 4T60-E and 4T80-E transaxles.

VISCOSITY: The ability of a fluid to flow. The lower the viscosity rating, the easier the fluid will flow. 10 weight motor oil will flow much easier than 40 weight motor oil.

VISCOSITY INDEX IMPROVERS: Keeps the viscosity nearly constant with changes in temperature. This is especially important at low temperatures, when the oil needs to be thin to aid in shifting and for cold-weather starting. Yet it must not be so thin that at high temperatures it will cause excessive hydraulic leakage so that pumps are unable to maintain the proper pressures.

VISCOUS CLUTCH: A specially designed torque converter clutch apply plate that, through the use of a silicon fluid, clamps smoothly and absorbs torsional vibrations.

VOLT: Unit used to measure the force or pressure of electricity. It is defined as the pressure needed to move one amp through the resistance of one ohm.

VOLTAGE: The electrical pressure that causes current to flow. Voltage is measured in volts (V).

VOLTAGE, APPLIED: The actual voltage read at a given point in a circuit. It equals the available voltage of the power supply minus the losses in the circuit up to that point.

VOLTAGE DROP: The voltage lost or used in a circuit by normal loads such as a motor or lamp or by abnormal loads such as a poor (high-resistance) lead or terminal connection.

VOLTAGE REGULATOR: A device that controls the current output of the alternator or generator.

VOLTMETER: An instrument used for measuring electrical force in units called volts. Voltmeters are always connected parallel with the circuit being tested.

VORTEX FLOW: The crosswise or circulatory flow of oil between the blades of the members caused by the centrifugal pumping action of the impeller.

WANKEL ENGINE: An engine which uses no pistons. In place of pistons, triangular-shaped rotors revolve in specially shaped housings.

WATER PUMP: A belt driven component of the cooling system that mounts on the engine, circulating the coolant under pressure.

WATT: The unit for measuring electrical power. One watt is the product of one ampere and one volt (watts equals amps times volts). Wattage is the horsepower of electricity (746 watts equal one horsepower).

WHEEL ALIGNMENT: Inclusive term to describe the front end geometry (caster, camber, toe-in/out).

WHEEL CYLINDER: Found in the automotive drum brake assembly, it is a device, actuated by hydraulic pressure, which, through internal pistons, pushes the brake shoes outward against the drums.

WHEEL WEIGHT: Small weights attached to the wheel to balance the wheel and tire assembly. Out-of-balance tires quickly wear out and also give erratic handling when installed on the front.

WHEELBASE: Distance between the center of front wheels and the center of rear wheels.

WIDE OPEN THROTTLE (WOT): Full travel of accelerator pedal.

WORK: The force exerted to move a mass or object. Work involves motion; if a force is exerted and no motion takes place, no work is done. Work per unit of time is called power. Work = force x distance = ft. lbs. 33,000 ft. lbs. in one minute = 1 horsepower

ZERO-THROTTLE COAST DOWN: A full release of accelerator pedal while vehicle is in motion and in drive range.

Commonly Used Abbreviations

2

2WD Two Wheel Drive

4

4WD Four Wheel Drive

A

A/C Air Conditioning
ABDC After Bottom Dead Center
ABS Anti-lock Brakes
AC Alternating Current
ACL Air cleaner
ACT Air Charge Temperature
AIR Secondary Air Injection
ALCL Assembly Line Communications Link
ALDL Assembly Line Diagnostic Link
AT Automatic Transaxle/Transmission
ATDC After Top Dead Center
ATF Automatic Transmission Fluid
ATS Air Temperature Sensor
AWD All Wheel Drive

B

BAP Barometric Absolute Pressure
BARO Barometric Pressure
BBDC Before Bottom Dead Center
BCM Body Control Module
BDC Bottom Dead Center
BPT Backpressure Transducer
BTDC Before Top Dead Center
BVSV Bimetallic Vacuum Switching Valve

C

CAC Charge Air Cooler
CARB California Air Resources Board
CAT Catalytic Converter
CCC Computer Command Control
CCCC Computer Controlled Catalytic Converter
CCCI Computer Controlled Coil Ignition
CCD Computer Controlled Dwell
CDI Capacitor Discharge Ignition
CEC Computerized Engine Control
CFI Continuous Fuel Injection
CIS Continuous Injection System
CIS-E Continuous Injection System - Electronic
CKP Crankshaft Position
CL Closed Loop
CMP Camshaft Position
CPP Clutch Pedal Position
CTOX Continuous Trap Oxidizer System
CTP Closed Throttle Position
CVC Constant Vacuum Control
CYL Cylinder

D

DBC Dual Bed Catalyst
DC Direct Current
DFI Direct Fuel Injection
DIS Distributorless Ignition System
DLC Data Link Connector
DMM Digital Multimeter
DOHC Double Overhead Camshaft
DRB Diagnostic Readout Box
DTC Diagnostic Trouble Code
DTM Diagnostic Test Mode
DVOM Digital Volt/Ohmmeter

E

EBCM Electronic Brake Control Module
ECM Engine Control Module
ECT Engine Coolant Temperature
ECU Engine Control Unit or Electronic Control Unit
EDIS Electronic Distributorless Ignition System
EEC Electronic Engine Control
EEPROM Electrically Erasable Programmable Read Only Memory
EFE Early Fuel Evaporation
EGR Exhaust Gas Recirculation
EGRT Exhaust Gas Recirculation Temperature
EGRVC EGR Valve Control
EPROM Erasable Programmable Read Only Memory
EVAP Evaporative Emissions
EVP EGR Valve Position

F

FBC Feedback Carburetor
FEEPROM Flash Electrically Erasable Programmable Read Only Memory
FF Flexible Fuel
FI Fuel Injection
FT Fuel Trim
FWD Front Wheel Drive

G

GND Ground

H

HAC High Altitude Compensation
HEGO Heated Exhaust Gas Oxygen sensor
HEI High Energy Ignition
HO2 Sensor Heated Oxygen Sensor

I

IAC Idle Air Control
IAT Intake Air Temperature
ICM Ignition Control Module
IFI Indirect Fuel Injection
IFS Inertia Fuel Shutoff
ISC Idle Speed Control
IVSV Idle Vacuum Switching Valve

Commonly Used Abbreviations

K

KOEO Key On, Engine Off
KOER Key ON, Engine Running
KS Knock Sensor

M

MAF Mass Air Flow
MAP Manifold Absolute Pressure
MAT Manifold Air Temperature
MC Mixture Control
MDP Manifold Differential Pressure
MFI Multiport Fuel Injection
MIL Malfunction Indicator Lamp or Maintenance
MST Manifold Surface Temperature
MVZ Manifold Vacuum Zone

N

NVRAM Nonvolatile Random Access Memory

O

O2 Sensor Oxygen Sensor
OBD On-Board Diagnostic
OC Oxidation Catalyst
OHC Overhead Camshaft
OL Open Loop

P

P/S Power Steering
PAIR Pulsed Secondary Air Injection
PCM Powertrain Control Module
PCS Purge Control Solenoid
PCV Positive Crankcase Ventilation
PIP Profile Ignition Pick-up
PNP Park/Neutral Position
PROM Programmable Read Only Memory
PSP Power Steering Pressure
PTO Power Take-Off
PTOX Periodic Trap Oxidizer System

R

RABS Rear Anti-lock Brake System
RAM Random Access Memory
ROM Read Only Memory
RPM Revolutions Per Minute
RWAL Rear Wheel Anti-lock Brakes
RWD Rear Wheel Drive

S

SBC Single Bed Converter
SBEC Single Board Engine Controller
SC Supercharger
SCB Supercharger Bypass
SFI Sequential Multiport Fuel Injection
SIR Supplemental Inflatible Restraint
SOHC Single Overhead Camshaft
SPL Smoke Puff Limiter
SPOUT Spark Output
SRI Service Reminder Indicator
SRS Supplemental Restraint System
SRT System Readiness Test
SSI Solid State Ignition
ST Scan Tool
STO Self-Test Output

T

TAC Thermostatic Air Cleamer
TBI Throttle Body Fuel Injection
TC Turbocharger
TCC Torque Converter Clutch
TCM Transmission Control Module
TDC Top Dead Center
TFI Thick Film Ignition
TP Throttle Position
TR Sensor Transaxle/Transmission Range Sensor
TVV Thermal Vacuum Valve
TWC Three-way Catalytic Converter

V

VAF Volume Air Flow, or Vane Air Flow
VAPS Variable Assist Power Steering
VRV Vacuum Regulator Valve
VSS Vehicle Speed Sensor
VSV Vacuum Switching Valve

W

WOT Wide Open Throttle
WU-TWC Warm Up Three-way Catalytic Converter

ENGLISH TO METRIC CONVERSION: TORQUE

To convert foot-pounds (ft. lbs.) to Newton-meters (Nm), multiply the number of ft. lbs. by 1.36
To convert Newton-meters (Nm) to foot-pounds (ft. lbs.), multiply the number of Nm by 0.7376

ft. lbs.	Nm	ft. lbs.	Nm	ft. lbs.	Nm	ft. lbs.	Nm
0.1	0.1	34	46.2	76	103.4	118	160.5
0.2	0.3	35	47.6	77	104.7	119	161.8
0.3	0.4	36	49.0	78	106.1	120	163.2
0.4	0.5	37	50.3	79	107.4	121	164.6
0.5	0.7	38	51.7	80	108.8	122	165.9
0.6	0.8	39	53.0	81	110.2	123	167.3
0.7	1.0	40	54.4	82	111.5	124	168.6
0.8	1.1	41	55.8	83	112.9	125	170.0
0.9	1.2	42	57.1	84	114.2	126	171.4
1	1.4	43	58.5	85	115.6	127	172.7
2	2.7	44	59.8	86	117.0	128	174.1
3	4.1	45	61.2	87	118.3	129	175.4
4	5.4	46	62.6	88	119.7	130	176.8
5	6.8	47	63.9	89	121.0	131	178.2
6	8.2	48	65.3	90	122.4	132	179.5
7	9.5	49	66.6	91	123.8	133	180.9
8	10.9	50	68.0	92	125.1	134	182.2
9	12.2	51	69.4	93	126.5	135	183.6
10	13.6	52	70.7	94	127.8	136	185.0
11	15.0	53	72.1	95	129.2	137	186.3
12	16.3	54	73.4	96	130.6	138	187.7
13	17.7	55	74.8	97	131.9	139	189.0
14	19.0	56	76.2	98	133.3	140	190.4
15	20.4	57	77.5	99	134.6	141	191.8
16	21.8	58	78.9	100	136.0	142	193.1
17	23.1	59	80.2	101	137.4	143	194.5
18	24.5	60	81.6	102	138.7	144	195.8
19	25.8	61	83.0	103	140.1	145	197.2
20	27.2	62	84.3	104	141.4	146	198.6
21	28.6	63	85.7	105	142.8	147	199.9
22	29.9	64	87.0	106	144.2	148	201.3
23	31.3	65	88.4	107	145.5	149	202.6
24	32.6	66	89.8	108	146.9	150	204.0
25	34.0	67	91.1	109	148.2	151	205.4
26	35.4	68	92.5	110	149.6	152	206.7
27	36.7	69	93.8	111	151.0	153	208.1
28	38.1	70	95.2	112	152.3	154	209.4
29	39.4	71	96.6	113	153.7	155	210.8
30	40.8	72	97.9	114	155.0	156	212.2
31	42.2	73	99.3	115	156.4	157	213.5
32	43.5	74	100.6	116	157.8	158	214.9
33	44.9	75	102.0	117	159.1	159	216.2

METRIC TO ENGLISH CONVERSION: TORQUE

To convert foot-pounds (ft. lbs.) to Newton-meters (Nm), multiply the number of ft. lbs. by 1.36
To convert Newton-meters (Nm) to foot-pounds (ft. lbs.), multiply the number of Nm by 0.7376

Nm	ft. lbs.	Nm	ft. lbs.	Nm	ft. lbs.	Nm	ft. lbs.	Nm	ft. lbs.
0.1	0.1	34	25.0	76	55.9	118	86.8	160	117.6
0.2	0.1	35	25.7	77	56.6	119	87.5	161	118.4
0.3	0.2	36	26.5	78	57.4	120	88.2	162	119.1
0.4	0.3	37	27.2	79	58.1	121	89.0	163	119.9
0.5	0.4	38	27.9	80	58.8	122	89.7	164	120.6
0.6	0.4	39	28.7	81	59.6	123	90.4	165	121.3
0.7	0.5	40	29.4	82	60.3	124	91.2	166	122.1
0.8	0.6	41	30.1	83	61.0	125	91.9	167	122.8
0.9	0.7	42	30.9	84	61.8	126	92.6	168	123.5
1	0.7	43	31.6	85	62.5	127	93.4	169	124.3
2	1.5	44	32.4	86	63.2	128	94.1	170	125.0
3	2.2	45	33.1	87	64.0	129	94.9	171	125.7
4	2.9	46	33.8	88	64.7	130	95.6	172	126.5
5	3.7	47	34.6	89	65.4	131	96.3	173	127.2
6	4.4	48	35.3	90	66.2	132	97.1	174	127.9
7	5.1	49	36.0	91	66.9	133	97.8	175	128.7
8	5.9	50	36.8	92	67.6	134	98.5	176	129.4
9	6.6	51	37.5	93	68.4	135	99.3	177	130.1
10	7.4	52	38.2	94	69.1	136	100.0	178	130.9
11	8.1	53	39.0	95	69.9	137	100.7	179	131.6
12	8.8	54	39.7	96	70.6	138	101.5	180	132.4
13	9.6	55	40.4	97	71.3	139	102.2	181	133.1
14	10.3	56	41.2	98	72.1	140	102.9	182	133.8
15	11.0	57	41.9	99	72.8	141	103.7	183	134.6
16	11.8	58	42.6	100	73.5	142	104.4	184	135.3
17	12.5	59	43.4	101	74.3	143	105.1	185	136.0
18	13.2	60	44.1	102	75.0	144	105.9	186	136.8
19	14.0	61	44.9	103	75.7	145	106.6	187	137.5
20	14.7	62	45.6	104	76.5	146	107.4	188	138.2
21	15.4	63	46.3	105	77.2	147	108.1	189	139.0
22	16.2	64	47.1	106	77.9	148	108.8	190	139.7
23	16.9	65	47.8	107	78.7	149	109.6	191	140.4
24	17.6	66	48.5	108	79.4	150	110.3	192	141.2
25	18.4	67	49.3	109	80.1	151	111.0	193	141.9
26	19.1	68	50.0	110	80.9	152	111.8	194	142.6
27	19.9	69	50.7	111	81.6	153	112.5	195	143.4
28	20.6	70	51.5	112	82.4	154	113.2	196	144.1
29	21.3	71	52.2	113	83.1	155	114.0	197	144.9
30	22.1	72	52.9	114	83.8	156	114.7	198	145.6
31	22.8	73	53.7	115	84.6	157	115.4	199	146.3
32	23.5	74	54.4	116	85.3	158	116.2	200	147.1
33	24.3	75	55.1	117	86.0	159	116.9	201	147.8

ENGLISH/METRIC CONVERSION: TEMPERATURE

To convert Fahrenheit (F°) to Celsius (C°), take F° temperature and subtract 32, multiply the result by 5 and divide the result by 9
To convert Celsius (C°) to Fahrenheit (F°), take C° temperature and multiply it by 9, divide the result by 5 and add 32

F°	C°	F°	C°	C°	F°	C°	F°
-40	-40.0	150	65.6	-38	-36.4	46	114.8
-35	-37.2	155	68.3	-36	-32.8	48	118.4
-30	-34.4	160	71.1	-34	-29.2	50	122
-25	-31.7	165	73.9	-32	-25.6	52	125.6
-20	-28.9	170	76.7	-30	-22	54	129.2
-15	-26.1	175	79.4	-28	-18.4	56	132.8
-10	-23.3	180	82.2	-26	-14.8	58	136.4
-5	-20.6	185	85.0	-24	-11.2	60	140
0	-17.8	190	87.8	-22	-7.6	62	143.6
1	-17.2	195	90.6	-20	-4	64	147.2
2	-16.7	200	93.3	-18	-0.4	66	150.8
3	-16.1	205	96.1	-16	3.2	68	154.4
4	-15.6	210	98.9	-14	6.8	70	158
5	-15.0	212	100.0	-12	10.4	72	161.6
10	-12.2	215	101.7	-10	14	74	165.2
15	-9.4	220	104.4	-8	17.6	76	168.8
20	-6.7	225	107.2	-6	21.2	78	172.4
25	-3.9	230	110.0	-4	24.8	80	176
30	-1.1	235	112.8	-2	28.4	82	179.6
35	1.7	240	115.6	0	32	84	183.2
40	4.4	245	118.3	2	35.6	86	186.8
45	7.2	250	121.1	4	39.2	88	190.4
50	10.0	255	123.9	6	42.8	90	194
55	12.8	260	126.7	8	46.4	92	197.6
60	15.6	265	129.4	10	50	94	201.2
65	18.3	270	132.2	12	53.6	96	204.8
70	21.1	275	135.0	14	57.2	98	208.4
75	23.9	280	137.8	16	60.8	100	212
80	26.7	285	140.6	18	64.4	102	215.6
85	29.4	290	143.3	20	68	104	219.2
90	32.2	295	146.1	22	71.6	106	222.8
95	35.0	300	148.9	24	75.2	108	226.4
100	37.8	305	151.7	26	78.8	110	230
105	40.6	310	154.4	28	82.4	112	233.6
110	43.3	315	157.2	30	86	114	237.2
115	46.1	320	160.0	32	89.6	116	240.8
120	48.9	325	162.8	34	93.2	118	244.4
125	51.7	330	165.6	36	96.8	120	248
130	54.4	335	168.3	38	100.4	122	251.6
135	57.2	340	171.1	40	104	124	255.2
140	60.0	345	173.9	42	107.6	126	258.8
145	62.8	350	176.7	44	111.2	128	262.4

LENGTH CONVERSION

To convert inches (in.) to millimeters (mm), multiply the number of inches by 25.4
To convert millimeters (mm) to inches (in.), multiply the number of millimeters by 0.04

Inches	Millimeters	Inches	Millimeters	Inches	Millimeters	Inches	Millimeters
0.0001	0.00254	0.005	0.1270	0.09	2.286	4	101.6
0.0002	0.00508	0.006	0.1524	0.1	2.54	5	127.0
0.0003	0.00762	0.007	0.1778	0.2	5.08	6	152.4
0.0004	0.01016	0.008	0.2032	0.3	7.62	7	177.8
0.0005	0.01270	0.009	0.2286	0.4	10.16	8	203.2
0.0006	0.01524	0.01	0.254	0.5	12.70	9	228.6
0.0007	0.01778	0.02	0.508	0.6	15.24	10	254.0
0.0008	0.02032	0.03	0.762	0.7	17.78	11	279.4
0.0009	0.02286	0.04	1.016	0.8	20.32	12	304.8
0.001	0.0254	0.05	1.270	0.9	22.86	13	330.2
0.002	0.0508	0.06	1.524	1	25.4	14	355.6
0.003	0.0762	0.07	1.778	2	50.8	15	381.0
0.004	0.1016	0.08	2.032	3	76.2	16	406.4

ENGLISH/METRIC CONVERSION: LENGTH

To convert inches (in.) to millimeters (mm), multiply the number of inches by 25.4

To convert millimeters (mm) to inches (in.), multiply the number of millimeters by 0.04

Inches		Millimeters	Inches		Millimeters	Inches		Millimeters
Fraction	Decimal	Decimal	Fraction	Decimal	Decimal	Fraction	Decimal	Decimal
1/64	0.016	0.397	11/32	0.344	8.731	11/16	0.688	17.463
1/32	0.031	0.794	23/64	0.359	9.128	45/64	0.703	17.859
3/64	0.047	1.191	3/8	0.375	9.525	23/32	0.719	18.256
1/16	0.063	1.588	25/64	0.391	9.922	47/64	0.734	18.653
5/64	0.078	1.984	13/32	0.406	10.319	3/4	0.750	19.050
3/32	0.094	2.381	27/64	0.422	10.716	49/64	0.766	19.447
7/64	0.109	2.778	7/16	0.438	11.113	25/32	0.781	19.844
1/8	0.125	3.175	29/64	0.453	11.509	51/64	0.797	20.241
9/64	0.141	3.572	15/32	0.469	11.906	13/16	0.813	20.638
5/32	0.156	3.969	31/64	0.484	12.303	53/64	0.828	21.034
11/64	0.172	4.366	1/2	0.500	12.700	27/32	0.844	21.431
3/16	0.188	4.763	33/64	0.516	13.097	55/64	0.859	21.828
13/64	0.203	5.159	17/32	0.531	13.494	7/8	0.875	22.225
7/32	0.219	5.556	35/64	0.547	13.891	57/64	0.891	22.622
15/64	0.234	5.953	9/16	0.563	14.288	29/32	0.906	23.019
1/4	0.250	6.350	37/64	0.578	14.684	59/64	0.922	23.416
17/64	0.266	6.747	19/32	0.594	15.081	15/16	0.938	23.813
9/32	0.281	7.144	39/64	0.609	15.478	61/64	0.953	24.209
19/64	0.297	7.541	5/8	0.625	15.875	31/32	0.969	24.606
5/16	0.313	7.938	41/64	0.641	16.272	63/64	0.984	25.003
21/64	0.328	8.334	21/32	0.656	16.669	1/1	1.000	25.400
			43/64	0.672	17.066